# TEACHER'S EDITION

## PRENTICE HALL

# MAGRUDER'S AMERICAN GOVERNMENT

**William A. McClenaghan**   Professor Emeritus, Oregon State University

## PEARSON

Boston, Massachusetts   Chandler, Arizona   Glenview, Illinois   Upper Saddle River, New Jersey

Acknowledgments appear on pages 861–864, which constitute an extension of this copyright page.

ISBN 13: 978-0-13-317364-2
ISBN 10:     0-13-317364-X
1 2 3 4 5 6 7 8 9 10 V063 15 14 13 12 11

# Revised yearly by William A. McClenaghan,

**Professor Emeritus, Oregon State University**

**In Memoriam** *During the production of this edition and after nearly 60 years of authoring* Magruder's American Government, *Bill McClenaghan passed away. This and every edition of* Magruder's American Government *since the death of Frank Abbott Magruder in 1949 are a tribute to Professor McClenaghan's depth of knowledge, passion for American government and politics, and insistence on excellence. Professor McClenaghan's strength of character and dynamic personality were inspiring to all who had the good fortune to know and work with him. Through both his teaching and this textbook, Bill McClenaghan influenced an extraordinary number of government students throughout the United States. Through those students and future readers of* Magruder's American Government, *his legacy goes on.*

**Magruder's American Government,** first published in 1917 and revised annually, is an enduring symbol of the author's faith in American ideals and American institutions. The life of Frank Abbott Magruder (1882–1949) was an outstanding example of Americanism at its very best. His career as a teacher, author, and tireless worker in civic and religious undertakings remains an inspiring memory to all who knew him.

## Grant Wiggins, Program Consultant

Grant Wiggins is the President of Authentic Education in Hopewell, New Jersey. He earned his Ed.D. from Harvard University and his B.A. from St. John's College in Annapolis. Grant consults with schools, districts, and state education departments on a variety of reform matters; organizes conferences and workshops; and develops print materials and Web resources on curricular change. He is the co-author, with Jay McTighe, of *Understanding By Design* and *The Understanding By Design Handbook,* the award-winning and highly successful materials on curriculum published by ASCD. His work has been supported by the Pew Charitable Trusts, the Geraldine R. Dodge Foundation, and the National Science Foundation.

Over the past twenty years, Wiggins has worked on some of the most influential reform initiatives in the country, including Vermont's portfolio system and Ted Sizer's Coalition of Essential Schools. He has established statewide Consortia devoted to assessment reform for the states of North Carolina and New Jersey. Grant is the author of *Educative Assessment* and *Assessing Student Performance*, both published by Jossey-Bass. His many articles have appeared in such journals as Educational Leadership and Phi Delta Kappan.

# Unit 1

## Foundations of American Government

**Essential Question** What should be the goals of government?

**Go online with Unit 1**
Find these interactive resources at
PearsonSchool.com/phgovt

**GOVERNMENT ONLINE**
**How Government Works**

- Checks and Balances
- Amending the Constitution
- Louisiana Becomes a State

**GOVERNMENT ONLINE**
**Government on the Go**

- Political Dictionary
- Audio Review
- Downloadable Interactivities

**GOVERNMENT ONLINE**
**WebQuest**

- Explore Essential Questions online

**GOVERNMENT ONLINE**
**Government Online**

- Interactivities
- In the News
- Citizenship Activity Pack
- Online Self-Test
- Audio Tours
- Updates
- Documents

Contents **v**

# Unit 2

## Political Behavior: Government By the People  119

**Essential Question** In what ways should people participate in public affairs?

**Go online with Unit 2**
Find these interactive resources at PearsonSchool.com/phgovt

**GOVERNMENT** ONLINE
**How Government Works**

- Significant Minor Parties
- Five Methods of Nomination
- What Happens to a Ballot
- Grass-roots Organizing

**GOVERNMENT** ONLINE
**Government on the Go**

- Political Dictionary
- Audio Review
- Downloadable Interactivities

**GOVERNMENT** ONLINE
**WebQuest**

- Explore Essential Questions online

**GOVERNMENT** ONLINE
**Government Online**

- Interactivities
- In the News
- Citizenship Activity Pack
- Online Self-Test
- Audio Tours
- Updates
- Documents

# Unit 3

**Essential Question** What makes a successful Congress?

**Go online with Unit 3**
Find these interactive resources at
PearsonSchool.com/phgovt

**GOVERNMENT** ONLINE
**How Government Works**

- Gerrymandering: Choosing Their Voters
- The Impeachment Process
- Congressional Checks on the Presidential Treaty-Making Power
- How a Bill Becomes a Law

**GOVERNMENT** ONLINE
**Government on the Go**

- Political Dictionary
- Audio Review
- Downloadable Interactivities

**GOVERNMENT** ONLINE
**WebQuest**

- Explore Essential Questions online

**GOVERNMENT** ONLINE
**Government Online**

- Interactivities
- In the News
- Citizenship Activity Pack
- Online Self-Test
- Audio Tours
- Updates
- Documents

# Unit 4

## The Executive Branch

**361**

**Essential Question** What makes a good President?

**Go online with Unit 4**
Find these interactive resources at **PearsonSchool.com/phgovt**

**GOVERNMENT** ONLINE
**How Government Works**

- Presidential Succession
- The Race to the Presidency
- Confirmation Process
- The Executive Branch
- The Executive Departments
- Regulatory Commissions
- Creating the Federal Budget
- The State Department
- Civilian Control of the Military
- Department of Homeland Security

**GOVERNMENT** ONLINE
**Government on the Go**

- Political Dictionary
- Audio Review
- Downloadable Interactivities

**GOVERNMENT** ONLINE
**WebQuest**

- Explore Essential Questions online

**GOVERNMENT** ONLINE
**Government Online**

- Interactivities
- In the News
- Citizenship Activity Pack
- Online Self-Test
- Audio Tours
- Updates
- Documents

# Unit 5

## The Judicial Branch

**Essential Question** What should be the role of the judicial branch?

**Go online with Unit 5**
Find these interactive resources at PearsonSchool.com/phgovt

**GOVERNMENT** ONLINE
**How Government Works**

- The Appellate Path in the Federal Courts
- How a Case Reaches the Supreme Court
- The *Lemon* Test
- Freedoms of Speech and Press
- Exceptions to the Exclusionary Rule
- Rights of the Accused

**GOVERNMENT** ONLINE
**Government on the Go**

- Political Dictionary
- Audio Review
- Downloadable Interactivities

**GOVERNMENT** ONLINE
**WebQuest**

- Explore Essential Questions online

**GOVERNMENT** ONLINE
**Government Online**

- Interactivities
- In the News
- Citizenship Activity Pack
- Online Self-Test
- Audio Tours
- Updates
- Documents

# Unit 6

## Comparative Political and Economic Systems
## 643

**Essential Question** How should a government meet the needs of its people?

**Go online with Unit 6**
Find these interactive resources at
PearsonSchool.com/phgovt

⟶ **GOVERNMENT** ONLINE
**How Government Works**

- The Federal Reserve System

⟶ **GOVERNMENT** ONLINE
**Government on the Go**

- Political Dictionary
- Audio Review
- Downloadable Interactivities

⟶ **GOVERNMENT** ONLINE
**WebQuest**

- Explore Essential Questions online

⟶ **GOVERNMENT** ONLINE
**Government Online**

- Interactivities
- In the News
- Citizenship Activity Pack
- Online Self-Test
- Audio Tours
- Updates
- Documents

# Unit 7

## Participating in State and Local Government

**705**

**Essential Question** What is the right balance of local, State, and federal government?

**Go online with Unit 7**
Find these interactive
resources at
PearsonSchool.com/phgovt

**GOVERNMENT** ONLINE
**How Government Works**

- Amending State
  Constitutions
- Initiative and Referendum
- Choosing Executive
  Officers
- Criminal and Civil Law
- Municipalities and
  Townships
- Alternate Forms of City
  Government
- State and Local Spending
- State and Local Revenues

**GOVERNMENT** ONLINE
**Government on the Go**

- Political Dictionary
- Audio Review
- Downloadable
  Interactivities

**GOVERNMENT** ONLINE
**WebQuest**

- Explore Essential
  Questions online

**GOVERNMENT** ONLINE
**Government Online**

- Interactivities
- In the News
- Citizenship Activity
  Pack
- Online Self-Test
- Audio Tours
- Updates
- Documents

# Learning With Essential Questions

*Magruder's American Government* is organized around Essential Questions. An essential question is a launching pad for exploring ideas. It doesn't have just one right answer. The answer to an essential question changes as you learn more or as circumstances change.

**GOVERNMENT** ONLINE
**Webquest**
To complete the Chapter Essential Question Webquest, visit **PearsonSchool.com/phgovt**

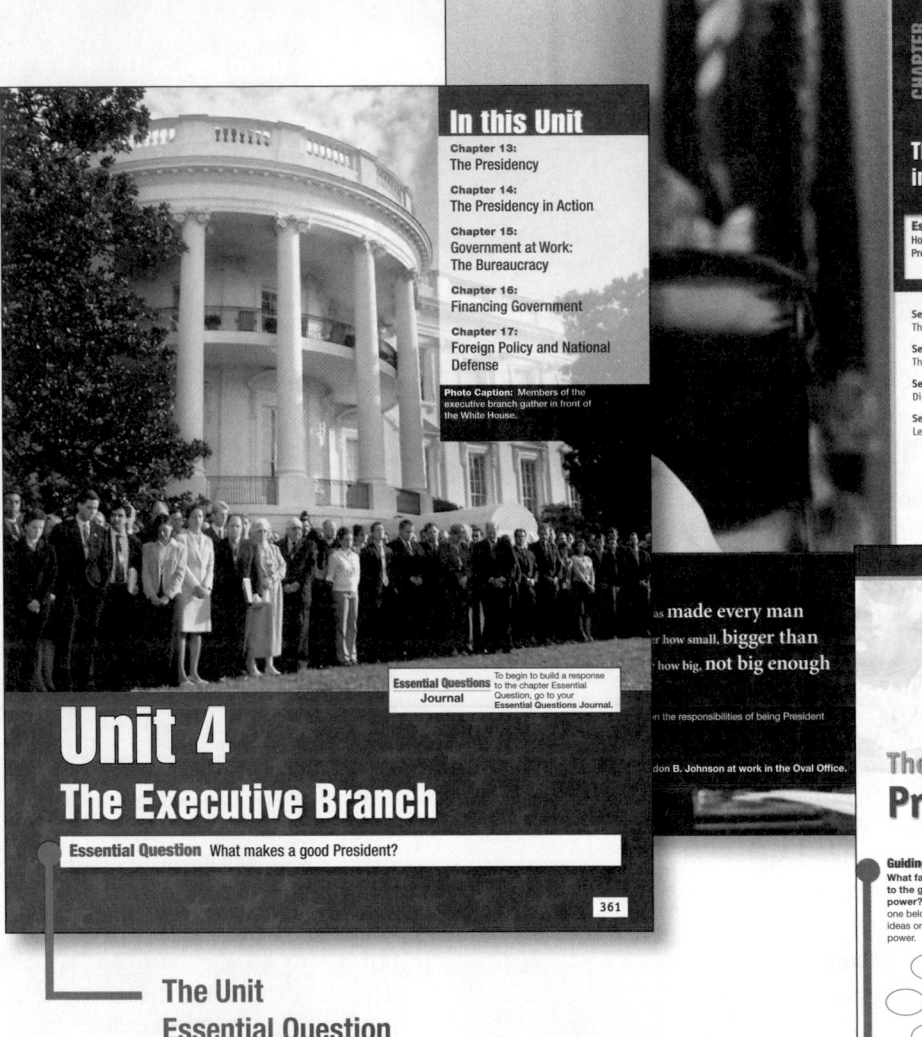

**In this Unit**

Chapter 13:
The Presidency

Chapter 14:
The Presidency in Action

Chapter 15:
Government at Work:
The Bureaucracy

Chapter 16:
Financing Government

Chapter 17:
Foreign Policy and National Defense

**Photo Caption:** Members of the executive branch gather in front of the White House.

**Essential Questions Journal**  To begin to build a response to the chapter Essential Question, go to your Essential Questions Journal.

## Unit 4
### The Executive Branch

**Essential Question**  What makes a good President?

361

**The Unit Essential Question** addresses the main idea of the unit.

CHAPTER **14**

**The Presidency in Action**

**Essential Question**
How much power should the President have?

Section 1:
The Growth of Presidential Power

Section 2:
The Executive Powers

Section 3:
Diplomatic and Military Powers

Section 4:
Legislative and Judicial Powers

**The Chapter Essential Question** addresses the main idea of each chapter. Answering the Chapter Essential Question helps you answer the Unit Essential Question.

...as made every man ...er how small, **bigger than** ...how big, **not big enough** ...in the responsibilities of being President

...don B. Johnson at work in the Oval Office.

The guiding questions steer you to the main ideas of each section of the chapter. Answering the section guiding questions helps you think about the Chapter Essential Question.

**SECTION 1**

## The **Growth** of **Presidential Power**

**Guiding Question**
**What factors have contributed to the growth of presidential power?** Use a concept web like the one below to keep track of the main ideas on the growth of presidential power.

Reasons for the Growth of Presidential Power

**Political Dictionary**
• Executive Article
• imperial presidency

**Objectives**
1. Explain why Article II of the Constitution can be described as "an outline" of the presidential office.
2. List several reasons for the growth of presidential power.
3. Explain how the Presidents' own views have affected the power of the office.

The presidency is regularly called "the most powerful office in the world," and it is. But is this what the Framers had in mind when they created the post in 1787? At Philadelphia, they purposely created a single executive with very broadly stated powers. Still, they agreed with Thomas Jefferson, who wrote in the Declaration of Independence that "a Tyrant is unfit to be the ruler of a free people." So, just as purposefully, they constructed a "checked," or limited, presidency.

### Article II
Article II of the Constitution is known as the **Executive Article**, which in only a few words established the presidency. It begins this way:

**FROM THE CONSTITUTION**
The executive Power shall be vested in a President of the United States of America.

—Article II, Section 1

With this one sentence, the Framers laid the basis for the vast power and influence the nation's chief executive possesses today.

The Constitution also sets out other, somewhat more specific grants of presidential power. Thus, the President is given the power to command the armed forces, to make treaties, to approve or veto acts of Congress, to send and receive diplomatic representatives, and to "take Care that the Laws be faithfully executed." [1]

Still, the Constitution lays out the powers of the presidency in a very sketchy fashion. Article II reads almost as an outline. It has been called "the most loosely drawn chapter" in the nation's fundamental law. [2] It does not

**Images Above:** President George Washington; Mount Rushmore (background)

1  Most of the specific grants of presidential power are found in Article II, Sections 2 and 3. A few are elsewhere in the Constitution—for example, the veto power, in Article I, Section 7, Clause 2.
2  Edward S. Corwin, *The President: Office and Powers.*

The guiding questions steer you to the main ideas of each section of the chapter. Answering the section guiding questions helps you think about the Chapter Essential Question.

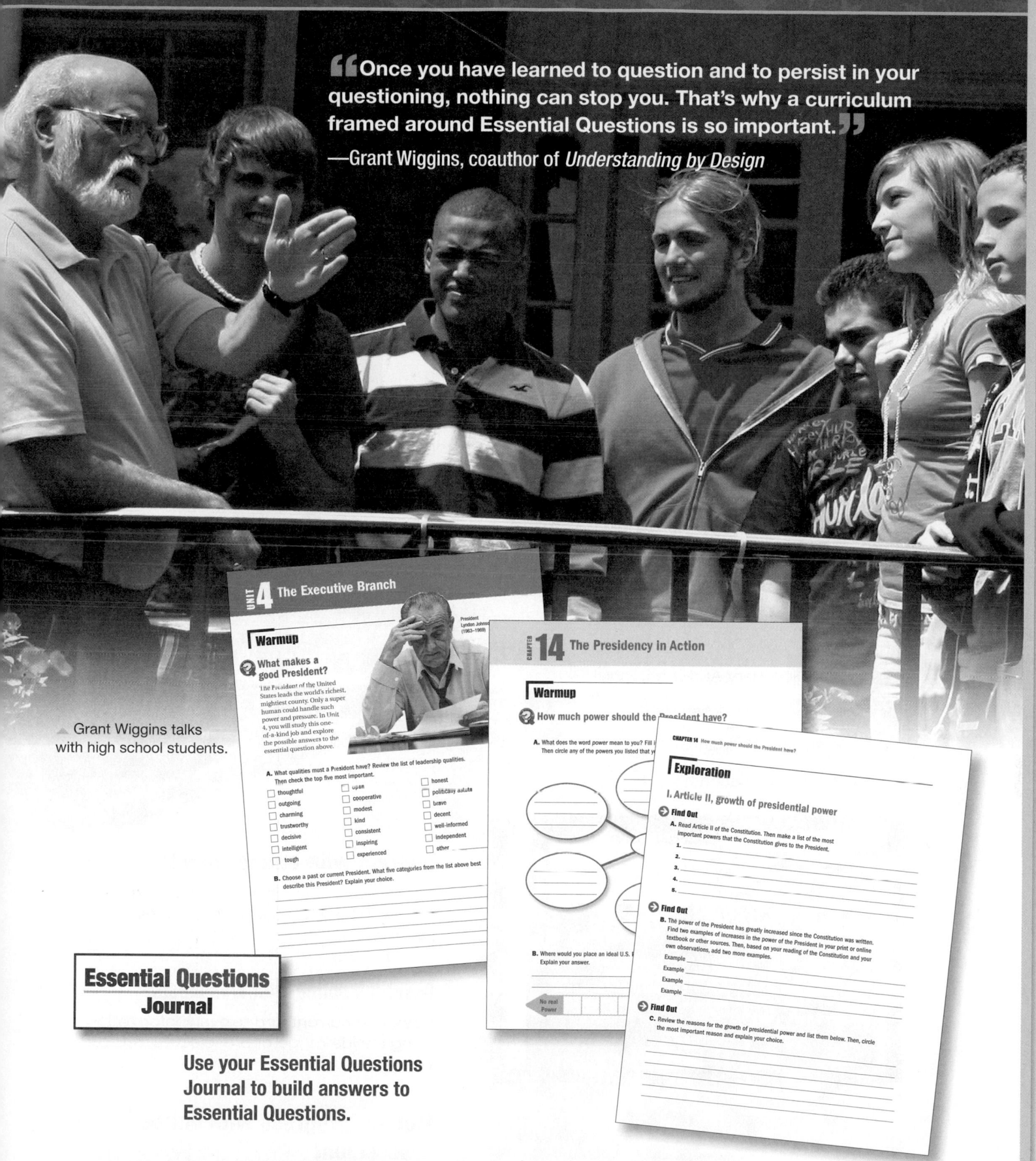

"Once you have learned to question and to persist in your questioning, nothing can stop you. That's why a curriculum framed around Essential Questions is so important."

—Grant Wiggins, coauthor of *Understanding by Design*

▲ Grant Wiggins talks with high school students.

## Essential Questions Journal

Use your Essential Questions Journal to build answers to Essential Questions.

## *Also available online at PearsonSchool.com/phgovt*

# Learning Online

## ▶ Online Student Center

It all starts with the Online Student Center! There you can access a wide array of 21st century learning tools to help personalize learning.

### Access *Magruder's American Government* Online

Go to the Online Student Center at PearsonSchool.com/phgovt to find your textbook.

### Connect with content using Government on the Go Audio and Video ▶

Study anywhere, anytime with downloadable audio and video files.

- Political Dictionary Audio in English
- Political Dictionary Audio in Spanish
- Audio Review in English
- Audio Review in Spanish
- Audio Tour Animations

**How Government Works**

🔊 **GOVERNMENT** ONLINE

For an **interactive** exploration of the confirmation process, visit PearsonSchool.com/phgovt

INTERACTIVE

**Confirmation Process**

# Who Gets the Job?

Most presidential nominations for high-level positions, such as Supreme Court justices, require Senate approval. This multi-step process can be long and drawn out, and at times grueling for the nominee. *Why is this multi-step process necessary?*

### ◀ Interact with online activities

Online features such as "How Government Works" help you visualize key concepts and information.

### Research online with Webquests

Research current and relevant information using a wide range of preselected, reliable Web sites.

### Monitor progress with online assessment

Online self-tests help you monitor your learning.

# Study Skills

## ▶ Prepare To Read

Get more from your reading by answering the guiding questions and filling in note-taking graphic organizers that appear at the beginning of each section.

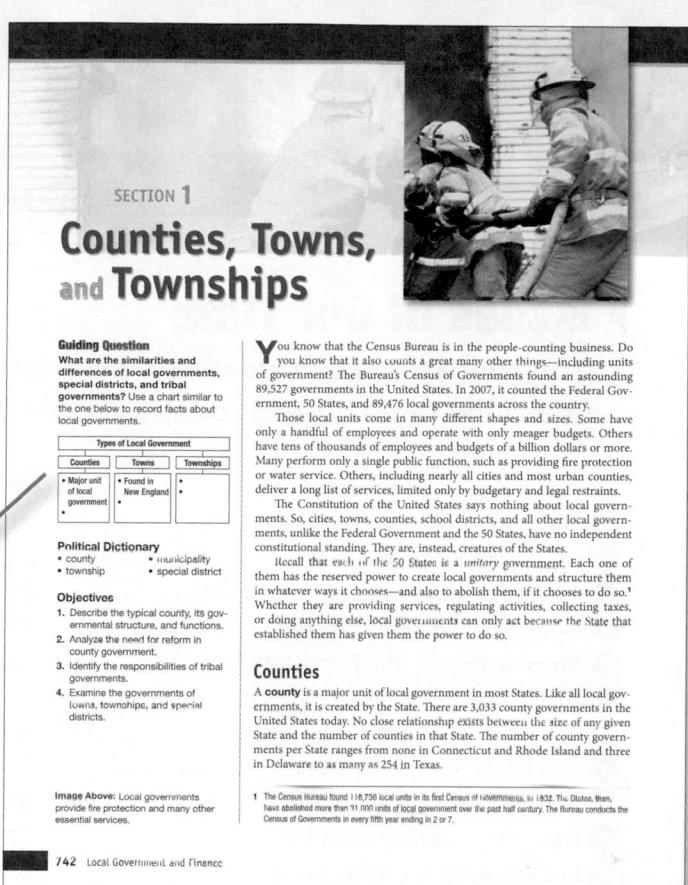

Graphic organizers help you answer the guiding question at the beginning of each section.

## ▶ Quick Study Guide

Review for tests with charts that organize unit and chapter Essential Questions, political dictionary terms, and the key concepts of each chapter.

A graphic organizer helps you see how the guiding questions for each chapter help you answer the chapter's Essential Question.

Charts, diagrams, and tables summarize key information.

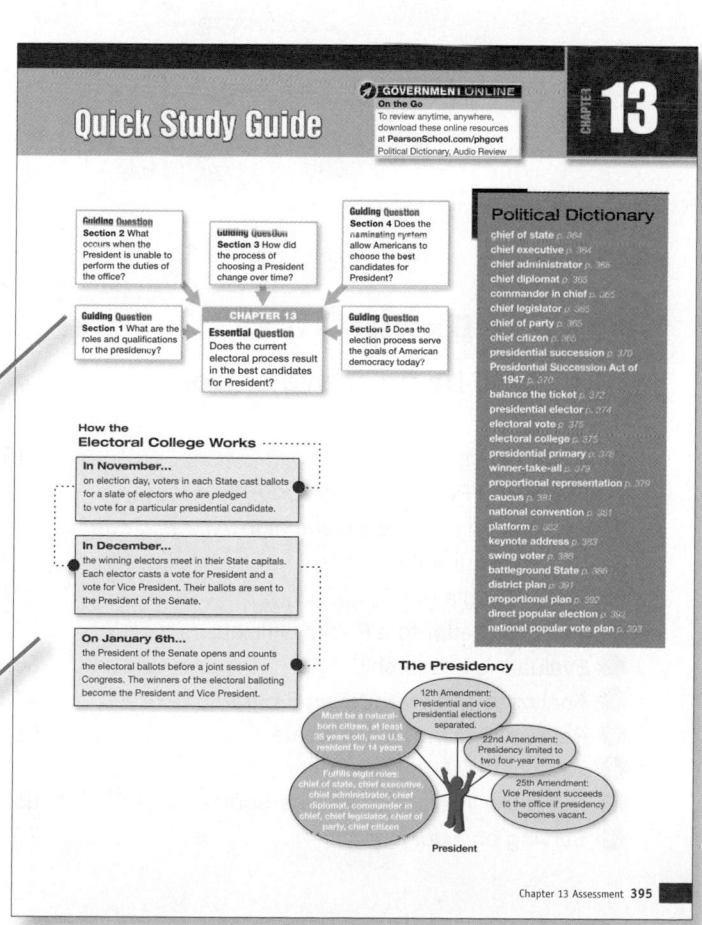

# Special Features

## ▶ Issues Of Our Time

Confront key issues from new perspectives.
Learn the facts behind today's debates.

### GOVERNMENT ONLINE
#### with Online Enhancement

Many charts, graphs, diagrams, and illustrations
are expanded online with interactivities, audio
tours, and updates. To view these enhanced
graphics, go to **PearsonSchool.com/phgovt**
The ⟳ on these pages indicates an online
enhancement.

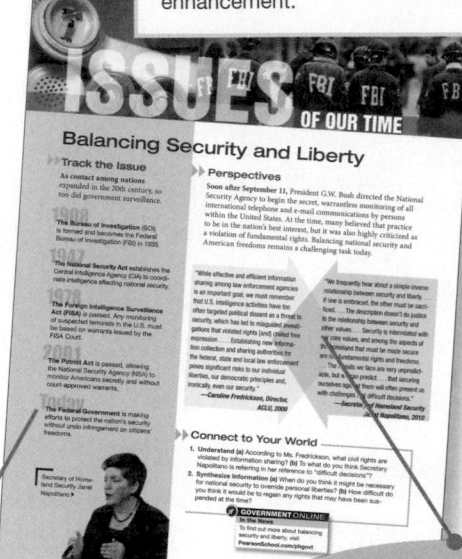

A timeline shows the
connection between today's
debate and past events.

Consider the viewpoints of
prominent Americans on the
issues that impact our lives.

## ▶ Citizenship 101

Learn to be an active citizen.

Practice your citizenship
skills with online activities.

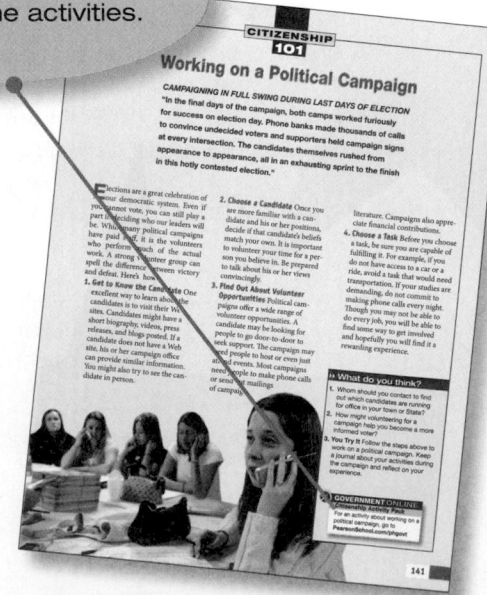

# Focus on the Supreme Court

## ▶ Landmark Decisions of the Supreme Court

Learn the complete story behind groundbreaking decisions of the U.S. Supreme Court.

Meet the Americans who inspired each case.

Evaluate opposing arguments and the impact of the Court's decision.

## ▶ Supreme Court-at-a-Glance

Identify the defining facts of important Supreme Court cases.

See the Supreme Court Glossary for summaries of key cases, p. 805.

**SUPREME COURT** at a glance

▶ **Case:** *Gideon v. Wainwright,* 1963

▶ **Issue:** 6th Amendment right to counsel

▶ **Decision:** Clarence Earl Gideon (below) defended himself at his trial and was found guilty. He wrote to the Supreme Court, saying that he had been unconstitutionally denied counsel. The Court agreed and ordered a new trial, holding that an attorney must be provided to those who cannot afford one.

# ▶ From The Constitution

Trace enduring government concepts to the words of the U.S. Constitution.

Focus on passages from the United States Constitution.

Learn the significance behind key constitutional principles.

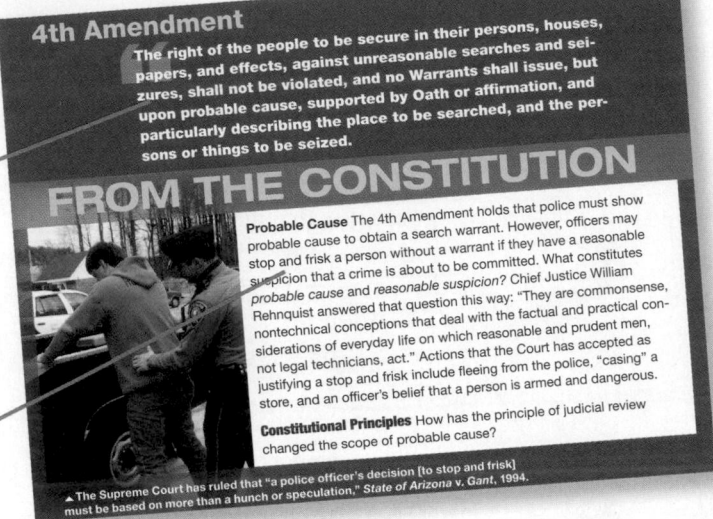

## 4th Amendment

The right of the people to be secure in their persons, houses, papers, and effects, against unreasonable searches and seizures, shall not be violated, and no Warrants shall issue, but upon probable cause, supported by Oath or affirmation, and particularly describing the place to be searched, and the persons or things to be seized.

## FROM THE CONSTITUTION

**Probable Cause** The 4th Amendment holds that police must show probable cause to obtain a search warrant. However, officers may stop and frisk a person without a warrant if they have a reasonable suspicion that a crime is about to be committed. What constitutes *probable cause* and *reasonable suspicion*? Chief Justice William Rehnquist answered that question this way: "They are commonsense, nontechnical conceptions that deal with the factual and practical considerations of everyday life on which reasonable and prudent men, not legal technicians, act." Actions that the Court has accepted as justifying a stop and frisk include fleeing from the police, "casing" a store, and an officer's belief that a person is armed and dangerous.

**Constitutional Principles** How has the principle of judicial review changed the scope of probable cause?

▲ The Supreme Court has ruled that "a police officer's decision [to stop and frisk] must be based on more than a hunch or speculation," *State of Arizona* v. *Gant*, 1994.

Recall the words and ideas behind today's government with excerpts from the Constitution throughout the text.

# ▶ How Government Works

## Find out about the processes by which our government functions through detailed diagrams and infographics.

Complex content is displayed visually to explain how our government works.

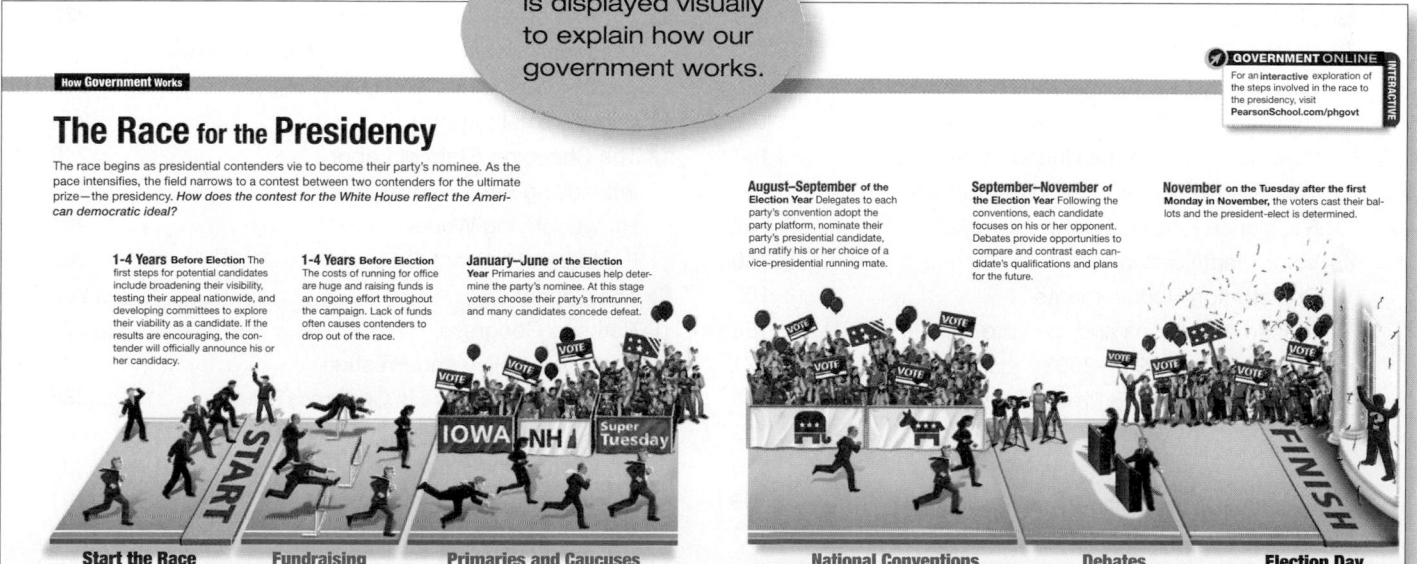

**How Government Works**

## The Race for the Presidency

The race begins as presidential contenders vie to become their party's nominee. As the pace intensifies, the field narrows to a contest between two contenders for the ultimate prize—the presidency. *How does the contest for the White House reflect the American democratic ideal?*

⚡ **GOVERNMENT** ONLINE
For an interactive exploration of the steps involved in the race to the presidency, visit PearsonSchool.com/phgovt

**1-4 Years Before Election** The first steps for potential candidates include broadening their visibility, testing their appeal nationwide, and developing committees to explore their viability as a candidate. If the results are encouraging, the contender will officially announce his or her candidacy.

**1-4 Years Before Election** The costs of running for office are huge and raising funds is an ongoing effort throughout the campaign. Lack of funds often causes contenders to drop out of the race.

**January–June of the Election Year** Primaries and caucuses help determine the party's nominee. At this stage voters choose their party's frontrunner, and many candidates concede defeat.

**August–September of the Election Year** Delegates to each party's convention adopt the party platform, nominate their party's presidential candidate, and ratify his or her choice of a vice-presidential running mate.

**September–November of the Election Year** Following the conventions, each candidate focuses on his or her opponent. Debates provide opportunities to compare and contrast each candidate's qualifications and plans for the future.

**November on the Tuesday after the first Monday in November,** the voters cast their ballots and the president-elect is determined.

**Start the Race**    **Fundraising**    **Primaries and Caucuses**    **National Conventions**    **Debates**    **Election Day**

# ▶ Infographics, Charts, Graphs, and Tables

Visualize key government concepts and interpret relevant data through infographics, charts, graphs, and tables.

Charts, graphs, and diagrams help deepen your understanding of important concepts.

# ▶ Political Cartoons

**Examine historical and modern political cartoons for insights into American government.**

# Document-Based Assessment

Analyze enduring issues and prepare for high-stakes tests by examining documents, data, and political cartoons.

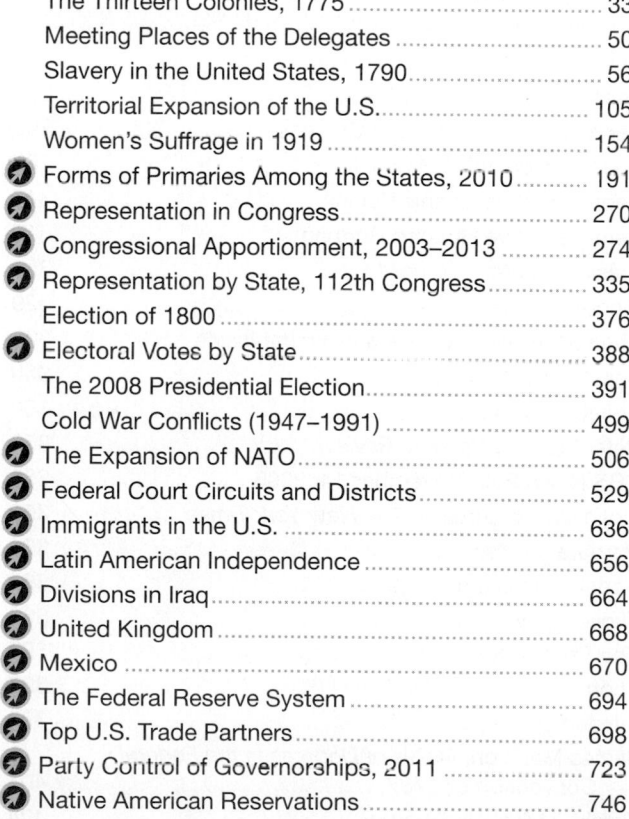
# Maps

Explore the intersection of government and geography.

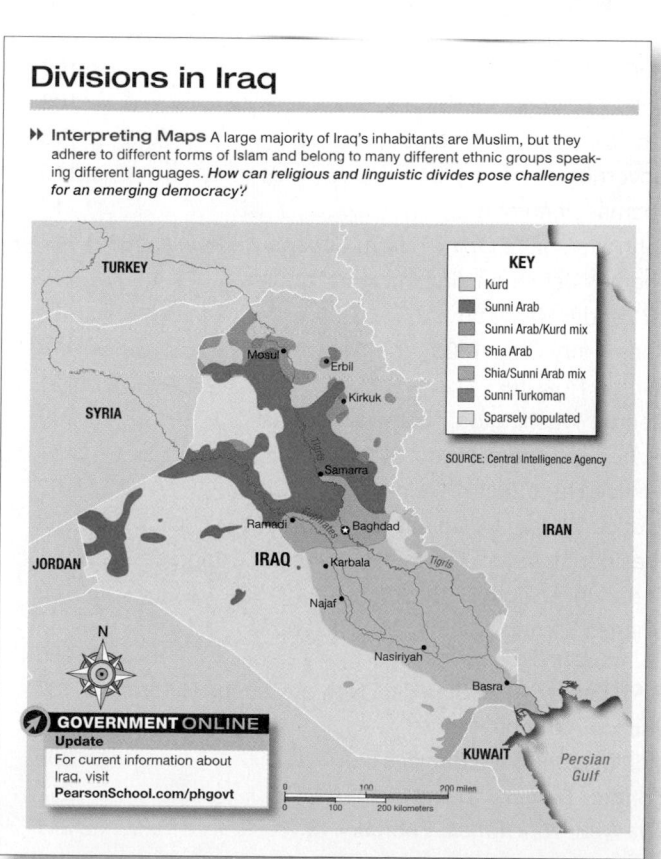

## Divisions in Iraq

▶▶ **Interpreting Maps** A large majority of Iraq's inhabitants are Muslim, but they adhere to different forms of Islam and belong to many different ethnic groups speaking different languages. *How can religious and linguistic divides pose challenges for an emerging democracy?*

**KEY**
- Kurd
- Sunni Arab
- Sunni Arab/Kurd mix
- Shia Arab
- Shia/Sunni Arab mix
- Sunni Turkoman
- Sparsely populated

SOURCE: Central Intelligence Agency

**GOVERNMENT** ONLINE
Update
For current information about Iraq, visit
PearsonSchool.com/phgovt

# ▶ Primary Sources

**Gain insights as you read through the words of people who shaped American government.**

## Contents

Raising the achievement level of all students is the number one challenge facing teachers today. To assist in meeting this challenge, we've enlisted a team of respected authors and consultants who specialize in government education, instructional design, and differentiated instruction. In these pages, you'll find explanations of the key elements that are woven throughout this program to assure teaching and learning success.

TEACHING
GOVERNMENT

PROGRAM
ORGANIZATION

DIFFERENTIATED
INSTRUCTION

ASSESSMENT

PLANNING YOUR
INSTRUCTION

## DIFFERENTIATED INSTRUCTION

## ASSESSMENT

## PLANNING YOUR INSTRUCTION

**DANIEL M. SHEA, PH.D.**

Daniel M. Shea is a professor of social science and director of the Center for Political Participation at Allegheny College. His research and teaching specializations are campaigns and elections, political parties, legislative dynamics, politics of popular culture, and youth mobilization.

Shea has written or edited some 12 books and dozens of articles. Along with two coauthors, he recently completed a text for American government offerings, published for Prentice Hall books. *Living Democracy* was released in December of 2007 and has been adopted at over 150 colleges and universities nationwide.

## Why Teach Government?

Many assume that young Americans are apathetic, self-absorbed, and indifferent to civic matters. It's a turned-off generation, we are sometimes told. They are too interested in having a good time, hanging out at the mall, downloading music, playing video games, and hooking up to care about civic matters. It's hard enough to get young folks off the couch to do some work around the house, much less convince them to volunteer in the community.

In fact, nothing could be further from the truth. Young Americans give their energy, time, and money to their schools, their communities and their nation. In fact, loads of data suggest that rates of volunteerism for those under 25 are now twice as high as for those over 55. Perhaps you see evidence of this trend in your daily interactions with high school students. Many of your students leave school to help at the literacy program, the soup kitchen, the retirement home, or the hospital. Perhaps *this* is the activist generation.

But you also understand that today's youth activism is perplexing and disconcerting because it generally does not extended to political involvement. Somehow this generation doubts the utility of politics and its place in the democratic process. The decline in election turnout among young Americans has been stark in recent decades, and the problem runs much deeper than simply not voting. As noted in a recent report by the Annette Strauss Institute for Civic Participation at the University of Texas at Austin, "By almost every measure, today's youth pale in comparison to the knowledge, engagement, and participation of their forebears when they were their age." They are less trusting, less interested in politics, less knowledgeable about political life, less likely to follow the news, and less likely to join groups geared toward solving public problems. Yes, those who work with America's youth day-in and day-out, such as civics teachers, understand that the withdrawal from politics has been rapid, deep, and broad.

In 2006, the National Assessment of Educational Progress (NAEP) issued a civic assessment report card, based on information from over 25,000 students. Among much else, the study found that only 27 percent of twelfth graders scored at or above the Proficient level, and 66 percent scored at or above the Basic level. As one commentator noted, "During the past several decades, education policy and practice appear to have focused more and more upon developing the 'worker' at the expense of the 'citizen.'"

Only recently have we started to understand the relationship between civic and political involvement for young Americans. Why would a generation so eager to be involved in civic life refrain from political involvement? My guess is that most young people characterize their volunteering as an alternative to politics, what they might call "service politics." They view traditional involvement as corrupt, ineffective, and unrelated to their deeper ideals. They have confidence in their own involvement; they are hardworking and can witness and take pride in the fruits of their labor. When volunteering for Make a Difference Day, the payoff is immediate. They have little confidence in public institutions, which they see as slow-moving, remote, and impossible to control. In other words, young Americans are disengaged from the policy process because they feel marginalized. They do not understand how the process works or how they might be viable players in the system.

This is a serious problem. As an instructor of American Government, you understand the fragility of democracy and the importance of broad political participation. A generation turned off from traditional politics is something to fret about. It mutes the democratic character of our government and distorts the outcome of the policy process. We teach this class because we care about our democracy, and we know how it works. So like it or not, the issue of youth political apathy lies at our doorstep.

Much to the surprise of pundits and scholars, there was a rise in youth political participation in the 2008 election. There was a swell of involvement in the primaries and caucuses, and turnout in the general election reached a two-decade high. Beyond voting, high school and college-age citizens

TEACHING
GOVERNMENT

PROGRAM
ORGANIZATION

DIFFERENTIATED
INSTRUCTION

ASSESSMENT

PLANNING YOUR
INSTRUCTION

rolled up their sleeves for Barack Obama and John McCain—as well as for many congressional and state-level candidates. Many discovered the power and potential of electoral politics, and our system surely benefited from their engagement.

Has the crisis been resolved? Not nearly. While we may have turned the corner, few believe we are out of the woods. More youth engagement is wonderful news, but far too many of our students still remain on the sidelines. And just because young Americans found their political voice in 2008 does not mean they will stay in the democratic choirs—especially if their candidate lost or if promised policy changes prove elusive. As teachers of government, we know that policy changes are often modest, incremental, and slow moving. As a famous social scientist once noted, "Politics is like boring holes in hard wood." But young activists expect grand changes, quickly. I dare say that many will be surprised and perhaps disappointed. Will they remain active when the field is void of dynamic candidates? Perhaps, but my guess is that we are certainly not out of the woods with youth apathy.

There are no quick fixes, of course, as the roots of youth disengagement are numerous and deep. Perhaps we can agree, however, that a course in American government, the very class you teach, offers a unique opportunity. There are numerous, complex objectives for this class, but surely some on the list should be the importance of political participation, the cultivation of civic skills, and an understanding of the potential of young people to make a difference. Yes, those who teach this important class appreciate its potential to engage students and are anxious to find better ways to make connections to real-world politics. There are hefty challenges: large classes, a wide range of student abilities, numerous important topics to cover, and cynical and unprepared students. Our job will not be easy, to be sure. But we can make a difference; we can help train young people for their duties as citizens in a democracy.

Thomas Dewey, the 20th-century education theorist, hit the nail on the head when he noted, "Democracy needs to be reborn in each generation, and education is its midwife."

Here's wishing you success in teaching this course. May your students be grateful for your efforts, and may they take what they learn in your class and head out to change the world—slowly, perhaps, but surely!

## What Makes *Magruder's American Government* Unique?

*Magruder's American Government* is a multidimensional program designed around Essential Questions. It helps students of all abilities gain an understanding of key concepts in government and recognize the application of those concepts in the real world. The print Student Edition, Teacher's Edition, and Essential Questions Journal are supported online by a rich array of resources in the Student Center and Teacher Center.

### Essential Questions for Each Unit

1. What should be the goals of government?

2. In what ways should people participate in public affairs?

3. What makes a successful Congress?

4. What makes a good President?

5. What should be the role of the judicial branch?

6. How should a government meet the needs of its people?

7. What is the right balance of federal, State, and local government?

### Based on Essential Questions

Prentice Hall, in partnership with Grant Wiggins, has created a government program that focuses on Essential Questions. Students have the opportunity to explore these timeless and timely questions in a variety of situations and formats.

1. **Chapter Essential Question Activities**
   These activities give students the opportunity to transfer their understanding of the principles of government to authentic situations. They are challenged to rethink their assumptions and modify their responses based on changing situations and new perspectives.

2. **Essential Questions Journal** Students work through the process of critical thinking in graphic, chart, question, and essay formats. This process helps develop students' abilities to organize and analyze information.

3. **WebQuests** Students develop 21st-century skills by using online resources to research topics related to the Essential Questions. These projects foster deeper understandings of key concepts.

## Accessible

Core content is made accessible through differentiated instruction. Lesson modifications are suggested to help students of all abilities and learning styles achieve understanding of key principles and ideas.

### 1. Leveled Instruction and Worksheets

Lessons provide options for reaching all students, using appropriate pedagogy and activities. When appropriate, teachers may choose from multiple levels of editable worksheets and assessments found on the Online Teacher Center and on the Resource Library CD-ROM. Levels are noted in the title bar for each worksheet.

### 2. Technology to Assist Learning

Rich digital assets such as audio, video, and animations on the Government Online Student Center provide multiple ways for learners to access the content. Interactive section and chapter assessments enable students to monitor their own progress.

## Personal and Relevant

Government is all around us. These special features help students become active citizens and understand current debates in government.

### 1. Citizenship 101

These features stimulate students' interest with real-life skills that allow students to get involved in government and politics. The Citizenship Activity Pack Online extension activities encourage students to further explore the rights and responsibilities of citizenship.

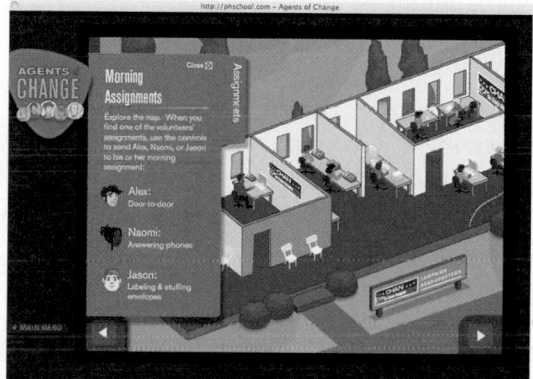

▲ Citizenship Activity Pack Online

### 2. Issues of Our Time

These features provide background and perspectives on thirteen contemporary issues, from globalization and free trade to campaign finance. Each student page includes a timeline showing the connection between today's debate and past events, a summary of the debate, and two quotations showing different sides of the issue.

## How Can Technology Help?

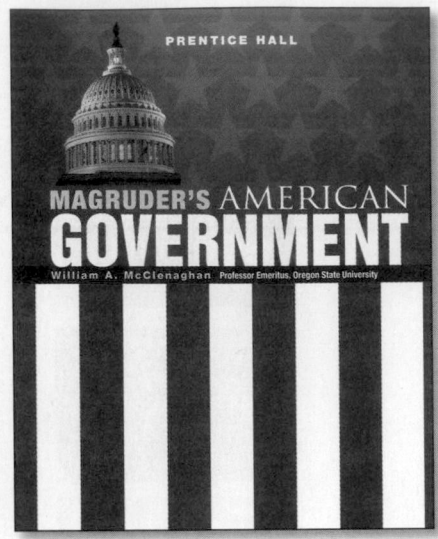

### Online Student Center

Students can use a wide array of 21st-century learning tools to personalize learning. No matter where they are or what time of day it is, students have access to their work.

**Online Student Edition** has rich digital assets. Two levels of the Student Edition teach core content, enabling students to use the version that matches their reading level (also available on CD-ROM)

**Interactivities** help students gain deeper understanding of key concepts.

**How Government Works** features focus on key American government processes and organization in each chapter. They include

- Checks and Balances

- Five Methods of Nomination

- How a Bill Becomes a Law

- Creating the Federal Budget

- How a Case Reaches the Supreme Court

- State and Local Spending

**Online Updates** provide students up-to-date information on elections and elected officials.

**Audio Tours** enrich graphics with step-by-step instruction.

**WebQuests** allow students to explore issues related to each chapter's Essential Question. They include research projects that use online resources to explore current issues in government and politics.

**American Government Essential Questions Videos** introduce and explore topics related to the Essential Questions for each of the seven units.

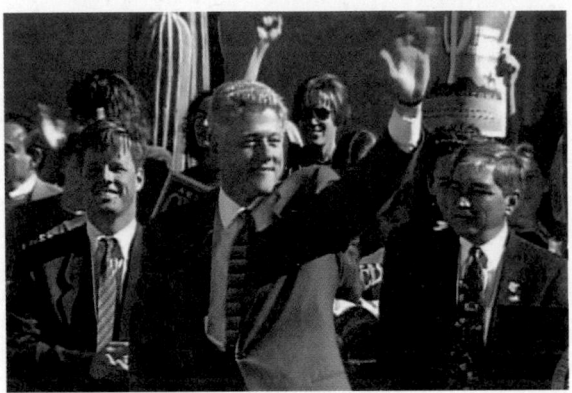

**Government on the Go** allows students to access audio and video files.

**Audio Review (English and Spanish)** lets students review anywhere, any time.

**Political Dictionary (English and Spanish)** builds vocabulary support.

**Interactivities** reinforce and enhance students' understanding of government principles through engaging animations.

**Online Self-Tests** are practice quizzes that allow students to check their understanding informally.

**In the News** provides updates related to Issues of Our Time feature topics and Landmark Cases of the Supreme Court.

TEACHING
GOVERNMENT

PROGRAM
ORGANIZATION

DIFFERENTIATED
INSTRUCTION

ASSESSMENT

PLANNING YOUR
INSTRUCTION

## Online Teacher Center

The Online Teacher Center is an instructional management tool that saves time by letting teachers plan, teach, assess, remediate, and manage the classroom quickly and easily.

This center provides a single point of access to both student and teacher materials, including two levels of the Teacher's Edition for built-in differentiation. These Teacher's Editions include the Student Editions and lessons in the side columns, as well as access to worksheets and other resources.

**Teacher's Resource Library** provides access to wide range of teaching support.

**Editable lesson plans** give teachers the ability to customize lessons according to their own classroom needs.

**Editable, leveled worksheets** permit teachers to adjust activities to match learning levels and content.

**Leveled quizzes and tests** support assessment for differentiated instruction.

**Color Transparencies** enrich lessons with visuals for teaching and engaging student interest.

**AYP Monitoring Assessments** provide diagnostic and leveled unit tests and remediation.

**Answer Keys** speed the assessment process.

**Assessment Rubrics** evaluate student understanding and performance.

**Blank graphic organizers** organize ideas and facilitate learning.

All these resources are also available on CD-ROM.

**Lecture Notes** offer multimedia in-class teaching aids of key concepts.

**Online Assessment** enables teachers to measure each student's progress by assigning tests and makes use of the needs of individual students.

**Alternative Lesson Plans** are lesson ideas from government teachers for one section of each chapter.

**In-Service On Demand and Professional Development** In addition to our on-site consultant support, Pearson offers online tutorials available 24/7, as well as scheduled instructor-led Webinars for selected products.

**VISIT** *my*PearsonTraining.com **FOR MORE INFORMATION.**

## HOW IS THE PROGRAM ORGANIZED?

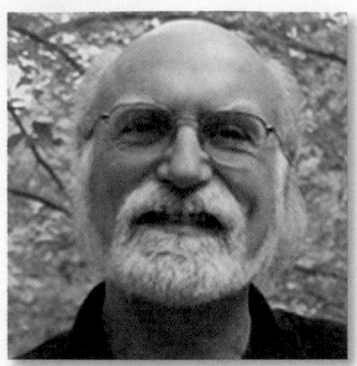

**GRANT WIGGINS, ED. D.**

Grant Wiggins advocates the use of Essential Questions to ensure in-depth and lasting learning. During the development of *Magruder's American Government,* Wiggins advised the product team in the creation of the essential questions and pedagogy that supports them.

> **Every textbook has questions for students. *Magruder's American Government* is different. It has been deliberately built around a few vital questions—Essential Questions**

### What are Essential Questions?

What is an "Essential Question"? An Essential Question is important, vital, at the heart of the matter. Whether in our teaching or our personal lives, when we wonder, for example, "How do we decide what is true?" "Whom shall we trust?"—then we are pondering Essential Questions.

Such questions form the basis of this textbook. A brief look at the table of contents in this book raises obvious questions: "What should be the goals of government?" "Why do voters act as they do?" "How should people participate in public affairs?" "What makes a good President?" "What should be the role of the judicial branch?" "Can and should the lawmaking process be improved?" "What is the right balance of federal, State, and local government?" For a study of government, these questions are key.

**Essential *vs.* Basic Questions** In what senses are these questions "essential"? An Essential Question is different from many of the questions teachers typically ask students in class. The most commonly asked questions in school are what may be called basic or factual questions—questions that seek or underscore a correct answer. There are definitive responses to basic questions, and they can typically be found in the textbook. There is nothing wrong with this type of question, of course. It just doesn't fit what we mean when we say, Let's consider the Essential Questions.

Essential Questions need to be asked and reasked as we learn more—because our answers to such are always provisional. It is never clear what the goals of government should be; it is never clear how we should balance individual rights against the common good. These vital issues remain alive over days, months, and years, unlike simple or superficial queries. The key questions are meant to be pondered and discussed as we go. The questions thus provide focus and a way to make sense of all that we learn in a good government course.

**Raising more questions** *For what purpose does the government collect taxes?* is a "basic" question. *How should a government meet the needs of its people?* is different. It is more conceptual than technical, and more a matter of judgment than of fact. Indeed, the more we consider the essential questions, the more questions we generate, and that makes learning more fun! *What are the needs of the people? What are the needs of the government? Who decides the needs? Who should be taxed and at what rates?* The questions deepen as well as broaden our inquiry as we read, and they inevitably raise more questions as the inquiry proceeds.

So it is with all essential questions. They don't seek a glib or thought-ending plausible answer. They properly raise *more* questions in our attempts to address them. They beg for inquiry; they rouse our minds to life.

Promotes inquiry

Fosters deep understanding

Allows for Transfer

**Essential Question**

Provokes lively debate

Stimulates rethinking

Connects prior learnings

## Essential Points

In my writing over the years with Jay McTighe for *Understanding by Design*, we remind readers that "essential" has a few different connotations:

- One meaning of "essential" involves **important questions that recur**. Such questions . . . are perpetually arguable . . . We may arrive at or be helped to grasp understandings for these questions but we soon learn that answers to them are invariably provisional. In other words, we are liable to change our minds in response to reflection and experience concerning such questions, and that such changes of mind are not only expected but beneficial. A good education is grounded in such life-long questions, even if we sometimes lose sight of them while focusing on content mastery. The big-idea questions signal that education is not just about learning "the answer" but about learning how to learn.

- A second connotation for "essential" refers to **key inquiries within a discipline**. Essential questions in this sense are those that informed citizens and policy-makers are constantly asking. They are historically important, and very much "alive" in the field . . .

- There is a third important connotation for the term "essential" that refers to what is needed for **learning core content**. In this sense, a question can be considered essential when it helps students make sense of important but complicated and confusing ideas—findings that may be understood by experts, but not yet grasped or seen as valuable by the learner. . . . By actively exploring such questions, the learners are helped to arrive at important understandings as well as greater coherence in their content knowledge and skill.

We summarized by saying a question is essential if it meets the following criteria:

### To what extent is the question meant to

- cause genuine and relevant inquiry into the big ideas and core content?

- provoke deep thought, lively discussion, sustained inquiry, and new understanding as well as more questions?

- require students to consider alternatives, weigh evidence, support their ideas, and justify their answers?

- stimulate vital, on-going rethinking of big ideas, assumptions, and prior lessons?

- spark meaningful connections with prior learning and personal experiences?

- naturally recur, creating opportunities for transfer to other situations and subjects?

From *Understanding by Design,* 2nd ed. by Wiggins & McTighe. © 2005 by ASCD

### How do Essential Questions frame *Magruder's American Government?*

Essential Questions provide the framework and core content of our government course. *Magruder's American Government* presents Essential Questions at the unit and chapter levels. Questions are scaffolded, with section guiding questions acting as building blocks to help students answer the chapter-level essential questions. Taken together, the thinking students do about the chapter-level questions will help them answer the unit-level question.

### Working with Essential Questions

**For Teachers** You will of course be teaching and clarifying content and in so doing, addressing basic questions of fact. But to help students understand the implications of what they are learning and make the subject their own, you will also be constantly posing Essential Questions. An Essential Question is more of a "why?" or "so what?" or "where?" question. We are not looking for a definitive answer; we are inviting inquiry and discussion in ways that make abstract ideas real for students.

An Essential Question sometimes confuses students who are used to a steady diet of factual questions. The Essential Question is supposed to slow students down, to make them stop and think! It invites more questions. Students thus learn that they must be active learners. The more we re-ask the Essential Questions and encourage students to do so also, the more it demonstrates that we all learn from reconsidering the same important questions as we read, discuss, experience, and reflect further. That's what keeps Essential Questions alive. That's what this book is designed to help you accomplish.

Your challenge is to make this shift in purpose clear to students – that the goal of the text reading and the activities is to pursue important questions. A key instructional goal in working with essential questions is to coach students in how to address such questions without trying to guess the teacher's preferred answer or giving up in despair. The answers to the Essential Questions will not be found "in the text" but "in our heads."

**For Students** Since there is not a single correct answer to complex questions, students need to think carefully and critically. They will have to consider plausible rival answers. They will see the need to become investigators, asking further questions and seeking information that will help them better understand and address an Essential Question. This work has great practical value. Students will be developing the skills commonly tested on high-stakes exams, such as analysis, comparison, making arguments backed up by evidence, and synthesis. By learning to take notes on the questions and their implications, and by being assessed on their growing sophistication in addressing the questions, students will be far better prepared for college.

**Long-term Goal** A key long-term purpose of the Essential Question is to make the question the student's own. As teachers, you ask Essential Questions repeatedly and build activities and assessments around them to cause transfer. You succeed in the long term, only if and when the Essential Questions are persistently and confidently asked and pursued by students on their own, without your prompts.

## What Is Understanding by Design and How Does It Incorporate Essential Questions?

This approach to organizing instruction around a question is a centerpiece of a more general and comprehensive approach to planning entitled Understanding by Design. As the title suggests, the two big ideas in Understanding by Design are to aim for understanding, not "coverage," and to aim at understanding by design—in other words, by deliberately crafting assessments and activities "backward" from the goal of understanding, not content recall, to make understanding more likely. In short, content mastery is the means, not the long-term goal of education. The point of education is to learn to use content wisely (transfer) and to be able to make sense of new tasks, situations, and texts on one's own. So, you must design backward from such transfer and sense-making, or it will only happen "by good fortune," not "by design."

It's really about common sense, then. If you want students to end up asking the Essential Questions on their own, then your courses have to be designed "backward" from that goal, using this text as a resource. Along the way in *Magruder's American Government,* teachers are expected to help students develop skills and strategies for analyzing government. But those are the *short-term goals. The point of political literacy is not to learn abstract principles of government, but to have a better understanding of the forces that affect them every day.* The value of understanding how government works is in helping people comprehend the modern world and to identify and evaluate the consequences of individual decisions and public policies. That understanding begins with questioning. So, you have to plan to meet this more challenging, *long-term* goal from the start. If you want students to learn from their reading, your methods have to foster that inquiry and meaning-making, and make it clear that success in the study of government requires it. If you aim to have students ponder the Essential Questions and transfer their prior thinking to new texts and discussions, then the course has to be planned to make that happen. So, in Understanding by Design, there is a deliberate process for achieving long-term understanding goals.

**Assessment of Essential Questions** A key to "backward" design: Make sure your assessments reflect the long-term goal of understanding. So, design your assessments before designing your lessons. This is easily done: Make the Essential Questions central to the assessments. "Is it going to be on the test?" This classic question signals, in no uncertain terms, that you had best practice what you preach, or the Essential Questions will be lost. But it must be done. The mantra in Understanding by Design is, If you value it, assess it. If you don't assess it, then you really don't value it. More practically, the kinds of essays, oral presentations, and Socratic seminars with scoring rubrics implied in such a call for higher-order assessment based on Essential Questions is what occurs in every good college in America.

## Application in the Classroom

| Types of Knowledge | Acquisition of Organized Knowledge | Development of Intellectual Skills | Increased Understanding of Ideas and Values |
|---|---|---|---|
| Teaching Style | Didactic Instruction | Coaching, Exercises, and Supervised Practice | Socratic Questioning and Active Participation |

## Understanding by Design in a Nutshell

1. Understanding by Design is a way of thinking purposefully about curricular planning, a set of helpful design tools, and design standards—not a rigid program or recipe.

2. The end goal is student understanding and the ability to transfer learnings—to enable learners to connect, make meaning of, and effectively use discrete knowledge and skills.

3. Evidence of understanding is revealed through performance—when learners transfer knowledge and skills effectively, in varied realistic situations, using one or more "facets"of understanding (explain, interpret, apply, shift perspective, empathize, and self-assess), with minimal scaffolding and prompting.

4. Educators are coaches of understanding, not mere purveyors of content or activity.

5. Planning is best done "backward" from the desired results and the transfer tasks that embody the goals. The 3 stages (Desired Results, Assessment, Learning Plan) must all align for the unit to be valid and potentially effective.

6. Understanding by Design "unpacks" and transforms content standards into focused learning targets based on "big ideas" and transfer tasks, as well as knowledge and skill.

## Backward Planning

As teachers plan their lessons, they are guided by various standards (national, state, etc.) that specify what content students are expected to know and what skills they are to develop. These standards are the framework of the course. Along with the standards, teachers consider the various needs, learning styles, and ability levels of their students. These all figure into class preparation.

Backward design focuses on the desired results first. Then it determines how students will demonstrate their learning. And last, it plans instructional activities that will enable students to be successful. "All the methods and materials we use are shaped by a clear conception of the vision of desired results. That means we should be able to state with clarity what the student should understand and be able to do as a result of any plan . . ." (From *Understanding by Design,* 2nd ed. by Wiggins & McTighe. © 2005 by ASCD, p. 14). Begin with the end in mind.

## Tools to Succeed

Essential Questions are at the core of a model government course. The challenge is to make this fact clear to students—that a major goal of information gathering is to pursue important questions. The questions are the purpose and rationale for learning. The text and activities are the vehicles to gain insight into these questions.

*Magruder's American Government* has been designed to help you make this aim and framework more transparent. The text and features are organized around the questions. The questions can and do recur, and the assessment requires the student to respond to these questions often and to improve in their response over time. The Understanding by Design template focuses lessons on the Essential Questions. The alignment of assessment, learning activities, and goals is at the core of the organization of this program. The template on the next page shows how you can focus instruction and assessment.

Students are challenged to answer the Essential Questions and are given the tools needed to do so. The Section Guiding questions break down the larger question, providing students with scaffolded support. The Essential Question Assessment requires students to transfer learning to authentic tasks. The Essential Questions Journal gives students guidelines to explore the Essential Questions, making them more accessible and manageable.

Circumstances always change and students need to prepare to deal with the unexpected and the unfamiliar. This program is designed to have students transfer skills and knowledge beyond the classroom.

## Stages of Backward Planning

1. Identify desired results. → 2. Determine acceptable evidence. → 3. Plan learning experiences and instruction.

## Backward Planning Template

### STAGE 1

**Begin with the end in mind by identifying what students should know, understand, and be able to do.**

- Long-term transfer goals, content standards, program objectives
- Enduring understandings
- Essential questions (EQ)
- Enabling knowledge and skills

> Identify the "big ideas" you want students to explore. These will be transformed into understandings and Essential Questions on the template.

### STAGE 2

**Determine needed evidence for the targeted knowledge, skill, and understanding in Stage 1, including**

- Performance task(s) involving transfer
- Other assessment evidence
- Rubrics as needed for performance task(s) and other open-ended assessments (e.g., writing prompt)

> Strive to make the performance task(s) authentic.

> Label each assessment in terms of which Essential Questions it assesses.

> Make sure that the rubrics focus on the most important traits related to the unit goals (Stage 1), not only on "surface features" (e.g., word count, neatness).

### STAGE 3

**Plan learning experiences and instruction that lead toward the desired understandings and transfer performances.**

- Preassess to find out prior knowledge, skill levels, and misconceptions
- Balance acquisition, meaning-making, and transfer-focused activities.
- Use ongoing (formative) assessments to check for understanding and make needed adjustments.

> Use diagnostic assessments to check for skill levels and predictable performance errors.

For more information about each stage of planning, go to the Online Teacher Center at PearsonSchool.com/phgovt

## The Value of Differentiated Instruction

It's basic, but it's true—not all students learn in the same manner and not all students have the same academic background or abilities. The "one size fits all" approach has not been proven the most successful strategy. As educators, we need to respond to a variety of student learning styles, readiness levels, and interests by developing and using instructional strategies that address the needs of diverse learners.

Under the *No Child Left Behind* mandate, educators are required to work to close the achievement gap. All students are expected to master state academic standards. Our goal as teachers is to enable 100 percent of students to achieve success on the high-stakes assessment tests.

It is critical to properly match the difficulty level of tasks with the ability level of students. Giving students tasks that they perceive as too hard lowers their expectations of success. However, giving students assignments that they think are too easy undermines their feelings of competence. Therefore, it is important for a program to give teachers leveled activities that allow them to match tasks with the abilities of their individual students.

### How Is Instruction Differentiated?

It is vital to determine the readiness, interests, and learning styles of all students. Diagnostic tests and assessments will help define the specific needs of students. Then, once strengths and weaknesses are determined, you can differentiate curriculum in several ways.

### Content

What students learn may be layered to fit their interests and talents. The level of concepts, enduring understandings, and skills students can acquire will often depend on the complexity of thinking skills required. All students must master the same standards, but depth of learning should be adjusted to meet the needs of diverse learners.

### Process

The process of instruction involves differentiating learning activities and strategies. Content can be accessed, or processed, through a combination of methods, such as direct instruction, inquiry-based learning, cooperative learning, and information processing models. It can be done as a class, in groups or pairs, or individually.

Differentiating instruction is also an essential tool for adapting technology into classroom activities. Technology, such as online activities, can provide an ideal opportunity for engaging students who struggle with a text-based curriculum. It also can be used to provide additional opportunities to access content. A complete social studies program makes content available in a variety of formats, including text, audio, visuals, and interactivities.

### Product

In the end, what students produce demonstrates skills and concepts they have learned. When evaluating student understanding, once again, we cannot assume that "one size fits all." The style, depth, and complexity of the product varies to match ability levels and learning styles. Various methods of assessment—activities, portfolios, performance-based assessment, rubrics, as well as standard tests—can measure students' progress in ways that are fair to many styles of learners.

### How Does This Improve Learning?

Differentiated instruction provides multiple paths for students to access, use, and transfer understanding of concepts. It integrates instructional strategies to meet the needs of a diverse population of students, and thereby enables all students to achieve success. By using differentiated instruction, we allow students to take more responsibility for learning and create a community of learners who cooperate and respect each other.

## How Do We Implement Differentiated Instruction?

The mission of *Magruder's American Government* is to provide standards-based instruction in ways that allow all students to participate and to achieve. Our program provides options so that diverse learners meet established goals, using different content, processes, and products to get there. Our effective support helps you close the achievement gap.

## Teaching Support Helps You Modify Instruction

The **Teacher's Edition** provides continuous professional development throughout the program, starting with strategies for specific populations at the beginning of this textbook.

The **Teacher's Edition** was designed to make it easy for teachers to modify instruction for diverse learners. Specific activities help you adapt instruction for individual students in five categories: less proficient readers, English language learners, advanced students, special needs, and the general population (all students). Resources are identified as being appropriate for use by each of these categories. All resources are also assigned a level—special needs, basic, all students, and advanced—so you know exactly how to assign tasks of appropriate difficulty.

---

**DISTRIBUTE CORE WORKSHEET**

Distribute the Chapter 10 Section 1 Core Worksheet (Unit 3 All-in-One, p. 15). Explain that students will predict the benefits and drawbacks of a bicameral system by using school government as an example. Ask a student to read the introductory paragraph on the worksheet aloud.

**L3** **Differentiate** If time is short, have half the class do benefits and half do drawbacks. Then have them explain their answers to the other half of the class.

**L1** **L2** **ELL Differentiate** Clarify the meaning of *benefits* (advantages) and of *drawbacks* (disadvantages).

---

**All-in-One Teaching Resources** Everything you need to provide differentiated instruction for each lesson is provided in one convenient location. Leveled worksheets enable students of varying abilities to participate equally in the classroom discussion. Where appropriate, worksheets for the general population are paired with lower-level worksheets; the topic and/or presentation is adapted to the ability of the students. In addition, there are activities to challenge advanced students, requiring more complexity or a higher level of critical thinking.

## Varied Resources Address Different Populations

The program also delivers content through a wide variety of formats—including text, transparencies, video, and interactive activities—appealing to all of your students.

- **Reading Comprehension Worksheets** help students understand key concepts.
- **Prereading and Vocabulary Worksheets** for each chapter prepare English language learners and less proficient readers to meet the demands of a government text and its specialized vocabulary.

Using technology as a tool to differentiate content enables students to access content in an engaging method. These include

- **How Government Works** features focus on key American government processes and organization.
- **Online Updates** provide students with up-to-date information on elections and elected officials.
- **Audio Tours** enrich graphics with step-by-step explanations.
- **WebQuests** ask students to do research online to explore the Essential Question.

## Leveled Assessments Give More Options

The program offers a variety of assessment methods. This allows you to choose the style and level of assessment to meet students' needs.

- **AYP Monitoring** provides diagnostic tests to determine student skills and readiness as well as leveled unit assessments to gain feedback on student understanding.
- **Exam*View*® Test Bank CD-ROM,** in English and Spanish, offers leveled tests and helps adapt tests to individual needs.
- **Rubrics** provide both students and teachers clear performance targets and criteria for evaluation.

# DIFFERENTIATED INSTRUCTION

## Strategies for Specific Student Populations

Differentiated instruction can be fostered through modifying instruction to address individual needs. To increase student achievement, teachers can use strategies for specific student populations to offer specialized support. Lesson plans in this **Teacher's Edition** provide differentiated instruction strategies and suggest ancillary support such as the **Reading Comprehension Worksheets**. The following pages provide general guidelines for modifying instruction for students with special needs, less-proficient readers, English Language Learners, and advanced learners.

### SPECIAL NEEDS

Students with special education needs are a highly heterogeneous group of learners, presenting unique cognitive, behavioral, social, and physical needs. To help create a classroom culture that supports the participation and achievement of students with such needs, set clear expectations and provide reasonable choices for all students. Lessons should be planned with individual adaptations and modifications. Offer instructional activities that foster the development of relationships among students and between students and teachers.

### Preteach

**Preteaching helps prepare students for learning.**

- Preteach critical social studies terms and high-use academic words using the Prereading and Vocabulary worksheet and by reviewing the key terms in the side columns.

- Provide preferred seating in the front of the class, face-to-face talk for students who read lips, interpreters, or space for a guide dog as necessary.

### Teach

**Using a variety of approaches enhances lessons.**

- Provide an overview of key ideas and concepts presented in the text using outlines, maps, or study guides.

- Present all ideas orally and visually, and when possible, incorporate tactile and kinesthetic experiences as well.

- Require students to demonstrate that they are listening and following along (e.g., taking notes, running a finger along the text).

- Incorporate active reading strategies (e.g., choral reading, paired reading) to assist in maintaining attention.

- Provide adaptive materials as appropriate (e.g., enlarged print, Braille edition, captions for the video program).

- Incorporate the same comprehension and learning strategies over time to allow for mastery.

### Assess

**Students need to know what is expected.**

- Assess students' understanding by asking them to write questions about what they have learned, identify what they find unclear or confusing, or complete short quick-writes of the key points.

- When having students work in groups or pairs, set up procedures that maintain each student's accountability (e.g., each student having to write, draw, or state a response).

- Make sure that you have adequately scaffolded tasks for special needs students and equipped them with writing instruction and practice that builds the prerequisite skills.

- When appropriate, have students manage and chart their academic performance, homework and assignment completion, and behavior.

- Provide outlines of what is to be done, with suggested dates and timelines for project completion.

## ENGLISH LANGUAGE LEARNERS

Students who are learning English are the fastest-growing segment of the school-age population. These students require frontloading, or preteaching, in order to grasp challenging literacy tasks, such as those encountered in a social studies textbook. Since English Language Learners may be approaching an assignment with limited background knowledge and weak English vocabulary, concentrate on activities that build strong conceptual and linguistic foundations, guide them through the text's organization, and model appropriate comprehension strategies. The following practices will support ELL students in making strides in their English literacy.

### Preteach

**English Language Learners require extra preparation.**

- Introduce essential words in meaningful contexts, through simple sentences drawing on familiar issues, scenarios, and vocabulary. Ask students to write the definitions in their own words and then identify the words when they occur within the reading.
- Utilize realia and visuals (e.g., photographs, objects, color transparencies) to make the concepts less abstract.
- Lead a quick text prereading, or "text tour," focusing student attention on illustrations, title and subtopics, and boldfaced words.
- Suggest students use the Political Dictionary Online, which is presented in both English and Spanish.

### Teach

**Many of these techniques will benefit all learners.**

- Get students physically involved with the page, using sticky notes or small pieces of cardboard to focus and guide their reading.
- Have students engage in repeated readings of the same brief passage to build word recognition, fluency, and reading rate.
- Praise students' efforts to experiment with new language in class, both in writing and in speaking.

### Assess

**Students will demonstrate learning in different ways.**

- Ask students to demonstrate their understanding by drawing upon different language skills: formal and informal writing assignments, posters, small group tasks, and oral presentations.
- Make sure students understand assessment criteria in advance. Distribute rubrics provided in the **All-in-One Teaching Resources**. Whenever possible, provide models of student work to emulate, along with an example of work that fails to meet the specified assessment criteria.

## LESS PROFICIENT READERS

Less-proficient readers are individuals who begin the year one or more years below grade level yet do not qualify for special education services. They may or may not be English Language Learners. They may be under-prepared for the academic challenges due to difficulties with attention and memory, learning strategies, or vocabulary and reading fluency. It is especially important to engage these students in challenging lessons while incorporating support or instructional scaffolding to increase their likelihood of success.

## Preteach

**Preteaching helps build students' confidence.**

- *For Difficulties With Attention and Memory:* Gain attention by requesting a simple physical response (e.g. "Everyone, eyes on me please"). Then keep the lesson pace brisk—a "perky not pokey" pace is helpful.

- *For Difficulties With Learning Strategies:* Clarify the rationale for learning a new strategy in terms the students value. Directly teach any requisite skills needed to perform the strategy.

- *For Difficulties With Vocabulary and Fluency:* Directly teach meanings of critical vocabulary required for full understanding of the lesson.

## Teach

**Lessons have to address specific, different needs.**

- *For Difficulties With Attention and Memory:* Emphasize connections between new and known information. Engage students in collaborative "read/reflect/discuss/note" cycle, filling out a graphic organizer in the section opener.

- *For Difficulties With Learning Strategies:* Explicitly model the use of the strategy, including a significant focus on thinking aloud during the execution of each step in the strategy. Discuss where else in or out of school students could use the strategy.

- *For Difficulties With Vocabulary and Fluency:* Intentionally revisit newly acquired vocabulary during discussion. Suggest that students use the Political Dictionary Online.

## Assess

**Assessment must accommodate special needs.**

- *For Difficulties With Attention and Memory:* Ask students to reorganize, prioritize, and otherwise reflect on the key aspects of the lesson. Have them explain their graphic organizers to a partner. Monitor and reteach as necessary.

- *For Difficulties With Learning Strategies:* Include explicit use of strategies taught as part of the quiz, report, project, and other formal assessments.

- *For Difficulties With Vocabulary and Fluency:* Randomly call on students to provide examples of the vocabulary word under examination.

## ADVANCED LEARNERS

Advanced Learners need modified instruction to achieve their highest potential. They tend to understand complex concepts quickly, learn more rapidly and in greater depth, and may have interests that are different from their peers. Teachers can modify pacing and offer enrichment to allow for exploring topics in-depth, manipulating ideas in novel ways, and making connections to other disciplines.

### Preteach

**These students may have extensive background.**

- Before beginning a new unit, have students write, verbalize, or draw what they know about the topic and present this information to peers.
- Ask students to brainstorm what they'd like to learn, and then work with them to create a plan for advanced study based on their interests.

### Teach

**Activate students' ability to think creatively and see connections.**

- Help students adjust the pace of their learning, speeding through concepts they master quickly or slowing down to study content in-depth. The **Teacher's Edition** provides ideas for ways to extend content in the Extend part of the lesson plan.
- Challenge students to tackle more complex topics and offer frequent opportunities to focus on abstract ideas.

- Provide opportunities for in-depth research on student-directed topics. Have students explore topics on the Internet under your direction.
- Encourage students to make connections between content they are learning and other disciplines such as language arts, science, and math. For example, students might want to read about the impact of technology on the government concept they are studying.

### Assess

**Assessment can take many forms.**

- Give students responsibility for part of the assessment of their learning. Allow them to plan, design, and monitor the project or assignment.
- Encourage students to apply standards-based understanding to new situations. Challenge them to take information and use it in novel ways.

# DIFFERENTIATED INSTRUCTION

## Strategies to Engage All Learners

All students may benefit from strategies that we often consider "differentiation." While these strategies are necessary for success with students with special needs, they also aid many on-level students who are kinesthetic or visual learners, or those who struggle with organization. Here are some tips to keep in mind as you plan.

- **Clarify behavioral expectations for the lesson.** Use rubrics and work with students to create rubrics for class activities and projects. Modeling what students are to do or providing students with examples of finished products are necessary for student success. Explicit instructions do not water down the curriculum; they make it clear so that all students can access it.

- **Use visuals throughout the lesson.** Outlining key ideas, writing key phrases, and vocabulary on the overhead projector or board, or putting notes on the overhead projector or board, are critical supports for many students. You may want to provide some students with a copy of your overheads or notes ahead of time so that they can follow along. For other students, make a partial or blank copy of the graphic or outline you will be using and require students to write in key information as it is discussed. It is very helpful if you model this filling-in procedure for students. It also helps them to overcome problems with spelling or with capturing complex ideas using only a few words.

- **Explicitly teach skills.** Model note taking as you present information to the classroom. Collect and review the students' notes and provide suggestions for improvement. Teach study skills, listening skills, and reading skills along with the content.

- **Incorporate active reading strategies.** Build vocabulary by teaching the meaning of prefixes and suffixes. Have students make study cards of unfamiliar words. Have students read and summarize the paragraph in their own words. Monitor their work to clarify any misunderstandings.

- **Use a variety of strategies to teach and assess understanding.** Present ideas orally and visually, and when possible, incorporate tactile and kinesthetic experiences. Think beyond the common modes of reading and writing. Students could present information orally, create a poster or visual representation of a work, record their ideas, or act out their understanding. These activities take into consideration multiple intelligences and can provide access for all learners in the classroom.

- **Assist in time management.** When requiring students to complete projects or long-term assignments, provide a calendar that breaks down the requirements by due dates. Review the checklist with students and monitor their use of the checklist and task completion as the assignment proceeds. Many students will experience significant difficulties in self-managing the time needed to complete complex and long-term assignments.

- **Incorporate students' strengths and interests.** Use the students' abilities to connect them to content and activities.

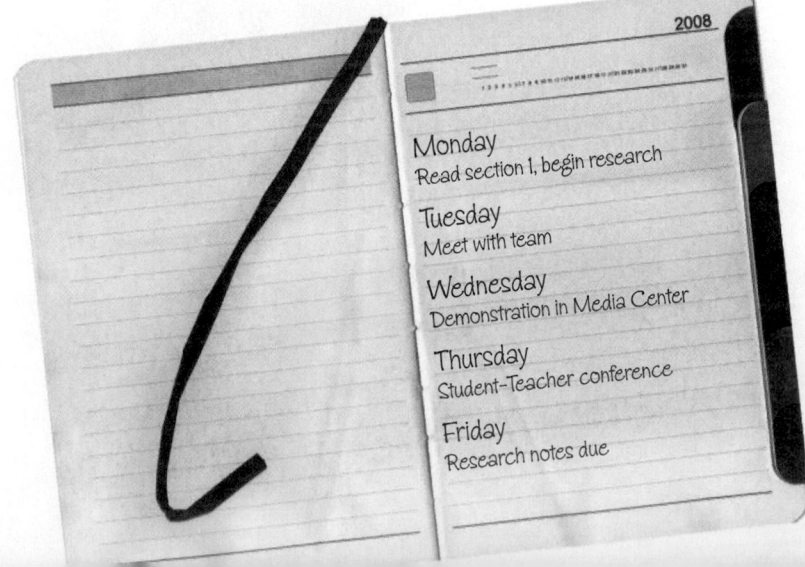

2008

Monday
Read section 1, begin research

Tuesday
Meet with team

Wednesday
Demonstration in Media Center

Thursday
Student-Teacher conference

Friday
Research notes due

# CLASSROOM MANAGEMENT

Creating a positive learning environment enables all students reach their full potential. In a supportive, respectful setting, students perform and behave better. Teachers who use effective motivational and management strategies that actively engage students and appeal to individual learning styles and needs create classrooms that enhance students' academic and personal lives.

## The following are some tips for classroom management.

- **Make learning relevant.** Help students make connections between their own lives and the classroom content. Ask students to list questions about the topic that they would like to learn about. Allow students to extend the lesson by exploring subtopics of their choice. Use the Essential Questions Journal to enable students to demonstrate understanding in their own words and through their own experiences.

- **Be organized—and help students be organized.** Many students have difficulty organizing their time. Break down assignments into short tasks. Require students to submit a plan for completing a large project. Teach skills such as notebook organization. Hand out assignment sheets ahead of time, allowing students to organize their time for the upcoming week or unit. Keep a master notebook with class notes, handouts, and homework that students may consult if they miss a day of class.

- **Have students begin individual work in class.** Prior to class dismissal, check to ensure that each student has a good start and understands what is expected.

- **Provide time for students to collect their thoughts.** This gives more reflective learners time to consider the answer. Explain this procedure to the class before using it. Tell students the questions that you will be asking during tomorrow's class in order to give them time overnight to prepare their responses.

- **Use an instructional warmup activity.** Use the bellringers to grab students' attention and immediately engage them in a task.

- **Use group activities.** Collaborative work encourages students to be supportive of each other, creating positive interdependence. Explain the task clearly. Teach collaborative skills (such as problem solving, time management, accepting criticism).

- **Use peer tutoring.** This technique helps teachers accommodate academic diversity. All students can be actively involved in tasks they can perform successfully. Students work in pairs to assist each other in learning, which leads to improved self-esteem, personal interaction, and positive attitudes about school. Steps for using this strategy are given on the next page.

---

**BELLRINGER**

Display Transparency 14G showing part of Article I, Section 7, Clause 2 of the Constitution. Write on the board: **(1) How does this clause relate to checks and balances? (2) Do you think the legislation approval process is sufficient to prevent abuse of power by the legislative or executive branch? Why or why not? Answer in your notebook.**

TEACHING GOVERNMENT

PROGRAM ORGANIZATION

DIFFERENTIATED INSTRUCTION

ASSESSMENT

PLANNING YOUR INSTRUCTION

# DIFFERENTIATED INSTRUCTION

## DISCUSSION STRATEGIES

Simple structures for discussion can help students extract and process meaning from reading the text. These strategies guide students to a more productive and inclusive class discussion while enabling students to "take ownership" of the information.

### Strategy: Idea Wave Discussion

**Purpose:** To support all students in actively listening and responding academically to a critical question within a more elaborate, unified class discussion.

**How to do it:**

1. Pose an open-ended question or task *(e.g., What do members of Congress do?)*.

2. Provide a model response on the board *(e.g., Members of Congress vote on bills.)*.

3. Give students time to consider what they know about the topic and record a number of responses.

   **L2 Differentiate** Provide two or three sentence starters and ask students to write one or two of their ideas using a sentence starter. These starters should include key academic vocabulary and sentence structures that students wouldn't ordinarily use in casual conversation *(e.g., In their role as legislators...)*.

4. As students jot down ideas, pick volunteers to jumpstart the subsequent class discussion.

   **L2 Differentiate** Get a few answers from students who wouldn't ordinarily respond voluntarily and bolster their confidence by affirming their idea prior to the actual discussion.

   **L2 Differentiate** Read aloud your model response and have students read along with you a second time to build reading fluency.

5. Have students share their responses with a partner to build confidence and accountability to respond, even if all students do not participate in the class discussion.

6. Move around the class in a fast-paced, but structured manner (e.g., down rows, around tables).

   **L4 Differentiate** After this structured debriefing, call on a few volunteers who have additional answers.

7. Provide an active listening and note-taking task during the discussion. Ask students to jot down two ideas, such as two perspectives with which you agree, two additional examples, etc.

8. If there tends to be repetition in responses, ask student to point out similarities rather than stating that their idea has already been mentioned. Require that students use language for acknowledging other ideas *(e.g., My idea builds upon _____'s idea. I also believe that ...)*.

### Strategy: Think-Write-Pair-Share

**Purpose:** To engage students in responding to instruction.

**How to do it:**

1. **Think** Students listen while the teacher poses a question or task related to the reading or classroom discussion. The level of questions should vary from lower level literal to higher order inferential or analytical.

   **L1 L2 ELL Differentiate** Write questions on the board or provide them on a piece of paper.

2. **Write** Provide quiet thinking or writing time for students to deal with the question and go back to the text or review notes. Have students record their ideas in their notebooks.

   **L1 L2 Differentiate** Consider providing academic sentence starters for students to complete as a means of encouraging more thoughtful and formal responses.

3. **Pair/Share** Cue students to find a partner and share their written response, noting similarities and differences. Teach students to encourage one another to clarify and justify their responses. To add more accountability for active listening, ask students to share their partner's idea during the structured debriefing and require that they begin their response with a citation expression *(e.g., My partner pointed out / emphasized / predicted that ...)*.

4. Randomly call on students to share during a class discussion after they have rehearsed answers with their partners.

5. Invite volunteers to contribute additional ideas and points of view to the discussion after calling on a reasonable number of students.

6. Direct students to go back to their notes and add any important information garnered during the partner and class discussions.

## Strategy: Numbered Heads

**Purpose:** To engage all students in responding to questions in order to assess reading comprehension and content understanding.

**How to do it:**

1. Seat students in groups of four and have them count off one through four.

2. After asking a question or assigning a task, give students a specified amount of time to discuss a response. This time should generally be no longer than ninety seconds to prevent students from wandering off task.

3. Remind students to pay attention to each member of the group because only one member will be chosen to represent the group's ideas.

4. Call a number, one through four, and ask students with that number to raise their hands to respond in a whole-class discussion.

5. Add comments, extend key ideas, ask follow-up questions, and make connections between students' comments. If you have a classroom with native English speakers and English Language Learners, you may ask an English speaker to take notes on the board as the discussion progresses, using key words and ideas.

6. Finish up by asking students to write a two-to-four sentence summary of the discussion and have a few students read their summaries out loud.

## Strategy: Click and Clunk

**Purpose:** To gauge student understanding of a reading selection or course content.

**How to do it:**

1. After students have read a selection or finished covering a topic in class, ask students to write down one or two pieces of information or ideas that "clicked," meaning that students feel that they understand well.

2. Then have them write down one or two pieces of information or ideas that "clunked," meaning they did not understand them.

3. Rotate around the room, asking students to list their "clicks" and "clunks." Use the information to guide your follow-up lessons, skipping information that students already understand and spending more time with the information they do not understand. Alternatively, you may collect their lists to read after class.

## Strategy: Peer Tutoring and Peer Feedback

**Purpose:** To pair students of the same or different abilities to help learn or practice educational tasks.

**How to do it:**

1. Give students directions and model appropriate methods of how to assist each other. List the do's and don'ts of helping someone with the work.

2. Pair students. Match students based on need and personality, or on ability. Students may alternate roles as tutor/tutee or the more advanced student may be assigned the tutor role to a struggling student. As the curriculum progresses, you may want to change the pairing.

3. Clearly define the objectives of peer tutoring. Give a specific assignment or task to work on. These tasks supplement classroom instruction; they do not teach new material or skills.

TEACHING GOVERNMENT

PROGRAM ORGANIZATION

**DIFFERENTIATED INSTRUCTION**

ASSESSMENT

PLANNING YOUR INSTRUCTION

4. The tutor should give immediate corrective feedback. Students should be reminded that the feedback should be constructive and positive.

5. Monitor the tutoring process to be sure students stay on task and assess student learning. Walk around the room and engage students frequently.

6. Ask students for feedback about the process. Checklists or self-reporting forms can give students opportunities to discuss the experience. Formal assessments can also provide evaluation of achievement.

## Strategy: Socratic Dialogue

**Purpose:** To encourage students to come to a consensus about ideas through structured discussion.

**How to do it:**

1. Pose a question about a text or other stimulus to the class. Emphasize that the class will try to reach a consensus (agreement) about the answer. If they can not come to agreement, they will still try to come to a deeper understanding together. Here are some questions to start a discussion.

   • What assumptions does the author make?

   • How does this connect to other things that we have learned?

   • What is the significance of the article?

2. Establish rules for the discussion.

   • Students must focus on ideas.

   • Information from readings and class materials must be used to substantiate claims. Every opinion needs proof.

   • Students may not disagree with one another. Instead, they must find something to build on or ask for clarification on a point.

   • Students should take notes so that when it is their turn to speak, they can comment accurately on the statements from which they would like to build.

3. Discuss. As much as possible, allow students to direct the discussion. Do not act as a participant. You may also consider a system for ensuring that all students participate. For example, you may give each student three paperclips to throw in a bucket when they contribute. A rule may be that everyone must contribute once before anyone may contribute three times.

4. Debrief. Following a Socratic dialogue, it is important to have an open discussion afterward in which students may discuss what they found difficult about the exercise and how it made them think differently.

**NOTE:** When possible, it is beneficial to use a defined text, such as a primary source, as the basis for a discussion. Students must, however, be given ample time to read and make notes about the text. When a text is the basis for a discussion, it is also important that students only discuss what is in that text, rather than bring in information they have learned in other settings.

**Modifications:** When a class is too large for a single discussion, break the class into two groups, with inner and outer circles. Partners may then take turns participating in the discussion. The one in the outside circle should take notes about the comments the partner made. For example, "One interesting point was ____ because . . . " or "I'd like to know more about . . ." Alternatively, have two discussions, one following the other.

## Strategy: Debate

**Purpose:** To help students learn to make arguments with strong points and counterpoints.

### How to do it:

1. Present a question to students that can be logically answered in several different ways. Whenever possible, debates should be based on readings rather than students' opinions alone.

2. Begin by assigning students to one of four groups: A1, A2, B1, or B2. Give each side its argument. Groups A1 and A2 will argue against groups B1 and B2. However, the groups will prepare differently. Hand out Debate Worksheet A.

3. Assign groups A1 and B1 to brainstorm and research the arguments FOR their positions and summarize them in a three- to four-sentence opening statement.

4. Assign groups A2 and B2 to brainstorm and research the arguments AGAINST their positions and come up with counterarguments to support their points.

5. Provide time for students to review sources and make notes on their own, then let each team (A and B) review their case as a group.

Worksheets like those below are available from the Online Teacher Center at **PearsonSchool.com/phgovt**

TEACHING GOVERNMENT

PROGRAM ORGANIZATION

**DIFFERENTIATED INSTRUCTION**

ASSESSMENT

PLANNING YOUR INSTRUCTION

## MAKING CLASS FUN AND MEANINGFUL

Too often, students become bored and listless in the classroom. The chief culprits for this are lessons that are filled with routine, lecture, and/or content that matters little to them. Students who experience classes that are provocative and animated are more engaged with learning and are more motivated.

**Here are some tips to manipulate the pace and rhythm of the class.**

### Strategy: Opinion Line

**Purpose:** To engage all students by making them active participants and able to defend their position on a given topic.

**How to do it:**

1. Ask students to write or think about their opinion on a topic that has answers at two extremes *(e.g., The government should use your tax money to help the poor.)*. Meanwhile, post the two extremes *(e.g., "Strongly agree" and "Strongly disagree")* at either end of the wall. If it makes sense, post "I don't know" or "neutral" in the middle.

2. After students write their answers, ask them to stand against the wall at the point where they think they stand in the opinion continuum.

3. Ask several students to explain their positions, either by choosing or asking for volunteers. Tell them that they may move if they are swayed by a classmate's argument.

4. Give students two minutes to revise their original opinion, allowing them to discuss their positions with each other and then repositioning themselves if necessary.

5. You may want to follow up by asking a question that invites students to explain their position or consider arguments made in the course of the activity.

TEACHING
GOVERNMENT

PROGRAM
ORGANIZATION

DIFFERENTIATED
INSTRUCTION

ASSESSMENT

PLANNING YOUR
INSTRUCTION

## Strategy: Jigsaw

**Purpose:** To allow students to cover one topic in-depth, becoming the instructors for the rest of the class, while allowing the class to cover large amounts of information.

### How to do it:

1. When you have many topics to cover in a short period of time, divide the class into numbered groups (e.g., 1, 2, 3, 4, . . .) and assign each group a different topic. These may be referred to as "expert groups," as the members will become "experts" in their topics.

2. Give each group a task (e.g., make a study guide, prepare a presentation) that demands that they summarize the key points and significance of the topic. For classes with lower level students, you may consider giving students a worksheet on which they record important information.

3. Divide the class into new, lettered groups (e.g., A, B, C, D. . . ) that include a member from each of the numbered groups (e.g., group A has one member from group 1, one from group 2, and so on).

4. Assign the new groups a new task that requires them to teach each other the information they learned in their numbered group (e.g., give a presentation) or requires collaboration (e.g., make a plan).

## Strategy: Conversation Wall

**Purpose:** To give students an opportunity to share ideas and reflect on the work of their classmates. (See sample below.)

### How to do it:

1. Post stimuli and "conversation boards" around the classroom. The stimuli may be student work (produced individually or in groups) or materials that are new to students, such as images or quotations. The conversation boards are blank posters or sheets of paper. Alternatively, students may be given a few sticky notes for comments.

2. Give students a set amount of time to look at the stimuli posted around the room. Each activity should have a defined objective, such as, "comment on the poster that you think is most informative and explain why" or "comment on a quotation that makes you think about the content in a different way." When possible, relate the activity to the Essential Questions for the unit or chapter.

3. Remind students that they may react to another comment as well as a stimulus.

4. Assign a student or groups of students to look at the comments from each stimulus and summarize the "conversation."

5. Use the summaries to launch a class discussion about the content.

I totally disagree with this quote. The author assumes that only political extremists vote.

"Mandatory voting would solve a lot of the problems with our current political system. Although it seems undemocratic, the result would be leaders who consider the needs of all Americans rather than those on the political extremes."
—Joe S., The Herald, Letter to the editor, 8/19/08

I would like to ask M. G. if an unexercised right means anything. What's the point of rights if we can't be bothered to vote?

Totally agree with this. We wouldn't really be free if the government forced it on us.

"Mandatory voting is in opposition to everything for which the United States stands. The option not to exercise our right to vote is just as important as the right to vote."
—M. G., The Herald, Letter to the editor, 8/19/08

I agree with Joe's solution for low voter turnout. But what other problems could mandatory voting address? That's not clear from the statement.

He probably means general lack of interest in government. If people had to vote, they would probably be more interested in the whole system.

While I agree in principle, I think it would be better for the nation if more people chose to vote.

## Understanding The Common Core State Standards: What They Mean for Social Studies Teachers

**Jeff Passe,** former president of NCSS; current Chair, Department of Secondary Education, Towson University

The Common Core State Standards Initiative was organized by the National Governors Association and the Council of Chief State School Officers to develop college and career readiness through K-12 standards in English language arts and mathematics. This enterprise is meant to be comprehensive and will ultimately include a set of social studies standards as well. The underlying principle behind the Common Core is that today's students need to develop the skills and knowledge to make them ready for college or careers after high school.

### Literacy Standards for Social Studies

A surprising twist in the language arts standards is the inclusion of literacy standards in history and social studies. This means that not only should historical and political texts be included in the language arts classroom, but language arts and reading teachers need to teach students how to apply their reading skills to primary and secondary social studies sources. Further, the Common Core standards in Language Arts set expectations for writing.

Writing standards include presenting and supporting arguments, writing informative or explanatory texts, and conducting and presenting the results of research. Writing should build in sophistication, clarity, and organization through the students' secondary years.

The inclusion of literacy standards in social studies could lead to collaboration between language arts and social studies colleagues. Consider the reading standard that requires students to determine "how Madison defines faction in Federalist No. 10." Standards such as this will challenge most language arts teachers, who may have only cursory knowledge of political and historical documents. So social studies teachers may be called upon to collaborate with their language arts colleagues.

### Helping Students Master the Common Core State Standards

Language arts teachers will not be the only ones affected by the Common Core Standards initiative. To help students master the new standards, social

> The Common Core State Standards provide a consistent, clear understanding of what students are expected to learn, so teachers and parents know what they need to do to help them. The standards are designed to be robust and relevant to the real world, reflecting the knowledge and skills that our young people need for success in college and careers. With American students fully prepared for the future, our communities will be best positioned to compete successfully in the global economy.
>
> — *Common Core State Standards Initiative*

TEACHING
GOVERNMENT

PROGRAM
ORGANIZATION

DIFFERENTIATED
INSTRUCTION

ASSESSMENT

PLANNING YOUR
INSTRUCTION

PEARSON                                                                    ALWAYS LEARNING

Understanding the Common Core   |   Why Pearson   |   How We Can Help   |   Webinars   |   Resources   |   Contact

THE COMMON CORE STATE STANDARDS

Helping Teachers and Students
Succeed in a Changing Environment

UNDERSTANDING THE COMMON CORE   |   WHY PEARSON   |   HOW WE CAN HELP

Get Help With:

Teacher Training

Pre K-12 Literacy Curriculum

Pre K-12 Math Curriculum

Assessments & Systems

School Improvement Planning

Mobile Solutions

One Source for Today & Tomorrow

Only Pearson offers complete and cohesive support to
implement the new Common Core State Standards
and provide the easiest possible transition. We
combine the resources and expertise of the world's
leading assessment company with evolving and
continually improving instructional materials, content
experts, and professional development to help you,
your teachers, and your students succeed at every
step along the way.

 • The Basics of Common Core
 • Connect with the Experts
 • Explore Aligned Literacy and Math Products
 • Your Common Core Timeline

How to Prepare

Many Pearson authors and experts helped create the
new standards. They explain, in practical terms, what
the change will mean for you.

GOING MOBILE!
Pearson eTexts for Grades 6-12 will
be available for the iPad® in 2011.
                                    LEARN MORE

START HERE
Teacher Training
See our range
of Professional
Development
courses.
            LEARN MORE

VIDEO FAQ
Experts Explain

                                    PLAY

Copyright © 2010 Pearson Education, Inc.or its affiliate(s). All rights reserved. Accessibility, Terms of Use, Privacy Statement, Rights and Permissions

For more information about how Pearson can help you implement the
Common Core State Standards, go to http://commoncore.pearsoned.com/

studies teachers will have to teach some reading
and writing skills. In the pages that follow, you
will find helpful suggestions for incorporating
literacy skills in your instruction. Success in reading social studies sources will require a curricular
plan based on gradual increases in text complexity. Without such a plan, students might have
difficulty reaching the level of reading proficiency
required by college and the workplace. Language
arts teachers can be partners in achieving the
right balance.

## Toward College and Career Readiness

Interdisciplinary collaboration is a welcome development. Secondary teachers who collaborate

will share in helping their students develop skills
that are essential to citizenship in a democracy.
Proficiency in reading historical and political texts
is required for college success and effective citizenship. Obviously, college social science courses
are filled with those types of reading, but so are
courses in business, nursing, and other professions. Because subjects like history, economics,
and law are relevant in many workplace decisions,
career success depends on one's ability to process
texts from those disciplines. Implementation may
transform the curriculum, and it may alter the very
essence of how secondary teachers work together
to achieve educational goals. Social Studies teachers can play a key role in this transformation.

## Developing Reading Skills

Due to the increased emphasis on reading required by the No Child Left Behind (NCLB) legislation, social studies teachers may be called on to help improve their students' reading skills. These skills are critical to prepare students for academic success. A teacher using a graph about exports and imports can teach math skills and social studies concepts at the same time. The connection between reading and government is especially important. Many state and local assessments require students to read and interpret informational texts. Therefore, social studies teachers may assist in raising scores by integrating reading instruction into their teaching of government content.

### How does *Magruder's American Government* Enhance Reading Skills?

Too often the text is too hard for some students, and far too easy for others. So educators "teach to the middle of the class," trying to keep everyone on board, but always worrying about all the students who are falling off both edges. By providing reading checks and differentiated instruction, *Magruder's American Government* helps all students access the material.

**Differentiated Instruction** helps meet the needs of students with reading difficulties or disabilities. By using strategies provided in the teacher lesson (such as scaffolding questions and allowing less-proficient readers to answer first), students of all levels can access the material and fully participate in class discussions.

**Reading Comprehension Worksheets** are available for each section. These help both on-level and below-level students take notes on the material and can serve as a study guide to review and reinforce learning.

**Prereading and Vocabulary Worksheets** teach students essential content terms they will need to understand and be able to use in reading, discussion, and writing tasks.

**Reading Checkpoints** help students monitor their comprehension of the text.

**Academic Vocabulary** is defined at point-of-use.

**Graphic Organizers** help struggling readers find the key points in the text and make visual connections between the section focus question and the supporting details.

**Bellringers** are warmup activities that help students recall prior knowledge or preview the content they will be learning about. The more a reader knows about the topic, context, or issue, the better his or her comprehension will be.

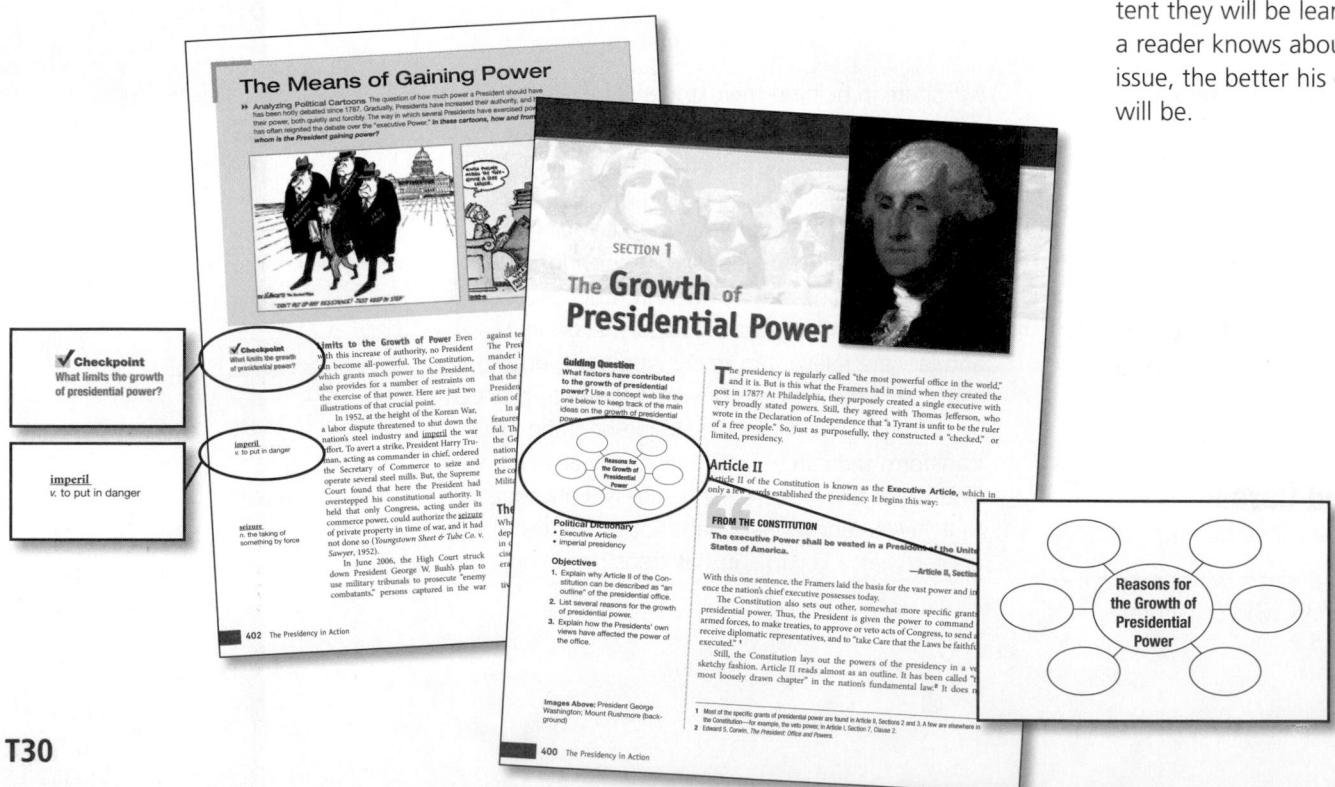

# Developing Writing Skills

Teachers often assume that if they teach content effectively, their students will be able to communicate what they have learned in writing on state assessments. However, many student falter when asked to write because they don't know how to construct a response that shows what they have learned. Teachers can help students improve their performance by embedding expository writing tasks in class activities, homework assignments, and tests throughout the year.

Take time with students to work through the process of analyzing the task and framing their response. To be successful, students will need to learn how to analyze the prompt, budget their time and answer space, plan and write their response, and then edit their first drafts. Good writing prompts are key to successful responses. A good prompt will

- test what students have been taught, whether defined by state standards or your own course outline
- communicate what is expected of students in terms of format, length, and level of detail, such as the number of examples or reasons and
- be doable in the time and space allocated for the task

A good prompt provides multiple access points to help students with different learning styles, backgrounds, and abilities engage with the task. This may be done by breaking the task into parts that build from lower- to higher- order thinking skills. This sequencing provides a point of entry for weaker students who may not be capable of completing the entire task and enables them to respond in a limited way.

## Assessing the Product

The goal of a writing program should be to empower students to assess and improve their own work. For this to happen, students need to have a clear vision of what good writing looks like and how to bring their own work up to that standard.

An effective way to communicate your expectations is through the consistent use of generic rubrics and/or scoring guides. Generic rubrics describe levels of performance on various aspects of a written task, such as writing mechanics or development of a clear thesis statement. Scoring guides, in contrast, describe levels of performance for each specific task. Teachers can use both of these tools to communicate efficiently with students about their written work.

## How Does *Magruder's American Government* Address Writing Skills?

Research shows that writing about what you read actually helps you learn new information. Government provides continuous opportunities for students to prepare and practice writing skills.

The **Skills Handbook** teaches the steps and skills needed to write informative essays. The handbook addresses several categories of writing: Expository and Research Writings, Persuasive Essays, and Writing for Assessment. The Skills Handbook contains a Writing Rubric, for students to assess and improve upon their own work.

**Document-Based Questions** provided at the end of every chapter and unit give students practice in writing.

**Assessment Rubrics** found in the unit-level All-in-One Resources, Teacher Center Online, or on CD-ROM allow teachers to provide clear expectations and consistent grading.

The **Essential Questions Journal** gives students opportunities to express their own opinions and personal experiences in essays addressing both chapter and unit level Essential Questions.

**Lesson Activities** often require students to use writing skills as they work on projects such as research papers or writing editorials or letters.

## Supporting Media Literacy

**"We are drowning in information but starved for knowledge.""**

—John Naisbitt,
*Megatrends: Ten New Directions Tranforming Our Lives*

### Defining Media Literacy

People define *media literacy* in many ways. Some educators understand it to mean teaching students how to use technology. Others see it as meaning teaching to them how to evaluate the media. In fact, we need to teach students both the technical and the critical thinking aspects of media literacy in order to equip them with the 21st Century Skills they need to navigate today's electronic and media-rich era.

Teenagers are spending more time using a wider array of technologies than ever before. What are the challenges for teachers?

- How do we channel this familiarity and time spent with technology toward technology that teaches and informs as well as entertains?

- How do we ensure that we and our students are taking full advantage of the opportunities for learning that technology in the classroom can provide?

- How do we make sure that our students are critical consumers of the media that they are surrounded by on a daily basis?

### Teaching With and About Technology

Studies indicate that students in "technology-rich environments" experience increased achievement in all major subject areas (Sivin-Kachela, 1998). By integrating technology into the classroom, teachers not only help students learn the critical tools they need to thrive in a digital age, they also enhance social studies content.

Technology provides easily accessible ways to both present core content and engage students. Audio and video bring dynamic moments to life. Primary sources provide the personal experience. The Internet unlocks a vast array of materials. Together, these materials make government come alive in the classroom.

### Teaching Critical Thinking About Media

Media can be a powerful tool not just to teach through technology, but also to teach critical thinking skills. Studies show that media literacy training increases students' ability to access, analyze, and evaluate media messages (Yates, 2001). Students need to learn to analyze what they see and hear as well as what they read. In a social studies course, sources include primary and secondary documents, quotations, political cartoons, and news reports on television, the Internet, and in newspapers. These are ideal instruments for fostering 21st Century Skills for critical thinking, including

- comparing viewpoints
- identifying bias
- evaluating evidence
- interpreting cause and effect
- decision making

By embedding these media skills into your course, you not only enhance key concepts, but also teach students key analysis skills, many of which are tested on high-stakes exams and in document-based assessments. In addition, media-literate students will become more effective consumers, decision-makers, and citizens, able to succeed in the classroom and beyond.

## Media Literacy Skills include the ability to

| Access | Analyze | Evaluate | Communicate |

### INFORMATION

Media literacy is essential for students in today's classroom as well as in the world at large. *Magruder's American Government* supports media literacy in an exciting variety of ways, helping students at all levels become more active and engaged learners. Assets on the Teacher Center Online and Student Center Online and lesson extension ideas provide opportunities to integrate media literacy.

## Access Content

Differentiated instruction is designed to help all students access content—no matter their levels of ability or learning styles. Technology is one method of information delivery that appeals to a variety of students through a variety of learning styles: visual/spatial, auditory/verbal, kinesthetic/body, and logical/mathematical. The program features multimedia assets for busy on-the-go learners and teachers.

- Student Edition Online (with English and Spanish audio)
- Political Dictionary (English and Spanish)
- Audio Review
- How Government Works
- Color Transparencies
- Audio Tours
- Interactivities

## Enrich and Reinforce Learning

Authentic learning means students will be able to transfer knowledge to new situations. When students use and apply their understandings or further explore concepts, learning becomes more real. Using technology to extend the lesson reinforces learning and improves the retention level of students. These activities make government more relevant and meaningful.

- WebQuests
- American Government Essential Questions Videos

## Assessment

Monitoring comprehension can take form in multiple ways. For some, using the online format is more engaging and therefore gives more motivation to succeed.

- Checkpoint Quiz Game
- Checkpoint Test
- Exam*View* Test Bank
- Online Student Self-Tests

For further information about these features, see the section on Assessment.

> " Media literacy is...absolutely critical. It's going to make the difference between whether the kids are a tool of the mass media or whether the mass media is a tool for kids to use. "
> —Linda Ellerbee, producer/host, *Nick News*

# The Need for Assessment

## Why Do We Need to Assess Student Learning?

Assessment should be viewed as a process, not an activity, that quickly evaluates instruction or student learning. As such, the goal of assessment is to focus, guide, and support instruction and, subsequently, learning. When making an assessment, the teacher isn't just "testing," but rather making thoughtful observations about the student's strengths and weaknesses. It is not a value judgment (good/bad), but an analysis of student performance against specific goals and criteria. Assessment is a process, whose goal is to assemble information from a variety of sources.

Assessment happens constantly, though you probably don't give a quiz every day. It takes a variety of formats. Traditional assessments focus on written work, such as essays. Performance assessments are geared toward students who prefer to show what they've learned in a less verbal or written format. Alternative assessments range from metacognitive activities, such as journals, to student-generated assessments, such as portfolios.

## Formative Assessment

Formative assessment may be self-assessment or informal assessment by the teacher. It provides feedback to modify teaching and learning activities. Formative assessments are conducted throughout the instructional process to monitor students' progress and provide feedback on strengths and weaknesses. The key is feedback. Feedback allows students to correct conceptual errors and encourages instructors to modify their methods. It provides students with an understanding of what they are doing well and links to classroom learning, and it gives specific input to adjust the learning process.

## Summative Assessment

Summative assessments are formal assessments used to judge progress. They are meant to gauge student learning at particular points in time. Common summative assessments occur at the ends of chapters or units or school terms to determine what students know and do not know. Like formative assessments, they reveal areas that need review before moving on to new topics.

## Balancing Assessments

Proper utilization of assessment tools in the classroom will lead to greater learning. Incorporating a variety of assessments (differing both in format and product), observations, and communications with and between students allows for a more fully developed picture of students' learning processes. The more information a teacher has about students, the better he or she can determine teaching effectiveness and the quality of student learning.

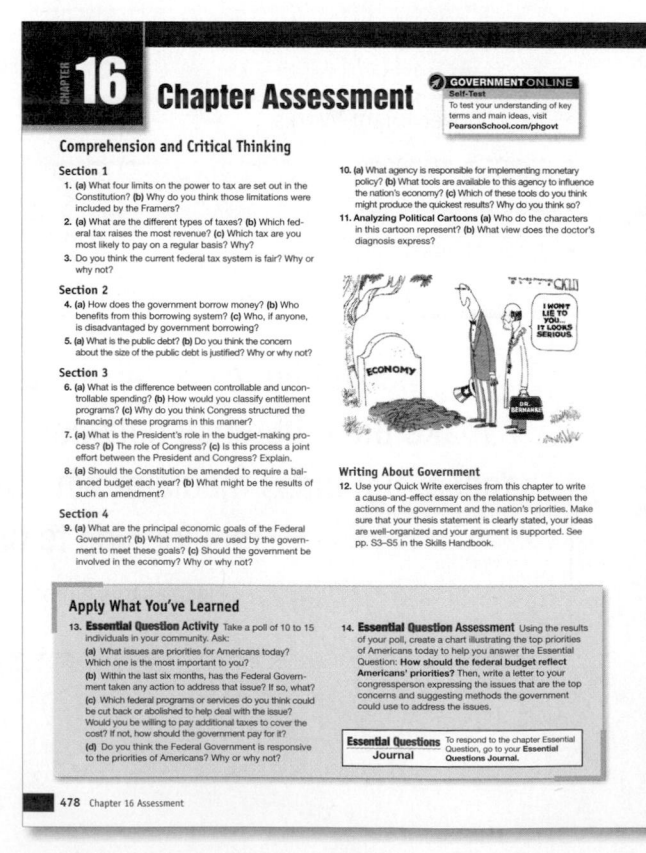

# Assessment Informs Instruction

Assessment is a never-ending cycle. With the spotlight now on improving student performance and providing differentiated instruction, it is essential to use assessment to target goals, identify strategies to achieve results, monitor progress, and assess results to inform lesson planning.

## Using AYP Monitoring Assessments

The key to success is using a variety of assessment tools coupled with data analysis and decision making. The AYP Monitoring Assessments in this program provides several types of assessments.

| Types of Assessment | AYP Monitoring Assessments |
|---|---|
| **Screening assessments** are brief procedures used to identify at-risk students who are not ready to work at grade level. | Screening tests identify students who are reading 2–3 years below grade level. |
| **Diagnostic assessments** provide a more in-depth analysis of strengths and weaknesses that can help teachers make instructional decisions and plan intervention strategies. | Diagnostic tests focus on social studies skills, including subtests in geographic literacy, visual analysis, critical thinking and reading, as well as vocabulary and writing. |
| **Progress monitoring assessments** (sometimes referred to as benchmark tests) provide an ongoing, longitudinal record of student achievement detailing individual student progress toward meeting end-of-year and end-of-schooling grade-level, district, or state standards. | Unit tests assess progress toward mastery of the content, and offer remediation recommendations tied to specific program content for each question. |
| **Summative assessments** judge students' achievement at a particular point in a course of study. Large-scale assessments, such as state tests and standardized tests, can be used to determine whether individual students have met the expected standards and whether a school system has made adequate progress in improving its performance. | Use the unit tests to measure student progress toward large-scale assessment goals. |

# ASSESSMENT

## Ongoing Assessment

Assessments may fall in either the formative or the summative category. However, depending on their use, the following evaluations may provide information for both categories.

### Formative Assessments

**AYP Monitoring Assessments,** as previously described, help you to understand where your students are in the learning process and to determine an effective strategy for moving them to the next stage.

**Quizzes** measure how students are progressing in their skills and understanding of subject matter. These provide snapshot assessments: What have students learned and what do you need to revisit? These quizzes can be found in the Teacher Resource Library Online and on CD-ROM, as well as in the Exam*View* Test Bank.

**Exam*View* Test Bank** questions assess understanding and foster remediation by providing text page numbers for quick references to content.

**Online Assessment** assigns content and tracks student progress to assess learning.

**Teacher's Edition** includes remediation suggestions for section assessments to reteach key concepts to struggling students.

**Section Assessment Questions** require students to apply the information they have learned to answer the section focus question and other content-based questions.

**Student Self-Assessments** give students frequent and varied opportunities to check comprehension and reflect on learning. By taking advantage of these opportunities for personal and peer feedback, students become aware of their strengths and weaknesses.

**Rubrics** enable students to evaluate their own

work. *Assessment Rubrics* found in the unit-level All-in-One Resources, on the Teacher Center Online, and on CD-ROM includes reproducible rubrics for students and instructions for teacher rubric use.

### Summative Assessment

**Exam*View* Test Bank** allows teachers to easily create tests from banks of thousands of questions, which can be sorted by difficulty levels to provide leveled quizzes and tests.

**Essential Questions Journal** provides students with the opportunity to examine and reflect upon what they have learned.

**WebQuests** encourage students to explore the Essential Questions using technology and the Internet. Students develop products that demonstrate their creativity and critical thinking processes.

**Chapter and Unit Activities** provide opportunities for students to transfer their learning and demonstrate their application of concepts to different situations.

**Document-Based Assessments** require students to synthesize information and draw conclusions. As they defend their positions, students demonstrate their critical thinking skills.

**Rubrics** can also be used as a summative evaluation of understanding.

**AYP Monitoring Assessments** test how well students have mastered the standards.

# Encouraging Student Self-Assessment

As mentioned earlier, formative assessment is self-assessment. An important aspect of the philosophy of *Understanding by Design* instruction, as explained by Grant Wiggins, is the "need to help students self-monitor, self-assess, and self-adjust their work, individually and collectively, as the work progresses . . . self-understanding is arguably the most important facet of understanding for lifelong learning." (See *Understanding by Design*, p. 214.) Successful people take time to reflect on what they have accomplished and what needs to be adjusted as they work toward their goals. Students need to evaluate their own progress and accept responsibility to manage and adjust their own learning. As part of the educational process, teachers must help students understand the importance of and methods used to achieve such reflection and self-evaluation.

### Ways To Develop Self-Assessment General Strategies

- Set aside a few minutes at the middle and end of the lesson to ask: What have we learned? What questions do you have about this?

- Require that a self-assessment be attached to every formal product or performance.

- Include a one-minute essay at the end of a class, in which students summarize the two or three main points and the questions that they still have.

- Have students write their questions on an index card as homework. Then, in small groups, have them find the common issues and use these questions to begin class.

## Checking Understanding

Students also should use the following checks of their understanding of skills and concepts offered by *Magruder's American Government* before moving on to the next topic.

**Reading Checkpoints** reinforce and confirm students' understanding.

**Caption Questions** enhance critical thinking skills and maximize the effectiveness of art, graphics, charts, and narrative.

**Checkpoint Quiz Game** lets students assess their understanding of content and find instant remediation online.

**Scaffolded Section Assessment** questions ease students into the review, then challenge them with more advanced questions.

**Quick Study Guide and Chapter Assessment** enable students to check their understanding and prepare for test-taking success.

**Rubrics** enable students to judge their own work against desired criteria.

TEACHING GOVERNMENT

PROGRAM ORGANIZATION

DIFFERENTIATED INSTRUCTION

ASSESSMENT

PLANNING YOUR INSTRUCTION

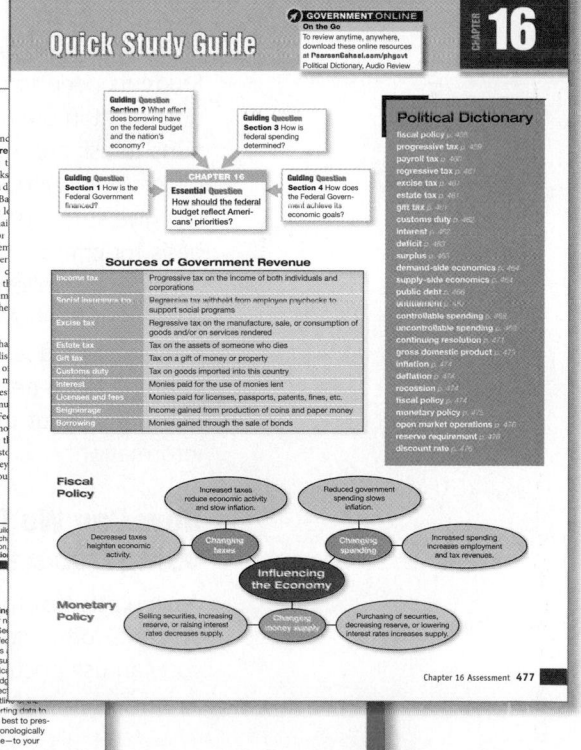

# The Value of Document-Based Assessment

For years, teachers have understood the value of having students read and analyze primary source documents to acquire knowledge and develop critical thinking skills. Document analysis has become an important assessment tool as well. Both the College Board Advanced Placement examinations and many state-mandated tests use document-based questions. Many of these include a writing task in which students think critically about a variety of sources, form opinions guided by a prompt, and then present their analyses in an essay.

Primary sources are records produced at the time of the event or period that they describe, or soon thereafter. These sources may include written accounts, such as diaries, speech transcripts, government records, and law codes. They can also include period cartoons and photographs. They are distinct from secondary sources, which are produced well after the events that they describe and interpret.

## How Do We Teach With Primary Sources?

Teaching students to examine primary and secondary sources involves asking the right questions. Students need to understand the purpose of a document in order to analyze it. The first questions to ask are those for which students can find concrete answers. The answers to these questions will give students the information that forms a basis for critical thinking. From there, students can consider the following questions: What kind of document is it? Who wrote this document? Who is the intended audience? Why was this document written? Ultimately, students need to ask their own questions about the document and evaluate the information.

## How Can We Differentiate Instruction Using Documents?

As you attempt to differentiate instruction for students' differing abilities and learning styles, you can use document analysis for small group or whole class discussion, individual written reports, in-class presentations, role-playing, or other instructional strategies. Students need direct instruction in using primary sources and handling conflicting interpretations, as well as repeated opportunities to practice these skills both in class and independently. Regardless of the strategy, teachers must generate one or two well-crafted questions about a document. This may be more difficult than it appears at first glance. The purpose of the questions is to help students find the kernel of information that the document offers. These questions can be used to spark a class discussion or as a focus for independent practice.

The documents can also be used to help students apply the concepts they are learning to new situations and to extend that learning beyond the textbook. The analysis of the documents can be a springboard to a plethora of activities, such as preparing oral presentations in which students take a stand on an issue, writing persuasive letters to an editor, designing posters to illustrate a point, and more.

## What Skills Are Developed?

Working with primary sources will not only increase students' critical thinking skills and their appreciation of government principles, but will also help to prepare them for the document-based questions on state and College Board examinations and reinforce the 21st Century Skills needed to become effective citizens. The skills students will develop include the following:

- Applying information they have learned in their study of government
- Evaluating the reliability of sources
- Identifying the point of view of those sources and determining bias
- Identifying problems and considering alternative solutions
- Considering issues from multiple perspectives
- Building support for a viewpoint by choosing accurate, relevant evidence

TEACHING
GOVERNMENT

PROGRAM
ORGANIZATION

DIFFERENTIATED
INSTRUCTION

ASSESSMENT

PLANNING YOUR
INSTRUCTION

# Document-Based Assessment

## Addressing the Rising Cost of Healthcare

The costs of entitlement programs and the constraints they place on the federal budget have been debated at great length. Most Americans agree that these programs are critical to the public's well-being, however. As the documents below illustrate, keeping these programs going without undermining others is proving to be a very difficult fiscal challenge.

### Document 1

*identify point of view*

In the United States a large and growing [share of] both federal and state expenditures is for [subsidized] health insurance. In 1975, federal spending [on Medicare] and Medicaid was about 6 percent of total [non-interest] federal spending. Today, that share is about 23 percent. Because of rising costs of health care and the aging of the population, the CBO projects that, without reform, Medicare and Medicaid will be about 35 percent of non-interest federal spending in 2025. This trend implies increasingly difficult tradeoffs for legislators and taxpayers, as higher government spending on health care spending will . . . require reductions in other government programs, higher taxes, or larger budget deficits.

—Ben S. Bernanke, Chairman,
Federal Reserve, 2008

### Document 2

[If th]e major entitlement programs grow as forecast, [our ch]ildren will be forced to choose between mas[sive ta]x increases, near-elimination of all government programs outside of entitlements (including defense and essential services), or some combination. . . . Because of these rising entitlement obligations, ensuring long-term fiscal stability requires much more than addressing current spending and deficits, important as that is. Also necessary is finding a means of controlling the costs of the major entitlement programs, without compromising their essential functions.

—Katherine Baicker,
Council of Economic Advisors, 2005

### Document 3

*media literacy*

*critical thinking and writing skills*

*comprehension questions*

**Federal Healthcare Expenditures**

SOURCE: Centers for Medicare & Medicaid Services      * Estimated

Use your knowledge of financing government and the documents above to answer Questions 1–3.

1. What is the main point of Document 3?
   A. Controllable expenditures are becoming uncontrollable.
   B. Entitlement programs are too costly.
   C. Revenue from healthcare has increased.
   D. Subsidized healthcare costs have risen considerably over time.

2. What concerns are discussed in both Document 1 and Document 2?

3. **Pull It Together** Given the increasing costs of entitlement programs, do you think the Federal Government should continue to provide subsidized healthcare? Why or why not?

*transfer knowledge*

**GOVERNMENT** ONLINE
**Documents**
To find more primary sources [on] the cost of healthcare, visit
**PearsonSchool.com/phgov**

Chapter 16 Assessment **479**

## Simplify Your Planning Using This Program

### Where Do I Start?

*Right here!* These pages will guide you through the program's unique organization and describe the many resources that will enrich your teaching.

### How Do I Teach the Unit?

Begin each unit with the Unit Opener, previewing the content to come with the students. Use the questions at the end of the Unit to prepare students to answer the Essential Question.

### What Should I Use to Plan and Prepare?

Start your planning with the Pacing Guide to give you a time frame for the year's curriculum. Then use the Lesson Planner before each section to give you a summary of the lesson plan in the Teacher's Edition, with suggestions for incorporating resources into your instruction.

### How Do I Differentiate Instruction?

*Magruder's American Government* provides unprecedented opportunities for differentiated instruction:

- **Teacher's Edition** provides a core lesson for the entire class, but within that lesson you will find strategies and modified instruction geared toward different levels of student ability and learning styles.
- **All-in-One** provides leveled resources for each section and chapter to support differentiation.
- **Graphic Organizers** on the section opener give struggling readers additional support.
- **Government Online** provides students with another format to access the material.

### What Are These Features?

- **Red Boxes** Within the core lesson plan, you will notice red boxes labeled **L1**, **L2**, **L3**, or **L4**. These denote differentiation suggestions for different levels of students. In planning your lesson, you should review the lesson plan and resources to determine which differentiation suggestions are appropriate for your class. "**ELL**" or "**LPR**" following the label denotes an activity tailored specifically for English Language Learners or Less Proficient Readers. Many teachers, however, find these strategies helpful for many students.

- **"Bellringer"** You have a lot to do at the beginning of the class: attendance, returning papers, and other housekeeping. These Bellringers are short activities that engage students upon their arrival, allowing you to get organized. They are best used consistently, providing a routine for students to begin working without explicit instructions to do so.

- **Pressed for Time** There is a lot of material to cover in *Magruder's American Government*. We know that most of you teach several subjects and may be new to teaching government. On the chapter level, we suggest an activity that will help you cover a chapter in a short amount of time.

- **Block Scheduling** This format allows for greater depth and flexibility in education. For you, we provide a variety of resources, strategies, and activities to stimulate and engage students.

- **Focus on the Basics** On the section level, we summarize the most important points to help you focus on the essential facts, concepts, and enduring understandings that students must grasp. This feature is designed to be a helpful reminder in the three minutes between periods, or when you choose to create your own lesson plan to cover the content.

## How Does the Program Help Me Develop as a Teacher?

**The Teacher's Edition provides these built-in professional development features:**

- **Lesson plans** Margin notes provide pedagogy, strategies, and activities to teach and extend the content.

- **Differentiated Instruction** Lessons provide leveled instruction, giving support for struggling students, modifications of lessons to address cultural differences, and enrichment for advanced students.

- **Background Notes** Notes provide background on the topic, historical development of issues, and connections to students' lives in order to enhance your effectiveness as a teacher.

- **Debates** Thought-provoking quotations offer a starting point for classroom debates.

## How Can I Use Technology In My Classroom?

*Magruder's American Government* allows you to teach the entire program without using the print products. It contains all of the components of the program in one central location: all of the print and activity-based materials *plus* integrated videos, animations, interactive practice activities, and audio. You will navigate through the program by the Table of Contents, exactly as you would in the textbook. In addition to serving as a stand-alone, the digital product can also support a print-based approach, providing material for classroom presentations, assessment, lesson planning, and reporting.

TEACHING
GOVERNMENT

PROGRAM
ORGANIZATION

DIFFERENTIATED
INSTRUCTION

ASSESSMENT

PLANNING
YOUR
INSTRUCTION

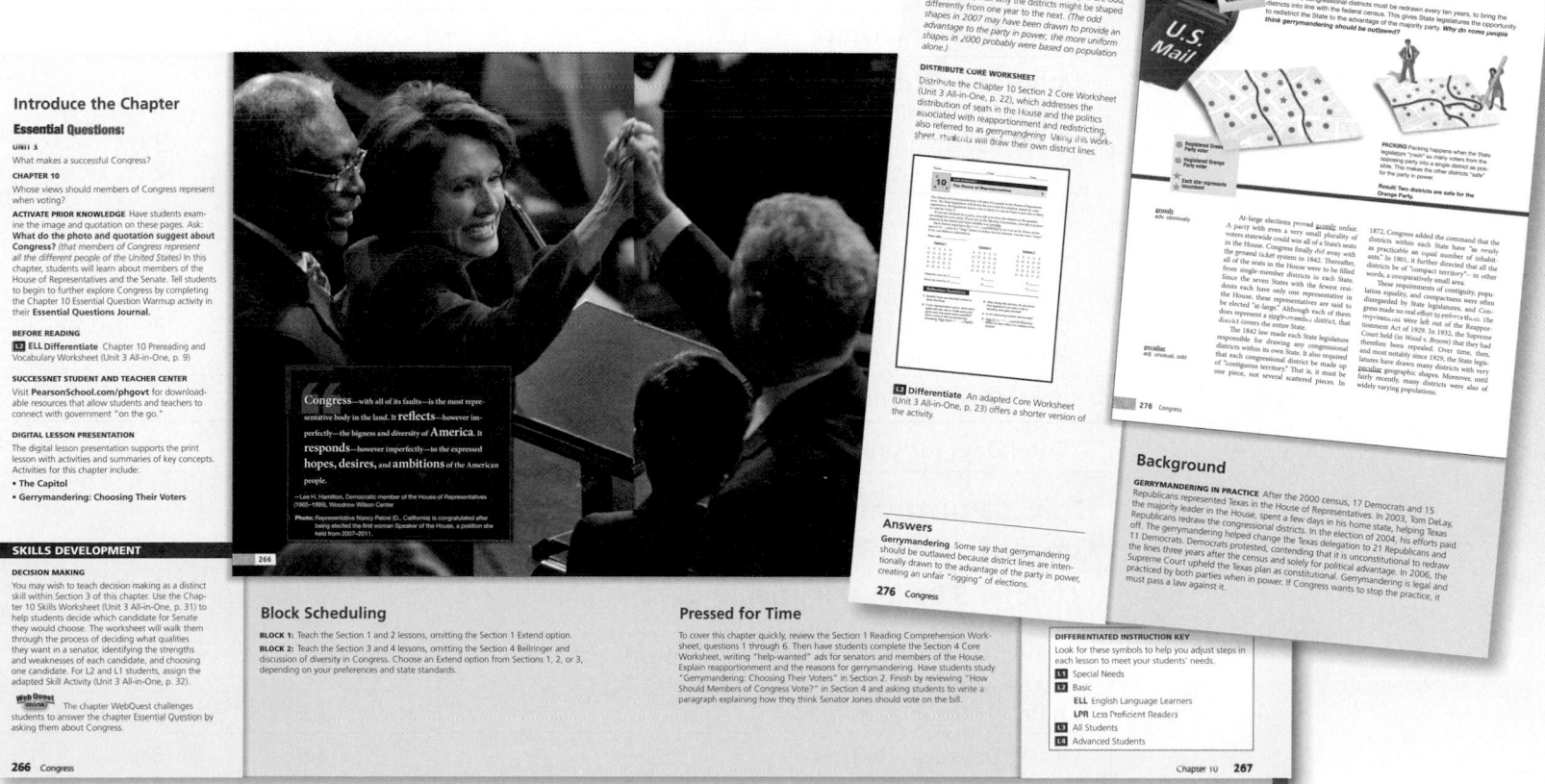

## Year and Semester Pacing Guides

The following pacing guides show how the units and chapters of *Magruder's American Government* can be adapted to fit your specific course focus and time constraints. The year guide is representative of a course based on 36 weeks or 180 days. The semester guide is representative of a course that lasts for 18 weeks or 90 days.

| 1 Period = 50 minutes<br>1 Block = 100 minutes | Semester Course | | Full-Year Course | |
|---|---|---|---|---|
| | Periods | Blocks | Periods | Blocks |
| **Unit 1 Foundations of American Government** | | | | |
| **Chapter 1 Principles of Government** | | | | |
| 1 Government and the State | 1.5 | .75 | 3 | 1.5 |
| 2 Forms of Government | 1 | .5 | 2 | 1 |
| 3 Basic Concepts of Democracy | 1.5 | .75 | 3 | 1.5 |
| Total Days for Chapter | 4 | 2 | 8 | 4 |
| **Chapter 2 Origins of American Government** | | | | |
| 1 Our Political Beginnings | 1 | .5 | 2 | 1 |
| 2 The Coming of Independence | 1 | .5 | 2 | 1 |
| Declaration of Independence | 1 | .5 | 2 | 1 |
| 3 The Critical Period | .5 | .25 | 1 | .5 |
| 4 Creating the Constitution | 1.5 | .75 | 3 | 1.5 |
| 5 Ratifying the Constitution | .5 | .25 | 1 | .5 |
| Total Days for Chapter | 5.5 | 2.75 | 11 | 5.5 |
| **Chapter 3  The Constitution** | | | | |
| 1 Basic Principles | 2 | 1 | 4 | 2 |
| 2 Formal Amendment | 1.5 | .75 | 3 | 1.5 |
| 3 Change by Other Means | 1 | .5 | 2 | 1 |
| Total Days for Chapter | 4.5 | 2.25 | 9 | 4.5 |
| **Chapter 4  Federalism** | | | | |
| 1 Federalism: Powers Divided | 1.5 | .75 | 3 | 1.5 |
| 2 The National Government and the 50 States | 1 | .5 | 2 | 1 |
| 3 Interstate Relations | 1 | .5 | 2 | 1 |
| Total Days for Chapter | 3.5 | 1.75 | 7 | 3.5 |
| Total Days for Unit | 17.5 | 8.75 | 35 | 17.5 |
| **Unit 2 Political Behavior:<br>Government By the People** | | | | |
| **Chapter 5 Political Parties** | | | | |
| 1 Parties and What They Do | .5 | .25 | 1 | .5 |
| 2 Two-Party System in American History | 1 | .5 | 2 | 1 |
| 3 The Minor Parties | 1 | .5 | 2 | 1 |
| 4 Party Organization | .5 | .25 | 1 | .5 |
| Total Days for Chapter | 3 | 1.5 | 6 | 3 |

| | Semester Course Periods | Blocks | Full-Year Course Periods | Blocks |
|---|---|---|---|---|
| **Chapter 6 Voters and Voter Behavior** | | | | |
| 1 The Right to Vote | 1 | .5 | 2 | 1 |
| 2 Voter Qualifications | 1 | .5 | 2 | 1 |
| 3 Suffrage and Civil Rights | 1.5 | .75 | 3 | 1.5 |
| 4 Voter Behavior | 1.5 | .75 | 3 | 1.5 |
| Total Days for Chapter | 5 | 2.5 | 10 | 5 |
| **Chapter 7 The Electoral Process** | | | | |
| 1 The Nominating Process | 1.5 | .75 | 3 | 1.5 |
| 2 Elections | 1.5 | .75 | 3 | 1.5 |
| 3 Money and Elections | 1 | .5 | 2 | 1 |
| Total Days for Chapter | 4 | 2 | 8 | 4 |
| **Chapter 8 Mass Media and Public Opinion** | | | | |
| 1 The Formation of Public Opinion | 1 | .5 | 2 | 1 |
| 2 Measuring Public Opinion | 1 | .5 | 2 | 1 |
| 3 The Mass Media | 1 | .5 | 2 | 1 |
| Total Days for Chapter | 3 | 1.5 | 6 | 3 |
| **Chapter 9 Interest Groups** | | | | |
| 1 The Nature of Interest Groups | .5 | .25 | 1 | .5 |
| 2 Types of Interest Groups | .5 | .25 | 1 | .5 |
| 3 Interest Groups at Work | 1 | .5 | 2 | 1 |
| Total Days for Chapter | 2 | 1 | 4 | 2 |
| Total Days for Unit | 17 | 8.5 | 34 | 17 |

## Unit 3 The Legislative Branch

| | Semester Course Periods | Blocks | Full-Year Course Periods | Blocks |
|---|---|---|---|---|
| **Chapter 10 Congress** | | | | |
| 1 The National Legislature | .5 | .25 | 1 | .5 |
| 2 The House of Representatives | 1 | .5 | 2 | 1 |
| 3 The Senate | 1 | .5 | 2 | 1 |
| 4 The Members of Congress | .5 | .25 | 1 | .5 |
| Total Days for Chapter | 3 | 1.5 | 6 | 3 |
| **Chapter 11 Powers of Congress** | | | | |
| 1 The Expressed Powers of Money and Commerce | 1.5 | .75 | 3 | 1.5 |
| 2 The Other Expressed Powers | 1 | .5 | 2 | 1 |
| 3 The Implied Powers | 1 | .5 | 2 | 1 |
| 4 The Nonlegislative Powers | .5 | .25 | 1 | .5 |
| Total Days for Chapter | 4 | 2 | 8 | 4 |
| **Chapter 12 Congress in Action** | | | | |
| 1 Congress Organizes | 1 | .5 | 2 | 1 |
| 2 Committees in Congress | .5 | .25 | 1 | .5 |
| 3 Making Law: The House | 1 | .5 | 2 | 1 |
| 4 Making Law: The Senate | 1 | .5 | 2 | 1 |
| Total Days for Chapter | 3.5 | 1.75 | 7 | 3.5 |
| Total Days for Unit | 10.5 | 5.25 | 21 | 10.5 |

TEACHING GOVERNMENT

PROGRAM ORGANIZATION

DIFFERENTIATED INSTRUCTION

ASSESSMENT

PLANNING YOUR INSTRUCTION

| | Semester Course | | Full-Year Course | |
|---|---|---|---|---|
| | Periods | Blocks | Periods | Blocks |
| **Unit 4 The Executive Branch** | | | | |
| **Chapter 13 The Presidency** | | | | |
| 1 The President's Job Description | .5 | .25 | 1 | .5 |
| 2 Presidential Succession and the Vice Presidency | .5 | .25 | 1 | .5 |
| 3 Presidential Selection: The Framers' Plan | .5 | .25 | 1 | .5 |
| 4 Presidential Nominations | 1.5 | .75 | 3 | 1.5 |
| 5 The Presidential Election | 1 | .5 | 2 | 1 |
| Total Days for Chapter | 4 | 2 | 8 | 4 |
| **Chapter 14 The Presidency in Action** | | | | |
| 1 The Growth of Presidential Power | .5 | .25 | 1 | .5 |
| 2 The Executive Powers | .5 | .25 | 1 | .5 |
| 3 Diplomatic and Military Powers | 1 | .5 | 2 | 1 |
| 4 Legislative and Judicial Powers | .5 | .25 | 1 | .5 |
| Total Days for Chapter | 2.5 | 1.25 | 5 | 2.5 |
| **Chapter 15 Government at Work: The Bureaucracy** | | | | |
| 1 The Federal Bureaucracy | .5 | .25 | 1 | .5 |
| 2 Executive Office of the President | .5 | .25 | 1 | .5 |
| 3 The Cabinet Departments | 1 | .5 | 2 | 1 |
| 4 Independent Agencies | 1 | .5 | 2 | 1 |
| Total Days for Chapter | 3 | 1.5 | 6 | 3 |
| **Chapter 16 Financing Government** | | | | |
| 1 Taxes and Other Revenue | .5 | .25 | 1 | .5 |
| 2 Borrowing and the Public Debt | .5 | .25 | 1 | .5 |
| 3 Spending and the Budget | .5 | .25 | 1 | .5 |
| 4 Fiscal and Monetary Policy | .5 | .25 | 1 | .5 |
| Total Days for Chapter | 2 | 1 | 4 | 2 |
| **Chapter 17 Foreign Policy and National Defense** | | | | |
| 1 Foreign Affairs and Diplomacy | 1 | .5 | 2 | 1 |
| 2 National Security | .5 | .25 | 1 | .5 |
| 3 American Foreign Policy Overview | 1.5 | .75 | 3 | 1.5 |
| 4 Foreign Aid and Alliances | 1 | .5 | 2 | 1 |
| Total Days for Chapter | 4 | 2 | 8 | 4 |
| Total Days for Unit | 15.5 | 7.75 | 31 | 15.5 |
| **Unit 5 The Judicial Branch** | | | | |
| **Chapter 18 The Federal Court System** | | | | |
| 1 The National Judiciary | .5 | .25 | 1 | .5 |
| 2 The Inferior Courts | .5 | .25 | 1 | .5 |
| 3 The Supreme Court | 1.5 | .75 | 3 | 1.5 |
| 4 The Special Courts | .5 | .25 | 1 | .5 |
| Total Days for Chapter | 3 | 1.5 | 6 | 3 |
| **Chapter 19 Civil Liberties: First Amendment Freedoms** | | | | |
| 1 The Unalienable Rights | 1.5 | .75 | 3 | 1.5 |
| 2 Freedom of Religion | 1.5 | .75 | 3 | 1.5 |
| 3 Freedom of Speech and Press | 1.5 | .75 | 3 | 1.5 |
| 4 Freedom of Assembly and Petition | 1 | .5 | 2 | 1 |
| Total Days for Chapter | 5.5 | 2.75 | 11 | 5.5 |

| | Semester Course Periods | Semester Course Blocks | Full-Year Course Periods | Full-Year Course Blocks |
|---|---|---|---|---|
| **Chapter 20 Civil Liberties: Protecting Individual Rights** | | | | |
| 1 Due Process of Law | 1 | .5 | 2 | 1 |
| 2 Freedom and Security of the Person | 1 | .5 | 2 | 1 |
| 3 Rights of the Accused | 1.5 | .75 | 3 | 1.5 |
| 4 Punishment | .5 | .25 | 1 | .5 |
| Total Days for Chapter | 4 | 2 | 8 | 4 |
| **Chapter 21 Civil Rights: Equal Justice Under Law** | | | | |
| 1 Diversity and Discrimination | .5 | .25 | 1 | .5 |
| 2 Equality Before the Law | 2 | 1 | 4 | 2 |
| 3 Federal Civil Rights Laws | 1.5 | .75 | 3 | 1.5 |
| 4 American Citizenship | 1 | .5 | 2 | 1 |
| Total Days for Chapter | 5 | 2.5 | 10 | 5 |
| Total Days for Unit | 17.5 | 8.75 | 35 | 17.5 |

## Unit 6 Comparative Political and Economic Systems

| | Semester Course Periods | Semester Course Blocks | Full-Year Course Periods | Full-Year Course Blocks |
|---|---|---|---|---|
| **Chapter 22 Comparative Political Systems** | | | | |
| 1 Origins of the Modern State | 1 | .5 | 2 | 1 |
| 2 Ideas and Revolutions | .5 | .25 | 1 | .5 |
| 3 Transitions to Democracy | .5 | .25 | 1 | .5 |
| 4 Case Studies in Democracy | .5 | .25 | 1 | .5 |
| Total Days for Chapter | 2.5 | 1.25 | 5 | 2.5 |
| **Chapter 23 Comparative Economic Systems** | | | | |
| 1 Capitalism | .5 | .25 | 1 | .5 |
| 2 Socialism and Communism | .5 | .25 | 1 | .5 |
| 3 The United States in a Global Economy | .5 | .25 | 1 | .5 |
| Total Days for Chapter | 1.5 | .75 | 3 | 1.5 |
| Total Days for Unit | 4 | 2 | 8 | 4 |

## Unit 7 Participating in State and Local Government

| | Semester Course Periods | Semester Course Blocks | Full-Year Course Periods | Full-Year Course Blocks |
|---|---|---|---|---|
| **Chapter 24 Governing the States** | | | | |
| 1 State Constitutions | 1 | .5 | 2 | 1 |
| 2 State Legislatures | .5 | .25 | 1 | .5 |
| 3 The Governor and State Administration | 1 | .5 | 2 | 1 |
| 4 In the Courtroom | .5 | .25 | 1 | .5 |
| 5 The Courts and Their Judges | 1 | .5 | 2 | 1 |
| Total Days for Chapter | 4 | 2 | 8 | 4 |
| **Chapter 25 Local Government and Finance** | | | | |
| 1 Counties, Towns, and Townships | 1 | .5 | 2 | 1 |
| 2 Cities and Metropolitan Areas | 1 | .5 | 2 | 1 |
| 3 Providing Vital Services | 1 | .5 | 2 | 1 |
| 4 Financing State and Local Government | 1 | .5 | 2 | 1 |
| Total Days for Chapter | 4 | 2 | 8 | 4 |
| Total Days for Unit | 8 | 4 | 16 | 8 |

## Chapter Resources

### Introduce the chapter
- American Government Essential Questions Video
- WebQuests
- Essential Questions Journal

### Additional Support
- All-in-One Teaching Resources
- Differentiation suggestions in each lesson
- Government Online interactivities
- Color Transparencies

### Assessment
- Document-Based Assessment
- ExamView Test Bank CD-ROM
- Online Assessment
- Online Student Self-Tests
- Section Quizzes (All-in-One Resources)
- Chapter Tests A and B (All-in-One Resources)
- AYP Monitoring Assessments
- Assessment Rubrics

---

## Essential Questions:

**UNIT 1** What should be the goals of government?
**CHAPTER 1** Is government necessary?

### Government Online Student Center includes
- Interactive textbook with audio
- American Government Essential Questions Video
- WebQuests
- Audio Tours
- Interactivities
- Student Self-Tests

### Government Online Teacher Center includes
- Online Teacher's Edition with lesson planner
- Online Lecture Notes
- Teacher's Resource Library with All-in-One Resources, color transparencies, and an alternative lesson plan
- Online Assessment

Teacher Center
at PearsonSchool.com/phgovt

---

## SECTION 1

### GOVERNMENT AND THE STATE

**Guiding Question:** What is government and what is its purpose?

### Summary of Teaching Strategies
Students will identify the characteristics and theories of the origins of states, and study the Preamble of the Constitution as a means of understanding the purpose of government.

### Differentiated Resources
- **L2 Prereading and Vocabulary Worksheet** (p. 7)
- **L3 L2 Reading Comprehension Worksheets** (pp. 10, 11)
- **L3 L2 Core Worksheets** (pp. 12, 14)
- **L4 L3 Extend Worksheet** (p. 16)
- **L2 Extend Activity** (p. 18)
- **L3 Quiz A** (p. 19)   **L2 Quiz B** (p. 20)

### Student Objectives
- Define government and the basic powers every government holds.
- Describe the four defining characteristics of a state.
- Identify four theories that attempt to explain the origin of the state.
- Understand the purpose of government in the United States and other countries.

---

## SECTION 2

### FORMS OF GOVERNMENT

**Guiding Question:** What are some forms of government in the world today?

### Summary of Teaching Strategies
Students will define various forms of government, including democracies and dictatorships.

### Differentiated Resources
- **L3 L2 Reading Comprehension Worksheets** (pp. 21, 22)
- **L3 Core Worksheet** (p. 23)
- **L3 Quiz A** (p. 25)   **L2 Quiz B** (p. 26)

### Student Objectives
- Classify governments according to three sets of characteristics.
- Define systems of government based on who can participate.
- Identify different ways that power can be distributed, geographically, within a state.
- Describe a government by the distribution of power between the executive branch and legislative branch.

TEACHING
GOVERNMENT

PROGRAM
ORGANIZATION

DIFFERENTIATED
INSTRUCTION

ASSESSMENT

PLANNING
YOUR
INSTRUCTION

## SECTION 3

### BASIC CONCEPTS OF DEMOCRACY

**Guiding Question:** What are the basic concepts of democracy?

### Summary of Teaching Strategies
Students will analyze the five basic concepts of democracy, and explore the free enterprise system.

### Differentiated Resources
- **L3 L2 Reading Comprehension Worksheets** (pp. 27, 28)
- **L3 L2 ELL Bellringer Worksheets** (pp. 29, 30)
- **L3 Core Worksheet** (p. 31)
- **L2 Extend Activity** (p. 35)
- **L3 L2 Skills Worksheets** (pp. 33, 34)
- **L3 Quiz A** (p. 36)   **L2 Quiz B** (p. 37)
- **L3 Chapter Test A** (p. 38)
- **L2 Chapter Test B** (p. 41)

### Student Objectives
- Understand the elements of democracy.
- Analyze the connections between democracy and the free enterprise system.

---

**DIFFERENTIATED INSTRUCTION KEY**

**L1** Special Needs             **L3** All Students

**L2** Basic includes            **L4** Advanced Students

**ELL** English Language Learners

**LPR** Less Proficient Readers

## Chapter Resources

**Introduce the chapter**
- American Government Essential Questions Video
- WebQuests
- Essential Questions Journal

**Additional Support**
- All-in-One Teaching Resources
- Differentiation suggestions in each lesson
- Government Online interactivities
- Color Transparencies

**Assessment**
- Document-Based Assessment
- ExamView Test Bank CD-ROM
- Online Assessment
- Online Student Self-Tests
- Section Quizzes (All-in-One Resources)
- Chapter Tests A and B (All-in-One Resources)
- AYP Monitoring Assessments
- Assessment Rubrics

## Essential Questions:

**UNIT 1** What should be the goals of government?

**CHAPTER 2** How does the Constitution reflect the times in which it was written?

**Government Online Student Center includes**
- Interactive textbook with audio
- American Government Essential Questions Video
- WebQuests
- Audio Tours
- Interactivities
- Student Self-Tests

**Government Online Teacher Center includes**
- Online Teacher's Edition with lesson planner
- Online Lecture Notes
- Teacher's Resource Library with All-in-One Resources, color transparencies, and an alternative lesson plan
- Online Assessment

**Teacher Center**
at PearsonSchool.com/phgovt

## SECTION 1

### OUR POLITICAL BEGINNINGS

**Guiding Question:** What ideas and traditions influenced government in the English colonies?

**Summary of Teaching Strategies**
Students will examine and analyze early English concepts of government, related landmark documents, and royal colonial governments.

**Differentiated Resources**
- **L2 Prereading and Vocabulary Worksheet** (p. 56)
- **L3 L2 Reading Comprehension Worksheets** (pp. 61, 62)
- **L3 Core Worksheet** (p. 64)
- **L3 Quiz A** (p. 66) **L2 Quiz B** (p. 67)

**Student Objectives**
- Identify the three concepts of government that influenced the American colonies.
- Explain the significance of three landmark English documents.
- Describe the three types of colonies that the English established in the American colonies.

## SECTION 2

### THE COMING OF INDEPENDENCE

**Guiding Question:** What events and ideas led to American independence?

**Summary of Teaching Strategies**
Students will analyze colonial reactions to British policies and examine events leading up to the Declaration of Independence.

**Differentiated Resources**
- **L3 L2 Reading Comprehension Worksheets** (pp. 68, 70)
- **L3 Core Worksheets A and B** (pp. 72, 74)
- **L3 L2 Skills Worksheets** (pp. 76, 77)
- **L2 Extend Activities** (pp. 78, 79)
- **L3 Quiz A** (p. 80) **L2 Quiz B** (p. 81)

**Student Objectives**
- Explain how Britain's colonial policies contributed to the growth of self-government in the colonies.
- Identify the major steps that led to growing feelings of colonial unity.
- Compare the First and the Second Continental Congresses.
- Analyze the ideas in the Declaration of Independence.
- Summarize the common features of the first State constitutions.

## SECTION 3

### THE CRITICAL PERIOD

**Guiding Question:** What weaknesses in the Articles of Confederation made a lasting government impossible?

**Summary of Teaching Strategies**
Students will assess the Critical Period of the 1780s by analyzing land claims in North America and weaknesses of the Articles of Confederation.

TEACHING
GOVERNMENT

PROGRAM
ORGANIZATION

DIFFERENTIATED
INSTRUCTION

ASSESSMENT

PLANNING
YOUR
INSTRUCTION

**Differentiated Resources**
- **L3 L2 Reading Comprehension Worksheets** (pp. 86, 87)
- **L3 L2 Core Worksheets** (pp. 88, 91)
- **L3 Quiz A** (p. 95)   **L2 Quiz B** (p. 96)

**Student Objectives**
- Describe the structure of the government set up under the Articles of Confederation.
- Explain why the weaknesses of the Articles led to a critical period for the country in the 1780s.
- Describe how a growing need for a stronger National Government led to plans for a Constitutional Convention.

## SECTION 4

### CREATING THE CONSTITUTION

**Guiding Question:** What compromises enabled the Framers to create the Constitution?

**Summary of Teaching Strategies**
Students will evaluate the major compromises made at the Constitutional Convention.

**Differentiated Resources**
- **L3 L2 Reading Comprehension Worksheets** (pp. 97, 98)
- **L3 Core Worksheet** (p. 99)
- **L4 L3 Extend Worksheet** (p. 101)
- **L2 Extend Activity** (p. 103)
- **L3 Quiz A** (p. 104)   **L2 Quiz B** (p. 105)

**Student Objectives**
- Identify the Framers of the Constitution and discuss how they organized the Philadelphia Convention.

- Compare and contrast the Virginia Plan and the New Jersey Plan.
- Summarize the convention's major compromises and the effects of those decisions.
- Describe the delegates' reactions to the Constitution.

## SECTION 5

### RATIFYING THE CONSTITUTION

**Guiding Question:** What issues aroused the vigorous debate over ratification of the Constitution?

**Summary of Teaching Strategies**
Students will analyze primary sources arguing for and against the ratification of the Constitution.

**Differentiated Resources**
- **L3 L2 Reading Comprehension Worksheets** (pp. 106, 107)
- **L3 Bellringer Worksheet** (p. 108)
- **L3 Core Worksheet** (p. 109)
- **L2 Extend Activity** (p. 113)
- **L3 Quiz A** (p. 114)   **L2 Quiz B** (p. 115)
- **L3 Chapter Test A** (p. 116)
- **L2 Chapter Test B** (p. 119)

**Student Objectives**
- Identify the opposing sides in the fight for ratification and describe the major arguments for and against the proposed Constitution.
- Describe the inauguration of the new government of the United States of America.

---

**DIFFERENTIATED INSTRUCTION KEY**

- **L1** Special Needs
- **L2** Basic includes
- **ELL** English Language Learners
- **LPR** Less Proficient Readers
- **L3** All Students
- **L4** Advanced Students

# PLANNING YOUR INSTRUCTION

## Chapter Resources

### Introduce the chapter
- American Government Essential Questions Video
- WebQuests
- Essential Questions Journal

### Additional Support
- All-in-One Teaching Resources
- Differentiation suggestions in each lesson
- Government Online interactivities
- Color Transparencies

### Assessment
- Document-Based Assessment
- ExamView Test Bank CD-ROM
- Online Assessment
- Online Student Self-Tests
- Section Quizzes (All-in-One Resources)
- Chapter Tests A and B (All-in-One Resources)
- AYP Monitoring Assessments
- Assessment Rubrics

## Essential Questions:

**UNIT 1** What should be the goals of government?

**CHAPTER 3** How has the Constitution lasted through changing times?

### Government Online Student Center includes
- Interactive textbook with audio
- American Government Essential Questions Video
- WebQuests
- Audio Tours
- Interactivities
- Student Self-Tests

### Government Online Teacher Center includes
- Online Teacher's Edition with lesson planner
- Online Lecture Notes
- Teacher's Resource Library with All-in-One Resources, color transparencies, and an alternative lesson plan
- Online Assessment

Teacher Center
at PearsonSchool.com/phgovt

## SECTION 1

### BASIC PRINCIPLES

**Guiding Question:** What are the six main principles on which the Constitution is based?

### Summary of Teaching Strategies
Students will define the six basic principles on which the Constitution is based.

### Differentiated Resources
- **L2 Prereading and Vocabulary Worksheet** (p. 129)
- **L3 L2 Reading Comprehension Worksheets** (pp. 133, 135)
- **L3 Core Worksheet** (p. 137)
- **L4 L3 Extend Worksheet** (p. 139)
- **L3 Quiz A** (p. 141)  **L2 Quiz B** (p. 142)

### Student Objectives
- Understand the basic outline of the Constitution.
- Understand the six basic principles of the Constitution: popular sovereignty, limited government, separation of powers, checks and balances, judicial review, and federalism.

## SECTION 2

### FORMAL AMENDMENT

**Guiding Question:** How has the Constitution been amended through the formal amendment process?

### Summary of Teaching Strategies
Students will summarize and compare the 27 amendments to the Constitution. This will be followed by a study of how an amendment is proposed and ratified.

### Differentiated Resources
- **L3 L2 Reading Comprehension Worksheets** (pp. 143, 145)
- **L3 Bellringer Worksheet** (p. 147)
- **L3 Core Worksheet** (p. 148)
- **L3 L2 Skills Worksheets** (pp. 149, 150)
- **L3 Quiz A** (p. 151)  **L2 Quiz B** (p. 152)

### Student Objectives
- Identify the four different ways by which the Constitution may be formally changed.
- Explain how the formal amendment process illustrates the principles of federalism and popular sovereignty.
- Understand that several amendments have been proposed but not ratified.
- Outline the 27 amendments that have been added to the Constitution.

TEACHING
GOVERNMENT

PROGRAM
ORGANIZATION

DIFFERENTIATED
INSTRUCTION

ASSESSMENT

PLANNING
YOUR
INSTRUCTION

## SECTION 3

### CHANGE BY OTHER MEANS

**Guiding Question:** How have the day-to-day workings of government affected how we interpret the Constitution?

### Summary of Teaching Strategies
Students will examine the five informal ways to change how the government operates.

### Differentiated Resources
- **L3** **L2** Reading Comprehension Worksheets (pp. 153, 155)
- **L3** Bellringer Worksheet (p. 157)
- **L3** **L2** Core Worksheets (pp. 158, 159)
- **L3** Quiz A (p. 161)  **L2** Quiz B (p. 162)
- **L3** Chapter Test A (p. 167)
- **L2** Chapter Test B (p. 170)

### Student Objectives
- Identify how basic legislation has added to our understanding of the Constitution over time.
- Describe the ways in which the executive and judicial branches have interpreted the Constitution.
- Analyze the role of party practices and custom in interpreting the Constitution.

---

**DIFFERENTIATED INSTRUCTION KEY**

**L1** Special Needs                    **L3** All Students

**L2** Basic includes                   **L4** Advanced Students

　　　**ELL** English Language Learners

　　　**LPR** Less Proficient Readers

## Chapter Resources

### Introduce the chapter
- American Government Essential Questions Video
- WebQuests
- Essential Questions Journal

### Additional Support
- All-in-One Teaching Resources
- Differentiation suggestions in each lesson
- Government Online interactivities
- Color Transparencies

### Assessment
- Document-Based Assessment
- ExamView Test Bank CD-ROM
- Online Assessment
- Online Student Self-Tests
- Section Quizzes (All-in-One Resources)
- Chapter Tests A and B (All-in-One Resources)
- AYP Monitoring Assessments
- Assessment Rubrics

---

## Essential Questions:

**UNIT 1** What should be the goals of government?

**CHAPTER 4** Is the federal system the best way to govern the United States?

### Government Online Student Center includes
- Interactive textbook with audio
- American Government Essential Questions Video
- WebQuests
- Audio Tours
- Interactivities
- Student Self-Tests

### Government Online Teacher Center includes
- Online Teacher's Edition with lesson planner
- Online Lecture Notes
- Teacher's Resource Library with All-in-One Resources, color transparencies, and an alternative lesson plan
- Online Assessment

Teacher Center
at PearsonSchool.com/phgovt

---

## SECTION 1

### FEDERALISM: POWERS DIVIDED

**Guiding Question:** How is power divided between the Federal Government and the States?

### Summary of Teaching Strategies
Students will identify the powers held by the Federal Government, by State governments, and concurrently by both.

### Differentiated Resources
- **L2** **Prereading and Vocabulary Worksheet** (p. 180)
- **L3 L2** **Reading Comprehension Worksheets** (pp. 184, 185)
- **L3** **Core Worksheet** (p. 186)
- **L3 L2** **Skills Worksheets** (pp. 187, 188)
- **L3** **Quiz A** (p. 189)   **L2** **Quiz B** (p. 190)

### Student Objectives
- Define *federalism* and explain why the Framers chose this system.
- Identify powers delegated to and denied to the National Government and powers reserved for and denied to the States.
- Explain the difference between exclusive and concurrent powers.
- Examine the Constitution as "the supreme Law of the Land."

---

## SECTION 2

### THE NATIONAL GOVERNMENT AND THE 50 STATES

**Guiding Question:** According to the Constitution, what must the National Government guarantee to each State?

### Summary of Teaching Strategies
Students will identify the responsibilities the National Government has to the States, as well as how States are admitted to the Union.

### Differentiated Resources
- **L3 L2** **Reading Comprehension Worksheets** (pp. 191, 193)
- **L3** **Bellringer Worksheet** (p. 195)
- **L3 L2** **ELL Core Worksheets** (pp. 196, 198)
- **L4 L3** **Extend Worksheet** (p. 200)
- **L3** **Quiz A** (p. 203)   **L2** **Quiz B** (p. 204)

### Student Objectives
- Summarize the obligations that the Constitution places on the National Government with regard to the States.
- Explain the process for admitting new States to the Union.
- Examine the many and growing areas of cooperative federalism.

TEACHING
GOVERNMENT

PROGRAM
ORGANIZATION

DIFFERENTIATED
INSTRUCTION

ASSESSMENT

PLANNING
YOUR
INSTRUCTION

# SECTION 3

## INTERSTATE RELATIONS

**Guiding Question:** How do the States work together to preserve the Union?

### Summary of Teaching Strategies
Students will explore constitutional provisions that promote cooperation among States.

### Differentiated Resources
- **L3** **L2** Reading Comprehension Worksheets (pp. 205, 206)
- **L3** Core Worksheet (p. 207)
- **L3** Quiz A (p. 208)    **L2** Quiz B (p. 209)
- **L3** Chapter Test A (p. 210)
- **L2** Chapter Test B (p. 213)

### Student Objectives
- Explain why States make interstate compacts.
- Understand the purpose of the Full Faith and Credit Clause.
- Describe the Extradition Clause and explain its purpose.
- Explain the purpose of the Privileges and Immunities Clause.

---

### DIFFERENTIATED INSTRUCTION KEY

**L1** Special Needs          **L3** All Students

**L2** Basic includes          **L4** Advanced Students

    **ELL** English Language Learners

    **LPR** Less Proficient Readers

## Chapter Resources

**Introduce the chapter**
• American Government Essential Questions Video
• WebQuests
• Essential Questions Journal

**Additional Support**
• All-in-One Teaching Resources
• Differentiation suggestions in each lesson
• Government Online interactivities
• Color Transparencies

**Assessment**
• Document-Based Assessment
• ExamView Test Bank CD-ROM
• Online Assessment
• Online Student Self-Tests
• Section Quizzes (All-in-One Resources)
• Chapter Tests A and B (All-in-One Resources)
• AYP Monitoring Assessments
• Assessment Rubrics

## Essential Questions:

**UNIT 2** In what ways should people participate in public affairs?
**CHAPTER 5** Does the two-party system help or harm democracy?

**Government Online Student Center includes**
• Interactive textbook with audio
• American Government Essential Questions Video
• WebQuests
• Audio Tours
• Interactivities
• Student Self-Tests

**Government Online Teacher Center includes**
• Online Teacher's Edition with lesson planner
• Online Lecture Notes
• Teacher's Resource Library with All-in-One Resources, color transparencies, and an alternative lesson plan
• Online Assessment

**Teacher Center**
at PearsonSchool.com/phgovt

## SECTION 1

### PARTIES AND WHAT THEY DO

**Guiding Question:** What are political parties, and how do they function in our two-party system?

### Summary of Teaching Strategies
Students will study the function of political parties and discuss the benefits and drawbacks of the two-party system.

### Differentiated Resources
• **L2** Prereading and Vocabulary Worksheet (p. 9)
• **L3 L2** Reading Comprehension Worksheets (pp. 13, 14)
• **L3 L2** Core Worksheets (pp. 15, 16)
• **L3** Quiz A (p. 17)  **L2** Quiz B (p. 18)

### Student Objectives
• Define a *political party*.
• Describe the major functions of political parties.
• Identify the reasons why the United States has a two-party system.
• Understand multiparty and one-party systems and how they affect the functioning of a political system.

## SECTION 2

### TWO-PARTY SYSTEM IN AMERICAN HISTORY

**Guiding Question:** How has the two-party system affected the history of American government?

### Summary of Teaching Strategies
Students will analyze the history of the two-party system, including each party's beliefs and the individuals and groups associated with each party. They will also learn how political cartoons are used to target a political party's audience.

### Differentiated Resources
• **L3 L2** Reading Comprehension Worksheets (pp. 19, 20)
• **L3** Core Worksheet (p. 21)
• **L3 L2** Skills Worksheets (pp. 23, 24)
• **L3** Quiz A (p. 25)  **L2** Quiz B (p. 26)

### Student Objectives
• Understand the origins of political parties in the United States.
• Identify and describe the three major periods of single-party domination and describe the current era of divided government.

## SECTION 3

### THE MINOR PARTIES

**Guiding Question:** What role have minor parties played in American politics?

#### Summary of Teaching Strategies
Students will read an article about a "get out the vote" campaign and then map out their own plan for a campaign.

#### Differentiated Resources
- **L3 L2 Reading Comprehension Worksheets** (pp. 27, 28)
- **L3 Core Worksheet** (p. 29)
- **L4 L3 Extend Worksheet** (p. 31)
- **L3 Quiz A** (p. 33)   **L2 Quiz B** (p. 34)

#### Student Objectives
- Identify the types of minor parties that have been active in American politics.
- Understand why minor parties are important despite the fact that none has ever won the presidency.

## SECTION 4

### PARTY ORGANIZATION

**Guiding Question:** How are political parties organized at the federal, State, and local levels?

#### Summary of Teaching Strategies
Students will discuss the organization and strategies of political parties, and then plan activities for a campaign at the federal, State, and local levels.

#### Differentiated Resources
- **L3 L2 Reading Comprehension Worksheets** (pp. 35, 36)
- **L3 Core Worksheets A and B** (pp. 37, 39)
- **L3 Quiz A** (p. 40)   **L2 Quiz B** (p. 41)
- **L3 Chapter Test A** (p. 42)
- **L2 Chapter Test B** (p. 45)

#### Student Objectives
- Understand why the major parties have a decentralized structure.
- Describe the national party machinery and party organization at the State and local levels.

TEACHING GOVERNMENT

PROGRAM ORGANIZATION

DIFFERENTIATED INSTRUCTION

ASSESSMENT

PLANNING YOUR INSTRUCTION

---

**DIFFERENTIATED INSTRUCTION KEY**

**L1** Special Needs

**L2** Basic includes

    **ELL** English Language Learners

    **LPR** Less Proficient Readers

**L3** All Students

**L4** Advanced Students

## Chapter Resources

**Introduce the chapter**
- American Government Essential Questions Video
- WebQuests
- Essential Questions Journal

**Additional Support**
- All-in-One Teaching Resources
- Differentiation suggestions in each lesson
- Government Online interactivities
- Color Transparencies

**Assessment**
- Document-Based Assessment
- ExamView Test Bank CD-ROM
- Online Assessment
- Online Student Self-Tests
- Section Quizzes (All-in-One Resources)
- Chapter Tests A and B (All-in-One Resources)
- AYP Monitoring Assessments
- Assessment Rubrics

---

## Essential Questions:

**UNIT 2** In what ways should people participate in public affairs?

**CHAPTER 6** Why do voters act as they do?

### Government Online Student Center includes
- Interactive textbook with audio
- American Government Essential Questions Video
- WebQuests
- Audio Tours
- Interactivities
- Student Self-Tests

### Government Online Teacher Center includes
- Online Teacher's Edition with lesson planner
- Online Lecture Notes
- Teacher's Resource Library with All-in-One Resources, color transparencies, and an alternative lesson plan
- Online Assessment

Teacher Center
at PearsonSchool.com/phgovt

---

## SECTION 1

### THE RIGHT TO VOTE

**Guiding Question:** How have voting rights changed over the course of American history?

### Summary of Teaching Strategies
Students will discuss who initially had the right to vote and the reasons for voting rights expansion. They will also create a poster about the history of voting rights expansion, illustrating the changing definition of the American electorate.

### Differentiated Resources
- **L2** Prereading and Vocabulary Worksheet (p. 57)
- **L3 L2** Reading Comprehension Worksheets (pp. 61, 62)
- **L3 L2** Core Worksheets (pp. 63, 65)
- **L3 L2** Skills Worksheets (pp. 67, 68)
- **L3** Quiz A (p. 69)   **L2** Quiz B (p. 70)

### Student Objectives
- Summarize the history of voting rights in the United States.
- Identify and explain constitutional restrictions on the States' power to set voting qualifications.

---

## SECTION 2

### VOTER QUALIFICATIONS

**Guiding Question:** What are the qualifications for voting, and how have they changed over time?

### Summary of Teaching Strategies
Students will analyze how voter qualifications have changed over time and examine a registration application from the 1960s. They will also evaluate an editorial about mandatory voting and respond with a letter to the editor.

### Differentiated Resources
- **L3 L2** Reading Comprehension Worksheets (pp. 71, 73)
- **L3** Core Worksheet A (p. 75)
- **L3 L2** Core Worksheets B (pp. 78, 80)
- **L3 L4** Extend Worksheet (p. 82)
- **L2** Extend Activity (p. 83)
- **L3** Quiz A (p. 84)   **L2** Quiz B (p. 85)

### Student Objectives
- Identify the universal qualifications for voting in the United States.
- Explain the other requirements that States use or have used as voting qualifications.

TEACHING
GOVERNMENT

PROGRAM
ORGANIZATION

DIFFERENTIATED
INSTRUCTION

ASSESSMENT

PLANNING
YOUR
INSTRUCTION

## SECTION 3

### SUFFRAGE AND CIVIL RIGHTS

**Guiding Question:** How did the U.S. fulfill the promise of the 15th Amendment?

### Summary of Teaching Strategies
Students will identify historical barriers that faced African American voters by examining a political cartoon, and analyze historical data on African American representation in Congress to understand the effects of discrimination and the civil rights movement.

### Differentiated Resources
- **L3** **L2** Reading Comprehension Worksheets (pp. 86, 87)
- **L3** Core Worksheet (p. 88)
- **L3** Quiz A (p. 91)  **L2** Quiz B (p. 92)

### Student Objectives
- Describe the tactics often used to deny African Americans the right to vote despite the command of the 15th Amendment.
- Understand the significance of the civil rights laws enacted in 1957, 1960, and 1964.
- Analyze the provisions and effects of the Voting Rights Act of 1965.

## SECTION 4

### VOTER BEHAVIOR

**Guiding Question:** What factors influence voter behavior?

### Summary of Teaching Strategies
Students will explore the factors that influence voting behavior by creating a television advertisement that encourages voter participation.

### Differentiated Resources
- **L3** **L2** Reading Comprehension Worksheets (pp. 93, 95)
- **L3** Core Worksheet (p. 97)
- **L3** Quiz A (p. 98)  **L2** Quiz B (p. 99)
- **L3** Chapter Test A (p. 100)
- **L2** Chapter Test B (p. 103)

### Student Objectives
- Examine the problem of nonvoting in this country.
- Identify those people who typically do not vote.
- Examine the behavior of those who vote and those who do not.
- Understand the sociological and psychological factors that affect voting and voter behavior.

---

**DIFFERENTIATED INSTRUCTION KEY**

**L1** Special Needs

**L2** Basic includes

    **ELL** English Language Learners

    **LPR** Less Proficient Readers

**L3** All Students

**L4** Advanced Students

## Chapter Resources

**Introduce the chapter**
- American Government Essential Questions Video
- WebQuests
- Essential Questions Journal

**Additional Support**
- All-in-One Teaching Resources
- Differentiation suggestions in each lesson
- Government Online interactivities
- Color Transparencies

**Assessment**
- Document-Based Assessment
- ExamView Test Bank CD-ROM
- Online Assessment
- Online Student Self-Tests
- Section Quizzes (All-in-One Resources)
- Chapter Tests A and B (All-in-One Resources)
- AYP Monitoring Assessments
- Assessment Rubrics

---

## Essential Questions:

**UNIT 2** In what ways should people participate in public affairs?

**CHAPTER 7** How fair and effective is the electoral process?

### Government Online Student Center includes
- Interactive textbook with audio
- American Government Essential Questions Video
- WebQuests
- Audio Tours
- Interactivities
- Student Self-Tests

### Government Online Teacher Center includes
- Online Teacher's Edition with lesson planner
- Online Lecture Notes
- Teacher's Resource Library with All-in-One Resources, color transparencies, and an alternative lesson plan
- Online Assessment

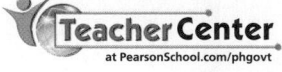
**Teacher Center**
at PearsonSchool.com/phgovt

---

## SECTION 1

### THE NOMINATING PROCESS

**Guiding Question:** What methods are used to choose candidates for public office?

### Summary of Teaching Strategies
Students will participate in a talk show simulation about the nominating process for choosing candidates. They will also evaluate the "blanket primary" by analyzing a Supreme Court ruling.

### Differentiated Resources
- **L2** **Prereading and Vocabulary Worksheet** (p. 116)
- **L3** **L2** **Reading Comprehension Worksheets** (pp. 120, 122)
- **L3** **Core Worksheet A** (p. 124)
- **L3** **L2** **Core Worksheets B** (pp. 125, 127)
- **L3** **Quiz A** (p. 129)   **L2** **Quiz B** (p. 130)

### Student Objectives
- Explain why the nominating process is a critical first step in the election process.
- Describe self-announcement, the caucus, and the convention as nominating methods.
- Discuss the direct primary as the principal nominating method used in the United States today.
- Understand why some candidates use the petition as a nominating device.

---

## SECTION 2

### ELECTIONS

**Guiding Question:** How are elections conducted in the United States?

### Summary of Teaching Strategies
Students will explore the types of election procedures and write a memorandum about issues raised in the 2000 Florida presidential voting to understand how voting procedures and equipment can affect elections.

### Differentiated Resources
- **L3** **L2** **Reading Comprehension Worksheets** (pp. 131, 133)
- **L3** **L2** **Core Worksheets** (pp. 135, 136)
- **L3** **L4** **Extend Worksheet** (p. 138)
- **L3** **Quiz A** (p. 140)   **L2** **Quiz B** (p. 141)

### Student Objectives
- Analyze how the administration of elections in the United States helps make democracy work.
- Define the role of local precincts and polling places in the election process.
- Describe the various ways in which voters can cast their ballots.
- Outline the role that voting devices play in the election process.

TEACHING
GOVERNMENT

PROGRAM
ORGANIZATION

DIFFERENTIATED
INSTRUCTION

ASSESSMENT

PLANNING
YOUR
INSTRUCTION

# SECTION 3

## MONEY AND ELECTIONS

**Guiding Question:** What role does money play in electoral politics?

### Summary of Teaching Strategies
Students will consider the potentially corrupting effect of money in politics by analyzing a political cartoon. Then they will debate campaign finance reform and create an editorial cartoon that expresses one of the views in the debate.

### Differentiated Resources
- **L3 L2** Reading Comprehension Worksheets (pp. 142, 144)
- **L3** Core Worksheet (p. 146)
- **L3** Skills Worksheet (p. 148)
- **L2** Skill Activity (p. 149)
- **L3** Quiz A (p. 150)  **L2** Quiz B (p. 151)
- **L3** Chapter Test A (p. 152)
- **L2** Chapter Test B (p. 155)

### Student Objectives
- Explain the issues raised by campaign spending.
- Describe the various sources of funding for campaign spending.
- Examine federal laws that regulate campaign finance.
- Outline the role of the Federal Election Commission in enforcing campaign finance laws.
- Distinguish hard money from soft money.

---

**DIFFERENTIATED INSTRUCTION KEY**

**L1** Special Needs                          **L3** All Students

**L2** Basic includes                         **L4** Advanced Students

     **ELL** English Language Learners

     **LPR** Less Proficient Readers

## Chapter Resources

### Introduce the chapter
- American Government Essential Questions Video
- WebQuests
- Essential Questions Journal

### Additional Support
- All-in-One Teaching Resources
- Differentiation suggestions in each lesson
- Government Online interactivities
- Color Transparencies

### Assessment
- Document-Based Assessment
- ExamView Test Bank CD-ROM
- Online Assessment
- Online Student Self-Tests
- Section Quizzes (All-in-One Resources)
- Chapter Tests A and B (All-in-One Resources)
- AYP Monitoring Assessments
- Assessment Rubrics

---

## Essential Questions:

**UNIT 2** In what ways should people participate in public affairs?

**CHAPTER 8** What is the place of the media and public opinion in a democracy?

### Government Online Student Center includes
- Interactive textbook with audio
- American Government Essential Questions Video
- WebQuests
- Audio Tours
- Interactivities
- Student Self-Tests

### Government Online Teacher Center includes
- Online Teacher's Edition with lesson planner
- Online Lecture Notes
- Teacher's Resource Library with All-in-One Resources, color transparencies, and an alternative lesson plan
- Online Assessment

Teacher Center
at PearsonSchool.com/phgovt

---

## SECTION 1

### THE FORMATION OF PUBLIC OPINION

**Guiding Question:** What is public opinion, and what factors help to shape it?

### Summary of Teaching Strategies
Students will discuss the concept of public opinion in a democracy and list key factors that influence it. They also will explain their opinions on five public issues and rank their sources of influence.

### Differentiated Resources
- **L2** Prereading and Vocabulary Worksheet (p. 168)
- **L3 L2** Reading Comprehension Worksheets (pp. 172, 173)
- **L3** Core Worksheet (p. 174)
- **L3** Quiz A (p. 177)    **L2** Quiz B (p. 178)

### Student Objectives
- Examine the term *public opinion* and understand why it is so difficult to define.
- Analyze how family and education help shape public opinion.
- Describe four other factors that shape public opinion.

---

## SECTION 2

### MEASURING PUBLIC OPINION

**Guiding Question:** How is public opinion measured and used?

### Summary of Teaching Strategies
Students will research the significance of how polling questions are worded and practice writing good polling questions. They will study the importance of scientific polling by examining a poll on issues from a recent presidential election.

### Differentiated Resources
- **L3 L2** Reading Comprehension Worksheets (pp. 179, 181)
- **L3** Core Worksheet (p. 183)
- **L2** Extend Activity (p. 184)
- **L3** Quiz A (p. 185)    **L2** Quiz B (p. 186)

### Student Objectives
- Describe the challenges involved in measuring public opinion.
- Explain why scientific opinion polls are the best way to measure public opinion.
- Identify the five steps in the polling process.
- Understand the problems in evaluating polls.
- Recognize the limits on the impact of public opinion in a democracy.

# SECTION 3

## THE MASS MEDIA

**Guiding Question:** How has the development of different media helped inform the public about politics?

### Summary of Teaching Strategies
Students will evaluate the Web site of a candidate for President, and then design their own candidate Web site with a visual layout and links.

### Differentiated Resources
- **L3** **L2** **Reading Comprehension Worksheets** (pp. 187, 189)
- **L3** **L2** **Core Worksheets** (pp. 191, 192)
- **L3** **L2** **Skills Worksheets** (pp. 194, 195)
- **L4** **L3** **Extend Worksheet** (p. 196)
- **L3** **Quiz A** (p. 198)   **L2** **Quiz B** (p. 199)
- **L3** **Chapter Test A** (p. 200)
- **L2** **Chapter Test B** (p. 203)

### Student Objectives
- Examine the role of the mass media in providing the public with political information.
- Explain how the mass media influence politics.
- Understand the factors that limit the influence of the media.

TEACHING GOVERNMENT

PROGRAM ORGANIZATION

DIFFERENTIATED INSTRUCTION

ASSESSMENT

PLANNING YOUR INSTRUCTION

---

**DIFFERENTIATED INSTRUCTION KEY**

**L1** Special Needs

**L2** Basic includes

    **ELL** English Language Learners

    **LPR** Less Proficient Readers

**L3** All Students

**L4** Advanced Students

## Chapter Resources

### Introduce the chapter
- American Government Essential Questions Video
- WebQuests
- Essential Questions Journal

### Additional Support
- All-in-One Teaching Resources
- Differentiation suggestions in each lesson
- Government Online interactivities
- Color Transparencies

### Assessment
- Document-Based Assessment
- ExamView Test Bank CD-ROM
- Online Assessment
- Online Student Self-Tests
- Section Quizzes (All-in-One Resources)
- Chapter Tests A and B (All-in-One Resources)
- AYP Monitoring Assessments
- Assessment Rubrics

## Essential Questions:

**UNIT 2** In what ways should people participate in public affairs?

**CHAPTER 9** To what extent do interest groups advance or harm democracy?

### Government Online Student Center includes
- Interactive textbook with audio
- American Government Essential Questions Video
- WebQuests
- Audio Tours
- Interactivities
- Student Self-Tests

### Government Online Teacher Center includes
- Online Teacher's Edition with lesson planner
- Online Lecture Notes
- Teacher's Resource Library with All-in-One Resources, color transparencies, and an alternative lesson plan
- Online Assessment

Teacher Center
at PearsonSchool.com/phgovt

## SECTION 1

### THE NATURE OF INTEREST GROUPS

**Guiding Question:** What roles do interest groups play in our political system?

#### Summary of Teaching Strategies
Students will describe the functions of interest groups and then create a brochure that represents their position either for or against interest groups.

#### Differentiated Resources
- **L2 Prereading and Vocabulary Worksheet** (p. 213)
- **L3 L2 Reading Comprehension Worksheets** (pp. 217, 218)
- **L3 L2 Core Worksheets A** (pp. 219, 221)
- **L3 Core Worksheet B** (p. 220)
- **L2 Extend Activity** (p. 223)
- **L3 Quiz A** (p. 224)    **L2 Quiz B** (p. 225)

#### Student Objectives
- Describe the role of interest groups in influencing public policy.
- Compare and contrast political parties and interest groups.
- Explain why people see interest groups as both good and bad for American politics.

## SECTION 2

### TYPES OF INTEREST GROUPS

**Guiding Question:** What are the different types of interest groups at work in American society?

#### Summary of Teaching Strategies
Students will write position statements based on one issue and present it to the class. They will also research the activities of specific interest groups and create a list of the groups' major issues.

#### Differentiated Resources
- **L3 L2 Reading Comprehension Worksheets** (pp. 226, 227)
- **L3 Core Worksheet** (p. 228)
- **L3 L2 Skills Worksheets** (pp. 231, 232)
- **L3 Quiz A** (p. 233)    **L2 Quiz B** (p. 234)

#### Student Objectives
- Explain how the American tradition of joining organizations has resulted in a wide range of interest groups.
- Describe four categories of groups based on economic interests.
- Outline the reasons other interest groups have been created.
- Identify the purpose of public-interest groups.

TEACHING
GOVERNMENT

PROGRAM
ORGANIZATION

DIFFERENTIATED
INSTRUCTION

ASSESSMENT

PLANNING
YOUR
INSTRUCTION

# SECTION 3

## INTEREST GROUPS AT WORK

**Guiding Question:** In what ways do interest groups attempt to influence government and public opinion?

## Summary of Teaching Strategies
Students will design an interest group campaign using direct and indirect approaches.

## Differentiated Resources
- **L3** **L2** **Reading Comprehension Worksheets** (pp. 235, 236)
- **L3** **Core Worksheet** (p. 237)
- **L3** **L4** **Extend Worksheet** (p. 238)
- **L2** **Extend Activity** (p. 240)
- **L3** **Quiz A** (p. 241)   **L2** **Quiz B** (p. 242)
- **L3** **Chapter Test A** (p. 243)
- **L2** **Chapter Test B** (p. 246)

## Student Objectives
- Understand the difference between the *direct* and *indirect* approaches of interest groups.
- Describe how lobbyists influence the legislative, executive, and judicial branches of government.
- Examine how interest groups use grass-roots lobbying.
- Identify how interest groups use media, propaganda, and political campaigns to influence public opinion and policy.

---

**DIFFERENTIATED INSTRUCTION KEY**

**L1** Special Needs

**L2** Basic includes

    **ELL** English Language Learners

    **LPR** Less Proficient Readers

**L3** All Students

**L4** Advanced Students

## Chapter Resources

**Introduce the chapter**
- American Government Essential Questions Video
- WebQuests
- Essential Questions Journal

**Additional Support**
- All-in-One Teaching Resources
- Differentiation suggestions in each lesson
- Government Online interactivities
- Color Transparencies

**Assessment**
- Document-Based Assessment
- ExamView Test Bank CD-ROM
- Online Assessment
- Online Student Self-Tests
- Section Quizzes (All-in-One Resources)
- Chapter Tests A and B (All-in-One Resources)
- AYP Monitoring Assessments
- Assessment Rubrics

## Essential Questions:

**UNIT 3** What makes a successful Congress?

**CHAPTER 10** Whose views should members of Congress represent when voting?

**Government Online Student Center includes**
- Interactive textbook with audio
- American Government Essential Questions Video
- WebQuests
- Audio Tours
- Interactivities
- Student Self-Tests

**Government Online Teacher Center includes**
- Online Teacher's Edition with lesson planner
- Online Lecture Notes
- Teacher's Resource Library with All-in-One Resources, color transparencies, and an alternative lesson plan
- Online Assessment

at PearsonSchool.com/phgovt

# SECTION 1

## THE NATIONAL LEGISLATURE

**Guiding Question:** Why does the Constitution establish a bicameral legislature?

## Summary of Teaching Strategies
Students will discuss the structure and reasons for a bicameral Congress, make comparisons to school government, and consider the benefits and drawbacks.

## Differentiated Resources
- **L2** **Prereading and Vocabulary Worksheet** (p. 9)
- **L3** **L2** **Reading Comprehension Worksheets** (pp. 13, 14)
- **L3** **Core Worksheet** (p. 15)
- **L3** **Quiz A** (p. 17)   **L2** **Quiz B** (p. 18)

## Student Objectives
- Explain why the Constitution provides for a bicameral Congress.
- Explain the difference between a term and a session of Congress.
- Describe a situation in which the President may convene or end a session of Congress.

# SECTION 2

## THE HOUSE OF REPRESENTATIVES

**Guiding Question:** How are the seats in the House distributed and what qualifications must members meet?

## Summary of Teaching Strategies
Students will study the House of Representatives and the qualifications for its members. They will also identify the reasons for and results of gerrymandering by role-playing the process of drawing district lines.

## Differentiated Resources
- **L3** **L2** **Reading Comprehension Worksheets** (pp. 19, 20)
- **L3** **L2** **Core Worksheets** (pp. 22, 23)
- **L3** **Quiz A** (p. 25)   **L2** **Quiz B** (p. 26)

## Student Objectives
- Explain how House seats are distributed and describe the length of a term in the House.
- Explain how House seats are reapportioned among the States after each census.
- Describe a typical congressional election and congressional district.
- Analyze the formal and informal qualifications for election to the House.

TEACHING
GOVERNMENT

PROGRAM
ORGANIZATION

DIFFERENTIATED
INSTRUCTION

ASSESSMENT

PLANNING
YOUR
INSTRUCTION

## SECTION 3

### THE SENATE

**Guiding Question:** How does the Senate differ from the House?

#### Summary of Teaching Strategies
Students will use a Venn diagram to compare the Senate to the House. Then they will assess the qualifications and characteristics of four real senators in a Socratic Dialogue.

#### Differentiated Resources
- **L3 L2** Reading Comprehension Worksheets (pp. 27, 28)
- **L3** Bellringer Worksheet (p. 29)
- **L3** Core Worksheet (p. 30)
- **L3 L2** Skills Worksheets (pp. 31, 32)
- **L3** Quiz A (p. 33)   **L2** Quiz B (p. 34)

#### Student Objectives
- Compare the size of the Senate to the size of the House of Representatives.
- Describe how senators are elected.
- Explain how and why a senator's term differs from a representative's term.
- Describe the qualifications for election to the Senate.

## SECTION 4

### THE MEMBERS OF CONGRESS

**Guiding Question:** What roles and functions do members of Congress perform?

#### Summary of Teaching Strategies
Students discuss the attributes of a "typical" member of Congress, and then write help-wanted ads for members of Congress. In their ads, they will write job descriptions and address qualifications, salary, and benefits.

#### Differentiated Resources
- **L3 L2** Reading Comprehension Worksheets (pp. 35, 36)
- **L3** Core Worksheet (p. 37)
- **L4 L3** Extend Worksheet (p. 39)
- **L3** Quiz A (p. 40)   **L2** Quiz B (p. 41)
- **L3** Chapter Test A (p. 42)
- **L2** Chapter Test B (p. 45)

#### Student Objectives
- Describe the personal and political backgrounds of present-day Congress.
- Identify the major roles played by those who serve in Congress.
- Describe the compensation and privileges of members of Congress.

---

**DIFFERENTIATED INSTRUCTION KEY**

**L1** Special Needs          **L3** All Students

**L2** Basic includes         **L4** Advanced Students

　　　**ELL** English Language Learners

　　　**LPR** Less Proficient Readers

---

## Chapter Resources

### Introduce the chapter
- American Government Essential Questions Video
- WebQuests
- Essential Questions Journal

### Additional Support
- All-in-One Teaching Resources
- Differentiation suggestions in each lesson
- Government Online interactivities
- Color Transparencies

### Assessment
- Document-Based Assessment
- ExamView Test Bank CD-ROM
- Online Assessment
- Online Student Self-Tests
- Section Quizzes (All-in-One Resources)
- Chapter Tests A and B (All-in-One Resources)
- AYP Monitoring Assessments
- Assessment Rubrics

## Essential Questions:

**UNIT 3** What makes a successful Congress?

**CHAPTER 11** What should be the limits on the powers of Congress?

### Government Online Student Center includes
- Interactive textbook with audio
- American Government Essential Questions Video
- WebQuests
- Audio Tours
- Interactivities
- Student Self-Tests

### Government Online Teacher Center includes
- Online Teacher's Edition with lesson planner
- Online Lecture Notes
- Teacher's Resource Library with All-in-One Resources, color transparencies, and an alternative lesson plan
- Online Assessment

**Teacher Center**
at PearsonSchool.com/phgovt

---

## SECTION 1

### THE EXPRESSED POWERS OF MONEY AND COMMERCE

**Guiding Question:** What powers over money and commerce does the Constitution give to Congress and what limits does it put on these powers?

### Summary of Teaching Strategies
Students will discuss, define, and complete a worksheet on the expressed, implied, and inherent powers of Congress. They also will consider limits on the powers of Congress through a Socratic Dialogue.

### Differentiated Resources
- **L2** Prereading and Vocabulary Worksheet (p. 57)
- **L3 L2** Reading Comprehension Worksheets (pp. 61, 63)
- **L3 L2** Core Worksheets (pp. 65, 67)
- **L3** Quiz A (p. 68)  **L2** Quiz B (p. 69)

### Student Objectives
- Describe the three types of powers delegated to Congress.
- Analyze the importance of the commerce power.
- Summarize key points relating to the taxing power.
- Explain how the bankruptcy and borrowing powers work.
- Explain why the Framers gave Congress the power to issue currency.

---

## SECTION 2

### THE OTHER EXPRESSED POWERS

**Guiding Question:** How do the expressed powers reflect the Framers' commitment to creating a strong but limited National Government?

### Summary of Teaching Strategies
Students will examine the division of war powers by analyzing a primary source document and will rank the top ten expressed powers of Congress.

### Differentiated Resources
- **L3 L2** Reading Comprehension Worksheets (pp. 70, 72)
- **L3** Bellringer Worksheet (p. 74)
- **L3** Core Worksheets A and B (pp. 75, 76)
- **L3 L2** Skills Worksheets (pp. 77, 78)
- **L3** Quiz A (p. 79)  **L2** Quiz B (p. 80)

### Student Objectives
- Identify the key sources of the foreign relations powers of Congress.
- Describe the power-sharing arrangement between Congress and the President on the issues of war and national defense.
- List other key domestic powers exercised by Congress.

TEACHING
GOVERNMENT

PROGRAM
ORGANIZATION

DIFFERENTIATED
INSTRUCTION

ASSESSMENT

PLANNING
YOUR
INSTRUCTION

## SECTION 3

### THE IMPLIED POWERS

**Guiding Question:** How has the doctrine of implied powers increased the powers of Congress?

### Summary of Teaching Strategies
Students will consider the meaning of implied powers, explore strict and liberal construction by evaluating congressional actions, and will decide upon and defend a position on implied powers.

### Differentiated Resources
- **L3** **L2** Reading Comprehension Worksheets (pp. 81, 82)
- **L3** **L2** Core Worksheets (pp. 83, 85)
- **L3** Quiz A (p. 87)  **L2** Quiz B (p. 88)

### Student Objectives
- Explain how the Necessary and Proper Clause gives Congress flexibility in lawmaking.
- Compare the strict construction and liberal construction positions on the scope of congressional power.
- Describe the ways in which the implied powers have been applied.

## SECTION 4

### THE NONLEGISLATIVE POWERS

**Guiding Question:** What nonlegislative powers does the Constitution delegate to Congress?

### Summary of Teaching Strategies
Students will evaluate the nonlegislative powers of Congress, using as an example the impeachment of President Clinton. Then they will use the Jigsaw strategy to learn and teach each other about the nonlegislative powers of Congress.

### Differentiated Resources
- **L3** **L2** Reading Comprehension Worksheets (pp. 89, 91)
- **L3** Bellringer Worksheet (p. 93)
- **L3** Core Worksheets A and B (pp. 95, 96)
- **L4** **L3** Extend Worksheet (p. 97)
- **L3** Quiz A (p. 98)  **L2** Quiz B (p. 99)
- **L3** Chapter Test A (p. 104)
- **L2** Chapter Test B (p. 107)

### Student Objectives
- Describe the role of Congress in amending the Constitution and its electoral duties.
- Describe the power of Congress to impeach, and summarize presidential impeachment cases.
- Identify the executive powers of Congress.
- Describe the investigatory powers of Congress.

---

**DIFFERENTIATED INSTRUCTION KEY**

**L1** Special Needs  **L3** All Students
**L2** Basic includes  **L4** Advanced Students
 **ELL** English Language Learners
 **LPR** Less Proficient Readers

## Chapter Resources

### Introduce the chapter
- American Government Essential Questions Video
- WebQuests
- Essential Questions Journal

### Additional Support
- All-in-One Teaching Resources
- Differentiation suggestions in each lesson
- Government Online interactivities
- Color Transparencies

### Assessment
- Document-Based Assessment
- ExamView Test Bank CD-ROM
- Online Assessment
- Online Student Self-Tests
- Section Quizzes (All-in-One Resources)
- Chapter Tests A and B (All-in-One Resources)
- AYP Monitoring Assessments
- Assessment Rubrics

## Essential Questions:

**UNIT 3** What makes a successful Congress?
**CHAPTER 12** Can and should the lawmaking process be improved?

### Government Online Student Center includes
- Interactive textbook with audio
- American Government Essential Questions Video
- WebQuests
- Audio Tours
- Interactivities
- Student Self-Tests

### Government Online Teacher Center includes
- Online Teacher's Edition with lesson planner
- Online Lecture Notes
- Teacher's Resource Library with All-in-One Resources, color transparencies, and an alternative lesson plan
- Online Assessment

**TeacherCenter**
at PearsonSchool.com/phgovt

## SECTION 1

### CONGRESS ORGANIZES

**Guiding Question:** How do constitutional and party officers keep Congress organized?

#### Summary of Teaching Strategies
Students will complete a flowchart showing opening-day events in the House and learn about congressional leaders by taking part in a press conference simulation.

#### Differentiated Resources
- **L2 Prereading and Vocabulary Worksheet** (p. 121)
- **L3 L2 Reading Comprehension Worksheets** (pp. 125, 127)
- **L3 Core Worksheet A** (p. 129)
- **L3 L2 Core Worksheet B** (p. 130)
- **L3 Quiz A** (p. 131)   **L2 Quiz B** (p. 132)

#### Student Objectives
- Describe how and when Congress convenes.
- Compare the roles of the presiding officers in the Senate and the House.
- Identify the duties of the party officers in each house.
- Describe how committee chairmen are chosen and explain their role in the legislative process.

## SECTION 2

### COMMITTEES IN CONGRESS

**Guiding Question:** How do committees help Congress do its work?

#### Summary of Teaching Strategies
Students will examine the need for committees to divide work by planning an event. Then they will match House committees with their jurisdictions and follow the path of a bill through the House.

#### Differentiated Resources
- **L3 L2 Reading Comprehension Worksheets** (pp. 133, 134)
- **L3 L2 Core Worksheets** (pp. 135, 137)
- **L4 L3 Extend Worksheet** (p. 139)
- **L3 Quiz A** (p. 141)   **L2 Quiz B** (p. 142)

#### Student Objectives
- Explain how standing committees function.
- Describe the responsibilities and duties of the House Rules Committee.
- Describe the role of select committees.
- Compare the functions of joint and conference committees.

TEACHING
GOVERNMENT

PROGRAM
ORGANIZATION

DIFFERENTIATED
INSTRUCTION

ASSESSMENT

PLANNING
YOUR
INSTRUCTION

## SECTION 3

### MAKING LAW: THE HOUSE

**Guiding Question:** What steps does a successful bill follow as it moves through the House?

### Summary of Teaching Strategies

Students will brainstorm a list of issues and laws at the federal level that affect them. Then they will select a topic and write a bill. These bills will then be sent to student committees. Finally, the full class will vote on bills that make it to the "floor."

### Differentiated Resources

- **L3** **L2** Reading Comprehension Worksheets (pp. 143, 145)
- **L3** Core Worksheets A and B (pp. 147, 149)
- **L3** Quiz A (p. 150) **L2** Quiz B (p. 151)

### Student Objectives

- Identify the first steps in the introduction of a bill to the House.
- Describe what happens to a bill once it is referred to a committee.
- Explain how House leaders schedule debate on a bill.
- Explain what happens to a bill on the House floor, and identify the final step in the passage of a bill in the House.

## SECTION 4

### MAKING LAW: THE SENATE

**Guiding Question:** What are the major differences in the lawmaking process in the House and the Senate?

### Summary of Teaching Strategies

Students will explore the meaning and purpose of a filibuster. Acting as conference committees, groups of students will try to negotiate a compromise version of a sample bill. In the activity, students will try to advance the agenda of their assigned party.

### Differentiated Resources

- **L3** **L2** Reading Comprehension Worksheets (pp. 152, 153)
- **L3** Bellringer Worksheet (p. 154)
- **L3** Core Worksheet (p. 155)
- **L3** **L2** Skills Worksheets (p. 156, 157)
- **L3** Quiz A (p. 158) **L2** Quiz B (p. 159)
- **L3** Chapter Test A (p. 160)
- **L2** Chapter Test B (p. 163)

### Student Objectives

- Describe how a bill is introduced in the Senate.
- Compare the Senate's rules for debate with those in the House.
- Describe the role of conference committees in the legislative process.
- Evaluate the actions the President can take after both houses have passed a bill.

---

### DIFFERENTIATED INSTRUCTION KEY

**L1** Special Needs

**L2** Basic includes

    **ELL** English Language Learners

    **LPR** Less Proficient Readers

**L3** All Students

**L4** Advanced Students

## Chapter Resources

**Introduce the chapter**
- American Government Essential Questions Video
- WebQuests
- Essential Questions Journal

**Additional Support**
- All-in-One Teaching Resources
- Differentiation suggestions in each lesson
- Government Online interactivities
- Color Transparencies

**Assessment**
- Document-Based Assessment
- ExamView Test Bank CD-ROM
- Online Assessment
- Online Student Self-Tests
- Section Quizzes (All-in-One Resources)
- Chapter Tests A and B (All-in-One Resources)
- AYP Monitoring Assessments
- Assessment Rubrics

## Essential Questions:

**UNIT 4** What makes a good President?

**CHAPTER 13** Does the current electoral process result in the best candidates for President?

### Government Online Student Center includes
- Interactive textbook with audio
- American Government Essential Questions Video
- WebQuests
- Audio Tours
- Interactivities
- Student Self-Tests

### Government Online Teacher Center includes
- Online Teacher's Edition with lesson planner
- Online Lecture Notes
- Teacher's Resource Library with All-in-One Resources, color transparencies, and an alternative lesson plan
- Online Assessment

Teacher Center
at PearsonSchool.com/phgovt

## SECTION 1

### THE PRESIDENT'S JOB DESCRIPTION

**Guiding Question:** What are the roles and qualifications of the office of the President?

**Summary of Teaching Strategies**
Students will describe the qualifications, roles, and activities of the President.

**Differentiated Resources**
- **L2** Prereading and Vocabulary Worksheet (p. 11)
- **L3 L2** Reading Comprehension Worksheets (pp. 15, 16)
- **L3** Core Worksheet (p. 17)
- **L3** Quiz A (p. 19) **L2** Quiz B (p. 20)

**Student Objectives**
- Describe the President's many roles.
- Understand the formal qualifications necessary to become President.
- Explain how the President's term of office has changed over time.
- Describe the President's pay and benefits.

## SECTION 2

### PRESIDENTIAL SUCCESSION AND THE VICE PRESIDENCY

**Guiding Question:** What occurs when the President is unable to perform the duties of the office?

**Summary of Teaching Strategies**
Students will evaluate scenarios and explain the order of presidential succession for each one.

**Differentiated Resources**
- **L3 L2** Reading Comprehension Worksheets (pp. 21, 22)
- **L3** Core Worksheet (p. 23)
- **L3 L4** Extend Worksheet (p. 24)
- **L3** Quiz A (p. 25) **L2** Quiz B (p. 26)

**Student Objectives**
- Explain how the Constitution provides for presidential succession.
- Understand the constitutional provisions relating to presidential disability.
- Describe the role of the Vice President.

## SECTION 3

### PRESIDENTIAL SELECTION: THE FRAMERS' PLAN

**Guiding Question:** How did the process of choosing a President change over time?

**Summary of Teaching Strategies**
Students will analyze the Framers' original plan for selecting the President and Vice President and how historical events led to changes.

TEACHING
GOVERNMENT

PROGRAM
ORGANIZATION

DIFFERENTIATED
INSTRUCTION

ASSESSMENT

PLANNING
YOUR
INSTRUCTION

**Differentiated Resources**
- **L3 L2 Reading Comprehension Worksheets** (pp. 27, 28)
- **L3 Core Worksheet** (p. 29)
- **L3 Quiz A** (p. 30) **L2 Quiz B** (p. 31)

**Student Objectives**
- Explain the Framers' original provisions for choosing the President.
- Understand how the rise of political parties changed the process of choosing a President as set out in the Constitution.

# SECTION 4

## PRESIDENTIAL NOMINATIONS

**Guiding Question:** Does the nominating system allow Americans to choose the best candidates for President?

### Summary of Teaching Strategies
Students will learn about primaries and caucuses in a jigsaw and analyze a presidential acceptance speech.

**Differentiated Resources**
- **L3 L2 Reading Comprehension Worksheets** (pp. 32, 34)
- **L3 Core Worksheets A and B** (pp. 36, 37)
- **L3 Primary Sources A and B** (pp. 38–41)
- **L3 Quiz A** (p. 42) **L2 Quiz B** (p. 43)

**Student Objectives**
- Describe the role of conventions in the presidential nominating process.
- Evaluate the importance of presidential primaries.

- Understand the caucus-convention process.
- Outline the events that take place during a national convention.
- Examine the characteristics that determine who is nominated as a presidential candidate.

# SECTION 5

## THE PRESIDENTIAL ELECTION

**Guiding Question:** Does the election process serve the goals of American democracy today?

### Summary of Teaching Strategies
Students will evaluate the impact of the electoral college system and proposed alternatives.

**Differentiated Resources**
- **L3 L2 Reading Comprehension Worksheet** (pp. 44, 46)
- **L3 Core Worksheets A and B** (pp. 48, 49)
- **L3 L2 Skills Worksheets** (pp. 50, 51)
- **L3 Quiz A** (p. 52) **L2 Quiz B** (p. 53)
- **L3 Chapter Test A** (p. 54)
- **L2 Chapter Test B** (p. 57)

**Student Objectives**
- Describe the features of the presidential campaign.
- Explain how the electoral college provides for the election of the President.
- Identify the major flaws in the electoral college system.
- Outline the advantages and disadvantages of proposed reforms of the electoral college.

**DIFFERENTIATED INSTRUCTION KEY**

**L1** Special Needs
**L2** Basic includes
   **ELL** English Language Learners
   **LPR** Less Proficient Readers

**L3** All Students
**L4** Advanced Students

## Chapter Resources

### Introduce the chapter
- American Government Essential Questions Video
- WebQuests
- Essential Questions Journal

### Additional Support
- All-in-One Teaching Resources
- Differentiation suggestions in each lesson
- Government Online interactivities
- Color Transparencies

### Assessment
- Document-Based Assessment
- ExamView Test Bank CD-ROM
- Online Assessment
- Online Student Self-Tests
- Section Quizzes (All-in-One Resources)
- Chapter Tests A and B (All-in-One Resources)
- AYP Monitoring Assessments
- Assessment Rubrics

## Essential Questions:

**UNIT 4** What makes a good President?

**CHAPTER 14** How much power should the President have?

### Government Online Student Center includes
- Interactive textbook with audio
- American Government Essential Questions Video
- WebQuests
- Audio Tours
- Interactivities
- Student Self-Tests

### Government Online Teacher Center includes
- Online Teacher's Edition with lesson planner
- Online Lecture Notes
- Teacher's Resource Library with All-in-One Resources, color transparencies, and an alternative lesson plan
- Online Assessment

Teacher Center
at PearsonSchool.com/phgovt

# SECTION 1

## THE GROWTH OF PRESIDENTIAL POWER

**Guiding Question:** What factors have contributed to the growth of presidential power?

### Summary of Teaching Strategies
Students will identify the presidential powers provided in the Constitution and discuss the use of these powers and their growth over time.

### Differentiated Resources
- **L2** **Prereading and Vocabulary Worksheet** (p. 69)
- **L3** **L2** **Reading Comprehension Worksheets** (pp. 73, 74)
- **L3** **L2** **Core Worksheets** (pp. 75, 77)
- **L2** **Extend Worksheet** (p. 80)
- **L3** **Quiz A (p. 81)** **L2** **Quiz B** (p. 82)

### Student Objectives
- Explain why Article II of the Constitution can be described as "an outline" of the presidential office.
- List several reasons for the growth of presidential power.
- Explain how various Presidents' views have shaped the powers of the office.

# SECTION 2

## THE EXECUTIVE POWERS

**Guiding Question:** What are the executive powers and how were they established?

### Summary of Teaching Strategies
Students will create a list of facts that apply to each executive power, and discuss the appointment power and confirmation process.

### Differentiated Resources
- **L3** **L2** **Reading Comprehension Worksheets** (pp. 83, 84)
- **L3** **Bellringer Worksheet** (p. 85)
- **L3** **Core Worksheet** (p. 86)
- **L3** **L4** **Extend Worksheet** (p. 87)
- **L3** **Quiz A** (p. 88) **L2** **Quiz B** (p. 89)

### Student Objectives
- Identify the sources of the President's power to execute federal law.
- Define the ordinance power.
- Explain how the appointment power works and describe the limits on the removal power.
- Examine the power of executive privilege.

TEACHING
GOVERNMENT

PROGRAM
ORGANIZATION

DIFFERENTIATED
INSTRUCTION

ASSESSMENT

PLANNING
YOUR
INSTRUCTION

## SECTION 3

### DIPLOMATIC AND MILITARY POWERS

**Guiding Question:** What tools are available to the President to implement foreign policy?

#### Summary of Teaching Strategies
Students will study the tools available to the President to carry out foreign policy, summarize the President's diplomatic and military powers, and identify checks and balances on these powers.

#### Differentiated Resources
- **L3 L2 Reading Comprehension Worksheets** (pp. 90, 91)
- **L3 Core Worksheet** (p. 92)
- **L3 L2 Skills Worksheets** (pp. 94, 95)
- **L3 Quiz A** (p. 96)  **L2 Quiz B** (p. 97)

#### Student Objectives
- Explain how treaties are made and approved.
- Explain why and how executive agreements are made.
- Summarize how the power of recognition is used.
- Describe the President's powers as commander in chief.

## SECTION 4

### LEGISLATIVE AND JUDICIAL POWERS

**Guiding Question:** How can the President check the actions of the legislative and judicial branches?

#### Summary of Teaching Strategies
Students will analyze the principle of checks and balances, define elements of the President's legislative and judicial powers, and evaluate the use of the presidential pardon.

#### Differentiated Resources
- **L3 L2 Reading Comprehension Worksheets** (pp. 98, 99)
- **L3 Core Worksheet** (p. 100)
- **L2 Extend Activity** (p. 102)
- **L3 Quiz A** (p. 103)  **L2 Quiz B** (p. 104)
- **L3 Chapter Test A** (p. 110)
- **L2 Chapter Test B** (p. 113)

#### Student Objectives
- Explain the President's legislative powers and how they are an important part of the system of checks and balances.
- Describe the President's major judicial powers.

---

### DIFFERENTIATED INSTRUCTION KEY

| | |
|---|---|
| **L1** Special Needs | **L3** All Students |
| **L2** Basic includes | **L4** Advanced Students |
| **ELL** English Language Learners | |
| **LPR** Less Proficient Readers | |

## Chapter Resources

### Introduce the chapter
- American Government Essential Questions Video
- WebQuests
- Essential Questions Journal

### Additional Support
- All-in-One Teaching Resources
- Differentiation suggestions in each lesson
- Government Online interactivities
- Color Transparencies

### Assessment
- Document-Based Assessment
- ExamView Test Bank CD-ROM
- Online Assessment
- Online Student Self-Tests
- Section Quizzes (All-in-One Resources)
- Chapter Tests A and B (All-in-One Resources)
- AYP Monitoring Assessments
- Assessment Rubrics

## Essential Questions:
**UNIT 4** What makes a good President?
**CHAPTER 15** Is the bureaucracy essential to good government?

### Government Online Student Center includes
- Interactive textbook with audio
- American Government Essential Questions Video
- WebQuests
- Audio Tours
- Interactivities
- Student Self-Tests

### Government Online Teacher Center includes
- Online Teacher's Edition with lesson planner
- Online Lecture Notes
- Teacher's Resource Library with All-in-One Resources, color transparencies, and an alternative lesson plan
- Online Assessment

Teacher Center
at PearsonSchool.com/phgovt

## SECTION 1

### THE FEDERAL BUREAUCRACY

**Guiding Question:** What is the structure and purpose of the federal bureaucracy?

### Summary of Teaching Strategies
Students will describe their school as a bureaucracy. Then they will identify the federal agencies responsible for resolving several scenarios.

### Differentiated Resources
- **L2 Prereading and Vocabulary Worksheet** (p. 124)
- **L3 L2 Reading Comprehension Worksheets** (pp. 128, 129)
- **L3 L2 Core Worksheets** (pp. 130, 132)
- **L3 Quiz A** (p. 133) **L2 Quiz B** (p. 134)

### Student Objectives
- Define a bureaucracy.
- Identify the major elements of the federal bureaucracy.
- Explain how groups within the federal bureaucracy are named.
- Describe the difference between a staff agency and a line agency.

## SECTION 2

### EXECUTIVE OFFICE OF THE PRESIDENT

**Guiding Question:** What agencies and advisors are part of the Executive Office of the President and what are their functions?

### Summary of Teaching Strategies
Students will investigate the importance of presidential advisors and then will summarize features and functions of agencies within the Executive Office of the President by using a Jigsaw activity.

### Differentiated Resources
- **L3 L2 Reading Comprehension Worksheets** (pp. 135, 136)
- **L3 Core Worksheet** (p. 137)
- **L3 Quiz A** (p. 139) **L2 Quiz B** (p. 140)

### Student Objectives
- Describe the Executive Office of the President.
- Explain the duties of The White House Office, the National Security Council, and the Office of Management and Budget.
- Identify the other agencies that make up the Executive Office of the President.

## SECTION 3

### THE CABINET DEPARTMENTS

**Guiding Question:** What is the Cabinet and what does it do?

#### Summary of Teaching Strategies
Students will study the services that the Federal Government provides American citizens. Then they will generate a list of the necessary qualifications for Cabinet-level department heads.

#### Differentiated Resources
- **L3** **L2** **Reading Comprehension Worksheets** (pp. 141, 142)
- **L3** **Core Worksheet** (p. 143)
- **L2** **Extend Activities** (pp. 144, 145)
- **L3** **Quiz A** (p. 146)   **L2** **Quiz B** (p. 147)

#### Student Objectives
- Describe the origin and work of the executive departments.
- Explain how the members of the Cabinet are chosen.
- Identify the role of the Cabinet in the President's decisions.

## SECTION 4

### INDEPENDENT AGENCIES

**Guiding Question:** What are the roles and structures of the independent agencies?

#### Summary of Teaching Strategies
Students will compare types of independent agencies and will research job opportunities within the civil service using information from the Office of Personnel Management.

#### Differentiated Resources
- **L3** **L2** **Reading Comprehension Worksheets** (pp. 148, 149)
- **L3** **L2** **Core Worksheets** (pp. 150, 155)
- **L3** **L2** **Skills Worksheets** (pp. 160, 161)
- **L3** **L4** **Extend Worksheet** (p. 162)
- **L2** **Extend Activity** (p. 163)
- **L3** **Quiz A** (p. 164)   **L2** **Quiz B** (p. 165)
- **L3** **Chapter Test A** (p. 166)
- **L2** **Chapter Test B** (p. 169)

#### Student Objectives
- Explain why Congress has created the independent agencies.
- Identify the characteristics of independent executive agencies.
- Describe the history and formation of NASA, the OPM, and the Selective Service System.
- Explain the structure and function of the independent regulatory commissions and government corporations.

---

**DIFFERENTIATED INSTRUCTION KEY**

**L1** Special Needs

**L2** Basic includes

    **ELL** English Language Learners

    **LPR** Less Proficient Readers

**L3** All Students

**L4** Advanced Students

---

## Chapter Resources

**Introduce the chapter**
- American Government Essential Questions Video
- WebQuests
- Essential Questions Journal

**Additional Support**
- All-in-One Teaching Resources
- Differentiation suggestions in each lesson
- Government Online interactivities
- Color Transparencies

**Assessment**
- Document-Based Assessment
- ExamView Test Bank CD-ROM
- Online Assessment
- Online Student Self-Tests
- Section Quizzes (All-in-One Resources)
- Chapter Tests A and B (All-in-One Resources)
- AYP Monitoring Assessments
- Assessment Rubrics

---

## Essential Questions:

**UNIT 4** What makes a good President?

**CHAPTER 16** How should the federal budget reflect Americans' priorities?

### Government Online Student Center includes
- Interactive textbook with audio
- American Government Essential Questions Video
- WebQuests
- Audio Tours
- Interactivities
- Student Self-Tests

### Government Online Teacher Center includes
- Online Teacher's Edition with lesson planner
- Online Lecture Notes
- Teacher's Resource Library with All-in-One Resources, color transparencies, and an alternative lesson plan
- Online Assessment

Teacher Center
at PearsonSchool.com/phgovt

## SECTION 1

### TAXES AND OTHER REVENUE

**Guiding Question:** How is the Federal Government financed?

**Summary of Teaching Strategies**
Students will examine the parameters the Constitution sets on the power to tax and who must pay taxes.

**Differentiated Resources**
- **L2** Prereading and Vocabulary Worksheet (p. 181)
- **L3 L2** Reading Comprehension Worksheets (pp. 185, 187)
- **L3** Bellringer Worksheet (p. 189)
- **L3 L2** Core Worksheets (pp. 190, 191)
- **L2** Extend Activity (p. 193)
- **L3** Quiz A (p. 194)   **L2** Quiz B (p. 195)

**Student Objectives**
- Explain how the Constitution gives Congress the power to tax and at the same time places limits on that power.
- Identify the most significant federal taxes collected today.
- Describe the nontax sources of federal revenue.

## SECTION 2

### BORROWING AND THE PUBLIC DEBT

**Guiding Question:** What effect does borrowing have on the federal budget and the nation's economy?

**Summary of Teaching Strategies**
Students will learn about federal borrowing by analyzing the annual deficits and surpluses, and the history of public debt by interpreting graphs and timelines.

**Differentiated Resources**
- **L3 L2** Reading Comprehension Worksheets (pp. 196, 197)
- **L3 L2** Core Worksheets (pp. 198, 199)
- **L3 L2** Skills Worksheets (pp. 200, 201)
- **L3 L4** Extend Worksheet (p. 202)
- **L3** Quiz A (p. 203)   **L2** Quiz B (p. 204)

**Student Objectives**
- Describe federal borrowing.
- Explain how the Federal Government's actions can affect the economy.
- Analyze the causes and effects of the public debt.

TEACHING
GOVERNMENT

PROGRAM
ORGANIZATION

DIFFERENTIATED
INSTRUCTION

ASSESSMENT

PLANNING
YOUR
INSTRUCTION

# SECTION 3

## SPENDING AND THE BUDGET

**Guiding Question:** How is federal spending determined?

### Summary of Teaching Strategies
Students will identify how the budget-making process works in Congress, and will rank the priority of funding specific federal programs.

### Differentiated Resources
- **L3** **L2** Reading Comprehension Worksheets (pp. 205, 207)
- **L3** Core Worksheets A and B (pp. 209, 210)
- **L3** Quiz A (p. 211)   **L2** Quiz B (p. 212)

### Student Objectives
- Identify the key elements of federal spending.
- Define controllable and uncontrollable spending.
- Explain how the President and Congress work together to create the federal budget.

# SECTION 4

## FISCAL AND MONETARY POLICY

**Guiding Question:** How does the Federal Government achieve its economic goals?

### Summary of Teaching Strategies
Students will discuss the nation's current economic situation, analyze the tools available to the government to address it, and suggest policy actions for economic goals.

### Differentiated Resources
- **L3** **L2** Reading Comprehension Worksheets (pp. 213, 214)
- **L3** Core Worksheet (p. 215)
- **L3** Quiz A (p. 217)   **L2** Quiz B (p. 218)
- **L3** Chapter Test A (p. 219)
- **L2** Chapter Test B (p. 222)

### Student Objectives
- Describe the overall goals of the Federal Government's actions in the economy.
- Explain the features and purposes of fiscal policy.
- Explain the features and purposes of monetary policy.

---

**DIFFERENTIATED INSTRUCTION KEY**

**L1** Special Needs
**L2** Basic includes
    **ELL** English Language Learners
    **LPR** Less Proficient Readers

**L3** All Students
**L4** Advanced Students

## Chapter Resources

**Introduce the chapter**
- American Government Essential Questions Video
- WebQuests
- Essential Questions Journal

**Additional Support**
- All-in-One Teaching Resources
- Differentiation suggestions in each lesson
- Government Online interactivities
- Color Transparencies

**Assessment**
- Document-Based Assessment
- ExamView Test Bank CD-ROM
- Online Assessment
- Online Student Self-Tests
- Section Quizzes (All-in-One Resources)
- Chapter Tests A and B (All-in-One Resources)
- AYP Monitoring Assessments
- Assessment Rubrics

## Essential Questions:

**UNIT 4** What makes a good President?

**CHAPTER 17** How should the United States interact with other countries?

### Government Online Student Center includes
- Interactive textbook with audio
- American Government Essential Questions Video
- WebQuests
- Audio Tours
- Interactivities
- Student Self-Tests

### Government Online Teacher Center includes
- Online Teacher's Edition with lesson planner
- Online Lecture Notes
- Teacher's Resource Library with All-in-One Resources, color transparencies, and an alternative lesson plan
- Online Assessment

Teacher Center
at PearsonSchool.com/phgovt

## SECTION 1

### FOREIGN AFFAIRS AND DIPLOMACY

**Guiding Question:** How is foreign policy made and conducted?

### Summary of Teaching Strategies
Students will explore the benefits and disadvantages of internationalist policies on U.S. interests and will study the role of the State Department in foreign affairs.

### Differentiated Resources
- **L2** **Prereading and Vocabulary Worksheet** (p. 234)
- **L3** **L2** **Reading Comprehension Worksheets** (pp. 238, 239)
- **L3** **Core Worksheets A and B** (pp. 240, 241)
- **L2** **Extend Activity** (p. 244)
- **L3** **Quiz A** (p. 245) **L2** **Quiz B** (p. 246)

### Student Objectives
- Explain the difference between isolationism and internationalism.
- Define foreign policy.
- Understand that a nation's foreign policy is composed of its many foreign policies.
- Describe the functions, components, and organization of the Department of State.

## SECTION 2

### NATIONAL SECURITY

**Guiding Question:** How does the Federal Government safeguard this nation's security?

### Summary of Teaching Strategies
Students will discuss the tension between freedom and security, and take a stand on government responses to potential security threats.

### Differentiated Resources
- **L3** **L2** **Reading Comprehension Worksheets** (pp. 247, 249)
- **L3** **L2** **Core Worksheets** (pp. 251, 252)
- **L3** **L2** **Skills Worksheets** (pp. 253, 254)
- **L3** **L4** **Extend Worksheet** (p. 255)
- **L3** **Quiz A** (p. 256) **L2** **Quiz B** (p. 257)

### Student Objectives
- Summarize the functions, components, and organization of the Department of Defense and the military departments.
- Explain how the Director of National Intelligence and the Department of Homeland Security contribute to the nation's security.

TEACHING
GOVERNMENT

PROGRAM
ORGANIZATION

DIFFERENTIATED
INSTRUCTION

ASSESSMENT

PLANNING
YOUR
INSTRUCTION

## SECTION 3

### AMERICAN FOREIGN POLICY OVERVIEW

**Guiding Question:** How has American foreign policy changed over time?

### Summary of Teaching Strategies
Students will describe and understand foreign policies from U.S. history and analyze the Truman Doctrine.

### Differentiated Resources
- **L3** **L2** **Reading Comprehension Worksheets** (pp. 258, 260)
- **L3** **Core Worksheets A and B** (pp. 262, 263)
- **L3** **Quiz A** (p. 265)  **L2** **Quiz B** (p. 266)

### Student Objectives
- Summarize American foreign policy from independence through World War I.
- Show how the two World Wars affected America's traditional policy of isolationism.
- Explain the principles of collective security and deterrence and their use during the cold war.
- Describe American foreign policy since the end of the cold war.
- Understand why the world remains a dangerous place.

## SECTION 4

### FOREIGN AID AND ALLIANCES

**Guiding Question:** In what ways does the United States cooperate with other nations?

### Summary of Teaching Strategies
Students will describe the effect of foreign aid programs and defense alliances on U.S. interests, and compare and contrast the UN Universal Declaration on Human Rights with the U.S. Constitution.

### Differentiated Resources
- **L3** **L2** **Reading Comprehension Worksheets** (pp. 267, 269)
- **L3** **Core Worksheets A and B** (pp. 271, 272)
- **L2** **Extend Activities** (pp. 275, 276)
- **L3** **Quiz A** (p. 277)  **L2** **Quiz B** (p. 278)
- **L3** **Chapter Test A** (p. 279)
- **L2** **Chapter Test B** (p. 282)

### Student Objectives
- Identify two types of foreign aid and describe the foreign aid policy of the United States.
- Describe the major regional security alliances developed by the United States.
- Examine the role and structure of the United Nations and the problems it addresses.

---

**DIFFERENTIATED INSTRUCTION KEY**

**L1** Special Needs

**L2** Basic includes

    **ELL** English Language Learners

    **LPR** Less Proficient Readers

**L3** All Students

**L4** Advanced Students

## Chapter Resources

### Introduce the chapter
- American Government Essential Questions Video
- WebQuests
- Essential Questions Journal

### Additional Support
- All-in-One Teaching Resources
- Differentiation suggestions in each lesson
- Government Online interactivities
- Color Transparencies

### Assessment
- Document-Based Assessment
- ExamView Test Bank CD-ROM
- Online Assessment
- Online Student Self-Tests
- Section Quizzes (All-in-One Resources)
- Chapter Tests A and B (All-in-One Resources)
- AYP Monitoring Assessments
- Assessment Rubrics

## Essential Questions:

**UNIT 5** What should be the role of the judicial branch?

**CHAPTER 18** Does the structure of the federal court system allow it to administer justice effectively?

### Government Online Student Center includes
- Interactive textbook with audio
- American Government Essential Questions Video
- WebQuests
- Audio Tours
- Interactivities
- Student Self-Tests

### Government Online Teacher Center includes
- Online Teacher's Edition with lesson planner
- Online Lecture Notes
- Teacher's Resource Library with All-in-One Resources, color transparencies, and an alternative lesson plan
- Online Assessment

Teacher Center
at PearsonSchool.com/phgovt

## SECTION 1

### THE NATIONAL JUDICIARY

**Guiding Question:** What are the structure and function of the national judiciary?

### Summary of Teaching Strategies
Students will analyze an excerpt from *The Federalist* No. 78; use graphic organizers to understand the structure, role, and jurisdiction of the federal courts; and create classified ads for a Supreme Court justice.

### Differentiated Resources
- **L2 Prereading and Vocabulary Worksheet** (p. 9)
- **L3 L2 Reading Comprehension Worksheets** (pp. 13, 15)
- **L3 L2 Core Worksheets** (pp. 17, 18)
- **L3 L4 Extend Worksheet** (p. 20)
- **L2 Extend Activity** (p. 22)
- **L3 Quiz A** (p. 23) **L2 Quiz B** (p. 24)

### Student Objectives
- Explain why the Constitution created a national judiciary, and describe its structure.
- Identify the criteria that determine whether a case is within the jurisdiction of a federal court, and compare the types of jurisdiction.
- Outline the process for appointing federal judges, and list their terms of office.
- Understand the impact of judicial philosophy.
- Examine the roles of court officers.

## SECTION 2

### THE INFERIOR COURTS

**Guiding Question:** What are the structure and jurisdiction of the inferior courts?

### Summary of Teaching Strategies
Students will identify the structure of the inferior constitutional courts by studying the various courts and their jurisdictions. Then they will learn how inferior courts function by constructing paths of appeals for various case scenarios.

### Differentiated Resources
- **L3 L2 Reading Comprehension Worksheets** (pp. 25, 26)
- **L3 Core Worksheet** (p. 27)
- **L2 Extend Activity** (p. 28)
- **L3 Quiz A** (p. 29) **L2 Quiz B** (p. 30)

### Student Objectives
- Describe the structure and jurisdiction of the federal district courts.
- Describe the structure and jurisdiction of the federal courts of appeals.
- Describe the structure and jurisdiction of the two other constitutional courts.

# SECTION 3

## THE SUPREME COURT

**Guiding Question:** What is the Supreme Court's jurisdiction, and how does the Court operate?

### Summary of Teaching Strategies
Students will learn about the scope of the Supreme Court's jurisdiction, the power of judicial review, and the Court's original and appellate jurisdiction. They also will identify how the Supreme Court operates by sequencing the appeals process, reading a transcript of a real case, and formulating opinions on controversial cases.

### Differentiated Resources
* **L3** **L2** Reading Comprehension Worksheets (pp. 31, 33)
* **L3** Core Worksheets A and B (pp. 35, 40)
* **L3** **L2** Skills Worksheets (pp. 41, 42)
* **L3** Quiz A (p. 43)  **L2** Quiz B (p. 44)

### Student Objectives
* Define the concept of judicial review.
* Outline the scope of the Supreme Court's jurisdiction.
* Examine how cases reach the Supreme Court.
* Summarize the way the Court operates.

# SECTION 4

## THE SPECIAL COURTS

**Guiding Question:** What are the special courts, and what are the jurisdictions of each?

### Summary of Teaching Strategies
Students will learn about the special courts and their jurisdictions. They will understand how special courts function by constructing paths of appeals for case scenarios. They will also analyze options in favor of and opposing military commissions.

### Differentiated Resources
* **L3** **L2** Reading Comprehension Worksheets (pp. 45, 46)
* **L3** **L2** Core Worksheets (pp. 47, 49)
* **L3** Quiz A (p. 51)  **L2** Quiz B (p. 52)
* **L3** Chapter Test A (p. 53)
* **L2** Chapter Test B (p. 56)

### Student Objectives
* Contrast the jurisdiction of the Court of Appeals for the Armed Forces and the Court of Appeals for Veterans Claims.
* Explain how a citizen may sue the United States government in the Court of Federal Claims.
* Examine the roles of the territorial courts and those of the District of Columbia courts.
* Explain what types of cases are brought to the Tax Court.

TEACHING GOVERNMENT

PROGRAM ORGANIZATION

DIFFERENTIATED INSTRUCTION

ASSESSMENT

PLANNING YOUR INSTRUCTION

---

**DIFFERENTIATED INSTRUCTION KEY**

**L1** Special Needs

**L2** Basic includes

    **ELL** English Language Learners

    **LPR** Less Proficient Readers

**L3** All Students

**L4** Advanced Students

## Chapter Resources

### Introduce the chapter
- American Government Essential Questions Video
- WebQuests
- Essential Questions Journal

### Additional Support
- All-in-One Teaching Resources
- Differentiation suggestions in each lesson
- Government Online interactivities
- Color Transparencies

### Assessment
- Document-Based Assessment
- ExamView Test Bank CD-ROM
- Online Assessment
- Online Student Self-Tests
- Section Quizzes (All-in-One Resources)
- Chapter Tests A and B (All-in-One Resources)
- AYP Monitoring Assessments
- Assessment Rubrics

## Essential Questions:

**UNIT 5** What should be the role of the judicial branch?

**CHAPTER 19** How can the judiciary balance individual rights with the common good?

### Government Online Student Center includes
- Interactive textbook with audio
- American Government Essential Questions Video
- WebQuests
- Audio Tours
- Interactivities
- Student Self-Tests

### Government Online Teacher Center includes
- Online Teacher's Edition with lesson planner
- Online Lecture Notes
- Teacher's Resource Library with All-in-One Resources, color transparencies, and an alternative lesson plan
- Online Assessment

Teacher Center
at PearsonSchool.com/phgovt

## SECTION 1

### THE UNALIENABLE RIGHTS

**Guiding Question:** How does the Constitution protect the rights of individuals against government?

### Summary of Teaching Strategies
Students will learn that rights are not absolute by debating issues in which rights and interests must be balanced. Then they will describe how the Constitution protects the rights of individuals by creating a diagram.

### Differentiated Resources
- **L2 Prereading and Vocabulary Worksheet** (p. 68)
- **L3 L2 Reading Comprehension Worksheets** (pp. 72, 74)
- **L3 Core Worksheet** (p. 76)
- **L3 L2 Skills Worksheets** (pp. 77, 78)
- **L2 Extend Activity** (p. 79)
- **L3 Quiz A** (p. 80)   **L2 Quiz B** (p. 81)

### Student Objectives
- Explain how Americans' commitment to freedom led to the creation of the Bill of Rights.
- Understand that the rights guaranteed by limited government are not absolute.
- Show how federalism affects individual rights.
- Describe how the 9th Amendment helps protect individual rights.

## SECTION 2

### FREEDOM OF RELIGION

**Guiding Question:** How does the 1st Amendment protect the freedom of religion?

### Summary of Teaching Strategies
Students will study the meaning of the Establishment Clause and its "wall of separation" through cases about freedom of religion. Then they will determine how the Supreme Court has interpreted the Establishment Clause and Free Exercise Clause by evaluating scenarios about freedom-of-religion conflicts.

### Differentiated Resources
- **L3 L2 Reading Comprehension Worksheets** (pp. 82, 84)
- **L3 Core Worksheet** (p. 86)
- **L3 Quiz A** (p. 88)   **L2 Quiz B** (p. 89)

### Student Objectives
- Examine why religious liberty is protected in the Bill of Rights.
- Describe the limits imposed by the Establishment Clause of the 1st Amendment.
- Summarize the Supreme Court rulings on religion and education as well as other Establishment Clause cases.
- Explain how the Supreme Court has interpreted and limited the Free Exercise Clause.

TEACHING
GOVERNMENT

PROGRAM
ORGANIZATION

DIFFERENTIATED
INSTRUCTION

ASSESSMENT

PLANNING
YOUR
INSTRUCTION

# SECTION 3

## FREEDOM OF SPEECH AND PRESS

**Guiding Question:** What are the limits on the guarantees of free speech and free press?

### Summary of Teaching Strategies
Students will identify the limits and protections of freedom of speech by charting restrictions on different forms of expression, analyzing prior restraint, summarizing court rulings on student speech, and interpreting political cartoons. Then they will identify the limits and protections of freedom of the press by participating in dramatizations of cases related to that freedom.

### Differentiated Resources
* **L3** **L2** Reading Comprehension Worksheets (pp. 90, 91)
* **L3** Core Worksheet (p. 92)
* **L3** **L4** Extend Worksheet (p. 95)
* **L2** Extend Activity (p. 96)
* **L3** Quiz A (p. 97)   **L2** Quiz B (p. 98)

### Student Objectives
* Explain the importance of the two basic purposes served by the guarantees of free expression.
* Summarize how the Supreme Court has limited seditious speech and obscenity.
* Examine the issues of prior restraint and press confidentiality, and describe the limits the Court has placed on the media.
* Define symbolic and commercial speech; describe the limits of their exercise.

# SECTION 4

## FREEDOM OF ASSEMBLY AND PETITION

**Guiding Question:** How has the Supreme Court ruled on assembly and petition cases?

### Summary of Teaching Strategies
Students will participate in scenarios about freedom of assembly and petition conflicts. Then they will study the restrictions on assembly and petition by applying time-place-manner regulations and content neutrality to assembly situations.

### Differentiated Resources
* **L3** **L2** Reading Comprehension Worksheets (pp. 99, 100)
* **L3** **L2** Core Worksheets (pp. 101, 105)
* **L3** Quiz A (p. 109)   **L2** Quiz B (p. 110)
* **L3** Chapter Test A (p. 111)
* **L2** Chapter Test B (p. 114)

### Student Objectives
* Explain the Constitution's guarantees of assembly and petition.
* Summarize how government can limit the time, place, and manner of assembly.
* Compare and contrast the freedom-of-assembly issues that arise on public versus private property.
* Explore how the Supreme Court has interpreted freedom of association.

---

**DIFFERENTIATED INSTRUCTION KEY**

**L1** Special Needs                    **L3** All Students

**L2** Basic includes                   **L4** Advanced Students

          **ELL** English Language Learners

          **LPR** Less Proficient Readers

## Chapter Resources

### Introduce the chapter
- American Government Essential Questions Video
- WebQuests
- Essential Questions Journal

### Additional Support
- All-in-One Teaching Resources
- Differentiation suggestions in each lesson
- Government Online interactivities
- Color Transparencies

### Assessment
- Document-Based Assessment
- ExamView Test Bank CD-ROM
- Online Assessment
- Online Student Self-Tests
- Section Quizzes (All-in-One Resources)
- Chapter Tests A and B (All-in-One Resources)
- AYP Monitoring Assessments
- Assessment Rubrics

## Essential Questions:

**UNIT 5** What should be the role of the judicial branch?

**CHAPTER 20** To what extent has the judiciary protected the rights of privacy, security, and personal freedom?

### Government Online Student Center includes
- Interactive textbook with audio
- American Government Essential Questions Video
- WebQuests
- Audio Tours
- Interactivities
- Student Self-Tests

### Government Online Teacher Center includes
- Online Teacher's Edition with lesson planner
- Online Lecture Notes
- Teacher's Resource Library with All-in-One Resources, color transparencies, and an alternative lesson plan
- Online Assessment

Teacher Center
at PearsonSchool.com/phgovt

## SECTION 1

### DUE PROCESS OF LAW

**Guiding Question:** Why is the concept of due process important to a free society?

### Summary of Teaching Strategies
Students will analyze examples of when due process was and was not followed, and will consider how government might function without due process. They also will evaluate how government balances its police power with individual freedoms.

### Differentiated Resources
- **L2** **Prereading and Vocabulary Worksheet** (p. 126)
- **L3** **L2** **Reading Comprehension Worksheets** (pp. 130, 131)
- **L3** **Core Worksheets A and B** (pp. 132, 134)
- **L3** **Quiz A** (p. 135)   **L2** **Quiz B** (p. 136)

### Student Objectives
- Explain the meaning of due process of law as set out in the 5th and 14th amendments.
- Define *police power* and understand its relationship to civil rights.
- Describe the right of privacy and its origins in constitutional law.

## SECTION 2

### FREEDOM AND SECURITY OF THE PERSON

**Guiding Question:** How does the Constitution protect the freedom and security of the person?

### Summary of Teaching Strategies
Students will discuss proper procedures of police officers. Then they will identify how Supreme Court rulings have narrowed the meaning of the exclusionary rule by analyzing Court opinions related to it.

### Differentiated Resources
- **L3** **L2** **Reading Comprehension Worksheets** (pp. 137, 139)
- **L3** **Core Worksheet** (p. 141)
- **L3** **L2** **Skills Worksheets** (pp. 142, 143)
- **L3** **Extend Worksheet** (p. 144)
- **L3** **Quiz A** (p. 146)   **L2** **Quiz B** (p. 147)

### Student Objectives
- Outline Supreme Court decisions regarding slavery and involuntary servitude.
- Explain the intent and application of the 2nd Amendment's protection of the right to keep and bear arms.
- Summarize the constitutional provisions designed to guarantee security of home and person.

TEACHING
GOVERNMENT

PROGRAM
ORGANIZATION

DIFFERENTIATED
INSTRUCTION

ASSESSMENT

PLANNING
YOUR
INSTRUCTION

## SECTION 3

### RIGHTS OF THE ACCUSED

**Guiding Question:** What protections does the Constitution set out for persons accused of crimes?

### Summary of Teaching Strategies

Students will identify the rights of people accused of crime and discuss a case related to habeas corpus. Then they will evaluate the guarantee against self-incrimination by analyzing a case related to the Miranda rule.

### Differentiated Resources

- **L3 L2** Reading Comprehension Worksheets (pp. 148, 149)
- **L3 L2** Core Worksheets A (pp. 151, 155)
- **L3 L2** Core Worksheets B (pp. 153, 158)
- **L3** Quiz A (p. 161)   **L2** Quiz B (p. 162)

### Student Objectives

- Define writ of habeas corpus, bills of attainder, and ex post facto laws.
- Outline how the right to a grand jury and the guarantee against double jeopardy help safeguard the rights of the accused.
- Describe issues that arise from guarantees of speedy and public trials.
- Determine what constitutes a fair trial by jury.
- Examine the right to an adequate defense and the guarantee against self-incrimination.

## SECTION 4

### PUNISHMENT

**Guiding Question:** How does the Constitution set limits on the punishments for crime?

### Summary of Teaching Strategies

Students will analyze court cases on the death penalty. Then they will evaluate arguments on the constitutionality of juvenile capital punishment by analyzing Supreme Court opinions and editorials on this issue.

### Differentiated Resources

- **L3 L2** Reading Comprehension Worksheets (pp. 163, 164)
- **L3** Core Worksheets A and B (pp. 165, 167)
- **L3** Quiz A (p. 171)   **L2** Quiz B (p. 172)
- **L3** Chapter Test A (p. 177)
- **L2** Chapter Test B (p. 180)

### Student Objectives

- Explain the purpose of bail and preventive detention.
- Describe the Court's interpretation of cruel and unusual punishment.
- Outline the history of the Court's decisions on capital punishment.
- Define the crime of treason.

---

**DIFFERENTIATED INSTRUCTION KEY**

**L1** Special Needs

**L2** Basic includes

**ELL** English Language Learners

**LPR** Less Proficient Readers

**L3** All Students

**L4** Advanced Students

---

## Chapter Resources

### Introduce the chapter
- American Government Essential Questions Video
- WebQuests
- Essential Questions Journal

### Additional Support
- All-in-One Teaching Resources
- Differentiation suggestions in each lesson
- Government Online interactivities
- Color Transparencies

### Assessment
- Document-Based Assessment
- ExamView Test Bank CD-ROM
- Online Assessment
- Online Student Self-Tests
- Section Quizzes (All-in-One Resources)
- Chapter Tests A and B (All-in-One Resources)
- AYP Monitoring Assessments
- Assessment Rubrics

---

## Essential Questions:

**UNIT 5** What should be the role of the judicial branch?

**CHAPTER 21** Why are there ongoing struggles for civil rights?

### Government Online Student Center includes
- Interactive textbook with audio
- American Government Essential Questions Video
- WebQuests
- Audio Tours
- Interactivities
- Student Self-Tests

### Government Online Teacher Center includes
- Online Teacher's Edition with lesson planner
- Online Lecture Notes
- Teacher's Resource Library with All-in-One Resources, color transparencies, and an alternative lesson plan
- Online Assessment

Teacher Center
at PearsonSchool.com/phgovt

---

## SECTION 1

### DIVERSITY AND DISCRIMINATION

**Guiding Question:** How have various minority groups in American society been discriminated against?

### Summary of Teaching Strategies
Students will study the ethnic composition of the U.S. and explore its history of race- and gender-based discrimination.

### Differentiated Resources
- **L2** **Prereading and Vocabulary Worksheet** (p. 192)
- **L3** **L2** **Reading Comprehension Worksheets** (pp. 196, 197)
- **L3** **Core Worksheet** (p. 198)
- **L3** **Quiz A** (p. 199)  **L2** **Quiz B** (p. 200)

### Student Objectives
- Understand what it means to live in a heterogeneous society.
- Summarize the history of race-based discrimination in the United States.
- Examine discrimination against women in the past and present.

---

## SECTION 2

### EQUALITY BEFORE THE LAW

**Guiding Question:** How has the interpretation of the guarantee of equal rights changed over time?

### Summary of Teaching Strategies
Students will examine historical data and tests used by the Supreme Court to analyze discrimination, and will explore school integration through timelines.

### Differentiated Resources
- **L3** **L2** **Reading Comprehension Worksheets** (pp. 201, 204)
- **L3** **Core Worksheet** (p. 207)
- **L3** **L4** **Extend Worksheet** (p. 208)
- **L3** **Quiz A** (p. 210)  **L2** **Quiz B** (p. 211)

### Student Objectives
- Explain the importance of the Equal Protection Clause.
- Describe the history of segregation in America.
- Examine how classification by gender relates to discrimination.

TEACHING
GOVERNMENT

PROGRAM
ORGANIZATION

DIFFERENTIATED
INSTRUCTION

ASSESSMENT

PLANNING
YOUR
INSTRUCTION

## SECTION 3

### FEDERAL CIVIL RIGHTS LAWS

**Guiding Question:** What is the history of civil rights legislation from Reconstruction to today?

### Summary of Teaching Strategies
Students will trace the development of civil rights legislation by reviewing States' actions to nullify African Americans' rights, and will analyze affirmative action by exploring the issues surrounding it.

### Differentiated Resources
- **L3 L2 Reading Comprehension Worksheets** (pp. 212, 213)
- **L3 Core Worksheet** (p. 215)
- **L3 L2 Skills Worksheets** (pp. 217, 218)
- **L3 Quiz A** (p. 219) **L2 Quiz B** (p. 220)

### Student Objectives
- Outline the history of civil rights legislation from the Reconstruction period on to today.
- Explore the issues surrounding affirmative action.

## SECTION 4

### AMERICAN CITIZENSHIP

**Guiding Question:** How can American citizenship be attained and how has immigration policy changed over the years?

### Summary of Teaching Strategies
Students will discuss ways individuals become citizens in the United States, and prepare arguments reflecting the controversy over immigration.

### Differentiated Resources
- **L3 L2 Reading Comprehension Worksheets** (pp. 221, 222)
- **L3 Core Worksheet A** (p. 223)
- **L3 L2 Core Worksheets B** (pp. 225, 226)
- **L3 Quiz A** (p. 227) **L2 Quiz B** (p. 228)
- **L3 Chapter Test A** (p. 233)
- **L2 Chapter Test B** (p. 236)

### Student Objectives
- Describe how people become American citizens by birth and by naturalization.
- Explain how an American can lose his or her citizenship.
- Illustrate how the United States is a nation of immigrants.
- Compare and contrast the status of undocumented aliens and legal immigrants.

---

**DIFFERENTIATED INSTRUCTION KEY**

L1 Special Needs

L2 Basic includes

    **ELL** English Language Learners

    **LPR** Less Proficient Readers

L3 All Students

L4 Advanced Students

## Chapter Resources

### Introduce the chapter
- American Government Essential Questions Video
- WebQuests
- Essential Questions Journal

### Additional Support
- All-in-One Teaching Resources
- Differentiation suggestions in each lesson
- Government Online interactivities
- Color Transparencies

### Assessment
- Document-Based Assessment
- ExamView Test Bank CD-ROM
- Online Assessment
- Online Student Self-Tests
- Section Quizzes (All-in-One Resources)
- Chapter Tests A and B (All-in-One Resources)
- AYP Monitoring Assessments
- Assessment Rubrics

## Essential Questions:

**UNIT 6** How should a government meet the needs of its people?

**CHAPTER 22** How should you measure different governments?

### Government Online Student Center includes
- Interactive textbook with audio
- American Government Essential Questions Video
- WebQuests
- Audio Tours
- Interactivities
- Student Self-Tests

### Government Online Teacher Center includes
- Online Teacher's Edition with lesson planner
- Online Lecture Notes
- Teacher's Resource Library with All-in-One Resources, color transparencies, and an alternative lesson plan
- Online Assessment

**Teacher Center**
at PearsonSchool.com/phgovt

## SECTION 1

### ORIGINS OF THE MODERN STATE

**Guiding Question:** On what early political ideas and traditions was modern government founded?

### Summary of Teaching Strategies
Students will compare the governments of ancient Athens and Rome, discuss the legitimacy of governments, and apply the concept to the Declaration of Independence.

### Differentiated Resources
- **L2** Prereading and Vocabulary Worksheet (p. 9)
- **L3 L2** Reading Comprehension Worksheets (pp. 13, 14)
- **L3 L2** Core Worksheets (pp. 16, 18)
- **L3 L2** Skills Worksheets (pp. 20, 22)
- **L3 L4** Extend Worksheet (p. 24)
- **L3** Quiz A (p. 26)  **L2** Quiz B (p. 27)

### Student Objectives
- Identify the ancient foundations of the state in Athens, in Rome, and in the feudal system.
- Analyze the rise of sovereign states.
- Explain how governments can achieve legitimacy.
- Understand why European nations turned to colonialism.

## SECTION 2

### IDEAS AND REVOLUTIONS

**Guiding Question:** How have some nations expanded popular sovereignty?

### Summary of Teaching Strategies
Students will review Enlightenment ideas, connect them with the spread of popular sovereignty, and illustrate the relationship of fascism or communism with popular sovereignty.

### Differentiated Resources
- **L3 L2** Reading Comprehension Worksheets (pp. 28, 30)
- **L3** Core Worksheet (p. 32)
- **L3** Quiz A (p. 34)  **L2** Quiz B (p. 35)

### Student Objectives
- Understand how Enlightenment ideas helped influence the expansion of popular sovereignty.
- Analyze the role of popular sovereignty in England, France, and around the world.
- Describe events in Latin America, Asia, and Africa that expanded popular sovereignty.
- Examine how fascism and communism distort the concept of popular sovereignty.

TEACHING
GOVERNMENT

PROGRAM
ORGANIZATION

DIFFERENTIATED
INSTRUCTION

ASSESSMENT

PLANNING
YOUR
INSTRUCTION

# SECTION 3

## TRANSITIONS TO DEMOCRACY

**Guiding Question:** How successfully have some nations achieved democratic government?

### Summary of Teaching Strategies
Students will discuss challenges to democratic transitions, list factors contributing to both greater and failed democracy, and analyze Haiti's and Iraq's transitions to democracy.

### Differentiated Resources
- **L3 L2 Reading Comprehension Worksheets** (pp. 36, 37)
- **L3 Core Worksheet** (p. 38)
- **L2 Extend Activity** (p. 39)
- **L3 Quiz A** (p. 40)  **L2 Quiz B** (p. 41)

### Student Objectives
- Understand how regimes can change from dictatorship to democracy.
- Describe the fall of the Soviet Union in the late 1980s and early 1990s.
- Explain the factors necessary for democratic consolidation.
- Analyze why some countries experience setbacks or failed transitions to democracy.

# SECTION 4

## CASE STUDIES IN DEMOCRACY

**Guiding Question:** What form does democratic government take in the UK and in Mexico?

### Summary of Teaching Strategies
Students will recognize variations in democracies by studying the governments of the UK and Mexico.

### Differentiated Resources
- **L3 L2 Reading Comprehension Worksheets** (pp. 42, 43)
- **L3 Core Worksheet** (p. 44)
- **L3 Quiz A** (p. 46)  **L2 Quiz B** (p. 47)
- **L3 Chapter Test A** (p. 48)
- **L2 Chapter Test B** (p. 51)

### Student Objectives
- Examine elements of the United Kingdom's parliamentary democracy.
- Describe regional and local government in the United Kingdom.
- Analyze the federal government of Mexico.

---

**DIFFERENTIATED INSTRUCTION KEY**

**L1** Special Needs

**L2** Basic includes

    **ELL** English Language Learners

    **LPR** Less Proficient Readers

**L3** All Students

**L4** Advanced Students

## Chapter Resources

### Introduce the chapter
- American Government Essential Questions Video
- WebQuests
- Essential Questions Journal

### Additional Support
- All-in-One Teaching Resources
- Differentiation suggestions in each lesson
- Government Online interactivities
- Color Transparencies

### Assessment
- Document-Based Assessment
- ExamView Test Bank CD-ROM
- Online Assessment
- Online Student Self-Tests
- Section Quizzes (All-in-One Resources)
- Chapter Tests A and B (All-in-One Resources)
- AYP Monitoring Assessments
- Assessment Rubrics

## Essential Questions:

**UNIT 6** How should a government meet the needs of its people?
**CHAPTER 23** To what extent should governments participate in the economy?

### Government Online Student Center includes
- Interactive textbook with audio
- American Government Essential Questions Video
- WebQuests
- Audio Tours
- Interactivities
- Student Self-Tests

### Government Online Teacher Center includes
- Online Teacher's Edition with lesson planner
- Online Lecture Notes
- Teacher's Resource Library with All-in-One Resources, color transparencies, and an alternative lesson plan
- Online Assessment

Teacher Center
at PearsonSchool.com/phgovt

## SECTION 1

### CAPITALISM

**Guiding Question:** What is the role of government in the American economy?

### Summary of Teaching Strategies
Students will examine the factors of production and the fundamental factors of free enterprise. Then they will create and present arguments advocating the free enterprise system.

### Differentiated Resources
- **L2 Prereading and Vocabulary Worksheet** (p. 61)
- **L3 L2 Reading Comprehension Worksheets** (pp. 65, 67)
- **L3 Core Worksheet** (p. 69)
- **L3 L4 Extend Worksheet** (p. 70)
- **L3 Quiz A** (p. 71)  **L2 Quiz B** (p. 72)

### Student Objectives
- Identify the factors of production.
- Describe the free enterprise system and laissez-faire theory.
- Analyze the role of government in a mixed economy.
- Compare and contrast three types of business organizations.
- Explain the role of profit and loss in a free enterprise system.

## SECTION 2

### SOCIALISM AND COMMUNISM

**Guiding Question:** What is the role of government under socialism and communism?

### Summary of Teaching Strategies
Students will discuss the theories of Karl Marx, compare and contrast economic systems, and write a dialogue to compare and contrast life under capitalism and communism.

### Differentiated Resources
- **L3 L2 Reading Comprehension Worksheets** (pp. 73, 75)
- **L3 Bellringer Worksheet** (p. 77)
- **L3 L2 Core Worksheets** (pp. 78, 79)
- **L3 Quiz A** (p. 80)  **L2 Quiz B** (p. 81)

### Student Objectives
- Summarize the theories of Karl Marx and their roots.
- Identify important characteristics of socialist economies.
- Outline the characteristics of Communist economies.
- Describe socialism and communism in action today.
- Evaluate the effects of socialism and communism.

TEACHING
GOVERNMENT

PROGRAM
ORGANIZATION

DIFFERENTIATED
INSTRUCTION

ASSESSMENT

PLANNING
YOUR
INSTRUCTION

# SECTION 3

## THE U.S. IN A GLOBAL ECONOMY

**Guiding Question:** How does the Federal Government support economic growth at home and abroad?

### Summary of Teaching Strategies

Students will determine ways in which government regulation of the economy affects their own lives. Then they will present economic news reports to the class in a mock television program.

### Differentiated Resources

- **L3 L2 Reading Comprehension Worksheets** (pp. 82, 84)
- **L3 Core Worksheet** (p. 86)
- **L3 L2 Skills Worksheets** (pp. 88, 90)
- **L3 Quiz A** (p. 92)   **L2 Quiz B** (p. 93)
- **L3 Chapter Test A** (p. 94)
- **L2 Chapter Test B** (p. 97)

### Student Objectives

- Describe the role of government in the domestic economy.
- Understand the reasons why nations participate in trade.
- Describe the role of the Federal Government in the global economy.
- Explain the causes of globalization and its effects on the American economy.

---

**DIFFERENTIATED INSTRUCTION KEY**

L1 Special Needs
L2 Basic includes
    **ELL** English Language Learners
    **LPR** Less Proficient Readers

L3 All Students
L4 Advanced Students

## Chapter Resources

**Introduce the chapter**
- American Government Essential Questions Video
- WebQuests
- Essential Questions Journal

**Additional Support**
- All-in-One Teaching Resources
- Differentiation suggestions in each lesson
- Government Online interactivities
- Color Transparencies

**Assessment**
- Document-Based Assessment
- ExamView Test Bank CD-ROM
- Online Assessment
- Online Student Self-Tests
- Section Quizzes (All-in-One Resources)
- Chapter Tests A and B (All-in-One Resources)
- AYP Monitoring Assessments
- Assessment Rubrics

## Essential Questions:

**UNIT 7** What is the right balance of federal, State, and local government?

**CHAPTER 24** How much power should State government have?

**Government Online Student Center includes**
- Interactive textbook with audio
- American Government Essential Questions Video
- WebQuests
- Audio Tours
- Interactivities
- Student Self-Tests

**Government Online Teacher Center includes**
- Online Teacher's Edition with lesson planner
- Online Lecture Notes
- Teacher's Resource Library with All-in-One Resources, color transparencies, and an alternative lesson plan
- Online Assessment

Teacher Center
at PearsonSchool.com/phgovt

## SECTION 1

### STATE CONSTITUTIONS

**Guiding Question:** What are the defining features of State constitutions?

**Summary of Teaching Strategies**
Students will examine the origins, features, and purposes of State constitutions.

**Differentiated Resources**
- **L2** Prereading and Vocabulary Worksheet (p. 11)
- **L3 L2** Reading Comprehension (pp. 15, 16)
- **L3** Core Worksheet (p. 17)
- **L3 L4** Extend Worksheet (p. 19)
- **L2** Extend Activity (p. 20)
- **L3** Quiz A (p. 21)  **L2** Quiz B (p. 22)

**Student Objectives**
- Examine the history, content, and significance of the first State constitutions.
- Describe the basic principles common to all State constitutions today.
- Explain the procedures used to change State constitutions.
- Analyze why State constitutions are in need of reform.

## SECTION 2

### STATE LEGISLATURES

**Guiding Question:** What are the defining traits and purpose of State legislatures?

**Summary of Teaching Strategies**
Students will compare and contrast features of State legislatures with those of the U.S. Congress.

**Differentiated Resources**
- **L3 L2** Reading Comprehension Worksheets (pp. 23, 25)
- **L3** Core Worksheet (p. 27)
- **L2** Extend Activity (p. 28)
- **L3** Quiz A (p. 29)  **L2** Quiz B (p. 30)

**Student Objectives**
- Describe State legislatures.
- Explain the election, terms, and compensation of legislators.
- Examine the powers and organization of State legislatures.
- Describe how voters may write and pass laws through direct legislation.

## SECTION 3

### THE GOVERNOR AND STATE ADMINISTRATION

**Guiding Question:** What are the roles and powers of a governor?

**Summary of Teaching Strategies**
Students will examine the powers of State governors, and will compare and contrast State governorships with the U.S. presidency.

TEACHING
GOVERNMENT

PROGRAM
ORGANIZATION

DIFFERENTIATED
INSTRUCTION

ASSESSMENT

PLANNING
YOUR
INSTRUCTION

## Differentiated Resources
- **L3** **L2** **Reading Comprehension Worksheets** (pp. 31, 33)
- **L3** **Core Worksheets A and B** (pp. 35, 36)
- **L3** **L2** **Skills Worksheets** (pp. 37, 38)
- **L3** **Quiz A** (p. 39)  **L2** **Quiz B** (p. 40)

## Student Objectives
- Describe the main features of the office of governor.
- Summarize a governor's roles, powers, duties, and the limitations of the office.
- List and describe the other executive offices at the State level.

- Describe the types and purposes of juries and juror selection.

# SECTION 4

### IN THE COURTROOM

**Guiding Question:** How do State and local courts apply different types of law?

### Summary of Teaching Strategies
Students will study the five forms of law, contrast civil and criminal law, and evaluate State court cases.

### Differentiated Resources
- **L3** **L2** **Reading Comprehension Worksheets** (pp. 41, 42)
- **L3** **L2** **Core Worksheets** (pp. 43, 46)
- **L3** **Quiz A** (p. 49)  **L2** **Quiz B** (p. 50)

### Student Objectives
- Identify and define the kinds of law applied in State courts.
- Compare and contrast criminal law and civil law.

# SECTION 5

### STATE COURTS AND THEIR JUDGES

**Guiding Question:** How are State and local courts organized and staffed?

### Summary of Teaching Strategies
Students will discuss the positive and negative aspects of electing or appointing judges, and will evaluate methods of judge selection.

### Differentiated Resources
- **L3** **L2** **Reading Comprehension Worksheets** (pp. 51, 52)
- **L3** **Core Worksheet** (p. 53)
- **L3** **Quiz A** (p. 57)  **L2** **Quiz B** (p. 58)
- **L3** **Chapter Test A** (p. 59)
- **L2** **Chapter Test B** (p. 62)

### Student Objectives
- Explain how State courts are organized and describe the work that each type of court does.
- Examine and evaluate the different methods by which judges are selected among the States.

---

### DIFFERENTIATED INSTRUCTION KEY

**L1** Special Needs

**L2** Basic includes

   **ELL** English Language Learners

   **LPR** Less Proficient Readers

**L3** All Students

**L4** Advanced Students

## Chapter Resources

### Introduce the chapter
- American Government Essential Questions Video
- WebQuests
- Essential Questions Journal

### Additional Support
- All-in-One Teaching Resources
- Differentiation suggestions in each lesson
- Government Online interactivities
- Color Transparencies

### Assessment
- Document-Based Assessment
- ExamView Test Bank CD-ROM
- Online Assessment
- Online Student Self-Tests
- Section Quizzes (All-in-One Resources)
- Chapter Tests A and B (All-in-One Resources)
- AYP Monitoring Assessments
- Assessment Rubrics

## Essential Questions:

**UNIT 7** What is the right balance of federal, State, and local government?

**CHAPTER 25** How local should government be?

### Government Online Student Center includes
- Interactive textbook with audio
- American Government Essential Questions Video
- WebQuests
- Audio Tours
- Interactivities
- Student Self-Tests

### Government Online Teacher Center includes
- Online Teacher's Edition with lesson planner
- Online Lecture Notes
- Teacher's Resource Library with All-in-One Resources, color transparencies, and an alternative lesson plan
- Online Assessment

Teacher Center
at PearsonSchool.com/phgovt

## SECTION 1

### COUNTIES, TOWNS, AND TOWNSHIPS

**Guiding Question:** What are the similarities and differences of local governments, special districts, and tribal governments?

### Summary of Teaching Strategies
Students will discuss the typical structure and variations in county governments, debate the need for county government, and complete a diagram about their local government structure.

### Differentiated Resources
- **L2** Prereading and Vocabulary Worksheet (p. 74)
- **L3 L2** Reading Comprehension Worksheets (pp. 77, 79)
- **L3 L2** Core Worksheets (pp. 81, 82)
- **L2** Extend Activity (p. 84)
- **L3** Quiz A (p. 85)  **L2** Quiz B (p. 86)

### Student Objectives
- Describe the typical county, its governmental structure, and functions.
- Analyze the need for reform in county government.
- Identify the responsibilities of tribal governments.
- Examine the governments of towns, townships, and special districts.

## SECTION 2

### CITIES AND METROPOLITAN AREAS

**Guiding Question:** How do city governments serve the needs of residents and other Americans?

### Summary of Teaching Strategies
Students will compare and contrast the three basic forms of city government. Then students will plan a city square.

### Differentiated Resources
- **L3 L2** Reading Comprehension Worksheets (pp. 87, 89)
- **L3** Core Worksheet (p. 91)
- **L3 L2** Skills Worksheets (pp. 94, 95)
- **L2** Extend Activity (p. 96)
- **L3** Quiz A (p. 97)  **L2** Quiz B (p. 98)

### Student Objectives
- Explain the process of incorporation and the function of city charters.
- Contrast the major forms of city government.
- Evaluate the need for city planning and list some major municipal functions.
- Outline the challenges that face suburbs and metropolitan areas.

TEACHING
GOVERNMENT

PROGRAM
ORGANIZATION

DIFFERENTIATED
INSTRUCTION

ASSESSMENT

PLANNING
YOUR
INSTRUCTION

## SECTION 3

### PROVIDING VITAL SERVICES

**Guiding Question:** What services do State and local governments provide?

### Summary of Teaching Strategies
Students will categorize services that they receive from State and local governments. They will then rank the importance of State and local services from several perspectives and compare their rankings to actual State and local spending.

### Differentiated Resources
- **L3** **L2** **Reading Comprehension Worksheets** (pp. 99, 100)
- **L3** **Core Worksheet** (p. 101)
- **L3** **Quiz A** (p. 102)  **L2** **Quiz B** (p. 103)

### Student Objectives
- Explain why State and local governments have a major role in providing important services.
- Identify State and local services in the fields of education, public welfare, public safety, and highways.

## SECTION 4

### FINANCING STATE AND LOCAL GOVERNMENT

**Guiding Question:** How do State governments raise money to pay for services?

### Summary of Teaching Strategies
Students will list and categorize taxes as progressive or regressive, and discuss sources of State and local revenue. Then they will evaluate different types of State and local taxes based on Adam Smith's four criteria for "a good tax."

### Differentiated Resources
- **L3** **L2** **Reading Comprehension Worksheets** (pp. 105, 107)
- **L3** **Core Worksheet** (p. 109)
- **L3** **L4** **Extend Worksheet** (p. 112)
- **L3** **Quiz A** (p. 115)  **L2** **Quiz B** (p. 116)
- **L3** **Chapter Test A** (p. 117)
- **L2** **Chapter Test B** (p. 120)

### Student Objectives
- Describe the major Federal and State limits on raising revenue.
- List the four principles of sound taxation.
- Identify major tax and nontax sources of State and local revenue.
- Explain the State budget process.

---

**DIFFERENTIATED INSTRUCTION KEY**

**L1** Special Needs

**L2** Basic includes

    **ELL** English Language Learners

    **LPR** Less Proficient Readers

**L3** All Students

**L4** Advanced Students

# Constitution Quick Study Guide

## Amendments

| | |
|---|---|
| 1st Amendment: | **Freedom of Religion, Speech, Press, Assembly, and Petition** |
| 2nd Amendment: | **Right to Keep, Bear Arms** |
| 3rd Amendment: | **Lodging Troops in Private Homes** |
| 4th Amendment: | **Search, Seizures, Proper Warrants** |
| 5th Amendment: | **Criminal Proceedings, Due Process, Eminent Domain** |
| 6th Amendment: | **Criminal Proceedings** |
| 7th Amendment: | **Jury Trials in Civil Cases** |
| 8th Amendment: | **Bail; Cruel, Unusual Punishment** |
| 9th Amendment: | **Unenumerated Rights** |
| 10th Amendment: | **Powers Reserved to the States** |
| 11th Amendment: | **Suits Against the States** |
| 12th Amendment: | **Election of President and Vice President** |
| 13th Amendment: | **Slavery and Involuntary Servitude** |
| Section 1. | Slavery and Involuntary Servitude Prohibited |
| Section 2. | Power of Congress |
| 14th Amendment: | **Rights of Citizens** |
| Section 1. | Citizenship; Privileges and Immunities; Due Process; Equal Protection |
| Section 2. | Apportionment of Representation |
| Section 3. | Disqualification of Officers |
| Section 4. | Public Debt |
| Section 5. | Powers of Congress |
| 15th Amendment: | **Right to Vote—Race, Color, Servitude** |
| Section 1. | Suffrage Not to Be Abridged |
| Section 2. | Power of Congress |
| 16th Amendment: | **Income Tax** |
| 17th Amendment: | **Popular Election of Senators** |
| Section 1. | Popular Election of Senators |
| Section 2. | Senate Vacancies |
| Section 3. | Inapplicable to Senators Previously Chosen |
| 18th Amendment: | **Prohibition of Intoxicating Liquors** |
| Section 1. | Intoxicating Liquors Prohibited |
| Section 2. | Concurrent Power to Enforce |
| Section 3. | Time Limit on Ratification |

| | |
|---|---|
| 19th Amendment: | **Equal Suffrage—Sex** |
| Section 1. | Suffrage Not to Be Abridged |
| Section 2. | Power of Congress |
| 20th Amendment: | **Commencement of Terms; Sessions of Congress; Death or Disqualification of President-Elect** |
| Section 1. | Terms of President, Vice President, members of Congress |
| Section 2. | Sessions of Congress |
| Section 3. | Death or Disqualification of President-Elect |
| Section 4. | Congress to Provide for Certain Successors |
| Section 5. | Effective Date |
| Section 6. | Time Limit on Ratification |
| 21st Amendment: | **Repeal of 18th Amendment** |
| Section 1. | Repeal of Prohibition |
| Section 2. | Transportation, Importation of Intoxicating Liquors |
| Section 3. | Time Limit on Ratification |
| 22nd Amendment: | **Presidential Tenure** |
| Section 1. | Restriction on Number of Terms |
| Section 2. | Time Limit on Ratification |
| 23rd Amendment: | **Inclusion of District of Columbia in Presidential Election Systems** |
| Section 1. | Presidential Electors for District |
| Section 2. | Power of Congress |
| 24th Amendment: | **Right to Vote in Federal Elections—Tax Payment** |
| Section 1. | Suffrage Not to Be Abridged |
| Section 2. | Power of Congress |
| 25th Amendment: | **Presidential Succession; Vice Presidential Vacancy; Presidential Inability** |
| Section 1. | Presidential Succession |
| Section 2. | Vice Presidential Vacancy |
| Section 3. | Presidential Inability |
| 26th Amendment: | **Right to Vote—Age** |
| Section 1. | Suffrage Not to Be Abridged |
| Section 2. | Power of Congress |
| 27th Amendment: | **Congressional Pay** |

The Preamble states the broad purposes the Constitution is intended to serve—to establish a government that provides for greater cooperation among the States, ensures justice and peace, provides for defense against foreign enemies, promotes the general well-being of the people, and secures liberty now and in the future. The phrase We the People emphasizes the twin concepts of popular sovereignty and of representative government.

## Legislative Department

### Section 1. Legislative power; Congress

Congress, the nation's lawmaking body, is bicameral in form; that is, it is composed of two houses: the Senate and the House of Representatives. The Framers of the Constitution purposely separated the lawmaking power from the power to enforce the laws (Article II, the Executive Branch) and the power to interpret them (Article III, the Judicial Branch). This system of separation of powers is supplemented by a system of checks and balances; that is, in several provisions the Constitution gives to each of the three branches various powers with which it may restrain the actions of the other two branches.

### Section 2. House of Representatives

♦ **Clause 1. Election** Electors means voters. Members of the House of Representatives are elected every two years. Each State must permit the same persons to vote for United States representatives as it permits to vote for the members of the larger house of its own legislature. The 17th Amendment (1913) extends this requirement to the qualification of voters for United States senators.

♦ **Clause 2. Qualifications** A member of the House of Representatives must be at least 25 years old, an American citizen for seven years, and a resident of the State he or she represents. In addition, political custom requires that a representative also reside in the district from which he or she is elected.

♦ **Clause 3. Apportionment** The number of representatives each State is entitled to is based on its population, which is counted every 10 years in the census. Congress reapportions the seats among the States after each census. In the Reapportionment Act of 1929, Congress fixed the permanent size of the House at 435 members with each State having at least one representative. Today there is one House seat for approximately every 700,000 persons in the population.

The words "three-fifths of all other persons" referred to slaves and reflected the Three-Fifths Compromise reached by the Framers at Philadelphia in 1787; the phrase was made obsolete, was in effect repealed, by the 13th Amendment in 1865.

---

\* The black lines indicate portions of the Constitution altered by subsequent amendments to the document.

♦ **Clause 4. Vacancies** The executive authority refers to the governor of a State. If a member leaves office or dies before the expiration of his or her term, the governor is to call a special election to fill the vacancy.

# United States Constitution

## PREAMBLE

We the People of the United States, in Order to form a more perfect Union, establish Justice, insure domestic Tranquility, provide for the common defence, promote the general Welfare, and secure the Blessings of Liberty to ourselves and our Posterity, do ordain and establish this Constitution for the United States of America.

## Article I.
### Section 1.

All legislative Powers herein granted shall be vested in a Congress of the United States, which shall consist of a Senate and House of Representatives.

### Section 2.

♦ 1. The House of Representatives shall be composed of Members chosen every second Year by the People of the several States, and the Electors in each State shall have the Qualifications requisite for Electors of the most numerous Branch of the State Legislature.

♦ 2. No Person shall be a Representative who shall not have attained to the age of twenty-five Years, and been seven Years a Citizen of the United States, and who shall not, when elected, be an Inhabitant of that State in which he shall be chosen.

♦ 3. ~~Representatives and direct Taxes~~\* shall be apportioned among the several States which may be included within this Union, according to their respective Numbers, ~~which shall be determined by adding to the whole Number of free Persons, including those bound to Service for a Term of Years and excluding Indians not taxed, three fifths of all other Persons.~~ The actual Enumeration shall be made within three Years after the first Meeting of the Congress of the United States, and within every subsequent term of ten Years, in such Manner as they shall by Law direct. The Number of Representatives shall not exceed one for every thirty Thousand, but each State shall have at Least one Representative; and, until such enumeration shall be made, the State of New Hampshire shall be entitled to choose three, Massachusetts eight, Rhode Island and Providence Plantations one, Connecticut five, New York six, New Jersey four, Pennsylvania eight, Delaware one, Maryland six, Virginia ten, North Carolina five, South Carolina five, and Georgia three.

♦ 4. When vacancies happen in the Representation from any State, the Executive Authority thereof shall issue Writs of Election to fill such Vacancies.

♦5. The House of Representatives shall choose their Speaker and other Officers; and shall have the sole Power of Impeachment.

## Section 3.

♦1. The Senate of the United States shall be composed of two Senators from each State ~~chosen by the Legislature thereof~~ for six Years; and each Senator shall have one Vote.

♦2. Immediately after they shall be assembled in Consequences of the first Election, they shall be divided, as equally as may be, into three Classes. The Seats of the Senators of the first Class shall be vacated at the Expiration of the second Year; of the second Class, at the Expiration of the fourth Year; and of the third Class, at the Expiration of the sixth Year; so that one-third may be chosen every second Year; ~~and if Vacancies happen by Resignation, or otherwise, during the Recess of the Legislature of any State, the Executive thereof may make temporary Appointments until the next Meeting of the Legislature, which shall then fill such Vacancies.~~

♦3. No Person shall be a Senator who shall not have attained to the Age of thirty Years, and been nine Years a Citizen of the United States, and who shall not, when elected, be an Inhabitant of that State for which he shall be chosen.

♦4. The Vice President of the United States shall be President of the Senate but shall have no Vote, unless they be equally divided.

♦5. The Senate shall choose their other Officers, and also a President pro tempore, in the Absence of the Vice President, or when he shall exercise the Office of President of the United States.

♦6. The Senate shall have the sole Power to try all Impeachments. When sitting for that Purpose, they shall be on Oath or Affirmation. When the President of the United States is tried, the Chief Justice shall preside: And no Person shall be convicted without the Concurrence of two thirds of the Members present.

♦7. Judgment in Cases of Impeachment shall not extend further than to removal from Office, and disqualification to hold and enjoy any Office of honor, Trust, or Profit under the United States: but the Party convicted shall nevertheless be liable and subject to Indictment, Trial, Judgment and Punishment, according to Law.

♦**Clause 5. Officers; impeachment** The House elects a Speaker, customarily chosen from the majority party in the House. Impeachment means accusation. The House has the exclusive power to impeach, or accuse, civil officers; the Senate (Article I, Section 3, Clause 6) has the exclusive power to try those impeached by the House.

## Section 3. Senate

♦**Clause 1. Composition, election, term** Each State has two senators. Each serves for six years and has one vote. Originally, senators were not elected directly by the people, but by each State's legislature. The 17th Amendment, added in 1913, provides for the popular election of senators.

♦**Clause 2. Classification** The senators elected in 1788 were divided into three groups so that the Senate could become a "continuing body." One-third of the Senate's seats are up for election every two years.

The 17th Amendment provides that a Senate vacancy is to be filled at a special election called by the governor; State law may also permit the governor to appoint a successor to serve until that election is held.

♦**Clause 3. Qualifications** A senator must be at least 30 years old, a citizen for at least nine years, and must live in the State from which elected.

♦**Clause 4. Presiding officer** The Vice President presides over the Senate, but may vote only to break a tie.

♦**Clause 5. Other officers** The Senate chooses its own officers, including a president pro tempore to preside when the Vice President is not there.

♦**Clause 6. Impeachment trials** The Senate conducts the trials of those officials impeached by the House. The Vice President presides unless the President is on trial, in which case the Chief Justice of the United States does so. A conviction requires the votes of two-thirds of the senators present.

No President has ever been convicted. In 1868 the House voted eleven articles of impeachment against President Andrew Johnson, but the Senate fell one vote short of convicting him. In 1974 President Richard M. Nixon resigned the presidency in the face of almost certain impeachment by the House. The House brought two articles of impeachment against President Bill Clinton in late 1998. Neither charge was supported by even a simple majority vote in the Senate, on February 12, 1999.

♦**Clause 7. Penalty on conviction** The punishment of an official convicted in an impeachment case has always been removal from office. The Senate can also bar a convicted person from ever holding any federal office, but it is not required to do so. A convicted person can also be tried and punished in a regular court for any crime involved in the impeachment case.

### Section 4. Elections and Meetings

♦ **Clause 1. Election In 1842** Congress required that representatives be elected from districts within each State with more than one seat in the House. The districts in each State are drawn by that State's legislature. Seven States now have only one seat in the House: Alaska, Delaware, Montana, North Dakota, South Dakota, Vermont, and Wyoming. The 1842 law also directed that representatives be elected in each State on the same day: the Tuesday after the first Monday in November of every even-numbered year. In 1914 Congress also set that same date for the election of senators.

♦ **Clause 2. Sessions Congress** must meet at least once a year. The 20th Amendment (1933) changed the opening date to January 3.

### Section 5. Legislative Proceedings

♦ **Clause 1. Admission of members; quorum** In 1969 the Supreme Court held that the House cannot exclude any member-elect who satisfies the qualifications set out in Article I, Section 2, Clause 2.

A majority in the House (218 members) or Senate (51) constitutes a quorum. In practice, both houses often proceed with less than a quorum present. However, any member may raise a point of order (demand a "quorum call"). If a roll call then reveals less than a majority of the members present, that chamber must either adjourn or the sergeant at arms must be ordered to round up absent members.

♦ **Clause 2. Rules** Each house has adopted detailed rules to guide its proceedings. Each house may discipline members for unacceptable conduct; expulsion requires a two-thirds vote.

♦ **Clause 3. Record** Each house must keep and publish a record of its meetings. The Congressional Record is published for every day that either house of Congress is in session, and provides a written record of all that is said and done on the floor of each house each session.

♦ **Clause 4. Adjournment** Once in session, neither house may suspend (recess) its work for more than three days without the approval of the other house. Both houses must always meet in the same location.

### Section 4.

♦ 1. The Times, Places and Manner of holding Elections for Senators and Representatives, shall be prescribed in each State by the Legislature thereof; but the Congress may at any time by law make or alter such Regulations, except as to the Places of choosing Senators.

♦ 2. The Congress shall assemble at least once in every Year, and such Meeting shall be on the first Monday in December, unless they shall by Law appoint a different Day.

### Section 5.

♦ 1. Each House shall be the Judge of the Elections, Returns and Qualifications of its own Members, and a Majority of each shall constitute a Quorum to do Business; but a smaller Number may adjourn from day to day, and may be authorized to compel the Attendance of absent Members, in such Manner, and under such Penalties, as each House may provide.

♦ 2. Each House may determine the Rules of its Proceedings, punish its Members for disorderly Behavior, and, with the Concurrence of two thirds, expel a Member.

♦ 3. Each House shall keep a Journal of its Proceedings, and from time to time publish the same, excepting such Parts as may in their Judgment require Secrecy; and the Yeas and Nays of the Members of either House on any question shall, at the Desire of one fifth of those Present, be entered on the Journal.

♦ 4. Neither House, during the Session of Congress, shall, without the Consent of the other, adjourn for more than three days, nor to any other Place than that in which the two Houses shall be sitting.

## Section 6.

♦ 1. The Senators and Representatives shall receive a Compensation for their Services, to be ascertained by Law, and paid out of the Treasury of the United States. They shall in all Cases, except Treason, Felony, and Breach of the Peace, be privileged from Arrest during their Attendance at the Session of their respective Houses, and in going to and returning from the same; and for any Speech or Debate in either House, they shall not be questioned in any other Place.

♦ 2. No Senator or Representative shall, during the Time for which he was elected, be appointed to any civil Office under the Authority of the United States, which shall have been created, or the Emoluments whereof shall have been increased during such time; and no Person holding any Office under the United States, shall be a Member of either House during his Continuance in Office.

## Section 7.

♦ 1. All Bills for raising Revenue shall originate in the House of Representatives; but the Senate may propose or concur with amendments as on other Bills.

♦ 2. Every Bill which shall have passed the House of Representatives and the Senate, shall, before it become a law, be presented to the President of the United States: If he approve, he shall sign it, but if not he shall return it, with his Objections to that House in which it shall have originated, who shall enter the Objections at large on their Journal, and proceed to reconsider it. If after such Reconsideration two thirds of the House shall agree to pass the Bill, it shall be sent, together with the Objections, to the other House, by which it shall likewise be reconsidered, and if approved by two thirds of that House, it shall become a Law. But in all such Cases the Votes of both Houses shall be determined by Yeas and Nays, and the Names of the Persons voting for and against the Bill shall be entered on the Journal of each House respectively. If any Bill shall not be returned by the President within ten Days (Sunday excepted) after it shall have been presented to him, the Same shall be a law, in like Manner as if he had signed it, unless the Congress by their Adjournment, prevent its Return, in which Case it shall not be a Law.

♦ 3. Every Order, Resolution, or Vote to which the Concurrence of the Senate and House of Representatives may be necessary (except on a question of adjournment) shall be presented to the President of the United States; and before the Same shall take Effect, shall be approved by him, or, being disapproved by him, shall be repassed by two thirds of the Senate and House of Representatives, according to the Rules and Limitations prescribed in the Case of a Bill.

## Section 6. Compensation, Immunities, and Disabilities of Members

♦ **Clause 1. Salaries; immunities** Each house sets its members' salaries, paid by the United States; the 27th Amendment (1992) modified this pay-setting power. This provision establishes "legislative immunity." The purpose of this immunity is to allow members to speak and debate freely in Congress itself. Treason is strictly defined in Article III, Section 3. A felony is any serious crime. A breach of the peace is any indictable offense less than treason or a felony; this exemption from arrest is of little real importance today.

♦ **Clause 2. Restrictions on office holding** No sitting member of either house may be appointed to an office in the executive or in the judicial branch if that position was created or its salary was increased during that member's current elected term. The second part of this clause—forbidding any person serving in either the executive or the judicial branch from also serving in Congress—reinforces the principle of separation of powers.

## Section 7. Revenue Bills, President's Veto

♦ **Clause 1. Revenue bills** All bills that raise money must originate in the House. However, the Senate has the power to amend any revenue bill sent to it from the lower house.

♦ **Clause 2. Enactment of laws; veto** Once both houses have passed a bill, it must be sent to the President. The President may (1) sign the bill, thus making it law; (2) veto the bill, whereupon it must be returned to the house in which it originated; or (3) allow the bill to become law without signature, by not acting upon it within 10 days of its receipt from Congress, not counting Sundays. The President has a fourth option at the end of a congressional session: If he does not act on a measure within 10 days, and Congress adjourns during that period, the bill dies; the "pocket veto" has been applied to it. A presidential veto may be overridden by a two-thirds vote in each house.

♦ **Clause 3. Other measures** This clause refers to joint resolutions, measures Congress often passes to deal with unusual, temporary, or ceremonial matters. A joint resolution passed by Congress and signed by the President has the force of law, just as a bill does. As a matter of custom, a joint resolution proposing an amendment to the Constitution is not submitted to the President for signature or veto. Concurrent and simple resolutions do not have the force of law and, therefore, are not submitted to the President.

### Section 8. Powers of Congress

♦ **Clause 1.** The 18 separate clauses in this section set out 27 of the many expressed powers the Constitution grants to Congress. In this clause Congress is given the power to levy and provide for the collection of various kinds of taxes, in order to finance the operations of the government. All federal taxes must be levied at the same rates throughout the country.

♦ **Clause 2.** Congress has power to borrow money to help finance the government. Federal borrowing is most often done through the sale of bonds on which interest is paid. The Constitution does not limit the amount the government may borrow.

♦ **Clause 3.** This clause, the Commerce Clause, gives Congress the power to regulate both foreign and interstate trade. Much of what Congress does, it does on the basis of its commerce power.

♦ **Clause 4.** Congress has the exclusive power to determine how aliens may become citizens of the United States. Congress may also pass laws relating to bankruptcy.

♦ **Clause 5.** has the power to establish and require the use of uniform gauges of time, distance, weight, volume, area, and the like.

♦ **Clause 6.** Congress has the power to make it a federal crime to falsify the coins, paper money, bonds, stamps, and the like of the United States.

♦ **Clause 7.** Congress has the power to provide for and regulate the transportation and delivery of mail; "post offices" are those buildings and other places where mail is deposited for dispatch; "post roads" include all routes over or upon which mail is carried.

♦ **Clause 8.** Congress has the power to provide for copyrights and patents. A copyright gives an author or composer the exclusive right to control the reproduction, publication, and sale of literary, musical, or other creative work. A patent gives a person the exclusive right to control the manufacture or sale of his or her invention.

♦ **Clause 9.** Congress has the power to create the lower federal courts, all of the several federal courts that function beneath the Supreme Court.

♦ **Clause 10.** Congress has the power to prohibit, as a federal crime: (1) certain acts committed outside the territorial jurisdiction of the United States, and (2) the commission within the United States of any wrong against any nation with which we are at peace.

### Section 8.

The Congress shall have Power

♦ 1. To lay and collect Taxes, Duties, Imposts and Excises to pay the Debts and provide for the common Defence and general Welfare of the United States; but all Duties, Imposts and Excises, shall be uniform throughout the United States;

♦ 2. To borrow Money on the credit of the United States;

♦ 3. To regulate Commerce with foreign Nations, and among the several States, and with the Indian Tribes;

♦ 4. To establish an uniform Rule of Naturalization, and uniform Laws on the subject of Bankruptcies throughout the United States;

♦ 5. To coin Money, regulate the Value thereof, and of foreign Coin, and fix the Standard of Weights and Measures;

♦ 6. To provide for the Punishment of counterfeiting the Securities and current Coin of the United States;

♦ 7. To establish Post Offices and post Roads;

♦ 8. To promote the Progress of Science and useful Arts, by securing, for limited Times to Authors and Inventors the exclusive Right to their respective Writings and Discoveries;

♦ 9. To constitute Tribunals inferior to the supreme Court;

♦ 10. To define and punish Piracies and Felonies committed on the high Seas, and Offences against the Law of nations;

11. To declare War, grant Letters of Marque and Reprisal, and make Rules concerning Captures on Land and Water;

12. To raise and support Armies; but no Appropriation of Money to that Use shall be for a longer Term than two Years;

13. To provide and maintain a Navy;

14. To make Rules for the Government and Regulation of the land and naval Forces;

15. To provide for calling forth the Militia to execute the Laws of the Union, suppress Insurrections and repel Invasions;

16. To provide for organizing, arming, and disciplining the Militia, and for governing such Part of them as may be employed in the Service of the United States, reserving to the States respectively the Appointment of the Officers, and the Authority of training the Militia according to the discipline prescribed by Congress;

17. To exercise exclusive Legislation in all Cases whatsoever, over such District (not exceeding ten Miles square) as may, by Cession of Particular States, and the Acceptance of Congress, become the Seat of the Government of the United States, and to exercise like Authority over all Places purchased by the Consent of the Legislature of the State in which the Same shall be, for the Erection of Forts, Magazines, Arsenals, Dockyards and other needful Buildings;—And

18. To make all Laws which shall be necessary and proper for carrying into Execution the foregoing Powers and all other Powers vested by this Constitution in the Government of the United States, or in any Department or Officer thereof.

## Section 9.

1. The Migration or Importation of such Persons as any of the States now existing shall think proper to admit, shall not be prohibited by the Congress prior to the Year one thousand eight hundred and eight, but a Tax or duty may be imposed on such Importation, not exceeding ten dollars for each Person.

♦ **Clause 11.** Only Congress can declare war. However, the President, as commander in chief of the armed forces (Article II, Section 2, Clause 1), can make war without such a formal declaration. Letters of marque and reprisal are commissions authorizing private persons to outfit vessels (privateers) to capture and destroy enemy ships in time of war; they were forbidden in international law by the Declaration of Paris of 1856, and the United States has honored the ban since the Civil War.

♦ **Clauses 12 and 13.** Congress has the power to provide for and maintain the nation's armed forces. It established the air force as an independent element of the armed forces in 1947, an exercise of its inherent powers in foreign relations and national defense. The two-year limit on spending for the army insures civilian control of the military.

♦ **Clause 14.** Today these rules are set out in three principle statutes: the Uniform Code of Military Justice, passed by Congress in 1950, and the Military Justice Acts of 1958 and 1983.

♦ **Clauses 15 and 16.** In the National Defense Act of 1916, Congress made each State's militia (volunteer army) a part of the National Guard. Today, Congress and the States cooperate in its maintenance. Ordinarily, each State's National Guard is under the command of that State's governor; but Congress has given the President the power to call any or all of those units into federal service when necessary.

♦ **Clause 17.** In 1791 Congress accepted land grants from Maryland and Virginia and established the District of Columbia for the nation's capital. Assuming Virginia's grant would never be needed, Congress returned it in 1846. Today, the elected government of the District's 69 square miles operates under the authority of Congress. Congress also has the power to acquire other lands from the States for various federal purposes.

♦ **Clause 18.** This is the Necessary and Proper Clause, also often called the Elastic Clause. It is the constitutional basis for the many and far-reaching implied powers of the Federal Government.

## Section 9. Powers Denied to Congress

♦ **Clause 1.** The phrase "such persons" referred to slaves. This provision was part of the Commerce Compromise, one of the bargains struck in the writing of the Constitution. Congress outlawed the slave trade in 1808.

**Clause 2.** A writ of habeas corpus, the "great writ of liberty," is a court order directing a sheriff, warden, or other public officer, or a private person, who is detaining another to "produce the body" of the one being held in order that the legality of the detention may be determined by the court.

**Clause 3.** A bill of attainder is a legislative act that inflicts punishment without a judicial trial. See Article I, Section 10, and Article III, Section 3, Clause 2. An ex post facto law is any criminal law that operates retroactively to the disadvantage of the accused. See Article I, Section 10.

**Clause 4.** A capitation tax is literally a "head tax," a tax levied on each person in the population. A direct tax is one paid directly to the government by the taxpayer—for example, an income or a property tax; an indirect tax is one paid to another private party who then pays it to the government—for example, a sales tax. This provision was modified by the 16th Amendment (1913), giving Congress the power to levy "taxes on incomes, from whatever source derived."

**Clause 5.** This provision was a part of the Commerce Compromise made by the Framers in 1787. Congress has the power to tax imported goods, however.

**Clause 6.** All ports within the United States must be treated alike by Congress as it exercises its taxing and commerce powers. Congress cannot tax goods sent by water from one State to another, nor may it give the ports of one State any legal advantage over those of another.

**Clause 7.** This clause gives Congress its vastly important "power of the purse," a major check on presidential power. Federal money can be spent only in those amounts and for those purposes expressly authorized by an act of Congress. All federal income and spending must be accounted for, regularly and publicly.

**Clause 8.** This provision, preventing the establishment of a nobility, reflects the principle that "all men are created equal." It was also intended to discourage foreign attempts to bribe or otherwise corrupt officers of the government.

## Section 10. Powers Denied to the States

**Clause 1.** The States are not sovereign governments and so cannot make agreements or otherwise negotiate with foreign states; the power to conduct foreign relations is an exclusive power of the National Government. The power to coin money is also an exclusive power of the National Government. Several powers forbidden to the National Government are here also forbidden to the States.

**Clause 2.** This provision relates to foreign, not interstate, commerce. Only Congress, not the States, can tax imports; and the States are, like Congress, forbidden the power to tax exports.

**2.** The Privilege of the Writ of Habeas Corpus shall not be suspended, unless when in Cases of Rebellion or Invasion the public safety may require it.

**3.** No Bill of Attainder or ex post facto Law shall be passed.

**4.** No Capitation, ~~or other direct, Tax~~ shall be laid, unless in Proportion to the Census of Enumeration hereinbefore directed to be taken.

**5.** No Tax or Duty shall be laid on Articles exported from any State.

**6.** No Preference shall be given by any Regulation of Commerce or Revenue to the Ports of one State over those of another: nor shall Vessels bound to, or from, one State, be obliged to enter, clear or pay Duties in another.

**7.** No Money shall be drawn from the Treasury, but in Consequence of Appropriations made by Law; and a regular Statement and Account of the Receipts and Expenditures of all public Money shall be published from time to time.

**8.** No Title of Nobility shall be granted by the United States: And no Person holding any Office of Profit or Trust under them, shall, without the Consent of the Congress, accept of any present, Emolument, Office, or Title, of any kind whatever, from any King, Prince, or foreign State.

### Section 10.

**1.** No State shall enter into any Treaty, Alliance, or Confederation; grant Letters of Marque and Reprisal; coin Money; emit Bills of Credit; make any Thing but gold and silver Coin a Tender in Payment of Debts; pass any Bill of Attainder, ex post facto Law, or Law impairing the Obligation of Contracts, or grant any Title of Nobility.

**2.** No State shall, without the Consent of the Congress, lay any Imposts or Duties on Imports or Exports, except what may be absolutely necessary for executing its inspection Laws; and the net Produce of all Duties and Imposts, laid by any State on Imports or Exports, shall be for the Use of the Treasury of the United States; and all such Laws shall be subject to the Revision and Control of the Congress.

♦ 3. No State shall, without the Consent of Congress, lay any Duty of Tonnage, keep Troops, or Ships of War in time of Peace, enter into any Agreement or Compact with another State, or with a foreign Power, or engage in War, unless actually invaded, or in such imminent Danger as will not admit of delay.

## Article II
### Section 1.

♦ 1. The executive Power shall be vested in a President of the United States of America. He shall hold his Office during the Term of four Years, and, together with the Vice President, chosen for the same Term, be elected as follows:

♦ 2. Each State shall appoint, in such Manner as the Legislature thereof may direct, a Number of Electors, equal to the whole Number of Senators and Representatives to which the State may be entitled in the Congress: but no Senator or Representative, or Person holding an Office of Trust or Profit, under the United States, shall be appointed an Elector.

♦ 3. The Electors shall meet in their respective States, and vote by Ballot for two Persons, of whom one at least shall not be an Inhabitant of the same State with themselves. And they shall make a List of all the Persons voted for, and of the Number of Votes for each; which List they shall sign and certify, and transmit sealed to the Seat of the Government of the United States, directed to the President of the Senate. The President of the Senate shall, in the Presence of the Senate and House of Representatives, open all the Certificates, and the Votes shall then be counted. The Person having the greatest Number of Votes shall be the President, if such Number be a majority of the whole Number of Electors appointed; and if there be more than one who have such Majority, and have an equal Number of Votes, then, the House of Representatives shall immediately choose by Ballot one of them for President; and if no Person have a Majority, then from the five highest on the List the said House shall in like Manner choose the President. But in choosing the President, the Votes shall be taken by States, the Representatives from each State having one Vote; a quorum for this Purpose shall consist of a Member or Members from two thirds of the States, and a Majority of all the States shall be necessary to a Choice. In every Case, after the Choice of the President, the Person having the greatest Number of Votes of the Electors shall be the Vice President. But if there should remain two or more who have equal Votes, the Senate shall choose from them by Ballot the Vice President.

♦ **Clause 3.** A duty of tonnage is a tax laid on ships according to their cargo capacity. Each State has a constitutional right to provide for and maintain a militia; but no State may keep a standing army or navy. The several restrictions here prevent the States from assuming powers that the Constitution elsewhere grants to the National Government.

## Executive Department
### Section 1. President and Vice President

♦ **Clause 1. Executive power, term** This clause gives to the President the very broad "executive power," the power to enforce the laws and otherwise administer the public policies of the United States. It also sets the length of the presidential (and vice-presidential) term of office; see the 22nd Amendment (1951), which places a limit on presidential (but not vice-presidential) tenure.

♦ **Clause 2. Electoral college** This clause establishes the "electoral college," although the Constitution does not use that term. It is a body of presidential electors chosen in each State, and it selects the President and Vice President every four years. The number of electors chosen in each State equals the number of senators and representatives that State has in Congress.

♦ **Clause 3. Election of President and Vice President** This clause was replaced by the 12th Amendment in 1804.

National convention to nominate candidates for President and Vice President

◆**Clause 4. Date** Congress has set the date for the choosing of electors as the Tuesday after the first Monday in November every fourth year, and for the casting of electoral votes as the Monday after the second Wednesday in December of that year.

◆**Clause 5. Qualifications** The President must have been born a citizen of the United States, be at least 35 years old, and have been a resident of the United States for at least 14 years.

◆**Clause 6. Vacancy** This clause was modified by the 25th Amendment (1967), which provides expressly for the succession of the Vice President, for the filling of a vacancy in the Vice Presidency, and for the determination of presidential inability.

◆**Clause 7. Compensation** The President now receives a salary of $400,000 and a taxable expense account of $50,000 a year. Those amounts cannot be changed during a presidential term; thus, Congress cannot use the President's compensation as a bargaining tool to influence executive decisions. The phrase "any other emolument" means, in effect, any valuable gift; it does not mean that the President cannot be provided with such benefits of office as the White House, extensive staff assistance, and much else.

◆**Clause 8. Oath of office** The Chief Justice of the United States regularly administers this oath or affirmation, but any judicial officer may do so. Thus, Calvin Coolidge was sworn into office in 1923 by his father, a justice of the peace in Vermont.

## Section 2. President's Powers and Duties

◆**Clause 1. Military, civil powers** The President, a civilian, heads the nation's armed forces, a key element in the Constitution's insistence on civilian control of the military. The President's power to "require the opinion, in writing" provides the constitutional basis for the Cabinet. The President's power to grant reprieves and pardons, the power of clemency, extends only to federal cases.

◆4. The Congress may determine the Time of choosing the Electors, and the Day on which they shall give their Votes; which Day shall be the same throughout the United States.

◆5. No Person except a natural born Citizen, or a Citizen of the United States, at the time of the Adoption of this Constitution, shall be eligible to the Office of President; neither shall any person be eligible to that Office who shall not have attained to the Age of thirty-five Years, and been fourteen Years a Resident within the United States.

◆6. ~~In Case of the Removal of the President from Office, or of his Death, Resignation, or Inability to discharge the Powers and Duties of the said Office, the Same shall devolve on the Vice President,~~ and the Congress may by Law provide for the Case of Removal, Death, Resignation or Inability, both of the President and Vice President, declaring what Officer shall then act as President, and such Officer shall act accordingly, until the Disability be removed, or a President shall be elected.

◆7. The President shall, at stated Times, receive for his Services, a Compensation, which shall neither be increased nor diminished during the Period for which he shall have been elected, and he shall not receive within that Period any other Emolument from the United States, or any of them.

◆8. Before he enter on the Execution of his Office, he shall take the following Oath or Affirmation:
"I do solemnly swear (or affirm) that I will faithfully execute the Office of President of the United States, and will to the best of my Ability, preserve, protect and defend the Constitution of the United States."

## Section 2.

◆1. The President shall be Commander in Chief of the Army and Navy of the United States, and of the Militia of the several States, when called into the actual Service of the United States; he may require the Opinion, in writing, of the principal Officer in each of the executive Departments, upon any Subject relating to the Duties of their respective Offices, and he shall have Power to Grant Reprieves and Pardons for Offences against the United States, except in Cases of Impeachment.

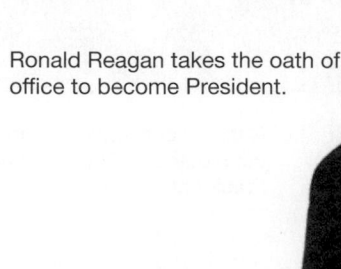

Ronald Reagan takes the oath of office to become President.

2. He shall have Power, by and with the Advice and Consent of the Senate, to make Treaties, provided two thirds of the Senators present concur; and he shall nominate, and by and with the Advice and Consent of the Senate, shall appoint Ambassadors, other public Ministers and Consuls, Judges of the supreme Court, and all other Officers of the United States, whose Appointments are not herein otherwise provided for, and which shall be established by Law: but the Congress may by Law vest the Appointment of such inferior Officers, as they think proper, in the President alone, in the Courts of Law, or in the Heads of Departments.

3. The President shall have Power to fill up all Vacancies that may happen during the Recess of the Senate, by granting Commissions which shall expire at the End of their next Session.

## Section 3.

He shall from time to time give to the Congress Information of the State of the Union, and recommend to their Consideration such Measures as he shall judge necessary and expedient; he may, on extraordinary Occasions, convene both Houses, or either of them, and in Case of Disagreement between them, with Respect to the Time of Adjournment, he may adjourn them to such Time as he shall think proper; he shall receive Ambassadors and other public Ministers; he shall take Care that the Laws be faithfully executed, and shall Commission all the Officers of the United States.

## Section 4.

The President, Vice President and all Civil Officers of the United States, shall be removed from Office on Impeachment for and Conviction of, Treason, Bribery, or other high Crimes and Misdemeanors.

# Article III
## Section 1.

The judicial Power of the United States, shall be vested in one supreme Court, and in such inferior Courts as the Congress may from time to time ordain and establish. The Judges, both of the supreme and inferior Courts, shall hold their Offices during good Behaviour, and shall, at stated Times, receive for their Services, a Compensation, which shall not be diminished during their Continuance in Office.

◆ **Clause 2. Treaties, appointments** The President has the sole power to make treaties; to become effective, a treaty must be approved by a two-thirds vote in the Senate. In practice, the President can also make executive agreements with foreign governments; these pacts, which are frequently made and usually deal with routine matters, do not require Senate consent. The President appoints the principal officers of the executive branch and all federal judges; the "inferior officers" are those who hold lesser posts.

◆ **Clause 3. Recess appointments** When the Senate is not in session, appointments that require Senate consent can be made by the President on a temporary basis, as "recess appointments." Recess appointments are valid only to the end of the congressional term in which they are made.

## Section 3. President's Powers and Duties

The President delivers a State of the Union Message to Congress soon after that body convenes each year. That message is delivered to the nation's lawmakers and, importantly, to the American people, as well. It is shortly followed by the proposed federal budget and an economic report; and the President may send special messages to Congress at any time. In all of these communications, Congress is urged to take those actions the Chief Executive finds to be in the national interest. The President also has the power: to call special sessions of Congress; to adjourn Congress if its two houses cannot agree for that purpose; to receive the diplomatic representatives of other governments; to insure the proper execution of all federal laws; and to empower federal officers to hold their posts and perform their duties.

## Section 4. Impeachment

The Constitution outlines the impeachment process in Article I, Section 2, Clause 5 and in Section 3, Clauses 6 and 7.

# Judicial Department
## Section 1. Judicial Power, Courts, Terms of Office

The judicial power conferred here is the power of federal courts to hear and decide cases, disputes between the government and individuals and between private persons (parties). The Constitution creates only the Supreme Court of the United States; it gives to Congress the power to establish other, lower federal courts (Article I, Section 8, Clause 9) and to fix the size of the Supreme Court. The words "during good Behaviour" mean, in effect, for life.

## Section 2. Jurisdiction

♦ **Clause 1. Cases to be heard** This clause sets out the jurisdiction of the federal courts; that is, it identifies those cases that may be tried in those courts. The federal courts can hear and decide—have jurisdiction over—a case depending on either the subject matter or the parties involved in that case. The jurisdiction of the federal courts in cases involving States was substantially restricted by the 11th Amendment in 1795.

♦ **Clause 2. Supreme Court jurisdiction** Original jurisdiction refers to the power of a court to hear a case in the first instance, not on appeal from a lower court. Appellate jurisdiction refers to a court's power to hear a case on appeal from a lower court, from the court in which the case was originally tried. This clause gives the Supreme Court both original and appellate jurisdiction. However, nearly all of the cases the High Court hears are brought to it on appeal from the lower federal courts and the highest State courts.

♦ **Clause 3. Jury trial in criminal cases** A person accused of a federal crime is guaranteed the right to trial by jury in a federal court in the State where the crime was committed; see the 5th and 6th amendments. The right to trial by jury in serious criminal cases in the State courts is guaranteed by the 6th and 14th amendments.

## Section 3. Treason

♦ **Clause 1. Definition** Treason is the only crime defined in the Constitution. The Framers intended the very specific definition here to prevent the loose use of the charge of treason—for example, against persons who criticize the government. Treason can be committed only in time of war and only by a citizen or a resident alien.

♦ **Clause 2. Punishment** Congress has provided that the punishment that a federal court may impose on a convicted traitor may range from a minimum of five years in prison and/or a $10,000 fine to a maximum of death; no person convicted of treason has ever been executed by the United States. No legal punishment can be imposed on the family or descendants of a convicted traitor. Congress has also made it a crime for any person (in either peace or wartime) to commit espionage or sabotage, to attempt to overthrow the government by force, or to conspire to do any of these things.

## Section 2.

♦ 1. The judicial Power shall extend to all Cases, in Law and Equity, arising under this Constitution, the Laws of the United States, and Treaties made, or which shall be made, under their Authority;— to all Cases affecting Ambassadors, other public ministers, and Consuls;— to all Cases of Admiralty and maritime Jurisdiction;— to Controversies to which the United States shall be a Party;— to Controversies between two or more States;— ~~between a State and Citizens of another State;~~ between Citizens of different States;— between Citizens of the same State claiming Lands under Grants of different States, ~~and between a State, or the Citizens thereof, and foreign States, Citizens, or Subjects.~~

♦ 2. In all Cases affecting Ambassadors, other public Ministers and Consuls, and those in which a State shall be a Party, the supreme Court shall have original Jurisdiction. In all the other Cases before mentioned, the supreme Court shall have appellate Jurisdiction, both as to Law and Fact, with such Exceptions, and under such Regulations as the Congress shall make.

♦ 3. The trial of all Crimes, except in Cases of Impeachment, shall be by Jury; and such Trial shall be held in the State where the said Crimes shall have been committed; but when not committed within any State, the Trial shall be at such Place or Places as the Congress may by Law have directed.

## Section 3.

♦ 1. Treason against the United States shall consist only in levying War against them, or in adhering to their Enemies, giving them Aid and Comfort. No Person shall be convicted of Treason unless on the Testimony of two Witnesses to the same overt Act, or on Confession in open Court.

♦ 2. The Congress shall have Power to declare the Punishment of Treason, but no Attainder of Treason shall work Corruption of Blood, or Forfeiture except during the Life of the Person attainted.

## Article IV

### Section 1.

Full Faith and Credit shall be given in each State to the public Acts, Records, and judicial Proceedings of every other State. And the Congress may by general Laws prescribe the Manner in which such Acts, Records and Proceedings shall be proved, and the Effect thereof.

### Section 2.

♦ 1. The Citizens of each State shall be entitled to all Privileges and Immunities of Citizens in the several States.

♦ 2. A Person charged in any State with Treason, Felony, or other Crime, who shall flee from justice, and be found in another State, shall on Demand of the executive Authority of the State from which he fled, be delivered up, to be removed to the State having Jurisdiction of the Crime.

♦ 3. No Person held to Service or Labor in one State, under the Laws thereof, escaping into another, shall, in Consequence of any Law or Regulation therein, be discharged from Service or Labor, but shall be delivered up on Claim of the Party to whom such Service or Labor may be due.

### Section 3.

♦ 1. New States may be admitted by the Congress into this Union; but no new State shall be formed or erected within the Jurisdiction of any other State; nor any State be formed by the Junction of two or more States, or Parts of States, without the Consent of the Legislatures of the States concerned as well as of the Congress.

♦ 2. The Congress shall have Power to dispose of and make all needful Rules and Regulations respecting the Territory or other Property belonging to the United States; and nothing in this Constitution shall be so construed as to Prejudice any Claims of the United States, or of any particular State.

### Section 4.

The United States shall guarantee to every State in this Union a Republican Form of Government, and shall protect each of them against Invasion; and on Application of the Legislature, or of the Executive (when the Legislature cannot be convened) against domestic Violence.

## Relations Among States

### Section 1. Full Faith and Credit

Each State must recognize the validity of the laws, public records, and court decisions of every other State.

### Section 2. Privileges and Immunities of Citizens

♦ **Clause 1. Residents of other States** In effect, this clause means that no State may discriminate against the residents of other States; that is, a State's laws cannot draw unreasonable distinctions between its own residents and those of any of the other States. See Section 1 of the 14th Amendment.

♦ **Clause 2. Extradition** The process of returning a fugitive to another State is known as "interstate rendition" or, more commonly, "extradition." Usually, that process works routinely; some extradition requests are contested however—especially in cases with racial or political overtones. A governor may refuse to extradite a fugitive; but the federal courts can compel an unwilling governor to obey this constitutional command.

♦ **Clause 3. Fugitive slaves** This clause was nullified by the 13th Amendment, which abolished slavery in 1865.

### Section 3. New States; Territories

♦ **Clause 1. New States** Only Congress can admit new States to the Union. A new State may not be created by taking territory from an existing State without the consent of that State's legislature. Congress has admitted 37 States since the original 13 formed the Union. Five States—Vermont, Kentucky, Tennessee, Maine, and West Virginia—were created from parts of existing States. Texas was an independent republic before admission. California was admitted after being ceded to the United States by Mexico. Each of the other 30 States entered the Union only after a period of time as an organized territory of the United States.

♦ **Clause 2. Territory, property** Congress has the power to make laws concerning the territories, other public lands, and all other property of the United States.

### Section 4. Protection Afforded to States by the Nation

The Constitution does not define "a republican form of government," but the phrase is generally understood to mean a representative government. The Federal Government must also defend each State against attacks from outside its border and, at the request of a State's legislature or its governor, aid its efforts to put down internal disorders.

## Provisions for Amendment

This section provides for the methods by which formal changes can be made in the Constitution. An amendment may be proposed in one of two ways: by a two-thirds vote in each house of Congress, or by a national convention called by Congress at the request of two-thirds of the State legislatures. A proposed amendment may be ratified in one of two ways: by three-fourths of the State legislatures, or by three-fourths of the States in conventions called for that purpose. Congress has the power to determine the method by which a proposed amendment may be ratified. The amendment process cannot be used to deny any State its equal representation in the United States Senate. To this point, 27 amendments have been adopted. To date, all of the amendments except the 21st Amendment were proposed by Congress and ratified by the State legislatures. Only the 21st Amendment was ratified by the convention method.

## National Debts, Supremacy of National Law, Oath

### Section 1. Validity of Debts

Congress had borrowed large sums of money during the Revolution and later during the Critical Period of the 1780s. This provision, a pledge that the new government would honor those debts, did much to create confidence in that government.

### Section 2. Supremacy of National Law

This section sets out the Supremacy Clause, a specific declaration of the supremacy of federal law over any and all forms of State law. No State, including its local governments, may make or enforce any law that conflicts with any provision in the Constitution, an act of Congress, a treaty, or an order, rule, or regulation properly issued by the President or his subordinates in the executive branch.

### Section 3. Oaths of Office

This provision reinforces the Supremacy Clause; all public officers, at every level in the United States, owe their first allegiance to the Constitution of the United States. No religious qualification can be imposed as a condition for holding any public office.

## Ratification of Constitution

The proposed Constitution was signed by George Washington and 37 of his fellow Framers on September 17, 1787. (George Read of Delaware signed for himself and also for his absent colleague, John Dickinson.)

## Article V

The Congress, whenever two thirds of both Houses shall deem it necessary, shall propose Amendments to this Constitution, or, on the Application of the Legislatures of two thirds of the several States, shall call a Convention for proposing Amendments, which, in either Case, shall be valid to all Intents and Purposes, as Part of this Constitution, when ratified by the Legislatures of three fourths of the several States, or by Conventions in three fourths thereof, as the one or the other Mode of Ratification may be proposed by the Congress; Provided ~~that no Amendment which may be made prior to the Year One thousand eight hundred and eight shall in any Manner affect the first and fourth Clauses in the Ninth section of the first Article; and~~ that no State, without its Consent, shall be deprived of its equal Suffrage in the Senate.

## Article VI

### Section 1.

All Debts contracted and Engagements entered into, before the Adoption of this Constitution, shall be as valid against the United States under this Constitution, as under the Confederation.

### Section 2.

This Constitution, and the Laws of the United States which shall be made in Pursuance thereof; and all Treaties made, or which shall be made, under the Authority of the United States, shall be the supreme Law of the Land; and the Judges in every State shall be bound thereby, anything in the constitution or Laws of any State to the Contrary notwithstanding.

### Section 3.

The Senators and Representatives before mentioned, and the Members of the several State legislatures, and all executive and judicial Officers, both of the United States and of the several States, shall be bound by Oath or Affirmation, to support this Constitution; but no religious Test shall ever be required as a Qualification to any Office or public Trust under the United States.

## Article VII

The ratification of the Conventions of nine States, shall be sufficient for the Establishment of this Constitution between the States so ratifying the same.

Nine States had to approve the Constitution before it could become effective.

Done in Convention by the Unanimous Consent of the States present the Seventeenth Day of September in the Year of our Lord one thousand seven hundred and Eighty-seven and of the Independence of the United States of America the twelfth. In witness whereof We have hereunto subscribed our Names.

**Attest:**
William Jackson,
*Secretary*
George Washington,
*President and Deputy from Virginia*

**New Hampshire**
John Langdon
Nicholas Gilman

**Massachusetts**
Nathaniel Gorham
Rufus King

**Connecticut**
William Samuel Johnson
Roger Sherman

**New York**
Alexander Hamilton

**New Jersey**
William Livingston
David Brearley
William Paterson
Jonathan Dayton

**Pennsylvania**
Benjamin Franklin
Thomas Mifflin
Robert Morris
George Clymer
Thomas Fitzsimons
Jared Ingersoll
James Wilson
Gouverneur Morris

**Delaware**
George Read
Gunning Bedford, Jr.
John Dickinson
Richard Bassett
Jacob Broom

**Maryland**
James McHenry
Dan of St. Thomas Jennifer
Daniel Carroll

**Virginia**
John Blair
James Madison, Jr.

**North Carolina**
William Blount
Richard Dobbs Spaight
Hugh Williamson

**South Carolina**
John Rutledge
Charles Cotesworth
    Pinckney
Charles Pinckney
Pierce Butler

**Georgia**
William Few
Abraham Baldwin

The first 10 amendments, the Bill of Rights, were each proposed by Congress on September 25, 1789, and ratified by the necessary three-fourths of the States on December 15, 1791. These amendments were originally intended to restrict the National Government—not the States. However, the Supreme Court has several times held that most of their provisions also apply to the States, through the 14th Amendment's Due Process Clause.

### 1st Amendment. Freedom of Religion, Speech, Press, Assembly, and Petition

The 1st Amendment sets out five basic liberties: The guarantee of freedom of religion is both a protection of religious thought and practice and a command of separation of church and state. The guarantees of freedom of speech and press assure to all persons a right to speak, publish, and otherwise express their views. The guarantees of the rights of assembly and petition protect the right to join with others in public meetings, political parties, interest groups, and other associations to discuss public affairs and influence public policy. None of these rights is guaranteed in absolute terms, however; like all other civil rights guarantees, each of them may be exercised only with regard to the rights of all other persons.

### 2nd Amendment. Bearing Arms

Each State has the right to maintain a militia, an armed force for its own protection—today, the National Guard. The National Government and the States can and do regulate the private possession and use of firearms.

### 3rd Amendment. Quartering of Troops

This amendment was intended to prevent what had been common British practice in the colonial period; see the Declaration of Independence. This provision is of virtually no importance today.

### 4th Amendment. Searches and Seizures

The basic rule laid down by the 4th Amendment is this: Police officers have no general right to search for or seize evidence or seize (arrest) persons. Except in particular circumstances, they must have a proper warrant (a court order) obtained with probable cause (on reasonable grounds). This guarantee is reinforced by the exclusionary rule, developed by the Supreme Court: Evidence gained as the result of an unlawful search or seizure cannot be used at the court trial of the person from whom it was seized.

### 5th Amendment. Criminal Proceedings; Due Process; Eminent Domain

A person can be tried for a serious federal crime only if he or she has been indicted (charged, accused of that crime) by a grand jury. No one may be subjected to double jeopardy—that is, tried twice for the same crime. All persons are protected against self-incrimination; no person can be legally compelled to answer any question in any governmental proceeding if that answer could lead to that person's prosecution. The 5th Amendment's Due Process Clause prohibits unfair, arbitrary actions by the Federal Government; a like prohibition is set out against the States in the 14th Amendment. Government may take private property for a legitimate public purpose; but when it exercises that power of eminent domain, it must pay a fair price for the property seized.

### 1st Amendment

Congress shall make no law respecting an establishment of religion, or prohibiting the free exercise thereof, or abridging the freedom of speech, or of the press; or the right of the people peaceably to assemble, and to petition the Government for a redress of grievances.

### 2nd Amendment

A well-regulated Militia being necessary to the security of a free State, the right of the people to keep and bear Arms, shall not be infringed.

### 3rd Amendment.

No Soldier shall, in time of peace be quartered in any house, without the consent of the Owner, nor, in time of war, but in a manner to be prescribed by law.

### 4th Amendment.

The right of the people to be secure in their persons, houses, papers, and effects, against unreasonable searches and seizures, shall not be violated, and no Warrants shall issue, but upon probable cause, supported by Oath or affirmation, and particularly describing the place to be searched, and the persons or things to be seized.

### 5th Amendment.

No person shall be held to answer for a capital, or otherwise infamous crime, unless on a presentment or indictment of a Grand Jury, except in cases arising in the land or naval forces, or in the Militia, when in actual service in time of War, or public danger; nor shall any person be subject for the same offence to be twice put in jeopardy of life or limb; nor shall be compelled in any criminal case to be a witness against himself, nor be deprived of life, liberty, or property, without due process of law; nor shall private property be taken for public use, without just compensation.

Jury swearing in

## 6th Amendment

In all criminal prosecutions, the accused shall enjoy the right to a speedy and public trial, by an impartial jury of the State and district wherein the crime shall have been committed, which district shall have been previously ascertained by law, and to be informed of the nature and cause of the accusation; to be confronted with the witnesses against him; to have compulsory process for obtaining witnesses in his favor, and to have the Assistance of Counsel for his defence.

## 7th Amendment

In Suits at common law, where the value in controversy shall exceed twenty dollars, the right of trial by jury shall be preserved, and no fact tried by a jury, shall be otherwise re-examined in any Court of the United States, than according to the rules of the common law.

## 8th Amendment

Excessive bail shall not be required, nor excessive fines imposed, nor cruel and unusual punishment inflicted.

## 9th Amendment

The enumeration in the Constitution, of certain rights, shall not be construed to deny or disparage others retained by the people.

## 10th Amendment

The powers not delegated to the United States by the Constitution, nor prohibited by it to the States, are reserved to the States respectively, or to the people.

### 6th Amendment. Criminal Proceedings

A person accused of crime has the right to be tried in court without undue delay and by an impartial jury; see Article III, Section 2, Clause 3. The defendant must be informed of the charge upon which he or she is to be tried, has the right to cross-examine hostile witnesses, and has the right to require the testimony of favorable witnesses. The defendant also has the right to be represented by an attorney at every stage in the criminal process.

### 7th Amendment. Civil Trials

This amendment applies only to civil cases heard in federal courts. A civil case does not involve criminal matters; it is a dispute between private parties or between the government and a private party. The right to trial by jury is guaranteed in any civil case in a federal court if the amount of money involved in that case exceeds $20 (most cases today involve a much larger sum); that right may be waived (relinquished, put aside) if both parties agree to a bench trial (a trial by a judge, without a jury).

### 8th Amendment. Punishment for Crimes

Bail is the sum of money that a person accused of crime may be required to post (deposit with the court) as a guarantee that he or she will appear in court at the proper time. The amount of bail required and/or a fine imposed as punishment must bear a reasonable relationship to the seriousness of the crime involved in the case. The prohibition of cruel and unusual punishment forbids any punishment judged to be too harsh, too severe for the crime for which it is imposed.

### 9th Amendment. Unenumerated Rights

The fact that the Constitution sets out many civil rights guarantees, expressly provides for many protections against government, does not mean that there are not other rights also held by the people.

### 10th Amendment. Powers Reserved to the States

This amendment identifies the area of power that may be exercised by the States. All of those powers the Constitution does not grant to the National Government, and at the same time does not forbid to the States, belong to each of the States, or to the people of each State.

### 11th Amendment. Suits Against States

Proposed by Congress March 4, 1794; ratified February 7, 1795, but official announcement of the ratification was delayed until January 8, 1798. This amendment repealed part of Article III, Section 2, Clause 1. No State may be sued in a federal court by a resident of another State or of a foreign country; the Supreme Court has long held that this provision also means that a State cannot be sued in a federal court by a foreign country or, more importantly, even by one of its own residents.

### 12th Amendment. Election of President and Vice President

Proposed by Congress December 9, 1803; ratified June 15, 1804. This amendment replaced Article II, Section 1, Clause 3. Originally, each elector cast two ballots, each for a different person for President. The person with the largest number of electoral votes, provided that number was a majority of the electors, was to become President; the person with the second highest number was to become Vice President. This arrangement produced an electoral vote tie between Thomas Jefferson and Aaron Burr in 1800; the House finally chose Jefferson as President in 1801. The 12th Amendment separated the balloting for President and Vice President; each elector now casts one ballot for someone as President and a second ballot for another person as Vice President. Note that the 20th Amendment changed the date set here (March 4) to January 20, and that the 23rd Amendment (1961) provides for electors from the District of Columbia. This amendment also provides that the Vice President must meet the same qualifications as those set out for the President in Article II, Section 1, Clause 5.

Vice President Joseph R. Biden, President Barack Obama

### 13th Amendment. Slavery and Involuntary Servitude

Proposed by Congress January 31, 1865; ratified December 6, 1865. This amendment forbids slavery in the United States and in any area under its control. It also forbids other forms of forced labor, except punishments for crime; but some forms of compulsory service are not prohibited—for example, service on juries or in the armed forces. Section 2 gives to Congress the power to carry out the provisions of Section 1 of this amendment.

## 11th Amendment

The Judicial power of the United States shall not be construed to extend to any suit in law or equity, commenced or prosecuted against one of the United States by Citizens of another State, or by Citizens or Subjects of any Foreign State.

## 12th Amendment

The Electors shall meet in their respective States and vote by ballot for President and Vice President, one of whom, at least, shall not be an inhabitant of the same State with themselves; they shall name in their ballots the person voted for as President, and in distinct ballots the person voted for as Vice President, and they shall make distinct lists of all persons voted for as President, and of all persons voted for as Vice President, and of the number of votes for each, which lists they shall sign and certify, and transmit sealed to the seat of the government of the United States, directed to the President of the Senate;— The President of the Senate shall, in the presence of the Senate and the House of Representatives, open all the certificates and the votes shall then be counted;— the person having the greatest Number of votes for President shall be the President, if such number be a majority of the whole number of Electors appointed; and if no person have such a majority, then, from the persons having the highest numbers not exceeding three on the list of those voted for as President, the House of Representatives shall choose immediately, by ballot, the President. But in choosing the President, the votes shall be taken by States, the representation from each State having one vote; a quorum for this purpose shall consist of a member or members from two thirds of the States, and a majority of all the States shall be necessary to a choice. And if the House of Representatives shall not choose a President whenever the right of choice shall devolve upon them, before the fourth day of March next following, then the Vice President shall act as President, as in case of death or other constitutional disability of the President. The person having the greatest number of votes as Vice President, shall be the Vice President, if such number be a majority of the whole number of Electors appointed, and if no person have a majority, then from the two highest numbers on the list, the Senate shall choose the Vice President; a quorum for the purpose shall consist of two thirds of the whole number of Senators, a majority of the whole number shall be necessary to a choice. But no person constitutionally ineligible to the office of President shall be eligible to that of Vice-President of the United States.

## 13th Amendment

**Section 1.** Neither slavery nor involuntary servitude, except as a punishment for crime whereof the party shall have been duly convicted, shall exist within the United States, or any place subject to their jurisdiction.

**Section 2.** Congress shall have power to enforce this article by appropriate legislation.

# 14th Amendment

**Section 1.** All persons born or naturalized in the United States and subject to the jurisdiction thereof, are citizens of the United States and of the State wherein they reside. No State shall make or enforce any law which shall abridge the privileges or immunities of citizens of the United States; nor shall any State deprive any person of life, liberty, or property, without due process of law; nor deny to any person within its jurisdiction the equal protection of the laws.

**Section 2.** Representatives shall be apportioned among the several States according to their respective numbers, counting the whole number of persons in each State, excluding Indians not taxed. But when the right to vote at any election for the choice of electors for President and Vice President of the United States, Representatives in Congress, the Executive and Judicial officers of a State, or the members of the Legislature thereof, is denied to any of the male inhabitants of such State, being twenty-one years of age and citizens of the United States, or in any way abridged, except for participation in rebellion, or other crime, the basis of representation therein shall be reduced in the proportion which the number of such male citizens shall bear to the whole number of male citizens twenty-one years of age in such State.

**Section 3.** No person shall be a Senator or Representative in Congress, or elector of President and Vice President, or hold any office, civil or military, under the United States, or under any State, who, having previously taken an oath, as a member of Congress, or as an officer of the United States, or as a member of any State legislature, or as an executive or judicial officer of any State, to support the Constitution of the United States, shall have engaged in insurrection or rebellion against the same, or given aid or comfort to the enemies thereof. But Congress may, by a vote of two thirds of each House, remove such disability.

**Section 4.** The validity of the public debt of the United States, authorized by law, including debts incurred for payment of pensions and bounties for services in suppressing insurrection or rebellion, shall not be questioned. But neither the United States nor any State shall assume or pay any debt or obligation incurred in aid of insurrection or rebellion against the United States, or any claim for the loss or emancipation of any slave; but all such debts, obligations and claims shall be held illegal and void.

**Section 5.** The Congress shall have power to enforce, by appropriate legislation, the provisions of this article.

## 14th Amendment. Rights of Citizens

Proposed by Congress June 13, 1866; ratified July 9, 1868. Section 1 defines citizenship. It provides for the acquisition of United States citizenship by birth or by naturalization. Citizenship at birth is determined according to the principle of jus soli—"the law of the soil," where born; naturalization is the legal process by which one acquires a new citizenship at some time after birth. Under certain circumstances, citizenship can also be gained at birth abroad, according to the principle of jus sanguinis—"the law of the blood," to whom born. This section also contains two major civil rights provisions: the Due Process Clause forbids a State (and its local governments) to act in any unfair or arbitrary way; the Equal Protection Clause forbids a State (and its local governments) to discriminate against, draw unreasonable distinctions between, persons.

Most of the rights set out against the National Government in the first eight amendments have been extended against the States (and their local governments) through Supreme Court decisions involving the 14th Amendment's Due Process Clause.

The first sentence here replaced Article I, Section 2, Clause 3, the Three-Fifths Compromise provision. Essentially, all persons in the United States are counted in each decennial census, the basis for the distribution of House seats. The balance of this section has never been enforced and is generally thought to be obsolete.

This section limited the President's power to pardon those persons who had led the Confederacy during the Civil War. Congress finally removed this disability in 1898.

Section 4 also dealt with matters directly related to the Civil War. It reaffirmed the public debt of the United States; but it invalidated, prohibited payment of, any debt contracted by the Confederate States and also prohibited any compensation of former slave owners.

### 15th Amendment. Right to Vote—Race, Color, Servitude

Proposed by Congress February 26, 1869; ratified February 3, 1870. The phrase "previous condition of servitude" refers to slavery. Note that this amendment does not guarantee the right to vote to African Americans, or to anyone else. Instead, it forbids the States from discriminating against any person on the grounds of his "race, color, or previous condition of servitude" in the setting of suffrage qualifications.

### 16th Amendment. Income Tax

Proposed by Congress July 12, 1909; ratified February 3, 1913. This amendment modified two provisions in Article I, Section 2, Clause 3, and Section 9, Clause 4. It gives to Congress the power to levy an income tax, a direct tax, without regard to the populations of any of the States.

### 17th Amendment. Popular Election of Senators

Proposed by Congress May 13, 1912; ratified April 8, 1913. This amendment repealed those portions of Article I, Section 3, Clauses 1 and 2 relating to the election of senators. Senators are now elected by the voters in each State. If a vacancy occurs, the governor of the State involved must call an election to fill the seat; the governor may appoint a senator to serve until the next election, if the State's legislature has authorized that step.

### 18th Amendment. Prohibition of Intoxicating Liquors

Proposed by Congress December 18, 1917; ratified January 16, 1919. This amendment outlawed the making, selling, transporting, importing, or exporting of alcoholic beverages in the United States. It was repealed in its entirety by the 21st Amendment in 1933.

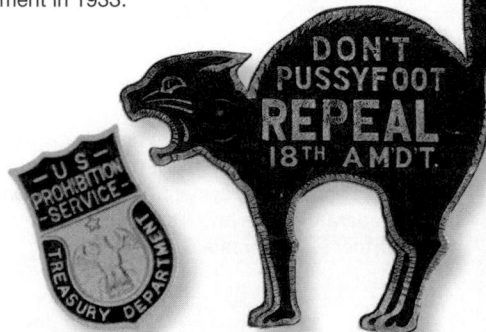

### 19th Amendment. Equal Suffrage—Sex

Proposed by Congress June 4, 1919; ratified August 18, 1920. No person can be denied the right to vote in any election in the United States on account of his or her sex.

## 15th Amendment

**Section 1.** The right of citizens of the United States to vote shall not be denied or abridged by the United States or by any State on account of race, color, or previous condition of servitude.

**Section 2.** The Congress shall have power to enforce this article by appropriate legislation.

## 16th Amendment

The Congress shall have power to lay and collect taxes on incomes, from whatever source derived, without apportionment among the several States, and without regard to any census or enumeration.

## 17th Amendment

The Senate of the United States shall be composed of two Senators from each State, elected by the people thereof, for six years; and each Senator shall have one vote. The electors in each State shall have the qualifications requisite for electors of the most numerous branch of the State legislatures.

When vacancies happen in the representation of any State in the Senate, the executive authority of such State shall issue writs of election to fill such vacancies: Provided, That the legislature of any State may empower the executive thereof to make temporary appointments until the people fill the vacancies by election as the legislature may direct.

This amendment shall not be so construed as to affect the election or term of any Senator chosen before it becomes valid as part of the Constitution

## 18th Amendment.

Section 1. After one year from the ratification of this article the manufacture, sale, or transportation of intoxicating liquors within, the importation thereof into, or the exportation thereof from the United States and all territory subject to the jurisdiction thereof for beverage purposes is hereby prohibited.

**Section 2.** The Congress and the several States shall have concurrent power to enforce this article by appropriate legislation.

Section 3. This article shall be inoperative unless it shall have been ratified as an amendment to the Constitution by the legislatures of the several States, as provided in the Constitution, within seven years of the date of the submission hereof to the States by Congress.

## 19th Amendment

The right of citizens of the United States to vote shall not be denied or abridged by the United States or by any State on account of sex.

Congress shall have power to enforce this article by appropriate legislation.

## 20th Amendment

**Section 1.** The terms of the President and Vice President shall end at noon on the 20th day of January, and the terms of Senators and Representatives at noon on the 3d day of January, of the years in which such terms would have ended if this article had not been ratified; and the terms of their successors shall then begin.

**Section 2.** The Congress shall assemble at least once in every year, and such meeting shall begin at noon on the 3d day of January, unless they shall by law appoint a different day.

**Section 3.** If, at the time fixed for the beginning of the term of the President, the President elect shall have died, the Vice President elect shall become President. If a President shall not have been chosen before the time fixed for the beginning of his term, or if the President-elect shall have failed to qualify, then the Vice President elect shall act as President until a President shall have qualified; and the Congress may by law provide for the case wherein neither a President elect nor a Vice President elect shall have qualified, declaring who shall then act as President, or the manner in which one who is to act shall be selected, and such person shall act accordingly until a President or Vice President shall have qualified.

**Section 4.** The Congress may by law provide for the case of the death of any of the persons from whom the House of Representatives may choose a President whenever the right of choice shall have devolved upon them, and for the case of the death of any of the persons from whom the Senate may choose a Vice President whenever the right of choice shall have devolved upon them.

**Section 5.** Sections 1 and 2 shall take effect on the 15th day of October following the ratification of this article.

**Section 6.** This article shall be inoperative unless it shall have been ratified as an amendment to the Constitution by the legislatures of three fourths of the several States within seven years from the date of its submission.

## 21st Amendment

**Section 1.** The eighteenth article of amendment to the Constitution of the United States is hereby repealed.

**Section 2.** The transportation or importation into any State, Territory, or possession of the United States for delivery or use therein of intoxicating liquors, in violation of the laws thereof, is hereby prohibited.

**Section 3.** This article shall be inoperative unless it shall have been ratified as an amendment to the Constitution by conventions in the several States, as provided in the Constitution, within seven years from the date of the submission hereof to the States by the Congress.

### 20th Amendment. Commencement of Terms; Sessions of Congress; Death or Disqualification of President-Elect

Proposed by Congress March 2, 1932; ratified January 23, 1933. The provisions of Sections 1 and 2 relating to Congress modified Article I, Section 4, Clause 2, and those provisions relating to the President, the 12th Amendment. The date on which the President and Vice President now take office was moved from March 4 to January 20. Similarly, the members of Congress now begin their terms on January 3. The 20th Amendment is sometimes called the "Lame Duck Amendment" because it shortened the period of time a member of Congress who was defeated for reelection (a "lame duck") remains in office.

This section deals with certain possibilities that were not covered by the presidential selection provisions of either Article II or the 12th Amendment. To this point, none of these situations has occurred. Note that there is neither a President-elect nor a Vice President-elect until the electoral votes have been counted by Congress, or, if the electoral college cannot decide the matter, the House has chosen a President or the Senate has chosen a Vice President.

Congress has not in fact ever passed such a law. See Section 2 of the 25th Amendment, regarding a vacancy in the vice presidency; that provision could some day have an impact here.

Section 5 set the date on which this amendment came into force.

Section 6 placed a time limit on the ratification process; note that a similar provision was written into the 18th, 21st, and 22nd amendments.

### 21st Amendment. Repeal of 18th Amendment

Proposed by Congress February 20, 1933; ratified December 5, 1933. This amendment repealed all of the 18th Amendment. Section 2 modifies the scope of the Federal Government's commerce power set out in Article I, Section 8, Clause 3; it gives to each State the power to regulate the transportation or importation and the distribution or use of intoxicating liquors in ways that would be unconstitutional in the case of any other commodity. The 21st Amendment is the only amendment Congress has thus far submitted to the States for ratification by conventions.

## 22nd Amendment. Presidential Tenure

Proposed by Congress March 21, 1947; ratified February 27, 1951. This amendment modified Article II, Section I, Clause 1. It stipulates that no President may serve more than two elected terms. But a President who has succeeded to the office beyond the midpoint in a term to which another President was originally elected may serve for more than eight years. In any case, however, a President may not serve more than 10 years. Prior to Franklin Roosevelt, who was elected to four terms, no President had served more than two full terms in office.

BETTER A THIRD TERMER THAN A THIRD RATER

Political button supporting FDR's third term.

## 23rd Amendment. Presidential Electors for the District of Columbia

Proposed by Congress June 16, 1960; ratified March 29, 1961. This amendment modified Article II, Section I, Clause 2 and the 12th Amendment. It included the voters of the District of Columbia in the presidential electorate; and provides that the District is to have the same number of electors as the least populous State—three electors—but no more than that number.

## 24th Amendment. Right to Vote in Federal Elections—Tax Payment

Proposed by Congress August 27, 1962; ratified January 23, 1964. This amendment outlawed the payment of any tax as a condition for taking part in the nomination or election of any federal officeholder.

## 25th Amendment. Presidential Succession, Vice Presidential Vacancy, Presidential Inability

Proposed by Congress July 6, 1965; ratified February 10, 1967. Section 1 revised the imprecise provision on presidential succession in Article II, Section 1, Clause 6. It affirmed the precedent set by Vice President John Tyler, who became President on the death of William Henry Harrison in 1841. Section 2 provides for the filling of a vacancy in the office of Vice President. The office had been vacant on 16 occasions and remained unfilled for the rest of each term involved. When Spiro Agnew resigned the office in 1973, President Nixon selected Gerald Ford per this provision; and, when President Nixon resigned in 1974, Gerald Ford became President and chose Nelson Rockefeller as Vice President.

## 22nd Amendment

**Section 1.** No person shall be elected to the office of the President more than twice, and no person who has held the office of President, or acted as President, for more than two years of a term to which some other person was elected President shall be elected to the office of the President more than once. But this Article shall not apply to any person holding the office of President, when this Article was proposed by the Congress, and shall not prevent any person who may be holding the office of President, or acting as President, during the term within which this Article becomes operative from holding the office of President or acting as President during the remainder of such term.

**Section 2.** This article shall be inoperative unless it shall have been ratified as an amendment to the Constitution by the legislatures of three fourths of the several states within seven years from the date of its submission to the States by the Congress.

## 23rd Amendment.

**Section 1.** The District constituting the seat of Government of the United States shall appoint in such manner as the Congress may direct:

A number of electors of President and Vice President equal to the whole number of Senators and Representatives in Congress to which the District would be entitled if it were a State, but in no event more than the least populous State; they shall be in addition to those appointed by the States, they shall be considered, for the purposes of the election of President and Vice President, to be electors appointed by a State; and they shall meet in the District and perform such duties as provided by the twelfth article of amendment.

## 24th Amendment.

**Section 1.** The right of citizens of the United States to vote in any primary or other election for President or Vice President, for electors for President or Vice President, or for Senator or Representative in Congress, shall not be denied or abridged by the United States or any State by reason of failure to pay any poll tax or other tax.

**Section 2.** The Congress shall have power to enforce this article by appropriate legislation.

## 25th Amendment.

**Section 1.** In case of the removal of the President from office or of his death or resignation, the Vice President shall become President.

**Section 2.** Whenever there is a vacancy in the office of the Vice President, the President shall nominate a Vice President who shall take office upon confirmation by a majority vote of both Houses of Congress.

**Section 3.** Whenever the President transmits to the President pro tempore of the Senate and the Speaker of the House of Representatives his written declaration that he is unable to discharge the powers and duties of his office, and until he transmits to them a written declaration to the contrary, such powers and duties shall be discharged by the Vice President as Acting President.

**Section 4.** Whenever the Vice President and a majority of either the principal officers of the executive departments or of such other body as Congress may by law provide, transmit to the President pro tempore of the Senate and the Speaker of the House of Representatives their written declaration that the President is unable to discharge the powers and duties of his office, the Vice President shall immediately assume the powers and duties of the office as Acting President.

Thereafter, when the President transmits to the President pro tempore of the Senate and the Speaker of the House of Representatives his written declaration that no inability exists, he shall resume the powers and duties of his office unless the Vice President and a majority of either the principal officers of the executive department or of such other body as Congress may by law provide, transmit within four days to the President pro tempore of the Senate and the Speaker of the House of Representatives their written declaration that the President is unable to discharge the powers and duties of his office. Thereupon Congress shall decide the issue, assembling within forty-eight hours for that purpose if not in session. If the Congress, within twenty-one days after receipt of the latter written declaration, or, if Congress is not in session, within twenty-one days after Congress is required to assemble, determines by two-thirds vote of both Houses that the President is unable to discharge the powers and duties of his office, the Vice President shall continue to discharge the same as Acting President; otherwise, the President shall resume the powers and duties of his office.

This section created a procedure for determining if a President is so incapacitated that he cannot perform the powers and duties of his office.

Section 4 deals with the circumstance in which a President will not be able to determine the fact of incapacity. To this point, Congress has not established the "such other body" referred to here. This section contains the only typographical error in the Constitution; in its second paragraph, the word "department" should in fact read "departments."

## 26th Amendment.

**Section 1.** The right of citizens of the United States, who are eighteen years of age or older, to vote shall not be denied or abridged by the United States or by any State on account of age.

**Section 2.** The Congress shall have the power to enforce this article by appropriate legislation.

### 26th Amendment. Right to Vote—Age

Proposed by Congress March 23, 1971; ratified July 1, 1971. This amendment provides that the minimum age for voting in any election in the United States cannot be more than 18 years. (A State may set a minimum voting age of less than 18, however.)

## 27th Amendment.

No law varying the compensation for the services of the Senators and Representatives, shall take effect, until an election of Representatives shall have intervened.

### 27th Amendment. Congressional Pay

Proposed by Congress September 25, 1789; ratified May 7, 1992. This amendment modified Article I, Section 6, Clause 1. It limits Congress's power to fix the salaries of its members—by delaying the effectiveness of any increase in that pay until after the next regular congressional election.

Use the lessons on these pages and the Skills Work-sheets and Activities for each chapter to teach students vital 21st Century Skills. The worksheets and activities can be found in the All-in-One Resources for each unit.

# Skills Handbook

The following pages provide you with the skills you need to learn and demonstrate your knowledge of American government.

# Writing

Writing is one of the most powerful communication tools you will use for the rest of your life. Beyond the ability of the written word to inspire, inform, and entertain, research also shows that writing about what you read actually helps you learn new information and form new ideas. A systematic approach to writing—including prewriting, drafting, revising, and proofreading—can help you write better, whether you are writing an essay or a research paper.

## Narrative Essay

Narrative writing tells a story, often about a personal experience. In a government or civics course, this story, for example, might be a narrative essay that recounts how participation in a campaign or a summer job working for a government agency affected you, your friends, or your family.

### ① Prewriting

**Choose a topic.** The focus of your essay should be an experience of significance to you. Use these suggestions as a guide.

- Look at photos that show you with friends or family. Perhaps you attended a political rally or worked on a community event for a cause or charity you cared about.
- Scan the news in print or through electronic media. Consider how current events, court decisions, or election results have affected you or people you know. Brainstorm with family or friends. How did you react or respond to these events? Jot down ideas like the ones below.

| Connections to Government and Politics This Year |
|---|
| - participated in a mock legislative assembly |
| - watched televised debates between candidates at election time |
| - attended a climate change rally and circulated a petition for stricter controls on greenhouse emissions |

**Consider audience and purpose.** As you write, think about who your reader will be.

- Keep the knowledge and experience level of your audience in mind. Make sure you provide any necessary background information.
- Think about the purpose of the essay. Is your goal to entertain or inform? If your goal is to inform, you might share insights, describe lessons learned, or convey how the experience changed you.

**Gather details.** Collect the facts and details you need to tell your story.

- Research and include any background information about the experience that readers might need to know to understand how it affected you.
- List details about your own perceptions of the experience.

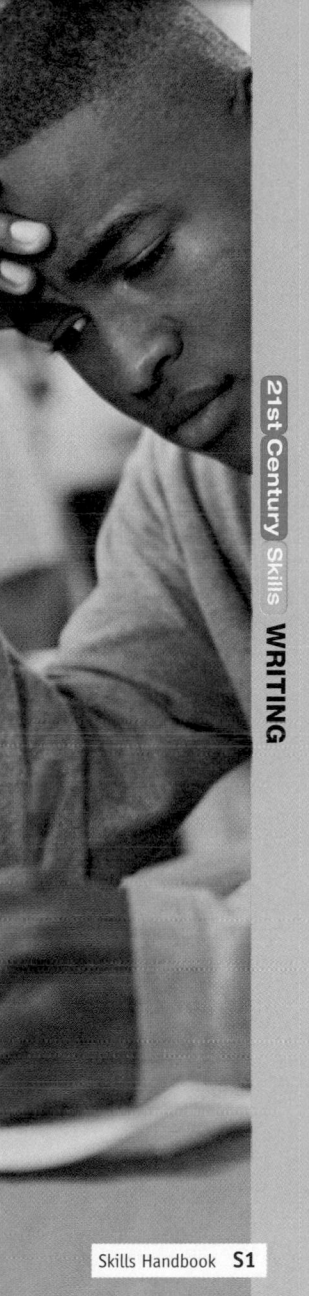

21st Century Skills **WRITING**

Skills Handbook **S1**

## LESSON GOALS

Students will . . .

- write a narrative essay using a four-step writing process: prewriting, drafting, revising, and publishing and presenting.
- identify the features that distinguish a narrative essay from other types of essay writing.
- write a narrative essay that is clearly organized to help the reader understand the order of events and their significance.

## Teach

### INTRODUCE

Explain that employers and colleges often require narrative essays on job and technical school or college applications. Such essays offer a way for applicants to explain how their personal experiences have prepared them for the position or assignment they hope to obtain. Point out that the purpose of a narrative essay is to reflect on a personal experience. It also offers a way of linking personal experiences to a broader topic. Often such essays offer the reader insight into the writer's hopes, fears, goals, or thought process. Many narrative essays tell a story about an experience that has influenced the choices the writer has made in his or her personal or professional life.

### ACTIVATE PRIOR KNOWLEDGE

Have students read the steps in the prewriting process. Have students choose a topic for a narrative essay about a recent experience that surprised them or changed their perspective in some way. Students might think about personal experiences that involved a community service project, running for office at school or in a club, campaigning for a candidate or cause, or meeting with government officials. They might think about a problem they have encountered, a choice they have made, a person they have met, or an experience that challenged their thinking or taught them a lesson. Have students brainstorm topics with peers.

### DISCUSS PREWRITING

Once students have chosen a topic, have them identify the audience for this essay. Ask: **Is the intended audience people who have shared similar experiences or people who know nothing about this topic?** The answer to this question tells the writer what background information or context might be needed and which aspects of this narrative might need to be explained in greater detail to make it meaningful to the reader.

## DISCUSS DRAFTING

Students may find it helpful to list the main events of their narratives in chronological order. They can then expand this list into an outline as they add details that will make the narrative more understandable to the reader by providing a context. They can also explore rearranging the events to allow for a flashback or other breaks in the chronological order of the narrative. Students might then list sensory details that can be included in the essay to make the narrative more vivid. Emphasize that a narrative essay is not just a listing of events. The writer's goal is to show the significance of these events.

## DISCUSS REVISING

Review the example in the chart. Then ask students to write simple sentences with general words on the board and work together to replace them with more specific, vivid options.

# Assess and Remediate

Have students write the narrative essay they have been drafting. Pair students to review each other's essays. Ask students to read aloud their essays to their partners. As one student speaks, encourage the partner who is listening to note any unclear or confusing statements as well as suggestions for improvements. Encourage peer reviewers to identify at least two successful aspects of their partner's work before focusing on areas needing further work. For additional practice, students might revise the Writing Rubric on page S13 to adapt the evaluation criteria to narrative writing.

##  Drafting

**Organize information.** Narratives are usually told in chronological order. Identify the climax of the decisive moment in your story. Then logically organize your work into a beginning, middle, and end.

**Write an opening sentence.** Open strongly with an engaging sentence that will catch your reader's attention.

**Use sensory details.** Use sights, sounds, or smells to make the story vivid for readers. Describe people's actions and gestures. Pinpoint and describe locations.

**Write a conclusion.** Sum up the significance of the experience.

A strong opening engages the reader. → Practicing my speech in front of my bedroom mirror wasn't so bad. Now, however, I was saying these same words out loud in a crowded high school auditorium filled with seniors who would rather be somewhere else.

Sensory details make the experience more vivid for the reader. → My heart pounded wildly. My first thought was "What am I doing here?" As I began to talk, some of those bored expressions began to change. Others, however, whispered to their neighbors or stared off into space. Couldn't they see that climate change might someday have a dramatic effect on their lives?

Insight or significance tells the reader what this event means to you. → I learned that day that knowing how you feel about an issue is easy. Convincing others to take that issue seriously is a much tougher challenge. My political education was just beginning.

##  Revising

**Add dialogue or description.** Dialogue (a person's thoughts or feelings in his or her own words) can make a narrative more convincing. Look for places in the story where the emotions are especially intense. In the model, this might be when the speaker first faces the bored audience.

| First Draft | Revision |
|---|---|
| Despite the many times I had practiced my speech in front of a mirror, I was still nervous. My heart was beating fast as I looked out at the auditorium. | Practicing my speech in front of my bedroom mirror wasn't so bad. Now, however, I was saying these same words in a crowded high school auditorium filled with seniors who would rather be somewhere else. My heart pounded wildly. |

**Revise word choice.** Replace general words with more specific, colorful ones. Choose vivid action verbs, precise adjectives, and specific nouns to convey your meaning. In the example above, notice how much more effective the revised version is at conveying the experience.

**Read your draft aloud.** Listen for grammatical errors and statements that are unclear. Revise your sentences as necessary.

## ④ Publishing and Presenting

Highlight text you want to emphasize, and then read your essay aloud to the class. Invite and respond to questions.

# Expository Writing

Expository writing explains ideas or information in detail. The strategies on these pages examine several expository writing styles.

## ① Prewriting

**Choose a topic.** In a government course, the focus of your writing might be explaining the process of a bill becoming law, comparing and contrasting the positions of political candidates, identifying a problem and proposing a solution, or examining the causes and effects behind policy changes. The following suggestions are a guide.

- For writing about a process, consider the question *how*. For example, you might ask, "How does a bill become a law?" Then you would identify the steps or procedures involved.

| |
|---|
| **Question:** How does a bill become a law? |
| **Answer:** A proposed law is introduced in the House or Senate, then sent to the appropriate committee to be studied. If the committee votes to pass the bill, it is debated by the full House or Senate. After debate, members vote on the bill. If passed, it is sent to the other house and goes through the same process. If it passes that house, it is sent to the President for his approval or veto. |

- With a partner, visit the Web site of two candidates for office. Choose three issues that both candidates address and note each candidate's viewpoint on the issues you've chosen.
- With a small group, write problems related to each of these challenges on slips of paper: global warming, universal healthcare, and energy alternatives. Have each person take a slip of paper and brainstorm possible solutions to each problem with the group.
- Write down questions to ask a school board member about policy or other changes they are considering. Ask why these changes are being considered. Understanding why is the basis of a cause-and-effect essay.

**Consider audience and purpose.** Consider how much your readers know about the process, comparison, problem, or event you will address. Adjust your writing to your audience's knowledge or provide explanations of unfamiliar ideas.

**Research the topic.** Use library and Internet resources and interviews with local officials or experts if possible. Also consider your personal experience. You might know about a local community problem from firsthand experience.

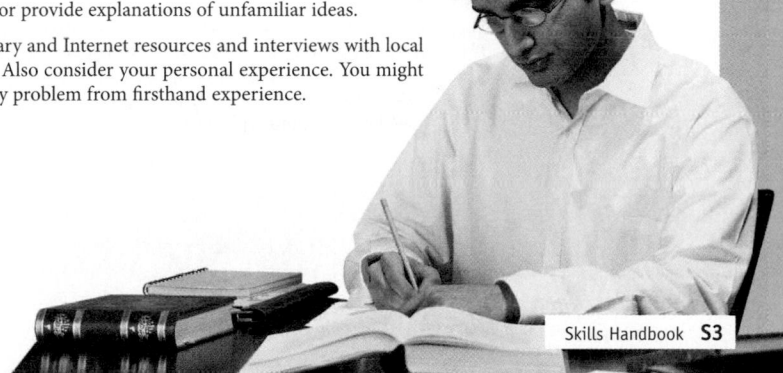

Skills Handbook **S3**

# Get Started

## LESSON GOALS

Students will . . .

- write an expository essay using a four-step writing process: prewriting, drafting, revising, and publishing and presenting.
- identify the features that distinguish expository writing from other types of essay writing.
- identify the writing strategies and structures that are most useful for writing different types of expository essays.

# Teach

## INTRODUCE

Point out that expository writing is also called explanatory writing. It is the type of writing students use most often in school. Unlike narrative writing, which may seek to entertain, persuade, or convey insights, the primary purpose of expository writing is to inform or explain something to the reader.

## ACTIVATE PRIOR KNOWLEDGE

Ask students to recall school assignments in which they had to explain a process; compare and contrast products, ideas, or policies; identify causes and effects; or describe a problem and solution. Point out that expository writing is a skill required by workers in a variety of jobs. People in technical or scientific fields often use expository writing to explain a process, write a journal article, or create instructions for programming computers or delivering medical services. Many jobs in business and finance require analysts to write reports that compare and contrast products, companies, and proposals. Government policymakers and analysts routinely write reports that explain cause and effect, define problems and recommend solutions, or compare and contrast policy options.

## DISCUSS PREWRITING

Lead students through the strategy of selecting slips of paper and brainstorming ideas, described in the text, for choosing a topic to compare and contrast. Then using the Venn diagram in the text as a model, help them create a similar graphic organizer to compare and contrast their topics.

## DISCUSS DRAFTING

Review the drafting steps with students. Invite several volunteers to tell the class the topics they have chosen. Write the topics on the board and ask students to suggest structures for organizing and presenting the information on this topic. Clarify for students the difference between a compare-and-contrast essay organized by subject and one organized by point. For example, a report on healthcare policy organized by subject might be structured as a comparison of a government-run and a private insurance healthcare plan. An essay on healthcare policy organized by point might introduce a category such as cost of healthcare program, comparing and contrasting the two healthcare plans based on their costs. Deciding on the structure of the essay will help students narrow their topics and decide what additional information is needed. Emphasize that regardless of structure, all explanatory essays should begin with a clear statement of the purpose of the essay.

## EXAMINE STRUCTURE

Model the steps in drafting an expository essay by working through the passage in the text on rising healthcare costs. Have students explain how this passage is structured. To give students additional practice in identifying different ways of organizing expository essays, bring examples of expository writing such as newspaper and newsmagazine editorials and op-ed pieces, computer or software instruction manuals, home remodeling magazines, or online sources. Display materials and have students take turns identifying the structure of each document.

**Candidate A**
- Favors expanding free trade agreements
- Wants government subsidies for private insurance companies
- Supports oil drilling on public lands to increase energy independence

**Shared by Both Candidates**
- Favors expanding healthcare benefits
- Supports increased energy independence

**Candidate B**
- Opposes international trade agreements
- Favors government-run healthcare programs
- Wants government to fund alternative energy programs to increase energy independence

**Create a graphic organizer.** For cause-and-effect or problem-solution essays, use a two-column chart. Process writing can be a bulleted list of steps. A Venn diagram can help you compare and contrast.

**Fine-tune your ideas.** For a problem-solution essay, choose a solution and narrow its scope to ensure that it is achievable in cost, effort, and timing. If your solution has been tried by others, describe successes or failures and how your approach will differ. Keep in mind that problem-solution and process writing often involve cause-effect relationships. Look for causes and effects as you organize your material.

### ② Drafting

**Match structure to purpose.** Typically, problem-solution essays benefit from block organization, which presents the entire problem and then proposes a solution. Put process and cause-and-effect essays in sequential order. Organize compare/contrast essays by subject or by point.

> **By subject:** Discuss the issues and viewpoints of Candidate A, and then compare and contrast them with those of Candidate B.
>
> **By point:** Introduce each issue, such as healthcare or trade agreements. Relate views of both candidates on the issue, comparing or contrasting them in your discussion. Then, move on to the next issue.

**Give background.** To discuss a policy, program, or process, orient the reader to context. Ensure readers know why a law was passed or what the court case was about. Choose the important facts, but don't overwhelm the reader with details.

**Elaborate for interest and emphasis.** Give details about each point in your essay. To clarify a cause-and-effect relationship, add facts that explain the link between the reason for a decision or action and its consequences. In a problem-solution essay, readers are more likely to support proposed solutions if essays clearly show how these solutions will solve the problem. Sum up in a brief conclusion.

One of the most serious problems Americans face today is the rising cost of healthcare. For several decades, the cost of healthcare has risen much faster than personal wages. At the same time, the number of Americans without health insurance continues to rise. In 2006, 14.8 percent of Americans were uninsured. To further complicate the problem, the retirement of the baby boom generation is just beginning. Experts predict that in the decade ahead these changes will greatly increase the demand for healthcare.

Healthcare policy analysts offer several strategies for reducing costs. First, allow the government to negotiate with drug companies for lower prescription prices, and allow cheaper drugs to be brought in from other countries. Second, pay doctors and other providers lower fees similar to those paid to providers in other industrialized nations. Finally, make consumers pay more of their own healthcare costs so that they will weigh the necessity of treatments. Many experts see consumers' reliance on high-cost specialists rather than primary care doctors as a key cost factor. A carefully implemented plan to put these ideas into action will give more Americans access to quality healthcare.

*Annotations:*
- Identify the topic to orient readers.
- Point out causes of the problem.
- List possible solutions.
- Conclude by summarizing the goal of the solution.

### ③ Revising

**Remember purpose.** Your essay should answer the question or thesis with which you began. In a problem-solution essay, your purpose is to convince readers to support your solution. Try to anticipate opposing arguments and respond to them.

**Review organization.** Number your main points. Reorganize these points until they flow in a logical order.

**Add transition words.** Make cause-and-effect relationships clear with such words as *because* and *so*. To compare and contrast, use linking words, such as *similarly* or *in contrast*. Use words such as *first* and *next* to show steps in a process.

| First Draft | Revision |
|---|---|
| The Federal Drug Administration monitors small clinical trials. These trials show the drug to be safe, and FDA officials conduct larger trials. | First, the Federal Drug Administration monitors small clinical trials. Next, if the results of these trials show the drug to be safe and effective enough for further study, FDA officials conduct larger trials. |

**Add details.** For a process essay, be sure to include all steps; don't assume readers will make connections. When writing about cause and effect, stress the way one event leads to the next. Add more background if necessary for clarity.

**Revise.** Vary sentence length. Scan for vague words, such as *good,* and replace them with specific words. Use technical terms sparingly and define them.

**Peer review.** Ask a classmate to review your draft. Revise areas of confusion.

### ④ Publishing and Presenting

**Create a government manual.** Contribute your explanation of a government process to a class manual of Government How-Tos.

21st Century Skills **WRITING**

### DISCUSS REVISING

Challenge students to use each transition word in the text in a sentence and to identify transition words that can be used in their own essays. Have them compare the first draft and revised passage in the text. Ask students to explain why the revised version is more effective than the original.

### REVIEW CONCLUDING PARAGRAPH

As a final step in the revision process, students should end with a concluding paragraph that restates the problem and summarizes the recommendations or options for solving it, summarizes how subjects are alike or different, or briefly restates the causes or effects of an event and how they are related to the outcome.

## Assess and Remediate

Have students write an expository essay. Essays might focus on a procedure in the legislative, judiciary, or executive branch such as the selection of a Supreme Court justice or on a current issue or concern in the school or community or in State or Federal government. Ask them to use one of the prewriting steps to choose the type of essay that best fits their topic. Circulate to make sure students have chosen topics and provide guidance with the planning and writing of the essays. As a concluding activity, have students review the Writing Rubric on page S13 and suggest ways of revising the evaluation criteria to create specific rubrics for different types of expository essays.

# Get Started

## LESSON GOALS

Students will . . .

- write a research paper using a four-step writing process: prewriting, drafting, revising, and publishing and presenting.
- identify the features that distinguish research reports from other types of writing.
- identify the challenges of evaluating Internet sources.

# Teach

## INTRODUCE

Point out that research writing is based heavily on information from outside sources beyond the writer's own knowledge. Research writing is often required in job settings as well as in schools. In private businesses and government offices, workers write research papers on a wide variety of topics from potential new markets for farm crops to the impact on the music industry of online sales of individual tunes.

## DISCUSS PREWRITING

Point out that finding a topic requires not only identifying a subject that interests the writer but also making sure that valid, accurate, and verifiable sources of information are available on this topic. Evaluating sources is a critical part of any research writing activity. Unlike reputable print sources, many Web sites do not have fact checkers or credentialed reviewers. Caution students that anyone with Internet access can create a Web site. Discuss with the class the sources that you consider to be acceptable for research papers. Make sure that the class understands the criteria that you use to decide whether or not a source can be used in writing a research report.

## BRAINSTORM

Before students choose their own topics, have them examine the Government and Internet topics web in the text. Ask them to suggest possible sources for researching the topics shown. Then divide students into groups to choose a topic and create a web like the one shown. Encourage students to choose topics that are of interest to them as writers. Research writing is time-consuming, and an interest in the topic will help students stay focused on the task. Remind students that they can use sources such as magazines, Web sites, and newspapers to get ideas.

# Research Writing

A research paper presents information about a particular topic from several different sources. The author must then tie this information together with a single unifying idea and present it to the reader.

## ① Prewriting

**Choose a topic.** Often, a teacher will assign your research topic. If not, you may have flexibility in choosing your focus, or you may have the opportunity to completely define your topic. The following suggestions are a guide.

- Using an online or electronic library catalog, search for topics that interest you. When a title looks promising, find the book on the shelves. Because libraries group research materials by subject, you should find other books on similar subjects that may help you decide on your final topic.
- Review your class notes. Jot down topics that you found interesting. For example, you might find a starting point for research into students' legal rights in schools from a Supreme Court case that you studied in class.
- Brainstorm topics with a group. List interesting current events issues such as the economy, healthcare, the environment, and privacy. Within each category, take turns adding subtopics. The chart below looks at different topics related to the Internet, politics, and government.

**Analyze the audience.** Your research and your paper should be strongly influenced by the audience. How much will readers already know about this topic and how much will you have to teach them?

**Gather details.** Collect the facts and details you need to write your paper. Use a variety of resources, including nonfiction books or journal articles, newspapers, newsmagazines, and government publications. Search the Internet for reliable information and opinions on your topic, starting with online encyclopedias and news organizations. Look for interviews with experts on your topic.

**Organize evidence and ideas.** Create notecards or a computer file on your topic to record information and to help you organize your thoughts. Start by writing down a possible thesis statement. Then begin reading and taking notes. Write a heading at the top of each notecard and add subtopics below. List your information sources on a separate card, giving each a number. Use that number to identify the source for each subtopic on your cards. In the examples below, the number 3 is used to identify the information source. Use the same number for additional topic cards derived from the same source.

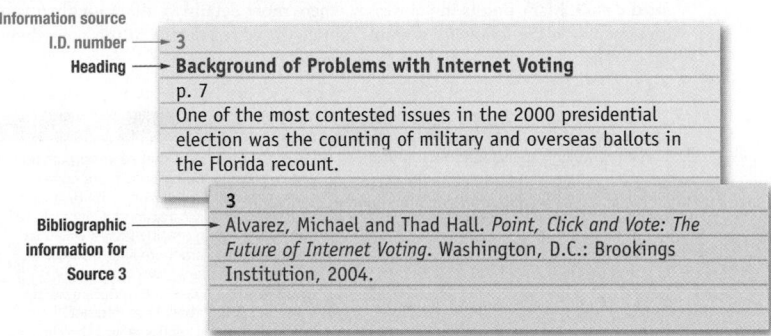

Information source
I.D. number → 3
Heading → **Background of Problems with Internet Voting**
p. 7
One of the most contested issues in the 2000 presidential election was the counting of military and overseas ballots in the Florida recount.

3
Bibliographic → Alvarez, Michael and Thad Hall. *Point, Click and Vote: The*
information for *Future of Internet Voting.* Washington, D.C.: Brookings
Source 3 Institution, 2004.

## ② Drafting

**Fine-tune your thesis.** Review your notes to find relationships between ideas. Shape a thesis that is supported by the majority of your information, then check that it is specific enough to address thoroughly in the time and space allotted. You can fine-tune your thesis further as you draft or even when you revise.

**Organize the information to fit your purpose.** Consider your reason for exploring this topic, and identify the structure that will best help you reach this goal. Decide whether you want to present arguments that will compare and contrast aspects of a topic, persuade readers to support your position on an issue or policy, or argue for a particular solution to a problem. Then organize appropriately. For example, if your goal is to persuade readers that electronic voting should be allowed in national elections, begin by stating arguments in favor of your position. Follow by presenting opposing views with your counterarguments or rebuttals to those points.

**Make an outline.** Create an outline in which you identify each topic and subtopic in a single phrase. Turn these phrases into sentences and then into the topic and supporting sentences of your draft paragraphs. Write an introduction, at least three body paragraphs, and a conclusion. Support all of your statements with the facts and details you gathered.

Skills Handbook **S7**

Direct students' attention to the sample note cards on the text page. Ask them to identify each piece of information on the cards. Point out that the researcher has identified sources by numbering the cards. Strongly encourage students to document facts as they write. Searching through a stack of index cards to find one piece of information or missing citation can be very time-consuming. Correct documentation of sources saves time and reduces errors.

**DISCUSS DRAFTING**

Explain that research papers often begin with a thesis statement. The thesis statement clearly states the purpose of the report and usually appears in the introductory paragraph. The statement provides the reader with a preview of what will be discussed in the paper. Explain to the students that a thesis statement for a research paper on Internet voting might be: "Internet voting has many benefits, but it also has several potentially serious drawbacks. In the United States, a country with a long and stable democratic tradition, the benefits outweigh the risks."

**ANALYZE OUTLINE**

Review the sample outline in the text. Have students paraphrase the thesis statement you discussed with the class. Ask students what kinds of facts or statistics the writer might use to support this thesis. Discuss each step in the outline, pointing out how the information is organized. Explain that each paragraph of a student's research paper should link to an outline entry. Note that the Introduction puts the topic in context and conveys the thesis statement, while the Conclusion recaps key points. Emphasize that students will make a stronger case for their thesis if they draw on several sources of information rather than relying on a single source to support their thesis.

## DISCUSS REVISING

Throughout the revision process, students should check their outlines against their paper to make sure that all statements are supported by evidence. Review the sample first draft and discuss the revision. Note that the revised version provides more information on who benefits from Internet voting and makes the criticisms of Internet voting easier to understand. An important step in revising a research paper is rereading it to confirm that each fact is documented. Stress the importance of documenting each fact. If a fact cannot be documented, it should not be included.

## PUBLISH AND PRESENT

Have students prepare a list of the topics of the research projects they will present to the class. Encourage students to review the list of topics to think of possible questions to ask the presenters. Presenters should anticipate questions classmates might ask and prepare answers. If possible, provide access to computers so that students can create accompanying visuals such as Power Point presentations.

# Assess and Remediate

Have students work in groups to consider and choose a topic for a research paper. Once they have selected a general topic, have them create a word web of possible subtopics and then list possible sources of information for researching the subtopics that interest them. Circulate to provide guidance with selecting topics and brainstorming subtopics and sources of information. Have students review the Writing Rubric on page S13 and suggest ways of revising the evaluation criteria to create a specific rubric for research writing.

An outline helps you organize your information.

Each body paragraph examines a part of the main topic.

| Internet Voting |
| --- |
| Outline |
| I. Introduction |
| II. What Are the Benefits of Internet Voting? |
|     A. Appeal to young voters and increased voter turnout |
|     B. Ease and convenience of voting |
| III. What Are the Risks of Internet Voting? |
|     A. Inequality of access (Counterargument: Computers in schools and libraries expand access) |
|     B. Potential for voter fraud and tampering (Counterargument: Technological improvements make Internet voting more secure) |
| IV. Conclusion: Benefits Outweigh Risks |

## ③ Revising

**Add detail.** Mark points in your essay where more details would strengthen your statements. In the following example, notice the added details in the revised version. When adding facts, be sure they are accurate.

| First Draft | Revision |
| --- | --- |
| Internet voting can increase voter participation by making it easier to cast a ballot. Even people who don't own computers can vote in schools and libraries. | Internet voting can increase voter participation by making the process more convenient, especially for citizens with disabilities and Americans living abroad. Critics argue that online voting unfairly favors wealthier Americans who are more likely to own computers. In many places, however, voters who do not own computers will be able to cast their ballots at Internet terminals in public schools and libraries. |

**Make the connection for readers.** Help readers find their way through your ideas. First, check that your body paragraphs and the information within them flow in a logical sequence. If they do not, revise to correct this. Then add transition words to link ideas and paragraphs.

**Give credit.** Check that you have used your own words or given proper credit to other sources. For quoted text, add parenthetical notes that include the author's last name and the relevant page number from the source. For example, you could cite the notecard on page S7 as (Alvarez and Hall, p. 7). The surest way to avoid plagiarism is to take notes in your own words, and then write from your notes, not from the original source.

## ④ Publishing and Presenting

**Share your research.** Gather a group of classmates and present your research projects. If time allows, create visual materials to accompany your presentations. After you share your papers, hold a question-and-answer session.

# Persuasive Essay

Persuasive writing supports an opinion and often takes the form of a position paper, editorial, blog, or Op-Ed piece. Persuasive essays in government often argue for or against government policies, candidates, or political issues.

## ① Prewriting

**Choose a topic.** Choose a topic that provokes discussion and has at least two sides. Use these suggestions as a guide.

- Talk with classmates in a round-table discussion about issues you have studied recently. Outline pro and con positions on these issues.
- Scan the table of contents or flip through the pages of your textbook. Focus on issues that interest you.
- Look at blogs, editorials, or Op-Ed pieces online or in current newspapers. Develop a position on an issue of importance today.

**Narrow your topic.** Choose a subsection of the topic to cover if the subject is complex. Write for five minutes on the general topic. Circle the most important idea. Then write for five minutes on that idea. Continue looping until the topic is manageable.

**Consider your audience.** Choose arguments that will appeal to your audience and that are likely to persuade readers to agree with your views.

**Gather evidence.** Collect evidence that will help you support your position convincingly.

**Identify pros and cons.** Use a graphic organizer like the one below to list points on both sides of the issue.

| Position: State and local governments should provide funds to build a new soccer stadium. | |
|---|---|
| **Pro** ◀ | ▶ **Con** |
| • Create new jobs, both temporary construction jobs and permanent service jobs<br>• Attract customers to local businesses<br>• Increase tax revenue<br>• Increase sense of community and civic pride | • Costly to build and maintain<br>• Money spent on this project will result in less money for schools, public transit, and other pressing needs.<br>• Increase in traffic and use of public facilities will require improved infrastructure and more cost. |

## ② Drafting

**State your thesis.** Clearly state your position, as in this example:

> Local and State government officials should provide funding for the construction of a new soccer stadium because of the economic and social benefits it will bring to the city and the region.

# Get Started

## LESSON GOALS

Students will . . .

- write a persuasive essay using a four-step writing process: prewriting, drafting, revising, and publishing or presenting.
- identify the features that distinguish a persuasive essay from other types of writing.
- clearly state a position on an issue and answer opposing arguments.

# Teach

## INTRODUCE

Read aloud or display a copy of an editorial from a current newspaper or magazine. Have students identify arguments and counterarguments. Point out that the main purpose of a persuasive essay is to convince other people to share your point of view. To be effective, the points the writer makes in a persuasive essay must be supported by accurate, reliable evidence and arguments.

## DISCUSS PREWRITING

Review suggestions for choosing a topic: round-table discussion, textbook flip, and looking at issues online or in newspapers. Divide students into small groups. Assign each group one of the prewriting strategies for choosing a topic. Have each group share its list of topics with the class. Encourage students to pick topics that they care about personally. It is also important to choose a topic that people disagree about. Debatable topics might include immigration policy, taxes, crime, human rights abuses, land use, responses to traffic congestion, responses to water or air pollution, gun control, teenage curfews, and dress codes.

## ANALYZE AND DISCUSS

Direct students' attention to the chart in the text about the construction of a new soccer stadium. Ask students to paraphrase the writer's position on this issue and the arguments the writer plans to use to support the position. Have the class brainstorm opposing positions.

## DISCUSS DRAFTING

Have a volunteer read aloud the sample thesis statement. Point out that it clearly takes a position on the stadium construction issue and states the writer's strongest argument in support of that position. Readers then know what to expect from the essay to follow and can assess whether other arguments advanced by this writer in the essay support this thesis.

## PROVIDE A CONTEXT

Emphasize the importance of providing a context for the issue. In the introductory paragraph, the writer should briefly cover the "who, what, when, where, and why" of the issue. Throughout the essay, students should use their research to provide specific supporting information. An argument supported by facts and careful reasoning is more effective than one that is unsupported. A factual argument appeals to readers' intelligence rather than their emotions.

## ANSWER COUNTERARGUMENTS

Writers should anticipate the arguments that might be made by those who disagree with their positions and include responses or rebuttals to these arguments in the essay. A review of the pros and cons listed on the graphic organizers students created in the prewriting activity will help them identify the counterarguments that need to be addressed in the essay.

## REVISING

Throughout the revision process, encourage students to check for areas where logic is faulty or information should be added to make arguments clearer. Have students assess their writing for clarity and coherence. Students should also check to make sure counterarguments have been addressed and identify places where transition words can help guide readers through the argument and clarify relationships among ideas or arguments. Then discuss the sample first draft and revision in the text. Ask students to explain in what ways the revision is an improvement over the first draft.

## PUBLISH AND PRESENT

Model for students how they can use emphasis, gesture, tone, volume, or speed in their presentations. Emphasize that persuasive speech should be delivered with feeling, but never involve anger, shouting, or the use of insulting or inappropriate language. Such behaviors distract listeners from the speaker's ideas.

# Assess and Remediate

Have students write persuasive essays about topics that matter to them. Pair students to discuss their positions. One partner can state his or her topic and position, and the other partner can try to refute it. Students will then switch roles and repeat the process. Circulate to make sure that students stay focused on their topics for their persuasive essays. Have students review the Writing Rubric on page S13 and suggest ways of revising the evaluation criteria to create a specific rubric for persuasive writing.

**Write your introduction** Use your introduction to provide context. Tell your readers when and why the issue arose, and identify the key decision makers involved.

**Acknowledge the opposition.** State, and then refute, opposing arguments.

**Use facts and details.** Include quotations, statistics, or comparisons to build your case. Include personal experiences or reactions to the topic, such as the opinions of officials who were interviewed.

**Write a conclusion.** Return to your thesis and close with a strong, compelling argument or a brief summary of the three strongest arguments.

| | |
|---|---|
| Background orients readers. | A plan to build a world-class soccer stadium has been proposed at both the State and local levels. Is this a good idea for our city? I believe that |
| Thesis identifies your main argument. | it is. Local and State government officials should provide funding for construction of a new soccer stadium because of the economic and social benefits it will bring to the city and the region. Those who oppose the |
| Acknowledging opposing argument and then refuting it solidifies your position. | stadium project focus mainly on its costs to the public. The new stadium will bring many benefits that don't show up on a balance sheet—entertainment, excitement, and most importantly, a sense of enhanced community pride. Studies show that cities with professional sports teams |
| Supporting argument clarifies your thesis and sums up your position. | attract more tourists. Equally important, residents get a positive message about their community every time they turn on their TVs and see the local team on the new playing field. |

##  Revising

**Add information.** Extra details can generate interest in your topic. For example, add a quotation from a news article supporting your argument.

**Review arguments.** Make sure your arguments are logical and clear. Avoid faulty logic such as circular reasoning (arguing a point by merely restating it differently). Evidence is the best way to support your points. Notice how much more effectively the revised version supports the argument in the following example.

| First Draft | Revision |
|---|---|
| Building a new stadium will bring money to the city, which will help residents. | A 2008 study commissioned by the city manager estimated that stadium construction would create 1,700 construction jobs and provide $2 million in tax revenues. The study also concluded that spending at local hotels, restaurants, and shops by visiting soccer teams and fans would bring in an additional $1.1 million per year. |

**Use transition words to guide readers.** To show contrast, use *although,* or *despite.* To point out a reason, use *because,* or *if.* To signal a conclusion, use *so,* or *then.*

## ④ Publishing and Presenting

**Persuasive speech.** Many persuasive essays are delivered orally. Prepare your essay as a speech, highlighting words for emphasis, and adding cues for changes in tone, volume, or speed.

# Writing for Assessment

Assessment writing allows fewer choices than other writing and usually imposes a time limit. In government and political science courses, you will be required to write both short-answer and extended responses.

## ① Prewriting

**Choose a topic.** Short-answer questions seldom offer a choice of topics. For extended response, however, you may have a choice of more than one question.

- Analyze what each question is asking. Identify key words such as those listed.

| Key Words | What You Need in an Answer |
|---|---|
| • Explain | • Give a clear, complete account. |
| • Compare/Contrast | • Show how two or more things are alike and different. |
| • Define | • Give examples to explain meaning. |
| • Argue, Convince, Support, Persuade | • Take a position on an issue and present strong reasons to support your opinion. |
| • Summarize | • Provide the most important elements. |
| • Evaluate/Judge | • Assign a value or explain an opinion. |

Notice in the examples below that the key words are underlined.

> **Short-Answer Question:** Explain why the ability to communicate is an important aspect of presidential leadership.
>
> **Extended-Response Question:** What leadership qualities have the nation's most outstanding Presidents displayed? Give examples to support your choices.

- After choosing a question, try to plot the answer quickly in your mind. If you cannot do so easily, choose another question.

**Measure your time.** Divide your time: one-quarter on prewriting, half on drafting, one-quarter on revising. For short-answer questions, decide how much of the overall test time you can spend on each question.

**Organize your response.** For extended-response questions, divide your topic into subtopics that fit the type of question. Jot down facts and details for each. For a question on presidential leadership, consider the following.

> **Leadership Qualities of Outstanding Presidents**
> - ability to communicate and build consensus on major policies (1)
> - ability to gain the trust and respect of the American public (2)
> - vision or clear idea of where to lead the nation (3)
> - openness to new ideas; flexibility in changing conditions (4)
>
> **Example of President Exhibiting Specific Leadership Qualities**
> - Franklin Roosevelt: ability to communicate, gain trust, try new ideas (New Deal)

# Get Started

## LESSON GOALS

Students will . . .

- be able to write for assessment using a four-step writing process: prewriting, drafting, revising, and publishing and presenting.
- identify the features that distinguish assessment writing from other types of writing.
- identify strategies for time management and for successfully completing writing assessments.

# Teach

## ACTIVATE PRIOR KNOWLEDGE

Ask students to name in-class assignments or different kinds of placement exams or achievement tests they have completed that included a writing component. Point out that many job applications and college exams require students to write for assessment.

## DISCUSS PREWRITING STEPS

Point out that many writing assessments require students to write either a narrative, expository, or persuasive essay. Writing tests sometimes provide test takers with several topics or questions to choose from. Students should select the questions that allow them to discuss their areas of greatest knowledge.

## CHOOSE A QUESTION

Review with students the chart of Key Words in the text. This chart will help them identify the structures associated with different types of test questions and topics. Ask students to suggest the appropriate organization for each of the question types shown in the Key Words list. For example, a topic that requires the writer to show how two or more things are alike or different calls for a compare-and-contrast structure.

## MANAGE THE TIME

Remind students that assessment writing requires them to meet time constraints. As students quickly decide which is the best question or questions to answer, caution them to be aware of how many questions they are expected to answer and to consider approximately how long it will take them to answer each question.

## DISCUSS DRAFTING

Have students compare the Extended Response question on presidential leadership with the graphic organizer outlining the answer. Note that the two underlined key elements have main headings in the organizer. This reminds the writer to provide supporting details or examples for each required point in the question.

## RESTATE QUESTION

Emphasize the importance of restating the question at the beginning of the essay. This clearly tells the reader what question the essay will answer. Have students link the opening sentence of the sample response in the text to the question about presidential leadership, noting words that appear in both texts. Then have them examine how the writer used the actions of Franklin Roosevelt as examples of specific presidential leadership qualities noted in the two-column graphic organizer in the text.

## DISCUSS REVISING

Have students read the First Draft and Revision examples from the essay on presidential leadership. Ask students to list the words and phrases added to the revised version, and then explain how each addition or change improves the passage. Point out that revising can be a critical step in assessment writing, and students should resist the impulse to omit it. Emphasize that in writing assessments, correct use of grammar, usage, and mechanics may be an essential part of the scoring.

Throughout the revision process, encourage students to check for areas where logic is faulty or information should be added to make arguments clearer or stronger. Students can also check to make sure all counterarguments have been addressed and identify places where transition words can help guide readers through the argument or explanation.

## PUBLISH AND PRESENT

Emphasize the importance of making sure that students have answered all the questions before turning in their assessments.

# Assess and Remediate

Give students a choice of three sample assessment questions for a practice test. Allow students a reasonable amount of time to choose and respond to the question chosen. Before beginning the practice assessment, ask students to read the Writing Rubric on page S13, which consists of the evaluation criteria for scoring the writing portion of the SAT test. At the start of the practice assessment, announce how much time students will have to write their essays. Give students a five-minute warning before completion time.

## ② Drafting

**Choose an appropriate organization.** For short-answer responses, write one to three complete sentences. Extended responses require a more elaborate structure. For an extended response on presidential leadership, describe the leadership qualities of each President, and give examples. For problem-solution questions, describe the problem, and propose a solution. For compare/contrast questions, present similarities first, then differences.

**Open and close strongly.** Start by using the question's language to state your position. This helps you focus and shows that you understand the question. Conclude by restating your position. For short answers, include language from the question in your response.

**Support your ideas.** Each paragraph should support your main idea.

> The opening restates the question and presents the main idea.
>
> The writer uses information from the graphic organizer to build an argument.
>
> The writer supports the second subtopic.
>
> The conclusion recaps the main idea and uses the question's language.

By itself, no single quality makes an exceptional leader. In the careers of the nation's most outstanding Presidents, many of their qualities built upon and complemented one another. Franklin Roosevelt was a highly effective communicator and flexible leader. (1) Despite his privileged upbringing, his skills as a communicator enabled him to convey his compassion for the poor and earned him the trust and respect of the American people. He used his communication skills to convince the people in his administration to work together. Roosevelt showed flexibility in responding to the difficult economic and social challenges of the Depression (2) by his advocacy of the many experimental programs and policies of his New Deal initiative. President Roosevelt provides an excellent example of several key qualities of an exceptional leader.

## ③ Revising

**Examine word choice.** Replace general words with specific words. Add transitions where they improve clarity. Read the following examples. The revised version shows the relative importance of the writer's supporting evidence.

| First Draft | Revision |
|---|---|
| No single quality makes a good leader. Qualities build upon and complement one another. Franklin Delano Roosevelt was a highly effective communicator because he won the trust and support of the American people. He convinced people to work together. | By itself no single quality makes an exceptional leader. In the careers of the nation's most outstanding Presidents, many qualities built upon and complemented one another. For example, Franklin Delano Roosevelt was a highly effective communicator, who won the trust and support of the American people; in addition, the President convinced the people in his administration to work together. |

**Check organization.** Make sure your introduction includes a main idea and briefly defines each subtopic. Review each paragraph for a single main idea. Check that your conclusion summarizes the information you have presented.

## ④ Publishing and Presenting

**Edit and proofread.** Check spelling, grammar, and mechanics. Make sure that tenses match, subjects agree with verbs, and all sentences include a subject and verb. Confirm that you have responded to all the questions you were asked.

After students have handed in their essays, have the class reflect on their experience. Ask students how they chose their topic and how they decided what structure to use in their responses. Then invite volunteers to explain how they managed their time, any problems they encountered, and how much time they spent on each step in the writing process.

# Writing Rubric

Use this chart, or rubric, to evaluate your writing.

| Criteria | Exceeds standard | Meets standard | Approaches standard | Does not meet standard |
|---|---|---|---|---|
| Thesis | Sharp, well-developed thesis with clear connection to topic | Sharp and mostly developed thesis with clear connection to topic | Somewhat clear thesis with limited connection to topic | No thesis, or unclear thesis, with little connection to topic |
| Introduction | Clear, direct focus; highly interesting and engaging; provides excellent context for discussing topic | Focused and interesting, provides context for discussing topic | Somewhat focused and interesting, provides some limited context for discussing topic | Too broad, provides little context for discussing topic; uses throwaway phrases like "throughout history" |
| Organization | Recognizable beginning, middle, and ending; logically organized with a variety of transitions | Clear beginning, middle, and ending; generally logical organization with some transition words used | Beginning, middle, and ending unclear; connections between ideas weak and few transition words used | No beginning, middle, or ending; no connections between ideas and no transition words used |
| Supporting evidence and facts | Substantial facts and evidence | Sufficient facts and evidence | Uneven use of facts and evidence | Insufficient facts and evidence |
| Analysis | Effective, logical, sophisticated analysis supported by facts and evidence; demonstrates keen insight into and understanding of topic | Effective, logical analysis supported by facts and evidence; demonstrates clear understanding of topic | General analysis only, and/or somewhat illogical or inconsistent; facts and evidence somewhat enhance analysis; demonstrates basic understanding of topic | Limited analysis and/or illogical; uses descriptive and storytelling format rather than analysis; demonstrates limited understanding of topic |
| Conclusion | Ties together main ideas to arrive at a logical and insightful conclusion that shows deep understanding of the topic | Ties together main ideas to arrive at a logical and insightful conclusion | Demonstrates some understanding of the topic and/or relies heavily on summary | Demonstrates general and shallow understanding of the topic or is summary only |
| Mechanics | Extremely few or no grammatical, spelling, punctuation, or other mechanical errors | A few grammatical and spelling errors, which do not distract from the overall quality of the paper | Some errors in spelling, grammar, punctuation, word choice, and capitalization; includes repetition, fragments, conversational prose | Many grammatical, spelling, punctuation, and other errors, which detract from the quality of the paper |

21st Century Skills WRITING

**LESSON GOAL**

• Students will identify and analyze the scoring process in the SAT writing assessment by examining the writing rubric for this test.

## Teach

### INTRODUCE

Poll the class to see how many students are familiar with the SAT exam. Explain that an important part of this exam involves essay writing. Explain that the Writing Rubric on this page shows students how graders score the essays on the SAT writing exam. Ask volunteers to name the seven criteria used to rate these essays. Then ask them to explain in their own words the characteristics of a strong essay and identify the evaluation criteria on the rubric that they think are their own greatest strengths or weaknesses.

## Assess and Remediate

Ask each student to choose the best essay they have written so far. Pair each student with a partner with similar writing skills. Ask pairs to work together to create self-evaluations of their essays. Students can begin by exchanging essays and evaluating each other's work using the rubric. Have them explain their assessments to their partners, starting with strengths. Then ask pairs to brainstorm how they can make their essays stronger and write self-evaluations of their essay writing skills.

Collect students' essays and self-evaluations. Meet with students to go over good points and areas for improvement.

# Get Started

## LESSON GOAL

- Students will distinguish between primary and secondary sources by examining two sources on the role of President Dwight Eisenhower in the conflict over the integration of Central High School in Little Rock, Arkansas.

# Teach

## ACTIVATE PRIOR KNOWLEDGE

Have students read the steps in the process of analyzing primary and secondary sources and share any questions they have. Ask them to recall events that have occurred during their lifetime or stories they have heard from older family members or friends about events that took place many years ago. Ask students how eyewitness accounts might differ from secondary sources about events. Point out that eyewitness accounts often provide a unique personal perspective, while secondary sources often identify and assess the effects or consequences of an event from the perspective of the passage of time.

## DISCUSS

Have students identify the point of view of the writer of each source in the text and the differences in the information each source gives the reader. Point out that the Little Rock crisis had many other participants who wrote eyewitness accounts including the African American students attempting to enter the high school, the Arkansas governor, U.S. soldiers protecting the students, and white protesters in the mob. Ask students how the point of view and bias of each of these groups might be different.

# Assess and Remediate

Have students complete the Practice and Apply the Skill questions. Discuss their responses as a class. Have students bring to class online or print examples of a primary and a secondary source. Have students write three questions about each source they have chosen, and exchange sources and questions with a partner.

# Critical Thinking

## Analyze Sources

A primary source is a firsthand account of an event. Examples include letters and photographs. A secondary source is an account based on primary sources. Follow these steps to analyze primary and secondary sources.

1. **Identify the document.** Identify the source of the document. Determine when, where, and why it was written. Is the document a primary or secondary source?

2. **Find the main idea.** After identifying the main idea, identify details or sections of text that support the main idea.

3. **Evaluate the source for point of view and bias.** Primary sources often have a strong point of view or bias. It is important to analyze primary sources critically.

> For three weeks in September 1957, . . . Little Rock became the focus of a showdown over integration as Gov. Orval Faubus blocked nine black students from enrolling at all-white Central. Although the U.S. Supreme Court had declared segregated classrooms unconstitutional in 1954 . . . Faubus said he feared violence if the races mixed in a public school. The showdown soon became a test for President Dwight D. Eisenhower, who has been derided by some historians as being silent on civil rights. . . .
> David A. Nichols, author of *A Matter of Justice: Eisenhower and the Beginning of the Civil Rights Revolution*, argues that the showdown . . . showed the 34th president's true feelings about desegregation. "I think the intervention in Little Rock revealed who Eisenhower really was on this issue," . . .
> —*USA Today*, September 22, 2007

> Newport, Rhode Island,
> September 27, 1957
>
> The Honorable Richard B. Russell [Georgia]
> United States Senate
> Washington, D.C.
>
> Few times in my life have I felt as saddened as when the obligations of my office required me to order the use of force [federal troops] within a state to carry out the decisions of a Federal Court. My conviction is that had the police powers of the State of Arkansas been utilized not to frustrate the orders of the Court but to support them, the ensuing violence and open disrespect for the law would never have occurred . . . . When a State, by seeking to frustrate the orders of a Federal Court, encourages mobs of extremists to flout the orders of a Federal Court, and when a State refuses to utilize its police powers to protect against mobs persons who are peaceably exercising their right under the Constitution . . . the oath of office of the President requires that he take action . . . ."

## Practice and Apply the Skill

Use the sources above to answer the following questions.

1. What makes the letter a primary source and the article a secondary source?

2. Based on the letter, what is Eisenhower's reason for sending federal troops?

3. What point does the article make about Eisenhower's role in the Little Rock crisis? How is this point supported by the letter?

# Answers

**1.** The letter is a primary source because it was written during the crisis by a participant in the event. The newspaper article is a secondary source because a reporter who did not have first-hand knowledge of the event wrote it 50 years later.

**2.** Eisenhower says that he sent in troops to enforce the decision of the Federal Court after the State failed to use its police powers to protect the constitutional rights of the black students.

**3.** The article says Eisenhower's stance showed his true feelings about desegregation and it implies that he supported it. In his letter, Eisenhower says that the State refused "to utilize its police powers to protect against mobs persons who are peaceably exercising their right under the Constitution."

# Compare Viewpoints

Many factors shape a person's viewpoint, including values, age, prejudices, gender, and past experiences. Comparing viewpoints will help you understand issues and form your own opinions. Use the following steps to learn about comparing viewpoints. Then analyze the speeches below and answer the questions.

**1 Identify the authors.** Determine when and where each person was speaking. Identify the intended audience for each speech and its purpose.

**2 Determine the author's frame of reference.** Consider how each speaker's attitudes; beliefs; values; social, economic, or political concerns and affiliations; as well as past experiences, might affect his or her viewpoint.

**3 Determine the author's bias.** Bias may be revealed in the use of emotionally charged words, faulty logic, or exaggerated claims. In written or spoken materials, be sure to identify which statements are facts and which are opinions.

**4 Compare and contrast.** Determine how the viewpoints are similar and different. Consider factors that might have contributed to differing positions.

### Passage A

It is time to check and reverse the growth of government which shows signs of having grown beyond the consent of the governed. It is my intention to curb the size and influence of the Federal establishment . . . . Now . . . it is not my intention to do away with government. It is, rather, to make it...stand by our side, not ride on our back.... It is no coincidence that our present troubles . . . are proportionate to the intervention and intrusion into our lives that result from unnecessary and excessive growth of government.

—Ronald Reagan, First Inaugural Address,
January 20, 1981

### Passage B

My view is to . . . recognize that [the federal government] has a role in our lives and a partnership role to play. We have made the Government smaller. . . . We have . . . been working . . . to reduce the burden of unnecessary regulation. But we believe Government has important work to do, to expand opportunity, to give people the tools they need to make the most of their own lives, to enhance our security. That's why we support adding 100,000 police . . . more affordable college loans . . . the minimum wage legislation now before Congress. . . .

—Bill Clinton, Press Conference, March 4, 1995

## Practice and Apply the Skill

Use the excerpts above to answer the following questions.

1. Who are the speakers, where did they speak, and who was the intended audience?

2. What issue are both Presidents addressing? How do Reagan and Clinton's viewpoints differ?

3. How do you think each President's political background influenced his viewpoint?

4. How does Reagan's statement that government should "not ride on our back" reflect a bias, if any, on this issue?

Skills Handbook **S15**

## Get Started

### LESSON GOAL

• Students will identify the steps in comparing viewpoints by examining excerpts from speeches by Presidents Reagan and Clinton on the role of government.

## Teach

### READ ALOUD

Have students read the steps in the process of comparing viewpoints and share any questions they have. Point out that comparing viewpoints is a valuable tool for making choices among political candidates. Recall a recent school, local, or national election. Identify for students a key issue in the debate between candidates during the campaign and the viewpoint expressed by each candidate on this issue. Then ask a student to read aloud each of the quotes. Ask class members to identify the main idea of the passage, the statements that are facts, and the statements that are opinions. Then ask students to identify one fact or argument from each quote that supports the speaker's point of view on the role of government in American life.

### COMPARE AND CONTRAST

Have students find two differing sources of opinion on the same topic. Statements by political candidates about their positions on specific issues can usually be found on their Web sites and on the Web sites of their political parties. Have students use the steps in comparing viewpoints to write a brief comparison of the positions taken by competing candidates or elected officials on a current issue.

## Assess and Remediate

Have students complete the Practice and Apply the Skill questions. Discuss their responses as a class.

## Answers

**1.** The speakers were U.S. Presidents. Reagan spoke at his inauguration. Clinton spoke to reporters at a press conference. The audience for both was the American public.

**2.** They are addressing the role of government. Clinton thinks that some government regulations are unnecessarily burdensome but asserts the Federal Government has a key role to play in insuring the welfare of citizens. Reagan argues that Federal Government should be reduced in size and have a smaller regulatory role in the economy.

**3.** Reagan was a Republican, and Republicans tend to favor smaller government. Clinton was a Democrat, and Democrats tend to favor larger government.

**4.** Reagan uses emotionally-charged language to express a belief that much government regulation is unnecessarily burdensome and intrusive.

# Get Started

## LESSON GOAL

- Students will identify the steps in analyzing cause and effect by examining an article on the effect of changes in driver's education on 16-year-olds.

# Teach

## BRAINSTORM

Have students read the steps in the process of analyzing cause and effect and share any questions they have. Then write the following events on the board: school wins top State academic ranking, funding for school athletic programs cut, reductions in parking spaces in student parking lot, enrollment triples, and price of fuel for school activity buses goes up sharply. Have class members identify the effects these events might have on students.

## IDENTIFY CAUSES AND EFFECTS

Make a list on the board of the causes and effects of the decrease in 16-year-olds obtaining driver's licenses. Mix the causes and effects. Have students take turns identifying each item on the list as a cause or an effect. Then have students predict which effects on the list are likely to be short-term or long-term effects, giving reasons for their opinions. Then have students make predictions about what effects a rise in the cost of gas might have on the number of 16-year-old drivers.

# Assess and Remediate

Have students complete the Practice and Apply the Skill questions. Discuss their responses as a class. Ask students to choose one of the landmark Supreme Court decisions discussed in the text and create a graphic organizer identifying effects of the Court's decision.

# Analyze Cause and Effect

Recognizing a cause-effect relationship means examining how one event or action brings about others. Government decision makers face a complex web of choices and often need to understand relationships among events to set or improve policy. Use the following steps to learn how to understand the relationships between causes and effects. Then read the passage below and answer the questions.

**1 Identify the central event.** Determine what event is the most important and decide if it is a cause or effect.

**2 Look for signal words and phrases.** Words and phrases such as *because, due to,* and *on account of* signal causes. Words and phrases such as *so, thus, therefore,* and *as a result* signal effects.

**3 Decide if an event has more than one cause or effect.** Most events have multiple causes and many have more than one effect.

**4 Identify events that are both causes and effects.** Events can form a chain of causes and effects. For example, a decrease in taxes might result in a decrease in State funding for new highway construction, which in turn might cause increased traffic delays.

## Fewer Youths Jump Behind the Wheel at 16
by Mary Chapman and Micheline Maynard, *The New York Times*, February 25, 2008

For generations, driver's licenses have been tickets to freedom for America's 16-year-olds, prompting many to line up at motor vehicle offices the day they were eligible to apply.

No longer. In the last decade, the proportion of 16-year-olds nationwide who hold driver's licenses has dropped from nearly half to less than one-third, according to . . . the Federal Highway Administration.

Reasons vary, including tighter state laws governing when teenagers can drive, higher insurance costs and a shift . . . . to expensive private driving academies. . . .

[E]xperts also add parents . . . willing to chauffeur their children to activities, and pastimes like surfing the Web that keep them indoors . . . .

The way students learn has undergone a major change, too. Twenty-five years ago most teenagers took driver's education in their local schools. But the number of school systems offering the program has plummeted to about 20 percent today, from 90 percent in the 1980s, said Allen Robinson, of American Driver and Traffic Safety Education Association. . . .

"High schools are out of the business because of the cost," said Henning Mortensen, owner of Bond Driving School in Sacramento. Commercial driving academies have stepped in to fill the gap. . . .

Driving schools charge higher rates. . . .

Graduated driver-licensing laws, which delay awarding a full license until a teenager spends time . . . driving under certain conditions, are also keeping down the number of 16-year-olds on the road, said Frederik R. Mottola . . . of the National Institute for Driver Behavior. . . .

## Practice and Apply the Skill

Use the article above to answer the following questions.

1. What is the issue discussed in this article?
2. According to the article, what are the causes of the decline in 16-year-old drivers?
3. What two causes are cited in paragraph four?

# Answers

**1.** decrease in number of 16-year-olds getting driver's licenses

**2.** Causes: tighter State laws governing when teenagers can drive, higher insurance costs, shift from school-run to more costly private driving schools, graduated driver-licensing laws

**3.** parents willing to drive their children, and indoor pastimes like surfing the Web

# Problem Solving

Every year elected officials at all levels of government face problems. Whether they are dealing with traffic congestion, airport safety, or hurricane relief, the ability to solve problems is a valuable skill. Use the following steps to learn more about problem solving. Then read the passage below and answer the questions.

**1 Identify the problem.** Begin by clearly identifying the problem. Write a statement or question that summarizes the problem you are trying to solve.

**2 Gather information and identify options.** Collect information and data, considering both the causes of the problem and strategies for addressing it. Most problems have multiple solutions. Identify as many options as possible.

**3 Consider advantages and disadvantages of each option.** Analyze each option by predicting benefits, drawbacks, and possible outcomes.

**4 Choose, implement, and evaluate a solution.** Pick the option with the most benefits and fewest drawbacks. Once the chosen option has been implemented, evaluate the outcome to decide if the strategy worked.

> "Like most large cities in America today, Minneapolis continues to face violent crime. . . .
>
> We have met the challenge of crime with a multi-faceted plan of attack. . . . The most. . . powerful tool in our crime fighting strategy has been increasing the visibility and presence of police officers on the street. We are growing our police force by over 100 officers. . . .
>
> To a larger more diverse, more visible police force, we added groundbreaking public safety technology. . . . The addition of dozens of safety cameras and dramatically increased police patrol has made our downtown one of the safest in America. The safety cameras. . . have helped provide essential evidence to arrest and successfully charge criminals. . . .
>
> The technology we are implementing increases prosecutions by providing needed court evidence, but we also invested in better prosecution with more funding for community prosecutors. . . . The number of our most chronic criminals. . . who were convicted has increased from 81 convictions in 2005 to 129 convictions in 2006—a 60% increase in one year. . . .
>
> Working. . . with our juvenile crime unit, we are identifying young offenders early and getting them into programs that offer a productive alternative to gangs. . . .
>
> We have also focused. . . efforts to get illegal guns off the street. . . .
> The results. . . are beginning to be seen. After a surge of crime during the summer of 2005 and first half of 2006, violent crime began trending down in the later months of 2006. As we end the first quarter of 2007, for the first time in years, violent crime is falling, down 22 percent city-wide. . . . "
>
> —Minneapolis Mayor R.T. Rybak,
> State of the City Address,
> March 19, 2007

## Practice and Apply the Skill

Use the passage above to answer the following questions.

1. What problem is the mayor concerned about, and what is his problem-solving goal?
2. What options does the mayor identify for solving this problem?
3. What are the advantages and drawbacks of the safety camera option?
4. How did the mayor assess the effectiveness of efforts to prosecute criminals?
5. What kinds of information can the mayor use to evaluate his solutions?

21st Century Skills **CRITICAL THINKING**

# Get Started

## LESSON GOAL

- Students will identify the steps in making a decision by examining the decision-making process to resolve the tardiness of students.

# Teach

## ACTIVATE PRIOR KNOWLEDGE

Have students read the steps in the process of decision making and share any questions they have. Ask students to identify an important decision each has made and write down the process they used to make their decision. Students might think about such events as choosing a summer job or activity, deciding which courses to take, picking colleges to apply to or a place for a family vacation, or making a major purchase. Have students compare the process they used to make their decisions with the steps outlined in the text.

## CREATE A GRAPHIC ORGANIZER

Divide students into groups. Ask each group to identify the goal the school wants to achieve in the scenario described in the text. Then ask each group to create a graphic organizer that shows a goal for a real or hypothetical situation in their own lives, the options for meeting this goal, and possible decisions. After completing the organizers, ask students to share their opinions about whether the decisions they suggest are good ones and what other choices they might have considered.

# Assess and Remediate

Have students complete the Practice and Apply the Skill questions. Discuss their responses as a class. Ask student groups to pick a current issue that has been recently addressed by State or local officials and do research to learn more about how officials reached decisions on the issue. Have each group create a graphic organizer that lists the steps used in the process of making the decisions.

# Decision Making

Decision making plays a key role in the political process in every branch of government. Although the types of decisions Presidents, cabinet heads, governors, and city councilors make differ, they all involve the steps below.

**1 Identify the problem and gather information.** Define and clarify what needs to be decided. Consider the goal or the intended outcome. Decide what information is needed to make an informed decision. Apply existing knowledge and research about the subject. Consider strategies others have used to address the issue.

**2 List and review possible options.** A decision requires choosing among two or more alternatives. List all possible options.

**3 Identify possible consequences and make a decision.** Consider the possible outcomes and predict the consequences of each option. Then review all options and choose those with the fewest drawbacks and greatest number of benefits. Read about one school's tardiness problem and possible solutions.

**The Problem**
A large portion of the student body has been tardy more than usual this semester.
- The city has cancelled bus service past the school due to budget cuts. The school is located on a low-use bus route, and student discount passes did not generate enough revenue to keep the bus route going.
- Since many parents now drive their children to school, traffic has increased, causing school buses and parents to be late.
- Many students are unable to walk because they live too far away from the school.
- Students are missing the first five to twenty minutes of their first-period class, when attendance is taken.
- Students are either marked as tardy, or absent if they come in excessively late.

**Potential Solutions**
- Require all students to take school buses.
- Circulate a petition, demanding the city reinstate its bus service.
- Work with city councilors to establish a reasonable fare, or a reduced schedule that will allow city buses to run during school hours.
- Create a car-pooling program for students who live close to one another.
- Establish first period as a study hall, and take attendance at the end of the period in order to allow students time to arrive at school.

## Practice and Apply the Skill

Use the list above to answer the following questions.
1. What is the major concern for the school?
2. What is the advantage of requiring all students to take the bus to school?
3. What are the disadvantages of turning first period into a study hall?
4. What do you think is the best solution to the problem? Why?

# Answers

**1.** that many students have been tardy during the semester

**2.** Students will have a means for arriving at the school.

**3.** It would eliminate the first period as actual class time for students.

**4.** Students' answers should indicate thoughtful consideration of the problem and a logical decision-making process to reach a solution.

# Draw Inferences and Conclusions

Drawing inferences means reading between the lines—that is, forming conclusions based on information that is not stated directly, but only suggested. Use the following steps to learn how to draw inferences and arrive at conclusions. Then read the passage below and answer the questions.

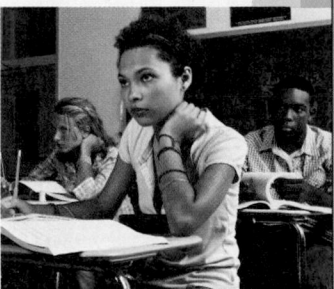

**1 Summarize information.** Confirm your understanding of the text by identifying the main idea. To find information that is suggested but unstated in a passage, you have to understand the stated content of the passage.

**2 Study the facts.** Determine what facts and information the text provides.

**3 Apply other facts or prior knowledge.** Consider what you know about the topic. Use this prior knowledge to evaluate the information. A combination of what you already know and what you learn from reading the passage can help you draw inferences.

**4 Summarize the information to form a conclusion.** Combine the inferences you made to form a conclusion about the topic.

### It's Time to Deal With the Debt

As of this moment, according to the Bureau of the Public Debt, the debt of the federal government is $13,795,134,710,938.49. I'm not sure I even know how to correctly pronounce that number, but I know that $13.8 trillion is an astounding amount.

Just ten years ago the federal debt was a mere $5 trillion but even then Americans were clamoring about the huge balance. We roared about how our children were going to have to pay for a debt that accumulated during our watch. We demanded that something be done. Congress may have listened but it did not act, and the debt continued to rise.

Now that the debt has nearly tripled, isn't it time for members of Congress to address the national debt in a manner that will actually reduce it? We have reached a critical moment wherein decisions must be made that are as difficult for the public to accept as they

are for career politicians to introduce. It is time to increase taxes, cut social services, and reform Social Security.

Earlier this month the bipartisan National Committee on Fiscal Responsibility and Reform made such a proposal. The committee admitted that "the solution is painful, there's no easy way out, [and] everything must be on the table." Now, we are all listening.

Today's economic woes and our government's fiscal irresponsibility make these drastic choices no longer options but necessities. Even if it would be the death knell for their political careers, the President must lead and Congress must act. And, Americans must be willing to accept. If we don't, the American way of life will disappear under the weight of trillions upon trillions of dollars.

## Practice and Apply the Skill

Use the editorial above to answer the following questions.

1. What is the main idea in this editorial?
2. To what is the National Committee on Fiscal Responsibility and Reform referring in their statement that "the solution is painful"?
3. What is the author implying by saying that the actions of Congress might be the death knell for its members' political careers?
4. What conclusion can you draw about the likelihood of resolving the problem of the national debt?

# Get Started

## LESSON GOAL

- Students will draw inferences about the need for a new GI Bill of Rights for veterans by analyzing an editorial on this topic.

# Teach

## SUMMARIZE

Have students read the steps in the process of drawing inferences and conclusions and share any questions they have. Then have students read the editorial, write a sentence that summarizes the main idea, and give three examples of facts or expert opinions that support the editorial's argument.

## ACTIVATE PRIOR KNOWLEDGE

Have students recall information they may know about the GI Bill of Rights during World War II, along with knowledge they may have about recent veterans' experiences after tours in Iraq or Afghanistan. Have students share their information with the class. Then ask what inferences or conclusions students can draw from their prior knowledge.

# Assess and Remediate

Have students complete the Practice and Apply the Skill questions. Discuss their responses as a class. Have students bring to class a newspaper article or editorial on a local problem or issue that makes inferences or draws conclusions about how this problem might be solved. Have students use the steps in the lesson to analyze the article. Have several students explain to the class what inferences and conclusions they drew from the article.

# Answers

**1.** the public debt and how Congress and the President need to address it

**2.** that any resolution to the increasing public debt will be a hardship to Americans as they will have to pay more in taxes and do with fewer public services

**3.** Usually when a politician supports a policy that is against the wishes of his or her constituents, it is unlikely that the politician will be re-elected.

**4.** Although the public and Congress are aware and concerned about the public debt and would like to address it, the solutions are so difficult to accept it is unlikely that the government will actually solve the problem.

# Get Started

## LESSON GOAL

• Students will identify and practice the steps in note taking by analyzing and taking notes on a speech about climate change.

# Teach

## ACTIVATE PRIOR KNOWLEDGE

Have students read the steps in the process of note taking and active listening and share any questions they have. Remind students that they use the skills of note taking and active listening daily, not only in the classroom but also in social settings with friends and in the workplace with employers and co-workers. Ask students what they mean when they describe someone as a "good listener." Point out that the traits most students associate with people they consider to be good listeners are those of an active listener. Active listening means focusing on what the person you are listening to is saying and listening to fit the situation. At different times, that might mean listening empathetically, appreciatively, or critically.

## IDENTIFY KEY POINTS

Divide students into small groups. Ask each group to choose a current political topic or issue of interest. Have each group present a short oral report on their topic. Each group can write its own report or read aloud a newspaper editorial or an excerpt from a speech by an expert on the topic chosen. Remind students that many speakers begin their talks by summarizing the topics or key points they will make and conclude their speech by summarizing the points they have covered in their talk. As each group gives its presentation, have the rest of the class take notes on the speech. After each speech, ask one or two students to share their notes with the class.

# Assess and Remediate

Have students complete the Practice and Apply the Skill questions. Discuss their responses as a class. Give students additional practice by showing a segment from a nightly newscast or television documentary on a topic of interest. Have student take notes on the presentation and share with the class what they identified as the key points and supporting details in the presentation.

---

# Note Taking and Active Listening

Note taking and active listening are two skills that can increase your ability to remember and understand a speech or lecture. Use the following steps to learn more about note taking and active listening. Then read the excerpted speech below and answer the questions.

**1 Identify the topic and main ideas.** The title of the text often gives clues to its content. Once you identify the topic, it is easier to identify main ideas. Many speakers start their speeches by listing the key points they will develop. At the conclusion of the talk, they often restate their main ideas and then summarize their conclusions.

**2 Take notes selectively.** Do not write down every word you hear. Instead, jot down important terms and summarize key points and details that support these points.

**3 Practice active listening.** Active listening is a key component of the communication process. Like all communication, it requires engaged participation. Look at and listen to the speaker. Think about what you hear and see.

**4 Listen for transitions, repetition, and emphasis.** Listen for words or phrases that indicate key points or transition from one point to the next. Be alert for repetition. Statements that are repeated or said with emphasis are important points. Pay attention for phrases, gestures, or expressions that suggest strong opinions.

## Speech On Stewardship of the Earth by James E. Hansen, NASA chief climate scientist, 2007

. . . Global warming differs from previous pollution problems in two fundamental ways. With water pollution or common air pollution, smog, the problems occur immediately. . . . If we . . . stop emitting them, the problem goes away. However, global warming is caused by greenhouse gases that have a lifetime of hundreds of years. . . .

The second major difference . . . is that the climate system responds slowly to the gases that we add to the air. . . . The Earth has warmed one and one-half degrees Fahrenheit so far. . . . Moreover, there are surely more gases in the pipeline, because of power plants . . . and vehicles. . . . One and one-half degrees! Who cares about that? . . . Well, we had better all care about it, because we have already brought the planet close to some tipping points. . . .

Let me mention three major consequences of global warming, if we go down the business-as-usual path. . . . First, there is the extermination of species. . . . [A] given mean temperature line is moving poleward, . . . about 35 miles per decade. That rate will accelerate under business-as-usual. Many species cannot migrate that fast. Besides, there is no place colder for polar species to go. . . . Second, there is potential instability of the ice sheets. If additional global warming exceeds two degrees Fahrenheit, the West Antarctic ice sheet and part of Greenland surely will become unstable, causing eventual sea level rise of several meters. . . . Third, there will be a noticeable increase in climate extremes. . . . Heavy rains and floods will increase, but so will . . . droughts and forest fires. . . .

## Practice and Apply the Skill

Use the excerpt above to answer the following questions.

1. What is the topic of this speech?
2. What three main points would you list as consequences of global warming?
3. What statements in this speech suggest greater emphasis or strong emotion?

# Answers

**1.** consequences of global warming

**2.** Consequences: many plant and animal species will become extinct, ice sheet will become unstable and melt, greater extremes in climate such as both droughts and floods are likely

**3.** such statements as "Who cares about that?," "Well, we had better all care," and "we have already brought the planet close to some tipping points"

# Give a Multimedia Presentation

Government officials are often asked to make presentations. You too will be asked to give presentations in school and at work. One key to an effective presentation is to combine text, video, audio, and graphics. Use these steps for an effective presentation.

**1 Define your topic.** When choosing a topic, consider the time allotted for the presentation and the complexity of the subject. Multimedia presentations lend themselves to topics that have several subtopics. However, a topic that is too broad is hard to cover adequately in a limited amount of time. Consider how to narrow the topic.

**2 Determine what types of media are available for the presentation.** Do you have a computer and the software to create a podcast, PowerPoint presentation, or slide show? Do you have access to video, film, or audio clips of speeches or historic events?

**3 Make a storyboard.** Create a storyboard by brainstorming ideas for covering your topic in various media. Then make a detailed outline of the information you will present. Identify the medium that will work best for each part of the presentation. Plan the transitions between each part of the presentation.

**4 Practice your presentation.** A trial run gives presenters a chance to time each segment, identify technical problems, and make sure all participants know their roles.

Below is a storyboard for a presentation on reducing traffic congestion.

---

**1** (2 mins)

Gridlock: Traffic cam of city at rush hour

Introduce issue by explaining how traffic congestion affects everyone in the audience.
- Wastes time
- Wastes gas
- Increases energy dependence

**2** (3 mins)

Graphs
- Rise in peak period travel times
- Costs of congestion
- Smog and poor air quality

1996 2000 2004 2008

**3** (4 mins)

Video clip of transportation expert or newscaster talking about possible solutions to traffic problems

**4** (4 mins)

Solutions
- More emphasis on public transportation: buses, light rail, metro
- Construction of Park and Ride lots
- Incentives by local businesses to encourage employees to carpool
- Fast passes

**5** (4 mins)

Solutions
- Toll roads
- HOV lanes
- Better signal control
- Businesses encourage employees to commute at different times through flextime

**6** (5 mins)

Summarize possible solutions in sections 4 and 5
What we recommend

---

## Practice and Apply the Skill

Use the storyboards above to answer the following questions.
1. What media will be used in the presentation?
2. How did the presenters narrow or focus the presentation of their topic?
3. How did the presenters stay within the time limit of the presentation?

---

# Get Started

### LESSON GOAL
- Students will analyze the steps in giving an effective presentation by examining a storyboard for a multimedia presentation.

# Teach

### ACTIVATE PRIOR KNOWLEDGE

Have students read the steps in giving a multimedia presentation and review the types of media available to students in their school. Ask students to describe multimedia presentations they have seen at school, online, or on television. Many national parks, State visitors' centers, and museums offer multimedia presentations. Assess the level of familiarity students have with the various forms of technology discussed in the text.

### BRAINSTORM

Have students divide into groups. Ask each group to brainstorm a list of current topics of concern. Groups might think of current local, State, or national issues or a school event, charity, or fundraising activity they would like to promote. Tell the class how much time groups will have for their presentations. Point out that topics should be narrow enough to be covered in the time allotted.

### MAKE A PRESENTATION

Ask each group to prepare a short presentation on their topic. Point out that multimedia presentations add interest by providing both visual and sound effects. Slides, photographs, audio and video clips, and maps can also be used to create multimedia presentations. Remind groups that the technology they use in their presentations is a tool for teaching, explaining, and communicating information rather than an end in itself. Students should focus on deciding which technology is best for presenting the information they want to convey.

# Assess and Remediate

Have students complete the Practice and Apply the Skill questions. Discuss their responses as a class.

---

# Answers

**1.** video from traffic cam, graphics in charts and graphs, video clip of traffic expert

**2.** by limiting the presentation to identification of the problem, options for solving problem, and recommendations for action

**3.** run-time for each segment noted on storyboard

# Get Started

## LESSON GOAL

• Students will identify the steps in analyzing political cartoons by analyzing a cartoon on the impact of funding cuts to Medicare.

# Teach

## DISCUSS

Have students read the steps in the process of analyzing political cartoons and share any questions they have. Make sure students know that Medicare is a Federal Government program under the Social Security Administration that reimburses doctors and hospitals for medical care provided to people over the age of 65. Point out that it is the primary form of healthcare insurance for many older Americans.

## ANALYZE A CARTOON

Ask students to write a sentence that explains the issue or problem the cartoonist is addressing and the opinion the cartoonist is expressing on this issue. Have students identify the symbols the cartoonist has used to make points about this issue. What does the cutting saw represent? Ask what will happen at the conclusion of the action in the cartoon. Conclude by asking students to identify what they think are the advantages and limitations of political cartoons as a way of expressing opinions on political issues.

## CREATE A CARTOON

Discuss with the class other concerns or opinions Americans have about healthcare today. Then divide students into groups, and ask each group to create a political cartoon on some aspect of healthcare.

# Assess and Remediate

Have students complete the Practice and Apply the Skill questions. Discuss their responses as a class. To give students additional practice with this skill, have students pick a cartoon from the text and analyze the cartoon for the class.

---

# Analyze Political Cartoons

Political cartoons express the cartoonist's opinion on a recent issue or current event. Often the cartoon's purpose is to influence public opinion about political leaders, government policies, or economic and political issues. To achieve this goal, cartoonists use humor and exaggeration. When analyzing a political cartoon, be sure to examine all words, images, and labels to help you fully understand the cartoon's intent. Use the following steps to analyze a political cartoon.

1 **Identify the symbols in the cartoon.** Analyze the cartoon to determine what each image or symbol represents. Read the title and any labels or captions.

2 **Analyze the meaning of the cartoon.** Consider how the cartoonist uses the images and symbols in the cartoon to express his or her opinion.

3 **Draw conclusions about the cartoon's intent.** Determine the main idea, message, or point of view expressed in the cartoon.

**Medicare Cuts**

## Practice and Apply the Skill

Use the cartoon above to answer the following questions.
1. Who does the figure in the bed represent?
2. What symbol represents cuts to the senior insurance program, Medicare?
3. According to the cartoon, what will be the result of Medicare cuts?
4. What is the main idea of this cartoon?

---

# Answers

1. people who are elderly and require healthcare
2. the saw
3. The elderly will be harmed.
4. that Medicare cuts will be so extreme as to hurt the elderly

# Innovate and Think Creatively

An innovation is a new idea that improves on an existing product or process. Use the steps below to learn how to think innovatively and creatively. Then read the passage below and answer the questions.

**1 Identify what it is that needs improving.** Describe a specific problem to be solved. Are there faster, better, or more efficient ways of getting a job or task done? Consider the intended outcome.

**2 Brainstorm solutions.** Generate as many ideas as possible. Be open to all ideas. If you are working in a group, don't criticize the ideas of others and don't hesitate to suggest ideas that might seem strange or impractical. Innovation often results from a chain of related ideas leading to an unexpected insight.

**3 Understand how to achieve the innovation.** Think about the skills, tools, or methods needed to realize the goal. Identify such factors as ease of use, resources, costs, and time. Get input from likely users. Involve people who are knowledgeable about the process, and work to build their support. Establish benchmarks for success and compare the results of the innovation with the original process.

## Homeless Project's Army of Citizens Calls Year Success
by Kevin Fagan, *San Francisco Chronicle*, 10/19/05

Barry Cowart stood in front of the Bill Graham Civic Auditorium, staring at the 200 homeless people in a line . . . .

"Last April, that was me in that line," he said. "I'd been sleeping in the Greyhound bus station for months, and then I came here to this *thing* they do every month. That day, they got me into a residential hotel room . . . .

The "thing" he referred to is Project Homeless Connect, San Francisco Mayor Gavin Newsom's monthly gathering of volunteers to help his city's street people . . . .

On Oct. 13, 2004, the mayor kicked off his concept . . . with a handful of participants and street counselors . . . . By the end of the day, they had placed 24 into shelter and housing . . .

Since that first foray, Project Homeless Connect became a veritable citizen army that assembles between 1,000 and 2,000 community and government volunteers from all over the nation at the auditorium every other

month to help more than 1,000 homeless people get into shelter, permanent housing, counseling and health care. While the homeless are being hooked up to those services, they get . . . food, clothing, blankets, and even kibble for their dogs or cats . . . .

. . . [R]epresentatives of cities from New York and Chicago to Los Angeles have come to check out the past few gatherings . . . .

"It's daunting . . . to even consider doing something this big," said Kathleen Gardipee, a representative of Portland, Ore., who came to help prepare her city for its own Connect . . . . "But this is amazing . . . ."

Over the past year . . . the Connect efforts have helped 6,822 homeless people, putting 646 into shelter or housing, 1,583 into medical or mental health care, and the rest into legal counseling, food programs or other services. A total 11,382 individual volunteers pitched in.

## Practice and Apply the Skill

Use the newspaper article to answer the following questions.

1. What problem did Mayor Newsom want to solve through the creation of PHC?

2. What was innovative about the mayor's solution?

3. Why do you think many cities are interested in San Francisco's innovation?

4. How did the mayor's office measure the effectiveness of this program?

# Get Started

## LESSON GOALS

Students will . . .

- define innovation and describe an example of innovation.
- think creatively about an innovation to school procedures and suggest ideas for innovations in education.

# Teach

Have students read the steps in the process of innovating and thinking creatively and share any questions they have. Explain that an innovation is an idea for improving upon an existing product or process. For example, year-round schools and public charter schools are innovations on the traditional school model. In many cities, HOV or high-occupancy-vehicle lanes for cars with more than one person are an innovation that is helping to reduce traffic congestion during peak driving hours.

## BRAINSTORM

Divide students into groups. Have each group brainstorm an idea for improving an existing process. In the school setting, possibilities might include school parking, cafeteria service, school security, use of gym and other facilities during after-school hours, use of Internet in classrooms, changing the role of student government, making peer or student-teacher tutoring more effective.

## EXPLAIN AND PRESENT

Have each group make a presentation to the class, explaining their proposed innovation, why it represents an improvement over the current procedure, and the criteria for assessing its usefulness.

# Assess and Remediate

Have students complete the Practice and Apply the Skill questions. Discuss their responses as a class. Have students do research to learn more about community and government volunteers.

# Answers

1. delivery of services to San Francisco's homeless

2. Instead of relying entirely on government workers, PHC involved local citizens as well, reducing the cost of providing the services, increasing the rate at which services were delivered, and solving the problem of insufficient staff to administer the program

3. Possible answer: Many cities had similar concerns about meeting the needs of the homeless and saw the San Francisco project as a model they could adapt to their own communities.

4. by collecting data on the number of homeless provided with housing or shelter, or other services, and number of volunteers who participated

# Get Started

## LESSON GOALS

Students will . . .

- learn how to write an e-mail.
- learn how to evaluate wikis.
- find and evaluate a blog entry.

# Teach

## ACTIVATE PRIOR KNOWLEDGE

Have students read the steps in the process of using the Internet to create e-mails, evaluate wikis, and read blogs. Point out that digital information is information represented in numerical form for use by a computer. Have students suggest reasons why digital literacy is becoming an increasingly essential 21st-century skill. Ask students to describe various ways they or people they know use the Internet. Responses might include ordering groceries, reading the newspaper, getting directions for travel, selling used furniture, job hunting, and buying concert tickets. List responses on the board and conduct a quick poll to see how many students use the Internet for the activities on the list.

## WRITE AN E-MAIL

Have students write an e-mail to apply for a part-time job, request information from a university library on a research topic, ask local businesses for donations to a charity, or request information about college scholarships. Have students exchange e-mails with a partner and analyze the language and tone of each other's e-mails.

# Digital Age Literacy

The Internet is a valuable research tool that provides links to millions of sources of information created by government agencies, schools, businesses, and individuals all over the world. E-mail, wikis, and blogs all provide ways for Internet users to share information and express opinions. Follow the steps below to learn how you can use e-mail, wikis, and blogs effectively.

## Writing an E-mail

① **Identify the purpose of the email.** Clearly indicate the topic in the subject line. A busy recipient is more likely to open the e-mail promptly if the subject is stated.

② **Focus on why you are writing.** Include the subject of your e-mail in the first sentence. State why you are writing and what you expect to receive in terms of information or action from the recipient. Try to limit messages to three or four key points and keep paragraphs short.

③ **Respect your reader.** If you are responding to or following up on an e-mail query or request that is more than a few days old, remind the recipient of why you are writing. It is often helpful to leave the original e-mail in your response for reference. Identify yourself clearly if the recipient is someone you don't know. If you are uncertain about whether your language and tone should be formal or informal, examine the e-mail received and take your cues from it.

④ **Proofread e-mails before sending.** Once you have composed your e-mail, use a spell checker or other tool to check grammar, punctuation, and spelling. Remember that e-mail is not private. Think carefully about sending messages that you would not want shared with others. Below is an example of an e-mail sent from one student to another.

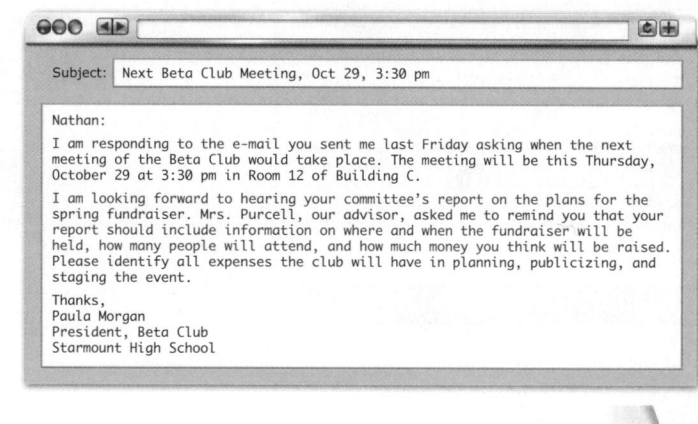

Subject: Next Beta Club Meeting, Oct 29, 3:30 pm

Nathan:

I am responding to the e-mail you sent me last Friday asking when the next meeting of the Beta Club would take place. The meeting will be this Thursday, October 29 at 3:30 pm in Room 12 of Building C.

I am looking forward to hearing your committee's report on the plans for the spring fundraiser. Mrs. Purcell, our advisor, asked me to remind you that your report should include information on where and when the fundraiser will be held, how many people will attend, and how much money you think will be raised. Please identify all expenses the club will have in planning, publicizing, and staging the event.

Thanks,
Paula Morgan
President, Beta Club
Starmount High School

## Understanding and Evaluating Wikis

A wiki is a Web site that allows users to make, edit, and link Web pages to create an online document. As communal Web sites, many wikis are used for collaborative writing and research activities. Each entry includes a list of changes made by successive writers or editors. While many Internet users are enthusiastic about wikis, critics question their reliability and fear that users will accept information without verifying its accuracy.

Follow the steps below to learn about evaluating wikis.

❶ **Identify the sources of the information on the Web site.** Scan the entry to find out who provided the information. Consider whether the writer has expertise or special knowledge of this topic that would make his or her opinion authoritative, or whether the author is not credible at all, making the information unreliable.

❷ **Determine when the article was written.** Look for a date indicating when the article was written or last updated. Does the entry reflect changing events or provide current information on this topic?

❸ **Verify information by looking at other sources.** Compare the information on the wiki with information from official sources such as government Web sites, Web sites sponsored by respected organizations, or traditional encyclopedias. Do further research if your sources disagree.

## Reading and Assessing Blogs

Blogs are online journals. The word *blog* is short for *weblog*. Most blogs are short posts expressing an author's opinions. Blog writers, or bloggers, typically focus on a particular subject. Blogs can be found on every topic from politics to fashion. Blogs usually include the writer's previous posts as well as links to posts on other blogs, Web sites, and news articles. Some also include photos and video or audio files. Most blogs are interactive, providing a space for readers to comment.

❶ **Identify the writer.** Look for the author's name and his or her professional affiliation, if any, as well as any biographical information.

❷ **Assess sources.** Evaluate the credibility and accuracy of recommended sources.

❸ **Identify the writer's bias.** Consider the arguments and evidence the writer presents. Are positions stated in rational language and presented in a balanced way that acknowledges other points of view, or is the language clearly one-sided? Do the posts contain frequent misspellings and grammatical errors? Scan reader comments to determine whether the blog allows opposing points of view.

### Practice and Apply the Skill

Use the information above to answer these questions.

1. How might the language in a business e-mail differ from the language in an e-mail sent to friends?

2. How are wikis useful for projects that require input from multiple participants?

3. How does a blog differ from an editorial in a newspaper?

## Answers

**1.** Business e-mail is formal and concise rather than informal or casual and chatty in language and tone.

**2.** Wikis allow users to share, update, and access information from diverse sources online so that all participants can become fully informed about all aspects of a project and cooperate more easily in problem solving and decision making.

**3.** Online blogs are interactive, allowing readers to comment on a blogger's post as soon as they read it and review other users' comments on the current posting. They can also view previous postings and reader comments. Newspaper editorials usually need to meet specific criteria before printing, while anyone can express an opinion in a personal blog.

# Get Started

## LESSON GOALS

Students will . . .

- analyze a line graph.
- compare and contrast types of graphic data and identify the types of graphic images that are most appropriate for displaying different kinds of data.

# Teach

## ACTIVATE PRIOR KNOWLEDGE

Have students read the steps in the process of analyzing graphic data and share any questions they have. Have students give examples of the ways they have seen data displayed in their textbooks, on television, online, and in newsmagazines and newspapers. Point out that local governments and utilities regularly send residents graphs of yearly budgets or water and electricity usage. Entertainment magazines have graphs of movie attendance or box office receipts. Ask students to explain the advantages of displaying data in graphic form.

## TAKE A POLL

Have students work in small groups to create a survey question for a classroom poll. Possible topics might include a question on the media sources students go to for news or election information, how leisure time is spent, or political party or candidate preferences.

## CREATE GRAPH AND ANALYZE DATA

Once groups have taken their polls, remind them to group responses or data by categories. For example, categories in a graph on how students spend their after-school hours might include working in part-time jobs, doing homework, participating in sports or after-school activities, surfing the net, watching TV, and playing video games. After completing their graphs, ask each group to exchange graphs with another group and use the steps listed in the lesson to analyze the graph they receive. Then have them display the same data in a different type of graph or chart.

# Assess and Remediate

Have students complete the Practice and Apply the Skill questions. Discuss their responses as a class. Have students bring to class graphs from newspapers, magazines, or advertisements. Give each student a graph and ask them to write three questions about the graph they received.

---

# Analyze Graphic Data

A graph is a useful way to visually present large amounts of data. Every day, government policymakers, economists, and statisticians use different kinds of graphs to present and summarize data. Line graphs describe changes over time. Bar graphs show the relationships between two or more sets of data, and suggest trends. Circle graphs show how individual parts relate to a whole. Use the steps below to analyze graphic data.

**1 Identify the type of information presented.** Before you can interpret the information in a graph, you must identify what is being shown. Note the title, all labels, and the key, if there is one. On a bar or line graph, use the graph title, the axis labels, and the key to interpret the data. On a circle graph, examine labels of all segments of the graphs. Identify the source of the data for the graph.

**2 Read the data.** Before studying overall patterns, look at specific elements on the graph. On line graphs and bar graphs, determine what the numbers on the $x$-axis (horizontal) and the $y$-axis (vertical) represent. Then determine the relationship between the numbers.

**3 Interpret the graph and draw conclusions.** Study the data in the graph to draw conclusions. Look for patterns or trends, such as changes over time or comparisons of different groups.

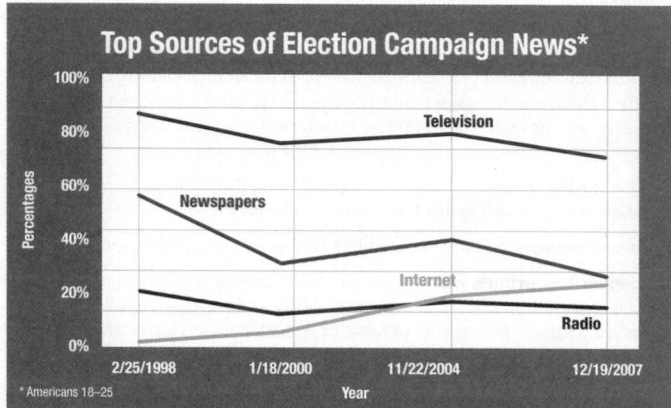

## Practice and Apply the Skill

Use the graph above to answer the questions below.

1. (a) What is the subject of the graph? (b) What is the time frame? (c) What do the numbers on the $x$-axis and $y$-axis represent?

2. What does the graph indicate about the relationship between Internet use and newspaper readership among 18- to 25-year-olds?

3. Based on the graph, what prediction can you make about the use of Internet and television as sources in the future?

---

# Answers

**1.** (a) sources of election campaign news for Americans ages 18-25; (b) February 1998 to December 2007; (c) x axis: date each poll was taken y axis: percentage of poll participants who chose each media as a key source of election news

**2.** As Internet use for election news has increased, use of newspapers as a source for election news has decreased.

**3.** Internet and television sources will be more popular sources of campaign news than newspapers.

# Analyze Maps

Maps bring information to life in a way that words alone cannot. Election maps, for example, can be valuable tools for identifying and understanding voting patterns. Political analysts often study voting patterns from previous elections to make predictions about winners and losers on election night. Use the steps below to analyze an election map.

### 2006 Missouri Senate Race Election Results by County

**KEY**

- Majority Democrat (Claire McCaskill)
- Majority Republican (James Talent)
- Counties won by Talent by a margin of 2% or less
- ● City with population over 300,000
- ● City with population over 100,000
- ○ City with population over 70,000
- ○ City with population over 50,000

① **Identify the purpose of the map.** Study the title to identify the purpose of the map and to make sure that you understand what information is shown.

② **Determine the scope of the analysis.** For a national election map, analysis might focus on voting by State or region. Analysis of a map of a State's election data might focus on voter turnout by county or by precinct. Here, it is by county.

③ **Use the key.** Analyze and apply the information in the map key to determine what data is shown. In an election map, you might look for color patterns. These might include areas of the State where voter turnout was strong for one political party or the other.

## Practice and Apply the Skill

Use the Missouri county election map above to answer the following questions.

1. What does the map's title tell you?
2. What does each color on the map represent?
3. What voting pattern can you find in the counties with the State's largest cities?
4. How was McCaskill able to win the election despite winning only the city of St. Louis and 25 of Missouri's 114 counties?

# Get Started

## LESSON GOAL

- Students will identify the steps in analyzing election maps by analyzing an election map on the 2006 Missouri Senate race.

# Teach

## IDENTIFY KEY IDEAS

Have students read the steps in the process of analyzing election maps and identify the purpose of the map. Remind students that Senate races are decided on the basis of the total popular vote in the State. Point out that special-purpose maps like this one can be used not only to analyze State election results but also to predict future trends in voter behavior. After studying the map key, have students identify the candidate who won the largest number of counties. Ask students to explain why Talent lost the election, despite winning a majority of the votes in many more counties than McCaskill. Based on the map, which candidate appealed more strongly to urban voters? How did their support help McCaskill win the election?

## PREDICTING FUTURE TRENDS

Have students use the map to make three predictions about where in the State each party might expect strong support for their candidates and which areas of the State each party may be weakest.

# Assess and Remediate

Have students complete the Practice and Apply the Skill questions. Discuss their responses as a class. In the library or on the Internet, have students find a map and data on election results for another State in a recent Senate election and analyze the voting patterns shown on the map using the steps in the lesson.

# Answers

**1.** The title indicates that the map provides election results for the 2006 Missouri Senate race by county.

**2.** Red and blue indicate whether the majority of voters in each county voted for McCaskill or Talent. Pink indicates counties in which Talent won by less than 2 percent of the vote.

**3.** Voters in most of the State's counties with large cities voted for the Democrat McCaskill.

**4.** The counties that gave McCaskill a majority of votes had the largest populations and most of the State's largest cities.

# Get Started

## LESSON GOALS

Students will . . .

- critically analyze two political campaign ads.
- assess the effectiveness of two political ads in informing or persuading the viewer.

# Teach

## BRAINSTORM

Have volunteers explain what form of media their most vivid or memorable images of political figures come from. Have students recall events in which public officials or political candidates became associated with positive or negative images in the media. Have students discuss the effect these images had on public perception of these figures. Emphasize that it is important to recognize and critically evaluate the message in every visual image, especially if the image is meant to persuade viewers as it is in political and commercial advertising.

## ANALYZE AND PRESENT

Have students read the steps in the process of analyzing images and share any questions they have. Divide students into two groups and assign each group one of the images. Have groups analyze the ad assigned, identifying the context of the ad, its message or purpose, and the group's conclusion on how effective or persuasive the image is.

# Assess and Remediate

Have students complete the Practice and Apply the Skill questions. Discuss their responses as a class. Have each student find a political ad for a candidate or cause and write a paper analyzing the image using the steps discussed in the text.

# Analyze Images

During elections, images of candidates and the issues they support fill television screens, newspapers, and Web sites. They seek to inform, persuade, and influence the viewer's opinion on a particular candidate or issue. It is important to be able to analyze an image, especially in advertising, for bias, emotional appeals, or inaccurate statements. Use the steps below to practice analyzing images.

**1 Identify the content.** When viewing an advertisement, look closely at the images and text and determine which information is most important. Identify themes or issues that the advertisement highlights. Notice how the images reinforce the overall message.

**2 Note emotions.** In analyzing the images of people, study facial expressions and body positions. Consider the emotions these expressions or positions suggest.

**3 Consider context.** Determine the context in which the image was created. Evaluate the accuracy of any information and supporting facts presented. Read all captions and credits. When possible, gather information about who produced or paid for the image or advertisement.

**4 Identify the purpose.** Determine whether the advertisement provides primarily factual information or opinions about a candidate or an issue. Does it emphasize a candidate's positive features or present an issue in a positive or balanced way, or is it intended to show an opponent or decision in a negative light?

**Image A**
This advertisement, paid for by a national organization that represents large private nursing home chains, refers to a Congressperson who voted in favor of a bill that might have reduced Medicare funding.

**Image B**
This poster is from Ronald Reagan's 1980 presidential campaign.

## Practice and Apply the Skill

Use the political ads above to answer the following questions.

1. (a) What issue does Image A focus on? (b) What is the purpose of Image A?
2. Why do you think the producers of Image A chose this image?
3. In what ways could Image A be considered a negative, or attack, ad?
4. (a) Does Image B make the candidate seem presidential? How? (b) What is the impact of the phrase at the bottom of the poster?
5. How does the purpose of Image B differ from the purpose of Image A?

# Answers

1. (a) healthcare legislation; (b) to make citizens concerned about Medicare

2. The woman's age suggests she is a member of the age group most likely to be directly affected by congressional decisions on healthcare for the elderly. It is likely that the group also thought that the photo would evoke sympathy.

3. It presents politicians in a negative light.

4. (a) yes; by placing around him images of the flag and White House, symbols associated with patriotism and presidency; (b) the phrase appeals to patriotism and implies that Reagan is able to to make America great

5. Image A is issue-oriented and intended to evoke sympathy; the purpose of Image B is to get Reagan elected.

# Analyze Timelines

A timeline allows readers to analyze a sequence of historical events in chronological order and to find relationships, such as causes and effects, among those events. Use the steps below to analyze a timeline.

**1** **Identify the topic and time period.** Read the timeline's title. Then determine the span of time represented by the entire timeline.

**2** **Determine how the timeline is divided.** Most timelines are divided into equal segments, or increments, of time—years, decades, or centuries.

**3** **Read each entry.** Read each caption carefully. Where possible, connect each one to the events before and after it. Note the date when each event occurred.

**4** **Look for relationships.** Decide if any of the events fall into a common category. Identify any recurring events. Look for events that might be causes and/or effects of other events.

### Voting Rights in the United States, 1964–2009

**1960**

**1964** Civil Rights Act bans use of any voter registration or literacy requirement in unfair or discriminatory manner.

**1965** Voting Rights Act seeks to end discrimination in *all* elections, establishes "preclearance" and "bail-out" processes.

**1970**

**1970** Voting Rights Act renewed for 5 years, bans literacy tests.
**1971** 26th Amendment lowers voting age to 18.
**1975** Voting Rights Act extended for 7 years; protection of voting by "language minorities" added to law.

**1980**

**1982** Voting Rights Act renewed for 25 years.

**1990**

**1990** Americans with Disabilities Act requires States to make it easier for disabled to vote.
**1993** Motor Voter Act provides for registration by mail or when one applies for or renews a driver's license.

**2000**

**2002** Help America Vote Act requires States to upgrade conduct of elections, bans punch-card and lever-operated voting devices.

**2006** Voting Rights Act extended to 2031.

**2010**

**2009** Supreme Court rebuffs challenge to "preclearance" and "bail-out" provisions of Voting Rights Act.

## Practice and Apply the Skill

Use the timeline above to answer the following questions.
1. What span of time does the timeline cover?
2. How many years is each segment of the timeline?
3. What was the impact of the Americans with Disabilities Act on voting rights?
4. What event recurs on the timeline?
5. What was the longest interval between renewals of the Voting Rights Act?

# Get Started

## LESSON GOALS

Students will . . .
- analyze a timeline on voting rights in the United States
- explain the usefulness of putting events in a visual sequence.

# Teach

Have students read the steps in the process of analyzing a timeline and share any questions they have.

## DISCUSS

Ask students to identify events on the timeline that are related to each other or indicate a trend or change over time, such as the expansion of voting rights. Then ask students how adding the assassinations of John Kennedy in 1963 and the assassination of Martin Luther King in 1968 would affect their understanding of the events on the timeline.

## CONSTRUCT A TIMELINE

Ask students to make timelines of their own lives or of someone they know or admire. After completing the timeline, have students write a paragraph explaining how one event or decision on their own timeline is related to or was influenced by other events on their timeline.

# Assess and Remediate

Have students complete the Practice and Apply the Skill questions. Discuss their responses as a class. Have students research the terms of Presidents in the White House during each decade on the timeline. Ask students to use this information to create a parallel timeline. After completing their parallel timelines, have students pick three events on their parallel timelines and explain how they are related to events on the timeline in the text.

# Answers

1. 1960–2010, 50 years
2. 10 years
3. made it easier for people with disabilities to vote by making voting places more accessible
4. reauthorization of the Voting Rights Act
5. 24 years

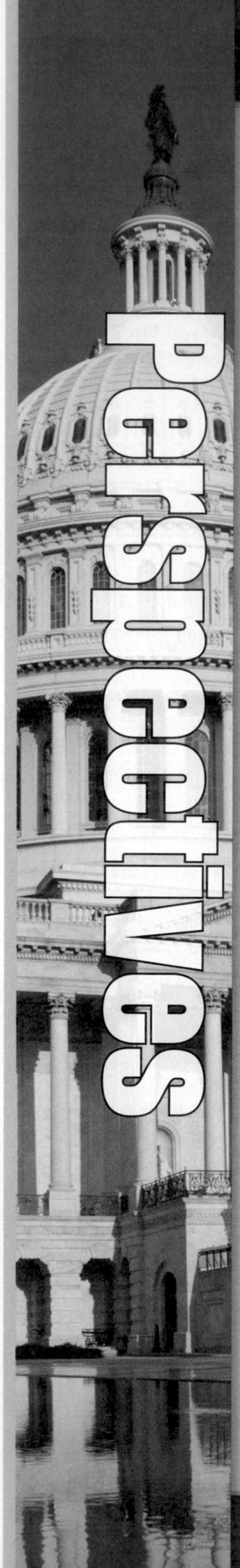

Perspectives

# PREFACE

This is a book about government—and, more particularly, about government in the United States. Over the course of its 25 chapters, you will consider the ways in which government in this country is organized, the ways in which it is controlled by the people, the many things that it does, and the various ways that it does them.

The American system of government is extraordinarily dynamic. Change—growth, adaptation, innovation—is the basic element of its character. While it is true that our government's fundamental principles and its basic structure have remained constant over time, many of its other characteristics have changed. They continue to do so—from year to year and, frequently, from one day to the next, and sometimes remarkably.

To underscore the critical importance of this fact of continuing change, dwell for a moment on the phrase "the American system of government." You will come across it again and again, for it is an apt description of government in the United States. As you will soon discover, that system is a very complex one.

It is complex because it is made up of many different parts, performing many different functions. It is a system because its many different parts are interrelated. The whole cannot be understood without a knowledge of its several interacting parts; and those parts cannot be understood without a knowledge of the whole. Given all of this, the vital effects of ongoing change in the system are obvious.

Every effort has been made to see that this book is as accurate, as up-to-date, as readable, and as interesting and usable as possible. The wealth of factual information it contains has been drawn from the most current and reliable of sources. This is not a book about current events, however. It does contain much data and draws many examples from the contemporary scene. But they are purposefully woven into the context of its primary objective: the description, analysis, and explanation of the American system of government.

— William A. McClenaghan

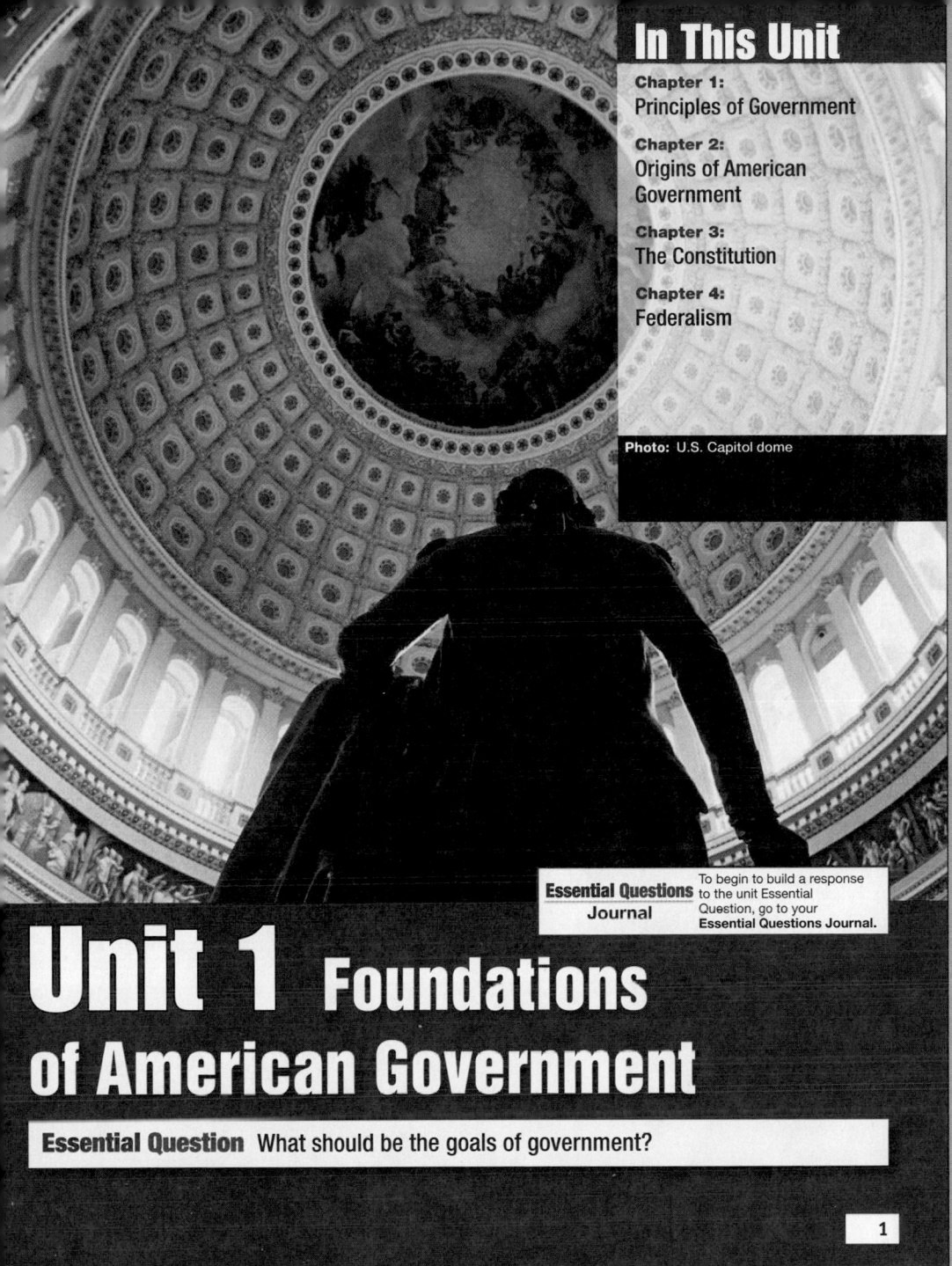

Photo: U.S. Capitol dome

**Essential Questions Journal** To begin to build a response to the unit Essential Question, go to your **Essential Questions Journal.**

# Unit 1 Foundations of American Government

**Essential Question** What should be the goals of government?

## Government Online Resources

Government Online Teacher Center at **PearsonSchool.com/phgovt** includes
- Online Teacher's Edition with lesson planner and lecture notes
- Teacher's Resource Library with All-in-One Resources, Color Transparencies, Adequate Yearly Progress Monitoring, and an alternative lesson plan for each chapter
- SuccessTracker Assessment

Government Online Student Center at **PearsonSchool.com/phgovt** includes
- Interactive textbook with audio
- American Government Essential Questions Video
- Chapter-level WebQuests
- Guided Audio Tours and Interactivities
- Student Self-Tests

**ESSENTIAL QUESTION PERSPECTIVES**

Essential questions frame each unit and chapter of study, asking students to consider big ideas about government. The question for this unit—**What should be the goals of government?**—demands that students ask further questions. How large or small should government be? How much should government regulate our lives? Does government have a responsibility to provide a safety net for the poor? Should government attempt to regulate the economy?

To begin this unit, assign the Unit 1 Warmup Activity on page 2 of the **Essential Questions Journal.** This will help students start to consider their position on the **Unit 1 Essential Question: What should be the goals of government?**

Show the **Unit 1 American Government Essential Questions Video** to help students begin thinking about the unit Essential Question and designate a classroom bulletin board for students to post news articles related to the unit Essential Question. Use the Conversation Wall strategy (p. T27) to encourage students to post articles and comments on other students' postings.

Later, students will further explore the chapter-level essential questions:

*Chapter 1:* **Is government necessary?**

*Chapter 2:* **How does the Constitution reflect the times in which it was written?**

*Chapter 3:* **How has the Constitution lasted through changing times?**

*Chapter 4:* **Is the federal system the best way to govern the United States?**

Use the **Essential Questions Journal** throughout the program to help students consider these and other big ideas about government.

# Introduce the Chapter

## Essential Questions:

**UNIT 1**

What should be the goals of government?

**CHAPTER 1**

Is government necessary?

### ACTIVATE PRIOR KNOWLEDGE

Have students examine the photo and quotation on these pages. Ask: **What is the purpose of government?** *(Students might suggest that government maintains order in society, provides services, maintains a military to defend the country, and performs functions that generally benefit everyone, such as building roads and making laws to protect the environment.)* In this chapter, students will learn about the purpose and forms of government and about the fundamental principles of democracy. Then tell students to begin to further explore the basic characteristics of government by completing the Chapter 1 Essential Question Warmup activity in their **Essential Questions Journal.** Discuss their responses as a class.

### BEFORE READING

**L2 ELL Differentiate** Chapter 1 Prereading and Vocabulary Worksheet (Unit 1 All-in-One, p. 7)

### SUCCESSNET STUDENT AND TEACHER CENTER

Visit **PearsonSchool.com/phgovt** for downloadable resources that allow students and teachers to connect with government "on the go."

### DIGITAL LESSON PRESENTATION

The digital lesson presentation supports the print lesson with activities and summaries of key concepts.

## SKILLS DEVELOPMENT

### NOTETAKING AND ACTIVE LISTENING

You may wish to teach notetaking and active listening as a distinct skill within Section 3 of this chapter. Use the Chapter 1 Skills Worksheet (Unit 1 All-in-One, p. 33) to help students learn to take notes selectively and practice active listening. The worksheet asks students to read an excerpt from John F. Kennedy's inaugural address, identify the general topic and main ideas, and identify transitions, repetition, and emphasis. For L2 and L1 students, assign the adapted Skill Activity (Unit 1 All-in-One, p. 34).

**WebQuest online** The chapter WebQuest challenges students to answer the chapter Essential Question by asking them about principles of government.

2

## Block Scheduling

**BLOCK 1:** Teach Section 1, omitting Extend the Discussion.

**BLOCK 2:** Teach Sections 2 and 3. Omit the Cartoon Mini-Lesson from Section 2. Choose one of the Extend activities from Section 2 or Section 3, depending on your preference and State standards.

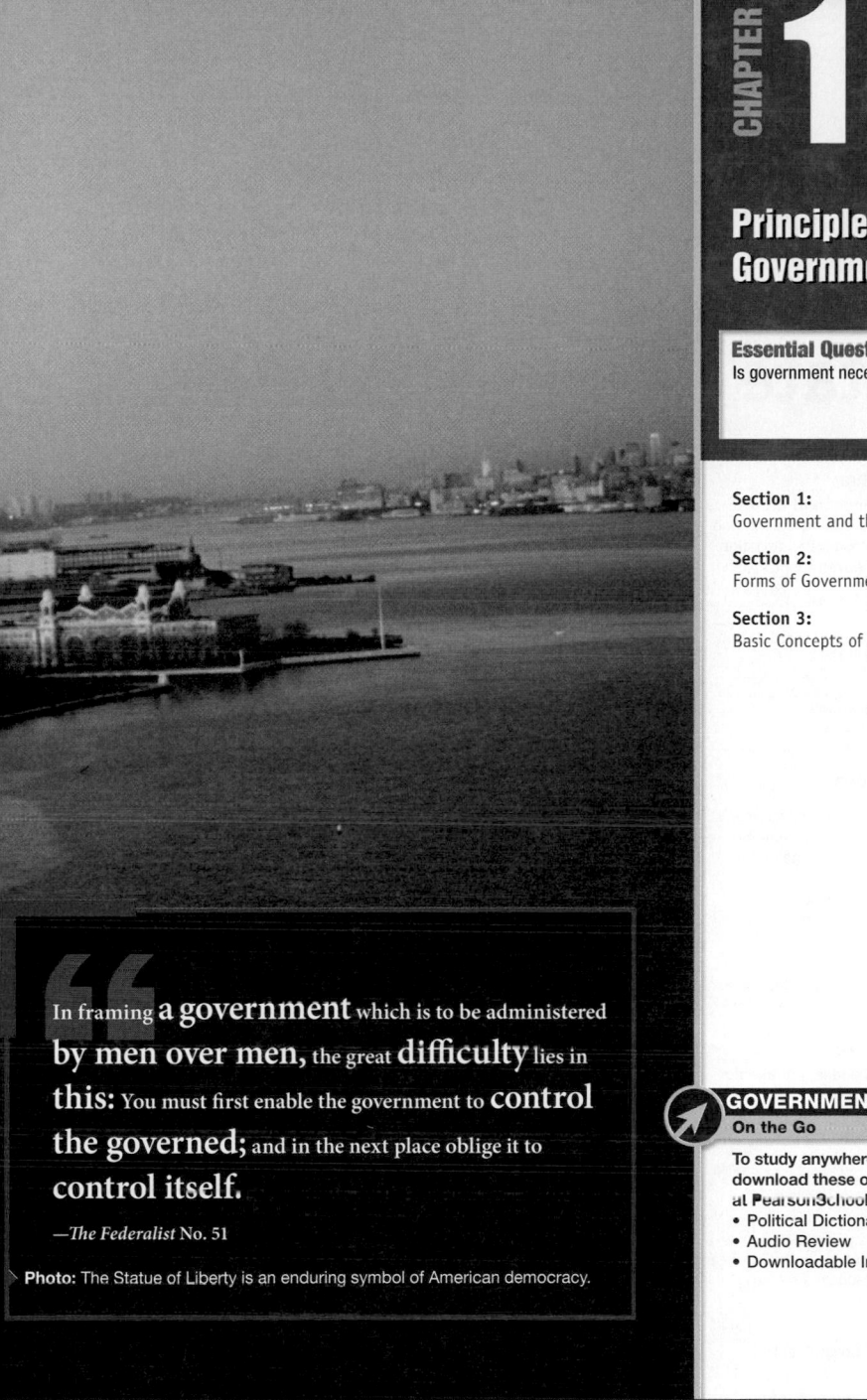

# Principles of Government

**Essential Question**
Is government necessary?

> In framing **a government** which is to be administered **by men over men,** the great **difficulty** lies in **this:** You must first enable the government to **control the governed;** and in the next place oblige it to **control itself.**
>
> —*The Federalist* No. 51

▶ **Photo:** The Statue of Liberty is an enduring symbol of American democracy.

**GOVERNMENT** ONLINE
**On the Go**

To study anywhere, anytime, download these online resources at Pearson3chool.com/phgovt
• Political Dictionary
• Audio Review
• Downloadable Interactivities

3

# Lesson Goals

**SECTION 1**
Students will...
• assess what they know and what they would like to learn about key concepts in American government by completing a chart.
• recall characteristics of states and theories of government by completing a worksheet.
• examine the purposes of American government by completing a chart about the Preamble of the Constitution.

**SECTION 2**
Students will...
• use a checklist to identify terms that describe the United States government, and define each term.
• compare and contrast democracies and dictatorships by predicting their responses in different situations.
• analyze different forms of government through discussion questions.

**SECTION 3**
Students will...
• identify and explain the five concepts of democracy by completing a chart.
• identify real-world examples of the five concepts by brainstorming and filling out a table.
• discuss the responsibilities and duties of citizenship.

# Pressed for Time

To cover this chapter quickly, review the Section 1 Reading Comprehension Worksheet, items 1 through 4 on characteristics of the state, and the Section 3 Reading Comprehension Worksheet on the five concepts of democracy. Then have students complete the Section 1 Core Worksheet, analyzing the Preamble to the Constitution, establishing its relevance today, and giving an opinion about the Framers' idea that government is necessary to keep order and guarantee freedom. Finish by having students make a table comparing the features of democracy versus dictatorship in Section 2.

**DIFFERENTIATED INSTRUCTION KEY**

Look for these symbols to help you adjust steps in each lesson to meet your students' needs.
**L1** Special Needs
**L2** Basic
    **ELL** English Language Learners
    **LPR** Less Proficient Readers
**L3** All Students
**L4** Advanced Students

## What is government and what is its purpose?

A. Definition of Government
   a. Institution through which society makes and enforces public policies
   b. Legislative, judicial, and executive power
   c. Dictatorship—power held by a person or small group
   d. Democracy—power held by the people
B. Characteristics of State
   a. Population
   b. Territory—land with known and recognized boundaries
   c. Sovereignty—supreme power within its territory
   d. Government—agency through which the state exerts its will and works toward its goals
C. Purposes of Government
   a. Form a more perfect union
   b. Establish justice
   c. Insure domestic tranquility
   d. Provide for the common defense
   e. Promote the general welfare
   f. Secure the blessings of liberty

# Get Started

### LESSON GOALS

Students will . . .

- assess what they know and what they would like to learn about key concepts in American government by completing a chart.
- recall characteristics of states and theories of government by completing a worksheet.
- examine the purposes of American government by completing a chart about the Preamble of the Constitution.

## SKILLS DEVELOPMENT

### ANALYZE SOURCES

To help students learn to analyze primary sources, have them turn to the Skills Handbook, p. S14, and use the information there to work with the primary sources referenced in this lesson.

---

## SECTION 1

# Government and the State

### Guiding Question

**What is government and what is its purpose?** Use an outline like the one below to take notes on the definition and purposes of government.

A. Definition of Government
   a. _____
   b. _____
B. Characteristics of a State
   a. _____
   b. _____
C. Purposes of Government
   a. _____
   b. _____

### Political Dictionary

- government
- public policies
- legislative power
- executive power
- judicial power
- constitution
- dictatorship
- democracy
- state
- sovereign

### Objectives

1. Define government and the basic powers every government holds.
2. Describe the four defining characteristics of a state.
3. Identify four theories that attempt to explain the origin of the state.
4. Understand the purpose of government in the United States and other countries.

**Image Above:** Flags representing several countries fly outside of the European Parliament in Strasbourg, France.

This is a book about government—and, more particularly, about government in the United States. Why should you read it? Why should you study government? These are legitimate questions, and they can be answered in several different ways—as you will see throughout the pages of this book. But, for now, consider this response: you should know as much as you possibly can about government because government affects you in an uncountable number of very important ways. It does so today, it did so yesterday, and it will do so every day for the rest of your life.

Think of the point in this light: What would your life be like *without* government? Who would protect you, and all of the rest of us, against terrorist attacks and against other threats from abroad? Who would provide for education, guard the public's health, and protect the environment? Who would pave the streets, regulate traffic, punish criminals, and respond to fires and other human-made and natural disasters? Who would protect civil rights and care for the elderly, the poor, and those who cannot care for themselves? Who would protect consumers and property owners?

Government does all of these things, of course—and much more. In short, if government did not exist, we would have to invent it.

## What Is Government?

**Government** is the institution through which a society makes and enforces its public policies. Government is made up of those people who exercise its powers, all those who have authority and control over people.

The **public policies** of a government are, in short, all of those things a government decides to do. Public policies cover matters ranging from taxation, defense, education, crime, and healthcare to transportation, the environment, civil rights, and working conditions. Indeed, the list of public policy issues handled by government is nearly endless.

Governments must have power in order to make and carry out public policies. Power is the ability to command or prevent action, the ability to achieve a desired end.

---

# Focus on the Basics

**FACTS:** • Society makes and enforces public policies through the institution of government. • A state has a population, a defined territory, sovereignty, and a government. • Basic concepts of American government evolved from the Social Contract Theory. • The Preamble of the Constitution established the basic goals of American government.

**CONCEPTS:** purpose and role of government, values and principles of civil society, popular sovereignty, justice, liberty

**ENDURING UNDERSTANDINGS:** • Government affects our daily lives by maintaining civil society, safeguarding rights, and preventing anarchy. • Liberty is not absolute; one person's freedom cannot infringe on the rights of others.

Every government has and exercises three basic kinds of power: (1) **legislative power**—the power to make laws and to frame public policies; (2) **executive power**—the power to execute, enforce, and administer laws; and (3) **judicial power**—the power to interpret laws, to determine their meaning, and to settle disputes that arise within the society. These powers of government are often outlined in a country's constitution. A **constitution** is the body of <u>fundamental</u> laws setting out the principles, structures, and processes of a government.

The ultimate responsibility for the exercise of these powers may be held by a single person or by a small group, as in a **dictatorship**. In this form of government, those who rule cannot be held responsible to the will of the people. When the responsibility for the exercise of these powers rests with a majority of the people, that form of government is known as a democracy. In a **democracy**, supreme authority rests with the people.

Government is among the oldest of all human inventions. Its origins are lost in the mists of time. But, clearly, government first appeared when human beings realized that they could not survive without some way to regulate their own actions, as well as those of their neighbors.

The earliest known evidences of government date from ancient Egypt and the sixth century B.C. More than 2,300 years ago, the Greek philosopher Aristotle observed that "man is by nature a political animal."[1] When he wrote those words, Aristotle was only recording a fact that, even then, had been obvious for thousands of years.

What did Aristotle mean by "political"? That is to say, what is "politics"? Although people often equate the two, politics and government are very different things. Politics is a process, while government is an institution.

More specifically, politics is the process by which a society decides how power and resources will be distributed within that society. Politics enables a society to decide who

---

[1] In most of the world's written political record, the words *man* and *men* have been widely used to refer to all of humankind. This text follows that form when presenting excerpts from historical writings or documents and in references to them.

---

will <u>reap</u> the benefits, and who will pay the costs, of its public policies.

The word *politics* is sometimes used in a way that suggests that it is somehow immoral or something to be avoided. But, again, politics is the means by which government is conducted. It is neither "good" nor "bad," but it is necessary. Indeed, it is impossible to conceive of government without politics.

## The State

Over the course of human history, the state has emerged as the dominant political unit throughout the world. The **state** can be

**reap**
*v.* to gain, receive, take in

**fundamental**
*adj.* basic, essential, primary

## The Three Basic Powers of Government

In the United States, the three basic powers of government are held in three separate branches. *Why do you think the Framers of the Constitution separated these powers?*

The President is the Head of State and executes the laws.

**Executive**

Congress creates the laws and frames public policy.

**Legislative**

The Supreme Court interprets the laws and determines their constitutionality.

**Judicial**

5

---

## Differentiated Resources

The following resources are located in the All-in-One, Unit 1, Chapter 1, Section 1:

**L2** Prereading and Vocabulary Worksheet (p. 7)
**L3** Reading Comprehension Worksheet (p. 10)
**L2** Reading Comprehension Worksheet (p. 11)
**L3** **L2** Core Worksheets (pp. 12, 13, 14, 15)
**L3** **L4** Extend Worksheet (p. 16)
**L2** Extend Activity (p. 18)
**L3** Quiz A (p. 19)
**L2** Quiz B (p. 20)

---

**BEFORE CLASS**

Assign the section, the graphic organizer in the text, and the Reading Comprehension Worksheet (Unit 1 All-in-One, p. 10) before class.

**L2** **Differentiate** Reading Comprehension Worksheet (Unit 1 All-in-One, p. 11)

**BELLRINGER**

Begin a two-column chart on the board with the headings "Prior Knowledge" at the top of one column and "Making Predictions" at the top of the other column. Write the following on the board:
**Write what you already know about these topics in column one: democracy, federalism, separation of powers, balance of power, constitutional government, Enlightenment thinkers. In column two, predict what you expect to learn about each topic.**

## Teach

To present this topic using online resources, use the lesson presentations at **PearsonSchool.com/phgovt**.

**ASSESS PRIOR KNOWLEDGE**

Draw a horizontal line on the board with markings from 0 to 10. Have students copy the scale in their notebooks and assess what they know about each of the topics in the Bellringer activity by assigning themselves a number on the scale for each topic. Then invite students to share their prior knowledge and predictions. Encourage students to keep their charts and scales; tell them that they will reassess their knowledge at the end of the unit.

## Answers

**The Three Basic Powers of Government** Possible response: to prevent one branch of government from gaining too much power, which might lead to dictatorship

Ask students to take out their Reading Comprehension Worksheets. First, review the four basic characteristics of the state, asking volunteers to identify and define each one. *(1. population: the people who live within the boundaries of the state; 2. territory: land with known and recognized boundaries; 3. sovereignty: the supreme and absolute power within a state's own territory; 4. government: the institution through which society makes and enforces public policies)* Follow the same process with Part 2, calling on volunteers to explain each theory about the origin of the state. *(5. Force Theory: The state was born when one person or a small group took control over people in an area. 6. Evolutionary Theory: The state evolved from the early families that united to form clans. Later, clans united to form tribes. As tribes settled into agricultural groups over time, they formed states. 7. Divine Right Theory: God created the state and gave those of royal birth the right to rule. 8. Social Contract Theory: People voluntarily agreed to create a state and give up to the government just enough power to promote the safety and well-being of all. Government exists to serve the will of the people and the people are the sole source of political power.)*

## EXTEND THE DISCUSSION

Use these questions to continue a discussion about the origin theories and characteristics of the state.

**1. Does a church qualify as a state? Why or why not?** *(A church is not a state, as it does not possess all four characteristics of a state; a church does not hold the supreme power within a territory.)*

**2. Does the largest State in the U.S. qualify as a sovereign state? Does the smallest? Why or why not?** *(Any State, regardless of its size, does not qualify as a state, although it does have population, territory, and government. However, a State does not have the fourth characteristic of a state: sovereignty. That power is reserved to the United States Government.)*

**3. Which of the following islands, or groups of islands, qualify as a state: Hawaii, Japan, Cuba, Australia? Explain.** *(Japan, Cuba, and Australia are all states that possess population, territory, sovereignty, and government. Hawaii, however, is part of the United States, and, therefore, it does not have sovereignty.)*

Tell students to go to the Audio Tour to listen to a guided audio tour of the four characteristics of a state.

## Answers

**Four Characteristics of a State** The characteristic of territory is denoted by the lines drawn to distinguish individual countries.

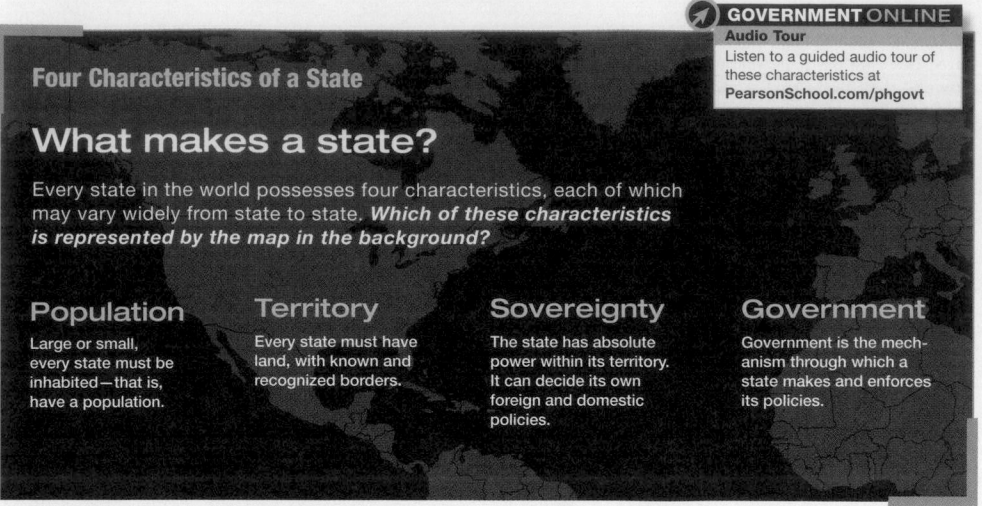

**GOVERNMENT** ONLINE
**Audio Tour**
Listen to a guided audio tour of these characteristics at **PearsonSchool.com/phgovt**

# What makes a state?

Every state in the world possesses four characteristics, each of which may vary widely from state to state. *Which of these characteristics is represented by the map in the background?*

**Population** Large or small, every state must be inhabited—that is, have a population.

**Territory** Every state must have land, with known and recognized borders.

**Sovereignty** The state has absolute power within its territory. It can decide its own foreign and domestic policies.

**Government** Government is the mechanism through which a state makes and enforces its policies.

---

**populous**
*adj.* relating to the number of people in a given region

defined as a body of people, living in a defined territory, organized politically (that is, with a government), and with the power to make and enforce law without the consent of any higher authority.

There are more than 200 states in the world today. They vary greatly in size, military power, natural resources, and economic importance. Still, each of them possesses all four of the characteristics of a state. That is, each of them has population, territory, sovereignty, and government.

Note that the word *state* describes a legal entity. In popular usage, a state is often called a "nation" or a "country." In a strict sense, however, the word *nation* is an ethnic term, referring to races or other large groups of people. The word *country* is a geographic term, referring to a particular place, region, or area of land.

**Population** Clearly, a state must have people—a population. The size of that population, however, has nothing directly to do with the existence of a state. One of the world's smallest states, in population terms, is San Marino. Bound on all sides by Italy, it has only some 30,000 people. The People's Republic of China is the world's most populous state, with more than 1.3 billion people—just about one fifth of all of the world's population. The more than 310 million people who live in the United States make it the world's third-most-populous state, after China and India.

The people who make up a state may or may not be homogeneous. The adjective *homogeneous* describes members of a group who share customs, a common language, and ethnic background. Today, the population of the United States includes people from a wide variety of backgrounds. Still, most Americans think of themselves as exactly that: Americans.

**Territory** Just as a state cannot exist without people, so it must have land—territory—with known and recognized boundaries. The states in today's world vary as widely in terms of territory as they do in population. Here, too, San Marino ranks among the world's smallest states. It covers less than 24 square miles, and so is smaller than thousands of cities and towns in the United States. The United States also recognizes the state of Vatican City, which is completely surrounded by the city of Rome. It has a permanent population of less than 900 and an area of only 109 acres.

# Debate

Ask: **Which theory of the origin of the state is most logical?** Have students hold a roundtable debate on this question. To prepare for the debate, small groups should each take one of the theories and brainstorm arguments in its favor. They might also research proponents of that theory to find additional support for their ideas.

Russia, the world's largest state, stretches across some 6.6 million square miles. The total area of the United States is slightly less than 3.8 million square miles.

**Sovereignty** Every state is **sovereign**—that is, it has supreme and absolute power within its own territory and can decide its own foreign and domestic policies. It is neither subordinate nor responsible to any other authority. Sovereignty is the one characteristic that distinguishes the state from all other, lesser political units in the world.

Thus, as a sovereign state, the United States can determine its form of government, frame its own economic system, and shape its own foreign policies. The States within the United States are not sovereign and so are not states in the international, legal sense. Each State is subordinate to the Constitution of the United States.[2]

**Government** Every state is politically organized. That is, every state has a government. Recall, a government is the institution through which society makes and enforces its public policies. A government is the agency through which the state exerts its will and works to accomplish its goals. Government includes the machinery and the <u>personnel</u> by which the state is ruled.

[2] In this book, *state* printed with a small *s* denotes a state in the family of nations, such as the United States, Great Britain, and Mexico. *State* printed with a capital *S* refers to a State in the American union.

Government is necessary to avoid what the English philosopher Thomas Hobbes (1588–1679) called "the war of every man against every man." Without government, said Hobbes, there would be "continual fear and danger of violent death and the life of man [would be] solitary, poor, nasty, brutish, and short." The world has seen a number of examples over recent years of what happens when a government disappears: In Lebanon, Bosnia, Somalia, and many other places, life became "nasty, brutish, and short."

## Origin of the State

For centuries, historians, philosophers, and others have pondered the question of the origin of the state. What set of circumstances first brought it into being?

Over time, many different answers have been offered, but history provides no conclusive evidence to support any of them. However, four theories have emerged as the most widely accepted explanations for the origin of the state.

**The Force Theory** Many scholars have long believed that the state was born of force. They hold that one person or a small group claimed control over an area and forced all within it to submit to that person's or group's rule. When that rule was established, all the basic elements of the state—population, territory, sovereignty, and government—were present.

✔ **Checkpoint**
What is the definition of *sovereignty*?

**personnel**
*n.* people who work for an organization

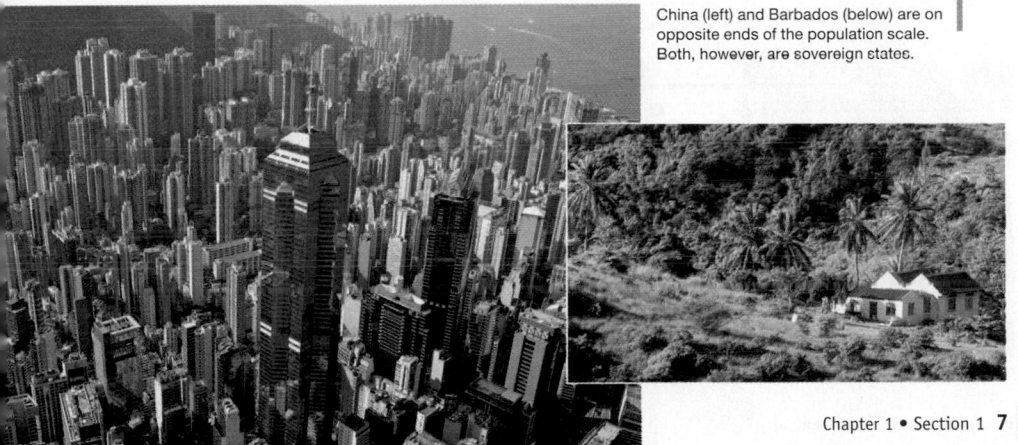

China (left) and Barbados (below) are on opposite ends of the population scale. Both, however, are sovereign states.

# Background

**STATES OF THE WORLD** Geographic boundaries have been changing since the creation of the state. Throughout the ancient world, conquerors created vast empires, and new states rose as these empires fell. Beginning in the sixteenth century, many European nations colonized other continents, carving out territories that would later become states of their own. Wars have always played a role in redrawing the map. In the twentieth century, Czechoslovakia, Austria, Hungary, and Yugoslavia were born out of the aftermath of WWI. After WWII, Israel was created, and Germany split in two. Between 1990 and 2008, 28 new states were formed. The Soviet Union, for example, broke into 15 states. Czechoslovakia peacefully separated into the Czech Republic and Slovakia. East and West Germany merged into a single state. It is likely that this pattern will continue: old states will fall, and new states will rise.

**4. Why do you think many scholars have long believed that the state was born of force?** *(Possible answer: History reveals a long record of conquest, conflict, and war in the struggle for power and dominion.)*

**L4** **Differentiate** Have students research Andorra and report on whether it qualifies as a state.

### DISTRIBUTE CORE WORKSHEET

Distribute the Chapter 1 Section 1 Core Worksheet (Unit 1 All-in-One, p. 12), which asks students to analyze the Preamble to the Constitution and to establish its relevance today. It also asks students whether they agree with the Framers that government is necessary to keep order and guarantee freedoms. Allow time for students to respond to this question after they complete the rest of the activity.

First, have students fill out the middle column on the worksheet, explaining why the Framers may have included each statement in the Preamble. You might ask students to share their responses before they complete the right-hand column. Then, have partners brainstorm ideas about how the Preamble is relevant to today's society. Encourage them to include questions and current examples that show how our Constitution continues to hold practical value today.

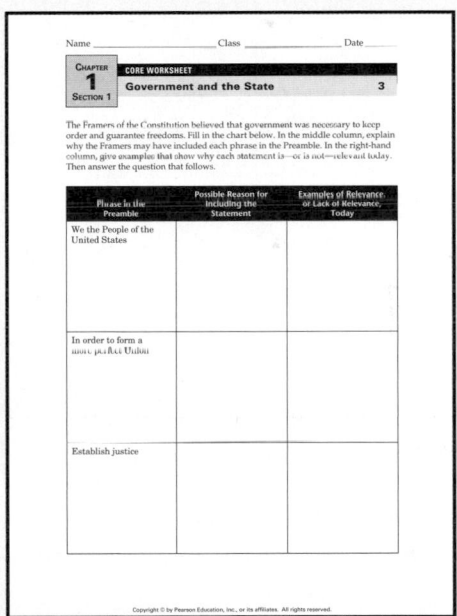

**L2** **ELL Differentiate** For these students, distribute the adapted Core Worksheet (Unit 1 All-in-One, p. 14), which includes an explanation of selected vocabulary.

**L4** **Differentiate** Have students memorize the Preamble. Encourage them to give a dramatic recitation to the class.

## Answers

**Checkpoint** the supreme and absolute power a state holds within its own territory and the ability to decide its own foreign and domestic policies

In *The Federalist* No. 51, James Madison wrote: "If men were angels, no government would be necessary." Write this quotation on the board, and call on a volunteer to read it. Invite students to share their reactions to this statement, based on their thinking about the Preamble and their reading of this section.

Tell students to go to the Audio Tour to listen to a guided audio tour of how the state formed.

**Government** *online*   *All print resources are available on the Teacher's Resource Library CD-ROM and online at* <u>PearsonSchool.com/phgovt</u>.

## Answers

**Origins of the State**  Possible response: the social contract theory, because the Constitution represents the social contract where the people gave some power to the government in exchange for security

---

**GOVERNMENT** **ONLINE**
**Audio Tour**
To listen to a guided audio tour of theories about how the state formed, visit
PearsonSchool.com/phgovt

## Origins of the State

There are four theories as to how the state came to be. Each theory brings together the four characteristics of the state in different ways. *Which of the theories best describes the origin of the United States? Why?*

### Force Theory
An individual or group claimed control over a **territory** and forced the **population** to submit. In this way, the state became **sovereign**, and those in control formed a **government.**

### Evolutionary Theory
A **population** formed out of primitive families. The heads of these families became the **government.** When these families settled in one **territory** and claimed it as their own, they became a **sovereign** state.

### Divine Right Theory
God created the state, making it **sovereign**. The **government** is made up of those chosen by God to rule a certain **territory**. The people **(population)** must obey their ruler.

### Social Contract Theory
A **population** in a given place **(territory)** gave up as much power to a **government** as needed to promote the well-being of all. In doing so, they created a **sovereign** state.

**The Evolutionary Theory** Others claim that the state developed naturally out of the early family. They hold that the primitive family, of which one person was the head and thus the "government," was the first stage in political development. Over countless centuries, the original family became a network of related families, a clan. In time, the clan became a tribe. When the tribe first turned to agriculture and gave up its nomadic, wandering ways, tying itself to the land, the state was born.

**The Divine Right Theory** The theory of **divine right** was widely accepted in much of the Western world from the fifteenth through the eighteenth centuries. It held that God created the state and that God had given those of royal birth a "divine right" to rule. The people were bound to obey their ruler as they would God; opposition to "the divine right of kings" was both treason and a mortal sin.

During the seventeenth century, philosophers began to question this theory. Much of the thought upon which present-day democracies rest began as a challenge to the theory of divine right.

The notion of divine right was not unique to European history. The rulers of many ancient civilizations, including the Chinese, Egyptian, Aztec, and Mayan civilizations, were held to be gods or to have been chosen by the gods. The Japanese emperor, the *mikado*, governed by divine right until 1945.

**The Social Contract Theory** In terms of the American political system, the most significant of the theories of the origin of the state is that of the "social contract." Philosophers such as Thomas Hobbes, James Harrington (1611–1677), and John Locke (1632–1704) in England and Jean Jacques Rousseau (1712–1778) in France developed this theory in the seventeenth and eighteenth centuries.

Hobbes wrote that in earliest history humans lived in unbridled freedom, that is in a "state of nature," in which no government existed and no person was subject to any superior power. That which people could take by force belonged to them. However, all people were similarly free in that state of nature. No authority existed to protect one

---

## Background

King James I of England was a firm believer in the divine right of kings. In 1598, James set forth his views in a document entitled *The True Law of Free Monarchies,* in which he declared: "The State of monarchy is the supreme thing on Earth . . . As to dispute what God may do is blasphemy, so is it treason in subjects to dispute what a king may do. . . . " In James's *Basilikon Doron* (1599), he stated that God gave political power directly to a monarch; that the monarch's power was absolute; and that those who opposed the monarch were guilty of treason, which was punishable by death. After England's "Glorious Revolution" of 1688, the theory of the divine right of kings was no longer taken seriously. However, the coronation ceremony for British monarchs still retains some of the divine right symbolism. The monarch is anointed with holy oils and crowned in a Christian ceremony.

person from the aggressive actions of another. Thus, individuals were only as secure as their own physical strength and intelligence could make them.

Human beings overcame their unpleasant condition, says the social contract theory, by agreeing with one another to create a state. By contract, people within a given area agreed to give up to the state as much power as was needed to promote the safety and well-being of all. In the contract (that is, through a constitution), the members of the state created a government to exercise the powers they had voluntarily given to the state.

In short, the social contract theory argues that the state arose out of a voluntary act of free people. It holds that the state exists only to serve the will of the people, that they are the sole source of political power, and that they are free to give or to withhold that power as they choose from the government. The theory may seem somewhat far-fetched today. The great concepts that this theory promoted, however—popular sovereignty, limited government, and individual rights—were immensely important to the shaping of the American governmental system.

The Declaration of Independence (see pages 43–47) justified its revolution through the social contract theory, arguing that King George III and his ministers had violated the contract. Thomas Jefferson called the document "pure Locke."

## The Purpose of Government

What does government do? You can find a very meaningful answer to that question in the Constitution of the United States. The American system of government was created to serve the purposes set out there.

" **FROM THE CONSTITUTION**

**We the People of the United States, in Order to form a more perfect Union, establish Justice, insure domestic Tranquility, provide for the common defence, promote the general Welfare, and secure the Blessings of Liberty to ourselves and our Posterity, do ordain and establish this Constitution for the United States of America.**
— Preamble to the Constitution

**Form a More Perfect Union** The United States, which had just won its independence from Great Britain, faced an altogether uncertain future in the postwar 1780s. In 1781, the Articles of Confederation, the nation's first constitution, created "a firm league of friendship" among the 13 States. That league soon proved to be neither very firm nor very friendly. The government created by the Articles was powerless to overcome the intense rivalries and jealousies among the States that marked the times.

The Constitution of today was written in 1787. The original States adopted it in order to link themselves, and the American people, more closely together. That Constitution was built in the belief that in union there is strength.

✔ **Checkpoint**
What is the Social Contract Theory?

▶▶ **Interpreting Cartoons** This cartoon pokes fun at organized government. *Which types of government might restrict people from "having it as good as this"? Why?*

CAN YOU STAND THE THOUGHT OF FUTURE GENERATIONS HAVING IT AS GOOD AS THIS?

NO.

GOOD! -- LET'S FORM A GOVERNMENT.

Reproduced by permission of Johnny Hart and Field Enterprises

**L3 Differentiate** Write on the board the following quotation from John Locke's *Second Treatise,* Chapter 9:

**"But though men when they enter into society, give up the equality, liberty and executive power they had in the state of nature, into the hands of the society, to be so far disposed of by the legislature, as the good of the society shall require; yet it being only with an intention to everyone the better to preserve himself his liberty and property."**

Have partners read and paraphrase the quotation together. Then ask them to identify John Locke's main ideas about the need for and role of government.

**L1 L2 Differentiate** Write on the board the following quote from Locke's *First Treatise,* Chapter 9, for students to analyze: **"Government being for the preservation of every man's right and property, by preserving him from the violence or injury of others, is for the good of the governed."**

**L1 L2 Differentiate** For these students, distribute the Extend Activity entitled "Concerns About Rules and Laws" (Unit 1 All-in-One, p. 18), which has students research rules and laws that people are concerned about today.

**L3 L4 Differentiate** Distribute the Chapter 1 Section 1 Extend Worksheet on "Second Treatise of Government" (Unit 1 All-in-One, p. 16). Have students analyze Locke's essay and answer the questions on their own.

**L3 L4 Differentiate** Distribute the Chapter 1 Section 1 Extend Worksheet entitled "Assess Prior Knowledge" (Unit 1 All-in-One, p. 17), which has students answer questions to assess their prior knowledge about constitutions in general and the U.S. Constitution in particular. Explain to students that they will learn about the U.S. Constitution in the next two chapters and throughout this book. Encourage them to return to these questions periodically to see how their understanding evolves.

# Constitutional Principles

**THE ENLIGHTENMENT** In many ways, the U.S. Constitution was a product of the Enlightenment, a seventeenth- and eighteenth-century intellectual movement. Scientific advances led European thinkers to realize that reason could uncover the best method in which to organize society. They began to question authoritarian rule and consider new ways to govern through natural rights and democracy. The idea of government as a social contract with the governed conflicted with the prevailing concept of government by divine right. As colonists arrived in America, they brought these radical ideas with them. Europeans viewed the Declaration of Independence and American Revolution as enlightened ideas put into practice for the first time. These ideas became the Constitution's basic principles: individual rights, popular sovereignty, limited government, separation of powers, and checks and balances.

## Answers

**Checkpoint** The Social Contract Theory holds that people within a given area agreed to create a state and give the state as much power as needed to promote the safety and well-being of all. The state exists only to serve the will of the people, and the people are the sole source of the government's power.

## Assess and Remediate

**L3** Collect the Core Worksheet and assess students' work.

**L3** Assign the Section 1 Assessment questions.

**L3** Section Quiz A (Unit 1 All-in-One, p. 19)

**L2** Section Quiz B (Unit 1 All-in-One, p. 20)

Have students complete the review activities in the digital lesson presentation and continue their work in the **Essential Questions Journal.**

A Coast Guard cutter stands guard in New York Harbor. *Against what kinds of threats does the Coast Guard defend the nation?*

**administration**
*n.* a performance of duties

**abundant**
*adj.* available in large quantity, plentiful

**Establish Justice** To provide justice, said Thomas Jefferson, is "the most sacred of the duties of government." No purpose, no goal of public policy, can be of greater importance in a democracy.

But what is justice? The term is difficult to define, for justice is a concept—an idea, an invention of the human mind. Like other concepts, such as truth, liberty, and fairness, justice means what people want it to mean.

As the concept of justice has developed over time in American thought and practice, it has come to mean this: The law, in both its content and its <u>administration,</u> must be reasonable, fair, and impartial. Those standards of justice have not always been met in this country. We have not attained our professed goal of "equal justice for all." However, this must be said: The history of this country can be told largely in terms of our continuing attempts to reach that goal.

"Injustice anywhere," said Martin Luther King, Jr., "is a threat to justice everywhere." You will encounter this idea again and again in this book.

**Insure Domestic Tranquility** Order is essential to the well-being of any society, and keeping the peace at home has always been a prime function of government. Most people can only imagine what it would be like to live in a state of anarchy—without government, law, or order. In fact, people do live that way in some parts of the world today. For years now, Somalia, located on the eastern tip of Africa, has not had a permanent functioning government; rival warlords control different parts of the country.

In *The Federalist* No. 51, James Madison observed: "If men were angels, no government would be necessary." Madison, who was perhaps the most thoughtful of the Framers of the Constitution, knew that most human beings fall far short of that standard.

**Provide for the Common Defense** Defending the nation against foreign enemies has always been one of government's major responsibilities. You can see its importance in the fact that defense is mentioned far more often in the Constitution than any of the other functions of government.

The nation's defense and its foreign policies are but two sides of the same coin: the security of the United States. To provide this security, the nation maintains an army, navy, air force, and coast guard. Departments such as the Department of Homeland Security keep watch for threats to the country and its people.

The United States has become the world's most powerful nation, but the world remains a dangerous place. This country must maintain its vigilance and its armed strength. Just a glance at today's newspapers or at one of this evening's television news programs will furnish <u>abundant</u> proof of that fact.

**Promote the General Welfare** Few people realize the extent to which government acts as the servant of its citizens, yet you can see examples everywhere. Public schools are one illustration of government's work to promote the general welfare. So, too, are its efforts to protect the quality of the air you breathe, the water you drink, and the food you eat. The list of tasks government performs for your benefit goes on and on.

Some governmental functions that are common in other countries—operating steel mills, airlines, and coal mines, for example—are not carried out by government in this country. In general, the services that government provides in the United States are those

## Political Cartoon Mini-Lesson

Display Transparency 1A, Security, when you discuss the purpose of government. This cartoon suggests that government creates security at a cost. Ask: **What government responsibilities stated in the Preamble does this cartoon portray?** *(establish justice, secure liberty, provide for the common defense)* **How does this cartoon suggest that the government is providing for the common defense?** *(by taking pieces away from liberty, justice, equality, and freedom)* **How do you think the cartoonist feels about the government's policies for providing security?** *(The cartoonist likely opposes government policies for providing security at the expense of the other important responsibilities of preserving liberty, justice, freedom, and equality.)*

## Answers

**Caption** possible response: terrorist threats, illegal activity that benefit all or most people. Many of them are the services that are not very likely to be provided by the voluntary acts of private individuals or groups.

**Secure the Blessings of Liberty** This nation was founded by those who loved liberty and prized it above all earthly possessions. They believed with Thomas Jefferson that "the God who gave us life gave us liberty at the same time." They subscribed to Benjamin Franklin's <u>maxim</u>: "They that can give up essential liberty to obtain a little temporary safety deserve neither liberty nor safety."

The American dedication to freedom for the individual recognizes that liberty cannot be absolute. It is, instead, a relative matter. No one can be free to do whatever he or she pleases, for that behavior would interfere with the freedoms of others. As Clarence Darrow, the great defense lawyer, once said: "You can only be free if I am free."

Both the Federal Constitution and the State constitutions set out many guarantees of rights and liberties for the individual in this country. That does not mean that those guarantees are so firmly established that they exist forever, however. To preserve and protect them, each generation must learn and understand them anew, and be willing to stand up for them when necessary.

For many people, the inspiration to protect our rights and liberties arises from deep

time to thank your lucky stars

▶▶ **Analyzing Political Cartoons** In this cartoon, some of the liberties secured by the Constitution are written on the flag. *What is the phrase "thank your lucky stars" referring to?*

feelings of patriotism. Patriotism is the love of one's country; the passion that drives one to serve one's country, either by defending it from invasion or by protecting its rights and maintaining its laws and institutions. Patriotism is the defining characteristic of a good citizen, the noblest passion that animates a man or a woman in the character of a citizen. As a good citizen, you, too, must agree with Thomas Jefferson: "Eternal vigilance is the price of liberty."

<u>maxim</u>
*n.* a general truth or rule of conduct

---

**Essential Questions Journal** To continue to build a response to the chapter Essential Question, go to your **Essential Questions Journal.**

---

# SECTION 1 ASSESSMENT

1. **Guiding Question** Use your completed outline to answer this question: What is government and what is its purpose?

**Key Terms and Comprehension**

2. What is the difference between a **state** and a nation?

3. **(a)** How is government conducted under a **dictatorship? (b)** How does a dictatorship differ from a **democracy?**

4. How does a **constitution** help to make it possible for a government to carry out its **public policies?**

**Critical Thinking**

5. **Summarize (a)** Summarize the four leading theories of the origin of the state. **(b)** Which two best describe the origin of dictatorships?

6. **Draw Inferences (a)** What is meant by "standards of justice have not always been met"? **(b)** What are some examples of efforts made to reach the goal of justice for all?

**Quick Write**

**Expository Writing: Ask Questions** When explaining a topic, you want to answer *Who, What, When, Where, Why,* and *How.* Develop these questions to explain the origins of either dictatorship or democracy. For example, if you choose dictatorship, you may ask these questions: *Who are some well-known dictators? When did dictatorships first develop?* You will answer these questions as you research the topic.

---

| If Your Students Have Trouble With | Strategies For Remediation |
|---|---|
| The purposes of government (Questions 1, 6) | Write the eight phrases that make up the Preamble onto strips of paper, along with four unrelated phrases. Have students eliminate the unrelated phrases, reconstitute the Preamble from the remaining strips, and highlight the six strips containing the purposes of government. |
| The five characteristics of the state (Question 2) | Write each characteristic and its definition on separate cards. Have students match characteristics with definitions. |
| The four theories of origin of the state (Question 5) | Write each theory and its definition on separate cards. Have students match theories with definitions. |

## Answers

**Analyzing Cartoons** The liberties are written on the flag to show that they are as much a part of our symbolism as are the stars and stripes. The phrase refers to the fact that Americans are fortunate to have these liberties.

---

# Assessment Answers

**1.** Government is used by society to create and carry out its public policies. The purposes of government are to form a union, provide justice, keep the peace, defend the state, promote general welfare, and secure liberty.

**2.** A state is a legal entity, whereas a nation is an ethnic entity.

**3. (a)** In a dictatorship, the ruler or rulers are not held responsible to the will of the people. **(b)** In a democracy, the government derives its power from the people. The people hold the government responsible for its actions.

**4.** A constitution is the body of laws that sets out the principles, structures, and processes of a government. It creates the framework on which government conducts public policies.

**5. (a) Force:** One person, or a small group, claimed control of an area and forced all within it to submit to that person's or group's rule. **Evolution:** Family units banded together into clans and later clans formed tribes. Eventually tribes formed states as they became agricultural. **Divine Right:** God bestowed the right to rule on an individual. The people obeyed their ruler as they would God. **Social Contract:** The people voluntarily agreed to create a state and give the government just enough power to promote the safety and well-being of all. **(b)** force theory and divine right theory

**6. (a)** Discrimination and oppression have deprived certain groups of justice. **(b)** Efforts to change the law, such as the suffrage movement and the abolition movement are examples of efforts to attain justice for all.

**QUICK WRITE** While researching, students should take notes to make sure they answer each question.

# What are some forms of government in the world today?

| Forms of Government | |
| --- | --- |
| **Democracy** | **Dictatorship** |
| • Political authority rests with the people<br>• Direct or indirect<br>• Presidential—powers separated into executive and legislative branch<br>• Parliamentary—executive branch part of legislature<br>• Federal—power shared by local and national government<br>• Confederate—power centered in local governments<br>• Unitary—power centered in national government | • Rulers not responsible to the people<br>• Government not accountable for policies or how they are carried out<br>• Autocracy—one person rules<br>• Oligarchy—small group rules<br>• All are authoritarian<br>• Most are totalitarian<br>• Militaristic |

# Get Started

## LESSON GOALS

Students will . . .

- use a checklist to identify terms that describe the United States Government, and define each term.

- compare and contrast democracies and dictatorships by predicting their responses in different situations.

- analyze different forms of government through discussion questions.

## BEFORE CLASS

Assign the section, the graphic organizer in the text, and the Reading Comprehension Worksheet (Unit 1 All-in-One, p. 21) before class.

**L2 Differentiate** Reading Comprehension Worksheet (Unit 1 All-in-One, p. 22)

## SKILLS DEVELOPMENT

### ANALYZE POLITICAL CARTOONS

Before the political cartoon mini-lesson in this section, you may want to review tips on analyzing political cartoons in the Skills Handbook, p. S22.

---

SECTION **2**

# Forms of Government

## Guiding Question
**What are some forms of government in the world today?**
Use a table like the one below to take notes on the different kinds of government in the world today.

| Forms of Government | |
| --- | --- |
| **Democracy** | **Dictatorship** |
| • | • |
| • | • |
| • | • |
| • | • |

## Political Dictionary

- autocracy
- oligarchy
- unitary government
- federal government
- division of powers
- confederation
- presidential government
- parliamentary government

## Objectives

1. Classify governments according to three sets of characteristics.
2. Define systems of government based on who can participate.
3. Identify different ways that power can be distributed, geographically, within a state.
4. Describe a government by the distribution of power between the executive branch and legislative branch.

**Image Above:** Members of the House of Lords in the British Parliament wear traditional robes and wigs.

**D**oes the form a government takes, the way in which it is structured, have any importance? Political scientists, historians, and other social commentators have long argued that question. The English poet Alexander Pope weighed in with this couplet in 1733:

**" PRIMARY SOURCE**
For Forms of Government let fools contest; Whate'er is best adminster'd is best. . . ."

*—Essay on Man*

Was Pope right? Does it matter what form a government takes? Pope thought not. You can form your own opinion as you read this section.

## Classifying Governments

No two governments are, or ever have been, exactly alike, for governments are the products of human needs and experiences. All governments can be classified according to one or more of their basic features, however. Over time, political scientists have developed many bases upon which to classify (and so to describe, compare, and analyze) governments.

Three of those classifications are especially important and useful. These are classifications according to (1) who can participate in the governing process, (2) the geographic distribution of governmental power within the state, and (3) the relationship between the legislative (lawmaking) and the executive (law-executing) branches of the government.[3]

## Who Can Participate

To many people, the most meaningful of these classifications is the one that depends on the number of persons who can take part in the governing process.

---

3  Note that these classifications are not mutually exclusive. For example, the government of the United States is federal in form, and it is also presidential and democratic.

---

# Focus on the Basics

**FACTS:** • Political scientists classify governments based on who participates, geographic distribution of power, and the relationship between the legislative and executive branches. • In a democracy, supreme political authority rests with the people. • In representative democracies, citizens choose representatives who act on their behalf. • In dictatorships, rulers are not accountable to the people.

**CONCEPTS:** federalism, limited government, popular sovereignty, dictatorship, separation of powers, checks and balances

**ENDURING UNDERSTANDINGS:** • The geographic distribution of power determines whether a government is unitary, federal, or confederate. • In presidential government, the executive and legislative branches share power. • In parliamentary government, the legislative branch dominates.

Here there are two basic forms to consider: democracies and dictatorships.

**Democracy** In a democracy, supreme political authority rests with the people. The people hold the sovereign power, and government is conducted only by and with the consent of the people.[4]

Abraham Lincoln gave immortality to this definition of democracy in his Gettysburg Address in 1863: "government of the people, by the people, for the people." Nowhere is there a better, more <u>concise</u> statement of the American understanding of democracy.

A democracy can be either direct or indirect in form. A direct democracy, also called a pure democracy, exists where the will of the people is translated into public policy (law) directly by the people themselves, in mass meetings. Clearly, direct democracy can work only in small communities, where the citizenry can meet in a central place, and where the problems of government are few and relatively simple.

Direct democracy does not exist at the national level anywhere in the world today. However, the New England town meeting, which you will read about in Chapter 25, and the *Landsgemeinde* in a few of the smaller Swiss <u>cantons</u> is an excellent example of direct democracy in action.[5]

Americans are more familiar with the indirect form of democracy—that is, with representative democracy. In a representative democracy, a small group of persons, chosen by the people to act as their representatives, expresses the popular will. These agents of the people are responsible for carrying out the day-to-day conduct of government—the making and executing of laws and so on. They are held accountable to the people for that conduct, especially at periodic elections.

At these elections, the people have an opportunity to express their approval or disapproval of their representatives by casting ballots for or against them. To put it another way, representative democracy is government by popular consent—government with the consent of the governed.

Some people insist that the United States is more properly called a republic rather than a democracy. They hold that in a republic the sovereign power is held by those eligible to vote, while the political power is exercised by representatives chosen by and held responsible to those citizens. For them, democracy can be defined only in terms of direct democracy.

---

4 The word *democracy* is derived from the Greek words *demos* meaning "the people" and *kratia* meaning "rule" or "authority." The Greek word *demokratia* means "rule by the people."

5 The *Landsgemeinde*, like the original New England town meeting, is an assembly open to all local citizens qualified to vote. In a more limited sense, lawmaking by initiative petition is also an example of direct democracy; see Chapter 24.

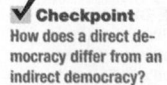
✔ **Checkpoint**
How does a direct democracy differ from an indirect democracy?

**concise**
*adj.* brief; to the point

**canton**
*n.* a local governmental unit in Switzerland

**Direct**
**Democracy**
● Also called pure democracy
● Occurs when the will of the people translates directly into public policy
● Works only on a small, local level
**Image:** Town meeting

**Direct and Indirect Democracy**
## Who governs?

Democratic government derives its power from the people. The picture above shows citizens of a small town voting. Below, a representative casts her vote. The board behind her records the votes of each representative. *Why might direct democracy be more appropriate for a smaller population? Why might indirect democracy be better for a larger population?*

**Indirect**
**Democracy**
● Also called representative democracy
● A group of persons chosen by the people express the will of the people.
● Widely used on a national, State, and local level
**Image:** A legislator votes.

# Differentiated Resources

The following resources are located in the All-in-One, Unit 1, Chapter 1, Section 2:

- **L3** Reading Comprehension Worksheet (p. 21)
- **L2** Reading Comprehension Worksheet (p. 22)
- **L3** Core Worksheet (p. 23)
- **L3** Quiz A (p. 25)
- **L2** Quiz B (p. 26)

**BELLRINGER**

**BELLRINGER**

Write on the board: **direct democracy, indirect democracy, dictatorship, unitary government, federal government, confederation, presidential government, parliamentary government.** Have students copy the list, circle each term that describes the U.S. Government, and define each circled term.

**L2** **ELL Differentiate** Write these terms and definitions in scrambled order on the board: *direct democracy* (all citizens meet to make the laws); *indirect democracy* (laws made by representatives chosen by the citizens); *dictatorship* (one person or a small group holds all the power); *unitary government* (all government powers belong to a single, central agency); *federal government* (the powers of government are divided between a central government and several local governments); *confederation* (an alliance of independent states); *presidential government* (the executive and legislative branches are separate, independent, and equal with one another); *parliamentary government* (the chief executive and cabinet are chosen by the legislature and are members of the legislature). Have students match each term to its definition.

# Teach

To present this topic using online resources, use the lesson presentations at **PearsonSchool.com/phgovt**.

**REVIEW BELLRINGER ANSWERS**

Invite volunteers to share their classifications of the U.S. Government. *(The U.S. Government is an indirect democracy that is federal and presidential.)* Then have them define each term. *(Indirect, or representative, democracy is a system of government in which a small group of officials, chosen by the people, act as the people's representatives and express the people's will. A federal government divides power between a central government and local governments. A presidential government separates power between coequal executive and legislative branches.)*

**L4** **Differentiate** Have students discuss recent U.S. issues, how they have been addressed here, and how they might be treated under other systems of government.

---

# Answers

**Checkpoint** In a direct democracy, the people transform their will into public policy directly through mass meetings. In an indirect democracy, the people elect representatives to create public policy.

**Direct and Indirect Democracy** Direct democracy is practical only when the population is small enough for all citizens to meet in one place. If mass meetings are not possible, then ruling through a smaller number of representatives is more practical.

## DISCUSS FORMS OF GOVERNMENT

Review students' definitions and examples on the Reading Comprehension Worksheet. Then use the following questions to discuss forms of government:

**1. Many dictatorships endure for a decade or longer. What characteristics of this form of government contribute to the longevity of dictators?** *(Dictators are often supported by strong groups, such as the army, religious leaders, and industrialists.)*

**2. In the parliamentary governments of some countries, the prime minister remains in office only a short time. What characteristics of this form of government contribute to the short duration of some prime ministers?** *(The prime minister is chosen by parliament. If parliament defeats the prime minister on an important matter, it can force the prime minister to resign by a vote of no confidence.)*

**3. Why do you think that the majority of governmental systems today are parliamentary?** *(Possible response: The parliamentary form of government predates the presidential form, which was invented in the United States.)*

**4. Why do you think dictatorships generally go hand-in-hand with military power?** *(The military provides the force to take and maintain control of the government for the dictator.)*

**5. What kinds of organizations other than states have some form of government?** *(Possible response: Most large groups have leaders who make policies for the group. For example, superintendents, principals, and school boards govern schools. Sports teams might be dictatorships, with the coach making all team rules. Religious organizations have a governing hierarchy. For example, the Pope and other top Catholic leaders make policy for Catholics.)*

**L4** **Differentiate** Assign each student a country and have them research its form of government. Encourage them to use their findings to create charts that show the relationship between the people and the leader, leaders, or representatives.

---

## Answers

**Checkpoint** An autocracy is a dictatorship by one person, whereas an oligarchy is a dictatorship by a small group.

---

✔ **Checkpoint**
What is the difference between an oligarchy and an autocracy?

**regimes**
*n.* particular governments

**prestige**
*n.* a reputation based on achievement

**elite**
*n.* a select group, a privileged class

Many Americans use the terms *democracy, republic, representative democracy,* and *republican form of government* interchangeably, although they are not the same. Whatever the terms used, remember that in a democracy the people are sovereign. They are the only source for any and all of government's power. In other words, the people rule.

**Dictatorship** A dictatorship exists where those who rule cannot be held responsible to the will of the people. The government is not accountable for its policies, nor for how they are carried out. Dictatorship is probably the oldest, and it is certainly the most common, form of government known to history.[6]

Dictatorships are sometimes identified as either autocracies or oligarchies. An **autocracy** is a government in which a single person holds unlimited political power. An **oligarchy** is a government in which the power to rule is held by a small, usually self-appointed <u>elite.</u>

All dictatorships are authoritarian; those in power hold absolute and unchallengeable authority over the people. Modern dictatorships have tended to be totalitarian, as well. That is, they exercise complete power over nearly every aspect of human affairs. Their power embraces all matters of human concern.

The leading examples of dictatorship in the modern era have been those in Fascist Italy (from 1922 to 1943), in Nazi Germany (from 1933 to 1945), in the Soviet Union (from 1917 until the late 1980s), and one that still exists in the People's Republic of China (where the present regime came to power in 1949).

Although they do exist, one-person dictatorships are not at all common today. A few close approaches to such a regime can now be found in Libya, which has been dominated by Muammar al-Qaddafi since 1969, and in some other Arab and African states.

Most present-day dictatorships are not nearly so absolutely controlled by a single person or by a small group as may appear to be the case. Outward appearances may hide the fact that several groups—the army, religious leaders, industrialists, and others—compete for power in the political system.

Dictatorships often present the outward appearance of control by the people. The people often vote in popular elections; but the vote is closely controlled, and ballots usually contain the candidates of but one political party. An elected legislative body often exists, but only to rubber-stamp the policies of the dictatorship.

Typically, dictatorial <u>regimes</u> are militaristic in character. They usually gain power by force. The military holds many of the major posts in the government. After crushing all effective opposition at home, these regimes may turn to foreign aggression to enhance the country's military power, political control, and <u>prestige.</u>

## Geographic Distribution of Power

In every system of government, the power to govern is located in one or more places geographically. From this standpoint, three basic forms of government exist: unitary, federal, and confederate.

**Unitary Government** A **unitary government** is often described as a centralized government. All powers held by the government belong to a single, central agency. The central (national) government creates local units of government for its own convenience. Those local governments have only those powers that the central government chooses to give them.

Most governments in the world are unitary in form. Great Britain is a classic illustration. A single central organization, the Parliament, holds all of the government's power. Local governments do exist—but solely to relieve Parliament of burdens it could perform only with much difficulty and inconvenience. Though unlikely, Parliament could do away with all local government in Britain at any time.

Be careful not to confuse the unitary form of government with a dictatorship. In the unitary form, all of the powers held by the government are concentrated in the central government.

---

**6** The word *dictatorship* comes from the Latin *dictare,* meaning "to dictate, issue orders," "to give authoritative commands." *Dictator* was the ancient Roman republic's title for the leader who was given extraordinary powers in times of crisis. Julius Caesar (100–44 B.C.) was the last of the Roman dictators.

---

# Political Cartoon Mini-Lesson

Display Transparency 1B, Robert Mugabe, President of Zimbabwe, when you discuss dictatorships. This cartoon shows the difference between elections in a democracy and in a dictatorship. Ask: **What is the woman doing?** *(voting)* **Why is the man holding up a sword?** *(to force the woman to vote in a certain way)* **What form of government does this cartoon illustrate?** *(a dictatorship)* **How do elections in a dictatorship differ from elections in a democracy?** *(Elections in a dictatorship are controlled by those in power. In a democracy, people are free to vote for the candidate of their choice.)*

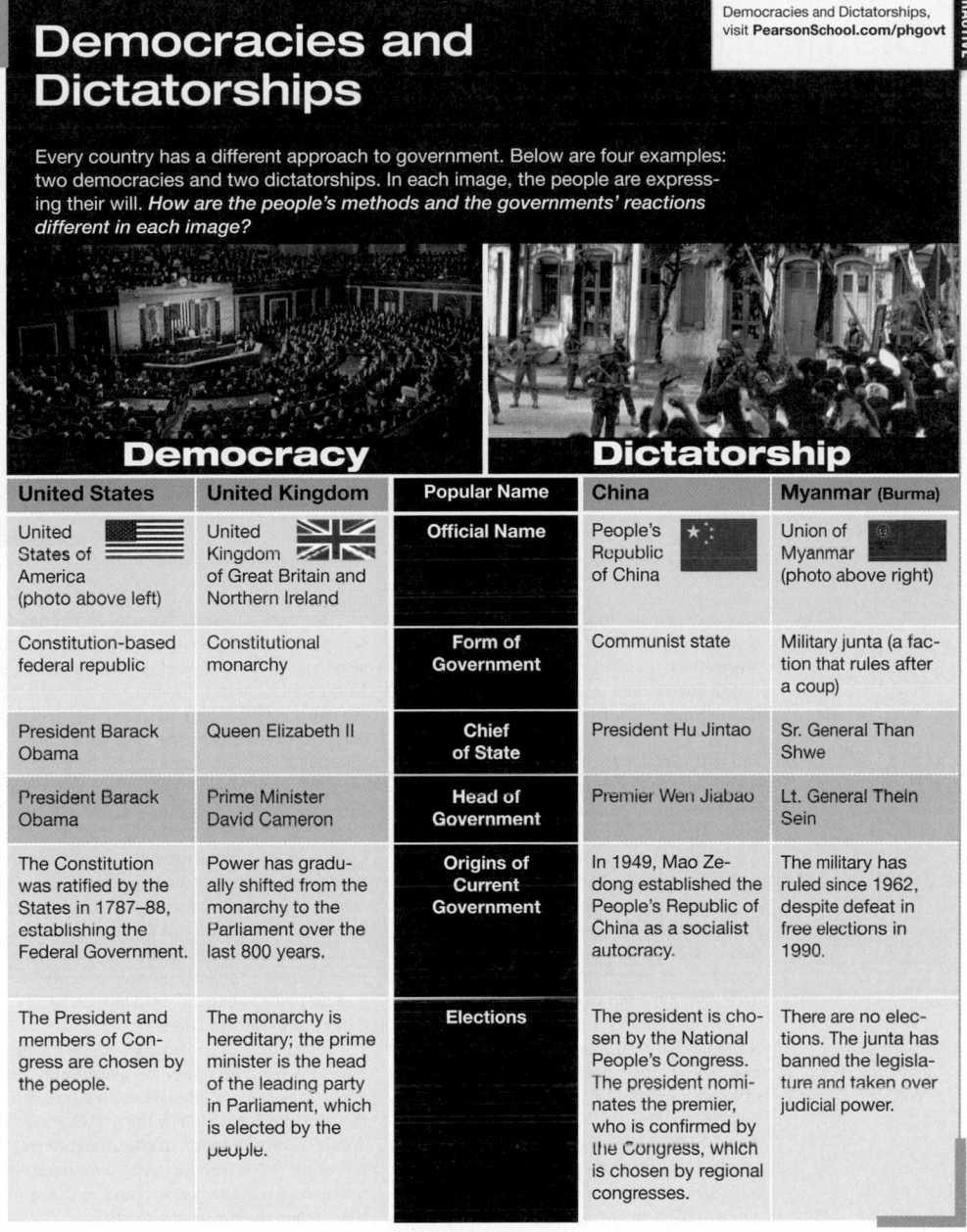

# Democracies and Dictatorships

GOVERNMENT ONLINE
For an **interactive** version of Democracies and Dictatorships, visit **PearsonSchool.com/phgovt**

INTERACTIVE

Every country has a different approach to government. Below are four examples: two democracies and two dictatorships. In each image, the people are expressing their will. *How are the people's methods and the governments' reactions different in each image?*

## Democracy | Dictatorship

| United States | United Kingdom | Popular Name | China | Myanmar (Burma) |
|---|---|---|---|---|
| United States of America (photo above left) | United Kingdom of Great Britain and Northern Ireland | **Official Name** | People's Republic of China | Union of Myanmar (photo above right) |
| Constitution-based federal republic | Constitutional monarchy | **Form of Government** | Communist state | Military junta (a faction that rules after a coup) |
| President Barack Obama | Queen Elizabeth II | **Chief of State** | President Hu Jintao | Sr. General Than Shwe |
| President Barack Obama | Prime Minister David Cameron | **Head of Government** | Premier Wen Jiabao | Lt. General Thein Sein |
| The Constitution was ratified by the States in 1787–88, establishing the Federal Government. | Power has gradually shifted from the monarchy to the Parliament over the last 800 years. | **Origins of Current Government** | In 1949, Mao Zedong established the People's Republic of China as a socialist autocracy. | The military has ruled since 1962, despite defeat in free elections in 1990. |
| The President and members of Congress are chosen by the people. | The monarchy is hereditary; the prime minister is the head of the leading party in Parliament, which is elected by the people. | **Elections** | The president is chosen by the National People's Congress. The president nominates the premier, who is confirmed by the Congress, which is chosen by regional congresses. | There are no elections. The junta has banned the legislature and taken over judicial power. |

## DISTRIBUTE CORE WORKSHEET

Number index cards 1 through 6. Write the word *Democracy* on cards 1 through 3 and *Dictatorship* on cards 4 through 6. Distribute the Chapter 1 Section 2 Core Worksheet (Unit 1 All-in-One, p. 23) and divide the class into six teams. Give each team one of the cards. Explain that teams should predict what would happen in the scenarios assigned to their team, under the form of government on their card. When students finish their worksheets, ask them to share their predictions. Invite students to generalize about how different forms of government react to disasters and challenges.

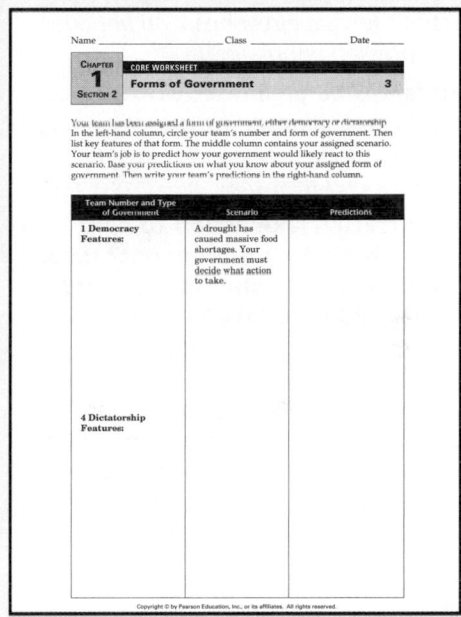

Tell students to go to the interactivity to learn more about democracies and dictatorships.

# Background

**CHOOSING A SYSTEM OF GOVERNMENT** The Framers of the Constitution had to deal with several critical matters as they drafted a new Constitution for the United States. None of the Framers favored a government based on the British model. The Revolutionary War had been fought in the name of local self-government, and the Framers were determined to preserve that cherished principle. But how could they create a central government that was strong enough to be effective and, at the same time, preserve the powers of the existing States? Having tried a confederation first, they realized that that form of government had failed to meet the needs of the new country. Their solution: federalism. The powers of government would be divided between the new Federal Government and the States.

## Answers

**Democracies and Dictatorships** In the democracy image, the people have sent representatives to discuss issues, and the government is holding a vote. In the dictatorship image, the people are protesting in the street, and the government is reacting with violence.

**CONTINUE CORE ACTIVITY**

Have students investigate the effects of dictatorship. Ask small groups to research modern dictators, such as Joseph Stalin, Vladimir Lenin, Benito Mussolini, Adolf Hitler, Mao Zedong, Ho Chi Minh, Muammar al-Qaddafi, Robert Mugabe, Augusto Pinochet, and Kim Jong-il. They should find out how each dictator came to power and held power and what effect dictatorship has had on each country. Invite students to share their findings. Based on this information, help them to create a chart showing similarities and differences. End the activity with the following discussion questions:

**1. What circumstances are most likely to create dictatorship?** *(possible response: an unhappy, economically depressed population)*

**2. Can dictatorships be prevented? How?** *(Possible response: Dictatorships can be prevented only when a government is established in which the people have a voice and their basic needs are met.)*

**3. Should democracies take action to help prevent dictatorship? Why or why not? If so, under what circumstances should they act? What actions should they take?** *(Some students might say no. Democracy is an evolutionary process. Removing a dictator by force, before the society is ready for democracy, will only lead to another dictatorship. Other students might say that democracies have a moral obligation to help oppressed people throw off their oppressors. Democratic governments can support dissenters in those countries with money, arms, and education about democratic processes.)*

**L4 Differentiate** Have students research a dictator on their own.

# Distribution of Power

Power can be distributed between central (national) and local governments in three different ways. *Which diagram best describes the distribution of power in the United States?*

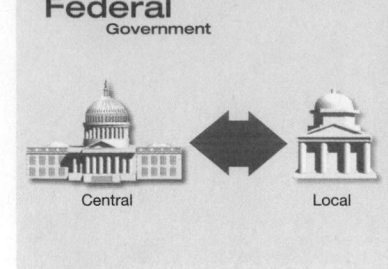

**Federal** Government

The National Government and the States are co-equal partners in a federal system.

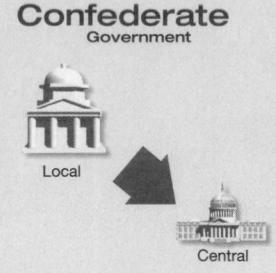

**Confederate** Government

Most power belongs to the local (regional) governments. The central government has only limited power.

**Unitary** Government

Power resides with the central government, which creates local governments.

That government might not hold all power, however. In Great Britain, for example, the powers held by the government are limited. British government is unitary and, at the same time, democratic.

**Federal Government** A **federal government** is one in which the powers of government are divided between a central government and several local governments. An authority superior to both the central and local governments makes this **division of powers** on a geographic basis; that division cannot be changed by either the local or national level acting alone. Both levels of government act directly on the people through their own sets of laws, officials, and agencies.

In the United States, for example, the National Government has certain powers, and the 50 States have others. This division of powers is set out in the Constitution of the United States. The Constitution stands above both levels of government; it cannot be changed unless the people, acting through both the National Government and the States, agree to the change.

Australia, Canada, Mexico, Switzerland, Germany, India, and some 20 other states also have federal forms of government today. In the United States, the phrase "the Federal Government" is often used to identify the National Government, the government headquartered in Washington, D.C. Note, however, that each of the 50 State governments in this country is unitary, not federal, in form.

**Confederate Government** A **confederation** is an alliance of independent states. A central organization, the confederate government, has the power to handle only those matters that the member states have assigned to it. Typically, confederate governments have had limited powers and only in such fields as defense and foreign affairs.

Most often, confederate governments have not had the power to make laws that apply directly to individuals, at least not without some further action by the member states. A confederate structure of government makes it possible for the several states to cooperate in matters of common concern and, at the same time, retain their separate identities.

# Debate

Display Transparency 1C, Choosing a Chief Executive. Ask: **What basic initial step does the population take to choose the chief executive of a presidential or parliamentary democracy?** *(vote)* Point out to students that voting is crucial in any democratic government. Present the following question for debate: **Should citizens be required by law to vote?** Divide students into two groups, and have them brainstorm benefits and drawbacks. Allow time for representatives from each group to debate the question.

## Answers

**Distribution of Power** federal

Confederations have been rare in the modern world. The European Union (EU) is the closest approach to one today. The EU, formed by 12 countries in 1993, has established free trade among its now 27 member-nations, launched a common currency, and seeks to coordinate its members' foreign and defense policies.

In our own history, the United States under the Articles of Confederation (1781–1789) and the Confederate States of America (1861–1865) also provide examples of this form of government.

## Legislative and Executive Branches

Political scientists also classify governments based on the relationship between their legislative and executive agencies. This grouping yields two basic forms of government: presidential and parliamentary.

**Presidential Government** A **presidential government** features a separation of powers between the executive and the legislative branches of the government. The two branches are independent of one another and <u>coequal.</u> The chief executive (the president) is chosen by the people, independently of the legislature. He or she holds office for a fixed term, and has a number of significant powers that are not subject to the direct control of the legislative branch.

The details of this separation of the powers of these two branches are almost always spelled out in a written constitution—as they are in the United States. Each of the branches is regularly given several powers with which it can block actions of the other branch.

✔ **Checkpoint**
How is the executive branch related to the legislative branch in a presidential government?

**coequal**
*adj.* equal with one another, of the same rank

# Choosing a Chief Executive

In a presidential democracy, the people choose their representatives as well as their President. In a parliamentary democracy, the representatives (members of parliament) choose the prime minister. *Which method seems best for choosing a chief executive? Why?*

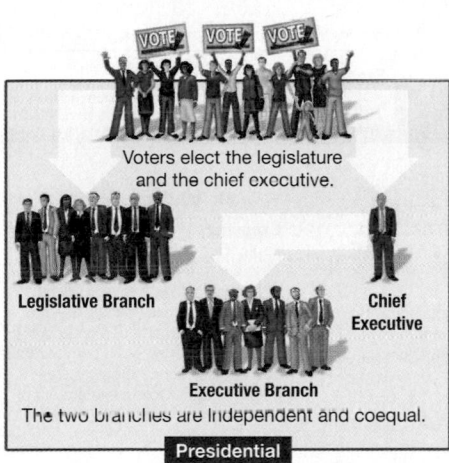

Voters elect the legislature and the chief executive.

**Legislative Branch**

**Chief Executive**

**Executive Branch**
The two branches are independent and coequal.

**Presidential**

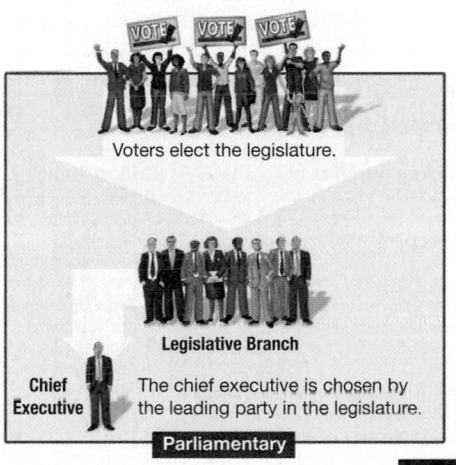

Voters elect the legislature.

**Legislative Branch**

**Chief Executive**
The chief executive is chosen by the leading party in the legislature.

**Parliamentary**

## EXTEND THE LESSON

At the beginning of this section, students read the following quote from Pope's "Essay on Man":

**"For Forms of Government let fools contest; Whate'er is best adminster'd is best."**

Write the quote on the board, and call on volunteers to paraphrase it. *(People are foolish to argue about the form of government; the best government is one that is well run.)* Ask students if their opinion has changed about whether the form of government matters. After a short discussion, assign students who hold similar opinions to small groups. Have each group write a response to Pope.

**L4** **Differentiate** Have students create a poem in response to Pope's assertion.

## Assess and Remediate

**L3** Collect the Core Worksheet and assess students' work.

**L3** Assign the Section 2 Assessment questions.

**L3** Section Quiz A (Unit 1 All-in-One, p. 25)

**L2** Section Quiz B (Unit 1 All-in-One, p. 26)

Have students complete the review activities in the digital lesson presentation and continue their work in the **Essential Questions Journal.**

# Teacher-to-Teacher Network

**ALTERNATIVE LESSON PLAN** Chemists use the periodic table to classify the elements. Biologists classify organisms into species. Political scientists classify governments of the world by their common characteristics. As students study this chapter, have them devise a classification system for governments and insert various governments into their system. They will need to define each classification using specific criteria.

To see this lesson plan, go to

**Teacher Center**
at PearsonSchool.com/phgovt

## Answers

**Checkpoint** The executive branch and the legislative branch are separate and coequal.

**Choosing a Chief Executive** Answers will vary. Students might note that popular election of the president makes the chief executive more accountable to the people and enables checks and balances between the branches. However, selection of the chief executive by the parliament avoids the prolonged conflict and deadlock that sometimes occurs between the executive and legislative branches in the presidential form.

| If Your Students Have Trouble With | Strategies For Remediation |
|---|---|
| The features of democracy versus dictatorship (Questions 1, 4) | Have students create word webs for *democracy* and *dictatorship*. |
| The geographic distribution of power (Questions 1, 2, 5) | Have students write and exchange quizzes about unitary, federal, and confederate forms of government. |
| The differences among presidential and parliamentary governments (Questions 3, 5) | Write individual features of each type of government on index cards. Have teams take turns picking cards and identifying the form of government. |

▲ Members of the South African parliament are sworn into office.

The United States is the world's leading example of presidential government. In fact, the United States invented the form. Nearly all of the other presidential systems that exist in the world today are also found in the Western Hemisphere.

**Parliamentary Government** In a **parliamentary government,** the executive branch is made up of the prime minister or premier, and that official's cabinet. The prime minister and cabinet are themselves members of the legislative branch, the parliament. The prime minister is the leader of the majority party or of a like-minded group of parties (a coalition) in parliament and is chosen by that body. With parliament's approval, the prime minister selects the members of the cabinet from among the members of parliament. The executive is thus chosen by the legislature, is a part of it, and is subject to its direct control.

The prime minister and the cabinet (often called "the government") remain in office only as long as their policies and administration have the support of a majority in parliament. If the parliament defeats the prime minister and cabinet on an important matter, the government may receive a "vote of no confidence," and the prime minister and his cabinet must resign from office. Then a new government must be formed. Either parliament chooses a new prime minister or, as often happens, all the seats in parliament go before the voters in a general election.

A majority of the governmental systems in the world today are parliamentary, not presidential, in form—and they are by a wide margin. Parliamentary government avoids one of the major problems of the presidential form: prolonged conflict and sometimes deadlock between the executive and legislative branches. However, the protections against arbitrary government found in the checks and balances of presidential government are not a part of the parliamentary system.

**Essential Questions Journal** To continue to build a response to the chapter Essential Question, go to your **Essential Questions Journal.**

## SECTION **2** ASSESSMENT

1. **Guiding Question** Use your completed table to answer this question: What are some forms of government in the world today?

### Key Terms and Comprehension

2. **(a)** How is power distributed in a **federal government? (b)** How does a federal state differ from a confederate state?

3. What is the relationship between the executive and legislative branches in a **parliamentary government?**

### Critical Thinking

4. **Draw Inferences** Why do some dictatorships adopt some of the features of democratic government— for example, popular elections and elected legislative bodies?

5. **Draw Conclusions** Explain why it is possible that a unitary government might be either democratic or dictatorial in form.

### Quick Write

**Expository Writing: Research Your Topic** Use several sources to find the answers to the questions you posed in Section 1. The answers will help you gather details you will need to fully explain either a democracy or a dictatorship. Then put all of your facts and details in chronological order to help the reader follow the growth of democracy or dictatorship.

## Assessment Answers

**1.** democracy (direct and indirect), dictatorship (autocracy and oligarchy), unitary, federal, confederate, presidential, parliamentary

**2. (a)** In a federal government, power is distributed between the central government and several local governments. **(b)** In a confederation, the central government is weak, and most of the power is held by the member states. In a federal government, the power is distributed equally between levels of government.

**3.** In a parliamentary government, the chief executive is chosen by the legislature, is a part of it, and is subject to its direct control. The chief executive selects the cabinet from among the members of the legislature. The legislature may remove the executive branch by a vote of no confidence.

**4.** Rulers might choose to take on these characteristics to appease their people and other nations, in order to remain in power.

**5.** In a unitary government, all powers held by the government belong to a single central agency. This central authority may be either democratic or dictatorial in nature.

**QUICK WRITE** Students should use several sources to research their topics. Putting their notes in chronological order will help them write their essays later.

# Volunteering

In one of his State of the Union addresses, President George W. Bush called on Americans to volunteer. He also announced the creation of USA Freedom Corps, an organization that links Americans to thousands of volunteer opportunities. USA Freedom Corps has helped many volunteer organizations—including Learn and Serve America, which supports student volunteers—gain recognition and support for their causes.

A substantial number of students volunteer their time and skills every year. According to the Department of Labor, about one in five citizens between the ages of 16 and 24 has volunteered in recent years.

While volunteering is not required of U.S. citizens, it is an important responsibility that many students fulfill in their spare time. More recently, the number of volunteers between 16 and 24 years old has fallen. Many essential programs suffer when the number of people willing to give time and money declines.

All citizens of the United States benefit from services provided by the government. Citizens can attend public schools, receive mail, and enjoy national parks. However, sometimes the government lacks funding or manpower to provide these services to their greatest extent.

Volunteers provide services that the government may not have the time or the resources to offer. A student may tutor a younger student after school. A volunteer group might maintain hiking trails in a national park.

In addition, volunteers fulfill services that the government is not required to provide. These include visiting the elderly or providing community theater. Volunteers are particularly necessary in times of war. The United Service Organizations (USO) support troops overseas with comforts such as entertainment, packages from home, and phone cards to call the United States.

1. **Make a List** To volunteer, make a list of activities that interest you and talents that you possess. Many people find it rewarding to share their talents and interests with others. For example, if you like to play soccer, you may be able to coach for a children's team.
2. **Seek Out Opportunities** Look for volunteer opportunities that are connected to your interests

and strengths. Ask your teacher or use the Internet to find organizations that fit your criteria.

3. **Make Contact** Write an e-mail to or call the contact person for your chosen organization. Some organizations require a résumé references, or a list of past experiences. Make sure you have these on hand.

## ▸▸ What do you think?

1. How does volunteering benefit all citizens? Why is volunteering an important civic responsibility?
2. The United States has seen a drop in the number of volunteers in the last few years. How could teenagers be persuaded to volunteer? Brainstorm two ways to get people interested in volunteering.
3. **You Try It** Locate some volunteer opportunities in your community. Make a list of the ones that interest you, and how you would get involved. Is it easy or difficult to get involved in these organizations? What are the steps that you must take? Are these causes ones to which you would give some of your time?

### GOVERNMENT ONLINE
**Citizenship Activity Pack**
For an activity to help you explore volunteering, go to **PearsonSchool.com/phgovt**

**19**

## Citizenship Activity Pack

**L1** **L2** If your students need extra support, use the Citizenship Activity Pack lesson *How to Volunteer.* It includes a lesson plan for you and worksheets to help students narrow their choices of volunteer opportunities. Scenario cards help groups of students brainstorm volunteer opportunities. Students may also access the Citizenship Activity Pack online for activities on How to Volunteer at **PearsonSchool.com/phgovt**.

---

**LESSON GOAL**
- Students will brainstorm personal interests and talents that might lead to volunteer opportunities.

# Teach

### READ

Have a volunteer read the introduction aloud. If students have Internet access, have them research USA Freedom Corps and Learn and Serve America to find out about student-volunteer experiences.

### SURVEY PRIOR EXPERIENCE

Make a list of organizations students have worked for. Was their experience rewarding? Why or why not? Invite students to tell about what they did and what they learned from their volunteer experience.

### MAKE A PLAN

Encourage students to create a step-by-step plan for finding a volunteer job. Offer the following chart as a sample that students might customize.

| |
|---|
| Brainstorm Interests: |
| Investigate Opportunities: |
| Narrow Prospects: |
| Follow Up: |

# Assess and Remediate

Collect and grade students' plans. You may also have them answer the What Do You Think questions.

---

## Answers

1. A strong answer will show an understanding that volunteers extend services provided by the government and promote the general welfare.
2. Point out to teenagers that volunteering rewards the volunteer. It adds value to a resumé, helps teenagers find a career, and brings satisfaction.
3. Student lists should reflect their personal interests and talents.

# What are the basic concepts of democracy?

# Get Started

## LESSON GOALS

Students will . . .

- identify and explain the five concepts of democracy by completing a chart.
- identify real-world examples of the five concepts by brainstorming and filling out a table.
- discuss the responsibilities and duties of citizenship.

## BEFORE CLASS

Assign the section, the graphic organizer in the text, and the Reading Comprehension Worksheet (Unit 1 All-in-One, p. 27) before class.

**L2 Differentiate** Reading Comprehension Worksheet (Unit 1 All-in-One, p. 28)

---

## SKILLS DEVELOPMENT

### NOTETAKING AND ACTIVE LISTENING

To practice notetaking and active listening in this section, use the Chapter 1 Section 3 Skills Worksheet (Unit 1 All-in-One, p. 33). You may teach the skill before the debate in this lesson. For L2 and L1 students, assign the adapted Skill Activity (Unit 1 All-in-One, p. 34).

---

SECTION **3**

# Basic **Concepts** of **Democracy**

## Guiding Question

**What are the basic concepts of democracy?** Use a concept web like the one below to take notes on the basic concepts of democracy.

## Political Dictionary

- majority rule
- compromise
- citizen
- free enterprise system

## Objectives

1. Understand the foundations of democracy.
2. Analyze the connections between democracy and the free enterprise system.

**Image Above:** Children gather to celebrate Flag Day in New York City.

**W**hat do you make of this assessment of democracy by British statesman James Bryce: "No government demands so much from the citizen as Democracy, and none gives so much back"? What does democratic government demand from you? What does it give you in return?

## Foundations

Democracy is not <u>inevitable.</u> It does not exist in the United States simply because Americans regard it as the best of all possible political systems. Rather, democracy exists in this country because the American people believe in its basic concepts. It will continue to exist only for as long as we, the people, continue to subscribe to and practice those concepts.

Sir Winston Churchill (1874–1965) once put the argument for democracy this way: "No one pretends that democracy is perfect or all-wise. Indeed, it has been said that democracy is the worst form of government except all those other forms that have been tried from time to time."

The American concept of democracy—what we believe democracy means—rests on these basic notions:

1. Recognition of the fundamental worth and dignity of every person;
2. Respect for the equality of all persons;
3. Faith in majority rule and an insistence upon minority rights;
4. Acceptance of the necessity of compromise; and
5. Insistence upon the widest possible degree of individual freedom.

Of course, these concepts can be worded in other ways. No matter what the wording, however, they form the very minimum with which anyone who professes to believe in democracy must agree.

**Worth of the Individual** Democracy is firmly based upon a belief in the fundamental importance of the individual. Each individual, no matter what his or her station in life, is a separate and distinct being.

---

# Focus on the Basics

**FACTS:** • Democracy is based on the concepts of individual worth, equality, majority rule with minority rights, compromise, and individual freedom. • Equality means all are entitled to equality of opportunity and equality before the law. • Individuals are free to do as they please as long as they do not violate the rights of others.

**CONCEPTS:** democratic principles, equality, majority rule, minority rights, freedom, citizenship, duties and responsibilities of citizens

**ENDURING UNDERSTANDINGS:** • Democracy depends on citizens' commitment and participation • Democratic governments work to balance the needs of society with individual rights. • Both democracy and free enterprise are based on individual freedom.

This concept of the dignity and worth of the individual is of overriding importance in democratic thought. At various times, of course, the welfare of one or a few individuals is <u>subordinated</u> to the interests of the many in a democracy. People can be forced to do certain things whether they want to or not. Examples range from paying taxes to registering for the draft to stopping at a stop sign.

When a democratic society forces people to pay a tax or obey traffic signals, it is serving the interests of the many. However, it is not simply serving the interests of the many who as a mass of people happen to outnumber the few. Rather, it is serving the many who, as individuals, together make up that society.

The distinction we are trying to make here between *an* individual and *all* individuals may be difficult to grasp. It is, however, critically important to a real understanding of the meaning of democracy.

**Equality of All Persons** Hand in hand with the belief in the worth of the individual, democracy stresses the equality of all individuals. It holds, with Jefferson, that "all men are created equal."

Certainly, democracy does not imply an equality of condition for all persons. Thus, it does not claim that all are born with the same mental or physical abilities. Nor does it hold

that all persons have a right to an equal share of worldly goods.

Rather, the democratic concept of equality means that every person is entitled to (1) equality of opportunity and (2) equality before the law. That is, the democratic concept of equality holds that no person should be held back for any such <u>arbitrary</u> reasons as those based on race, color, religion, or gender. It states that each person must be free to develop himself or herself as fully as he or she wishes to, and that each person should be treated as the equal of all other persons under the law.

We have come a great distance toward the goal of equality for all in this country. It is clear, however, that we are still a considerable distance from a genuine, universally recognized and respected equality for all of America's people.

**Majority Rule, Minority Rights** In a democracy, the will of the people and not the dictate of the ruling few determines public policy. But what is the popular will, and how is it determined? Some device must exist by which these crucial questions can be answered. The only satisfactory device democracy knows is that of **majority rule.** Democracy holds that a majority will be right more often than it will be wrong, and that the majority will also be right more often than any one person or small group will.

✔ **Checkpoint**
To what are citizens entitled under the democratic concept of equality?

**subordinate**
*v.* of lesser rank

**arbitrary**
*adj.* based on unsupported opinion, random choice

**inevitable**
*adj.* unavoidable, sure to happen

In *Brown v. Board of Education,* (1954) the Supreme Court ruled that segregation denied African Americans equality guaranteed by the Constitution and the democratic system. Arkansas fought the integration of its schools. Elizabeth Eckford (inset) was one of nine African Americans who enrolled at Central High School in Little Rock in 1957. Below, seven of the students known as the Little Rock Nine sit with Thurgood Marshall, who argued the case.

## Differentiated Resources

The following resources are located in the All-in-One, Unit 1, Chapter 1, Section 3:

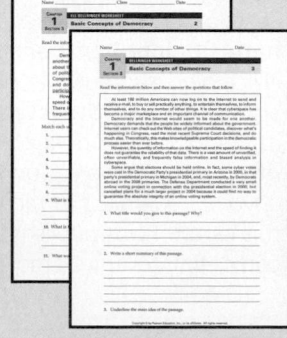

Distribute the Bellringer Worksheet (Unit 1 All-in-One, p. 29), which is a passage about the role of the Internet in democracy. Have students read the selection and answer the questions.

**L2** **ELL Differentiate** Have students complete the adapted Bellringer Worksheet (Unit 1 All-in-One, p. 30), which presents a simpler version of the passage and has students match vocabulary words and determine the main ideas of the text.

# Teach

To present this topic using online resources, use the lesson presentations at **PearsonSchool.com/phgovt.**

**COVER THE BASICS**

Tell students that today you will discuss the five basic concepts of democracy. You will return to their Bellringer answers later in the lesson. Then ask them to take out their Reading Comprehension Worksheets.

First, call on a volunteer to identify the five basic concepts of democracy. *(individual worth, equality, majority rule and minority rights, compromise, individual freedom)* Then have volunteers tell what each concept means to them. *(possible answers: **individual worth:** all people have value and deserve to be treated with dignity; **equality:** every individual is entitled to an equal chance to take advantage of life's opportunities and to the same treatment before the law as everyone else; **majority rule and minority rights:** decisions of the majority hold, but the majority must be willing to listen to the views of the minority; **compromise:** a process of give-and-take among conflicting views to come to a decision that is acceptable to most people; **individual freedom:** all individuals may do as they like as long as their actions do not violate the rights of others)*

Ask students the meaning of the term *free enterprise system.* Write this term on the board with student definitions. *(**free enterprise system:** an economic system characterized by private ownership of capital goods; investments made by private decision, not by government directive; and success or failure determined by competition in the marketplace)*

## Answers

**Checkpoint** All citizens are entitled to equality of opportunity and equality before the law.

## DISTRIBUTE CORE WORKSHEET

Distribute the Chapter 1 Section 3 Core Worksheet (Unit 1 All-in-One, p. 31). Direct students' attention to Part 1, which asks students to identify real-world situations from daily life, showing the five concepts of democracy in action. Then have students fill in the chart in Part 2, which has them consider differences between the duties and responsibilities of citizenship.

**L1 L2 Differentiate** For Part 1, use the Jigsaw strategy (p. T27) and have students work in groups of three to focus on one concept. Have the students jigsaw into a second group with students who reviewed each of the other concepts and have them review their ideas together. For Part 2, have students meet as one group to discuss duties and responsibilities of citizenship.

**L4 Differentiate** Have students work individually to find real-world situations from history for each concept of democracy. An historical example that reflects the concept of equality: the Civil Rights Act of 1964. An historical example that shows reality falling short of the ideal of equality: the Japanese-American internments during World War II.

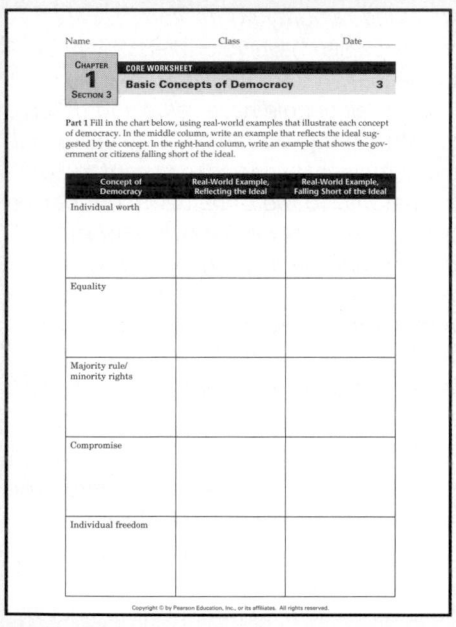

Democracy can be described as an experiment or a trial-and-error process designed to find satisfactory ways to order human relations. Democracy does not dictate that the majority will always arrive at the best decisions on public matters. In fact, the democratic process is not meant to come up with "right" or "best" answers. Rather, the democratic process is a search for *satisfactory* solutions to public problems.

Of course, in a democracy the majority's decisions will usually be more, rather than less, satisfactory. Democracy does admit the possibility of mistakes; there is the possibility that "wrong" or less satisfactory answers will sometimes be found. Democracy also recognizes that seldom is any solution to a public problem so satisfactory that it cannot be improved upon, and that circumstances can change over time. So, the process of experimentation, of seeking answers to public questions, is a never-ending one.

Certainly, a democracy cannot work without the principle of majority rule. Unchecked, however, a majority could destroy its opposition and, in the process, destroy democracy itself. Thus, democracy requires majority rule restrained by minority rights. The majority must always recognize the right of any minority to become, if it can by fair and lawful means, the majority. The majority must always be willing to listen to a minority's argument, to hear its objections, to bear its criticisms, and to welcome its suggestions.

**Necessity of Compromise** In a democracy, public decision making must be largely a matter of give-and-take among the various competing interests. It is a matter of compromise in order to find the position most acceptable to the largest number. **Compromise** is the process of blending and adjusting competing views and interests.

Compromise is an essential part of the democratic concept for two major reasons. First, remember that democracy puts the individual first and, at the same time, insists that each individual is the equal of all others. In a democratic society made up of many individuals and groups with many different opinions and interests, how can the people make public decisions except by compromise?

Second, few public questions have only two sides. Most can be answered in several ways. Take the apparently simple question of how a city should pay for the paving of a public street. Should it charge those who own property along the street? Or should the costs be paid from the city's general treasury? Or should the city and the adjacent property owners share the costs? What about those who will use the street but do not live in the city? Should they have to pay a toll?

Remember, compromise is a process, a way of achieving majority agreement. It is never an end in itself. Not all compromises are good, and not all are necessary.

**Individual Freedom** It should be clear by this point that democracy can thrive only in an atmosphere of individual freedom. However, democracy does not and cannot insist on complete freedom for the individual. Absolute freedom can exist only in a state of anarchy—the total absence of government. Anarchy can only lead, inevitably and quickly, to rule by the strong and ruthless.

Democracy does require that each individual must be as free to do as he or she pleases as far as the freedom of all will allow. Justice Oliver Wendell Holmes once had this to say about the relative nature of each individual's rights: "The right to swing my fist ends where the other man's nose begins."

▶▶ **Analyzing Cartoons** *Who do the chefs represent in this cartoon?*

# Political Cartoon Mini-Lesson

Display Transparency 1D, Equality, when you discuss the democratic concept of equality. This cartoon illustrates equal opportunity. Ask: **What is the setting of this cartoon?** *(a school civics class)* **Who is the woman?** *(teacher)* **To whom do the hands belong?** *(students)* **What is the significance of the colors of the hands?** *(The colors suggest that people of all races aspire to become president.)* **What is the significance of the jewelry?** *(The jewelry suggests gender—both boys and girls aspire to the presidency.)* **How does this cartoon reflect the democratic concept of equality?** *(The cartoon suggests equality of opportunity—in the United States, anyone, regardless of race or gender, can grow up to be President.)* Tell students that this cartoon was published when Senators Hillary Clinton and Barack Obama were competing for the Democratic nomination for President.

## Answers
**Analyzing Cartoons** competing views and interests

Drawing the line between the rights of one individual and those of another is not easy. Still, the drawing of that line is a continuous and vitally important function of democratic government. As John F. Kennedy put it: "The rights of every man are diminished when the rights of one man are threatened."

Striking the proper balance between freedom for the individual and the rights of society as a whole is similarly difficult—and vital. Abraham Lincoln described democracy's problem in these words:

**PRIMARY SOURCES**
Must a government, of necessity, be too *strong* for the liberties of its own people, or too *weak* to maintain its own existence?
—Message to Congress, July 4, 1861

Human beings desire both liberty and authority. Democratic government must work constantly to strike the proper balance between the two. The authority of government must be <u>adequate</u> to the needs of society. At the same time, that authority must never be allowed to become so great that it restricts the individual beyond what is absolutely necessary.

## Duties and Responsibilities of Citizenship

Over the centuries, any number of statesmen, philosophers, and others have told us that citizenship carries with it both duties and responsibilities. Theodore Roosevelt put that point this way in 1902: "The first requisite of a good citizen in our republic is that he should be able and willing to pull his weight."

In a democratic society, the *duties* of "a good citizen" all revolve around his or her commitment to obey the law—a point long accepted in this country. In his Farewell Address in 1796, George Washington put that obligation this way: "the very idea of the power and right of the People to establish Government presupposes the duty of every individual to obey the established Government."

The several *responsibilities* of "a good citizen" in a free society all come down to this: an abiding respect for each of the core beliefs on which democracy is based in this country. A **citizen** is one who holds both rights and responsibilities in a state. Look again at page 20 and then ask yourself this question: Do I understand and am I committed to honoring the basic concepts of American democracy?

## Democracy and the Free Enterprise System

The American commitment to freedom for the individual is deep-rooted, and it is as evident in the nation's economic system as it is in the political system. The American economic system is often called the **free enterprise system**. It is an economic system characterized by the private ownership of capital goods; investments made by private decision, not by government directive; and success or failure determined by competition in the marketplace. The free enterprise system is based on four fundamental factors: private ownership, individual <u>initiative</u>, profit, and competition.

✔ **Checkpoint**
Name two duties of every U.S. citizen.

**adequate**
*adj.* enough to meet the needs of a situation

**initiative**
*n.* enterprise, resourcefulness

## Duties and Responsibilities of Citizenship

| Duties | Responsibilities |
|---|---|
| • Serving on a **jury**<br>• Serving as a **witness** when called<br>• Attending **school**<br>• Paying **taxes**<br>• Registering for the **draft** (men only)<br>• **Obeying** local, State, and national **laws**<br>• Respecting the **rights of others** | • **Voting**<br>• **Volunteering**<br>• **Participating** in civic life<br>• **Understanding** the workings of **our government** |

▸ **Analyzing Charts** Many duties and responsibilities come with being a citizen. *Why might obeying the law be a duty rather than a responsibility?*

**REVIEW BELLRINGER ANSWERS**

Invite volunteers to share their answers to the Bellringer questions. (*Possible answers: 1. "Democracy and the Internet"; it is a simple statement of the basic idea. 2. With nearly 200 million Americans using it, the Internet holds great potential for keeping citizens informed about their government and for holding online elections. However, the reliability of information and integrity of results remain issues of concern. 3. "Democracy and the Internet would seem to be made for one another;" or "There is a vast amount of unverified, often unverifiable, and frequently false information and biased analysis in cyberspace."*)

**EXTEND THE DISCUSSION**

Use these questions to continue the discussion about the duties and responsibilities of citizenship:

1. Why might going to school be a duty instead of a responsibility?
2. Should volunteering be a duty rather than a responsibility?
3. What would be the benefits of making voting a duty?
4. What might happen if serving on a jury was a responsibility rather than a duty?

**EXTEND THE LESSON**

**L3** **Differentiate** Tell students that they will be submitting art for an exhibit. Students may work alone, with partners, or in small groups to create artwork about some aspect of the section, such as the meaning of democracy, the responsibilities and duties of citizenship, or the free enterprise system. Their work might contain relevant words from the section, as well as pictures and illustrations. Hold a gallery "opening" to display student art, and allow time for a question-and-answer session.

**L2** **Differentiate** Distribute and have students complete the Extend Activity (Unit 1 All-in-One, p. 35), "Volunteering to Improve Your Community."

# Debate

Ask: **Should the government support online elections?** Divide students into two groups and have them list arguments, based on the discussion, about the risks and benefits of holding online elections. Use the Debate strategy (p. T25) to organize the groups. Allow time for representatives from each group to debate the question.

## Answers

**Checkpoint** Possible answer: Every U.S. citizen must pay taxes and attend school to a certain age.

**Analyzing Charts** Possible answer: A duty is required of every citizen, while responsibilities are only strongly encouraged. Everyone has a duty to obey the law.

# Assess and Remediate

**L3** Collect the Core Worksheet and assess students' work.

**L3** Assign the Section 3 Assessment questions.

**L3** Section Quiz A (Unit 1 All-in-One, p. 36)

**L2** Section Quiz B (Unit 1 All-in-One, p. 37)

Have students complete the review activities in the digital lesson presentation and continue their work in the **Essential Questions Journal.**

## REMEDIATION

| If Your Students Have Trouble With | Strategies For Remediation |
|---|---|
| The five concepts of democracy (Questions 1, 2, 3, 4, 5) | Have students create and exchange cross-word puzzles that include clues about each concept of democracy. |
| The free enterprise system (Question 6) | Find real-world examples when the demand for a product dictated the price (tickets to a concert or sporting event). |

## Answers

**Checkpoint** private ownership, individual initiative, profit, and competition

---

✔ **Checkpoint**
What are the four factors of the free enterprise system?

**antitrust laws**
*n.* laws that regulate business practices in order to promote competition

**zoning ordinances**
*n.* laws that regulate the uses of property in certain areas

**How the System Works** The free enterprise system is often called capitalism. It is also known as the private enterprise system and as a market-based system. It does not rely on government to decide what items are to be produced, how much of any particular item should be produced, or how much any item is to sell for. Rather, those decisions are made in the marketplace. Millions of producers and consumers obey the unwritten law of supply and demand: When supplies of goods and services become plentiful, prices will tend to drop; when, on the other hand, supplies become scarce, prices will very likely rise.

Democracy and the free enterprise system are not the same thing. One is a political system, and the other is an economic system. However, both are firmly based on the concept of individual freedom. America's experience with both systems clearly suggests that the two reinforce one another in practice.

**Government and the Free Enterprise System** The basis of the American economic system is the free market. However, government does play a role in the American economy, and it always has. Government's participation in the economy serves a two-fold purpose: to protect the public and to preserve private enterprise.

Government's participation in the economy can be seen at every level in this country: national, State, and local. Here are but a few examples: Economic activities are regulated by government through antitrust laws, pure food and drug laws, antipollution standards, and city and county zoning ordinances and building codes.

The nation's economic life is promoted in a great number of public ways. The government grants money for transportation systems and the growing of particular food crops, builds roads and operates public schools, provides services such as the postal system and weather reports, and much more.

Thus, some activities that might be carried out privately are in fact conducted by government. Public education, local fire departments, and city bus systems are long-standing examples of the point.

How much should government participate, regulate, promote, police, and serve? Many heated debates in American politics center on that question, and we are often reminded of Abraham Lincoln's advice:

> **" PRIMARY SOURCES**
> **The legitimate object of government, is to do for a community of people, whatever they need to have done, but can not do, *at all,* or can not, *so well do,* for themselves—in their separate, and individual capacities.**
> —Abraham Lincoln

---

| **Essential Questions** **Journal** | To continue to build a response to the chapter Essential Question, go to your **Essential Questions Journal.** |
|---|---|

## SECTION 3 ASSESSMENT

**1. Guiding Question** Use your completed concept web to answer this question: What are the basic concepts of democracy?

**Key Terms and Comprehension**

**2. (a)** In what two ways does democracy require the equality of all persons? **(b)** What kind of equality is *not* guaranteed by democracy?

**3.** Why is **compromise** so important in a democracy?

**4.** What does it mean to be a good **citizen?**

**Critical Thinking**

**5. Predict Consequences (a)** What must a good citizen do in order to help preserve democracy? **(b)** What might be the consequences if citizens were not required to pay taxes? To serve on a jury?

**6. Draw Conclusions** How might the government react to a downturn in the economy?

**Quick Write**

**Quick Write Expository Writing: Create an Outline** Using the notes from the research you conducted in Section 2, create an outline to help you further organize your information. The outline should follow the chronological order you established.

---

## Assessment Answers

**1.** worth of the individual; equality of all persons; majority rule, minority rights; necessity of compromise; and individual freedom

**2. (a)** Citizens are guaranteed equality of opportunity and equality before the law. **(b)** Democracy does not guarantee an equality of condition or of worldly goods.

**3.** Democracy values individual rights, yet a democratic society includes many individuals with many opinions. Compromise is needed to blend and adjust competing views to find the position most acceptable to the majority.

**4.** Being a good citizen means fulfilling the duties and responsibilities of citizenship. Duties include paying taxes, obeying the law, and respecting the rights of others. Responsibilities include voting, volunteering, and participating in civic life.

**5. (a)** Democracy can exist only if citizens continue to practice democratic concepts. Citizens can do this by respecting the rights and equality of others, fulfilling their duties and responsibilities, accepting the will of the majority while respecting minority rights, and being willing to compromise. **(b)** If citizens were not required to pay taxes, the government would not have the money to provide essential services. If citizens did not serve on juries, the right to a fair trial by one's peers might not be possible for every accused person.

**6.** The government might take steps to stimulate the economy.

**QUICK WRITE** Students' outlines should follow the chronological order of their notes.

# Quick Study Guide

**GOVERNMENT** ONLINE
**On the Go**
To review anytime, anywhere, download these online resources at **PearsonSchool.com/phgovt**
Political Dictionary, Audio Review

CHAPTER **1**

**Guiding Question
Section 2** What are some forms of government in the world today?

**Guiding Question
Section 1** What is government and what is its purpose?

**CHAPTER 1
Essential Question**
Is government necessary?

**Guiding Question
Section 3** What are the basic concepts of democracy?

## Political Dictionary

government *p. 4*
public policies *p. 4*
legislative power *p. 5*
executive power *p. 5*
judicial power *p. 5*
constitution *p. 5*
dictatorship *p. 5*
democracy *p. 5*
state *p. 5*
sovereign *p. 7*
autocracy *p. 14*
oligarchy *p. 14*
unitary government *p. 14*
federal government *p. 16*
division of powers *p. 16*
confederation *p. 16*
presidential government *p. 17*
parliamentary government *p. 18*
majority rule *p. 21*
compromise *p. 22*
citizen *p. 23*
free enterprise system *p. 23*

**Elements of a Democratic Government**
- Worth of the Individual
- Equality of All Persons
- Individual Freedom
- Majority Rule, Minority Rights
- Necessity of Compromise

### Major Political Ideas

| Force Theory | Evolutionary Theory | Divine Right Theory | Social Contract Theory |
|---|---|---|---|
| One person or a small group took control of a population by force. | The state developed naturally out of the early family. | God created the state and gave those of royal birth the "divine right" to rule. | Hobbes: People agreed to give up as much freedom as needed to create a state that provided safety and well-being for all. |

# For More Information

To learn more about democracy, refer to these sources or assign them to students:

**L1** **Fandel, Jennifer.** *Dictatorship.* The Creative Company, 2007.

**L2** **Lindop, Edmund.** *Presidents Versus Congress: Conflict and Compromise.* Scholastic Library Publishing, 1994.

**L3** **Butler, Nicholas Murray.** *Why Should We Change Our Form of Government?* Girvin Press, 2007.

**L4** **Diamond, Larry.** *The Spirit of Democracy: The Struggle to Build Free Societies Throughout the World.* Times Books, 2008.

---

Have students download the digital resources available at Government on the Go for review and remediation.

## STUDY TIPS

**Essay Tests** When faced with an essay test, students should scan the test and note the number of questions and the point value of each. They should then budget their time accordingly. Before beginning to write, encourage students to read the question carefully and be sure to do what it asks. Key words to look for include *analyze, explain, identify, demonstrate, compare, contrast,* and *define.* Jotting down an outline can help students organize their thoughts and may get them some points if they run out of time. Stress that if the test is handwritten, neatness counts. They may find it preferable to draw a line through mistakes rather than erasing. This tends to be quicker and easier to read. If students are having trouble understanding the question, suggest they try to put it in their own words. When they've finished writing, have students proofread their work if at all possible, and make sure they have answered all the parts of each question.

## ASSESSMENT AT A GLANCE

### Tests and Quizzes
Section Assessments
Section Quizzes A and B, Unit 1 **All-in-One**
Chapter Assessment
Chapter Tests A and B, Unit 1 **All-in-One**
Document-Based Assessment
Progress Monitoring Online
Exam*View* Test Bank

### Performance Assessment
Essential Questions Journal
Debates, pp. 6, 16, 23
Assessment Rubrics, **All-in-One**

# Chapter Assessment

## COMPREHENSION AND CRITICAL THINKING

### SECTION 1

1. legislative, judicial, and executive powers

2. **(a)** Every state possesses population, territory, sovereignty, and government. **(b)** Under the force theory, a single person or a group takes control of a territory and its population by force. Government is created when the person or group declares authority to rule. **(c)** The social contract theory seems best for fostering democracy, because the authority to rule comes from the people.

3. **(a)** According to the Constitution, the six purposes of government are to form a more perfect union, establish justice, ensure domestic tranquility, provide for the common defense, promote the general welfare, secure the blessings of liberty. **(b)** Answers will vary. Sample response: provides a postal service, maintains roads, and provides aid during natural disasters

4. **(a)** The king represents a dictatorship. **(b)** The king is implying that he does not have any decision-making power because he does not have the right to vote. **(c)** This statement is misleading because under a dictatorship, the king makes all of the decisions. He doesn't have to vote.

### SECTION 2

5. **(a)** In a democracy, the government rules by the consent of the people. Decisions are made by the rule of the majority. **(b)** In a republic, the sovereign power is held by those who are eligible to vote, and the will of the people is carried out by representatives elected by voters. The people do not rule directly. **(c)** For those people, democracy can be defined only in terms of direct democracy.

6. **(a)** In an autocracy, the power to rule is held by one person. In an oligarchy, the power to rule is held by a small group of people. **(b)** You are more likely to find oligarchies today.

7. **(a)** In a presidential government, the president and members of Congress are chosen separately, and are independent of one another. The president holds powers that are not under the control of the legislature. **(b)** In a parliamentary government, the prime minister and the cabinet belong to the legislative branch. He or she is chosen by the legislature and is under its direct control. **(c)** The parliamentary system seems to give more power to the legislative branch.

---

# Chapter Assessment

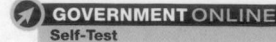 **GOVERNMENT** ONLINE
**Self-Test**
To test your understanding of key terms and main ideas, visit
PearsonSchool.com/phgovt

## Comprehension and Critical Thinking

### Section 1

1. What are the three basic powers exercised by government?

2. **(a)** What four characteristics does every state possess? **(b)** How does the force theory account for those four characteristics? **(c)** Which of those theories best explains the rise of democratic states? Why?

3. **(a)** What are the six purposes of government established by the Constitution? **(b)** Cite three ways in which the Federal Government promotes the general welfare that are not listed in the text.

4. **Analyze Political Cartoons (a)** What form of government does the king represent? **(b)** What is the king implying when he says that he doesn't get to vote either? **(c)** Is this a misleading statement? Why or why not?

"So what? — I don't get to vote *either*, you know!"

### Section 2

5. **(a)** Explain the fundamental ideas of democracy. **(b)** How is a republic different from a democracy? **(c)** Why do some people hold that the United States is more properly called a republic rather than a democracy?

6. **(a)** What is the difference between an autocracy and an oligarchy? **(b)** According to the text, which of these types of dictatorship are you more likely to find today?

7. **(a)** How is power distributed in a presidential government? **(b)** How is power distributed in a parliamentary government? **(c)** Which system seems to give the most power to the legislative branch?

### Section 3

8. **(a)** When looking at majority rule versus minority rights, why would some people argue that the United States is not a true democracy? **(b)** How are the rights of the individual protected in a true democracy? **(c)** How are they protected in the United States?

9. **(a)** How might the application of purely democratic ideas to a functioning government cause a problem for a large federal state? **(b)** How might it cause a problem for minority groups within that state?

10. Explain how the following duties and responsibilities of citizenship contribute to the good of all: **(a)** paying taxes, **(b)** voting, and **(c)** volunteering. **(d)** Which do you think is most important? Why?

### Writing About Government

11. Use your Quick Write activities to write an expository piece explaining democracy or dictatorship. Use your outline as a basis for your expository piece. See pp. S3–S5 in the Skills Handbook.

---

## Apply What You've Learned

12. **Essential Question Activity** You are the leaders of a group of formerly independent states now coming together to form a new country. The new country will be large in area, with a large population. Choose a form of government (federal, confederate, or unitary) that you think would best suit this situation.

    **(a)** Work out the details of your new government based on information from the chapter. Answer the following questions: Will the country run under a free enterprise system? Will it be a direct or representative democracy? What major functions will the government be required to perform?

    **(b)** Write an organizational plan for your government and present it to the class. Allow time for questions. Revise your plan according to issues your classmates point out.

13. **Essential Question Assessment** Use the work from the activity and the content of this chapter to help you write a paragraph that answers the Essential Question: **Is government necessary?** Then, as a class, discuss your responses. Discuss why or why not government is necessary.

**Essential Questions Journal** To respond to the chapter Essential Question, go to your **Essential Questions Journal.**

---

### SECTION 3

8. **(a)** Some people would say that the United States is not a true democracy because the rights and opinions of the minority are protected from possible abuses that could arise from majority rule. In other words, the majority can only rule as far as the minority's rights are not infringed. **(b)** The rights of the individual are protected by restricting individual freedoms. Individuals are free to do what they want as long as they don't infringe on the rights of other individuals. **(c)** In the United States, the rights of the individual are protected by various Constitutional amendments and Federal and State laws.

9. **(a)** In a pure democracy, the people would have direct control of the government. However, in a state with many people from different regions, it is impossible to have direct control. **(b)** If the majority ruled unrestricted, minorities would become unequal and their individual rights might be infringed upon.

10. **(a)** By paying taxes, citizens are helping fund schools, police forces, and other government-run programs. **(b)** When citizens vote, they are deciding who will represent

# Document-Based Assessment

## The Roots of Democracy

Its invention is usually attributed to ancient Greece, but democracy existed well before the Greeks coined the term around 2,500 years ago. However, the Greek philosophers wrote extensively on the subject. Some supported it, while others—like Plato—did not.

### Document 1

" Thus it is manifest that the best political community is formed by citizens of the middle class, and that those states are likely to be well-administered in which the middle class is large, and stronger if possible than both the other classes, or at any rate than either singly; for the addition of the middle class turns the scale, and prevents either of the extremes from being dominant. Great then is the good fortune of a state in which the citizens have a moderate and sufficient property; for where some possess much, and the others nothing, there may arise an extreme democracy, or a pure oligarchy; or a tyranny may grow out of either extreme—either out of the most rampant democracy, or out of an oligarchy; but it is not so likely to arise out of the middle constitutions and those akin to them. . . . The mean condition of states is clearly best, for no other is free from faction; and where the middle class is large, there are least likely to be factions and dissensions [disagreements].

—Discussion on the mean condition from Aristotle's *Politics*, Part XI

### Document 2

" How grandly does [democracy] trample all these fine notions of ours under her feet, never giving a thought to the pursuits which make a statesman, and promoting to honor any one who professes to be the people's friend. . . .

And when they [democratic principles] have emptied and swept clean the soul of him [the individual] who is now in their power and who is being initiated by them in great mysteries, the next thing is to bring back to their house insolence [ill-mannered behavior] and anarchy [lawlessness, chaos] and waste and impudence [disrespect] in bright array having garlands on their heads, and a great company with them, hymning their praises and calling them by sweet names; insolence they term breeding, and anarchy liberty, and waste magnificence, and impudence courage.

—Discussion about democracy from Plato's *Republic*, Book 8

---

**Use your knowledge of the concepts of democracy, other forms of government, and Documents 1 and 2 to answer Questions 1–3.**

1. According to Aristotle, what is the best condition for political stability?
   A. extreme democracy
   B. moderate democracy
   C. pure oligarchy
   D. tyranny

2. Based on the excerpt from Plato's *Republic*, what is Plato's attitude toward democracy? Cite two supporting details from the passage.

3. **Pull It Together** How might Aristotle address Plato's concerns? Write a paragraph from Aristotle's point of view.

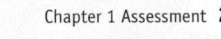

**GOVERNMENT** ONLINE
**Documents**
To find more primary sources on democracy, visit
**PearsonSchool.com/phgovt**

---

**DOCUMENT-BASED ASSESSMENT**

1. B

2. Plato sees democracy as the next step toward anarchy. He writes about democracy "trampling the notions" of the statesman. Once the ideas of democracy have emptied the soul of the citizen, they bring anarchy to his house.

3. Possible response: Aristotle might tell Plato that the people of the middle class are best at ruling because they are the most moderate. Democracy would not lead to anarchy. There would be fair laws that all would obey. Democracy would not lead to a new ruling elite "having garlands on their heads." Instead, the people would rule together, making decisions by sharing ideas.

**L2 Differentiate** Students use all the documents on the page to support their thesis.

**L3 Differentiate** Students include additional information available online at **PearsonSchool .com/phgovt.**

**L4 Differentiate** Students use materials from the textbook, the online information at **PearsonSchool .com/phgovt,** and do additional research to support their views.

**Go Online to PearsonSchool.com/phgovt** for a student rubric and extra documents.

---

them or what policies the government should make. They are telling the government how to act in the citizens' best interest. **(c)** By volunteering, citizens provide services that help others, such as distributing food or building houses. **(d)** Answers will vary.

### WRITING ABOUT GOVERNMENT

11. Students should explain the origins and basic ideas behind democracy or dictatorship. Their essays should cite details from the chapter and from their individual research.

### APPLY WHAT YOU'VE LEARNED

12. Students should use what they have learned to set up a basic governmental system for their state. Details should include the kind of government, the restrictions on individual freedoms, and the kind of economic system.

13. Students should take either side of the question "Is government necessary?" They should back up their opinions with facts from the text and with what they learned in the activity.

# Introduce the Chapter

## Essential Questions:

**UNIT 1**

What should be the goals of government?

**CHAPTER 2**

How does the Constitution reflect the times in which it was written?

**ACTIVATE PRIOR KNOWLEDGE**

Have students examine the image and quotation on these pages. Ask: **What do the image and quotation suggest about the origins of American government?** *(that the colonists had to fight to establish the American government)* In this chapter, students will learn how the American system of government came into being. Then tell students to begin to further explore American independence and the creation of the Constitution by completing the Chapter 2 Essential Question Warmup activity in their **Essential Questions Journal.** Discuss their responses as a class.

**BEFORE READING**

**L2** **ELL Differentiate** Chapter 2 Prereading and Vocabulary Worksheet (Unit 1 All-in-One, p. 56)

**SUCCESSNET STUDENT AND TEACHER CENTER**

Visit **PearsonSchool.com/phgovt** for download-able resources that allow students and teachers to connect with government "on the go."

**DIGITAL LESSON PRESENTATION**

The digital lesson presentation supports the print lesson with activities and summaries of key concepts.

## SKILLS DEVELOPMENT

**COMPARE VIEWPOINTS**

You may wish to teach comparing viewpoints as a distinct skill within Section 2 of this chapter. Use the Chapter 2 Skills Worksheet (Unit 1 All-in-One, p. 76) to help students learn how to compare viewpoints. The worksheet asks students to read two opposing statements about the taxation of the American colonists by the British government, decide how the viewpoints differ, and consider how the viewpoints were influenced by frames of reference. For L2 and L1 students, assign the adapted Skill Activity (Unit 1 All-in-One, p. 77).

**WebQuest online** The chapter WebQuest challenges students to answer the chapter Essential Question by asking about the origins of American government.

28

# Block Scheduling

**BLOCK 1:** Teach the Section 1 and 2 lessons. Choose either the debate in Lesson 2 or one of the Extend options, depending on your preferences and State standards. You may wish to use the alternate lesson for Lesson 2.

**BLOCK 2:** Teach the Section 3, 4, and 5 lessons, omitting one of the Extend options for Lesson 4.

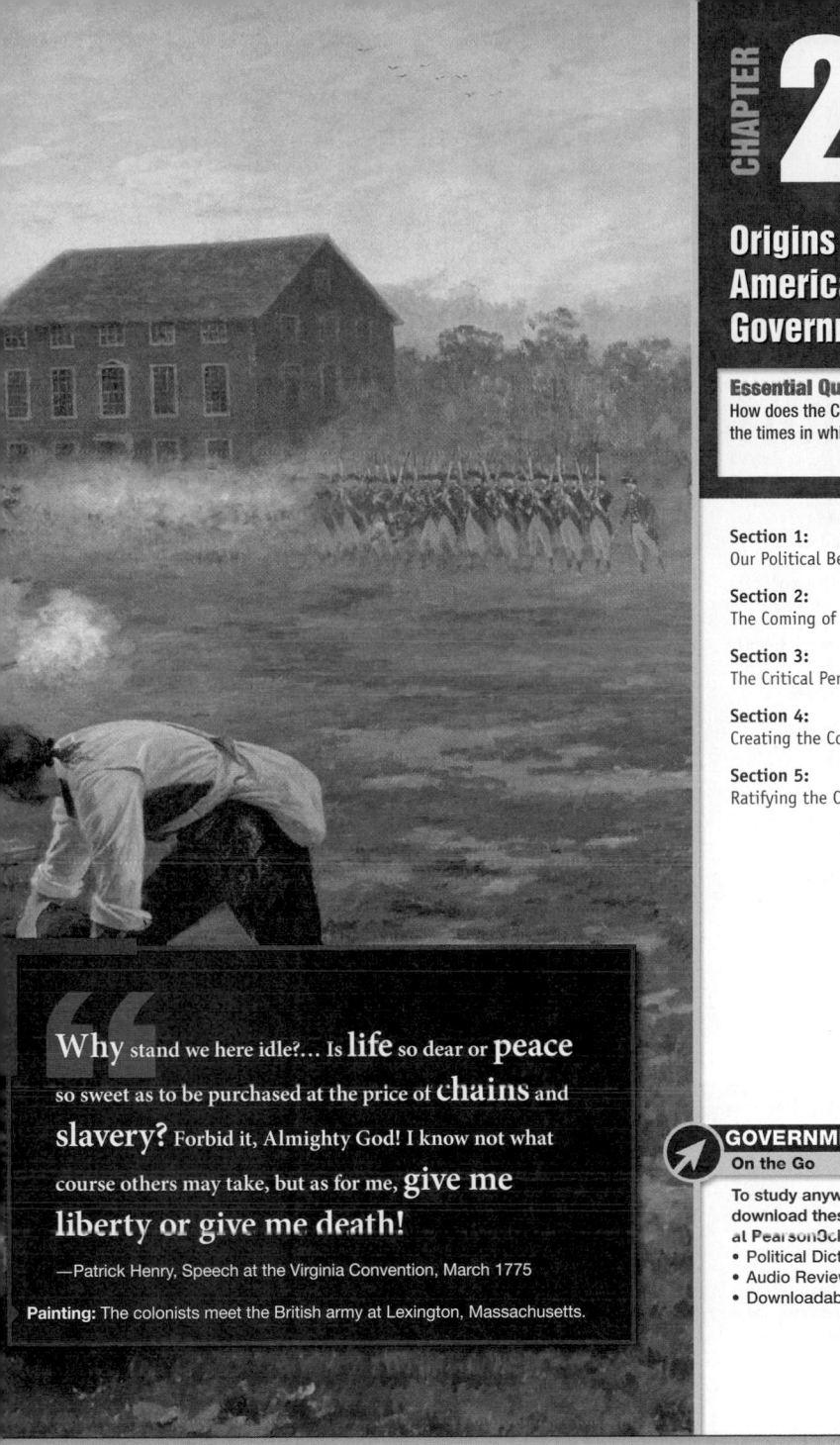

**Essential Question**
How does the Constitution reflect the times in which it was written?

> "Why stand we here idle?... Is life so dear or peace so sweet as to be purchased at the price of chains and slavery? Forbid it, Almighty God! I know not what course others may take, but as for me, give me liberty or give me death!

—Patrick Henry, Speech at the Virginia Convention, March 1775

**Painting:** The colonists meet the British army at Lexington, Massachusetts.

**GOVERNMENT ONLINE**
**On the Go**

To study anywhere, anytime, download these online resources at Pearson3chool.com/phgovt
• Political Dictionary
• Audio Review
• Downloadable Interactivities

## Lesson Goals

**SECTION 1**

Students will . . .

• examine early English concepts of government.
• analyze the influences of the Magna Carta, Petition of Right, and English Bill of Rights on American ideas about government and freedom.
• compare the structure of royal colony governments to our National Government.

**SECTION 2**

Students will . . .

• analyze British policies and colonial reactions as causes and effects.
• examine events leading up to the Declaration of Independence through political cartoons and a firsthand account from that era.
• identify, define, and analyze propaganda in political cartoons.

**SECTION 3**

Students will . . .

• identify and analyze weaknesses of the Articles of Confederation by completing a worksheet.
• analyze the issue of land claims by examining a map.

**SECTION 4**

Students will . . .

• use worksheets to analyze the different plans and compromises in creating the Constitution.
• use primary and secondary sources to evaluate the major compromises made at the Constitutional Convention.

**SECTION 5**

Students will . . .

• analyze the positions of the Federalists and the Anti-Federalists, using primary sources.
• use primary sources to evaluate arguments in favor of and opposed to a bill of rights.

## Pressed for Time

To cover this chapter quickly, review the Bellringer flowchart in Section 1, and explain the rights found in each document. Then have students complete the Section 2 Reading Comprehension Worksheet, identifying the events that led to the Revolution. Explain that the colonists revolted when the rights under the English documents were taken away. Point out these rights in the Declaration of Independence. Have students answer the questions that appear after the Declaration of Independence. Review the Articles of Confederation, and have students fill out the Section 3 Reading Comprehension Worksheet. Review the New Jersey and Virginia plans and the compromises. Have students complete the Section 4 Extend options, creating a yearbook for the Framers and discussing the Enlightenment thinkers. Finally, have them complete the Section 5 Bellringer Worksheet and Extend option, comparing the Federalist and Anti-Federalist Papers.

**DIFFERENTIATED INSTRUCTION KEY**

Look for these symbols to help you adjust steps in each lesson to meet your students' needs.

**L1** Special Needs

**L2** Basic

　　**ELL** English Language Learners
　　**LPR** Less Proficient Readers

**L3** All Students

**L4** Advanced Students

## What ideas and traditions influenced government in the English colonies?

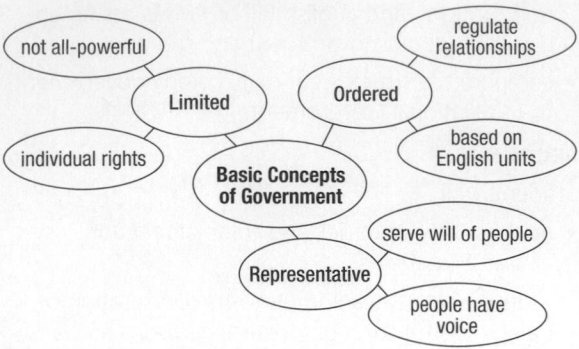

- not all-powerful
- Limited
- individual rights
- Ordered
- regulate relationships
- based on English units
- **Basic Concepts of Government**
- Representative
- serve will of people
- people have voice

# Get Started

## LESSON GOALS

Students will . . .

- examine early English concepts of government.
- analyze the influences of the Magna Carta, Petition of Right, and English Bill of Rights on American ideas about government and freedom.
- compare the structure of royal colony governments to our National Government.

## BEFORE CLASS

Assign the section, the graphic organizer in the text, and the Reading Comprehension Worksheet (Unit 1 All-in-One, p. 61) before class.

**L2** **Differentiate** Reading Comprehension Worksheet (Unit 1 All-in-One, p. 62)

# SKILLS DEVELOPMENT

## DRAW INFERENCES AND CONCLUSIONS

To help students learn to draw inferences and conclusions, have them turn to the Skills Handbook, p. S19, and use the steps, as they evaluate the importance of the landmark documents in their own lives and answer interpretive questions, in Parts 1 and 2 of the Core Worksheet. The steps are:

- summarize information;
- study the facts;
- apply other facts or prior knowledge;
- decide if the information suggests an unstated fact or conclusion.

## SECTION 1

# Our **Political Beginnings**

### Guiding Question

**What ideas and traditions influenced government in the English colonies?** Use a concept web like the one below to take notes on the ideas that shaped American colonists' concepts of government.

- Limited
- Ordered
- **Basic Concepts of Government**
- Representative

### Political Dictionary

- limited government
- representative government
- Magna Carta
- due process
- Petition of Right
- English Bill of Rights
- charter
- bicameral
- proprietary
- unicameral

### Objectives

1. Identify the three concepts of government that influenced the American colonies.
2. Explain the significance of three landmark English documents.
3. Describe the three types of colonies that the English established in the American colonies.

**Image Above:** King John signs the Magna Carta, limiting his own power.

The American system of government did not suddenly spring into being with the signing of the Declaration of Independence in 1776. Nor was it created by the Framers of the Constitution in 1787.

The beginnings of what was to become the United States can be found in the mid-sixteenth century when explorers, traders, and settlers first made their way to North America. The French, Dutch, Spanish, Swedes, and others came to explore and settle what would become this nation—and to dominate those Native Americans who were here for centuries before the arrival of the first Europeans. It was the English, however, who came in the largest numbers. And it was the English who soon controlled the 13 colonies that stretched for some 1,300 miles along the Atlantic seaboard.

## Basic Concepts of Government

The earliest English settlers brought with them knowledge of a political system—of established laws, customs, practices, and institutions—that had been developing in England for centuries.

Some aspects of that governing system had come to England from other times and places. Thus, the concept of the rule of law that influenced English political ideas has roots in the early civilizations of Africa and Asia.[1] More directly, the ancient Romans occupied much of England from A.D. 43 to 410. They left behind a legacy of law, religion, and custom. From that rich political history, the English colonists brought to North America three basic notions that were to loom large in the shaping of government in the United States.

**Ordered Government** The English colonists saw the need for an orderly regulation of their relationships with one another—that is, a need for government. They created local governments, based on those they had known in England.

1 For example, King Hammurabi of Babylonia developed a system of laws known as Hammurabi's Code around 1750 B.C. Its 282 legal rules covered real estate, trade, and business transactions, as well as criminal law. The code distinguished between major and minor offenses, established the state as the authority to enforce the law, and tried to guarantee social justice. Because of the Babylonians' close contact with the Hebrews, many of their laws became part of Hebrew law and thus later a part of the Old Testament of the Bible—for example, "An eye for an eye." The English were quite familiar with and devoutly attracted to this Biblical concept of the rule of law.

# Focus on the Basics

Here is the information that your students need to learn in this section.

**FACTS:** • Early English settlers brought with them the tradition of ordered, limited, and representative government. • The Magna Carta, the Petition of Right, and the English Bill of Rights established basic concepts of government and rights of individuals. • The English colonies were of three types: royal, proprietary, and charter.

**CONCEPTS:** limited government, popular sovereignty, representative government

**ENDURING UNDERSTANDINGS:** • Early colonists in America benefited from English traditions of government. • The colonies served as a school for learning about government.

Many of the offices and units of government they established are with us yet today: the offices of sheriff and justice of the peace, the grand jury, counties, and several others.

**Limited Government** The colonists also brought with them the idea that government is restricted in what it may do, and every individual has certain rights that government cannot take away. This concept is called **limited government,** and it was deeply rooted in English belief and practice by the time the first English ships set sail for America. It had been planted in England centuries earlier, and had been developing there for nearly 400 years before Jamestown was settled in 1607.

**Representative Government** The early English settlers also carried another important concept across the Atlantic: **representative government.** This idea that government should serve the will of the people had also been developing in England for several centuries. With it had come a growing insistence that the people should have a voice in deciding what government should and should not do. As with the concept of limited government, the idea of "government of, by, and for the people" flourished in America.

## Landmark English Documents

These basic notions of ordered government, limited government, and representative government can be traced to several <u>landmark</u> documents in English history.

**The Magna Carta** A group of determined barons forced King John to sign the **Magna Carta**—the Great Charter—at Runnymede in 1215. Weary of John's military campaigns and heavy taxes, the barons who prompted the Magna Carta were seeking protection against heavy-handed and <u>arbitrary</u> acts by the king.

The Magna Carta included guarantees of such fundamental rights as trial by jury and **due process** of law (protection against the arbitrary taking of life, liberty, or property). Those protections against the absolute power of the king were originally intended for the

privileged classes only. Over time, however, they became the rights of all English people and were incorporated into other documents. The Magna Carta established the critical idea that the monarchy's power was not absolute.

**The Petition of Right** The Magna Carta was respected by some monarchs and ignored by others for 400 years. Over that period, England's Parliament slowly grew in influence. In 1628, when Charles I asked Parliament for more money in taxes, Parliament refused until he agreed to sign the **Petition of Right.**

The Petition of Right limited the king's power in several ways. Most importantly, it demanded that the king no longer imprison or otherwise punish any person but by the lawful judgment of his peers or by the law of the land. The document also insisted that the king may not impose martial law, or military rule, in times of peace, or require homeowners to shelter the king's troops without their consent. The Petition declared that no man should be

> **PRIMARY SOURCE**
> compelled to make or yield any gift, loan, benevolence, tax, or such like charge, without common consent by act of parliament.

—Petition of Right

Commemorative coin from the reign of Charles I

The Petition challenged the idea of the divine right of kings, declaring that even a monarch must obey the law of the land.

**The English Bill of Rights** In 1689, after years of revolt and turmoil, Parliament offered the crown to William and Mary of Orange. The events surrounding their ascent to the throne are known as the Glorious Revolution. To prevent abuse of power by William and Mary and all future monarchs, Parliament, in 1689, drew up a list of provisions to which William and Mary had to agree.

This document, the **English Bill of Rights,** prohibited a standing army in peacetime, except with the consent of Parliament,

**landmark**
*adj.* historical, pivotal, highly significant

**arbitrary**
*adj.* not restrained or limited in the exercise of power

✔ **Checkpoint**
What is representative government?

---

# Differentiated Resources

The following resources are located in the All-in-One, Unit 1, Chapter 2, Section 1:

- **L2** Prereading and Vocabulary Worksheet (p. 56)
- **L3** Reading Comprehension Worksheet (p. 61)
- **L2** Reading Comprehension Worksheet (p. 62)
- **L3** Core Worksheet (p. 64)
- **L3** Quiz A (p. 66)
- **L2** Quiz B (p. 67)

---

Display Transparency 2A, Three Basic Concepts of English Government. Write on the board: **Copy this flowchart in your notebook. Then write a brief definition of each concept in the boxes.**

# Teach

To present this topic using online resources, use the lesson presentations at **PearsonSchool.com/phgovt.**

### INTRODUCE THE TOPIC

Tell students that today they will discuss the influence of English traditions and ideas on colonial governments. Have students share their definitions from the Bellringer in a brainstorm session. Write their ideas on the board, and help students reach a consensus about each definition. *(Ordered government: Government regulates affairs between people and maintains order and predictability. Limited government: Government is restricted in what it may do, and each individual has rights that the government cannot take away. Representative government: Government should serve the will of the people, and people should have a voice in what the government can and cannot do.)* Help students connect these concepts to their own experience. Ask: **What kind of government do you live under? What rights do you have that the government cannot take away? How does the government help you in your everyday life?**

### DISCUSS LANDMARK DOCUMENTS

Point out that the three basic concepts of English government can be traced to three documents. Ask: **What are these three landmark documents?** *(the Magna Carta, the Petition of Right, and the English Bill of Rights)* Discuss the reforms established under each document. Students can take out their Reading Comprehension Worksheet (Unit 1 All-in-One, p. 61) at this time and use their answers to Part 1 to start the discussion. Help students connect the three basic concepts of government with the documents. *(Magna Carta: limited government, ordered government; Petition of Right and English Bill of Rights: limited, ordered, and representative government)*

### DISTRIBUTE CORE WORKSHEET

Distribute the Chapter 2 Section 1 Core Worksheet (Unit 1 All-in-One, p. 64). Explain that students will assess the importance of the landmark documents in their own lives. Ask a student to read the introductory paragraph in Part 1 of the worksheet aloud.

---

## Answers

**Checkpoint** Government should serve the will of the people and people should have a voice in deciding what government should and should not do.

Display Transparency 2B, Foundation of American Rights. Call on volunteers to define each right. *(trial by jury: right to trial by a jury of peers; due process: prohibits unfair, arbitrary [random] actions by government; private property: prohibits taking property except for legitimate public purpose and only for a fair price; no cruel punishment: punishment must bear a reasonable relationship to the seriousness of the crime and should be humane; no excessive bail or fines: bail or fines must bear a reasonable relationship to the seriousness of the crime; right to bear arms: right of each State to maintain a militia for its own protection; right to petition: right to join with others in public meetings, political parties, interest groups, and other associations to discuss public affairs and influence public policy; no unreasonable searches and seizures: police cannot search, seize evidence, or arrest people without a warrant or probable cause; freedom of speech and of the press: right to speak, publish, and express views; freedom of religion: right to hold personal religious ideas and practices and also the separation of church and state)*

**L1 L2 Differentiate** Pair less proficient students with more proficient students for Part 2.

### REVIEW WORKSHEET AND SURVEY OPINIONS

Survey students' opinions about the importance of each right. Have them support their opinions.

**L1 L2 Differentiate** Ask students to look at the list of rights on the Core Worksheet. Have them choose between one and three rights that they consider most important and write a sentence explaining their reason. Write each of the rights on the board or on separate pieces of paper that can be posted around the room. Have students write their names under the rights that they chose. You will be able to see clearly which rights the class considers most important and then call on students to explain their answers.

**L2 ELL Differentiate** Have students use the list of rights on the Core Worksheet to create quizzes that they exchange with classmates.

Tell students to go to the Audio Tour for a guided audio tour of the foundations of American rights.

---

## Answers

**Foundations of American Rights** Possible answer: With sufficient public support, a petition could pressure a monarch to change a behavior viewed by the people as an abuse of power.

**Checkpoint** prohibited standing army in peacetime, suspension of laws, and taxes without consent of Parliament; banned excessive bail or fines and cruel punishment; guaranteed right to free elections, to petition, to bear arms, to trial by jury, and to due process

---

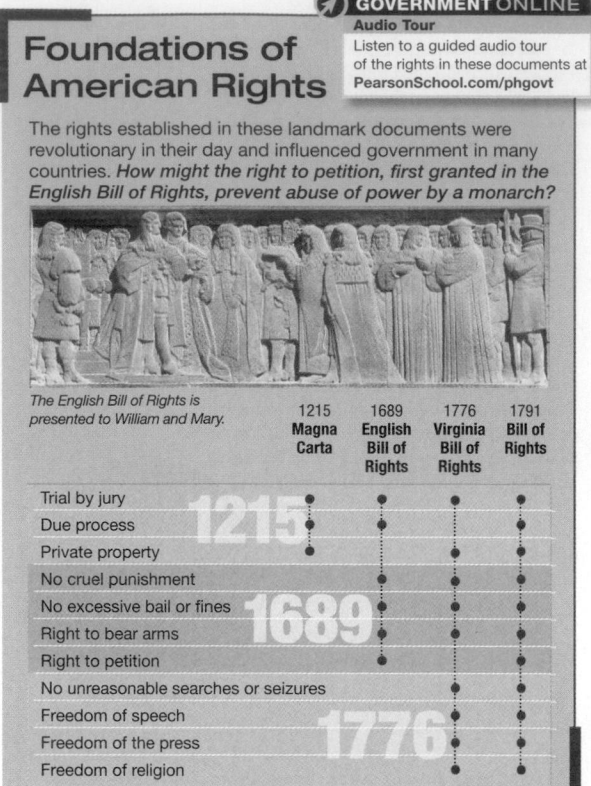

# Foundations of American Rights

The rights established in these landmark documents were revolutionary in their day and influenced government in many countries. *How might the right to petition, first granted in the English Bill of Rights, prevent abuse of power by a monarch?*

The English Bill of Rights is presented to William and Mary.

| | 1215 Magna Carta | 1689 English Bill of Rights | 1776 Virginia Bill of Rights | 1791 Bill of Rights |
|---|---|---|---|---|
| Trial by jury | ● | ● | ● | ● |
| Due process | | ● | ● | ● |
| Private property | | | ● | ● |
| No cruel punishment | | ● | ● | ● |
| No excessive bail or fines | | ● | ● | ● |
| Right to bear arms | | ● | ● | ● |
| Right to petition | | ● | ● | ● |
| No unreasonable searches or seizures | | | ● | ● |
| Freedom of speech | | | ● | ● |
| Freedom of the press | | | ● | ● |
| Freedom of religion | | | ● | ● |

✔ **Checkpoint**
What were the limitations set by the English Bill of Rights?

**venture**
*n.* an undertaking involving risk

**levy**
*v.* to impose, to collect by legal authority

and required that all parliamentary elections be free. In addition, the document declared

> **PRIMARY SOURCE**
>
> that the pretended power of suspending the laws, or the execution of laws, by regal authority, without consent of Parliament is illegal . . .
>
> that **levying** money for or to the use of the Crown . . . without grant of Parliament . . . is illegal . . .
>
> that it is the right of the subjects to petition the king . . . and that prosecutions for such petitioning are illegal . . .
>
> —English Bill of Rights

The English Bill of Rights also included such guarantees as the right to a fair trial, as well as freedom from excessive bail and from cruel and unusual punishment.

Our nation has built upon, changed, and added to those ideas and institutions that settlers brought here from England. Still, much in American government and politics today bears the stamp of those early English ideas. Surely, this is not so strange when you recall that the colonial period of American history lasted for some 170 years and that the United States has existed as an independent nation for only a slightly longer period.

## The Thirteen Colonies

England's colonies in North America have been described as "13 schools of government." The colonies were the settings in which Americans first began to learn the difficult art of government.[2]

The 13 colonies were established, separately, over a span of some 125 years. During that long period, outlying trading posts and isolated farm settlements developed into organized communities. The first colony, Virginia, was founded with the first permanent English settlement in North America at Jamestown in 1607.[3] Georgia was the last to be formed, with the settlement of Savannah in 1733.

Each of the colonies was born out of a particular set of circumstances. Virginia was originally organized as a commercial **venture**. Its first colonists were employees of the Virginia Company of London (also called the London Company), a private trading corporation. Massachusetts was first settled by

---

2 The English and other Europeans brought their own notions of government, but that is not to say that they introduced the idea of government to the Americas. Several Native American societies had developed systems of government. Some Native American political organizations were very complex. For example, five Native American tribes in what is now New York State—the Seneca, Cayuga, Oneida, Onondaga, and Mohawk—formed a confederation known as the Iroquois League. The League was originally created to end conflicts among the tribes. It proved so successful as a form of government that it lasted for some 200 years.

3 St. Augustine, Florida, is the oldest continuously populated European settlement in what is now the United States. St. Augustine was founded by Pedro Menéndez de Aviles in 1565 to establish Spanish authority in the region.

---

# Background

**EARLY COLONIAL GOVERNMENTS** The earliest English settlers in America recognized the need to establish orderly societies under the rule of law. Before the *Mayflower* landed in 1620, the Pilgrims signed the Mayflower Compact, an agreement to enact laws and abide by them for the general good of the colony. The government of Plymouth Colony was later based on this document. In 1639, the Puritans in Connecticut adopted the Fundamental Orders of Connecticut, the first written constitution in the American colonies. The plan of government set out in the Fundamental Orders included a representative legislature and governor elected by male landowners. These founding documents reflected the concepts of ordered, limited, and representative government the colonists brought with them from England.

people who came to North America in search of greater personal and religious freedom. King George granted Georgia to 21 trustees, who governed the colony.

But the differences among the colonies are of little importance. Of much greater significance is the fact that all of them were shaped by their English origins. The many similarities among all 13 colonies far outweighed their differences.

Each colony was established on the basis of a **charter,** a written grant of authority from the king. This grant gave colonists or companies a grant of land and some governing rights, while the Crown retained a certain amount of power over a colony. Over time, these instruments of government led to the development of three different types of colonies: royal, proprietary, and charter.

**Royal Colonies** The royal colonies were subject to the direct control of the Crown. On the eve of the American Revolution in 1775, there were eight: New Hampshire, Massachusetts, New York, New Jersey, Virginia, North Carolina, South Carolina, and Georgia. The Virginia colony did not enjoy the quick success its sponsors had promised. In addition, the colony's government was evolving into one of popular rule. The king disapproved of the local government's methods, as well as their attempt to grow tobacco. So, in 1624, the king revoked the London Company's charter, and Virginia became the first of the royal colonies. Later, as the charters of other colonies were canceled or withdrawn for a variety of reasons, they became royal colonies.

A pattern of government gradually emerged for each of the royal colonies. The king named a governor to serve as the colony's chief executive. A council, also named by the king, served as an advisory body to the royal governor. Later, the governor's council became both the upper house of the colonial legislature and the colony's

highest court. The lower house of a **bicameral** (two-house) legislature was elected by those property owners qualified to vote.[4] It owed much of its influence to the fact that it shared with the governor and his council the power of the purse—the power to tax and spend. The governor, advised by the council, appointed judges for the colony's courts.

The laws passed by the legislature had to be approved by the governor and the Crown. Royal governors often ruled with a stern hand, following instructions from London. Much of the resentment that finally flared into revolution was fanned by their actions.

**The Proprietary Colonies** By 1775, there were three **proprietary** colonies: Maryland,

---

[4] The Virginia legislature held its first meeting in Jamestown on July 30, 1619, and was the first representative body to meet in the North American English colonies. It was made up of burgesses—that is, representatives—elected from each settlement (each borough) in the colony. Virginia called the lower house of its colonial legislature the House of Burgesses; South Carolina, the House of Commons; Massachusetts, the House of Representatives.

---

## The Thirteen Colonies, 1775

▶▶ **Analyzing Maps** Despite the differing government systems within the colonies, they were all influenced by their English roots. *How many royal colonies were left at this time? How were royal colonies and charter colonies different?*

---

**L4 Differentiate** Ask: **What would happen if we didn't have these rights?** Have partners or small groups work together to act out a scenario in which one of the basic rights does not exist. Assign one of the following scenarios: (1) A student is stopped for speeding, and protection against cruel punishment and excessive bail or fines does not exist. (2) A student's family home is in the middle of a spot planned for a new highway, and the right to private property does not exist. (3) A student has been unfairly accused of destroying parking meters, and the rights to trial by jury and due process do not exist. Alternatively, students could create a scenario of their own choosing.

**REVIEW FACTS**

Ask students to turn to the "Structure of the Royal Colonies" organization chart in Part 2 of the Reading Comprehension Worksheet (Unit 1 All-in-One, p. 61). Re-create the flowchart on the board. Call on volunteers to fill in the information.

**L2 Differentiate** If students have a weak background in American history, pause and have them study the map of the colonies in the text.

**L4 Differentiate** Have partners create a compare-contrast chart, showing similarities and differences between the royal colony governments and our National Government today. *(similarities: bicameral legislature and distinct executive and legislative branches; differences: today separate judicial and legislative branches and no king)*

**EXTEND THE LESSON**

**L3** Provide copies of the Fundamental Orders of Connecticut, the first constitution in the American colonies. Assign a section to each pair of students to summarize the key points in their own words.

**L3 L4** Ask small groups to debate the following idea: Had Britain allowed other colonies the same freedoms and self-government as Connecticut and Rhode Island enjoyed, the Revolutionary War might never have occurred.

**L4** Have students talk about why Britain did not allow other colonies to govern themselves.

---

# Background

**JOHN LOCKE** The ideas of English philosopher John Locke were so radical that he could not publish his *Treatises on Government* until 1690, ten years after its completion. Locke believed that all people are born with natural rights, including life, liberty, and property. People establish governments to protect these rights. If the government fails in this duty, the people have a right to change the government. This idea challenged the divine right of kings, and was used to justify the Glorious Revolution. Locke's ideas of natural rights, government by and for the people, and religious toleration greatly influenced the Framers of the U.S. Constitution.

This information also appears on the Extend Worksheet for Section 4, along with information about other influential philosophers covered in this chapter.

---

## Answers

**Analyzing Maps** 8; A royal colony was subject to direct control of the monarch, who appointed the governor. The governor of a charter colony was elected by the white, male property owners in the colony. Charter colonies were largely self-governing.

# Assess and Remediate

**L3** Collect the Core Worksheets and assess the students' class participation, using the Rubric for Assessing a Graph, Chart, or Table (Unit 1 All-in-One, p. 217).

**L3** Assign the Section 1 Assessment questions.

**L3** Section Quiz A (All-in-One, p. 66)

**L2** Section Quiz B (All-in-One, p. 67)

Have students complete the review activities in the digital lesson presentation and continue their work in the **Essential Questions Journal.**

## REMEDIATION

| If Your Students Have Trouble With | Strategies For Remediation |
|---|---|
| The rights and protections in the three landmark documents (Questions 3, 5) | Create a chart on the board with a column for each document. Have students work together and write the rights and protections on note cards and then put the note cards in the correct columns. |
| The three kinds of colonies (Questions 4, 6) | Have pairs create concept webs with each kind of colony in the center. Each pair should write the characteristics of each colony in the outlying circles. |

## Answers

**Checkpoint** Proprietary colonies were organized by, and the governor was appointed by, a proprietor to whom the king had granted land. Charter colonies were self-governing, and the governors were elected.

---

✔**Checkpoint**
What is the difference between a proprietary colony and a charter colony?

**haven**
*n.* a place of safety

Pennsylvania, and Delaware. These colonies were organized by a proprietor, a person to whom the king had made a grant of land. By charter, that land could be settled and governed much as the proprietor chose. In 1632, the king granted Maryland to Lord Baltimore, which was intended as a <u>haven</u> for Catholics. In 1681, Pennsylvania was granted to William Penn. In 1682, Penn also acquired Delaware. **5**

The governments of these three colonies were much like those in the royal colonies. The governor, however, was appointed by the proprietor. In Maryland and Delaware, the legislatures were bicameral. In Pennsylvania, the legislature was a **unicameral** body. It consisted of only one house. The Frame of Government, a constitution that William Penn drew up for that colony in 1682, was, for its time, exceedingly democratic. As in the royal colonies, appeals of decisions in the proprietary colonies could be carried to the king in London.

**The Charter Colonies** The Massachusetts Bay Colony was established as the first charter colony in 1629. Its charter was later

---

**5** New York, New Jersey, North Carolina, South Carolina, and Georgia also began as proprietary colonies. Each later became a royal colony.

---

revoked, and Massachusetts became a royal colony in 1691.

Connecticut and Rhode Island were charter colonies founded by religious dissidents from Massachusetts. Connecticut was founded in 1633, and granted a charter in 1662. Rhode Island was founded in 1636, and granted a charter in 1663. Both colonies were largely self-governing.

The governors of Connecticut and Rhode Island were elected each year by the white, male property owners in each colony. Although the king's approval was required before the governor could take office, it was not often asked. Laws made by their bicameral legislatures were not subject to the governor's veto, nor was the Crown's approval needed. Judges in the charter colonies were appointed by the legislature, but appeals could be taken from the colonial courts to the king.

The Connecticut and Rhode Island charters were so liberal for their time that, after independence, they were kept with only minor changes as State constitutions until 1818 and 1843, respectively. In fact, many historians say that if Britain had allowed the other colonies the same freedoms and self-government found in the charter colonies, the Revolution might never have occurred.

---

**Essential Questions Journal** To continue to build a response to the chapter Essential Question, go to your **Essential Questions Journal.**

# SECTION 1 ASSESSMENT

1. **Guiding Question** Use your completed concept web to answer this question: What ideas and traditions influenced government in the English colonies?

### Key Terms and Comprehension

2. Define the concept of **representative government.**

3. Explain why the barons forced King John to sign the **Magna Carta.**

4. **(a)** What is a **bicameral** legislature? **(b)** How was the lower house of the legislature chosen in the royal colonies?

### Critical Thinking

5. **Make Comparisons** What principles do the Magna Carta, the Petition of Right, and the English Bill of Rights have in common?

6. **Predict Consequences** The English Crown gave Connecticut and Rhode Island many freedoms not enjoyed by other colonies. Do you agree with the historians who say that the Revolution may have never happened if all colonies enjoyed the same freedoms? Why or why not?

### Quick Write

**Narrative Writing: Choose a Colony** Choose one of the 13 colonies and write questions about its founding, its original government, and how it changed throughout the Revolutionary period. You will later research answers for these questions and write a narrative nonfiction piece. For example, if you choose Connecticut, you might ask: What was Connecticut's reaction to the English government's treatment of the colonies?

---

# Assessment Answers

1. ordered government; limited government; representative government; trial by jury; due process; private property; no cruel punishment; no excessive bail; right to bear arms; right to petition; no martial law in peacetime; no requirement to shelter troops; no levying money without consent

2. Government serves the will of the people, and the people have a voice in determining what their government can and cannot do.

3. The barons wanted to protect themselves from heavy-handed and arbitrary acts by the king. The document guaranteed trial by jury and due process of law.

4. **(a)** a legislature made up of two houses **(b)** elected by property owners qualified to vote

5. limited government, trial by jury, due process of law

6. Students should back up their responses with evidence from the text. Possible response: Yes, I agree. Connecticut and Rhode Island essentially governed themselves, while the governments of the other colonies were more

restrictive. If the other colonies had been given representation and the ability to make their own laws, then perhaps they would not have objected to remaining a part of Great Britain.

**QUICK WRITE** A strong assignment will include in-depth questions that go beyond the scope of the text. These questions should lead to good research, and a well-planned narrative of the colony's story.

# ISSUES OF OUR TIME

## Transitions to Democracy

### ▶▶ Track the Issue

The battle against oppressive government has been fought around the globe for centuries. Whether symbolic or violent, it is citizen action that more often than not has brought change.

**1776**

**Declaration of Independence** is signed, marking the start of the American Revolution against British tyranny.

**1804**

**Following a successful slave revolt,** Haiti is the first Latin American country to declare independence from colonial rule.

**1917**

**The Russian Revolution** ends the harsh, centuries-long tsarist rule.

**1989**

**Tiananmen Square** protestors call for economic and political reform in China, but the protests are forcibly subdued by the communist government.

**2009**

**Iranian voters angrily dispute** presidential election results, weakening the legitimacy of the ruling theocratic regime.

Myanmar's junta chief, Senior General Than Shwe ▼

### ▶▶ Perspectives

**Since the sudden overthrow** of the government in 1962, Burma, also known as the Union of Myanmar, has been under military control. The nation has since been frequently on the verge of revolution as citizens have risen up in protest against the regime. In 1990, the government held its first multi-party elections. The opposition party won by a landslide, but the junta—the military faction in power—refused to accept the results and did not relinquish control. Continued unrest has led the government to promise to transition to a more democratic government depending on the results of upcoming parliamentary elections.

"Preparations are being made to be ready in every aspect for a gentle transition to democracy and market oriented economic systems. Failure to make a systemic step-by-step transition from one system to another may endanger the nation and the people. During the transition to an unfamiliar system, countries with greater experience usually interfere and take advantage for their own interest. For this reason, it is an absolute necessity to avoid relying on external powers."

**—Senior General Than Shwe, Myanmar's junta chief, March 2010**

"The tone in [General Shwe's] speech strongly suggests that the junta will control every step in the process and ensure that political affiliations, especially the opposition, do not manage to muster up enough support from the international community to derail its plans of entrenching itself in the new order for a long time to come."

**—Altafur Rahman, Executive Director, Human Security Alliance, March 2010**

### ▶▶ Connect to Your World

1. **Predict Consequences (a)** Considering its election history, what do you think will be the outcome of the elections in Burma? **(b)** Would the presence of international monitors at the polls ensure fair and legitimate results? **(c)** Why is legitimacy important?

2. **Draw Conclusions** Is it possible to change government by casting a vote?

**⊘ GOVERNMENT ONLINE**
In the News
For updates about transitions to democracy, visit
PearsonSchool.com/phgovt

35

## Background

**EUROPE'S CONSTITUTIONAL BATTLE** French president Jacques Chirac believed that the constitution proposed for the European Union would bind Europe into a political and economic powerhouse—positioning the EU to compete with the United States. But in 2005, French voters soundly defeated the proposal. Dutch voters soon followed suit. With France's growing unemployment, voters feared that closer ties would increase competition among EU nations, resulting in French jobs going to cheaper eastern European workers. Dutch voters objected to the EU's expanding power over their lives and believed the pact would open their country to a flood of immigrants. "No" voters in both nations pointed to loss of their country's generous social benefits and erosion of their national identities. Like the United States, the EU will have to address the competing interests of its component states in order to unify under one constitution.

---

# What events and ideas led to American independence?

| The Albany Plan | The Stamp Act | New Restrictive Laws |
|---|---|---|
| • congress of colonial delegates<br>• powers: raise military, make war/peace and regulate trade with Native Americans, tax, collect customs<br>• plan rejected by colonies and Crown | • tax stamp on documents and newspapers<br>• Stamp Act Congress<br>• Declaration of Rights and Grievances<br>• Repealed by Parliament | • boycott<br>• Boston Massacre<br>• Boston Tea Party |

| First Continental Congress | Second Continental Congress | Declaration of Independence |
|---|---|---|
| • prompted by Intolerable Acts<br>• Declaration of Rights to king<br>• urged boycotts | • first national government<br>• created continental army<br>• raised military, borrowed, created money system, made treaties | • Jefferson main author<br>• equality<br>• unalienable rights<br>• consent of governed |

## COMPARE VIEWPOINTS

To practice comparing viewpoints in this section, use the Chapter 2 Skills Worksheet (Unit 1 All-in-One, p. 76). You may teach the skill explicitly either before or after filling out the Bellringer chart. For L2 and L1 students, assign the adapted Skill Activity (Unit 1 All-in-One, p. 77).

---

SECTION **2**

# The **Coming of Independence**

## Guiding Question

**What events and ideas led to American independence?** Use a flowchart like the one below to record major events that led to American independence.

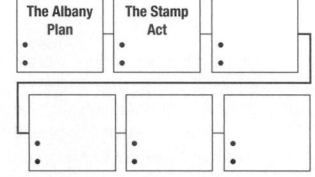

| The Albany Plan | The Stamp Act | |
|---|---|---|
| •<br>•<br>• | •<br>•<br>• | •<br>• |

| | | |
|---|---|---|
| •<br>• | •<br>• | • |

## Political Dictionary

- confederation
- Albany Plan of Union
- delegate
- popular sovereignty

## Objectives

1. Explain how Britain's colonial policies contributed to the growth of self-government in the colonies.
2. Identify the major steps that led to growing feelings of colonial unity.
3. Compare the First and the Second Continental Congresses.
4. Analyze the ideas in the Declaration of Independence.
5. Summarize the common features of the first State constitutions.

**Image Above:** Benjamin Franklin was a leading member of the Second Continental Congress.

"**W**e must all hang together, or assuredly we shall all hang separately." Benjamin Franklin is said to have spoken these words on July 4, 1776, as he and the other members of the Second Continental Congress approved the Declaration of Independence. Those who heard him may have chuckled. But they also may have felt a shiver, for Franklin's humor carried a deadly serious message.

In this section, you will follow the events that led to the momentous decision to break with Great Britain.[7] You will also consider the new State governments that were established with the coming of independence.

## Britain's Colonial Policies

The 13 colonies were separately controlled under the king, largely through the Privy Council and the Board of Trade in London. Parliament took little part in the management of the colonies. Although it did become interested in matters of trade, it often left administrative matters to the Crown.[8]

Over the century and a half that followed the first settlement at Jamestown, the colonies developed within that framework of royal control. In theory, they were governed from London. But London was more than 3,000 miles away, and it took nearly two months to sail that distance. The colonists became used to a large measure of self-government.

Each colonial legislature began to assume broad lawmaking powers. Many found the power of the purse to be very effective. They often bent a royal governor to their will by not voting the money for his salary until he came to terms with them. As one member of New Jersey's assembly put it: "Let us keep the dogges poore, and we'll make them do as we please."

By the mid-1700s, the relationship between Britain and the colonies had become, in fact if not in form, federal. This meant that the central government

---

[7] England became Great Britain by the Act of Union with Scotland in 1707.

[8] Much of British political history can be told in terms of the centuries-long struggle for supremacy between the monarch and Parliament. That conflict was largely settled by England's Glorious Revolution of 1688, but it did continue through the American colonial period and into the nineteenth century. However, Parliament paid little attention to the American colonies until very late in the colonial period.

---

# Focus on the Basics

**FACTS:** • Britain became more involved in trying to govern the colonies in the 1760s. • Delegates joined the First Continental Congress to plan opposition to British policy. • The Second Continental Congress proclaimed independence and served as the first United States government. • After the Declaration of Independence, most of the 13 States adopted written constitutions, which later influenced the U.S. Constitution.

**CONCEPTS:** limited government, popular sovereignty, civil rights and liberties, constitutional government

**ENDURING UNDERSTANDINGS:** • More restrictive British policies ignited resentment in the colonies and led to the American Revolution. • Principles expounded in early State constitutions influenced the development of our current system of government.

in London was responsible for colonial defense and for foreign affairs. It also provided a uniform system of money and credit and a common market for colonial trade. Beyond that, the colonies were allowed a fairly wide amount of self-rule. Little was taken from them in direct taxes to pay for the central government. The few regulations set by Parliament, mostly about trade, were largely ignored.

This was soon to change. Shortly after George III came to the throne in 1760, Britain began to deal more firmly with its colonies. Restrictive trading acts were expanded and enforced. New taxes were imposed, mostly to support British troops in North America.

Many colonists took strong exception to those policies. They objected to taxes imposed on them from afar. That arrangement, they claimed, was "taxation without representation." They saw little need for the costly presence of British troops on North American soil, since the French had been defeated and their power broken in the French and Indian War (1754–1763). Yet, the colonists still considered themselves British subjects loyal to the Crown.

The king's ministers were poorly informed and stubborn. They pushed ahead with their policies, despite the resentments they stirred in America. Within a few years, the colonists faced a fateful choice: submit or revolt.

## Growing Colonial Unity

A decision to revolt was not one to be taken lightly—or alone. The colonies would need to learn to work together if they wanted to succeed. Indeed, long before the 1770s, several attempts had been made to promote cooperation among the colonies.

**Early Attempts** In 1643, the Massachusetts Bay, Plymouth, New Haven, and Connecticut settlements formed the New England Confederation, a "league of friendship" for defense against Native American tribes. A **confederation** is a joining of several groups for a common purpose. As the danger passed and frictions among the settlements grew, the confederation lost importance and finally dissolved in 1684.

In 1696, William Penn offered an elaborate plan for intercolonial cooperation, largely in trade, defense, and criminal matters. It received little attention and was very quickly forgotten.

**The Albany Plan** In 1754, the British Board of Trade called a meeting of seven of the northern colonies at Albany. The main purpose of the meeting was to discuss the problems of colonial trade and the danger of attacks by the French and their Native American allies. Here, Benjamin Franklin offered what came to be known as the **Albany Plan of Union.**

In his plan, Franklin proposed the creation of an annual congress of **delegates** (representatives) from each of the 13 colonies. That body would have the power to raise military and naval forces, make war and peace with the Native Americans, regulate trade with them, tax, and collect customs <u>duties</u>.

✔ **Checkpoint**
How did Britain's dealings with the colonies change? When did they change?

<u>duty</u>
*n.* a tax on imports

① 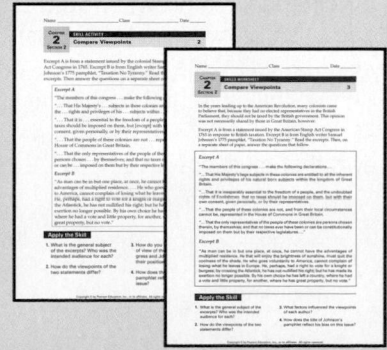 ②

▶▶ **Analyzing Political Cartoons** (1) A colonial cartoonist mocks British Lord William on stilts fishing for popularity in the Atlantic after the Stamp Act disaster. (2) A British cartoon depicts the colonists, forcing tea down the throat of a tarred-and-feathered tax collector. Both Britain and the colonies had their own opinions about the taxes. *How does the British cartoon depict the colonists? How does this differ from the colonial cartoon?*

## Differentiated Resources

The following resources are located in the All-in-One, Unit 1, Chapter 2, Section 2:

**L3** Reading Comprehension Worksheet (p. 68)
**L2** Reading Comprehension Worksheet (p. 70)
**L3** Core Worksheets A and B (pp. 72, 74)
**L3** Skills Worksheet (p. 76)
**L2** Skill Activity (p. 77)
**L2** Extend Activities (pp. 78, 79)
**L3** Quiz A (p. 80)
**L2** Quiz B (p. 81)

# Get Started

## LESSON GOALS
Students will . . .

- analyze British policies and colonial reactions as causes and effects.
- examine events leading up to the Declaration of Independence through political cartoons and a firsthand account from that era.
- identify, define, and analyze propaganda in political cartoons.

## BEFORE CLASS
Assign the section, the graphic organizer in the text, and the Reading Comprehension Worksheet (Unit 1 All-in-One, p. 68) before class.

**L2** **Differentiate** Reading Comprehension Worksheet (Unit 1 All-in-One, p. 70)

## BELLRINGER
Display Transparency 2C, The Road to Revolution. Write on the board: **In your notebook, use a chart like this to identify each event leading to the Revolutionary War as a British or Colonial action or reaction. Use the Cause-Effect Chains from your Reading Comprehension Worksheet and the timeline in the text to help you.**

# Teach

To present this topic using online resources, use the lesson presentations at **PearsonSchool.com/phgovt.**

## INTRODUCE THE TOPIC
Tell students that today they will discuss the events that led to war and independence. Ask students to help fill out the Bellringer chart.

| British Actions/Reactions | Colonial Actions/Reactions |
| --- | --- |
| • British troops stay in America | • Outrage, anger, defiance |
| • Taxes on Colonies to pay for troops | • Stamp Act Congress |
| • Stamp Act | • Boston Tea Party |
| • Boston Massacre | • Mob violence |
| • Intolerable Acts | • First Continental Congress |
| • Battles of Lexington and Concord | • Declaration of Rights |
| • Refusal to back down | • Battles of Lexington and Concord |
| • Stricter measures | • Second Continental Congress |
| | • Declaration of Independence |
| | • State Constitutions |

## Answers

**Checkpoint** Shortly after George III became king in 1760, Britain began imposing restrictive trading acts and new taxes.

**Analyzing Political Cartoons** As a mob of bullies; each side makes the other side look foolish.

Point out that each action and reaction had momentous effects. Ask: **What was the effect of the Stamp Act and other English taxes on the colonies?** *(colonists: outraged, sent delegates to Stamp Act Congress, organized boycotts; British: refused to back down, enacted further restrictions; Both: tension mounted)* **Why did the British adopt these taxes?** *(They needed money to support British troops in America.)* **Why did the colonists oppose taxes for these troops?** *(They believed that British troops were unnecessary, and that "taxation without representation" was unfair.)* **Why did the colonists react so strongly to this tax?** *(The colonists had enjoyed a long history of self-government in America; these new taxes, levied by a distant Parliament that did not represent them, shocked and dismayed them.)* Discuss the causes and effects of each item on the chart. You may want to review students' cause-effect chains in the Reading Comprehension Worksheet (Unit 1 All-in-One, p. 68) at this time.

**L1 L2 Differentiate** Review the timeline in the textbook. Ask: **What events does the timeline show?** *(the events leading up to the War for Independence)* **What happened in 1773?** *(The Tea Act was passed, sparking the Boston Tea Party.)* **What happened in 1775?** *(The Battles of Lexington and Concord started the Revolutionary War.)* You might want to compare and contrast timelines and cause-effect chains. *(A timeline shows events in chronological order; a cause-effect chain shows the relationship of one event to another. A timeline is useful for visualizing and remembering a series of events; a cause-effect chart is helpful for understanding the impact of each event within a series and its influence on outcomes.)*

**L4 Differentiate** Point out that by the end of the costly French and Indian War, Britain was in the midst of financial crisis, while the colonies were prospering. As a result, Britain passed a series of acts that led to the Revolutionary War. Invite students to consider both sides of the growing crisis. Have students research Britain's financial woes as well as the taxes and other acts that Britain passed to ease this emergency at home (for example, Sugar Act, Stamp Act, Quartering Act, Declaratory Act, Townshend Acts, Tea Act, Intolerable Acts). Then have a roundtable discussion about this question: **Was Britain justified in imposing taxes on the colonies?**

After students discuss this question, have them create a journal entry about their findings. Ask them whether their understanding of Britain's viewpoint changed during this investigation.

## Answers

**Interpreting Timelines** Colonists organized their own governments, and colonies moved toward unity. New taxes sparked protest and later armed conflict, resulting in the Declaration of Independence.

# The Road to Independence

**The New World**

**1607** Jamestown, Virginia, the first successful English settlement, is founded.

**1620** The Pilgrims sign the Mayflower Compact.

**1669** John Locke contributes to the constitution for the Carolina colony.

**The Colonies Unite**

**1754** The Albany Congress proposes that the colonies unite.

JOIN, or DIE.

**1765** The Stamp Act is passed.

**1770** Five colonists are killed by the British at the Boston Massacre.

▶▶ **Interpreting Timelines** English colonists brought with them the ideas of the Enlightenment and limited government. In time, these ideas began to shape the ideals of American government and the actions of the colonists. *How did early events contribute to the signing of the Declaration of Independence?*

**repeal**
*v.* to cancel

**boycott**
*n.* a refusal to buy or sell certain goods

Franklin's plan was ahead of its time. It was agreed to by the representatives attending the Albany meeting, but it was turned down by the colonies and by the Crown.

**The Stamp Act Congress** Britain's harsh tax and trade policies fanned resentment in the colonies. Parliament had passed a number of new laws, among them the Stamp Act of 1765. That law required the use of tax stamps on all legal documents, on certain business agreements, and on newspapers.

The new taxes were widely denounced, in part because the rates were perceived as severe, but largely because they amounted to "taxation without representation." In October of 1765, nine colonies—all except Georgia, New Hampshire, North Carolina, and Virginia—sent delegates to a meeting in New York, the Stamp Act Congress. There, they prepared a strong protest, called the Declaration of Rights and Grievances, against the new British policies and sent it to the king. The Stamp Act Congress marked the first

time a significant number of the colonies had joined to oppose the British government.

Parliament repealed the Stamp Act, but frictions still mounted. New laws were passed and new policies made to tie the colonies more closely to London. Colonists showed their resentment and anger by completely evading the laws. Mob violence erupted at several ports, and many colonists supported a boycott of English goods. On March 5, 1770, British troops in Boston fired on a jeering crowd, killing five, in what came to be known as the Boston Massacre.

Organized resistance was carried on through Committees of Correspondence, which had grown out of a group formed by political leader Samuel Adams in Boston in 1772. Those committees soon spread throughout the colonies, providing a network for cooperation and the exchange of information among the patriots.

Protests multiplied. The Boston Tea Party took place on December 16, 1773. A group of men, disguised as Native Americans, boarded

# Debate

Divide the class into patriots and loyalists. Have them debate this question from their assigned point of view: **Should we declare independence from Britain?** Use the quotation below from loyalist clergyman Charles Inglis to start the debate.

"Suppose we were to revolt from Great-Britain, declare ourselves Independent, and set up a Republic of our own—what would be the consequence? — I stand aghast at the prospect — my blood runs chill when I think of the calamities, the complicated evils that must ensue . . ."

**—Charles Inglis**
*The True Interest of America Impartially Stated* (1776)

**GOVERNMENT** ONLINE
**Audio Tour**
Listen to a guided audio tour of the road to independence at
**PearsonSchool.com/phgovt**

## War Begins

**1773** The Tea Act is passed. Colonists respond with the Boston Tea Party.

**1775** The battles of Lexington and Concord spark the Revolution.

## Independence

**1776** The Declaration of Independence is signed.

three tea ships in Boston Harbor. They broke open the chests and dumped the ship's cargo into the sea to protest British control of the tea trade.

### First Continental Congress

In the spring of 1774, Parliament passed yet another set of laws, this time to punish the colonists for the troubles in Boston and elsewhere. These new laws, denounced in America as the Intolerable Acts, prompted widespread calls for a meeting of the colonies.

Delegates from every colony except Georgia met in Philadelphia on September 5, 1774. Many of the <u>ablest</u> men of the day were there: Samuel Adams and John Adams of Massachusetts; Roger Sherman of Connecticut; Stephen Hopkins of Rhode Island; John Dickinson and Joseph Galloway of Pennsylvania; John Jay and Philip Livingston of New York; George Washington, Richard Henry Lee, and Patrick Henry of Virginia; and John Rutledge of South Carolina.

For nearly two months, the members of that First Continental Congress discussed the worsening situation and debated plans for action. They sent a Declaration of Rights,

protesting Britain's colonial policies, to King George III. The delegates urged the colonies to refuse all trade with England until the hated taxes and trade regulations were repealed. The delegates also called for the creation of local committees to enforce that boycott.

The meeting adjourned on October 26, 1774, with a call for a second congress to be convened the following May. Over the next several months, all 13 colonial legislatures gave their support to the actions of the First Continental Congress.

### Second Continental Congress

During the fall and winter of 1774–1775, the British government continued to refuse to compromise, let alone reverse, its colonial policies. It reacted to the Declaration of Rights as it had to other expressions of colonial discontent—with even stricter and more repressive measures.

The Second Continental Congress met in Philadelphia on May 10, 1775. By then, the Revolution had begun. The "shot heard 'round the world" had been fired. The battles of Lexington and Concord had been fought three weeks earlier, on April 19.

✓ **Checkpoint**
What did the First Continental Congress accomplish?

**ablest**
*adj.* the most talented, capable, competent, skillful

# Teacher-to-Teacher Network

**ALTERNATE LESSON PLAN** Revolutionary War-era propaganda was instrumental in uniting the colonies and for winning foreign support. Analyzing historical materials from institutions such as the Library of Congress or the National Archives can help students understand the role propaganda played before and during the Revolution. By learning about propaganda during the time period covered by this chapter, students can develop critical awareness in dealing with propaganda in their own lives.

To see this lesson plan, go to

**Teacher Center**
at PearsonSchool.com/phgovt

**DISTRIBUTE CORE WORKSHEET A**

Distribute the Chapter 2 Section 2 Core Worksheet A (Unit 1 All-in-One, p. 72). Explain that students will now examine the people and events of the Revolutionary War era through the prism of political cartoons. Cartoons were important tools in the propaganda war, used to sway public opinion, strengthen unity, and promote both the colonial and British causes. By studying the cartoons closely, students will appreciate what a potent weapon propaganda can be. Ask a student to read the directions and questions on the worksheet.

Tell students to go to the Audio Tour for a guided audio tour of the Road to Independence timeline.

**Government** online
*All print resources are available on the Teacher's Resource Library CD-ROM and online at PearsonSchool.com/phgovt.*

## Answers

**Checkpoint** It unified colonial response to British policies by organizing a boycott of trade, calling for local committees to enforce the boycott, and calling for a second congress.

## DISCUSS THE IMPACT OF PROPAGANDA

Point out that political cartoons are a form of propaganda and that both the patriots and the British used this tool to promote their own agenda. Call on volunteers to define *propaganda*. (*Propaganda is a form of persuasion that appeals to emotions in order to convince people about the truth of a particular idea or point of view.*) Ask: **What are some kinds of propaganda?** (*advertisements, editorials, political speeches and writing, testimonials, other persuasive writing*) **How are political cartoons different from other forms of propaganda?** (*Political cartoons use visual humor and visual exaggeration as persuasive devices; cartoons seldom use reason or evidence to bolster opinions or point of view.*) **How are political cartoons similar to other forms of propaganda?** (*Like all propaganda, political cartoons promote a point of view and use techniques such as exaggeration and emotional appeals.*)

Students can work with partners or individually to answer the questions for each cartoon on the worksheet. They can also answer the same questions for the cartoons that appear in Chapter 2, Section 2 of the textbook.

**L1 L2 Differentiate** Divide the class into three groups and assign each group one political cartoon. Have the groups complete the questions for their cartoons. Allow time for groups to share their findings with the class.

**L4 Differentiate** Ask students to write a brief persuasive argument in favor of the point of view presented in one of the cartoons they studied. They should use logic and evidence along with persuasive techniques to support their opinions. Students' written argument should get across the same idea as the cartoon.

### DISTRIBUTE CORE WORKSHEET B

Have a student read the article about the Boston Massacre in Core Worksheet B. Then call on volunteers to answer the questions.

**L4 Differentiate** Have students investigate the trial of Captain Preston and President John Adams's defense of the British soldier.

**L1 L2 ELL Differentiate** Preview difficult vocabulary from the article to support comprehension: *circumstances* (situation, condition); *outrage* (wrongdoing, crime); *enormous* (huge); *slaughter* (killing); *issued* (came out from); *dispersed* (went away, disappeared).

---

## Answers

**Checkpoint** to proclaim the existence of a new nation

---

**The Delegates** Each of the 13 colonies sent representatives to the Congress. Most of those who had attended the First Continental Congress were again present. Most notable among the newcomers were Benjamin Franklin of Pennsylvania and John Hancock of Massachusetts.

Hancock was chosen president of the Congress.[9] Almost at once, a continental army was created, and George Washington was appointed its commander-in-chief. Thomas Jefferson then took Washington's place in the Virginia delegation.

**Our First National Government** The Second Continental Congress became, by force of circumstance, the nation's first national government. However, it rested on no constitutional base. It was condemned by the British as an unlawful assembly and a den of traitors. But it was supported by the force of public opinion and practical necessity.

The Second Continental Congress served as the first government of the United States for five fateful years, from the formal adoption of the Declaration of Independence in July 1776 until the Articles of Confederation went into effect on March 1, 1781. During that time, the Second Continental Congress fought a war, raised armies and a navy, borrowed funds, bought supplies, created a money system, made treaties with foreign powers, and did other things that any government would have had to do in those circumstances.

The unicameral Congress exercised both legislative and executive powers. In legislative matters, each colony—later, State—had one vote. Executive functions were handled by committees of delegates.

## The Declaration of Independence

Slightly more than a year after the Revolution began, Richard Henry Lee of Virginia proposed to the Congress:

---

9  Peyton Randolph, who had also served as president of the First Continental Congress, was originally chosen to the office. He resigned on May 24, however, because the Virginia House of Burgesses, of which he was the speaker, had been called into session. Hancock was then elected to succeed him.

---

**PRIMARY SOURCE**
Resolved, That these United Colonies are, and of right ought to be, free and independent States, that they are absolved from all allegiance to the British Crown, and that all political connection between them and the State of Great Britain is, and ought to be, totally dissolved.

—Resolution of June 7, 1776

Congress named a committee of five—Benjamin Franklin, John Adams, Roger Sherman, Robert Livingston, and Thomas Jefferson—to prepare a proclamation of independence. Their momentous product, the Declaration of Independence, was very largely the work of Jefferson.

On July 2, the final break came. The delegates agreed to Lee's resolution—but only after spirited debate, for many of the delegates had serious doubts about the wisdom of a complete separation from England. Two days later, on July 4, 1776, they adopted the Declaration of Independence, proclaiming the existence of the new nation.

At its heart, the Declaration proclaims:

**PRIMARY SOURCE**
We hold these truths to be self-evident, that all men are created equal, that they are endowed by their Creator with certain unalienable Rights, that among these are Life, Liberty and the pursuit of Happiness. That to secure these rights, Governments are instituted among Men, deriving their just powers from the consent of the governed; That whenever any Form of Government becomes destructive of these ends it is the Right of the People to alter or to abolish it, and to institute new Government, laying its foundations on such principles and organizing its powers in such form, as to them shall seem most likely to effect their Safety and Happiness.

—The Unanimous Declaration of the Thirteen United States of America

---

# Background

**BARON DE MONTESQUIEU** In his work *The Spirit of the Laws* (1748), French philosopher Baron de Montesquieu examined different forms of government. He observed that corruption can creep into any government. ". . . [C]onstant experience shows us that every man invested with power is apt to abuse it . . . it is necessary from the very nature of things that power should be a check to power." Montesquieu concluded that abuse of power can be prevented by separating legislative, executive, and judicial powers among different bodies. Each body would restrain the power of the others, and all would be bound by the rule of law.

This information also appears on the Extend Worksheet for Section 4, along with information about other influential philosophers covered in this chapter.

> "And for the support of this Declaration, with a firm reliance on the protection of Divine Providence, we mutually pledge to each other, our lives, our Fortunes, and our sacred Honor.
> — Declaration of Independence

The members of the Second Continental Congress signed the Declaration of Independence on July 4, 1776. *By signing this document, what were these men risking? Why were they willing to sign it?*

No political system had ever been founded on the notion that the people should rule instead of being ruled, nor on the idea that every person is important as an individual, "created equal," and endowed with "certain unalienable rights." The Declaration was also groundbreaking because it was founded on the concept of "the consent of the governed," not divine right or tradition as the basis for the exercise of power.

With the adoption of the Declaration, the United States was born. The 13 colonies became free and independent States.

## The First State Constitutions

In January 1776, New Hampshire adopted a constitution to replace its royal charter. Less than three months later, South Carolina followed suit. Then, on May 10, nearly two months before the adoption of the Declaration of Independence, the Congress urged each of the colonies to adopt "such governments as shall, in the opinion of the representatives of the people, best conduce to the happiness and safety of their constituents."

**Drafting State Constitutions** In 1776 and 1777, most of the States adopted written constitutions—bodies of fundamental laws setting out the principles, structures, and processes of their governments. Assemblies or conventions were commonly used to draft and then adopt these new documents.

Massachusetts set a lasting example in the constitution-making process. There, a popularly elected convention submitted its work to the voters for ratification. The Massachusetts constitution of 1780 is the oldest of the present-day State constitutions, and the oldest written constitution in force in the world today.[10]

**Common Features** The first State constitutions differed, sometimes widely, in their details. Yet they were on the whole more alike than not. The most common features were the principles of **popular sovereignty** (a government that exists only with the consent of the governed), limited government, civil rights and liberties, separation of powers, and checks and balances.

*Popular Sovereignty.* Everywhere, the people were recognized as the only source of

---

[10] From independence until that constitution became effective in 1780, Massachusetts relied on its colonial charter, in force prior to 1691, as its fundamental law.

Ask students to turn to the "Common Features of State Constitutions" chart in Part 2 of the Reading Comprehension Worksheet (Unit 1 All-in-One, p. 69). Recreate the chart on the board. Call on volunteers to fill in the information.

**L4** **Differentiate** Have students write a one-page essay on this question: **Why did many first State constitutions share several common features?**

**EXTEND THE LESSON**

**L3** If you have time, have students draw a political cartoon with a clear point of view, either pro-colonist or pro-British. It should describe one of the key events or concepts covered in this section. Their cartoon should use exaggeration and humor and should express a point of view about a specific idea or event. Ask students to annotate their cartoons, explaining who, what, when, and where.

**L3** Display Transparency 2E, Excerpt from a Letter to John Adams from Dr. Benjamin Rush, about the signing of the Declaration of Independence. Ask: **What risk did the patriots face in defying Britain?** *(execution)* **Based on their reaction to Harrison's statement, did the patriots believe they really might be executed? Explain.** *(Yes. The macabre joke brought only a momentary smile.)*

**L1** **L2** **ELL** Have these students complete one or both of the Extend Activities (Unit 1 All-in-One, pp. 78, 79), on the topics of "Making a Difference" and "Patriotism."

**L4** Have students work in small groups to create outlines for the constitution of a fifty-first state. Allow time for students to compare their results.

# Background

**CAPTAIN PRESTON'S ACCOUNT** After students analyze the colonist's account of the Boston Massacre in Core Worksheet B, have them compare it to this account from Thomas Preston, the commander of the British troops: "The mob still increased and were more outrageous, striking their clubs . . . one against another, and calling out, come on you rascals, you bloody backs, you lobster scoundrels, fire if you dare. . . . [I was] endeavouring all in my power to persuade them to retire peaceably, but to no purpose. They advanced to the points of the bayonets. . . . [O]ne of the soldiers having received a severe blow with a stick . . . instantly fired, on which turning to and asking him why he fired without orders, I was struck with a club on my arm. . . . On this a general attack was made on the men by a great number of heavy clubs and snowballs being thrown at them, by which all our lives were in imminent danger."

## Answers

**Caption** their lives, wealth, and honor; they believed that their cause was just and, because it was, that God would protect them

# Assess and Remediate

**L3** Collect the Core Worksheets and assess students' work.

**L3** Assign the Section 2 Assessment questions.

**L3** Section Quiz A (Unit 1 All-in-One, p. 80)

**L2** Section Quiz B (Unit 1 All-in-One, p. 81)

Have students complete the review activities in the digital lesson presentation and continue their work in the **Essential Questions Journal.**

## REMEDIATION

| If Your Students Have Trouble With | Strategies For Remediation |
|---|---|
| The events leading up to the Declaration of Independence (Questions 1, 2, 3, 4, 5) | Have students work in pairs to create their own timelines. Write a list of events from the text on the board, including the First and Second Continental Congresses. Students should plot the events in sequential order and include a sentence or two describing each event. |

## Answer

**Checkpoint** Power was divided among executive, legislative, and judicial branches.

---

## Common Features of State Constitutions

▶ Popular Sovereignty    ▶ Separation of Powers
▶ Limited Government      ▶ Checks and Balances
▶ Civil Rights and Liberties

Once the seat of Massachusetts government, the Old State House in Boston has endured just as the State constitution has. Shown here: the Old State House as seen in 1870 and present day.

✔ **Checkpoint**
How did the State constitutions separate governmental power?

**unalienable**
*adj.* cannot be surrendered or transferred, sacred

governmental authority. In the new United States, government could be conducted only with the consent of the governed.

*Limited Government.* The new State governments could exercise only those powers granted to them by the people through the constitution. The powers that were given were hedged with many restrictions.

*Civil Rights and Liberties.* In every State, it was made clear that the sovereign people held certain rights that government must at all times respect. Seven of the new documents began with a bill of rights, setting out the "<u>unalienable</u> rights" held by the people.

*Separation of Powers, Checks and Balances.* The powers granted to the new State governments were divided among three distinct branches: executive, legislative, and judicial. Each branch was given powers with which to check, or restrain the actions of, the other branches of the government.

Beyond those basics, the new State constitutions were rather brief documents. They were, for the most part, declarations of principle and statements of limitation on governmental power. Memories of the royal governors were fresh, and State governors were given little real power. Most of the authority that was granted to government was placed in the legislature. Elective terms of office were made purposely short, seldom more than one or two years. The right to vote was limited to those adult white males who could meet rigid qualifications, including property ownership.

We shall come back to the State constitutions later, in Chapter 24. For now, note this very important point: The earliest of those documents were, within a very few years, to have a marked impact on the drafting of the Constitution of the United States.

**Essential Questions Journal** To continue to build a response to the chapter Essential Question, go to your **Essential Questions Journal.**

## SECTION 2 ASSESSMENT

1. **Guiding Question** Use your completed flowchart to answer this question: What events and ideas led to American independence?

**Key Terms and Comprehension**
2. **(a)** What is a **confederation**? **(b)** What was the purpose of the New England Confederation?
3. In your own words, explain what "taxation without representation" means.

**Critical Thinking**
4. **Summarize** What major events led to the calling of the First Continental Congress?
5. **Make Comparisons (a)** Compare the goals of the First and Second Continental Congresses. **(b)** What challenges did each meeting face?

**Quick Write**

**Narrative Writing: Research Your Colony** Using the questions you drafted in Section 1, conduct preliminary research to find the answers. Add any additional questions that you may have after reading Section 2. Browse the Internet or other sources and take notes on what you find. Use the information to begin a story about your colony's involvement in the shaping of the American government.

---

# Assessment Answers

**1.** Albany Plan, Stamp Act, Boston Massacre, Boston Tea Party, Intolerable Acts, First Continental Congress, Second Continental Congress, Declaration of Independence

**2. (a)** A confederation is a joining of several groups for a common purpose. **(b)** The New England Confederation was formed to defend several settlements against Native Americans.

**3.** Parliament passed laws to tax the colonies, but the colonists had no elected representatives in Parliament to give them a voice in the passage of those laws.

**4.** Britain's restrictive laws fueled unrest in the colonies. Protests, boycotts, and mob violence broke out. When Britain passed additional laws, called the Intolerable Acts, to punish the colonies, the First Continental Congress was called to discuss the situation.

**5. (a)** The goals of the First and Second Continental Congresses were to address the growing restrictions on the colonies by Britain. **(b)** Each meeting faced the challenge of attracting enough delegates, coming to a consensus on issues, and keeping their meetings secret.

**QUICK WRITE** A strong assignment will show research from reputable sources. Questions should lead to a basic summary of the colony's involvement in the Revolution.

Thomas Jefferson was the primary author of the Declaration of Independence. *What principles from the three British documents did he incorporate in the Declaration?*

# The Declaration of Independence

The Declaration of Independence is composed of four parts: a Preamble, a Declaration of Natural Rights, a List of Grievances, and a Resolution of Independence.

**IN CONGRESS, JULY 4, 1776**
**The Unanimous Declaration of the Thirteen United States of America**

43

## Focus on the Basics

**FACTS:** • The Declaration of Independence has four parts: the Preamble, the Declaration of Natural Rights, the List of Grievances, and the Resolution of Independence. • The Preamble explains reasons for separating. • The Declaration of Natural Rights lists basic rights to which people are entitled. • The List of Grievances offers evidence that King George has violated the colonists' rights. • The Resolution of Independence asserts that the colonies are now independent from Britain.

**CONCEPTS:** popular sovereignty, civil rights and liberties

**ENDURING UNDERSTANDINGS:** • The Declaration of Independence expresses the political ideals that underlie American democracy. • The Declaration of Independence has had an enduring influence on American government and culture.

# Get Started

## Answers

**Caption** the right to petition the government, freedom from cruel punishment, the right to trial by jury, the right to due process, the right to private property

## SKILLS DEVELOPMENT

# Teach

To present this topic using online resources, use the lesson presentations at **PearsonSchool.com/phgovt**.

## INTRODUCE THE TOPIC

Tell students that today they will analyze one of the most important political documents in the world. Have students share their paraphrase from the Bell-ringer activity. *(Possible answer: All people are born with basic rights that cannot be taken from them, including the freedom to live and search for happiness as they see fit. People establish governments to safeguard their basic rights. If a government does not protect these rights, people have the right to end that government and establish a new one.)*

Point out that Thomas Jefferson was the principal author of the Declaration of Independence. Ask: **Why did Jefferson begin his case for independence with a statement of natural rights?** *(Jefferson wanted to establish a philosophical foundation for his argument that the colonies had the right and duty to sever their ties to England. In the eighteenth century, Enlightenment thinkers were famous, influential, and respected. Using a philosophical foundation based on Enlightenment thinking gave weight and influence to the colonial argument.)*

Ask students to name Enlightenment thinkers who influenced Jefferson and the other Founders. *(Locke, Rousseau, Montesquieu, Hobbes, Voltaire, Blackstone)* Review the ideas of these philosophers. Information can be found in the Background notes in the Chapter 2 teacher's edition and on the Section 4 Extend Worksheet for students (Unit 1 All-in-One, p. 101).

## REVIEW READING COMPREHENSION WORKSHEET

Have students take out their Reading Comprehension worksheets (Unit 1 All-in-One, p. 82) and share their answers to be sure they understand the four parts of the Declaration.

**L1** **L2** **Differentiate** Write sentences from the Declaration of Independence on index cards. Have students take turns picking a card and identifying from which part of the document (Preamble, Declaration of Natural Rights, List of Grievances, or Resolution of Independence) each sentence comes.

**L4** **Differentiate** Point out to students that Jefferson and many signers of the Declaration of Independence held slaves. Ask them to do research about one of these men and explain how he reconciled the ideals of the Declaration with his role as a slaveholder. Then ask them to explain what the Declaration left unsaid or unresolved.

---

## DECLARATION OF INDEPENDENCE

▶ **Preamble:** The Preamble explains why the Declaration was written.

▶ **Declaration of Natural Rights:** This paragraph lists the basic rights to which all people are entitled. It describes those rights as being unalienable. They cannot be taken away. The government gets its power from the people. When the government usurps (takes) power from the people and does not protect their rights, the people have the right and responsibility to throw off that government and to create a new one.

▶ **List of Grievances:** This section lists the colonists' 27 complaints against the British Crown. In essence, King George III had chosen to rule as a tyrant rather than govern with the people's well-being in mind.

▶ The people refuse to give up their right to representation—a right the colonists considered vital.

▶ The king had dissolved representative houses and refused to allow the election of new legislators. Without legislators, the colonists were without protection from foreign invasion or convulsions (riots) from within.

**When in the Course of human events** it becomes necessary for one people to dissolve the political bands which have connected them with another, and to assume among the powers of the earth, the separate and equal station to which the Laws of nature and of nature's God entitle them, a decent respect to the opinions of mankind requires that they should declare the causes which impel them to the separation.

▶ We hold these truths to be self-evident, that all men are created equal, that they are endowed by their Creator with certain unalienable Rights, that among these are Life, Liberty and the Pursuit of Happiness. That to secure these rights, Governments are instituted among Men, deriving their just powers from the consent of the governed; That whenever any Form of Government becomes destructive of these ends it is the Right of the People to alter or to abolish it, and to institute new Government, laying its foundation on such principles and organizing its powers in such form, as to them shall seem most likely to effect their Safety and Happiness. Prudence, indeed, will dictate that Governments long established should not be changed for light and transient causes; and accordingly all experience hath shown, that mankind are more disposed to suffer, while evils are sufferable, than to right themselves by abolishing the forms to which they are accustomed. But when a long train of abuses and usurpations, pursuing invariably the same Object evinces a design to reduce them under absolute Despotism, it is their right, it is their duty, to throw off such Government, and to provide new Guards for their future security.

▶ Such has been the patient sufferance of these Colonies; and such is now the necessity which constrains them to alter their former Systems of Government. The history of the present King of Great Britain is a history of repeated injuries and usurpations, all having in direct object the establishment of an absolute Tyranny over these States. To prove this, let Facts be submitted to a candid world.

He has refused his Assent to Laws, the most wholesome and necessary for the public good.

He has forbidden his Governors to pass Laws of immediate and pressing importance, unless suspended in their operation till his Assent should be obtained; and when so suspended, he has utterly neglected to attend to them.

▶ He has refused to pass other Laws for the accommodation of large districts of people, unless those people would relinquish the right of Representation in the Legislature, a right inestimable to them and formidable to tyrants only.

He has called together legislative bodies at places unusual, uncomfortable, and distant from the depository of their Public Records, for the sole purpose of fatiguing them into compliance with his measures.

▶ He has dissolved Representative Houses repeatedly, for opposing with manly firmness his invasions on the rights of the people.

He has refused for a long time, after such dissolutions, to cause others to be elected; whereby the Legislative powers, incapable of Annihilation, have returned to the People at large for their exercise; the State remaining in the mean time exposed to all the dangers of invasions from without, and convulsions within.

---

# Differentiated Resources

The following resources are located in the All-in-One, Unit 1, Chapter 2, Declaration of Independence:

**L2** Prereading and Vocabulary Worksheet (p. 57)

**L3** Reading Comprehension Worksheet (p. 82)

**L2** Reading Comprehension Worksheet (p. 83)

**L3** Core Worksheet (p. 84)

Even the Declaration of Independence had revisions.

Thomas Jefferson

▶ He has endeavored to prevent the population of these States; for that purpose obstructing the Laws for Naturalization of Foreigners; refusing to pass others to encourage their migration hither, and raising the conditions of new Appropriations of Lands.

He has obstructed the Administration of Justice, by refusing his Assent to Laws for establishing Judiciary powers.

▶ He has made Judges dependent on his Will alone for the tenure of their offices, and the amount and payment of their salaries.

He has erected a multitude of New Offices, and sent hither swarms of Officers to harass our people and eat out their substance.

He has kept among us in time of peace, Standing Armies, without the Consent of our legislatures.

He has affected to render the Military independent of, and superior to, the Civil Power.

He has combined with others to subject us to a jurisdiction foreign to our constitutions, and unacknowledged by our laws; giving his Assent to their Acts of pretended Legislation:

▶ For quartering large bodies of armed troops among us;

For protecting them, by a mock Trial, from punishment for any Murders which they should commit on the Inhabitants of these States;

For cutting off our Trade with all parts of the world;

For imposing Taxes on us without our Consent;

For depriving us, in many cases, of the benefits of Trial by Jury;

For transporting us beyond Seas to be tried for pretended offenses;

▶ For abolishing the free System of English Laws in a neighboring Province, establishing therein an Arbitrary government, and enlarging its Boundaries so as to render it at once an example and fit instrument for introducing the same absolute rule into these Colonies;

For taking away our Charters, abolishing our most valuable Laws, and altering fundamentally the Forms of our Governments;

For suspending our own Legislatures, and declaring themselves invested with Power to legislate for us in all cases whatsoever.

▶ The king had tried to slow population growth by preventing individuals from other countries from becoming citizens of the colonies.

▶ This grievance was later addressed in Article III, Section 1 of the Constitution, which states that federal judges shall hold office "during good Behaviour."

▶ The king forced colonists to lodge British soldiers in their homes. The Bill of Rights addressed this in the 3rd Amendment, which states that no soldier can be lodged in "any house" without the consent of the owner.

▶ Here, the Declaration refers to Canada. The colonists feared that they, too, would fall under absolute rule. Britain extended the border of Quebec to the Ohio Valley, cutting it off to colonial settlers.

Declaration of Independence **45**

# Background

**EQUALITY** In 1775, reacting to colonial charges of British oppression, British author Samuel Johnson wrote, "How is it that we hear the loudest yelps for liberty from the drivers of Negroes?" Indeed, many signers of the Declaration of Independence, including its author—Thomas Jefferson—held slaves. Yet Jefferson's words "all men are created equal" would become a rallying cry for groups seeking equality. Abolitionists before the Civil War cited these words to support their calls to end slavery. Civil Rights leader Dr. Martin Luther King, Jr., quoted these words in a 1963 speech: "I have a dream that one day this nation will rise up and live out the true meaning of its creed: 'We hold these truths to be self-evident, that all men are created equal.'" The Women's Rights convention at Seneca Falls in 1848 adapted Jefferson's words, asserting that "all men and women are created equal."

## DISTRIBUTE THE CORE WORKSHEET

Distribute the Chapter 2 Declaration of Independence Core Worksheet (Unit 1 All-in-One, p. 84), which asks students to consider the role of the Declaration as an idealistic statement of human rights, as a statement of grievances, and as propaganda. Students may work with partners or individually to complete Part 1 by rating the Declaration of Independence in terms of its various purposes and then explaining their reasons for each ranking.

After students share their responses, have partners complete Part 2 of the Core Worksheet to analyze how different groups might have reacted to the Declaration because of their differing viewpoints.

**L1 L2 Differentiate** Have groups of students represent each group listed in Part 2 of the Core Worksheet. Ask them to make a public statement about the Declaration from their perspective. You may extend the activity by letting the groups respond to each other's public statements.

**L2 ELL Differentiate** Ask students to represent another group: "recently arrived colonials" or "new Americans." Encourage them to explain the viewpoint of this group to the class.

**L4 Differentiate** Have students write a response to the Declaration of Independence from an opposing point of view in the form of a propaganda brochure.

Show a Revolutionary War movie in class, or assign a movie to students or partners to watch at home on a DVD. Encourage students to rate the movie with one to four stars, with four stars as the top rating. Have students write a review of the movie.

**L4** **Differentiate** Have groups of students prepare a script for an additional short scene for the movie. Tell them that they can plan their scene to go into any point in the movie, not just the beginning or end. They should use the same characters, and their scene should be consistent with the plot of the movie. After students in each group perform their scene, have the class discuss what the scene contributed to the plot or character development of the movie.

## DECLARATION OF INDEPENDENCE

▶ The king had forced captive sailors to fight against their own people, or die.

▶ The colonists tried repeatedly to petition the king to correct his wrongs. However, their protests were met by harsh laws. Therefore, he does not deserve to rule the colonies.

▶ The colonists still felt a common identity with citizens of Britain. However, their fellow British subjects ignored their appeals for help.

▶ **The Resolution of Independence:** The colonies declare themselves free and independent States, by authority of the people of the States and of God. Therefore, the States have the power to declare war, make peace, create alliances and trade with foreign powers, and do all other acts afforded to independent States.

He has abdicated Government here, by declaring us out of his Protection, and waging War against us.

He has plundered our seas, ravaged our Coasts, burned our towns, and destroyed the lives of our people.

He is at this time transporting large Armies of foreign mercenaries to complete the works of death, desolation and tyranny, already begun with circumstances of Cruelty and perfidy scarcely paralleled in the most barbarous ages, and totally unworthy the Head of a civilized nation.

▶ He has constrained our fellow Citizens taken Captive on the high Seas to bear Arms against their Country, to become the executioners of their friends and Brethren, or to fall themselves by their Hands.

He has excited domestic insurrections amongst us, and has endeavored to bring on the inhabitants of our frontiers the merciless Indian Savages whose known rule of warfare, is an undistinguished destruction of all ages, sexes, and conditions.

▶ In every stage of these Oppressions We have Petitioned for Redress in the most humble terms. Our repeated Petitions have been answered only by repeated injury. A Prince, whose character is thus marked by every act which may define a Tyrant, is unfit to be the ruler of a free People.

▶ Nor have We been wanting in attentions to our British brethren. We have warned them from time to time of attempts by their legislature to extend an unwarrantable jurisdiction over us. We have reminded them of the circumstances of our emigration and settlement here. We have appealed to their native justice and magnanimity, and we have conjured them by the ties of our common kindred to disavow these usurpations, which, would inevitably interrupt our connections and correspondence. They too have been deaf to the voice of justice and of consanguinity. We must, therefore, acquiesce in the necessity, which denounces our Separation, and hold them, as we hold the rest of mankind, Enemies in War, in Peace Friends.

▶ We, therefore, the Representatives of the United States of America, in General Congress, Assembled, appealing to the Supreme Judge of the world for the rectitude of our intentions, do, in the Name, and by the Authority of the good People of these Colonies, solemnly publish and declare, That these United Colonies are, and of right ought to be Free and Independent States; that they are Absolved from all Allegiance to the British Crown, and that all political connection between them and the State of Great Britain, is and ought to be totally dissolved, and that as Free and Independent States, they have full Power to levy War, conclude Peace, contract Alliances, establish Commerce, and to do all other Acts and Things which Independent States may of right do. And for the support of this Declaration, with a firm reliance on the protection of Divine Providence, we mutually pledge to each other our Lives, our Fortunes, and our sacred Honor.

# Background

**JOHN ADAMS** When the Second Continental Congress opened in May 1775, John Adams arrived ready for action. Armed conflict had already occurred at Lexington and Concord. Adams wanted Congress to prepare for war. Impatient with the slow progress, Adams took the floor. He proposed the formation of a Continental Army, under the command of George Washington. He also urged the colonies to form their own governments. As Congress debated the Declaration of Independence in June 1776, Adams's passionate support won over the hesitant delegates. On July 3, 1776, the day after Congress approved Richard Henry Lee's resolution to pursue independence, Adams wrote to his wife Abigail: "The Second Day of July . . . will be celebrated, by succeeding Generations, as the great anniversary Festival . . . with Pomp and Parade, . . . Guns, Bells, Bonfires and Illuminations. . . ."

New Hampshire:
**Josiah Bartlett**
**William Whipple**
**Mathew Thornton**

Massachusetts Bay:
**John Hancock**
**Samuel Adams**
**John Adams**
**Robert Treat Paine**
**Elbridge Gerry**

Rhode Island:
**Stephan Hopkins**
**William Ellery**

Connecticut:
**Roger Sherman**
**Samuel Huntington**
**William Williams**
**Oliver Wolcott**

New York:
**William Floyd**
**Philip Livingston**
**Francis Lewis**
**Lewis Morris**

New Jersey:
**Richard Stockton**
**John Witherspoon**
**Francis Hopkinson**
**John Hart**
**Abraham Clark**

Delaware:
**Caesar Rodney**
**George Read**
**Thomas M'Kean**

Maryland:
**Samuel Chase**
**William Paca**
**Thomas Stone**
**Charles Carroll**
  **of Carrollton**

Virginia:
**George Wythe**
**Richard Henry Lee**
**Thomas Jefferson**
**Benjamin Harrison**
**Thomas Nelson, Jr.**
**Francis Lightfoot Lee**
**Carter Braxton**

Pennsylvania:
**Robert Morris**
**Benjamin Rush**
**Benjamin Franklin**
**John Morton**
**George Clymer**
**James Smith**
**George Taylor**
**James Wilson**
**George Ross**

North Carolina:
**William Hooper**
**Joseph Hewes**
**John Penn**

South Carolina:
**Edward Rutledge**
**Thomas Heyward, Jr.**
**Thomas Lynch, Jr.**
**Arthur Middleton**

Georgia:
**Button Gwinnett**
**Lyman Hall**
**George Walton**

As president of the Second Continental Congress, John Hancock was the first to sign the Declaration of Independence, approving it with his now-famous signature.

**DECLARATION OF INDEPENDENCE**

# Reviewing the Declaration

**Vocabulary**
Choose ten unfamiliar words in the Declaration. Look them up in the dictionary. Then, on a piece of paper, copy the sentence in the Declaration in which each unfamiliar word is used. After the sentence, write the definition of the unfamiliar word.

**Comprehension**
1. Name the three "unalienable rights" listed in the Declaration.
2. From what source do governments derive their "just powers"?
3. According to the Declaration, what powers belong to the United States as "Free and Independent States"?

**Critical Thinking**
4. **Recognize Cause and Effect** Why do you think the colonists were unhappy with the fact that their judges' tenure and salaries were dependent on the king?
5. **Identifying Assumptions** Do you think that the words "all men are created equal" were intended to apply to all those who lived in the colonies? Which groups were most likely not included?
6. **Drawing Conclusions** What evidence is there that the colonists had already and unsuccessfully voiced their concerns to the king?

Declaration of Independence **47**

# Assess and Remediate

**L3** Collect the Core Worksheet and assess students' class participation, using the Rubric for Assessing Performance of an Entire Group (Unit 1 All-in-One, p. 218).

**L3** Assign the Declaration of Independence Assessment questions.

Have students complete the review activities in the digital lesson presentation and continue their work in the **Essential Questions Journal.**

**REMEDIATION**

| If Your Students Have Trouble With | Strategies For Remediation |
| --- | --- |
| The Declaration of Natural Rights (Questions 1, 2) | Write in your own words the rights listed in this section. Have students work in pairs to find their location in the text. Have volunteers read aloud the sentence that contains each right. |
| The List of Grievances (Questions 4, 6) | Work with students to write the grievances in their own words. List them on the board, and provide any relevant historical information that might clarify the grievances. |

# Assessment Answers

Vocabulary answers should reflect an understanding of the selected words.

**1.** life, liberty, and the pursuit of happiness

**2.** Governments derive their "just powers" from the consent of the governed.

**3.** They have the power to declare war, conclude peace, contract alliances, establish commerce, and do everything else that independent States have a right to do.

**4.** Judges were likely to favor the king over the colonists in order to keep their jobs.

**5.** Possible answer: No; many of the signers, including Jefferson, owned slaves and were unwilling to extend these basic rights to African Americans. In addition, Native Americans and women were also excluded.

**6.** Just before the Resolution of Independence, the Declaration claims that the colonists petitioned the king several times and that they also appealed to the British people for justice.

## What weaknesses in the Articles of Confederation made a lasting government impossible?

I. The Articles of Confederation
   A. Weaknesses
      1. Congress lacked power to tax, regulate trade between States, and make States obey its laws or the Articles
      2. Laws required approval of 9 of 13 States
      3. Change to Articles required approval of all 13 States
   B. Effects of the Weaknesses
      1. Congress had to ask States for funds or borrow, neither of which raised enough money
      2. States bickered among themselves; made treaties with other nations; raised own military; taxed one another's goods and banned some trade; and printed own money with little backing, causing economic chaos
      3. Violence—Shays' Rebellion
      4. Congress too weak to deal with problems

# Get Started

## LESSON GOALS

Students will . . .

- identify and analyze weaknesses of the Articles of Confederation by completing a worksheet.
- analyze the issue of land claims by examining a map.

## ANALYZE MAPS

To teach the skills of analyzing maps, have students read Analyze Maps in the Skills Handbook, p. S27. Then have them examine the map in the Core Worksheet and answer the questions.

---

SECTION 3

# The **Critical Period**

### Guiding Question
**What weaknesses in the Articles of Confederation made a lasting government impossible?** Use an outline like the one below to take notes on the reasons why the Articles of Confederation failed.

I. The Articles of Confederation
   A. Weaknesses
      1. _____
      2. _____
   B. Effects of the Weaknesses
      1. _____
      2. _____

### Political Dictionary
- Articles of Confederation
- ratification

### Objectives
1. Describe the structure of the government set up under the Articles of Confederation.
2. Explain why the weaknesses of the Articles led to a critical period for the country in the 1780s.
3. Describe how a growing need for a stronger national government led to plans for a Constitutional Convention.

**Image Above:** Daniel Shays' rebellion made the need for a stronger government clear.

The First and Second Continental Congresses rested on no legal base. They were called in haste to meet an emergency, and they were intended to be temporary. Something more regular and permanent was clearly needed. In this section, you will look at the first attempt to establish a lasting government for the new nation.

## The Articles of Confederation

Richard Henry Lee's resolution that led to the Declaration of Independence also called on the Second Continental Congress to propose "a plan of confederation" to the States. Off and on, for 17 months, Congress debated the problem of uniting the former colonies. Finally, on November 15, 1777, the **Articles of Confederation** were approved.

The Articles of Confederation established "a firm league of friendship" among the States. Each State kept "its sovereignty, freedom, and independence, and every Power, Jurisdiction, and right . . . not . . . expressly delegated to the United States, in Congress assembled." The States came together "for their common defense, the security of their Liberties, and their mutual and general welfare. . . ." In effect, the Articles created a structure that more closely resembled an alliance of independent states than a government "of the people."

The Articles did not go into effect immediately, however. The **ratification** (formal approval) of each of the 13 States was needed first. Eleven States approved the document within a year. Delaware added its approval in February 1779. Maryland did not ratify until March 1, 1781. The Second Continental Congress declared the Articles effective on that date.

**Governmental Structure** The government set up by the Articles was quite simple. A Congress was the sole body created. It was unicameral, made up of delegates chosen yearly by the States in whatever way their legislatures might direct. Each State had only one vote in the Congress, no matter its population or wealth.

The Articles established no executive or judicial branch. These functions were to be handled by committees of the Congress. Each year the Congress would choose one of its members as its president. That person would be its

---

# Focus on the Basics

**FACTS:** • The Second Continental Congress adopted the Articles of Confederation to establish a more lasting form of government. • Under the Articles, each State had one vote in Congress; no executive or judicial branches existed. • Congress did not have the power to tax, regulate commerce, or make the States obey the Articles. • The Articles' weaknesses led to bickering among the States. • The growing need for a stronger National Government led to plans for a Constitutional Convention.

**CONCEPTS:** limited government, federalism, States' rights

**ENDURING UNDERSTANDINGS:** • The Articles of Confederation set up a central government that was too weak to solve the nation's problems. • The chaos of the 1780s led to a movement favoring a more powerful central government.

presiding officer, but not the president of the United States. Civil officers such as postmasters were to be appointed by the Congress.

**Powers of Congress** Several important powers were given to the Congress. It could make war and peace, send and receive ambassadors, make treaties, borrow money, set up a money system, establish post offices, build a navy, raise an army by asking the States for troops, fix uniform standards of weights and measures, and settle disputes among the States.

**State Obligations** By agreeing to the Articles, the States pledged to obey the Articles and acts of the Congress. They promised to provide the funds and troops requested by Congress; treat citizens of other States fairly and equally within their own borders; and give full faith and credit to the public acts, records, and judicial proceedings of every other State. In addition, the States agreed to surrender fugitives from justice to one another, submit their disputes to Congress for settlement, and allow open travel and trade among the States.

Beyond those few obligations, the States retained those powers not explicitly given to the Congress. They, not the Congress, were primarily responsible for protecting life and property, and for promoting "the safety and happiness of the people."

**Weaknesses** The powers of the Congress appear, at first glance, to have been considerable. Several important powers were missing, however. Their omission, together with other weaknesses, soon proved the Articles inadequate for the needs of the time.

The Congress did not have the power to tax. It could raise money only by borrowing and by asking the States for funds. Borrowing was, at best, a poor source. The Second Continental Congress had borrowed heavily to support the Revolution, and many of those debts had not been paid. And, while the Articles remained in force, not one State came close to meeting the financial requests made by the Congress.

Nor did the Congress have the power to regulate trade between the States. This lack of a central mechanism to regulate the young

☑ **Checkpoint**
What powers did Congress hold under the Articles of Confederation?

**jurisdiction**
*n.* legal authority

**presiding officer**
*n.* the chair of a meeting

**Weaknesses of the Articles of Confederation**

## "WHO WILL TREAT WITH US ON SUCH TERMS?"

George Washington's frustration with the Articles of Confederation is reflected in his quote above. The Articles were too weak to bind the States together, thus presenting a quarreling group of States rather than a unified nation to the rest of the world. *What were the consequences of these weaknesses?*

- Only a **"firm league of friendship"** among States
- **Only one vote** for each State, regardless of size
- Congress **powerless to levy taxes** or duties
- Congress **powerless to regulate commerce**
- **No executive power** to enforce acts of Congress
- **No national court system**
- Amendments require **the consent of all States**
- A **9/13 majority** required to pass laws

## Differentiated Resources

The following resources are located in the All-in-One, Unit 1, Chapter 2, Section 3:

- **L3** Reading Comprehension Worksheet (p. 86)
- **L2** Reading Comprehension Worksheet (p. 87)
- **L3** Core Worksheet (p. 88)
- **L2** Core Worksheet (p. 91)
- **L3** Quiz A (p. 95)
- **L2** Quiz B (p. 96)

### BEFORE CLASS

Assign the section, the graphic organizer in the text, and the Reading Comprehension Worksheet (Unit 1 All-in-One, p. 86) before class.

**L2 Differentiate** Reading Comprehension Worksheet (Unit 1 All-in-One, p. 87)

### BELLRINGER

Display Transparency 2G. Write on the board:
**(1) Which government issued this currency?**
**(2) What problems did local currencies create? Answer in your notebook.**

**L4 Differentiate** Add to the directions: **What features of the Articles of Confederation contributed to the currency disaster?** *(Lacking the power to tax, Congress had no funds to establish a national money system. Lacking the power to enforce the Articles, Congress could not stop the States from issuing their own currency.)*

## Teach

To present this topic using online resources, use the lesson presentations at **PearsonSchool.com/phgovt**.

### INTRODUCE THE TOPIC

Have students share their answers to the Bellringer activity. *(1. Pennsylvania; 2. Local currencies hampered interstate trade, because their value and acceptability varied from State to State. This would interfere with the development of a national economy.)* The printing of State currency was one of many State actions that weakened the new government. Ask students what other State actions undermined national unity. *(States refused to meet financial requests of Congress, made agreements with foreign governments, organized their own military forces, and taxed or banned goods from other States.)*

**L2 ELL Differentiate** Write the answers on the board or print the worksheet onto a transparency to allow students to copy the correct answers.

## Answers

**Checkpoint** make war and peace, send and receive ambassadors, make treaties, borrow money, set up a money system, establish post offices, build a navy, raise an army by asking the States for troops, fix uniform standards of weights and measures, settle disputes among States

**Weaknesses of the Articles of Confederation** possible response: a loose alliance of independent States rather than a cohesive nation

## DISTRIBUTE CORE WORKSHEET

Distribute the Chapter 2 Section 3 Core Worksheet (Unit 1 All-in-One, page 88). The map shows land claims of the States and foreign nations after the Revolution. Have student pairs examine the map and answer the questions.

**L2 Differentiate** Distribute the adapted Chapter 2 Section 3 Core Worksheet (Unit 1 All-in-One, p. 91).

## DISCUSS

Display Transparency 2H. Ask why the Articles were adopted, given their many flaws. To what extent were colonists reacting to English abuses that led to war? Were the Articles appropriate for their time?

**L2 ELL Differentiate** Use the Think-Pair-Share strategy (p. T22) to allow students to verbalize their answers before starting the class discussion.

## PREDICT CONSEQUENCES

Explain that Part 2 of the Core Worksheet asks students to consider what might have happened had the Articles of Confederation remained the national constitution. Students will make predictions about five scenarios on the worksheet. After they finish, allow time to compare and contrast predictions.

## DISCUSS SHAYS' REBELLION

Ask students to explain the significance of Shays' Rebellion. *(It showed the weakness of the National Government under the Articles and led to calls for a Constitutional Convention.)* Then ask why some of Shays' contemporaries might have seen his rebellion as an extension of the War for Independence. *(They might have said that he was rebelling against a government that was taxing people unfairly and using arbitrary power, just as the colonists had rebelled against British abuses.)*

**L4 Differentiate** Ask: **Was Shays a traitor? Did he deserve to be pardoned?** Students might work in teams to debate both sides of these questions.

## EXTEND THE LESSON

Have students work in small groups to invent a game called "Government under the Articles." Their games might be board games, card games, or other games. Students' games should reflect the weaknesses and challenges presented by the Articles. For example, the point of the game might involve trying to pass a bill or act to benefit one or many States.

**L1 L2 Differentiate** Provide an outline of a game for students to work out in groups. For example: "Pass a bill to build an interstate road" card with 20 to 30 cards. A small number of cards would say "Nine states agree" or "Bill passes." The other cards would have actions allowed under the Articles, which worked against passage. The point of the game might be to get approval first, or some other variation.

---

nation's growing commerce was one of the major factors that soon led to the adoption of the Constitution.

The Congress was further limited by a lack of power to make the States obey the Articles of Confederation or the laws it made. Congress could exercise the powers it did have only with the consent of 9 of the 13 State delegations. Finally, the Articles themselves could be changed only with the consent of all 13 of the State legislatures.

**arsenal**
*n.* a store of arms or military equipment

## The Critical Period, the 1780s

The long Revolutionary War finally ended on October 19, 1781. America's victory was confirmed by the signing of the Treaty of Paris in 1783. Peace, however, brought the new nation's economic and political weaknesses into sharp focus. Problems, made even more difficult by the weaknesses of the Articles, soon surfaced.

With a central government unable to act, the States bickered among themselves. They grew increasingly jealous and suspicious of one another. They often refused to support the new central government, financially and in almost every other way. Several of them made agreements with foreign governments without the approval of the Congress, even though that was forbidden by the Articles. Most organized their own military forces. George Washington complained, "…we are one nation today and 13 tomorrow. Who will treat with us on such terms?"

The States taxed one another's goods and even banned some trade. They printed their own money, often with little backing. Economic chaos spread throughout the colonies as prices soared

Delegates met first at Alexandria. They met again at Annapolis. The First and Second Continental Congresses met at Philadelphia.

and sound credit vanished. Debts, public and private, went unpaid. Violence broke out in a number of places.

The most spectacular of these events played out in western Massachusetts in a series of incidents that came to be known as Shays' Rebellion. As economic conditions worsened there, property holders, many of them small farmers, began to lose their land and possessions for lack of payment on taxes and other debts. In the fall of 1786, Daniel Shays, who had served as an officer in the War for Independence, led an armed uprising that forced several State judges to close their courts. Early the next year, Shays mounted an unsuccessful attack on the federal arsenal at Springfield. State forces finally moved to quiet the rebellion and Shays fled to Vermont. In response to the violence, the Massachusetts legislature eventually passed laws to ease the burden of debtors.

## A Need for Stronger Government

The Articles had created a government unable to deal with the nation's troubles. Inevitably, demand grew for a stronger, more effective national government. Those who were most threatened by economic and political instability—large property owners, merchants, traders, and other creditors—soon took the lead in efforts to that end. The movement for change began to take concrete form in 1785.

**Mount Vernon** Maryland and Virginia, plagued by bitter trade disputes, took the first step in the movement for change. Ignoring the Congress, the two States agreed to a conference to resolve conflicts over commerce and navigation on the Potomac River and Chesapeake Bay. Representatives from the two States met at Alexandria, Virginia, in March 1785. At George Washington's invitation, they moved their sessions to his home at nearby Mount Vernon.

Their negotiations proved so successful that on January 21, 1786, the Virginia General Assembly called for "a joint meeting of [all of] the States to consider and recommend a federal plan for regulating commerce."

**Annapolis** That joint meeting opened at Annapolis, Maryland, on September 11, 1786. Turnout was poor, with representatives from only five of the 13 States attending: New York, New Jersey, Pennsylvania, Delaware, and

---

# Background

**VOLTAIRE** François-Marie Arouet, known as Voltaire, was one of the most vocal of the French Enlightenment thinkers. He wrote scathing attacks on religious bigotry and fanaticism, for which he was jailed and eventually exiled. In place of traditional religion, Voltaire promoted *deism*—a religious philosophy that acknowledged God but rejected specific teachings of any church. Deists argued for religious freedom and toleration. As Voltaire wrote in *A Treatise on Toleration* (1763), "We ought to look upon all men as our brothers." Deist views migrated to America and were adopted by leaders such as Thomas Jefferson, Benjamin Franklin, and George Washington.

This information also appears on the Extend Worksheet for Section 4, along with information about other influential philosophers covered in this chapter.

Virginia. Although New Hampshire, Massachusetts, Rhode Island, and North Carolina had appointed delegates, none attended the Annapolis meeting. Disappointed but still hopeful, Alexander Hamilton, a delegate from New York, and Virginia's James Madison persuaded the gathering to call for yet another meeting of the States.

By mid-February of 1787, seven of the States had named delegates to the Philadelphia meeting: Delaware, Georgia, New Hampshire, New Jersey, North Carolina, Pennsylvania, and Virginia. On February 21, the Congress, which had been hesitating, also called upon the States to send delegates to Philadelphia

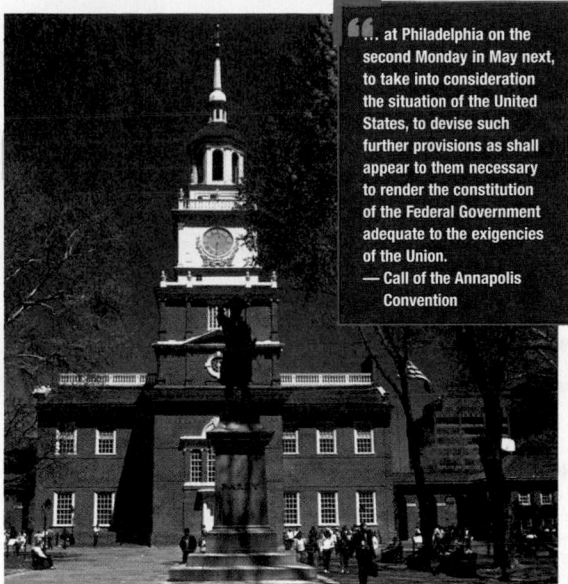

" . . at Philadelphia on the second Monday in May next, to take into consideration the situation of the United States, to devise such further provisions as shall appear to them necessary to render the constitution of the Federal Government adequate to the exigencies of the Union.
— Call of the Annapolis Convention

Independence Hall served as the meeting place for both the Second Continental Congress and the Constitutional Convention. **What significance might this building have had for the Constitutional Convention?**

## Primary Source

. . . for the sole and express purpose of revising the Articles of Confederation and reporting to Congress and the several legislatures such alterations and provisions therein as shall when agreed to in Congress and confirmed by the States render the [Articles] adequate to the exigencies of Government and the preservation of the Union.

—The United States in Congress Assembled, February 21, 1787

That Philadelphia meeting became the Constitutional Convention. What began as an assembly to revise the existing Articles

of Confederation soon evolved into a meeting dedicated to a different purpose—the creation of an entirely new kind of government for the United States of America. This government would derive its power from a constitution.

**Essential Questions Journal** To continue to build a response to the chapter Essential Question, go to your **Essential Questions Journal.**

# SECTION 3 ASSESSMENT

1. **Guiding Question** Use your completed outline to answer this question: What weaknesses in the Articles of Confederation made a lasting government impossible?

**Key Terms and Comprehension**

2. What was the goal of the **Articles of Confederation?**

3. (a) Under the Articles of Confederation, was Congress unicameral or bicameral? (b) How were representatives chosen to serve in Congress?

**Critical Thinking**

4. **Synthesize Information** When the States ratified the Articles, they agreed to obey the Articles and all acts of Congress. (a) Did the States honor their agreement? (b) How do you know?

5. **Identify Point of View** Washington was referring to foreign affairs when he complained, "We are one nation today and 13 tomorrow. Who will treat with us on such terms?" (a) What did Washington fear would happen? (b) Do you agree with his point of view? Why or why not?

**Quick Write**

**Narrative Writing: Details and Anecdotes** When writing narrative nonfiction, it is important to have details and anecdotes to keep your reader's interest. Choose some important dates or events that you wish to highlight. Research them further to find personal accounts or interesting examples from that time.

---

# Assess and Remediate

**L3** Collect the Core Worksheet and assess students' work.

**L3** Assign the Section 3 Assessment questions.

**L3** Section Quiz A (All-in-One, p. 95)

**L2** Section Quiz B (All-in-One, p. 96)

Have students complete the review activities in the digital lesson presentation and continue their work in the **Essential Questions Journal.**

## REMEDIATION

| If Your Students Have Trouble With | Strategies For Remediation |
|---|---|
| The structure of the government under the Articles of Confederation (Question 3) | Draw a diagram that depicts the structure of the Federal Government under the Articles of Confederation, and create a list of its powers. Compare it with a diagram of the three branches of the current Federal Government and a list of their powers. Ask students to point out differences. |
| The need for the Framers to create a stronger government (Questions 1, 4, 5) | Refer back to the diagrams. Ask students to point out reasons why specific features of the Federal Government under the Articles of Confederation (such as the existence of a Congress only) might make for a weak government. |

## Answers

**Caption** The Declaration of Independence was signed in Independence Hall, and so it served as a symbol of the birth of the nation.

---

# Assessment Answers

**1. Weaknesses:** Congress lacked power to tax, regulate trade between States, or make States obey its laws or the Articles. Laws required approval of 9 of 13 States. Changes to Articles required approval of all 13 States. **Effects of the weaknesses:** Congress had to ask States for funds or borrow, neither of which raised enough money. States bickered among themselves, made treaties with other nations, raised their own military forces, taxed one another's goods and banned some trade,

and printed their own money with little backing, causing economic chaos. Violence broke out, including Shays' Rebellion. Congress was too weak to deal with the problems.

**2.** The goal was to unite the colonies (now States) under one central, though weak, government. The States kept their sovereignty but came together for matters such as defense and trade.

**3. (a)** unicameral **(b)** chosen yearly from each State by whatever method the State chose

**4. (a)** no **(b)** The States failed to support the

central government, made alliances with foreign countries, and created their own money.

**5. (a)** that foreign countries would see each State as sovereign, and deal with them individually, rather than with Congress **(b)** Possible response: I agree. Foreign nations would see the States, not the nation, as capable of entering and enforcing agreements. This would undermine the United States as a nation.

**QUICK WRITE** Students should find personal accounts or interesting examples for their chosen dates or events.

# What compromises enabled the Framers to create the Constitution?

**Constitutional Compromises**

| Three-Fifths Compromise | Connecticut Compromise | Commerce and Slave Trade Compromise |
|---|---|---|
| • three fifths of slaves counted for representation<br>• three fifths of slaves counted for taxation | • bicameral Congress<br>• equal representation in Senate<br>• representation by State population in House | • Congress forbidden to tax exports<br>• Congress forbidden to interfere with slave trade until 1808<br>• Congress could regulate commerce |

## Get Started

### LESSON GOALS

Students will . . .

- use worksheets to analyze the different plans and compromises in creating the Constitution.
- use primary and secondary sources to evaluate the major compromises made at the Constitutional Convention.

## SKILLS DEVELOPMENT

### GIVE A MULTIMEDIA PRESENTATION

Before the debate in this lesson, you may want to review tips on giving a multimedia presentation in the Skills Handbook, p. S21.

---

**SECTION 4**

## Creating the
# Constitution

### Guiding Question

**What compromises enabled the Framers to create the Constitution?** Use a flowchart like the one below to record details about the Framers' compromises.

**Constitutional Compromises**

| Three-Fifths Compromise | Compromise | Compromise |
|---|---|---|
| •<br>•<br>• | •<br>•<br>• | •<br>•<br>• |

### Political Dictionary

- Framers
- Virginia Plan
- New Jersey Plan
- Connecticut Compromise
- Three-Fifths Compromise
- Commerce and Slave Trade Compromise

### Objectives

1. Identify the Framers of the Constitution and discuss how they organized the Philadelphia Convention.
2. Compare and contrast the Virginia Plan and the New Jersey Plan.
3. Summarize the convention's major compromises and the effects of those decisions.
4. Describe the delegates' reactions to the Constitution.

**Image Above:** George Washington was president of the Constitutional Convention.

---

Picture the scene. It is hot—sweltering, in fact. Yet all of the windows of the State House are closed and shuttered to discourage eavesdroppers. Outside, soldiers keep curious onlookers and others at a distance. Inside, the atmosphere is frequently tense as 50 or so men exchange sometimes heated views. Indeed, some who are there become so upset that they threaten to leave the hall, and a few actually do so.

This was often the scene at the Philadelphia meeting, which finally began on May 25, 1787.[11] Over the long summer months, until mid-September, the Framers of what was to become the Constitution worked to build a new government that could meet the needs of the nation. In this section, you will consider that meeting and its outcome.

### The Framers

Twelve of the 13 States, all but Rhode Island, sent delegates to Philadelphia.[12] In total, 74 delegates were chosen by the legislatures in those 12 states. For a number of reasons, however, only 55 of them actually attended the convention.

Of that 55, this much can be said: Never, before or since, has so remarkable a group been brought together in this country. Thomas Jefferson, who was not among them, later called the delegates "an assembly of demi-gods."

The delegates who attended the Philadelphia Convention, known as the **Framers** of the Constitution, included many outstanding individuals. These were men of wide knowledge and public experience. Many of them had fought in the Revolution; 46 had been members of the Continental Congress or the Congress of the Confederation, or both. Eight had served in constitutional conventions in their own States, and seven had been State governors. Eight had signed the Declaration of Independence. Thirty-four of the delegates had attended college in a day when there were but a few colleges in the land. Two were to become

---

11 Not enough States were represented on the date Congress had set, May 14, to begin the meeting. The delegates who were present met and adjourned each day until the 25th, when a quorum (a majority) of the States was on hand.

12 The Rhode Island legislature was controlled by the soft-money forces, mostly debtors and small farmers, who were helped by inflation and so were against a stronger central government. The New Hampshire delegation, delayed mostly by lack of funds, did not reach Philadelphia until late July.

---

## Focus on the Basics

**FACTS:** • The Constitutional Convention convened in Philadelphia to revise the Articles of Confederation. • The Virginia Plan and the New Jersey Plan each offered an approach to organizing a new government. • Delegates accepted compromises that led to agreement on the configuration of Congress and other issues.

**CONCEPTS:** compromise, constitutional government, limited government

**ENDURING UNDERSTANDINGS:** • The Framers produced one of the world's landmark documents. • The new plan of government addressed the major concerns of the States. • While the Framers made significant compromises, they agreed on the fundamental principles of popular sovereignty, limited government, separation of powers, and checks and balances.

Presidents of the United States, and one a Vice President. Nineteen later served in the Senate and thirteen in the House of Representatives.

Is it any wonder that the product of such a gathering was described by the English statesman William E. Gladstone, nearly a century later, as "the most wonderful work ever struck off at a given time by the brain and purpose of man"?

Remarkably, the average age of the delegates was only 42, and most of the leaders were in their 30s—James Madison was 36, Gouverneur Morris 35, Edmund Randolph 34, and Alexander Hamilton, 30. At 81, Benjamin Franklin was the oldest. His health was failing, however, and he was not able to attend many of the meetings. George Washington, at 55, was one of the few older members who played a key role at the Convention. Jonathan Dayton of New Jersey was, at 26, the youngest delegate.

By and large, the Framers of the Constitution were of a new generation in American politics. Several of the leaders of the Revolutionary period were not in Philadelphia. Patrick Henry said he "smelt a rat" and refused to attend. Samuel Adams, John Hancock, and Richard Henry Lee were not selected as delegates by their States. Thomas Paine was in Paris. So was Thomas Jefferson, as American minister to France. John Adams was the <u>envoy</u> to England and Holland at the time.

## Organization and Procedure

The Framers met in the State House (now Independence Hall), probably in the same room in which the Declaration of Independence had been signed 11 years earlier.

They organized immediately on May 25, unanimously electing George Washington president of the convention. Then, and at the second session on Monday, May 28, they adopted several rules of procedure. A majority of the States would be needed to conduct

✓ **Checkpoint**
What were some of the Framers' accomplishments?

**envoy**
*n.* a representative, especially in diplomatic affairs

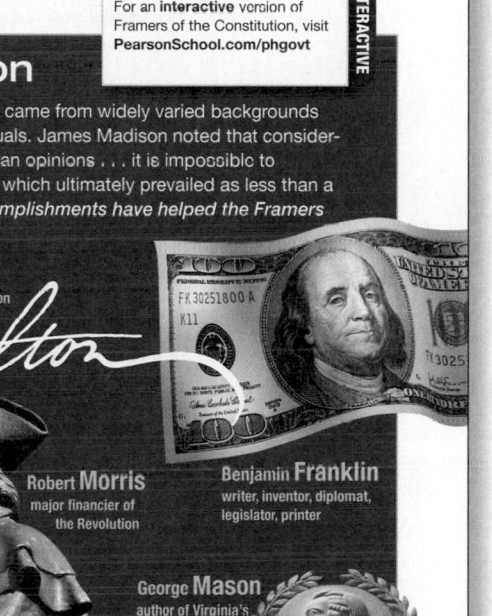

> GOVERNMENT ONLINE
> For an **interactive** version of Framers of the Constitution, visit **PearsonSchool.com/phgovt**

# Framers of the Constitution

The Framers of the Constitution came from widely varied backgrounds and were accomplished individuals. James Madison noted that considering "the natural diversity of human opinions . . . it is impossible to consider the degree of concord which ultimately prevailed as less than a miracle." *How might their accomplishments have helped the Framers to create the Constitution?*

George **Washington**
commander of the Continental Army

Alexander **Hamilton**
lawyer, signer of the Declaration of Independence

James **Madison**
major figure in the movement to replace the Articles of Confederation

Robert **Morris**
major financier of the Revolution

Benjamin **Franklin**
writer, inventor, diplomat, legislator, printer

George **Mason**
author of Virginia's Declaration of Rights

# Differentiated Resources

The following resources are located in the All-in-One, Unit 1, Chapter 2, Section 4:

- **L3** Reading Comprehension Worksheet (p. 97)
- **L2** Reading Comprehension Worksheet (p. 98)
- **L3** Core Worksheet (p. 99)
- **L3 L4** Extend Worksheet (p. 101)
- **L2** Extend Activity (p. 103)
- **L3** Quiz A (p. 104)
- **L2** Quiz B (p. 105)

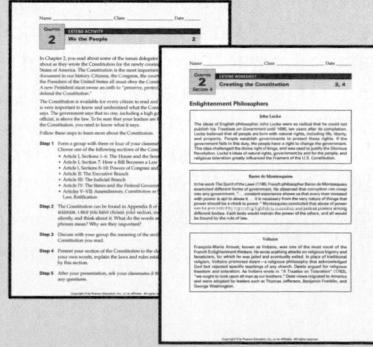

## BEFORE CLASS

Assign the section, the graphic organizer in the text, and the Reading Comprehension Worksheet (Unit 1 All-in-One, p. 97) before class.

**L2 Differentiate** Reading Comprehension Worksheet (Unit 1 All-in-One, p. 98)

## BELLRINGER

Display Transparency 2I. Write on the board: **Answer these questions in your notebook: (1) What is Franklin's main point? (2) What does he mean by "local interests" and "selfish views"? (3) What does his statement suggest about the difficulties faced by the Convention? (4) How would you paraphrase this statement?**

**L2 ELL Differentiate** Read the quote aloud, and have students paraphrase each clause's meaning.

# Teach

To present this topic using online resources, use the lesson presentations at **PearsonSchool.com/phgovt**.

## INTRODUCE THE TOPIC

Ask students to volunteer answers to the Bellringer questions. (*1. To form a government, every delegate made compromises that ran counter to his personal and sectional interests. 2. He means that each delegate had different ideas based on the concerns, needs, and demands of his State. 3. The Convention faced significant conflict, and compromises were crucial to success in resolving these issues and forming a government. 4. Possible paraphrase: The Constitution may not be flawless, but I accept and embrace it, because we need a government and no group could produce a better constitution. When you bring together such a diverse group, you get the benefit of their combined intelligence and judgment, but you also get their biases and concerns. Thus, it is remarkable that the Constitution comes so close to ideal.*)

**L1 L2 Differentiate** Review the text's photo essay about the Framers. Ask students what similarities, differences, and strengths they see in the background of these important people.

Tell students to go to the interactivity to learn more about the Framers of the Constitution.

---

# Answers

**Checkpoint** fought in the Revolution, served in Continental Congress or Congress of the Confederation, attended State constitutional conventions, served as State governors, signed Declaration of Independence, attended college

**Framers of the Constitution** Their accomplishments gave them the skills they needed to face such a task and to consider the issues from various points of view.

**L4 Differentiate** Which "local interests" and "selfish views" might this sampling of Framers reflect? Have students write a paragraph on this topic.

## COVER THE BASICS

Ask students to take out the Reading Comprehension Worksheet. Review the New Jersey Plan and the Virginia Plan. Ask: **What is the basic conflict underlying the differences between the two plans?** (Should the States be represented in Congress equally or by population?) **What problem did small States have with the Virginia Plan?** (States with large populations, which gave more money to the central government, would have more power to make laws that favored their own interests.) **What problem did large States have with the New Jersey Plan?** (States with small populations could thwart the will of the majority by blocking laws that did not benefit them.)

## SUMMARIZE

On the board, recreate the chart of compromises in Part 2 of the Reading Comprehension Worksheet. Call on volunteers to complete the chart. Point out that despite conflict, the Framers agreed on most basic principles. Ask students to identify these principles. (popular sovereignty, limited government, representative government, separation of powers, checks and balances)

**L2 Differentiate** Use the Jigsaw strategy (p. T27) and have students work in groups of three to become "experts" on one compromise. Have the students jigsaw into a second group with one "expert" on each compromise and have them review their answers together.

**Government** online *All print resources are available on the Teacher's Resource Library CD-ROM and online at* PearsonSchool.com/phgovt.

business. Each State delegation was to have one vote on all matters, and a majority of the votes cast would carry any proposal.

The Framers met on 92 of the 116 days from May 25 through their final meeting on September 17. They did most of their work on the floor of the convention. They handled some matters in committees, but the full body ultimately settled all questions.[13]

**A Momentous Decision** Remember, Congress had called the Philadelphia Convention "for the sole and express purpose" of recommending revisions to the Articles of Confederation. However, almost at once the delegates agreed that they were meeting to create an entirely new government for the United States. On May 30 they adopted this proposal:

> ## PRIMARY SOURCE
> **Resolved, . . . that a national Government ought to be established consisting of a supreme Legislative, Executive and Judiciary.**
> —Edmund Randolph, Delegate from Virginia

With this momentous decision, the Framers redefined the purpose of the convention. From that point on, they set about writing a new constitution, intended to replace the Articles of Confederation. (However, much that would go into this new constitution would come directly from the Articles of Confederation.) Their debates were spirited, even bitter. At times the convention seemed near collapse. Once they had passed Randolph's resolution, however, the resolve of most of the delegates never wavered.

## Proposals

Once the Framers resolved to replace the Articles of Confederation, two major plans were offered for the new government, the Virginia Plan and the New Jersey Plan.

---

[13] Twenty-nine delegates from seven States were present on the first day. The full number of 55 was not reached until August 6, when John Francis Mercer of Maryland arrived. In the meantime, some delegates had departed, and others were absent from time to time. Some 40 members attended most of the daily sessions of the convention.

**Virginia Plan** No State had more to do with the calling of the convention than Virginia. It was not surprising, then, that its delegates should offer the first plan for a new constitution. On May 29, the **Virginia Plan,** largely the work of Madison, was presented by Randolph.

The Virginia Plan called for a new government with three separate branches: legislative, executive, and judicial. The legislature—Congress—would be bicameral. Representation in each house was to be based either on each State's population or on the amount of money it gave for the support of the central government. The members of the lower house, the House of Representatives, were to be popularly elected in each State. Those of the upper house, the Senate, were to be chosen by the House from lists of persons nominated by the State legislatures.

Congress was to be given all of the powers it held under the Articles. In addition, it would have the power "to legislate in all cases to which the separate States are incompetent" to act, to veto any State law in conflict with national law, and to use force if necessary to make a State obey national law.

Under the proposed Virginia Plan, Congress would choose a "National Executive" and a "National Judiciary." Together, these two branches would form a "Council of revision." They could veto acts passed by Congress, but a veto could be overridden by the two houses. The executive would have "a general authority to execute the National laws." The judiciary would "consist of one or more supreme tribunals [courts], and of inferior tribunals."

The Virginia Plan also provided that all State officers should take an oath to support the Union, and that each State be guaranteed a republican form of government. Under the plan, Congress would have the exclusive power to admit new States to the Union.

The Virginia Plan, then, would create a new constitution by thoroughly revising the Articles. Its goal was the creation of a truly national government with greatly expanded powers and, importantly, the power to enforce its decisions.

The Virginia Plan set the agenda for much of the convention's work. But some delegates—especially those from New York

## Background

**JEAN-JACQUES ROUSSEAU** "Man is born free, but everywhere is in chains." Thus began Rousseau's *The Social Contract* (1762). Rousseau believed that a social contract exists between a government and the governed. The people agree to obey the laws and submit to the general will of society. In exchange, government agrees to protect the rights and equality of all people. Current governments, he argued, broke this contract by protecting only the wealthy and powerful, enslaving the common people. In such cases, the people should change the government. This idea of social contract underlies the Bill of Rights and the concept of consent of the governed.

This information also appears on the Extend Worksheet for Section 4, along with information about other influential philosophers covered in this chapter.

and the smaller States of Delaware, Maryland, and New Jersey—found it too radical.[14] Soon they developed their counterproposals. On June 15, William Paterson of New Jersey presented the position of the small States.

**The New Jersey Plan** Paterson and his colleagues offered several amendments to the Articles, but not nearly so thorough a revision as that proposed by the Virginia Plan. The **New Jersey Plan** retained the unicameral Congress of the Confederation, with each of the States equally represented. In addition to those powers Congress already had, the plan would add closely limited powers to tax and to regulate trade between the States.

The New Jersey Plan also called for a "federal executive" of more than one person. This plural executive would be chosen by Congress and could be removed by it at the request of a majority of the States' governors. The "federal judiciary" would be composed of a single "supreme Tribunal," appointed by the executive.

Among their several differences, the major point of disagreement between the two plans centered on this question: How should the States be represented in Congress? Would it be on the basis of their populations or financial contributions, as in the Virginia Plan? Or would it be on the basis of State equality, as in the Articles and the New Jersey Plan?

For weeks the delegates returned to this conflict, debating the matter again and again. The lines were sharply drawn. Several delegates on both sides of the issue threatened to withdraw. Finally, the dispute was settled by one of the key compromises the Framers were to make as they built the Constitution.

## Compromises

The disagreement over representation in Congress was critical. The larger States expected to dominate the new government. The smaller States feared that they would not be able to protect their interests. Tempers flared on both sides. The debate became so

---

[14] The Virginia Plan's major support came from the three most populous States: Virginia, Pennsylvania, and Massachusetts. New York was then only the fifth most populous State.

## The Enlightenment and American Government

**GOVERNMENT** ONLINE
**Audio Tour**
Listen to a guided audio tour of these philosophers' words at
**PearsonSchool.com/phgovt**

The 17th and 18th centuries are known as the Enlightenment; a period where thinkers based their philosophies on reason. This movement greatly influenced the leaders of the new American government. Read these quotes from four Enlightenment thinkers.

***In what ways do they parallel the principles of American Government?***

" The end of law is not to abolish or restrain, but to preserve and enlarge freedom. For in all the states of created beings capable of law, where there is no law, there is no freedom. — *The Second Treatise of Government*, 1690

john **Locke**

" The people, in whom the supreme power resides, ought to have the management of everything within their reach: that which exceeds their abilities must be conducted by their ministers. But they cannot be said to have their ministers [agents], without the power of nominating them: . . . therefore . . . the people should choose their ministers. — *The Spirit of Laws*, 1748

baron de **Montesquieu**

" If we enquire wherein lies precisely the greatest good of all, which ought to be the goal of every system of law, we shall find that it comes down to two main objects, *freedom* and *equality*: freedom because any individual dependence means that much strength drawn from the body of the state, and equality because freedom cannot survive without it. — *The Social Contract*, 1762

jean jacques **Rousseau**

" The absolute rights of man . . . are usually summed up in one general appellation [name] . . . of acting as one thinks fit, without any restraint or control, unless by the law of nature: being a right inherent in us by birth, and one of the gifts of God to man at his creation, when he endued [provided] him with the faculty of free-will. — *Commentaries on the Laws of England*, 1765–1769

william **Blackstone**

---

**DISTRIBUTE THE CORE WORKSHEET**

Distribute the Chapter 2 Section 4 Core Worksheet (Unit 1 All-in-One, p. 99), which asks students to examine a population chart of the original States and to analyze in detail two issues that led to key constitutional compromises: size of population and slavery.

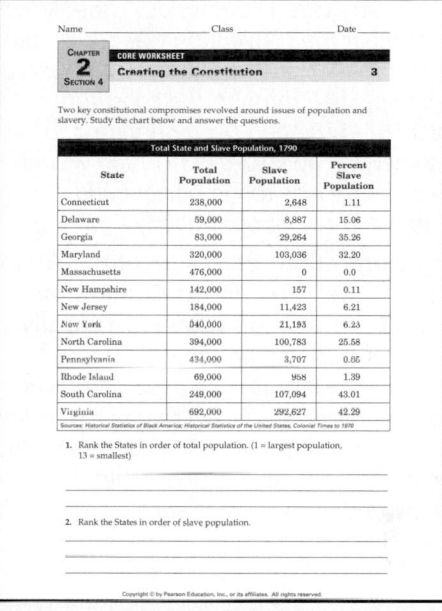

**L1 L2 Differentiate** Walk through the lesson as a class, rather than having students work alone.

**L4 Differentiate** James Madison reported that "The States were divided into different interests not by their differences of size, but principally from them having or not having slaves. . . . It did not lie between the large and small States: it lay between the Northern and Southern." Ask students to write a paragraph about how this difference in interests influenced the framing of the Constitution.

Tell students to go to the Audio Tour for a guided audio tour of Enlightenment thinkers' words.

---

# Debate

Divide the class in half, with one group representing Framers in favor of the Virginia Plan and the other half representing Framers proposing the New Jersey Plan. Have students debate the following questions: **How should States be represented in Congress? Should it be on the basis of their populations or financial contributions, or on the basis of State equality?** After students have debated, ask them how the Connecticut Compromise finally settled the conflict.

---

## Answers

**The Enlightenment and American Government**
Locke: purpose of law to protect freedom; Montesquieu: popular sovereignty, representative government; Rousseau: freedom, equality; Blackstone: natural rights

Use these questions to continue a discussion about constitutional compromises:

**1. In the Three-Fifths Compromise, the Constitution never uses the words "slave" or "slavery." Instead it refers to "free persons" and "three fifths of all other persons." Why do you think this was so?** *(Slavery was a contentious issue. Much of the deliberation at the convention was secret, but according to the book* Founding Brothers: *"If political leaders who had pushed through the constitutional settlement of 1787–1788 had been permitted to speak, their somewhat awkward conclusion would have been that slavery was too important and controversial a subject to talk about publicly." [p. 84])*

**2. What misgivings might each side of the Great Compromise and the Three-Fifths Compromise have held? Did their worries prove historically true?** *(Small States were worried that they could not protect their interests against the power of large States. States dependent on slavery feared that other States would push through laws banning slavery. The latter fear did prove valid, as sectional rivalries over slavery eventually led to the Civil War.)*

## Slavery in the United States, 1790

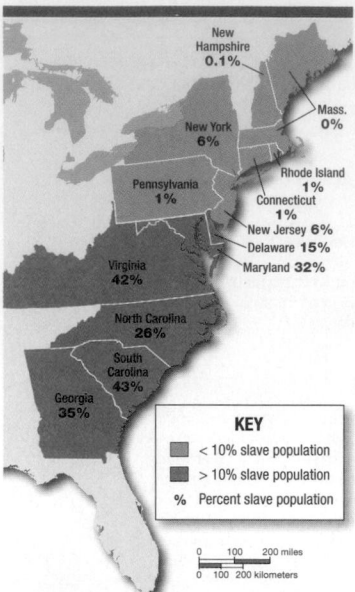

New Hampshire 0.1%
Mass. 0%
New York 6%
Rhode Island 1%
Pennsylvania 1%
Connecticut 1%
New Jersey 6%
Delaware 15%
Maryland 32%
Virginia 42%
North Carolina 26%
South Carolina 43%
Georgia 35%

**KEY**
- < 10% slave population
- > 10% slave population
- **%** Percent slave population

0    100    200 miles
0  100  200 kilometers

▶▶ **Analyzing Maps** The southern States had a larger slave population than did the northern States at the time of the Constitutional Convention. *How might this have affected their stance on the Three-Fifths and Commerce and Slave Trade compromises?*

✔ **Checkpoint**
What was the Connecticut Compromise?

intense that Benjamin Franklin was moved to suggest that "henceforth prayers imploring the assistance of Heaven . . . be held in this Assembly every morning before we proceed to business."

**Connecticut Compromise** The conflict was settled by a compromise suggested by the Connecticut delegation. In the **Connecticut Compromise,** it was agreed that Congress should be composed of two houses. In the smaller Senate, the States would be represented equally. In the House, the representation of each State would be based upon its population.

By combining basic features of the plans, the convention's most serious dispute was resolved. The agreement satisfied the smaller States in particular, allowing them to support the creation of a strong central government.

The Connecticut Compromise was so pivotal to the writing of the Constitution that it has often been called the Great Compromise.

**Three-Fifths Compromise** Once it had been agreed to base the seats in the House on each State's population, this question arose: Should slaves be counted in figuring the populations of the States?

Again debate was fierce. Most delegates from the southern States argued that slaves should be counted. Most of the northerners took the opposing view. All could see the contradictions between slavery and the sentiments expressed in the Declaration of Independence, but slavery was legal in every State except

Massachusetts. The slave population was concentrated in the southern States, however, as you can see from the map on this page.

Finally, the Framers agreed to the **Three-Fifths Compromise.** It provided that all "free persons" should be counted, and so, too, should "three fifths of all other persons" (Article I, Section 2, Clause 3). For "all other persons," read "slaves." For the three fifths won by the southerners, the northerners exacted a price. That formula was also to be used in fixing the amount of money to be raised in each State by any direct tax levied by Congress. In short, the southerners could count their slaves, but they would have to pay for them.

This odd compromise disappeared from the Constitution with the adoption of the 13th Amendment, abolishing slavery, in 1865. For nearly 150 years, there have been no "all other persons" in this country.

**Commerce and Slave Trade Compromise** The Framers generally agreed that Congress must have the power to regulate foreign and interstate trade. To many southerners, that power carried a real danger, however. They worried that Congress, likely to be controlled by northern commercial interests, would act against the interests of the agricultural South.

They were particularly fearful that Congress would try to pay for the new government out of export duties, and southern tobacco was the major American export of the time. They also feared that Congress would interfere with the slave trade.

Before they would agree to the commerce power, the southerners insisted on certain protections. So, according to the **Commerce and Slave Trade Compromise,** Congress was forbidden the power to tax the export of goods from any State. It was also forbidden the power to act on the slave trade for a period of at least 20 years. It could not interfere with "the migration or importation of such persons as any State now existing shall think proper to admit," except for a small head tax, at least until the year 1808.[15]

---

**15** Article I, Section 9, Clause 1. Congress promptly banned the importation of slaves in 1808, and, in 1820, it declared the slave trade to be piracy. The smuggling of the enslaved into this country continued until the outbreak of the Civil War, however.

# Background

**WILLIAM BLACKSTONE** William Blackstone was no fan of American independence. Yet his *Commentaries on the Laws of England* would greatly influence America's founding documents, including the Declaration of Independence and Constitution. In his *Commentaries,* he distilled the vast bulk on English common law into four clearly written, understandable volumes. Once Americans had won their rights on the battlefield, they turned to the *Commentaries* for a summary of those rights. Readers included John Adams, John Jay, and James Wilson. Despite their disdain for Blackstone's politics, the Framers often referred to his work as they laid the nation's legal foundation.

This information also appears on the Extend Worksheet for Section 4, along with information about other influential philosophers covered in this chapter.

## Answers

**Analyzing Maps** Southern States wanted slaves counted for representation but not taxation. To win southern support of commerce power, northern States had to agree to forbid Congress to interfere with the slave trade for 20 years.

**Checkpoint** agreement establishing a bicameral Congress, with equal representation in the Senate and representation by State population in the House

## The Connecticut Compromise

"All legislative Powers herein granted shall be vested in a Congress of the United States, which shall consist of a Senate and House of Representatives." —Article 1, Section 1

# FROM THE CONSTITUTION

**The Great Compromise** The Connecticut delegates Roger Sherman, Oliver Ellsworth, and William Samuel Johnson presented their compromise to the Philadelphia Convention as a means to end the deadlock between supporters of the rival New Jersey and Virginia Plans. The compromise incorporated parts of each plan in order to resolve the dispute over representation.

**Constitutional Principles**
In what ways did each plan propose to limit the powers of the legislative and executive branches?

▲ Seated at the table are William Samuel Johnson (left) and Roger Sherman at the signing of the Constitution.

**A "Bundle of Compromises"** The convention spent much of its time, said Franklin, "sawing boards to make them fit." The Constitution drafted at Philadelphia has often been called a "bundle of compromises." Those descriptions are apt, if they are properly understood.

There were differences of opinion among the delegates, certainly. After all, the delegates came from 12 different States widely separated in geographic and economic terms, and the delegates often reflected the particular interests of their own States. Bringing those interests together did require compromise. Indeed, final decisions on issues such as the selection of the President, the treaty-making process, the structure of the national court system, and the amendment process were all reached as a result of compromise.

But by no means did all, or even most, of what shaped the document come from compromises. The Framers were agreed on many of the basic issues they faced. Thus, nearly all the delegates were convinced that a new national government, a federal government, had to be created, and that it had to have the

powers necessary to deal with the nation's grave social and economic problems. The Framers were also dedicated to the concepts of popular sovereignty and limited government. None questioned for a moment the wisdom of representative government. The principles of separation of powers and of checks and balances were accepted almost as a matter of course.

Many disputes did occur, and the compromises by which they were resolved came only after hours, days, and even weeks of heated debate. The point here, however, is that the differences were not over the most fundamental of questions. They involved, instead, such vital but lesser points as these: the details of the structure of Congress, the method by which the President was to be chosen, and the practical limits that should be put on the several powers to be given to the new central government.

For several weeks, through the hot Philadelphia summer, the delegates took up resolution after resolution. On September 8, a committee was named "to revise the stile of and arrange the articles which had been agreed to" by the

**apt**
*adj.* appropriate, correct, fit

# Political Cartoon Mini-Lesson

Display Transparency 2K, Steps in the Establishment of a More Stable Government, as a wrap-up activity. This mid-20th century cartoon depicts the three conventions as steps taking America out of the morass of the Articles of Confederation up to higher, more stable ground with the Constitution. Ask: **What do the steps represent?** *(the three conventions leading to the Constitution)* **How does the cartoonist depict the Articles of Confederation? Why?** *(as dark flowing water, to symbolize the instability of the Articles)* **How does the color of the sky change as Uncle Sam ascends?** *(from darker to lighter)* **How does this detail contribute to the message of the cartoon?** *(America is emerging out of the darkness, or turmoil, under the Articles into a brighter future under the Constitution.)*

---

## EXTEND THE LESSON

Display the "Selected Framers of the Constitution" chart on Transparency 2J. Survey students about how many names they recognize. Point out that all these Framers were distinguished in their day. Ask students what similarities they see in their backgrounds. What strengths did they bring to the Philadelphia convention? Assign partners or small groups one of the Framers. Allow time for students to find portraits and biographical information about each Framer. Much of this information is available from the National Archives Web site. They should use the information to create a "yearbook page" for the Framer of their choice. This page should include the following information: the Framer's State and occupation, his contribution to the Constitutional Convention, his attitude toward the different compromises, and his contribution to American politics and government before and after the convention.

**L2 Differentiate** Assign students one of the more recognizable Framers, who will be easier to research, such as Washington, Franklin, Madison, or Hamilton.

**L2 L1 Differentiate** For these students, distribute the Extend Activity entitled "We the People" (Unit 1 All-in-One, p. 103).

**L3 L4 Differentiate** Have students review "The Enlightenment and American Government" feature in the text along with the Extend Worksheet (Unit 1 All-in-One, p. 101) on Locke, Montesquieu, Voltaire, Rousseau, and Blackstone. Have students create a chart identifying ideas from each philosopher that contributed to the framing of the Constitution.

**L4 Differentiate** Ask students how these philosophers would have viewed the process of framing a constitution. Which compromises would these philosophers have found out of step with Enlightenment thinking? Have students write a brief response to these questions from the point of view of one of the philosophers in this group.

**L4 Differentiate** Have students review the information on the Extend Worksheet about the philosophers. Then students should use the information to make a "superlatives" yearbook page, with categories such as "most likely to" and "best philosopher." Students should come up with the categories and explain them.

---

## Answers

**Constitutional Principles** Each plan proposed separate branches, each with the power to veto acts of the other two.

# Assess and Remediate

**L3** Collect the Core Worksheet and assess students' work.

**L3** Assign the Section 4 Assessment questions.

**L3** Section Quiz A (All-in-One, p. 104)

**L2** Section Quiz B (All-in-One, p. 105)

Have students complete the review activities in the digital lesson presentation and continue their work in the **Essential Questions Journal.**

## REMEDIATION

| If Your Students Have Trouble With | Strategies For Remediation |
|---|---|
| The goals and structure of the Philadelphia Convention. (Questions 2, 3) | Have students reread the content under "Organization and Procedure" in this section. |
| The plans and compromises (Questions 1, 5) | Have groups become experts on one of the plans or compromises. Then have them explain it to the rest of the class. |
| The merit of the Articles of Confederation (Question 4) | Have students brainstorm the strengths and weaknesses of the Articles and list them on the board. Then lead a discussion on the merits of the Articles of Confederation. |

## Answers

**Checkpoint** Delegates agreed on the most fundamental principles, but many vital lesser points required compromise.

---

✔ **Checkpoint**
Why was the Constitution called "a bundle of compromises"?

convention. That committee, the Committee of Stile and Arrangement, put the Constitution into its final form. Finally, on September 17, the convention approved its work and 39 names were placed on the finished document.[16] Because not all of the delegates were willing to sign the Constitution, its final paragraph was very carefully worded to give the impression of unanimity: "Done in Convention by the Unanimous Consent of the States present. . . ."

Perhaps none of the Framers was completely satisfied with their work. Nevertheless, wise old Benjamin Franklin put into words what many of them must have thought on that final day:

"Sir, I agree with this Constitution with all its faults, if they are such; because I think a general Government necessary for us . . . I doubt . . . whether any other Convention we can obtain, may be able to make a better Constitution. For when you assemble a number of men to have the advantage of their joint wisdom, you inevitably assemble with those men, all their prejudices, their passions, their errors of opinion, their local interests,

---

[16] Three of the 41 delegates present on that last day refused to sign the proposed Constitution: Edmund Randolph of Virginia, who later supported ratification and served as Attorney General and then Secretary of State under President Washington; Elbridge Gerry of Massachusetts, who later became Vice President under Madison; and George Mason of Virginia, who continued to oppose the Constitution until his death in 1792. George Read of Delaware signed both for himself and for his absent colleague John Dickinson.

---

and their selfish views. From such an assembly can a perfect production be expected? It therefore astonishes me, Sir, to find this system approaching so near to perfection as it does . . . "

—*Notes* of Debates in the Federal Convention of 1787, James Madison

On Franklin's motion, the Constitution was signed. Madison tells us that

### " PRIMARY SOURCE

. . . Doctor Franklin, looking towards the President's chair, at the back of which a rising sun happened to be painted, observed to a few members near him, that painters had found it difficult to distinguish in their art a rising sun from a setting sun. 'I have,' said he, 'often and often in the course of the Session . . . looked at that behind the President without being able to tell whether it was rising or setting: But now at length I have the happiness to know that it is a rising and not a setting Sun.'

—*Notes* of Debates in the Federal Convention of 1787, James Madison

---

**Essential Questions Journal** To continue to build a response to the chapter Essential Question, go to your **Essential Questions Journal.**

## SECTION 4 ASSESSMENT

1. **Guiding Question** Use your completed flowchart to answer this question: What compromises enabled the Framers to create the Constitution?

**Key Terms and Comprehension**

2. **(a)** What was the goal of the **Framers** when they met at Independence Hall? **(b)** How did that goal change?

3. What was the purpose of keeping the discussions within the Constitutional Convention a secret?

**Critical Thinking**

4. **Test Conclusions** The Framers abandoned the Articles of Confederation in favor of an entirely new constitution. Do you agree with their decision? Why or why not?

5. **Identify Central Issues** Explain the differences between the Virginia Plan and the New Jersey Plan. How were these differences resolved?

**Quick Write**

**Narrative Writing: Choose a Main Idea** When writing narrative nonfiction, it is important to have a main idea. This idea will help you stay on track as you write the story of your colony. Look through your notes and write a main idea.

---

# Assessment Answers

1. **Connecticut Compromise:** bicameral Congress, with States represented equally in the Senate and by population in the House; **Three-Fifths Compromise:** three fifths of all slaves counted for voting and taxing; **Commerce and Slave Trade Compromise:** Congress cannot tax exports or interfere with slave trade for at least 20 years

2. **(a)** to revise the Articles of Confederation **(b)** They realized they needed to create an entirely new constitution.

3. The talks were kept secret to encourage the free exchange of ideas and to protect the delegates from outside pressures.

4. Possible response: I agree with the Framers' decision to abandon the Articles. The government set up under it was too weak to sustain a nation. For example, Congress did not have the power to tax, so it could not pay debts. States made their own money, which caused radical inflation.

5. The Virginia Plan called for a bigger central government with a bicameral legislature. Each State would be represented by population or by the amount of money it contributed. The New Jersey Plan proposed a central government with closely limited powers and a unicameral legislature. Each State would be equally represented. The Connecticut Compromise resolved the plans' differences by creating a Congress with two houses. Each State is represented equally in the Senate and by population in the House of Representatives.

**QUICK WRITE** Students should find a central idea that unites their facts and details into one story.

## SECTION 5

# Ratifying the Constitution

### Guiding Question

**What issues aroused the vigorous debate over the ratification of the Constitution?** Use an outline like the one below to keep track of the issues debated during ratification.

I. Ratification of the Constitution
  A. Federalist Arguments
    1. _____
    2. _____
  B. Anti-Federalist Arguments
    1. _____
    2. _____

### Political Dictionary
• Federalist     • Anti-Federalist

### Objectives
1. Identify the opposing sides in the fight for ratification and describe the major arguments for and against the proposed Constitution.
2. Describe the inauguration of the new government of the United States of America.

**Image Above:** This poster celebrates the bicentennial of Virginia's ratification of the Constitution.

Today, the Constitution of the United States is the object of unparalleled admiration and respect, both here and abroad. But in 1787 and 1788, it was widely criticized, and in every State there were many who opposed its adoption. The battle over the ratification of the document was not easily decided.

## The Fight for Ratification

Remember, the Articles of Confederation provided that changes could be made to them only if *all* of the State legislatures agreed. But the Framers had determined that the new Constitution would replace, not <u>amend</u>, the Articles. They had seen how crippling the requirement of unanimity could be. So, the new Constitution provided that

### FROM THE CONSTITUTION

**The ratification of the conventions of nine States shall be sufficient for the establishment of this Constitution between the States so ratifying the same.**

—Article VII

The Congress of the Confederation agreed to this irregular procedure. On September 28, 1787, it sent copies of the new document to the States.

**Federalists and Anti-Federalists** The Constitution circulated widely and was debated vigorously. Two groups quickly emerged in each of the States: the **Federalists,** who favored ratification, and the **Anti-Federalists,** who opposed it.

The Federalists were led by many of those who attended the Philadelphia Convention. Among the most active were James Madison and Alexander Hamilton. The opposition was headed by such well-known Revolutionary War figures as Patrick Henry, Richard Henry Lee, John Hancock, and Samuel Adams.

The Federalists stressed the weaknesses of the Articles. They argued that the many difficulties facing the Republic could be overcome only by the creation of new government based on the Constitution.

## Focus on the Basics

**FACTS:** • The Constitution took effect after 11 States voted for ratification. • The Federalists promoted ratification of the Constitution. • The Anti-Federalists opposed the Constitution for its strong central government and lack of a bill of rights. • Alexander Hamilton, James Madison, and John Jay wrote essays known as the *Federalist Papers,* supporting the Constitution. • In March 1789, the new Congress convened in New York City, the temporary capital.

**CONCEPTS:** limited government, compromise

**ENDURING UNDERSTANDINGS:** • The Federalists supported a strong central government while the Anti-Federalists opposed increasing the powers of central government.
• The *Federalist* papers influenced public opinion in favor of ratification.

## What issues aroused the vigorous debate over ratification of the Constitution?

I. Ratification of the Constitution
  A. Federalist Arguments
    1. Articles too weak
    2. strong government needed to solve nation's problems
    3. liberties protected in State constitutions
    4. separation of powers would prevent abuse
  B. Anti-Federalist Arguments
    1. ratification process flawed
    2. presidency could become monarchy
    3. Congress could become too powerful
    4. lacked bill of rights
    5. States lacked power to print money

## Get Started

### LESSON GOALS

Students will . . .

• analyze the positions of the Federalists and the Anti-Federalists, using primary sources.

• use primary sources to evaluate arguments in favor of and opposed to a bill of rights.

### BEFORE CLASS

Assign the section, the graphic organizer in the text, and the Reading Comprehension Worksheet (Unit 1 All-in-One, p. 106) before class.

**L2 Differentiate** Reading Comprehension Worksheet (Unit 1 All-in-One, p. 107)

## SKILLS DEVELOPMENT

### ANALYZE POLITICAL CARTOONS

To help students learn to analyze political cartoons when the class discusses the cartoon in the textbook, have them turn to the Skills Handbook, p. S22, and use the steps explained there.

## BELLRINGER

Distribute the Bellringer Worksheet (Unit 1 All-in-One, p. 108). Ask students to study the chart about ratification and answer the questions.

# Teach

To present this topic using online resources, use the lesson presentations at **PearsonSchool.com/phgovt.**

## INTRODUCE THE TOPIC

Today students will discuss the struggle for ratification of a new constitution and the establishment of a new government. Point out that the table from the Bellringer reflects how contentious and emotionally charged the battle for ratification was. Have students share their answers.

## DISCUSS

Display Transparency 2L and ask: **What important issues divided the Federalists and the Anti-Federalists?** *(Federalists believed that a strong central government with powers divided among executive, legislative, and judicial branches was necessary to hold the new country together. The Anti-Federalists favored a weaker central government, more power for State governments, and strong protections of individual rights.)*

Direct students' attention to the text's cartoon showing columns with State labels. What point is the cartoon making? *(The proposed Constitution will form a strong foundation for the nation. If the States don't ratify it, the nation will fail.)*

**L1 L2 Differentiate** Write the Federalist and Anti-Federalist positions on the board in a table format.

**L4 Differentiate** Have students create a cartoon that presents the Anti-Federalist position and answers the cartoon on this page.

## DISTRIBUTE THE CORE WORKSHEET

Distribute the Chapter 2 Section 5 Core Worksheet (Unit 1 All-in-One, p. 109), which asks students to analyze primary source excerpts about ratification of the Constitution. Students can work with partners or individually to complete Part 1. After students share their answers, have them complete the ranking activity in Part 2.

Tell students to go to the Audio Tour to listen to a guided audio tour of the ratification arguments.

---

## Answers

**Checkpoint** Ratification would require approval of nine instead of all thirteen States.

**Two Sides of Ratification** The Federalists emphasized the nation as a whole, while the Anti-Federalists wanted to preserve more power for the States.

---

**amend**
*v.* to change or modify

The Anti-Federalists attacked nearly every part of the document. Many objected to the ratification process. Several worried that the presidency could become a monarchy and that Congress would become too powerful. In Massachusetts, Amos Singletary, a delegate to the ratifying convention, condemned the Federalists:

"These lawyers, and men of learning, and monied men, that talk so finely and gloss over matters so smoothly, to make us poor illiterate people, swallow down the pill, expect to get into Congress themselves; they expect to . . . get all the power and all the money into their own hands, and then they will swallow up all us little folks . . . just as the whale swallowed up Jonah."[17]
—**Amos Singletary**

17 S.B. Harding, "The Contest Over the Ratification of the Federal Constitution in the State of Massachusetts," 1896, as quoted in Carl Van Doren, *The Great Rehearsal,* 1948.

The lack of one major feature of the proposed Constitution drew the heaviest fire: a bill of rights. The new document did contain some protections of individual rights—for example, a provision for the writ of habeas corpus, which is a protection against arbitrary arrest. The Framers had made no provision for such basic liberties as freedom of speech, press, and religion, however—largely because those matters were covered by the existing State constitutions. They also believed that because the powers to be granted to the new government would be fragmented among three branches, no branch of the government could become powerful enough to threaten the rights of the people.

Everywhere, the Anti-Federalists bore down on the absence of a bill of rights. At Virginia's ratifying convention, Patrick Henry said of the proposed Constitution, "I look on that paper as the most fatal plan that could possibly be conceived to enslave a free

**GOVERNMENT ONLINE**
**Audio Tour**
Listen to a guided audio tour of these arguments at PearsonSchool.com/phgovt

### The Federalist/Anti-Federalist Argument
# Two Sides of Ratification

The Federalists and Anti-Federalists felt very strongly about the proposed Constitution. Ratification was fiercely debated in letters, articles, cartoons, and public forums. *Read the arguments for each side and the comments by Alexander Hamilton and Patrick Henry. What do these comments reveal about the sentiments of the time?*

**Federalist**
- The Articles of Confederation are too weak.
- Only a stronger national government can overcome the difficulties the Republic faces.
- Liberties that could be included in a bill of rights are covered in the State constitutions.

**Anti-Federalist**
- The States would no longer have the power to print money.
- The national government would be given too much power.
- There should be a bill of rights.

"The subject speaks its own importance; comprehending in its consequences **nothing less than the existence of the UNION,** the safety and welfare of the parts of which it is composed, the fate of an empire in many respects the most interesting in the world."
— Alexander Hamilton,
*The Federalist,* No. 1, 1787

"The fate of this question and America may depend on this: **Have they said, we the States?** Have they made a proposal of a compact between States? If they had this would be a confederation..."
— Patrick Henry,
Speech before the
Virginia Ratifying
Convention,
June 5, 1788

---

# Differentiated Resources

The following resources are located in the All-in-One, Unit 1, Chapter 2, Section 5:

**L3** Reading Comprehension Worksheet (p. 106)
**L2** Reading Comprehension Worksheet (p. 107)
**L3** Bellringer Worksheet (p. 108)
**L3** Core Worksheet (p. 109)
**L2** Extend Activity (p. 113)
**L3** Quiz A (p. 114)   **L2** Quiz B (p. 115)
**L3** Chapter Test A (p. 116)
**L2** Chapter Test B (p. 119)

United we stand—Divided we fall.

► Columns representing the States that had ratified the Constitution are placed in a row by the hand of God. **Is this a Federalist or Anti-Federalist cartoon? In which States was ratification won by only a narrow margin?**

## Ratification of the Constitution

| State | Date | Vote |
|---|---|---|
| Delaware | Dec. 7, 1787 | 30–0 |
| Pennsylvania | Dec. 12, 1787 | 46–23 |
| New Jersey | Dec. 18, 1787 | 38–0 |
| Georgia | Jan. 2, 1788 | 26–0 |
| Connecticut | Jan. 9, 1788 | 128–40 |
| Massachusetts | Feb. 6, 1788 | 187–168 |
| Maryland | April 28, 1788 | 63–11 |
| South Carolina | May 23, 1788 | 149–73 |
| New Hampshire | June 21, 1788 | 57–46 |
| Virginia | June 25, 1788 | 89–79 |
| New York | July 26, 1788 | 30–27 |
| North Carolina* | Nov. 21, 1789 | 195–77 |
| Rhode Island | May 29, 1790 | 34–32 |

\* Second vote; ratification was originally defeated on August 4, 1788, by a vote of 184–84.

people." Stung by the criticism, the Federalists promised that the Constitution, once adopted, would be amended to overcome this fault.

Over the course of the struggle for ratification, an extraordinary number of essays, speeches, letters, and other commentaries were printed. Of them all, the most remarkable were a series of 85 essays that first appeared in various newspapers in New York in the fall of 1787 on into the spring of 1788. Those essays, supporting the Constitution, were written by Alexander Hamilton, James Madison, and John Jay, and they were soon published in book form as *The Federalist: A Commentary on the Constitution of the United States*. All of the essays bore the pen name "Publius" (Latin for "Public Man"), and they were reprinted throughout the 13 States. They remain an excellent commentary on the Constitution and rank among the finest of all political writings in the English language.

The Anti-Federalists' attacks were also published widely. Among the best of their works were several essays usually attributed to Robert Yates, who had been one of New York's delegates to the Philadelphia Convention; they were signed by "Brutus" and appeared in the *New York Journal* at the same time that the paper carried several of the *Federalist* essays. The Anti-Federalists' views were also presented in pamphlets and letters written by

Richard Henry Lee of Virginia, who used the pen name "The Federal Farmer."

**Nine States Ratify** Ratification came fairly quickly in a few States and only after a bitter struggle in others. Delaware was the first to approve the Constitution, on December 7. Pennsylvania followed five days later. In Pennsylvania, however, where the legislature had been slow to call a ratifying convention, several Federalists, angered by Anti-Federalist delays, took matters into their own hands. They broke into a Philadelphia boarding house, seized two legislators hiding there, and forcibly marched them to the State house so the assembly could vote to schedule the convention.

The contest for ratification was close in several States, but the Federalists finally prevailed in all of them. On June 21, 1788, New Hampshire brought the number of ratifying States to nine.

Under Article VII, New Hampshire's ratification should have brought the Constitution into effect, but it did not. Neither Virginia nor New York had yet ratified. Without either of those key States the new government could not hope to succeed.

**Virginia's Ratification** Virginia's vote for ratification followed New Hampshire's by just four days. The brilliant debates in its convention were followed closely throughout the

✔ **Checkpoint**
Why did the Framers not include a bill of rights in the original Constitution?

## Constitutional Principles

**FEDERALISM AND STATES' RIGHTS** The delegates to the Constitutional Convention agreed on the fundamental principle of federalism—power divided between the central government and the States. But controversy emerged over how much power each should have. Anti-Federalists preferred more power to the States, a position later known as States' rights. States' rights advocates favored limiting the powers of the National Government to those specifically assigned to it in the Constitution. The States would retain all powers not explicitly forbidden them. This controversy would not be solved with ratification of the new Constitution. Because the issue of States' rights was tightly intertwined with slavery, it would continue to cause heated debate and violent clashes, culminating in the Civil War. Today, States' rights advocates try to limit national power through strict interpretation of the terms in the Constitution.

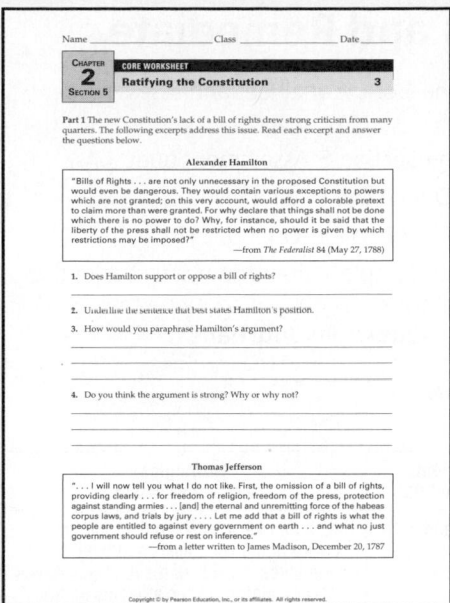

**L1 L2 Differentiate** The excerpts by Thomas Jefferson and Charles Cotesworth Pinckney are most appropriate for lower-level students. Have them work with partners or in small groups to read these two excerpts and answer the questions.

**L2 ELL Differentiate** Preview vocabulary from the Jefferson and Pinckney excerpts to support student comprehension: *omission* (lack); *unremitting* (never stopping); *are entitled to* (deserve); *insertion* (addition); *consists* (is made of).

**L4 Differentiate** Have students write an editorial that would appear in the Providence Journal on May 28, 1790, the day before Rhode Island voted for ratification. The editorial should argue one of the following points: (1) The Constitution should be ratified with a bill of rights. (2) The Constitution should be ratified without a bill of rights.

### EXTEND THE LESSON

Have partners research the positions expressed in either the Federalist or Anti-Federalist papers on one of these issues: checks and balances, reserved powers, absence of the mention of God in the Constitution, the denial of the power to print money, or the power of the presidency. If the position resulted in a compromise or resolution, they should explain that as well. Encourage partners to share and compare their findings on their issue.

**L2 Differentiate** Distribute the Extend Activity "Influence of the Press" (Unit 1 All-in-One, p. 113).

## Answers

**Interpreting Tables** Federalist cartoon; Rhode Island, New York, Virginia

**Checkpoint** They believed liberties were protected by the State constitutions.

# Assess and Remediate

**L3** Collect the Core Worksheet and assess students' work.

**L3** Assign the Section 5 Assessment questions.

**L3** Section Quiz A (All-in-One, p. 114)

**L2** Section Quiz B (All-in-One, p. 115)

Have students complete the review activities in the digital lesson presentation and continue their work in the **Essential Questions Journal.**

## REMEDIATION

| If Your Students Have Trouble With | Strategies For Remediation |
|---|---|
| The Federalist and Anti-Federalist arguments (Questions 2, 3, 4) | Hold a debate, in which one group takes the side of the Federalists and the other group takes the side of the Anti-Federalists. Act as mediator to keep students on track. |
| The ratification process (Question 5) | List the States in no particular order. As a class, create a timeline on the board, plotting when each State ratified the Constitution. |

## Answers

**Checkpoint** New York was a large commercial State that effectively separated New England from the rest of the nation.

---

✔ **Checkpoint**
Why was New York such a key ratification State?

**inauguration**
*n.* a ceremonial induction into office

**quorum**
*n.* a majority

**unanimous**
*adj.* having the approval or consent of all

State. The Federalists were led by Madison, John Marshall, and Governor Edmund Randolph (even though he had refused to sign the Constitution at Philadelphia). Patrick Henry, leading the opposition, was joined by James Monroe, Richard Henry Lee, and George Mason (another of the nonsigners).

Although George Washington was not one of the delegates to Virginia's convention, his strong support for ratification proved vital. With Madison, he was able to get a reluctant Thomas Jefferson to support the document. Had Jefferson fought as did other Anti-Federalists, Virginia might never have ratified the Constitution.

**New York, The Last Key State** In New York, the ratifying convention was bitterly divided. The Anti-Federalists were led by Governor George Clinton and two of the State's three delegates to the Philadelphia convention: Robert Yates and John Lansing, who had quit Philadelphia in late July, claiming that the convention had gone beyond its authority.

New York's approval of the Constitution was absolutely necessary, for that large commercial State effectively separated New England from the rest of the nation. Its ratification of the Constitution, on July 26, brought the number of ratifying States to 11. The victory there was largely won by Alexander Hamilton.

## Inauguration

On September 13, 1788, with 11 of the 13 States "under the federal roof," the Congress of the Confederation paved the way for its successor.[18] It chose New York City as the temporary capital.[19] It set the first Wednesday in January as the date on which the States would choose presidential electors. The first Wednesday in February was set as the date on which those electors would vote, and the first Wednesday in March as the date for the inauguration of the new government.

The new Congress convened on March 4, 1789. It met in Federal Hall, on Wall Street in New York City. But because it lacked a quorum, it could not count the electoral votes until April 6. Finally, on that day, it found that George Washington had been elected President by a unanimous vote. John Adams was elected Vice President by a large majority.

On April 30, after a historic trip from Mount Vernon to New York, Washington took the oath of office as the first President of the United States.

---

[18] Neither North Carolina nor Rhode Island had ratified the new Constitution before it became effective. The Constitution failed in a first convention in North Carolina and was finally approved by a second one in late November of 1789. Rhode Island did not hold a ratifying convention until May of 1790.

[19] The District of Columbia did not become the nation's capital until 1800.

---

| Essential Questions Journal | To continue to build a response to the chapter Essential Question, go to your **Essential Questions Journal.** |
|---|---|

## SECTION 5 ASSESSMENT

**1. Guiding Question** Use your completed outline to answer this question: What issues aroused the vigorous debate over the ratification of the Constitution?

**Key Terms and Comprehension**

2. Explain why the **Anti-Federalists** opposed the presidency.

3. Explain the importance of adding a bill of rights to the Constitution.

**Critical Thinking**

4. **Identify Point of View** Reread the quote by Amos Singletary in this section. According to Singletary, why did the Federalists support ratifying the Constitution?

5. **Make Inferences** Recall Virginia's role in writing the Declaration of Independence and in the Second Continental Congress. Why do you think it was important for Virginia to ratify the Constitution?

**Quick Write**

**Narrative Writing: Create an Outline** When writing a narrative nonfiction piece, it helps to have an outline of your thoughts and ideas. Create an outline using your main ideas and supporting details. Revise your outline as needed to make sure that the story progresses in an interesting and clear way.

---

# Assessment Answers

**1.** Federalists and Anti-Federalists divided over these key issues: how much power to give the central government versus the States, how to prevent the president or Congress from becoming too powerful, and whether or not the Constitution needed a bill of rights to protect individual liberties.

**2.** The Anti-Federalists feared that a presidency would become a monarchy.

**3.** A bill of rights guarantees citizens certain basic rights, such as the right to free speech and the right to a fair trial. These rights were not guaranteed explicitly in the Constitution itself, and some feared that their basic rights could, therefore, be threatened.

**4.** Singletary accused the Federalists of using the ratification of the Constitution to satisfy their own ends. He feared that the Federalists would use their victory as a way to gain power and money from the new government.

**5.** Virginia played an important role in calling for the Constitutional Convention and in creating the Constitution itself. Several of America's most prominent leaders were Virginians, including George Washington, James Madison, and Thomas Jefferson, the author of the Declaration of Independence. Because Virginia was so large and influential, the new government needed Virginia's support to succeed.

**QUICK WRITE** Students' outlines should tell a clear and comprehensive story of their State.

# Quick Study Guide

**GOVERNMENT** ONLINE
**On the Go**
To review anytime, anywhere, download these online resources at PearsonSchool.com/phgovt
Political Dictionary, Audio Review

CHAPTER **2**

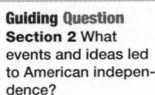

**Guiding Question**
**Section 2** What events and ideas led to American independence?

**Guiding Question**
**Section 3** What weaknesses in the Articles of Confederation made a lasting government impossible?

**Guiding Question**
**Section 4** What compromises enabled the Framers to create the Constitution?

**Guiding Question**
**Section 1** What ideas and traditions influenced government in the English colonies?

**CHAPTER 2**
**Essential Question**
How does the Constitution reflect the times in which it was written?

**Guiding Question**
**Section 5** What issues aroused the vigorous debate over the ratification of the Constitution?

## Political Dictionary

limited government *p. 31*
representative government *p. 31*
Magna Carta *p. 31*
due process *p. 31*
Petition of Right *p. 31*
English Bill of Rights *p. 31*
charter *p. 33*
bicameral *p. 33*
proprietary *p. 33*
unicameral *p. 34*
confederation *p. 37*
Albany Plan of Union *p. 37*
delegate *p. 37*
popular sovereignty *p. 41*
Articles of Confederation *p. 48*
ratification *p. 48*
Framers *p. 52*
Virginia Plan *p. 54*
New Jersey Plan *p. 55*
Connecticut Compromise *p. 56*
Three-Fifths Compromise *p. 56*
Commerce and Slave Trade Compromise *p. 56*
Federalist *p. 59*
Anti-Federalist *p. 59*

## Key Documents

### Declaration of Independence: Key Facts

- In 1776, the Second Continental Congress approved the Declaration of Independence.

- Written by Thomas Jefferson, the Declaration proclaimed the natural rights of all citizens, and outlined how the king had violated those rights.

- With the approval of the Declaration, the 13 colonies became free and independent States.

### Constitution: Key Facts

- The New Jersey Plan: A unicameral Congress with each State equally represented

- The Virginia Plan: A bicameral Congress with representation based on population or the amount of money each State contributed to Congress each year

- The Connecticut Compromise: A bicameral Congress with each State equally represented in the Senate and represented by population in the House

- The Three-Fifths Compromise: Three fifths of the slave population was counted for representation in the House and for taxation.

- The Constitution was hotly debated by Federalists and Anti-Federalists.

## The Road to the Constitution

**1215:** Magna Carta
**1628:** Petition of Right
**1689:** English Bill of Rights

**1765:** Parliament passes the Stamp Act.
**1774:** The First Continental Congress meets.
**1775:** The American Revolution begins.
**1776:** The Declaration of Independence
**1777:** Articles of Confederation approved.

**1787:** The Framers sign the Constitution.
**1789:** The Constitution takes effect.

Chapter 2 Assessment **63**

---

Have students download the digital resources available at Government on the Go for review and remediation.

**STUDY TIPS**

**Choosing a Place to Study** Explain to students that *where* they study can be as important as *how* they study. A good study spot has several important features. It should be a quiet place, with a minimum of distractions. Distractions can come in many forms, including noise, conversation, visitors, and telephone calls. Studying in a place where temptations to play video or computer games exist can make it harder to concentrate. Instead, students should choose a spot in which there is little else to do besides study. In addition, the study area should have good lighting and not be too comfortable. Studying in bed can prompt even those with the best intentions to drop off to sleep! Have students make a list of five possible study spots and ask them to try each one. Have them rate each spot on a scale from one to ten.

**ASSESSMENT AT A GLANCE**

**Tests and Quizzes**
Section Assessments
Section Quizzes A and B, Unit 1 **All-in-One**
Chapter Assessment
Chapter Tests A and B, Unit 1 **All-in-One**
Document-Based Assessment
Progress Monitoring Online
Exam*View* Test Bank

**Performance Assessment**
Essential Questions Journal
Extend the Lesson, p. 57
Assessment Rubrics, **All-in-One**

# For More Information

To learn more about the origins of American government, refer to these sources or assign them to students:

**L1** **Fradin, Dennis Brindell.** *The Founders: The 39 Stories Behind the U.S. Constitution.* Walker Books for Young Readers, 2005.

**L2** **Jordan, Terry L.** *The U.S. Constitution: And Fascinating Facts About It.* Oak Hills Publishing Company, 1999.

**L3** **Ellis, Joseph.** *Founding Brothers: The Revolutionary Generation.* Vintage Books, 2002.

**L4** **Shaara, Jeff.** *Rise to Rebellion.* Ballantine Books, 2001.

# Chapter Assessment

## COMPREHENSION AND CRITICAL THINKING

### SECTION 1

1. **(a) Ordered government:** When the colonists first arrived, they saw the need to regulate relationships among one another. They created governments like they had known in England. **Limited government:** People have certain rights that cannot be taken away, and the government's power is restricted. **Representative government:** Government may rule only with the consent of the people. **(b)** The colonists rebelled against taxation without representation and what they saw as violations of their rights by the British government. These ideas formed the basis of the Articles of Confederation and the Constitution.

2. **(a) Magna Carta:** trial by jury, due process, private property **(b) Petition of Right:** king may not punish citizens without trial by peers, declare martial law in peacetime, require home owners to house troops without their consent, or impose taxes without an act of Parliament **(c) English Bill of Rights:** no standing army in peacetime; free parliamentary elections; king may not suspend laws or levy taxes without consent of Parliament; subjects have right to petition king; right to a fair trial; freedom from excessive bail or fines and from cruel and unusual punishment; right to bear arms

3. In royal colonies, the colonists elected the lower house, but the king or his appointed governor could strike down any laws passed. This lack of power to shape their own laws led to resentment.

### SECTION 2

4. This kind of government is representative government.

5. **(a)** high tax rates and taxation without representation **(b)** The colonists had no representatives in Parliament and therefore no say in the tax laws imposed on them.

6. **(a)** as wild and bucking, trying to throw off its rider **(b)** as wild and uncontrollable

### SECTION 3

7. **(a)** make war and peace, send and receive ambassadors, make treaties, borrow money, set up a money system, establish post offices, build a navy, raise an army by asking the States for troops, fix uniform standards of weights and measures, settle disputes among States **(b)** The States began to make treaties with foreign coun-

---

# Chapter Assessment

GOVERNMENT ONLINE
Self-Test
To test your understanding of key terms and main ideas, visit
PearsonSchool.com/phgovt

## Comprehension and Critical Thinking

### Section 1

1. **(a)** Name and explain the three concepts of government that the English brought with them to the colonies. **(b)** How did these ideas shape the creation of the 13 colonies?

2. Describe the limitations on the monarchy imposed by these documents: **(a)** the Magna Carta, **(b)** the Petition of Right, **(c)** the English Bill of Rights.

3. In the royal colonies, why might the colonists resent the "stern hand" of a royal governor?

### Section 2

4. The Declaration of Independence states, "Governments are instituted among Men, deriving their just powers from the consent of the governed." What kind of government is this?

5. **(a)** What were the complaints of the Stamp Act Congress? **(b)** What was meant by "taxation without representation"?

6. **Analyze Political Cartoons** Look at the cartoon below. **(a)** How has the artist drawn the horse "America"? **(b)** How does this reflect British attitudes toward the American colonies?

THE HORSE AMERICA, throwing his Master.

### Section 3

7. **(a)** Explain the responsibilities of Congress under the Articles of Confederation. **(b)** Which of these responsibilities were taken over by the States? **(c)** Why did this cause a problem?

### Section 4

8. **(a)** Why did the Framers consider it necessary to replace the Articles of Confederation? **(b)** What obstacles did they face in creating a strong central government?

9. How did the Constitution improve upon the Articles of Confederation? Give examples from the text.

10. Look at the population density map in Section 4 and reread the paragraphs concerning the Three-Fifths Compromise. Why, in addition to moral reasons, might the northern States have wished to abolish slavery?

### Section 5

11. **(a)** Why was a bill of rights not included in the original Constitution? **(b)** Why might the Anti-Federalists have wanted a bill of rights in the document?

### Writing About Government

12. Use your Quick Write exercises to write a narrative non-fiction piece about a State's role in the formation of the national government. Make sure that you use your outline as the frame of your story. Include interesting details and anecdotes wherever possible. See pp. S1–S2 in the Skills Handbook.

---

## Apply What You've Learned

13. **Essential Question Activity** Research a recently created constitution for a foreign nation or international association.
    **(a)** Identify the writer(s) of the constitution, and what their qualifications were.
    **(b)** Research the process through which the constitution was created. How did the writers decide on what to include? What did they think were the most important rights to protect?
    **(c)** Did the constitution go through a ratification process? How was the process conducted?

14. **Essential Question Assessment** Based on your research and this chapter, make a chart comparing the process used to create the U.S. Constitution with a more recently written constitution. This comparison will help you answer the Essential Question: **How does the Constitution reflect the times in which it was written?** Include details such as the concerns of the creators, and the process of ratification in your chart.

**Essential Questions Journal** To respond to the chapter Essential Question, go to your **Essential Questions Journal.**

---

tries, make their own money, and settle disputes among themselves. **(c)** Foreign countries began to see the States, not the nation, as sovereign, weakening national unity. Trade disputes among States and unrestrained production of money led to inflation and economic chaos. Sound credit vanished, and debts went unpaid. Violence broke out in many places.

### SECTION 4

8. **(a)** The central government was too weak to solve the nation's problems. **(b)** reconciling a diversity of opinions, overcoming State and sectional biases, overcoming fear of a strong central government after just throwing off the oppressive British government

9. The Constitution created a more powerful central government. It gave the federal government the power to tax and to regulate foreign and interstate commerce. Tax revenue would enable the federal government to operate without depending on State funding. The commerce power would reduce trade disputes among States and provide national unity in dealing with foreign nations. The Constitution also established three separate branches of government, creating

# Document-Based Assessment

## The Constitution and the Revolutionary War Era

The Declaration of Independence espoused the highest principles of Enlightenment thinking. However, a significant percent of the new nation's population remained disenfranchised under their new Constitution. The text below refers to two of those groups.

### Document 1

I long to hear that you have declared an independency — and by the way in the new code of Laws which I suppose it will be necessary for you to make I desire you would Remember the Ladies, and be more generous and favourable to them than your ancestors. Do not put such unlimited power into the hands of the Husbands. Remember all Men would be tyrants if they could. If perticular care and attention is not paid to the Ladies we are determined to foment a Rebelion, and will not hold ourselves bound by any Laws in which we have no voice, or Representation.

—Letter from Abigail Adams to John Adams, March 31, 1776

### Document 2

Would any one believe that I am Master of Slaves, of my own purchase! I am drawn along by the general inconvenience of living here without them. I will not, I cannot justify it. However culpable my Conduct, I will so far pay my devoir to Virtue, as to own the excellence & rectitude of her Precepts, & lament my want of conforming to them.

I believe a time will come when an opportunity will be offered to abolish this lamentable Evil. Every thing we can do is to improve it, if it happens in our day; if not, let us transmit to our descendants, together with our Slaves, a pity for their unhappy Lot, & our abhorrence for Slavery. If we cannot reduce this wished for Reformation to practice, let us treat the unhappy victims with lenity. It is the furthmost advance we can make towards Justice. It is a debt we owe to the purity of our Religion, to show that it is at variance with that Law which, warrants Slavery.

—Patrick Henry on slavery, in a letter to Robert Pleasants, January 18, 1773

---

**Use your knowledge of the social reality of the Revolutionary War era and the documents above to answer Questions 1–3.**

1. What warning did Abigail Adams issue to her husband in Document 1?
   A. The new nation will fail if slaves are not freed.
   B. Families will fail if women are not equal partners with their husbands.
   C. Women will rise up if their rights are not answered.
   D. The War for Independence will fail if women do not join the battle.

2. How do Patrick Henry's comments reflect the differences between the ideals of the War for Independence and the reality of life in those times?

3. **Pull It Together** Does the culture of the time in which the Constitution was written excuse inequalities that the document allowed?

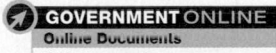

**GOVERNMENT** ONLINE
Online Documents
To find more primary sources on colonial suffrage, visit
**PearsonSchool.com/phgovt**

---

1. C

2. The War for Independence touted the ideals of liberty and equality for all. However, slaves were not included in these ideals. While many people opposed slavery, the Framers saw it as a necessary evil they could not address at that time.

3. Students' answers should give a clear opinion, supported by what they have learned in the chapter.

**L2 Differentiate** Students use all the documents on the page to support their thesis.

**L3 Differentiate** Students include additional information available online at **PearsonSchool .com/phgovt.**

**L4 Differentiate** Students use materials from the textbook the online information at **PearsonSchool .com/phgovt,** and do additional research to support their views.

 **Go Online to PearsonSchool.com/phgovt** for a student rubric and extra documents.

---

checks and balances, and established fair State representation in Congress.

10. Most slaves lived in the South. Under the compromise, three fifths of a State's slave population counted toward the total population. This allowed States like Virginia to send more representatives to Congress. The North may have wanted to abolish slavery to gain more representatives and thus more power in Congress.

## SECTION 5

11. **(a)** The Framers believed that State constitutions already protected basic rights and that

separation of powers would prevent government from becoming powerful enough to threaten people's rights. **(b)** to ensure that this new, stronger central government would not overstep its powers, as Britain had

### WRITING ABOUT GOVERNMENT

12. Students should combine their research and outline to write a short narrative piece about a State's role in creating the new American government.

### APPLY WHAT YOU'VE LEARNED

13. Students should thoroughly research the process of writing the constitution of an-

other country. Students may want to look back at Issues of Our Time for ideas.

14. The Constitution is a collection of the beliefs and laws of England, philosophies of the Enlightenment, and solutions to grievances against the Crown that led to the American Revolution. Students should use their research on a more recently written constitution to compare the process to that of the U.S. Constitution. They should explain how the constitution they researched reflects its times.

# Introduce the Chapter

## Essential Questions:

**UNIT 1**

What should be the goals of government?

**CHAPTER 3**

How has the Constitution lasted through changing times?

**ACTIVATE PRIOR KNOWLEDGE**

Have students examine the photo and quotation. Ask: **What do the photo and quotation suggest about the Constitution?** *(The historical principles on which the Constitution was created provided guidance for the Framers.)* In this chapter, students will learn about the articles and amendments that make up the Constitution, as well as how the Constitution is changed and interpreted. Tell students to explore the Constitution by completing the Chapter 3 Essential Question Warmup Activity in their **Essential Questions Journal.** Discuss their responses as a class.

**BEFORE READING**

**L2** **ELL Differentiate** Chapter 3 Prereading and Vocabulary Worksheet (Unit 1 All-in-One, p. 129)

**SUCCESSNET STUDENT AND TEACHER CENTER**

Visit **PearsonSchool.com/phgovt** for downloadable resources that allow students and teachers to connect with government "on the go."

**DIGITAL LESSON PRESENTATION**

The digital lesson presentation supports the print lesson with activities and summaries of key concepts.

## SKILLS DEVELOPMENT

**ANALYZE SOURCES**

You may wish to teach analyzing sources as a distinct skill within Section 2 of this chapter. Use the Chapter 3 Skills Worksheet (Unit 1 All-in-One, p. 149) to help students learn the steps in analyzing sources. The worksheet asks students to read source excerpts about women's suffrage and then answer questions about the sources. For L2 and L1 students, assign the adapted Skill Activity (Unit 1 All-in-One, p. 150).

**WebQuest online** The chapter WebQuest challenges students to answer the chapter Essential Question by asking them about the Constitution.

66

# Block Scheduling

**BLOCK 1:** Teach Section 1.

**BLOCK 2:** Teach Sections 2 and 3, choosing either the Political Cartoon Mini-Lesson or the Debate in Section 2.

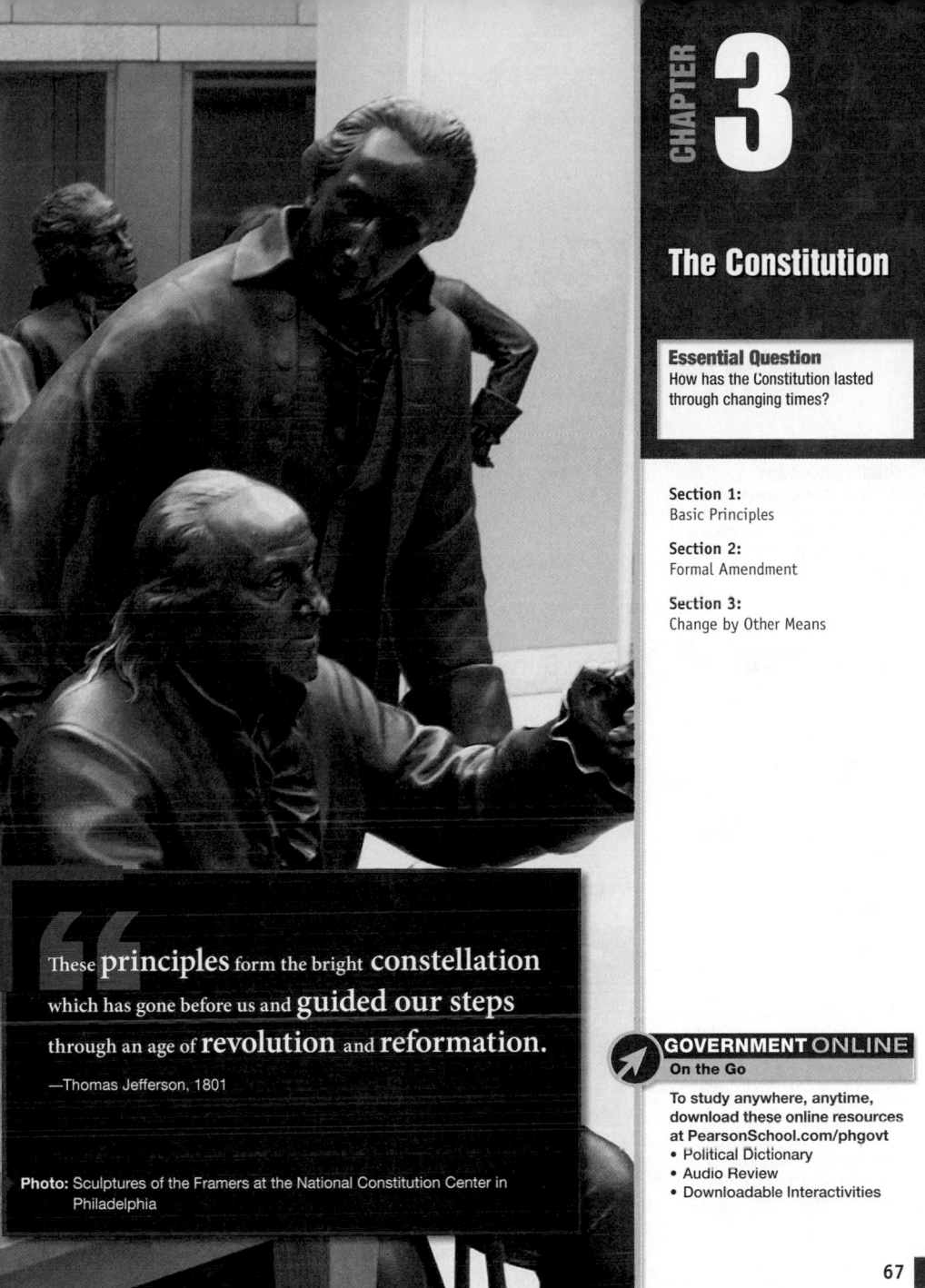

# 3

## The Constitution

### Essential Question
How has the Constitution lasted through changing times?

**Section 1:**
Basic Principles

**Section 2:**
Formal Amendment

**Section 3:**
Change by Other Means

> These **principles** form the bright **constellation** which has gone before us and **guided our steps** through an age of **revolution** and **reformation**.

—Thomas Jefferson, 1801

**Photo:** Sculptures of the Framers at the National Constitution Center in Philadelphia

### GOVERNMENT ONLINE
On the Go

To study anywhere, anytime, download these online resources at PearsonSchool.com/phgovt
- Political Dictionary
- Audio Review
- Downloadable Interactivities

67

## Lesson Goals

**SECTION 1**

Students will . . .

- identify a key problem facing the Framers, as expressed from different viewpoints in two primary source quotes.
- define the six basic principles around which the Constitution is built.
- read the Constitution and identify where in the document the basic principles are reflected.

**SECTION 2**

Students will . . .

- compare the process of ratification of amendments by studying a chart.
- examine the meaning of several amendments by creating and performing a skit.
- debate the merits of three unsuccessful amendments, using primary sources.

**SECTION 3**

Students will . . .

- identify the informal methods of change used in example scenarios.
- apply the informal methods of change by writing example scenarios.

## Pressed for Time

To cover this chapter quickly, explain the six basic principles of the Constitution, and have students work through the Section 1 Reading Comprehension Worksheet. Use the chart in Section 2 of the textbook to describe the methods of formal amendment. Then have students work through the Section 2 Bellringer Worksheet and the Section 2 Core Worksheet. Finally, distribute the Section 3 Core Worksheet to students, and work through it with them to identify the methods of change by other means.

**DIFFERENTIATED INSTRUCTION KEY**

Look for these symbols to help you adjust steps in each lesson to meet your students' needs.

**L1** Special Needs

**L2** Basic

    **ELL** English Language Learners

    **LPR** Less Proficient Readers

**L3** All Students

**L4** Advanced Students

What are the six main principles on which the Constitution is based?

# Get Started

## LESSON GOALS

Students will . . .

• identify a key problem facing the Framers, as expressed from different viewpoints in two primary source quotes.

• define the six basic principles around which the Constitution is built.

• read the Constitution and identify where in the document the basic principles are reflected.

## BEFORE CLASS

Assign the section, the graphic organizer in the text, and the Reading Comprehension Worksheet (Unit 1 All-in-One, p. 133) before class.

**L2** **Differentiate** Reading Comprehension Worksheet (Unit 1 All-in-One, p. 135)

## SKILLS DEVELOPMENT

### PROBLEM SOLVING

Before students do the Bellringer activity, you may want to review tips on problem solving in the Skills Handbook, p. S17.

---

## SECTION 1

# Basic Principles

### Guiding Question

**What are the six main principles on which the Constitution is based?**
Use a concept web like the one below to take notes on the six basic principles of the Constitution.

### Political Dictionary

• popular sovereignty
• limited government
• constitutionalism
• rule of law
• separation of powers

• checks and balances
• veto
• judicial review
• unconstitutional
• federalism

### Objectives

1. Understand the basic outline of the Constitution.
2. Understand the six basic principles of the Constitution: popular sovereignty, limited government, separation of powers, checks and balances, judicial review, and federalism.

**Image Above:** Voters express their will to the government. This concept is called popular sovereignty.

The Constitution of the United States dates from the latter part of the eighteenth century. Written in 1787, it took effect in 1789. The fact that it is more than 220 years old does not mean, however, that in the twenty-first century, it is only an interesting historical artifact, best left to museums and dusty shelves. On the contrary, it remains a vitally important and vibrant document.

The Constitution is this nation's fundamental law. It is, by its own terms, "the supreme Law of the Land"—the highest form of law in the United States.

## An Outline of the Constitution

The Constitution sets out the basic principles upon which government in the United States was built and operates today. The document lays out the ways in which the Federal Government is organized, how the leaders of that government are selected, and many of the procedures those leaders must follow as they perform their duties. Of utmost importance, it sets out the limits within which government must conduct itself.

The Constitution also lays out the basic rules of American politics. By doing so, it helps to determine who wins and who loses in the political arena. To really understand government and politics in this country, we must know a good deal about the Constitution and how it has been interpreted and applied throughout our history.

Even with its 27 amendments, the Constitution is a fairly brief document. Its little more than 7,000 words can be read in half an hour. You will find the text of the Constitution at the beginning of the book. As you read it, remember that this document has successfully guided this nation through more than two centuries of tremendous growth and change. One of the Constitution's greatest strengths is that it deals largely with matters of basic principle. Unlike most other constitutions—those of the 50 States and those of other nations—the Constitution of the United States is not weighted down with detailed and cumbersome provisions.

As you read the Constitution, you will also see that it is organized in a simple and straightforward way. It begins with a short introduction, the Preamble. The balance of the original document is divided into seven numbered

## Focus on the Basics

**FACTS:** • The Constitution is the supreme law of the land. • It sets the framework of government. • The people are sovereign and government is limited. • The Constitution distributes powers among three branches of government. • Each branch has the power to check the other branches.

**CONCEPTS:** separation of powers, popular sovereignty, federalism, limited government, judicial review, checks and balances, constitutionalism, rule of law

**ENDURING UNDERSTANDINGS:** • The Constitution has guided American government for more than 200 years. • The Constitution is based on six principles: limited government, popular sovereignty, separation of powers, checks and balances, judicial review, and federalism.

sections called articles. The first three articles deal with the three branches of the National Government: Congress, the presidency, and the federal court system. These articles outline the basic organization and powers of each branch, and the methods by which the members of Congress, the President and Vice President, and federal judges are chosen. Article IV deals mostly with the place of the States in the American Union and their relationships with the National Government and with one another. Article V indicates how formal amendments may be added to the document. Article VI declares that the Constitution is the nation's supreme law; Article VII provided for the ratification of the Constitution.

The seven articles of the original document are followed by 27 amendments, printed in the order in which each provision was adopted.

The Constitution is built around six basic principles. They are popular sovereignty, limited government, separation of powers, checks and balances, judicial review, and federalism.

## Popular Sovereignty

In the United States, all political power resides in the people, a concept known as **popular sovereignty.** The people are the *only* source for any and all governmental power. Government can govern only with the consent of the governed.

The principle of popular sovereignty is woven throughout the Constitution. In its opening words—the Preamble—that document declares: "We the People of the United States . . . do ordain and establish this Constitution for the United States of America."

The people have given the United States Government whatever powers it has, through the Constitution. That government exercises those powers through popularly elected leaders who are chosen by the people to represent them in the exercise of the people's power.

## Limited Government

The principle of **limited government** holds that no government is all-powerful. That government may do *only* those things that the people have given it the power to do.

✔**Checkpoint**
What is the purpose of the Preamble of the Constitution?

**political arena**
*n.* the setting in which political activity occurs

**provision**
*n.* a clause in a document or agreement

**The Seven Articles**
# Outline of Government

The body of the Constitution is made up of seven articles. These articles set out the basic shape of the Federal Government. *What is the purpose of the first three articles?*

### Articles of the Constitution

| Section | Subject |
|---|---|
| Preamble | States the purpose of the Constitution |
| Article I | Creates the Legislative branch |
| Article II | Creates the Executive branch |
| Article III | Creates the Judicial branch |
| Article IV | Relations among the States |
| Article V | Amending the Constitution |
| Article VI | National debts, supremacy of national law, and oaths of office |
| Article VII | Ratifying the Constitution |

# Differentiated Resources

The following resources are located in the All-in-One, Unit 1, Chapter 3, Section 1:

**L2** Prereading and Vocabulary Worksheet (p. 129)
**L3** Reading Comprehension Worksheet (p. 133)
**L2** Reading Comprehension Worksheet (p. 135)
**L3** Core Worksheet (p. 137)
**L3** **L4** Extend Worksheet (p. 139)
**L3** Quiz A (p. 141)
**L2** Quiz B (p. 142)

**BELLRINGER**
Display Transparency 3A, A Question of Power, showing quotations from both a Federalist and an Anti-Federalist perspective. Write on the board:
**(1) What problem do both of these quotations address? (2) Which of the six principles help to solve this problem? Answer in your notebook.**

**L2** **ELL Differentiate** Define these words on the board to help students understand the quotes: *denied* (declared untrue), *encroaching* (intruding), *effectually* (effectively), *restrained* (limited), *assigned* (given), *discriminating* (noting differences in), *invasion* (intrusion), *vested in* (given to), *annihilate* (destroy), *absorb* (swallow up), *consolidated* (combined), *iron-handed* (powerful), *despotism* (tyranny), and *supremacy* (domination).

# Teach

To present this topic using online resources, use the lesson presentations at **PearsonSchool.com/phgovt.**

**INTRODUCE THE TOPIC**

Tell students that today they will discuss the six important ideas upon which the Constitution is based. You will return to their Bellringer answers later in the lesson.

## Answers

**Checkpoint** to state the Constitution's purpose

**The Seven Articles** to lay out the powers of the three branches: legislative, executive, and judicial

Distribute the Chapter 3 Section 1 Core Worksheet (Unit 1 All-in-One, p. 137), which lists the six principles. Display Transparencies 3C, Popular Sovereignty and Limited Government, 3D, Separation of Powers and Checks and Balances, and 3E, Judicial Review and Federalism, and ask students to interpret each cartoon. Have students offer definitions of the principles in a brainstorming session. Write down a definition next to each principle and have students record these on the Core Worksheet. *(Possible definitions are shown in the Core Worksheet solutions.)*

**L1 L2 Differentiate** Have students label six index cards with one principle on each card. In pairs, have them write a simple definition of each term on the back of the card. Ask students to share their definitions and try to reach a consensus about each one. Based on this discussion, write a definition on the board for them to record on the Core Worksheet. They may keep these cards to refer to throughout their study of American government.

**L4 Differentiate** Ask students to think of an example of each principle in action.

## Answers

**Basic Principles of the Constitution** judicial branch: to act as a check on the other branches and to be the referees to determine when the government has overstepped the bounds of the Constitution; citizens: to communicate their will to the government and to keep the government in check

# Basic Principles of the Constitution

These cartoons illustrate the six principles of government set out in the Constitution. *According to the cartoons, what is the role of the judicial branch? What are the roles of citizens?*

**Popular Sovereignty**

**Limited Government**

**Separation of Powers**

**enshrined**
*v.* set out with respect; honored

In effect, the principle of limited government is the other side of the coin of popular sovereignty. It is that principle stated the other way around: The people are the only source of any and all of government's authority; and government has only that authority the people have given to it.

The concept of limited government can be put another way: Government must obey the law. Stated this way, the principle is often called **constitutionalism**—that is, government must be conducted according to constitutional principles. The concept of limited government is also frequently described as the **rule of law,** which holds that government and its officers, in all that they do, are always subject to—never above—the law.

**prohibition**
*n.* a denial; a ban

In large part, the Constitution is a statement of limited government. Much of it reads as <u>prohibitions</u> of power to government. For example, notice the Constitution's guarantees of freedom of expression. Those great guarantees—of freedom of religion, of speech, of the press, of assembly, and of petition—are

vital to democratic government. They are <u>enshrined</u> in the 1st Amendment, which begins with the words: "Congress shall make no law. . . ."

## Separation of Powers

Recall from Chapter 1 that in a parliamentary system, the legislative, executive, and judicial powers of government are all gathered in the hands of a single agency. British government is a leading example of the form. In a presidential system, these basic powers are distributed—separated—among three distinct and independent branches of the government.

This concept is known as **separation of powers.** The idea had been written into each of the State constitutions adopted during the Revolution. A classic expression of the doctrine can be found in the Massachusetts constitution written in 1780 (Part the First, Article XXX):

"In the government of this commonwealth, the legislative department shall never

# Myths and Misconceptions

**POPULAR SOVEREIGNTY** Not every Framer enthusiastically embraced the great principle of popular sovereignty set forth in the Constitution. In fact, the idea of granting the people as a whole too much say in government frightened many of them. Alexander Hamilton, for example, wrote that the "turbulent and changing" opinions of the masses "seldom judge or determine right," and referred to the "imprudence of democracy." Thomas Jefferson held a different opinion, however. "I know no safe depository of the ultimate powers of the society but the people themselves," he wrote in 1820, "and if we think them not enlightened enough to exercise their control with a wholesome discretion, the remedy is not to take it from them, but to inform their discretion by education. This is the true corrective of abuses of constitutional power."

**GOVERNMENT** ONLINE
**Audio Tour**
Listen to a guided audio tour of these principles at
**PearsonSchool.com/phgovt**

**Checks and Balances**

**Judicial Review**

**Federalism**

exercise the executive and judicial powers, or either of them: The executive shall never exercise the legislative and judicial powers, or either of them: The judicial shall never exercise the legislative and executive powers, or either of them: to the end it may be a government of laws and not of men."

The Constitution of the United States distributes the powers of the National Government among the Congress (the legislative branch), the President (the executive branch), and the courts (the judicial branch). This separation of powers is clearly set forth in the opening words of each of the first three Articles of the Constitution.

Article I, Section 1 declares: "All legislative Powers herein granted shall be <u>vested</u> in a Congress of the United States. . . ." Thus, Congress is the lawmaking branch of the National Government.

Article II, Section 1 declares: "The executive Power shall be vested in a President of the United States of America." Thus, the President is given the law-executing, law-

enforcing, and law-administering powers of the National Government.

Article III, Section 1 declares: "The judicial Power of the United States shall be vested in one supreme Court, and in such inferior Courts as the Congress may from time to time ordain and establish." Thus, the federal courts, and most importantly the Supreme Court, interpret and apply the laws of the United States in cases brought before them.

Remember, the Framers intended to create a stronger central government for the United States. Yet they also intended to limit the powers of that government. The doctrine of separation of powers was designed to accomplish just that.

In *The Federalist,* No. 47, James Madison wrote of this arrangement: "The accumulation of all powers, legislative, executive, and judiciary, in the same hands, whether of one, a few, or many . . . may justly be pronounced the very definition of tyranny."

The earliest of the State constitutions provided for a separation of powers among the

✔ **Checkpoint**
How does the separation of powers keep government from becoming too powerful?

**vested**
*v.* given to, conferred upon

# Constitutional Principles

**GOVERNMENT BY THE PEOPLE** Our representative government arises from the principle of popular sovereignty. The people exercise their sovereignty by electing representatives to carry out their will. However, the Constitution left it to the States to decide which citizens would be allowed to vote. The Constitution says only that those entitled to vote for the "most numerous Branch of the State Legislature" can also vote for members of the House of Representatives (Article I, Section 2, Clause 1). At first, our government represented only *some* of the people, for the States allowed only white male property owners to vote. Hard times in the early nineteenth century led men to demand an end to the property requirement. Over time, immigrants, African Americans, Native Americans, and women gained voting rights, creating a government more truly "by the people."

## MAKE CONNECTIONS

Ask students to review the list of six basic principles and identify patterns. Ask: **What issues do the principles address, as a group?** *(Possible answer: All six principles are concerned with the power of government, with limiting that power, with protecting individual rights and States' rights, and with preventing abuse and corruption of power.)* Then ask them to think back to what they know about the causes of the Revolutionary War and the weaknesses of the Articles of Confederation. Ask: **What experiences made the Framers build these six principles into the Constitution?** *(Possible answer: King George undermined the colonial judiciary and suspended their legislatures; he imposed taxes without representation, abolished laws arbitrarily, and deprived colonists of jury trials; under the Articles of Confederation, Congress was the sole body created; there was no executive or judicial branch; the Congress itself was hobbled by restrictions on its power.)*

Finish by asking students to read their Bellringer answers aloud. *(1. Both quotes address the problem of preventing the central government from becoming too powerful. 2. limited government, separation of powers, checks and balances, federalism)*

## ANALYZE THE CONSTITUTION

Explain that students will be using the Constitution itself as a primary source to find where in the document the major principles are reflected. Remind them that the principle of judicial review does not appear specifically in the Constitution. However, Federalist writings suggest that the Framers intended for the federal courts to have this power. Direct students to the Constitution reproduced in the textbook. Have them work in pairs to find statements in the Constitution that relate to each principle, and record the locations on the Core Worksheet. Then call on partners to share their responses for each section.

**L1** **L2** **Differentiate** Have students work in small groups. Assign each group one principle to locate in the Constitution. Call on groups to present information about their principle to the class.

**L4** **Differentiate** Have students work individually to find as many places as possible where each principle is addressed.

Tell students to go to the Audio Tour to listen to a guided tour of the Basic Principles of the Constitution.

## Answers

**Checkpoint** by preventing the concentration of legislative, executive, and judicial powers in one branch

**L3 Differentiate** Use these questions to continue students' search of and discussion about the Constitution.

1. **Which section and clause of Article I contains the Three-Fifths Compromise?** *(Section 2, Clause 3)* **What other compromise related to slavery appears in Article I? In what Section and Clause is it located?** *(Section 9, Clause 1: Congress may not interfere with the importation of enslaved people until 1808.)* **Why did the Framers include these compromises in Article I?** *(The Three-Fifths Compromise relates to representation in the House of Representatives, the subject of Article I. The agreement that Congress would not interfere with the slave trade helped to win the South's agreement to the Three-Fifths Compromise.)*

2. **What military power does Article II grant the President?** *(to serve as commander in chief)*

3. **According to Article III, how long is the term for a federal judge?** *(for life)* **Why do you think the Framers saw fit to make the terms of judges different from those of other offices?** *(probably to allow judges to make objective decisions, free of the influence of politics and public opinion)*

4. **Which section of Article IV deals with the formation of new States?** *(Section 3)*

5. **According to Article V, what fraction of the States must approve an amendment before it becomes part of the Constitution?** *(three fourths)*

6. **What is the purpose of Article VI, Section 2?** *(to establish the Constitution as the supreme law of the land)*

## Answers

**Checkpoint** by vetoing an act of Congress

---

✔ **Checkpoint**
Name one of the ways in which the President can check the powers of Congress.

legislative, executive, and judicial branches of the new governments they established. This was a reflection of the mistrust and suspicion toward any government common to the people of the new United States in the late 1700s. Thus, the inclusion of the doctrine of separation of powers was both natural and inevitable in the writing of the Constitution.

## Checks and Balances

The National Government is organized around three separate branches. As you have just seen, the Constitution gives to each branch its own field of governmental authority: legislative, executive, and judicial.

These three branches are not entirely separated nor completely independent of one another. Rather, they are tied together by a complex system of **checks and balances.** This means that each branch is subject to a number of constitutional checks, or restraints, by the other branches. In other words, each branch has certain powers with which it can check the operations of the other two.

Congress has the power to make laws, but the President may **veto** (reject) any act of Congress. In its turn, Congress can <u>override</u> a presidential veto by a two-thirds vote in each house. Congress can refuse to provide funds requested by the President, or the Senate may refuse to approve a treaty or an appointment made by the chief executive. The President is the commander in chief of the armed forces, but Congress provides that military force; and so on.

**override**
*v.* to overturn, reverse, cancel

The system of checks and balances links the judicial branch to the legislative and the executive branches. The President has the power to name all federal judges. Each appointment, however, must be approved by a majority vote in the Senate. At the same time, the courts have the power to determine the constitutionality of acts of Congress and of presidential actions, and to strike down those they find unconstitutional.

Head-on clashes between the branches of government do not often happen. The check-and-balance system operates all the time, however, and in routine fashion. The very fact that it exists affects much of what happens in Washington, D.C.

**partisan**
*n.* loyalty to a particular political party

For example, when the President picks someone to serve in some important office in the executive branch—as, say, secretary of state or director of the Office of National Intelligence—the President is quite aware that the Senate must confirm that appointment. So, the chief executive is apt to pick someone who very likely will be approved by the Senate. In a similar sense, when Congress makes a law, it does so with a careful eye on both the President's veto power and the power of the courts to review its actions.

Spectacular clashes—direct applications of the check-and-balance system—do sometimes occur, of course. The President does veto some acts of Congress. On rare occasions, Congress does override a veto. And, even more rarely, the Senate does reject a presidential appointee. Twice in our history, the House of Representatives has impeached (brought charges against) a President, seeking his removal: Andrew Johnson in 1868 and Bill Clinton in 1998. On both occasions the President was acquitted by the Senate.

But, again, these and other direct confrontations are not common. Congress, the President, and even the courts try to avoid them. The check-and-balance system makes compromise necessary—and, remember, compromise is a vital part of democratic government.

Over time, the check-and-balance system has worked quite well. It has done what the Framers intended it to do; it has prevented "an unjust combination of a majority." At the same time, the system of checks and balances has not often forestalled a close working relationship between the executive and legislative branches of the Federal Government.

Note, however, that that working relationship runs more smoothly when the President and a majority in both houses of Congress are of the same political party. When the other party controls one or both houses, <u>partisan</u> friction and conflict play a larger-than-usual part in that relationship.

Through most of our history, the President and a majority of the members of both houses of Congress have been of the same party. Over the past 50 years or so, however, the American people have become quite familiar with divided government—that is, a political

# Checks and Balances

**GOVERNMENT ONLINE**
For an **interactive** version of Checks and Balances, visit PearsonSchool.com/phgovt

- May veto legislation
- May call special sessions of Congress

**EXECUTIVE BRANCH**
Carries out the law
- Appoints Supreme Court justices
- Appoints other federal judges

- May override a President's veto
- May impeach the President
- Approves appointments of judges
- Approves treaties

**LEGISLATIVE BRANCH**
Makes the law
- May impeach federal judges
- Creates lower courts

- May declare executive acts unconstitutional

**JUDICIAL BRANCH**
Interprets the law

- May declare acts of Congress unconstitutional

▶▶ **Interpreting Diagrams** Under the system of checks and balances, each branch of government can check the actions of the others. *In what ways can the power of the executive be checked by the other two branches?*

environment in which one party occupies the White House and the other controls one or both houses of Congress.

That was not the situation in 2008, when Democrat Barack Obama captured the White House and his party took control of both houses of Congress. But divided government returned with the 2010 midterm elections, when the Republicans gained control of the House while the Democrats retained their majority in the Senate.

## Judicial Review

One aspect of the principle of checks and bal ances is of such importance in the American constitutional system that it stands by itself, as one of that system's basic principles. The

power of **judicial review** may be defined as the power of a court to determine the consti- tutionality of a governmental action.

In part, then, judicial review is the power to declare **unconstitutional**—to declare ille- gal, null and void, of no force and effect—a governmental action found to violate some provision in the Constitution. The power of judicial review is held by all federal courts and by most State courts, as well.[1]

The Constitution does not provide for judicial review in so many words. Yet it seems

---

1 Generally, the power is held by all courts of record—courts that keep a record of their proceedings and have the power to punish for contempt. Usually, only the lowest courts in a State (justice of the peace courts, for example) are not courts of record.

# How Government Works

## Answers

**Interpreting Diagrams** The judicial branch may declare executive acts unconstitutional. The legisla- tive branch may override the President's veto, may impeach the President, must approve presidential appointments, and approves treaties.

# Assess and Remediate

**L3** Display Transparency 3G, Who Has the Power? Have students draw conclusions about why this diagram represents the principle of federalism. Students should then present their conclusions to the class. *(The powers show a division among a central government and several regional [State] governments, with powers shared between levels of government.)*

**L3** Collect the Core Worksheets and assess students' work.

**L3** Assign the Section 1 Assessment questions.

**L3** Section Quiz A (Unit 1 All-in-One, p. 141)

**L2** Section Quiz B (Unit 1 All-in-One, p. 142)

Have students complete the review activities in the digital lesson presentation and continue their work in the **Essential Questions Journal.**

## Answers

**Interpreting Diagrams** possible response: to make trade rules uniform across the nation and to prevent trade disputes between States

---

clear that the Framers intended that the federal courts, and in particular the Supreme Court, should have that power. In *The Federalist* No. 51, James Madison described the judicial power as one of the "<u>auxiliary</u> precautions" against the possible domination of one branch of the government over another.

In *The Federalist* No. 78, Alexander Hamilton wrote:

> "The interpretation of the laws is the proper and peculiar province of the courts. A constitution is, in fact, and must be regarded by the judges as a fundamental law. It therefore belongs to them to ascertain its meaning, as well as the meaning of any particular act proceeding from the legislative body. If there should happen to be an irreconcilable variance between the two, that which has the superior obligation and validity ought, of course, to be preferred; or, in other words, the Constitution ought to be preferred to the statute. . . ."

In practice, the Supreme Court established the power of judicial review in the landmark case of *Marbury* v. *Madison* in 1803. Since *Marbury,* the Supreme Court and other federal and State courts have used the power in thousands of cases. For the most part, those courts have upheld challenged governmental actions. That is, in most cases in which the power of judicial review is exercised, the actions of government are found to be constitutional.

That is not always the case, however. To date, the Supreme Court has decided some 150 cases in which it has found an act or some part of an act of Congress to be unconstitutional. It has struck down several presidential and other executive branch actions as well. The Court has also voided hundreds of actions of the States and their local governments, including some 1,200 State laws and local ordinances.

## Federalism

As you know, the American governmental system is federal in form. The powers held by government are distributed on a territorial basis. The National Government holds some of those powers. Others belong to the 50 States.

**auxiliary**
*adj.* extra; supportive; supplemental

### Federalism
## Who Has the Power?

**FEDERAL POWERS**
- To maintain an army and a navy
- To declare war
- To coin money
- To regulate trade between States and with foreign nations
- To make treaties

**SHARED POWERS**
- To enforce laws
- To establish courts
- To borrow money
- To secure the population
- To build an infrastructure
- To collect taxes
- To make laws

**STATE POWERS**
- To conduct elections
- To establish schools
- To regulate business within a State
- To establish local governments
- To regulate marriage, divorce
- To assume other powers not given to the Federal Government nor denied to the States, by the Constitution

**Interpreting Diagrams** The Constitution divides power among the State and Federal governments. ***Why does the Constitution give the power to regulate trade among the States to the Federal Government?***

---

## Teacher-to-Teacher Network

**ALTERNATE LESSON PLAN** Have students learn about our nation's constitutional foundation by playing the "Constitution Game." Teams will study the Constitution and prepare game cards containing clues to facts in the Constitution. During the game, teams will alternate giving clues and identifying constitutional facts from the clues. After a team identifies a fact, it will look up the passage in the Constitution where the fact is revealed. Then a team member will read the passage aloud.

To see this lesson plan, go to

The principle of **federalism**—the division of power among a central government and several regional governments—came to the Constitution out of both experience and necessity. At Philadelphia, the Framers faced a number of difficult problems, not the least of them: How to build a new, stronger, more effective National Government while preserving the existing States and the concept of local self-government.

The colonists had rebelled against the harsh rule of a powerful and distant central government. They had fought for the right to manage their own local affairs without the meddling and dictation of the king and his ministers in far-off London. Surely, the colonists would not now agree to another such government.

The Framers found their solution in federalism. In short, they constructed the federal arrangement, with its division of powers, as a compromise. It was an alternative to both the system of nearly independent States, loosely tied to one another in the weak Articles of Confederation, and to a much feared, too powerful central government.

We shall explore the federal system at length in the next chapter. For now, keep in mind that among so many other reasons, federalism is an important part of the Constitution's web of protections of individual freedom. Remember, the Framers were dedicated to the concept of limited government. They were convinced (1) that governmental power poses a threat to individual liberty, (2) that, therefore, the exercise of governmental power must be restrained, and (3) that to divide governmental power, as federalism does, is to curb it and to prevent its abuse. James Madison addressed this point in this passage from *The Federalist Papers*:

> ## PRIMARY SOURCE
>
> **In the compound republic of America, the power surrendered by the people is first divided between two distinct governments, and then the portion allotted to each is subdivided among distinct and separate departments. Hence a double security arises to the rights of the people. The different governments will control each other, at the same time that each will be controlled by itself.**
>
> —*The Federalist* No. 51

✔ **Checkpoint**
Identify two powers that the States hold, but that the Federal Government does not.

## REMEDIATION

| If Your Students Have Trouble With | Strategies For Remediation |
| --- | --- |
| The articles of the Constitution (Question 2) | Work with students to create an outline of the articles, breaking down their most important elements. |
| The six principles of the Constitution (Questions 1, 3, 4, 5, 6) | Look at the cartoons representing the principles on pages 70 and 71. Work with students to understand how each cartoon represents a principle, and how the elements of each principle are depicted. |
| The separation of powers among the three branches of government (Question 3) | Divide students into three groups, and assign each group a branch of the government. Have each group become an "expert" in their branch, and teach the other groups about it. |

**Essential Questions Journal** To continue to build a response to the chapter Essential Question, go to your **Essential Questions Journal.**

# SECTION 1 ASSESSMENT

1. **Guiding Question** Use your completed concept web to answer this question: What are the six main principles on which the Constitution is based?

**Key Terms and Comprehension**

2. How do the first three **articles** differ from the other four articles?

3. **(a)** Into what three branches are the powers of the Federal Government separated? **(b)** Give a brief summary of the **checks and balances** in place for each of the three branches.

4. **(a)** Explain the concept of the **rule of law. (b)** Why would this concept have been important for the Framers? **(c)** What might happen if there were no rule of law?

**Critical Thinking**

5. **Summarize (a)** Explain the concept of judicial review. **(b)** How was this power formally established?

6. **Express Problems Clearly** What issues might arise when the legislative and executive branches are controlled by different parties?

**Quick Write**

**Writing for Assessment: Develop a Main Idea** Some essay tests provide a list of topics from which you must choose. Try to select a topic for which you can quickly develop a main idea. For example:
**(a)** The relationship between the separation of powers, checks and balances, and judicial review
**(b)** The importance of federalism to the survival of the U.S. government
**(c)** The importance of separating powers between the State and Federal governments

## Answers

**Checkpoint** to conduct elections, establish schools, regulate business within the State, establish local government, regulate marriages

# Assessment Answers

**1.** popular sovereignty, limited government, separation of powers, checks and balances, judicial review, federalism

**2.** The first three articles are the only ones that deal specifically with the organization of the Federal Government.

**3. (a)** executive, judicial, and legislative
**(b) judicial:** may declare a law or presidential action unconstitutional; **executive:** appoints judges, may veto a law, may call special sessions of Congress; **legislative:** may override a veto, may impeach a president or a judge, approves treaties and presidential appointments, creates lower courts

**4. (a)** The government and its officers are always subject to the law. **(b)** The Framers wanted to avoid absolute rule similar to that exercised by the British government over the colonists. **(c)** Government would have unlimited power. It could act arbitrarily and for its own interests.

**5. (a)** the power of the judicial branch to declare acts of Congress or the President unconstitutional **(b)** Although intended by the Framers, the concept became official when the Supreme Court decided *Marbury* v. *Madison* in 1803.

**6.** Possible response: Conflict between party agendas would make checks and balances more apparent, with more frequent vetoes and battles over judicial appointees. The legislative process could become gridlocked as confrontations between the branches prevent legislation on politically charged issues from passing into law.

**QUICK WRITE** Sample main idea: Constitutional change by other means has allowed branches of government to work around checks and balances.

# Get Started

## LESSON GOAL

- Students will discuss the Supreme Court case *Marbury* v. *Madison,* and then write a letter to the editor of a 19th-century newspaper.

# Teach

Write *judicial review* on the board. Ask students to define the term and write their answers on the board. Judicial review is the power of a court to determine the constitutionality of a government action. Point out that most courts may exercise judicial review. Emphasize that judges cannot rule against a legislative or executive action based on their own ideas of fairness or morality; they must decide based on whether or not the Constitution allows the action.

**L2 ELL Differentiate** To help students define the key term, have them define *judge* (a public official authorized to decide questions put before a court). Then have students apply their definition to *judicial* (of or relating to a judgment). Next, have them define *review* (a critical evaluation). Finally, have them define the key term *judicial review.*

## CREATE A CONCEPT WEB

Draw a concept web on the board. Write *Marbury* v. *Madison* in the center circle. Have students identify the results of the Court's decision, and write them in circles around the center circle. For example, students might suggest that the Supreme Court reprimanded the President, but did not order him to do anything; and that the Supreme Court struck down the Judiciary Act of 1789. Ask: **What was the significance of the Court's decision?** *(The Court established the power of judicial review.)*

## SKILLS DEVELOPMENT

## DRAW INFERENCES AND CONCLUSIONS

Before students begin the Landmark Decisions of the Supreme Court Worksheet (Unit 1 AiO, pp. 163–166), you may want to review tips on drawing inferences and conclusions in the Skills Handbook p. S19.

---

# What is judicial review?

"It is emphatically the province and duty of the Judicial Department to say what the law is."

Those words, penned by Chief Justice John Marshall, lie at the heart of the Supreme Court's decision in *Marbury* v. *Madison* in 1803—the landmark case in which the High Court established the principle of judicial review. The Constitution does not, in so many words, grant that power to the courts. Yet its exercise has long since become a major feature of the American system of constitutional government.

*Marbury* arose in the aftermath of the contentious elections of 1800, in which Thomas Jefferson and his Democratic-Republicans captured both the presidency and control of Congress. The Federalists, stung by defeat, tried to pack the federal courts with loyal party members. The outgoing Congress created dozens of new judgeships, and President John Adams promptly filled those posts with tried-and-true Federalists.

William Marbury had been named a justice of the peace for the District of Columbia, and the Senate had confirmed that appointment. President Adams signed his and several other commissions of office late the night of March 3, 1801. Jefferson became President at noon the following day, and he found that Marbury's and the other commissions had not yet been delivered. Angered by the Federalists' court-packing scheme, he directed the new secretary of state, James Madison, not to deliver those documents to the "midnight justices."

Secretary of State James Madison refused to deliver William Marbury's commission of office.

Marbury asked the Supreme Court to order Madison to make delivery of Marbury's commission.

Refusing Marbury's request, Chief Justice John Marshall established the power of judicial review.

# Supreme Court Notes

**FLETCHER V. PECK, 1810** In *Marbury* v. *Madison,* the Supreme Court first asserted its power to strike down a federal law. Seven years later, the Court extended the power of judicial review to State laws. Then, in 1795, the Georgia State legislature passed a law granting land to four companies but later repealed the law. John Peck acquired some land under the original grant. He later sold the land to Robert Fletcher. Fletcher sued, arguing that Peck had no legal right to sell the land. The case reached the Supreme Court. Noting that the Constitution does not allow ex post facto (after the fact) laws, the Court ruled that the Georgia legislature could not void grants made by the previous law. Thus Georgia's repeal of its law was unconstitutional. By asserting the power of judicial review over both federal and State laws, the Supreme Court secured its authority as chief interpreter of the Constitution.

Angered in turn, Marbury went to the Supreme Court, seeking a writ of mandamus—a court order directing an officer of government to perform a lawfully required duty. Congress had authorized such suits in the Judiciary Act of 1789. A section of that law gave the Supreme Court the power to hear them in its original jurisdiction—that is, directly, not on appeal from a lower court.

Marbury's suit put Chief Justice Marshall in a most difficult position. His Court had yet to become the coequal of the President and Congress in the still quite new Federal Government. If it granted the writ, the President would almost certainly ignore the action. The Court had no power with which it could enforce its decision, and its place in the system of separation of powers would surely suffer. On the other hand, to deny the writ meant that Marbury would not receive the commission to which he was clearly entitled.

Finally, after sitting on the case for nearly two years, Marshall hit upon a shrewd—indeed, a brilliant and calculatingly farsighted—solution. Unanimously, the Court rejected Marbury's plea. It found that the section of the Judiciary Act on which Marbury depended was in conflict with a provision of the Constitution and was, therefore, invalid. Said the Court: "A law repugnant [completely unacceptable] to the Constitution is void; and the courts, as well as the other departments, are bound by that instrument."

With this ruling, the Court established its power to determine the constitutionality of governmental actions. In doing so, it had in effect upheld President Jefferson's refusal to deliver Marbury's commission. However, that short-term success pales in the light of John Marshall's triumph: the Supreme Court had acquired the power of judicial review.

**GOVERNMENT** ONLINE
**In the News**
To learn more about the relevance of the case today, go to **PearsonSchool.com/phgovt**

---

**Think Critically**

1. Should the Supreme Court have the power to declare an act of Congress unconstitutional? Why or why not?
2. **Constitutional Principles** Explain why the power of judicial review is an important part of the system of checks and balances.

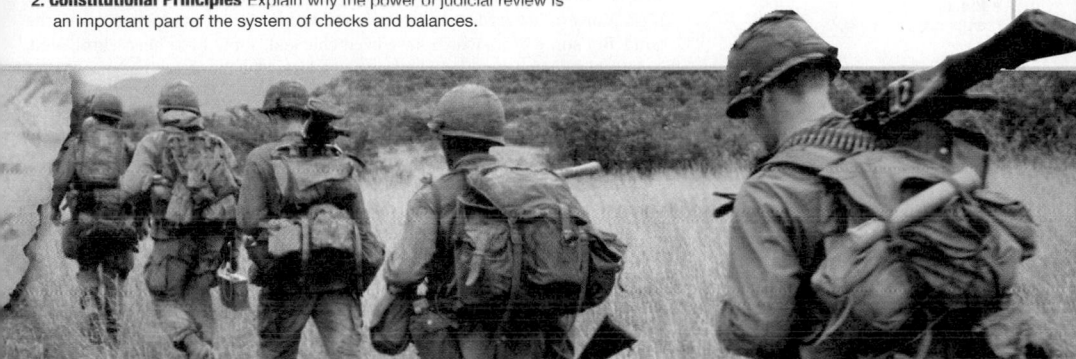

Exercising its power of judicial review, the High Court has found several congressional and presidential actions unconstitutional. Thus, in *New York Times* v. *United States*, 1971, the Court held that the government could not bar the publication of secret documents relating to the war in Vietnam.

77

# Supreme Court Notes

**JUDICIARY ACT OF 1789** Article III, Section 1 of the new Constitution left to Congress the responsibility to "ordain and establish" a federal court system. Congress wasted little time. Senate Bill Number One of the First Session of the First Congress became the Judiciary Act of 1789. This act established the federal district and circuit courts and the authority of judges and court officials. Section 13 of the act authorized the Supreme Court to issue writs of mandamus in original jurisdiction, rather than upon appeal from a lower court. In *Marbury* v. *Madison,* John Marshall pointed out that Article III, Section 2 of the Constitution lists specific situations in which the Court has original jurisdiction, and issuing writs of mandamus was not one of them. Therefore, he concluded, anything not listed in this section of the Constitution must go through the lower courts first. Section 13 of the Judiciary Act was unconstitutional.

# How has the Constitution been amended through the formal amendment process?

I. **Formal Amendment Process**
  A. First Method
    1. proposed by two-thirds vote of each house of Congress
    2. ratified by three fourths of State legislatures
  B. Second Method
    1. proposed by two-thirds vote of each house of Congress
    2. ratified by conventions in three fourths of States
  C. Third Method
    1. proposed by national convention called by Congress at request of two thirds of State legislatures
    2. ratified by three fourths of State legislatures
  D. Fourth Method
    1. proposed by national convention called by Congress at request of two thirds of State legislatures
    2. ratified by conventions in three fourths of States

## Get Started

### LESSON GOALS

Students will . . .

- compare the process of ratification of amendments by studying a chart.
- examine the meaning of several amendments by creating and performing a skit.
- debate the merits of three unsuccessful amendments, using primary sources.

## SKILLS DEVELOPMENT

### ANALYZE SOURCES

To practice analyzing sources in this section, use the Chapter 3 Skills Worksheet (Unit 1 All-in-One, p. 149). You may teach the skill explicitly either before or after beginning the chapter. For L2 and L1 students, assign the adapted Skill Activity (Unit 1 All-in-One, p. 150).

---

## SECTION 2

# Formal Amendment

### Guiding Question

**How has the Constitution been amended through the formal amendment process?** Use an outline like the one below to take notes on how the Constitution can be amended.

I. Formal Amendment Process
  A. First Method
    1. _____
    2. _____
  B. Second Method
    1. _____
    2. _____

### Political Dictionary

- amendment
- ratification
- formal amendment
- Bill of Rights

### Objectives

1. Identify the four different ways by which the Constitution may be formally changed.
2. Explain how the formal amendment process illustrates the principles of federalism and popular sovereignty.
3. Understand that several amendments have been proposed, but not ratified.
4. Outline the 27 amendments that have been added to the Constitution.

**Image Above:** Inez Milholland fought to amend the Constitution to allow women's suffrage.

The Constitution of the United States has now been in force for more than 200 years—longer than the written constitution of any other nation in the world.[2]

When the Constitution became effective in 1789, the United States was a small agricultural nation of fewer than four million people. That population was scattered for some 1,300 miles along the eastern edge of the continent. The 13 States, joined together mostly by travel on horseback and sailing ships, struggled to stay alive in a generally hostile world.

Today, well over 300 million people live in the United States. The now 50 States stretch across the continent and beyond, and the country has many far-flung commitments. The United States is the most powerful nation on Earth, and its modern, highly industrialized and technological society has produced a standard of living that has long been the envy of many other countries.

How has the Constitution, written in 1787, endured and kept pace with that astounding change and growth? The answer lies in this highly important fact: The Constitution of today is, and at the same time is not, the document of 1787. Many of its words are the same, and much of their meaning remains the same. But some of its words have been changed, some have been eliminated, and some have been added. And, very importantly, the meanings of many of its provisions have been modified, as well.

This process of constitutional change, of modification and growth, has come about in two basic ways: (1) by formal amendment and (2) by other, informal means. In this section, you will look at the first of them: the addition of formal amendments to the Constitution.

## Formal Amendment Process

The Framers knew that even the wisest of constitution makers cannot build for all time. Thus, the Constitution provides for its own **amendment**—that is, for changes in its written words.

2 The British constitution dates from well before the Norman Conquest of 1066, but it is not a single, written document. Rather, it is an "unwritten constitution," a collection of principles, customs, traditions, and significant parliamentary acts that guide British government and practice. Israel, which has existed only since 1948, is the only other state in the world without a written constitution.

---

## Focus on the Basics

**FACTS:** • The formal amendment process established in Article V emphasizes federalism. • An amendment may be proposed by a two-thirds vote in both houses of Congress or by a national convention called by Congress at the request of two thirds of State legislatures. • An amendment may be ratified by three fourths of State legislatures or by conventions in three fourths of the States.

**CONCEPTS:** constitutional government, federalism, popular sovereignty

**ENDURING UNDERSTANDINGS:** • The amendment process enables constitutional modification as the nation changes. • The Bill of Rights guarantees freedom of belief and expression, security, and fair and equal treatment before the law.

Article V sets out two methods for the proposal and two methods for the **ratification** of amendments. So, there are four possible methods of **formal amendment**—changes or additions that become part of the written language of the Constitution itself. The diagram below sets out these two methods of proposal and two methods of ratification.

First, an amendment may be proposed by a two-thirds vote in each house of Congress and ratified by three fourths of the State legislatures. Today, at least 38 State legislatures must approve an amendment to make it a part of the Constitution. Of the Constitution's 27 amendments, 26 were adopted in this manner.

Second, an amendment may be proposed by Congress and ratified by <u>conventions</u>, called for that purpose, in three fourths of the States. Only the 21st Amendment (1933) was adopted in this way.

When Congress proposes an amendment, it chooses the method of ratification.

State conventions were used to ratify the 21st Amendment, largely because the lawmakers felt that the conventions' popularly elected delegates would be more likely to reflect public opinion on the question of the repeal of nationwide prohibition than would State legislators.

Third, an amendment may be proposed by a national convention, called by Congress at the request of two thirds of the State legislatures—today, 34. As you can see in the diagram, it must then be ratified by three fourths of the State legislatures. To this point, Congress has not called such a convention.[3]

3 The calling of a convention was a near thing twice over the past 40 years or so. Between 1963 and 1969, 33 State legislatures, one short of the necessary two thirds, sought an amendment to erase the Supreme Court's "one-person, one-vote" decisions; see Chapter 24. Also, between 1975 and 1983, 32 States asked for a convention to propose an amendment that would require that the federal budget be balanced each year, except in time of war or other national emergency.

**convention**
*n.* a meeting to deal with matters of common concern

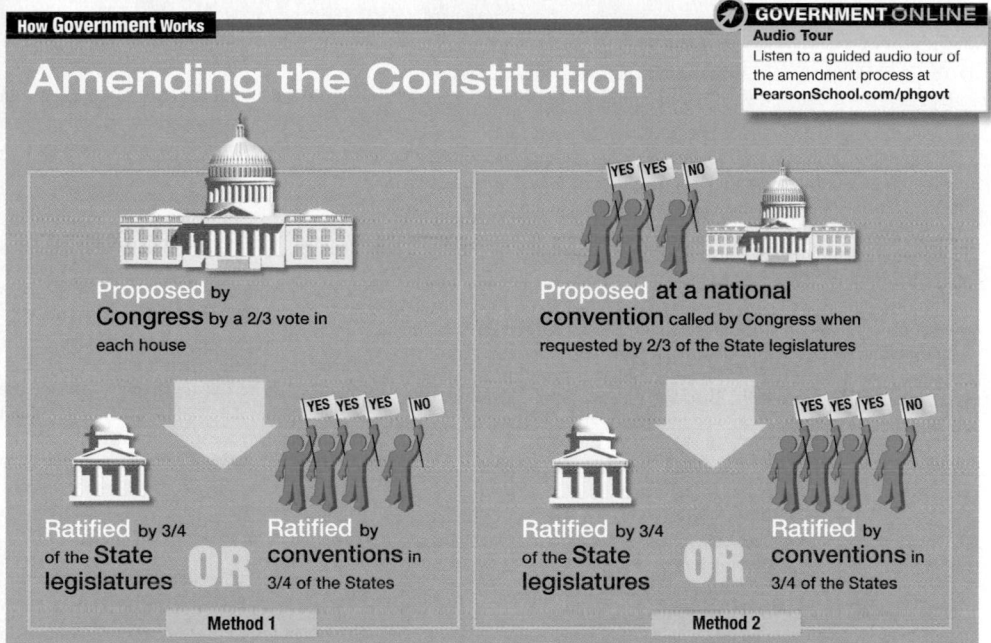

How Government Works

GOVERNMENT ONLINE
Audio Tour
Listen to a guided audio tour of the amendment process at PearsonSchool.com/phgovt

# Amending the Constitution

**Proposed by Congress** by a 2/3 vote in each house

**Ratified** by 3/4 of the **State legislatures** OR **Ratified** by **conventions** in 3/4 of the States

**Method 1**

**Proposed at a national convention** called by Congress when requested by 2/3 of the State legislatures

**Ratified** by 3/4 of the **State legislatures** OR **Ratified** by **conventions** in 3/4 of the States

**Method 2**

▶ **Interpreting Diagrams** There are two ways to propose an amendment, each with two means of ratification. ***Which method has been used to ratify most amendments?***

# Differentiated Resources

The following resources are located in the All-in-One, Unit 1, Chapter 3, Section 2:

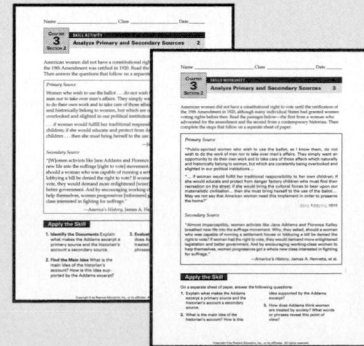

Assign the section, the graphic organizer in the text, and the Reading Comprehension Worksheet (Unit 1 All-in-One, p. 143) before class.

**L2 Differentiate** Reading Comprehension Worksheet (Unit 1 All-in-One, p. 145)

**BELLRINGER**

Distribute the Bellringer Worksheet (Unit 1 All-in-One, p. 147) and instruct students to answer the questions about the constitutional amendments.

# Teach

To present this topic using online resources, use the lesson presentations at **PearsonSchool.com/phgovt.**

**INTRODUCE THE TOPIC**

Tell students that today they will discuss the formal amendment of the Constitution. Before reviewing answers to the Bellringer worksheet, have students divide into teams for a "Quick-Check" game. Instruct the teams to consult on each question, and have a team captain raise a hand when the team has the answer. The first team with the correct answer wins one point. Ask: **How many amendments to the Constitution are there?** *(27)* **How many formal methods of amendment does the Constitution provide?** *(four)* **Which method of amendment has been used most frequently?** *(The Amendment is proposed in Congress and ratified by State legislatures.)* **How many amendments were ratified this way?** *(26 of 27)* **Which amendment was ratified differently?** *(the 21st Amendment)* **What method was used to ratify the 21st Amendment?** *(The 21st Amendment was proposed in Congress and ratified by State conventions.)* **What was the purpose of the 21st Amendment?** *(repeal of Prohibition)* **What are the other two methods of amendment?** *(The amendment is proposed at a national convention called by Congress and ratified by State legislatures or State conventions.)* **How many amendments have been ratified by these methods?** *(none)* You may want students to take out their Reading Comprehension worksheets (Unit 1 All-in-One, p. 143) at this time. Then review students' answers to the Bellringer worksheet.

Tell students to go to the Audio Tour for a guided tour of the processes of formal amendment.

# Answers

**Amending the Constitution** Most successful amendments have been proposed by Congress by a two-thirds vote in both houses and ratified by three fourths of the State legislatures

Distribute Chapter 3 Section 2 Core Worksheet (Unit 1 All-in-One, p. 148), and divide the class into teams. Assign each team one of the following amendments: 3rd, 11th, 14th, 15th, 16th, 19th, 22nd, 24th, 26th, or 27th. Instruct them not to reveal their amendment to other teams. Explain that each team will create a skit to act out the subject of their assigned amendment. The rest of the class will try to guess the amendment being depicted. Tell students that the skits may be set in the past or present and may depict a real event or realistic fictional event. Explain that when they serve as the audience, they will use their Core Worksheet to record the number of the amendment depicted in each skit and evidence from the skit that led them to that conclusion.

**L1** **L2** **Differentiate** Some amendments are easier to address than others. Assign less-skilled students one of these more concrete amendments: 14th, 15th, 19th, 24th, or 26th.

## DISCUSS

Use these questions to continue the discussion of the amendments to the Constitution.

1. **What changes in the United States made the 13th, 14th, and 15th Amendments necessary?** *(The Civil War ended slavery.)* **Do these amendments help to explain the Constitution's durability? Give your reasons.** *(Possible response: Yes. Slavery was reflected in the original Constitution in the Three-Fifths Compromise. When slavery ended, the Constitution needed to be adjusted to guarantee full voting rights and citizenship for the newly freed African Americans.)*

2. **Did your skit, or another team's skit, change the way you think about an amendment? Give your reasons.**

3. **How did the two world wars and the Vietnam War contribute to the passage of the 26th Amendment?** *(Many Americans felt that if 18-year-olds were old enough to fight, they should be old enough to vote.)*

4. **Which amendment affects you most today? Why?**

5. **Which amendment affects you least today? Why?**

## Answers

**The Amendments** It is written in such a broad manner that its provisions can cover issues as they arise, and, therefore, requires few amendments.

# The 27 Amendments

**1700s**

The first ten amendments are known as the Bill of Rights.

**1791 Amendments 1–10** Bill of Rights

**1795 Amendment 11 States** immune from certain lawsuits

**1800s**

**1804 Amendment 12 Changes in** electoral college procedures

**1865 Amendment 13 Abolition of slavery**

**1868 Amendment 14 Citizenship, equal** protection, and due process

**1870 Amendment 15 No denial of vote** because of race, color, or previous enslavement

A symbol of the anti-slavery movement

**1900s**

**1913 Amendment 16 Congress** given the power to tax incomes

**Amendment 17 Popular** election of U.S. Senators

**1919 Amendment 18** Prohibition of alcohol

**1920 Amendment 19 Women's** suffrage

The first women to vote in Brooklyn, Ne

▸▸ **The Amendments** Only 27 amendments have been added to the Constitution thus far. *Why do you think the Constitution has been amended so infrequently since 1789?*

And fourth, an amendment may be proposed by a national convention and then ratified by conventions in three fourths of the States. Remember, the Constitution itself was adopted in much this same way.

## Federalism and Popular Sovereignty

Note that the formal amendment process emphasizes the federal character of the governmental system. Proposal takes place at the national level and ratification is a State-by-State matter. Also note that when the Constitution is amended, that action represents the expression of the people's sovereign will.

Some criticize the practice of sending proposed amendments to the State legislatures rather than to ratifying conventions, especially because it permits a constitutional change without a clear-cut expression by the people.

The critics point out that State legislators, who do the ratifying, are elected to office for a mix of reasons, including party membership, name familiarity, and their stands on certain issues. They are almost never chosen because of their stand on a proposed amendment. On the other hand, the delegates to a ratifying convention would be chosen by the people on the basis of only one factor: a yes-or-no stand on the proposed amendment.

The Supreme Court has held that a State cannot require an amendment proposed by Congress to be approved by a vote of the people of the State before it can be ratified by that State's legislature. It made that ruling in *Hawke* v. *Smith,* in 1920. However, a State legislature can call for an advisory vote by the people before it acts, as the Court held in *Kimble* v. *Swackhamer,* in 1978.

## Proposed Amendments

The Constitution places only one restriction on the subjects with which a proposed amendment may deal. Article V declares

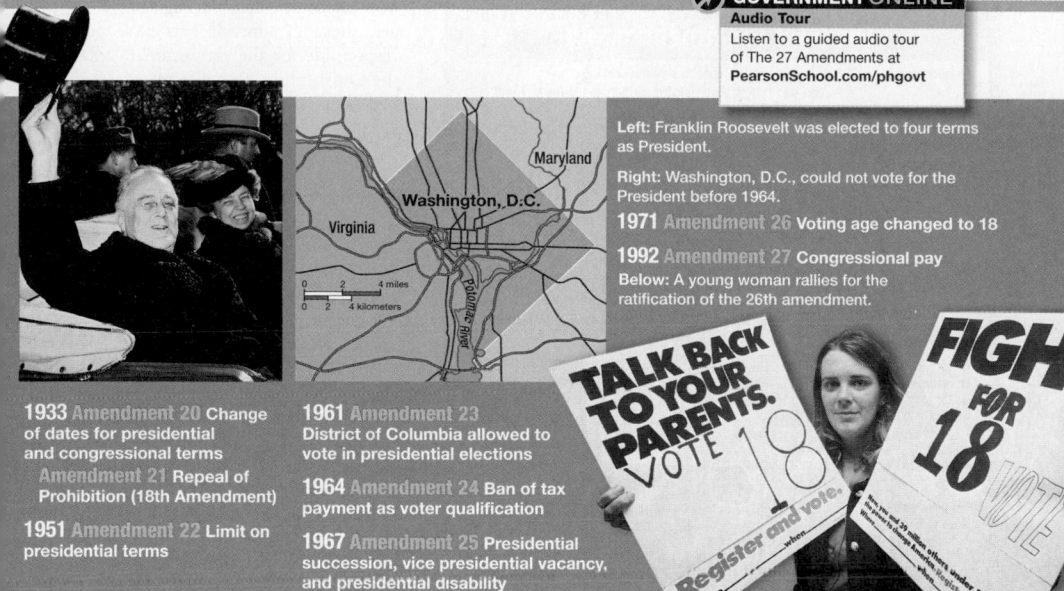

GOVERNMENT ONLINE
Audio Tour
Listen to a guided audio tour
of The 27 Amendments at
PearsonSchool.com/phgovt

Left: Franklin Roosevelt was elected to four terms as President.

Right: Washington, D.C., could not vote for the President before 1964.

**1971** Amendment 26 Voting age changed to 18

**1992** Amendment 27 Congressional pay

Below: A young woman rallies for the ratification of the 26th amendment.

Maryland

Washington, D.C.

Virginia

Potomac River

0    2    4 miles
0    2    4 kilometers

**1933** Amendment 20 Change of dates for presidential and congressional terms
Amendment 21 Repeal of Prohibition (18th Amendment)

**1951** Amendment 22 Limit on presidential terms

**1961** Amendment 23 District of Columbia allowed to vote in presidential elections

**1964** Amendment 24 Ban of tax payment as voter qualification

**1967** Amendment 25 Presidential succession, vice presidential vacancy, and presidential disability

TALK BACK TO YOUR PARENTS. VOTE 18

Register and vote.

FIGHT FOR 18

---

that "no State, without its Consent, shall be deprived of its equal Suffrage in the Senate."

When both houses of Congress pass a resolution proposing an amendment, Congress does not send it to the President to be signed or vetoed, though the Constitution would seem to require it[4]—because when Congress proposes an amendment, it is not making law (not legislating). Although the chief executive has no formal role in the amendment process, his or her political influence can affect the success or failure of any attempt to amend the Constitution, of course.

If a State rejects a proposed amendment, it is not forever bound by that action. It may later reconsider and ratify the proposal. Most constitutional scholars agree that the reverse is not true, however. Once a State has approved an amendment, that action cannot be undone; and no governor's veto power

extends to the ratification of a proposed amendment.

Some 15,000 joint resolutions calling for amendments to the Constitution have been proposed in Congress since 1789. Only 33 of them have been sent on to the States. Of those, only 27 have been finally ratified. One of the unratified amendments had been offered by Congress in 1789—along with 10 other proposals that became the Bill of Rights in 1791, and another that became the 27th Amendment in 1992.

The unratified amendment of 1789 dealt with the distribution of seats in the House of Representatives. A second, proposed in 1810, would have voided the citizenship of anyone accepting any foreign title or other honor. Another, in 1861, would have prohibited forever any amendment relating to slavery. A fourth, in 1924, was intended to give Congress the power to regulate child labor. A fifth one, proclaiming the equal rights of women (ERA), was proposed in 1972; it fell three States short of ratification and died in 1982. An amendment to give the District of

---

4   See Article I, Section 7, Clause 3. This practice of not submitting proposed amendments to the President is an example of the many changes in the Constitution that have been made by means other than formal amendment, a matter addressed in the next section.

✓ **Checkpoint**
How does the formal amendment process reflect the concept of federalism?

---

# Debate

In 2006, the Senate defeated a constitutional amendment, preventing it from passing to the States for a ratification vote. Known as the Flag Desecration Amendment, the measure would have banned the burning of the American flag. Supporters intended the amendment as a way to overrule the Supreme Court, which had twice struck down similar laws. In *Texas* v. *Johnson* (1989), the Court overturned a Texas law, arguing that burning a flag in protest is symbolic speech. "[I]f there is a bedrock principle underlying the First Amendment, it is that the Government may not prohibit the expression of an idea simply because society finds the idea itself offensive or disagreeable." Today, the debate continues over whether flag burning is hate speech and should be banned or is simply a distasteful exercise of free expression. Have students debate the issue. Ask: **Should flag burning be banned?**

## Answers

**Checkpoint** In all four methods of amending the Constitution, proposals occur at the national level and ratification occurs at the State level.

# Assess and Remediate

**L3** Display Transparency 3J, Changing Views of Free Speech. Ask: **What are some of the debates resulting from the guarantees of freedom of speech and press?** *(possible answer: debates over the right to criticize the government or over the right to wear protest armbands in school)*

**L3** Collect the Core Worksheets and assess the students' class participation using the Rubric for Assessing a Role Play (Unit 1 All-in-One, p. 220).

**L3** Assign the Section 2 Assessment questions.

**L3** Section Quiz A (Unit 1 All-in-One, p. 151)

**L2** Section Quiz B (Unit 1 All-in-One, p. 152)

Have students complete the review activities in the digital lesson presentation and continue their work in the **Essential Questions Journal.**

---

## Answers

**The First Ten Amendments** These rights were not included in the original Constitution. They were added to make sure they were guaranteed, as well as to appease Anti-Federalists.

**Checkpoint** Anti-Federalists feared that a strong central government would trample individual rights. They wanted the protection of rights written into the Constitution.

---

## The First Ten Amendments

| | |
|---|---|
| Amendment 1 | • Freedom of religion, speech, and the press<br>• Freedom to peaceably assemble and to petition the government |
| Amendment 2 | • The right to maintain a militia<br>• The right to bear arms |
| Amendment 3 | • Protection from having to quarter (house) soldiers in time of peace without the consent of the owner, nor in time of war except as provided by law |
| Amendment 4 | • Protection against arbitrary searches and seizures without proper warrant or probable cause |
| Amendment 5 | • Protection from prosecution without an indictment<br>• Protection from being tried for the same crime twice<br>• Protection from having to testify against oneself<br>• Protection from the loss of life, liberty, or property without due process of law<br>• Protection from loss of property without just compensation |
| Amendment 6 | • The right to a speedy trial by an impartial jury<br>• The right to be informed of the charges, to cross-examine witnesses, and to present favorable witnesses<br>• The right to an attorney |
| Amendment 7 | • The right to a trial by jury in any civil case where the amount of money involved is $20 or more |
| Amendment 8 | • Protection from excessive bail or fines<br>• Protection from cruel and unusual punishment |
| Amendment 9 | • The fact that the Constitution spells out a number of civil rights does not mean that there are not other, unwritten, rights held by the people. |
| Amendment 10 | • The powers not delegated to the Federal Government may be exercised by the States, as long as they are not prohibited by the Constitution. |

▶▶ The first ten amendments protect many fundamental rights held by the people. *Why is it important to spell out these rights?*

✔ **Checkpoint**
What is the purpose of the Bill of Rights?

Columbia seats in Congress was proposed in 1978; it died in 1985.

When Congress proposed the 18th Amendment in 1917, it set a seven-year deadline for its ratification. The Supreme Court held that Congress can place "a reasonable time limit" on the ratification process, in a case from California, *Dillon* v. *Gloss,* in 1921. Congress has set a similar limit on the ratification period for each of the amendments (except the 19th) that it has proposed since then. It also granted a three-year extension of the deadline for the Equal Rights Amendment in 1979.

## The 27 Amendments

The Constitution's 27 amendments are summarized on pages 80 and 81, and in the table above. As you review them, note this important fact: As significant as they are, those 27 amendments have not been responsible for the extraordinary vitality of the Constitution. That is to say, they have not been a major part of the process by which the Constitution has kept pace with more than two centuries of change.

**The Bill of Rights** The first ten amendments were added to the Constitution less than three years after it became effective. They were proposed by the first session of the First Congress in 1789 and were ratified by the States in late 1791. Each of these amendments arose out of the controversy surrounding the ratification of the Constitution itself. Many people, including Thomas Jefferson, had agreed to support the Constitution only if a listing of the basic rights held by the people were added to it, immediately.

Collectively, the first ten amendments are known as the **Bill of Rights.** They set out the great constitutional guarantees of freedom of belief and expression, of freedom and security of the person, and of fair and equal treatment before the law.

The first ten amendments were added to the Constitution so quickly that, for all intents and purposes, they might just as well be regarded as a part of the original Constitution. In point of fact, they were not. We shall look at the 1st through the 9th amendments at some length in Chapters 19 and 20. The 10th Amendment does not deal with civil rights, as such. Rather, it spells out the concept of reserved powers held by the States in the federal system.

**The Later Amendments** Each of the other amendments that have been added to the Constitution over the past 200 years also grew out of some particular, and often interesting, set of circumstances. For example, the 11th Amendment declares that no State may be sued in the federal courts by a citizen of another State or by a citizen of any foreign state. It was proposed by Congress in 1794 and ratified in 1795, after the State of Georgia had lost a case in the United States Supreme Court. The case (*Chisholm* v. *Georgia,* decided by the Court in 1793) arose out of a dispute over the ownership of some land in Georgia.

---

## Background

**27TH AMENDMENT** The remarkable history of the 27th Amendment began during the debate over ratification of the Constitution. Pointing out that the Constitution was silent on congressional pay, James Madison proposed an amendment that forbade Congress from voting itself a pay raise during that term. It failed to win ratification. The amendment remained dormant until college student Gregory Watson made it the topic of his research paper in 1982. Watson began to lobby State legislatures to ratify this forgotten amendment. Eventually he succeeded, and the 27th Amendment took effect in 1992, nearly 203 years after it was proposed. In 1989, however, Congress passed a law that established automatic cost-of-living pay increases for Congress. Twice, in 1994 and 2001, federal courts ruled that the automatic raises did not violate the 27th Amendment. This finding has yet to be tested in the Supreme Court.

It had been brought to the brand new federal court system by a man who lived in South Carolina.

The 12th Amendment was added in 1804 after the electoral college had failed to produce a winner in the presidential election of 1800. Thomas Jefferson became the third President of the United States in 1801, but only after a long, bitter fight in the House of Representatives.

The 13th Amendment, added in 1865, provides another example. It abolished slavery in the United States and was a direct result of the Civil War. The 14th Amendment, with its definition of citizenship (in 1868), and the 15th Amendment on the right to vote (in 1870) also resulted from that conflict.

The 18th Amendment, establishing a nationwide prohibition of alcohol, was ratified in 1919. Known as "the noble experiment," it lasted fewer than 14 years. The 18th Amendment was repealed by the 21st in 1933.

The 22nd Amendment (1951), limiting the number of terms in which a President may serve to two, was proposed in 1947, soon after the Republican Party had gained control of Congress for the first time in 16 years. Over that period, Franklin D. Roosevelt, a Democrat, had won the presidency four times.

The 26th Amendment was added in 1971. It lowered the voting age to 18 in all elections in the United States. Many who

HE'S GOT A WARRANT!

offthemark.com

▸▸ **Analyzing Political Cartoons** This cartoon illustrates the 4th Amendment. *What is this cartoon conveying about that amendment?*

backed the amendment began to work for its passage during World War II, creating the slogan "Old enough to fight, old enough to vote." Its ratification was spurred by the war in Vietnam.

The most recent amendment, the 27th, was written by James Madison and was among the first to be offered by Congress, in 1789. It forbids members of Congress from raising their own pay during that term. It finally became a part of the Constitution in 1992, when the 38th State, Michigan, ratified it.

# SECTION 2 ASSESSMENT

1. **Guiding Question** Use your completed outline to answer this question: How has the Constitution been amended through the formal amendment process?

**Key Terms and Comprehension**

2. **(a)** Which method of **formal amendment** has been used only once? **(b)** For which **amendment** was it used?

3. Explain how the **ratification** process is an example of popular sovereignty.

**Critical Thinking**

4. **Predict Consequences (a)** Why was the Bill of Rights added to the Constitution? **(b)** What rights do these amendments protect? **(c)** How might news reports differ if freedom of speech and the press were not part of the Constitution?

5. **Identify Central Issues** Some people have criticized the ratification of amendments by State legislatures instead of by popularly elected delegates. **(a)** Why has this process been criticized? **(b)** Do you agree? Why or why not?

**Quick Write**

**Writing for Assessment: Gather Details** Reread the topic you chose in the previous section. What is this question asking for? For example, when you see the word *effect* in a question, you know you are looking for a cause-and-effect relationship. Gather details from the reading that specifically answer the question. Leave out unnecessary details.

| If Your Students Have Trouble With | Strategies For Remediation |
|---|---|
| The 27 Amendments (Questions 1, 2, 3) | Provide historic background to give each of the amendments context. |
| The Bill of Rights (Question 4) | Review Chapter 2 to give students an understanding of the purpose of the Bill of Rights. Work through each amendment to simplify the wording. |
| The Formal Amendment Process (Question 5) | Create a "timeline" for each method of ratification. Have volunteers place the steps for each method on their respective timelines. |

## Answers

**Analyzing Political Cartoons** The 4th Amendment prohibits searches without probable cause. The cartoon conveys the opinion that a warrant and probable cause can be used for questionable motives.

## Assessment Answers

**1. Method 1:** amendment proposed by a two-thirds vote in Congress and ratified by three quarters of State legislatures; **Method 2:** amendment proposed by two-thirds vote in Congress and ratified by conventions in three quarters of States; **Method 3:** amendment proposed by national convention called by Congress at request of two thirds of State Legislatures and ratified by three quarters of State legislatures; **Method 4:** amendment proposed by national convention called by Congress at request of two thirds of State Legislatures and ratified by conventions in three quarters of the States

**2. (a)** amendment proposed by two-thirds vote in Congress and ratified by conventions in three quarters of States **(b)** 21st

**3.** Popularly elected congressional representatives propose amendments, which are ratified by elected representatives in State legislatures or elected delegates to State conventions.

**4. (a)** to gain support from Anti-Federalists who wanted a list of basic rights **(b)** guarantees of freedom of belief and expression, of freedom and security of the person, and of fair and equal treatment before the law **(c)** The government could dictate content of the news reporters.

**5. (a)** because people elect convention delegates based solely on the delegates' views on the proposed amendment; the people elect State legislators for many other reasons **(b)** Sample response: I agree. Ratification by delegates chosen by the people for that purpose would better represent the people's will.

**QUICK WRITE** Details should support the topic.

## LESSON GOAL

- Students will research an issue of interest and conduct an opinion poll.

# Teach

### SURVEY

Have students read the introduction to Citizenship 101. Ask students to rate each question in terms of its significance to their lives, giving the most significant issue three points and the least significant one point. Record their responses. Invite students to comment on why each issue was more or less significant to them as a group.

### RESEARCH

Have students research in groups or on their own one of the issues. They should find information on both sides of the issue, as well as recent national opinion polls. Ask: **What do people in different parts of the country think about this issue? How do different political parties react to this issue?** Ask them to create a chart of their findings, detailing the results of the opinion polls.

### CONDUCT A POLL

Have students who conducted research on the same issue work together to create polling questions. Have students ask their questions of a sample of students in the school, and record responses. Allow time for groups to share the results of their polls. Did these results differ from or reflect national polls that they found in their research? Can they explain why?

# Assess and Remediate

Have students write two or three paragraphs on what they learned about how political roots affect public opinion. Students should be able to extrapolate a response from their research and responses to their poll questions.

## Answers

1. A strong answer will show an understanding of how family, friends, party affiliations, geography, or other sources influenced the student's political attitudes.

2. A strong answer will show an understanding of how a family's party affiliation or cultural background influenced the student's political attitudes.

3. Interview questions should address the influence of family, friends, party affiliations, geography, and cultural background.

---

# Identifying Political Roots and Attitudes

**What is your position on these questions:**
- **Should Congress concentrate on paying down the national debt?**
- **Should the Federal Government do more to protect the environment?**
- **Has outsourcing jobs to other countries harmed the nation's economy?**

Your position on these issues probably reflects a number of factors, especially your background and personal experiences. Family, friends, and teachers, as well as their party affiliations, may also influence you. The part of the country in which you live may be at the root of your political attitudes, as well.

Political attitudes evolve from a variety of sources. People settle in different parts of the country. They belong to different ethnic and cultural groups. Career paths and education also have a major impact.

These political attitudes affect the way a citizen votes. They also affect the way senators and representatives vote, and how Presidents choose the issues they support or oppose. Use these steps to determine where your classmates stand on one of the above issues.

1. **Choose a Question** Look at the questions above. Do you have opinions about these issues? Where do you think your opinions came from? Have you read articles about these issues? Have you heard others talking about them?

2. **Choose One Question** Choose one of these questions and look at opinion polls from various sources to see how people across the country feel about the issue. Do you notice trends? For example, how do people in the city feel about the environment and how do people from rural areas feel about it? What is the opinion of each of the political parties?

3. **Create and Ask Polling Questions** Now, create your own polling questions on the issue. Ask fellow students their opinion on the subject. Make sure your questions are neutral in nature.

Ask them how much they have read or heard about the matter, as well as how they think of themselves politically. Are they conservative? Liberal? With which party do they most often identify? How did they come to identify with this party?

Collect your information to present to the class. Then, review what you've learned. Where do your political roots originate? Has your opinion on this issue changed? Understanding your own political roots and attitudes can help you judge where you stand on an issue, and how you would make the best choice when voting.

### ▸▸ What do you think?

1. What personal experiences and individuals have influenced your political attitudes?

2. What has had the greatest effect on your political attitudes: the place where you live, your family's party affiliation, or your cultural background? Explain your answer.

3. **You Try It** Write five interview questions about political roots and attitudes. Answer each question yourself. Then interview a friend or family member about their views.

**GOVERNMENT** ONLINE
**Citizenship Activity Pack**
For an activity on political roots and attitudes, go to **PearsonSchool.com/phgovt**

**84**

# Citizenship Activity Pack

**L1** **L2** If your students need extra support, use the Citizenship Activity Pack lesson *Political Roots and Attitudes*. It includes a lesson plan for you and materials to help students understand how political roots and attitudes are formed. First, students will take a self-test to identify their existing views on three important issues: public assistance, capital punishment, and immigration. You can tabulate the results and write them on a poster showing the spectrum of political views—from far left to far right. In the core activity, students will assess their views based on additional information about the issues provided on card handouts. Students may also access the Citizenship Activity Pack online for activities on Political Roots and Attitudes at **PearsonSchool.com/phgovt**.

## SECTION 3

# Change by Other Means

### Guiding Question

**How have the day-to-day workings of government affected how we interpret the Constitution?** Use a cause-and-effect chart like the one below to take notes on the workings of government.

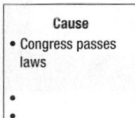

| Cause | Effect |
|-------|--------|
| • Congress passes laws | • Vague parts of the Constitution are clarified |
| • | • |
| • | • |

### Political Dictionary

- executive agreement
- treaty
- electoral college
- Cabinet
- senatorial courtesy

### Objectives

1. Identify how basic legislation has added to our understanding of the Constitution over time.
2. Describe the ways in which the executive and judicial branches have interpreted the Constitution.
3. Analyze the role of party practices and custom in interpreting the Constitution.

**Image Above:** The Constitution makes no mention of either political parties or their national conventions.

---

**S**urely, the Framers would be surprised to learn that only 17 amendments have been added to their handiwork since the adoption of the Bill of Rights more than two centuries ago. That so few formal changes have been made is, in part, a tribute to the wisdom of the Framers. But it is also due, in no small part, to the fact that many of the Constitution's provisions are cast in almost outline-like form; they are brief and seldom very detailed or specific. In short, their skeletal nature virtually guarantees interpretation.

So, to understand the Constitution, you must grasp this key point: There is much in that document—in fact, a great deal—that cannot be seen with the naked eye.

To put this essential point another way: Over time, many interpretations have been made in the Constitution that have not involved any changes in its written words. This vital process of constitutional change by means other than formal amendment has taken place—and continues to occur—in five key ways: through (1) the passage of basic legislation by Congress; (2) actions taken by the President; (3) key decisions of the Supreme Court; (4) the activities of political parties; and (5) custom and usage.

## Basic Legislation

Congress has been a major agent of constitutional change in two important ways. First, it has passed a number of laws to clarify several of the Constitution's brief provisions. That is, Congress has added flesh to the bones of those sections of the Constitution that the Framers left purposely skeletal—provisions they left for Congress to detail as circumstances required.

Take the structure of the federal court system as an example. In Article III, Section 1, the Constitution provides for "one supreme Court, and . . . such inferior Courts as the Congress may from time to time <u>ordain</u> and establish." Beginning with the Judiciary Act of 1789, all of the federal courts, except the Supreme Court, have been created by acts of Congress. Or, similarly, Article II creates only the offices of President and Vice President. The many departments, agencies, and offices in the now huge executive branch have been created by acts of Congress.

### GUIDING QUESTION

## How have the day-to-day workings of government affected how we interpret the Constitution?

| Cause | Effect |
|-------|--------|
| • Congress passes laws<br>• Congress uses its expressed powers<br>• President uses power as commander in chief to deploy troops<br>• President makes an executive agreement with another country<br>• President acts on a broad interpretation of "executive power" in Section 1, Article II<br>• Courts, especially the Supreme Court, interpret and apply the Constitution to cases<br>• Political parties nominate candidates<br>• Congress and President make decisions based on party affiliation<br>• Government follows unwritten customs, such as senatorial courtesy | • Vague parts of the Constitution are clarified<br>• Broad terms in the Constitution become more defined<br>• American troops enter conflicts without a declaration of war<br>• A binding agreement is created without a formal treaty<br>• Executive powers are expanded without amending the Constitution<br>• Actions that are and are not addressed in the Constitution are clarified<br>• A nominating system not stated in the Constitution is established<br>• Government governs through parties<br>• Customs take on the force of written law |

## Get Started

### LESSON GOALS

Students will . . .

- identify the informal methods of change used in example scenarios.
- apply the informal methods of change by writing example scenarios.

---

**SKILLS DEVELOPMENT**

### DECISION MAKING

Before students begin the Core Worksheet in this lesson, you may want to review tips on decision making in the Skills Handbook, p. S18.

---

## Focus on the Basics

**FACTS:** • Over time, change has occurred through interpretation and practice. • There are five informal means of change: basic legislation, executive action, court decisions, party practices, and custom and usage.

**CONCEPTS:** judicial review, checks and balances, constitutional government, rule of law

**ENDURING UNDERSTANDINGS:** • The provisions of the Constitution are cast in almost outline-like form. • Over the years, the Constitution's brief provisions have been fleshed out and reshaped as a result of the day-to-day workings of government, without formal amendment.

Assign the section, the graphic organizer in the text, and the Reading Comprehension Worksheet (Unit 1 All-in-One, p. 153) before class.

**L2 Differentiate** Reading Comprehension Worksheet (Unit 1 All-in-One, p. 155)

**BELLRINGER**

Distribute the Bellringer Worksheet (Unit 1 All-in-One, p. 157), and write on the board: **Identify each statement on the worksheet as true or false and explain your answer.**

# Teach

To present this topic using online resources, use the lesson presentations at **PearsonSchool.com/phgovt.**

**INTRODUCE THE TOPIC**

Tell students that today they will discuss the process of constitutional change by means other than formal amendment. Before reviewing the Bellringer questions, ask students to use their Reading Comprehension Worksheets to review the five ways in which informal changes occur. Then encourage students to give examples of each method. (***basic legislation:*** *Judiciary Act of 1789 created a federal court system;* ***executive action:*** *the President has sent troops abroad without a formal declaration of war from Congress;* ***court decisions:*** Marbury v. Madison *established the power of judicial review;* ***party practices:*** *parties nominate candidates for office;* ***custom and usage:*** *Cabinet is made up of the 15 executive department heads*)

Review answers to the Bellringer activity. *(1. false; 2. true; 3. true; 4. false; 5. true; 6. true; 7. false)*

## Answers

**Constitutional Principles** The constitutional requirement that the President report to Congress about the state of the Union establishes a check on executive power by the legislative branch.

**Checkpoint** by passing laws that spell out brief provisions in the Constitution and by using its powers in ways that help define the meaning of the broad terms in the Constitution

---

## The State of the Union

" The President shall from time to time give to Congress information of the State of the Union and recommend to their Consideration such measures as he shall judge necessary and expedient.

—**Article II, Section 3**

# FROM THE CONSTITUTION

**Creating a Custom** While an address to Congress is required by the Constitution, the method of address is left to each President. Both George Washington and then John Adams delivered their speeches to joint sessions of Congress. But Thomas Jefferson submitted a written document in 1801 and set a precedent that lasted for more than a century. In 1913 Woodrow Wilson revived the practice of appearing before Congress, and every President since then has followed his lead. Calvin Coolidge's 1923 speech was the first broadcast by radio and Harry Truman's 1947 address was the first to be televised.

**Constitutional Principles** How does the State of the Union address reflect the system of checks and balances?

▲ President Harry Truman delivers the first televised State of the Union.

---

✔**Checkpoint**
Name the two methods by which Congress has shaped the government.

**succession**
*n.* the process by which one follows in order (succeeds) to an office

**ordain**
*v.* to order, direct, decree

As an additional example, the Constitution deals with the matter of presidential succession, but only up to a point. The 25th Amendment says that if the presidency becomes vacant, the Vice President automatically succeeds to the office. Who becomes President if both the presidency and the vice presidency are vacant? Thus, the Constitution leaves the answer to that question to Congress.

Second, Congress has added to the Constitution by the way in which it has used many of its powers. The Constitution gives to Congress the expressed power to regulate foreign and interstate commerce.[5] But what is "foreign commerce" and "interstate commerce"? What, exactly, does Congress have the power to regulate? The Constitution does not say. Congress has done much to

define those words, however, by exercising its commerce power with the passage of literally thousands of laws. As it has done so, Congress has, in a very real sense, expanded the Constitution.

## Executive Action

The manner in which various Presidents, especially the more vigorous ones, have used their powers has also contributed to the growth of the Constitution. For example, the document says that only Congress can declare war.[6] But the Constitution also makes the President the commander in chief of the nation's armed forces.[7] Acting under that authority, several Presidents have made war without a declaration of war by

---

5  See Article I, Section 8, Clause 3.

6  See Article I, Section 8, Clause 11.
7  See Article II, Section 2, Clause 1.

---

# Differentiated Resources

The following resources are located in the All-in-One, Unit 1, Chapter 3, Section 3:

**L3** Reading Comprehension Worksheet (p. 153)

**L2** Reading Comprehension Worksheet (p. 155)

**L3** Bellringer Worksheet (p. 157)

**L3** Core Worksheet (p. 158)

**L2** Core Worksheet (p. 159)

**L3** Quiz A (p. 161)    **L2** Quiz B (p. 162)

**L3** Chapter Test A (p. 167)

**L2** Chapter Test B (p. 170)

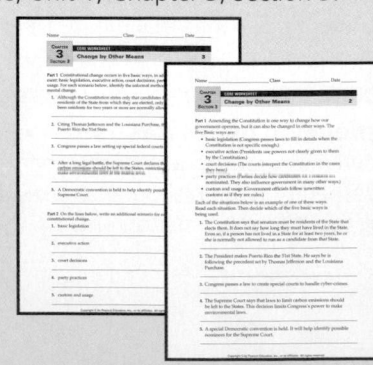

Congress. In fact, Presidents have used the armed forces abroad in combat without such a declaration on several hundred occasions in our history.

Take the use of executive agreements in the conduct of foreign affairs as another example. An **executive agreement** is a pact made by the President directly with the head of a foreign state. A **treaty,** on the other hand, is a formal agreement between two or more sovereign states. The principal difference between agreements and treaties is that executive agreements need not be approved by the Senate. They are as legally binding as treaties, however. Recent Presidents have often used them in our dealings with other countries, instead of the much more cumbersome treaty-making process outlined in Article II, Section 2 of the Constitution.

Additionally, most Presidents have insisted that the phrase "executive Power" in Section 1 of Article II includes much more than the particular presidential powers set out in that article. Thus, Thomas Jefferson engineered the Louisiana Purchase in 1803, doubling the size of the United States—even though the Constitution does not say that the President has the power to acquire territory.

## Court Decisions

The nation's courts, most tellingly the United States Supreme Court, interpret and apply the Constitution in many of the cases they hear. You have already encountered several of these instances of constitutional interpretation by the Court, most notably in *Marbury* v. *Madison,* 1803.

Recall that the Court established the power of judicial review—which is not specifically mentioned in the Constitution. You will find many more instances throughout the pages of this book—for the Supreme Court is, as Woodrow Wilson once put it, "a constitutional convention in continuous session."

## Party Practices

The nation's political parties have been a major agent of constitutional change over the course of our political history, despite the fact that the Constitution makes no mention

of them. In fact, most of the Framers were opposed to political parties. In his Farewell Address in 1796, George Washington warned the people against what he called "the baneful effects of the spirit of party." He and many others feared the divisive effect of party politics on government. Yet, even as he spoke, parties were developing. They have had a major place in the shaping of government and its processes ever since. Illustrations of that point are almost endless.

Neither the Constitution nor any law provides for the nomination of candidates for the presidency. From the 1830s on, however, the major parties have held national conventions to do just that. The parties have converted the **electoral college,** the body that makes the formal selection of the nation's President, from what the Framers intended into a "rubber stamp" for each State's popular vote in presidential elections. Both houses of Congress are organized and conduct much of their business on the basis of party. The President makes appointments to office with an eye to party politics. In short, government in the United States is in many ways government through party.

## Custom and Usage

Unwritten customs may be as strong as written law, and many of them have developed in our governmental system. Again, there are many examples. By custom, not because the Constitution says so, the heads of the 15 executive departments make up the **Cabinet,** an advisory body to the President.

On each of the eight occasions when a President died in office, the Vice President succeeded to that office—most recently Lyndon Johnson, following John Kennedy's assassination in 1963. Yet, the written words of the Constitution did not provide for this practice until the adoption of the 25th Amendment in 1967. Until then, the Constitution said only that the powers and duties of the presidency—but *not* the office itself—"shall devolve on" (be transferred to) the Vice President.[9]

---

8  Read carefully Article II, Section 1, Clause 6, and then read Section 1 of the 25th Amendment.

---

✔ **Checkpoint**
Why did the Framers make no provision for political parties?

**tellingly**
*adv.* striking, with marked effect

## Background

**TITLE IX** Display Transparency 3K. The role of women in American society has expanded dramatically, exposing the need to extend constitutional protections to the rights of women. Congress passed a landmark law that helped open to women the full range of educational opportunities. Title IX of the Higher Education Act (1972) states that "No person . . . shall, on the basis of sex, be excluded from participation in . . . any educational program or activity." Now, more women are attending college and serving on faculties. Medical schools and law schools are accepting women on an equal basis with men. Support for the law remains strong. Before Title IX, only 300,000 high school girls participated in the few competitive sports available to them. By 2005, 2.95 million girls were playing sports of all kinds. Title IX has helped extend to women the constitutional protections against discrimination.

---

**DISTRIBUTE CORE WORKSHEET**

Distribute the Chapter 3 Section 3 Core Worksheet (Unit 1 All-in-One, p. 158), which asks students to consider scenarios involving informal change. Students can work individually to identify the informal method of change used in each scenario in Part 1. Then have partners work together to complete Part 2. Encourage them to come up with examples not given in the text. Have students read their scenarios aloud to the class.

**L2** **LPR Differentiate** Distribute the adapted Chapter 3 Section 3 Core Worksheet (Unit 1 All-in-One, p. 159) to these students.

**L4** **Differentiate** Have students do research to come up with specific, real examples of change for each informal method.

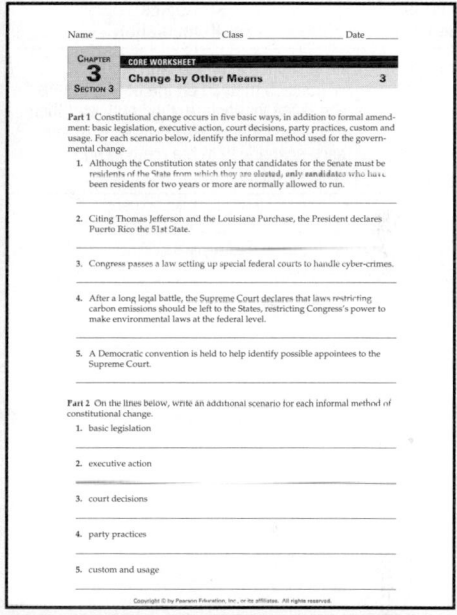

**EXTEND THE LESSON**

Remind students that Woodrow Wilson once described the Supreme Court as "a constitutional convention in continuous session." Call on volunteers to explain his meaning. Then direct students to the Supreme Court Glossary at the back of the textbook. Have them read the brief descriptions of these 1st Amendment cases: *Dennis* v. *United States,* 1951; *Schenck* v. *United States,* 1919; and *United States* v. *Eichman,* 1990. After they read each case description, ask: **In what way does this decision reflect Wilson's description?**

**L1** **L2** **Differentiate** Have a student read the description of the Court's ruling in *Schenck* v. *United States,* 1919, aloud. Then ask students to explain how this decision interpreted the Constitution.

---

## Answers

**Checkpoint** The Framers made no provision for political parties because they were opposed to them and they feared their divisive effect on government.

# Assess and Remediate

**L3** Collect the Core Worksheets and assess the students' class participation, using the Rubric for Assessing a Writing Assignment (Unit 1 All-in-One, p. 221).

**L3** Assign the Section 3 Assessment questions.

**L3** Section Quiz A (Unit 1 All-in-One, p. 161)

**L2** Section Quiz B (Unit 1 All-in-One, p. 162)

Have students complete the review activities in the digital lesson presentation and continue their work in the **Essential Questions Journal.**

### REMEDIATION

| If Your Students Have Trouble With | Strategies For Remediation |
|---|---|
| Change by other means (Questions 1, 2, 3, 4, 5) | Review each subhead with students. Write each method on the board. Create scenarios for each method and read them aloud to students. Have students match each scenario with the method under which it falls. |

## Answers

**Checkpoint** 22nd: limit on the number of presidential terms; 25th: presidential succession

▲ The President and three Cabinet secretaries (from left): Eric Shinseki (Veterans Affairs), Shaun Donovan (Education), and Ken Salazar (Interior).

✔ **Checkpoint**
Which two customs did the 22nd and 25th amendments establish as law?

amounts to an unwritten rule that is closely followed in the Senate. Notice that its practical effect is to shift a portion of the appointing power from the President, where the formal wording of the Constitution puts it, to certain members of the Senate.

Both the strength and the importance of unwritten customs can be seen in the reaction to the rare circumstances in which one of them has not been observed. For nearly 150 years, the "no-third-term tradition" was a closely followed rule in presidential politics. The tradition began in 1796, when George Washington refused to seek a third term as President, and several later Presidents followed that lead. In 1940, and again in 1944, however, Franklin Roosevelt broke the no-third-term custom. He sought and won a third and then, four years later, a fourth term in the White House. As a direct result, the 22nd Amendment was added to the Constitution in 1951, limiting the President to two terms. What had been an unwritten custom, an informal rule, became part of the written Constitution itself.

It is a long-established custom that the Senate will approve only those presidential appointees, such as a federal judge or a United States marshal, who are acceptable to the senator or senators of the President's party from the State involved. This practice is known as **senatorial courtesy,** and it

**Essential Questions Journal** To continue to build a response to the chapter Essential Question, go to your **Essential Questions Journal.**

## SECTION 3 ASSESSMENT

**1. Guiding Question** Use your completed cause-and-effect chart to answer this question: How have the day-to-day workings of government affected how we interpret the Constitution?

**Key Terms and Comprehension**

**2. (a)** Did the Framers lay out the provisions of the Constitution in a general or specific manner? **(b)** In what way has the Framers' plan eased change throughout the last two centuries?

**3.** In what two ways has Congress "added flesh to the bones" of the Constitution? Give an example of each.

**Critical Thinking**

**4. Predict Consequences** Several Presidents have deployed troops to various conflicts without asking Congress for a declaration of war. What might be the consequences of setting aside this check **(a)** on the executive branch? **(b)** on Congress? **(c)** How might it change the interpretation of the Constitution?

**5. Draw Conclusions (a)** Name two examples of customs that have endured despite their absence in the Constitution. **(b)** How important is custom in the workings of the Federal Government? Why?

**Quick Write**

**Writing for Assessment: Outline and Answer** Once you have gathered the details you need for the topic you selected in Section 1, write an outline to organize the information. Remember, you may not have much time. Make your outline brief and to the point. Use the outline as a framework to write your response.

## Assessment Answers

**1.** Legislation, executive action, court decisions, political parties, and customs can influence our interpretation of the Constitution. Laws passed by Congress flesh out and define broad provisions in the Constitution. The President's use of executive agreements, power as commander in chief, and other interpretations of powers granted under the Constitution can expand executive power. By interpreting and applying the Constitution to cases, the courts clarify what actions are and are not permissible. Parties nominate candidates and influence much of the work of government. Government

follows unwritten customs that take on the force of written law.

**2. (a)** general **(b)** This enabled the flexibility to change through interpretation and practice.

**3.** First, Congress has passed laws to spell out the provisions of the Constitution. For example, the Judiciary Act of 1789 set up the federal court system. Second, Congress has added to the Constitution by the way it has used its powers. For example, Congress has defined what commerce it has the power to regulate by the way it exercises its commerce power.

**4. (a)** broadens the President's powers as commander in chief **(b)** reduces Congress's ability to control use of troops **(c)** It could negate the constitutional power Congress holds to declare war.

**5. (a)** sample response: the makeup of the Cabinet and senatorial courtesy **(b)** Very important. Custom provides rules that were not laid down in the Constitution but are still important to a smoothly-running government.

**QUICK WRITE** Students should write an outline using the details they gathered, and then use the outline to write their assessment essay.

# Quick Study Guide

**GOVERNMENT** ONLINE

**On the Go**
To review anytime, anywhere, download these online resources at **PearsonSchool.com/phgovt**
Political Dictionary, Audio Review

CHAPTER **3**

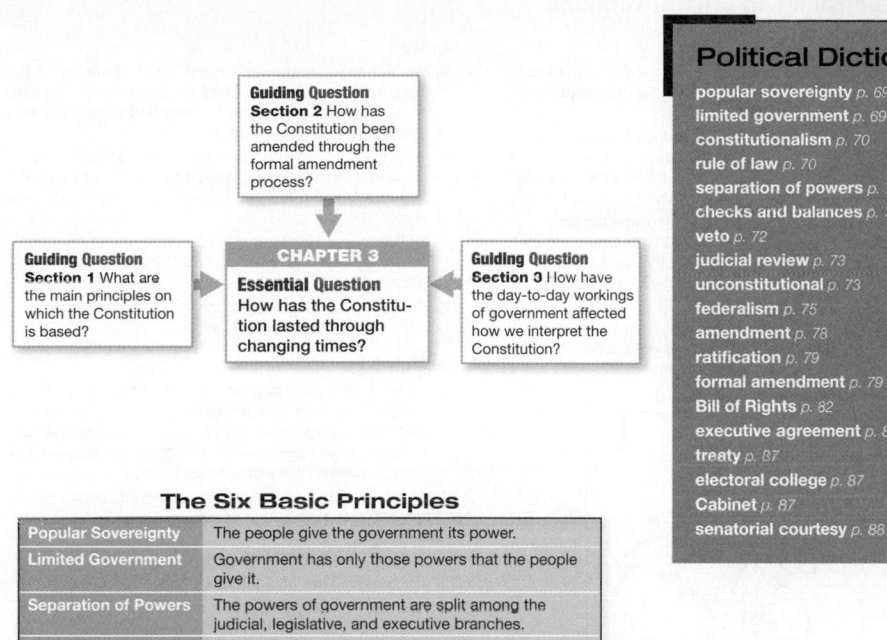

## Political Dictionary

popular sovereignty *p. 69*
limited government *p. 69*
constitutionalism *p. 70*
rule of law *p. 70*
separation of powers *p. 70*
checks and balances *p. 72*
veto *p. 72*
judicial review *p. 73*
unconstitutional *p. 73*
federalism *p. 75*
amendment *p. 78*
ratification *p. 79*
formal amendment *p. 79*
Bill of Rights *p. 82*
executive agreement *p. 87*
treaty *p. 87*
electoral college *p. 87*
Cabinet *p. 87*
senatorial courtesy *p. 88*

### The Six Basic Principles

| | |
|---|---|
| Popular Sovereignty | The people give the government its power. |
| Limited Government | Government has only those powers that the people give it. |
| Separation of Powers | The powers of government are split among the judicial, legislative, and executive branches. |
| Checks and Balances | Each branch has the power to check the other two branches. |
| Judicial Review | The courts have the power to determine if government actions violate the Constitution. |
| Federalism | The powers of government are divided between the Federal Government and the States. |

### The Formal Amendment Process

**By Congress**
- **Proposal** by a 2/3 vote in each house of Congress
- **Ratification** by 3/4 of State legislatures or by conventions in 3/4 of the States

**By a National Convention**
- **Proposal** by a national convention called by Congress
- **Ratification** by 3/4 of State legislatures or by conventions in 3/4 of the States

---

Have students download the digital resources available at Government on the Go for review and remediation.

**STUDY TIPS**

**Test-Taking Skills** A few simple strategies should help most students improve their performance on tests. A positive attitude toward the test and their own abilities is top priority. Beyond that, students should scan the entire test before beginning to work. Using this approach, they should answer the easiest questions first, and then focus on the more difficult ones. This strategy boosts confidence, and the simpler questions may contain information that helps with the more difficult ones. When answering questions, students should be sure to read the entire question before answering and to read any instructions thoroughly. If they find a question confusing, they should ask the teacher for clarification. Focusing on one question at a time can help with concentration. Finally, if students find themselves getting anxious, they should stop working and take a few deep breaths to help them relax.

**ASSESSMENT AT A GLANCE**

**Tests and Quizzes**
Section Assessments
Section Quizzes A and B, Unit 1 **All-in-One**
Chapter Assessment
Chapter Tests A and B, Unit 1 **All-in-One**
Document-Based Assessment
Progress Monitoring Online
Exam*View* Test Bank

**Performance Assessment**
Essential Questions Journal
Debate, p. 81
Assessment Rubrics, **All-in-One**

---

# For More Information

To learn more about the Constitution, refer to these sources or assign them to students:

**L1** **Sobel, Syl.** *The U.S. Constitution and You.* Barron's Educational Series, 2001.

**L2** **Bjornlund, Lydia.** *The U.S. Constitution: Blueprint for Democracy.* Lucent Books, Inc., 1999.

**L3** **Lane, Eric and Michael Oreskes.** *The Genius of America: How the Constitution Saved Our Country—and Why It Can Again.* Bloomsbury USA, 2007.

**L4** **Amar, Akhil Reed.** *America's Constitution: A Biography.* Random House, 2005.

# Chapter Assessment

**COMPREHENSION AND CRITICAL THINKING**

## SECTION 1

**1. (a)** The executive branch may veto legislation and call special sessions of Congress. The legislative branch may override a President's veto, impeach a President, and approve appointments and treaties. **(b)** The Framers feared that one branch would gain too much power, or that the presidency would become a monarchy. These checks protect against such abuses of power.

**2. (a)** The Massachusetts constitution restricts each branch of government from performing the duties of the other two branches. **(b)** By preventing the concentration of power in any one group, this separation of powers will require government officials to operate within the law.

**3. (a)** The Framers wanted to make sure that the people would be the source of government power and that government would remain under the rule of law. **(b)** judicial branch **(c)** through presidential power to name federal judges and the Senate's right to approve those appointments

**4. (a)** It suggests the judicial branch's ability to declare laws made by Congress as unconstitutional. **(b)** The members of Congress are not above the law of the Constitution when they create legislation.

## SECTION 2

**5. (a)** through proposal by a two-thirds vote in each house of Congress and ratification by three fourths of the State legislators **(b)** Both national and State levels are involved in the amendment process.

**6. (a)** the Civil War **(b)** election of Franklin D. Roosevelt to four terms as President

**7. (a)** When Congress proposes an amendment, it is not making law, so the proposal need not go to the President to sign or veto. **(b)** Possible response: I agree. Ratification of an amendment requires popular support. A veto is a check by the President on the power of Congress. It was not intended as a check on the will of the people.

**8.** The Framers provided an amendment process to give the Constitution flexibility to meet future needs. They promoted federalism by including both the national and State levels in the amendment process. Their goal of popular sovereignty is reflected in the fact that an amendment requires broad popular support to win ratification by 38 of the 50 States.

---

# CHAPTER 3 — Chapter Assessment

## Comprehension and Critical Thinking

### Section 1

**1. (a)** What checks exist between the legislative and executive branches? **(b)** How do these checks represent the intentions of the Framers?

**2.** Reread the excerpt from the Massachusetts Constitution in Section 1. **(a)** What restrictions does it put on the three branches of the State government? **(b)** What is meant by "a government of laws and not of men"?

**3. (a)** Why were the Framers so careful to limit the powers of the Federal Government? **(b)** Which branch of the Federal Government seems to have the least amount of checks against its power? **(c)** How might the power of this branch be further limited?

**4. Analyze Political Cartoons (a)** Which checks on government does this cartoon suggest? **(b)** How does it reflect "a government of laws and not of men"?

"How come everything I like is always unconstitutional?"

### Section 2

**5. (a)** Of the four methods of formal amendment, which has been used the most to amend the Constitution? **(b)** How does this method preserve the intention of the Framers to create a federal government?

**6.** In most cases, amendments have been added as the result of a specific issue. What issue gave rise to **(a)** the 13th, 14th, and 15th amendments? **(b)** the 22nd Amendment?

**7. (a)** When an amendment is proposed, why is it not sent to the President to sign or veto? **(b)** Do you agree with this practice? Why or why not?

**8.** How does the process of constitutional amendment reflect the goals of the Framers?

### Section 3

**9. (a)** How have party practices changed the way we interpret the Constitution? **(b)** How did the Framers—in particular, George Washington—feel about political parties? **(c)** Do you agree with Washington's assessment of political parties? Why or why not?

**10. (a)** List two ways in which custom has influenced government. **(b)** How important is custom to our government?

### Writing About Government

**11.** Use your Quick Write exercises to write a brief essay answering the question you chose. Make sure that you use your outline as the frame for your essay. Try to make your point in three or four paragraphs, with an introduction, a body, and a conclusion. See pp. S11–S12 in the Skills Handbook.

## Apply What You've Learned

**12. Essential Question Activity** Propose your own amendment to the Constitution.

**(a)** Research a current government issue, something that you feel should be made a permanent part of the Constitution.

**(b)** Create an outline of arguments for and against your proposed addition to the Constitution.

**(c)** Create a plan detailing which method you would use to get your amendment proposed and ratified.

**(d)** Bring your amendment before the class and explain why it should be passed.

**13. Essential Question Assessment** Based on your work from the activity and the content you have learned in this chapter, hold a group discussion to help you answer the Essential Question: **How has the Constitution lasted through changing times?** Take notes on your ideas from the discussion.

**Essential Questions Journal** To respond to the chapter Essential Question, go to your **Essential Questions Journal.**

**90** Chapter 3 Assessment

---

## SECTION 3

**9. (a)** Political parties have determined the system for nominating candidates, changed the original intent of the electoral college, and influenced the way the government operates. **(b)** The Framers were against political parties. **(c)** Possible response: I agree. Political parties influence the government without having a constitutional check on their power.

**10. (a)** Possible response: The president's cabinet was established; presidents choose only those appointees that the Senate will approve. **(b)** Possible response: Custom is very important to our government. Though it doesn't really affect the processes of government, it has affected the way in which the government carries out its processes.

## WRITING ABOUT GOVERNMENT

**11.** Students should follow their outline to answer their chosen essay question.

## APPLY WHAT YOU'VE LEARNED

**12.** Students should clearly describe the intent of their amendment and choose one of the formal amendment methods. They should present persuasive arguments for adopting

# Document-Based Assessment

## Amendments for a Growing City

In 1790, Congress chose a site along the Potomac River for the nation's capital. The map illustrates the plan for the new city. This site would belong to no State. It would be under the authority of Congress. The image reflects the city's small population at its beginnings. In 1950, Washington, D.C., was home to over 800,000 residents, who could not vote for their President. Document 1 shows the amendment that changed that situation.

### Document 1

"**Section 1.** The District constituting the seat of Government of the United States shall appoint in such manner as the Congress may direct:

A number of electors of President and Vice President equal to the whole number of Senators and Representatives in Congress to which the District would be entitled if it were a State, but in no event more than the least populous State; they shall be in addition to those appointed by the States, they shall be considered, for the purposes of the election of President and Vice President, to be electors appointed by a State; and they shall meet in the District and perform such duties as provided by the twelfth article of Amendment.

**Section 2.** Congress shall have the power to enforce this article by appropriate legislation.

—23rd Amendment

### Document 2

—Washington, D.C., circa 1790

Use your knowledge of the Constitution, the amendment process, and Documents 1 and 2 to answer Questions 1–3.

1. What was the purpose of the 23rd Amendment to the Constitution?
   A. to include voters of Washington, D.C., in all elections
   B. to include voters of Washington, D.C., in presidential elections
   C. to include members of Congress, living in Washington, D.C., in presidential elections
   D. to include members of Congress, living in Washington, D.C., in all elections

2. Why did the Constitution not address the issue of voters in the national capital?

3. **Pull It Together** How does the example of Washington, D.C., help to explain why the Constitution has endured through changing times?

**GOVERNMENT** ONLINE
**Online Documents**
To find more primary sources on Washington, D.C., visit
PearsonSchool.com/phgovt

---

## DOCUMENT-BASED ASSESSMENT

1. B

2. At the time it was built, Washington, D.C., was a sparsely populated town. In addition, the city was meant as a seat of government, under the authority of Congress and belonging to no State. It was not intended to be home to many people.

3. Because Washington, D.C., grew and its citizens wanted the right to vote, the Constitution had to be amended. The flexibility of the Constitution allowed for an amendment to allow Washington, D.C., citizens to vote in presidential elections.

**L2 Differentiate** Students use all the documents on the page to support their theses.

**L3 Differentiate** Students include additional information available online at **PearsonSchool .com/phgovt.**

**L4 Differentiate** Students use materials from the textbook, the online information at **PearsonSchool .com/phgovt,** and do additional research to support their views.

**Go Online to PearsonSchool.com/phgovt** for a student rubric and extra documents.

---

their amendment and have prepared arguments to counter anticipated objections.

13. Possible discussion points: The Framers created the Constitution to be a flexible document. They formed it around basic principles rather than try to detail every possible situation. Therefore, changes can be made based on enduring principles rather than on specifics that could become outdated. The formal amendment process reflects two of these principles: popular sovereignty and federalism. Also, the almost-outline form of the Constitution leaves room for change through interpretation and practice to reflect growth and change in the nation.

# Introduce the Chapter

## Essential Questions:

**UNIT 1**

What should be the goals of government?

**CHAPTER 4**

Is the federal system the best way to govern the United States?

**ACTIVATE PRIOR KNOWLEDGE**

Have students examine the image and quotation on these pages. Ask: **What governments in our country make laws that you must obey?** *(National and State)* **How do these different governments know which responsibilities belong to them?** *(The Constitution divides powers between the National and State governments.)* In this chapter, students will learn about our nation's dual system of government called *federalism.* Then tell students to begin to further explore federalism by completing the Chapter 4 Essential Question Warmup Activity in their **Essential Questions Journal.** Discuss their responses as a class.

**BEFORE READING**

**L2 ELL Differentiate** Chapter 4 Prereading and Vocabulary Worksheet (Unit 1 All-in-One, p. 180)

**SUCCESSNET STUDENT AND TEACHER CENTER**

Visit **PearsonSchool.com/phgovt** for downloadable resources that allow students and teachers to connect with government "on the go."

**DIGITAL LESSON PRESENTATION**

The digital lesson presentation supports the print lesson with activities and summaries of key concepts.

## SKILLS DEVELOPMENT

**PROBLEM SOLVING**

You may wish to teach problem solving as a distinct skill within Section 1 of this chapter. Use the Chapter 4 Skills Worksheet (Unit 1 All-in-One, p. 187) to help students learn how to solve a problem. The worksheet asks students to read information about the Framers of the Constitution, determine the main problem they had to solve at the Constitutional Convention of 1787, and choose possible solutions to the problem. For L2 and L1 students, assign the adapted Skill Activity (Unit 1 All-in-One, p. 188).

**WebQuest online** The chapter WebQuest challenges students to answer the chapter Essential Question by asking them about federalism.

92

## Block Scheduling

**BLOCK 1:** Teach Section 1, omitting the debate.

**BLOCK 2:** Teach Sections 2 and 3, and choose one Extend the Lesson feature.

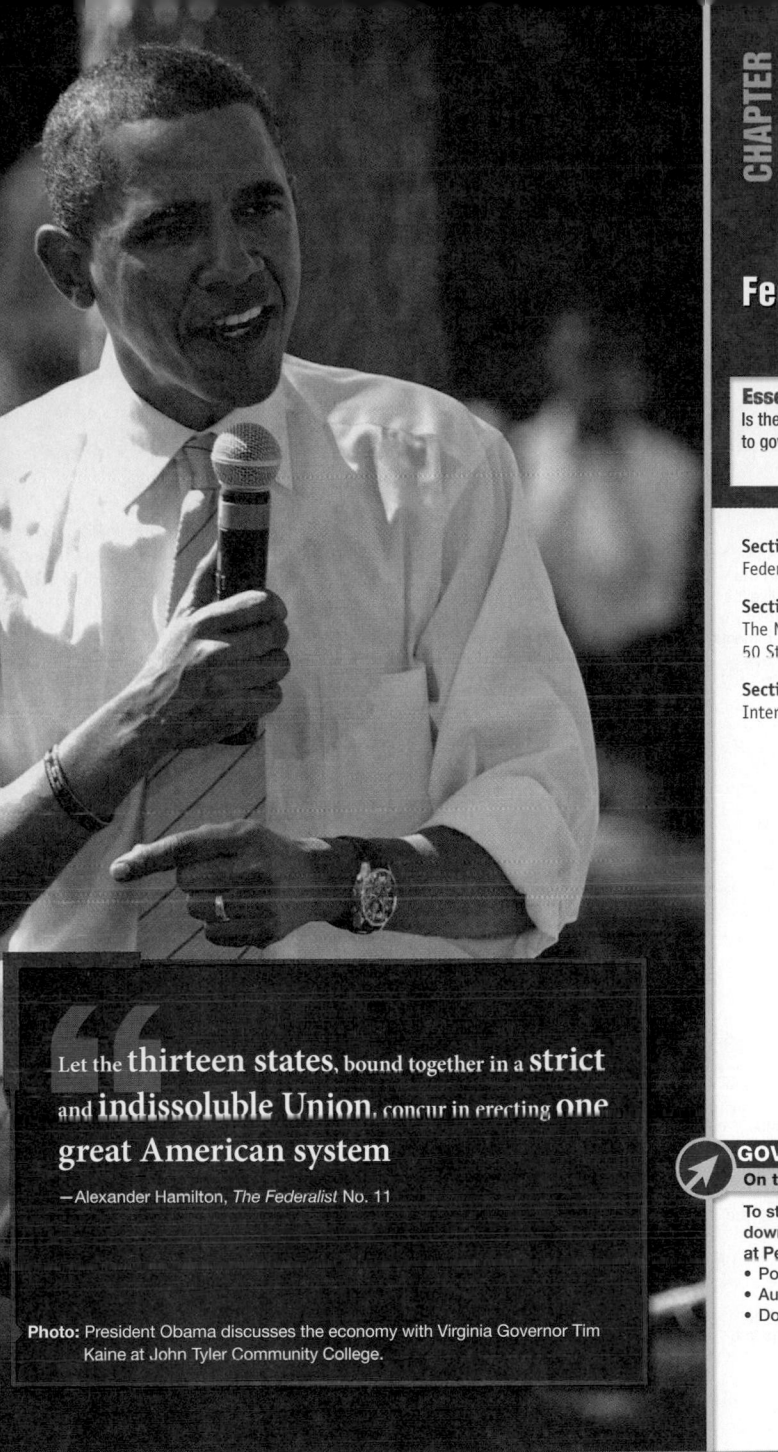

**Essential Question**
Is the federal system the best way to govern the United States?

**Section 1:**
Federalism: Powers Divided

**Section 2:**
The National Government and the 50 States

**Section 3:**
Interstate Relations

"
Let the **thirteen states**, bound together in a **strict** and **indissoluble Union**, concur in erecting **one** great American system

—Alexander Hamilton, *The Federalist* No. 11

**GOVERNMENT**ONLINE
**On the Go**

**To study anywhere, anytime, download these online resources at PearsonSchool.com/phgovt**
• Political Dictionary
• Audio Review
• Downloadable Interactivities

**Photo:** President Obama discusses the economy with Virginia Governor Tim Kaine at John Tyler Community College.

93

## Lesson Goals

**SECTION 1**

Students will...

• define and give examples of national and State powers by completing a chart.

• examine scenarios and identify the type of power.

**SECTION 2**

Students will...

• analyze the process of admission to the Union.

• identify and define types of federal aid to the States.

• understand how federal grants blur the division of power in our federal system by analyzing an article about the No Child Left Behind law.

**SECTION 3**

Students will...

• define and give the location of the constitutional provisions that deal with States' interrelations.

• analyze scenarios in which States interact with other States to identify the constitutional provision that prohibits each action.

## Pressed for Time

To cover this chapter quickly, have students write definitions only for the powers in Section 1 and the grants in Section 3 Reading Comprehension worksheets, skipping the examples (Section 1) and location (Section 3). Then have students complete the first half of each chart on the Section 1 and Section 3 Core worksheets, identifying the power or clause covered by each scenario. Finish by drawing a flowchart on the board and having students fill in the seven steps in the process of admitting States to the Union (from the Section 2 Reading Comprehension Worksheet).

**DIFFERENTIATED INSTRUCTION KEY**

Look for these symbols to help you adjust steps in each lesson to meet your students' needs.

**L1** Special Needs

**L2** Basic

    **ELL** English Language Learners

    **LPR** Less Proficient Readers

**L3** All Students

**L4** Advanced Students

# How is power divided between the Federal Government and the States?

### Federal
- Coin money
- Regulate foreign and interstate commerce
- Raise and maintain armed forces
- Declare war
- Fix standards of weights and measures
- Grant patents and copyrights
- Make treaties
- Make laws "necessary and proper" for carrying out expressed powers
- Regulate immigration
- Acquire territory
- Grant diplomatic recognition
- Protect against rebellion or overthrow of government
- Lay duties on imports

### Concurrent
- Levy and collect taxes
- Borrow money
- Establish courts
- Define crimes and set punishments
- Set environmental and health standards
- Claim private property for public use
- Establish a police force
- Protect national borders

### State
- Set marriage laws
- Issue licenses
- Confiscate property used in illicit activities
- Establish public schools
- Enact land use laws
- Regulate public utilities
- Protect and promote public health, public morals, public safety, and general welfare
- Powers the Constitution does not grant to the National Government nor deny to the States

---

## SKILLS DEVELOPMENT

### PROBLEM SOLVING

To practice problem solving in this section, use the Chapter 4 Skills Worksheet (Unit 1 All-in-One, p. 187). You may wish to teach the skill explicitly before you discuss the Framers and the Constitutional Convention of 1787. For L2 and L1 students, assign the adapted Skill Activity (Unit 1 All-in-One, p. 188).

---

**SECTION 1**

# Federalism: Powers Divided

### Guiding Question
**How is power divided between the Federal Government and the States?** Use a Venn diagram like the one below to take notes on the powers of the Federal and State Governments.

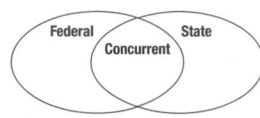

### Political Dictionary
- federalism
- division of powers
- delegated powers
- expressed powers
- implied powers
- inherent powers
- reserved powers
- exclusive powers
- concurrent powers
- Supremacy Clause

### Objectives
1. Define federalism and explain why the Framers chose this system.
2. Identify powers delegated to and denied to the National Government, and powers reserved for and denied to the States.
3. Explain the difference between exclusive and concurrent powers.
4. Examine the Constitution as "the supreme Law of the Land."

**Image Above:** Members of the California National Guard reporting to assist federal agents in border patrol.

Yoou know that federal law requires young men to register for military service at age 18, that most employers must pay their workers at the least a minimum wage set by act of Congress, and that no person can be denied a job on the basis of his or her race or ethnicity.

You also know that State law says that you must have a driver's license in order to drive a car, that it is illegal for anyone under 21 to buy alcoholic beverages, and that only those persons who can satisfy certain requirements can buy or own firearms.

Those three examples illustrate a very complex matter: the division of the powers of government in this country between the National Government, on the one hand, and the 50 States on the other. This section will help you to better understand that sometimes complicated, but very important, arrangement.

## The Framers Choose Federalism

When the Framers of the Constitution met at Philadelphia in 1787, they faced a number of difficult questions. Not the least of them: How could they possibly create a new central government that would be strong enough to meet the needs of the day and would, at the same time, preserve the already existing States?

Few of the Framers favored a strong central government based on the British model, and all of them knew that the Revolution had been fought in the name of local self-government. They also knew that the government established under the Articles of Confederation had proved too weak to deal with the new nation's many problems.

While the Framers favored a stronger national government, they also knew firsthand the importance of limiting federal powers. They were convinced that (1) governmental power inevitably poses a threat to individual liberty, (2) that therefore the exercise of governmental power must be restrained, and (3) that to divide governmental power, as federalism does, is to prevent its abuse.

## Federalism Defined

**Federalism** is a system of government in which a written constitution divides the powers of government on a territorial basis, between a central government and several regional governments, usually called states or provinces. Each of

---

## Focus on the Basics

Here is the information that your students need to learn in this section.

**FACTS:** • The Framers created a federal system, with two levels of government: national and State. • The Constitution delegates powers to the National Government. • The States exercise reserved powers—those not assigned to the National Government nor denied to the States. • The National Government and the States exercise some concurrent powers. • The Constitution is the supreme law of the land.

**CONCEPTS:** federalism, limited government, division of powers, judicial review

**ENDURING UNDERSTANDINGS:** • Dividing the powers of government helps prevent abuse of power. • Federalism promotes national unity, while giving States control over State and local matters.

those basic levels of government has its own substantial set of powers. Neither level, acting alone, can change the basic division of powers the constitution has created. Additionally, each level of government operates through its own agencies and acts directly through its own officials and laws.

The American system of government stands as a prime example of federalism. The basic design of that system is set out in the Constitution. The document provides for a **division of powers** between the National Government and the governments of the 50 States. That is, it assigns certain powers to the National Government and reserves others to the States. This division of powers was implied in the original Constitution and then spelled out in the 10th Amendment.

In effect, federalism produces a dual system of government. That is, it provides for two basic levels of government, each with its own field of authority, and each operating over the same people and the same territory at the same time.

In the American federal system, each of the two basic levels of government can make certain decisions and do certain things that the other level cannot. For example, only the Federal Government can regulate interstate commerce—that is, trade conducted between and among the various States. On the other hand, each of the States decides for itself whether those who commit certain crimes in that State can be put to death.

Federalism's major strength lies in this central fact: It allows local action in matters of local concern and national action in matters of wider concern. Local traditions, needs, and desires vary from one State to another, and federalism allows for differing circumstances among the States.

Illustrations of this point are nearly endless. For example, in 48 States most gas stations are self-service; in New Jersey and Oregon, the law forbids motorists to pump their own gas. Only one State—North Dakota—does not require voters to register in order to cast their ballots. Only Nebraska

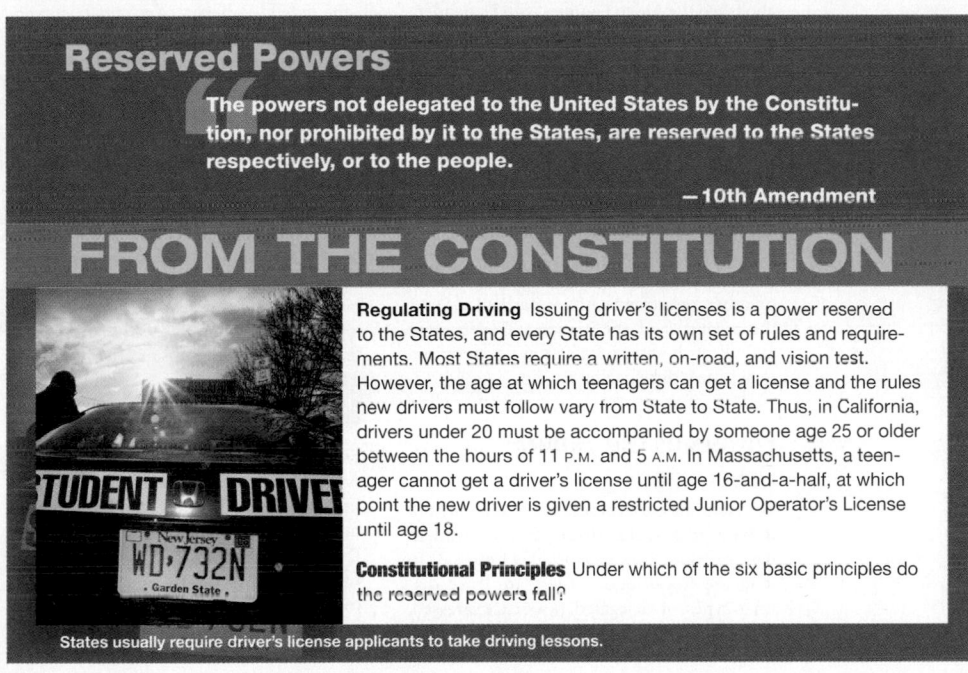

**Reserved Powers**

"The powers not delegated to the United States by the Constitution, nor prohibited by it to the States, are reserved to the States respectively, or to the people.

—10th Amendment

**FROM THE CONSTITUTION**

**Regulating Driving** Issuing driver's licenses is a power reserved to the States, and every State has its own set of rules and requirements. Most States require a written, on-road, and vision test. However, the age at which teenagers can get a license and the rules new drivers must follow vary from State to State. Thus, in California, drivers under 20 must be accompanied by someone age 25 or older between the hours of 11 P.M. and 5 A.M. In Massachusetts, a teenager cannot get a driver's license until age 16-and-a-half, at which point the new driver is given a restricted Junior Operator's License until age 18.

**Constitutional Principles** Under which of the six basic principles do the reserved powers fall?

States usually require driver's license applicants to take driving lessons.

# Differentiated Resources

The following resources are located in the All-in-One, Unit 1, Chapter 4, Section 1:

- **L2** Prereading and Vocabulary Worksheet (p. 180)
- **L3** Reading Comprehension Worksheet (p. 184)
- **L2** Reading Comprehension Worksheet (p. 185)
- **L3** Core Worksheet (p. 186)
- **L3** Skills Worksheet (p. 187)
- **L2** Skill Activity (p. 188)
- **L3** Quiz A (p. 189)
- **L2** Quiz B (p. 190)

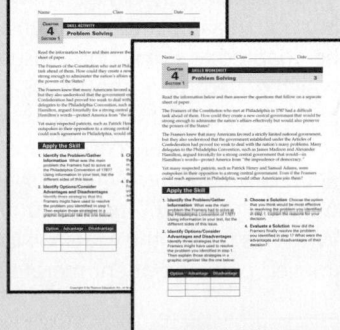

# Get Started

**LESSON GOALS**

Students will . . .

- define and give examples of national and State powers by completing a chart.
- examine scenarios and identify the type of power.

**BEFORE CLASS**

Assign the section, the graphic organizer in the text, and the Reading Comprehension Worksheet (Unit 1 All-in-One, p. 184) before class.

**L2** **Differentiate** Reading Comprehension Worksheet (Unit 1 All-in-One, p. 185)

**BELLRINGER**

Write on the board: **Read Article I, Section 8 of the Constitution in your text and note the clause(s) granting Congress each of these powers:**

1. raise and maintain armed forces
2. decide how citizens of other countries can become U.S. citizens
3. mint money
4. set up a court system
5. borrow money
6. declare war
7. set up a mail system
8. impose taxes
9. make laws as needed to carry out expressed powers
10. regulate foreign and interstate trade

---

# Answers

**Constitutional Principles** federalism

# Teach

## INTRODUCE THE TOPIC

Tell students that today they will discuss different types of powers assigned to the National Government and to the States under the federal system. You will return to their Bellringer answers later in the lesson.

To present this topic using online resources, use the lesson presentations at **PearsonSchool.com/phgovt**.

## COVER THE BASICS

Ask students to take out the Reading Comprehension Worksheet. Point out that the first three powers listed on the chart are types of delegated powers. Call on a volunteer to define *delegated powers*. *(powers granted to the National Government by the Constitution)* Then have students define each power listed on the chart. (**expressed powers:** *specific powers assigned to the National Government;* **implied powers:** *powers that are not expressly stated in the Constitution but that are reasonably suggested by the expressed powers;* **inherent powers:** *powers that belong to the National Government because it is a sovereign state in the world community;* **reserved powers:** *powers that the Constitution does not grant to the National Government nor deny to the States;* **concurrent powers:** *powers that both the National Government and the States possess and exercise;* **exclusive powers:** *powers that can be exercised by the National Government alone)* Call on volunteers to give examples of each power and write these on the board. Display Transparency 4A, Federal Reserve Districts. Ask: **What type of delegated power does the map represent?** *(implied power— It falls under the "Necessary and Proper Clause," which gives Congress the right to establish the Federal Reserve System of banks.)*

## Answers

**Checkpoint** The 10th Amendment delegates those powers not given to the Federal Government and not denied to the States by the Constitution to the States.

---

**enumerated**
*adj.* specified, listed, identified

**reprieve**
*n.* postponement or delay in the execution of a sentence

has a unicameral (one-house) legislature. Oregon and Washington are the only States that have legalized physician-assisted suicide. Only five States—Alaska, Delaware, New Hampshire, Montana, and Oregon—do not impose a general sales tax.

Federalism also allows for experimentation and innovation in solving public policy problems. Indeed, the several States have long been described as so many "laboratories of government." New approaches to difficult matters may originate in one State and then be adopted in another or even be put in place at the national level.

The Welfare Reform Act passed by Congress in 1996 affords a useful illustration of the point. That landmark statute revolutionized the Federal Government's approach to providing welfare assistance to millions of Americans on the lower rungs of the nation's economic ladder—and its basic features were first suggested by welfare administrators in the States of Wisconsin, California, and Michigan.

In its most noteworthy provisions, the law abolished the Aid to Families with Dependent Children (AFDC) program, replacing it with block grants to the States. The several States now have wide discretion in the determination of eligibility for financial assistance.

While federalism allows individual States to handle State and local matters, it also provides for the strength that comes from union. National defense and foreign affairs offer useful illustrations of this point. So, too, do domestic affairs. Take, for example, a natural disaster. When a flood, drought, hurricane, or other catastrophe hits a particular State, the resources of the National Government and all of the other States can be mobilized to aid the stricken area.

## Powers of the Federal Government

The National Government is a government of **delegated powers.** That is, that government has only those powers delegated (granted) to it in the Constitution. There are three distinct types of delegated powers: expressed, implied, and inherent.

**The Expressed Powers** The **expressed powers** are those powers delegated to the National Government in so many words— spelled out, expressly, in the Constitution. Those powers are also sometimes called the "enumerated powers."

You can find most of the expressed powers in Article I, Section 8. There, in 18 separate clauses, the Constitution expressly gives 27 powers to Congress. They include the power to lay and collect taxes, to coin money, to regulate foreign and interstate commerce, to raise and maintain armed forces, to declare war, to fix standards of weights and measures, to grant patents and copyrights, and to do many other things.

Several other expressed powers are set out elsewhere in the Constitution, as well. Article II, Section 2 gives several powers to the President—including the power to act as commander in chief of the armed forces, to grant reprieves and pardons, to make treaties, and to appoint major federal officials. Article III grants "the judicial Power of the United States" to the Supreme Court and other courts in the federal judiciary. And, finally, several expressed powers also are found in various amendments to the Constitution; thus, the 16th Amendment gives Congress the power to levy an income tax.

**The Implied Powers** The **implied powers** are not expressly stated in the Constitution, but they are reasonably suggested—implied— by the expressed powers. The constitutional basis for the implied powers is found in one of the expressed powers. Article I, Section 8, Clause 18 gives Congress the "necessary and proper power." The Necessary and Proper Clause says that Congress has the power

> **FROM THE CONSTITUTION**
>
> to make all Laws which shall be necessary and proper for carrying into Execution the foregoing Powers and all other Powers vested by this Constitution in the Government of the United States, or in any Department or Officer thereof.
>
> —Article I, Section 8, Clause 18

---

# Supreme Court Notes

**IMPLIED POWERS** Chief Justice John Marshall recognized the importance of the Necessary and Proper Clause. In *McCullough* v. *Maryland,* 1819, he wrote: "This provision is made in a constitution intended to endure for ages to come, and, consequently, to be adapted to the various crises of human affairs. To have prescribed the means by which government should, in all future time, execute its powers, would have been to change, entirely, the character of the instrument, and give it the properties of a legal code." The Framers could not spell out every power the National Government might need in the future. With the Necessary and Proper Clause, they built in flexibility that would allow adaptation to future needs, thus enabling the Constitution to endure. With this ruling, the Marshall Court established that the National Government has implied powers not enumerated in the Constitution.

Expressed Powers

Implied Powers

Congress has the expressed power to provide for naturalization—the process by which aliens become citizens. Its implied powers allow it to do such things as create hydroelectric dams. *Where does the Constitution provide for dam-building?*

Through decades of congressional and court interpretation, the words *necessary and proper* have come to mean, in effect, "convenient and useful." Indeed, the Necessary and Proper Clause is sometimes called the Elastic Clause, because, over time, it has been stretched to cover so many different situations.

Here are but a few of the thousands of examples of the exercise of implied powers: Congress has provided for the regulation of labor-management relations, the building of hydroelectric power dams, and the building of the 42,000-mile interstate highway system. It has made federal crimes of such acts as moving stolen goods, gambling devices, and kidnapped persons across State lines. It has prohibited racial discrimination in granting all people access to such places as restaurants, theaters, hotels, and motels. Congress has taken these actions, and many more, because the power to do so is reasonably implied by just one of the expressed powers: the power to regulate interstate commerce.[1]

**The Inherent Powers** The **inherent powers** are those powers that belong to

the National Government because it is the national government of a sovereign state in the world community. Although the Constitution does not expressly provide for them, they are powers that, over time, all national governments have come to possess. It stands to reason that the Framers of the Constitution intended the National Government they created would also hold those several constitutional powers.

The inherent powers are few in number. The major ones include the power to regulate immigration, to <u>deport</u> aliens, to acquire territory, to grant diplomatic recognition to other states, and to protect the nation against rebellion or other attempts to overthrow the government by force or violence.

One can argue that most of the inherent powers really are implied by one or more of the expressed powers. For example, the power to regulate immigration is suggested by the expressed power to regulate foreign trade. The power to acquire territory can be drawn from the treaty-making power and the several war powers. But the doctrine of inherent powers holds that it is not necessary to go to these lengths to find these powers in the Constitution. In short, these powers exist because the United States exists.

✔ **Checkpoint**
Why is the Necessary and Proper Clause sometimes referred to as the Elastic Clause?

**deport**
*v.* to order that one be sent to another country

---

1 Article I, Section 8, Clause 3. The doctrine of implied powers is treated in greater detail in Chapter 11.

Chapter 4 • Section 1 **97**

---

**EXTEND THE DISCUSSION**
Use these questions to continue a discussion about federalism:

**1. What are the main advantages of federalism?** *(possible response: creates strong National Government while allowing States to handle local concerns; restrains government power by dividing it among levels of government)*

**2. How does the Constitution settle conflicts that may arise between national law and State law?** *(It establishes the Constitution as the supreme law of the land.)*

**3. How does the central government in a federal system differ from the central government in a confederation?** *(Possible response: The central government is stronger in a federal system because it heads a sovereign state. In a confederation, the central government coordinates a loose alliance of independent groups.)*

**4. Is federalism an effective way to govern?** *(Possible response: Yes. It divides power, preventing abuses, while enabling local action in matters of local concern and national action in matters of wider concern.)*

**L4** **Differentiate** Have groups of students use the Internet or a library to find five news articles that provide examples of federalism. Examples may include any aspects of State, national, or shared powers. Have each group draw conclusions about federalism, based on their research.

# Constitutional Principles

**LIMITED GOVERNMENT** Although the Necessary and Proper Clause of the Constitution seems to give Congress an almost unlimited power to make laws, there are limitations. The power of judicial review, established under Chief Justice John Marshall in *Marbury* v. *Madison,* allows the nation's courts to determine which laws are unconstitutional. This judicial power serves as a check on the power of the National Government by limiting the types of laws that Congress can enact to only those that are necessary and proper. The Court has declared many laws passed by Congress to be unconstitutional.

## Answers

**Powers of Federal Government** the Necessary and Proper Clause, also called the Elastic Clause

**Checkpoint** It is stretched to give Congress the power to legislate in many different areas.

Invite volunteers to share their answers from the Bellringer activity, which asks students to locate the clause or clauses in Article I, Section 8 that grant specific powers to Congress. *(1. Clauses 12–16; 2. Clause 4; 3. Clause 5; 4. Clause 9; 5. Clause 2; 6. Clause 11; 7. Clause 7; 8. Clause 1; 9. Clause 18; 10. Clause 3)*

## Powers Denied to the Federal Government

Although the Constitution delegates certain powers to the National Government, it also *denies* certain powers to that level of government in order to keep federalism intact. It does so in three distinct ways.

First, the Constitution denies some powers to the National Government in so many words—*expressly*.[2] Among them are the powers to levy duties on exports; to take private property for public use without the payment of just compensation; to prohibit freedom of religion, speech, press, or assembly; to conduct illegal searches or seizures; and to deny to any person accused of a crime a speedy and public trial or a trial by jury.

Second, several powers are denied to the National Government because of the *silence* of the Constitution. Recall that the National Government is a government of delegated powers; it has only those powers the Constitution gives to it.

Among the many powers not granted to the National Government are the powers to do such things as create a public school system for the nation, enact uniform marriage and divorce laws, and set up units of local government. The Constitution says nothing that would give the National Government the power to do any of those things, expressly, implicitly, or inherently. In short, the lack of any such provision—the silence of the Constitution—denies power to the National Government.

Third, some powers are denied to the National Government because of the federal system itself. Clearly the Constitution does not intend that the National Government should have the power to take any action that would threaten the existence of that system. For example, in the exercise of its power to tax, Congress cannot tax any of the States or any of their local units in the conduct of their various governmental functions. If it could, it would have the power to destroy—tax out of existence—one or more, or all, of the States.[3]

---

2  Most of the expressed denials of power are found in Article I, Section 9 and in the 1st through the 8th amendments.

3  But notice that when a State, or one of its local units, performs a so-called nongovernmental function—for example, maintains liquor stores, runs a bus system, or operates a farmers market—it is liable to federal taxation. We shall return to this point later, in Chapter 25.

Inherent Powers

▲ President Barack Obama meets with Italian Prime Minister Silvio Berlusconi and other world leaders at the 2010 G8 Summit as part of his diplomatic role.

# Background

**LABORATORY OF GOVERNMENT**  About 45 million Americans lack health insurance. So far, no federal administration has succeeded in solving this important, but politically charged, problem. The power of States to enact their own laws in our federal system enables them to experiment with innovative solutions that could become a model for other States and for the nation as a whole. In 2006, Massachusetts became a "laboratory of government" on health insurance reform. It passed a bill requiring all residents to buy health insurance. Under this plan, insurance companies are providing a range of inexpensive policies from which to choose. People with low incomes can purchase plans subsidized by the State government, based on ability to pay. If the Massachusetts plan succeeds, it can serve as an important step toward universal healthcare in the United States.

## The States

The 50 States are the other half of the very complicated equation we call federalism. Their many-sided role in the American federal system is no less important than that of the National Government.

**Powers Reserved to the States** Recall, the 10th Amendment states that the States are governments of **reserved powers.** The reserved powers are those powers that the Constitution does not grant to the National Government and does not, at the same time, deny to the States.

Thus, any State can forbid persons under 18 to marry without parental consent. It can ban the sale of pornography, outlaw prostitution, and permit some forms of gambling and prohibit others. A State can require that doctors, lawyers, hairdressers, and plumbers be licensed in order to practice in the State. It can <u>confiscate</u> automobiles and other property used in connection with such <u>illicit</u> activities as drug trafficking. It can establish public schools, enact land use laws, regulate the services and restrict the profits of such public utilities as natural gas, oil, electric power, and telephone companies, and do much, much more.

In short, the sphere of powers held by each State—the scope of the reserved powers—is huge. The States can do all of those things just mentioned, because the Constitution does not give the National Government the power to do those things, and it does not deny the States the power to do them.

How broad the reserved powers really are can be understood from this fact: Most of what government does in this country today is done by the States (and their local governments), not by the National Government. The point can also be seen from this fact: The reserved powers include the vitally important police power—the power of a State to protect and promote the public health, the public morals, the public safety, and the general welfare.

The Constitution does not grant expressed powers to the States, with one notable exception. Section 2 of the 21st Amendment gives the States a virtually unlimited power to regulate the manufacture, sale, and consumption of alcoholic beverages.

**Powers Denied to the States** Just as the Constitution denies many powers to the National Government, so it denies many powers to the States. Some of those powers are denied to the States in so many words.[4] For example, no State can enter into any treaty, alliance, or confederation. Nor can a State print or coin money or deprive any person of life, liberty, or property without due process of law.

Some powers are denied to the States inherently—that is, by the existence of the federal system. Thus, no State (and no local government) can tax any of the agencies or functions of the National Government. Remember, too, each State has its own constitution. Those documents also deny many powers to the States.[5]

## The Exclusive and the Concurrent Powers

Most of the powers that the Constitution delegates to the National Government are **exclusive powers.** That is, they can be exercised only by the National Government; they cannot be exercised by the States under any circumstances.

Some of these powers are expressly denied to the States—for example, the power to coin money, to make treaties with foreign states, and to lay duties (taxes) on imports. Some of them are not expressly denied to the States but are, nonetheless, among the exclusive powers of the Federal Government because of the nature of the particular power involved. The power to regulate interstate commerce is a leading example of this point.

---

4  Most of those expressed prohibitions of powers to the States (and so, too, to their local governments) are found in Article I, Section 10 and in the 13th, 14th, 15th, 19th, 24th, and 26th Amendments.

5  Note the many provisions in your own State's constitution that deny various powers to your State and its many local governments. As you do, note the significance of these too-little noticed words in the 10th Amendment of the Federal Constitution: "or to the people." We shall look at State constitutions later, and in more detail, in Chapter 24.

**confiscate**
*v.* to take or seize legally

**illicit**
*adj.* illegal, unlawful, outlawed

---

### DISTRIBUTE CORE WORKSHEET

Distribute the Chapter 4 Section 1 Core Worksheet (Unit 1 All-in-One, p. 186), which asks students to identify the type of power illustrated by various scenarios. Divide the class into groups. Explain that they should study each scenario in the first column and determine what type of power it illustrates. When students finish their worksheets, ask them to share their findings and explain their reasoning.

**L1 L2 Differentiate** Walk through the lesson as a class. Alternatively, divide the chart into several parts; have each team complete a few examples.

**L4 Differentiate** Have students complete the worksheet individually.

**L4 Differentiate** Give partners two index cards. Ask them to write down a new scenario on the front of each card and the type of power it illustrates on the back. Students might return to the examples on the Reading Comprehension Worksheet to help them generate ideas for new scenarios. When they finish, have students share their cards. Ask them to read the new scenarios and challenge students to identify the power illustrated.

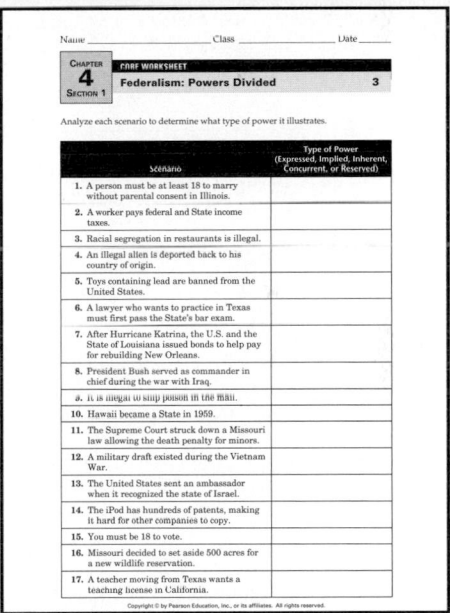

### Answers

**Checkpoint** The States hold some powers in order to preserve the federal system. Their powers provide a check on Federal Government, so it will not become too powerful.

---

# Debate

"It is my intention to curb the size and influence of the Federal establishment and to demand recognition of the distinction between the powers granted to the Federal Government and those reserved to the States or to the people. All of us need to be reminded that the Federal Government did not create the States; the States created the Federal Government."

—President Ronald Reagan, First Inaugural Address

Ask students what President Reagan meant in the last sentence. Divide students into two teams and use the Debate strategy (p. T25) to organize a debate.

Thomas Jefferson, a strong supporter of States' rights, once observed: "Were we directed from Washington when to sow and when to reap, we should soon want for bread." Ask students what Jefferson meant by this remark. Then have students create a cartoon about federalism's "tug-of-war" between the States and the National Government. Cartoons might address Jefferson's comment or stand on their own.

**L4 Differentiate** Have students research Jefferson's terms as President and write a short essay about whether or not he applied his federalist principles to his presidency.

Concurrent Powers
## Sharing Responsibility

Some powers are exercised by both levels of government, as you can see in the circle. *Why do both levels of government have the power to establish law enforcement agencies?*

- Levy and collect taxes
- Borrow money
- Establish courts
- Define crimes and set punishments
- Set environmental and health standards
- Claim private property for public use
- Establish a police force
- Protect national borders

An Idaho State trooper patrols a **STATE** highway.

FBI and volunteers look for evidence of a **FEDERAL** crime.

If the States could exercise that power, trade between and among the States would be at best chaotic and at worst impossible.[6]

Some of the powers delegated to the National Government are **concurrent powers.** That is, they are powers that both the National Government and the States possess and exercise. Those powers include the power to levy and collect taxes, to define crimes and set punishments for them, and to condemn (take) private property for public use.

The concurrent powers are held and exercised separately and simultaneously by the two basic levels of government. That is, the concurrent powers are those powers that the Constitution does not grant exclusively to the National Government and that, at the same time, does not deny to the States. The concurrent powers, in short, are those powers that make it possible for a federal system of government to function.

Although government in the United States is often discussed in terms of three levels—national, State, and local—there are, in fact, only two basic levels in the federal system: the National Government and the State governments. The more than 87,000 units of local government in the United States today are subunits of the various State governments. Local governments can provide services, regulate activities, collect taxes, and do many other things only because the State has given them the power to do so. In short, when local governments exercise their powers, they are actually exercising State powers.

Another way of putting all of this is to remind you of a point that we first made in Chapter 1. Each of the 50 States has a *unitary* form of government—an arrangement in which a central government that creates local units of government for its own convenience.

---

6 The States cannot regulate interstate commerce as such, but they can and do *affect* that trade. For example, in regulating highway speeds, the States regulate not only those vehicles operating within the State, but also those operating from State to State. Generally, the States can *affect* interstate commerce but they cannot impose an unreasonable burden upon it.

## Supreme Law of the Land

As you have just seen, the division of powers in the American federal system produces a dual system of government, one in which two basic

## Answers

**Concurrent Powers** Possible response: Crimes can occur in local areas or across State lines. Also, both National and State governments enact laws. Police forces are needed to investigate crimes wherever they occur and to enforce both national and State laws.

levels of government operate over the same territory and the same people at the same time. Such an arrangement is bound to result in conflicts between national and State law.

**The Supremacy Clause** The Framers anticipated those conflicts—and so they wrote the **Supremacy Clause** into the Constitution. That provision declares that

> ❝
> **FROM THE CONSTITUTION**
>
> **This Constitution, and the Laws of the United States which shall be made in <u>Pursuance</u> thereof; and all Treaties made, or which shall be made, under the Authority of the United States, shall be the supreme Law of the Land; and the Judges in every State shall be bound thereby, anything in the Constitution or Laws of any State to the Contrary notwithstanding.**
>
> **—Article VI, Section 2**

The Constitution and the laws and treaties of the United States are "the supreme Law of the Land." This means that the Constitution ranks above all other forms of law in the United States. Acts of Congress and treaties stand immediately beneath the Constitution.[7]

The Supremacy Clause has been called the "linchpin of the Constitution" because it joins the National Government and the States into a single governmental unit, a federal government. In other words, the Supremacy Clause is the provision in the Constitution that makes the complex federal system a working reality.

Our political history is studded with challenges to the concept of national supremacy. Recall that this nation fought a horrific Civil War over that very matter in the years 1861 to 1865. Those who have rejected the concept of national supremacy have insisted that the

Constitution is, at base, a compact among sovereign States, rather than one between and among "We the People of the United States." They believe that the powers that compact does give to the National Government are to be very narrowly defined and applied. Echoes of that view can still be found in contemporary American politics.

**The Supreme Court and Federalism** The Supreme Court is the umpire in the federal system. One of its chief duties is to apply the Constitution's Supremacy Clause to the conflicts that the dual system of government inevitably produces.

The Court was first called to settle a clash between a national and a State law in 1819. The case, *McCulloch* v. *Maryland*, involved the controversial Second Bank of the United States. The bank had been chartered by Congress in 1816. In 1818, the Maryland legislature, hoping to cripple the bank, placed a tax on all notes issued by its Baltimore branch. James McCulloch, the branch cashier, refused to pay the tax, and the Maryland courts convicted him for that refusal. (See pp. 310–311.)

The Supreme Court unanimously reversed the Maryland courts. Speaking for the Court, Chief Justice John Marshall based

---

7 Acts of Congress and treaties stand on equal planes with one another. Neither can conflict with any provision in the Constitution. In the rare case of conflict between the provisions of an act and those of a treaty, the one more recently adopted takes precedence as the latest expression of the sovereign people's will. The Supreme Court has regularly held to that position from the first cases it decided on the point, *The Head Money Cases*, in 1884.

✓ **Checkpoint**
How is a local government different from a State government?

**pursuance**
*n.* a carrying out of an execution of something

THIS LITTLE BOY WOULD PERSIST IN HANDLING BOOKS ABOVE HIS CAPACITY.

AND THIS WAS THE DISASTROUS RESULT.

▸▸ **Analyzing Cartoons** This cartoon ran in *Harper's Weekly* when Congress attempted to remove President Andrew Johnson. ***How does the "disastrous result" illustrate the Supremacy Clause?***

# Myths and Misconceptions

**REVERSE DELEGATION** The Constitution reserves a number of powers to the States. But would you be surprised to learn that some of these powers are surrendered back to the National Government? The reason is simply that billions of dollars are at stake. The National Government often attaches preconditions to federal grants-in-aid. If a State wants the money, it has to comply with those preconditions and give up certain decision-making powers in the process. For example, the National Highway System Designation Act of 1995 repealed a law that had required that States, as a condition of receiving federal-aid highway assistance, adhere to a national maximum speed limit.

---

# Assess and Remediate

**L3** Collect the Core Worksheet and assess students' work.

**L3** Assign the Section 1 Assessment questions.

**L3** Section Quiz A (Unit 1 All-in-One, p. 189)

**L2** Section Quiz B (Unit 1 All-in-One, p. 190)

Have students complete the review activities in the digital lesson presentation and continue their work in the **Essential Questions Journal**.

---

## Answers

**Checkpoint** A local government derives its powers from the State government and governs only by the consent of the State government. A State government derives powers from the Constitution, and those powers cannot be taken away.

**Analyzing Cartoons** When the "boy" (Andrew Johnson) tries to handle the large Constitution book, it falls on him, signifying that even the President must acknowledge the supremacy of the Constitution.

| If Your Students Have Trouble With | Strategies For Remediation |
|---|---|
| Division of powers (Questions 1, 2) | Have students summarize the 10th Amendment in their own words. |
| Delegated powers (Question 3) | Write several examples of each type of delegated power on cards. Have students separate them into categories: expressed, implied, inherent. |
| Reserved powers (Questions 4, 5, 6) | Write examples of reserved powers on cards along with powers denied to the States. Have students pick a card and identify whether it is an example of a reserved or a denied power. |
| Concurrent powers (Question 1) | Have students create a word web of concurrent powers, with specific examples on each spoke. |

the decision squarely on the Constitution's Supremacy Clause:

imperil
*v.* to endanger, put at risk, threaten

> **PRIMARY SOURCE**
> [If] any one proposition could command the universal assent of mankind, we might expect it would be this—that the government of the Union, though limited in its powers, is supreme within its sphere of action. . . . [T]he states have no power . . . to retard, impede, burden, or in any manner control, the operations of the constitutional laws enacted by Congress. . . . [8]
>
> —*McCulloch v. Maryland*, 1819

Since the decision in this landmark case, it has been impossible to overstate the significance of the role of the Court as the umpire of the federal system. Had the Court not assumed this role, the American federal system and probably the United States itself could not have survived its early years. Justice Oliver Wendell Holmes once made that point in these words:

[8] The case is also critically important in the development of the constitutional system because, in deciding it, the Court for the first time upheld the doctrine of implied powers. It also held that the National Government is immune from any form of State taxation, a point we shall return to in Chapter 25.

> **PRIMARY SOURCE**
> I do not think the United States would come to an end if we [the Court] lost our power to declare an Act of Congress void. I do think the Union would be imperiled if we could not make that declaration as to the laws of the several States.
>
> —*Collected Legal Papers*

The Supreme Court first held a State law to be unconstitutional in a case from Georgia, *Fletcher v. Peck,* in 1810. The Court found that a Georgia law passed in 1794 that sold some 35 million acres of public land for 1.5 cents an acre amounted to a contract between the State and Peck and other buyers. Despite the obvious corruption involved, it found that the legislature's later (1796) repeal of the law violated the Constitution's Contract Clause (Article I, Section 10, Clause 1). That provision prohibits the States the power to pass any "Law impairing the Obligation of Contracts." Over the centuries since then, the High Court has found thousands of State laws and local ordinances unconstitutional, but it has upheld the constitutionality of thousands of others.

**Essential Questions Journal** To continue to build a response to the chapter Essential Question, go to your **Essential Questions Journal.**

## SECTION 1 ASSESSMENT

**1. Guiding Question** Use your completed Venn diagram to answer this question: How is power divided between the Federal Government and the States?

**Key Terms and Comprehension**

**2. (a)** How is power divided under the concept of **federalism? (b)** What is the purpose of this **division of powers?**

**3. (a)** What are the three kinds of **delegated powers** held by the Federal Government? **(b)** Cite two examples of **inherent powers.**

**4. (a)** Cite two examples of **reserved powers** held by the States. **(b)** How does the Constitution determine which powers are to be held by the States?

**Critical Thinking**

**5. Draw Conclusions (a)** Why might the Framers have wanted to reserve specific powers for the States? **(b)** Why might they have wanted to deny certain powers, such as the power to make alliances or enter into treaties, to the States?

**6. Make Comparisons (a)** What purpose does government at a local level serve? **(b)** How does the source of the powers given to governments at the local level differ from the source of the delegated powers of the Federal Government?

### Quick Write

**Compare and Contrast: Choose and Research a Topic** A compare-contrast essay holds two subjects side-by-side and looks at their differing and similar aspects. For this exercise, compare and contrast State powers with the powers of the Federal Government. Research and take notes on the various powers held by the State and Federal Governments.

# Assessment Answers

**1.** The Constitution grants specific powers, such as controlling interstate trade, to the National Government. It reserves to the States all powers not expressly granted to the National Government nor denied to the States. National and State governments share concurrent powers, such as the power to tax.

**2. (a)** Power is divided on a territorial basis, between a central government and several regional governments. **(b)** The division of powers helps prevent abuse of power.

**3. (a)** expressed, implied, and inherent

**(b)** regulate immigration, deport aliens, acquire territory, grant diplomatic recognition to foreign states, protect against rebellion or violent overthrow of the government

**4. (a)** establish public schools; issue licenses; enact land use laws; regulate public utilities; protect and promote public health, public morals, public safety, and general welfare **(b)** The Constitution reserves to the States all powers not expressly granted to the National Government nor denied to the States.

**5. (a)** Possible response: The Framers wanted

to limit the National Government to only those powers expressly granted to it, and give broad authority to the States. **(b)** The Framers wanted to preserve the Union by denying the States powers that only a national government should have.

**6. (a)** to exercise powers delegated by the State **(b)** Federal powers are defined by the Constitution. Local government exercises the constitutional powers granted to the States.

**QUICK WRITE** Students should research and take notes on federal and State powers.

## SECTION 2

# The National Government and the 50 States

**Guiding Question**

According to the Constitution, what must the National Government guarantee to each State? Use a chart like the one below to take notes on the Federal Government's responsibilities.

**Responsibilities of the Federal Government**

| Republican Government | | |
|---|---|---|
| • | • | • |
| | • | • |
| | • | • |

**Political Dictionary**

- enabling act
- act of admission
- grants-in-aid program
- categorical grant
- block grant
- project grant

**Objectives**

1. Summarize the obligations that the Constitution places on the National Government with regard to the States.
2. Explain the process for admitting new States to the Union.
3. Examine the many and growing areas of cooperative federalism.

**Image Above:** Residents of Hawaii celebrate their newly acquired Statehood in 1959.

Have you ever really focused on the words *United States,* and what those two words say? The United States is a union of States, the several States joined together, the States united.

The Framers of the Constitution created that union of States, and they intended to preserve it. To that end, the Constitution (1) requires the National Government to guarantee certain things to the States and (2) makes it possible for the National Government to do certain things for the States.

## The Nation's Obligations

The Constitution places several obligations on the National Government for the benefit of the States. Most of them are found in Article IV.

**Republican Form of Government** The Constitution requires the National Government to "guarantee to every State in this Union a Republican Form of Government."[9] The Constitution does not define "Republican Form of Government," and the Supreme Court has regularly refused to do so. The term is generally understood to mean a "representative government."

The Supreme Court has held that the question of whether a State has a republican form of government is a "political question." That is, it is one to be decided by the political branches of the government—the President and Congress—and not by the courts.[10]

The only extensive use ever made of the republican-form guarantee came in the years immediately following the Civil War. Congress declared that several southern States did not have governments of a republican form, and refused to admit senators and representatives from those States until they had ratified the 13th, 14th, and 15th amendments and broadened their laws

---

9  Article IV, Section 4. The provision is sometimes called "the Guarantee Clause."
10  The leading case here is *Luther v. Borden* (1849). This case grew out of Dorr's Rebellion, a revolt led by Thomas W. Dorr against the State of Rhode Island in 1841–1842. Dorr and his followers had written a new constitution for the State. When they tried to enforce the new document, the governor in office under the original constitution declared martial law (temporary rule by military authorities), and called on the Federal Government for help. President John Tyler took steps to put down the revolt, and it quickly collapsed. Although the question of which of the competing governments was the legitimate one was a major issue in *Luther v. Borden,* the Supreme Court refused to decide the matter.

# Focus on the Basics

Here is the information that your students need to learn in this section.

**FACTS:** • The National Government guarantees the States representative government, protection from invasion and internal disorder, and territorial integrity. • Congress has the power to admit new States. • The federal system involves a range of powers shared between the Federal Government and the States.

**CONCEPTS:** federalism, representative government, cooperation

**ENDURING UNDERSTANDINGS:** • Federalism produces a dual system of government under which the States and the Federal Government govern the same people and same territory at the same time. • The Federal Government and the States operate in a spirit of cooperation, with some inevitable conflict.

---

## According to the Constitution, what must the National Government guarantee to each State?

**Responsibilities of the Federal Government**

| Republican Government | Protection from Invasion and Internal Disorder | Respect for Territory |
|---|---|---|
| • Representative government | • Protect each State against foreign attack<br>• Restore order within States | • Recognize legal existence of States<br>• Recognize physical boundaries of States |

# Get Started

**LESSON GOALS**

Students will . . .

- analyze the process of admission to the Union.
- identify and define types of federal aid to the States.
- understand how federal grants blur the division of power in our federal system by analyzing an article about the No Child Left Behind law.

**BEFORE CLASS**

Assign the section, the graphic organizer in the text, and the Reading Comprehension Worksheet (Unit 1 All-in-One, p. 191) before class.

**L2 Differentiate** Reading Comprehension Worksheet (Unit 1 All-in-One, p. 193)

## SKILLS DEVELOPMENT

**DRAW INFERENCES AND CONCLUSIONS**

There are several opportunities in this section's activities for students to do research. You may want to review tips on drawing inferences and conclusions in the Skills Handbook, p. S19.

## BELLRINGER

Distribute the Bellringer Worksheet (Unit 1 All-in-One, p. 195), which examines one aspect of the cooperative relationship between the National Government and the States. Have students study the table and answer the questions.

**L1 L2 Differentiate** Have students answer only questions 1 through 3.

# Teach

To present this topic using online resources, use the lesson presentations at **PearsonSchool.com/ phgovt.**

## COVER THE BASICS

Call students' attention to the map on the territorial expansion of the United States on p.105. Ask: **When did our State join the Union? How many States were part of the United States at that time? How much of the nation's present area did the United States cover at that time?**

Then ask students to take out the Reading Comprehension Worksheet. Call on a volunteer to explain grants-in-aid programs. *(The Federal Government gives money or other resources to the States and/or their cities, counties, and other local units.)* Have students name the three types of grants-in-aid *(categorical grants, block grants, project grants).* Then ask them to define and give examples of each type of federal aid to the States.

---

## Answers

**Checkpoint** representative government

**104** Federalism

---

✔ **Checkpoint**
What is another term for "republican form of government"?

**integrity**
*n.* a single, undivided whole

**insurrection**
*n.* a revolt against a government

---

to recognize the voting and other rights of African Americans.

**Invasion and Internal Disorder** The Constitution states that the National Government must also

> ❝ **FROM THE CONSTITUTION**
>
> **protect each of them [the States] against Invasion; and on Application of the Legislature, or of the Executive (when the Legislature cannot be convened) against domestic Violence.**
>
> —**Article IV, Section 4**

Today it is clear that an invasion of any one of the States would be met as an attack on the United States itself. This constitutional guarantee is therefore now of little significance.

That was not the case in the late 1780s. Then it was not at all certain that all 13 States would stand together if a foreign power attacked one of them. So, before the States agreed to give up their war-making powers, each demanded that an attack on any one of the States would be met as an attack on all of them.

The federal system assumes that each of the 50 States will keep the peace within its own borders. Thus, the primary responsibility for curbing insurrection, riot, or other internal disorder rests with the individual States. However, the Constitution does recognize that a State might not be able to control some situations. It therefore guarantees protection against internal disorder, or what the Constitution calls "domestic Violence."

The use of federal force to restore order within a State has been a rare event historically. Several instances did occur in the 1960s, however. When racial unrest exploded into violence in Detroit during the "long, hot summer" of 1967, President Lyndon Johnson ordered units of the United States Army into the city. He acted at the request of the governor of Michigan, George Romney, and only after Detroit's police and firefighters, supported by State police and National Guard units, could not control riots, arson, and looting in the city. In 1968, again at the request of the governors involved, federal troops were sent into Chicago and Baltimore to help put

down the violence that erupted following the assassination of Martin Luther King, Jr. In 1992, President George H.W. Bush ordered members of the National Guard, the Army, and the Marines to Los Angeles to restore order after three days of rioting. The violence was sparked by the acquittal of four white officers charged with beating Rodney King, a black motorist, after he led them on a high-speed chase.

Normally, a President has sent troops into a State only in answer to a request from its governor or legislature. If national laws are being broken, national functions interfered with, or national property endangered, however, a President does not need to wait for such a plea.[11]

The ravages of nature—storms, floods, drought, forest fires, and the like—can be far more destructive than human violence. Here, too, acting to protect the States against "domestic Violence," the Federal Government stands ready to aid stricken areas.

**Respect for Territorial Integrity** The National Government is constitutionally bound to respect the territorial integrity of each of the States. That is, the National Government must recognize the legal existence and the physical boundaries of each State.

The basic scheme of the Constitution imposes this obligation. Several of its provisions do so, as well. For example, Congress must include, in both of its houses, members chosen in each one of the States.[12] Recall, too, that Article V of the Constitution declares that no State can be deprived of its equal representation in the United States Senate without its own consent.

---

11 President Grover Cleveland ordered federal troops to end rioting in the Chicago rail yards during the Pullman Strike in 1894 despite the objections of Illinois Governor William Altgeld. The Supreme Court upheld his actions in *In re Debs* (1895). The Court found that rioters had threatened federal property and impeded the flow of the mail and interstate commerce. Thus, more than "domestic Violence" was involved. Since then, several Presidents have acted without a request from the State involved. Most recently, President Dwight Eisenhower did so in Little Rock, Arkansas, in 1957, and President John Kennedy did so at the University of Mississippi in 1962 and at the University of Alabama in 1963. In each of those instances, the President acted to halt the unlawful obstruction of school integration orders issued by the federal courts.

12 In the House, Article I, Section 2, Clause 1; in the Senate, Article I, Section 3, Clause 1 and the 17th Amendment.

**104** Federalism

---

# Differentiated Resources

The following resources are located in the All-in-One, Unit 1, Chapter 4, Section 2:

**L3** Reading Comprehension Worksheet (p. 191)
**L2** Reading Comprehension Worksheet (p. 193)
**L3** Bellringer Worksheet (p. 195)
**L3** Core Worksheet (p. 196)
**L2** **ELL** Core Worksheet (p. 198)
**L3** **L4** Extend Worksheet (p. 200)
**L3** Quiz A (p. 203)
**L2** Quiz B (p. 204)

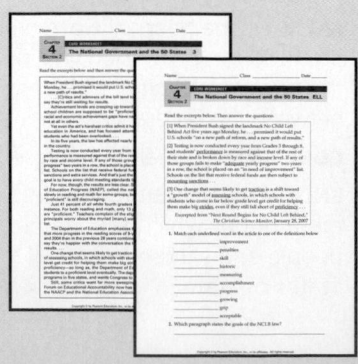

## Admitting New States

That new States would soon join the original 13 as members of the new United States was generally accepted as fact in the 1780s. To that end, the Congress of the Confederation, meeting as the Framers were drafting what was to become the Constitution, enacted the Northwest Ordinance of 1787—clearly, the most important measure passed by that body in its eight years as the government of the United States.

The ordinance anticipated the creation of new States in what was then known as the Northwest Territory—a roughly defined area lying north of the Ohio River and west of New York, Pennsylvania, and Virginia. The measure provided for the eventual Statehood of any sector in that region that acquired a population of at least 60,000 persons. It made provision for local self-government, for civil and political rights, and for the support of education. An earlier measure, the Ordinance of 1785, had created the township system for the dividing of land for the support of local schools. Its provisions were folded into the 1787 enactment.

The Northwest Ordinance was readopted by the new Congress under the Constitution in 1790, and it served as the basis for later legislation regarding the nation's territorial possessions. It established that those territories were not to be kept in a second-class

## Territorial Expansion of the U.S.

**GOVERNMENT** ONLINE
**Audio Tour**
Listen to a guided audio tour on the political spectrum at **PearsonSchool.com/phgovt**

➤➤ **Analyzing Maps** For more than a century, the United States acquired the lands out of which new States were created (indicated by dates). *From which 19th-century acquisition were the most States formed?*

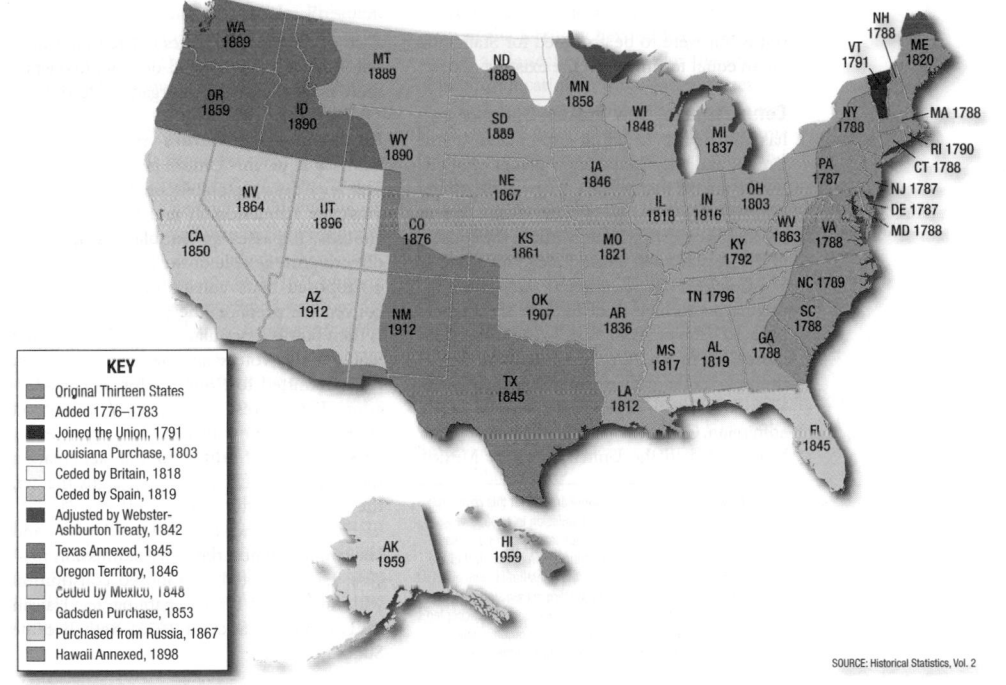

**KEY**
- Original Thirteen States
- Added 1776–1783
- Joined the Union, 1791
- Louisiana Purchase, 1803
- Ceded by Britain, 1818
- Ceded by Spain, 1819
- Adjusted by Webster-Ashburton Treaty, 1842
- Texas Annexed, 1845
- Oregon Territory, 1846
- Ceded by Mexico, 1848
- Gadsden Purchase, 1853
- Purchased from Russia, 1867
- Hawaii Annexed, 1898

SOURCE: Historical Statistics, Vol. 2

## Background

**PUERTO RICO: OUR 51ST STATE?** As a U.S. commonwealth, Puerto Rico is not quite a State and not quite an independent nation. Puerto Ricans are U.S. citizens and can vote for local officials, but not for the President. They can elect a representative to Congress, who can vote in committee but not on the House floor. In 1967, 1993, and 1998, Puerto Rico held local plebiscites, asking voter preference: Statehood, independence, or commonwealth. Each time, voters chose commonwealth. In 2008, the Puerto Rico Democracy Act emerged from congressional committee. Display Transparency 4C, Puerto Rico Democracy Act of 2007. If the bill passes into law, Puerto Ricans will be able to hold a U.S.-authorized vote on Statehood for the first time. Ask: **What is the purpose of the Act?** *(to allow the people of Puerto Rico to vote on the future status of the commonwealth)*

## DISCUSS

Use these questions to facilitate a discussion of federal aid.

1. **Why are grants from the Federal Government important?** *(Possible response: In our federal system, the States and National Government share responsibility for the same citizens, and therefore should share the costs. Also, the Federal Government has a greater ability to raise funds than do State governments.)*

2. **In what ways does federal aid help your community?** *(Answers will vary.)*

3. **How can federal aid help to eliminate disparities among regions, States, and communities?** *(Possible response: Communities of lower-income residents cannot raise as much tax money as can wealthier communities. Federal aid to lower-income communities can make up the difference, providing greater equality in services.)*

4. **Critics say that grants give the Federal Government too much power in making public policy at State and local levels. Do you agree or disagree? Give your reasons.** *(Possible answers: I agree because many of the grants come with strings attached, which forces the States to comply in order to receive the grants. OR: I disagree, because State and local governments can decide whether or not to accept federal aid.)*

### DISCUSS THE BELLRINGER ACTIVITY

Ask volunteers to share their answers about the FEMA disaster process. *(1. Steps 1, 2, 4; 2. Steps 5, 6; 3. Step 3; 4. Although the States hold primary responsibility for dealing with local issues, occasions occur when they cannot fulfill these obligations alone. At those times, the Constitution provides for the intervention, support, or cooperation of the National Government. 5. Article IV, Section 4: the Invasion and Internal Disorder provision)*

Tell students to go to the Audio Tour for a guided tour on the territorial expansion of the U.S.

## Answers

**Analyzing Maps** the Louisiana Purchase (1803)

# Assess and Remediate

**L3** Collect the Core Worksheet and assess students' work.

**L3** Assign the Section 2 Assessment questions.

**L3** Section Quiz A (Unit 1 All-in-One, p. 203)

**L2** Section Quiz B (Unit 1 All-in-One, p. 204)

Have students complete the review activities in the digital lesson presentation and continue their work in the **Essential Questions Journal.**

## Answers

**Three Types of Federal Grants** possible answers: State healthcare initiatives; welfare programs; homeland security

---

### Three Types of Federal Grants
# Where Does the Money Go?

Its taxing power gives Congress the implied power to make grants-in-aid to States and their local governments. *What kinds of organizations might receive a block grant?*

**CATEGORICAL**
Tens of billions of dollars fund interstate roads each year.

**BLOCK**
Congress gives millions of dollars to the States for homeland security purposes.

**PROJECT**
Federal money supports hundreds of State and local projects each year.

mass transit, highway construction, healthcare, and many others.

Grants-in-aid are based on the National Government's taxing power. The Constitution gives Congress that power in order

**unwarranted**
*adj.* without legal authority

> ## FROM THE CONSTITUTION
>
> **to pay the Debts and provide for the common Defense and general Welfare of the United States. . . .**
> —Article I, Section 8, Clause 1

Today, these grants total about $400 billion, and account for about a third of all State and local government spending each year.

In effect, grants-in-aid blur the division-of-powers line in the federal system. They make it possible for the Federal Government to operate in many policy areas in which it would otherwise have no constitutional authority—for example, in such fields as education, low-income housing, local law enforcement, and mental health.

Critics of grants-in-aid have long made this point. They also argue that the grants, which usually come with strings attached, often give Washington a major—and, they say, an <u>unwarranted</u>—voice in the making of public policy at the State and local levels.

**Types of Federal Grants** Today, Congress appropriates money for three types of grants-in-aid: categorical grants, block grants, and project grants.

Over time, most grants have been categorical. **Categorical grants** are made for some specific, closely defined purpose—for school lunches or for the construction of airports or wastewater treatment plants, for example. Categorical grants are usually made with conditions attached. These "strings" require the State to (1) use the federal monies only for the specific purpose involved; (2) make its own monetary contribution, often a matching amount but sometimes much less; (3) provide an agency to administer the grant; and (4) obey a set of guidelines

---

# Debate

After students read about No Child Left Behind in the Core Worksheet, have them debate the issue. Ask: **Should Congress renew the No Child Left Behind Act?** Encourage additional research, if time permits.

tailored to the particular purpose for which the monies are given.

**Block grants** have come into wide use over the last several years. They are made for much more broadly defined purposes than are categorical grants—for healthcare, social services, or welfare, for example. They are also made with fewer strings attached, so State and local governments have greater freedom in deciding just how and on what to spend block grant dollars. From the 1980s on, many programs once supported by separate and fragmented categorical grants have been merged into broader block grants.

Congress also provides money for **project grants.** These are grants made to States, localities, and sometimes private agencies that apply for the grants. The Department of Health and Human Services makes many project grants—through its National Institutes of Health, for example, to support scientists engaged in research on cancer, diabetes, neurological disease, and other medical issues. Many State and local governments also apply for these grants to fund their job training and employment programs.

**Other Forms of Federal Aid** The National Government aids the States in several other important ways. For example, the FBI gives extensive help to State and local police. The army and the air force equip and train each State's National Guard units. The Census Bureau's data are essential to State and local school, housing, and transportation officials as they plan for the future.

Many other forms of aid are not nearly so visible. "Lulu payments," for example, are federal monies that go to local governments in those areas in which there are large federal landholdings. These direct payments are made in lieu of (to take the place of) the property taxes that those local governments cannot collect from the National Government. These payments are also known as PILTs (payment in lieu of taxes).

### State Aid to the National Government
Intergovernmental cooperation is a two-way street. That is, the States and their local governments also aid the National Government in many ways.

Thus, State and local election officials conduct national elections. These elections are financed with State and local funds, and they are regulated largely by State laws. The legal process by which aliens can become citizens, called naturalization, takes place most often in State courts. The examples go on and on.

**Essential Questions Journal** To continue to build a response to the chapter Essential Question, go to your **Essential Questions Journal.**

## SECTION 2 ASSESSMENT

1. **Guiding Question** Use your completed chart to answer this question: According to the Constitution, what must the National Government guarantee to each State?

**Key Terms and Comprehension**

2. **(a)** What is the purpose of an **enabling act? (b)** What does Congress do once the requirements of the enabling act are met?

3. **(a)** Why does the Federal Government make **grants-in-aid** to the States? **(b)** Why are grants-in-aid controversial?

4. **(a)** What are the three main types of grants-in-aid? **(b)** For what is the money used in each type?

**Critical Thinking**

5. **Draw Conclusions (a)** Why might the Framers have included standards in the Constitution that each territory must meet before it can become a State? **(b)** Why is Congress barred from including conditions concerning a State's government? **(c)** How is this restriction an example of the federalist system?

6. **Summarize (a)** What is cooperative federalism? **(b)** How does this practice help the States to fulfill their several responsibilities?

**Quick Write**

**Compare and Contrast: Create a Venn Diagram** Use a Venn diagram to organize the research you gathered in Section 1. Put examples of the States' powers on one side, examples of the Federal Government's powers on the other, and examples of concurrent powers in the middle. You will use the Venn Diagram to create your final essay.

### REMEDIATION

| If Your Students Have Trouble With | Strategies For Remediation |
|---|---|
| The National Government's obligations to the States (Question 1) | As a class, have students complete the section's graphic organizer on the board. |
| The admission procedure for a new State (Questions 2, 5) | Write each step on an index card, mix them up, and have students put them in order. |
| The types of federal grants (Questions 3, 4) | Have students create and exchange crossword puzzles that include clues about each type of grant. |
| Cooperative federalism (Question 6) | Draw a rough outline on the board of the U.S. and your State within it. Ask students what citizens your State government serves. Draw diagonal lines through your State to indicate these citizens. Then ask what citizens the U.S. Government serves. Draw opposite diagonals through the entire country, including your State. Ask why cooperation is needed. *(because both governments serve the same citizens)* |

## Assessment Answers

**1.** The Constitution requires the Federal Government to provide a republican, or representative, form of government; protect each State from invasion and internal disorder; and recognize the legal existence of the States and their physical boundaries.

**2. (a)** directs a territory desiring Statehood to draft a State constitution **(b)** passes an act of admission, creating a new State

**3. (a)** to help States run programs for their citizens **(b)** The conditions attached to the grants enable the Federal Government to operate in policy areas generally reserved to the States, such as education.

**4. (a)** categorical grants, block grants, and project grants **(b)** categorical grant: closely defined purpose, such as school lunches; block grant: broadly defined purpose, such as healthcare; project grant: specific purpose for which a State, locality, or private agency applies, such as to support scientists conducting cancer research

**5. (a)** to make sure that new States entered the Union on equal footing with existing States **(b)** The Supreme Court ruled that political conditions would compromise the State's independence in managing its own internal affairs. **(c)** This ruling protects the integrity of the States within our federal system.

**6. (a)** The two levels of government—State and national—have many shared powers through which they work together to serve the citizens. **(b)** Federal grants-in-aid supplement State resources in supporting State and local programs.

**QUICK WRITE** Students' Venn diagrams should identify State, federal, and concurrent powers.

## LESSON GOAL

- Students will examine the conflict between States' rights and federal control in the context of environmental protection.

## Teach

### ACTIVATE PRIOR KNOWLEDGE

Ask students to name some environmental issues that their State is facing. Do they know what their State is doing to address these issues? Then ask students to identify the role of the EPA. *(The Environmental Protection Agency is a federal agency charged with the care and protection of the nation's environment.)*

### SUMMARIZE THE ISSUE

Display Transparency 4E, Environment and States' Rights. Have students read the quotes. Ask them to summarize the issue and the views expressed in the quotes.

**L2 ELL Differentiate** Have students look up these words in the dictionary: *leverage, precedent,* and *undermine.*

### PREDICT

Point out that States' rights versus the power of the Federal Government has played out in many arenas, not just the environment. Refer to the writings of the Federalists and Anti-Federalists to show students that this issue has been discussed since the nation's birth. Then, have students read the timeline. Ask them whether they think federal regulations will be placed on the oil industry, based on what they see in the timeline.

## Assess and Remediate

Have students select one quote on this page and write a short paragraph explaining why they agree or disagree.

## Answers

1. **(a)** He suggests that the disaster is due in part to the lack of federal regulations. **(b)** He uses the disaster to illustrate how the Federal Government has overreached its authority and that States could perform a better job. **(c)** Answers will vary.

2. Sample answer: They cause friction because what happens within a State should be controlled by the State. If a State wants harsher or more lenient rules, it should have the authority to make that determination.

---

# ISSUES OF OUR TIME

## The Environment and States' Rights

### ▶▶ Track the Issue

**The Federal Government,** over time, has taken many, often controversial, steps to protect the environment.

**1872**
**Congress sets aside land** in three States for Yellowstone National Park, the nation's and world's first national park.

**1907**
**Theodore Roosevelt sets aside 16** million acres of new forest preserves by presidential proclamation.

**1948**
**The Clean Water Act is passed** by Congress. It has been amended several times since.

**1963**
**Congress passes the Clean Air Act.** It, too, has been amended several times.

**2010**
**The explosion of a BP oil rig** in the Gulf of Mexico spurs efforts to increase drilling regulations to protect communities as well as the environment.

Governor of Texas Rick Perry ▶

### ▶▶ Perspectives

**In April 2010,** a Deepwater Horizon oil rig exploded in the Gulf of Mexico, killing eleven workers and causing a massive oil leak that lasted almost four months. Over that time, an estimated 39.1 million gallons of oil spilled into the Gulf, threatening both wildlife and livelihoods along the Gulf coast. This major environmental disaster reignited the controversy over regulation of the oil industry by the Federal Government.

"I've heard people speaking about the dangers of too much government regulation. And I think . . . there have been times in history when the government has overreached. But in this instance, the oil industry's . . . sometimes corrupt relationship with government regulators meant little or no regulation at all. . . . What's been made clear from this disaster is that for years the oil and gas industry has . . . effectively been allowed to regulate themselves. . . . Congress needs to address these issues . . . and my administration will work with them to do so."
**—President Barack Obama, May 2010**

"The Deepwater Horizon disaster . . . occurred on the federal government's watch. . . . [I]t is incomprehensible that . . . Congress is entertaining proposals that expand federal authority over oil and gas drilling in state waters and lands long regulated by states. . . . [P]utting the federal government in charge of energy production on state lands and waters not only breaks years of successful precedent and threatens the 10th Amendment to the . . . Constitution, but it also . . . threatens the environmental and economic security of our state's citizens."
**—Republican Governor of Texas Rick Perry, May 2010**

### ▶▶ Connect to Your World

1. **Understand (a)** How does President Obama use the Deepwater Horizon disaster to support his argument for reforming oil industry regulations? **(b)** How does Governor Perry? **(c)** Who do you think should have the authority to regulate the oil industry?

2. **Synthesize Information** Why do you think environmental issues cause friction between Federal and State governments?

**GOVERNMENT ONLINE**
**In the News**
For updates on the environment and states' rights, visit
**PearsonSchool.com/phgovt**

## Background

**CALIFORNIA VERSUS THE EPA** The Clean Air Act allows California to set anti-pollution standards higher than required nationally, with EPA-approved waivers. In the last 40 years, the EPA approved every waiver California requested—more than 40 in all. California became an innovator in pollution control, requiring carmakers to install equipment to reduce tailpipe emissions and gasoline evaporation. Following California's lead, many States enacted similar regulations. In 2005, California requested another waiver to further limit car emissions. Despite repeated urging from Governor Schwarzenegger, the EPA refused to rule on the waiver for two years. Then in April 2007, the Supreme Court denied the Federal Government's effort to block State regulation of greenhouse gases in *Massachusetts* v. *EPA*. The way seemed clear for the EPA to grant the waiver—but it refused. California sued.

## SECTION 3

# Interstate Relations

### Guiding Question

**How do the States work together to preserve the Union?** Use an outline like the one below to take notes on how the States cooperate.

I. The States Work Together
  A. Interstate Compacts
    1. _____
    2. _____
  B. _____
    1. _____
    2. _____
  C. _____

### Political Dictionary

- interstate compact
- Full Faith and Credit Clause
- extradition
- Privileges and Immunities Clause

### Objectives

1. Explain why States make interstate compacts.
2. Understand the purpose of the Full Faith and Credit Clause.
3. Describe the Extradition Clause and explain its purpose.
4. Explain the purpose of the Privileges and Immunities Clause.

**Image Above:** A person stands where the borders of Utah, Colorado, Arizona, and New Mexico meet to create "The Four Corners."

You know that rivalries, conflicts, and jealousies among the newly independent States was a principal reason for the writing and the adoption of the Constitution. The fact that the new document strengthened the hand of the National Government, especially with regard to trade among the States, reduced many of those frictions. So, too, did several of the new Constitution's provisions dealing with the States' relationships with one another.

## Interstate Compacts

No State can enter into any treaty, alliance, or confederation, says the Constitution. However, the States can, with the consent of Congress, enter into **interstate compacts**—agreements among themselves and with foreign states.[14]

The States made few of these agreements for several decades—only 36 of them by 1920. The number has grown steadily since then, however. New York and New Jersey led the way in 1921 with a pact creating what is now the Port Authority of New York and New Jersey to manage the harbor facilities bordering both States. More than 200 compacts are now in force, and many involve several States. In fact, all 50 States have joined in two of them: the Compact for the Supervision of Parolees and Probationers and the Compact on Juveniles. These two compacts enable States to share important law-enforcement data.

Other agreements cover a widening range of subjects. They include pacts that coordinate the development and conservation of such resources as water, oil, wildlife, and fish; counter the effects of global climate change; and encourage the cooperative use of public universities.

## Full Faith and Credit

In Article IV, Section 1, the Constitution commands that: "Full Faith and Credit shall be given in each State to the public Acts, Records, and judicial Proceedings of every other State."

---

**14** Article 1, Section 10, Clause 3: The Supreme Court has held that congressional consent is not needed for any compact that does not tend to increase the political power of a State (*Virginia* v. *Tennessee*, 1893). But it is often difficult to decide whether an interstate agreement is political or nonpolitical in nature. So, nearly all compacts are submitted to Congress as a matter of course.

## Focus on the Basics

Here is the information that your students need to learn in this section.

**FACTS:** • States can make interstate compacts for matters of mutual concern. • The Constitution requires each State to respect the laws, official records, and court actions of other States. • The Constitution requires each State to return fugitives from other States. • No State can draw unreasonable distinctions between its own residents and residents of other States.

**CONCEPTS:** federalism, cooperation

**ENDURING UNDERSTANDINGS:** • Several key provisions of the Constitution promote cooperation between and among the States.

## How do the States work together to preserve the Union?

I. The States Work Together
  A. Interstate Compacts
    1. Agreements among States
    2. Cooperate in areas such as law enforcement and resource conservation
  B. Full Faith and Credit
    1. States respect validity of public acts, records, and judicial proceedings of other States
    2. Applies only to civil, not criminal, matters
    3. Divorce recognized only if granted by State where person is legal resident
  C. Extradition
    1. Fugitive from one State can be returned by another
    2. Federal courts can compel unwilling governor to extradite
  D. Privileges and Immunities
    1. No State can draw unreasonable distinctions between own residents and those of other States
    2. Reasonable distinctions may be drawn, such as higher tuition for out-of-State students at State colleges

## Get Started

### LESSON GOALS

Students will . . .

- define and give the location of the constitutional provisions that deal with States' interrelations.
- analyze scenarios in which States interact with other States to identify the constitutional provision that prohibits each action.

## SKILLS DEVELOPMENT

### INNOVATE AND THINK CREATIVELY

Before students prepare their posters for the Extend the Lesson portion of this section, you may want to review tips on innovating and thinking creatively in the Skills Handbook, p. S23.

Assign the section, the graphic organizer in the text, and the Reading Comprehension Worksheet (Unit 1 All-in-One, p. 205) before class.

**L2 Differentiate** Reading Comprehension Worksheet (Unit 1 All-in-One, p. 206)

## BELLRINGER

Write on the board: **What should be the goals of government? (Unit 1 Essential Question) Is the federal system the best way to govern the United States? (Chapter 4 Essential Question) Has your thinking about these questions changed since the start of Unit 1? Write your assessment for each question in one or two paragraphs.**

# Teach

To present this topic using online resources, use the lesson presentations at **PearsonSchool.com/phgovt.**

## DISCUSS THE BELLRINGER ACTIVITY

Invite students to share their responses to the Bellringer activity and discuss their assessments of what they have learned about these Essential Questions.

## DISCUSS THE BASICS

Tell students that today you will discuss constitutional provisions that promote cooperation among the States. Ask them to take out their Reading Comprehension worksheet. Call on volunteers to define the purpose and location of each important provision.

## Answers

**Checkpoint** possible answers: compacts to regulate water resources and compacts to prevent and fight forest fires; by creating these compacts, States share the burden of solving problems that span more than one State

---

✔**Checkpoint**
Name two examples of interstate compacts. How do the States benefit from these compacts?

**probate**
*v.* to establish the validity of a will

The term *public acts* refers to the laws of a State. *Records* refers to such documents as birth certificates, marriage licenses, deeds to property, car registrations, and the like. The words *judicial proceedings* relate to the outcome of court actions: damage awards, the probating of wills, divorce decrees, and so forth.

The **Full Faith and Credit Clause** most often comes into play in court matters. Take this example: Allen sues Bill in Florida, and the Florida court awards Allen $50,000 in damages. Bill cannot escape payment of the damages by moving to Georgia, because Allen could simply ask the Georgia courts to enforce the damage award. Nor would the case have to be retried in Georgia. Instead, the Georgia courts would have to give full faith and credit to—recognize and respect the validity of—the judgment made by the Florida court.

In a similar vein, a person can prove age, place of birth, marital status, title to property, and similar facts by securing the necessary documents from the State where the record was made. The validity of these documents will be recognized in each of the 50 States.

**Exceptions** The Full Faith and Credit Clause is regularly observed, and it usually operates routinely between the States. There are two notable exceptions to the rule, however. First,

The Full Faith and Credit Clause ensures that all States recognize public records, such as these.

it applies only to *civil,* not *criminal,* matters. One State cannot enforce another State's criminal law. Second, full faith and credit need not be given to certain divorces granted by one State to residents of another State.

On the second exception, the key question is always this: Was the person who obtained the divorce in fact a resident of the State that granted it? If so, the divorce will be accorded full faith and credit in other States. If not, the State granting the divorce did not have the authority to do so, and another State can refuse to recognize it.

**Marriage and Divorce** The matter of interstate "quickie" divorces has been troublesome for decades, and especially since the Supreme Court's decision in a 1945 case, *Williams* v. *North Carolina.* In that case, a man and a woman traveled to Nevada, where each wanted to obtain a divorce so they could marry one another. They lived in Las Vegas for six weeks, the minimum period of State residence required by Nevada's divorce law. The couple were granted their divorces, were married, and returned to North Carolina the next day.

Problems arose when that State's authorities refused to recognize their Nevada divorces. North Carolina brought the couple to trial and a jury convicted each of them of the crime of bigamous cohabitation (marrying and living together while a previous marriage is still legally in effect).

On appeal, the Supreme Court upheld North Carolina's denial of full faith and credit to the Nevada divorces. It ruled that the couple had not in fact established *bona fide*—good faith, valid—residence in Nevada. Rather, the Court held that the couple had remained legal residents of North Carolina. In short, it found that Nevada lacked the authority to grant their divorces.

A divorce granted by a State court to a *bona fide* resident of that State must be given full faith and credit in all other States. To become a legal resident of a State, a person must intend to reside there permanently, or at least indefinitely. Clearly, the Williamses had not intended to do so.

The *Williams* case, and later ones like it, have cast dark clouds of doubt over the validity of thousands of other interstate divorces.

---

# Differentiated Resources

The following resources are located in the All-in-One, Unit 1, Chapter 4, Section 3:

**L3** Reading Comprehension Worksheet (p. 205)
**L2** Reading Comprehension Worksheet (p. 206)
**L3** Core Worksheet (p. 207)
**L3** Quiz A (p. 208)
**L2** Quiz B (p. 209)
**L3** Chapter Test A (p. 210)
**L2** Chapter Test B (p. 213)

The later marriages of people involved in these divorces, and the frequently tangled estate problems produced by their deaths, suggest the serious nature of the matter.

Even the legality of some marriages differs among the States. Today, most States and the Federal Government prohibit same-sex unions. However, six States do provide that such marriages can be legally performed within their borders.

In 2003, Massachusetts' Supreme Judicial Court held that that State's constitutional guarantees of equal rights to all persons in the State means that same-sex couples have exactly the same marriage rights as those enjoyed by all male-female couples in Massachusetts.

Since then, by court decision or legislation, five other States and the District of Columbia have come to the same position. Connecticut did so in 2008; Iowa, Maine, Vermont, and the District in 2009; and New Hampshire in 2010.

New York and Maryland are among the many jurisdictions that do not allow for the marriage of gay or lesbian couples. Both, however, do recognize the validity of such weddings performed elsewhere.

If a same-sex couple, legally married to one another in one State, moves to a State where those unions are outlawed, does the Full Faith and Credit Clause require the second State to recognize the validity of that couple's marriage? That thorny question has not yet (2011) reached the Supreme Court, but it almost certainly will—and soon.

Congress stepped into this building controversy in its early stages with the passage of the Defense of Marriage Act (DOMA) in 1996. That law declares that only those marriages that unite a man and a woman are legal in the United States. And it also provides that no State can be required to give full faith and credit to any same-sex marriage performed in any other State.

For several years now, critics of same-sex unions have urged Congress to propose a federal marriage amendment to the Constitution. That amendment would, in effect, write DOMA into the nation's fundamental law. To this point at least, those efforts have not been successful in either house.

## Extradition

The Constitution makes provisions for those who flee to another State to avoid punishment for a crime:

> **FROM THE CONSTITUTION**
>
> **A Person charged in any State with Treason, Felony, or other Crime, who shall flee from Justice, and be found in another State, shall on Demand of the executive Authority of the State from which he fled, be delivered up, to be removed to the State having <u>Jurisdiction</u> of the Crime.**
> —Article IV, Section 2, Clause 2

This clause refers to **extradition,** the legal process by which a <u>fugitive</u> from justice in one State can be returned to that State. Extradition is designed to prevent a person from escaping justice by fleeing a State.

The return of a fugitive from justice is usually a routine matter; governors regularly approve the extradition requests they receive from other States' chief executives. Some of those requests, however, are contested. This is especially true in cases with strong racial or political overtones, and in cases of parental kidnapping of children involved in custody disputes.

Until the 1980s, governors could, and on occasion did, refuse to return fugitives. In *Kentucky* v. *Dennison* (1861) the Supreme Court had held that the Constitution did not give the Federal Government any power with which to compel a governor to act in an extradition case. So, for more than a century,

▲ In 1958, Richard and Mildred Loving married in Washington, D.C., but were subsequently arrested in their home State of Virginia, where their interracial marriage was illegal. The Supreme Court ruled the Virginia law unconstitutional, and that all States must recognize interracial marriage.

**jurisdiction**
*n.* the authority to interpret and apply the law

**fugitive**
*n.* one who flees

## DISTRIBUTE CORE WORKSHEET

Distribute the Chapter 4 Section 3 Core Worksheet (Unit 1 All-in-One, p. 207). On the board, list three constitutional provisions: **Full Faith and Credit, Extradition,** and **Privileges and Immunities.** Divide the class into groups. Explain that students should review each situation in the first column of the worksheet. Then they should decide which clause listed on the board prohibits that situation from occurring. When students finish their worksheets, ask them to share their findings and explain their reasoning.

**L1** **L2** **Differentiate** Walk through the activity as a class. Alternatively, divide the chart into several parts and assign one team to each part.

**L4** **Differentiate** Have students complete the worksheet individually.

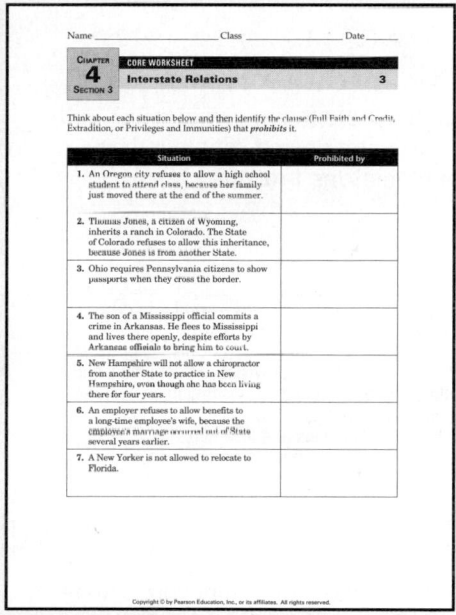

**L3** **Differentiate** Display Transparency 4F, The Process of Extradition. Have students analyze the extradition process. Then have them write a letter to a friend, explaining the stages of the process that a suspected felon would go through before that person finally went to trial.

# Teacher-to-Teacher Network

**ALTERNATE LESSON PLAN** In an advanced class, you might discuss challenges to the Full Faith and Credit Clause regarding marriage. In *Loving* v. *Virginia,* 1967, an interracial married couple sued the State of Virginia after they were arrested for breaking a State law banning marriage between people of different races. The Supreme Court struck down the Virginia law. Have students review the facts of the case and discuss the challenges that arise when one State does not recognize marriages that are legal in another.

To see this lesson plan, go to

at PearsonSchool.com/phgovt

Remind students that more than 200 interstate compacts now exist between the States. Ask partners to research one of these agreements: New York-New Jersey Port Authority Compact; Emergency Management Assistance Compact; Washington Metro Area Transit Authority Compact; Multistate Tax Compact; Southern Dairy Compact; Colorado River Compact; Interstate Compact on the Placement of Children; Interstate Compact on the Placement of Juveniles. Have students use their findings to create a poster explaining the compact.

# Assess and Remediate

**L3** Collect the Core Worksheet and assess students' work.

**L3** Assign the Section 3 Assessment questions.

**L3** Section Quiz A (Unit 1 All-in-One, p. 208)

**L2** Section Quiz B (Unit 1 All-in-One, p. 209)

Have students complete the review activities in the digital lesson presentation and continue their work in the **Essential Questions Journal.**

## REMEDIATION

| If Your Students Have Trouble With | Strategies For Remediation |
|---|---|
| The constitutional provisions that shape interstate relations (Questions 1–5) | Write each provision, its definition, and its location in the Constitution on separate cards. Have students match provisions with definitions and locations. |

## Answers

**Checkpoint** By making such distinction, a State would be violating the democratic principle that all citizens are equal.

---

the Constitution's word *shall* in the Extradition Clause had to be read as "may."

The Court overturned that ruling in 1987, however. In *Puerto Rico* v. *Branstad*, a unanimous Court held that the federal courts can indeed order an unwilling governor to extradite a fugitive.

## Privileges and Immunities

The Constitution also protects citizens who move between the States.

### FROM THE CONSTITUTION

**The Citizens of each State shall be entitled to all Privileges and Immunities of Citizens in the several States.**
—Article IV, Section 2, Clause 1[15]

This clause, known as the **Privileges and Immunities Clause,** means that no State can draw unreasonable distinctions between its own residents and those persons who happen to live in another State.

Each State must recognize the right of any American to travel in or become a resident of that State. It must also allow any citizen, no matter where he or she lives, to use its courts and make contracts; buy, own, rent, or sell property; or marry within its borders.

---

15 The provision is reinforced in the 14th Amendment.

---

However, a State cannot do such things as try to relieve its unemployment problems by requiring employers to hire in-State residents first. Thus, the Supreme Court struck down an Alaskan law requiring employers to prefer Alaskan workers to construct that State's oil and gas pipelines (*Hicklin* v. *Orbeck*, 1978). The Court overturned a California law that set the welfare benefits for newly arrived residents from States with lower welfare benefit levels at a lower level than those paid to long-term residents (*Saenz* v. *Roe*, 1999).

However, the Privileges and Immunities Clause does allow States to draw *reasonable* distinctions between its own residents and those of other States. Thus, any State can require that a person live within the State for some time before he or she can vote or hold public office. It also can require some period of residence before one can be licensed to practice law, medicine, dentistry, and so on.

In another example, the wild fish and game in a State are considered the common property of the people of that State. So, a State can require nonresidents to pay higher fees for fishing or hunting licenses than those paid by residents—who pay taxes to provide fish hatcheries, enforce game laws, and so on. By the same token, State colleges and universities regularly set higher tuition rates for out-of-State students.

---

**Essential Questions Journal** To continue to build a response to the chapter Essential Question, go to your **Essential Questions Journal.**

## SECTION 3 ASSESSMENT

1. **Guiding Question** Use the completed outline to answer this question: How do the States work together to preserve the Union?

### Key Terms and Comprehension

2. **(a)** Cite two **interstate compacts.** **(b)** What purpose do these compacts serve?

3. **(a)** Cite two examples of records that a State must recognize under the **Full Faith and Credit Clause.** **(b)** What are the two exceptions to that recognition?

### Critical Thinking

4. **Synthesize Information** If a person commits a felony in one State and flees to another, why might that person face extradition? Why wouldn't he or she be tried for his or her crime in the second State?

5. **Summarize (a)** How does the Privileges and Immunities Clause protect the rights of U.S. citizens? **(b)** Give three examples of rights that may be protected under this clause.

### Quick Write

**Compare and Contrast: Draft Your Essay** Use the Venn diagram you created in Section 2 as the outline for your essay. You may want to order your outline by first describing one set of powers, followed by the second set of powers, and finally putting the concurrent powers at the end.

---

# Assessment Answers

**1.** States make compacts with other States to cooperate in many areas, such as law enforcement and resource conservation. All States respect the validity of public acts, records, and judicial proceedings of other States. States extradite fugitives from other States. States afford the same rights and privileges to residents of other States as to their own residents.

**2. (a)** possible response: the Compact for the Supervision of Parolees and Probationers and the Compact on Juveniles **(b)** These compacts allow States to share law-enforcement information.

**3. (a)** possible response: marriage licenses and divorces **(b)** The clause applies only to civil, not criminal, law. Also, a State recognizes divorces only if granted by the State where the person is a legal resident.

**4.** The Full Faith and Credit Clause requires extradition to prevent someone from escaping justice by fleeing. The clause does not require a State to enforce another State's criminal law.

**5. (a)** The clause prevents States from treating residents of other States unequally. **(b)** possible response: the right to marry, the right to own

property, the right to make a contract

**QUICK WRITE** Students should use their Venn diagram to write their outline before they write the full essay.

# Quick Study Guide

**GOVERNMENT** ONLINE
**On the Go**
To review anytime, anywhere, download these online resources at **PearsonSchool.com/phgovt**
Political Dictionary, Audio Review

**CHAPTER 4**

**Guiding Question Section 2** According to the Constitution, what must the National Government guarantee to each State?

**Guiding Question Section 1** How is power divided between the Federal Government and the States?

**CHAPTER 4**
**Essential Question**
Is the federal system the best way to govern the United States?

**Guiding Question Section 3** How do the States work together to preserve the Union?

Republican form of government

**The Nation's Obligations to the States**

Protection from invasion and internal disorder

Respect for territorial integrity

## Political Dictionary

federalism *p. 94*
division of powers *p. 95*
delegated powers *p. 96*
expressed powers *p. 96*
implied powers *p. 96*
inherent powers *p. 97*
reserved powers *p. 99*
exclusive powers *p. 99*
concurrent powers *p. 100*
Supremacy Clause *p. 101*
enabling act *p. 106*
act of admission *p. 106*
grants-in-aid program *p. 107*
categorical grant *p. 108*
block grant *p. 109*
project grant *p. 109*
interstate compact *p. 111*
Full Faith and Credit Clause *p. 112*
extradition *p. 113*
Privileges and Immunities Clause *p. 114*

## Division of Power

| Federal Powers | Concurrent Powers | State Powers |
|---|---|---|
| Coin money | Levy and collect taxes | License marriage |
| Control commerce with foreign nations | Borrow money | License professionals |
| Determine standards of weight and measure | Establish courts | Maintain public schools |
| Declare war | Define crimes and set punishments | License drivers |
| Make laws that are "necessary and proper" | Claim private property for public use | Ratify amendments to the Constitution |
| Regulate interstate commerce | Establish a police force | Regulate elections |
| Control immigration | Set environmental and health standards | Oversee intrastate commerce |
| Acquire territory | | Set speed limits |
| Conduct diplomatic relations with other countries | | Establish standards of health and safety |
| | | Exercise those powers not given to the Federal Government and not restricted by the Constitution |

---

Have students download the digital resources available at Government on the Go for review and remediation.

## STUDY TIPS

**Organization** Point out to students that organizing their personal spaces and items, such as desks, backpacks, lockers, and study spaces, will save time and help avoid the frustration caused by searching fruitlessly for missing assignments or notebooks. Organizing information will help make studying easier and more productive. Suggest that students use three-ring binders, pouches, and boxes to organize their personal space. Give them time each week to sort through old papers, deciding which to keep and which to discard. Those that are kept should be filed in an appropriate location for easy reference later.

## ASSESSMENT AT A GLANCE

### Tests and Quizzes
Section Assessments
Section Quizzes A and B, Unit 1 **All-in-One**
Chapter Assessment
Chapter Tests A and B, Unit 1 **All-in-One**
Document-Based Assessment
Progress Monitoring Online
Exam*View* Test Bank

### Performance Assessment
Essential Questions Journal
Debates, pp. 99, 108
Assessment Rubrics, **All-in-One**

---

# For More Information

To learn more about federalism, refer to these sources or assign them to students:

**L1** **Cefrey, Holly.** *The Interstate Commerce Act: The Government Takes Control of Trade Between the States.* The Rosen Publishing Group, Inc., 2003.

**L2** **Roberts, Russell.** *Texas Joins the United States.* Mitchell Lane Publishers, 2007.

**L3** **Monk, Linda R.** *The Words We Live By: Your Annotated Guide to the Constitution.* Hyperion, 2004.

**L4** **Gerston, Larry N.** *American Federalism: A Concise Introduction.* M. E. Sharpe, 2007.

# Chapter Assessment

## COMPREHENSION AND CRITICAL THINKING

### SECTION 1

1. **(a)** Federalism is a system of government in which a written constitution divides the powers of government on a territorial basis, between a central government and several regional governments. **(b)** The Constitution grants certain specific powers to each level of government, some of which are to be exercised concurrently, and reserves to the States those powers not granted to the National Government nor denied to the States. **(c)** Leaving some powers to the States allows action on matters of State concern and allows for differing circumstances among States.

2. possible responses: **(a)** act as commander in chief, grant reprieves and pardons, make treaties, appoint major federal officials **(b)** lay and collect taxes, coin money, regulate foreign and interstate commerce, maintain armed forces, declare war **(c)** judicial power of the United States **(d)** delegated powers

3. **(a)** the Necessary and Proper Clause; Article I, Section 8, Clause 18 **(b)** It gives Congress the power to make all laws that are "necessary and proper" to carry out its expressed powers; that is, it gives Congress implied powers. **(c)** Possible response: Yes. "Necessary and proper" can be interpreted to be nearly unlimited. For example, the power to ban discrimination in public places is far removed from any expressed power, yet the ban was accomplished through implied powers.

4. **(a)** reserved power **(b)** favors State anti-pollution laws; the dark, unpleasant air of the more polluted State **(c)** financial concerns as well as differing needs and philosophies **(d)** Possible response: the Federal Government so there is consistency across the nation

### SECTION 2

5. **(a)** guarantee a republican, or representative, government; protect each State against foreign attack and internal disorder; recognize the legal existence and physical boundaries of each State **(b)** Possible response: Under federalism, the States are legal entities with established boundaries, but they also belong to a national union for mutual defense and benefit.

6. **(a)** Territory asks Congress for admission; Congress passes enabling act; territorial

---

# Chapter Assessment

**GOVERNMENT** ONLINE
**Self-Test**
To test your understanding of key terms and main ideas, visit
PearsonSchool.com/phgovt

## Comprehension and Critical Thinking

### Section 1

1. **(a)** Define federalism. **(b)** How are powers divided among the States and the National Government? **(c)** Why are certain powers left to the States rather than given to the National Government?

2. Give an example of an expressed power that the Constitution gives to **(a)** the President; **(b)** Congress; **(c)** the courts. **(d)** Under what Constitutional principle do these powers fall?

3. **(a)** What is the Elastic Clause? **(b)** What powers does this clause give to Congress? **(c)** Do you think that the Elastic Clause is broad enough to cover some of the powers that Congress has assumed? Why or why not? Cite specific examples.

4. **Analyze Political Cartoons (a)** Is the subject of this cartoon an example of reserved, exclusive, or concurrent powers? **(b)** Does the cartoonist favor or oppose State anti-pollution laws? How can you tell? **(c)** Why do you think one State may have different policies than another

on the same issue? **(d)** Which level of government do you think should have the basic responsibility for regulating the quality of the environment? Why?

### Section 2

5. **(a)** Name three obligations that the National Government has with regard to the States. **(b)** How do these obligations illustrate the concept of federalism?

6. **(a)** Briefly describe the process by which a new State can be admitted to the Union. **(b)** What types of conditions may not be imposed by the Federal Government on a territory as it becomes a State?

7. **(a)** Define cooperative federalism. **(b)** Name two types of federal aid given to the States. **(c)** How might federal aid be used to heighten the Federal Government's influence on State matters?

### Section 3

8. **(a)** Until 1987, a governor could challenge an extradition order. Under what circumstances was this allowed? **(b)** According to *Puerto Rico* v. *Branstad*, who can order an unwilling governor to extradite a fugitive? **(c)** Do you think this infringes on States' rights? Why or why not?

9. **(a)** Under the Privileges and Immunities Clause, what reasonable distinctions can a State make between its own residents and those of other States? **(b)** What distinction may a State not draw?

### Writing About Government

10. Use your Quick Write exercises to write a compare-and-contrast essay that compares State and federal powers. Refer back to your Venn diagram if you need help organizing your essay. See pp. S3–S5 in the Skills Handbook.

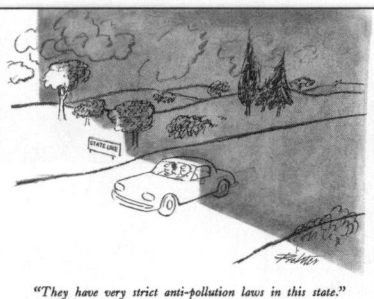

*"They have very strict anti-pollution laws in this state."*

## Apply What You've Learned

11. **Essential Question Activity** Create a federal grant proposal.

    **(a)** Identify some local activity (education, law enforcement, traffic control, etc.) that could be, but is not currently, supported by a federal grant.

    **(b)** Create a grant proposal for that activity. How large would the grant be? What strings might be attached?

    **(c)** Present your grant proposal to the class for its consideration.

12. **Essential Question Assessment** Based on your work from the grant proposal activity, write an Op-Ed for a local newspaper that addresses the Essential Question: **Is the federal system the best way to govern the United States?** Apply what you learned about grants and the grant process to answer this question. Make sure you back up your opinion with facts from the textbook and from your research.

**Essential Questions Journal** To respond to the chapter Essential Question, go to your **Essential Questions Journal.**

---

convention prepares a State constitution; constitution approved by popular vote in territory; approved constitution submitted to Congress; Congress passes act of admission; President signs act. **(b)** It may not impose political conditions or conditions that compromise the ability of the State to manage its own affairs.

7. **(a)** Cooperative federalism is a dual-level system of government that includes shared powers, requiring the levels of government to cooperate with one another. **(b)** categorical grants, block grants, project grants **(c)** Grants typically come with conditions

that States must meet to get the grant money. In effect, these conditions make it possible for the Federal Government to operate in policy areas that are constitutionally reserved to the States.

### SECTION 3

8. **(a)** Governors sometimes contested extradition in cases with strong racial or political overtones and in cases of parental kidnapping of children involved in custody disputes. **(b)** federal courts **(c)** possible response: no, because the Constitution requires States to extradite OR yes, because

# Document-Based Assessment

## The Power Divide

Debate over the extent of the powers of the new National Government in the federal system continued beyond the ratification of the Constitution in 1789. Thomas Jefferson and John Marshall were leading participants in that debate.

### Document 1

". . . to take from the states all the powers of self-government, & transfer them to a general & consolidated government, . . . is not for the peace, happiness or prosperity of these states: and that therefore this commonwealth [Kentucky] is determined, . . . to submit to undelegated & consequently unlimited powers in no man, or body of men on earth: that in cases of an abuse of the delegated powers . . . a change by the people would be the constitutional remedy; but where powers are assumed which have not been delegated a nullification of the act is the rightful remedy: that every state has a natural right, . . . to nullify . . . all assumptions of power by others within their limits . . ."

—Opposition to the Alien and Sedition Act from Thomas Jefferson's draft of the "Kentucky Resolution," 1798

### Document 2

"America has chosen to be, in many respects and to many purposes, a nation; and for all these purposes her government is complete; to all these objects, it is competent. The people have declared that in the exercise of all powers given for these objects, it is supreme. It can, then, in effecting these objects, legitimately control all individuals or governments within the American territory. The Constitution and laws of a State, so far as they are repugnant to the Constitution and laws of the United States, are absolutely void. These States are constituent parts of the United States. They are members of one great empire—for some purposes sovereign, for some purposes subordinate."

—John Marshall's Opinion from Cohens v. Virginia, 1821

---

**Use your knowledge of the Constitution, the federal system, and Documents 1 and 2 to answer Questions 1–3.**

1. Jefferson's resolution declares
   A. the right of the States to nullify a federal statute or federal law.
   B. the right of the States to initiate amendments to the Constitution.
   C. the absolute power of the Federal Government over the States.
   D. the authority of the Supreme Court to review State court judgments.

2. According to Marshall, what is the test of the constitutionality of State laws?

3. **Pull It Together** Which of these arguments best describes our government today? Why?

**GOVERNMENT** ONLINE

**Documents**
To find more primary sources on federalism, visit
PearsonSchool.com/phgovt

---

## DOCUMENT-BASED ASSESSMENT

1. A

2. State laws must not violate the Constitution nor federal laws.

3. Possible response: Document 2 better describes our government today, because the States can no longer refuse to obey a federal law. The law's constitutionality must be decided in the courts. Until such time as it is declared unconstitutional, the law must be obeyed.

**L2 Differentiate** Students use all the documents on the page to support their thesis.

**L3 Differentiate** Students include additional information available online at **PearsonSchool.com/phgovt**

**L4 Differentiate** Students use materials from the textbook, the online information at **PearsonSchool.com/phgovt,** and do additional research to support their views.

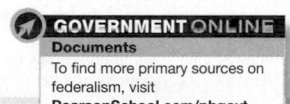

**Go Online to PearsonSchool.com/phgovt** for a student rubric and extra documents.

---

States have a right to enforce their own laws, even if they differ from those of other States

9. **(a)** possible response: require a person to live within the State for some time before he or she can vote, hold public office, or be licensed to practice a profession; require nonresidents to pay higher fees for fishing and hunting licenses and higher tuition to attend State colleges **(b)** unreasonable distinctions, such as require employers to give hiring preference to in-State residents or set welfare benefits lower for newcomers

### WRITING ABOUT GOVERNMENT

10. Students should compare and contrast the powers of the State and Federal governments.

### APPLY WHAT YOU'VE LEARNED

11. Students should design a grant to pay for something that will benefit their community. They should explain the requirements to obtain their grant, the amount of money, what it is for, and who it benefits.

12. Students should use grants as an example plus facts from the text to support their opinion about whether the federal system is the best way to govern the United States.

## ANSWERS TO ESSENTIAL QUESTION WARMUP

Before assigning these questions, distribute the Rubric for Assessing a Writing Assignment (Unit 1 All-in-One, p. 221). Use the criteria and the guidelines below to grade students' answers to the Essential Question Warmup questions. Then send students to the **Essential Questions Journal** to answer the unit Essential Question.

**1.** To answer this question, students must understand the various forms that a government can take, including democracy, dictatorship, unitary, federal, confederate, presidential, and parliamentary. A good answer will show an understanding that a major goal of a democracy, for example, is preserving the rights of the people, while the goal of a dictatorship is to keep power in the hands of an individual.

**2.** Some additional factors that might determine a government's goals are the country's relative wealth, levels of education, need for supporting agriculture, industry, or services, level of employment, natural resources, and expectations for social supports such as healthcare.

**3.** Answers may include support for democratic institutions, the rights of individuals, individual freedom, and free enterprise.

**4.** They looked to the Enlightenment thinkers such as John Locke and to English documents such as the Magna Carta and the English Bill of Rights for ideas that supported democracy and popular sovereignty as well as to their own experiences as colonists under a monarchy.

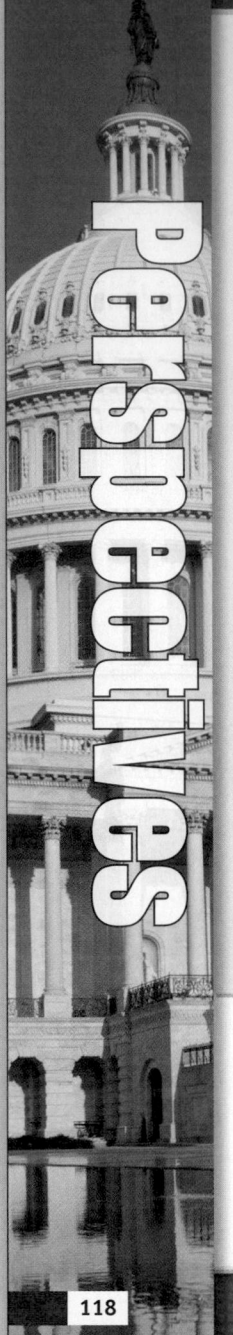

_Perspectives_

### Essential Question
# What should be the goals of government?

For every government, there exists a set of goals unique to the country's needs and history. For the United States government, those goals have been discussed and debated for the more than 200 years of the nation's existence.

**ON THE GOALS OF GOVERNMENT:**

**A wise and frugal [thrifty] government . . . shall restrain men from injuring one another, shall leave them otherwise free to regulate their own pursuits of industry and improvement, and shall not take from the mouth of labor the bread it has earned. This is the sum of good government.**
—Thomas Jefferson, First Inaugural Address, March 4, 1801

**ON WHERE GOVERNMENT DERIVES ITS POWER:**

**Here, sir, the people govern; here they act by their immediate representatives.**
—Alexander Hamilton, on ratifying the Constitution, June 27, 1788

**ON WHAT MAKES A GOOD GOVERNMENT:**

**Good government is a trust, and the officers of the government are trustees; and both the trust and the trustees are created for the benefit of the people.**
—Sen. Henry Clay,
   Speech at Ashland, Kentucky, 1829

### Essential Question Warmup

Throughout this unit, you studied the origins and elements of various governments, including those of the United States. Use what you have learned and the quotations above to answer the following questions. Then, go to your **Essential Questions Journal.**

**1.** How might a government's goals be affected by that government's form?

**2.** What are some other factors that might determine a government's goals?

**3.** What are the goals of the U.S. government?

**4.** How did the Framers develop these goals?

**Essential Questions Journal** To continue to build a response to the unit Essential Question, go to your **Essential Questions Journal.**

# Assessment Resources

Unit 1 AYP Monitoring Assessment
Exam*View* Test Bank CD-ROM
SuccessTracker Assessment
Online Student Self-Tests
Chapter Tests
Section Quizzes
Chapter-level Document-Based Assessment

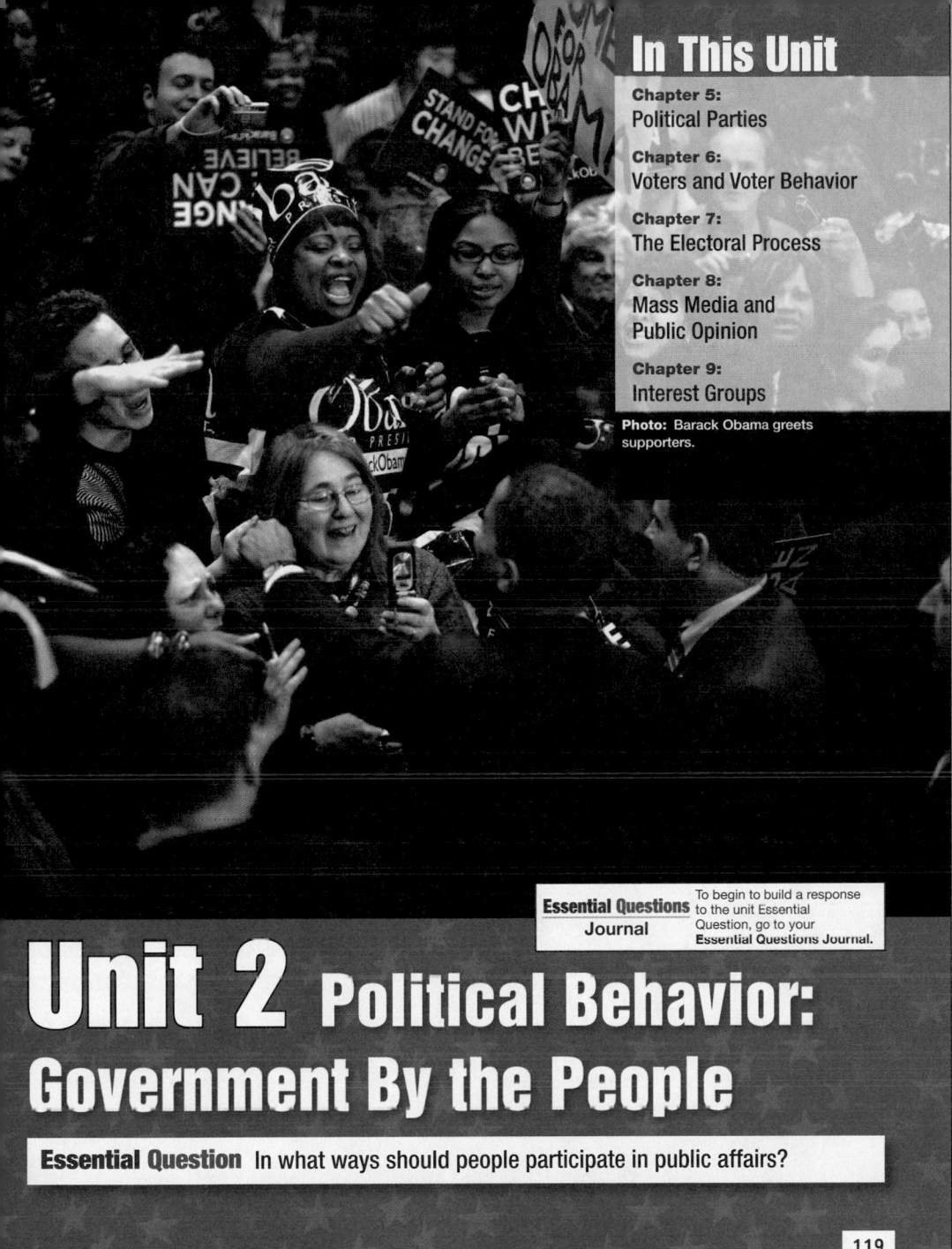

**Photo:** Barack Obama greets supporters.

**Essential Questions Journal**
To begin to build a response to the unit Essential Question, go to your **Essential Questions Journal.**

# Unit 2 Political Behavior: Government By the People

**Essential Question** In what ways should people participate in public affairs?

## Government Online Resources

Government Online Teacher Center at **PearsonSchool.com/phgovt** includes
• Online Teacher's Edition with lesson planner and lecture notes
• Teacher's Resource Library with All-in-One Resources, Color Transparencies, Adequate Yearly Progress Monitoring, and an alternative lesson plan for each chapter
• SuccessTracker Assessment

Government Online Student Center at **PearsonSchool.com/phgovt** includes
• Interactive textbook with audio
• American Government Essential Questions Video
• Chapter-level WebQuests
• Guided Audio Tours and Interactivities
• Student Self-Tests

---

**ESSENTIAL QUESTION PERSPECTIVES**

Essential questions frame each unit and chapter of study, asking students to consider big ideas about government. The question for this unit—**In what ways should people participate in public affairs?**—demands that students ask further questions. Is voting alone enough participation? Are interest groups helpful or harmful? How much does one vote matter? How can you participate if you are too young to vote? What is the best way to participate?

To begin this unit, assign the Unit 2 Warmup Activity on page 35 of the **Essential Questions Journal.** This will help students start to consider their position on the **Unit 2 Essential Question: In what ways should people participate in public affairs?**

Show the **Unit 2 American Government Essential Questions Video** to help students begin thinking about the unit Essential Question and designate a classroom bulletin board for students to post news articles related to the unit Essential Question. Use the Conversation Wall strategy (p. T27) to encourage students to post articles and comments on other students' postings.

Later, students will further explore the chapter-level essential questions:

*Chapter 5:* **Does the two-party system help or harm democracy?**

*Chapter 6:* **Why do voters act as they do?**

*Chapter 7:* **How fair and effective is the electoral process?**

*Chapter 8:* **What is the place of the media and public opinion in a democracy?**

*Chapter 9:* **To what extent do interest groups advance or harm democracy?**

Use the **Essential Questions Journal** throughout the program to help students consider these and other big ideas about government.

# Introduce the Chapter

## Essential Questions:

**UNIT 2**

In what ways should people participate in public affairs?

**CHAPTER 5**

Does the two-party system help or harm democracy?

### ACTIVATE PRIOR KNOWLEDGE

Have students examine the photo and quotation on these pages. Ask: **What do the image and quotation suggest about political parties?** *(that political parties involve citizen participation and are an important part of politics and of American democracy)* In this chapter, students will learn about the role of the two-party system in our democracy. Then tell students to begin to further explore political parties by completing the Chapter 5 Essential Question Warmup activity in their **Essential Questions Journal.** Discuss their responses as a class.

### BEFORE READING

**L2** **ELL Differentiate** Chapter 5 Prereading and Vocabulary Worksheet (Unit 2 All-in-One, p. 9)

### SUCCESSNET STUDENT AND TEACHER CENTER

Visit **PearsonSchool.com/phgovt** for download-able resources that allow students and teachers to connect with government "on the go."

### DIGITAL LESSON PRESENTATION

The digital lesson presentation supports the print lesson with activities and summaries of key concepts.

## SKILLS DEVELOPMENT

### ANALYZE POLITICAL CARTOONS

You may wish to teach analyzing political cartoons as a distinct skill within Section 2 of this chapter. Use the Chapter 5 Skills Worksheet (Unit 2 All-in-One, p. 23) to help students learn how to analyze political cartoons. The worksheet asks students to study a political cartoon and answer questions about it. For L2 and L1 students, assign the adapted Skill Activity (Unit 2 All-in-One, p. 24).

**WebQuest online** The chapter WebQuest challenges students to answer the chapter Essential Question by asking them about political parties.

120

## Block Scheduling

**BLOCK 1:** Teach the Section 1 and Section 2 lessons in their entirety.
**BLOCK 2:** Teach the Section 3 and Section 4 lessons in their entirety.

# 5

## Political Parties

### Essential Question

Does the two-party system help or harm democracy?

**Section 1:**
Parties and What They Do

**Section 2:**
Two-Party System in American History

**Section 3:**
The Minor Parties

**Section 4:**
Party Organization

"
No **America** without **democracy**, no democracy without **politics**, no politics without **parties**, no parties without **compromise** and **moderation**....

—Clinton Rossiter, *Parties and Politics in America*

**Photo:** Republican convention delegates cheer their party's 2008 presidential and vice presidential nominees, Sen. John McCain (R., Arizona) and Gov. Sarah Palin (R., Alaska).

**GOVERNMENT ONLINE**
**On the Go**

To study anywhere, anytime, download these online resources at PearsonSchool.com/phgovt
• Political Dictionary
• Audio Review
• Downloadable Interactivities

121

## Lesson Goals

**SECTION 1**

Students will . . .

• brainstorm their own associations with the terms *Republican* and *Democrat*.

• differentiate among the five main functions of political parties by categorizing examples of political actions under each function.

**SECTION 2**

Students will . . .

• explore the origin and uses of the symbols for the Democratic and Republican parties by analyzing political cartoons.

• review the history of political parties in the United States by answering questions.

**SECTION 3**

Students will . . .

• describe the categories of minor parties by examining an illustration.

• learn about minor parties by creating an identity and a campaign flyer for a fictitious minor party.

• examine the possible impact of minor parties on a recent presidential election.

**SECTION 4**

Students will . . .

• learn about the activities of party organizations by analyzing an excerpt from a periodical.

• design political activities for a campaign at the local, State, and national levels.

## Pressed for Time

Organize the class into three groups representing one of the following: Republicans, Democrats, or a minor third party. Have each group create and deliver a presentation that explains their roles in the American political system, including their major goals and challenges. As groups give their presentations, create a study guide on the board that explains the roles of major and minor parties in the American political system.

**FOLLOW UP** Have students create a diagram of the functions of political parties in the American political system.

---

**DIFFERENTIATED INSTRUCTION KEY**

Look for these symbols to help you adjust steps in each lesson to meet your students' needs.

**L1** Special Needs

**L2** Basic

**ELL** English Language Learners

**LPR** Less Proficient Readers

**L3** All Students

**L4** Advanced Students

## GUIDING QUESTION

What are political parties, and how do they function in our two-party system?

I. What Parties Do
  A. Definition: group that seeks to control government through winning elections and holding public office
  B. Functions
    1. nominate candidates and work for their election
    2. inform and activate supporters
    3. bonding agent
    4. governing
    5. watchdog
II. Types of Party Systems
  A. two party
  B. multiparty
  C. one party

## Get Started

### LESSON GOALS

Students will . . .

- brainstorm their own associations with the terms *Republican* and *Democrat*.

- differentiate among the five main functions of political parties by categorizing examples of political actions under each function.

### BEFORE CLASS

Assign the section, the graphic organizer in the text, and the Reading Comprehension Worksheet (Unit 2 All-in-One, p. 13) before class.

**L2 Differentiate** Reading Comprehension Worksheet (Unit 2 All-in-One, p. 14)

## SKILLS DEVELOPMENT

### COMPARE VIEWPOINTS

To teach the skill of comparing viewpoints, have students read Compare Viewpoints in the Skills Handbook, p. S15. Then have them conduct the debate described in this lesson.

---

SECTION **1**

# Parties and What They Do

### Guiding Question

**What are political parties, and how do they function in our two-party system?** Use an outline to organize the main features of political parties, their roles, and types of party systems.

I. What Parties Do
  A. Definition:
  B. Functions
II. Types of Party Systems
  A. Two Party
  B. _____
  C. _____

### Political Dictionary

- political party
- political spectrum
- partisanship
- single-member districts
- plurality
- bipartisan
- consensus
- coalition

### Objectives

1. Define a *political party*.
2. Describe the major functions of political parties.
3. Identify the reasons why the United States has a two-party system.
4. Understand multiparty and one-party systems and how they affect the functioning of a political system.

**Image Above:** National party conventions are opportunities for parties to show their support.

"**W**inning isn't everything; it's the only thing." So said legendary football coach Vince Lombardi. Lombardi was talking about teams in the National Football League. He might just as well have had the Republican and Democratic parties in mind. They, too, are in the business of competing and winning.

## What Is a Party?

A **political party** is a group of persons who seek to control government through the winning of elections and the holding of public office. This definition of a political party is broad enough to cover any party, including the two major parties in American politics, the Republicans and the Democrats. Another, more specific definition can be used to describe most political parties, both here and abroad: A group of persons, joined together on the basis of certain common principles, who seek to control government in order to secure the adoption of certain public policies and programs.

This latter definition, with its emphasis on principles and policy positions, will not fit the two major parties in the United States, however. The Republican and Democratic parties are not primarily principle- or issue-oriented. They are, instead, *election*-oriented.

You can better understand our two major parties if you recognize that each of them is an organization made up of three separate but closely related elements, three separate groups of party loyalists:

**1.** *The party organization.* This element of the party includes its leaders, its other activists, and its many "hangers-on"—all those who give their time, money, and skills to the party. In short, these are the party "professionals," those who run the party at the national, State, and local levels.

**2.** *The party in government.* This component includes the party's candidates and officeholders, those thousands of persons who run for or hold elective or appointive offices in the executive, legislative, and judicial branches at the federal, State, and local levels of government.

**3.** *The party in the electorate.* These are the millions of people who call themselves Republicans or Democrats, and who support the party and its candidates

## Focus on the Basics

**FACTS:** • A political party is a group of people with common principles, who seek to control government. • Political parties work to get their candidates elected. • Parties inform people and activate their participation in public affairs. • Parties are the main means by which the will of the people is made known to the government. • The U.S. has a two-party system (Democrats and Republicans); however, third parties sometimes play a role in elections. • Multiparty systems provide more choice but less stability.

**CONCEPTS:** sharing power, types of government, electoral system

**ENDURING UNDERSTANDINGS:** • Political parties are essential to democratic government. • Parties work to elect candidates in order to help their members influence government policies and programs.

through thick and thin. Many of them cast their votes on the basis of the party label, without regard to candidates or issues in an election. Observers sometimes criticize this kind of voting behavior as thoughtless. Yet knowing that a candidate is a Republican or Democrat often provides useful clues about where a candidate stands on key issues.

## What Parties Do

It is clear from our history, and from the histories of other peoples as well, that political parties are absolutely essential to democratic government. They are a vital link between the people and their government, between the governed and those who govern. Indeed, many observers argue that political parties are the principal means by which the will of the people is made known to government and by which government is held accountable to the people.

Parties serve the democratic ideal in another significant way: They work to blunt conflict; they are "power brokers." Political parties seek to modify the contending views of various interests and groups, encourage compromise, and so help to unify, rather than divide, the American people. They are very often successful in their attempts to soften the impact of extremists at both ends of the **political spectrum,** the range of political views.

Again, parties are indispensable to democratic government and, so, to American government. That fact is underscored by the several significant functions they perform.

**Nominating Candidates** The major function of a political party is to nominate—name—candidates for public office. That is, parties select candidates and present them to the voters. Then the parties work to help those nominees win elections.

In a functioning democracy, there must be some way to find (choose and recruit) candidates for office. There must also be some mechanism to gather support for those

---

1 The exceptions are in nonpartisan elections and in those rare instances in which an independent candidate enters a partisan contest. Nominations are covered at length in Chapter 7.

candidates. Parties are the best device yet found to do these jobs.

The nominating function is almost exclusively a party function in the United States.[1] It is the one activity that most clearly sets political parties apart from all of the other groups that operate in the political process.

**Informing and Activating Supporters**
Parties inform the people, and inspire and activate their interest and their participation in public affairs. Other groups also perform this function—in particular, the news media and interest groups.

Parties try to inform and inspire voters in several ways. Mostly, they do so by campaigning for their candidates, taking stands on current issues and criticizing opposing candidates and the positions they adopt.

Each party tries to inform the people as it thinks they should be informed—that is, to its own advantage. It conducts its "educational" efforts through pamphlets, signs, buttons, and stickers; advertisements in newspapers and magazines and via radio, television, the Internet, and text messaging; at speeches, rallies, and conventions; and in a variety of other ways.

Remember, both parties want to win elections, and that consideration has much to do with the stands they take on most issues. Both Republicans and Democrats try to shape positions that will attract as many voters as possible—and at the same time, offend as few as possible.

### ✓ Checkpoint
The two major parties are made up of what three elements?

**extremist**
*n.* one on the extreme right or left in politics

During the 2010 elections, the Tea Party gained nationwide attention as it rallied for lower taxes and smaller government. ▼

123

---

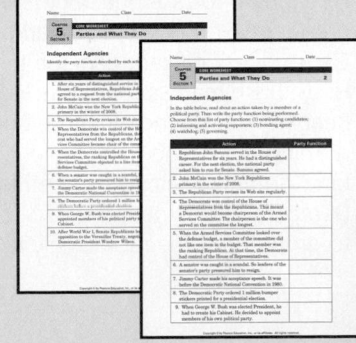
---

Display Transparency 5A, Five Functions of Political Parties. Ask: **How do parties today carry out these functions?** *(They nominate through primaries and caucuses and inform with ads, phone banks, signs, and flyers. As bonding agents, they back their best performers. They govern by appointing and voting along party lines. As watchdogs, they make sure the media hears about missteps by opposing party members.)* Then ask students to consider how the functions of parties relate to the chapter's Essential Question: Does the two-party system help or hurt democracy? Ask: **Compared to multiparty systems, how does our two-party system help our democracy?** *(Our two-party system modifies extreme views and provides more stability than do the coalitions that result from multiparty systems.)* **How does our two-party system limit democracy?** *(It limits the number of candidates and parties from which to choose.)*

**L4** **Differentiate** Have students research the role of political parties in a multiparty system—for example, Canada's or Italy's—and create a graphic organizer that compares and contrasts the multiparty system with the system in the United States.

---

**✓ Checkpoint**
How do parties perform the watchdog function?

**rascal**
*n.* a mean, unprincipled, or dishonest person

**The Bonding Agent Function** In the business world, a bond is an agreement that protects a person or a company against loss caused by a third party. In politics, a political party acts as a "bonding agent," to ensure the good performance of its candidates and elected officeholders. In choosing its candidates, the party tries to make sure that they are men and women who are both qualified and of good character—or, at the least, that they are not unqualified for the public offices they seek.

The party also prompts its successful candidates to perform well in office. The democratic process imposes this bonding agent function on a party, whether the party really wants to perform it or not. If it fails to assume the responsibility, both the party and its candidates may suffer the consequences of that failure in future elections.

**Governing** In several respects, government in the United States is government by party. For example, public officeholders—those who govern—are regularly chosen on the basis of party. Congress and the State legislatures are organized on party lines, and they conduct much of their business on the basis of **partisanship**—the strong support of their party and its policy stands. Most appointments to executive offices, at both the federal and State levels, are made with an eye to party.

In yet another sense, parties provide a basis for the conduct of government. In the complicated separation of powers arrangement, the executive and legislative branches must cooperate with one another if government is to accomplish anything. It is political parties that regularly provide the channels through which these two branches are able to work together.

Political parties have also played a role in the process of constitutional change. Consider this important example: The Constitution's <u>cumbersome</u> system for choosing a President works principally because political parties reshaped it in its earliest years, and they have made it work ever since.

**cumbersome**
*adj.* unwieldy; clumsy

**The Watchdog Function** Parties act as watchdogs over the conduct of the public's business. This is particularly true of the party out of power. It plays this role as it criticizes the policies and behavior of the party in power. In American politics, the party in power is the party that controls the executive branch of government—the presidency at the national level or the governorship at the State level.

In effect, the party out of power attempts to convince the voters that they should "throw the rascals out," that the "outs" should become the "ins" and the "ins" the "outs." The scrutiny and criticism by the "out" party tends to make the "<u>rascals</u>" more careful of their public charge and more responsive to the wishes and concerns of the people. In short, the party out of power plays the important role of "the loyal opposition"—opposed to the party in power but loyal to the people and the nation.

Again, these functions performed by political parties and, particularly, the two major parties, testify to the important role they play in making democracy work in this country. You might well remember that point the next time a comedian on late-night television ridicules some candidate, party, or officeholder.

There was a time when the parties played an even larger role in the nation's affairs than they do today. For example, in what has been called "the golden age of parties," from roughly the late nineteenth to the mid-twentieth century, party organizations operated as major welfare organizations in many places in the United States. They regularly helped newly arrived immigrants and many others among the poor to obtain food, housing, and jobs. Often they did this to win the support of these people at the polls. That once important welfare function has long since been taken over by a number of government programs put in place in the twentieth century.

## The Two-Party System

Two major parties, the Republicans and the Democrats, dominate American politics. That is to say, this country has a two-party system. In a typical election in the United States, only the Republican or the Democratic Party's candidates have a reasonable chance of winning public office.

It is true that in some States, and in many local communities, one of the two

---

# Background

**RIVALRY WITHIN THE PARTY** Sometimes the process of nominating a candidate can appear to cause deep divisions in a party, at least for a time. During the 1980 presidential primaries, for example, a Democratic challenge to then-President Jimmy Carter did significant damage to his reelection effort. On the Republican side, George H. W. Bush made strong attacks on eventual candidate Ronald Reagan. Yet after Reagan won the nomination, Bush ended his criticisms, agreed to serve as Reagan's running mate, and helped the Republicans capture the White House. In 2008, the long, sometimes testy competition between Barack Obama and Hillary Clinton for the Democratic nomination led some Democratic leaders to call for one of the candidates to drop out of the race simply for the good of the party.

---

## Answers

**Checkpoint** by publicly criticizing the party in power and making them more aware of the concerns of the people

Parties have created their own Web sites and tried to connect with voters by joining popular social networking sites.

## How Parties Communicate

For the better part of two centuries now, political parties have used a wide variety of strategies to communicate with voters. *How do the images shown here reflect attempts to reach potential voters?*

At recent national conventions, both parties gave limited edition macaroni and cheese to press and delegates.

---

major parties may be overwhelmingly dominant, winning election after election. And it may do so for a long time—as, for example, the Democratic Party dominated the politics of the South from the years after the Civil War into the 1960s. But, on the whole, and through most of our history, the United States has been a two-party nation.

Several factors explain why America has had and continues to have a two-party system. No one of these factors, alone, offers a wholly satisfactory explanation for the phenomenon. Taken together, however, they are quite persuasive.

**The Historical Basis** The two-party system in the United States is rooted in the beginnings of the nation itself. The Framers of the Constitution were opposed to political parties. As you know, the ratification of the Constitution gave rise to America's first two parties: the Federalists, led by Alexander Hamilton, and the Anti-Federalists. In short, the American party system *began* as a two-party system.

The Framers hoped to create a unified country; they sought to bring order out of the chaos of the Critical Period of the 1780s. To most of the Framers, parties were "factions," and therefore agents of divisiveness and disunity. George Washington reflected this view when, in his Farewell Address in 1796, he warned the new nation against "the <u>baneful</u> effects of the spirit of party."

In this light, it is hardly surprising that the Constitution made no provision for political parties. The Framers could not foresee the ways in which the governmental system they created would develop. Thus, they could not possibly know that two major parties

✓ **Checkpoint**
How did the Framers view political parties?

**baneful**
*adj.* troubling, distressing

---

## DISTRIBUTE CORE WORKSHEET

Distribute the Chapter 5 Section 1 Core Worksheet (Unit 2 All-in-One, p. 15). Instruct students to complete the activity, which asks them to categorize various party actions by function. Invite volunteers to share their answers and explain why they categorized each action as they did.

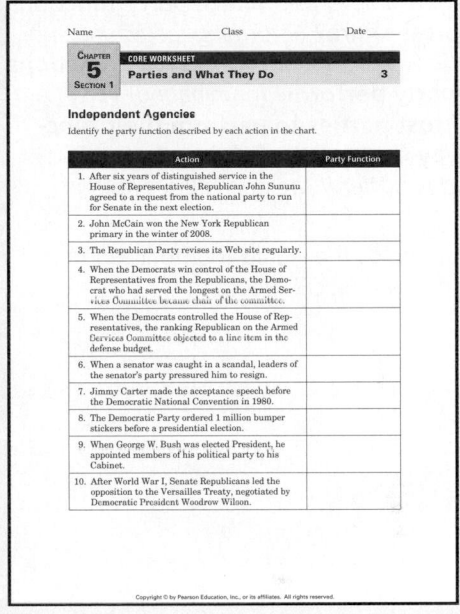

**L1 L2 Differentiate** Distribute the adapted Chapter 5 Section 1 Core Worksheet (Unit 2 All-in-One, p. 16).

**L4 Differentiate** Have students come up with additional examples of actions to illustrate each party function.

## Answers

**How Parties Communicate** Parties can reach the public through classic methods such as a speech or press conference. Today, they can also reach voters through general Web sites and specific groups by using social networking sites. They can target advertising to specific groups. These ads on boxes of macaroni and cheese would reach parents of young children.

**Checkpoint** The Framers saw political parties as factions that would divide rather than unify.

After students have completed the activity, have students discuss the importance of the different party functions. Remind students of the section's Guiding Question: **What are political parties, and how do they function in our two-party system?** Ask students if there are other institutions or organizations in American public life that perform some of these jobs. For example, ask: **Which party functions might the press share?** (informing, activating supporters, or the watchdog function) **Which functions can only a party perform?** (nominating) **Why should we trust parties to perform their functions in a way that is beneficial to the nation?** (Parties stand to suffer if the public loses faith in them.)

Tell students to go to the Audio Tour to listen to a guided tour of the political spectrum.

---

would emerge as prime instruments of government in the United States. Nor could they know that those two parties would tend to be moderate, most often choose "middle-of-the-road" positions, and so help to unify rather than divide the nation.

**The Force of Tradition** Once established, human institutions are likely to become self-perpetuating. So it has been with the two-party system. The very fact that the nation began with a two-party system has been a leading reason for the retention of a two-party system in this country. Over time, it has become an increasingly important, self-reinforcing reason as well.

The point can be made this way: Most Americans accept the idea of a two-party system simply because there has always been one. This inbred support for the arrangement is a principal reason why challenges to the system—by minor parties, for example—have made so little headway. In other words, America has a two-party system because America has a two-party system.

**The Electoral System** Several features of the American electoral system tend to promote the existence of but two major parties. The basic shape, and many of the details, of the election process work in that direction and to discourage minor parties.

**GOVERNMENT ONLINE**
**Audio Tour**
Listen to a guided audio tour on the political spectrum at **PearsonSchool.com/phgovt**

**Political Spectrum**

## Where Do the Parties Stand?

**LEFT ← CENTER → RIGHT**

**Radical**
Favors extreme change to create an altered or entirely new social system.

**Liberal**
Believes that government must take action to change economic, political, and ideological policies thought to be unfair.

**Moderate**
Holds beliefs that fall between liberal and conservative views, usually including some of each.

**Conservative**
Seeks to keep in place the economic, political, and social structures of society.

**Reactionary**
Favors extreme change to restore society to an earlier, more conservative state of affairs.

### Democratic Platform 2008

**Labor**
"Democrats are committed to an economic policy that produces good jobs with good pay and benefits. That is why we support the right to organize. We know that when unions are allowed to do their job of making sure that workers get their fair share, they pull people out of poverty and create a stronger middle class."

**Healthcare**
"The American people understand that good health is the foundation of individual achievement and economic prosperity. Ensuring quality, affordable health care for every single American is essential to children's education, workers' productivity, and businesses' competitiveness. We believe that covering all is absolutely necessary to making our health care system workable and affordable."

### Republican Platform 2008

**Labor**
"We affirm both the right of individuals to voluntarily participate in labor organizations and bargain collectively and the right of States to enact Right-to-Work laws. But the nation's labor laws . . . should be modernized to make it easier for employers and employees to plan, execute, and profit together."

**Healthcare**
"Americans have the best doctors, the best hospitals, the most innovative medical technology, and the best facilities anywhere in the world. Our challenge and opportunity is to build around them the best health-care system. Republicans believe the key to real reform is to give control of the health-care system to patients and their health-care providers, not bureaucrats in government or business."

▶▶**Critical Thinking** How do the platforms differ on the issues of labor and healthcare? How are they similar? How do the party platforms reflect the political spectrum?

---

## Answers

**Critical Thinking** Each party's platform reflects the political spectrum because it shows that Republicans tend to be more conservative about issues while Democrats tend to be more liberal and to accept government intervention. Differences: Although both support unions, Republicans emphasize more federal involvement in employment policy. Democrats want to increase access to healthcare in part through government programs. Republicans oppose government involvement in health insurance. Similarities: Both accept the right of workers to organize and recognize the need to make affordable healthcare available.

## Debate

"There are many [people] of principle in both parties in America, but there is no party of principle."

—Alexis de Tocqueville

Use this quotation to start a debate in your classroom. Ask: **Do party affiliations corrupt otherwise principled public servants?**

**L1 L2 ELL Differentiate** Have students look up the word principle in a dictionary and identify the meaning of the word used in this quote. (integrity, or driven by a desire to do what is right and proper)

The prevalence of **single-member districts** is one of the most important of these features. Nearly all of the elections held in this country—from the presidential contest to those at the local levels—are single-member district elections. That is, they are contests in which only one candidate is elected to each office on the ballot. They are winner-take-all elections. The winning candidate is the one who receives a **plurality,** or the largest number of votes cast for the office. Note that a plurality need not be a majority, or more than half of all votes cast in any given election.

The single-member district pattern works to discourage minor parties. Because only one winner can come out of each contest, voters usually face only two <u>viable</u> choices: They can vote for the candidate of the party holding the office, or they can vote for the candidate of the party with the best chance of replacing the current officeholder. In short, the single-member district arrangement has led many voters to think of a vote for a minor party candidate as a "wasted vote."

Another important aspect of the electoral system works to the same end. Much of American election law is purposely written to discourage non-major-party candidates.[2] The GOP and the Democrats regularly act in a **bipartisan** way in this matter.[3] That is, the two major parties find common ground here. They work together to shape election laws in such a way that minor party or independent candidates have a much harder time winning elective office.

Every four years, the presidential contest offers a striking illustration of this situation. In 2008, Republican John McCain and Democrat Barack Obama were listed on the ballots

of all 50 States and the District of Columbia. However, none of the other serious presidential hopefuls—the non-major parties' candidates—made it to the ballot in every State.

Independent candidate Ralph Nader was on the ballots of 45 States and the District of Columbia in 2008; and the Libertarian Party's Bob Barr also made it to the ballot in 45 States. The Green Party's Cynthia McKinney was listed in 41 States and the Constitution Party's Chuck Baldwin in 38. All of the other minor party candidates fell far short of those totals, however. Indeed, most suffered their usual fate: they managed to make the ballots of only one or a few States.

### The American Ideological Consensus
Americans are, on the whole, an <u>ideologically</u> homogeneous people. That is, over time, the American people have shared many of the same ideals, the same basic principles, and the same patterns of belief.

This is not to say that Americans are all alike. Clearly, this is not the case. The United States is a pluralistic society—one consisting of several distinct cultures and groups. Increasingly, the members of various ethnic, racial, religious, and other social groups compete for and share in the exercise of political power in this country. Still, there is a broad **consensus**—a general agreement among various groups—on matters of fundamental importance.

Nor is it to say that Americans have always agreed with one another in all matters. The nation has been deeply divided at times: during the Civil War and in the years of the Great Depression, for example, and over such critical issues as racial discrimination, the war in Vietnam, and abortion.

Still, note this very important point: This nation has not been regularly plagued by sharp and unbridgeable political divisions. The United States has been free of long-standing, bitter disputes based on such factors as economic class, social status, religious beliefs, or national origin.

Those conditions that could produce several strong rival parties simply do not exist in this country. In this way, the United States differs from most other democracies. In short, the realities of American society and

---

2  Nearly all election law in this country is State law, not federal law—a point discussed at length in the next two chapters. However, note this very important point: Almost all of the nearly 7,400 State legislators—nearly all of those persons who make State law—are either Democrats or Republicans. Only a handful of minor party members or independents now sit, or have ever sat, in State legislatures.

3  GOP is common shorthand for the Republican Party. The initials stand for Grand Old Party, a nickname acquired in the latter part of the 19th century. The nickname may owe its origins to British politics. Prime Minister William Gladstone was dubbed "the Grand Old Man," often abbreviated "GOM," by the English press in 1882. Soon after, "GOP" appeared in headlines in the *New York Tribune,* the *Boston Post,* and other American papers.

✔ **Checkpoint**
What is a plurality and how does it differ from a majority?

**viable**
*adj.* reasonable, practical, sensible

**ideologically**
*adv.* relating to or concerned with ideas

Have students use newspapers, magazines, or the Internet to find examples from the present day of political leaders performing the five functions of political parties. Have students share their examples with the class.

**L2** **Differentiate** Have students find examples for two of the five functions.

**L1** **L2** **Differentiate** Help students locate results from the last two presidential elections and create two color-coded maps that show which parties carried which states. Ask students if they can see any patterns in the different elections.

**L3** **L4** **Differentiate** Have students obtain copies of each major party's platform for the most recent presidential election. Have them create a chart that compares and contrasts the two parties' views on major issues.

# Background

**OUR FIRST PRESIDENT** The first presidential election in 1789 was really not much of an election at all. There were no political parties, and there was no race among competing candidates. Revolutionary war hero and president of the Constitutional Convention George Washington was the unanimous choice of all the electors. By 1792 and the second presidential election, the first parties had begun to emerge. Washington reluctantly chose to seek the presidency a second time. Among his reasons was to prevent a party clash. By agreeing to a second term, Washington made the 1792 election a one-candidate race; he again received a unanimous electoral college vote.

## Answers

**Checkpoint** the largest number of votes cast for an office; a plurality need not be a majority (more than half of all votes cast in any given election)

# Assess and Remediate

**L3** Collect the Core Worksheets and assess the students' work.

**L3** Assign the Section 1 Assessment questions.

**L3** Section Quiz A (Unit 2 All-in-One, p. 17)

**L2** Section Quiz B (Unit 2 All-in-One, p. 18)

Have students complete the review activities in the digital lesson presentation and continue their work in the **Essential Questions Journal.**

## Answers

**Analyzing Charts** political parties join together to form a coalition

---

politics simply do not permit more than two major parties.

This ideological consensus has had another very important impact on American parties. It has given the nation two major parties that often look very much alike. Both tend to be moderate. Both are built on compromise and usually try to occupy "the middle of the road." Both parties seek the same prize: the votes of a majority of the electorate. To do so, they must win over essentially the same people. Each party usually takes policy positions that do not differ a great deal from those of the other major party.

This is not to say that there are no significant differences between the two major parties today. There are many. For example, the Democratic Party, and those who usually vote for its candidates, are more likely to support such things as social welfare programs, government regulation of business practices, and efforts to improve the status of minorities. On the other hand, the Republican Party and its supporters are much more likely to favor the play of private market forces in the economy and to argue that the Federal Government should be less extensively involved in social welfare programs.

## Multiparty Systems

Some critics argue that the American two-party system should be scrapped. They would replace it with a multiparty arrangement, a system in which several major and many lesser parties exist, seriously compete for, and actually win public offices. Multiparty systems have long been a feature of most European democracies, and they are now found in many other democratic societies elsewhere in the world.

In the typical multiparty system, the various parties are each based on a particular interest, for example on economic class, religious belief, sectional attachment, or political ideology. Those who favor such an arrangement for this country say that it would provide for a broader representation of the electorate and be more responsive to the will of the people. They claim that a multiparty system would give voters a much more meaningful choice among candidates and policy alternatives than the present two-party system does.

Multiparty systems do tend to produce a broader, more diverse representation of the electorate. That strength, however, is also a major weakness of a multiparty system. It often leads to instability in government. One party is often unable to win the support of a majority of the voters. As a result, the power to govern must be shared by a number of parties in a **coalition.** A coalition is a temporary alliance of several groups who come together to form a working majority and so

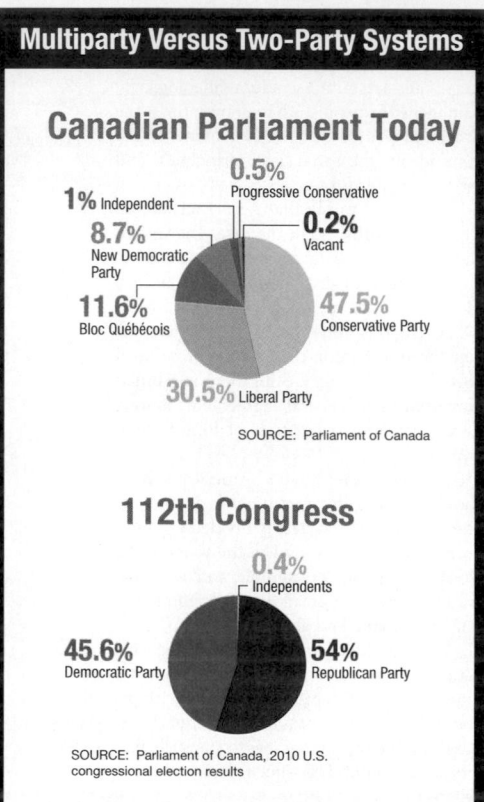

**Multiparty Versus Two-Party Systems**

**Canadian Parliament Today**

- 1% Independent
- 0.5% Progressive Conservative
- 0.2% Vacant
- 8.7% New Democratic Party
- 11.6% Bloc Québécois
- 47.5% Conservative Party
- 30.5% Liberal Party

SOURCE: Parliament of Canada

**112th Congress**

- 0.4% Independents
- 45.6% Democratic Party
- 54% Republican Party

SOURCE: Parliament of Canada, 2010 U.S. congressional election results

▶▶ **Analyzing Charts** In Canada's multiparty system, power is shared by several parties, none with a majority. In the American system, two parties have a monopoly on power. **_How are majorities built in the Canadian Parliament?_**

---

# Teacher-to-Teacher Network

**ALTERNATE LESSON PLAN** Have students research political parties in another country in order to answer such questions as the following: Does the country have a two-party system? What is the historical basis of the parties? What role do the parties play in the country's government?

To see this lesson plan, go to

**Teacher Center**

at PearsonSchool.com/phgovt

to control a government. Several of the multiparty nations of Western Europe have experienced frequent changes in party control as coalitions shift and dissolve.

Historically, the American people have shunned a multiparty approach to politics. They have refused to give substantial support to any but the two major parties and their candidates. Two of the factors mentioned here—single-member districts and the American ideological consensus—seem to make the multiparty approach impossible in the United States.

## One-Party Systems

In the typical dictatorship, only one political party, the party of the ruling clique, is allowed to exist. For all practical purposes, the resulting one-party system really amounts to a "no-party" system.

Many Americans are quite familiar with one-party systems of a quite different sort. What are often called "modified one-party systems" are found in roughly a fourth of the States today. That is, in those States one of the two major parties—either the Republicans or the Democrats—consistently wins most of the elections held there. Although in the remaining States there is more or less vigorous two-party competition at the Statewide level, there are also many locales in most of them where the political landscape is regularly dominated by a single party.

*"My goodness, if I'd known how badly you wanted democracy I'd have given it to you ages ago."*

▶▶ **Analyzing Political Cartoons** *What is this cartoon saying about one-party systems?*

From the 1870s into the 1960s, the Democratic Party was so dominant throughout the southern States that that quarter of the country came to be known as the Solid South. Over the past 40 years or so, however, the GOP has become the leading party in that part of the country.

**Essential Questions**
Journal

To continue to build a response to the chapter Essential Question, go to your **Essential Questions Journal.**

## SECTION 1 ASSESSMENT

1. **Guiding Question** Use your completed outline to answer this question: What are political parties, and how do they function in our two-party system?

**Key Terms and Comprehension**

2. How do **political parties** help to unify the American people?

3. Explain the bonding agent function of political parties in your own words.

4. What is a **single-member district**?

5. How is the ideological **consensus** of the American electorate reflected in the membership of the major parties?

**Critical Thinking**

6. **Recognize Propaganda** Do you think political parties are a valid source of information about candidates and their views? Why or why not?

7. **Compare Points of View** Explain why a person might consider a vote for a minor-party candidate even knowing that candidate is not likely to win.

**Quick Write**

**Persuasive Writing: Choose a Topic** The first step in writing a persuasive essay is to explore a topic. Make a list of five controversial national issues from history or the present that you feel strongly about or are familiar with. Examples might include immigration, labor, intervention in international affairs, education, the environment, or healthcare.

**REMEDIATION**

| If Your Students Have Trouble With | Strategies For Remediation |
|---|---|
| The definition of a political party (Question 1) | Write the definition of *political party* on the board, and ask students to rephrase this definition in their own words. |
| The roles of political parties (Questions 2, 3, 6) | Make a table of the different functions of parties. Have students offer examples of how parties fill each role. |
| The reasons why the United States has a two-party system (Questions 4, 5, 7) | Have students create an outline of the portion of the section headed "The Two-Party System." |

## Answers

**Analyzing Political Cartoons** The cartoon is ironic because one-party systems are undemocratic by nature.

# Assessment Answers

**1.** Political parties are groups who try to control government through winning elections and holding public office. Their functions include nominating candidates and working for their election, informing and activating supporters, acting as bonding agents, assisting in the job of governing, and acting as watchdogs.

**2.** by modifying contending views of various interests and groups and encouraging compromise

**3.** The parties will be held accountable at election time for the performance of their officeholders. Therefore, the parties try to choose candidates with integrity and strong qualifications, and encourage them to perform well in office.

**4.** a district in which only one candidate is elected to each office, or in which winner-take-all elections occur

**5.** Although Democrats and Republicans belong to different parties, they have similar stances on many issues and try to stay as moderate as possible to appeal to the largest number of voters.

**6.** A strong answer will note that parties are likely to promote information that favors their candidates and to try to prejudice voters against other parties' candidates.

**7.** Possible answer: A person may feel that it is important to send a signal about dissatisfaction with the views of the major parties.

**QUICK WRITE** Students should compile a thoughtful list of five controversial national issues from history or the present.

## How has the two-party system affected the history of American government?

| Two-Party System in American History | |
|---|---|
| Early Parties | began with battle over ratification; Federalists—Alexander Hamilton, strong national government, liberal interpretation of Constitution; Anti-Federalists/Jeffersonian Republicans/Democratic Republicans/Democratic Party—Thomas Jefferson, limited national government, strict construction of Constitution |
| 1800–1860 | era of Democrats; Federalist Party disappears; National Republican (Whig) Party emerges for brief time in 1830s–1850s; Republican Party—former Whigs and antislavery Democrats, Abraham Lincoln |
| 1860–1932 | era of Republicans; Democrats survived on support of Solid South; Theodore Roosevelt—Bull Moose Party; Democrat Woodrow Wilson; Republicans Harding, Coolidge, Hoover |
| 1932–1968 | return of Democrats; Depression; Franklin Roosevelt—New Deal revolutionary economic and social welfare programs, 4 terms |
| 1968–Present | Vietnam War divided Democrats; Republican Richard Nixon—resigned over Watergate, era of divided government |

# Get Started

### LESSON GOALS

Students will . . .

- explore the origin and uses of the symbols for the Democratic and Republican parties by analyzing political cartoons.
- review the history of political parties in the United States by answering questions.

## SKILLS DEVELOPMENT

### ANALYZE POLITICAL CARTOONS

To practice analyzing political cartoons in this section, use the Chapter 5 Skills Worksheet (Unit 2 All-in-One, p. 23). You may teach the skill explicitly before or after teaching the Political Cartoon Mini-Lesson. For L2 and L1 students, assign the adapted Skill Activity (Unit 2 All-in-One, p. 24).

---

SECTION **2**

# Two-Party System in American History

### Guiding Question

How has the two-party system affected the history of American government? Use the table to record details about the history of the two-party system in American history.

| Two-Party System in American History |  |
|---|---|
| Early Parties | |
| 1800–1860 | |
| 1860–1932 | |
| 1932–1968 | |
| 1968–Present | |

### Political Dictionary

- incumbent
- faction
- spoils system
- electorate
- sectionalism

### Objectives

1. Understand the origins of political parties in the United States.
2. Identify and describe the three major periods of single-party domination and describe the current era of divided government.

**Images Above:** James Madison (left) and Alexander Hamilton were founders of the nation's two earliest political parties.

Henry Ford, the great auto maker, once said that all history is "bunk." Mr. Ford knew a great deal about automobiles and mass production, but he did not know much about history, or its importance.

Listen, instead, to William Shakespeare: "What's past is prologue." Today is the product of yesterday. You are what you are today because of your history. The more you know about your past, the better prepared you are for today, and for tomorrow.

Much the same can be said about the two-party system in American politics. The more you know about its past, the better you will understand its workings today.

## The Nation's First Parties

The beginnings of the American two-party system can be traced to the battle over the ratification of the Constitution. The conflicts of the time, centering on the proper form and role of government in the United States, were not stilled by the adoption of the Constitution. Rather, those disputes were carried over into the early years of the Republic, and they led directly to the formation of the nation's first full-blown political parties.

The Federalist Party was the first to appear. It formed around Alexander Hamilton, who served as secretary of the treasury in the new government organized by George Washington. The Federalists were, by and large, the party of "the rich and the well-born." Most of them had supported the Constitution.

Led by Hamilton, the Federalists worked to create a stronger national government. They favored vigorous executive leadership and a set of policies designed to correct the nation's economic ills. The Federalists' program appealed to financial, manufacturing, and commercial interests. To reach their goals, they urged a liberal interpretation of the Constitution.

Thomas Jefferson, the nation's first secretary of state, led the opposition to the Federalists.[4] Jefferson and his followers were more sympathetic to the

---

4  As you recall, George Washington was opposed to political parties. As President, he named arch foes Hamilton and Jefferson to his new Cabinet to get them to work together—in what proved to be an unsuccessful attempt to avoid the creation of formally organized and opposing groups.

# Focus on the Basics

**FACTS:** • The first two political parties—the Federalists and the Anti-Federalists—emerged from the battle over ratification of the Constitution. • Thomas Jefferson's Anti-Federalists became the Democratic Party in 1828. • The Republican Party formed in 1854 from antislavery Democrats and former Whigs. • One party has dominated American government in three eras. • The fourth and current era is marked by divided government.

**CONCEPTS:** representative democracy, types of government

**ENDURING UNDERSTANDINGS:** • The United States has had three eras of one-party domination. • Historically, the major parties have alternated prolonged periods of dominance.

"common man" than were the Federalists. They favored a very limited role for the new government created by the Constitution. In their view, Congress should dominate that new government, and its policies should help the nation's small shopkeepers, laborers, farmers, and planters. The Jeffersonians insisted on a strict construction of the provisions of the Constitution.

Jefferson resigned from Washington's Cabinet in 1793 to concentrate on organizing his party. Originally, the new party took the name Anti-Federalist. Later it became known as the Jeffersonian Republicans or the Democratic-Republicans. Finally, by 1828, it became the Democratic Party.

These two parties first clashed in the election of 1796. John Adams, the Federalists' candidate to succeed Washington as President, defeated Jefferson by just three votes in the electoral college. Over the next four years, Jefferson and James Madison worked tirelessly to build the Democratic-Republican Party. Their efforts paid off in the election of 1800. Jefferson defeated the **incumbent,** the current officeholder, President Adams; Jefferson's party also won control of both houses of Congress. The Federalists never returned to power.

## Four Major Eras

The history of the American party system since 1800 can be divided into four major periods. Through the first three of these periods, one or the other of the two major parties was dominant, regularly holding the presidency and usually both houses of Congress. The nation is now in a fourth period, much of it marked by divided government.

In the first of these periods, from 1800 to 1860, the Democrats won 13 of 15 presidential elections. They lost the office only in the contests of 1840 and 1848. In the second era, from 1860 to 1932, the Republicans won 14 of 18 elections, losing only in 1884, 1892, 1912, and 1916.

The third period, from 1932 to 1968, began with the Democrats' return to power and Franklin Roosevelt's first election to the presidency. The Democrats won seven of the nine presidential elections, losing only in

1952 and 1956. Through the fourth and current period, which began in 1968, the Republicans have won seven of eleven presidential elections. Today, the Democrats occupy the White House, however, and they also control the Senate, but lost control of the House during the off-year elections in 2010.

## The Era of the Democrats

Thomas Jefferson's election in 1800 marked the beginning of a period of Democratic domination that was to last until the Civil War. The Federalists, soundly defeated in 1800, had disappeared altogether by 1816.

For a time, through the "Era of Good Feeling," the Democratic-Republicans were unopposed in national politics. However, by the mid-1820s they had split into a number of **factions,** or competing groups. By the time of Andrew Jackson's administration (1829–1837), a potent party had arisen to challenge the Democrats, known as the National Republicans and then Whigs. The major issues of the day—conflicts over public lands, the Second Bank of the United States, high tariffs, and slavery—all had made new party alignments inevitable.

**potent**
*adj.* powerful, strong

**alignment**
*n.* arrangement, grouping

✔ **Checkpoint**
How are the politics of today different from past eras?

▶ **Analyzing Political Cartoons** This cartoon ridiculed the fighting in Congress between Federalists and Anti-Federalists soon after John Adams, a Federalist, was elected President in 1796. *Why was the election of 1796 so significant to each party?*

---

## Differentiated Resources

The following resources are located in the All-in-One, Unit 2, Chapter 5, Section 2:

- **L3** Reading Comprehension Worksheet (p. 19)
- **L2** Reading Comprehension Worksheet (p. 20)
- **L3** Core Worksheet (p. 21)
- **L3** Skills Worksheet (p. 23)
- **L2** Skill Activity (p. 24)
- **L3** Quiz A (p. 25)
- **L2** Quiz B (p. 26)

---

**BEFORE CLASS**

Assign the section, the graphic organizer in the text, and the Reading Comprehension Worksheet (Unit 2 All-in-One, p. 19) before class.

**L2** **Differentiate** Reading Comprehension Worksheet (Unit 2 All-in-One, p. 20)

**BELLRINGER**

Display Transparency 5C, Two-Party Politics. Write on the board: **What qualities are associated with these animals? Answer in your notebook.**

**L1** **L2** **Differentiate** Ask students to describe what is happening in the cartoon.

## Teach

To present this topic using online resources, use the lesson presentations at **PearsonSchool.com/phgovt.**

**DISCUSS**

Have students share their responses to the Bellringer. *(Qualities include strength, size, intelligence, and clumsiness for the elephant; endurance, braying, and stubbornness for the donkey.)* Point out that cartoonist Thomas Nast popularized the symbols of the elephant for Republicans and the donkey for Democrats, beginning in the 1870s. Ask: **What did the cartoonist hope to accomplish by using an elephant and a donkey in this cartoon?** *(The cartoonist was trying to show how Democrats and Republicans differed on a policy question, and the donkey and the elephant quickly made that point.)*

**L3** **L4** **Differentiate** Have students draw a political cartoon using the elephant, donkey, or both. Instruct them to portray the party symbol(s) in a way that either supports or opposes the party's stand on a current issue. Encourage them to use characteristics of the animal to help get their message across.

---

## Answers

**Checkpoint** In past eras, government was dominated by one party or the other. Today, government control is divided between the two parties.

**Analyzing Political Cartoons** It was the first truly contested election between the two parties.

## DISTRIBUTE CORE WORKSHEET

Distribute the Chapter 5 Section 2 Core Worksheet (Unit 2 All-in-One, p. 21), in which students test their knowledge of American political history. Tell students that they can use their textbooks to help them find the information. You may wish to have students work in groups in which each group member works on one part of the activity and then shares his or her findings with the other members.

**L1 L2 Differentiate** Group L1 and L2 students with L3 and L4 students.

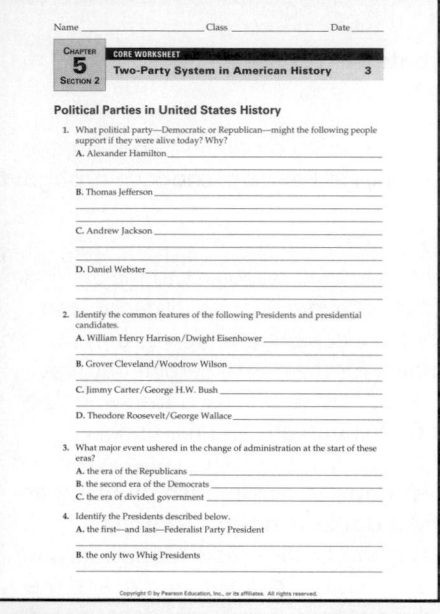

## CREATE A CARTOON

After completing their worksheets, have students create a political cartoon about a key event in American political history. Distribute the Rubric for Assessing Political Cartoons (Unit 2 All-in-One, p. 250).

**L1 L2 Differentiate** Have students work in teams to locate an event to illustrate and to design their cartoons.

## Answers

**Checkpoint** conflicts over public lands, the Second Bank of the United States, high tariffs, and slavery

---

**sway**
*n.* influence, power

**tenet**
*n.* principle, belief, conviction

The Democrats, led by Jackson, were a coalition of small farmers, debtors, frontier pioneers, and slaveholders. They drew much of their support from the South and West. The years of Jacksonian democracy produced three fundamental changes in the nation's political landscape: (1) voting rights for all white males, (2) a huge increase in the number of elected offices around the country, and (3) the spread of the **spoils system**—the practice of awarding public offices, contracts, and other governmental favors to those who supported the party in power.

The Whig Party was led by the widely popular Henry Clay and the great orator Daniel Webster. The party consisted of a loose coalition of eastern bankers, merchants and industrialists, and many owners of large southern plantations. The Whigs were opposed to the tenets of Jacksonian democracy and strongly supported a high tariff. However, the Whigs' victories were few. Although they were the other major party from the mid-1830s to the 1850s, the Whigs were able to elect only two men to the White House, both of them war heroes: William Henry Harrison in 1840 and Zachary Taylor in 1848.

By the 1850s, the growing crisis over slavery split both major parties. Left leaderless by the deaths of statesmen Clay and Webster, the Whig Party fell apart. Meanwhile, the Democratic Party split into two sharply divided camps, in the North and South. Through the decade, the nation drifted toward civil war.

Of the several groupings that arose to compete for supporters among the former Whigs and the fragmented Democrats, the Republican Party was the most successful. Founded in 1854, it drew many Whigs and antislavery Democrats to its ranks. The Republicans nominated their first presidential candidate, John C. Frémont, in 1856; and they elected their first President, Abraham Lincoln, in 1860.

With Abraham Lincoln's election, the Republican Party became the only party in the history of American politics to make the jump from third-party to major-party status. As you will see, even greater things were in store for the Republicans.

## The Era of the Republicans

The Civil War signaled the beginning of the second era of one-party sway. For nearly 75 years, the Republicans were to dominate the national political scene. They were supported by business and financial interests, and by farmers, laborers, and newly freed African Americans.

The Democrats, crippled by the war, were able to survive as a national party largely because of their hold on the Solid South in the years following the end of Reconstruction in the mid-1870s. Southern resentment of the Republicans' role in the defeat of the South, coupled with fears that the Federal Government would act to advance the rights of African Americans, meant that the Democrats would monopolize southern politics for the next 100 years.

For the balance of the century, the Democratic Party struggled to rebuild its national electoral base. In all that time, they were able to place only one candidate in the White House: Grover Cleveland in 1884 and again in 1892. His two victories marked only short breaks in Republican control, however. Riding the crest of popular acceptance and unprecedented prosperity, the GOP remained the dominant party well into the twentieth century.

The election of 1896 was especially critical in the development of the two-party system. It climaxed years of protest by small business owners, farmers, and the emerging labor unions against big business, financial monopolies, and the railroads. The Republican Party nominated William McKinley and supported the gold standard. The Democratic candidate was William Jennings Bryan, a supporter of free silver, who was also endorsed by the Populist Party.

With McKinley's victory in 1896, the Republicans regained the presidency. In doing so, they drew a response from a broader range of the **electorate**—the people eligible to vote. This new strength allowed the GOP to maintain its role as the dominant party in national politics for another three decades.

The Democratic Party lost the election of 1896, but it won on another score. Bryan, its young, dynamic presidential nominee,

---

# Political Cartoon Mini-Lesson

Display Transparency 5E, The Third Term Panic, when you discuss party symbols. Explain that Thomas Nast is accusing Democrats of scaring voters into thinking Republican President Ulysses S. Grant would seek an unprecedented third term. Ask: **What is the donkey wearing?** *(a lion skin labeled "Caesarism"—a reference to the dictatorial emperor of Rome)* **Whom was Nast comparing to Caesar? Why?** *(He was comparing Grant to Caesar, suggesting that Grant wanted to become an emperor by seeking a third term.)* **How are Republican voters reacting?** *(In a panic, they are jumping toward an abyss labeled "chaos.")* **Is Nast confirming or denying that Grant will seek a third term?** *(denying—he sees it as a Democratic ploy, represented by the donkey dressed in a lion's skin)*

# Party Identity: Past and Present

▸▸ **Analyzing Political Cartoons**
Cartoonist Thomas Nast has been credited with creating the party symbols in his 1874 cartoons for the magazine *Harper's Weekly*. Originally, neither party adopted his ideas. Over time, each party assumed and revised the symbols, which have since become synonymous with party identity. *What characteristics of the donkey and elephant do you think appeal to Democrats and Republicans? How have the parties modernized the symbols since the publication of Nast's cartoons?*

Democrats ▸

◂ Republicans

campaigned throughout the country as the champion of the "little man." He helped to push the nation's party politics back toward the economic arena, and away from the divisions of **sectionalism** that had plagued the nation for so many years. Sectionalism emphasizes a devotion to the interests of a particular region.

The Republicans suffered their worst setback of the era in 1912, when they renominated incumbent President William Howard Taft. Former President Theodore Roosevelt, denied the nomination of his party, left the Republicans to become the candidate of his "Bull Moose" Progressive Party. Traditional Republican support was divided between Taft and Roosevelt. As a result, the Democratic nominee, Woodrow Wilson, was able to capture the presidency although with less than fifty percent of the popular vote. Wilson also managed to keep the office four years later by a very narrow margin.

Again, however, the Democratic successes of 1912 and 1916 proved only a brief **interlude**. The GOP reasserted its control of the nation's politics by winning each of the next three presidential elections: Warren Harding of Ohio in 1920, Calvin Coolidge of Vermont in 1924, and Herbert Hoover of California in 1928.

## The Return of the Democrats

The Great Depression, which began in 1929, had a massive impact on nearly all aspects of American life including the political landscape. The landmark presidential election of 1932 brought Franklin Roosevelt and the Democrats back to power at the national level. That election also marked a basic shift in the public's attitude toward the proper role of government in the nation's social and economic life.

Franklin Roosevelt and the Democrats won in 1932 with a new electoral base, built largely of southerners, small farmers, organized labor, and big-city political organizations. Roosevelt's revolutionary economic and social welfare programs further strengthened that coalition. It also brought increasing support from African Americans and other minorities to the Democrats.

The historic election of 1932 made the Democratic Party the clear majority party in American politics—a position it was to keep for the better part of the next 40 years. President Roosevelt won overwhelming reelection in 1936, an unprecedented third term in 1940, and another term in the midst of World War II, in 1944. Vice President Harry S Truman completed that fourth term, following FDR's death in April of 1945. President Truman was elected to a full term of his own in 1948

**✔ Checkpoint**
What third-party candidate had an influence on the election of 1912? Explain.

**interlude**
*n.* intervening time

---

# Background

**THE DEMOCRATIC DONKEY** In the campaign for the presidency in 1828, Andrew Jackson's opponents called him a jackass for his views. Jackson turned this label into an advantage. He used the donkey in his campaign posters. The donkey appeared in a cartoon for the first time to represent Jackson's stubbornness during the battle over the Second Bank of the United States. In the cartoon on this page, Thomas Nast associated the donkey with the Democratic Party for the first time. Nast intended the donkey as a criticism of the Copperheads, an anti-war faction of the Democratic Party. The lion is Secretary of War Edwin Stanton, who had died. The cartoon is titled "A Live Jackass Kicking a Dead Lion." The donkey symbol caught on, and Nast continued to use it to represent Democrats.

---

## Answers

**Analyzing Political Cartoons** The donkey seems stubborn, tough, and fearless. The elephant may be seen as mighty and courageous. The modern symbols are more iconic and patriotic and less realistic than the older cartoon images.

**Checkpoint** Theodore Roosevelt and his Bull Moose Party split the Republicans and may have helped the Democrats win the election.

**L3 Differentiate** Have students create a timeline of the most recent era—the Era of Divided Government—that combines election information with key events discussed in the section. Students may add events from their own research and knowledge to the timeline. Where appropriate, students should indicate how they think events may have influenced political developments.

**L1 L2 Differentiate** Ask students to examine the timeline "Political Parties from 1800 to Today" and write their own caption for the illustration.

**L4 Differentiate** Have students write an essay in which they predict which party, if any, will gain and hold control of the White House in the next era of political parties. Students should also predict what issues will help shape the era.

# Political Parties From 1800 to Today

## Era of Democrats 1800–1860

**1800** Thomas Jefferson (below) is elected President, ushering in an era of Democratic domination that lasted until the Civil War.

**1828** President Andrew Jackson's (right) Democratic Party includes small farmers, debtors, frontier pioneers, and slaveholders.

**1854** The Republican Party is born, attracting many former Whigs and antislavery Democrats.

## Era of Republicans, 1860–1932

**1860** The election of Abraham Lincoln (below) and the start of the Civil War mark the beginning of 75 years of Republican Party supremacy.

▶▶ **Analyzing Timelines** This timeline shows which parties have dominated the presidency since the election of 1800. *What issues or events had an impact on elections held before the current era?*

in a close election against GOP challenger Thomas E. Dewey of New York. The Republicans regained the White House in 1952, and kept it in 1956, with World War II hero Dwight Eisenhower. Both times, the widely popular Eisenhower defeated the Democrat Adlai Stevenson.

The GOP's return to power was brief, however. Senator John F. Kennedy recaptured the presidency for the Democrats in 1960. He did so with a razor-thin victory over the Republican Party's standard bearer, and then Vice President Richard M. Nixon.

Lee Harvey Oswald shot and killed President Kennedy in Dallas, Texas, on November 22, 1963, and so Vice President Lyndon B. Johnson became President. Mr. Johnson won a full term of his own in 1964, crushing Republican Barry Goldwater of Arizona.

## Era of Divided Government

Richard Nixon made a successful return to presidential politics eight years after his narrow loss to John Kennedy in 1960. In 1968 he defeated Vice President Hubert Humphrey, the candidate of a Democratic Party torn apart by conflicts over the war in Vietnam, civil rights, and a variety of social issues. That election also had a strong third-party effort from American Independent Party candidate George Wallace. Mr. Nixon won only a slim plurality of the votes cast in that election.

President Nixon retained the White House in 1972, routing the choice of the still-divided Democrats, Senator George McGovern of South Dakota. However, the Watergate scandal forced him from office in August of 1974.

Vice President Gerald Ford then became President and served the remainder of the second Nixon term in the White House. Beset by problems in the economy, by the continuing effects of Watergate, and by his pardon of former President Nixon, Mr. Ford lost the presidency in 1976. In a very close election, the voters rejected his bid for a full term, preferring instead the Democratic Party's candidate, Jimmy Carter, the former governor of Georgia.

# Debate

Use this quotation to start a debate in your classroom.

"Divided government seemed to lead to deadlocks that threatened our ability to govern."

—"Divided Government—Gridlock or Godsend" from the *Wisconsin Academy Review,* 1996

Ask: **Do you agree with this observation about divided government?**

# Answers

**Analyzing Timelines** slavery, Civil War, Great Depression

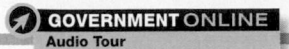

**GOVERNMENT** ONLINE
**Audio Tour**
Listen to a guided audio tour of this timeline at
**PearsonSchool.com/phgovt**

Tell students to go to the Audio Tour for a guided tour of this timeline about the parties in history.

## Assess and Remediate

**L3** Collect the Core Worksheets and assess the students' class participation, using the Rubric for Assessing Individual Performance in a Group (Unit 2 All-in-One, p. 251).

**L3** Assign the Section 2 Assessment questions.

**L3** Section Quiz A (Unit 2 All-in-One, p. 25)

**L2** Section Quiz B (Unit 2 All-in-One, p. 26)

Have students complete the review activities in the digital lesson presentation and continue their work in the **Essential Questions Journal.**

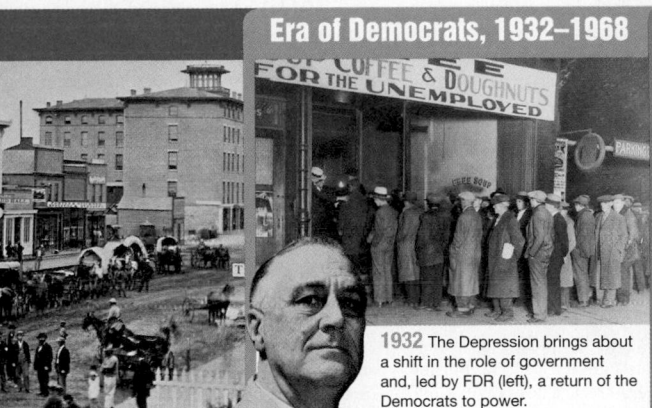

### Era of Democrats, 1932–1968

**1932** The Depression brings about a shift in the role of government and, led by FDR (left), a return of the Democrats to power.

### Era of Divided Government, 1968–Today

**1968** From this election on, neither party consistently holds the presidency, and Congress is often controlled by the opposing party.

**The Republican Advantage** A steadily worsening economy, political fallout from the Iranian hostage crisis, and his own inability to establish himself as an effective President spelled defeat for Jimmy Carter in 1980. Led by Ronald Reagan, the former governor of California, the Republicans scored an impressive victory over President Carter and the independent bid of former Republican Congressman John Anderson of Illinois. Mr. Reagan won a second term by a landslide in 1984; the Democratic candidate Vice President Walter Mondale could carry only his home State of Minnesota and the District of Columbia.

The GOP kept the White House with a third straight win in 1988. Their candidate, George H.W. Bush of Texas, had served as Vice President through the Reagan years and became the first sitting Vice President to win the presidency since Martin Van Buren in 1836. Mr. Bush trounced his Democratic opponent, Governor Michael Dukakis of Massachusetts.

The Reagan and Bush victories of the 1980s triggered wide-ranging efforts to alter many of the nation's foreign and domestic policies. Despite the hugely successful Persian Gulf War of 1990–1991, Mr. Bush was done in by problems that plagued the nation's economy in the 1980s into the 1990s. He was defeated in 1992 by Democrat Bill Clinton, then governor of Arkansas, who also turned back an independent challenge by Texas billionaire H. Ross Perot.

**Into the Twenty-First Century** Bill Clinton won a second term in 1996, handily defeating the Republican candidate, longtime senator from Kansas, Bob Dole, and, at the same time, underlined thwarting a third-party bid by Mr. Perot. The Republican-controlled Congress mounted an unsuccessful attempt to impeach and remove President Clinton in the midst of his second term.

The GOP did regain the White House in the exceedingly close presidential contest of 2000. Their candidate, George W. Bush, son of the former Republican President, was then the governor of Texas. The younger Mr. Bush failed to win the popular vote contest in 2000, but he did capture a bare majority of the electoral votes and so the White House. His Democratic opponent, Vice President Al Gore, became the first presidential nominee since 1888 to win the popular vote and yet

✔ **Checkpoint**
What factors contributed to Jimmy Carter's defeat in the 1980 election?

**thwart**
*v.* to defeat, stop

## Fast Facts

The following table gives information about party control of state legislatures and governor's mansions.

|  | 2000 | 2002 | 2004 | 2006 |
|---|---|---|---|---|
| State Legislatures* | D=16 R=17 Divided=16 | D=17 R=21 Divided=11 | D=19 R=20 Divided=10 | D=23 R=15 Divided=11 |
| Governors | D=19 R=29 Other=2 | D=24 R=26 | D=22 R=28 | D=22 R=28 |

*Nebraska's legislature has one chamber and is nonpartisan.

## Answers

**Checkpoint** steadily worsening economy, political fallout from the Iranian hostage crisis, and own inability to establish himself as an effective President

| If Your Students Have Trouble With | Strategies For Remediation |
|---|---|
| Knowing when and why the two-party system first emerged (Questions 1 and 5) | Have students write a brief biographical profile of both Alexander Hamilton and Thomas Jefferson, explaining their role in the founding of the government and their beliefs about its basic forms and purposes. |
| Identifying and understanding the four major eras of political parties (Questions 2 and 3) | Have students create a table that shows for each era the party that dominated and the major issues that faced the nation during that era. |
| Recognizing the causes and features of the current era of divided government (Questions 4 and 6) | Have students identify the times between 1968 and the present in which one party has controlled both the Congress and the presidency. |

## Answers

**Checkpoint** one major party occupies the White House while other party holds majority of seats in one or both houses of Congress

---

✔ **Checkpoint**
What does "divided government" mean?

**prodigious**
*adj.* of great size, power, extent

fail to win the presidency; you will read more about this in Chapter 13.

The years since Richard Nixon won the presidency in 1968 have been marked by divided government—that is, by a situation in which one of the major parties occupies the White House and the other party holds a majority of the seats in one or both houses of Congress. Over much of the past 40 years, Republicans have lived in the White House and Democrats have controlled Capitol Hill.[5] That circumstance was reversed from 1995 to 2001, however.

Through much of our history, newly elected Presidents have regularly swept many of their party's candidates into office with them—"on their coattails." Thus, the Democrats gained 62 seats in the House of Representatives when Woodrow Wilson won his first term in 1912, and they picked up 97 seats when FDR was first elected in 1932. But the victories of several recent Presidents—like George W. Bush in 2000—have not carried the coattail effect.

The Republicans lost seats in the House and Senate in 2000 but did manage to keep a narrow hold on both chambers. The Democrats reclaimed the upper house in 2001, when a senator switched parties.

---

5 The Democrats held almost uninterrupted control of Congress from 1933 to 1995. Over those years, the Republicans controlled both houses of Congress for only two two-year periods—first, after the congressional elections of 1946, and then after those of 1952. The GOP did win control of the Senate (but not the House) in 1980; the Democrats recaptured the upper chamber in 1986.

Sparked by the prodigious campaign efforts of President Bush, the Republicans won back the Senate and padded their slim majority in the House in the off-year elections of 2002 and continued their winning ways in 2004. Mr. Bush defeated his Democratic opponent, Senator John Kerry of Massachusetts, and his party kept its narrow grip on both the House and Senate in the hard-fought congressional elections of that year.

The GOP suffered significant losses in the off-year elections that followed, however. The Democrats, riding the wave of increasing dissatisfaction with several Bush administration policies and, in particular, mounting opposition to the war in Iraq, regained control of both houses of Congress in the November 2006 elections.

The Democrat's slim margins in the House and Senate were strengthened considerably in the elections of 2008, as they took even more seats away from the Republicans in both chambers. And in the presidential contest, their candidate, Senator Barack Obama of Illinois, bested his Republican rival, Senator John McCain of Arizona.

In the midterm elections of 2010, however, the Democrats succumbed to voter frustration over the nation's continuing economic troubles and other thorny issues. The GOP won a strong majority in the House, marking the biggest gain in that chamber by either major party since 1948. The Democrats did manage to retain their majority in the Senate, however.

**Essential Questions Journal** To continue to build a response to the chapter Essential Question, go to your **Essential Questions Journal.**

## SECTION 2 ASSESSMENT

1. **Guiding Question** Use your completed table to answer the question: How has the two-party system affected the history of American government?

**Key Terms and Comprehension**
2. Briefly describe the overall pattern in the way the two major parties have competed for and held power in American history.
3. What is **sectionalism**?
4. What characterizes the present political era that began in 1968?

**Critical Thinking**
5. **Draw Conclusions** Do you think one-party rule or divided government comes closer to the ideal the Framers had when they envisioned a government without political parties?
6. **Synthesize Information** How do political and economic crises hinder or help candidates get elected? Use specific examples from the section to support your answer.

**Quick Write**

**Persuasive Writing: Gather Details** Using the Internet or other resources, carry out research to find out how political parties view (or viewed) one of the issues that you listed in Section 1. Take notes on your findings.

## Assessment Answers

**1.** A strong answer will explain that the struggle between the two parties to gain power has created four distinct eras in American history, each hinging on a significant historical event.

**2.** In general, the history of American government can be divided into four eras, three of which were dominated by one or the other major party. In the current era, neither party has managed to gain lasting control.

**3.** devotion to the interests of a particular region

**4.** divided government, in which one major party holds the presidency while the other holds the majority of seats in one or both houses of Congress

**5.** Sample answer: Divided government more closely represents the Framers' ideal of no party. Since no one party has firm control, the parties must compromise to get anything done. The Framers intended members of government to cooperate. When one party controls both the White House and Congress, then it has little incentive to listen to the ideas of the opposing party.

**6.** Sample answer: Political or economic crises create discontent and a demand for political change. The Great Depression helped Franklin Roosevelt win. Conflicts over the Vietnam War and civil rights opened the door for Richard Nixon, but Watergate forced him out. Gerald Ford pardoned Nixon, helping to doom his re-election bid. Economic troubles and the Iranian hostage crisis led to Jimmy Carter's reelection defeat.

**QUICK WRITE** Students will research their issue to find out how political parties viewed it.

# SECTION 3
# The Minor Parties

**Guiding Question**

**What role have minor parties played in American politics?** Use a flowchart to take notes on the role of minor parties in American politics.

| Minor Parties | | | |
|---|---|---|---|
| Ideological | Single-Issue | Economic Protest | Splinter |
| • • | • • | • • | • • |
| • | • | • | • |

**Political Dictionary**
- ideological parties
- single-issue parties
- economic protest parties
- splinter parties

**Objectives**
1. Identify the types of minor parties that have been active in American politics.
2. Understand why minor parties are important despite the fact that none has ever won the presidency.

**Images Above:** George C. Wallace, governor of Alabama, campaigned for President in 1968 as a member of the American Independent Party.

Libertarian, Reform, Socialist, Prohibition, Natural Law, Communist, American Independent, Green, Constitution—these are only some of the many parties that have fielded presidential candidates in recent years and continue to do so. You know that none of these parties or their candidates has any real chance of winning the presidency. But this is not to say that minor parties are unimportant. The bright light created by the two major parties too often blinds us to the vital role several minor parties have played in American politics.

## Minor Parties in the United States

Their number and variety make minor parties difficult to describe and classify. Some have limited their efforts to a particular locale, others to a single State, and some to one region of the country. Still others have tried to woo the entire nation. Most have been short-lived, but a few have existed for decades. And, while most have lived, mothlike, around the flame of a single idea, some have had a broader, more practical base. Still, four distinct types of minor parties can be identified.

**Ideological Parties** The **ideological parties** are those based on a particular set of beliefs—a comprehensive view of social, economic, and political matters. Most of these minor parties have been built on some shade of Marxist thought; the Socialist, Socialist Labor, Socialist Worker, and Communist parties are leading examples of that fact.

A few ideological parties have had a quite different approach, however—especially the Libertarian Party of today, which emphasizes individualism and calls for doing away with most of government's present functions and programs. The ideological parties have seldom been able to win many votes. As a rule, however, they have been long-lived.

**Single-Issue Parties** The **single-issue parties** focus on a single public question. Their names have usually indicated their primary concern. Thus, the Free Soil Party opposed the spread of slavery in the 1840s and 1850s; the American Party, also called the "Know Nothings," opposed Irish-Catholic immigration in the 1850s; and the Right to Life Party opposes abortion today.

# Focus on the Basics

**FACTS:** • There are four types of minor parties: ideological, single-issue, economic protest, and splinter. • Even though minor parties do not win most elections, they play an important role as critics and innovators. • Minor parties affect election outcomes mainly by taking votes away from the major parties.

**CONCEPTS:** popular sovereignty, role of government in public policy

**ENDURING UNDERSTANDINGS:** • Minor parties rarely win elections but can have a significant impact on election outcomes. • Minor parties represent views and calls for change that are not embraced by the major parties and that otherwise might be overlooked.

**GUIDING QUESTION**

## What role have minor parties played in American politics?

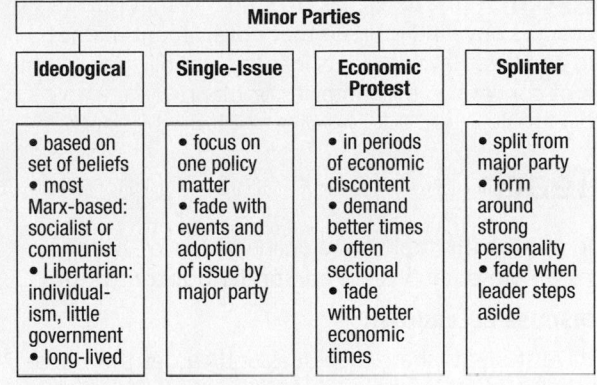

| Minor Parties | | | |
|---|---|---|---|
| **Ideological** | **Single-Issue** | **Economic Protest** | **Splinter** |
| • based on set of beliefs<br>• most Marx-based: socialist or communist<br>• Libertarian: individualism, little government<br>• long-lived | • focus on one policy matter<br>• fade with events and adoption of issue by major party | • in periods of economic discontent<br>• demand better times<br>• often sectional<br>• fade with better economic times | • split from major party<br>• form around strong personality<br>• fade when leader steps aside |

# Get Started

**LESSON GOALS**

Students will . . .

- describe the categories of minor parties by examining an illustration.
- learn about minor parties by creating an identity and a campaign flyer for a fictitious minor party.
- examine the possible impact of minor parties on a recent presidential election.

**BEFORE CLASS**

Assign the section, the graphic organizer in the text, and the Reading Comprehension Worksheet (Unit 2 All-in-One, p. 27) before class.

**L2 Differentiate** Reading Comprehension Worksheet (Unit 2 All-in-One, p. 28)

## SKILLS DEVELOPMENT

**INNOVATE AND THINK CREATIVELY**

To teach the skill of thinking creatively, have students read Innovate and Think Creatively in the Skills Handbook, p. S23. Then have them create their own minor political parties using the Core Worksheet.

## BELLRINGER

Write on the board: **In your notebook, list three current political or public policy issues or causes that interest you. Then rank them in order of importance to American society.**

**L2 Differentiate** Explain to students that public policy is any kind of issue that government might try to address. Have students identify a public policy that is of concern to their families or friends.

# Teach

To present this topic using online resources, use the lesson presentations at **PearsonSchool.com/phgovt.**

### DISCUSS BELLRINGER

Have students share the issues and causes they identified in the Bellringer activity. *(Some might include climate change, taxes, or government ethics.)* List them on the board.

Tell students that in this lesson, they will create their own minor political parties. Each party will focus on a particular issue or cause. They can use the Bellringer lists to help them decide on the focus of their party.

### DISPLAY TRANSPARENCIES

Display Transparency 5F, Four Types of Minor Political Parties. Discuss how each illustration relates to the descriptions of the four types of parties in the textbook.

Display Transparency 5G, Presidential Election of 1912. Tell students that this election highlights the role of minor parties in our political system. Ask: **What is the significance of the fact that there are three figures in the cartoon?** *(Man on elephant: Republican William Howard Taft; man on donkey: Democrat Woodrow Wilson; man on moose: Theodore Roosevelt of Bull Moose Party—a splinter party)* **What is the cartoon's message?** *(The cartoon shows Wilson pulling ahead because Roosevelt's Bull Moose Party, which split off from the Republican Party, is holding Taft back.)*

Review answers to the Reading Comprehension Worksheet to ensure that students understand the differences between the types of parties.

## Answers

**Checkpoint** Economic protest parties focus on broad economic concerns—"hard times"—while single-issue parties are intently focused on a specific policy issue.

**138** Political Parties

---

✔**Checkpoint**
How are economic protest parties different from single-issue parties?

**smorgasbord**
*n.* widely varied assortment or collection

**agrarian**
*adj.* relating to the land or its cultivation

Most of the single-issue parties have faded into history. They died away as events have passed them by, as their themes have failed to attract voters, or as one or both of the major parties have taken their key issues as their own.

**Economic Protest Parties** The **economic protest parties** have been rooted in periods of economic discontent. Unlike the socialist parties, these groups have not had any clear-cut ideological base. Rather, they have proclaimed their disgust with the major parties and demanded better times, and have focused their anger on such real or imagined enemies as the monetary system, "Wall Street bankers," the railroads, or foreign imports.

Often, they have been sectional parties, drawing their strength from the agricultural South and West. The Greenback Party tried to take advantage of <u>agrarian</u> discontent from 1876 through 1884. It appealed to struggling farmers by calling for the free coinage of silver, federal regulation of the railroads, an income tax, and labor legislation. A descendant of the Greenbacks, the Populist Party of the 1890s also demanded public ownership of railroads, telephone and telegraph companies, lower tariffs, and the adoption of the initiative and referendum.

Each of these economic protest parties has disappeared as the nation has climbed out of the difficult economic period in which that party arose.

**Splinter Parties** Those that have split away from one of the major parties are known as **splinter parties.** Most of the more important minor parties in our politics have been splinter parties. Among the leading groups that have split away from the Republicans are Theodore Roosevelt's "Bull Moose" Progressive Party of 1912 and Robert La Follette's Progressive Party of 1924. From the Democrats have come Henry Wallace's Progressive Party and the States' Rights (Dixiecrat) Party, both of 1948, and George Wallace's American Independent Party of 1968.

Most splinter parties have formed around a strong personality—most often someone who has failed to win his or her major party's presidential nomination. These parties

have faded or collapsed when that leader has stepped aside. Thus, the Bull Moose Progressive Party passed away when Theodore Roosevelt returned to the Republican fold after the election of 1912. Similarly, the American Independent Party lost nearly all of its brief strength when Governor George Wallace rejoined the Democrats after his strong showing in the presidential race in 1968.

Like many minor parties in American politics, the Green Party, founded in 1996, is difficult to classify. The Green Party began as a classic single-issue party but, as the party has evolved, it simply will not fit into any of the categories set out here. The Green Party came to prominence in 2000, with Ralph Nader as its presidential nominee. His campaign was built around a <u>smorgasbord</u> of issues—environmental protection, of course, but also universal healthcare, campaign finance reform, restraints on corporate power, and much more.

The Greens refused to nominate Ralph Nader in either 2004 or 2008. In 2004, they instead chose attorney and political activist David Cobb—who built his presidential campaign around most of the positions the Greens had supported in 2000.

In 2008, the Green Party nominated Cynthia McKinney, a former Democratic congresswoman from Georgia. Among the positions supported by McKinney were an end to the war in Iraq, universal health care, and repeal of the Patriot Act.

## Why Minor Parties Are Important

Even though most Americans do not support them, minor parties have still had a considerable impact on American politics and on the major parties. For example, it was a minor party, the Anti-Masons, that first used a national convention to nominate a presidential candidate in 1831. The National Republicans and then the Democrats followed suit in 1832. Ever since, national conventions have been used by both the Democrats and the Republicans to pick their presidential tickets.

Minor parties can have a telling effect in other ways. Thus, a strong third-party candidacy can play a decisive role—often a

**138** Political Parties

---

# Differentiated Resources

The following resources are located in the All-in-One, Unit 2, Chapter 5, Section 3:

**L3** Reading Comprehension Worksheet (p. 27)
**L2** Reading Comprehension Worksheet (p. 28)
**L3** Core Worksheet (p. 29)
**L3** **L4** Extend Worksheet (p. 31)
**L3** Quiz A (p. 33)
**L2** Quiz B (p. 34)

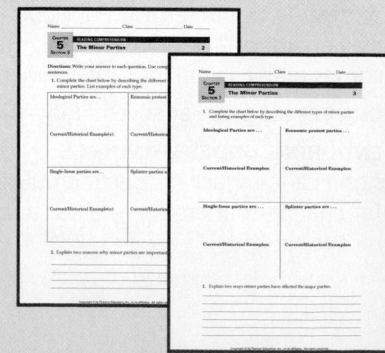

# How Government Works

## Significant Minor Parties

**GOVERNMENT ONLINE**

For an **interactive** version of Significant Minor Parties, visit PearsonSchool.com/phgovt

**INTERACTIVE**

Minor parties have played important roles in our political history, sometimes forcing one or both major parties to adopt new positions on public policy matters. *Have any third-party candidates had an impact on presidential elections in recent years? Explain.*

▶ Eugene Debs, pictured far right on this 1912 campaign button, led the Socialist Party, an ideological party founded in 1900.

▲ The Free Soil Party is an example of a single-issue party. It campaigned against the spread of slavery into the western States and territories. Former Democratic President Martin Van Buren ran as the party's presidential candidate in 1848.

▶ In 1924, Robert La Follette led the Progressive Party, a splinter party that broke away from the Republican Party.

*Robt. M. La Follette*

### Strong Minor Party Efforts, 1848 to Today*

| Year | Party | % Popular Vote | Electoral Votes |
|------|-------|----------------|-----------------|
| 1848 | Free Soil | 10.13 | --- |
| 1856 | Whig-American | 21.55 | 8 |
| 1860 | Constitutional Union | 12.64 | 39 |
| 1880 | Greenback | 3.36 | --- |
| 1888 | Prohibition | 2.19 | --- |
| 1892 | Populist | 8.54 | 22 |
|      | Prohibition | 2.19 | --- |
| 1904 | Socialist | 2.98 | --- |
| 1908 | Socialist | 2.82 | --- |
| 1912 | Progressive (Bull Moose) | 27.39 | 88 |
|      | Socialist | 5.99 | --- |
| 1916 | Socialist | 3.17 | --- |
| 1920 | Socialist | 3.45 | --- |
| 1924 | Progressive | 16.61 | 13 |
| 1932 | Socialist | 2.22 | --- |
| 1948 | States' Rights (Dixiecrat) | 2.41 | 39 |
|      | Progressive | 2.37 | --- |
| 1968 | American Independent | 13.53 | 46 |
| 1996 | Reform | 8.40 | --- |
| 2000 | Green | 2.74 | --- |

*Includes all minor parties that polled at least 2% of the popular vote. SOURCE: U.S. Census Bureau; *Historical Statistics of the United States, Colonial Times to 1970*

▶▶ **Analyzing Charts** Minor parties have sometimes had significant impact on presidential elections. *Using the data in the chart, which of these minor parties may have changed election results?*

## Debate

Ross Perot became a popular phenomenon in the 1992 presidential campaign. In 30-minute infomercials, he expressed his dissatisfaction with the government's performance on issues such as deficit spending and corrupt campaign financing. That year he received 19 percent of the national vote. He ran again in 1996, but his support had waned, and he received only 8 percent of the vote.

"Exit polls also show that more people would have voted for Perot if they thought he had a chance to win—his vote total could have approached 40 percent."

—*New York Times Magazine,* March 31, 1996

Use this quote to start a debate. Ask: **Should people base their vote for a candidate on whether or not they think that candidate can win?**

## DISTRIBUTE CORE WORKSHEET

Distribute the Chapter 5 Section 3 Core Worksheet (Unit 2 All-in-One, p. 29), in which students create their own minor political parties. Have students work through the steps to create an identity and a flyer for their own minor political party. Have students present their flyers to the class. Students should explain the reasons for their decisions and choices.

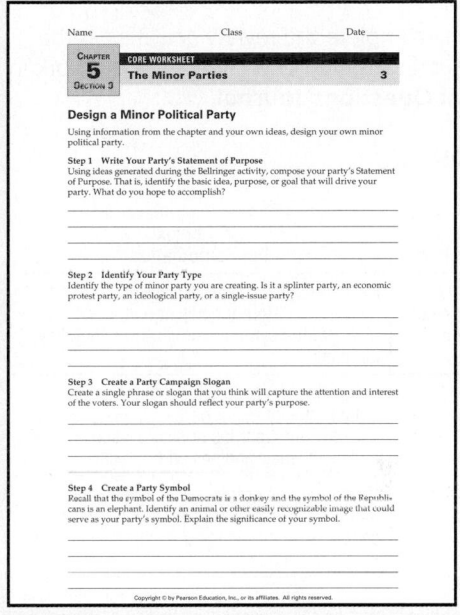

**L1 L2 Differentiate** Allow students to select specific steps in the activity to work on as an alternative to the entire activity.

**L3 L4 Differentiate** Have students answer the bonus question to the activity and share their answers with the class during their flyer presentations.

## EXTEND THE LESSON

**L3 L4 Differentiate** Distribute the Chapter 5 Section 3 Extend Worksheet (Unit 2 All-in-One, p. 31). This worksheet provides the vote counts for major and minor parties in Florida and the nation for the 2000 elections. The questions lead the students to consider how minor parties might have affected the outcome of the election.

Tell students to go to the interactivity to learn more about minor parties.

## Answers

**Significant Minor Parties** Students might mention Ralph Nader (Green Party), who helped make the 2000 election one of the closest and most controversial in U.S. history.

**Analyzing Charts** The most obvious example is the Progressive (Bull Moose) Party, which took a substantial share of electoral votes, but other parties include the Constitutional Union in 1860, the Dixiecrats in 1948, and the American Independent Party in 1968.

# Assess and Remediate

**L3** Collect the Core Worksheets and assess the students' class participation, using the Rubric for Assessing Student Performance on a Project (Unit 2 All-in-One, p. 252).

**L3** Assign the Section 3 Assessment questions.

**L3** Section Quiz A (Unit 2 All-in-One, p. 33)

**L2** Section Quiz B (Unit 2 All-in-One, p. 34)

Have students complete the review activities in the digital lesson presentation and continue their work in the **Essential Questions Journal.**

## REMEDIATION

| If Your Students Have Trouble With | Strategies For Remediation |
|---|---|
| Identifying the different types of minor parties (Question 2) | Have students create an illustrated table that shows the different types of minor parties, along with a symbol that captures their key qualities. |
| Distinguishing between the different types of minor parties (Questions 2, 3) | Have students compare and contrast different pairings of minor parties, such as economic protest parties or single issue parties, and share their findings with the class. |
| Understanding the possible impact of minor parties (Question 4) | Have students create a scenario in which a minor-party candidate prevents major party candidates from winning a majority in the electoral college. |
| Understanding the roles of minor parties (Questions 1, 5, 6) | Have students create an outline for the portion of the section entitled "Why Minor Parties Are Important." |

## Answers

**Caption** Possible response: A moose is a huge, powerful animal. This image would play up Roosevelt's strength and vigor.

**Checkpoint** by drawing attention to important or controversial issues that the major parties may have ignored

Former President Theodore Roosevelt became the Progressive or "Bull Moose" party's nominee in 1912 after losing the Republican Party's nomination. *How might this image have been used by the Progressive Party in the 1912 election?*

### ✓ Checkpoint
How do minor parties act as critics of the major parties?

"spoiler role"—in an election. In a presidential contest, even if a minor party ticket fails to win any electoral votes, it can still pull enough support away from one of the major parties to affect the outcome of the election. Many analysts think that Ralph Nader and the Green Party did exactly that to Al Gore and the Democratic Party in 2000. The spoiler effect can occur in any national, State, or local election.

In 1912, a split in the Republican Party resulted in Theodore Roosevelt's third-party candidacy. Almost certainly, if Roosevelt had not quit the Republican Party, William Howard Taft would have fared much better, and Woodrow Wilson would not have become President.

**innovator**
*n.* one who introduces a new approach

Historically, however, minor parties have been most important in their roles of critic and innovator. Unlike the major parties, they have been ready, willing, and able to take quite clear-cut stands on controversial issues. Many of the more important issues of American politics were first brought to the public's attention by a minor party—among them, the progressive income tax, women's suffrage, and railroad and banking regulation. Oddly enough, this very important innovator role of the minor parties has also been a major source of their frustration. When their proposals have gained any real degree of popular support, one and sometimes both of the major parties have taken over those ideas. The late Norman Thomas, who was six times the Socialist Party's candidate for President, often complained that "the major parties are stealing from my platform."

Altogether, 21 minor-party and independent presidential candidates, some of them nominated by more than one party, appeared on the ballots of at least one State in 2008. The most visible minor-party presidential campaigns in the most recent election were those of the Green, Libertarian, Constitution, and Socialist parties. More than a thousand minor-party and independent candidates also sought seats in Congress and ran for various State and local offices around the country.

**Essential Questions Journal** To continue to build a response to the chapter Essential Question, go to your **Essential Questions Journal.**

## SECTION 3 ASSESSMENT

1. **Guiding Question** Use your completed flowchart to answer the question: What role have minor parties played in American politics?

**Key Terms and Comprehension**

2. How do **ideological parties** differ from **single-issue parties**?

3. (a) Why do **splinter parties** develop? (b) What usually happens to these break-away parties?

4. In what ways can minor parties impact elections in this country?

**Critical Thinking**

5. **Identify Points of View** Why do you think a leader or group might seek to create a minor party even though their chances for winning are less than those of a major party?

6. **Express Problems Clearly** A minor party is likely to be a victim of its own success. Explain the meaning of this statement.

**Quick Write**

**Persuasive Writing: Review Arguments** Make a list of each party's most persuasive arguments on the issue you selected in Sections 1 and 2. Review your lists and decide with which party you most agree or disagree. Note any arguments from the opposing party that you find compelling.

# Assessment Answers

**1.** Minor parties have played the role of spoiler and innovator. They often draw attention to important and controversial issues that the major parties avoid. When a minor party has gathered enough public support, the major parties often adopt the minor party's issue as their own.

**2.** Ideological parties are generally organized around a broad set of beliefs, whereas single-issue parties are focused only on one issue.

**3.** (a) Splinter parties develop when a smaller group splits away from one of the major parties. They usually form around a strong personality. (b) Splinter parties often fade when the leader steps aside, typically to rejoin a major party.

**4.** Typically, minor parties don't have a strong impact on elections, although several minor party candidates have played a spoiler role, taking votes away from a major party candidate. Minor parties serve as innovators and draw attention to important and controversial issues that major parties might then add to their own platforms.

**5.** Possible answer: They may hope to gain enough public support to create change or pressure the major parties into adopting the issue.

**6.** Possible answer: A minor party will not become too successful, because as soon as it achieves some success, a major party will likely take over its ideas.

**QUICK WRITE** Students should review the parties' arguments and decide with which party they most agree or disagree.

# Working on a Political Campaign

**CAMPAIGNING IN FULL SWING DURING LAST DAYS OF ELECTION**

"In the final days of the campaign, both camps worked furiously for success on election day. Phone banks made thousands of calls to convince undecided voters and supporters held campaign signs at every intersection. The candidates themselves rushed from appearance to appearance, all in an exhausting sprint to the finish in this hotly contested election."

Elections are a great celebration of our democratic system. Even if you cannot vote, you can still play a part in deciding who our leaders will be. While many political campaigns have paid staff, it is the volunteers who perform much of the actual work. A strong volunteer group can spell the difference between victory and defeat. Here's how:

1. **Get to Know the Candidate** One excellent way to learn about the candidates is to visit their Web sites. Candidates might have a short biography, videos, press releases, and blogs posted. If a candidate does not have a Web site, his or her campaign office can provide similar information. You might also try to see the candidate in person.

2. **Choose a Candidate** Once you are more familiar with a candidate and his or her positions, decide if that candidate's beliefs match your own. It is important to volunteer your time for a person you believe in. Be prepared to talk about his or her views convincingly.

3. **Find Out About Volunteer Opportunities** Political campaigns offer a wide range of volunteer opportunities. A candidate may be looking for people to go door-to-door to seek support. The campaign may need people to host or even just attend events. Most campaigns need people to make phone calls or send out mailings of campaign literature. Campaigns also appreciate financial contributions.

4. **Choose a Task** Before you choose a task, be sure you are capable of fulfilling it. For example, if you do not have access to a car or a ride, avoid a task that would need transportation. If your studies are demanding, do not commit to making phone calls every night. Though you may not be able to do every job, you will be able to find some way to get involved and hopefully you will find it a rewarding experience.

## ▸▸ What do you think?

1. Whom should you contact to find out which candidates are running for office in your town or State?
2. How might volunteering for a campaign help you become a more informed voter?
3. **You Try It** Follow the steps above to work on a political campaign. Keep a journal about your activities during the campaign and reflect on your experience.

**GOVERNMENT ONLINE**
**Citizenship Activity Pack**
For an activity about working on a political campaign, go to **PearsonSchool.com/phgovt**

141

## Citizenship Activity Pack

**L1 L2** If your students need extra support, use the Citizenship Activity Pack lesson *How to Work on a Political Campaign*. It includes a lesson plan for you and campaign strategy briefs and worksheets for students. Student teams will prepare a campaign strategy for a fictitious candidate, based on their assigned campaign brief. Teams will present their strategies to the teacher/candidate. Students will use worksheets to assess strategies and to write a letter of introduction to a campaign manager. Students may also access the Citizenship Activity Pack online for another activity about working on a political campaign at **PearsonSchool.com/phgovt.**

## LESSON GOAL

• Students will identify and explore opportunities for volunteer involvement in a political campaign.

# Teach

## BRAINSTORM

Have students read the news story about the election campaign at the beginning of the Citizenship 101 lesson. As a class, have students generate a list of activities that are mentioned in the news article that might be performed by volunteers. Students should identify such campaign activities as participating in phone banks, holding signs at intersections, and helping organize and hold campaign appearances.

## EXPLORE CANDIDATES

As a class, discuss ways students can identify and learn about candidates in an election. Have students generate a list of possible sources of information—candidate Web sites, campaign offices, newspapers, and appearances. If students have computer access, have them bring in examples of campaign Web sites.

## EXPLORE OPPORTUNITIES

Have students follow steps 3 and 4 to generate a list of possible volunteer opportunities. Then have them select one that they feel they would be qualified to perform. Ask students to write a paragraph explaining why their choice was appropriate for them.

# Assess and Remediate

Collect the students' paragraphs and assess them. You may also wish to have them answer the What Do You Think questions at the bottom of the page.

## Answers

1. Students can contact local or state election officials to find out who is on the ballot. They may also find this information through reliable print or online sources.

2. A strong answer should consider how getting involved in a campaign might allow a volunteer to learn about issues in the campaign and about the different views of the candidates.

3. Strong responses should describe the tasks students did and what they learned from the experience.

## How are political parties organized at the federal, State, and local levels?

| Party Organization | | |
| --- | --- | --- |
| **National** | **State** | **Local** |
| • National convention<br>• National committee<br>• National chairperson | • Central committee<br>• State chairperson | • Vary widely<br>• Units in each electoral district |

# Get Started

## LESSON GOALS

Students will . . .

- learn about the activities of party organizations by analyzing an excerpt from a periodical.
- design political activities for a campaign at the local, State, and national levels.

## BEFORE CLASS

Assign the section, the graphic organizer in the text, and the Reading Comprehension Worksheet (Unit 2 All-in-One, p. 35) before class.

**L2** **Differentiate** Reading Comprehension Worksheet (Unit 2 All-in-One, p. 36)

## BELLRINGER

Write on the board: **In your notebook, explain what this means: "[Both parties] are highly decentralized, fragmented, and often plagued by factions and internal squabbling."**

**L2** **ELL Differentiate** Help students define any unfamiliar words in the statement.

# SKILLS DEVELOPMENT

## PROBLEM SOLVING

Before students work on Core Worksheet B in this lesson, you may want to review tips on problem solving in the Skills Handbook, p. S17.

---

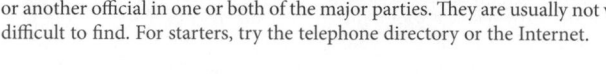

SECTION **4**

## Party
# Organization

**How are political parties organized at the federal, State, and local levels?** Use a table to take notes on how political parties are organized.

| Party Organization | | |
| --- | --- | --- |
| **National** | **State** | **Local** |
| • | • | • |
| • | • | • |
| • | • | • |

**Political Dictionary**
- ward
- precinct

**Objectives**
1. Understand why the major parties have a decentralized structure.
2. Describe the national party machinery and party organization at the State and local levels.

**Image Above:** Howard Dean served as the Democratic Party's national chairperson in the 2008 election.

**H**ow strong, how active, and how well organized are the Republican and Democratic parties in your community? Contact the county chairperson or another official in one or both of the major parties. They are usually not very difficult to find. For starters, try the telephone directory or the Internet.

## The Decentralized Nature of the Parties

The two major parties are often described as though they were highly organized, close-knit, well-disciplined groups. However, neither party is anything of the kind. They are, instead, highly decentralized, fragmented, and often plagued by factions and internal squabbling.

Neither party has a chain of command running from the national through the State to the local level. Each of the State party organizations is only loosely tied to the party's national structure. By the same token, local party organizations are often quite independent of their parent State organizations. These various party units usually cooperate with one another, of course—but that is not always the case.

**The Role of the Presidency** The President's party is almost always more solidly united and better organized than the other major party. The President is automatically the party's leader, and asserts that leadership with such tools as ready access to the media, personal popularity, the power to make appointments to federal office, and the ability to dispense other favors.

The other party has no one in an even faintly comparable position. Indeed, in the American party system, there is seldom any one person who can truly be called the leader of the party out of power. Rather, a number of personalities, frequently in competition with one another, form a loosely identifiable leadership group in that party.[6]

---

6 The party out of power does have a temporary leader for a brief time every fourth year: its presidential candidate, from nomination to election day. A defeated presidential candidate is often called the party's "titular leader"—a leader in title, by custom, but not in fact. What's more, if he or she lost by a wide margin, the defeated nominee may have little or no role to play in ongoing party affairs.

---

# Focus on the Basics

**FACTS:** • Federalism and the nominating process contribute to a decentralized party structure. • Neither major party has a strong chain of command from the national to the local level. • Nationally, each major party has these basic elements: convention, committee, chairperson, and two congressional campaign committees. • A central committee, headed by a chairperson, typically leads State party organizations.

**CONCEPTS:** party decentralization, elements of party structure

**ENDURING UNDERSTANDINGS:** • Both major parties are decentralized and fragmented. • There are distinct national and State party organizations. • The President's leadership helps unify the party in power.

**The Impact of Federalism** Federalism is a major reason for the decentralized nature of the two major political parties. Remember, the basic goal of the major parties is to gain control of government by winning elective offices.

Today there are more than *half a million* elective offices in the United States. We elect more people to public office in this country than do the voters of any other country on the planet. In the American federal system, those offices are widely distributed over the national, State, and local levels. In short, because the governmental system is highly decentralized, so too are the major parties that serve it.

**The Nominating Process** The nominating process is also a major cause of party decentralization. Recall, from Section 1, that the nominating process has a central role in the life of political parties. You will consider the selection of candidates at some length in Chapter 7, but, for now, look at two related aspects of that process.

First, candidate selection is an intraparty process. That is, nominations are made *within* the party. Second, the nominating process can be, and often is, a <u>divisive</u> one. Where there is a fight over a nomination, that contest pits members of the same party against one another: Republicans fight Republicans; Democrats battle Democrats. In short, the prime function of the major parties—the making of nominations—is also a prime cause of their highly fragmented character.

## National Party Machinery

At the national level, both major parties are composed of five basic elements. They are structured around a national convention, a national committee, a national chairperson, and two congressional campaign committees.

**The National Convention** The national convention, often described as the party's national voice, meets in the late summer of every presidential election year to pick the party's presidential and vice-presidential candidates. It also performs a few other functions, as you will see in Chapter 13, including

the adoption of the party's rules and the writing of its platform.

Beyond that, however, the convention has little authority. It has no control over the party's selection of candidates for any other offices nor over the policy stands those nominees take. Often, a national convention does play a role in making peace among various factions in the party, helping them to accept a party platform that will appeal to a wide range of voters in the general election.

**The National Committee** Between conventions, the party's affairs are handled, at least in theory, by the national committee and by the national chairperson. For years, each party's national committee was composed of a committeeman and a committeewoman from each State and several of the territories. They were chosen by the State's party organization. Over the past several years, however, both parties have expanded the committee's membership.

Today, the Republican National Committee (RNC) also seats the party chairperson from each State and members from the District of Columbia, Guam, American Samoa, Puerto Rico, and the Virgin Islands.

✔ **Checkpoint**
How does the nomination process contribute to intraparty conflict?

**divisive**
*adj.* causing disagreement

➤ **Analyzing Political Cartoons** *How does this cartoon illustrate the decentralized nature of political parties?*

## Differentiated Resources

The following resources are located in the All-in-One, Unit 2, Chapter 5, Section 4:

- **L3** Reading Comprehension Worksheet (p. 35)
- **L2** Reading Comprehension Worksheet (p. 36)
- **L3** Core Worksheet A (p. 37)
- **L3** Core Worksheet B (p. 39)
- **L3** Quiz A (p. 40)
- **L2** Quiz B (p. 41)
- **L3** Chapter Test A (p. 42)
- **L2** Chapter Test B (p. 45)

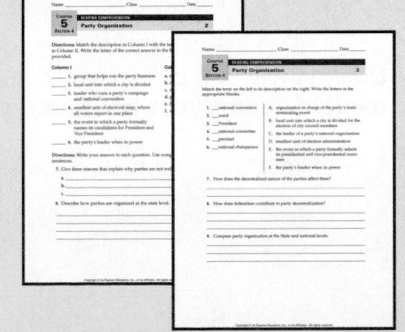

# Teach

To present this topic using online resources, use the lesson presentations at **PearsonSchool.com/phgovt.**

### DISCUSS BELLRINGER

Have students share their answers to the Bellringer question. *(The parties are not well-organized, cohesive groups. Instead, they are a loose-knit confederation of small pieces, and members often fight among themselves.)*

### DISTRIBUTE CORE WORKSHEET A

Distribute the Chapter 5 Section 4 Core Worksheet A (Unit 2 All-in-One, p. 37), in which students read a news report about a "get out the vote" campaign. This worksheet will stimulate their thinking about party activities, which will help them complete Core Worksheet B.

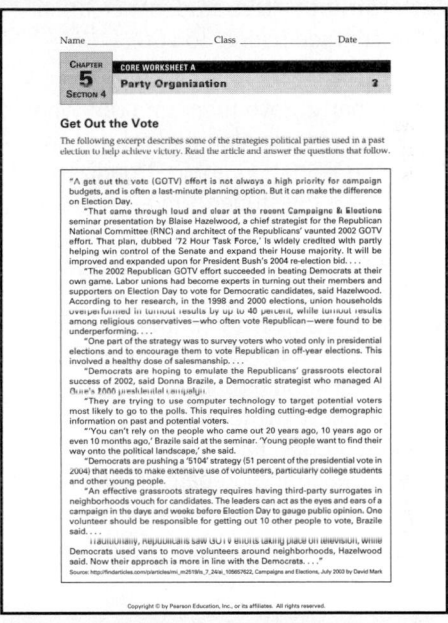

## Answers

**Checkpoint** by placing members of the same party against each other

**Analyzing Political Cartoons** by showing that each party is made up of different factions, each with its own agenda

## DISTRIBUTE CORE WORKSHEET B

Distribute the Chapter 5 Section 4 Core Worksheet B (Unit 2 All-in-One, p. 39), in which students map out a national campaign. Point out that a successful campaign requires activity on the national, State, and local levels. Divide students into groups representing each major party to plan their activities together. Encourage them to list specific activities targeted to specific goals.

**L1 L2 Differentiate** Have students focus on only one of the three levels—national, State, or local.

## EXTEND THE LESSON

**L3 Differentiate** Have students create a plan for organizing political activity at their school. Student plans should include components for identifying and registering possible voters, identifying possible volunteers, sharing information about candidates, and getting out the vote.

**L1 L2 ELL Differentiate** Have students create a poster that will encourage people to vote.

**L4 Differentiate** Divide students into two groups, one for each major party. Have them find out who leads their local party organization and ask for an interview. Display the T-Chart Graphic Organizer Transparency, and have the students in each group collaborate to create their own T-Chart to assist during the interview process. Tell groups that they should write a title on their chart, and suggest writing "Questions" and "Responses" in the column headers. Of course, the charts can be expanded as needed. Each group should prepare interview questions to find out how the local organization is structured and what it does. Each group should then interview the party leader and prepare an oral report for the class.

Tell students to go to the Audio Tour for a guided tour of the costs of running for office.

## Answers

**Checkpoint** The parties select their presidential and vice-presidential candidates, adopt party rules, and write the platform.

**Raising Funds for Public Office** Spending has grown significantly, suggesting that fundraising has become increasingly important in elections. Inviting well-known speakers to dinners could attract more possible contributors to the party.

---

✓**Checkpoint**
What happens at each party's national convention?

Representatives of such GOP-related groups as the National Federation of Republican Women also serve on the RNC.

The Democratic National Committee (DNC) is an even larger body. In addition to the committeeman and -woman from each State, it now includes the party's chairperson and vice-chairperson from every State and the territories. Moreover, its ranks now include a few dozen members from the party organizations of the larger States, and up to 75 at-large members chosen by the DNC itself. Several members of Congress, as well as governors, mayors, and members of the Young Democrats, also have seats on the DNC.

On paper, the national committee appears to be a powerful organization loaded with many of the party's leading figures. In fact, it does not have a great deal of clout. Most of its work centers on the staging of the party's national convention every four years.

**The National Chairperson** In each party, the national chairperson is the leader of the national committee. He or she is chosen to a four-year term by the national committee, at a

**GOVERNMENT** ONLINE
**Audio Tour**
Listen to a guided audio tour about fundraising at
PearsonSchool.com/phgovt

# Raising Funds for Public Office

Both parties spend a great deal of effort to make sure the party's officeholders stay in power. They raise money by holding large-scale dinners, soliciting donations on their Web sites, and in a wide variety of other ways. *What does the chart show about spending over the last several years? Why might well-known party members be invited to speak at dinners?*

**Fundraising Dinners** Parties invite donors to extravagant fundraising dinners to honor past Presidents and current party leaders.

**Spending for Congressional Campaign Committees**

Republicans: **$630**
Democrats: **$733**

Republicans: **$299**
Democrats: **$376**

(Millions of dollars)

300 — 250 — 200 — 150 — 100 — 50 — 0

1990    2006

SOURCE: Federal Election Commission

**Web Sites** For the 2008 election, the Democratic Party encouraged its supporters to purchase "Democracy Bonds."

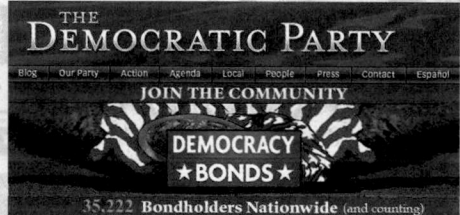

THE
**DEMOCRATIC PARTY**
Blog  Our Party  Action  Agenda  Local  People  Press  Contact  Español
**JOIN THE COMMUNITY**
**DEMOCRACY ★ BONDS ★**
35,222 **Bondholders Nationwide** (and counting)

---

# Debate

Use this quotation to start a debate in your classroom.

"All politics is local."

—"The Last Liberal" from *The New York Times,* March 11, 2001

Divide students into debate teams. Ask: **Do you agree or disagree with this statement? Support your position.**

meeting held right after the national convention. The choice is made by the just-nominated presidential candidate and is then ratified by the national committee.

Only two women have ever held that top party post. Jean Westwood of Utah chaired the DNC from her party's 1972 convention until late 1972; and Mary Louise Smith of Iowa headed the RNC from 1974 until early 1977. Each lost her post soon after her party lost a presidential election. To this point, only two African Americans have served as major party chairmen: Ron Brown, who headed the DNC from 1989 to 1993, and Michael Steele, who chaired the RNC from 2009–2011.

The national chairperson directs the work of the party's headquarters and its professional staff in Washington. In presidential election years, the committee's attention is focused on the national convention and then the campaign. In between presidential elections, the chairperson and the committee work to strengthen the party and its fortunes. They do so by promoting party unity, raising money, recruiting new voters, and otherwise preparing for the next presidential season. Both parties have lately established state-of-the-art technical facilities to help their candidates and officeholders better communicate with voters. Those sophisticated facilities include such things as television studios, satellite uplinks, constantly updated Web sites, and computerized voter registration lists.

## Congressional Campaign Committees
Each party also has a campaign committee in each house of Congress.[7] These committees work to reelect incumbents and to make sure that "open seats," seats given up by retiring members, remain in the party. The committees also take a hand in carefully selected campaigns to unseat incumbents in the other party, in those races where the chances for success seem to justify those efforts.

In both parties and in both houses, the members of these congressional campaign committees are chosen by their colleagues.

---

7 In the House: the National Republican Congressional Committee and the Democratic Congressional Campaign Committee; in the Senate: the National Republican Senatorial Campaign Committee and the Democratic Senatorial Campaign Committee

## Local Party Organization

Third Level:
Wards are divided into **precincts**.

**Precinct**

Second Level:
Cities and towns are divided into **wards**.

**Ward**

First Level:
States are divided into **congressional districts**.

**Congressional District**

▶▶ **Analyzing Diagrams** Local party organization can vary from State to State, but a common example is shown here. *What kind of party jobs do you think exist at each level of organization?*

They serve for two-year terms—that is, for a term of Congress.

## State and Local Party Machinery

National party organization is largely the product of custom and of rules adopted by the party's national conventions over time. At the State and local levels, on the other hand, party structure is largely determined by State law.

**The State Organization** In most States, party structure is decentralized, much as it is at the national level. It is usually built around

✔ **Checkpoint**
What do the national committees do between presidential elections?

---

# Assess and Remediate

**L3** Collect the Core Worksheets and assess the students' class participation, using the Rubric for Assessing Individual Performance in a Group (Unit 2 All-in-One, p. 251).

**L3** Assign the Section 4 Assessment questions.

**L3** Section Quiz A (Unit 2 All-in-One, p. 40)

**L2** Section Quiz B (Unit 2 All-in-One, p. 41)

Have students complete the review activities in the digital lesson presentation and continue their work in the **Essential Questions Journal.**

**Government**
**online**
*All print resources are available on the Teacher's Resource Library CD-ROM and online at PearsonSchool.com/phgovt.*

# Background

**Political Machines** In the 1900s, a type of local political organization began to appear in large American cities: the machine. Urban political machines are organizations run by a single "boss" or small group of powerful leaders. They use a variety of means, including legal and sometimes illegal control of jobs and contracts, to build broad political support. Once in control of a local government, the machine uses its power to expand its base and strengthen its grip on power. One infamous machine was New York's Tammany Hall of the late 1800s. Richard Daly's machine ruled Chicago for a period in the mid-1900s.

# Answers

**Analyzing Diagrams** Precinct-level jobs probably involve direct work with voters. Ward-level jobs may involve coordinating the work of precinct-level workers. District-level jobs may involve more strategic planning with the state-level organization in addition to coordinating activities.

**Checkpoint** promote party unity, fundraise, recruit new voters, and prepare for the next presidential election

| If Your Students Have Trouble With | Strategies For Remediation |
|---|---|
| Recognizing the causes of decentralized nature of parties (Questions 5 and 6) | Have students create a cause-and-effect diagram for each of the subheadings under "The Decentralized Nature of the Parties." |
| Identifying the main elements of major party national organization (Questions 1 and 3) | Have students create an illustrated diagram that shows in visual format the roles and purposes of the different parts of party machinery. |
| Identifying state and local party machinery (Question 4) | Have students create a pyramid-shaped diagram showing how parties are organized at the State and local levels. |
| Understanding the role of the President in uniting the party (Question 2) | Have students create a two-column table, listing leadership tools available to the President on the left and ways the President can use each tool to benefit individual party members on the right. |

## Answers

**Caption** State delegates should be an accurate reflection of the population of their state, and that would include people of different ethnic backgrounds, genders, and ages.

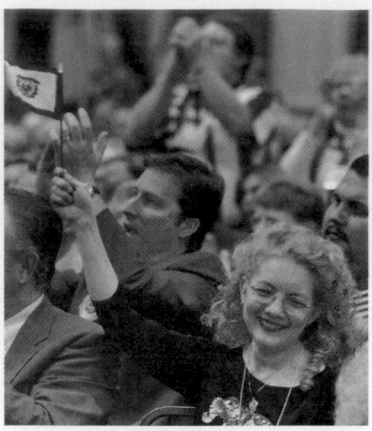

State delegates attending national conventions generally must represent the population demographics of their State. *Why might the gender, age, or ethnic background of a State delegate be important?*

**defy**
*v.* resist, frustrate

Because most of these committees meet only infrequently, the chairperson has great independence in conducting the party's affairs.

Together, the chairperson and the central committee work to further the party's interests in the State. Most of the time, they attempt to do this by building an effective organization and promoting party unity, finding candidates and campaign funds, and so on. Remember, however, both major parties are highly decentralized, fragmented, and sometimes torn by struggles for power. This can really complicate the chairperson's and the committee's job.

**Local Organization** Local party structures vary so widely that they nearly <u>defy</u> even a brief description. Generally, they follow the electoral map of the State, with a party unit for each district in which elective offices are to be filled: congressional and legislative districts, counties, cities and towns, wards, and precincts. A **ward** is a unit into which cities are often divided for the election of city council members. A **precinct** is the smallest unit of election administration; the voters in each precinct cast their ballots at one polling place located within the precinct.

In most larger cities, a party's organization is further broken down by residential blocks and sometimes even by apartment buildings. In some places, local party organizations are active year-round, but most often they are inactive except for those few hectic months before an election.

a State central committee, headed by a State chairperson. The chairperson, chosen by the committee, may be an important political figure in his or her own right. More often than not, however, he or she fronts for the governor, a U.S. senator, or some other powerful figure or group in the politics of the State.

The party's State central committee is almost everywhere composed of members who represent major geographic subdivisions, usually counties. They are chosen in primary elections, by local caucuses, or at State conventions.

> **Essential Questions Journal** To continue to build a response to the chapter Essential Question, go to your **Essential Questions Journal.**

## SECTION 4 ASSESSMENT

1. **Guiding Question** Use your completed table to answer the question: How are political parties organized at the federal, State, and local levels?

**Key Terms and Comprehension**

2. Describe the place of the presidency in national party organization.
3. Describe the role of the congressional campaign committees for each party.
4. What is the difference between a **ward** and a **precinct**?

**Critical Thinking**

5. **Recognize Cause and Effect** Why is party unity harder to achieve for the party out of power than it is for the party in power?
6. **Expressing Problems Clearly** Why do you think direct primaries create more conflict within parties than the other forms of the nominating process?

**Quick Write**

**Persuasive Writing: Decide on a Structure** Using the list of arguments from Section 3, arrange them in order from most persuasive to least persuasive or vice versa. Decide whether you would be more likely to persuade a reader by starting with weaker reasons and building to the best argument or, conversely, leading with your best argument.

## Assessment Answers

**1.** Organization at the federal level is structured around a national convention, committee, chairperson, and congressional campaign committee in each house. State-level organization centers on a central committee and a chairperson. Local organizations vary widely but generally have a party unit for each elective district.

**2.** The President helps unite the party with tools such as access to the media, personal popularity, and ability to make federal appointments and distribute other favors.

**3.** These committees exist in each house of Congress and work to reelect party members, make sure that seats abandoned by retiring members remain in the party, and to try to unseat incumbents of the opposing party in selected campaigns.

**4.** A ward is a larger division than a precinct. Wards are divided into precincts, the smallest unit of election administration.

**5.** The party in power has a clear leader—the President—who can use media attention and political clout to unify the party. The party out

of power has no clear leader. Its ill-defined leadership group consists of personalities often in competition with one another.

**6.** Direct primaries pit members of the same party against each other, causing division within the party as party members side with one candidate or the other.

**QUICK WRITE** Students will use their list of arguments to decide on a structure for persuasive writing.

# Quick Study Guide

**GOVERNMENT** ONLINE

**On the Go**
To review anytime, anywhere, download these online resources at **PearsonSchool.com/phgovt**
Political Dictionary, Audio Review

CHAPTER **5**

**Guiding Question**
**Section 2** How has the two-party system affected the history of American government?

**Guiding Question**
**Section 3** What role have minor parties played in American politics?

**Guiding Question**
**Section 1** What are political parties, and how do they function in our two-party system?

**CHAPTER 5**
**Essential Question**
Does the two-party system help or harm democracy?

**Guiding Question**
**Section 4** How are political parties organized at the federal, State, and local levels?

Rooted in American history and political tradition

Promoted by the electoral system and single-member districts

**Two-party System in American Government**

Characterized by eras of one-party domination

Encouraged by American ideological consensus

## Political Dictionary

political party *p. 122*
political spectrum *p. 123*
partisanship *p. 124*
single-member district *p. 127*
plurality *p. 127*
bipartisan *p. 127*
consensus *p. 127*
coalition *p. 128*
incumbent *p. 131*
faction *p. 131*
spoils system *p. 132*
electorate *p. 132*
sectionalism *p. 133*
ideological parties *p. 137*
single-issue parties *p. 137*
economic protest parties *p. 138*
splinter parties *p. 138*
ward *p. 146*
precinct *p. 146*

## Political Parties in the United States

| Major Parties | Minor Parties |
| --- | --- |
| • Historically, one of two parties with a realistic chance to win elections | • Have difficulty winning elections in the American party system |
| • Currently Democratic and Republican parties | • May form based on an ideology or single issue, as a result of bad economic times, or from an existing party |
| • One party may dominate national elections at times. | • Though rarely successful, they influence elections and the major parties. |
| • Both parties agree on some important issues and disagree on others. | |

Have students download the digital resources available at Government on the Go for review and remediation.

**STUDY TIPS**

**Making Outlines** Point out that preparing a good outline before starting to write ensures that writing goes more quickly and is more focused. An outline also will help students identify whether they have too much or not enough information and how their ideas connect. Have students first identify the topic of their essay, such as "Minor Parties in the most recent Presidential Election," and then list the main points they want to make. Under each main point, students should list the details that support that point. Generally speaking, each detail in their outline will translate into at least one paragraph in their final essay. After students have completed these steps, have them review the items and place them in the most logical order. Explain that, once they begin writing, they may decide to make changes in the outline, but the outline will serve as the general plan for their essays.

**ASSESSMENT AT A GLANCE**

**Tests and Quizzes**
Section Assessments
Section Quizzes A and B, Unit 2 **All-in-One**
Chapter Assessment
Chapter Tests A and B, Unit 2 **All-in-One**
Document-Based Assessment
Progress Monitoring Online
Exam*View* Test Bank

**Performance Assessment**
Essential Questions Journal
Debates, pp. 126, 134, 139, 144
Assessment Rubrics, **All-in-One**

# For More Information

To learn more about political parties, refer to these sources or assign them to students:

**L1** **Smalley, Carol Parenzan.** *Elections and Political Parties.* Perfection Learning, 2005.

**L2** **Burgan, Michael.** *Political Parties.* Graphic Library, 2008.

**L3** **Maisel, L. Sandy.** *American Political Parties and Elections: A Very Short Introduction.* Oxford University Press, 2007.

**L4** **Adkins, Randall E., ed.** *The Evolution of Political Parties, Campaigns, and Elections: Landmark Documents from 1787–2008.* CQ Press, 2008.

# Chapter Assessment

**COMPREHENSION AND CRITICAL THINKING**

## SECTION 1

1. Possible examples: **(a)** a caucus in Iowa, **(b)** holding a rally for a candidate, **(c)** a party recruiting a candidate for a vacant seat in Congress, **(d)** a party that controls Congress choosing the Speaker of the House to regulate House activities, **(e)** creating a TV commercial critical of an opposing party's position on tax reform

2. **(a)** Single-member districts and the fact that elected officials write election laws make it hard for minor-party and independent candidates to win elections. **(b)** Sample answer: Because only one winner can come out of each contest in single-member districts, voters tend to think that a vote for a minor-party candidate is a wasted vote.

3. In general parties in a multiparty system are based on a particular issue, providing voters more meaningful choices as well as more choices overall. Multiparty systems also tend to produce a broader, more diverse representation of the electorate. However, two-party systems are more stable because they don't result in coalition governments.

## SECTION 2

4. **(a)** two Republicans, parent and child **(b)** Possible answer: Party loyalty is often inherited or passed down through families. **(c)** Many people are loyal to certain parties with which they identify.

5. **(a)** The Federalists and Anti-Federalists emerged out of early debates over the ratification of the Constitution, as people took sides on the proper role of government. **(b)** Sample answer: Political parties have strengthened U.S. democracy by providing a vital link between the people and their government. Parties are the main means by which the will of the people is made known to government and by which government is held accountable to the people. Parties also blunt conflict, modify extreme views, encourage compromise, and help unify the people. For example, parties recruit qualified candidates and help ensure good performance in office. A party also informs the public of missteps of the opposing party.

6. A strong answer will consider that transitions tend to occur during times of national crisis, such as the Civil War and the Great Depression.

---

# Chapter Assessment

## Comprehension and Critical Thinking

### Section 1

1. Provide an example of a political party performing in the following roles: **(a)** nominating, **(b)** informing and activating, **(c)** serving as a bonding agent, **(d)** governing, **(e)** serving as a watchdog.

2. **(a)** What features of the electoral system support the existence of a two-party system? **(b)** Analyze one of these features and explain its role.

3. Compare and contrast two-party with multiparty systems, noting the strengths and weaknesses of each.

### Section 2

4. **Analyze Political Cartoons (a)** Who is represented in the political cartoon below? **(b)** What does this cartoon imply about party loyalty? **(c)** Do you think people are loyal to a certain party?

*"Yes, son, we're Republicans."*

### Section 1

5. **(a)** Describe the circumstances that led to the development of the first two political parties in American history. **(b)** Explain, using specific examples, how political parties strengthen or weaken U.S. democracy.

6. Consider the eras of one-party domination. What factors are necessary to cause a transition from one era to another?

### Section 3

7. Explain what type of minor party is likely to develop around the following: **(a)** a strong personality, **(b)** the collapse of the stock market, **(c)** a specific theory about government, **(d)** growing concern about climate change.

8. **(a)** State three reasons why a person might wish to vote for a minor party candidate in a presidential election. **(b)** How do minor parties strengthen or weaken the two-party system?

### Section 4

9. **(a)** What does it mean to say that the major parties in American politics are decentralized? **(b)** Would a more centralized political party be more or less effective in winning elections? Explain your answer.

10. **(a)** Define **ward** and **precinct**. **(b)** How does party organization contribute to the strength of the two-party system?

### Writing About Government

11. Use your Quick Write exercises from the chapter to write a newspaper editorial persuading others to support or oppose a political party on the issue you selected. Begin your editorial with the following prompt: I agree (or disagree) with the _____ party on the issue of _____. Cover both sides of the issue but take a clear stand on one side. See pp. S9–S10 of the Skills Handbook.

### Apply What You've Learned

12. **Essential Question Activity** Interview close friends or relatives who voted in the last election. Ask them if they identify themselves as members of a political party. Consider:

    **(a)** If they do not identify themselves as a member of a party, ask them why not.

    **(b)** If they do identify themselves as a party member, ask on what issues do they most agree and/or disagree with the party.

    **(c)** Ask them what might make them change their party affiliation. Then have them consider whether or not the two-party system helps or harms democracy.

13. **Essential Question Assessment** Based on your interviews and the content you have learned in this chapter, write an anonymous magazine profile about the people you interviewed that helps answer the Essential Question: **Does the two-party system help or harm democracy?**

**Essential Questions Journal** To respond to the chapter Essential Question, go to your **Essential Questions Journal.**

---

## SECTION 3

7. **(a)** splinter party **(b)** economic protest party **(c)** ideological party **(d)** single-issue party

8. **(a)** possible answer: to support a strong belief in the minor party's ideals, to express dissatisfaction with both major parties, or to influence the major parties in hopes of bringing about change **(b)** Sample answer: Minor parties strengthen the two-party system by initiating innovations and forcing the major parties to deal with important issues. They can weaken the two-party system by drawing away members or by acting as spoilers in elections.

## SECTION 4

9. **(a)** The parties do not have a single, strong, unified organization, but are instead composed of many small organizations at the national, State, and local levels. **(b)** A strong answer will consider that a centralized party would be able to coordinate efforts for maximum efficiency but could also be unwieldy and unable to respond to the needs or opinions of people in different parts of the country.

10. **(a)** A ward is a political unit into which cities are often divided for the election of city council members. A precinct is the

# Document-Based Assessment

## Political Parties

The Constitution says nothing about political parties. Yet they soon developed and quickly became a significant part of the governmental system—sometimes, a controversial part, as illustrated by the documents below.

### Document 1

"Let me now take a more comprehensive view, and warn you in the most solemn manner against the baneful effects of the spirit of party generally.

This spirit, unfortunately, is inseparable from our nature, having its root in the strongest passions of the human mind. It exists under different shapes in all governments, more or less stifled, controlled, or repressed; but, in those of the popular form, it is seen in its greatest rankness, and is truly their worst enemy.

The alternate domination of one faction over another, sharpened by the spirit of revenge, natural to party dissension, which in different ages and countries has perpetrated the most horrid enormities, is itself a frightful despotism . . . and sooner or later the chief of some prevailing faction, more able or more fortunate than his competitors, turns this disposition to the purposes of his own elevation, on the ruins of public liberty.

Without looking forward to an extremity of this kind (which nevertheless ought not to be entirely out of sight), the common and continual mischiefs of the spirit of party are sufficient to make it the interest and duty of a wise people to discourage and restrain it."

—George Washington, *Farewell Address,* September 17, 1796

### Document 2

Use your knowledge of political parties and Documents 1 and 2 to answer Questions 1–3.

1. Which answer best summarizes the point of Document 1?
   A. Political parties promote good government
   B. Parties are likely to lead to the rise of a despot in the long run.
   C. Party conflict and rivalry is a necessary evil in government.
   D. Parties work best in a government that is not based on democratic principles.

2. What does Document 2 suggest about the view of the two major political parties in the United States?

3. **Pull It Together** What are the advantages and disadvantages of political parties?

 **GOVERNMENT** ONLINE
**Documents**
To find more primary sources on political parties, visit PearsonSchool.com/phgovt

---

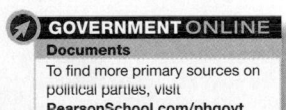

---

smallest unit of election administration and a subset of a ward. Voters in each precinct use the same polling place. **(b)** Students might note that decentralization enables party activities to focus on each electoral unit—national, State, district, county, ward, and precinct.

### WRITING ABOUT GOVERNMENT

11. Students will write a persuasive editorial, promoting or opposing a political party on the issue they selected.

### APPLY WHAT YOU'VE LEARNED

12. Students should record the responses to their interview questions.

13. Student profiles should use the specific responses from their interview subject to make generalizations about the two-party system, supported by content from the chapter.

# Introduce the Chapter

## Essential Questions:

**UNIT 2**

In what ways should people participate in public affairs?

**CHAPTER 6**

Why do voters act as they do?

### ACTIVATE PRIOR KNOWLEDGE

Have students examine the image and quotation on these pages. Ask: **Have all adult Americans always had the right to vote?** *(no)* **Which groups had been excluded from voting earlier in U.S. history?** *(African Americans, women)* In this chapter, students will learn about the right to vote—how it has been extended and denied to certain groups, how it is regulated, and how it is exercised. Then tell students to begin to further explore the topic of voting by completing the Chapter 6 Essential Question Warmup activity in their **Essential Questions Journal.** Discuss their responses as a class.

### BEFORE READING

**L2 ELL Differentiate** Chapter 6 Prereading and Vocabulary Worksheet (Unit 2 All-in-One, p. 57)

### SUCCESSNET STUDENT AND TEACHER CENTER

Visit **PearsonSchool.com/phgovt** for downloadable resources that allow students and teachers to connect with government "on the go."

### DIGITAL LESSON PRESENTATION

The digital lesson presentation supports the print lesson with activities and summaries of key concepts.

## SKILLS DEVELOPMENT

### DRAW INFERENCES AND CONCLUSIONS

You may wish to teach drawing inferences and conclusions as a distinct skill within Section 1 of this chapter. Use the Chapter 6 Skills Worksheet (Unit 2 All-in-One, p. 67) to help students learn how to draw inferences and conclusions. The worksheet asks students to read an article about the passage of the 26th Amendment and draw conclusions about its impact on American political life. For L2 and L1 students, assign the adapted Skill Activity (Unit 2 All-in-One, p. 68).

**WebQuest online** The chapter WebQuest challenges students to answer the chapter Essential Question by asking them about voting.

150

# Block Scheduling

**BLOCK 1:** Teach the lessons for Section 1, including the Bellringer, Core Worksheet, and Extend activities for Section 1 and the Bellringer, Core Worksheet A, and Extend activities for Section 2.

**BLOCK 2:** Teach the entire lesson for Section 3.

**BLOCK 3:** Teach the Bellringer and Core Worksheet for Section 4.

CHAPTER

# 6

## Voters and Voter Behavior

**Essential Question**
Why do voters act as they do?

**Section 1:**
The Right to Vote

**Section 2:**
Voter Qualifications

**Section 3:**
Suffrage and Civil Rights

**Section 4:**
Voter Behavior

> " People often say that in a **democracy**, decisions are made by a majority of the **people**. . . . Decisions are made by a **majority** of those who make **themselves heard** and who **vote**—a very different thing.
>
> —Walter Judd, *Wit and Wisdom of Politics*

**Photo:** A college student casts her first-ever vote in a presidential election in Springfield, Missouri.

**GOVERNMENT** ONLINE
**On the Go**

To study anywhere, anytime, download these online resources at PearsonSchool.com/phgovt
• Political Dictionary
• Audio Review
• Downloadable Interactivities

151

## Lesson Goals

**SECTION 1**
Students will . . .
• examine a primary source photograph and discuss the reasons for the expansion of voting rights.
• illustrate the changing definition of the American electorate by creating a poster of the history of voting rights expansion in the United States.

**SECTION 2**
Students will . . .
• examine a political cartoon to begin a discussion of the benefits and drawbacks of voter identification laws.
• analyze how voter qualifications have changed over time by examining a registration application from the 1960s.
• evaluate and respond to an editorial about mandatory voting.

**SECTION 3**
Students will . . .
• identify historical barriers that faced African American voters by examining a political cartoon.
• analyze historical data on African American representation in Congress to understand the effects of widespread voter discrimination and its removal.

**SECTION 4**
Students will . . .
• analyze a political cartoon in order to understand the effects of and reasons for nonvoting.
• explore the factors that influence voting behavior by creating a television advertisement that encourages voter participation.

## Pressed for Time

Organize the class into four groups. Assign each group a section from the chapter. (Note that Section 4 is nine pages, considerably longer than the other sections.) Have each group create a presentation detailing the main points of the assigned section. As groups give their presentations, create a study guide on the board outlining each section's main points.

**FOLLOW UP** Have students create a flyer that summarizes key information about voting rights, including qualifications, history, and voter behavior.

**DIFFERENTIATED INSTRUCTION KEY**

Look for these symbols to help you adjust steps in each lesson to meet your students' needs.

**L1** Special Needs

**L2** Basic
    **ELL** English Language Learners
    **LPR** Less Proficient Readers

**L3** All Students

**L4** Advanced Students

# How have voting rights changed over the course of American history?

| History of Voting Rights | |
|---|---|
| Early 1800s | religious, property, and tax qualifications begin to disappear |
| 1870 | 15th Amendment removes restrictions based on race or color |
| 1920 | 19th Amendment removes restrictions based on sex |
| 1960s | Voting Rights Act of 1965 and other civil rights legislation enforces racial equality at polling places; 23rd Amendment enables citizens of District of Columbia to vote in presidential elections; 24th Amendment eliminates poll tax |
| 1970s | 26th Amendment sets minimum voting age at 18 |

# Get Started

## LESSON GOALS

Students will . . .

- examine a primary source photograph and discuss the reasons for the expansion of voting rights.
- illustrate the changing definition of the American electorate through history by creating a poster of the history of voting rights expansion in the United States.

## BEFORE CLASS

Assign the section, the graphic organizer in the text, and the Reading Comprehension Worksheet (Unit 2 All-in-One, p. 61) before class.

**L2 Differentiate** Reading Comprehension Worksheet (Unit 2 All-in-One, p. 62)

# SKILLS DEVELOPMENT

## DRAW INFERENCES AND CONCLUSIONS

To practice drawing inferences and conclusions in this section, use the Chapter 6 Skills Worksheet (Unit 2 All-in-One, p. 67). You may teach the skill explicitly either before or after reviewing the Bell-ringer. For L2 and L1 students, assign the adapted Skill Activity (Unit 2 All-in-One, p. 68).

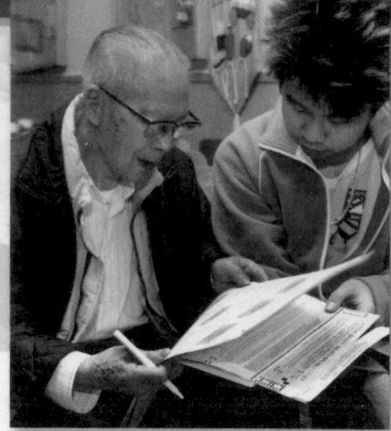

# SECTION 1
# The Right to Vote

**Guiding Question**
**How have voting rights changed over the course of American history?** Use a graphic organizer to take notes on the history of voting rights in this country.

| History of Voting Rights | |
|---|---|
| Early 1800s | |
| 1870 | |
| 1920 | |
| 1960s | |
| 1970s | |

**Political Dictionary**
- suffrage
- franchise
- electorate
- disenfranchised
- poll tax

**Objectives**
1. Summarize the history of voting rights in the United States.
2. Identify and explain constitutional restrictions on the States' power to set voting qualifications.

**Image Above:** A volunteer helps a voter with instructions to vote.

Soon, you will be eligible to vote—but will you exercise that right? The record suggests that while you may do so, many of your friends will not, at least not for some time. The record also suggests that some of your friends will never vote. Yet, clearly, the success of democratic government depends on popular participation and, in particular, on the regular and informed exercise of the right to vote.

## The History of Voting Rights

The Framers of the Constitution purposely left the power to set suffrage qualifications to each State. **Suffrage** means the right to vote. **Franchise** is a synonym for the right to vote.[1]

**Expansion of the Electorate** When the Constitution went into effect in 1789, the right to vote was generally restricted to white male property owners. In fact, probably not one in fifteen adult white males could vote in elections in the various States. Benjamin Franklin often made fun of this situation. He told of a man whose only property was a jackass and noted that the man would lose the right to vote if his jackass died. "Now," asked Franklin, "in whom is the right of suffrage? In the man or the jackass?"

Today, the size of the American **electorate**—the potential voting population—is truly impressive. More than 230 million people, nearly all citizens who are at least 18 years of age, qualify to vote. That huge number is a direct result of the legal definition of suffrage. In other words, it is the result of those laws that determine who can and cannot vote. It is also the result of more than 200 years of continuing, often bitter, and sometimes violent struggle over the right to vote.

The history of American suffrage since 1789 has been marked by two long-term trends. First, the nation has experienced the gradual elimination of

1 Originally, the Constitution had only two suffrage provisions. Article I, Section 2, Clause 1 requires each State to allow anyone qualified to vote for members of "the most numerous Branch" of its own legislature to vote as well for members of the national House of Representatives. Article II, Section 1, Clause 2 declares that presidential electors be chosen in each State "in such Manner as the Legislature thereof may direct."

# Focus on the Basics

Here is the information that your students need to learn in this section.

**FACTS:** • Expansion of the electorate occurred in five stages: elimination of religious, property, and tax qualifications; addition of the 15th and 19th amendments; passage of civil rights laws; and addition of the 23rd, 24th, and 26th amendments. • States determine voting qualifications but must not deny a person aged 18 or over the right to vote on the basis of race, color, or sex, nor may they impose a poll tax in federal elections.

**CONCEPTS:** rights and responsibilities as citizens, equal protection

**ENDURING UNDERSTANDINGS:** • The history of the United States has been marked by steady expansion of the electorate. • States can set voting qualifications under various restrictions set by the Federal Government.

several restrictions on the right to vote. Those restrictions were based on a variety of factors, including religious belief, property ownership, tax payment, race, and gender. Second, a significant share of what was originally the States' power over the right to vote has been gradually assumed by the Federal Government.

**Extending Suffrage: The Five Stages** The growth of the American electorate has come in five identifiable stages. The two trends described above—growing federal control over suffrage and the elimination of voting restrictions—are woven through those stages.

**1.** The first stage of the struggle to extend voting rights came in the early 1800s. Religious qualifications, put in place in colonial days, quickly disappeared. No State has had a religious test for voting since 1810. Then, one by one, States began to eliminate property ownership and tax payment qualifications.

By mid-century, almost all white adult males could vote in every State.

**2.** The second major effort to broaden the electorate followed the Civil War. The 15th Amendment, ratified in 1870, was intended to protect any citizen from being denied the right to vote because of race or color. Still, for nearly another century, African Americans were systematically <u>barred</u> from voting, and they remained the largest group of **disenfranchised** citizens, or citizens denied the right to vote, in the nation's population.

**3.** The 19th Amendment prohibited the denial of the right to vote because of sex. Its ratification in 1920 completed the third expansion of suffrage. Wyoming, while still a territory, had given women the vote in 1869.[2]

---

2 Women did vote in some elections in this country before Wyoming acted in 1869, however—notably in New Jersey, where women could and did vote in all elections from 1776 to 1807.

✔**Checkpoint**
What was the first voting qualification to disappear?

**bar**
*v.* to prevent, prohibit, ban

---

## The Five Stages of Expanding Suffrage

Suffrage was gradually expanded over a period of nearly 200 years. *As more and more Americans gained the right to vote, how might election results have been affected?*

**Early 1800s**
Religious, property, and tax qualifications begin to disappear in every State.

**1870**
15th Amendment prohibits voting restrictions based on race or color.

**1920**
19th Amendment removes voting restrictions based on sex.

**1965**
The Voting Rights Act of 1965 enforces racial equality at polling places.

**1971**
26th Amendment sets the minimum voting age at 18.

---

## Differentiated Resources

The following resources are located in the All-in-One, Unit 2, Chapter 6, Section 1:

**L2** Prereading and Vocabulary Worksheet (p. 57)
**L3** Reading Comprehension Worksheet (p. 61)
**L2** Reading Comprehension Worksheet (p. 62)
**L3** Core Worksheet (p. 63)
**L2** Core Worksheet (p. 65)
**L3** Skills Worksheet (p. 67)
**L2** Skill Activity (p. 68)
**L3** Quiz A (p. 69)  **L2** Quiz B (p. 70)

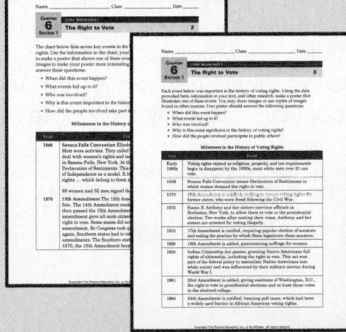

---

**BELLRINGER**

Display Transparency 6A, Women's Suffrage. Write on the board: **A suffragette is a woman who supports women's voting rights. In your notebook, write your answers to the questions that appear below the picture.**

**L1** **L2** **Differentiate** Point out that at the time of the illustration, women were not allowed to vote in the United States.

# Teach

To present this topic using online resources, use the lesson presentations at **PearsonSchool.com/phgovt.**

**DISCUSS THE PHOTOGRAPH**

Discuss student response to the Bellringer photo. Explain that there appears to be a vote upcoming in the State in which voters—all of whom are men at this point—will have a chance to vote on a measure that would give women in Ohio the vote. Ask students to share their answers to the questions. *(The office probably contains information for voters that might persuade them to support the cause of woman suffrage in an upcoming vote. The women are taking part in public affairs by helping to educate the public and promoting a particular cause that is important to them—the vote for women.)*

**INTRODUCE THE TOPIC**

Tell students that today they will learn about the history of voting rights in the United States. Explain that this history has followed a clear trend—the steady expansion of the electorate.

**L2** **ELL Differentiate** Explain that the word *franchise* means "vote," *suffrage* means "voting," and *electorate* means "people who have the right to vote."

---

## Answers

**Checkpoint** Religious qualifications were the first to disappear.

**The Five Stages of Expanding Suffrage** Possible response: Winning candidates would be more sympathetic to the concerns of the poor, African Americans, and women.

## DISTRIBUTE CORE WORKSHEET

Distribute the Chapter 6 Section 1 Core Worksheet (Unit 2 All-in-One, p. 63), which lists significant events in the history of voting rights and directs students to make a poster describing one of these events and its significance. First review the events quickly as a class. Then divide students into pairs or triads and assign each group an event. Students may use information from the chapter and other sources, if they wish. Remind students to divide tasks—for example, designing the overall poster, drawing individual illustrations, writing captions for each image, and so on.

**L1 L2 Differentiate** Distribute the adapted Core Worksheet (Unit 2 All-in-One, p. 65).

**L4 Differentiate** Have students perform research to find additional examples of events or trends in the history of the expansion of voting rights.

## REFLECT AND DISCUSS

When completed, use the Conversation Wall strategy (p. T27) to have students display their posters. Give students time to circulate and review their classmates' work. Ask students to choose one event (not their own) and explain in a few sentences why they think it is the most interesting. Use these reflections as a basis for a class discussion in which you focus on the Unit 2 Essential Question: **In what ways should people participate in public affairs?** Explain that these events illustrate how people participate in public affairs when denied the vote. Ask students if they see any patterns, or if some tactics seem more effective than others.

## EXTEND THE LESSON

**L3 Differentiate** Have students debate the following question: **Is it reasonable to require voters to be able to read and understand English?** Divide students into teams to argue both sides of the question. Students should be sure to consider the potential for misuse of such restrictions, as demonstrated by history. Have students use the Internet or other resources to find information on this topic, and use the Debate strategy (p. T25) to help them organize their thoughts before beginning the debate.

**L2 Differentiate** Have students use the Internet or library resources to research and create a timeline that traces the women's suffrage movement in the United States.

Tell students to go to the Audio Tour to learn more about women's suffrage.

## Answers

**Interpreting Maps** The Western States were much more likely to have granted suffrage to women than States in the East.

---

# Women's Suffrage in 1919

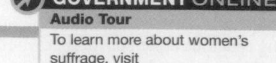 GOVERNMENT ONLINE
Audio Tour
To learn more about women's suffrage, visit
PearsonSchool.com/phgovt

➤➤ **Interpreting Maps** Women could vote in some or all elections in several States before the adoption of the 19th Amendment in 1920. *In which part of the country was their right to vote most widely supported?*

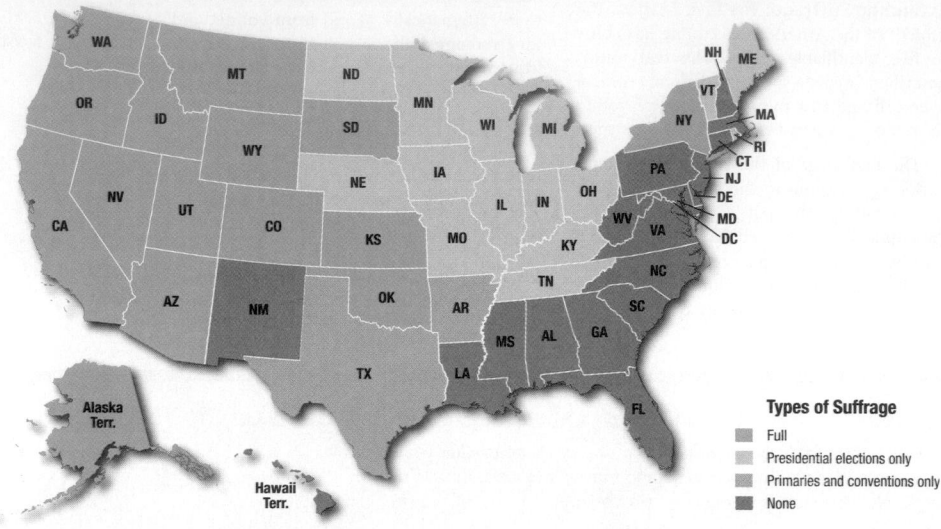

**Types of Suffrage**
- Full
- Presidential elections only
- Primaries and conventions only
- None

By 1920, more than half of the States had followed that lead.

**4.** A fourth major extension took place during the 1960s. During that time, federal legislation and court decisions focused on securing African Americans a full role in the electoral process in all States. With the passage and <u>vigorous</u> enforcement of a number of civil rights acts, especially the Voting Rights Act of 1965 and its later extensions, racial equality finally became fact in polling booths throughout the country.

The 23rd Amendment, passed in 1961, added the voters of the District of Columbia to the presidential electorate. The 24th Amendment, ratified in 1964, eliminated the poll tax (and any other tax) as a condition for voting in any federal election. A **poll tax** was a tax imposed by several States as a qualification for voting.

**5.** The fifth and latest expansion of the electorate came with the adoption of the 26th Amendment in 1971. It provides that no State can set the minimum age for voting at more than 18 years of age. In other words, those 18 and over were given the right to vote by this amendment.

## The Power to Set Voting Qualifications

Again, the Constitution does not give the Federal Government the power to set suffrage qualifications. Rather, that matter is reserved to the States. The Constitution does,

<u>vigorous</u>
*adj.* strong or powerful

---

# Background

**THE FRAMERS AND VOTING RIGHTS** The Framers of the Constitution clearly had concerns about allowing voters too much power in choosing their government. The methods for electing the President were designed to limit the influence of a voting public that the Framers of the Constitution did not fully trust. In addition, the Framers originally sought to have the Senate chosen by state legislatures rather than by direct popular vote. Only the House of Representatives was to be elected by the voters directly.

however, place five restrictions on the ability of the States to exercise that power:

**1.** Any person whom a State allows to vote for members of the "most numerous Branch" of its own legislature must also be allowed to vote for representatives and senators in Congress.[3] This restriction is of little real meaning today. With only minor exceptions, each of the States allows the same voters to vote in all elections within the State.

**2.** No State can deprive any person of the right to vote "on account of race, color, or previous condition of servitude" (15th Amendment).[4]

**3.** No State can deprive any person of the right to vote on account of sex (19th Amendment).[5]

**4.** No State can require payment of any tax as a condition for taking part in the nomination or election of any federal officeholder. That is, no State can levy any tax in connection with the selection of the President, the Vice President, or members of Congress (24th Amendment).

---

**3** Article I, Section 2, Clause 1; the 17th Amendment extended the "most numerous Branch" provision to the election of senators.

**4** The phrase "previous condition of servitude" refers to slavery. This amendment does not guarantee the right to vote to African Americans, or to anyone else. Instead, it forbids discrimination on these grounds when the States set suffrage qualifications.

**5** This amendment does not guarantee the right to vote to women as such. Technically, it forbids States the power to discriminate against males or females in establishing suffrage qualifications.

**5.** No State can deprive any person who is at least 18 years of age of the right to vote because of age (26th Amendment).[6]

Beyond these five restrictions, remember that no State can violate any other provision in the Constitution in the setting of suffrage qualifications—or in anything else that it does. A case decided by the Supreme Court in 1975, *Hill* v. *Stone*, illustrates the point.

There, the Court struck down a section of the Texas constitution that declared that only those persons who owned taxable property could vote in city bond elections. The Court found the drawing of such a distinction for voting purposes—between those who do and those who do not own taxable property—to be an unreasonable classification prohibited by the 14th Amendment's Equal Protection Clause.

---

**6** This amendment does not prevent any State from allowing persons younger than age 18 to vote. It does prohibit a State from setting a maximum age for voting, however.

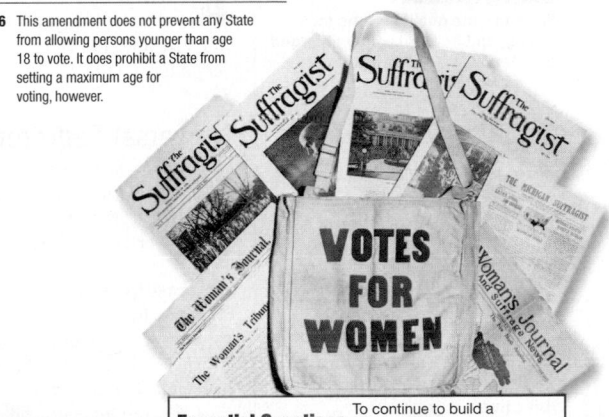

Suffragists published newspapers and pamphlets in support of their cause. *How might weekly or daily publications help in the fight for women's suffrage?*

✔ **Checkpoint**
What did the 26th Amendment do?

---

## SECTION 1 ASSESSMENT

**1. Guiding Question** Use your completed graphic organizer to answer this question: How have voting rights changed over the course of American history?

**Key Terms and Comprehension**

**2.** Briefly summarize the history of **suffrage** qualifications in this country.

**3. (a)** What is a **poll tax**? **(b)** Which amendment eliminated it?

**4. (a)** What is the American **electorate**? **(b)** Approximately how large is it?

**Critical Thinking**

**5. Identify Central Issues (a)** What was the voting experience of African Americans after the Civil War? **(b)** What does this suggest about the legal expansion of voting rights?

**6. Recognize Ideologies (a)** What does the Constitution say about suffrage qualifications? **(b)** How does this reflect the Framers' ideas about the role of the Federal Government in the nation's political system?

**Quick Write**

**Narrative Essay: Choose a Topic** Choose a significant event in the history of suffrage such as the coming of women's suffrage or the abolition of the poll tax. You may want to do preliminary research online or at the library. Write a paragraph summarizing the event and its importance. Include details such as who, what, when, where, and why.

**Essential Questions Journal** To continue to build a response to the chapter Essential Question, go to your **Essential Questions Journal.**

---

## Assess and Remediate

**L3** Collect the Core Worksheet and assess student performance using the Rubric for Assessing a Student Poster (Unit 2 All-in-One, p. 253).

**L3** Assign the Section 1 Assessment questions.

**L3** Section Quiz A (Unit 2 All-in-One, p. 69)

**L2** Section Quiz B (Unit 2 All-in-One, p. 70)

Have students complete the review activities in the digital lesson presentation and continue their work in the **Essential Questions Journal.**

### REMEDIATION

| If Your Students Have Trouble With | Strategies For Remediation |
|---|---|
| The two long-term trends in the history of suffrage (Questions 1, 2, 4) | Write the words *eliminating barriers* and *extending voting rights* on the board, and have students find examples of each phenomenon in the section. |
| The five distinct stages of growth in the American electorate (Questions 1, 2) | Have students create a timeline of the expansion of voting rights as described in the text |
| Ways in which government has expanded voting rights (Questions 3, 5) | Have students create a table of government actions aimed at expanding voting rights. |
| The constitutional restrictions on setting suffrage qualifications by the States (Question 6) | Have students write and exchange among themselves a quiz about the power of the States to establish voting qualifications. |

## Answers

**Checkpoint** It effectively lowered the voting age to 18.

**Caption** Newspapers might inform voters and influence public opinion.

---

## Assessment Answers

**1.** Originally, voting rights were generally limited to white male property owners. Over time, voting rights expanded to include all adult white men, then African American men, and finally women. Now most citizens 18 and over can vote.

**2.** The trend in suffrage has been a steady expansion of the electorate.

**3. (a)** a tax a person must pay in order to vote **(b)** the 24th Amendment

**4. (a)** It is the potential voting population. **(b)** It is more than 230 million.

**5. (a)** After the 15th Amendment legally enfranchised African Americans in 1870, their voting rights remained restricted until the 1960s when civil rights legislation and enforcement assured racial equality at polling places. **(b)** A good answer will recognize that expansion of voting rights by law can be frustrated if there is significant opposition of the people.

**6. (a)** Originally it said little, specifying only that States must allow those eligible to vote for representatives to the most numerous branch of the State legislature to vote in House elections, though later amendments ensured that people could not be denied the vote based on race, gender, age 18 or older, or payment of taxes. **(b)** The Framers wanted to leave the settings of voting qualifications to the States, but they also believed in democracy and equality, and that government should represent the people. The later expansion of voting rights reflects these early core values.

**QUICK WRITE** Student summaries should include important details about their chosen event.

## GUIDING QUESTION

What are the requirements for voting, and how have they changed over time?

**Voting Requirements**

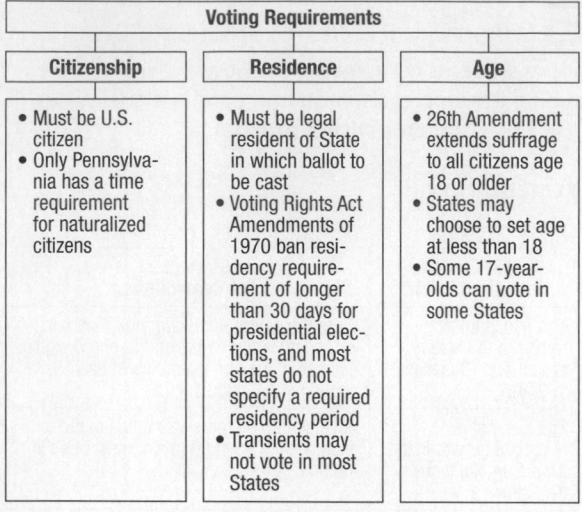

| Citizenship | Residence | Age |
|---|---|---|
| • Must be U.S. citizen<br>• Only Pennsylvania has a time requirement for naturalized citizens | • Must be legal resident of State in which ballot to be cast<br>• Voting Rights Act Amendments of 1970 ban residency requirement of longer than 30 days for presidential elections, and most states do not specify a required residency period<br>• Transients may not vote in most States | • 26th Amendment extends suffrage to all citizens age 18 or older<br>• States may choose to set age at less than 18<br>• Some 17-year-olds can vote in some States |

## Get Started

### LESSON GOALS

Students will . . .

- examine a political cartoon to begin a discussion of the benefits and drawbacks of voter identification laws.
- analyze how voter qualifications have changed over time by examining a registration application from the 1960s.
- evaluate and respond to an editorial about mandatory voting.

## SKILLS DEVELOPMENT

### ANALYZE POLITICAL CARTOONS

To help students learn to analyze political cartoons, have them turn to the Skills Handbook, p. S22, and use the information there to complete the Bellringer activity.

---

### SECTION 2

# Voter Qualifications

**Guiding Question**

**What are the qualifications for voting, and how have they changed over time?** Use the flowchart to record information about voter qualifications in the United States.

**Voting Qualifications**

| Citizenship | Residence | Age |
|---|---|---|
| •<br>•<br>• | •<br>•<br>• | •<br>•<br>• |

### Political Dictionary

- alien
- transient
- registration
- purge
- poll books
- literacy

### Objectives

1. Identify the universal qualifications for voting in the United States.
2. Explain the other requirements that States use or have used as voting qualifications.

**Image Above:** Members of the armed forces stationed abroad vote by absentee ballot.

**A**re you qualified to vote? Probably not—at least not yet. Do you know why? In this section, you will see how the States, including yours, determine who can vote. You will also see that the various qualifications they set are not very difficult to meet.

## Universal Requirements

Today, every State requires that any person who wants to vote must be able to satisfy qualifications based on three factors: (1) citizenship, (2) residence, and (3) age. The States have some leeway in shaping the details of the first two of these factors; they have almost no discretion with regard to the third one.

**Citizenship** **Aliens,** foreign-born residents who have not become citizens, are generally denied the right to vote in this country. Still, nothing in the Constitution says that aliens cannot vote, and any State could allow them to do so if it chose. At one time, about a fourth of the States permitted those aliens who had applied for naturalization—that is, applied for citizenship—to vote. Typically, the western States did so to help attract settlers.[7]

States may draw a distinction between native-born and naturalized citizens with regard to suffrage. The Pennsylvania constitution says that one must have become a citizen at least one month before an election in order to vote in that State.

**Residence** In order to vote in this country today, one must be a legal resident of the State in which he or she wishes to cast a ballot. In many States, a person must have lived in the State for at least a certain period of time before he or she can vote.

The States adopted residence requirements for two reasons: (1) to keep a political machine from bringing in enough outsiders to affect the outcome of an election (a once common practice), and (2) to allow new voters at least some time in which to become familiar with the candidates and issues in an upcoming election.

---

7 Arkansas, the last State in which aliens could vote, adopted a citizenship requirement in 1926. In a few States, local governments can permit noncitizens to vote in local contests—e.g., city council elections—and a handful do.

## Focus on the Basics

**FACTS:** • Throughout our history, different States have imposed different qualifications for voting. • The three current universal requirements are citizenship, residency, and age. • People can be denied the right to vote based on mental incapability, imprisonment for some crimes, or dishonorable discharge from the armed forces. • Literacy tests and poll taxes used to disenfranchise certain groups have been eliminated.

**CONCEPTS:** rights and responsibilities as citizens, democratic values/principles

**ENDURING UNDERSTANDINGS:** • All States have citizenship, residence, and age requirements for voting. • Other qualifications differ from State to State. • Some voting requirements used to disenfranchise certain groups have been eliminated.

## Residence Requirements

# Where You Live Determines Where You Vote

In order to vote in elections today, voters must be citizens with established residence in their voting locations. *Why does every State require that a voter be a resident of that State?*

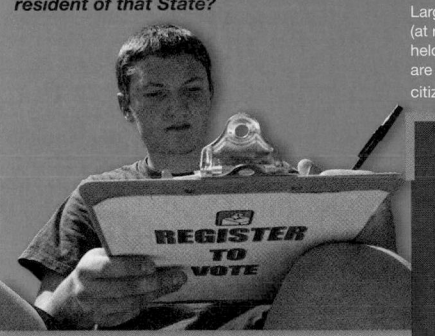

Large ceremonies (at right) are often held when people are sworn in as citizens.

▸ States require voters to be residents.

▸ A person can have only one residence.

▸ Some States have provided registration qualifications that require people to have lived in a place for a certain amount of time.

▸ Naturalized citizens are eligible to vote.

For decades, every State imposed a fairly lengthy residence requirement—typically, a year in the State, 60 or 90 days in the county, and 30 days in the local precinct or ward.[8] The requirement was longer in some southern States—for example, one year in the State, six months in the county, and three months in the precinct in Alabama, Louisiana, and South Carolina, and in Mississippi a year in the State, a year in the county, and six months in the precinct.

Residence requirements are not nearly so long today. In fact, most States now require that a voter be a legal resident but do not attach a time period to that qualification. About a third of them say that a voter must have lived in the State for at least 30 days. In a few, the period is somewhat shorter—for example, 29 days in Arizona, 20 in Minnesota, and 10 in Wisconsin.[9]

Today's much shorter requirements are a direct result of a 1970 federal law and a 1972 Supreme Court decision. In the Voting Rights Act Amendments of 1970, Congress banned any requirement of longer than 30 days for voting in presidential elections.[10] And in *Dunn* v. *Blumstein*, 1972, the Court found Tennessee's requirement—at the time, a year in the State and 90 days in the county—unconstitutional. The Court found such a lengthy requirement to be an unsupportable discrimination against new residents and so in conflict with the 14th Amendment's Equal Protection Clause. The Supreme Court said that "30 days appears to be an ample period of time." Election law and practice among the States quickly accepted that standard.

Nearly every State does prohibit **transients,** persons who plan to live in a State for only a short time, from gaining legal residence status there. Thus, a traveling sales agent, a member of the armed services, or a college student usually cannot vote in a State

✔ **Checkpoint**
When and why did residence requirements begin to get shorter?

---

8 Recall from Chapter 5, the precinct is the smallest unit of election administration. The ward is a unit into which cities are often divided for the election of members of the city council.

9 Until recently, Arizona imposed a 50-day requirement period. The Supreme Court upheld Arizona's residence law in *Marston* v. *Lewis* in 1973, but it also declared in another case that a similar law "approaches the outer constitutional limits."

10 The Supreme Court upheld this provision in the law in *Oregon* v. *Mitchell* in 1970.

---

Assign the section, the graphic organizer in the text, and the Reading Comprehension Worksheet (Unit 2 All-in-One, p. 71) before class.

**L2 Differentiate** Reading Comprehension Worksheet (Unit 2 All-in-One, p. 73)

**BELLRINGER**

Write on the board: **(1) What is the purpose of voter ID laws? (2) How might voter ID laws discourage voting? Answer in your notebook.**

# Teach

To present this topic using online resources, use the lesson presentations at **PearsonSchool.com/phgovt.**

**DISCUSS THE BELLRINGER**

Ask students to share their responses to the Bellringer questions. *(1. to prevent voter fraud by requiring voters to prove their identity 2. Some otherwise qualified voters, such as people who are elderly, poor, or disabled, may not have a driver's license or other photo ID.)* Ask: **Do you think people should be required to show a photo ID in order to vote? Why or why not? Is it a concern that these requirements may prevent some people from voting?**

**INTRODUCE THE TOPIC**

Tell students that today they will learn about the ways in which the Federal and State governments establish qualifications for voting. Have students scan the headings and subheadings of the section to see what these qualifications are. *(universal requirements of citizenship, residence, and age; registration, and tax payment and literacy.)* Tell students that literacy and tax requirements are no longer in use.

---

# Differentiated Resources

The following resources are located in the All-in-One, Unit 2, Chapter 6, Section 2:

**L3** Reading Comprehension Worksheet (p. 71)

**L2** Reading Comprehension Worksheet (p. 73)

**L3** Core Worksheet A (p. 75)

**L3** Core Worksheet B (p. 78)

**L2** Core Worksheet B (p. 80)

**L3 L4** Extend Worksheet (p. 82)

**L2** Extend Activity (p. 83)

**L3** Quiz A (p. 84)   **L2** Quiz B (p. 85)

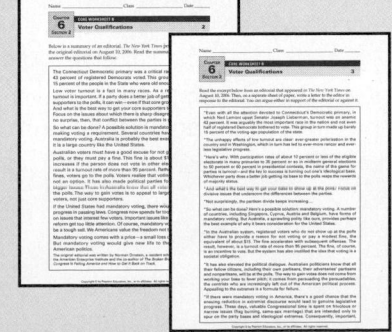

## Answers

**Residence Requirements** Possible response: States with a history of newcomers interfering in local politics might set longer residency requirements than other States.

**Checkpoint** Requirements began to get shorter in the early 1970s, in response to a federal law and a subsequent Supreme Court ruling.

## DISTRIBUTE CORE WORKSHEET A

Distribute the Chapter 6 Section 2 Core Worksheet A (Unit 2 All-in-One, p. 75), which is a sample voter registration application. Have students work independently to read the application and complete the questions that follow. After students have completed the activity, review the answers as a class. Invite students to respond to each other's answers.

**L1 L2 Differentiate** Read the questions in the registration application aloud. Then ask students to choose two questions to answer at the bottom of the page.

**L4 Differentiate** Have students attempt to fill in the application.

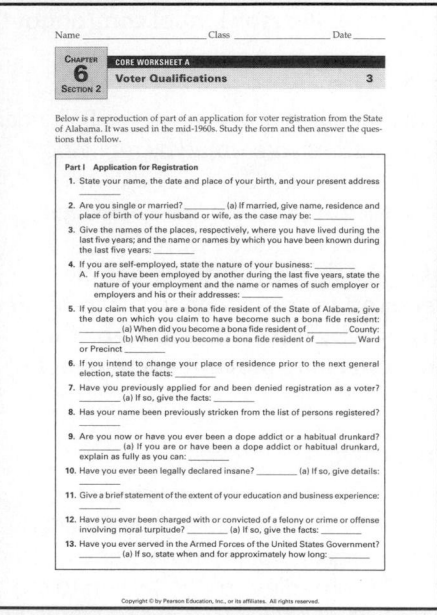

## INVITE STUDENT REACTION

Tell students that the application was one of several available to registrars in Alabama prior to 1965, when the federal Voting Rights Act made such tests illegal. The law was aimed at breaking down barriers to voting faced by African Americans in the South. Tell students that parts of this application were especially aimed at African Americans. Ask: **Do you think the average 18-year-old could pass this test? Do you think a person who could not pass this test would nevertheless be able to cast an informed vote?**

## Answers

**Checkpoint** the Vietnam War

---

✔ **Checkpoint**
What event was significant to lowering the voting age?

**infirmity**
*n.* physical or mental weakness

where he or she has only a temporary physical presence. In several States, however, the courts have held that college students who claim the campus community as their legal residence must be allowed to vote there.

**Age** The 26th Amendment, added to the Constitution in 1971, declares,

### FROM THE CONSTITUTION

> The right of citizens of the United States, who are eighteen years of age or older, to vote shall not be denied or abridged by the United States or by any State on account of age.
>
> —26th Amendment

**fraudulent**
*adj.* deceitful; false

Thus, no State can set the minimum age for voting in any election at more than 18. In other words, the amendment extends suffrage to citizens who are at least 18 years of age. Notice, however, that any State can set the age at less than 18, if it chooses to do so.

**eligibility**
*n.* qualifications

Until the 26th Amendment was adopted, the generally accepted age requirement for voting was 21. In fact, until 1970, only four States had put the age at less than 21. Georgia was the first State to allow 18-year-olds to vote; it did so in 1943, in the midst of World War II. Kentucky followed suit in 1955. Alaska entered the Union in 1959 with the voting age

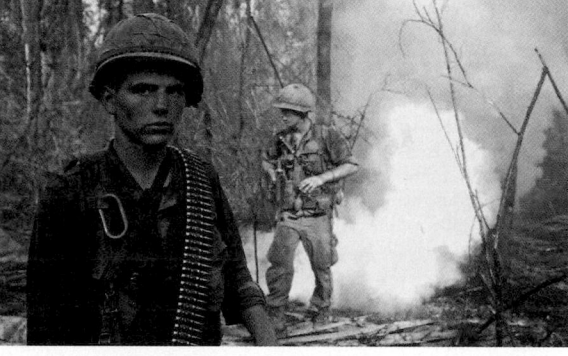

The Vietnam War spurred the lowering of the voting age to 18.

set at 19, and Hawaii became a State later that same year with a voting age of 20.

Both Alaska and Hawaii set the age above 18 but below 21 to avoid potential problems caused by high school students voting in local school-district elections. Whatever the fears at the time, there have been no such problems in any State since the passage of the 26th Amendment.

Efforts to lower the voting age to 18 nationwide began in the 1940s, during World War II. Those efforts were capped by the adoption of the 26th Amendment in 1971, during the war in Vietnam. That amendment was ratified more quickly than any other amendment to the Constitution. This fact is testament to the emotional weight of the principal argument in its favor: "Old enough to fight, old enough to vote."

How have 18 to 20-year-olds responded to the 26th Amendment? In short, not very well. In election after election, young voters are much less likely to vote than any other age group in the electorate. In 1972, 48 percent of the 18-to-20 age group voted, but by 2000 that figure had plummeted to 28 percent. It rose again, substantially, in 2004 and topped 48 percent in 2008. But contrast that figure with the turnout of Americans 65 and older. Despite the infirmities that may accompany their age, their voting rate regularly exceeds 60 percent, and it did so again in the presidential election of 2008.

In a growing number of States, some 17-year-olds can now cast ballots in primary elections. Those States allow anyone whose 18th birthday falls after the primary but before the general election to vote in the primary election.

Several states have come very close to effectively lowering the voting age to 17 for *all* elections. In Nebraska, for example, any person who will be 18 by the Tuesday following the first Monday in November can qualify to vote in any election held during that calendar year.

## Registration

One other significant qualification, registration, is nearly universal among the States today. **Registration** is a procedure of voter

---

## Debate

"Disenfranchisement seems a particularly appropriate punishment for felons. The murderer, rapist, or thief has expressed contempt for his fellow citizens and broken the rules of society in the most unmistakable way."

—"Should Felons Vote?" by Edward Feser from *City Journal,* Spring 2005

Use this quotation to start a debate in your classroom. Ask: **Should convicted felons be allowed to regain their right to vote after they serve their sentences?**

identification intended to prevent <u>fraudulent</u> voting. It gives election officials a list of those persons who are qualified to vote in an election. Several States also use voter registration to identify voters in terms of their party preference and, thus, their <u>eligibility</u> to take part in closed primaries.

**Requirements** Forty-nine States—all except North Dakota—require that most, and usually all, voters be registered in order to cast ballots. Voter registration became a common feature of State election law in the early 1900s. Today, most States require all voters to register in order to vote in any election held within the State. A few, however, do not impose the requirement for all elections.

Maine and Wisconsin allow voters to register at any time, up to and including election day. Elsewhere, a voter must be registered by a certain date, often 20 or 30 days before an election.[11] That cutoff gives election officials time to prepare the poll books for an upcoming election.

Typically, a prospective voter must register his or her name, age, place of birth, present address, length of residence, and similar facts. The information is logged by a local official, usually a registrar of elections or the county clerk. A voter typically remains registered unless or until he or she moves, dies, is convicted of a serious crime, or is committed to a mental institution.

State law directs local election officials to review the lists of registered voters and to remove the names of those who are no longer eligible to vote. This process, known as **purging,** is usually done every two or four years. Unfortunately, the requirement is often ignored. When it is, the **poll books** (the official lists of qualified voters in each precinct) soon become clogged with the names of many people who, for one reason or another, are no longer eligible to vote.

**Controversies** There are some who think that the registration requirement should be abolished everywhere. They see the qualifica-

11 In Idaho, Minnesota, New Hampshire, and Wyoming, a person who is qualified to vote but misses the deadline can register (and then vote) on election day.

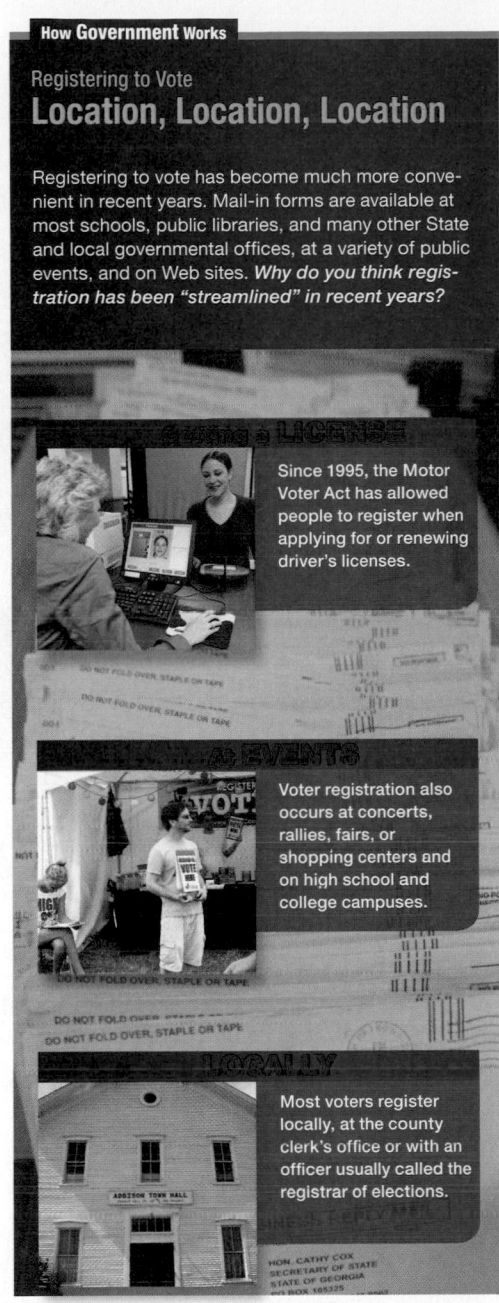

**How Government Works**

Registering to Vote
## Location, Location, Location

Registering to vote has become much more convenient in recent years. Mail-in forms are available at most schools, public libraries, and many other State and local governmental offices, at a variety of public events, and on Web sites. *Why do you think registration has been "streamlined" in recent years?*

Since 1995, the Motor Voter Act has allowed people to register when applying for or renewing driver's licenses.

Voter registration also occurs at concerts, rallies, fairs, or shopping centers and on high school and college campuses.

Most voters register locally, at the county clerk's office or with an officer usually called the registrar of elections.

# Myths and Misconceptions

**VOTING RIGHTS IN ANCIENT GREECE** Ancient Greece is widely regarded as the birthplace of democracy. Yet even at its height, Athenian democracy empowered only a small percentage of the population. Only citizens were allowed to vote, and only men could become citizens. In addition, voting was typically restricted to the most affluent members of Athenian society. Never in the history of Ancient Greece were any more than one out of seven Athenians able to cast a ballot.

**DISTRIBUTE CORE WORKSHEET B**

Give students copies of the Chapter 6 Section 2 Core Worksheet B (Unit 2 All-in-One, p. 78). This worksheet includes an excerpt from a *New York Times* editorial arguing for mandatory voting. Have students read the excerpt and summarize the main message. *(Possible summary: Mandatory voting would be a good way to get candidates to focus on all voters rather than those people on the fringes that consistently vote.)* Then ask them to underline the evidence that supports the argument and circle the portion of the editorial that addresses the counter-argument. *(the last paragraph)* Briefly discuss the arguments and attributes that make this an effective or ineffective editorial.

Have students write their own letters to the editor that either echo the demand in the editorial or take a contrary view. Distribute and review the Rubric for Assessing a Letter to the Editor (Unit 2 All-in-One, p. 254).

**L1 L2 Differentiate** Distribute the adapted Core Worksheet B (Unit 2 All-in-One, p. 80), and have students read the summary of the editorial and answer the questions.

**L3 L4 Differentiate** Have students take both positions on the question of mandatory voting.

## Answers

**Registering to Vote** Possible answer: Concern over low turnout has spurred efforts to make registration easier.

Distribute the student letters to the class, so that each student has an editorial written by another student. Have students offer a critique of the letter in which they identify what they think is the strongest point and the weakest point in the author's argument. Students should also make suggestions for improvements to the letters, using the criteria identified in the rubric.

**L1 L2 Differentiate** Create student teams to review the letters to the editor and offer suggestions.

**DEBRIEF**

Have students discuss what they have learned about the possible benefits and drawbacks of mandatory voting. Tell students to consider this question in light of the Unit 2 Essential Question: **In what ways should people participate in public affairs?** Ask: **Is voting a valid way to participate in public affairs? Should people be required to participate in this way?**

Tell students to go to the Audio Tour to learn more about voter identification.

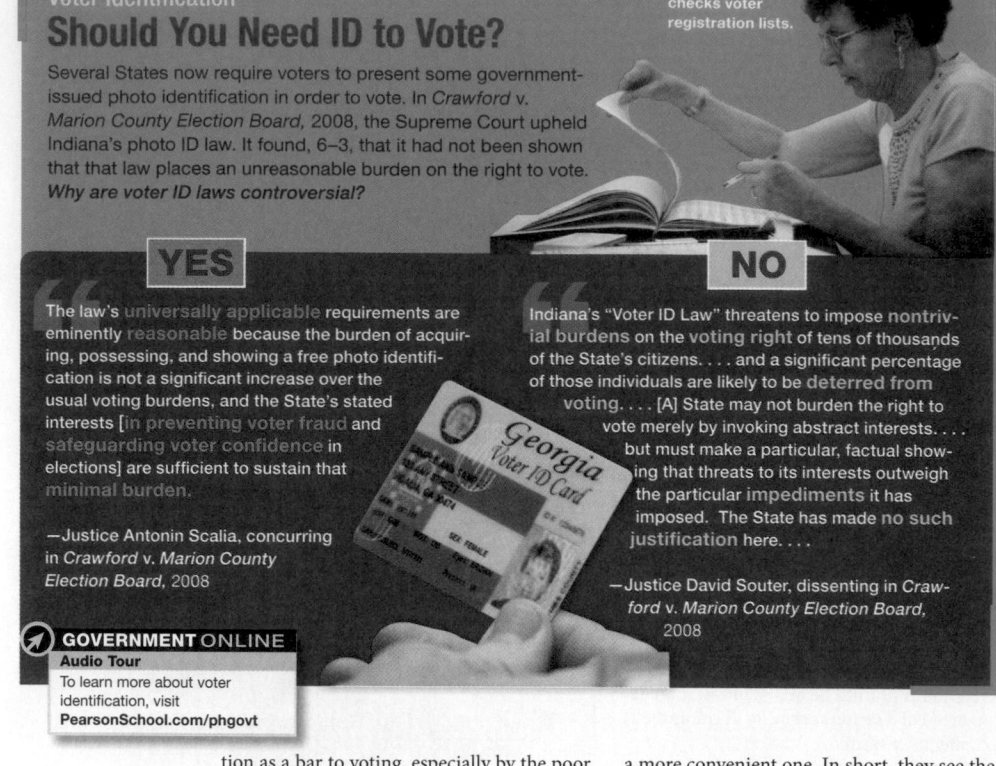

## Voter Identification
### Should You Need ID to Vote?

Several States now require voters to present some government-issued photo identification in order to vote. In *Crawford* v. *Marion County Election Board*, 2008, the Supreme Court upheld Indiana's photo ID law. It found, 6–3, that it had not been shown that that law places an unreasonable burden on the right to vote. *Why are voter ID laws controversial?*

A poll worker checks voter registration lists.

**YES**

The law's universally applicable requirements are eminently reasonable because the burden of acquiring, possessing, and showing a free photo identification is not a significant increase over the usual voting burdens, and the State's stated interests [in preventing voter fraud and safeguarding voter confidence in elections] are sufficient to sustain that minimal burden.

—Justice Antonin Scalia, concurring in *Crawford* v. *Marion County Election Board*, 2008

**NO**

Indiana's "Voter ID Law" threatens to impose nontrivial burdens on the voting right of tens of thousands of the State's citizens. . . . and a significant percentage of those individuals are likely to be deterred from voting. . . . [A] State may not burden the right to vote merely by invoking abstract interests. . . . but must make a particular, factual showing that threats to its interests outweigh the particular impediments it has imposed. The State has made no such justification here. . . .

—Justice David Souter, dissenting in *Crawford* v. *Marion County Election Board*, 2008

**GOVERNMENT** ONLINE
**Audio Tour**
To learn more about voter identification, visit
**PearsonSchool.com/phgovt**

**buttress**
*v.* to support, reinforce, strengthen

tion as a bar to voting, especially by the poor and less educated.

Those critics <u>buttress</u> their case by noting that voter turnout began to decline in the early 1900s, just after most States adopted a registration requirement. They also point to the fact that voter turnout is much higher in most European democracies than in the United States. In those countries, voter registration is not a matter of individual choice but is the law. Public officials must enter the names of all eligible citizens on registration lists. The United States is the only democratic country in which each person decides whether or not to register to vote.

Most people who have studied the problem favor keeping the registration requirement as a necessary defense against fraud. However, they also favor making the process

a more convenient one. In short, they see the problem in these terms: Where is the line between making it so easy to vote that fraud is encouraged, and making it so difficult that legitimate voting is discouraged?

Most States have eased the registration process over the last several years. In 1993, Congress passed a law that required every State (but North Dakota) to do so. That law, dubbed the "Motor Voter Act," became effective in 1995. It directs the States to (1) allow all eligible citizens to register to vote when they apply for or renew a driver's license; (2) provide for voter registration by mail; and (3) make registration forms available at the local offices of State employment, welfare, and other social service agencies. The Federal Election Commission reported that by the year 2000, approximately 8 mil-

## Background

**AUSTRALIAN BALLOT** Although the use of paper ballots in the U.S. dates back to colonial times, the growth of political parties in the early 1800s led to widespread abuses. The law at that time allowed parties to print and distribute ballots to voters before elections. These ballots listed the party's candidates only. To vote for another candidate, voters would have to cross out the printed name and write in another. Voting was not always secret, and corruption was common. Parties often paid election officials to stuff ballot boxes. Heeding calls for reform, Massachusetts in 1888 adopted the Australian Ballot System, which originated in Australia in 1856. Under this system, ballots list all candidates and are prepared by government agencies. Voters receive one ballot at the polling place, which they mark in the privacy of a voting booth. Today, all States use a form of this system.

## Answers

**Voter Identification** Possible answer: The requirement is controversial because, while some believe it is a reasonable effort to stop fraud, others see it as an unnecessary barrier to voting.

lion persons had registered to vote as a direct result of the Motor Voter Law.

The law also requires every State to mail a questionnaire to each of its registered voters every four years, so that the poll books can be purged for deaths and changes of residence. It also forbids the States to purge for any other reason, including failure to vote.

Several States now have so-called voter ID laws that require people to prove their identity when they seek to register or vote. Some government-issued photo ID—a passport or a driver's license, for example—will usually satisfy the requirement to confirm their identity at the polls.

The statutes are quite controversial. Their sponsors, usually Republican State legislators, insist that the measures are intended to prevent people from voting under false identities, also known as fraudulent voting. Fraudulent voting, they argue, weakens the value of legally-cast votes by diluting them with illegitimate votes. Critics, mostly Democrats, say that they are really designed to discourage voting by the elderly, disabled, poor, and minority groups, who are less likely to have State-issued driver's licenses or federally issued passports. They also argue that very few cases of voter fraud have been identified and prosecuted in recent years.

The Supreme Court upheld Indiana's photo ID law in *Crawford* v. *Marion County Election Board* in 2008. The Court ruled, 6–3, that the opponents of the law had not shown that it puts so unreasonable a burden on some groups of voters that it violates the 14th Amendment's Equal Protection Clause. The Court will likely hear other challenges to these laws as they are applied in future elections.

## Literacy, Tax Payment

Suffrage qualifications based on two other factors—literacy and tax payment—were once fairly common among the States. They had a fairly long history but are no longer to be found anywhere.

**Literacy** Today, no State has a suffrage qualification based on voter **literacy**—a person's ability to read and write. At one time, the literacy requirement could be, and in many places was, used to make sure that a qualified voter had the capacity to cast an informed ballot. Some States asked potential voters to prove that they could read; others asked for the ability to both read and write. And still others required those who registered to vote to show that they could read and write and also understand some piece of printed material—often, a passage from the State or Federal Constitution.

Connecticut adopted the first literacy qualifications in 1855. Massachusetts followed in 1857. Both States were trying to limit voting by Irish Catholic immigrants. Mississippi adopted a literacy requirement in 1890, and soon after, most of the other southern States followed suit. The literary qualification in most southern States included an "understanding" clause. Often, whites were asked to "understand" some short, plainly worded constitutional provision; but African Americans had to interpret a long, complex passage to the satisfaction of local election officials.

While those qualifications had been aimed at disenfranchising African Americans, they sometimes had unintended effects. Several States soon found that they needed to adjust their voting requirements by adding so-called grandfather clauses to their constitutions. These grandfather clauses were designed to enfranchise those white males who were unintentionally disqualified by their failure to meet the literacy or taxpaying requirements.

A grandfather clause was added to the Louisiana constitution in 1898; Alabama, Georgia, Maryland, North Carolina, Oklahoma, and Virginia soon added them as well. These clauses stated that any man, or his male descendants, who had voted in the State before the adoption of the 15th Amendment (1870) could become a legal voter without regard to any literacy or taxpaying qualifications. The Supreme Court found the Oklahoma provision, the last to be adopted (in 1910), in conflict with the 15th Amendment in *Guinn* v. *United States* in 1915.

A number of States outside the South also adopted literacy qualifications, including Wyoming, California, Washington, New

✔ **Checkpoint**
What are the requirements of the "Motor Voter Law Act?"

## Background

**LEGAL LITERACY TEST** The use of literacy tests as a requirement for registration was brought to an end in 1970, yet some voters must still meet certain basic literacy requirements. Immigrants to the United States must demonstrate the ability to read, speak, and write English in order to become United States citizens. Since citizenship is a requirement for voting in the United States, people who are not born citizens of the United States do, in fact, face a kind of literacy test before they can cast a ballot.

### EXTEND THE LESSON

**L3 Differentiate** Distribute the Extend Worksheet (Unit 2 All-in-One, p. 82). Tell students that this is a copy of a standardized application that is widely accepted among States that require voter registration. Have students fill out the form to the best of their ability. Then have students write a brief paragraph that explains how this form differs from the form on Core Worksheet A. *(Students should observe that the form asks only basic information necessary to confirm a potential voter's identity and the universal qualifications of citizenship, residency, and age, whereas the form on Core Worksheet A required would-be voters to know detailed information about government and to provide personal information.)*

**L4 Differentiate** Have students use the Internet to locate the specific instructions for their State and prepare a valid registration application for themselves or someone in their family. If applicable, they can use the National Mail Registration Form, on which the worksheet is based. They should leave a blank for Social Security Number to avoid compromising their identity security.

**L2 Differentiate** Distribute the Extend Activity "Registering to Vote" (Unit 2 All-in-One, p. 83) and have students follow the instructions on it.

---

## Answers

**Checkpoint** The law requires States to allow people to register when they apply for or renew their driver's licenses; to provide for registration by mail; to make registration forms available in certain specific places; to mail voters questionnaires for purposes of purging poll books; and to limit purging to those who have died or changed residence.

## Assess and Remediate

**L3** Collect the letters to the editor and assess students' work using the Rubric for Assessing a Letter to the Editor (Unit 2 All-in-One, p. 254).

**L3** Assign the Section 2 Assessment questions.

**L3** Section Quiz A (Unit 2 All-in-One, p. 84)

**L2** Section Quiz B (Unit 2 All-in-One, p. 85)

Have students complete the review activities in the digital lesson presentation and continue their work in the **Essential Questions Journal.**

## Answers

**Registration Requirements** Lengthy or complex test questions could intimidate and discourage registrants.

**Checkpoint** the 24th Amendment

---

## Registration Requirements

Literacy tests (below) were used in many places to try to deny African Americans the right to vote. The questions below are reproduced from one of the many versions of those tests in use during that time. The tests were changed frequently, making it impossible to study for them. *How might these questions discourage eligible citizens from registering to vote?*

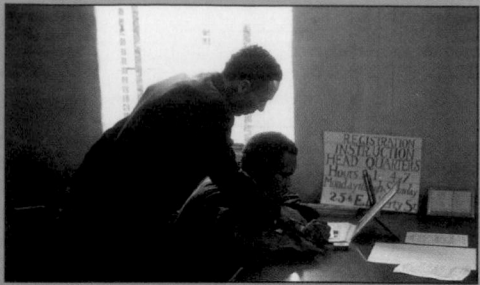

A voter fills out a registration form. ▶

## Can you answer these?

**1.** If you have been employed by another during the last five years, state the nature of your employment and the name or names of such employer or employers and his or their addresses.

**2.** Give the names of the places, respectively, where you have lived during the last five years; and the name or names by which you have been known during the last five years.

**3.** Are you now or have you ever been affiliated with any group or organization which advocates the overthrow of the Unites States Government or the government of any State of the United States by unlawful means?

**4.** Name some of the duties and obligations of citizenship. Do you regard those duties and obligations as having priority over the duties and obligations you owe to any other secular organization when they are in conflict?

Source: The Honorable Rufus A. Lewis Collection at Trenholm State Technical College Archives

---

✔ **Checkpoint**
Which amendment outlawed the poll tax?

Hampshire, Arizona, New York, Oregon, and Alaska. Its unfair use finally led Congress to ban literacy qualifications in 1970. The Court agreed in *Oregon* v. *Mitchell,* 1970:

> **PRIMARY SOURCE**
> In enacting the literacy test ban . . . Congress had before it a long history of the discriminatory use of literacy tests to disfranchise voters on account of their race.
> —Justice Hugo Black, Opinion of the Court

Some form of the literacy requirement was in place in 18 States when Congress finally banned its use.

**Tax Payment** Property ownership, proved by the payment of property taxes, was once a very common suffrage qualification. For decades, several States also demanded the payment of a special tax, called the poll tax, as a condition for voting. Those requirements and others that

called for the payment of a tax in order to vote have disappeared over the years.

The poll tax was once found throughout the South. Beginning with Florida in 1889, each of the 11 southern States adopted the poll tax as part of the effort to discourage voting by African Americans. The device proved to be of only limited effectiveness, however. That fact, and opposition to the use of the poll tax from within the South as well as elsewhere, led most of those States to abandon it. By 1966, the tax was still in use in only Alabama, Mississippi, Texas, and Virginia.[12]

The 24th Amendment, ratified in 1964, outlawed the poll tax, or any other tax, as a condition for voting in any federal election. The Supreme Court finally eliminated the poll tax in 1966 as a qualification for voting in all elections. In *Harper* v. *Virginia Board of Elections,* the Court held the Virginia poll tax to be

---

12 By that time, the poll tax had been abolished in North Carolina (1920), Louisiana (1934), Florida (1937), Georgia (1945), South Carolina (1951), Tennessee (1953), and Arkansas (1965).

---

## Background

**AFRICAN AMERICAN VOTING RIGHTS** The introduction of discriminatory voter restrictions came about in the years after Reconstruction, the post-Civil War period in which the Southern states were brought back into the Union and the newly freed African Americans were granted voting and other civil rights. During that time, African American populations in some places were a majority of voters. New African American voters succeeded in helping elect representatives to local and State governments throughout the South and also to Congress. But with the end of Reconstruction in 1877, the Federal Government turned its attention away from the South—and many whites began a systematic program of terror and intimidation to drive African Americans out of the political process. That job accomplished, many southern states passed discriminatory laws, such as literacy tests and poll taxes.

in conflict with the 14th Amendment's Equal Protection Clause. The Court could find no reasonable relationship between the act of voting on one hand and the payment of a tax on the other. Justice William O. Douglas, writing for the majority, put the point this way:

### PRIMARY SOURCE

"Once the franchise is granted to the electorate, lines may not be drawn which are inconsistent with the Equal Protection Clause. . . . Voter qualifications have no relation to wealth nor to paying this or any other tax. . . . Wealth, like race, creed, or color, is not germane to one's ability to participate intelligently in the electoral process.

—Justice William O. Douglas,
Opinion of the Court

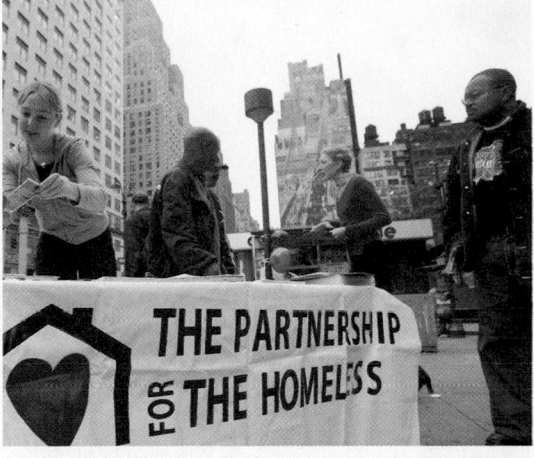

▲ Several groups hold voter registration drives targeting the homeless, especially in larger cities. **Why might it be important to register the homeless in a large city?**

**Persons Denied the Vote** Clearly, democratic government can exist only where the right to vote is widely held. Still, every State does purposely deny the vote to certain persons. For example, few of the 50 States allow people in mental institutions, or any other persons who have been legally found to be mentally incompetent, to vote.

Most States disqualify, at least temporarily, those persons who have been convicted of serious crimes. Until fairly recently, that disqualification was almost always a permanent one. Over recent years, however, most States have made it possible for the majority of convicted felons to regain the right to vote, although those guilty of such election-related offenses as bribery and ballot-box stuffing, however, are still regularly banned. A few States also do not allow anyone dishonorably discharged from the armed forces to cast a ballot.

---

**Essential Questions Journal** To continue to build a response to the chapter Essential Question, go to your **Essential Questions Journal.**

## SECTION 2 ASSESSMENT

1. **Guiding Question** Use your completed flowchart to answer the question: What are the qualifications for voting, and how have they changed over time?

### Key Terms and Comprehension

2. What does the Constitution say about the voting rights of **aliens?**

3. (a) What is the purpose of laws requiring voter **registration?** (b) How do registration laws vary among States?

4. Why should election officials regularly **purge** voter lists?

### Critical Thinking

5. **Express Problems Clearly (a)** What are the pros and cons of voter registration? **(b)** Do you think the "Motor Voter Law" has had a positive or negative impact on voting? Explain.

6. **Draw Inferences (a)** Why were literacy requirements originally added to some State's voting requirements? **(b)** How did the establishment of "grandfather clauses" call into question the motives of States that had literacy test requirements?

### Quick Write

**Narrative: Consider Audience and Purpose** Once you have chosen an event, think about who your audience is. Will you be writing for your fellow classmates, your teacher, or someone outside of your class? Consider how much background information you need to provide to your reader. Write a brief paragraph describing your audience.

---

# How did the U.S. fulfill the promise of the 15th Amendment?

| 15th Amendment | Civil Rights |
|---|---|
| • Ratified 1870<br>• Vote cannot be denied any U.S. citizen because of race, color, or previous condition of servitude<br>• Southern whites used violence, threats, social pressures, literacy tests, poll taxes, white primaries, and gerrymandering to deny African Americans their 15th Amendment rights<br>• *Smith* v. *Allwright* (1944) banned white primaries, and *Gomillion* v. *Lightfoot* (1960s) banned gerrymandering for purposes of racial discrimination, but use of literacy tests and poll taxes remained into the 1960s | • Civil Rights Act of 1957 set up commission to investigate voter discrimination and enabled attorney general to enforce voting rights<br>• Civil Rights Act of 1960 provided for federal voting referees to serve where voter discrimination existed and help eligible voters register and vote<br>• Civil Rights Act of 1964 banned discrimination in jobs and other areas and discriminatory voter registration or literacy requirements<br>• Voting Rights Act of 1965 prompted by civil rights march in Selma, Alabama; applied 15th Amendment to all elections, not just federal; challenged poll taxes and literacy tests; authorized voting examiners; required federal preclearance for any changes to State election laws<br>• *South Carolina* v. *Katzenbach* upheld Voting Rights Act of 1965<br>• Voting Rights Act Amendments of 1970 extended the Act for five years; banned literacy tests<br>• *Oregon* v. *Mitchell* upheld ban on literacy tests and the residency requirements in the law<br>• Law extended in 1975; ban on literacy tests made permanent; applied provisions to language minorities |

**Equal Voting Rights**

## SKILLS DEVELOPMENT

### ANALYZE TIMELINES

Before students study the timeline in this section, you may want to review information on analyzing timelines in the Skills Handbook, p. S29.

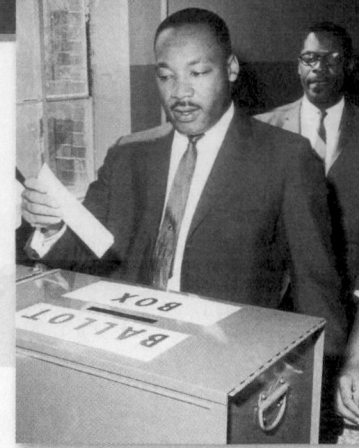

## SECTION 3

# Suffrage and Civil Rights

### Guiding Question

**How did the U.S. fulfill the promise of the 15th Amendment?** Use the chart to record details of the history of voting rights for African Americans.

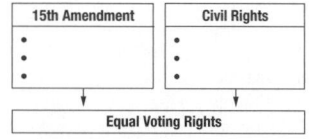

| 15th Amendment | Civil Rights |
|---|---|
| •<br>•<br>• | •<br>•<br>• |

**Equal Voting Rights**

### Political Dictionary
• gerrymandering
• injunction
• preclearance

### Objectives
1. Describe the tactics often used to deny African Americans the right to vote despite the command of the 15th Amendment.
2. Understand the significance of the civil rights laws enacted in 1957, 1960, and 1964.
3. Analyze the provisions and effects of the Voting Rights Act of 1965.

**Image Above:** Dr. Martin Luther King, Jr., casts his ballot in Atlanta, Georgia, on November 3, 1964.

How important is the right to vote? For those who do not have it, that right can seem as important as life itself. Indeed, in the Deep South of the 1960s, civil rights workers suffered arrest, beatings, shocks with electric cattle prods, even death—all in the name of the right to vote. Their efforts inspired the nation and led to large-scale federal efforts to secure that right for African Americans and other minority groups in the United States.

## The 15th Amendment

The effort to extend the franchise to African Americans began with the 15th Amendment, which was ratified in 1870. It declares that the right to vote cannot be denied to any citizen of the United States because of "race, color, or previous condition of servitude." The amendment was plainly intended to ensure that African American men, nearly all of them former slaves and nearly all of them living in the South, could vote.

The 15th Amendment is not self-executing, however. In other words, simply stating a general principle without providing for a means of enforcement was not enough to carry out the intention of the amendment. To make it effective, Congress had to act. Yet for nearly 90 years the Federal Government paid little attention to the voting rights of African Americans.

**History** During that period, African Americans were generally and systematically kept from the polls in much of the South. White supremacists employed a number of tactics to that end. Their major weapon was violence. Other tactics included more subtle threats and social pressures—for example, firing an African American man who tried to register or vote, or denying his family credit at local stores.

More formal "legal" devices were used, as well. The most effective were literacy tests. White officials regularly manipulated those tests to disenfranchise African Americans. Registration laws served the same end. As written, they applied to all potential voters. In practice, however, they were often administered to keep African Americans from qualifying to vote. Poll taxes, "white primaries," gerrymandering, and several other devices were also used.

## Focus on the Basics

**FACTS:** • The 15th Amendment, ratified in 1870, forbade denial of voting rights due to race. • Some southern whites used unfair laws, intimidation, and other discriminatory practices to circumvent the 15th Amendment. • Supreme Court cases and civil rights laws beginning in the 1950s finally helped fulfill the purpose of the 15th Amendment.

**CONCEPTS:** equal protection, rights and responsibilities of citizens, values and principles of a civil society, personal and civic rights and responsibilities

**ENDURING UNDERSTANDINGS:** • Whites in the South and elsewhere took actions to deny African Americans their civil rights starting in the late 1800s. • Civil rights workers, the judiciary, and Congress finally reversed these injustices.

**Gerrymandering** is the practice of drawing electoral district lines (the boundaries of the geographic area from which a candidate is elected to a public office) in order to limit the voting strength of a particular group or party.

The white primary arose out of the decades-long Democratic domination of politics in the South. It was almost a given that the Democratic candidate for an office would be elected. Therefore, only the Democrats ordinarily nominated candidates, generally in primaries. In several southern States, political parties were defined by law as "private associations" that could exclude whomever they chose, and the Democrats regularly refused to admit African Americans. Because only party members could vote in the party's primary, African Americans were then excluded from a critical step in the public election process.

**Court Rulings** The Supreme Court outlawed the white primary in a case from Texas, *Smith v. Allwright,* in 1944. The Court held that nominations are an integral part of the election process. So, when a political party holds a primary, it is performing a public function and is bound by the 15th Amendment.

The Supreme Court outlawed gerrymandering used for purposes of racial discrimination in *Gomillion* v. *Lightfoot,* 1960. There, the Alabama legislature had redrawn the electoral district boundaries of Tuskegee, effectively excluding blacks from the city limits. The Court ruled that the legislature's action violated the 15th Amendment, because the irregularly shaped district clearly was created to deprive blacks of political power.

Led by these decisions, the lower federal courts struck down many practices designed to deny the vote to African Americans in the 1940s and 1950s. Still, the courts could act only when those who claimed to be victims of discrimination sued. That case-by-case method was, at best, agonizingly slow.

## Early Civil Rights Legislation

Finally, largely in response to the civil rights movement led by Dr. Martin Luther King, Jr., Congress was moved to act. In the late 1950s, it began to enact civil rights laws specifically intended to implement the 15th Amendment.

**Acts of 1957 and 1960** The first of the laws Congress passed to enforce the 15th Amendment was the Civil Rights Act of 1957, which created the United States Commission on Civil Rights. One of the Commission's major duties is to inquire into claims of voter discrimination. The Commission reports its findings to Congress and the President and, through the media, to the public. The 1957 law also gave the attorney general the power to seek federal court orders to prevent interference with any person's right to vote in any federal election.

The Civil Rights Act of 1960 added an additional safeguard. It provided for the appointment of federal voting referees. Those officers were to serve anywhere a federal court found voter discrimination. They were given the power to help qualified persons to register and vote in federal elections.

**The Civil Rights Act of 1964** The Civil Rights Act of 1964 is much broader and more effective than either of the two earlier measures. It outlaws discrimination in several areas, especially in job-related matters. With regard to voting rights, its most important section forbids the use of any voter registration or literacy requirement in an unfair or discriminatory manner.

The 1964 law continued a pattern set in the earlier laws. It relied on judicial action to overcome racial barriers and emphasized the use of federal court orders called injunctions. An **injunction** is a court order that either compels or restrains the performance of some act by a private individual or public official. The violation of an injunction amounts to contempt of court, a crime punishable by fine and/or imprisonment.

Dramatic events in Selma, Alabama, soon revealed the shortcomings of this approach. Dr. King mounted a voter registration drive in that city in early 1965. He and his supporters hoped that they could focus national attention on the issue of African American voting rights—and they most certainly did.

Their registration efforts were met with insults and violence by local white civilians, by city and county police, and then by State troopers. Three civil rights workers were murdered, and many were beaten when they attempted a peaceful march to the State

✔ **Checkpoint**
What is gerrymandering and how was it used to keep African Americans from voting?

**white supremacist**
*n.* advocate of the superiority of the white race, racist

**compel**
*v.* to force, require

**civilian**
*n.* any person not an active member of the armed forces or having police power

# Differentiated Resources

The following resources are located in the All-in-One, Unit 2, Chapter 6, Section 3:

**L3** Reading Comprehension Worksheet (p. 86)

**L2** Reading Comprehension Worksheet (p. 87)

**L3** Core Worksheet (p. 88)

**L3** Quiz A (p. 91)

**L2** Quiz B (p. 92)

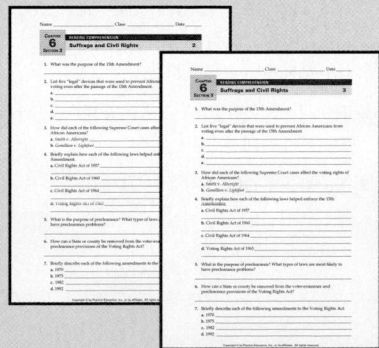

# Get Started

## LESSON GOALS

Students will . . .

• identify historical barriers that faced African American voters by examining a political cartoon.

• analyze historical data on African American representation in Congress to understand the effects of widespread voter discrimination and its removal.

## BEFORE CLASS

Assign the section, the graphic organizer in the text, and the Reading Comprehension Worksheet (Unit 2 All-in-One, p. 86) before class.

**L2** **Differentiate** Reading Comprehension Worksheet (Unit 2 All-in-One, p. 87)

## BELLRINGER

Display Transparency 6C, Voting Rights, a political cartoon that symbolizes the challenges to African Americans' voting rights. On the board, write: **Examine the cartoon and record the answers to the questions in your notebook.**

**L1 L2** **Differentiate** Review the explanations of literacy tests, poll taxes, and grandfather clauses. *(Literacy tests were tests of people's ability to read and write, which a person had to pass in order to vote. Poll taxes were taxes required as a condition for voting. Both limited the ability of African Americans to vote, because most had little money or education. However, some white males could not pass the literacy test or pay the poll tax. Grandfather clauses were designed to allow these white males to vote anyway.)*

# Teach

To present this topic using online resources, use the lesson presentations at **PearsonSchool.com/phgovt.**

## DISCUSS

Ask students to share their Bellringer answers. *(1. The African American voter faced barriers that the white voter did not. 2. These included poll taxes, literacy tests, grandfather clauses, and intimidation.)* Explain that students will learn about how African Americans and sympathetic whites responded to this reality. Ask: **How can people who cannot vote still take part in public affairs?** *(They can protest, they can seek to influence lawmakers, and they can try to get courts to take action.)*

## Answers

**Checkpoint** Gerrymandering is the drawing of district lines in ways that weaken specific groups. It was used to weaken African Americans' voting power.

Ask students to examine this section's timeline. Have them create titles for each of the three colored segments. *(possible title for the green section: "High Hopes—and Disappointment"; for the blue section: "Some Barriers Fall"; for the orange section: "Victory at Last.")* Be sure students recognize that the history of African Americans and voting rights included a long period of rights denied, followed by gradual progress toward the successes of the 1960s.

**DISTRIBUTE CORE WORKSHEET**

Distribute the Chapter 6 Section 3 Core Worksheet (Unit 2 All-in-One, p. 88), which asks students to examine data and draw conclusions about African American representation in Congress. Help students recognize the general pattern in the data—a brief period of modest success at electing African American candidates following the 1870 ratification of the 15th Amendment, followed by a long period in which there were very few candidates elected, followed finally by a steady trend upward, beginning in the 1960s. Explain that the data reflect representation from all the States, including those in the North.

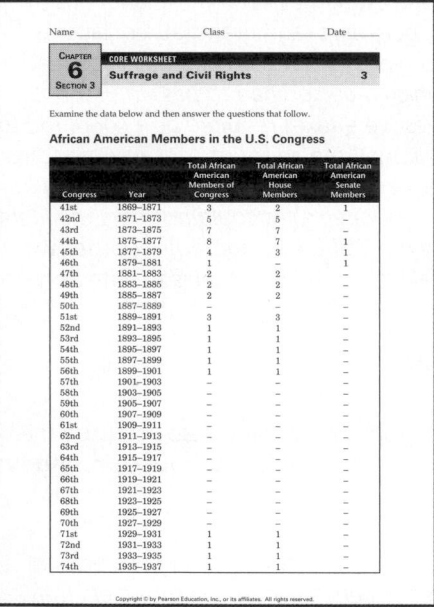

Name _____ Class _____ Date _____

CHAPTER **6** SECTION 3 — CORE WORKSHEET
**Suffrage and Civil Rights** 3

Examine the data below and then answer the questions that follow.

**African American Members in the U.S. Congress**

| Congress | Year | Total African American Members of Congress | Total African American House Members | Total African American Senate Members |
|---|---|---|---|---|
| 41st | 1869–1871 | 3 | 2 | 1 |
| 42nd | 1871–1873 | 5 | 5 | – |
| 43rd | 1873–1875 | 7 | 7 | – |
| 44th | 1875–1877 | 8 | 7 | 1 |
| 45th | 1877–1879 | 4 | 3 | 1 |
| 46th | 1879–1881 | 1 | – | 1 |
| 47th | 1881–1883 | 2 | 2 | – |
| 48th | 1883–1885 | 2 | 2 | – |
| 49th | 1885–1887 | 2 | 2 | – |
| 50th | 1887–1889 | – | – | – |
| 51st | 1889–1891 | 3 | 3 | – |
| 52nd | 1891–1893 | 1 | 1 | – |
| 53rd | 1893–1895 | 1 | 1 | – |
| 54th | 1895–1897 | 1 | 1 | – |
| 55th | 1897–1899 | 1 | 1 | – |
| 56th | 1899–1901 | 1 | 1 | – |
| 57th | 1901–1903 | – | – | – |
| 58th | 1903–1905 | – | – | – |
| 59th | 1905–1907 | – | – | – |
| 60th | 1907–1909 | – | – | – |
| 61st | 1909–1911 | – | – | – |
| 62nd | 1911–1913 | – | – | – |
| 63rd | 1913–1915 | – | – | – |
| 64th | 1915–1917 | – | – | – |
| 65th | 1917–1919 | – | – | – |
| 66th | 1919–1921 | – | – | – |
| 67th | 1921–1923 | – | – | – |
| 68th | 1923–1925 | – | – | – |
| 69th | 1925–1927 | – | – | – |
| 70th | 1927–1929 | – | – | – |
| 71st | 1929–1931 | 1 | 1 | – |
| 72nd | 1931–1933 | 1 | 1 | – |
| 73rd | 1933–1935 | 1 | 1 | – |
| 74th | 1935–1937 | 1 | 1 | – |

## Answers

**Analyzing Timelines** Since the 15th Amendment did not provide a means of enforcing the law, the significant public resistance prevented the amendment's provisions from taking hold.

# African Americans and the Vote

**1800s**

**1870** The 15th Amendment declares that the right to vote cannot be denied on the basis of race.

**1871** For the first time, African Americans, including Senator Hiram R. Revels (R., Miss.), shown at right, serve in Congress.

**1896** First literacy tests and grandfather clauses enacted in some southern States; soon voting by African Americans virtually disappeared in much of the South.

**Early 1900s**

**1915** The Supreme Court rules an Oklahoma grandfather clause unconstitutional in *Guinn* v. *United States.*

**1944** In *Smith* v. *Allwright,* the Supreme Court finds that the Texas white primary—which excluded African American voters—is unconstitutional.

▶▶ **Analyzing Timelines** The 15th Amendment did not really become an effective part of the Constitution until the 1960s. **Why do you think it took so long for the 15th Amendment to become truly effective?**

Capitol. The nation saw much of the drama on television and was shocked. An outraged President Lyndon Johnson urged Congress to pass new and stronger legislation to ensure the voting rights of African Americans. Congress responded, and quickly.

## Voting Rights Act of 1965

The Voting Rights Act of 1965 made the 15th Amendment, at long last, a truly effective part of the Constitution. Unlike its predecessors, this act applied to *all* elections held anywhere in this country—State and local, as well as federal.

Originally, the Voting Rights Act was to be in effect for a period of five years. Congress has extended its life on four occasions, in the Voting Rights Act Amendments of 1970, 1975, 1982, and, most recently, 2006. The present version of the law was made effective for 25 years; its provisions will not expire until 2031.

**predecessor**
*n.* one who goes before, forerunner

The 1965 law directed the attorney general to challenge the constitutionality of the remaining State poll-tax laws in the federal courts. That provision led directly to *Harper* v. *Virginia Board of Elections,* 1966, as you may recall from Section 2.

The law also suspended the use of any literacy test or similar device in any State or county where less than half of the electorate had been registered or had voted in the 1964 presidential election. The law authorized the attorney general to appoint voting examiners to serve in any of those States or counties. It also gave these federal officers the power to register voters and otherwise oversee the conduct of elections in those areas.

**Preclearance** The Voting Rights Act of 1965 imposed another restriction on those States where a majority of the electorate had not voted in 1964. The act declared that no new election laws, and no changes in existing election laws, could go into effect in any

## Fast Facts

- Number of African Americans who have been members of Congress: 123 (118 in the House and 5 in the Senate)
- Number of African American members of Congress by party: 96 Democrats and 27 Republicans
- The first African American woman in Congress: Shirley Chisholm, who served from 1969 until 1983
- Number of Africans Americans serving in the 111th Congress (2009–2011): 42

## Today

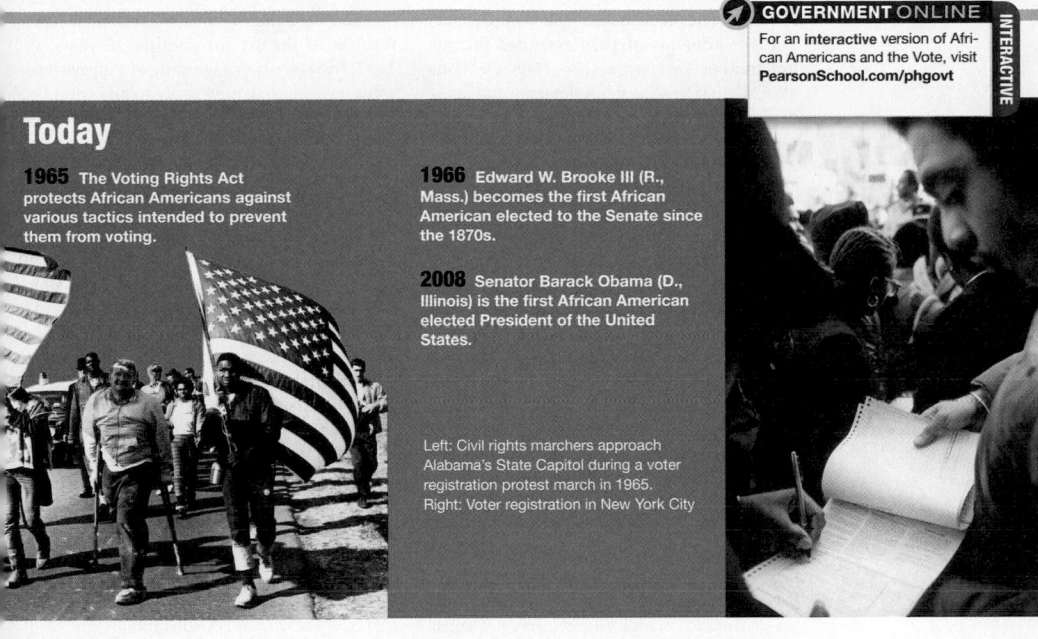

**1965** The Voting Rights Act protects African Americans against various tactics intended to prevent them from voting.

**1966** Edward W. Brooke III (R., Mass.) becomes the first African American elected to the Senate since the 1870s.

**2008** Senator Barack Obama (D., Illinois) is the first African American elected President of the United States.

Left: Civil rights marchers approach Alabama's State Capitol during a voter registration protest march in 1965.
Right: Voter registration in New York City

**GOVERNMENT** ONLINE

For an **interactive** version of African Americans and the Vote, visit **PearsonSchool.com/phgovt**

INTERACTIVE

---

of those States unless first approved—given **preclearance**—by the Department of Justice. Only those new or revised laws that do not <u>dilute</u> the voting rights of minority groups can survive the preclearance process and take effect.

The preclearance hurdle has produced a large number of court cases over the years. Those cases show that the laws most likely to <u>run afoul</u> of the preclearance requirement are those that make these kinds of changes: (1) the location of polling places; (2) the boundaries of election districts; (3) the deadlines in the election process; (4) a shift from ward or district election to at-large elections; or (5) the qualifications candidates must meet in order to run for office.

Any State or county subject to the voter-examiner and preclearance provisions can be removed from the law's coverage through a "bail-out" process. That relief can come if the State shows the United States District Court in the District of Columbia that it has not

applied any voting procedures in a discriminatory way for at least 10 years.

The voter-examiner and preclearance provisions of the 1965 Voting Rights Act originally applied to six entire States: Alabama, Georgia, Louisiana, Mississippi, South Carolina, and Virginia. In addition, these provisions applied to 40 counties in North Carolina.

The Supreme Court upheld the Voting Rights Act in 1966. In *South Carolina* v. *Katzenbach*, a unanimous Court rejected the claim that the law—and, most particularly, its preclearance provisions—violated the reserved power of each State to shape its own electoral system. Instead the Court found the Voting Rights Act to be a proper exercise of the power granted to Congress in Section 2 of the 15th Amendment. That provision authorizes Congress to enact "appropriate legislation" to enforce the constitutional prohibition against racial discrimination in voting set out in Section 1 of the amendment.

✔ **Checkpoint**
What provision about literacy tests was in the Voting Rights Act of 1965?

**dilute**
*v.* to weaken, diminish, water down

**run afoul**
*v.* to come into conflict with, be at odds with

---

**L1 L2 Differentiate** Help students read the table, making clear that the middle column shows totals, the second column from the right shows representation in the House, and the far-right column shows representation in the Senate.

**L4 Differentiate** To challenge students, have them research and provide data about the electoral success of women and other minority groups in Congress.

### DISCUSS WORKSHEET ANSWERS

Review the answers to the Core Worksheet questions as a class. Make sure students correctly recognize the impact of the 15th Amendment (Question 1), the systematic effort to deny African American voting rights (Question 2), and the impact of the civil rights movement (Question 3). When discussing Question 4, point out that Senate elections are statewide and most House elections are not. Invite classroom debate of student answers to Question 5.

### EXTEND THE LESSON

**L3** Have students use the Internet to research the life of one African American who served or serves in the United States Congress. Students may choose a subject from the post-Civil War era or a more contemporary example. Using the information they collect, students should create a brief biographical sketch of their subject. The sketch should specifically address what kind of obstacles—if any—the politician experienced as an African American candidate, and how he or she overcame those challenges.

**L1 L2 Differentiate** Help students identify a possible subject for their research, and have them compile biographical information about their subject and present their findings as a list of facts and highlights about the person's career.

**L4 Differentiate** Have students research and report on the 91st Congress, which featured a dramatic jump in the number of African American members over the 90th Congress.

Tell students to go to the Interactivity to learn more about African American voting rights over time.

## Background

**EXTENDING THE VOTING RIGHTS ACT** The Voting Rights Act was reauthorized in 2006. This action extended the basic features of the law for 25 years. The reauthorization was named in honor of three leading women of the civil rights movement—Fannie Lou Hamer, Coretta Scott King, and Rosa Parks. During the debate, some lawmakers argued that the original Voting Rights Act had already achieved its purpose. In addition, others objected to provisions that required bilingual ballots or interpreters for voters who do not speak English well.

## Answers

**Checkpoint** The act suspended the use of literacy tests in places where less than half of the electorate was registered or voted in 1964.

# Assess and Remediate

**L2 L3** Assess students' work on the Core Worksheet.

**L3** Assign the Section 3 Assessment questions.

**L3** Section Quiz A (Unit 2 All-in-One, p. 91)

**L2** Section Quiz B (Unit 2 All-in-One, p. 92)

Have students complete the review activities in the digital lesson presentation and continue their work in the **Essential Questions Journal.**

## REMEDIATION

| If Your Students Have Trouble With | Strategies For Remediation |
|---|---|
| The many legal means of denying African Americans the vote (Questions 2, 4) | Have students create flash cards with definitions of the terms *gerrymandering, grandfather clause, white primary, poll tax,* and *literacy test.* |
| The key Supreme Court rulings that helped end voter discrimination (Questions 1, 5) | Have student pairs write quiz questions for each other on the major cases mentioned in this section. |
| The key features of the Civil Rights Act of 1964 and the Voting Rights Act of 1965 (Questions 3, 5) | Have students create a table that lists the key features of each law and its impact. |

**Amendments to the Act** The Voting Rights Act Amendments of 1970 extended the law for another five years. The 1968 elections were taken into account in determining jurisdictions with concerns; the result was that a number of counties in six more States (Alaska, Arizona, California, Idaho, New Mexico, and Oregon) were included in the law's coverage.

That 1970 law also provided that, for five years, no State could use literacy as the basis for any voting requirement. That temporary ban as well as residence provisions outlined in the law were upheld by the Supreme Court in *Oregon* v. *Mitchell* in 1970.

In 1975, the law was extended again, this time for seven years, and the five-year ban on literacy tests was made permanent. Since 1975, no State has been able to apply *any* sort of literacy qualification to *any* aspect of the election process. The law's voter-examiner and preclearance provisions were also broadened in 1975. Since then, they have also covered any State or county where more than 5 percent of the voting-age population belongs to certain "language minorities." These groups are defined to include all persons of Spanish heritage, Native Americans, Asian Americans, and Alaskan Natives.

This addition expanded the law's coverage to all of Alaska and Texas and to several counties in 24 other States, as well. In these areas, all ballots and other official election materials must be printed both in English and in the language of the minorities involved.

The 1982 amendments extended the basic features of the act for another 25 years. In 1992, the law's language-minority provisions were revised: they now apply to any community that has a minority-language population of 10,000 or more.

Over the years, several States and a handful of counties in a few other States have been removed from the law's coverage, through the "bail-out" process. Today, eight entire States remain subject to the Voting Rights Act: Alabama, Alaska, Arizona, Georgia, Louisiana, Mississippi, South Carolina, and Texas. At least some counties in six other States are also covered by the statute: California, Florida, New York, North Carolina, South Dakota, and Virginia, as well as two townships in Michigan and ten towns in New Hampshire.

The Court still faces challenges to the Voting Rights Act, most recently in *Northwest Austin Municipal Utility District* v. *Holder* in 2009. There, a small Texas water district argued that, given the many significant changes in race relationships over the past 40 years, the 2006 extension of the law was unnecessary and is, therefore, unconstitutional.

In deciding the case, the Court sidestepped the question of the law's constitutionality. It did so by holding, 8–1, that because the water district had no history of race-based discrimination it was not subject to the law's preclearance provisions. Clearly, the future holds more challenges to the validity of the Voting Rights Act.

---

**Essential Questions Journal** To continue to build a response to the chapter Essential Question, go to your **Essential Questions Journal.**

## SECTION 3 ASSESSMENT

1. **Guiding Question** Use your completed chart to answer the question: **How did the United States fulfill the promise of the 15th Amendment?**

### Key Terms and Comprehension

2. How has **gerrymandering** been used to prevent the fulfillment of the 15th Amendment?

3. (a) What is **preclearance**? (b) What is the process meant to prevent?

### Critical Thinking

4. **Synthesize Information** Why, for nearly a century, was the 15th Amendment largely ineffective?

5. **Make Comparisons (a)** In what key way did the Voting Rights Act of 1965 differ from earlier civil rights laws? **(b)** How have more recent legislation and court decisions helped further refine that Act?

### Quick Write

**Narrative: Gather Details** Gather any additional details about the event you chose in Section 1 that may be important to your essay. List details in order of importance.

---

# Assessment Answers

**1.** After the 15th Amendment passed, widespread resistance to African American suffrage in the South led to effective limits to African American voting, but legal rulings and legislative action overcame these barriers.

**2.** Gerrymandering has been used to create electoral districts that weaken the voting strength of African Americans.

**3. (a)** Certain States could not institute or alter election law without prior approval of the Department of Justice. **(b)** the denial of voting rights through government action

**4.** The lack of an enforcement provision within the 15th Amendment allowed the overwhelming public resistance to effectively deny African Americans the basic freedoms granted by the amendment for nearly a century.

**5. (a)** The Voting Rights Act applied to State and local elections, not just national elections. The Act did not rely on injunctions to stop illegal practices, but instead involved the federal government proactively in registering voters, monitoring elections, and challenging discriminatory laws and practices. **(b)** *South Carolina* v.

*Katzenbach* upheld the act. *Oregon* v. *Mitchell* upheld the act's ban on literacy tests and its residency requirements. Later amendments extended the life of the act, banned literacy tests permanently, and broadened voter-examiner and preclearance provisions to include language minorities.

**QUICK WRITE** Students should gather enough details to support a strong essay.

# Casting Your Vote

**Voting is one of the greatest privileges a citizen enjoys. It means that you have a role in deciding who your elected officials will be. Yet voting is a big responsibility. It takes some planning to ensure your eligibility, prepare yourself to become an informed voter, and eventually cast your vote.**

Casting your vote in an election requires two different kinds of preparation. First, you must become aware of the rules and procedures concerning registering to vote and submitting your ballot where you live. Beyond that, you must consider several factors and examine the issues and candidates involved in the election in order to make an informed decision.

1. **Understand Eligibility Rules** In order to vote, you must be a United States citizen. You must be of age. This generally means being 18, though some States allow people to vote at a younger age in some circumstances. Be sure to find out what the rules are where you live. Also find out about residence requirements.

You must be a resident of the place where you plan to vote, though how you prove residency does vary.

2. **Register to Vote** You can register to vote by visiting the city or town election offices, or when you get or renew a driver's license. You can also register by mail or online. Find out what you must do in your State to register as well as how soon before the election. Pay close attention to whether or not you will need to declare a political party when registering.

3. **Educate Yourself** As the election approaches, research the candidates and issues that will appear on the ballot. Read newspaper and online news coverage. Watch televised debates. Review candidate

Web sites to learn about views and positions. By doing these things and thinking critically about what you learn, you are closer to being an informed voter.

4. **Vote** Finally, you must make the effort to come to the polling place on election day and cast your ballot. Find out ahead of time when the polls will be open, and make plans to take the time necessary to meet this responsibility. If you think you will not be present on election day, find out about absentee voting. If advance voting is used where you live, be sure you understand the rules and procedures for casting a ballot.

## ▸▸ What do you think?

1. Of the steps listed, which do you think is most important to casting a vote?

2. Why is it important to be an informed voter?

3. **You Try It** Follow the steps above and write a step-by-step description of how you would cast a ballot, using details specific to your community.

**GOVERNMENT ONLINE**
**Citizenship Activity Pack**
For an activity to help you learn more about voting, go to **PearsonSchool.com/phgovt**

169

# Citizenship Activity Pack

**L1** **L2** If your students need extra support, use the Citizenship Activity Pack lesson *How to Cast Your Vote*. It includes a lesson plan for you, a poster offering a brief history of voting in the United States, and a fill-in-the-blank activity to test students' basic voting vocabulary. Students will complete a sample voter registration card. Then they will consider and vote on three ballot initiatives related to the classroom. Students may also access the Citizenship Activity Pack online for activities on How to Cast Your Vote at **PearsonSchool.com/phgovt.**

## LESSON GOAL

- Students will analyze the process for casting a vote, including identifying the specific rules for their State and community.

# Teach

## READ

Have students read the introduction to Citizenship 101 aloud. If students have computer access, you may have them search for information about the registration and voting rules for their State.

## DISCUSS

Discuss the importance of advance preparation to vote. Ask: **What factors make it necessary to begin planning to vote well in advance of an election?** *(Local laws about registration and establishing residency can vary, so it is important to investigate voting procedures well ahead of the actual election. You should plan ahead if you will be away from home on Election Day. Advanced planning can also ensure that you can make it to the polls on Election Day or that you obtain and properly submit an absentee ballot.)*

## EXPLORE THE IMPORTANCE OF BEING AN INFORMED VOTER

Explain to students that voting is a responsibility and that voters have an obligation to cast an informed ballot. Ask: **What might happen if voters did not have adequate knowledge of the candidates or issues being contested in an election?** *(They could not make wise choices that served their own or the public interest.)*

# Assess and Remediate

Have students answer the What Do You Think questions at the bottom of the page. Collect and assess student plans for registering to vote.

## Answers

1. Registration is a prerequisite to voting, so it is most important.

2. Being informed is necessary for making wise choices.

3. A strong plan will identify where the student can register, what is needed in order to register, when to register to ensure participation in any upcoming election, when and where voting will take place, and what is needed to cast a ballot.

## What factors influence voter behavior?

I. Factors That Influence Voters
  A. Sociological
    1. Income
    2. Occupation
    3. Education
    4. Gender
    5. Age
    6. Religion
    7. Ethnic background
    8. Geography
    9. Family and other groups
  B. Psychological
    1. Party identification
    2. Views on candidates
    3. Views on issues

# Get Started

## LESSON GOALS

Students will . . .

- analyze a political cartoon in order to understand the effects of and reasons for nonvoting.
- explore the factors that influence voting behavior by creating a television advertisement that encourages voter participation.

## BEFORE CLASS

Assign the section, the graphic organizer in the text, and the Reading Comprehension Worksheet (Unit 2 All-in-One, p. 93) before class.

**L2 Differentiate** Reading Comprehension Worksheet (Unit 2 All-in-One, p. 95)

# SKILLS DEVELOPMENT

## INNOVATE AND THINK CREATIVELY

In this section, students will create a television advertisement to encourage voter participation. You may want to refer them to the Skills Handbook, p. S23, for information on innovating and thinking creatively.

---

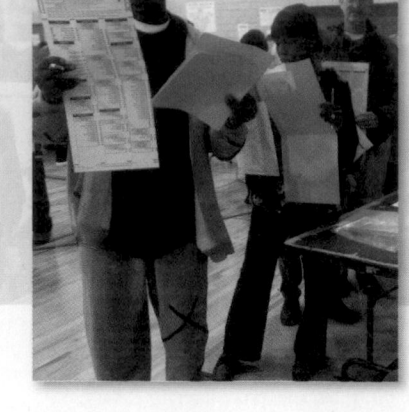

SECTION 4

# Voter Behavior

## Guiding Question

**What factors influence voter behavior?** Use the outline to record details about voter behavior.

Factors that Influence Voters
  A. Sociological
    1. _____
    2. _____
    3. _____
  B. Psychological

## Political Dictionary

- off-year election
- ballot fatigue
- political efficacy
- political socialization
- gender gap
- party identification
- straight-ticket voting
- split-ticket voting
- independent

## Objectives

1. Examine the problem of nonvoting in this country.
2. Identify those people who typically do not vote.
3. Examine the behavior of those who vote and those who do not.
4. Understand the sociological and psychological factors that affect voting and voter behavior.

**Image Above:** Reviewing a ballot on election day

**"Your vote is your voice. Use it."** That's the advice of Rock the Vote, an organization that encourages young voters ages 18 to 25 to participate in the election process. In the United States, and in other democratic countries, we believe all voices should be heard. That is, we believe in voting.

Most elections in this country are built around two-candidate contests. How many choices does a voter have in a two-candidate race? More than most people think. Not just two but, in fact, *five* options. He or she can (1) vote FOR Candidate A, (2) vote AGAINST Candidate A, (3) vote FOR Candidate B, (4) vote AGAINST Candidate B, or (5) decide not to vote for either candidate.

Over the next several pages, you will look at voter behavior in this country—at who votes and who does not, and at why those people who do vote cast their ballots as they do.

## Nonvoting

The word *idiot* came to our language from the Greek. In ancient Athens, idiots *(idiotes)* were those citizens who did not vote or otherwise take part in public life.

Tens of millions of Americans vote in presidential and congressional elections; in State elections; and in city, county, and other public elections. Still, there are many millions of other Americans who, for one reason or another, do not vote. There are some quite valid reasons for not voting, as you will see. But this troubling fact remains: Most of the millions of Americans who could—but do not—go to the polls cannot claim any of those justifications. Indeed, they would have been called idiots in the Greece of 2500 years ago.

On election day in 2008, there were an estimated 228 million persons of voting age in the United States. Yet only some 131 million of them—only 60 percent—actually voted in the presidential election. Nearly 100 million persons who might have voted did not.

In 2008, some 121 million votes were cast in the elections held across the country to fill the 435 seats in the House of Representatives. That is, only some 53 percent of the electorate voted in those congressional contests. (Notice the even lower rates of turnout in the **off-year elections**—that is, in the congressional elections held in the even-numbered years, between presidential elections.)

# Focus on the Basics

**FACTS:** • Many eligible voters do not vote for reasons ranging from illness to lack of interest. • Sociological factors such as income, occupation, education, gender, age, religion, ethnicity, geography, and family and other group affiliation influence voting behavior. • Psychological factors such as a person's party identification and perception of candidates and issues affect voter behavior.

**CONCEPTS:** values and principles of a civil society, rights and responsibilities as citizens, personal and civic rights and responsibilities, democratic values/principles

**ENDURING UNDERSTANDINGS:** • Nonvoting affects election outcomes. • Voting behavior results from a combination of several psychological and sociological factors.

Several facets of the nonvoter problem are not very widely known. Take, for example, this striking fact: There are millions of nonvoters *among those who vote*. Some 10 million persons who voted in the last presidential election could also have voted for a congressional candidate, but they did not choose to do so.

"Nonvoting voters" are not limited to federal elections. In fact, they are much more common in State and local elections. As a general rule, the farther down the ballot an office is, the fewer the number of votes that will be cast for it. This phenomenon is sometimes called **ballot fatigue.** The expression suggests that many voters exhaust their patience and/or their knowledge as they work their way down the ballot. More votes are generally cast for the governorship than for other Statewide offices, such as lieutenant governor or secretary of state. More voters in a county usually vote in the races for Statewide offices than vote in the contests for such county offices as sheriff, county clerk, and so on.

There are other little-recognized facets of the nonvoter problem, too. Turnout in congressional elections is consistently higher in presidential years than it is in off-year elections. That same pattern holds among the States in terms of the types of elections; more people vote in general elections than in either primary or special elections.

## Why People Do Not Vote

Why so many nonvoters? Why, even in a presidential election, do as many as half of those who could vote stay away from the polls?

Clearly, the time that it takes to vote should not be a significant part of the answer. For most people, it takes more time to choose a DVD to watch than it does to go to their neighborhood polling place and cast a ballot. So we must look elsewhere for answers.

**"Cannot-Voters"** To begin with, look at another of those little-recognized aspects of the nonvoter problem. Several million persons who are regularly identified as nonvoters can be much more accurately described as "cannot-voters." That is, although it is true that they do not vote, the fact is that they cannot do so.

The 2008 data support the point. Included in that figure of nearly 100 million who did not vote in the last presidential election are at least 10 million who are resident aliens. Remember, they are barred from the polls in

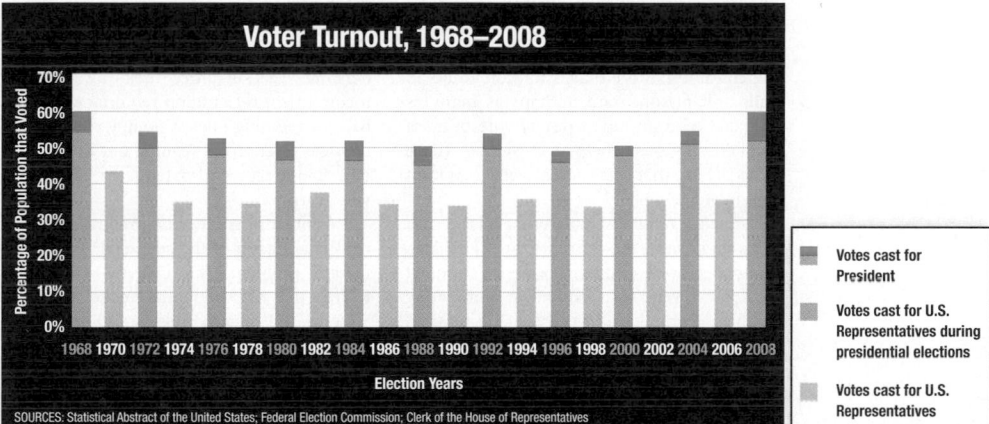

**Voter Turnout, 1968–2008**

Legend:
- Votes cast for President
- Votes cast for U.S. Representatives during presidential elections
- Votes cast for U.S. Representatives

SOURCES: Statistical Abstract of the United States; Federal Election Commission; Clerk of the House of Representatives

▶▶ **Analyzing Graphs** Voter turnout varies from election to election, but presidential elections always draw more voters than off-year elections. *What factor does the blue at the top of each bar represent, and what is this factor called?*

## Differentiated Resources

The following resources are located in the All-in-One, Unit 2, Chapter 6, Section 4:

- **L3** Reading Comprehension Worksheet (p. 93)
- **L2** Reading Comprehension Worksheet (p. 95)
- **L3** Core Worksheet (p. 97)
- **L3** Quiz A (p. 98)
- **L2** Quiz B (p. 99)
- **L3** Chapter Test A (p. 100)
- **L2** Chapter Test B (p. 103)

**BELLRINGER**

Write on the board: **What reason might someone give for not voting? Answer in your notebook.**

## Teach

To present this topic using online resources, use the lesson presentations at **PearsonSchool.com/phgovt.**

### REVIEW BELLRINGER ANSWERS

Discuss students' answers to the Bellringer activity. *(Sample answers: nonvoters may believe their vote will not make a difference, nonvoters may not approve of any of the candidates, nonvoters may not care about politics, nonvoters may not trust politicians or the political system)* Ask: **In what ways can nonvoters affect an election?** *(Sample answer: If nonvoters outweigh the voters, it is possible that a candidate or policy that is supported by only a minority of the public could actually be elected or passed.)*

**L1 L2 Differentiate** Organize a group of students to explore the meaning of the nonvoting by acting out a brief skit in which a growing number of voters declare, "My vote won't make a difference," eventually overwhelming a smaller group of voters.

**L4 Differentiate** Have students create a political cartoon that expresses the importance of voting.

## Answers

**Checkpoint** voters who do not mark a choice for every office on the ballot

**Analyzing Graphs** It represents voters who vote in the presidential race and not in the congressional race, and it illustrates the problem of nonvoting voters.

Tell students that this section is about the behavior of the American electorate. Explain that voting is considered a central right of citizenship—and a key responsibility, as well. Voting is the main way that people make their wishes known about public policy and have a say in their government. For this reason, those who choose not to vote are a major concern in a democratic government. Direct student attention to the graph on voter turnout. Ask students to react to the information presented there. Does it surprise them to see the turnout for presidential elections? What about off-year elections?

▶ **Analyzing Political Cartoons** Until the 2008 election, voter participation had not broken the 60 percent mark since the 1960s. *What does this cartoon suggest about voter apathy?*

✔ **Checkpoint**
Why do people choose not to vote?

**alienate**
*vt.* to feel unfriendly or hostile to, isolated from

**idolatry**
*n.* excessive devotion to some person or thing

every State. Another 5 to 6 million citizens were so ill or otherwise physically disabled that they simply could not vote in an election. An additional 2 to 3 million persons were traveling suddenly and unexpectedly, and so could not vote.

Other groups of cannot-voters can be discovered in the nonvoting group. They include some 500,000 persons in mental health care facilities or under some other form of legal restraint because of their mental condition; more than 2 million adults in jails and prisons; and perhaps as many as 100,000 who do not (cannot) vote because of their religious beliefs—for example, those who believe that acts such as voting amount to <u>idolatry</u>.

Racial, religious, and other biases still play a part here, too—despite the many laws, court decisions, and enforcement actions of the past several years aimed at eliminating such discrimination in the political process. An unknown but certainly significant number of people cannot vote today because of (1) the purposeful administration of election laws to keep them from doing so, and/or (2) various "informal" local pressures applied to that same end.

**Actual Nonvoters** Even so, there are millions of actual nonvoters in the United States. Thus, in 2008, more than 80 million Americans who could have voted in the presidential election did not. There are any number of reasons for that behavior. As a leading example: Many who could go to the polls do not because they are convinced that it makes little real difference which candidate wins a particular election.

That fairly large group includes two quite different groups of nonvoters. On the one hand, there are many who generally approve of the way the public's business is being managed—that is, many who believe that no matter who wins an election, things will continue to go well for themselves and for the country.

On the other hand, that group also includes many people who feel <u>alienated</u>—that is, many who deliberately refuse to vote because they don't trust political institutions and processes. They either fear or scorn "the system." To them, elections are meaningless, choiceless exercises.

Another large group of nonvoters is composed of people who have no sense of **political efficacy.** That is, they lack any feeling of influence or effectiveness in politics. They do not believe that they or their votes can have any real impact on what government does or does not do.

Other factors can also dictate whether voters show up at the polls or not. Cumbersome election procedures—for example, inconvenient registration requirements, long ballots, and long lines at polling places—discourage voters from turning out on election day. Bad weather also tends to discourage voter turnout.

Another possible, though somewhat controversial, factor is the so-called "time-zone fallout" problem. This expression refers to the fact that, in presidential elections, polls in States in the Eastern and Central time zones close an hour or more before polls in States in the Mountain and Pacific time zones. Based on early returns from the East and Midwest, the news media often project the outcome of the presidential contest before all voters in the West have gone to the polls. Some people

## Answers

**Analyzing Political Cartoons** The cartoon suggests that voters are apathetic because they take the right to vote for granted.

**Checkpoint** possible answers: because they think it makes little difference which candidate wins an election; because they feel alienated; because they have no sense of political efficacy; because of cumbersome election procedures; because of time-zone fallout; because of lack of interest

# Teacher-to-Teacher Network

**ALTERNATE LESSON PLAN** Ask students to research voting requirements in their State and in five others of their choosing from various parts of the country. Have them create a graphic organizer to compare and contrast these requirements. Then ask them to write a brief essay summarizing their results and explaining how State control of voting requirements reflects the principle of federalism. They should conclude their essays with their opinion as to whether the States or the Federal Government should control voting requirements and explain the reasons for their choice.

To see this lesson plan, go to

**Teacher Center** at PearsonSchool.com/phgovt

fear that such reports discourage western voters from casting their ballots.

Of all the reasons that may be cited, however, the chief cause for nonvoting is, purely and simply, a lack of interest. Those who are indifferent, who just cannot be bothered, are usually woefully uninformed. Most often, they know little or nothing about the candidates and issues in an election. There are many who argue that the democratic process is well served by the fact that most of these people do not go to the polls.

**Comparing Voters and Nonvoters** One useful way to get a handle on the problem of nonvoting is to contrast those persons who tend to go to the polls regularly with those who do not.

The people most likely to vote display such characteristics as higher levels of income, education, and occupational status. They are usually well integrated into community life. They tend to be long-time residents who are active in, or at least comfortable with, their surroundings. They are likely to have a strong sense of party identification, and to believe that voting is an important act. They are also likely to live in those areas where laws, customs, and competition between the parties all promote turnout.

The opposite characteristics produce a profile of those less likely to vote. Nonvoters are likely to be younger than age 35, unmarried, and unskilled. More nonvoters live in the South and in rural locales. Men are less likely to vote than women—a fact that first became apparent in the 1980s.

A few of the factors that help determine whether or not a person will vote are so important that they influence turnout even when they conflict with other factors. For example, those persons with a high sense of political efficacy are likely to vote—no matter what their income, education, age, race, and so on may be. The degree of two-party competition also has an extraordinary impact on participation. Thus, the greater the competition between candidates, the more likely people will be to go to the polls, regardless of other factors.

Despite the greater weight of some of these factors, however, note this point: It is the combined presence of several factors, not one of them alone, that tends to determine whether a person will or will not vote.

## Voters and Voting Behavior

As you have read, tens of millions of potential voters do not go to the polls in this country. But many millions more do. How do those who do vote behave? What prompts many to vote most often for Republicans and many others to support the Democratic Party? Research has produced a huge amount of information about why people tend to vote as they do.

**Studying Voting Behavior** Most of what is known about voter behavior comes from three sources.

**1.** *The results of particular elections.* How individuals vote in a given election is secret in the United States. However, careful study of the returns from areas populated largely by, say, African Americans or Catholics or high-income families will indicate how those groups voted in a given election.

**2.** *The field of survey research.* The polling of scientifically determined cross sections of the population is the method by which public opinion is most often identified and measured. The Gallup Organization and the Pew Research Center conduct perhaps the best known of these polls today.

**3.** *Studies of political socialization.* **Political socialization** is the process by which people gain their political attitudes and opinions. That complex process begins in early childhood and continues through each person's life. Political socialization involves all of the experiences and relationships that lead people to see the political world, and to act in it, as they do.

**Factors That Influence Voters** Observers still have much to learn about voter behavior, but many sociological and psychological factors clearly influence the way people cast their ballots. Sociology is the study of groups and how people behave within groups. The sociological factors affecting voter behavior are really the many pieces of a voter's social and economic life. Those pieces are of two

✔ **Checkpoint**
What three sources are used to gather data about voter behavior?

**indifferent**
*adj.* uninterested, uncaring, not concerned

**CONSIDER ALTERNATIVES**

Ask students what, if any, problem they see with low voter turnout. Ask: **Is it a bad thing? Why or why not?** Point out that many countries, including many democracies, have considerably higher turnout of 80 or even 90 percent or more. Some countries also have laws that require people to vote. Ask: **Should voters be required to take part in elections? What are the possible benefits and drawbacks of such a step?** *(A possible benefit would be that all people would feel a greater sense of responsibility for their government, and government would feel responsible to a greater range of people. A drawback might be that many uninterested and uninformed voters might make poor choices at the polls.)*

**L1 L2 Differentiate** Provide assistance in reading the graph. Explain what each bar on the graph measures *(The combined green and blue bars represent voter turnout in presidential years, with the blue portion showing the larger vote for President than for members of congress. The yellow bar represents turnout in national elections in years where there is no presidential race.)* Check student understanding of the graph by having them identify the voter turnout for selected years.

**L4 Differentiate** Have students research turnout for statewide elections, such as those for governor and state legislator. Students should use this data to create their own graph.

## Background

**UNCOUNTED VOTES** Today, elections regularly feature complaints from people who want to vote but who are unable to for some reason. Problems range from unopened polling places to malfunctioning voting equipment to charges of intimidation. While many complaints lack merit, it is a fact that many people cast votes that are not counted due to voter error in marking a ballot or using equipment or equipment malfunction. Most famously, the 2000 presidential election shined a light on this problem. In Florida, thousands of voters entered polling booths and tried to cast a vote, only to have their ballots rejected by vote-counting machines. The presence of these unread ballots created controversy with the extremely close returns in that State and in the presidential election nationwide.

## Answers

**Checkpoint** results of elections, the field of survey research, and studies of political socialization

## DISTRIBUTE CORE WORKSHEET

Distribute the Chapter 6 Section 4 Core Worksheet and the Rubric for Assessing a Television Advertisement (Unit 2 All-in-One, pp. 97, 255). Have students work in small groups to create a television advertisement to encourage voter participation among a nonvoting group. Students can work collaboratively on all aspects of the presentation, or they may divide up the tasks among themselves. The entire group, however, is responsible for the group's presentation. If possible, have students create a multimedia presentation, incorporating video, sound, and Web pages. All groups should also make a storyboard that outlines each portion of the advertisement. The frame should include a sketch of what would appear on the screen, with the text of the message written below. On the reverse side of the paper, students should explain the intended message and how the frame accomplishes it.

**L1 L2 Differentiate** Allow students to choose roles at which they may excel or feel most comfortable.

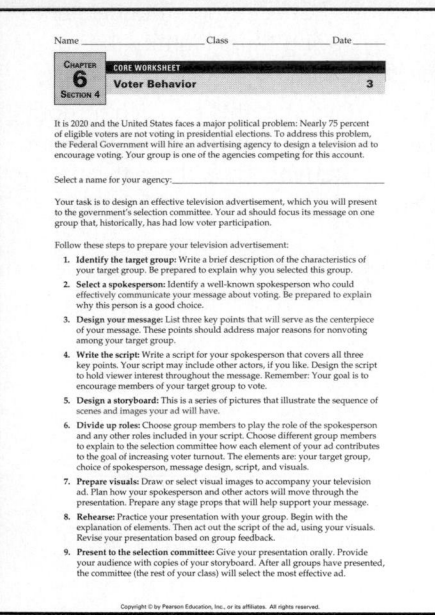

broad kinds: (1) a voter's personal characteristics—age, race, income, occupation, education, religion, and so on; and (2) a voter's group affiliations—family, co-workers, friends, and the like.

Psychology is the study of the mind and individual behavior. The psychological factors that influence voter behavior are a voter's perceptions of politics—that is, how the voter sees the parties, the candidates, and the issues in an election.

The differences between these two kinds of influences are not nearly so great as they might seem. In fact, they are closely related and they constantly interact with one another. How voters look at parties, candidates, or issues is often shaped by their own social and economic backgrounds.

## Sociological Factors

Using data from past elections, you can draw a composite picture of the American voter in terms of a number of sociological factors. A word of caution here: Do not make too much of any one of these factors. Remember, each voter possesses not just one, but in fact *several* of the many characteristics involved here.

To illustrate the point: College graduates are more likely to vote Republican. So are persons over age 50. African Americans, on the other hand, are more likely to vote for Democrats. So are members of labor unions. How, then, would a 55-year-old, college-educated African American who belongs to the AFL-CIO decide to vote?

**Income and Occupation** Voters in lower income brackets are more likely to be Democrats. Voters with higher incomes tend to be Republicans. This pattern has held up over time, no matter whether a particular election was a cliffhanger or a blow-out. The 2008 election proved to be an exception, however. In that contest, those making under $50,000 did favor Democrat Barack Obama by an overwhelming majority. However, those with incomes of $50,000 and up were fairly evenly divided between the two candidates, and President Obama made significant inroads among those who make over $200,000, winning 52 percent of their votes.

Most often, how much one earns and what one does for a living are closely related. Professional and business people, and others with higher incomes, regularly tend to vote for Republican candidates. Manual workers, and others in lower income groups, usually vote for Democrats. Thus, with the exception of 1964 and 2008, professional and business people have voted heavily Republican in every presidential election in the modern era.

**Education** Studies of voter behavior reveal that there is also a close relationship between the level of a voter's education and how he or she tends to vote. College graduates vote for Republicans in higher percentages than high-school graduates; and high-school graduates vote Republican more often than those who have only gone through grade school. Again, however, the 2008 election proved an exception to this trend.

**Gender, Age** There are often measurable differences between the partisan choices of men and women today. This phenomenon is known as the **gender gap,** and it first appeared in the 1980s. Women generally tend to favor the Democrats by a margin of five to ten percent, and men often give the GOP a similar edge. In 2008, however, President Obama won 56 percent of all votes cast by women, while men's votes were evenly split between the candidates.

A number of studies show that men and women are most likely to vote differently when such issues as abortion, health care or other social welfare matters, or military involvements abroad are prominent in an election.

Traditionally, younger voters have been more likely to vote Democratic than Republican. Older voters are likely to find the GOP and its candidates more attractive. Thus, in every presidential election from 1960 through 1980, the Democrats won a larger percentage of the votes of the under-30 age group than of the 50-and-over age bracket.

That long-standing pattern was broken by Ronald Reagan's appeal to younger voters in 1984, and by George H.W. Bush in 1988. However, Bill Clinton restored the Democrats' claim to those voters in 1992 and 1996.

# Debate

"In this country, you are free to vote or not vote. And Americans want it that way.... Our right not to vote is sacred, too."

—"Crock the Vote" by Knute Berger from the *Seattle Weekly,* June 23, 2004

Use this quotation to start a debate in your classroom. Ask: **Would a legal requirement to vote violate our basic freedoms?**

And John Kerry won the major slice of the votes of that age group—54 percent—in 2004. The 2008 election upheld this tradition of younger voters favoring the Democrats, and in a big way, with Barack Obama winning 66 percent of the under 30 vote.

**Religion, Ethnic Background** Historically, a majority of Protestants have most often preferred the GOP. Catholics and Jews have tended to be Democrats.[14] The 2008 elections supported this trend, with President Obama winning just 45 percent of the votes cast by all

Protestants and only 34 percent of those cast by white Protestants. Fifty-four percent of all Catholic voters backed the President, and he won a huge 78 percent of the ballots cast by Jewish voters.

Moral issues, notably same-sex marriage, were unusually prominent in 2004 and 2008. Church attendance has also emerged as a major indicator of partisan

14 In 1960, John F. Kennedy became the first Roman Catholic President. His election marked a sharper split between Catholic and Protestant voters than in any other recent election.

✔ **Checkpoint**
How do sociological factors affect voting?

**GOVERNMENT** ONLINE
**Audio Tour**
Listen to a guided audio tour on voting at
PearsonSchool.com/phgovt

## Group Voting, 2008 Presidential Election

▶▶ **Analyzing Charts** This chart reports the voting behavior of several major segments of the American electorate in the most recent presidential election. As you analyze this data, remember that every voter belongs to not just one, but all of these groups. *How might a 45-year-old, college-educated, Hispanic woman who makes $60,000 per year vote? Explain your reasoning.*

| | GROUPS (percentage of total) | REPUBLICAN | DEMOCRATIC |
|---|---|---|---|
| | All voters (100%)* | 45% | 53% |
| **GENDER** Women vote Democratic more often than men. | Men (46%) | 48% | 49% |
| | Women (54%) | 43% | 56% |
| **RACE** African Americans vote heavily Democratic. | White (74%) | 55% | 43% |
| | African American (13%) | 4% | 95% |
| | Latino/a (9%) | 31% | 67% |
| | Asian (2%) | 35% | 62% |
| **AGE** Older people vote more heavily Republican. | 18–29 years (18%) | 32% | 66% |
| | 30–44 years (29%) | 46% | 52% |
| | 45–64 years (37%) | 49% | 50% |
| | 65 years (16%) | 53% | 45% |
| **INCOME** People with higher incomes tend to vote Republican. | Less than $50,000/year (38%) | 38% | 60% |
| | $50,000 or more/year (62%) | 49% | 49% |
| **EDUCATION** Republican voting tends to increase with level of education. | No high school (4%) | 35% | 63% |
| | High school graduate (20%) | 46% | 52% |
| | Some college (31%) | 47% | 51% |
| | College graduate (28%) | 48% | 50% |
| | Postgraduate study (17%) | 40% | 58% |
| **PARTY IDENTIFICATION** Most significant predictor of how one will vote. | Democratic (39%) | 10% | 89% |
| | Republican (32%) | 90% | 9% |
| | Independent (29%) | 44% | 52% |

SOURCE: CNN.com 2008

*Exit poll results may not match vote totals.

# Myths and Misconceptions

**TURNOUT AMONG YOUNG VOTERS** It is true that young people historically have been poor participants in the electoral process. Yet recent elections suggest that the trend may be turning around. Display Transparency 6E, Reported Rates of Voting. It gives data about the voting rates of young people in recent elections. The percentage of eligible voters age 18 to 24 jumped sharply in the 2004 presidential election to 47 percent and has been rising steadily in presidential elections. Though still below the turnout of older voters, the increase in this age group was larger than in any other group. The 2006 off-year elections also saw an increase in voter participation among younger voters.

## REVIEW PRESENTATIONS

Have groups deliver their presentations to the class. Presentations should begin with an explanation of how the advertisement contributes to the goal of increasing voter turnout. Presentations should end with a skit in which the spokesperson (and possibly students playing other roles) acts out the television script for the ad or presents their storyboards. After each group presents, ask the other class members to write their evaluations on a sheet of paper, using the rubric provided with the activity. Evaluations should also address the following questions: **What is most effective about the advertisement? What is least effective?** After all groups have presented, ask the class to vote on which advertisement would be most effective in increasing voter turnout, and discuss why.

Tell students to go to the Audio Tour to listen to a guided tour on voter data.

## Answers

**Checkpoint** Sociological factors include income, occupation, education, gender, age, religion, ethnic background, geography, family, and other groups. Any of these factors can influence people in how they make voting decisions.

**Analyzing Charts** Possible answer: Because this person belongs to several groups that generally vote in conflicting ways, the person may vote based more on family history or on the tendencies of her peer group.

**L3** Have students design and carry out a survey of at least five adults that assesses voting attitudes and participation. Students should seek information about past participation in voting and about what factors influenced their interviewees' political views and affiliations. Be sure students understand that it is not appropriate to ask subjects to reveal certain personal information, such as income. Students should also respect subjects' wish not to share information about specific candidates supported. Once students have collected their data, they should write a brief summary of their findings.

**L2 ELL Differentiate** For students who have recently lived in other countries, have them instead interview family members and write a brief report about voting procedures and behaviors in that country and compare it to behaviors here.

**L4 Differentiate** Have students pool the class's findings and organize and present the information in a graph.

**L3 Differentiate** Display Transparency 6F, Voting by Groups in Presidential Election 2008. Have students select one voting group and create a pie chart or bar graph that represents the percentage of Republican and Democratic voters. Have them draw a conclusion based on their chart or graph and share it with the class.

## Answers

**Analyzing Political Cartoons** Possible answer: All citizens have the right to complain because participation in public affairs is not limited to voting alone.

▶▶ **Analyzing Political Cartoons** *Is it really true that only those persons who vote have a right to complain? Why or why not?*

preference. Fifty-five percent of voters who go to church at least once a week marked their ballots for Mr. McCain in 2008.

For decades now, African Americans have supported the Democratic Party consistently and massively. They form the only group that has given the Democratic candidate a clear majority in every presidential election since 1952. There are now more than 40 million African Americans, and they make up the second largest minority in the country.

In the North, African Americans generally voted Republican until the 1930s, but, with the coming of the New Deal, they moved away from the party of Abraham Lincoln. The civil rights movement of the 1960s led to much greater African American participation in the politics of the South. Today, African Americans vote overwhelmingly Democratic in that region, too.

The United States is now home to more than 45 million Latinos, people with Spanish-speaking backgrounds. Latinos generally favor Democratic candidates. Note, however, that the label "Latino" conceals differences among Cuban Americans, who most often vote Republican, and Mexican Americans and Puerto Ricans, who are strongly Democratic. While the rate of turn-out among Latinos increased significantly in the

historic election of 2008, it was still comparatively low—well below 50 percent.

**Geography** Geography—the part of the country, State, and/or locale in which a person lives—also has a measurable impact on voter behavior. After the Civil War, the States of the old Confederacy voted so consistently Democratic that the southeast quarter of the nation became known as the Solid South. For more than a century, most Southerners, regardless of any other factor, identified with the Democratic Party.

The Solid South is now a thing of the past. Republican candidates have been increasingly successful throughout the region over the past half-century. The GOP now carries at least most of the Southern States in the presidential contest every four years, and it is now widely successful at the State and local levels across the region, too.

Those States that have most consistently supported Republican candidates over time have been Idaho, Wyoming, and Utah in the West and Kansas, Nebraska, and the Dakotas in the Midwest. The Democrats have made significant inroads in former Republican strongholds in New England, over the past two decades or so.

Voters' attitudes also vary in terms of the size of the communities in which they live. Generally, the Democrats draw strength from the big cities of the North and East and on the Pacific Coast. Many white Democrats have moved from the central cities and taken their political preferences with them, but Republican voters still dominate much of suburban America. Voters in smaller cities and rural areas are also likely to be Republicans.

**Family and Other Groups** To this point, you have seen the American voter sketched in terms of several broad social and economic characteristics. The picture can also be drawn on the basis of much smaller and more personal groupings, especially such primary groups as family, friends, and co-workers.

Typically, the members of a family vote in strikingly similar ways. Nine out of ten married couples share the same partisan leanings. As many as two out of every three voters follow the political attachments of their

## Background

**NIXON AND THE SOLID SOUTH** The decline of the Solid South is often traced to the 1968 election and the so-called "southern strategy" of Republican candidate Richard Nixon. Nixon and his team tried to take advantage of public reaction among some whites in the South against Democratic support for major civil rights laws in 1964 and 1965. The southern strategy stressed "states rights" and is thought to have succeeded in attracting many long-time Democrats to the Republican Party.

parents. Those who work together and circles of friends also tend to vote very much alike.

This like-mindedness is hardly surprising. People of similar social and economic backgrounds tend to associate with one another. In short, a person's group associations usually reinforce the opinions he or she already holds.

## Psychological Factors

Although they are quite important, it would be wrong to give too much weight to the sociological factors in the voting mix. For one thing, those factors are fairly static. That is, they tend to change only gradually and over time. To understand voter behavior, you must look beyond such factors as occupation, education, ethnic background, and place of residence. You must also take into account a number of psychological factors. That is, you must look at the voters' perceptions of politics: how they see and react to the parties, the candidates, and the issues in an election.

**Party Identification** A majority of Americans identify themselves with one or the other of the two major parties early in life. Many never change. They support that party, election after election, with little or no regard for either the candidates or the issues involved in a particular election.

The hefty impact of **party identification**—the loyalty of people to a particular political party—is the single most significant and lasting predictor of how a person will vote. A person who is a Democrat or a Republican will, for that reason, very likely vote for all or most of that party's candidates in any given election. The practice of voting for candidates of only one party in an election is called **straight-ticket voting.**

Party identification is, therefore, a key factor in American politics. Among many other things, it means that each of the major parties can regularly count on the votes of millions of faithful supporters in every election.

Several signs suggest that, while it remains a major factor, party identification has lost some of its impact in recent years. One of those signs is the weakened condition of the parties themselves. Another is the marked increase in **split-ticket voting**—the practice of voting for the candidates of more than one party in an election. That behavior, which began to increase in the 1960s, is fairly common today.

Another telling sign is the large number of voters who now call themselves **independents.** That term is regularly used to identify those people who have no party affiliation. It includes voters who are independent of both the Republicans and the Democrats (and of any minor party as well). "Independent" is a tricky term, however.[15] Many who claim to be independents actually vote most often for the candidates of one or the other of the major parties.

The loose nature of party membership makes it difficult to determine just what proportion of the American electorate is independent. However, the best guesses put the number of independents at somewhere between a fourth and a third of all voters today. The role that these independent voters play is especially critical in those elections

[15] Note that the term "Independent" is sometimes mistakenly used to suggest that independents form a more or less cohesive group that can be readily compared with Republicans and Democrats. In short, independents in American politics are not only independent of Republicans and Democrats; each of them is also independent of all other independents.

✔ **Checkpoint**
What is straight-ticket voting?

Family can influence party identification.

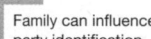

# Background

**VOTING A STRAIGHT TICKET** Straight-ticket voting technically involves voting for all the candidates of one party. But in a number of States, voters have the option of casting a straight-ticket vote with a single mark or punch on the ballot. That is, by responding in one specific spot on the ballot, the voter casts a ballot for every single candidate of the designated party that appears on the ballot. The option was available in 17 States in 2008, though its use was limited in some cases—for example, to only primaries or only general elections. The number of States offering the option has declined in recent years.

# Assess and Remediate

**L2 L3** Grade students' work according to the rubric for the Core Worksheet activity.

**L3** Assign the Section 4 Assessment questions.

**L3** Section Quiz A (Unit 2 All-in-One, p. 98)

**L2** Section Quiz B (Unit 2 All-in-One, p. 99)

Have students complete the review activities in the digital lesson presentation and continue their work in the **Essential Questions Journal.**

## Answers

**Checkpoint** voting only for members of a single party

## REMEDIATION

| If Your Students Have Trouble With | Strategies For Remediation |
|---|---|
| The size of the nonvoting problem (Questions 2, 3) | Have students review and summarize the graph on Voter Turnout. |
| Why people do not vote (Questions 1, 2, 3, 6) | Have students create a web diagram that identifies and describes the major reasons for nonvoting. |
| The sociological factors that affect voting behavior (Questions 1, 3, 4, 6) | Have students create a sociological profile of a "typical" Democrat and Republican. |
| The psychological factors that affect voting behavior (Questions 1, 3) | Create a table that lists the major psychological factors affecting voting behavior. Ask students to explain how each factor listed might influence a potential voter. |

## Answers

**Checkpoint** the candidates and issues involved in the election

---

**tumultuous**
*adj.* chaotic, stormy, agitated

where the opposing major party candidates are more or less evenly matched.

Until fairly recently, the typical independent was less concerned, less well informed, and less active in politics than those voters who identified themselves as Republicans or Democrats. That unflattering description still fits many independents.

However, a new breed of independent voter began to appear in the 1960s and 1970s, and their ranks have grown over the years since then. Largely because of the political events and personalities of that period, these "new" independents preferred not to join either of the two major parties. Today, these independents are often young and above average in education, income, and job status.

**Candidates and Issues** Party identification is a long-term factor. While most voters identify with one or the other of the major parties and most often support its candidates, they do not always vote that way. One or more short-term factors can cause them to switch sides in a particular election, or at least vote a split ticket. Thus, in 2008, several exit polls indicated that about 10 percent of those voters who regularly identify themselves as Democrats actually marked their ballots for the Republican nominee, Senator John McCain. And just about that same

percentage of Republicans crossed over and voted for the Democratic senator from Illinois, Barack Obama, in that election.

The most important of these short-term factors are the candidates and the issues in an election. Clearly, the impression a candidate makes on the voters can have an impact on how they vote. What image does a candidate project? How do the voters see that candidate in terms of personality, character, style, appearance, past record, abilities, and so on? And how do voters see the opposing candidate?

Just as clearly, issues can also have a large impact on voter behavior. The role of issues varies, however, depending on such things as the emotional content of the issues themselves, the voters' awareness of them, and the ways in which the contending candidates present them to the electorate.

Issues have become increasingly important to voters over the past 40 years or so. The <u>tumultuous</u> nature of politics over the period—highlighted by the civil rights movement, the Vietnam War, the feminist movement, the Watergate scandal, economic problems, and, over recent years, such critical matters as a severe economic recession and the ongoing wars in Iraq and Afghanistan—is most likely responsible for this heightened voter concern.

---

## SECTION 4 ASSESSMENT

**Essential Questions Journal** To continue to build a response to the chapter Essential Question, go to your **Essential Questions Journal.**

1. **Guiding Question** Use your completed outline to answer this question: What factors influence voter behavior?

**Key Terms and Comprehension**

2. What are **off-year elections?**

3. **(a)** How does a person's sense of **political efficacy** affect voting behavior? **(b)** What other factors affect how a person will vote?

4. What is the meaning and significance of the **gender gap?**

**Critical Thinking**

5. **Predict Consequences (a)** In some democracies, voters are required to vote. Do you think such mandatory voting would work in the United States? **(b)** Why or why not?

6. **Draw Inferences (a)** How do factors such as income and level of education impact rates of voter participation? **(b)** Why do you think this is the case?

**Quick Write**

**Narrative: Select a Narrative Structure** Using your research and the list of details, identify what the climax, or most interesting and vivid part of your story, is. Narratives are usually told in chronological order with the climax near the end. Organize the details you collected for your essay into a beginning, middle, and end.

---

# Assessment Answers

**1.** Sociological factors include income, occupation, education, gender, age, religion, ethnicity, geographic location, and family and other group affiliation. For example, people from suburbs and with high incomes and education tend to vote Republican. African Americans, Catholics, and women favor Democrats. Psychological factors include the voter's party affiliation and views on the candidates and issues.

**2.** elections in which there is no presidential race

**3. (a)** A person who lacks any feeling of influence on politics is less likely to vote. **(b)** Possible response: Inconvenient registration requirements, long ballots, long lines at polling places, and bad weather can cause people to not vote.

**4.** Women and men differ in their voting behavior, with more women today favoring Democrats and more men favoring Republicans.

**5. (a)** Possible answer: Mandatory voting would be very unpopular. **(b)** because Americans value the freedom to make their own choice about whether or not to vote. Nonvoting can also send a message to political leaders.

**6. (a)** Wealthier and better educated voters tend to vote in higher numbers. **(b)** Wealthy people are more likely to have a sense of political efficacy because they have been successful in the system. They also have a high stake in keeping politicians in power who will support favorable policies.

**QUICK WRITE** Students should identify the chronology and the beginning, middle, and end of their story.

# Quick Study Guide

**GOVERNMENT** ONLINE
**On the Go**
To review anytime, anywhere, download these online resources at **PearsonSchool.com/phgovt**
Political Dictionary, Audio Review

**CHAPTER 6**

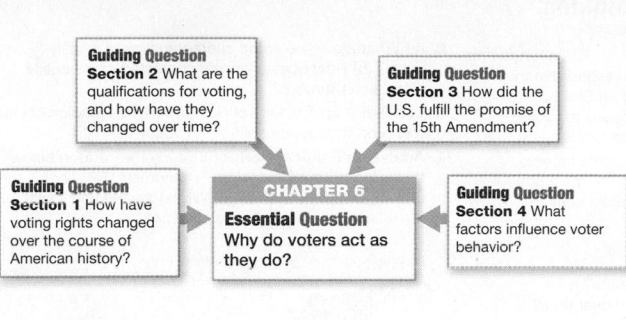

**Guiding Question**
**Section 2** What are the qualifications for voting, and how have they changed over time?

**Guiding Question**
**Section 3** How did the U.S. fulfill the promise of the 15th Amendment?

**Guiding Question**
**Section 1** How have voting rights changed over the course of American history?

**CHAPTER 6**
**Essential Question**
Why do voters act as they do?

**Guiding Question**
**Section 4** What factors influence voter behavior?

## Political Dictionary

**suffrage** *p 152*
**franchise** *p. 152*
**electorate** *p. 152*
**disenfranchised** *p. 153*
**poll tax** *p. 154*
**alien** *p. 156*
**transient** *p. 157*
**registration** *p. 158*
**purge** *p. 159*
**poll book** *p. 159*
**literacy** *p. 161*
**gerrymandering** *p. 165*
**injunction** *p. 165*
**preclearance** *p. 167*
**off-year election** *p. 170*
**ballot fatigue** *p. 171*
**political efficacy** *p. 172*
**political socialization** *p. 173*
**gender gap** *p. 174*
**party identification** *p. 177*
**straight-ticket voting** *p. 177*
**split-ticket voting** *p. 177*
**independent** *p. 177*

### Expansion of Voting Rights in the U.S.

**Original Electorate**
Voting generally limited to white male property owners.

**Expansion Era #1**
Religious qualifications and property-ownership requirements eliminated; by the mid 1800s most white males could vote.

**Expansion Era #2**
After the Civil War, the 15th Amendment intended to protect any male citizen from being denied the vote because of race or color.

**Expansion Era #3**
The 19th Amendment, ratified in 1920, gave women the right to vote in every State.

**Expansion Era #4**
Court decisions and federal legislation, especially the Voting Rights Act of 1965 and its later extensions, finally made the 15th Amendment truly effective.

**Expansion Era #5**
In 1971, the 26th Amendment lowered the voting age to 18.

### Influences on Voter Behavior

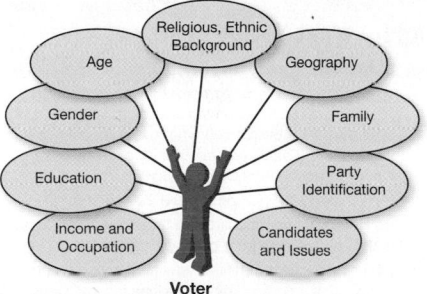

Religious, Ethnic Background — Age — Geography — Gender — Family — Education — Party Identification — Income and Occupation — Candidates and Issues

**Voter**

Chapter 6 Assessment **179**

---

Have students download the digital resources available at Government on the Go for review and remediation.

**STUDY TIPS**

**Short-Answer Tests** Explain that when preparing for a short-answer test, students should focus on key terms, dates, and concepts. Flashcards are a good way to study for this type of test. Stress that simplicity is the rule for short answers. Introductions and conclusions are not necessary; instead, answers should be brief and to the point. It may help students to focus their thoughts if they underline key words in the question. For each statement they make, they should provide an example, reason, or explanation. Short-answer tests usually ask questions that begin with such words as *list, define, name,* or *identify.* Students might think in these terms as they study for the test.

**ASSESSMENT AT A GLANCE**

**Tests and Quizzes**
Section Assessments
Section Quizzes A and B, Unit 2 **All-in-One**
Chapter Assessment
Chapter Tests A and B, Unit 2 **All-in-One**
Document-Based Assessment
Progress Monitoring Online
Exam*View* Test Bank

**Performance Assessment**
Essential Questions Journal
Debates, pp. 158, 174
Assessment Rubrics, **All-in-One**

---

# For More Information

To learn more about voting, refer to these sources or assign them to students:

**L1** **De Capua, Sarah.** *Voting.* Children's Press, 2002.

**L2** **Adams, Colleen.** *Women's Suffrage: A Primary Source History of the Women's Rights Movement in America.* Rosen Publishing Group, Inc., 2002.

**L3** **Laney, Garrine P.** *The Voting Rights Act of 1965: Historical Background and Current Issues.* Novinka Books, 2004.

**L4** **Kaufmann, Karen M., Petrocik, John R., and Shaw, Daron R.,** *Unconventional Wisdom: Facts and Myths About American Voters.* Oxford University Press, 2008.

Chapter 6 Assessment **179**

# Chapter Assessment

**COMPREHENSION AND CRITICAL THINKING**

## SECTION 1

**1. (a)** The States have the primary role of setting voter qualifications, within basic guidelines set by the Federal Government. **(b)** In some cases, States have been unwilling to observe the basic principles that the Constitution lays down—for example, by denying African Americans the vote in spite of the 15th Amendment.

**2. (a)** Restrictions include property ownership, religion, age, race, gender, and taxes. **(b)** possible response: greater federal involvement in removing restrictions, such as by constitutional amendment along with active federal enforcement **(c)** Possible answer: Federal action or a constitutional amendment all at once affects practices across the entire country, and it effectively overcomes local or State resistance to basic principles of the Constitution.

## SECTION 2

**3. (a)** to prevent a political machine from bringing in outsiders to vote in local elections and to allow time for new voters to become familiar with the candidates and issues **(b)** The trend is to require shorter residency requirements. **(c)** Court rulings found that periods longer than 30 days were unreasonable for accomplishing the objectives and so an unnecessary hindrance to voting.

**4. (a)** The argument was "old enough to fight, old enough to vote." **(b)** They tend to vote in smaller numbers than older groups. **(c)** Possible answer: Young voters don't see politics as relevant to their lives.

**5. (a)** Originally, literacy tests were used to make sure that a voter had the capacity to cast an informed ballot. **(b)** Some whites, especially in the South, used difficult literacy tests as a means of unfairly preventing African Americans from voting.

## SECTION 3

**6. (a)** to ensure that freed African American men would not be denied the vote on the basis of race **(b)** There was strong resistance among some white southerners, who used discriminatory laws and practices as well as intimidation to prevent African Americans from voting.

**7. (a)** Laws such as literacy tests and poll taxes were used to block access to the polls. **(b)** Would-be African American

voters were kept from the polls through threats and violence. **(c)** Over time, the courts struck down many legal barriers, and strong federal laws, a constitutional amendment, and active federal enforcement also helped.

## SECTION 4

**8. (a)** A nonvoting voter is a person who casts a ballot but does not make a choice in every race. **(b)** People exhaust their patience or knowledge as they work through the ballot.

**9. (a)** older; higher levels of income, educa-

tion, and occupational status; long-time residents who are well integrated into the community **(b)** Tighter races tend to produce more turnout.

**10. (a)** Split-ticket voting is voting for candidates of more than one party on the same ballot. **(b)** differing opinions on individual candidates and issues

**11. (a)** Individuals fought and sacrificed for the United States and its way of life, and therefore people should not say that they are "too busy" to vote. **(b)** The soldier represents the ultimate sacrifice of giving one's life for one's country.

---

# Chapter Assessment

**GOVERNMENT** ONLINE
Self-Test
To test your understanding of key terms and main ideas, visit PearsonSchool.com/phgovt

## Comprehension and Critical Thinking

### Section 1

**1. (a)** Which level of government is primarily responsible for establishing voter qualifications in the United States? **(b)** Why has the Federal Government gradually assumed a larger role in the setting of those qualifications?

**2. (a)** Identify the restrictions that prevented some citizens from voting in the past. **(b)** What has been the most effective and common way to overturn those restrictions? **(c)** Why do you think this is?

### Section 2

**3. (a)** Why do States set residence requirements? **(b)** How have those requirements changed over time? **(c)** Why have those changes occurred?

**4. (a)** What was the primary argument made in favor of lowering the voting age to 18? **(b)** How has youth participation in elections changed since then? **(c)** Why do you think this is?

**5. (a)** What was the original purpose of literacy tests? **(b)** What prompted the removal of literacy requirements?

### Section 3

**6. (a)** Why was the 15th Amendment adopted? **(b)** Why was that amendment largely ineffective for nearly a century?

**7. (a)** What were some of the legal means used to keep African Americans from voting? **(b)** What were some of the illegal means used? **(c)** How were the efforts to disenfranchise African Americans finally overcome?

### Section 4

**8. (a)** What is a nonvoting voter? **(b)** What is the cause of ballot fatigue?

**9. (a)** What are some of the characteristics of a likely voter? **(b)** How does a closely contested race usually affect voter turnout?

**10. (a)** What is split-ticket voting? **(b)** What psychological factors tend to produce split-ticket voting?

**11. Analyzing Political Cartoons** Study the cartoon below that references a World War II monument. **(a)** What is the message of the cartoon? **(b)** Why does the cartoonist use a soldier as the voice of this cartoon?

### Writing About Government

**12.** Use your Quick Write exercises from the chapter to write a narrative essay about an important event in the history of suffrage. You should review the paragraph you wrote about your audience before you begin. See pp. SH9–10 of the Writing Handbook.

## Apply What You've Learned

**13. Essential Question Activity** Conduct research on voter registration and participation in your community. Find out what a person who wishes to vote must do in order to cast a ballot, and what may disqualify a person from voting. Then interview friends or relatives about why they do or do not vote. Ask:

**(a)** What must a person who wishes to vote do?

**(b)** How easy or difficult is the registration process? If it is difficult, how might it be made easier?

**(c)** If the friends or relatives you interviewed do not vote, ask what, if anything, might be done to encourage voting.

**14. Essential Question Assessment** Based on your research and what you learned in this chapter, create a brochure explaining the registration process for someone who has recently moved into your community. You might also include statistics or some information about why people do or do not vote. Your brochure should help you to answer the Chapter Essential Question: **Why do voters act as they do?**

**Essential Questions Journal** To respond to the chapter Essential Question, go to your **Essential Questions Journal.**

# Document-Based Assessment

## The American Electorate

Since the nation's founding, the size of the electorate has grown remarkably. Much of that growth has involved extending the right to vote to such originally disenfranchised groups as African Americans and women. To many, efforts to expand the electorate represent the highest ideals of the American system of government, as illustrated by the documents below.

### Document 1

" This was the first nation in the history of the world to be founded with a purpose. The great phrases of that purpose still sound in every American heart, North and South: "All men are created equal." "Government by consent of the governed." "Give me liberty or give me death." Well, those are not just clever words, or those are not just empty theories. In their name Americans have fought and died for two centuries, and tonight around the world they stand there as guardians of our liberty, risking their lives.

Those words are promised to every citizen that he shall share in the dignity of man. This dignity cannot be found in a man's possessions. It cannot be found in his power or in his position. It really rests on his right to be treated as a man equal in opportunity to all others. It says that he shall share in freedom. He shall choose his leaders, educate his children, provide for his family according to his ability and his merits as a human being....

Many of the issues of civil rights are very complex and most difficult. But about this there can and should be no argument: every American citizen must have an equal right to vote.

—President Lyndon Johnson
Address to Congress, March 15, 1965

### Document 2

—Thomas Nast,
*Harper's Weekly*, November 22, 1869

---

**Use your knowledge of voting rights and Documents 1 and 2 to answer Questions 1–3.**

1. Which answer best summarizes the point of Document 1?
   A. Voting rights are only one of the many important civil rights guaranteed to the American people.
   B. The right to vote is one of the most basic rights possessed by the American people.
   C. Only those people who are well informed should be allowed to vote.
   D. More people will have to fight and die in order to secure voting rights.

2. What are the people celebrating in Document 2, and what does the picture suggest will result?

3. **Pull It Together** Why do you think that securing voting rights for African Americans was essential to securing equal rights as citizens of the United States?

 **GOVERNMENT** ONLINE
**Online Documents**
To find more primary sources on the electorate, visit
PearsonSchool.com/phgovt

---

## DOCUMENT-BASED ASSESSMENT

1. B
2. They are celebrating universal suffrage, and they are suggesting that the result will be greater harmony among different racial and ethnic groups.
3. A good answer will explore how freedom depends on true equality.

**L2 Differentiate** Students use all the documents on the page to support their thesis.

**L3 Differentiate** Students include additional information available online at **PearsonSchool.com/phgovt.**

**L4 Differentiate** Students use materials from the textbook, the online information at **PearsonSchool.com/phgovt,** and do additional research to support their views.

**Go Online to PearsonSchool.com/phgovt** for a student rubric and extra documents.

---

### WRITING ABOUT GOVERNMENT

12. In their essays, students should provide background for their chosen event and include key details, organized in chronological order.

### APPLY WHAT YOU'VE LEARNED

13. **(a)** A good answer will include all the necessary steps for the student's community. **(b)** Students should identify any requirements, such as proof of residency or citizenship or identification, that may require advance planning by a person wishing to register. **(c)** A good answer will give specific suggestions, including explanations for how they would improve the process and prevent misuse.

14. The brochure should carefully list all the steps. Students should consider how registration requirements in the community either help or hinder voter participation.

# Introduce the Chapter

## Essential Questions:

**UNIT 2**

In what ways should people participate in public affairs?

**CHAPTER 7**

How fair and effective is the electoral process?

### ACTIVATE PRIOR KNOWLEDGE

Have students examine the image and quotation on these pages. Ask: **How does the power of the vote promote equality?** *(Each vote counts equally, regardless of the voter's race, religion, or other differences. Thus, to win office, candidates must address the concerns of diverse voters, not just an influential few.)* In this chapter, students will learn about the electoral process. Tell students to begin to further explore the electoral process by completing the Chapter 7 Essential Question Warmup activity in their **Essential Questions Journal.**

### BEFORE READING

**L2** **ELL Differentiate** Chapter 7 Prereading and Vocabulary Worksheet (Unit 2 All-in-One, p. 116)

### SUCCESSNET STUDENT AND TEACHER CENTER

Visit **PearsonSchool.com/phgovt** for download-able resources that allow students and teachers to connect with government "on the go."

### DIGITAL LESSON PRESENTATION

The digital lesson presentation supports the print lesson with activities and summaries of key concepts.

## SKILLS DEVELOPMENT

### ANALYZE MAPS

You may wish to teach analyzing maps as a distinct skill within Section 3 of this chapter. Use the Chapter 7 Skills Worksheet (Unit 2 All-in-One, p. 148) to help students learn how to analyze maps. The worksheet asks students to analyze maps of presidential campaign contributions in 2000 and 2004 and then answer questions about the maps. For L2 and L1 students, assign the adapted Skill Activity (Unit 2 All-in-One, p. 149).

**WebQuest** **online** The chapter WebQuest challenges students to answer the chapter Essential Question by asking them about the electoral process.

182

## Block Scheduling

**BLOCK 1:** Teach all the Section 1 lesson plan. Begin Teaching the Section 2 lesson plan, including the Bellringer and the following discussion, and the Core Worksheet.

**BLOCK 2:** Complete Section 2, starting with the discussion of student memoranda and continuing through the lesson. Then teach the Section 3 lesson plan in its entirety.

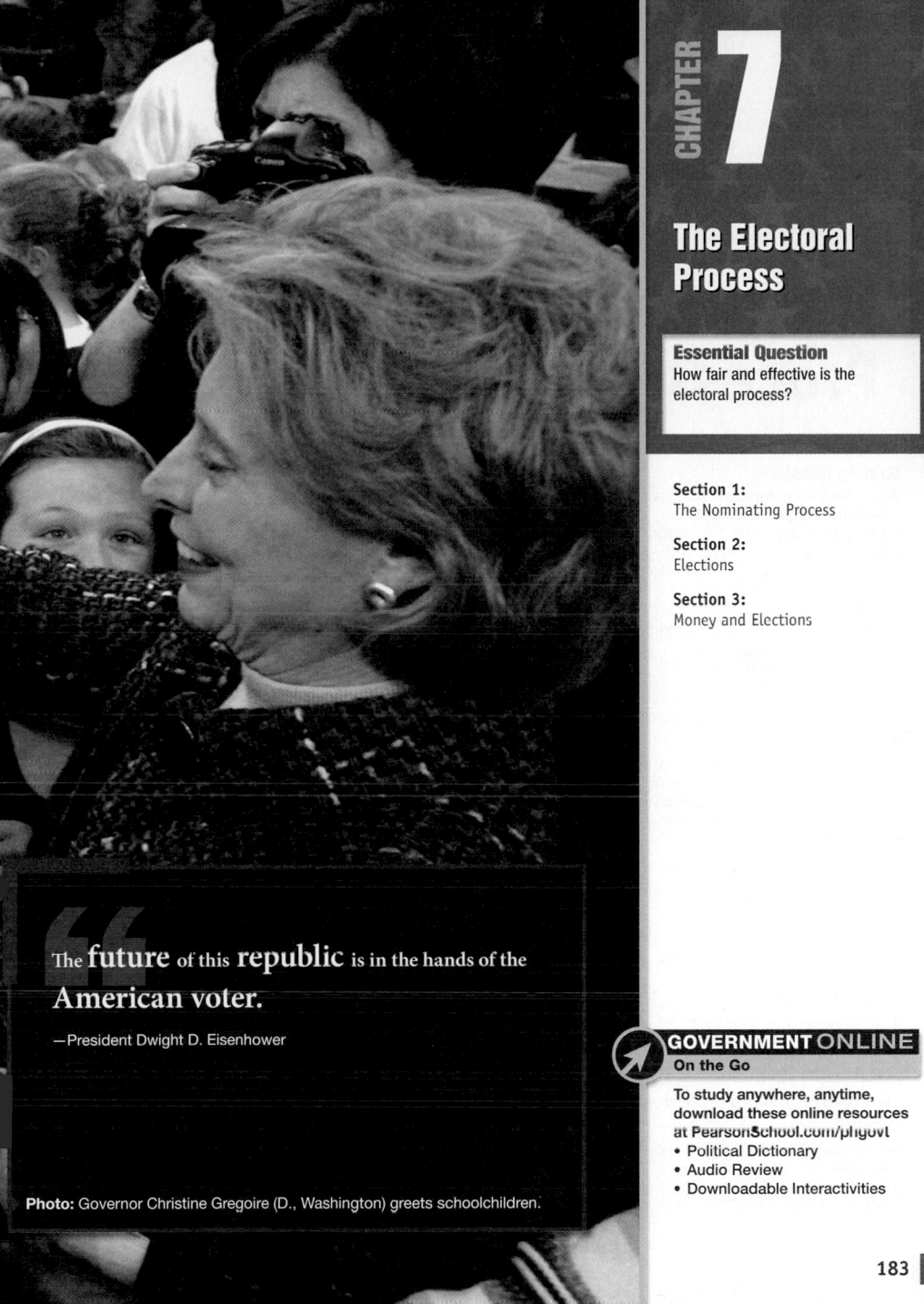

CHAPTER 7

# The Electoral Process

## Essential Question
How fair and effective is the electoral process?

> The **future** of this **republic** is in the hands of the **American voter.**
>
> —President Dwight D. Eisenhower

**GOVERNMENT** ONLINE
On the Go

To study anywhere, anytime, download these online resources at PearsonSchool.com/phgovt
• Political Dictionary
• Audio Review
• Downloadable Interactivities

**Photo:** Governor Christine Gregoire (D., Washington) greets schoolchildren.

183

## Lesson Goals

**SECTION 1**

Students will . . .

• participate in a talk show simulation to build understanding about the nominating process and methods.

• evaluate the fairness of the nominating process by analyzing a Supreme Court ruling.

**SECTION 2**

Students will . . .

• explore the variation in types of election procedures used nationwide in order to understand how election laws vary by State.

• examine issues raised in the 2000 Florida presidential voting to gain understanding of how voting procedures and equipment can affect elections.

**SECTION 3**

Students will . . .

• consider the potentially corrupting effect of money in politics by analyzing a political cartoon.

• prepare for and carry out a debate on campaign finance reform.

• produce a political cartoon about campaign finance laws.

## Pressed for Time

Have students create an outline of the chapter using the main headings and subheadings, adding other useful information to the outline as appropriate.

Then have students create a flowchart that covers the electoral process—from nominating to elections. Annotations on the flowchart should explain the role of money in the process.

**DIFFERENTIATED INSTRUCTION KEY**

Look for these symbols to help you adjust steps in each lesson to meet your students' needs.

**L1** Special Needs

**L2** Basic

  **ELL** English Language Learners

  **LPR** Less Proficient Readers

**L3** All Students

**L4** Advanced Students

# What methods are used to choose candidates for public office?

## Get Started

### LESSON GOALS

Students will . . .

- participate in a talk show simulation to build understanding about the nominating process and methods.
- evaluate the fairness of the nominating process by analyzing a Supreme Court ruling.

### BEFORE CLASS

Assign the section, the graphic organizer in the text, and the Reading Comprehension Worksheet (Unit 2 All-in-One, p. 120) before class.

**L2 Differentiate** Reading Comprehension Worksheet (Unit 2 All-in-One, p. 122)

## SKILLS DEVELOPMENT

### INNOVATE AND THINK CREATIVELY

Before students prepare their talk show presentations in this section, you may want to review the information in the Skills Handbook, p. S23, on innovating and thinking creatively.

---

### SECTION 1

# The Nominating Process

### Guiding Question
**What methods are used to choose candidates for public office?** Use the diagram to write down information about the various methods of nominating candidates to run for office.

### Political Dictionary
- nomination
- general election
- caucus
- direct primary
- closed primary
- open primary
- blanket primary
- runoff primary
- nonpartisan election

### Objectives
1. Explain why the nominating process is a critical first step in the election process.
2. Describe self-announcement, the caucus, and the convention as nominating methods.
3. Discuss the direct primary as the principal nominating method used in the United States today.
4. Understand why some candidates use the petition as a nominating device.

**Image Above:** Jesse Ventura, the first Reform Party nominee to win a governorship, celebrates his election as governor of Minnesota in 1999.

Suppose your teacher stood in front of the class and said: "Here's a $1,000 bill. Who'd like to have it?" You, and everyone else in the room, would promptly say, or at least think: "Me!" Suppose the teacher then said: "Okay, we'll hold an election. The person who wins the most votes gets the money."

What would happen? If the election were held immediately, it is likely that each member of the class would vote for himself or herself. A few might vote for a friend. Almost certainly, however, the election would end in a tie. No one would win the money.

But suppose the teacher said: "We'll hold the election tomorrow." What do you suppose would happen then? As you think about the answer to that question, you begin to get a sense of the practical importance of the nominating process—the first step in the process of electing candidates for public office.

### A Critical First Step

The nominating process is the process of candidate selection. **Nomination**—the naming of those who will seek office—is a critically important step in the election process.

You have already seen two major illustrations of the significance of the nominating process. In Chapter 5, you read about the making of nominations (1) as a prime function of political parties in American politics, and (2) as a leading reason for the decentralized character of the two major parties in the United States.

The nominating process also has a very real impact on the right to vote. In the typical election in this country, voters can choose between only two candidates for each office on the ballot. They can vote for the Republican or they can vote for the Democratic candidate.[1] This is another way of saying that we have a two-party system in the United States. It is also another way to say that the nominating stage is a critically important step in the electoral process. Those who make nominations place real, very practical limits on the choices that voters can make in the general election.

---

1 Other choices are sometimes listed, of course—minor party or independent nominees. These are not often meaningful alternatives, however; most voters choose not to "waste" their votes on candidates who cannot win. Also, nonpartisan elections are an exception to this statement, of course, since candidates are not identified by party labels.

## Focus on the Basics

Here is the information that your students need to learn in this section.

**FACTS:** • Five major nominating methods are used in American politics: self-announcement, caucus, convention, direct primary, and petition. • The most widely used method today is the direct primary.

**CONCEPTS:** representative government, will of the people

**ENDURING UNDERSTANDINGS:** • The nominating process is vital to democratic government. • Corruption spurred changes in the American political process and led to the development of the modern nominating procedure. • The nominating process determines which candidates can appear on the ballot in local, State, and national elections.

In one-party constituencies (those areas where one party regularly wins elections), the nominating process is usually the only point at which there is any real contest for public office. Once the dominant party has made its nomination, the general election is little more than a formality.

Dictatorial regimes point up the importance of the nominating process. Many of them hold **general elections**—regularly scheduled elections at which voters make the final selection of officeholders—much as democracies do. But, typically, the ballots used in those elections list only one candidate for each office—the candidate of the ruling clique; and those candidates regularly win with majorities approaching 100 percent.

Nominations are made in five different ways in this country. Candidates are named to the ballot by (1) self-announcement, (2) caucus, (3) convention, (4) direct primary, and (5) petition.

## Self-Announcement

Self-announcement is the oldest form of the nominating process in American politics. First used in colonial times, it is still often found at the small-town and rural levels in many parts of the country.

The method is quite simple. A person who wants to run for office simply announces that fact. Modesty or local custom may dictate that someone else actually makes the candidate's announcement, but, still, the process amounts to the same thing.

Self-announcement is sometimes used by someone who failed to win a regular party nomination or by someone unhappy with the party's choice. Note that whenever a write-in candidate appears in an election, the self-announcement process has been used.

In recent history, four prominent presidential contenders have made use of the process: George Wallace, who declared himself to be the American Independent Party's nominee in 1968; and independent candidates Eugene McCarthy in 1976; John Anderson in 1980; and Ross Perot in 1992. And all of the 135 candidates who sought to replace Governor Gray Davis of California in that State's recall election in 2003—including the winner, Arnold Schwarzenegger—were self-starters.

## The Caucus

As a nominating device, a **caucus** is a group of like-minded people who meet to select the candidates they will support in an upcoming election. The first caucus nominations were made during the later colonial period, probably in Boston in the 1720s. John Adams described the caucus this way in 1763:

### PRIMARY SOURCE

" This day learned that the Caucus Club meets, at certain times, in the garret of Tom Dawes, the Adjutant of the Boston Regiment. He has a large house, and he has a moveable partition in his garret which he takes down, and the whole club meets in one room. There they smoke tobacco till you cannot see from one end of the garret to the other. There they drink flip, I suppose, and they choose a moderator, who puts questions to the vote regularly; and selectmen, assessors, collectors, wardens, fire-wards, and representatives, are regularly chosen before they are chosen in the town. "

—Charles Francis Adams (ed.)
*The Works of John Adams* (1856)

▶▶ **Analyzing Cartoons** Ross Perot launched his 1992 presidential campaign via self-announcement. *Why might self-announcement attract candidates with the personal wealth to finance their own campaigns?*

clique
*n.* an exclusive group

---

## Differentiated Resources

The following resources are located in the All-in-One, Unit 2, Chapter 7, Section 1:

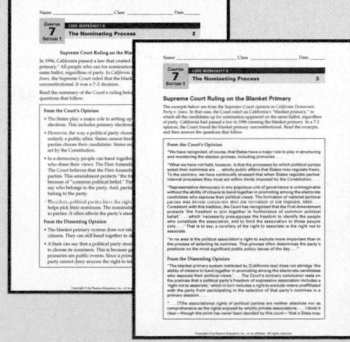

---

### BELLRINGER

Display Transparency 7A, Presidential Bandwagon, which is a political cartoon about the nominating process. Have students write a brief, one- or two-sentence description of the cartoon. Descriptions should explain the major message of the cartoon and how the elements of the cartoon achieve this message.

**L2** **Differentiate** Tell students that *bandwagon* has two meanings. A bandwagon can be a vehicle on which musicians perform during a parade. It can also mean a popular movement, such as a political campaign.

## Teach

To present this topic using online resources, use the lesson presentation at **PearsonSchool.com/phgovt.**

### INTRODUCE THE TOPIC

Tell students that they will be learning about the process by which the candidates who run for office are selected. Say that this process is called *nomination,* which comes from a Latin word meaning "name." Ask: **Why do you think it is necessary to have a process for naming candidates for office?** *(A nominating process may help prevent unqualified people from appearing on the ballot. Also, it pares down the number of candidates on the ballot to a reasonable number.)* **How does the fact that we have a two-party system increase the importance of nomination?** *(Voters generally face a choice of only two candidates, so it is important that those two candidates be of very high quality.)*

Next, review student responses to the Bellringer. Invite volunteers to share their summaries. Review the major message of the cartoon. *(It suggests that the nominating process is too crowded, with so many candidates that it is impossible to build excitement for any one candidate.)* Review also the elements of the cartoon. *(The crowded bandwagon represents the large number of candidates. The band represents excitement for a candidate.)*

---

## Answers

**Checkpoint** the naming of those who will seek office

**Analyzing Cartoons** because such a candidate might not need the support of a major party

## DISTRIBUTE CORE WORKSHEET A

Distribute the Chapter 7 Core Worksheet A (Unit 2 All-in-One, p. 124), which helps students build understanding of the nominating process by guiding them through a talk show segment on the process. Arrange students in groups of three to four. Tell students to use their textbooks and any other available resources, such as the Internet, to prepare for their presentation.

**L1 L2 Differentiate** Group L1 and L2 students with L3 and L4 students.

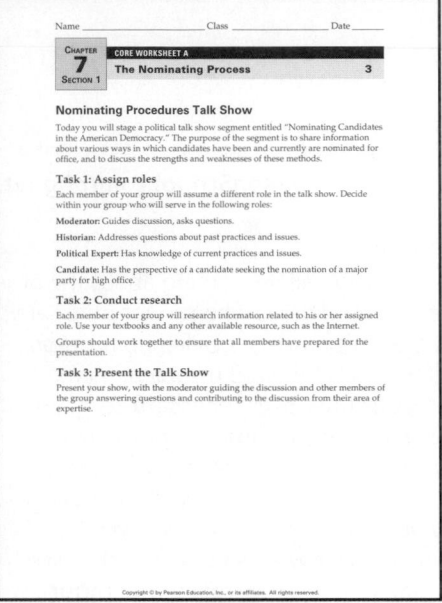

Tell students to go to the Audio Tour to listen to a guided audio tour of the five methods of nomination.

## Answers

**Five Methods of Nomination** possible response: the direct primary, because all qualified voters may participate directly in selecting candidates by private ballot

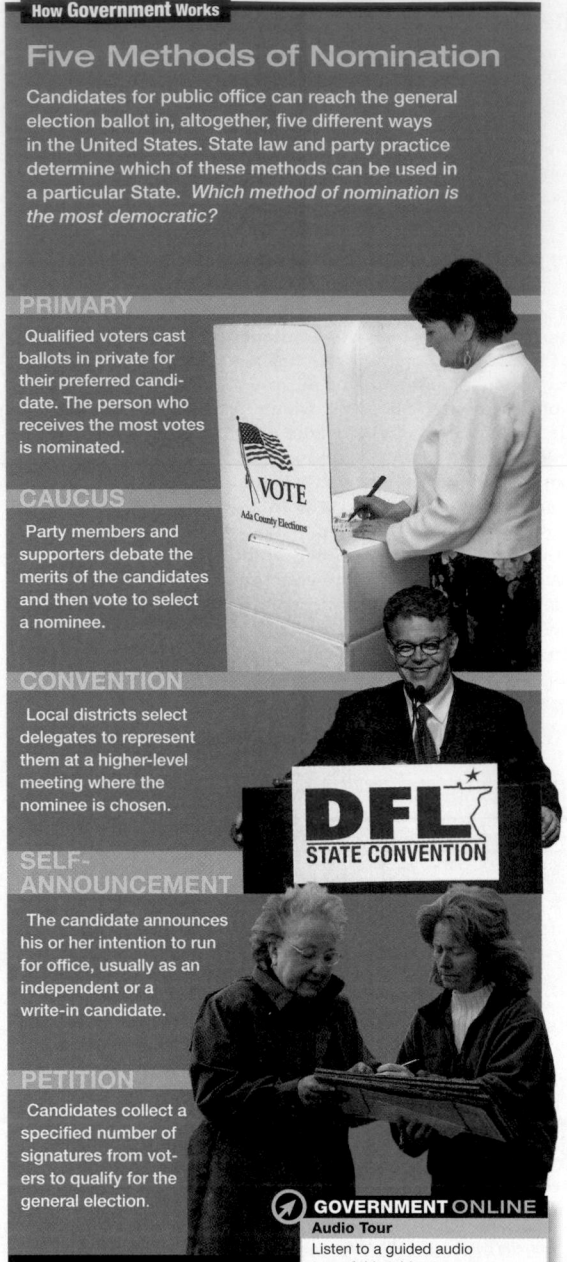

### How Government Works
## Five Methods of Nomination

Candidates for public office can reach the general election ballot in, altogether, five different ways in the United States. State law and party practice determine which of these methods can be used in a particular State. *Which method of nomination is the most democratic?*

**PRIMARY**
Qualified voters cast ballots in private for their preferred candidate. The person who receives the most votes is nominated.

**CAUCUS**
Party members and supporters debate the merits of the candidates and then vote to select a nominee.

**CONVENTION**
Local districts select delegates to represent them at a higher-level meeting where the nominee is chosen.

**SELF-ANNOUNCEMENT**
The candidate announces his or her intention to run for office, usually as an independent or a write-in candidate.

**PETITION**
Candidates collect a specified number of signatures from voters to qualify for the general election.

**GOVERNMENT ONLINE**
**Audio Tour**
Listen to a guided audio tour of this table at
**PearsonSchool.com/phgovt**

Originally the caucus was a private meeting of a few influential figures in the community.[2] As political parties began to appear in the late 1700s, they took over the device and soon broadened the membership of the caucus considerably.

The coming of independence brought the need to nominate candidates for State offices: governor, lieutenant governor, and others above the local level. The legislative caucus—a meeting of a party's members in the State legislature—took on the job. At the national level, both the Federalists and the Democratic-Republicans in Congress were, by 1800, choosing their presidential and vice-presidential candidates through the congressional caucus.

The legislative and congressional caucuses were quite practical in their day. Transportation and communication were difficult at best. Since legislators were already gathered regularly in a central place, it made sense for them to take on the nominating responsibility. The spread of democracy, especially in the newer States on the frontier, spurred opposition to the use of caucuses, however. They were widely condemned for their closed, unrepresentative character.

Criticism of the caucus reached its peak in the early 1820s. The supporters of three of the leading contenders for the presidency in 1824—Andrew Jackson, Henry Clay, and John Quincy Adams—boycotted the Democratic-Republicans' congressional caucus that year. In fact, Jackson and his supporters made "King Caucus" a leading campaign issue. The other major contender, William H. Crawford of Georgia, became the caucus nominee at a meeting attended by fewer than one third of the Democratic-Republican Party's members in Congress.

Crawford ran a poor third in the electoral college balloting in 1824, and the reign of

---

2 The origin of the term *caucus* is not clear. Most authorities agree that it comes from the word *caulkers*, because the Boston Caucus Club met in a room formerly used as a meeting place by caulkers in the Boston shipyards. (Caulkers made ships watertight by filling seams or cracks in the hulls of sailing vessels with tar or oakum.) The term is also used to refer to a group whose members (often members of a legislative body) unite to promote some particular interest—for example, in Congress today, the Congressional Black Caucus.

## Background

**GETTING ON THE BALLOT** Achieving nomination by any method does not automatically or necessarily place a person's name on the ballot for an election. In each State, laws determine the process a candidate must go through in order to get his or her name on the actual general election ballot. For example, different State laws may require the completion of petitions, the payment of a filing fee, or other such measures. For minor parties, the requirements can be especially difficult to meet. For example, minor party candidates need thousands more signatures than candidates of the major parties must provide.

King Caucus at the national level was ended. With its death in presidential politics, the caucus system soon withered at the State and local levels, as well.

The caucus is still used to make local nominations in some places, especially in New England. There, a caucus is open to all members of a party, and it only faintly resembles the original closed and private process.

## The Convention

As the caucus method collapsed, the convention system took its place. The first national convention to nominate a presidential candidate was held by a minor party, the Anti-Masons, in Baltimore in 1831. The newly formed National Republican (soon to become Whig) Party also held a convention later that same year. The Democrats picked up the practice in 1832. All major-party presidential nominees have been chosen by conventions ever since. By the 1840s, conventions had become the principal means for making nominations at every level in American politics.

On paper, the convention process seems perfectly suited to representative government. A party's members meet in a local caucus to pick candidates for local offices and, at the same time, to select delegates to represent them at a county convention.[3]

At the county convention, the delegates nominate candidates for county offices and select delegates to the next rung on the convention ladder, usually the State convention. There, the delegates from the county conventions pick the party's nominees for governor and other Statewide offices. State conventions also send delegates to the party's national convention, where the party selects its presidential and vice-presidential candidates.

In theory, the will of the party's rank and file membership is passed up through each of its representative levels. Practice soon pointed up the weaknesses of the theory, however, as party bosses found ways to manipulate the

---

[3] The meetings at which delegates to local conventions are chosen are still often called caucuses. Earlier, they were also known as primaries—that is, first meetings. The use of that name gave rise to the term *direct primary*, to distinguish that newer nominating method from the convention process.

---

process. By playing with the selection of delegates, usually at the local levels, they soon dominated the entire system.

As a result, the caliber of most conventions declined at all levels, especially during the late 1800s. How low some of them fell can be seen in this description of a Cook County (Chicago), Illinois, convention in 1896:

> **PRIMARY SOURCE**
> Of [723] delegates, those who had been on trial for murder numbered 17; sentenced to the penitentiary for murder or manslaughter and served sentence, 7; served terms in the penitentiary for burglary, 36; served terms in the penitentiary for picking pockets, 2; served terms in the penitentiary for arson, 1; . . . jailbirds identified by detectives, 84; keepers of gambling houses, 7; keepers of houses of ill-fame, 2; convicted of mayhem, 3; ex-prize fighters, 11; poolroom proprietors, 2; saloon keepers, 265; . . . political employees, 148; no occupation, 71; . . .
> —R.M. Easley
> "The Sine qua Non of Caucus Reform"
> *Review of Reviews* (Sept. 1897)

Many people had hailed the change from caucus to convention as a major change for the better in American politics. The abuses of the new device soon dashed their hopes. By the 1870s, the convention system was itself under attack as a major source of evil in the nation's politics. By the 1910s, the direct primary had replaced the convention in most States as the principal nominating method in American politics.

Conventions still play a major role in the nominating process in some States—notably, Connecticut, Michigan, South Dakota, Utah, and Virginia. And, as you will see, no adequate substitute for the device has yet been found at the presidential level.

## The Direct Primary

A **direct primary** is an *intra*party election. It is held within a party to pick that party's candidates for the general election. Wisconsin

✔ **Checkpoint**
What is the caucus and how has its popularity changed?

---

As students present their talk shows, encourage them to raise questions for the talk show members. If the talk show panel is unable to answer a question, ask other members of the class to volunteer answers.

---

**Government** *online*  *All print resources are available on the Teacher's Resource Library CD-ROM and online at* PearsonSchool.com/phgovt.

---

# Background

**NOMINATION AT A NATIONAL CONVENTION** At a national convention for one of the major parties, there will be several thousand delegates. Most of these may be pledged to cast their first vote for a specific candidate based on the results of State primaries, caucuses, and conventions. Some of the delegates—usually party officials—are unpledged, however. If a candidate captures a majority of the delegates before the convention, he or she can be certain of winning the nomination. If no candidate has secured a majority of delegates before the convention, however, the delegates themselves decide whom they will nominate. This decision can involve much negotiation and deal making.

---

## Answers

**Checkpoint** The caucus is a group of like-minded people who meet to select the candidates they will support in an upcoming election. After criticism of the caucus reached its peak in the 1820s, the method withered at the national, State, and local levels.

Tell students that the primary has emerged as a leading method of nominating major candidates. Remind students that the use of primaries in the presidential selection process is somewhat different than that used for other offices. Ask: **How are primaries different from other nominating processes?** *(Primaries are generally open to all of the electorate and not as subject to the control of party officials.)* **How does this fact affect the fairness and effectiveness of elections at nominating qualified candidates?** *(It may make them longer and more contentious, which may not necessarily improve the quality of candidates eventually nominated. But it does make them more participatory, which may make them at least appear more fair.)*

✔ **Checkpoint**
What happens at a convention?

adopted the first Statewide direct primary law in 1903; several other States soon followed its lead. Every State now makes at least some provision for its use.

In most States, State law requires that the major parties use the primary to choose their candidates for the United States Senate and House of Representatives, for the governorship and all other Statewide offices, and for most local offices as well. In a few States, however, different combinations of convention and primary are used to pick candidates for the top offices.

In Michigan, for example, the major parties choose their candidates for the U.S. Senate and House, the governorship, and the State legislature in primaries. Nominees for lieutenant governor, secretary of state, and attorney general are picked by conventions.[4]

Although the primaries are party-nominating elections, they are closely regulated by law in most States. The State usually sets the dates on which primaries are held, and it regularly conducts them, too. The State, not the parties, provides polling places and election officials, registration lists and ballots, and otherwise polices the process.

Caucuses are also found in the presidential selection process. They are used to select national convention delegates in a handful of States, as you will see in Chapter 13.

Two basic forms of the direct primary are in use today: (1) the closed primary and (2) the open primary. The major difference between the two lies in the answer to this question: Who can vote in a party's primary—*only* those qualified voters who are party members, or *any* qualified voter?

**The Closed Primary** Today, 25 States provide for the **closed primary**—a party's nominating election in which only declared party members can vote. The party's primary is closed to all but those party members.[5]

In most of the closed primary States, party membership is established by registration. When voters appear at their polling places on primary election day, their names are checked against the poll books and each voter is handed the primary ballot of the party in which he or she is registered. The voter can mark only that party's ballot; he or she can vote only in that party's primary.

In some of the closed primary States, however, a voter can change his or her party registration on election day. In those States, then, the primary is not as completely "closed" as it is elsewhere.

**The Open Primary** The **open primary**—also known as the crossover primary—is a party's nominating election in which *any* qualified voter can cast a ballot. Although it is the form in which the direct primary first appeared, it is now found in only 17 States.

When voters go to the polls in some open primary States, they are handed a ballot of each party holding a primary. Usually, they receive only two ballots, those of the Republican and

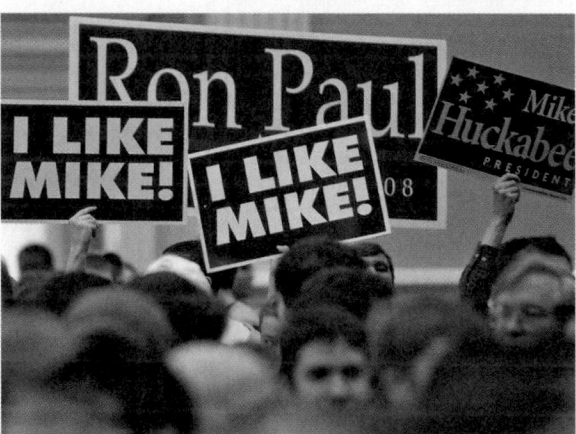

Volunteers wave signs for candidates Rep. Ron Paul (R., Texas) and Gov. Mike Huckabee (R., Arkansas) during the 2008 Republican presidential primaries.

4 In most States, minor parties are required to make their nominations by other, more difficult processes, usually in conventions or by petition. This is another of the several ways in which State election laws often, purposely, make life difficult for minor parties.

5 The Supreme Court has held that a State's closed primary law cannot forbid a party to allow independent voters to participate in its primary if the party itself chooses to allow them to do so. In *Tashjian* v. *Republican Party of Connecticut*, 1986, the Court struck down such a State law. Note that the Court did not outlaw the closed primary in this case, nor did it hold that a political party *must* allow independents to vote in its primary. The Court found that the Connecticut law violated the 1st and 14th Amendments' guarantees of the right of association—here the right of Connecticut Republicans to associate with independents (invite independents to join them) in making GOP nominations.

## Background

**"WHITE PRIMARIES"** Primary elections are held within political parties—which are technically private organizations. During the Jim Crow era, this fact was exploited as one of the techniques by which whites in some southern States denied African Americans a meaningful role in electoral politics. With the so-called "white primary," African American and other minority voters in some states were barred from taking part in Democratic primary elections. Since the Democratic Party dominated politics in these States, keeping voters out of the primary effectively deprived them of any say in the election of public officials. The use of the white primary was outlawed by the Supreme Court ruling in *Smith* v. *Allwright* in 1944.

## Answers

**Checkpoint** At a convention, delegates nominate candidates for offices at higher levels.

the Democratic parties. Then, in the privacy of the voting booth, each voter marks the ballot of the party in whose primary he or she chooses to vote. In other open primary States, a voter must ask for the ballot of the party in whose primary he or she wants to vote. That is, each voter must make a *public* choice of party in order to vote in the primary.

Through 2000, three States used a different version of the open primary—the **blanket primary,** sometimes called the "wide-open primary." Washington adopted the first blanket primary law in 1935. Alaska followed suit in 1970, and California did so in 1996. In a blanket primary, every voter received the same ballot—a long one that listed *every* candidate, regardless of party, for every nomination to be made at the primary. Voters could participate however they chose. They could confine themselves to one party's primary; or they could switch back and forth between the parties' primaries, voting to nominate a Democrat for one office, a Republican for another, and so on down the ballot.

The Supreme Court found California's version of the blanket primary unconstitutional in 2000, however. In *California Democratic Party* v. *Jones,* the High Court held that that process violated the 1st and 14th amendments' guarantees of the right of association. It ruled that a State cannot force a political party to associate with outsiders—that is, with members of other parties or with independents—when it picks its candidates for public office.

The Court's decision in *Jones* made the blanket primary a thing of the past. Alaska responded by adopting a more traditional version of the open primary. But California and Washington have gone quite another way.

Those two States now provide for the "top two" form of the open primary. In both States, the names of *all* those who seek nomination are listed, by office, on a single primary ballot. Then the top two vote getters for each office, regardless of party, face one another in the general election. Thus, two Republicans, or two Democrats, may battle one another in November.

Louisiana uses yet another version of the open primary, under what is sometimes called its "open-election law." There, as in Washington, all candidates for nomination are listed on a single ballot, and the top two

## Nominating a President

The two major parties name their presidential and vice-presidential candidates at national conventions held every fourth year. *How do those national conventions differ from the nominating conventions held in some States?*

### MAJOR PARTIES
Modern-day national conventions formally nominate a presidential candidate, but his or her victory has been predetermined by wins in State primaries and caucuses held earlier in the year.

2008 Democratic National Convention

### OTHER CANDIDATES
Independent and minor party candidates often must submit signed petitions to win a place on the general election ballot in several States.

Libertarian candidate
Bob Barr

vote getters, regardless of party, face off in the general election. But if a candidate wins a majority of the votes in the primary, he or she is declared the winner of the office involved—so, the primary becomes, in effect, the election.[6]

**Closed vs. Open Primaries** The merits of the two basic forms of the direct primary have been argued for decades. Those who support the closed primary rely on three major arguments. They regularly claim that:

---

6 Louisiana's "open-election" primary law applies to its State and local elections, which are held in November of the *odd*-numbered years. Since 1872, federal law has directed that congressional elections be held in November of the *even*-numbered years, and Louisiana abides by that law. It holds traditional closed primaries in the *even*-numbered years to choose candidates for seats in the U.S. House and Senate.

# Background

**THE EVOLUTION OF THE PRIMARY** The primary system emerged from the Progressive Era of the late 1800s and early 1900s. It was an attempt to give voters a greater say in the political process. Other Progressive Era reforms of the time were the initiative and referendum, by which voters have a direct say on the passage of specific laws; the recall, by which voters can remove an elected official from office before the end of his or her term; and the popular election of United States senators.

## Answers

**Nominating a President** In a State convention, delegates for the national convention are chosen. Nomination actually takes place at the national convention.

**L3 Differentiate** Have students write a newspaper editorial in which they make an argument in favor of one method of nomination as the preferred method for the whole nation. The editorial should clearly identify their preferred method and explain why it is superior to the other methods at producing fair elections between quality candidates.

**L1 L2 Differentiate** Have students identify the method of nomination that they feel is the most fair and effective. Have them write or speak a brief statement explaining their choice.

---

✓**Checkpoint**
What is the difference between an open primary and a closed primary?

**1.** The closed primary prevents one party from "raiding" the other's primary in the hope of nominating weaker candidates in the opposition party.

**2.** It helps to make candidates more responsive to the party, its platform, and its members.

**3.** It helps make voters more thoughtful, because they must choose between the parties in order to vote in the primaries.

Those who criticize the closed primary usually contend that:

**1.** It compromises the secrecy of the ballot, because it forces voters to make their party preferences known in order to participate, and

**2.** It tends to exclude independent voters from the nominating process.[7]

The advocates of the open primary believe that that nominating arrangement addresses both of those objections to the closed primary. They say that in the typical open primary (1) voters are not forced to make their party preferences a matter of public record, and (2) independent voters are not excluded from the nominating process.

**The Runoff Primary** In most States, candidates need to win only a plurality of the votes cast in the primary to win their party's nomination.[8] (Remember, a *plurality* is the greatest number of votes won by any candidate, whether a *majority* or not.) In 8 States, however, an absolute majority is needed to carry a primary.[9] If no one wins a majority in a race, a **runoff primary** is held a few weeks later. In that runoff contest, the two top vote getters in the first primary face one another to determine the party's nomination,

and the winner of that vote becomes the party's nominee.

**The Nonpartisan Primary** In most States all or nearly all of the elected school and municipal offices are filled in **nonpartisan elections**. These are elections in which candidates are not identified by party labels. About half of all State judges are chosen on nonpartisan ballots, as well. The nomination of candidates for these offices takes place on a nonpartisan basis, too, and most often in nonpartisan primaries.

Typically, a contender who wins a clear majority in a nonpartisan primary then runs unopposed in the general election, subject only to write-in opposition. In many States, however, a candidate who wins a majority in the primary is declared elected at that point. If there is no majority winner, the names of the two top contenders are placed on the general election ballot.

The primary first appeared as a partisan nominating device. Many have long argued that it is not well suited for use in nonpartisan elections. Instead, they favor the petition method, as you will see in a moment.

**The Presidential Primary** The presidential primary developed as an offshoot of the direct primary. It is *not* a nominating device, however. Rather, the presidential primary is an election that is held as one part of the process by which presidential candidates are chosen.

The presidential primary is a very complex process that was in place in a large majority of States in the most recent presidential election. It is one or both of two things, depending on the State involved. It is a process in which a party's voters elect some or all of a State party organization's delegates to that party's national convention; and/or it is a preference election in which voters can choose (vote their preference) among various contenders for the grand prize, the party's presidential nomination.

Much of what happens in presidential politics in the early months of every fourth year centers on this very complicated process. (See Chapter 13 for an extended discussion of the presidential primary.)

---

**7** See the discussion of *Tashjian* v. *Republican Party of Connecticut*, 1986, in footnote 5. The closed primary States have amended their election laws to comply with that decision.

**8** In Iowa, if no candidate wins at least 35 percent of the votes in a primary, the party must then nominate its candidate for that office by convention.

**9** Alabama, Arkansas, Georgia, Mississippi, Oklahoma, South Carolina, Texas—and Louisiana under its unique "open election" law. In North Carolina a runoff is held when no candidate wins 40 percent of the primary vote. In South Dakota, if no one who seeks a party's nomination for governor, U.S. senator, or U.S. representative wins at least 35 percent, the party's candidate for that office must be picked in a runoff primary two weeks later.

# Debate

"The privilege of membership in a party may be . . . no concern of a state. But when . . . that privilege is also the essential qualification for voting in a primary to select nominees for a general election, the state makes the action of the party the action of the state . . ."

—Supreme Court decision in *Smith* v. *Allwright*

Use this quotation to start a debate in your classroom.

---

## Answers

**Checkpoint** In an open primary, any qualified voter can cast a ballot. In a closed primary, only declared party members can vote.

## Forms of Primaries Among the States, 2010

**GOVERNMENT** ONLINE
**Audio tour**
Listen to a guided audio tour of this map at
PearsonSchool.com/phgovt

**Analyzing Maps** The direct primary, whatever its form, intends to put the nominating function in the hands of a party's rank-and-file membership. *What form of the primary is used in your State?*

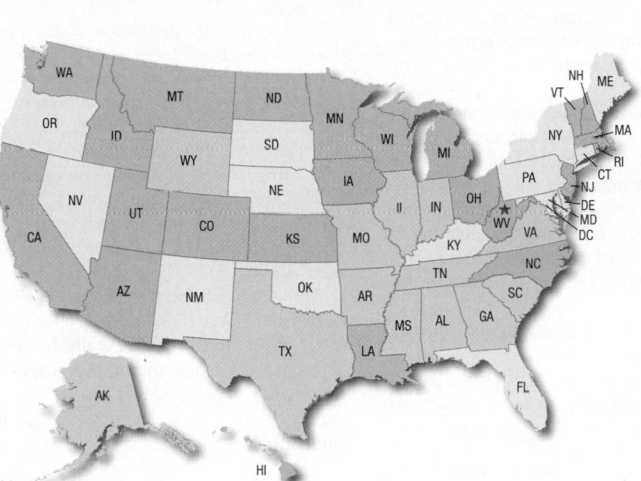

**KEY**

☐ **Closed Primary**
*Unaffiliated Voters Excluded*
Primaries are limited to voters registered with that party. Unaffiliated voters cannot vote in primaries.

☐ **Closed Primary**
*Unaffiliated Voters Permitted*
Primaries are limited to voters registered with that party and unaffiliated voters, who may vote in any party's primary.

☐ **Open Primary**
*Private Choice*
Voters may vote in any party's primary. Their choice of party remains private.

☐ **Open Primary**
*Public Declaration*
Voters may vote in any party's primary. Election officials record which party's ballot they choose.

☐ **Open Election**
All candidates appear on a single ballot open to all voters. If no candidate receives 50 percent, the top two vote getters proceed to a run-off.

★ Unaffiliated voters permitted to vote in Republican race only

## Evaluation of the Primary

The direct primary, whether open or closed, is an *intra*party nominating election. It came to American politics as a reform of the boss-dominated convention system. It was intended to take the nominating function away from the party organization and put it in the hands of the party's rank-and-file membership.

The basic facts about the primary have never been very well understood by most voters, however. So, in closed primary States, many voters resent having to declare their party preference in order to vote in the primary. And, in both open and closed primary States, many are upset because they cannot express their support for candidates in more than one party. Many are also annoyed by the "bed-sheet ballots" they regularly see in primary elections—not realizing that the use of the direct primary almost automatically

means a long ballot. And some are concerned because the primary (and, in particular, its closed form) tends to exclude independents from the nominating process.

All of these factors, combined with a lack of appreciation of the important role that primaries play in the election process, result in this unfortunate and significant fact: Nearly everywhere, voter turnout in primary elections is usually less than half what it is in the general elections in November.

Primary contests can be quite costly. The fact that successful contenders must then wage—and finance—a general election campaign adds to the money problems that <u>bedevil</u> American politics. Unfortunately, the financial facts of political life in the United States mean that some well-qualified people refuse to seek public office simply because they cannot muster the funding absolutely necessary to finance a campaign.

**bedevil**
*v.* irritate, bother

---

Tell students to go to the Audio Tour to listen to a guided audio tour of the map showing forms of primaries in State elections.

## Assess and Remediate

**L3** Collect the Core Worksheet and assess students' class participation using the Rubric for Assessing the Performance of an Entire Group (Unit 2 All-in-One, p. 256).

**L3** Assign the Section 1 Assessment questions.

**L3** Section Quiz A (Unit 2 All-in-One, p. 129)

**L2** Section Quiz B (Unit 2 All-in-One, p. 130)

Have students complete the review activities in the digital lesson presentation and continue their work in the **Essential Questions Journal.**

## Background

**LOW VOTER TURNOUT IN PRIMARIES** One concern about low primary election turnout is that the results will not reflect the full range of public opinion. The concern is that a small but active and organized wing of a party or some special interest could be able to have a strong influence in a low-turnout primary election. In the primaries leading up to the 2008 presidential election, turnout was often around 20 to 30 percent. Turnout for caucuses was generally in the single digits. Presidential primaries and caucuses generally enjoy higher turnout than those for lower offices.

## Answers

**Analyzing Maps** Answers will vary, depending on the students' State.

| If Your Students Have Trouble With | Strategies For Remediation |
|---|---|
| The importance of the nomination process (Question 2) | Have students work in pairs to write and administer a quiz about the text section "A Critical First Step." |
| The different methods of nomination (Questions 1, 3, 4) | Review with students the diagram about ways to nominate a candidate that appears in this section. |
| The different types of primaries (Questions 4, 5) | Have students create their own diagram that illustrates the differences between a closed and open primary. |
| Criticisms of the primary (Questions 6, 7) | Have student pairs prepare for and engage in a debate on this question: "Primaries should be replaced as a method of nomination in the United States." |

## Answers

**Checkpoint** Benefits of primaries include putting the nominating function in the hands of the party's rank-and-file membership and giving party members the opportunity to participate at the core of the political process. Drawbacks include the possibility of having to declare party preferences in order to vote in the primary; long ballots; costly primaries; possible divisiveness in parties; and advantages for well-known contenders.

✔ **Checkpoint**
What are the benefits and drawbacks of primaries?

The nominating process, whatever its form, can have a very divisive effect on a party. Remember, the process takes place *within* the party—so, when there is a contest for a nomination, that is where the contest occurs: Republicans fight with Republicans, Democrats do battle with Democrats. A bitter fight in the primaries can so wound and divide a party that it cannot recover in time to present a united front for the general election. Many a primary fight has cost a party an election.

Finally, because many voters are not very well informed, the primary places a premium on name familiarity. That is, it often gives an edge to a contender who has a well-known name or a name that sounds like that of some well-known person. But, notice, name familiarity in and of itself usually has little or nothing to do with a candidate's qualifications for public office.

Obviously, the primary is not without its problems, nor is any other nominating device. Still, the primary does give a party's members the opportunity to participate at the very core of the political process.

## Petition

One other nominating method is used fairly widely at the local level in American politics today—nomination by petition. Where this process is used, candidates for public office are nominated by means of petitions signed by a certain number of qualified voters in the election district.[10]

Nomination by petition is found most widely at the local level, chiefly for non-partisan school posts and municipal offices in medium-sized and smaller communities and, increasingly, for judgeships. It is also the process usually required by State law for nominating minor party and independent candidates in many of the States. (Remember, the States often purposely make the process of getting on the ballot difficult for those candidates.)

The details of the petition process vary widely from State to State, and even from one city or county to the next. Usually, however, the higher the office and/or the larger the constituency represented by the office, the greater the number of signatures needed for nomination by petition.

---

**10** The petition device is also an important part of the recall and the initiative and referendum processes; see Chapter 24.

---

## SECTION 1 ASSESSMENT

**Essential Questions Journal** To continue to build a response to the chapter Essential Question, go to your **Essential Questions Journal.**

1. **Guiding Question** Use your completed diagram to answer this question: What methods are used to choose candidates for public office?

**Key Terms and Comprehension**

2. What is the purpose of **nomination** in the electoral system?

3. In addition to primaries, what nominating methods are used in the United States?

4. What is the difference between a **closed primary** and an **open primary**?

5. How does the presidential primary differ from those primaries used in State and local nominations?

**Critical Thinking**

6. **Express Problems Clearly** Summarize the relationship between the will of the people and the power of party organizations. How has this relationship changed the way that parties nominate candidates?

7. **Draw Inferences** What do you think explains the usually low level of turnout in primary elections in most States?

**Quick Write**

**Explanatory Essay: Choose a Topic** Using the Internet, other media sources, and your textbook, find an example of a recent election that took place at the national level or in your State or local community. Write a brief summary of the election—who the candidates were and when the race took place.

## Assessment Answers

**1.** Methods of nominating candidates are self-announcement, caucus, convention, direct primary, and petition.

**2.** Nomination is the process for choosing candidates to run for office.

**3.** self-announcement, caucus, convention, and petition

**4.** Closed primaries are limited to members of a particular party, and open primaries are open to any qualified voter.

**5.** Presidential primaries are not a nominating step in and of themselves, as are primaries at the State and local levels. Presidential primaries are merely one step in a larger process, which culminates in a nominating convention.

**6.** The caucus and convention systems were criticized because they helped give rise to party machines with powerful party bosses that dominated the nominating process, leading to elections that did not reflect the will of the people. The direct primary system was instituted to take the nominating function away from the party organization and put it in the hands of the people.

**7.** Possible answer: Many voters don't understand the primary system or recognize its importance. In closed primaries, voters may resent having to declare their party preference. In closed and open primary States, many voters may get upset because they cannot vote for candidates of more than one party. Long ballots irritate some voters, and primaries tend to exclude independents.

**QUICK WRITE** Students should choose an election about which they have plenty of information.

# SECTION 2
# Elections

## Guiding Question

**How are elections conducted in the United States?** Use the chart to record information about how elections are administered and conducted.

```
                Elections
   ┌──────────────┬──────────┬──────────────┐
Administration  Ballots    Voting
                           Procedures
   •              •          •
   •              •          •
   •              •          •
```

## Political Dictionary

• ballot
• absentee voting
• coattail effect
• precinct
• polling place

## Objectives

1. Analyze how the administration of elections in the United States helps make democracy work.
2. Define the role of local precincts and polling places in the election process.
3. Describe the various ways in which voters can cast their ballots.
4. Outline the role that voting devices play in the election process.

**Image Above:** Campaign lawn signs express support for specific candidates.

Most high school students are not old enough to vote. In some parts of the country, though, high school students can serve on local election boards. First in Hawaii and Oregon and now in several States, 16- and 17-year-olds can become full-fledged members of the panels that administer local elections.

We hold more elections in this country and we vote more often than most people realize. Indeed, Sundays and holidays are about the only days of the year on which people do not go to the polls somewhere in the United States. We also elect *far* more officeholders than most people realize—in fact, more than 500,000 of them, more than in any other country in the world.

## The Administration of Elections

Democratic government cannot possibly hope to succeed unless its elections are free, honest, and accurately reported. Many people see the details of the election process as much too complicated, too legalistic, too dry and boring to worry about. Those who do really miss the vital part that those details play in making democracy work. *How* something can be done very often shapes *what* is in fact done—and that fact is as true in politics as it is in all other areas of human concern.

**Extent of Federal Control** Nearly all elections in the United States are held to choose the more than 500,000 persons who hold elective office in the more than 89,000 units of government at the State and local levels. It is quite understandable, then, that most election law in the United States is *State*—not federal—law.

Even so, a body of federal election law does exist. The Constitution gives Congress the power to fix "[t]he Times, Places, and Manner of holding Elections" of members of Congress.[11] Congress also has the power to set the time for choosing presidential electors, to set the date for casting the electoral votes, and to regulate other aspects of the presidential election process.[12]

---

**11** Article I, Section 4, Clause 1; 17th Amendment
**12** Article II, Section 1, Clause 4; 12th Amendment

## GUIDING QUESTION

## How are elections conducted in the United States?

| Elections | | |
|---|---|---|
| **Administration** | **Ballots** | **Voting Procedures** |
| • most election law is State law | • instrument on which voter registers choice | • voting machine, often electronic |
| • Congress sets time, place and manner of congressional and presidential elections | • forms include paper, optical scanner, touch screens | • optical scanning—voters fill in and scanners read and record |
| • congressional elections—first Tuesday following first Monday in November of every even-numbered year | • secret ballots | • direct response electronic voting—voters touch screen or push buttons and votes recorded electronically |
| • presidential election—same date every fourth year | • based on Australian ballot—printed at public expense, all candidates listed, given only at polls, marked in secret | • vote by mail |
| • Help America Vote Act—upgrade voting machines and training of election officials; computerize registration; allow provisional voting | • office-group ballot—candidates for an office grouped together; order of names rotated | • online voting |
| • most elections for State offices on same date as national elections | • party-column ballot—candidates listed in column under party name | |
| • absentee voting | • sample ballots help voters prepare | |
| • early voting | • bed-sheet ballot—lengthy | |
| • precinct—voting district | | |
| • polling place—place votes cast | | |
| • precinct election board supervises | | |
| • poll watchers—one per party at each polling place | | |

## SKILLS DEVELOPMENT

### DRAW INFERENCES AND CONCLUSIONS

In this section's Core Worksheet, students are asked to analyze information about balloting problems in the 2000 presidential election. Before they complete this activity, they may review information in the Skills Handbook, p. S19, about drawing inferences and conclusions.

## Focus on the Basics

**FACTS:** • Elections are regulated mostly by State law, though federal laws apply to federal elections. • Most voting takes place at precincts across the country, though some occurs by mail, by absentee ballot, or by early voting procedures. • All States now use the Australian ballot, usually with the office-group format, though sometimes with a party-column format. • Electronic voting and vote counting are common now.

**CONCEPTS:** representative government, political participation, civic duty

**ENDURING UNDERSTANDINGS:** • Voting gives Americans the chance to participate in the democratic process. • Voting procedures have been refined over the years to reduce fraud and corruption and to increase fairness and accuracy of results.

# Get Started

## LESSON GOALS

Students will . . .

- explore the variation in types of election procedures used nationwide in order to understand how election laws vary by State.
- examine issues raised in the 2000 Florida presidential voting to gain understanding of how voting procedures and equipment can affect elections.

## BEFORE CLASS

Assign the section, the graphic organizer in the text, and the Reading Comprehension Worksheet (Unit 2 All-in-One, p. 131) before class.

**L2 Differentiate** Reading Comprehension Worksheet (Unit 2 All-in-One, p. 133)

## BELLRINGER

Display Transparency 7B, How America Votes. Ask students to examine the transparency and answer the questions in their notebook.

# Teach

To present this topic using online resources, use the lesson presentation at **PearsonSchool.com/phgovt.**

## DISCUSS BELLRINGER

Have students share their reactions to the Bellringer questions: **What do these graphs suggest about the way Americans vote nationally?** (Overall, most voters cast their ballots at the polls.) **What does the transparency suggest about election laws?** (Possible response: The transparency suggests that election laws and voting methods vary from State to State.) Continue the discussion by asking: **Do you think different voting procedures might affect the outcome of elections?** (Different procedures may affect who does and does not take part in elections, which could affect outcome. For example, distributing ballots to all voters by mail could increase voter participation.) **Do you think the voting procedures in use matter in producing fair and effective elections?** (The procedure used may affect the fairness of elections by altering turnout or making it relatively harder or easier for certain groups to take part, or by affecting the way votes are counted.)

Tell students to go to the Audio Tour to listen to a guided audio tour of the diagram "What Happens to a Ballot?"

## Answers

**Checkpoint** Most election law in the U.S. is State law; however, a body of federal law does exist.

**What Happens to a Ballot?** to ensure an accurate, uncorrupted voting process

---

Congress has set the date for holding congressional elections as the first Tuesday following the first Monday in November of every even-numbered year. It has set the same date every fourth year for the presidential election.[13] Thus, the next presidential election will be held on November 6, 2012, and the next (off-year) congressional contests will be decided on November 4, 2014.

Congress has required the use of secret ballots and allowed the use of voting machines and similar devices in federal elections. It has also acted to protect the right to vote, as you saw in Chapter 6. Congress has also prohibited various corrupt practices and regulates the financing of campaigns for federal office, as you will see in the pages ahead.

Congress expanded the body of federal election law with the passage of the Help America Vote Act of 2002. That law came in response to the many ballot and voter registration problems that plagued several States

in the presidential election in 2000. A **ballot**[14] is the medium by which a voter registers a choice in an election.

In its major provisions, the law requires the States to

**1.** replace all their lever-operated and punch-card voting devices by 2006—a deadline that, in fact, most States failed to meet;

**2.** upgrade their administration of elections, especially through the better training of local election officials and of those more than 2 million (mostly low-paid workers and volunteers) who work in precinct polling places on election day;

**3.** centralize and computerize their voter registration systems, to facilitate the identification of qualified voters on election day and so minimize fraudulent voting;

**4.** provide for provisional voting, so a person whose eligibility to vote has been challenged

---

**13** Congress has made an exception for Alaska. Because of the possibility of severe weather in much of Alaska in early November, that State may, if it chooses, elect its congressional delegation and cast its presidential vote in October. To this point, however, Alaska has chosen to use the November date.

**14** The word comes from the Italian *ballotta*, "little ball," and reflects the practice of dropping black or white balls into a box to indicate a choice. The term *blackball* also comes from that practice. The ancient Romans used paper ballots as early as 139 B.C.

---

> **GOVERNMENT** ONLINE
> **Audio tour**
> Listen to a guided audio tour of this diagram at PearsonSchool.com/phgovt

**How Government Works**

## What Happens to a Ballot?

The several States offer voters different ways to cast their votes, in both paper formats and electronically, and on election day or earlier. *Why is it important for local officials to guard and track ballots after they are cast?*

**Paper Ballot**
Usually collected at polling place, taken to counting facility

**Absentee Ballot**
Mailed to the counting facility
OR
Brought to the polling place and combined with other ballots

**Electronic Ballot**
Data transported manually on disks or drives
OR
Votes transmitted electronically to counting facility

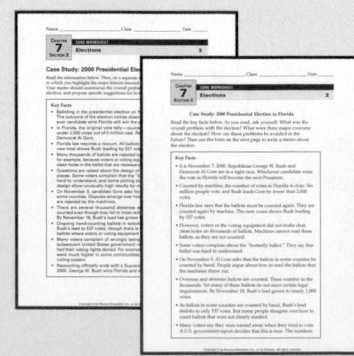

**Counting Facility**
Ballots usually are counted in a central location and stored in case a recount is required.

---

# Differentiated Resources

The following resources are located in the All-in-One, Unit 2, Chapter 7, Section 2:

- **L3** Reading Comprehension Worksheet (p. 131)
- **L2** Reading Comprehension Worksheet (p. 133)
- **L3** Core Worksheet (p. 135)
- **L2** Core Worksheet (p. 136)
- **L3 L4** Extend Worksheet (p. 138)
- **L3** Quiz A (p. 140)
- **L2** Quiz B (p. 141)

can nonetheless cast a ballot that will be counted if it is later found that he or she is, in fact, qualified to vote.

State law deals with all other matters relating to national elections—and with all of the details of State and local elections as well.

**Election Day** Most States hold their elections to fill State offices on the same date Congress has set for national elections: in November of every even-numbered year. The "Tuesday-after-the-first-Monday" formula prevents election day from falling on (1) Sundays (to maintain the principle of separation of church and state) and (2) the first day of the month, which is often payday and therefore peculiarly subject to campaign pressures.

Some States do fix other dates for some offices, however. Louisiana, Mississippi, New Jersey, and Virginia elect the governor, other executive officers, and State legislators in November of *odd*-numbered years. In Kentucky, the governor and other executive officers are chosen in odd-numbered years, but legislators are elected in even-numbered years. City, county, and other local election dates vary from State to State. When those elections are not held in November, they generally take place in the spring.

**Early Voting** Millions of Americans cast their ballots before election day. Indeed, some 32 million did so in 2008. Many of them did so by **absentee voting**—a process by which they could vote without going to their polling places on election day. Congress was responsible for the first instance of absentee voting. In the midst of the Civil War, it provided for the casting of absentee ballots by federal troops in the elections of 1864. Over the years, every State has made at least some provision for the process.

Now, almost everywhere, voters can apply for an absentee ballot some weeks before an election. They mark those ballots and return them to the local election office, usually by mail, in a sealed envelope, and before election day.

State absentee voting was originally intended to serve a relatively small group of voters, especially the ill or disabled and those who expected to be away from home on election day. Most States have broadened their

laws over recent years, however—to the point where, in most of them, any qualified voter can cast an absentee ballot simply because he or she wants to vote that way.

Two thirds of the States have now formalized early voting. They allow any voters who choose to do so to cast their ballots at any time over a period of several days before an election—not as an absentee ballot but as though they were voting on election day itself. Indeed, in many places, election day is now just the final day on which votes can be cast.

**The Coattail Effect** The **coattail effect** occurs when a strong candidate running for an office at the top of the ballot helps attract voters to other candidates on the party's ticket. In effect, the lesser-known office seeker "rides the coattails" of the more prestigious personality—for example, a Franklin Roosevelt, a Ronald Reagan, or a Barack Obama. The coattail effect is usually most apparent in presidential elections. However, a popular candidate for senator or governor can have the same kind of pulling power in State and local elections.

A reverse coattail effect can occur, too. This happens when a candidate for some major office is less than popular with many voters—for example, Barry Goldwater as the Republican presidential nominee in 1964, and George McGovern for the Democrats in 1972. President Jimmy Carter's coattails were also of the reverse variety in 1980.

Some have long argued that all State and local elections should be held on dates other than those set for federal elections. This, they say, would help voters pay more attention to State and local candidates and issues and lessen the coattail effect a presidential candidate can have.

## Precincts and Polling Places

A **precinct** is a voting district. Precincts are the smallest geographic units for the conduct of elections. State law regularly restricts their size, generally to an area with no more than 500 to 1,000 or so qualified voters. A **polling place**—the place where the voters who live in a precinct actually vote—is located somewhere in or near each precinct.

✔ **Checkpoint**
What is early voting?

## Myths and Misconceptions

**PUBLIC VOTING** While the secret ballot is a cherished tradition in American elections, there are still circumstances in which citizens are asked to vote publicly. For example, at New England town meetings, it is common for votes to be cast by voice, by standing, and/or by a show of hands. In general, citizens can request a written ballot for specific questions, but the town meeting must vote to approve this request.

### DISTRIBUTE CORE WORKSHEET

Distribute the Chapter 7 Section 2 Core Worksheet (Unit 2 All-in-One, p. 135), which asks students to analyze information about the problems with the balloting in Florida during the 2000 presidential election. Instruct students to read the material and follow the instructions for writing a memorandum about the election. Tell students to think as they read about the qualities of a fair and effective election. Give students ample time to complete the activity.

**L2 Differentiate** Distribute the adapted version of the Chapter 7 Section 2 Core Worksheet (Unit 2 All-in-One, p. 136), which offers more structure for writing.

**L4 Differentiate** Have students perform additional research and write a follow-up to their memoranda, explaining how the issues raised during the Florida vote were resolved.

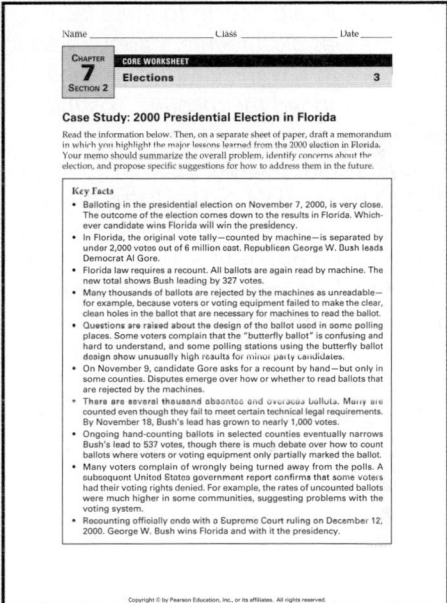

## Answers

**Checkpoint** Early voting is the process by which any voters who choose to do so may cast their ballots at any time over a period of several days before an election.

Ask: **How did the Florida voting measure up to the standard of a fair and effective election?** *(Both fairness and effectiveness are in question, since there were many questions about the casting and counting of ballots, and the election there was so close and so significant. The problems in Florida might also prompt citizens to look with suspicion on voting and counting methods elsewhere in the country.)*

**DISCUSS**

Invite students to share their memoranda with the class. On the board, keep a running list of the various issues identified as well as specific solutions proposed. *(Possible issues: Machine recount did not match original machine count. The machines could not read thousands of ballots. The ballot design was confusing to some. Many absentee and overseas ballots were counted despite failing to meet legal requirements. There was disagreement about how to count the ballots rejected by the counting machines. The Supreme Court stopped the recount. Possible solutions: Have representatives of both parties test and certify voting machines before each election. Do away with punch-card voting. Use focus groups to test different ballot designs.)* With students, rank the issues from most important to address to least important. Ask: **Why is it important to address concerns about the fairness of elections?** *(It is vital to maintain public belief in the integrity of the election in order for the public to accept its results.)* **How would addressing some of the issues on the list and implementing some of the solutions increase fairness?**

A precinct election board supervises the polling place and the voting process in each precinct. Typically, the county clerk or county board of elections draws precinct lines, fixes the location of each polling place, and picks the members of the precinct boards.

The precinct board opens and closes the polls at the times set by State law. In most States, the polls are open from 7:00 or 8:00 A.M. to 7:00 or 8:00 P.M. The precinct election board must also see that the ballots and the ballot boxes or voting devices are available. It must make certain that only qualified voters cast ballots in the precinct. Often the board also counts the votes cast in the precinct and then sends the results to the proper place, usually to the county clerk or county board of elections.

Poll watchers, one from each party, are allowed at each polling place. They may challenge any person they believe is not qualified to vote, check to be sure that their own party's supporters do vote, and monitor the whole process, including the counting of the ballots.

## Casting the Ballot

A ballot can take a number of different forms, ranging from a piece of paper to optical scanners and touch screens. Whatever its form, however, it is clearly an important and sensitive part of the election process.

Each State now provides for a secret ballot. That is, State law requires that ballots be cast in such manner that others cannot know how a person has voted.

Voting was a quite public process through much of the nation's earlier history, however. Paper ballots were used in some colonial elections, but voting was more commonly *viva voce*—by voice. Voters simply stated their choices, in public, to an election board. With suffrage limited to the privileged few, many people defended oral voting as the only "manly" way in which to participate. Whatever the merits of that view, the expansion of the electorate brought with it a marked increase in intimidation, vote buying, and other corruptions of the voting process.

Mechanical voting machines like the one below were outlawed by Congress in 2002.

196

Paper ballots were in general use by the mid-1800s. The first ones were unofficial—slips of paper that voters prepared themselves and dropped in the ballot box. Soon candidates and parties began to prepare ballots and hand them to voters to cast, sometimes paying them to do so. Those party ballots were often printed on distinctively colored paper, and anyone watching could tell for whom voters were voting.

Political machines—local party organizations capable of mobilizing or "manufacturing" large numbers of votes on behalf of candidates for political office—flourished in many places in the latter 1800s. They fought all attempts to make voting a more dependably fair and honest process. The political corruption of the post–Civil War years brought widespread demand for ballot reforms.

**The Australian Ballot** A new voting arrangement was devised in Australia, where it was first used in an election in Victoria in 1856. Its successes there led to its use in other countries. By 1900 nearly all of the States were using it, and it remains the basic form of the ballot in this country today.

The Australian Ballot has four essential features: It (1) is provided at public expense; (2) lists the names of all candidates in an election; (3) is given out only at the polls, one to each qualified voter; and (4) can be marked in secret.

Two basic forms of the Australian ballot, shown on p. 197, have been used in this country over the past century. Most States now use the office-group ballot; only a handful of them rely on the party-column ballot.

**Sample Ballots** Sample ballots, clearly marked as such, are available in most States before an election. In some States they are mailed to all voters, and they appear in most newspapers and on the Internet. They cannot be cast, but they can help voters prepare for an election.

First in Oregon (1907), and now in several States, an official voter's pamphlet is mailed to voters before every election. It lists all candidates and measures that will appear on the ballot. In Oregon, each candidate is allowed space to present his

## Background

**THE AUSTRALIAN BALLOT** The move to the use of the Australian ballot was part of a larger reform effort led in part by a group known as the Mugwumps. The Mugwumps—which is a Native American term for "big chief" or "person of honor"—came into being in the presidential election of 1884. They were Republicans who rejected their party's selection of the allegedly corrupt James G. Blaine. Instead, the Mugwumps chose to support the reputedly honest and reforming Grover Cleveland, who narrowly won the election. The term was originally used sarcastically to make fun of the moralistic Blaine opponents.

## Answers

**Checkpoint** a voting district that is the smallest geographic unit for the conduct of elections or her qualifications and position on the issues. Supporters and opponents of ballot measures are allowed space to present their arguments as well.

**Bed-sheet Ballots** The ballot in a typical American election is lengthy, often and aptly called a "bed-sheet" ballot. It frequently lists so many offices, candidates, and ballot measures that even the most well-informed voters have a difficult time marking it intelligently.

The long ballot came to American politics in the era of Jacksonian Democracy in the 1830s. Many held the view at the time that the greater the number of elective offices, the more democratic the governmental system. That idea remains widely accepted today.

Generally, the longest ballots are found at the local level, especially among the nation's 3,000-odd counties. The list of elected offices is likely to include several commissioners, a clerk, a sheriff, one or more judges, a prosecutor, coroner, treasurer, assessor, surveyor, school superintendent, engineer, sanitarian, and even the proverbial dogcatcher.

Critics of the bed-sheet ballot reject the notion that the more people you elect, the more democratic the system. Instead, they say, the fewer the offices voters have to fill, the better they can know the candidates and their qualifications. Those critics often point to the factor of "ballot fatigue"—that is, to the drop-off in voting that can run as high as 20 to 30 percent at or near the bottom of the typical (lengthy) ballot.

There seems little, if any, good reason to elect such local officials as clerks, coroners, surveyors, and engineers. Their jobs do not carry basic policy-making responsibilities. Rather, they carry out policies made by others. Many believe that to shorten the ballot and promote good government, the rule should be: Elect those who make public policies; appoint those whose basic job it is to administer those policies.

## Automated Voting

Well over half the votes now cast in national elections are cast on some type of voting machine—and, increasingly, on some type of electronic voting device.

## Ballot Types

Also called the Massachusetts ballot, from its early use (1888) in that State, the office-group ballot is the most common form of the ballot in use in the United States today. *How does a party-column ballot encourage voters to vote along party lines?*

### OFFICE-GROUP BALLOT

All candidates for an office are grouped together under the title of that office. It is sometimes called the "office block" ballot because the names appear as a block. Names may be listed in random order to avoid giving any candidate an unfair advantage.

Favored by many authorities because voters consider each choice, office by office.

| OFFICIAL BALLOT |
| --- |
| **FOR PRESIDENT AND VICE PRESIDENT OF THE UNITED STATES (VOTE FOR ONE ONLY)** |
| (Republican Party) |
| John S. McCain, III / Sarah Palin ..................... ( ) |
| (Democratic Party) |
| Barack Obama / Joseph Biden ......................... ( ) |
| (Libertarian Party) |
| Bob Barr / Wayne Root ................................. ( ) |
| (Green Party) |
| Cynthia McKinney / Rosa Clemente ................. ( ) |
| **FOR UNITED STATES SENATOR (VOTE FOR ONE ONLY)** |
| (Republican Party) |
| Brett Locker ............................................ ( ) |
| (Democratic Party) |
| Paula Robinson .......................................... ( ) |
| (Green Party) |
| Phoebe J. Bowne ....................................... ( ) |

### PARTY-COLUMN BALLOT

Also known as the Indiana ballot, from its early use (1889) in that State, the party-column ballot lists all candidates under their party's name.

| OFFICIAL BALLOT | | | | |
| --- | --- | --- | --- | --- |
| OFFICE TITLE | A LIBERTARIAN | B DEMOCRAT | C REPUBLICAN | D GREEN |
| President and Vice President of the United States *Vote for One* | Bob BARR Wayne ROOT ☐ | Barack OBAMA Joseph BIDEN ☐ | John S. McCAIN III Sarah PALIN ☐ | Cynthia McKINNEY Rosa CLEMENTE ☐ |
| United States Senator *Vote for One* | | Paula ROBINSON ☐ | Brett LOCKER ☐ | Phoebe J. BOWNE ☐ |

Favored by *politicians* because it encourages straight-ticket voting and the coattail effect.

## EXTEND THE LESSON

**L2 Differentiate** Have students create a timeline of major developments in the history of elections and balloting in the United States. The timeline should highlight and explain the significance of new methods or technologies.

**L4 Differentiate** Have students research noteworthy presidential election controversies in United States history and add them to their timelines.

**L3 L4 Differentiate** You may choose to distribute the Chapter 7 Section 2 Extend Worksheet (Unit 2 All-in-One, p. 138), which asks students to evaluate information about absentee votes rejected in a recent national election.

**L3 Differentiate** Have small groups of students make a voting handbook for new citizens. The handbook should describe what happens at polling stations on election day and the types of ballots and voting machines they may encounter. Handbooks should be organized and easy to follow.

**L3 Differentiate** Ask students to skim the section and note the ways in which elections are administered. Divide the class into small groups, and tell them to suppose Congress has charged them with the task of increasing voter turnout. They must evaluate the current methods for administering elections, brainstorm ideas for new ones, and then make recommendations to Congress.

Tell students to go to the Audio Tour to listen to a guided audio tour of the diagram "Ballot Types."

## Background

**BILINGUAL VOTING** The 1975 amendments to the Voting Rights Act introduced the requirement that States use bilingual ballots and election materials in places where there are 10,000 members of a single-language minority group, or a number greater than 5 percent of all voting-age citizens. This requirement has stirred some controversy and was the basis of some resistance to the 2006 vote to reauthorize and amend the Voting Rights Act.

## Answers

**Ballot Types** A party-column ballot makes it easier to identify candidates by party, which may encourage straight-ticket voting.

## Assess and Remediate

**L3** Collect the Core Worksheet and assess students' class participation using the Rubric for Assessing a Writing Assignment (Unit 2 All-in-One, p. 257).

**L3** Assign the Section 2 Assessment questions.

**L3** Section Quiz A (Unit 2 All-in-One, p. 140)

**L2** Section Quiz B (Unit 2 All-in-One, p. 141)

Have students complete the review activities in the digital lesson presentation and continue their work in the **Essential Questions Journal.**

▲ Memory cards record votes cast on electronic voting machines.

Thomas Edison patented the first voting machine—the first mechanical device for the casting and counting of votes—in 1868, and the Myers Automatic Booth was first used in a public election in Lockport, New York, in 1892. The use of similar but much-improved devices soon spread to polling places across the country.

For the better part of a century, most voting machines were lever-operated, and quite cumbersome. Voters had to pull various levers in order to cast their ballots—one lever to open (unlock) the machine, others to indicate their choices of candidates, and yet another to close (lock) the machine and record their votes.

Those lever-operated machines did speed up the voting process; and they reduced both fraud and counting errors. The machines were quite expensive, however, and they also posed major storage and transport problems from one election to the next.

**Electronic Vote Counting** Electronic data processing (EDP) techniques were first applied to the voting process in the 1960s. California and Oregon led the way and EDP is now a vital part of that process in most States.

For some years, the most widely used adaptations of EDP involved punch-card ballots, counted by computers. But punch-card ballots often produced problems—most frequently because voters failed to make clean punches. Their incomplete perforations left "hanging chads" that made the cards difficult or impossible for computers to read.

Punch-card ballots played a major role in the disputed presidential election vote count in Florida in 2000; and that fiasco led to the passage of the Help America Vote Act of 2002. As we noted on page 194, that law required the elimination of all punch-card voting devices (and all lever-operated voting machines, as well).

Most States have turned to two other EDP-based voting systems. One of them involves the same optical-scanning technology used to grade the standardized tests students take in school. Voters mark their ballots by filling in circles, ovals, or rectangles or by completing arrows. A computer scans the marked ballots, counting and recording the votes cast.

The other system utilizes direct response electronic voting machines (DREs). Those machines are much like ATMs or cash machines. Voters make their choices on most models by touching a screen or, on some, by pushing buttons. Their votes are recorded electronically.

DREs have proved troublesome in many places. Some models have malfunctioned and some do not provide a paper record of voters' choices. Many computer scientists insist that DREs can be easily compromised by hackers. Several States abandoned them for 2008. They turned, instead, to optical-scanning systems or went back to hand-counted paper ballots.

**Vote-by-Mail Elections** A number of States now conduct at least some of their elections by mail. Voters receive a ballot in the mail, mark them, and mail the ballots back to election officials. The first such election was held in Monterey County, California, in 1977; and the first large-scale use of mail-in ballots took place in San Diego in 1981.

## Debate

"Part of me thinks inconvenience in voting isn't such a bad thing. People ought to sacrifice a little for our republic. But another part of me says we should move into the 21st century and increase convenience."

—blogger writing about attempts to make voting more convenient through early voting and other measures

Use the quotation to begin a debate in your classroom.

To this point, most vote-by-mail elections have been confined to the local level and to voting on city or county measures, not on candidates for local offices. But, recall, as we noted a few pages ago, vote-by-mail is an integral part of the absentee voting process, and voting by absentee ballot is becoming an increasingly common practice in many places.

In fact, one State, Oregon, now holds *all* of its elections by mail, and it has done so since 1998. That State held the first-ever all-mail primary election and then the first all-mail general election (including the presidential election) in 2000.

Voting by mail has stirred controversy, of course. Critics fear that the process threatens the secret ballot principle. They worry about fraud, especially the possibility that some voters may be subjected to undue pressures when they mark their ballots at home or any place other than a secure voting booth.

Supporters, on the other hand, say that more than ten years of voting by mail in Oregon indicates that that process can be as fraud-proof as any other method of voting. They also make this point: The mail-in process increases voter participation in elections and, at the same time, reduces the costs of conducting them.

**Online Voting** Online voting—casting ballots via the Internet—has attracted considerable attention and some support in recent years. Will e-voting become widespread, even

commonplace, as some predict? Obviously, only time will tell.

Online voting is not an entirely new phenomenon. The first e-vote was cast in November 1997. Election officials in Harris County, Texas, allowed astronaut David Wolf to vote in Houston's city election by e-mail from the space station *Mir*.

The first public election in which some votes were cast by computer was held in 2000, in Arizona's Democratic presidential primary. The Defense Department enabled 84 members of the military stationed abroad to vote electronically in the general election that year, but chose not to repeat the program because of worries about ballot security. In 2010, a minor party, the Independent Party of Oregon, became the first political party to nominate its candidates in a primary election that was held entirely online.

A number of public officials and private companies promote online voting. They claim that it will make participation much more convenient, increase voter turnout, and reduce election costs.

Many skeptics believe that the electronic infrastructure is not ready for e-voting. Some fear digital disaster: jammed phone lines, blocked access, hackers, viruses, denial-of-service attacks, fraudulent vote counts, and violations of voter secrecy. Critics also point out that because not everyone can afford home computers, online voting could undermine the basic American principle of equality.

✔ **Checkpoint**
How successful have vote-by-mail and online voting been?

**Essential Questions Journal**

To continue to build a response to the chapter Essential Question, go to your **Essential Questions Journal.**

## SECTION 2 ASSESSMENT

1. **Guiding Question** Use your completed chart to answer the question: How are elections conducted in the United States?

**Key Terms and Comprehension**

2. What is the Federal Government's role in the administration of elections?

3. What is the role of the **precinct** in elections?

4. How have **ballots** changed over time?

5. What factors have complicated the move to automated voting?

**Critical Thinking**

6. **Predict Consequences** What might happen if people lost confidence that their ballots were being counted and recorded properly?

7. **Synthesize Information** Present an argument for or against a proposal to use only hand-counted ballots in all elections.

**Quick Write**

**Explanatory Essay: Research the Topic** Use the Internet or other resources to collect information about the election you chose in Section 1. Gather as much information as you can about the candidates and the balloting. Record your information carefully.

---

**REMEDIATION**

| If Your Students Have Trouble With | Strategies For Remediation |
|---|---|
| Understanding the administration of elections in the United States (Questions 1, 2, 3, 6) | Have students work in pairs to create a brochure for new voters that gives frequently asked questions about voting, including the role of the federal government, when elections are held, how absentee balloting works, and where people vote. |
| The significance of different types of ballots (Questions 4, 7) | Have students create examples of different types of voting procedures and ballots, with captions explaining the basic strengths and weaknesses of each type. |
| Issues related to automated voting (Question 5) | Have students design the "perfect" voting machine, and describe its key features. |

---

## Answers

**Checkpoint** Vote-by-mail is an integral part of the absentee voting process, and voting by absentee ballot is becoming increasingly more common. Online voting has some support now and may become widespread in the future.

---

## Assessment Answers

**1.** Congressional elections are held the first Tuesday following the first Monday in November of every even-numbered year. Presidential elections are held on the same date every fourth year. Most elections for State offices are held on the same date as national elections. Voters cast secret ballots at their precinct polling place. The precinct election board supervises. Voters may choose to cast absentee ballots or vote early.

**2.** Congress sets the date for federal elections.

Congress has passed laws to require secret ballots, allow voting machines, protect voting rights, prohibit corrupt practices, and regulate campaign financing.

**3.** A precinct is a voting district. The precinct election board opens and closes the polls, ensures availability of ballots and ballot boxes or voting devices, makes sure only qualified voters cast ballots, and some count votes.

**4.** Ballots have changed from slips of paper prepared by voters to paper ballots distributed by parties to adoption of the Australian ballot. Today, most ballots are electronic.

**5.** machine malfunction; lack of paper record; potential for hacking

**6.** Possible answer: People might not bother to vote and might lose trust in government.

**7.** Possible answers: Hand counting is a straightforward process and is not subject to technological failure. OR: Hand counting may take too long, be subject to human error or corruption, and be costly.

**QUICK WRITE** Students should record detailed information about their subjects carefully.

- Students will examine the issue of money in the electoral process, using a contemporary example.

## Teach

### ACTIVATE PRIOR KNOWLEDGE

Ask students to define *bribery. (the use of money to influence the behavior of a public official)* Ask: **Why does bribery create problems for a government?** *(Bribery can influence government to behave in ways that do not benefit the community as a whole. It can also undermine people's faith in government.)* **Why do elections create a special challenge with regard to bribery and similar types of behaviors?** *(In elections, candidates need a lot of money, and if elected, they will have the power to grant favors to their contributors.)*

### SUMMARIZE THE ISSUE

Have students read the feature and summarize the issue. Have volunteers share their opinion on whether or not the BCRA violates the 1st Amendment. Ask them to explain how soft money and attempts to limit it illustrate the tension between protecting the integrity of government and enabling people to take part in politics.

**L1 L2 Differentiate** Have students review the discussion of hard and soft money in Section 3.

**L3 L4 Differentiate** Have students research reactions to the Supreme Court's decision in *Citizens United* and create a pro-and-con chart from their findings.

## Assess and Remediate

Have students write and deliver a speech in which they weigh the importance of protecting the right of people to participate in government through campaign contributions with the need to maintain the integrity of the electoral process.

## Answers

1. (a) The electorate has access to corporate disclosure statements that voters can use to determine the extent of a corporation's political influence. (b) by claiming that the electorate through Congress has fought corporate influence and that the Court's decision rejects the voice of American citizens (c) Answers will vary.

2. Sample answer: Money is a very powerful tool. Wealthy corporations can use their wealth to sway political policy decisions unfairly and hinder the democratic process.

# Issues OF OUR TIME

## Campaign Finance

### ▶▶ Track the Issue

**When regulating campaign finance,** the Federal Government has tried to balance free speech rights against the potential for corruption.

**1907**
**Congress bans** corporate contributions to federal candidates.

**1947**
**The Taft-Hartley Act** blocks labor unions from donating to candidates. In response, unions donate through political action committees (PACs).

**1974**
**Congress creates** the Federal Election Commission to enforce strict new laws on campaign fundraising.

**2002**
**The Bipartisan Campaign Reform Act** is passed and signed, placing strict limits on the use of so-called soft money.

**2010**
**The Supreme Court** holds that a provision in the Bipartisan Campaign Reform Act violates the 1st Amendment.

Supreme Court Justice Anthony M. Kennedy ▶

### ▶▶ Perspectives

**An historic and controversial decision** by the Supreme Court in early 2010 virtually negated years of bipartisan efforts to control campaign spending. In *Citizens United* v. *Federal Election Commission*, Citizens United claimed its rights were violated when the BCRA was applied to its film on presidential candidate Hillary Clinton. The Court, by a vote of 5–4, sided with Citizens United. Reactions to the decision were both swift and heated.

"With the advent of the Internet, prompt disclosure of expenditures can provide shareholders and citizens with the information needed to hold corporations and elected officials accountable for their positions and supporters. Shareholders can determine whether their corporation's political speech advances the corporation's interest in making profits, and citizens can see whether elected officials are 'in the pocket' of so-called moneyed interests."
—*Justice Anthony M. Kennedy, majority opinion, 2010*

"[T]he Court's opinion is…a rejection of the common sense of the American people, who have recognized a need to prevent corporations from undermining self-government since the founding, and who have fought against the distinctive corrupting potential of corporate electioneering . . . . It is a strange time to repudiate [reject] that common sense. While American democracy is imperfect, few outside the majority of this Court would have thought its flaws included a dearth of corporate money in politics."
—*Justice John Paul Stevens, Dissenting opinion, 2010*

### ▶▶ Connect to Your World

1. **Understand (a)** What is the basis of Justice Kennedy's argument? **(b)** How does Justice Stevens dispute this claim? **(c)** Whose view do you agree with? Why?
2. **Synthesize Information** Why is allowing a voice in government to corporations so controversial?

**GOVERNMENT** ONLINE
**In the News**
For updates about campaign finance, visit **PearsonSchool.com/phgovt**

**200**

## Background

**ISSUE ADVERTISING** One way that soft money has been widely used in political campaigns is the creation of so-called issue advertisements. These are ads that focus on a particular issue or policy—without ever mentioning a candidate by name. Yet such ads can be crafted in a way that clearly benefits specific candidates in specific races. For example, an ad about gun control can clearly aid a particular candidate when it is aired during a campaign in which gun control has been a major issue. Recent efforts at campaign finance reform have sought to limit the use of soft money for such advertisements.

## SECTION 3

# Money
## and Elections

### Guiding Question
**What role does money play in electoral politics?** Use a flowchart to record information about the role of money in electoral politics and the efforts of government to regulate it.

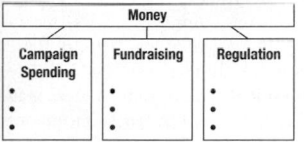

### Political Dictionary

- political action committee (PAC)
- subsidy
- hard money
- soft money

### Objectives

1. Explain the issues raised by campaign spending.
2. Describe the various sources of funding for campaign spending.
3. Examine federal laws that regulate campaign finance.
4. Outline the role of the Federal Election Commission in enforcing campaign finance laws.
5. Distinguish hard money from soft money.

**Image Above:** Senator Russ Feingold (D., Wisconsin) has led efforts to regulate campaign contributions.

Running for public office costs money—and often quite a lot of it. That fact creates some very real problems. It presents the possibility that candidates will try to buy their way into office. It also makes it possible for special interests to try to buy favors from those who hold office.

Clearly, government by the people must be protected from those dangers. But how? Parties and candidates must have money. Without it, they cannot campaign or do any of the many other things they must do to win elections.

In short, dollars are absolutely necessary campaign resources. Yet, the getting and spending of campaign funds can corrupt the entire political process.

## Campaign Spending

No one really knows how much money is spent on political campaigns in the United States. Remember, there are more than 500,000 elective offices in this country—most of them at the State and particularly the local level. More or less reliable estimates of total spending in presidential election years—on all efforts to win nominations and to gain offices at all levels—can be seen in the table on the next page.

The presidential election consumes by far the largest share of campaign dollars. For 2008, total spending for all of the major and minor party presidential efforts—for primaries and caucuses, conventions, general election campaigns, for everything—reached a mind-boggling $2.5 billion.

The vast sums spent on congressional campaigns also continue to climb, election after election. That spending has doubled over the past decade. A candidate must now raise and spend at least $1 million in a typical race for a seat in the House. A Senate campaign can cost as much as twenty times that amount. All told, some $1.5 billion was spent on House and Senate contests in 2010.

Radio and television time, professional campaign managers and consultants, newspaper advertisements, pamphlets, buttons, posters and bumper stickers, office rent, polls, data processing, mass mailings, Web sites, travel—these and a host of other items make up the huge sums spent in campaigns. Television ads are far and away the largest item in most campaign budgets

## What role does money play in electoral politics?

| Money | | |
|---|---|---|
| **Campaign Spending** | **Fundraising** | **Regulation** |
| • campaign managers and consultants <br> • television, radio, newspaper ads <br> • pamphlets, buttons, posters, bumper stickers <br> • office rent <br> • mass mailings <br> • Web sites <br> • travel | • small contributors <br> • wealthy contributors <br> • candidates and their families <br> • political appointees <br> • political action committees <br> • temporary organizations <br> • fundraising events <br> • mail, telethon, Internet solicitations <br> • public subsidies <br> • contributors often want something in return—appointments, social recognition, certain laws or administrative actions | • Federal Election Campaign Act of 1971 <br> • FECA Amendments <br> • Bipartisan Campaign Reform Act <br> • Federal Election Commission <br> • no contributions in another's name <br> • cash gifts limited <br> • single campaign committee collects and spends contributions <br> • contributions, loans, or spending of more than $200 must be documented <br> • must report contributions of more than $5,000 <br> • individual contribution limits <br> • public funding for presidential races <br> • if accept public money, can spend no more than amount of the subsidy in general election and cannot accept funds from other sources <br> • soft money loophole |

## SKILLS DEVELOPMENT

### ANALYZE MAPS

To practice analyzing maps in this section, use the Chapter 7 Skills Worksheet (Unit 2 All-in-One, p. 148). You may teach the skill explicitly either before or after reviewing the Bellringer. For L2 and L1 students, assign the adapted Skill Activity (Unit 2 All-in-One, p. 149).

# Focus on the Basics

**FACTS:** • Money has always played a key role in politics. • Campaign money comes from public and private sources, including political action committees, or PACs. • The Federal Election Commission administers federal election laws. • Candidates and contributors sometimes use loopholes in campaign finance laws to avoid regulation.

**CONCEPTS:** campaign spending, representative democracy

**ENDURING UNDERSTANDINGS:** • Money plays a critical role in political campaigns but raises the danger of corruption. • Abuses of campaign finance regulations and attempts to reform them are ongoing.

## LESSON GOALS

Students will . . .

- consider the potentially corrupting effect of money in politics by analyzing a political cartoon.
- prepare for and carry out a debate on campaign finance reform.
- produce a political cartoon about campaign finance laws.

## BEFORE CLASS

Assign the section, the graphic organizer in the text, and the Reading Comprehension Worksheet (Unit 2 All-in-One, p. 142) before class.

**L2** **Differentiate** Reading Comprehension Worksheet (Unit 2 All-in-One, p. 144)

## BELLRINGER

Write on the board: **How do politicians get money to run for office? Brainstorm a list and record it in your notebook.**

**L2** **ELL Differentiate** Students who are unfamiliar with electoral financing in this country can list ways that politicians raise money and pay for political campaigns in their countries of origin.

# Teach

To present this topic using online resources, use the lesson presentation at **PearsonSchool.com/phgovt.**

## DISCUSS THE BELLRINGER

Tell students that today they will discuss campaign finance. Display Transparency 7C, Political Organization Report of Finances. Ask: **Do political organizations have to account for their money?** *(yes)* Then have students share their Bellringer lists with the class. *(Possible responses include individual donations, corporate donations, government funding, and funding raised by special interest groups.)* Ask: **What impact does money in government have upon the fairness of government?** *(Money's prominent role has the potential to make government unfair—by giving power to the wealthy and shutting out those with fewer resources.)*

## Answers

**Analyzing Charts** Rising costs for advertising, especially television ads, have added to the huge sums spent during campaigns.

| Total Campaign Spending, 1964–2008 | | | |
| --- | --- | --- | --- |
| Year | Estimated spending | Voter turnout* | Spending per voter |
| 1964 | $200 million | 70.6 million | $2.83 |
| 1968 | $300 million | 73.2 million | $4.10 |
| 1972 | $425 million | 77.7 million | $5.47 |
| 1976 | $540 million | 81.6 million | $6.62 |
| 1980 | $1.2 billion | 86.6 million | $13.87 |
| 1984 | $1.8 billion | 92.7 million | $19.42 |
| 1988 | $2.7 billion | 91.6 million | $29.48 |
| 1992 | $3.2 billion | 104.4 million | $30.65 |
| 1996 | $4.0 billion | 96.5 million | $41.45 |
| 2000 | $5.1 billion | 105.4 million | $48.39 |
| 2004 | $6.0 billion | 120.2 million | $49.92 |
| 2008 | $7.0 billion | 130.9 million | $53.48 |

*Presidential elections
SOURCES: Federal Election Commission; Herbert E. Alexander, *Financing Politics*

**Analyzing Charts** Total campaign spending has risen dramatically in recent elections. ***What factors may account for this rise?***

today, even at the local level. As humorist Will Rogers put it years ago, "You have to be loaded just to get beat."

The total amount spent in particular races varies widely, of course. How much depends on several things: the office involved, the candidate and whether he or she is the incumbent or the challenger, the nature of the opposition, and much more—including, not least, the availability of campaign funds.

## Sources of Funding

Parties and their candidates draw their money from two basic sources: private contributors and the public treasury.

**Private and Public Sources** Private givers have always been the major source of campaign funds in American politics. They come in various shapes and sizes:

**1.** Small contributors—those who give $5 or $10 or so, and only occasionally. Only about 10 percent of people of voting age ever make a campaign contribution, so parties and candidates must look to other places for much of their funding.

**2.** Wealthy individuals and families—the "fat cats," who can make large donations and find it in their best interest to do so.

**3.** Candidates—both incumbents and challengers, their families, and, importantly, people who hold and want to keep appointive public offices. Ross Perot holds the all-time record in this category. He spent some $65 million of his own money on his independent bid for the presidency in 1992.

**4.** Various nonparty groups—especially **political action committees (PACs).** Political action committees are the political arms of special-interest groups and other organizations with a stake in electoral politics.

**5.** Temporary organizations—groups formed for the immediate purposes of a campaign, including fundraising. Hundreds of these short-lived units spring up every two years, and at every level in American politics.

Then, too, parties and their candidates often hold fundraisers of various sorts. The most common are $100-, $500-, and $1,000-a-plate luncheons, dinners, picnics, receptions, and similar gatherings. Some of these events now reach the $100,000-or-more level in presidential campaigns. Direct mail requests, telethons, and Internet solicitations are also among the oft-used tools of those who raise campaign money.

Over recent years, the Internet has become, by far, the most productive of those tools. Often, donations spiked immediately after an important speech or primary election victory or when the candidate challenged donors to give. Web sites including Daily Kos and Act Blue identified and profiled congressional candidates for their readers to support.

Public funds—subsidies from the federal and some State treasuries—are now another prime source of campaign money. A **subsidy** is a grant of money, usually from a government. Subsidies have so far been most important at the presidential level, as you will see shortly. Several States also provide some form of public funding of parties and/or candidacies.

**Why People Give** Campaign donations are a form of political participation. Those who

# Differentiated Resources

The following resources are located in the All-in-One, Unit 2, Chapter 7, Section 3:

**L3** Reading Comprehension Worksheet (p. 142)
**L2** Reading Comprehension Worksheet (p. 144)
**L3** Core Worksheet (p. 146)
**L3** Skills Worksheet (p. 148)
**L2** Skill Activity (p. 149)
**L3** Quiz A (p. 150)    **L2** Quiz B (p. 151)
**L3** Chapter Test A (p. 152)
**L2** Chapter Test B (p. 155)

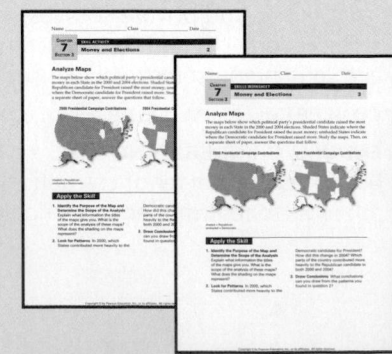

donate do so for a number of reasons. Many small donors give simply because they believe in a party or in a candidate. Many of those who give, however, want something in return. They want access to government, and hope to get it by helping their "friends" win elections. And, notice, some contributors give to both sides in a contest: Heads they win and tails they still win.

## Regulating Finance

Congress first began to regulate the use of money in federal elections in 1907. In that year, it became unlawful for any corporation or national bank to make "a money contribution in any election" to candidates for federal office. Since then, Congress has passed several laws to regulate the use of money in presidential and congressional campaigns. Today, these regulations are found in four detailed laws: the Federal Election Campaign Act (FECA) of 1971, the FECA Amendments of 1974 and of 1976, and the Bipartisan Campaign Reform Act (BCRA) of 2002.

The earliest federal laws were loosely drawn, not often obeyed, and almost never enforced. The 1971 law replaced them. The 1974 law was the major legislative response to the Watergate scandal of the Nixon years. The 1976 law was passed in response to a landmark Supreme Court decision, *Buckley* v. *Valeo*, in 1976. The 2002 law attempted to close the "soft-money" loophole in the 1974 and 1976 statutes; it was upheld by the High Court in *McConnell* v. *FEC* in 2003.

In 2010, the Supreme Court issued a stunning and controversial ruling that struck down part of the BCRA and called into question portions of the 1907 and 1971 laws. In *Citizens United* v. *Federal Election Commission*, a divided Court ruled, 5–4, that the government ban on political spending by corporations or labor unions violated the 1st Amendment right to free speech. Some supported the ruling. Others feared that it would, in the words of President Obama, "open the floodgates for special interests." As of 2010, Congress had yet to craft legislation in response to the ruling.

**✓ Checkpoint**
Where do campaign contributions come from?

**GOVERNMENT** ONLINE
**Audio Tour**
Listen to a guided audio tour of this diagram at PearsonSchool.com/phgovt

### Internet Fundraising
## A Trickle Becomes a Flood

Candidates use the Internet to raise more money, faster, from many more donors than in the past. Insurgent candidates, not those favored by party leaders and traditional donors, have made the greatest leaps in Internet fundraising. *Why did outside candidates like McCain, Dean, and Obama need to find new ways to raise money?*

**New Hampshire Surprise**
**2000 $1 Million**
John McCain raised $1 million via the Internet after an upset in the New Hampshire primary.

**Gov. Dean Leads the Way**
**2004 $20 Million**
Howard Dean raised $20 million for the Democratic primaries, creating a comprehensive Internet strategy later adopted by other candidates.

**Obama Shatters Records**
**2008 $230 Million**
Barack Obama raised some $230 million via the Internet for his primary campaign. More than 80 percent of that amount came in sums of less than $100.

---

## Teacher-to-Teacher Network

**ALTERNATE LESSON PLAN** Have students conduct a mock election for a local, State, or congressional office. First ask students to work in pairs or small groups to conduct research on the candidates and the important issues in the race. Encourage students to contact candidates' headquarters and to conduct voter and campaign worker interviews. After they have completed their research, divide students into teams of supporters for the candidates of their choice and help each team devise a campaign strategy for their candidate. Finish with a class election.

To see this lesson plan, go to

**Teacher Center**
at PearsonSchool.com/phgovt

---

**DESCRIBE THE DILEMMA**

Tell students that money creates a dilemma for our democratic system of government. Point out that elections today are very costly, so candidates need access to a lot of money to mount a successful campaign. In other words, money is an integral part of our electoral system. It also is a way for citizens to get involved with their government. Ask: **How might a citizen use money as a way of getting involved with politics and government?** *(A citizen can make contributions to candidates he or she supports and help them win elections.)* At the same time, the role of money introduces the potential for corruption. Ask: **How might money have a corrupting influence on government?** *(Candidates might offer to do favors in return for campaign contributions. A candidate with a lot of money might use it to buy votes or otherwise improperly influence an election.)* Tell students that government has sought to address the dilemma by placing some limits on how campaign money is raised and spent.

Tell students to go to the Audio Tour to listen to a guided audio tour of the diagram "A Trickle Becomes a Flood."

---

## Answers

**Checkpoint** from private sources (small contributors, wealthy persons, candidates themselves, political action committees, and temporary organizations) and from public funds (subsidies)

**A Trickle Becomes a Flood** Possible response: They probably did not receive as much funding from traditional funding sources as did the party's favored candidates.

Divide the class into two teams, Team 1 and Team 2. Within each team, create a Group A and a Group B. Then distribute the Chapter 7 Section 3 Core Worksheet (Unit 2 All-in-One, p. 146), which asks students to explore and debate the two sides of the issue of campaign finance reform. Have students read the excerpts and complete the assignment for their particular group and team. Then have students engage in a structured debate. Each team will have four minutes to present their main argument. After each team's presentation, the other team will have one minute to prepare and two minutes to deliver a rebuttal to the opening argument. Tell students to take notes on the other team's main arguments. Distribute the Debate worksheets, available in the Teacher Center at **PearsonSchool.com/phgovt,** to help students organize their thoughts.

**L1 L2 Differentiate** Assign L1 and L2 students to investigate arguments for their own side.

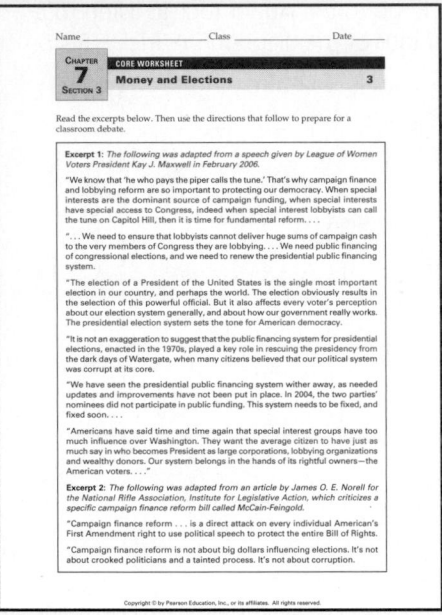

Tell students to go to the Interactivity for an interactive view of campaign spending.

## Answers

**Rising Campaign Costs** Television ads are far and away the largest item in most campaign budgets, reflecting the major influence of media in American life. This makes it essential that any candidate who hopes to succeed takes advantage of television as a campaign tool.

---

Congress cannot regulate the use of money in State and local elections. Every State now regulates at least some aspects of campaign finance, however—some of them do so more effectively than others.[15]

## Federal Election Commission

The Federal Election Commission (FEC) administers all federal law dealing with campaign finance. Set up by Congress in 1974, the FEC is an independent agency in the executive branch. Its six members are appointed by the President, with Senate confirmation.

Federal campaign finance laws are both strongly worded and closely detailed. But they are not very well enforced. In large part this is because the FEC has been both underfunded and understaffed. That is to say, members of Congress—who, remember, raise and spend campaign money—have made it practically impossible for the FEC to do an effective job. In short, the FEC finds itself in a situation much like that of the chickens who must guard the fox house.

The laws that the FEC is supposed to enforce cover four broad areas. They (1) require the timely disclosure of campaign finance data, (2) place limits on campaign contributions, (3) place limits on campaign expenditures, and (4) provide public funding for several parts of the presidential election process.

**Disclosure Requirements** Congress first required the reporting of certain campaign finance information in 1910. Today, the disclosure requirements are intended to spotlight the place of money in federal campaigns, and they were not affected by the Court's ruling in *Citizens United* in 2010. Those requirements are so detailed that most candidates for federal office must now include at least one certified public accountant in their campaign organization.

No individual or group can make a contribution in the name of another. Cash gifts of more than $100 are prohibited, as are contributions and spending from foreign sources.

---

**15** State campaign finance laws are summarized in *The Book of the States,* an annual publication of the Council of State Governments.

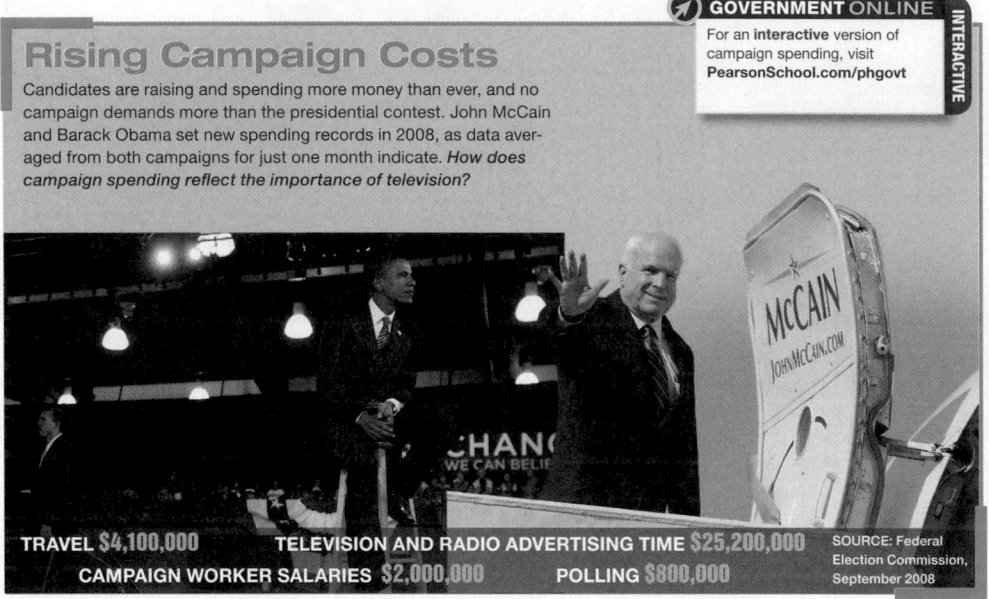

### Rising Campaign Costs

Candidates are raising and spending more money than ever, and no campaign demands more than the presidential contest. John McCain and Barack Obama set new spending records in 2008, as data averaged from both campaigns for just one month indicate. *How does campaign spending reflect the importance of television?*

**GOVERNMENT** ONLINE
For an **interactive** version of campaign spending, visit **PearsonSchool.com/phgovt**

TRAVEL $4,100,000    TELEVISION AND RADIO ADVERTISING TIME $25,200,000
CAMPAIGN WORKER SALARIES $2,000,000    POLLING $800,000

SOURCE: Federal Election Commission, September 2008

## Background

**THE FEDERAL ELECTION COMMISSION** The Federal Election Commission (FEC) is the agency responsible for administering and enforcing federal laws about financing federal elections. Congress established the agency in 1975. It is an independent and nonpartisan commission. Though its six members are appointed by the President and confirmed by the Senate, they serve fixed terms (of six years), and by law no more than three members can belong to the same political party. The terms of the commissioners are staggered so that only two seats are open every two years. Leadership of the commission also rotates among the members.

All contributions to a candidate for federal office must be made through a single campaign committee. Only that committee can spend that candidate's campaign money. All contributions and spending must be closely accounted for by that one committee. Any contribution or loan of more than $200 must be identified by source and by date. Any spending over $200 must also be identified by the name of the person or firm to whom payment was made, by date, and by purpose.

Any contribution of more than $5,000 must be reported to the FEC no later than 48 hours after it is received. So, too, must any sum of $1,000 or more received in the last 20 days of a campaign.

**Limits on Contributions** Congress first began to regulate campaign contributions in 1907, when it outlawed donations by corporations and national banks. A similar ban was first applied to labor unions in 1943. Individual contributions have been regulated since 1939.

Today, no person can give more than $2,300 to any federal candidate in a primary election, and no more than $2,400 to any federal candidate's general election campaign. Also, no person can give more than $5,000 in any year to a political action committee (PAC), or $28,500 to a national party committee. The total of any person's contributions to federal candidates and committees now must be limited to no more than $108,200 in an election cycle (the two years from one general election to the next one). The FEC adjusts those figures, to account for inflation, every two years.

Those limits may seem generous; in fact, they are very tight. Before limits were imposed in 1974, many wealthy individuals gave far larger amounts. In 1972, for example, W. Clement Stone, a Chicago insurance executive, contributed more than $2 million (equal to more than $20 million in today's money) to President Richard Nixon's reelection campaign.

**PAC Contributions** Neither corporations nor labor unions can contribute directly to any candidate for federal office. Their political action committees, however, can and do.

Political action committees (PACs) seek to affect the making of public policy, and so they are very interested in the outcome of elections in the United States. Some 4,400 PACs are active today, and those organizations are of two distinct types:

**1.** Most PACs are the political arms of special interest groups—and especially of business associations, labor unions, and professional organizations. These groups are known in the law as "segregated fund committees." They can raise funds *only* from their members—from the executives, the employees, and the stockholders of a corporation, from the members of a labor union, and so on. They *cannot* seek contributions from the general public. Each of these PACs is a part of its parent organization.

BIPAC (the Business-Industry Political Action Committee) and COPE (the AFL-CIO's Committee on Political Education) are among the most active of these groups.

**2.** A few hundred PACs are "unconnected committees." Each of them was established as an independent entity, not as a unit in some larger organization. Many are ideologically based. These PACs can raise money from the public at large. One major example is EMILY's List, which actively recruits and funds pro-choice women as Democratic candidates. (The group takes its name from this political maxim: Early Money Is Like Yeast, it makes the dough rise.)

PACs fill their war chests with contributions from the members of the PAC's parent organization or with the dollars they raise from the public. They "bundle" the money they gather—that is, each PAC pools its many contributions into a single large fund. Then they distribute that money to those candidates who (1) are sympathetic to the PAC's policy goals, and (2) have a reasonable chance of winning their races.

No PAC can give more than $5,000 to any one federal candidate in an election, or $10,000 per election cycle (primary and general election). However, there is no overall limit on PAC giving to candidates. Each PAC can give up to $5,000 per election to each of as many candidates as it chooses. A PAC may also contribute up to $15,000 a year to a political party.

Barack Obama refused PAC contributions in 2008. Even so, those groups poured $416 million into the presidential and congressional

**DEBRIEF**

Review the debate activity with the class. Invite students from opposing teams to give their thoughts about which opposing arguments were most effective. Were any arguments left out?

**FOLLOW UP THE ACTIVITY**

Have students create an editorial cartoon that expresses one of the points of view presented in the debate. The cartoon should include an image and a caption. Students should be able to explain the elements and features of their cartoon.

**L1 L2 Differentiate** Have students work in teams to come up with a design for their cartoon.

**L3 L4 Differentiate** Have students create a cartoon for both points of view.

# Background

**WATERGATE AND CAMPAIGN FINANCE LAWS** The Watergate scandal of 1972–1974 ultimately led to the resignation of President Richard Nixon. As it unfolded, Congress and the public learned of a host of corrupt campaign practices used by Nixon's reelection team. For example, the campaign sought and used large, illegal corporate donations to create secret "slush funds," which were then used to pay for other illegal activities—including an attempt to break into and bug Democratic National Committee headquarters and subsequent attempts to cover up the crime. Some campaign donors were alleged to have received ambassadorships or other government favors. In the aftermath of this scandal, Congress established the basic laws that govern campaign financing today.

## Answers

**Checkpoint** administers all federal law dealing with campaign finance

**L3** Have students research and write a short essay on the following topic: How might the Internet change political fundraising and campaigning in the future? Students should include details from recent elections to support their argument.

**L1 L2 Differentiate** Have students locate information on the total amount of money raised by the most recent presidential candidates via the Internet.

**L4 Differentiate** Have students include in their essays historical information about the role of the Internet in politics, using data from the earliest days of Internet fundraising.

▲ Former Massachusetts governor Mitt Romney promoted his bid for the GOP presidential nomination with a widely publicized telethon in 2008. *Why must candidates spend significant time on fundraising activities?*

spending limit along with them, as part of their deal with the FEC.[16]

**Public Funding for Presidential Campaigns** Congress first began to provide for the public funding of presidential campaigns in the Revenue Act of 1971. It broadened sections of that law in 1974 and again in 1976.

The 1971 law created the Presidential Election Campaign Fund. Every person who files a federal income tax return can "check off" (assign) three dollars of his or her tax bill (six dollars on a joint return) to the fund. The money in the fund is used every four years to subsidize preconvention campaigns (including the primary campaigns), national conventions, and presidential election campaigns. The FEC administers the various subsidies involved.

*Preconvention Campaigns.* Presidential primary and caucus campaigns are supported by private contributions and, if the candidate applies for them, the public money he or she receives from the FEC. To be eligible for the public funds, a contender must raise at least $100,000 in contributions from individuals (not organizations). That amount must be gathered in $5,000 lots in each of at least 20 States, with each lot built from individual donations of no more than $250. That convoluted requirement is meant to discourage frivolous candidacies.

For each presidential hopeful who passes that test and applies for the subsidy, the FEC will match the first $250 of each individual contribution to the candidate, up to a total of half of the overall limit on preconvention spending. So, in 2008, the FEC could give a contender about $21 million, because the preconvention ceiling was slightly more than $42 million. The FEC does not match contributions from PACs or from any other political organizations.

In 2008, Senator John McCain spent about $100 million to win the GOP nomination—some $7 million of it from the FEC. Senator Barack Obama, on the other hand, refused the public money. He raised and

campaigns that year. And they funneled untold other millions into State and local contests around the country, as well.

**Limits on Expenditures** Congress first began to limit federal campaign spending in 1925. Most of the limits now on the books apply only to presidential (not congressional) elections. This fact is due mostly to the Supreme Court's decision in *Buckley* v. *Valeo*, 1976.

In *Buckley*, the High Court struck down all but one of the spending limits set by the FECA Amendments of 1974. It held each of the other restrictions to be contrary to the 1st Amendment's guarantees of free expression. In effect, said the Court, in politics "money is speech."

The one limit the Court did uphold is a cap on spending by those presidential contenders who accept FEC subsidies for their preconvention and/or their general election campaigns. As you will see in a moment, those who seek the presidency can either accept or reject that public money for their campaigns. In *Buckley*, the Court said that those who take the subsidies must take a

---

[16] Until 2008, only a handful of major party aspirants refused the public money. George W. Bush, in 2000 and again in 2004, and his Democratic opponent in 2004, John Kerry, won nomination without the public money. However, both Bush and Kerry did take the FEC funds for their general election campaigns.

## Supreme Court Notes

***BUCKLEY V. VALEO*** The Supreme Court ruling in *Buckley* v. *Valeo,* 1976, was important in several respects. It upheld Congress' right to set limits on individual contributions to political campaigns. Here the Court reasoned that the government's interest in maintaining the integrity of government was strong enough to support limiting the freedom of speech—that is, the spending of money for political purposes. However, the Court ruled that Congress could not limit how much of his or her own money a candidate could spend. Neither could Congress set a cap on the total amount a campaign spends. The Court reasoned that spending personal money or simply spending more for a campaign did not inherently threaten the integrity of government. Therefore, Congress did not have a strong enough basis for limiting 1st Amendment freedoms.

## Answers

**Caption** To be eligible for public funds, candidates must raise at least $100,000 in contributions from individuals. Also, the cost of campaigning is such that candidates must rely on donations to fund the expense.

spent more than $230 million in private contributions in his campaign for the Democratic Party's nomination.[17]

*National Conventions.* If a major party applies for the money, it automatically receives a grant to help pay for its national convention. The FEC gave the Republicans and the Democrats $16.4 million each for that purpose in 2008.

*Presidential Election Campaigns.* Each major party nominee automatically qualifies for a public subsidy to pay for the general election campaign. For 2008, that subsidy was $84.1 million. A candidate can refuse that funding, of course, and, in that event, be free to raise however much he or she can from private sources.

Until 2008, the nominees of both major parties took the public money each time. Because they did, each (1) could spend no more than the amount of the subsidy in the general election campaign and (2) could not accept campaign funds from any other source.

For 2008, only Republican John McCain ran with the FEC money and so could spend only that $84.1 million in the fall campaign. The Republican National Committee, other party organizations, and several independent groups also backed the McCain effort, however—to the tune of some $210 million.

Barack Obama, on the other hand, became the first presidential nominee in the 32-year history of the program to reject the public money. He raised and spent more than $500 million on his successful ten-week post-convention campaign.

The fact that several contenders, in both parties, rejected the FEC money for their pre-convention campaigns and Senator Obama's abstention for the general election have led many to predict the collapse of the public funding arrangements in federal law. That development is a direct result of two major factors: (1) a continuing decline in the number of taxpayers willing to contribute to the Presidential Election Campaign Fund and, especially, (2) the continuing and accelerating rise in the costs of campaigning.

The massive effect of that second factor, soaring costs, on the whole matter of campaign

[17] His chief opponent for the Democratic nomination, Senator Hillary Clinton, also refused FEC funds. She raised and spent nearly $200 million in her unsuccessful bid.

finance and its regulation can be seen in this stunning fact: For 2008, just one item, television advertising, accounted for at least $300 million in presidential campaign spending.

A minor party's candidate can also qualify for the FEC funding, but none does so automatically. For a minor party nominee to be eligible, his or her party must either (1) have won at least five percent of the popular vote in the last presidential election, or (2) win at least that much of the total vote in the current election. Since 1972, only Ross Perot in 1992 and 1996 has come even close to qualifying.

In the latter case, the public money is received *after* the election and so could not possibly help the candidate win votes in that election. (Remember, many provisions in both federal and State election law are purposely drawn to discourage the efforts of minor party and independent candidacies.)

## Hard Money, Soft Money

More than 40 years ago, President Lyndon Johnson described the then-current body of

✔ **Checkpoint**
How are presidential campaigns financed?

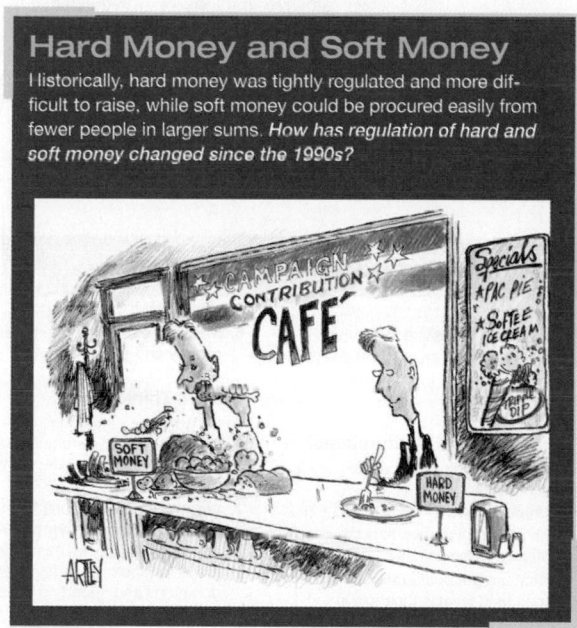

### Hard Money and Soft Money

Historically, hard money was tightly regulated and more difficult to raise, while soft money could be procured easily from fewer people in larger sums. *How has regulation of hard and soft money changed since the 1990s?*

## Supreme Court Notes

***MCCONNELL* V. *FEC*** The Bipartisan Campaign Reform Act's limits on soft money were examined by the Supreme Court in *McConnell* v. *FEC,* 2003. In a narrow 5-4 ruling, the Court held that Congress' desire to prevent the perceived or real corruption of candidates was a legitimate reason to limit the 1st Amendment exercise of spending soft money.

# Assess and Remediate

**L3** Collect the Core Worksheet and assess students' class participation using the Rubric for Assessing a Debate (Unit 2 All-in-One, p. 258).

**L3** Assign the Section 3 Assessment questions.

**L3** Section Quiz A (Unit 2 All-in-One, p. 150)

**L2** Section Quiz B (Unit 2 All-in-One, p. 151)

Have students complete the review activities in the digital lesson presentation and continue their work in the **Essential Questions Journal.**

## Answers

**Checkpoint** through public subsidies, party organizations, independent groups, and private contributions

**Hard Money and Soft Money** In the 1980s and 1990s, major parties raised huge amounts of money by exploiting the soft-money loophole, resulting in the need for the reform of campaign finance laws. Although such laws as the BCRA have been enacted, loopholes still remain.

| If Your Students Have Trouble With | Strategies For Remediation |
|---|---|
| Understanding the importance and sources of money in electoral politics (Questions 1, 2, 4, 6, 7) | Assign student pairs to read and create quizzes for the two sections on "Campaign Spending" and "Sources of Funding." Then have them exchange their quizzes with each other. |
| The history of efforts to control campaign financing (Questions 3, 7) | Have students create a timeline of major events in the history of campaign finance regulation, using material from the section. |
| The difference between hard and soft money (Question 5) | Have students create a script for a television commercial that uses hard money and soft money. |

federal campaign finance law as "more loophole than law." Over recent years, we have come dangerously close to the point where LBJ's description can be applied to the federal election money statutes of today—particularly because of soft money.

Since the 1970s, federal law has placed limits on **hard money**—that is, those contributions that are given directly to candidates for their campaigns for Congress or the White House, are limited in amount, and must be reported. That kind of campaign money is usually more difficult to raise than **soft money**—funds given to parties or to other political organizations, in unlimited amounts, to be used for such "party-building activities" as voter registration or get-out-the-vote drives or for campaigns for or against particular public policies, for example, gun control or minimum wage hikes.

Both major parties began to raise soft money (began to exploit the soft-money loophole) in the 1980s and they intensified their efforts in the 1990s. The Republican and Democratic National Committees and their House and Senate campaign committees gathered millions of unregulated dollars from wealthy individuals, labor unions, corporations, and other interest groups. Officially, those funds were to be used for party-building purposes; but both parties found it easy to filter them into their presidential and congressional campaigns.

The torrent of money rushing through the soft-money loophole rose from about $19 million in 1980 to some $500 million in 2000. Those huge numbers finally prompted Congress to enact the Bipartisan Campaign Reform Act (the BCRA) of 2002, after years of debate and delay. The measure is also known as the McCain-Feingold Law, after its chief Senate sponsors.

The BCRA was aimed principally at the soft-money problem. It bans soft-money contributions to political parties. But the law does not say that other political organizations cannot raise and spend those dollars.

Almost immediately, a number of independent groups—organizations with no formal ties to any party—sprang up to do just that. In short, creative minds in both parties quickly found ways to skirt the ban on soft money. Many of these independent organizations are known as "527s," after the section in the Internal Revenue code under which they operate as tax-free entities. It remains to be seen what effect, if any, the Court's 2010 ruling in *Citizens United* will have on these groups and their spending.

Some $200 million poured through that loophole in 2004 and even more for the congressional elections of 2006 and the presidential campaigns in 2008. In 2008, Senator Obama initially discouraged the help of 527 organizations, while his opponent, Republican Senator John McCain, encouraged that help.

**Essential Questions Journal** To continue to build a response to the chapter Essential Question, go to your **Essential Questions Journal.**

## SECTION 3 ASSESSMENT

1. **Guiding Question** Use your completed chart to answer the question: What role does money play in electoral politics?

### Key Terms and Comprehension

2. Why do people contribute to political campaigns?

3. What are the four ways in which the FEC attempts to regulate the role of money in campaigns?

4. What are **political action committees,** and what is their role in the political process?

5. What is the difference between **hard money** and **soft money**?

### Critical Thinking

6. **Summarize** Why do the huge amounts of money required for most political campaigns concern many observers?

7. **Identify Central Issues** The Supreme Court has ruled that "Money is speech." What does this observation mean for efforts to regulate and limit donations and spending in political campaigns?

### Quick Write

**Explanatory Essay: Write a Thesis Statement** A thesis statement sets out what, specifically, you will cover in your essay. Write a thesis statement for an explanatory essay about the election you chose in Section 1.

# Assessment Answers

**1.** Money is necessary to conduct a campaign. Its sources include private contributions and public financing. Government has tried to regulate the collection and spending of money for elections. Contributors and parties have found ways around the regulations.

**2.** People contribute to express their belief in a candidate or party, for social status, to influence policy, or to get something in return.

**3.** The FEC oversees disclosure of campaign finance data, contribution and expenditure limits, and public funding for presidential elections.

**4.** Political action committees are political arms of special interest groups and other organizations with a stake in electoral politics. They seek to influence elections as a means of affecting public policy.

**5.** Hard money is given directly to candidates for their campaigns. It is limited and must be reported. Soft money is given to parties or other political organizations for party-building or for policy campaigns. It is unlimited and represents a loophole through which unregulated money can enter the political process.

**6.** Money, which is so essential to a successful campaign, has the potential to enable contributors to buy influence and wealthy candidates to buy their way into office.

**7.** Freedom of speech is protected in the Bill of Rights. If campaign contributions and spending are forms of speech, then government may not impose undue limits on these activities.

**QUICK WRITE** Thesis statements should clearly identify the essay's main point and content.

# Quick Study Guide

**GOVERNMENT** ONLINE
**On the Go**
To review anytime, anywhere, download these online resources at **PearsonSchool.com/phgovt**
Political Dictionary, Audio Review

Have students download the digital resources available at Government on the Go for review and remediation.

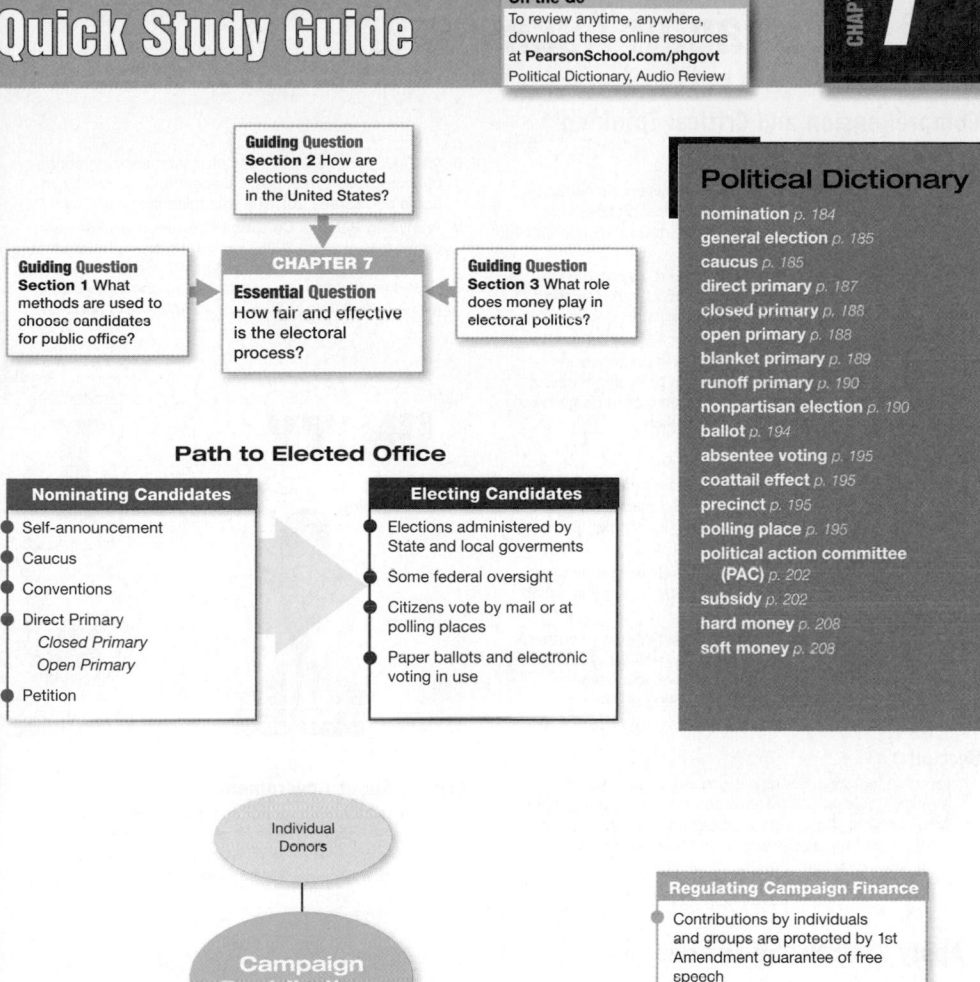

**Guiding Question**
**Section 2** How are elections conducted in the United States?

**Guiding Question**
**Section 1** What methods are used to choose candidates for public office?

**CHAPTER 7**
**Essential Question**
How fair and effective is the electoral process?

**Guiding Question**
**Section 3** What role does money play in electoral politics?

## Political Dictionary

nomination *p. 184*
general election *p. 185*
caucus *p. 185*
direct primary *p. 187*
closed primary *p. 188*
open primary *p. 188*
blanket primary *p. 189*
runoff primary *p. 190*
nonpartisan election *p. 190*
ballot *p. 194*
absentee voting *p. 195*
coattail effect *p. 195*
precinct *p. 195*
polling place *p. 195*
political action committee (PAC) *p. 202*
subsidy *p. 202*
hard money *p. 208*
soft money *p. 208*

### Path to Elected Office

**Nominating Candidates**
- Self-announcement
- Caucus
- Conventions
- Direct Primary
  - Closed Primary
  - Open Primary
- Petition

**Electing Candidates**
- Elections administered by State and local goverments
- Some federal oversight
- Citizens vote by mail or at polling places
- Paper ballots and electronic voting in use

Individual Donors

**Campaign Contributions**

Political Action Committees (PACs)

Public Financing by Government

**Regulating Campaign Finance**
- Contributions by individuals and groups are protected by 1st Amendment guarantee of free speech
- Direct contributions by unions and corporations to campaigns are illegal
- Federal campaigns must record donations and report regularly to Federal Election Commission

## STUDY TIPS

**Making and Keeping a Schedule** Schedules are indispensable tools for staying focused, getting things done, and not letting obligations or important tasks slip through the cracks. Suggest to students that they use a large monthly calendar for long-terms items, such as test dates and project due dates. A separate weekly or even daily schedule should list every hour in the day. On this schedule, students should first block out time for those commitments that are inflexible, such as class time, work schedules, or practices. The time left each day is their "free time," which must be used for meals, studying, errands, relaxation and everything else. Explain that the more detailed and realistic a schedule is, the more useful it will be.

## ASSESSMENT AT A GLANCE

**Tests and Quizzes**
Section Assessments
Section Quizzes A and B, Unit 2 **All-in-One**
Chapter Assessment
Chapter Tests A and B, Unit 2 **All-in-One**
Document-Based Assessment
Progress Monitoring Online
Exam*View* Test Bank

**Performance Assessment**
Essential Questions Journal
Debates, pp. 190, 198
Assessment Rubrics, **All-in-One**

# For More Information

To learn more about voting, refer to these sources or assign them to students:

**L1** **Giddens-White, Bryon.** *National Elections and the Political Process.* Heinemann, 2005.

**L2** **Kallen, Stuart A., ed.** *Are American Elections Fair?* Greenhaven Press, 2006.

**L3** **Maisel, L. Sandy.** *American Political Parties and Elections: A Very Short Introduction.* Oxford University Press, USA, 2007.

**L4** **Thurber, James A. and Candice J. Nelson.** *Campaigns and Elections American Style,* 2d edition. Westview Press, 2004.

# Chapter Assessment

**COMPREHENSION AND CRITICAL THINKING**

## SECTION 1

1. **(a)** Nomination is the process of selecting candidates who will appear on the ballot in the general election. **(b)** The two-party system means that nomination is the step at which voters are likely to have the largest number of choices—or in some cases, the only meaningful choice.

2. **(a)** Originally, caucuses were practical. Transportation and communications were difficult. As democracy spread, citizens criticized caucuses for being undemocratic. The caucus system died after a boycott of a party caucus led to the nomination of a weak candidate in the election of 1824. **(b)** At first, the convention system seemed like a good choice for a representative government. Party members would meet locally to select candidates for local offices and choose delegates to a county convention. County delegates would choose State delegates, and so on. However, party bosses manipulated delegate selection and soon dominated the entire system. By the 1910s, the direct primary had replaced the convention in most States.

3. **(a)** Political parties use primaries to choose their candidates for the general election. **(b)** A party might object to a blanket primary because voters who are not members of the party would participate in choosing the party's candidates. **(c)** Possible responses: Closed primaries are fair because they prevent one party from raiding the other's primary to nominate a weak candidate. Closed primaries also help make candidates responsive to the party and require voters to think about party differences. OR: Closed primaries are not fair because they compromise secrecy of the ballot by requiring voters to declare a party preference. Also, closed primaries tend to exclude independent voters.

## SECTION 2

4. **(a)** Federal election laws establish when federal elections will occur, require the use of secret ballots in federal elections, allow the use of voting machines, protect the right to vote, prohibit various corrupt practices, and regulate election financing. **(b)** The goal of regulation is to assure free, honest, and accurate elections.

5. **(a)** intimidation of voters and vote buying **(b)** The Australian ballot is printed at public

---

# Chapter Assessment

## Comprehension and Critical Thinking

### Section 1

1. **(a)** What is the essential difference between the nominating and the election stages in the political process? **(b)** Explain why the two-party system makes the nominating process especially significant.

2. **(a)** What factors led to the convention replacing the caucus as a widely used nominating method? **(b)** How well did the convention method succeed in improving upon the caucus method?

3. **(a)** What is the role of political parties in primary elections? **(b)** Why do you think a political party might object to the use of a blanket primary? **(c)** Are closed primaries a fair way to nominate candidates? Explain.

### Section 2

4. **(a)** Provide three examples of areas in which the Federal Government has established election law. **(b)** What are the goals of the Federal Government in regulating elections?

5. **(a)** What are some of the problems that the secret ballot is designed to prevent? **(b)** How did the Australian ballot improve the voting process?

6. **(a)** Why do you think there has been an interest in automating the voting process in recent times? **(b)** What are the possible benefits and drawbacks of voting via the Internet? **(c)** Do the advantages of voting via the Internet outweigh its drawbacks? Explain.

### Section 3

7. **(a)** What factors affect how much money is spent in a political campaign? **(b)** How do campaign contributions help candidates running for office? **(c)** Does the private rather than the public financing of campaigns make elections more effective? Why or why not?

8. **(a)** The Supreme Court has held that campaign contributions are a form of political speech. Explain why you agree or disagree. **(b)** Why was this ruling significant?

9. **Analyzing Political Cartoons** The cartoon below was drawn following the 2008 Democratic presidential primaries in which Senator Obama defeated Senator Clinton. **(a)** Why is Senator Obama holding a sign reading "Unity"? **(b)** What does this cartoon say about primary rivalries?

THE TIMES-PICAYUNE © 2008 CKLLY

### Writing About Government

10. Use the Quick Write exercises from this chapter to complete a 3–5 paragraph explanatory essay that describes and explains the key steps and features of the election you selected. See pages S3–S5 of the Skills Handbook.

---

## Apply What You've Learned

11. **Essential Question Activity** Prepare an outline for each side of a debate about the topic: Money is essential to the electoral process.
    **(a)** Develop a compelling argument both for and against the statement.
    **(b)** Describe existing efforts to regulate the role of money in elections.
    **(c)** Identify the main sources of campaign funding and analyze the impact each source has on elections.
    **(d)** Analyze the potential effects of removing all money from the political process, or, alternatively, removing all regulation of money.

12. **Essential Question Assessment** After you have considered and written about both sides of the question about the role of money in government, write a brief essay explaining your own views on the role of money in the electoral process today. Your essay should help you answer the Essential Question: **How fair and effective is the electoral process?**

**Essential Questions**
**Journal**
To respond to the chapter Essential Question, go to your **Essential Questions Journal.**

---

expense, lists the name of all candidates, is given out only at the polls, and is marked in secret. This type of ballot reduces party pressure on voters and corrupt practices.

6. **(a)** Thanks to new technologies, automation can make voting faster and easier, and it may offer the opportunity for greater accuracy and security. **(b)** Benefits include ease of voting and cost savings. Drawbacks include the potential for fraudulent vote counts, blocked access, hackers, viruses, denial of service attacks, and violations of voter secrecy. **(c)** Possible response: No. The infrastructure for online voting is not yet capable of ensuring fair and accurate elections. OR: Yes, the potential problems with Internet voting are no greater than those present in more traditional methods, and the benefits are clear.

## SECTION 3

7. **(a)** Factors include the office, the candidate, whether he or she is the incumbent, and the availability of funds. **(b)** Candidates need money to buy advertising, hire staff and consultants, rent office space, maintain Web sites, travel to campaign events, and send mass mailings. **(c)** Possible responses:

# Document-Based Assessment

## Nominating Candidates in Our Electoral System

Nominating candidates to run for office is a function of political parties. It is also a key step in the democratic process. This dual quality of the nominating process can create tension, as the party's wishes and the voice of the people do not always agree.

### Document 1

" Tonight, after fifty-four hard-fought contests, our primary season has finally come to an end. Sixteen months have passed since we first stood together on the steps of the Old State Capitol in Springfield, Illinois. Thousands of miles have been traveled. Millions of voices have been heard. . . .

There are those who say that this primary has somehow left us weaker and more divided. Well I say that because of this primary, there are millions of Americans who have cast their ballot for the very first time.

—Senator Barack Obama, June 3, 2008

### Document 2

" President [George H.W.] Bush received a jarring political message in the New Hampshire primary today, scoring a less-than-impressive victory over Patrick J. Buchanan, the conservative commentator. . . .

The signal to Mr. Bush was unmistakable. Even though Mr. Buchanan's support represented more than 63,000 actual votes, it amounted to a roar of anger from those who voted in the Republican primary, and it showed the power of a "send a message" campaign against him in times of economic distress. . . .

Republicans loyal to Mr. Bush tried to play down the results. . . . But there was alarm in the White House. . . .

—The New York Times, February 19, 1992

### Document 3

" Senator [Warren G.] Harding's nomination was the outcome of a complex situation that did not begin to clear until last evening. After four ineffective ballots yesterday the convention had adjourned until this morning. Four additional ballots in the forenoon and early afternoon of today had developed Harding strength, but General Leonard Wood and Governor Frank O. Lowden had remained in the lead. . . .

Interesting, and even thrilling, as the open proceedings in the convention were, moves behind the scenes, of which most of the convention knew nothing, had their dramatic side. The nomination of the candidate for President was arranged in conferences in hotel rooms.

—The New York Times, June 12, 1920

---

**Use your knowledge of the nominating process and Documents 1, 2, and 3 to answer Questions 1–4.**

1. According to Barack Obama in Document 1, which of the following is **not** an advantage of the primary process?
   A. The candidates competed in many States across the country.
   B. Primaries divided the party and upset many voters.
   C. Primaries brought millions of new voters into the nomination process.
   D. The candidates met many voters in their travels.

2. In Document 2, why do you think the message received by President Bush was so jarring?

3. Does the nominating process described in Document 3 seem democratic? Explain your answer.

4. **Pull It Together** How do the interests of voters and the interests of party officials sometimes come into conflict during the nomination process?

 **GOVERNMENT**ONLINE
**Online Documents**
To find more primary sources on the nominating process, visit
PearsonSchool.com/phgovt

---

1. B

2. As the incumbent, George H. W. Bush should have expected to receive more support and less of a challenge from within his own party.

3. Possible response: The process was democratic because the delegates had a chance to make their choice but failed. OR: The process of having a small group of people in a hotel room decide the nomination is clearly not democratic.

4. Possible response: Party officials and candidates would like to see the process produce a quick and clear result that does not divide the party or hint at disagreement. Voters naturally vote for their favorites, even though it might make other candidates and the party leaders uncomfortable.

**L2 Differentiate** Students use all the documents on the page to support their thesis.

**L3 Differentiate** Students include additional information available online at **PearsonSchool .com/phgovt**.

**L4 Differentiate** Students use materials from the textbook, the online information at **PearsonSchool .com/phgovt,** and do additional research to support their views.

**Go Online to PearsonSchool.com/phgovt** for a student rubric and extra documents.

---

Yes, because private financing enables citizens to participate in the election process. OR: No, because private financing enables wealthy donors, corporations, and special interests to buy influence.

8. **(a)** Possible response: I agree. Supporting a candidate financially is a way for citizens to express their political preferences. **(b)** The ruling applied constitutional protection to political donations, limiting the ability of Congress to regulate campaign financing.

9. **(a)** Sen. Obama wanted the Democratic party to unite behind his candidacy. **(b)** Primary rivalries can be intense. Once the candidate has been chosen, the party needs to come together to ensure that candidate's success.

### WRITING ABOUT GOVERNMENT

10. Students should use their Quick Write exercises from this chapter to complete a three- to five-paragraph explanatory essay that explains the key steps and features of the election they selected. See pages WH9–10 of the Writing Handbook.

### APPLY WHAT YOU'VE LEARNED

11. Student outlines should contain arguments for each side and contain all required elements.

12. Essays should express students' own views on the importance of money in the electoral process, and they should explain how their view of financing promotes fair and effective elections.

# Introduce the Chapter

## Essential Questions:

### UNIT 2

In what ways should people participate in public affairs?

### CHAPTER 8

What is the place of the media and public opinion in a democracy?

### ACTIVATE PRIOR KNOWLEDGE

Have students examine the image and quotation on these pages. Ask: **What do the photo and quotation suggest about the impact of the media?** *(The media play a major role in providing information about a wide range of topics, but what people really understand depends on their evaluation and use of that information.)* In this chapter, students will learn about how public opinion is formed and measured, and the media's influence on it. Tell students to further explore public opinion and the media by completing the Chapter 8 Essential Question Warmup activity in their **Essential Questions Journal.**

### BEFORE READING

**L2** **ELL Differentiate**  Chapter 8 Prereading and Vocabulary Worksheet (Unit 2 All-in-One, p. 168)

### SUCCESSNET STUDENT AND TEACHER CENTER

Visit **PearsonSchool.com/phgovt** for downloadable resources that allow students and teachers to connect with government "on the go."

### DIGITAL LESSON PRESENTATION

The digital lesson presentation supports the print lesson with activities and summaries of key concepts.

## SKILLS DEVELOPMENT

### DIGITAL AGE LITERACY

You may wish to teach digital age literacy as a distinct skill within Section 3 of this chapter. Use the Chapter 8 Skills Worksheet (Unit 2 All-in-One, p. 194) to help students learn about digital age literacy. The worksheet asks students to visit a political and current affairs blog, identify possible bias, and verify information. For L2 and L1 students, assign the adapted Skill Activity (Unit 2 All-in-One, p. 195).

**WebQuest online**   The chapter WebQuest challenges students to answer the chapter Essential Question by asking them about the media.

212

## Block Scheduling

**BLOCK 1:** Teach all of the Section 1 lesson plan and the Bellringer and Core Worksheet Activity in the Section 2 lesson plan.

**BLOCK 2:** Teach the Section 3 lesson plan in its entirety.

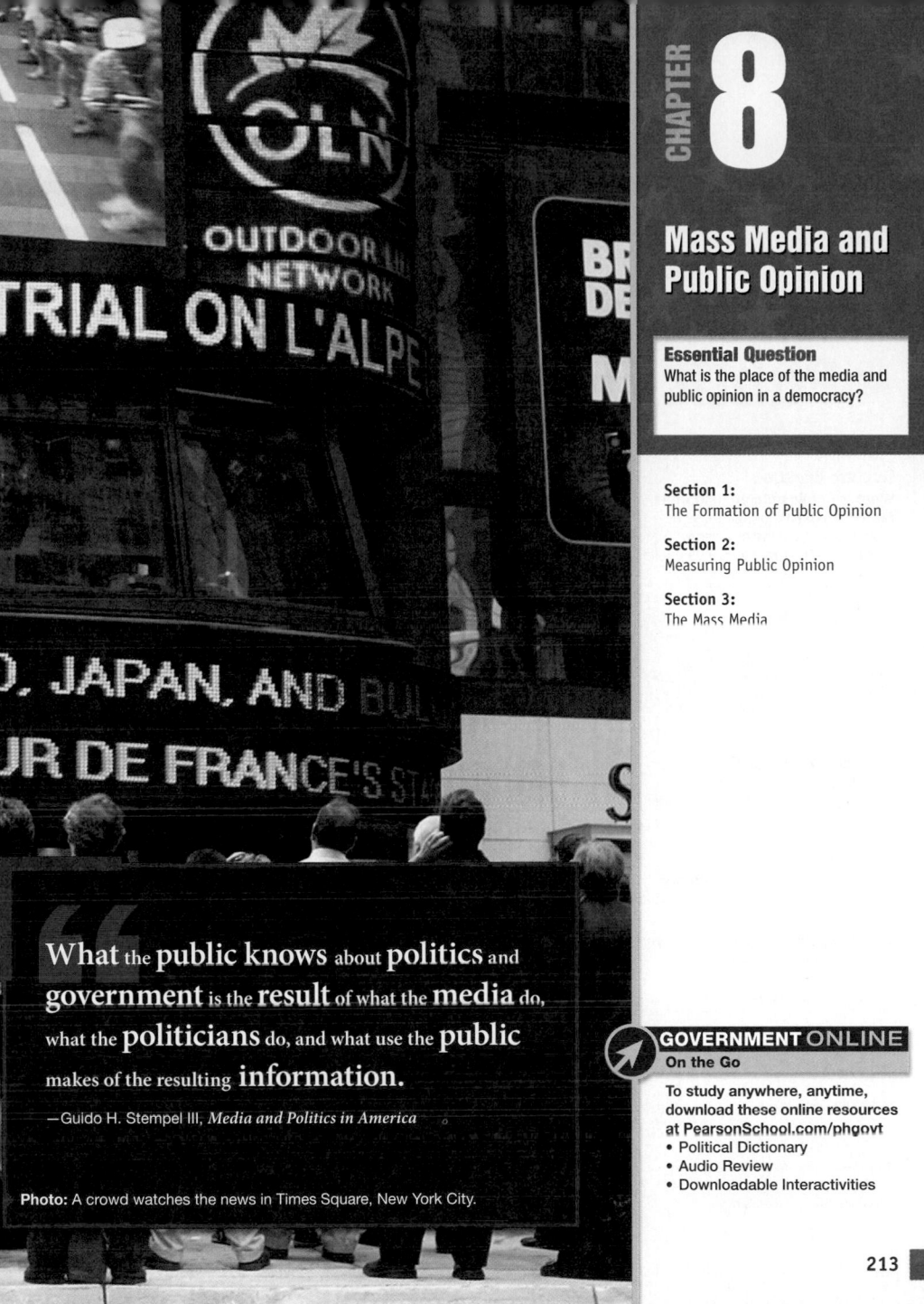

# Mass Media and Public Opinion

**Essential Question**
What is the place of the media and public opinion in a democracy?

> What the **public knows** about **politics** and **government** is the **result** of what the **media** do, what the **politicians** do, and what use the **public** makes of the resulting **information.**

—Guido H. Stempel III, *Media and Politics in America*

**Photo:** A crowd watches the news in Times Square, New York City.

**GOVERNMENT ONLINE**
On the Go

To study anywhere, anytime, download these online resources at PearsonSchool.com/phgovt
• Political Dictionary
• Audio Review
• Downloadable Interactivities

213

## Lesson Goals

### SECTION 1

Students will . . .

• discuss the concept of public opinion and its place in a democracy.

• explain how key factors influence public opinion by completing a chart.

• identify and explain their opinions on five public issues.

• explore the roots of their opinions by ranking their sources of influence on the five public issues.

### SECTION 2

Students will . . .

• examine the significance of how polling questions are worded and practice writing good polling questions.

• understand the importance of scientific polling by examining a poll on issues of concern to voters in a recent presidential election.

• evaluate the accuracy and usefulness of polls by examining a famous photograph.

### SECTION 3

Students will . . .

• understand the impact of the Internet as a political medium by examining study findings.

• evaluate the use of the Internet for electoral politics by analyzing a candidate's Web site.

• recognize the strengths of the Internet as a campaign medium by designing a home page for a candidate's Web site.

## Pressed for Time

To cover the chapter quickly, review the Section 1 Reading Comprehension Worksheet. Then have students complete Part 1 of the Section 1 Core Worksheet, in which they explain various influences on public opinion. Discuss which influences students consider most important and ask them to explain the reasons behind their choices. Then discuss any polls that students have seen in the media and explain that polls, when conducted properly, are the best way to measure public opinion. Have students examine "Questions to Ask About Polls" in Section 2 and ask them to explain why these questions are important in evaluating a poll's accuracy. List the various types of media on the board (newspapers, television, the Internet, radio, and magazines) and discuss their role in students' lives. Then use the cartoons in text Section 3 to discuss the influence of the media on politics and public opinion.

**DIFFERENTIATED INSTRUCTION KEY**

Look for these symbols to help you adjust steps in each lesson to meet your students' needs.

**L1** Special Needs
**L2** Basic
   **ELL** English Language Learners
   **LPR** Less Proficient Readers
**L3** All Students
**L4** Advanced Students

# What is public opinion, and what factors help to shape it?

## Get Started

### LESSON GOALS

Students will . . .

- discuss the concept of public opinion and its place in a democracy.
- explain how key factors influence public opinion by completing a chart.
- identify and explain their opinions on five public issues.
- explore the roots of their opinions by ranking their sources of influence on the five public issues.

### BEFORE CLASS

Assign the section, the graphic organizer in the text, and the Reading Comprehension Worksheet (Unit 2 All-in-One, p. 172) before class.

**L2 Differentiate** Reading Comprehension Worksheet (Unit 2 All-in-One, p. 173)

## SKILLS DEVELOPMENT

### COMPARE VIEWPOINTS

Before your classroom discussion of students' opinions about the topics in this section's Core Worksheet, you may want to review information on comparing viewpoints in the Skills Handbook, p. S15.

---

### SECTION 1

# The Formation of Public Opinion

### Guiding Question

**What is public opinion, and what factors help to shape it?** Use a concept web like the one below to show the factors that influence public opinion.

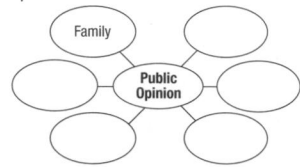

### Political Dictionary

- public affairs
- public opinion
- mass media
- peer group
- opinion leader

### Objectives

1. Examine the term *public opinion* and understand why it is so difficult to define.
2. Analyze how family and education help shape public opinion.
3. Describe four other factors that shape public opinion.

**Image Above:** *Meet the Press* host David Broder and guest discuss the 2008 presidential election.

**D**o you like broccoli? Blue fingernail polish? Tattoos? Hard rock music? What about sports? Old cars? You almost certainly have an opinion on each of those things. On some of them, you may hold strong opinions, and those opinions may be very important to you. Still, each of those opinions is your own view, your *private* opinion. None of them qualifies as *public* opinion.

## What Is Public Opinion?

Few terms in American politics are more widely used, and less well understood, than the term *public opinion*. It appears regularly in newspapers and magazines and on blogs, and you hear it frequently on radio and television.

Quite often, the phrase is used to suggest that all or most of the American people hold the same view on some public issue, such as global warming or deficit spending. Thus, time and again, politicians say that "the people" want such and such, television commentators tell us that "the public" favors this or opposes that, and so on.

In fact, there are very few matters about which all or nearly all of "the people" think alike. "The public" holds many different and often conflicting views on nearly every public issue.

To understand what public opinion is, you must recognize this important point: Public opinion refers to a complex collection of the opinions of many different people. It is the sum of all of their views. It is *not* the single and undivided view of some mass mind.

**Different Publics** Many publics exist in the United States—in fact, too many to be counted. Each public is made up of all those individuals who hold the same view on some particular public issue. Each group of people with a differing point of view is a *separate* public with regard to that issue.

For example, the people who think that Congress should concentrate on paying down the national debt belong to the public that holds that view. People who believe that the President is doing an excellent job as chief executive, or that capital punishment should be abolished, or that prayer should be permitted in public school, are members of separate publics with those particular opinions. Clearly, many people can and do belong to more than one of those publics; but

## Focus on the Basics

**FACTS:** • Public opinion refers to the attitudes of a significant number of people on matters of government and politics. • Family and education are two important factors in shaping people's political opinions. • Additional factors that shape public opinion include peer groups, opinion leaders, historic events, and mass media.

**CONCEPTS:** representative democracy, rights and responsibilities of citizens

**ENDURING UNDERSTANDINGS:** • Public opinion is not a single opinion, but a complex collection of opinions of many different publics. • Public opinion includes only views that relate to public affairs and that are expressed publicly.

almost certainly only a very few belong to all four of them.

Notice this important point: Not many issues capture the attention of all—or even nearly all—Americans. In fact, those that do are few and far between. Instead, most public issues attract the interest of *some* people (and sometimes millions of them), but those same issues are of little or no interest to many (and sometimes millions of) other people.

This point is crucial, too: In its proper sense, public opinion includes only those views that relate to public affairs. **Public affairs** include politics, public issues, and the making of public policies—those events and issues that concern the people at large. To be a *public* opinion, a view must involve something of general concern and of interest to a significant portion of the people as a whole.

Of course, the American people as a whole are interested in many things—rock groups and symphony orchestras, the New York Yankees and the Dallas Cowboys, candy bars and green vegetables, and a great deal more. Many people have opinions on each of these things, views that are sometimes loosely called "public opinion." But, again, in its proper sense, public opinion involves only those views that people hold on such things as political parties and candidates, taxes, unemployment, welfare programs, national defense, foreign policy, and so on.

**Definition** Clearly, public opinion is so complex that it cannot be readily defined. From what has been said about it to this point, however, **public opinion** can be described this way: those attitudes held by a significant number of people on matters of government and politics.

As we have suggested, you can better understand the term in the plural—that is, as public opinions, the opinions of different publics. Look at it this way: public opinion is made up of expressed group attitudes.

A view must be *expressed* in order to be an opinion in the public sense. Otherwise, it cannot be identified with any public. That expression need not be oral (spoken). It can take any number of other forms, as well: a protest demonstration, a film, a billboard, a vote for or against a candidate, and so on. The point is that a person's private thoughts on an issue enter the stream of public opinion only when those thoughts are expressed publicly.

## Family and School

No one is born with a set of attitudes about government and politics. Instead, each of us learns our political opinions, and we do so in a lifelong "classroom" and from many different "teachers." In other words, public opinion is formed out of a very complex process. The factors involved in it are almost <u>infinite.</u>

✔ **Checkpoint**
What do public affairs include?

**Infinite**
*adj.* uncountable, never ending, limitless

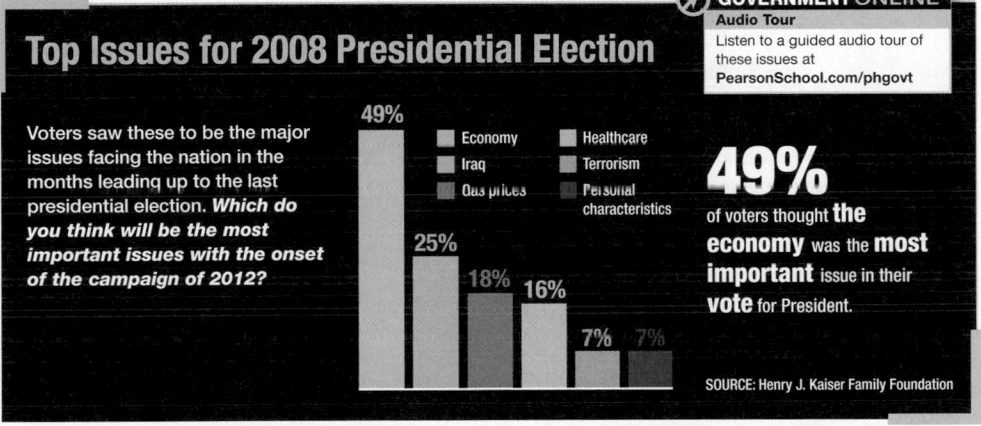

**GOVERNMENT ONLINE**
**Audio Tour**
Listen to a guided audio tour of these issues at PearsonSchool.com/phgovt

### Top Issues for 2008 Presidential Election

Voters saw these to be the major issues facing the nation in the months leading up to the last presidential election. *Which do you think will be the most important issues with the onset of the campaign of 2012?*

| | |
| Economy | Healthcare |
| Iraq | Terrorism |
| Gas prices | Personal characteristics |

49%
25%
18% 16%
7% 7%

**49%** of voters thought **the economy** was the **most important** issue in their **vote** for President.

SOURCE: Henry J. Kaiser Family Foundation

## Differentiated Resources

The following resources are located in the All-in-One, Unit 2, Chapter 8, Section 1:

**L2** Prereading and Vocabulary Worksheet (p. 168)
**L3** Reading Comprehension Worksheet (p. 172)
**L2** Reading Comprehension Worksheet (p. 173)
**L3** Core Worksheet (p. 174)
**L3** Quiz A (p. 177)
**L2** Quiz B (p. 178)

Write the following on the board. (Note: You may wish to modify the following list or provide your own list of issues, depending on particular sensitivities in your classroom.) **What do you think most Americans believe about the following issues?**

• **health insurance for all**
• **prayer in school**
• **the death penalty**

# Teach

To present this topic using online resources, use the lesson presentations at **PearsonSchool.com/phgovt.**

### INTRODUCE THE TOPIC

Display Transparency 8A, Whose Opinions Are They? Ask: **What does television have to do with the public's opinion on issues?** *(It can portray the event or issue in a way to bias the public.)* **What does this cartoon imply about forming an opinion based on a news issue?** *(The public has to come up with its own opinion because the breaking news is so fresh that it is being reported exactly as it happens without the media having the chance to slant the information.)*

Tell students that they will learn about the formation of public opinion. To help focus the class, ask a student volunteer to read aloud and summarize the text under the heading "What Is Public Opinion?" Then have another volunteer read aloud and summarize the first paragraph under the heading "Definition." Explain that students will focus on the question of how public opinion is formed and why it matters.

### REVIEW THE BELLRINGER

Turn students' attention to the Bellringer. Lead a discussion on the differences between private opinion and public opinion, and how public opinion shapes public policy. Use the Think-Write-Pair-Share strategy (p. T22) and ask students: **What is the place of public opinion in a democracy?** You may wish to write the following quotation on the board as a discussion starter: **"If forty million people say a foolish thing, it does not become a wise one."** **—W. Somerset Maugham, British writer**

Tell students to go to the Audio Tour for a guided audio tour of the top issues in the 2008 presidential election.

## Answers

**Checkpoint** politics, public issues, and the making of public policies

**Top Issues for 2008 Presidential Election** Possible response: The economy could improve, making it less of an issue, or a terrorist attack could lift terrorism to the top of the list.

## DISTRIBUTE CORE WORKSHEET

Distribute the Chapter 8 Section 1 Core Worksheet (Unit 2 All-in-One, p. 174), which asks students to explore factors that influence their own opinions. Have students work individually on this worksheet.

**L2 Differentiate** Briefly review the various controversies surrounding the issues raised in the Core Worksheet. Make sure students understand in broad terms the range of viewpoints involved.

---

Name _____ Class _____ Date _____

**CHAPTER 8 SECTION 1 · CORE WORKSHEET**
**The Formation of Public Opinion** 3

**Part 1 Public Opinion and You**

For each statement below, circle "Agree" or "Disagree" and explain the reasons for your belief.

1. The President is doing a great job carrying out his duties. (Agree/Disagree)

2. The death penalty should be an option for people convicted of murder. (Agree/Disagree)

3. People should be allowed to own handguns. (Agree/Disagree)

4. Smoking cigarettes in public places should be banned. (Agree/Disagree)

5. The drinking age should be lowered to age 18. (Agree/Disagree)

---

Name _____ Class _____ Date _____

**CORE WORKSHEET (continued)**
**The Formation of Public Opinion** 3

**Part 2 Influences on Your Opinions**

Why do you believe the things you do? For each question in Part 2, rank how much each source listed below has influenced your beliefs. Rank them from 1 (most influential) to 7 (least influential). If another source influenced your beliefs on the issue, identify the source, rank it, and explain its influence.

6. Presidential Approval—Sources influencing your beliefs:
   ____Family        ____Peer Groups
   ____School        ____Opinion Leaders
   ____Mass Media    ____Historic Events
   ____Parent's Occupation  ____Other:

7. Death Penalty—Sources influencing your beliefs:
   ____Family        ____Peer Groups
   ____School        ____Opinion Leaders
   ____Mass Media    ____Historic Events
   ____Parent's Occupation  ____Other:

8. Handguns—Sources influencing your beliefs:
   ____Family        ____Peer Groups
   ____School        ____Opinion Leaders
   ____Mass Media    ____Historic Events
   ____Parent's Occupation  ____Other:

9. Smoking in Public Places—Sources influencing your beliefs:
   ____Family        ____Peer Groups
   ____School        ____Opinion Leaders
   ____Mass Media    ____Historic Events
   ____Parent's Occupation  ____Other:

10. Drinking Age—Sources influencing your beliefs:
   ____Family        ____Peer Groups
   ____School        ____Opinion Leaders
   ____Mass Media    ____Historic Events
   ____Parent's Occupation  ____Other:

---

## Answers

**Checkpoint** age, race, income, occupation, residence, group affiliations, family, education

---

✔ **Checkpoint**
What are several agents of political socialization?

**monopoly**
*n.* dominant or exclusive control

**impressionable**
*adj.* easily influenced, receptive

**indoctrinate**
*v.* to teach, instruct

You have already considered that point. Recall the detailed look at why people vote as they do in Chapter 6. Those pages amounted to an extensive look at how public opinion is formed. Also in that chapter, you considered the process by which each person acquires his or her political opinions—the process of *political socialization*. That complex process begins in early childhood, and it continues on through one's lifetime. It involves all of the many experiences and relationships that lead each of us to see the political world and to act in it as we do.[1]

There are many different agents of political socialization at work in the opinion-shaping process. Again, you looked at these agents in Chapter 6: age, race, income, occupation, residence, group affiliations, and many others. Here, look again at two of them, the family and school. They have so large an impact that they deserve another and slightly different discussion here.

**Family** Most parents do not think of themselves as agents of political socialization, nor do other members of most families. Parents and other family members do nonetheless play an important part in this process.

Children first see the political world from within the family and through the family's eyes. They begin to learn about politics much as they begin to learn about most other things in life. They learn from what their parents have to say, from the stories that their older brothers and sisters bring home from school, from watching television with the family, and so on.

Most of what smaller children learn in the family setting cannot really be described as political opinions. Clearly, toddlers are not concerned with the wisdom of spending billions of dollars on an antimissile defense system, with the causes of global warming, or the pros and cons of the monetary policies of the Federal Reserve Board.

Young children do pick up some fundamental attitudes, however. With those attitudes, they acquire a basic slant toward such things as authority and rules of behavior, property, neighbors, people of other racial or religious backgrounds, and the like. In short, children lay some foundations on which they will later build their political opinions.

A large number of scholarly studies report what common sense also suggests. The strong influence the family has on the development of political opinions is largely a result of the near monopoly the family has on the child in his or her earliest, most impressionable years. Those studies also show that:

"Children raised in households in which the primary caregivers are Democrats tend to become Democrats themselves, whereas children raised in homes where their caregivers are Republican tend to favor the GOP."

—**Benjamin Ginsberg, Theodore Lowi, and Margaret Weir,** *We the People*

**School** The start of formal schooling marks the initial break in the influence of the family. For the first time, children become regularly involved in activities outside the home.

From the first day, schools teach children the values of the American political system. They work to indoctrinate the young, to instill in them loyalty to a particular cause or idea. In fact, preparing students to become good citizens is an important part of our educational system.

Students may salute the flag, recite the Pledge of Allegiance, and sing patriotic songs. They learn about George Washington, Abraham Lincoln, Susan B. Anthony, Martin Luther King, Jr., and other great Americans. From the early grades on, they pick up growing amounts of specific political knowledge, and they begin to form political opinions. In high school, they are often required to take a course in American government and even to read books such as this one.

School involves much more than books and classes, of course. It is a complex bundle of experiences and a place where a good deal of informal learning occurs—about the similarities and differences among individuals

---

1  The concept of socialization comes from the fields of sociology and psychology. There, it is used to describe all of the ways in which a society transforms individuals into members of that society. To put this another way: Socialization is the multi-sided, lifelong process in which people come to know, accept, and follow the beliefs and practices of their society. *Political socialization* is a part of that much broader process.

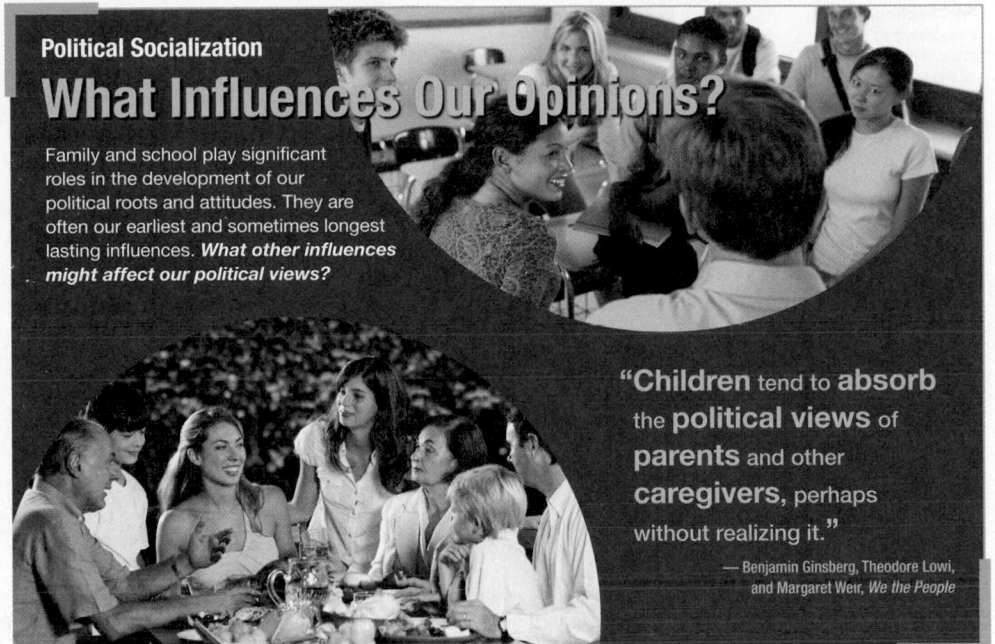

## Political Socialization
# What Influences Our Opinions?

Family and school play significant roles in the development of our political roots and attitudes. They are often our earliest and sometimes longest lasting influences. *What other influences might affect our political views?*

"**Children** tend to **absorb** the **political views** of **parents** and other **caregivers**, perhaps without realizing it."

— Benjamin Ginsberg, Theodore Lowi, and Margaret Weir, *We the People*

and groups, about the various ways in which decisions can be made, and about the process of compromise that must often occur in order for ideas to move forward.

Once again, the family and school are *not* the only forces at work in the process by which opinions are formed. A number of other influences are part of the mix. These two factors are singled out here to highlight their leading roles in that process.

## Other Factors

No factor, taken by itself, shapes a person's opinion on any single issue. Some factors do play a much larger role than others in that process, however. Thus, in addition to family and school, occupation and race are usually much more significant than, say, gender or place of residence.

For example, on the question of paying down the public debt, what a person does for a living and his or her level of income will almost certainly have a much greater

impact on his or her views than will gender or where he or she happens to live.

On the other hand, the relative weight of each factor that influences public opinion also depends on the issue in question. If the issue involves, say, equal pay for women or the effects of a major oil spill in the Gulf of Mexico, then gender or where one lives will almost certainly loom larger in the opinion-making mix.

Besides family, school, and such factors as occupation and race, four other factors have a major place in the opinion making process. They are the mass media, peer groups, opinion leaders, and historic events.

**Mass Media** The **mass media** include those means of communication that reach large, widely <u>dispersed</u> audiences (masses of people) simultaneously. No one needs to be told that the mass media, including newspapers, magazines, radio, and in particular, television and the Internet, have a huge effect on the formation of public opinion.

<u>dispersed</u>
*adj.* scattered, spread out

# Debate

Form teams to debate the issues in the Core Worksheet, Part 2. Omit any issues that are too sensitive for your class. Allow students to choose the issue they want to debate and the position they want to take—either "Agree" or "Disagree." Allow teams time to prepare. Advise them to prepare rebuttals for points they expect the opposing team to make. After teams debate each issue, ask if anyone's opinion changed based on the points the teams made. Use the Debate strategy (p. T25) to organize the debate.

## REFLECT ON WORKSHEET RESPONSES

While students respond to the remaining questions on the worksheet, you may wish, depending on classroom sensitivities, to have them submit their answers from Part 1 to you anonymously. On the board, keep a tally of the different answers to the questions. Ask: **Are you surprised to see the range of opinions—or to see that the opinions on some topics are the same among all class members?** Next, you may wish to have students present their top influences from Part 2—again, anonymously. Write the results on the board. Ask: **Are you surprised to see the range of influences on public opinions?** Lead a discussion on how the range, or lack of range, of opinions would influence public policy on these issues.

## EXTEND THE LESSON

**L3** Ask students to recall their answer to Reflection Question 13 from the Core Worksheet. Have students write an essay that explores the ways in which this particular influence has affected their lives and opinions.

**L1 L2 Differentiate** Have students describe verbally the ways in which their most important influences have affected their lives.

**L4 Differentiate** For each issue listed in Part 1 of the Core Worksheet, have students describe different backgrounds and experiences that might lead other people to form opinions different from their own. For example, a victim of gun-related crime would be less likely to support gun ownership than would a hunting enthusiast.

**L2 Differentiate** Divide the class into four groups. Assign each group one of the following factors that shape public opinion: peer groups, opinion leaders, historic events, and mass media. Have groups discuss people, events, and experiences within their category that have had a significant influence on their political opinions. Each group should elect a spokesperson to share the highlights of their discussion, including which factor the group felt was the most influential and why.

## Answers

**What Influences Our Opinions?** possible response: occupation, race, mass media, peer groups, opinion leaders, historic events

# Assess and Remediate

**L3** Collect the Core Worksheet and assess students' work.

**L3** Assign the Section 1 Assessment questions.

**L3** Section Quiz A (Unit 2 All-in-One, p. 177)

**L2** Section Quiz B (Unit 2 All-in-One, p. 178)

Have students complete the review activities in the digital lesson presentation and continue their work in the **Essential Questions Journal.**

---

**Government** online  *All print resources are available on the Teacher's Resource Library CD-ROM and online at PearsonSchool.com/phgovt.*

---

## Answers

**Checkpoint** Most people trust the views of their friends and want to be liked by their friends and associates, so they seldom stray too far from the opinions of their peer groups.

**Analyzing Cartoons** The cartoonist is implying that the mass media generally presents biased information—it tells people what to think.

---

✔ **Checkpoint**
How does one's peer group shape his or her attitudes?

Take this as but one indication: There is at least one television set in more than 98 percent of the nation's 115 million households. There are two or more sets in more than 80 million homes and millions more in many other places. Most of those sets are turned on for at least eight hours a day, for a mind-boggling total of more than a *billion* hours a day. You will take a longer look at the influence of the mass media later in this chapter.

**Peer Groups** People with whom one regularly associates, including friends, classmates, neighbors, co-workers, and the like, make up one's **peer group.** When a child enters school, friends and classmates become important agents in shaping his or her attitudes and behavior. The influence of peer groups continues on through adulthood.

Belonging to a peer group usually reinforces what a person has already come to believe. One obvious reason for this is that most people trust the views of their friends. Another is that the members of a peer group have shared many of the same socializing experiences, and so tend to think along the same or similar lines.

To put this observation another way, contradictory or other unsettling opinions are not often heard within a peer group. Most people want to be liked by their friends and associates. As a result, they are usually reluctant to stray too far from what their peers think and how they behave.

**Opinion Leaders** The views expressed by **opinion leaders** also bear heavily on the formation of public opinion. An opinion leader is any person who, for any reason, has an unusually strong influence on the views of others. These opinion shapers are a distinct minority in the total population, of course, but they are found everywhere.

Many opinion leaders hold public office. Some write for newspapers or magazines, or express their opinions on radio or television or the Internet. Others are prominent in business, labor, agriculture, and civic organizations. Many are professionals—doctors, lawyers, teachers, ministers, and rabbis—and have regular contact with large numbers of people. Many others are active members of their neighborhood or church, or have leadership roles in their local communities.

Whoever they may be—the President of the United States, a network television commentator, the governor, the head of a local citizens committee, or even a local talk-show host—these opinion leaders are people to whom others listen and from whom others draw ideas and convictions. Whatever their political, economic, or social standing or outlook may be, opinion leaders play a significant role in the formation of public opinion.

**Historic Events** Historic events can have a major impact on the views of large numbers of people—and so have a major impact on the content and direction of public policy. Clearly, the events of September 11, 2001, and the onset of the global war on terror constitute a leading illustration of that point. American views on national security and foreign policy have undergone dramatic shifts as a result of those events.

Our history affords many other examples, as well—not the least of them the Great Depression, which began in 1929 and lasted for the better part of a decade.

The Depression was a shattering national experience. Almost overnight, need and

"WE DO WANT TO WARN YOU THAT THIS NEWS HAS YET TO BE SPUN, SO YOU MAY HAVE TO FORMULATE YOUR OWN OPINION."

▶▶ **Analyzing Cartoons** An effort to shape the public's response is known as "spin." **What is the cartoonist implying about the media here?**

---

## Background

**Celebrity Endorsements** Before every election, celebrities of various stripes endorse candidates. Polls by the Pew Research Center, however, suggest that celebrity endorsements do little to sway voter opinion—at least not directly. "[Endorsements] generate free media attention, fundraising, and get people talking about the endorsements to their friends," said Professor Kelli Lammie, of SUNY-Albany, in a *US News* article from October 24, 2008. A Pew poll in 2007 found that the most influential endorsements come from local religious leaders and State governors. In the 2008 Democratic primaries, however, Oprah Winfrey's endorsement of Barack Obama may have played a key role. Winfrey's television show, magazine, and radio show reach 49 million people a week. A University of Maryland study found that Winfrey's endorsement brought Obama over a million votes in the primaries.

poverty became massive national problems. Hunger and despair stalked the land. In 1929, some two million people were unemployed in the United States. By just four years later, that number had climbed to 13.5 million. In 1935, some 18 million men, women, and children were wholly dependent on public emergency relief programs. Some 10 million workers had no employment other than that provided by temporary public projects.

All of this changed people's view of the proper place of government in the United States. The Depression persuaded a large majority of Americans to support an expanded role for government—in particular, for the National Government—in the nation's economic and social life.

The Great Depression also prompted a majority of Americans to shift their loyalties from the Republicans to the Democrats. The Republicans had dominated the national political scene from Lincoln's election in 1860 to the onset of the Depression. That situation changed abruptly when Franklin D. Roosevelt's landslide victory in 1932 began nearly 40 years of Democratic domination.

The turbulent politics of the 1960s and early 1970s furnish another example of the way in which significant occurrences can impact and shape opinions. The American people had emerged from World War II and the prosperity of the 1950s with a largely optimistic view of the future and of the

United States' place in the world. That rose-colored outlook was reflected in a generally favorable, even respectful, attitude toward government in this country.

The 1960s and early 1970s changed all that. Those years were highlighted by a number of traumatic events. Of special note were the assassinations of President John Kennedy in 1963 and of the Reverend Martin Luther King, Jr., and Senator Robert Kennedy in 1968. This period also included the civil rights movement and the Vietnam War, with all of the protests, violence, and strong emotions that accompanied both of those chapters in this nation's life. The era ended with the Watergate scandal and the near-impeachment and subsequent resignation of President Richard Nixon in 1974.

Those years of turmoil and divisiveness produced a dramatic decline in the American people's estimate of their government—and most especially in their evaluation of its trustworthiness.

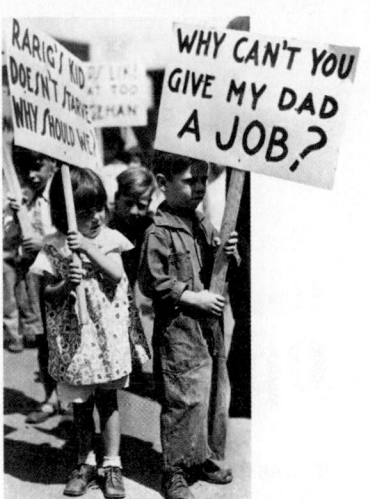

Many Americans became Democratic voters as a result of the Great Depression.

**divisiveness**
*n.* result of disagreement, tending to divide

Essential Questions Journal — To continue to build a response to the chapter Essential Question, go to your Essential Questions Journal.

# SECTION 1 ASSESSMENT

1. **Guiding Question** Use your completed concept web to answer this question: What is public opinion, and what factors help to shape it?

## Key Terms and Comprehension

2. What does it mean to say that there are different "publics" that help make up **public opinion?**

3. To what kinds of issues and affairs is **public opinion** limited?

4. What are the two most important early influences on many people's political socialization?

5. What are the roles of **mass media, peer groups,** and **opinion leaders** in influencing public opinion?

## Critical Thinking

6. **Make Generalizations** What features of peer groups explain why they tend to reinforce rather than challenge what a person believes?

7. **Identify Central Issues** What are some of the public issues that were brought to the forefront of public opinion in the wake of the terrorist attacks of September 11, 2001?

### Quick Write

**Cause-and-Effect Essay: Choose a Topic** Using the Internet, other sources, and your textbook, identify a public affairs issue, such as the environment or energy, about which there are strong public opinions. Write a brief summary of the issue and cite at least two of the more prominent public opinions about the topic.

---

## How is public opinion measured and used?

| Measuring Public Opinion | |
|---|---|
| Elections | Voting results can sometimes reflect public opinion. |
| Interest Groups | Key way public opinion made known, but difficult to know number of people and strength of views |
| Media | Mirror and mold public opinion, but often reflect views of vocal minority |
| Personal Contacts | Officials gauge views through interactions, but can fall into trap of finding only views that agree with their own |
| Public Opinion Polls | Collect information by asking people questions—best measure of opinion |
| Straw Vote | Asks large number of people same question—unreliable because not based on scientific techniques |
| Scientific Polling | Define the survey universe, construct a sample, prepare valid questions, select and control how poll will be taken, analyze and report findings |

# Get Started

### LESSON GOALS

Students will . . .

- examine the significance of how polling questions are worded and practice writing good polling questions.
- understand the importance of scientific polling by examining a poll on issues of concern to voters in a recent presidential election.
- evaluate the accuracy and usefulness of polls by examining a famous photograph.

## SKILLS DEVELOPMENT

### ANALYZE IMAGES

Before displaying the image in Transparency 8E to the class, you may want to review the information on analyzing images in the Skills Handbook, p. S28.

---

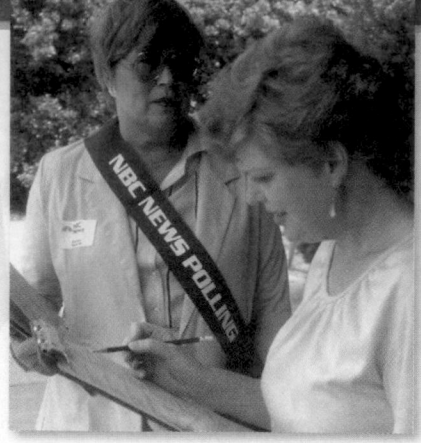

SECTION **2**

# Measuring **Public Opinion**

### Guiding Question

**How is public opinion measured and used?** Use a table like the one below to take notes on the section.

| Measuring Public Opinion | |
|---|---|
| Elections | Voting results can sometimes reflect public opinion. |
| | |
| | |
| | |

### Political Dictionary

- mandate
- interest group
- public opinion poll
- straw vote
- universe
- sample
- random sample
- quota sample

### Objectives

1. Describe the challenges involved in measuring public opinion.
2. Explain why scientific opinion polls are the best way to measure public opinion.
3. Identify the five steps in the polling process.
4. Understand the problems in evaluating polls.
5. Recognize the limits on the impact of public opinion in a democracy.

**Image Above:** NBC News pollster conducts an election exit poll.

H ow often have you heard the phrase: "According to a recent poll . . ."? Probably more than you can count, especially in the months leading up to an election. Polls are one of the most common means of gauging public opinion.

If public policy is to reflect public opinion, one needs to be able to find the answers to these questions: What are people's opinions on a particular issue? How many people share a given view on that issue? How firmly do they hold that view? In other words, there must be a way to "measure" public opinion.

## Measuring Public Opinion

The general shape of public opinion on an issue can be found through a number of key indicators. They include voting; lobbying; books; pamphlets; magazine and newspaper articles; editorial comments in the press and on radio, television, and the Internet; paid advertising; letters to editors and public officials; and so on.

These and other means of expression are the devices through which the general direction of public opinion becomes known. Usually though, the means by which a view is expressed tells little—and often nothing reliable—about the size of the group that holds that opinion or how strongly it is held. In the American political system, this information is critically important. To find it, some effort must be made to measure public opinion. Elections, interest groups, the media, and personal contacts with the public all—at least to some degree—provide the means by which that measurement can be done.

**Elections** In a democracy, the voice of the people is supposed to express itself through the ballot box. Election results are thus very often said to be indicators of public opinion. The votes cast for the various candidates are regularly taken as evidence of the people's approval or rejection of the stands taken by those candidates and their parties. As a result, a party and its victorious candidates regularly claim to have received a mandate to carry out their campaign promises. In American politics, a **mandate** refers to the instructions or commands a constituency gives to its elected officials.[2]

---

2 The term *mandate* comes from the Latin *mandatum*, meaning "a command."

# Focus on the Basics

**FACTS:** • Elections, interest groups, the media, and personal contacts reflect public opinion but do not provide accurate measurements of it. • The most reliable measure of public opinion is scientifically conducted opinion polls. • Scientific polls define the universe, construct a sample, prepare valid questions, select and control how the poll will be taken, and analyze and report findings.

**CONCEPTS:** democratic values/principles

**ENDURING UNDERSTANDINGS:** • To achieve reliable results, pollsters must use a random sample from the target population and avoid bias in the wording of their questions. • Democracy is more about thoughtful participation than mere measurement of public opinion.

In reality, however, election results are seldom an accurate measure of public opinion. Voters make choices in elections for any of several reasons, as you have seen. Very often, those choices have little or nothing to do with the candidates' stands on public questions. Then, too, candidates often disagree with some of the planks of their party's platform. And, as you know, candidates and parties often express their positions in broad, generalized terms.

In short, much of what you have read about voting behavior, and about the nature of parties, adds up to this: Elections are, at best, only useful indicators of public opinion. To call the typical election a mandate for much of anything other than a general direction in public policy is to be on very shaky ground.

**Interest Groups** Private organizations whose members share certain views and objectives, and who work to shape the making and the content of public policy are called **interest groups.** These organizations are also very aptly known as pressure groups and special-interest groups.

Interest groups are a chief means by which public opinion is made known. They present their views (exert their pressures) through their lobbyists, by letters, telephone calls, and e-mails, in political campaigns, and by other methods. In dealing with them, however, public officials often have difficulty determining two things: How many people does an interest group really represent? How strongly do those people hold the views that an organization says they hold?

**The Media** Earlier, you read some impressive numbers about television that help describe the place of the media in the opinion process; you will read more of those numbers later. Here, recognize this point: The media are also a gauge for assessing public opinion.

The media are frequently said to be "mirrors" as well as "molders" of opinion. It is often claimed that the views expressed in newspaper editorials, syndicated columns, news magazines, television commentaries, and blogs are fairly good indicators of public opinion. In fact, however, the media are not very accurate mirrors of public opinion, often reflecting only the views of a vocal minority.

**Personal Contacts** Most public officials have frequent and wide-ranging contacts in many different forms with large numbers of people. In each of these contacts, they try to read the public's mind. Indeed, their jobs demand that they do so.

✓**Checkpoint**
How do interest groups present their views?

aptly
*adv.* fittingly, appropriately, suitably

### How Government Works

## Using Public Opinion

Public officials seek to measure public opinion through a variety of sources, as shown below. Whether or not a public official gets reelected may depend on how he or she responds to public opinion. **For what reasons is public opinion measured?**

| Media | Serve as mirrors and molders of public opinion |
| The People | Convey their opinions in e-mails, letters, phone calls, or public meetings |
| Interest Groups | Share the views of their members in hopes of influencing policy |

A candidate for office shakes hands with a voter on his way into a polling place. ▶

Chapter 8 • Section 2 **221**

## Differentiated Resources

The following resources are located in the All-in-One, Unit 2, Chapter 8, Section 2:

- **L3** Reading Comprehension Worksheet (p. 179)
- **L2** Reading Comprehension Worksheet (p. 181)
- **L3** Core Worksheet (p. 183)
- **L2** Extend Activity (p. 184)
- **L3** Quiz A (p. 185)
- **L2** Quiz B (p. 186)

**BEFORE CLASS**

Assign the section, the graphic organizer in the text, and the Reading Comprehension Worksheet (Unit 2 All-in-One, p. 179) before class.

**L2 Differentiate** Reading Comprehension Worksheet (Unit 2 All-in-One, p. 181)

**BELLRINGER**

Display Transparency 8D, which shows the effects of wording on poll questions. Have students answer the question in their notebook.

## Teach

To present this topic using online resources, use the lesson presentations at **PearsonSchool.com/phgovt.**

**REVIEW BELLRINGER**

Have students share their reactions to the Bellringer. Point out that the only difference in the wording of the last two questions is the order in which the options are presented. The results, however, are vastly different. This suggests that the order significantly influenced the responses. The first question requiring a simple "agree" or "disagree" response will likely bring the most accurate results. Ask: **What do these examples tell you about polls and polling?** (*How questions are worded can change the results of a poll, so polls may not always be an accurate measure of public opinion.*)

Then write the following topic on the board: **Protecting the Environment.** Ask students to work in pairs to write a poll question two different ways—one designed to elicit a particular response and another designed to be neutral and unbiased. Have volunteers share their questions, and write them on the board. Discuss how the wording of particular questions could influence the answers, and point out which questions would be most appropriate to use in a poll.

**L2 Differentiate** Start by underlining the parts that differ among the questions on the board and choose questions with the clearest differences in wording to discuss first. Provide help with any difficult vocabulary words.

## Answers

**Checkpoint** Interest groups present their views using lobbyists, letters, telephone calls, and e-mails, as well as in political campaigns.

**Using Public Opinion** to shape public policy and to win elections

Explain that measuring public opinion is a complicated task that is of great interest to public officials.
Ask: **Why would officials be interested in public
opinion?** *(Knowing public opinion is key to being
elected, and it can also help guide officials to form
public policy that the people want.)* **Why is this
information important to the American political
system?** *(The system is based on public officials
carrying out the people's wishes.)* Then write the
following headings on the board: **Elections, Interest Groups, Media,** and **Personal Contacts.** Ask
students to explain how each reflects public opinion
and discuss the limitations of each as a measurement
tool. Tell students that scientific opinion polls provide
the most reliable measure of public opinion.

▸▸ **Analyzing Cartoons** A pollster is a person or group who researches
public opinion. *What do you think the cartoonist is saying about
pollsters here?*

**mishap**
*n.* calamity, disaster,
misfortune

Members of Congress receive bags of
mail and hundreds of phone calls and e-mails
every day. Many of them make frequent trips
"to keep in touch with the folks back home."
Top administration figures are often on the
road, too, selling the President's programs
and gauging the people's reactions. Even the
President does some of this, with speaking
trips to different parts of the country.

Governors, State legislators, mayors, and
other officials also have any number of contacts with the public. These officials encounter
the public in their offices, in public meetings,
at social gatherings, community events, and
even at ball games.

Can public officials find "the voice of the
people" in all of those contacts? Many can
and do, and often with surprising accuracy.
But some public officials cannot. They fall
into an ever-present trap: They find only what
they want to find, only those views that support and agree with their own.

## Public Opinion Polls

Public opinion is best measured by **public
opinion polls,** devices that attempt to collect
information by asking people questions.[3] The
more accurate polls are based on scientific
polling techniques.

**Straw Votes** Public opinion polls have
existed in this country for more than a century. Until the 1930s, however, they were far
from scientific. Most earlier polling efforts
were of the **straw vote** variety.[4] That is, they
were polls that sought to read the public's
mind simply by asking the same question of
a large number of people. Straw votes are still
fairly common. Many radio talk-show hosts
pose questions that listeners can respond
to by telephone, and television personalities
regularly invite responses by e-mail.

The straw-vote technique is highly unreliable, however. It rests on the mistaken
assumption that a relatively large number
of responses will provide a fairly accurate
picture of the public's views on a given question. The problem is this: The respondents are
self-selected. Nothing in the process ensures
that those who respond will represent a reasonably accurate cross section of the total
population. The straw vote emphasizes the
quantity rather than the quality of the sample
to which its question is put.

The most famous of all straw-polling
mishaps took place in 1936. A widely read
periodical, the *Literary Digest,* mailed postcard
ballots to more than 10 million people and
received answers from more than 2 million
of them. Based on that huge return, the
magazine confidently predicted the outcome
of the presidential election that year. It said
that Governor Alfred Landon, the Republican nominee, would easily defeat incumbent
Franklin Roosevelt. Instead, Roosevelt won
in a landslide. He captured more than 60
percent of the popular vote and carried every
State but Maine and Vermont.

The *Digest* had drawn its sample on a faulty
basis: from automobile registration lists and
telephone directories. The *Digest* had failed
to consider that in the mid-Depression year
of 1936, millions of people could not afford to
own cars or have private telephones.

The *Digest* poll failed to reach most of
the vast pool of the poor and unemployed,

---

3  *Poll* comes from the old Teutonic word *polle,* meaning "the top
or crown of the head," the part that shows when heads are
counted.

4  The odd name comes from the fact that a straw, thrown up in
the air, will indicate which way the wind is blowing.

## Background

**EXIT POLLS** On presidential election night, results pour into television and Internet
news sources. Their U.S. maps begin lighting up with red and blue as reporters
"call," or project, a winner in each State—even before most votes are counted. News
sources project winners based largely on exit polls, which are carried out during the
balloting. Interviewers stand outside randomly selected polling places in each State
and interview voters as they leave the polls. They select interviewees at set intervals,
such as every fourth or eighth voter. The exit poll typically asks voters for whom they
voted and why. Pollsters also collect demographic data, such as the gender, race, and
age to analyze voting patterns. To avoid influencing voter turnout, the major news
sources have agreed not to project the winner in a State until the polls close in that
State.

## Answers

**Analyzing Cartoons** The cartoonist is saying that
pollsters do a poor job of predicting future actions or
events.

**222**  Mass Media and Public Opinion

millions of blue-collar workers, and most of the ethnic minorities in the country. Those were the very segments of the population from which Roosevelt and the Democrats drew their greatest support. The magazine had predicted the winner of each of the three previous presidential elections, but its failure to do so in 1936 was so colossal that it ceased publication not long thereafter.

**Scientific Polling** Serious efforts to take the public's pulse on a scientific basis date from the mid-1930s. They began with the work of such early pollsters as George Gallup and Elmo Roper. The techniques that they and others have developed over the decades since then have reached a highly sophisticated level.

There are now more than 1,000 national and regional polling organizations in this country. Many of them do mostly commercial work. That is, they tap the public's preferences on everything from toothpastes and headache remedies to television shows and thousands of other things. However, at least 200 of these polling organizations also poll the political preferences of the American people.

Among the best known of the national pollsters today are the Gallup Organization (the Gallup Poll) and the Pew Research Center for People and the Press.

A number of the leading national polls are joint efforts of major news-gathering and professional polling organizations. Their polls regularly report public attitudes on matters of current interest—including, for example, the level of public support of the President and/or Congress or, in election seasons, candidates running for such major offices as governor or member of the House or Senate. Those joint ventures that can most frequently be found in print and on television and the Internet include the ABC News/*The Washington Post* poll, the CBS News/*The New York Times* poll, the NBC/*The Wall Street Journal* poll, and the CNN/*USA Today*/Gallup poll.

## The Polling Process

Scientific poll-taking is an extremely complex process that can best be described in five basic steps. In their efforts to discover and report public opinion, pollsters must

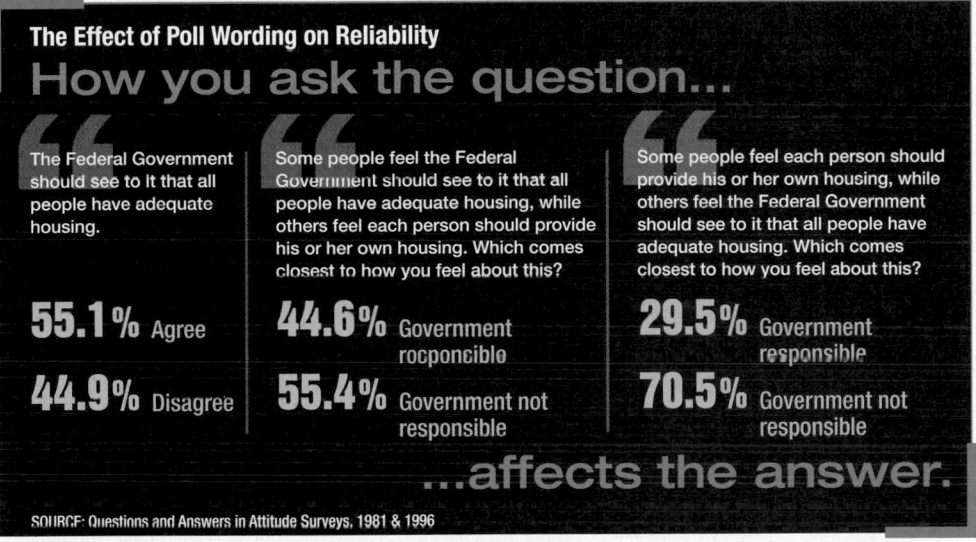

**The Effect of Poll Wording on Reliability**

## How you ask the question...

"The Federal Government should see to it that all people have adequate housing.

**55.1%** Agree

**44.9%** Disagree

"Some people feel the Federal Government should see to it that all people have adequate housing, while others feel each person should provide his or her own housing. Which comes closest to how you feel about this?

**44.6%** Government responsible

**55.4%** Government not responsible

"Some people feel each person should provide his or her own housing, while others feel the Federal Government should see to it that all people have adequate housing. Which comes closest to how you feel about this?

**29.5%** Government responsible

**70.5%** Government not responsible

### ...affects the answer.

SOURCE: Questions and Answers in Attitude Surveys, 1981 & 1996

▸▸ **Analyzing Charts** This chart demonstrates the importance of carefully wording each question in a poll. *Which question is worded in the least biased manner? How can you tell?*

---

# Background

**TRUMAN-DEWEY ELECTION, 1948** When you display the famous photograph of Truman holding up the *Chicago Tribune* with the headline "Dewey Defeats Truman," point out that this was not the only leading publication that relied too heavily on pre-election polls. *The New York Times* had boldly predicted "Thomas E. Dewey's Election as President Is a Foregone Conclusion." The *Life Magazine* cover pictured Dewey with the caption "The Next President of the United States." Polls had shown Dewey ahead by 5 percent to 15 percent. Post-election analysis suggested that the polls had been taken too early, missing the last-minute swing in voter opinion. The erroneous polls might have helped Truman win by making Republicans overconfident and energizing Democratic efforts to get out the vote. The error proved disastrous for the young opinion polling organization, Gallup, which had to work to regain credibility.

---

Ask students if they have ever participated in a poll or if they look at polls online or on television news shows. Point out that, while interesting to a casual viewer, many of these are straw votes that do not accurately measure public opinion. Ask students to explain how scientific polls differ from straw votes. *(The sample in a straw vote is self-selected. It consists of people who decide to call in or email a response to the poll question. Such a sample is not random and so does not represent an accurate cross section of the total population. A scientific poll uses a random sample of the universe, questions that are carefully worded to avoid bias, and an interview process designed to avoid influencing replies.)* Ask: **Why might policymakers care about how a poll is constructed?** *(They want to know the true nature of public opinion and how accurately the poll measures it.)* **How might a poll be misused?** *(A group might intentionally introduce bias into the polling process to create a favorable rating for their candidate or cause.)*

**DISTRIBUTE CORE WORKSHEET**

Distribute the Chapter 8, Section 2 Core Worksheet (Unit 2 All-in-One, page 183), in which students evaluate a poll about voters' concerns prior to the 2008 presidential election. Ask students to study the poll on the worksheet and answer the questions that follow.

## Answers

**Checkpoint** National polls measure the public's preferences for a wide variety of products as well as political preferences.

**Analyzing Charts** possible answer: the first question, because even though the last two questions are the same, their wording produced vastly different results, suggesting bias

Review students' answers to the worksheet, using the following questions to guide the discussion: **Why is it important to know who took the poll?** *(The source is an indicator of the poll's reliability. We can assume that a reputable source, such as Gallup, used scientific methods, whereas a biased source, such as a special interest group, or an unfamiliar source, such as the one on the worksheet, might have skewed the results toward the candidate it favors.)* **Why is the poll's date important?** *(Circumstances may have changed since the poll was taken, making the data no longer relevant.)* **What is the significance of the number of people who responded to the poll?** *(The sample must be large enough to yield results that are statistically accurate within a small margin of error.)* **What information about the respondents is relevant to interpreting poll results?** *(It is important to know if this sample was random and large enough to accurately represent the target universe.)* **Does this seem to be a scientific poll?** *(No, although the questions were rotated to avoid influencing results and it includes enough people for an accurate sampling with a standard margin of error ±3, the source is unfamiliar and may be biased.)* **How might a presidential candidate use this poll?** *(to craft the campaign message to focus on the issues of most concern to voters)*

## DISPLAY TRANSPARENCY

Display Transparency 8E, Truman-Dewey Election, 1948. Point out that the man in the photograph is Harry S. Truman. Explain that this photograph dramatizes a famous case of a newspaper incorrectly predicting the outcome of a presidential race. Although polls had predicted that Dewey would win, Truman in fact became President. Ask: **What does this situation suggest about polls?** *(While they can attempt to make predictions, they can be wrong.)* Discuss whether students themselves are influenced by polls. Then ask: **Are polls good for democracy?** *(Yes, they are useful tools to help candidates and policymakers act based on public opinion; No, they do not reflect thoughtful, nuanced responses and could influence voter turnout at the polls.)*

## Answers

**Checkpoint** The *universe* is the whole population that the poll aims to measure.

✔**Checkpoint**
Who does the *universe* refer to in the polling process?

**sufficient**
*adj.* adequate, enough

**deliberately**
*adv.* on purpose, knowingly, intentionally

(1) define the universe to be surveyed; (2) construct a sample; (3) prepare valid questions; (4) select and control how the poll will be taken; and (5) analyze and report their findings to the public.

**Defining the Universe** The **universe** is a term that means the whole population that the poll aims to measure. It is the group whose opinions the poll will seek to discover. That universe can be all voters in Chicago, or every high school student in Texas, or all Republicans in New England, or all Democrats in Georgia, or all Catholic women over age 35 in the United States, and so on.

**Constructing a Sample** If the universe is very small—say, the 30 members of a high school class—the best way to discover what that entire universe thinks about some matter would be to question all of its members. Most polls involve much larger universes, however—for example, all of the people who live in a particular city or State or the United States. Clearly, each of those universes is so large that it would be impossible to interview all of its members. So pollsters construct a **sample**—a representative slice of the total universe.

Most pollsters draw random samples (often called probability samples). A **random sample** is composed of randomly selected people, and so it is one in which all the members of its universe stand an equal chance of being interviewed. Recall, the sample used for the infamous *Literary Digest* poll in 1936 was not picked at random and so did not accurately reflect the universe it sought to measure.

Most major national polls regularly use samples composed of some 1,500 or so people to represent the nation's adult population (of more than 200 million people) today. How can the views of so few people possibly represent the views of so many?

The answer to that question lies in the mathematical law of probability. Flip a coin a thousand times. The law of probability says that, given an honest coin and an honest flip, heads will come up 500 times. The results of that exercise will be the same no matter how often it is repeated.

The law of probability is regularly applied in any number of situations—by insurance companies to compute life expectancies, by food quality inspectors to grade a farmer's truckload of beans, and by many others who "play the odds," including pollsters when they draw random samples.

In short, if the sample is of sufficient size and is properly selected at random from the entire universe, the law of probability says that the result will be accurate to within a small and predictable margin of error. Mathematicians tell us that a properly drawn random sample of some 1,500 people will reflect the opinions of the nation's entire adult population and be accurate to within a margin of plus or minus (±) 3 percent.

Pollsters agree that it is impossible to construct a sample that would be an absolutely accurate reflection of a large universe. Hence, the allowance for error. A margin of error of ±3 percent means a spread of 6 percentage points, of course. To reduce the sampling error from ±3 percent to ±1 percent, the size of the sample would have to be at least 9,500 people. The time and expense to interview so huge a sample make that impractical.

Some pollsters do use a less complicated, but less reliable, sampling method. They draw quota samples. A **quota sample** is one deliberately constructed to reflect the major characteristics of a given universe.

For example, if 51.3 percent of a universe is female, 17.5 percent of it is African American, and so on, then the quota sample will be made up of 51.3 percent females, 17.5 percent African Americans, and so on. Most of the people in the sample will belong to more than one of the categories used to build the sample. That fact is a major reason why such samples are less reliable than random samples.

**Asking Well-Drawn Questions** The way in which the questions are phrased is critically important to the reliability of any poll. To illustrate that point, most will probably say "yes" to a question put this way: "Should local taxes be reduced?" Many will also answer "yes" if asked this question: "Should the size of the city's police force be increased to fight the rising tide of crime in our community?" Yet, expanding the police force would almost certainly require more local tax dollars.

# Background

**SAMPLING** Up to 1948, polls used quota sampling. Interviewers could choose their respondents, as long as they satisfied quotas for certain characteristics, such as male, female, young, and old. However, the interviewers tended to choose people who were most convenient to interview, introducing bias into the sample. The polling disaster in the Truman-Dewey election of 1948 led to the adoption of sampling based on probability—random sampling. Random sampling takes the choice of respondents out of the hands of humans. For example, telephone polls today typically use random-digit dialing, in which a computer generates phone numbers from known area codes and digits selected by chance. Interviewing every fourth voter leaving the polls is another form of random sampling. Random sampling techniques ensure that all members of the target universe have an equal chance of being selected.

# Questions to Ask About Polls

**GOVERNMENT** ONLINE

For an **interactive** version of Evaluating Polls, visit **PearsonSchool.com/phgovt**

INTERACTIVE

Poll results are often published in newspapers, magazines, or online. You should learn to analyze such results carefully. Use the following questions as a starting point. *Why is it important to read poll results critically?*

| WHO? | WHAT? | HOW? | WHY? | WHEN? |
|---|---|---|---|---|
| **Who is responsible for the poll?** | **What is the poll's universe?** | **How was the sample chosen?** | **Why is the poll being conducted?** | **When was the data collected?** |
| Polls sponsored by political campaigns may aim to mislead as much as inform. | The universe is the population the poll aims to measure. This allows you to judge whether the sample is truly representative. | Samples should be selected randomly. How were questions written and asked? The method of creating and asking questions can alter the results. | Polls meant to boost a candidate's approval ratings are not reliable. | Opinions change quickly during elections—so knowing when the data was collected is important. |

Responsible pollsters recognize the problem and construct their questions with great care. They try to avoid "loaded," emotionally charged words and terms that are difficult to understand. They also try to avoid questions that are worded in a way that tends to shape the answers that will be given to them.

**Interviewing** How pollsters communicate with respondents can also affect accuracy. For decades, most polls were conducted door-to-door, face-to-face. That is, the interviewer questioned the respondent in person. Today, however, most pollsters do their work by telephone, with a sample selected by *random digit dialing*. Calls are placed to randomly chosen numbers within randomly chosen area codes around the country. Telephone surveys are less labor intensive and less expensive than door-to-door polling. Still, most professional pollsters see advantages and drawbacks to each approach. But they all agree that only one technique, not a combination of the two, should be used in any given poll.

The interview itself is a very sensitive point in the process. An interviewer's tone of voice or the emphasis he or she gives to certain words can influence a respondent's replies and so affect the validity of a poll. If the questions are not carefully worded, some of the respondent's replies may be snap judgments or emotional reactions. Others may be answers that the person being interviewed thinks "ought" to be given. Thus, polling organizations try to hire and train their interviewing staffs very carefully.

**Analyzing Findings** Polls, whether scientific or not, try to measure people's attitudes. To be of any real value, however, someone must analyze and report the results. Scientific polling organizations today collect huge amounts of raw data. In order to handle these data, computers and other electronic hardware have become routine parts of the process. Pollsters use these technologies to tabulate and interpret their data, draw their conclusions, and then publish their findings.

## Evaluating Polls

How good are polls? On balance, the major national polls are fairly reliable. So, too, are most of the regional surveys around the country. Still, they are far from perfect. Fortunately,

# How Government Works

**USING PUBLIC OPINION** Franklin Roosevelt was the first President to use polling data. He worked to gain public support for his Lend-Lease program and used private polls to track his progress. John F. Kennedy made polling an essential component of campaign strategy. He worked with Louis Harris (founder of the Harris Poll) in several key areas, including education and religion. When the results of one poll showed that 30 percent of families were sending their children to college while 80 percent hoped to do so, Kennedy incorporated the idea of improved educational opportunities in his campaign speeches. When he found that 30 States strongly opposed his candidacy based on his Roman Catholic upbringing, Kennedy eliminated those States from his campaign schedule, focusing instead on those States where he stood a better chance. Today, nearly all candidates use polls to plan their campaign strategies.

---

Tell students to go to the interactivity to learn more about questions about polls.

**EXTEND THE LESSON**

**L4 Differentiate** Have students use the Internet or other sources to research a recent presidential or other major election. Ask them to write a brief report comparing polling results to the actual outcome of the race.

**L1 L2 Differentiate** Distribute the Extend Activity entitled "Study a Political Poll" (Unit 2 All-in-One, p. 184), which asks students to find the results of a political poll, study the information, and answer questions about it.

**L3 Differentiate** Have students find examples of public opinion polls in newspapers, in news magazines, or on the Internet. Ask them to explain in writing (1) whether the polls are scientific and how they know, (2) what the polls show about public opinion, and (3) who would use these results and for what purpose.

---

## Answers

**Questions to Ask About Polls** Possible response: A poll can contain bias if the pollsters did not follow proper scientific techniques or if the poll was sponsored by an organization that is trying to boost its candidate's approval rating.

# Assess and Remediate

**L3** Collect the Core Worksheet and assess students' work.

**L3** Assign the Section 2 Assessment questions.

**L3** Section Quiz A (Unit 2 All-in-One, p. 185)

**L2** Section Quiz B (Unit 2 All-in-One, p. 186)

Have students complete the review activities in the digital lesson presentation and continue their work in the **Essential Questions Journal.**

## REMEDIATION

| If Your Students Have Trouble With | Strategies For Remediation |
|---|---|
| The different expressions of public opinion (Questions 1, 2, 3, 7) | Have students work in groups of four, and have each student study and give a lesson to the others in his or her group about one of the sections under the heading "Measuring Public Opinion" (elections, interest groups, media, and personal contacts). |
| The role of polls in measuring public opinion (Questions 4, 6) | Have students create a Venn diagram that compares and contrasts the straw vote technique and scientific polling. |
| The process of opinion polling (Question 5) | Have students create an illustrated diagram of the different steps in scientific polling. |

## Answers

**Checkpoint** the intensity, stability, and relevance of the opinions they report

---

**Checkpoint** What do pollsters have difficulty measuring?

most responsible pollsters readily acknowledge the limits of their polls. Many of them are involved in continuing efforts to refine every aspect of the polling process.

Pollsters know that they have difficulty measuring the intensity, stability, and relevance of the opinions they report. *Intensity* is the strength of feeling with which an opinion is held. *Stability* (or fluidity) is the relative permanence or changeableness of an opinion. *Relevance* (or pertinence) is how important a particular opinion is to the person who holds it.

Polls and pollsters are sometimes said to shape the opinions they are supposed to measure. Some critics say that in an election, for example, pollsters often create a "bandwagon effect." That is, some voters, wanting to be with the winner, jump on the bandwagon of the candidate who is ahead in the polls.

In spite of these criticisms, it is clear that scientific polls are the most useful tools there are for the difficult task of measuring public opinion. Although they may not always be precisely accurate, they do offer reasonably reliable guides to public thought. Moreover, they help to focus attention on public questions and to stimulate the discussion of them.

## Limits on the Impact

More than a century ago, the Englishman Lord Bryce described government in the United States as "government by public opinion." Clearly, the energy devoted to measuring public opinion in this country suggests something of its powerful role in American politics. However, Lord Bryce's observation is true only if it is understood to mean that public opinion is the major, but by no means the only, force at work to influence public policy in this country.

Most importantly, remember that our system of constitutional government is not designed to give free, unrestricted play to public opinion—and especially not to majority opinion. In particular, the doctrines of separation of powers and of checks and balances, and the constitutional guarantees of civil rights and liberties are intended to protect minority interests against the excesses of majority views and actions.

Finally, polls are not elections, nor are they substitutes for elections. It is when faced with a ballot that the voter must decide for himself or herself what is important and what is not. He or she must be able to tell the difference between opinions and concrete information, and appreciate the difference between personalities and platforms.

Democracy involves far more than a simple measuring of the various opinions people hold. At base, democracy is all about making careful choices among leaders and their positions on public issues, and among the actions that may flow from those choices.

**Essential Questions Journal** To continue to build a response to the chapter Essential Question, go to your **Essential Questions Journal.**

---

# SECTION 2 ASSESSMENT

1. **Guiding Question** Use your completed table to answer the question: How is public opinion measured and used?

**Key Terms and Comprehension**

2. Why do victorious candidates sometimes claim a **mandate?**

3. Why is it difficult to determine much about public opinion based on the actions of **interest groups?**

4. Why are **straw votes** a generally unreliable form of measuring public opinion?

5. Identify the five steps in the polling process.

**Critical Thinking**

6. **Analyze Information** What are the benefits and drawbacks of releasing to the public the results of public opinion polls on upcoming elections?

7. **Recognize Ideologies** Give an example of how our system of government works to minimize the influence of public opinion on certain types of decisions.

**Quick Write**

**Cause-and-Effect Essay: Research the Topic** Use the Internet and other resources to collect information about the history of the topic you chose in Section 1. Find out when the topic first gained prominence in American social life and what events, trends, or factors have had a significant impact on public opinion about that topic.

226 Mass Media and Public Opinion

---

# Assessment Answers

**1.** Public opinion can be measured through elections and through the opinions put forth by interest groups, the media, and personal contacts, but the most accurate way of measuring public opinion is through polls.

**2.** Candidates claim a mandate when they see their election as a clear statement of public approval of their stands on issues or those of their party.

**3.** It is not always clear how many people are represented by an interest group and how strongly those people hold particular views.

**4.** Straw votes do not use scientifically drawn random samples of the population being studied.

**5.** (1) define the universe, (2) construct a sample, (3) prepare valid questions, (4) select and control how the poll will be taken, (5) analyze and report results

**6.** Possible benefits: encourage voter turnout if the race is tight; focus attention on public questions and stimulate discussion of them. Possible drawbacks: may shape opinions they intend to measure; can create a bandwagon

effect that brings more votes to the candidate who is ahead in the polls; can discourage turnout if people believe the election already has a clear winner

**7.** Possible examples: The 1st Amendment guarantee of freedom of speech and assembly enable minority views to be heard. Also, many government positions are appointed, not elected.

**QUICK WRITE** Students should collect information from reliable sources on their chosen topic.

**226** Mass Media and Public Opinion

# Conducting a Poll

We live in a representative democracy in which the voters elect representatives to act on their behalf. Your school's student government may operate the same way. One way representatives can gain insight into the thoughts and feelings of their constituents—that is, understand public opinion—is to conduct a poll. A well-constructed poll can help provide solid information about what a group of people thinks. Yet putting together a good poll requires knowledge and skill.

Follow these simple steps to conduct an effective poll.

1. **Define the universe.** In polling, the universe is the group of people whose opinion you are interested in learning about. For a presidential candidate, it may be all the voters in the country. For a candidate for student council, it may be all the students in a school, and so on.

2. **Construct your sample.** In some cases, you may be able to poll every person in the universe. If that is not possible, you must identify whom you will poll—your *sample*. Your sample should be a number of people chosen randomly from the universe. The goal is to poll a group that represents the whole universe in its views and attitudes.

Note: The people who volunteer to be polled or who walk by a specific corner of your school or community are not a random sample.

3. **Prepare valid questions.** Good poll questions do not lead people to an answer or convey a strong attitude about an issue. They provide enough information to frame the question properly, but not so much that they promote one response or another. Before you conduct your poll, invite friends or colleagues to review your questions to help ensure their reliability and objectivity.

4. **Conduct interviews carefully.** Just as a pollster must prepare questions carefully, he or she must ask questions carefully. Remember, the goal is to get answers that truly reflect people's attitudes at the time. An interviewer must be careful not to seem to lead respondents to a particular answer.

5. **Interpret the results.** Polls are not perfect. If you have used a random sample, your results will contain a margin of error. When you interpret your results, remember to analyze the intensity, the stability, and the relevance of the opinions you collect.

## ▸▸ What do you think?

1. Why do you think that selecting your sample from volunteers or from a group that passes by a specific hallway or corner might not be a valid random sample?

2. Explain how an interviewer's behavior affects the way people respond to a poll question.

3. **You Try It** Follow the steps laid out here, and design a public opinion poll about an issue in your school or community with detailed descriptions of the universe, how you will construct your sample, and what questions you will ask.

**GOVERNMENT ONLINE**
**Citizenship Activity Pack**
For activities on conducting polls, go to
**PearsonSchool.com/phgovt**

227

## Citizenship Activity Pack

**L1** **L2** If your students need extra support, use the Citizenship Activity Pack lesson *How to Conduct a Poll.* It includes a lesson plan, assessment rubrics, a student survey, and a poster with examples of forced-choice, scaled, and ranked questions. Students may also access the Citizenship Activity Pack online for activities on How to Conduct a Poll at **PearsonSchool.com/phgovt.**

## LESSON GOAL

- Students will analyze the process for constructing and conducting an opinion poll.

# Teach

### READ

Have students read the introduction aloud. If students have computer access, you may have them search for more about scientific polling.

### DISCUSS

Have students discuss ways to create a random sample. *(Methods might include interviewing every fourth student entering the school or scrambling a list of all students and choosing every tenth name.)* Ask students how the wording of questions might lead people to respond in a particular way. *(Questions might not provide proper context or might include "loaded" language that creates an emotional response. For example, people tend to react more negatively to "bureaucrat" than to "public servant.")*

### IDENTIFY LIMITS OF POLLS

Ask: **What is margin of error?** *(It is the mathematical range within which a poll result might vary from the actual result. For example, a poll with a margin of error of plus or minus 3 is expected to be no more than 3 percent higher or lower than the actual opinion of the universe.)* Have students describe the proper way to use polls. *(Polls are estimates, not perfect measures. They can focus attention on public questions and help politicians plan campaign strategy and craft public policy.)*

# Assess and Remediate

Collect and assess student plans for a public opinion poll. Have students answer the What Do You Think questions.

## Answers

1. In both of these cases, not all members of the universe have an equal chance of being interviewed. People who ask to be interviewed are self-selecting. A specific location excludes people who do not routinely use that hallway.

2. An interviewer's tone of voice or the emphasis given to certain words can influence replies.

3. A strong plan will include an accurate definition of the universe, a means of obtaining a random sample, and well-crafted questions.

## How has the development of different media helped inform the public about politics?

| Newspapers | Magazines | Radio |
|---|---|---|
| • America's first regular newspaper 1704<br>• first daily newspaper 1783<br>• today more than 10,000<br>• daily newspapers declining for decades<br>• most now local | • into early 1900s, mostly literature and social graces<br>• first political magazines mid-1800s<br>• muckraking early 1900s<br>• only national medium before radio and television<br>• most today trade or personal interest | • began 1920<br>• by 1930s major entertainment medium<br>• convenient availability helped it survive arrival of television<br>• satellite radio receives signals nationwide<br>• most local<br>• some all-news stations<br>• talk radio—political comment |

| Television | The Internet |
|---|---|
| • boomed in 1950s<br>• early 1960s replaced newspapers as main source of political information<br>• now main news source for 80 percent of population<br>• independent broadcasting, cable, PBS | • roots in Defense Department Cold War research<br>• by early 2000s mass medium<br>• now second to television as source of political news<br>• almost all government and political organizations have sites<br>• weblogs usually devoted to specific subject<br>• podcasts—downloadable digital recordings |

## SKILLS DEVELOPMENT

### DIGITAL AGE LITERACY

To practice digital age literacy in this section, use the Chapter 8 Skills Worksheet (Unit 2 All-in-One, p. 194). You may teach the skill explicitly either before or after discussing the role of electronic media in politics. For L2 and L1 students, assign the adapted Skill Activity (Unit 2 All-in-One, p. 195).

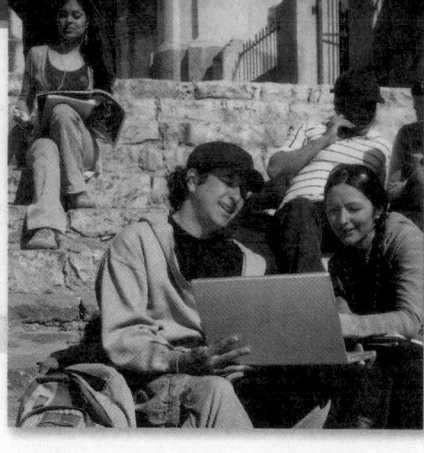

### SECTION 3

# The Mass Media

### Guiding Question

**How has the development of different media helped inform the public about politics?** Use the flowchart like the one below to take notes on the development of different media.

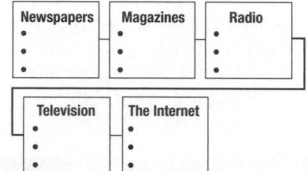

### Political Dictionary
- medium
- weblog
- public agenda
- sound bite

### Objectives
1. Examine the role of the mass media in providing the public with political information.
2. Explain how the mass media influence politics.
3. Understand the factors that limit the influence of the media.

**Image Above:** People get their news from various media outlets, such as the Internet.

How much television do you watch each day? Little or none? Two hours a day? Three hours? More? However much you watch, you no doubt know that your peers spend a great deal of time in front of the TV. Studies show that by the time the average student graduates from high school today, he or she will have spent nearly 11,000 hours in classrooms and nearly 15,000 hours watching television. On average, high school students now watch more than 20 hours of TV programming each week.

Television has an extraordinary impact on the lives of everyone in this country. So do all of the other elements of the mass media.

### The Role of Mass Media

A **medium** is a means of communication; it transmits some kind of information. *Media* is the plural of medium. The *mass media* include those means of communication that can reach large, widely dispersed audiences simultaneously.

Five major elements of the mass media are especially significant in American politics today. Ranked in terms of their impact, they are television, the Internet, newspapers, radio, and magazines. Other forms of the media, including books, films, and satellite radio, play a lesser but still relevant role in the political process.

Importantly, the mass media do not function as an arm of government in the United States. They are, instead, almost entirely privately owned and operated. And, unlike political parties and interest groups, their prime goal is *not* that of influencing the course of public affairs. They are, nonetheless, an extremely potent force in American politics.

Along with entertainment, the media provide political information. They do so directly when they report the news, in a television newscast or in the news columns of a newspaper, for example. The media also provide a large amount of political information less directly—for example, in radio and television programs, magazine articles, and blogs. These venues often deal with such public topics as crime, healthcare, climate change, or some aspect of American foreign policy. Either way, people acquire most of what they know about government and politics from the various forms of media.

## Focus on the Basics

**FACTS:** • The public gets information on issues of public interest through the mass media—television, newspapers, radio, magazines, and the Internet. • The media influence the public agenda by focusing attention on certain issues and helping candidates appeal directly to voters. • The media influence is limited because of limited coverage of public affairs.

**CONCEPTS:** democratic values, rights and responsibilities of citizenship

**ENDURING UNDERSTANDINGS:** • Mass media influence the public agenda and electoral politics. • To be informed, citizens must seek out in-depth coverage of public affairs.

**Television** Politics and television have gone hand in hand since the technology first appeared. The first public demonstration of television occurred at the New York World's Fair in 1939. President Franklin Roosevelt opened the fair on camera, and a <u>comparative</u> handful of local viewers watched him do so on tiny five- and seven-inch screens.

World War II interrupted the development of the new medium, but it began to become generally available in the late 1940s. Television boomed in the 1950s. The first transcontinental broadcast came in 1951, when President Harry Truman, speaking in Washington, D.C., addressed the delegates attending the Japanese Peace Treaty Conference in San Francisco.

Today, television is <u>all-pervasive.</u> As you read earlier, there is at least one television set in 98 percent of the nation's 115 million households. Just a few years ago, there were more homes in this country with television sets than with indoor plumbing facilities!

Television replaced newspapers as the principal source of political information for a majority of Americans in the early 1960s. Now, television is the principal source of news for an estimated 80 percent of the population.

The more than 1,700 television stations in this country include more than 1,400 commercial outlets and some 350 public broadcasters. Three major national networks have dominated television from its infancy: the Columbia Broadcasting System (CBS), the American Broadcasting Company (ABC), and the National Broadcasting Company (NBC). Those three giants furnish most of the programming for more than 500 local stations, and that programming accounts for nearly half of all television viewing time today.

The major networks' audience share has declined over recent years, however. Their main challenges have come from three general sources: (1) the 24/7 programming of cable broadcasters—notably, Turner Broadcasting's Cable News Network (CNN) and the Fox Network, (2) the Internet, and, to a lesser extent, (3) the Public Broadcasting System (PBS) and its more than 350 local television stations.[5]

**Newspapers** The first regularly published newspaper in America, the *Boston News-Letter,* appeared in 1704.[6] Other papers soon followed, in Boston and then in Philadelphia, New York, Annapolis, and elsewhere. By 1775, 37 newspapers were being published

✔ **Checkpoint**
What is the principal news source for the majority of Americans?

**comparative**
*adj.* by comparison

**all-pervasive**
*adj.* spread throughout

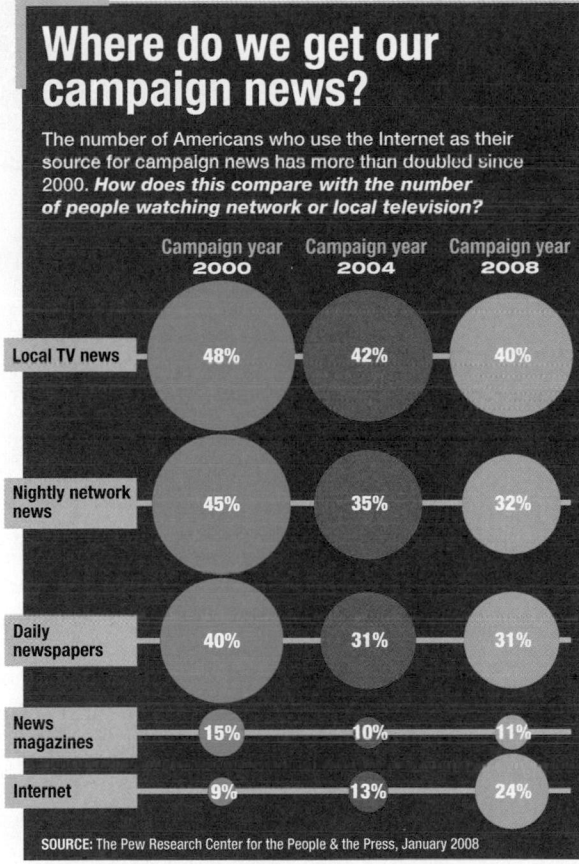

**Where do we get our campaign news?**

The number of Americans who use the Internet as their source for campaign news has more than doubled since 2000. *How does this compare with the number of people watching network or local television?*

| | Campaign year 2000 | Campaign year 2004 | Campaign year 2008 |
|---|---|---|---|
| Local TV news | 48% | 42% | 40% |
| Nightly network news | 45% | 35% | 32% |
| Daily newspapers | 40% | 31% | 31% |
| News magazines | 15% | 10% | 11% |
| Internet | 9% | 13% | 24% |

**SOURCE:** The Pew Research Center for the People & the Press, January 2008

---

5 C-SPAN, the Cable-Satellite Public Affairs Network, is sponsored by the cable industry. C-SPAN, C-SPAN2, and C-SPAN3 cover a broad range of public events—including major floor debates and committee hearings in Congress, presidential and other press conferences, and speeches by notable public figures.
6 The world's first newspaper was almost certainly the *Acta Diurna,* a daily gazette in Rome dating from 59 B.C. Another very early forerunner of today's newspapers was *Tsing Pao,* a court journal in Beijing. Press historians believe that its first issues, printed from stone blocks, were published beginning in A.D. 618; its last issue appeared in 1911.

# Get Started

## LESSON GOALS
Students will . . .

- understand the impact of the Internet as a political medium by examining study findings.
- evaluate the use of the Internet for electoral politics by analyzing a candidate's Web site.
- recognize the strengths of the Internet as a campaign medium by designing a home page for a candidate's Web site.

## BEFORE CLASS
Assign the section, the graphic organizer in the text, and the Reading Comprehension Worksheet (Unit 2 All-in-One, p. 187) before class.

**L2 Differentiate** Reading Comprehension Worksheet (Unit 2 All-in-One, p. 189)

## BELLRINGER
Display Transparency 8F, The Internet and the 2008 Election at a Glance. Explain that this table lists key findings in a research study. Have students examine the findings and answer the question in their notebook.

**L3 L4 Differentiate** Have students do research to find out how online donations affected the 2008 presidential campaign, and write a brief report.

---

# Differentiated Resources

The following resources are located in the All-in-One, Unit 2, Chapter 8, Section 3:

- **L3** Reading Comprehension Worksheet (p. 187)
- **L2** Reading Comprehension Worksheet (p. 189)
- **L3 L2** Core Worksheets (pp. 191, 192)
- **L3** Skills Worksheet (p. 194)
- **L2** Skill Activity (p. 195)
- **L3 L4** Extend Worksheet (p. 196)
- **L3** Quiz A (p. 198)   **L2** Quiz B (p. 199)
- **L3** Chapter Test A (p. 200)   **L2** Chapter Test B (p. 203)

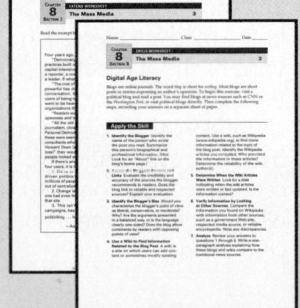

---

# Answers
**Checkpoint** television

**Where do we get our campaign news?** Local and network television have both declined as a source for campaign news since 2000 but still exceed the Internet.

To present this topic using online resources, use the lesson presentations at **PearsonSchool.com/phgovt.**

### REVIEW BELLRINGER RESPONSES

Invite students to offer their response to the Bellringer question: **If you were a candidate for President, how would you apply the results of this study to your campaign?** *(possible responses: create a very attractive Web site; include lots of opportunities for citizens to interact with the site and express their opinions; include videos of television appearances and audio clips of speeches; include an easy way to donate online; collect e-mail addresses of visitors and send them regular e-mail updates; encourage site visitors to volunteer to work for the campaign; constantly update the site with campaign news and documents supporting the candidate's positions; sponsor conversations about issues on social networking sites)*

Point out that the Internet has drawbacks for campaigns as well. If a candidate makes a political mistake, the news will spread widely and quickly over the Internet. Also, rumors spread quickly online, so campaigns must closely monitor online chatter and respond to negative posts quickly.

## Answers

**The Power of the Press** Possible response: Yes; Tabloids use dramatic headlines and sensational stories with only a loose connection to facts.

## The Power of the Press

The phrase "yellow journalism" was born in the late 1800s when competing newspaper owners William Randolph Hearst and Joseph Pulitzer used dramatic headlines, news photos, and editorials instead of factual reporting to stir up public opinion in favor of war with Spain—and to sell more papers. Historians say that "nothing better illustrates the power of the press and the misuse of that power" as well as the Spanish-American War. ***Does yellow journalism exist today?***

### "You furnish the pictures . . . I'll furnish the war."

—William Randolph Hearst, 1897

in the colonies. All of them were weekly papers, and they were printed on one sheet that was usually folded to make four pages. The nation's first daily newspaper, the *Pennsylvania Evening Post and Daily Advertiser,* began publication in 1783.

Those first papers regularly carried political news. Several spurred the colonists to revolution, carrying the news of independence and the text of the Declaration of Independence to people throughout the colonies. Thomas Jefferson marked the vital role of the press in the earliest years of the nation when, in 1787, he wrote to a friend:

> ### PRIMARY SOURCE
> . . . were it left to me to decide whether we should have a government without newspapers or newspapers without a government, I should not hesitate a moment to prefer the latter.
>
> —Thomas Jefferson, Letter to Colonel Edward Carrington, January 16, 1787

The 1st Amendment, added to the Constitution in 1791, made the same point regarding the importance of newspapers with its guarantee of the freedom of the press.

Today, nearly 10,000 newspapers are published in the United States, including some 1,300 dailies, more than 7,000 weeklies and 500 semiweeklies, and several hundred foreign-language papers. They have a combined circulation of more than 140 million copies per issue. More than 40 percent of the nation's adult population reads a newspaper every day, and they spend, on average, a half hour doing so.

The number of daily newspapers has been declining for decades, however, from more than 2,000 in 1920 to 1,745 in 1980 and 1,480 in 2000, to just about 1,300 today. Radio and television, and more recently the Internet, have been major factors in that downward trend.

Nevertheless, newspapers are still an important source of information about government and politics. Most papers cover stories in greater depth than television does, and many try to present various points of view

## Background

**CAMPAIGN MISINFORMATION** The strategic use of rumors, half-truths, and outright falsehoods has long been part of political campaigns. Political organizations unleash barrages of "attack ads"—strongly negative comments about an opponent placed in the media. Often such ads turn out to be less than truthful. Yet multiple repetitions of the accusations, accompanied by powerful images, influence many voters. In the 2008 campaign, a new trend emerged. The media increasingly reported on the truthfulness of political statements made in debates, speeches, interviews, and ads, based on evaluations by nonpartisan organizations. Many sites devoted to debunking campaign assertions appeared on the Web. In some cases, politicians backed down when their statements proved false. Still, powerful attack ads can overshadow the corrections.

in their editorial sections. Those newspapers that have the most substantial reputations and national influence today include *The New York Times, The Washington Post, The Wall Street Journal,* and *USA Today.*

Most newspapers are local papers. That is, most of their readers live in or near the communities in which those papers are published. While many local papers do provide some national and international news coverage, most of them focus on events closer to home.

Advances in telecommunications and computerized operations are changing that basic fact, however. Now, each day's editions of *USA Today, The New York Times,* and *The Wall Street Journal* are generally available on the day of publication around the country.

**Radio** Radio as it exists today began in 1920. On November 2 of that year, station KDKA in Pittsburgh went on the air with presidential election returns. The new medium soon became immensely popular.

By the 1930s, radio had assumed much of the role in American society that television has today. It was a major entertainment medium, and millions of people planned their daily schedules around their favorite programs. The networks also provided the nation with dramatic coverage of important events, and radio exposed the American people to national and international politics as never before.

President Franklin Roosevelt was the first major public figure to use radio effectively. The late author David Halberstam described the impact of FDR's famous fireside chats:

**PRIMARY SOURCE**

❝ He was the first great American radio voice. For most Americans of [that] generation, their first memory of politics would be of sitting by a radio and hearing that voice, strong, confident, totally at ease. . . . Most Americans in the previous 160 years had never even seen a President; now almost all of them were hearing him, in their own homes. It was literally and figuratively electrifying. ❞

—David Halberstam, *The Powers That Be*

Many thought that the arrival of television would bring the end of radio as a major medium. Radio has survived, however, in large part because it is so conveniently available. People can hear music, news, sports, and other radio programs in a great many places where they cannot watch television—in their cars, at work, in remote areas, and in any number of other places and situations. The arrival of satellite radio has added to radio's popularity. With this new technology, digital radio signals are beamed from a communications satellite, allowing subscribers to tune in to their favorite station anywhere in the country, and often with no commercial interruptions.

Radio remains a major source of news and other political information. The average person hears some 15 hours of radio each week. No one knows how many millions of radios there are in this country—in homes, offices, cars, backpacks, and a great many other places. Those radios can pick up some 14,000 stations on the AM and FM dials.

Many AM stations are affiliated with one or another of the national networks. Unlike television, however, most radio programming is local. There are also some 700 public radio stations, most of them on the FM dial. These noncommercial outlets are part of National Public Radio (NPR), which is radio's counterpart of television's PBS.

Most radio stations spend little time on public affairs today. Many do devote a few minutes every hour to "the news"—really, to a series of headlines. All-news stations are now found in most of the larger and many medium-sized communities. They are usually on the air 24 hours a day, and they do provide somewhat more extensive coverage of the day's events. A growing number of stations now serve the preferences of Latino Americans, African Americans, and other minority listeners.

Over recent years, talk radio has become an important source of political comment. The opinions and analyses offered by a number of talk show hosts can be found on hundreds of stations across the United States. Among the most prominent talk broadcasters today are conservatives Rush Limbaugh, Sean Hannity, and Bill O'Reilly, and liberals Thom Hartmann and Rachel Maddow. Their

**ANALYZE A CANDIDATE WEB SITE**

Display Transparency 8G, Candidate Web Site, which shows a page from a candidate's Web site during an election campaign. Barack Obama was the first candidate to use the Internet as an effective media resource, setting the standard for future campaigns to follow. This site also makes use of the Internet as an effective media resource. Ask: **What forms of media does this candidate use to reach voters?** *(The Web site offers video clips, photographs, speeches, written information about issues in Spanish as well as English, an e-mail link, biographies, YouTube, blog, and a link for making a contribution.)* Discuss how this site illustrates ways in which the Internet can be used to help a candidate get elected. *(It is a campaign Web site, with the purpose of influencing voters. At the Hot Topics link, the candidate could educate voters about his position on issues. The photos and links to biographical information about himself, his wife, and his running mate would help site visitors relate to them as people. The site includes ways for visitors to participate by e-mail, on the blog, or through contributions.)*

Ask: **What characteristics of the Internet make it an effective medium for electoral politics?** *(The Internet is a mass medium that can spread the candidate's message widely and quickly. Unlike television or the radio, the content remains available online for visitors to access at their convenience, and can be updated constantly. The Internet also offers a convenient, inexpensive way to solicit donations and identify supporters.)*

# Background

**EVALUATING WEB PAGES** Barack Obama's use of the Internet is being hailed as a key tool in his successful presidential campaign. As students' use of the Internet continues to grow, the skills to critically evaluate Web pages become more important. Cornell University offers Jim Kapoun's "Five Criteria for Evaluating Web Pages." The questions to ask include: What is the purpose of the document and why was it produced? What institution publishes the document? What opinions (if any) are expressed by the author? When was it produced? Is the information presented cited correctly? Who wrote the page, and can you contact him or her? Does the publisher list his or her qualifications? Learning to ask the right questions about Web pages can help students find the best of what the Internet has to offer.

Distribute the Chapter 8 Section 3 Core Worksheet (Unit 2 All-in-One, p. 191), which provides guidelines for students to design a home page for a candidate's Web site, aimed at reaching today's voter. At the same time, distribute the Rubric for Assessing the Design of a Web Site (Unit 2 All-in-One, p. 259).

**L2 L1 Differentiate** For these students, distribute the adapted Chapter 8 Section 3 Core Worksheet (Unit 2 All-in-One, p. 192), which is a simplified version and which gives step-by-step guidance.

## Answers

**The Transformation of Mass Media** The Internet has enabled anyone to join the political discussion.

**232** Mass Media and Public Opinion

---

programs air nationally and attract millions of listeners every weekday.

**Magazines** Several magazines were published in colonial America. Benjamin Franklin began one of the very first, his *General Magazine*, in Philadelphia in 1741. On into the early 1900s, most magazines published in the United States were generally devoted to literature and the social graces. The first political magazines—among them, *Harper's Weekly* and the *Atlantic Monthly*—appeared in the mid-1800s.

The progressive reform period in the early 1900s spawned several journals of opinion, including a number that featured articles by the day's leading muckrakers.[7] For decades before radio and television, magazines constituted the only national medium.

Some 12,000 magazines are published in the United States today. Most are trade publications, such as *Veterinary Forum* and the *Automotive Executive*, or periodicals that target some special personal interest, such as *Golf Digest*, *Teen*, and *American Rifleman*. Among magazines with the highest circulation today: *AARP the Magazine*, *Reader's Digest*, and *National Geographic*. They each sell some 10 to 20 million or more copies per issue.

Three news magazines, *Time*, *Newsweek*, and *U.S. News & World Report*, rank in the top 35 periodicals in terms of circulation. They have a combined circulation of nearly 10 million copies a week, and they are important sources of political news and comment. There are a number of other magazines devoted to public affairs, most of them vehicles of opinion, including the *Nation*, the *New Republic*, the *National Review*, and the *Weekly Standard*.

**The Internet** The Internet is fast becoming a leading source of political news and information for the American people. Its roots can be traced to a Defense Department research project of the Cold War era. In 1969, the DoD's Advanced Research Projects Agency established a four-computer network in the

---

7 The *muckrakers* were journalists who exposed wrongdoing in politics, business, and industry. The term was coined by Theodore Roosevelt in 1906 and is derived from the raking of muck—that is, manure and other barnyard debris. The muckrakers set the pattern for what is now called investigative reporting.

# The Transformation of Mass Media

As media have changed, so too has the way that people participate. *What has been the impact of the Internet on political discussion?*

**Radio** spread widely in the 1920s and 1930s, giving a national voice to elected officials and gifted speakers.

The "big three" networks, ABC, CBS, and NBC, dominated the limited channels of early television. Nightly news programs by respected anchors, such as Walter Cronkite (right), commanded large audiences and set the agenda for the nation.

THEN... A Few Voices Imparting Information

## Constitutional Principles

**LIMITED GOVERNMENT AND A FREE PRESS** Freedom of the press—and of all media—is at the very heart of the American system of limited government. Its roots extend back even to colonial times. In 1735, John Peter Zenger was arrested in New York for printing strong political opinions. He was put on trial, but the jury of local New Yorkers found him not guilty. The trial marked a major moment in the development of a free press.

Today, for the first time in history, a single person, with a minimal investment, can put his or her views out, not only before the local populace but before the entire world. Some individuals have formed Internet news services that provide specialized information instantaneously about politics, weather, the stock market, sports, and entertainment. In addition to the print and broadcast media, the world now has a third branch of the press—the online service.

Pentagon designed to protect military secrets from hostile actions. Two years later that grid (ARPANET) had grown to include some two dozen computers at 15 widely scattered locations across the country.

From those beginnings, the Internet has grown phenomenally, and it continues to do so. By the 1990s, it had expanded into the private sector, and by the beginning of the 21st century, it had become a mass medium. Today, more than 75 percent of the American people report that they have access to a computer at home, in the workplace, or at school, and nearly two-thirds of them say they go online on a regular basis.

Television remains the most widely used source for political news and information, but the Internet is now in second place, ahead of newspapers, radio, and magazines. One of every four people say they regularly go online to "get the news." Younger people are especially <u>inclined</u> to do so.

Other media have recognized the Internet's capabilities. Nearly all newspapers have Web sites where all or most of the stories carried in their print versions can be found. Most magazines are also available online, and most television stations maintain home pages that provide links to many other sources. With only a few exceptions, media outlets allow visitors to view their Web sites free of charge.

Much the same can be said of virtually all government agencies, interest groups, political parties, elected officials, and candidates' campaign organizations. The extraordinary range of printed, audio, and visual information available on the Internet really defies description. To the point, much of the updated factual content of this textbook has been drawn from reliable Internet sources.

The Internet has <u>spawned</u> the growth of **weblogs**—"blogs"—Web site postings usually devoted to some specific subject. There were some 12,000 active blogs in 2000 and more than 141 million by 2010. Most are written by single authors, some have several contributors, and many allow visitors to add comments. Those devoted to public affairs typically feature links to a variety of sources. Podcasts, digital recordings that are posted and can be downloaded from the Internet, have also grown spectacularly over recent years.

**✔ Checkpoint**
What are weblogs?

**spawned**
*v.* produced, brought forth

**inclined**
*adj.* more likely, tend toward

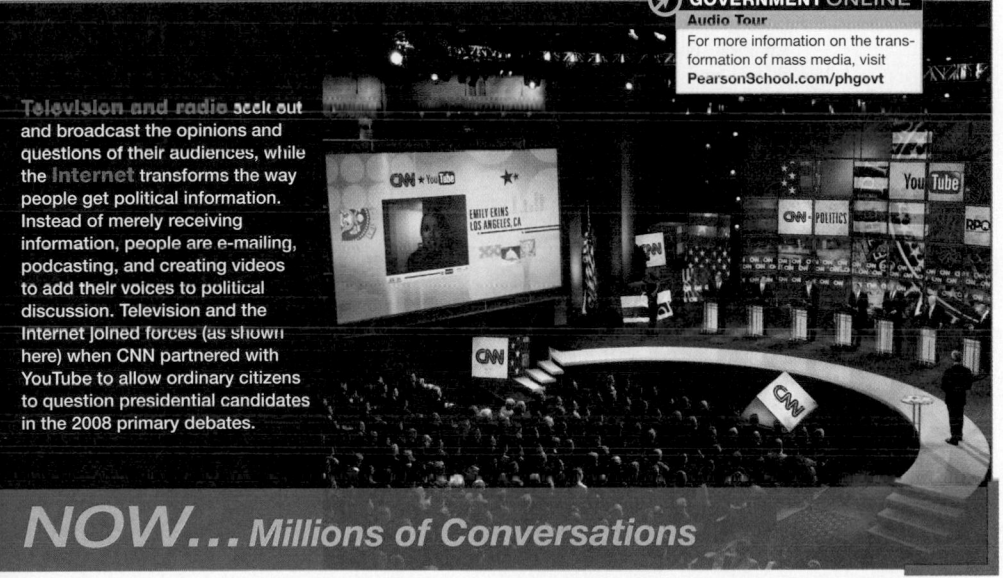

**🔊 GOVERNMENT** ONLINE
**Audio Tour**
For more information on the transformation of mass media, visit PearsonSchool.com/phgovt

Television and radio seek out and broadcast the opinions and questions of their audiences, while the Internet transforms the way people get political information. Instead of merely receiving information, people are e-mailing, podcasting, and creating videos to add their voices to political discussion. Television and the Internet joined forces (as shown here) when CNN partnered with YouTube to allow ordinary citizens to question presidential candidates in the 2008 primary debates.

**NOW... Millions of Conversations**

# Background

**MEDIA INFLUENCE** According to a study published by the Annenberg Public Policy Center in late 2008, many Americans were unable to identify the stands that major party candidates took on various issues such as abortion, free trade, the Iraq War, and children's health insurance. It appeared that not much education about the candidates' positions had taken place in the election campaign. Interestingly, in 2004 a similar study found that people who watched late-night comedy shows such as those hosted by David Letterman, Jay Leno, and Jon Stewart knew more about the candidates and their positions than those who did not watch such programs. Young viewers of the Daily Show with Jon Stewart scored particularly well on campaign knowledge—even better than young people who watched network news programs, and just as well as those who watched cable news programs or read newspapers.

## DESIGN A HOME PAGE

Tell students that they will create a pencil-and-paper version of a home page for an imaginary candidate for President. Point out that a home page is the gateway to the rest of the information on the Web site. They will not create the entire site content. Instead, they will decide the kinds of content they would include, so they can provide links to it on their home page. Remind them that Web sites can include a range of media—video clips, sound files, in-depth articles, photos, even campaign-related music and ring tones. Explain that their goal is to attract support—and ultimately votes—for their candidate.

As a first step, have students discuss ideas for Web site content with a partner to help them create their content list on the worksheet. Explain that they should create links on their home page to each piece of site content on their list. Circulate to offer suggestions and refocus student effort as needed. Remind students to consult their Web site home page rubrics for guidance as they move on to designing their home page.

Part 2 of the worksheet asks students to write a memo that explains the thinking behind their home page design. In their memo, students should describe the content visitors would find when they follow each link.

**L4 Differentiate** Have students choose two links on their home page and create a content page that would appear on visitors' screens when they follow each of these links.

Tell students to go to the Audio Tour for more information on the transformation of mass media.

## Answers

**Checkpoint** Weblogs are Web site postings usually devoted to some specific subject that may be written by one or many contributors. Many allow visitors to post comments.

## REVIEW HOME PAGE DESIGNS AND MEMOS

Have students post their home page designs at their desks or on a bulletin board or wall, along with their memos explaining their design and links to site content. Then have students move through the classroom reviewing each other's work.

## SHARE STUDENT REACTION

After students have had an opportunity to review their classmates' efforts, have them identify examples that seemed especially impressive and explain why. For example, did the home page include a clear, compelling message about the candidate? Did it link to information presented in a variety of media forms? Did the home page make them want to follow the links to learn more about the candidate?

## INTERNET GROWTH

Display Transparency 8H, U.S. IP and Internet Traffic Projection. Point out what the text says about the American people's online computer use. In addition, point out that a phenomenal growth of use and data traffic is projected to take place in the near future. Analysts predict that by 2015 there will be an "exaflood"—or a tsunami of bytes—of IP (an Internet protocol address of devices participating in computer networks) and Internet traffic. The flood could even reach one million million billion bytes. (Byte is the lowest familiar size for measuring data, such as one character. Measurements of kilobytes, where one kilobyte equals 1,024 bytes, are probably most familiar.) Look at the scale. Consider that the size of a student's ten-page research paper e-mailed to school is approximately only 86 kilobytes. Consider then that one photo from a digital camera can equal 3 megabytes of Internet traffic. Have students examine the graph now. Then hypothesize what possible uses could cause the growth. *(faster, bigger games; TV shows; videos; digital publishing)*

## Answers

**Media Influence** Possible response: The first cartoon suggests that popular talk show hosts have as much political influence as both houses of Congress. The second cartoon suggests that listeners tend to "parrot," or repeat, the political opinions they hear on the radio.

# Media Influence

The mass media have a great impact on the issues that people focus on and how they think about the world around them. *What do these cartoons say about media influence?*

"That's not my political opinion. That's just stuff I hear on the radio."

## The Media and Politics

Clearly, the media play a significant role in American politics. Just how significant that role is, and just how much influence the media have, is the subject of a long, still unsettled debate.

Whatever its weight, the media's influence can be seen in any number of situations. It is most visible in two particular areas: (1) the public agenda and (2) the field of electoral politics.

**The Public Agenda** The media play a very large role in shaping the **public agenda,** the societal problems that the nation's political leaders and the general public agree need government attention. As they report and comment on events, issues, policies, and personalities, the media determine to a very large extent what public matters the people will think and talk about—and, so, those matters about which public-policy makers will be most concerned.

Put another way, the media have the power to focus the public's attention on a specific issue. They do so by emphasizing some things and downplaying others. For example, they feature certain items on the front page or at the top of the newscast and bury others in the latter pages or segments of the program.

It is not correct to say that the media tell the people *what* to think; but it is clear that they tell the people what to think *about.* A look at any issue of a daily newspaper or a quick review of the content of any television or Internet news story will demonstrate that point. Remember, people rely on the media for most of the information they receive on public issues.

The mass media also have a direct impact on the nation's leaders. Some years ago, Stephen Hess, a widely respected authority on the media, identified several news organizations that form the "inner ring" of influence in Washington, D.C. He cited the three major television networks, CBS, ABC, and NBC; three newspapers, *The New York Times, The Washington Post,* and *The Wall Street Journal;* the leading news wire service, the Associated Press (AP); and the three major news weeklies, *Time, Newsweek,* and *U.S. News & World Report.* CNN, MSNBC, Fox News, Reuters, and *USA Today* have since joined that select group.

Top political figures in and out of government pay close and continuing attention to these sources. In fact, the President receives a daily digest of the news reports, analyses, and editorial comments that these and other sources broadcast and publish.

**Electoral Politics** You have seen several illustrations of the media's importance in electoral politics as you have read this book. Recall, for example, the fact that the media, and in particular television, have contributed to a decline in the place of political parties in American politics.

Television has made candidates far less dependent on party organizations than they once were. Before television, the major parties generally dominated the election process. They recruited most candidates who ran for office, and they ran those candidates' campaigns. The candidates depended on party organizations in order to reach the voters.

Now, both television and the Internet allow candidates to appeal directly to the people, without the help of a party organization. Candidates for office need not be experienced politicians who have worked their way up a party's political ladder over the course of several elections. It is not unusual for candidates to assemble their own campaign organizations and operate with only loose connections to their political parties.

Remember, too, that how voters see a candidate—the impressions they have of that candidate's personality, character, abilities, and so on—is one of the major factors that influence voting behavior. Candidates and professional campaign managers are quite aware of this fact. They know that the kind of "image" a candidate projects in the media can have a telling effect on the outcome of an election.

Candidates regularly try to manipulate media coverage to their advantage. Campaign strategists understand that, even with the Internet, most people learn almost everything they know about a candidate from

television. They therefore plan campaigns that emphasize television exposure. Such technical considerations as timing, location, lighting, and camera angles loom large, often at the expense of such substantive matters as the issues involved in an election or a candidate's qualifications for public office.

Good campaign managers also know that most television news programs are built out of stories that (1) take no more than a minute or two of air time, and (2) show people doing something interesting or exciting. Newscasts seldom feature "talking heads," speakers who drone on and on about some complex issue.

Instead, newscasts featuring candidates are usually short, sharply focused **sound bites**—snappy reports that can be aired in 30 or 45 seconds or so. Staged and carefully orchestrated visits to historic sites, factory gates, toxic-waste dumps, football games, and the like, have become a standard part of the electoral scene.

## Limits on Media Influence

Having said all this, it is all too easy to overstate the media's role in American politics. A number of built-in factors work to limit the media's impact on the behavior of the American voting public.

For one thing, few people follow international, national, or even local political events very closely. Many studies of voting behavior show that in the typical election, only about 10 percent of those who can vote and only about 15 percent of those who do vote are well informed on the many candidates and issues involved in that election. In short, only a small part of the public actually takes in and understands much of what the media have to say about public affairs.

Moreover, most people who do pay some attention to politics are likely to be selective about it. That is, they most often watch, listen to, and read those sources that generally agree with their own viewpoints. They regularly ignore those sources with which they disagree. Thus, for example, many Democrats do not watch the televised campaign appearances or visit the Web sites of Republican candidates. Nor do many Republicans

✓ **Checkpoint**
How do candidates use media coverage to their advantage?

**L3 Differentiate** Separate the class into three groups, with one group representing television, one newspapers, and one news magazines. Choose a story currently receiving broad media coverage and ask one group to watch coverage on three television news programs, one to read coverage in three different newspapers, and one to read coverage in three different news magazines. As a group, have students compare coverage in the various media.

**L2 ELL Differentiate** Have students prepare a two-page "Guide for Using the Mass Media to Find Out About Public Issues" that would be useful to a newcomer to the United States. Ask them to include the names of newspapers, magazines, and TV and radio networks available locally. The guide should provide brief descriptions of what each source offers relating to public issues.

**L3 L4 Differentiate** Distribute the Chapter 8 Section 3 Extend Worksheet (Unit 2 All-in-One, p. 196), which includes an excerpt from an article about the impact of the Internet on American politics. Have students read the article and then answer the reflection questions. As a class, discuss the answers. You may also wish to have students collect data and write a brief report on the use of the Internet in the most recent presidential election.

# Teacher-to-Teacher Network

**ALTERNATE LESSON PLAN** Students will act in the role of consultants hired by major newspapers to help them improve coverage of government-related news and attract younger readers. In this role, they will choose an article, rewrite it, and then write a memo suggesting ways to improve current events coverage and offering strategies for attracting younger readers.

To see this lesson plan, go to

**Teacher Center**
at PearsonSchool.com/phgovt

## Answers

**Checkpoint** Mass media allow candidates to appeal directly to the people, with less help from party organizations. Campaign strategists plan television exposure to project a favorable image.

# Assess and Remediate

**L4** Have students write a brief essay on what they consider to be the best sources of news and information and why. Their essays should include specific examples to support their points.

**L3** Collect the Core Worksheet and assess students' work.

**L3** Assign the Section 3 Assessment questions.

**L3** Section Quiz A (Unit 2 All-in-One, p. 198)

**L2** Section Quiz B (Unit 2 All-in-One, p. 199)

Have students complete the review activities in the digital lesson presentation and continue their work in the **Essential Questions Journal.**

## REMEDIATION

| If Your Students Have Trouble With | Strategies For Remediation |
|---|---|
| The role of the mass media (Questions 1, 2, 3) | Have students create an "infographic" that describes the "American media," with images and captions that illustrate its different features. |
| The impact of the media in politics (Question 4) | Have students work in pairs to read through the section "The Media and Politics," and then create three quiz questions for their partner on one of the subsections ("The Public Agenda" and "Electoral Politics"). |
| The limits on media influence (Questions 5, 6, 7) | Have students read and create an outline for the last section, "Limits on Media Influence." |

---

read newspaper stories about the campaign efforts of Democratic candidates.

Another important limit on the media's impact is the content the media carries. This is especially true of radio and television. Most television programs, for example, have little or nothing to do with public affairs, at least not directly. (A number of popular programs do relate to public affairs in an indirect way, however. Thus, many are "crime shows," and crime is certainly a matter of public concern. Many also carry a political message—for example, that the police are hard-working public servants.)

Advertisers who pay the high costs of television air time want to reach the largest possible audiences. Because most people are more interested in being entertained than in being informed about public issues, few public-affairs programs air in prime time. There are exceptions, however, including *60 Minutes, 20/20, Dateline,* and *Anderson Cooper 360.*

Radio and television mostly "skim" the news. They report only what their news editors determine to be the most important or the most interesting stories of the day. Even on widely watched evening news programs, most reports are presented in 60- to 90-second time slots. In short, the broadcast media seldom give the kind of in-depth coverage that a good newspaper can supply.

Newspapers are not as <u>hampered</u> as many other media in their ability to cover public affairs. Still, much of the content of most newspapers is nonpolitical. Like nearly all of television and radio, newspapers depend on their advertising revenues, which in turn depend on producing a product with the widest possible appeal. Newspaper readers are often more interested in the sports pages and the social, travel, advertising, and entertainment sections of a newspaper than they are in its news and editorial pages.

In-depth coverage of public affairs is available in the media to those who want it and will seek it out. There are a number of good newspapers around the country. In-depth coverage can also be found on the Internet, in several magazines, and on a number of radio and television stations, including public broadcast outlets. Remember, however, that there is nothing about democracy that guarantees an alert and informed public. Like voting and other forms of political participation, being an informed citizen requires some effort.

**hampered**
*v.* restricted, curbed, limited

---

## SECTION 3 ASSESSMENT

1. **Guiding Question** Use your completed flowchart to answer this question: How has the development of different media helped inform the public about politics?

### Key Terms and Comprehension

2. Cite an example of an influential **medium** in our society.

3. What is the status of newspapers today compared to, say, 1980, and what are the likely explanations for the change that has occurred?

4. What is the media's role in shaping the **public agenda?**

5. What are **sound bites,** and what do they suggest about the limits of the media's influence?

### Critical Thinking

6. **Predict Consequences** What might happen to the influence of the media if the 1st Amendment guarantee of freedom of the press were to be repealed?

7. **Recognize Cause and Effect** What are some of the effects of the fact that most television viewers want to be entertained rather than informed?

> **Essential Questions Journal** To continue to build a response to the chapter Essential Question, go to your **Essential Questions Journal.**

> **Quick Write**
>
> **Cause-and-Effect Essay: Write a Thesis Statement** A thesis outlines the subject of your essay. Write a thesis statement for a cause-and-effect essay on the topic you chose in Section 1. You will use your thesis to develop an organizational structure for your essay.

---

# Assessment Answers

**1.** The development of mass media enabled political news to be spread more widely and more quickly. Early newspapers spurred colonists toward revolution. Magazines communicated news nationally until radio and television arrived. Magazines promoted reforms in the early 1900s, and top news magazines remain an important source today. Radio enabled Franklin Roosevelt to speak directly to the people during the Depression and war years. Today, all-news stations cover politics, and talk radio offers political opinion. The development of television enabled people to see and hear political figures. Today television is our main source of political information. The Internet is a growing source. Most other media also have an online presence. The Internet allows citizens easily to join the political discussion.

**2.** Examples include television, the Internet, newspapers, radio, and magazines.

**3.** Newspapers have been declining, due mainly to competition from radio, television, and the Internet.

**4.** The media focus public attention on particular issues by emphasizing some things and ignoring or downplaying others.

**5.** Sound bites are snappy reports that can be aired in about 30 or 45 seconds. They suggest that media coverage often stresses style more than substance.

**6.** Possible answer: Powerful interests or the government might control the information people receive. Dissent could be blunted.

**7.** Possible answer: Television airs little public affairs programming, and staying informed requires effort.

**QUICK WRITE** Students should structure their essay around a clear, concise thesis statement.

# Quick Study Guide

**GOVERNMENT** ONLINE
**On the Go**
To review anytime, anywhere, download these online resources at **PearsonSchool.com/phgovt**
Political Dictionary, Audio Review

CHAPTER 8

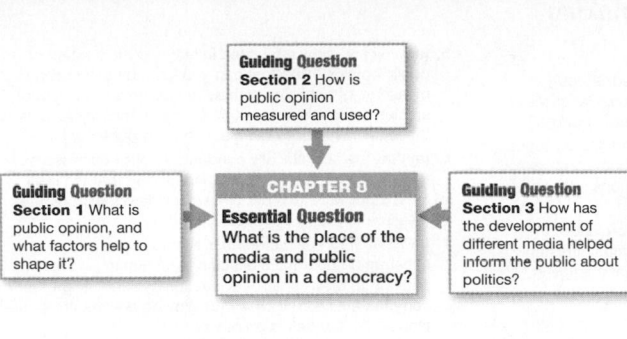

**Guiding Question Section 2** How is public opinion measured and used?

**Guiding Question Section 1** What is public opinion, and what factors help to shape it?

**CHAPTER 8 Essential Question** What is the place of the media and public opinion in a democracy?

**Guiding Question Section 3** How has the development of different media helped inform the public about politics?

## Political Dictionary

public affairs *p. 215*
public opinion *p. 215*
mass media *p. 217*
peer group *p. 218*
opinion leader *p. 218*
mandate *p. 220*
interest group *p. 221*
public opinion poll *p. 222*
straw vote *p. 222*
universe *p. 224*
sample *p. 224*
random sample *p. 224*
quota sample *p. 224*
medium *p. 228*
weblog *p. 233*
public agenda *p. 234*
sound bite *p. 235*

### The Mass Media's Impact on Public Opinion

| Benefits | Limits |
|---|---|
| • Help shape the public agenda | • Only a small number of people follow media very closely. |
| • Influence electoral politics | • People tend to be selective in choosing political coverage. |
| • In-depth media coverage is available to those who look for it, particularly on the Internet. | • Much media content is shallow and unrelated to political affairs. |
| • Changing nature of the media allows for more people to actively participate in discussions. | • Media, such as radio and television, tend to carry only short reports on general news and politics. |
| • Publication of poll results allows media to show how public opinion is measured. | • Newspapers and television depend on advertising revenue, which can sometimes dictate coverage. |

### Media Influence on American Politics

| Public Agenda | Electoral Politics |
|---|---|
| • Direct the public's attention to certain issues | • Allow candidates to be less dependent on political parties |
| • Influence public officials through editorials, analyses, and news reports | • Help candidates reach people directly through television and the Internet |

## For More Information

To learn more about the media and public opinion, refer to these sources or assign them to students:

**L1 Hibbert, Adam.** *The Power of the Media.* Smart Apple Media, 2006.

**L2 Kallen, Stuart A., ed.** *Media Bias.* Greenhaven Press, 2004.

**L3 Moore, David W.** *The Opinion Makers: An Insider Exposes the Truth Behind the Polls.* Beacon Press, 2008.

**L4 Bishop, George F.** *The Illusion of Public Opinion: Fact and Artifact in American Public Opinion Polls.* Rowman & Littlefield Publishers, Inc., 2004.

---

Have students download the digital resources available at Government on the Go for review and remediation.

### STUDY TIPS

**Choosing Partners for a Study Group** Explain that study groups are an excellent way to review information and study for tests. When deciding whom to include in their groups, students should consider which of their peers (1) have similar goals, (2) have comparable study habits, including the time of day they prefer to study (or are available) and their learning style, and (3) have a personality that will complement their own. Suggest that students avoid including friends in their study groups. This choice can lead to more visiting than studying. Students should also consider partners who will balance their own skills and knowledge, who are able to stay on track, and who are self-motivated and can motivate others to learn.

### ASSESSMENT AT A GLANCE

**Tests and Quizzes**
Section Assessments
Section Quizzes A and B, Unit 2 **All-in-One**
Chapter Assessment
Chapter Tests A and B, Unit 2 **All-in-One**
Document-Based Assessment
Progress Monitoring Online
Exam*View* Test Bank

**Performance Assessment**
Essential Questions Journal
Debate, p. 217
Assessment Rubrics, **All-in-One**

# Chapter Assessment

**COMPREHENSION AND CRITICAL THINKING**

## SECTION 1

1. **(a)** people who hold the same opinion on some particular public issue **(b)** because public opinion includes only those views that relate to public affairs—politics, public issues, and the making of public policies

2. **(a)** family and school **(b)** the mass media, peer groups, opinion leaders, and historic events

3. **(a)** possible response: being well liked, respected, prominent, trusted; having authority **(b)** crises, such as an economic downturn or war

## SECTION 2

4. **(a)** The cartoon suggests that pollsters keep asking the same questions. A "second opinion" suggests that if the pollster doesn't like the first response, he'll see if he can get a different response the next time. **(b)** The cartoonist suggests that polls are mainly about producing a particular result rather than finding out true opinion.

5. **(a)** Politicians want to know public opinion to plan campaign strategy and to craft policies that people want. **(b)** Possible answer: You can learn about the views of the individuals who wrote these opinions, but you cannot learn how many people share the opinions. **(c)** Voters can express their opinion in elections by voting for candidates with whom they agree on the issues. However, elections are an inaccurate measure of public opinion because voters often choose candidates based on factors other than the issues.

6. **(a)** because they use valid scientific techniques in an attempt to identify the true opinion of a particular population **(b)** It must define the universe, include a representative sample of the chosen universe, include valid questions, be skillfully administered in a way that does not prejudice the results, and be accurately analyzed and reported.

7. **(a)** Polls have trouble measuring the intensity, stability, and relevance of the opinions they report. **(b)** that polls shape the opinions they are supposed to measure **(c)** Polls measure a sample, not the whole universe, and projections based on samples have a margin of error. Also, events might occur between the poll and the election that change voters' minds.

---

# Chapter Assessment

## Comprehension and Critical Thinking

### Section 1

1. **(a)** What constitutes a "public" in the United States? **(b)** Why is the opinion of the public about a popular movie or television program not a good example of public opinion?

2. **(a)** What are the earliest influences on a person's attitudes about public matters? **(b)** What are some of the factors that might influence a person's public opinions after he or she leaves school?

3. **(a)** What factors do you think give an opinion leader the ability to shape public opinion? **(b)** What kinds of historic events are most likely to lead to a significant change in public opinion?

### Section 2

4. **Analyze Political Cartoons (a)** What does this cartoon suggest about opinion polls? **(b)** How does the cartoon exaggerate or downplay the import of opinion polls?

5. **(a)** Why are many interested in learning the content of public opinion? **(b)** What can you learn by examining such measures of public opinion as magazine and newspaper articles, editorials, and letters to the editor? **(c)** What is the relationship between elections and public opinion?

6. **(a)** Why are scientifically conducted polls described as the best measure of public opinion? **(b)** What features must a poll have in order to be considered an accurate measure of public opinion?

7. **(a)** What are three factors that even scientifically constructed polls have difficulty accounting for? **(b)** In addition to their occasional inaccuracy, what is another common criticism of polls? **(c)** Why do poll results sometimes differ from election outcomes?

### Section 3

8. **(a)** What makes television perhaps the most effective of the different forms of media? **(b)** How has the growth of the Internet affected other media?

9. **(a)** What are the two ways the media affect politics? **(b)** How does the concept of the "sound bite" illustrate how the media affect politicians and how they work today?

10. **(a)** How does the content of most media programming limit the media's influence on public opinion? **(b)** How do the attitudes of the American people affect the influence of the media on public opinion?

### Writing About Government

11. Use your Quick Write exercises from each Section Assessment to write a cause-and-effect essay about the public affairs issue you selected in Section 1. Be sure to clearly highlight the causes and effects of the issue. Note that there can be multiple causes. See pp. S3–S5 in the Skills Handbook.

## Apply What You've Learned

12. **Essential Question Activity** For five days, keep a log of all the time you spend viewing or otherwise interacting with a form of mass media. In addition to keeping track of the number of hours you spend, record:
    **(a)** what programs you watch or listen to, and what articles you read;
    **(b)** whether the program discusses any public affairs topics (include entertainment programs that deal with public affairs topics); and
    **(c)** what you learned about public affairs.

13. **Essential Question Assessment** Based on your research and what you have learned in this chapter, write a newspaper editorial that helps to answer the Essential Question: **What is the place of the media and public opinion in a democracy?** Your editorial should focus on your interaction with the media and how or whether it had any impact on your opinions on public affairs.

**Essential Questions**
**Journal**
To respond to the chapter Essential Question, go to your **Essential Questions Journal.**

---

## SECTION 3

8. **(a)** Possible answer: People are exposed to television more than any other media. **(b)** The growth of the Internet has caused other media to develop their own presence on the Web.

9. **(a)** The media play a large role in shaping the public agenda and influencing elections. **(b)** To gain media exposure, politicians must focus less on delivering comprehensive information and more on crafting interesting sound bites that fit easily into the brief story format of newscasts.

10. **(a)** Most media content contains little on public affairs, and many media just skim the news rather than provide in-depth coverage. Limited and shallow coverage reduces the media's influence on public opinion. **(b)** Most Americans rely on the major media for entertainment more than for information. Advertisers want the media to give people what they want. As a result, the most widely used media provide little information on public affairs, and people who want information must seek it out.

# Document-Based Assessment

## The Impact of Television on Political Events

In 1960, most people who listened to the Nixon-Kennedy debates on the radio thought the candidates performed equally well, but those who watched the debates on television, thought John Kennedy looked vibrant while Richard Nixon looked pale and listless. The power of the media to influence public opinion—and shape history—is well demonstrated throughout our history, as shown in the documents below.

### Document 1

" The Nixon-Kennedy debates' significance extended well beyond 1960. The use of television to transmit an image or idea instantly to millions soon made presidential campaigns more of a spectator sport—leading to campaign concepts and phrases such as 'catchy sound bites,' the 'likability' factor and mass marketing.

—Excerpt from "JFK, Nixon usher in marriage of TV, politics" by Greg Botelho from cnn.com

### Document 2

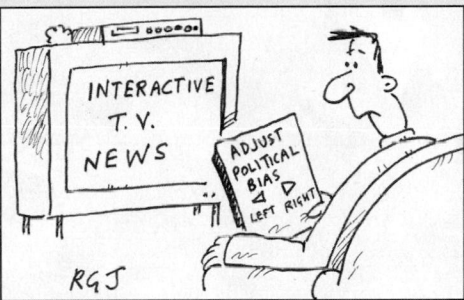

### Document 3

" In the area of political affairs, the impact of television has been widely condemned. As the dominant form of mass communication, television is said to have contributed to a variety of maladies including reduced voter turnout, discounting of substantive issues in political campaigns, decline of the political parties, [and] automatic reelection of incumbents. . . . As the public's 'mind's eye,' television effectively sets the political agenda; the themes and issues that are repeated in television news coverage become the priorities of viewers.

—Excerpt from *Is Anyone Responsible?: How Television Frames Political Issues* by Shanto Iyengar

---

**Use your knowledge of the media and Documents 1–3 to answer the following questions.**

1. Which statement best summarizes Document 1?
   A. The use of television in the Nixon-Kennedy debates led to increased voter turnout.
   B. The Nixon-Kennedy debates had a huge impact on television programming.
   C. Presidential campaigns as they were known changed dramatically when television began to broadcast the debates.
   D. The phrase "catchy sound bites" came out of the debates.

2. In Document 2, what is the cartoonist's point of view regarding television news?

3. What does Document 3 suggest about the influence of television?

4. **Pull It Together** How do you think the impact of television, and the media in general, will change over time? Consider audience, users, and technology.

 **GOVERNMENT ONLINE**
**Documents**
To find additional primary sources on the impact of the media, visit
**PearsonSchool.com/phgovt**

---

## DOCUMENT-BASED ASSESSMENT

1. C

2. The cartoon suggests that the news has a political bias. "Interactive" news could allow the user to "adjust" that bias to get news that is more liberal or more conservative.

3. It suggests that television has had a negative impact on public affairs in several ways. It has depressed voter turnout, discounted campaign issues, contributed to the decline of political parties, and determined public priorities.

4. A good response will acknowledge both sides of the issue and argue persuasively for one or another viewpoint.

**L2 Differentiate** Students use all the documents on the page to support their thesis.

**L3 Differentiate** Students include additional information available online at **PearsonSchool.com/phgovt**.

**L4 Differentiate** Students use materials from the textbook, the online information at **PearsonSchool.com/phgovt,** and do additional research to support their views.

**Go Online to PearsonSchool.com/phgovt** for a student rubric and extra documents.

---

## WRITING ABOUT GOVERNMENT

11. Students' essays should show cause-and-effect relationships for their selected issue.

## APPLY WHAT YOU'VE LEARNED

12. Students should keep a thorough record of their media usage.

13. A good student editorial will use findings and information from the chapter to answer the question, "What is the place of the media and public opinion in a democracy?"

# Introduce the Chapter

## Essential Questions:

**UNIT 2**

In what ways should people participate in public affairs?

**CHAPTER 9**

To what extent do interest groups advance or harm democracy?

**ACTIVATE PRIOR KNOWLEDGE**

Have students examine the image and quotation on these pages. Ask: **What do you think this group of people is doing?** *(demonstrating to pressure authorities to get something they want)* **This event was probably organized by a special interest group. Think about an organization to which you belong. Why did you choose to join?** *(Students should recognize that they join organizations because they share interests or goals with the group's members.)* In this chapter, students will learn about interest groups. Tell students to begin to explore interest groups by completing the Chapter 9 Essential Question Warmup Activity in the **Essential Questions Journal.** Discuss their responses as a class.

**BEFORE READING**

**L2** **ELL Differentiate** Chapter 9 Prereading and Vocabulary Worksheet (Unit 2 All-in-One, p. 213)

**SUCCESSNET STUDENT AND TEACHER CENTER**

Visit **PearsonSchool.com/phgovt** for downloadable resources that allow students and teachers to connect with government "on the go."

**DIGITAL LESSON PRESENTATION**

The digital lesson presentation supports the print lesson with activities and summaries of key concepts.

## SKILLS DEVELOPMENT

**COMPARE VIEWPOINTS**

You may wish to teach comparing viewpoints as a distinct skill within Section 2 of this chapter. Use the Chapter 9 Skills Worksheet (Unit 2 All-in-One, p. 231) to help students learn the steps in comparing viewpoints. The worksheet presents the viewpoints of two different interest groups. Students must read the excerpts and then answer questions. For L2 and L1 students, assign the adapted Skill Activity (Unit 2 All-in-One, p. 232).

**WebQuest online** The chapter WebQuest challenges students to answer the chapter Essential Question about interest groups and their effect on democracy.

## Block Scheduling

**BLOCK 1:** Teach the Section 1 lesson and the Section 2 lesson in their entirety. Include the Extend activity for Section 2.

**BLOCK 2:** Teach the Section 3 lesson in its entirety. Assign the Extend activities.

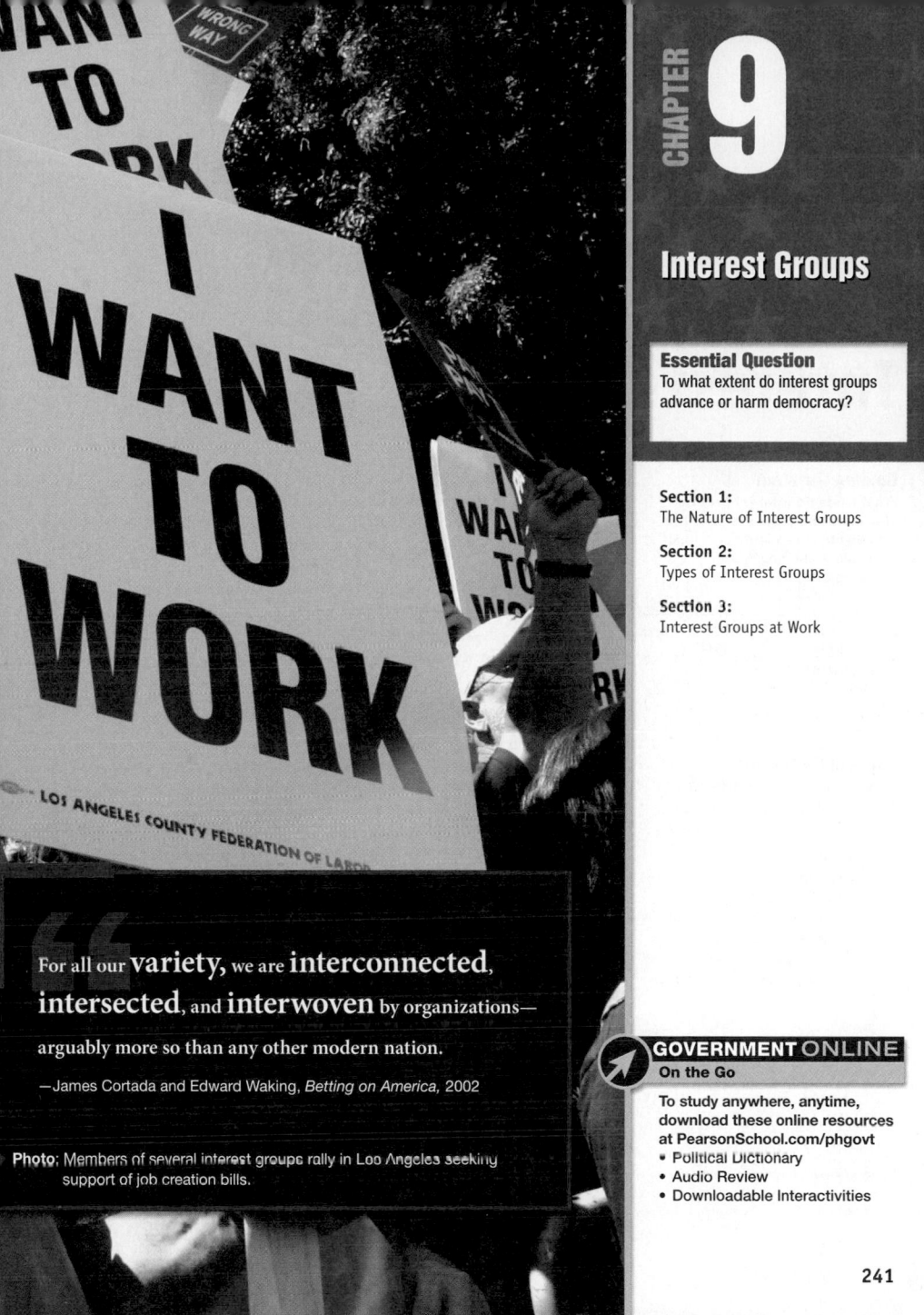

For all our **variety**, we are **interconnected**, **intersected**, and **interwoven** by organizations—arguably more so than any other modern nation.

—James Cortada and Edward Waking, *Betting on America*, 2002

**Photo:** Members of several interest groups rally in Los Angeles seeking support of job creation bills.

# CHAPTER 9

# Interest Groups

**Essential Question**
To what extent do interest groups advance or harm democracy?

**GOVERNMENT ONLINE**
On the Go

**To study anywhere, anytime,** download these online resources at PearsonSchool.com/phgovt
• Political Dictionary
• Audio Review
• Downloadable Interactivities

241

## Lesson Goals

**SECTION 1**

Students will . . .

- identify functions of interest groups in a worksheet of examples.
- examine the positive and negative functions of interest groups by creating a persuasive brochure.
- write a persuasive letter encouraging or discouraging participation in interest groups.

**SECTION 2**

Students will . . .

- recognize the role of interest groups in their lives by identifying and categorizing those to which they belong.
- examine excerpts from different interest groups expressing opposing views on the same issue.
- research the activities and interests of a specific interest group discussed in the section.

**SECTION 3**

Students will . . .

- create an interest group campaign for influencing public policy and opinion, using direct and indirect approaches.
- practice influencing public opinion by composing a persuasive fundraising letter for their interest group campaign.

## Pressed for Time

Organize the class into three groups, assigning each group a section from the chapter. Have each group create a study guide detailing the main points of the assigned section. Then, have students present their study guides to the other groups.

**FOLLOW UP** Have students create a Venn diagram that compares and contrasts the roles and purposes of special interest groups with political parties in the American political system.

**DIFFERENTIATED INSTRUCTION KEY**

Look for these symbols to help you adjust steps in each lesson to meet your students' needs.

**L1** Special Needs

**L2** Basic

    **ELL** English Language Learners

    **LPR** Less Proficient Readers

**L3** All Students

**L4** Advanced Students

# What roles do interest groups play in our political system?

| Functions of Interest Groups | |
| --- | --- |
| **Positive** | **Negative** |
| • Awareness of public affairs<br>• Represent members based on shared attitudes, rather than geography<br>• Provide useful, specialized, and detailed information to government<br>• Enable people to participate in political process<br>• Monitor public agencies and officials, ensuring accountability<br>• Compete with each other to influence public policy | • Push own special interests, which may not be in best interests of other Americans<br>• Influence out of proportion to their size or importance to public good<br>• Hard to tell who or how many people in the group<br>• May not represent views of all people for whom they speak<br>• Some use unethical tactics |

## Get Started

### LESSON GOALS

Students will . . .

- identify functions of interest groups on a worksheet of examples.
- examine the positive and negative functions of interest groups by creating a persuasive brochure.
- write a persuasive letter encouraging or discouraging participation in interest groups.

### BEFORE CLASS

Assign the section, the graphic organizer in the text, and the Reading Comprehension Worksheet (Unit 2 All-in-One, p. 217) before class.

**L2 Differentiate** Reading Comprehension Worksheet (Unit 2 All-in-One, p. 218)

## SKILLS DEVELOPMENT

### ANALYZE POLITICAL CARTOONS

To help students learn to analyze political cartoons, have them turn to the Skills Handbook, p. S22, and use the steps explained there to complete the Bellringer activity.

---

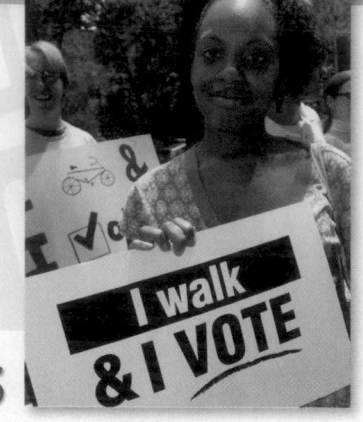

SECTION **1**

# The **Nature** of Interest Groups

### Guiding Question

**What roles do interest groups play in our political system?** Use the table to note information about the positive and negative effects of interest groups.

| Functions of Interest Groups | |
| --- | --- |
| **Positive** | **Negative** |
| • Awareness of public affairs | • |
| • | • |
| • | • |

### Political Dictionary

- interest group
- public policy
- public affairs

### Objectives

1. Describe the role of interest groups in influencing public policy.
2. Compare and contrast political parties and interest groups.
3. Explain why people see interest groups as both good and bad for American politics.

**Image Above:** Members of an environmental group express their support for a "greener" city.

**A**n **interest group** is a collection of people who share certain views on public matters and work to shape public policy to their benefit. They try to persuade public officials to respond to their positions favorably. You may not think that you belong to this sort of group, but as you read this section you will likely discover that you do. You might, in fact, belong to several of them. You will probably also realize that you will become a member of many more of these groups in the years to come—because these organizations provide one of the most effective ways in which Americans can get government to react to their needs and wants.

## The Role of Interest Groups

Where do you stand on the question of gun control? What about global warming? Campaign finance reform? Abortion? Prayer in public schools? What can you do to promote your views on these and other public questions? How can you increase the chance that your positions will carry the day?

Joining with others who share your opinions is both practical and democratic. Organization can provide the route to power, and organized efforts to further group interests are a fundamental part of the democratic process. Moreover, the right to do so is protected by the Constitution. Remember, the 1st Amendment guarantees "the right of the people peaceably to assemble, and to petition the Government for a redress of grievances."

Interest groups are sometimes called "pressure groups" and often "organized interests" or "special interests." They try to influence what government does in some specific area of special interest to them. They give themselves a variety of labels: leagues, associations, clubs, federations, unions, committees, and so on. But whatever they call themselves, every interest group seeks to influence the making and content of **public policy.** Used in this general sense, public policy includes all of the goals that a government pursues in the many areas of human affairs in which it is involved—everything from seat belts, speed limits, and zoning to flood control, old-age pensions, and the use of military force in international affairs.

Because interest groups exist to shape public policy, they can be found wherever those policies are made or can be influenced. They operate at every

## Focus on the Basics

**FACTS:** • Interest groups exist in many forms and by many names, but they all share the purpose of influencing public policy. • Interest groups promote knowledge about public matters and help people take part in the political process. • Interest groups are often criticized for their tactics or impact on society and government.

**CONCEPTS:** representative government

**ENDURING UNDERSTANDINGS:** • Interest groups play a major role in the shaping of public policy and enabling citizen involvement. • Interest groups have positive and negative impacts.

level of government—on Capitol Hill and elsewhere in Washington, D.C., in every one of the 50 State capitals, in thousands of city halls and county courthouses, and in many other places at the local level all across the country. In short, as diplomat and historian Lord Bryce put it somewhat indelicately more than a century ago: "Where the body is, there will the vultures be gathered."

Remember, our society is <u>pluralistic</u>. It is not dominated by any one <u>elite</u>. It is, instead, composed of several distinct cultures and groups. Increasingly, the members of various ethnic, racial, religious, and other groups compete for and share in the exercise of political power in the United States.

## Parties and Interest Groups

Interest groups are made up of people who join together for some political purpose, much like political parties. Parties and interest groups overlap in a number of ways. They differ from each other in three significant ways, however: (1) with respect to the making of nominations, (2) in their basic focus, and (3) in the scope of their interests.

*First*, parties nominate candidates for public office; interest groups do not. Recall, the making of nominations is a prime function of political parties. If an interest group were to nominate candidates, it would, in effect, become a political party.

Interest groups do attempt to affect the outcome of primaries and other nominating contests. They do not pick candidates who then run for office under their labels, however. It may be widely known that a particular interest group supports this or that candidate, but the candidate seeks votes as a Republican or a Democrat.[1]

*Second*, parties are chiefly interested in winning elections and thereby controlling government. Interest groups are chiefly concerned with controlling or influencing the policies of government. Unlike parties, those groups do not face the problems involved in trying to appeal to the largest possible

number of people. In short, political parties are mostly interested in the *who*, and interest groups are mostly concerned with the *what*, of government. To put it another way, parties focus mostly on the candidate; interest groups focus mostly on policy questions.

*Third*, political parties are necessarily concerned with the whole range of public affairs, with everything of concern to voters. Interest groups almost always concentrate only on those issues that most directly affect the interests of their members.

In addition, interest groups are private organizations. Unlike political parties, they are not accountable to the public. Their members, not the voters, pass judgment on their performance.

## Interest Groups: Good or Bad?

Do interest groups pose a threat to the well-being of the American political system? Or are they, instead, a valuable part of that system? The argument over the merit of interest groups goes back to the beginnings of the Republic.

**Two Early Views** Many have long viewed interest groups with suspicion and <u>foreboding</u>. They have feared that some would become so powerful that they would be able to shape public policies to their own narrow and selfish ends. James Madison gave voice to that view in 1787. In *The Federalist* No. 10, he argued that, inevitably, people join together to pursue common interests. They form "factions," Madison's term for what we now call interest groups. He warned that those factions, left unchecked, could dominate public decision making because of size, resources, and/or leadership.

---

1 Note that this discussion centers on the differences between interest groups and the *major* parties. There are many striking parallels between interest groups and most minor parties—for example, in terms of their scope of interest.

✔**Checkpoint**
Where do interest groups operate?

<u>pluralistic</u>
*adj.* made up of several groups with different ethnic, religious, or political backgrounds

<u>elite</u>
*n.* select, privileged group in a society

<u>foreboding</u>
*n.* an expectation of trouble

▶▶ **Analyzing Political Cartoons**
AARP is a well-known interest group for people over 50; it responds to the needs of older Americans. *What is this cartoon saying about AARP and similar interest groups?*

---

## Teach

To present this topic using online resources, use the lesson presentations at **PearsonSchool.com/phgovt.**

**DISCUSS BELLRINGER**

Review students' answers to the Bellringer activity. Tell students that an interest group is any group that seeks to influence public policy. Point out that interest groups come in many forms and represent a diverse range of interests, such as the oil industry, mine workers, health insurance reformers, gun control advocates, tax reformers, and many others.

**L2 ELL Differentiate** Write *interest group* and *public policy* and their definitions on the board.

---

# Differentiated Resources

The following resources are located in the All-in-One, Unit 2, Chapter 9, Section 1:

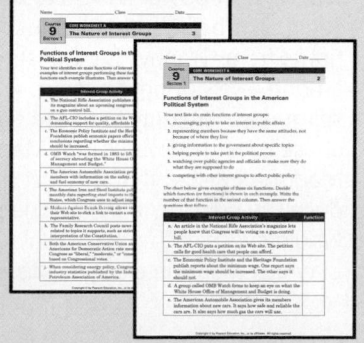

## Answers

**Checkpoint** at all levels of government and anywhere public policy is made

**Analyzing Political Cartoons** Possible response: It is saying that interest groups actively seek new members among any who might be interested in their cause. The American Association of Retired Persons (AARP) vigorously recruits new members as they approach retirement age.

## REVIEW FUNCTIONS OF INTEREST GROUPS

Review Question 6 on the Reading Comprehension Worksheet, which asks students to list the six functions of interest groups:

1. encourage interest in public affairs
2. represent members based on shared attitudes rather than geography
3. offer specialized, detailed information to the government
4. enable people to participate in the political process
5. monitor public agencies and officials, ensuring accountability
6. compete with each other to influence public policy

## DISTRIBUTE CORE WORKSHEET A

Distribute the Chapter 9 Section 1 Core Worksheet A (Unit 2 All-in-One, p. 219), in which students will read and analyze examples of interest group behavior. Instruct students to identify the interest group function illustrated by each example and answer the reflection questions.

**L1 L2 Differentiate** Distribute the adapted Core Worksheet A (Unit 2 All-in-One, p. 221).

**L3 L4 Differentiate** Have students use newsmagazines, newspapers, or the Internet to find out more about one interest group and write a brief summary of the group's recent activities.

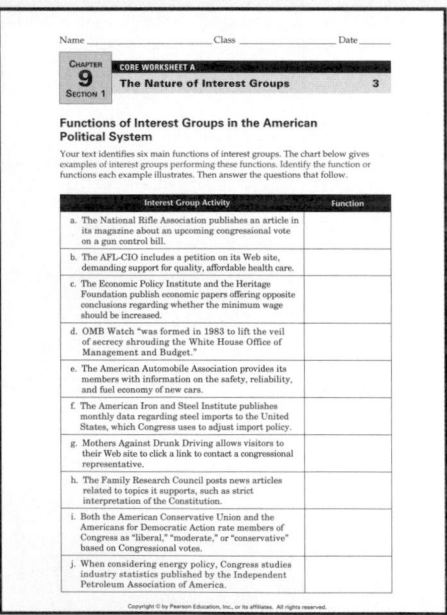

Tell students to go to the Audio Tour to learn more about early interest groups.

## Answers

**Early Interest Groups** They might have created literature, made speeches, held meetings, and petitioned the government in support of their causes.

---

**mischief**
*n.* troublesome conduct, misbehavior

Madison believed that a society could eliminate factions only by eliminating the people's fundamental freedoms. He argued that "the <u>mischiefs</u> of factions" could best be controlled by a political system in which the powers of government, or the ability to make public policies, are fragmented. That is a major reason why, he said, the Constitution provides for a separation of powers and checks and balances, and for a federal system of government—to make it unlikely that one group can override the interests of other (competing) groups.[2]

2 You can read the full text of *The Federalist* No. 10 in the historic documents section at the end of this book.

Nearly fifty years later, Alexis de Tocqueville was deeply impressed by the vast number of organizations he found in this country. Tocqueville, a Frenchman, toured much of what was the United States in the 1830s. In his work, *Democracy in America*, he wrote that

### PRIMARY SOURCE
**In no country in the world has the principle of association been more successfully used, or more unsparingly applied to a multitude of different objects, than in America.**

—Alexis de Tocqueville

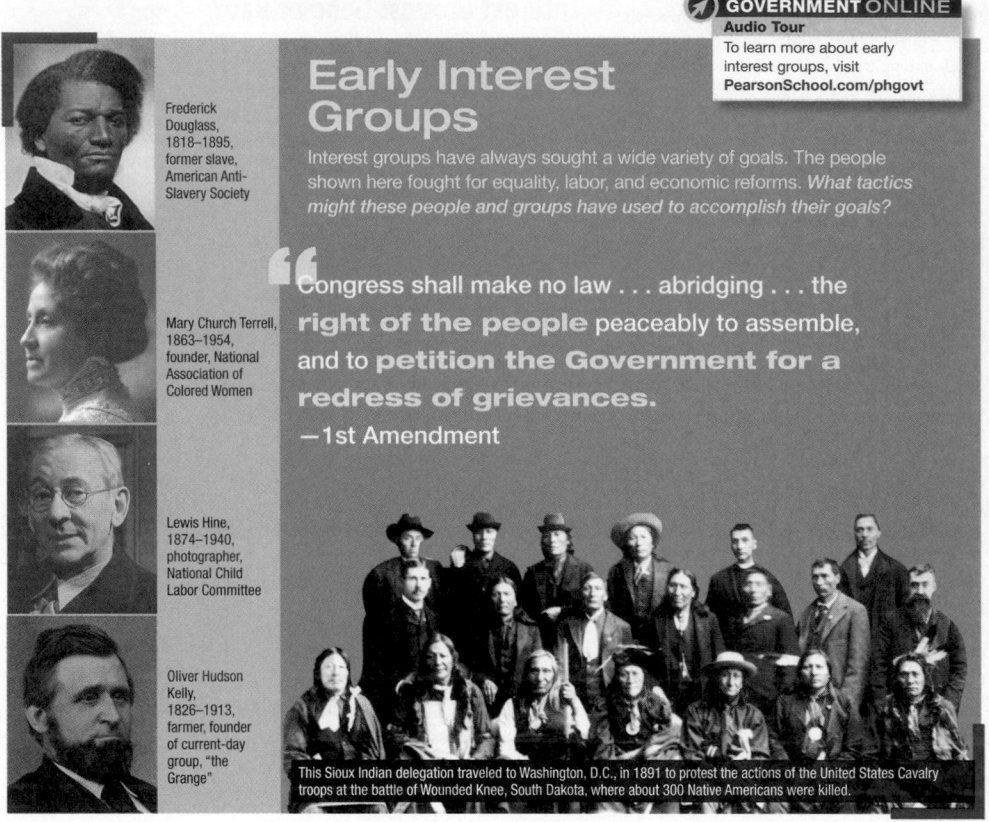

**GOVERNMENT** ONLINE
**Audio Tour**
To learn more about early interest groups, visit PearsonSchool.com/phgovt

# Early Interest Groups

Interest groups have always sought a wide variety of goals. The people shown here fought for equality, labor, and economic reforms. *What tactics might these people and groups have used to accomplish their goals?*

**"Congress shall make no law . . . abridging . . . the right of the people peaceably to assemble, and to petition the Government for a redress of grievances.**
—1st Amendment

Frederick Douglass, 1818–1895, former slave, American Anti-Slavery Society

Mary Church Terrell, 1863–1954, founder, National Association of Colored Women

Lewis Hine, 1874–1940, photographer, National Child Labor Committee

Oliver Hudson Kelly, 1826–1913, farmer, founder of current-day group, "the Grange"

This Sioux Indian delegation traveled to Washington, D.C., in 1891 to protest the actions of the United States Cavalry troops at the battle of Wounded Knee, South Dakota, where about 300 Native Americans were killed.

# Constitutional Principles

**FEDERALISM** Much of the debate over ratification of the Constitution swirled around where most power should reside—with the States or central government. Anti-Federalists believed that maintaining State sovereignty would best protect individual rights from tyranny. The Constitution proposed a federal system, with power shared among levels of government. In *The Federalist* No. 9, Alexander Hamilton argued that splitting sovereignty between national and State governments would protect against abuse by either level. James Madison continued the argument in *The Federalist* No. 10. Madison insisted that the vast size and diverse interests in a large republic would reduce the risk of tyranny by one powerful group, as factions with conflicting interests would check each other. Display Transparency 9B, Excerpt from *The Federalist* No. 10, in which Madison explains this view.

And, in a similar vein, he also observed that

"Americans of all ages, all conditions, and all dispositions, constantly form associations . . . not only commercial and manufacturing . . . but . . . of a thousand other kinds—religious, moral, serious, futile, extensive or restricted, enormous or diminutive."
—Alexis de Tocqueville

Are those "associations," or interest groups, good or bad? To answer that question you must weigh, on the one hand, the functions those groups perform in American politics and, on the other, the various criticisms often leveled at them.

**Their Valuable Functions** *First,* among their several commendable functions, organized interests help to stimulate awareness of and interest in **public affairs.** Public affairs are those issues and events that concern the people at large. Interest groups raise awareness of public affairs mostly by developing and publicizing those policy positions they favor and by opposing those they see as threats to the interests of their members.

*Second,* interest groups represent their members on the basis of shared attitudes rather than on the basis of geography—by what their members think as opposed to where they happen to live. Public officials are elected from districts drawn on maps. But many of the issues that concern and unite people today have less to do with where they live than with, say, how they make a living. A labor union member who lives in Chicago may have much more in common with someone who does the same kind of work in Seattle than he or she does with someone who owns a business in Chicago or runs a farm in another part of Illinois.

*Third,* organized interests often provide useful, specialized, and detailed information to government—for example, on employment, price levels, or the sales of new and existing homes. These data are important to the making of public policy, and government officials often cannot obtain them from any other source. This flow of information works both ways: interest groups frequently get useful information from public agencies and pass it along to their members.

*Fourth,* interest groups are vehicles for political participation. Most people are not inclined to run for and hold public office, or even to volunteer for a campaign. For many Americans, then, interest groups are a convenient and less time-consuming way to help shape public policy. They are a means through which like-minded citizens can pool their resources and channel their energies into collective political action. One mother concerned about drunk driving cannot accomplish very much acting alone. Thousands of people united in an organization like MADD (Mothers Against Drunk Driving) certainly can and do.

*Fifth,* interest groups add another element to the checks-and-balances feature of the political process. Many of them keep close tabs on the work of various public agencies and officials and thus help to make sure that they perform their tasks in responsible and effective ways.

*Finally,* interest groups regularly compete with one another in the public arena. That competition places a very real limit on the lengths to which some groups might otherwise go as they seek to advance their own interests. For example, the automotive industry may work to weaken or postpone auto emission standards imposed under the Clean Air Act. Their efforts may be opposed—and to some extent counterbalanced—by environmental and health-related organizations.

**Criticisms** All of what has just been said is not meant to suggest that interest groups are above reproach. On the contrary, they can be, and often are, criticized on several counts.

The potentially negative side of interest groups is sometimes all too apparent. Many groups push their own special interests which, despite their claims to the contrary, are not always in the best interests of other Americans. Their critics often make several more specific charges.

*First,* some interest groups have an influence far out of proportion to their size, or, for that matter, to their importance or contribution to the public good. Thus, the

✔ **Checkpoint**
How do interest groups increase political participation?

**commendable**
*adj.* admirable, praiseworthy

**reproach**
*n.* blame, criticism

# Background

**DEMOCRACY IN AMERICA** When Alexis de Tocqueville left France for America in 1831, France, like the rest of Europe, was emerging from its historical monarchy into a more democratic future. Tocqueville wanted to find out why democracy thrived in America and learn how it might be applied in France. "I looked for an image of democracy itself, its penchants, its character, its prejudices, and its passions. I wanted to know it, if only to know what we ought to hope or fear from it." In America, Tocqueville found a unique sense of social equality. America had no aristocracy. Instead of government by a powerful ruling class, Americans formed self-governing units— towns, States, and later an association of States. Tocqueville concluded that such popular sovereignty was possible for France, but only if the classes could overcome their traditional conflict and cooperate to form free institutions.

## DISTRIBUTE CORE WORKSHEET B

Distribute the Chapter 9 Section 1 Core Worksheet B (Unit 2 All-in-One, p. 220). This worksheet asks students to create a brochure to persuade people that interest groups are either a threat to the American political system or a valuable part of that system. The worksheet breaks the task into steps to help students create their brochure. Have students work in teams, dividing up tasks involved with writing, designing, and creating the brochure. All elements of their brochure should support their position for or against interest groups.

**L1 L2 Differentiate** Review with students the list of pros and cons of interest groups presented in the text.

## SHARE AND REFLECT

Post students' brochures around the room. Give students time to evaluate the other groups' work. Students should take turns viewing work and standing at their own work to answer questions about it. Ask students to reflect on which brochure they think would most influence the public's opinion of interest groups and explain why.

## EXTEND THE LESSON

**L3** Extend the lesson by having students write a letter to the editor in which they offer a defense or a criticism of the role of interest groups in American society. Student letters should draw on material from the section, acknowledge different points of view about interest groups, and include their own thoughts about the benefits or drawbacks of interest groups. Distribute the Rubric for Assessing a Letter to the Editor (Unit 2 All-in-One, p. 254).

**L1 L2 Differentiate** Give students an outline from which to write their letters:

1. my opinion about interest groups

2. roles of interest groups in society

3. positive functions of interest groups

4. criticisms

5. conclusion

**L1 L2 Differentiate** Another option would be to have students complete the Extend Activity titled "A Civil Society" (Unit 2 All-in-One, p. 223), which guides students through an interview with a member of an interest group.

## Answers

**Checkpoint** They give people another way of accessing the policy-making process.

# Assess and Remediate

**L3** Collect the Core Worksheets and assess students' brochures, using the Rubric for Assessing a Cooperative Learning Project (Unit 2 All-in-One, p. 260).

**L3** Assign the Section 1 Assessment questions.

**L3** Section Quiz A (Unit 2 All-in-One, p. 224)

**L2** Section Quiz B (Unit 2 All-in-One, p. 225)

Have students complete the review activities in the digital lesson presentation and continue their work in the **Essential Questions Journal.**

## REMEDIATION

| If Your Students Have Trouble With | Strategies For Remediation |
|---|---|
| The role of interest groups (Questions 1, 2, 4, 7) | Have students create an outline of the sections that appear under the headings "The Role of Interest Groups" and "Their Valuable Functions." |
| The difference between political parties and interest groups (Question 3) | Have students create a Venn diagram that compares and contrasts political parties and interest groups. |
| Positive and critical views of interest groups (Questions 5, 6) | Have students form pairs and then prepare for and deliver a mini-debate over the benefits and drawbacks of interest groups. Each side will have one minute to present its argument, and 30 seconds to rebut the other's initial presentation. |

## Answers

**Caption** Possible response: College campuses and high schools are places where there are large groups of young people who could be easily recruited by interest groups.

---

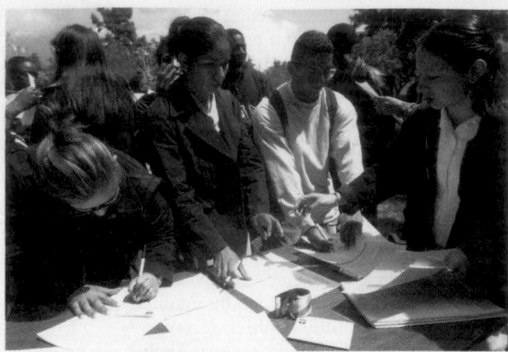

▲ Colleges and high schools often hold events where interest groups try to recruit new members. **Why might those places be good locations for recruiting?**

**overt**
*adj.* open, observable

**dole**
*vt.* to give or distribute

*Third,* many groups do not in fact represent the views of all of the people for whom they claim to speak. Very often, both in and out of politics, an organization is dominated by an active minority who conduct the group's affairs and make its policy decisions.

*Finally,* some groups use tactics that, if they were to become widespread, would undermine the whole political system. These practices include bribery and other heavy-handed uses of money, <u>overt</u> threats of revenge, and so on. Instances of that sort of behavior are not at all common; they are not altogether unknown, however.

The illegal behavior of a number of representatives of special interests was exposed in Washington during the Abramoff scandal. Jack Abramoff, several of his associates, and a member of Congress were sent to federal prison, convicted of bribery and other offenses. Abramoff and the other special interest representatives funneled hundreds of thousands of dollars into congressional campaigns, provided all-expense-paid trips to resorts, and <u>doled</u> out such things as skybox tickets to professional football games, free dinners, and even jobs for some congressional spouses—all in exchange for legislative favors. Those favors included the introduction of bills written to benefit Abramoff's clients and other attempts to shape lawmaking to that same end.

contest over "who gets what, when and how" is not always a fair fight. The more highly organized and better-financed groups often have a decided advantage in that struggle.

*Second,* it is sometimes hard to tell just who or how many people a group really represents. Many groups have titles that suggest that they have thousands—even millions—of dedicated members. Some organizations that call themselves such things as "The American Citizens Committee for . . ." or "People United Against . . ." are, in fact, only "fronts" for a very few people with very narrow interests.

---

## SECTION 1 ASSESSMENT

**Essential Questions Journal** To continue to build a response to the chapter Essential Question, go to your **Essential Questions Journal.**

**1. Guiding Question** Use your completed table to answer this question: What roles do interest groups play in our political system?

### Key Terms and Comprehension

**2.** What are **interest groups** and how do they attempt to shape **public policy?**

**3.** How do political parties and interest groups differ from one another?

**4.** How do interest groups raise awareness of **public affairs?**

**5. (a)** Summarize public attitudes about interest groups. **(b)** What is their role in the American political system?

### Critical Thinking

**6. Express Problems Clearly (a)** What were James Madison's concerns about "factions" in *The Federalist* No. 10? **(b)** Do you think Madison's concerns were justified? Use evidence from the text and your personal observations to support your point of view.

**7. Understand Point of View** What does it mean to say that joining interest groups is both practical and democratic?

### Quick Write

**Assessment Writing: Gather Details** Writing for assessment often means that you have a limited time to answer an essay question. It may help to plan your response carefully using a graphic organizer. As you have read, interest groups are seen as both positive and negative. What do you think? To answer this question, gather details and list the positive and negative points of interest groups on a graphic organizer.

---

# Assessment Answers

**1.** Interest groups try to influence government in specific areas. They create awareness of public affairs, represent members, provide information to government, allow people to participate in politics, monitor public agencies and officials, and compete with each other to influence policy.

**2.** Interest groups are people who share views and work to shape public policy at any level of government where policy is made.

**3.** Interest groups have no direct role in nominating candidates. They work to influence policy, not elections. They are narrowly focused on their own interests. Parties are concerned with the whole range of public affairs.

**4.** by publicizing policies they favor or oppose and by encouraging civic participation

**5. (a)** There is wide suspicion of interest groups, yet most people belong to one or more. **(b)** create public awareness, represent members, provide information to government, offer a way to participate in politics, monitor public agencies and officials, compete with each other to influence policy

**6. (a)** He believed factions were inevitable and, if unchecked, could dominate public decision making. **(b)** Possible response: Yes, Well-financed interest groups, such as drug company lobbies, can influence policy with huge donations to election campaigns.

**7.** Possible answer: Expressing views to government is part of the democratic process. Interest groups help people express shared views.

**QUICK WRITE** Lists should include all positive and negative points described in the section.

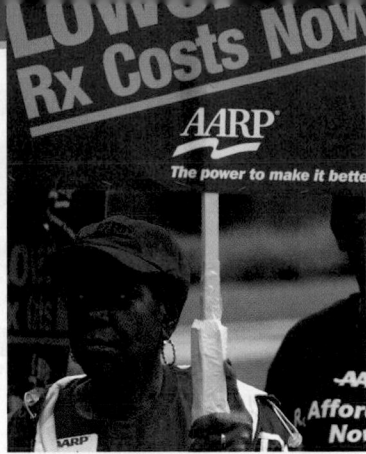

# SECTION 2

# Types of Interest Groups

**Guiding Question**
**What are the different types of interest groups at work in American society?** Use the outline to record notes about different types of interest groups.

I. Types of Interest Groups
   A. Economic Interests
      1. _____
      2. _____
   B. Other Interest Groups
   C. Public-Interest Groups

**Political Dictionary**
- trade association
- labor union
- public-interest group

**Objectives**
1. Explain how the American tradition of joining organizations has resulted in a wide range of interest groups.
2. Describe four categories of groups based on economic interests.
3. Outline the reasons other interest groups have been created.
4. Identify the purpose of public-interest groups.

**Image Above:** Members of AARP gather to urge lawmakers to pass prescription medication bill.

"Everything from A to Z." That expression can certainly be applied to the many interest groups in this country. They include, among thousands of others, AAA (the American Automobile Association), ACLU (the American Civil Liberties Union), Amnesty International, the Zionist Organization of America, and the Zoological Association of America. All of those thousands of organizations can be more or less readily classified and, so, usefully described as interest groups.

## An American Tradition

The United States has often been called "a nation of joiners." Recall Alexis de Tocqueville's observations cited in the previous section. His comments, true when he made them, have become even more accurate over time.

No one really knows how many associations exist in the United States today. There are thousands upon thousands of them, however, and at every level in society. Each one becomes an interest group whenever it tries to influence the actions of government in order to promote its own goals.

Interest groups come in all shapes and sizes. They may have thousands or even millions of long-established members or only a handful of new or temporary members. They may be well or little known, highly structured or quite loose and informal, wealthy or with few resources. No matter what their characteristics, they are found in every field of human activity in this country.

The largest number of these groups has been founded on the basis of an economic interest, and especially on the bases of business, labor, agricultural, and professional interests. Some groups are grounded in a geographic area.

Others have been born out of a cause or an idea, such as prohibition of alcohol, environmental protection, or gun control. Many groups seek to influence some aspect of the nation's foreign policy. Still others exist to promote the welfare of certain groups of people—veterans, senior citizens, a racial minority, the homeless, women, people with disabilities, and so on.

Many people belong to a number of local, regional, or national interest groups—often without realizing they do. A car dealer, for example, may belong to the local Chamber of Commerce, a car dealers' association, the

---

## Focus on the Basics

**FACTS:** • Citizen involvement in interest groups has a long tradition in the United States. • Most interest groups are based on economic interests, such as business, labor, agriculture, and professional interests. • Other groups are centered on certain causes, the welfare of specific groups, religious views, or the public good.

**CONCEPTS:** representative government

**ENDURING UNDERSTANDINGS:** • Americans have long participated in society and government through interest groups. • Groups represent a wide array of interests, and most people belong to one or more interest groups.

---

What are the different types of interest groups at work in American society?

I. Types of Interest Groups
   A. Economic Interests
      1. Business
      2. Labor
      3. Agriculture
      4. Professions
   B. Other Interest Groups
      1. Issue-oriented
      2. For specific communities
      3. Religious
   C. Public-Interest Groups

## Get Started

**LESSON GOALS**

Students will . . .

- recognize the role of interest groups in their lives by identifying and categorizing those to which they belong.
- examine excerpts from different interest groups expressing opposing views on the same issue.
- research the activities and interests of a specific interest group discussed in the section.

**BEFORE CLASS**

Assign the section, the graphic organizer in the text, and the Reading Comprehension Worksheet (Unit 2 All-in-One, p. 226) before class.

**L2 Differentiate** Reading Comprehension Worksheet (Unit 2 All-in-One, p. 227)

## SKILLS DEVELOPMENT

**COMPARE VIEWPOINTS**

To practice comparing viewpoints in this section, use the Chapter 9 Skills Worksheet (Unit 2 All-in-One, p. 231). You may teach the skill explicitly either before or after students do the Core Worksheet. For L2 and L1 students, assign the adapted Skill Activity (Unit 2 All-in-One, p. 232).

Write on the board: **In your notebook, list the interest groups to which you and your family belong.**

**L1 L2 Differentiate** Review with students the first paragraph of this section, to help them get a sense of the wide range of organizations that qualify as interest groups.

# Teach

To present this topic using online resources, use the lesson presentations at **PearsonSchool.com/phgovt.**

## COMPILE AND CATEGORIZE

Write these three broad categories across the top of the board: "Economic Interest Groups," "Other Interest Groups," and "Public Interest Groups." Ask: **What sub-types of interest groups does the text list under these categories?** (*Economic Interest Groups: business, labor, agricultural, professional; Other Interest Groups: issue-oriented, specific communities, religious; Public-Interest Groups: no sub-types given.*) Record the sub-types under the broad categories as students identify them. Ask students to explain the meaning of each category and sub-type.

Have students share the lists of interest groups they created in the Bellringer activity. (Be sure to respect the privacy of students who do not wish to provide information about groups to which they and their family belong.) Have students identify the category to which each group belongs. Write the groups in the proper categories on the board to create a master list for the class.

Display Transparency 9C, Membership in Labor Unions. Ask: **Into what category does the sub-type discussed in this graph fall?** (*economic interest groups*) **What trend do you see in this sub-type of interest group?** (*Membership in labor unions has declined since 1945.*)

You can continue the discussion by having students brainstorm and categorize other interest groups with which they are familiar. They can add any unique information they know about the group.

## Answers

**Checkpoint** to promote and protect the interests of specific businesses

---

**✓ Checkpoint**
Why are business groups formed?

American Legion, a local taxpayers' league, a garden club, a church, and the American Cancer Society. All of these are, to one degree or another, interest groups—including the church and the garden club, even though the car dealer may never think of these groups in that light.[3]

Many people may belong to groups that take conflicting stands on political issues. For example, the taxpayers' league may endorse a plan to eliminate plantings in traffic islands while the garden club wants to keep and even enlarge them.

## Economic Interest Groups

Most interest groups are formed on the basis of economic interests. Among those groups, the most active—and certainly the most effective—are those representing business, labor, agriculture, and certain professions.

**Business Groups** Business has long looked to government to promote and protect its interests. Recall that it was merchants, <u>creditors</u>, and property owners who were most responsible for calling the Constitutional Convention in 1787. In the early years of the Republic, business interests fought for and won the <u>protective tariff</u>. Along with organized labor, many of them continue to work to maintain it, even now.

The United States Brewers Association, the oldest organized interest group at work in national politics today, was born in 1862 when Congress first levied a tax on beer. The association's stated purpose was to assure the brewing trade that its interests would be "vigorously <u>prosecuted</u> before the legislative and executive departments."

Hundreds of business groups now operate in Washington, D.C., in the 50 State capitals, and at the local level across the country. The two best-known business organizations are

**creditor**
*n.* one to whom money is owed

**protective tariff**
*n.* import duty, imposed to give advantage to domestic industries

**prosecute**
*vt.* to follow up or pursue

**ebb**
*vi.* to weaken or lessen

3 Churches often take stands on such public issues as drinking, curfew ordinances, and legalized gambling, and they often try to influence public policy on those matters. Garden clubs frequently try to persuade cities to do such things as improve public parks and beautify downtown areas. Not every group to which people belong can properly be called an interest group, of course. But the point is that many groups that are not often thought to be interest groups are, in fact, just that.

the National Association of Manufacturers (NAM) and the Chamber of Commerce of the United States.

Formed in 1895, NAM now represents some 12,000 firms. It generally speaks for "big business" in public affairs. The U.S. Chamber of Commerce, founded in 1912, is a major voice for the nation's thousands of smaller businesses. It has some 3,000 local chambers with about 3 million total members.

The Business Roundtable, founded in 1972, is made up of the chief executive officers of the nation's largest companies. It, too, plays a major role in promoting and defending the business community.

Most segments of the business community also have their own interest groups, often called **trade associations.** They number in the hundreds and include the American Trucking Association, the Association of American Railroads, the National Restaurant Association, and many more. The several trade associations that represent the pharmaceutical, oil, and natural gas industries are generally regarded as the most powerful and effective interest groups today.

Despite their common goal of promoting business interests, business groups do not always present a solid front. In fact, they often disagree and sometimes fight among themselves. The trucking industry, for example, does its best to get as much federal aid as possible for highway construction. The railroads, however, are unhappy with what they see as "special favors" for their competition. At the same time, the railroads see federal taxes on gasoline, oil, tires, and other "highway users' fees" as legitimate sources of federal income. The truckers disagree, of course.

**Labor Groups** A **labor union** is an organization of workers who share the same type of job or who work in the same industry. Labor unions press for government policies that will benefit their members.

The strength of organized labor has <u>ebbed</u> over the past several years. Some 15 million Americans, only about 12 percent of the nation's labor force, belong to labor unions today. In the 1940s and 1950s, as many as a third of all working Americans were union members; as recently as 1975,

---

# Differentiated Resources

The following resources are located in the All-in-One, Unit 2, Chapter 9, Section 2:

- **L3** Reading Comprehension Worksheet (p. 226)
- **L2** Reading Comprehension Worksheet (p. 227)
- **L3** Core Worksheet (p. 228)
- **L3** Skills Worksheet (p. 231)
- **L2** Skill Activity (p. 232)
- **L3** Quiz A (p. 233)
- **L2** Quiz B (p. 234)

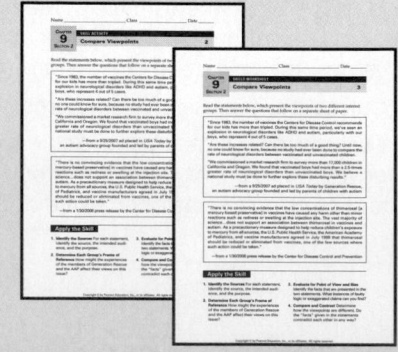

# The Changing State of Labor

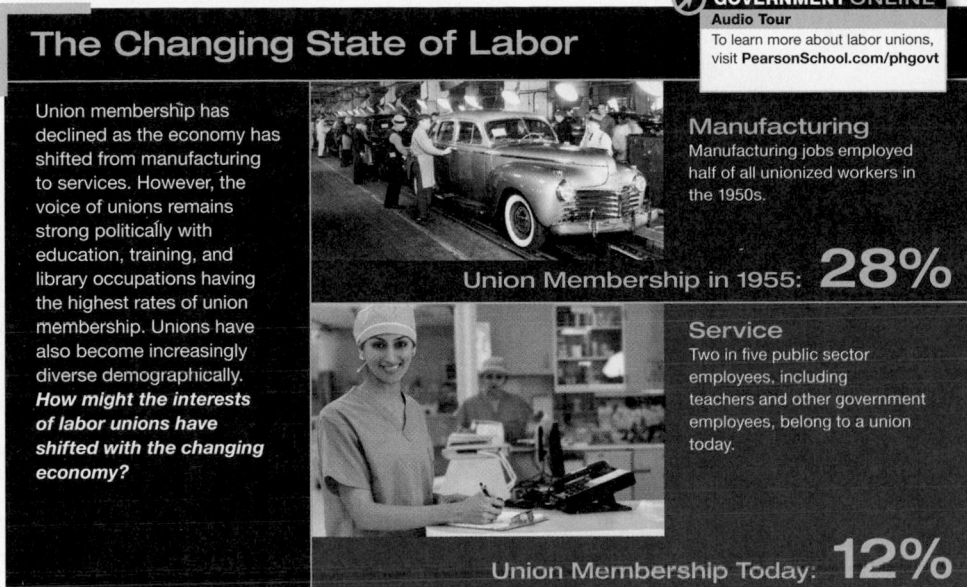

**GOVERNMENT ONLINE**
**Audio Tour**
To learn more about labor unions, visit PearsonSchool.com/phgovt

Union membership has declined as the economy has shifted from manufacturing to services. However, the voice of unions remains strong politically with education, training, and library occupations having the highest rates of union membership. Unions have also become increasingly diverse demographically. *How might the interests of labor unions have shifted with the changing economy?*

**Manufacturing**
Manufacturing jobs employed half of all unionized workers in the 1950s.

Union Membership in 1955: **28%**

**Service**
Two in five public sector employees, including teachers and other government employees, belong to a union today.

Union Membership Today: **12%**

---

union membership accounted for about a fourth of the labor force.

Organized labor is composed of a host of groups today. The AFL-CIO (the American Federation of Labor and Congress of Industrial Organizations) is by far the largest.[4] It is now made up of more than fifty separate unions, including, for example, the International Brotherhood of Electrical Workers (the IBEW) and the International Union of Automotive, Aerospace, and Agricultural Implement Workers (the UAW). All told, the AFL-CIO has 10 million dues-paying members today. Each of its member-unions is, like

[4] The AFL was formed in 1886 as a federation of craft unions. A craft union is made up of those workers who have the same craft or skill—for example, carpenters, plumbers, or electricians. The growth of mass-production industries created a large class of workers not skilled in any particular craft, however. The AFL found it difficult to organize those workers. Many of its craft unions opposed the admission of unions of unskilled workers to the AFL. In 1935, after years of bitter fighting, a group led by John L. Lewis of the United Mine Workers was expelled from the AFL. They formed the independent CIO in 1938. The rivalries between these unions eased to the point where a merger took place in 1955, creating the AFL-CIO.

the AFL-CIO itself, organized on a national, State, and local basis.

The industrial sector of the nation's economy has declined over recent years. Because of this, <u>blue-collar workers</u> in such basic industries as automobiles and steel now represent a decreasing percentage of the working population. That decline has forced organized labor leaders to look elsewhere for new members. The AFL-CIO has been particularly active in efforts to unionize migrant farm workers, service workers, and, most recently, public employees.

In fact, the overall decline in union membership has been partially offset by an upswing in the unionization of government workers in recent years. Public-sector unions now have nearly 8 million members, and that number is likely to continue to grow.

Quarrels over how to <u>rejuvenate</u> the labor movement led several unions to leave the AFL-CIO in 2005. Chief among them were the Service Employees International Union (the SEIU), with 2 million members, and the International Brotherhood of Teamsters (the

✓ **Checkpoint**
Give an example of a situation in which business groups might disagree with one another.

**blue-collar worker**
*n.* one who does manual or industrial work—e.g., a miner, mechanic

**rejuvenate**
*vt.* restore, breathe new life into

---

**DISTRIBUTE CORE WORKSHEET**

Distribute the Chapter 9 Section 2 Core Worksheet (Unit 2 All-in-One, p. 228). This worksheet provides two readings with opposing views on the issue of raising the minimum wage. After students examine the readings, they will write position statements on the issue from the viewpoints of different interest groups described on the worksheet. Remind students that there are many interest groups and that any policy issue can inspire a variety of opinions. Have students read the excerpts and identify which category of interest group likely made the statement. *(Both readings come from economic interest groups.)* Encourage students to think about what conclusion the interest groups want the audience to draw from each reading. *(Reading 1: The minimum wage should be raised. Reading 2: The minimum wage should not be raised.)*

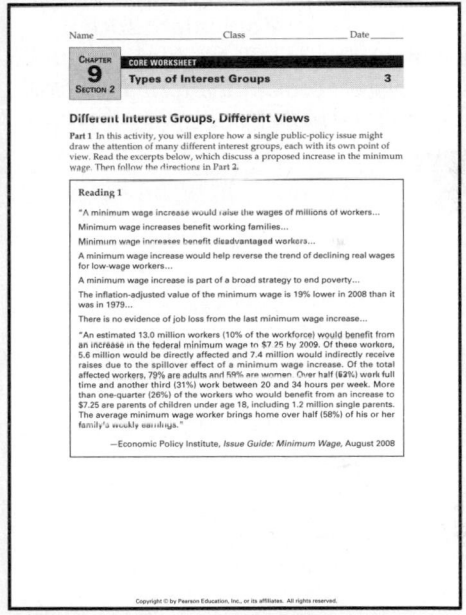

Tell students to go to the Audio Tour to listen to a guided tour on the changing state of labor.

## Answers

**The Changing State of Labor** Possible response: Globalization and loss of manufacturing jobs to overseas suppliers might focus union attention on international trade policies. Increased unionization in education and services might prompt union efforts on issues such as school funding, healthcare, and salary.

**Checkpoint** Possible answer: The trucking industry and the railroads disagree over taxes and the federal aid that the other group receives.

✓ **Checkpoint**
What issues are important to agricultural groups?

IBT), with 1.4 million members, who formed a new 5-million-member group, the Change to Win Coalition.

There are also several independent unions not associated with either the AFL-CIO or Change to Win. Among the largest of them is the Communications Workers of America (the CWA), with approximately 700,000 members.

Organized labor generally speaks with one voice on such social welfare and job-related matters as Social Security, minimum wages, and unemployment. Labor does sometimes oppose labor, however. White-collar and blue-collar workers, for example, do not always share the same economic interests. Sectional interests (East-West, urban-rural, and so on) sometimes divide labor. Production and transportation interests (trucks versus railroads versus airplanes, for example) can create divisions, as well.

**Agricultural Groups** For much of our history, most Americans lived in rural areas on farms. The First Census, taken in 1790, set the nation's population at 3,929,214. It found that nearly all Americans then—94.9 percent of them—lived outside any city or town.

**plummet**
*vi.* fall or drop

The nation's population has increased dramatically since 1790, of course—to well over 300 million today. Over that period the farm population has <u>plummeted</u>. Less than two percent of the population live on farms today. Still, farmers' influence on the government's agricultural policies has been and is enormous. Many powerful associations serve the interests of agriculture. They include several broad-based farm groups and organizations that represent farmers who raise particular <u>commodities</u>.

**commodity**
*n.* anything bought and sold

The most prominent farm groups today are the National Grange, the American Farm Bureau Federation, and the National Farmers Union. The Grange, which was established in 1867, is now as much a social as a political organization. Most of its 300,000 farm-family members live in the Northeast and Mid-Atlantic States.

The Farm Bureau, formed in 1919, is the largest and most effective of the three major agricultural groups. It has over 5 million members today and is especially strong in the Midwest.

The National Farmers Union draws its strength from smaller and less prosperous farmers. The NFU often calls itself the champion of the dirt farmer, and it is frequently at odds with the Grange and the Farm Bureau.

Many other groups speak for the producers of specific farm products—these include the National Association of Wheat Growers, the National Cattlemen's Beef Association, the National Milk Producers Federation, and many others. Then, too, farm-related businesses such as pesticide manufacturers and farm implement dealers have their own organizations.

As with business and labor, farm groups sometimes find themselves at odds with one another. Thus, cotton, corn, soybean, and dairy associations compete as each of them tries to influence State laws regulating margarine and yogurt. California and Florida citrus growers are sometimes pitted against one another, and so on.

**Professional Associations** The professions are generally defined as those occupations that require extensive formal training, and, often government licensing—for example, medicine, law, and teaching. Most professional associations are not nearly as large, well-organized, well-financed, or effective as most business, labor, and farm groups.

Three professional groups are exceptions, however: the American Medical Association (AMA), the American Bar Association (ABA), and the National Education Association (NEA). Each has a very real impact on public policies, and at every level of government.

There are hundreds of less well-known professional groups. Most pharmacists join the National Association of Retail Druggists, librarians join the American Library Association, optometrists join the American Optometric Association, and so on. Still, not all professionals are members of the organizations that claim to represent them. Thus, fewer than half of all licensed medical doctors in the United States belong to the AMA.

## Additional Interest Groups

Again, most organized interests are born out of economic concerns. Many others have

# Background

**GRANGER MOVEMENT** Oliver Hudson Kelley, an Agriculture Department employee, saw a need to bring farmers together to share sound farm practices. In 1867, Kelley founded the National Grange. Soon local Granges formed. At this time, railroads had broad power to set rates for transporting and storing farm products, and many took advantage of the situation to charge high prices. The Granger movement united farmers into a political force. The farmers influenced several States to pass laws limiting the rates railroads and storage facilities could charge. Challenges to these "Granger laws" reached the Supreme Court. In the landmark case *Munn* v. *Illinois,* 1876, the Court upheld the State law, arguing that government could regulate private business if needed for the public good. Although most Granger laws were soon modified or repealed, some became the basis for later antitrust and regulatory laws.

## Answers

**Checkpoint** policies that affect the welfare of farm families, pricing, and State laws regulating specific commodities been formed for other reasons, however, and many of these other groups have a good deal of political <u>clout</u>.

**Issue-Oriented Groups** Many groups exist to promote a cause or an idea. It would take several pages just to list them here, and so what follows is just a sampling of the more important ones.

The American Civil Liberties Union was born in 1920. It fights in and out of court to protect civil and political rights. Common Cause dates from 1970, calls itself "the citizen's lobby," and works for major reforms in the political process. The League of Women Voters and its many local leagues have been dedicated to stimulating participation in and greater knowledge about public affairs since 1919.

The list of groups devoted to causes goes on and on. Many, such as the National Women's Political Caucus, carry the women's rights banner. Others, including the National Wildlife Federation, the Sierra Club, and the Wilderness Society, are pledged to conservation and environmental protection.

Some groups are devoted to opposing or supporting certain causes. The National Right-to-Life Committee, Women Exploited by Abortion, and other groups oppose abortion. They are countered by the National Abortion and Reproduction Rights Action League, Planned Parenthood, and their allies. Similarly, the National Rifle Association (NRA) fights most forms of gun control; Handgun Control, Inc., works for it.

Washington's many "think tanks"— research institutions staffed by scholars and experts in a variety of fields—also qualify as interest groups. They promote their particular policy views and oppose those of others in books, newspaper articles, journals, and tele-

**✔ Checkpoint**
How do professional associations differ from business, labor, and farm groups?

<u>clout</u>
*n.* power, influence

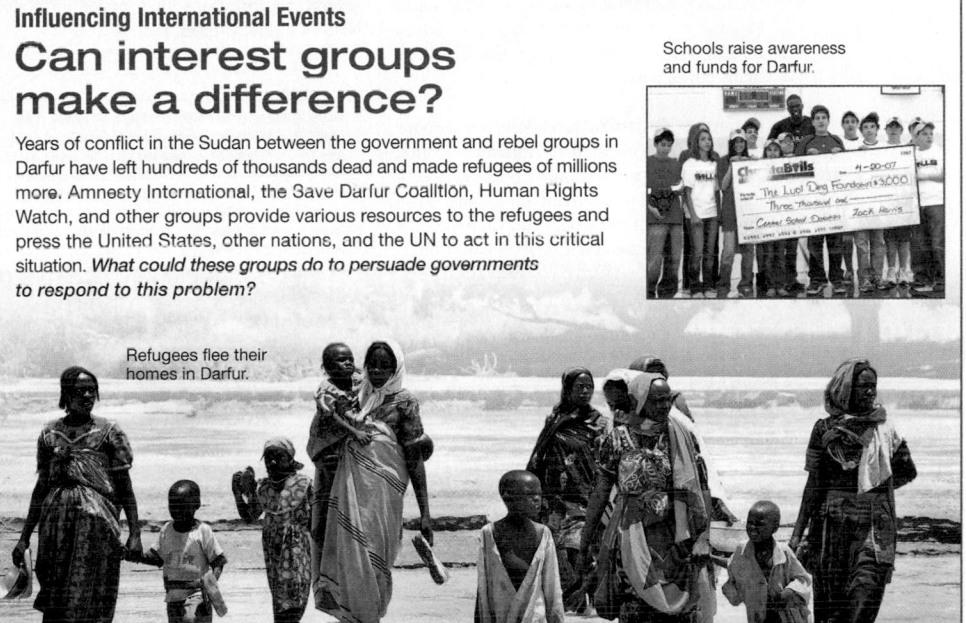

## Influencing International Events

# Can interest groups make a difference?

Years of conflict in the Sudan between the government and rebel groups in Darfur have left hundreds of thousands dead and made refugees of millions more. Amnesty International, the Save Darfur Coalition, Human Rights Watch, and other groups provide various resources to the refugees and press the United States, other nations, and the UN to act in this critical situation. *What could these groups do to persuade governments to respond to this problem?*

Schools raise awareness and funds for Darfur.

Refugees flee their homes in Darfur.

**EXTEND THE LESSON**

**L3** Have students research a specific interest group discussed in the text. Encourage them to visit the Web site of their chosen interest group and create a list of the group's major issues.

**L1 L2 Differentiate** Pair students with L3 or L4 students for this activity.

**L3 L4 Differentiate** Have students write a speech or position paper stating their chosen group's policies. Remind students that representatives of interest groups often testify before Congress, so their speeches and papers should be well written.

## Assess and Remediate

**L3** Collect the Core Worksheets and assess students' work.

**L3** Assign the Section 2 Assessment questions.

**L3** Section Quiz A (Unit 2 All-in-One, p. 233)

**L2** Section Quiz B (Unit 2 All-in-One, p. 234)

Have students complete the review activities in the digital lesson presentation and continue their work in the **Essential Questions Journal.**

## Background

**A FORCE FOR CIVIL RIGHTS** The oldest and largest civil rights interest group in the United States is the National Association for the Advancement of Colored People (NAACP). The NAACP has been committed to the "elimination of all barriers to political, educational, social, and economic equality" of African Americans and other minority groups since its founding in 1909. The NAACP has emphasized legal action to combat discrimination and brought many landmark cases before the Supreme Court. In *Brown* v. *Board of Education of Topeka, Kansas,* 1954, the NAACP's brilliant young lawyer, Thurgood Marshall, successfully convinced the Court to overturn segregation in public schools. Marshall would later become the first African American to serve on the Supreme Court. Today, the NAACP remains a potent force for civil rights and equality for all Americans.

## Answers

**Checkpoint** Professional groups represent specific, highly trained and often regulated professions, rather than whole industrial sectors.

**Influencing International Events** public protests, lobbying campaigns, public education campaigns

| If Your Students Have Trouble With | Strategies For Remediation |
|---|---|
| The American tradition of interest groups (Questions 1, 2) | Have students write a two-sentence summary of the section entitled "An American Tradition." |
| The range and purpose of economic interest groups (Questions 3, 5, 6) | Have students create a web diagram of the section entitled "Groups Based on Economic Interests." The diagram should include and describe the different types of groups discussed in the section. |
| The range and purpose of other types of interest groups (Question 4) | Have students create an illustrated diagram of the other types of groups discussed under the heading "Other Interest Groups." |

## Answers

**Checkpoint** They are research institutions staffed by scholars that promote particular policy views.

---

✔ **Checkpoint**
What are "think tanks"?

**centrist**
*adj.* having moderate views

**pension**
*n.* retirement or other benefit payment

vision appearances. The more prominent among them include the more conservative Cato Institute and the Heritage Foundation; the more liberal Institute for Policy Studies; and the <u>centrist</u> American Enterprise Institute and Brookings Institution.

**Organizations for Specific Groups** Hundreds of interest groups seek to promote the welfare of certain segments of the population. Among the best known and most powerful are the American Legion and the Veterans of Foreign Wars, which work to advance the interests of the country's veterans. Groups like Older Americans, Inc., and AARP are very active in such areas as <u>pensions</u> and medical care for senior citizens.

Several organizations—notably the National Association for the Advancement of Colored People (NAACP) and the National Urban League—are concerned with public policies affecting African Americans. Other organizations, such as the Japanese American Citizens League, the Mexican American Legal Defense Fund, and the National Association of Arab Americans, support the country's many ethnic groups.

**Religious Organizations** Religious groups have long been involved in American politics, and many work to affect public policy in several important areas today. Many Protestants do so through the National Council of Churches, the Christian Voice, and the Christian Coalition.

The National Catholic Welfare Council speaks for the interests of Roman Catholics. The American Jewish Congress and B'nai B'rith's Anti-Defamation League promote the interests of the Jewish community.

## Public-Interest Groups

The typical interest group seeks public policies that are of special benefit to its members and works against policies seen as threats. Some organizations have a broader focus and work for the "public good." That is, a **public-interest group** is an organization that works for the best interests of the overall community, rather than the narrower interests of one segment. It seeks policies that benefit all or most people, whether or not they belong to or support the organization.[5]

Public-interest groups have become quite visible over the past 30 years or so. Among the best known and most active are Common Cause, the League of Women Voters, and the several organizations that make up Ralph Nader's Public Citizen, Inc.

---

5 Nearly all interest groups claim that they work for the "public good." Thus, the National Association of Manufacturers (NAM) says that lower taxes on business will stimulate the economy and so help everyone. The AFL-CIO says the same thing about spending public dollars for public works programs. But, as a general rule, most interest groups support or oppose public policies on a much narrower basis: on what they see to be the best interests of their members.

**Essential Questions Journal** To continue to build a response to the chapter Essential Question, go to your **Essential Questions Journal.**

## SECTION 2 ASSESSMENT

**1. Guiding Question** Use your completed outline to answer this question: What are the different types of interest groups at work in American society?

**Key Terms and Comprehension**

2. What factor distinguishes an interest group from other associations or organizations?

3. **Labor unions** and **trade associations** are formed on the basis of what interest?

4. What is a **public-interest group,** and how does it differ from other types of interest groups?

**Critical Thinking**

**5. Determine Cause and Effect**
(a) How have economic changes in the United States transformed the nature and types of labor unions in the country? (b) What are the results of those changes?

**6. Draw Conclusions** Why do you think that groups involved with economic interests are the most numerous type of interest group in the United States today?

**Quick Write**

**Assessment Writing: Write Strong Opening and Closing Statements** When writing for assessment, it is important to craft strong opening and closing statements. Using the graphic organizer you created in Section 1, begin to draft complete sentences that expand your argument. Remember: Your opening sentences should clearly state your position and your closing statement should complete your argument with a clear and logical conclusion.

## Assessment Answers

**1.** The largest number of groups have formed around economic interests, such as business, labor, agriculture, and certain professions. Other groups have organized around specific issues, communities, or religions. Public-interest groups work for the broader public good rather than for the narrow interests of a segment of the population.

**2.** An interest group tries to influence the government to act in ways that promote the group's goals or interests.

**3.** economic interests

**4.** A public-interest group works for the best interests of the overall community, unlike other interest groups, which promote mainly the interests of their members.

**5.** Possible response: **(a)** Economic changes have eroded the sectors of the economy from which unions once drew their greatest strength. **(b)** Today, unions are drawing a growing share of their members from sectors such as government and service workers.

**6.** Possible response: Most people spend a majority of their time pursuing their economic

security and so are keenly interested in how policies may affect their well-being.

**QUICK WRITE** Students' opening sentence should clearly state their view of interest groups, and their closing statement should summarize their argument.

# ISSUES OF OUR TIME

# Lobbying the Federal Government

## ▶ Track the Issue

**The 1st Amendment,** which guarantees the right to peaceably assemble and petition the government for a redress of grievances, protects the rights of interest groups to lobby government.

**1876**
**The House** passes a temporary measure that, for the first time, requires all lobbyists to register with the clerk of the House.

**1906**
**A series of articles** entitled "The Treason of the Senate" appears in *Cosmopolitan,* alleging widespread corruption on the part of interest groups in Congress.

**1946**
**Congress** passes the Federal Regulation of Lobbying Act.

**1995**
**Congress** attempts to address short-comings of the 1946 law with the Lobbying Disclosure Act.

**2007**
**Congress and the President** respond to a major lobbying scandal with the Honest Leadership and Open Government Act.

President Barack Obama discusses his Administration policy. ▶

## ▶▶ Perspectives

**Recent scandals involving** several lobbyists and some members of Congress and other public officials have raised questions about the influence of lobbyists and interest groups. Amid charges that lobbyists had improperly used gifts and travel to gain support in government, the nation again debated the benefits and drawbacks of lobbying.

"My Administration is committed to reducing the undue influence of special interests that for too long has shaped the national agenda and drowned out the voices of ordinary Americans. Special interests exert this disproportionate influence, in part, by relying on lobbyists who have special access that is not available to all citizens. Although lobbyists can sometimes play a constructive role ..., their service in privileged positions within the executive branch can perpetuate the culture of special interest access that I am committed to changing."
—*President Barack Obama, June 18, 2010*

"Many lobbyists ... embody what government reform efforts seem to consider the noble lobbyist; one who does not attempt to influence with political contributions, but relies solely on the strength of their argument ... New reforms which treat these lobbyists like any other "special interest" promise to ... marginalize these professionals and their causes. ... These current reforms are curtailing the ability of these lobbyists to state their cases. This ... marginalization has exponential impacts on the voices of many Americans who will now be more unlikely than ever to be heard."
—*Darrell K. Smith, Executive Vice President, IMA-NA, February 3, 2010*

## ▶▶ Connect to Your World

1. **Understand (a)** How does the Obama directive limit lobbyist influence in Federal Government? **(b)** What does Mr. Smith suggest limits most lobbyists? **(c)** Are both concerns valid? Why or why not?
2. **Draw Conclusions (a)** Does lobbying reform violate the 1st Amendment? **(b)** Which do you think poses a greater danger: restricting lobbyists or giving them practically free reign? Why?

**GOVERNMENT ONLINE**
**In the News**
For updates about the regulation of lobbyists, visit
**PearsonSchool.com/phgovt**

President Barack Obama discusses his Administration policy. ▶

253

## In what ways do interest groups attempt to influence government and public opinion?

| How Interest Groups Work | |
| --- | --- |
| **Direct Approach** | **Indirect Approach** |
| • Talk to government officials at all levels<br>• Testify at congressional committee meetings<br>• Submit position statements on proposed legislation<br>• Provide useful information to Congress<br>• Make campaign contributions<br>• Write speeches<br>• Draft legislation<br>• Lobby senior White House aides and executive agencies<br>• Try to influence agency appointments<br>• Rely on networks of contacts in government<br>• Bring lawsuits<br>• File *amicus curiae* briefs<br>• Try to influence judicial appointments | • Grass-roots pressure<br>• Letters, postcards, phone calls, faxes, e-mails from local supporters<br>• Internet—Web site, e-mail lists, blogging<br>• Fundraising for candidates<br>• Get-out-the-vote efforts<br>• Demonstrations and protest marches<br>• Publish ratings of members of Congress<br>• Mold public opinion<br>• Use of advertising<br>• Promotion by group members and celebrities<br>• News items in mass media—press releases, interviews, studies<br>• Propaganda<br>• Electioneering—PACs |

# Get Started

## LESSON GOALS

Students will . . .

- create an interest group campaign for influencing public policy and opinion, using direct and indirect approaches.
- practice influencing public opinion by composing a persuasive fundraising letter for their interest group campaign.

# SKILLS DEVELOPMENT

## INNOVATE AND THINK CREATIVELY

Before students begin on the Core Worksheet, you may want to review information on innovating and thinking creatively in the Skills Handbook, p. S23.

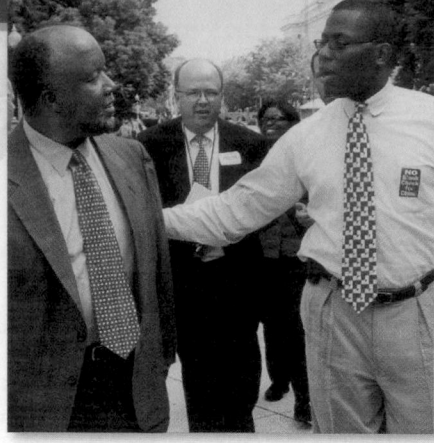

## SECTION 3

# Interest Groups at Work

### Guiding Question

**In what ways do interest groups attempt to influence government and public opinion?** Use the chart to record details of how interest groups work in our government and society.

| How Interest Groups Work | |
| --- | --- |
| **Direct Approach** | **Indirect Approach** |
| •<br>•<br>• | •<br>•<br>• |

### Political Dictionary

- lobbying
- lobbyist
- *amicus curiae* brief
- grass-roots pressures

### Objectives

1. Understand the difference between the *direct* and *indirect* approaches of interest groups.
2. Describe how lobbyists influence the legislative, executive, and judicial branches of government.
3. Examine how interest groups use grass-roots lobbying.
4. Identify how interest groups use media, propaganda, and political campaigns to influence public opinion and policy.

**Image Above:** Lobbyist Jack James of the AFL-CIO (right) speaks with Bennie Thompson (D., Miss.), chairman of the House committee on Homeland Security.

Interest groups exist to influence the making and the content of public policy, and they do so in a great many ways and in a great many places. They are, in effect, an excellent illustration of political scientist Harold D. Lasswell's notion that politics is all about "who gets what, when and how."

Interest groups approach government both directly and indirectly in their attempts to influence policy. Their *direct* efforts involve immediate, face-to-face contacts with policymakers. Their *indirect* efforts entail more subtle tactics—for example, mobilizing "the folks back home" to contact their members of Congress with letters, phone calls, faxes, and e-mails for or against a particular bill.

## The Direct Approach

Again, the direct approach, bringing group pressures to bear directly on public policymakers, is another way of saying "lobbying." **Lobbying** is the process by which organized interests attempt to affect the decisions and actions of public officials.[6] **Lobbyists** are those people who try to persuade public officials to do those things that interest groups want them to do.

Lobbying occurs wherever public policy is made, including Washington, D.C., every State capital, and all of the county courthouses and city halls across the country. It is a big business today. Every important interest and many lesser ones—business groups, labor unions, farm organizations, the professions, churches, veterans, environmental groups, and many more—maintain lobbyists in Washington. Best estimates put the number of people who earn at least part of their living by lobbying Congress at no fewer than 30,000, and they spend well over $3 billion per year on their efforts.

Most lobbyists are professionals. Some are freelancers, "hired guns" who will use their contacts and talents for anyone willing to pay what they charge.

---

6 The term was first used in Great Britain some 200 years ago, referring to journalists and special-interest pleaders who waited in the public lobbies of the House of Commons to talk with members of Parliament. The term *lobby-agent* was being used to identify favor-seekers at sessions of New York's legislature in Albany by the late 1820s. By the 1830s it had been shortened to *lobbyist* and was in wide use in Washington, D.C., and elsewhere. Lobbying is still frequently defined in terms of legislators and legislation. As we note, however, it has a much broader application today.

# Focus on the Basics

**FACTS:** • Interest groups apply direct pressure in the form of lobbying at all three branches of government and at all levels of government. • Interest groups apply indirect pressure by promoting grass-roots support and seeking to influence public opinion through propaganda and other techniques.

**CONCEPTS:** representative government

**ENDURING UNDERSTANDINGS:** • Lobbying occurs at any level of government at which public policy is made. • Interest groups try to capture and harness the power of public opinion.

Most larger companies and labor unions have their own full-time lobbyists. Many work for the hundreds of Washington law firms and public relations agencies, concentrated along K Street, that specialize in that kind of work.

The Abramoff scandal prompted Congress to tighten the statutes regulating lobbyists' behavior in 2007. As the law now stands, all persons and organizations that seek to influence members of Congress, their staffers, or any policy-making officer in the executive branch must register with the clerk of the House and the secretary of the Senate. They are required to supply such basic information as name, address, and principal place of business, plus a general description of their activities. Every lobbyist must describe his or her ongoing work in detail and account for the income from it in quarterly reports.

Former senators and top-level executive branch officials must now wait two years, but ex-House members wait only one year, before they can become lobbyists. And, since 2007, no member of Congress can receive *any* gift from lobbyists or their clients.

**Lobbying Congress** The benefits of maintaining close relationships with members of Congress are fairly obvious, for Congress is the prime place for the making of public policy in the Federal Government. Some lobbying efforts target individual lawmakers and their staffs, but most are aimed at the standing committees of the House and Senate. More than a century ago, Woodrow Wilson described "Congress in its committee rooms" as "Congress at work," and that remains the case today, as you will see in Chapter 12.

Lobbyists testify before congressional committees and regularly submit prepared statements that set out their organization's views on proposed legislation. What happens in a legislative body often excites the interest of several different and competing groups. For example, if the House Committee on the Judiciary is considering a bill to regulate the sale of firearms, those companies that make guns, those that sell them, and those that produce or sell ammunition and a host of other related products all will have a clear stake in the bill's contents and its fate. So, too, do law enforcement agencies, hunters, wildlife

conservationists, such groups as the National Rifle Association and the American Civil Liberties Union, and several others. Representatives of all of these groups are certain to be invited, or to ask for the opportunity, to present their views to the committee.

Lobbyists often provide useful information to Congress. To the point, John F. Kennedy, who served three terms in the House and was in his second term in the Senate when he won the presidency, observed:

> **PRIMARY SOURCE**
> Competent lobbyists can present the most persuasive arguments in support of their positions. Indeed, there is no more effective manner of learning all important arguments and facts on a controversial issue than to have the opposing lobbyists present their case.
>
> —John F. Kennedy

Lobbyists are ready to do such things as make campaign contributions, provide information, write speeches, and even draft legislation. The contributions are welcome,

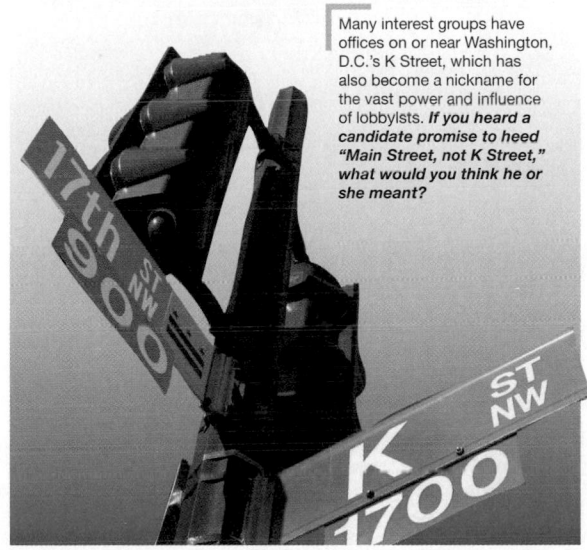

Many interest groups have offices on or near Washington, D.C.'s K Street, which has also become a nickname for the vast power and influence of lobbyists. *If you heard a candidate promise to heed "Main Street, not K Street," what would you think he or she meant?*

---

# Differentiated Resources

The following resources are located in the All-in-One, Unit 2, Chapter 9, Section 3:

- **L3** Reading Comprehension Worksheet (p. 235)
- **L2** Reading Comprehension Worksheet (p. 236)
- **L3** Core Worksheet (p. 237)
- **L3** **L4** Extend Worksheet (p. 238)
- **L2** Extend Activity (p. 240)
- **L3** Quiz A (p. 241)   **L2** Quiz B (p. 242)
- **L3** Chapter Test A (p. 243)
- **L2** Chapter Test B (p. 246)

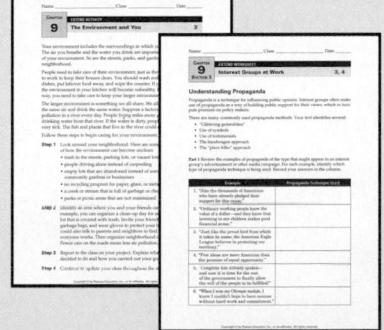

---

Assign the section, the graphic organizer in the text, and the Reading Comprehension Worksheet (Unit 2 All-in-One, p. 235) before class.

**L2** **Differentiate** Reading Comprehension Worksheet (Unit 2 All-in-One, p. 236)

**BELLRINGER**

Write the following on the board; **1. What three issues do you think should be the main focus of the Federal Government? 2. What would you be willing to do to ensure they were high on the government's agenda?**

# Teach

To present this topic using online resources, use the lesson presentations at **PearsonSchool.com/phgovt.**

**DISCUSS BELLRINGER**

Ask students to share their answers to question 1 of the Bellringer activity. *(Possible answers: the economy, the environment, Social Security, healthcare)* Then have them share their answers to question 2. Tell them that the public has a number of options available to influence the focus of the Federal Government. These include writing letters to public officials, taking part in marches or protests, giving money to interest groups, signing petitions, or volunteering to be an active member of an interest group. The amount of involvement often depends on how strongly an individual feels about a specific issue.

**Government** online | *All print resources are available on the Teacher's Resource Library CD-ROM and online at PearsonSchool.com/phgovt.*

---

# Answers

**Checkpoint** Lobbyists testify at hearings, provide information, make campaign contributions, and draft laws.

**Caption** The candidate intended to follow the will of the constituents, not the desires of lobbyists.

## DISTRIBUTE CORE WORKSHEET

Distribute the Chapter 9 Section 3 Core Worksheet (Unit 2 All-in-One, p. 237), which asks students to design an interest group campaign. In this activity, students will construct a multifaceted interest group campaign that uses both direct and indirect approaches. Help students identify a cause that is suitable for the project. Make sure they understand the difference between direct approaches, such as lobbying, and indirect approaches, such as propaganda designed to influence public opinion. Encourage students to consult their text for examples of different causes.

**L1 L2 Differentiate** Have students provide one or two examples of different types of interest group activities.

**L3 L4 Differentiate** Have students research an actual interest group and write a brief report describing the group's mission, the policies it is currently targeting, and some direct and indirect methods the group is using.

Tell students to go to the interactivity to learn more about how lobbying works.

## Answers

**Checkpoint** Lobbyists work to influence the executive branch because the executive branch can regulate the ways laws are carried out, as well as have an impact on who receives federal appointments.

**Lobbying in Action** Groups may conduct advertising campaigns to influence the public and lobby government officials.

256 Interest Groups

---

✔ **Checkpoint**
Why do lobbyists target the executive branch?

the information is usually quite accurate, the speeches are forceful, and the bills are well drawn. Most lobbyists know that if they behaved otherwise (gave false or misleading information, for example), they would damage, if not destroy, their credibility and so their overall effectiveness.

Lobbyists work hard to influence committee action, floor debate, and then the final vote in a legislative body. If they fail in one house, they carry their fight to the other. If they lose there, too, they may turn to the executive branch, and perhaps to the courts, as well.

**nurture**
*vt.* to foster, encourage, promote

**GOVERNMENT** ONLINE
For an **interactive** exploration of lobbying, visit
PearsonSchool.com/phgovt

**How Government Works**

# Lobbying in Action

An electricity company has recently announced plans to build a wind farm in a coastal location. There are a number of competing interests involved, and each is taking steps to make sure their influence is felt. *What actions might these interest groups take to build public support and further their views?*

**Step 1 A Proposal**
A project for building an electricity-generating wind farm in waters off the shores of an upscale vacation area is announced. The plan promises a nonpolluting source of electricity.

**Step 2 Debate Begins**
Some environmental interest groups favor the project as a source of clean energy. Others oppose the project because it may harm birds or ocean life. Each side tries to build public support.

**Step 3 Government Action**
The project requires approval of several State and Federal Government agencies. Those agencies consider everything from environmental impact to effects on the electric power industry. Interest groups mobilize to influence the views of the many agencies involved.

**Step 4 Final Decision**
Public agencies issue their rulings on the project, which might require legislative action.

**Lobbying the Executive Branch** A vast amount of public policy is made by those who administer the law—that is, by the executive branch. Many of the laws that Congress enacts are written in fairly broad terms. More specific details, such as the day-to-day enforcement of the measure, are left to be worked out in the executive branch. As a practical matter, Congress cannot do such things as prescribe the design specifications for military aircraft, or dictate the advice that federal extension agents are to give to farmers, or determine which of several vaccines will be most effective in the next flu season.

Because meetings with the President and Cabinet officers are difficult to arrange, most executive-branch lobbying focuses, instead, on senior aides in the White House and on the various agencies in the President's administration. The primary job of one of those White House aides, the Director of Public Liaison, is to nurture good relations with major interest groups, especially those that support the President's policies.

Organized interests regularly try to influence the President's appointment of the top officials in various agencies. If an industry group is successful in such efforts, it can improve its chances for favorable treatment by, for example, the Federal Communications Commission or the Bureau of Reclamation in the Department of the Interior.

The most successful lobbyists rely on their networks of contacts as they deal with federal agencies. Ed Rollins, sometime lobbyist and major White House aide in recent Republican administrations, puts that point this way:

> **PRIMARY SOURCE**
> I've got many friends all through the agencies and equally important, I don't have many enemies. . . . I tell my clients I can get your case moved to the top of the pile.
>
> —Ed Rollins

**Lobbying and the Courts** Organized interests have only recently recognized the fact that they can use the courts to realize their policy goals. You almost certainly know that in 1954, in *Brown* v. *Topeka Board of Education,* the United States Supreme Court held that segregation by race in public schools is unconstitutional. But do you know that *Brown* was taken to the Supreme Court by an interest group, the National Association for the Advancement of Colored People? The massive impact that that case has had made the special-interest community realize just how useful the courts can be.

Lawsuits brought by interest groups are not at all uncommon today. For some, like the American Civil Liberties Union, legal action is the primary means by which they seek to influence public policy. The ACLU regularly takes on unpopular causes—for example, those involving the free speech rights of <u>fringe groups.</u> Those causes usually have little chance of success in legislative bodies, but they may prevail in a courtroom.

An interest group may also file an ***amicus curiae*** ("friend of the court") **brief** in a case to which it is not itself a party but in which it does have a stake. An *amicus* brief consists of written arguments presented to a court in support of one side in a dispute. More than 100 different organizations submitted *amicus* briefs to the Supreme Court in 2003, arguing for or against the University of Michigan's affirmative action policies in *Gratz* v. *Bollinger* and *Grutter* v. *Bollinger.*

Organized interests often try to influence the selection of federal judges. Thus, over recent years, both pro-life and pro-choice organizations have urged Republican and Democratic administrations to make nominees' stances on abortion a major condition for appointment to the federal bench.

## The Indirect Approach

Organized interests also approach government in a number of indirect ways. No matter the particular tactic used, however, the goal is exactly the same as it is when they approach public officials directly—that is, to shape policies to their liking. Not infrequently, interest groups try to mask their involvement in some indirect approach, hoping to make the effort appear to be spontaneous. Their indirect approaches include what is often called "grass-roots lobbying," the molding of public opinion, and various election-related activities.

**Grass-roots Lobbying** Most lobbyists know how to bring **grass-roots pressures**—pressures from members of an interest group or from the people at large, often beginning at a very basic level—to bear on public officials. Many of the groups that the lobbyists speak for can mount campaigns using letters, postcards, phone calls, faxes, and e-mails from their supporters, often on very short notice.

Some members of Congress downplay the effectiveness of such efforts, and all of them know that groups orchestrate outpourings of letters, phone calls, e-mails, and the like. Still, every congressional office monitors those communications as a way of tracking <u>constituents'</u> opinions.

No organization uses grass-roots lobbying more effectively than AARP, a group originally known as the American Association of Retired Persons. Founded in 1958, it now has more than 39 million members and a staff of more than 1,600. Whenever legislation or some administrative action that affects retirees is pending, AARP swings into action. Members of Congress receive more letters, phone calls, and e-mails from members of AARP than they do from any other group.

The Internet has been a real <u>boon</u> to interest groups, and to cause-related organizations in particular. Nearly every organized interest has a Web site and an expanding e-mail list, as well. Blogging is used by many groups and has proved most effective in reaching people in younger age groups.

Cyberspace has been especially useful to those who want to organize a group but can do so only on a low-budget. Left-leaning MoveOn.org is a prime example of the Internet's capacity to organize. It was started by a handful of activists working out of a garage in Berkeley, California, in 1998. By 2004, they had formed an Internet network linking hundreds of thousands of citizens who could be mobilized to support liberal candidates and causes. MoveOn.org raised more than $3 million for Democratic

✔ **Checkpoint**
How does the indirect approach to lobbying differ from the direct approach?

**fringe group**
*n.* a group holding less popular, often extreme, views

**constituent**
*n.* one who is represented by a legislator

**boon**
*n.* welcome benefit, stroke of good fortune

# Teacher-to-Teacher Network

**ALTERNATE LESSON PLAN** To help students acquire real-life experience in influencing government, divide the class into groups and have them follow these steps: (1) Identify a problem in their community that they care about, such as maintaining recreational areas or issues surrounding safety for teens. (2) Propose solutions to the problem they have identified. (3) Create an "interest group" devoted to solving the problem. (4) Propose an action plan for the interest group to follow.

To see this lesson plan, go to

**Teacher Center**
at PearsonSchool.com/phgovt

**DISCUSS STUDENT PLANS**

After students have completed the activity, have them share their plans with the class. On the board, list the variety of activities identified in student plans. Review with students the difference between direct approaches to changing public policy and opinion and indirect approaches. Ask students to identify the differences between these two approaches. *(Direct approaches involve direct interaction with government officials. For example, lobbyists talk to members of Congress, provide information to committees, and bring lawsuits to the courts. Indirect approaches appeal to the people, so that public opinion can pressure policymakers.)*

## Answers

**Checkpoint** Indirect approaches do not involve direct contact with policymakers by interest-group representatives, whereas direct approaches do.

**L3 Differentiate** Extend the lesson by having students compose fundraising letters as part of their interest group campaign. Have them begin by thinking about who their target audience is and what appeals might persuade that audience to contribute money to the cause. If students have Internet access, have them examine fundraising pages at some interest group sites for ideas. Ask students to note their ideas and then use their notes to compose the letter.

**L1 L2 Differentiate** Distribute the Extend Activity "The Environment and You" (Unit 2 All-in-One, p. 240).

**L3 L4 Differentiate** Distribute the Extend Worksheet "Understanding Propaganda" (Unit 2 All-in-One, p. 238) and have students create their own piece of propaganda.

Tell students to go to the Audio Tour to learn more about grass-roots organizing.

## Answers

**Going Digital** Possible response: Technology-based efforts will miss segments of the population that do not have the technology. Also, government officials might discount the flood of incoming electronic transmissions out of suspicion they don't represent "real" constituents.

**GOVERNMENT** ONLINE

**Audio Tour**
To learn more about grass-roots organizing, visit
PearsonSchool.com/phgovt

### Grass-roots Organizing
# Going Digital

Advances in technology, notably the Internet, have drastically changed the way that interest groups organize on a grass-roots level. Having access to instantaneous and convenient communication tools allows smaller groups to mobilize and raise money as quickly as larger, more influential interests do. *What might be the potential drawbacks of relying on technology to organize?*

**Appeals**
to government officials can be made using cell phones, PDAs or other mobile technologies.

**Members**
organize faster and easier online, as well as being able to send important data to one another on the move.

**Petitions**
are a way for groups to quickly garner a large number of signatures and increase interest instantly online.

AVAAZ.ORG
HELP SUPPORT OUR WORK

**Fundraising**
can be conducted more easily with credit cards and online donation forms.

**Organizers**
can set up Web sites based on their interests and connect with other members remotely.

congressional candidates in 2006 and even more in 2008; and it also conducted a massive get-out-the-vote effort in both elections.

Demonstrations and protest marches are another form of grass-roots lobbying. Most are efforts to show public officials that some group's cause does have broad public support. Some involve an element of political theater or an eye-catching gimmick to attract media (especially television) coverage. Thus, for example, peace groups often stage "die-ins" to protest war, and farmers might drive their tractors to Washington in "tractorcades" to dramatize their opposition to some agricultural policy.

Several groups now publish ratings of members of Congress. These rankings are based on the votes cast on measures these groups regard as crucial to their interests. Among the more prominent organizations that do so are such liberal groups as Americans for Democratic Action (ADA) and the American Civil Liberties Union (ACLU) and such conservative ones as the American Conservative Union (ACU) and the Chamber of Commerce of the United States.

Each of these groups sees to it that the mass media publicize their ratings. They also distribute them to the group's membership. Their ultimate objective is either to persuade less-than-friendly legislators to change their voting behavior or to help bring about their defeat in future elections.

**Shaping Public Opinion** Many organized interests spend much of their time and energy on attempts to mold public opinion. Groups that can make enough people regard them and their cause in the best possible way, and can persuade enough people to convey that feeling to public officials, have taken a major step toward achieving their policy goals.

Television screens, newspapers, and magazines are filled with costly advertisements by oil, cell phone, drug, and insurance companies, and many others—all seeking to cast the sponsor of the ad in a favorable light. Most of those ads go well beyond promoting some particular product and try also to suggest that the organizations behave as good citizens or defend family values or protect the environment, and so on.

# Debate

Use the quotation below to start a debate in your class. Use the debate rules on page T25 to structure the class.

"The people of this country, not special interest big money, should be the source of all political power."

—Senator Paul Wellstone

Ask students to take a position on this statement: **Special interest groups undermine popular sovereignty.**

A group's own membership can be used to shape opinions. Thus, in its decades-long opposition (since abandoned) to national health insurance proposals, the American Medical Association persuaded many doctors to put literature condemning those proposals as "socialized medicine" in their waiting rooms and to talk with patients about the issue. Using those tactics, the AMA capitalized on the tendency of most patients to respect their own physicians and regard them as experts.

Many groups use well-regarded personalities or trusted public figures to persuade people to support the group's cause. The late Charlton Heston served two terms as president of the NRA. Mr. Heston had a long record of support for the 2nd Amendment, but he was much better known from his long career as an actor. The wide recognition of his name and the moral authority associated with many of the characters he played in movies were extremely helpful to the NRA in its efforts to protect and expand the rights of Americans to keep and bear arms.

Almost certainly, though, the most effective vehicle for the molding of opinions and attitudes is the mass media. Interest groups know that people are more likely to regard their positions favorably if their activities are covered by the media as news rather than presented to the public in paid advertisements. With that in mind, interest groups produce a veritable flood of press releases, interviews, studies, and other materials, hoping to attract media coverage.

**Propaganda** Interest groups try to create the public attitudes they want by using propaganda.[7] Propaganda is a technique of persuasion aimed at influencing individual or group behaviors. Its goal is to create a particular belief among the audience. That belief may be completely true or false, or it may lie somewhere between those extremes. Today, people tend to think of propaganda as a form of lying and deception. As a technique,

▲ Muhammad Ali (left) and Michael J. Fox lend their names to raising money for Parkinson's disease, an illness from which both men suffer. **How might Ali's and Fox's celebrity status help their cause?**

however, propaganda is neither moral nor immoral; it is, instead, amoral.

Propaganda does not use objective logic. Rather, it begins with a conclusion. Then it brings together any evidence that will support that conclusion and disregards information that will not. Propagandists are advertisers, persuaders—and occasionally even brainwashers—who are interested in influencing others to agree with their point of view.

The development of the mass media in this country encouraged the use of propaganda, first in the field of commercial advertising, and then in politics. To be successful, propaganda must be presented in simple, interesting, and credible terms. Talented propagandists almost never attack the logic of a policy they oppose. Instead, they often attack it with name-calling. That is, they attach such labels as "communist" or "fascist." Other labels include "ultraliberal," "ultraconservative," "pie-in-the-sky," or "greedy." Or, they try to discredit a policy or person by card-stacking—that is, presenting only one side of the issue.

Policies that propagandists support receive labels that will produce favorable reactions. They use such glittering generalities as "American," "sound," "fair," and "just." Symbols are often used to elicit those positive reactions from people, too: Uncle Sam and the American flag are favorites. So, too,

---

7  The term comes from the Latin *propagare*—to propagate, to spread, to disseminate. It has been part of the American political vocabulary since the 1930s.

---

# Assess and Remediate

**L3** Collect the Core Worksheets and assess students' interest group campaigns using the Rubric for Assessing Student Performance on a Project (Unit 2 All-in-One, p. 252).

**L3** Assign the Section 3 Assessment questions.

**L3** Section Quiz A (Unit 2 All-in-One, p. 241)

**L2** Section Quiz B (Unit 2 All-in-One, p. 242)

Have students complete the review activities in the digital lesson presentation and continue their work in the **Essential Questions Journal.**

# Background

**INTERNET FUNDRAISING** Display Transparency 9G, Development of PACs, to give students a perspective on PAC membership. Today, traditional fundraising for political candidates can involve costly private events staged for big-money donors. But the political action committee ActBlue is turning the fundraising process upside down. By harnessing the power of the Internet, ActBlue has collected millions of dollars from thousands of small donors. ActBlue allows Democratic candidates for office at any level—national, State, or local—to use its Web site to solicit donations. In response, a PAC called Right-Roots was formed as a conservative Republican counter to ActBlue. The primary goal of RightRoots is to act as an Internet channel to raise money for Republican candidates for federal office. The money contributed by donors is passed directly to the candidates, who pay a percentage to cover the credit card processing fee.

# Answers

**Caption** Possible response: Celebrities can bring favorable attention if viewers hold positive feelings toward the particular person. In addition, celebrities have ready access to the media and so can raise public awareness of an issue.

| If Your Students Have Trouble With | Strategies For Remediation |
|---|---|
| The ways interest groups influence policy directly (Questions 1, 2) | Have students identify specific lobbying actions described under "The Direct Approach" and categorize them under "Congress," "Executive Branch," and "Courts" in a three-column chart. |
| The ways interest groups influence policy indirectly (Questions 1, 2, 7, 8) | Have student pairs write and exchange quiz questions for the section entitled "The Indirect Approach." |
| The meaning and methods of propaganda (Question 5) | Have students create a web diagram that identifies the definition of propaganda and the different techniques that are often employed in propaganda campaigns. |
| The functions of lobbyists (Questions 3, 4, 6) | Have students review the section and write a job description listing the main activities and qualifications of lobbyists. |

▶▶ **Analyzing Political Cartoons** This cartoon shows a politician kissing the hand of a political action committee member rather than a baby. *What is this cartoonist saying about the influence of PACs on candidates for office?*

speeches—in fact, through every form of mass communication. The more controversial or less popular a group's position, the more necessary the propaganda campaign becomes.

**Electioneering** The most useful and the most appreciated thing that an interest group can do for a public official is to help that person win office. From the group's perspective, electing officeholders like members of Congress, State legislators, governors, and other State and local policymakers sympathetic to their interests is among the most effective things it can do. Once elected, these individuals can shape legislation and allocate money to meet the needs of the interest groups.

Groups can and do help those who run for office, and they do so in a variety of ways. Many do so through their political action committees. Recall that PACs are, as we said in Chapter 7, political arms of interest groups. They make financial contributions and hold fundraisers for candidates. They conduct voter registration and get-out-the-vote drives, supply professional campaign consultants, and provide information to be used in campaign speeches. Occasionally they even provide audiences to hear those speeches. And PACs do such other things as help staff local campaign offices, distribute campaign literature, work phone banks, and take voters to the polls on election day.

are testimonials—endorsements, or supporting statements, from such well-known personalities as television stars or professional athletes. The bandwagon approach, which urges people to follow the crowd, is another favorite technique. The plain-folks approach, in which the propagandist pretends to be one of the common people, gets heavy use, too.

Propaganda is spread through newspapers, radio, television, the Internet, movies, billboards, books, magazines, pamphlets, posters,

**Essential Questions Journal** To continue to build a response to the chapter Essential Question, go to your **Essential Questions Journal.**

## SECTION 3 ASSESSMENT

1. **Guiding Question** Use your completed chart to answer this question: In what ways do interest groups attempt to influence government and public opinion?

### Key Terms and Comprehension
2. How do direct and indirect approaches to **lobbying** differ?
3. What is a **lobbyist?**
4. At what levels of government does lobbying take place?
5. How do interest groups use the media and propaganda to influence the public?

### Critical Thinking
6. **Predict Consequences (a)** What might happen if nothing were done to limit the role of lobbyists in the governing process? **(b)** Do you think government should regulate lobbyists' behavior?
7. **Draw Inferences** Why do interest groups value a positive public image?
8. **Identify Central Issues** Using celebrity spokespeople is a commonly used way for interest groups to try to influence policymakers. Do interest groups gain undue influence when celebrities back their causes? Explain.

### Quick Write
**Assessment Writing: Support and Revise Ideas** As you begin to draft your complete essay, review what you have written and check to make sure that each paragraph includes a main idea. Build further upon the details gathered in Section 1 and compose a coherent, specific argument. Review word choice and write clear transitions between paragraphs.

## Answers

**Analyzing Political Cartoons** It suggests that PACs have become the focus of politicians.

# Assessment Answers

**1.** Direct approaches involve face-to-face contact with policymakers. Lobbyists testify before committees, talk to White House aides, and try to influence appointments. They help provide information, draft legislation, and write speeches. They lobby the courts by bringing lawsuits and filing *amicus curiae* briefs. Indirect strategies include grass-roots pressure and demonstrations. Groups mold public opinion through advertising, celebrity promotions, and press releases. Some use propaganda techniques. Interest groups also electioneer.

**2.** Direct approaches involve face-to-face contact with policymakers. Indirect approaches try to get the public to pressure policymakers.

**3.** a person who tries to persuade public officials to do things that his or her interest group wants

**4.** at any level that public policy is made

**5.** They publish ads and celebrity promotions. They try to attract media coverage with press releases, interviews, and studies. Many use propaganda techniques.

**6. (a)** Government could become corrupt, with special interests influencing policymaking, perhaps through illegal means. **(b)** Sample answer: Yes, to prevent special interests from undermining policymaking based on the greater good and to prevent use of illegal tactics

**7.** Public opinion influences policy decisions.

**8.** Sample answer: Yes, celebrities may give an interest group influence out of proportion to the group's size.

**QUICK WRITE** Essays should argue the positive and negative aspects of interest groups.

# Quick Study Guide

**GOVERNMENT** ONLINE

**On the Go**

To review anytime, anywhere, download these online resources at **PearsonSchool.com/phgovt**
Political Dictionary, Audio Review

**Guiding Question**
**Section 2** What are the different types of interest groups at work in American society?

**Guiding Question**
**Section 1** What roles do interest groups play in our political system?

**CHAPTER 9**
**Essential Question**
To what extent do interest groups advance or harm democracy?

**Guiding Question**
**Section 3** In what ways do interest groups attempt to influence government and public opinion?

## Political Dictionary

interest group *p. 242*
public policy *p. 242*
public affairs *p. 245*
trade association *p. 248*
labor union *p. 248*
public-interest group *p. 252*
lobbying *p. 254*
lobbyist *p. 254*
*amicus curiae* brief *p. 257*
grass-roots pressures *p. 257*

## How Lobbying Works

**Lobbying occurs . . .**
wherever public policy is made—at the national, State, and local levels of government all across the country.

**Lobbyists are . . .**
the representatives of a wide variety of interest groups.

**Lobbying involves . . .**
writing speeches, providing information to officeholders, making campaign contributions, drafting legislation, filing court briefs, and much more.

**Lobbyists use . . .**
a variety of techniques to shape opinions, including grass-roots pressures, propaganda, and election-related activities.

## Features of Interest Groups

| Positive | Negative |
|---|---|
| ● Provide ways to participate in public life | ● Focus on special (narrow) interests of group |
| ● Inform and raise interest in public matters | ● Often represent small segment of population |
| ● Promote interests important to group members | ● Occasionally use unethical tactics |

---

# For More Information

To learn more about interest groups, refer to these sources or assign them to students:

**L1** **Sandak, Cass R.** *Lobbying (Inside Government).* 21st Century, 1997.

**L2** **Spangenburg, Ray, Kit Moser, and Diane Moser.** *Propaganda: Understanding the Power of Persuasion (Teen Issues).* Enslow Publishers, 2002.

**L3** **Thomson, Stuart and Steve John.** *Public Affairs in Practice: A Practical Guide to Lobbying (PR in Practice).* Kogan Page, 2007.

**L4** **DeKieffer, Donald E.** *The Citizen's Guide to Lobbying Congress.* Chicago Review Press, 2007.

---

Have students download the digital resources available at Government on the Go for review and remediation.

## STUDY TIPS

**SETTING PRIORITIES** Many students get derailed in their studying by an inability to set priorities. Explain to students that doing so can help them focus on the right tasks at the right time, and for the right amount of time. The first step in setting priorities is to write down all assignments and tasks that must be completed, along with the date by which each must be accomplished. Stress that students should *write down* (or input into a software program) their assignments, not rely on memory. Have students look at their assignment list. Which items must be done first? Which can wait? Point out that all tasks do not have equal urgency, nor should easy tasks be given first priority merely because they are less difficult to perform. Next, ask students to rewrite their list in order of importance. They can then use this list to schedule their time each day. Suggest that they check off each task as it is accomplished.

## ASSESSMENT AT A GLANCE

### Tests and Quizzes
Section Assessments
Section Quizzes A and B, Unit 1 **All-in-One**
Chapter Assessment
Chapter Tests A and B, Unit 1 **All-in-One**
Document-Based Assessment
Progress Monitoring Online
Exam*View* Test Bank

### Performance Assessment
Essential Questions Journal
Debate, p. 258
Assessment Rubrics, **All-in-One**

# Chapter Assessment

**COMPREHENSION AND CRITICAL THINKING**

## SECTION 1

1. **(a)** Possible answer: Expressing views to government is part of the democratic process. Interest groups provide a practical way for people to join together to express shared views. **(b)** Interest groups behave practically by organizing on the basis of shared beliefs and reaching out to all levels and branches of government where policies are made. They behave democratically by stimulating interest in public affairs, informing voters about the issues, and providing a way for citizens to participate in politics.

2. **(a)** Groups create awareness of public affairs, represent members based on shared attitudes, provide useful information to government, offer a way for people to participate in politics, and monitor public agencies and officials. **(b)** Groups push their own interests, which may not be in the best interest of other Americans. Their influence can be out of proportion to their size or importance to the public good. They may not represent the views of all people for whom they speak. Some use heavy-handed tactics. **(c)** Possible response: I find the criticisms most persuasive. Too often, big money from powerful interest groups results in policies that are not in the best interests of society as a whole.

3. **(a)** Interest groups monitor the work of public agencies and officials, helping to assure responsible performance. Also, groups on different sides of the same issue check each other by competing for influence. **(b)** yes **(c)** possible answer: because interest groups will publicize wrongdoing by public officials, which helps voters make informed decisions

## SECTION 2

4. **(a)** Not all members of every group are sincere in their interest. **(b)** The cartoonist does not see interest groups as always representing a sincere, deeply felt concern.

5. possible answers: **(a)** groups representing business, labor, agriculture, or professions, such as labor unions and professional associations **(b)** groups organized around issues, such as Planned Parenthood and the National Rifle Association; around segments of the population, such as the American Legion and AARP; or around religious beliefs, such as the National Council of Churches **(c)** groups focused on the broad public good, such as Common Cause and League of Women Voters

6. **(a)** groups based on economic interests **(b)** because the need to earn a living is common to almost everyone, and government policies can significantly impact this area **(c)** possible answer: yes, because most people consider economic well-being a priority

7. **(a)** Possible answer: The groups might have different opinions on certain policies or multiple, conflicting interests. **(b)** Disagreements can make it more difficult to persuade policymakers.

## SECTION 3

8. **(a)** Lobbyists talk with policymakers face to face, testify before congressional committees, submit prepared statements on proposed legislation, provide useful information to members of Congress, make campaign contributions, write speeches, and draft legislation. **(b)** Possible response: Talking with policymakers could provide useful information. **(c)** by being careful to provide accurate information so as not to destroy their credibility

9. **(a)** They try to mold public opinion to favor their cause, so that public opinion can put

---

# Chapter Assessment

## Comprehension and Critical Thinking

### Section 1

1. **(a)** Explain how interest groups are both practical and democratic. **(b)** Give examples of interest groups behaving in both practical and democratic ways.

2. Consider the role of interest groups in American society and in your own life. **(a)** Identify some positive impacts of these groups. **(b)** Summarize some common criticisms. **(c)** Which argument do you think is more persuasive?

3. **(a)** How do interest groups contribute to the checks-and-balances feature of the political process? **(b)** Do you think their contribution adds to the democratic process? **(c)** Why or why not?

### Section 2

5. Give an example of each of the following: **(a)** a group based on economic interests, **(b)** a group based on other special interests, and **(c)** a public interest group.

6. **(a)** What is the biggest category of interest group? **(b)** Why do you think this is? **(c)** Do you think this category is representative of the most important American interests?

7. **(a)** Why might interest groups with shared interests sometimes disagree with one another? **(b)** How might these disagreements affect their ability to influence policy?

### Section 3

8. **(a)** What techniques might a lobbyist use to influence Congress? **(b)** Which of these techniques might be most effective, and why? **(c)** How do lobbyists balance ethics with effectiveness?

9. **(a)** How do lobbyists use public opinion? **(b)** How is this similar to advertising? **(c)** Would you be more or less likely to support a special interest group if it garnered positive public opinion?

10. **(a)** What involvements do lobbyists have in political campaigns? **(b)** How does this affect campaign finance?

### Writing About Government

11. Use your Quick Write exercises from this chapter to complete a 3–5 paragraph essay supporting your argument concerning interest groups. See pages S11–S12 of the Skills Handbook.

4. **Analyze Political Cartoons (a)** What is the cartoon at left saying about interest groups? **(b)** Do you think the cartoonist sees interest groups as a positive or negative influence in society? Explain.

*"Well, if you feel so left out, why don't you join one of those Citizens Concerned About Something groups?"*

## Apply What You've Learned

12. **Essential Question Activity** Study the role of an interest group in your school or community and then investigate the role of a larger lobbying firm, such as those found on K Street in Washington, D.C. Then, answer the following:

   **(a)** What are the goals of these groups?

   **(b)** How does each group pursue its goals?

   **(c)** Do you think these groups are effective in their attempts to shape policy?

13. **Essential Question Assessment** Based on your research and what you have learned in this chapter, stage a press conference with some classmates acting as reporters and others as members of interest groups presenting their points of view. At a press conference, reporters are given the opportunity to ask questions, so allow time for both groups to participate. Try to answer the Essential Question: **To what extent do interest groups advance or harm democracy?**

**Essential Questions**
**Journal**
To respond to the chapter Essential Question, go to your **Essential Questions Journal.**

# Document-Based Assessment

## Regulating Special Interests

In 2007, Congress passed a new law limiting the reach of lobbyists. Several members were very concerned about "earmarks" (funding for specific projects in appropriations bills) and the fact that former members often become well-paid lobbyists.

### Document 1

*Here are some earmarks from 2008 appropriations bills:*

Alaska Native Education Equity Assistance Program ($34,500,000)

AFL-CIO Working for American Institute ($1,500,000)

YMCA of Central Stark County, Ohio ($500,000)

Detroit Renaissance ($231,000)

Coastal Wind, Ohio ($100,000)

—Taxpayers for Common Sense, FY2008 Appropriations Bills database

Facilities and Equipment for Hudson Alpha Institute for Biotechnology ($310,000)

—Office of Management and Budget

### Document 2

"This bill won't even begin to stop corruption in Washington, because the earmark favor factory will remain open and ready for business. Politicians will still be able to use these secret earmarks to direct millions of taxpayer dollars to special interests. You can hear the champagne bottles being uncorked all over K Street, because the lobbyists know it will be business as usual.

—Senator Jim DeMint (R., South Carolina), press release from his Web site

### Document 3

### Document 4

"What we did today was momentous. The link between lobbyists and legislation that we have broken is something that will make a difference in the lives of the American people. . . We are free to act in the people's interest instead of the special interest.

—House Speaker Nancy Pelosi (D., California), quoted in *USA Today*, August 1, 2007

---

**Use your knowledge of lobbying, and Documents 1, 2, 3 and 4 to answer Questions 1–3.**

1. Summarize Documents 2 and 4.
   A. Both speakers think the new law will have little effect on lobbyists.
   B. Both speakers feel it will make a big difference.
   C. Speaker 4 sees it as an important step to regulate special interests whereas Speaker 2 doesn't think the law will have any effect on corruption.
   D. Speaker 2 thinks the law will be ineffective; Speaker 4 sees it as a very positive step in the regulation of lobbying.

2. How does Document 3 illustrate the link between Congress and lobbyists?

3. How might some of the earmarks in Document 1 show the influence of special interests?

4. **Pull It Together** Do you think lobbying regulation will be effective? Why or why not?

 **GOVERNMENT ONLINE**
Documents
To find more primary sources on lobbyists and interest groups, visit
**PearsonSchool.com/phgovt**

---

## DOCUMENT-BASED ASSESSMENT

1. C

2. The cartoon suggests that many lobbyists are former members of Congress.

3. The earmarks may have come about as a result of lobbying by an interest group.

4. Some students might suggest that regulation will be effective because rules have been established to control specific behaviors. Other students might believe that lobbyists will find ways around the rules. No matter which position students take, they should provide supporting reasons.

**L2 Differentiate** Students use all the documents on the page to support their thesis.

**L3 Differentiate** Students include additional information available online at **PearsonSchool .com/phgovt.**

**L4 Differentiate** Students use materials from the textbook, the online information at **PearsonSchool .com/phgovt,** and do additional research to support their views.

**Go Online to PearsonSchool.com/phgovt** for a student rubric and extra documents.

---

pressure on policymakers. **(b)** Advertising is another way of producing favorable public opinion. **(c)** more likely, because positive public opinion can be a strong influence on an individual's thinking and decision making

10. **(a)** They form PACs that make financial contributions and hold fundraisers for candidates who support their cause. They also conduct get-out-the-vote drives, supply professional campaign consultants, provide information for speeches and audiences to hear the speeches, help staff local campaign offices, distribute

campaign literature, and participate in phone banks. **(b)** All of these activities either bring money into the campaign or lower campaign costs for the candidate.

### WRITING ABOUT GOVERNMENT

11. Student essays should clearly state a position on whether interest groups have an overall positive or negative effect on society, and provide supporting details.

### APPLY WHAT YOU'VE LEARNED

12. Students should select a local or school interest group, clearly state its goals, and describe its strategies for achieving these

goals. Students should be able to list the group's goals, how it pursues goals, and judge the effectiveness of the group by citing policies the group influenced.

13. In the student press conference, reporters should ask thoughtful questions, and the answers from interest group members should display an understanding of the issue and the group's goals.

Before assigning these questions, distribute the Rubric for Assessing a Writing Assignment (Unit 2 All-in-One, p. 257). Use the criteria and the guidelines below to grade students' answers to the Essential Question Warmup questions. Then send students to the **Essential Questions Journal** to answer the unit Essential Question.

**1.** A good answer to this question will demonstrate an understanding of the tremendous influence the media have on public opinion. Most students will probably believe that the media has a responsibility to be accurate, fair, and unbiased. More nuanced answers will recognize that a gray area exists around reporting on events and information that could endanger individuals or national security.

**2.** Students should recognize the importance of voting, but also point to the importance of the many other ways of participating in good government, including working on campaigns, joining interest groups, making opinions known through writing to members of Congress, and staying informed.

**3.** Students' answers should recognize that interest groups are democratic in that they strive to make the voices of the people heard; however, they can be un-democratic if they exert undue pressure or influence.

**4.** Answers should recognize that being an active member of a political party, like being an active member of an interest group, is one way that a citizen can influence government. This is especially true in the case of many minor parties that are devoted to one particular cause.

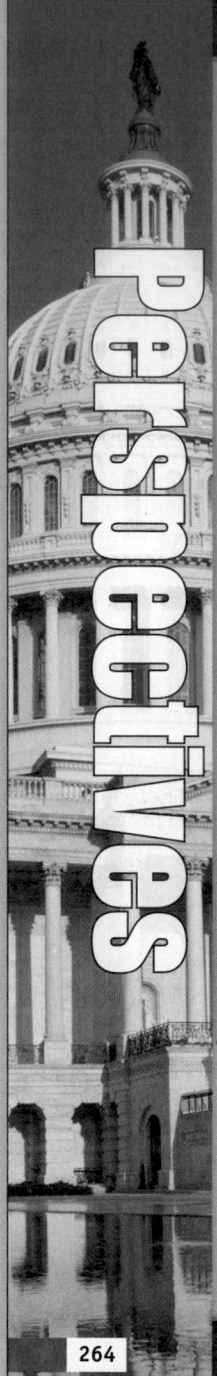

## Essential Question
# In what ways should people participate in public affairs?

Political parties, the media, voting, belonging to interest groups—Americans today have unprecedented opportunities to take part in public affairs. How and why should we do so?

**ON THE FREE PRESS:**

Freedom of expression—in particular, freedom of the press—guarantees popular participation in the decisions and actions of government, and popular participation is the essence of . . . democracy.

—Corazon Aquino, former President of the Philippines

**ON A VOTER'S RESPONSIBILITIES:**

"I'm undecided, but that doesn't mean I'm apathetic or uninformed."

**ON GOVERNMENT AND THE PEOPLE:**

It is not the function of our Government to keep the citizen from falling into error; it is the function of the citizen to keep the Government from falling into error.

—Justice Robert H. Jackson, *American Communications Association* v. *Douds*, 1950

### Essential Question Warmup

Throughout this unit, you studied how people and government interact. Use what you have learned and the quotations and opinions above to answer the following questions. Then go to your **Essential Questions Journal.**

**1.** What responsibilities do the media have, if any?

**2.** Can citizens "keep the Government from falling into error" through voting alone?

**3.** Are interest groups vital to democratic government?

**4.** How successfully do political parties link citizens with their government?

**Essential Questions Journal**
To continue to build a response to the unit Essential Question, go to your **Essential Questions Journal.**

## Assessment Resources

Unit 2 AYP Monitoring Assessment
Exam*View* Test Bank CD-ROM
SuccessTracker Assessment
Online Student Self-Tests
Chapter Tests
Section Quizzes
Chapter-level Document-Based Assessment

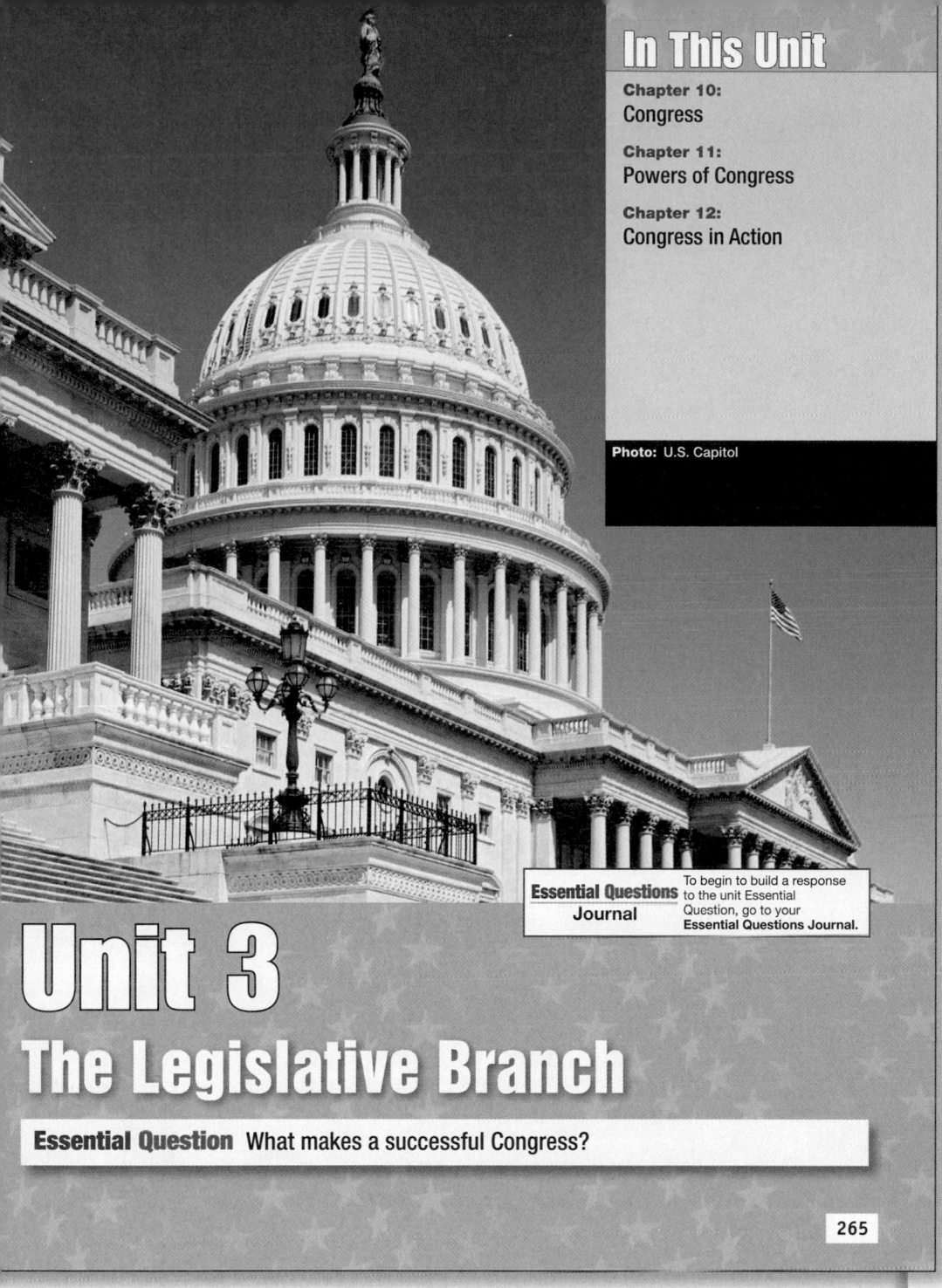

**Photo:** U.S. Capitol

**Essential Questions Journal** — To begin to build a response to the unit Essential Question, go to your **Essential Questions Journal.**

# Unit 3
# The Legislative Branch

**Essential Question** What makes a successful Congress?

265

## Government Online Resources

Government Online Teacher Center at **PearsonSchool.com/phgovt** includes
• Online Teacher's Edition with lesson planner and lecture notes
• Teacher's Resource Library with All-in-One Resources, Color Transparencies, Adequate Yearly Progress Monitoring, and an alternative lesson plan for each chapter
• SuccessTracker Assessment

Government Online Student Center at **PearsonSchool.com/phgovt** includes
• Interactive textbook with audio
• American Government Essential Questions Video
• Chapter-level WebQuests
• Guided Audio Tours and Interactivities
• Student Self-Tests

### ESSENTIAL QUESTION PERSPECTIVES

Essential questions frame each unit and chapter of study, asking students to consider big ideas about government. The question for this unit—**What makes a successful Congress?**—demands that students ask further questions. How do they define "successful"? What criteria should be used to judge Congress? Should Congress be judged as a whole, or should members be judged individually? Can success be measured immediately, or must we rely on historical perspective to make a judgment?

To begin this unit, assign the Unit 3 Warmup Activity on page 77 of the **Essential Questions Journal.** This will help students start to consider their position on the **Unit 3 Essential Question: What makes a successful Congress?**

Show the **Unit 3 American Government Essential Questions Video** to help students begin thinking about the unit Essential Question and designate a classroom bulletin board for students to post news articles related to the unit Essential Question. Use the Conversation Wall strategy (p. T27) to encourage students to post articles and comments on other students' postings.

Later, students will further explore the chapter-level essential questions:

*Chapter 10:* **Whose views should members of Congress represent when voting?**

*Chapter 11:* **What should be the limits on the powers of Congress?**

*Chapter 12:* **Can and should the lawmaking process be improved?**

Use the **Essential Questions Journal** throughout the program to help students consider these and other big ideas about government.

# Introduce the Chapter

## Essential Questions:

**UNIT 3**

What makes a successful Congress?

**CHAPTER 10**

Whose views should members of Congress represent when voting?

**ACTIVATE PRIOR KNOWLEDGE** Have students examine the image and quotation on these pages. Ask: **What do the photo and quotation suggest about Congress?** *(that members of Congress represent all the different people of the United States)* In this chapter, students will learn about members of the House of Representatives and the Senate. Tell students to begin to further explore Congress by completing the Chapter 10 Essential Question Warmup activity in their **Essential Questions Journal.**

**BEFORE READING**

**L2 ELL Differentiate** Chapter 10 Prereading and Vocabulary Worksheet (Unit 3 All-in-One, p. 9)

**SUCCESSNET STUDENT AND TEACHER CENTER**

Visit **PearsonSchool.com/phgovt** for downloadable resources that allow students and teachers to connect with government "on the go."

**DIGITAL LESSON PRESENTATION**

The digital lesson presentation supports the print lesson with activities and summaries of key concepts. Activities for this chapter include:

- **The Capitol**
- **Gerrymandering: Choosing Their Voters**

## SKILLS DEVELOPMENT

**DECISION MAKING**

You may wish to teach decision making as a distinct skill within Section 3 of this chapter. Use the Chapter 10 Skills Worksheet (Unit 3 All-in-One, p. 31) to help students decide which candidate for Senate they would choose. The worksheet will walk them through the process of deciding what qualities they want in a senator, identifying the strengths and weaknesses of each candidate, and choosing one candidate. For L2 and L1 students, assign the adapted Skill Activity (Unit 3 All-in-One, p. 32).

**WebQuest online** The chapter WebQuest challenges students to answer the chapter Essential Question by asking them about Congress.

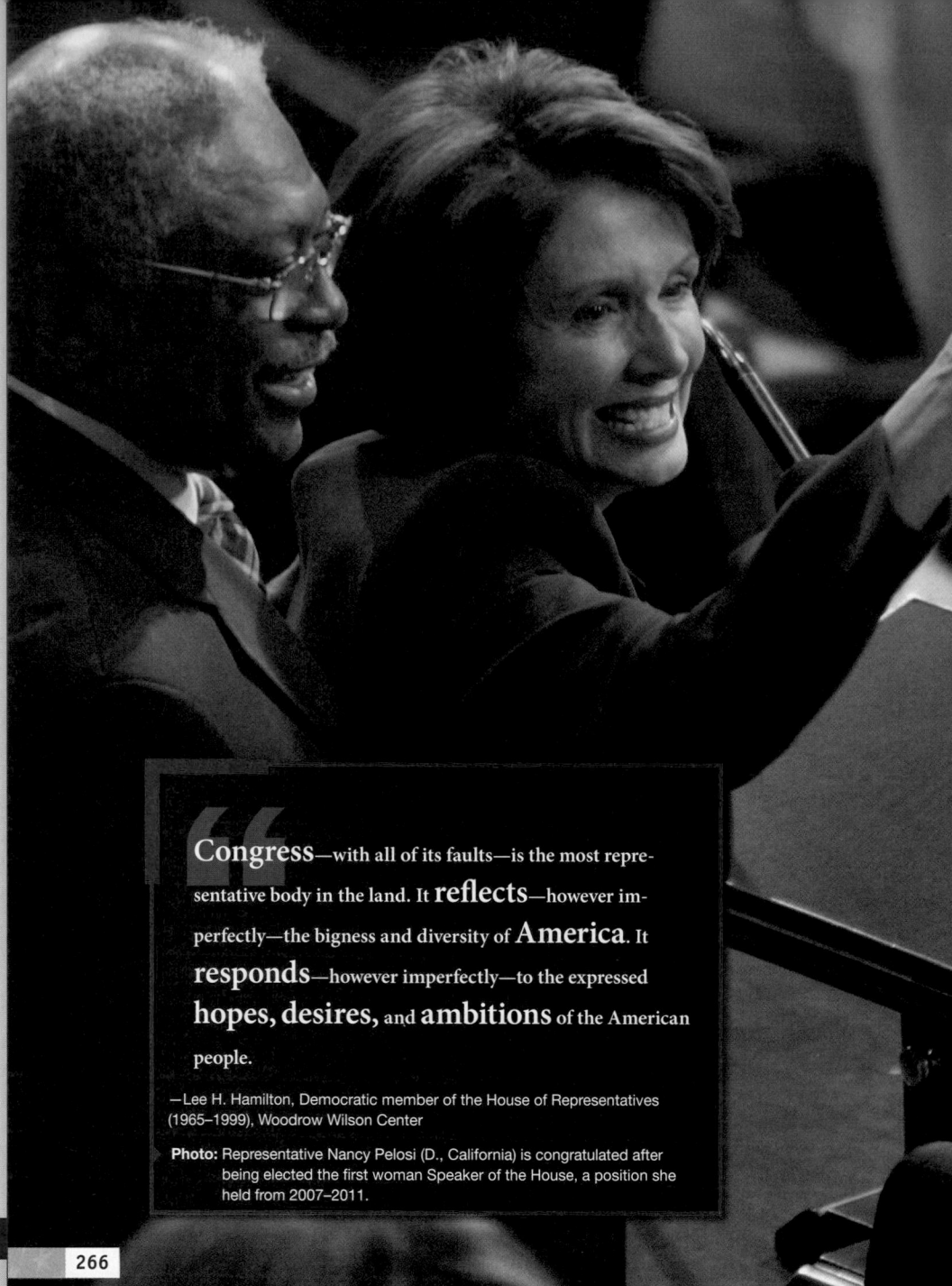

"**Congress**—with all of its faults—is the most representative body in the land. It **reflects**—however imperfectly—the bigness and diversity of **America**. It **responds**—however imperfectly—to the expressed **hopes, desires,** and **ambitions** of the American people."

—Lee H. Hamilton, Democratic member of the House of Representatives (1965–1999), Woodrow Wilson Center

**Photo:** Representative Nancy Pelosi (D., California) is congratulated after being elected the first woman Speaker of the House, a position she held from 2007–2011.

266

## Block Scheduling

**BLOCK 1:** Teach the Section 1 and 2 lessons, omitting the Section 1 Extend option.

**BLOCK 2:** Teach the Section 3 and 4 lessons, omitting the Section 4 Bellringer and discussion of diversity in Congress. Choose an Extend option from Sections 1, 2, or 3, depending on your preferences and state standards.

## Congress

**Essential Question**
Whose views should members of Congress represent when voting?

Section 1:
The National Legislature

Section 2:
The House of Representatives

Section 3:
The Senate

Section 4:
The Members of Congress

**GOVERNMENT** ONLINE
**On the Go**

To study anywhere, anytime, download these online resources at PearsonSchool.com/phgovt
• Political Dictionary
• Audio Review
• Downloadable Interactivities

267

# Lesson Goals

### SECTION 1
Students will . . .

• explain the structure of Congress and describe the controversy over the equity of the distribution of seats through a class discussion.

• predict the benefits and drawbacks of a bicameral Congress by drawing comparisons between a National Government and a school government.

### SECTION 2
Students will . . .

• identify the States with the most and fewest representatives in the House and review the challenges the Framers faced in creating a functioning government.

• describe the House of Representatives.

• analyze the qualifications for members of the House through brainstorming and class discussion.

• identify the reasons for and results of gerrymandering by simulating the process of drawing district lines.

### SECTION 3
Students will . . .

• use a Venn diagram to compare the job and qualifications of senators and members of the House.

• assess the characteristics and qualifications of senators through four real-life examples.

### SECTION 4
Students will . . .

• address the composition of Congress by describing an "average" member and discussing ways the composition might be altered to reflect the population.

• identify and analyze the formal and informal qualifications for members of Congress by writing help-wanted ads.

# Pressed for Time

To cover this chapter quickly, review the Section 1 Reading Comprehension Worksheet, questions 1 through 6. Then have students complete the Section 4 Core Worksheet, writing "help-wanted" ads for senators and members of the House. Explain reapportionment and the reasons for gerrymandering. Have students study "Gerrymandering: Choosing Their Voters" in Section 2. Finish by reviewing "How Should Members of Congress Vote?" in Section 4 and asking students to write a paragraph explaining how they think Senator Miller should vote on the bill.

**DIFFERENTIATED INSTRUCTION KEY**

Look for these symbols to help you adjust steps in each lesson to meet your students' needs.

**L1** Special Needs

**L2** Basic

**ELL** English Language Learners

**LPR** Less Proficient Readers

**L3** All Students

**L4** Advanced Students

# Why does the Constitution establish a bicameral legislature?

| Reason | Summary |
|---|---|
| Historical | Americans familiar with bicameral British Parliament |
| Practical | compromise between Virginia and New Jersey Plans |
| Theoretical | each house can check power of the other; prevents Congress from overpowering other branches |

# Get Started

## LESSON GOALS

Students will . . .

- explain the structure of Congress and describe the controversy over the equity of the distribution of seats through a class discussion.
- predict the benefits and drawbacks of a bicameral Congress by drawing comparisons between a National Government and a school government.

## BEFORE CLASS

Assign the section, the graphic organizer in the text, and the Reading Comprehension Worksheet (Unit 3 All-in-One, p. 13) before class.

**L2 Differentiate** Reading Comprehension Worksheet (Unit 3 All-in-One, p. 14)

## BELLRINGER

Display Transparency 10A, Representation in Congress, and have students answer these questions in their notebook: **Is the distribution of senators fair? Why or why not?**

## SKILLS DEVELOPMENT

### DRAW INFERENCES AND CONCLUSIONS

Before students work on this section's Core Worksheet, you may want to review the information on drawing inferences and conclusions in the Skills Handbook, p. S19.

---

## SECTION 1

# The National Legislature

### Guiding Question

**Why does the Constitution establish a bicameral legislature?**
Use a table to take notes on the reasons for a bicameral legislature.

| Reason | Summary |
|---|---|
| Historical | |
| Practical | |
| Theoretical | |

### Political Dictionary

- bicameral
- term
- session
- convene
- adjourn
- recess
- prorogue
- special session

### Objectives

1. Explain why the Constitution provides for a bicameral Congress.
2. Explain the difference between a term and a session of Congress.
3. Describe a situation in which the President may convene or end a session of Congress.

**Image Above:** Senators Steny Hoyer (D., Maryland) and Max Baucus (D., Montana)

You live in a democracy, and you know that in a democracy the people rule. But what does that really mean? You are one of "the people," but you do not rule, at least not in the literal, hands-on sense. You do not make laws, collect taxes, arrest criminals, or decide court cases.

You do not do those or all of the many other things that government does because you live in a representative democracy. Here, it is the representatives of the people who do the day-to-day, hands-on work of government.

Congress stands as a prime example of that point. It is the nation's lawmaking body, the legislative branch of its National Government. It is charged with the most basic of governmental functions in a democratic society: Translating the public will into public policy in the form of law.

Yet Congress has never been very widely admired by the American people. Mark Twain amused his audiences with comments like, "Suppose you were an idiot. And suppose you were a member of Congress. But I repeat myself." Television personalities such as Jay Leno or Jon Stewart often make similar comments.

Still, despite those belittlings, Congress is immensely important in the American scheme of democratic government. James Madison called Congress "the first branch" of the National Government. Just how profoundly important he and the other Framers thought Congress to be is indicated by this fact: The very first and longest of the articles of the Constitution is devoted to it.

### FROM THE CONSTITUTION

All legislative Powers herein granted shall be vested in a Congress of the United States, which shall consist of a Senate and House of Representatives.

—Article I, Section 1

## A Bicameral Congress

Immediately, the Constitution establishes a **bicameral** legislature—that is, a legislature made up of two houses. It does so for historical, practical, and theoretical reasons.

# Focus on the Basics

Here is the information that your students need to learn in this section.

**FACTS:** • Congress is bicameral. • In the House of Representatives, States are represented according to population. • Each State has two senators. • Congress meets for two-year terms, divided into two one-year sessions.

**CONCEPTS:** separation of powers, checks and balances, federalism

**ENDURING UNDERSTANDINGS:** • The Constitution provides for a bicameral Congress for historical, practical, and theoretical reasons. • The bicameral structure of Congress is a compromise between two models of representation that the Framers developed to accommodate the needs of both large and small States.

**Historical** The British Parliament had consisted of two houses since the 1300s. The Framers and most other Americans knew the British system of bicameralism quite well. Most of the colonial assemblies and, in 1787, all but two of the new State legislatures were also bicameral. Among the original thirteen colonies, only Georgia and Pennsylvania had unicameral colonial and then State legislatures. Georgia's legislature became bicameral in 1789 and Pennsylvania's in 1790. (Only one State, Nebraska, has a unicameral legislature today.)

**Practical** The Framers had to create a two-chambered body to settle the conflict between the Virginia and the New Jersey Plans at Philadelphia in 1787. Recall, the most <u>populous</u> States wanted to distribute the seats in Congress in proportion to the population of each State, while the smaller States demanded an equal voice in Congress.

Bicameralism is a reflection of federalism. Each of the States is equally represented in the Senate and each is represented in line with its population in the House.

**Theoretical** The Framers favored a bicameral Congress in order that one house might act as a check on the other.

A leading constitutional historian recounts a conversation between Thomas Jefferson and George Washington at Mount Vernon. Jefferson, who had just returned from France, told Washington that he was opposed to a two-chambered legislature. As he made his point, he poured his coffee into his saucer, and Washington asked him why he did so. "To cool it," replied Jefferson. "Even so," said Washington, "we pour legislation into the senatorial saucer to cool it."[1]

The Framers were generally convinced that Congress would dominate the new National Government. As Madison observed,

### Primary Source
" In a republican government, the legislative authority necessarily <u>predominates</u>. The remedy for this inconveniency is to divide the legislature into different branches.

—*The Federalist* No. 51

[1] Max Farrand, *The Framing of the Constitution* (1913).

**✔ Checkpoint**
What practical problem did the Framers solve by creating a bicameral legislature?

**populous**
*adj.* with many people

**predominates**
*v.* holds controlling power or influence

## The Capitol

Congress meets in the Capitol, which houses the chambers of the bicameral Congress. It has undergone several additions as both the nation and Congress have grown.
***Why do the two houses meet in the same building?***

▼ House Chamber

**GOVERNMENT**ONLINE
For an animated, **interactive** exploration of the Capitol and its chambers, visit
**PearsonSchool.com/phgovt**

House Chamber — **435** members

Old House Chamber (Statuary Hall) — The Rotunda — Old Senate Chamber

Senate Chamber — **100** members

---

# Teach

To present this topic using online resources, use the lesson presentations at **PearsonSchool.com/phgovt**.

### INTRODUCE THE TOPIC

Tell students that today they will discuss the structure of Congress and the reasons for it. Tell them that Congress is bicameral and ask what that means. *(It is made up of two legislative chambers or houses: the Senate and the House of Representatives.)*

**L2 ELL Differentiate** Write the word *bicameral* on the board and break it down into parts. *Bi-* means "two" and *camera* is the Latin word for "chamber," or "room." Explain that *bicameral* is a political word that refers to governments with two legislative chambers.

### REVIEW THE STRUCTURE OF THE HOUSES

Review representation in Congress: two senators per State, representatives allotted according to population. Ask students to explain why Congress is set up this way *(for historical, practical, and theoretical reasons)*.

You may also discuss what the author means when he says, "Remember, had the States not been equally represented in the Senate, there might never have been a Constitution." *(The large States would not have agreed to a Congress with equal representation, while the small States would not have agreed to a Congress with representation based on population.)* Review responses to the Bellringer questions.

**L2 Differentiate** Model note-taking skills by drawing a chart like the one shown on the previous page. Record notes on the board, asking students where on the chart their responses should be written.

---

# Differentiated Resources

The following resources are located in the All-in-One, Unit 3, Chapter 10, Section 1:

- **L2** Prereading and Vocabulary Worksheet (p. 9)
- **L3** Reading Comprehension Worksheet (p. 13)
- **L2** Reading Comprehension Worksheet (p. 14)
- **L3** Core Worksheet (p. 15)
- **L2** Extend Activity (p. 16)
- **L3** Quiz A (p. 17)
- **L2** Quiz B (p. 18)

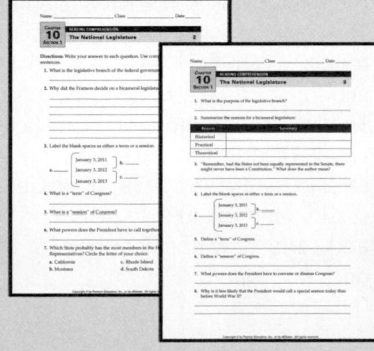

## Answers

**Checkpoint** It solved the conflict between large- and small-population States over how to distribute the seats in Congress.

**The Capitol** The houses are two parts of one National Government. Therefore, the two chambers must reside close together so that members can work together.

## DISTRIBUTE CORE WORKSHEET

Distribute the Chapter 10 Section 1 Core Worksheet (Unit 3 All-in-One, p. 15). Explain that students will predict the benefits and drawbacks of a bicameral system by using school government as an example. Ask a student to read the introductory paragraph on the worksheet aloud.

**L3 Differentiate** If time is short, have half the class do benefits and half do drawbacks. Then have them explain their answers to the other half of the class.

**L1 L2 ELL Differentiate** Clarify the meaning of *benefits* (advantages) and of *drawbacks* (disadvantages).

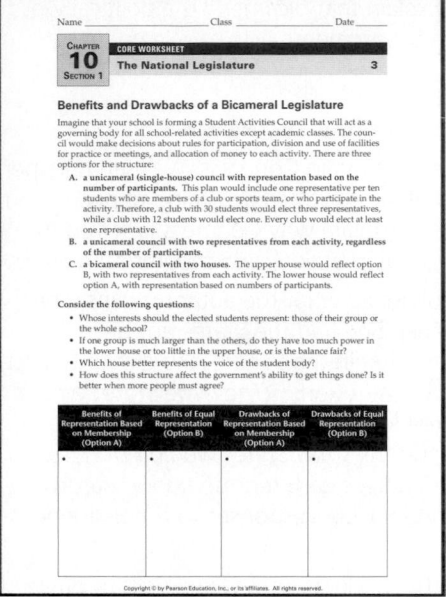

## REVIEW WORKSHEET AND DRAW PARALLELS

After students complete their charts, draw a chart on the board. Ask students to share their predictions and discuss. Ask students to draw parallels between the theoretical school government and Congress. They are:

School = nation

Team or club = State

Upper house = Senate

Lower house = House of Representatives

## REVIEW FACTS

Review the answers to the Reading Comprehension Worksheet (Unit 3 All-in-One, p. 13). Emphasize questions 2, 4, and 7.

## Answers

**Interpreting Maps** California has a much larger population than Wyoming, yet both States have two members in the Senate. This system prevents large States like California from dominating small States in the Senate's decision making.

---

# Representation in Congress

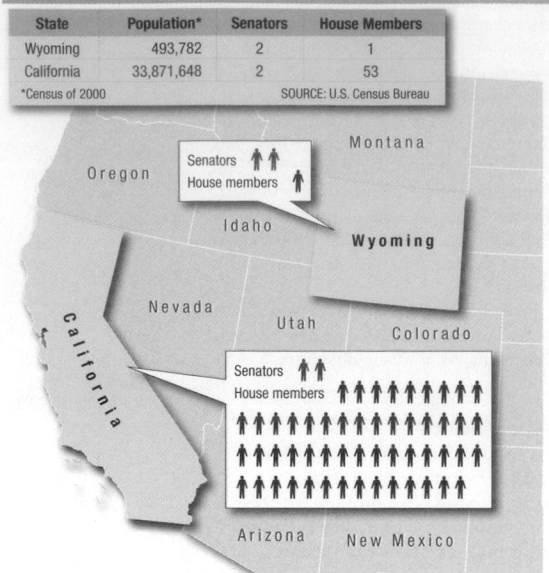

| State | Population* | Senators | House Members |
|---|---|---|---|
| Wyoming | 493,782 | 2 | 1 |
| California | 33,871,648 | 2 | 53 |

*Census of 2000     SOURCE: U.S. Census Bureau

➤➤ **Interpreting Maps** California and Wyoming each elect two senators, despite a huge difference in their populations. *How does the distribution of Senate seats among the States illustrate the principle of federalism?*

**diffuse**
*v.* to spread out

The Framers saw bicameralism as a way to <u>diffuse</u> the power of Congress and so prevent it from overwhelming the other two branches of government.

For more than 200 years now, some people have argued that equal representation of the States in the Senate is undemocratic and should be eliminated.[2] They often point to the two extremes to make their case. The State with the least population, Wyoming, has only some 550,000 residents. The most populous State, California, now has a population of nearly 37 million. Yet each of these States has two senators.

Those who object to State equality in the Senate ignore a vital fact. The Senate was purposely created as a body in which the States would be represented as coequal members and partners in the Union. Remember, if the Framers had been unable to agree that the States would be equally represented in the Senate, there might never have been a Constitution.

## Terms and Sessions

It is said that a woman, incensed at something her senator had done, said to him, "You know, the 535 of you people in Congress meet every two years. Well, Senator, there are some of us who think that it would be much better if just two of you met every 535 years."

Whether that story is true or not, that woman's advice has never been followed. Ever since 1789, Congress has met for two-year terms.

**Terms of Congress** Each **term** of Congress lasts for two years, and each of those two-year terms is numbered consecutively.[3] Congress began its first term on March 4, 1789. That term ended two years later, on March 3, 1791.

The date for the start of each new term was changed by the 20th Amendment in 1933. In an earlier era, the several months from election to March 4 allowed for delays in communicating election results, and it gave newly chosen lawmakers time to arrange their affairs and travel to Washington. The March date gave Congress less time to accomplish its work each year, however, and by the 1930s travel and communications were no longer an issue. The start of each new two-year term is now "noon of the 3d day of January" of every odd-numbered year. So the scheduled term of the 112th Congress runs for two years—from noon on January 3, 2011, to noon on January 3, 2013.

**Sessions** A **session** of Congress is that period of time during which, each year, Congress assembles and conducts business. There are two sessions to each term of Congress—one session each year. The Constitution provides that:

---

2   There is not the remotest chance that that would ever be done. Recall, the Constitution provides in Article V that "no State, without its Consent, shall be deprived of its equal Suffrage in the Senate."

3   Article I, Section 2, Clause 1 dictates the two-year term by providing that members of the House "shall be . . . chosen every second Year."

---

# Background

**SPECIAL SESSIONS** When President Franklin D. Roosevelt took office in March 1933, the nation was in the Great Depression. Millions of Americans were out of work. The banking system had collapsed. Roosevelt did not wait until Congress went into regular session in December. He immediately called a special session to address the economic crisis, and Congress passed a remarkable range of important legislation. The Depression, however, was not the only crisis Roosevelt faced. In the late 1930s, German aggression was pushing Europe toward war. The American policy was to remain neutral. In 1939, after Germany invaded Poland, Roosevelt called a special session and asked Congress to lift the ban on the sale of arms. The resulting "cash-and-carry" law enabled the U.S. to supply arms to the Allies without formally declaring war.

## FROM THE CONSTITUTION

**The Congress shall assemble at least once in every year, and such meeting shall begin at noon on the 3d day of January, unless they shall by law appoint a different day.**

—20th Amendment, Section 2

In fact, Congress often does "appoint a different day." The second session of each two-year term frequently **convenes** (begins) a few days or even a few weeks after the third of January.

Congress **adjourns**, or suspends until its next session, each regular session as it sees fit. Until World War II, the nation's lawmakers typically met for four or five months each year. Today, the many pressing issues facing Congress force it to remain in session through most of each year. Both houses do **recess** for several short periods during a session. That is, they temporarily suspend business.

Neither house may adjourn *sine die* (finally, ending a session) without the other's consent. The Constitution provides that

## FROM THE CONSTITUTION

**Neither House . . . shall, without the Consent of the other, adjourn for more than three days, nor to any other Place than that in which the two Houses shall be sitting.**

—Article I, Section 5, Clause 4

Article II, Section 3 of the Constitution does give the President the power to **prorogue** (end, discontinue) a session, but only when the two houses cannot agree on a date for adjournment. No President has ever had to use that power.

**Special Sessions** Only the President may call Congress into **special session**—a meeting to deal with some emergency situation.[4] Only 27 of these special joint sessions of Congress have ever been held. President Harry Truman called the most recent one in 1948, to consider anti-inflation and welfare measures in the aftermath of World War II.

Note that the President can call Congress or either of its houses into a special session. The Senate has been called alone on 46 occasions, to consider treaties or presidential appointments, but not since 1933. The House has never been called alone.

Of course, the fact that Congress now meets nearly year-round reduces the likelihood of special sessions. That fact also lessens the importance of the President's power to call one. Still, as Congress nears the end of a session, the President sometimes finds it useful to threaten a special session if the two chambers do not act on some measure high on the administration's legislative agenda.

---

4 Article II, Section 3 says that the President "may, on extraordinary Occasions, convene both Houses, or either of them...."

✔**Checkpoint**
How many sessions make up each congressional term?

**agenda**
*n.* list of things to be done

**Essential Questions Journal**
To continue to build a response to the chapter Essential Question, go to your **Essential Questions Journal.**

## SECTION 1 ASSESSMENT

1. **Guiding Question** Use your completed table to answer this question: Why does the Constitution establish a bicameral legislature?

**Key Terms and Comprehension**

2. What is a **bicameral** legislature?

3. What is the difference between a **term** and a **session** of Congress?

4. How is a congressional **recess** different from an **adjournment**?

**Critical Thinking**

5. **Determine Cause and Effect** What might have happened if the Framers had created a legislature with only one house?

6. **Draw Inferences** Why is the President's power to convene and dismiss Congress very limited?

7. **Make Comparisons** The Articles of Confederation provided for a Congress that met for one-year terms. Why do you suppose the Framers created a Congress that meets for two-year terms?

**Quick Write**

**Expository Writing: Gather Information** Do research to gather information about Britain's two houses of Parliament. Include information about historical background, formal qualifications for office, salary and benefits of members, terms, and elections. Make a parallel list for the U.S. Congress. Continue to add information to your list as you read.

---

## EXTEND THE LESSON

Ask students to make a fact sheet on the current term and session of Congress. They should include the names of their representatives and the dates for the start, end, adjournment, and recesses.

**L2 L1 Differentiate** For these students, distribute the Extend Activity "Write to Your Senator or Representative" (Unit 3 All-in-One, p. 16).

## Assess and Remediate

**L3** Collect the Core Worksheet and assess students' work.

**L3** Assign the Section 1 Assessment questions.

**L3** Section Quiz A (Unit 3 All-in-One, p. 17)

**L2** Section Quiz B (Unit 3 All-in-One, p. 18)

Have students complete the review activities in the digital lesson presentation and continue their work in the **Essential Questions Journal.**

### REMEDIATION

| If Your Students Have Trouble With | Strategies For Remediation |
|---|---|
| Explaining reasons for bicameralism (Questions 1, 5) | Write the section graphic organizer on the board and have students explain it. |
| Understanding terms and sessions (Questions 2, 3, 4, 6, 7) | Have students make a timeline of the last session of Congress using the relevant Political Dictionary words. |

## Answer

**Checkpoint** two

---

## Assessment Answers

**1. Historical:** familiarity with British Parliament, which was bicameral **Practical:** compromise between the Virginia and New Jersey Plans **Theoretical:** The Framers believed that bicameralism would enable each house of Congress to check the power of the other and would help to prevent Congress from overpowering the other branches of government.

**2.** one that has two houses

**3.** A *term* is the period from noon of January 3 of the year following a congressional election (every odd-numbered year) to noon of January 3 after the next election. It lasts two years. A *session* is the period in a given year during which Congress is conducting business. Each term has two sessions, one each year of the term.

**4.** *recess:* a temporary break; *adjournment:* business is ended until the next session

**5.** The large and small States might not have agreed to a National Government.

**6.** Under a monarchy, the executive (king) was very powerful. The Framers chose to create a republic, in which the legislators, as the people's representatives, would hold greater power than the executive (President).

**7.** A good answer will include the possibility that experience had taught the Framers that a one-year term was too short to allow Congress to accomplish much, so they decided to lengthen it to two years.

**QUICK WRITE** Students' lists should show evidence of thoughtful research and evaluation of information.

## LESSON GOAL

- Students will identify an issue being debated by Congress in which they are interested and write a letter to one of their representatives in Congress.

# Teach

### READ

Have students read the introduction to Citizenship 101 aloud. If students have computer access, you may have them research bills on the current congressional calendars. Alternatively, students may read newspapers or watch the news to collect ideas about what issues Congress is currently debating.

### BRAINSTORM

As a class, have students brainstorm a list of issues that affect them. Compare this with a list of bills that have recently or will soon be debated by Congress. If there is no bill that students feel strongly about, they could propose one. Read Step 1 aloud. Use the Internet or a local newspaper to identify the students' representatives in Congress, including both senators and representatives.

### DRAFT AND WRITE LETTERS

In groups or on their own, have students follow the remaining steps to write a letter to a member of Congress. Work with individual students to address problems with their letters.

# Assess and Remediate

Collect the students' letters and grade them. You may also wish to have them answer the What Do You Think questions at the bottom of the page.

## Answers

1. Possible answers: Officials try to represent their constituents' views. Unless constituents write to them, officials may not know the views of the people in their districts.

2. A strong answer will explain that elected officials receive a lot of mail or that a short letter can be more effective than a long one.

3. A strong letter will address the correct recipient, clearly state the reasons for the letter, explain the writer's position on the issue, call for action, and use good grammar.

---

# Writing a Letter to a Public Official

Terrorism, drunk driving, climate change, discrimination, immigration—Do you have a strong opinion about an issue that's being debated in Congress? A brief, well-written letter or e-mail is a very effective way to let your representative and senators know about it. Members of Congress pay attention to constituents who take the time to write to them.

Follow these simple steps when writing your letter:

1. **Find out who represents you in Congress.** If you don't know who your representative and senators are, look in your local newspaper, which may have a weekly record of how they voted on recent bills. You could also go to the Senate or House of Representatives Web site and type your zip code or State in the Search box. You can be sure you are using an official government Web site if the address ends in *.gov*. You can also use the blue (government) pages of your phone book to look up your members of Congress and their office addresses.

2. **Organize your thoughts.** Identify your issue clearly. Before you write, list the reasons you hold your opinion and arrange them in order of importance. Choose only the top two or three to include in your letter.

3. **Clearly state what action you want your member of Congress to take.** For example, you might say, "I am writing to urge you to vote for Senate Bill 244, the bill that will continue funding for Job Corps." If you don't know the number of a bill, identify it as closely as you can by name.

4. **Explain your reasons.** Tell your member of Congress why you think he or she should support your position. Be sure to include specific details and personal experiences that have led you to your position: "I dropped out of high school in tenth grade and couldn't get a job. My cousin learned auto mechanics in Job Corps and ended up with a really good job, so I applied. Job Corps turned my life around. I earned my GED and trained as a computer technician. This year I'm working part time and going to college. I'm writing to you to say that this is a great program. Please vote for funding to make sure it will continue to help young people who want a chance to succeed."

5. **Prepare your letter.** Make sure to address your letter correctly. Include your full name, phone number, and mailing address on the letter or in the e-mail.

### ▸▸ What do you think?

1. Why might an elected official want to hear about your experiences?
2. Why might it be important to limit yourself to explaining only the top two or three reasons for the position you hold?
3. **You Try It** Follow the steps above to write a letter on an issue that is important to you.

**GOVERNMENT** ONLINE
**Citizenship Activity Pack**
For an activity to help you write a letter to a public official, go to **PearsonSchool.com/phgovt**

# Citizenship Activity Pack

**L1** **L2** If your students need extra support, use the Citizenship Activity Pack lesson *How to Write a Letter to a Public Official*. It includes a lesson plan for you and four Mission Briefs for students, which provide a script and instructions for writing effective letters. The Template and Checklist for a Letter to a Public Official may be helpful for students who do not need the full support of the Mission Briefs. Students may also access the Citizenship Activity Pack online for activities on How to Write a Letter to a Public Official at **PearsonSchool.com/phgovt**.

# SECTION 2

# The **House** of **Representatives**

## Guiding Question

**How are the seats in the House distributed and what qualifications must members meet?** Use a concept web to take notes on the House of Representatives.

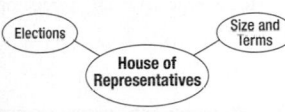

## Political Dictionary

- apporton
- reapportion
- off-year election
- single-member district
- at-large
- gerrymander
- incumbent

## Objectives

1. Explain how House seats are distributed and describe the length of a term in the House.
2. Explain how House seats are reapportioned among the States after each census.
3. Describe a typical congressional election and congressional district.
4. Analyze the formal and informal qualifications for election to the House.

**Image Above:** Members of the media follow Rep. John Conyers (D., Mich.) (front right), the chairman of the House Judiciary Committee.

Every other autumn, hundreds of men and women seek election to the House of Representatives. Most of them try to attract supporters and win votes with posters, yard signs, billboards, flyers, buttons, and other eye-catching campaign materials. Nearly all make their "pitches" with radio and television spots, newspaper ads, and Web sites. In this section, you will discover the general shape of the office that all of those candidates so eagerly pursue.

## Size and Terms

The exact size of the House of Representatives—today, 435 members—is not fixed by the Constitution. Rather, it is set by Congress. The Constitution provides that the total number of seats in the House of Representatives shall be **apportioned** (distributed) among the States on the basis of their respective populations.[5] Each State is guaranteed at least one seat no matter what its population. Today, seven States have only one representative apiece: Alaska, Delaware, Montana, North Dakota, South Dakota, Vermont, and Wyoming.

Voters in the District of Columbia, Guam, the Virgin Islands, and American Samoa each elect a delegate to represent them in the House, and Puerto Rico chooses a resident commissioner. Those officials are not, however, full-fledged members of the House of Representatives and do not vote on bills.

Article I, Section 2, Clause 1 of the Constitution provides that "Representatives shall be . . . chosen every second Year"—that is, they are elected for two-year terms. This rather short term means that, for House members, the next election is always just around the corner. That fact tends to make them pay close attention to "the folks back home."

There is no constitutional limit on the number of terms any member of Congress may serve. A considerable effort was made in the 1990s to persuade Congress to offer a constitutional amendment to limit congressional terms. Most versions of such an amendment would have put a three- or four-term limit on service in the House and a two-term limit for the Senate.[6]

---

5 Article I, Section 2, Clause 3.
6 The States do not have the power to limit the number of terms their members of Congress may serve, *United States v. Thornton*, 1995.

---

## Focus on the Basics

**FACTS:** • Members of the House represent districts of roughly equal population and serve two-year terms. • After each census, the 435 seats in the House are redistributed among the States to reflect changes in population. • Elections are held on the Tuesday following the first Monday in November of even-numbered years. • Members of the House must be at least 25 years old, must have been a U.S. citizen for at least seven years, and must live in the State he or she represents.

**CONCEPTS:** judicial review

**ENDURING UNDERSTANDINGS:** • Congressional districts can be gerrymandered to provide an advantage to the dominant party in a State's legislature. • The right combination of formal and informal qualifications helps members of the House get elected.

---

**GUIDING QUESTION**

## How are the seats in the House distributed and what qualifications must members meet?

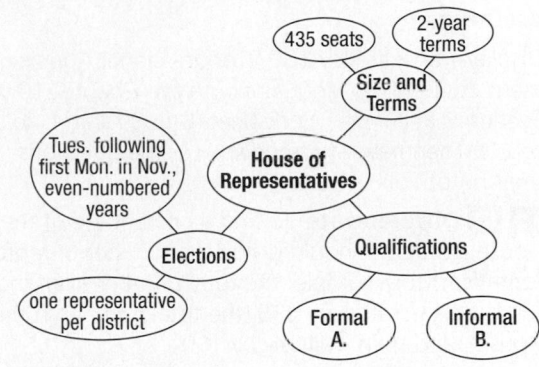

**A.** age 25; citizen 7 years; inhabit State where elected

**B.** name familiarity; gender; ethnicity; experience; incumbency; fundraising ability

## Get Started

### LESSON GOALS

Students will . . .

- identify the States with the most and fewest representatives in the House and review the challenges the Framers faced in creating a functioning government.
- describe the House of Representatives.
- analyze the qualifications for members of the House through brainstorming and class discussion.
- identify the reasons for and results of gerrymandering by simulating the process of drawing district lines.

### SKILLS DEVELOPMENT

**GIVE A MULTIMEDIA PRESENTATION**

To help students with the debates in this lesson, you may want to review the information on giving a multimedia demonstration in the Skills Handbook, p. S21.

Assign the section, the graphic organizer in the text, and the Reading Comprehension Worksheet (Unit 3 All-in-One, p. 19) before class.

**L2 Differentiate** Reading Comprehension Worksheet (Unit 3 All-in-One, p. 20).

## BELLRINGER

Display Transparency 10C, Congressional Apportionment 2003–2013, and distribute the Chapter 10 Section 2 Bellringer Worksheet (Unit 3 All-in-One, p. 21). Then have students answer the questions in their notebook.

**L1 L2 Differentiate** To find a percentage of the House, students should divide the number of representatives (for example, the total number from the four largest States) by 435 (the total number in the House), and then multiply by 100.

# Teach

To present this topic using online resources, use the lesson presentations at **PearsonSchool.com/phgovt.**

## INTRODUCE THE TOPIC

Answer the Bellringer questions on the board:

1. The four States with the most representatives are California (53), Texas (32), New York (29), and Florida (25). These States represent about 32 percent of the seats in the House of Representatives (139 seats held by these states divided by 435 total).

2. The seven States with one representative each are Alaska, Delaware, Montana, North Dakota, South Dakota, Vermont, and Wyoming. These States represent 1.6 percent of the House seats.

3. Larger States have more representatives and, therefore, a louder voice in the House than the smaller States. If students claim that this is an unfair situation, remind them that the organization of the Senate addresses the issue.

Ask students who elects members of the House. *(voters in each congressional district)*

**L4 Differentiate** To challenge students, ask: **Whose interests should members of the House represent: their State, their district, or the entire nation? Which group is "the people"?**

## Answers

**Checkpoint** The House had grown too large for effective action, but it was politically difficult to reapportion without adding seats. This would have caused some States to lose seats. No reapportionment took place following the 1920 census.

**Interpreting Maps** Population is declining in several North Central and Northeastern States. Population is increasing in the South and Southwest.

**274** Congress

---

✔ **Checkpoint**
What problem did the House face after the census of 1920?

## Reapportionment

Article I of the Constitution directs Congress to **reapportion** (redistribute) the seats in the House every ten years, after each census.[7] Until a first census could be taken, the Constitution set the size of the House at 65 seats. That many members served in the First and Second Congresses (1789–1793). The census of 1790 showed a national population of 3,929,214 persons; so in 1792 Congress increased the number of House seats by 41, to 106.

**A Growing Nation** As the nation's population grew over the decades, and as the number of States also increased, so did the size of the House. It went to 142 seats after the census of 1800, to 182 seats 10 years later, and so on.[8] By 1912, following the census of 1910 and the admission of Arizona and then New Mexico to the Union, the House had grown to 435 seats.

---

[7] Article I, Section 2, Clause 3. A decennial census is one taken every ten years.
[8] Once, following the census of 1840, the size of the House was reduced from 242 to 232 seats.

With the census of 1920, Congress found itself in a difficult political position. The House had long since grown too large for effective floor action. To reapportion without adding more seats, however, would mean that some States would have to lose seats.

Congress met the problem by doing nothing. So, despite the Constitution's command, there was no reapportionment on the basis of the 1920 census.

**Reapportionment Act of 1929** Faced with the 1930 census, Congress avoided repeating its earlier lapse by passing the Reapportionment Act of 1929. That law, still on the books, sets up what is often called an "automatic reapportionment." It provides:

1. The "permanent" size of the House is 435 members. Of course, that figure is permanent only so long as Congress does not decide to change it. Congress did enlarge the House temporarily in 1959 when Alaska and then Hawaii became States. Today each of the 435 seats in the House represents an average of some 700,000 persons.

## Congressional Apportionment 2003-2013

🔊 **GOVERNMENT** ONLINE
**Audio Tour**
Listen to a guided audio tour of this map at **PearsonSchool.com/phgovt**

➤➤ **Interpreting Maps** The 435 seats in the House are reapportioned among the States every ten years. *What regions are gaining or losing population?*

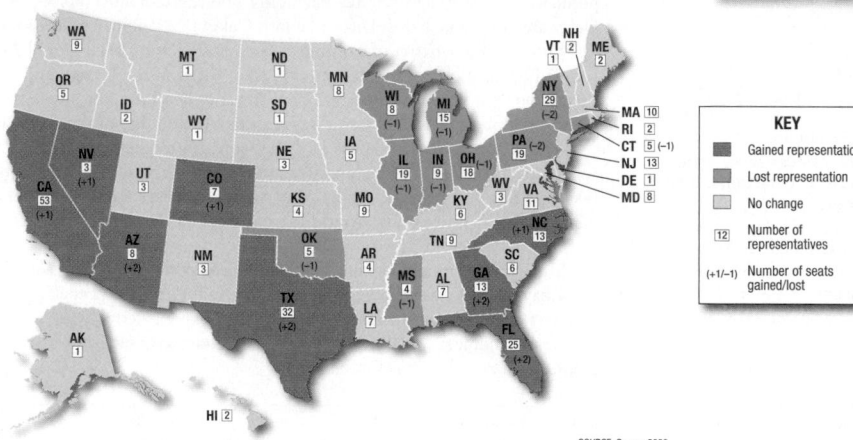

SOURCE: Census 2000

**274** Congress

---

# Differentiated Resources

The following resources are located in the All-in-One, Unit 3, Chapter 10, Section 2:

- **L3** Reading Comprehension Worksheet (p. 19)
- **L2** Reading Comprehension Worksheet (p. 20)
- **L3** Bellringer Worksheet (p. 21)
- **L3** Core Worksheet (p. 22)
- **L2** Core Worksheet (p. 23)
- **L2** Extend Activity (p. 24)
- **L3** Quiz A (p. 25)
- **L2** Quiz B (p. 26)

**2.** Following each census, the Census Bureau is to determine the number of seats each State should have.

**3.** When the Bureau's plan is ready, the President must send it to Congress.

**4.** If, within 60 days of receiving it, neither house rejects the Census Bureau's plan, it becomes effective.

The plan set out in the 1929 law has worked quite well through eight reapportionments. The law leaves to Congress its constitutional responsibility to reapportion the House, but it gives to the Census Bureau the mechanical chores and the political "heat" that go with that task.

## Congressional Elections

According to the Constitution, any person whom a State allows to vote for members of "the most numerous Branch" of its own legislature is qualified to vote in congressional elections.[9] The Constitution also provides that

> ### FROM THE CONSTITUTION
>
> **The Times, Places and Manner of holding [Congressional] Elections . . . shall be prescribed in each State by the Legislature thereof; but the Congress may at any time by Law make or alter such Regulations. . . .**[10]
> —Article I, Section 4, Clause 1

**Date** Congressional elections are held on the same day in every State. Since 1872 Congress has required that those elections be held on the Tuesday following the first Monday in November of each even-numbered year. Congress has made an exception for Alaska, which may hold its election in October. To date, however, Alaskans have chosen to use the November date.

In that same 1872 law, Congress directed that representatives be chosen by written or printed ballots. The use of voting machines was approved in 1899. Today, most votes cast in congressional elections are cast on some type of (usually electronic) voting device.

**Off-Year Elections** Those congressional elections that occur in nonpresidential years—that is, between presidential elections—are called **off-year elections.** The next ones will occur in 2014 and 2018.

Far more often than not, the party that holds the presidency loses seats in the off-year elections. The most recent exception occurred in 2002, in the first election to be held after the terrorist attacks on September 11, 2001. The Republicans, sparked by the campaign efforts of President Bush, regained control of the Senate and padded their slim majority in the House. The party in power lost seats in the 2010 off-year elections, however. The Republicans, riding a wave of popular dissatisfaction with a stubbornly sluggish economy, captured control of the House, while the Democrats retained their hold on the Senate.

**Districts** The 435 members of the House are chosen by the voters in 435 separate congressional districts across the country. Recall that seven States each have only one seat in the House. There are, then, 428 congressional districts within the other 43 States.

The Constitution makes no mention of congressional districts. For more than half a century, Congress allowed each State to decide whether to elect its members by a general ticket system or on a **single-member district** basis. Under the single-member district arrangement, the voters in each district elect one of the State's representatives from among a field of candidates running for a seat in the House from that district.

Most States quickly set up single-member districts. However, several States used the general ticket system. Under that arrangement, all of the State's seats were filled **at-large**—that is, elected from the State as a whole, rather than from particular districts. Every voter could vote for a candidate for each one of the State's seats in the House.

9 Article I, Section 2, Clause 1.
10 The Constitution allows only one method for filling a vacancy in the House—by a special election, which may be called only by the governor of the State involved (Article I, Section 2, Clause 4).

✓ **Checkpoint**
Which party typically gains seats in off-year elections?

---

**COVER THE BASICS**

Ask students to take out the Reading Comprehension Worksheet. Review the answers to questions 1, 3, and 13 to make sure they know the size of the House *(435)*, length of term *(two years)*, and formal qualifications for members *(at least 25 years old, a citizen of the United States for at least seven years, and live in the State he or she represents; informal: party identification, name familiarity, gender, ethnic characteristics, political experience, and incumbency)*.

Allow students to ask questions related to these topics.

**BRAINSTORM**

Remind students that there are informal qualifications for members of the House. List students' ideas for other qualifications on the board. Ask them to explain why they identified these qualifications. Tell them to write down these qualifications in their notebooks, as they will use them for reference after reading Section 4. They will spend the rest of this lesson focusing on how districts may be drawn to the advantage of the party in power.

**L2 Differentiate** Draw students' attention to the paragraphs below the heading "Informal Qualifications" at the end of the section. Ask them to find the informal qualifications listed by the author.

**L4 Differentiate** Ask students to make a distinction between the qualifications that people look for—such as experience—and the qualifications people may not recognize as influencing their votes—such as gender, race, and fundraising ability.

---

## Answers

**Checkpoint** The party that is not in power typically gains seats in off-year elections.

## COMPARE DISTRICT MAPS

Show Transparency 10E, Congressional Districts. Ask what this map shows. *(the congressional districts in Louisiana)* Direct them to examine the size and shape of the districts. Ask what they notice about the shapes. *(They should notice that the shapes are odd, not uniform.)* Ask why the districts might be shaped differently from one year to the next. *(The odd shapes in 2007 may have been drawn to provide an advantage to the party in power; the more uniform shapes in 2000 probably were based on population alone.)*

## DISTRIBUTE CORE WORKSHEET

Distribute the Chapter 10 Section 2 Core Worksheet (Unit 3 All-in-One, p. 22), which addresses the distribution of seats in the House and the politics associated with reapportionment and redistricting, also referred to as *gerrymandering*. Using this worksheet, students will draw their own district lines.

**L2** **Differentiate** An adapted Core Worksheet (Unit 3 All-in-One, p. 23) offers a shorter version of the activity.

## Answers

**Gerrymandering** Some say that gerrymandering should be outlawed because district lines are intentionally drawn to the advantage of the party in power, creating an unfair "rigging" of elections.

---

### Gerrymandering
# Choosing Their Voters

Each State's congressional districts must be redrawn every ten years, to bring the districts into line with the federal census. This gives State legislatures the opportunity to redistrict the State to the advantage of the majority party. *Why do some people think gerrymandering should be outlawed?*

**PACKING** Packing happens when the State legislators "pack" as many voters from the opposing party into a single district as possible. This makes the other districts "safe" for the party in power.

**Result: Two districts are safe for the Orange Party.**

● Registered Green Party voter

● Registered Orange Party voter

★ Each star represents incumbent

**grossly**
*adv.* obviously

At-large elections proved <u>grossly</u> unfair. A party with even a very small plurality of voters statewide could win all of a State's seats in the House. Congress finally did away with the general ticket system in 1842. Thereafter, all of the seats in the House were to be filled from single-member districts in each State. Since the seven States with the fewest residents each have only one representative in the House, these representatives are said to be elected "at-large." Although each of them does represent a single-member district, that district covers the entire State.

The 1842 law made each State legislature responsible for drawing any congressional districts within its own State. It also required that each congressional district be made up of "contiguous territory." That is, it must be one piece, not several scattered pieces. In

**peculiar**
*adj.* unusual, odd

1872, Congress added the command that the districts within each State have "as nearly as practicable an equal number of inhabitants." In 1901, it further directed that all the districts be of "compact territory"—in other words, a comparatively small area.

These requirements of contiguity, population equality, and compactness were often disregarded by State legislatures, and Congress made no real effort to enforce them. The requirements were left out of the Reapportionment Act of 1929. In 1932, the Supreme Court held (in *Wood* v. *Broom*) that they had therefore been repealed. Over time, then, and most notably since 1929, the State legislatures have drawn many districts with very <u>peculiar</u> geographic shapes. Moreover, until fairly recently, many districts were also of widely varying populations.

---

# Background

**GERRYMANDERING IN PRACTICE** After the 2000 census, 17 Democrats and 15 Republicans represented Texas in the House of Representatives. In 2003, Tom DeLay, the majority leader in the House, spent a few days in his home state, helping Texas Republicans redraw the congressional districts. In the election of 2004, his efforts paid off. The gerrymandering helped change the Texas delegation to 21 Republicans and 11 Democrats. Democrats protested, contending that it is unconstitutional to redraw the lines three years after the census and solely for political advantage. In 2006, the Supreme Court upheld the Texas plan as constitutional. Gerrymandering is legal and practiced by both parties when in power. If Congress wants to stop the practice, it must pass a law against it.

**GOVERNMENT** ONLINE

For an **interactive** exploration of gerrymandering, visit PearsonSchool.com/phgovt

INTERACTIVE

**CRACKING** Cracking happens when the party in power splits up (spreads out) the voters who support the opposing party. This results in the minority party winning fewer seats.

**Result: The Orange Party wins three districts.**

**KIDNAPPING** Kidnapping happens when the party in power redraws the district lines to move a minority-party incumbent into a different district where she or he is less likely to win reelection.

**Result: The Orange Party wins three seats. The Green Party incumbent "loses" his district.**

**Gerrymandering** Congressional district maps in several States show one and sometimes several districts of very odd shapes. Some look like the letters S or Y, some resemble a dumbbell or a squiggly piece of spaghetti, and some defy description. Those districts have usually been **gerrymandered**. That is, they have been drawn to the advantage of the political party that controls the State's legislature.

Gerrymandering is widespread today—and not just at the congressional district level. Districts for the election of State legislators are regularly drawn for the advantage of one party. In fact, gerrymandering can be found in most places where lines are drawn for the election of public officeholders—in cities, counties, school districts, and elsewhere.

Most often gerrymandering takes one of two forms. The lines are drawn either (1) to concentrate the opposition's voters in one or a few districts, thus leaving the other districts comfortably safe for the dominant party; or (2) to spread the opposition as thinly as possible among several districts, limiting the opposition's ability to win anywhere in the region. Gerrymandering's main goal is to create as many "safe" districts as possible—districts almost certain to be won by the party in control of the line-drawing process. And the computer-driven map-making techniques of today make the practice more effective than ever in its storied past.

Gerrymandering is the principle reason why, presently, only a handful of seats in the House are actually at risk in an election. In most elections, no more than 40 members now represent districts that cannot be classified as more or less safe districts.

For decades, gerrymandering produced congressional districts that differed widely

✔ **Checkpoint**
What is gerrymandering and what are its purpose and result?

# Debate

In March 2006, as the Supreme Court was considering a case concerning gerrymandering in Texas, an editorial appeared in *The New York Times.* It ended with this strong statement: "If the Supreme Court permits those drawing legislative lines to use high-powered computers to create district lines that predetermine the outcomes of all but a handful of Congressional races, America may need to come up with another word for its form of government, because 'democracy' will hardly apply." ("The Texas Gerrymander" from *The New York Times,* March 1, 2006) Ask: **Do you agree with this opinion? Why or why not? What would you do to make the redistricting process more "democratic"?**

## REVIEW KEY INFORMATION

Tell students that today they will learn about *gerrymandering,* or drawing district lines to benefit the party in control of the State legislature.

Ask: **Whom does each member of the House represent?** *(the people of his or her district)* **What is a district?** *(an area of about 700,000 people)* **If your State has more than one representative in the House, do you get to vote for each representative from your state?** *(no, only the one who represents your district)* **Why are district lines redrawn?** *(because population patterns shift)* **How can gerrymandering benefit the party in control?** *(The dominant party can make sure its members win by concentrating opposition voters into a few districts or by spreading opposition voters thin.)*

**L2** **Differentiate** Display Transparency 10F, Gerrymandering: Choosing Their Voters. Explain that the graphic shows three ways in which the orange party may gerrymander a district. Discuss those ways.

## BEGIN THE ACTIVITY

Ask a student to read the directions aloud. Divide students into groups and assign each group one of three roles: Party X legislators, Party O legislators, or Election Commission officers. Give them time to discuss their plans and draw district lines.

**L2** **Differentiate** Students who work more slowly should be assigned to the Election Commission because Commission members do not need to decide how to concentrate or spread the opposition.

**L4** **Differentiate** Advanced students may draw districts from all three perspectives.

## STUDENTS POST AND EXPLAIN DISTRICTS

When students finish drawing their districts on the Core Worksheet, have each group choose one map to post and explain below it why they chose those divisions. Choose a wall for each interest (Party X, Party O, and Election Commission) and have groups post their maps together.

Tell students to go to the Interactivity for an interactive version of *Gerrymandering.*

## Answers

**Checkpoint** *Gerrymandering* is drawing electoral districts (congressional and otherwise) with the goal of maximizing the number of seats held by the party that controls the State's legislature.

Have students discuss the reflection questions on the Core Worksheet in small groups. This will help them make connections to the unit Essential Question (What should determine the balance between partisanship and consensus in Congress?).

After students have answered the questions on their own, discuss them as a class. Display Transparency 10G, The Gerry-mander. Ask: **How did this cartoon get its name?** *(from Massachusetts governor Gerry when he and his supporters redrew districts)* You may choose to emphasize the Court cases discussed in the text and their effect on gerrymandering since then. The cases are as follows:

- *Wesberry* v. *Sanders* said that districts must have substantially equal populations.
- *Gomillion* v. *Lightfoot* said that gerrymandering solely on race is unconstitutional. *Bush* v. *Vera* and *United Latin American Citizens* v. *Perry* also struck down race-based districts.
- *Hunt* v. *Cromartie* said that race may be one of a mix of factors that shape the districting process.
- *Davis* v. *Bendemer* said that under some circumstances, gerrymandering may be unconstitutional.
- *United Latin American Citizens* v. *Perry* said that nothing in the Constitution prevents a State from redrawing district lines to give advantage to the party in control of the legislature.

### EXTEND THE LESSON

Have students do research to find a map that shows the electoral districts in their State before and after the most recent reapportionment. They should find out which party was in power at the time of the reapportionment and the results of the elections just before and just after the new district lines were drawn. They should then draw conclusions about whether redistricting benefited the dominant party.

**L4 Differentiate** Have advanced students do further research on the demographics of particular districts to determine what criteria the legislature may have used to draw the lines.

**L2** Assign the Extend Activity "The Importance of Congress" (Unit 3 All-in-One, p. 24).

## Answers

**Checkpoint** The *Wesberry* decision said that all congressional districts must have roughly the same population. This is often summarized as "one person, one vote."

---

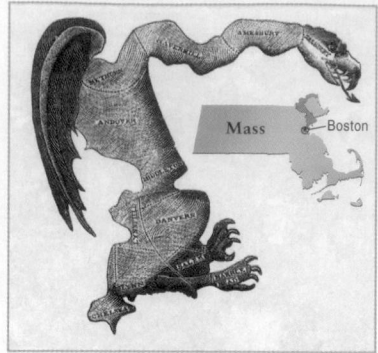

**Gerrymandering** takes its name from Massachusetts Governor Elbridge Gerry, who in 1812, drew the State's legislative districts to favor his party. A noted painter added a head, wings, and claws to a district map hanging over the desk of a newspaper editor. "That will do for a salamander," the artist said. "Better say Gerrymander," growled the editor. ▶

✔ **Checkpoint**
What did the Supreme Court rule in the 1964 case of *Wesberry* v. *Sanders*?

**gouging**
*v.* cheating, swindling

in the number of people they included. State legislatures were responsible for this situation, of course. A number of them regularly drew district lines on a partisan basis—with the Republicans <u>gouging</u> the Democrats in those States where the GOP controlled the legislature, and the Democrats did the same thing to the Republicans where they held sway. In fact, that circumstance exists in several States today. Historically, most States were carved up on a rural versus urban basis as well as a partisan one—because, through much of history, the typical State legislature was dominated by the less-populated (and over-represented) rural areas of the State.[11]

***Wesberry v. Sanders*, 1964** The long-standing pattern of congressional districts of widely varying populations and, as a result, the long-standing fact of rural overrepresentation in the House came to an abrupt end in the mid to late 1960s. That dramatic change was the product of an historic Supreme Court decision in 1964. In a case from Georgia, *Wesberry* v. *Sanders*, the Supreme Court held that the Constitution demands that the States draw congressional districts of substantially equal populations.

---

[11] The pattern of rural overrepresentation in the State legislatures has now all but disappeared as a consequence of the Supreme Court's several "one person, one vote" decisions of the 1960s and 1970s. In the leading case, *Reynolds* v. *Sims*, 1964, the Court held that the 14th Amendment's Equal Protection Clause commands that the seats in both houses of a State's legislature must be apportioned on the basis of population equality.

The Court's "one person, one vote" decision in *Wesberry* had an immediate and extraordinary impact on the makeup of the House, on the content of public policy, and on the shape of electoral politics in general. The nation's cities and suburbs now speak with a much louder voice in Congress than they did before that decision. But notice, it remains quite possible for States to draw their congressional (or any other) district lines in accord with the "one person, one vote" rule and, at the same time, gerrymander those districts.

Gerrymandering based solely on race, however, is a violation of the 15th Amendment, *Gomillion* v. *Lightfoot*, 1960. So-called "majority-minority districts" were drawn in some States following the census in 1990 and again in 2000. Those districts were crafted to include a majority of African Americans and/or Latinos and so were likely to send African Americans and Latinos to Congress. The Supreme Court struck down those race-based districts in several cases—most notably in two cases from Texas, *Bush* v. *Vera*, 1996 and *United Latin American Citizens* v. *Perry*, 2006. However, the Court has also held this: While race cannot be the controlling factor in drawing district lines, race can be one of the mix of factors that shape that process. It did so in a case from North Carolina, *Hunt* v. *Cromartie*, in 2001.

The Court has said that under some circumstances, which it has never spelled out, excessively partisan gerrymandering might be unconstitutional. It did so for the first time in a 1986 case, *Davis* v. *Bandemer*. In 2003, Texas became the first State to redistrict between censuses, with the purpose of increasing the number of Republican-held Texas seats in the U.S. House of Representatives. In a dramatic showdown, the Republican governor called a special session of the legislature. Democratic legislators fled the State, but ultimately they were unable to stop the redistricting. In a 2006 decision, a bare majority of the Court ruled that neither the Constitution nor any act of Congress prevents a State from redrawing its district lines whenever the party in control of the legislature believes that it might be to its advantage to do so, *United Latin American Citizens* v. *Perry*.

## Supreme Court Notes

**GERRYMANDERING IS LEGAL** *United Latin American Citizens* v. *Perry* (2006) arose from the Texas redistricting plan crafted by Tom DeLay in 2003. The plan passed by the Texas State legislature replaced one created by a federal court after the 2000 census. Opponents charged that the plan violated the Voting Rights Act because it diluted the voting power of racial minorities and was designed to gain partisan advantage. The Court held that the Texas plan was constitutional. Justice Anthony Kennedy wrote, "There was nothing inherently suspect about a legislature's decision to replace mid-decade a court-ordered plan with one of its own." However, the Court struck down one district for diluting the voting power of Latinos. Gerrymandering based solely on race is illegal, but race may be considered as one factor.

## Qualifications for Office

You know that there are 435 members of the House of Representatives, and that each one of them had to win an election to get there. Each one of them also had to meet two quite different sets of qualifications to win office: the formal qualifications for membership in the House set out in the Constitution and a number of informal qualifications imposed by the realities of politics.

**Formal Qualifications** The Constitution says that a member of the House must (1) be at least 25 years of age, (2) have been a citizen of the United States for at least seven years, and (3) be an inhabitant of the State from which he or she is elected.[12]

Custom, not the Constitution, also requires that a representative must live in the district he or she represents. The custom is based on the belief that the legislator should be familiar with the locale he or she represents, its people, and its problems. Rarely, then, does a district choose an outsider to represent it.

The Constitution makes the House "the Judge of the Elections, Returns and Qualifications of its own Members."[13] Thus, when the right of a member-elect to be seated is challenged, the House has the power to decide the matter. Challenges are rarely successful.

The House may refuse to seat a member-elect by majority vote. It may also "punish its Members for disorderly Behavior" by majority vote, and "with the Concurrence of two thirds, expel a Member."[14]

For decades, the House viewed its power to judge the qualifications of members-elect as the power to impose additional standards. It did so several times. In 1900, it refused to seat Brigham H. Roberts of Utah because he was a polygamist—that is, he had more than one wife. In 1919 and again in 1920, the House excluded Victor L. Berger of Wisconsin, the first Socialist Party candidate

---

12 Article I, Section 2, Clause 2; see also Article I, Section 6, Clause 2.
13 Article I, Section 5, Clause 1.
14 Article I, Section 5, Clause 2.

✔ **Checkpoint**
What are the formal qualifications for members of the House?

# Paths to Congress

More members of Congress are lawyers by profession than any other occupation. Voters, however, have seen fit to elect representatives with widely varying backgrounds. *What qualifications do these representatives bring to their positions?*

▶▶ **Heath Shuler** (D., North Carolina) Unlike many members of Congress, Heath Shuler had no political experience before his first election to the House in 2006. Shuler had been a quarterback in the National Football League and, later, started a real estate business. Both parties approached Shuler to run for public office. In Congress, he is a member of the Blue Dog Coalition, a group of fiscally conservative Democrats who, among other goals, are dedicated to balancing the budget.

▶▶ **Ileana Ros-Lehtinen** (R., Florida) In 1989, Ileana Ros-Lehtinen became the first Cuban American and Hispanic woman elected to the House of Representatives. Born in Havana, her family fled to Florida when she was seven years old. She graduated from community college before earning master's and doctoral degrees in education. After founding a private elementary school, she was elected to the Florida legislature in 1982. She is the ranking member of the House Committee on Foreign Affairs and an advocate for human rights.

# Debate

In 1919, Victor L. Berger's (Socialist Party, Wisconsin) outspoken opposition to America's involvement in World War I prompted the House to refuse to seat him. In fact, Berger was under indictment for sedition at the time. A special House committee concluded that "Victor L. Berger . . . did obstruct, hinder, and embarrass the Government of the United States in the prosecution of the war and did give aid and comfort to the enemy." Ask: **Do you think the House had good reason to exclude Berger? For what reasons do you think the House would be justified in refusing to seat an elected representative? What possible abuses could arise from the power of the House to exclude a member?**

# Assess and Remediate

**L3** Collect the Core Worksheet and assess the students' reflections using the Rubric for Assessing Individual Performance in a Group (Unit 3 All-in-One, p. 167).

**L3** Assign the Section 2 Assessment questions.

**L3** Section Quiz A (Unit 3 All-in-One, p. 25)

**L2** Section Quiz B (Unit 3 All-in-One, p. 26)

Have students complete the review activities in the digital lesson presentation and continue their work in the **Essential Questions Journal.**

---

**Government** online *All print resources are available on the Teacher's Resource Library CD-ROM and online at PearsonSchool.com/phgovt.*

---

## Answers

**Checkpoint** House candidates must be at least 25 years old, have been citizens of the United States for at least seven years, and be inhabitants of the States in which they run for office.

**Paths to Congress** Shuler: experience in real estate and in working as part of a team; Ros-Lehtinen: experience in education, knowledge of Hispanic community

| If Your Students Have Trouble With | Strategies For Remediation |
|---|---|
| Explaining the distribution of seats in the House (Questions 1, 2, 5) | Review the Congressional Apportionment map and ask students to infer which States have the largest populations. |
| Understanding gerrymandering and redistricting (Question 4) | Use Transparency 10E, Congressional Districts, and Transparency 10F, Gerrymandering: Choosing Their Voters, to explain the process of gerrymandering and the result on the size and shape of districts. Remind students that districts must be of approximately equal size and of compact territory. |
| Explaining qualifications (Question 6) | Ask students to make an outline of the text under the textbook heading "Qualifications for Office" and compare it with a partner's. |
| Describing congressional elections (Question 3) | Model a graphic organizer on the board that includes information about dates, off-year elections, and districts. |

✔ **Checkpoint**
What "informal qualifications" affect a candidate's electability?

**sedition**
*n.* attempt to overthrow the government by force

to win a House seat. During World War I, Mr. Berger wrote several newspaper articles denouncing America's participation in that conflict. In 1919, he was convicted of <u>sedition</u> for obstructing the war effort and sentenced to twenty years in prison. The Supreme Court reversed that conviction in 1921. Mr. Berger was reelected to the House three more times and seated each time without challenge.

In *Powell* v. *McCormack,* 1969, however, the Supreme Court held that the House could not exclude a member-elect who meets the Constitution's standards of age, citizenship, and residence. The House has not excluded anyone since that decision.

Over more than 200 years, the House has expelled only five members. Three were ousted in 1861 for their "support of rebellion." Michael Myers (D., Penn.) was expelled for corruption in 1980. James Traficant (D., Ohio) was ejected after his conviction for bribery, fraud, and tax evasion in 2002. Over time, a few members have resigned to avoid almost certain expulsion. Thus, Randy "Duke" Cunningham (R., Calif.) resigned after pleading guilty to bribery charges in 2005.

The House has not often punished a member for "disorderly Behaviour," but such actions are not nearly so rare as expulsions. For example, the House voted to "censure" Charles Rangel (D., New York) in 2010 for improper fundraising activities, among other charges. The reprimand came just weeks after Mr. Rangel had been easily reelected to the House, despite the upcoming ethics hearing.

**Informal Qualifications** The realities of politics produce a number of informal qualifications for membership in the House, beyond those requirements set out in the Constitution. Those informal yardsticks vary from time to time, sometimes from State to State, and even from one congressional district to another within the same State. Clearly, some of those factors that attract or repel voters in a heavily urbanized district differ from some of those that influence how voters see candidates in a largely rural setting.

These informal qualifications have to do with a candidate's vote-getting abilities. They include such considerations as party identification, name familiarity, gender, ethnic characteristics, and political experience. Being the **incumbent,** the person who currently holds the office, almost always helps. Regularly, well over 90 percent of those members of the House who seek reelection do so successfully.

Much more so today than in the past, a candidate's fundraising abilities also figure into the mix of informal qualifications. Like all other races, congressional campaigns have become very expensive. The average amount spent on a winning bid for the House topped the million dollar mark in 2008. Several winners, and some losers, spent a good deal more than that.

The "right" combination of these informal measurements will help a candidate win nomination and then election to the House of Representatives. The "wrong" mix will almost certainly spell defeat.

**Essential Questions Journal**
To continue to build a response to the chapter Essential Question, go to your **Essential Questions Journal.**

## SECTION 2 ASSESSMENT

1. **Guiding Question** Use your completed concept web to answer this question: How are seats in the House distributed and what qualifications must members meet?

**Key Terms and Comprehension**

2. How are seats in the House of Representatives **apportioned**?

3. How do elections in a **single-member district** differ from elections in States that filled their seats **at-large**?

4. Why do politicians **gerrymander** electoral districts?

**Critical Thinking**

5. **Draw Inferences** How did *Wesberry* v. *Sanders* change the makeup of the House?

6. **Make Comparisons** Explain how informal qualifications for House membership might vary in rural areas versus urban areas within the same State, in different States, and at different times in history.

**Quick Write**

**Expository Writing: Compare and Contrast** Using the lists you started in Section 1 about the British Parliament and the U.S. Congress, draw a Venn diagram in which you can organize features unique to the British Parliament, features unique to the U.S. Congress, and overlapping or shared features. Add to the diagram as you read Sections 3 and 4.

## Answers

**Checkpoint** Informal qualifications include party identification, name familiarity, gender, ethnic characteristics, political experience, incumbency, and fundraising ability.

## Assessment Answers

**1.** Seats are distributed according to State population, with each State guaranteed at least one seat. **Formal qualifications:** must be at least 25, have been a citizen of the U.S. for at least seven years, and be an inhabitant of the State represented. **Informal qualifications:** party identification, name familiarity, gender, ethnic characteristics, political experience, incumbency, and fundraising ability.

**2.** based on each State's population

**3.** **Single-member district:** Voters from each district choose one representative. **At-large:** Voters choose representatives for the State as a whole.

**4.** to increase their party's chances of winning elections

**5.** By ruling that congressional districts must represent a roughly equal number of people, *Wesberry* changed the balance of power between rural and urban areas, and residents of cities and suburbs gained greater representation in the House.

**6.** Informal qualifications include such factors as party identification, name familiarity, gender, ethnic characteristics, and political experience. They vary from time to time, from State to State, and even from district to district.

**QUICK WRITE** Students' Venn diagrams should be logically arranged.

## SECTION 3

# The Senate

**Guiding Question**
**How does the Senate differ from the House?** Use a concept web to take notes on the Senate.

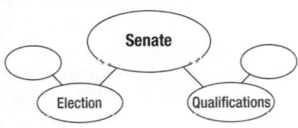

**Political Dictionary**
• continuous body
• constituency

**Objectives**
1. Compare the size of the Senate to the size of the House of Representatives.
2. Describe how senators are elected.
3. Explain how and why a senator's term differs from a representative's term.
4. Describe the qualifications for election to the Senate.

**Image Above:** The late Senator Edward Kennedy (D., Massachusetts) was first elected to Congress in 1962.

You should not be very surprised by these facts: Nearly a third of the present members of the Senate once served in the House of Representatives; none of the current members of the House has ever served in the Senate. Indeed, many of the men and women who now serve in the House look forward to the day when, they hope, they will sit in the Senate. As you read this section, you will come to see why the Senate is often called the "upper house."

## Size, Election, and Terms

Why are there 100 members of the United States Senate? Have the members of the Senate always been elected by the voters of their States? Why do senators serve six-year terms? What qualifications must candidates for the Senate meet? Read on to find the answers to these and other questions.

**Size** The Constitution says that the Senate "shall be composed of two Senators from each State," and so the Senate is a much smaller body than the House of Representatives.[15] Today, however, the Senate is a much larger body than the Framers imagined. The Senate had only 22 members when it held its first session in March of 1789, and 26 members by the end of the 1st Congress in 1791. Like the House, the size of the upper chamber has grown with the country. Today, 100 senators represent the 50 States.

The Framers hoped that the smaller Senate would be a more enlightened and responsible body than the House. Many of them thought that the House would be too often swayed by the immediate impact of events and by the passions of the moment, mostly because of the short term of office for members of the lower chamber. They reinforced that hope by giving senators a longer term of office and by setting the qualifications for membership in the Senate a cut above those they set for the House.

James Madison saw those provisions as "a necessary fence" against the "fickleness and passion" of the House of Representatives. Nearly a century later, Woodrow Wilson agreed with Madison:

15 Article I, Section 3, Clause 1 and the 17th Amendment.

# Focus on the Basics

**FACTS:** • The Senate includes 100 members, two from each State, who are elected to six-year terms. • Senators must be at least 30 years old, must have been citizens of the U.S. for at least nine years, and must live in the State from which they are elected. • Only one third of the Senate is up for election at any one time, so the Senate is a continuous body.

**CONCEPTS:** popular sovereignty

**ENDURING UNDERSTANDINGS:** • Senators represent a larger group of people—and therefore a broader range of interests—than members of the House, and are more often viewed as national political leaders. • Senators usually have more experience, power, and prestige than their colleagues in the House. • Senators are protected from some political pressures because they serve for a longer term.

# How does the Senate differ from the House?

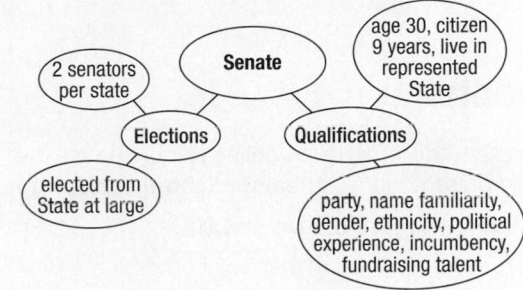

# Get Started

**LESSON GOALS**

Students will . . .

• use a Venn diagram to compare the job and qualifications of senators and members of the House.

• assess the characteristics and qualifications of senators through four real-life examples.

**BEFORE CLASS**

Assign the section, the graphic organizer in the text, and Reading Comprehension Worksheet (Unit 3 All-in-One, p. 27) before class.

**L2 Differentiate** Reading Comprehension Worksheet (Unit 3 All-in-One, p. 28)

## SKILLS DEVELOPMENT

**DECISION MAKING**

To practice decision making in this section, use the Chapter 10 Skills Worksheet (Unit 3 All-in-One, p. 31). You may teach the skill explicitly after students do the Core Worksheet. For L2 and L1 students, assign the adapted Skill Activity (Unit 3 All-in-One, p. 32).

Distribute the Chapter 10 Section 3 Bellringer Worksheet (Unit 3 All-in-One, p. 29). Have students fill in the Venn diagram comparing the House and Senate.

**L2 Differentiate** Have students work in pairs to complete the diagram.

# Teach

To present this topic using online resources, use the lesson presentations at **PearsonSchool.com/phgovt.**

### COMPARE THE HOUSE AND SENATE

Tell students that today they will compare the job and qualifications for members of the House of Representatives with the job and qualifications for members of the Senate. Draw a blank Venn diagram on the board. Let students take turns giving you information to fill in the diagram. Ask students to explain why the houses are different as you write the comparisons on the board.

**L1 Differentiate** Call on certain students early in the activity, giving them an opportunity to contribute to the class before the more standard answers are given.

### DISTRIBUTE CORE WORKSHEET

Distribute the Chapter 10 Section 3 Core Worksheet (Unit 3 All-in-One, p. 30), which describes four candidates for the Senate. Ask a student to read the directions aloud. Answer any questions that students may have about the activity. Give students several minutes to decide, on their own, which candidate they would select.

**L2 LPR Differentiate** Choose one student to act out the role of each candidate, presenting his or her qualifications.

### THINK-PAIR-SHARE

Use the Think-Pair-Share strategy (p. T22) to let students verbalize their thoughts.

### TAKE A POLL

Ask which candidate each student would vote for and why. Choose a student to record arguments. Ask if anyone would make a different decision if he or she were voting for a member of the House. Ask students to explain the qualities they find attractive in each candidate.

---

## Answers

**Senators: Policy and Prestige** Senators serve as representatives of the people of an entire State and tend to have a higher profile than representatives.

---

# Senators: Policy and Prestige

Senators are Washington celebrities—members of what is often called "the world's most exclusive club." Their names are frequently household words and their activities draw media coverage that allows them to call attention to issues they consider important. Many senators make use of the spotlight to launch campaigns for the presidency. *In what ways are senators national leaders?*

**From left:** Maria Cantwell (D., Washington) is known for her environmentalism; presidential campaign buttons; a bipartisan group of senators holds a press conference

---

"It is indispensable that besides the House of Representatives which runs on all fours with popular sentiment, we should have a body like the Senate which may refuse to run with it at all when it seems to be wrong—a body which has time and security enough to keep its head, if only now and then and but for a little while, till other people have had time to think."

—**Woodrow Wilson, Congressional Government**

**maneuvering**
*n.* deal-making or strategy

Each one of the 100 members of the upper house represents an entire State. That same thing can be said of only a few members of the lower house—the seven representatives from those States with only one seat in the House. Consequently, nearly all of the members of the Senate represent a much larger and more diverse population and a much broader range of interests than do the several representatives from their State. If you look at your own State—at the size, diversity, and major characteristics of its population and at its history, geography, and economy—you will see the point.

**Election** Originally, the Constitution provided that the members of the Senate were to be chosen by the State legislatures. Since the ratification of the 17th Amendment in 1913,

however, senators have been picked by the voters in each State at the regular November elections. Only one senator is elected from a State in any given election, except when the other seat has been vacated by death, resignation, or expulsion.[16]

Before the coming of popular election, the State legislatures often picked well-liked and qualified men to be senators. On other occasions, however, their choice was the result of <u>maneuvering</u> and infighting among the leaders of various factions in the State. These personalities all spent a great deal of energy trying to gain (and sometimes buy) enough legislators' votes to win a seat in the United States Senate. In fact, by the late 1800s, the Senate was often called the "Millionaires' Club," because so many wealthy party and business leaders sat in that chamber.

The Senate twice defeated House-passed amendments to provide for popular election. In 1912, it finally bowed to public opinion and agreed to what became the 17th Amendment the next year. The Senate was also

---

[16] The 17th Amendment gives each State a choice of methods for filling a Senate vacancy. A State may (1) fill the seat at a special election called by the governor or (2) allow the governor to appoint someone to serve until the voters fill the vacancy at such a special election or at the next regular (November) election. Most States use the appointment–special election method.

---

# Differentiated Resources

The following resources are located in the All-in-One, Unit 3, Chapter 10, Section 3:

- **L3** Reading Comprehension Worksheet (p. 27)
- **L2** Reading Comprehension Worksheet (p. 28)
- **L3** Bellringer Worksheet (p. 29)
- **L3** Core Worksheet (p. 30)
- **L3** Skills Worksheet (p. 31)
- **L2** Skill Activity (p. 32)
- **L3** Quiz A (p. 33)
- **L2** Quiz B (p. 34)

persuaded by the fact that several States had already devised ways to ensure that their legislatures would choose senators who were supported by the people of the State.

Each senator is elected from the State at-large. The 17th Amendment declares that all persons whom the State allows to vote for members of "the most numerous Branch" (the larger house) of its legislature are automatically qualified to vote for candidates for the U.S. Senate.

**Term** Senators serve for six-year terms, three times the length of those for which members of the House are chosen.[17] The Constitution puts no limit on the number of terms any senator may serve. The late Robert C. Byrd (1917–2010), a Democrat from West Virginia, was first elected to the upper house in 1958 and holds the all time record there—more than 51 years.

Senators' terms are staggered. Only a third of them—33 or 34 terms—expire every two years. The Senate is, then, a **continuous body.** That is, all of its seats are never up for election at the same time.

The six-year term gives senators a somewhat greater degree of job security than that enjoyed by members of the lower house. Those six years give senators some insulation from the rough-and-tumble of day-to-day politics. The six-year term also tends to make senators less subject to the pressures of public

opinion and less <u>susceptible</u> to the pleas of special interests than their colleagues in the House.

The larger size and the geographic scope of their **constituencies**—the people and interests the senators represent—are designed to have much the same effect. That is to say, senators are supposed to be less concerned with the interests of some particular small locality and more focused on the "big picture" of national concerns. Indeed, senators are much more likely to be regarded as national political leaders than are most House members.

The large size of the House generally prevents representatives from gaining as much notice and public exposure as most members of the Senate attract. Senators, and especially those who have presidential ambitions, are better able to capture national media attention. Over the past several elections, the Senate has emerged as a prime source of contenders for the presidential nomination in both parties. Senators also find it easier to establish themselves as the champions of public policies that appeal to large segments of the American people—for example, social security or national health care.

Senators are also more likely to be covered by the media in their States. And they tend to have more <u>clout</u> in their State's politics than that enjoyed by members of the House of Representatives.

## Qualifications for Office

A senator must meet a higher level of qualifications for office than those the Constitution sets for a member of the House. A senator must (1) be at least 30 years of age, (2) have been a citizen of the United States for at least nine years, and (3) be an inhabitant of the State from which he or she is elected.[18]

Senators must satisfy a number of informal qualifications for office—various <u>extralegal</u> yardsticks based on such factors as party, name familiarity, gender, ethnic characteristics, and political experience. Both

✔ **Checkpoint**
How were senators chosen before and after the passage of the 17th Amendment?

**susceptible**
*adj.* likely to be affected by, vulnerable

**clout**
*n.* power, influence

**extralegal**
*adj.* informal, not covered by law

---

17 Article I, Section 3, Clause 1.

18 Article I, Section 3, Clause 3. Under the inhabitant qualification, a senator need not have lived in the State for any particular period of time. Most often, of course, senators have been longtime residents of their States.

# Background

**HOW MANY SENATORS?** After intense debate, the delegates to the Constitutional Convention in 1787 resolved a thorny issue: States would have equal representation in the Senate. Now the delegates had to decide how many senators. The delegates quickly agreed that one per State was not enough. If that person were ill or absent, the State would go unrepresented. The Senate needed to be large enough to counter the influence of the House, yet not so large as to lose its distinctive nature. This realization narrowed the discussion to two or three. Gouverneur Morris and Rufus King circulated this statement for delegates to fill in the blank: "That the representation in the second branch consist of _____ members from each State, who shall vote per capita." Only Pennsylvania filled in "three." The decision was made.

## MAKE A DECISION USING SOCRATIC DIALOGUE

Discuss which characteristics of candidates (both positive and negative) students find most important. Tell students that they will now have ten minutes to decide which candidate they can all support, using the Socratic Dialogue strategy (p. T24).

**L3 Differentiate** Have students rank the candidates from fourth choice to first, using positive and negative characteristics for support.

## FOLLOW UP THE DISCUSSION

Ask students to reflect on the Socratic Dialogue in a journal entry. If they agreed on a candidate, they should answer these questions: What criteria were important in choosing a candidate? How did you eliminate candidates? If they were unable to agree, ask: Why were you not able to agree on a candidate? Do you think the class could have settled on a candidate with qualifications and characteristics different from those described here?

## WRAP UP THE LESSON

Tell students the identity of each candidate.

Candidate A: Daniel Inouye, Hawaii, 1963–

Candidate B: Elizabeth Dole, North Carolina, 2003–2009

Candidate C: Barack Obama, Illinois, 2005–2008

Candidate D: Hillary Rodham Clinton, New York, 2001–2009

Ask if they are surprised by any of these and why. Ask students to read their Bellringer answers aloud. Discuss their answers and emphasize how the length of a senator's term affects his or her actions. Display Transparency 10H, What Are the Pollsters Saying?, and ask which congressional house this cartoon applies to. *(the House)* Senators are not as responsive to public opinion as representatives because they have a long period of time before they are up for reelection.

## EXTEND THE LESSON

**L3 Differentiate** Have students research a current senator, write a short biography, and then analyze the senator's qualifications and actions.

**L4 Differentiate** Have students work in small groups to create a graphic organizer identifying key issues facing the Senate today and the positions taken on these issues by the senators they researched.

## Answers

**Checkpoint** Before: State legislatures chose the senators for their State. After: Voters of the State elect senators.

# Assess and Remediate

**L3** Collect the Core Worksheets and assess students' work.

**L3** Assign the Section 3 Assessment questions.

**L3** Section Quiz A (Unit 3 All-in-One, p. 33)

**L2** Section Quiz B (Unit 3 All-in-One, p. 34)

Have students complete the review activities in the digital lesson presentation and continue their work in the **Essential Questions Journal**.

## REMEDIATION

| If Your Students Have Trouble With | Strategies For Remediation |
|---|---|
| Describing differences between the House and Senate (Questions 1, 3, 4, 6, 7) | Have students make a chart or Venn diagram detailing differences. |
| Explaining a continuous body (Question 2) | Have students do research to find out when their senators are up for reelection, and point out that it's not the same year. |
| The 17th Amendment (Question 5) | Compare the pre-1913 situation with teachers choosing class officers instead of students. |

## Answers

**Analyzing Political Cartoons** The Capitol in the background indicates Washington, D.C. The discussion of a campaign budget implies an elected official, such as a member of Congress.

---

*"According to our estimates, a campaign budget around six point two million is needed to successfully sing your praises."*

▸▸ **Analyzing Political Cartoons** In this cartoon, a campaign manager talks to a candidate. *What clues in the cartoon tell you where this is taking place and who the characters may be?*

**incumbency**
*n.* the current holding of the office

**concurrence**
*n.* agreement

incumbency and a talent for fundraising are also major assets in Senate races.

The Senate can also judge the qualifications of its members when and if they are challenged, and it may exclude a member-elect by a majority vote.[19] The upper house has refused to seat someone on three occasions. It has not exercised that power since 1867, however. The chamber may also "punish its Members for disorderly Behaviour" by

majority vote and "with the Concurrence of two thirds, expel a Member."[20]

Fifteen members of the Senate have been expelled by that body, one in 1797 and 14 during the Civil War. Senator William Blount of Tennessee was expelled in 1797 for conspiring to lead two Native American tribes, supported by British warships, in attacks on Spanish Florida and Louisiana. The 14 senators ousted in 1861 and 1862 were all from States of the Confederacy and had supported secession.

Over time, a few senators have resigned in the face of almost certain expulsion. In 1995, the Senate's Ethics Committee found that four-term senator Bob Packwood (R., Oregon) had been involved in several instances of blatant sexual harassment, and it urged his dismissal. Senator Packwood fought the charges for a time but resigned when it became apparent that his colleagues had had more than enough of his behavior.

The punishing of a senator for "disorderly Behaviour" has also been rare. In the most recent case, in 1990, the Senate formally "denounced" Senator David Durenberger (R., Minnesota). The Ethics Committee had found him guilty on several counts of financial misconduct. The Senate called Senator Durenberger's conduct "reprehensible" and declared that he had "brought the Senate into dishonor and disrepute." Senator Durenberger chose not to seek reelection to a third term in 1994.

**19** Article I, Section 5, Clause 1.
**20** Article I, Section 5, Clause 2.

**Essential Questions Journal** To continue to build a response to the chapter Essential Question, go to your **Essential Questions Journal.**

## SECTION **3** ASSESSMENT

1. **Guiding Question** Use your completed concept web to answer this question: How does the Senate differ from the House?

### Key Terms and Comprehension
2. Why is the Senate called a **continuous body**?
3. How does a senator's **constituency** differ from that of a typical member of the House?
4. Why do most senators receive more public attention than their colleagues in the House?

### Critical Thinking
5. **Determine Cause and Effect** Based on your reading, why do you think the 17th Amendment gained wide public support?
6. **Make Comparisons** How do the different terms of office for the House and Senate allow each house of Congress to make a unique contribution to national decision-making?
7. **Draw Inferences** Do the differences between the Senate and the House of Representatives ensure that the people are well represented?

### Quick Write
**Expository Writing: Make an Outline** Using the Venn diagram you started in Section 2, make a detailed outline for an essay describing similarities and differences between the British Parliament and Congress. Organize your points into a logical order so that, when you are ready to write your essay, your outline can serve as a guide.

---

# Assessment Answers

**1.** The Senate is a smaller and continuous body. Senators must meet a higher standard of formal qualifications. They serve a longer term, represent an entire State, and get more media attention and public exposure.

**2.** It is always in session because only one third of its seats change hands in any election.

**3.** Most senators represent a larger and more diverse constituency.

**4.** Senators are fewer in number, more powerful, and more prestigious than their House colleagues. They tend to focus on national rather than local concerns.

**5.** A strong answer will raise concerns about corrupt practices in the selection of senators by State legislatures and will note that only wealthy men were usually selected.

**6.** The House has two-year terms and must be more attuned to constituents' opinions. It more closely reflects popular opinion. The Senate is more insulated from public pressures and special interests by its six-year terms, enabling senators to tackle riskier issues.

**7.** The differences between the two chambers complement each other, ensuring representation on local, State, and national issues. Students should judge whether this system best represents the people and should support their position.

**QUICK WRITE** Outlines should be detailed and logically organized, with supportive information for preparing an essay.

# SECTION 4

# The **Members** of **Congress**

## Guiding Question

**What roles and functions do members of Congress perform?**
Use a concept web to take notes on the roles and functions of members of Congress.

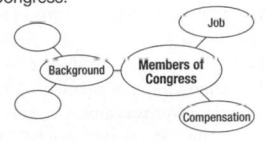

## Political Dictionary
- delegate
- trustee
- partisan
- politico
- bill
- floor consideration
- oversight function
- franking privilege

## Objectives
1. Describe the personal and political backgrounds of present-day members of Congress.
2. Identify the major roles played by those who serve in Congress.
3. Describe the compensation and privileges of members of Congress.

**Image Above:** GOP congressional leaders: Representative John Boehner (Ohio) and Senators John Kyl (Arizona) and Mitch McConnell (Kentucky)

Can you name your two senators? Your representative? Regrettably, most Americans cannot—let alone tell you much about the backgrounds, qualifications, or voting records of those who represent them in Congress.

## Personal and Political Background

Whatever else they may be, the 535 members of Congress are *not* a representative cross section of the American people. Rather, the "average" member is a white male in his late 50s. The average age of the members of the House is 56 and about 62 for those in the Senate.

The number of women in Congress fell for the first time in thirty years in the 112th Congress. Seventy-one women now serve in the House of Representatives, while 17 sit in the Senate. Several women hold leadership positions. Nancy Pelosi (D., Calfornia), who became the first woman Speaker of the House in 2007, is now Minority Leader. One standing committee in the House and four in the Senate are chaired by women today.

There are now 42 African Americans, 22 Hispanics, seven Asian Americans, and one Native American in the House. Two Hispanics, one Asian American, and one Native Hawaiian sit in the Senate. No African Americans serve in the upper house today. The one African American senator in the 111th Congress, Roland Burris (D., Illinois), was appointed in 2009 to fill Barack Obama's seat. Senator Burris, who did not run in 2010, was only the sixth African American ever to be a member of the upper house.

Nearly all members are married, a few are divorced, and they have, on average, two children. Only a few members say they have no religious affiliation. Just over half are Protestants, nearly three in ten are Roman Catholics, less than one in ten are Jewish, two are Muslim, and one is a Quaker.

Well over a third of the members of the House and over half the senators are lawyers. Ninety-five percent have a college degree and most, in fact, have advanced degrees. Most senators and representatives were born in the States they represent. Only a handful were born outside the United States. Sprinkled among the members of Congress are several millionaires. A surprisingly large number of the men and women who sit in the House depend on their congressional salaries as their major source of income, however.

# Focus on the Basics

**FACTS:** • Members of Congress juggle a number of roles, including those of legislator, constituents' representative, committee member, constituents' servant, and politician. • Members of Congress are compensated with a salary and many privileges. • The Constitution provides for legislative immunity from prosecution in the courts and protects lawmakers in carrying out their duties.

**CONCEPTS:** Federalism

**ENDURING UNDERSTANDINGS:** • Though Congress has become more diverse in recent years, members are likely to be older and wealthier than the average American, and most are white men. • Members of Congress must fill several roles as lawmakers, politicians, and servants of their constituents. Their most important role is as legislators.

# What roles and functions do members of Congress perform?

1. legislators, representatives of constituents, committee members, servants of constituents, politicians
2. $174,000 per year, Speaker $223,500, Senate leaders $193,400; many fringe benefits

# Get Started

## LESSON GOALS

Students will . . .

- address the composition of Congress by describing an "average" member and discussing ways the composition might be altered to reflect the population.
- identify and analyze the formal and informal qualifications for members of Congress by writing help-wanted ads.

## BEFORE CLASS

Assign the section, the graphic organizer in the text, and the Reading Comprehension Worksheet (Unit 3 All-in-One, p. 35) before class.

**L2 Differentiate** Reading Comprehension Worksheet (Unit 3 All-in-One, p. 36)

## SKILLS DEVELOPMENT

### INNOVATE AND THINK CREATIVELY

To help students learn to innovate and think creatively, have them turn to the Skills Handbook, p. S23, and use the information there to complete the Core Worksheet.

Write the following directions on the board:

**In your notebook, describe a "typical" member of Congress. To what extent do the members of Congress reflect the general population?**

**L2** **Differentiate** Substitute the following directions for those above:

**In your notebook, describe the median age of a member of Congress, the ethnic breakdown of Congress, and the jobs that many members of Congress had before running for office.**

# Teach

To present this topic using online resources, use the lesson presentations at **PearsonSchool.com/phgovt.**

### DISCUSS THE COMPOSITION OF CONGRESS

Ask students to read their descriptions of a "typical" member of Congress. As they read, note the characteristics on the board. Display Transparency 10I, Minority Members in Congress—Consistent Growth. Use their responses to assess whether they understand that Congress is relatively less diverse than the nation as a whole. Students should understand that a typical member of Congress is a white upper-middle-class male in his late 50s or early 60s, married, college educated, religious, and a lawyer. Ask: **What trend related to minority members in Congress has developed since the 1950s?** *(greater diversity)* Students may add more detail to this portrait.

## Answers

**Analyzing Charts** Some students might suggest that Congress should closely reflect the population because its members are there to represent the people. Other students might suggest that government would work most effectively if the most able candidates are elected, regardless of demographic characteristics.

**Checkpoint** The "average" member of Congress is a white male in his late 50s. Members of the House include 71 women, 42 African Americans, 22 Hispanics, 7 Asian Americans, and 1 Native American. The Senate includes 17 women, no African Americans, 2 Hispanics, 1 Asian American, and 1 Native Hawaiian. Just over half are Protestants, 30 percent are Roman Catholics, and nearly 10 percent are Jewish. Two members are Muslim and one is a Quaker.

---

# How Representative Is Congress?

| COLLEGE DEGREES | WOMEN | AGE 60 AND OLDER | FOREIGN-BORN |
|---|---|---|---|
| **29%** of Americans | **51%** of Americans | **18%** of Americans | **13%** of Americans |
| **95%** of 111th Congress | **17%** of 111th Congress | **53%** of 111th Congress | **2%** of 111th Congress |
| In the 1st Congress, elected in 1789, only 48.4% of the members had college degrees. Today, 42% of senators and representatives have law degrees. | The first woman in Congress was Jeanette Rankin (R., Montana), a suffragist and peace activist first elected in 1916. | The 111th Congress was, on average, the oldest that has ever served. The oldest member was 87, the youngest was 29. | Foreign-born members of Congress have come from Canada, Cuba, India, Japan, Mexico, the Netherlands, Pakistan, Taiwan, and many other places. |

SOURCES: U.S. Census Bureau; Congressional Research Service; Biographical Directory of the United States Congress; *Politics in the First Congress, 1789–1791*

▸▸ **Analyzing Charts** Over time, the membership of Congress has become more educated, older, and more diverse. *To what extent should the composition of Congress reflect that of the general population? Why?*

✔**Checkpoint**
Describe the gender, ethnic, and religious diversity of members of Congress.

Most members of Congress have had considerable political experience. The average senator is serving a second term, and the typical representative has served four terms. Nearly a third of the senators once sat in the House. Several senators are former governors. A few senators have held Cabinet seats or other high posts in the executive branch of the Federal Government. The House includes a large number of former State legislators and prosecuting attorneys among its members.

Again, Congress is not an accurate cross section of the nation's population. Rather, it is made up of upper-middle-class Americans, who are, on the whole, quite able and hardworking people.

## The Job
One leading commentary on American politics describes Congress and the job of a member of Congress this way:

"Congress has a split personality. On the one hand, it is a lawmaking institution and makes policy for the entire nation. In this capacity, all the members are expected to set aside their personal ambitions and perhaps even the concerns of their constituencies. Yet Congress is also a representative assembly, made up of 535 elected officials who serve as links between their constituents and the National Government. The dual roles of making laws and responding to constituents' demands forces members to balance national concerns against the specific interests of their States or districts."

—James M. Burns, et al.,
*Government by the People*

Members of both houses of Congress play five major roles. They are most importantly (1) legislators and (2) representatives of their constituents. Beyond those roles, they are also (3) committee members, (4) servants of their constituents, and (5) politicians. You will take a close look at their lawmaking function in the next two chapters. Here, we consider their representative, committee member, and servant functions.

**Representatives of the People** Senators and representatives are elected to represent the people. What does that really mean? The members of both houses cast hundreds of votes during each session of Congress. Many of those votes involve quite routine, relatively unimportant matters; for example, a bill to designate a week in May as National Wildflower Week. But many of those votes,

---

# Differentiated Resources

The following resources are located in the All-in-One, Unit 3, Chapter 10, Section 4:

**L3** Reading Comprehension Worksheet (p. 35)
**L2** Reading Comprehension Worksheet (p. 36)
**L3** Core Worksheet (p. 37)
**L3** **L4** Extend Worksheet (p. 39)
**L3** Quiz A (p. 40)
**L2** Quiz B (p. 41)
**L3** Chapter Test A (p. 42)
**L2** Chapter Test B (p. 45)

including some on matters of organization and procedure, do involve questions of far-reaching importance.

Therefore, no questions about the lawmaking branch can be more vital than these: How do the people's representatives represent the people? On what basis do they cast their votes?

In broadest terms, each lawmaker has four voting options. He or she can vote as a delegate, a trustee, a partisan, or a politico.

**Delegates** see themselves as the agents of the people who elected them. They believe that they should discover what "the folks back home" think about an issue and vote that way. They are often willing to suppress their own views, ignore those of their party's leadership, and turn a deaf ear to the arguments of their colleagues and of special interests from outside their constituencies.

**Trustees** believe that each question they face must be decided on its merits. Conscience and judgment are their guides. They reject the notion that they must act as robots or rubber stamps. Instead, they call issues as they see them, regardless of the views held by a majority of their constituents or by any of the other groups that seek to influence their decisions.

**Partisans** believe that they owe their first allegiance to their political party. They feel duty-bound to cast their votes in line with the party platform and the views of their party's leaders. Most studies of legislators' voting behavior indicate that partisanship is the leading factor influencing lawmakers' votes on most important questions.

**Politicos** attempt to combine the basic elements of the delegate, trustee, and partisan roles. They try to balance these often conflicting factors: their own view of what is best for their constituents and/or the nation as a whole, the political facts of life, and the peculiar pressures of the moment.

**Committee Members** In every session of Congress, proposed laws, known as **bills**, are referred to the various committees in each chamber. As committee members, senators and representatives must screen those proposals. They decide, in committee, which measures will go on to **floor consideration**—that is, be considered and acted upon by the full membership of the House or Senate.

✔ **Checkpoint**
What is the leading factor in how legislators vote?

**peculiar**
*adj.*, unique, special, particular

## How Should Members of Congress Vote?

The Senate must vote on an appropriations (spending) bill passed by the House. The measure includes earmarks (funds designated for specific projects) for hospitals and the State college system in Senator Miller's home State, as well as projects in other States. Senator Miller may decide to act as a delegate, a trustee, a partisan, or a politico. *How should he vote?*

### What are the options?

| DELEGATE | TRUSTEE | PARTISAN | POLITICO |
|---|---|---|---|
| Although Senator Miller personally thinks that it is bad policy to run a deficit, polls show that his constituents support this bill. As a delegate, he would vote **for the bill**. | Senator Miller favors a balanced budget. His constituents trust him. As a trustee, he would vote **against this bill** because it would contribute to another year of deficits. | Senator Miller believes that it is important for his party to show that it can get things done. As a partisan, he would **follow the party leadership** and vote to pass the bill. | As a politico, Senator Miller attempts to **balance the views** of his constituents, his own views, those of his party, and other considerations. |

---

Ask: **"To what extent do members of Congress reflect the general population?"** If students say that Congress does not represent the population, they may jump to conclusions of racism or sexism as the cause. Point out that Congress has become more diverse over time and note the numbers mentioned in the reading. Direct the conversation to solutions, asking them to recall the profiles of candidates in a recent election. Point out that presidential elections, especially, often feature a choice among upper-middle-class white men. Urge them to consider why some individuals run for office and others do not. Remind them that voters elect members of Congress. You may also ask them how they would change the composition of Congress. If they are stuck, remind them that the United States has low levels of voter participation. Transition by telling students that in order to choose the best candidates, they need to understand the job of a member of Congress.

**INTRODUCE THE ACTIVITY**

Ask students if they have ever looked at job listings in the newspaper or online. Ask them to describe what types of information might be included in a listing for a restaurant server. They should mention information that a job seeker would want to know (salary, hours, benefits) and skills that the person hiring will be looking for. Tell them that today they will be using these same categories to create a "help wanted" listing for a representative and a senator.

**L1 L2 Differentiate** For lower-level students, write the two categories on the board: (1) Information for the Job Seeker and (2) Description of Skills and Experiences the Job Seeker Needs.

## Background

**CONGRESSIONAL PAGE PROGRAM** Each year, 100 lucky high school juniors get a first-hand look at what members of Congress do. These students are congressional pages. Pages chiefly serve as messengers, carrying documents between buildings on Capitol Hill. They also prepare the House and Senate chambers each day by distributing the Congressional Record and other documents needed for the day's work. During sessions, pages sit near the podium, and members of Congress call them for assistance. To become a page, students must be at least 16 and must apply to their senator or representative for sponsorship. Competition is intense. Only students with high grades are considered. Those who succeed gain valuable insight into the inner workings of our National Government.

## Answers

**Checkpoint** partisanship

**How Should Members of Congress Vote?** Senator Miller must consider such factors as his constituents' wishes, his own views, and his party's position.

Distribute the Chapter 10 Section 4 Core Worksheet (Unit 3 All-in-One, p. 37). Using the worksheet, have students work alone or in pairs to write a want ad for a senator. Then they can use the worksheet as a model to write a want ad for a member of the House on a separate page. Remind them to look at the list of qualifications that they started in the lesson for Section 3.

**L1 L2 Differentiate** Walk through the lesson as a class, rather than letting students work on their own. Alternatively, you may walk through one role and let students do the other on their own.

**L4 Differentiate** Have students use information in their completed want ads to create a flier that might be posted on a university bulletin board to attract applicants. Have them use a word processing or desktop publishing software and include graphics to draw attention.

## Answers

**Caption** servant of the people

Rep. José Serrano (D., New York), far right, takes part in the ceremonial first delivery of a program to bring discounted heating oil from Venezuela to his constituents. He worked with nonprofit groups and foreign officials to get the program started. *What role is Serrano fulfilling?*

**appropriate**
*v.*, provide funds for a public purpose

Although Congress enacts laws and <u>appropriates</u> the money to implement them, the Constitution assigns the task of executing those laws to the executive branch. Congress must see that executive agencies carry out those laws faithfully and spend that money properly. It does so through the exercise of its critically important **oversight function**, the process by which Congress, through its committees, checks to see that the executive branch agencies are carrying out the policies that Congress has set by law.

**Servants of the People** Members of both the House and the Senate act as servants of their constituents. Most often, they do this as they (and their staff aides) try to help people in various dealings with the federal bureaucracy. Those interactions may involve a Social Security benefit, a passport application, a small business loan, or any one of a thousand other matters.

Some of "the folks back home" seem to think that members of Congress are sent to Washington mostly to do favors for them. Most members are swamped with constituent requests from the moment they take office. The range of these requests is almost without limit—everything from help in securing a government contract or an appointment to a military academy, to asking for a free sightseeing tour of Washington

or even a personal loan. Consider this job description offered only half-jokingly by a former representative:

"A Congressman has become an expanded messenger boy, an employment agency, getter-outer of the Navy, Army, Marines, ward heeler, wound healer, trouble shooter, law explainer, bill finder, issue translator, resolution interpreter, controversy oil pourer, gladhand extender, business promoter, convention goer, civil ills skirmisher, veterans' affairs adjuster, ex-serviceman's champion, watchdog for the underdog, sympathizer with the upper dog, namer and kisser of babies, recoverer of lost luggage, soberer of delegates, adjuster for traffic violators, voter straying into Washington and into toils of the law, binder up of broken hearts, financial wet nurse, Good Samaritan, contributor to good causes—there are so many good causes—cornerstone layer, public building and bridge dedicator, ship christener—to be sure he does get in a little flag waving—and a little constitutional hoisting and spread-eagle work, but it is getting harder every day to find time to properly study legislation—the very business we are primarily here to discharge, and that must be done above all things."

—**Rep. Luther Patrick (D., Alabama)**

Most members of Congress know that to deny or fail to respond to most of these requests would mean to lose votes in the next election. This is a key fact, for all of the roles a member of Congress plays—legislator, representative, committee member, constituent servant, and politician—are related, at least in part, to their efforts to win reelection.

## Compensation

The Constitution says that members of Congress "shall receive a Compensation for their Services, to be ascertained by Law...."[21] That is, the Constitution says that Congress fixes its own pay. The late Senator Russell Long (D., Louisiana) once characterized this provision as one that gives to members of Congress "a power that no good man would want and no bad man should have."

## Background

**EARMARKS** One way members of Congress fulfill their role as servants of the people is through earmarks. *Earmarks* are funds set aside by Congress to pay for projects in the sponsoring legislators' home States. Earmarks are typically included in spending bills. For example, Representative Thomas Reynolds (R., New York) sponsored an earmark to spend $1.6 million for a crime laboratory in his district. This laboratory may mean little to most people, but it is important to the people Reynolds represents. Earmarks have stirred controversy, however. The 2008 budget bill contained almost 9,000 of them, totaling an estimated $8 billion. Opponents of the practice argue that earmarks supporting local pet projects drain money away from national priorities, such as national defense. Supporters insist that earmarks are a legitimate way for legislators to advocate for their constituents.

**Salary** Today, senators and representatives are paid $174,000 per year. A few members are paid somewhat more. The Speaker of the House makes $223,500 per year. The Vice President makes $227,300 per year. The Senate's president pro tem and the floor leaders in both houses receive $193,400 per year.

**Nonsalary Compensation** Members receive a number of "fringe benefits," and some are quite substantial. Thus, each member has a special tax deduction. That deduction recognizes the fact that most members of Congress must maintain two residences, one in his or her home State and one in Washington.

Generous travel allowances offset the cost of several round trips each year between home and Washington. Members pay relatively small amounts for life and health insurance and for outpatient care by a medical staff on Capitol Hill; they can get full medical care, at very low rates, at any military hospital. They also have a generous retirement plan, to which they contribute. The plan pays a pension based on years of service in Congress, and longtime members can retire with an income of $150,000 or more per year. The lawmakers are also covered by Social Security's retirement and Medicare programs.

Members are also provided with offices in one of the several Senate and House office buildings near the Capitol and allowances for offices in their home State or district. Each member is given funds for hiring staff and for the operating costs related to running those offices. The **franking privilege** is a well-known benefit that allows them to mail letters and other materials postage-free by substituting their facsimile signature (frank) for the postage.

Congress has also provided its members with the free printing—and through franking, the free distribution—of speeches, newsletters, and the like. Radio and television tapes can be produced at very low cost. Each member can choose among several fine restaurants and two first-rate gymnasiums. Members receive still more privileges, including such things as the

21 Article I, Section 6, Clause 1. The 27th Amendment modified this pay-setting authority. It declares that no increase in members' pay can take effect until after the next congressional election—that is, not until after voters have had an opportunity to react to the pay raise.

help of the excellent services of the Library of Congress and free parking in spaces reserved for them at the Capitol and also at Washington's major airports.[22]

**The Politics of Pay** There are only two real limits on the level of congressional pay. One is the President's veto power. The other and more potent limit is the fear of voter backlash, an angry reaction by constituents at the ballot box. That fear of election-day fallout has always made most members reluctant to vote to raise their own salaries.

Congress has often tried to skirt the politically sensitive pay question. It has done so by providing for such fringe benefits as a special tax break for those who must maintain two residences, a liberal pension plan, more office and travel funds, and other perquisites, or "perks"—items of value that are much less apparent to "the folks back home."

22 For decades, many members of Congress supplemented their salaries with honoraria—speaking fees and similar payments from private sources, mainly special interest groups. Critics long attacked that widespread practice as at least unseemly and, at its worst, a form of legalized bribery. The House finally prohibited its members from accepting honoraria in 1989, and the Senate did so in 1991.

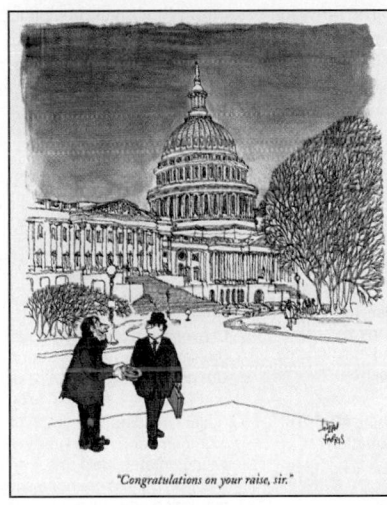

"Congratulations on your raise, sir."

▶▶ **Analyzing Political Cartoons** The nation's current economic difficulties have persuaded both the House and Senate to forego any salary increase over the past few years. *What does the cartoon say about the power of Congress to set its own pay?*

✓ **Checkpoint**
Name five "fringe benefits" for members of Congress.

**fringe benefits**
*n.*, compensation in addition to a base salary

**offset**
*v.*, to balance, counteract, or compensate for

**FOLLOW UP THE DISCUSSION**

After students finish the want ads, ask several to read their qualifications out loud. Use these questions to start a discussion:

• **Do you agree with the different formal qualifications for the House and Senate?**

• **Are the informal qualifications any different?**

• **Do you look for different backgrounds or experiences for senators versus members of the House?**

• **Is the age limit for the House (25 years old) too young?**

• **What specific aspects of the job require specific skills or experience?**

**EXTEND THE LESSON**

Distribute the Extend Worksheet about Jeannette Rankin, the first woman elected to the House of Representatives (Unit 3 All-in-One, p. 39). Have students read the biography and answer the questions. Point out that for members of Congress, voting their conscience sometimes conflicts with the desires of their constituents. Rankin's decision to vote against entry into World War II ended her political career, but she had voted her conscience. Ask students if they think she made a good choice.

Ask: **Should an elected representative always vote the way the majority of constituents want, or do constituents elect the representative because they trust the person's judgment?**

**L2** **ELL Differentiate** Define difficult words in the biography of Jeannette Rankin: *pacifist* (person who opposes war), *suffrage* (right to vote), and *conviction* (firm belief).

**L3** **Differentiate** Display Transparency 10J, Congressional Pay Raise. Ask: **What does the man holding out his hat represent?** *(voters, who cannot count on an automatic pay raise, expecting help from members of Congress)*

# Teacher-to-Teacher Network

**ALTERNATE LESSON PLAN** Have students explore the different ways members of Congress represent the people. In this lesson plan, students will research a recent issue before Congress. They will analyze the position of members of Congress on this issue and identify those who voted as delegates, trustees, partisans, and politicos.

To see this lesson plan, go to

**Teacher Center**
at PearsonSchool.com/phgovt

# Answers

**Checkpoint** Benefits include a special tax deduction, travel allowances, low-cost life and medical insurance, low-cost healthcare, generous retirement plan, Social Security benefits, offices near the Capitol and allowances for offices in their home State or district, funds for office operation, franking privileges, free printing, restaurants, exercise facilities, library services, and free parking.

**Analyzing Political Cartoons** that it is possible, even in hard economic times, that Congress can give its members a raise whereas the public does not have that opportunity

# Assess and Remediate

**L3** Collect the Core Worksheet and assess students' want ads using the Rubric for Assessing a Writing Assignment (Unit 3 All-in-One, p. 168).

**L3** Assign the Section 4 Assessment questions.

**L3** Section Quiz A (Unit 3 All-in-One, p. 40)

**L2** Section Quiz B (Unit 3 All-in-One, p. 41)

Have students complete the review activities in the digital lesson presentation and continue their work in the **Essential Questions Journal.**

## REMEDIATION

| If Your Students Have Trouble With | Strategies For Remediation |
|---|---|
| Roles of members of Congress (Questions 1, 4) | Review the five major roles listed under textbook heading "The Job." |
| The oversight function (Question 2) | Read aloud the section following the textbook heading "Committee Members" and discuss the oversight function. |
| The difference between a bill and a law (Question 3) | Have students look up the definitions in the glossary and explain them in a sentence. |
| Informal qualifications and members' backgrounds (Question 5) | Have students use the first page of this section to make graphs and charts showing aspects of the backgrounds of members of Congress. |
| Voting options (Question 6) | Review the graphic "How Should Members of Congress Vote?" |

## Answers

**Checkpoint** Immunity is intended to ensure that members of Congress know they can speak their minds freely in legislative debates on often controversial issues.

---

✔ **Checkpoint**
Why does the Constitution grant members of Congress immunity from prosecution for anything they say in committee or on the floor?

**contentious**
*adj.*, likely to cause argument

The debate over congressional pay is not likely to end soon—at least not as long as the current method of establishing salaries remains in effect. All sides of the issue present reasonable arguments. Certainly, decent salaries—pay in line with the responsibilities of the job—will not automatically bring the most able men and women to Congress, or to any other public office. But certainly, decent salaries can make public service much more appealing to qualified people.

**Membership Privileges** Beyond the matter of their salaries and other compensation, members of Congress enjoy several privileges. The Constitution commands that senators and representatives

> ## FROM THE CONSTITUTION
>
> **shall in all Cases, except Treason, Felony and Breach of the Peace, be privileged from Arrest during their Attendance at the Session of their respective Houses, and in going to and returning from the same. . . .**
> —Article I, Section 6, Clause 1

The provision dates from English and colonial practice, when the king's officers often harassed legislators on petty grounds. It has been of little importance in our national history, however.[23]

Another much more important privilege is set out in the same place in the Constitution.

The Speech or Debate Clause of Article I, Section 6, Clause 1 declares ". . . for any Speech or Debate in either House, they shall not be questioned in any other Place." The words "any other Place" refer particularly to the courts.

The privilege is intended to "throw a cloak of legislative immunity" around members of Congress. The clause protects members from suits for libel or slander arising out of their official conduct. The Court has held that the immunity applies "to things generally done in a session of the House [or Senate] by one of its members in relation to the business before it."[24] The protection includes work in committees and all other things generally done by members of Congress in relation to congressional business.

The important and necessary goal of this provision is to protect freedom of legislative debate. Clearly, members must not feel restrained in their vigorous discussion of the sometimes contentious issues of the day. However, this provision is not designed to give members unbridled freedom to attack others verbally or in writing. Thus, a member is not free to defame another person in a public speech, an article, a conversation, or otherwise.

---

**23** The courts have held that "Breach of the Peace" covers criminal offenses. So the protection covers only arrest for civil (noncriminal) offenses while engaged in congressional business.

**24** The leading case is *Kilbourn v. Thompson*, 1881. The holding has been affirmed many times since. In *Hutchinson v. Proxmire*, 1979, however, the Court held that members of Congress may be sued for libel for statements they make in news releases or in newsletters.

> **Essential Questions Journal** To continue to build a response to the chapter Essential Question, go to your **Essential Questions Journal.**

---

## SECTION 4 ASSESSMENT

1. **Guiding Question** Use your completed concept web to answer this question: What roles and functions do members of Congress perform?

**Key Terms and Comprehension**

2. What is the **oversight function**?
3. What is the difference between a **bill** and a law?
4. What are the five major roles played by members of Congress in their jobs?

**Critical Thinking**

5. **Draw Inferences** What does the profile of the average member of Congress tell you about the informal qualifications for the office?
6. **Make Decisions** Rank the options that members of Congress have when voting: trustee, delegate, partisan, and politico. Number one should be the option you would want your representatives and senators to use when voting. For each, explain why you would or would not favor each option.

**Quick Write**

**Expository Writing: Write Topic Sentences** Extend the outline you began in Section 3. Then write a topic sentence for each of the major headings in your outline. Topic sentences should introduce the information under that heading. If your headings are too broad to write a comprehensive topic sentence, revise the outline so that each topic sentence serves as an introduction to what follows.

---

# Assessment Answers

1. Members of Congress act as legislators, representatives of their constituents, committee members, servants of their constituents, and politicians. When they vote, they may act as delegates, trustees, partisans, or politicos.

2. Congress exercises its oversight function when, through its committees, it checks to see that the executive branch is carrying out the laws Congress has passed.

3. A bill is a proposed law; a law is a bill that has been passed by both houses of Congress and signed by the President.

4. representatives of the people, committee members, servants of the people, legislators, politicians

5. A good answer should indicate awareness that the characteristics of the "average" member of Congress are an indication of informal qualifications for office. Students may mention that the public seems to favor older white males with political experience; being a lawyer or having another advanced degree, being married with children, being religiously affiliated, and so on.

6. Students should present a reasonable explanation for their preferences.

**QUICK WRITE** Students' topic sentences should correlate to the major outline headings, which should not be too broad.

# Quick Study Guide

**GOVERNMENT ONLINE**

**On the Go**

To review anytime, anywhere, download these online resources at **PearsonSchool.com/phgovt**
Political Dictionary, Audio Review

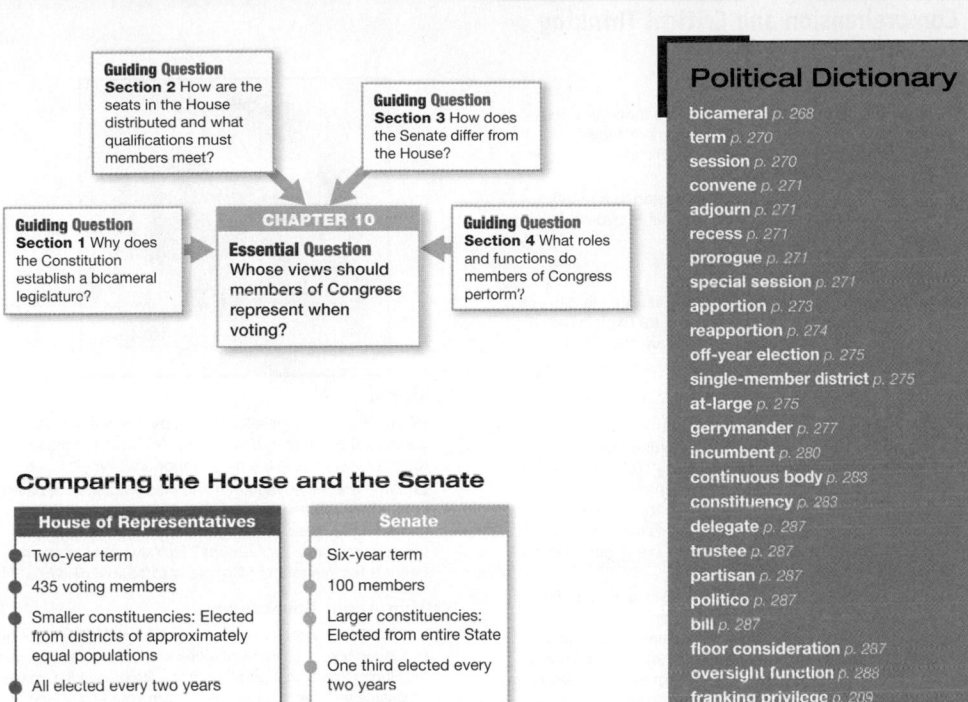

**Guiding Question Section 2** How are the seats in the House distributed and what qualifications must members meet?

**Guiding Question Section 3** How does the Senate differ from the House?

**Guiding Question Section 1** Why does the Constitution establish a bicameral legislature?

**CHAPTER 10**
**Essential Question** Whose views should members of Congress represent when voting?

**Guiding Question Section 4** What roles and functions do members of Congress perform?

### Political Dictionary

bicameral *p. 268*
term *p. 270*
session *p. 270*
convene *p. 271*
adjourn *p. 271*
recess *p. 271*
prorogue *p. 271*
special session *p. 271*
apportion *p. 273*
reapportion *p. 274*
off-year election *p. 275*
single-member district *p. 275*
at-large *p. 275*
gerrymander *p. 277*
incumbent *p. 280*
continuous body *p. 283*
constituency *p. 283*
delegate *p. 287*
trustee *p. 287*
partisan *p. 287*
politico *p. 287*
bill *p. 287*
floor consideration *p. 287*
oversight function *p. 288*
franking privilege *p. 289*

## Comparing the House and the Senate

| House of Representatives | Senate |
| --- | --- |
| • Two-year term | • Six-year term |
| • 435 voting members | • 100 members |
| • Smaller constituencies: Elected from districts of approximately equal populations | • Larger constituencies: Elected from entire State |
| • All elected every two years | • One third elected every two years |
| • Modest prestige, less national media attention | • High prestige, more media attention |

## Reasons for a Bicameral Congress

| Historical | Practical | Theoretical |
| --- | --- | --- |
| • Most colonies had bicameral legislatures. | • Larger States wanted representation based on population; smaller States favored equal representation. | • The Framers wanted to divide the lawmaking power so that the legislative branch would not become too powerful. |
| • British Parliament was bicameral. | | |

## For More Information

To learn more about Congress, refer to these sources or assign them to students:

**L1** **Heath, David.** *The Congress of the United States.* Capstone Press, 2000.

**L2** **Cohen Bell, Lauren.** *The United States Congress: A Simulation for Students.* Wadsworth Publishing, 2004.

**L3** **Hamilton, Lee.** *How Congress Works and Why You Should Care.* Indiana University Press, 2004.

**L4** **Baker, Ross K.** *House and Senate.* W. W. Norton, 2000.

Have students download the digital resources available at Government on the Go for review and remediation.

**STUDY TIPS**

**Summarizing** To help students prepare for college, have students practice summarizing. Give them several minutes to summarize one section of the chapter in one to three sentences. In groups of three, they should share their summaries and work together to agree on the most succinct summary possible. Share these summaries with the class and see if it is possible to write a better one. A good summary should identify the main idea(s) and conclusions of the section without including too many details or examples.

**ASSESSMENT AT A GLANCE**

**Tests and Quizzes**
Section Assessments
Section Quizzes A and B, Unit 3 **All-in-One**
Chapter Assessment
Chapter Tests A and B, Unit 3 **All-in-One**
Document-Based Assessment
Progress Monitoring Online
Exam*View* Test Bank

**Performance Assessment**
Essential Questions Journal
Debates, pp. 277, 279
Assessment Rubrics, **All-in-One**

## Chapter Assessment

**COMPREHENSION AND CRITICAL THINKING**

**SECTION 1**

1. **(a) Historical:** Americans accustomed to British bicameral legislature; most colonial and State legislatures were bicameral. **Practical:** compromise between large and small States. **Theoretical:** Framers wanted bicameral legislature so each house could check the power of the other. **(b)** States had vastly unequal populations and could not agree on a single form of representation that would be fair to all. Bicameralism was a compromise that allowed equal representation to the States in the Senate and proportional representation based on population in the House.

2. **(a)** There are two sessions to each term of Congress—one session each year. **(b)** The President may call a special session to deal with an emergency situation. The President can end a session but only when the two houses cannot agree on a date for adjournment.

**SECTION 2**

3. **(a)** Voters elect one candidate from among a field of candidates running for a single seat. **(b)** After each decennial census, Congress redistributes, or reapportions, the seats in the House to adjust to changes in the population. The legislature of each State then redraws its congressional district lines to adjust for the new number of seats. Gerrymandering is the drawing of these new lines with the goal of maximizing the seats held by the majority party. **(c)** A good answer will include an awareness of the complexity of the process and recognition that reformers must be careful not to introduce new kinds of unfairness.

**SECTION 3**

4. **(a)** Senators must be older and be citizens longer. **(b)** Longer terms insulate senators from political pressures because they don't have to campaign frequently. This allows greater freedom to act according to what is best for the nation rather than what will be most popular with constituents. **(c)** A good answer should note that a policy may be good for the nation but not good for a senator's State.

5. **(a)** a bag containing $1 million **(b)** The original method of choosing senators (appointment by State legislatures) had been

## Comprehension and Critical Thinking

**Section 1**

1. **(a)** Give a historical, a practical, and a theoretical reason why the Framers created a bicameral legislature. **(b)** Explain the following statement: *Bicameralism is an expression of federalism.*

2. **(a)** How is a session of Congress related to a term? **(b)** Under what circumstances may the President convene or end a session of Congress?

**Section 2**

3. **(a)** Describe how members of Congress are elected in a single-member district arrangement. **(b)** Explain how the terms *reapportion* and *gerrymander* are related. **(c)** In your opinion, what criteria should legislators use when drawing district lines?

**Section 3**

4. **(a)** How do the qualifications for membership in the Senate differ from those of the House? **(b)** How does the length of their term of office tend to insulate senators from the political pressures faced by the members of the House? **(c)** Under what circumstances might a senator's role as a national leader conflict with his or her role as a representative of a State?

5. **Analyze Political Cartoons** The 1890 cartoon to the right is a commentary on the selection of senators by State legislatures prior to the 17th Amendment. **(a)** What is the candidate placing in the box? **(b)** What point is the artist making? **(c)** Compare the role of money in elections before the passage of the 17th Amendment to its role today.

**Section 4**

6. **(a)** List the five major roles played by members of Congress as they perform their duties. **(b)** Which of these roles do you think is the most important? Why?

7. **(a)** What are the advantages and disadvantages of paying our elected representatives a salary? **(b)** How much do you think members of Congress should be paid in comparison with other professions? Explain. **(c)** How important is it for members of Congress to be well paid?

**Writing About Government**

8. Use the Quick Write exercises from this chapter to write an expository essay citing similarities and differences between the British Parliament and Congress. Before writing, make an outline and decide how to organize your essay. See pp. S3–S5 in the Skills Handbook.

## Apply What You've Learned

9. **Essential Question Activity** Members of Congress are national legislators, yet they must please their local constituents in order to be reelected. One way to do that is through earmarks.
**(a)** Research earmarks using news stories and other current media. Summarize the controversy over the use of earmarks. Why do some people oppose them? What effect do earmarks have on the nation?
**(b)** Would the earmarks sponsored by your members of Congress make you more likely to vote for them? Would you support the earmarks if they benefited another State?

10. **Essential Question Assessment** Based on the results of your research and the content you learned in this chapter, write a paragraph answering this question: How should members of Congress balance their roles as national leaders and State or local leaders? This question will help you think about the chapter Essential Question: **Whose views should members of Congress represent when voting?**

**Essential Questions Journal** To respond to the chapter Essential Question, go to your **Essential Questions Journal.**

corrupted and those who had the money could buy a seat in the Senate. **(c)** Answers will vary. A good answer will recognize that, today, many people believe that money still plays a large role in the election process.

**SECTION 4**

6. **(a)** legislator, representative, committee member, servant of constituents, politician **(b)** The text states that the most important roles are those of legislator and representative. Students should support their opinions.

7. **(a)** If congressional salaries were eliminated, many qualified people would be unwilling or unable to serve. **(b)** Students should support their opinions. **(c)** Students should recognize that compensation influences the kinds of people who will be willing to run for office.

**WRITING ABOUT GOVERNMENT**

8. Students' outlines and essays should show evidence of awareness of the similarities and differences between both legislative bodies. The essays should be organized correctly by subject or by point.

# Document-Based Assessment

## Members of Congress Cast Their Votes

Members of Congress must decide how to vote on any number of issues during each session. As Document 1 shows, voters would prefer that members of Congress act as delegates. However, members may feel that it is in their constituents' best interest to vote as trustees or politicos.

### Document 1

**When your representative in Congress votes on an issue, which should be more important?**

The Representative's own principles and judgment about what is best for the country

**25% AGREE**

The way voters in your district feel about that issue

**68% AGREE**

SOURCE: The Center on Policy Attitudes, 1999

### Document 2

" I am now here in Congress . . . I am at liberty to vote as my conscience and judgment dictates to be right, without the yoke of any party on me . . . Look at my arms, you will find no party hand-cuff on them! . . . But you will find me . . . the people's faithful representative, and the public's most obedient, very humble servant.

**—Davy Crockett, Representative from Tennessee, 1834**

### Document 3

Of course, both major parties today seek to serve the national interest. They would do so in order to obtain the broadest base of support, if for no nobler reason. But when party and officeholder differ as to how the national interest is to be served, we must place first the responsibility we owe not to our party or even to our constituents but to our individual consciences."

**—Senator John F. Kennedy, *Profiles in Courage*, 1956**

**Use your knowledge of Congress and Documents 1, 2, and 3 to answer Questions 1–3.**

1. Which statement does Document 1 support?
   A. Members of Congress should vote in the best interest of large corporations.
   B. Members of Congress should vote in the best interests of the nation.
   C. Members of Congress should vote in line with their constituents' wishes.
   D. Members of Congress should vote for what they consider to be morally correct.

2. What factors would Crockett and Kennedy have considered when voting on bills?

3. **Pull It Together** Based on these documents, what factors do you think are most important for members of Congress to consider when casting their votes? Why?

**GOVERNMENT ONLINE**

**Documents**

To find more primary sources on Congress, visit
**PearsonSchool.com/phgovt**

---

**DOCUMENT-BASED ASSESSMENT**

1. C

2. Crockett would likely have considered conscience, judgment, and the views of his constituents. Kennedy would have voted according to his conscience more than in the interest of his party or constituents.

3. Answers will vary, but students should consider the various voting options and the advantages and disadvantages of each.

**L2 Differentiate** Students use all the documents on the page to support their thesis.

**L3 Differentiate** Students include additional information available online at **PearsonSchool .com/phgovt.**

**L4 Differentiate** Students use materials from the textbook, the online information at **PearsonSchool .com/phgovt,** and do additional research to support their views.

**Go Online to PearsonSchool.com/phgovt** for a student rubric and extra documents.

---

**APPLY WHAT YOU'VE LEARNED**

9. **Essential Question Activity (a)** and **(b)** Answers will vary. Students' research and responses should be thoughtful and should synchronize information learned from the chapter along with their own thoughts.

10. **Essential Question Assessment** Students' paragraphs should reflect what they have learned about voting as a delegate, trustee, partisan, or politico.

# Introduce the Chapter

## Essential Questions:

**UNIT 3**

What makes a successful Congress?

**CHAPTER 11**

What should be the limits on the powers of Congress?

### ACTIVATE PRIOR KNOWLEDGE

Have students examine the image and quotation on these pages. Ask: **In what way is Congress "the people"?** (*Members are elected by the people to represent their interests.*) **In what way is Congress the President's commander?** (*Congress has some powers that can check the President's power.*) Tell students to begin to further explore the powers of Congress by completing the Chapter 11 Essential Question Warmup activity in their **Essential Questions Journal.** Discuss their responses as a class.

### BEFORE READING

**L2** **ELL Differentiate** Chapter 11 Prereading and Vocabulary Worksheet (Unit 3 All-in-One, p. 57)

### SUCCESSNET STUDENT AND TEACHER CENTER

Visit **PearsonSchool.com/phgovt** for downloadable resources that allow students and teachers to connect with government "on the go."

### DIGITAL LESSON PRESENTATION

The digital lesson presentation supports the print lesson with activities and summaries of key concepts. Activities for this chapter include:

- **Federal Spending: Where Do Our Taxes Go?**
- **The Implied Powers of Congress**
- **The Impeachment Process**

## SKILLS DEVELOPMENT

### DRAW INFERENCES AND CONCLUSIONS

You may wish to teach drawing inferences and conclusions as a distinct skill within Section 2 of this chapter. Use the Chapter 11 Skills Worksheet (Unit 3 All-in-One, p. 77) to help students learn how to draw inferences and conclusions. The worksheet asks students to read an excerpt about eminent domain and then answer questions about the reading. For L2 and L1 students, assign the adapted Skill Activity (Unit 3 All-in-One, p. 78).

**WebQuest online** The chapter WebQuest challenges students to answer the chapter Essential Question by asking them about Congress.

294

## Block Scheduling

**BLOCK 1:** Begin with the heading "Introduce the Delegated Powers" in Section 1 and teach the rest of the lesson, choosing one Extend activity. Then have students complete Chapter 11 Section 2 Core Worksheets A and B. Finish by reviewing "The Expressed Powers of Congress" chart in Section 2 and having students read *The Federalist* No. 41, in which James Madison describes the reasons the National Government has certain powers.

**BLOCK 2:** Teach the full lesson for Section 3 and then have students do research and present information associated with modern conflicts related to the powers of the National Government. Then have them do the Section 4 Jigsaw activity and choose one Extend activity for students to complete.

# Powers of Congress

## Essential Question
What should be the limits on the powers of Congress?

**Section 1:**
The Expressed Powers of Money and Commerce

**Section 2:**
The Other Expressed Powers

**Section 3:**
The Implied Powers

**Section 4:**
The Nonlegislative Powers

> "Though the President is Commander in Chief, **Congress** is **his commander;** ... this is **not** a Government of **kings** ..., but a Government **of the people**, and ... Congress **is the people.**
>
> —Rep. Thaddeus Stevens, 1867

**Photo:** Members of the House of Representatives are sworn in.

**GOVERNMENT** ONLINE
On the Go

To study anywhere, anytime, download these online resoures at PearsonSchool.com/phgovt
• Political Dictionary
• Audio Review
• Downloadable Interactivities

295

## Lesson Goals

### SECTION 1
Students will . . .

• explain what is meant by the expressed, implied, and inherent powers of Congress.

• identify the expressed powers of Congress by examining the Constitution and recognizing their application in scenarios.

• consider limits on the powers of Congress through a Socratic Dialogue.

### SECTION 2
Students will . . .

• examine the division of war powers by analyzing a primary source document.

• evaluate the expressed powers of Congress by determining which powers they feel are most important.

• examine the domestic powers by using photographs illustrating each power.

### SECTION 3
Students will . . .

• use the example of a teacher's powers in the classroom to consider the meaning of implied powers.

• explore strict and liberal construction by evaluating congressional actions.

• decide upon and defend a position on implied powers.

### SECTION 4
Students will . . .

• evaluate the impeachment process by examining primary sources and data about the impeachment of President Clinton.

• examine the nonlegislative duties of Congress, using the Jigsaw strategy.

## Pressed for Time

To cover the chapter quickly, begin with Section 1, asking students to outline Article I, Section 8 of the Constitution. Then ask them to complete the Chapter 11 Section 1 Core Worksheet and Chapter 11 Section 2 Core Worksheet A. Introduce the implied powers using Transparency 11D, Implied Powers of Congress, which lists some expressed and implied powers. Review Landmark Decisions of the Supreme Court: *McCulloch* v. *Maryland,* and discuss modern conflicts related to strict and liberal construction of the Constitution. To cover Section 4, do the Core Worksheets as a group.

**DIFFERENTIATED INSTRUCTION KEY**

Look for these symbols to help you adjust steps in each lesson to meet your students' needs.

**L1** Special Needs
**L2** Basic
    **ELL** English Language Learners
    **LPR** Less Proficient Readers
**L3** All Students
**L4** Advanced Students

What powers over money and commerce does the Constitution give to Congress and what limits does it put on these powers?

| Money and Commerce | |
| --- | --- |
| Expressed Power | Limits on Power |
| • regulate interstate and foreign trade<br>• tax<br>• borrow<br>• establish uniform bankruptcy laws<br>• coin money and regulate its value | • cannot favor ports of one State over those of any other State in regulating trade; • cannot require vessels bound to or from one State to be obliged to enter, clear, or pay duties in another; • could not interfere with slave trade until 1808<br>• may tax only for public purposes; • cannot tax exports; • direct taxes (except income taxes) must be apportioned among States according to population; • indirect taxes must be levied at same rate in every part of country |

# Get Started

## LESSON GOALS

Students will . . .

- explain what is meant by the expressed, implied, and inherent powers of Congress.
- identify the expressed powers of Congress by examining the Constitution and recognizing their application in scenarios.
- consider limits on the powers of Congress through a Socratic Dialogue.

## SKILLS DEVELOPMENT

### ANALYZE SOURCES

Before students analyze Article I, Sections 8 and 9 of the Constitution in this lesson, you may want to have students turn to the Skills Handbook, p. S14, to read the information there.

---

SECTION **1**

# The **Expressed Powers**
## of Money and Commerce

### Guiding Question

What powers over money and commerce does the Constitution give to Congress and what limits does it put on these powers? Use a table to keep track of the powers of Congress and their limits.

| Money and Commerce | |
| --- | --- |
| Expressed Power | Limits on Power |
| •<br>•<br>• | •<br>•<br>• |

### Political Dictionary

- expressed powers
- implied powers
- inherent powers
- commerce power
- tax
- public debt
- deficit financing
- bankruptcy
- legal tender

### Objectives

1. Describe the three types of powers delegated to Congress.
2. Analyze the importance of the commerce power.
3. Summarize key points relating to the taxing power.
4. Explain how the bankruptcy and borrowing powers work.
5. Explain why the Framers gave Congress the power to issue currency.

**Image Above:** Congress has the expressed power to coin money and regulate its value.

A typical day in either chamber of Congress might suggest that there is no limit to what Congress can do. On any given day, the House might consider bills dealing with such varying matters as the interstate highway system, an increase in the minimum wage, and grazing on public lands. Meanwhile, the Senate might be considering aid to a famine-stricken country in Africa, the President's nomination of someone to fill a vacancy on the Supreme Court, or any number of other matters.

Still, remember, there are very real limits on what Congress can do. Recall that (1) government in the United States is limited government, and (2) the American system of government is federal in form. These two fundamental facts work to shape and also to limit the powers of Congress.

## The Delegated Powers

Remember, Congress has only those powers delegated (granted, given) to it by the Constitution. Large areas of power are denied to Congress (1) in so many words in the Constitution, (2) by the Constitution's silence on many matters, and (3) because the Constitution creates a federal system.

There is much that Congress cannot do. It cannot create a national public school system, require people to vote or attend church, or set a minimum age for marriage or drivers' licenses. It cannot abolish jury trials, confiscate all handguns, or authorize the censorship of newspapers or radio or television broadcasts. Congress cannot do these and a great many other things because the Constitution does not delegate to it any power to do so.

Still, Congress does have the power to do many things. The Constitution grants it a number of specific powers—and, recall, it delegates those powers in three different ways: (1) explicitly, in its specific wording—the **expressed powers;** (2) by reasonable deduction from the expressed powers—the **implied powers;** and (3) by creating a national government for the United States—the **inherent powers.**

The Framers very purposefully created a limited government. Given that fact, it is understandable that the existence and the scope of both the implied and the inherent powers have been the subject of dispute ever since the adoption

---

# Focus on the Basics

**FACTS:** • Congress has expressed, implied, and inherent powers. • The Constitution spells out 27 expressed powers of Congress. • The commerce power allows Congress to regulate trade. • Congress levies taxes to meet public needs and to protect domestic industry and public health and safety. • The currency power allows the Federal Government to coin money and regulate its value. Congress may borrow on the credit of the United States and establish uniform bankruptcy laws.

**CONCEPTS:** enumerated powers, implied powers, federalism

**ENDURING UNDERSTANDINGS:** • Much of the meaning of the expressed powers is found in the ways in which these powers have been carried out. • The commerce power is the basis for many of the implied powers. • The taxing power is vital to the functioning of government.

of the Constitution. Later in the chapter, we shall examine the conflict between the strict constructionists, who interpret congressional power narrowly, and the liberal constructionists, who favor a broader interpretation.

## The Expressed Powers

Most, but not all, of the expressed powers of Congress are found in Article I, Section 8 of the Constitution. There, in 18 separate clauses, 27 different powers are explicitly given to Congress.[1]

These grants of power are brief. What they do and do not allow Congress to do often cannot be discovered by merely reading the few words involved. Rather, their meaning is found in the ways in which Congress has exercised its powers since 1789, and in scores of Supreme Court cases arising out of the measures Congress has passed.

As a case in point, take the Commerce Clause, in Article I, Section 8, Clause 3. It gives Congress the power "to regulate Commerce with foreign Nations, and among the several States, and with the Indian Tribes." What do these words mean? Over the past two centuries, Congress and the Court have had to answer hundreds of questions about the scope of the Commerce Clause. Here are but a few examples: Does "commerce" include people crossing State lines or entering or leaving the country? What about business practices? Working conditions? Radio and television broadcasts? The Internet? Does Congress have the power to ban the shipment of certain goods from one State to another? To prohibit discrimination? What trade is "foreign" and what is "interstate"? And what trade is neither?

In answering these and dozens of other questions arising out of this one provision, Congress and the Court have defined—and are still defining—the meaning of the

Commerce Clause. So it is with most of the other constitutional grants of power to Congress.

The commerce power and, with it, the expressed power to tax have provided much of the basis upon which Congress and the courts have built nearly all of the implied powers. Most of what the Federal Government does, day to day and year to year, it does as the result of legislation enacted by Congress in the exercise of those two powers.

## The Commerce Power

Commerce, generally, is the buying and selling of goods and services. The **commerce power**—the power of Congress to regulate interstate and foreign trade—is vital to the welfare of the nation. Its few words have prompted the growth of the greatest open market in the world. The Commerce Clause proved to be more responsible for the building of a strong and *United* States out of a weak confederation than any other provision in the Constitution.

*Gibbons v. Ogden,* **1824** The first case involving the Commerce Clause to reach the Supreme Court, *Gibbons* v. *Ogden,* was decided in 1824. The case arose out of a clash over the regulation of steamboats by the State of New York, on the one hand, and the Federal Government, on the other. In 1807, Robert Fulton's steamboat, the *Clermont,* had made its first successful run up the Hudson River, from New York City to Albany. The State legislature then gave Fulton an exclusive, long-term grant to navigate the waters of the State by steamboat. Fulton's monopoly then gave Aaron Ogden a permit for steamboat navigation between New York City and New Jersey.

Thomas Gibbons, operating with a coasting license from the

✔ **Checkpoint**
Who defines the meaning of the Commerce Clause?

**Inherent** powers are those that belong to all sovereign nations—for example, the power to control a nation's borders.

**Expressed** powers are those stated in the Constitution—for example, the power to regulate both foreign and interstate commerce.

**Implied** powers are not stated in the Constitution, but drawn from the expressed powers. Based on the expressed power to regulate commerce, Congress has set a minimum wage for hourly workers.

▶▶ This chart gives an example of each type of congressional power. *From which type of power does Congress derive most of its current authority?*

---

1 Several of the expressed powers of Congress are set out elsewhere in the Constitution. Thus, Article IV, Section 3 grants Congress the power to admit new States to the Union (Clause 1) and to manage and dispose of federal territory and other property (Clause 2). The 16th Amendment gives Congress the power to levy an income tax. The 13th, 14th, 15th, 19th, 24th, and 26th amendments grant Congress the "power to enforce" the provisions of the amendments "by appropriate legislation."

# Differentiated Resources

The following resources are located in the All-in-One, Unit 3, Chapter 11, Section 1:

- **L2** Prereading and Vocabulary Worksheet (p. 57)
- **L3** Reading Comprehension Worksheet (p. 61)
- **L2** Reading Comprehension Worksheet (p. 63)
- **L3** Core Worksheet (p. 65)
- **L2** Core Worksheet (p. 67)
- **L3** Quiz A (p. 68)
- **L2** Quiz B (p. 69)

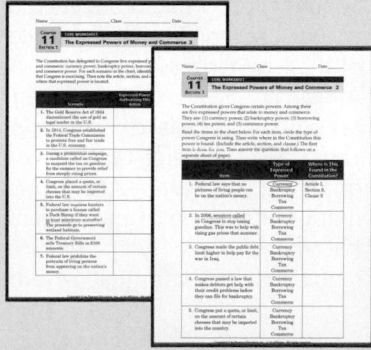

## BEFORE CLASS

Assign the section, the graphic organizer in the text, and the Reading Comprehension Worksheet (Unit 3 All-in-One, p. 61) before class.

**L2 Differentiate** Reading Comprehension Worksheet (Unit 3 All-in-One, p. 63)

## BELLRINGER

Write **Article I, Section 8,** and **Should Internet purchases be taxed?** on the board. Have students review this part of the Constitution and then write down the clause that gives Congress the power to answer this question.

# Teach

To present this topic using online resources, use the lesson presentation at **PearsonSchool.com/phgovt.**

## REVIEW BELLRINGER

Discuss students' Bellringer answers. Point out Article I, Section 8, Clause 3 and explain that it is from this clause that Congress may derive the power to regulate the Internet, if the regulation deals with commerce. Explain that regulation of commerce is an *expressed* power, because it is stated directly in the Constitution. Regulation of the Internet is not stated directly, and therefore is an implied power.

## INTRODUCE THE DELEGATED POWERS

Explain to students that *delegated* means "granted" or "given" and that Congress has only those powers delegated to it by the Constitution. Direct students' attention to the graphic on this page describing the three types of powers that the Constitution delegates to Congress. Ask students to name the three types of powers *(inherent, expressed, and implied)* and to define each. *(Inherent powers are those that all sovereign nations have. Expressed powers are those directly stated in the Constitution. Implied powers are drawn from the expressed powers.)*

**L2 ELL Differentiate** Help students understand the term *inherent* by providing the following concrete examples: "John had an inherent ability to excel at math." "Anti-lock brakes were an inherent part of the car's braking system." Provide the following synonym: *built-in.* Then ask students to offer a synonym of their own *(included, integrated, inseparable).*

# Answers

**Checkpoint** Congress and the Supreme Court

**Caption** the implied powers, based on the expressed powers of commerce and tax

## OUTLINE ARTICLE I, SECTION 8 OF THE CONSTITUTION

Have students read Article I, Section 8, Clauses 1–6 of the Constitution and list the powers related to money and commerce. They are: Clause 1—the taxing power; Clause 2—the borrowing power; Clause 3—the power to regulate foreign and interstate commerce; Clause 4—the bankruptcy power; Clause 5—the power to coin money; and Clause 6—the power to punish counterfeiters.

## DISTRIBUTE CORE WORKSHEET

Distribute the Chapter 11 Section 1 Core Worksheet (Unit 3 All-in-One, p. 65), which asks students to identify the power Congress is exercising in several scenarios.

**L2 ELL Differentiate** Distribute the adapted Core Worksheet (Unit 3 All-in-One, p. 67), which has similar scenarios but fewer for students to address.

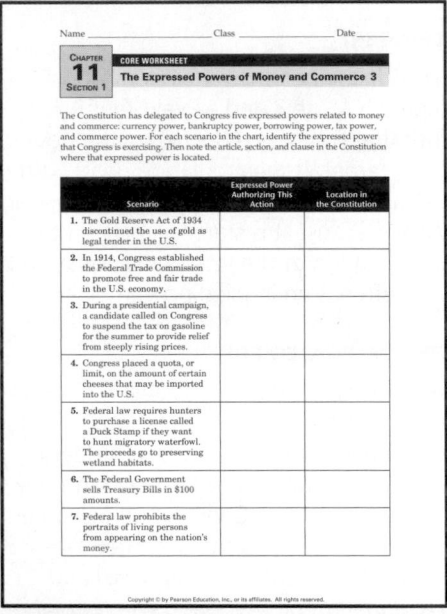

## Answers

**Checkpoint** The Court found in favor of Gibbons, establishing a broad definition of "commerce."

**Constitutional Principles** The Commerce Clause places authority over commerce between States in the hands of the Federal Government rather than State governments.

---

✔ **Checkpoint**
What was the Court's decision in *Gibbons* v. *Ogden*?

**sweeping**
*adj.* wide-ranging

Federal Government, began to carry passengers on a competing line. Ogden sued, and the New York courts ruled in his favor, holding that Gibbons could not sail by steam in New York waters.

Gibbons appealed that ruling to the Supreme Court. He claimed that the New York grant conflicted with the congressional power to regulate interstate commerce. The Court agreed. It rejected Ogden's argument that "commerce" should be defined narrowly, as simply "traffic" or the mere buying and selling of goods. Instead, the Court read the Commerce Clause in very broad terms:

### PRIMARY SOURCE

" Commerce, undoubtedly, is traffic, but it is something more; it is intercourse. It describes the commercial intercourse between nations, and parts of nations, in all its branches, and is regulated by prescribing rules for carrying on that intercourse.

—Chief Justice John Marshall

The Court's ruling was widely popular at the time because it dealt a death blow to steamboat monopolies. Freed from restrictive State regulation, many new steamboat companies came into existence. As a result, steam navigation developed rapidly. Within a few years, the railroads were similarly freed, which revolutionized transportation within the United States.

Over the decades, the Court's sweeping definition of commerce has brought an extension of federal authority into many areas of American life—a reach of federal power beyond anything the Framers could have imagined. As another of the many examples of the point, note this: It is on the basis of the commerce power that the Civil Rights Act of 1964 prohibits discrimination in access to or service in hotels, motels, theaters, restaurants, and in other public accommodations on grounds of race, color, religion, or national origin.[2]

2 The Supreme Court upheld this use of the commerce power in *Heart of Atlanta Motel* v. *United States* in 1964. The unanimous Court noted that there was "overwhelming evidence of the disruptive effect that racial discrimination has had on commercial intercourse." You will look at this case again in Chapter 21.

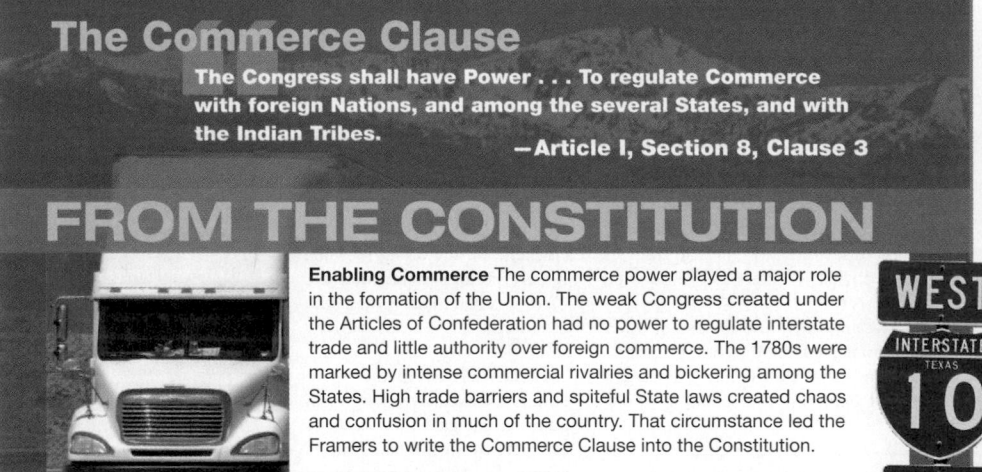

## The Commerce Clause

The Congress shall have Power . . . To regulate Commerce with foreign Nations, and among the several States, and with the Indian Tribes.

—Article I, Section 8, Clause 3

## FROM THE CONSTITUTION

**Enabling Commerce** The commerce power played a major role in the formation of the Union. The weak Congress created under the Articles of Confederation had no power to regulate interstate trade and little authority over foreign commerce. The 1780s were marked by intense commercial rivalries and bickering among the States. High trade barriers and spiteful State laws created chaos and confusion in much of the country. That circumstance led the Framers to write the Commerce Clause into the Constitution.

**Constitutional Principles** *How does the Commerce Clause reflect the principle of federalism?*

▲ Acting under its commerce power, Congress created the interstate highway system.

---

## Background

**CIVIL RIGHTS AND THE COMMERCE CLAUSE** During the first half of the 1900s, the Supreme Court had broadened the scope of the Commerce Clause to allow Congress to regulate more areas of the economy, including interstate commerce. Supporters of the Civil Rights Act of 1964 believed that discrimination in public places had kept African Americans from traveling around the country. Both Title II and Title VII of the act prohibited racial discrimination by businesses that affected interstate commerce. Thus, the Commerce Clause became the foundation for affirming the constitutionality of the act. In *Heart of Atlanta Motel* v. *United States,* 1964, the Supreme Court found that Congress could regulate a business that served mainly interstate travelers. In *Katzenbach* v. *McClung,* 1964, the Court ruled that federal civil rights legislation could regulate a restaurant that served food that had previously crossed state lines.

## The Americans with Disabilities Act

Based on the commerce power, Congress passed the Americans with Disabilities Act (ADA) in 1990. It prohibits discrimination against people with disabilities in areas such as employment, public accommodation, public transportation, and access to commercial buildings. *How do these photographs illustrate problems addressed by the ADA?*

**Limits on the Commerce Power** The congressional power to regulate commerce is not unlimited. It, too, must be exercised in accord with all other provisions in the Constitution. As but one example: the Supreme Court struck down the Gun-Free School Zone Act of 1990 in *United States* v. *Lopez*, 1995. That act had made it a federal crime for anyone other than a police officer to possess a firearm in or around a school. The Court could find no useful connection between interstate commerce and guns at school. It held that Congress had in this case invaded the reserved powers of the States.

In more specific terms, the Constitution places four explicit limits on the use of the commerce power. The Constitution declares that Congress

1. cannot tax exports (Article I, Section 9, Clause 5);

2. cannot favor the ports of one State over those of any other in the regulation of trade (Article I, Section 9, Clause 6);

3. cannot require that "Vessels bound to, or from, one State, be obliged to enter, clear, or pay Duties in another" (Article I, Section 9, Clause 6); and, finally,

4. could not interfere with the slave trade, at least not until the year 1808 (Article I, Section 9, Clause 1). This last limitation, part of the curious Slave-Trade Compromise the Framers struck at Philadelphia, has been a dead letter for more than two centuries.

## The Power to Tax

The Constitution gives Congress the power

> **FROM THE CONSTITUTION**
>
> To lay and collect Taxes, Duties, Imposts and Excises, to pay the Debts and provide for the common Defense and general Welfare of the United States. . . .
>
> —Article I, Section 8, Clause 1

Remember, the Articles of Confederation had not given Congress the power to tax. Congress did have the power to requisition funds from the States; that is, Congress could ask (in reality, beg) each of the 13 States for money. But, through the 1780s, not a single State came even remotely close to meeting the few requests that Congress made, and a number of them paid nothing at all. The government was <u>impotent</u>, and the lack of a power to tax was a leading cause for the creation of the Constitution.

**impotent**
*adj.* powerless

**The Purpose of Taxes** We shall take another and longer look at the taxing power in Chapter 16. But, here, a number of important points: The Federal Government will take in some $2.1 trillion in fiscal year 2010, and almost certainly an even larger sum in 2011. Most of that money—well over 95 percent of it—will come from the various taxes levied by Congress.

Be sure students understand the sequence of events and import of the *Gibbons* v. *Ogden* case. Ask *who, where, what, when,* and *how* questions to check understanding of sequence. Then ask: **What was the long-term impact of the case on the commerce power of Congress?** *(Its broad definition of* commerce *extended federal authority into many areas of American life; for example, the ban on discrimination in public places and services set forth in the Civil Rights Act of 1964 is based on the commerce power.)*

**DISCUSS LIMITS ON THE POWERS OF CONGRESS**

Distribute copies of Article I, Section 8, Clauses 1–6, and Section 9 of the Constitution. Have students underline those clauses or parts of clauses that place limits on Congress. *(Article I, Section 8, Clause 1 and Article I, Section 9, all Clauses)* Use this question to lead a Socratic Dialogue (p. T24) about the powers of Congress: **Using the Constitution as your primary source and this section of the book for examples, discuss how far the powers of Congress should extend. Has Congress gone beyond the limits the Framers intended?**

**L2 Differentiate** Implement a ten- to fifteen-minute wait time between comments. The break will allow all students to formulate a response.

## Background

**PROTECTIVE TARIFF** In the early 1800s, Congress imposed protective tariffs to help fledgling U.S. industries compete with the more established industries of Europe. A protective tariff works by increasing the price of an imported product. For example, suppose a hat made in Britain cost $1 in the U.S. Because the U.S. hat industry was less efficient, the American-made hat might cost $1.05. To induce Americans to buy U.S.-made hats, Congress might place a 10 cent tariff on British hats, raising the cost to $1.10 and giving U.S. hat makers a price advantage. Consumers, however, were not happy about paying higher prices. Most U.S. manufacturing was located in the North. The agricultural South depended on buying manufactured products, putting the burden of higher prices disproportionately on Southerners. Southern opposition to the Tariff of 1828 led to the Nullification Crisis, which nearly split the Union.

## Answers

**Caption** Steps can prevent persons with disabilities from holding certain jobs or entering public buildings. By requiring ramps, the ADA reduces discrimination against persons with disabilities by enabling equal access.

**L4 Differentiate** Assign students a mock newscast in which they highlight the main points of the 1824 *Gibbons* v. *Ogden* case and then interview major participants, such as a member of the New York State legislature, Aaron Ogden, and Thomas Gibbons. The newscast should cover the facts in the case, including the position of each side and the Supreme Court decision, the participants' reactions to that decision, and the long-term impact of the case.

**L3 Differentiate** Ask students to find recent newspaper articles that discuss instances in which Congress has exercised its money and commerce powers. Have them summarize their articles and identify the power(s) of Congress that are discussed. Post these around the room and have students choose two other articles to analyze.

**L3 Differentiate** Have students look at the textbook graphic "Federal Spending." Ask students to identify the categories of the 2010 federal budget that did not exist in 1800 and 1900. Then have them do research and make a presentation explaining what these programs are, why they were created, and how Congress pays for them. Reports should also analyze the origin of the legislation and discuss whether the Framers would have accepted it as being under the jurisdiction of Congress.

**L2 Differentiate** Have students begin a chart with three main headings: "Expressed Powers," "Implied Powers," and "Inherent Powers." Under the heading "Expressed Powers," have them list the powers described in this section. As they read later sections, students can complete their charts.

**L4 Differentiate** Remind students that the debate over how the Constitution should be interpreted has its roots in the early years of the nation. Have students refer to chapters 2 and 4 of their textbooks, and summarize the debates of the Federalists and the Anti-Federalists. Then have students research recent examples of the strict v. liberal construction debate, summarize the issue, politicians' positions on it (one on each side), and the student's position, based on his or her understanding of the Constitution.

## Answers

**Interpreting Cartoons** The cartoon suggests that the government keeps tax money rather than using it for the public good.

**Checkpoint** Taxes are used to raise revenue for public purposes, to protect domestic industry against foreign competition, and to protect public health and safety.

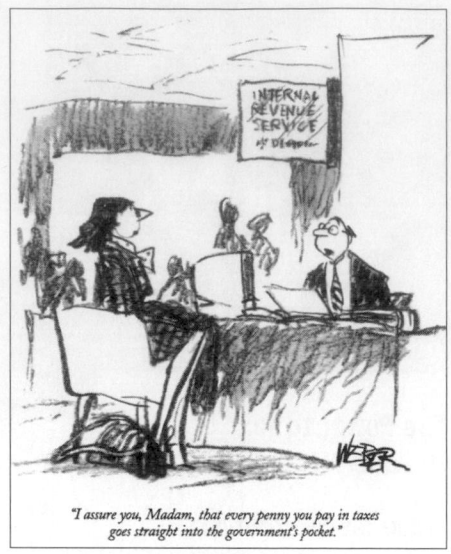

*"I assure you, Madam, that every penny you pay in taxes goes straight into the government's pocket."*

▶▶ **Interpreting Cartoons** Congress levies taxes and created the Internal Revenue Service to collect them. This cartoon shows a taxpayer and an IRS agent. *In what ways does this cartoon show a negative attitude toward taxes?*

✔ **Checkpoint**
Name three purposes for which the government collects taxes.

A **tax** is a charge levied by government on persons or property to raise money to meet public needs. But notice, Congress does sometimes impose taxes for other purposes as well. The protective tariff is perhaps the oldest example of this point. Although it does bring in some revenue every year, its real goal is to "protect" domestic industry against foreign competition by increasing the cost of imported goods.

Taxes are also sometimes levied to protect the public health and safety. The Federal Government's regulation of narcotics is a case in point. Only those who have a proper federal license can legally manufacture, sell, or deal in those drugs—and licensing is a form of taxation.

**Limits on the Taxing Power** Congress does not have an unlimited power to tax. As with all other powers, the taxing power must be used in accord with all other provisions of the Constitution. Thus, Congress cannot lay a tax on church services, for example—because such a tax would violate the 1st Amendment. Nor could it lay a poll tax as a condition for voting in federal elections, for that would violate the 24th Amendment.

More specifically, the Constitution places four explicit limitations on the congressional power to tax:

1. Congress may tax only for public purposes, not for private benefit. Article I, Section 8, Clause 1 says that taxes may be levied only "to pay the Debts and provide for the common Defence and general Welfare of the United States. . . ."

2. Congress may not tax exports. Article I, Section 9, Clause 5 declares "[n]o Tax or Duty shall be laid on Articles exported from any State." Thus, customs duties (tariffs), which are taxes, can be levied only on goods brought into the country (imports), not on those sent abroad (exports).

3. Direct taxes must be apportioned among the States, according to their populations:

> ❝ **FROM THE CONSTITUTION**
>
> No Capitation, or other direct, Tax shall be laid, unless in Proportion to the Census of enumeration herein before directed to be taken.
>
> —Article I, Section 9, Clause 4

A direct tax is one that must be paid directly to the government by the person on whom it is imposed—for example, a tax on the ownership of land or buildings, or a capitation (head or poll) tax.

An income tax is a direct tax, but it may be laid without regard to population:

> ❝ **FROM THE CONSTITUTION**
>
> The Congress shall have power to lay and collect taxes on incomes, from whatever source derived, without apportionment among the several States, and without regard to any census or enumeration.
>
> —16th Amendment

## Debate

Most State constitutions place restrictions on borrowing by State and local governments. Yet the U.S. Constitution places no limit on federal borrowing. This lack of imposed restraint worried Thomas Jefferson:

"[We should] all consider ourselves unauthorized to saddle posterity with our debts, and morally bound to pay them ourselves. . . ."

—Thomas Jefferson, letter to John Wayles Eppes, 1813

Use the Debate strategy (p. T25) to have students argue this point: **We need a constitutional amendment requiring the Federal Government to balance the budget.**

Wealth (which translates to the ability to pay taxes) is not evenly distributed among the States. So, a direct tax levied in proportion to population would fall more heavily on the residents of some States than it would on others—and would, therefore, be grossly unfair. Consequently, Congress has not levied any direct tax—except for the income tax—outside the District of Columbia since 1861.

4. Article I, Section 8, Clause 1 provides that "all Duties, Imposts and Excises shall be uniform throughout the United States." That is, all indirect taxes levied by the Federal Government must be levied at the same rate in every part of the country. Those indirect taxes include the federal levies on gasoline, alcoholic beverages, and tobacco products.

As a general rule, an indirect tax is one first paid by one person but then passed on to another. It is indirectly paid by that second person. Take, for example, the federal tax on cigarettes. It is paid to the Treasury by the tobacco company but is then passed on through the wholesaler and retailer to the person who finally buys the cigarettes.

## The Borrowing Power

Article I, Section 8, Clause 2 gives Congress the power "[t]o borrow Money on the credit of the United States." There are no constitutional limits on the amount of money Congress may borrow and no restrictions on the purposes for borrowing.

The Treasury does the actual borrowing. Usually, it issues Treasury Notes (T-bills) for short-term borrowing and bonds for long-term purposes. Those securities are, in effect, promissory notes—IOUs—for which the government agrees to pay investors a certain sum plus interest on a certain date.

Congress has put a statutory ceiling on the public debt, however. The **public debt** is all of the money borrowed by the Federal Government over the years and not yet repaid, plus the accumulated interest on that money. That legal ceiling has never amounted to much more than a political gesture, however. Congress regularly raises the limit whenever the debt threatens to overtake it. The public debt now exceeds $13 trillion.

For decades, the Federal Government has practiced **deficit financing.** That is, it regularly spends more than it takes in each year and then borrows to make up the difference. Thus, the government has relied on deficit financing—on borrowing—to deal with the economic Depression of the 1930s, to meet

**GOVERNMENT** ONLINE
**Audio Tour**
Listen to a guided tour on federal spending at
**PearsonSchool.com/phgovt**

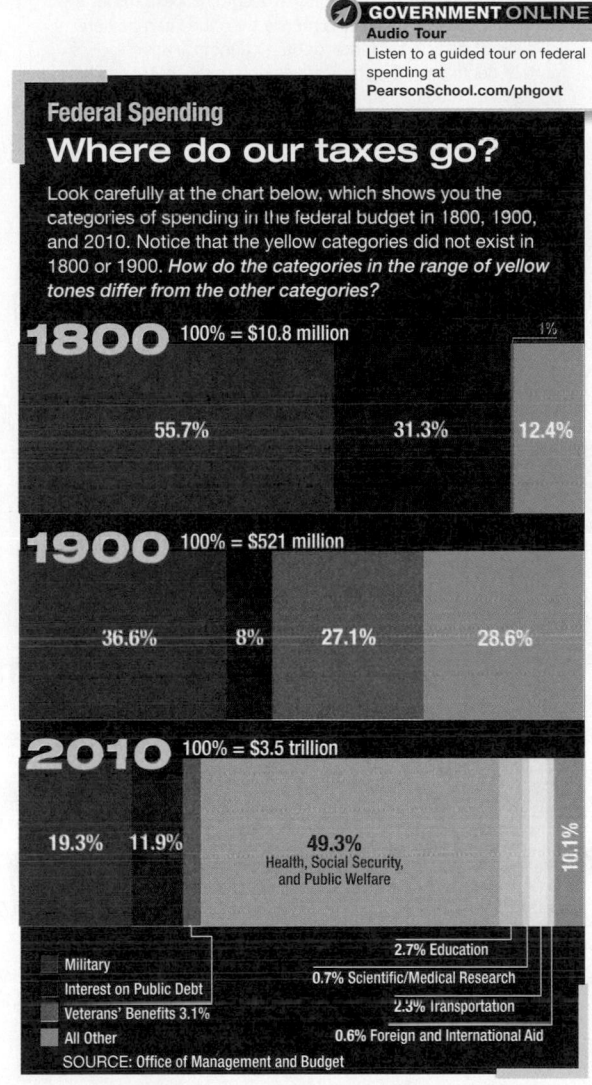

**Federal Spending**

## Where do our taxes go?

Look carefully at the chart below, which shows you the categories of spending in the federal budget in 1800, 1900, and 2010. Notice that the yellow categories did not exist in 1800 or 1900. *How do the categories in the range of yellow tones differ from the other categories?*

**1800** 100% = $10.8 million
1%
55.7% | 31.3% | 12.4%

**1900** 100% = $521 million
36.6% | 8% | 27.1% | 28.6%

**2010** 100% = $3.5 trillion
19.3% | 11.9% | 49.3% Health, Social Security, and Public Welfare | 10.1%

Military
Interest on Public Debt
Veterans' Benefits 3.1%
All Other

2.7% Education
0.7% Scientific/Medical Research
2.3% Transportation
0.6% Foreign and International Aid

SOURCE: Office of Management and Budget

**L2 Differentiate** Ask students how the designs of coins and bills have changed in recent years. Show an example of a newly designed five dollar bill or State quarter. Ask students to do research and make a poster explaining the changes to the new currency and reasons for those changes. They may find these Web sites helpful:

www.bep.treas.gov

www.moneyfactory.gov

www.usmint.gov

**L4 Differentiate** Ask students to investigate *Gibbons* v. *Ogden* and *United States* v. *Lopez* to see how the Court's interpretation of the Commerce Clause and the purpose of the laws in question shaped its opinion. Have students summarize this information and explain why they agree or disagree with the Court's decision.

**L4 Differentiate** Have students write a position paper addressing the borrowing power of Congress. They should answer this question: **Should there be a limit on the borrowing power of Congress? Why or why not?**

**Government** online
*All print resources are available on the Teacher's Resource Library CD-ROM and online at PearsonSchool.com/phgovt.*

## Answers

**Federal Spending** The range of yellow categories represents benefits for the general public, such as social programs. These programs did not exist in 1800 and 1900.

## Assess and Remediate

**L3** Collect the Core Worksheet and assess students' work.

**L3** Assign the Section 1 Assessment questions.

**L3** Section Quiz A (Unit 3 All-in-One, p. 68)

**L2** Section Quiz B (Unit 3 All-in-One, p. 69)

Have students complete the review activities in the digital lesson presentation and continue their work in the **Essential Questions Journal.**

---

## Answers

**What Is Personal Bankruptcy?** to apply bankruptcy rules uniformly across the country

---

### What Is Personal Bankruptcy?

**GOVERNMENT** ONLINE
**Audio Tour**
Listen to a guided audio tour about bankruptcy at
PearsonSchool.com/phgovt

Tell students to go to the Audio Tour for a guided audio tour about bankruptcy.

Regulating bankruptcy is one of the expressed powers of Congress. Declaring bankruptcy is a legal process through which people who owe more money than they can pay are relieved of part or all of their debt. It cannot be used for certain debts, including mortgages and taxes, but it can be used for medical expenses and other debts. *Why is bankruptcy a function of the Federal Government?*

### Steps in Filing for Bankruptcy

**1** A debtor must choose one of two kinds of bankruptcy: | *The debtor gives up most of his or her property, which is then sold to pay creditors, people who are owed money.* → **Chapter 7** Liquidation Bankruptcy

OR

*The debtor works out a payment plan with creditors, who may accept a reduced amount in exchange for total repayment over time.* → **Chapter 13** Individual Debt Adjustment

**2** The application for bankruptcy requires detailed documentation of income, expenses, assets, liabilities, and all recent financial transactions.

**3** When a bankruptcy application is filed, the court assumes responsibility for the debtor's finances and issues an order informing all creditors and stopping them from taking steps to collect their debts without court permission.

**4** With a court-appointed trustee, the debtor meets with creditors to negotiate and agree on how much each will be paid. The trustee's job is to recover as much money as possible for creditors.

**5** At a hearing, a federal judge then declares the debt discharged—that is, the debtor is free of debt.

---

the extraordinary costs of World War II, and to pay for wars and social programs over the decades since then.

In fact, the government's books showed a deficit in all but seven years from 1930 to 1969. And they were in the red *every* year from 1969 to 1998. As a result, the public debt climbed to more than $5.5 trillion at the beginning of fiscal year 1998.

A concerted effort by a Republican-controlled Congress and President Bill Clinton did curb the soaring debt. In fact, it produced four straight years of budget surpluses from 1998 to 2002.

Deficits are once again the order of the day, however. The Treasury has reported a deficit for every fiscal year since 2002. The shortfall reached nearly $1.3 trillion in 2010—as you will see when we return to this whole matter of government finance in Chapter 16.

### The Bankruptcy Power

Article I, Section 8, Clause 4 gives Congress the power "[t]o establish . . . uniform Laws on the subject of Bankruptcies throughout the United States." A bankrupt individual or company or other organization is one a court has found to be insolvent—that is, unable to pay debts in full. **Bankruptcy** is the legal proceeding in which the bankrupt's assets—however much or little they may be—are distributed among those to whom a debt is owed. That proceeding frees the bankrupt from legal responsibility for debts acquired before bankruptcy.

The States and the National Government have concurrent power to regulate bankruptcy. Today, however, federal bankruptcy law is so broad that it all but excludes the States. Nearly all bankruptcy cases are now heard in federal district courts.

### The Currency Power

Article I, Section 8, Clause 5 gives Congress the power "[t]o coin Money [and] regulate the Value thereof." The States are expressly denied that power.[3]

---

**3** Article I, Section 10, Clause 1 forbids the States the power to coin money, issue bills of credit (paper money), or make anything but gold and silver legal tender.

---

## Background

**CONSEQUENCES OF BANKRUPTCY** Personal bankruptcy offers a fresh start for people with severe financial problems. However, point out to students that bankruptcy is not a step to be taken lightly. It carries significant consequences. If a person files for bankruptcy, he or she may have to give up most possessions. Also, not all debts are discharged. The person would still have to pay student loans, child support, and taxes. His or her credit report would show the bankruptcy for up to ten years, seriously limiting the ability to get a loan or credit card. The individual may have to buy with cash only, which could put large purchases, such as a car, out of reach. If able to obtain credit, the rates and fees would be very high. As a credit risk, a bankrupt person would have difficulty finding a landlord who would rent an apartment to him or her.

Until the Revolution, the English money system, built on the shilling and the pound, was in general use in the colonies. With independence, that stable currency system collapsed. The Second Continental Congress and then the Congress under the Articles issued paper money. Without sound backing, and with no taxing power behind it, however, the money was practically worthless. Each of the 13 States also issued its own currency. Adding to the confusion, people still used English coins, and Spanish money circulated freely in the southern States.

Nearly all the Framers agreed on the need for a single, national system of "hard" money. So the Constitution gave the currency power to Congress, and it all but excluded the States from that field. Currency is money in any form when it is in use as a medium of exchange. From 1789 on, among the most important of all of the many tasks performed by the Federal Government has been that of providing the nation with a uniform, stable monetary system.

From the beginning, the U.S. has issued coins in gold, silver, and other metals. Congress chartered the first Bank of the United States in 1791 and gave it the power to issue bank notes—that is, paper money. Those notes were not legal tender, however. **Legal tender** is any kind of money that a creditor must by law accept in payment for debts.

Congress did not create a national paper currency, and make it legal tender, until 1862. Its new national notes, known as Greenbacks, had to compete with other paper currencies already in the marketplace. Although the States could not issue paper money themselves, State governments could and did charter (license) private banks, whose notes did circulate as money. When those private bank notes interfered with the new national currency, Congress (in 1865) laid a ten percent tax on their production. The private bank notes soon disappeared. The Supreme Court upheld the 1865 law as a proper exercise of the taxing power in *Veazie Bank* v. *Fenno*, 1869.

At first, the Greenbacks could not be redeemed for gold or silver. Their worth fell to less than half their face value on the open market. Then, in 1870, the Supreme Court held their issuance to be unconstitutional. In *Hepburn* v. *Griswold* it said "to coin" meant to stamp metal and so the Constitution did not authorize the National Government to issue paper money.

The Court soon changed its mind, however, in the *Legal Tender Cases* in 1871 and again in *Juliard* v. *Greenman* in 1884. In both cases, it held the issuing of paper money as legal tender to be a proper use of the currency power. The Court also declared this a power properly implied from both the borrowing and the war powers.

**✓ Checkpoint**
How did Congress stop private bank notes from interfering with the national currency?

**creditor**
*n.* person to whom money is owed

---

**Essential Questions**
**Journal**
To continue to build a response to the chapter Essential Question, go to your **Essential Questions Journal.**

## SECTION 1 ASSESSMENT

1. **Guiding Question** Use your completed table to answer this question: What powers over money and commerce does the Constitution give to Congress and what limits does it put on these powers?

**Key Terms and Comprehension**

2. Explain the difference between the **expressed powers** and the **implied powers.**

3. What is the **commerce power** and why is it important?

**Critical Thinking**

4. **Make Decisions** Based on your understanding of the commerce power, explain whether Congress has the power to regulate the Internet.

5. **Draw Inferences** Why did the Framers place limits on the power of Congress to levy taxes?

6. **Express Problems Clearly** Why did the Framers explicitly grant the powers of currency, borrowing, and bankruptcy to Congress?

**Quick Write**

**Persuasive Writing: Gather Evidence** Choose one power of Congress described in this section. Then list the pros and cons of Congress exercising that power. Use your list to help you form an opinion on whether Congress has taken use of that power too far or not far enough.

---

**REMEDIATION**

| If Your Students Have Trouble With | Strategies For Remediation |
|---|---|
| Understanding the differences among the delegated powers (Question 2) | Review the graphic describing inherent, expressed, and implied powers. Have students give an example of each type of power. Examples should be different from those given in the textbook. |
| Identifying the long-term importance of *Gibbons* v. *Ogden* and *McCulloch* v. *Maryland* (Questions 3, 4) | Teach students to ask themselves: "How did things change after this event/decision/development?" |
| The need for limits on the money and commerce powers of Congress (Questions 1, 3, 4, 5, 6) | Discuss: What might happen if Congress did not have these limits? |

## Answers

**Checkpoint** It laid a ten percent tax on private bank notes.

---

# Assessment Answers

**1. Commerce:** must be exercised in accordance with other constitutional limitations; can't tax exports; can't favor the ports of one State over another; can't require that vessels bound to or from one State be obliged to enter, clear, or pay duties in another State; could not interfere in the slave trade until 1808
**Tax:** can't conflict with any other constitutional provision; must tax only for public purposes; may not tax exports; direct taxes must be apportioned among the States according to population; indirect taxes must be levied at same rate
**Power to borrow:** no specific limitations
**Bankruptcy:** no limits
**Currency:** no limits

**2.** those stated in Constitution; those that can reasonably be deduced from the expressed powers

**3.** Congress can regulate foreign and interstate trade. It has been the basis for expanding the powers of Congress.

**4.** The broad definition of *commerce* given since *Gibbons* v. *Ogden* might allow Congress to regulate the Internet.

**5.** The Framers were concerned about a Congress that might use the taxing power unfairly.

**6.** The National Government needed the currency and borrowing powers to ensure a stable national currency. They needed the bankruptcy power to create uniform laws for all debtors seeking bankruptcy protection.

**QUICK WRITE** Students' lists should relate correctly to the powers of Congress they selected.

## How do the expressed powers reflect the Framers' commitment to creating a strong but limited National Government?

| Powers of Congress | |
|---|---|
| Foreign Policy | Domestic Policy |
| • From inherent powers as sovereign nation in matters affecting national security<br>• Shares power with President<br>• Can declare war<br>• Can raise and maintain military forces<br>• Can grant letters of marque and reprisal<br>• War Powers Act | • Naturalization laws<br>• Copyrights and patents<br>• Post offices<br>• Establishes crimes based on postal power<br>• Fixes standards of weights and measures<br>• Acquires, manages, and disposes of federal areas<br>• Eminent domain<br>• Can admit new States<br>• Creates federal courts below Supreme Court<br>• Defines federal crimes and sets punishments |

# Get Started

## LESSON GOALS

Students will . . .

- examine the division of war powers by analyzing a primary source document.

- evaluate the expressed powers of Congress by determining which powers they feel are most important.

- examine the domestic powers by using photographs illustrating each power.

## SKILLS DEVELOPMENT

### DRAW INFERENCES AND CONCLUSIONS

To practice drawing inferences and conclusions in this section, use the Chapter 11 Skills Worksheet (Unit 3 All-in-One, p. 77). You may teach the skill explicitly either before or after this lesson's class discussion about downloading from the Internet. For L2 and L1 students, assign the adapted Skill Activity (Unit 3 All-in-One, p. 78).

---

SECTION **2**

# The **Other** Expressed Powers

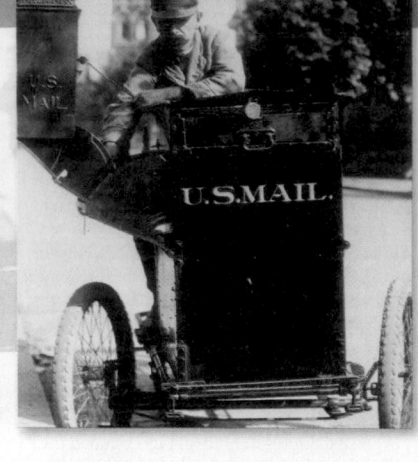

**How do the expressed powers reflect the Framers' commitment to creating a strong but limited National Government?** Use a table to organize information about the expressed powers of Congress.

| Powers of Congress | |
|---|---|
| Foreign Policy | Domestic Policy |
| •<br>•<br>• | • Naturalization laws<br>•<br>• |

**Political Dictionary**
- copyright
- patent
- territory
- eminent domain
- naturalization

**Objectives**
1. Identify the key sources of the foreign relations powers of Congress.
2. Describe the power-sharing arrangement between Congress and the President on the issues of war and national defense.
3. List other key domestic powers exercised by Congress.

**Image Above:** Congress has the expressed power to establish post offices and post roads.

We have just reviewed the several expressed powers that Congress has with regard to money and to foreign and interstate commerce. The Constitution gives Congress a number of other—and very important—expressed powers, and they are the focus of this section.

## Congress and Foreign Policy

The Federal Government has greater powers in the field of foreign affairs than it does in any other area of public policy. The 50 States that comprise the Union are not sovereign, so they have no standing in international law. In short, the Constitution does not allow them to take part in foreign relations.[4]

The Constitution gives the President primary responsibility for the conduct of American foreign policy. As the Supreme Court put that point in a leading case, *United States* v. *Curtiss-Wright Export Corp.* in 1936, the chief executive is "the sole organ of the Federal Government in the field of international relations."

Still, the Constitution does give Congress a significant place in the field of foreign affairs. Its authority in that area arises from two sources: (1) from a number of the expressed powers, most especially the spending, the commerce, and the war powers; and (2) from the fact that the United States is a sovereign state in the world community. As the lawmaking body of the sovereign United States, Congress has the inherent power to act on matters affecting the security of the nation—for example, the regulation of immigration and the enactment of measures to combat terrorism here and abroad. We shall return to this vitally important subject—foreign policy—in Chapter 17.

## The War Powers

Six of the 27 expressed powers set out in Article I, Section 8 deal explicitly with the subject of war and national defense.[5] Remember that here, too, Congress shares power with the chief executive. The Constitution makes the

---

4  See Article I, Section 10, Clauses 1 and 3.
5  The war powers of Congress are contained in Clauses 11 through 16.

---

# Focus on the Basics

**FACTS:** • Congress derives its foreign affairs powers from the expressed powers and from its position as the lawmaking body of a sovereign nation. • Congress shares power with the President in the areas of defense and foreign affairs. • Congress regulates the postal system, copyrights, patents, and weights and measures. • Congress has the power to acquire and manage federal territories, to oversee naturalization laws, and to create federal courts.

**CONCEPTS:** balance of power, enumerated powers, checks and balances

**ENDURING UNDERSTANDINGS:** • Some expressed powers of Congress serve to check the powers of the President and the courts. • The fact that the States do not have any powers in the field of foreign affairs is a reflection of the federal system. • The domestic powers of Congress have a direct impact on the daily lives of all Americans.

President commander in chief of the nation's armed forces,[6] and, as such, the President dominates the field.

The congressional war powers are, however, both extensive and substantial. Only Congress can declare war. It alone has the power to raise and support armies, to provide and maintain a navy, and to make rules for the governing of the nation's military forces. Congress also has the power to provide for "calling forth the Militia" (today, the National Guard), and for the organizing, arming, and disciplining of that force. And Congress is also given the power to grant letters of marque and reprisal,[7] and to make rules concerning captures on land and water.

We shall return to the war powers in Chapter 14 and there consider, at some length, this question: Does the Constitution give the President the power to make war in the absence of a declaration of war by Congress? Many argue that it does not, but more than 200 years of American history argue otherwise. Indeed, most Presidents have used the armed forces of the United States abroad, in combat, without a congressional declaration of war.

---

6 Article II, Section 2, Clause 1.

7 A few of the expressed powers are of little importance today. Thus, Congress has the power to grant letters of marque and reprisal (Article I, Section 8, Clause 11), and the States are denied the power to issue them (Article I, Section 10, Clause 1). Letters of marque and reprisal are written grants of power authorizing private persons to outfit vessels to capture and destroy enemy vessels in time of war. In effect, they authorize a form of legalized piracy. Letters of marque and reprisal are forbidden in international law by the Declaration of Paris, 1856, and the United States honors the rule.

✔ **Checkpoint**
What war powers does Congress have?

### The Expressed Powers of Congress
# Why These Powers?

Of all the many powers the Framers could have granted to Congress, why did they choose these? In the *Federalist Papers*, James Madison answered this question by grouping the enumerated powers into the five categories below. Only Clause 9, bestowing the power to create courts inferior to the Supreme Court, was not included. *Which of these powers do you think is most important? Explain.*

**Security against foreign danger:**
**Clause 1** levy taxes, duties, and excises
**Clause 2** borrow money
**Clause 11** declare war
**Clauses 12, 13, 14** raise, regulate and provide for armies and a navy
**Clauses 15 and 16** organize, arm, discipline, and call forth the militia to execute federal laws, suppress uprisings, and repel invasions

**Regulation of the intercourse with foreign nations:**
**Clause 3** regulate foreign commerce
**Clause 10** define and punish crimes committed on the high seas and offenses against the law of nations

**Maintenance of harmony and proper intercourse among the States:**
**Clause 3** regulate commerce among the several States and the Indian tribes
**Clause 4** establish a uniform rule of naturalization and uniform laws of bankruptcy
**Clause 5** coin money, regulate the value of domestic and foreign coin, fix the standard of weights and measures
**Clause 6** provide for the punishment of counterfeiting
**Clause 7** establish post offices and post roads

**Miscellaneous objects of general utility:**
**Clause 8** establish patent and copyright laws
**Clause 17** legislate for the seat of the federal capital and other federal territories

**Provisions for giving due efficacy to all these powers:**
**Clause 18** The Necessary and Proper Clause

The powers delegated by the proposed Constitution to the federal government are few and defined. Those which are to remain in the State governments are numerous and indefinite. The former will be exercised principally on external objects, . . .
— James Madison, *The Federalist* No. 45

---

# Differentiated Resources

The following resources are located in the All-in-One, Unit 3, Chapter 11, Section 2:

**L3** Reading Comprehension Worksheet (p. 70)
**L2** Reading Comprehension Worksheet (p. 72)
**L3** Bellringer Worksheet (p. 74)
**L3** Core Worksheets A and B (pp. 75, 76)
**L3** Skills Worksheet (p. 77)
**L2** Skill Activity (p. 78)
**L3** Quiz A (p. 79)
**L2** Quiz B (p. 80)

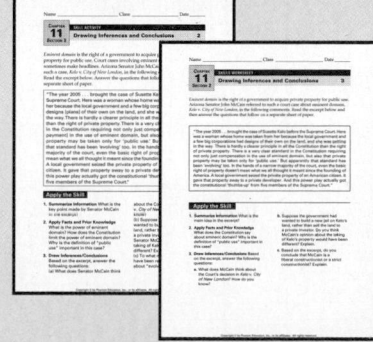

---

## BEFORE CLASS

Assign the section, the graphic organizer in the text, and the Reading Comprehension Worksheet (Unit 3 All-in-One, p. 70) before class.

**L2** **Differentiate** Reading Comprehension Worksheet (Unit 3 All-in-One, p. 72)

## BELLRINGER

Distribute the Bellringer Worksheet, which is an excerpt from the U.S. declaration of war on Germany in 1917.

**L2** **Differentiate** Define the word *resolved* (decided) on the board. Add these scaffolding questions before students answer the questions on the worksheet: **What group of people declared war? (Hint: Look after the words "Resolved by.") Who was given permission to carry out the war?**

# Teach

To present this topic using online resources, use the lesson presentation at **PearsonSchool.com/phgovt.**

## DISCUSS THE BELLRINGER

Discuss students' answers to the Bellringer questions. *(The excerpt suggests that the President implements war, but this power is balanced by Congress's power to authorize the use of resources for war.)* Make sure they understand that the Framers granted Congress the power to declare war to prevent the President from gaining too much power. Tell them that they will read more about the role of Congress in the conduct of war in "Issues of Our Time" in this chapter.

**L4** **Differentiate** Challenge students to describe other examples of Congress working with or against the President in carrying out its war powers.

## IDENTIFY THE WAR POWERS

Have students list the war powers of Congress and the President, including the provisions of the War Powers Resolution. Then ask them to use the textbook to answer this question: **What limits are placed on the President's war powers?** *(Only Congress can formally declare war and raise and maintain military forces. The President can use military forces in response to an attack, but must then report to Congress within 48 hours. The military commitment ends in 60 days unless Congress extends it.)*

---

# Answers

**Checkpoint** declare war; raise and support armies, provide and maintain a navy; make rules for the governing of the nation's military forces; call forth and organize, arm, and discipline the militia (National Guard)

**The Expressed Powers of Congress** Students should support their answers with evidence.

Have students list an example of an action that Congress might take under each of the following powers: foreign affairs; war; postal; copyrights and patents; weights and measures; territories; naturalization; and judicial. Then ask students to trade papers with a partner. Did their partner choose different examples? If so, have students jot down those examples as well. Have students continue to trade papers with different students until they have two or three examples for each power.

**L2 Differentiate** Photocopy and distribute the pages of Section 2. Have students underline, highlight, or circle one or two examples of actions Congress might take using each expressed power. Then ask students to think of laws that Congress might pass using these powers. For example, for the naturalization power, Congress might pass a law changing the requirements for citizenship.

**How Government Works**

# How does copyright law affect me?

The Internet makes sharing information easier than ever, but laws regulate what information can or cannot be shared freely. Copyright protection may be inconvenient for those who want music or other content for free, but it is important to protect the rights of writers and artists. *What determines fair use?*

**Alex, Ryan, and Chris form a band.** They practice their favorite popular songs and sometimes play for their friends after school. They are asked to play at a school dance. **WARNING:** Although they do not charge for their performance and they are not taking money away from the copyright holder, the band could be sued for using someone else's copyrighted work.

**Ryan suggests they record an album of cover songs and distribute it for free. WARNING:** The band could lose its case if sued in court for copyright infringement. If they record current songs, some people might download their version instead of buying it. That would take money from the original artist or copyright holder.

**GOVERNMENT ONLINE**
For an **interactive** exploration of copyright law, visit **PearsonSchool.com/phgovt**

**INTERACTIVE**

In today's world, no one can doubt that the President must have the power to respond, rapidly and effectively, to any threat to the nation's security. Still, many people have long warned of the dangers inherent in a presidential power to involve the country in undeclared wars.

Again, we shall revisit this matter in Chapter 14. But here, in the context of the war powers of Congress, we must examine the War Powers Resolution, a statute enacted by Congress in 1973.

The war-making power as it was exercised by Presidents Johnson and Nixon during the undeclared war in Vietnam (1964–1973) moved Congress to enact the War Powers Resolution. That law provides that the chief executive can commit American military forces to combat abroad only (1) if Congress has declared war, or (2) when Congress has specifically authorized a military action, or (3) when an attack on the United States or any of its armed forces has occurred.

If troops are ordered into combat in the third circumstance, the President is directed to report that fact to Congress within 48 hours. Any such commitment of military forces must end within 60 days, unless Congress agrees to a longer involvement. And Congress can end a commitment at any time.

The constitutionality of the War Powers Resolution remains in dispute. A determination of the question must await a situation in which Congress demands that its provisions be obeyed but the President refuses to do so.

## Domestic Powers

The other expressed powers relate to domestic matters. Each of them has a direct and a considerable effect on the daily lives of the American people.

**Copyrights and Patents** The Constitution gives Congress the power

### FROM THE CONSTITUTION

**To promote the Progress of Science and useful Arts, by securing for limited Times to Authors and Inventors the exclusive Right to their respective Writings and Discoveries.**

—Article I, Section 8, Clause 8

## Answers

**How does copyright law affect me?** Fair use is determined by the purpose and character of the use, the nature of the copyrighted work, the amount and substantiality of the portion used, and the effect of the use on the value of the copyrighted work. It also depends on whether a new work is transformative.

The band sells their songs over the Internet, but discover that some people are sharing the songs with friends who have not paid. **WHAT CAN THEY DO?** They can sue those who are illegally distributing and copying their compositions. If they do not take action, they could forfeit their copyright.

The band members write songs and record them. They should then copyright their compositions, registering them with the Copyright Office. **CAUTION:** The band must protect their copyrights by suing anyone who uses their songs without permission.

A rival band records one of Ryan, Chris, and Alex's songs and sells the CDs at school. **WHAT CAN THEY DO?** They can sue the other band for copyright infringement. If they can prove that they wrote the song or recorded it first, they could win and force the other band to pay damages.

**Fair Use** Determining an infringement of copyright depends upon whether the test of "fair use" is met. The factors considered are: **1** the purpose and character of the use, **2** the nature of the copyrighted work, **3** the amount and substantiality of the portion used, and **4** the effect of the use on the value of the copyrighted work. In addition, the Supreme Court has held that the courts should focus on the extent that the new work is transformative—that is, does it alter the work with new expression, meaning, or message? The more transformative the new work, the less will be the significance of the other factors.

A **copyright** is the exclusive right of an author to reproduce, publish, and sell his or her creative work. That right may be assigned—transferred by contract—to another, as to a publishing firm by mutual agreement between the author and the other party.

Copyrights are registered by the Copyright Office in the Library of Congress. Under present law, they are good for the life of the author plus 70 years. They cover a wide range of creative efforts: books, magazines, newspapers, musical compositions and lyrics, dramatic works, paintings, sculptures, cartoons, maps, photographs, motion pictures, sound recordings, and much more.[8] The Office registers more than 500,000 copyrights each year.

The Copyright Office does not enforce the protections of a copyright. If the holder thinks a copyright has been violated, he or she may bring a suit for damages in the federal courts.

A **patent** grants a person the sole right to manufacture, use, or sell "any new and useful process, machine, manufacture, or composition of matter, or any new and useful improvement thereof." A patent is good for up to 20 years. The term of a patent may be extended only by a special act of Congress. The Patent and Trademark Office in the Department of Commerce administers patent laws.[9]

**The Postal Powers** Article I, Section 8, Clause 7 gives Congress the power "[t]o establish Post Offices and Post roads"—in effect, the power to provide for the carrying of the mail. "Post roads" are all postal routes, including rail lines, airways, and waters within the United States, during the time mail is being carried on them.

Carrying the mail is among the oldest of all governmental functions. Its origins date back at least to Egyptian practice before

✔ **Checkpoint**
Who enforces copyrights?

---

8 Not all publications can be protected by copyright. Thus, the Supreme Court has held that such "factual compilations" as telephone directories "lack the requisite originality" for copyright protection (*Feist Publications, Inc.*, v. *Rural Telephone Service Co.*, 1991).

9 The power to protect trademarks is an implied power drawn from the commerce power. A trademark is some distinctive word, name, symbol, or device used by a manufacturer or merchant to identify his goods or services and distinguish them from those made or sold by others. A trademark need not be original, merely distinctive. The registration of a trademark carries the right to its exclusive use in interstate commerce for 10 years. The right may be renewed an unlimited number of times.

---

# How Government Works

**FAIR USE** The fair-use rule allows the limited use of someone's creative work without asking for permission from the copyright holder. Point out to students that they must always cite their sources. However, citing sources is not enough. They still must follow fair-use guidelines. The guidelines continue to evolve as the courts apply the four factors to specific cases. Generally, the courts have allowed teachers and students to copy small amounts of copyrighted material for educational purposes, without obtaining permission. However, they may not sell the materials. Students may use quotations in their papers without requesting permission. The amount of lifted material matters, however. The courts are more likely to allow the use of 20 words from a 500-page book than 20 words from a 40-word poem. Advise students to use common sense: Does their use seem fair or like stealing?

---

## DISTRIBUTE CORE WORKSHEET A

Tell students that today they will look closely at the powers of Congress and rank them according to their importance. Point out that some of the expressed powers are very important, yet controversial, while others, though important for the nation to run smoothly, are not at all controversial. Divide students into groups of two or three and distribute the Chapter 11 Section 2 Core Worksheet A (Unit 3 All-in-One, p. 75), which asks students to rank the top ten expressed powers of Congress. Remind them to use the chart "The Expressed Powers of Congress: Why These Powers?" which summarizes the powers.

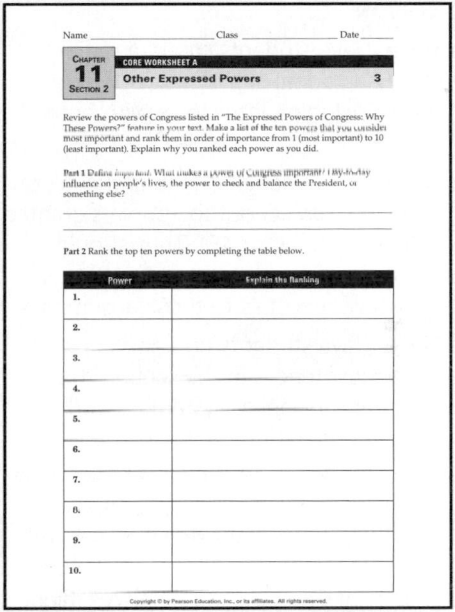

## DISTRIBUTE CORE WORKSHEET B

After students have completed Core Worksheet A, distribute the Chapter 11 Section 2 Core Worksheet B (Unit 3 All-in-One, p. 76), which asks students to compare their lists to those of other groups. They should rotate around the room, looking for students whose lists differ from their own to answer the questions. Finish the class by discussing students' answers on the Core Worksheets.

**L2 ELL Differentiate** Pair ELLs with partners to complete Core Worksheet B.

---

## Answers

**Checkpoint** If the copyright holder thinks a copyright has been violated, he or she may sue for damages in the federal courts.

Challenge students to take or find five photographs, each relating to a different domestic power of Congress discussed in the section. Display all photos, and have the students explain how each of their photos relates to a domestic power of Congress. If students cannot access a digital camera, they can cut photographs from magazines and newspapers.

**L4 Differentiate** Have students research congressional and presidential speeches, news articles on laws passed by Congress, and other primary sources to find quotations to pair with their photographs. The quotations can be attached to the photos.

## EXTEND THE LESSON

**L3 Differentiate** Have students create a radio news segment on a fictional copyright or patent infringement case, including interviews with both sides in the case.

**L4 Differentiate** Ask students to read and analyze one of *The Federalist* essays about the powers granted to Congress (No. 41, 42, 43, or 45). They should make an outline of Madison's arguments and then make a list of possible rebuttals to those arguments.

**L2 Differentiate** Have students find and copy into their notebooks the sentences in the section that explain the checks-and-balances system at work in the areas of war powers and judicial powers.

**L4 Differentiate** Have students create a board game called "Power." The game should include rewards for the constitutional use of congressional power and penalties for unconstitutional use. Players can be real or fictional members of Congress. Game pieces might include cards describing various scenarios and a board with steps leading to the capture of the prize, which might be the recognition of the player as an "expert on congressional power" and an invitation to appear on a panel discussion. These are suggestions only.

**L3 Differentiate** Have students write a letter from a former President to a member of Congress. The letter should express the President's views on the division of the war-making power between the two branches. It should include a summary of the war powers of the President and those of Congress and a discussion of the War Powers Resolution. The letter should indicate whether the division of power is appropriate and necessary.

**L3 Differentiate** Have students research a recent copyright or patent infringement case and create a graphic organizer in which they show the main facts, players, and outcome of the case.

## Answers

**Caption** the fact that the residents of the District of Columbia do not have a voting representative or senator

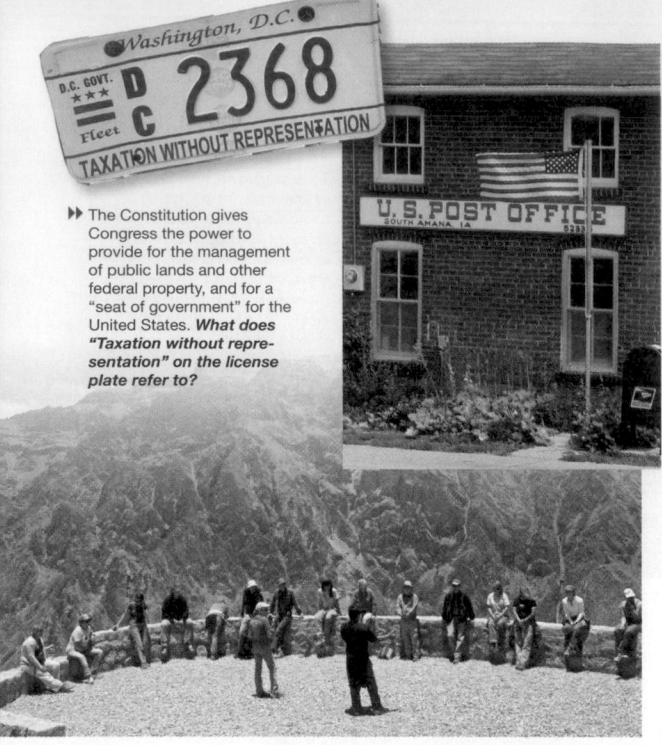

▶▶ The Constitution gives Congress the power to provide for the management of public lands and other federal property, and for a "seat of government" for the United States. *What does "Taxation without representation" on the license plate refer to?*

4000 B.C. The first post office in America was established in Boston in 1639, by the General Court of the Massachusetts Bay Colony. The first successful postal system in the colonies, the Penn Post, was begun by William Penn in 1683. He established a post office in Philadelphia and provided a regular weekly service along a thirty-mile route from there to New Castle, Delaware.

The United States Postal Service traces its history back to the early colonial period. The remarkable Benjamin Franklin is generally recognized as the father of the present-day postal system. He served as Co-Deputy Postmaster of the British Colonies in North America from 1753 to 1774, when the British removed him from office because of his political activities. In 1775, he became, by unanimous choice of the Second Continental Congress, the first Postmaster General of the United States.

Today, the Postal Service functions as an independent agency in the executive branch. It serves the nation through some 37,000 post offices. The more than 650,000 career employees of the Postal Service handle nearly 200 billion pieces of mail every year.

Congress has established a number of crimes based on the postal power. It is, for example, a federal crime for anyone to obstruct the mails or to use the mails to commit any criminal act. It has also prohibited the mailing of many items, among them poisons, explosives, intoxicating liquors, some live animals, libelous or obscene matter, lottery tickets, and any articles dangerous to the mails or postal workers. Any article prohibited by a State's laws—for example, switchblade knives or firecrackers—cannot be sent into that State by mail.

The States and their local governments cannot interfere with the mails in any unreasonable way. Nor can they require licenses for Postal Service vehicles, tax the gas they use, or tax post offices or any other property of the United States Postal Service.

**Territories and Other Areas** In two places—in Article I, Section 8, Clause 17 and in Article IV, Section 3, Clause 2—the Constitution delegates to Congress the power to acquire, manage, and dispose of various federal areas. That power relates to the District of Columbia and to the several federal **territories,** parts of the United States that are not admitted as States and that have their own systems of government, including Puerto Rico, Guam, and the Virgin Islands. It also covers hundreds of military and naval installations, arsenals, dockyards, post offices, prisons, parks and forest preserves, and many other federal holdings.

The Federal Government may acquire property by purchase or gift. It may also do so through the exercise of the power of **eminent domain,** the inherent power to take private property for public use. Notice that the Taking Clause in the 5th Amendment restricts the Federal Government's use of the power with these words: "nor shall private property be taken for public use, without just compensation." Private property may be taken

# Background

**EMINENT DOMAIN** Governments have long used eminent domain to obtain property for public works, such as a highway or power plant. But could your local government take your home to make way for a shopping center? Quite possibly! The government of New London, Connecticut, was looking for a way to revitalize the city's sagging economy. A developer presented a plan to build a hotel and conference center in the city's Fort Trumbull neighborhood. The new complex would create jobs and yield greater tax revenue than did the modest homes in the area, so the city agreed to take the home owners' property by eminent domain. A group of home owners sued, arguing that seizing property to sell to private developers was not public use. In *Kelo* v. *City of New London,* 2005, the Supreme Court ruled for the city, interpreting "public use" broadly to mean a "public purpose," such as economic development.

by eminent domain only (1) for a public use, (2) with proper notice to the owner, and (3) for a fair price. What in fact constitutes a public use, proper notice, or a fair price often becomes a matter for courts to decide.

Territory may also be acquired from a foreign state as the result of the exercise of the power of Congress to admit new States (in Article IV), the war powers, or the President's treaty-making power (in Article II). Under international law, any sovereign state may acquire unclaimed territory by discovery.

**Weights and Measures**  Article I, Section 8, Clause 5 gives Congress the power to "fix the Standard of Weights and Measures" throughout the United States. The power reflects the absolute need for accurate, uniform gauges of time, distance, area, weight, volume, and the like.

In 1838, Congress set the English system of pound, ounce, mile, foot, gallon, quart, and so on, as the legal standards of weights and measures in this country. In 1866, Congress also legalized the use of the metric system of gram, meter, kilometer, liter, and so on.

In 1901, Congress created the National Bureau of Standards in the Commerce Department. Now known as the National Institute of Standards and Technology, the agency keeps the original standards for the United States. It is these standards by which all other measures in the United States are tested and corrected.

**Naturalization**  Citizens of one country become citizens of another through a process called **naturalization.** Article I, Section 8, Clause 4 gives Congress the exclusive power "[t]o establish an uniform Rule of Naturalization." Today, the nation's population includes more than 14 million naturalized citizens.

**Judicial Powers**  As a part of the system of checks and balances, the Constitution gives Congress several judicial powers. Thus, it has the power to create all of the federal courts below the Supreme Court and otherwise provide for the organization and composition of the federal judiciary. The federal court system is treated at length in Chapter 18.

Congress also has the power to define federal crimes and set the punishments that may be imposed on those who violate federal law. The Constitution mentions only four offenses. Three are found in Article I, Section 8: counterfeiting, piracies and felonies committed on the high seas, and offenses against international law. Treason is listed in Article III, Section 3. But, as you will see, Congress has used its implied powers to establish more than 100 other federal crimes.

✔ **Checkpoint**
What restrictions does the Constitution place on the exercise of the power of eminent domain?

---

## SECTION 2 ASSESSMENT

**Essential Questions Journal**  To continue to build a response to the chapter Essential Question, go to your **Essential Questions Journal.**

1. **Guiding Question**  Use your completed table to answer this question: How do the expressed powers reflect the Framers' commitment to creating a strong but limited National Government?

**Key Terms and Comprehension**

2. In what ways do Congress and the President share power in foreign policy and defense?

3. How does a **copyright** differ from a **patent**?

4. What judicial powers does the Constitution give to Congress?

**Critical Thinking**

5. **Predict Consequences**  How might the foreign policy of the United States be different if the Constitution had not forbidden the individual States from making treaties or alliances with foreign powers?

6. **Draw Conclusions**  Some people believe that the U.S. Postal Service should be abolished because its functions could be performed more efficiently by for-profit mail companies. Do you agree? Explain.

**Quick Write**

**Persuasive Writing: Identify Your Audience**  Think about who you would like to persuade to share your point of view about the power of Congress that you selected in Section 1. For example, a group of students may be interested in how Congress affects education. Make a list of the strongest evidence to persuade your audience that Congress has used that power too little or too much.

---

## Assess and Remediate

[L3] Collect the Core Worksheets and assess students' work.

[L3] Assign the Section 2 Assessment questions.

[L3] Section Quiz A (Unit 3 All-in-One, p. 79)

[L2] Section Quiz B (Unit 3 All-in-One, p. 80)

Have students complete the review activities in the digital lesson presentation and continue their work in the **Essential Questions Journal.**

### REMEDIATION

| If Your Students Have Trouble With | Strategies For Remediation |
|---|---|
| Understanding how the foreign affairs powers of Congress are limited (Questions 1, 2, 5) | Have them list the President's foreign affairs powers in one column and the powers of Congress in another |
| Recognizing the importance of the postal, copyright, or weights and measures powers (Questions 3, 6) | Have them write a scenario in which these matters operate without government control |
| The judicial powers of Congress (Question 4) | Provide specific questions relating to these powers and direct students to the appropriate subsection to answer those questions |

---

## Answers

**Checkpoint**  Property can be taken only for a public use, with proper notice to the owner, and for a fair price.

---

## Assessment Answers

**1.** The Framers gave Congress important powers, but imposed limits on those powers.

**2.** The President is the commander in chief and has primary responsibility for foreign policy. Only Congress can declare war, but the President can deploy the military in response to an attack on U.S. interests. The President must report to Congress and must end military involvement unless Congress agrees to extend it.

**3.** A copyright protects creative works, such as art, music, and literature. A patent protects inventions, such as a new machine.

**4.** to create federal courts below the Supreme Court; to define federal crimes and punishments

**5.** If every State had a different foreign policy, the U.S. would have been less of a nation and more of a confederation of States, each pursuing its own goals. The Union might not have held together.

**6.** Possible responses: I agree, because competition among carriers might lead to lower rates. I disagree, because businesses might not find it profitable to deliver mail to thinly populated areas, leaving people in some parts of the country without service or force them to pay higher rates.

**QUICK WRITE**  Evidence students list should be appropriate for their chosen audience.

# Get Started

## LESSON GOAL

• Students will discuss the significance of the Court's decision in *McCulloch* v. *Maryland* on the power of the National Government.

# Teach

Have students read the feature as homework or at the beginning of class.

## INTRODUCE THE CONTENT

The decision in *McCulloch* v. *Maryland* is important because it established the meaning of the Necessary and Proper Clause—the Elastic Clause—of the Constitution. The Court authorized a broad reading of the Constitution that has allowed Congress to pass laws relating to issues not specifically mentioned in the Constitution. In other words, the ruling confirmed the existence of implied powers.

## ESTABLISH THE FACTS

Have students work in pairs to sequence the main events in the case (not the events on the bottom of the page). The events are:

**1.** Congress charters the Second Bank of the United States.
**2.** A branch opens in Baltimore.
**3.** Maryland levies a tax on the bank.
**4.** McCulloch refuses to pay.
**5.** The case goes to the Maryland court, which rules in the State's favor.
**6.** The case is appealed to the Supreme Court.

## SKILLS DEVELOPMENT

### ANALYZE POLITICAL CARTOONS

To teach the skill of analyzing political cartoons, have students read Analyze Political Cartoons in the Skills Handbook, p. S22. Then have them work the Landmark Decisions of the Supreme Court Worksheet (All-in-One, p. 100).

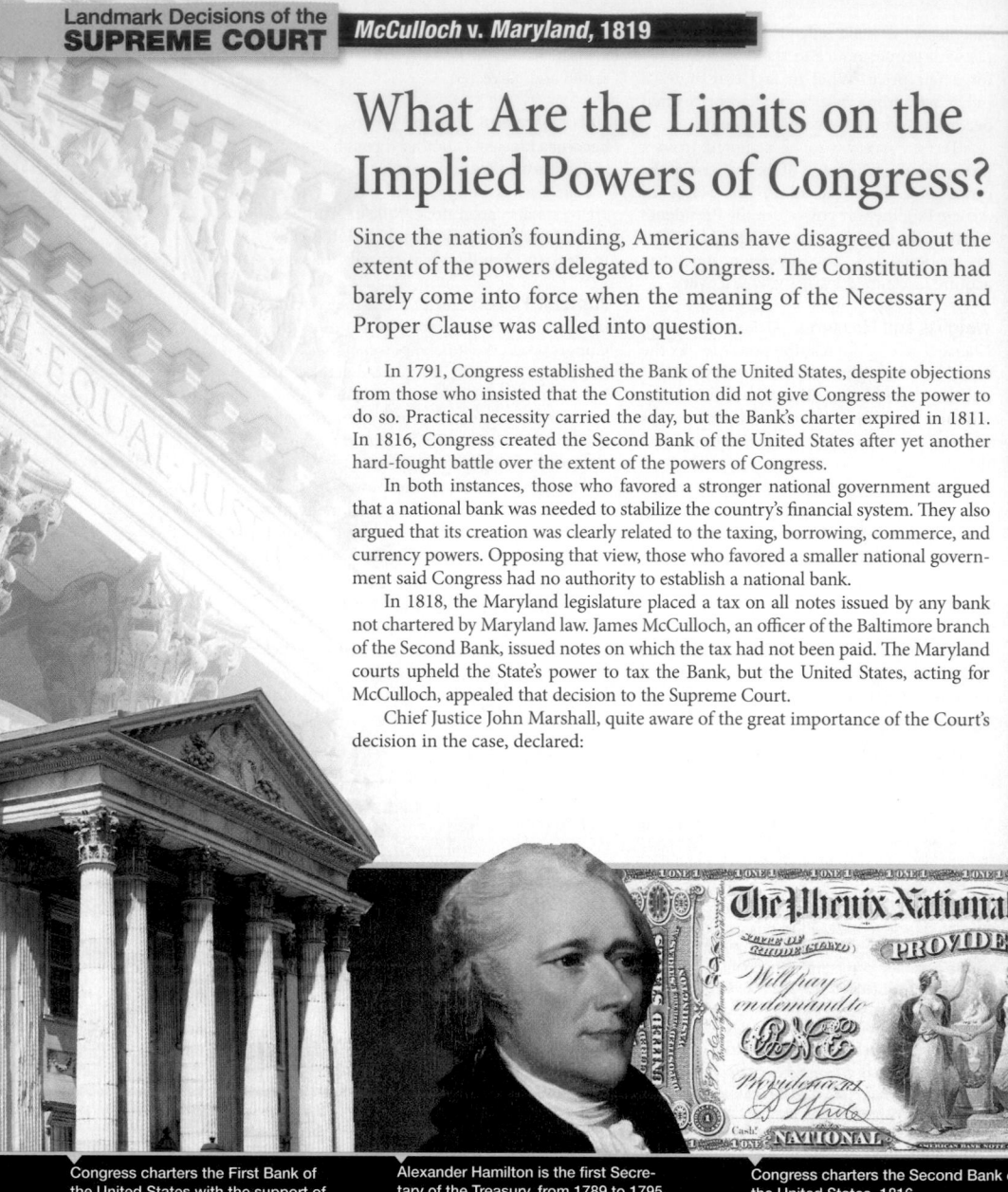

# What Are the Limits on the Implied Powers of Congress?

Since the nation's founding, Americans have disagreed about the extent of the powers delegated to Congress. The Constitution had barely come into force when the meaning of the Necessary and Proper Clause was called into question.

In 1791, Congress established the Bank of the United States, despite objections from those who insisted that the Constitution did not give Congress the power to do so. Practical necessity carried the day, but the Bank's charter expired in 1811. In 1816, Congress created the Second Bank of the United States after yet another hard-fought battle over the extent of the powers of Congress.

In both instances, those who favored a stronger national government argued that a national bank was needed to stabilize the country's financial system. They also argued that its creation was clearly related to the taxing, borrowing, commerce, and currency powers. Opposing that view, those who favored a smaller national government said Congress had no authority to establish a national bank.

In 1818, the Maryland legislature placed a tax on all notes issued by any bank not chartered by Maryland law. James McCulloch, an officer of the Baltimore branch of the Second Bank, issued notes on which the tax had not been paid. The Maryland courts upheld the State's power to tax the Bank, but the United States, acting for McCulloch, appealed that decision to the Supreme Court.

Chief Justice John Marshall, quite aware of the great importance of the Court's decision in the case, declared:

Congress charters the First Bank of the United States with the support of Alexander Hamilton, 1791

Alexander Hamilton is the first Secretary of the Treasury, from 1789 to 1795.

Congress charters the Second Bank of the United States, 1816.

310

# Supreme Court Notes

**ON TAXING THE BANK** One key question in *McCulloch* v. *Maryland* was whether the constitutional power of the States to tax included the power to tax the National Bank. In the opinion, Chief Justice John Marshall stated that "the power to tax involves the power to destroy." He went on to explain: "If the States may tax one instrument, employed by the Government in the execution of its powers, they may tax any and every other instrument. They may tax the mail; they may tax the mint; they may tax patent rights; they may tax the papers of the custom house; they may tax judicial process; they may tax all the means employed by the Government to an excess which would defeat all the ends of Government. This was not intended by the American people. They did not design to make their Government dependent on the States."

"The conflicting powers of the government of the Union … are to be discussed; and an opinion given, which may essentially influence the great operations of the government. No tribunal can approach such a question without a deep sense of its importance, and of the awful responsibility involved in its decision. But it must be decided peacefully, or remain a source of hostile legislation, perhaps of hostility of a still more serious nature; . . ."

In one of its most important decisions, the Court unanimously reversed the Maryland courts, upholding the concept of implied powers. It held that the Constitution need not expressly empower Congress to create a bank. The creation of the Second Bank of the United States, said the Court, was "necessary and proper" to the execution of the taxing, borrowing, currency, and commerce powers.

As to the question of whether Maryland had the right to tax the Bank, the Court said, "the power to tax involves the power to destroy." If States had the power to tax the Federal Government, they could destroy it. This was not, said the Court, the intention of the people when they ratified the Constitution.

**GOVERNMENT** ONLINE
In the News
To learn more about the relevance of the case today, go to
PearsonSchool.com/phgovt

### Arguments for Maryland

- The Constitution gives the Federal Government no right to establish a bank.
- The power to establish banks is therefore reserved to the States.
- States are sovereign and may tax any bank within their borders.

### Arguments for McCulloch and the National Bank

- The Necessary and Proper Clause gives Congress the right to do what is necessary to carry out any of its expressed powers.
- No State can lawfully tax any agency of the Federal Government.

**Thinking Critically**

1. What standard should be used to decide whether an act of Congress is or is not "necessary and proper"?
2. **Constitutional Principles** Did the decision in *McCulloch v. Maryland* strengthen or weaken the federal system?

President Andrew Jackson vetoes a bill to renew the charter of the Second Bank of the United States, 1832.

The National Banking Act creates a uniform currency for the United States, 1863.

President Woodrow Wilson signs the Federal Reserve Act, creating the Federal Reserve System, 1913.

311

## Supreme Court Notes

**ON EXECUTING EXPRESSED POWERS** The opinion written by Chief Justice John Marshall in *McCullough v. Maryland* broadened the scope of federal power. The Court concluded that the Constitution's expressed powers naturally included the implied powers to carry them out. "Although, among the enumerated powers of Government, we do not find the word 'bank' or 'incorporation,' we find the great powers, to lay and collect taxes; to borrow money; to regulate commerce; to declare and conduct a war; and to raise and support armies and navies. . . . But it may with great reason be contended that a Government entrusted with such ample powers, on the due execution of which the happiness and prosperity of the Nation so vitally depends, must also be entrusted with ample means for their execution. The power being given, it is the interest of the Nation to facilitate its execution."

## DISCUSS

Ask students to summarize the arguments of the two sides in *McCulloch* and remind them that the Court found in favor of McCulloch. Then ask students to list ways in which society today differs from that of the Framers. You may discuss how the Internet, telephones, television, prescription drugs, and other important facets of today's life did not exist until recently. Ask: **What would have happened if the National Government could only legislate based on what is specifically in the Constitution?** *(The National Government would likely still make laws regarding commerce but might be limited in how it could regulate new developments, such as the Internet, television advertising, or prescription drugs.)* Tell students that they will learn more about implied powers in the next section of the chapter.

**L2 ELL Differentiate** Give students prompts, asking them describe how business and communications are different than in the past.

### CONNECT TO THE ESSENTIAL QUESTION

To end the discussion, ask students to consider the chapter Essential Question: **What should be the limits on the powers of Congress?** Students may want to discuss how implied powers can and should be defined.

### EXTEND THE LESSON

**L3 L4 Differentiate** Assign the Landmark Decisions of the Supreme Court Worksheet (Unit 3 All-in-One, p. 100).

**L2 Differentiate** Assign the adapted Landmark Decisions of the Supreme Court Worksheet (Unit 3 All-in-One, p. 102).

## Assess and Remediate

Have students answer the Thinking Critically questions in the student edition.

### IN THE NEWS

Point out to students that they can learn about more cases involving implied powers by visiting **PearsonSchool.com/phgovt.**

## Answers

1. The act of Congress must be needed to carry out its expressed powers without violating any other provisions of the Constitution.
2. The decision strengthened the federal system by shifting significant power to the Federal Government.

## How has the doctrine of implied powers increased the powers of Congress?

**Implied Powers**

| Liberal Construction | Necessary and Proper Clause | Expressed Powers |
|---|---|---|
| • Broad interpretation of congressional powers<br>• Upheld in *McCulloch* v. *Maryland*<br>• Led to growth in national power<br>• Eliminated need for frequent amendment of Constitution to meet changing needs<br>• Based on expressed powers | • Congress may choose means for carrying out its expressed powers<br>• Stretched so much that it is called "Elastic Clause" | • Commerce interpreted to include almost all economic activity<br>• Congress may not pass law solely to promote general welfare<br>• War powers include defense and waging war<br>• Power to raise military grants implied power to conduct a draft |

# Get Started

## LESSON GOALS

Students will . . .

- use the example of a teacher's powers in the classroom to consider the meaning of implied powers.
- explore strict and liberal construction by evaluating congressional actions.
- decide upon and defend a position on implied powers.

## SKILLS DEVELOPMENT

### DECISION MAKING

To help students learn to make decisions, have them turn to the Skills Handbook, p. S18, and use the information explained there to complete this lesson's Core Worksheet.

---

SECTION **3**

# The **Implied Powers**

**Guiding Question**

**How has the doctrine of implied powers increased the powers of Congress?** Use a chart to record information about the implied powers.

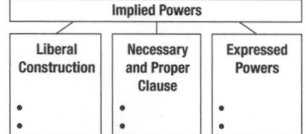

**Political Dictionary**

- Necessary and Proper Clause
- strict constructionist
- liberal constructionist
- consensus
- appropriate

**Objectives**

1. Explain how the Necessary and Proper Clause gives Congress flexibility in lawmaking.
2. Compare the strict construction and liberal construction positions on the scope of congressional power.
3. Describe the ways in which the implied powers have been applied.

**Image Above:** Congress established the United States Border Patrol in 1924. Today, it is a major federal police agency.

What does the Constitution have to say about education? Nothing, not a word. Still, Congress provides tens of billions of dollars every year for the United States Department of Education to spend in a variety of ways throughout the country. Look around you. What indications of these federal dollars can you find in your school? If you attend a public school anywhere in the United States, that evidence should not be hard to spot.

How can this be? You know that Congress has only those powers delegated to it by the Constitution, and that document says nothing about education. The answer to that question lies in the central topic of this section: the implied powers of Congress.

## The Necessary and Proper Clause

Remember, the implied powers are those powers that are not set out in so many words in the Constitution but are, rather, implied by (drawn from) those that are. The constitutional basis for the existence of the implied powers is found in one of the expressed powers. The **Necessary and Proper Clause,** the final clause in the lengthy Section 8 of Article I in the Constitution, gives to Congress the expressed power

**FROM THE CONSTITUTION**

**To make all Laws which shall be necessary and proper for carrying into Execution the foregoing Powers, and all other Powers vested by this Constitution in the Government of the United States, or in any Department or Officer thereof.**

—Article I, Section 8, Clause 18

Much of the vitality and adaptability of the Constitution can be traced directly to this provision, and even more so to the ways in which both Congress and the Supreme Court have interpreted and applied it over the years. In effect, the Necessary and Proper Clause allows Congress to choose the means "for carrying into Execution" the many powers given to it by the Constitution.

---

# Focus on the Basics

**FACTS:** • The Necessary and Proper Clause allows Congress to exercise powers not expressly defined in the Constitution. • The scope of implied powers remains a subject of debate. • Liberal constructionists believe that the Constitution should be interpreted loosely, allowing Congress to do many things not expressly stated. • Strict constructionists believe that Congress should have only those implied powers absolutely necessary to carry out its expressed powers.

**CONCEPTS:** limited government, implied powers

**ENDURING UNDERSTANDING:** • The concept of implied powers has been a major factor in the growth of the powers of Congress. • The Necessary and Proper Clause has helped avoid the need for frequent amendments to the Constitution.

The manner in which Congress has viewed the concept, together with the supporting decisions of the Supreme Court, have made the final clause in Article I, Section 8, truly the "Elastic Clause." It has earned that name, for it has been stretched so far and made to cover so much over the years.

**Strict Versus Liberal Construction** The Constitution had barely come into force when the meaning of the Elastic Clause became the subject of one of the most important disputes in American political history. The Framers of the Constitution intended to create a new and stronger National Government. The ratification of their plan was opposed by many, and that opposition was not stilled by the adoption of the Constitution. Rather, the conflict between the Federalists and the Anti-Federalists continued into the early years of the Republic. Much of that conflict centered on the powers of Congress and the meaning of the Elastic Clause. Just how broad, in fact, were those powers?

The **strict constructionists,** led by Thomas Jefferson, continued to argue the Anti-Federalist position from the ratification period. They insisted that Congress should be able to exercise (1) its expressed powers and (2) only those implied powers absolutely necessary to carry out those expressed powers. They maintained that the States should keep as much power as possible. They agreed with Jefferson that "that government is best which governs least."

Most of these Jeffersonians did acknowledge a need to protect interstate trade, and they recognized the need for a strong national defense. At the same time, they feared the consequences of a strong National Government. They believed, for instance, that the interests of the people of Connecticut were

✓**Checkpoint**
What was the argument of the strict constructionists?

## The Implied Powers of Congress

Many of the laws Congress makes today stem from the Necessary and Proper Clause. The Framers could not have made provisions for every situation that might arise in the modern world. *Without its implied powers, how effectively could Congress address new situations?*

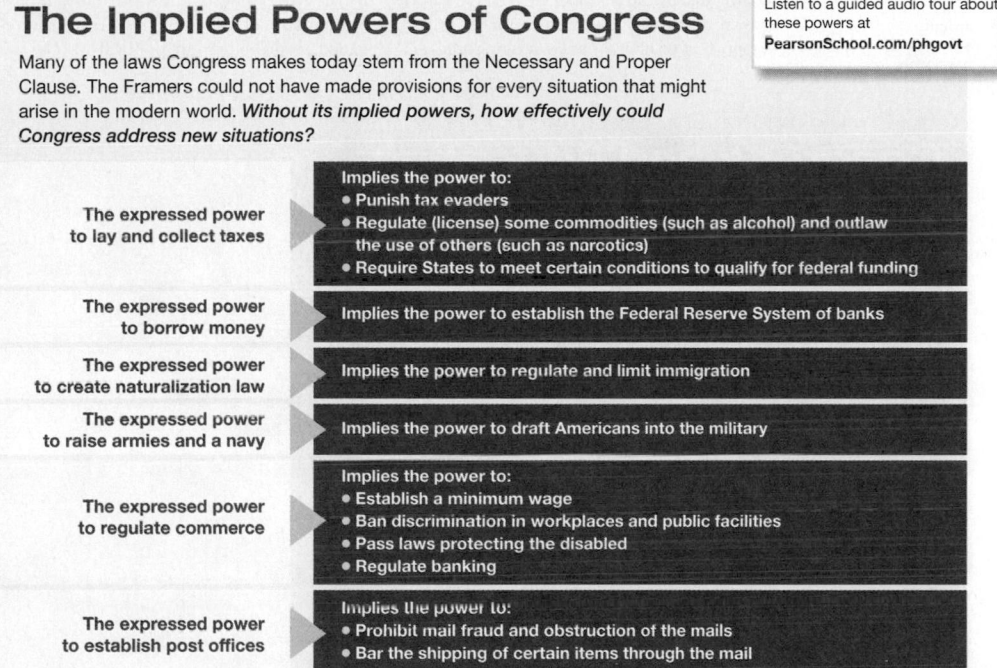

> **GOVERNMENT** ONLINE
> **Audio Tour**
> Listen to a guided audio tour about these powers at **PearsonSchool.com/phgovt**

| | Implies the power to: |
|---|---|
| The expressed power to lay and collect taxes | • Punish tax evaders<br>• Regulate (license) some commodities (such as alcohol) and outlaw the use of others (such as narcotics)<br>• Require States to meet certain conditions to qualify for federal funding |
| The expressed power to borrow money | Implies the power to establish the Federal Reserve System of banks |
| The expressed power to create naturalization law | Implies the power to regulate and limit immigration |
| The expressed power to raise armies and a navy | Implies the power to draft Americans into the military |
| The expressed power to regulate commerce | Implies the power to:<br>• Establish a minimum wage<br>• Ban discrimination in workplaces and public facilities<br>• Pass laws protecting the disabled<br>• Regulate banking |
| The expressed power to establish post offices | Implies the power to:<br>• Prohibit mail fraud and obstruction of the mails<br>• Bar the shipping of certain items through the mail |

## Differentiated Resources

The following resources are located in the All-in-One, Unit 3, Chapter 11, Section 3:

- **L3** Reading Comprehension Worksheet (p. 81)
- **L2** Reading Comprehension Worksheet (p. 82)
- **L3** Core Worksheet (p. 83)
- **L2** Core Worksheet (p. 85)
- **L3** Quiz A (p. 87)
- **L2** Quiz B (p. 88)

### BEFORE CLASS

Assign the section, the graphic organizer in the text, and the Reading Comprehension Worksheet (Unit 3 All-in-One, p. 81) before class.

**L2** **Differentiate** Reading Comprehension Worksheet (Unit 3 All-in-One, p. 82)

### BELLRINGER

Write on the board: **Teachers will maintain order in the classroom. (1) What does this mean? (2) What would such a rule allow teachers to do? Give examples. (3) What would it not allow teachers to do? Give examples. (4) Why are there limits on a teacher's power? Answer in your notebook.**

# Teach

To present this topic using online resources, use the lesson presentations at **PearsonSchool.com/phgovt**.

### REVIEW BELLRINGER ANSWERS

Ask about ways in which teachers can maintain order in class. *(using grading systems, calling parents, or sending students to the principal)* Ask students if they can think of any strategies that fall into a gray area. *(Some teachers might find ridiculing a disruptive student to be appropriate, while others might find that technique objectionable.)*

**L2** **ELL** **Differentiate** Clarify the word *implied* (not stated, but suggested or understood).

### DRAW PARALLELS WITH POWERS OF CONGRESS

Display Transparency 11D, Implied Powers of Congress. Ask: **What provision of the Constitution allows Congress to take these actions?** *(Article I, Section 8, Clause 18, known as the Necessary and Proper Clause)* **Why is this also called the Elastic Clause?** *(It has allowed Congress to stretch its powers to meet changing needs.)* **What limits the power of teachers to impose discipline?** *(laws, school rules, and community standards for acceptable behavior)* **How is this similar to the implied powers of Congress?** *(Congress, too, may do what is necessary and proper to carry out its duties as long as it respects the Constitution.)*

Tell students to go to the Audio Tour for a guided audio tour of the implied powers of Congress.

## Answers

**The Implied Powers of Congress** Congress could not effectively address new situations.

**Checkpoint** that Congress should exercise its expressed powers and only those implied powers necessary to carry out the expressed powers

### DISTRIBUTE CORE WORKSHEET

Distribute the Chapter 11 Section 3 Core Worksheet (Unit 3 All-in-One, p. 83). Tell students that they will look at some specific actions by Congress to identify the expressed powers that form the basis for each implied power. Then they will evaluate each action and decide whether they think Congress overstepped its constitutional authority.

**L2** **Differentiate** Distribute the adapted Chapter 11 Section 3 Core Worksheet (Unit 3 All-in-One, p. 85), which is shorter than the on-level version.

### REVIEW CASES

Walk through each congressional action on the worksheet. Ask: **How is an act of Congress determined to be constitutional or unconstitutional?** *(A case challenging the law must be brought to court.)* Tell students which actions were overturned by the courts. Point out that not all of these actions were challenged, and many were controversial.

### EXPLORE LIBERAL AND STRICT CONSTRUCTION

Have students use their notes on the Core Worksheet to consider their position on how Congress uses its powers—Do they tend to agree more with strict constructionists or liberal constructionists? Point out that they are probably not completely one or the other. Use the Opinion Line strategy (p. T26) to gauge student understanding of the concept. Provide the following "talking points": (1) The States need to keep as much power as possible in order to protect their varying interests. (2) If Congress becomes too powerful, the States will have no say in matters that affect their residents directly. (3) The National Government should focus solely on protecting interstate and foreign trade and defending the nation. (4) The National Government needs broad powers in the areas of war, economic issues, and national emergencies. (5) There are some issues on which the States should have no power, such as immigration.

## Answers

**Congress and Education** Examples may include: integrated school systems, NCLB, funding for special programs

---

not the same as those of South Carolinians or Marylanders or Pennsylvanians. They argued that only the States—not the far-off National Government—could protect and preserve those differing interests.

The **liberal constructionists,** led by Alexander Hamilton, had led the fight to adopt the Constitution. Now they favored a liberal interpretation of that document, a broad construction of the powers it gives to Congress. They believed that the country needed, as Hamilton put it in *The Federalist* No. 70, "an energetic government."

The strict constructionists were sorely troubled by that broad view of the powers of Congress. They were sure that it would all but destroy the reserved powers of the States.

**Liberal Construction Prevails** You know that the Supreme Court upheld the concept of implied powers in *McCulloch* v. *Maryland* in 1819. That victory for the liberal constructionists set a pattern that, in general, has been followed ever since. Over the years, the powers wielded by the National Government have grown to a point that even the most <u>ardent</u> supporters of liberal construction could not

**ardent**
*adj.* committed, passionate

have imagined. It is impossible to see how the United States could have developed as it has over the past two centuries had the Court not ruled as it did in *McCulloch*.

Several factors, working together with the liberal construction of the Constitution, have been responsible for that marked growth in national power. They have included wars, economic crises, and other national emergencies. Spectacular advances, especially in transportation and communication, have also had a real impact on the size and the scope of government. Equally important have been the demands of the people for more and still more services from government.

Congress has been led by these and other factors to view its powers in broader and broader terms. Most Presidents have regarded their powers in like fashion. The Supreme Court has generally taken a similar position in its decisions in cases involving the powers of the National Government.

Moreover, the American people have generally agreed with a broader rather than a narrow reading of the Constitution. This **consensus,** or general agreement, has prevailed even though our political history has

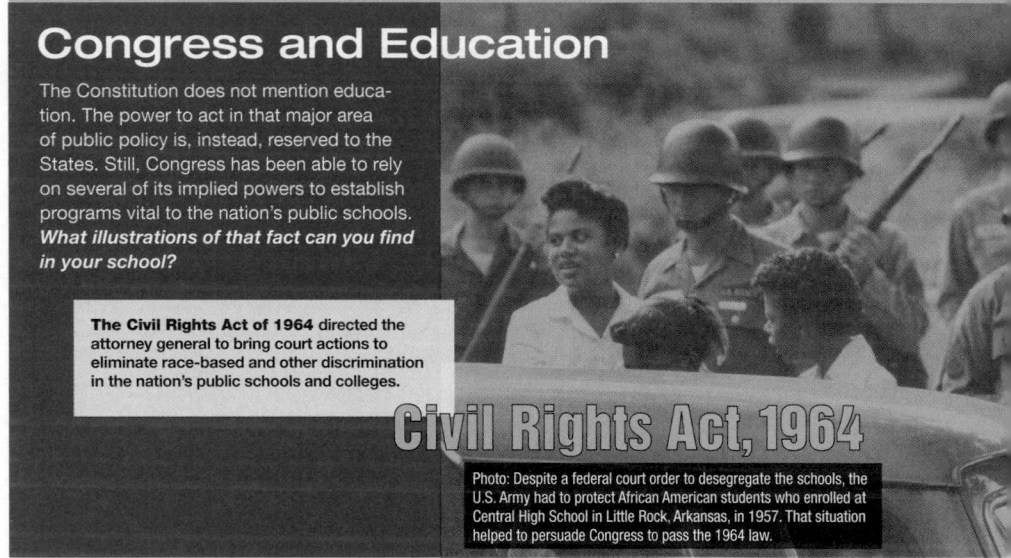

# Congress and Education

The Constitution does not mention education. The power to act in that major area of public policy is, instead, reserved to the States. Still, Congress has been able to rely on several of its implied powers to establish programs vital to the nation's public schools. *What illustrations of that fact can you find in your school?*

**The Civil Rights Act of 1964** directed the attorney general to bring court actions to eliminate race-based and other discrimination in the nation's public schools and colleges.

Civil Rights Act, 1964

Photo: Despite a federal court order to desegregate the schools, the U.S. Army had to protect African American students who enrolled at Central High School in Little Rock, Arkansas, in 1957. That situation helped to persuade Congress to pass the 1964 law.

## Constitutional Principles

**FEDERALISM AND IMPLIED POWERS** The Constitution delegates expressed powers to the National Government and reserves the remaining powers to the States. Congress's use of implied powers, however, sometimes encroaches into the realm of the States. Judicial interpretation of the expressed powers helps to establish the division of authority between State and National Governments in our federal system. The Court's decision in *Gibbons* v. *Ogden* interpreted the Commerce Clause broadly, allowing Congress to regulate many activities that are only indirectly related to commerce. In *United States* v. *Lopez,* the Court reined in congressional regulatory power by ruling that the federal firearms law depended on an overly broad definition of "commerce." Future cases will no doubt continue to adjust the line where federal authority ends and State powers begin.

been marked, and still is, by controversies over the proper limits of national power.

## The Doctrine in Practice

The ways in which the Necessary and Proper Clause has been construed (interpreted) and applied over the last 200 years has enabled the National Government to meet the changing needs of the times. As a result, it has virtually eliminated the need for frequent amendment of the Constitution.

Instances of the exercise of the <u>doctrine</u> of implied powers are almost too numerous to count. The concept of implied powers has made it possible for the Government of the United States to meet any number of problems that could not possibly have been foreseen by the Framers. It does not stretch matters too much to say that, today, the Constitution's words "necessary and proper" really mean "convenient and useful."

Every exercise of implied powers must be based on at least one of the expressed powers. Thus, in *McCulloch* v. *Maryland* the Supreme Court found that the creation of the Bank of the United States was "necessary and proper"

to the execution of four expressed powers held by Congress: the taxing, borrowing, currency, and commerce powers.

Over the years, Congress has most often found a basis for the exercise of implied powers in (1) the commerce power, (2) its power to tax and spend, and (3) the war powers.

**The Commerce Clause** As you know, the Commerce Clause gives Congress the power to regulate both foreign and interstate trade. And you are aware, too, of the Supreme Court's hugely expansive reading of that provision, beginning with *Gibbons* v. *Ogden* in 1824. The word "commerce" has been held to include the production and the buying and selling of goods as well as the transportation of people and commodities. Commerce has been defined so broadly that it encompasses virtually every form of economic activity today. Congress has the authority to regulate manufacturing, wages and hours, labor-management relations, foods and drugs, air travel, and much more. It can provide for the building of interstate highways, consumer protection, the protection of the environment—the list goes on and on. In 1998,

✔ **Checkpoint**
What factors have led to the growth of national power?

**doctrine**
*n.* a principle or concept

Title IX of the Education Amendments to the Civil Rights Act forbids gender discrimination in federally funded education programs. Its most visible effect has been in girls' and women's athletics. Since 1970, the number of female high school athletes has increased from fewer than 300,000 to more than 3 million.

**Title IX, 1972**

Photo: The Mossyrock, Washington, girls' high school basketball team celebrates a tournament victory.

The **Individuals with Disabilities Education Act (IDEA)** is a federal civil rights law designed to prevent discrimination and enable individuals with disabilities to participate fully in all aspects of education.

The education gap between people with and without disabilities is shrinking. People with disabilities are attending postsecondary institutions in greater numbers.

**IDEA, 1990**

Photo: Schools today must be accessible to students with wheelchairs.

## Political Cartoon Mini-Lesson

Display Transparency 11F, Power to Tax and Spend, when you discuss the power of Congress to appropriate funds. Give students a moment to analyze the cartoon. Point out that funding decisions always require tradeoffs. If the Congressional Ways and Means Committee decides more money is necessary for public use, it can exercise both expressed powers and implied powers to raise money. Ask: **What is the setting for the cartoon?** *(the Washington, D.C., government office of the Committee on Ways and Means)* **How would you describe the tone of this cartoon?** *(as a slur by economic opponents of greater government spending on public programs)* **What does the cartoon suggest has happened to the Ways and Means Committee?** *(The committee is controlled by spending liberals now.)*

**L2 ELL Differentiate** Define *liberal* and *strict* in the context of Section 3. *(liberal:* broad, generous, loose; *strict:* kept within narrow limits, exact, precise) Have students say the words aloud and then write a sentence using each. Be sure students know what *elastic* means. If possible, demonstrate how an elastic stretches and explain again why the Necessary and Proper Clause is referred to as the Elastic Clause.

### REVIEW *MCCULLOCH* V. *MARYLAND*

If you didn't cover *McCulloch* v. *Maryland* in another class, have students read about that case now in this chapter's Landmark Decisions of the Supreme Court feature. Explain that the case established the constitutionality of implied powers and a broad interpretation of the Constitution. This ruling helped shape the way in which the Necessary and Proper Clause has been interpreted in the years since 1819.

**L2 Differentiate** Make signs with these labels: "McCulloch," "State of Maryland," "Chief Justice Marshall," "Arguments for Maryland," and "Arguments for McCulloch." Tell the story of the case, while students holding the signs act it out. You may ask the student playing Marshall to read a segment of the Court's decision, and those holding the Arguments signs to read the arguments for each side.

**L4 Differentiate** Have students write a brief dialogue that might have taken place between a member of the Maryland State legislature and James McCulloch in 1818. The dialogues should reflect the basic facts in the case.

### EXTEND THE LESSON

**L3 Differentiate** Have students do research to find recent legislation. They should identify the power by which Congress made the legislation and describe any controversy surrounding it.

**L4 Differentiate** Ask students to identify types of laws that the Framers could not have anticipated—such as environmental protection laws—and make a presentation giving their examples, reasons the need for such laws could not have been anticipated, and an argument for either national or State power in the arena.

## Answers

**Checkpoint** wars, economic crises, national emergencies, advances in transportation and communications, and people's demands for more services

# Assess and Remediate

**L3** Ask students to write a journal entry arguing that liberal construction of the Constitution has been either good or bad for the United States. Suggest that students look at the chart "The Implied Powers of Congress" in their textbook for ideas.

**L3** Collect the Core Worksheet and assess students' work.

**L3** Assign the Section 3 Assessment questions.

**L3** Section Quiz A (Unit 3 All-in-One, p. 87)

**L2** Section Quiz B (Unit 3 All-in-One, p. 88)

Have students complete the review activities in the digital lesson presentation and continue their work in the **Essential Questions Journal**.

### REMEDIATION

| If Your Students Have Trouble With | Strategies For Remediation |
|---|---|
| Understanding the importance of the Necessary and Proper Clause (Questions 2, 4, 6) | Have them re-read the text material under that heading and answer this question: Congress may make laws that are necessary and proper for what? *(to carry out its expressed powers)* |
| Recognizing how liberal construction has affected American history (Questions 1, 3, 5) | Direct them to the chart "The Implied Powers of Congress" and point out that some of these actions may have been ruled unconstitutional under strict construction. |

## Answers

**Caption** the power to declare war

---

*"I do want a war, but I'd like to be asked nicely."*

▸▸ **Interpreting Cartoons** Congress has several war powers, but the President has primary responsibility for the conduct of wars. **To which war power does this cartoon refer?**

**moratorium**
*n.* temporary suspension

Congress used the Commerce Clause to impose a three-year <u>moratorium</u> on State taxation of e-commerce and other Internet activities; that freeze was extended in 2007.

**Limits on the Commerce Power** Still, Congress is not free to use the Commerce Clause to do whatever it chooses. The Constitution places four explicit limitations on the exercise of the commerce power. And the Supreme Court does, at least on occasion, find that the lawmaking branch has overstepped its authority under that provision.

Congress cannot pass a law based solely on the grounds that a measure will somehow promote "the general Welfare of the United States." But it can and does levy taxes and provide for the spending of money for that purpose. Thus, for example, as we said on the opening page of this section, Congress **appropriates**—assigns to a particular use—tens of billions of dollars per year to support education. And, similarly, it does so to provide for such things as farm subsidies, unemployment compensation, Social Security, Medicare, and a host of other programs.

**The War Powers** The several war powers reflect the fact that the National Government is responsible for the protection of this country against aggression and, when necessary, for the waging of war. As with its other expressed powers, Congress has the authority to do whatever is necessary and proper for the execution of its war power—with the exception that, in doing so, it cannot violate any other provision of the Constitution. Among many other examples of the point, Congress has the power to provide for compulsory military service—a draft—because Article I, Section 8 gives it the expressed power "[t]o raise and support Armies" (in Clause 12) and "[t]o provide and maintain a Navy" (in Clause 13). The Supreme Court originally upheld the constitutionality of a draft in a series of cases challenging the Selective Service Act of 1917 (*Selective Draft Law Cases*, 1918).

**Essential Questions Journal** To continue to build a response to the chapter Essential Question, go to your **Essential Questions Journal**.

## SECTION **3** ASSESSMENT

1. **Guiding Question** Use your completed chart to answer this question: How has the doctrine of implied powers increased the powers of Congress?

**Key Terms and Comprehension**
2. What is the **Necessary and Proper Clause** and why is it important?
3. Summarize the main disagreements between **strict constructionists** and **liberal constructionists**.

**Critical Thinking**
4. **Draw Inferences** How have war and economic crises increased the power of the National Government?
5. **Predict Consequences** If the strict constructionists had won the battle to limit the implied powers, how might the United States be different today?
6. **Draw Conclusions** Why is the Commerce Clause, written in 1787, still adequate to meet the needs of the nation in the 21st century?

**Quick Write**

**Persuasive Writing: Make an Outline** Write a thesis statement expressing your view and explaining the power you chose in Section 1. Explain why the Framers delegated this power to Congress and how it has been interpreted. Then use your lists from Sections 1 and 2 to make an outline of the arguments you will use to support it.

---

# Assessment Answers

**1.** Possible response: The doctrine of implied powers has enabled Congress to apply the narrowly worded expressed powers to broad areas of American life. For example, the expressed power to regulate commerce led to the implied power to ban discrimination in public places.

**2.** Article I, Section 8 Clause 18 allows Congress to make all laws that are necessary and proper to carry out the expressed powers. It is important because it has allowed the Congress to choose a wide variety of means to carry out its delegated powers.

**3.** Strict constructionists believe that the implied powers are limited to only those that are absolutely necessary to carry out the expressed powers. Liberal constructionists believe that the Necessary and Proper Clause gives Congress power to do anything that is reasonably related to carrying out its expressed powers.

**4.** Students should recognize that wars and economic crises lead to public support for strong national leadership and expanded national power to deal with the crises.

**5.** Possible response: The States would operate more like sovereign nations. Laws would be less uniform nationwide. The Federal Government might have been too weak to adjust to new situations.

**6.** The Commerce Clause, which is very broad, combined with the Necessary and Proper Clause allows Congress to address 21st-century issues without amending the Constitution.

**QUICK WRITE** Students should write a thesis sentence and outline of supporting arguments.

# ISSUES OF OUR TIME

# Congressional War Powers

## ► Track the Issue

**The Constitution** divides the war powers between Congress and the President. However, it remains unclear whether Congress may control the conduct of war.

### 1770s–1780s

**Continental Congress** acts as the civilian authority over the armed forces.

### 1860s

**President Abraham Lincoln** clashes with Congress over the conduct of the Civil War, the appointment of generals, and the freeing of slaves.

### 1969

**The War Powers Resolution** limits the President's ability to send troops abroad without Congressional approval.

### 2001

**President George W. Bush** requests military authority to combat terrorism; Congress approves force only against those involved in the 9/11 attacks.

### 2010

**Representative Dennis Kucinich** proposes a resolution to withdraw U.S. forces from Afghanistan by December 2010. The resolution is not passed.

Representative Dennis Kucinich (D., Ohio) ►

## ►► Perspectives

**In August 2010, the American combat mission** in Iraq was declared a success and effectively ended by President Barack Obama. However, the fight against terrorism and the Taliban continues in Afghanistan. Many Americans, including members of Congress, feel that the time has come to re-evaluate the war in Afghanistan and the President's authority to continue it.

> "[I]t has become clear that the authorization for the use of military force is being used carte blanche for circumventing Congress' role as a coequal branch of government. Both the Bush and Obama administrations have cited that the 2001 authorization of the use of military force is justification for the military escalation in Afghanistan. … As [we] begin the first in a series of large military operations in Afghanistan, this House must … reclaim [its] constitutional responsibility and [its] responsibility to the American people."
> —**Rep. Dennis Kucinich**
> **(D., Ohio), 2010**

> "[President Obama] has … examined numerous options over the course of several months and consulted with all relevant military leaders and allies. He really left no stone unturned … He deserves an opportunity now to implement his strategy. He has given us the timeline for when he expects to see results, and there will be a reassessment of our strategy in 18 months. … I am not endorsing an open-ended commitment. I am not advocating that we remain without assessing our progress. But I do believe this strategy of our President deserves support."
> —**Rep. Howard Berman**
> **(D., California), 2010**

## ►► Connect to Your World

1. **Understand (a)** To what is Representative Kucinich referring in his reference to "its constitutional responsibility"? **(b)** How does Representative Berman defend the current policy in Afghanistan?
2. **Identify Central Issues (a)** Why is there an ongoing struggle between Congress and the President on the exercise of the war powers? **(b)** Who do you think should have the ultimate authority? Why?

**GOVERNMENT ONLINE**
**In the News**
For updates about congressional war powers, visit
**PearsonSchool.com/phgovt**

317

# Background

**WAR FUNDING, WITH STRINGS** With the approach of the 2008 election, which would end the administration of George W. Bush and Richard Cheney, the Democrat-controlled Congress passed a huge funding bill for the Iraq War. Congress, however, exacted some concessions from the White House in exchange for war funding. In the bill, Congress included funds for college scholarships for veterans and an extension of unemployment benefits—both measures that the President opposed. The bill also prohibited the use of the funds to reconstruct Iraq unless the Iraqi government matched every dollar spent. Passage of the war funding bill assured that the war would continue into the administration of the next President, who would then have to deal with the knotty problem of how to end the war and bring the troops home.

## LESSON GOAL
- Students will evaluate the war powers of Congress and justify their positions.

# Teach

## INTRODUCE THE CONTENT

Point out that the war powers are divided between Congress and the President. This division of powers has been contentious, as Congress must raise and provide for the armed forces, while the President is the commander in chief of those forces. The Constitution, however, gives no details about the duties of the commander in chief. Have students review the war powers by reading Article I, Section 8, Clauses 11-16 and Article II, Section 2, Clause 1 of the Constitution.

## READ THE POSITIONS

Have a student read the introduction below "Perspectives." Then have different students read each quotation. Ask students to practice summarizing by writing a one-sentence summary of each argument and then read a few aloud. You may wish to spend a few minutes discussing the ambiguity in the Constitution.

## OPINION LINE

Use the Opinion Line strategy (p. T26) to have students take a position on whether the role of Congress has been circumvented with regard to the war in Afghanistan.

# Assess and Remediate

Have students answer the Connect to Your World questions.

# Answers

1. **(a)** the war powers as defined by the Constitution **(b)** by indicating that President Obama was thorough in his decision making and his strategy should be seen through

2. **(a)** Sample answer: Using the war powers affects the security and well-being of the nation. Its use should not be taken lightly and should be checked by both branches to ensure power is not abused. **(b)** Answers will vary. Students should support their positions.

# What nonlegislative powers does the Constitution delegate to Congress?

1. Senate chooses Vice President if no one wins electoral majority
2. Confirm President's choice to fill vacancy in vice presidency
3. Senate confirms presidential appointments
4. House elects President if no one receives electoral majority
5. Senate advises on and confirms treaties
6. Oversee executive agencies
7. Propose amendment
8. Gather information for laws
9. Call national convention to propose amendment
10. Focus public attention on issue

# Get Started

## LESSON GOALS

Students will . . .

- evaluate the impeachment process by examining primary sources and data about the impeachment of President Clinton.
- examine the nonlegislative duties of Congress, using the Jigsaw strategy.

## SKILLS DEVELOPMENT

### GIVE A MULTIMEDIA PRESENTATION

Before students complete this lesson's Core Worksheet, you may want to review tips on giving a multimedia presentation in the Skills Handbook, p. S21.

---

## SECTION 4

# The Nonlegislative Powers

**Guiding Question**
**What nonlegislative powers does the Constitution delegate to Congress?** Use a concept web to record the congressional powers described in this section.

### Political Dictionary

- successor
- impeach
- acquit
- perjury
- censure
- subpoena

### Objectives

1. Describe the role of Congress in amending the Constitution and its electoral duties.
2. Describe the power of Congress to impeach, and summarize presidential impeachment cases.
3. Identify the executive powers of Congress.
4. Describe the investigatory powers of Congress.

**Image Above:** Bill Gates testifies at a congressional hearing on technological innovation.

**C**ongress is a legislative body; its primary function is to make law. But the Constitution does give it some other chores—several nonlegislative duties—to perform as well.

## Constitutional Amendments

Article V says that Congress may propose amendments to the Constitution by a two-thirds vote in each house. All 33 of the amendments thus far added to the document have been proposed by Congress. Article V also provides that Congress may call a national convention of delegates from each of the States to propose an amendment—but only if requested to do so by at least two thirds (34) of the State legislatures. No such convention has ever been called.

In recent years, several State legislatures have petitioned Congress for amendments—among them measures that would require Congress to balance the federal budget each year, prohibit flag burning, permit prayer in public schools, outlaw abortions, impose term limits on members of Congress, and prohibit same-sex marriages.

## Electoral Duties

The Constitution gives certain electoral duties to Congress. But they are to be exercised only in very unusual circumstances.

The House may be called on to elect a President. The 12th Amendment says that if no one receives a majority of the electoral votes for President, the House, voting by States, is to decide the issue. It must choose from among the three highest contenders in the electoral college balloting. Each State has but one vote to cast, and a majority of the States is necessary for election.

The Senate must choose a Vice President if no candidate wins a majority of the electoral votes for that office. In that situation, the vote is by individual senators, with a majority of the full Senate necessary for election.[10]

---

**10** Notice that the 12th Amendment makes it possible for the President to be of one party and the Vice President another. On the matter of presidential and vice-presidential selection, see Chapter 13.

---

# Focus on the Basics

**FACTS:** • Congress may propose constitutional amendments by a two-thirds vote in each house. • Congress must choose a President or Vice President if no candidate wins a majority of the electoral votes. • The House can impeach, or accuse, government officials, but the Senate conducts the trial. • The Senate has the power to confirm or reject presidential appointments and give advice and consent for treaties. • Congress may investigate any matter that falls within the scope of its legislative powers.

**CONCEPTS:** checks and balances, enumerated powers

**ENDURING UNDERSTANDING:** • Many nonlegislative duties of Congress help maintain the balance of power among the branches of government.

The House has had to choose a President twice: Thomas Jefferson in 1801 and John Quincy Adams in 1825. The Senate has had to pick a Vice President only once: Richard M. Johnson in 1837.

Remember that the 25th Amendment provides for the filling of a vacancy in the vice presidency. When one occurs, the President nominates a **successor**—a replacement, someone to fill the vacancy, subject to a majority vote in both houses of Congress. That process has also been used twice: Gerald Ford was confirmed as Vice President in 1973 and Nelson Rockefeller in 1974.

## Impeachment

The Constitution provides that the President, Vice President, and all civil officers of the United States may "be removed from Office on Impeachment for, and Conviction of, Treason, Bribery, or other high Crimes and Misdemeanors."[11] A close reading of those words suggests that the Framers expected that only serious criminal offenses, not political disagreements, would lead to impeachment. Politics has, nevertheless, been at the root of most impeachment controversies.

The House has the sole power to **impeach**—to accuse, bring charges. The Senate has the sole power to try—to judge, to sit as a court—in impeachment cases.[12]

Impeachment requires only a majority vote in the House; conviction requires a two-thirds vote in the Senate. The Chief Justice presides over the Senate when a President is to be tried. The penalty for conviction is removal from office. The Senate may also prohibit a convicted person from ever holding federal office again; and he or she can be tried

11 Article II, Section 4. Military officers are not considered "civil officers," nor are members of Congress.
12 Article I, Section 2, Clause 5; Section 3, Clause 6.
13 Seven other federal judges were impeached by the House but later acquitted by the Senate. Four federal judges impeached by the House resigned before the Senate could act in their cases. In one case, that of Louisiana district judge Thomas Porteous, the Senate vote was still pending after impeachment by the House in early 2010. One of the seven judges removed from office was later elected to Congress. The only other federal officer ever impeached was William W. Belknap, President Grant's Secretary of War, who had been accused of accepting bribes. Although he had resigned from office, he was impeached by the House in 1876 and later acquitted by the Senate.

in the regular courts for any crime involved in the events that led to the impeachment. To date, there have been 19 impeachments and seven convictions; all seven persons removed by the Senate were federal judges.[13]

Two Presidents have been impeached by the House: Andrew Johnson in 1868 and Bill Clinton in 1998. The Senate voted to **acquit** both men—that is, it found them not guilty.

**Andrew Johnson** The unsuccessful attempt to remove Andrew Johnson grew out of the turmoil that followed the Civil War. Mr. Johnson had become the nation's 17th President when Abraham Lincoln was assassinated in April of 1865, and he soon became

✔ **Checkpoint**
What is the penalty if a President is impeached and convicted?

### How Government Works

### Electoral Duties of Congress
## Who Wins?

Presidents regularly come from the two major parties. No law says that only two people may run in the general election, but the Constitution does say that the winner must receive a majority of the electoral college votes, now 270. *What would happen if a minor party candidate won enough electoral votes to prevent any candidate winning a majority?*

**STEP 1:**
No candidate receives a majority of the **electoral college votes.**

**246    25    267**

**STEP 2:**
Each State's **House** delegation must decide which of the top three candidates to support. Each State has **one vote** in the contest. Failure to agree means the loss of that State's vote.

**STEP 3:**
A candidate who wins a **majority** (26) of the votes of the States' delegations **wins the presidency.** If no candidate wins a majority of the States' votes, another vote must be taken.

**Winner!**

# Differentiated Resources

The following resources are located in the All-in-One, Unit 3, Chapter 11, Section 4:

- **L3** Reading Comprehension Worksheet (p. 89)
- **L2** Reading Comprehension Worksheet (p. 91)
- **L3** Bellringer Worksheet (p. 93)
- **L3** Core Worksheets A and B (pp. 95, 96)
- **L3** **L4** Extend Worksheet (p. 97)
- **L3** Quiz A (p. 98)   **L2** Quiz B (p. 99)
- **L3** Chapter Test A (p. 104)
- **L2** Chapter Test B (p. 107)

**BEFORE CLASS**

Assign the section, the graphic organizer in the text, and the Reading Comprehension Worksheet (Unit 3 All-in-One, p. 89) before class.

**L2 Differentiate** Reading Comprehension Worksheet (Unit 3 All-in-One, p. 91)

**BELLRINGER**

Distribute the Bellringer Worksheet (Unit 3 All-in-One, p. 93), which investigates the role of partisanship in the Clinton impeachment.

# Teach

To present this topic using online resources, use the lesson presentations at **PearsonSchool.com/phgovt.**

**DEVELOP THE BELLRINGER**

Review students' answers to the Bellringer questions: **Which house of Congress has the power to impeach?** (the House) **Which house conducts the trial?** (the Senate) **How many votes are required to convict an impeached official?** (67 votes, or two thirds of the Senate) **Was President Clinton impeached?** (yes, on two articles) **Was he convicted?** (no) Then ask these additional questions: **Why did the House vote on four articles of impeachment, while the Senate voted on only two?** (The other two articles did not receive enough votes in favor of impeachment in the House and so were not sent on to the Senate.) **How is Alexander's Hamilton's concern expressed in the excerpt from *The Federalist* No. 65 reflected in the data shown in the charts?** (Hamilton expressed a concern that members of Congress would tend to let partisanship cloud their judgment during an impeachment trial. The data shows that President Clinton's impeachment trial did follow strict party lines—the Democrats overwhelmingly voted against the charges, while the Republicans overwhelmingly voted for impeachment and conviction.)

**L2 ELL Differentiate** Have students look up the definitions of these words in the Bellringer Worksheet excerpt from Hamilton: *impeachment, faction, animosity, partiality.* Then have them read the excerpt again, this time substituting the definitions in place of these words.

## Answers

**Checkpoint** removal from office

**Electoral Duties of Congress** The House would choose the President and the Senate would choose the Vice President.

## EMPHASIZE CHECKS AND BALANCES

Tell students that today they will discuss the nonlegislative roles of Congress. Emphasize that Congress has many important functions related to checks and balances. Ask students to explain why Congress has the ultimate authority to override the President on many matters or propose amendments to the Constitution. *(The Framers saw Congress as being most responsive to the needs and wishes of the people, because they are elected by the people and represent the diversity of each State. The Framers wanted the United States to have a government by and for the people.)*

**L1 Differentiate** Help students understand the phrase *checks and balances* with a visual example. Place a flat rectangular block on top of a small block, so that the ends of the rectangular block extend well past the smaller block. Place three small blocks on each end of the rectangular block, so that the block remains balanced. Explain that this is how the Framers intended checks and balances to work, with each of the three branches keeping the government in balance. Then remove two blocks from one end so that the rectangular block crashes to one side. Explain that without checks and balances, the government might also become unbalanced, with one branch having more power than the others.

---

✔ **Checkpoint**
Why was President Johnson impeached?

**enmeshed**
*v.* entangled; caught up in

**conciliatory**
*adj.* producing agreement

enmeshed in a series of disputes with the Radical Republicans who controlled both houses of Congress. Many of those disagreements centered around the treatment of the defeated Southern States in the immediate post-war period.

President Johnson sought to carry out the conciliatory Reconstruction policies favored by Abraham Lincoln—policies that Mr. Lincoln had summarized in these memorable words in his Second Inaugural Address on March 4, 1865: "With malice toward none, with charity for all. . . ." The Radical Republicans supported a much harsher approach to Reconstruction.

Matters came to a head when Congress passed the Tenure of Office Act, over the President's veto, in 1867. President Johnson's violation of that law triggered his impeachment by a House bent on political revenge. The Senate fell just one vote short of removing him from office.

**Bill Clinton** Bill Clinton was impeached by the House in 1998. In proceedings steeped

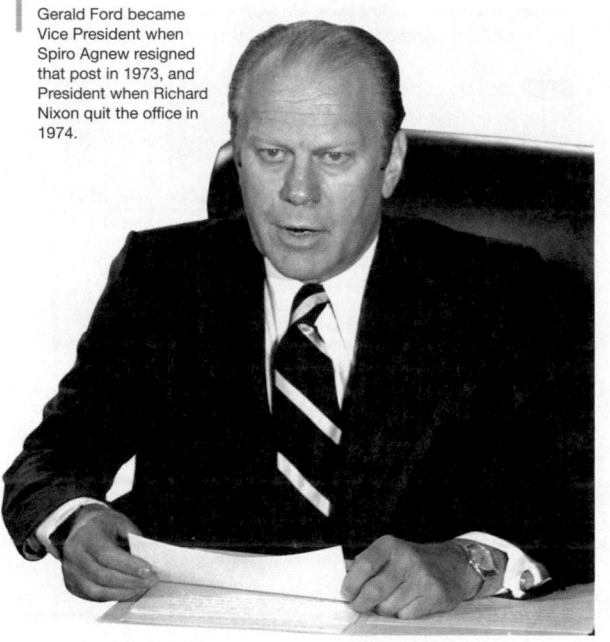

Gerald Ford became Vice President when Spiro Agnew resigned that post in 1973, and President when Richard Nixon quit the office in 1974.

in partisanship, the House voted two articles of impeachment against him on December 19. Both articles arose out of the President's admitted "inappropriate relationship" with a White House intern. The first article charged the President with **perjury**—that is, lying under oath. The second article accused him of obstruction of justice because he had withheld information about his affair with the intern.

Members of the House who supported the articles of impeachment contended that the acts of lying under oath and of withholding evidence were within the meaning of the Constitution's phrase "other high Crimes and Misdemeanors." Therefore, they argued, the President's immediate removal from office was justified.

Their opponents argued that the facts involved in the case did not justify either charge. They insisted that, while the President's conduct was deplorable and should be condemned, that conduct did not rise to the level of an impeachable offense. Many of them pressed, instead, for a resolution to **censure** the President—that is, for a formal condemnation of his behavior.

The Senate received the articles of impeachment when the new Congress convened in 1999, and it began to sit in judgment of the President on January 7.

**Richard Nixon** A few officeholders have resigned in the face of almost certain impeachment—most notably, Richard Nixon, who resigned the presidency in mid-1974. President Nixon's second term in office was cut short by the Watergate scandal.

The term *Watergate* comes from a June 1972 attempt by Republican operatives to break into the Democratic Party's national headquarters in the Watergate office complex in Washington, D.C. The investigation of that incident, by the *Washington Post* and then by other media, led to official investigations by the Department of Justice and by the Senate's Select Committee on Presidential Campaign Activities, popularly known as the Senate Watergate Committee.

The probes unearthed a long list of illegal acts, including bribery, perjury, income tax fraud, and illegal campaign contributions.

**320** Powers of Congress

---

# Debate

After students have studied the feature on "President Clinton's Impeachment," divide the class into two groups and use the Debate strategy (p. T25) to have them debate this question: **Did President Clinton commit "high crimes and misdemeanors," as required for conviction?**

---

## Answers

**Checkpoint** his violation of the Tenure of Office Act

GOVERNMENT ONLINE
**Audio Tour**
Listen to a guided audio tour about impeachment at
PearsonSchool.com/phgovt

## The Impeachment Process
# President Clinton's Impeachment

This chronology details the complex impeachment process and shows how the process worked in the impeachment of President Bill Clinton. *What measures did the Framers build into the impeachment process to ensure its fairness? Why do you think the attempt to remove President Clinton failed?*

## 1998

*The House Judiciary Committee considers charges* against the accused and votes on whether to send articles of impeachment to the full House. A simple majority vote is needed to start the process. ▼

**December 11–12, 1998** After three months of hearings, the House Judiciary Committee approves four articles.

*Acting much like a grand jury, the House considers the charge(s) brought by the Judiciary Committee.* It can subpoena witnesses and evidence. It hears and debates arguments. ▼

**December 18–19, 1998** The House holds 13 hours of bitter, partisan debate, in which more than 200 House members speak. Democrats briefly walk out to protest Republican leaders' refusal to consider the lesser punishment of censure.

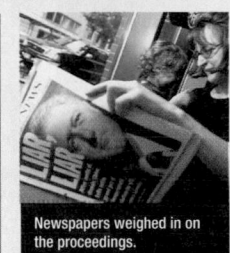
Newspapers weighed in on the proceedings.

*The House votes on each article.* If any article is approved by a majority vote, the official is impeached, which is similar to being indicted. The House sends the article(s) of impeachment to the Senate. ▼

**December 19, 1998** The House votes to impeach Mr. Clinton on two counts. The votes are 228-206 on the count of perjury and 221-212 on obstruction of justice. Voting is mostly along party lines.

## 1999

*The Senate tries the case.* If the President is to be tried, the Chief Justice of the United States presides. Selected members of the House act as managers (prosecutors). ▼

**January 7, 1999** Chief Justice William Rehnquist opens a televised trial. Representative Henry Hyde of Illinois leads a team of 13 House managers. White House Counsel Charles Ruff leads the defense.

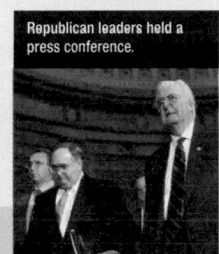
Republican leaders held a press conference.

*Senators hear testimony and evidence.* House prosecutors and lawyers for both sides present their cases. Additional witnesses may be called. Senators may also vote to curb testimony. ▼

**January 7–February 11, 1999** With public distaste for impeachment growing, the Senate limits testimony to three witnesses, the intern among them. Closing arguments follow. For three days, the Senate deliberates in secret (despite Democrats' objections).

Protesters rallied outside the Capitol.

*The Senate debates the articles, publicly or privately.* It need not render a verdict. It could, for example, vote to drop the case and instead censure the official. A two-thirds vote is required for conviction. ▼

**February 12, 1999** In a televised session, the Senate acquits the President on both charges, falling well short of the two-thirds vote needed for conviction. There are 55 Republicans and 45 Democrats in the Senate. On the perjury count, 45 Democrats and 10 Republicans vote not guilty. On the obstruction charge, 5 Republicans break with their party to vote with all of the Democrats against conviction.

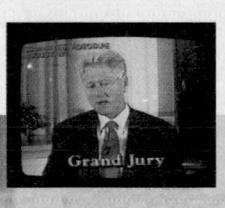

Top: Congress reviewed tapes of President Clinton's testimony.
Bottom: House Democrats walked out to protest the impeachment resolution.

# How Government Works

**ELECTORAL DUTIES** Four candidates ran for President in 1824. The electoral vote was as follows: Andrew Jackson, 99; John Quincy Adams, 84; William Crawford, 41; and Henry Clay, 37. Since no candidate received a majority of the electoral vote, the decision went to the House of Representatives. The Constitution requires the House to choose among the top three candidates in the electoral vote. This requirement knocked Clay, the powerful speaker of the House, out of the running. Clay threw his support to Adams, assuring a majority vote in the House to elect Adams. Shortly after his election, Adams offered Clay the job of secretary of state, which Clay accepted. Jackson's supporters were outraged. They charged Adams and Clay of entering into a "corrupt bargain," robbing Jackson of the presidency. This charge cast a cloud over Adams' administration and helped Jackson defeat Adams in the election of 1828.

---

## DISTRIBUTE CORE WORKSHEETS

Explain that students will use the Jigsaw strategy (p. T27) to learn about the nonlegislative duties of Congress. Distribute Chapter 11 Section 4 Core Worksheet A (Unit 3 All-in-One, p. 95) to some students and Core Worksheet B (Unit 3 All-in-One, p. 96) to others. These worksheets give students directions about what type of information to include in their presentation. Divide students into groups and assign each group one of the topics listed on their worksheet (Worksheet A: "Appointments," "Treaties," or "Investigatory Powers"; Core Worksheet B: "Amending the Constitution," "Electoral Duties," or "Impeachment").

**L2 Differentiate** Give these students Core Worksheet B (Unit 3 All-in-One, p. 96) and assign "Electoral Duties" or "Impeachment."

**L3 Differentiate** Any of the topics are appropriate for on-level students. The topics on Core Worksheet B are more straightforward but no less important for all students to learn. Refer students using Core Worksheet A to Unit 4 for more information. Refer students using Core Worksheet B to Chapter 3 for more information.

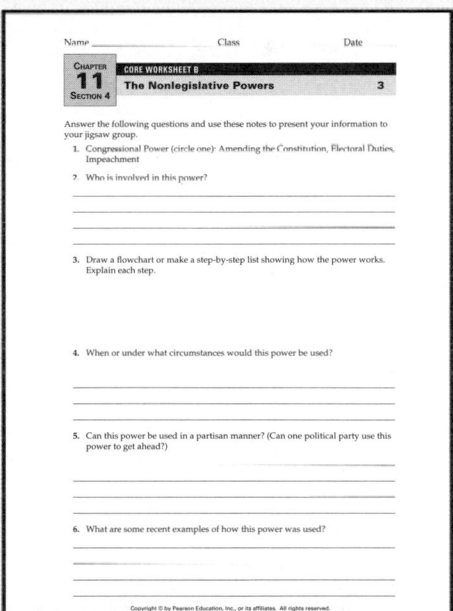

Tell students to go to the Audio Tour for a guided audio tour of The Impeachment Process.

---

## Answers

**The Impeachment Process** The Framers divided the process, giving the power to impeach to the House and power to convict to the Senate. Conviction requires a two-thirds vote, which is a high bar. Also, the Chief Justice presides over the trial. The attempt to remove Clinton probably failed because it was more politically motivated than based on "high crimes and misdemeanors."

## JIGSAW

After students have time to answer the questions with their "expert" group, jigsaw the groups and let students explain their topic to their new group. Instruct students to ask at least one question of an "expert." Experts will record these questions to discuss with their expert groups.

## RECONVENE EXPERT GROUPS

Expert groups should reconvene and discuss the questions they were asked after their jigsaw presentations. One group member should stand up and address these questions for the class. To finish, ask each group to submit three quiz questions on their topic.

**L2** **Differentiate** Have students use the Click and Clunk strategy (p. T23) to assess which topics from the jigsaw they understood and which need further clarification.

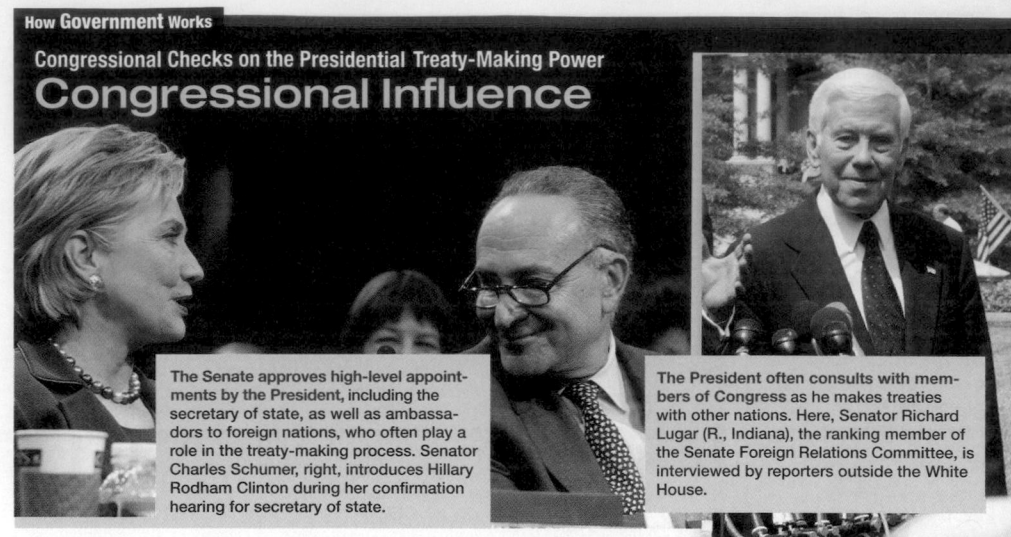

**How Government Works**

Congressional Checks on the Presidential Treaty-Making Power

## Congressional Influence

The Senate approves high-level appointments by the President, including the secretary of state, as well as ambassadors to foreign nations, who often play a role in the treaty-making process. Senator Charles Schumer, right, introduces Hillary Rodham Clinton during her confirmation hearing for secretary of state.

The President often consults with members of Congress as he makes treaties with other nations. Here, Senator Richard Lugar (R., Indiana), the ranking member of the Senate Foreign Relations Committee, is interviewed by reporters outside the White House.

They also revealed the use of the Federal Bureau of Investigation, the Internal Revenue Service, and other government agencies for personal and partisan purposes.

The House Judiciary Committee voted three articles of impeachment against President Nixon in late July 1974. He was charged with obstruction of justice, abuse of power, and failure to respond to the Judiciary Committee's **subpoenas.** A committee's subpoena is a legal order directing one to appear before that body and/or to produce certain evidence. Mr. Nixon had ignored the committee's subpoena of several tape recordings of Watergate-related conversations in the Oval Office.

It was quite apparent that the full House would impeach the President and that the Senate would convict him. Those facts prompted Mr. Nixon to resign the presidency on August 9, 1974.

Beyond doubt, the Watergate scandal involved the most extensive and the most serious violations of public trust in the nation's history. Among its other consequences, several Cabinet officers, presidential assistants, and others were convicted of various felonies and misdemeanors—and many of them served jail time.

## Executive Powers

The Constitution gives two executive powers to the Senate. One of those powers has to do with appointments to office, and the other with treaties made by the President.[14]

**Appointments** All major appointments made by the President must be confirmed by the Senate by majority vote. Each of the President's nominations is referred to the appropriate standing committee of the Senate. That committee may then hold hearings to decide whether or not to make a favorable recommendation to the full Senate for that appointment. When the committee's recommendation is brought to the floor of the Senate, it may be, but seldom is, considered in executive (secret) session.

The appointment of a Cabinet officer or of some other top member of the President's "official family" is rarely rejected by the Senate. The Senate has rejected only 12

**14** Article II, Section 2, Clause 2

**15** The first was Roger B. Taney, Andrew Jackson's choice for secretary of the treasury in 1832. Jackson later named Taney Chief Justice. The most recent rejection came in 1989, when the Senate refused President George H.W. Bush's nomination of John Tower as secretary of defense.

# Teacher-to-Teacher Network

**ALTERNATE LESSON PLAN** Have student groups examine the impeachment process in the cases of Andrew Johnson, Bill Clinton, and Richard Nixon. Each group will research and write a speech either supporting or opposing impeachment of these Presidents. After all groups present their speeches, the class will vote on the President who they think most deserved impeachment and conviction.

To see this lesson plan, go to

Teacher Center

at PearsonSchool.com/phgovt

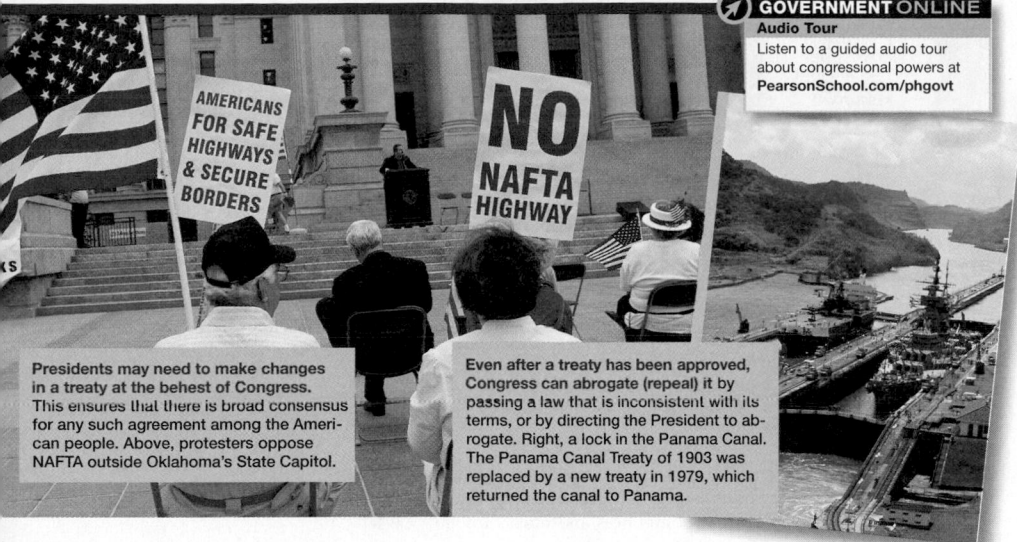

**GOVERNMENT** ONLINE
**Audio Tour**
Listen to a guided audio tour about congressional powers at PearsonSchool.com/phgovt

Presidents may need to make changes in a treaty at the behest of Congress. This ensures that there is broad consensus for any such agreement among the American people. Above, protesters oppose NAFTA outside Oklahoma's State Capitol.

Even after a treaty has been approved, Congress can abrogate (repeal) it by passing a law that is inconsistent with its terms, or by directing the President to abrogate. Right, a lock in the Panama Canal. The Panama Canal Treaty of 1903 was replaced by a new treaty in 1979, which returned the canal to Panama.

of more than 600 Cabinet appointments.[15] More commonly, the President will withdraw a nomination if the Senate sends signals that it will reject the nominee in a confirmation vote. For example, President George W. Bush withdrew the nomination of Harriet Miers, his White House Counsel, to the Supreme Court. Bush later nominated Samuel Alito, who was confirmed by the Senate.

It is with the President's appointment of federal officers who serve in the various States (for example, U.S. attorneys and federal marshals) that the unwritten rule of "senatorial courtesy" comes into play. The Senate will turn down such a presidential appointment if it is opposed by a senator of the President's party from the State involved. The Senate's observance of this unwritten rule has a significant impact on the President's exercise of the power of appointment; in effect, this rule means that some senators virtually dictate certain presidential appointments.

**Treaties** The President makes treaties "by and with the Advice and Consent of the Senate, . . . provided two thirds of the Senators present concur."[16] For a time after the adoption of the Constitution, the President asked the advice of the Senate when a treaty

was being negotiated and prepared. Now the President most often consults the members of the Senate Foreign Relations Committee and other influential senators of both parties.

The Senate may accept or reject a treaty as it stands, or it may decide to offer amendments, reservations, or understandings to it. Treaties are sometimes considered in executive session. Because the House has a hold on the public purse strings, influential members of that body are often consulted in the treaty-making process, too.

### The Power to Investigate

Congress has the power to investigate—to inquire into, or inform itself on—any matter that falls within the scope of its lawmaking authority. The authority to do so is implied by the Constitution's grant of the legislative power to Congress, in Article I, Section 1. As

16 Article II, Section 2, Clause 2. It is often said that the Senate "ratifies" a treaty. It does not. The Senate may give or withhold its "advice and consent" to a treaty made by the President. Once the Senate has consented to a treaty, the President ratifies it by exchanging "instruments of ratification" with other parties to the agreement. We discuss the treaty-making process at some length in Chapter 14.

✔ **Checkpoint**
What is the unwritten rule known as "senatorial courtesy"?

**concur**
v. agree

---

**L3** **L4** **Differentiate** Distribute Chapter 11 Section 4 Extend Worksheet (Unit 3 All-in-One, p. 97), which asks students to research the path of a treaty sent to the Senate for ratification or a Senate confirmation hearing and write a summary of the proceedings and the media coverage.

**L3** **Differentiate** Have students research one instance in which Congress has recently exercised its nonlegislative powers. Ask them to write a critique explaining whether Congress used its power wisely and how partisanship affected the action.

**L4** **Differentiate** Have students find and read a portion of a recent congressional hearing in which members question a presidential appointee or investigate a matter of national concern. Evaluate the hearing for partisan motives and evaluate the quality of the hearing. Students should explain whether they would have asked different questions or think that members of Congress should have investigated an issue further.

**Government** online *All print resources are available on the Teacher's Resource Library CD-ROM and online at PearsonSchool.com/phgovt.*

Tell students to go to the Audio Tour for a guided audio tour of Congressional Influence.

## Assess and Remediate

**L3** Compile students' questions into a quiz and give it to the class.

**L3** Collect the Core Worksheet and assess each student's work in the Jigsaw activity, using the Rubric for Assessing Individual Performance in a Group (Unit 3 All-in-One, p. 167).

**L3** Assign the Section 4 Assessment questions.

**L3** Section Quiz A (Unit 3 All-in-One, p. 98)

**L2** Section Quiz B (Unit 3 All-in-One, p. 99)

Have students complete the review activities in the digital lesson presentation and continue their work in the **Essential Questions Journal.**

---

### Answers

**Checkpoint** The Senate will reject a presidential appointment if it is opposed by a senator of the President's party from the State involved.

| If Your Students Have Trouble With | Strategies For Remediation |
|---|---|
| Identifying the nonlegislative powers of Congress (Questions 1, 4, 5, 6) | Have them write the five main headings in this text section across the top of a broadside sheet of paper. Ask them to add a bullet list of powers under each heading as they review the section. |
| Remembering how a President and Vice President are chosen if no candidate wins a majority of electoral votes (Question 2) | Have them draw a flowchart showing the steps in the electoral process, using information provided in the text. |
| Understanding the impeachment and conviction processes (Question 3) | Suggest they create a chart, comparing the reasons for the impeachment of Johnson, Clinton, and Nixon, the results, and the reasons for these results. |

CONGRESSIONAL OVERSIGHT

"I'M WARNING YOU. KEEP IT UP AND YOU'LL GET ANOTHER STRONGLY WORDED NONBINDING RESOLUTION!"

▸▸ **Interpreting Cartoons** In February 2007, the House passed a nonbinding resolution opposing the President's plan to send more troops to Iraq. *What point does the cartoonist make?*

✔ **Checkpoint**
What are some of the reasons that Congress holds hearings?

we noted, both the House and Senate exercise that power through the standing committees and their subcommittees and often through special committees, as well.

Both houses may choose to conduct investigations for any one or a number of reasons. Most often, those inquiries are held to (1) gather information necessary to the framing of legislation, (2) oversee the operations of various agencies in the executive branch, (3) focus public attention on some particular matter, (4) expose the questionable activities of some public official or private

person or group, and/or (5) promote the particular interests of some members of Congress. Notice that the second of these motives, oversight, is a little-noted but quite important aspect of the constitutional system of checks and balances. Note, too, that Congress is more inclined to exercise its oversight function when one or both of its chambers is controlled by the party that does not hold the presidency, most recently in 2011 and 2012.

Over recent years, Congress has improved its ability both to inform itself and to perform its oversight responsibilities by increasing the staff resources available to the standing committees of both houses. The three little-known agencies in the legislative branch which also add to that capability are:

1. the Congressional Budget Office, which committees of both houses rely on quite heavily in taxing, spending, and other budget-related matters;

2. the Congressional Research Service, in the Library of Congress, whose several hundred staff specialists provide members with factual information on virtually any subject; and

3. the Government Accountability Office, also called Congress' watchdog because it has broad authority to monitor the work of the Federal Government and report its findings to Congress.

**Essential Questions Journal** To continue to build a response to the chapter Essential Question, go to your **Essential Questions Journal.**

## SECTION 4 ASSESSMENT

1. **Guiding Question** Use your completed concept web to answer this question: What nonlegislative powers does the Constitution delegate to Congress?

**Key Terms and Comprehension**

2. If the vice presidency becomes vacant, how is a **successor** chosen?
3. Summarize the circumstances of President Richard Nixon's resignation from office.
4. Outline the process by which Congress approves or rejects presidential appointments.

5. What powers does Congress have with regard to treaties negotiated by the President?

**Critical Thinking**

6. **Draw Conclusions** In what two ways may Congress propose amendments to the Constitution? Do you think the Framers made amending the Constitution too difficult? Explain.
7. **Determine Cause and Effect** How do each of the nonlegislative powers of Congress illustrate the principle of checks and balances?

**Quick Write**

**Persuasive Writing: Review and Revise** Review and revise your outline from Section 3, making sure that your points are presented in a logical sequence. Use transition words, such as *although, because,* and *then* to guide readers through your ideas. Add details that will make your presentation more interesting.

## Answers

**Interpreting Cartoons** The cartoonist is making fun of congressional oversight by suggesting that a nonbinding resolution doesn't amount to much of a threat to the President.

**Checkpoint** to gather information for legislation, oversee executive agencies, focus public attention on a matter, expose questionable activities of a public official or a private person or group, and/or promote the interests of some members of Congress

# Assessment Answers

**1.** amending the Constitution; electoral duties; impeachment; appointments and treaties; power to investigate

**2.** President nominates successor, and a majority vote of both houses of Congress confirms

**3.** People with ties to the White House broke into the Democratic Party's national headquarters. Investigations found evidence of illegal activities and abuses of power. Congress subpoenaed tape recordings from Nixon, who refused to turn them over. Realizing he would be impeached and convicted, Nixon resigned.

**4.** Each presidential nomination is referred to the appropriate standing committee of the Senate. The committee may hold hearings before making a recommendation to the full Senate. The Senate approves or rejects by majority vote.

**5.** The President makes treaties with the "advice and consent" of the Senate. A two-thirds vote of the Senate is required for approval.

**6.** by a two-thirds vote in each house or by calling a national convention of State delegates; possible answer: No, it is best that

constitutional amendments not be passed too easily, lest ill-considered changes have a negative effect on American government.

**7.** Each nonlegislative power involves more than one branch or level of government, or divides responsibilities between houses of Congress. This design enables one part of government to check the power of another.

**QUICK WRITE** Students will sequence their outlines logically and add transitions and details.

# Quick Study Guide

**GOVERNMENT** ONLINE
**On the Go**
To review anytime, anywhere, download these online resources at **PearsonSchool.com/phgovt**
Political Dictionary, Audio Review

CHAPTER **11**

**Guiding Question**
**Section 2** How do the expressed powers reflect the Framers' commitment to creating a strong but limited national government?

**Guiding Question**
**Section 3** How has the doctrine of implied powers increased the powers of Congress?

**Guiding Question**
**Section 1** What powers over money and commerce does the Constitution give to Congress and what limits does it put on these powers?

**CHAPTER 11**
**Essential Question**
What should be the limits on the powers of Congress?

**Guiding Question**
**Section 4** What nonlegislative powers does the Constitution delegate to Congress?

## Political Dictionary

**expressed powers** p. 296
**implied powers** p. 296
**inherent powers** p. 296
**commerce power** p. 297
**tax** p. 300
**public debt** p. 301
**deficit financing** p. 301
**bankruptcy** p. 302
**legal tender** p. 303
**copyright** p. 307
**patent** p. 307
**territory** p. 308
**eminent domain** p. 308
**naturalization** p. 309
**Necessary and Proper Clause** p. 312
**strict constructionist** p. 313
**liberal constructionist** p. 314
**consensus** p. 314
**appropriate** p. 316
**successor** p. 319
**impeach** p. 319
**acquit** p. 319
**perjury** p. 320
**censure** p. 320
**subpoena** p. 322

## Legislative Checks and Balances

| On the Executive Branch | On the Judicial Branch |
|---|---|
| • Provides funding for the armed forces | • Congress creates courts inferior to the Supreme Court |
| • The power to declare war | • Senate must confirm appointments of federal judges |
| • Senate must approve treaties | |
| • Senate must approve appointments | |

## Comparing the House and the Senate

| Only the House has the power to | Only the Senate has the power to |
|---|---|
| • Impeach executive and judicial officers | • Try impeachments |
| • Originate tax bills | • Approve or reject treaties |
| | • Confirm the appointment of all federal judges, Cabinet members, and other top-level officers |

# For More Information

To learn more about the powers of Congress, refer to these sources or assign them to students:

**L1 Skog, Jason.** *The Civil Rights Act of 1964.* Compass Point Books, 2007.

**L2 Murphy, John.** *The Impeachment Process (The U.S. Government: How It Works).* Chelsea House Publications, 2007.

**L3 Abernathy, Scott.** *No Child Left Behind and the Public Schools.* University of Michigan Press, 2007.

**L4 Ellis, Richard E.** *Aggressive Nationalism: McCulloch v. Maryland and the Foundation of Federal Authority in the Young Republic.* Oxford University Press, USA, 2007.

---

Have students download the digital resources available at Government on the Go for review and remediation.

**STUDY TIPS**

**Active Reading** Effective readers interact with the material they are reading to help them absorb and comprehend information. Before reading each section in Chapter 11, have students scan the section by reading the introduction, headings, and conclusion. Ask them to look at the photographs, charts, and other visuals. Then have them write a question about the material, such as "How important are the expressed powers of Congress?" As they read, students should look for an answer to their question; this will give them a purpose for reading. Additional strategies include chunking the material into short segments and paraphrasing that section before continuing to read, and drawing diagrams, flowcharts, or other graphic organizers to map ideas visually. Students might also consider reading aloud or photocopying the material so they can highlight or underline key points. The Checkpoint questions in the margins will also keep students engaged as they read.

**ASSESSMENT AT A GLANCE**

**Tests and Quizzes**
Section Assessments
Section Quizzes A and B, Unit 3 **All-in-One**
Chapter Assessment
Chapter Tests A and B, Unit 3 **All-in-One**
Document-Based Assessment
Progress Monitoring Online
Exam*View* Test Bank

**Performance Assessment**
Essential Questions Journal
Debates, pp. 300, 320
Assessment Rubrics, **All-in-One**

# Chapter Assessment

## COMPREHENSION AND CRITICAL THINKING

### SECTION 1

1. **(a)** expressed powers, implied powers, inherent powers **(b)** Congress cannot: favor different State ports; require vessels bound to or from one State to be obliged to enter, clear, or pay duties in another; tax for private benefit; tax exports; tax at different rates in different parts of the country.

2. **(a)** the power of Congress to regulate interstate and foreign trade **(b)** to build a strong and united country **(c)** It established a broad definition of *commerce*.

3. **(a)** to ensure that the Federal Government would obtain revenue **(b)** to raise money to meet public needs, but also to protect domestic industry against foreign competition **(c)** They are both expressed powers.

4. With independence, the former currency system collapsed. Congress needed to provide a uniform, stable monetary system for the nation.

### SECTION 2

5. **(a)** Congress can: declare war; raise and support armies and a navy; make rules for the governing of the nation's military forces; call forth, organize, arm, and discipline the militia; grant letters of marque and reprisal and make rules concerning captures on land and water. **(b)** Students should recognize that Congress' power to declare war serves as a check on the President's power as commander in chief. **(c)** The President must be able to respond rapidly and effectively to national security threats. However, there could be dangers inherent in a presidential power to involve the country in undeclared wars.

6. **(a)** Copyrights and patents provide a financial incentive for progress in the arts and sciences by granting exclusive rights to a work for a period of time. **(b)** to provide a centralized process for registering copyrights and patents across the country

7. **(a)** Article I, Section 8 of the Constitution **(b)** Answers will vary.

### SECTION 3

8. **(a)** The meaning of the clause led to conflict between the strict constructionists (who wanted a limited interpretation of the Constitution) and the liberal constructionists (who favored a broad interpretation).

---

# Chapter Assessment

**GOVERNMENT** ONLINE
**Self-Test**
To test your understanding of key terms and main ideas, visit
PearsonSchool.com/phgovt

## Comprehension and Critical Thinking

### Section 1

1. **(a)** Identify the three different types of congressional powers. **(b)** Explain how the Constitution limits the power of Congress.

2. **(a)** Describe the commerce power. **(b)** Why did the Framers grant this power to Congress? **(c)** What was the significance of the Supreme Court's decision in *Gibbons* v. *Ogden*?

3. **(a)** Why did the Framers grant Congress the power to tax? **(b)** What is the purpose of taxes? **(c)** How is the borrowing power related to the taxing power?

4. Why did Congress create a national currency?

### Section 2

5. **(a)** What powers does the Constitution grant to Congress affecting war and national defense? **(b)** Why do you think the Framers gave Congress the sole power to declare war? **(c)** What tensions may arise from the division of the war powers between the Congress and the President?

6. **(a)** How do copyrights and patents "promote the Progress of Science and useful Arts"? **(b)** Why do you think the Framers granted these powers to Congress?

7. **(a)** List five of the expressed powers of Congress set out in the Constitution. **(b)** Are there any powers which, in your view, Congress should possess, but does not? Explain.

### Section 3

8. **(a)** Describe the conflict over the meaning of the Necessary and Proper Clause. **(b)** Why is that clause also called the Elastic Clause?

9. **(a)** What is the significance of the Court's decision in *McCulloch* v. *Maryland*? **(b)** Does the concept of implied powers undercut federalism? Why or why not?

### Section 4

10. **(a)** What nonlegislative powers does the Constitution grant to Congress? **(b)** How does each of those powers check or balance the executive branch?

11. **(a)** Outline the steps of the impeachment process. **(b)** Has the definition of "high crimes and misdemeanors" as impeachable offenses been stretched too far? Explain.

### Writing About Government

12. **Persuasive Writing** Use your Quick Write exercises from this chapter to write a persuasive essay arguing that Congress has used its power too little or too much. Remember that your writing will be most effective if you emphasize arguments your audience will find convincing. See pp. S9—S10 in the Skills Handbook.

---

## Apply What You've Learned

13. **Essential Question Activity** Do research to identify the major pieces of legislation that Congress enacted in a recent session. Choose two pieces of legislation that are based on the expressed powers of Congress and two pieces that are based on its implied powers. Summarize each of the measures and indicate on which power(s) the measure is based.

14. **Essential Question Assessment** Based on your summaries and the content of this chapter, explain in a paragraph how current congressional activity might be different if the Constitution were interpreted strictly. This will help you think about the chapter Essential Question: **What should be the limits on the powers of Congress?**

**Essential Questions Journal** To respond to the chapter Essential Question, go to your **Essential Questions Journal.**

---

**(b)** It has been stretched very far and been made to cover so much over the years.

9. **(a)** The Court upheld the concept of implied powers, which set a pattern over the years of the National Government wielding wide powers. **(b)** possible answer: no, because the doctrine of implied powers has enabled the Federal Government to deal with problems that have evolved over time and which the Framers could not have anticipated.

### SECTION 4

10. **(a)** Congress can: propose or call a national convention to propose amendments to Constitution; elect President or Vice President if no candidate receives electoral majority; confirm President's choice to fill vacancy in vice presidency; impeach (House) and try impeached officials (Senate); confirm President's appointments and give advice and consent for treaties (Senate); and conduct investigations to frame legislation, oversee executive agencies, focus attention on issues, expose questionable activities, and promote interests of members of Congress. **(b)** Congress' confirmation powers ensure that the President must appoint people

# Document-Based Assessment

## Strict v. Liberal Construction of the Constitution

The dispute over the extent of the powers the Constitution grants to the National Government has continued to the present day. As you can see in Document 1, some make the argument that big government can be dangerous. Others see small government as insufficient to meet the needs of the people, as in Document 2.

### Document 1

"[Americans] are a lot better economists than most economists care to admit. They know that a government big enough to give you everything you want is a government big enough to take from you everything you have.

—President Gerald R. Ford, Remarks to a Joint Session of Congress, August 12, 1974

### Document 2

How much pruning can we do and still get apples?

---

**Use your knowledge of the debate over the limits of federal power and these two documents to answer Questions 1–3.**

1. In Document 2, what do "apples" represent?
   - A. Supreme Court rulings
   - B. wasteful federal programs
   - C. things people want from government
   - D. taxes

2. What did President Ford mean when he said that "a government big enough to give you everything you want is a government big enough to take from you everything you have"?

3. **Pull It Together** Compare the viewpoints of each document. How do you think the Federal Government should balance these points of view?

**GOVERNMENT** ONLINE
Documents
To find more primary sources on interpreting the Constitution, visit **PearsonSchool.com/phgovt**

---

## DOCUMENT-BASED ASSESSMENT

1. C

2. President Ford meant that, in order to get services from government, the people have to give it increasing power, which is a potential threat to their liberty. He was warning Americans to think carefully about how much power the Federal Government should have.

3. A good answer will explain that Ford warns of granting too much power to government, while the cartoon warns of the risk of taking too much away. Students should then explain their own viewpoint using these documents and what they learned in this chapter.

**L2 Differentiate** Students use all the documents on the page to support their thesis.

**L3 Differentiate** Students include additional information available online at **PearsonSchool.com/phgovt.**

**L4 Differentiate** Students use materials from the textbook, the online information at **PearsonSchool.com/phgovt,** and do additional research to support their views.

**Go Online to PearsonSchool.com/phgovt** for a student rubric and extra documents.

---

acceptable to Congress. Impeachment allows Congress to remove officials from office. Congress also oversees executive agencies and can investigate questionable activities, assuring executive branch accountability.

11. **(a)** A majority of the House Judiciary Committee sends articles of impeachment to the full House, which hears evidence and then votes on each charge. Articles approved by a majority of the House are sent to the Senate for trial. Members of the House act as managers (prosecutors). House managers and lawyers for both sides present their cases. The Senate debates the articles and decides to drop the case, censure, or convict the official. A two-thirds vote is required to convict. **(b)** Students should consider the difficulty of drafting this wording so that it would cover a wide range of potential misconduct by federal officials.

### WRITING ABOUT GOVERNMENT

12. Students' essays should reflect the principles of good persuasive writing.

### APPLY WHAT YOU'VE LEARNED

13. A good answer will show a firm grasp of the meaning of the concept of expressed and implied powers.

14. Students should understand both strict and liberal construction and the complexities of deciding how much power Congress needs to do its work effectively.

# Introduce the Chapter

## Essential Questions:

### UNIT 3

What makes a successful Congress?

### CHAPTER 12

Can and should the lawmaking process be improved?

### ACTIVATE PRIOR KNOWLEDGE

Have students examine the image and quotation on these pages. Ask: **What does this photograph tell you about Congress "on exhibition"?** *(Much of what Congress does is scrutinized by the public and the media.)* In this chapter, students will learn about the organization of Congress and how a bill becomes a law. Tell students to begin to explore Congress in action by completing the Chapter 12 Essential Question Warmup Activity in their **Essential Questions Journal.** Discuss their responses as a class.

### BEFORE READING

**L2** **ELL Differentiate** Chapter 12 Prereading and Vocabulary Worksheet (Unit 3 All-in-One, p. 121)

### SUCCESSNET STUDENT AND TEACHER CENTER

Visit **PearsonSchool.com/phgovt** for download-able resources that allow students and teachers to connect with government "on the go."

### DIGITAL LESSON PRESENTATION

The digital lesson presentation supports the print lesson with activities and summaries of key concepts. Activities for this chapter include:

• **Congressional Committee Staffers**

• **How a Bill Becomes a Law**

## SKILLS DEVELOPMENT

### GIVE AN EFFECTIVE PRESENTATION

You may wish to teach giving an effective presentation as a distinct skill within Section 4 of this chapter. Use the Chapter 12 Skills Worksheet (Unit 3 All-in-One, p. 156) to help students learn how to give an effective presentation. The worksheet asks students to create a multimedia presentation demonstrating how a bill becomes a law. For L2 and L1 students, assign the adapted Skill Activity (Unit 3 All-in-One, p. 157).

**WebQuest online** The chapter WebQuest challenges students to answer the chapter Essential Question by asking them about the lawmaking process.

328

## Block Scheduling

**BLOCK 1:** Review the "Leadership in the 112th Congress" chart and explain the role of each congressional leader. An online update for this chart is available at **PearsonSchool.com/phgovt.** Then introduce committees and have students do the Chapter 12 Section 2 Core Worksheet, which describes the standing committees of Congress, before beginning the Section 3 lesson.

**BLOCK 2:** Finish teaching the lessons for Sections 3 and 4 in their entirety.

> "Congress **in session** is Congress on **public exhibition**, whilst Congress in its **committee-rooms** is Congress **at work**.

—Woodrow Wilson, *Congressional Government: A Study in American Politics*, 1885

**Photo:** Members of the press at work at a Senate Select Committee on Intelligence session.

CHAPTER

**12**

**Congress in Action**

**Essential Question**
Can and should the lawmaking process be improved?

**GOVERNMENT ONLINE**
On the Go

To study anywhere, anytime, download these online resources at PearsonSchool.com/phgovt
• Political Dictionary
• Audio Review
• Downloadable Interactivities

329

## Lesson Goals

**SECTION 1**

Students will . . .

• complete a flowchart of opening-day events in the House.
• describe the leadership roles in Congress by taking part in a press conference simulation.

**SECTION 2**

Students will . . .

• examine the need for committees to divide work by creating an organization for an event.
• identify jurisdictions of House committees by matching committee names to descriptions.
• trace the path of the 2007 Food and Energy Security bill through the House.

**SECTION 3**

Students will . . .

• recognize the need for committees by examining a transparency showing the volume of bills flowing through Congress.
• write a bill using guidelines and following a sample.
• simulate how a bill passes through the House, using a bill created by students.

**SECTION 4**

Students will . . .

• use a dramatization to learn about filibusters.
• examine the work of conference committees by simulating negotiations to iron out differences between versions of a bill.
• identify a bill's final steps toward becoming law by completing a flowchart.

## Pressed for Time

To cover this chapter quickly, direct students to the "Leadership in the 112th Congress" chart in the text or the online update to review the current congressional leaders. Briefly explain the role of each congressional leader and the seniority system in Congress. Then use "A Bill in the House" to explain how a bill moves through the House. Complete the Chapter 12 Section 2 Core Worksheet and Extend Worksheet to explain the role of committees and committee chairmen, the division of labor, and jurisdiction. Then review "How a Bill Becomes a Law" in detail.

**DIFFERENTIATED INSTRUCTION KEY**

Look for these symbols to help you adjust steps in each lesson to meet your students' needs.

**L1** Special Needs

**L2** Basic

   **ELL** English Language Learners

   **LPR** Less Proficient Readers

**L3** All Students

**L4** Advanced Students

## How do constitutional and party officers keep Congress organized?

| Congressional Leaders and Their Duties | |
|---|---|
| House | Senate |
| **Speaker of the House**<br>• presides and keeps order<br>• chairs sessions<br>• allows members to speak by recognizing them<br>• interprets and applies the rules<br>• refers bills to committee<br>• rules on points of order<br>• puts motions to a vote and decides outcome<br>• names members of select and conference committees<br>• signs all bills and resolutions passed by House | **President of the Senate**<br>• presides<br>• Vice President<br>• cannot speak or debate on Senate floor<br>• may vote only to break tie<br><br>**President *pro tempore***<br>• presides in Vice President's absence<br><br>**Majority Leader**<br>• controls order of business on floor<br>• carries out decisions of party's caucus |
| **Majority Leader**<br>• controls order of business on floor<br>• carries out decisions of party's caucus | **Minority Leader**<br>• carries out decisions of party's caucus |
| **Minority Leader**<br>• carries out decisions of party's caucus | **Majority and Minority Whips**<br>• liaison between party leaders and members<br>• make sure party members are present for important votes<br>• influence party members to vote with leaders |
| **Majority and Minority Whips**<br>• same as in Senate | **Committee Chairmen**<br>• head standing committees<br>• have major say in which bills the committee will consider, in what order, and at what length, and what witnesses the committee will call<br>• manage debate and steer passage on floor |
| **Committee Chairmen**<br>• same as in Senate | |

---

## SKILLS DEVELOPMENT

### COMPARE VIEWPOINTS

Before students begin the role-playing activity in this section, you may want to review tips on comparing viewpoints in the Skills Handbook, p. S15.

---

SECTION **1**

# Congress Organizes

### Guiding Question

**How do constitutional and party officers keep Congress organized?**
Use a table like the one below to keep track of the officers in each house.

| Congressional Leaders and Their Duties | |
|---|---|
| House | Senate |
| **Speaker of the House**<br>• presides and keeps order | |

### Political Dictionary

- Speaker of the House
- President of the Senate
- President *pro tempore*
- party caucus
- floor leader
- majority leader
- minority leader
- whip
- committee chairman
- seniority rule

### Objectives

1. Describe how and when Congress convenes.
2. Compare the roles of the presiding officers in the Senate and the House.
3. Identify the duties of the party officers in each house.
4. Describe how committee chairmen are chosen and explain their role in the legislative process.

**Image Above:** John Boehner (R., Ohio), became Speaker of the House in 2011.

What comes to mind when you hear the word *Congress?* The Capitol? Your members of Congress? Some particular bill? Those senators and representatives you often see on the evening news? Of course, you know that the nation's lawmaking body is much more than that. It is in fact a very complex enterprise, and much larger than most people realize. Some 30,000 men and women work for the legislative branch today, and Congress appropriates some $4 billion every year to finance its own many-sided operations.[1]

## Congress Convenes

Congress convenes—begins a new term—every two years, on January 3 of every odd-numbered year. Each new term follows the general elections in November.

**Opening Day in the House** Every other January, the 435 men and women who have been elected to the House come together at the Capitol to begin a new term. At that point, they are, in effect, just so many representatives-elect. Because all 435 of its seats are up for election every two years, the House technically has no sworn members, no rules, and no organization until its opening-day ceremonies are held.

Senator Sherrod Brown (D., Ohio) sat in the House of Representatives for seven terms before he won election to the Senate in 2006. He remembers his first opening day, in 1993, this way:

### PRIMARY SOURCE

> Walking around the chamber the first day, I was awed and nervous. . . . [Q]uestions gnawed at me when I walked into that august [grand] room, when I met several members about whom I had read and whom I had seen on television. And then I thought about the President of the United States coming to address us— 'Do I deserve to be here with all these people? How did I get here? Will I measure up? How was I chosen for this privilege?'
>
> —Sherrod Brown, *Congress From the Inside*

---

# Focus on the Basics

**FACTS:** • Congress begins each new term in early January of every odd-numbered year. • The Speaker of the House controls the agenda in the House of Representatives. • The Vice President is the President of the Senate but votes only to break a tie. • The majority and minority leaders of each house carry out the decisions of their party's caucus. • Party whips act as liaisons between members and leadership. • Committee chairmen are usually chosen by seniority.

**CONCEPTS:** continuous body, seniority rule

**ENDURING UNDERSTANDINGS:** • The Speaker of the House and the majority leaders and committee chairmen in both houses are members of the majority party, and wield the most power in Congress.

The clerk of the House in the preceding term presides at the beginning of the first day's session.[2] The clerk calls the chamber to order and checks the roll of representatives-elect. Those members-to-be then choose a Speaker, who will be their permanent presiding officer. By custom, the Speaker is a long-standing member of the majority party, and election on the floor is only a formality. The majority party's members in the House have settled the matter beforehand.

The Speaker then takes the oath of office. By tradition, the oath is administered by the Dean of the House, the member-elect with the longest record of service in the House.[3] With that accomplished, the Speaker swears in the rest of the members, as a body. The Democrats take their seats to the right of the center aisle; the Republicans, to the left.

Next, the House elects its clerk, parliamentarian, sergeant at arms, chief administrative officer, and chaplain. None of these people are members of the House, and their elections are also a formality. The majority party has already decided the matter.

Then, the House adopts the rules that will govern its proceedings through the term. The rules of the House have been developing for over 200 years, and they are contained in a volume of about 400 pages. They are readopted, most often with little or no change, at the beginning of each term, though they are occasionally and sometimes extensively amended during a term. Thus, in 2009, the rules were amended to repeal a limit on the number of terms any member can chair any House committee. That controversial limit (of three terms, six years) had been adopted by a newly elected Republican majority at the beginning of the 104th Congress in 1995.

Finally, members of the 20 permanent committees of the House are appointed by a floor vote. With that, the House is organized.

**Opening Day in the Senate** The Senate is a continuous body. It has been organized without interruption since its first session in 1789. Recall that only one third of the seats are up for election every two years. Two thirds of the Senate's membership is carried over from one term to the next. As a result, the Senate does not face large organizational problems at the beginning of a term. Its first-day session is nearly always fairly short and routine, even when the elections have brought a change in the majority party. Newly elected and reelected members must be sworn in, vacancies in Senate organization and on committees must be filled, and a few other details attended to.

**State of the Union Message** When the Senate is notified that the House of Representatives is organized, a joint committee of the two chambers is appointed and instructed "to wait upon the President of the United States and inform him that a quorum of each House is assembled and that the Congress is ready to receive any communication he may be pleased to make."

Within a few weeks—in late January or early February—the President delivers the

**preside**
*v.* to act in the role of chairperson

**quorum**
*n.* a minimum number of members required to do business

Opening day in the House of Representatives, February 8, 1906

---

1 More than 15,000 of those who work in the legislative branch have jobs in the House or Senate—in members' offices, as committee staff, or in some part of the congressional administrative organization. The other 15,000 or so work in the various support agencies Congress has, over time, established within the legislative branch—including the Library of Congress, the Government Printing Office, the Congressional Budget Office, and the Government Accountability Office.

2 The clerk, a nonmember officer of the House, is picked by the majority party and usually keeps the post until that party loses control of the chamber.

3 Today, John D. Dingell (D., Michigan), who first became a member of the House on December 13, 1955.

# Get Started

## LESSON GOALS

Students will . . .

- complete a flowchart of opening-day events in the House.

- describe the leadership roles in Congress by taking part in a press conference simulation.

## BEFORE CLASS

Assign the section, the graphic organizer in the text, and the Reading Comprehension Worksheet (Unit 3 All-in-One, p. 125) before class.

**L2 Differentiate** Reading Comprehension Worksheet (Unit 3 All-in-One, p. 127)

## BELLRINGER

Display Transparency 12A, Opening Day in the House of Representatives. Ask students to copy and complete the flowchart in their notebook.

---

# Differentiated Resources

The following resources are located in the All-in-One, Unit 3, Chapter 12, Section 1:

- **L2** Prereading and Vocabulary Worksheet (p. 121)
- **L3** Reading Comprehension Worksheet (p. 125)
- **L2** Reading Comprehension Worksheet (p. 127)
- **L3** Core Worksheet A (p. 129)
- **L3 L2** Core Worksheet B (p. 130)
- **L3** Quiz A (p. 131)
- **L2** Quiz B (p. 132)

# Teach

To present this topic using online resources, use the lesson presentations at **PearsonSchool.com/phgovt.**

### DISCUSS OPENING-DAY ACTIVITIES

Tell students that today's lesson will introduce them to the organization of Congress and the details of how that organization helps it get its work done. Display Transparency 12B, Opening Day in the House of Representatives, which contains the solutions to the Bellringer transparency. Discuss each step in the process of organizing the House on opening day. Ask: **What happens in the Senate on opening day?** *(New and reelected members are sworn in. Organizational and committee vacancies are filled.)* **Why is opening day in the Senate so different from opening day in the House?** *(In the House, all seats are up for election each term. Therefore, the House needs to be organized each term. In the Senate, only a third of the seats are up for election, so only one third of the Senate needs to be sworn in and few positions need to be filled, making opening-day activities shorter and more routine than in the House.)*

### PRESENT THE TOPIC

Direct students to the "Leadership in the 112th Congress" chart in this section (or to the updated version at **PearsonSchool.com/phgovt**). Walk through these positions, pointing out the differences between the constitutional officers (Speaker, President of the Senate, and President *pro tempore*) and the party officers *(the remainder)*. Ask: **Why does Congress have party officers in addition to constitutional officers?** *(Constitutional officers facilitate the work of the entire chamber as well as their own party's agenda. Party officers focus on party business. They organize members to prepare and pass measures on the party's legislative agenda.)*

**L4 Differentiate** In a classroom with a number of advanced students, you may wish to extend the discussion to cover the reasons that parties and party officers evolved. *(Parties are not part of the Constitution, but have existed since it was signed. The size of Congress has grown tremendously and requires more organization than is specified in the Constitution. Congress also has the power to organize itself.)*

---

## Answers

**Checkpoint** The State of the Union address reports on the status of the nation, as the President sees it, in terms of domestic and foreign policy. The address also lays out the broad policies the administration expects to follow and includes specific legislative recommendations.

**332** Congress in Action

---

*judicious*
*adj.* reasonable

annual State of the Union message to a joint session of Congress. The speech is a major political event and is based on this constitutional command:

> ### FROM THE CONSTITUTION
>
> **He shall from time to time give to the Congress Information of the State of the Union, and recommend to their Consideration such Measures as he shall judge necessary and expedient . . .**
>
> —**Article II, Section 3**

From Woodrow Wilson's first message in 1913, the President has almost always presented his annual assessment in person. Members of Congress, together with the members of the Cabinet, the justices of the Supreme Court, the foreign diplomatic corps, and other dignitaries, assemble in the House chamber to hear him.

In the address, the President reports on the state of the nation as he or she sees it, in both domestic and foreign policy terms. The message is widely covered by the news media, and it is very closely followed both here and abroad. In fact, the chief executive's speech is as much a message to the American people, and to the world, as it is an address to Congress. In it, the President lays out the broad shape of the policies the administration expects to follow and the course the chief executive has charted for the nation. The message regularly includes a number of specific legislative recommendations, along with a plea that Congress will enact them. Its presentation is soon followed by scores of bills drawn up in the executive branch and introduced in the House and Senate by various members of the President's party.

With the conclusion of the speech, the joint session is adjourned. Each house then separately turns to the legislative business that will come before it.

## The Presiding Officers

The Constitution provides for the presiding officers of each house of Congress—the Speaker of the House and the President of the Senate. Article I, Section 2, Clause 5 directs that "The House of Representatives shall choose their Speaker and other Officers. . . ." And Article I, Section 3, Clause 4 declares: "The Vice President of the United States shall be President of the Senate. . . ."

**The Speaker of the House** Of the two positions, the **Speaker of the House** is by far the more important and more powerful within the halls of Congress. This is particularly so because the Speaker is both the elected presiding officer of the House and the acknowledged leader of its majority party.

Although neither the Constitution nor its own rules require it, the House has always chosen the Speaker from among its own members. Today, the post is held by John Boehner (R., Ohio). He was first elected to the House in 1990 and became Speaker in 2011.[4]

The Speaker is expected to preside in a fair and _judicious_ manner and regularly does. The Speaker is also expected to aid the fortunes of the majority party and its legislative goals, and regularly does that, too.

Nearly all of the Speaker's powers revolve around two duties: to preside and to keep order. The Speaker chairs most sessions of the House but often appoints another member as temporary presiding officer. No member may speak until he or she is recognized by the Speaker. The presiding officer also interprets and applies the rules, refers bills to committee, rules on points of order (questions of procedure raised by members), puts motions to a vote, and decides the outcome of most votes taken on the floor of the House. (The Speaker can be overridden by a vote of the House, but that almost never happens.) The Speaker also names the members of all select and conference committees and must sign all bills and resolutions passed by the House.

As an elected member of the House, the Speaker may debate and vote on any matter

---

4 Speaker Boehner is the 53rd person to hold the post. The first Speaker, elected in 1789, was Frederick A. C. Muhlenburg, a Federalist from Pennsylvania. Sam Rayburn (D., Texas) held the office for a record of nearly ten terms in the period from 1940 to 1961. Mr. Boehner succeeded Nancy Pelosi (D., California), who was the first woman to ever hold the post (2007–2011). In the past 55 years, three Republicans—Newt Gingrich of Georgia (1995–1999), Dennis Hastert of Illinois (1999–2007), and Mr. Boehner—have held the Speakership.

---

# Political Cartoon Mini-Lesson

After discussing opening-day activities, display Transparency 12C, State of the Union Message, to begin a discussion of the President's annual address to Congress. Point out that the man in the cartoon is President George W. Bush. Ask: **Why is the dog snarling?** *(The dog has identified President Bush's energy proposals as a bomb.)* **How do you think members of Congress will react to the President's proposals?** *(The cartoon suggests that members of Congress will react negatively, like the dog.)* **Based on this cartoon, do you think the President's party controls Congress? How do you know?** *(No. Members of the President's party usually agree with his proposals, so he would get a warmer reception if his party were the majority.)*

## Leadership in the 112th Congress

GOVERNMENT ONLINE
**Update**
Check out who holds these offices today at
**PearsonSchool.com/phgovt**

**HOUSE**      **SENATE**

### Presiding Officer and Party Leader

**Speaker of the House**
JOHN BOEHNER
(R., Ohio)

### Presiding Officers

**President of the Senate**
JOE BIDEN
(D., Delaware)

**President Pro Tempore**
DANIEL K. INOUYE
(D., Hawaii)

### Party Officers

**Majority Floor Leader**
ERIC CANTOR
(R., Virginia)

**Minority Floor Leader**
NANCY PELOSI
(D., California)

**Majority Whip**
KEVIN MCCARTHY
(R., California)

**Minority Whip**
STENY HOYER
(D., Maryland)

### Party Officers

**Majority Floor Leader**
HARRY REID
(D., Nevada)

**Minority Floor Leader**
MITCH MCCONNELL
(R., Kentucky)

**Majority Whip**
DICK DURBIN
(D., Illinois)

**Minority Whip**
JON KYL
(R., Arizona)

▶▶ **Interpreting Charts** Party and constitutional leadership roles are very important in both houses of Congress. **How can you tell which party holds power in the House? The Senate?**

---

before that body. That seldom happens, but when it does, the Speaker appoints another member as the temporary presiding officer and he or she then occupies the Speaker's chair. The Speaker does not often vote, and the House rules say only that the Speaker *must* vote to break a tie. Notice then, that because a tie vote defeats a question, the Speaker occasionally votes to cause a tie and so defeat a proposal.

The Speaker of the House follows the Vice President in the line of succession to the presidency. That fact is a considerable testimony to the power and importance of both the office and the person who holds it.

**The President of the Senate** The Constitution makes the Vice President the **President of the Senate,** the Senate's presiding officer. This means that (1) unlike the House, the Senate does not choose its own presiding

officer and (2) unlike the Speaker of the House, the Senate's presiding officer is not in fact a member of that body. Indeed, the Vice President might not even be a member of the party that controls the Senate.

All of this adds up to the major reason why the Vice President plays a much less powerful role in the Senate than that played by the Speaker in the House. Also note this important point: the Vice President's career path, the route traveled to the post, is a much different path than the one the Speaker has followed. The Vice President has not become the Senate's presiding officer out of long service in that body. He has, instead, come to the post out of a much different process—as you will see when we take a more detailed look at the vice presidency in Chapter 13.

The president of the Senate does have the usual powers of a presiding officer: to recognize members, put questions to a vote, and so

✔ **Checkpoint**
When must the Speaker vote?

---

# Leadership Mini-Lesson

**LEADERS OF CONGRESS** Use the chart on this page or the online update at PearsonSchool.com/phgovt as a starting point for students to research the current congressional leaders. In groups or individually, ask students to research the backgrounds of these leaders, which can be found on their personal Web sites at www.house.gov or www.senate.gov. Then have students present a brief summary of each member's background and discuss what these leaders have in common.

---

## INTRODUCE THE ACTIVITY

Tell students that today they will learn about the organization of Congress by playing the role of a congressional leader or a member of the media during a press conference.

**L2 ELL Differentiate** Explain what a press conference is, who attends, and what happens there. If possible, play a video clip of a national press conference.

## ASSIGN ROLES FOR PRESS CONFERENCE

Assign each student a role to play for a simulated press conference. Tell students that the press conference is for foreign journalists unfamiliar with the U.S. legislative system. The media's goal is to ask questions that would help them write a story for a foreign newspaper, describing the roles of congressional leaders.

Assign students to these roles:

- Speaker of the House
- Majority floor leader (House)
- Majority whip (House)
- Minority floor leader (House)
- Minority whip (House)
- President of the Senate
- President *pro tempore*
- Majority floor leader (Senate)
- Majority whip (Senate)
- Minority floor leader (Senate)
- Minority whip (Senate)
- Members of the media

**L1 L2 Differentiate** Assign students to be members of the media.

**L2 ELL Differentiate** Assign ELLs a native-speaking partner to help address errors in grammar and to practice questions before asking them in front of the full class.

Tell students to go to the Update to find out who the congressional leaders are today.

---

## Answers

**Interpreting Charts** The Speaker of the House and the President *pro tempore* of the Senate are always members of the majority party.

**Checkpoint** to break a tie

# DISTRIBUTE CORE WORKSHEET

To congressional leaders, distribute the Chapter 12 Section 1 Core Worksheet A (Unit 3 All-in-One, p. 129), which guides students in preparing for their role.

To members of the media, distribute the Chapter 12 Section 1 Core Worksheet B (Unit 3 All-in-One, p. 130), which guides students in preparing questions for the congressional leaders.

Give students adequate time to prepare their roles.

Tell students to go to the Online Update to learn about party strength in Congress today.

---

## Answers

**Analyzing Charts** Democrats: 269 members in the House (1983–1985) and 58 members in the Senate (2009–2011); Republicans: 242 members in the House (2011–2013) and 55 members in the Senate (1997–1999, 1999–2001, 2005–2007)

**Checkpoint** the President *pro tempore*

**334** Congress in Action

---

# Party Strength in House and Senate

| House 435 Members (Dem) | House (Rep) | Term | Senate 100 Members (Dem) | Senate (Rep) |
|---|---|---|---|---|
| 269 | 166 | 1983 – 1985 | 46 | 54 |
| 253 | 182 | 1985 – 1987 | 47 | 53 |
| 258 | 177 | 1987 – 1989 | 55 | 45 |
| 260 | 175 | 1989 – 1991 | 55 | 45 |
| 267 (1) | 167 | 1991 – 1993 | 56 | 44 |
| 258 | 176 | 1993 – 1995 | 57 | 43 |
| 204 (1) | 230 | 1995 – 1997 | 48 | 52 |
| 207 (1) | 227 | 1997 – 1999 | 45 | 55 |
| 211 (1) | 223 | 1999 – 2001 | 45 | 55 |
| 212 (1) | 221 (1) | 2001 – 2003 | 50 | 50 |
| 205 (1) | 229 | 2003 – 2005 | 48 | 51 (1) |
| 202 (1) | 232 | 2005 – 2007 | 44 | 55 (1) |
| 233 | 202 | 2007 – 2009 | 49 (2) | 49 |
| 257 | 178 | 2009 – 2011 | 58 (2) | 40 |
| 193 | 242 | 2011 – 2013 | 51 (2) | 47 |

Democrat    Republican    Independent
Majority Republican    Majority Democrat

SOURCE: Clerk of the House; Secretary of the Senate: Election returns

▸▸ **Analyzing Charts** This chart shows the strength of each party at the start of the past fifteen terms of Congress. Independents are placed with their caucus party. *What is the largest majority that each party has held in each house over the past 30 years?*

---

✔ **Checkpoint**
Who presides over the Senate if the Vice President is absent?

on. However, the Vice President cannot take the floor to speak or debate and may vote *only* to break a tie.

Any influence a Vice President may have in the Senate is largely the result of personal abilities and relationships. Several of the more recent Vice Presidents came to that office from the Senate: Harry Truman, Alben Barkley, Richard Nixon, Lyndon Johnson, Hubert Humphrey, Walter Mondale, Dan Quayle, Al Gore, and, today, Joe Biden. Each was able to build at least some power into the position out of that earlier experience.

The Senate does have another presiding officer, the **President pro tempore,** who serves in the Vice President's absence. The President *pro tempore,* or President *pro tem* for short, is elected by the Senate itself and is always a leading member of the majority party—usually its longest serving member. Today, the post is occupied by Senator Daniel K. Inouye (D., Hawaii). Senator Inouye, who was elected to his first term in the upper house in 1963, became President *pro tempore* in 2010.

The President *pro tem* follows the Speaker of the House in the line of presidential succession. Other senators do frequently preside over the Senate, on a temporary basis; newly elected members regularly do so early in their terms.

## Party Officers

Congress is a *political* body. This is so for two leading reasons: (1) Congress is the nation's central *policy*-making body, and (2) Congress is *partisan*. Reflecting its political character, both houses of Congress are organized along party lines.

**The Party Caucus** The **party caucus** is a closed meeting of the members of each party in each house. These meetings are regularly held just before Congress convenes in January and occasionally during a session. In recent years

---

# Background

**PORTRAIT OF A SPEAKER** Physically, Sam Rayburn was not a big man. But as Speaker of the House for a record 17 years, "Mr. Sam" cast a long shadow. Becoming Speaker in 1940, Rayburn, a staunch Democrat, presided at a time when most formal power in the House resided with the committee chairs, not the Speaker. According to Mr. Sam, "You cannot lead people by trying to drive them. Persuasion and reason are the only ways to lead them." Rayburn put his considerable persuasive skills to work in his famous "Board of Education," a room tucked away beneath the House chamber. There he regularly summoned influential Democrats to discuss issues and twist arms. Today, as Congress organizes each new term, members vie for newly vacated offices. But one room is not up for grabs. By tradition, the new Speaker inherits Rayburn's legendary hideaway.

the Republicans have called their caucus in each house the party conference, and the Democrats now use this term in the Senate, too.

A caucus deals mostly with matters related to party organization, such as the selection of the party's floor leaders and questions of committee membership. It sometimes takes stands on particular bills, but neither party tries to force its members to follow its caucus decisions, nor can it.[5]

The policy committee is composed of the party's top leadership. It acts as an executive committee for the party caucus. That body is known as the policy committee in each party's structure in the Senate and in the Republicans' organization in the House. However, it is called the steering and policy committee by the Democrats in the lower chamber.

**✔ Checkpoint**
What is a party caucus?

5 A number of informal groupings of members of Congress meet to discuss matters of mutual interest. Some are partisan, others are bipartisan, and several use the word *caucus* in their titles. Some of these groups include, for example, the Congressional Black Caucus, the House Republican Study Committee, the Pro-Life Caucus, and the Congressional Hispanic Caucus.

## Representation by State, 112th Congress

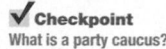

**GOVERNMENT** ONLINE
**Update**
Check out updated representation by State at
**PearsonSchool.com/phgovt**

The colors on these maps indicate the party composition of each State's delegation in the House and Senate. **Which States are the same color on both maps?**

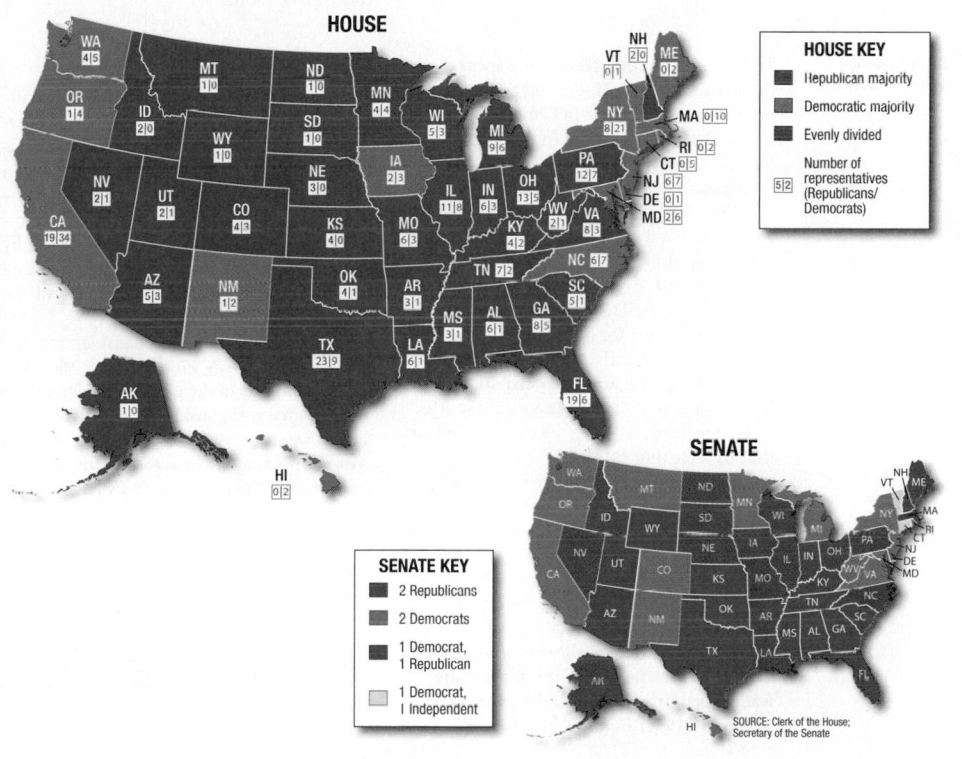

**HOUSE KEY**
- Republican majority
- Democratic majority
- Evenly divided
- 5|2 Number of representatives (Republicans/Democrats)

**SENATE KEY**
- 2 Republicans
- 2 Democrats
- 1 Democrat, 1 Republican
- 1 Democrat, 1 Independent

SOURCE: Clerk of the House; Secretary of the Senate

# Background

**RED STATES, BLUE STATES** As election results roll in, television viewers see States on a map turn red for a Republican win and blue for a Democratic win. News outlets also regularly refer to "red States" and "blue States." This has not always been the case. Earliest red-blue references date back to 1900, when the *Chicago Tribune* followed the traditional European practice of associating red with liberal parties and blue with conservative parties. In the aftermath of the disputed 2000 election, news sources began to reach consensus on the current color scheme. However, stereotyping a State as "red" or "blue" ignores the diversity within each State. For example, California has gone Democratic in all recent presidential elections, yet it had a Republican governor from 2003 until 2011. In using these polarizing designations, we must keep in mind that no State is all red or all blue.

## Answers

**L3 Differentiate** Display Transparency 12D, Representation by State, 112th Congress. Use this map and the information in the Background Note to lead a discussion about the "red state" and "blue state" labels used by the media.

**L4 Differentiate** Have students go to www.house.gov to research each party's position on a specific issue. For example, how does each party stand on the issue of the rising cost of healthcare? Students will be able to gather information by following links to the office of the Speaker, majority and minority leaders and whips, and the caucuses for each party. Have students present a summary of the issue and the parties' positions to the class.

**L2 Differentiate** Display Transparency 12E, Party Strength of House and Senate. Help students read the graph. Point out that there are actually two graphs—one representing the House and the other, the Senate. Ask: **Which party was the majority in the House between 2009 and 2011?** (Democrats) **How do you know? Name three ways.** (blue bar is longer than red bar; number on blue bar is larger than number on red bar; the blue donkey symbol means majority Democrat)

**L4 Differentiate** Have students conduct research on the changing role of the Speaker of the House. Ask them to summarize their research in brief reports.

## Answers

**Analyzing Cartoons** Congress often asks difficult questions, making those who are called to testify uncomfortable.

**Checkpoint** Floor leaders carry out decisions of their parties' leadership and steer floor action to their parties' benefit.

▶▶ **Interpreting Cartoons** Congressional committees hold hearings about a wide variety of matters. *What does the cartoon say about the feelings of those who are asked to give testimony?*

✔**Checkpoint**
What do floor leaders do?

**The Floor Leaders** Next to the Speaker, the **floor leaders** in the House and Senate are the most important officers in Congress. They do not hold official positions in either chamber. Rather, they are party officers, picked for their posts by their party colleagues.

The floor leaders are legislative strategists. Assisted by paid staff, they try to carry out the decisions of their parties' caucuses and steer floor action to their parties' benefit. Each of them is also the chief spokesman for his party in his chamber. All of that calls for political skills of a high order. Senator Howard Baker (R., Tennessee), one of the Senate's most effective floor leaders, often likened his job to that of "herding cats."

The floor leader of the party that holds the majority of seats in each house of Congress is known as the **majority leader.** The floor leader of the party that holds the minority of seats in each house is the **minority leader.** The majority leader is the more powerful in each house—for the obvious reason that the majority party has more seats (more votes) than the other party has. And, the majority leader very largely controls the order of business on the floor in his or her chamber.

The two floor leaders in each house are assisted by party **whips.** The majority whip and the minority whip are, in effect, assistant floor leaders. Each of them is chosen at the party caucus, almost always at the floor leader's recommendation. A number of assistant whips serve in the House.

Whips serve as a liaison—a two-way link—between the party's leadership and its rank-and-file members.[6] The whips check with party members and tell the floor leader which members, and how many votes, can be counted on in any particular matter. The whips also see that all members of the party are present for important votes and that they vote with the party leadership. If a member must be absent for some reason, a whip sees that that member is paired with a member of the other party who will also be absent that day or who agrees not to vote on certain measures at that day's session—so one nonvote cancels out another.

## Committee Chairmen

The bulk of the work of Congress, especially in the House, is really done in committee. Thus, **committee chairmen**—those members who head the standing committees in each chamber—hold very strategic posts. The chairman of each of these permanent committees is chosen from the majority party by the majority party caucus.[7] These men and women are always ranking members of the majority party.

Although committee chairmen are less powerful now than in years past, they still have a major say in such matters as which bills a committee will consider and in what order and at what length, whether public hearings are to be held, and what witnesses the committee will call. When a committee's bill has been

---

6  The term *whip* was borrowed from British politics. There, it came from the "whipper-in" in a fox hunt, the rider who is supposed to keep the hounds bunched in a pack.
7  The title *chairman* is used here because this is the form used in both houses of Congress today, both officially and informally. Only 29 women (11 in the Senate, 18 in the House) have chaired a standing committee. Five standing committees (four in the Senate, one in the House) are chaired by women today, as you can see in the tables in Section 2, where the current chairmen of the standing committees are identified.

# Background

**BEHIND THE SCENES** At age 85, Representative Ralph Hall (R., Texas) was the oldest member of the House in 2008—but not the oldest to have ever been elected to Congress (he was elected at age 57). That honor goes to Representative Isaac Bloom of New York, who was elected in 1803 at the age of 87. Second in line is Representative James Bowler, a Chicago Democrat, who won a special election for a seat left vacant by Representative Al Sabath's death. Long before that event, Bowler and Sabath had served together on the city council. The council reached a deadlock over which of the two men should run for a congressional seat. Finally, the two men tossed a coin. Sabath won, with Bowler agreeing to fill the seat when Sabath left. Forty-six years later, he did. Bowler was sworn into Congress for his first term in the early 1950s, at the age of 78.

reported—approved for consideration—to the floor, the chairman usually manages the debate and tries to steer it to final passage.

We shall take a closer look at committees and their chairs in a moment. But, first, consider the seniority rule.

**The Seniority Rule** The **seniority rule** is, in fact, an unwritten custom. It dates from the late 1800s, and is still more or less closely followed in both houses today. The seniority rule provides that the most important posts in Congress, in both the formal and the party organizations, will be held by those party members with the longest records of service. (Notice that seniority rule does not apply to the presiding officers or to the floor leaders in either chamber. As you've seen, their selection is otherwise provided for.)

The rule is applied most strictly to the choice of committee chairmen. The head of each committee is almost always the longest-serving majority party member of that committee. The rule is also followed quite closely in the selection of those members who chair the several subcommittees into which nearly all the standing committees are divided.

**Criticism of the Seniority Rule** Critics of the seniority rule are many, and they do make a strong case. They insist that the seniority system ignores ability, rewards mere length of service, and works to discourage younger members. Its opponents also note that the rule means that a committee head often comes from a "safe" constituency—a State or district in which one party regularly wins the seat. With no play of fresh and conflicting forces in those places, critics claim, the chairman of a committee is often out of touch with current public opinion.

Defenders of the seniority rule argue that it ensures that a powerful and experienced member will head each committee. They also say that the rule encourages members to stay on a particular committee and so, over time, gain a wide-ranging knowledge of matters that fall within that committee's jurisdiction. In addition, they note that the rule is fairly easy to apply and that it very nearly eliminates the possibility of fights within the party.

The rule's opponents have gained some ground in recent years. Thus, the House Republican Conference (caucus) now picks several GOP members of House committees by secret ballot. House Democrats use secret ballots to choose a committee chairman whenever 20 percent of their caucus requests that procedure.

Whatever the arguments against the seniority rule, it is unlikely to be eliminated. Those members with the real power to abolish the rule are also the ones who reap the largest benefits from it.

**jurisdiction**
*n.* the range of matters under the committee's control

---

**Essential Questions Journal**
To continue to build a response to the chapter Essential Question, go to your **Essential Questions Journal.**

## SECTION 1 ASSESSMENT

1. **Guiding Question** Use your completed table to answer this question: How do constitutional and party officers keep Congress organized?

**Key Terms and Comprehension**

2. Describe opening day in the House.

3. Summarize the duties of the **floor leaders** in each house.

4. (a) What is the **seniority rule**? (b) What are the arguments for and against it?

**Critical Thinking**

5. **Understand Point of View (a)** Senator Howard Baker likened his job as majority leader to that of "herding cats." What does that mean? **(b)** What problems do majority leaders face?

6. **Make Comparisons** Compare and contrast the positions of Speaker of the House and President of the Senate. Which is more powerful, and why?

7. **Draw Conclusions** How important are committee chairmen in Congress? Explain.

**Quick Write**

**Persuasive Essay: Gather Details** The structure of Congress has evolved over time. As you read the chapter, take notes on the organizational structure and how it affects the lawmaking process.

---

# Assess and Remediate

**L3** Distribute the Rubric for Assessing a Newspaper Article (Unit 3 All-in-One, p. 169). Have students write an article explaining the U.S. legislative system.

**L1** **L2** **ELL** Distribute the rubric noted above. Have students write an article about one leadership position in either the House or Senate.

**L3** Ask students to construct an organizational chart that shows the hierarchy of power in Congress.

**L3** Assign the Section 1 Assessment questions.

**L3** Section Quiz A (Unit 3 All-in-One, p. 131)

**L2** Section Quiz B (Unit 3 All-in-One, p. 132)

Have students complete the review activities in the digital lesson presentation and continue their work in the **Essential Questions Journal.**

### REMEDIATION

| If Your Students Have Trouble With | Strategies For Remediation |
|---|---|
| The organization of Congress (Question 1) | Make a chart showing the leadership roles. |
| The duties of floor leaders (Questions 3, 5, 6) | Have students make posters comparing leadership in the House with leadership in the Senate. |
| The seniority rule and committee chairmen (Questions 4, 7) | Make a T chart showing the arguments for and against the seniority rule. |
| Opening day in the House (Question 2) | Lead students in a exercise in which they portray opening day in the House. Divide students into two groups: Democrats and Republicans. |

---

# Assessment Answers

**1.** Constitutional officers preside and keep formal order over the proceedings. Party officers keep legislative order by explaining party positions and educating party members on bills coming before each chamber.

**2.** The members choose a Speaker, who administers the oath to the rest of the House. Then they elect officers, adopt the rules, and select members of standing committees.

**3.** Floor leaders are legislative strategists who carry out the decisions of their party's caucuses.

Majority leaders control the order of business on the floor.

**4. (a)** custom in which most important posts go to party members with the longest service **(b)** Arguments for: ensures a powerful, experienced member will head each committee; prevents fights within party. Arguments against: discourages younger members; rewards longevity instead of merit; chairmen often come from "safe" seats and are thus out of touch with public opinion

**5. (a)** and **(b)** It is often hard to get Congress members to go along with the party position.

**6.** The President of the Senate is the Vice President, who is not a member and holds little power there. He or she cannot speak in floor debate and may vote only to break a tie. The Speaker is the most powerful member of Congress, because he or she is the elected presiding officer and leader of the majority party.

**7.** Committee chairs have great influence over what bills Congress will pass in their committee's jurisdiction.

**QUICK WRITE** Students should note organizational structures and their effects on lawmaking.

# How do committees help Congress do its work?

| Standing Committee | Select Committee | Joint Committee | Conference Committee |
|---|---|---|---|
| • permanent; considers all bills of similar subject matter<br>• 20 in House; 16 in Senate<br>• decides fate of most bills<br>• divided into subcommittees<br>• House Rules Committee controls flow of bills to floor and sets conditions for their consideration there | • usually temporary<br>• set up for special purpose<br>• Speaker or President of Senate appoints members<br>• investigate current issue | • composed of members of both houses<br>• some are temporary select committees<br>• some are permanent<br>• some investigate and issue periodic reports | • temporary joint committee<br>• resolves differences in House and Senate versions of a bill<br>• produces compromise bill that both houses will accept |

# Get Started

## LESSON GOALS

Students will . . .

- examine the need for committees to divide work by creating an organization for an event.
- identify jurisdictions of House committees by matching committee names to descriptions.
- trace the path of the 2007 Farm Bill through the House.

## SKILLS DEVELOPMENT

### DECISION MAKING

Before students begin the Bellringer activity, you may want to review the information on decision making in the Skills Handbook, p. S18.

---

# Committees in Congress

## Guiding Question

**How do committees help Congress do its work?** Use a table to keep track of the purpose and characteristics of each type of congressional committee.

| Standing Committee | Select Committee | Joint Committee | Conference Committee |
|---|---|---|---|
| • | • usually temporary | • | • |
| • | | • | • |
| • | | • | • |
| • | | | |

## Political Dictionary

- standing committee
- subcommittee
- select committee
- joint committee
- conference committee

## Objectives

1. Explain how standing committees function.
2. Describe the responsibilities and duties of the House Rules Committee.
3. Describe the role of select committees.
4. Compare the functions of joint and conference committees.

**Image Above:** Former Secretary of Defense Donald Rumsfeld testifying at a defense appropriations hearing

Do you know the phrase "a division of labor"? It means dividing the work to be done, assigning the several parts of the overall task to various members of the group. The House and the Senate are both so large, and their agendas are so crowded with so many different matters, that both chambers must rely on a division of labor. That is to say, much of the work that Congress does is in fact done by committees. Indeed, Representative Clem Miller (D., Calif.) once described Congress as "a collection of committees that come together in a chamber periodically to approve of one another's actions."

## Standing Committees

In 1789, the House and Senate each adopted the practice of naming a special committee to consider each bill as it was introduced. By 1794, there were more than 300 committees in each chamber. Each house then began to set up permanent panels, **standing committees,** to which all similar bills can be sent. The number of these committees has varied over the years. There are 20 standing committees in the House and 17 in the Senate today. Each House committee has from 10 to as many as 75 members, and each Senate committee has from 14 to 28. Representatives are normally assigned to one or two standing committees and senators to three or four.

The pivotal role these committees play in the lawmaking process cannot be overstated. Most bills receive their most thorough consideration in these bodies. Members of both houses regularly respect the decisions and follow the recommendations they make. Thus, the fate of most bills is usually decided in the various standing committees, not on the floor of either house. More than a century ago, Woodrow Wilson described "Congress in its committee rooms" as "Congress at work," and that remains true today.

Some panels are more prominent and more influential than others. As you would expect, most members try to win assignments to one of these major panels. The leading committees in the House are the Rules, Ways and Means, Appropriations, Armed Services, Judiciary, Foreign Affairs, and Agriculture committees. In the Senate, senators usually compete for places on the Foreign Relations; Appropriations; Finance; Judiciary; Armed Services; and Banking, Housing, and Urban Affairs committees.

# Focus on the Basics

**FACTS:** • Standing committees decide the fate of most bills. • The powerful House Rules Committee can speed, delay, or even prevent House action on a bill. • Both houses create temporary select committees to investigate current issues. • Joint committees are composed of members of both houses. • The majority party holds the majority in each committee. • Conference committees resolve differences in House and Senate versions of a bill to produce a single compromise bill.

**CONCEPTS:** separation of powers, role of government in public policy

**ENDURING UNDERSTANDINGS:** • Most work in Congress is divided among committees that focus on particular policy areas. • Most bills never make it out of committee. • Bills must pass both houses in identical form to go to the President.

Of course, some of the other committees are particularly attractive to some members. Thus, a representative whose district lies wholly within a major city might want to sit on the House Committee on Education and the Workforce. A senator from one of the western States might angle for assignment to the Senate's Committee on Energy and Natural Resources.

Most of the standing committees review bills dealing with particular policy matters—say, public lands, taxes, or veterans' affairs. However, there are four standing committees that are not organized as subject-matter bodies: in the House, the Rules Committee, the Committee on House Administration, and the Committee on Standards of Official Conduct, and in the Senate, the Committee on Rules and Administration.

When a bill is introduced in either house, the Speaker or the President of the Senate refers the measure to the appropriate standing committee. Thus, the Speaker sends all tax measures to the House Ways and Means Committee; in the Senate, tax measures go to the Finance Committee. A bill dealing with the creation of additional federal district judgeships will be sent to the Judiciary Committee in both chambers, and so on.

Recall that the chairman of each of the standing committees is chosen according to the seniority rule. As a consequence, most committee chairmen have served in Congress for at least 12 years and some much longer. The seniority rule is also closely applied in each house when it elects the other members of each of its committees.

The members of each standing committee are formally elected by a floor vote at the beginning of each term of Congress. In fact, each party has already drawn up its own committee roster before that vote, and the floor vote merely ratifies those party choices.

The majority party always holds a majority of the seats on each standing committee.[8] The other party is well represented, however.

8 The only exception is the House Committee on Standards of Official Conduct, with five Democrats and five Republicans. Often called the House Ethics Committee, it investigates allegations of misconduct by House members. In the Senate, a six-member bipartisan Select Committee on Ethics plays a similar role.

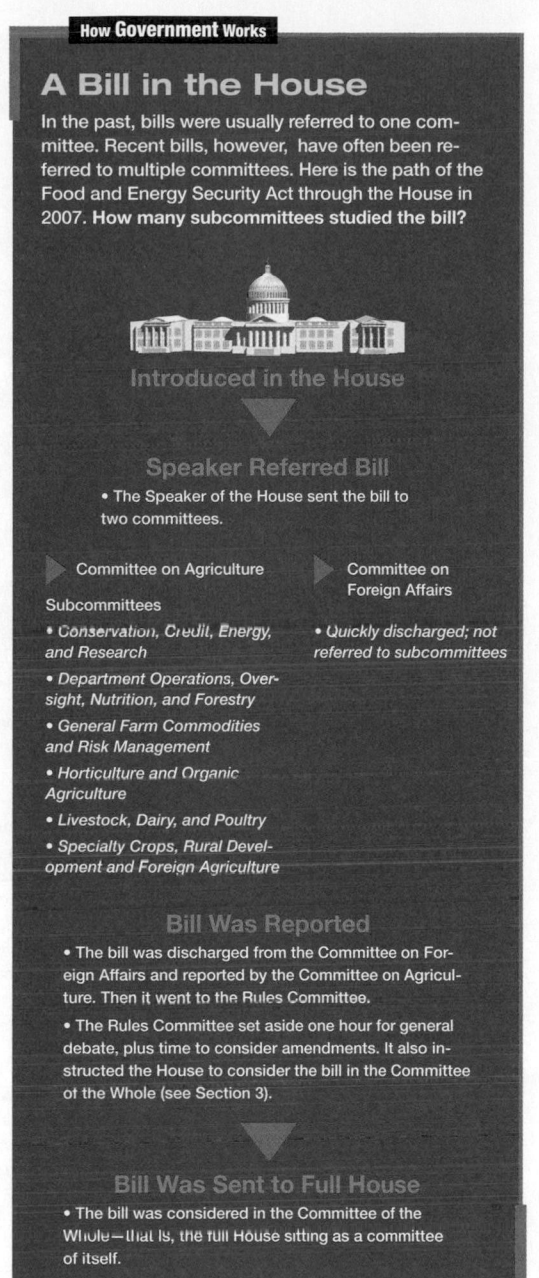

### How Government Works

## A Bill in the House

In the past, bills were usually referred to one committee. Recent bills, however, have often been referred to multiple committees. Here is the path of the Food and Energy Security Act through the House in 2007. How many subcommittees studied the bill?

**Introduced in the House**

**Speaker Referred Bill**
• The Speaker of the House sent the bill to two committees.

**Committee on Agriculture**

Subcommittees
• *Conservation, Credit, Energy, and Research*
• *Department Operations, Oversight, Nutrition, and Forestry*
• *General Farm Commodities and Risk Management*
• *Horticulture and Organic Agriculture*
• *Livestock, Dairy, and Poultry*
• *Specialty Crops, Rural Development and Foreign Agriculture*

**Committee on Foreign Affairs**
• *Quickly discharged; not referred to subcommittees*

**Bill Was Reported**
• The bill was discharged from the Committee on Foreign Affairs and reported by the Committee on Agriculture. Then it went to the Rules Committee.
• The Rules Committee set aside one hour for general debate, plus time to consider amendments. It also instructed the House to consider the bill in the Committee of the Whole (see Section 3).

**Bill Was Sent to Full House**
• The bill was considered in the Committee of the Whole—that is, the full House sitting as a committee of itself.

## Differentiated Resources

The following resources are located in the All-in-One, Unit 3, Chapter 12, Section 2:

- **L3** Reading Comprehension Worksheet (p. 133)
- **L2** Reading Comprehension Worksheet (p. 134)
- **L3** Core Worksheet (p. 135)
- **L2** Core Worksheet (p. 137)
- **L3** **L4** Extend Worksheet (p. 139)
- **L3** Quiz A (p. 141)
- **L2** Quiz B (p. 142)

Assign the section, the graphic organizer in the text, and the Reading Comprehension Worksheet (Unit 3 All-in-One, p. 133) before class.

**L2 Differentiate** Reading Comprehension Worksheet (Unit 3 All-in-One, p. 134)

**BELLRINGER**

Write on the board: **Think of a big event that you might like to plan, such as homecoming, a fundraiser, a science fair, or a sports tournament. Suppose you are the chairperson of the planning committee. Make a list of tasks required to plan and carry out the event. Then develop a system of committees and divide up the tasks among them. You may use paragraph or chart form.**

## Teach

To present this topic using online resources, use the lesson presentations at **PearsonSchool.com/phgovt.**

**REVIEW BELLRINGER**

Review students' organizational plans for their event. Ask them what committees they would form and the duties they would assign to each committee. Tell students that, similarly, Congress is broken down into committees to divide up the huge volume of work into manageable portions. Tell students that in Congress, committees do the bulk of the work. Ask: **Why does Congress use committees, rather than the full House or Senate, to shape bills?** *(With so many people, it would be difficult to get anything done. In addition, committees allow more work to be done because different committees address different issues.)*

**REVIEW COMMITTEES**

Write the following terms and definitions on the board, or ask students to provide definitions: *standing committees:* **permanent groups set up to consider bills on similar topics;** *select committees:* **temporary groups established for a specific purpose, usually for a limited time;** *joint committees:* **committees with members from both houses;** *conference committees:* **temporary joint committees that work out differences in bills passed in each house**

Spend a few minutes discussing why each type of committee is needed.

## Answer

**A Bill in the House** six

## DISTRIBUTE CORE WORKSHEET

Distribute the Chapter 12 Section 2 Core Worksheet (Unit 3 All-in-One, p. 135), which asks students to match committees to their jurisdictions. Explain that *jurisdiction* means "area of authority." Point out that a committee's name gives clues to its jurisdiction.

**L1 L2 Differentiate** Distribute the adapted Chapter 12 Section 2 Core Worksheet (Unit 3 All-in-One, p. 137), which asks students to identify fewer committees and employs simpler vocabulary to describe the committees.

**L2 ELL Differentiate** Explain the meanings of difficult words in committee names, such as *agriculture* (farming), *appropriations* (spending), *armed services* (military), *commerce* (business), *judiciary* (having to do with the courts, or judicial branch), and *infrastructure* (basic public facilities and services, such as transportation and communications systems, water lines, and power plants).

Tell students to go to the Online Update to check out House standing committee chairs today.

## Answers

**Analyzing Charts** Example predictions: The Appropriations Committee authorizes the use of money. The Natural Resources Committee reviews bills dealing with the management and conservation of the nation's forests, oil and coal reserves, and other natural resources.

### House Standing Committee Chairs

| Committee | Name, Party, State, Year Elected |
| --- | --- |
| Agriculture | Frank D. Lucas (R., Oklahoma), 1994 |
| Appropriations | Harold Rogers (R., Kentucky), 1980 |
| Armed Services | Howard P. "Buck" McKeon (R., California), 1992 |
| Budget | Paul D. Ryan (R., Wisconsin), 1998 |
| Education and Labor | John Kline (R., Minnesota), 2002 |
| Energy and Commerce | Fred Upton (R., Michigan), 1986 |
| Financial Services | Spencer Bachus (R., Alabama), 1992 |
| Foreign Affairs | Ileana Ros-Lehtinen (R., Florida), 1988 |
| Homeland Security | Peter T. King (R., New York), 1992 |
| House Administration | Dan Lungren (R., California), 1978 |
| Judiciary | Lamar Smith (R., Texas), 1986 |
| Natural Resources | Doc Hastings (R., Washington), 1994 |
| Oversight and Government Reform | Darrell Issa (R., California), 2000 |
| Rules | David Dreier (R., California), 1980 |
| Science and Technology | Ralph M. Hall (R., Texas), 1980 |
| Small Business | Sam Graves (R., Missouri), 2000 |
| Standards of Official Conduct | Jo Bonner (R., Alabama), 2002 |
| Transportation and Infrastructure | John L. Mica (R., Florida), 1992 |
| Veterans' Affairs | Jeff Miller (R., Florida), 2001 |
| Ways and Means | Dave Camp (R., Michigan), 1990 |

SOURCE: *Congressional Directory* and Clerk of the House

▸▸ **Analyzing Charts** These are the House standing committees and their chairs. *What predictions can you make about the committees' jurisdiction based on their titles?*

**⊙ GOVERNMENT** ONLINE
**Update**
To check out who holds these positions today, go to PearsonSchool.com/phgovt

**Subcommittees** Most standing committees are divided into **subcommittees**—divisions of standing committees that do most of the committees' work. Each subcommittee is responsible for a portion of the committee's workload. There are now more than 150 subcommittees in the two houses—nearly 70 in the Senate and about 100 in the House.

Take a quick look at the Senate's 19-member Judiciary Committee (currently composed of 11 Democrats and 8 Republicans). It does most of its work in its seven subcommittees. Each member serves on at least two of these bodies, and their titles describe their focuses: Administrative Oversight and the Courts; Antitrust, Competition Policy and Consumer Rights; The Constitution; Crime and Drugs; Human Rights and the Law; Immigration, Refugees and Border Security; and Terrorism and Homeland Security.

**gauge**
*v.* to measure; judge

**The House Rules Committee** The House Committee on Rules is the Speaker's "right arm." It controls the flow of bills to the floor and sets the conditions for their consideration there. The panel is often described as the "traffic cop" in the lower house. So many measures are introduced in the House each term that some sort of screening device is absolutely necessary.

Most bills die in the committees to which they are referred. Still, several hundred are reported out every year. So, before most of these bills can reach the floor of the House, they must also clear the Rules Committee.

Normally, a bill gets to the floor only if it has been granted a rule—been scheduled for floor consideration—by the Rules Committee. The committee decides whether and under what conditions the full House will consider a measure. As you will see, this means that the powerful 13-member Rules Committee can speed, delay, or even prevent House action on a measure. In the smaller Senate, where the process is not so closely regulated, the majority leader controls the appearance of bills on the floor.

## Select Committees

At times, each house finds a need for a **select committee**, sometimes called special committees. They are panels set up for some specific purpose and, most often, for a limited time. The Speaker of the House or the President of the Senate appoints the members of these special committees, with the advice of the majority and minority leaders.

The congressional power to investigate is an essential part of the lawmaking function. Congress must decide on the need for new laws and gauge the adequacy of those already on the books. It also must exercise its vital oversight function, to ensure that federal agencies are following the laws it has already passed. At times, too, a committee may conduct an investigation of an issue—for example, the threat of domestic terrorism—in order to focus public attention on that matter. Most investigations are conducted by standing committees, or by their subcommittees.

However, select committees are sometimes formed to investigate a current issue,

## How Government Works

**FARM BILL** In addition to continuing current farm subsidies, the 2007 Farm Bill specified billions of dollars of new spending for anti-hunger and conservation programs, fruit and vegetable growers, dairy farmers, and the biofuel industry. The bill passed both houses of Congress. When it reached President Bush's desk, he vetoed it. He objected to what he saw as the bill's wasteful spending: "Americans sent us to Washington to achieve results and be good stewards of their hard-earned taxpayer dollars. This bill violates that fundamental commitment." Breaking with the President, House Republican Conference Chairman Adam Putnam (Florida) supported the bill, explaining: "The principal purpose of agriculture policy in the United States is to guarantee we're not as dependent on other countries for our food as we are for our fuel." Both the House and Senate overrode the veto, and the bill is now law.

as the Senate's Select Committee on Indian Affairs recently did. That 15-member panel spent nearly three years investigating the behavior of a number of well-connected lobbyists who represented several Native American tribes as they sought to establish gambling casinos. The committee's extensive probe uncovered massive instances of fraud, bribery, tax evasion, and other illegal activities for which several offenders began to serve long prison sentences in 2006 and 2007. The most prominent of those miscreants were Washington-based lobbyist Jack Abramoff and a member of Congress, Representative Robert Ney (R., Ohio), who had been chairman of the House Committee on Administration.

At times, select committees have been spectacularly important. This happened, for example, with the Senate's Select Committee on Presidential Campaign Activities, popularly known as the Senate Watergate Committee. As the Watergate scandal began to unfold in 1973, the Senate created that committee. Chaired by Senator Sam Ervin (D., North Carolina), its job was to investigate "the extent, if any, to which illegal, improper, or unethical activities were engaged in by any persons . . . in the presidential election of 1972." Its sensational hearings riveted the nation for months. Eventually, they formed a key link in the chain of events that led to President Richard Nixon's resignation from office in mid-1974.

Another notable instance came in 1987, with the work of two panels: the Senate's Select Committee on Secret Military Assistance to Iran and the Nicaraguan Opposition, and the House Select Committee to Investigate Covert Arms Transactions with Iran. These twin committees, often referred to jointly as the Iran-Contra Committee, probed the Reagan administration's conduct of two highly secret projects abroad: the sale of arms to Iran and efforts to give military aid to the Contra rebels in Nicaragua. The operation in Iran was intended, at least in part, as an arms-for-hostages deal, and it failed. The aid to the Contras was funded in part with money from the Iranian arms sales, despite an act of Congress that expressly prohibited such aid by the United States.

Most congressional investigations are not nearly so visible, nor so historic. Their more usual shape can be seen when, for example, the House Committee on Agriculture probes the spruce budworm problem (an infestation affecting trees in the Pacific Northwest) or the Senate's Armed Services Committee looks at the Army's recruiting programs.

## Joint and Conference Committees

A **joint committee** is one composed of members of both houses. Some of these are select committees set up to serve some temporary purpose. Most are permanent groups that serve on a regular basis. Because the standing committees of the two houses often duplicate one another's work, many have long urged that Congress make much greater use of the joint committee device.

Some joint committees are investigative in nature and issue periodic reports to the

miscreants
*n.* criminals, wrongdoers

### Senate Standing Committee Chairs

| Committee | Name, Party, State, Year Elected |
|---|---|
| Agriculture, Nutrition, and Forestry | Debbie Stabenow (D., Michigan), 1996 |
| Appropriations | Daniel Inouye (D., Hawaii), 1962 |
| Armed Services | Carl Levin (D., Mich.), 1978 |
| Banking, Housing, and Urban Affairs | Christopher C. Dodd (D., Conn.),1980 |
| Budget | Kent Conrad, (D., N.D.), 1986 |
| Commerce, Science, and Transportation | Jay Rockefeller (D., W.Va.), 1984 |
| Energy and Natural Resources | Jeff Bingaman (D., N.M.), 1982 |
| Environment and Public Works | Barbara Boxer (D., Calif.), 1992 |
| Finance | Max Baucus (D., Mont.), 1978 |
| Foreign Relations | John Kerry, Jr. (D., Mass.), 1984 |
| Health, Education, Labor, and Pensions | Tom Harkin (D., Iowa), 1984 |
| Homeland Security and Governmental Affairs | Joseph L. Lieberman (I., Conn.), 1988 |
| Indian Affairs | Maria Cantwell (D. Washington), 1992 |
| Judiciary | Patrick T. Leahy (D., Vt.), 1974 |
| Rules and Administration | Charles Schumer (D., N.Y.), 1998 |
| Small Business and Entrepreneurship | Mary Landrieu (D., La.), 1996 |
| Veterans' Affairs | Daniel K. Akaka (D., Hawaii), 1990 |

SOURCE: *Congressional Directory* and Secretary of the Senate

▶▶ **Analyzing Charts** This chart lists the Senate's committees and their chairs. *Why do you think the Senate has fewer committees than the House?*

**GOVERNMENT ONLINE**
**Update**
To check out who holds these positions today, go to
PearsonSchool.com/phgovt

---

## Background

**WAYS AND MEANS COMMITTEE** Ways and Means is the oldest standing committee in Congress. Yet the idea of a committee to handle public finances is even older. Britain established a ways and means committee in 1641. America's colonial and early State legislatures adopted the British practice. Congress created a Ways and Means Committee in its first session in 1789. As a select committee, it was disbanded and reinstituted each session. Congress redefined it as a standing committee in 1802. Its jurisdiction has changed many times through its history. At first its duties included appropriations as well as revenues. In 1865, Congress created new committees on banking and appropriations to relieve Ways and Means of some of its huge workload. Today, Ways and Means remains one of the most powerful committees in Congress, with responsibilities for government revenues, borrowing, and Social Security.

---

### FOLLOW A BILL THROUGH THE HOUSE

Direct students to the chart in the text showing the path of the 2007 Food and Energy Security bill in the House. Point out that while most of the work of Congress happens in committees, most of the work of committees happens in subcommittees. Follow the path of the bill through the House. Students may be interested to learn that the bill included provisions for foreign food aid, which led to the referral to the Committee on Foreign Affairs. During this portion of the lesson, be sure to point out that bills are *referred,* or sent, to committees by the Speaker or President of the Senate.

**L2 ELL Differentiate** Teach the prefix *sub-,* which means "under" or "subordinate."

**L4 Differentiate** If you have classroom Internet access, you may have students access current legislation through GPOaccess.gov and trace its path through committees and subcommittees. Students should then make a flowchart showing the path of one of those bills.

### EXTEND THE LESSON

**L3 L4 Differentiate** Distribute the Chapter 12 Section 2 Extend Worksheet (Unit 3 All-in-One, p. 139), which summarizes bills referred to House committees. Have students use the descriptions of committee jurisdictions in the Core Worksheet to predict which committees worked on each bill.

**L3 Differentiate** Assign student groups one committee of Congress. Have them create a poster that explains the jurisdiction of each committee, its history, its chairman, and its ranking member.

**L2 Differentiate** Have students research and identify the committees on which their representative and senators serve, and in what capacity.

Tell students to go to the Online Update to check out Senate standing committee chairs today.

**Government online** *All print resources are available on the Teacher's Resource Library CD-ROM and online at* PearsonSchool.com/phgovt.

### Answers

**Checkpoint** A select committee is a committee appointed for a specific purpose, often for a limited time.

**Analyzing Charts** The Senate has fewer members than the House.

# Assess and Remediate

**L3** Collect the Core Worksheet and assess students' work.

**L3** Assign the Section 2 Assessment questions.

**L3** Section Quiz A (Unit 3 All-in-One, p. 141)

**L2** Section Quiz B (Unit 3 All-in-One, p. 142)

Have students complete the review activities in the digital lesson presentation and continue their work in the **Essential Questions Journal.**

## REMEDIATION

| If Your Students Have Trouble With | Strategies For Remediation |
|---|---|
| The role of committees (Questions 1, 2, 3, 5, 6) | Review the Chapter 12 Section 2 Core Worksheet, which lists committee jurisdictions. Refer students to the graphic in Section 3 showing how many bills become laws. Ask students to propose ways that Congress could review all these bills on a vast range of topics without committees. |
| The power to investigate (Question 4) | Draw a triangle with each of the branches of government on the board. Point out that Congress can investigate the other branches, which is part of the system of checks and balances. |

## Answers

**Checkpoint** A joint committee is any committee that is made up of members from both houses. A conference committee is a particular type of joint committee that has the job of reconciling House and Senate versions of a bill.

**Analyzing Charts** to avoid duplication of efforts between standing committees in each house

---

✔**Checkpoint**
What is the difference between a joint committee and a conference committee?

### Joint Committees of Congress

- The **Joint Economic Committee** holds hearings, performs research, and makes recommendations on matters related to the U.S. economy.

- The **Joint Committee on the Library** oversees the operations of the Library of Congress and manages the congressional art collection and the U.S. Botanic Garden.

- The **Joint Committee on Printing** is the oldest joint committee of Congress. It oversees other printing by the Federal Government.

- The **Joint Committee on Taxation** is involved in legislation about taxes. The chair position rotates between the chair of the House Ways and Means Committee and the Senate Finance Committee.

▸▸ **Analyzing Charts** The Joint Committees of Congress include members from both houses. *Why do you think these matters are dealt with by joint committees?*

perform more routine duties—for example, the Joint Committee on the Library oversees the administration of that remarkable institution, the Library of Congress.

Before a bill may be sent to the President, each house must pass it in identical form. Sometimes, the two houses pass differing versions, and the first house will not agree to the changes the other has made. When this happens, a **conference committee**—a temporary, joint body—is created to iron out the differences in the bill. Its job is to produce a compromise bill that both houses will accept—as you will see shortly.

Senator Dick Durbin (D., Illinois) listens to testimony during a Senate Judiciary Committee hearing in 2010. ▼

House and Senate—for example, the Joint Committee on Taxation. It conducts in-depth studies of the federal tax system and presents its findings to the House Ways and Means Committee and the Senate's Finance Committee. Most often, those committees

**Essential Questions Journal** To continue to build a response to the chapter Essential Question, go to your **Essential Questions Journal.**

## SECTION 2 ASSESSMENT

1. **Guiding Question** Use your completed table to answer this question: How do committees help Congress to do its work?

### Key Terms and Comprehension

2. **(a)** What are **standing committees? (b)** What rule determines which members of Congress will serve as chairs and which as members of each committee?

3. Describe the role of **(a) select committees, (b) joint committees,** and **(c) conference committees.**

4. Why is the power of Congress to investigate a vital part of its legislative functions?

### Critical Thinking

5. **Predict Consequences** What might happen if all proposed bills were sent directly to the full House for a vote?

6. **Express Problems Clearly** What are the benefits and drawbacks of the committee and subcommittee system used by Congress?

### Quick Write

**Persuasive Essay: Establish a Point of View** Make a graphic organizer to keep track of the pros and cons of each aspect of congressional organization. Start thinking about whether you would change any aspect of how Congress is organized to make it more efficient or effective.

---

# Assessment Answers

**1.** Committees help by dividing up the labor. Each committee and its subcommittees specialize in evaluating bills in a specific area. Each house forms temporary select committees to investigate current issues. Conference committees reconcile differences between House and Senate versions of a bill before it is sent to the President.

**2. (a)** permanent panels to which all bills within their subject area are referred **(b)** seniority

**3. (a)** Select committees are temporary committees set up for a specific purpose. **(b)** Joint committees are composed of members of both houses; most are permanent and perform routine duties. **(c)** Conference committees reconcile differences between House and Senate versions of a bill.

**4.** Congress investigates to gauge the adequacy of existing laws, decide whether new ones are needed, determine whether the executive branch is carrying out the existing laws, and focus public attention on important problems.

**5.** Members of Congress would be overwhelmed. It is not possible for each member to have expertise in every policy area or time to investigate every proposed bill.

**6.** Benefits: committee members gain expertise by specializing; cuts down workload; provides flexibility; allows members of both houses to work together. Drawbacks: most bills never receive a floor vote; majority party controls agenda of every committee.

**QUICK WRITE** Students will make a pro-con graphic organizer to evaluate congressional organization.

# Making Law:
# The House

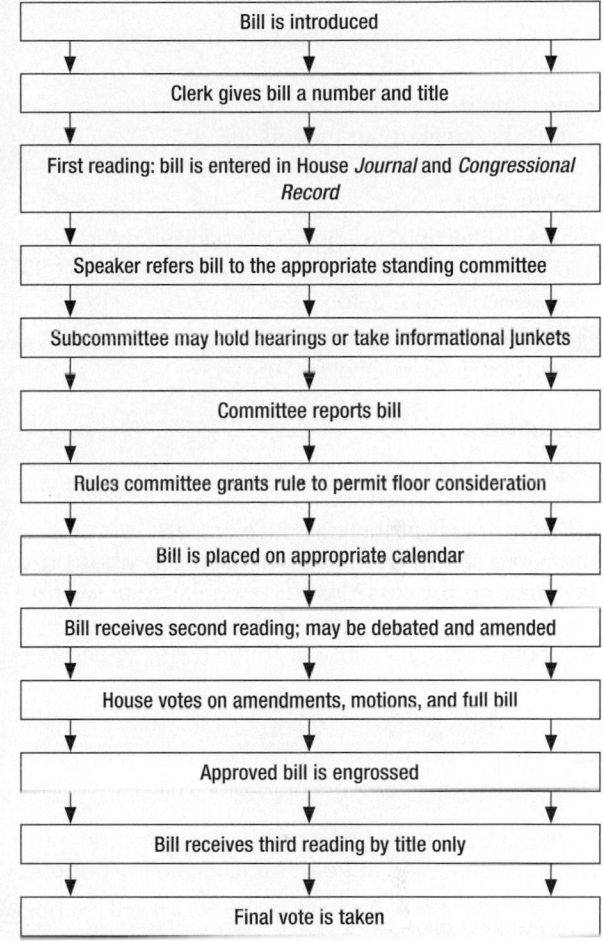

## Guiding Question
**What steps does a successful bill follow as it moves through the House?** Use a flowchart to keep track of the progress of a bill through the House.

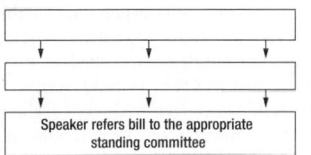

| |
|---|
| Speaker refers bill to the appropriate standing committee |

## Political Dictionary
- bill
- joint resolution
- concurrent resolution
- resolution
- rider
- pigeonhole
- discharge petition
- quorum
- engrossed

## Objectives
1. Identify the first steps in the introduction of a bill to the House.
2. Describe what happens to a bill once it is referred to a committee.
3. Explain how House leaders schedule debate on a bill.
4. Explain what happens to a bill on the House floor, and identify the final step in the passage of a bill in the House.

**Image Above:** Rep. Greg Walden (R., Ore.) waves a bill during a committee work session.

These numbers may surprise you: From 6,000 to 9,000 bills and resolutions are introduced in the House and Senate during each session of Congress. Fewer than 10 percent become law. Where do all those measures come from? Why are so few of them passed? How, by what process, does Congress make law?

## The First Steps
A **bill** is a proposed law presented to the House or Senate for consideration. Most bills introduced in either house do not originate with members themselves. Instead, however, many of the most important bills are born somewhere in the executive branch. Business, labor, agriculture, and other special interest groups often draft measures, as well. And some bills, or at least the ideas for them, come from private citizens who think "there ought to be a law. . . ." Many others are born in the standing committees of Congress.

According to Article I, Section 7, Clause 1 of the Constitution, "bills for raising Revenue shall originate in the House." In other words, tax bills must first be acted upon by the House. Measures dealing with any other matter may be introduced in either chamber. Only members can introduce bills in the House, and they do so by dropping them into the hopper, a box hanging on the edge of the clerk's desk. [9]

Often, before a member introduces a bill, he or she will circulate a letter informing other members about the measure and why its sponsor thinks it should become law. That is, he or she hopes to persuade several other members to become cosponsors, thereby increasing the chances that the bill will be passed. By the time many measures are introduced, in either house, a number of members are listed on them as cosponsors.

**Types of Bills and Resolutions** The thousands of measures—bills and resolutions—Congress considers take several forms. To begin with, there are two types of bills: public bills and private bills.

---
[9] Puerto Rico's resident commissioner and the delegates from the District of Columbia, Guam, the Virgin Islands, American Samoa, and the Northern Mariana Islands also may introduce measures in the House. Only a senator may introduce a measure in the upper house. He or she does so by addressing the chair.

## What steps does a successful bill follow as it moves through the House?

| |
|---|
| Bill is introduced |
| Clerk gives bill a number and title |
| First reading: bill is entered in House *Journal* and *Congressional Record* |
| Speaker refers bill to the appropriate standing committee |
| Subcommittee may hold hearings or take informational junkets |
| Committee reports bill |
| Rules committee grants rule to permit floor consideration |
| Bill is placed on appropriate calendar |
| Bill receives second reading; may be debated and amended |
| House votes on amendments, motions, and full bill |
| Approved bill is engrossed |
| Bill receives third reading by title only |
| Final vote is taken |

## SKILLS DEVELOPMENT

### INNOVATE AND THINK CREATIVELY
Since the activities in this section require students to brainstorm and debate issues, you may want to have students review the information on innovating and thinking creatively in the Skills Handbook, p. S23.

# Focus on the Basics

**FACTS:** • Only a member can introduce a bill in either house. • Bills approved by the appropriate committee and the Rules Committee are given floor consideration. • Measures that win House approval are sent to the Senate. • All bills are scheduled on the appropriate calendar.

**CONCEPTS:** checks and balances, public policy

**ENDURING UNDERSTANDINGS:** • Only a small fraction of the bills introduced become laws. • Bills are referred to standing committees and most to subcommittees. • Important bills are referred to the Committee of the Whole to speed business on the floor with rules that are less strict than those of the House itself.

# Get Started

## LESSON GOALS

Students will . . .

- recognize the need for committees by examining a transparency showing the volume of bills flowing through Congress.
- write a bill using guidelines and following a sample.
- simulate how a bill passes through the House, using a bill created by students.

## BEFORE CLASS

Assign the section, the graphic organizer in the text, and the Reading Comprehension Worksheet (Unit 3 All-in-One, p. 143) before class.

**L2** **Differentiate** Reading Comprehension Worksheet (Unit 3 All-in-One, p. 145)

## BELLRINGER

Display Transparency 12F, Number of Bills that Become Laws, which shows the number of bills at different stages of the legislative process. Write on the board: **What do these numbers say about the lawmaking process?** Instruct students to answer the transparency questions in their notebooks. Then tell them to write an answer to the question on the board.

# Teach

To present this topic using online resources, use the lesson presentation at **PearsonSchool.com/phgovt.**

## REVIEW BELLRINGER

Have a volunteer answer the first two Bellringer questions. *(bills introduced: 11,228; number that became law: 460)* Then have several students read their answer to the third question. *(Possible responses: Congress does a good job weeding out frivolous bills. Members of Congress have a huge workload. Work must be divided up because the volume is too great for all members to be able to work on all bills.)*

Remind students of the chapter Essential Question: **Can and should the lawmaking process be improved?** Tell them to think about this question as they study the last two sections of the chapter.

---

## Answers

**Caption** Possible response: to gain public support for the bill which would put pressure on other members of Congress to vote in favor of it

**Checkpoint** by the addition of multiple riders

---

The Democratic House leadership held a rally before an all-night debate on a bill that would withdraw U.S. troops from Iraq. *Why might members of Congress hold a public rally before holding a debate on a bill?*

✔ **Checkpoint**
How does an appropriations bill become a "Christmas tree"?

**voluminous**
*adj.* massive; lengthy

Public bills are measures applying to the nation as a whole—for example, a tax measure. Private bills are measures that apply to certain persons or places rather than to the entire nation. As an example, Congress once passed an act to give a sheep rancher $85,000 for his losses resulting from attacks by grizzly bears. The bears had been moved from Yellowstone National Park to other public lands on which the rancher grazed his flock.

**Joint resolutions** are similar to bills, and, when passed, have the force of law. They most often deal with unusual or temporary matters—for example, to appropriate money for the presidential inauguration ceremonies. Joint resolutions are used, too, to propose constitutional amendments, and they have also been used to annex territories.

**Concurrent resolutions** deal with matters in which the House and Senate must act jointly. However, they do not have the force of law and do not require the President's signature. Concurrent resolutions are used most often by Congress to state a position on some matter—for example, in foreign affairs.

**Resolutions,** often called "simple resolutions," deal with matters concerning either house alone and are taken up only by that body. They are regularly used for such matters as the adoption of a new rule of procedure or the amendment of some existing rule. Like concurrent resolutions, a resolution does not have the force of law and is not sent to the President for approval.

A bill or resolution usually deals with a single subject, but sometimes a rider dealing with an unrelated matter is included. A **rider** is a provision not likely to pass on its own merit that is attached to an important measure certain to pass. Its sponsors hope that it will "ride" through the legislative process on the strength of the main measure.

Most riders are tacked onto appropriations measures, and are often called "earmarks." In fact, some money bills have so many riders attached that they are called "Christmas trees." The opponents of those "decorations" and the President are almost always forced to accept them if they want the bill's major provisions to become law.

**Introduction and First Reading** The clerk of the House numbers each bill as it is introduced. Thus, H.R. 3410 would be the 3,410th measure introduced in the House during the congressional term. Bills originating in the Senate receive the prefix S.—such as S. 210. Resolutions are similarly identified in each house in the order of their introduction.[10]

The clerk also gives each bill a short title—a brief summary of its principal contents. Having received its number and title, the bill is then entered in the House *Journal* and in the *Congressional Record* for the day.

The *Journal* contains the minutes, the official record, of the daily proceedings in the House or Senate. The *Congressional Record* is a voluminous account of the daily proceedings (speeches, debates, other comments, votes, motions, etc.) in each house. The *Record* is not quite a word-for-word account, however. Members have five days in which to make changes in each temporary edition. They often insert speeches that were in fact never made, reconstruct "debates," and revise thoughtless or inaccurate remarks.

With these actions the bill has received its first reading. All bills are printed immediately after introduction and distributed to all members of the House.

Each bill that is finally passed in either house is given three readings along the legislative route. In the House, second reading

---

# Differentiated Resources

The following resources are located in the All-in-One, Unit 3, Chapter 12, Section 3:

- **L3** Reading Comprehension Worksheet (p. 143)
- **L2** Reading Comprehension Worksheet (p. 145)
- **L3** Core Worksheet A (p. 147)
- **L3** Core Worksheet B (p. 149)
- **L3** Quiz A (p. 150)
- **L2** Quiz B (p. 151)

comes during floor consideration, if the measure gets that far. Third reading takes place just before the final vote on the measure. Each reading is usually by number and title only: "H.R. 3410, A bill to provide. . . ." However, the more important or controversial bills are read in full and taken up line by line, section by section, at second reading.

The three readings, an ancient parliamentary practice, are intended to ensure careful consideration of bills. Today, the readings are little more than way stations along the legislative route. They were quite important in the early history of Congress, however, when some members could not read.

After the first reading, the Speaker refers the bill to one or more of the standing committees. A bill's content largely determines where it will go. The Speaker does have some discretion, however, particularly over complex measures with provisions covering a number of subjects. Which committee gets a bill can matter. For example, a controversial provision in the bill might receive a more favorable welcome in one committee than it might in another.

## The Bill in Committee

The Constitution makes no mention of standing committees. These bodies do play an absolutely essential role in the lawmaking process, however—and in both houses of Congress. Indeed, their place is so pivotal that they are sometimes called "little legislatures."

The standing committees act as <u>sieves</u>. They sift through all of the many bills referred to them—rejecting most, considering and reporting only those they find to be worthy of floor consideration. In short, the fate of most bills is decided in these committees rather than on the floor of either house.

---

10 Thus, H.J. Res. 12 would be the 12th joint resolution introduced in the House during the term, and similarly in the Senate, S.J. Res. 19. Concurrent resolutions are identified as H. or S. Con. Res., and simple resolutions as H. or S. Res.

11 The term comes from the old-fashioned rolltop desks with pigeonholes—slots into which papers were put and often soon forgotten. Most "by request" bills are routinely pigeonholed; they are the measures that members introduce but only because some constituent or some interest group has asked them to do so.

## The Number of Bills That Become Laws

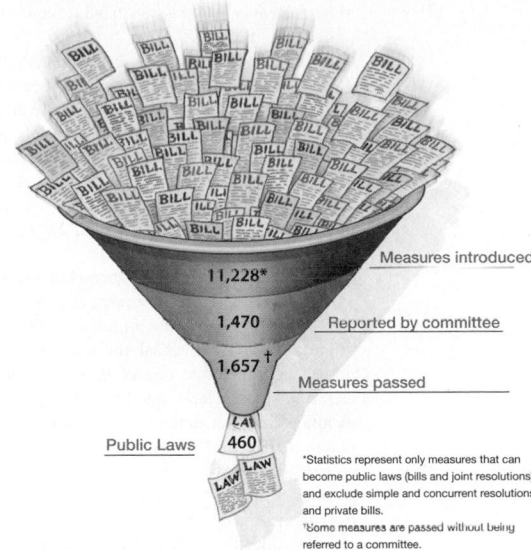

| | |
|---|---|
| 11,228* | Measures introduced |
| 1,470 | Reported by committee |
| 1,657† | Measures passed |
| 460 | Public Laws |

*Statistics represent only measures that can become public laws (bills and joint resolutions) and exclude simple and concurrent resolutions and private bills.
†Some measures are passed without being referred to a committee.

SOURCE: Library of Congress. Figures are for the 110th Congress.

▸▸ **Interpreting Charts** A bill must pass through many steps before it becomes law. *After which step do most bills die?*

Most of the thousands of bills introduced in each session of Congress are **pigeonholed.**[11] That is, they are buried; they die in committee. They are simply put away, never to be acted upon.

Most pigeonholed bills deserve their fate. On occasion, however, a committee buries a measure that a majority of the members of the House want to consider. When that happens, the bill can be blasted out of the committee with a discharge petition.

A **discharge petition** enables members to force a bill that has remained in committee 30 days (7 in the Rules Committee) onto the floor for consideration. Any member may file a discharge motion. If that motion is signed by a majority (218) of House members, the committee has seven days to report the bill. If it does not, any member who signed the motion may, on the second and fourth Mondays of each month, move that the bill be

✓**Checkpoint**
What happens to the majority of bills that are introduced?

<u>sieve</u>
*n.* a sitting device, gatekeeper

---

## Political Cartoon Mini-Lesson

Display Transparency 12G, Spending Bill, when you discuss riders. Explain that riders are commonly called "pork." Ask: **Who is the man driving the sled?** *(President George W. Bush)* **Whom does the elf represent?** *(Congress)* **What has Congress done?** *(attached a lot of pork, or riders, to the President's spending bill)* **Why do you think Congress chose to attach the riders to this particular bill?** *(Riders are typically attached to appropriations bills because such bills are important and likely to pass. The fact that the President is steering this bill means that it is important to him.)* **Why do you think the cartoonist shows the riders pulling the sled?** *(The President will have to accept the riders if he wants his spending bill to move forward toward passage.)*

---

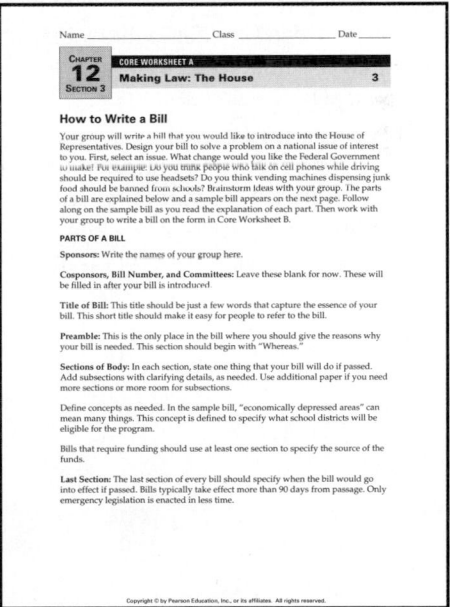

---

## Answers

**Interpreting Charts** after introduction, when they've been referred to committee

**Checkpoint** Most are pigeonholed.

## MAKE IT VISUAL

After students have finished writing their bills, choose one bill to use as an example. The least controversial would be the easiest for the activity. Tell students that you will walk this bill through the legislative process in the House of Representatives. Write the summary title of the group's bill on a large piece of paper. Holding the bill, tell students that you hold a bill that has been written to address a current issue. Ask what you should do with it. *(They should tell you that a member of the House needs to submit it.)*

Then tell students to suppose that they are all members of the House. Ask members who support the bill to come sign their names as cosponsors. Then ask if any students oppose the bill. If so, ask what it would take to make them support it, including adding unrelated provisions. Write these provisions on sticky notes and stick them to the paper. Explain that these provisions are riders, which may not pass on their own. If these riders will persuade students to support the bill, have them add their names to the list of cosponsors. Point out that the bill's sponsors just gained support for their bill.

## WALK THROUGH THE STEPS

Tell students that you will walk their bill through the steps of the first reading. Assign the bill a number, H.R.1, for example, and write the number on the bill. Then ask a sponsor to read the title. Ask students what happens next. *(The entire bill is entered into the House* Journal *and* Congressional Record. *Then the Speaker refers it to a committee.)* Point out that bills are no longer "read" in their entirety upon introduction. Entering the text of the bill into the *Congressional Record* serves a similar purpose.

Explain that the bill gets a second and third reading. Ask: **Why were these readings important in the early days of Congress?** *(At that time, not all members could read.)*

Post the bill, including riders, on the board for the whole class to see.

---

## Answers

**Checkpoint** a motion to force a bill out of committee for floor consideration

---

discharged from the committee—that is, sent to the floor. If the motion carries, the rules require the House to consider the bill at once. This maneuver is not often tried, and it seldom succeeds.

The process was most recently successful in 2002, however. What went on to become the Bipartisan Campaign Reform Act of 2002 was blasted out of the Committee on House Administration—where the House leadership had managed to bury it for several years. That measure marked the first major change in federal campaign finance law in 23 years.

**The Committee at Work** Once a bill reaches a committee, the chairman almost always refers it to one of several subcommittees. For an important or controversial measure, a committee, or most often one of its subcommittees, holds public hearings. Interested parties, including the representatives of interest groups, public officials, and others, are invited to testify at these information-gathering sessions. If necessary, a committee can issue a subpoena, forcing a witness to testify. [12]

Occasionally, a subcommittee will make a trip to locations affected by a measure. Thus, several members of the House Foreign Affairs Committee's Subcommittee on the Western Hemisphere may visit Rio de Janero for a first-hand look at Brazil's successful efforts to reduce that country's dependence on foreign oil.

These trips are made at public expense, and members of Congress are sometimes criticized for taking them. Some of these junkets deserve criticism. But an on-the-spot investigation often proves to be among the best ways a committee can inform itself.

**Committee Actions** When a subcommittee has completed its work on a bill, the measure goes to the full committee. At the chairman's direction, that body may do one of several things. It may:

1. Report the bill favorably, with a "do pass" recommendation. It is then the chairman's job to steer the bill through debate on the floor.

---

12 A subpoena is an order compelling one to testify and/or produce evidence. Failure to obey a subpoena may lead the House or Senate to cite the offender for contempt of Congress—a federal crime punishable by fine and/or imprisonment.

2. Refuse to report the bill—that is, pigeonhole it. Again, this is the fate suffered by most measures in both houses.

3. Report the bill in amended form. Many bills are changed in committee, and several bills on the same subject may be combined into a single measure.

4. Report the bill with an unfavorable recommendation. This does not often happen. Occasionally, however, a committee feels that the full House should have a chance to consider a bill or does not want to take the responsibility for killing it.

5. Report a committee bill. The panel produces a substantially rewritten measure as a substitute for one or several of the bills referred to it.

## Scheduling Floor Debate

Before it goes to the floor for consideration, a bill reported by a standing committee is placed on one of several calendars in the House. A calendar is a schedule of the order in which bills will be taken up on the floor.

**Calendars** There are five calendars in the lower house. The *Calendar of the Committee of the Whole House on the State of the Union,* commonly known as the *Union Calendar,* is for all bills having to do with revenues, appropriations, or government property. The *House Calendar* is for all other public bills. The *Private Calendar* is for all private bills. The *Corrections Calendar* is for all bills from the Union or House Calendar taken out of order by unanimous consent of the House of Representatives. These are most often minor bills to which there is no opposition. The *Discharge Calendar* is for petitions to discharge bills from committee.

Under the rules of the House, bills are taken from each of these calendars for consideration on a regularly scheduled basis. For example, bills from the Corrections Calendar are supposed to be considered on the second and fourth Tuesdays of each month. Measures relating to the District of Columbia can be taken up on the second and fourth Mondays, and private bills on the first and third Tuesdays. On "Calendar Wednesdays," the various committee chairmen may each call

---

# Background

**BATTLE FOR POWER** Following Democratic victories in the 2008 election, the House Energy and Commerce Committee witnessed a fight for control that tested the seniority system. The chair of the committee was expected to shape important environmental legislation by working with Democrats in the Senate and President Obama. The incoming chair, Rep. John Dingell (D., Michigan), had served more than 50 years in the House and often represented the interests of the auto industry and its workers against stricter environmental laws. Rep. Henry Waxman (D., California), who supported strong moves toward energy efficiency and lower CO2 emissions, challenged Dingell for control of the committee. Waxman defeated Dingell in a vote of all Democratic representatives, 137-122, unexpectedly unseating the veteran legislator. In exchange, Waxman named Dingell to lead the committee's efforts on healthcare reform.

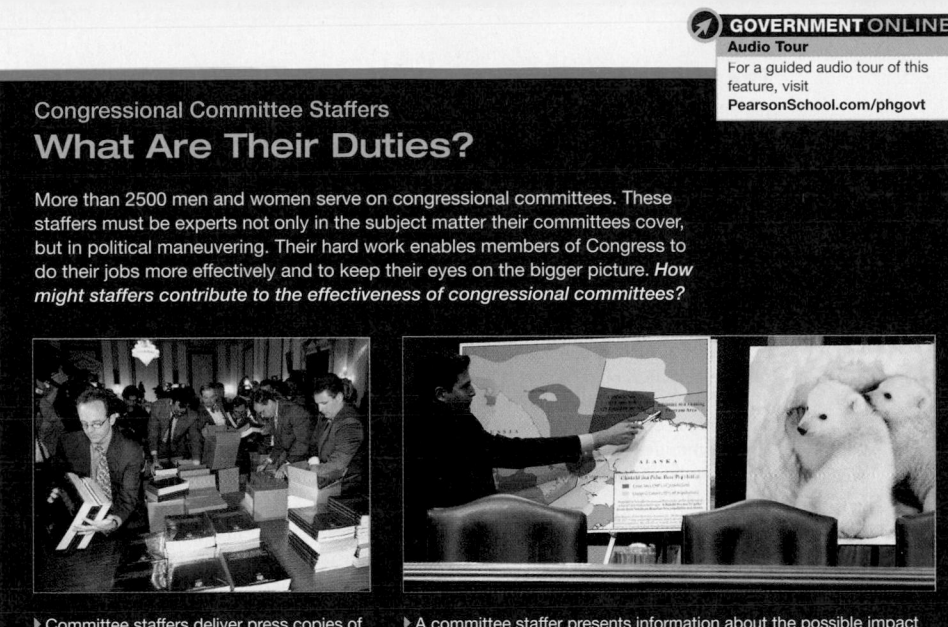

GOVERNMENT ONLINE
**Audio Tour**
For a guided audio tour of this feature, visit
PearsonSchool.com/phgovt

Congressional Committee Staffers
# What Are Their Duties?

More than 2500 men and women serve on congressional committees. These staffers must be experts not only in the subject matter their committees cover, but in political maneuvering. Their hard work enables members of Congress to do their jobs more effectively and to keep their eyes on the bigger picture. *How might staffers contribute to the effectiveness of congressional committees?*

▶ Committee staffers deliver press copies of a Special Committee report on China's theft of U.S. nuclear weapons secrets.

▶ A committee staffer presents information about the possible impact of oil exploration on Alaska's polar bears.

---

up one bill from the House or Union calendars that has cleared their committees.

**Rules** None of these arrangements is followed too closely, however. What most often happens is even more complicated. Remember that the Rules Committee plays a critical role in the legislative process in the House. It must grant a rule before most bills can in fact reach the floor. That is, before most measures can be taken from a calendar, the Rules Committee must approve that step and set a time for its appearance on the floor.

By not granting a rule for a bill, the Rules Committee can effectively kill it. Or, when the Rules Committee does grant a rule, it may be a special rule—one setting conditions under which the members of the House will consider the measure. A special rule often sets a time limit on floor debate. It may even prohibit amendments to certain, or even to any, of the bill's provisions.

Then, too, certain bills are privileged. That is, they may be called up at almost any time, ahead of any other business before the House. The most privileged measures include major appropriations (spending) and general revenue (tax) bills, conference committee reports, and special rules granted by the Rules Committee.

On certain days, the House may suspend its rules. A motion to that effect must be approved by a two-thirds vote of the members present. When that happens, as it sometimes does, the House moves so far away from its established operating procedures that a measure can go through all the many steps necessary to enactment in a single day.

All of these—the calendars, the role of the Rules Committee, and the other complex procedures—have developed over time to help members of the House manage their heavy workload. Because of the large size of the House and the sheer number and variety of bills its members introduce, no one member could possibly know the contents, let alone the merits, of every bill on which he or she has to vote.

✔ **Checkpoint**
What power makes the Rules Committee so important?

---

**FORM COMMITTEES**

Have students identify the committee(s) to which their bill should be sent. Write the name(s) of the committees on the bill and on the board.

Divide the class into three committees. Each committee will debate the bill. They can change the bill according to their discussions or leave the bill the same. Throughout their debate, the following could happen:

**1.** The bill could die in committee. If most committee members dislike the bill and disagree with the ideas behind it, they can vote to kill it.

**2.** The bill could pass as is. If most committee members agree with the bill as it stands, they can vote to move it on to the whole class for a vote.

**3.** The bill could change and the committee will have to defend that change. Committee members should propose their changes during debate, and the full committee should vote on whether to make the change.

The three actions above are the most likely to happen with this simulation, but you could remind the students of the other routes a bill might take.

**VOTE ON THE BILLS**

When the class comes back together, set rules for debate as the Committee of the Whole. Then spend a short time debating the bill. Have students vote on each version, or allow students to add amendments from one version to another version.

Tell students to go to the Audio Tour for a guided audio tour of the "Congressional Committee Staffers" feature.

---

# Debate

Explain that virtually all bills introduced in the House go to committee, and most of them die there. Have students consider whether this demonstrates a fundamental problem in the House. Organize the class into two teams: one will argue that the pigeonholing of so many bills reveals a failure of the legislative process, and the other will argue that it contributes to its success. Ask: **Does the fact that most bills fail to become law represent a basic flaw in the legislative process?**

---

## Answers

**What Are Their Duties?** Possible response: Staffers can do the research and political arm-twisting for the members of Congress. Also, by specializing, the staffers can contribute expert knowledge to the committee's decision making.

**Checkpoint** the power to allow or prevent a bill from reaching the House floor

**L4 Differentiate** Have students research current legislation and its progress through the House and write a news article summarizing the key points of the bill and its current status.

**L3 Differentiate** Ask students to watch a floor debate on cable television or the Internet and summarize the proceedings.

**L2 Differentiate** Have students make a flowchart that shows the steps of a bill through the House.

## The Bill on the Floor

If a bill finally reaches the floor, it receives its second reading in the House. Many bills the House passes are minor ones, with little or no opposition. Most of these less important measures are called from the Corrections Calendar, get their second reading by title only, and are quickly disposed of.

Nearly all of the more important measures are dealt with in a much different manner. They are considered in the Committee of the Whole, an old parliamentary device for speeding business on the floor.

The Committee of the Whole includes all the members of the House, sitting as one large committee of the House, not as the House itself. The rules of the Committee of the Whole are much less strict than the rules of the House, and floor action moves along at a faster pace. For example, a **quorum,** which is a majority of the full membership (218), must be present in order for the House to do business. Only 100 members need be present in the Committee of the Whole.

When the House resolves itself into the Committee of the Whole, the Speaker steps down because the full House of Representatives is no longer in session. Another member presides. General debate begins, and the bill receives its second reading, section by section. As each section is read, amendments may be offered. Under the five-minute rule, supporters and opponents of each amendment have just that many minutes to make their cases. Votes are taken on each section and its amendment as the reading proceeds.

When the bill has been gone through—and many run to dozens and sometimes hundreds of pages—the Committee of the Whole has completed its work. It then rises, that is, dissolves itself. Presto! The House is now back in session. The Speaker resumes the chair, and the House formally adopts the committee's work.

**Debate** Its large size has long since forced the House to impose severe limits on floor debate. A rule first adopted in 1842 forbids any member from holding the floor for more than one hour without unanimous consent to speak for a longer time. Since 1880, the Speaker has had the power to force any member who strays from the subject at hand to give up the floor.

The majority and minority floor leaders generally decide in advance how they will split the time to be spent on a bill. But at any time, any member may "move the previous question." That is, any member can demand a vote on the issue before the House. If that motion is adopted, debate ends. An up-or-down vote must be taken. This device is the only motion that can be used in the House to close (end) debate, but it can be a very effective one.

**Voting** A bill may be the subject of several votes on the floor. If amendments are offered, as they frequently are, members must vote on each of them. Then, too, a number of procedural motions may be offered, for example, one to table the bill (lay it aside), another for the previous question, and so on. The members must vote on each of these motions. These several other votes are very often a better guide to a bill's friends and foes than is the final vote itself. Sometimes, a member votes for a bill that is now certain to pass, even though he or she had supported amendments to it that, had they been adopted, would have in fact defeated the measure.

*"The only solution I can see is to hold a series of long and costly hearings in order to put off finding a solution."*

▸ **Analyzing Political Cartoons** This cartoon mocks the lawmaking process. *Is the cartoon a reference to how Congress actually works or how people think it works? Explain.*

## Answers

**Analyzing Political Cartoons** The cartoon probably refers to the way people think Congress works. Hearings may seem like a lengthy diversion to many people, but they are an important way for Congress to gather information to find a solution.

# Background

**CONGRESSIONAL STAFF** Because of the volume and complexity of their work, members of Congress rely on congressional staff. Each member has a personal staff. An administrative assistant or chief of staff runs the office. Legislative assistants analyze bills under consideration and present the pros and cons to their boss. Legislative assistants often specialize in specific areas, such as taxes or energy issues. The press secretary promotes the member's views in communications with the media and the public. The appointment secretary allocates the member's time and may arrange travel or speaking engagements. Caseworkers solve problems and fulfill requests from constituents. In addition to personal staff, more than 2,500 staff members serve specific congressional committees or subcommittees. These staffers assist in writing, analyzing, and amending legislation within committee jurisdiction.

The House uses four different methods for taking floor votes:

1. Voice votes are the most common. The Speaker calls for the "ayes" and then the "noes," the members answer in chorus, and the Speaker announces the result.

2. If any member thinks the Speaker has erred in judging a voice vote, he or she may demand a standing vote, also known as a division of the House. All in favor, and then all opposed, stand and are counted by the clerk.

3. One fifth of a quorum (44 members in the House or 20 in the Committee of the Whole) can demand a teller vote. When this happens, the Speaker names one teller from each party. The members pass between the tellers and are counted, for and against. Teller votes are rare today. The practice has been replaced by electronic voting.

4. A roll-call vote, also known as a record vote, may be demanded by one fifth of the members present.[13]

In 1973, the House installed a computerized voting system for all quorum calls and record votes to replace the roll call by the clerk. Members now vote at any of the 48 stations on the floor by inserting a personalized plastic card in a box and then pushing one of three buttons: "Yea," "Nay," or "Present." The "Present" button is most often used for a quorum call—a check to make sure that a quorum of the members is in fact present.

Otherwise, it is used when a member does not wish to vote on a question but still wants to be recorded as present.[14]

A large master board above the Speaker's chair shows instantly how each member has voted. The House rules allow the members 15 minutes to answer quorum calls or cast record votes. Voting ends when the Speaker pushes a button to lock the electronic system, producing a permanent record of the vote at the same time. Under the former roll-call process, it took the clerk up to 45 minutes to call each member's name and record his or her vote. Before 1973, roll calls took up about three months of House floor time each session.

Voting procedures are much the same in the Senate. The upper house uses voice, standing, and roll-call votes, but does not take teller votes or use an electronic voting process. Only six or seven minutes are needed for a roll-call vote in the smaller upper chamber.

**Final Steps in the House** Once a bill has been approved at second reading, it is **engrossed,** or printed in its final form. Then it is read a third time, by title, and a final vote is taken. Invariably, a bill is approved at third reading, and then the Speaker signs it. A page—a legislative aide—then carries it to the Senate side of the Capitol and places it on the Senate president's desk.

✔ **Checkpoint**
What are the four types of votes that the House can take?

13 The Constitution (Article I, Section 7, Clause 2) requires a record vote on the question of overriding a presidential veto. No record votes are taken in the Committee of the Whole.

14 A "present" vote is not allowed on some questions—for example, a vote to override a veto.

---

## SECTION 3 ASSESSMENT

**Essential Questions Journal** To continue to build a response to the chapter Essential Question, go to your **Essential Questions Journal.**

1. **Guiding Question** Use your completed flowchart to answer this question: What steps does a successful bill follow as it moves through the House?

**Key Terms and Comprehension**

2. Compare and contrast a **simple resolution,** a **joint resolution,** and a **concurrent resolution.**

3. What happens to most bills in committee? Why?

**Critical Thinking**

4. **Make Decisions** Congressional committees are sometimes called "little legislatures." Explain this expression. Is it an accurate one? Why or why not?

5. **Draw Inferences** Why does the House use such a complicated calendar system?

**Quick Write**

**Persuasive Essay: Make an Outline** Using your graphic organizer from Section 2, choose one aspect of congressional organization that you think is very effective or one aspect that you think should be changed. Describe that point in a thesis statement and write an outline that includes at least three supporting points.

---

## Assess and Remediate

**L3** Collect Core Worksheet B and assess students' work.

**L3** Assign the Section 3 Assessment questions.

**L3** Section Quiz A (Unit 3 All-in-One, p. 150)

**L2** Section Quiz B (Unit 3 All-in-One, p. 151)

Have students complete the review activities in the digital lesson presentation and continue their work in the **Essential Questions Journal.**

### REMEDIATION

| If Your Students Have Trouble With | Strategies For Remediation |
|---|---|
| Identifying the steps of a bill as it moves through the House (Questions 1, 3) | Make a flowchart showing the steps |
| Identifying types of resolutions (Question 2) | Review the text under the heading, "Types of Bills and Resolutions" |
| Understanding the work of committees (Question 4) | Make a list of pros and cons of the committee system |
| Understanding the role of the calendar system (Question 5) | Make a real calendar with sample days |

## Answers

**Checkpoint** voice vote, standing vote, teller vote, roll-call vote

---

## Assessment Answers

**1.** A bill is introduced. The clerk numbers and titles it. The first reading consists of entering the bill into the *Journal* and *Congressional Record*. The Speaker refers the bill to committee. The committee reports the bill favorably, unfavorably, or in amended or new form. The Rules Committee grants it a rule. It is placed on a calendar. On the floor, it receives its second reading. It is debated by the whole House. A vote is taken on each amendment offered. The approved bill is engrossed. It is read a third time by title. A final vote is taken. The Speaker signs it. It is delivered to the president of the Senate.

**2.** A simple resolution deals with a matter concerning only one house, is dealt with by that house, and does not have the force of law. A joint resolution has the force of law, but usually deals with a temporary or unusual matter. A concurrent resolution is usually used to declare a position on a policy matter; it involves both houses but does not have the force of law or require the President's signature.

**3.** Most bills die in committee, because committees report only those bills they think are worthy of floor consideration.

**4.** Possible response: The expression is accurate because committees do most of the work and decide the fate of most bills. Congress takes committee recommendations seriously because committee members are experts.

**5.** The calendars help House members manage their workload. Bills are grouped by type on different calendars, helping Congress prioritize.

**QUICK WRITE** Students should write a thesis statement and outline with supporting points.

## LESSON GOAL

- Students will formulate and defend an opinion on whether the filibuster protects minority rights or gives the minority too much power.

## Teach

### INTRODUCE THE TOPIC

Ask a volunteer to define *filibuster*. *(It is a tool used by senators to hold up legislation they oppose by "talking a bill to death" and holding up floor action by following certain rules.)* Then ask students how a filibuster can be forced to end. *(The Senate can invoke cloture, in which 60 senators vote to end debate.)*

### SUMMARIZE THE ISSUE

Have students read the feature and summarize the two views expressed at right. Ask: **How does the filibuster protect the rights of the minority?** *(Possible response: A filibuster forces the majority to consider the minority's point of view. Under cloture rules, a filibuster can be stopped by a three-fifths vote. If the majority does not have that many votes, they will have to compromise with the minority. This prevents domination by a slim majority and assures stronger bipartisan support.)*

### OPINION LINE

Use the Opinion Line strategy (p. T26) to have students declare an opinion on this question: **Does the filibuster protect minority rights, or does it allow a tyranny of the minority?** Label the sides of the line "protects minority rights" and "tyranny of the minority." Ask students to defend their positions.

## Assess and Remediate

Have students support their view on this issue in a letter addressed to one of the quoted senators.

## Answers

1. **(a)** because he believes the filibuster is being used more as a tool of obstruction rather than an extension of debate **(b)** by stating that the Framers created the legislative branch to ensure no majority rule and thus the filibuster is key to the legislative process **(c)** Sample answer: No, the Framers would expect debate but not to the degree that it makes the Senate ineffective.

2. Answers will vary, but should show an understanding of the pros and cons of the filibuster rule.

# ISSUES OF OUR TIME

## Minority Rights: The Filibuster

### ▶▶ Track the Issue

**A minority in the Senate** has used strategies such as the filibuster to ensure its voice will be heard.

**1790**
**Southern senators used the first filibuster** to oppose the move of the First Congress to Philadelphia.

**Early 1800s**
**Congress admitted new States** in pairs of one slave State and one free State to ensure a balance in the Senate.

**1917**
**The Cloture Rule,** requiring a two-thirds vote of the Senate to end debate, arose from a filibuster against arming American merchant ships.

**1960s**
**A newly introduced two-track** option allowed the Senate to continue its work during a filibuster.

**1975**
**The number of votes** needed for cloture was reduced to three fifths.

**Today**
**Today's Senate** is often referred to as the 60-vote Senate, a reference to the number needed to invoke cloture.

Senator Pat Roberts (R., Kansas) ▶

### ▶▶ Perspectives

**The term** *filibuster* **was used first** in 1851 to describe the tactic of talking a bill to death. In recent years, the filibuster has been used more than ever. The majority has criticized its use, claiming that it prevents the Senate from fulfilling its responsibilities to the people. Yet, the minority adopts the same argument to validate its use. It is unlikely that the debate over the filibuster rule will be easily resolved.

"[B]oth parties in recent years have shown their willingness to use it [the filibuster] as a tool of obstruction, rather than a means to extend debate.... There are many great traditions in this body that should be kept and respected, but stubbornly clinging to ineffective and unproductive procedures should not be one of them. We can ... ensure that minority rights are protected and that the Senate remains a uniquely deliberative body. But we must also ensure that it is a functional body, regardless of which party is in the majority."

—*Senator Mark Udall
(D., Colorado), 2010*

"The founding fathers had the foresight to create an institution that was based not on majority rule, but where each state ... had two Senators to speak out on their behalf. It is that power to speak ... that is the hallmark of the Senate.... The filibuster is ... meant to foster great consultation, consensus, and cooperation between the parties. It is a means for the minority to make its voice heard.... In this way it is impossible to abuse the filibuster because it is an expression of the people against the majority's attempt to shut them out of the process."

—*Senator Pat Roberts
(R., Kansas), 2010*

### ▶▶ Connect to Your World

1. **Understand (a)** Why does Senator Udall believe reforming the rules of the Senate is necessary? **(b)** How does Senator Roberts use tradition to defend his argument for the filibuster? **(c)** Do you think the filibuster reflects the Framers' idea of debate in the Senate?

2. **Demonstrate Reasoned Judgment** Do you think the filibuster rule should be revised? Why or why not?

**GOVERNMENT** ONLINE
**In the News**
For updates about minority rights, visit **PearsonSchool.com/phgovt**

350

## SECTION 4

# Making Law:
# The Senate

### Guiding Question

**What are the major differences in the lawmaking process in the House and the Senate?** Use a Venn diagram to keep track of ways the House and Senate procedures compare.

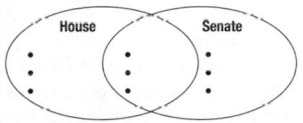

### Political Dictionary

- filibuster
- cloture
- veto
- pocket veto

### Objectives

1. Describe how a bill is introduced in the Senate.
2. Compare the Senate's rules for debate with those in the House.
3. Describe the role of conference committees in the legislative process.
4. Evaluate the actions the President can take after both houses have passed a bill.

**Image Above:** Senate pages carry copies of a bill to the Senate floor.

The House and the Senate really are two quite different places. Overall, however, the basic steps in the lawmaking process are much the same in the two chambers. Still, there are a few critical differences in their processes.

## The Senate Floor

The chief differences in House and Senate procedures involve the consideration of measures on the floor. With introduction by a senator formally recognized for the purpose, a measure is given a number, read twice, and then referred to a standing committee, where it is dealt with much as are bills in the House. The Senate's proceedings are less formal and its rules less strict than those in the much larger lower house. For example, the Senate has only one calendar for all bills reported out of its committees. (Recall, there are five of these schedules in the House.) Bills are called to the Senate floor by the majority leader, usually, but not always, in consultation with the minority leader.[15]

## Rules for Debate

Where debate in the House is strictly limited, it is almost unrestrained in the Senate. Indeed, most members of the Senate are intensely proud of belonging to what has often been called "the greatest deliberative body in the world."

As a general matter, a senator may speak on the floor for as long as he or she pleases. Unlike the House, the Senate has no rule that requires a member to speak only to the measure before the chamber. In short, a senator can talk about anything he or she wants to. And the Senate's rules do not allow any member to move the previous question.

Many bills, and particularly the most important pieces of legislation, come to the Senate floor under a unanimous consent agreement. The majority leader regularly negotiates these agreements with the minority leader, and they become effective only if no senator objects. Unanimous consent agreements usually limit the amount of floor time to be devoted to a particular measure

---

[15] The Senate does have one other calendar, the Executive Calendar, for treaties and appointments made by the President. The majority leader controls that schedule, too.

# What are the major differences in the lawmaking process in the House and the Senate?

| House | | Senate |
|---|---|---|
| • Five calendars<br>• Rules Committee<br>• Restricted debate<br>• Members must speak to the bill before the chamber<br>• Members may move the previous question | • Member introduces bill<br>• Bill referred to committee<br>• Most bills die in committee<br>• Bill must pass full floor vote<br>• Conference committee | • Proceedings less formal<br>• Rules less strict<br>• One calendar<br>• Majority leader calls bill to floor<br>• Nearly unrestricted debate<br>• Members may speak on anything<br>• Unanimous consent agreement limits consideration time and amendments<br>• Two speech rule<br>• Filibuster |

## SKILLS DEVELOPMENT

### GIVE AN EFFECTIVE PRESENTATION

To practice giving an effective presentation in this section, use the Chapter 12 Skills Worksheet (Unit 3 All-in-One, p. 156). You may want to teach the skill before the Core Worksheet activity. For L2 and L1 students, assign the adapted Skill Activity (Unit 3 All-in-One, p. 157).

# Focus on the Basics

**FACTS:** • Debate in the Senate is largely unrestricted. • After both houses approve a bill, it is sent to the President. • The President can sign the bill, allow it to become law without signing, veto it, or apply a pocket veto. • The House of Representatives and the Senate must pass a bill in the same form for it to become law.

**CONCEPTS:** checks and balances

**ENDURING UNDERSTANDINGS:** • Senate procedures are less formal and its rules less restrictive than in the House. • The lawmaking process is intentionally cumbersome in order to ensure that each law has been thoroughly considered.

# Get Started

## LESSON GOALS

Students will . . .

- use a dramatization to learn about filibusters.
- examine the work of conference committees by simulating negotiations to iron out differences between versions of a bill.
- identify a bill's final steps toward becoming law by completing a flowchart.

## BEFORE CLASS

Assign the section, the graphic organizer in the text, and the Reading Comprehension Worksheet (Unit 3 All-in-One, p. 152) before class.

**L2** **Differentiate** Reading Comprehension Worksheet (Unit 3 All-in-One, p. 153)

## BELLRINGER

Show the filibuster scene from the famous movie *Mr. Smith Goes to Washington* or distribute the Chapter 12 Section 4 Bellringer Worksheet (Unit 3 All-in-One, p. 154), which is a Senate historical minute essay about the film. Ask students to answer the questions on the worksheet. If you show the scene from the movie, write the worksheet questions on the board for students to answer in their notebooks.

▶ Senator Strom Thurmond (D., South Carolina) held up the Civil Rights Act of 1957 with the longest filibuster in history.

and the number and content of amendments that may be offered to it.

The Senate does have a "two-speech rule." No senator may speak more than twice on a given question on the same legislative day. By recessing rather than adjourning a day's session, the Senate can prolong a "legislative day" indefinitely. Thus, the two-speech rule can successfully limit the amount of time the Senate spends on some matters.

The Senate's dedication to freedom of debate is almost unique among modern legislative bodies. That freedom is intended to encourage the fullest possible discussion of matters on the floor. But, notice, the great <u>latitude</u> it allows also gives rise to the filibuster.

**latitude**
*n.* leeway, range of action

**The Filibuster** Essentially, a **filibuster** is an attempt to "talk a bill to death." It is a stalling tactic by which a minority of senators seeks to delay or prevent Senate action on a measure. The filibusterers try to so monopolize the Senate floor and its time that the Senate must either drop the bill or change it in some manner acceptable to the minority.

Talk—and more talk—is the filibusterers' major weapon. In addition, senators may use time-killing motions, quorum calls, and other parliamentary maneuvers. Indeed, anything to delay or obstruct is grist for the minority's mill as it works to block a bill that would very likely pass if brought to a vote.

Among the many better-known filibusterers, Senator Huey Long (D., Louisiana) spoke for more than 15 hours in 1935. He stalled by reading from the Washington telephone directory and giving his colleagues his recipes for "pot-likker," corn bread, and turnip greens. Senator Strom Thurmond (R., South Carolina) set the current filibuster record. He held the floor for 24 hours and 18 minutes in an unsuccessful, one-person effort against what, despite his arguments, became the Civil Rights Act of 1957.

No later efforts have come close to matching Senator Thurmond's record. In fact, both in the past and today, nearly all filibusters are team efforts, with a number of senators taking turns on the floor, relieving one another as they monopolize the Senate's time. Well over 300 measures have been killed by filibusters. Just the *threat* of a filibuster has resulted in the Senate's failure to consider a number of bills and the amending of many others.

The Senate often tries to beat off a filibuster with lengthy, even day-and-night, sessions to wear down the participants. At times, some little-observed rules are strictly enforced. Among them are the requirements that senators stand—not sit, lean on their desks, or walk about—as they speak and that they not use "unparliamentary language" on the floor. These countermeasures seldom work.

**The Cloture Rule** The Senate's real check on the filibuster is its Cloture Rule, Rule XXII in the Standing Rules of the Senate. It was first adopted in 1917, after one of the most notable of all filibusters in Senate history. That filibuster, which lasted for three weeks, took place less than two months before the United States entered World War I.

German submarines had renewed their attacks on shipping in the North Atlantic, so President Wilson asked Congress to permit the arming of American merchant vessels. The bill, widely supported in the country, quickly passed the House, by a vote of 403–13. The measure died in the Senate, however, because

# Differentiated Resources

The following resources are located in the All-in-One, Unit 3, Chapter 12, Section 4:

**L3** Reading Comprehension Worksheet (p. 152)
**L2** Reading Comprehension Worksheet (p. 153)
**L3** Bellringer Worksheet (p. 154)
**L3** Core Worksheet (p. 155)
**L3** Skills Worksheet (p. 156)
**L2** Skill Activity (p. 157)
**L3** Quiz A (p. 158)   **L2** Quiz B (p. 159)
**L3** Chapter Test A (p. 160)   **L2** Chapter Test B (p. 163)

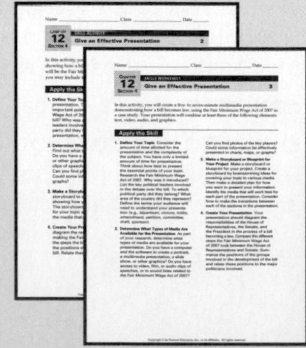

twelve senators filibustered it until the end of the congressional term on March 4th.

The public was outraged. President Wilson declared: "A little group of willful men, representing no opinion but their own, has rendered the great Government of the United States helpless and contemptible." The Senate passed the Cloture Rule at its next session.

Rule XXII provides for **cloture**—limiting debate. The rule is not in regular, continuing force; it can be brought into play only by a special procedure. A vote to invoke the rule must be taken two days after a petition calling for that action has been submitted by at least 16 members of the Senate. If at least 60 senators—three fifths of the full Senate—vote for the motion, the rule becomes effective. From that point, no more than another 30 hours of floor time may be spent on the measure. Then it *must* be brought to a final vote.

Of more than 700 attempts to invoke the rule, less than a third have been successful. Many senators hesitate to vote for cloture because (1) they honor the tradition of free debate and/or (2) they worry that frequent use of cloture will undercut the value of the filibuster that they may someday want to use.

**The Situation Today** Filibusters have become much more common in recent years because, for more than a decade now, party control of the upper house has been a very narrow thing. The Democrats enjoyed a reasonably comfortable majority in the 111th Congress (2009–2011): 58 Democrats (plus two independent members, Joe Lieberman of Connecticut and Bernie Sanders of Vermont, who chose to support the Democrats), to the GOP's 40 seats. Even so, the 60 votes needed to beat back a filibuster were at times hard to come by.

Today, the Democrats have a much smaller margin of control in the Senate: 51 seats and the two independents to the GOP's 47 seats. This means the Democrats currently do not have the 60 votes needed to invoke cloture.

Over the past several years, the minority party, at times the Democrats, currently the Republicans, has made frequent use of the filibuster to block legislation backed by the majority party. And their filibusters have been regularly successful. They have because, given the Cloture Rule, the minimum number of votes necessary to pass an important bill in the Senate today is not 51 or a simple majority of the members present and voting. It is, instead, 60, the minimum number of votes necessary to invoke cloture (end debate). It is true that filibusters can protect the minority and prevent hasty and ill-considered legislation. It is also true that they can promote gridlock, and public ridicule.

## Conference Committees

As you have seen, a bill must survive any number of challenges in order to become a law. Most don't. A measure can be killed, or simply buried, in a subcommittee, in the full committee, in the House Rules Committee, or in any of the parallel committees in the Senate. The remainder must make it through votes on the floor in both houses.

Any measure that does survive the legislative process *must* have been passed by both houses in identical form. Most often, a bill approved by one house and then passed by the other is left unchanged by the second. When the House and Senate do pass different versions of the same bill, the first house usually concurs in the other's amendments, and congressional action is completed.

When one house will not accept the other's version of a bill, the measure is sent to a conference committee—a temporary joint committee of the two chambers. It seeks to produce a compromise bill acceptable to both houses.

The conferees—managers—are named by the respective presiding officers. Mostly, they are leading members of the standing committee that first handled the measure in each house.

Both chambers' rules say that a conference committee can consider only those parts of a bill on which the two houses have disagreed. In practice, however, conferees often add provisions never considered in either the House or Senate.

Once the conferees agree, their report, the compromise bill, is submitted to both houses. It must be accepted or rejected without amendment. Only rarely does either house turn down a conference committee's work. This is not surprising, for two major

**✓ Checkpoint**
What caused the Senate to pass the Cloture Rule in 1917?

## Political Cartoon Mini-Lesson

Display Transparency 12I, Bipartisan Filibuster Compromise, when you discuss the effects of a filibuster. Explain that this cartoon was published at the end of a Democratic filibuster that delayed a confirmation vote on the Republican President's judicial nominees. Ask: **What do the paint colors represent?** (the conflicting viewpoints—blue for Democratic and red for Republican) **In the process of their fight, what are the adversaries creating?** (compromise—As they fling paint at each other, they are painting the word "compromise.") **What can you infer about Republican strength in the Senate at this time, based on the cartoon? How do you know?** (The Republicans must have held either a minority of seats or only a slim majority at this time, because they could not gather 60 votes for cloture and had to compromise.)

# Teach

To present this topic using online resources, use the lesson presentation at **PearsonSchool.com/phgovt.**

## DISCUSS THE FILIBUSTER

Ask students to identify the tool that Mr. Smith used on the floor of the Senate. (the filibuster) Ask: **What is a filibuster?** (an attempt by a minority of senators to delay or defeat a bill, especially by making extended speeches) Have students share their answers to the Bellringer questions. Make sure they understand that the objection of a single senator will defeat a unanimous consent agreement.

## COMPARE THE HOUSE AND SENATE

Explain that filibusters and unanimous consent agreements are two differences between the House and Senate. Direct students to open their books to "How a Bill Becomes a Law." Ask volunteers to read each step aloud and then describe each step in more detail, based on their reading and previous classes. At step 7, discuss the differences between the House and Senate and reasons for them. Specifically, discuss the less formal rules and the role of the filibuster. Ask: **Does the filibuster improve the lawmaking process?**

## INTRODUCE THE ACTIVITY

When students reach step 8 on the chart, distribute the Chapter 12 Section 4 Core Worksheet (Unit 3 All-in-One, p. 155), which provides a different version of the sample bill from the Section 3 Core Worksheet A. Briefly describe a conference committee. (A committee made up of powerful members of both houses, formed when each house passes a different version of the same bill; the committee must write a compromise bill.)

Divide students into groups of four or five. Explain that each group is a conference committee. The bill on the Core Worksheet has been passed by the Senate. However, the version that passed in the House is the one shown in Section 3 Core Worksheet A. Each conference committee should compare the two versions to identify the differences. Then they should negotiate to come up with a compromise bill.

Before they begin, divide each committee in half. Designate one half as members of Party Y and the other half as members of Party Z. Party Y is dedicated to reducing government spending. Party Z is dedicated to improving science and math education.

## Answers

**Checkpoint** The Cloture Rule was passed after a filibuster prevented Congress from passing a popular bill that would have allowed the arming of American merchant ships in 1917.

## BEGIN NEGOTIATIONS

Have the conference committees begin by identifying the differences in the bills. Then have them begin negotiations. Remind them that they must produce one compromise bill that is acceptable to all. Have students record their group's compromises at the bottom of the worksheet.

**L2 ELL Differentiate** Have students place the two versions side by side and compare each sentence individually. Whenever they find a difference, have them circle it on both bills.

**L4 Differentiate** In addition to negotiating compromises, have students propose new amendments from their party's viewpoint and negotiate passage of the amendments in committee.

## DISCUSS THE PROCESS

After the committees finish their negotiations, have them share their compromises with the class. Ask: **Which original bill was more restrictive: the House version or Senate version?** *(The Senate version—it would have paid out much less in benefits than would the House bill.)* Ask students how the conflicting goals of the two parties affected the negotiations.

Tell students to go to the Interactivity for an interactive of "How a Bill Becomes a Law."

## Answers

**How a Bill Becomes a Law** In the House, the Rules Committee sets conditions for debate and amendment on the floor. Senate debate is less restricted.

---

# How a **Bill** Becomes a Law

**A** bill may be introduced in either chamber. The path to the right is that of a bill that begins in the House. If a bill were to start in the Senate, steps 5, 6, and 7 would precede steps 1, 2, 3, and 4. *In what ways does the lawmaking process in the House differ from that in the Senate?*

**1 H.R. 1 INTRODUCED IN HOUSE.**

**2 COMMITTEE ACTION** H.R. 1 referred to standing committee for study, hearings, revisions, and approval.

**3 RULES COMMITTEE** The Rules Committee sets conditions for debate and amendment on the floor.

**5 S. 1 INTRODUCED IN SENATE.**

**4 FLOOR ACTION** H.R. 1 debated, then passed or defeated. If passed, it goes to the Senate.

**6 COMMITTEE ACTION** S. 1 referred to standing committee for study, hearings, revisions, and approval.

**7 FLOOR ACTION** S. 1 debated, then passed or defeated.

**8 CONFERENCE COMMITTEE** Conference committee resolves differences between House and Senate versions of bill.

President Eisenhower signs a bill into law.

**9 CONGRESSIONAL APPROVAL** House and Senate vote on final passage. Approved bill is sent to the President.

**10 PRESIDENTIAL ACTION** The President signs or vetoes the bill or allows it to become law without signing. A vetoed bill returns to Congress; the veto may be (but seldom is) overridden.

---

## Teacher-to-Teacher Network

**ALTERNATE LESSON PLAN** Divide the class into groups to make a timeline showing a "typical" day for a student. Compile a list of daily activities on the board. Then have students write down the events in the timelines that would be affected by laws—for example, FDA regulations on the foods they eat or the products they use, laws affecting education, etc. Help students identify the laws and decide which are federal, State, or local. Should any of the federal laws be changed? Should there be more federal laws, or fewer? How do federal laws get added or changed?

To see this lesson plan, go to

**Teacher Center**

at PearsonSchool.com/phgovt

# Lawmaking Behind the Scenes

The simplified path on the facing page does not fully reveal the complexity of the lawmaking process or the subtle changes to the process over the past several decades. As partisanship has increased in Congress, the majority party leaders in both houses have taken a much more important role, and lawmakers have introduced several unofficial, informal steps to the process. *How does the majority leadership influence legislation?*

A House-Senate conference committee ▲

## ▶▶ Before a Bill Is Submitted

**Building Support** Much work happens before a member of Congress submits a bill. Members may work with their own staff, experts in the field, interest groups, or the executive branch to draft the bill. They revise and edit the measure to ensure broad support and ask other members to announce their support by cosponsoring the bill. Negotiating behind the scenes is vital to the success of a proposed bill.

**Getting It Right** The exact wording of the bill determines its future in more ways than one. If a bill deals with matters that fall within the jurisdiction of more than one committee, the sponsors of the measure may tweak its wording to ensure that the primary responsibility for the bill will fall to the committee most likely to report it favorably.

The Hopper in the House

Howard McKeon, (R., Calif. ) and Roscoe G. Bartlett (R., Md.) talk during a House Armed Services Committee markup. ▼

## ▶▶ Committee Action

**Multiple Committees** The most important measures are now often referred to more than one committee. This reduces the clout of members of each committee by adding more voices to the committee debate.

**Majority Rules** The majority leadership in the House regularly uses the Rules Committee to advance its party's agenda. For example, the Rules Committee may restrict debate on a bill when it reaches the floor. In an emergency situation, the leadership may even bypass committees and bring a bill directly to the floor for a vote. This seldom happens, but it illustrates the increased power of party leaders over committees.

# How Government Works

**BUILDING SUPPORT BEHIND THE SCENES** Each party's leaders work behind the scenes to rally members to support measures that advance the party's agenda. This is not an easy task. Members of Congress have responsibilities to their constituents as well as to their party, and these responsibilities sometimes conflict. Much of the leader's influence is based on exchange. The leader is in a position to help individual party members achieve their political goals. For example, in exchange for a senator's cooperation, the party's floor leader might help the senator gain a seat on a desirable committee or might support legislation that benefits the senator's constituents. Party leaders must persuade rather than command, because they are elected and reelected by the same people they lead.

---

## TRACK THE BILL'S FINAL STEPS

Display Transparency 12J, which shows the start of a flowchart. Complete the flowchart as you review the bill's remaining steps with the class. The completed flowchart is shown below. Begin by telling students that the conference committee has produced a compromise bill. Ask: **What happens next?** *(The compromise bill goes to the floor of both houses for a vote.)* **The bill passes both houses. What's next?** *(It goes to the President.)* **What options does the President have?** *(sign, veto, allow the bill to become law without signing, pocket veto).*

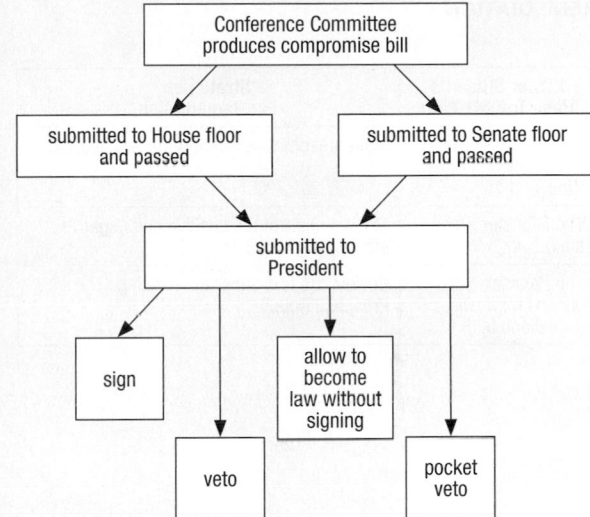

## DISCUSS THE ESSENTIAL QUESTION

Discuss the chapter's Essential Question with students: **Can and should the lawmaking process be improved?**

## EXTEND THE LESSON

**L3 Differentiate** Have students take the role of the President, who vetoed a compromise bill passed by the House and Senate. Have them write a veto message, explaining to Congress why they rejected the bill.

**L2 Differentiate** Prepare flash cards on which various stages that a bill goes through in the Senate are written. For stages that have several possible outcomes, write each outcome on a separate card and stack them. Have students take turns choosing necessary cards to enact the path of a bill.

**L4 Differentiate** Have students research the Civil Rights Act of 1964 and the filibuster surrounding that passage. Then have a follow-up discussion in class.

---

## Answers

**Lawmaking Behind the Scenes** Majority leadership in the House uses the Rules Committee to advance their party's agenda. They may even bypass committees and bring a bill directly to the floor.

# Assess and Remediate

**L3** Collect the compromise bills and ask students to write a paragraph explaining how their party compromised.

**L3** Assign the Section 4 Assessment questions.

**L3** Section Quiz A (Unit 3 All-in-One, p. 158)

**L2** Section Quiz B (Unit 3 All-in-One, p. 159)

Have students complete the review activities in the digital lesson presentation and continue their work in the **Essential Questions Journal.**

### REMEDIATION

| If Your Students Have Trouble With | Strategies For Remediation |
|---|---|
| Differences between the House and Senate (Question 1) | Make a T-chart comparing the two houses. |
| The filibuster (Questions 2, 4) | Make a chart of the positive and negative effects of a filibuster. |
| The President's options for a bill (Questions 3, 5) | Review the text under the heading "The President Acts." |

## Answers

**Checkpoint** A conference committee composed of members of both houses irons out the differences and presents a compromise bill for a floor vote in both houses.

---

reasons: (1) the powerful membership of the typical conference committee, and (2) the fact that its report usually comes in the midst of the rush to adjournment at the end of a congressional session.

The conference committee stage is a most strategic step. A number of major legislative decisions and compromises are often made at that point. Indeed, the late Senator George Norris (R., Nebraska) once quite aptly described conference committees as "the third house of Congress."

## The President Acts

The Constitution requires that bills and resolutions be sent to the President after they have passed both houses of Congress. The President has four options at this point:

1. The President may sign the bill, and it then becomes law.

Nancy Reagan and members of Congress watch the President sign the Ronald Reagan Centennial Commission Act of 2009. ▼

2. The President may **veto**—refuse to sign—the bill. The measure must then be returned to the house in which it originated, together with the President's objections (a veto message). Although it seldom does, Congress may then pass the bill over the President's veto, by a two-thirds vote of the full membership of each house.

3. The President may allow the bill to become law without signing it—by not acting on it within 10 days, not counting Sundays, of receiving it.

4. The fourth option is a variation of the third, called the **pocket veto.** If Congress adjourns its session within 10 days of submitting a bill to the President, and the President does not act, the measure dies. (Sundays are not counted.)

Congress added another element to the President's veto power with the passage of the Line Item Veto Act of 1996. That law gave the chief executive the power to reject individual items in appropriations bills. The Supreme Court held the law unconstitutional, however, in *Clinton* v. *City of New York,* 1998.

Because Congress can seldom muster enough votes to override a veto, the power can play an extremely effective part in the President's dealings with Congress. The weight of that power in the executive-legislative relationship is underscored by this fact: The mere threat of a veto is often enough to defeat a bill or to prompt changes in its provisions as it moves through the legislative process.

**Essential Questions Journal** To continue to build a response to the chapter Essential Question, go to your **Essential Questions Journal.**

## SECTION 4 ASSESSMENT

1. **Guiding Question** Use your completed Venn diagram to answer this question: What are the major differences in the lawmaking process in the House and the Senate?

**Key Terms and Comprehension**

2. **(a)** What is a **filibuster? (b)** How can it be ended?

3. What are the four options a President has when a bill reaches his desk?

**Critical Thinking**

4. **Draw Inferences** Consider what you have read about the filibuster. Identify two reasons why it has become a valued Senate tradition.

5. **Understand Point of View** Why might some Presidents have used the veto power frequently, while others have not used it very often?

**Quick Write**

**Persuasive Essay: Consider Your Audience** Look at your outline from Section 3. Suppose that the audience for your essay is members of Congress. Add details to your outline that will help you present your view in the most persuasive way. Begin with a clear statement of your argument. Be sure to address the various opposing points of view.

---

# Assessment Answers

**1.** The Senate's proceedings are less formal and its rules less strict than those of the larger House. The Senate has one calendar; the House has five. During floor debate, House members must speak to the bill at hand and follow certain conditions. Senators may speak on any topic in nearly unlimited debate. House members can move the previous question. Senators cannot; they must use cloture to end a filibuster.

**2. (a)** A filibuster is the use of long speeches by senators to delay or prevent a floor vote on a bill likely to pass. It is intended to kill the bill or force changes acceptable to the minority.
**(b)** It can be ended by cloture, which requires a three-fifths Senate vote.

**3.** sign the bill into law; veto the bill; allow the bill to become law without signing it by not taking action on it within ten days of receiving it; kill the bill with a "pocket veto" if Congress adjourns within ten days of submitting it

**4.** The filibuster protects the rights of the minority by pressuring the majority to compromise. A filibuster prevents passage of ill-considered legislation or legislation supported by only a narrow majority. Also, senators are proud of their strong tradition of free debate.

**5.** Possible response: A President whose party holds a majority in Congress will have less reason to use a veto than a President whose party is in the minority.

**QUICK WRITE** Students will state their argument, add supporting details to their outlines, and address opposing views.

# Quick Study Guide

**GOVERNMENT** ONLINE
**On the Go**
To review anytime, anywhere, download these online resources at **PearsonSchool.com/phgovt**
Political Dictionary, Audio Review

**Guiding Question**
**Section 2** How do committees help Congress do its work?

**Guiding Question**
**Section 3** What steps does a successful bill follow as it moves through the House?

**Guiding Question**
**Section 1** How do constitutional and party officers keep Congress organized?

**CHAPTER 12**
**Essential Question**
Can and should the lawmaking process be improved?

**Guiding Question**
**Section 4** What are the major differences in the lawmaking process in the House and the Senate?

## Political Dictionary

Speaker of the House *p. 332*
President of the Senate *p. 333*
President *pro tempore* *p. 334*
party caucus *p. 334*
floor leader *p. 336*
majority leader *p. 336*
minority leader *p. 336*
whip *p. 336*
committee chairman *p. 336*
seniority rule *p. 337*
standing committee *p. 338*
subcommittee *p. 340*
select committee *p. 340*
joint committee *p. 341*
conference committee *p. 342*
bill *p. 343*
joint resolution *p. 344*
concurrent resolution *p. 344*
resolution *p. 344*
rider *p. 344*
pigeonhole *p. 345*
discharge petition *p. 345*
quorum *p. 348*
engrossed *p. 349*
filibuster *p. 352*
cloture *p. 353*
veto *p. 356*
pocket veto *p. 356*

## Comparing the House and the Senate

| House of Representatives | Senate |
|---|---|
| Smaller personal staffs | Larger personal staffs |
| Fewer committee assignments | More committee assignments |
| More formal, less flexible rules | Fewer, more flexible rules |
| Committee work usually more important than floor debate in shaping outcome of legislation | Floor debate often more important than committee work in shaping outcome of legislation |
| Floor debate strictly limited | Floor debate largely unlimited, but subject to cloture vote by 60 senators to end debate |

### Types of Bills and Resolutions

| | |
|---|---|
| **Bill** | A proposed law: a public bill applies to the entire nation; a private bill applies only to certain people or places |
| **Joint Resolution** | A proposal for some action that has the force of law when passed; usually deals with special circumstances or temporary matters |
| **Concurrent Resolution** | A statement of position on an issue, adopted by the House and Senate in identical form |
| **Resolution** | A measure dealing with some matter in one house; does not have the force of law and does not require the President's signature |

# For More Information

To learn more about the lawmaking process, refer to these sources or assign them to students:

**L1** **Donovan, Sandra.** *Making Laws: A Look at How a Bill Becomes a Law.* Lerner Publishing Group, 2004.

**L2** **Fish, Bruce and Becky Durost Fish.** *The Speaker of the House of Representatives.* Chelsea House Publications, 2001.

**L3** **Anderson, Janet.** *The Senate.* Chelsea House Publishers, 2007.

**L4** **Sinclair, Barbara.** *Unorthodox Lawmaking: New Legislative Processes in the U. S. Congress.* Congressional Quarterly, Inc., 2000.

Have students download the digital resources available at Government on the Go for review and remediation.

## STUDY TIPS

**Taking Notes** Perhaps the most important point for students to remember when taking notes in class is that they should *not* attempt to write down everything the teacher is saying. Rather than writing in sentences, students should use phrases or even a single word when that will suffice. Abbreviations and symbols should be used whenever possible. Caution students, however, that they *should* copy anything the teacher writes on the board, anything the teacher repeats, and all terms and definitions. It is a good idea to leave space between ideas so that students can go back and add information later. As they write, students should highlight important ideas by underlining, circling, or starring them. If the teacher is talking too fast, suggest that students jot down nouns and verbs only and fill in the rest after class.

## ASSESSMENT AT A GLANCE

### Tests and Quizzes
Section Assessments
Section Quizzes A and B, Unit 3 **All-in-One**
Chapter Assessment
Chapter Tests A and B, Unit 3 **All-in-One**
Document-Based Assessment
Progress Monitoring Online
Exam*View* Test Bank

### Performance Assessment
Essential Questions Journal
Debate, p. 347
Assessment Rubrics, **All-in-One**

# Chapter Assessment

## COMPREHENSION AND CRITICAL THINKING

### SECTION 1

1. (a) every two years (b) The House must be reorganized each opening day because all seats are up for election each term. All members must be sworn in. All officers must be selected and committee seats filled. Opening day activities in the Senate are shorter and more routine than in the House, because the Senate is a continuous body. Only a third of the seats are up for election each term. Only new and reelected members must be sworn in and only a few committee vacancies must be filled.

2. (a) Chairmen are chosen by the majority party caucus, based on seniority. (b) Constitutional officers serve the chamber as a whole. Party officers focus on advancing their party's agenda.

### SECTION 2

3. (a) Standing committees are permanent panels that address bills pertaining to matters within a specific jurisdiction. (b) the party that holds the majority of seats in that chamber (c) Most committees review bills dealing with particular policy matters. When a bill is introduced, the Speaker or President of the Senate refers it to the appropriate committee.

4. (a) The parties choose committee members, and a floor vote ratifies their choices. (b) Some committees are more prestigious or powerful than others. Also, members of Congress whose constituents are heavily influenced by the actions of a particular committee may seek a seat on that committee.

### SECTION 3

5. (a) resolution (b) joint resolution (c) private bill

6. (a) report the bill favorably, report it unfavorably, refuse to report it, report it in amended form, or report a committee bill—a new bill substituted for one or more bills referred to the committee (b) when the committee feels that the full House should have a chance to consider the bill or when the committee does not want to take responsibility for killing it (c) Possible response: Killing a bill that is popular with constituents can have political consequences. By reporting the bill unfavorably rather than killing it, committee members can share the blame with the other members of Congress.

---

# Chapter Assessment

**GOVERNMENT ONLINE**
Self-Test
To test your understanding of key terms and main ideas, visit
PearsonSchool.com/phgovt

## Comprehension and Critical Thinking

### Section 1

1. (a) How often does a new term of Congress begin? (b) Compare opening day in the House and the Senate.

2. (a) How are House and Senate committee chairmen chosen? (b) Why are there both constitutional and party officers in Congress?

### Section 2

3. (a) What are the standing committees in the House and Senate? (b) Which party holds the majority of seats on each committee? (c) What factors determine which committee will deal with a bill?

4. (a) Who determines who will serve on each congressional committee? (b) Why are some committee assignments more desirable than others?

### Section 3

5. What type of measure would the House or Senate use if it wanted to (a) amend one of its rules? (b) express an opinion that would have the force of law on some temporary matter? (c) make a law affecting only one person?

6. (a) What are the five options a committee has when it has finished work on a bill? (b) Describe a situation in which a committee might decide to report a bill with an unfavorable recommendation rather than pigeonhole it. (c) Evaluate the usefulness of this practice.

7. Why might a member of Congress vote in favor of a bill once it is certain to pass even though he or she had supported previous attempts to scuttle it?

### Section 4

FILIBUSTED.

8. (a) **Analyzing Political Cartoons** Study the cartoon above. (a) What point is the cartoon making? (b) Do you agree or disagree with its point of view?

9. (a) Why are conference committees rarely necessary? (b) Why are their recommendations usually accepted?

10. Compare and contrast the rules for debate in the House and Senate.

### Writing About Government

11. Use your Quick Write exercises from this chapter to write a persuasive essay about the organization of Congress. Make sure that your thesis is stated clearly and that it is illustrated with specific examples and supported by your arguments. When you are finished, ask a friend to read the essay and give you feedback about its clarity and persuasiveness. Use this feedback to fine tune your writing. See pp. S9–S10 of the Skills Handbook.

## Apply What You've Learned

12. **Essential Question Activity** Go online to find information about bills recently introduced in Congress. Find a bill that became law and another that died in committee. Make a flowchart to show the progression of each bill through Congress and explain how that process compares to the chart "How a Bill Becomes a Law" in Section 4.

13. **Essential Question Assessment** Look at your flowchart from Question 12. Using these two bills as examples, write an essay in which you evaluate the success of the current lawmaking process. This will help you answer the chapter Essential Question: **Can and should the lawmaking process be improved?**

**Essential Questions Journal** To respond to the chapter Essential Question, go to your **Essential Questions Journal.**

---

7. Possible response: Attempts to kill a bill often occur behind the scenes, but the record of final votes is highly visible. If a member's constituents favor the bill, the member might want to go on record as supporting it when his less-visible attempts to kill it fail. Also, there may be political advantages to voting with the winning side.

### SECTION 4

8. (a) The cartoon suggests that Congress is broken because of the filibuster. (b) Possible response: I disagree. Although the filibuster allows a minority to stall legislation, it also ensures broad support and sufficient consideration for bills that reach the Senate floor.

9. (a) Most bills passed in one house are then passed in the other unchanged. When different versions do pass, the first house usually concurs with the other's amendments, so no conference committee is needed to resolve differences. (b) because the members of conference committees are usually powerful

10. The House has more restrictive rules to control the flow of business and limit debate. The Senate's rules are less formal and more flexible and debate is almost unlimited.

# Document-Based Assessment

## Divided Government

Over recent decades, the majority party in Congress has often not been the President's party. Americans disagree about this state of divided government. As Document 2 shows, independents generally favor divided government. Critics, however, point out that divided government allows each party to blame the other for government failures, as the author of Document 3 argues.

### Document 1

One fallacious viewpoint too often expressed this election season is that a Democrat takeover of one or both houses of Congress would be desirable, since we then would have "divided government," with each party holding a share of power. Given the problems our nation faces today, this would be disastrous for America. . . . [T]he fundamental problems our nation faces today require a full commitment to coherent solutions, not a little of the left and a little of the right jumbled together.

—Peter Ferrara, *National Review Online,*
November 1, 2006

### Document 2

The voters gave the country divided government last week, [in the 2006 congressional elections] and Americans tend to believe divided government is a good thing, although the belief is not overwhelming. 42% say it's better for the country when one party controls the Presidency and the other the Congress, while 33% (and even more Republicans) favor one party government. Independents [51%] are particularly happy with divided control.

—CBS News Poll, November 14, 2006

### Document 3

[D]ivided government is the main reason voters should be mistrustful of the decisions and nondecisions made in Washington. Division produces deadlock. Deadlock produces a mélange [mix] of actions and nonactions that no elected official can or will defend, and for which every elected official in each party blames the elected officials in the other.

—Lloyd Cutler, Counsel to President Carter,
Letter to *The New York Times,* September 16, 1992

### Document 4

Use your knowledge of Congress and Documents 1–4 above to answer Questions 1–3.

1. Which statement does Document 2 support?
   A. Independents are most likely to support divided government.
   B. Republicans are most likely to support divided government.
   C. Democrats are most likely to support divided government.
   D. A majority of Americans support divided government.

2. What point does Document 4 make?

3. **Pull It Together** Using these documents, explain whether divided government enhances or hinders the lawmaking process.

**GOVERNMENT** ONLINE
**Documents**
To find more resources on divided government, visit **PearsonSchool.com/phgovt**

---

## DOCUMENT-BASED ASSESSMENT

1. A

2. Partisanship in Congress has brought the work of government to a halt, and some people view that as positive.

3. Possible response: Some people support divided government because it slows down the pace of legislation in Congress.

**L2 Differentiate** Students use all the documents on the page to support their thesis.

**L3 Differentiate** Students include additional information available online at **PearsonSchool.com/phgovt.**

**L4 Differentiate** Students use materials from the textbook, the online information at **PearsonSchool.com/phgovt,** and do additional research to support their views.

**Go Online to PearsonSchool.com/phgovt** for a student rubric and extra documents.

---

### WRITING ABOUT GOVERNMENT

**11.** Persuasive essays should include a clear thesis statement with supporting details and specific examples.

### APPLY WHAT YOU'VE LEARNED

**12.** Students' flowcharts should show a grasp of the lawmaking process and its variations.

**13.** Students' answers should reflect a thoughtful assessment of the lawmaking process.

Perspectives

## Essential Question
# What makes a successful Congress?

There are many ways to define a successful Congress. The following examples offer perspectives on different qualities.

**"ON SETTING PRIORITIES:**

**Congress should pass laws that reflect the will of the people; that is, Congress should be responsive to popular majorities. Congress should pass laws that deal promptly and effectively with pressing national problems. . . . Only in a perfect world would what the majority wants always accord with what policy experts deem most likely to be effective. When a conflict exists, which should take priority?"**

—Barbara Sinclair, *An Effective Congress and Effective Members: What Does It Take?*, 1996

**ON COMPROMISE:**

**"ON EFFICIENCY:**

**. . . Congress simply isn't set up to be efficient. . . . Its job is to understand [issues] thoroughly, weigh the beliefs and interests of an astounding variety of Americans, and consider carefully how to move forward.**

—Rep. Lee Hamilton (D., Indiana), 2004

### Essential Question Warmup

Throughout this unit, you studied the powers and functions of Congress. Use what you have learned and the quotations and opinions above to answer the following questions. Then go to your **Essential Questions Journal.**

**1.** How should members of Congress balance their roles as representatives of what voters want and as trustees who promote the best interests of the nation as a whole?

**2.** How should members of Congress balance their roles as party members with the need to compromise?

**3.** What should be the role of debate in Congress?

**Essential Questions Journal** — To continue to build a response to the unit Essential Question, go to your **Essential Questions Journal.**

## Assessment Resources

Unit 3 AYP Monitoring Assessment
Exam*View* Test Bank CD-ROM
SuccessTracker Assessment
Online Student Self-Tests
Chapter Tests
Section Quizzes
Chapter-level Document-Based Assessment

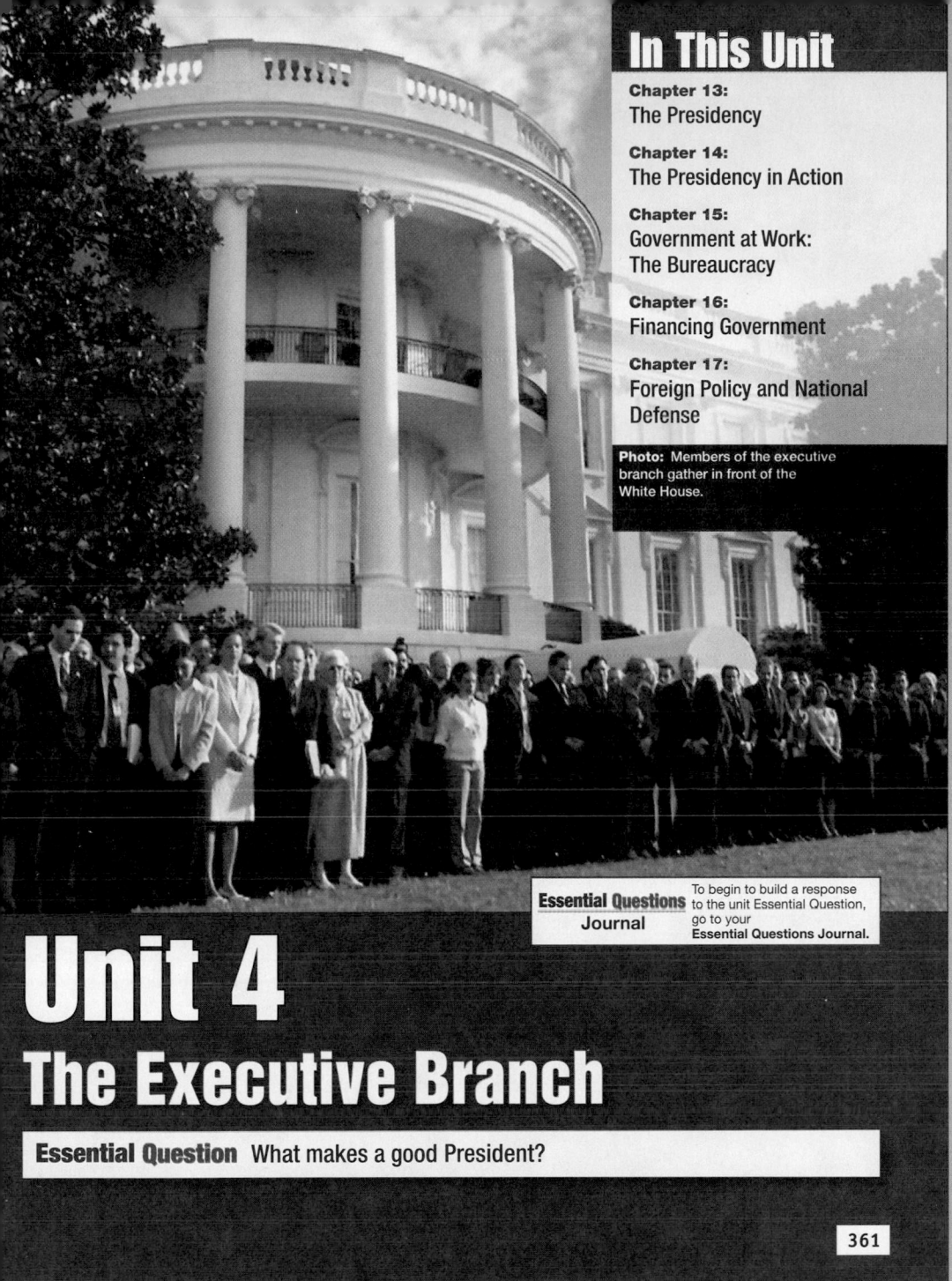

**Photo:** Members of the executive branch gather in front of the White House.

**Essential Questions Journal** To begin to build a response to the unit Essential Question, go to your **Essential Questions Journal.**

# Unit 4
# The Executive Branch

**Essential Question** What makes a good President?

361

---

**ESSENTIAL QUESTION PERSPECTIVES**

Essential questions frame each unit and chapter of study, asking students to consider big ideas about government. The question for this unit—**What makes a good President?**—demands that students ask further questions. How closely does a good President follow the advice of others? Is firm leadership more or less important than consensus building? Should a President's governing style change in times of crisis? What qualities have made for our greatest Presidents? Do the qualities that make for a good candidate also make for a good President?

To begin this unit, assign the Unit 4 Warmup Activity on page 103 of the **Essential Questions Journal.** This will help students start to consider their position on the **Unit 4 Essential Question: What makes a good President?**

Show the **Unit 4 American Government Essential Questions Video** to help students begin thinking about the unit Essential Question and designate a classroom bulletin board for students to post news articles related to the unit Essential Question. Use the Conversation Wall strategy (p. T27) to encourage students to post articles and comments on other students' postings.

Later, students will further explore the chapter-level essential questions:

*Chapter 13:* **Does the current electoral process result in the best candidates for President?**

*Chapter 14:* **How much power should the President have?**

*Chapter 15:* **Is the bureaucracy essential to good government?**

*Chapter 16:* **How should the federal budget reflect Americans' priorities?**

*Chapter 17:* **How should the United States interact with other countries?**

Use the **Essential Questions Journal** throughout the program to help students consider these and other big ideas about government.

---

# Government Online Resources

Government Online Teacher Center at **PearsonSchool.com/phgovt** includes
- Online Teacher's Edition with lesson planner and lecture notes
- Teacher's Resource Library with All-in-One Resources, Color Transparencies, Adequate Yearly Progress Monitoring, and an alternative lesson plan for each chapter
- SuccessTracker Assessment

Government Online Student Center at **PearsonSchool.com/phgovt** includes
- Interactive textbook with audio
- American Government Essential Questions Video
- Chapter-level WebQuests
- Guided Audio Tours and Interactivities
- Student Self-Tests

# Introduce the Chapter

## Essential Questions:

### UNIT 4

What makes a good President?

### CHAPTER 13

Does the current electoral process result in the best candidates for President?

### ACTIVATE PRIOR KNOWLEDGE

Have students examine the image and quotation on these pages. Ask: **In what way is the presidency "the people's office"?** *(The President is elected by a vote of citizens nationwide, making him or her the representative of all Americans.)* In this chapter, students will learn about the job of the President and the election process. Tell students to begin to further explore the presidency by completing the Chapter 13 Essential Question Warmup Activity in their **Essential Questions Journal.** Discuss their responses as a class.

### BEFORE READING

**L2** **ELL Differentiate** Chapter 13 Prereading and Vocabulary Worksheet (Unit 4 All-in-One, p. 11)

### SUCCESSNET STUDENT AND TEACHER CENTER

Visit **PearsonSchool.com/phgovt** for downloadable resources that allow students and teachers to connect with government "on the go."

### DIGITAL LESSON PRESENTATION

The digital lesson presentation supports the print lesson with activities and summaries of key concepts. Activities for this chapter include:

- **Who Is Next in Line?**
- **The 2008 Presidential Election**

## SKILLS DEVELOPMENT

### ANALYZE POLITICAL CARTOONS

You may wish to teach analyzing political cartoons as a distinct skill within Section 5 of this chapter. Use the Chapter 13 Skills Worksheet (Unit 4 All-in-One, p. 50) to help students learn to analyze political cartoons. The worksheet asks students to study a cartoon and then answer questions about it. For L2 and L1 students, assign the adapted Skill Activity (Unit 4 All-in-One, p. 51).

**WebQuest online** The chapter WebQuest challenges students to answer the chapter Essential Question by asking them about the presidential electoral process.

362

## Block Scheduling

**BLOCK 1:** Teach the Section 1, 2, and 3 lessons, omitting the Section 1 Core Worksheet activity, the Section 2 political cartoon analysis, and the sections' extend activities.

**BLOCK 2:** Teach the Section 4 and 5 lessons, omitting the Section 4 Core Worksheet B activity, the Section 4 debate, and both sections' extend activities.

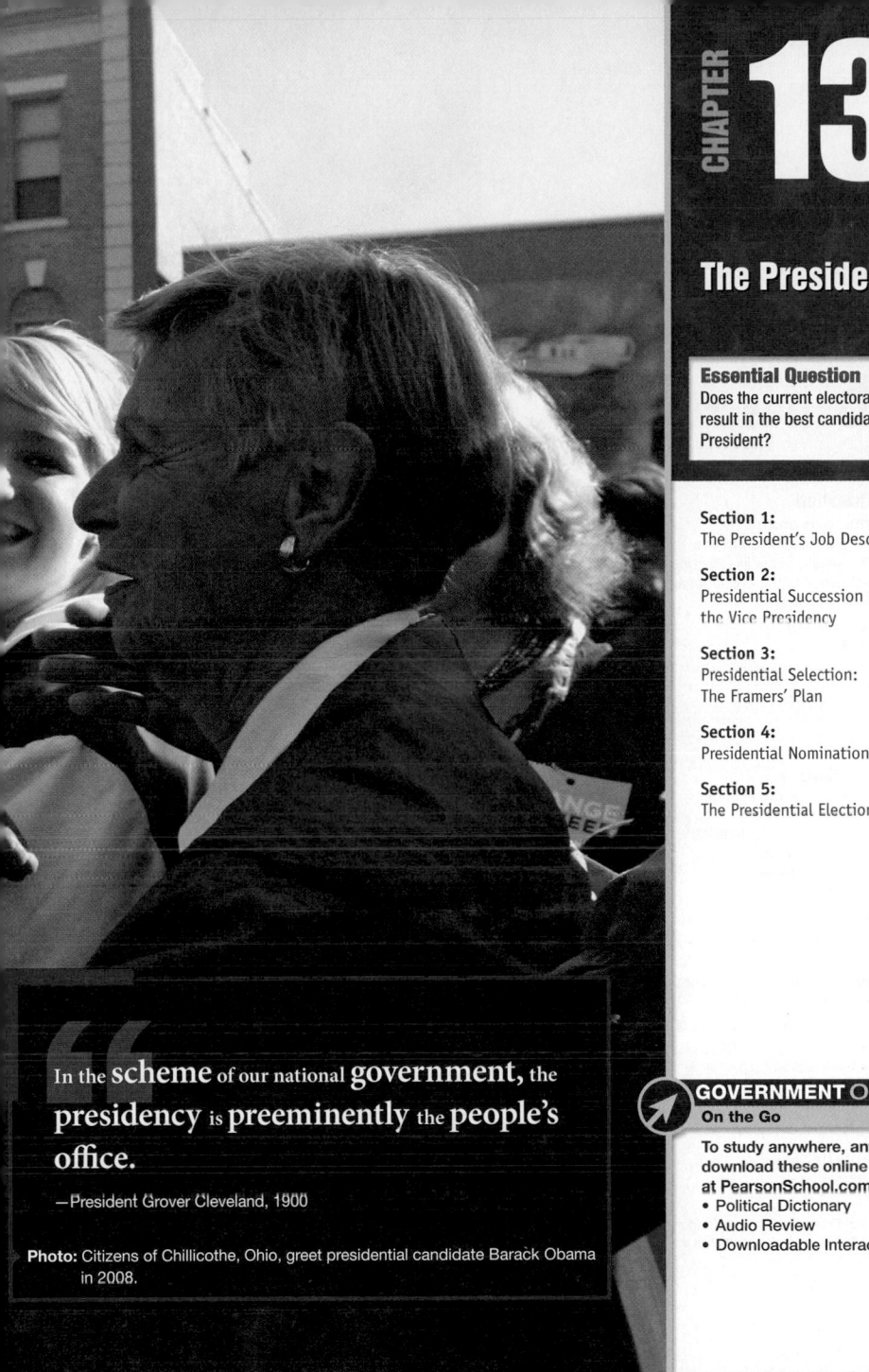

### Essential Question
Does the current electoral process result in the best candidates for President?

> In the **scheme** of our national **government**, the **presidency** is **preeminently** the **people's office.**
>
> —President Grover Cleveland, 1900

**Photo:** Citizens of Chillicothe, Ohio, greet presidential candidate Barack Obama in 2008.

**GOVERNMENT** ONLINE
**On the Go**

To study anywhere, anytime, download these online resources at PearsonSchool.com/phgovt
• Political Dictionary
• Audio Review
• Downloadable Interactivities

363

## Lesson Goals

**SECTION 1**

Students will . . .

• describe the roles and formal qualifications of the President.

• categorize each activity on a President's actual appointment schedule, according to the roles involved.

• compile a list of informal qualifications for a President, based on an analysis of roles.

**SECTION 2**

Students will . . .

• evaluate the importance of the position of Vice President.

• describe the process of succession.

• reflect on the importance of the Vice President's role as presidential successor.

**SECTION 3**

Students will . . .

• describe the Framers' original plan for selecting the President and Vice President.

• analyze how historical events led to changes in the way the President and Vice President are selected.

**SECTION 4**

Students will . . .

• discuss the influence of early primaries on the presidential nomination process.

• compare the nomination process in different States by researching and completing a chart.

• explore the goals of national conventions by analyzing nomination acceptance speeches.

**SECTION 5**

Students will . . .

• examine the distribution of electoral votes.

• recognize the influence of the electoral system on campaign strategy, using a map of pre-election opinion poll results.

• evaluate proposals to reform the electoral college system, using a Jigsaw strategy.

## Pressed for Time

Begin the class with a brainstorming session on the roles of the President and the qualifications and skills students think a President needs. Then, review the election process, clarifying how the primary and caucus elections work and the part the electoral college plays in the election system. Divide the class into groups of four and have each group research the results of the primary/caucus in their State or a State of their choosing and the results of the most recent presidential election with a focus on the Essential Question: **Does the current electoral process result in the best candidates for President?** Have students share their research results and opinion on the Essential Question with the class.

**FOLLOW UP** Have students write an essay expressing how their research illustrates the success or failure of the presidential election system in the United States.

**DIFFERENTIATED INSTRUCTION KEY**

Look for these symbols to help you adjust steps in each lesson to meet your students' needs.

**L1** Special Needs

**L2** Basic

  **ELL** English Language Learners

  **LPR** Less Proficient Readers

**L3** All Students

**L4** Advanced Students

## What are the roles and qualifications of the office of the President?

I. The President's Roles
   A. chief of state
      1. ceremonial head of government
      2. symbol of the people
   B. chief executive
      1. executive power
      2. limited by checks and balances
   C. chief administrator of executive branch
   D. chief diplomat
      1. main architect of foreign policy
      2. nation's chief spokesman to world
   E. commander in chief
      1. head of military
      2. dominant in military and foreign affairs
   F. chief legislator
      1. main author of public policy
      2. shapes congressional agenda
   G. chief of party
      1. leads party that controls executive branch
      2. role not mentioned in Constitution
   H. chief citizen
      1. representative of all the people
      2. champions public over private interests
      3. role not mentioned in Constitution
II. Formal Qualifications
   A. natural born citizen
   B. at least 35 years old
   C. resident at least 14 years

## SKILLS DEVELOPMENT

### ANALYZE SOURCES

The Core Worksheet activity in this section asks students to analyze President Truman's appointment schedule. Before doing the activity, you may want to have students review the steps in analyzing sources on page S14 of the Skills Handbook.

---

SECTION **1**

# The **President's** Job Description

### Guiding Question
**What are the roles and qualifications of the office of the President?** Use an outline like the one below to keep track of the presidential roles and qualifications.

I. The President's Roles
  A. Chief of state
    1. _____
    2. _____
  B. _____
    1. _____
    2. _____

### Political Dictionary
• chief of state
• chief executive
• chief administrator
• chief diplomat
• commander in chief
• chief legislator
• chief of party
• chief citizen

### Objectives
1. Describe the President's many roles.
2. Understand the formal qualifications necessary to become President.
3. Explain how the President's term of office has changed over time.
4. Describe the President's pay and benefits.

**Image Above:** President Ronald Reagan addresses U.S. troops in South Korea in 1983.

Do you know who the youngest person ever to be President of the United States was? The oldest? Who held the presidency for the longest time? The shortest? Can a person born abroad become President? You will find the answers to these questions, and much more, in this section, which provides a basic overview of the presidential office.

## Presidential Roles

At any given time, of course, only one person is the President of the United States. The office, with all of its awesome powers and duties, belongs to that one individual. Whoever that person may be, he—and most likely someday she[1]—must fill several different roles, and all of them at the same time. The President is simultaneously (1) chief of state, (2) chief executive, (3) chief administrator, (4) chief diplomat, (5) commander in chief, (6) chief legislator, (7) chief of party, and (8) chief citizen.

**1.** To begin with, the President is **chief of state,** the ceremonial head of the government of the United States. He or she is, then, the symbol of all of the people of the nation—in President William Howard Taft's words, "the personal embodiment and representative of their dignity and majesty."

In many countries, the chief of state reigns but does not rule. That is certainly true of the queens of England, Denmark, and the Netherlands; the kings of Norway, Sweden, and Belgium; the emperor of Japan; and the presidents of Italy and Germany. It is just as certainly *not* true of the President of the United States. The President both reigns and rules.

**2.** The President is the nation's **chief executive,** vested by the Constitution with "the executive Power" of the United States. That power is immensely broad in both domestic and foreign affairs. Indeed, the American presidency is often described as "the most powerful office in the world."

But remember, the President is not all-powerful. He or she lives in an environment filled with constitutional checks and balances in which there are

---

1   To this point, all of the Presidents have been men, but nothing in the Constitution precludes the possibility of a woman in that office.

## Focus on the Basics

**FACTS:** • The Constitution establishes the President's roles as chief of state, chief executive, chief administrator, chief diplomat, commander in chief, and chief legislator. • The President's roles of chief of party and chief citizen developed over time. • The Constitution requires the President to be a natural born citizen, at least 35 years old, and a U.S. resident for at least 14 years. • The 22nd Amendment limits a President to two full terms and no more than ten years.

**CONCEPTS:** leadership, separation of powers, checks and balances

**ENDURING UNDERSTANDINGS:** • The Constitution defines the roles and qualifications of the President. • Term limits check the power of the President.

many practical limits on what he or she can and cannot do.

**3.** The President is also the **chief administrator,** the director of the huge executive branch of the Federal Government. He or she heads one of the largest governmental machines the world has ever known. Today, the President directs an administration that employs more than 2.7 million civilians and spends more than $3 trillion a year.

Managing the <u>sprawling</u> executive branch is only one of the President's several jobs. Harry Truman complained that he had to spend too much of his time "flattering, kissing, and kicking people to get them to do what they were supposed to do anyway."

**4.** Every President is also the nation's **chief diplomat,** the main architect of American foreign policy and the nation's chief spokesman to the rest of the world. "I make foreign policy," President Truman once said—and he did. Everything the President says and does is closely followed, both here and abroad.

**5.** In close <u>concert</u> with the President's role in foreign affairs, the Constitution also makes him or her the **commander in chief** of the nation's armed forces. The 1.4 million men and women in uniform and all of the nation's military might are subject to the President's direct and immediate control. The Constitution does give Congress some significant powers in foreign affairs and over the military, but the President has long since become dominant in both fields.

**6.** The President is also the nation's **chief legislator,** the principal author of its public policies. Most often, it is the President who sets the overall shape of the congressional agenda—initiating, suggesting, requesting, insisting, and demanding that Congress enact most of the major pieces of legislation that it does.

The President and Congress do sometimes clash, and the President does not always get his or her way on Capitol Hill. Still, working with Congress occupies a major part of the President's time.

These six presidential roles all come directly from the Constitution. Yet they do not complete the list. The President has still other vital roles to play.

**7.** The President is, automatically, the **chief of party,** the acknowledged leader of the political party that controls the executive branch—and is virtually unchallengeable in that role. As you know, parties are not mentioned in the Constitution, but they do have a vital place in the workings of the American governmental system. Much of the real power and influence of the President depends on his or her ability to play this critical role.

**8.** The office also automatically makes its occupant the nation's **chief citizen.** The President is expected to be "the representative of all the people." He or she is expected to take the high road and <u>champion</u> the public interest against the many different and competing private interests. "The presidency," said Franklin Roosevelt, "is not merely an administrative office. That is the least of it. It is, preeminently, a place of moral leadership."

Listing the President's several roles is a useful and convenient way to describe the President's job. But, remember, the President

✓ **Checkpoint**
What are the President's responsibilities as the nation's chief legislator?

<u>sprawling</u>
*adj.* spreading out over a large area

<u>concert</u>
*n.* with all in agreement, together as one

<u>champion</u>
*v.* to fight for, defend, or promote

President Bill Clinton meets with Israeli and Palestinian leaders at Camp David in 2000 to conduct peace talks. *What role is President Clinton fulfilling here?*

# Get Started

## LESSON GOALS
Students will . . .

- describe the roles and formal qualifications of the President.
- categorize each activity on a President's actual appointment schedule according to the roles involved.
- compile a list of informal qualifications for a President based on an analysis of roles.

## BEFORE CLASS
Assign the section, the graphic organizer in the text, and the Reading Comprehension Worksheet (Unit 4 All-in-One, p. 15) before class.

**L2 Differentiate** Reading Comprehension Worksheet (Unit 4 All-in-One, p. 16)

## BELLRINGER
Write on the board: **In your notebook, list five specific examples of things a President does as part of the job.**

**L2 ELL Differentiate** Provide prompts, such as "meet with foreign leaders," "sign bills into law," "give the State of the Union address," and "throw out the ceremonial first pitch in a baseball game."

# Teach

To present this topic using online resources, use the lesson presentations at **PearsonSchool.com/phgovt.**

## REVIEW BELLRINGER
Write students' examples of the President's activities on the board. Then, have students categorize each example according to one or more of the presidential roles.

**L1 L2 Differentiate** Ask students to share their answers early in the discussion.

# Differentiated Resources

The following resources are located in the All-in-One, Unit 4, Chapter 13, Section 1:

**L2** Prereading and Vocabulary Worksheet (p. 11)
**L3** Reading Comprehension Worksheet (p. 15)
**L2** Reading Comprehension Worksheet (p. 16)
**L3** Core Worksheet (p. 17)
**L3** Quiz A (p. 19)
**L2** Quiz B (p. 20)

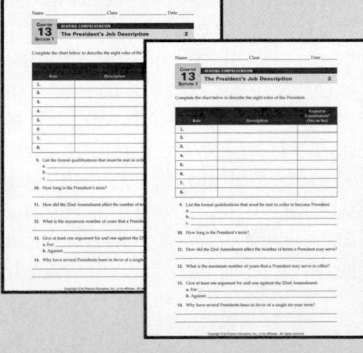

# Answers

**Checkpoint** being principal author of the nation's public policies and setting the overall shape of the congressional agenda

**Caption** chief diplomat and chief citizen

## DISTRIBUTE CORE WORKSHEET

Distribute the Chapter 13 Section 1 Core Worksheet (Unit 4 All-in-One, p. 17), which uses President Truman's actual appointment schedule for a day during his administration. Have students read the schedule and categorize each activity by the presidential role(s) it fulfills. Remind students that some activities may fulfill more than one role.

**L4 Differentiate** For each role the students identify, have them locate the text in the Constitution that spells out that presidential role. Have students include in the second column of the worksheet the Article and Section of the Constitution in which it is located. Remind students that not all roles are delineated by the Constitution.

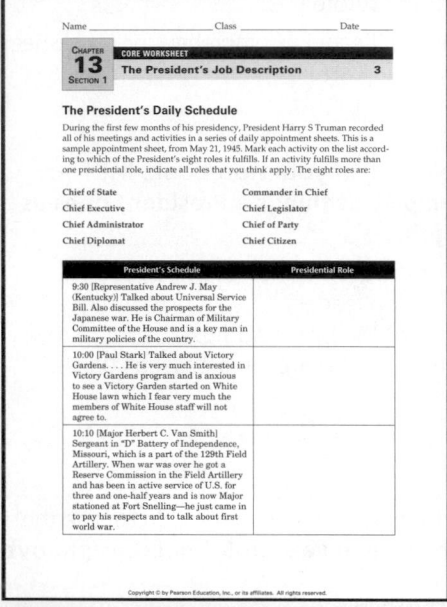

## COMPARE WORKSHEET ANSWERS

Read the schedule items one by one, and for each item, call on a student to state the presidential role(s) he or she assigned to this activity. After each item, have the other students in the class raise their hand if they categorized the item differently. If so, ask the student to explain his or her own answer. Then discuss both answers with the class until the group has agreed on a category (or categories).

## Answers

**Checkpoint** a natural born citizen, at least 35 years of age, been a U.S. resident for 14 years

---

**agonizing**
*adj.* painful, distressing

**sordid**
*adj.* shameful

must play all of these roles simultaneously, and they are all interconnected. None of them can be performed in isolation. The manner in which a President plays any one role can have a real effect on his or her ability to play another and even all of them.

As but two illustrations of the point, take the experiences of Presidents Lyndon Johnson and Richard Nixon. Each was a strong and relatively effective President during his first years in office. But Mr. Johnson's actions as commander in chief during the <u>agonizing</u> and increasingly unpopular war in Vietnam seriously damaged his stature and effectiveness in the White House. In fact, the damage was so great that it helped persuade LBJ not to run for reelection in 1968.

The many-sided and <u>sordid</u> Watergate scandal brought President Nixon's downfall. The manner in which he filled the roles of party leader and chief citizen so destroyed Mr. Nixon's presidency that he was forced to leave office in disgrace in 1974.

## Formal Qualifications

Whatever else a President must be, the Constitution says that he—and, again, likely one day she—must meet three formal qualifications for office.[2] The President must:

**1.** Be "a natural born Citizen . . . of the United States." Do the words "natural born" mean "native born"—that is, born in the United States? By law, a person born abroad to an American-citizen parent becomes an American citizen at birth. That law leads many to argue that it is therefore possible for a person born outside the United States to become President.[3] Some dispute that view, however. The question of what the Constitution means here cannot be answered until someone born a citizen, but born abroad, does in fact become President.

---

2 Article II, Section 1, Clause 5.
3 Martin Van Buren, who was born December 5, 1782, was the first President actually born in the United States. His seven predecessors (and his immediate successor) were each born in the colonies, before the Revolution—that is, before there was a United States. But notice, the Constitution anticipated that circumstance with these words: "or a Citizen of the United States, at the time of the Adoption of this Constitution."

---

**2.** "[H]ave attained . . . the Age of 35 years." John F. Kennedy, at 43, was the youngest person ever elected to the office. Theodore Roosevelt reached the White House by succession at age 42. Only seven other chief executives took the oath of office before age 50: James K. Polk in 1845, Franklin Pierce in 1853, Ulysses S. Grant in 1869, James Garfield in 1881, Grover Cleveland in 1885, Bill Clinton in 1993, and Barack Obama in 2009.

Ronald Reagan, who was 69 when he was first elected in 1980, was the oldest candidate ever to win the office; and, when he left office in 1989 at age 77, he was the oldest person ever to hold the presidency. Most chief executives have been in their 50s when they gained the White House.

**3.** "[H]ave . . . been fourteen years a Resident within the United States." Given the elections of Herbert Hoover (in 1928) and Dwight Eisenhower (in 1952), we know that here the Constitution means any 14 years in a person's life. Both Mr. Hoover and General Eisenhower spent several years outside the country before winning the White House.

While these formal qualifications do have some importance, they are really not very difficult to meet. Indeed, well over 100 million Americans do so today. There are several other *informal* and important qualifications for the presidency, as you will see in Section 4.

## The Presidential Term

The Framers considered a number of different limits on the length of the presidential term. Most of their debate centered on a four-year term, with the President eligible for reelection, versus a single six-year or seven-year term without being eligibile for reelection. They finally settled on a four-year term.[4] They agreed, as Alexander Hamilton wrote in *The Federalist* No. 71, that four years was a long enough period for a President to have gained experience, demonstrated his abilities, and established stable policies.

Until 1951, the Constitution placed no limit on the number of terms a President might serve. Several Presidents, beginning

---

4 Article II, Section 1, Clause 1.

---

# Debate

Arnold Schwarzenegger, California's former governor, would like to run for President, but he is not eligible. Fearing the influence of foreign powers, the Framers wrote into the Constitution a requirement that the President be native-born. Schwarzenegger, born in Austria, became a naturalized U.S. citizen in 1983. He believes the restriction is outdated. "Look at the kind of contribution that people like Henry Kissinger have made, Madeleine Albright," Schwarzenegger said, referring to two former secretaries of state who were foreign-born. In the post-9/11 climate, however, many Americans want to tighten, not loosen, restrictions on immigrants. The former governor's supporters launched a drive for a constitutional amendment that would allow an immigrant who has been a naturalized citizen for 20 years to run for President. To begin a class debate, ask: **Would you support this amendment?**

## Term Limits

"No person shall be elected to the office of the President more than twice, and no person who has held the office of President, or acted as President, for more than two years of a term to which some other person was elected President shall be elected to the office of the President more than once.

—22nd Amendment

# FROM THE CONSTITUTION

NO FOURTH TERM EITHER

BETTER A THIRD TERMER THAN A THIRD RATER

**Shattering Precedent** George Washington's refusal to seek another term as President in 1796 soon gave rise to the "no-third-term tradition" in presidential politics. That unwritten rule was followed for nearly 150 years. In 1940, however, in an election in which the third-term question was a major issue, Franklin D. Roosevelt won another term in the White House; and, four years later, in the midst of World War II, FDR won a fourth term. In 1947, Congress proposed what in 1951 became the 22nd Amendment. It says that no President may serve more than two elected terms or, at the most, ten years in office.

**Constitutional Principles** How does the 22nd Amendment reflect the principles of popular sovereignty, limited government, and checks and balances?

Franklin D. Roosevelt campaigning for his third term in 1940

with George Washington, refused to seek more than two terms, however. Soon, the "no-third-term tradition" became an unwritten rule.

Franklin D. Roosevelt broke the tradition by seeking and winning a third term in 1940, and then a fourth in 1944. To prevent this from recurring, the 22nd Amendment made the unwritten custom limiting presidential terms a part of the written Constitution.

Each President may now serve a maximum of two full terms—eight years—in office. A President who succeeds to the office after the midpoint in a term could possibly serve for more than eight years. In that case, the President may finish out the predecessor's term and then seek two full terms of his or her own. However, no President may serve more than ten years in the office.

Many people, including Presidents Truman, Eisenhower, and Reagan, have called for the repeal of the 22nd Amendment. They insist that the two-term rule is undemocratic because it places an <u>arbitrary</u> limit on the people's right to decide who should be President. Critics also say that it undercuts the authority of a two-term President, especially in the latter part of a second term. Supporters of the amendment defend it as a reasonable safeguard against "executive tyranny."

Several Presidents have urged a single six-year term. They and others have argued that a single, nonrenewable term would free a President from the pressures of a campaign for a second term—and so would allow the chief executive to focus on the pressing demands of the office.

**arbitrary**
*adj.* high-handed, unreasonable

## Political Cartoon Mini-Lesson

Display Transparency 13A, President Calvin Coolidge, to begin a discussion about term limits. Ask: **The cartoonist portrays President Coolidge as what historical leader?** *(Julius Caesar)* **Why do you think the cartoonist chose this portrayal?** *(possibly to show respect for Coolidge as a leader and because Rome at that time was a republic, not a monarchy)* **What is President Coolidge doing?** *(refusing the offer of a third term)* **What is the significance of the crown?** *(It suggests that a third term would turn the President into a king.)* **Based on the cartoon, why do you think Americans approved the 22nd Amendment?** *(From the nation's early days, Americans feared that the President might gain so much power that he would become a monarch. Term limits established by the 22nd Amendment removed that possibility.)*

Ask: **Why is it important for a citizen to understand the roles of the President?** Have students suggest reasons, and then lead a discussion about how knowing the President's roles helps voters determine whether an individual has the personal qualities to be President.

List the three formal qualifications required by the Constitution on the board. *(natural born citizen, at least 35 years old, U.S. resident at least 14 years)* Then, have students reflect on the job of the President and determine qualifications beyond those listed in the Constitution that they believe an individual should have in order to be President. Allow students to expand their list to personal traits such as leadership skills, integrity, and so on.

**L1 L2 Differentiate** Help students by providing them with prompts, such as "Is experience in foreign affairs important?" or "What characteristics do you look for in a leader?" Allow a few minutes for students to think and write some notes before beginning the discussion.

**EXTEND THE LESSON**

**L2 Differentiate** Have students make a graphic organizer showing the roles of the President.

**L3 Differentiate** Assign two presidential roles for each student to illustrate through drawings or photographs taken from newspapers, magazines or the Internet. Each illustration should have a one-sentence caption explaining the presidential role shown. Post each in the classroom for students to review. Make sure to assign all eight roles.

**L4 Differentiate** Have students create a list of the ways discussed in this section that the Constitution provides Congress with checks on the President's job. Then, in a brief essay, have students describe which check they think is the most important and why.

## Assess and Remediate

**L3** Collect the Core Worksheet and assess students' work.

**L3** Assign the Section 1 Assessment questions.

**L3** Section Quiz A (Unit 4 All-in-One, p. 19)

**L2** Section Quiz B (Unit 4 All-in-One, p. 20)

Have students complete the review activities in the digital lesson presentation and continue their work in the **Essential Questions Journal.**

## Answers

**Constitutional Principles** The publicly elected members of Congress deemed term limits necessary in order to prevent a President from gaining too much power.

| If Your Students Have Trouble With | Strategies For Remediation |
|---|---|
| Determining the roles and qualifications of the President (Question 1) | Create a graphic organizer on the board of the eight roles and the three formal qualifications. |
| Describing the roles of chief of state, chief diplomat, and chief citizen (Question 2) | Brainstorm with students activities in which the President performs these roles. |
| Listing the roles not defined by the Constitution (Question 3) | Have students reread content under #7 and #8 of the "Presidential Roles." |
| Understanding the 22nd Amendment (Question 4) | Review the "From the Constitution" feature. |
| Drawing conclusions about the formal qualifications (Question 5) | Review the three formal qualifications and create a list of undesirable scenarios these qualifications would prevent. |
| Judging the salary and benefits provided to the President (Question 6) | Discuss with students the compensation that film and sports celebrities enjoy, and weigh them against the work they perform. Then compare them with the responsibilities of the President. |

**Government** online
*All print resources are available on the Teacher's Resource Library CD-ROM and online at* PearsonSchool.com/phgovt.

## Answers

**Caption** The security of the President is of the utmost importance and providing transportation services ensures his or her security. Also, these services enhance the prestige and authority that come with the presidency.

▲ *Air Force One* and a fleet of automobiles are some of the benefits that come with the presidency. *Why is it necessary for these services to be made available to the President?*

1789.[5] It is now $400,000 a year. Congress set that figure in 1999, and it became effective on January 20, 2001.

Congress has also provided the President with a $50,000-a-year expense allowance. That money may be spent however the President chooses. This allowance is, in effect, a part of his or her pay, and it is taxed as part of his or her income.

The Constitution forbids the President "any other emolument [payment for work] from the United States, or any of them." This provision does not prevent the President from being provided with a great many extras, however.

They include the White House, a magnificent 132-room mansion set on an 18.3-acre estate in the heart of the nation's capital; a sizable suite of offices and a large staff to assist him; a fleet of automobiles; the lavishly fitted Air Force One and several other planes and helicopters; Camp David, the resort hideaway in the Catoctin Mountains in Maryland; the finest medical, dental, and other healthcare available; generous travel and entertainment funds; and many other fringe benefits.

### Pay and Benefits

Congress determines the President's annual salary, which can neither be increased nor decreased during a presidential term. The President's pay was first set at $25,000 a year, in

5 Article II, Section 1, Clause 7. At Philadelphia, Benjamin Franklin argued that, as money and power might corrupt a man, the President ought to receive nothing beyond his expenses; his suggestion was not put to a vote at the Convention.

**Essential Questions Journal**
To continue to build a response to the chapter Essential Question, go to your **Essential Questions Journal.**

## SECTION 1 ASSESSMENT

1. **Guiding Question** Use your completed outline to answer this question: What are the roles and qualifications of the office of the President?

**Key Terms and Comprehension**

2. **(a)** How does the President function as **chief of state? (b)** In what manner might this role be performed simultaneously with those of **chief diplomat** and **chief citizen?**

3. **(a)** Which two presidential roles do not come from the Constitution? **(b)** How did they come about?

4. What is the purpose of the 22nd Amendment?

**Critical Thinking**

5. **Draw Conclusions** Why do you think the Framers chose to provide formal qualifications for the office of the President?

6. **Demonstrate Reasoned Judgment** Do you think the pay and benefits with which the President is compensated are adequate and appropriate for the job? Why or why not?

**Quick Write**

**Research Writing: Explore a Topic** Choose three Presidents from this section and write a list of questions about each one for which you will research to find the answers. Focus on their personal backgrounds and political experience prior to their election. For example, you might ask: What partisan political experience did President Dwight Eisenhower have before his election?

## Assessment Answers

1. **roles:** chief of state, chief executive, chief administrator, chief diplomat, commander in chief, chief legislator, chief of party, and chief citizen; **qualifications:** a natural born citizen, at least 35 years old, has been a resident for 14 years

2. **(a)** greeting foreign dignitaries, giving a college commencement address, attending the Olympic Games, lighting the national Christmas tree, and awarding medals for national service **(b)** In any international interaction, the President is acting as chief of state and chief

diplomat simultaneously. The President also serves as chief citizen in performing ceremonial duties.

3. **(a)** chief of party, chief citizen **(b)** They developed over time and with the rise of parties.

4. to limit the number of terms a President can serve

5. Sample answer: The Framers created the formal qualifications to ensure that the President would be a solid U.S. citizen, without loyalties to another nation, and would bring years of life experience to the office.

6. Yes. As leader of a powerful nation, the President has one of the most complex jobs in the world. The high compensation and generous benefits are appropriate for the difficulty of the job. OR: No. With excessive benefits and salary, the President lives like a king rather than an elected public servant. He should have to pay for rent, food, and necessities not related to his job.

**QUICK WRITE** Questions should focus on the background and experience of three Presidents.

# Evaluating Leadership

"Tuesday's election for the State Assembly seat in Gloucester County is going to be a close one. Recent polls show that Jane Arbino is leading among voters who say that coalition-building is a key factor in their choice, but that voters who favor fiscal responsibility are much more likely to vote for her opponent, Keith James."

What qualities do you consider important when you choose whom to vote for in an election? Many different factors can make someone the right candidate for you, and your factors might not be the ones that matter to someone else. It is important to decide what you consider essential before you cast your ballot.

1. **Decide what factors are most important to you.** Before you begin evaluating leadership abilities, you should determine which qualities you care about the most. Do you want a leader with a proven track record? Past actions can be a good indicator of what someone will do in the future. It can be important for a leader to have demonstrated his or her ability to get things done. You may wish to evaluate a candidate based on aspects of his or her personality or character. Does the candidate have the ability to motivate or inspire others? Does this person share your beliefs and values?

2. **Match the skills to the job.** Your evaluation of a candidate may depend on what leadership position is being filled. Your town mayor may need different leadership qualities than, say, the town clerk, and the qualities of a good senator might differ from those of a good Board of Education member. For some positions, it is important for a leader to have a strong vision and the ability to unite conflicting groups. For others, you might be looking for someone who can stand his or her ground in the face of opposition. A candidate might be a good choice for one position but not another, so you should make sure to think about the specific requirements of the job when you evaluate leadership abilities.

3. **Compare their qualifications.** Once you have determined the factors that are important to you and have evaluated the skills necessary for the position, you will need to compare each candidate against those factors. Who meets most of your requirements? Does your list of requirements reduce your options to one candidate? If not, you will need to compare the several choices against each other to determine who you think is the best choice for the position.

### ▸▸ What do you think?

1. What do you think is the most important leadership quality for a United States senator? What about for a high school principal?

2. Do you think it's a good idea for a leader to admit when he or she has made a mistake?

3. **You Try It** Make a list of the criteria that you think make someone a good leader. Choose someone in a leadership position, such as a member of Congress or the President. Evaluate that person using the leadership criteria that you selected.

**GOVERNMENT ONLINE**
**Citizenship Activity Pack**
For activities on evaluating leadership, go to
**PearsonSchool.com/phgovt**

369

# Citizenship Activity Pack

**L1** **L2** If your students need extra support, use the Citizenship Activity Pack lesson *How to Evaluate Leadership*. It includes a lesson plan for you and materials that help students identify leadership styles. Each student group will make a poster supporting a fictional leader profiled on a Build a Leader Card. Then you will give each group a News Flash Bulletin containing a surprise disclosure about their leader. Students will write a paragraph describing whether the news altered their perception of their leader and, if so, how. Students may also access the Citizenship Activity Pack online for activities on How to Evaluate Leadership at **PearsonSchool.com/phgovt.**

---

## LESSON GOAL

• Students will identify and evaluate qualities for different leadership roles.

# Teach

### CREATE A LIST

Ask students: **What qualities do you think are important for your class president?** *(experience, intelligence, responsibility, listening skills, popularity, attractiveness)* Record the list on the board. Then ask: **Which of these qualities really matter in the class president's ability to do the job?** Cross off factors that students say are not job-related.

### DEFINING LEADERSHIP QUALITIES

Divide the class into six groups. Assign each group one of these leadership positions: U.S. senator, town mayor, school principal, football coach, film director, or business owner. Have each group determine the qualities they think are important for that person.

### DISCUSS

Have a volunteer from each group share the results of their discussion. Create a list on the board of the qualities that are repeated in one column and those that are unique in another. Ask: **Why do these leadership positions have these qualities in common?** *(because they are important skills for most leaders)* Pointing at the unique list, ask: **Why don't all the positions have these qualities?** *(because they are unique to each position)* Then have students add to the common list the qualities that they think are important for the President. Then ask: **Would you vote for a presidential candidate who had all of these qualities?**

# Assess and Remediate

Have students choose the five most important qualities for a President and explain their choices.

Correct answers to the What Do You Think questions.

---

# Answers

1. **U.S. senator:** political experience, legal knowledge, trustworthiness, integrity; **school principal:** understanding, fairness, patience

2. yes, because it shows that the person is honest

3. Students should evaluate a leader based on criteria appropriate to the position.

GUIDING QUESTION

What occurs when the President is unable to perform the duties of the office?

| Presidential Succession | | |
|---|---|---|
| **Constitution** | **Congress** | **Vice President** |
| • powers and duties of President transfer to Vice President if President unable to serve<br>• 25th Amendment establishes that Vice President becomes President in succession<br>• 25th Amendment provides for disability of President<br>• 25th Amendment provides for vice presidential vacancy | • sets order of succession following Vice President<br>• Presidential Succession Act of 1947: after VP, Speaker of House, President pro tem of Senate, secretary of state, each head of other Cabinet departments in the order of precedence<br>• decides if President can resume duties if Vice President and majority of Cabinet disagree with President's declaration that no inability exists<br>• confirms President's nomination to fill vacancy of office of Vice President | • succeeds to presidency if President dies, resigns, or is removed by impeachment<br>• becomes Acting President if President or Vice President and majority of Cabinet inform Congress in writing that President is incapacitated<br>• vacancy filled by President's nominee confirmed by Congress |

## SKILLS DEVELOPMENT

### DECISION MAKING

Before students begin the Core Worksheet activity on deciding presidential and vice presidential succession, have them review the information on decision making in the Skills Handbook, p. S18.

---

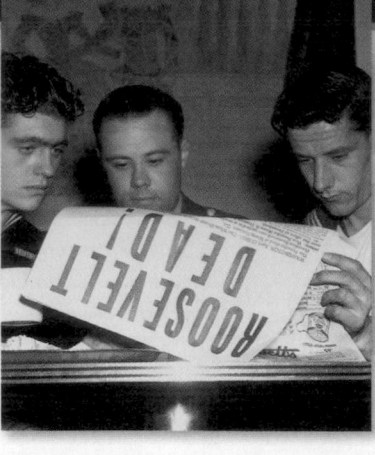

SECTION **2**

# Presidential **Succession** and the **Vice Presidency**

## Guiding Question

**What occurs when the President is unable to perform the duties of the office?** Use a chart like the one below to keep track of the main ideas about presidential succession.

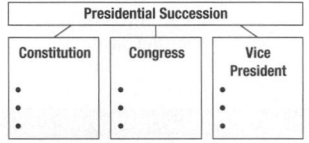

| Presidential Succession | | |
|---|---|---|
| **Constitution** | **Congress** | **Vice President** |
| • | • | • |
| • | • | • |
| • | • | • |

## Political Dictionary

• presidential succession
• Presidential Succession Act of 1947
• balance the ticket

## Objectives

1. Explain how the Constitution provides for presidential succession.
2. Understand the constitutional provisions relating to presidential disability.
3. Describe the role of the Vice President.

**Image Above:** Servicemen read of President Franklin Roosevelt's death in a newspaper, April 12, 1945.

Consider these facts. To this point, forty-eight people have served as Vice President. Fourteen of them have reached the Oval Office—most recently, George H.W. Bush in 1989. Indeed, five of the last twelve Presidents were once Vice President.

## The Constitution and Succession

**Presidential succession** is the scheme by which a presidential vacancy is filled. If a President dies, resigns, or is removed from office by impeachment, the Vice President succeeds to the office.

Originally, the Constitution did not provide for the succession of a Vice President. Rather, it declared that "the powers and duties" of the office—not the office itself—were to "devolve on [transfer to] the Vice President."[6]

In practice, however, the Vice President did succeed to the office when it became vacant. Vice President John Tyler was the first to do so. He set the precedent in 1841 when he succeeded President William Henry Harrison, who died of pneumonia just one month after taking office. What had been practice became a part of the written Constitution with the 25th Amendment in 1967, which states, "In case of the removal of the President from office or of his death or resignation, the Vice President shall become President."

Congress fixes the order of succession following the Vice President, as you can see in the table on the next page.[7] The present law on the matter is the **Presidential Succession Act of 1947.** By its terms, the Speaker of the House and then the President *pro tempore* of the Senate are next in line. They are followed, in turn, by the secretary of state and then by each of the other 14 heads of the Cabinet departments, in order of each position's precedence—that is, the order in which their offices were created by Congress.[8]

---

6 Read carefully Article II, Section 1, Clause 6.
7 Article II, Section 1, Clause 6. On removal of the President by impeachment, see Chapter 11.
8 A Cabinet member is to serve only until a Speaker or a president pro tem is available and qualified. Notice that the 25th Amendment also provides for the filling of any vacancy in the vice presidency. In effect, that provision makes the Presidential Succession Act a law with little real significance—except in the highly unlikely event of simultaneous vacancies in the presidency and vice presidency.

## Focus on the Basics

**FACTS:** • If a President dies, resigns, or is removed from office, presidential powers and duties transfer to the Vice President. • The 25th Amendment officially makes the Vice President the President's successor. • Congress fixed the order of succession after the Vice President with the Presidential Succession Act of 1947. • The Constitution lists only two formal duties of the Vice President: preside over the Senate and help decide presidential disability.

**CONCEPTS:** leadership, separation of powers, checks and balances

**ENDURING UNDERSTANDINGS:** • The order of succession is Vice President, Speaker of the House, President *pro tem* of the Senate, secretary of state, followed by the other Cabinet heads. • The Vice President is the President's successor and must be prepared to serve.

## Presidential Disability

Until the 25th Amendment was adopted in 1967, there were serious gaps in the arrangement for presidential succession. Neither the Constitution nor Congress had made any provision for deciding when a President was so disabled that he could not perform the duties of the office. Nor was there anything to indicate by whom such a decision was to be made.

For nearly 180 years, then, the nation played with fate. President Eisenhower suffered three serious but temporary illnesses while in office: a heart attack in 1955, ileitis in 1956, and a mild stroke in 1957. Two other Presidents were disabled for much longer periods. James Garfield lingered for 80 days before he died from an assassin's bullet in 1881. Woodrow Wilson suffered a paralytic stroke in September of 1919 and was an invalid for the rest of his second term. In fact, he was so ill that he could not meet with his Cabinet for seven months after his stroke. And, in 1981, Ronald Reagan was gravely wounded in an assassination attempt.

Sections 3 and 4 of the 25th Amendment fill the disability gap, and in detail. The Vice President is to become Acting President if (1) the President informs Congress, in writing, "that he is unable to discharge the powers and duties of his office," or (2) the Vice President and a majority of the members of the Cabinet inform Congress, in writing, that the President is so incapacitated.[9]

The President may resume the powers and duties of the office by informing Congress by "written declaration" that no inability exists. However, the Vice President and a majority of the Cabinet may challenge the President on this score. If they do, Congress has 21 days in which to decide the matter.

Thus far, the disability provisions of the 25th Amendment have come into play on three occasions: In 1985, Ronald Reagan transferred the powers of the presidency to Vice President George H.W. Bush for nearly

✔ **Checkpoint**
How did the 25th Amendment fill the gaps in the Presidential Succession Act of 1947?

---

**9** The 25th Amendment gives this authority to the Vice President and the Cabinet or to "such other body as Congress may by law provide." To this point, no "such other body" has been created.

---

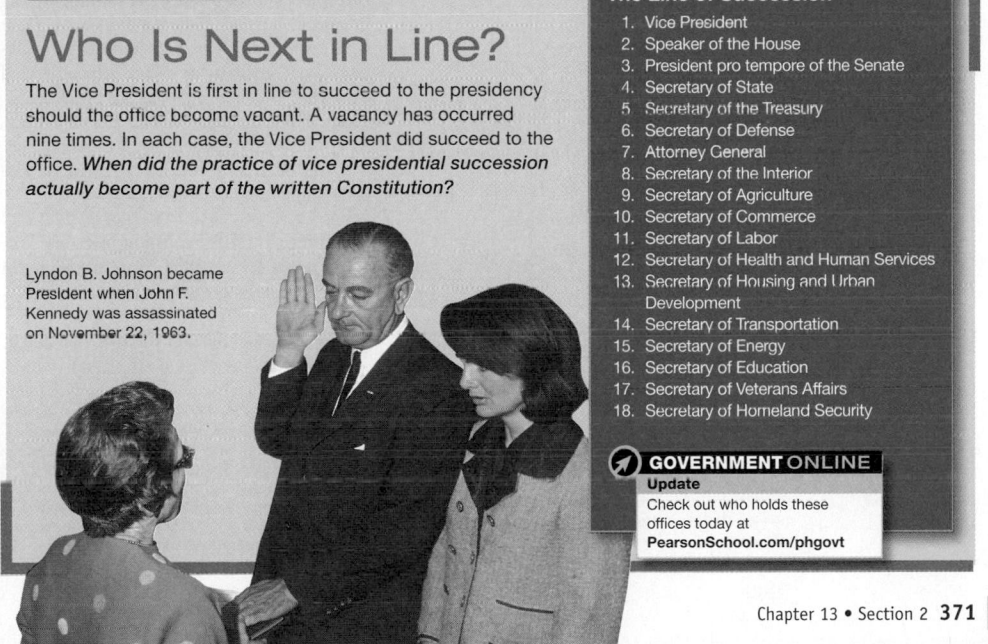

### How Government Works

## Who Is Next in Line?

The Vice President is first in line to succeed to the presidency should the office become vacant. A vacancy has occurred nine times. In each case, the Vice President did succeed to the office. *When did the practice of vice presidential succession actually become part of the written Constitution?*

Lyndon B. Johnson became President when John F. Kennedy was assassinated on November 22, 1963.

**The Line of Succession**
1. Vice President
2. Speaker of the House
3. President pro tempore of the Senate
4. Secretary of State
5. Secretary of the Treasury
6. Secretary of Defense
7. Attorney General
8. Secretary of the Interior
9. Secretary of Agriculture
10. Secretary of Commerce
11. Secretary of Labor
12. Secretary of Health and Human Services
13. Secretary of Housing and Urban Development
14. Secretary of Transportation
15. Secretary of Energy
16. Secretary of Education
17. Secretary of Veterans Affairs
18. Secretary of Homeland Security

➡ **GOVERNMENT ONLINE**
**Update**
Check out who holds these offices today at
**PearsonSchool.com/phgovt**

---

## Differentiated Resources

The following resources are located in the All-in-One, Unit 4, Chapter 13, Section 2:

- **L3** Reading Comprehension Worksheet (p. 21)
- **L2** Reading Comprehension Worksheet (p. 22)
- **L3** Core Worksheet (p. 23)
- **L3 L4** Extend Worksheet (p. 24)
- **L3** Quiz A (p. 25)
- **L2** Quiz B (p. 26)

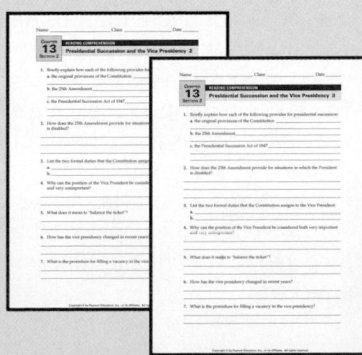

---

# Get Started

### LESSON GOALS

Students will . . .

- evaluate the importance of the position of Vice President.
- describe the process of succession using a variety of scenarios.
- reflect on the importance of the Vice President's role as presidential successor by analyzing a political cartoon.

### BEFORE CLASS

Assign the section, the graphic organizer in the text, and the Reading Comprehension Worksheet (Unit 4 All-in-One, p. 21) before class.

**L2 Differentiate** Reading Comprehension Worksheet (Unit 4 All-in-One, p. 22)

### BELLRINGER

Write on the board: **Describe the duties of the Vice President. In your opinion, how important is the position? Support your answer with evidence from the chapter. Answer in your notebooks.**

# Teach

To present this topic using online resources, use the lesson presentations at **PearsonSchool.com/phgovt.**

### REVIEW BELLRINGER

Using the Opinion Line strategy (p. T26), write at one end of the board "Very Important," at the other end "Not At All Important," and in the middle "Somewhat Important." Have students take a position along the opinion line based on their answer to the second part of the Bellringer question. Ask a few students at each position on the line to explain the reasons for their position.

**L1 L2 Differentiate** Write key phrases from students' responses on the board, and have students copy the phrases in their notebooks.

Tell students to go to the Online Update to check out who holds the offices in the line of succession today.

---

## Answers

**Caption** with the adoption of the 25th Amendment in 1967

**Checkpoint** It extends the list of successors beyond the Vice President through specific members of Congress and the Cabinet in order of precedence.

## DISTRIBUTE CORE WORKSHEET

Distribute the Chapter 13 Section 2 Core Worksheet (Unit 4 All-in-One, p. 23), which describes situations involving potential presidential and vice presidential succession. Have students read the scenarios and describe how the vacancy would be filled in each case.

**L1 Differentiate** Read each scenario to the class and ask volunteers to explain how the vacancy would be filled in each case. Discuss correct answers with the class.

**L2 ELL Differentiate** Pair students and have them work together to complete the worksheet.

## ANALYZE A POLITICAL CARTOON

Begin a discussion of presidential succession by displaying Transparency 13B, a political cartoon about Vice President Dick Cheney temporarily assuming presidential powers. Point out that the man in the bed is President George W. Bush. Ask: **In the cartoon, what happened to President Bush?** (He underwent a medical procedure while under anesthesia.) **What role of the Vice President does this cartoon illustrate?** (The Vice President assumes presidential powers while the President is temporarily disabled.) **What comment is the cartoonist making about Vice President Cheney?** (that he assumes more power than he should) Have students reflect on the scenarios in the Core Worksheet and the chance that the Vice President could be elevated to President at a moment's notice. Ask them if they still hold firm to their view of the Vice President's importance from the Opinion Line activity at the beginning of class.

## EXTEND THE LESSON

**L3 L4 Differentiate** Give students a copy of the Chapter 13 Section 2 Extend Worksheet (Unit 4 All-in-One, p. 24), which lists the offices in the chain of succession to the presidency. Have students use the Internet or the library to identify who currently occupies each position and answer the Reflection Questions.

**L3 Differentiate** Have each student select a Vice President from the last 40 years and research how that person helped balance the ticket in the presidential election. Then ask students to write a paragraph stating whether they think the President made a good choice for running mate.

## Answers

**Checkpoint** preside over Senate and help decide question of presidential disability

**Analyzing Political Cartoons** The cartoonist is suggesting that the current Vice President is actually running the country.

---

**contrive**
*v.* to create or bring about

eight hours, while surgeons removed a tumor from Mr. Reagan's large intestine. In 2002, and again in 2007, George W. Bush conveyed his powers to Vice President Dick Cheney for some two hours, while Mr. Bush was anesthetized during a routine medical procedure.

## The Vice Presidency

"I am Vice President. In this I am nothing, but I may be everything." So said John Adams, the nation's first Vice President. Those words could have been repeated, very appropriately, by each of the 47 Vice Presidents who have followed him in that office.

**Importance of the Office** The Constitution pays little attention to the office of the Vice President. It assigns the position only two formal duties: (1) to preside over the Senate[10] and (2) to help decide the question of presidential disability.[11] Beyond those duties, the Constitution makes the Vice President, in effect, a "President-in-waiting."

Throughout much of the nation's history, in fact, the vice presidency was treated as an

**ideological**
*adj.* having to do with the beliefs or ideas of a person or group

10 Article I, Section 3, Clause 4; see Chapter 12.
11 25th Amendment, Sections 3 and 4.

*"Dad, who runs the country if anything happens to the Vice-President?"*

➤➤ **Analyzing Political Cartoons** Today, there is some criticism regarding the growth of the power of the Vice President. *How does this cartoon illustrate this attitude?*

---

office of little real consequence and, often, as the butt of jokes. Indeed, many Vice Presidents themselves had a hand in this undermining of the office. John Adams described his post as "the most insignificant office that ever the invention of man contrived or his imagination conceived."

John Nance Garner, who served for two terms as Franklin D. Roosevelt's Vice President (1933–1941), once declared, "The vice presidency isn't worth a warm pitcher of spit." Alben Barkley, who served during Harry Truman's second term, often told the story of a woman who had two sons. One of them, Barkley said, went away to sea and the other one became Vice President, "and neither of them was ever heard from again."[12]

Despite these and a great many other unkind comments, the office is clearly an important one. Its occupant is literally "only a heartbeat away" from the presidency. Remember, eight Presidents have died in office, and one was forced to resign.

Much of the blame for the low status of the vice presidency can be laid on the two major parties and the way they choose their candidates for the office. Traditionally, each national convention names the handpicked choice of its just-nominated presidential candidate. Usually, the newly minted presidential candidate picks someone who will **"balance the ticket."** That is, the nominee chooses a running mate who can strengthen his or her chance of being elected by virtue of certain ideological, geographic, racial, ethnic, gender, or other characteristics. In short, fate—presidential succession—does not very often have a high priority in the vice presidential candidate selection process.

**The Vice President Today** Although the vice presidency is still at times the target of late-night television humor, recent Presidents have made much greater use of their Vice Presidents than did any of their predecessors. In effect, the office has been reinvented.

12 Indeed, one Vice President, William Rufus King, never actually served in the office. A five-term senator from Alabama, he was elected with President Franklin Pierce in 1852. Shortly after the election, he became ill and went to Cuba hoping the climate would aid his health. His condition worsened, however, and he could not return to Washington for the inauguration. Although sworn in while in Cuba, he died upon his return to the United States.

---

# Background

**CABINET SUCCESSION** The line of succession to the presidency has long been legally defined. Throughout most of American history, however, there were no formal provisions for what would happen to other offices in the executive branch in the event that one of their officers dies, resigns, or otherwise is unable to perform his or her duties. This is no longer the case. One effect of the September 11, 2001, terrorist attacks on the United States was a series of executive orders signed by President George W. Bush that leave no question as to who is to fulfill a vacancy in any of the Cabinet departments. Bush's action was prompted by the feeling of many in the executive branch and elsewhere that the unpredictable nature of terrorist attacks requires the nation to be prepared to continue to function regardless of which government official or building is attacked.

Indeed, Dick Cheney (2001–2009) is widely seen as the most influential occupant of the office in the nation's history.

Barack Obama chose Joe Biden of Delaware as his running mate in 2008, in no small part on the basis of his long record of public service. Vice President Biden's 36 years in the Senate were capped by his chairmanship of the Senate's Foreign Relations Committee—a qualification that seems particularly fitting in today's crisis-filled world.

Still, even with the elevation of the office in recent years, no President has been willing to make his Vice President a true "Assistant President." The major reason: Of all the President's official family, only the Vice President is not subject to the ultimate discipline of removal from office by the President. No matter what the circumstances, the President cannot fire the Vice President.

**Vice-Presidential Vacancy** The vice presidency has been vacant 18 times thus far: nine times by succession to the presidency, twice by resignation, and seven times by death.[13] Yet not until 1967 and the 25th Amendment did the Constitution deal with the matter. The amendment provides, in part:

---

**13** John C. Calhoun resigned to become a senator from South Carolina in 1832. Spiro T. Agnew resigned in 1973, after a conviction for income tax evasion. The seven who died in office were George Clinton (1812), Elbridge Gerry (1814), William R. King (1853), Henry Wilson (1875), Thomas A. Hendricks (1885), Garret A. Hobart (1899), and James S. Sherman (1912).

## FROM THE CONSTITUTION

**Whenever there is a vacancy in the office of the Vice President, the President shall nominate a Vice President who shall take office upon confirmation by a majority vote of both Houses of Congress.**

—25th Amendment, Section 2

This provision was first implemented in 1973. In that year, President Richard Nixon selected and Congress confirmed Gerald R. Ford to succeed Spiro Agnew as Vice President. It came into play again in 1974 when, following Mr. Nixon's resignation, President Ford named and Congress approved Nelson Rockefeller for the post.

Vice President Joe Biden addresses the press.

Essential Questions
Journal

To continue to build a response to the chapter Essential Question, go to your **Essential Questions Journal.**

## SECTION 2 ASSESSMENT

1. **Guiding Question** Use your completed chart to answer this question: What occurs when the President is unable to perform the duties of the office?

**Key Terms and Comprehension**

2. **(a)** How does the Constitution address **presidential succession? (b)** In what way did the **Presidential Succession Act of 1947** deal with this matter?

3. What duties does the Constitution assign to the Vice President?

**Critical Thinking**

4. **Demonstrate Reasoned Judgment** Do you think an attempt to "balance the ticket" is an acceptable method of selecting a Vice President? Why or why not?

5. **Synthesize Information** How has the office of the Vice President changed in recent years?

**Quick Write**

**Research Writing: Narrow a Topic** Using the questions you drafted in the Section 1 Quick Write, conduct preliminary research to find the answers to your questions. Browse the Internet or other sources and take notes on what you find. Then use this information to determine which President you are most interested in researching further.

---

# Assess and Remediate

**L3** Collect the Core Worksheet and assess the students' work.

**L3** Assign the Section 2 Assessment questions.

**L3** Section Quiz A (Unit 4 All-in-One, p. 25)

**L2** Section Quiz B (Unit 4 All-in-One, p. 26)

Have students complete the review activities in the digital lesson presentation and continue their work in the **Essential Questions Journal.**

### REMEDIATION

| If Your Students Have Trouble With | Strategies For Remediation |
|---|---|
| Describing the process of succession (Question 1) | Have students read the 25th Amendment and summarize each Section in their own words. |
| Explaining the manner in which the Constitution and the Presidential Succession Act address succession (Question 2) | Review with students this section's feature on "Who Is Next in Line?" |
| Describing the duties of the Vice President (Question 3) | Have students read the only locations in the Constitution where the Vice President's duties are defined: Article 1, Section 3, Clause 4, and the 25th Amendment, Sections 3 and 4. |
| Making a judgment on balancing the ticket (Question 4) | Lead a discussion on how the current President and Vice President illustrate this point. |
| Explaining how the vice presidency has changed in recent years (Question 5) | Have students look through newspapers, magazines, and the Internet to find articles on the current activities of the Vice President. |

---

# Assessment Answers

**1.** The Vice President becomes President if the President dies, resigns, or is removed by impeachment. The new President then nominates someone to fill the vice presidential vacancy, upon confirmation of Congress. If a President becomes incapacitated, the Vice President becomes Acting President until the President informs Congress, in writing, that the inability no longer exists.

**2. (a)** Initially, the Constitution simply stated that the President's duties would devolve to the Vice President. The 25th Amendment establishes that the Vice President would become President. This amendment also provides for presidential disability and for filling a vacancy as Vice President. **(b)** The Act provides the order of succession after the Vice President.

**3.** to preside over the Senate and to help decide the question of presidential disability

**4.** Sample answers: Yes, a balanced ticket ensures that the views of the majority of Americans are represented in the two highest offices. OR: No, the Vice President is a heartbeat away from the presidency and must have the qualifications to serve effectively, if needed.

**5.** Sample answer: Although the Constitution created the vice presidency as a relatively unimportant position with few responsibilities, recent Presidents have made greater use of their Vice Presidents. Still, the Vice President's role has not risen to the level of an Assistant President.

**QUICK WRITE** Students will conduct research to answer their questions and select a President to research further.

# How did the process of choosing a President change over time?

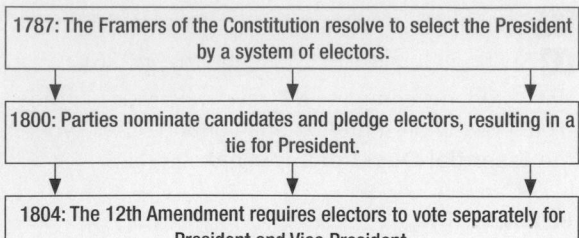

1787: The Framers of the Constitution resolve to select the President by a system of electors.

↓

1800: Parties nominate candidates and pledge electors, resulting in a tie for President.

↓

1804: The 12th Amendment requires electors to vote separately for President and Vice President.

# Get Started

## LESSON GOALS

Students will . . .

- describe the Framers' original plan for selecting the President and Vice President.
- analyze how historical events led to changes in the way the President and Vice President are selected.

## BEFORE CLASS

Assign the section, the graphic organizer in the text, and the Reading Comprehension Worksheet (Unit 4 All-in-One, p. 27) before class.

**L2 Differentiate** Reading Comprehension Worksheet (Unit 4 All-in-One, p. 28)

## BELLRINGER

Display Transparency 13C, the Election of 1800 map. Instruct students to study the map and answer the question in their notebook.

# SKILLS DEVELOPMENT

## ANALYZE MAPS

If students have difficulty analyzing maps, refer them to page S27 of the Skills Handbook as they do the Bellringer activity.

---

SECTION **3**

# Presidential Selection: The Framers' Plan

## Guiding Question

**How did the process of choosing a President change over time?** Use a flowchart like the one below to keep track of the main ideas about selecting a President.

1787: The Framers of the Constitution resolve to select the President by a system of electors.

↓ ↓ ↓

## Political Dictionary

- presidential elector
- electoral vote
- electoral college

## Objectives

1. Explain the Framers' original provisions for choosing the President.
2. Understand how the rise of political parties changed the process of choosing a President as set out in the Constitution.

**Images Above:** 1800 Presidential candidates Aaron Burr (left) and Thomas Jefferson

In formal terms, the President is chosen according to the provisions of the Constitution.[14] In practice, however, the President is elected through an altogether extraordinary process—one that is not very well understood by most Americans. It is a combination of constitutional provisions, State and federal laws, and a number of practices born of the nation's political parties. To make sense of this very complex system, you must first understand what the Framers had in mind when they designed the presidential election process.

## Original Provisions

The Framers gave more time to the method for choosing the President than to any other matter. It was, said James Wilson of Pennsylvania, "the most difficult of all on which we have had to decide." The difficulty arose largely because most of the Framers were against selecting the President by either of the obvious ways: by Congress or by a direct vote of the people.

Early in the Convention, most of the delegates did favor selection by Congress. Later, nearly all of them came to believe that congressional selection would, as Alexander Hamilton said, put the President "too much under the legislative thumb." Only a few of the Framers favored choosing the President by popular vote. Nearly all agreed that that process would lead to "tumult and disorder." Most delegates felt, too, that the people, scattered over so wide an area, could not possibly know enough about the available candidates to make wise, informed choices. George Mason of Virginia spoke for most at the convention: "The extent of the Country renders it impossible that the people can have the requisite capacity to judge of the respective pretensions of the Candidates."

After weeks of debate, the Framers finally agreed on a plan first put forward by Hamilton. Under it, the President and Vice President were to be chosen by a special body of **presidential electors.** These electors would be chosen in each State in a manner the State legislature directed, and each State would have as many electors as it has senators and representatives in Congress.

---

14 The Constitution deals with the process of presidential selection in several places: Article II, Section 1, Clauses 2, 3, and 4; and the 12th, 20th, and 23rd amendments.

---

# Focus on the Basics

**FACTS:** • The Framers determined that electors selected by each State would cast two votes each for different candidates for President, with the winner becoming President and the runner-up, Vice President. • The election of 1800 introduced party nomination of candidates, pledged electors, and electoral votes cast as pledged. • The 12th Amendment requires electors to vote separately for President and Vice President.

**CONCEPTS:** popular sovereignty, separation of powers, representative democracy

**ENDURING UNDERSTANDINGS:** • The rise of political parties created a need to alter the Framers' electoral plan. • The election of 1800 led to changes, including the 12th Amendment, that form the framework for today's presidential election system.

Once selected, these electors would each cast two **electoral votes,** each for a different candidate. The candidate with the most votes would become President. The person with the second-most votes would become Vice President.

The Framers intended the electors to be "the most enlightened and respectable citizens" from each State. They were to act as "free agents" in choosing the people best qualified to fill the nation's two highest offices.

## The Rise of Parties

The **electoral college,** then, is the group of people (electors) chosen from each State and the District of Columbia to formally select the President and Vice President. The original version of the electoral college worked as the Framers intended only as long as George Washington was willing to seek and hold the presidency. He did so twice, and was unanimously elected President, in 1789 and in 1792.

Flaws began to appear in the system in 1796, however, with the rise of political parties. John Adams, the Federalist candidate, was elected to the presidency. Thomas Jefferson, an arch-rival and Democratic-Republican, lost to Adams by just three votes in the electoral balloting. Jefferson then became Adams's Vice President.

**The Election of 1800** The system broke down altogether in the election of 1800. By then there were two well-defined parties: the Federalists, led by Adams and Hamilton, and the Democratic-Republicans, headed by Jefferson. Each of these parties nominated presidential and vice-presidential candidates. They also nominated candidates to serve as presidential electors in the several States. Those elector-candidates were picked with the clear understanding that, if elected, they would vote for their party's presidential and vice-presidential nominees.

Each of the 73 Democratic-Republicans who won posts as electors voted for his party's nominees: Thomas Jefferson and Aaron Burr. In doing so, they produced a tie for the presidency. Remember that the Constitution

**flaw**
*n.* a defect, shortcoming, weakness

---

## The Electoral College

# Crisis Causes Change

The Framers saw the electoral college as an appropriate way to select the President and Vice President. They did not foresee the development of political parties, however, and the parties' participation in the election of 1800 caused a serious breakdown in the Framers' presidential selection process. *What did the Framers hope to accomplish by designing the electoral college system as they did?*

### The 12th Amendment

Separate elections

President    Vice President

### 1787
**The Framers' Original Plan**

- Each elector casts two electoral votes, each for a different person for President.
- The person receiving a majority of the electoral votes becomes President.
- The person with the second-highest number of electoral votes becomes Vice President.

### 1800
**The Crisis**

In accord with the Framers' original plan, in 1800 the electors cast their two votes for two different persons. Each of the 73 Democratic-Republican electors voted for that party's two nominees, Thomas Jefferson and Aaron Burr, producing a tie. In the end, it took 36 separate votes in the House of Representatives to finally select the President and, by default, the Vice President.

### 1804
**Changes to the Original Plan**

- The 12th Amendment to the Constitution separates the presidential and vice-presidential elections.
- Each presidential elector now casts one vote for President and one vote for Vice President.

---

# Differentiated Resources

The following resources are located in the All-in-One, Unit 4, Chapter 13, Section 3:

- **L3** Reading Comprehension Worksheet (p. 27)
- **L2** Reading Comprehension Worksheet (p. 28)
- **L3** Core Worksheet (p. 29)
- **L3** Quiz A (p. 30)
- **L2** Quiz B (p. 31)

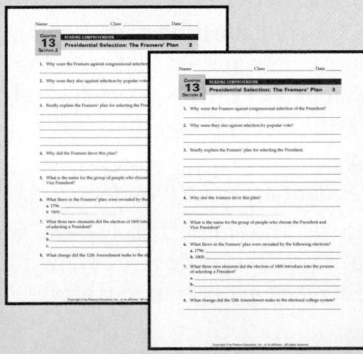

---

# Teach

To present this topic using online resources, use the lesson presentations at **PearsonSchool.com/phgovt.**

## REVIEW BELLRINGER

Distribute the Chapter 13 Section 3 Core Worksheet (Unit 4 All-in-One, p. 29), which shows milestones in the development of the presidential election process. Have students share their answers to the Bellringer question, and as they do so, have them categorize the information under the four headings on the Core Worksheet. If students have missed any important issues, make sure to discuss them and have students categorize the additions on the worksheet.

## EXTEND THE LESSON

**L2** **L3** **Differentiate** Pair students and have them create a map that illustrates the distribution of electoral votes in the most recent presidential election.

**L4** **Differentiate** Have students conduct research on the method used today in the selection of the President and Vice President. Then have them create a graphic organizer that compares and contrasts the Framers' plan with the actual events as they occur today.

# Assess and Remediate

**L3** Collect the Core Worksheet and assess the students' work.

**L3** Assign the Section 3 Assessment questions.

**L3** Section Quiz A (Unit 4 All-in-One, p. 30)

**L2** Section Quiz B (Unit 4 All-in-One, p. 31)

Have students complete the review activities in the digital lesson presentation and continue their work in the **Essential Questions Journal.**

---

# Answers

**Crisis Causes Change** Possible response: They hoped the process would ensure the equitable selection of the best possible candidate for the office of President.

| If Your Students Have Trouble With | Strategies For Remediation |
|---|---|
| Determining how the process of selecting the President has changed over time (Question 1) | Review with students this section's "Crisis Causes Change" feature. |
| Explaining the Framers' plan for selecting presidential electors (Question 2) | Review Article II, Section 1, Clause 2 and have students summarize the clause in their own words. |
| Determining the makeup and function of the electoral college (Question 3) | Create a flowchart showing how electors are nominated and selected, and how they vote to elect the President and Vice President. |
| Understanding the 12th Amendment (Question 4) | Have students compare the content in Article II, Section 1, Clause 3 and the 12th Amendment. |
| Explaining the Framers' view of the presidential electors (Question 5) | Brainstorm the characteristics of the typical voter at that time to identify reasons why the Framers thought electors would produce a better result than would a direct popular vote. |
| Determining the effect of parties on the election of 1800 (Question 6) | Create a chronological list of the events of the election on the board. |

## Answers

**Analyzing Maps** The map illustrates how the States were virtually (and in two cases literally) divided in two by the political division. The charts indicate that the electoral college was also almost equally divided along party lines.

---

# The Election of 1800

Differing attitudes on the role of the government and the interpretation of the Constitution gave rise to political parties in the United States. *How do the map and chart below illustrate these political divisions?*

**Election of 1800**

47% Federalist
53% Democratic-Republican

| Candidate and Party | Electoral Votes |
|---|---|
| Thomas Jefferson Democratic-Republican | 73 |
| Aaron Burr Democratic-Republican | 73 |
| John Adams Federalist | 65 |
| Charles C. Pinckney Federalist | 64 |
| John Jay Federalist | 1 |

SOURCE: National Archives and Records Administration

gave each elector two votes, each to be cast for a different person, but each to be cast for someone as President. Popular opinion clearly favored Jefferson. Still, the House of Representatives had to take 36 separate ballots before it finally settled on Mr. Jefferson as the third President of the United States.

The spectacular election of 1800 marked the introduction of three new elements into the process of selecting a President: (1) party nominations for the presidency and vice presidency, (2) nominations of candidates for presidential electors in the States who pledged to vote for their party's presidential ticket, and (3) automatic casting of the electoral votes in line with those pledges.

**The 12th Amendment** The election of 1800 produced another notable result: the 12th Amendment. This amendment was added to the Constitution in 1804 to make certain there would never be another such fiasco. The amendment is lengthy, but it made only one major change in the electoral college system. It separated the presidential and vice-presidential elections: "The Electors . . . shall name in their ballots the person voted for as President, and in distinct ballots the person voted for as Vice-President. . . ."[15]

With the appearance of parties, the election of 1800, and the 12th Amendment, the constitutional framework had been laid for the presidential selection system as it exists today. That system is, indeed, a far cry from what was agreed to in 1787, as you will see in the sections ahead.

[15] Not only does the amendment mean there cannot be a repeat of the circumstances that produced a tie in 1800, it also almost certainly guarantees that the President and Vice President will be of the same party.

**Essential Questions Journal** To continue to build a response to the chapter Essential Question, go to your **Essential Questions Journal**.

## SECTION 3 ASSESSMENT

1. **Guiding Question** Use your completed flowchart to answer this question: How did the process of choosing a President change over time?

**Key Terms and Comprehension**

2. How were **presidential electors** to be selected in the Framers' plan?
3. **(a)** Who makes up the **electoral college? (b)** What does it do?
4. What change did the 12th Amendment make in the presidential selection process?

**Critical Thinking**

5. **Recognize Bias** The Framers believed that the presidential electors would be "the most enlightened and respectable citizens" in each State. How does this statement reflect the voting population of the time?
6. **Determining Relevance** How did party allegiances complicate the election of 1800?

**Quick Write**

**Research Writing: Gather Details** When writing a research report, you should include facts, examples, descriptions, and other information to help explain your findings. Use the library and reliable Internet sources to do more in-depth research on the President you selected in Section 2. Record information on notecards to help you organize your thoughts.

---

# Assessment Answers

**1.** In 1787, the Framers developed a presidential selection plan centered on a body of electors who would vote for two different candidates for President. The winner would become President and the second-place candidate, Vice President. By 1800, two well-defined parties had evolved, and each party nominated candidates and electors pledged to vote for their party's candidates. During the 1800 election, the electors voted along party lines and caused a tie for the presidency. In 1804, the 12th Amendment was added to the Constitution, requiring electors to cast separate ballots

for President and Vice President.

**2.** Electors would be chosen in each State in a manner set by the State legislature.

**3. (a)** people nominated by the parties and chosen by popular vote in each State and the District of Columbia **(b)** casts votes to formally elect the President and Vice President

**4.** The 12th Amendment separated the election of the President and Vice President.

**5.** Sample answer: The Framers likely believed that the average citizen was not well enough informed or educated enough to make wise

choices for President and Vice President.

**6.** Parties nominated the candidates and electors who pledged to vote for the party's candidates. Each elector voted once for the party's presidential candidate and once for the party's vice presidential candidate. Since the highest vote-getter was to be President, the electoral votes created a tie for President. It took 36 ballots to make the final selection.

**QUICK WRITE** Students should record their research data on notecards.

# Does the nominating system allow Americans to choose the best candidates for President?

| Presidential Nominee | | |
|---|---|---|
| **Personal Characteristics** | **Primaries and Caucuses** | **National Conventions** |
| • Seen as most electable<br>• Broad appeal<br>• Record free of controversies<br>• Held elective office<br>• Most from larger States<br>• Pleasant and healthy appearance<br>• Most happily married<br>• Well-developed speaking ability | • Primary—party's voters choose convention delegates or express preference for presidential nominee<br>• Delegates awarded in proportion to votes candidate received in primary<br>• Republican Party holds winner-take-all primaries in a few States<br>• Preference primaries—party chooses delegates later, in line with preference vote<br>• Precinct caucus chooses delegates to local or district convention, which chooses delegates to State convention, which chooses delegates to national convention | • National committees number of delegates per State<br>• Delegates choose party nominees predetermined by caucus and primary votes<br>• Presidential nominee named through roll-call vote of State delegations |

## SECTION 4

# Presidential Nominations

## Guiding Question
**Does the nominating system allow Americans to choose the best candidates for President?** Use a chart like the one below to keep track of the main ideas about the nomination process.

| Presidential Nominee | | |
|---|---|---|
| Personal Characteristics | Primaries and Caucuses | National Conventions |
| •<br>•<br>• | •<br>•<br>• | •<br>•<br>• |

## Political Dictionary
- presidential primary
- winner-take-all
- proportional representation
- caucus
- national convention
- platform
- keynote address

## Objectives
1. Describe the role of conventions in the presidential nominating process.
2. Evaluate the importance of presidential primaries.
3. Understand the caucus-convention process.
4. Outline the events that take place during a national convention.
5. Examine the characteristics that determine who is nominated as a presidential candidate.

**Image Above:** Delegates cheer on a speaker at the 2008 Democratic National Convention.

The Constitution makes no provision for the nomination of candidates for the presidency. Rather, the Framers designed a system in which presidential electors would select the "wisest and best man" to be President. But the rise of political parties and the election of 1800 altered that system drastically. In this section, you will examine what emerged from that historic revision of the Framers' plan: the modern-day presidential nominating process.

## National Conventions
Recall, the congressional caucus was the first method the parties developed to pick their presidential candidates. The closed, unrepresentative character of that arrangement led to its downfall in the mid-1820s. For the election of 1832, both major parties turned to the national convention as their presidential nominating device, and it has continued to serve them ever since.

**Convention Arrangements** Not only does the Constitution say nothing about presidential nominations, but there is, as well, almost no federal or State statutory law on the matter. The convention process has been built over the years almost entirely by the two major parties.

In both parties, the national committee makes the arrangements for the party's convention. The committee picks the place and also sets the date for that meeting. Several of the nation's larger cities regularly bid for the honor (and the financial boost to local business) of hosting the quadrennial gatherings. For their 2008 meeting, the Democrats picked Denver, and the GOP opted for Minneapolis–St. Paul.

**Apportioning Delegates** With the date and the location set, the national committee issues its "call" for the convention. That formal announcement names the time and place. It also tells the party's State organizations how many delegates the States may send to the national gathering.

By tradition, both parties give each State party a certain number of delegates based on that State's electoral vote. Over the past several conventions, both parties have developed complicated formulas that also award bonus delegates to those States that have supported the party's candidates in recent elections.

---

## SKILLS DEVELOPMENT

### DRAW INFERENCES AND CONCLUSIONS
To teach the skill of drawing inferences and conclusions, have students read the information on p. S19 in the Skills Handbook. In this section's Core Worksheet B activity, students will analyze and discuss speeches by presidential candidates.

---

# Focus on the Basics

**FACTS:** • The major parties, not the Constitution, define the nomination process. • In primaries and caucuses, party voters express a preference among potential nominees or select delegates to the party's national convention. • At the national conventions, each party adopts a platform, officially selects its presidential and vice presidential candidates, and attempts to unify the party.

**CONCEPTS:** popular sovereignty, federalism

**ENDURING UNDERSTANDINGS:** • Delegate selection systems differ from State to State.
• Primaries and caucus-conventions help narrow the field of presidential candidates.
• In addition to selecting the presidential nominee, national conventions strive to capture national attention and generate support for the party ticket.

# Get Started

## LESSON GOALS

Students will . . .

- discuss the influence of early primaries on the presidential nomination process by analyzing a political cartoon.
- compare the nomination process in different States by researching and completing a chart.
- explore the goals of national conventions by analyzing nomination acceptance speeches.

## BEFORE CLASS

Assign the section, the graphic organizer in the text, and the Reading Comprehension Worksheet (Unit 4 All-in-One, p. 32) before class.

**L2** **Differentiate** Reading Comprehension Worksheet (Unit 4 All-in-One, p. 34)

## BELLRINGER

Display Transparency 13D, The United States of America, Revised. This cartoon comments on the oversized influence of the early Iowa caucuses and New Hampshire primary. Explain to students that this cartoon appeared while the nation was in the process of nominating candidates for the presidency. Have students answer the questions on the transparency in their notebooks.

---

For 2008, the GOP's formula produced a convention of 2,380 delegates. The Democrats' more complicated plan called for 4,233 delegates. Given those large numbers, it should be fairly clear that neither party's national convention can be called "a deliberative body," an assembly able to give each of its decisions thoughtful consideration.

**Selecting Delegates** There are really *three* campaigns for the presidency every four years. One is the final contest between the Republican candidate and the Democratic candidate in the fall, leading up to the election in November. The other two occur earlier and are quite different affairs. They take place *within* each of the major parties: the struggles for Republican and, separately, for Democratic convention delegates.

State laws and/or party rules fix the procedures for picking delegates in each State. That system is a reflection of federalism, and it has produced a jigsaw puzzle of presidential primaries, conventions, and caucuses among the 50 States.

To a large extent, the Republican Party leaves the matter of delegate selection to its State organizations and to State law. The Democratic Party, on the other hand, has adopted several national rules to govern the process. Most of those rules reflect the Democratic Party's attempts to broaden participation in the delegate selection process, especially by the young, African Americans, other minorities, and women.

## Presidential Primaries

More than three fourths of all the delegates to both parties' conventions come from States that hold presidential primaries. Many of those primaries are major media events. Serious contenders in both the Democratic and Republican parties must make the best possible showing in at least most of them.

Depending on the State, a **presidential primary** is an election in which a party's voters (1) choose some or all of a State party organization's delegates to their party's national convention, and/or (2) express a preference among various contenders for their party's presidential nomination.[16]

**History of the Presidential Primary** The presidential primary first appeared in the early 1900s as part of the reform movement aimed at the party boss–dominated convention system. Wisconsin passed the first presidential primary law in 1905, providing for the popular election of national convention delegates. Several States soon followed that lead, and Oregon added the preference feature in 1910. By 1916 half the States had adopted presidential primary laws.

For a time, the primary system fell into disfavor so that by 1968, primaries were found in only 16 States and the District of Columbia. Efforts to reform the national convention process, especially in the Democratic Party, reversed that downward trend in the 1970s, however. Some form of the presidential primary can now be found in most States. For 2008, the device was in place in 40 States, and in the District of Columbia and Puerto Rico, as well.[17]

**Primaries Today** Recall, a presidential primary is either or both of two things: a delegate-selection process and/or a candidate preference election. Once that much has been said, however, the system becomes very hard to describe, except on a State-by-State basis.

The difficulty comes largely from two sources: (1) the fact that in each State the details of the delegate-selection process are set by State law—and those details vary from State to State, and (2) the ongoing reform efforts in the Democratic Party.

Ever since 1968, when the Democratic Party was shattered by disputes over Vietnam and civil rights policies, the Democratic National Committee has written and rewritten

---

16 Both parties allot delegates to the District of Columbia, Puerto Rico, the Virgin Islands, Guam, and American Samoa; the Democrats also provide for delegates who represent Democrats Abroad. The Democratic convention also includes a large number of "superdelegates"—mostly party officers and Democrats who hold major elective offices, and other party activists. More than 750 superdelegates were seated at the 2008 Democratic convention.

17 In a few States—South Carolina, for example—only one party held a primary. Presidential primaries were not held in ten States in 2008: Alaska, Colorado, Hawaii, Iowa, Kansas, Maine, Nebraska, Nevada, North Dakota, and Wyoming. In some States, the law permits but does not require a major party to hold a primary. In South Carolina the presidential primary is a product of party rules, not State law.

---

# Differentiated Resources

The following resources are located in the All-in-One, Unit 4, Chapter 13, Section 4:

the party's rules in an effort to promote greater grass-roots participation in the Democratic primaries. Most States treat the two major parties alike in their election laws; so, as States have responded to the Democratic Party's reform efforts, the Republicans have had to revise some of their procedures, as well.

Even a matter that seems as simple as the date for the primary illustrates the <u>crazy-quilt</u> pattern of State laws. New Hampshire holds the first of the presidential primaries every four years, and it has done so since 1920. The State guards its first-in-the-nation title with a law that provides that its primary is to be held at least a week before the date any other State picks for its contest.

Most States have come to prefer an early date, so the primary schedule has become heavily "front-loaded" in recent elections. In 2008, the scramble for an earlier date meant that 16 States held their primaries on the same day—"Super Tuesday," February 5— and three fourths of the contests had been held by mid-March.

Name recognition and money have always been important factors in the primary process, and front-loading has multiplied their importance. Until lately, a candidate who was not very well-known nationally could hope to build a following from primary to primary over several weeks—as, for example, Bill Clinton did in 1992. The front-loaded process leaves little or no time for that strategy now. Contenders have to mount (and pay for) campaigns in a number of widely separated States that hold their primaries early and, often, on the same day or within a few days of one another.

**Proportional Representation** For decades, most presidential primaries were both delegate-selection and preference exercises. Several were also **winner-take-all** contests: The candidate who won the preference vote automatically won the support of all of the delegates chosen at that primary.

Winner-take-all primaries have now all but disappeared, however. The Democratic Party's rules actually prohibit them. Instead, the Democrats now have a complex **proportional representation** rule. Any candidate who seeks the party's presidential nomination who wins at least 15 percent of the votes cast in a primary gets the number of that State's Democratic convention delegates that corresponds to his or her share of that primary vote. Take, for example, a State that has 40 convention delegates. If a candidate wins 45 percent of the primary vote, he or she automatically gains the support of at least 18 of the delegates.

Most States had to change their primary laws to account for the Democrats' proportional representation rule. So in many States, Republican delegates are also chosen on a proportional representation basis. Still, a few States do permit winner-take-all primaries, and the Republicans hold them where they can—in California, for example.

The proportional representation rule had another major impact on the shape of presidential primaries. It led several States—among them Oregon and Wisconsin, the States that had pioneered the presidential primary—to give up the popular selection of delegates. More than half of the presidential primary States now hold only a preference primary. The delegates themselves are actually chosen

✔ **Checkpoint**
How do State laws affect the presidential primary system?

**crazy-quilt**
*adj.* made up of a mixture of things, hodgepodge

**Winner-Take-All vs. Proportional Representation**

In **winner-take-all** States, the delegates are awarded only to the candidate who wins the preference vote.

40% of vote = 0 delegates    60% of vote = 100% delegates

In a State with **proportional representation**, delegates are awarded to candidates who win at least 15% of the vote.

40% of vote = 40% delegates    60% of vote = 60% delegates

▶▶ **Analyzing Charts** As political parties' rules have changed, so has the manner in which primaries have been conducted. *Why do you think candidates who receive less than 15% of the vote are not assigned delegates?*

---

# Teach

To present this topic using online resources, use the lesson presentations at **PearsonSchool.com/phgovt.**

**REVIEW BELLRINGER**

Ask for student volunteers to share their Bellringer answers with the class. Tell students that since 1952, New Hampshire has been the first State in the nation to hold its presidential primary and since 1976, Iowa has been the first to hold its caucuses. Because these are the contenders' first opportunities to showcase their candidacy on a major political stage, they focus a great deal of their time and energy campaigning in both States. Critics feel that the early States have too much influence on the presidential nomination process. Because there is a sense that States with early primaries or caucuses have greater influence on who wins the nomination, many States have jockeyed for an early date in recent campaigns.

**INTRODUCE ACTIVITY**

Explain that the methods as well as the dates of nominating events differ from State to State. Most States use primaries but some use caucuses, and there are even different types of primaries and caucuses.

**L2** **ELL Differentiate** Discuss the meanings of the terms *primary* and *caucus*. Tell students that primary means "first, basic, main," and provide examples such as *primary colors* (three basic colors), *primary school* (the first grades taught in school), *primary tooth* (a child's first tooth). Tell students that the word *caucus* may come from an Indian word for *counsel,* or advisory group. Provide examples such as *counselor* (legal advisor) and *guidance counselor* (career and education advisor).

# Background

**BLANKET PRIMARY** The "blanket primary" is an alternative to the open or closed primaries described in the chapter. Until recently, a few States used the blanket primary, in which primary voters were allowed to choose among all registered candidates, regardless of party affiliation. In 2000, the Supreme Court found California's version of the blanket primary unconstitutional, saying that it violated parties' free-association rights. After that decision, California and Alaska both moved away from blanket primaries. Washington stayed with the blanket primary system for a few more years, despite a State court ruling it unconstitutional. In 2004, the Supreme Court refused to hear Washington's appeal of that State court ruling, and Washington now uses what is called the "pick-a-party" primary system, a semi-open primary.

# Answers

**Checkpoint** In each State, the details of the delegate-selection process are set by State law, and those details vary from State to State. Most States have had to change their primary laws to account for the Democrats' proportional representation rule.

**Analyzing Charts** Possible answer: An individual who receives less than 15 percent of the vote is most likely going to eventually drop out of the race and the parties need to draw a line at a reasonable percentage that would be both democratic and realistic.

## CONDUCT A JIGSAW ACTIVITY

Use the Jigsaw strategy (p. T27) to evaluate the process of selecting convention delegates. Divide students into four groups, and assign a particular State to each group. Assign one group a State with a closed primary (such as California, Massachusetts, Florida, or Utah), assign one a State with an open primary (such as Wisconsin, Michigan, Ohio, or Vermont), assign one a State with caucuses (such as Iowa or Nevada), and assign the fourth group the State in which your school is located. Do not tell the students at this point that each group has a State with a different type of delegate-selection process. They will figure this out as part of the activity. Distribute the Chapter 13 Section 4 Core Worksheet A (Unit 4 All-in-One, p. 36), which lists questions each group should use to guide their research.

After the groups complete their research, put the students in new groups, each containing one member from each of the previous groups. Have the students share the results of their research with their new groups to complete the chart in their worksheet. Ask students to discuss with their group the differences between the nominating processes in each of the assigned States.

When the students finish sharing their results with the Jigsaw groups, conduct a brief class discussion on the different types of primaries and caucuses. Ask: **Which process do you think best expresses the wishes of the voters? Why?**

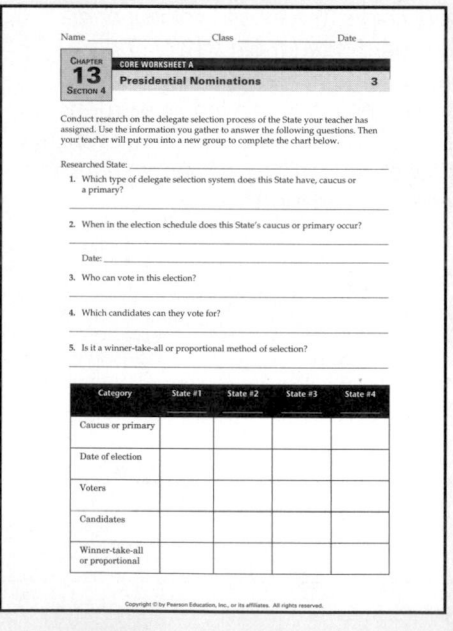

## Answers

**Analyzing Political Cartoons** The emphasis of the delegate-selection process in Iowa and New Hampshire is such that both States are more prominent and important than any other State in the Union.

**Checkpoint** They have played the major part in deciding the presidential nominating contests in both parties.

---

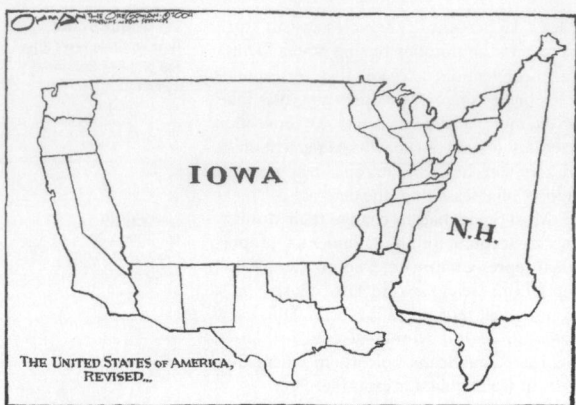

▶▶ **Analyzing Political Cartoons** The first delegate-selection event in a presidential election by caucus is held in Iowa, followed afterward by the first scheduled primary in New Hampshire. *How does this cartoon illustrate the emphasis placed on the elections held in these two States?*

✔ **Checkpoint**
Why are the primaries considered vital to the nomination process?

**vie**
*v.* to compete with someone to achieve something

later, at party conventions. In most of these States, the delegates must be picked in line with the results of the preference primary—for example, for the Republicans in 2008, so many delegates for John McCain, so many for Mitt Romney, so many for Mike Huckabee, and so on. In a few States, the preference vote does not govern the choice of the delegates. In those States—Nebraska, for example—the preference primary is often called a "beauty contest."

Most of the preference contests are also "all-candidate" primaries. These are contests in which all generally recognized contenders for a party's presidential nomination must be listed on that party's preference ballot.

## Primary Appraisal

No one who has surveyed the presidential primary system needs to be told that it is complicated, or that it is filled with confusing variations. Still, these primaries are vital. For half a century now, they have played *the* major part in deciding the presidential nominating contests in both parties—and particularly in the party out of power.

**Evaluation of the Primary** Presidential primaries tend to democratize the delegate-

selection process. And, importantly, they force would-be nominees to test their candidacies in actual political combat. For the party out of power, especially, the primaries are often "knock-down, drag-out" affairs. Without the unifying force of the President as party leader, several top personalities and factions in the party <u>vie</u> with one another, vigorously, for the presidential nomination. Here, a key function of the presidential primary can be seen: the screening out of the lesser possibilities to the point where only one or a few contenders for the nomination remain in the contest.

Such hard-fought contests do occur, but are not common, in the party in power. This tends to be true either because the President (1) is himself seeking reelection, or (2) has given his backing to someone he favors for the nomination. In either case the President regularly gets his way.

A sitting President is seldom challenged for his renomination, but that situation does sometimes happen. Thus, for example, Ronald Reagan made a stiff run at President Gerald Ford in the Republican Party in 1976, and Senator Edward Kennedy gave President Carter a real fight in 1980.

**Reform Proposals** The fact that so many States now hold presidential primaries places large demands on contenders in terms of time, effort, money, scheduling, and, not least, fatigue. The lengthy primary season tests the public's endurance, as well.

Some think that each of the major parties should hold a single, nationwide primary, and have both parties choose their presidential candidates in those contests. National conventions would be done away with—except perhaps to pick their vice-presidential nominees and/or write party platforms.

Most often, however, critics of the present arrangement favor one version or another of a regional primary plan. A series of primaries would be held at two- or three-week intervals across the country.

The prospects for reform are uncertain at best. Major changes would require joint action by Congress, the several States, and both major parties. Neither major party has ever expressed any interest in abandoning

---

# Background

**VOTING DAY** For years, Americans have cast their ballots for President on the Tuesday after the first Monday in November. The tradition of voting in November originally developed in order to accommodate the schedules of farmers, who were often too busy to vote before the harvest was in for the year. The religious practices of early Americans contributed to the designation of Tuesday as the election day of choice; voting could not take place on a Sunday or Monday because voters from outlying areas would be forced to break the Christian Sabbath in order to travel to central polling locations.

its national convention. Both parties see the conventions as a device to promote compromise and, out of it, party unity.

## Caucuses

In those States that do not hold presidential primaries, delegates to the national conventions are selected in a system of local caucuses and district and/or State conventions. A **caucus** is a closed meeting of members of a political party who gather to select delegates to the national convention. The process works basically as it is described here, but the details do differ from State to State.

A party's voters meet in local caucuses, most often at the precinct level. There they often express a preference among the contenders for the party's presidential nomination and select delegates to a local or district convention, where delegates to a State convention are elected. At the State level, and sometimes in the district conventions as well, delegates to the national convention are chosen.

The caucus-convention process dates back to the 1840s and is the oldest method for choosing national convention delegates. Its use has declined significantly over the years, however. In 2008, less than a fourth of all delegates to either party's national convention came from States that still use this method of delegate choice.

The Iowa caucuses generally get the most attention, largely because they are now the first delegate-selection event held in every presidential election season. Iowa schedules the start of its caucus process early, and has purposely done so ever since 1972. In 2008 the event took place on January 3, five days before New Hampshire held its first-in-the-nation presidential primary.

The national conventions are organized so that the energy and fervor heighten in intensity with each passing day. **Why do you think the conventions are designed to stir the emotions of party members?**

## Securing the Nomination

Once all the primaries and caucuses have been held and all of the delegates have been chosen, another event <u>looms</u> large. The two major parties hold their **national conventions,** the <u>quadrennial</u> meetings at which the delegates select their presidential and vice-presidential candidates.

For over a century, those gatherings were highly dramatic, often chaotic, and even stormy affairs at which, after days of heated bargaining, the party would finally nominate its presidential and vice-presidential candidates. Both parties' meetings have become much tamer in recent years—largely because there is now little doubt about who will win the party's grand prize. Regularly, the leading contender has won enough delegates in the primaries and caucuses to lock up the nomination long before the convention meets.

Each party's convention remains a major event, nonetheless. The conventions have three major goals: (1) naming the party's presidential and vice-presidential candidates,

✔ **Checkpoint**
Who are the voters electing in the system of caucuses and conventions?

<u>loom</u>
*v.* to take shape, emerge

<u>quadrennial</u>
*adj.* occurring every fourth year

## DISCUSS THE CONVENTIONS

Review with students the "Race for the Presidency" graphic in the text. Have volunteer students read one of the captions in each step of the race. Tell students that the climax of the primaries and caucuses is the national conventions. Have volunteers list the goals of the conventions and write them on the board *(adopt the party platform, name the presidential and vice presidential nominees, promote party unity, mobilize support for the party ticket, and capture the interest and attention of the nation).* Ask: **How do the conventions meet these goals?** *(showing solidarity through the presence of other candidates and different factions of the party, delegate enthusiasm, barnburner speeches, disparaging the other party, media coverage, patriotic adornment, showcasing the party's nominees and their acceptance speeches)*

## DISTRIBUTE CORE WORKSHEET B

Distribute the Chapter 13 Section 4 Core Worksheet B (Unit 4 All-in-One, p. 37), which asks students to answer questions about a presidential nomination acceptance speech. Divide the class into pairs, and assign each pair either the Democratic or Republican Party. Then distribute Primary Source A (Unit 4 All-in-One, p. 38) to those assigned to the Democratic Party and Primary Source B (Unit 4 All-in-One, p. 40) to those assigned to the Republican Party. Have students read their assigned speech and answer the questions in the worksheet.

**L2** **ELL Differentiation** Either read or have volunteers read one of the excerpts aloud. With each paragraph, have a volunteer summarize the general idea as well as describe the emotion they think it evokes. Then work with the class as a whole to answer the questions on the worksheet.

## Debate

"One of the expedients [methods] of party to acquire influence within particular districts is to misrepresent the opinions and aims of other districts. You cannot shield yourselves too much against the jealousies and heart burnings which spring from these misrepresentations. They tend to render alien to each other those who ought to be bound together by fraternal affection."

This quote from George Washington's Farewell Address was a warning against the growth of political parties. Use it to start a classroom debate. Ask: **Have political parties had a positive or a negative impact on our political process?**

## Answers

**Checkpoint** Precinct caucuses select delegates to the local or district convention. Those delegates select delegates to the State convention, who then select the delegates to the national convention.

**Caption** Possible answer: Encouraging party unity and enthusiasm bolsters the party spirit during the convention and into the upcoming campaign, increasing the members' desire and efforts to help ensure the election of their party's candidate.

Have student volunteers brainstorm adjectives to describe the acceptance speech they read. *(sample answers: patriotic, partisan, enthusiastic, visionary, disparaging, unifying, resolute, nationalistic)* Then have students share their answers to the questions on the worksheet, making sure to get input on each party's speech. Ask: **Based on the acceptance speech, would you vote for the nominee?** Then lead a discussion on whether students felt that the speech they read successfully achieved the goals of the national convention, expressed the goals of the nominee, and provided insight into the vision and qualities of the nominee.

**L3 Differentiation** Have students read both speeches and compare the two on what they say about the nominee's policies, the reasons they should be elected, and the other candidate. Then have students create a poster supporting the candidate of his or her choice.

**L4 Differentiation** Have students select one of the parties. Ask them to read that party's platform and compare its contents to the contents of the acceptance speech of that party's nominee. Then have them write a brief essay describing how the speech and the platform are similar and how they are different.

## Answers

**The Race for the Presidency** Voters express their preferences throughout the race, through contributions and through votes in primaries and caucuses. To win, a candidate must attract strong popular support.

---

# The Race for the Presidency

The race begins as presidential contenders vie to become their party's nominee. As the pace intensifies, the field narrows to a contest between two contenders for the ultimate prize—the presidency. *How does the contest for the White House reflect the American democratic ideal?*

**1-4 Years** Before Election The first steps for potential candidates include broadening their visibility, testing their appeal nationwide, and developing committees to explore their viability as a candidate. If the results are encouraging, the contender will officially announce his or her candidacy.

**1-4 Years** Before Election The costs of running for office are huge and raising funds is an ongoing effort throughout the campaign. Lack of funds often causes contenders to drop out of the race.

**January–June** of the Election Year Primaries and caucuses help determine the party's nominee. At this stage voters choose their party's frontrunner, and many candidates concede defeat.

**Start the Race** **Fundraising** **Primaries and Caucuses**

(2) bringing the various factions and the leading personalities in the party together in one place for a common purpose, and (3) adopting the party's **platform**—its formal statement of basic principles, stands on major policy matters, and objectives for the campaign and beyond.

Both parties hope that their convention will do a number of other things, as well. They want the meeting to promote party unity, capture the interest and attention of the country at large, and generate support for the party's ticket in the upcoming campaign.

**The First Days** Each party's convention now meets in one or two sessions per day over three or four days. Each of those sessions is tightly scheduled and closely scripted. In short, they are now made for television.

The first day is dedicated to welcoming the delegates and organizing the convention, and to dozens of short speeches by an array of party figures. The second day sees a continuing parade of speakers but is highlighted by two major events: the adoption of the party's platform and the delivery of the keynote address.

The platform comes to the convention floor as a report by the committee on platform and resolutions. In fact, it has been drawn up by the party's leadership beforehand.

Platform-writing is a fine art. Recall, the platform is a statement of party principles and stands on policy matters. But it is also an important campaign document aimed at appealing to as many people and as many groups as possible. So both parties tend to produce somewhat generalized comments on some of the hard questions facing the nation at

---

# Teacher-to-Teacher Network

Pass out a primary source document related to each step of a presidential election. Have groups of students create a tableau based on one of the documents from the set. The other groups will try to guess which step in the process the tableau represents. A tableau is a frozen image illustrating the sense and feel of a primary source. As students present their tableau, have the class write down their impressions of the scene. The audience will ask questions, and student actors will answer in single sentences. At this point, the audience should be able to guess which step or event the actors are acting out.

To see this lesson plan, go to

**GOVERNMENT** ONLINE
For an **interactive** exploration of
the steps involved in the race to
the presidency, visit
PearsonSchool.com/phgovt

**L3 Differentiate** Divide the class into groups of
four or five and tell students that their group is forming a new political party and must come up with a
platform. Have groups use library or online resources
to find copies of the most recent party platforms.
Although party platforms tend to be very long and
comprehensive, tell students that their platforms
should state at least five political ideas or principles
held by their new political party. Have a member
from each group present the platform to the class.
Discuss which platform "planks" are the most common and which are the most controversial.

**L4 Differentiate** Using the Internet or the library,
have students conduct research to determine what
percentage of eligible voters in their State participated in the most recent presidential primaries or
caucuses, and what percentage voted in the most
recent presidential election. Students should present
their findings in the form of a graph, accompanied
by a short essay explaining what difference (if any)
exists between the two participation rates and a
possible explanation for that difference. Does this
difference in participation rates affect their opinion
on whether the presidential nomination and election
process fairly represents the wishes of the voters?

Tell students to go to the Interactivity to learn more
about the race to the presidency.

**August–September** of the
**Election Year** Delegates to each
party's convention adopt the
party platform, nominate their
party's presidential candidate,
and ratify his or her choice of a
vice-presidential running mate.

**September–November** of
**the Election Year** Following the
conventions, each candidate
focuses on his or her opponent.
Debates provide opportunities to
compare and contrast each candidate's qualifications and plans
for the future.

**November** on the Tuesday after the first
**Monday in November,** the voters cast their ballots and the president-elect is determined.

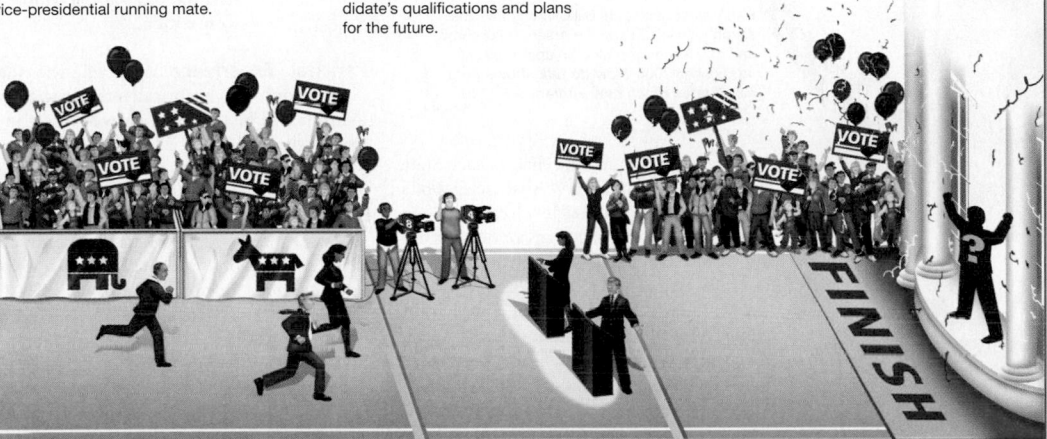

**National Conventions**     **Debates**     **Election Day**

the time. Platforms are regularly criticized for
blandness. Still, the platforms are important.
They do set out a number of hard-and-fast
stands in many policy areas. They also reflect
the compromising nature of American politics
and of the two major parties.

The **keynote address** is usually a <u>barn-
burner</u>, delivered by one of the party's most
accomplished orators. The address, like nearly
all the speeches the delegates hear, follows a
predictable pattern. It glorifies the party, its history, its leaders, and its programs, blisters the
other party, and predicts a resounding victory
for the party and its candidates in November.

**The Last Two Days** The convention turns to
its chief task on the third day: the nomination
of the party's candidates for President and Vice
President. The delegates turn first to the vice-

presidential choice. Historically, that task often
involved some suspense and a good deal of
bargaining among party factions. Nowadays,
however, the soon-to-be-nominated presidential candidate sometimes announces his or
her choice of a running mate before the convention meets—and the delegates ratify that
choice with little or no dissent.

The vice-presidential candidate then
delivers his or her acceptance speech—
another effort to fire up the party faithful and
appeal to as many other voters as possible.

The third day's session <u>culminates</u> with
the selection of the party's presidential candidate. The names of several contenders may be
offered, especially in the party out of power.
Once the nominating (and several second-
ing) speeches are made, the delegates vote.
The convention secretary calls the States in

**barnburner**
*n.* an event that is very
exciting or intense

**culminate**
*v.* to reach the highest
point, climax

# Background

**FRONTLOADING** In the 2008 campaign, Florida and Michigan moved their primaries earlier, ruining the primary schedules that both parties had carefully planned
to allow a diverse group of States to participate early. Both parties imposed penalties
for violating party rules. The Republican Party cut in half these States' convention
votes, but this mattered little because McCain had already clinched the nomination.
With its nomination still in doubt, the Democratic Party imposed harsher penalties.
The Florida and Michigan primaries would be nonbinding—no convention delegates
would be awarded based on the results. Also, no Democratic candidates would campaign
in these States. As the convention neared, frontrunner Barack Obama agreed to
restore full voting rights to promote party unity. However, the problem remains—How
can parties prevent frontloading in future elections?

# Assess and Remediate

**L3** Have students draw a flowchart illustrating the different steps in the nomination process, and ask them to note at each step on the flowchart what qualities a candidate must possess in order to succeed in that step.

**L3** Assign the Section 4 Assessment questions.

**L3** Section Quiz A (Unit 4 All-in-One, p. 42)

**L2** Section Quiz B (Unit 4 All-in-One, p. 43)

Have students complete the review activities in the digital lesson presentation and continue their work in the **Essential Questions Journal.**

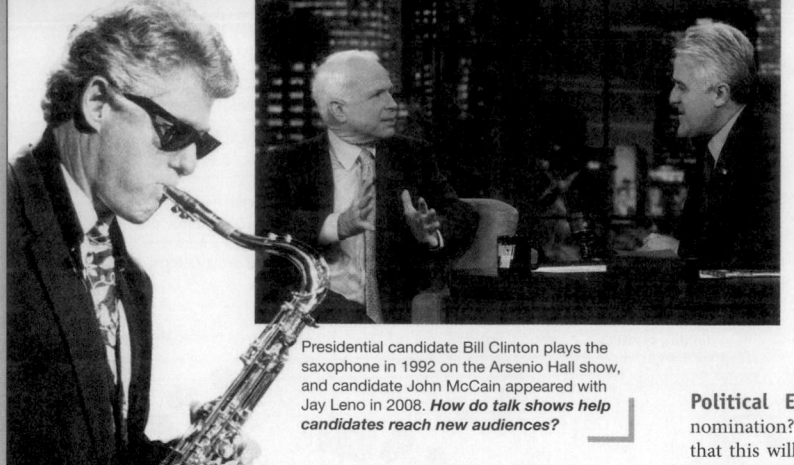

Presidential candidate Bill Clinton plays the saxophone in 1992 on the Arsenio Hall show, and candidate John McCain appeared with Jay Leno in 2008. *How do talk shows help candidates reach new audiences?*

alphabetical order, and the chair of each State delegation announces how that delegation's votes are cast. Each complete roll call is known as a ballot, and the balloting continues until one of the contenders wins a majority of the delegates' votes.

Most often, the first ballot produces a winner. Over the 28 conventions held by each party since 1900, the Republicans have made a first ballot choice 24 times and the Democrats 23 times. Indeed, the GOP has not had to take a second ballot since 1948, and the Democrats since 1952.[18]

With its candidates named, the convention comes to the final major item on its agenda: the presidential candidate's acceptance speech. That speech caps the convention and launches the party's general election campaign.

## Who Is Nominated?

If an incumbent President wants another term, and the 22nd Amendment is not in play, the convention's choice is easily made. The sitting President is virtually certain to gain the nomination, and usually with no real opposition from within the party. The President's advantages are immense: the majesty and publicity of the office and close control of the party's machinery.[19]

When the President is not in the field, up to a dozen or more contenders may surface in the preconvention period. At most, two or three of them may survive to contest the prize at the national convention.

**Political Experience** Who will win the nomination? The historical record suggests that this will be the usual answer: The contender who is the most electable. Both parties want to pick candidates who can win, those with the broadest possible appeal, within the party and in the electorate.

Most presidential candidates come to their nominations with substantial, well-known records in public office. Thus, in 2008, the Republicans picked John McCain, who had spent 26 years in Congress. But, notice, his Democratic opponent did not have nearly so lengthy a record. Barack Obama had served only four years in the Senate. However long the record, it is usually free of controversies that could have antagonized key elements in the party and the voting public.

Almost always, the major party candidates have served in elective offices, where they have demonstrated vote-getting abilities. Only rarely does a candidate step from the private world or from the military directly into a presidential candidacy—although Wendell Willkie did in 1940, and Dwight Eisenhower in 1952, both in the Republican Party.

Historically, the governorships of the larger States have produced the largest number of presidential candidacies. Of the 36 men nominated by the two major parties from 1908 to 2008, fifteen were either serving or had once served as a governor.

It is true that neither party picked a governor in 2008; but, notice, several governors

---

18 A convention can become deadlocked. In that case, a "dark horse"—that is, someone who did not seem a likely choice before the convention—may finally emerge as the nominee. The most spectacular deadlock in convention history occurred at the Democratic convention in New York in 1924. That convention took 103 ballots before John W. Davis of West Virginia won the nomination.

19 In fact, only four sitting Presidents have ever been denied nomination: John Tyler (1844), Millard Fillmore (1852), Franklin Pierce (1856), and Chester Arthur (1884).

---

## Political Cartoon Mini-Lesson

Display Transparency 13E, Change, as a wrap-up activity after students read the candidates' acceptance speeches. Tell students that this cartoon appeared shortly after the candidates gave their acceptance speeches at their party's national convention in 2008. Ask: **According to the cartoon, how were the two speeches alike?** *(both focused on change)* **What was the main difference in the two speeches?** *(the tone, or the way the candidates expressed their message of change)* **According to the cartoon, how did the tone of the two speeches differ?** *(Obama expressed his message optimistically, as a bright future through change. McCain's message was less hopeful, expressing change as a way to fix what's broken.)* **Which tone do you think would appeal most to voters? Why?** *(probably Obama's, because a happy vision of the future is appealing during economic hard times)*

## Answers

**Caption** Talk shows have specific audiences to which they are directed and candidates can use these forums as a method to reach those audiences.

were among the also-rans that year. The major party tickets were also notable in this respect in 2008: For the first time, both major parties selected sitting members of the United States Senate as their standard bearers.

**Other Characteristics** Most of the leading contenders for the nomination have been Protestants. The most notable exceptions to that statement, all Democrats and all Catholics, are Alfred E. Smith (1928), John F. Kennedy (1960), and John Kerry (2004).

Most nominees have also come from the larger States. So hopefuls from such pivotal States as New York, Ohio, Illinois, Texas, and California tend to have an advantage.

Television and now the Internet have reshaped this consideration, however. Thus, the Republicans nominated Bob Dole of Kansas in 1996 and John McCain of Arizona in 2008. And the Democrats selected Jimmy Carter of Georgia in 1976 and Bill Clinton of Arkansas in 1992.

Nominees usually have a pleasant and healthy appearance, seem to be happily married, and have an attractive (and exploitable) family. Only five have ever been divorced.

A well-developed speaking ability has always been a plus in American politics. The ability to project well over television, pioneered by John F. Kennedy in 1960, has long since become a must, as well.

**Shattering Barriers** Until 2008, neither major party had ever seriously considered a woman or nominated a member of any minority group as its presidential candidate. The Democrats broke with tradition in the most recent election, however.

Senator Hillary Clinton of New York came remarkably close to being the Democratic Party's presidential candidate in 2008. It is generally thought that the longstanding barrier to a woman at the top of a major party's national ticket has now been shattered.

The Democratic Party's presidential candidate in 2008, Barack Obama, was the child of a white mother from Kansas and a black father from Kenya. His historic election in 2008 shattered the racial barrier for the nation's highest office.

The Republicans also defied the historical record in 2008. Over time, most major party presidential candidates have been in their 50s or early 60s, with only a few in their 40s, when nominated. But none has ever been as old as John McCain, who turned 72 only a few weeks before he became the GOP's candidate in 2008. Indeed, the age spread between the two major party candidates was greater than it had been in any presidential election.

✔ **Checkpoint**
What characteristics of the presidential nominees have influenced the voting public?

**standard bearer**
*v.* a leader of a movement or party

---

## REMEDIATION

| If Your Students Have Trouble With | Strategies For Remediation |
|---|---|
| Judging the American nominating system (Question 1) | Brainstorm with students the advantages and disadvantages of the nominating system. |
| Understanding a primary and caucus and how they differ (Question 2) | Create a diagram on the board showing each at work and have students describe how they differ. |
| Describing the importance of early primaries (Question 3) | Work with students to create a list of reasons why a State might prefer an early primary. |
| Listing the main goals of the national conventions (Question 4) | Have students review the content under the heading "Securing the Nomination." |
| Expressing their opinion on proportional representation (Question 5) | Create a Pros and Cons table for the winner-take-all and proportional representation contests. |
| Explaining the characteristics that a good candidate should have (Question 6) | Remind students of the list of qualifications they created in Section 1 and have them help re-create the list on the board. |

---

**Essential Questions Journal**
To continue to build a response to the chapter Essential Question, go to your Essential Questions Journal.

## SECTION 4 ASSESSMENT

1. **Guiding Question** Use your completed chart to answer this question: Does the nominating system allow Americans to choose the best candidates for President?

**Key Terms and Comprehension**

2. **(a)** What is the purpose of a **presidential primary** and a **caucus**? **(b)** How do these processes differ?

3. **(a)** Where is the first presidential primary held? **(b)** Why do you think there is such a great desire for a State to hold its primary as early as possible?

4. What are the three main goals of the **national conventions**?

**Critical Thinking**

5. **Draw Conclusions** Do you think the proportional representation rule promotes a more democratic delegate selection process? Why or why not?

6. **Demonstrate Reasoned Judgment (a)** What characteristics are common to those who have been nominated to run for President by a major party? **(b)** What other characteristics would you like to see in a presidential nominee? **(c)** Explain how these characteristics would help a President perform the job more effectively.

**Quick Write**

**Research Writing: Write a Thesis Statement** As in other types of essays and reports, the backbone for a research report is the thesis, or main idea. Review your notes to find relationships between ideas. Focusing on his qualifications and administration, write a thesis statement that is supported by the majority of the information that you have found on the President you chose.

---

## Answers

**Checkpoint** possible answers: political experience, service in elected offices, Protestants, residents of larger States, well-developed speaking ability

---

# Assessment Answers

**1.** The nomination process assures strong candidates by putting contenders through many tests along the way. The candidates who survive these tests will likely have broad appeal and a high degree of electability.

**2. (a)** to select delegates to the party's national convention or express a preference among contenders for nomination **(b)** A primary is a vote by party members. A caucus-convention process is a series of meetings of party members at the precinct, local, district, and State levels.

**3. (a)** New Hampshire **(b)** Candidates spend a lot of time and money in early States. Some late primary voters feel their votes are unimportant because early States have already decided the nominee.

**4.** naming the party's presidential and vice-presidential candidates, bringing party factions and the leading personalities together, adopting the party's platform

**5.** Compared to the winner-take-all contests, proportional representation seems more democratic. The delegate selection more closely represents the voice of the people.

**6. (a)** record free of controversies, held elective office, many were governors, Protestant, from big States, good speakers **(b)** Sample answer: I would like a presidential nominee to hold an advanced degree and to have graduated near the top of his or her college class. **(c)** These characteristics are a measure of above-average intelligence, which would help a President decide complex issues.

**QUICK WRITE** The thesis statement should express the main idea supported by research.

GUIDING QUESTION

Does the election process serve the goals of American democracy today?

| Electoral College | |
|---|---|
| **Defects** | **Significance** |
| • winner-take-all system | • winner of popular vote not guaranteed presidency |
| • two electors in each State allotted based on Senate seats | • allotment of electoral votes does not match population and voter distribution<br>• winner of popular vote not guaranteed presidency |
| • electors not required to vote in accord with popular vote | • electors who break their pledge could influence outcome |
| • House may have to decide election | • House votes by State, so States with small or large populations have equal weight<br>• State loses vote if no candidate favored by majority of that State's representatives<br>• election requires majority of States, so third-party candidate could prevent decision |

## Get Started

### LESSON GOALS

Students will . . .

- examine the distribution of electoral votes, using a table.
- recognize the influence of the electoral system on campaign strategy, using a map of pre-election opinion poll results.
- evaluate proposals to reform the electoral college system, using a Jigsaw strategy.

## SKILLS DEVELOPMENT

### ANALYZE POLITICAL CARTOONS

To practice analyzing political cartoons in this section, use the Chapter 13 Skills Worksheet (Unit 4 All-in-One, p. 50). You may teach the skill explicitly before or after discussing the electoral college. For L2 and L1 students, assign the adapted Skill Activity (Unit 4 All-in-One, p. 51).

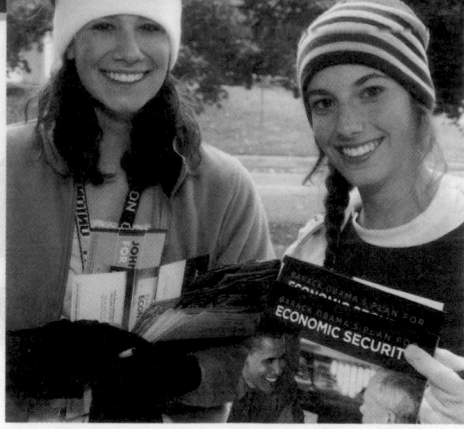

SECTION 5

# The Presidential Election

### Guiding Question

**Does the election process serve the goals of American democracy today?** Use a table like the one below to keep track of the main ideas about the election process.

| Electoral College | |
|---|---|
| **Defects** | **Significance** |
| • Winner-take-all system | • |
| • | • |
| • | • |

### Political Dictionary

- swing voter
- battleground State
- district plan
- proportional plan
- direct popular election
- national popular vote plan

### Objectives

1. Describe the features of the presidential campaign.
2. Explain how the electoral college provides for the election of the President.
3. Identify the major flaws in the electoral college system.
4. Outline the advantages and disadvantages of proposed reforms of the electoral college.

**Image Above:** Young volunteers canvas door-to-door in the 2008 presidential election.

As you know, the Constitution calls for a presidential election to be held every four years. The first one was held in 1789, and, like clockwork, 55 of those contests have followed along, right on schedule. That remarkable fact is unmatched in the history of any other nation in the world. Even during a civil war, two world wars, several economic depressions, and various other crises, the Constitution's command has been met.

## The Presidential Campaign

The presidential campaign is an all-out effort to win the votes of the American people. For decades, that slugfest began soon after the two parties' conventions had adjourned. But, over recent decades, it has been quite apparent some weeks, or even a month or more, before the conventions who the delegates would nominate. So those campaigns have in fact begun at some point before the candidates were formally nominated.

The campaign itself is organized chaos, and it dominates the national news scene up to election day. The candidates' campaign organizations work to show their standard bearers in the best possible light and, with negative jabs, to undercut the claims of the opposition. The voters are bombarded with radio and television interviews, speeches and advertisements, direct mail, Internet messages, "whistle-stop" tours, press conferences and press releases, rallies and party dinners, stickers and buttons, pamphlets, balloons, and billboards. The candidates pose for hundreds of photographs and shake thousands of hands as each of them tries to convince the voters that he (and, one day, she) is the best bet for the country.

Both campaigns focus much of their efforts on **swing voters**—the roughly one third of the electorate who have not made up their minds at the start of the campaign and are open to persuasion by either side. Campaign strategy is also driven by the electoral college, as you will see in a moment. The would-be Presidents target the **battleground States**—those States in which the outcome is "too close to call" and either candidate could win. Both campaigns tend to concentrate their organizational efforts, campaign funds, and candidate appearances in those States.

## Focus on the Basics

**FACTS:** • Voters do not vote directly for the President, but for presidential electors. • In most States, electors are chosen on a winner-take-all basis, so the party with the largest popular vote in a State wins all of that State's electors. • Today's electors are pledged to vote for their party's candidates, contrary to the Framers' intent. • Some people say that the electoral college is flawed and are working to reform it.

**CONCEPTS:** popular sovereignty, representative democracy

**ENDURING UNDERSTANDINGS:** • Although the popular vote represents the people's choice, the electoral college actually elects the President. • A candidate can win the popular vote and fail to win the presidency. • Supporters of the electoral college say that, although it may be flawed, it is a known system that works in most cases.

A series of presidential debates now highlights the campaign. An incumbent President, or a candidate ahead in the polls, may not really want to debate, but both major party contenders now regularly agree to do so. [20]

The first presidential debates, in 1960, featured then-Vice President Richard Nixon and his Democratic opponent, Senator John F. Kennedy. Their four televised debates, which were really little more than joint appearances, generated a great deal of interest, and many analysts credit John Kennedy's strong performance in them as one of the keys to his very narrow victory in the election that year.

The next set of debates came in 1976, between President Gerald Ford and his Democratic opponent, Jimmy Carter; with another involving their vice-presidential running mates, Bob Dole and Walter Mondale. That general pattern has been followed in every campaign since then. Thus, in 2008, there were three debates between John McCain and Barack Obama and one that pitted Sarah Palin against Joe Biden.

The most recent presidential debates—still more joint appearances than real debates—included one on foreign policy, a second with a "town hall" format, and a third on domestic and economic policy. Whether or not, and how much, the candidates' performances in those debates affected their ratings is open to question. In all, an average of 57 million people watched each debate. Surprisingly, more viewers watched the single vice-presidential debate between Senator Joe Biden and Governor Sarah Palin of Alaska than watched any of the Obama-McCain debates.

The presidential campaign finally comes to an end on election day. Millions of voters go to the polls in all 50 States and the District of Columbia. But the President, whoever that is to be, is not formally elected until the presidential electors' votes are cast and counted, several weeks later.

## The Election

You have arrived at one of the least understood points in the American political process. As the people vote in the presidential election, they do not cast a vote directly for one of the contenders for the office of the President. They vote, instead, for presidential electors.

Recall, the Constitution provides for the election of the President by the electoral college, in which each State has as many electors as it has members of Congress. The Framers expected the electors to use their own judgment in selecting a President. Today the electors, once chosen, are, in fact, just "rubber stamps." They are expected to vote automatically for their party's candidates for President and Vice President. In short, the electors go through the form set out in the Constitution in order to meet the letter of the Constitution, but their behavior is far from the original intent of that document.

**Choosing Electors** The electors are chosen by popular vote in every State on the same day everywhere: the Tuesday after the first Monday in November every fourth year.[21] So the 2012 presidential election is set for November 6, 2012. In every State except Maine and Nebraska, the electors are chosen at large.[22] That is, they are chosen on

---

20 The debates are now sponsored by an independent, nonpartisan body created by Congress in 1987, the Commission on Presidential Debates. The participants must be party-nominated candidates who are (1) supported by at least 15 percent of the respondents in five national polls and (2) listed on the ballot of States which, taken together, will cast at least a majority (270) of the electoral votes in the upcoming election. In effect, the Commission's rules exclude minor party and independent candidates from the debates.

21 The Constitution (Article II, Section 1, Clause 2) says that the electors are to be chosen in each State "in such Manner as the Legislature thereof may direct." In several States the legislatures themselves chose the electors in the first several elections. By 1832, however, every State except South Carolina had provided for popular election. The electors were picked by the legislature in South Carolina through 1860. Since then, all presidential electors have been chosen by popular vote in every State, with two exceptions. The State legislatures chose the electors in Florida in 1868 and in Colorado in 1876.

22 Maine (beginning in 1972) and Nebraska (1992) use the "district plan." In those States, two electors are chosen from the State at large and the others are picked in each of the State's congressional districts. The district plan was used by several States in the first few presidential elections, but every State except South Carolina had provided for the choice of electors from the State at large by 1832. Since then, the district plan has been used only by Michigan in 1892 and by Maine and Nebraska. In 2008, Barack Obama won one electoral vote from Nebraska's 2nd congressional district.

**✓ Checkpoint**
What role does the popular vote play in a presidential election?

---

## Differentiated Resources

The following resources are located in the All-in-One, Unit 4, Chapter 13, Section 5:

---

### BEFORE CLASS

Assign the section, the graphic organizer in the text, and the Reading Comprehension Worksheet (Unit 4 All-in-One, p. 44) before class.

**L2 Differentiate** Reading Comprehension Worksheet (Unit 4 All-in-One, p. 46)

### BELLRINGER

Display Transparency 13F, which shows a quotation supporting direct election of the President. Have students answer the question in their notebooks.

**L2 Differentiate** Explain key terms from the Bellringer quote: *thwarts* (blocks or prevents), *distorts* (twists out of shape), and *bipartisan* (including members of both parties).

## Teach

To present this topic using online resources, use the lesson presentations at **PearsonSchool.com/phgovt.**

### REVIEW BELLRINGER

On opposite sides of the board, write "Agree" and "Disagree." Call on students to say which side they chose, and have each student you call on give one of his or her specific facts in support of the position. As students name facts, write them on the board under the relevant header. *(Possible arguments for direct election: most democratic; each vote counts equally; the winner will always be the majority choice; loser of popular vote has actually become President in past elections; most Americans support this plan. Possible arguments against direct election: abolishes Framers' original plan; weakens federalism because the States, as States, would lose their role in choosing a President; weakens the voice of small States; could lead to electoral dominance of large States; would require widespread campaigning that would strain electoral resources; could lead to voter fraud and post-election challenges)*

---

## Answers

**Checkpoint** The popular vote elects presidential electors who will actually vote for the President and Vice President.

## DISTRIBUTE CORE WORKSHEET

Distribute the Chapter 13 Section 5 Core Worksheet A (Unit 4 All-in-One, p. 48) containing a table of electoral college votes by State. Have students read the table and answer the questions on the worksheet. When they have completed the worksheet, review the answers with the class.

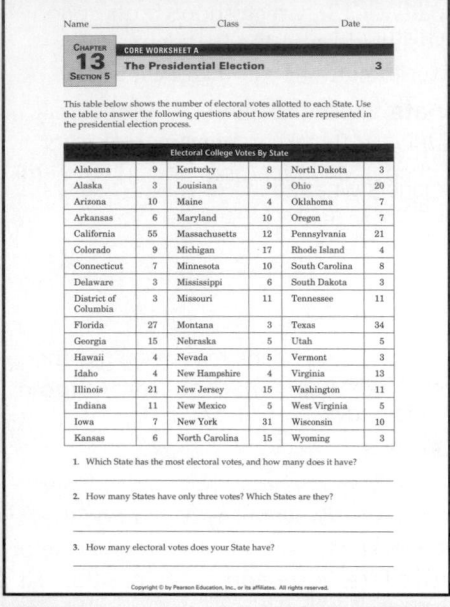

## CALCULATE ELECTORAL COLLEGE VOTES

Display Transparency 13G, Electoral Vote Projection. Explain that this map represents the results of opinion polling shortly before the 2008 election. Based on this map, ask students how many electoral votes are either "solid" or "leaning" toward each candidate. *(Obama: 164 solid, 38 leaning; McCain: 163 solid, 26 leaning)*

Next, have students identify the States that were considered "battleground" States, meaning that their electoral votes could have gone to either candidate at the time this map was created. *(Nevada, Colorado, Minnesota, Wisconsin, Michigan, Indiana, Ohio, Pennsylvania, New Hampshire, Virginia, Florida)* Ask students how many electoral votes were at stake in these battleground States. *(147)*

Tell students to go to the Audio Tour to learn more about the nation's electoral votes.

## Answers

**Checkpoint** The electors meet at their State capital and each cast a vote, one for President and one for Vice President. The ballots are signed and sealed and sent via registered mail to the President of the Senate in Washington, D.C. to be counted.

**Analyzing Maps** The States in the northeast have much larger electoral strength than other States relative to their actual size.

**388** The Presidency

---

✓ **Checkpoint**
What is the procedure for casting electoral votes?

**slate**
*n.* a list of candidates in an election

a winner-take-all basis. The presidential candidate—technically, the <u>slate</u> of elector-candidates nominated by his party—who receives the largest number of popular votes in a State regularly wins all of that State's electoral votes.

Today, the names of the individual elector-candidates appear on the ballot in only a handful of States. In most States, only the names of the presidential and vice-presidential candidates are listed. They stand as "shorthand" for the elector slates.

**Counting the Electoral Votes** The Constitution provides that the date Congress sets for the electors to meet "shall be the same throughout the United States."[23] The 12th

Amendment provides that "the Electors shall meet in their respective States." The electors thus meet at their State capital on the date set by Congress, now the Monday after the second Wednesday in December. There they each cast their electoral votes, one for President and one for Vice President. The electors' ballots, signed and sealed, are sent by registered mail to the President of the Senate in Washington.

Who has won a majority of the electoral votes, and who then will be the next President of the United States, is usually known by midnight of election day, more than a month before the electors cast their ballots. But the *formal* election of the President and Vice President finally takes place in early January.[24]

---

[24] Usually on January 6th. Congress can choose another day in early January, however—and it did so when it moved the date to January 8 for 2009.

[23] Article II, Section 1, Clause 4.

**GOVERNMENT ONLINE**
**Audio Tour**
To learn more about the nation's electoral votes, visit
**PearsonSchool.com/phgovt**

## Electoral Votes by State

A cartogram is a thematic map that shows a relationship between two factors, distorted to convey the data. The large map below shows the electoral vote strength of each State. Note that several small, populous States have more electoral votes than many larger, rural States. ***What do these maps suggest about the electoral vote strength of the Northeast?***

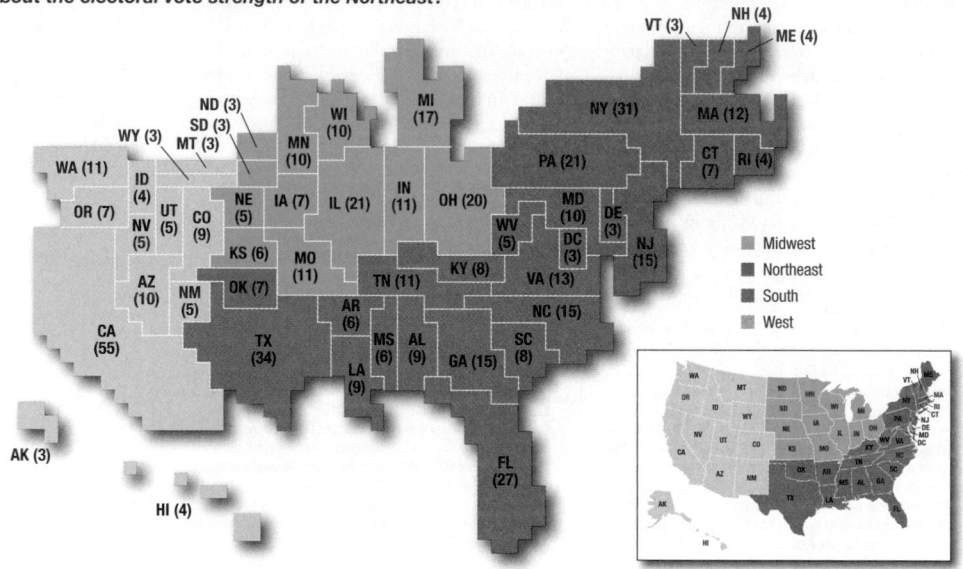

## Background

**ALLOCATION OF ELECTORAL VOTES** In the electoral college, each State has the same number of electors as it has members of Congress (both senators and House representatives). Each State has at least three electors, because each State has two senators and at least one representative. After each census, when the distribution of congressional representatives changes, the distribution of electors also changes. The exception to this rule is the District of Columbia, which does not have senators or representatives but nonetheless has three votes in the electoral college.

On that date, the president of the Senate opens the electoral votes from each State and counts them before a joint session of Congress. The candidate who receives a majority of the electors' votes for President is declared elected, as is the candidate with a majority of the votes for Vice President.

If no candidate has won a majority—at least 270 of the 538 electoral votes today—the election is thrown into the House of Representatives. This happened in 1800 and again in 1824. The House chooses a President from among the top three candidates voted for by the electoral college. Each State delegation has one vote, and it takes a majority of 26 to elect. If the House fails to choose a President by January 20, the 20th Amendment provides that the newly elected Vice President shall act as President until a choice is made.

The 20th Amendment also says that "the Congress may by law provide for the case wherein neither a President elect nor a Vice President elect shall have qualified" by Inauguration Day. Congress has done so, in the Presidential Succession Act of 1947. The Speaker of the House would "act as President . . . until a President or Vice President shall have qualified."

If no person receives a majority of the electoral votes for Vice President, the Senate decides between the top two candidates. It takes a majority of the whole Senate to elect. The Senate has chosen a Vice President only once: Richard M. Johnson in 1837.

## Flaws in the Electoral College

The electoral college system is plagued by three major defects: (1) the winner of the popular vote is not guaranteed the presidency; (2) electors are not required to vote in <u>accord</u> with the popular vote; and (3) any election might have to be decided in the House of Representatives.

**The First Major Defect** There is the ever-present threat that the winner of the popular vote will not win the presidency. This continuing danger is largely the result of two factors. The most important is the winner-take-all

feature of the electoral college system. That is, the winning candidate customarily receives all of a State's electoral votes. Thus, in 2008, Barack Obama won just 51.5 percent of the popular vote in Ohio. Still, he won all of that State's 20 electoral votes—despite the fact that nearly 2.7 million Ohioans voted for his Republican opponent, John McCain.

The other major culprit here is the way the electoral votes are distributed among the States. Remember, two of the electors in each State are allotted because of a State's two Senate seats, regardless of population. So the distribution of electoral votes among the States does not match the facts of population and voter distribution.

Take an extreme case to illustrate this point: California, the country's most populous State, has 55 electoral votes, one for each 615,848 persons in the State, based on its 2000 population of 33,871,648 residents. Wyoming has three electoral votes, one for each 164,594 persons, based on its 2000 population of 493,782 residents.

The popular vote winner has, in fact, failed to win the presidency four times: in 1824, 1876, 1888, and most recently 2000.[25] In that latest instance, the Democratic candidate, Vice President Al Gore, won 50,999,897 popular votes—543,895 more votes than his Republican opponent, the then-governor of Texas, George W. Bush. However, Mr. Bush received 271 electoral votes—one more than the bare majority in the electoral college, and so he became the nation's 43rd President.

Florida's 25 electoral votes proved to be decisive in the 2000 election. The popular vote results in several Florida counties were challenged immediately after the polls closed there. The next five weeks were filled with partisan infighting, several recounts, and a number of court disputes.

[25] The election of 1876, pitting Republican Rutherford B. Hayes against Democrat Samuel J. Tilden, is often called the "Stolen Election." Two conflicting sets of electoral votes were received from Florida (4 votes), Louisiana (8 votes), and South Carolina (7 votes), and the validity of one vote from Oregon was disputed. Congress created an Electoral Commission to decide the matter. It was composed of five senators, five representatives, and five Supreme Court justices. The Commissioners, eight Republicans and seven Democrats, voted on strict party lines, so all 20 disputed votes were awarded to Hayes, who won the presidency with 185 electoral votes to Tilden's 184.

✔ **Checkpoint**
What three flaws affect the electoral college system?

**accord**
*n.* agreement

---

### CREATE ELECTION STRATEGY

Remind students that a candidate needs 270 electoral votes to win the presidential election. Based on their analysis of the transparency, ask them how many votes each candidate needed from battleground States to become President. (*Assuming that both candidates won all their "solid" and "leaning" States, Obama would need 68 additional votes from battleground States and McCain would need 81.*)

Designate each student as either a Democrat or a Republican. Tell students that they are the campaign managers for their party's 2008 candidate in the last weeks of this election. Based on the map and the electoral vote projections, ask the Democratic campaign managers what advice they would give to their candidate. Write their answers on the board. Then repeat for the Republican campaign managers. Discuss the answers as a class, finding the similarities and differences between the two parties' strategies.

**L2 Differentiate** Pair students and use the Think-Write-Pair-Share strategy (p. T22) to have students come up with their advice for both candidates.

### DISPLAY TRANSPARENCY

Display Transparency 13H, which is a map of the 2008 election results. Ask students to think about the ways that the results map differs from the previous transparency of the opinion poll map.

Ask: **How many States did each candidate actually win?** (*Obama: 28; McCain: 22*) **What was the final count of electoral votes for each candidate?** (*Obama: 365; McCain: 173*) **Which battleground States did each candidate win?** (*Obama: Florida, Indiana, North Carolina, Ohio; McCain: North Dakota, Montana, Missouri*) **How many total votes did each candidate gain from battleground States?** (*Obama: 73; McCain: 17*) **Based on these results, how effective were the winning candidate's campaign efforts in the final weeks before the election?**

---

# Political Cartoon Mini-Lesson

Display Transparency 13I, I Survived Campaign 2004, when you discuss campaign strategies in battleground States. This cartoon illustrates how campaigns target battleground States. Ask: **Who does the man represent?** (*a typical voter in a battleground State*) **What happened to the voter?** (*He was hit with a barrage of campaign-related messages.*) **Why?** (*Candidates focus a lot of attention and resources on battleground States, because these States are still up for grabs.*) **Based on the cartoon, how do voters in battleground States feel when the election finally arrives?** (*They feel beat up or worn out.*)

---

## Answers

**Checkpoint** the winner of the popular vote may not win the presidency; the electors are not required to vote in accord with the popular vote; any election might be decided by the House

## JIGSAW ACTIVITY

Discuss the relationship between the popular vote and the electoral college vote, and the reasons why the electoral vote does not always reflect the popular vote. Ask: **Do you feel that this issue represents a flaw with the electoral college system?**

Distribute the Chapter 13 Section 5 Core Worksheet B (Unit 4 All-in-One, p. 49), which has a chart for students' use in this exercise. Use the Jigsaw strategy (p. T27) to conduct an activity on possible reforms to the electoral college system. Divide the students into five groups, one for each of the four major reform plans discussed in the chapter (district plan, proportional plan, direct popular election, and national popular vote) and one for the current electoral college system. Instruct them to work with their group to complete the part of the chart for their assigned election plan. Give each group five or ten minutes to discuss the advantages and disadvantages, and record their notes on the chart. While they discuss, circulate through the classroom and help any groups that are having difficulty.

At the end of the discussion time, have the students form new groups, each composed of one student from each previous group. In their new configuration, have students share the results of their previous discussions and complete the remaining parts of the chart. Finally, have them work with their group to answer the question at the end of the worksheet. This question asks them to choose which of the five options they think is the best method for selecting a President.

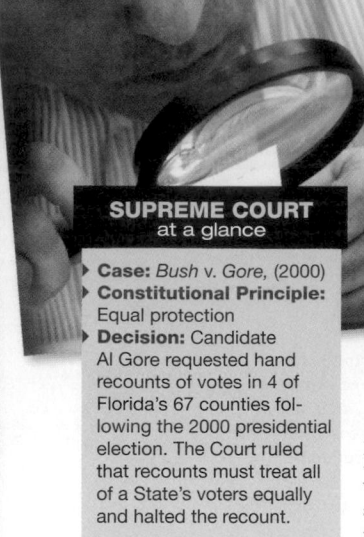

The United States Supreme Court finally brought an end to the bitter contest on December 12. It ruled, in *Bush* v. *Gore*, that the differing ways in which various counties were recounting votes violated the 14th Amendment's Equal Protection Clause. The Court's 5–4 decision ended those recounts. It also preserved Mr. Bush's 537-vote lead in the Statewide count, and so gave him Florida's 25 electoral votes. The High Court's split decision in *Bush* v. *Gore* remains highly controversial.

To this point, 15 Presidents have won the White House with less than a majority of the popular votes cast in their elections. The most recent of these "minority Presidents" were Bill Clinton in both 1992 and 1996, and George W. Bush in 2000.

By now, you see the point: The winner-take-all factor produces an electoral vote that is, at best, only a distorted reflection of the popular vote.

**The Second Major Defect** Nothing in the Constitution, nor in any federal statute, requires the electors to vote for the candidate favored by the popular vote in their States. Several States do have such laws, but they are of doubtful constitutionality, and none has ever been enforced.

To this point, however, electors have "broken their pledges," refused to vote for their party's presidential nominee, on only eleven occasions—most recently in 2004. That year, one Minnesota elector, a Democrat, did not cast his ballot for his party's presidential candidate, John Kerry.

He voted, instead, for the Democrats' vice-presidential choice, John Edwards. In fact, he voted for Senator Edwards twice—once for President and then, again, on his other ballot, for Vice President.

In no case has the vote of a "faithless elector" had a bearing on the outcome of a presidential election. But the potential is most certainly there.

**The Third Major Defect** In any presidential election, it is possible that the contest will be decided in the House. This has happened only twice, and not since 1824. In several other elections, however—most recently, 1968—a strong third-party bid has threatened to make it impossible for either major party candidate to win a majority in the electoral college, and so throw the election into the House of Representatives.

Three serious objections can be raised regarding election by the House. First, the voting in such cases is by States, not by individual members. A State with a small population, such as Alaska, Wyoming, or Vermont, would have as much weight as the most populous State. Second, if the representatives from a State were so divided that no candidate was favored by a majority, that State would lose its vote. Third, the Constitution requires a majority of the States for election in the House—today, 26 States. If a strong third-party candidate were involved, there is a real possibility that the House could not make a decision by Inauguration Day.

In such a case, Section 3 of the 20th Amendment states that "the Vice President elect shall act as President until a President shall have qualified." If no Vice President elect is available, the Presidential Succession Act would come into play. Note that it is even mathematically possible for the minority party in the House to have control of a

## Background

**COLORADO ATTEMPTS REFORM** In 2000, Al Gore won the popular vote but lost the election to George W. Bush by five electoral votes. The closeness of this race renewed attention on the electoral college system. In Colorado, a group proposed a State constitutional amendment, Amendment 36, which would make Colorado the first State to adopt a proportional plan. Had Amendment 36 been in place in 2000, Al Gore would have become President. Colorado has nine electoral votes. Under the proportional plan, a candidate who wins 60 percent of Colorado's popular vote would take five electoral votes, with the other four going to the loser. Supporters pointed out that Amendment 36 would make each individual's vote count. Critics argued that it would take away Colorado's influence. Candidates would not campaign in the State if they might win only one vote more than their opponent. Amendment 36 failed.

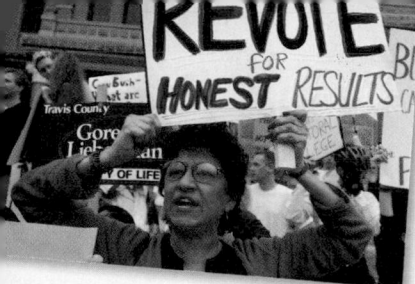

**Far Left:** An election official uses a magnifying glass to decipher whether a "chad" was punched through on a Florida ballot in 2000. **Middle and Right:** Voters take to the streets to express their views on the contested 2000 election.

majority of the individual State delegations. That party could then elect its candidate, even though he or she may have run second or even third in both the popular and the electoral vote contests.

## Proposed Reforms

The several shortcomings of the electoral college have long been recognized. To that point, Thomas Jefferson once called its original version "the most dangerous blot" on the

Constitution. Amendments to revise or eliminate the electoral college have been introduced in every term of Congress since 1789. Most of the proposals fall under four headings: the district plan, the proportional plan, direct popular election, and the national popular vote plan. Over recent years, most advocates of change have supported proposals for the direct election of the President.

**District and Proportional Plans** Under the **district plan,** each State would choose its electors much as it chooses its members of Congress. That is, two electors would be chosen from the State at large, and they would be required to cast their electoral votes in

🔊 **GOVERNMENT** ONLINE
**Audio Tour**
Listen to a tour of this map at
**PearsonSchool.com/phgovt**

The 2008 Presidential Election
# McCain vs Obama

Although John McCain won more than 45 percent of the popular vote in the 2008 election, the Republican received only 32 percent of the electoral votes. *How do these results illustrate the significance of the winner-take-all factor in State contests?*

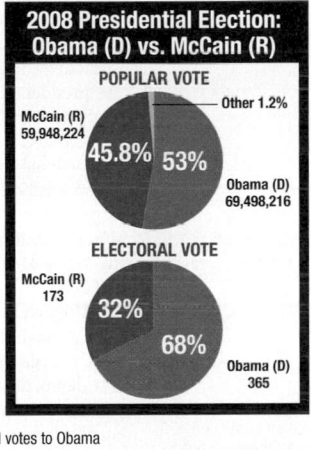

**2008 Presidential Election: Obama (D) vs. McCain (R)**

**POPULAR VOTE**
McCain (R) 59,948,224 — 45.8%
Other 1.2%
53% — Obama (D) 69,498,216

**ELECTORAL VOTE**
McCain (R) 173 — 32%
68% — Obama (D) 365

■ Barack Obama (D)
■ John McCain (R)
\* One of five electoral votes to Obama

SOURCE: Federal Election Commission

# Background

**FAITHLESS ELECTORS** Electors are expected to vote for the candidate who carries their State, and they usually do. However, electors have broken ranks with their parties and voted for other candidates a few times in American history. Electors who do this are known as "faithless electors." Some faithless electors have even voted for people who were not officially declared candidates. In 1976, one Republican elector voted for Ronald Reagan instead of the party's candidate, incumbent Gerald Ford. Reagan, though he had competed in the primary, was not on the ticket. That elector seemed to have a good instinct, though—Reagan was elected President four years later.

## Answers

**Caption** Although McCain won nearly 50 percent of the popular vote, he only acquired about one third of the electoral vote, which would not have been the case had the winner-take-all element not been in place.

**L3** **Differentiate** As the national popular vote plan is gaining momentum throughout the nation, have students research the progress of this plan. Have students write a newspaper article, describing the proposed plan and reporting its history, current status, and prospects for eventual adoption.

**L4** **Differentiate** Divide the class into four groups and assign a country to each group (suggested countries to assign: the United Kingdom, Mexico, France, and Germany). Have the groups research, either in the library or online, how their assigned country chooses its head of government. Each group should then present the results of its research to the rest of the class.

---

**scheme**
*n.* a plan or system in which things are put together

line with the popular vote in their State. The State's other electors would be chosen, separately, in each of that State's congressional districts. The votes of these electors would be cast in accord with the popular vote in their districts. Remember, two States—Maine and Nebraska—now choose their electors on a district plan basis.

Under the **proportional plan,** each presidential candidate would receive a share of each State's electoral vote equal to his or her share of that State's popular vote. So a candidate who won, say, 62 percent of the votes cast in a State with 20 electors would receive 12.4 of that State's electoral votes.

In their basic forms, neither the district nor the proportional plan would require a constitutional amendment to become effective. Remember, the Constitution leaves the manner of selecting the electors up to the State legislatures. Any of them could decide to allocate the State's electoral votes by districts or on a proportional basis.

The Constitution would have to be amended to accomplish direct popular election, however. If the goal of reform is to ensure that the winner of the national popular vote would in fact win the presidency, only direct election would guarantee that result. Neither the district nor the proportional plan would do so.

If the district plan had been in place in 1960, Richard Nixon, not John F. Kennedy, would have won the presidency. And in 1976 the presidential election would almost certainly have had to be decided by the House.

If the Constitution had provided for a proportional plan in 1960, the Kennedy-Nixon election would very likely have had to go to the House. And, the House would almost certainly have had to decide who won the White House in 1968, 1976, 1992, 1996, and 2000.

Moreover, neither a district plan nor a proportional plan would overcome the electoral college arrangement that violates the core democratic value of equality. The district scheme prevents the weighing of all votes equally. It does, in major part, because, recall, every State has two electoral votes because it has two seats in the Senate, no matter what its population.

The proportional plan does do a better job of weighing popular votes equally. Still, because each of the smaller States is over-represented by its two Senate-based electors, that arrangement would make it possible for the loser of the popular vote to win the White House in the electoral vote. And, again, the proportional plan would often throw the election into the House.

**Direct Popular Election** Proposals for **direct popular election** would not reform but, instead, abolish the electoral college system. The voters in all 50 States and the District of Columbia would be given the power to actually choose the President and the Vice President. Each vote, cast anywhere in the country, would count equally in the national result. The winner would, therefore, always be the choice of a majority or at least a plurality of the nation's voters.

A majority of the American people have consistently supported direct popular election for several decades now. The fact that the loser of the popular vote nevertheless won the presidency in 2000 has given added weight to the case for direct election.

Several obstacles stand in the way of that plan, however. Not the least of them is the constitutional amendment process itself. Recall, the smaller States are heavily over-represented in the electoral college. They would lose that advantage with direct election. It is altogether likely that enough senators, or representatives, from smaller States would oppose a direct election amendment to kill it. [26]

Some argue that direct election would weaken the federal system because the States, as States, would lose their role in the choice of a President. Others believe that direct election would put too great a load on the election process. They believe this because every vote, no matter where it was cast, would count in the national result. And so candidates would have to campaign strenuously everywhere. The impact that would have on campaign

---

[26] The House did approve a direct election amendment by the required two-thirds majority in 1969; a Senate filibuster killed the measure in 1970. A similar proposal was defeated in a Senate floor vote in 1979.

---

# Debate

"[The national popular vote initiative] is basically an end run around the Constitution. The appropriate way would be to actually amend the Constitution. But [the plan's supporters] know that they can't do that because they wouldn't have the popular support, they wouldn't be able to get it through [Congress]."

— Michael Hough, American Legislative Exchange Council
from "Obama-McCain Contest: Should Winner of Popular Vote Always Win the White House?" *Christian Science Monitor* (September 3, 2008)

Use this quotation to begin a debate in your class. Ask: **Should an amendment to the U.S. Constitution be required to abolish the electoral college system?**

# The Electoral College Today

▶ **Analyzing Political Cartoons** Defenders of the electoral college say that it identifies the President-elect both quickly and certainly. Critics insist that the system can and has given the presidency to candidates who did not win the popular vote. **What is this cartoon's objection to the electoral college?**

With 20 electoral college votes at stake, hotly contested Ohio was a major battleground State in the 2008 election.

time, effort, and finances would be huge and, opponents argue, probably unmanageable.

Some claim that, inevitably, direct election would spur various forms of voter fraud. That, they predict, would lead to lengthy, bitter, and highly explosive post-election challenges.

In several States, a Statewide election often hinges on the behavior of some particular group in the electorate. The overall result in the State depends in large part on how that group of voters cast their ballots or, often more importantly, on how heavily they do or do not turn out to vote. As but one of many examples of the point, the African American vote in Cook County (Chicago) is regularly decisive in a presidential election in Illinois. With direct election, those key groups would not have the critical power they now enjoy, and so many of them oppose direct election of the President.

Given all of this, there seems little chance that the electoral college will be abolished and direct election put in its place any time in the near future.

**The National Popular Vote Plan** A quite different approach to electoral college reform has recently surfaced: the **national popular vote plan**—in effect, a proposal to bring about the direct popular election of the President—and to do so without making any change in the words of the Constitution.

This new plan looks to the State legislatures to take the lead in electoral college reform. It calls upon each State's lawmaking body to (1) amend State election laws to provide that all of a State's electoral votes are to be awarded to the presidential candidate who wins the national popular vote and (2) enter into an interstate compact, the Agreement Among the States to Elect the President by National Popular Vote. That compact, and with it each State's election law changes, would come into force only if and when the compact has been agreed to by enough States to account for a majority (at least 270) of the 538 electoral votes.

The national popular vote plan is the only proposal to reform the electoral college that attracts any significant amount of public

---

# Assess and Remediate

**L3** Have the students write a paragraph explaining how the electoral college system has influenced American politics.

**L3** Collect the Core Worksheets and assess the students' work.

**L3** Assign the Section 5 Assessment questions.

**L3** Section Quiz A (Unit 4 All-in-One, p. 52)

**L2** Section Quiz B (Unit 4 All-in-One, p. 53)

Have students complete the review activities in the digital lesson presentation and continue their work in the **Essential Questions Journal.**

---

# Background

**BUTTERFLY BALLOT** Display Transparency 13J, Butterfly Ballot in Palm Beach County, Florida, when you discuss *Bush* v. *Gore.* In the 2000 election, Republican George W. Bush defeated Democrat Al Gore in Florida by a mere 537 votes. Gore called for a recount in four Florida counties, including Palm Beach County, where the Reform Party candidate, Pat Buchanan, received an unexpectedly high vote total. This result did not match the demographics of Palm Beach County, which was home to many elderly, mostly Democratic voters. The county used the butterfly ballot illustrated in the transparency. Gore's name was listed second on the ballot, but to select Gore, voters had to punch the third hole. This confused many voters, who punched the second hole for Buchanan by mistake. Many people still believe that the confusing butterfly ballot cost Gore the election.

---

# Answers

**Analyzing Political Cartoons** The cartoon suggests that the electoral college is an outdated system for today's voters.

| If Your Students Have Trouble With | Strategies For Remediation |
|---|---|
| Judging the election process (Question 1) | Brainstorm the advantages and disadvantages of the current election system. |
| Understanding the focus of candidates on swing and battleground States (Question 2) | Review this section's Core Worksheet A, and discuss the importance of each electoral college vote. |
| Describing the election process (Question 3) | On the board, create a list showing each step in election process. |
| Identifying and evaluating the options for reforming the electoral college (Questions 4, 5) | Review this section's Core Worksheet B. |
| Explaining how the popular and electoral votes can differ (Question 6) | Review the content under the header "The First Major Defect." |

## Answers

**Checkpoint** It is a known process, it identifies the President-to-be quickly and certainly, and it helps promote the nation's two-party system.

---

✔ Checkpoint
What are the principal arguments for keeping the present electoral college system?

attention today. By early 2009, it had been approved by four States—Hawaii, Illinois, Maryland, and New Jersey—and is under serious consideration in several others.

This innovative plan is sponsored by a number of prominent Republicans, Democrats, and independents. It has attracted the support of several nonpartisan groups and major newspapers around the country. It has, in large part because (1) it appears to satisfy the major objections that have been raised to the electoral college as it currently operates, and (2) it does so without the need for an amendment to the Constitution.

## Defending the Electoral College

Although their case is not often heard, the present electoral college system does have its defenders. They react to the several proposed reforms by raising the various objections to them you have just read. Beyond that, most of these supporters argue that critics regularly exaggerate the "dangers" they see in the present system. Thus, they note that only two presidential elections

have ever gone to the House of Representatives and that none has gone there in more than 180 years.

Those who support the present electoral college system do grant the point that the candidate who loses the popular vote has in fact won the presidency four times—and as recently as 2000. But, they note, that circumstance has happened only four times over the course of 56 presidential elections, and they add that it has happened only once in more than a century.

Supporters also say that the present arrangement, whatever its warts, has three major strengths:

1. It is a *known* process. Each of the proposed, but untried, reforms may very well have defects that could not be known until they appeared in practice.

2. In nearly every instance, the present system identifies the President-to-be quickly and certainly. Rarely does the nation have to wait very long to know the outcome of the presidential election.

3. Although it does present an enormous obstacle to minor party candidates, the present arrangement does help promote the nation's two-party system.

**Essential Questions Journal** To continue to build a response to the chapter Essential Question, go to your **Essential Questions Journal.**

## SECTION 5 ASSESSMENT

1. **Guiding Question** Use your table to answer this question: Does the election process serve the goals of American democracy today?

**Key Terms and Comprehension**

2. Why do presidential campaigns focus heavily on **swing voters** and **battleground States**?

3. **(a)** How are the members of the electoral college chosen? **(b)** What role do they play in the presidential selection process?

4. What are the four major options suggested as alternatives to the electoral college?

**Critical Thinking**

5. **Demonstrate Reasoned Judgment (a)** Which of the alternatives to the electoral college system do you think is the most democratic? **(b)** Considering its several defects, do you think that the existing system should be reformed?

6. **Express Problems Clearly** In four presidential elections, most recently in 2000, the candidate who lost the popular vote nonetheless became President. **(a)** Why is that possible? **(b)** Do you believe that fact to be a persuasive argument for electoral college reform? Why or why not?

**Quick Write**

**Research Writing: Make an Outline** To help you structure a research report on the President you selected in Section 2, create an outline in which you identify each topic and subtopic in a single phrase. When you are ready to write your research report on how that President's professional and political experience influenced his administration, you can use the outline as a guide.

---

## Assessment Answers

**1.** Although the electoral college system has flaws, the suggested reforms also have serious flaws. Until a less-flawed method is devised, the current system serves our democratic goals best.

**2.** Swing voters and battleground States are undecided and can be swayed.

**3. (a)** Electoral college members are chosen in each State in the manner the state legislature directs. **(b)** Voters select electors in the popular election, and then the electoral college delegates cast their votes and officially elect the President and Vice President.

**4.** district plan, proportional plan, direct popular election, national popular vote plan

**5. (a)** national popular vote plan **(b)** Yes. This plan is most democratic because each vote counts equally and the choice of the majority will be President. Also, candidates should campaign everywhere—not just in States with disproportionate influence.

**6. (a)** Because of the winner-take-all system and the distribution of the electoral votes among the States, a candidate who wins the popular vote could lose the electoral vote.

**(b)** Answers will vary, but students should show an understanding about the advantages and disadvantages of reforming the electoral college system.

**QUICK WRITE** Students should create an outline and structure their essay based on it.

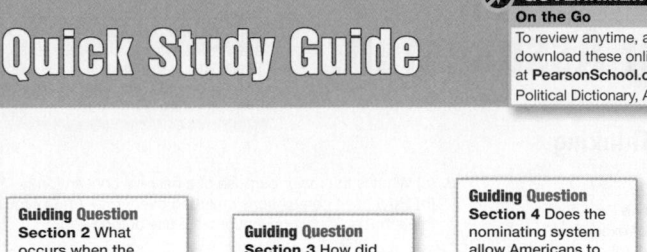

# Quick Study Guide

**⊘ GOVERNMENT** ONLINE

**On the Go**
To review anytime, anywhere, download these online resources at PearsonSchool.com/phgovt
Political Dictionary, Audio Review

CHAPTER **13**

**Guiding Question**
**Section 2** What occurs when the President is unable to perform the duties of the office?

**Guiding Question**
**Section 3** How did the process of choosing a President change over time?

**Guiding Question**
**Section 4** Does the nominating system allow Americans to choose the best candidates for President?

**Guiding Question**
**Section 1** What are the roles and qualifications for the presidency?

**CHAPTER 13**
**Essential Question**
Does the current electoral process result in the best candidates for President?

**Guiding Question**
**Section 5** Does the election process serve the goals of American democracy today?

## Political Dictionary

chief of state *p. 364*
chief executive *p. 364*
chief administrator *p. 365*
chief diplomat *p. 365*
commander in chief *p. 365*
chief legislator *p. 365*
chief of party *p. 365*
chief citizen *p. 365*
presidential succession *p. 370*
**Presidential Succession Act of 1947** *p. 370*
balance the ticket *p. 372*
presidential elector *p. 374*
electoral vote *p. 375*
electoral college *p. 375*
presidential primary *p. 378*
winner-take-all *p. 379*
proportional representation *p. 379*
caucus *p. 381*
national convention *p. 381*
platform *p. 382*
keynote address *p. 383*
swing voter *p. 386*
battleground State *p. 386*
district plan *p. 391*
proportional plan *p. 392*
direct popular election *p. 392*
national popular vote plan *p. 393*

## How the Electoral College Works

**In November...**
on election day, voters in each State cast ballots for a slate of electors who are pledged to vote for a particular presidential candidate.

**In December...**
the winning electors meet in their State capitals. Each elector casts a vote for President and a vote for Vice President. Their ballots are sent to the President of the Senate.

**On January 6th...**
the President of the Senate opens and counts the electoral ballots before a joint session of Congress. The winners of the electoral balloting become the President and Vice President.

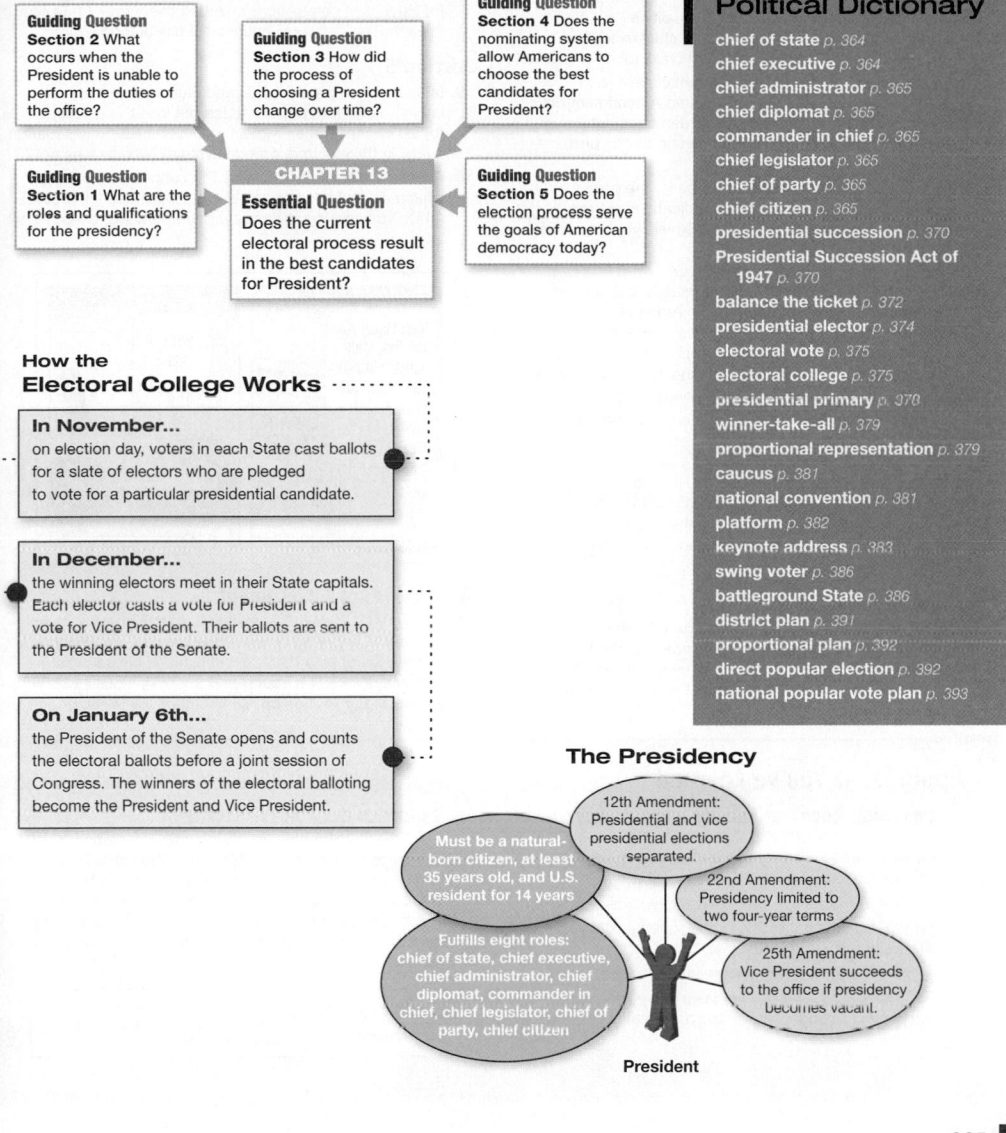

**The Presidency**

12th Amendment: Presidential and vice presidential elections separated.

Must be a natural-born citizen, at least 35 years old, and U.S. resident for 14 years

22nd Amendment: Presidency limited to two four-year terms

Fulfills eight roles: chief of state, chief executive, chief administrator, chief diplomat, commander in chief, chief legislator, chief of party, chief citizen

25th Amendment: Vice President succeeds to the office if presidency becomes vacant.

**President**

Chapter 13 Assessment **395**

---

Have students download the digital resources available at Government on the Go for review and remediation.

**STUDY TIPS**

**Create Graphic Organizers** To review for a test, divide the class into groups of three to five students. Give each group a large piece of paper with a topic written at the top and a set period of time to create a graphic organizer related to the topic, such as a web diagram, a Venn diagram, a table, or a flowchart. Then ask students to pass their paper to the next group, which must expand the organizer. Continue until each group has worked on each topic. If the class is large, two organizers can be prepared for each topic and later compared. Post the completed organizers around the classroom.

**ASSESSMENT AT A GLANCE**

**Tests and Quizzes**
Section Assessments
Section Quizzes A and B, Unit 4 **All-in-One**
Chapter Assessment
Chapter Tests A and B, Unit 4 **All-in-One**
Document-Based Assessment
Progress Monitoring Online
Exam*View* Test Bank

**Performance Assessment**
Essential Questions Journal
Debates, pp. 366, 381, 392
Assessment Rubrics, **All-in-One**

---

# For More Information

To learn more about the presidency, refer to these sources or assign them to students:

**L1** **Levert, Suzanne.** *The Electoral College.* Children's Press, 2005.

**L2** **Morris-Lipsman, Arlene.** *Presidential Races: The Battle for Power in the United States.* Twenty-First Century Books, 2007.

**L3** **Kincade, Vance R.** *Heirs Apparent: Solving the Vice Presidential Dilemma.* Praeger Publishers, 2000.

**L4** **Amy, Douglas J.** *Real Choices/New Voices: How Proportional Representation Elections Could Revitalize American Democracy.* Columbia University Press, 2002.

# Chapter Assessment

**COMPREHENSION AND CRITICAL THINKING**

## SECTION 1

1. **(a)** political experience, managerial skills, decisiveness, integrity, vision, ability to work with others **(b)** diplomatic experience, cultural understanding, communication skills, patience, willingness to consider different viewpoints **(c)** military experience, intelligence, decision-making skills, calmness, ability to build alliances **(d)** integrity, principled, tolerant, open-minded, fair

2. **(a)** limits a President to two full terms **(b)** yes, because it disqualifies a current two-term President from running again; OR no, because a multi-term President could become too powerful

3. **(a)** natural born citizen, at least 35 years old, U.S. resident for at least 14 years **(b)** Sample answers: These formal qualifications are too loose because they do not sufficiently restrict the type of individual who can run nor define the prerequisites that should be required to hold the office. OR: These formal qualifications are neither too restrictive nor too loose as they merely ensure that candidates are U.S. citizens and old enough to have some life experience.

## SECTION 2

4. **(a)** The Presidential Succession Act of 1947 sets the order of succession following the Vice President. The 25th Amendment establishes that the Vice President becomes President if the President dies, resigns, or is removed from office. It also provides for presidential disability and for filling a vacancy in the vice presidency. **(b)** Sample answer: Yes. The voters should have evaluated the vice presidential candidate's credentials for succeeding the President before electing him or her. **(c)** Answers will vary but should show an understanding of government leadership and the democratic system.

5. **(a)** to preside over the Senate and to help decide the question of presidential disability **(b)** The vice presidency has held low status, because the Constitution gives the Vice President few formal duties and because the parties choose a vice presidential candidate to balance the ticket. Recent Vice Presidents have wielded more influence because of their impressive credentials.

## SECTION 3

6. **(a)** Each State selected electors by a means established by the State legislature. Each

---

## Comprehension and Critical Thinking

### Section 1

1. Identify character traits that would qualify a President to best perform each of these roles: **(a)** chief executive, **(b)** chief diplomat, **(c)** commander in chief, **(d)** chief citizen.

2. Some critics of the 22nd Amendment claim it is undemocratic. **(a)** What does the 22nd Amendment do? **(b)** Does it put an unreasonable burden on the ability of voters to pick the most qualified person for the presidency?

3. **(a)** What are the formal qualifications for the presidency? **(b)** Do you think these qualifications are too loosely worded or too restrictive? Explain your reasoning.

### Section 2

4. **(a)** What are the provisions of the Presidential Succession Act of 1947 and of the 25th Amendment? **(b)** Do they provide for the best replacement for a President? **(c)** Suggest an alternative approach, and identify one advantage and one disadvantage of your alternative.

5. **(a)** What are the duties of the Vice President? **(b)** How has the overall nature of the vice presidency changed over time?

### Section 3

6. **(a)** What were the original provisions for the electoral college? **(b)** What changes in the electoral college system were prompted by the presidential election of 1800?

### Section 4

7. **(a)** What is a presidential primary? **(b)** What happens to the number of presidential contenders as the primaries continue? **(c)** Is a primary vote more valuable than a general election vote in selecting a President? Explain.

8. **(a)** What is the major purpose of a national convention? **(b)** How have conventions changed over time? **(c)** Do you think that national conventions are useful today?

### Section 5

9. **(a)** How can a presidential candidate receive the largest number of popular votes but lose the election. **(b)** Do you think the Framers would consider this situation a flaw in the electoral college system? Why or why not?

10. **Analyze Political Cartoons (a)** This cartoon pokes fun at what aspect of the presidential candidate selection process? **(b)** Do you agree or disagree with the view expressed here? Why?

### Writing About Government

11. Use your Quick Write exercises from this chapter to write a research paper on how the political and professional experience of your President influenced his administration. Make sure that your report supports your thesis with accurate details. See pp. S6–S7 in the Skills Handbook.

## Apply What You've Learned

12. **Essential Question Activity** With a partner, conduct research on either the Republican or Democratic primary/caucus results in your State in the most recent presidential election. Research the following:
    **(a)** Which method of delegate selection was used?
    **(b)** Where in the national election schedule did your State's primary or caucuses fall?
    **(c)** How many candidates were in the race?
    **(d)** What percentage of your State's population voted in the primary or caucuses? In the presidential election?

13. **Essential Question Assessment** Based on your research and the content of this chapter, create a chart that illustrates how your findings show the success or failure of the American presidential selection system. Then write a letter to your governor expressing how this research helps you answer the Essential Question: **Does the current electoral process result in the best candidates for President?**

**Essential Questions Journal** To respond to the chapter Essential Question, go to your **Essential Questions Journal**.

---

State would have the same number of electors as it has members in the Senate and House. Each elector would cast two votes, one vote for two different candidates for President. The candidate with the most votes would be President. The second-place candidate would be Vice President. **(b)** The emergence of parties by 1800 led to electors pledged to vote for their party's candidates. Pledged voting created a tie for President in the election of 1800, and the House cast 36 ballots to choose a President. The complications in this election led to enactment of

the 12th Amendment, which separated the electoral vote for President and Vice President.

## SECTION 4

7. **(a)** an election in which a party's voters choose some or all of a State party organization's delegates to the national convention and/or express a presidential preference **(b)** the number dwindles **(c)** In a general election, the choice is limited to mainly two candidates from the major parties. The primary offers more choices and determines the candidates in the general election.

# Document-Based Assessment

## The President's Term of Office

The tradition limiting a President to two terms in office was begun by George Washington in 1796. In 1951, the 22nd Amendment formally restricted a President to two terms, following Franklin D. Roosevelt's unique four terms in office. As the documents below illustrate, the issue of term limits remains debatable.

### Document 1

Nothing appears more plausible at first sight, nor more ill-founded upon close inspection, than a scheme . . . of continuing the Chief Magistrate in office for a certain time, and then excluding him from it, either for a limited period or forever after. This exclusion . . . would be for the most part rather pernicious [destructive] than salutary [beneficial].

One ill effect . . . would be the depriving the community of the advantage of the experience gained by the Chief Magistrate in the exercise of his office. . . .

[Another] ill effect . . . would be the banishing men from stations in which, in certain emergencies of the State, their presence might be of the greatest moment to the public interest or safety.

—Alexander Hamilton, *The Federalist*, No. 72, 1788

### Document 2

[T]he United States ought to be able to choose for its President anybody that it wants, regardless of the number of terms he has served. . . . Now, some people have said "You let him get enough power and this will lead toward a one-party government." That, I don't believe. I have got the utmost faith in the long-term common sense of the American people.

—Dwight D. Eisenhower, 1956

### Document 3

If some termination to the services of the chief magistrate be not fixed by the Constitution or supplied in practice, his office, nominally for years, will in fact become for life; and history shows how easily that degenerates into an inheritance."

—Thomas Jefferson, 1807

---

**Use your knowledge of the presidential term limits and Documents 1–3 to answer Questions 1–3.**

1. What is the main point of Document 1?
   A. Excluding candidates from reelection is democratic.
   B. Term limits deprive the voters of qualified leaders.
   C. Presidential term limits ensure that no individual can control the country in the manner of a monarch.
   D. The benefits of term limits outweigh its drawbacks.

2. What basic anxiety about leadership in a democratic system does Document 3 exploit? Explain.

3. **Pull It Together** Do you approve or disapprove of presidential term limits? Write a three-paragraph essay explaining your point of view.

 **GOVERNMENT** ONLINE
**Documents**
To find more primary sources on presidential term limits, visit PearsonSchool.com/phgovt

---

**DOCUMENT-BASED ASSESSMENT**

1. B

2. The idea that one person would gain complete control of the government and rule as a monarch or tyrant.

3. Example answers: Yes, I approve of presidential term limits. The policy ensures that no one President will acquire so much power that he or she could ignore minority viewpoints and squash dissent. Past Presidents could still serve as consultants, if needed, during times of crisis. OR: No, I do not agree with presidential term limits, because I believe a good leader should continue in the presidency as long as voters approve of that person's leadership.

**L2 Differentiate** Students use all the documents on the page to support their thesis.

**L3 Differentiate** Students include additional information available online at **PearsonSchool .com/phgovt.**

**L4 Differentiate** Students use materials from the textbook, the online information at **PearsonSchool .com/phgovt,** and do additional research to support their views.

**Go Online to PearsonSchool.com/phgovt** for a student rubric and extra documents.

---

8. **(a)** naming the party's vice presidential and presidential candidates, bringing the party together, and adopting the party platform **(b)** Originally, the convention was the site of serious negotiation over whom to nominate. Today the event is mainly a media event to garner support for the party and its candidate. **(c)** Yes, national conventions unify each party behind a platform of shared principles and goals. OR: No, national conventions no longer decide the nominees.

### SECTION 5

9. **(a)** In most States, the winner of the popular vote takes all of the State's electoral votes, even if the margin of victory is slim. Also, the distribution of electoral seats among States does not match population. The winner of the popular vote could lose the electoral vote. **(b)** Sample answer: No, because the Framers allotted electoral votes for Senate seats to preserve some power for less-populous States.

10. **(a)** physical, unimportant traits of a candidate **(b)** Sample answer: The cartoonist is saying that unlike 150 years ago, voters are choosing candidates based on trivial qualities that are unrelated to the ability to do the job.

### WRITING ABOUT GOVERNMENT

11. Papers should relate the President's background to the success of his administration.

### APPLY WHAT YOU'VE LEARNED

12. Students' research should uncover facts about their State's primary/caucus and election results.

13. In their letters, students should support their assessment with facts.

# Introduce the Chapter

## Essential Questions:

**UNIT 4**

What makes a good President?

**CHAPTER 14**

How much power should the President have?

**ACTIVATE PRIOR KNOWLEDGE** Have students examine the photo and quotation on these pages. Ask: **What do the image and quotation suggest about the presidency?** *(that although the presidency is the highest office a person can hold, it is a tremendously difficult position)* In this chapter, students will learn about the powers of the President and the limits on those powers. Tell students to begin to explore presidential powers by completing the Chapter 14 Essential Question Warmup activity in their Essential Questions Journal. Discuss their responses as a class.

### BEFORE READING

**L2** **ELL Differentiate** Chapter 14 Prereading and Vocabulary Worksheet (Unit 4 All-in-One, p. 69)

### SUCCESSNET STUDENT AND TEACHER CENTER

Visit **PearsonSchool.com/phgovt** for downloadable resources that allow students and teachers to connect with government "on the go."

### DIGITAL LESSON PRESENTATION

The digital lesson presentation supports the print lesson with activities and summaries of key concepts. Activities for this chapter include:

- **The Confirmation Process**
- **Expanding Executive Power**

## SKILLS DEVELOPMENT

### PROBLEM SOLVING

You may wish to teach problem solving as a distinct skill within Section 3 of this chapter. Use the Chapter 14 Skills Worksheet (Unit 4 All-in-One, p. 94) to help students learn the steps in solving a problem. The worksheet asks students to identify the problem President Roosevelt faced in 1933, identify options to solve it, consider the pros and cons of each option, choose a solution, and evaluate it. For L2 and L1 students, assign the adapted Skill Activity (Unit 4 All-in-One, p. 95).

**WebQuest online** The chapter WebQuest challenges students to answer the chapter Essential Question by asking them to take part in a newscast or talk show about the Watergate scandal.

398

## Block Scheduling

**BLOCK 1:** Teach the Section 1, 2, and 4 lessons, omitting the Section 2 Modeling a Graphic Organizer, and the Section 1 and 4 Extend options.

**BLOCK 2:** Teach the Section 3 lesson. Select an Extend option from Section 1, 2, 3, or 4, depending on your preferences and State standards.

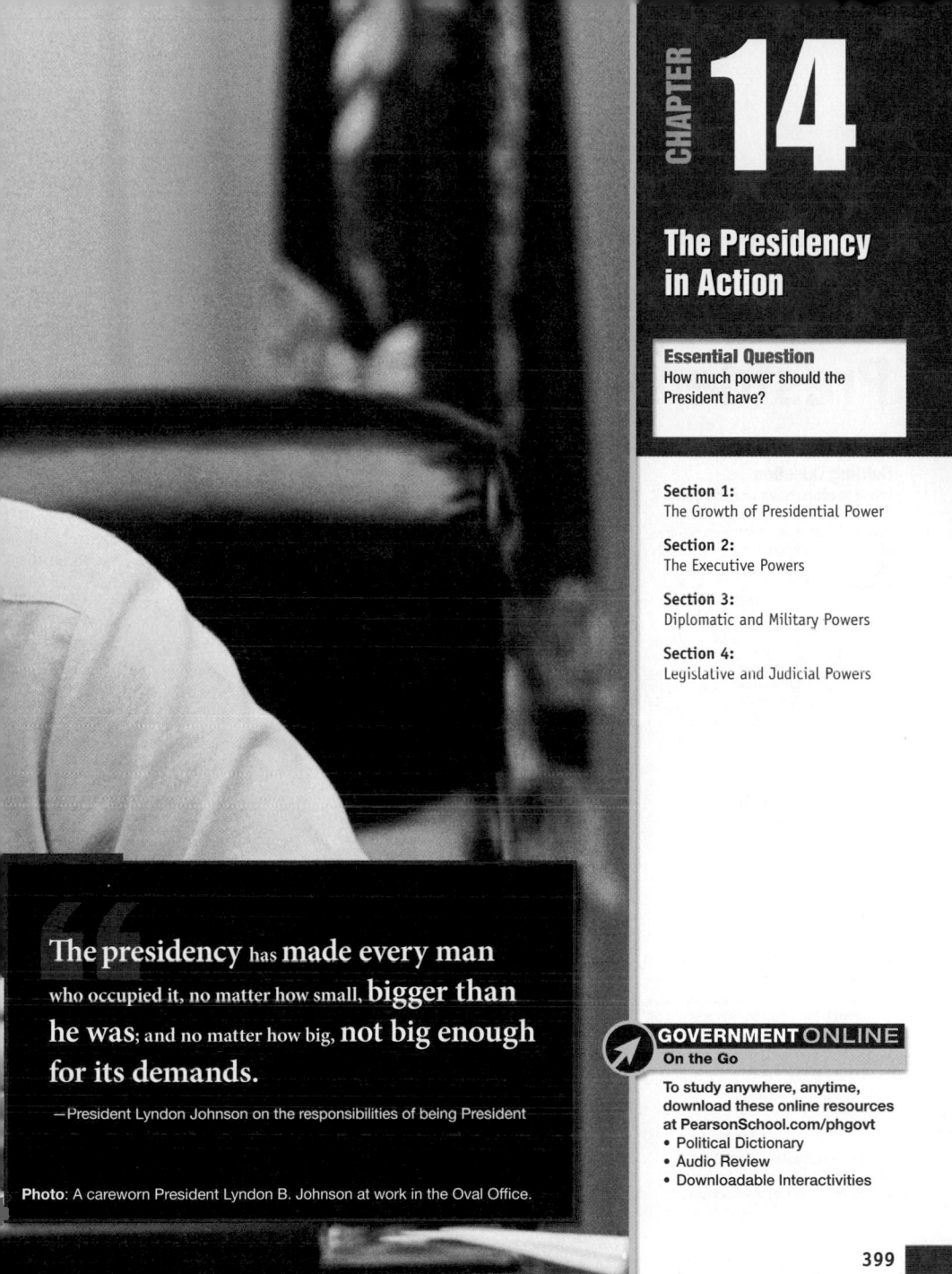

## The Presidency in Action

**Essential Question**
How much power should the President have?

**Section 1:**
The Growth of Presidential Power

**Section 2:**
The Executive Powers

**Section 3:**
Diplomatic and Military Powers

**Section 4:**
Legislative and Judicial Powers

> " The presidency has **made every man** who occupied it, no matter how small, **bigger than he was**; and no matter how big, **not big enough for its demands.**

—President Lyndon Johnson on the responsibilities of being President

**Photo:** A careworn President Lyndon B. Johnson at work in the Oval Office.

**GOVERNMENT** ONLINE
**On the Go**

To study anywhere, anytime, download these online resources at PearsonSchool.com/phgovt
• Political Dictionary
• Audio Review
• Downloadable Interactivities

399

## Lesson Goals

**SECTION 1**

Students will . . .

• evaluate the controversy over the growth of presidential power by analyzing a historic political cartoon.

• examine Article II, Sections 2 and 3, of the Constitution to determine the powers granted to the President.

• determine whether a President's action in selected scenarios reflects the Framers' intent in Article II.

**SECTION 2**

Students will . . .

• analyze Executive Order 9981 to learn about the ordinance power.

• identify the executive powers used in various scenarios and will determine how each is checked by the other branches.

**SECTION 3**

Students will . . .

• analyze a hypothetical scenario to learn about the tools available to the President to carry out foreign policy.

• summarize the President's diplomatic and military powers, and identify checks and balances on these powers.

**SECTION 4**

Students will . . .

• analyze the principle of checks and balances using Article I, Section 7, Clause 2 of the Constitution.

• define elements of the President's legislative and judicial powers.

• use primary sources to evaluate a President's use of the power to pardon.

## Pressed for Time

Begin the class with the Introduce the Chapter activity on the previous page. Then, organize the class into groups of three, with one person covering the President's executive powers; another, the diplomatic and military powers; and the third, the legislative and judicial powers. Have each group create a chart outlining the President's powers in each of these categories. Have each group present its chart to the class.

**FOLLOW UP** Have students consider the President's powers and list real-life examples of each next to the appropriate power in their chart. Then, have volunteers share their examples and have the class determine to which power the example relates.

**DIFFERENTIATED INSTRUCTION KEY**

Look for these symbols to help you adjust steps in each lesson to meet your students' needs.

**L1** Special Needs
**L2** Basic
    **ELL** English Language Learners
    **LPR** Less Proficient Readers
**L3** All Students
**L4** Advanced Students

## What factors have contributed to the growth of presidential power?

Reasons for the Growth of Presidential Power

1. Unity of presidency; 2. Authority delegated by Congress; 3. Citizens' demand for leadership; 4. President's ability to act quickly during crises; 5. President's views and way of fulfilling roles; 6. President's ability to use media

# Get Started

## LESSON GOALS

Students will . . .

- evaluate the controversy over the growth of presidential power by analyzing a historic political cartoon.

- examine Article II, Sections 2 and 3, of the Constitution to determine the powers granted to the President.

- determine whether a President's action in selected scenarios reflects the Framers' intent in Article II.

# SKILLS DEVELOPMENT

## ANALYZE POLITICAL CARTOONS

To help students learn to analyze political cartoons, have them turn to the Skills Handbook, p. S22, and use the steps explained there to complete the Bell-ringer activity. The steps are:

- identify the symbols in the cartoon;

- analyze the meaning of the cartoon;

- draw conclusions about what the cartoon conveys.

---

## SECTION 1

# The Growth of Presidential Power

### Guiding Question

**What factors have contributed to the growth of presidential power?** Use a concept web like the one below to keep track of the main ideas on the growth of presidential power.

Reasons for the Growth of Presidential Power

### Political Dictionary

- Executive Article
- imperial presidency

### Objectives

1. Explain why Article II of the Constitution can be described as "an outline" of the presidential office.
2. List several reasons for the growth of presidential power.
3. Explain how various Presidents' views have shaped the powers of the office.

**Images Above:** President George Washington, with the sculptures on Mount Rushmore in the background

The presidency is regularly called "the most powerful office in the world," and it is. But is this what the Framers had in mind when they created the post in 1787? At Philadelphia, they purposely created a single executive with very broadly stated powers. Still, they agreed with Thomas Jefferson, who wrote in the Declaration of Independence that "a Tyrant is unfit to be the ruler of a free people." So, just as purposefully, they constructed a "checked," a limited presidency.

## Article II

Article II of the Constitution is known as the **Executive Article,** which in only a few words established the presidency. It begins this way:

### FROM THE CONSTITUTION

**The executive Power shall be vested in a President of the United States of America.**

—Article II, Section 1

With this one sentence, the Framers laid the basis for the vast power and influence the nation's chief executive possesses today.

The Constitution also sets out other, somewhat more specific grants of presidential power. Thus, the President is given the power to command the armed forces, to make treaties, to approve or veto acts of Congress and call special sessions of that body, to send and receive diplomatic representatives, and to "take Care that the Laws be faithfully executed." [1]

Still, the Constitution lays out the powers of the presidency in a very sketchy fashion. Article II reads almost as an outline. It has been called "the most loosely drawn chapter" in the nation's fundamental law.[2] It does not

---

1 Most of the specific grants of presidential power are found in Article II, Sections 2 and 3. A few are elsewhere in the Constitution—for example, the veto power, in Article I, Section 7, Clause 2.
2 Edward S. Corwin, *The President: Office and Powers.*

**400** The Presidency in Action

---

# Focus on the Basics

Here is the information that your students need to learn in this section.

**FACTS:** • Article II of the Constitution establishes and empowers the presidency. • The brief outline of the presidential powers eternally pits advocates of a weaker presidency against those of a strong presidency. • Presidential power has grown as the nation's social and economic life has become more complex. • The power of the President is checked by the legislative and judicial branches.

**CONCEPTS:** checks and balances, limited government, separation of powers

**ENDURING UNDERSTANDINGS:** • The system of checks and balances helps prevent Presidents from overstepping their bounds. • Debate is ongoing regarding the interpretation of Article II and the extent of executive power.

define "the executive Power," and the other grants of presidential power are <u>couched</u> in similarly broad terms.

Much of our political history can be told in terms of the struggle over the meaning of the constitutional phrase "executive Power"—that is, over the extent of presidential power. That struggle has pitted those who have argued for a weaker presidency, subordinate to Congress, against those who have pressed for a stronger, independent, co-equal chief executive.

That never-ending contest began at the Philadelphia Convention in 1787. There, several of the Framers agreed with Roger Sherman of Connecticut, who, according to James Madison,

**Primary Source**
"considered the Executive Magistracy as nothing more than an institution for carrying the will of the legislature into effect, that the person or persons [occupying the presidency] ought to be appointed by and accountable to the Legislature only, which was the depository of the supreme will of the Society.

—James Madison, *Notes of Debates in the Federal Convention of 1787*

As you know, those delegates who argued for a stronger executive carried the day. The Framers established a single executive, chosen independently of Congress and with its own distinct field of powers.

## The Growth of Power

The Constitution's formal grants of power to the President have not been changed since 1789. Yet presidential power has grown remarkably over the past 200 years.

**Reasons for the Expansion** That extraordinary expansion has come, in no small part, because of the *unity* of the presidency. The office, and its powers, are held by one person. The President is the single, commanding chief executive. In contrast, Congress is composed of two houses, and both must agree

before Congress can do anything. Moreover, one of those two houses is made up of 100 separately elected members, and the other of 435.

Several other factors have also been at work here. Not least among them have been the Presidents themselves, and especially the stronger ones—Abraham Lincoln and the two Roosevelts, for example.

The nation's increasingly complex economic and social life has also had a telling effect on presidential power. As the United States has become more industrialized and technologically advanced, the people have demanded that the Federal Government take a larger and still larger role in transportation, communications, health, welfare, employment, education, civil rights, and a host of other fields. And they have looked especially to the President for leadership in those matters.

Clearly, the need for immediate and decisive action in times of crisis, and most notably in times of war, has also had a major impact here. The ability of the President—the single, commanding chief executive—to act in those situations has done much to strengthen "the executive Power."

Congress has also been involved, as it has passed the thousands of laws that have been a key part of the historic growth of the Federal Government. Congress has neither the time nor the specialized knowledge to provide much more than basic outlines of public policy. Out of necessity, it has delegated substantial authority to the executive branch to carry out the laws it has enacted.

A number of other factors have also fed the growth of executive power. Among them have been the ways several Presidents have played their roles as chief legislator, party leader, and chief citizen. Another is the huge amount of staff support a President has, both in the White House and throughout the executive branch of the Federal Government. Still another lies in the unique position from which the President can attract and hold the public's attention, and so build support for policies and actions. Every President, from Franklin Roosevelt's day to this, has purposely used the mass media—forms of communication, especially radio, television, and the Internet—to that end.

✔ **Checkpoint**
What two views of the presidency were debated by the Framers?

<u>couch</u>
*v.* to express using a particular style

---

# Differentiated Resources

The following resources are located in the All-in-One, Unit 4, Chapter 14, Section 1:

**L2** Prereading and Vocabulary Worksheet (p. 69)

**L3** Reading Comprehension Worksheet (p. 73)

**L2** Reading Comprehension Worksheet (p. 74)

**L3** Core Worksheet (p. 75)

**L2** Core Worksheet (p. 77)

**L2** Extend Activity (p. 80)

**L3** Quiz A (p. 81)

**L2** Quiz B (p. 82)

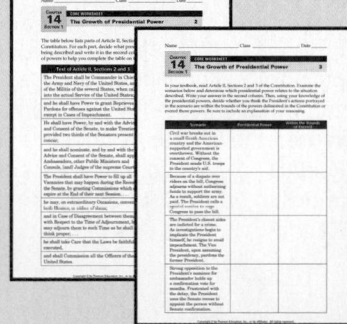

---

Assign the section, the graphic organizer in the text, and the Reading Comprehension Worksheet (Unit 4 All-in-One, p. 73) before class.

**L2 Differentiate** Reading Comprehension Worksheet (Unit 4 All-in-One, p. 74)

**BELLRINGER**

Write the following on the board: **Examine the two political cartoons on page 402 of your textbook. Answer the questions in the feature in your notebook.**

# Teach

To present this topic using online resources, use the lesson presentation at **PearsonSchool.com/phgovt.**

**DISCUSS**

Have students discuss their responses to the Bellringer activity. Possible answers: *(left cartoon: strong presidential powers are shown controlling the smaller, weaker Congress; right cartoon: a perceived weak and meek President subtly uses his authority to gain power over a willing Congress)* Write common aspects of students' analyses on the board. Have students look at the section's "The Means of Gaining Power." Ask: **Should the President's power have limits?** List students' opinions on the board under "Reasons For" and "Reasons Against."

**L1 Differentiate** Ask students to share ideas early in the discussion.

**L4 Differentiate** Select a volunteer to write and categorize student opinions on the board.

**DISTRIBUTE CORE WORKSHEET**

Distribute the Chapter 14 Section 1 Core Worksheet (Unit 4 All-in-One, p. 75), which presents several scenarios illustrating the use of the presidential powers. Have a volunteer read the directions aloud.

**L1 L2 ELL Differentiate** For lower-level students, distribute the adapted Core Worksheet (Unit 4 All-in-One, p. 77). Students will use this worksheet to take notes and complete the activity.

## Answers

**Checkpoint** (a) a weaker presidency, subordinate to Congress (b) a stronger, independent, co-equal chief executive

Have students read Article II, Sections 2 and 3 of the Constitution in their textbook.

**L2 LPR Differentiate** Have student volunteers read a paragraph of each Section aloud, including the annotation. After each paragraph, ask a different volunteer to paraphrase the powers granted to the President. Write the powers on the board.

**L2 ELL Differentiate** Have language learners record information in the graphic organizer on the Core Worksheet.

### IDENTIFY THE PRESIDENT'S POWERS

Have students complete the Core Worksheet by identifying the power granted by the Constitution to the President as it applies to each scenario. Then, have students determine whether the situation described is within or beyond the prescribed powers and explain their reasoning in the chart.

**L1 L2 ELL Differentiate** Pair lower-level students with higher-level students to complete the worksheet.

### REVIEW ACTIVITY

Have students share their answers with the class. Discuss any scenarios that may have proved difficult to associate with a specific presidential power and how this may relate to the growth of presidential power over time.

### EXTEND THE LESSON

**L2 ELL Differentiate** Have students find print or online images of the current President that illustrate three presidential powers granted by the Constitution. Students should say which power is shown.

**L2 Differentiate** Distribute the Extend Activity "Information about the White House" (Unit 4 All-in-One, p. 80).

**L3 Differentiate** Have students read the presidential quotes at the end of this section and write an essay supporting one of them.

**L4 Differentiate** Have students compare the powers granted to the executive branch with those granted to the legislative and judicial branches by reading Articles I and III of the Constitution. Have them present their findings in a chart.

## Answers

**Analyzing Political Cartoons** In the left cartoon, strong presidential power is shown controlling the smaller, weaker Congress. In the right cartoon, the smaller, weaker President asks Congress for greater presidential authority.

**Checkpoint** The Constitution provides for a number of restraints on the exercise of presidential power.

# The Means of Gaining Power

▶▶ **Analyzing Political Cartoons** The question of how much power a President should have has been hotly debated since 1787. Gradually, Presidents have increased their authority, and hence their power, both quietly and forcibly. The way in which several Presidents have exercised power has often reignited the debate over the "executive Power." *In these cartoons, how and from whom is the President gaining power?*

'DON'T PUT UP ANY RESISTANCE! JUST KEEP IN STEP'

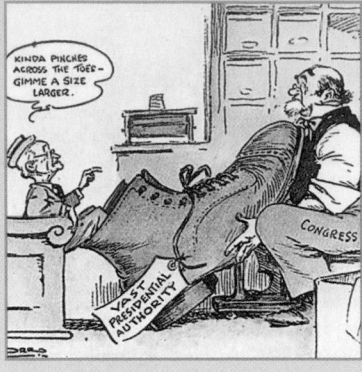

✔ **Checkpoint**
What limits the growth of presidential power?

**imperil**
*v.* to put in danger

**seizure**
*n.* taking by force

**Limits to the Growth of Power** Even with this increase of authority, no President can become all-powerful. The Constitution, which grants much power to the President, also provides for a number of restraints on the exercise of that power. Here are just two illustrations of that crucial point.

In 1952, at the height of the Korean War, a labor dispute threatened to shut down the nation's steel industry and <u>imperil</u> the war effort. To avert a strike, President Harry Truman, acting as commander in chief, ordered the Secretary of Commerce to seize and operate several steel mills. But, the Supreme Court found that here the President had overstepped his constitutional authority. It held that only Congress, acting under its commerce power, could authorize the <u>seizure</u> of private property in time of war, and it had not done so, *Youngstown Sheet & Tube Co.* v. *Sawyer*, 1952.

In June 2006, the High Court struck down President George W. Bush's plan to use military tribunals to prosecute "enemy combatants," persons captured in the war against terrorism, held at Guantanamo Bay. The President, citing his powers as commander in chief, had ordered the formation of those tribunals. However, the Court held that the Constitution gives Congress, not the President, the power to provide for the creation of such court-like bodies.

In addition, the Court found that several features of the President's plan violated several provisions in an act of Congress (the Uniform Code of Military Justice, enacted in 1950) and a treaty of the United States (the Geneva Conventions of 1949, dealing with the treatment of prisoners of war), *Hamdan* v. *Rumsfeld,* 2006.

## The Presidential View

What the presidency is at any given time depends, in large part, on how the President in office at the time sees the office and exercises its several powers. Presidents have generally taken one of two contrasting views.

The stronger, more effective chief executives have seen the office in a broad light—a

# Background

**RECESS APPOINTMENT** In 2005, President George W. Bush nominated John Bolton as ambassador to the United Nations. Bolton's confrontational style made him a controversial choice for a post that typically requires tactful negotiating skills. But President Bush wanted to reform the United Nations, and he believed the tough Bolton could push through changes. Senate Democrats fought the nomination, holding up the confirmation vote for five months. Citing "partisan delaying tactics," Bush circumvented the Senate by appointing Bolton during recess. Senate Minority Leader Harry Reid (D., Nev.) said that Bush abused a presidential power intended for unusual situations in order to install "a seriously flawed and weakened candidate" in the United Nations.

view that Theodore Roosevelt called "the stewardship theory":

"My view was that every executive officer . . . was a steward of the people bound actively and affirmatively to do all that he could for the people. . . . I declined to adopt the view that what was imperatively necessary for the Nation could not be done by the President unless he could find some specific authorization to do it."

—Theodore Roosevelt,
*Theodore Roosevelt: An Autobiography,*
1913

Ironically, the most strongly worded presidential statement of the opposing view came from Roosevelt's handpicked successor in the office, William Howard Taft. Looking back on his years in the White House, Mr. Taft had this to say:

"[T]he President can exercise no power which cannot be fairly and reasonably traced to some specific grant of power or justly implied and included within such express grant. . . . Such specific grant must be either in the Federal Constitution or in an act of Congress passed in pursuance thereof. There is no undefined residuum [remnant] of power which he can exercise because it seems to him to be in the public interest."

—William Howard Taft,
*Our Chief Magistrate and His Powers,*
1916

In more recent times, critics of what they see as a too-powerful President have condemned what has been called the **"imperial presidency."** The term paints a picture of the chief executive as a strong-willed emperor, taking various actions without consulting Congress or seeking its approval—sometimes acting in secrecy to evade or even deceive Congress. Critics of the imperial presidency worry that Presidents have become isolated policymakers who are unaccountable to the American people and their elected representatives in Congress.

Theodore Roosevelt (left) and William Howard Taft held opposing views on the presidency. **Which view has most often prevailed?** ▾

**Essential Questions Journal** To continue to build a response to the chapter Essential Question, go to your **Essential Questions Journal.**

## SECTION 1 ASSESSMENT

1. **Guiding Question** Use your completed concept web to answer: What factors have contributed to the growth of presidential power?

**Key Terms and Comprehension**

2. How has the **Executive Article** fueled debate on presidential power?

3. How can the President use the **mass media** as a tool for the expansion of executive power?

4. How have the legislative and judicial branches influenced the growth of the power of the President?

**Critical Thinking**

5. **Draw Conclusions** Why do you think some people are concerned that the presidency has become too powerful?

6. **Compare Points of View** Compare and contrast the comments by Presidents Roosevelt and Taft on this page. **(a)** Which view do you favor? Why? **(b)** Whose view do you think most modern-day Presidents have favored? Explain.

**Quick Write**

**Persuasive Writing: Take a Position** The scope of presidential power has been debated for over 200 years. How do you feel about the extent of the power of the presidency? Write a thesis statement that expresses your point of view. Make sure that your thesis states your position and specifies the conclusion you intend to persuade your audience to support.

---

# Assess and Remediate

**L3** Collect the Core Worksheets and assess the students' class participation using the Rubric for Assessing a Graph, Chart, or Table (Unit 4 All-in-One, p. 286).

**L3** Assign the Section 1 Assessment questions.

**L3** Section Quiz A (Unit 4 All-in-One, p. 81)

**L2** Section Quiz B (Unit 4 All-in-One, p. 82)

Have students complete the review activities in the digital lesson presentation and continue their work in the **Essential Questions Journal.**

### REMEDIATION

| If Your Students Have Trouble With | Strategies For Remediation |
|---|---|
| Determining contributing factors to growth of power (Questions 1, 4) | Make a table on the board listing the source and the motive. |
| Identifying the debate over the Executive Article (Question 2) | Review the Core Worksheet discussion and reiterate how interpretations of the Constitution may differ. |
| Understanding the use of mass media (Question 3) | Have students write a television spot advocating a specific presidential policy. |
| Illustrating public concern about a too-powerful President (Question 5) | Have students create a chart indicating the advantages and disadvantages of limiting presidential power. |
| Determining their view on the presidency (Question 6) | Have pairs work together to paraphrase each excerpt. |

## Answers

**Caption** Roosevelt's view of "the stewardship theory" has prevailed, although critics of too-powerful Presidents have condemned the "imperial presidency."

---

# Assessment Answers

**1.** looseness of the Executive Article, unity of the presidency, delegation of authority by Congress, citizens' demand for leadership, ability of President to act quickly during crises, huge executive staff, President's own views and way of fulfilling roles, and President's ability to use the media

**2.** The sketchy nature of the Executive Article leaves much room for interpretation.

**3.** Because the media reaches most Americans, the President can use it to build public support for policies and actions.

**4.** Congress has increased presidential power by delegating more authority to the executive branch to carry out the laws, but the President still must abide by the laws. The courts restrict presidential power by reviewing presidential actions.

**5.** Sample answer: Some people believe Presidents have become isolated policymakers who do not listen to Congress and are thus unaccountable to the public.

**6.** Answers will vary, but should be supported with sound reasoning and specific examples.

**QUICK WRITE** Students' thesis statements should illustrate an understanding of presidential power and clearly express the students' point of view on the issue.

**LESSON GOAL**

- Students will examine and debate the President's ability to expand his or her power, using a contemporary example.

# Teach

### TAKE A POLL

Ask: **Does the President have the constitutional authority to interfere in the country's industries and businesses in an effort to protect the nation from an economic crisis?**

### SUMMARIZE THE ISSUE

Have students read the feature and summarize the issue and views expressed in the quotes. Then, have volunteers read Article II of the Constitution aloud. Ask: **Is there any reference to business or the economy?**

**L2 ELL Differentiate** Have students read the annotations in the textbook's reprint of these amendments.

### DISCUSS

Tell students that Congress has increased the President's power significantly during national emergencies in an effort to secure economic, national, and personal security. Ask: **Is the President's action justified in this situation? Does the President have the legal authority to take such action?** Make sure students use the quotes and Article II to support their opinions. Then, using the initial question at the beginning of the lesson, take another poll. If students have changed their stance, ask why.

# Assess and Remediate

Have students select one quote on this page and write a short paragraph explaining why they agree or disagree with the speaker's opinion.

---

## Answers

1. **(a)** Sample answer: He claimed that he had to act or the situation would have worsened. **(b)** Sample answer: He claims that the government is incapable of taking care of itself and incapable of taking over responsibility for industries that are outside federal jurisdiction.

2. Answers will vary but should express an understanding of the powers granted by the Constitution and how the use of those powers has evolved over time.

# ISSUES OF OUR TIME

## Expanding Presidential Powers

### ▶▶ Track the Issue

**Article II of the Constitution** provides only a framework for the duties and powers of the presidency. Most Presidents have tried to extend their powers in order to perform their jobs more effectively.

**1787**
**The Constitution** designs a strong National Government with an independent presidency.

**1930s**
**President Franklin D. Roosevelt** strengthens the executive branch to overcome the effects of the Great Depression.

**1950s**
**President Dwight Eisenhower** claims executive privilege to shield conversations from the courts and Congress.

**1970s**
**The term "imperial presidency,"** meaning a President who ignores or misleads Congress, is used to describe the Nixon administration.

**Today**
**In the 21st century,** Presidents have found it necessary to expand their powers to solve national security and economic crises.

Senator Mitch
McConnell
(R., Kentucky) ▶

### ▶▶ Perspectives

**Upon entering the Oval Office in 2009,** President Barack Obama faced the worst economic crisis since the Great Depression. Major industries were on the verge of bankruptcy, banks were failing, and millions of Americans were unemployed. Like President Roosevelt before him, President Obama had to take action. Critics claimed his actions overstepped his powers, while others praised him for leading the nation in avoiding even greater economic difficulty.

"I had just inherited a $1.3 trillion deficit from the previous administration, so that the last thing I wanted to do was to spend money on a recovery package, or help the American auto industry keep its doors open, or prevent the collapse of Wall Street banks . . . But what I knew was if I didn't act boldly and I didn't act quickly, . . . we could have risked an even greater disaster. . . . I'm absolutely confident that if we continue to take responsibility to invest in our future that our brightest days are still ahead of us."
**—President Barack Obama, 2010**

"Washington can't even pay its bills, yet over the last 16 months it's taken over banks, insurance companies, car companies, the student loan business, and health care. And now it's got its sights set on anyone in America who engages in a financial transaction. . . . The administration . . . [is] using the financial crisis as a way to intrude into the lives of people and business. . . and to hire thousands of government employees and spend billions of dollars in taxpayer money to pay for it all."
**—Sen. Mitch McConnell (R., Kentucky), 2010**

### ▶▶ Connect to Your World

1. **Understand (a)** How does President Obama defend his actions to alleviate the economic crisis? **(b)** Why does Senator McConnell criticize those actions?

2. **Draw Conclusions** Why might President Obama's response to the economic crisis be considered an expansion of his presidential powers? Do you agree? Why or why not?

**GOVERNMENT ONLINE**
**In the News**
For updates about the expansion of presidential powers, visit
**PearsonSchool.com/phgovt**

404

# Background

**WARRANTLESS WIRETAPPING** In 1978, Congress passed the Foreign Intelligence Surveillance Act to protect Americans from unauthorized government spying. This law requires a warrant to conduct domestic wiretapping. After a judge declared warrantless wiretapping by the National Security Agency illegal in 2007, the Bush administration pushed Congress to amend the surveillance law. The result was the Protect America Act. This law greatly expanded the government's power to monitor communications without court oversight. Privacy-rights groups say the law goes too far. The law was intended as a stopgap measure to keep the surveillance program operating while Congress considers more permanent guidelines. The law will expire unless Congress decides to make it permanent.

# SECTION 2

# The **Executive Powers**

## Guiding Question
**What are the executive powers and how were they established?** Use a flowchart like the one below to keep track of the supporting details of the President's executive powers.

| Executive Powers | | |
|---|---|---|
| Power to Execute the Law | Ordinance Power | Appointment and Removal Power |
| • | • | • |
| • | • | • |

## Political Dictionary
• executive order
• ordinance power
• executive privilege

## Objectives
1. Identify the sources of the President's power to execute federal law.
2. Define the ordinance power.
3. Explain how the appointment power works and describe the limits on the removal power.
4. Examine the power of executive privilege.

**Image above:** President Ronald Reagan takes the oath of office in 1985.

Thomas Jefferson wrote this to a friend in 1789: "The execution of the laws is more important than the making of them." Whether Jefferson was right about that or not, in this section you will see that the President's power to execute the law endows the chief executive with extraordinary authority.

## Executing the Law

As chief executive, the President executes (enforces, administers, carries out) the provisions of federal law. The power to do so rests on two brief constitutional provisions. The first of them is the oath of office sworn by the President on the day he or she takes office:

### FROM THE CONSTITUTION

**I do solemnly swear (or affirm) that I will faithfully execute the Office of President of the United States, and will to the best of my Ability, preserve, protect and defend the Constitution of the United States.**

—Article II, Section 1, Clause 8

The other provision is the Constitution's command that "he shall take Care that the Laws be faithfully executed."[3]

The President's power to execute the law covers all federal laws. In fact, the Constitution requires the President to execute *all* federal laws no matter what the chief executive's own views of any of them may be. Their number, and the many subjects they cover, nearly boggle the mind. Social security, gun control, affirmative action, immigration, minimum wages, terrorism, environmental protection, taxes—these only begin the list. There are scores of others.

The President—and, importantly, the President's subordinates—have much to say about the meaning of laws, as do Congress and the courts. In executing and enforcing law, the executive branch also interprets it.

3 Article II, Section 3; this provision gives the President what is often called the "take care power."

---

## What are the executive powers and how were they established?

| Executive Powers | | |
|---|---|---|
| Power to Execute the Law | Ordinance Power | Appointment and Removal Power |
| • To execute, enforce, and interpret all federal laws<br>• Oath of office<br>• "Take care" clause | • To administer government using executive orders<br>• Implied in Constitution<br>• Delegated by Congress | • To appoint high-ranking officials<br>• To remove any officer (except federal judges)<br>• Article II, Section 2, Clause 2; First Congress |

## Get Started

### LESSON GOALS
Students will . . .
• analyze Executive Order 9981 to learn about the ordinance power.
• identify the executive powers used in various scenarios and determine how each is checked by the other branches.

### BEFORE CLASS
Assign the section, the graphic organizer in the text, and the Reading Comprehension Worksheet (Unit 4 All-in-One, p. 83) before class.

**L2** **Differentiate** Reading Comprehension Worksheet (Unit 4 All-in-One, p. 84)

## SKILLS DEVELOPMENT

### ANALYZE SOURCES
To help students learn to analyze sources, have them turn to the Skills Handbook, p. S14, and use the steps explained there to complete the Bellringer activity. The steps are:
• identify the author or source of the document;
• find the main idea;
• evaluate the document for point of view and bias.

---

# Focus on the Basics

Here is the information that your students need to learn in this section.

**FACTS:** • Article II gives the President the power and responsibility to execute the laws. • The executive power gives the President a great deal of flexibility in deciding how laws are carried out. • Among the President's key powers are appointing and removing key federal officials.

**CONCEPTS:** checks and balances, enumerated and implied powers, separation of powers

**ENDURING UNDERSTANDING:** • Much of the power of the presidency rests on the discretion the President has in the use of his or her powers to issue executive orders, execute the laws, and appoint key federal officials.

Have students read Executive Order 9981 on the Bellringer Worksheet (Unit 4 All-in-One, p. 85) and answer the questions in their notebook.

**L1 L2 ELL Differentiate** For students who may need help with the vocabulary in the primary source, write the following terms and definitions on the board: *vested* (legally assigned to a person), *statute* (an established rule or law), *effectuate* (to put into operation), *impair* (to damage or weaken), *designate* (to choose or appoint), *confer* (to meet to discuss), and *furnish* (to provide or supply).

# Teach

To present this topic using online resources, use the lesson presentations at **PearsonSchool.com/phgovt.**

## MODEL A GRAPHIC ORGANIZER

Create a four-column table on the board with the following headings: "Executing the Law," "Ordinance Power," "Appointment Power," and "Removal Power." Have students create a list of four facts that apply to each of the executive powers, such as:

*Executing the Law:* defined by Constitution, covers all federal laws, allows interpretation of federal law, details of a law are determined by executive branch

*Ordinance Power:* power to issue executive orders, equivalent to law, power is implied, allows executive branch to refine details of policies and programs

*Appointment Power:* allows President to name top-ranking officers of Federal Government, Senate must confirm appointments, President can bypass Senate confirmation with recess appointments, most executive branch employees are not appointed

*Removal Power:* President can remove any individual he or she appointed (except for federal judges) without Senate consent, reasons for removal are not clearly defined, Congress has tried to restrict the removal power, Supreme Court rulings have put some limitations on removal power

When discussing the appointment power, display Transparency 14C, which portrays the How Government Works visual about the confirmation process. Tell students to go to the Interactivity for an interactive version of actual confirmation hearings.

**L2 ELL Differentiate** Provide students with definitions of the following: *execute* (to put into effect), *ordinance* (a law made by an authority), and *appointment* (the selection of a person for a position or office).

## Answers

**Caption** Possible answer: An executive order has the effect of law and is more immediate than the congressional approval process.

▲ President Bill Clinton, with Vice President Al Gore, signs the executive order establishing Utah's Grand Staircase-Escalante National Monument. **Why do you think an executive order was used for this purpose?**

**discretion**
*n.* the freedom to act according to one's judgment

To look at the point more closely: Many laws that Congress enacts are written in fairly broad terms. Congress sets out the basic policies and standards to be followed. The specific details—much of the fine print necessary to the actual, day-to-day administration of the law—are usually left to be worked out by the executive branch.

For example, immigration laws require that all immigrants seeking permanent admission to this country must be able to "read and understand some dialect or language." But what does this broadly worded requirement mean in day-to-day practice? How well must an alien be able to "read and understand"? The law does not say. Rather, the details come from within the executive branch—from the U.S. Citizenship and Immigration Services in the Department of Homeland Security.

## The Ordinance Power

The job of administering and applying most federal law is the day-to-day work of all of the many departments, commissions, and other agencies of the Federal Government. All of the some 2.7 million civilian men and women who staff those agencies are subject to the President's control and direction.

The chief executive has the power to issue **executive orders,** which are directives, rules, or regulations that have the effect of law. The power to issue these orders, the **ordinance power,** arises from two sources: the Constitution and acts of Congress.

The Constitution does not mention the ordinance power in so many words, but that power is clearly intended. In granting certain powers to the President, the Constitution obviously anticipates their use. In order to exercise those powers, the chief executive must have the power to issue the necessary orders, and, as well, the power to implement them.[4]

The number, the scope, and the complexity of the problems that face the government of the United States have grown over the course of more than two centuries. As a result, Congress has found it necessary to delegate more and yet more <u>discretion</u> to the President and to top-level subordinates in the executive branch to spell out the policies and programs it has approved.

## The Appointment Power

A President cannot hope to succeed without loyal subordinates who support the policies of the President's administration. To that end, the Constitution says that the President

> **FROM THE CONSTITUTION**
>
> **by and with the Advice and Consent of the Senate . . . shall appoint Ambassadors, other public Ministers and Consuls, Judges of the supreme Court, and all other Officers of the United States, whose Appointments are not herein otherwise provided for . . . but the Congress may by Law vest the Appointment of such inferior Officers, as they think proper, in the President alone, in the Courts of Law, or in the Heads of Departments.**
>
> **—Article II, Section 2, Clause 2**

Those "Officers of the United States whose Appointments are . . . otherwise provided for" are the Vice President, members of Congress, and presidential electors.

---

4 All executive orders are published in the *Federal Register,* which appears five times per week. At least once per year, all orders currently in force are published in the *Code of Federal Regulations.* Both of these publications are issued by the National Archives and Records Administration.

# Differentiated Resources

The following resources are located in the All-in-One, Unit 4, Chapter 14, Section 2:

**L3** Reading Comprehension Worksheet (p. 83)
**L2** Reading Comprehension Worksheet (p. 84)
**L3** Bellringer Worksheet (p. 85)
**L3** Core Worksheet (p. 86)
**L3 L4** Extend Worksheet (p. 87)
**L3** Quiz A (p. 88)
**L2** Quiz B (p. 89)

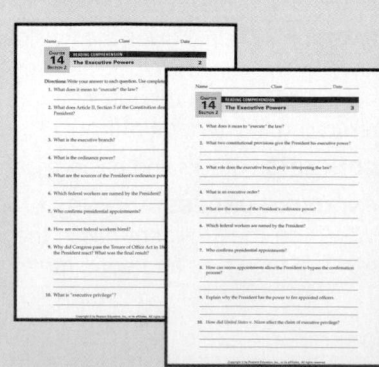

Acting alone, the President names only some 3,000 of the 2.7 million civilians who work for the Federal Government. The vast majority of the rest of the federal work force is hired under the civil service laws.

**Appointees** The President names most of the top-ranking officers of the Federal Government. Among them are (1) ambassadors and other diplomats; (2) Cabinet members and their top aides; (3) the heads of independent agencies; (4) all federal judges, U.S. marshals, and attorneys; and (5) all officers in the armed forces. When the President makes one of these appointments, the nomination is sent to the Senate. There, the support of a majority of the senators present and voting is needed for confirmation.

The unwritten rule of senatorial courtesy plays an important part in this process. That rule applies to the choice of those federal officers who serve within a State—a federal district judge or a U.S. marshal, for example. The rule holds that the Senate will approve only those federal appointees acceptable to the senator or senators of the President's party from the State involved. The practical effect of this custom, which is closely followed in the Senate, is to place a meaningful part of the President's appointing power in the hands of particular senators.

**Recess Appointments** The Constitution does allow the President to make "recess appointments," that is, appointments "to fill up all Vacancies that may happen during the Recess of the Senate."[5] Any such appointment automatically expires at the end of the congressional term in which it is made.

Recess appointments have often been a matter of contention—in particular, because they make it possible for the President to bypass the Senate confirmation process. So, as a rule, Presidents have not usually given these appointments to highly controversial personalities or to someone whom the Senate has previously rejected. Over time, Presidents

[5] Article II, Section 2, Clause 3. Over time, the words "may happen" have come to mean "may happen to exist" and "the Recess of the Senate" has come to include both the period between regular sessions of Congress and the several short recesses during a session.

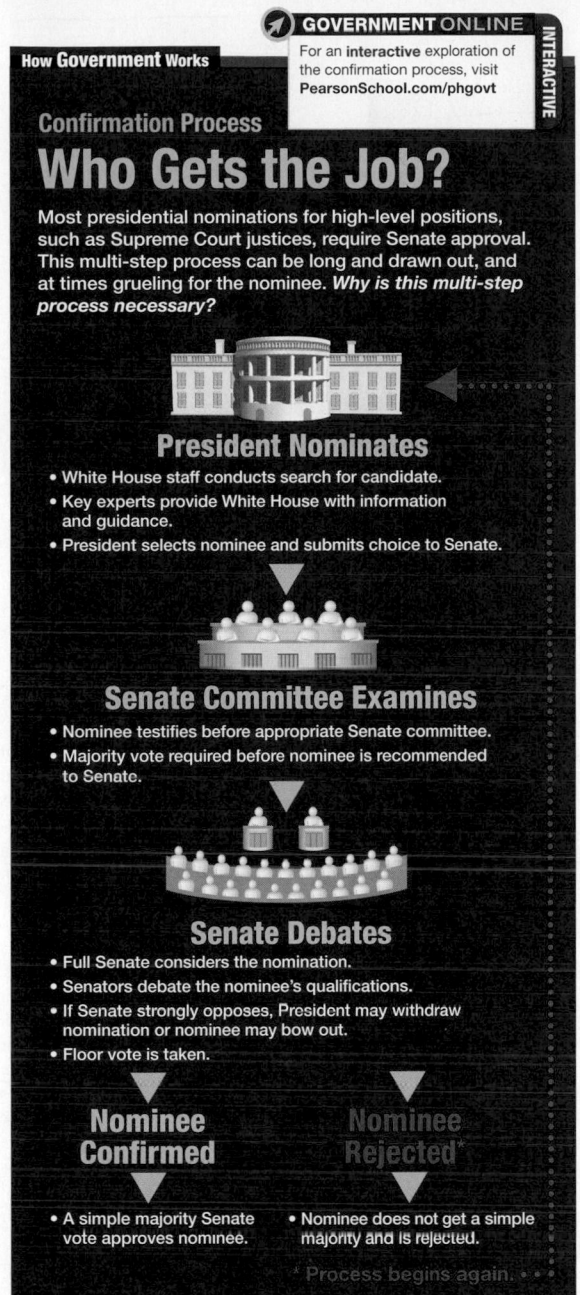

**How Government Works**

GOVERNMENT ONLINE
For an **interactive** exploration of the confirmation process, visit PearsonSchool.com/phgovt

**Confirmation Process**

# Who Gets the Job?

Most presidential nominations for high-level positions, such as Supreme Court justices, require Senate approval. This multi-step process can be long and drawn out, and at times grueling for the nominee. *Why is this multi-step process necessary?*

### President Nominates
- White House staff conducts search for candidate.
- Key experts provide White House with information and guidance.
- President selects nominee and submits choice to Senate.

### Senate Committee Examines
- Nominee testifies before appropriate Senate committee.
- Majority vote required before nominee is recommended to Senate.

### Senate Debates
- Full Senate considers the nomination.
- Senators debate the nominee's qualifications.
- If Senate strongly opposes, President may withdraw nomination or nominee may bow out.
- Floor vote is taken.

### Nominee Confirmed
- A simple majority Senate vote approves nominee.

### Nominee Rejected*
- Nominee does not get a simple majority and is rejected.

*Process begins again.*

## Background

**THE GRAND STAIRCASE** With the stroke of a pen in 1996, President Bill Clinton issued an executive order setting aside a vast area of Southern Utah as the Grand Staircase-Escalante National Monument. Many Utah residents were outraged. This order would block a planned coal mine and other development, which would have created over 1,000 jobs for local residents. Several lawsuits ensued. In 2004, a Utah district judge upheld the order, ruling that President Clinton acted within his rights in using the Antiquities Act of 1906 to create the monument. In fact, several Presidents had used the act this way before, starting with Theodore Roosevelt, who used it 18 times. Since 1996, the people of Utah have warmed up to their monument. Tourists have flocked to this remote area to experience the beauty of its multicolored cliffs and twisting canyons—spending their money at local businesses in the process.

**REVIEW BELLRINGER ANSWERS**

As students begin to list the facts under the "Ordinance Power" column, remind them of the Bellringer activity. Answers to the Bellringer are as follows:

1. two goals: (a) the immediate desegregation of the armed services and (b) the creation of an advisory committee to determine needed changes in the rules, procedures, and practices of the armed forces to carry out this new policy

2. the ordinance power, or the presidential power to issue executive orders

**DISTRIBUTE CORE WORKSHEET**

Distribute the Chapter 14 Section 2 Core Worksheet (Unit 4 All-in-One, p. 86). Students will review various scenarios illustrating a President's use of one of the executive powers. They will then determine which power is illustrated, what step or steps will follow each situation, and which branch is responsible for those next steps.

**L1 L2 ELL Differentiate** Pair lower-level students with higher-level students to complete the worksheet.

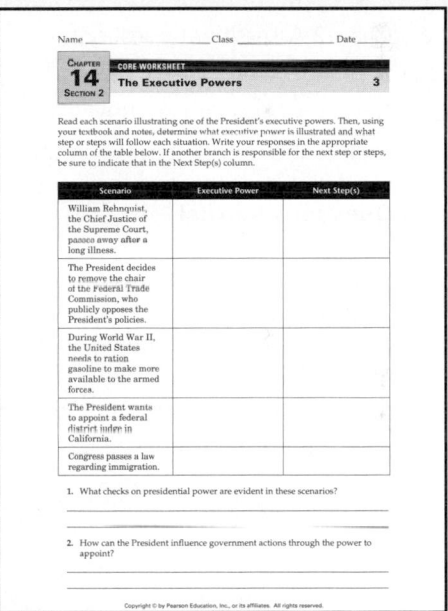

**L1 L2 ELL Differentiate** Focus students' attention on the specific portion or paragraph in the textbook that will help them determine the answers to the scenarios.

Tell students to go to the interactivity to learn more about the confirmation process.

## Answers

**Confirmation Process** possible answer: to ensure that Presidents make appointments fairly, rather than for purely political or personal reasons

**L1 L2 Differentiate** Have lower-level students work with more advanced students to create a graphic organizer to capture the main ideas and supporting details of this section.

**L3 Differentiate** Have students revisit the Guiding Question. As you say each power aloud, have them identify how the power was established. For powers that arise directly from the Constitution, ask students to read the appropriate clauses aloud.

**L3 L4 Differentiate** Have students use the Chapter 14 Section 2 Extend Worksheet (Unit 4 All-in-One, p. 87) to research a recent presidential appointee who required Senate confirmation. Then, have them create a timeline of the events from the appointee's nomination to confirmation (or rejection).

## Assess and Remediate

**L3** Collect the Core Worksheets and assess the students' class participation using the Rubric for Assessing a Graph, Chart, or Table (Unit 4 All-in-One, p. 286).

**L3** Assign the Section 2 Assessment questions.

**L3** Section Quiz A (Unit 4 All-in-One, p. 88)

**L2** Section Quiz B (Unit 4 All-in-One, p. 89)

Have students complete the review activities in the digital lesson presentation and continue their work in the **Essential Questions Journal.**

---

**Government online** *All print resources are available on the Teacher's Resource Library CD-ROM and online at PearsonSchool.com/phgovt.*

---

## Answers

**Analyzing Political Cartoons** Possible answer: Reiterating (or parroting) the President's views implies that the President has political and public support.

**Checkpoint** (1) If an appointment requires Senate approval, Senate consent should also be required for removal. (2) The President cannot execute laws without a free hand to dismiss those who are unsuited to office.

---

MR.FISH

▸▸ **Analyzing Political Cartoons** Presidential appointees are sometimes criticized for parroting the views of the President without expressing their own opinions. *How might this actually benefit the President?*

✔**Checkpoint**
What are the two sides of the removal power debate?

have made very few recess appointments. The number tends to increase when the President's party does not control the Senate.

## The Removal Power

The power to remove is the other side of the appointment coin, and is as important to presidential success as is the power to appoint. Yet, except for mention of the little-used impeachment process, the Constitution says nothing about how, by whom, or why an appointed officer may be dismissed.[6]

**depose**
*v.* to remove from a position of power

**The Historical Debate** The matter was hotly debated in the first session of Congress, in 1789. Several members argued that, if an appointment required Senate approval, Senate consent should also be required for removal. They insisted that this restriction on presidential authority was essential to congressional supervision (oversight) of the executive branch. But others argued that the President could not "take Care that the Laws be faithfully executed" without a free hand to dismiss those who were incompetent or otherwise unsuited to office.

---

6  In Article I, Section 2, Clause 5 and Section 3, Clauses 6 and 7, and Article II, Section 4.

The latter view prevailed. The First Congress gave the President the power to remove any officer he appointed, except federal judges. Over the years since then, Congress has sometimes tried, with little success, to restrict the President's freedom to dismiss.

One notable instance occurred in 1867. Locked with Andrew Johnson in the fight over Reconstruction, Congress passed the Tenure of Office Act. That law's plain purpose was to prevent President Johnson from removing several top officers in his administration, in particular the secretary of war, Edwin M. Stanton. The law provided that any person holding an office by presidential appointment with Senate consent should remain in that office until a successor had been confirmed by the Senate.

The President vetoed the bill, charging that it was an unconstitutional invasion of executive authority. The veto was overridden, but Mr. Johnson ignored Congress and fired Stanton anyway. The veto and Stanton's removal sparked the move for Johnson's impeachment. Ultimately, the President was acquitted, and the law was ignored in practice. It was finally repealed in 1887.

**Removal and the Court** The question of the President's removal power did not reach the Supreme Court until *Myers* v. *United States*, 1926. In 1876, Congress had passed a law requiring Senate consent before the President could dismiss any first-class, second-class, or third-class postmaster.

In 1920, without consulting the Senate, President Woodrow Wilson removed Frank Myers as the postmaster at Portland, Oregon. The deposed postmaster then sued for the salary for the rest of his four-year term. He based his claim on the point that he had been removed in violation of the 1876 law.

The Court, led by a former President, Chief Justice Taft, found the law unconstitutional. It held that the removal power was an essential part of executive power, clearly necessary to the faithful execution of the laws.

The Supreme Court did place some limits on the President's removal power in 1935, in *Humphrey's Executor* v. *United States*. President Herbert Hoover had appointed William Humphrey to a seven-year term on the

---

## Myths and Misperceptions

**EXECUTIVE PRIVILEGE** Contrary to popular belief, neither the term nor the concept of executive privilege appears anywhere in the Constitution. Legal historian Raoul Berger called it one of the greatest "constitutional myths." Yet Presidents as far back as George Washington have claimed the right to withhold certain information from public scrutiny, even when served a subpoena. Dwight D. Eisenhower was the first President to use the term. Eisenhower asserted executive privilege more than 40 times in refusing to allow his aides to testify during the McCarthy hearings. Presidents contend that executive privilege is implied in the Constitution's principle of separation of powers—they need candid and confidential advice from their aides to do their jobs.

Federal Trade Commission (FTC) in 1931. When Franklin D. Roosevelt took office in 1933, he found Commissioner Humphrey to be in sharp disagreement with many of his policies. He asked the commissioner to resign, saying that his administration would be better served with someone else on the FTC. When Mr. Humphrey refused, President Roosevelt removed him. Humphrey soon died, but his heirs filed a suit for back salary.

The Supreme Court upheld the heirs' claim. It based its decision on the act creating the FTC. That law provides that a member of the commission may be removed only for "inefficiency, neglect of duty, or malfeasance in office."

The Court further held that Congress does have the power to set the conditions under which a member of the FTC and other such agencies might be removed by the President. It did so because those agencies, the independent regulatory commissions, are not purely executive agencies (see Chapter 15).

As a general rule, the President may remove those whom the President appoints. Occasionally, a presidential appointee does have to be fired. Most often, however, what was in fact a dismissal is called a "resignation."

## Executive Privilege

At times, the nation's chief executives have insisted that the Constitution gives to the President the inherent power to refuse to disclose certain information to Congress or to the federal courts. That is, they have claimed the power of **executive privilege.** Most often, a claim of executive privilege has been made with regard to conversations and other communications between the President and his or her closest advisors.

The chief executive must, of necessity, rely on the information and advice he or she receives from key staff and their ability to speak with utmost candor, which depends on the confidential nature of their relationship with the President. These officials must be sure that what they say will become known publicly only if and when the President chooses to disclose that information.

Congress has never recognized executive privilege. It has often tried to compel executive officials to testify at congressional committee hearings, and Presidents have frequently resisted those efforts, citing executive privilege.

The federal courts have been reluctant to become involved in this dispute between the executive and legislative branches. However, the Supreme Court has recognized both the existence of and the need for executive privilege in a historic case, *United States* v. *Nixon*, in 1974. There, a unanimous Court said that although the President might legitimately claim executive privilege in matters involving national security, that privilege cannot be used to prevent evidence from being heard in a criminal proceeding. This decision was a key factor in Mr. Nixon's resignation.

**✓ Checkpoint**
What is the Court's stand on executive privilege?

**candor**
*n.* the quality of being open and honest in speaking

**malfeasance**
*n.* wrong or illegal conduct by a public official

---

| If Your Students Have Trouble With | Strategies For Remediation |
|---|---|
| Identifying the executive powers and how they were established (Questions 1, 3) | As a class, have the students complete this section's graphic organizer on the board. |
| Describing the executive branch's influence on law interpretation (Question 2) | Have groups of students write a one-sentence classroom law; then exchange laws and have each group add details clarifying the scope of the law. |
| Determining the officers appointed by the President and the confirmation process (Question 4) | Have students create an outline of the Appointment Power content of the section. |
| Identifying the controversial nature of executive privilege (Question 5) | Review and discuss the Landmark Decisions of the Supreme Court feature. |
| Determining the importance of the appointment power (Question 6) | Have pairs work together to create a list of the benefits of selecting high-ranking officers. |
| Identifying their view on senatorial courtesy (Question 7) | Review with students the principle of separation of powers and the definition of senatorial courtesy. |

---

**Essential Questions Journal**

To continue to build a response to the chapter Essential Question, go to your **Essential Questions Journal.**

## SECTION 2 ASSESSMENT

**1. Guiding Question** Use your completed flowchart to answer this question: What are the executive powers and how were they established?

**Key Terms and Comprehension**

**2.** How can the executive branch influence the meaning of a particular law?

**3.** What is the **ordinance power** and from what sources does it arise?

**4. (a)** What officers does the President appoint? **(b)** What is the Senate's role in the appointment process?

**5.** What is **executive privilege** and why is it controversial?

**Critical Thinking**

**6. Identify Central Issues** Why is the President's power of appointment so important to the success of his or her administration?

**7. Demonstrate Reasoned Judgment** Consider this statement: The unwritten rule of senatorial courtesy contradicts the principle of separation of powers. Do you agree or disagree?

### Quick Write

**Persuasive Writing: Generate Arguments** An effective way to persuade an audience is to address both sides of the issue. Using your thesis statement from Section 1, create a chart to record facts about the debate on presidential power. In one column, record the facts that support your position, and, in the second column, note arguments that could be used against your position.

## Answers

**Checkpoint** The Court has recognized both the existence of and the need for executive privilege.

---

# Assessment Answers

**1.** power to execute the law, established by oath of office and "take care" clause; ordinance power, implied in Constitution and delegated by Congress; appointment power, established by Article II, Section 2, Clause 2; removal power, established by First Congress

**2.** Laws are written in broad terms. It is up to the President and the President's subordinates to work out the details and the day-to-day administration of the laws.

**3.** President's power to issue executive orders; from the Constitution and acts of Congress

**4. (a)** ambassadors, diplomats, Cabinet members and their top aides, heads of independent agencies, federal judges, attorneys, marshals, and all officers of the armed forces **(b)** to confirm all the presidential nominations by a majority vote

**5.** power of President to refuse to disclose certain information to Congress or to the federal courts; controversial because executive privilege limits Congress's ability to check the power of the President

**6.** Loyal subordinates who support the President's policies and actions help ensure the administration's success.

**7.** Some students may disagree, saying senatorial courtesy falls within the Senate's right to offer advice and consent. Others may agree, saying it enables select senators' influence in the presidential appointment process.

**QUICK WRITE** Charts should illustrate appropriate supporting facts and arguments against each student's thesis statement.

- Students will debate the claim of executive privilege from the perspectives of the executive and legislative branches.

## Teach

Have students read the feature as homework or at the beginning of class.

### DEFINE EXECUTIVE PRIVILEGE

Write *executive privilege* on the board. Ask students to provide a definition. Display Transparency 14D. Tell students that executive privilege is a claim by the executive branch that it can refuse to disclose information and/or documents requested by Congress or the courts.

**L2 ELL Differentiate** Have students define *executive* (the senior manager responsible for making and implementing decisions—in this case, the President) *and privilege* (the right to special treatment or benefits). Then, have them define the key term *executive privilege*.

### CREATE A TIMELINE

Create a timeline on the board. Have students sequence the events from the Watergate break-in to Nixon's resignation. *(Order should be: Watergate break-in, Senate hearing, existence of tapes revealed, Nixon ordered to provide tapes, Nixon denies request claiming executive privilege, Supreme Court overrules executive privilege claim, tapes released, Nixon resigns.)* Ask: **What is the significance of the Supreme Court ruling?** *(The Court recognized executive privilege, but ruled that it is acceptable only as it relates to military and diplomatic matters.)*

## SKILLS DEVELOPMENT

### ANALYZE CAUSE AND EFFECT

Before the debate in this lesson, you may want to review tips on analyzing cause and effect in the Skills Handbook, p. S16.

**410**

---

# What Are the Limits on Executive Privilege?

A number of chief executives have argued that the Constitution gives the President the authority to refuse to disclose certain information to Congress or to the federal courts. That authority, known as "executive privilege," was first recognized by the Supreme Court in the historic case, *United States v. Nixon*, in 1974.

"Richard Milhous Nixon announced last night that he will resign as the 37th President of the United States at noon today. . . . After two years of bitter public debate over the Watergate scandals, President Nixon bowed to pressures from the public and leaders of his party to become the first President in American history to resign.

"'By taking this action,' he said in a subdued yet dramatic television address from the Oval Office, 'I hope that I will have hastened the start of the process of healing which is so desperately needed in America.'"
—Carroll Kilpatrick, "Nixon Resigns," *The Washington Post*, 9 August 1974

What could possibly have led the President of the United States to resign his office? The answers to that question begin with a botched attempt to break into the Democratic National Committee's headquarters in the Watergate complex in Washington, D.C., in June of 1972, in the midst of the presidential campaign. The burglars, it turned out, were working for President Nixon's chief campaign organization, CREEP—the Committee to Re-Elect the President. Over the next two years the President and many of the major figures in his administration steadfastly denied any involvement in what came to be known as the Watergate scandal.

During Senate hearings on the issue, a White House aide revealed that the President had secretly taped most of his telephone calls and personal conversations

Burglars break into the Watergate complex, June 1972.

President Nixon denies any knowledge of the break-in, April 1973.

President Nixon refuses to turn over the White House audio tapes, July 1973.

**410**

## Supreme Court Notes

***UNITED STATES v. NIXON*** Nixon's lawyers argued that the courts should accept executive privilege without question. Writing for the majority, Chief Justice Warren Burger asserted the right of the courts to decide whether the President's need for confidential communications outweighed the courts' need for the evidence in the communications. To support this assertion, Burger quoted from *Marbury v. Madison*: "[I]t is emphatically the province and duty of the judicial department to say what the law is." The *Nixon* decision, however, did not rule out executive privilege. The Court recognized "the valid need for protection of communications between high Government officials and those who advise and assist them in the performance of their manifold duties." This acknowledgment leaves the door open to valid claims of executive privilege by future Presidents.

in the Oval Office. When both the special prosecutor and a federal district court ordered Mr. Nixon to release those tapes, he refused, asserting that executive privilege gave him the right to withhold the information. The Constitution does not provide for executive privilege in so many words; the concept is, instead, derived from the principle of separation of powers.

The matter was then carried to the Supreme Court. There, in a unanimous decision, the Court ruled that although the confidentiality of communications between the President and his closest aides is important, their protection is not absolute. If the President possessed an absolute executive privilege, the Court held, the executive branch would, in effect, be unchecked, and it ordered that the tapes be released. President Nixon resigned shortly after he obeyed the Court's order.

**GOVERNMENT** ONLINE

**In the News**

To learn more about the relevance of the case today, go to **PearsonSchool.com/phgovt**

### Arguments for Nixon

- Under the doctrine of separation of powers, no court has the authority to question executive privilege.
- The President must have the power to keep his various communications with his aides secret.
- The forced disclosure of communications between the President and his advisors could threaten the nation's security.

### Arguments for the United States

- Separation of powers does not mean that the three branches are absolutely independent of one another.
- Withholding critical evidence damages the 6th Amendment guarantees of a fair trial to all defendants.
- While the secrecy of presidential communications is important, that protection should be limited to military and diplomatic matters.

### Thinking Critically

1. Should the President have the right to keep all communications with advisors private? Why or why not?
2. **Constitutional Principles** How does the decision in this case reflect the principle of separation of powers?

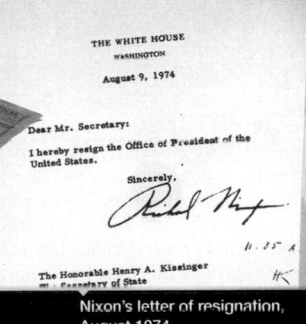

A woman reads a newspaper announcing Nixon's intention to resign, August 1974.

Nixon's letter of resignation, August 1974.

Nixon boards *Air Force One*. When the plane lands in California, he will no longer be President.

411

## Supreme Court Notes

**CHENEY v. U.S. DISTRICT COURT FOR THE DISTRICT OF COLUMBIA** In 2001, President George W. Bush created an advisory task force on energy policy, headed by Vice President Dick Cheney. The task force included top executives from the energy industry, while excluding environmentalists. In secret proceedings, the task force produced recommendations for policies favorable to the energy industry. The Sierra Club and Judicial Watch sued, seeking to require the task force to make its records public. In 2004, the Supreme Court upheld the Bush administration's claim for privacy. However, in the majority opinion, Justice Anthony Kennedy issued this warning: "Executive privilege is an extraordinary assertion of power 'not to be lightly invoked'. . . . Once executive privilege is asserted, coequal branches of the Government are set on a collision course."

---

**DISCUSS**

Tell students that Presidents other than Richard Nixon have claimed executive privilege. Although the term was coined during the Eisenhower administration to fend off the anti-communist inquiries of Senator Joseph McCarthy, George Washington asserted the ability to withhold information from Congress regarding a treaty with England. Ask students for examples of when they think the claim of executive privilege would seem justified. *(examples: when disclosure could endanger national policies, offend a foreign nation, or risk revealing national secrets)*

**LEAD A DEBATE**

Divide the class into two groups. One group will argue for the view of the executive branch; the other, for Congress. Give each group ten minutes to prepare their arguments. Using the debate strategy on p. T25 as a basic structure, begin the debate by asking: **Should the executive branch have the power to keep communications secret?**

**L1 L2 Differentiate** Have students raise their hands, and call on lower-level students first to ensure that they participate in the debate.

## Assess and Remediate

**L3 L4 L2** Have students read and complete the Landmark Decisions of the Supreme Court Worksheet (Unit 4 All-in-One, pp. 105, 107).

**L3** Have students write a brief paragraph on whether they think Nixon's claim of executive privilege and his subsequent resignation have affected the public's view of the claim by later Presidents.

**IN THE NEWS**

Point out to students that they can learn about more cases in which a President has claimed executive privilege by visiting **PearsonSchool.com/phgovt**.

### Answers

1. Sample for private communications: The executive branch needs to be able to discuss matters candidly without concern for public disclosure, especially related to issues of diplomacy and national security. Sample against private communications: Executive privilege can be used to conceal inappropriate or criminal activities and, as the executive branch is not above the law, it should be held responsible for its activities.

2. The case demonstrates how Congress and the Court can check as well as define the action and powers of the executive branch.

**411**

## What tools are available to the President to implement foreign policy?

# Get Started

## LESSON GOALS

Students will . . .

- analyze a hypothetical scenario to learn about the tools available to the President to carry out foreign policy.
- summarize the President's diplomatic and military powers, and identify checks and balances on these powers.

## BEFORE CLASS

Assign the section, the graphic organizer in the text, and the Reading Comprehension Worksheet (Unit 4 All-in-One, p. 90) before class.

**L2 Differentiate** Reading Comprehension Worksheet (Unit 4 All-in-One, p. 91)

# SKILLS DEVELOPMENT

## PROBLEM SOLVING

To practice problem solving in this section, use the Chapter 14 Skills Worksheet (Unit 4 All-in-One, p. 94). You may teach the skill explicitly either before or after reviewing the Bellringer. For L2 and L1 students, assign the adapted Skill Activity (Unit 4 All-in-One, p. 95).

---

## SECTION 3

# Diplomatic and Military Powers

### Guiding Question

**What tools are available to the President to implement foreign policy?** Use a concept web to keep track of the main ideas and supporting details on foreign policy tools.

### Political Dictionary

- treaty
- executive agreement
- recognition
- *persona non grata*

### Objectives

1. Explain how treaties are made and approved.
2. Explain why and how executive agreements are made.
3. Summarize how the power of recognition is used.
4. Describe the President's powers as commander in chief.

Images Above: President Jimmy Carter and Chinese leader Deng Xiaoping

**J**ohn F. Kennedy described the pressures of the presidency this way:

> **Primary Source**
> When I ran for the presidency . . . I knew the country faced serious challenges, but I could not realize—nor could any man who does not bear the burdens of this office—how heavy and constant would be those burdens.
>
> —John F. Kennedy, radio broadcast (1961)

When President Kennedy made that comment, he had in mind the subject of this section: the President's awesome responsibilities as chief diplomat and as commander in chief.

## Chief Diplomat

The Constitution does not say, in so many words, that the President is the nation's chief diplomat. Rather, Presidents have come to dominate the field of foreign affairs through the use of the powers of the office. In major part, they were able to do so because the Constitution makes the President the commander in chief of the nation's armed forces—and several centuries of relationships between sovereign states tells us that military force is the ultimate language of diplomacy.

**The Power to Make Treaties** A **treaty** is a formal agreement between two or more sovereign states. The President, usually acting through the secretary of state, negotiates these international agreements. The Senate must give its approval by a two-thirds vote of the members present before a treaty made by the President can become effective. Recall, the Constitution, in Article VI, makes treaties a part of "the supreme Law of the Land."

Contrary to popular belief, the Senate does not ratify treaties. The Constitution requires the Senate's "Advice and Consent" to a treaty made by the President. Once the Senate has given its consent, the President ratifies a treaty by the exchange of formal notifications with the other party or parties to the agreement.

---

# Focus on the Basics

Here is the information that your students need to learn in this section.

**FACTS:** • The President negotiates treaties, but the Senate must approve them by a two-thirds vote before the President can ratify them. • Sovereign states can recognize other states or deny recognition. • Presidents have used the armed forces without declaring war and without a congressional resolution. • Debate continues over the constitutionality of the War Powers Resolution.

**CONCEPTS:** checks and balances, enumerated and implied powers, separation of powers

**ENDURING UNDERSTANDING:** • The President shares diplomatic and military powers with Congress; however, in practice, the President's power as commander in chief is almost unlimited.

Treaties have the same legal standing as acts of Congress, and their provisions are enforceable in the courts. Congress may abrogate (repeal) a treaty by passing a law contrary to its provisions, and an existing law may be repealed by the terms of a treaty. When the provisions of a treaty and an act of Congress conflict, the courts consider the latest enacted to be the law (*The Head Money Cases*, 1884). The terms of a treaty cannot conflict with any provision in the Constitution (*Missouri* v. *Holland*, 1920); but the Supreme Court has never found a treaty provision to be unconstitutional.

**Treaties and the Senate** The Framers considered the Senate—with, originally, only 26 members—a suitable council to advise the President in foreign affairs. Secrecy was thought to be necessary and was seen as an impossibility in a body as large as the House.

The two-thirds rule for treaty approval creates the possibility that a relatively small Senate minority can kill an international agreement. For example, in 1920, the Senate rejected the Treaty of Versailles, the general peace agreement negotiated by Woodrow Wilson to end World War I. The treaty included provisions for the League of Nations. Forty-nine senators voted for the pact and 35 against, but the vote was 7 short of the necessary two thirds. More than once, a President has been forced to bow to the views of a few senators in order to get a treaty approved, even when this has meant making concessions opposed by the majority.

At times, a President has had to turn to roundabout methods in order to achieve his goals. When a Senate minority defeated a treaty to annex Texas, President John Tyler was able to bring about annexation in 1845 by encouraging passage of a joint resolution—a move that required only a majority vote in each house. In 1898, President William McKinley used the same tactic to annex Hawaii, again after a treaty his administration had negotiated failed in the Senate.

**Executive Agreements** Recent Presidents have relied more heavily on executive agreements than on formal treaties in their dealings with foreign governments, especially in

routine matters. An **executive agreement** is a pact between the President and the head of a foreign state, or their subordinates. Unlike treaties, these agreements do not have to be approved by the Senate.

These pacts have the same standing as treaties in the relationships between sovereign states, but they do not <u>supersede</u> federal law or the laws of any State. However, they are otherwise binding on the United States.

Most executive agreements flow out of legislation already passed by Congress or out of treaties to which the Senate has agreed. However, the President can make these agreements without any congressional action. Treaties, once made, become a permanent part of American law. Executive agreements do not. When a change of administrations occurs, only those the new President agrees to remain in force.

A few executive agreements have been extraordinary, most notably, the destroyers-for-bases deal of 1940. Under its terms, the United States gave Great Britain 50 "over-age" U.S. destroyers, naval vessels that the British needed to combat German submarine attacks in the North Atlantic. In return, the United

✓ **Checkpoint**
How do executive agreements differ from treaties?

**supersede**
*v.* to take the place of something previously in use

Secretary of State Madeleine Albright with Israeli Prime Minister Ehud Barak during Middle East peace discussions in 1999. *Why does the President rely on the secretary of state to perform diplomatic duties?*

413

**Differentiated Resources**

The following resources are located in the All-in-One, Unit 4, Chapter 14, Section 3:

**L3** Reading Comprehension Worksheet (p. 90)
**L2** Reading Comprehension Worksheet (p. 91)
**L3** Core Worksheet (p. 92)
**L3** Skills Worksheet (p. 94)
**L2** Skill Activity (p. 95)
**L3** Quiz A (p. 96)
**L2** Quiz B (p. 97)

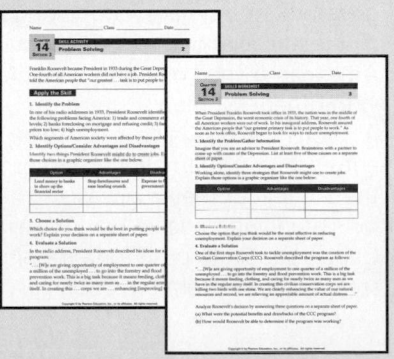

**BELLRINGER**

Display Transparency 14E, Diplomatic and Military Powers: A Scenario, which describes a hypothetical scenario involving foreign policy. Have students write their answers to the questions in their notebooks.

**L1** **L2** **Differentiate** Give students a choice of answering one or both questions.

## Teach

To present this topic using online resources, use the lesson presentations at **PearsonSchool.com/phgovt.**

**REVIEW BELLRINGER ANSWERS**

Go around the class and have each student read one option from his or her list of options. Write each option on the board. Remind students to consider Congress's response to each action. Allow one minute for students to review the options listed on the board. Then, have each student assume the role of President and choose the option he or she considers best. Have volunteers share with the class their decision and why they chose it.

**L2** **Differentiate** Create three columns on the board labeled "Option," "Pros," and "Cons." As students explain their options, write them in the first column. Discuss the pros and cons, reminding students to consider the response of Congress.

**DISTRIBUTE CORE WORKSHEET**

Divide the class into pairs. Designate each pair as either a Diplomatic Power or a Military Power team. Give each pair the Chapter 14 Section 3 Core Worksheet (Unit 4 All-in-One, p. 92). Have pairs research their assigned power and complete the chart for that power.

**L1** **L2** **ELL Differentiate** Assign lower-level students the Diplomatic Powers chart.

**L3** **L4** **Differentiate** Assign on-level or higher-level students the Military Powers chart.

## Answers

**Checkpoint** Executive agreements do not need Senate approval and do not supercede federal or State law.

**Caption** Possible answer: The President has many other administrative duties to handle and so must delegate some of these responsibilities to others.

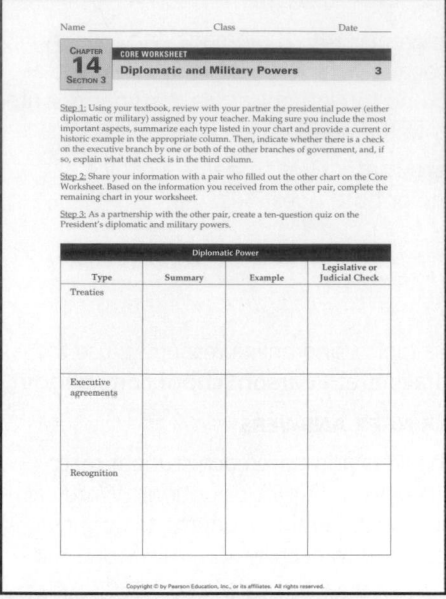

## COMBINE PAIRS TO CREATE A QUIZ

When all pairs have completed their chart, create groups of four that contain one pair from each team. Have pairs that researched the Diplomatic Power share their information with their new teammates, who should then complete their Diplomatic Power chart. Then, have the Military Power pairs share their information, which their new teammates will use to complete their chart.

Next, have each group use their charts to create a ten-question quiz. Tell them that they can create any type of question, including multiple-choice, short answer, and fill-in-the-blank. Once each quiz is complete, have groups exchange quizzes and answer a quiz from a different group.

## Answers

**Expanding Executive Power** Possible answer: In a crisis, the President may be aware of confidential information that is unknown to Congress, he or she can act more quickly than Congress, and Congress needs to be conscious of public sentiment.

# Expanding Executive Power

By dividing the military powers, the Framers created an enduring tension between Congress and the President as they battle over their war power authority. However, in times of national emergency, when our safety and national interests are threatened, there is a marked shift of power to the President. *Why might Congress yield to a President's decisions regarding military actions?*

## 1950 Korea

**President Truman** orders the use of military force to defend South Korea against communist North Korea. He claims that United Nations resolutions give him the legal authority for his actions.
**Congress** is not consulted by the President, but makes no attempt to block his "police action."

## 1964 Vietnam

**President Johnson,** citing a report of a North Vietnamese attack on an American destroyer, asks Congress to give him the authority to do whatever he considers necessary to deal with the threat.
**Congress** gives the President that authority by enacting the Gulf of Tonkin Resolution.

States received 99-year leases to a string of air and naval bases extending from Newfoundland to the Caribbean.

**The Power of Recognition** When the President receives the diplomatic representatives of another sovereign state, the President exercises the power of **recognition.** That is, the chief executive, acting for the United States, acknowledges the legal existence of that country and its government. The President's action indicates that the United States accepts that country as an equal member of the family of nations. Sovereign states generally recognize one another through the exchange of diplomatic representatives.[7]

Recognition does not mean that one government approves the character or the conduct of another. The United States recognizes several governments about which it has serious misgivings. Among the most notable examples today is the People's Republic of China. The facts of life in world politics make relations with these governments necessary.

Recognition can be used to gain some advantage in world affairs. President Theodore Roosevelt's quick recognition of Panama in 1903 is a classic example of that point. He recognized the new state less than three days after the Panamanians had begun a revolt against Colombia, of which Panama had been a part. Roosevelt's action guaranteed their success. Similarly, President Harry Truman's dramatic recognition of Israel, within minutes of its creation in 1948, helped that new state to survive among its hostile Arab neighbors.

The President may show American displeasure with the conduct of another country by asking for the recall of that nation's ambassador or other diplomatic representatives in this country. The official recalled is declared to be *persona non grata*, an unwelcome person. The same point can be made by the recalling of an American diplomat from a post in another country. The withdrawal of recognition is the sharpest diplomatic rebuke one government may give to another and has often been a step on the way to war.

## Commander in Chief

The Constitution makes the chief executive the commander in chief of the nation's armed forces, although Congress does have extensive war powers.[8] However, the President

**rebuke**
*n.* an expression of sharp disapproval

---

7 Recognition may be accomplished by other means, such as proposing to negotiate a treaty, since in international law only sovereign states can make such agreements.

8 Article II, Section 2, Clause 1; see also Chapter 17.

# Background

**RECOGNITION** A President's decision to end diplomatic recognition of a foreign government can have long-lasting effects. In 1961, President Eisenhower cut off diplomatic relations with Cuba, primarily in response to Fidel Castro's appropriation of American-owned property there. Although the United States has established relations with other Communist states—most notably, the People's Republic of China—formal relations with Cuba have yet to be resumed. The U.S. has continued to oppose Cuba's entrance into international groups such as the Organization of American States and the Summit of the Americas. In 2007, President George W. Bush refused to lift the long-standing trade embargo against the island. Instead, he appealed directly to the Cuban people to push for a transition to democracy. In 2008, due to ill health, Castro stepped down from the Cuban leadership in favor of his brother, Raul.

**Left:** The U.S.S. *Constellation* gears up in response to the Gulf of Tonkin incident.
**Right:** President George W. Bush rallying support for military action against Iraq.

**2002** **Iraq**
**President George W. Bush** plans preemptive combat operations against Iraq in reaction to reports of the stockpiling of weapons of mass destruction. **Congress** passes the Iraq Resolution authorizing the President to use military force, which he exercises in 2003.

**2010**
**President Barack Obama** escalates the number of U.S. troops in Afghanistan in an effort to end the threat posed by the extremist Taliban and al Qaeda organizations in that country. Congress had authorized that action in a 2001 resolution allowing the President to use force against those nations involved in the terrorist attacks of September 1, 2001.

**GOVERNMENT ONLINE**
**Audio Tour**
Listen to a guided audio tour of Expanding Executive Power at PearsonSchool.com/phgovt

dominates the field of military policy. In fact, the President's powers as commander in chief are almost without limit.

Consider this illustration of the point: In 1907, Theodore Roosevelt sent the Great White Fleet around the world. He did so partly as a training exercise for the Navy but mostly to impress other nations with America's naval might. Several members of Congress objected to the cost and threatened to block funds for the President's project. To this, Roosevelt is said to have replied, "Very well, the existing appropriation will carry the Navy halfway around the world and if Congress chooses to leave it on the other side, all right." Congress was forced to give in.

Presidents delegate much of their command authority to military subordinates. They are not required to do so, however. George Washington actually took command of federal troops and led them into Pennsylvania during the Whiskey Rebellion of 1794. Abraham Lincoln often visited the Army of the Potomac and instructed his generals in the field during the Civil War.

Most Presidents have not become so directly involved in military operations. Still, the President has the final authority over and responsibility for all military matters, and the most critical decisions are <u>invariably</u> made by the commander in chief.

**Making Undeclared War** Does the Constitution give the President the power to make war without a declaration of war by Congress? Although many argue that it does not, 200 years of American history argue otherwise. Presidents have often used the armed forces abroad, in combat, without a declaration of war.[9] In fact, most Presidents have done so, and on several hundred occasions.

John Adams was the first to do so, in 1798. At his command, the Navy fought and won a number of battles with French warships harassing American merchantmen in the Atlantic and the Caribbean. There have been a great many other foreign adventures since then. The long military conflicts in Korea, Vietnam, and now in Afghanistan and Iraq stand as the most extensive of these "undeclared wars."

**Congressional Resolutions** Congress has not declared war since World War II. On eight occasions since then, however, it has enacted joint resolutions to authorize the President to meet certain international crises with military force.

**✔ Checkpoint**
To whom does the Constitution give the power to declare war?

9  Congress has declared war 11 times. It did so against Great Britain in 1812; Mexico in 1848; Spain in 1898; Germany and Austria-Hungary in 1917; Japan, Germany, and Italy in 1941; and Bulgaria, Hungary, and Romania in 1942.

**invariably**
*adv.* always, without exception

# Debate

Use the quotation below to start a debate in your class. Use the debate rules on page T25 to structure the class.

"The President today believes he is free to pursue any policy he wants in the Balkans and the Persian Gulf without Congressional approval. It shouldn't be that way. It's dangerous politically, militar[ily], morally, and above all else undermines our entire system of the rule of law."

—Representative Ron Paul (R, Texas)

on sending troops to Kosovo, *Congressional Record* (March 17, 1999)

Ask students to take a position on this statement: **Congress should act as a stronger check on the President's power to deploy American troops.**

---

**DISCUSS**

Tell students that the skillful use of diplomatic and military powers is critical in keeping good relationships with other nations as well as in dealing with tense and precarious relationships. Have students predict what the outcome would be to some of the options in the Bellringer. Then, ask students to reflect on the unit Essential Question: **What makes a good President?** Have students discuss the characteristics a President needs in order to perform well in foreign relations. Write the Essential Question on the board and use the Idea Wave strategy (p. T22) to create a list of characteristics. Write them on the board as well.

**L1 L2 Differentiate** To help students brainstorm, ask: **How much should a President listen to advisors and experts? Should a President take time to consider options or take action immediately? Should a President have experience dealing with foreign nations?**

**EXTEND THE LESSON**

**L1 L2 Differentiate** Have students look through newspapers or news magazines to find images of the President using one of the powers discussed in this section. Students should select three images, affix them to paper, identify the power illustrated, and state why they believe the image reflects this power.

**L3 Differentiate** To extend students' understanding of "Expanding Presidential Power," have them select one of the incidents described and write a brief essay on whether they believe the President's actions were appropriate at the time.

**L4 Differentiate** Display Transparency 14F, and discuss each President's war powers. Then have students research the controversy surrounding the War Powers Resolution. Divide students into two groups for a debate. Assign one group to support the constitutionality of the resolution and the other to oppose it.

Tell students to go to the Audio Tour for a guided audio tour of "Expanding Executive Power."

---

**Answers**
**Checkpoint** Congress

# Assess and Remediate

**L3** Collect the Core Worksheet and student-created quizzes. Assess student participation using the Rubric for Assessing Performance of an Entire Group (Unit 4 All-in-One, p. 287).

**L3** Assign the Section 3 Assessment questions.

**L3** Section Quiz A (Unit 4 All-in-One, p. 96)

**L2** Section Quiz B (Unit 4 All-in-One, p. 97)

Have students complete the review activities in the digital lesson presentation and continue their work in the **Essential Questions Journal**.

## REMEDIATION

| If Your Students Have Trouble With | Strategies For Remediation |
|---|---|
| Identifying foreign policy tools (Question 1) | Provide students with a matching exercise with a list of the tools and a historic example of each. |
| Describing the President's role as chief diplomat (Questions 2–4) | Work with the class to make a concept web on the board of the President's diplomatic tools. |
| Determining the purpose of the War Powers Resolution (Question 5) | Describe to students the actions of Presidents Johnson and Nixon during the Vietnam War to illustrate the reasons behind the resolution's enactment by Congress. |
| Evaluating the unlimited military power of the President (Question 6) | Have pairs review the "Expanding Executive Powers" feature and in one sentence describe the President's action in each undeclared war. |
| Determining the constitutionality of the War Powers Resolution (Question 7) | Review with students Article I, Section 8, Clause 11 and Article II, Section 2, Clause 1 of the Constitution. |

## Answers

**Checkpoint** to limit the President's war-making power without congressional approval

---

✔ **Checkpoint**
Why did Congress enact the War Powers Resolution?

President Dwight Eisenhower sought the first of these measures in 1955, to block the designs the People's Republic of China had (and still has) on Taiwan. That show of American resolve, and the presence of American warships, defused the situation.

In 2002, Congress agreed that President George W. Bush should take those measures "necessary and appropriate" to eliminate the threat posed by Saddam Hussein and his Iraqi dictatorship. In March 2003, an international coalition, led by the United States, launched Operation Iraqi Freedom—a military campaign that ousted Saddam Hussein and his government from power. Some 150,000 American troops served in Iraq, engaged in the difficult, often dangerous task of stabilizing that country. President Obama declared "the end of our combat mission in Iraq" in August of 2010. Some 50,000 U.S. troops remain there "to advise and assist" the Iraqis as they rebuild their homeland.

**Other Uses of Military Power** Since the end of World War II, there have been many other critical situations in which Presidents have deployed the nation's armed forces—without a congressional resolution to support the action. Certainly, the Korean War stands as the foremost illustration of that fact. Among the other more notable instances: the attack on Grenada, ordered by President Ronald Reagan in 1983, to frustrate a military coup in that Caribbean island nation; the invasion of Panama, at the command of President George H.W. Bush in 1989, to oust the dictatorship of General Manuel Noriega and protect American interests there; and the dispatch of American forces to the Balkans by President Bill Clinton (to Bosnia in 1995 and to Kosovo in 1999) as part of NATO's response to a vicious civil war and the horrific "ethnic cleansing" campaign conducted by the forces of Serbian President Slobodan Milosevic.

**War Powers Resolution** The war-making power as it was exercised by Presidents Johnson and Nixon during the undeclared war in Vietnam moved Congress to enact (over President Nixon's veto) the War Powers Resolution of 1973. That statute provides that the President can commit American military forces to combat only (1) if Congress has declared war, (2) if Congress has authorized that action, or (3) when an attack on the nation or its armed forces has occurred.

If troops are ordered into combat in the third circumstance, the President must report it to Congress within 48 hours. Any such commitment of American forces must end within 60 days, unless Congress agrees to a longer involvement. At any time, Congress can end a commitment by the passage of a concurrent resolution (which is not subject to veto). The constitutionality of the War Powers Resolution remains in dispute.

---

## SECTION 3 ASSESSMENT

**Essential Questions Journal** To continue to build a response to the chapter Essential Question, go to your **Essential Questions Journal**.

1. **Guiding Question** Use your completed concept web to answer this question: What tools are available to the President to implement foreign policy?

### Key Terms and Comprehension

2. Describe the treaty-making process.

3. What is the difference between a **treaty** and an **executive agreement**?

4. What is the power of **recognition** and how can the President use it as a diplomatic tool?

5. Why did Congress enact the War Powers Resolution?

### Critical Thinking

6. **Synthesize Information** Why can the military powers of the President be described as almost without limit?

7. **Demonstrate Reasoned Judgment** Do you think the War Powers Resolution is constitutional? Why or why not?

### Quick Write

**Persuasive Writing: Sequence Your Arguments** Do you want to give the audience your strongest statement first or save it until the end? In order to sequence your arguments appropriately, you will need to determine the strength of each. Using your chart from Section 2, rank the arguments that support your thesis from strongest to weakest. Then, make an outline that shows where your arguments will appear in your essay.

---

# Assessment Answers

**1.** exchange diplomats, recognize nations, recall diplomats, make executive agreements, seek congressional resolutions, deploy troops, and make treaties

**2.** The President, usually through the secretary of state, negotiates a treaty. The Senate then must approve the treaty by a two-thirds vote of members present, after which the President ratifies it.

**3.** Unlike a treaty, an executive agreement does not require Senate approval, supersede federal and State laws, or become a permanent part of U.S. law. A subsequent President can end it.

**4.** Recognition is the acknowledgement of a country or government's legal existence. Quick recognition serves as a diplomatic seal of approval, while withholding recognition is a diplomatic rebuke.

**5.** to limit the President's power to make war without congressional approval

**6.** because the President always has the final authority over all military matters and may exert it without the approval of Congress

**7.** Students should support their opinion with facts from the War Powers Resolution and well-reasoned arguments.

**QUICK WRITE** Students should rank their arguments from strongest to weakest and order them appropriately in an outline to defend their thesis statement.

# SECTION 4
# Legislative and Judicial Powers

**Guiding Question**

**How can the President check the actions of the legislative and judicial branches?** Use a flowchart like the one below to keep track of the checks the President has on the other branches.

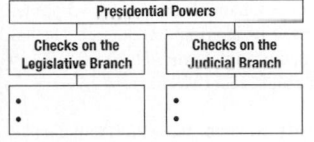

| Presidential Powers | |
|---|---|
| **Checks on the Legislative Branch** | **Checks on the Judicial Branch** |
| • <br> • | • <br> • |

**Political Dictionary**
- pocket veto
- line-item veto
- reprieve
- pardon
- clemency
- commutation
- amnesty

**Objectives**
1. Explain the President's legislative powers and how they are an important part of the system of checks and balances.
2. Describe the President's major judicial powers.

**Image Above:** President Barack Obama delivers his first State of the Union Address in January 2010.

In *The Federalist* No. 51, James Madison analyzes the Constitution's elaborate system of checks and balances. Its "constant aim," he says, "is to divide and arrange the several [branches] in such a manner as that each may be a check on the other." And he adds, "the great security against a gradual concentration of the several powers in the same department consists in giving to those who administer each department the necessary constitutional means and personal motives to resist encroachments of the others. . . . "

The Constitution gives the President certain legislative and judicial powers. They are, in Madison's phrase, "the constitutional means" that make it possible for the President to check the actions of Congress or the federal courts.

## Legislative Powers

The President's legislative powers, exercised in combination with a skillful playing of the roles of chief of party and chief citizen, have made the President, in effect, the nation's chief legislator. It is the President who initiates, suggests, and demands that Congress enact much of the major legislation that it produces. However, a President whose party controls both houses on Capitol Hill may have an easier time of it than one who faces a hostile Congress.

**Recommending Legislation** The Constitution says that the President

> **FROM THE CONSTITUTION**
>
> **shall from time to time give to the Congress Information of the State of the Union, and recommend to their Consideration such Measures as he shall judge necessary and expedient. . . .**
> —Article II, Section 3

This provision gives the President what is often called the message power.

The chief executive regularly sends three major messages to Capitol Hill each year. The first is the State of the Union message, a speech almost always delivered in person to a joint session of Congress. The President's budget message and then

## Focus on the Basics

Here is the information that your students need to learn in this section.

**FACTS:** • The President's legislative powers allow him or her considerable influence over the actions of Congress. • The President's key legislative powers are to submit legislation for Congress to consider and, using the veto power, to reject legislation that he or she opposes. • The presidential power to issue a pardon or reprieve applies only to federal offenses, but when given and accepted, is absolute.

**CONCEPTS:** checks and balances, enumerated and implied powers, separation of powers

**ENDURING UNDERSTANDING:** • The Constitution gives the President strong legislative and judicial powers as a part of the system of checks and balances.

---

**GUIDING QUESTION**

## How can the President check the actions of the legislative and judicial branches?

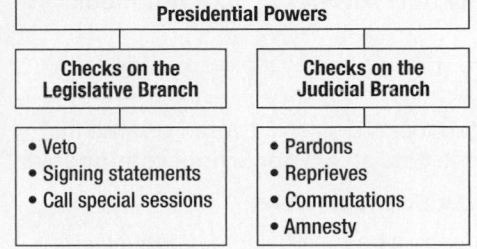

| Presidential Powers | |
|---|---|
| **Checks on the Legislative Branch** | **Checks on the Judicial Branch** |
| • Veto <br> • Signing statements <br> • Call special sessions | • Pardons <br> • Reprieves <br> • Commutations <br> • Amnesty |

## Get Started

### LESSON GOALS

Students will . . .

- analyze the principle of checks and balances using Article I, Section 7, Clause 2 of the Constitution.
- define elements of the President's legislative and judicial powers.
- use primary sources to evaluate a President's use of the power to pardon.

### BEFORE CLASS

Assign the section, the graphic organizer in the text, and the Reading Comprehension Worksheet (Unit 4 All-in-One, p. 98) before class.

**L2 Differentiate** Reading Comprehension Worksheet (Unit 4 All-in-One, p. 99)

## SKILLS DEVELOPMENT

### COMPARE VIEWPOINTS

To teach the skill of comparing viewpoints, have students read Compare Viewpoints in the Skills Handbook, p. S15. Then have them identify and evaluate the two viewpoints described in the article on the Core Worksheet.

Display Transparency 14G showing part of Article I, Section 7, Clause 2 of the Constitution. Write on the board: **(1) How does this clause relate to checks and balances? (2) Do you think the legislative approval process is sufficient to prevent abuse of power by the legislative or executive branch? Why or why not? Answer in your notebook.**

# Teach

To present this topic using online resources, use the lesson presentations at **PearsonSchool.com/phgovt.**

### REVIEW BELLRINGER ANSWERS

Have volunteers share their Bellringer answers. *(1. establishes power of executive branch to check Congress using the veto and power of Congress to check the President using the override 2. No—the requirement for override is too high, giving the President too much power. Yes—the process requires all parties to consider legislation and resolve objections.)*

### DISCUSS

Display Transparency 14H. Point out that checks and balances prevent abuse of power. The Constitution sets rules for each branch, and if any branch oversteps these rules, the other branches act as referees to rein in the offending branch. Ask: **How do the President's legislative and judicial powers check the actions of the other branches?** *(legislative: veto can block a law; judicial: can alter court decisions through reprieve, pardon, commutation, or amnesty)*

**L2 ELL Differentiate** Ask students if they have heard the terms *reprieve* and *pardon* used in a different context. For example, *pardon* may be used as a way to say "excuse me." Have volunteers define these terms in the context of presidential power.

### PLAY "WHERE DO YOU STAND?"

The United States drafted many men to serve in the Vietnam War. Many Americans opposed the war. Men who refused to report for service were arrested. Ask: **Should people have a right to refuse to serve in the military if they believe the war is unjust?** Using the Opinion Line strategy (p. T26), write on the board: **"Yes," "I Don't Know,"** and **"No."** Have students stand according to their answer and explain their decision. Then allow them to rethink their stance and relocate. Ask students who moved why they did so.

## Answers

**Checkpoint** (1) sign the bill, making it law; (2) veto the bill, which returns to Congress; (3) allow a bill to become law by not acting on it, neither signing nor vetoing it, within ten days; (4) use a pocket veto at the end of a congressional session

---

**✔ Checkpoint**
What options are available to a President when presented with a bill?

the annual Economic Report soon follow. The President often sends the lawmakers a number of other messages on a wide range of topics.

**The Veto Power** The Constitution says that "Every Bill" and "Every Order, Resolution, or Vote to which the Concurrence of the Senate and House of Representatives may be necessary (except on a question of Adjournment) shall be presented to the President."[10] Remember, the Constitution presents the President with four options once a measure has been approved by Congress.

First, he may sign the bill, making it law, which is what usually happens. Or he can veto the bill, and the measure must then be returned to Congress.[11] Congress can then override that veto, by a two-thirds vote in each of its two chambers, but it seldom does.

As a third option, the President may allow a bill to become law by not acting on it, neither signing nor vetoing it, within ten days (excluding Sundays). This rarely happens.

The fourth option, the **pocket veto,** can be used only at the end of a congressional session. If Congress adjourns within ten days (not counting Sundays) of sending a bill to the White House and the chief executive does not act on it, the measure dies.

The veto power is an exceedingly valuable tool in the President's dealings with the legislative branch. Even the mere *threat* of a veto can defeat a bill or, at the least, prompt changes in its provisions as it moves through the legislative mill. When the chief executive makes such a threat, congressional leaders must do the math: Can they find enough votes in both houses to overcome a presidential veto?

George Washington rejected only two measures in his eight years in the presidency, and for nearly seven decades his successors also used their veto pens infrequently. But from Andrew Johnson in the 1860s onward, most chief executives have been much more willing to reject measures.

---

10 Article I, Section 7, Clauses 2 and 3. Recall that, despite these words, joint resolutions proposing constitutional amendments and concurrent resolutions, which do not have the force of law, are not sent to the President.
11 *Veto,* from the Latin meaning "I forbid."

---

**Signing Statements** From James Monroe in the 1820s to today, various Presidents have issued "signing statements" as they approved some measures. On occasion, those statements were used to point out constitutional or other problems the President saw in a newly enacted law. More often, the statements have been used to do such things as to direct the manner in which a new law is to be enforced.

President George W. Bush stirred controversy by issuing signing statements far more often than any of his predecessors, using them to question the constitutionality of more than 1,200 provisions in various measures he signed. In doing so, he claimed a power, on one hand, to refuse to enforce those provisions or, on the other, to interpret them "in a manner consistent with" his view of "the constitutional authority of the President." His critics claim that Mr. Bush, in effect, used these statements as a substitute for the veto power, deciding which new laws he would execute and how those laws would be interpreted and applied.

President Obama has rejected his predecessor's view of signing statements. He has used them sparingly, in much the same way as earlier chief executives have.

**The Line-Item Veto** If the President decides to veto a bill, he must reject the *entire* measure. He cannot veto only a portion of it.

Since Ulysses S. Grant's day, most Presidents have favored expanding the veto power to include a **line-item veto.** That is, they have sought the power to cancel out some provisions in a measure while approving others. Most often, those who have proposed this device would restrict its application to specific dollar amounts (line items) in spending bills enacted by Congress. Many supporters argue that the line-item veto would be a potent weapon against wasteful and unnecessary federal spending.

Opponents of the line-item veto have long argued that the move would bring a massive and dangerous shift of power from the legislative branch to the executive branch. To this point, efforts to persuade Congress to propose a line-item veto amendment to the Constitution have failed.

# Differentiated Resources

The following resources are located in the All-in-One, Unit 4, Chapter 14, Section 4:

L3 Reading Comprehension Worksheet (p. 98)
L2 Reading Comprehension Worksheet (p. 99)
L3 Core Worksheet (p. 100)
L2 Extend Activity (p. 102)
L3 Quiz A (p. 103)
L2 Quiz B (p. 104)
L3 Chapter Test A (p. 110)
L2 Chapter Test B (p. 113)

# The Power of the Veto

When the President and the majority of Congress are of the same party, vetoes tend to be rare. They tend to be more frequent during periods of divided government. *Do you think the veto gives the President too much authority?*

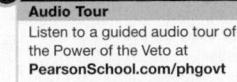
**GOVERNMENT ONLINE**
**Audio Tour**
Listen to a guided audio tour of the Power of the Veto at
PearsonSchool.com/phgovt

President Gerald Ford prepares to address the nation about his decision to veto a tax cut.

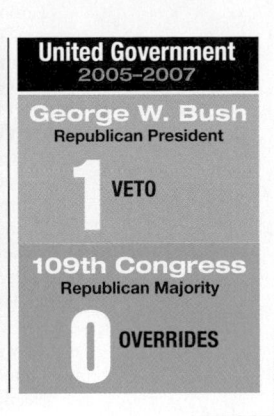

| Divided Government 1975–1977 | United Government 2005–2007 |
|---|---|
| **Gerald R. Ford** Republican President | **George W. Bush** Republican President |
| **39** VETOES | **1** VETO |
| **94th Congress** Democratic Majority | **109th Congress** Republican Majority |
| **8** OVERRIDES | **0** OVERRIDES |

In 1996, Congress did pass a Line-Item Veto Act. The Supreme Court struck it down, however, holding that Congress lacked the power to give the President a line-item veto, *Clinton v. New York City,* 1998. If the chief executive is to have that authority, said the Court, it can come only as the result of an amendment to the Constitution.

**Other Legislative Powers** According to Article II, Section 3 of the Constitution, only the President can call Congress into special session. The fact that Congress is now in session through most of each year practically eliminates the likelihood of special sessions and also lessens the importance of the President's power to call one. Still, as Congress nears the end of a regular session, Presidents have sometimes found it useful to threaten a special session if lawmakers do not act on some particular measure. President Harry Truman called the most recent special session in 1948, in an effort to force Congress to consider anti-inflation and welfare measures in the post–World War II period.

The same constitutional provision also gives the chief executive the power to prorogue (adjourn) Congress in the event the two houses cannot agree on a date for their adjournment. That has never happened.

## Judicial Powers

The Constitution gives the President the power to

### FROM THE CONSTITUTION

> . . . Grant Reprieves and Pardons for Offenses against the United States, except in Cases of Impeachment.
> —Article II, Section 2, Clause 1

A **reprieve** is the postponement of the execution of a sentence. A **pardon** is legal forgiveness of a crime.

The President's power to grant reprieves and pardons is <u>absolute</u>, except in cases of impeachment, where they may never be granted. These powers of **clemency** (mercy

✔ **Checkpoint**
How does a line-item veto differ from a regular veto?

**absolute**
*adj.* final, not subject to appeal

Chapter 14 • Section 4 **419**

## Teacher-to-Teacher Network

**ALTERNATE LESSON PLAN** Divide the students into three groups, one representing the President and the Cabinet, another representing the Senate, and the other one as the House of Representatives. Each group proposes a solution to a problem or an issue in the class, the school, or the country. As the groups debate solutions, they also have to find out what is happening in the other groups. Finally, the President has to decide to sign the legislation or veto it.

To see this lesson plan, go to

**Teacher Center**
at PearsonSchool.com/phgovt

---

### DISTRIBUTE CORE WORKSHEET

Distribute the Chapter 14 Section 4 Core Worksheet (Unit 4 All-in-One, p. 100). Divide the class into pairs. Have pairs work together to answer the questions.

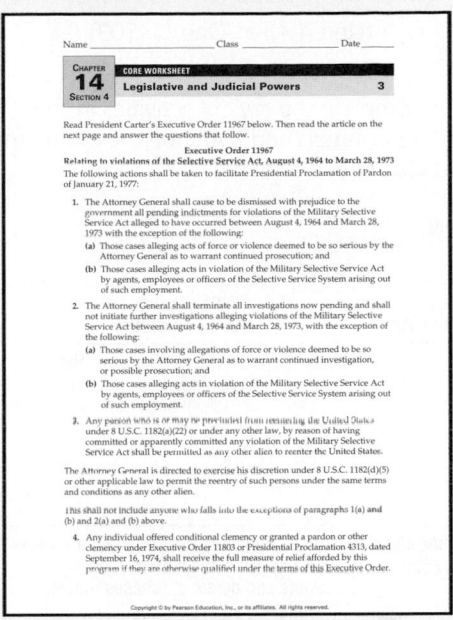

**L2 ELL Differentiate** Have students write the main idea of each numbered point in the Executive Order.

### DISCUSS STUDENTS' OPINIONS

Ask volunteers to read their answer to question 3 of the Core Worksheet for class discussion.

### EXTEND THE LESSON

**L4 Differentiate** Have students select a President, research the number of vetoes and overrides of that President, and determine the party in control of Congress during the President's administration(s). Display Transparency 14I. Have students write a brief paragraph on whether they think there is a correlation between the party in power and the number of presidential vetoes.

**L2 Differentiate** Distribute the Extend Activity "State of the Union" (Unit 4 All-in-One, p. 102).

Tell students to go to the Audio Tour for a guided tour of the power of the veto.

---

## Answers

**The Power of the Veto** sample answers: yes, because veto power enables the President to stop legislation supported by most representatives; no, because the veto is part of checks and balances

**Checkpoint** Unlike a regular veto, a line-item veto would allow the President to cancel some provisions in a measure while approving others.

# Assess and Remediate

**L3** Collect the Core Worksheet and assess students' work.

**L3** Assign the Section 4 Assessment questions.

**L3** Section Quiz A (Unit 4 All-in-One, p. 103)

**L2** Section Quiz B (Unit 4 All-in-One, p. 104)

Have students complete the review activities in the digital lesson presentation and continue their work in the **Essential Questions Journal.**

## REMEDIATION

| If Your Students Have Trouble With | Strategies For Remediation |
|---|---|
| Identifying presidential checks and balances (Questions 1, 5) | Write the section's key terms on the board and have students suggest the legislative or judicial action to which they are in response. |
| Determining the purpose of signing statements (Question 2) | Review Document 2 of the Document-Based Assessment with the class. |
| Identifying the line-item veto controversy (Question 3) | Have students create a budget for spending $100. Then, have them exchange budgets and delete purchases they think are unnecessary. |
| Differentiating the judicial powers (Question 4) | Create a table on the board listing the similarities and differences among the key terms. |
| Determining the value of the veto power (Question 6) | Review the process of overriding a veto. |

## Answers

**Checkpoint** the power to grant conditional pardons, the power of commutation, and the power of amnesty

---

or leniency) may be used only in cases involving *federal* offenses.

Presidential pardons are usually granted after a person has been convicted in court. Yet the President may pardon a federal offender before that person is tried, or even before that person has been formally charged.

Pardons in advance of a trial or charge are rare. The most noteworthy pardon, by far, was granted in 1974. In that year, President Gerald Ford gave "a full, free and absolute pardon unto Richard Nixon for all offenses against the United States which he . . . has committed or may have committed or taken part in during the period from January 20, 1969, through August 9, 1974." Of course, that pardon referred to the Watergate scandal.

To be effective, a pardon must be accepted by the person to whom it is granted. When a pardon is granted prior to a charge or conviction, as in the Nixon case, its acceptance is regularly seen as an admission of guilt by the person to whom it is given.

Nearly all pardons are accepted, of course, and usually gratefully. A few have been rejected, however. One of the most dramatic refusals led to a Supreme Court case, *Burdick* v. *United States,* 1915. George Burdick, a New York newspaper editor, had refused to testify before a federal grand jury regarding the sources for certain news stories his paper had printed. Those stories reported fraud in the collection of customs duties. He invoked the 5th Amendment, claiming that his testimony could incriminate him.

President Woodrow Wilson then granted Burdick "a full and unconditional pardon for all offenses against the United States" that he might have committed in obtaining material for the news stories.

Interestingly, Burdick refused to accept the pardon, and he continued to refuse to testify. With that, the federal judge in that district fined and jailed him for contempt. The judge ruled that (1) the President's pardon was fully effective, with or without Burdick's acceptance and (2) there was, therefore, no basis for Burdick's continued claim of protection against self-incrimination.

The Supreme Court overturned the lower court's action. It unanimously upheld the rule that a pardon must be accepted in order to be effective, and it ordered Burdick's release from jail.

The pardoning power includes the power to grant conditional pardons, provided the conditions are reasonable. It also includes the power of **commutation,** or the power to reduce a fine or the length of a sentence imposed by a court.

The pardoning power also includes the power of **amnesty,** which is in effect a blanket pardon offered to a group of law violators. Thus, in 1893, President Benjamin Harrison issued a proclamation of amnesty forgiving all Mormons who had violated the antipolygamy (multiple marriage) laws in the federal territories. And in 1977, President Jimmy Carter granted amnesty to those who evaded the draft during the war in Vietnam.

**Essential Questions Journal** To continue to build a response to the chapter Essential Question, go to your **Essential Questions Journal.**

## SECTION **4** ASSESSMENT

1. **Guiding Question** Use your completed flowchart to answer this question: How can the President check the actions of the legislative and judicial branches?

### Key Terms and Comprehension

2. Why do Presidents sometimes issue signing statements?

3. What is the **line-item veto** and why is it controversial?

4. Explain how these presidential judicial powers differ: **reprieve, pardon, clemency, commutation, amnesty.**

### Critical Thinking

5. **Determine Relevance** How do the President's legislative and judicial powers illustrate the principle of checks and balances?

6. **Identify Central Issues** Why do you think the threat of a veto is an important presidential tool?

### Quick Write

**Persuasive Writing: Use Facts and Details** To help build your case in your persuasive essay, you should have facts, statistics, quotations, and other details that support your thesis. Select the top three arguments you ranked in Section 3 and locate at least two specific details that you can use to support each of your arguments.

---

## Assessment Answers

**1.** The President can check Congress by using the veto power, issuing signing statements, or calling special sessions. The President can check the judicial branch by issuing pardons and reprieves, commuting an individual's sentence, or granting amnesty.

**2.** Signing statements are a President's way to point out problems in a new law or direct the manner in which the law will be enforced.

**3.** A line-item veto is a proposed power that would enable the President to cancel some parts of a bill while accepting others. It is controversial because it potentially shifts a great deal of power to the President.

**4.** A reprieve postpones the execution of a sentence; a pardon legally forgives a crime; clemency refers to grants of mercy, which include pardons and reprieves; commutation reduces a sentence or fine; amnesty pardons a group of law violators rather than an individual.

**5.** These powers help balance the power among branches by serving as a check by the President on the other branches.

**6.** Because a two-thirds vote to override is difficult to achieve, the President can use the threat of a veto to defeat a bill before it even passes or to pressure Congress to address the President's concerns about the bill.

**QUICK WRITE** Students should gather supporting details that enhance the top three arguments they intend to use in their essay.

# Quick Study Guide

**GOVERNMENT ONLINE**
**On the Go**
To review anytime, anywhere, download these online resources at
**PearsonSchool.com/phgovt**
Political Dictionary, Audio Review

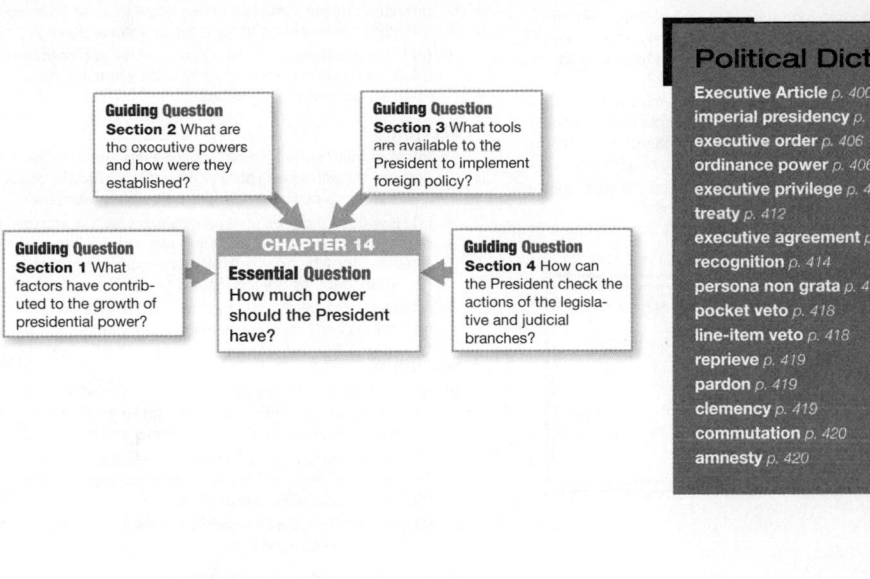

**Guiding Question**
**Section 2** What are the executive powers and how were they established?

**Guiding Question**
**Section 3** What tools are available to the President to implement foreign policy?

**Guiding Question**
**Section 1** What factors have contributed to the growth of presidential power?

**CHAPTER 14**
**Essential Question**
How much power should the President have?

**Guiding Question**
**Section 4** How can the President check the actions of the legislative and judicial branches?

## Political Dictionary

Executive Article *p. 400*
imperial presidency *p. 403*
executive order *p. 406*
ordinance power *p. 406*
executive privilege *p. 409*
treaty *p. 412*
executive agreement *p. 413*
recognition *p. 414*
persona non grata *p. 414*
pocket veto *p. 418*
line-item veto *p. 418*
reprieve *p. 419*
pardon *p. 419*
clemency *p. 419*
commutation *p. 420*
amnesty *p. 420*

**Diplomatic and Military Powers**
• Make treaties and executive agreements
• Recognize other sovereign states
• Act as commander in chief of the armed forces

**Legislative Powers**
• Recommend legislation
• Veto legislation
• Call Congress into special session

**Executive Powers**
• Execute the law
• Direct the administration
• Appoint key officials
• Remove officials

**Judicial Powers**
• Grant reprieves
• Grant pardons
• Commute sentences
• Grant amnesty

**The Powers of the President**

# For More Information

To learn more about the presidency, refer to these sources or assign them to students:

**L1** **L2** **Walker, Diana.** *Public & Private: Twenty Years of Photographing the Presidency.* National Geographic, 2002.

**L3** **Hargrove, Erwin.** *The Effective Presidency: Lessons on Leadership from John F. Kennedy to George W. Bush.* Paradigm Publishers, 2007.

**L4** **Graff, Garret M.** *The First Campaign: Globalization, the Web, and the Race for the White House.* Farrar, Straus, and Giroux, 2007.

---

Have students download the digital resources available at Government on the Go for review and remediation.

## STUDY TIPS

**When to Study** Part of effective studying includes choosing the best time to study. Each of us has a time of day when we are at our best, whether it's early in the morning, during the evening, or some other time. Explain to students that once they identify this time of day for themselves, they should try to study during those hours. Additionally, tell students to keep in mind that shorter study sessions of one or two hours are usually more effective than marathon sessions. Even during short study sessions, students should remember to take a break every hour or so. Whenever possible, encourage students to take time to review class notes as soon after class as possible in order to identify problem areas and questions and to fix the information in their minds. Have students make a study schedule for the week, keeping in mind these pointers.

## ASSESSMENT AT A GLANCE

### Tests and Quizzes
Section Assessments
Section Quizzes A and B, Unit 4 **All-in-One**
Chapter Assessment
Chapter Tests A and B, Unit 4 **All-in-One**
Document-Based Assessment
Progress Monitoring Online
Exam*View* Test Bank

### Performance Assessment
Essential Questions Journal
Debate, p. 415
Assessment Rubrics, **All-in-One**

# Chapter Assessment

## COMPREHENSION AND CRITICAL THINKING

### SECTION 1

**1. (a)** One view argued for a weaker presidency subordinate to Congress; the other, for a stronger, independent, and co-equal chief executive. **(b)** the stronger presidency **(c)** sample answers: no, because the Framers included methods within the Constitution to check the President's actions; yes, because the Framers did not define the executive powers clearly enough, which allowed the President to expand his powers beyond the prescribed expectations

**2. (a)** Factors include: looseness of the Executive Article, unity of the presidency, delegation of authority by Congress, citizens' demand for leadership, ability of the President to manage crises, President's own view of the presidency and way of fulfilling his or her roles, and President's use of the media. **(b)** Americans have looked to the President for leadership in a variety of fields. **(c)** Students might state that voters will look for qualities such as leadership and decision-making skills, government experience, and views on major issues.

**3.** Sample answer: It shows that presidential power has grown so much that today the other branches are subordinate to the executive branch.

### SECTION 2

**4. (a)** Article II Section 3 and the Oath of Office **(b)** by his or her interpretation of the law and the way in which subordinates work out the details **(c)** Some students might say yes, because administrators can interpret the broadly written laws to suit their own views. Other students might say no, because Congress should concentrate on the issue of the law and leave the execution to the executive branch.

**5. (a)** a presidential directive that has the effect of law; arises from the Constitution's implied ordinance power **(b)** because the Framers granted certain powers to the President, and to exercise those powers, the President must have the power to issue and implement the necessary orders

**6. (a)** ambassadors and other diplomats, Cabinet members and their top aides, independent agency heads, federal judges, U.S. marshals and attorneys, and all officers of the armed forces **(b)** Vice President, members of Congress, presidential electors **(c)** Some students might say the Framers

---

# Chapter Assessment

## Comprehension and Critical Thinking

### Section 1

**1. (a)** What competing views of the presidency were held by the Framers? **(b)** Which view did they finally adopt? **(c)** Do you think the Framers' decision helped to shape the nature of presidential power? Why?

**2. (a)** What factors have led to the growth of presidential power? **(b)** In what way have the people contributed to that growth? **(c)** How might this increased power affect the way voters view the qualifications of a President?

**3. Analyze Political Cartoons** How does this cartoon illustrate the presidential power controversy?

SEPARATION OF POWERS

THEN / NOW

### Section 2

**4. (a)** From what two sources in the Constitution does the President get the power to execute the law? **(b)** How can a President affect the meaning of a law? **(c)** Do you think Congress gives the executive branch too much authority to interpret laws?

**5. (a)** What is an executive order, and how is it related to the ordinance power? **(b)** How do we know that the Framers intended the President to have the ordinance power?

**6. (a)** What positions are filled by presidential appointment? **(b)** What positions are not? **(c)** Why do you think the Framers made this distinction?

### Section 3

**7. (a)** What methods are available to the President to make agreements with foreign states? **(b)** Is it necessary to check the President's power to make international agreements?

**8. (a)** How does the President usually exercise the power of recognition? **(b)** How can the power be used as a weapon? **(c)** Why do you think it is important to other countries that they are recognized by the United States?

**9. (a)** What tools are available to the President as commander in chief? **(b)** How have they been limited?

### Section 4

**10. (a)** What are the President's legislative powers? **(b)** What are the President's judicial powers? **(c)** How do these powers illustrate the principle of checks and balances?

**11. (a)** What is the difference between a veto and a line-item veto? **(b)** How would a line-item veto increase the President's legislative powers?

**12.** Why do you think the President's judicial powers are included in the Constitution?

### Writing About Government

**13.** Use your Quick Write exercises from this chapter to write a persuasive essay regarding the debate on the extent of presidential powers. Make sure to state your position clearly in the introduction and support it with detailed arguments. See pp. S9–S10 in the Skills Handbook.

## Apply What You've Learned

**14. Essential Question Activity** Take a survey of at least 10 voters (Democratic, Republican, and independent) in your community. Ask:

**(a)** Over the past decade, do you think the President has overstepped his authority? If so, when?

**(b)** Over the past decade, do you think the President needed more authority? If so, when?

**(c)** Over your lifetime, do you think the power of the presidency has changed? If so, how?

**15. Essential Question Assessment** Use the results of your survey and the content of this chapter to write a paragraph that helps answer the Essential Question:

**How much power should a President have?** Then, as a group, work with your classmates to create a chart that consolidates the results of each survey. Using the completed chart and your prepared paragraph, discuss the Essential Question as a class and reflect on the variety of answers that arise in response to the query. Following the discussion, if you find your opinion has changed, revise your paragraph accordingly.

**Essential Questions Journal** To respond to the chapter Essential Question, go to your **Essential Questions Journal.**

---

wanted to prevent a President from filling positions that should be democratically elected. Others might say the Framers wanted to allow the President to appoint subordinates with whom he will work.

### SECTION 3

**7. (a)** treaties and executive agreements **(b)** Sample answer: Treaties and agreements are binding on the United States and far-reaching in effect. Such decisions should not be made by one person unchecked.

**8. (a)** by exchanging diplomats **(b)** Quick rec-

ognition supports a government, helping it survive; removing recognition is a rebuke and often a step toward war. **(c)** Sample answer: Recognition by the strongest nation in the world lends legitimacy to a new government and may influence other nations to recognize it as well.

**9. (a)** can deploy troops with or without a declaration of war; can seek a congressional resolution to deploy troops in a crisis **(b)** The Constitution gives Congress the power to declare war. Also, Congress has enacted the War Powers Resolution, which sets limits on a President's military actions.

# Document-Based Assessment

## Presidential Signing Statements

Although the practice has been around since the mid 1800s, the use of presidential signing statements recently became quite controversial. As these documents show, the already existing tensions between the executive and legislative branches became more intense as they quarreled over the proper use of these statements.

### Document 1

We are at a pivotal moment in our Nation's history, where Americans are faced with a President who makes sweeping claims for almost unchecked Executive power. One of the most troubling aspects of such claims is the President's unprecedented use of signing statements. Historically, these statements have served as public announcements containing comments from the President on the enactment of laws. But [the George W. Bush] Administration has taken what was otherwise a press release and transformed it into a proclamation stating which parts of the law the President will follow and which parts he will simply ignore. . . .

Under our constitutional system of government, when Congress passes a bill and the President signs it into law, that should be the end of the story. It is the law of the land unless and until repealed by Congress or invalidated by the courts. For this reason, there are grave and inherent dangers to the extensive and unprecedented use of signing statements

When the President uses signing statements to unilaterally rewrite the laws enacted by the people's representatives in Congress, he creates doubt about what the rule of law means in our Nation.

—Senator Patrick Leahy (D., Vermont), 2006

### Document 2

Presidential signing statements are . . . an essential part of the constitutional dialogue between the branches that has been a part of the etiquette of government since the early days of the Republic. . . . Many constitutional signing statements are an attempt to preserve the enduring balance between co-equal branches, but this preservation does not mean that the President will not enforce the provision as enacted. . . .

[S]igning statements do not diminish congressional power, because Congress has no power to enact unconstitutional laws. . . . [Also,] the statements do not augment presidential power. Where Congress, perhaps inadvertently, exceeds its own power in violation of the Constitution, the President is bound to defer to the Constitution. The President cannot adopt the provisions he prefers and ignore those he does not; he must execute the law as the Constitution requires. . . .

These statements are an established part of the President's responsibility to "take Care that the Laws be faithfully executed." Members of Congress and the President will occasionally disagree on a constitutional question. This disagreement does not relieve the President of the obligation to interpret and uphold the Constitution, but instead supports the candid public announcement of the President's views.

—Michelle E. Boardman,
Deputy Assistant Attorney General, 2006

---

**Use your knowledge of the controversy surrounding signing statements and Documents 1 and 2 to answer Questions 1–3.**

1. How does each commentator cite the Constitution to his or her benefit?
   A. Both speakers claim signing statements are unconstitutional.
   B. Each speaker believes the Constitution supports signing statements.
   C. Each speaker uses it to defend his or her stance on the issue.
   D. Both take the Constitution out of context.

2. Why do you think a President would choose to approve a law with a signing statement attached rather than vetoing the measure?

3. **Pull It Together** Do you think the use of signing statements follows the Framers' intention in Article II of the Constitution?

**GOVERNMENT ONLINE**
**Documents**
To find more primary sources on signing statements, visit
**PearsonSchool.com/phgovt**

---

## DOCUMENT-BASED ASSESSMENT

1. C

2. Sample answer: A veto rejects the entire law, including the provisions the President wants. A signing statement can function like a line-item veto, using interpretation to void provisions the President doesn't like. Signing statements are also a way to get around a hostile Congress. Instead of negotiating with Congress to settle their disagreements, the President simply uses a signing statement to refuse to enforce parts of the law or to enforce it in ways that were not intended by Congress.

3. Sample answer: No. The Framers intended Presidents to veto laws in which they saw problems, sending these laws back to Congress to address the concerns. Signing statements sidestep this reconsideration process, which is an essential part of checks and balances. Also, the constitutionality of a law is a matter for the courts to decide—not the President.

**L2 Differentiate** Students use all the documents on the page to support their thesis

**L3 Differentiate** Students include additional information available online at **PearsonSchool .com/phgovt.**

**L4 Differentiate** Students use materials from the textbook, the online information at **PearsonSchool .com/phgovt,** and do additional research to support their views.

**Go Online to PearsonSchool.com/phgovt** for a student rubric and extra documents.

---

### SECTION 4

10. (a) message power and veto power
    (b) power to grant pardons and reprieves
    (c) The presidential legislative and judicial powers allow for the President's review of the actions of the other branches, and, if deemed necessary, override them.

11. (a) A veto rejects an entire bill. A line-item veto cancels some provisions in a bill while approving others. (b) Sample answer: A line-item veto would make Congress subordinate to the executive branch, allowing the President to write the law according to his or her views.

12. Sample answer: The powers are included in the Constitution to check the power of the judicial branch.

13. Essays should reflect all the steps in this chapter's section assessments and should be well-structured, with detailed arguments, a strong thesis statement, and an effective conclusion.

### APPLY WHAT YOU'VE LEARNED

14. Students' surveys should include well-documented results of the interviews of ten individuals and should be neat and comprehensive.

15. Students should actively participate in the creation of the consolidated chart and share their thoughts on the results. Their paragraphs should be well-thought out and their answers well-reasoned, showing an understanding of the issues involved in defining presidential power.

# Introduce the Chapter

## Essential Questions:

**UNIT 4**

What makes a good President?

**CHAPTER 15**

Is the bureaucracy essential to good government?

**ACTIVATE PRIOR KNOWLEDGE**

Have students examine the photo and quotation on these pages. Ask: **What do the image and quotation suggest about the role of the federal bureaucracy in American government?** *(that the federal bureaucracy is an expected part of living in a democracy and that the bureaucracy consists of many employees whose service supports the administration of government)* In this chapter, students will learn how the federal bureaucracy functions in our government. Tell students to begin to further explore the role of the federal bureaucracy by completing the Chapter 15 Essential Question Warmup Activity in their **Essential Questions Journal.** Discuss their responses as a class.

**BEFORE READING**

**L2** **ELL Differentiate** Chapter 15 Prereading and Vocabulary Worksheet (Unit 4 All-in-One, p. 124)

**SUCCESSNET STUDENT AND TEACHER CENTER**

Visit **PearsonSchool.com/phgovt** for downloadable resources that allow students and teachers to connect with government "on the go."

**DIGITAL LESSON PRESENTATION**

The digital lesson presentation supports the print lesson with activities and summaries of key concepts.

## SKILLS DEVELOPMENT

**DECISION MAKING**

You may wish to teach decision making as a distinct skill within Section 4 of this chapter. Use the Chapter 15 Skills Worksheet (Unit 4 All-in-One, p. 160) to help students learn how to make decisions. The worksheet asks students to read information about the draft and to decide whether the draft should be reinstated. For L2 and L1 students, assign the adapted Skill Activity (Unit 4 All-in-One, p. 161).

**WebQuest online** The chapter WebQuest challenges students to answer the chapter Essential Question by asking them about the bureaucracy.

424

## Block Scheduling

**BLOCK 1:** Teach the Section 1 and Section 2 lessons, omitting the Section 1 Describe a Bureaucracy activity and the Section 2 Extend options.

**BLOCK 2:** Teach the Section 3 and Section 4 lessons, omitting the political cartoon mini-lessons and the Section 3 Extend options.

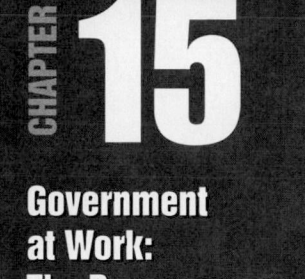

## CHAPTER 15
# Government at Work: The Bureaucracy

### Essential Question
Is the bureaucracy essential to good government?

**GOVERNMENT** ONLINE
On the Go

To study anywhere, anytime, download these online resources at PearsonSchool.com/phgovt
• Political Dictionary
• Audio Review
• Downloadable Interactivities

425

## Lesson Goals

### SECTION 1
Students will…

• define a bureaucracy using the existing structure of their school.

• illustrate the bureaucratic structure using a specific organization they have chosen.

• determine the federal agency and its hierarchical level responsible for a specific activity using scenarios.

### SECTION 2
Students will…

• understand the importance of advisors by imagining themselves as President and choosing areas of expertise for their advisors.

• summarize features and functions of three agencies within the Executive Office of the President by using a Jigsaw activity.

### SECTION 3
Students will…

• list the top five services they think the Federal Government provides American citizens.

• work in pairs/groups to generate a list of the qualifications the President should take into consideration when nominating a specific Cabinet-level department head.

### SECTION 4
Students will…

• understand the need for regulatory agencies by reading an excerpt from *The Jungle*.

• compare types of independent agencies using a Venn diagram.

• research job opportunities within the civil service using information from the Office of Personnel Management.

## Pressed for Time

Review the features of a bureaucracy and the major elements of the federal bureaucracy. Then divide the class into six groups and assign them one of these topics: Executive Office of the President, the Cabinet departments, independent executive agencies, independent regulatory commissions, government corporations, and the civil service. Groups should create a concept web or summary capturing the main ideas of their assigned topic. Using the Jigsaw strategy (p. T27), place one member of each group into a new group, so the class is organized with one representative for each topic. Students should share their expertise on their topic with the group.

**FOLLOW UP** Have students brainstorm a list of the benefits and drawbacks in the structure of the federal bureaucracy. Then lead a discussion on this chapter's Essential Question: **Is the bureaucracy essential to good government?**

### DIFFERENTIATED INSTRUCTION KEY

Look for these symbols to help you adjust steps in each lesson to meet your students' needs.

**L1** Special Needs

**L2** Basic

    **ELL** English Language Learners

    **LPR** Less Proficient Readers

**L3** All Students

**L4** Advanced Students

## What is the structure and purpose of the federal bureaucracy?

| Federal Bureaucracy | | |
|---|---|---|
| **Principles** | **Purpose** | **Structure** |
| • hierarchical authority<br>• job specialization<br>• formalized rules | • organizes people to work together on large and complex tasks<br>• reduces conflicts by clarifying power relationships<br>• promotes efficiency through specialization<br>• enables work to continue through changes of personnel | • Executive Office of the President<br>• 15 Cabinet departments<br>• many independent agencies |

# Get Started

### LESSON GOALS

Students will . . .

- define a bureaucracy using the existing structure of their school.

- illustrate the bureaucratic structure using a specific organization they have chosen.

- determine the federal agency and its hierarchical level responsible for a specific activity using scenarios.

## SKILLS DEVELOPMENT

### INNOVATE AND THINK CREATIVELY

Before students participate in this lesson's activity of describing how an organization could be arranged as a bureaucracy, you may want to review tips on thinking creatively in the Skills Handbook, p. S23.

---

## SECTION 1

# The **Federal Bureaucracy**

**Guiding Question**
**What is the structure and purpose of the federal bureaucracy?** Use a chart like the one below to keep track of the main ideas about the federal bureaucracy.

| Federal Bureaucracy | | |
|---|---|---|
| **Principles** | **Purpose** | **Structure** |
| • | • | • |
| • | • | • |
| • | • | • |

**Political Dictionary**
- bureaucracy
- bureaucrat
- administration
- staff agency
- line agency

**Objectives**
1. Define a bureaucracy.
2. Identify the major elements of the federal bureaucracy.
3. Explain how groups within the federal bureaucracy are named.
4. Describe the difference between a staff agency and a line agency.

The Federal Government is an immense organization. Its employees deliver the mail, regulate business practices, collect taxes, defend the nation, administer Social Security programs, manage the national forests, explore outer space, and do dozens of other things every day. Indeed, you cannot live through a single day without somehow encountering the federal bureaucracy.

## What Is a Bureaucracy?

A **bureaucracy** is a large, complex administrative structure that handles the everyday business of an organization.[1] To many Americans, the word *bureaucracy* suggests such things as waste, red tape, and delay. While that image is not altogether unfounded, it is quite lopsided. Basically, bureaucracy is an efficient and an effective way to organize people (bureaucrats) to do work.

Bureaucracies are found wherever there are large organizations, in both the public and the private sectors of this country. Thus, the United States Air Force, McDonald's, the Social Security Administration, MTV, your city government, Yahoo!, the Boy Scouts of America, and the Roman Catholic Church are all bureaucracies. Even your school is a bureaucracy.

**Three Features of a Bureaucracy** By definition, a bureaucracy is a system of organization built on three principles: hierarchical authority, job specialization, and formalized rules.

*Hierarchical authority.* The word *hierarchical* describes any organization structured as a pyramid, with a chain of command running from the top of the pyramid on down to its base. The few officials and units at the top of the structure have authority over those officials and units at the larger middle level, who in turn direct the activities of the many at the bottom level.

*Job specialization.* Each **bureaucrat,** each person who works for the organization, has certain defined duties and responsibilities. There is, then, a precise division of labor within the organization.

1 The term *bureaucracy* is a combination of the French word *bureau,* which originally referred to the desk of a government official and later to the place where an official works, and the suffix *-cracy,* signifying a type of social structure.

---

# Focus on the Basics

**FACTS:** • A bureaucracy features hierarchical authority, job specialization, and set rules. • The federal bureaucracy consists of all agencies, people, and procedures through which the government operates, and is the means by which the government makes and administers public policy. • The names given to agencies, including *commission, administration,* and *corporation,* may indicate the nature of the agency.

**CONCEPTS:** enumerated and implied powers, role of government

**ENDURING UNDERSTANDINGS:** • Although often believed to be slow and disorganized, bureaucracies are in fact an efficient and effective way to organize people to do work. • The bureaucratic structure allows the government to function properly even through changes of personnel and presidential administrations.

*Formalized rules.* The bureaucracy does its work according to a number of established regulations and procedures. Those rules are set out in written form and so can be known by all who are involved in that work.

**The Benefits of a Bureaucracy** Those three features—hierarchical authority, job specialization, and formalized rules—make bureaucracy the most effective way for people to work together on large and complex tasks, whether public or private.

The hierarchy can speed action by reducing conflicts over who has the power and the appropriate authority to make decisions. The higher a person's rank in the organization, the greater the decision-making power he or she has.

Job specialization promotes efficiency because each person in the organization is required to focus on one particular job. Each worker thus gains a set of specialized skills and knowledge.

Formalized rules mean that workers can act with some speed and precision because decisions are based on a set of known standards, not on someone's likes, dislikes, or inclinations. Those rules also enable work to continue with little interruption even as some workers leave an organization and new workers are hired to replace them.

Recognize this very important point about public bureaucracies: their bureaucrats hold appointive offices. Bureaucrats are *unelected* makers and implementers of public policy. This is not to say that bureaucracies are undemocratic. However, in a democracy much depends on how effectively the bureaucracy is controlled by those whom the people do elect—the President and Congress. Listen to James Madison on the point:

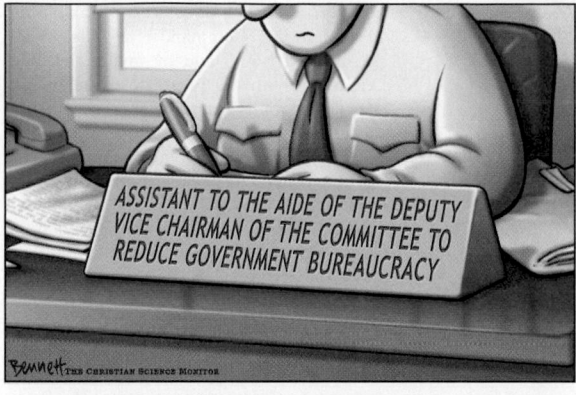

**Analyzing Political Cartoons** Although a bureaucracy may be the most effective governmental structure, the number of employees and time devoted to bureaucratic procedures are often criticized as a messy way to run the government. *How does this cartoon illustrate this point?*

## The Federal Bureaucracy

The federal bureaucracy is all of the agencies, people, and procedures through which the Federal Government operates. It is the means by which the government makes and administers public policy—the sum of all of its decisions and actions. Nearly all of that huge bureaucracy is located in the executive branch. Not all of it, however, because both Congress and the federal court system are bureaucracies, as well.

The Constitution makes the President the chief administrator of the Federal Government. Article II, Section 3 declares that "he shall take Care that the Laws be faithfully executed." But the Constitution makes only the barest mention of the administrative machinery (the bureaucracy) through which the President is to exercise that power.

Article II does suggest executive departments by giving to the President the power to "require the Opinion, in writing, of the principal Officer in each of the executive Departments."[2]

Article II anticipates two departments in particular, one for military and one for

✓ **Checkpoint**
What are the benefits of the bureaucratic structure?

**inclination**
*n.* a tendency, preference, attitude

---

2 Article II, Section 2, Clause 1. There is also a reference to "Heads of Departments" in Clause 2, and to "any Department or Officer" of the government in Article I, Section 8, Clause 18.

## Differentiated Resources

The following resources are located in the All-in-One, Unit 4, Chapter 15, Section 1:

- **L2** Prereading and Vocabulary Worksheet (p. 124)
- **L3** Reading Comprehension Worksheet (p. 128)
- **L2** Reading Comprehension Worksheet (p. 129)
- **L3** Core Worksheet (p. 130)
- **L2** Core Worksheet (p. 132)
- **L3** Quiz A (p. 133)
- **L2** Quiz B (p. 134)

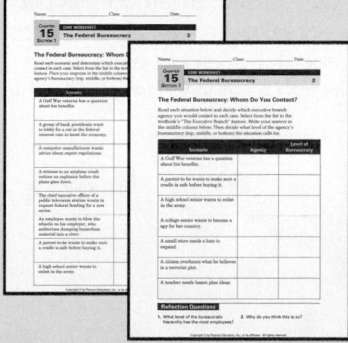

**BEFORE CLASS**

Assign the section, the graphic organizer in the text, and the Reading Comprehension Worksheet (Unit 4 All-in-One, p. 128) before class.

**L2 Differentiate** Reading Comprehension Worksheet (Unit 4 All-in-One, p. 129)

**BELLRINGER**

Write on the board: **Answer these questions in your notebook: (1) What are some departments in this school? (2) Why do you think the school is organized into different departments?**

# Teach

To present this topic using online resources, use the lesson presentations at **PearsonSchool.com/phgovt.**

**REVIEW BELLRINGER**

List students' answers to the first Bellringer question on the board. *(Common answers will probably include the Math Department, and so on.)* Then use students' answers to the second question to discuss the ways in which your school is a bureaucracy and how its structure helps (or hurts) its effective operation.

**DESCRIBE A BUREAUCRACY**

Display Transparency 15A, Federal Bureaucracy. Ask: **What is the result of bureaucracy in the cartoon?** *(U.S. food isn't distributed to the world's hungry people.)* Students should each think of a group that could be organized as a bureaucracy—such as a club or business. Using the description of the features in the textbook, the students should describe in their notebooks the hierarchical structure of their organization, what kinds of specific roles people occupy, how they are assigned, and what formal regulations govern the operation of the organization.

**L1 L2 Differentiate** Get students started by using your own classroom as the example. In this hierarchical organization, the teacher is the head of the bureaucracy. Describe for them the different specific roles that the teacher and the students have, and some of the rules that govern the operation of your classroom.

## Answers

**Analyzing Political Cartoons** The cartoon suggests that a bureaucracy seems inefficient by showing a nameplate that implies a vast number of employees are working to combat the size of government.

**Checkpoint** Action can be faster because the hierarchy clarifies decision-making power, and formalized rules base decisions on known standards. Job specialization enables each worker to gain specialized skills and knowledge.

## PAIR AND SHARE

Once students have completed their descriptions, divide them into pairs and have them exchange notebooks. Each student should read through his or her partner's bureaucratic description. Make sure to give them time to ask questions about the structure and purpose of the bureaucracy. Then call on a few students to explain to the class how their partner's bureaucratic structure benefits the organization in question. Ask students to think about whether all types of organizations benefit from bureaucratic structure, and why or why not.

## DISTRIBUTE CORE WORKSHEET

Hand out the Chapter 15 Section 1 Core Worksheet (Unit 4 All-in-One, p. 130), which uses scenarios to help students understand the federal bureaucracy. Explain that students will identify which units of the federal bureaucracy are responsible for different types of activities as well as determine what level of the bureaucracy should be contacted by the merits of each scenario. Have the students complete the table and the reflection question.

**L2 Differentiate** Distribute the adapted Chapter 15 Section 1 Core Worksheet (Unit 4 All-in-One, p. 132).

## REVIEW CORE WORKSHEET

Once students have completed their worksheets, have volunteers share their answers and explain their reasoning. If students disagree on what agency or level is responsible, have them discuss their analysis. Advise them that it might be possible that there could be multiple answers in some cases.

## Answers

**Checkpoint** Executive Office of the President, 15 Cabinet departments, many independent agencies

**428** Government at Work: The Bureaucracy

---

checkpoint**✔ Checkpoint**
What three main groups make up the executive branch?

foreign affairs. It does so by making the President the "Commander in Chief of the Army and Navy," and by giving the chief executive both the power to make treaties and to appoint "Ambassadors, other public Ministers, and Consuls."[3]

Beyond those references, the Constitution is silent on the organization of the executive branch. The Framers certainly intended that administrative agencies be created, however. They understood that no matter how wise the President and Congress, their decisions still had to be carried out in order to be effective. Without an **administration**—the government's many administrators and agencies—even the best policies would amount to just so many words and phrases. The President and Congress need millions of men and women to put policies into action in Washington, D.C., and in offices all around the country and the world.

The chief organizational feature of the federal bureaucracy is its division into areas of specialization. As you can see on the next page, the executive branch is composed of three broad groups of agencies: (1) the Executive Office of the President, (2) the 15 Cabinet departments, and (3) a large number of independent agencies.[4]

### The Name Game

The titles given to the many units that make up the executive branch vary a great deal. The name *department* is reserved for agencies of Cabinet rank. Beyond the title of *department,* however, there is little standardized use of titles among the agencies.

The most commonly used titles for units in the executive branch include *agency, administration, commission, corporation, authority, bureau, service, office, branch,* and *division.*

The term *agency* is often used to refer to any governmental body. It is sometimes used to identify a major unit headed by

**uniformity**
*n.* sameness, regularity

**standardize**
*v.* to set up according to a rule or model

a single administrator of near-cabinet status, such as the Environmental Protection Agency. But so, too, is the title *administration;* for example, the National Aeronautics and Space Administration and the General Services Administration.

The name *commission* is usually given to agencies charged with the regulation of business activities, such as the Federal Communications Commission and the Securities and Exchange Commission. Top-ranking officers called commissioners head these units. The same title, however, is given to some investigative, advisory, and reporting bodies, including the U.S. Commission on Civil Rights and the Federal Election Commission.

Either *corporation* or *authority* is the title most often given to those agencies that conduct businesslike activities. Corporations and authorities are regularly headed by a board and a manager—as is the case with the Federal Deposit Insurance Corporation, the Commodity Credit Corporation, and the Tennessee Valley Authority.

Within each major agency, the same confusing lack of uniformity in the use of names is common. *Bureau* is the name often given to the major elements in a department, but *service, administration, office, branch,* and *division* are often used for the same purpose. For example, the major units within the Department of Justice include the Federal Bureau of Investigation, the United States Marshals Service, the Drug Enforcement Administration, the Office of the Pardon Attorney, the Criminal Division, and the National Drug Intelligence Center.

Many federal agencies are often referred to by their initials. The EPA, IRS, FBI, CIA, FCC, NASA, and TVA are but a few of the dozens of familiar examples we hear and read about every day.[5] A few are also known by nicknames. For example, the Government National Mortgage Association is often called "Ginnie Mae," and the National Railroad Passenger Corporation is better known to us as Amtrak.

---

3  Article II, Section 2, Clauses 1 and 2.

4  The chart is adapted from the current edition of the *United States Government Manual,* published each year by the Office of the Federal Register in the National Archives and Records Administration. The Manual includes a brief description of every agency in each of the three branches of the Federal Government. More than 580 of its now nearly 700 pages are devoted to the executive branch.

5  The use of acronyms can sometimes cause problems. When the old Bureau of the Budget was reorganized in 1970, it was also renamed. It is now the Office of Management and Budget (OMB). However, it was for a time slated to be known as the Bureau of Management and Budget (BOMB).

**428** Government at Work: The Bureaucracy

---

# Myths and Misconceptions

**WASHINGTON BUREAUCRATS** You will sometimes hear people refer to the federal bureaucracy as "those people in Washington." In fact, of the approximately 3 million federal civilian employees, most of whom work for executive branch agencies, only about 15 percent work in the District of Columbia. Every major city in the country is home to at least some "Washington bureaucrats."

# The Executive Branch

**GOVERNMENT** ONLINE

For an **interactive** exploration of several agencies in the executive branch, visit

PearsonSchool.com/phgovt

INTERACTIVE

The executive branch of the Federal Government is composed of a large number of agencies, all of them created by act of Congress to execute the laws of the United States. Nearly 90 percent of all of the men and women who work for those agencies in fact work some place other than Washington, D.C. *Why do you think the executive branch makes up the majority of the federal bureaucracy?*

## INDEPENDENT
### Agencies*

These agencies are not attached to any of the Cabinet departments and exercise a wide range of responsibilities.

- Amtrak
- Central Intelligence Agency
- Consumer Financial Protection Bureau
- Consumer Product Safety Commission
- Environmental Protection Agency
- Equal Employment Opportunity Commission
- Farm Credit Administration
- Federal Communications Commission
- Federal Deposit Insurance Corporation
- Federal Election Commission
- Federal Reserve System
- Federal Trade Commission
- National Aeronautics and Space Administration
- National Endowment for the Arts
- National Labor Relations Board
- National Science Foundation
- National Transportation Safety Board
- Nuclear Regulatory Commission
- Office of Government Ethics
- Office of Personnel Management
- Peace Corps
- Securities and Exchange Commission
- Small Business Administration
- Social Security Administration
- Tennessee Valley Authority
- United States Postal Service

## EXECUTIVE OFFICE
### of the President

The Executive Office of the President is an umbrella agency composed of several sub-agencies staffed by the President's closest advisors and assistants.

- The White House
- Office of the Vice President
- Council of Economic Advisers
- Council on Environmental Quality
- National Security Council
- Office of Administration
- Office of Management and Budget
- Office of National Drug Control Policy
- Office of Science and Technology Policy
- Office of the United States Trade Representative

## EXECUTIVE
### Departments

Often called the Cabinet departments, the executive departments and their subunits carry out much of the work of the Federal Government.

- Department of State
- Department of the Treasury
- Department of Defense
- Department of Justice
- Department of the Interior
- Department of Agriculture
- Department of Commerce
- Department of Labor
- Department of Health and Human Services
- Department of Housing and Urban Development
- Department of Transportation
- Department of Energy
- Department of Education
- Department of Veterans Affairs
- Department of Homeland Security

*The agencies listed are just a sampling of the more than 150 independent agencies.

429

## Background Note

**BUREAUCRATIC RED TAPE** Historically, early bureaucrats in Europe used red cloth ribbons, commonly called "red tape," to hold together official records and documents. These actual red ribbons are the origin of the phrase "red tape" used to describe the delays and excessive paperwork that many people associate with bureaucratic organizations. Elected officials will often say that they plan on "cutting through the red tape" when they are promising greater speed and efficiency in government action.

**L1 L2 Differentiate** Pair lower-level and higher-level students to work together to complete their worksheet.

**L4 Differentiate** To challenge higher-level students, have them determine whether the agencies listed in the middle column of their worksheet function as a staff or line agency.

Tell students to go to the Interactivity to learn more about the executive branch agencies.

### EXTEND THE LESSON

**L3 Differentiate** Assign each student one executive branch agency from the chart in the textbook, and have them research that agency, either in the library or online. Tell them that they should be looking for the agency's main functions, the name of the chief administrator, the number of employees, the year it was founded, and whether it is a staff or line agency. Once they have completed their research, divide them into groups of four or five. Each student should share the results of his or her research with the group, and the members of the group should work together to create a table listing all of their agencies and the relevant facts about them.

**L4 Differentiate** Have students select an executive department and research the agencies that are subunits of the department they selected. Then, have them create an organization chart that illustrates the hierarchical structure of that executive department.

## Assess and Remediate

**L3** Collect the Core Worksheets and assess the students' work.

**L3** Assign the Section 1 Assessment questions.

**L3** Section Quiz A (Unit 4 All-in-One, p. 133)

**L2** Section Quiz B (Unit 4 All-in-One, p. 134)

Have students complete the review activities in the digital lesson presentation and continue their work in the **Essential Questions Journal.**

## Answers

**The Executive Branch** because a vast number of offices and personnel are required to execute and administer public policy

| If Your Students Have Trouble With | Strategies For Remediation |
|---|---|
| Describing the purpose and structure of the federal bureaucracy (Question 1) | Make a concept web on the board that illustrates the organization of the federal bureaucracy. |
| Defining the features of bureaucracy (Questions 2, 5, 6) | Have students make an illustration depicting each feature of a bureaucracy. |
| Identifying the names of government units (Question 3) | With students, create a chart on the board using this section's Name Game, describing each and how they can at times overlap. |
| Contrasting staff and line agencies (Question 4) | Have students review the graphic organizer in this chapter's Quick Study Guide. |

**Government** online
*All print resources are available on the Teacher's Resource Library CD-ROM and online at PearsonSchool.com/phgovt.*

## Answers

**Checkpoint** A staff agency offers advice or other support to the administrators. A line agency performs the tasks for which the organization exists.

---

✓ **Checkpoint**
How do staff agencies differ from line agencies?

## Staff and Line Agencies

The units that make up any administrative organization can be classified as either staff or line agencies. The Federal Government units are also described as such.

**Staff agencies** serve in a support capacity. They aid the chief executive and other administrators by offering advice and assistance in the management of the organization. **Line agencies,** on the other hand, actually perform the tasks for which the organization exists.

Congress and the President give the line agencies goals to meet, and the staff agencies help the line agencies meet these goals as effectively as possible through advising, budgeting, purchasing, management, and planning. The general public is much more aware of the work of line agencies than it is of that of most of the staff units. It is for a rather obvious reason: it is the line agencies that carry out public policies and, in doing so, deal directly with the public.

**distinction**
*n.* a difference between two or more things

Two illustrations of the <u>distinction</u> here can be found in the several agencies that make up the Executive Office of the President and, in contrast, the Environmental Protection Agency. The agencies that make up the Executive Office of the President (The White House, the National Security Council, the Office of Management and Budget, the Office of Policy Development, and others, as you will see in the next section) each exist as staff support to the President. Their primary mission is to assist the President in the exercise of the executive power and in the overall management of the executive branch. They are not operating agencies. That is, they do not actually administer public programs.

The Environmental Protection Agency (EPA), on the other hand, has an altogether different mission. It is responsible for the day-to-day enforcement of the many antipollution laws Congress has enacted over the years. The EPA operates "on the line," where the action is.

This difference between staff agencies and line agencies can help you find your way through the complex federal bureaucracy. The distinction between the two can be oversimplified, however. For example, most line agencies do have staff units to aid them in their line operations. Thus, the Environmental Protection Agency's Office of Civil Rights is a staff unit. Its job is to ensure that the agency's hiring and other personnel practices do not violate the Federal Government's antidiscrimination policies.

---

## SECTION 1 ASSESSMENT

**Essential Questions Journal**
To continue to build a response to the chapter Essential Question, go to your **Essential Questions Journal.**

1. **Guiding Question** Use your completed chart to answer this question: What is the structure and purpose of the federal bureaucracy?

**Key Terms and Comprehension**

2. Describe the three defining features of a **bureaucracy.**

3. List some of the more common names given to the various agencies in the executive branch.

4. What is the key difference between a **staff agency** and a **line agency?**

**Critical Thinking**

5. **Analyze Information** Explain how the defining features of a bureaucracy both help and hurt the effectiveness and efficiency of the Federal Government.

6. **Categorize** Think of a bureaucracy that you encounter or work with on a regular basis, and describe each of the three major features of bureaucracies in that organization.

7. **Express Problems Clearly** The bureaucrats who carry out government policy are appointed, not elected. Does this mean that bureaucracies are, therefore, undemocratic? Why or why not?

**Quick Write**

**Research Writing: Ask Questions** The numerous agencies that make up the federal bureaucracy administer public policy in a variety of fields. Think about subjects that you are interested in, for example, the economy, environment, defense, farming, transportation, or communication. Select the topic that interests you most. Then, write three questions that you would like to answer about the subject you selected as it relates to the Federal Government.

---

# Assessment Answers

**1.** The federal bureaucracy is all of the agencies, employees, and procedures through which the Federal Government operates. It is structured using hierarchical authority, job specialization, and formal rules. It is composed of the Executive Office of the President, 15 Cabinet departments, and many independent agencies. It organizes people to work on large, complex tasks.

**2. hierarchical authority:** pyramid-shaped, with a chain of command and each unit answering to a unit above it; **job specialization:** each person has a specific set of responsibili-

ties; **formalized rules:** written work regulations and procedures

**3. department:** Cabinet-level agency; **agency** or **administration:** often a major unit headed by single administrator of near-cabinet rank; **commission:** regulates business; **corporation** or **authority:** conducts business-like activities

**4. staff agency:** offers advice or other support to the administrators; **line agency:** performs the tasks for which the organization exists.

**5.** Bureaucracy helps by allowing many people to work efficiently on complex projects. It hurts

when there are too many levels or procedures that slow down the governing process.

**6.** Answers should include a description of the organization's hierarchy, job specialization, and rules.

**7.** Elected officials answer to the public but serve fixed terms in office. Appointed bureaucrats answer to elected officials, but they can be appointed or dismissed anytime.

**QUICK WRITE** Questions should relate to students' topics and to Federal Government involvement.

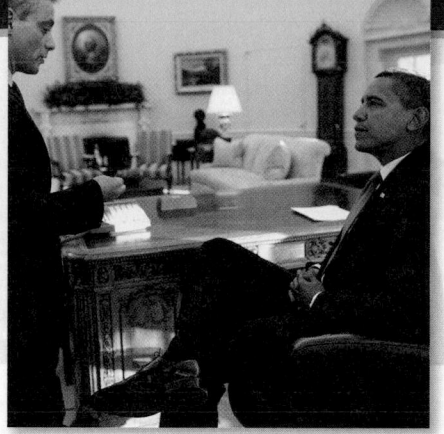

# SECTION 2

# Executive Office
## of the President

**Guiding Question**
What agencies and advisors are part of the Executive Office of the President and what are their functions? Use a table like the one below to keep track of those units and their functions within the Executive Office of the President.

| Executive Office of the President | |
| --- | --- |
| Agency | Function |
| • | • |
| • | • |
| • | • |

**Political Dictionary**
- Executive Office of the President
- federal budget
- fiscal year
- domestic affairs

**Objectives**
1. Describe the Executive Office of the President.
2. Explain the duties of The White House, the National Security Council, and the Office of Management and Budget.
3. Identify the other agencies that make up the Executive Office of the President.

**Image Above:** President Barack Obama meets with his chief of staff Rahm Emanuel.

Thomas Jefferson performed his presidential duties with the help of two aides, one a messenger and the other his secretary. Like other early Presidents, he paid their salaries out of his own pocket. Indeed, Congress did not provide any money for presidential staff until 1857, when it gave President James Buchanan $2,500 for one clerk.

President Jefferson presided over an executive branch that employed, altogether, only some 2,100 people. The situation is remarkably different today. Approximately 2.7 million men and women work in the Obama administration. Two institutions—the Executive Office of the President and the President's Cabinet—are at the center of today's huge executive branch.

## The Executive Office of the President

Every officer, every employee, and every agency in the executive branch of the Federal Government is legally subordinate to the President. They all exist to help the President—the chief executive—in the exercise of the executive power.

The President's right arm, however, is the **Executive Office of the President** (the EOP). The Executive Office of the President is, in fact, an umbrella agency, a complex organization of several separate agencies staffed by some 900 of the President's closest advisors and assistants.

President Franklin Roosevelt persuaded Congress to establish the EOP in 1939. It has been reorganized in every administration since then, including the Obama Administration.

## The White House

The EOP's nerve center—in fact, the nerve center of the entire executive branch—is an agency now called The White House. Most of the President's key personal and political aides work there.

The two wings on either side of the White House hold the offices of most of the President's staff. These presidential assistants occupy much of the crowded West Wing, which the public seldom sees and where the legendary Oval Office and the Cabinet Room are located.

**GUIDING QUESTION**

What agencies and advisors are part of the Executive Office of the President and what are their functions?

| Executive Office of the President | |
| --- | --- |
| Agency | Function |
| • White House Office | • President's inner circle; advises on foreign policy, defense, homeland security, the economy, and other areas |
| • National Security Council | • advises President on domestic, foreign, and military matters related to national security |
| • Office of Management and Budget | • prepares federal budget; monitors spending; keeps President up to date on work of all agencies |
| • Office of National Drug Control Policy | • prepares national drug control strategy; coordinates war on drugs |
| • Council of Economic Advisors | • advises on state of nation's economy; helps prepare annual Economic Report |
| • Office of Policy Development | • advises on domestic affairs |
| • Council on Environmental Quality | • advises on environmental policy and in writing annual state of the environment report |
| • Office of the Vice President | • supports duties of Vice President |
| • Office of United States Trade Representatives | • advises on foreign trade; represents President in foreign trade negotiations |
| • Office of Science and Technology Policy | • advises on scientific, engineering, and other technological matters related to national policies and programs |

## SKILLS DEVELOPMENT

**ANALYZE SOURCES**

The Extend Activity in this section asks students to do research using television, radio, or print sources about the executive department. Have students turn to the Skills Handbook, p. S14, to learn how to analyze sources.

# Focus on the Basics

**FACTS:** • The Executive Office of the President is a complex organization of separate agencies staffed by the President's closest advisors and assistants. • The White House Office is the nerve center of the EOP and of the entire executive branch. • The agencies of the EOP, including the National Security Council and the Office of Management and Budget, make sure the President's policies are being carried out in areas such as trade, the environment, legislation, and foreign and domestic affairs.

**CONCEPTS:** checks and balances, role of government

**ENDURING UNDERSTANDINGS:** • The Executive Office of the President is composed of the President's closest advisors and several support agencies. • The EOP is the President's right arm in the formation and execution of the nation's public policies.

# Get Started

## LESSON GOALS

Students will . . .

- understand the importance of advisors by imagining themselves as President and choosing areas of expertise for their advisors.
- summarize features and functions of three agencies within the Executive Office of the President by using a Jigsaw activity.

## BEFORE CLASS

Assign the section, the graphic organizer in the text, and the Reading Comprehension Worksheet (Unit 4 All-in-One, p. 135) before class.

**L2** **Differentiate** Reading Comprehension Worksheet (Unit 4 All-in-One, p. 136)

## BELLRINGER

Write on the board: **The President's advisors help plan policy in different areas. If you were President, what areas of expertise would you like your advisors to have? Answer in your notebook.**

# Teach

To present this topic using online resources, use the lesson presentations at **PearsonSchool.com/phgovt**.

## REVIEW BELLRINGER

Ask volunteers to read their list of advisors' areas of expertise. Have them discuss why they chose those particular kinds of expertise.

## EXECUTIVE AGENCIES JIGSAW

Conduct a Jigsaw activity (p. T27) on the agencies of the executive branch. Divide students into three groups. Distribute the Chapter 15 Section 2 Core Worksheet (Unit 4 All-in-One, p. 137) and assign each group either the White House Office, National Security Council, or Office of Management and Budget. Have groups use the information in the chapter to complete their worksheet and answer the discussion questions related to their agency.

---

## Answers

**Checkpoint** The chief of staff directs the EOP operations and is among the most influential presidential aides.

**The West Wing** Such close proximity allows the President quick access to the information and advice of the key advisors.

---

✔ **Checkpoint**
What is the role of the chief of staff of The White House?

**inner circle**
*n.* those most influential, closest to the center of power

The White House chief of staff to the President directs all of the operations of the EOP and is among the most influential presidential aides. The counselor to the President and a number of senior advisors are also key members of the President's <u>inner circle.</u>

Several top officials work in The White House. A number of assistants and deputy assistants to the President aid the chief executive in such vital areas as foreign policy, defense, homeland security, the economy, political affairs, congressional relations, speech writing, and contacts with the news media and the public.

The staff of The White House also includes such major presidential aides as the press secretary, the appointments and scheduling assistant, and the President's physician. The first lady's very visible place in public life today is reflected by the fact that one of the assistants to the President serves as her chief of staff and one of the several deputy assistants is her press secretary.

Some 500 men and women now serve in The White House. The titles of some of the subunits they work for indicate the scope of their responsibilities: the Office of Energy and Climate Change Policy, the Office of Political Affairs, the Office of the First Lady, the Office of Cabinet Affairs, and the Office of Public Engagement and Intergovernmental Affairs.

## National Security Council

Most of the President's major steps in foreign affairs are taken in close consultation with the National Security Council (NSC). It meets at the President's call, often on short notice, to advise him in all domestic, foreign, and military matters that relate to the nation's security.

The President chairs the Council. Its other members include the Vice President and the secretaries of state, treasury, and defense. The Director of National Intelligence and the chairman of the Joint Chiefs of Staff regularly attend its meetings.

The NSC has a small staff of foreign and military policy experts. They work under the direction of the President's national security advisor. The government's several intelligence agencies do much of their often super-secret work at the direction of the National Security Council.

The National Security Council is a staff agency. That is, its job is to advise the

### The West Wing

The White House is a vast structure that includes two office buildings and the President's residence. The East and West wings extend from the residence and host key presidential aides and advisors. The President's closest assistants are located in the West Wing only steps away from the Oval Office. *Why is it important that these advisors be so close at hand?*

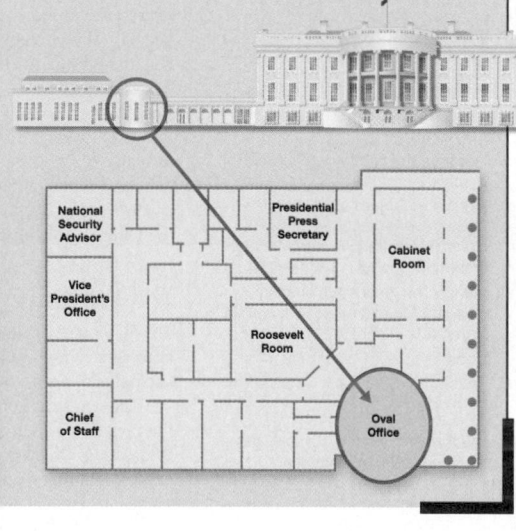

# Differentiated Resources

The following resources are located in the All-in-One, Unit 4, Chapter 15, Section 2:

- **L3** Reading Comprehension Worksheet (p. 135)
- **L2** Reading Comprehension Worksheet (p. 136)
- **L3** Core Worksheet (p. 137)
- **L3** Quiz A (p. 139)
- **L2** Quiz B (p. 140)

President in all matters affecting the nation's security. However, during the Reagan administration in the 1980s, the NSC's staff actually conducted a number of secret operations, including the sale of arms to Iran. The disclosure of the NSC's role in this sale led to the Iran-Contra scandal of the mid-1980s.

## Office of Management and Budget

The Office of Management and Budget (OMB) is the largest and, after The White House, the most influential unit in the Executive Office. The OMB is headed by a director who is appointed by the President and confirmed by the Senate. The OMB's major task is the preparation of the federal budget, which the President must submit to Congress every year.

The **federal budget** is a very detailed estimate of receipts and expenditures, an anticipation of federal income and outgo, during the next fiscal year. A **fiscal year** is the 12-month period used by government and business for record keeping, budgeting, and other financial management purposes. The Federal Government's fiscal year runs from October 1 through September 30.

The budget is more than just a financial document. It is a plan—a carefully drawn, closely detailed work plan for the conduct of government. It is an annual statement of the public policies of the United States, expressed in dollar terms.

The creation of each fiscal year's budget is a lengthy process that begins more than a year before the start of the fiscal year for which it is intended. Each federal agency prepares detailed estimates of its spending needs for that 12-month period. The OMB reviews those proposals and gives agency officials the opportunity to defend their dollar requests. Following that agency-by-agency review, the revised (and usually lowered) spending estimates are fitted into the President's overall program before it is sent to Congress. The OMB then monitors the spending of the funds Congress appropriates.

Beyond its budget chores, the OMB is a sort of presidential "handy-man" agency. It

makes continuing studies of the organization and management of the executive branch and keeps the President up to date on the work of all its agencies. The OMB checks and clears agency stands on all legislative matters to make certain they agree with the President's policy positions. It also helps prepare the hundreds of executive orders the President must issue each year and the veto messages the chief executive occasionally sends to Congress.

## Other EOP Agencies

The EOP's umbrella covers several other—and quite important—agencies. Each of those agencies provides essential staff help to the chief executive.

Chapter 15 • Section 2 **433**

---

### How Government Works

**Federal Budget**

## How is the President's budget created?

The Office of Management and Budget must consider a variety of factors before it creates the President's final budget proposals. Detailed analyses of those elements help the OMB determine the appropriate level of funding for each agency. *Which of these factors might be the most difficult to quantify?*

**What can the Government spend?**
The OMB must estimate how much income, principally from taxes, the government will receive in an upcoming fiscal year. Much of that sum must be spent for purposes and at levels previously set by Congress (mandatory spending).

**What do the People want?**
The people expect the Federal Government to maintain most existing programs. Only about 20 percent of all federal spending can be directed to expanding these programs and/or the creation of new ones (discretionary spending).

**What does the President want?**
Some spending has a higher priority in the give-and-take of the budget-making process than others—in particular, spending for those programs which are, for whatever reason, important to the President.

✔ **Checkpoint**
What are the duties of the Office of Management and Budget?

---

## How Government Works

**PREPARE A BUDGET** Have the class prepare a week's budget for a typical student. Ask: **What categories of items do you spend your money on each week?** *(clothes, movies, eating out)* Write the categories on the board. Then have the class agree on a reasonable amount they might spend for each category in a week and add them up. Then ask: **How much money do you have to spend each week?** Write an average amount on the board. If expected spending exceeds income, ask what students can do about the shortfall. *(reduce spending, increase income, or borrow)* If income exceeds expected spending, ask what they can do with the excess. *(spend more or save)* The Federal Government faces the same budget choices (see How is the President's budget created?). When revenue falls short, it can cut programs, raise taxes, or borrow. With a surplus, it can spend more or pay down the national debt.

---

Then have students form new groups comprised of one student from each previous group. Have students share the information on their agency and the results of their discussion with their new group. Tell students that each of them should be able to act as an "expert" on his or her agency and teach that material to the new group.

**L3** **L4** **Differentiate** Have the groups do research on their agency to include information in their core worksheet beyond that provided in the text. Encourage them to add more categories to the chart for additional information they find. Then conduct the peer-teaching part of the jigsaw.

**L2** **ELL** **Differentiate** Assign students who work more slowly the White House Office as the agency on which they should focus in this activity.

**L4** **Differentiate** Assign higher-level students the OMB on which to focus in this activity.

### DISCUSS

Display Transparency 15B, Agencies of the Executive Branch, which contains a blank version of the table in the Jigsaw activity. For each agency, select a student who was not an expert on that agency. Ask these students to provide the details on the agency that were "taught" to them by that agency's expert. Write the answers on the transparency and have students check the accuracy of their worksheets.

### EXTEND THE LESSON

**L1** **L2** **Differentiate** Ask students to use print or online resources to find an article about one of the executive branch agencies in the text. Have students write a short summary of the article.

**L3** **Differentiate** Ask students to use print or online resources to find an article about one of the executive branch agencies in the text. Ask them to prepare a brief oral presentation for the class based on their article. Presentations should focus on what they learned about how the agency operates and its role in the Federal Government.

**L4** **Differentiate** Have students research the career of a person who currently heads one of the executive branch agencies described in the text. Have them write a short biography, which should focus on accomplishments and qualifications for the office.

---

## Answers

**How Is the President's Budget Created?** possible response: what Americans want; predicted strength of economy

**Checkpoint** prepares federal budget, monitors spending, informs President on work of all agencies, checks agency stands on legislative matters to assure consistency with President's views, helps prepare executive orders and veto messages

# Assess and Remediate

**L3** Have students write a summary of the major activities of The White House, National Security Council, and Office of Management and Budget.

**L3** Collect the Core Worksheets and assess the students' class participation, using the Rubric for Assessing Individual Performance in a Group (Unit 4 All-in-One, p. 288).

**L3** Assign the Section 2 Assessment questions.

**L3** Section Quiz A (Unit 4 All-in-One, p. 139)

**L2** Section Quiz B (Unit 4 All-in-One, p. 140)

Have students complete the review activities in the digital lesson presentation and continue their work in the **Essential Questions Journal.**

## REMEDIATION

| If Your Students Have Trouble With | Strategies For Remediation |
|---|---|
| Identifying the EOP agencies and functions (Question 1) | Have students create an outline of the section using the red and blue heads as a structure. |
| Describing OMB responsibilities (Question 3) | Make a concept web on the board that tracks the main ideas in the section's Office of Management and Budget. |
| Understanding how the budget reflects presidential priorities (Question 4) | Review the section's How is the President's budget created? feature. |
| Examining the purpose of the EOP (Questions 2, 5, 6) | Review the Executive Branch graphic in Section 1 while leading a discussion on the purpose of the federal bureaucracy. |
| Determining how the agencies maintain the principle of checks and balances (Question 7) | Remind students about the principle and have them find references in the section that mention the legislative or judicial branch. |

## Answers

**Checkpoint** approves the President's appointments to top positions

---

**clout**
*n.* influence, power

**realm**
*n.* a particular field or area

## Office of National Drug Control Policy

The Office of National Drug Control Policy was established in 1988. It is headed by a director who is appointed by the President, with Senate approval. The Office prepares an annual national drug control strategy, which the President sends on to Congress. The director also coordinates the ongoing efforts of the more than 50 federal agencies that participate in the continuing war on drugs.

**Council of Economic Advisers** Three of the country's leading economists, chosen by the President with Senate consent, make up the Council of Economic Advisers. The Council is the chief executive's major source of information and advice on the state of the nation's economy. It also helps the President prepare the annual Economic Report to Congress, which goes to Capitol Hill in late January or early February each year.

**Other EOP Units** A number of other agencies in the Executive Office house key presidential aides. These men and women make it possible for the President to meet the many-sided responsibilities of the presidency.

The Domestic Policy Council advises the chief executive on all matters relating to the nation's **domestic affairs**—that is, all matters not directly connected to the realm of foreign affairs.

The Council on Environmental Quality aids the President in environmental policy and in writing the annual "state of the environment" report to Congress. It sees that federal agencies comply with presidential policy and the nation's environmental laws. The council's three members are appointed by the President, with the Senate's consent.

The Office of the Vice President houses the now more than fifty men and women who help the Vice President perform the duties of that office. The marked growth in the size of that staff in recent years illustrates the increase in the importance and political clout of the vice presidency.

The Office of United States Trade Representative advises the chief executive in all matters of foreign trade. The trade representative, appointed by the President and confirmed by the Senate, carries the rank of ambassador and represents the President in foreign trade negotiations.

The Office of Science and Technology Policy is the President's major advisor in all scientific, engineering, and other technological matters. Its director is drawn from the nation's scientific community.

The Office of Administration is the general housekeeping agency for all the other units in the Executive Office. It provides them with the many support services they must have in order to do their jobs.

---

**Essential Questions Journal** To continue to build a response to the chapter Essential Question, go to your **Essential Questions Journal.**

## SECTION 2 ASSESSMENT

1. **Guiding Question** Use your completed table to answer this question: What agencies and advisors are part of the Executive Office of the President and what are their functions?

### Key Terms and Comprehension

2. Which agency in the **Executive Office of the President** has the largest impact on foreign affairs?

3. Describe the major duties of the **Office of Management and Budget.**

4. How can the **federal budget** be used to advance the President's policy agenda?

### Critical Thinking

5. **Summarize** How does the White House Office help the President fulfill the role of chief administrator?

6. **Demonstrate Reasoned Judgment** Do you think that the number of agencies within the Executive Office of the President is too large, too small, or just right? Explain your answer.

7. **Draw Conclusions** Which particular agency in the executive branch do you think best illustrates the concept of checks and balances?

### Quick Write

**Research Writing: Gather Details** When writing a research report, you should include facts, examples, and other information to help support your findings. Make a list of details related to the research topic you selected in the Quick Write of Section 1. Make sure to indicate how your topic is specific to a government agency, how the agency is organized, and what its responsibilities are.

---

# Assessment Answers

1. **The White House:** advises on foreign policy, defense, homeland security, the economy; **National Security Council:** advises on domestic, foreign, and military matters related to national security; **Office of Management and Budget:** prepares federal budget, monitors spending, and informs President on work of all agencies; **Office of National Drug Control Policy:** prepares national drug control strategy and coordinates war on drugs; **Council of Economic Advisors:** advises on state of nation's economy; **Office of Policy Development:** advises on domestic affairs; **Council on Environmental Quality:** advises on environmental policy; **Office of the Vice President:** supports Vice President; **Office of United States Trade Representatives:** advises on foreign trade and negotiates trade deals; **Office of Science and Technology Policy:** advises on technological matters related to national policies and programs

2. National Security Council

3. prepares federal budget, monitors spending, and reports on work of all agencies

4. allocates funds to programs based on the President's priorities

5. includes the President's most trusted advisors, who consult on policy making

6. Answers should weigh the administrative costs of so many agencies against the benefits of bureaucratic specialization.

7. The OMB checks the legislative branch through creating the federal budget and monitoring federal spending. Some agencies are checked by the legislative branch by Senate approval on the selection of agency heads.

**QUICK WRITE** Details should relate a government agency to the student's chosen topic.

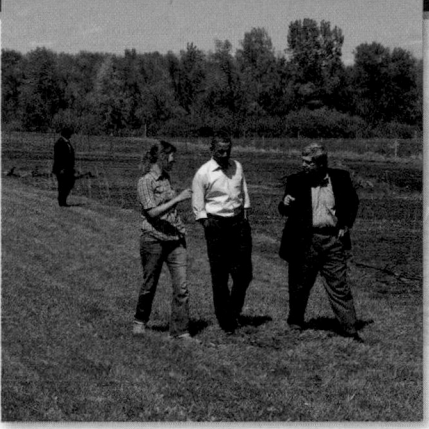

# SECTION 3

# The Cabinet Departments

## Guiding Question
**What is the Cabinet and what does it do?** Use a concept web like the one below to keep track of the supporting details about the Cabinet.

## Political Dictionary
- executive department
- civilian
- secretary
- attorney general

## Objectives
1. Describe the origin and work of the executive departments.
2. Explain how the members of the Cabinet are chosen.
3. Identify the role of the Cabinet in the President's decisions.

**Image Above:** Agriculture Secretary Tom Vilsack and President Barack Obama tour an Iowan organic farm in 2010.

In *The Federalist* No. 76, Alexander Hamilton declared that "the true test of a good government is its aptitude and tendency to produce a good administration." Given that comment, it seems strange that Hamilton and the other Framers of the Constitution spent so little time on the organization of the executive branch of the government they were creating. Instead, the machinery of federal administration has been built over time to meet the changing needs of the country.

## Executive Departments

Much of the work of the Federal Government is done by the 15 **executive departments.** Often called the Cabinet departments, they employ nearly two-thirds of the Federal Government's **civilian,** or nonmilitary, workforce. They are the traditional units of federal administration, and each of them is built around some broad field of activity.

The First Congress created three of these departments in 1789: the Departments of State, Treasury, and War. As the size and the workload of the Federal Government grew, Congress added new departments, as you can see in the chart on the next two pages. Some of the newer ones took over various duties originally assigned to older departments, and gradually assumed new functions, as well. Over time, Congress has also created and later combined or abolished some departments.

**Chief Officers and Staff** Each department is headed by a **secretary,** except for the Department of Justice, whose work is directed by the **attorney general.** As you will see, those department heads serve in the President's Cabinet. Their duties as the chief officers of their specific department take up most of their time, however.

Each department head is the primary link between presidential policy and his or her own department. Just as importantly, each of them also strives to promote and protect his or her department with the White House, with Congress and its committees, with the rest of the federal bureaucracy, and with the media and the public.

## What is the Cabinet and what does it do?

1. others as President desires: often Vice President, director of OMB, domestic policy advisor, President's counselor, chief of staff, trade representative, heads of Office of National Drug Control Policy and Environmental Protection Agency

## Get Started

### LESSON GOALS
Students will . . .
- list the top five services they think the Federal Government provides American citizens.
- work in pairs/groups to generate a list of the qualifications the President should take into consideration when nominating a specific Cabinet-level department head.

## SKILLS DEVELOPMENT

### DRAW INFERENCES AND CONCLUSIONS
To help students learn to draw inferences and conclusions, have them turn to the Skills Handbook, p. S19, and use the steps explained there to complete this lesson's Core Worksheet.

## Focus on the Basics

**FACTS:** • The federal administration has been built over time to meet the changing needs of the country. • Each executive department manages federal policy in a broad field. • The 15 executive department heads make up the President's Cabinet. • The President appoints department heads; the Senate confirms.

**CONCEPTS:** checks and balances, role of government

**ENDURING UNDERSTANDINGS:** • Although most employees of the executive departments are career civil servants, the President appoints those who will fill the top positions with Senate approval. • The Cabinet is an informal advisory body to the President; however, its influence on policies and decision making has varied from President to President.

Assign the section, the graphic organizer in the text, and the Reading Comprehension Worksheet (Unit 4 All-in-One, p. 141) before class.

**L2** **Differentiate** Reading Comprehension Worksheet (Unit 4 All-in-One, p. 142)

**BELLRINGER**

Write on the board: **What do you think are the five most important services provided to American citizens by the Federal Government? Answer in your notebook.**

# Teach

To present this topic using online resources, use the lesson presentations at **PearsonSchool.com/phgovt.**

**REVIEW BELLRINGER**

Ask students to share their answers to the Bellringer and write them on the board. Then, refer students to the "Executive Departments" diagrams in the textbook, which show the 15 executive branch departments, and have students determine which branch is responsible for the services they considered the most important. Write the answers on the board. Tell students that most of the Federal Government's work is completed by the various agencies and working groups that make up the executive departments.

**L2** **ELL Differentiate** Help students make their lists by providing them with prompts such as: Do you think healthcare for seniors is an important service? How important is national security? Should the quality of meat and vegetables be controlled? How would you rate protecting the environment?

---

## Answers

**The Executive Departments** Answers will vary, but should reflect an understanding of what areas are already under Cabinet department auspices and those that they think should be covered.

---

**How Government Works**

# The Executive Departments

Each of the now 15 executive departments was created by Congress. Their respective areas of responsibility generally reflect the conditions of the period and the major issues facing the nation when each of them was established. *What new department(s) do you think might be created in the 21st century?*

### Federalist Era

At its first session following the adoption of the Constitution, Congress established four key departments in the executive branch.

**State 1789**
- Advises the President on foreign policy
- Negotiates agreements with foreign countries
- Represents the United States abroad and in international organizations

**Treasury 1789**
- Produces coins and bills
- Borrows money and manages public debt
- Collects taxes

**Justice 1789**
- Founded as the Office of the Attorney General; renamed in 1870
- Prosecutes those accused of violating federal law
- Provides legal advice to the President
- Represents the United States in court
- Operates federal prisons

**Defense 1789**
- Founded as the National Military Establishment; renamed in 1949
- Provides military forces to deter war and protect the nation's security

### Expansion Era

As the United States expands to the west, two new departments are established to manage those lands and their use.

**Interior 1849**
- Manages public lands, wildlife refuges, and national parks
- Operates hydroelectric power plants
- Helps Native Americans manage their affairs

**Agriculture 1889**
- Assists farmers and ranchers
- Administers food stamp and school lunch programs
- Inspects food and ensures quality standards
- Manages national forests

### Industrial Era

Congress creates two new departments to address issues arising from industrialization and a growing economy.

**Commerce 1903**
- Founded as the Department of Commerce and Labor; separated in 1913
- Promotes international trade, economic growth, and technological development
- Grants patents and registers trademarks
- Conducts census

**Labor 1913**
- Enforces federal laws on minimum wages, maximum hours, and safe working conditions
- Administers unemployment insurance and workers' compensation programs

**multidimensional** *adj.* having several parts

An under secretary or deputy secretary and several assistant secretaries aid the secretary in his or her **multidimensional** role. These officials are also named by the President and confirmed by the Senate. Staff support for the secretary comes from assistants and aides with a wide range of titles in such areas as personnel, planning, legal advice, budgeting, and public relations.

**Subunits** Each department is made up of a number of subunits, both staff and line. Each of these subunits, or agencies, is usually further divided into smaller working units. Thus, the Criminal Division in the Department of Justice is composed of a number

of sections, including, for example, the Fraud Section and the Narcotic and Dangerous Drug Section. Approximately 80 percent of the men and women who head the bureaus, divisions, and other major units within each of the executive departments are career people, not political appointees.

Many of the agencies in executive departments are structured geographically. Much of their work is done through regional and/or district offices, which, in turn, direct the activities of the agency's employees in the field. In fact, nearly 90 percent of all of the men and women who work as civilian employees of the Federal Government are stationed outside the nation's capital.

---

# Differentiated Resources

The following resources are located in the All-in-One, Unit 4, Chapter 15, Section 3:

**L3** Reading Comprehension Worksheet (p. 141)
**L2** Reading Comprehension Worksheet (p. 142)
**L3** Core Worksheet (p. 143)
**L2** Extend Activities (pp. 144, 145)
**L3** Quiz A (p. 146)
**L2** Quiz B (p. 147)

## Postwar Era

Following World War II, the Cabinet expands to match the Federal Government's larger role in the nation's economy, social services, and education.

### Health and Human Services 1953
- Founded as the Department of Health, Education, and Welfare; separated and renamed in 1979
- Funds healthcare research programs
- Conducts programs to prevent and control disease
- Enforces pure foods and drug laws
- Administers Medicare and Medicaid

### Housing and Urban Development 1965
- Operates home-financing and public housing programs
- Enforces fair housing laws

### Transportation 1967
- Administers programs to promote and regulate highways, mass transit, railroads, waterways, air travel, and oil and gas pipelines
- Works with State and local levels on land, energy, resource, and technology programs

### Energy 1977
- Promotes production of renewable energy, fossil fuels, and nuclear energy
- Transmits and sells hydroelectric power
- Conducts nuclear weapons research and production

### Education 1979
- Administers federal aid to schools
- Ensures equal access to education
- Conducts educational research

### Veterans Affairs 1989
- Administers benefits, pensions, and medical programs for veterans of the armed forces
- Oversees military cemeteries

## 21st Century

The 9/11 attacks bring a new focus on national security and the newest executive department is established.

### Homeland Security 2002
- Ensures border and transportation security
- Develops emergency preparedness and response programs
- Safeguards national infrastructure and information systems

---

Take the Veterans Health Administration, part of the Department of Veterans Affairs, to illustrate the point. That administration does nearly all of its work providing medical care to eligible military veterans at some 150 medical centers, more than 800 outpatient clinics, and a large number of other facilities throughout the country.

**The Executive Departments Today** Today, the executive departments vary a great deal in terms of visibility, size, and importance. The Department of State is the oldest and the most prestigious department; but it is also among the smallest, with only some 30,000 employees. The Department of Defense is the largest, with nearly 700,000 civilian workers, and another 1.4 million men and women in the military services.

The Department of Health and Human Services has the largest budget; it accounts for just about a fourth of all federal spending each year. In contrast, the Department of Commerce has the smallest budget and contributes to less than one percent of all federal expenditures.

The Department of Homeland Security became the newest of the executive departments when Congress created it in 2002. The 15 departments, the dates they were established, and their principal functions are profiled in the chart above.

## How Government Works

**NAME THAT DEPARTMENT** To help students understand the functions of the executive departments, have them create an identification game. Ask each student to choose one department from "The Executive Departments" feature in the textbook without revealing the name. Instruct them to write a scenario that relates to the department's functions. Have students read their scenario aloud. After each reading, ask the class to identify the department that should handle the situation. Provide this example to get them started: "Ranchers near Yellowstone Park are angry that the park's wolves have killed some of their sheep." Ask: **What department should handle this situation?** *(the Department of the Interior)*

---

## DISTRIBUTE CORE WORKSHEET

Remind students that most employees of the executive departments are career civil servants, who, in many cases, have the background and education as well as years of experience in a field related to their department. The President, with Senate approval, selects those individuals who will hold high-level positions in each department. Divide the class into pairs or into groups of three, and give each pair/group the name of one executive department on which to focus. Make sure each department is covered in this exercise. Tell students that they are career employees for their department and they have been asked to provide the President with the qualifications to look for in determining the best candidate for their department head. Distribute the Chapter 15 Section 3 Core Worksheet (Unit 4 All-in-One, p. 143), which provides prompts to help them with this activity.

**L2 Differentiate** When designating executive departments, assign lower-level students to departments that may be more familiar and therefore easier to qualify, such as the Department of Defense or the Department of Education.

**L4 Differentiate** When designating executive departments, assign higher-level students to departments that may be less familiar and therefore more difficult to qualify, such as the Department of the Interior or the Department of Commerce.

**L2 ELL Differentiate** Go over the functions of the students' assigned department, using the lists in the textbook feature. Have students restate each function in their own words to check understanding.

Tell students to go to the Audio Tour to listen to a guided tour on the Cabinet departments.

---

Name _____ Class _____ Date _____

CHAPTER 15 SECTION 3 — CORE WORKSHEET
The Cabinet Departments          3

**Executive Department Head Qualifications**

You are a career employee in the executive department that your teacher has assigned to you and your partner(s). You have been asked to provide the President with the personal and professional qualifications that you feel the candidate he or she nominates should possess. Use the worksheet below to help you complete the activity.

Executive Department: _____

**Major Department Functions:**
_____
_____
_____

Title of Department Head: _____

Which qualities do you think are important for the head of your executive department?

Keep in mind the following:
- Responsibilities of the department
- Department size
- Field expertise

**Personal Qualifications:**
1. _____
2. _____
3. _____

**Professional Qualifications:**
1. _____
2. _____
3. _____

**Discussion Question**

Which qualifications seem to be common among all the recommendations?

Have volunteers read their lists of department head qualifications they created for the President. Write them on the board. Ask: **Are there any similarities among the lists of qualifications? What are the common denominators?** (personal: leadership, decision making, and managerial skills; professional: extensive experience in the department's field, respect and/or admiration by peers) Remind students that each department head is a member of the President's Cabinet, an informal advisory board. As such, the department heads provide the expert advice needed to help determine foreign and domestic policy. Ask: **Do you think the Cabinet should be the key advisors of the President? Why or why not?** (yes: because the department heads' expertise should help the President in decision making; no: because the Cabinet secretaries are too focused on their departments and the President should rely on a smaller group of close friends and advisors)

**L4 Differentiate** Have a volunteer write the qualifications on the board and categorize them by personal and professional as well as indicating those that are common among the recommendations.

## The Cabinet

The Cabinet is an informal advisory body brought together by the President to serve his needs. The Constitution makes no mention of this group of advisors, nor did Congress create it.[6] Instead, the Cabinet is the product of custom and usage.

At its first session in 1789, Congress established four top-level executive posts: secretary of state, secretary of the treasury, secretary of war, and attorney general. By his second term, President George Washington was regularly seeking the advice of the four outstanding people he had named to those offices: Thomas Jefferson (State), Alexander Hamilton (Treasury), Henry Knox (War), and Edmund Randolph (attorney general). So the Cabinet was born, and it has grown over time.

By tradition, the heads of the now 15 executive departments form the Cabinet. Each of the last several Presidents has regularly added a number of other top officials to the group, including the director of the Office of Management and Budget and the President's chief domestic policy advisor. The Vice President is a regular participant, and several other major figures usually attend Cabinet meetings—today, in particular, the counselor to the President, the White House chief of staff, the United States trade representative, the director of the Office of National Drug Control Policy, and the administrator of the Environmental Protection Agency.

**Choosing Cabinet Members** The President appoints the head of each of the 15 executive departments. Each of these appointments is subject to confirmation by the Senate, but rejections have been exceedingly rare. Of the more than 600 appointments made since 1789, only 12 have been rejected. The most recent rejection occurred in 1989, when the Senate refused to confirm President George H.W. Bush's selection of John Tower as secretary of defense.

---

6 The closest approach to it is in Article II, Section 2, Clause 1, where the President is given the power to "require the Opinion, in writing, of the principal Officer in each of the executive Departments, upon any Subject relating to the duties of their respective Offices." The Cabinet was first mentioned in an act of Congress in 1907, well over a century after its birth.

Many factors influence the President's Cabinet choices. Party is almost always important. Republican Presidents do not often pick Democrats, and vice versa. One or more of a new President's appointees invariably come from among those who played a major role in the recent presidential campaign.

Of course, professional qualifications and practical experience are also taken into account in the selection of Cabinet secretaries. Geography also plays a part. Each President tries to give some regional balance to the Cabinet. Thus, the secretary of the interior regularly comes from the West, where most of that department's wide-ranging work is carried out. The secretary of agriculture usually comes from one of the farm States in the Midwest and the secretary of housing and urban development often comes from one of the nation's major metropolitan centers.

Interest groups care about Cabinet appointments, and they influence some choices. The secretary of the treasury regularly comes out of the financial world, the secretary of commerce from the ranks of business, the secretary of education from among professional educators, the attorney general from the legal community, and so on.

Other considerations also guide the President's choices. Gender and race, management abilities and experience, and other personal characteristics—these and a host of other factors play a part in the process.

Today, a President makes Cabinet choices with an eye to racial, ethnic, and gender balance. But this has not always been the case. Thirty-one Presidents had named more than 300 Cabinet officers before Franklin Roosevelt appointed the first woman to that body: Frances T. ("Ma") Perkins, who served as secretary of labor from 1933 to 1945. In 1966, the first African American, Robert C. Weaver, was selected by Lyndon Johnson to head the Department of Housing and Urban Development. Ronald Reagan named the first Hispanic Cabinet officer, Lauro F. Cavazos, as secretary of education in 1988.

Barack Obama's Cabinet is quite diverse. It includes four women: Hillary Clinton as secretary of state, Janet Napolitano (Homeland Security), Hilda Solis (Labor), and Kathleen Sebelius (Health and Human Services).

## Answers

**Checkpoint** heads of the 15 executive departments

Attorney General Eric Holder is the first African American to hold his post.

Two Hispanics sit in the Cabinet: Labor Secretary Solis and Kenneth Salazar, who heads the Interior Department. They are joined by three Asian Americans: Steven Chu (Energy), Gary Locke (Commerce), and Eric Shinseki (Veterans Affairs). The other six Cabinet officers are white males: Shaun Donovan (Housing and Urban Development), Arne Duncan (Education), Robert Gates (Defense), Timothy Geithner (Treasury), Ray LaHood (Transportation), and Tom Vilsack (Agriculture).

Four Obama Cabinet members served in Congress, two in the Senate and two in the House, and four were governors. Energy Secretary Chu is a Nobel Prize winner, in physics in 1997; and Veterans Affairs Secretary Shinseki is a retired four-star general and former Army Chief of Staff.

Defense Secretary Gates, a registered Independent, is a holdover from the Bush Cabinet; and Transportation Secretary LaHood is a former seven-term Republican member of the House of Representatives.

**The Cabinet's Role** Cabinet members have two major responsibilities. Individually, each is the administrative head of one of the executive departments. Collectively, they are advisors to the President.

Once a central <u>cog</u> in presidential government, the overall importance of the Cabinet has declined in recent years. Through much of our history, the Cabinet was a principal source of presidential advice. It met frequently, sometimes as often as twice a week, to offer counsel to the chief executive, and its influence could be seen in virtually all areas of public policy.

The growth of other presidential resources—particularly the vast amount of staff assistance centered in the Executive Office of the President—has <u>eclipsed</u> the Cabinet's role, however. Indeed, during his presidency, John Kennedy said that he could see no need to discuss, say, Defense Department matters with his secretaries of labor and agriculture, and he found Cabinet meetings to be "a waste of time."

Still, Presidents do continue to call Cabinet meetings, though certainly not nearly

✔ **Checkpoint**
What factors are considered in the selection of executive department heads?

**cog**
*n.* part, element of an organization

**eclipse**
*v.* overshadow, surpass, outshine

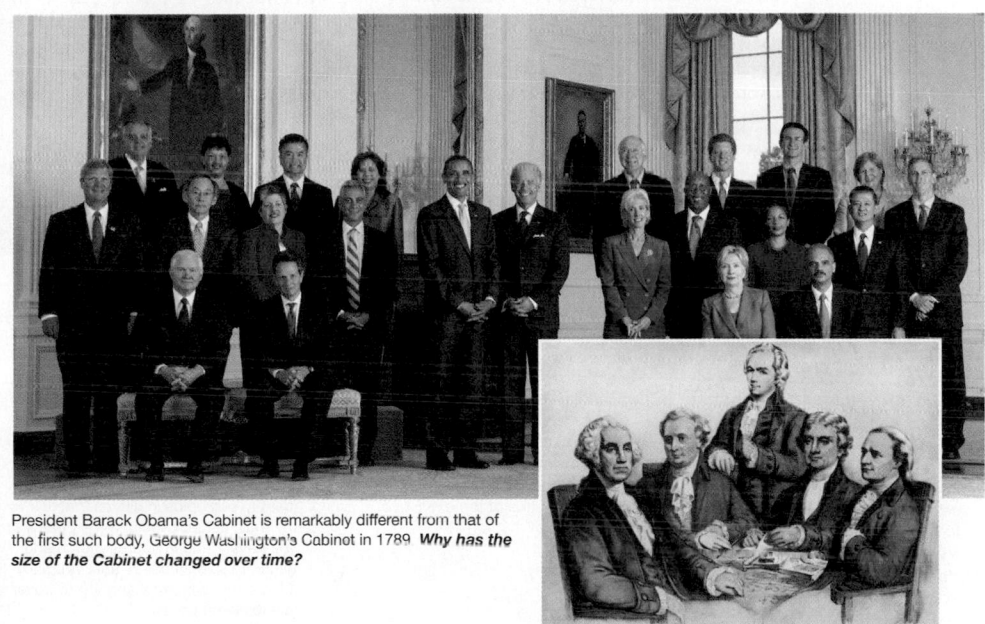

President Barack Obama's Cabinet is remarkably different from that of the first such body, George Washington's Cabinet in 1789 **Why has the size of the Cabinet changed over time?**

---

**L3 Differentiate** Have students research the Cabinet members of the current administration and select five individuals on which to do additional research. Students should look into the background of these five department heads and, in a brief paragraph for each, describe the factors that played a role in the President's nomination of each person.

**L2 ELL Differentiate** Have students research one Cabinet member of the current administration. Have them create a poster that includes the name of the department, an image of the department head, his/her title, a list of three agencies that are sub-units of the department, and a brief description of what each agency does.

**L2 Differentiate** Distribute the Extend Activities "The Executive Departments" and "The President's Cabinet in the News" (Unit 4 All-in-One, pp. 144, 145).

**L4 Differentiate** Ask students to choose a department in which they might like to work. Have them do research to identify one job in that department that appeals to them and find out the credentials they would need to qualify. Ask them to use their research to write a brief description of the job, including the job title and department, duties, and requirements. They should conclude by explaining why this job might be a good fit for their skills and interests.

## Assess and Remediate

**L3** Have each student identify three executive departments and list their primary functions.

**L3** Collect the Core Worksheets and assess students' work.

**L3** Assign the Section 3 Assessment questions.

**L3** Section Quiz A (Unit 4 All-in-One, p. 146)

**L2** Section Quiz B (Unit 4 All-in-One, p. 147)

Have students complete the review activities in the digital lesson presentation and continue their work in the **Essential Questions Journal.**

---

# Background

**LABOR RULES FOR TEENS** The Department of Labor enforces the provisions of the Fair Labor Standards Act. State laws also apply, so work rules vary from State to State. In general, nonfarm workers age 14 or 15 can work only outside school hours. They can work 3 hours on a school day and no more than 18 hours in a school week. They may work in jobs such as offices, grocery or retail stores, restaurants, amusement parks, and movie theaters. They may not work in jobs such as construction, mining, manufacturing, and warehousing. Young people age 16 to 18 can work any hours and in any jobs not declared hazardous by the Secretary of Labor. Teen work rules are designed to protect young workers from workplace hazards, ensure sufficient time for school, yet still allow them to gain skills and experience. To learn more about how the Department of Labor affects teen employment, have students visit the YouthRules! link on the DOL Web site.

---

## Answers

**Checkpoint** party, role in presidential campaign, professional qualifications, practical experience, management abilities, geography, gender, race, ethnicity

**Caption** The Cabinet has grown as the number of departments grew. Recent Presidents have included more diversity in appointments.

| If Your Students Have Trouble With | Strategies For Remediation |
|---|---|
| Describing the Cabinet and its function (Questions 1, 4) | Have students write a one- or two-sentence summary of each red and blue head in "The Cabinet" portion of this section. |
| Determining how the executive departments were established (Question 2) | Have students review this section's Executive Department graphic and lead a discussion on how the issues of the time resulted in the creation of additional Cabinet departments. |
| Summarizing the appointment process of the department heads (Questions 3, 6) | Have students reread the text on the appointment power in Chapter 14, Section 2. |
| Comparing the first and current Cabinets (Question 5) | Create a list on the board of obvious similarities and differences between the Cabinets using the photo montage in this section. |

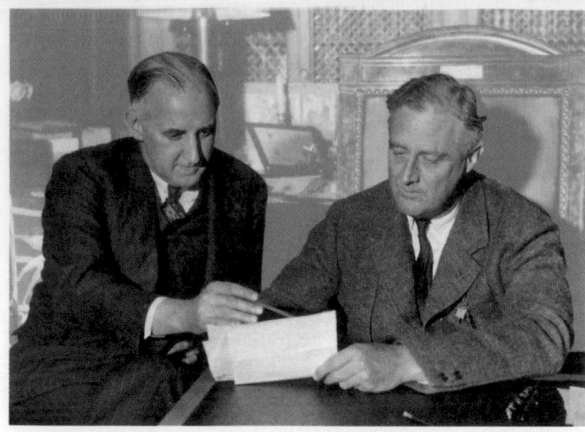

▲ President Franklin Roosevelt meets with Raymond Moley, a member of his "Brain Trust," in 1933. *Why might a President rely on the advice of people outside of the Cabinet?*

who was for it, declared: "Seven nays, one aye: the ayes have it."

William Howard Taft put the role of the President's Cabinet in its proper light nearly a century ago:

**PRIMARY SOURCE**

The Constitution . . . contains no suggestion of a meeting of all the department heads, in consultation over general governmental matters. The Cabinet is a mere creation of the President's will. . . . It exists only by custom. If the President desired to dispense with it, he could do so.

—William Howard Taft, *Our Chief Magistrate and His Powers*

as frequently as was once the case. More often than not, those sessions are held to do such things as show the administration's unified support for some particular presidential policy, rather than to thrash out the details of that matter. Cabinet members still do offer their advice—which need not be taken, of course—to the chief executive. President Abraham Lincoln once laid a proposition he favored before his seven-member Cabinet. Each member opposed it, whereupon Lincoln,

No President has ever suggested eliminating the Cabinet. However, several Presidents have leaned on other, unofficial advisory groups and sometimes depended upon them more heavily than on the Cabinet. Andrew Jackson began the practice when he became President in 1829. Several of his close friends often met with him in the kitchen at the White House and, inevitably, came to be known as the Kitchen Cabinet. Franklin Roosevelt's Brain Trust of the 1930s and Harry Truman's Cronies in the late 1940s were in the same mold.

**Essential Questions Journal** — To continue to build a response to the chapter Essential Question, go to your **Essential Questions Journal.**

## SECTION 3 ASSESSMENT

1. **Guiding Question** Use your completed concept web to answer this question: What is the Cabinet and what does it do?

**Key Terms and Comprehension**

2. How were the **executive departments** created?

3. **(a)** How are the executive department **secretaries** and **attorney general** selected? **(b)** What personal and professional factors are considered in the selection process?

4. How have various Presidents differed in their reliance on the Cabinet?

**Critical Thinking**

5. **Make Comparisons** Compare the Cabinet of today with the first Cabinet under President Washington. **(a)** How are the two alike? **(b)** How do they differ? **(c)** Why do you think the size of the Cabinet has grown since Washington's day?

6. **Synthesize Information** Why do you think it is important that the President select the heads of the executive departments?

**Quick Write**

**Research Writing: Narrow Your Topic** The Federal Government's involvement in the subject you selected in this chapter's Quick Writes can vary greatly. Create a concept web to help you narrow your topic to a more manageable focus. Write your subject in the middle circle, then identify subtopics in circles that link to the main subject. Include the details you have found in your research and generate specific ideas until you find a topic that is narrow enough to cover in a research paper.

## Answers

**Caption** Cabinet members may be selected for political reasons and be unfamiliar personally, so the President may prefer to rely on the advice of trusted and long-standing friends instead.

# Assessment Answers

**1.** The Cabinet consists of the heads of each executive department in addition to top officials that the President selects. Its function is to advise the President on matters relative to foreign and domestic policy.

**2.** over time, as needed, by Congress

**3. (a)** appointed by President with confirmation by the Senate **(b) personal:** party affiliation, relationship to the presidential campaign, race, gender, ethnicity; **professional:** practical experience, professional qualifications, management abilities

**4.** The President's reliance on the Cabinet has changed over time from regular meetings to less frequent ones. Some have felt that each department does not need to supply input on issues unrelated to their department, and, in some cases, the President has relied on a separate inner circle of advisors.

**5. (a) alike:** made up of the heads of the existing executive departments and act as advisors to the President **(b) different:** today, 15 department heads instead of 4 and diverse in race, gender, and ethnicity **(c)** Sample answer:

Departments have been added over time and the President has included other trusted advisors. Also, the President needs access to expertise in more areas than in earlier times.

**6.** sample answer: to ensure that these key people will support the President's policies and are people whose advice the President values

**QUICK WRITE** Students' concept webs should illustrate a clear connection between the subtopics and the main idea that guided them to their research topic.

# Independent Agencies

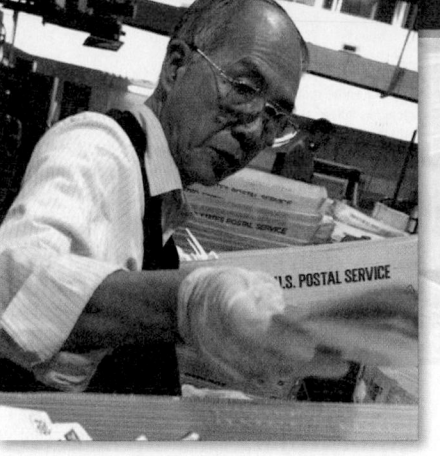

## Guiding Question

**What are the roles and structures of the independent agencies?** Use a table like the one below to keep track of the distinctions among the three categories of independent agencies.

| Federal Independent Agencies | | |
|---|---|---|
| Executive | Regulatory | Corporation |
| • | • | • |
| • | • | • |
| • | • | • |

## Political Dictionary

- independent agency
- independent executive agency
- civil service
- patronage
- spoils system
- draft
- independent regulatory commission
- government corporation

## Objectives

1. Explain why Congress has created the independent agencies.
2. Identify the characteristics of Independent executive agencies.
3. Describe the history and formation of NASA, the OPM, and the Selective Service System.
4. Explain the structure and function of the independent regulatory commissions and government corporations.

**Image Above:** A Postal Service employee sorts through the day's mail.

Until the 1880s, nearly all that the Federal Government did was done through its Cabinet departments. Since then, however, Congress has created a large number of additional agencies—the **independent agencies**—located outside the departments. Today, they number more than 150. Some of the more important ones are included in the chart on page 447.

Several independent agencies administer programs similar to those of the Cabinet departments. The work of the National Aeronautics and Space Administration (NASA), for example, is not unlike that of a number of agencies in the Department of Defense. NASA's responsibilities are also not very far removed from those of the Department of Transportation.

Neither the size of an independent agency's budget nor the number of its employees provides a good way to distinguish these agencies from the executive departments. Thus the Social Security Administration (SSA) is the largest of the independent agencies today. Only one Cabinet department, Health and Human Services, has a larger budget. The SSA now employs some 62,000 people—more than work for several Cabinet departments.

## Why Independent Agencies?

The reasons these agencies exist outside of the Cabinet departments are nearly as many as the agencies themselves. A few major reasons stand out, however. Some have been set up outside the regular departmental structure simply because they do not fit well within any of the departments. The General Services Administration (GSA) is a leading example of the point.

The GSA is the Federal Government's major housekeeping agency. Its main chores include the construction and operation of public buildings, purchase and distribution of supplies and equipment, management of real property, and a host of similar services to most other federal agencies.

Congress has given some agencies, such as the Social Security Administration, the Federal Election Commission, and the U. S. Commission on Civil Rights, an independent status to protect them from the influence of both partisan and pressure politics. But, notice, this point can be turned on its head: Congress has located some of these agencies outside any of the Cabinet departments

## Focus on the Basics

**FACTS:** • Independent agencies can be categorized as independent executive agencies, independent regulatory commissions, and government corporations. • Independence gives these agencies some freedom from political pressure. • Today, most federal employees are hired and promoted on the basis of merit.

**CONCEPTS:** checks and balances, separation of powers, role of government

**ENDURING UNDERSTANDINGS:** • Most independent agencies are executive, organized like Cabinet agencies to perform specific functions. • Regulatory commissions have the power to make, administer, and enforce rules within their field of authority.
• Government corporations are organized like private corporations, but are made up of public employees and are financed by public funds.

## What are the roles and structures of the independent agencies?

| Federal Independent Agencies | | |
|---|---|---|
| Executive | Regulatory | Corporation |
| • most non-Cabinet agencies<br>• organized like Cabinet departments<br>• executive bodies that administer programs for which they were created, such as NASA (space programs), OPM (civil service), and Selective Service System (conscription) | • not under presidential control<br>• monitor/police aspects of economy<br>• headed by board of 5–7 members appointed by President with Senate consent<br>• terms of board members are long and staggered<br>• have executive, legislative, and judicial powers | • under presidential control<br>• carry out business-like activities<br>• structured like a business<br>• run by a board of directors and general manager<br>• produce income that folds back into the business<br>• President selects top officials with Senate approval<br>• financed by public funds |

## Get Started

### LESSON GOALS

Students will . . .

- understand the need for regulatory agencies by reading an excerpt from *The Jungle*.
- compare types of independent agencies using a Venn diagram.
- research job opportunities within the civil service using information from the Office of Personnel Management.

### DECISION MAKING

To practice decision making in this section, use the Chapter 15 Skills Worksheet (Unit 4 All-in-One, p. 160). You may teach the skill explicitly either before or after discussing the Selective Service System. For L2 and L1 students, assign the adapted Skill Activity (Unit 4 All-in-One, p. 161).

Assign the section, the graphic organizer in the text, and the Reading Comprehension Worksheet (Unit 4 All-in-One, p. 148) before class.

**L2 Differentiate** Reading Comprehension Worksheet (Unit 4 All-in-One, p. 149)

## BELLRINGER

Display Transparency 15D, showing an excerpt from Upton Sinclair's *The Jungle.* Write on the board: **Could these conditions exist in a U.S. meatpacking plant today? Why or why not? Are regulatory commissions still needed? Answer in your notebook.**

**L2 ELL Differentiate** On the board, define difficult words in the excerpt: *dung* (animal droppings), *nuisance* (a thing that causes trouble), *hopper* (a funnel that, in this case, leads into a meat grinder).

# Teach

To present this topic using online resources, use the lesson presentations at **PearsonSchool.com/phgovt.**

### REVIEW BELLRINGER ANSWERS

Discuss students' answers to the Bellringer. *(Regulatory agencies make such conditions less likely to occur today. Most students will likely think that regulatory commissions still perform needed functions.)* Tell them that although *The Jungle* was written as a piece of fiction, its graphic details of the conditions within the meatpacking industry in 1906 caused great public and political outrage. In fact, the book is thought to have helped influence the creation of the Food and Drug Administration (FDA), which regulates the safety of cosmetics, blood products, and sanitation in addition to regulating food and drugs. The FDA is one of the many independent agencies that exist within the executive branch. Ask: **What are independent agencies?** *(They are government bodies that work outside the realm of the executive departments. They have been set up by Congress because they do not fit within the Cabinet departments and/or to protect them from the influence of partisan politics. There are three types of independent agencies: independent executive agencies, independent regulatory commissions, and government corporations.)*

## Answers

**Checkpoint** They are not located within any of the 15 Cabinet departments. Only a few are largely free of presidential control.

---

✔**Checkpoint**
Why are some federal agencies considered independent agencies?

**limelight**
*n.* the focus of attention

**catchall**
*n.* all-inclusive, covering a wide range of possibilities

because that is exactly where certain special interest groups want them.

Some agencies were born as independents largely by accident. In short, no thought was given to the problems of administrative confusion when they were created. Finally, some agencies are independent because of the peculiar and sensitive nature of their functions. This is especially true of the independent regulatory commissions.

The label *independent agency* is really a catchall. Most of these agencies are independent only in the sense that they are not located within any of the 15 Cabinet departments. But they are not independent of the President and the executive branch. A handful of them are independent in a much more concrete way, however. For most purposes, they do lie outside the executive branch and are largely free of presidential control.

Perhaps the best way to understand all of these many independent agencies is to divide them into three main groups: (1) the independent executive agencies, (2) the independent regulatory commissions, and (3) the government corporations.

## The Independent Executive Agencies

The **independent executive agencies** include most of the non-Cabinet agencies. Some are huge, with thousands of employees, multimillion-dollar or even multibillion-dollar budgets, and extremely important public tasks to perform.

The GSA, NASA, and the Environmental Protection Agency (EPA) are, for example, three of the largest of the independent executive agencies. They are organized much like the Cabinet departments: they are headed by a single administrator with subunits operating on a regional basis, and so on. The most important difference between these independent executive agencies and the 15 executive departments is simply in the fact that they do not have Cabinet status.

Some of these bureaucracies are not administrative or policy giants. But they do important work and they do sometimes attract public notice. The U. S. Commission on Civil Rights, the Peace Corps, the Small Business

Administration, and the National Transportation Safety Board fall into that category.

Most independent executive agencies operate far from the limelight. They have few employees, comparatively small budgets, and rarely attract any attention. The American Battle Monuments Commission, the Citizens' Stamp Advisory Committee, and the National Indian Gaming Commission are typical of the dozens of these seldom seen or heard public bodies.

Neither the scope nor the importance of the many tasks performed by a number of these independent bureaucracies can be overstated. To make the point, take a quick look at three specific examples.

**NASA** The National Aeronautics and Space Administration (NASA) was created by Congress in 1958 to handle this nation's space programs. Today, the scope of those programs is truly astounding. NASA's work ranges from basic scientific research focusing on the origin, evolution, and structure of the universe, to ongoing explorations of outer space.

The military importance of NASA's work can hardly be exaggerated. Still, Congress has directed the space agency to bend its efforts "to peaceful purposes for the benefit of all humankind," as well. Its wide-ranging research and development efforts have opened new frontiers in a great many areas: in astronomy, physics, and the environmental sciences; in communication, medicine, and weather forecasting; and many more. Many scientific advances, pioneered by NASA, have been put to productive use in the civilian realm.

In the 1980s, NASA developed the space shuttle program wherein ships were reused for regular spaceflights in an effort to conduct research more efficiently. This and other NASA programs were so successful that its spaceflights and other extraterrestrial projects became fairly routine and attracted little public notice. However, NASA's space activities were put on hold for several years following the shocking and tragic explosions of the shuttle *Challenger* in 1986 and then the shuttle *Columbia* in 2003.

For 30 years, shuttles have delivered personnel and supplies to the international

---

# Differentiated Resources

The following resources are located in the All-in-One, Unit 4, Chapter 15, Section 4:

**L3** Reading Comprehension Worksheet (p. 148)

**L2** Reading Comprehension Worksheet (p. 149)

**L3 L2** Core Worksheets (pp. 150, 155)

**L3 L2** Skills Worksheets (pp. 160, 161)

**L3 L4** Extend Worksheet (p. 162)

**L2** Extend Activity (p. 163)

**L3** Quiz A (p. 164)  **L2** Quiz B (p. 165)

**L3** Chapter Test A (p. 166)  **L2** Chapter Test B (p. 169)

# Modifying Space Innovations

Since its creation in 1958, NASA has made numerous technological advances that ensure successful space travel. Many of these innovations have been modified and are now in wide-spread public use. **Why do you think NASA has shared these innovations?**

▲ Modifying NASA's welding visors led to the production of UV protective sunglasses.

◀ NASA spacesuit technology has been adapted for public use.

▲ Lifesaving heart and other monitoring systems were originally created to observe the effects of space travel on astronauts.

▲ Spacesuit materials created to guard an astronaut against extreme temperatures now give race car drivers and the general public the same protection.

---

space station. This permanently occupied station now tops NASA's to-do list. Rotating three-member international crews have lived aboard the outpost since late 2000. By 2020, in addition to the completion of this advanced research laboratory in space, NASA plans to have more robotic missions exploring Mars and other planets in the solar system and eventually return to the moon as well.

**The Office of Personnel Management (OPM)** The Federal Government is the nation's largest employer. Nearly 2.7 million civilians now work for Uncle Sam (and, recall, another 1.4 million men and women serve in the military today). While many people tend to stereotype all civilian employees as "faceless paper pushers" they are, in fact, a quite diverse lot. Their ranks include computer programmers, forest rangers, electricians, chemists, physicists, FBI agents, security guards, engineers, librarians, truck drivers, botanists,

and men and women in literally hundreds of other occupations.

Most of the civilians who work for the Federal Government are members of the **civil service.** That is, they are career employees who were hired, and who are paid and promoted, in accord with acts of Congress administered by an independent agency, the Office of Personnel Management.

**The History of the Civil Service** For most of the first century following the adoption of the Constitution, federal employees were hired according to the **patronage** system—the practice of dispensing jobs, contracts, and other favors of government to political supporters and friends. That practice is often known, too, as the **spoils system.** The phrase comes from a comment on the floor of the Senate in 1832. Senator William Learned Marcy of New York, defending President Andrew Jackson's appointment of an

✔ **Checkpoint**
Who makes up the civil service?

**stereotype**
v. to regard or classify some persons or things in an oversimplified way

---

# Teacher-to-Teacher Network

**ALTERNATE LESSON PLAN** To save money, Congress is thinking about discontinuing an independent agency. Divide students into groups, and allow each group to select one agency mentioned in this section. Tell the students that they are the top officials in their agency. Their task is to prepare a presentation to Congress to justify their agency's continued existence. The groups will do research to learn more about the functions of their agency. Each group will prepare an oral presentation, with visuals, to describe to Congress the vital functions the agency performs for American society.

To see this lesson plan, go to

**Teacher Center**
at PearsonSchool.com/phgovt

---

## COMPARE INDEPENDENT AGENCIES

Explain that although the three types of independent agencies are distinctly different, they do have features in common. To help students compare and contrast the three types, display Transparency 15E, Independent Agencies. Each circle in this Venn diagram is labeled as one type of independent agency: executive, regulatory, or government corporation. Read the following characteristics, and have students identify where each characteristic belongs on the diagram.

A. **most common type** (executive)

B. **under President's control** (executive and government corporation)

C. **structured like a business** (government corporation)

D. **located outside Cabinet departments** (all three)

E. **exercises executive, legislative, and judicial powers** (regulatory)

F. **organized like Cabinet departments** (executive)

G. **produces income that is reinvested in the agency** (government corporation)

H. **headed by board of directors and general manager** (government corporation)

I. **monitors parts of the economy** (regulatory)

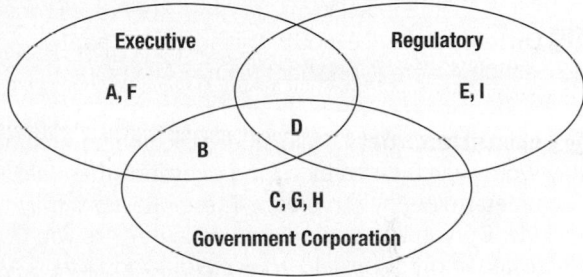

Executive — A, F
Regulatory — E, I
B
D
C, G, H
Government Corporation

**L2 ELL Differentiate** Explain that a regulation is a rule. Regulatory agencies make sure businesses follow certain rules. Point out that a corporation is a type of business. A government corporation works like a business.

**L3 Differentiate** Have students name specific agencies that belong to each category.

---

## Answers

**Modifying Space Innovations** Possible response: Part of NASA's mission is to benefit the public. Also, patents might bring in money and help justify continued funding of the space program.

**Checkpoint** most civilians who work for the Federal Government

Distribute the Chapter 15 Section 4 Core Worksheet (Unit 4 All-in-One, p. 150), which illustrates how the OPM helps prospective employees find work in the civil service. Remind students that nearly all employees of the various independent agencies, as well as the rest of the Federal Government for that matter, are members of the civil service. Most of these civil servants are career employees who found a permanent career within a specific field in the Federal Government. The OPM Web site provides an excellent tool for soon-to-be graduates to find opportunities within all aspects of the bureaucracy. Ask: **What do you think of when you think of civil service jobs?** *(Answers may include park rangers, security guards, IRS agents, or postal clerks.)* To give students a sense of the diversity of civil service jobs, refer them to the Careers in the Civil Services in this section. Then ask: **Have you ever considered a career in the civil service? Why or why not?** Have students follow the instructions on the worksheet and complete the activity and the questions provided.

If students do not have Internet access, provide the handouts included with the Core Worksheet (Unit 4 All-in-One, pp. 152–154). These handouts describe three jobs related to an interest in writing, each at a different employment level and setting within the government. Have students do additional research in the library to compile a list of government jobs that appeal to their interests.

**L2 Differentiate** Distribute the adapted Chapter 15 Section 4 Core Worksheet (Unit 4 All-in-One, p. 155).

**L2 ELL Differentiate** Help students come up with key-word search terms by asking questions that help them determine their interests. These questions may include: Do you like to work with wildlife? Are you interested in office or field work? Would you like to work in a foreign country? Are you interested in space travel?

## Answers

**Caption** Possible answer: Many Americans do not know about the variety of job opportunities in the civil service and assume that most government employees are paper-pushing bureaucrats.

**Checkpoint** Patronage spawned inefficiency and corruption. When a disappointed office-seeker assassinated President Garfield, the nation was outraged, and Congress pushed for reform.

## Careers in the Civil Service

Contrary to what many think, the civil service has a great variety of career opportunities in a wide range of fields. *With such variety in its workforce, why is working for the civil service often negatively stereotyped as paper pushing?*

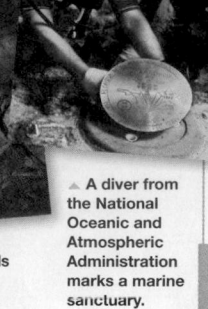

The National Zoo's chief veterinarian treats a baby panda. ▶

▲ A National Park Ranger leads visitors on a climbing tour in Mammoth Cave National Park.

▲ A diver from the National Oceanic and Atmospheric Administration marks a marine sanctuary.

**✔ Checkpoint**
Why was there a push to reform the civil service in the 1800s?

ambassador, declared: "To the victor belongs the spoils of the enemy."

Every change of administration brought a new round of patronage-based rewards and punishments. Inefficiency, even corruption, became the order of the day. Huge profits were made on public contracts, at the people's expense. Political power became centered in officeholders and others who owed their livelihoods to the party in power. Able people, in and out of government, pressed for reform, but little came of their efforts.

Unfortunately, it was a tragedy that at last brought about fundamental changes in the hiring and other staffing practices of the Federal Government. In 1881, President James Garfield was fatally shot by a disappointed office seeker, Charles J. Guiteau. Garfield had rejected the mentally unstable Guiteau's request that he be appointed to a high diplomatic post. The nation was horrified and outraged. Congress, pushed hard by Garfield's successor, Chester Arthur, passed the Pendleton Act—the Civil Service Act of 1883.

The Pendleton Act laid the foundation for the present federal civil service system. Its main purpose was to make merit—the quality of one's work—the basis for hiring, promotion, and other personnel actions in the federal workforce.

The law set up two categories of employment in the executive branch: the classified and the unclassified services. All hiring for positions in the classified service was to be based on merit. That quality was to be measured by "practical" examinations given by an independent agency, the Civil Service Commission (since 1978, the OPM).

The Pendleton Act placed only about 10 percent of the Federal Government's then 130,000 employees in the classified service; it did give the President the power to extend that coverage, however. Theodore Roosevelt championed the merit system, and by the end of his term in 1909 the classified umbrella covered two thirds of the federal workforce. Today, nearly 90 percent of all of the men and women who work for executive branch agencies are covered by the merit system.[7]

**The Civil Service Today** The first goal of civil service reform—the elimination of the spoils system—was largely achieved in the early years of the last century. Gradually, a new purpose emerged: recruiting and keeping the

7 This number does not take into account employees of the United States Postal Service and a few other federal agencies. The Postal Service is the largest agency not covered by the civil service system. It is the only federal agency in which employment policies are set by collective bargaining and labor union contracts.

## Political Cartoon Mini-Lesson

Display Transparency 15F, Government Job, to help explain why the civil service system is an improvement over the patronage system. This cartoon pokes fun at political appointees. Ask: **How did the speaker get his government job?** *(by appointment)* **What is the cartoonist saying about political appointees?** *(They don't have to work hard.)* **If the man had to get his job through the civil service system, how might his attitude toward the job change? Why?** *(Civil service jobs are based on merit. He would realize that he has to perform well, or he would be fired.)*

best available people in the federal workforce. On the whole, efforts to reach that newer goal have succeeded. Today, most federal employees are hired through a competitive process. They are paid and promoted on the basis of written evaluations by their superiors. They are generally protected from disciplinary actions or dismissal for partisan reasons.

Still, the federal civil service is not perfect. Critics often claim that not enough attention is paid to merit in the merit system. Another independent agency, the Merit Systems Protection Board, actually enforces the merit principle in the federal bureaucracy. The Board is bipartisan—that is, its five members, appointed by the President and Senate, must include members of both major political parties. It hears appeals from those federal workers who have complaints about personnel actions—for example, denials of pay increases, demotions, or firings.

**The Selective Service System** Through most of our history, the nation's armed forces have depended on voluntary enlistments to fill their ranks. From 1940 to 1973, however, the **draft**—also called conscription, or compulsory military service—was a major source of military manpower.

Conscription has a long history in this country. Several colonies and later nine States required all able-bodied males to serve in their militia. However, in the 1790s, Congress rejected proposals for national compulsory military service.

Both the North and the South did use limited conscription programs during the Civil War. It was not until 1917, however, that a national draft was first used in this country, even in wartime. More than 2.8 million of the 4.7 million men who served in World War I were drafted under the terms of the Selective Service Act of 1917.

The nation's first peacetime draft came with the Selective Training and Service Act of 1940, as World War II raged in Europe but before the United States entered the war. Eventually, more than 10 million of the 16.3 million Americans in uniform during World War II entered the service under that law.

The World War II draft ended in 1947. The crises of the postwar period, however, quickly moved Congress to revive the draft, which was reestablished by the Selective Service Act of 1948. From 1948 through 1973, nearly 5 million young men were drafted.

Mounting criticisms of compulsory military service, fed by opposition to our Vietnam policy, led many Americans to call for an end to the draft in the late 1960s. By 1972, fewer than 30,000 men were being drafted per year, and selective service was suspended in 1973. Nevertheless, the draft law is still on the books, and is administered by an independent agency, the Selective Service System.

The draft law places a military obligation on all males in the United States between the ages of 18 and 26. During the years in which the draft operated, it was largely conducted through hundreds of local selective service boards. All young men had to register for service at age 18. The local boards then selected those who were to enter the armed forces.

In 1980, President Jimmy Carter reactivated the registration requirement, and his executive order is still in force. All young males are required to sign up soon after they reach their 18th birthday. However, the President's power to order the actual <u>induction</u> of men into the armed forces expired on June 30, 1973. If the draft is ever to be reactivated, Congress must first renew that presidential authority. [8]

## Independent Regulatory Commissions

The **independent regulatory commissions** stand out among the independent agencies because they are largely beyond the reach of presidential direction and control. There are twelve of these agencies today, each created to regulate—monitor, police—important aspects of the nation's economy. Their vital statistics appear in the table on page 447.

**Structured for Independence** The independent regulatory commissions' large measure of independence from the White House comes mainly from the way in which Congress has structured them. Each is headed by a board

✔ **Checkpoint**
What agency manages the draft?

**induction** *n.* the process of installing somebody into military service

---

[8] The Supreme Court upheld the constitutionality of the draft in the *Selective Draft Law Cases* in 1918. The Court also found its all-male features constitutional in *Rostker* v. *Goldberg* in 1981.

**L4 Differentiate** Have students focus on the duties and qualifications of each position. Then have them determine what they would need to do after high school in order to become a valid candidate for the position available.

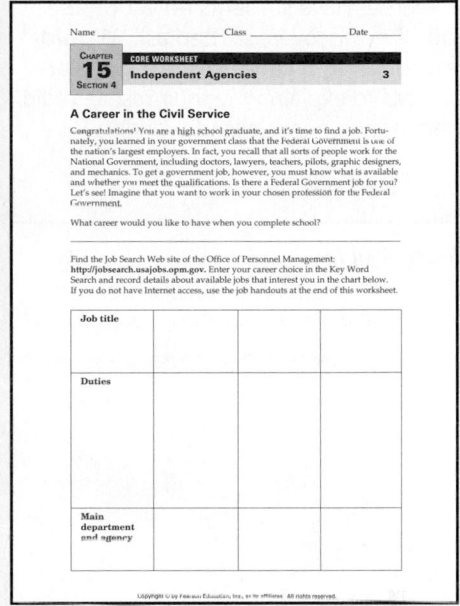

**REVIEW THE ACTIVITY**

Create a list on the board of the various types of careers and employment opportunities that students found of interest in their research. Ask the following questions:

**1. Were you surprised by the number and variety of jobs available in the civil service?**

**2. Were there any types of jobs that you discovered that you didn't expect to find in the Federal Government?**

**3. What, if any, key-word searches did not result in a listing?**

## Debate

"And so, my fellow Americans: ask not what your country can do for you—ask what you can do for your country." Soon after John F. Kennedy issued this challenge in 1961, he created the Peace Corps. Since then, thousands of Americans have served worldwide. Initially part of the State Department, the Peace Corps was made an independent agency in 1981. In 1964, Lyndon Johnson created Volunteers in Service to America (VISTA). Now AmeriCorps, it is part of the Corporation for National & Community Service, a government corporation. The idea of community service for all young Americans was a campaign issue in 2008. Some candidates favored community service as a requirement for high school graduation, while others proposed incentives, such as money for college, in exchange for either volunteer or military service. Ask: **Should some form of national service be mandatory?**

## Answers

**Checkpoint** Selective Service System

Remind students that the Federal Government is the largest employer in the country. As they have found, the types of jobs available can run from postal clerks to park rangers and doctors to mathematicians to foreign language teachers. The variety of jobs available is immense. Have students reflect on the diversity of jobs they discovered. Then ask: **Would you consider pursuing a career in the civil service?** Ask students to explain why their research did or did not change their minds about working for the government.

**Government** online

*All print resources are available on the Teacher's Resource Library CD-ROM and online at PearsonSchool.com/phgovt.*

---

**stagger**
*v.* to arrange something so that it does not occur at the same time

or commission made up of five to seven members appointed by the President with Senate consent; and those officials have terms of such length that it is unlikely a President will gain control over any of these agencies through the appointment process, at least not in a single presidential term.

Several other features of these boards and commissions put them beyond the reach of presidential control. No more than a bare majority of the members of each board or commission may belong to the same political party. Thus, several of those officers must belong to the party out of power.

Moreover, the appointed terms of the members are <u>staggered</u> so that the term of only one member on each board or commission expires in any one year. In addition, the officers of five of these agencies can be removed by the President only for those causes Congress has specified.[9]

As with the other independent agencies, the regulatory commissions are executive bodies. That is, Congress has given them the power to administer the programs for which they were created. However, unlike other independent agencies, the regulatory commissions are also quasi-legislative and quasi-judicial bodies.[10] That is, Congress has also given these agencies certain legislative-like and judicial-like powers.

These agencies exercise their quasi-legislative powers when they make rules and regulations. Those rules and regulations have the force of law. They implement and spell out the details of the laws that Congress has directed these regulatory bodies to enforce.

To illustrate the point: Congress has said that those who want to borrow money by issuing stocks, bonds, or other securities must provide a "full and fair disclosure" of all pertinent information to prospective investors. The Securities and Exchange Commission (SEC) makes that requirement effective and indicates how those who offer securities are to meet it by issuing rules and regulations.

---

9  Recall the Supreme Court's holding in *Humphrey's Executor* v. *United States*, 1935. Congress has provided that the members of six of these bodies (the SEC, FCC, EEOC, CPSC, NRC, and CFTC) can be removed at the President's discretion.

10 The prefix *quasi-* is from the Latin, meaning "in a certain sense, resembling, seemingly."

The regulatory commissions exercise their quasi-judicial powers when they decide disputes in those fields in which Congress has given them policing authority. For example, if an investor in Iowa thinks a local stockbroker has cheated him, he may file a complaint with the SEC's regional office in Chicago. SEC agents will investigate and report their findings, and the agency will judge the merits of the complaint much as a court would do. Decisions made by the SEC, and by the other independent regulatory bodies, can be appealed to the United States courts of appeals.

In a sense, Congress has created these agencies to act in its place. Congress could hold hearings and set interest rates, license radio and TV stations and nuclear reactors, check on business practices, and do the many other things it has directed the regulatory commissions to do. These activities are complex and time-consuming, however, and they demand constant and expert attention. If Congress were to do all of this work, it would have no time for its other and important legislative work.

Note that these regulatory bodies possess all three of the basic governmental powers: executive, legislative, and judicial. They are, then, exceptions to the principle of separation of powers. Technically, they should not be grouped with the other independent agencies. Instead, they should, somehow, be located somewhere between the executive and legislative branches, and between the executive and judicial branches, as well.

**Rethinking Regulation** Several authorities, and most recent Presidents, have urged that at least some of the administrative functions of the independent regulatory bodies be given to executive department agencies. Critics have raised other serious questions about these regulatory commissions and many think that they should be either abolished or, at the least, redesigned.

The most troubling questions are these: Have some of the regulatory commissions been unduly influenced by the special interests they are expected to regulate? Are all of the many and detailed rules created by these agencies really needed? Do some of those regulations have the effect of stifling

---

# Background

**OVERSIGHT OR OVERLOOK?** To do their job properly, government regulators need to understand the industry they monitor. As a result, regulatory agencies often hire executives from companies they regulate, and vice versa. For example, an executive at an airline might become a top official of the Federal Aviation Administration, or an FAA official might one day be CEO of an airline or a lobbyist for the airline industry. Critics point out that this relationship can turn regulators into industry advocates rather than watchdogs. This relationship came under renewed scrutiny in 2008 when two federal inspectors accused top officials at the FAA of ignoring safety violations at Southwest Airlines. "We need an FAA that actually fixes problems as they are found, rather than one that rushes into a public relations campaign to assure everyone that there isn't a problem," said Senator Patty Murray (D., Wash.).

---

## Answers

**Checkpoint**  They are largely beyond the reach of presidential control. Also, they have executive, legislative, and judicial powers.

# Regulatory Commissions

**GOVERNMENT** ONLINE
Audio Tour
Listen to a guided tour about the regulatory commissions at PearsonSchool.com/phgovt

The focus of the independent regulatory commissions is to ensure the stability of the nation's economy. Twelve federal agencies have been established to set and enforce standards on financial markets, employment, business practices, and public safety. *Should the government regulate these industries?*

## Protecting
### Financial Security

**Federal Reserve System (The FED) est. 1913** Formulates and administers the nation's credit and monetary policy by regulating the money supply, influencing the availability of credit, and supervising banking system practices.

**Securities and Exchange Commission (SEC) 1934** Regulates securities and other financial markets, investment companies, and brokers to ensure fair and honest transactions.

**Commodity Futures Trading Commission 1974** Protects investors from fraud and improper practices related to the sale of commodity futures. Its regulations encourage sound markets and competition as well as ensure market integrity.

**Consumer Financial Protection Bureau (CFPB) 2010** Formulates and enforces rules and regulations on consumer financial services, such as credit cards, online banking, and loans. The CFPB is charged with protecting consumers from dishonest financial products and practices.

Equality in the workplace is enforced by the EEOC.

## Ensuring
### Workplace Equality

**National Labor Relations Board (NLRB) 1935** Administers federal laws on labor-management and is responsible for the prevention or remedy of unfair labor practices by employers and unions.

**Equal Employment Opportunity Commission (EEOC) 1964** Enforces laws prohibiting discrimination based on race, color, religion, sex, national origin, disability, or age in employment.

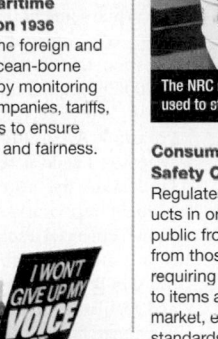
Workplace disputes are settled by the NLRB.

## Securing
### Business Integrity

**Federal Trade Commission (FTC) 1914** Ensures consumer welfare and protects competition by regulating pricing, preventing monopolies and false advertising, stopping fraud, and protecting consumers from unfair business practices.

**Federal Communications Commission (FCC) 1934** Regulates interstate and foreign communications by radio, television, wire, satellite, and cable while ensuring reasonable rates.

**Federal Maritime Commission 1936** Regulates the foreign and domestic ocean-borne commerce by monitoring shipping companies, tariffs, and services to ensure compliance and fairness.

**Federal Energy Regulatory Commission 1977** Regulates the transport and sale of electricity, natural gas, and oil by pipeline, licenses hydroelectric power projects, and oversees environmental issues related to energy resources.

## Guarding
### Public Safety

The NRC regulates the means used to store nuclear waste.

**Consumer Product Safety Commission 1972** Regulates consumer products in order to protect the public from risks of injury from those products by requiring corrective action to items already on the market, establishing labeling standards, and advising the public of product recalls.

**Nuclear Regulatory Commission (NRC) 1974** Licenses, regulates the use of nuclear energy to protect public health, safety, and the environment; sets rules and standards for nuclear reactors, facilities, and waste materials.

# Debate

Ben Stein, economist and columnist for *The Wall Street Journal,* blames deregulation for financial crises past and present. Use this quote to start a debate in your class:

"Deregulation has made Wall Street into a casino."

—Ben Stein

Ask students to explain the meaning of Stein's words. *(He means that with reduced regulatory protection, investing in the stock market has become a risky gamble.)* Have students take a position on this statement: **Regulation is good for the economy.** Have them do research on the positive and negative aspects of regulation to prepare for the debate.

---

Tell students to go to the Audio Tour for a guided tour on the regulatory commissions.

**EXTEND THE LESSON**

**L1 L2 Differentiate** NASA is an independent executive agency that encompasses a variety of civil service careers. The research and development group has come up with a number of innovations for NASA that have transferred to the public's use. Have students use the Internet, library, or news magazines to find images that reflect how innovations developed by NASA have affected our everyday lives. Then, have students create a collage of these products and post them around the room.

**L2 Differentiate** Distribute the Extend Activity "Getting Information from Independent Agencies" (Unit 4 All-in-One, p. 163).

**L3 L4 Differentiate** The Selective Service System is an independent executive agency that administers military manpower and coordinates the draft. Give students the Extend Worksheet (Unit 4 All-in-One, p. 162), which provides a list of questions about Selective Service to which they need to find the answers. Tell students to visit their local post office or library, or access the Selective Service System Web site (www.sss.gov/) to obtain the information they need to complete their worksheet.

**L4 Differentiate** To ensure the safety of consumers, some independent agencies establish standards and regulations that need to be met by businesses and industries. Display Transparency 15G, U.S. Consumer Product Safety Commission. Ask: **How can you learn of recalled products if you do not have access to the Internet?** *(radio, television, newspaper)* Have students conduct research on a recent product that has been recalled due to health and/or safety hazards to consumers. Students should write a newspaper article detailing what the issues surrounding the product are, when the public was alerted, which federal agency is involved, who the manufacturer is, and how the manufacturer and the government responded.

## Answers

**Regulatory Commissions** Possible response: Yes, citizens and the economy need protection from dishonest, unsafe, or anticompetitive practices.

# Assess and Remediate

**L3** Have students identify the three types of independent agencies, summarize the basic function of each, and include one example of each type.

**L3** Collect the Core Worksheets and assess students' work.

**L3** Assign the Section 4 Assessment questions.

**L3** Section Quiz A (Unit 4 All-in-One, p. 164)

**L2** Section Quiz B (Unit 4 All-in-One, p. 165)

Have students complete the review activities in the digital lesson presentation and continue their work in the **Essential Questions Journal.**

---

## Answers

**Analyzing Political Cartoons** Using a pun on books on tape, the cartoonist is able to humorously express discontent with regulations.

**Checkpoint** Congress

---

▶▶ **Analyzing Political Cartoons** Red tape is a term often used to describe a perceived excess of bureaucratic rules, complicated procedures, and unnecessary paperwork. *How does the use of this term convey the cartoonist's attitude toward government regulations?*

✔**Checkpoint**
Who is ultimately responsible for regulatory agency reform?

legitimate competition in the free enterprise system? Do some of them add unreasonably to the costs of doing business and therefore to the prices that consumers must pay?

Congress sets the basic policies of these agencies, and so it has a major responsibility to answer these questions. It has done so in recent years, particularly by deregulating much of the transportation industry. Airlines, bus companies, truckers, and railroads have greater freedom to operate today than they did only a few years ago. The same trend can be seen in the field of communications, notably with regard to cable television.

While some industries require less regulation today, others demand more. The severe recession that struck the nation's economy in 2007 prompted the passage of the Dodd-Frank Wall Street Reform and Consumer Protection Act in 2010. In addition to the most sweeping financial reforms since the Great Depression, the law established a new independent regulatory commission, the Consumer Financial Protection Bureau (CFPB). As a "watchdog for the American consumer," the CFPB has the authority to make rules and regulations for all institutions that offer consumer financial services or products, as well as the task of educating consumers on financial matters. The new commission will be funded by the Federal Reserve, rather than by Congress, in an effort to keep it free from the influence of special interests.

### Government Corporations

A number of independent agencies are **government corporations.** They, too, are located within the vast executive branch and are subject to the presidential direction and control. Unlike the other independent agencies, however, they were set up by Congress to carry out certain businesslike activities.

Congress established the first government corporation when it chartered the Bank of the United States in 1791. However, government corporations were little used until World War I and then the Great Depression. In both periods Congress set up dozens of corporations to carry out emergency programs. Several still exist—among them, the Federal Deposit Insurance Corporation (FDIC), which insures bank deposits, and the Export-Import Bank of the United States (Eximbank), which makes loans to help the export and sale of American goods abroad.

There are now more than 50 of these corporations. They do such things as deliver the mail (the U.S. Postal Service); provide intercity rail passenger service (the National Railroad Passenger Corporation, Amtrak); protect pension benefits (the Pension Benefit Guaranty Corporation); and generate, sell, and distribute electric power (the Tennessee Valley Authority). [11]

**Government v. Private Corporations** The typical government corporation is set up much like a corporation in the private sector. It is run by a board of directors, with a

---

[11] State and local governments maintain their own government corporations, most often called authorities, to operate airports, turnpikes, seaports, power plants, liquor stores, and housing developments, and to conduct many other corporate activities. The Port Authority of New York and New Jersey is one of the best known.

---

## Background

**FEDERAL DEPOSIT INSURANCE CORPORATION** The Federal Deposit Insurance Corporation (FDIC) is a government corporation managed by a five-person board of directors, all appointed by the President with Senate approval. No more than three directors can be from one political party. The FDIC was created in 1933 during the Great Depression, when thousands of bank failures threatened the U.S. financial system. The FDIC insures bank deposits up to at least $100,000 and monitors risks in the industry. The FDIC receives no public funds. Banks pay for this insurance out of their earnings. When a bank fails, the FDIC sells the bank's loans and deposits to another bank. The failed bank's customers automatically become customers of the healthy bank. The FDIC's activities limit the effects on the economy of bank failures, thus promoting confidence in, and the stability of, the banking system.

general manager who directs the corporation's operations according to the policies laid down by the board. Most government corporations produce income that is plowed back into the agency's programs.

There are several differences between government and private corporations, however. Congress decides the purpose for which the public agencies exist and the functions they perform. Their officers are public officers; in fact, all who work for these corporations are public employees. The President selects most of the top officers of government corporations with Senate approval.

In addition, these public agencies are financed by public funds appropriated by Congress, not by private investors. The Federal Government, representing the American people, owns the stock.

The advantage most often claimed for these agencies is their flexibility. It is said that the government corporation, freed from the controls of regular departmental organization, can carry on its activities with the incentive, efficiency, and ability to experiment that make many private concerns successful. Whether that claim is valid or not is open to question. At the very least, it raises this complex issue: Is a public corporation's need for flexibility compatible with the basic democratic requirement that all public agencies be held responsible and accountable to the people?

**Degrees of Independence** The degree of independence and flexibility government corporations have varies considerably. In fact, some corporations are not independent at all. They are attached to an executive department.

The Commodity Credit Corporation (CCC), for example, is the government's major crop-loan and farm-subsidy agency. It is located within the Department of Agriculture, and the secretary of agriculture chairs its seven-member board. The CCC carries out most of its functions through a line agency in the Department of Agriculture—the Farm Service Agency—which is also subject to the direct control of the secretary.

Some corporations do have considerable independence, however. The Tennessee Valley Authority (TVA) is a case in point. It operates under a statute that gives it considerable discretion over its own programs. Although its budget is subject to review by the OMB, the President, and Congress, the TVA has a large say in the uses of the income its several operations produce.[12]

✓ **Checkpoint**
How do government and private corporations differ?

---

12 Congress established the TVA in the Tennessee Valley Authority Act of 1933. Its operations include electric power, flood control, reforestation, soil conservation, agricultural research, recreational facilities, and the promotion of industrial growth. The TVA's power program is self-supporting. Much of its other activities are supported by Congress.

**Essential Questions Journal** To continue to build a response to the chapter Essential Question, go to your Essential Questions Journal.

# SECTION 4 ASSESSMENT

1. **Guiding Question** Use your completed table to answer this question: What are the roles and structures of the independent agencies?

**Key Terms and Comprehension**

2. Why has Congress created **independent agencies**?

3. What was the **spoils system** and what replaced it?

4. How do **independent regulatory commissions** differ from the many other independent agencies?

5. (a) How are **government corporations** similar to private corporations? (b) How are they different?

**Critical Thinking**

6. **Identify Central Issues** Why do you think Congress purposefully structured a few independent agencies so that they are largely beyond the control of the President?

7. **Draw Conclusions** Why do you think special interest groups become involved in the structure and function of independent agencies?

**Quick Write**

**Research Writing: Develop a Thesis** A thesis statement summarizes the main idea of your research paper. Use the research you gathered and the activities you have completed for this chapter's Quick Writes and look for an idea that can be supported by the information you found. Determine how the details are related and decide on the idea that best summarizes your research. Then, write a sentence that sums up the main idea on which you will focus your paper.

---

REMEDIATION

| If Your Students Have Trouble With | Strategies For Remediation |
|---|---|
| Identifying the roles and structures of the independent agencies (Questions 1, 2, 6) | Have students create an outline of the section using the red and blue heads as the main structure. |
| Describing the spoils system (Question 3) | Have students create a political cartoon illustrating the spoils system. |
| Explaining how regulatory commissions differ from other agencies (Question 4) | Recreate or review the Venn diagram illustrated earlier in this section. |
| Comparing government and private corporations (Question 5) | Review the *Government* v. *Private Corporation* portion in this section and help students find the terms or phrases that indicate comparison in the text. |
| Determining why interest groups are involved with independent agencies (Question 7) | Brainstorm a list of reasons why students think interest groups would benefit from being involved in the work of independent agencies. |

## Answers

**Checkpoint** Congress decides the purpose of government corporations and their functions. All employees are public. The President selects most top officials, with Senate approval. Government corporations are financed by public funds.

---

# Assessment Answers

1. Executive agencies administer specific programs and are structured like Cabinet departments. Regulatory commissions are structured to remove them from partisan influence, and use executive, legislative, and judicial powers to monitor and police aspects of the economy. Government corporations have business-like functions and are structured with a board of directors and general manager. They produce income that is folded back into the business. They are financed by public funds, not private investors.

2. main reasons: some agencies do not fit in the department structure; to protect agencies from partisan and political influence; and some agencies have sensitive responsibilities

3. The spoils system was the practice of giving jobs, contracts, and other government favors to friends and political supporters. It was replaced by the civil service, based on the merit system.

4. Regulatory commissions have quasi-legislative powers to make the rules and regulations that they enforce, and quasi-judicial powers to decide disputes in their fields of authority.

5. (a) **Similarities:** board of directors, general manager, income is folded back into the business (b) **Differences:** Government corporations consist of public officials, are publicly funded, and have purposes set by Congress.

6. to ensure that their actions are not influenced by partisan policy or political pressures

7. Special interest groups have expertise and economic interest in the functions of the agency.

**QUICK WRITE** Thesis statements should articulate the main ideas of the research papers.

## Teach

### TAKE A POLL

Ask: **Which level of government should be responsible for the quality of your education? (a) federal (b) State (c) local (d) none of these**

### SUMMARIZE THE ISSUE

Have students read the feature and summarize the issue and the views expressed in the quotes.

**L2 ELL Differentiate** Write these terms and definitions on the board: *accountable* (responsible), *curriculum* (the course of study in a school), *mandate* (an order or command), *accessible* (that can be approached).

### DISCUSS

Since the enactment of No Child Left Behind in 2002, there has been continuing debate on the program's value. Display Transparency 15H, No Child Left Behind. Supporters claim that it makes schools accountable for the quality of their education, while critics state that it promotes lower achievement goals. The program has also revived the debate on whether the Federal Government is interfering in a realm that should be a State and local responsibility. Ask: **Should the Federal Government control the quality of our education system?** *(yes: because education affects the nation's competitive edge; no: because federal funding to states should not be tied to students' test results)* **Does this program overstep the scope of National Government?** *(Answers will vary.)* Then take another poll using the question at the beginning of the lesson. If students have changed their stance, ask why.

## Assess and Remediate

Have students select one of the quotes and write a paragraph opposing the speaker's opinion.

## Answers

1. **(a)** managing the accountability of quality in schools **(b)** None, he feels education is the responsibility of local and State governments. **(c)** Answers will vary.
2. Answers will vary but should show an understanding of how federal involvement in education has grown over time and the debate over how much governmental control is acceptable in some realms.

---

- Students will examine the debate on the size of government using the question of the extent of the government's involvement in education.

---

# ISSUES OF OUR TIME

# The Size of Government

## Track the Issue

**The Constitution** makes no provisions for federal involvement in education, but in the last few decades, the Federal Government has taken an increasingly larger role in funding and supervising local schools.

**1787**
**Thomas Jefferson** argues that a democratic state must educate its citizens in order to survive.

**1865**
**Congress establishes** the Freedmen's Bureau that builds over 1,000 schools for newly freed black Americans.

**1979**
**Congress creates** the Department of Education to oversee federal funding of educational programs.

**2002**
**The No Child Left Behind Act (NCLB)** gives the Federal Government unprecedented influence over local schools.

**Today**
**The Federal Government** aims to provide students with an education that will make them competitive and successful in the 21st century workplace.

Secretary of Education Arne Duncan ▼

450

## Perspectives

**The issue of federal involvement in schools** is closely related to the larger question of the size and purpose of the Federal Government. People who favor a government with a more limited scope often point to agencies like the Department of Education as an example of unnecessary "big government" policies. However, others believe that the Federal Government has an important role to play in education.

"Under NCLB, the federal government greatly expanded its role in holding schools accountable. . . . But [NCLB] allows—even encourages—states to lower standards. It doesn't measure growth or reward excellence. . . . Our proposal will make significant improvements on accountability. . . . [W]e will change the accountability system to make it fairer. We will start by holding not just schools and teachers accountable for student success, but districts and states, as well. . . . ."
*—Arne Duncan, Secretary of Education, 2010*

"It's important to remember that state and local governments exercise primary control over education—building schools, hiring teachers, deciding curriculum, and setting standards for students to meet. . . . [M]ost educators would agree that maintaining local control, free of federal government mandates, is vitally important. . . . Most decisions should continue to be made locally by those who know children best and who are most accessible and accountable to parents, rather than by bureaucrats in Washington, D.C."
*—Senator Jon Kyl (R., Arizona), 2010*

## Connect to Your World

1. **Understand (a)** According to Secretary Duncan, what is the role of the Federal Government in education? **(b)** What level of government does Senator Kyl feel is responsible for education? **(c)** With which opinion do you agree? Why?
2. **Identify Central Issues** Why do you think education is considered an example of the Federal Government becoming too big?

**GOVERNMENT** ONLINE
**In the News**
For updates about education and the Federal Government, visit
**PearsonSchool.com/phgovt**

---

# Background

**GOVERNMENT ROLE IN EDUCATION** In the United States, education remains mostly a State and local responsibility. Local school boards oversee community schools—approve budgets, hire the superintendent, approve curricula, and establish policies for the district. In the 2007–2008 school year, over 91 percent of funds for elementary and secondary schools came from nonfederal sources, especially State taxes and local property taxes. Local funding gives communities a greater say in the operation of their schools. However, it also leads to inequalities. In communities with high real estate values, more property tax money will be available for schools than in communities with low real estate values. State spending for education varies from State to State as well. The U.S. Department of Education tries to fill gaps in State and local support for education by targeting areas where the funds can do the most good.

# Quick Study Guide

**GOVERNMENT ONLINE**
**On the Go**
To review anytime, anywhere, download these online resources at PearsonSchool.com/phgovt
Political Dictionary, Audio Review

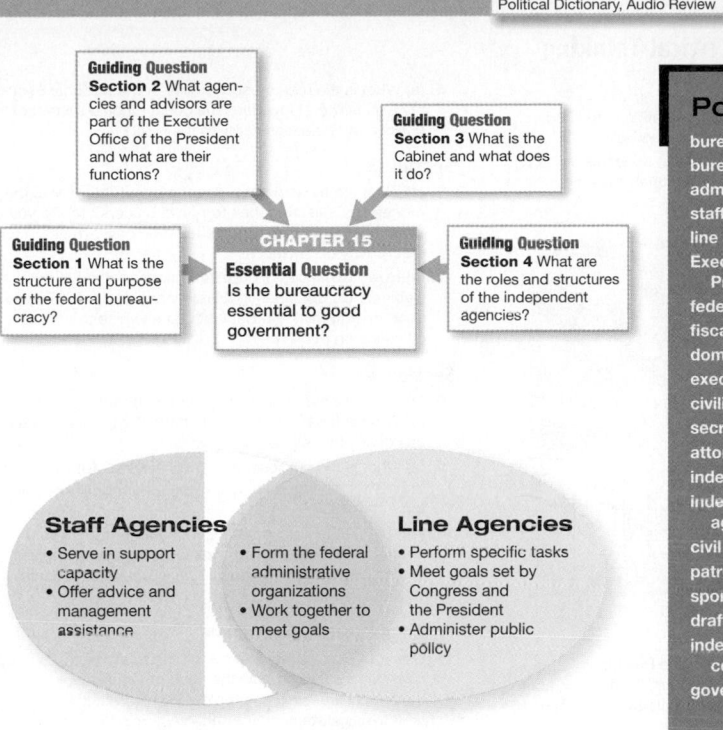

**Guiding Question**
**Section 2** What agencies and advisors are part of the Executive Office of the President and what are their functions?

**Guiding Question**
**Section 3** What is the Cabinet and what does it do?

**Guiding Question**
**Section 1** What is the structure and purpose of the federal bureaucracy?

**CHAPTER 15**
**Essential Question**
Is the bureaucracy essential to good government?

**Guiding Question**
**Section 4** What are the roles and structures of the independent agencies?

### Staff Agencies
- Serve in support capacity
- Offer advice and management assistance

- Form the federal administrative organizations
- Work together to meet goals

### Line Agencies
- Perform specific tasks
- Meet goals set by Congress and the President
- Administer public policy

## Political Dictionary

bureaucracy *p. 426*
bureaucrat *p. 426*
administration *p.428*
staff agency *p. 430*
line agency *p. 430*
Executive Office of the President *p. 431*
federal budget *p. 433*
fiscal year *p. 433*
domestic affairs *p. 434*
executive department *p. 435*
civilian *p. 435*
secretary *p. 435*
attorney general *p. 435*
independent agency *p. 441*
independent executive agency *p. 442*
civil service *p. 443*
patronage *p. 443*
spoils system *p. 443*
draft *p. 445*
independent regulatory commission *p. 445*
government corporation *p. 448*

## Executive Branch

### Executive Office of the President
- The White House comprises the President's key personal and political staff.
- National Security Council advises on matters relating to national security.
- OMB prepares federal budget and assists in executive branch management.
- Other units provide advice on issues ranging from the economy to foreign affairs.

### Executive Departments
- Traditional units of the federal administration
- Built around broad fields of authority
- Headed by a department secretary, serving as link between presidential policy and department
- Structured geographically, with much work done through regional offices

### Independent Agencies
- Located outside the executive departments
- Created by Congress to perform specific functions
- Nature and purpose vary from agency to agency.

# For More Information

To learn more about the federal bureaucracy, refer to these sources or assign them to students:

**L1** **Buckwalter, Stephanie.** *Independent Government Agencies: Working for America.* Enslow Publishers, Incorporated, 2008.

**L2** **Damp, Dennis V.** *The Book of U.S. Government Jobs: Where They Are, What's Available & How to Get One (9th Edition).* Bookhaven Press, 2008.

**L3** **Sollenberger, Mitchel A.** *The President Shall Nominate: How Congress Trumps Executive Power.* University Press of Kansas, 2008.

**L4** **Lewis, David E.** *The Politics of Presidential Appointments: Political Control and Bureaucratic Performance.* Princeton University Press, 2008.

---

Have students download the digital resources available at Government on the Go for review and remediation.

## STUDY TIPS

**Listening in Class** Be sure students understand the difference between *hearing* and *listening*. Listening requires effort and concentration. To enhance their listening skills, have students practice the following steps. Before they even arrive at class, students should make sure they have reviewed their notes from the previous class, finished assignments, and kept up with the reading. As they listen, students should watch for main ideas and notice how the details fit into them. To stay focused, suggest that students maintain eye contact with the speaker and try to ignore their physical surroundings. It will also help students stay focused if they are active listeners, which means taking notes, marking content about which they have a question, and asking questions when appropriate. To avoid daydreaming, students can try to anticipate what the speaker will say next as well as mentally evaluating and summarizing what they hear.

## ASSESSMENT AT A GLANCE

### Tests and Quizzes
Section Assessments
Section Quizzes A and B, Unit 4 **All-in-One**
Chapter Assessment
Chapter Tests A and B, Unit 4 **All-in-One**
Document-Based Assessment
Progress Monitoring Online
Exam*View* Test Bank

### Performance Assessment
Essential Questions Journal
Debates, pp. 445, 447
Assessment Rubrics, **All-in-One**

# Chapter Assessment

**COMPREHENSION AND CRITICAL THINKING**

**SECTION 1**

1. possible response: more effective, because the hierarchical structure reduces conflicts, job specialization develops specific expertise, and standard work rules enable work to continue as personnel changes; OR: less effective, because the sheer size requires navigation through a maze of bureaucrats before anything gets done

2. **(a)** Possible response: It implies that bureaucracy complicates matters that may be quite simple. **(b)** Answers will vary, but should show an understanding of advantages and disadvantages of a bureaucracy.

**SECTION 2**

3. **(a)** The Executive Office is the branch of the government that most directly executes the President's wishes. **(b)** Answers will vary, but should reflect an understanding of the different activities undertaken by the Executive Office.

4. **(a)** The Office of Management and Budget **(b)** The OMB monitors the spending of the funds Congress appropriates.

5. **(a)** The National Security Council advises the President on all domestic, foreign, and military matters related to national security. **(b)** Because the other branches often do not know about the NSC's secret work, the system of checks and balances sometimes cannot operate, which may lead to situations like the Iran-Contra scandal.

**SECTION 3**

6. **(a)** 15 Cabinet-level departments built around some broad field of activity **(b)** appointed by President with approval of Congress **(c)** Possible responses: Yes, because they would be more familiar with the work and processes of the department and have extensive experience in the organization. No, because the President needs advisors whom he or she trusts.

7. **(a)** The executive department heads make up the Cabinet. **(b)** Possible responses: Yes, because they likely hold the same views as the President, who needs to hear opposing views to consider all sides of an issue. No, because the people elected the President for his or her policy views, and the Cabinet of close advisors helps the President implement these policies.

---

**Chapter Assessment**

**GOVERNMENT** ONLINE
Self-Test
To test your understanding of key terms and main ideas, visit PearsonSchool.com/phgovt

## Comprehension and Critical Thinking

### Section 1

1. Do you think the bureaucratic organization of the Federal Government makes it more or less effective?

2. **Analyze Political Cartoons (a)** What does this cartoon say about bureaucracy? **(b)** Do you think it is an accurate portrayal? Why or why not?

### Section 2

3. **(a)** Why is the Executive Office of the President sometimes called the President's "right arm"? **(b)** Which activity of the EOP do you think has the greatest impact on the lives of the American people?

4. **(a)** Which unit of the EOP is responsible for preparing the federal budget? **(b)** What responsibility does that agency have once Congress has appropriated funds to the executive branch?

5. **(a)** What is the major responsibility of the National Security Council? **(b)** How does the constitutional system of checks and balances apply to the NSC?

### Section 3

6. **(a)** What are the executive departments? **(b)** What is the process for selecting their top-level officers? **(c)** Do you think the department heads should be career bureaucrats? Why or why not?

7. **(a)** How are executive departments connected to the Cabinet? **(b)** Considering its relationship with the President, do you think the Cabinet can exercise too much influence on public policy?

### Section 4

8. **(a)** What are the three types of independent agencies? **(b)** What is the basic role of each type? **(c)** Which type do you think affects your life the most?

9. **(a)** What is the purpose of the civil service? **(b)** How has the service changed since the enactment of the Pendleton Act in 1883?

10. **(a)** What is the function of the independent regulatory commissions? **(b)** Do you think laws regulating specific industries affect our personal and economic freedoms? Why or why not?

### Writing About Government

11. Use your Quick Write exercises from this chapter to write a research paper on how the government is involved in the administration of the topic you selected. Make sure your thesis statement is clear and supported with well-researched details, and that your conclusion reviews the key points of your thesis. See pp. S6–S7 in the Skills Handbook.

---

## Apply What You've Learned

12. **Essential Question Activity** Look through the government pages of a local telephone book or online to locate the federal agencies in your area. Select one that interests you and conduct an interview of a civil servant who works for that agency. Ask:

   **(a)** In which Cabinet department is your agency located? Is it one of the larger agencies of that department?
   **(b)** What are the agency's key responsibilities?
   **(c)** How and by whom are the agency's decisions made?
   **(d)** Do you think the organizational structure of the agency is efficient? Could it be improved? If so, how?

13. **Essential Question Assessment** Based on your interview and this chapter's content, make a graphic organizer that illustrates the hierarchy of the agency you selected. Then, write a short essay on how this chart helps answer the Essential Question: **Is the bureaucracy essential to good government?**

**Essential Questions Journal** To respond to the chapter Essential Question, go to your **Essential Questions Journal.**

---

**SECTION 4**

8. **(a)** independent executive agencies, independent regulatory commissions, government corporations **(b) executive:** perform tasks related to a specific area of authority, such as the space program or the budget; **regulatory:** monitor aspects of the economy; **government corporations:** carry out business-like activities **(c)** Answers will vary, but should be supported.

9. **(a)** to recruit and keep the best available people in the federal work force **(b)** The Pendleton Act set up hiring and promotion practices for classified employees based on merit. The Act placed about 10 percent of federal employees in the classified designation. Since then, coverage has been extended. Today, merit rules apply to nearly 90 percent of executive branch employees.

10. **(a)** to ensure the stability of the nation's economy **(b)** Possible responses: Regulations interfere with the freedom of business owners to choose how they want to run their businesses. Free market forces will prevent most abuses. OR: While regulations do interfere with freedom in some ways, they are necessary to protect

# Document-Based Assessment

## Protecting the Environment

Ecologist Rachel Carson's groundbreaking study, *Silent Spring,* was one of the earliest and most persuasive warnings of the urgent need to protect the environment, both here and abroad. As these documents show, the Federal Government and the public have since then become more actively involved in addressing the issue.

### Document 1

"Since 2001, our nation has funded nearly $10 billion in developing energy sources that are cleaner, cheaper and more reliable. [The] EPA has played a substantial role in this effort. . . . But we're not doing it alone.

Today, instead of having only 17-thousand EPA employees working to protect the environment, we now have over 300 million Americans as environmental partners. Americans from all sectors of society—communities, businesses and individuals—have begun to embrace the fact that environmental responsibility is everyone's responsibility.

—Stephen Johnson, EPA Administrator, 2007

### Document 2

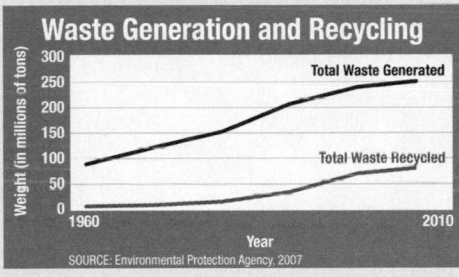

**Waste Generation and Recycling**

Weight (in millions of tons)

Total Waste Generated

Total Waste Recycled

1960 — 2010

Year

SOURCE: Environmental Protection Agency, 2007

### Document 3

"The most alarming of all man's assaults upon the environment is the contamination of air, earth, rivers, and sea with dangerous and even lethal materials. This pollution is for the most part irrecoverable. . . . In this now universal contamination of the environment, chemicals are the sinister and little-recognized partners . . . in changing the very nature of the world. . . . Many [of them] are used in man's war against nature.

These sprays, dusts, and aerosols are now applied almost universally to farms, gardens, forests, and homes—nonselective chemicals that have the power to kill every insect, the "good" and the "bad," to still the song of birds and the leaping of fish in the streams. . . . [W]e have allowed these chemicals to be used with little or no advance investigation of their effect on soil, water, wildlife, and man himself. Future generations are unlikely to condone our lack of prudent concern for the integrity of the natural world that supports all life.

—Rachel Carson, *Silent Spring,* 1962

---

Use your knowledge of the independent agencies and Documents 1–3 to answer Questions 1–3.

1. What is the main point of Document 3?
   A. Chemicals are the cause of all our environmental problems.
   B. People need to take responsibility for protecting the environment.
   C. Government must regulate the chemical industry.
   D. Insecticides are good for the environment.

2. How do Documents 1 and 2 illustrate the growing emphasis on environmental concerns?

3. **Pull It Together** Should the Federal Government become more heavily involved in efforts to protect the environment? Why or why not?

 **GOVERNMENT** ONLINE

**Documents**
To find more primary sources on the environment, visit
PearsonSchool.com/phgovt

---

**DOCUMENT-BASED ASSESSMENT**

1. B

2. Document 1 illustrates the growing emphasis on environmental concern by the shear amount of funds allocated to the effort as well as stating how citizens, in addition to the government, are making an effort to protect the environment. Document 2 shows that recycling has been increasing since 1960.

3. Possible responses: Yes, because environmental problems extend beyond State boundaries, affecting all of us, so we need policies applied uniformly across the nation. No, because environmental regulations increase business costs, making American businesses less competitive in world markets.

**L2 Differentiate** Students use all the documents on the page to support their thesis.

**L3 Differentiate** Students include additional information available online at **PearsonSchool .com/phgovt.**

**L4 Differentiate** Students use materials from the textbook, the online information at **PearsonSchool .com/phgovt,** and do additional research to support their views.

 **Go Online to PearsonSchool.com/phgovt** for a student rubric and extra documents.

---

consumers and the economy from unscrupulous or unsafe business practices.

### WRITING ABOUT GOVERNMENT

11. Students' papers should discuss agency involvement in their chosen topic. Students should focus on the thesis statement and draw a conclusion supported by details from their research.

### APPLY WHAT YOU'VE LEARNED

12. Student interviews should include comprehensive answers to the questions provided in the text and document the information gathered.

13. Graphic organizers should illustrate an understanding of the organization of the agency the student selected. Student essays should be well thought out and their answers well-reasoned, showing an understanding of the federal bureaucracy.

# Introduce the Chapter

## Essential Questions:

### UNIT 4

What makes a good President?

### CHAPTER 16

How should the federal budget reflect Americans' priorities?

### ACTIVATE PRIOR KNOWLEDGE

Have students examine the image and quotation on these pages. Ask: **What is the main source of funds for the Federal Government?** *(taxes)* **Each year the Federal Government creates a plan for how it will spend its revenue in the coming year. What is this plan called?** *(the federal budget)* In this chapter, students will learn how government acquires revenue and creates a plan for spending it. Then tell students to begin to further explore the financing of the Federal Government by completing the Chapter 16 Essential Question Warmup Activity in their **Essential Questions Journal.** Discuss their responses as a class.

### BEFORE READING

**L2 ELL Differentiate** Chapter 16 Prereading and Vocabulary Worksheet (Unit 4 All-in-One, p. 181)

### SUCCESSNET STUDENT AND TEACHER CENTER

Visit **PearsonSchool.com/phgovt** for download-able resources that allow students and teachers to connect with government "on the go."

### DIGITAL LESSON PRESENTATION

The digital lesson presentation supports the print lesson with activities and summaries of key concepts.

## SKILLS DEVELOPMENT

### ANALYZE GRAPHIC DATA

You may wish to teach analyzing graphic data as a distinct skill within Section 2 of this chapter. Use the Chapter 16 Skills Worksheet (Unit 4 All-in-One, p. 200) to help students learn how to analyze graphic data. The worksheet asks students to interpret a graph about U.S. federal budget surpluses and deficits and then draw conclusions. For L2 and L1 students, assign the adapted Skill Activity (Unit 4 All-in-One, p. 201).

**WebQuest online** The chapter WebQuest challenges students to answer the chapter Essential Question by asking them about the federal budget.

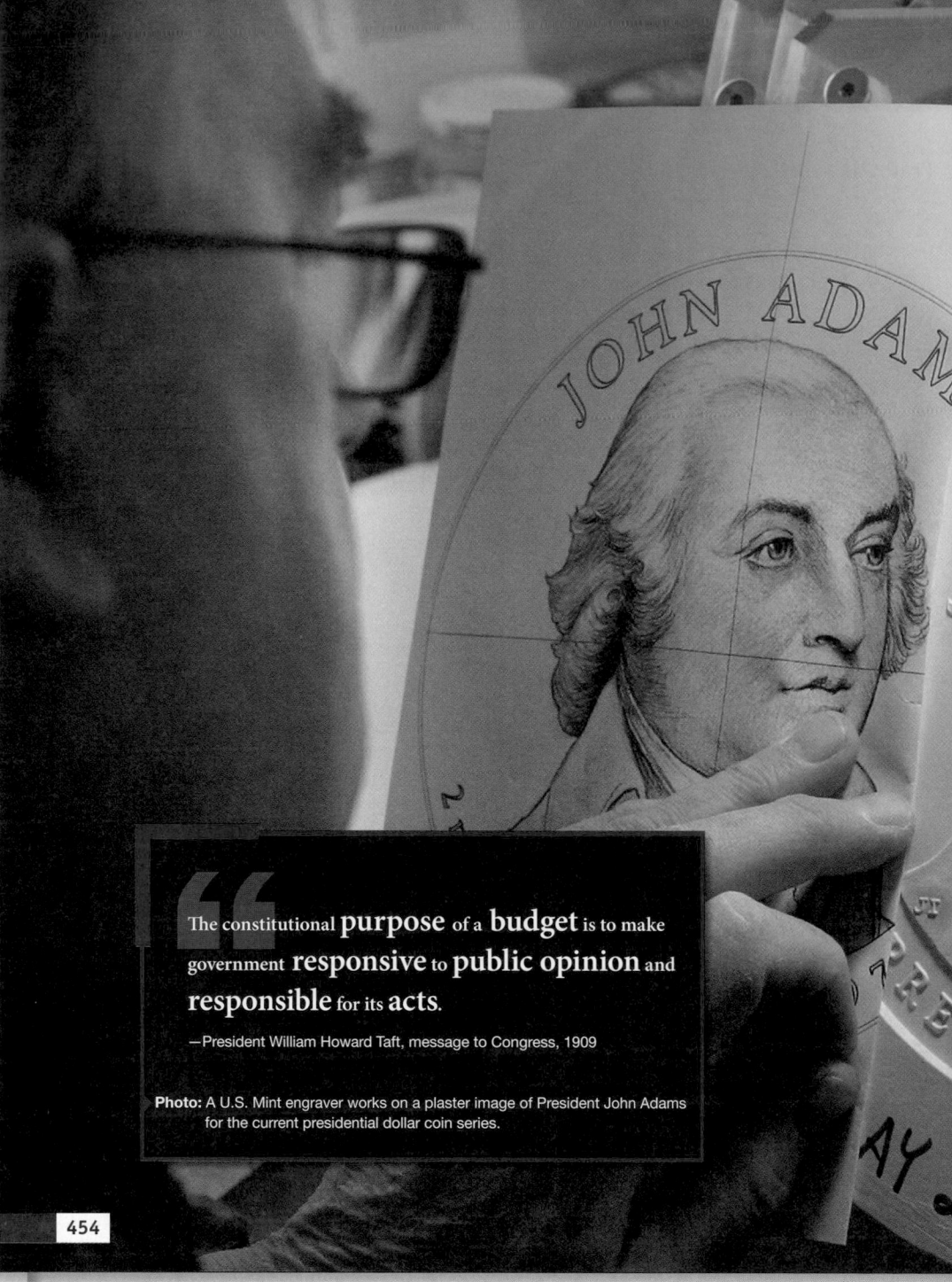

> " The constitutional **purpose** of a **budget** is to make government **responsive** to **public opinion** and **responsible** for its **acts**.
>
> —President William Howard Taft, message to Congress, 1909

**Photo:** A U.S. Mint engraver works on a plaster image of President John Adams for the current presidential dollar coin series.

454

## Block Scheduling

**BLOCK 1:** Teach the Section 1 and Section 2 lessons, omitting the political cartoon mini-lessons, extend activities and the Section 1 debate.

**BLOCK 2:** Teach the Section 3 and 4 lessons, omitting both sections' extend activities.

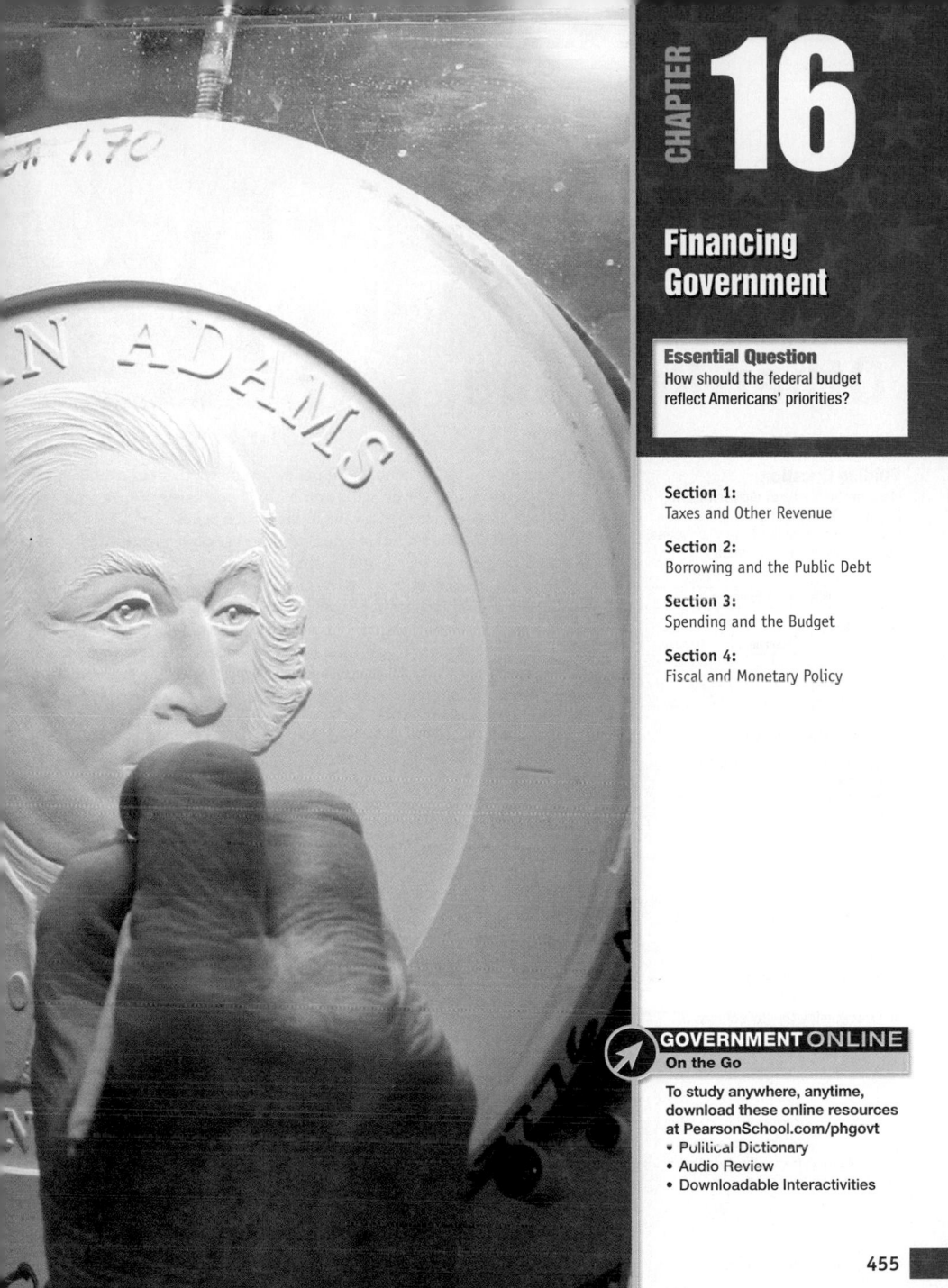

**Essential Question**
How should the federal budget reflect Americans' priorities?

**GOVERNMENT** ONLINE
**On the Go**

To study anywhere, anytime, download these online resources at PearsonSchool.com/phgovt
- Political Dictionary
- Audio Review
- Downloadable Interactivities

455

## Lesson Goals

**SECTION 1**

Students will . . .

- examine how taxes affect wages by calculating withholding and net pay using a sample paycheck.
- discuss how and why government raises money.
- examine sources of government funding using scenarios about the types of federal taxes.

**SECTION 2**

Students will . . .

- analyze the annual deficits and surpluses and the public debt by interpreting graphs.
- describe the federal borrowing process.
- analyze key events in the history of the public debt by examining a timeline.

**SECTION 3**

Students will . . .

- distinguish between controllable and uncontrollable spending categories on a federal budget circle graph.
- understand the difficulty of setting budget priorities by completing a ranking activity.

**SECTION 4**

Students will . . .

- discuss the nation's current economic situation and the tools available to the government to address it.
- analyze monetary and fiscal policy tools, using a transparency.
- analyze graphs of economic performance on the government's main economic goals and suggest policy actions.

## Pressed for Time

Discuss how the Federal Government acquires revenue. Then have students brainstorm the types of programs and government activities this revenue funds and list them on the board. Help students understand controllable and uncontrollable spending by categorizing each item on the board as one or the other. Review the government's budget-creation process. Then conduct the Section 3 Core Worksheet activity.

**FOLLOW UP** Have students write a summary of the process by which their group resolved the steps in each task in the activity. Students should keep in mind the chapter's Essential Question: **How should the federal budget reflect Americans' priorities?,** and should include in their summary how their group's choices were informed by the priorities of their constituents.

**DIFFERENTIATED INSTRUCTION KEY**

Look for these symbols to help you adjust steps in each lesson to meet your students' needs.

**L1** Special Needs
**L2** Basic
    **ELL** English Language Learners
    **LPR** Less Proficient Readers
**L3** All Students
**L4** Advanced Students

# How is the Federal Government financed?

| Financing Government | | |
|---|---|---|
| **Constitution** | **Tax Revenue** | **Nontax Revenue** |
| • grants Congress power to tax <br> • taxes may not violate other provisions <br> • tax only for public purposes <br> • no export taxes <br> • direct taxes must be equally apportioned among States by population <br> • income tax may be laid without regard to population <br> • indirect taxes must be same rate throughout country <br> • Federal Government may not tax State or local governmental activities | • individual income taxes <br> • corporate income taxes <br> • social insurance taxes <br> • excise taxes <br> • estate taxes <br> • gift taxes <br> • customs duties | • Federal Reserve interest charges <br> • other interest, tolls, fees <br> • sale or lease of public lands <br> • fines imposed by federal courts <br> • "conscience fund" <br> • seigniorage from minting coins <br> • stamps sold to collectors |

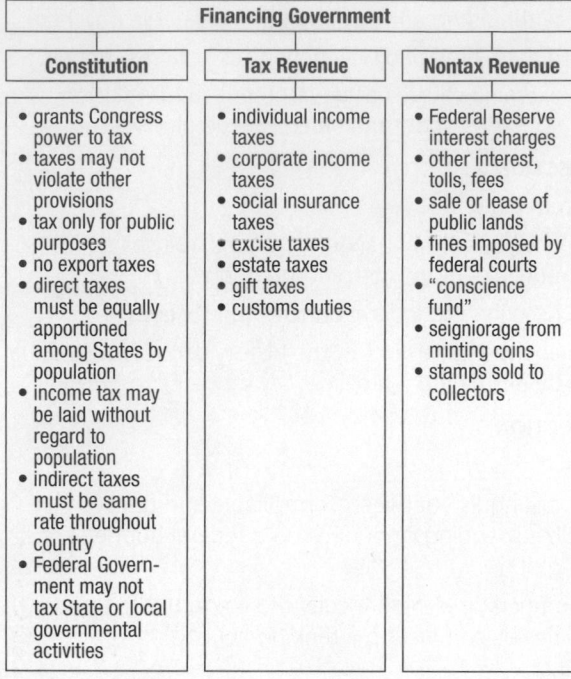

# Get Started

## LESSON GOALS

Students will . . .

- examine how taxes affect wages by calculating withholding and net pay using a sample paycheck.
- discuss how and why government raises money.
- examine sources of government funding using scenarios about the types of federal taxes.

## SKILLS DEVELOPMENT

### PROBLEM SOLVING

Before students do this section's Core Worksheet, which contains tax calculations, you may wish to review the information on problem solving in the Skills Handbook, p. S17.

---

## SECTION 1

# Taxes and Other Revenue

### Guiding Question

**How is the Federal Government financed?** Use a chart like the one below to keep track of the main ideas about financing government.

| Financing Government | | |
|---|---|---|
| Constitution | Tax Revenue | Nontax Revenue |
| • <br> • | • <br> • | • <br> • |

### Political Dictionary

- fiscal policy
- progressive tax
- payroll tax
- regressive tax
- excise tax
- estate tax
- gift tax
- customs duty
- interest

### Objectives

1. Explain how the Constitution gives Congress the power to tax and at the same time places limits on that power.
2. Identify the most significant federal taxes collected today.
3. Describe the nontax sources of federal revenue.

**Image Above:** Taxpayers filing their federal income tax forms.

This chapter is mostly about fiscal policy—a subject that has a tendency to make most people's eyes glaze over.[1] It is, nonetheless, a matter of very considerable importance to everyone in the United States.

A government's **fiscal policy** consists of the various means it uses to raise and spend money and thereby influence the nation's economy. No one needs to be told that the rate at which government takes in money and the level at which it spends that income have a very substantial impact on economic conditions. In simplest terms, it comes to this: A cut in taxes means more money in the hands of consumers, and their increased spending power means more jobs. An increase in taxes takes money away from consumers and so tends to slow the economy and reduce inflation.

In this section, we turn to taxes. Later, we shall look at borrowing—another source of governmental income, how the government spends what it takes in, and, finally, how the government's fiscal policy affects the economy.

## The Power to Tax

No one really likes taxes—except, perhaps, late-night television personalities who often find fodder for their monologues in that subject. They are far from the first to joke about taxes, however. More than two centuries ago, Benjamin Franklin famously said that "in this world nothing can be said to be certain, except death and taxes."

The Constitution underscores the central importance of the power to tax by listing it first among all of the many powers granted to Congress. The Constitution gives to Congress the power

> ### FROM THE CONSTITUTION
>
> To lay and collect Taxes, Duties, Imposts and Excises, to pay the Debts and provide for the common Defence and general Welfare of the United States. . . .
> —Article I, Section 8, Clause 1

---

1 The word *fiscal* comes from the Latin word *fiscus*, meaning originally a reed basket and later a purse or treasury. In ancient Rome, the *fiscus* was the public treasury, the emperor's purse.

## Focus on the Basics

**FACTS:** • Article I gives Congress the power to levy taxes to operate the Federal Government. • The Constitution states that Congress may tax only for public purposes, may not tax exports, must apportion direct taxes equally among the States, and must set indirect taxes at the same rate across the country. • Progressive taxes impose higher rates for higher incomes. • Regressive taxes apply the same rate to all, regardless of income.

**CONCEPTS:** enumerated and implied powers, limited government, federalism

**ENDURING UNDERSTANDINGS:** • The power to tax is used not only to raise revenue to operate the government, but also to regulate and even discourage some activities.

First and foremost, Congress exercises the taxing power in order to raise the money needed to operate the Federal Government. However, Congress does sometimes exercise that power for purposes other than the raising of revenue. Usually, that other purpose is to regulate, even discourage, some activity that the government believes to be harmful to the general public.

Thus, much of the Federal Government's regulation of narcotics and other dangerous drugs is based on the taxing power. Federal law provides that only those who hold a valid license can legally manufacture, sell, or otherwise deal in those drugs—and licensing is a form of taxation. The government also regulates a number of other things by licensing—including, for example, the sale and purchasing of certain firearms, prospecting on public lands, and the hunting of migratory birds.

In 1912, Congress used its taxing power to destroy a part of the domestic match industry. It did so by levying a tax of two cents a hundred on matches made with white or yellow phosphorus. Those highly poisonous substances were harmful to workers who produced the matches. Matches made from other substances commonly sold for a penny a hundred at the time. So, as a result, the two-cent tax drove phosphorus matches from the market.

The Supreme Court first upheld the use of the taxing power for nonrevenue purposes in *Veazie Bank* v. *Fenno*, 1869. In 1861, Congress had created a national paper money system to provide a single, sound currency for the country. Private bank notes, which also circulated as money, soon interfered with the government's new "greenbacks." So, in 1865, Congress imposed a 10 percent tax on the issuing of those private notes—and they soon disappeared.

**Constitutional Limitations** The power to tax is not unlimited. As with all of its other powers, Congress must exercise the taxing power in accord with every provision in the Constitution. Thus, for example, Congress cannot levy a tax on church services—clearly, such a tax would violate the 1st Amendment. In more specific terms, the Constitution puts

four expressed limits—and one very significant implied limit—on the power to tax.

First, it declares that Congress is given the power to tax in order to "pay the Debts and provide for the common Defence and general Welfare of the United States." That is, taxes can be levied *only* for public purposes, not for the benefit of some private interest.

The second expressed limit is the prohibition of export taxes. Article I, Section 9, Clause 5 declares that "No Tax or Duty shall be laid on Articles exported from any State." Thus, customs duties (tariffs) can be applied only to imports—goods brought into the United States. They may not be applied to exports, goods sent out of the country. Recall, this restriction was a part of the Commerce Compromise made by the Framers at Philadelphia in 1787.

While Congress cannot tax exports, it can and does *prohibit* the export of certain items. It does so under its expressed power to regulate foreign commerce, usually for reasons of national security. For example, Congress has banned the export of computer software that allows people to encrypt files in a code no government can crack.

✓ **Checkpoint**
How does the Constitution limit the power to tax?

**levy**
*v.* to charge, impose

**encrypt**
*v.* to encode, especially to prevent unauthorized access

"GIBBS, I SUBTRACTED YOUR FEDERAL, STATE AND SOCIAL SECURITY TAXES AND MEDICAL FROM YOUR PAYCHECK, AND YOU OWE THE FIRM $50."

▸▸ **Analyzing Political Cartoons** Taxes fund the programs and services the public expects from the government. Yet, some criticize the financial burden placed on taxpayers to provide government funding. *How does this cartoon illustrate this issue?*

---

**BEFORE CLASS**

Assign the section, the graphic organizer in the text, and the Reading Comprehension Worksheet (Unit 4 All-in-One, p. 185) before class.

**L2 Differentiate** Reading Comprehension Worksheet (Unit 4 All-in-One, p. 187)

**BELLRINGER**

Distribute the Bellringer Worksheet (Unit 4 All-in-One, p. 189), which shows a sample paycheck and earnings statement for Chris Torres, a weekend employee. Have students follow the directions to complete Chris's earnings statement and paycheck.

**L2 ELL Differentiate** Help students with the earnings statement terminology by writing the following terms and definitions on the board: ***deductions:*** **amounts subtracted from pay;** ***gross pay:*** **total pay before any deductions are subtracted;** ***net pay:*** **remaining pay after deductions are subtracted.**

# Teach

To present this topic using online resources, use the lesson presentations at **PearsonSchool.com/phgovt.**

**REVIEW BELLRINGER**

Display Transparency 16A, Earnings Statement, which shows the completed earnings statement and paycheck from the Bellringer Worksheet. Go over the calculation of gross pay, deductions, and net pay. Students should have found the rates of 6.2% for OASDI and 1.45% for Medicare in their text. Make sure students recognize that net pay on the earnings statement is the amount that they should write on the paycheck. This is the employee's take-home pay. Ask: **Which deductions are federal withholdings?** *(Federal Income Tax, OASDI, Medicare)* **Why does the government require employees to pay OASDI and Medicare taxes?** *(so that the government can provide financial aid and medical care to the elderly and to people with disabilities)*

# Differentiated Resources

The following resources are located in the All-in-One, Unit 4, Chapter 16, Section 1:

- **L2** Prereading and Vocabulary Worksheet (p. 181)
- **L3** Reading Comprehension Worksheet (p. 185)
- **L2** Reading Comprehension Worksheet (p. 187)
- **L3** Bellringer Worksheet (p. 189)
- **L3** Core Worksheet (p. 190)
- **L2** Core Worksheet (p. 191)
- **L2** Extend Activity (p. 193)
- **L3** Quiz A (p. 194)　**L2** Quiz B (p. 195)

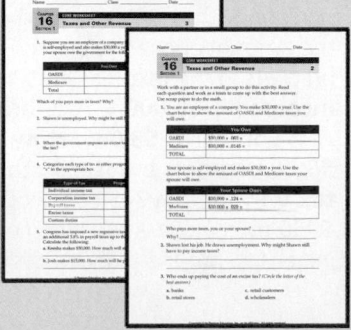

# Answers

**Checkpoint** Taxes can be levied only for public purposes, exports cannot be taxed, direct taxes must be equally apportioned among the States, and all indirect taxes must be set at the same rate across the country.

**Analyzing Cartoons** The taxpayer is so heavily taxed that his salary cannot actually pay for all taxes due.

## DISCUSS TYPES OF TAXES

Have students look at the earnings statement. Tell them that the federal income tax is a *progressive tax,* or a tax that applies a higher rate to higher incomes. The social insurance taxes—OASDI (Social Security) and Medicare on the statement—are *regressive taxes,* or taxes that apply the same rate to everyone.

Point out that no tax for unemployment compensation appears on the earnings statement. Explain that this is a type of payroll tax. However, the federal tax and almost all State taxes to support this joint program are paid completely by the employer. Nothing is deducted from the employee's pay. The amount the employer pays for this tax is based on wages paid to employees.

Remind students that in addition to these payroll taxes, the government imposes several others, including excise taxes, estate and gift taxes, and customs duties—all of which produce revenue. However, the government also imposes taxes for reasons other than to raise revenue. For example, the government places an excise tax on tobacco to discourage people from smoking. It requires licenses to hunt migratory birds to limit the number of birds taken in order to protect the species from overhunting.

**L1** **L2** **Differentiate** Write the definitions of the terms *progressive tax* and *regressive tax* on the board. Have students label the taxes on their Bellringer Worksheet with the appropriate type of tax, and have them include the definitions on their worksheet.

---

---

✓ **Checkpoint**
How does a direct tax differ from an indirect tax?

**FROM THE CONSTITUTION**

No Capitation, or other direct, Tax shall be laid, unless in Proportion to the Census or Enumeration herein before directed to be taken.

—Article I, Section 9, Clause 4

This restriction was a part of the Three-Fifths Compromise at the Philadelphia Convention. In effect, delegates from the northern States insisted that if slaves were to be counted in the populations of the southern States, those States would have to pay for them.

Recall that a direct tax is one that must be <u>borne</u> by the person upon whom it is levied. Examples include a tax on land or buildings, which must be paid by the owner of the property; or a capitation tax—a head or poll tax—laid on each person. Other taxes are indirect taxes, levies that may be shifted to another for payment—as, for example, the federal tax on liquor. That tax, placed initially on the distiller, is ultimately paid by the person who buys the liquor.

The direct tax restriction means, in effect, that any direct tax that Congress levies (except for the income tax) must be apportioned among the States according to their populations. Thus, a direct tax that raised, say, $1 billion would have to produce just about $120 million in California and close to $10 million in Mississippi, because California has about 12 percent of the nation's population and Mississippi nearly 1 percent.

Wealth is not evenly distributed among the States, of course. So, a direct tax laid in proportion to population would be <u>grossly</u> unfair; the tax would fall more heavily on the residents of some States than it would on others. As a result, Congress has not imposed a direct tax—except for the income tax—outside the District of Columbia since 1861.

An income tax is a direct tax, but it may be laid without regard to population:

**borne**
*v.* carried as a burden

**grossly**
*adv.* very badly, glaringly

Third, direct taxes must be equally apportioned—that is, evenly distributed, among the States. The Constitution originally provided that

**FROM THE CONSTITUTION**

The Congress shall have power to lay and collect taxes on incomes, from whatever source derived, without apportionment among the several States, and without regard to any census or enumeration.

—16th Amendment

Congress first levied an income tax in 1861, to help finance the Civil War. That tax, which expired in 1872, was later upheld by the Supreme Court in *Springer* v. *United States,* 1881. A unanimous Court found that that income tax was an indirect rather than a direct tax.

However, a later income tax law, enacted in 1894, was declared unconstitutional in *Pollock* v. *Farmers' Loan and Trust Co.,* 1895. There, the Court held that the 1894 law imposed a direct tax that Congress should have apportioned among the several States. The impossibility of taxing incomes fairly in accord with any plan of apportionment led to the adoption of the 16th Amendment, in 1913.

The fourth and final limit, in Article I, Section 8, Clause 1, declares that "all Duties, Imposts and Excises shall be uniform throughout the United States." That is, all of the indirect taxes levied by the Federal Government must be set at the same rate in all parts of the country.

**The Implied Limitation** The Federal Government cannot tax the States or any of their local governments in the exercise of their proper governmental functions. That is, federal taxes cannot be imposed on those governments when they are performing such tasks as providing public education, protecting the public health, providing police protection, or building streets and highways.

Recall, the Supreme Court laid down that rule in *McCulloch* v. *Maryland* in 1819, when it declared that "the power to tax involves the power to destroy." If the Federal Government could tax the governmental activities of the States or their local units, it could conceivably tax them out of existence and so destroy the federal system.

The Federal Government can and does tax those State and local activities that are of a nongovernmental character, however. For

---

# Myths and Misconceptions

**TAX BRACKETS** Tax brackets are widely misunderstood. Many people believe that if a pay raise bumps them up to the 15 percent tax bracket, then they will have to pay 15 percent of their entire income in taxes. In fact, they will pay the higher rate only on the amount above the previous bracket. To help students understand the use of tax brackets in the text feature "Progressive Taxes," write these brackets on the board: **Income $0–$8,000 = 10% bracket; Income $8,001–$32,000 = 15% bracket.** Ask: **Lori earns $8,000. How much income tax will she pay?** *($8,000 × 0.1 = $800)* **Lori gets a raise, so the next year she earns $9,000. How much income tax will she pay?** *($8,000 × 0.1 = $800; $1,000 × 0.15 = $150; $800 + $150 = $950 total income tax)* Income taxes are progressive—rates increase as total income increases, but the higher rates apply only to the "extra," not total, earnings.

example, in 1893, South Carolina created a State monopoly to sell liquor, and it claimed that each of its liquor stores was exempt from the federal saloon license tax. But in *South Carolina* v. *United States*, 1905, the Supreme Court held that the State was liable for the tax, because the sale of liquor is not a necessary or usual governmental activity. Today, most State and many local governments are engaged in a variety of businesslike enterprises.

## Current Federal Taxes

Oliver Wendell Holmes once described taxes as "what we pay for civilized society." Society does not appear to be much more civilized today than it was when Justice Holmes made that observation in 1927. However, "what we pay" has certainly gone up. In 1927, the Federal Government's tax collections altogether came to less than $3.4 billion. Compare that figure with the figures in the chart on this page.

**Income Tax**  You will recall that the income tax was authorized by the 16th Amendment, in 1913. It is the largest source of federal revenue today. It first became the major source in 1917 and 1918. And, except for a few years in the midst of the Depression of the 1930s, it has remained so.

Several features of the income tax fit its dominant role. It is a flexible tax, because its rates can be adjusted to produce whatever amount of money Congress thinks is necessary. The income tax is also easily adapted to the principle of ability to pay. It is a **progressive tax**—that is, the higher one's income, the higher the tax rate. The tax is levied on the earnings of both individuals and corporations.

**Individual Income Tax**  The tax on individuals' incomes regularly produces the largest amount of federal revenue. For fiscal year 2011, the individual income tax was expected to provide just over $1 trillion.

The tax is levied on each person's taxable income—that is, one's total income in the previous year less certain exemptions and deductions. On returns filed in 2011, covering income received in 2010, most taxpayers had a personal exemption of $3,650, and another

GOVERNMENT ONLINE
Audio Tour
For a guided tour on federal tax revenue, visit
PearsonSchool.com/phgovt

How Government Works

# Taxes At-a-Glance

The Federal Government acquires most of its revenue through taxes. The OMB reported that the government received just over $2 trillion in tax revenue in fiscal year 2010. *Who bears the greatest burden in providing funding for the Federal Government?*

**Individual Income Tax**
A tax levied on each person's total income during the previous year, less exemptions and deductions.

**43.5%** of tax revenue  **$899** billion

**Payroll Taxes**
A tax applied to a percentage of a person's salary, matched by the employer, to fund specific social insurance programs conducted by the government.

**41.9%** of tax revenue  **$865** billion

**Corporation Income Tax**
A tax levied on all the earnings of a business, less its operating costs and authorized deductions.

**9.3%** of tax revenue  **$191** billion

**Excise Taxes**
A tax placed on the manufacture, sale, or use of goods and/or for services rendered.

**3.2%** of tax revenue  **$67** billion

**Customs Duties**
Taxes levied on goods imported into the United States from other countries.

**1.2%** of tax revenue  **$25** billion

**Estate/Gift Taxes**
Taxes applied to the estate of a recently deceased person and to sizeable monetary gifts between living individuals.

**0.9%** of tax revenue  **$19** billion

SOURCE: Department of the Treasury

# Political Cartoon Mini-Lesson

Display Transparency 16B, Tax Cuts, when you discuss income taxes. This cartoon illustrates the general public attitude toward tax cuts. Ask: **Whom do the people represent?** *(taxpayers)* **What is the significance of the people's clothing?** *(The clothes show people in different walks of life, such as business people, construction worker, and teacher.)* **What is the message in the cartoon?** *(Everyone wants his or her taxes cut.)* **What problems does this attitude create for politicians who make tax policy?** *(It is difficult to make tax policies that everyone views as fair. Cutting taxes would please everyone, but would cost the government needed revenue. However, raising taxes would be politically risky, because the increase would displease whatever group has to pay it. As a result, candidates for office often promise tax cuts but seldom tax increases.)*

## DISTRIBUTE CORE WORKSHEET

Distribute the Chapter 16 Section 1 Core Worksheet (Unit 4, All-In-One, p. 190), which provides scenarios and prompts allowing students to delve more deeply into the types of taxes imposed by the Federal Government. Pair students or divide the class into small groups to complete the worksheet. As students do so, circulate and answer questions to keep them on track.

**L2** **ELL Differentiate**  For these students, distribute the adapted Core Worksheet (Unit 4 All-in-One, p. 191), which uses easier vocabulary and provides help with the calculations.

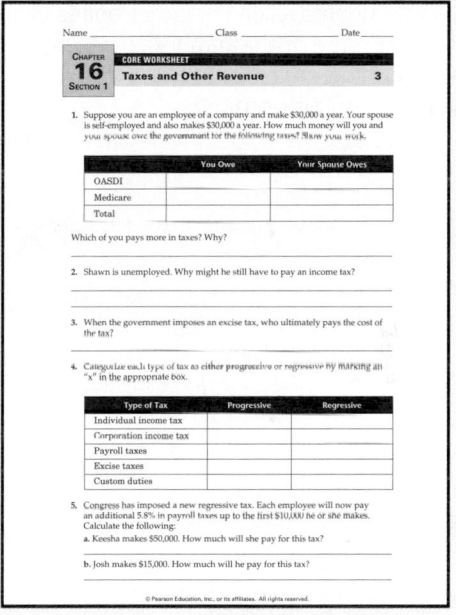

## REVIEW THE CORE WORKSHEET

Have students share their worksheet answers with the class. Tell students that the government receives most of its revenue from income taxes paid by individual citizens. However, these funds go toward programs that benefit the whole population. Have students create a list of five government programs or services that benefit Americans. *(examples: national defense, national parks, school funding, college scholarships, grants for medical research, community health centers, aid for people with disabilities, low-cost housing for people living in poverty, airport security, Social Security aid for the elderly, food stamps, disaster relief)* Ask: **Do you think the value of these programs justifies the amount of money that you must pay in taxes?**

Tell students to go to the Audio Tour to listen to a guided tour on federal tax revenue.

## Answers

**Taxes At-a-Glance** individuals

**L2 Differentiate** Distribute the Extend Activity "Taxes" (Unit 4 All-in-One, p. 193) to lower-level students. It asks them to use the Internet to find information about income taxes.

**L3 Differentiate** Have students use the library or Internet to research some of the licenses the government issues in order to regulate activities. Then, have them create a collage illustrating the variety of activities that the government regulates through licenses.

**L4 Differentiate** Some people in the United States maintain that the federal income tax is unconstitutional, and that by taxing individual wages and earnings, the national government is overstepping its bounds. Have students research, either online or in the library, what some of these anti-tax arguments are, and write a paragraph explaining why they agree or disagree with this position.

---

**Government**
online

*All print resources are available on the Teacher's Resource Library CD-ROM and online at PearsonSchool.com/phgovt.*

---

## Answers

**Checkpoint** OASDI, Medicare, and unemployment compensation

---

of the same amount for each dependent. The personal exemption is adjusted to account for inflation each year. Deductions are allowed for a number of things, including the cost of some medical care, most State and local taxes (except sales taxes), interest paid on home mortgages, and charitable contributions.

By April 15 of any given year, everyone who earned taxable income in the preceding calendar year must file a tax return—a declaration of that income and of the exemptions and deductions he or she claims. The returns are filed, by mail or online, with the Internal Revenue Service. The IRS now receives more than 180 million returns each year; more than 70 million of them are e-filed.

At President George W. Bush's urging, Congress passed major tax-cut legislation in 2001, 2002, and again in 2003. As a result, all taxable income earned in 2009 was taxed (in 2010) at one of six rates (brackets). Those rates ranged from 10 percent in the lowest bracket (up to $8,350) on up to 35 percent on the highest incomes (over $372,950). The Bush-era tax cuts were set to expire by the end of 2010, but majorities in both parties strongly supported the continuation of at least some aspects of the measure.

Most people who pay income taxes do so through withholding, a pay-as-you-go plan. Employers are required to withhold a certain amount from each employee's paycheck and send that money to the IRS. When the employee files a tax return, he or she receives a refund if the employer withheld more money than the employee owed in taxes, or must pay an additional amount if too little was withheld. Those who earn income from sources not subject to withholding (for example, rent or royalties) must estimate the tax they will owe and make quarterly payments on that amount through the year.

**Corporation Income Tax** Each corporation must pay a tax on its net income—that is, on all of its earnings above the costs of doing business. The corporate tax is the most complicated of all federal taxes because of the many deductions allowed. Nonprofit organizations such as churches and charitable foundations are not subject to the corporation income tax.

For 2011, the corporate tax rates ran from 15 percent on the first $50,000 of taxable earnings up to a top rate of 35 percent on taxable incomes of more than $15 million.

**Social Insurance Taxes** The Federal Government collects huge sums to finance three major social welfare programs: (1) the Old-Age, Survivors, and Disability Insurance (OASDI) program—the basic Social Security program, established by the Social Security Act of 1935; (2) Medicare—healthcare for the elderly, added to the Social Security program in 1965; and (3) the unemployment compensation program—benefits paid to jobless workers, a program also established by the Social Security Act in 1935.

OASDI and Medicare are supported by taxes imposed on nearly all employers and their employees, and on self-employed persons. These levies are often called **payroll taxes** because the amounts owed by employees are withheld from their paychecks. For 2011, employees paid an OASDI tax of 6.2 percent on the first $106,800 of their salary or wages for the year, and their employers had to match that amount. The self-employed were taxed at 12.4 percent on the first $106,800 of their income.

For Medicare, employees pay a 1.45 percent tax on their total annual income. Employers must match the amounts withheld from their employees' paychecks. The self-employed pay the full 2.9 percent Medicare tax on their annual incomes.

The unemployment insurance program is a joint federal–State operation that makes payments to workers who lose their jobs for reasons beyond their control. The program now covers most workers in this country. Each State and the District of Columbia, Puerto Rico, and the Virgin Islands have their own unemployment compensation laws. The amount of a worker's weekly benefits, and how many weeks these benefits last, are determined by State law.

The unemployment compensation program is financed by both federal and State taxes. The federal tax is 6.2 percent of the first $7,000 an employer pays to each employee in a year. Each employer is given a credit of up to 5.4 percent against that tax for unemployment

---

# Background

**STATE INCOME TAXES** All citizens are required to pay federal income taxes, but individual State governments may also levy personal and corporate income taxes against their residents. A number of States have chosen not to have individual income taxes, including Alaska, Florida, Nevada, South Dakota, Texas, Washington, and Wyoming. In addition, Tennessee and New Hampshire apply only limited personal income taxes, taxing dividend and interest income but not earned wages. While individual States do have the power to tax their residents, they are also bound by certain limitations. States cannot impose taxes for the purpose of impeding interstate commerce, and they cannot impose taxes that discriminate among taxpayers on the basis of age, race, religion, gender, or nationality. States also cannot use the payment of taxes as a criterion for voting eligibility.

# Progressive Taxes

GOVERNMENT ONLINE
**Audio Tour**
To find out more about how progressive taxes work, visit
PearsonSchool.com/phgovt

A progressive tax is structured so that the higher a taxpayer's income is, the greater percentage he or she must pay in taxes. The federal income tax is progressive and, in principle, works like the simplified, hypothetical example shown below. *What percentage of total income would be paid on salaries of $30,000 and $95,000?*

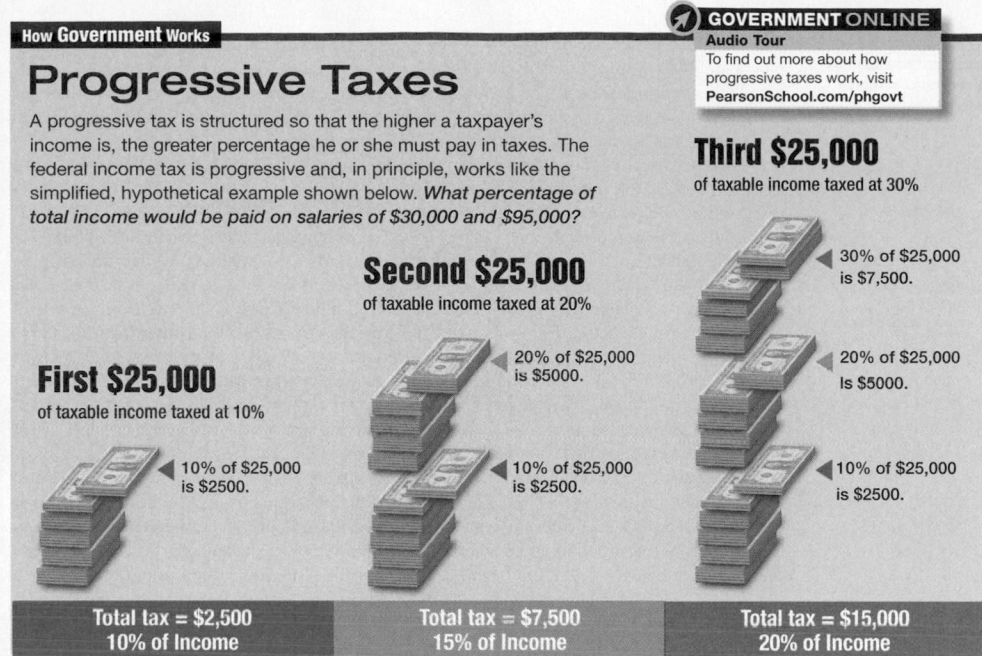

**First $25,000**
of taxable income taxed at 10%

10% of $25,000 is $2500.

**Second $25,000**
of taxable income taxed at 20%

20% of $25,000 is $5000.

10% of $25,000 is $2500.

**Third $25,000**
of taxable income taxed at 30%

30% of $25,000 is $7,500.

20% of $25,000 is $5000.

10% of $25,000 is $2500.

Total tax = $2,500
10% of Income

Total tax = $7,500
15% of Income

Total tax = $15,000
20% of Income

---

taxes that the employer pays to the State. So, the federal tax amounts to 0.8 percent on taxable wages.

Notice that these social insurance taxes for OASDI, Medicare, and unemployment compensation are not progressive taxes. They are, instead, **regressive taxes**—taxes levied at a fixed rate, without regard to the level of a taxpayer's income or his or her ability to pay them. In fact, the regressive OASDI and Medicare taxes now take more money out of the paychecks of many low- and middle-income workers than does the progressive federal income tax.

The IRS collects these social insurance taxes. The money is then credited to trust accounts maintained by the Treasury, and Congress appropriates funds for the social insurance programs as they are needed.

**Excise Taxes** An **excise tax** is a tax laid on the manufacture, sale, or consumption of goods and/or the performance of services. The Federal Government has imposed

and collected excise taxes since Congress acquired its taxing power in 1789.

Today, federal excise taxes are imposed on a long list of items, including gasoline, oil, tires, tobacco, alcohol, firearms, telephone services, airline tickets, and more. Many excise taxes are called "hidden taxes" because they are collected from producers who then figure them into the price that the retail customer finally pays. Some are called "luxury taxes" because they are imposed on goods not usually considered necessities. And some excise taxes are known as "sin taxes," particularly those laid on tobacco, alcohol, and gambling.

**Estate and Gift Taxes** An **estate tax** is a levy imposed on the assets (the estate) of someone who dies.[2] A **gift tax** is one imposed on a gift from one living person to another. Congress first provided for the estate

---

2 An inheritance tax is another form of the so-called death tax. It is not levied on the entire net estate but, instead, on the portion inherited by each heir. Most States impose inheritance, not estate, taxes; most States also levy gift taxes.

---

Tell students to go to the Audio Tour to find out more about how progressive taxes work.

## Assess and Remediate

**L3** Collect the Core Worksheet and assess students' work.

**L3** Assign the Section 1 Assessment questions.

**L3** Section Quiz A (Unit 4 All-in-One, p. 194)

**L2** Section Quiz B (Unit 4 All-in-One, p. 195)

Have students complete the review activities in the digital lesson presentation and continue their work in the **Essential Questions Journal.**

# Debate

"There is no such thing as a good tax." — Winston Churchill

Use this quote and the Debate strategy (p. T25) to start a class debate on the merits of taxation. Ask students who agree with the quote to explain what happens to social services (such as public schools, road maintenance, and police and fire departments) in the absence of taxes. Are these programs and services cut? If not, how do they propose funding them? Ask students who disagree with the quote to explain how the tax burden should be distributed among the population, what limits they believe should be imposed on taxation, and how much involvement individual citizens should be given in determining tax policy.

## Answers

**Progressive Taxes** $30,000 salary: 11.7 percent; $95,000 salary: 15.7 percent

| If Your Students Have Trouble With | Strategies For Remediation |
|---|---|
| Listing the revenue sources of the Federal Government (Question 1) | Have students make an outline of the section using the headings. |
| Explaining the difference between progressive and regressive taxes (Question 2) | Review this section's "Progressive Tax" feature and lead a discussion on the two types of taxes. |
| Determining the three social welfare programs supported by payroll taxes (Question 3) | Have students reread the first paragraph of the "Social Insurance Taxes" portion of the section. |
| Listing the four constitutional limitations to taxation (Question 4) | Have students reread the direct quotes from the Constitution in the section and rewrite them in their own words. |
| Describing their opinion on the equity of direct and indirect taxes (Question 5) | Remind students of the definition of the two taxes (introduced in Chapter 11), and lead a discussion on the advantages and disadvantages of both. |
| Explaining their opinion on using taxes for regulatory purposes (Question 6) | Have students create a Pros and Cons chart to list the positive and negative aspects of regulating through taxes. |
| Identifying reasons for withholding monies from paychecks instead of lump sum payments (Question 7) | Conduct a debate on paycheck withholding vs. annual payments. |

## Answers

**Checkpoint** any three of the following: interest, tolls, fees, sale or lease of public lands, federal court fines, seigniorage, postage stamps

---

✔ **Checkpoint**
What are three examples of federal nontax revenues?

**bequest**
*n.* something left, handed down, passed on

**dutied**
*adj.* subjected to a tax by the government

tax In 1916. It added the gift tax in 1932 to plug a loophole in the estate tax that allowed people to avoid the estate tax by giving away money or other property before death.

Most estates are not subject to the federal tax, however, because those valued below a certain threshold are exempt. For 2009, that threshold was set at $3.5 million. (For 2010, the estate tax was repealed completely.) In addition, deductions are allowed for such things as State death taxes and bequests to religious and charitable groups. Anything a husband or wife leaves to the other is taxed, if at all, only when the surviving spouse dies.

Any person may now make up to $13,000 in tax-free gifts to any other person in any one year. Gifts that spouses make to each other are not taxed, regardless of value.

The estate and gift taxes are separate federal taxes, but they are levied at the same rates. The entire issue of an estate tax is controversial, and it remains to be seen how Congress will adjust rates and thresholds for 2011 and beyond.

**Customs Duties** Customs duties are taxes laid on goods brought into the United States from abroad. Customs duties are also known as tariffs, import duties, or imposts. Congress decides which imports will be dutied and at what rates. Most imports are dutied, but some are not—for example, Bibles, coffee, bananas, and up to $800 of a tourist's purchases abroad. Once the major source of income for the Federal Government, customs duties now only produce just over 1 percent of government revenue taken in each year.

## Nontax Revenues

Large sums of money reach the federal treasury from a multitude of nontax sources. These miscellaneous receipts now total nearly $50 billion a year and come from dozens of places. A large portion comes from the earnings of the Federal Reserve System, mostly in interest charges. **Interest** is a charge for borrowed money, generally a percentage of the amount borrowed. The interest on other loans, canal tolls, and fees for such items as passports, copyrights, patents, and trademarks also generate large sums. So do the sale or lease of public lands and such other items as the fines imposed by the federal courts.

The Treasury Department maintains a "conscience fund" for the money that people pay to ease their minds over past taxpaying mistakes. Another little-known source of nontax money is *seigniorage*—the profit the United States Mint makes on the production of coins. The U.S. Postal Service sells more than $100 million in mint-condition stamps to collectors each year, and collectors spend untold millions more at local post offices.

**Essential Questions Journal** To continue to build a response to the chapter Essential Question, go to your **Essential Questions Journal.**

## SECTION 1 ASSESSMENT

1. **Guiding Question** Use your completed chart to answer this question: How is the Federal Government financed?

### Key Terms and Comprehension

2. What is the difference between a **progressive tax** and a **regressive tax**?
3. **Payroll taxes** support which three major social welfare programs?
4. (a) What are the four constitutional limitations placed on the power to tax? (b) What is the one implied limitation on that power?

### Critical Thinking

5. **Demonstrate Reasoned Judgment** Which do you think is more fair, a direct or an indirect tax? Explain.
6. **Draw Conclusions** Do you think it is appropriate for the Federal Government to use taxes for regulatory purposes? Why or why not?
7. **Identify Central Issues** Why do you think the Federal Government requires employers to withhold money from each paycheck instead of allowing taxpayers to pay their taxes in one annual payment?

### Quick Write

**Cause-and-Effect Writing: Ask Questions** To determine what our national priorities are today or once were, one must reflect on the conditions of the time. Select an administration in office between 1952 and today. Write five questions that you think will help you determine what might have influenced the Federal Government in its allocation of funds for that period. Think about subjects such as the economy, national security, and the environment.

---

## Assessment Answers

**1.** The Constitution gives Congress the power to tax to pay for the operation of government, defense, and national welfare, but only in accord with other constitutional provisions. Revenue comes from taxes (individual income, corporation income, social insurance, excise, estate, gift, and customs duties) and nontax sources (such as interest, tolls, fees, sale or lease of public lands, and federal court fines).

**2.** A progressive tax imposes a higher rate on people with higher incomes; a regressive tax places an equal rate on everyone, regardless of income.

**3.** OASDI (Old Age, Survivor, Disability Insurance), Medicare, unemployment compensation

**4. (a)** (1) may tax only for the public purposes; (2) no taxes on exports; (3) direct taxes must be distributed evenly among the States; (4) indirect tax rates must be uniform throughout country **(b)** The Federal Government cannot tax State or local governmental functions.

**5.** The income tax is the only direct tax the Federal Government has imposed since 1861, because a direct tax laid in proportion to population, as required by the Constitution, would be grossly unfair. A direct tax would fall more heavily on the residents of some States than on others.

**6.** Possible answer: Yes; the Federal Government is responsible for protecting the public's best interests.

**7.** Withholding provides the government with monies throughout the year and spreads out the tax burden on individuals.

**QUICK WRITE** Students' questions should target budget priorities, such as national security, healthcare, and the environment.

# Borrowing and the Public Debt

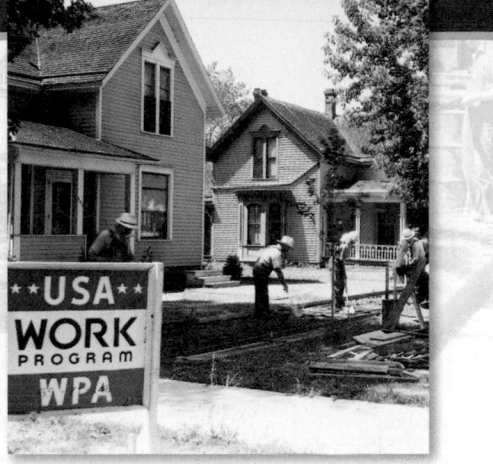

**Guiding Question**
**What effect does borrowing have on the federal budget and the nation's economy?** Use a concept web like the one below to keep track of the main ideas about the government's influence on the economy.

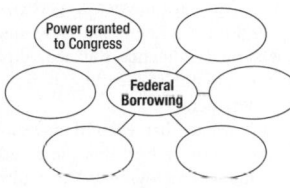

**Political Dictionary**
- deficit
- surplus
- demand-side economics
- supply-side economics
- public debt

**Objectives**
1. Describe federal borrowing.
2. Explain how the Federal Government's actions can affect the economy.
3. Analyze the causes and effects of the public debt.

**Image Above:** Work Projects Administration (WPA) workers built sidewalks during the Great Depression.

I n *Hamlet*, Shakespeare wrote, "Neither a borrower nor a lender be." That advice may make good sense in many situations. However, it most certainly has *not* been followed by the government of the United States, which has been both a borrower and a lender for more than 200 years now.

## Borrowing

The Constitution gives Congress the power "[t]o borrow Money on the credit of the United States" in Article I, Section 8, Clause 2. Congress first exercised that power in 1790, and it has done so hundreds of times since then. For the better part of 150 years, the power to borrow was seen as a way for the government to (1) meet the costs of crisis situations, most notably wars, and/or (2) pay for large-scale projects that could not be financed out of current income— for example, the construction of the Panama Canal in the early 1900s.

Beginning with the Depression years of the 1930s, the Federal Government has borrowed, regularly and heavily, for yet another purpose: to finance budget deficits. In nearly every one of the last 80 years, it has spent more than it has collected from taxpayers. That is, the government has run up a **deficit** (the shortfall between income and outgo) in each of those years—and it has borrowed to make up the difference.

Indeed, the government's financial books did not show a **surplus** (more income than outgo) in any fiscal year from 1970 to 1998.[3] For fiscal year 2011, which extends from October 1, 2010, to September 30, 2011, the government expects to spend some $3.5 trillion—and it will take in some $1.3 trillion less than that stupendous sum. It will have to borrow to cover that shortfall.

**The Depression and Deficit Spending** The collapse of the stock market in October 1929 triggered the Great Depression of the 1930s. To meet that catastrophe, deficit financing became a constant element of federal fiscal policy.

A few statistics begin to suggest the depths of that economic calamity and the miseries that accompanied it. Two million Americans were unemployed in

[3] From 1930 to 2009, the Federal Government ended only 13 fiscal years "in the black"—that is, with a budget surplus: fiscal years 1930, 1947, 1948, 1949, 1951, 1956, 1957, 1960, 1969, 1998, 1999, 2000, and 2001.

## Focus on the Basics

**FACTS:** • Article I gives Congress the power to borrow money, which allows the government to meet the costs of crisis situations and finance large-scale projects through deficit spending. • The public debt is the government's total outstanding indebtedness, including money borrowed and not yet repaid, plus accrued interest. • Years of deficit spending have resulted in a monumental public debt.

**CONCEPTS:** enumerated and implied powers

**ENDURING UNDERSTANDINGS:** • Federal Government revenue seldom exceeds its spending, requiring it to borrow heavily almost every year. • The ever-increasing public debt raises concerns about the burden on future taxpayers.

---

## What effect does borrowing have on the federal budget and the nation's economy?

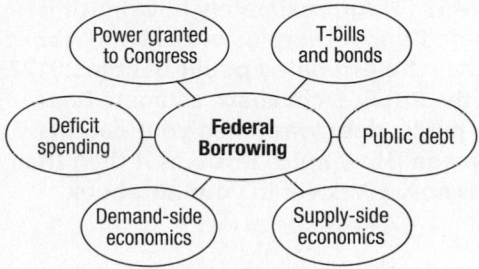

## Get Started

**LESSON GOALS**

Students will . . .
- analyze the annual deficits and surpluses and the public debt by interpreting graphs.
- describe the federal borrowing process.
- analyze key events in the history of the public debt by examining a timeline.

**BEFORE CLASS**

Assign the section, the graphic organizer in the text, and the Reading Comprehension Worksheet (Unit 4 All-in-One, p. 196) before class.

**L2 Differentiate** Reading Comprehension Worksheet (Unit 4 All-in-One, p. 197)

## SKILLS DEVELOPMENT

**ANALYZE GRAPHIC DATA**

To practice analyzing graphic data in this section, use the Chapter 16 Skills Worksheet (Unit 4 All-in-One, p. 200). You may wish to teach the skill before or after reviewing the Bellringer. For L2 and L1 students, assign the adapted Skill Activity (Unit 4 All-in-One, p. 201).

## BELLRINGER

Display Transparency 16C, Federal Receipts and Outlays and Public Debt, which shows a graph of federal receipts and outlays and a graph showing the growth of the public debt. Write on the board: **(1) Approximately how much was the annual deficit in 1945? (2) About how much was the public debt in 1945? (3) Approximately how much is the estimated annual surplus in 2012? (4) About how much is the estimated public debt in 2012? (5) Using the Public Debt chart, estimate how much the public debt was when your parents were your age. How much less was it then than the debt is now? Answer in your notebook.**

# Teach

To present this topic using online resources, use the lesson presentations at **PearsonSchool.com/phgovt.**

### REVIEW BELLRINGER

Review with students the answers to the Bellringer questions. *(1. about $450 billion 2. about $260 million 3. about $45 billion 4. nearly $11.5 trillion 5. Answers will vary, but students should recognize that the public debt now is much larger than when their parents were their age.)* Ask: **Do you think it is fair to put the responsibility of paying back the public debt on future generations? Why or why not?**

**L2 ELL Differentiate** Write these terms and definitions on the board: *interest* **(fee that a borrower owes to the lender),** *deficit* **(shortage; shortfall between revenue and spending),** *surplus* **(extra; amount by which income exceeds spending),** *public debt* **(total amount that the Federal Government owes).** Discuss each term and how it relates to government spending. Have students write the terms and definitions in their notebook.

### DISCUSS

Ask: **If the government needs more money to operate than it takes in, how does it acquire extra funds?** *(The government borrows by issuing securities, such as Treasury notes and bills, to investors—mostly individuals, banks, investment companies, and other financial institutions.)* **Why do investors lend to the U.S. Government?** *(because Treasury securities are very safe and investors receive interest on the amount they lend)*

## Answers

**Surpluses and Deficits** possible response: wars, because they are expensive and do not add anything productive to the economy

**464** Financing Government

---

1929. By 1933, that number had climbed to 13.5 million. One fifth of the nation's labor force was out of work—and millions more were working for, literally, pennies a day. By 1935, 18 million people, including children and the aged, were completely dependent on emergency public relief programs. Between 1929 and 1932, more than 5,000 banks—one of every five in the country—had failed, and their customers' deposits had vanished. By 1932, net farm income had plunged to 33 percent of its level in 1929.

Few States had made any provision for such a crisis, and those that had were overwhelmed. So, too, were churches and other private charities. Poverty and need had become national problems overnight.

**stimulate**
*v.* encourage, spur, whip up

In the elections of 1932, the voters overwhelmingly rejected the tentative efforts of President Herbert Hoover and a Republican-controlled Congress to solve the nation's economic woes. Mr. Hoover and his advisors were committed to the traditional view of the place of government in the economy. They held that government had only a very limited power to deal with what they believed was a private economic crisis. Government, they thought, should ensure a stable money supply; beyond that, the success or failure of businesses was a matter best left to the workings of the free market.

The voters turned, instead, to the Democrats. Franklin D. Roosevelt won the presidency in a landslide, and his party captured huge majorities in both houses of Congress.

**Keynesian Economics** Almost immediately, the President and Congress launched the New Deal—a series of government spending and jobs programs designed to <u>stimulate</u> the economy and put Americans back to work. That response to the Depression was built largely on the theories advanced by British economist John Maynard Keynes. In particular, it was based on the Keynesian view that government should influence the economy by large increases in public spending in times of high unemployment.[4]

Keynesians argue that even if government must borrow to support that increased spending, the higher employment that results will soon produce higher tax revenues. This element of Keynesian economics is sometimes called **demand-side economics.**

Keynesian economic thinking continues to influence federal fiscal policy. However, President Ronald Reagan (1981–1989) and more recently George W. Bush (2001–2009) insisted that lower taxes, not greater spending, provide the best route to a stronger economy. This view, which is sometimes called **supply-side economics** or "Reaganomics," is based on the assumption that tax cuts increase the supply of money in private hands and so stimulate the economy.

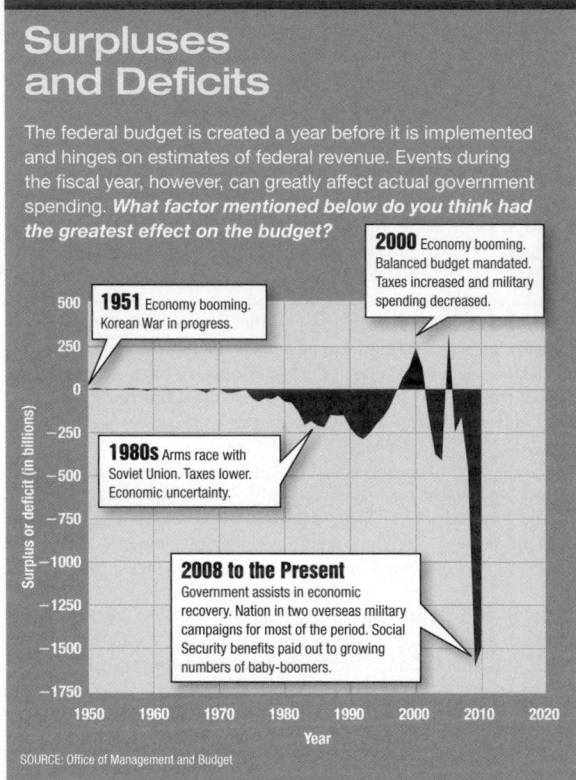

## Surpluses and Deficits

The federal budget is created a year before it is implemented and hinges on estimates of federal revenue. Events during the fiscal year, however, can greatly affect actual government spending. *What factor mentioned below do you think had the greatest effect on the budget?*

**1951** Economy booming. Korean War in progress.

**2000** Economy booming. Balanced budget mandated. Taxes increased and military spending decreased.

**1980s** Arms race with Soviet Union. Taxes lower. Economic uncertainty.

**2008 to the Present** Government assists in economic recovery. Nation in two overseas military campaigns for most of the period. Social Security benefits paid out to growing numbers of baby-boomers.

SOURCE: Office of Management and Budget

---

4  John Maynard Keynes' (1883–1946) economic theories were most fully developed in his work *The General Theory of Employment, Interest, and Money,* published in 1936.

**464**  Financing Government

# Differentiated Resources

The following resources are located in the All-in-One, Unit 4, Chapter 16, Section 2:

- **L3** Reading Comprehension Worksheet (p. 196)
- **L2** Reading Comprehension Worksheet (p. 197)
- **L3** Core Worksheet (p. 198)
- **L2** Core Worksheet (p. 199)
- **L3** Skills Worksheet (p. 200)
- **L2** Skill Activity (p. 201)
- **L3 L4** Extend Worksheet (p. 202)
- **L3** Quiz A (p. 203)  **L2** Quiz B (p. 204)

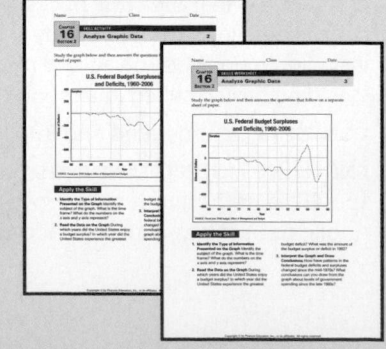

# The Public Debt

Congress has the power to "borrow Money on the credit of the United States," and it has exercised that power ever since 1789. The public debt produced by that borrowing now exceeds $13 trillion. **To whom does the Federal Government owe the most today?**

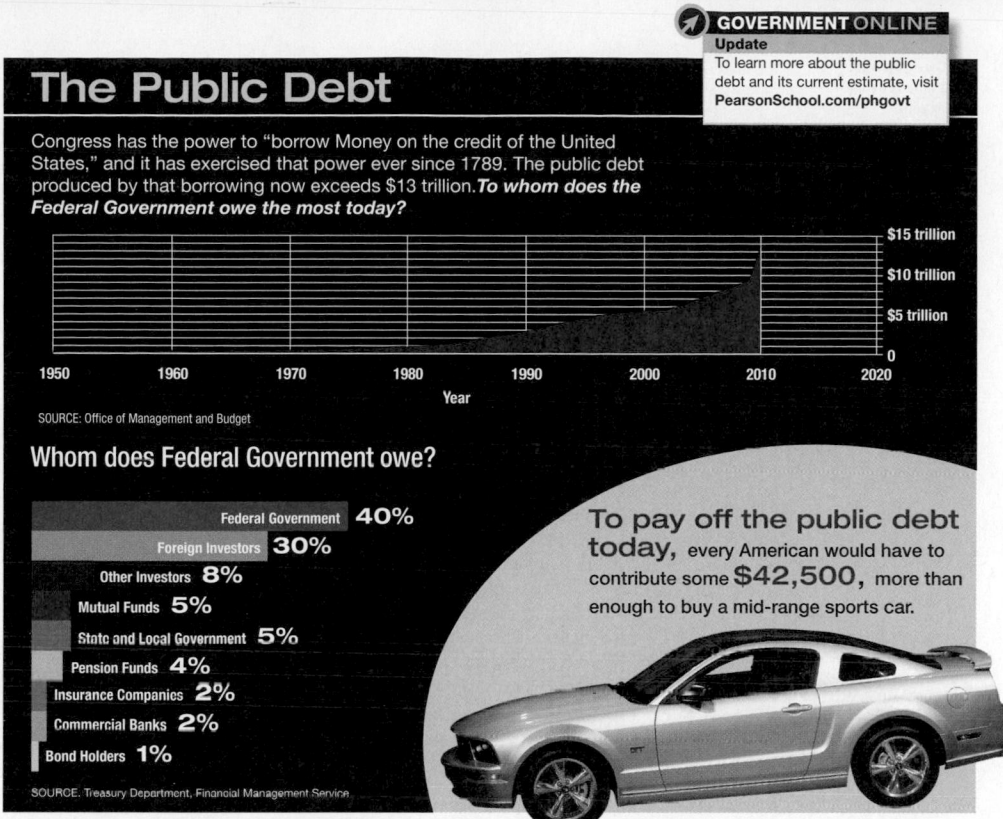

SOURCE: Office of Management and Budget

## Whom does Federal Government owe?

| | |
|---|---|
| Federal Government | **40%** |
| Foreign Investors | **30%** |
| Other Investors | **8%** |
| Mutual Funds | **5%** |
| State and Local Government | **5%** |
| Pension Funds | **4%** |
| Insurance Companies | **2%** |
| Commercial Banks | **2%** |
| Bond Holders | **1%** |

SOURCE: Treasury Department, Financial Management Service

**To pay off the public debt today,** every American would have to contribute some **$42,500,** more than enough to buy a mid-range sports car.

**GOVERNMENT ONLINE**
Update
To learn more about the public debt and its current estimate, visit **PearsonSchool.com/phgovt**

A steep downturn in the nation's economy that began in 2007 and continued into 2009 led President Bush and then President Obama to persuade Congress to enact a series of "economic stimulus" plans—pump-priming measures that could very well have been written by John Maynard Keynes himself. Those laws were variously designed to inject more than $1.5 *trillion* into the nation's ailing economy in order to (1) shore up the loan-making capacities of the nation's banks and other financial institutions, (2) overcome a marked decline in consumer spending, and (3) combat a rising tide of unemployment.

**How Borrowing Occurs** Congress must authorize all federal borrowing. The actual borrowing is done by the Treasury Department, which issues various kinds of securities to investors. These investors are principally individuals, banks, and other financial institutions, and, of late, the government of China. The securities usually take the form of Treasury notes or bills, often referred to as T-bills, for short-term borrowing, and bonds for long-term purposes. They are, in effect, IOUs—promissory notes in which the government agrees to repay a certain sum, plus interest, on a certain date.

The Federal Government is regularly able to borrow money at lower rates of interest than the rates charged to private borrowers. This is true largely because investors can find no safer securities than those issued by the United States. If this country could not pay its debts, no one else would be able to do so, either. Federal securities are also attractive because the interest they earn cannot

**✓ Checkpoint**
How does the federal government borrow money?

---

Distribute the Chapter 16 Section 2 Core Worksheet (Unit 4 All-In-One, p. 198). Have students review the chronology and answer the questions.

**L2 ELL Differentiate** Distribute the adapted Core Worksheet (Unit 4 All-in-One, p. 199).

**REVIEW WORKSHEET ANSWERS**

Have volunteers share their answers to the Core Worksheet questions. Ask: **What do you think the government can do to control the public debt?** *(enact balanced budget legislation, reduce some social services, require the government to operate using only the revenue it receives, increase taxes)*

**EXTEND THE LESSON**

**L1 L2** Use this example to help students understand surpluses and deficits: **You have $10 to spend on a movie ticket and popcorn. When you get to the theater, you find that the ticket costs $7 and the popcorn, $5, for a total of $12. Do you have a budget deficit or surplus? How do you know?** *(deficit; you have less money than you need)* **What choices do you have?** *(You can give up the popcorn and just buy the ticket, borrow $2 to get the popcorn, or find a way to earn the extra $2.)* **What are the government's choices when it has a budget deficit?** *(The government can spend less, borrow, or bring in more money by raising taxes.)*

**L3 L4** Have students complete the Extend Worksheet (Unit 4, All-in-One, p. 202), which contains excerpts on the tax cut debate. Discuss students' answers as a class.

Tell students to go to the Online Update to learn more about the public debt.

## Assess and Remediate

**L3** Collect the Core Worksheet and assess students' work.

**L3** Assign the Section 2 Assessment questions.

**L3** Section Quiz A (Unit 4 All-in-One, p. 203)

**L2** Section Quiz B (Unit 4 All-in-One, p. 204)

Have students complete the review activities in the digital lesson presentation and continue their work in the **Essential Questions Journal.**

---

## Answers

**The Public Debt** The Federal Government owes most to individual Americans, because it has borrowed from its own programs, such as Social Security and federal pension funds.

**Checkpoint** The Treasury Department issues various securities that are invested in by individuals, banks, and other financial institutions.

| If Your Students Have Trouble With | Strategies For Remediation |
|---|---|
| Determining the effects of government borrowing (Question 1) | Review the data on the "Surpluses and Deficits" graphic in this section. |
| Understanding the difference between the deficit and public debt (Question 2) | Compare the graph of annual deficits in "Surpluses and Deficits" to the graph of accumulated debt in "The Public Debt" to illustrate the difference. |
| Describing government borrowing (Question 3) | Have students create a concept web illustrating the main points described in "How Borrowing Occurs." |
| Explaining how the government can create a budget surplus (Questions 4, 6) | Define surplus and remind students of the concept of a balanced budget. |
| Determining their opinion on deficit financing (Question 5) | Create a list of government programs that people expect and lead a discussion on how these programs can be cut or funded without deficit financing. |
| Understanding the ramifications of deficit spending (Question 7) | Review the graphic on public debt. |

## Answers

**Checkpoint** all the money the government has borrowed and not yet repaid, plus accrued interest

---

✔ **Checkpoint**
What makes up the public debt?

be taxed by any of the States or their local governments.

## The Public Debt

Borrowing produces a debt, of course. The public debt is the result of the Federal Government's borrowing over time. More precisely, the **public debt** is the total outstanding indebtedness of the Federal Government. It includes all of the money the government has borrowed and not yet repaid, plus the accrued interest on that borrowing.[5]

**accrue**
v. to increase in amount or value over time

The Federal Government has built up a huge debt over the years. Indeed, in the years since the first federal budget was formulated in 1789, the government has recorded a surplus in only 19 years. Recall, the Federal Government first went into debt during George Washington's administration. Still, it took 192 years—from 1789 to 1981—for the public debt to reach $1 trillion. As you can see from the graph on the previous page, the debt has literally exploded over the past three decades and now (2011) exceeds $13 trillion.

**ceiling**
n. upper limit

The amounts involved here are absolutely mind-boggling. In 1981, as the debt approached $1 trillion, President Reagan said

that he found "such a figure—a trillion dollars—incomprehensible." He then drew this verbal picture: "[I]f you had a stack of $1,000 bills in your hand only four inches high, you'd be a millionaire. A trillion dollars would be a stack 67 miles high." Mr. Reagan's stack would have to be nearly 900 miles high to equal the national debt today!

There is no constitutional limit on the amount that may be borrowed, and so there is no constitutional limit on the public debt. Congress has put a statutory ceiling on the debt, but simply raises that ceiling whenever fiscal realities seem to call for it.

The debt has always been controversial, and its rapid rise in recent years has fueled the fire. The annual interest on the debt is the amount that must be paid each year to those from whom the government has borrowed. That interest came to some $414 billion in fiscal year 2010. Given the vast amounts now being spent to combat the current economic difficulties, that figure will be considerably higher for each of the next several fiscal years.

Most of those who are concerned about the size of the debt are worried about its impact on future generations of Americans. They say that years of shortsightedness and failure to operate government on a pay-as-you-go basis has produced monumental debt and interest obligations that will have to be met by tomorrow's taxpayers.

---

5 The Treasury Department's Bureau of the Public Debt acts as the Federal Government's borrowing agent. It issues Treasury bills, notes, and bonds and manages the U.S. Savings Bond Program.

---

**Essential Questions**
**Journal**
To continue to build a response to the chapter Essential Question, go to your **Essential Questions Journal.**

## SECTION 2 ASSESSMENT

1. **Guiding Question** Use your completed concept web to answer this question: What effect does borrowing have on the federal budget and the nation's economy?

### Key Terms and Comprehension

2. What is the difference between an annual **deficit** and the **public debt?**

3. **(a)** How does the Federal Government borrow money? **(b)** Why can it do so at a lower interest rate than can private borrowers?

4. How could the Federal Government create a budget **surplus?**

### Critical Thinking

5. **Demonstrate Reasoned Judgment** Do you think deficit financing is an acceptable method to fund the Federal Government? Explain why or why not.

6. **Analyze Information** Why do you think that for many years Congress and the President have chosen to borrow money rather than balance the federal budget?

7. **Draw Conclusions** What do you think are the long-term consequences of ongoing deficit spending?

### Quick Write

**Cause-and-Effect Writing: Gather Details** Using magazines, newspapers, and that fiscal year's federal budget, conduct research on the presidential administration you selected for the Section 1 Quick Write. Did any of the questions you developed reflect the conditions and priorities of the time? How did the Federal Government respond to those priorities? Record the results of your research relating to each of your questions in your notebook.

---

# Assessment Answers

**1.** Borrowing over more than 200 years has run up a huge public debt, requiring even more borrowing just to pay the interest on the debt. The monumental debt and interest obligations will have to be paid by future taxpayers.

**2.** The annual deficit is the amount that spending exceeds revenue for one year. The public debt is the accumulation of annual deficits, or the total indebtedness of the Federal Government.

**3. (a)** The Treasury Department issues securities, such as bonds or Treasury bills, to investors. **(b)** because investors consider U.S.

Government securities to be the safest investment available

**4.** By spending less on government programs and operations to reduce outgo, or by raising taxes to increase income; either way, the government must take in more than it spends to produce a surplus.

**5.** Students should note that deficit financing provides services the public expects, but also creates a debt burden on future generations.

**6.** Students should note that balancing the budget would require making unpopular deci-

sions, such as raising taxes or cutting government programs. Politicians risk getting voted out of office for such decisions. Borrowing is politically safer.

**7.** Students should recognize that ongoing deficit spending results in an ever-increasing debt burden on future generations and a drag on the economy. The money spent on debt interest could be spent more productively in other ways.

**QUICK WRITE** Students should research the answers to the questions on their note cards.

# SECTION 3

# Spending and the Budget

**Guiding Question**
**How is federal spending determined?** Use a concept web like the one below to keep track of how the federal budget is determined.

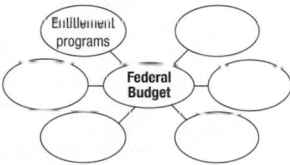

**Political Dictionary**
- entitlement
- controllable spending
- uncontrollable spending
- continuing resolution

**Objectives**
1. Identify the key elements of federal spending.
2. Define controllable and uncontrollable spending.
3. Explain how the President and Congress work together to create the federal budget.

**Image Above:** An elderly patient receives medical care financed by Medicare.

The Federal Government will spend some $3.5 trillion in fiscal year 2011. If you were to place 3.5 trillion $1 bills end to end, they would stretch out nearly 280 million miles, which is more than the distance from Earth to the sun and back again. In this section, you will see how the Federal Government spends that vast amount of money and how it plans for that spending through the budget process.

## Federal Spending

For more than half of our national history—from independence in 1776 to the mid-1930s—the government's income and spending were so comparatively small that they had little real impact on the nation's economy. That situation changed, dramatically, with the coming of the Great Depression of the 1930s and then World War II in the early 1940s.

Today, the Federal Government takes nearly $4 trillion from some segments of the national economy. It then pumps those trillions back into other segments of the economy—all with huge effects on the economy as a whole, of course.

**Spending Priorities** Look at the right-hand side graph on the next page. As you can see, the Department of Health and Human Services now spends more money than any other federal agency—over $854 billion a year, in fact. Most of this department's spending goes for Medicare, Medicaid, and other entitlement programs.

**Entitlements** are benefits that federal law says *must* be paid to all those who meet the eligibility requirements—for example, being above a certain age or below a certain income level. OASDI (the Old Age, Survivors, and Disability Insurance program)—often called "Social Security"—is the largest entitlement program today, and, recall, is funded by the social insurance taxes withheld from the paychecks of American workers. Other major examples include Medicare, Medicaid, food stamps, unemployment insurance, and veterans' pensions and other benefits. The government guarantees assistance for all who qualify for those benefits. In effect, the law says that the people who receive those benefits are *entitled* (that is, have a right) to them.

## Focus on the Basics

**FACTS:** • The largest categories of federal spending are entitlements, defense, and interest on the public debt. • The Constitution gives Congress the power to control federal financing. • The President initiates the budget, which then goes to Congress. • Various House and Senate committees review and revise the budget into final appropriations bills sent to the President to sign into law.

**CONCEPTS:** enumerated and implied powers, separation of powers, limited government, balance of power

**ENDURING UNDERSTANDINGS:** • The budget is a major political statement of the public policies of the U.S. • The budget is a joint effort of the President and Congress. • Lobbying by special interest groups influences the budget and thereby influences public policy.

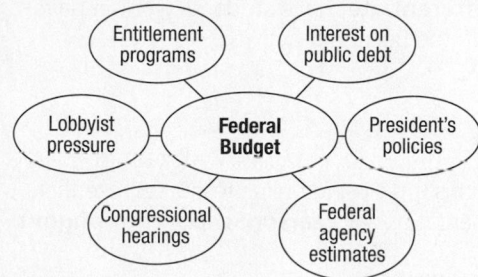

## Get Started

**LESSON GOALS**

Students will . . .

- distinguish between controllable and uncontrollable spending categories on a federal budget circle graph.

- understand the difficulty of setting budget priorities by completing a ranking activity.

**BEFORE CLASS**

Assign the section, the graphic organizer in the text, and the Reading Comprehension Worksheet (Unit 4 All-in-One, p. 205) before class.

**L2** **Differentiate** Reading Comprehension Worksheet (Unit 4 All-in-One, p. 207)

## SKILLS DEVELOPMENT

**DECISION MAKING**

Before students do the Core Worksheets in this section, have them turn to the Skills Handbook, p. S18, to review information on decision making.

GOVERNMENT ONLINE
Audio Tour
To learn more about Federal Government revenue spending, visit
PearsonSchool.com/phgovt

## BELLRINGER

Display Transparency 16E, Government Spending 2010, which contains a pie graph showing outlays of the federal government. Have students answer the questions on the transparency.

**L2 ELL Differentiate** Have students work in pairs to complete the Bellringer activity.

# Teach

To present this topic using online resources, use the lesson presentations at **PearsonSchool.com/phgovt.**

## REVIEW BELLRINGER

Have students share their answers to the Bellringer questions. Write the answers on the board. *(1. Discretionary spending is controllable—Congress and the President can decide how much to spend on these programs in any given year. Mandatory spending is uncontrollable. These budget items are written into law and must be paid unless the law is changed. Congress and the President cannot directly alter these costs. 2. Medicare, Medicaid, Social Security, other Health and Human Services programs, interest on the debt 3. Department of Defense and other services and programs 4. More is spent on mandatory programs.)*

## DISCUSS

Remind students of this chapter's Essential Question: **How should the federal budget reflect Americans' priorities?** Ask: **If the budget is supposed to reflect Americans' priorities, why is it so difficult to create?** Point out that Americans don't agree on spending priorities. For example, social service spending for programs such as food stamps or Medicaid makes up a significant portion of the budget. Some people believe that the size of those programs represents unnecessary federal spending, while others believe that the Federal Government has a responsibility to provide for the needy in our society. Any federal budget decision requires taking into account both of these positions, which are conflicting, but both represent American priorities.

Tell students to go to the Audio Tour for a guided tour on Federal Government revenue spending.

## Answers

**Federal Spending Comparison** Defense was the largest expenditure in 1970 because the Vietnam War and the cold war were in progress. Healthcare costs and the beginning of baby-boomer access to Medicare made Health and Human Services the highest spender in 2010.

# Federal Spending Comparison

The ways in which the Federal Government spends its monies hinge on the events of the time and the priorities set by Congress and the President. *What trends in that spending can you see from these pie charts?*

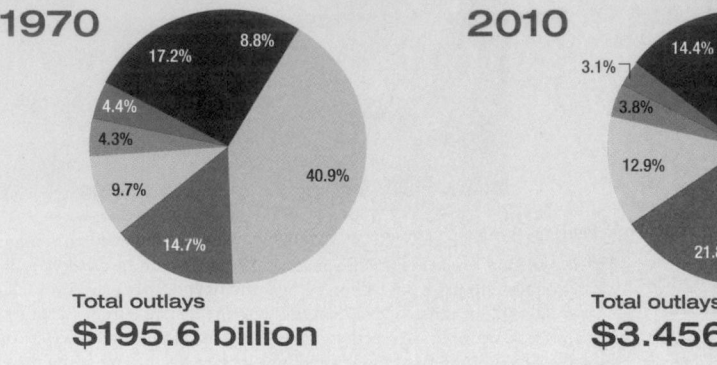

**1970**

8.8%
17.2%
4.4%
4.3%
9.7%
14.7%
40.9%

Total outlays
**$195.6 billion**

**2010**

14.4%
3.1%
3.8%
12.9%
24.7%
19.3%
21.8%

Total outlays
**$3.456 trillion**

- ■ Health and Human Services
- ▫ Defense
- ▪ Social Security Administration
- ▫ Treasury
- ▪ Agriculture
- ▪ Veterans Affairs
- ■ All other

SOURCE: Office of Management and Budget

OASDI is administered by an independent agency, the Social Security Administration (SSA). The department's outlays on OASDI—$706.4 billion in 2010—make SSA the third-largest government spender.

Outlays for national defense now account for a much larger share of the budget than they have over the past decade. The Department of Defense (DOD) spent more than $636 billion in 2010, and it will likely spend even more in 2011.

The defense-spending percentage in the graph is somewhat misleading, however. It does not include the defense-related expenditures of several other federal agencies, notably the nuclear weapons development work of the Department of Energy and many of the functions of the Department of Homeland Security.

Interest on the public debt is now the fourth-largest category of federal spending. Stoked by years of deficit financing, it has consumed a larger and still larger part of the

__stoke__
*v.* feed, stir up

federal budget over the last several years. In the graph above, interest on the debt is included in the Treasury Department's spending. For fiscal year 2010, the net interest on the debt came to some $414 billion.

**Controllable and Uncontrollable Spending** What the Federal Government spends can be described in terms of **controllable spending** and **uncontrollable spending.** Most specific items in the federal budget are controllable. That is, Congress and the President can decide each year just how much will be spent on many of the things that the Federal Government does—for example, on national parks, highway projects, aid to education, civil service pay, and so on. Defense spending is by far the largest controllable item in the federal budget today. Economists often use the term "discretionary spending" to describe spending on those budget items about which Congress and the President can make choices.

# Differentiated Resources

The following resources are located in the All-in-One, Unit 4, Chapter 16, Section 3:

**L3** Reading Comprehension Worksheet (p. 205)
**L2** Reading Comprehension Worksheet (p. 207)
**L3** Core Worksheet A (p. 209)
**L3** Core Worksheet B (p. 210)
**L3** Quiz A (p. 211)
**L2** Quiz B (p. 212)

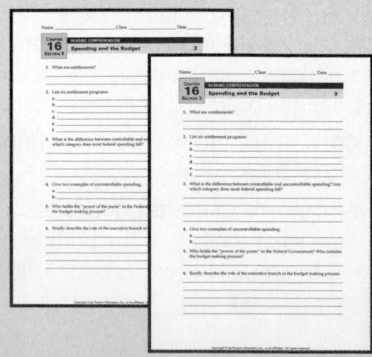

Much federal spending is uncontrollable, however. It is because "mandatory spending" was built into many public programs when Congress created them. That level of spending cannot be changed unless Congress changes the law(s) that set the funding for those programs.

Take the interest on the public debt as a leading example of uncontrollable spending. That interest amounts to a fixed charge; once the Federal Government borrows the money, the interest on that loan must be paid when it comes due—and at the rate the government promised to pay.

Social Security benefits, food stamps, and most other entitlements are also largely uncontrollable. Once Congress has set the standards of eligibility for those programs, it really has no control over just how many people will meet those standards. Thus, Congress does not—really cannot—determine how many people covered by Social Security will become eligible for retirement benefits each year.

Those expenditures are not completely uncontrollable, however. Congress could redefine eligibility standards, or it could reduce the amount of money each beneficiary is to receive. But, clearly, those actions would be politically difficult.

In general, the percentage of federal spending that is uncontrollable has grown in recent years, while the percentage of controllable spending has decreased. In fact, the Office of Management and Budget estimates that over 60 percent of all federal spending today falls into the uncontrollable category. These trends cause concern to those officials who are responsible for maintaining control of the budget.

## The Federal Budget

The Constitution gives to Congress the fabled "power of the purse"—the very significant power to control the financing of the Federal Government and all of its operations:

> ### FROM THE CONSTITUTION
>
> **No Money shall be drawn from the Treasury, but in Consequence of Appropriations made by Law. . . .**
> —Article I, Section 9, Clause 7

Congress—and only Congress—has the power to provide the enormous sums that the government consumes each year. In short, it is Congress that decides *how much* the government can spend and, just as importantly, for exactly *what* it can spend that money.

Still, despite the fact that Congress holds the power of the purse, it is the President who initiates the process by which the Federal Government spends its money. The chief executive does so by submitting (proposing) a budget to Congress soon after that body begins each of its yearly sessions.[6]

Remember, the federal budget is a hugely important document. It is, of course, a financial statement—a lengthy and detailed estimate of federal income and proposed outgo for the upcoming fiscal year. But it is also much more than that, much more than a dry listing of so many dollars from this and so many dollars for that. The budget is a major political statement, a declaration of the public policies of the United States. Put another way, the federal budget is the President's work plan for the conduct of the government and the execution of its public policies in the next fiscal year.

The annual budget-making process is a joint effort of the President and both houses of Congress. The President prepares the budget and submits it to Congress. Congress then reacts to the President's budget proposals, over a period of several months. It usually enacts most of those proposals, many of them in some altered form, in a number of appropriations measures.

**The President and the Budget** The process of building the budget is a lengthy one. In fact, it begins at least eighteen months before the start of the fiscal year for which the budget is intended. First, each federal agency prepares detailed estimates of its spending needs for that twelve-month period. Each agency then submits its spending plans to the President's budget-making agency, the Office of Management and Budget (OMB). (See Chapter 15, Section 2.)

6  The word *budget* comes from the French *bougette*, meaning a small pouch or bag with its contents. In the eighteenth century, the budget was the bag in which the British chancellor of the exchequer (the treasurer) carried financial documents.

## Background

**SPENDING WORRIES** Uncontrollable spending on government programs such as Social Security and Medicare has increased sharply in recent years. Expenditures are predicted to rise even more dramatically as the baby boom generation reaches retirement age, leading to worries about whether these programs can continue to meet their financial obligations. Politicians from across the political spectrum—including President George W. Bush—have offered plans to "save Social Security," using methods that range from cutting benefits to borrowing money for the establishment of personal investment accounts.

## PRIORITIZE SPENDING OPTIONS

Distribute the Chapter 16 Section 3 Core Worksheet A (Unit 4 All-In-One, p. 209), which has students work through the budgeting process. Have each student complete Task 1, according to his or her own opinion. Then distribute Core Worksheet B (Unit 4 All-in-One, p. 210) and assign each student to one of the districts. Explain that they are now acting as representatives of different congressional districts. Ask them to read the description of their district on the worksheet. Then have the students return to Core Worksheet A and revise their spending priority rankings based on this new information. They should record their new rankings in the Task 2 column.

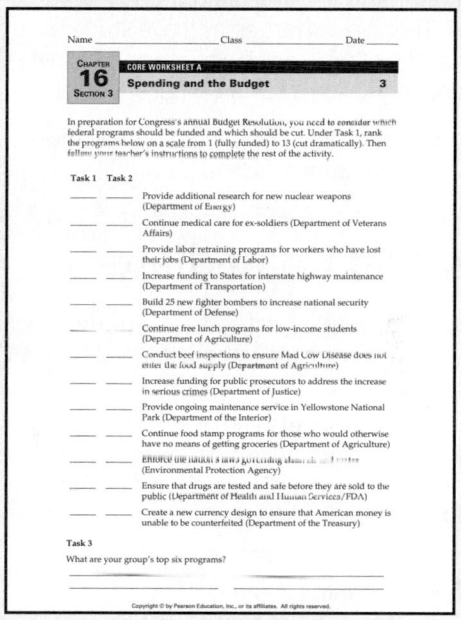

## NEGOTIATE SPENDING PRIORITIES

After students revise their priorities, have them work in groups of four to determine which programs to fund. Groups should have a representative from each district and need to produce a list of the top six programs they wish to fund. Ask them to record their list under Task 3 on their worksheet. Then have the groups share with the class their list and explain why they allocated their priorities in that manner.

Next, tell the groups that for Task 4, they have two options: They can choose to fund only two of the six programs on their list, or they can choose to raise taxes and fund all six programs. Once the groups have finished making this choice, have volunteers share their results with the class, explaining their reasoning. Ask students to discuss the difficulties in coming up with a unified spending list.

## Answers

**Checkpoint** It is the President's work plan for the government as well as an estimate of federal income and outgo.

**L2 Differentiate** Assign congressional districts A and B to struggling students.

**L3 L4 Differentiate** Assign congressional districts C and D to stronger students.

**EXTEND THE LESSON**

**L2 ELL Differentiate** Pair English Language Learners with more advanced students to create a graphic organizer that details the steps involved in the creation of the federal budget.

**L3 L4 Differentiate** Have students select the agency that was the highest priority on their Core Worksheet and research that agency's actual budget allocation from its initial request, the amount allocated by the President, and the final amount approved by Congress. Then, in a short essay, have students describe what they think may have influenced any changes made in the steps toward final approval.

Tell students to go to the Interactivity to learn more about the budget creation process.

# Assess and Remediate

**L3** Have students write a brief summary of the class activity and how it illustrates why the federal budget process is so difficult.

**L3** Collect Core Worksheets and assess students' class participation, using the Rubric for Assessing Individual Performance in a Group (Unit 4, All-in-One, p. 288).

**L3** Assign the Section 3 Assessment questions.

**L3** Section Quiz A (Unit 4 All-in-One, p. 211)

**L2** Section Quiz B (Unit 4 All-in-One, p. 212)

Have students complete the review activities in the digital lesson presentation and continue their work in the **Essential Questions Journal.**

## Answers

**Creating the Federal Budget** Although Congress has the "power of the purse," the Constitution requires that any bill created in Congress needs to be presented and approved by the President. Because of this, the budget-creation process illustrates the constitutional principle of checks and balances.

**470** Financing Government

---

**How Government Works**

**GOVERNMENT ONLINE** For an **interactive** exploration to learn more about the budget creation process, visit PearsonSchool.com/phgovt

# Creating the Federal Budget

Individually and then as one body, the House and Senate spend eight months or so determining the final allocation of federal funds. *Why are both the legislative and executive branches involved in this process?*

## 1 Presenting the Budget

On the first Monday in February, the President proposes a budget outlining the administration's policy and funding priorities and estimating spending, income, and borrowing for the coming fiscal year.

- President submits budget request to Congress.

## 2 Creating a Budget Resolution

Using the President's budget as a guide, the House and Senate work individually and then together to determine the size of the budget, estimate revenue, and set discretionary spending levels.

- House and Senate Budget Committees conduct hearings on a Budget Resolution.
- House and Senate debate and vote on their respective committee's Budget Resolution.
- Conference committee works to blend both chambers' resolutions into one final resolution.
- Each house votes on final version of the Budget Resolution.

## 3 Setting Appropriations

Guided by the Budget Resolution, the House and Senate work individually and then in conference to divide monies among federal agencies. Appropriations measures set out the budgets of the federal agencies in detail and provide the legal authority to spend their funds.

- House and Senate Appropriations Committees each develop 13 separate massive spending bills.
- Conference committee settles on one bill for each of the 13 appropriations measures.
- Each house votes on final version of each appropriations bill.

## 4 Approving the Final Budget

As each appropriations bill is approved by Congress, it is presented to the President to veto or sign into law.

- President signs or vetoes the appropriations bills. If a bill is not approved by October 1st, Congress must pass a continuing resolution for unfunded agencies to ensure their continued operation.

---

The OMB reviews all of the many agency proposals, often in budget hearings at which agency officials must defend their dollar requests. Following the OMB's review, revised and usually lowered spending plans for all of the agencies in the executive branch are fitted into the President's overall program. They become a part of the budget document—a part of the political statement—the President sends to Capitol Hill.[7]

**Congress and the Budget** Remember, Congress depends upon and works through its standing committees. The President's budget proposals, therefore, are referred to the Budget Committee in each chamber. There, in both the House and Senate committees, those money requests are studied and dissected with the help of the Congressional Budget Office (CBO).

The CBO is a staff agency created by Congress in 1974. It provides both houses of Congress and their committees with basic budget and economic data and analyses. The information that the CBO supplies is independent of the information provided by the OMB, which, recall, is the President's budget agency.

The President's budget is also sent to both the House and the Senate Appropriations Committees.[8] Their subcommittees hold extensive hearings in which they examine agency requests, quiz agency officials, and take testimony from a wide range of interested parties. Lobbyists for many of the interest groups' discussed earlier (in Chapter 9) are actively involved in those hearings. They testify, bring grass-roots pressures to bear on committee members, and otherwise work to promote the interests of the organizations they represent. (And campaign contributions from these groups often find their way to members of those subcommittees—in particular, to their chairmen and ranking members.)

The two Appropriations Committees shape measures that later are reported to the

---

7 Congress enacts a separate budget to cover its own expenses. The federal courts' spending requests are prepared by the Administrative Office of the United States Courts and sent directly to Congress.

8 All tax proposals included in the President's budget are referred to the House Ways and Means Committee and, separately, to the Senate's Finance Committee.

**470** Financing Government

---

# Teacher-to-Teacher Network

**ALTERNATE LESSON PLAN** To help students understand the federal budget, give them a summary budget showing the major categories of entitlement and discretionary spending and figures for what the Federal Government spends on each. Then give students the major categories of federal revenue and how much money the government receives. Ask them to balance the budget without raising taxes. They must justify what they did, and then evaluate if they would raise revenue instead of just cutting spending.

To see this lesson plan, go to

**Teacher Center** at PearsonSchool.com/phgovt

floor of each house. Those measures are the bills that actually appropriate the funds on which the government will operate.

The two Budget Committees propose a concurrent resolution on the budget to their respective chambers. That measure, which must be passed by both houses by May 15, sets overall targets for federal receipts and spending in the upcoming fiscal year. The estimates are intended to guide the committees in both houses as they continue to work on the budget.

The two Budget Committees propose a second budget resolution in early September. Congress must pass that resolution by September 15, just two weeks before the beginning of the next fiscal year. That second budget resolution sets <u>binding</u> expenditure limits for all federal agencies in that upcoming year. No appropriations measure can provide for any spending that exceeds those limits.

Congress passes thirteen major appropriations bills each year. Recall, each of these measures must go to the White House for the President's action. Every year, Congress hopes to pass all thirteen of the appropriations measures by October 1—that is, by the beginning of the Federal Government's fiscal year.

It seldom does so, however. Congress must then pass emergency spending legislation to

Singer and songwriter John Legend testifies before a House Appropriations hearing on funding for the arts. **Why do you think the congressional appropriations hearings are almost always open to the public?**

avoid a shutdown of those agencies for which appropriations have not yet been signed into law. That legislation takes the form of a **continuing resolution.** When signed by the President, the measure allows the affected agencies to continue to function on the basis of the previous year's appropriations. Should Congress and the President fail to act, many agencies of the Federal Government would, in fact, have to suspend their operations.

**binding**
*adj.* imposing an obligation or duty

---

## SECTION 3 ASSESSMENT

**Essential Questions Journal** To continue to build a response to the chapter Essential Question, go to your **Essential Questions Journal.**

1. **Guiding Question** Use your completed concept web to answer this question: How is federal spending determined?

**Key Terms and Comprehension**

2. (a) What are **entitlement** programs? (b) List three examples of those government programs.

3. Why is **controllable spending** sometimes referred to as "discretionary spending?"

4. What is the purpose of a **continuing resolution?**

5. Describe the basic steps involved in creating the federal budget.

**Critical Thinking**

6. **Identify Central Issues (a)** What programs do you think are considered high priorities by most Americans? **(b)** How are these priorities taken into account during the creation of the federal budget?

7. **Predict Consequences (a)** What might occur if the OMB accepted all agency funding requests without holding budget hearings? **(b)** What would be the advantages and disadvantages if this were to occur?

**Quick Write**

**Cause-and-Effect Writing: Identify Causes and Effects** Using your research for the Section 2 Quick Write, create a graphic organizer to help you determine how government spending priorities were affected by the needs of the nation at the time and identify possible explanations for the government's actions. Were programs created? Were taxes affected? Did the actions remedy the problem? Keep in mind that there can be multiple causes and effects.

## LESSON GOALS

- Students will analyze news programs by selecting stories to air from a newspaper.

# Teach

## SURVEY

Ask students what television news programs they watch and list them on the board. Have students explain why he or she chooses to watch that specific program. Is it because it covers local stories? Is it unbiased? Is it sensational? Is it the most popular program? Ask: **Which of these programs do you think is the best at delivering the news?** Record the results on the board.

## SELECT NEWS STORIES

Divide the class into four groups, and provide each group with a section of this morning's newspaper: international news, local news, sports, or entertainment. Have each group select five stories from their section that they think should be covered in that morning's television news program. Then, divide the class into new groups so that one individual from each section is a member of the new group. Assign each group to either a local or national program. Have groups select eight stories to cover and determine in which order they will be aired.

## DEFEND THE SELECTIONS

Have each group share the results of their discussion and explain the reasoning for their choices. Ask: **How did limiting the number of stories to air affect their selection process? Which stories got cut and why? How did their group's designation as a local or national news program affect their decision making?**

# Assess and Remediate

You may wish to have students answer the What Do You Think questions.

## Answers

1. Sample answer: The producers may differ in their opinion of the story's importance to their audience or to the producers' political agenda.

2. sample answer: to shape viewer opinion in one direction or another

3. Summaries should reflect an understanding of the differing goals of local and national news programs and should express an opinion on program quality.

**472** Chapter 16 • Citizenship 101

---

## CITIZENSHIP 101

# Analyzing Television News Programs

"Welcome to the Channel Four Evening News. Tonight's top story is the slashing of interest rates by the Fed for the second time in as many weeks to address the nation's economic woes. But first, some early speculation about the Academy Awards. . . ."

Television news programs are one of the major ways that most Americans keep up with local, national, and world events. These news programs are a valuable resource for people who want to stay aware of current events, but they also have the potential to influence public opinion.

Whenever you watch a television news program, you should think critically about how the information is presented to you.

1. **Think about the choice of stories.** There are more news events in any given day than a single news program can hope to cover. The producers of news shows have to choose which stories to report, and how long to spend on each story. By keeping track of which stories are covered, and for how long, you can get a sense of the priorities of that particular television news program.

2. **Pay attention to headlines and pictures.** Television news programs often use pictures and headline graphics to shape viewer reactions. For each news story, look closely at the headline graphics. Which words are the biggest? Are there any visual elements that are used just for entertainment or shock value?

3. **Compare with news coverage on other stations.** It can be very interesting to watch several television news programs on the same day to see how they handle the news. Are they covering the same stories? Do they describe those stories the same way? Does one program include information in a news story that another program does not?

4. **Look for signs of bias.** You will often hear people talk about a "liberal bias" or a "conservative bias" in certain television news programs. Whatever their intentions may be, all news programs have to make choices about which stories to cover and how to report them, and sometimes these choices might be shaped by political opinions.

### ▶▶ What do you think?

1. What might it mean when one television news program spends more time on a story than does a competing news program?

2. Other than time constraints, why would a television news program choose to leave some information out of a particular story?

3. **You Try It** Watch the coverage of one local and one national television news program and compare their coverage of the same day's news. Then, write a brief summary of your findings and indicate which of the two you think is the more useful and informative news broadcast.

**GOVERNMENT** ONLINE
**Citizenship Activity Pack**
For activities on analyzing television news programs, go to **PearsonSchool.com/phgovt**

472

# Citizenship Activity Pack

**L1** **L2** If your students need extra support, use the Citizenship Activity Pack lesson *How to Analyze Television News Programs.* It includes a lesson plan for you and worksheets to help students analyze news for content, structure, and point of view. Breaking News scenario cards supply each team with details of a breaking story to guide their own newscast. Students may also access the Citizenship Activity Pack online for activities on How to Analyze Television News Programs at **PearsonSchool.com/phgovt.**

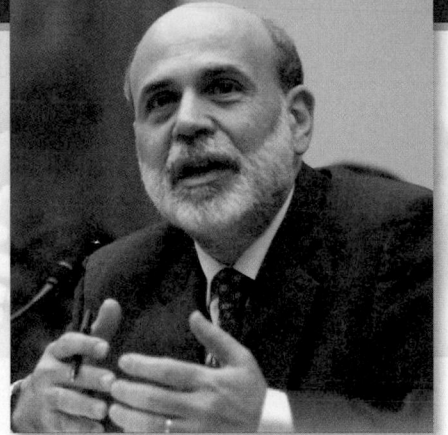

# SECTION 4

# Fiscal and Monetary Policy

## Guiding Question

**How does the Federal Government achieve its economic goals?**
Use a table like the one below to keep track of the methods used by the government to meet its broad economic goals.

| Types of Economic Policy | | |
|---|---|---|
| Goal | Fiscal Policy | Monetary Policy |
| • Full employment | • | • |
| • | • | • |

## Political Dictionary

- gross domestic product
- inflation
- deflation
- recession
- fiscal policy
- monetary policy
- open market operations
- reserve requirement
- discount rate

## Objectives

1. Describe the overall goals of the Federal Government's actions in the economy.
2. Explain the features and purposes of fiscal policy.
3. Explain the features and purposes of monetary policy.

**Image Above:** Federal Reserve Chairman Ben Bernanke testifies on monetary policy at a congressional hearing.

"It's the economy, stupid." That slogan has become a watchword in electoral politics. It first appeared during the presidential campaign of 1992, on a sign that hung on the wall of political advisor James Carville's office in Bill Clinton's campaign headquarters. Mr. Clinton, the Democratic Party's nominee, faced a daunting challenge in that election: How could he possibly convince the voters that he, not incumbent George H.W. Bush, should sit in the White House?

Mr. Bush, the 41st President of the United States, brought a substantial record to the contest—a record highlighted by the end, at long last, of the cold war and a stunning victory in the Persian Gulf War. Mr. Clinton, and Carville and Paul Begala, his chief campaign advisors, were convinced that the key to success in November lay in the domestic, not the foreign policy realm. The nation's economy was in shambles and, to their minds, the incumbent President was vulnerable on that score, and events proved them right.

The successful management of the economy is vital not only to a President's political survival. It has a very direct and immediate effect on the well being of every man, woman, and child in this country. In this section, we explore the Federal Government's key economic goals and the principal mechanisms with which it attempts to achieve those ends.

## Overall Economic Goals

The American economy is enormously complex. The nation's **gross domestic product** (GDP)—the total value of all final goods and services produced in the country each year—now exceeds $14 trillion. Over recent decades, the American people have come to expect that the government will actively and effectively control the behavior of this gigantic beast. The fortunes of presidencies, of members of Congress, and of political parties rise and fall in no small part on the basis of the economy's performance. In response to popular demand, the Federal Government seeks to achieve three main goals in the economic realm: full employment, price stability, and economic growth.

Full employment, as you might guess, means that there are enough jobs available to employ all those who are able and willing to work. The Bureau of Labor Statistics, in the Department of Labor, compiles employment and

---

## How does the Federal Government achieve its economic goals?

| Types of Economic Policy | | |
|---|---|---|
| Goal | Fiscal Policy | Monetary Policy |
| • Full employment<br>• Price stability<br>• Economic growth | • Increase government spending or cut taxes to stimulate economic activity<br>• Cut government spending or raise taxes to slow economic activity | • Increase money supply to stimulate economic and employment growth<br>• Decrease money supply to slow inflation<br>• Fed can increase money supply by buying back government securities, decreasing reserve requirement, or lower discount rate<br>• Fed can decrease money supply by selling securities, increasing reserve requirement, or raising discount rate |

## Get Started

### LESSON GOALS

Students will . . .

- discuss the nation's current economic situation and the tools available to the government to address it.

- analyze monetary and fiscal policy tools, using a transparency.

- analyze graphs of economic performance on the government's main economic goals and suggest policy actions.

## SKILLS DEVELOPMENT

### DRAW INFERENCES AND CONCLUSIONS

Before distributing this section's Core Worksheet to students, have them review the information in the Skills Handbook, p. S19, about drawing inferences and conclusions.

---

# Focus on the Basics

**FACTS:** • Since the Great Depression, Americans have grown to expect the Federal Government to take action to influence the economy. • The Federal Government has three broad economic goals: full employment, price stability, and economic growth. • Fiscal policy influences the economy by adjusting taxes and government spending. • Monetary policy influences the economy by using open market operations, reserve requirements, and the discount rate to adjust the supply of money in circulation.

**CONCEPTS:** enumerated and implied powers, separation of powers

**ENDURING UNDERSTANDINGS:** • The Federal Government uses fiscal and monetary policy as tools to promote full employment, price stability, and economic growth.

Assign the section, the graphic organizer in the text, and the Reading Comprehension Worksheet (Unit 4 All-in-One, p. 213) before class.

**L2 Differentiate** Reading Comprehension Worksheet (Unit 4 All-in-One, p. 214)

## BELLRINGER

Write on the board: **What is our current economic situation? What tools can the government use to address the situation? Answer in your notebook.**

# Teach

To present this topic using online resources, use the lesson presentations at **PearsonSchool.com/phgovt.**

## REVIEW BELLRINGER

Ask for volunteers to read their responses to the Bellringer questions. Make sure the tools suggested are applicable to the current situation.

## DISCUSS ECONOMIC POLICY TOOLS

Ask: **When the Fed buys back securities from banks or sells securities to banks, what are these operations called?** *(open market operations)* Display Transparency 16F, Government's Economic Tools, which is a diagram of the uses of fiscal and monetary policies. Ask: **What actions might the government consider in a recession?** *(increasing government spending, cutting taxes, buying back securities, decreasing reserve requirement, reducing discount rate)* **What is the reserve requirement?** *(the amount of money that the Fed requires banks to hold in reserve)* **How does lowering the reserve requirement increase the amount of money in circulation?** *(Banks must hold less in reserve, freeing up more money for loans. Increased borrowing puts more money into circulation.)* **What actions might the government consider if prices rise too fast?** *(cutting government spending, increasing taxes, selling securities, increasing reserve requirement, raising discount rate)* **What is the discount rate?** *(the rate of interest a bank must pay to borrow money from a Federal Reserve Bank)* **How does raising the discount rate decrease the money supply?** *(Higher interest rates make borrowing more expensive for banks and their customers. As a result, borrowing decreases—resulting in less money flowing into the economy.)*

## Answers

**Checkpoint** Increased prices due to inflation can reduce the purchasing power of consumers.

**Caption** fiscal policy

---

✓ **Checkpoint**
How can inflation affect the economy?

**dampen**
*v.* to deaden or check

**tamp**
*v.* to push down, press

unemployment data. Its reports are a major indicator of the nation's economic health.

Price stability refers to the absence of significant ups and downs in the prices of goods and services. A general increase in prices throughout the economy is called **inflation.** A general decrease in prices is known as **deflation.** The Consumer Price Index (the CPI), also reported by the Bureau of Labor Statistics, tracks trends in the prices of consumer goods.

Both inflation and deflation have harmful effects on the economy. Higher prices due to inflation rob consumers of purchasing power because their dollars buy less than they once did. Deflation makes it difficult for people and businesses to borrow money because the assets they use to borrow against decline in value. Deflation also hurts farmers and other producers, who receive less for their products. This makes it difficult for them to pay off their loans, which in turns hurts banks and investors.

A growing economy is one in which the GDP constantly increases. That growth helps produce a higher standard of living. When there is an absence of growth and the economy shrinks, a **recession** occurs.

President Barack Obama signs the American Recovery and Reinvestment Act in 2009, which provided funds for projects like the one below. *What economic policy do these images reflect?*

PUTTING AMERICA TO WORK
PROJECT FUNDED BY THE
American Recovery
and
Reinvestment Act
TIGER

474

---

# Fiscal Policy

**Fiscal policy** is a major tool with which the Federal Government seeks to achieve its broad economic goals. Fiscal policy consists of the government's powers to tax and spend to influence the economy.

Earlier in this chapter, you read about the generating of revenue and the making of spending decisions through the federal budget process. In addition to deciding how to raise and how to spend money, policymakers must consider what effects their taxing and spending decisions will have on the overall economy. Federal spending represents about 20 percent of the nation's GDP. How money is collected and spent can have a real effect throughout the economy—on employment, on prices, and on growth.

As a general matter, an increase in government spending means heightened economic activity; spending cuts tend to <u>dampen</u> that activity. Tax increases take money out of people's pockets and can slow economic growth. Tax cuts can boost economic activity.

For the better part of 150 years, the Federal Government did not make vigorous use of fiscal policy. Federal income and outgo represented just a bare fraction of GDP. As recently as 1930, that fraction amounted to just over 3 percent of GDP. The Federal Government simply stood by as ups and downs rippled through the economy. Those ups and downs were seen by most economists as an inevitable and even a healthy feature of a free enterprise system.

The Great Depression of the 1930s was a particularly severe downturn. Recall that, in the midst of that crisis, British economist John Maynard Keynes advocated an increase in governmental spending and a decrease in taxes to help end the economic misery. Over time, Keynes's ideas have gained wide acceptance. Now, during a downturn, policymakers usually seek to expand the economy with greater spending and/or lower taxes. This is precisely what happened in 2008 and 2009. Recall, Congress, pressed by President Bush and then by President Obama, enacted a number of economic stimulus measures.

Fiscal policy can also be used to slow inflation. In theory, cuts in government spending and/or tax increases can <u>tamp</u> down inflation across the entire economy.

# Differentiated Resources

The following resources are located in the All-in-One, Unit 4, Chapter 16, Section 4:

- **L3** Reading Comprehension Worksheet (p. 213)
- **L2** Reading Comprehension Worksheet (p. 214)
- **L3** Core Worksheet (p. 215)
- **L3** Quiz A (p. 217)
- **L2** Quiz B (p. 218)
- **L3** Chapter Test A (p. 219)
- **L2** Chapter Test B (p. 222)

" I BOUGHT BILLY AN EDUCATIONAL TOY..."

WHAM!

POP!

WHAM!

POP!

WHAM! WHAM!!!

POP! POP! POP!

" I'M HOPING HE GROWS UP TO BE FED CHAIRMAN."

ECONOMIC GROWTH   INTEREST RATES

▶▶ **Analyzing Political Cartoons** Influencing the economy can be an extremely delicate matter. A small action can result in an unexpected outcome requiring a change in policy that may lead to unexpected results. ***How does this cartoon illustrate the complexity of monetary policy?***

Fiscal policy does have its limits. For one thing, it takes time for policy changes—for example, an increase or reduction in spending—to have a measurable effect on the economy. Timing the delivery of hikes or cuts is a very tricky matter. So policymakers often resort to other means to influence economic activity.

## Monetary Policy

Monetary policy is the most significant of those other means by which the Federal Government can influence the nation's economy. **Monetary policy** involves the money supply (the amount of currency in circulation) and the availability of credit in the economy.

The Federal Reserve Board (the Fed) was created in 1913. It is responsible for the execution of the government's monetary policy. Its seven members are appointed by the President and Senate to serve overlapping 14-year terms. The Board directs the work of the Federal Reserve System as an independent agency created by Congress. It was established to function as the nation's central bank.

Congress intended the Fed to impose some order on a patchwork banking system that had become increasingly prone to panics.[9] Panics occur when depositors lose confidence in banks and rush to recover their funds. If enough customers do so, a bank can be overrun and driven out of business. A panic can spread to infect other banks and, conceivably, an entire banking system. The Fed was designed to avert such a calamity. It serves as a source of emergency funding to prevent panics.

Again, the key function of the Fed is to frame monetary policy. By taking steps to increase the money supply, it can provide a short-term boost to the economy, leading to economic growth and an increase in employment. The Fed can produce the opposite

**patchwork**
*n.* something made up of many different parts

**prone**
*adj.* likely, subject or liable to

---

9 *Panic* comes from the Latin *panicus*, meaning "terrified"; also from, Pan, the Greek god of nature, thought to inspire fear.

## Background

**INFLATION AND FISCAL POLICY** The government's fiscal tools—taxing and spending—influence the economy by affecting demand for goods and services. When overall demand rises, prices rise. This is inflation—a general increase in prices throughout an economy. When demand declines, prices decline. The Federal Government is a huge consumer. Its spending represents about 20 percent of the economy. When the government wants to reduce inflation, it can decrease its own spending. This drop in demand for products slows price increases. The government can also increase taxes to control inflation. Higher taxes leave less money for consumers to spend—decreasing demand and inflation. Fiscal policy is not a popular way to control inflation. Cuts in government spending can mean less money for education, highways, and other programs, and no one likes to pay higher taxes.

**DISTRIBUTE CORE WORKSHEET**

Distribute the Chapter 16 Section 4 Core Worksheet (Unit 4 All-in-One, p. 215), which shows data about the performance of the U.S. economy in three areas. Divide the class into groups to complete the worksheet.

**L2** **Differentiate** Group students with higher-level students to help them interpret the data shown.

**L2** **ELL Differentiate** Review each graph as a class and discuss the information shown.

**REVIEW CORE WORKSHEET**

Have groups share their proposal for addressing economic concerns. Tell students that in 2008 President George W. Bush approved a tax rebate and the Fed dropped the discount rate several times to help stabilize the economy. Display the Bellringer transparency again and ask: **Did the Bush Administration use fiscal or monetary policy, or both?** *(both—tax rebates are fiscal policy; reducing the discount rate is a monetary policy)* **What economic goals did the Bush policies target?** *(Both cutting taxes and reducing the discount rate promote full employment and economic growth.)* **How might these government actions affect inflation?** *(Both actions would be expected to increase inflation. Reducing inflation requires the opposite actions—increasing taxes and raising the discount rate.)* **Why is making economic policy challenging?** *(Actions to improve some aspects of the economy may worsen others. Also, it takes some time for actions to influence the economy, and it is difficult to determine whether changes in the economy resulted from the government's actions or from other factors.)*

**EXTEND THE LESSON**

**L1** **L2** **Differentiate** List on the board each fiscal and monetary policy option discussed in the text. Have students draw a cause-and-effect diagram for each government action.

**L4** **Differentiate** Have students research an effort by the Federal Government to influence the economy using fiscal policy or monetary policy between 1970 and 2000. Then, have them determine whether those efforts were successful and write a brief summary of their conclusions.

## Answers

**Analyzing Political Cartoons** Addressing one economic issue can result in a larger problem with another.

# Assess and Remediate

**L3** Collect the Core Worksheets and assess students' work.

**L3** Assign the Section 4 Assessment questions.

**L3** Section Quiz A (Unit 4 All-in-One, p. 217)

**L2** Section Quiz B (Unit 4 All-in-One, p. 218)

Have students complete the review activities in the digital lesson presentation and continue their work in the **Essential Questions Journal.**

## REMEDIATION

| If Your Students Have Trouble With | Strategies For Remediation |
|---|---|
| Understanding how fiscal and monetary policy can influence the economy (Questions 1, 4) | Create a flowchart illustrating how specific government actions affect elements of the economy. |
| Understanding gross domestic product (Question 2) | Have students create a graphic illustrating how to calculate a nation's GDP. |
| Understanding the difference between inflation and deflation (Question 3) | Have students look up each term in the glossary or other sources and write their definition in their own words. |
| Explaining how economic goals are critical to economic stability (Question 5) | Have students brainstorm a list of reasons why these goals are critical to a stable economy. |
| Determining government involvement in the economy (Questions 6, 7) | Create a list of the actions the government can take and brainstorm possible results if the government did not take action. |

## Answers

**Checkpoint** buy back government securities, decrease reserve requirements, cut discount rate

---

✔ **Checkpoint**
In what ways can the Fed increase the money supply?

effect by decreasing the supply of money and consequently slowing inflationary pressures.

The Fed can alter the money supply through three major mechanisms. Its tools for that purpose are open market operations, reserve requirements, and the discount rate.

**Open Market Operations** When the Fed seeks to alter the money supply, it does not simply send out trucks that carry bundles of cash to or from member banks. Its operations are far more sophisticated. It operates through what are called **open market operations**—a process that involves the buying or selling of government securities, such as bonds, from and to the nation's banks. By buying these government securities back from the banks, the Fed provides money to banks, which can then make loans to individuals and to businesses. If its aim is to decrease the money supply, the Fed sells government bonds through its open market operations. As it receives money from the banks that buy those securities, money is removed from circulation. Subsequently, the banks have less money to loan or invest, and so business activity slows.

**Reserve Requirements** The Fed can also influence or alter the amount of money in circulation by changing the reserve requirements

that all banks and similar financial institutions must meet. The **reserve requirement** is the amount of money that the Federal Reserve Board determines banks must keep "in reserve" in their vaults or on deposit with one of the 12 Federal Reserve Banks. Those funds cannot be used to make loans or for any other purpose. They remain, instead, out of circulation, available for use in the event of sudden, unexpected demand.

If the Fed sees a need to lower the money supply, on the other hand, it can require that banks increase the amount they have in reserve. Or the reserve requirement can be relaxed by the Fed to increase the amount of money in circulation.

**Discount Rate** The third mechanism available to the Fed involves the discount rate. The **discount rate** is the rate of interest a bank must pay when it borrows money from a Federal Reserve Bank. Interest, recall, is the cost borrowers incur and must repay in order to borrow money. If the Fed raises the discount rate, banks find it more difficult to obtain money. Banks must then charge higher interest rates to their customers; borrowing decreases and less money flows into the economy. Cutting the discount rate has the opposite effect.

---

# SECTION 4 ASSESSMENT

**Essential Questions Journal** To continue to build a response to the chapter Essential Question, go to your **Essential Questions Journal.**

1. **Guiding Question** Use your completed table to answer this question: How does the Federal Government achieve its economic goals?

### Key Terms and Comprehension

2. What is the **gross domestic product?**

3. What is the difference between **inflation** and **deflation?**

4. How can the use of **fiscal policy** and **monetary policy** influence the overall national economy?

### Critical Thinking

5. **Identify Central Issues (a)** What are the three main economic goals the government aims to achieve? **(b)** Why do you think these goals are critical to a healthy economy?

6. **Drawing Conclusions** Should the Federal Government have the authority to take actions that can alter the nation's economy? Why or why not?

7. **Predict Consequences** Why might policymakers hesitate to use fiscal policy to influence the nation's economy?

### Quick Write

**Cause-and-Effect Writing: Create an Outline** Review your notes and graphic organizer from Section 3 to clarify the cause-and-effect relationships between the issues and the data you found. What issues seemed to be important to Americans at the time? Did the federal budget and government actions reflect those concerns? Create an outline of the relationships with supporting data to help you determine how best to present the information—chronologically or by order of importance—to your audience.

---

# Assessment Answers

**1.** The Federal Government uses fiscal and monetary policy to adjust taxes, government spending, and the money supply to achieve its goals of full employment, price stability, and economic growth.

**2.** the total value of all final goods and services produced by a nation in a year

**3.** Inflation is a general increase in prices throughout an economy, while deflation is a general decrease in prices.

**4.** Fiscal policy adjusts the level of taxes and government spending to increase economic activity

or slow inflation. Monetary policy uses open market operations, reserve requirements, and the discount rate to adjust the money supply in order to stimulate economic growth or slow inflation.

**5. (a)** full employment, price stability, economic growth **(b)** Full employment, stable prices (and therefore stable purchasing power), and a growing economy promote a high standard of living for the nation's citizens, leading to a stable nation.

**6.** Yes, because government actions can promote economic stability by reducing the

extremes in the economy's ups and downs; OR No, because the free market will make the necessary economic adjustments more efficiently without government interference

**7.** Fiscal policy takes a long time to work. How the government taxes and spends can also have unintended consequences on the overall economy—affecting employment, prices, and growth. Cutting programs and raising taxes are politically unpopular.

**QUICK WRITE** Outlines should show a chronological or a rank-order organization.

# Quick Study Guide

**GOVERNMENT** ONLINE

**On the Go**
To review anytime, anywhere, download these online resources at **PearsonSchool.com/phgovt**
Political Dictionary, Audio Review

**CHAPTER 16**

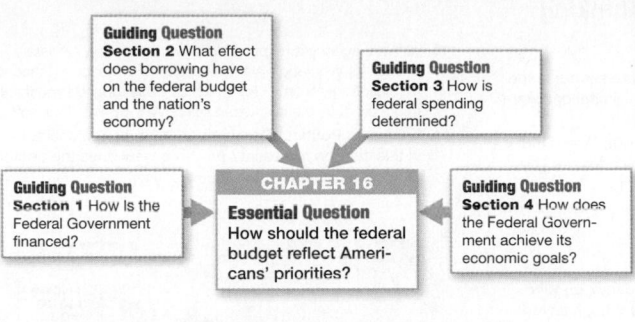

**Guiding Question Section 2** What effect does borrowing have on the federal budget and the nation's economy?

**Guiding Question Section 3** How is federal spending determined?

**Guiding Question Section 1** How is the Federal Government financed?

**CHAPTER 16 Essential Question** How should the federal budget reflect Americans' priorities?

**Guiding Question Section 4** How does the Federal Government achieve its economic goals?

## Political Dictionary

fiscal policy *p. 456*
progressive tax *p. 459*
payroll tax *p. 460*
regressive tax *p. 461*
excise tax *p. 461*
estate tax *p. 461*
gift tax *p. 461*
customs duty *p. 462*
interest *p. 462*
deficit *p. 463*
surplus *p. 463*
demand-side economics *p. 464*
supply-side economics *p. 464*
public debt *p. 466*
entitlement *p. 467*
controllable spending *p. 468*
uncontrollable spending *p. 468*
continuing resolution *p. 471*
gross domestic product *p. 473*
inflation *p. 474*
deflation *p. 474*
recession *p. 474*
fiscal policy *p. 474*
monetary policy *p. 475*
open market operations *p. 476*
reserve requirement *p. 476*
discount rate *p. 476*

## Sources of Government Revenue

| | |
|---|---|
| Income tax | Progressive tax on the income of both individuals and corporations |
| Social insurance tax | Regressive tax withheld from employee paychecks to support social programs |
| Excise tax | Regressive tax on the manufacture, sale, or consumption of goods and/or on services rendered |
| Estate tax | Tax on the assets of someone who dies |
| Gift tax | Tax on a gift of money or property |
| Customs duty | Tax on goods imported into this country |
| Interest | Monies paid for the use of monies lent |
| Licenses and fees | Monies paid for licenses, passports, patents, fines, etc. |
| Seigniorage | Income gained from production of coins and paper money |
| Borrowing | Monies gained through the sale of bonds |

**Fiscal Policy**

Increased taxes reduce economic activity and slow inflation.

Reduced government spending slows inflation.

Decreased taxes heighten economic activity.

Changing taxes

Changing spending

Increased spending increases employment and tax revenues.

**Influencing the Economy**

**Monetary Policy**

Selling securities, increasing reserve, or raising interest rates decreases supply.

Changing money supply

Purchasing of securities, decreasing reserve, or lowering interest rates increases supply.

# For More Information

To learn more about the federal budget, refer to these sources or assign them to students:

**L1** **De Capua, Sarah.** *Paying Taxes.* Children's Press, 2002.

**L2** **Grote, Joann A.** *The Internal Revenue Service.* Chelsea House, 2001.

**L3** **Boortz, Neal and John Linder.** *The FairTax Book: Saying Goodbye to the Income Tax and the IRS.* HarperCollins Publishers, 2006.

**L4** **Bittle, Scott and Jean Johnson.** *Where Does the Money Go?: Your Guided Tour to the Federal Budget Crisis.* HarperCollins Publishers, 2008.

Have students download the digital resources available at Government on the Go for review and remediation.

## STUDY TIPS

**Making Audio Study Guides** For auditory learners, there is no better way to review and absorb information than an audio study guide. In fact, most types of learners can benefit from listening to information while they are performing other tasks. Even if students are not actively paying attention to the content, they will still retain some of it. Tell students they can make their own audio study guide by using a computer, a CD burner, or an MP3 player and audio software. Students can record their own voices reading summaries of text information or lectures, asking questions and then providing the answers, reciting terms or key dates followed by their definitions or meanings, and more. The audio files can be listened to while traveling to school, waiting in line, exercising, or during any "down time."

## ASSESSMENT AT A GLANCE

**Tests and Quizzes**
Section Assessments
Section Quizzes A and B, Unit 4 **All-in-One**
Chapter Assessment
Chapter Tests A and B, Unit 4 **All-in-One**
Document-Based Assessment
Progress Monitoring Online
Exam*View* Test Bank

**Performance Assessment**
Essential Questions Journal
Debate, p. 461
Assessment Rubrics, **All-in-One**

# Chapter Assessment

## COMPREHENSION AND CRITICAL THINKING

### SECTION 1

1. **(a)** Taxes must be for public purposes only; export taxes are prohibited; direct taxes must be equally apportioned among States by population; and all indirect taxes must be levied at the same rates nationwide. **(b)** Students might suggest that these provisions help limit the power of government and preserve federalism by ensuring that federal taxes are applied equally to all States. Students might also note that the Framers included the export-tax restriction as part of the Commerce Compromise and the direct-tax restriction as part of the Three-Fifths Compromise.

2. **(a)** individual income tax, corporation income tax, social insurance taxes, excise tax, estate/gift taxes, and customs duties **(b)** individual income tax **(c)** Excise tax is paid practically on a daily basis because the retail price of many consumer purchases contains some form of excise tax.

3. Answers will vary, but should show an understanding that federal regressive taxes do require some individuals to pay more proportionally, but that the progressive income tax requires those with more income to pay more than those with less.

### SECTION 2

4. **(a)** The government borrows money through the sale of federal securities, such as Treasury notes, bills, and bonds. **(b)** Answers will vary, but should note that monies borrowed by the government are often used to fund programs that benefit the public. **(c)** Answers will vary, but should note that government borrowing increases the public debt, which future taxpayers will have to pay.

5. **(a)** the total amount of money the government owes, including interest **(b)** Yes, the huge and increasing debt puts a drag on the economy and unfairly transfers the burden of payment to future generations. OR No, the government's need to raise revenue to fund necessary programs and provide for national security is more important than the increasing debt.

### SECTION 3

6. **(a)** Controllable spending refers to items for which Congress and the President can decide how much to spend. Uncontrollable spending refers to spending that neither

---

 **GOVERNMENT** ONLINE
Self-Test
To test your understanding of key terms and main ideas, visit
PearsonSchool.com/phgovt

## Comprehension and Critical Thinking

### Section 1

1. **(a)** What four limits on the power to tax are set out in the Constitution? **(b)** Why do you think those limitations were included by the Framers?

2. **(a)** What are the different types of taxes? **(b)** Which federal tax raises the most revenue? **(c)** Which tax are you most likely to pay on a regular basis? Why?

3. Do you think the current federal tax system is fair? Why or why not?

### Section 2

4. **(a)** How does the government borrow money? **(b)** Who benefits from this borrowing system? **(c)** Who, if anyone, is disadvantaged by government borrowing?

5. **(a)** What is the public debt? **(b)** Do you think the concern about the size of the public debt is justified? Why or why not?

### Section 3

6. **(a)** What is the difference between controllable and uncontrollable spending? **(b)** How would you classify entitlement programs? **(c)** Why do you think Congress structured the financing of these programs in this manner?

7. **(a)** What is the President's role in the budget-making process? **(b)** The role of Congress? **(c)** Is this process a joint effort between the President and Congress? Explain.

8. **(a)** Should the Constitution be amended to require a balanced budget each year? **(b)** What might be the results of such an amendment?

### Section 4

9. **(a)** What are the principal economic goals of the Federal Government? **(b)** What methods are used by the government to meet these goals? **(c)** Should the government be involved in the economy? Why or why not?

10. **(a)** What agency is responsible for implementing monetary policy? **(b)** What tools are available to this agency to influence the nation's economy? **(c)** Which of these tools do you think might produce the quickest results? Why do you think so?

11. **Analyzing Political Cartoons (a)** Who do the characters in this cartoon represent? **(b)** What view does the doctor's diagnosis express?

### Writing About Government

12. Use your Quick Write exercises from this chapter to write a cause-and-effect essay on the relationship between the actions of the government and the nation's priorities. Make sure that your thesis statement is clearly stated, your ideas are well-organized and your argument is supported. See pp. S3–S5 in the Skills Handbook.

---

## Apply What You've Learned

13. **Essential Question Activity** Take a poll of 10 to 15 individuals in your community. Ask:
    **(a)** What issues are priorities for Americans today? Which one is the most important to you?
    **(b)** Within the last six months, has the Federal Government taken any action to address any issue? If so, what?
    **(c)** Which federal programs or services do you think could be cut back or abolished to help deal with the issue? Would you be willing to pay additional taxes to cover the cost? If not, how should the government pay for it?
    **(d)** Do you think the Federal Government is responsive to the priorities of Americans? Why or why not?

14. **Essential Question Assessment** Using the results of your poll, create a chart illustrating the top priorities of Americans today to help you answer the Essential Question: **How should the federal budget reflect Americans' priorities?** Then, write a letter to your congressperson expressing the issues that are the top concerns and suggesting methods the government could use to address the issues.

**Essential Questions Journal** To respond to the chapter Essential Question, go to your **Essential Questions Journal.**

---

Congress nor the President has the power to change. **(b)** uncontrollable **(c)** Entitlement programs are structured to ensure that the programs continue to run from administration to administration, and that those eligible for the programs continue to get the services needed.

7. **(a)** Through the work of the OMB, the President makes the initial proposal for the federal budget to Congress. The President also signs the finished legislation. **(b)** Through their budget and appropriations committees, both houses of Congress review the President's budget and fashion bills to appropriate funds. Both houses vote on these bills. **(c)** Yes. The budget process is a negotiation between the President and both houses of Congress to arrive at a final spending plan. OR No. Although Congress creates the appropriation bills, the President can veto any appropriations, which gives the President the power to control the results of the budgetary process.

8. **(a)** Yes, because an amendment would force the government to balance the budget, which it won't do on its own; OR No, because an amendment would take away the flexibility needed to raise funds

# Document-Based Assessment

## Addressing the Rising Cost of Healthcare

The costs of entitlement programs and the constraints they place on the federal budget have been debated at great length. Most Americans agree that these programs are critical to the public's well-being, however. As the documents below illustrate, keeping these programs going without undermining others is proving to be a very difficult fiscal challenge.

### Document 1

In the United States a large and growing portion of both federal and state expenditures is for subsidized health insurance. In 1975, federal spending on Medicare and Medicaid was about 6 percent of total non-interest federal spending. Today, that share is about 23 percent. Because of rising costs of health care and the aging of the population, the CBO projects that, without reform, Medicare and Medicaid will be about 35 percent of non-interest federal spending in 2025. This trend implies increasingly difficult tradeoffs for legislators and taxpayers, as higher government spending on health care spending will . . . require reductions in other government programs, higher taxes, or larger budget deficits.

—Ben S. Bernanke, Chairman,
Federal Reserve, 2008

### Document 2

If the major entitlement programs grow as forecast, our children will be forced to choose between massive tax increases, near-elimination of all government programs outside of entitlements (including defense and essential services), or some combination. . . . Because of these rising entitlement obligations, ensuring long-term fiscal stability requires much more than addressing current spending and deficits, important as that is. Also necessary is finding a means of controlling the costs of the major entitlement programs, without compromising their essential functions.

—Katherine Baicker,
Council of Economic Advisors, 2005

### Document 3

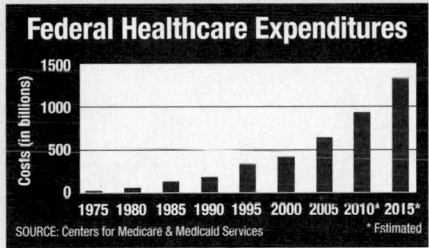

**Federal Healthcare Expenditures**

Costs (in billions): 0, 500, 1000, 1500

1975 1980 1985 1990 1995 2000 2005 2010ᴬ 2015*

SOURCE: Centers for Medicare & Medicaid Services    * Estimated

---

Use your knowledge of financing government and the documents above to answer Questions 1–3.

1. What is the main point of Document 3?
   A. Controllable expenditures are becoming uncontrollable.
   B. Entitlement programs are too costly.
   C. Revenue from healthcare has increased.
   D. Subsidized healthcare costs have risen considerably over time.

2. What concerns are discussed in both Document 1 and Document 2?

3. **Pull It Together** Given the increasing costs of entitlement programs, do you think the Federal Government should continue to provide subsidized healthcare? Why or why not?

**GOVERNMENT ONLINE**
**Documents**
To find more primary sources on the cost of healthcare, visit
PearsonSchool.com/phgovt

---

## DOCUMENT-BASED ASSESSMENT

1. D
2. Both documents are concerned with the fact that without reform, the cost of entitlement programs will have dire effects on other programs and the federal budget.
3. Possible response: Yes, the Federal Government should continue to subsidize healthcare, because our society has a responsibility to provide the necessities of life to citizens in need. Also, in the end, those with insurance will be forced to pay for those without insurance through their own premiums. OR No, the federal government should not continue to subsidize healthcare, because buying insurance should be the responsibility of the individual—not the government.

**L2 Differentiate** Students use all the documents on the page to support their thesis.

**L3 Differentiate** Students include additional information available online at **PearsonSchool.com/phgovt.**

**L4 Differentiate** Students use materials from the textbook, the online information at **PearsonSchool.com/phgovt,** and do additional research to support their views.

**Go Online to PearsonSchool.com/phgovt** for a student rubric and extra documents.

---

quickly in crisis situations **(b)** A balanced budget would require painful cuts in some programs and the elimination of some altogether. It would also likely require large tax increases.

### SECTION 4

9. **(a)** full employment, price stability, and economic growth **(b)** altering taxes, the money supply, and spending **(c)** Answers will vary, but should take into account the pros and cons of government involvement.

10. **(a)** the Federal Reserve Board **(b)** The Fed can alter the supply of money in circulation by buying or selling federal securities, changing the required reserve amount, and adjusting the discount rate. **(c)** Answers will vary but students should show an understanding that economic policies take time to show results especially in times of economic slumps since people are less likely to spend money even if they have it.

11. **(a)** Uncle Sam (the U.S.) and the Fed chairman Ben Bernanke **(b)** that the American economy is seriously ill

### WRITING ABOUT GOVERNMENT

12. Essays should follow the organization students outlined in an earlier step, show clear cause-and-effect relationships, and be well supported with appropriate details.

### APPLY WHAT YOU'VE LEARNED

13. Student polls should summarize opinions on economic priorities and government actions to address these priorities.

14. Letters should state the priorities that the student found to be of greatest importance, and the methods of addressing the issues should be reasonable and practical.

# Introduce the Chapter

## Essential Questions:

**UNIT 4**

What makes a good President?

**CHAPTER 17**

How should the United States interact with other countries?

### ACTIVATE PRIOR KNOWLEDGE

Have students examine the image and quotation on these pages. Ask: **How does this image reflect Americans' aspiration for peace?** *(A visiting foreign dignitary shows the American desire to use diplomacy to promote international interaction and peace while the ritual of reviewing the troops is a symbolic illustration of the U.S. military's strength and power to maintain peace.)* In this chapter, students will learn about U.S. foreign policy and its role in national security. Have students further explore U.S. foreign policy and national defense by completing the Chapter 17 Essential Question Warmup activity in their **Essential Questions Journal.** Discuss their responses as a class.

### BEFORE READING

**L2** **ELL Differentiate** Chapter 17 Prereading and Vocabulary Worksheet (Unit 4 All-in-One, p. 234)

### SUCCESSNET STUDENT AND TEACHER CENTER

Visit **PearsonSchool.com/phgovt** for download-able resources that allow students and teachers to connect with government "on the go."

### DIGITAL LESSON PRESENTATION

The digital lesson presentation supports the print lesson with activities and summaries of key concepts.

## SKILLS DEVELOPMENT

### INNOVATE AND THINK CREATIVELY

You may wish to teach thinking creatively and innovating as a distinct skill within Section 2 of this chapter. Use the Chapter 17 Skills Worksheet (Unit 4 All-in-One, p. 253) to help students learn to think creatively and to innovate. The worksheet asks students to read an excerpt about the redeployment of U.S. troops in Iraq, identify the problem, brainstorm solutions, and understand the factors involved. For L2 and L1 students, assign the adapted Skill Activity (Unit 4 All-in-One, p. 254).

**WebQuest online** The chapter WebQuest challenges students to answer the chapter Essential Question by asking them about foreign policy and national security.

480

# Block Scheduling

**BLOCK 1:** Teach the Section 1 and Section 2 lessons, but instead of the Section 1 skit, complete the first Section 1 Extend activity in class. Omit the Section 2 Extend activities and Debate.

**BLOCK 2:** Teach the Section 3 and Section 4 lessons, omitting the Bellringers, Debates, and Extend activities.

CHAPTER

# 17

## Foreign Policy and National Defense

**Essential Question**
How should the United States interact with other countries?

> " ... **peace** is the **highest aspiration** of the **American people**. We **will negotiate** for it, **sacrifice** for it; we will **not surrender** for it, now or **ever.**

—Ronald Reagan, Inaugural Address, January 20, 1981

**Photo:** President Reagan escorts British Prime Minister Margaret Thatcher as she reviews the honor guard at the White House in 1988.

**GOVERNMENT** ONLINE
On the Go

To study anywhere, anytime, download these online resources at PearsonSchool.com/phgovt
• Political Dictionary
• Audio Review
• Downloadable Interactivities

481

## Lesson Goals

**SECTION 1**
Students will . . .
• list examples of internationalist policies and discuss whether these policies have benefitted or harmed U.S. interests.
• explore the State Department's role in protecting Americans by role-playing and writing a newspaper article on an incident involving American travelers abroad.

**SECTION 2**
Students will . . .
• explore the tension between security and personal liberty by analyzing a quotation.
• analyze possible government responses to potential security threats.

**SECTION 3**
Students will . . .
• describe foreign policies from U.S. history, using a transparency.
• understand U.S. foreign policies as they relate to historic events by creating a timeline.
• analyze primary source passages from the Truman Doctrine, using a worksheet.

**SECTION 4**
Students will . . .
• describe how foreign aid programs and defense alliances promote U.S. interests.
• evaluate current international issues and how foreign aid benefits the region affected as well as the United States.
• compare and contrast the rights delineated in the UN Universal Declaration on Human Rights with those in the U.S. Constitution.

## Pressed for Time

Divide the class into six groups and assign each group one of the following: the State Department, the army, the air force, the navy, the Department of Homeland Security, or the Director of National Intelligence. Have students use the textbook and other sources to research each of these groups, focusing on how they are involved in the formulation and implementation of foreign policy. Then, review the history of American foreign policy using Section 3 and have students correlate the appropriate policy with the research they conducted on their assigned department or organization. Have each give a brief summary of their findings to the class.

**FOLLOW UP** Have students create a list of the key foreign policies of the United States and provide examples and/or summaries of what methods the Federal Government used or uses in exercising these policies.

**DIFFERENTIATED INSTRUCTION KEY**

Look for these symbols to help you adjust steps in each lesson to meet your students' needs.

**L1** Special Needs
**L2** Basic
**ELL** English Language Learners
**LPR** Less Proficient Readers
**L3** All Students
**L4** Advanced Students

## How is foreign policy made and conducted?

| Foreign Policy | | |
|---|---|---|
| **President** | **Secretary of State** | **State Department** |
| • Interacts with foreign officials as chief diplomat<br>• Responsible for military actions as commander in chief<br>• Responsible for making and conducting foreign policy<br>• Appoints secretary of state and ambassadors<br>• May handle foreign policy matters directly, but often relies heavily on the secretary of state | • Leads State Department<br>• Advises President on foreign policy | • Carries out foreign policy<br>• Bureaus organized geographically and functionally<br>• Foreign Service members represent U.S. abroad<br>• Ambassadors stationed at capital of each recognized state<br>• Ambassadors also represent U.S. at the UN, NATO, and international conferences |

# Get Started

### LESSON GOALS

Students will . . .

- list examples of internationalist policies and discuss whether these policies have benefited or harmed U.S. interests.
- explore the State Department's role in protecting Americans by role playing and writing a newspaper article on an incident involving American travelers abroad.

## SKILLS DEVELOPMENT

### DRAW INFERENCES AND CONCLUSIONS

To help students learn to draw inferences and conclusions, have them turn to the Skills Handbook, p. S19, and use the information there to write a newspaper article about the Core Worksheet activity in this lesson.

---

SECTION **1**

# Foreign Affairs and Diplomacy

### Guiding Question

**How is foreign policy made and conducted?** Use a chart like the one below to keep track of the main themes in the conduct of American foreign policy.

| Foreign Policy | | |
|---|---|---|
| **President** | **Secretary of State** | **State Department** |
| • | • | • |
| • | • | • |
| • | • | • |

### Political Dictionary

- domestic affairs
- foreign affairs
- isolationism
- foreign policy
- right of legation
- ambassador
- diplomatic immunity
- passport
- visa

### Objectives

1. Explain the difference between isolationism and internationalism.
2. Define foreign policy.
3. Understand that a nation's foreign policy is composed of its many foreign policies.
4. Describe the functions, components, and organization of the Department of State.

**Image Above:** Secretary of State John Foster Dulles meets with General Chiang Kai-Shek.

In *The Federalist* No. 72, Alexander Hamilton noted that the "actual conduct" of America's foreign affairs would be in the hands of "the assistants or deputies of the chief magistrate," the President. Today, most of the President's "assistants or deputies" in the field of foreign affairs are located within the Department of State.

Foreign affairs have been of prime importance from the nation's very beginnings, more than a dozen years before Hamilton penned his comment in *The Federalist*. Indeed, it is important to remember that the United States would have been hard pressed to win its independence without the aid of a foreign ally, France.

## Isolationism to Internationalism

With the coming of independence, and then for more than 150 years, the American people were chiefly concerned with **domestic affairs**—with events at home. **Foreign affairs,** this nation's relationships with other nations, were of little or no concern to them. Through that period, America's foreign relations were very largely shaped by a policy of **isolationism**—a purposeful refusal to become generally involved in the affairs of the rest of the world.

The period from the 1940s onward, however, has been marked by a profound change in the place of the United States in world affairs. The coming of World War II finally convinced the American people that neither they nor anyone else can live in isolation—that, in many ways, and whether we like it or not, the world of today is indeed "one world." The well-being of everyone in this country—in fact, the very survival of the United States—is affected by much that happens elsewhere on the globe. If nothing else, the realities of ultra-rapid travel and instantaneous communications make it clear that we now live in a "global village."

Wars and other political upheavals abroad have an impact on the United States and on the daily lives of the American people. Five times over the past century, the United States fought major wars abroad; and in several other instances, it has committed its armed forces to lesser, but significant, foreign conflicts. The ongoing war in Afghanistan, terrorists' plots in Europe, Asia, and at home, the continuing Arab-Israeli disputes in the Middle East, threats posed by

# Focus on the Basics

Here is the information that your students need to learn in this section.

**FACTS:** • Foreign policy consists of all stands and actions a nation takes in its relationships with other nations. • The President is responsible for making and conducting foreign policy. • The State Department is led by the secretary of state appointed by the President. • State Department officials promote U.S. interests abroad.

**CONCEPTS:** enumerated powers, limited government, separation of powers

**ENDURING UNDERSTANDINGS:** • The United States has been moving away from isolationism toward more involvement in world affairs. • U.S. internationalist foreign policy reflects the belief that world events affect the well-being of Americans.

"rogue states" like Iran—these and other circumstances around the globe threaten the security of the United States.

Economic conditions elsewhere in the world also have a direct and often immediate effect on and in this country. The American economy has become an intertwined part of a truly global economy, linked by international banking, multinational corporations, and worldwide investments that transcend national boundaries.

Clearly, today's world cannot be described as "one world" in all respects, however. The planet remains, in many ways, a very <u>fractured</u> and dangerous place. In the interconnected yet divided world of today, only those policies that protect and promote the security of all nations can assure the security and well-being of the United States.

## Foreign Policy Defined

Every nation's **foreign policy** is actually many different policies on many different topics. It is made up of all of the stands and actions that a nation takes in every aspect of its relationships with other countries—diplomatic, military, commercial, and all others. To put the point another way, a nation's foreign policy includes everything that that nation's government says and everything that it does in world affairs.

Thus, American foreign policy consists of all of the Federal Government's official statements and all of its actions as it conducts this nation's foreign relations. It involves treaties and alliances, international trade, the defense budget, foreign economic and military aid, the United Nations and other international organizations, nuclear weapons testing, and disarmament negotiations. It also includes the American position on oil imports, grain exports, human rights, immigration, climate change, space exploration, fishing rights, cultural exchange programs, economic <u>sanctions,</u> computer technology exports, and a great many other matters.

Some aspects of foreign policy remain largely unchanged over time. For example, an insistence on freedom of the seas has been a basic part of American policy from the nation's beginnings. Other policies are more

flexible. Two decades ago, resisting the ambitions of the Soviet Union was a basic part of American foreign policy. Since the fall of the Soviet Union, the United States and Russia have built close, if not always friendly, political, military, and economic ties; the United States has also developed close relations with several other former Soviet republics.

The President is both the nation's chief diplomat and the commander in chief of its armed forces. Constitutionally and by tradition, the President bears the major responsibility for both making and conducting foreign policy. The President depends on a number of officials and agencies—Hamilton's "assistants or deputies"—to meet the immense responsibilities that come with this dual role. Here we will examine the President's diplomatic support. In the next section, we will look at the defense and military departments.

## The State Department

The State Department, headed by the secretary of state, is the President's right arm in foreign affairs. The President names the secretary of state, subject to confirmation by the Senate. It is to the secretary of state and to the Department of State that the President

### ✔ Checkpoint
What is foreign policy?

**rogue state**
*n.*, state or nation acting outside accepted international norms and policies

**fractured**
*adj.* divided, split

**sanction**
*n.* penalty imposed for some hostile act(s)

▶▶ **Analyzing Political Cartoons** In an effort to bring peace to the region, several Presidents have brokered talks between Palestinian and Israeli leaders. *According to this cartoon, why have these diplomatic efforts not been wholly successful?*

## Differentiated Resources

The following resources are located in the All-in-One, Unit 4, Chapter 17, Section 1:

- **L2** Prereading and Vocabulary Worksheet (p. 234)
- **L3** Reading Comprehension Worksheet (p. 238)
- **L2** Reading Comprehension Worksheet (p. 239)
- **L3** Core Worksheets A and B (pp. 240, 241)
- **L2** Extend Activity (p. 244)
- **L3** Quiz A (p. 245)
- **L2** Quiz B (p. 246)

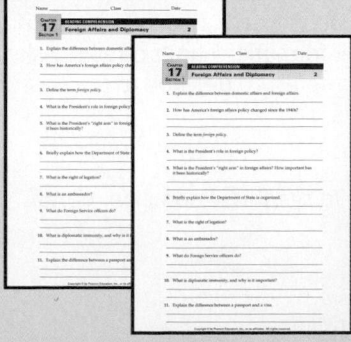

## BEFORE CLASS

Assign the section, the graphic organizer in the text, and the Reading Comprehension Worksheet (Unit 4 All-in-One, p. 238) before class.

**L2 Differentiate** Reading Comprehension Worksheet (Unit 4 All-in-One, p. 239)

## BELLRINGER

Write the following on the board: **After World War II, American foreign policy shifted from an isolationist position to an internationalist one. What types of foreign policy activities demonstrate internationalism? Answer in your notebook.**

**L2 Differentiate** For students who might have difficulty with some of the vocabulary in the Bellringer statement, write these terms and definitions on the board: *internationalism* (active involvement with the concerns and interests of other nations) and *isolationism* (staying out of the concerns and interests of other nations).

**L4 Differentiate** Have higher-level students complete the Bellringer activity, but add the following to the statement on the board: **Has the policy of internationalism been helpful or harmful to the United States?**

## Teach

To present this topic using online resources, use the lesson presentations at **PearsonSchool.com/phgovt.**

### REVIEW BELLRINGER

Read the Bellringer question aloud and ask for student volunteers to read their responses. Encourage a classroom discussion of students' opinions; any students who strongly disagree with the responses that are read out loud should read their own responses, as a way of stimulating discussion.

## Answers

**Checkpoint** It is made up of all the stands and actions that a nation takes in every aspect of its relationships with other countries.

**Analyzing Political Cartoons** The cartoon portrays the peace deal as standing on a house of cards, which is not a firm foundation, and illustrates the unstable ground that makes the diplomatic efforts problematic.

## PERFORM A GUIDED SKIT

Distribute the Chapter 17 Section 1 Core Worksheets A and B (Unit 4 All-in-One, pp. 240, 241). Explain that Core Worksheet A lists roles that students will play in a skit about an incident involving Americans in the fictional country of Zabrin. Assign a student to each role. Then explain that students without acting roles are reporters who will write a newspaper article about the incident. Instruct them to use Core Worksheet B to take notes as they watch the skit to help them write their article.

The teacher-only worksheet "Scenario: Incident in Zabrin" (Unit 4 All-in-One, p. 242) provides the sequence of events as the incident unfolds. Have students who are playing roles stand up and take their positions around the room. Explain that as you narrate the unfolding incident, you will pause after each event for the actors to act it out. Explain that the actors should move around as needed to play the scenes.

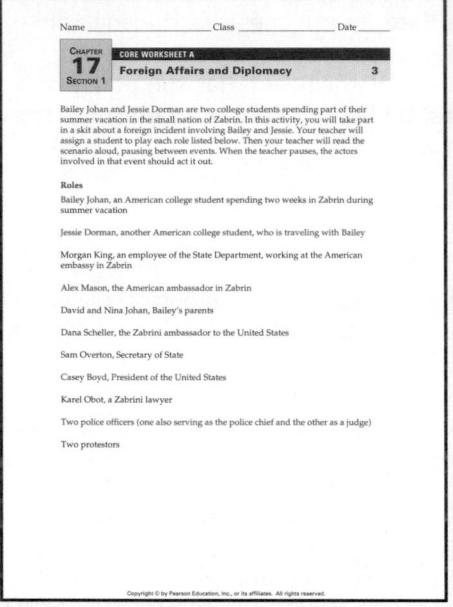

Tell students to go to the Audio Tour to learn more about implementing foreign policy.

## Answers

**Implementing Foreign Policy** Possible response: Promoting American values helps advance the other goals of advancing democracy, protecting America, and supporting the efforts of diplomatic officials. If people in other nations gain a better understanding of American values, hopefully they will become allies rather than adversaries.

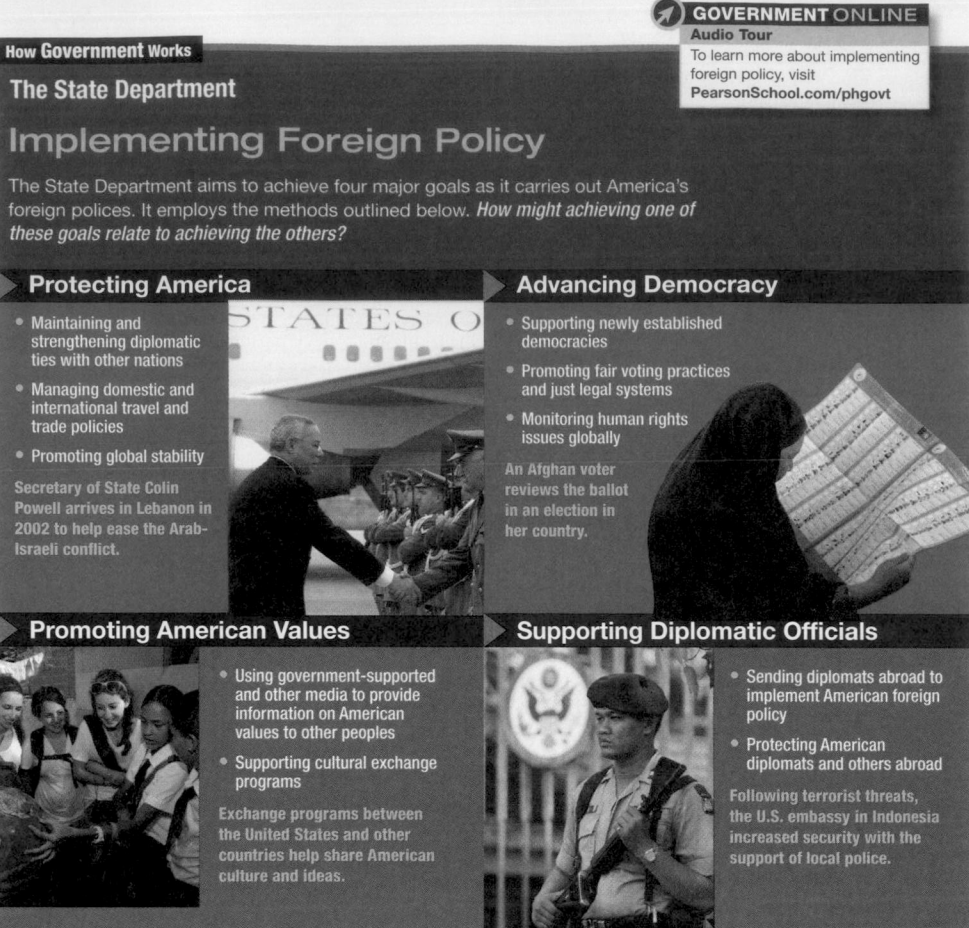

# Implementing Foreign Policy

The State Department aims to achieve four major goals as it carries out America's foreign polices. It employs the methods outlined below. *How might achieving one of these goals relate to achieving the others?*

### Protecting America

- Maintaining and strengthening diplomatic ties with other nations
- Managing domestic and international travel and trade policies
- Promoting global stability

Secretary of State Colin Powell arrives in Lebanon in 2002 to help ease the Arab-Israeli conflict.

### Advancing Democracy

- Supporting newly established democracies
- Promoting fair voting practices and just legal systems
- Monitoring human rights issues globally

An Afghan voter reviews the ballot in an election in her country.

### Promoting American Values

- Using government-supported and other media to provide information on American values to other peoples
- Supporting cultural exchange programs

Exchange programs between the United States and other countries help share American culture and ideas.

### Supporting Diplomatic Officials

- Sending diplomats abroad to implement American foreign policy
- Protecting American diplomats and others abroad

Following terrorist threats, the U.S. embassy in Indonesia increased security with the support of local police.

looks for advice and assistance in both the formulation and the conduct of the nation's foreign policy.

**The Secretary of State** The secretary of state ranks first among the members of the President's Cabinet. That ranking speaks to the importance of the office, and also to the fact that the State Department was the first of the now 15 executive departments that Congress created.

A Department of Foreign Affairs had first been created in 1781 under the Articles of Confederation. Congress re-created it in 1789 as the first major unit in the executive branch under the Constitution. Later that year, its name was changed to the Department of State.

President George Washington appointed Thomas Jefferson as the nation's first secretary of state, in 1789. Bill Clinton appointed the first woman to hold the post, Madeleine Albright, in 1997. Colin Powell, who served as secretary of state in George W. Bush's first term (2001 to 2005) became the first African American to occupy the office; and his

## Teacher-to-Teacher Network

**ALTERNATE LESSON PLAN** The U.S. Department of State Web site (www.state.gov/) has a wealth of information that can give students a first-hand glimpse into State Department affairs, including biographies, videos, press releases, virtual tours, and information about careers. Ask students to explore the site and choose an area of interest to describe to the class through a poster, a brochure, or an oral report.

To see this lesson plan, go to

at PearsonSchool.com/phgovt

successor, Condoleezza Rice, who is both a woman and an African American, served from 2005 to 2009. Today, the post is held by another major personality—former first lady and former senator from New York, Hillary Rodham Clinton.

Today, the duties of the secretary relate almost entirely to foreign affairs. That is, they center on the making and conduct of policy and on the management of the department, its many overseas posts, and its workforce of more than 30,000 men and women.[1]

Some Presidents—most famously, Woodrow Wilson and Franklin Roosevelt—have tended to ignore their secretaries of state and have handled many foreign policy matters personally and quite often directly. Others, notably Richard Nixon, Gerald Ford, and both Bushes, have chosen instead to rely on their national security advisors. Some chief executives—in particular, the earlier ones—have chosen to delegate a large share of the responsibility for matters of foreign policy to the secretary. President Obama has made it clear that Secretary Clinton is a major figure in both the formation and the conduct of American foreign policy.

**Organization and Components** The State Department is organized along both geographic and functional lines. Some of its agencies, such as the Bureau of African Affairs and the Bureau of Near Eastern Affairs, deal with matters involving particular regions of the world.

Other agencies have broader missions—for example, the Bureau of International Narcotics and Law Enforcement Affairs, sometimes called "Drugs 'n' Thugs." Most bureaus are headed by an assistant secretary and include several offices. Thus, both the Office of Passport Services and the Office of Visa Services are found in the Bureau of Consular Affairs.

▲ The U.S. Embassy in Beijing opened in 2008. Its design reflects the high-security needs of today. **Why does the United States maintain relationships with many countries with which we have significant disagreements?**

## Overseas Representatives

✔ **Checkpoint**
How are ambassadors selected?

Some 12,000 men and women now represent the United States as members of the Foreign Service, many of them serving abroad. Under international law, every nation has the **right of legation**—the right to send and receive diplomatic representatives. International law consists of those rules and principles that guide sovereign states in their dealings with one another and in their treatment of foreign nationals (private persons and groups). Its sources include treaties, decisions of international courts, and custom. Treaties are the most important source today. The right of legation is an ancient practice. Its history can be traced back to the Egyptian civilization of 6,000 years ago.

The Second Continental Congress named this nation's first foreign service officer in 1778. That year, it chose Benjamin Franklin to be America's minister to France. He served in that capacity for nearly eight years.

**Ambassadors** An **ambassador** is the official representative of a sovereign state in the conduct of its foreign affairs.[2] For some five

---

1 The secretary does have some domestic responsibilities. Thus, when Richard Nixon resigned the presidency on August 9, 1974, his formal, legal announcement of that fact had to be submitted to Secretary of State Henry Kissinger. Over the years, the secretary and the department have had (and been relieved of) a fairly wide range of domestic functions—including publishing the nation's laws, issuing patents, and supervising the decennial census.

2 See Chapter 14, Section 3. An ambassador's official title is Ambassador Extraordinary and Plenipotentiary. When the office is vacant or the ambassador is absent, the post is usually filled by the next-ranking Foreign Service officer in the embassy. That officer, temporarily in charge of embassy affairs, is known as the chargé d'affaires.

Conduct a brief discussion with the class about the guided skit activity. Ask students to describe their reactions to the events that occurred, and ask them whether the actions of the characters in the skit illustrated the qualities needed to be a good diplomat.

## WRITE A NEWSPAPER ARTICLE

Divide students into small groups, making sure that each group has some students who played roles in the guided skit and some students who were observers. Tell them that they are reporters for the local newspaper and that they have been assigned to write an article on the incident in Zabrin. They should work as a group to produce their newspaper article. Group members should share their notes on Core Worksheet B to help the group identify significant moments to include in the article. Encourage students to include quotes from the characters in the skit in their articles.

**L2 Differentiate** Before students begin writing their articles, have students who observed the skit (rather than acting in it) recap the major events. Use their descriptions to write a timeline on the board.

---

**Government** online *All print resources are available on the Teacher's Resource Library CD-ROM and online at PearsonSchool.com/phgovt.*

---

# Debate

"An ambassador is an honest man sent to lie abroad for the good of his country."
                                                                    —Henry Wotton

Use this quote to start a classroom debate on the role of diplomacy in implementing foreign policy. Prompt students to consider situations in which an ambassador (or other diplomat or foreign service official) might feel a conflict between the best interests of his or her home country and the country in which he or she is stationed.

## Answers

**Caption** Although the U.S. may have differences with other nations, it is important to keep diplomatic channels open for political, social, and economic reasons.

**Checkpoint** Ambassadors are appointed by the President with the consent of Congress. Although they are now being selected more frequently based on their background, they are sometimes chosen for their support of the President.

**L1 L2 Differentiate** Have each student bring in one article involving U.S. foreign policy. Students can find the article in print or online resources. Display Transparency 17A, Implementing Foreign Policy. Have a volunteer read aloud the State Department's goals listed. Then ask students to summarize the foreign policy actions described in their article. After each summary, have the class identify the foreign policy goals that the actions promote.

**L2 Differentiate** Distribute the Extend Activity "U.S. Foreign Relations" (Unit 4 All-in-One, p. 244), which has students research the media for reports about U.S. involvement in foreign countries.

**L3 L4 Differentiate** Have students choose a nation and research, either online or in the library, the United States ambassador to that nation. Ask students to write a short biography of their research subject.

## Assess and Remediate

**L3** Collect the Core Worksheet and assess students' class participation using the Rubric for Assessing a Newspaper Article (Unit 4 All-in-One, p. 290).

**L3** Assign the Section 1 Assessment questions.

**L3** Section Quiz A (Unit 4 All-in-One, p. 245)

**L2** Section Quiz B (Unit 4 All-in-One, p. 246)

Have students complete the review activities in the digital lesson presentation and continue their work in the **Essential Questions Journal.**

## Answers

**The Iran Hostage Crisis** Possible response: Diplomats can help work out our differences with these nations and promote better relationships.

---

**Diplomatic Immunity**

# The Iran Hostage Crisis

An **American hostage** is paraded in front of the media by Iranian militants in 1979.

Although an embassy serves a specific diplomatic function, it is also a symbol of the nation it represents. Occasionally, tensions between nations can cause citizens of one country to protest or even attack another country's embassy to express their anger at that country.

In 1979, Iranian students occupied the U.S. embassy in the capital, Tehran, and held embassy staff hostage for 444 days. The Iran Hostage Crisis was an unusual assault against both a nation and international law. **Why does the United States send diplomats to posts where political conditions are unstable?**

For the first time, **yellow ribbons** were tied to trees to symbolize public support for the hostages.

**accredit**
*v.* to send a diplomatic representative with proper credentials

centuries now, most of the formal contacts between sovereign nations—that is, most of their diplomatic relationships—have been conducted through their duly appointed ambassadors.

In this country, ambassadors are appointed by the President, with Senate consent, and they serve at his pleasure. Today, the United States is represented by an ambassador stationed at the capital of each sovereign state this nation recognizes. Thus, American embassies are now located in more than 180 countries around the world.

The United States now maintains over 260 diplomatic and consular offices abroad as well. There, Foreign Service officers promote American interests in a multitude of ways—for example, encouraging trade, gathering intelligence data, advising persons who seek to enter this country, and aiding American citizens who are abroad and in need of legal advice or other help.

Some ambassadorships are much desired political plums, and whenever a new President moves into the White House, he typically makes many new appointments. Too often, Presidents have appointed people to ambassadorships and other major diplomatic posts as a reward for those individuals' support—financial and otherwise—of the President's election to office. However, in many cases these ranks are filled with career diplomats in the Foreign Service.

President Harry Truman named the first African American, Edward R. Dudley, as an ambassador to Liberia, in 1949. Later that same year President Truman also appointed the first woman, Eugenie Anderson, as our ambassador to Denmark.

**Special Diplomats** Those persons whom the President names to certain other top diplomatic posts also carry the rank of ambassador. Examples include the United States representative to the UN and the American member of the North Atlantic Treaty Council. The President also often assigns the personal rank of ambassador to those diplomats who take on special assignments abroad—for example, representing the United States in the ongoing efforts to resolve Arab-Israeli differences.

**Diplomatic Immunity** In international law, every sovereign state is supreme within its own boundaries. All persons or things found within that state's territory are subject to its jurisdiction.

As a major exception to that rule, ambassadors are regularly granted **diplomatic immunity**—they are not subject to the laws of the state to which they are accredited. They cannot be arrested, sued, or taxed. Their official residences (embassies) cannot be entered or searched without their consent, and all official communications and other properties are

---

# Myths and Misconceptions

**AMBASSADORS** Most Americans are surprised to learn that the United States did not have ambassadors for nearly half of its history. The Constitution called for the establishment of embassies abroad, and the United States did send diplomatic representatives to many countries. But these representatives were ministers or consulate officials, not ambassadors. Why the delay? In the early years of the country, ambassadors were associated with monarchies, and anything viewed as a tool of the monarchy was something the United States understandably tried to stay far away from.

protected. All other embassy personnel and their families receive this same immunity.

Diplomatic immunity is essential to the ability of every nation to conduct its foreign relations. The practice assumes that diplomats will not abuse their privileged status. If a host government finds a diplomat's conduct unacceptable, that official may be declared *persona non grata* and expelled from the country. The mistreatment of diplomats is considered a major breach of international law.

Diplomatic immunity is a generally accepted practice. There are exceptions, however. The most serious breach in modern times occurred in Iran in late 1979. Militant followers of the Ayatollah Khomeini seized the American embassy in Tehran on November 4 of that year; 66 Americans were taken hostage and 52 were held for 444 days. The Iranians finally released the hostages moments after Ronald Reagan became President on January 20, 1981.

**Passports** A **passport** is a legal document issued by a state that identifies a person as a citizen of that state. It grants that person a right of protection while traveling abroad and the right to return to the homeland. Passports entitle their holders to the privileges accorded to them by international custom and treaties. Few countries will admit persons who do not hold valid passports.

## Travel Documents

Some years ago, a valid passport was all one needed to travel abroad and enter most other countries. Today, most countries also require a visa. *Why do you think this is now the case?*

### Passports

- Issued by a government and identifies the bearer as a citizen or national of the issuing country
- Entitles the bearer to consular protection abroad and to return to his or her country of citizenship
- Valid for 10 years
- Three types: diplomatic, official, tourist

### Visas

- Issued by the country the individual requests permission to enter
- Permits the traveler to remain in a country for a specified period of time, but does not guarantee entry
- Valid only for the time period stated
- Of many types, including: transit, tourist, business, and student

The State Department's Office of Passport Services now issues more than ten million passports to Americans each year. Do not confuse passports with visas. A **visa** is a permit to enter another state and must be obtained from the country one wishes to enter. Trips to most foreign countries require visas today. Most visas to enter this country are issued at American consulates abroad.

**Essential Questions Journal** To continue to build a response to the chapter Essential Question, go to your **Essential Questions Journal.**

## SECTION 1 ASSESSMENT

1. **Guiding Question** Use your completed chart to answer this question: How is foreign policy made and conducted?

### Key Terms and Comprehension
2. Why did the United States abandon a policy of **isolationism** and move to one of internationalism?
3. (a) What is **foreign policy?** (b) List three examples of topics covered by American foreign policy.
4. Why is it most often advisable that an **ambassador** come from the ranks of career diplomats?

### Critical Thinking
5. **Demonstrate Reasoned Judgment** Do you think it would be possible for the United States to return to a policy of isolationism? Why or why not?
6. **Draw Conclusions** Why do you think it is necessary that an American representative be assigned to work and live in each state the United States recognizes?
7. **Draw Inferences** Why is diplomatic immunity considered essential to relationships between and among nations?

### Quick Write
**Expository Writing: Define a Problem** In order to write a problem-and-solution essay, you need to define the problem you intend to solve. Think about the types of issues the world struggles with today—economic instability, environmental destruction, famine, political unrest, and so on. What issue do you think is most important? Write a brief description of the problem you select.

---

| If Your Students Have Trouble With | Strategies For Remediation |
|---|---|
| Describing how foreign policy is made and conducted (Question 1) | Work with students to create on the board the graphic organizer shown at the beginning of the section. |
| Explaining the U.S. move from isolationism to internationalism. (Questions 2, 5) | Have students brainstorm ways in which nations are tied together more closely today than ever before; for example, global trade, instant communication through the Internet, terrorist organizations operating across borders. |
| Identifying foreign policies (Question 3) | Have students look through newspapers or magazines to find images and articles on American foreign policies. |
| Analyzing the selection and roles of diplomats (Questions 4, 6) | Have pairs of students brainstorm the benefits of career diplomats and the reasons for stationing American diplomats abroad. |
| Understanding diplomatic immunity (Question 7) | Have students suggest scenarios about what might happen if diplomats did not have immunity in a foreign country. |

## Answers

**Caption** Possible response: As visas are provided by the admitting country, that country's government can place limits on the number of people coming into the country and can control and keep track of those who are actually permitted to enter the country.

---

# Assessment Answers

**1.** Foreign policy goals and agendas are set by the President, who relies on the secretary of state and the State Department to determine the best ways to implement them.

**2.** because the nations of the world have become increasingly interconnected, both politically and economically, and it is now clear that the problems in other nations can directly affect our safety and well-being

**3. (a)** all stands and actions that a nation takes in relationships with other countries—diplomatic, military, commercial, and all others **(b)** possible examples: treaties, alliances, nuclear weapons agreements, import and export policies, economic sanctions, economic aid, military aid

**4.** A career diplomat would have the skills and experience needed for the job.

**5. Yes.** Foreign conflicts are costing the lives of American soldiers and economic resources that could be better used at home. Economic globalization is costing American jobs. **No.** Globalization is happening and cannot be stopped. What happens in one country affects us all, whether we like it or not. Isolationist policy is simply putting our heads in the sand.

**6.** Possible response: Foreign relationships are complex. The people implementing foreign policy can better assess the diplomatic situation when they are present in the foreign country.

**7.** Diplomatic immunity allows diplomatic officials to act as official representatives of their home nations without fear of harassment or coercion.

**QUICK WRITE** Students should clearly describe the problem they selected.

## How does the Federal Government safeguard this nation's security?

| Protecting National Security | |
|---|---|
| Secretary of Defense | • President's chief advisor on defense policy<br>• Leads Defense Department |
| Joint Chiefs of Staff | • Military advisors to secretary of defense, President, and National Security Council |
| **Military Departments:** | |
| Department of the Army | • Military operations on land<br>• Defends the U.S. if attacked<br>• Protects American interests abroad |
| Department of the Navy | • Defends the nation through sea warfare |
| Marine Corps | • Provides support to navy and air force operations<br>• Carries out land operations to reinforce naval campaigns |
| Department of the Air Force | • Protects the U.S. from enemy air, ground, or sea forces<br>• Provides support for land and sea operations |
| Director of National Intelligence | • President's chief advisor on national security<br>• Directs and supervises intelligence agencies<br>• Gathers intelligence and dispenses it as necessary |
| Department of Homeland Security | • Protects U.S. against terrorism<br>• Conducts border and transportation security<br>• Protects national infrastructure<br>• Prepares for and responds to national emergencies<br>• Defends the nation against chemical, biological, radiological, and nuclear attack |

## SKILLS DEVELOPMENT

### INNOVATE AND THINK CREATIVELY

To practice thinking creatively and innovating in this section, use the Chapter 17 Skills Worksheet (Unit 4 All-in-One, p. 253). You may teach the skill before the Opinion Line activity in this lesson. For L2 and L1 students, assign the adapted Skill Activity (Unit 4 All-in-One, p. 254).

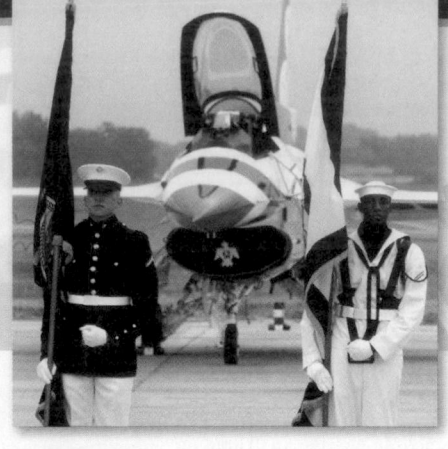

SECTION 2

# National Security

### Guiding Question
**How does the Federal Government safeguard this nation's security?**
Use a table like the one below to keep track of the methods used to safeguard the nation.

| Protecting National Security | |
|---|---|
| Secretary of Defense | •<br>•<br>• |
| | • |

### Political Dictionary
• espionage
• terrorism

### Objectives
1. Summarize the functions, components, and organization of the Department of Defense and the military departments.
2. Explain how the Director of National Intelligence and the Department of Homeland Security contribute to the nation's security.

**Image Above:** Two members of the Joint Service Color Guard present the colors at a military ceremony.

How many federal agencies, in addition to the Department of State, are involved with the nation's foreign affairs? Dozens of them. Thus, the FBI combats terrorism and espionage here and abroad. The Public Health Service works with the United Nations and foreign governments to conquer diseases and meet other health problems in many parts of the world. The United States Agency for International Development (USAID) provides economic help to foreign countries. The Office of the United States Trade Representative promotes this country's interests in international trade.

A recitation of this sort could go on and on. But, as you will see, this section deals with those agencies most directly involved in the areas of foreign and defense policy.

## The Defense Department
Congress established what is today called the Department of Defense (DoD) in the National Security Act of 1947. It is the present-day successor to two historic Cabinet-level agencies: the War Department, created by Congress in 1789, and the Navy Department, created in 1798.

Congress created the Defense Department in order to unify the nation's armed forces. It wished to bring the then-separate army (including the air force) and the navy under the control of a single Cabinet department. Today, there are nearly 1.4 million men and women on active duty in the military, over one million in the National Guard and Reserves, and some 650,000 civilians employed by the Defense Department.

**Civil Control of the Military** The authors of the Constitution understood the importance of the nation's defense. They emphasized that fact clearly in the Preamble, and they underscored it in the body of the Constitution by mentioning defense more frequently than any other governmental function.

The Framers also recognized the dangers inherent in military power and the potential of its abuse. They knew that its very existence can pose a threat to free government. And, therefore, the Constitution is studded with provisions to make sure that the military is always subject to the control of the nation's civilian authorities.

# Focus on the Basics

**FACTS:** • The secretary of defense is the President's chief advisor on military matters. • The military departments protect the U.S. domestically and internationally. • The DNI advises the President on national security issues. • The Department of Homeland Security coordinates public and private organizations on issues related to national emergencies.

**CONCEPTS:** role and purpose of government

**ENDURING UNDERSTANDINGS:** • The Constitution ensures civilian control of the military by making the President the commander in chief and granting broad military powers to Congress. • U.S. intelligence agencies covertly acquire information to help secure the nation. • The size and extensive infrastructure of the U.S. makes it nearly impossible to protect against all terrorist activities.

Thus, the Constitution makes the elected President the commander in chief of the armed forces. To the same end, it gives broad military powers to Congress—that is, to the elected representatives of the people.[3]

The principle of civilian control has always been a major factor in the making of defense policy and in the creation and staffing of the various agencies responsible for the execution of that policy. The importance of civilian control is clearly illustrated by this fact: The National Security Act of 1947 provides that the secretary of defense cannot have served on active duty in any of the armed forces for at least 10 years before being named to that post.

**The Secretary of Defense** The Department of Defense is headed by the secretary of defense, whose appointment by the President is subject to confirmation by the Senate. The secretary, who serves at the President's

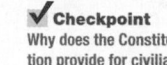 **Checkpoint**
Why does the Constitution provide for civilian control of the military?

---

3 Recall that the Constitution makes defense a national function and practically excludes the States from that field. Each State does have a militia, which it may use to keep the peace within its own borders. Today, the organized portion of the militia is the National Guard. Congress has the power (Article I, Section 8, Clauses 15 and 16) to "provide for calling forth the Militia" and to provide for organizing, arming, and disciplining it. Congress first delegated to the President the power to call the militia into federal service in 1795, and the commander in chief has had that authority ever since. Today, the governor of each State is the commander in chief of that State's units of the Army and the Air National Guard, except when the President orders those units into federal service.

**How Government Works**

## Civilian Control of the Military

 **GOVERNMENT ONLINE**
**Audio Tour**
Take a guided tour of this constitutional principle at PearsonSchool.com/phgovt

**President**
Directs the activities of the armed forces as constitutional commander in chief and is the nation's senior military authority

**Secretary of Defense**
Implements the President's national security policy by managing and directing the activities of the Defense Department

**Congress**
Provides structure and funding for each of the armed forces

**CIVILIAN / MILITARY**

**Military Departments**
Provide the Unified Commanders with the army, navy, and air force units for combat, peacekeeping, and humanitarian missions

**Joint Chiefs of Staff**
Provide advice to the President, the National Security Council, and the Secretary of Defense on all military matters

**Unified Commanders**
Command the U.S. armed forces around the globe. Are the direct link between the military forces and the President, and conduct military operations per their instruction

Civilian control of the military ensures that the military is always subordinate to the elected civilian leadership. Although the military participates in the making of key military decisions, ultimate authority lies in the hands of the President and Congress. *Why is the principle of civilian control of the military important?*

**KEY**
Chain of Command
Chain of Communication

---

# Differentiated Resources

The following resources are located in the All-in-One, Unit 4, Chapter 17, Section 2:

- **L3** Reading Comprehension Worksheet (p. 247)
- **L2** Reading Comprehension Worksheet (p. 249)
- **L3** Core Worksheet (p. 251)
- **L2** Core Worksheet (p. 252)
- **L3** Skills Worksheet (p. 253)
- **L2** Skill Activity (p. 254)
- **L3** **L4** Extend Worksheet (p. 255)
- **L3** Quiz A (p. 256)  **L2** Quiz B (p. 257)

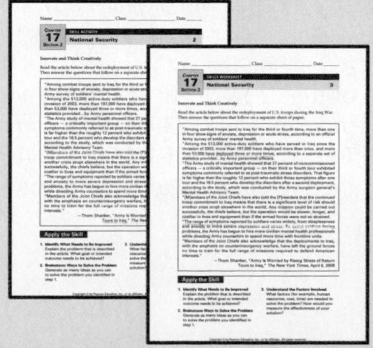

---

# Get Started

## LESSON GOALS

Students will . . .

- explore the tension between security and personal liberty by analyzing a quotation.
- analyze possible government responses to potential security threats.

## BEFORE CLASS

Assign the section, the graphic organizer in the text, and the Reading Comprehension Worksheet (Unit 4 All-in-One, p. 247) before class.

**L2** **Differentiate** Reading Comprehension Worksheet (Unit 4 All-in-One, p. 249)

## BELLRINGER

Write on the board: **"Our history has shown us that insecurity threatens liberty. Yet, if our liberties are curtailed, we lose the values that we are struggling to defend."** Do you agree or disagree with this statement? Why or why not? Answer in your notebook.

**L2** **ELL Differentiate** For students who might have difficulty with some of the vocabulary in the Bellringer statement, provide definitions on the board for *insecurity* (the feeling of being unsafe or vulnerable) and *curtail* (reduce or restrict).

Tell students to go to the Audio Tour for a guided audio tour of the constitutional principle of civilian control of the military.

---

# Answers

**Checkpoint** The Framers recognized the inherent dangers in the power of the military and its potential abuse, so they made sure the Constitution clearly ensures that the military is always subject to civilian control.

**Civilian Control of the Military** Military power can pose a threat to free government. Civilian control reduces the risk that the military might overpower the civilian government.

# Teach

To present this topic using online resources, use the lesson presentations at **PearsonSchool.com/phgovt**.

## REVIEW BELLRINGER

Ask volunteers to read their responses to the Bellringer activity. Guide a class discussion of the quotation by asking students to consider the statement in the context in which it was published, as part of the 9/11 Report, an analysis of the attacks on the United States on September 11, 2001. It may help to separate some of the premises behind the statement: that freedom and security are necessarily in conflict with each other, that giving up some measure of freedom can increase our security, and that giving up some measure of security is one of the prices we pay for living in a free society. Remind students that there are no easy or right answers here—no society yet, ours included, has found an easy balance between freedom and security.

## DISCUSS

The security of the United States is monitored and guarded by a variety of government agencies. These agencies endeavor to keep the nation secure to the best of their abilities, but sometimes security and freedom conflict. Tell students that a good example of this tension between freedom and security is flying on commercial airplanes.

Use the Think-Write-Pair-Share strategy (p. T22) to lead this class discussion. Tell students a few of the ways that commercial airline travel has changed since September 11, 2001. Specifically, explain that the Federal Government put in place much stricter security procedures for airline passengers. Passengers are now required to present a government-issue ID before flying, and must take off shoes, belts, hats, jackets, and other personal items for a security screening. Also, passengers cannot carry more than three ounces of liquid through the security checkpoints, and cannot have sharp objects with them on the plane.

Remind students that all of these measures represent some degree of a loss of privacy, but the government implemented them in response to specific threats to the security of aircraft and passengers. Then, for the Think-Write-Pair-Share activity, ask: **Can we safeguard the nation without giving up too much personal freedom?**

## Answers

**Checkpoint** the secretary of defense and the Joint Chiefs of Staff

---

pleasure, is charged with two major responsibilities. He is simultaneously (1) the President's chief aide and advisor in making and carrying out defense policy, and (2) the operating head of the Defense Department.

The secretary's huge domain is often called the Pentagon—because of its massive five-sided headquarters building in Virginia, across the Potomac River from the Capitol. Its operations have regularly taken a large slice of the federal budget every year for more than 70 years—and nearly a fourth of all federal spending today. The global war on terrorism has forced vast increases in expenditures for the military. The Department of Defense spent nearly $300 billion in fiscal year 2001, the year of the September 11 attacks. It will almost certainly spend well over twice that amount in fiscal year 2011.

**Chief Military Aides** The six members of the Joint Chiefs of Staff serve as the principal military advisors to the secretary of defense, and to the President and the National Security Council. This collective body is made up of the chairman of the Joint Chiefs, the vice chairman, the army chief of staff, the chief of naval operations, the commandant of the Marine Corps, and the air force chief of staff. The highest ranking uniformed officers in the armed services, the members of the Joint Chiefs are named by the President, subject to Senate approval.

## The Military Departments

The three military departments—the Departments of the Army, the Navy, and the Air Force—are major units and sub-Cabinet departments within the Department of Defense. A civilian secretary, named by the President and directly responsible to the secretary of defense, leads each military department. The nation's armed forces—the army, the navy, and the air force—operate within that unified structure.

**spearhead**
*v.* to lead a military force; to take the lead in

**The Department of the Army** The army is the largest of the armed services, and the oldest. The American Continental Army, now the United States Army, was established by the Second Continental Congress on June 14, 1775—more than a year before the Declaration of Independence.

The army is essentially a ground-based force, and it is responsible for military operations on land. It must be ready (1) to defeat any attack on the United States itself, and (2) to take swift and forceful action to protect American interests in any other part of the world. To these ends, it must organize, train, and equip its active duty forces—the Regular Army, the Army National Guard, and the Army Reserve.

Over 400,000 Army National Guard soldiers and reservists have been called to service since September 11, 2001, many of them for the wars in Afghanistan and Iraq. All of the army's active duty personnel are under the direct command of the army's highest ranking officer, the army chief of staff.

The Regular Army is the nation's standing army, the heart of its land forces. There are now more than 550,000 soldiers on active duty—officers and enlisted personnel, professional soldiers, and volunteers. The army has been downsized in the post–cold war era, however. At the time of the collapse of the Soviet Union in 1991, there were more than 700,000 men and women on active duty.

Women make up about 14 percent of the Army and now serve in all Regular Army units, except the Special Forces. Over recent years, women's roles have come to include many combat-related duties in the army and in each of the other armed services, as well.

The army trains and equips its combat units to fight enemy forces. The infantry takes, holds, and defends land areas. The artillery supports the infantry, seeks to destroy enemy concentrations with its heavier guns, and gives anti-aircraft cover. The armored cavalry also supports the infantry, using armored vehicles and helicopters to spearhead assaults and oppose enemy counteroffensives.

Other units of the army provide the many services and supplies in support of combat troops. Those soldiers could not fight without the help of members of the engineer, quartermaster, signal, ordnance, transportation, military police, and medical corps.

**The Department of the Navy** The United States Navy was first formed as the Continental Navy—a fledgling naval force created by

---

# Background

**THE COST OF DEFENDING THE NATION** The cost of supplying our armed forces is enormous. In fiscal year 2007 alone, the U.S. Government spent nearly $90 billion on weapons systems and supplies for the armed forces. If Pentagon procurement were a Cabinet agency, it would rank fifth, with a budget about $15 billion less than that of the Department of Agriculture. Navy procurement ($32.6 billion) and Air Force procurement ($33.4 billion) combined exceed the budget for the Department of Transportation ($61.4 billion). Army procurement, at nearly $20 billion, was closest to the budget for the Department of Energy ($20.3 billion).

## The Armed Forces Overseas

# Major Military Deployments

Protecting the nation's security does not end at the nation's borders. In fact, nearly one fourth of the armed forces of the United States is now stationed abroad. Today, the top five areas to which the men and women of the American military are deployed are in East Asia, Southwest Asia, and Europe. *Why is it necessary to post the armed forces overseas in order to protect national security?*

|  | Total | Army | Navy | Marine Corps | Air Force |
|---|---|---|---|---|---|
| **East Asia** | | | | | |
| Japan | 35,588 | 2,677 | 3,539 | 17,002 | 12,380 |
| South Korea* | 24,655 | 16,507 | 242 | 112 | 7,794 |
| **Europe** | | | | | |
| Germany | 53,130 | 37,828 | 225 | 369 | 14,708 |
| **Southwest Asia** | | | | | |
| Afghanistan | 95,800 | 60,500 | 6,500 | 19,500 | 9,300 |
| Iraq | 80,650 | 70,400 | 2,200 | 150 | 7,900 |

SOURCE: Department of Defense,
Personnel and Procurement Statistics, June 2010
*2008 data

A soldier attends a farewell event prior to his deployment.

the Second Continental Congress on October 13, 1775. Ever since, its major responsibility has been sea warfare.

The chief of naval operations is the navy's highest ranking officer and is responsible for its preparations and readiness for war and for its use in combat. Similar to the army, the navy's ranks also have been thinned in the post–cold war period. Today, some 330,000 officers and enlisted personnel serve in the navy, with women making up about 15 percent of the force.

The Second Continental Congress established the United States Marine Corps (USMC) on November 10, 1775. Today, it operates as a separate armed service within the Navy Department, but it is not under the control of the chief of naval operations. Its commandant answers directly to the secretary of the navy.

The marines are a combat-ready land force for the navy. They have two major combat missions: (1) to seize or defend land bases from which the ships of the fleet and the air

power of the navy and marines can operate, and (2) to carry out other land operations essential to a naval <u>campaign.</u> Today, some 200,000 men and women serve in the USMC. The proportion of women in the marines is lower than it is in the other service branches—about 6 percent.

**The Department of the Air Force** The air force is the youngest of the military services. Congress established the United States Air Force (USAF) and made it a separate branch of the armed forces in the National Security Act of 1947. However, its history dates back to 1907, when the army assigned an officer and two enlisted men to a new unit called the Aeronautical Division of the Army Signal Corps. Those three men were ordered to take "charge of all matters pertaining to military ballooning, air machines and all kindred subjects."

Today, the USAF is the nation's first line of defense. It has primary responsibility for military air and aerospace operations. In time

✔ **Checkpoint**
What are the main responsibilities of each of the military departments?

**campaign**
*n.* a series of military actions taken toward a specific goal

---

## CONDUCT AN OPINION LINE

Write "Agree" on the left side of the board, "Disagree" on the right side, and "Not Sure" in the center. (For more direction on the Opinion Line strategy, see p. T26.) Then, hand out the Chapter 17 Section 2 Core Worksheet (Unit 4 All-in-One, p. 251). In this activity, you will read a series of statements, and students will stand on the side of the room that applies to their opinion of the statement you have read. Tell students that they should be prepared to explain why they chose their position and should write their explanations on their Core Worksheet next to each statement.

**L2 Differentiate** For these students, distribute the adapted Chapter 17 Section 2 Core Worksheet (Unit 4 All-in-One, p. 252).

Name _____ Class _____ Date _____

**CHAPTER 17 SECTION 2** | CORE WORKSHEET
National Security 3

Read each statement and decide whether you agree or disagree. Below each statement, explain why you agree or disagree.

1. In times of national crisis, such as war or an imminent terrorist attack, the news media should not report information that might be useful to the enemy, even if that information affects the rights of ordinary American citizens.

2. The United States government should be allowed to tap your phone, read your mail, and read your e-mail in the interests of national security.

3. The United States government should be allowed to hold persons believed to be terrorists or enemy spies without filing charges or holding a trial.

4. When an intelligence agency acquires information that indicates a potential threat to the public, the public should be informed immediately.

5. During times of civil unrest, the Federal Government should be allowed to impose curfews and deploy the military to implement martial law in the region affected.

Copyright © by Pearson Education, Inc., or its affiliates. All rights reserved.

---

# Background

**ORIGIN OF THE NATIONAL SECURITY ACT** The National Security Act of 1947, widely considered to be one of the most important pieces of defense legislation ever passed, was born at the end of World War II. America's experience in that war pointed to the need for more coordinated and efficiently run armed forces. President Harry Truman spearheaded the effort to devise a plan that would not only coordinate all branches of the armed forces, but would also ensure that the executive branch and Congress were given powers equal to those of the military. The act created the National Security Council to coordinate domestic, foreign, and military policies relating to national security, and the CIA to fill the need for gathering and disseminating intelligence. Additionally, the act merged the War Department and Navy Department with the newly created Department of the Air Force into a single Department of Defense.

---

## Answers

**Major Military Deployments** Overseas bases position American forces to protect our national interests abroad and to counter threats arising from other nations or extremist groups within other nations.

**Checkpoint** Army: responsible for military land operations domestically and where American interests lie abroad; Navy: responsible for warfare at sea and national defense; Air Force: responsible for military air and aerospace operations

Read the statements aloud one at a time and give students time to think about their answers, write their explanation in the space provided on their worksheet, and then move to the appropriate part of the room. After each statement, call on one student from each position and ask him or her to explain his or her choice. For statements 2 and 3, ask students if their opinions would vary if the country were facing a major security crisis.

After one student from each side has explained his or her reasoning, ask the class to take a moment to think about what they have just heard and to consider whether they would like to change their own positions. If students do change positions, ask one or two of these students what new information persuaded them to change their minds. At the end of the activity, have students revise their written explanations as needed.

**OPINION LINE REVIEW**

Tell students that each decision they made about the statements in the Opinion Line activity represents the type of decisions made regularly by members of the Office of the Director of National Intelligence and the Department of Homeland Security. Many important decisions about protecting our nation's security involve the possibility of compromising individual liberties. Conduct a brief class discussion about why these types of decisions are difficult, and have students use their experiences in the Opinion Line activity as the basis for the discussion.

---

**Answers**

**Checkpoint** to ensure that intelligence is received, evaluated, and shared in a timely and efficient manner among government agencies

Foreign Policy and National Defense

---

✔ **Checkpoint**
Why was the Office of the Director of National Intelligence established?

**shroud**
*v.* to hide from view

**ideological**
*adj.* having to do with the ideas or beliefs of a group

of war, its major duties are to defend the United States; attack and defeat enemy air, ground, and sea forces; strike military and other war-related targets in enemy territory; and provide transport and combat support for land and naval operations.

Reduced by 150,000 since 1991, the air force now has about 340,000 officers and enlisted personnel, about 20 percent of whom are women. All who serve in the USAF are under the direct command of the chief of staff of the air force.

## The Director of National Intelligence

The Director of National Intelligence (DNI) heads the Office of the Director of National Intelligence, established in 2005. The Office was born out of the pre-9/11 failure of the government's several intelligence agencies to collect and share information that might have warned of al Qaeda's coming attacks.

The President, with Senate approval, appoints the DNI, who is now the President's chief advisor in all matters relating to intelligence. The DNI supervises the operations of the 16 separate agencies that make up the federal intelligence community and directs the work of the National Counterterrorism Center (NCTC). The NCTC's hundreds of specialists receive and evaluate all information gathered by the intelligence community and relay it to all those who have "the need to know." As the first DNI, John Negroponte, put it: "Our job is to integrate foreign, military, and domestic intelligence in defense of the homeland and of United States interests abroad."

Some of the agencies controlled by the DNI are fairly well known, among them the FBI, the DEA, and the CIA. Indeed, for more than half a century, one of them, the Central Intelligence Agency, was—as its title suggests—the government's principal, its central, intelligence gathering organization. The CIA remains a major "cloak and dagger" agency, but the DNI now holds its once leading role in the intelligence community.

Some of the agencies in the intelligence community are little known, however, including the National Geospatial Agency,

the Defense Intelligence Agency, and the world's largest spy organization, the National Security Agency. Much of their work involves **espionage**—spying—and is shrouded in deepest secrecy. Even Congress has generally shied away from more than a passing check on their activities, and their operating funds are disguised at several places in the federal budget each year.

Nearly all Americans agree that the work of the several agencies that comprise the intelligence community is absolutely essential to the security of the United States. At the same time, however, it is essential that both the policymaking leaders in the government and the American people clearly recognize the potential dangers of a complex of government agencies whose operations are conducted in utmost secrecy.

## Department of Homeland Security

The Department of Homeland Security (DHS) is charged with the awesome and complex task of protecting the United States against terrorism. **Terrorism** is the use of violence to intimidate a government or a society, usually for political or ideological reasons.

Congress created the department in 2002, and it became operational in 2003. It is responsible for the coordination and the direction of all antiterrorist activities of all of the public agencies that operate in the field of domestic security—including thousands of police departments, fire departments, emergency medical and search and rescue units, and other disaster response agencies across the country.

The Homeland Security Act of 2002 gives the department major operating responsibilities in five specific areas:

- border and transportation security
- infrastructure protection
- emergency preparedness and response
- chemical, biological, radiological, and nuclear defense
- information analysis (intelligence)

The department was built mostly of agencies transferred to it from other Cabinet departments. Those agencies include

---

# Myths and Misconceptions

**THE NATIONAL GUARD** The National Guard, part of U.S. reserve forces, is in many ways a direct descendent of the colonial-era State militias. The oversight and training of National Guard forces are under the direction of the individual States in addition to the Federal Government. Throughout their history, Guard forces have played a major role in military campaigns. National Guard units deployed overseas in both World War I and World War II; in World War I, nearly 40 percent of the American units stationed in France were National Guard rather than Regular Army. More recently, many Americans came to think of the National Guard primarily in terms of domestic service, as Guard units were often deployed both for defense and emergency response, but National Guard units also make up a significant percentage of the combat troops deployed in Iraq and Afghanistan.

## Department of Homeland Security

# Safeguarding the Nation's Security

**GOVERNMENT** ONLINE
**Audio Tour**
To learn more about the Department of Homeland Security, visit
**PearsonSchool.com/phgovt**

The attacks of September 11, 2001 illustrated the vulnerability of this nation and its people. Since those tragic events, the Department of Homeland Security was created and charged with the large and complicated task of protecting the security of this vast country. Achieving this goal requires the coordinated effort of the department's several agencies, State and local governments, and the American people. *Why do you think coordinating the efforts of all levels of government is necessary in the safeguarding of the nation's security?*

San Francisco's Golden Gate Bridge

## Prevention

To detect and deter threats to the United States, the department

- Secures the nation's borders against terrorists, means of terrorism, illegal drugs, and other illegal activity
- Develops technology to detect and prevent the illegal possession and use of chemical, biological, radiological and nuclear materials
- Coordinates the collection and sharing of information
- Strengthens the security of the Nation's transportation system
- Enforces the nation's immigration laws

U.S. Border Patrol agent examines a pedestrian barrier in New Mexico.

## Protection

To safeguard the nation's infrastructure, economy, and citizens from acts of terrorism, or other emergencies, the department

- Implements a plan to protect both the nation's physical infrastructure and cyber infrastructure
- Combats financial and electronic crimes and identity theft
- Protects the President and other key government officials
- Works with other agencies to protect governmental activities
- Administers a unified preparedness strategy affecting all levels of government and the private sector

Secret Service agents ensure the President's safety.

## Response

To lead, manage, and coordinate the national response to acts of terrorism or other emergencies, the department

- Maintains catastrophic all-hazard plans focusing on the nation's most vulnerable communities
- Promotes response readiness through integrated planning to meet such crises as health and medical emergencies or acts of terrorism
- Provides emergency housing following major disasters
- Partners with other agencies and the private sector to assist mariners in distress and to protect property

A U.S. Coast Guard officer searches for survivors of Hurricane Katrina.

493

## Debate

"This concept of 'national defense' cannot be deemed an end in itself, justifying any exercise of legislative power designed to promote such a goal. Implicit in the term 'national defense' is the notion of defending those values and ideals which set this Nation apart."

—Chief Justice Earl Warren, 1967

Use this quote to begin a classroom debate. Explain that this was part of a Supreme Court ruling, and the heart of the issue was whether national security should be more important than personal liberty. In that context, Warren argued that the core values expressed in the Constitution were more important than the immediate problems of defense and security. Ask students to think about the quotation in that context and to debate whether they agree with Warren that security is less important than liberty.

## EXTEND THE LESSON

**L3** **Differentiate** Display Transparency 17B, U.S. Overseas Troop Deployment by Country, which shows the U.S. overseas troops' changing demographics in specific locations over time. Explain that armed forces overseas defend and protect the national security of the United States. Have students analyze the graph and then write a brief paragraph utilizing their historical knowledge to determine why those locations were the focus of American troop deployment and buildup. Have them discuss their reasoning.

**L3** **L4** **Differentiate** Distribute the Chapter 17 Section 2 Extend Worksheet (Unit 4 All-in-One, p. 255), which asks students to answer questions about the Department of Homeland Security and come up with examples of how the government meets its security responsibilities.

**L2** **ELL Differentiate** Ask students to review the text material under "Department of Homeland Security" while you distribute the Chapter 17 Section 2 Extend Worksheet (Unit 4 All-in-One, p. 255). Help students identify the five areas of responsibility of the Department of Homeland Security to write in the first column of the worksheet. *(1. border and transportation security; 2. infrastructure protection; 3. emergency preparedness and response; 4. chemical, biological, radiological, and nuclear defense; 5. information analysis)* Define difficult words in this list: *infrastructure* (important structures and systems serving a society, such as dams, power plants, and subways); *radiological* (radioactive substances, or things that give off waves that could be harmful). Have students work in pairs to complete the worksheet. Discuss their responses as a class.

**L4** **Differentiate** Have students write a letter to one of their senators or representatives that expresses their opinion on the questions of security and freedom covered in this chapter.

Tell students to go to the Audio Tour for a guided tour of the Department of Homeland Security.

## Answers

**Safeguarding the Nation's Security** The United States is a vast nation. No centralized agency could hope to protect it all. However, reasonable security can be achieved by enlisting the help of local public and private organizations to gather intelligence, secure key structures, and respond to emergencies.

# Assess and Remediate

**L3** Collect the Core Worksheet and assess students' work.

**L3** Assign the Section 2 Assessment questions.

**L3** Section Quiz A (Unit 4 All-in-One, p. 256)

**L2** Section Quiz B (Unit 4 All-in-One, p. 257)

Have students complete the review activities in the digital lesson presentation and continue their work in the **Essential Questions Journal.**

## REMEDIATION

| If Your Students Have Trouble With | Strategies For Remediation |
|---|---|
| Describing how the Federal Government safeguards security (Question 1) | Have students create a concept web of the main ideas of the section. |
| Identifying key defense advisors (Question 2) | Review with students the content under the Defense Department heading. |
| Describing the main duties of the military departments (Question 3) | Create a graphic organizer of the military departments on the board. |
| Explaining why espionage is a tool in protecting national security (Question 4) | Ask students for another word for *espionage* (spying) and have them brainstorm the kinds of information spies might discover. |
| Defining terrorism (Question 5) | Have students list examples of recent terrorist acts and help them determine the similarities between these actions. |
| Understanding civil control of the military (Question 6) | Review the Civilian Control of the Military infographic with students. |
| Describing the duties and responsibilities of the Department of Homeland Security (Question 7) | Have students complete the Extend Worksheet. |

## Answers

**Caption** to guard against threats of bioterrorism and to protect the nation's oil supply

---

The State of Alaska and DHS jointly protect this 800-mile pipeline that carries crude oil to a seaport. *Why is the integrity of the Alaska pipeline important to national security?*

the Secret Service and the newly entitled U.S. Immigration and Customs Enforcement (ICE), from the Treasury Department; the Coast Guard and the Transportation Security Administration, from the Transportation Department; the renamed U.S. Citizenship and Immigration Services, from the Justice Department; and the independent Federal Emergency Management Agency (FEMA).

The threat of bioterrorism—the use of such biological agents as smallpox or anthrax as weapons—dramatizes the immensity of the problems facing the Department of Homeland Security. So, too, do these facts: There are nearly 600,000 bridges, 170,000 water systems, and more than 5,000 power plants (104 of them nuclear) in the United States. There are also 220,000 miles of rail lines, 1.5 million miles of natural gas pipelines, 25,000 miles of inland waterways, and 1,000 harbor channels. Additionally, there

**foment**
*v.* to stir up, provoke

are some 470 skyscrapers (each over 500 feet high), nearly 19,000 airports (including some 300 major facilities), thousands of stadiums and other large gathering places, and nearly 20,000 miles of international border.

Add to those fundamental facts such critical matters as the nation's food and water supply, its healthcare system, and its communications networks, and this point becomes clear: This country cannot be protected—completely and absolutely—against terrorist acts. Terrorism thrives on unpredictability and uses it as a weapon to <u>foment</u> fear and anxiety.

It seems quite apparent that the best that can be hoped for in current circumstances is that (1) most—nearly all—terrorist attacks will be thwarted or their impacts will at least be minimized; and (2) those responsible for the attacks will be rooted out and brought to justice.

> **Essential Questions Journal** To continue to build a response to the chapter Essential Question, go to your **Essential Questions Journal.**

## SECTION 2 ASSESSMENT

1. **Guiding Question** Use your completed table to answer this question: How does the Federal Government safeguard this nation's security?

### Key Terms and Comprehension

2. Who are the key advisors to the President on issues of defense?

3. Describe the main duties of each military department.

4. Why might **espionage** be considered an important tool in protecting national security?

5. What is **terrorism?**

### Critical Thinking

6. **Identify Central Issues (a)** Why do you think the Framers thought civilian control of the military to be so important? **(b)** Do you think it remains a matter of valid concern today?

7. **Analyze Information (a)** What are the five areas of responsibility tasked to the Department of Homeland Security? **(b)** How might the supervision of those areas help prevent terrorist attacks in the United States?

### Quick Write

**Expository Writing: Brainstorm Possible Solutions** Recognizing that a problem exists may be quite simple, but coming up with a solution is often a difficult task. Using the description you wrote in Section 1, brainstorm ideas for possible solutions to the problem you selected. Then, organize your list to rank the solutions from most effective to least effective.

---

# Assessment Answers

**1.** America's defense consists of federal agencies and military departments under civilian control. The President makes defense policy and the Defense Department implements it. The Joint Chiefs of Staff advise the President, National Security Council, and secretary of defense. The military departments are responsible for protecting the United States domestically as well as its interests and citizens in other parts of the world. The Office of the Director of National Intelligence oversees the nation's intelligence agencies. The Department of Homeland Security coordinates efforts against terrorism and other national emergencies.

**2.** secretary of defense, secretary of state, Director of National Intelligence, Joint Chiefs of Staff

**3.** Army: land operations; Navy: sea warfare and defense; Air Force: air and aerospace

**4.** Possible answer: Espionage can help uncover secret plots targeting the United States.

**5.** the use of violence to intimidate a government or a society

**6. (a)** to prevent a powerful military from taking control of the government **(b)** Possible response: Yes. Military coups still occur today.

**7. (a)** border and transportation security; infrastructure protection; emergency preparedness and response; chemical, biological, radiological, and nuclear defense; information analysis **(b)** by reducing risk of terrorists entering the country, guarding critical targets; preparing local groups for quick response; developing technology to detect chemical, biological, radiological, and nuclear weapons

**QUICK WRITE** Solutions should be realistic and student rankings well-reasoned.

# SECTION 3

# American **Foreign Policy** Overview

| Washington declares isolationist policy in Farewell Address | Open Door Policy declared | U.S. becomes involved in Latin America through the Roosevelt Corollary | U.S. enters World War I | U.S. returns to isolationist policy |
|---|---|---|---|---|
| **1796** | **1899** | **1900s** | **1917** | **1918** |

| U.S. endeavors to ease tensions with Latin America with Good Neighbor Policy | U.S. isolationist policy ends with the Pearl Harbor attack and entry into World War II | U.S. confirms acceptance of internationalism policy by joining the United Nations | Truman Doctrine begins as do the policies of deterrence and containment |
|---|---|---|---|
| **1930s** | **1941** | **1945** | **1947** |

| U.S. provides foreign aid during Berlin blockade | Korean War begins as U.S. attempt to contain communism | U.S. commits to war in Vietnam in attempt to contain communism | Efforts toward détente begin when Nixon visits China and Soviet Union; signs SALT I pact |
|---|---|---|---|
| **1948** | **1950** | **1965** | **1972** |

## Guiding Question

**How has American foreign policy changed over time?** Use a timeline to keep track of the major changes in American foreign policy.

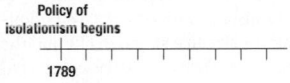

## Political Dictionary

- collective security
- deterrence
- cold war
- containment
- détente

## Objectives

1. Summarize American foreign policy from independence through World War I.
2. Show how the two World Wars affected America's traditional policy of isolationism.
3. Explain the principles of collective security and deterrence and their use during the cold war.
4. Describe American foreign policy since the end of the cold war.
5. Understand why the world remains a dangerous place.

**Image Above:** American diplomat Ben Franklin is received at the French court in Versailles in 1778.

The basic purpose of American foreign policy has always been to protect the security and well-being of the United States—and so it is today. It would be impossible to present a full-blown, detailed history of America's foreign relations in these pages, of course. But we can review its major themes and highlights here.

Why should you know as much as you can about the history of the United States? Because history is not "bunk," as automaker Henry Ford once described it. Let Robert Kelly, a leading historian, tell you what history really is: "History is our social memory. Our memories tell us who we are, where we belong, what has worked and what has not worked, and where we seem to be going."[4]

## Foreign Policy Through World War I

From its beginnings, and for 150 years, American foreign policy was very largely built on a policy of isolationism. Throughout that period, the United States refused to become generally and permanently involved in the affairs of the rest of the world.

Isolationism arose in the earliest years of this nation's history. In his Farewell Address in 1796, George Washington declared that "our true policy" was "to steer clear of permanent alliances with any portion of the foreign world." Our "detached and distant situation," Washington said, made it desirable for us to have "as little political connection as possible" with other nations.

At the time, and for decades to come, isolationism seemed a wise policy to most Americans. The United States was a new and relatively weak nation with a great many problems, a huge continent to explore and settle, and two oceans to separate it from the rest of the world.

The policy of isolationism did not demand a *complete* separation from the rest of the world, however. From the first, the United States developed ties abroad by exchanging diplomatic representatives with other nations, making treaties with many of them, and building an extensive foreign commerce. In fact, isolationism was, over time, more a statement of our desire for

---

4 *The Shaping of the American Past*, 2nd ed.

# Focus on the Basics

**FACTS:** • The Monroe Doctrine and the concept of Manifest Destiny, which focused on isolationism and national growth, shaped American foreign policy through World War I. • The two world wars ended America's traditional policy of isolationism and led to a policy of internationalism. • Victory in World War II made the U.S. one of two world superpowers and led to the policies of collective security, deterrence, and containment.

**CONCEPTS:** role and purpose of government, democratic values and principles

**ENDURING UNDERSTANDINGS:** • Knowledge of the history of American foreign policy is essential to understanding the foreign policy issues facing the U.S. today. • Although the cold war is over, the world is still a dangerous place requiring continued vigilance.

## SKILLS DEVELOPMENT

### ANALYZE TIMELINES

To help students learn to analyze timelines, have them turn to the Skills Handbook, p. S29, and use the information explained there to complete this lesson's Core Worksheet A.

# Get Started

## LESSON GOALS

Students will . . .

- describe foreign policies from U.S. history.
- understand U.S. foreign policies as they relate to historic events by creating a timeline.
- analyze primary source passages from the Truman Doctrine, using a worksheet.

## BEFORE CLASS

Assign the section, the graphic organizer in the text, and the Reading Comprehension Worksheet (Unit 4 All-in-One, p. 258) before class.

**L2** **Differentiate** Reading Comprehension Worksheet (Unit 4 All-in-One, p. 260)

## BELLRINGER

Write the following on the board: **isolationism, Monroe Doctrine, Manifest Destiny, Roosevelt Corollary to Monroe Doctrine, Good Neighbor Policy, Open Door Policy, internationalism, collective security, deterrence, containment, détente. Write brief descriptions of three of these policies in your notebook.**

**L2** **ELL Differentiate** Allow students to choose two policies to describe.

**L4** **Differentiate** Challenge students to describe as many policies as they can in the allotted time.

## Answers

**Checkpoint** to advise foreign nations that although the U.S. will maintain a policy of isolationism it will take action against any nation that threatens the security of North and South America

**Remember the *Maine*** The Monroe Doctrine was intended to prevent European domination in the Western Hemisphere. The U.S. applied this doctrine when American forces became involved in Cuba's struggle for independence from Spain.

---

✔ **Checkpoint**
What was the intent of the Monroe Doctrine?

**doctrine**
*n.* a rule or principle that forms the basis of a policy or belief

noninvolvement outside the Western Hemisphere than a description of United States policy within our own hemisphere.

**The Monroe Doctrine** James Monroe gave the policy of isolationism a clearer shape in 1823. In a historic message to Congress, he proclaimed what has been known ever since as the Monroe Doctrine.

A wave of revolutions had swept Latin America, destroying the old Spanish and Portuguese empires there. The United States viewed the prospect that other European powers would now help Spain and Portugal to take back their lost possessions as a threat to this country's security and a challenge to its economic interests.

In his message, President Monroe restated America's intentions to stay out of European affairs. He also warned the nations of Europe to stay out of the affairs of both North and South America. He declared that the United States would look on

> ## Primary Source
> **any attempt on their part to extend their system to any portion of this hemisphere as dangerous to our peace and safety.**
> —Speech by President James Monroe to Congress, December 2, 1823

At first, most Latin Americans took little notice of this doctrine. They knew that it was really the Royal Navy and British interest in Latin American trade that protected them from European domination. But in 1867, the Monroe Doctrine got its first real test. While Americans were immersed in the Civil War, France invaded Mexico. The French leader, Napoleon III, installed Archduke Maximilian of Austria as Mexico's puppet emperor. In 1867, the United States backed the Mexicans in forcing the French to withdraw, and the Maximilian regime fell.

Later, as the United States became more powerful, many Latin Americans came to view the Monroe Doctrine as a selfish policy designed to protect the political and economic interests of the United States, not the independence of other nations in the Western Hemisphere.

**A World Power** Following its victory in the Revolutionary War, the United States began to expand across the continent almost at once. The Louisiana Purchase in 1803 doubled the nation's size in a single stroke and the Florida Purchase Treaty in 1819 completed its expansion to the south.

Through the second quarter of the nineteenth century, the United States pursued what most Americans believed was this nation's "Manifest Destiny": the mission to

## Remember the *Maine*

Images of the **sunken battleship** and the **"Remember the *Maine*" battle cry** led to American intervention in Cuba.

The battleship U.S.S. *Maine* was sent to Cuba to protect American interests there during Cuba's struggle for independence from Spain. Its mysterious sinking in 1898 caused American outrage and demand for action. With its victory in the Spanish-American War, the United States itself became a colonial power by acquiring Guam, Puerto Rico, and the Philippines. *How are these events examples of the application of the Monroe Doctrine?*

---

# Differentiated Resources

The following resources are located in the All-in-One, Unit 4, Chapter 17, Section 3:

**L3** Reading Comprehension Worksheet (p. 258)

**L2** Reading Comprehension Worksheet (p. 260)

**L3** Core Worksheet A (p. 262)

**L3** Core Worksheet B (p. 263)

**L3** Quiz A (p. 265)

**L2** Quiz B (p. 266)

expand its boundaries across the continent to the Pacific Ocean. By 1900, the nation had not only accomplished that task, it had spread its influence beyond the continental boundaries to become both a colonial and a world power. The nation's interests now extended to Alaska, to the tip of Latin America, and across the Pacific to the Philippines.

**The Good Neighbor Policy** The threat of European intervention in the Western Hemisphere that troubled President Monroe declined in the second half of the nineteenth century. That threat was replaced by problems within the hemisphere. Political instability, revolutions, unpaid foreign debts, and injuries to citizens and property of other countries plagued Central and South America.

Under what came to be known as the Roosevelt Corollary to the Monroe Doctrine, the United States began to police Latin America in the early 1900s. Several times, the marines were used to quell revolutions and other unrest in Nicaragua, Haiti, Cuba, and elsewhere in Latin America.

In 1903, Panama revolted and became independent of Colombia, with America's blessing. In the same year, the United States gained the right to build a canal across the Isthmus of Panama. In 1917, the United States purchased the Virgin Islands from Denmark to help guard the canal. Many in Latin America resented these and other steps. They complained of "the Colossus of the North," of "Yankee imperialism," and of "dollar diplomacy"—and many still do.

This country's Latin American policies took a dramatic turn in the 1930s. Theodore Roosevelt's Corollary was replaced by Franklin Roosevelt's Good Neighbor Policy, a conscious attempt to win friends to the south by reducing this nation's political and military interventions in the region.

Today, the central provision of the Monroe Doctrine—the warning against foreign encroachments in the Western Hemisphere—is set out in the Inter-American Treaty of Reciprocal Assistance (the Rio Pact) of 1947. Still, the United States is, without question, the dominant power in the Western Hemisphere, and the Monroe Doctrine remains a vital part of American foreign policy.

THE WORLD CONSTABLE

▸▸ **Analyzing Political Cartoons** To prevent European intervention in Latin America, President Theodore Roosevelt proclaimed that the United States should be the only policeman of the western hemisphere. *According to this cartoon, what is involved in implementing this policy?*

**The Open Door in China** Historically, American foreign-policy interests have centered on Europe and Latin America. But America has also been involved in Asia since the mid-1800s. Forty-five years before the United States acquired territory in the Pacific, the U.S. Navy's Commodore Matthew Perry had opened Japan to American trade.

By the late nineteenth century, however, America's thriving trade in Asia was being seriously threatened. The British, French, Germans, and Japanese were each ready to take slices of the Chinese coast as their own exclusive trading preserves. In 1899, Secretary of State John Hay announced this country's insistence on an Open Door policy in China. That doctrine promoted equal trade access for all nations, and demanded that China's independence and sovereignty over its own territory be preserved.

The other major powers came to accept the American position, however reluctantly. Relations between the United States and Japan worsened from that point on, up to the climax at Pearl Harbor in 1941. Over the same period, the United States built increasingly strong ties with China; but those ties were cut when communists won control of the Chinese mainland in 1949. For nearly 30 years, the United States and the People's

✔ **Checkpoint**
How did the Good Neighbor policy differ from Roosevelt's Corollary?

plague
*v.* to cause continuing trouble, distress

quell
*v.* to put down

# Teach

To present this topic using online resources, use the lesson presentations at **PearsonSchool.com/phgovt**.

**REVIEW BELLRINGER**

Go through the list of foreign policies. Ask volunteers to describe each policy. Discuss the policies with the class. (*isolationism: purposeful refusal to become generally involved in the affairs of the rest of the world;* **Monroe Doctrine**: *warning to Europe to stay out of affairs of North and South America;* **Manifest Destiny**: *mission to expand U.S. boundaries across the continent to the Pacific Ocean;* **Roosevelt Corollary to Monroe Doctrine**: *U.S. would police Latin America to quell revolutions and other unrest;* **Good Neighbor Policy**: *attempt to win friends in Latin America by reducing U.S. political and military intervention in the region;* **Open Door Policy**: *equal trade access to China for all nations and preservation of China's independence and sovereignty;* **internationalism**: *greater involvement with other nations, due to the recognition that events in other parts of the world affect the well-being of the United States;* **collective security**: *acting together with other nations against any nation that threatens world peace;* **deterrence**: *strategy of maintaining military might so great that no nation would dare to attack;* **containment**: *prevent communism from expanding beyond its existing boundaries, leading to its eventual collapse;* **détente**: *purposeful attempt to improve relations with the Soviet Union and China*)

Ask: **Up to World War II, U.S. foreign policy was based on which broad concept?** (*isolationism*) **After World War II, which foreign policy concept dominated?** (*internationalism*)

# Background

**MONROE DOCTRINE** The Monroe Doctrine was initially intended as a warning to European nations, particularly Spain and Russia, but appears to have had little effect on the actions of those nations. The United States was not generally recognized as a military force to be reckoned with at the time of President Monroe's proclamation. While aimed at a European audience, the Monroe Doctrine's real impact was felt domestically, since it outlined a general belief that the political affairs on this side of the Atlantic Ocean should be kept separate from affairs on the European side.

# Answers

**Analyzing Political Cartoons** Possible answer: The United States needs to act as intermediary between Europe and Latin America as well as arbitrate what needs are addressed for both sides.

**Checkpoint** It reduced American interference in Latin America and encouraged a more diplomatic and less forceful relationship.

## DISCUSS

Tell students that in order to understand the foreign policy issues of today, they must understand the historical evolution of U.S. foreign policy. The foreign policy of the United States has changed dramatically over time and, subsequently, so have its relationships with other nations. Remind students that after the American Revolution, our political relationship with Great Britain was tenuous at best, but in the years since then that country has become one of our closest allies.

To illustrate foreign policy evolution further, ask: **How would you describe the relationship between the U.S. and Soviet Union following World War II?** *(tense, competitive, dangerous)* **What foreign policy toward the Soviet Union did the U.S. adopt at that time?** *(containment)*, **After the Vietnam War, what was the American policy on handling the Soviet Union?** *(détente)* **What major event ended the cold war relationship between the U.S. and Soviet Union?** *(the fall of the Soviet Union)* **What is our relationship with Russia today?** *(relatively friendly, but cautious)*

**L2** **ELL Differentiate** To help students understand the key terms used in this section, review the definitions with them. Have students write down the definition and then, next to the definition, include a drawing that helps them understand the concept.

---

## Answers

**Checkpoint** The U.S. needed to discard the policy of isolationism and be an active participant in world affairs and accept the policy of internationalism.

**498** Foreign Policy and National Defense

---

✔ **Checkpoint**
How did World War II change the foreign policy position of the United States?

**scourge**
*n.* something that causes great trouble or suffering

Republic of China refused diplomatic recognition of one another.

## World At War

Germany's submarine campaign against American shipping in the North Atlantic forced the United States out of its isolationist cocoon in 1917. America entered World War I "to make the world safe for democracy." However, with the defeat of Germany and the Central Powers, America pulled back from the involvements brought on by the war. The United States refused to join the League of Nations, and many Americans strongly believed that problems in Europe and the rest of the world were no concern of ours.

America's historic commitment to isolationism was finally ended by World War II. The United States became directly involved in the war when the Japanese attacked the American naval base at Pearl Harbor in Hawaii on December 7, 1941. From that point on—along with the British, the Russians, the Chinese, and our other Allies—the United States waged an all-out effort to defeat the Axis Powers (Germany, Italy, and Japan).

Under the direction and leadership of President Franklin Roosevelt, the United States became the "arsenal of democracy." American resources and industrial capacity supplied most of the armaments and other materials we and our Allies needed to win World War II. Within a very short time, the United States was transformed into the mightiest military power in the world—and it has remained so ever since.

## Two New Principles

The coming of World War II brought a historic shift from a position of isolationism to one of internationalism. This nation's foreign policy has been cast in that newer direction for more than 60 years now. Even so, the overall objective of that policy remains what it has always been: the protection of the security and well-being of the United States.

**Collective Security** Following World War II, the United States and most of the rest of a war-weary world looked to the principle of **collective security** to keep international peace and order. America hoped to forge a world community in which at least most nations would agree to act together against any nation that threatened the peace.

To that end, this country took the lead in creating the United Nations in 1945. The organization's charter declares that the UN was formed to promote international cooperation and so "to save succeeding generations from the scourge of war . . . and to maintain international peace and security."

It soon became clear, however, that the UN would not shape the future of the world. Rather, international security would depend largely on the nature of the relations between the two superpowers, the United States and the Soviet Union. Those relations, never very close, quickly deteriorated—and for the next 40 years, American foreign policy was built around that fact.

With the breakup of the Soviet Union, the United States became the only superpower in today's world. Still, collective security remains a cornerstone of American policy. The United States has supported the United Nations and other efforts to further international cooperation. This country has also taken another path to collective security: the building of a network of regional security alliances.

**Deterrence** The principle of deterrence has also been a part of American foreign policy since World War II. Basically, **deterrence** is the strategy of maintaining military might at so great a level that that very strength will deter—discourage, prevent—an attack on this country by any hostile power.

President Harry Truman initiated deterrence as U.S.–Soviet relations worsened after World War II. Every President since President Truman's day has reaffirmed the strategy, and deterrence was a key factor in the collapse of the Soviet Union.

## Resisting Soviet Aggression

One cannot hope to understand either recent or current American foreign policy without a knowledge of the long years of the cold war. The **cold war** was a period of more than 40 years during which relations

---

**498** Foreign Policy and National Defense

---

## Political Cartoon Mini-Lesson

Display Transparency 17D, U.S. Foreign Policy, May 1941, when you discuss World War II as a turning point in U.S. foreign policy. Ask: **What is happening in this cartoon?** *(Nazi aggression has toppled many European nations.)* **What is the U.S. foreign policy toward these events?** *(isolationism)* **What is the cartoonist's view toward American isolationism?** *(The cartoonist suggests that isolationism is unrealistic. When the energetic Nazi bird finishes with the England tree, it will likely start on the U.S. tree.)* Explain that before the attack on Pearl Harbor on December 7, 1941, many Americans believed strongly that the U.S. should stay out of the conflict in Europe. Ask students if they can identify the cartoonist. Many students might recognize the style of Dr. Seuss (Theodor Geisel), the famous writer of children's books. Students may not realize that Geisel also drew political cartoons.

between the two superpowers were at least tense and, more often than not, distinctly hostile. It was, for the most part, not a "hot war" of military action, but rather a time of threats, posturing, and military buildup.

At the Yalta Conference in early 1945, Soviet Premier Josef Stalin had agreed with President Franklin Roosevelt and British Prime Minister Winston Churchill to promote the establishment of "democratic governments" by "free elections" in the liberated countries of Eastern Europe. Instead, the Soviets imposed dictatorial regimes on those countries. The Soviets also looked to exploit postwar chaos in other nations, as well. In 1946, Churchill declared that "an iron curtain" had descended across the continent.

**The Truman Doctrine** The United States began to counter the aggressive actions of

the Soviet Union in the early months of 1947. Both Greece and Turkey were in danger of falling under Soviet control. At President Harry Truman's urgent request, Congress approved a massive program of economic and military aid, and both countries remained free. In his message to Congress, the President declared that it was now

### Primary Source
the policy of the United States to support free peoples who are resisting attempted subjugation by armed minorities or by outside pressures.

— Speech by President Harry S Truman to Congress, March 12, 1947

The Truman Doctrine soon became part of a broader American plan for dealing with

✔ **Checkpoint**
What policy developed to deter the spread of communism?

**posture**
*v.* to adopt a pose, usually intended to deceive

**counter**
*v.* to oppose, contradict

**Cold War Conflicts, 1947–1991**

GOVERNMENT ONLINE
For an **interactive** exploration of this map and to find out more about these conflicts visit PearsonSchool.com/phgovt

The ideological differences and competition for power between the two superpowers became the source of political tension worldwide. Many nations chose to side with one or the other of the superpowers. Several became battlefields and others political flashpoints where Soviet aggression and the American desire to contain communism clashed. *What do most of these locations have in common?*

**KEY**
- United States and allies
- Soviet Union and allies
- Other communist states
- Cold War hot spots (with dates)

Berlin (1948–1949, 1961)
Czechoslovakia (1968) · Hungary (1956)
Turkey (1947)
Greece (1947)
Afghanistan (1979–1989)
Korea (1950–1953)
Laos (1960–1962)
Taiwan (1954–1955, 1958)
Vietnam (1946–1954, 1959–1975)
Malaya (1948–1960)
Cuba (1962)
Dominican Republic (1965)
Guatemala (1954)
Nicaragua (1979)
Angola (1974–1990)
Namibia (1975–1991)
Chile (1973)

SOVIET UNION
UNITED STATES
ATLANTIC OCEAN
PACIFIC OCEAN
INDIAN OCEAN

## Background

**TURNING POINTS IN FOREIGN POLICY** Only a few single events in U.S. history have brought about major and lasting changes to our foreign policy. The attack on Pearl Harbor was one of those events. The same can be said of the attacks of September 11, 2001. Addressing Congress nine days after the terrorist attacks on the World Trade Center and the Pentagon, President George W. Bush said, "Americans have known the casualties of war—but not at the center of a great city on a peaceful morning. Americans have known surprise attacks—but never before on thousands of civilians. All of this was brought upon us in a single day—and night fell on a different world, a world where freedom itself is under attack." The September 11 attacks led the Bush administration to develop a policy aimed at defeating global terrorism.

### CREATE A TIMELINE

Distribute a copy of the Chapter 17 Section 3 Core Worksheet A (Unit 4 All-in-One, p. 262) to each student. In this activity, students will create a timeline of specific historical events and determine which American policy applied to that event.

When students have completed the timeline, divide them into small groups to share their answers. Ask them to discuss events that marked changes in foreign policy. Explain that some disagreement is possible, since foreign policy changes often happen gradually rather than in response to any single event. Then come together as a class to discuss ways in which U.S. foreign policy changed over time.

**L2** **ELL Differentiate** Display Transparency 17C, which contains a blank version of the timeline for this activity. Have students work as a class to place the events and policies from Core Worksheet A in their proper locations on the transparency timeline.

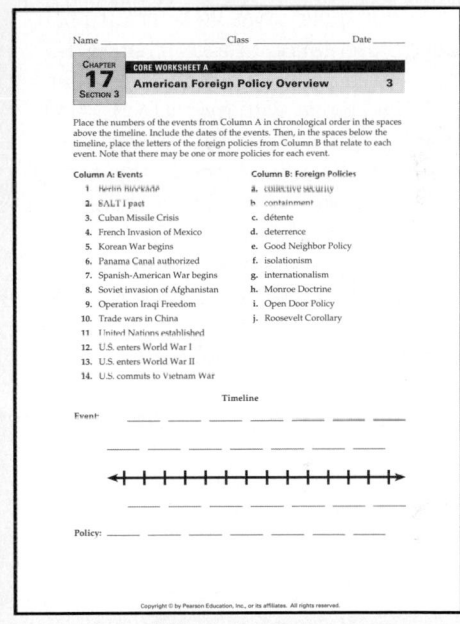

Tell students to go to the Interactivity to find out more about cold war conflicts.

---

## Answers

**Checkpoint** containment

**Cold War Conflicts, 1947–1991** Each conflict is near a communist-controlled region or an ally of the U.S.S.R.

Distribute copies of the Chapter 17 Section 3 Core Worksheet B (Unit 4 All-in-One, p. 263). This worksheet contains passages from President Truman's speech outlining a foreign policy known as the Truman Doctrine. Assign students one of the excerpts to read. Then, in the space provided, have students rephrase the text in their own words. Have student volunteers read their version of the excerpt. Write these on the board so that students have a revised version of each excerpt.

**L2 ELL Differentiate** Assign Passage C. Before students read it, define the words *subjugation* (takeover), *assist* (help), *destiny* (fate or fortune), *primarily* (mainly), *essential* (important), *orderly* (organized).

**L4 Differentiate** Assign all four excerpts to advanced students and have them complete Core Worksheet B in its entirety.

**DISCUSS CORE WORKSHEET B**

Tell students that this speech was President Truman's first major public presentation of a key change in American foreign policy, and remind the class that the Truman Doctrine, along with most U.S. foreign policy in the decades after World War II, was developed as a response to what was seen as the immediate threat of communism and the Soviet Union. Use the Think-Write-Pair-Share strategy (p. T22) to lead a discussion on Truman's speech by asking students whether they believe that the Truman Doctrine has any significance to U.S. foreign policy today. Student answers may vary, and good reasons can be offered on both sides. If students are having difficulty formulating a response, ask them to consider whether there are meaningful parallels to be drawn between the threat posed by communism and the threat posed by terrorism today.

## Answers

**Caption** The U.S. will live up to its policy of helping nations resist subjugation from outside pressures.

Grateful citizens of Berlin wave to an American plane delivering badly needed supplies during the Berlin airlift. *How did the Berlin airlift symbolize America's commitment to the Truman Doctrine?*

**armistice**
*n.* an agreement to stop fighting for a time, a cease-fire

the Soviet Union. From mid-1947 through the 1980s, the United States followed the policy of **containment.** That policy was rooted in the belief that if communism could be kept within its existing boundaries, it would collapse under the weight of its own internal weaknesses.

The United States and the Soviet Union confronted one another often during the cold war years. Two of those confrontations were of major, near-war proportions. The first, the Berlin blockade, occurred in 1948–1949, when the Soviets tried to force the United States and its allies to abandon the German city of Berlin to Soviet domination. The other major incident, the Cuban missile crisis, arose in 1962. The United States threatened war over the placement of Soviet nuclear missiles on the island of Cuba. In both cases, the Soviets backed down in the face of determined American resistance.

Not all cold war conflicts ended peacefully, however. During the postwar period, the United States fought two hot wars against communist forces in Asia.

**The Korean War** The Korean War began on June 25, 1950. Communist North Korea (the People's Democratic Republic of Korea) attacked South Korea (the UN-sponsored Republic of Korea). Immediately, the UN's Security Council called on all UN members to help South Korea repel the invasion.

The war lasted for more than three years. It pitted the United Nations Command, largely made up of American and South Korean forces, against Soviet-trained and Soviet-equipped North Korean and communist Chinese troops. Cease-fire negotiations began in July 1951, but fighting continued until an armistice was signed on July 27, 1953.

The long and bitter Korean conflict did not end in a clear-cut UN victory. Still, the invasion was turned back, and the Republic of Korea remained standing. For the first time in history, armed forces of several nations fought under an international flag against aggression. There is no telling how far the tide of that aggression might have been carried had the United States not come to the aid of South Korea.

**The War in Vietnam** In the years following World War II, a nationalist movement arose in French Indochina—today, Vietnam. Vietnamese nationalists were seeking independence from their French colonial rulers. Made up mostly of communist forces led by Ho Chi Minh, the nationalists fought and defeated the French in a lengthy conflict. Under truce agreements signed in 1954, the country was divided into two zones. The communist-dominated North Vietnam, with its capital in Hanoi, and an anticommunist South Vietnam, with its capital in Saigon.

Almost at once, communist guerrillas (the Viet Cong), supported by the North Vietnamese, began a civil war in South Vietnam. Because President Dwight Eisenhower and other foreign policy experts believed that South Vietnam was critical to the security of all of Southeast Asia, the Eisenhower administration responded with economic and then military aid to Saigon. President John Kennedy increased that aid, and President Lyndon Johnson committed the United States to full-scale war in early 1965.

In 1969, President Richard Nixon began what he called the "Vietnamization" of the war. Over the next four years, the United States gradually pulled troops out of combat. Finally, the two sides reached a cease-fire agreement in early 1973, and the United States withdrew its last units.

## Debate

During the 2008 election campaign, the views of candidates Barack Obama and John McCain differed significantly on continuing the Iraq War. Use the quotes below to start a debate. Ask: **Would continued involvement in Iraq promote U.S. security?**

"[F]ighting in a war without end will not make the American people safer. . . . I will end this war . . . because it is the right thing to do for our national security. . . ."

—Barack Obama

"It would be a grave mistake to leave before Al Qaeda in Iraq is defeated. . . . The best way to secure long-term peace and security is to establish a stable, prosperous, and democratic state in Iraq. . . ."

—John McCain

The ill-fated war in Vietnam cost the United States more than 58,000 American lives. As the war dragged on, millions of Americans came to oppose American involvement in Southeast Asia—and traces of the divisiveness of that period can still be seen in the politics of today.

## American Policies Succeed

As the United States withdrew from Vietnam, the Nixon administration embarked on a policy of **détente.** The term is French, meaning "a relaxation of tensions." In this case, the policy of détente included a purposeful attempt to improve relations with the Soviet Union and, separately, with China.

**Improving Relations** President Richard Nixon flew to Beijing in 1972 to begin a new era in American-Chinese relations. His visit paved the way for further contacts and, finally, for formal diplomatic ties between the United States and the People's Republic of China. Less than three months later, Mr. Nixon journeyed to Moscow. There, he and Soviet Premier Leonid Brezhnev signed the first Strategic Arms Limitations Talks agreement, SALT I—a five-year pact in which both sides agreed to a measure of control over their nuclear weapons.

Relations with mainland China have improved in fits and starts since the 1970s. Efforts at détente with the Soviets, however, proved less successful. Moscow continued to apply its expansionist pressures and provided economic and military aid to revolutionary movements around the world.

In 1979, an effort by the Soviet Union to impose a communist regime in Afghanistan was met by unexpectedly stiff resistance of armed groups of Afghans and their supporters around the region. The United States, acting largely in secret through the CIA, provided support to some of the groups resisting communist expansion. This type of war by proxy between the United States and the Soviet Union became common during the cold war. After the aggression against Afghanistan, the Carter and then the Reagan administrations placed a renewed emphasis on the containment of Soviet power.

**The Cold War Ends** Relations between the United States and the USSR improved remarkably after Mikhail Gorbachev came to power in Moscow in 1985. He and President Reagan met in a series of summit conferences that helped pave the way to the end of the cold war. Those meetings, focused on arms limitations, eased long-standing tensions.

Certainly, Mikhail Gorbachev deserves much credit for the fundamental change in the Soviets' approach to world affairs. But, just as certainly, that historic change was prompted by deepening political and economic chaos in Eastern Europe and within the Soviet Union itself—by conditions that ultimately brought the collapse of the Soviet Union in late 1991.

The fact that the cold war is now a matter of history should also be seen in this light:

✔ **Checkpoint**
What led to the end of the cold war?

**divisiveness**
*n.* disagreement, hostility, split

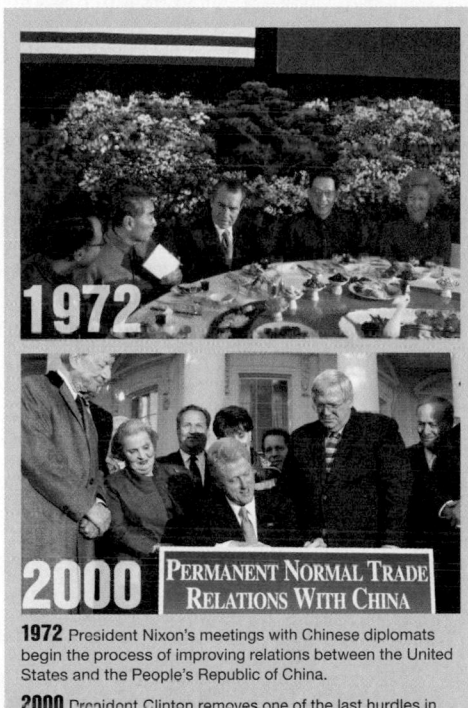

**1972** President Nixon's meetings with Chinese diplomats begin the process of improving relations between the United States and the People's Republic of China.

**2000** President Clinton removes one of the last hurdles in American-Chinese relations by approving a law permitting freer trade between the two nations.

**EXTEND THE LESSON**

**L2 Differentiate** Have students use print or online resources to research the current administration's foreign policies and find images that correspond to them. Then, have students create a collage of the current U.S. foreign policies.

**L2 Differentiate** Have students make a poster explaining how U.S. foreign policy affects a country of their choosing.

**L3 Differentiate** Divide the class into groups of three or four, and have each group choose one foreign policy discussed in this section. Ask the groups to draw a political cartoon that represents some aspect of that foreign policy. Display the cartoons on the classroom wall.

**L4 Differentiate** President Truman's address to Congress in 1947 included the following statement: "One of the primary objectives of the foreign policy of the United States is the creation of conditions in which we and other nations will be able to work out a way of life free from coercion." Have students write a brief essay in response to this statement as it relates to American foreign policy today.

# Myths and Misconceptions

**HOT LINE** The Cuban missile crisis shook the U.S. and Soviet leaders. Both realized that the incident brought them to the brink of nuclear war and mutual annihilation. After the crisis, the leaders agreed to set up a hot line for emergency communication. Contrary to popular myth, the hot line is not two red telephones connecting the White House to the Kremlin. At first, it was a set of teletype machines, on which operators punched in messages. In the 1970s, the two superpowers became linked by satellite and undersea cable. The American end is located in the Pentagon, not in the White House. Messages are transmitted by coded text, not voice or video. Despite the fall of the Soviet Union, the hot line remains in effect. It is tested hourly, with operators on each side sending a test message. The operators practice their translation skills by deciphering recipes and book excerpts sent in the other's native language.

**Answers**
**Checkpoint** the collapse of the Soviet Union

# Assess and Remediate

**L3** Collect the Core Worksheets and grade students' work.

**L3** Assign the Section 3 Assessment questions.

**L3** Section Quiz A (Unit 4 All-in-One, p. 265)

**L2** Section Quiz B (Unit 4 All-in-One, p. 266)

Have students complete the review activities in the digital lesson presentation and continue their work in the **Essential Questions Journal.**

---

## Answers

**Checkpoint** terrorism, nuclear proliferation, civil wars, cultural and religious conflict

**Caption** collective security and the Truman Doctrine

---

**✔Checkpoint**
What major international concerns challenge the world today?

The American policies of deterrence and containment, first put in place in 1947, finally realized their goals. As President Reagan put it, the Soviet Union was left "on the ash heap of history."

## Today's Dangerous World

The sudden collapse of the Soviet Union and, with it, the end of the cold war, did not mean that the world had suddenly become a peaceful place. Far from it. The planet is still plagued by conflicts and it remains a very dangerous place. Osama bin Laden, al Qaeda and other terrorist groups, and the global war against them certainly testify to that daunting fact.

Then, too, there is the worrisome fact that Iran, Iraq's neighbor in the Middle East, appears bent upon becoming a nuclear power. North Korea's nuclear aspirations may also threaten worldwide security. And there are a number of seemingly endless quarrels elsewhere in today's world—not the least of them the protracted civil wars in Africa, and repeated clashes between India and Pakistan, both nuclear powers.

In our own neighborhood, the rise of Venezuela's president Hugo Chávez raises concerns. A vocal critic of American policy, Chávez has managed to win wide support in the region. Many consider him the prime source of much anti-American feeling in Latin America today.

**The Middle East** The Middle East is both oil rich and conflict ridden. America's foreign policy interests in the Middle East have, for decades, been torn in two quite opposite directions: by its long-standing support of Israel and by the critical importance of Arab oil.

The United Nations created Israel as an independent state on May 14, 1948, and the United States recognized the new Jewish state within a matter of minutes. The day after it was established, Israel was invaded by Egypt, Jordan, Syria, Lebanon, and Iraq. The Israelis won that first Arab-Israeli war, decisively. Over the years since then, Israel has successfully defended itself in wars with various Arab states and against numerous terrorist attacks.

The United States has been Israel's closest friend for more than 60 years now. At the same time, however, this country has attempted to strengthen its ties with most of the Arab states in that volatile region.

With the active involvement of President Carter, Israel and Egypt negotiated a groundbreaking peace agreement, which became effective in 1979. That agreement, the Camp David Accords, led to the end of more than 30 years of hostilities between those two countries. Israel and Jordan signed a similar pact in 1994.

Israel and the Palestine Liberation Organization (PLO) took a huge, but so far unfulfilled, step toward peace in 1993. In the Oslo Accords, the PLO at last recognized Israel's right to exist. Israel recognized the PLO as the legitimate agent of the Palestinian people, and it also agreed to limited Palestinian self-rule under an autonomous Palestinian Authority.

The promise of the Oslo Accords remains to be realized. Both the United States and the UN have tried to bring the two parties together in a continuing dialogue. But recurring Palestinian terrorist attacks and Israeli military responses continue.

**Afghanistan** The Soviet Union's invasion of Afghanistan in 1979 introduced an era of war

U.S. Special Forces and Afghan National Army personnel travel from town to town working together to bring stability to Afghanistan. *Which American foreign policy does this effort illustrate?*

502

---

## Background

**NUCLEAR PROLIFERATION** The cold war arms race raised concern among the world's nuclear powers about how to control the spread of the fearsome weapons they had created. Negotiations led to the Nuclear Non-Proliferation Treaty (1970). The nuclear powers—the U.S., Britain, Russia (and now France and China)—agreed not to give nuclear weapons or the technology to make them to any state without nuclear capability. Non-nuclear signers would receive help in developing nuclear power, but must accept on-site monitoring to verify peaceful use only. Nearly all nations have joined the treaty. Recent concern has focused on Iran and North Korea. In 2003, North Korea withdrew from the treaty and returned to weapons development. International pressure persuaded North Korea to begin dismantling its nuclear program in 2007. Iran continued its program, insisting on its peaceful intent.

and devastation to that Central Asian country. Although the Soviets left Afghanistan in defeat in 1989, fighting in the country continued. The groups that had defeated the Soviets now competed for power. Among the factions to emerge from this civil war was an Islamic fundamentalist movement, the Taliban. By the late 1990s, the Taliban had gained control over most of Afghanistan.

In 2001, following the terrorist attacks of September 11, the United States moved to topple the Taliban regime, which had sheltered Osama bin Laden and the al Qaeda terrorists who had carried out the attack. Initially, the war was a marked success. After a few short weeks of fighting, the Taliban took flight. The United States and its allies helped orchestrate the creation of a popularly elected government. The United States removed many of its troops, and a NATO force took the lead in providing security for the fledgling Afghan government.

In subsequent years, however, the Taliban reemerged as an increasingly effective foe, prompting the United States to rebuild its military presence in that country. By late 2010, U.S. troops were at their highest levels ever. The Obama administration has said that those troops will remain until at least 2014.

**Iraq** At the end of the first Gulf War in 1991, Iraq's president, Saddam Hussein, agreed to destroy his country's stock of chemical and biological weapons and to abandon his efforts to acquire nuclear capability.

Convinced that Hussein had not honored those promises and that Iraq had secretly amassed large stores of weapons, President George W. Bush sought to hold Iraq to account in 2002. Efforts to persuade the UN Security Council to support that move proved unsuccessful. But, at his urging, both houses of Congress did adopt a joint resolution authorizing the President to take those actions "necessary and appropriate" to eliminate Iraq's "continuing threat to the national security of the United States and to international peace."

In March 2003, the United States and Great Britain, supported by a number of smaller nations, launched the second Gulf War. Iraq was conquered, and Saddam Hussein's regime toppled in less than six weeks.

Subsequent efforts to stabilize and rebuild Iraq, and to establish a democratic government there, proved extremely difficult. For a time, much of the country bordered on civil war, and the Iraqi government, led by Prime Minister Nouri al-Maliki, was hard put to control it. By 2009, the situation had improved enough for President Obama to announce a timetable for the withdrawal of American troops. Some 18 months later, the last U.S. combat brigade left Iraq. Today, a sizeable American force—about 50,000 troops—remains in that country to advise and assist the young Iraqi government.

| If Your Students Have Trouble With | Strategies For Remediation |
|---|---|
| Describing the change in American foreign policy over time (Question 1) | Review with students the timelines created in class on Core Worksheet A. |
| Explaining the goal of American foreign policy (Question 2) | Write each key foreign policy mentioned in this section on the board and have students supply a one-line summary of each. Then have students identify the common element among them. |
| Describing how the UN reflects collective security (Question 3) | Write the definition of collective security on the board. Then have students brainstorm current UN activities that illustrate this principle. |
| Defining and analyzing deterrence (Question 4) | Have students read the chapter's Document-Based Assessment and lead a discussion on how deterrence may be used today. |
| Explaining the cold war policy of containment (Question 5) | Have students review the Cold War Conflicts map and lead a discussion on how the fear of communism affected American policy. |
| Analyzing the responsibility of the U.S. in maintaining freedom (Question 6) | Create a list of the places where the United States has fought to maintain freedom around the globe. Have students make inferences about how each location might be different today had the United States not become involved. |

**Essential Questions Journal** To continue to build a response to the chapter Essential Question, go to your **Essential Questions Journal.**

# SECTION 3 ASSESSMENT

1. **Guiding Question** Use your completed timeline to answer this question: How has American foreign policy changed over time?

**Key Terms and Comprehension**

2. What is the principal aim of American foreign policy?

3. How did the creation of the United Nations reflect the principle of **collective security?**

4. (a) What is the policy of **deterrence?** (b) Is it in force today?

5. Why was **containment** a major American policy during the **cold war?**

**Critical Thinking**

6. **Recognize Ideologies** In 1947, President Truman said, "The free peoples of the world look to us for support in maintaining their freedoms. If we falter in our leadership, we may endanger the peace of the world, and we shall surely endanger the welfare of this nation." (a) Was that belief valid in 1947? (b) Do you think that belief remains valid in the world today? Why or why not?

**Quick Write**

**Expository Writing: Gather Evidence** Using your list of solutions from Section 2, select the one you believe is best suited to resolving the issue. Then, conduct research to find evidence that supports your proposed solution. Keep in mind which organizations you may need to carry out your solution and how your solution may affect the region concerned.

# Assessment Answers

**1.** U.S. foreign policy has shifted from isolationist to internationalist over time. In the 19th century, the U.S. focused on territorial expansion as the nation's "Manifest Destiny." Using the Monroe Doctrine, the U.S. protected its own security by opposing European domination in Latin America. World War I briefly brought the U.S. out of isolation, but it returned to that policy after the war. Entry into World War II ended isolationism and began a policy of internationalism that continues today. Since World War II, the U.S. has pursued collective security through the UN and regional alliances. Today the U.S. and its allies work to oppose global terrorism.

**2.** to protect the security of the U.S.

**3.** The UN was intended to be a world community in which most nations would act together against any nation that threatened peace.

**4. (a)** strategy of maintaining such military might that no nation will risk attacking **(b)** The policy is still useful in preventing attacks from other nations, but is less useful against terrorist attacks or rogue states.

**5.** The cold war was a period of tension between the U.S. and Soviet Union. Containment was intended to prevent the Soviet Union from expanding communism.

**6. (a)** In 1947, the U.S. was seen as the defender of freedom against communist aggression. **(b)** Possible response: Yes. Our actions in Afghanistan and Iraq reflect a belief that establishing democratic governments there will bolster world peace and U.S. security.

**QUICK WRITE** Students should consider groups needed to carry out the solution and effects on the region.

## Teach

### DEFINE FOREIGN POLICY

Ask: **What is foreign policy?** *(a group of policies made up of all the stands and actions that a nation takes in every aspect of its relationships with other countries)* Have students brainstorm examples of American foreign policies (current or historical).

**L2 Differentiate** Provide news articles or have students search the Internet for articles that illustrate current foreign policies of the United States.

### SUMMARIZE THE ISSUE

Have students read the feature and summarize the issue and the views expressed in the quotes.

**L2 ELL Differentiate** Write these terms and their definitions on the board: *preemptive* (done before someone else has an opportunity to act), *adversary* (opponent, enemy), *legitimacy* (the quality of being allowed by law or custom), *unilateral* (done by only one of several nations).

### DEBATE THE ISSUE

Divide the class into small groups and assign one quote to each group. Allow the groups time to discuss the position assigned and to come up with ways to defend that opinion. Then, divide the class by those defending President Bush and those defending President Obama. Lead a short debate. Ask: **When should force be used to protect national security?**

## Assess and Remediate

Have students summarize the argument made during the debate that they felt was the strongest and explain why.

___

### Answers

1. **(a)** Merely having the policy of preemption would deter terrorists and rogue states. **(b)** the legal authority to act in a specific manner, especially with international approval; because it means the U.S. will not act unilaterally, but within the boundaries of international law

2. Answers will vary but should show an understanding of both policies and how they can be viewed by the nation and the international community.

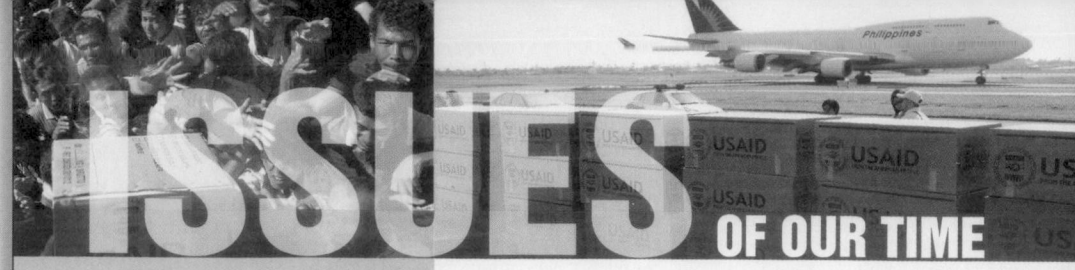

# ISSUES OF OUR TIME

## America's Role in the World

### Track the Issue

**United States foreign policy** deals not just with issues that affect the nation's foreign interests, but also both its global and national security.

**1796**
**George Washington,** in his Farewell Address, cautions the nation against any significant involvement in foreign affairs.

**1898**
**The Spanish-American** War is fought to help Cuba gain independence from Spain.

**1945**
**By dropping two atomic bombs,** President Truman causes Japan to admit defeat and ends World War II.

**1962**
**President Kennedy** averts outright war between the United States and the Soviet Union during the Cuban Missile Crisis.

**Today**
**The United States** remains a defender of democracy, human rights, and peace, yet encourages international cooperation and responsibility in achieving these ends.

Defense Secretary Robert Gates with Commander of International Security Assistance Forces Afghanistan General David Petraeus in 2010. ▾

### ▶▶ Perspectives

The main goal of American foreign policy is to serve our foreign interests and ensure this nation's security. As the world's most powerful nation, the United States has often taken on the role of global peacemaker. However, how the United States deals with threats to the nation and its allies can vary depending on the events of the time and the views of the President.

"We must be prepared to stop rogue states and their terrorist clients before they are able to threaten . . . the United States and our allies and friends. . . . The United States has long maintained the option of preemptive actions to counter a sufficient threat to our national security. The greater the threat, the greater is the risk of inaction—and the more compelling the case for taking anticipatory action to defend ourselves, even if uncertainty remains as to the time and place of the enemy's attack."

—**President George W. Bush's National Security Policy, 2002**

"Military force, at times, may be necessary to defend our country and allies or to preserve broader peace and security. . . . When force is necessary, we will continue to do so in a way that reflects our values and strengthens our legitimacy, and we will seek broad international support, working with such institutions as NATO and the U.N. . . . [We] must reserve the right to act unilaterally if necessary to defend our nation and our interests, yet we will also seek to adhere to standards that govern the use of force."

—**President Barack Obama's National Security Policy, 2010**

### ▶▶ Connect to Your World

1. **Understand (a)** According to President Bush, how would the option of using preemptive action deter rogue states? **(b)** What does President Obama mean by the term "legitimacy"? Why do you think he uses it?
2. **Draw Inferences** Of which of these opinions do you think the American public would approve? The international community? Explain your reasoning.

**In the News**
For updates about American foreign policy, visit
**PearsonSchool.com/phgovt**

## Background

**HUMANITARIAN AID** The United States has historically been the world's largest provider of emergency food aid during international disasters. For example, after Hurricane Mitch destroyed food supplies and the food distribution system in Honduras in 1998, the U.S. provided $67 million of food aid from the U.S. Agency for International Development, along with $63 million of commodity surpluses from the U.S. Department of Agriculture. As a result of such actions by the U.S., there is an assumption that, especially in the case of emergencies, the U.S. will make the largest contribution. However, there is often strong competition for U.S. food aid resources. After the 2004 Indian Ocean tsunami, the U.S. pledged millions of dollars in aid but was also faced with large demands for food resources in response to other emergencies in Sudan, Chad, and the Caribbean.

# SECTION 4

# Foreign Aid and Alliances

## Guiding Question

**In what ways does the United States cooperate with other nations?** Use a chart like the one below to keep track of the methods used in international cooperation.

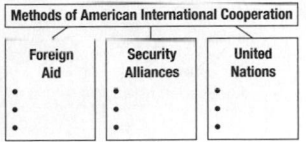

| Foreign Aid | Security Alliances | United Nations |
|---|---|---|
| • | • | • |
| • | • | • |
| • | • | • |

## Political Dictionary

- foreign aid
- regional security alliance
- NATO
- United Nations
- Security Council

## Objectives

1. Identify two types of foreign aid and describe the foreign aid policy of the United States.
2. Describe the major regional security alliances developed by the United States.
3. Examine the role and structure of the United Nations and the problems it addresses.

**Image Above:** Marshall Plan funding helped to rebuild West Berlin after World War II.

**D**o you know this ancient saying: "Those who help others help themselves"? You will see that that maxim underlies two basic elements of present-day American foreign policy: foreign aid and regional security alliances.

## Foreign Aid

**Foreign aid**—the economic and military aid given to other countries—has been a basic feature of American foreign policy for more than sixty years. It began with the Lend-Lease program of the early 1940s, through which the United States gave nearly $50 billion in food, munitions, and other supplies to its allies in World War II. Since then, this country has sent more than $500 billion in aid to more than 100 countries around the world.

Foreign aid became an important part of the containment policy beginning with American aid to Greece and Turkey in 1947. The United States also helped its European allies rebuild after the devastation of World War II. Under the Marshall Plan, named for its author, Secretary of State George C. Marshall, the United States poured some $13 billion into 16 nations in Western Europe between 1948 and 1952.

Foreign aid has taken several different directions over the years. Immediately after World War II, American aid was primarily economic. Since that time, however, military assistance has assumed a larger role in aid policy. Until the mid-1950s, Europe received the lion's share of American help. Since then, the largest amounts have gone to nations in Asia, the Middle East, and Latin America.

Most aid, which makes up less than 1 percent of the federal budget, has been sent to those nations regarded as the most critical to the realization of this country's foreign policy objectives. In recent years, Israel, Egypt, the Philippines, and various Latin American countries have been the major recipients of American help, both economic and military.

Most foreign aid money must be used to buy American goods and services. So, most of the billions spent for that aid amounts to a substantial subsidy to both business and labor in this country. The independent United States Agency for International Development (USAID) administers most of the economic aid programs, in close cooperation with the Departments of State and Agriculture. Most military aid is channeled through the Defense Department.

---

## In what ways does the United States cooperate with other nations?

### Methods of American International Cooperation

| Foreign Aid | Security Alliances | United Nations |
|---|---|---|
| • Economic and military aid to other countries<br>• Most aid to nations critical to U.S. policy goals<br>• Most aid must be spent on U.S. products<br>• United States Agency for International Development administers most economic aid | • mutual defense treaties in different regions<br>• NATO—defend Europe and North America; peacekeeping in Balkans, Afghanistan, Darfur<br>• Inter-American Treaty of Reciprocal Assistance (Rio Pact)—defend the Americas<br>• ANZUS Pact with Australia and New Zealand<br>• Japanese Pact<br>• Philippines Pact<br>• Korean Pact with South Korea | • U.S. and all other members have one vote in General Assembly<br>• The Security Council, of which the U.S. is one of 5 permanent members with veto power, has the main responsibility for international peace<br>• The U.S. funds over 20% of UN operating budget for work that includes peacekeeping; promoting development in poorer nations; protecting health, environment, and human rights; partnering with NGOs |

---

## SKILLS DEVELOPMENT

### ANALYZE SOURCES

Core Worksheet B in this section asks students to analyze excerpts from the United Nations Universal Declaration of Human Rights. Have students turn to the Skills Handbook, p. S14, to learn how to analyze sources.

---

# Focus on the Basics

**FACTS:** • The United States sends economic and military foreign aid to countries regarded as critical to American interests. • The U.S. belongs to several regional security alliances, including NATO. • The U.S. is a permanent member of the UN Security Council and provides a large portion of UN funding.

**CONCEPTS:** role and purpose of government, democratic values, and principles

**ENDURING UNDERSTANDINGS:** • The United States works with other nations for peace and political stability around the world. • Security alliances seek to deter aggression. • The purpose of the United Nations is to promote peace among nations and to improve living conditions around the world.

# Get Started

## LESSON GOALS

Students will . . .

- describe how foreign aid programs and defense alliances promote U.S. interests.
- evaluate current international issues and how foreign aid benefits the region affected as well as the United States.
- compare and contrast the rights delineated in the UN Universal Declaration on Human Rights with those in the U.S. Constitution.

## BEFORE CLASS

Assign the section, the graphic organizer in the text, and the Reading Comprehension Worksheet (Unit 4 All-in-One, p. 267) before class.

**L2** **Differentiate** Reading Comprehension Worksheet (Unit 4 All-in-One, p. 269)

## BELLRINGER

Write the following assignment on the board: **Foreign aid programs and regional security alliances are ways that the United States can protect its own interests by helping other nations protect their interests. List one type of foreign aid program and one regional security alliance, and describe how each may benefit both the recipient and the United States. Write your response in your notebook.**

**L2** **Differentiate** Write this short list of key programs and alliances on the board, and have students choose one from the list for this activity: **Alliances: NATO, Rio Pact, Japanese Pact, ANZUS, Philippines Pact; Programs: economic, military, and humanitarian aid**

Tell students to go to the Audio Tour to find out more about the members of NATO.

## Answers

**Analyzing Maps** Sample answer: Because there are still ideological differences between most NATO members and Russia, it seems unlikely that Russia will be invited to join NATO anytime soon.

---

# The Expansion of NATO

**GOVERNMENT** ONLINE
**Audio Tour**
To find out more about the members of NATO, visit
PearsonSchool.com/phgovt

▸▸ **Analyzing Maps** Membership in the North Atlantic Treaty Organization has extended beyond western Europe with the addition of several nations that were once part of the Soviet-dominated Eastern Bloc. *Do you think an invitation to join will ever be extended to Russia?*

**KEY**

- Founding member in 1949
- Joined between 1952–1990
- Joined after 1990
- Former Soviet Union
- Former Soviet republics
- Former Soviet satellites

## Security Alliances

Since World War II, the United States has constructed a network of **regional security alliances** built on mutual defense treaties. In each of those agreements, the United States and the other countries involved have agreed to take collective action to meet aggression in a particular part of the world.

**NATO** The North Atlantic Treaty, signed in 1949, established **NATO,** the North Atlantic Treaty Organization. The alliance was formed initially to promote the collective defense of Western Europe, particularly against the threat of Soviet aggression. NATO was originally composed of the United States and 11 other countries (see map above).

With the collapse of the Soviet Union, NATO's mutual security blanket was extended to cover much of Eastern Europe. Though it has grown in size, the alliance remains dedicated to the basic goal of protecting the freedom and security of its members through political and military action. Each of the now 28 member countries has agreed that "an armed attack against one or more of them in Europe or in North America shall be considered an attack against them all."

What has changed with NATO since its founding? Clearly, the threat of Soviet (if not Russian) aggression has lessened, yet the

---

# Differentiated Resources

The following resources are located in the All-in-One, Unit 4, Chapter 17, Section 4:

- **L3** Reading Comprehension Worksheet (p. 267)
- **L2** Reading Comprehension Worksheet (p. 269)
- **L3** Core Worksheets A and B (pp. 271, 272)
- **L2** Extend Activities (pp. 275, 276)
- **L3** Quiz A (p. 277)
- **L2** Quiz B (p. 278)
- **L3** Chapter Test A (p. 279)
- **L2** Chapter Test B (p. 282)

basic function of the alliance is the same. NATO was formed for defensive purposes and—if defense includes military intervention in conflicts that may <u>destabilize</u> Europe, and with it, the prevention of humanitarian disasters—defense remains its basic charge.

Increasingly, however, NATO is focused on what it calls "crisis management and peacekeeping." Its involvement in the Balkans provides a leading illustration of this role. First in Bosnia in 1995 and then in Kosovo in 1999, NATO forces, drawn mostly from the United States, Great Britain, and Canada, ended years of vicious civil war in what was once Yugoslavia. Those military interventions also put an end to the horrific campaigns of "ethnic cleansing," directed by Serbia's President Slobodan Milosevic. NATO troops continue to maintain a fragile peace in the Balkans today.

In mid-2003, NATO took command of the International Security Assistance Force (ISAF) in Afghanistan. The United Nations established this multinational peacekeeping force in late 2001 in the wake of the American-led war that <u>ousted</u> Afghanistan's Taliban regime.

Today, ISAF is composed of over 130,000 combat and support troops drawn from 48 nations, with American troops supplying almost 70 percent of that force. The NATO coalition has assumed the leading role in rebuilding Afghanistan, weakening the Taliban, and training an Afghan security force. Those efforts continue nine years after the war began. In 2009, President Obama announced his intention to send an additional 30,000 U.S. troops to the region, and his administration targeted July 2011 to begin withdrawing American troops. However, both the U.S. and NATO plan to keep a presence in the country to 2014 and beyond, to support the Afghan government and people as they continue their struggle against a <u>resilient</u> Taliban.

From 2005 through 2007, NATO also played a small peacekeeping role in Darfur. This conflict-plagued region of the African nation of Sudan has been the scene of what observers have described as a campaign of <u>genocide</u>, with government-backed militia targeting rival ethnic groups. NATO forces helped train and transport troops taking part in a multinational peacekeeping mission to end the bloodshed in Darfur.

**Other Alliances** The Inter-American Treaty of Reciprocal Assistance, the Rio Pact, was signed in 1947. It pledges the United States, Canada, and now 32 Latin American countries to treat any "armed attack . . . against an American state . . . as an attack against all the American states." The treaty is built on the Monroe Doctrine and commits those nations to the peaceful settlement of their disputes. Cuba is not a party to the agreement.

Beyond NATO and the Rio Pact, the United States is party to several other regional alliances. Thus, the ANZUS Pact of 1951 unites Australia, New Zealand, and the United States to ensure their collective security in the Pacific region.

The Japanese Pact also dates from 1951. After six years of American military occupation, the allies of World War II (with the exception of the Soviet Union) signed a peace treaty with Japan. At the same time, the United States and Japan signed a mutual defense treaty. In return for American protection, Japan permits the United States to maintain land, sea, and air forces in and around its territory.

The Philippines Pact was ratified in 1951 as well. It, too, is a mutual defense agreement. The pact remains in force, but disagreements over its redrafting prompted the withdrawal of all American military forces from the Philippines in 1992. The Korean Pact, signed in 1953, pledges the United States to come to the aid of South Korea should it be attacked again.

The Taiwan Pact was in effect between the United States and Nationalist China from 1954 to 1980. When the United States and the People's Republic of China established full diplomatic relations in 1979, the United States withdrew its recognition of the Nationalist Chinese government, and the Taiwan pact became obsolete.

## The United Nations

You know that a fundamental change occurred in American foreign policy during and immediately after World War II. That dramatic shift from isolationism to internationalism, is strikingly illustrated by this country's participation in the United Nations. Remember, the United States refused to join the League of Nations

✔ **Checkpoint**
How has NATO's purpose changed?

<u>destabilize</u>
*v.* to make something unstable, undermine, upset

<u>oust</u>
*v.* drive out, remove by force

<u>resilient</u>
*adj.* able to resume its original condition, bounce back

<u>genocide</u>
*n.* the deliberate extermination of a people or nation

# Teach

To present this topic using online resources, use the lesson presentations at **PearsonSchool.com/phgovt.**

### REVIEW BELLRINGER

Group students into pairs, and have each student read his or her partner's response to the Bellringer. Then call on four or five students to read and explain one of their partner's answers, either a foreign aid program or a regional security alliance. List the answers on the board, including the name of the program or alliance and a short description of its benefits. When you have recorded the answers, ask students if they see any patterns or commonalities between the answers, such as the proximity of aggressive nations near nations with whom the U.S. has security alliances.

**L2 Differentiate** Direct students to the world political map at the back of the textbook. As you review the Bellringer activity, use the map to help students locate the regions or nations involved so they can more easily visualize locations and influences.

# Background

**MARSHALL PLAN** In June 1947, Secretary of State George Marshall unveiled a large-scale plan for American aid to war-torn Europe. The Marshall Plan achieved several strategic goals at one time. By providing humanitarian aid during a time of severe economic and agricultural crisis, the Marshall Plan helped ensure that America's allies would not fall prey to political chaos. By encouraging recipients to spend the aid money on American-made goods, the plan also benefited the domestic economy. Finally, Marshall attached a significant condition to the aid package: Before they could receive any financial support, recipient nations had to work together to develop a plan for spending the money. This required European nations to cooperate with each other at a time when relations on the continent were under severe pressure, and it may have helped ensure peace during the turbulent decades that followed.

# Answers

**Checkpoint** Originally created to promote collective defense of Western Europe, NATO has extended its focus to assisting in peacekeeping around the world.

## BRAINSTORM

Distribute the Chapter 17 Section 4 Core Worksheet A (Unit 4 All-in-One, p. 271), which is a graphic organizer in which to categorize different types of aid. Divide the class into pairs, and have each reflect on current international issues. Have pairs identify one issue for each category on the organizer: environmental, humanitarian, or economic. Then they should determine the region or country affected, any government or nongovernmental organization providing aid, and the type of aid. Then, have pairs brainstorm how the aid benefits the region and the United States. *(some benefits to region: alleviates potential political or civil unrest or war, ensures the continuation of democratic governments, improves standard of living, assists economic development, reduces the spread of disease; some benefits to the U.S.: aid money often spent on U.S. products, new markets for U.S. trade, safeguards access to critical resources in that region such as oil, strengthens foreign relations, friendly governments more likely to partner with the U.S. in fighting terrorism)* Have volunteers share their answers with the class.

**L1 L2 Differentiate** Display Transparency 17E, Foreign Aid, which is a blank version of the graphic organizer used in this activity. As a class, brainstorm international issues and the benefits of the aid provided. Write students' answers on the transparency as they complete their worksheet.

**L4 Differentiate** Have students do research to learn more about the issues and then complete the worksheet in greater detail.

Tell students to go to the Audio Tour to learn more about the United Nations and its programs.

## Answers

**The UN by the Numbers** Sample answer: Peacekeeping is a major focus and expenditure of the UN.

**508** Foreign Policy and National Defense

---

## The UN by the Numbers

Data can provide a great deal of insight into the nature of an organization. *What does the information below tell you about the UN?*

### Membership

**192** Member countries today

**15** Security Council members

Membership by year: 1945: 51; 1965: 116; 1985: 155; Today: 192

### Operating Budget

Pie chart: United States 24%, Japan 12.2%, Germany 7.8%, United Kingdom 6.4%, France 6%, Italy 4.9%, Other 38.7%

**$5.05 billion** Current 2-year operating budget (2010–2011)

**24%** Operating budget share contributed by the United States

### UN Peacekeeping

**$7.9 billion** Current budget for UN peacekeeping operations

**16** Peacekeeping operations in progress

**88,000** UN troops deployed in peacekeeping missions around the world

SOURCE: The United Nations

**508** Foreign Policy and National Defense

---

after World War I. With the end of World War II, however, the American people realized that America was a world power with worldwide interests and responsibilities.

The **United Nations** (UN) came into being at the United Nations Conference on International Organization, which met in San Francisco from April 25 to June 26, 1945. There, the representatives of 50 nations—the victorious allies of World War II—drafted the United Nations Charter.[5] The charter is a treaty among all of the UN's member-states, and it serves as the body's constitution.

The United States became the first nation to ratify the UN Charter. The Senate approved it by an overwhelming vote, 89–2, on July 24, 1945. The other states that had taken part in the San Francisco Conference then ratified the charter in quick order, and it went into force on October 24, 1945. The UN held the first session of its General Assembly in London on January 10, 1946.

**Charter and Organization** The UN's charter is a lengthy document. It opens with an eloquent preamble which reads in part:

> **Primary Source**
> We, the peoples of the United Nations
>
> Determined to save succeeding generations from the scourge of war, which twice in our lifetime has brought untold sorrow to mankind, and . . .
>
> To practice tolerance and live together in peace with one another as good neighbors, and
>
> To unite our strength to maintain international peace and security . . .
>
> Have resolved to combine our efforts to accomplish these aims.
> —**Charter of the United Nations**

The body of the document begins in Article I with a statement of the organization's purposes: the maintenance of international peace

5 Fifty nations attended the San Francisco conference. Poland did not attend, but it did sign the charter on October 15, 1945, and is considered an original member of the UN.

---

## Background

**COUNTERING TERRORISM WITH AID** From the end of the cold war until the early 1990s, the major focus of U.S. foreign aid programs was the defeat of communism. During the presidency of George W. Bush, the majority of U.S. foreign aid was directed toward the global fight against terrorism. Toward this end, foreign aid programs were organized around three core principles or "strategic pillars": (1) encouraging economic growth through boosting agriculture and trade, (2) global health initiatives, and (3) humanitarian aid and peacekeeping support in the service of encouraging democracy. The State Department and other agencies overseeing foreign aid programs believe that this multilayered approach is the most promising for combating global terrorism.

Worksheet (small reproduction):

CHAPTER 17 SECTION 4 — CORE WORKSHEET A — Foreign Aid and Defense Alliances — 3

With your partner, identify current international issues, such as famine, political unrest, and deforestation. In the first row, write one issue for each category—environmental, humanitarian, and economic. Then complete the remaining rows by listing the region or country affected, any government or nongovernmental organization providing aid, and the type of aid (such as military, monetary, medical, or food). Then work with your partner to brainstorm how the aid benefits the region and the United States.

| | Environmental | Humanitarian | Economic |
|---|---|---|---|
| Issue | | | |
| Country or region | | | |
| Type of aid and organizations providing it | | | |
| Benefits to region affected | | | |
| Benefits to the United States | | | |

Copyright © by Pearson Education, Inc., or its affiliates. All rights reserved.

and security, the development of friendly relations between and among all nations, and the promotion of justice and cooperation in the solution of international problems.

The UN has 192 members today. Membership is open to those "peace-loving states" that accept the obligations of the charter and are, in the UN's judgment, able and willing to carry out those obligations. New members may be admitted by a two-thirds vote of the General Assembly, upon recommendation by the Security Council.

The charter sets forth the complicated structure of the UN. It is built around six principal organs: the General Assembly, the Security Council, the Economic and Social Council, the Trusteeship Council, the International Court of Justice, and the Secretariat.

**The General Assembly** The UN's General Assembly has been called "the town meeting of the world." Each of the UN's members has a seat and a vote in the Assembly. It meets once a year, and sessions take place at the UN's permanent headquarters in New York City. The secretary-general may call special sessions, at the request of either the Security Council or a majority of the UN's members.

The Assembly may take up and debate any matter within the scope of the charter, and it may make whatever recommendation it chooses to the Security Council, the other UN organs, and any member-state.[6] The recommendations it makes to UN members are not legally binding on them, but these recommendations do carry some considerable weight, for they have been approved by a significant number of the governments of the world.

The Assembly elects the 10 nonpermanent members of the Security Council, the 54 members of the Economic and Social Council, and the elective members of the Trusteeship Council. In conjunction with the Security Council, it also selects the secretary-general and the 15 judges of the International Court of Justice. The Assembly shares with the Security Council the power to admit, suspend, or expel members. But the Assembly alone may propose amendments to the charter.

[6] Except those matters currently under consideration by the Security Council.

**The Security Council** The UN's **Security Council** is made up of 15 members. Five—the United States, Britain, France, Russia (originally the Soviet Union's seat), and China—are permanent members. The General Assembly chooses the 10 nonpermanent members for two-year terms; they cannot be immediately reelected. The council meets in continuous session.

The Security Council bears the UN's major responsibility for maintaining international peace. It may take up any matter involving a threat to or a breach of that peace, and it can adopt measures ranging from calling on the parties to settle their differences peacefully to placing economic and/or military sanctions on an offending nation. The only time the Security Council has undertaken a military operation against an aggressor came in Korea in 1950. It has, however, provided peacekeeping forces in several world trouble spots, with varying degrees of success.

On procedural questions—routine matters—decisions of the Security Council can be made by the affirmative vote of any nine members. On the more important matters—substantive questions—at least nine affirmative votes are also needed. However, a negative vote by any one of the permanent members is enough to kill any substantive resolution. Because of that *veto power*, the Security Council is effective only when and if the permanent members are willing to cooperate with one another.

The veto does not come into play in a situation in which one or more of the permanent members abstains. When, on June 25, 1950, the Security Council called on all UN members to aid South Korea in repelling the North Korean invasion, the Soviet delegate was boycotting sessions of the Security Council and so was not present to veto that action.

**Economic and Social Council** The Economic and Social Council (ECOSOC) is made up of 54 members elected by the General Assembly to three-year terms. It is responsible to the Assembly for carrying out the UN's many economic, cultural, educational, health, and related activities. It coordinates the work of the UN's specialized agencies—a number of independent international

✔ **Checkpoint**
Which members of the Security Council have the veto power?

**organ**
*n.* a unit of organization that performs a specific function

**abstain**
*v.* to choose not to participate

---

## Debate

"Instead of breaking the 'endless cycle of poverty,' foreign aid has become the opiate of the Third World. [Foreign aid agencies] have encouraged Third World governments to rely on handouts instead of on themselves for development."

—James Bovard, Cato Institute, "The Continuing Failure of Foreign Aid

Use this quote to provoke a classroom debate. Ask: **Can foreign aid help poor nations rise out of poverty?**

---

## RESPOND TO READING

Distribute Core Worksheet B (Unit 4 All-in-One, p. 272) to the class. Have a volunteer read aloud the Preamble of the United Nations Universal Declaration of Human Rights from the first page of the worksheet. Ask: **According to the Preamble, how might people respond if their rights are not protected?** *(They might resort to rebellion against their oppressors.)* Have students create a list on their worksheet of what they believe to be essential human rights. *(Answers may include freedom of speech, freedom of religion, equality for all without discrimination, freedom from fear and want.)* After students have completed their lists individually, have them share their lists with the class.

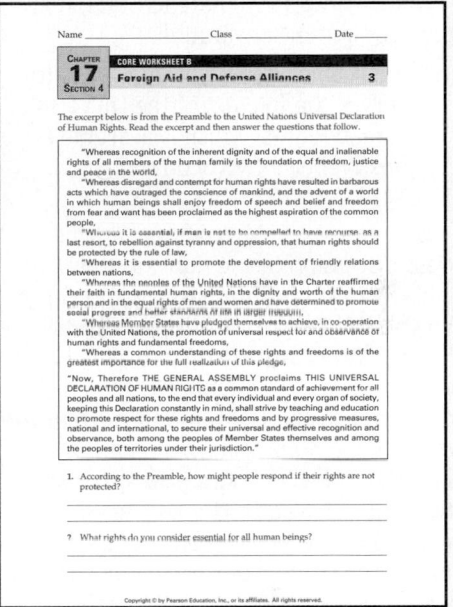

## Answers

**Checkpoint** U.S., Britain, France, Russia, and China

The next page of Core Worksheet B contains excerpts from the UN's Universal Declaration of Human Rights. Have each student read aloud one passage from the Declaration. As the passages are read aloud, students should mark each with a *Y* (if they think the right is guaranteed by the U.S. Constitution) or an *N* (if they do not think the right is guaranteed by the U.S. Constitution). After all passages have been read aloud, go through the list again, this time asking students to raise their hand to indicate whether they marked a *Y* or an *N* for each item. Keep a tally on the board. If students are having difficulty correctly identifying any passage as a *Y* or an *N*, have them consult the U.S. Constitution in their text. Point out that some rights that we take for granted, such as the right to move from State to State, may not actually appear in the Constitution.

**L4 Differentiate** If time allows, you may wish to have students analyze the full text of the Universal Declaration of Human Rights, which is available at the United Nations Web site (www.un.org).

**DISCUSS**

Conduct a class discussion of the rights in the UN Declaration. Ask: **What distinguishes some rights contained in the UN Declaration from rights found in the U.S. Constitution?** *(For example: the Declaration refers to some economic and social rights not mentioned in the Constitution, such as the right to hold a job, the right to form a union, the right to education, and so on.)* **Are you surprised by any of the rights listed in the Declaration?** *(Rights such as the ability to move around the country or to hold a job appear so universal that it seems unnecessary to list them; however, the fact that these rights are listed indicates that they are not universally available.)* Then have students reflect on this section's activities. Ask: **Why is foreign aid vital to the well-being of the United States?** *(Possible response: Oppression and lack of the basic necessities of life in parts of the world breed violence that can endanger the security and interests of all nations in the global community.)*

Tell students to go to the Audio Tour to listen to a guided tour on the specialized agencies of the UN.

---

## Answers

**The Specialized Agencies** Possible response: These agencies work to solve international problems, such as poverty, hunger, illiteracy, and low living standards. Such problems often underlie regional conflicts. By alleviating these conditions, the agencies are contributing to the other UN goals of international peace and friendly relations.

---

bodies that have a working relationship with the world organization. There are now 15 of these independent bodies—among the most notable: the World Health Organization (WHO), the International Monetary Fund (IMF), the World Bank Group, and the Food and Agriculture Organization (FAO). (See the feature below.)

**Trusteeship Council** The United Nations Charter requires each member to promote the well-being of the peoples of all "non-self-governing territories" as a "sacred trust." To that end, and for several decades, the Trusteeship Council monitored the way in which various UN members met that responsibility in their administration of (originally) eleven Trust

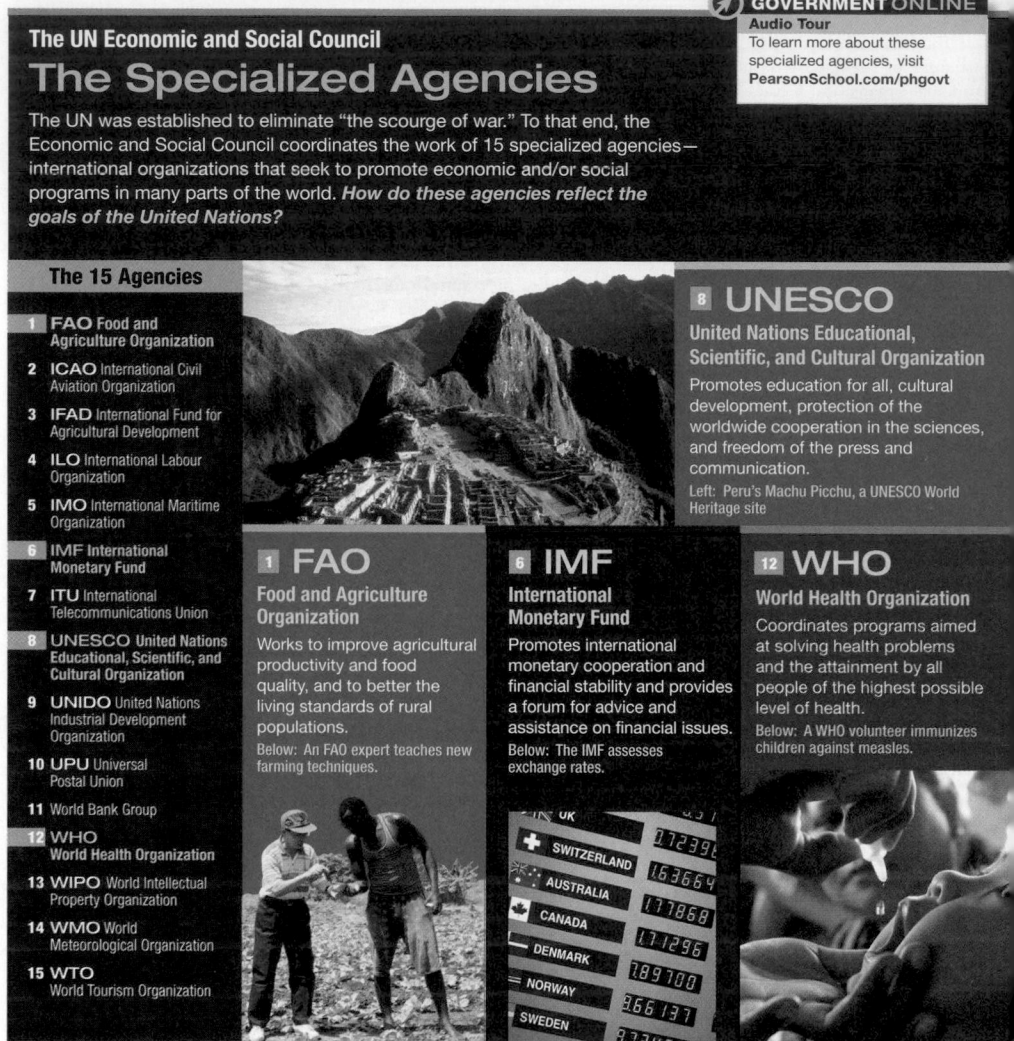

**The UN Economic and Social Council**

# The Specialized Agencies

The UN was established to eliminate "the scourge of war." To that end, the Economic and Social Council coordinates the work of 15 specialized agencies—international organizations that seek to promote economic and/or social programs in many parts of the world. *How do these agencies reflect the goals of the United Nations?*

**The 15 Agencies**

1. **FAO** Food and Agriculture Organization
2. **ICAO** International Civil Aviation Organization
3. **IFAD** International Fund for Agricultural Development
4. **ILO** International Labour Organization
5. **IMO** International Maritime Organization
6. **IMF** International Monetary Fund
7. **ITU** International Telecommunications Union
8. **UNESCO** United Nations Educational, Scientific, and Cultural Organization
9. **UNIDO** United Nations Industrial Development Organization
10. **UPU** Universal Postal Union
11. World Bank Group
12. **WHO** World Health Organization
13. **WIPO** World Intellectual Property Organization
14. **WMO** World Meteorological Organization
15. **WTO** World Tourism Organization

**8 UNESCO**

**United Nations Educational, Scientific, and Cultural Organization**

Promotes education for all, cultural development, protection of the worldwide cooperation in the sciences, and freedom of the press and communication.

Left: Peru's Machu Picchu, a UNESCO World Heritage site

**1 FAO**

**Food and Agriculture Organization**

Works to improve agricultural productivity and food quality, and to better the living standards of rural populations.

Below: An FAO expert teaches new farming techniques.

**6 IMF**

**International Monetary Fund**

Promotes international monetary cooperation and financial stability and provides a forum for advice and assistance on financial issues.

Below: The IMF assesses exchange rates.

**12 WHO**

**World Health Organization**

Coordinates programs aimed at solving health problems and the attainment by all people of the highest possible level of health.

Below: A WHO volunteer immunizes children against measles.

---

# Background

**UN AT WORK** Many diplomatic observers have noted a "renaissance" of the United Nations. Of the 63 UN peacekeeping operations set up since 1948, nearly three quarters have been established since 1991. In that time, the UN has played a key role in shaping the Gulf War coalition and in aiding Kurdish refugees after the war. In the early 1990s, the UN also helped Namibia achieve independence and mediated civil strife in Angola, Nicaragua, El Salvador, and Yugoslavia. As of 2010, the United Nations was involved in 16 active peace missions with more than 100,000 people serving worldwide. The UN election support missions in nations such as Afghanistan, Burundi, Iraq, Liberia, and the Democratic Republic of Congo have contributed to over 56 million voters having the opportunity to exercise their right to vote.

Territories. Those entities included (1) several colonies that had been mandates under the League of Nations in the years between World War I and World War II, (2) colonial possessions taken from enemy nations in World War II, and (3) some colonial areas voluntarily placed under the UN's trusteeship system by UN members. By 1994, however, the last of those Trust Territories had achieved self-governing status and so, today, the Trusteeship Council exists in name only.

**International Court of Justice** The International Court of Justice (ICJ), also known as the World Court, is the UN's judicial arm. All members of the UN are automatically parties to the ICJ Statute. Under certain conditions, the services of the court are also available to nonmember states. A UN member may agree to accept the court's jurisdiction over cases in which it may be involved either unconditionally or with certain reservations (exceptions that may not conflict with the ICJ Statute).

The ICJ is made up of 15 judges selected for nine-year terms by the General Assembly and the Security Council. It sits in permanent session at the Peace Palace in The Hague, the Netherlands, and handles cases brought to it voluntarily by both members and nonmembers of the UN. The ICJ also advises the other UN bodies on legal questions arising out of their activities. If any party to a dispute fails to obey a judgment of the court, the other party may take that matter to the Security Council.

**The Secretariat** The civil service branch of the UN is the Secretariat. It is headed by the secretary-general, who is elected to a five-year term by the General Assembly on the recommendation of the Security Council.

The secretary-general heads a staff of some 40,000 men and women who conduct the day-to-day work of the UN in New York and elsewhere around the globe. Beyond administrative chores, the Charter gives this vital power to the secretary-general: to bring before the Security Council any matter that he or she believes poses a serious threat to international peace and security.

The secretary-general prepares the UN's two-year budget, which must be approved by the General Assembly. For 2010–2011, the operating budget came to $5.05 billion. The Assembly apportions the UN's expenses for each two-year period among its member-states.

Early on, the secretary-general was seen as little more than the UN's chief clerk. The post amounts to much more than that, however, because the eight men who have thus far held it transformed the office into a major channel for the negotiated settlement of international disputes.[7]

## The Work of the UN

The purpose of the United Nations can be summed up this way: to make the world a better place. To that end, the UN is involved in a wide variety of activities.

Peacekeeping is a primary function of the United Nations. More than 120,000 military and civilian personnel provided by some 115 member countries are currently engaged in 16 UN global peacekeeping operations.

The UN's specialized agencies spend some several billion dollars a year for economic and social programs to help the world's poorest nations. Those monies are beyond that loaned by the World Bank, the International Monetary Fund, and the other UN agencies that further development in poorer countries.

Health is the major concern of several UN agencies. A joint program of UNICEF and WHO has immunized 80 percent of the world's children against six killer diseases, and it is estimated that this program saves the lives of more than 2 million children a year. Smallpox, which plagued the world for centuries, has now been all but eliminated by a WHO-led campaign. Today, that organization coordinates a massive global effort to control the spread of AIDS.

The health of the environment is also a significant concern of the world organization. United Nations environmental conventions have helped reduce acid rain, lessened marine pollution, and phased out the production of

---

[7] The eight secretaries-general: Trigve Lie (Norway, 1946–1953), Dag Hammarskjold (Sweden, 1953–1961), U Thant (Burma, 1962–1972), Kurt Waldheim (Austria, 1972–1982), Javier Perez de Cuellar (Peru, 1982–1992), Boutros Boutros-Ghali (Egypt, 1992–1997), Kofi Annan (Ghana, 1997–2006), and Ban Ki-moon (South Korea, 2007– ).

**✓ Checkpoint**
What is the secretary-general's role in the UN organization?

**jurisdiction**
*n.* authority of a court to hear and decide a dispute

---

**L1 L2 ELL Differentiate** Have students select a region—Europe, Asia, South America, Africa, or the Middle East—and research one alliance that exists between the United States and countries of that region. Then, have students create a map of the region, highlighting the members of the alliance and noting when each nation became a member.

**L2 Differentiate** Distribute the Extend Activities "Foreign Aid" and "The United Nations" (Unit 4 All-in-One, pp. 275, 276), which have students research to learn more about foreign assistance and the role of the UN around the world.

**L3 Differentiate** Have students create an advertisement, commercial, jingle, or poster for the UN, promoting the need to guarantee one of the rights in the UN Declaration.

**L3 Differentiate** Have students visit the United States Agency of International Development Web site (www.usaid.gov) and research the types of assistance provided by the agency. Then, students should create a poster to illustrate the work of this government agency.

**L4 Differentiate** Have students research, either online or in the library, the reactions to the United Nations Universal Declaration of Human Rights at the time the document was created and any issues relating to it today. Students should prepare a short oral presentation based on their research.

## Assess and Remediate

**L3** Collect the Core Worksheets and grade students' work.

**L3** Assign the Section 4 Assessment questions.

**L3** Section Quiz A (Unit 4 All-in-One, p. 277)

**L2** Section Quiz B (Unit 4 All-in-One, p. 278)

Have students complete the review activities in the digital lesson presentation and continue their work in the **Essential Questions Journal.**

---

**Government** online *All print resources are available on the Teacher's Resource Library CD-ROM and online at PearsonSchool.com/phgovt.*

---

# Background

**DOCTORS WITHOUT BORDERS** The nongovernmental organization Doctors Without Borders provides humanitarian medical assistance in nations where epidemics, malnutrition, conflict, and natural disasters threaten survival. It fields more than 27,000 health professionals and support staff of many nationalities, including more than 200 Americans. In recent years, medical teams have responded to pandemics of AIDS and tuberculosis. They have cared for victims of floods in Mexico and cyclones in Bangladesh. They have brought essential medical services to refugees, street children, and migrants who otherwise would have no access to healthcare. When their teams witness atrocities in the course of their work, they speak out to focus international attention on the situation. The group alerted the UN Security Council to the crisis in Darfur. In 1999, the group received the Nobel Peace Prize.

## Answers

**Checkpoint** heads the UN administrative staff, prepares the organization's budget, and is a major channel in the settlement negotiations of international disputes

| If Your Students Have Trouble With | Strategies For Remediation |
|---|---|
| Describing how the U.S. cooperates with other nations (Question 1) | Create a version of the section's graphic organizer on the board and review the answers with the class. |
| Defining and providing examples of foreign aid (Question 2) | Have students look through newspapers and magazines to find examples of the types of foreign aid. |
| Explaining how NATO has changed over time (Question 3) | Have students re-read the text material on NATO and create a concept web of the main ideas. |
| Summarizing the function of the UN Security Council (Question 4) | Have students write a summary of each Security Council paragraph in the text. |
| Understanding the purpose of regional alliances (Question 5) | Use the world political map at the back of the book to review the regional alliances mentioned in the section. |
| Analyzing the General Assembly (Question 6) | Define a "town hall meeting" and discuss the similarities and differences. |
| Comparing American attitudes on foreign policy (Question 7) | Define the terms *isolationist* and *internationalist* on the board and have students create a list of reasons why the U.S. has become more involved with other nations today. |

## Answers

**Checkpoint** international peace, economic development, solving health and environmental problems, protecting human rights

---

✓ **Checkpoint**
What global issues are the focus of the work of the UN?

gases that destroy the ozone layer. The UN also helped establish the Intergovernmental Panel on Climate Change. That body was created to examine the large volume of information about climate change generated by the scientific community and to help provide government decision-makers with accurate, balanced analysis of this data.

Human rights have long been a leading priority for the United Nations. In 1948, the UN drafted the Universal Declaration of Human Rights, and it has sponsored more than 80 treaties that help protect specific rights. Various United Nations agencies work to aid and protect refugees and displaced persons, and the international organization raises more than $1 billion a year for assistance to victims of war and natural disasters.

The UN also works closely with nongovernmental organizations, NGOs, around the world. As the name suggests, NGOs are independent of governments, and the list of issues and topics that they exist to address is nearly endless. On issues ranging from public health to the environment to the status of women, these groups perform valuable work around the world. The United Nations actively seeks to partner with those organizations as a means of achieving its goals. A prime example is the International Committee of the Red Cross, a humanitarian NGO with which the UN works to assist victims of

disasters ranging from military conflicts to those inflicted by Mother Nature.

## The UN and the U.S.

The United States has a long and close relationship with the UN. It was President Franklin Roosevelt who, with Britain's Winston Churchill, first proposed the formation of the UN. The United States occupies a permanent place on the Security Council. Though the United States is one of 192 members of the UN, it funds some 24 percent of the UN budget. (Each member's contribution is roughly equal in proportion to its share of the world's gross domestic product.)

The relationship with the UN is complex, however. The United States has at times been critical of the UN. In fact, the United States has even withheld payment of funds to the institution. Also, the United States has not always agreed with some formal policy positions taken by the UN. In 2003, for example, the Bush administration was frustrated in its efforts to win UN support for military action against Iraq. Yet, the United States often works closely with the UN on a variety of issues to further policies that are important to both, including environmental and humanitarian causes. For example, the UN is now closely involved with American efforts to bring peace and stability to Iraq.

---

**Essential Questions Journal** To continue to build a response to the chapter Essential Question, go to your **Essential Questions Journal.**

## SECTION 4 ASSESSMENT

1. **Guiding Question** Use your completed chart to answer this question: In what ways does the United States cooperate with other nations?

**Key Terms and Comprehension**

2. **(a)** What is **foreign aid? (b)** Cite two examples of that policy.

3. **(a)** What is **NATO? (b)** How has it changed over the years?

4. Summarize the organization and function of the UN **Security Council.**

**Critical Thinking**

5. **Identify Central Issues** Why do you think the U.S. has formed regional security alliances around the globe?

6. **Demonstrate Reasoned Judgment** Do you think the United Nations General Assembly deserves to be called "the town meeting of the world"? Why or why not?

7. **Make Comparisons (a)** Compare the basic foreign policy of the United States early on to that of today. **(b)** How do this nation's alliances illustrate this change?

**Quick Write**

**Expository Writing: Write a Thesis Statement** A thesis statement can summarize the focus of your problem-solution essay. To help you determine your thesis statement, use the problem you identified in Section 1, the solution you selected, and its supporting research to determine how best to summarize your findings. Then, write a sentence that clearly states the purpose and goal of your essay.

## Assessment Answers

**1.** The U.S. provides economic and military aid to other countries. The U.S. belongs to several regional mutual defense alliances, including NATO, the Rio Pact, ANZUS, and pacts with Japan, the Philippines, and South Korea. The U.S. is a founding member of the UN, which aims to maintain global peace and security through international cooperation.

**2. (a)** military and economic aid to other nations **(b)** possible examples: providing food, medicines, funds, and military training and supplies

**3. (a)** an alliance for the collective defense of Europe and North America **(b)** The original goal was to protect Western Europe, the U.S., and Canada against Soviet aggression. Since the collapse of the Soviet Union, NATO has expanded to include Eastern European nations. It now focuses on peacekeeping around the world.

**4.** The Security Council has five permanent members (the U.S., Britain, France, Russia, and China), and ten elected nonpermanent members. It is mainly responsible for maintaining international peace. It evaluates security threats and can take actions such as placing economic

or military sanctions and sending UN forces to stop aggression or keep the peace.

**5.** to promote U.S. security by partnering with other nations for mutual defense

**6.** Possible response: Yes, because each member nation has one seat and one vote

**7. (a)** Early American policymakers were more isolationist than policymakers now. **(b)** American alliances illustrate how the U.S. has become more active in international affairs.

**QUICK WRITE** Thesis statements should clearly state the essay's purpose and goal.

# Quick Study Guide

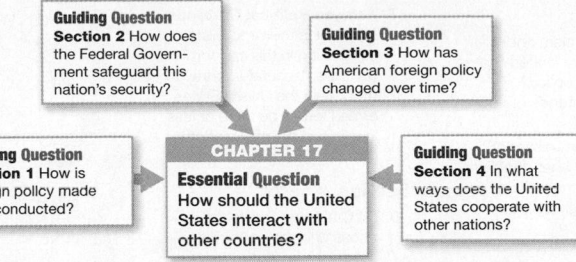

**Guiding Question**
**Section 2** How does the Federal Government safeguard this nation's security?

**Guiding Question**
**Section 3** How has American foreign policy changed over time?

**Guiding Question**
**Section 1** How is foreign policy made and conducted?

**CHAPTER 17**
**Essential Question**
How should the United States interact with other countries?

**Guiding Question**
**Section 4** In what ways does the United States cooperate with other nations?

## Political Dictionary

domestic affairs *p. 482*
foreign affairs *p. 482*
isolationism *p. 482*
foreign policy *p. 483*
right of legation *p. 485*
ambassador *p. 485*
diplomatic immunity *p. 486*
passport *p. 487*
visa *p. 487*
espionage *p. 492*
terrorism *p. 492*
collective security *p. 498*
deterrence *p. 498*
cold war *p. 498*
containment *p. 500*
détente *p. 501*
foreign aid *p. 505*
regional security alliance *p. 506*
NATO *p. 506*
United Nations *p. 508*
Security Council *p. 509*

## Key American Foreign Policies

| | |
|---|---|
| Monroe Doctrine | Isolates the U.S. from international affairs unless North or South America is threatened. |
| Roosevelt Corollary | Extends the Monroe Doctrine by giving the U.S. the authority to intervene in the affairs of Latin America. |
| Good Neighbor Policy | Reduces American political and military interference in Latin America. |
| Deterrence | Maintains that superior military strength will deter hostile powers from attacking the nation. |
| Truman Doctrine | Affirms that the U.S. will oppose any aggressor's attempt to control another nation and its people. |
| Containment | Prevents the spread of communism by assisting threatened nations. |
| Détente | Reduces tensions between the United States and both the Soviet Union and China. |
| Collective Security | Brings nations together to resist any nation that threatens the peace. |

## U.S. Foreign Policy Positions

### Isolationism

- American foreign policy until World War II
- Purposeful detachment from world affairs
- Domestic affairs are primary focus
- Allows for some ties with foreign nations
- Extended by the Monroe Doctrine to include regions of North and South America

### Internationalism

- American foreign policy since World War II
- Economic and political involvement in international affairs
- Focuses on collective security
- Acknowledges impact of global events on the United States
- Embodied in the Truman Doctrine

# For More Information

To learn more about foreign policy and national defense, refer to these sources or assign them to students:

**L1** **Ross, Stewart.** *United Nations.* Heinemann, 2003.

**L2** **Kallen, Stuart A., ed.** *What Are the Most Serious Threats to National Security?* Greenhaven Press, 2005.

**L3** **Renehan, Edward J.** *The Monroe Doctrine: The Cornerstone of American Foreign Policy.* Chelsea House Publications, 2007.

**L4** **Kissinger, Henry.** *Does America Need a Foreign Policy?: Toward a Diplomacy for the 21st Century.* Simon & Schuster, 2002.

---

Have students download the digital resources available at Government on the Go for review and remediation.

## STUDY TIPS

**True/False Tests** There are a few concrete strategies students can use when taking true/false tests. First, point out that every part of a statement must be true in order for the answer to be "true." If any part of the statement is false, the answer is "false." Words that qualify a statement, such as *sometimes, often, generally,* and *most,* often indicate a true answer because they make a statement more accurate. Conversely, qualifiers such as *never, always, all,* and *every* often indicate a false answer because they are too broad. If a sentence uses negatives, try dropping the negative and re-reading it. Decide if that answer is true or false, and then choose the opposite for your real answer. Finally, be sure students realize they should guess at answers they don't know on a true/false test. They have a 50 percent chance of being right.

## ASSESSMENT AT A GLANCE

### Tests and Quizzes

Section Assessments
Section Quizzes A and B, Unit 4 **All-in-One**
Chapter Assessment
Chapter Tests A and B, Unit 4 **All-in-One**
Document-Based Assessment
Progress Monitoring Online
Exam*View* Test Bank

### Performance Assessment

Essential Questions Journal
Debates, pp. 485, 493, 500, 509
Assessment Rubrics, **All-in-One**

# Chapter Assessment

## COMPREHENSION AND CRITICAL THINKING

### SECTION 1

**1. (a)** Isolationism is the purposeful refusal to become generally involved in the affairs of the rest of the world. Internationalism is a policy to become involved with the problems of other nations. **(b)** during and after World War II, because it became clear that the problems of other nations affected U.S. security and prosperity **(c)** possible advantages: promotes U.S. security by promoting political and economic stability around the world, increases markets for U.S. products; possible disadvantages: foreign aid reduces funds available for domestic programs, interfering in the affairs of other nations can involve us in armed conflicts

**2. (a)** to represent the U.S. in diplomatic matters **(b)** Ambassadors are appointed by the President with Senate consent. Appointees may have experience as career diplomats, but often their only qualification is their support for the President. **(c)** Ambassadors are located in foreign nations, so they can promote policy goals by negotiating with foreign governments and monitoring U.S. programs within those nations.

### SECTION 2

**3. (a)** The ultimate authority over the military lies with civilian branches of government. **(b)** The Constitution makes the President, a civilian, commander in chief, and gives broad military powers to Congress, the civilian elected representatives of the people. The Department of Defense implements the President's national security policies, and the department head cannot have served on active military duty for at least ten years before being named to the post. **(c)** The military might use its power to overthrow the civilian government.

**4. (a)** mostly the Office of the Director of National Intelligence and the Department of Homeland Security **(b)** The U.S. has a vast number of potential terrorist targets that could not be fully secured.

### SECTION 3

**5. (a)** the strategy of maintaining such military might that no nation would risk attacking **(b)** Deterrence is believed to have been a key factor in the downfall of the Soviet Union. **(c)** Deterrence is still useful now in preventing attacks from other

---

# Chapter Assessment

**GOVERNMENT** ONLINE
**Self-Test**
To test your understanding of key terms and main ideas, visit
**PearsonSchool.com/phgovt**

## Comprehension and Critical Thinking

### Section 1

**1. (a)** What is the difference between isolationism and internationalism? **(b)** When and why did the United States stop pursuing a largely isolationist foreign policy? **(c)** What are the advantages and disadvantages of an internationalist foreign policy?

**2. (a)** What is the major responsibility of an ambassador? **(b)** How are ambassadors appointed, and what qualifications do they usually have? **(c)** How does the work of an ambassador help advance American foreign policy?

### Section 2

**3. (a)** What does "civilian control of the military" mean? **(b)** How is civilian control of the military guaranteed in the United States? **(c)** What are the dangers of a military not under civilian control?

**4. (a)** Which executive branch agencies are primarily responsible for protecting the United States from terrorist attacks? **(b)** Why is it so difficult to protect this nation completely against terrorist attacks?

### Section 3

**5. (a)** What is the policy of deterrence? **(b)** How effective has it been as a tool in American foreign policy? **(c)** Do you think it is still an effective policy in today's world? Why or why not?

**6. (a)** What is the basic goal of American foreign policy? **(b)** How does the history of American foreign policy illustrate that goal? **(c)** What do you think should be the overall goal of American foreign policy?

### 7. Analyze Political Cartoons

**(a)** What is the cartoonist suggesting in this cartoon? **(b)** Is it an accurate portrayal? **(c)** Should the United States armed forces be more or less involved in the affairs of other nations? Explain.

### Section 4

**8. (a)** Cite three regional alliances and the countries associated with them. **(b)** What effect do you think a pact between the United States and countries in the Middle East would have on world affairs today?

**9. (a)** What is the main purpose of the United Nations? **(b)** What are the six main bodies of the UN and how do they support that purpose? **(c)** Do you think the United Nations should be a means of advancing American international policy? Why or why not?

### Writing About Government

**10.** Use your Quick Write exercises from this chapter to write a problem-and-solution essay on a current international issue. Make sure you clearly define the problem, explain your solution, and provide supporting details illustrating how your solution could succeed. See pp. S3–S5 in the Writing Handbook.

---

## Apply What You've Learned

**11. Essential Question Activity** Select a country to which the United States has provided humanitarian, military, or economic aid within the last 20 years. Conduct research and use the following questions to help you create a cause-and-effect chart:

**(a)** What event led to U.S. involvement? For how long did the United States provide support?

**(b)** Was American support military or humanitarian in nature? Did its purpose change over time?

**(c)** Were other organizations involved? If so, which ones?

**(d)** What were the results of American aid?

**12. Essential Question Assessment** Use the results of your research and the content of this chapter to write an editorial piece that helps express your opinion on the Essential Question: **How should the United States interact with other countries?** Remember that an Op-Ed is a form of persuasive essay. Your opinion should be well thought out and include accurate details that support the view you want to express.

**Essential Questions Journal** To respond to the chapter Essential Question, go to your **Essential Questions Journal.**

---

nations, but is less useful as a strategy against terrorist attacks or rogue states.

**6. (a)** to protect the security and well-being of the U.S. **(b)** Originally, isolationist policies were designed to keep the U.S. safe by staying out of foreign conflicts. Over time, more internationalist policies were designed to keep the U.S. safe by entering into collective security agreements. **(c)** Some students might agree with the current goal of protecting U.S. security and well-being. Others might suggest that humanitarian aid should be part of the overall goal of U.S. foreign policy.

**7. (a)** that the U.S. military bears the burden of supporting the world **(b)** Possible response: Yes; the U.S. military is involved in so many actions around the globe. **(c)** Possible response: The armed forces should be less involved in the affairs of other nations unless the security of the U.S. is genuinely at risk.

### SECTION 4

**8. (a)** Answers may include: NATO (Canada, the U.S., and most European nations), the Rio Pact (nations of North, South, and Central America), the ANZUS Pact (Australia,

# Document-Based Assessment

## Deterrence and Foreign Policy

The destructive force of a nuclear weapon is horrifying, not only in its actual detonation but in the mere possibility of its use. As illustrated by the following documents, having and stockpiling weapons with such destructive capabilities became the American foreign policy of deterrence that continues to this day.

### Document 1

The Japanese began the war from the air at Pearl Harbor. They have been repaid many fold. And the end is not yet. With this bomb we have now added a new and revolutionary increase in destruction to supplement the growing power of our armed forces. In their present form these bombs are now in production and even more powerful forms are in development. . . .

We are now prepared to obliterate more rapidly and completely every productive enterprise the Japanese have above ground in any city. We shall destroy their docks, their factories, and their communications. Let there be no mistake; we shall completely destroy Japan's power to make war.

**President Harry Truman,
on the bombing of Hiroshima, 1945**

### Document 2

Our reluctance for conflict should not be misjudged as a failure of will. When action is required to preserve our national security, we will act. We will maintain sufficient strength to prevail if need be, knowing that if we do so we have the best chance of never having to use that strength.

**—President Ronald Reagan,
first Inaugural Address, 1981**

### Document 3

Recall that earlier generations [of Americans] faced down fascism and communism not just with missiles and tanks, but with sturdy alliances and enduring convictions. They understood that our power alone cannot protect us, nor does it entitle us to do as we please. Instead, they knew that our power grows through its prudent use. Our security emanates from the justness of our cause, the force of our example, [and] the tempering qualities of humility and restraint.

We are the keepers of this legacy; guided by these principles once more, we can meet those new threats that demand even greater effort, even greater cooperation and understanding between nations. . . . With old friends and former foes we'll work tirelessly to lessen the nuclear threat and roll back the specter of a warming planet. . . .

For those who seek to advance their aims by inducing terror and slaughtering innocents, [and] to those leaders around the globe who seek to sow conflict or blame their society's ills on the West, know that your people will judge you on what you can build, not what you destroy. To those who cling to power through corruption and deceit and the silencing of dissent, know that you are on the wrong side of history, but that we will extend a hand if you are willing to unclench your fist.

**—President Barack Obama,
Inaugural Address, January 20, 2009**

---

**Use your knowledge of American foreign policy and Documents 1–3 to answer Questions 1–3.**

1. What is the main point of Documents 2 and 3?
   A. Deterrence, by itself, cannot deter aggression.
   B. The United States should reduce military spending.
   C. New methods of deterrence are necessary.
   D. Military strength will ensure national security.

2. How might President Truman's comments in Document 1 have helped deter other nations from attacking the United States?

3. **Put It Together** Do you think that nuclear weapons and weapon stockpiling have helped the United States achieve its foreign policy objectives? Why or why not?

**GOVERNMENT ONLINE**
**Documents**
To find more primary sources on deterrence, visit
**PearsonSchool.com/phgovt**

---

## DOCUMENT-BASED ASSESSMENT

1. D

2. If other nations believed that the United States would be able to use the new and immensely powerful atomic bombs against any nation that attacked it, they would not provoke the U.S. into retaliating against them.

3. Possible response: Arms stockpiling did help deter Soviet attack during the cold war and contributed to the collapse of the Soviet Union. Huge stores of nuclear and conventional weapons can still deter hostile nations. However, they will have little deterrent effect on terrorist organizations that are dispersed across many nations, not massed in one location where huge bombs can annihilate them and their war-making capabilities. Also, rogue states and terrorist groups might gain access to nuclear weapons and use them against us.

**L2 Differentiate** Students use all the documents on the page to support their thesis.

**L3 Differentiate** Students include additional information available online at **PearsonSchool.com/phgovt.**

**L4 Differentiate** Students use materials from the textbook, the online information at **PearsonSchool.com/phgovt,** and do additional research to support their views.

 **Go Online to PearsonSchool.com/phgovt** for a student rubric and extra documents.

---

New Zealand, and the U.S.), the Japanese Pact (Japan and the U.S.), the Philippines Pact (the Philippines and the U.S.), and the Korean Pact (South Korea and the U.S.). **(b)** The Middle East is a potentially explosive region. If the U.S. forms a pact with some nations there, resentment could lead to war.

9. **(a)** to maintain international peace and security, develop friendly relations, and promote justice and cooperation **(b)** General Assembly: representatives from all member nations discuss issues; Security Council: responsible for maintaining peace; Economic and Social Council: helps solve international economic, cultural, educational, and health problems; Trusteeship Council: intended to assure just treatment of non-self-governing territories; International Court of Justice: tries cases involving international law; Secretariat: secretary-general alerts Security Council to threats to peace and helps settle international disputes **(c)** Possible response: Yes. As the UN's major funder and a permanent member of the Security Council, the U.S. can influence UN actions. For example, a UN mandate supported the extended presence of U.S. troops in Iraq. This helped advance U.S. policy to reshape Iraq into a democracy.

### WRITING ABOUT GOVERNMENT

10. Essays should define a problem and give a viable solution with supporting details.

### APPLY WHAT YOU'VE LEARNED

11. Charts should show causes leading to U.S. foreign aid and the results of that aid.

12. Students should state their opinion clearly and support it with well-reasoned details.

## ANSWERS TO ESSENTIAL QUESTION WARMUP

Before assigning these questions, distribute the Rubric for Assessing a Writing Assignment (Unit 4 All-in-One, p. 291). Use the criteria and the guidelines below to grade students' answers to the Essential Question Warmup questions. Then send students to the **Essential Questions Journal** to answer the unit Essential Question.

**1.** Students may point out that voters often judge candidates based on rather superficial characteristics such as speaking style and appearance. Voters should, however, judge candidates by such criteria as experience, vision, reaction to pressure, intelligence, leadership qualities, and how closely a candidate's views on the issues match those of the voter. Answers may differ on the relative importance students assign to these criteria.

**2.** The passage of time results in perspective. For example, what might have been seen as a crisis at one time may turn out to be a relatively minor event with little bearing on a President's entire term of office. In addition, decisions might result in unexpected consequences later on.

**3.** A President who is popular—has the will of the people behind him or her—will be more effective than an unpopular President. However, sometimes a President must make an unpopular decision if it is for the greater good of the country. Presidents who are overly concerned about their popularity will likely not make good long-term decisions.

**4.** Sample answer: Those Presidents who are considered "great," such as Washington or Lincoln, were tested by extraordinary events that allowed them to rise to the occasion and show heroism. Not every potentially "great" President governs under such adverse circumstances, suggesting that one should look deeply into a presidency to see whether greatness in vision or decision making is evidenced under more ordinary circumstances.

## Perspectives

### Essential Question
# What makes a good President?

The more familiar you are with each of the now 44 presidencies, the better equipped you will be to identify the several factors that define a good President.

**ON THE QUALITIES OF A GREAT PRESIDENT:**

" . . . [R]esearch indicate[s] that great presidents, besides being stubborn and disagreeable, are more extraverted, open to experience, assertive, achievement striving, excitement seeking and more open to fantasy, aesthetics, feelings, actions, ideas and values. Historically great presidents were low on straightforwardness, vulnerability and order.

—American Psychological Association, August 2000

**ON HISTORY'S JUDGMENT OF THE PRESIDENT:**

In a pun on the names of cars and Presidents, Gerald Ford joked during his presidency that he was "a Ford, not a Lincoln."

**ON THE OPPORTUNITY TO BECOME A GREAT PRESIDENT:**

All our great presidents were leaders of thought at times when certain ideas in the life of the nation had to be clarified.

—Franklin D. Roosevelt, 1932

### Essential Question Warmup

Throughout this unit, you studied the office and the job of the President. Use what you have learned and the opinions expressed above to answer the following questions. Then go to your **Essential Questions Journal.**

**1.** How do voters evaluate candidates?

**2.** Why does history often judge a President somewhat differently from how he was judged while in office?

**3.** Should a President strive to be popular or, instead, strive to be effective?

**4.** Can a President be great if conditions present no real opportunity to show greatness?

**Essential Questions Journal** To continue to build a response to the unit Essential Question, go to your **Essential Questions Journal.**

# Assessment Resources

Unit 4 AYP Monitoring Assessment
*ExamView* Test Bank CD-ROM
SuccessTracker Assessment
Online Student Self-Tests
Chapter Tests
Section Quizzes
Chapter-level Document-Based Assessment

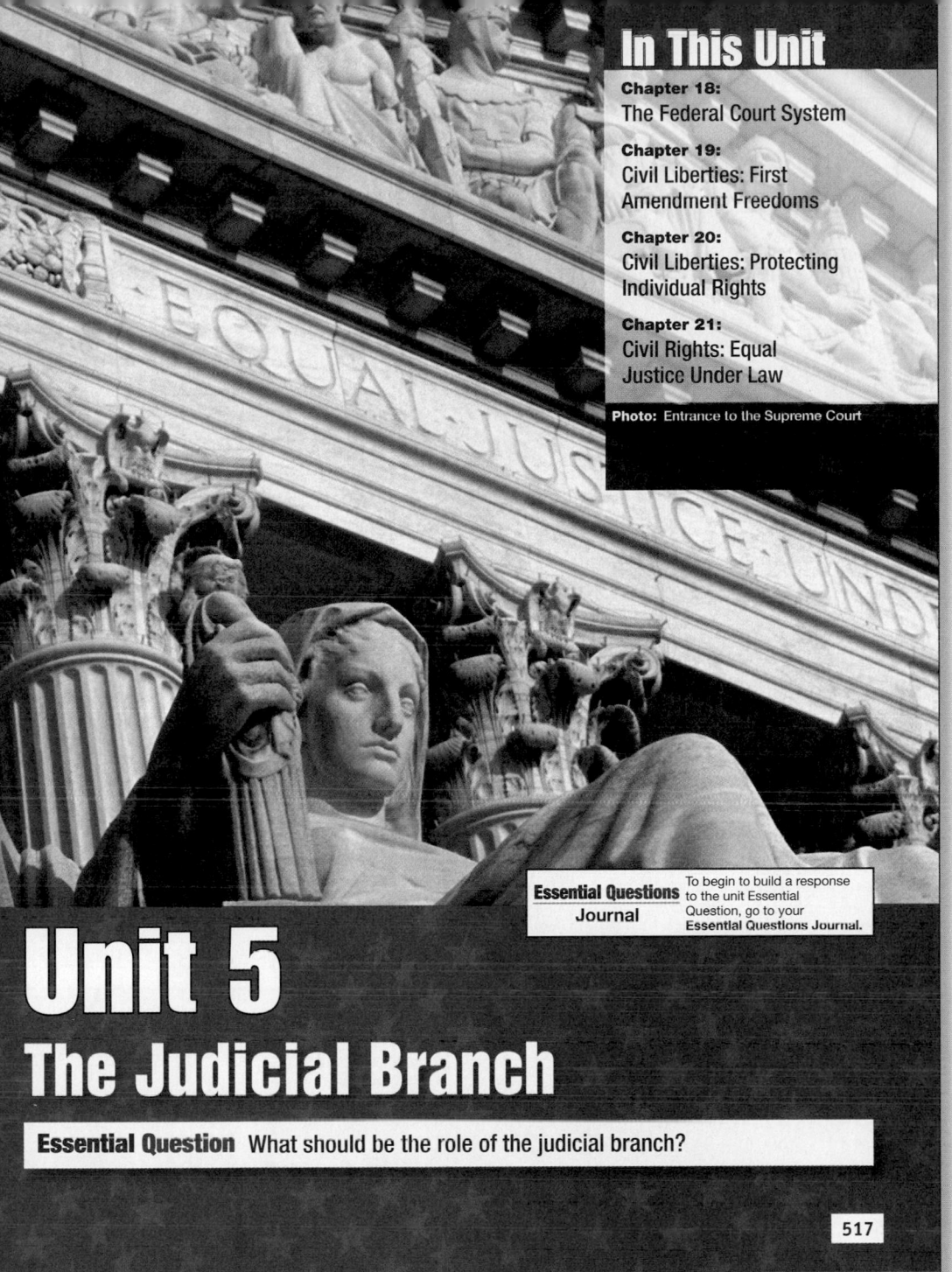

**Essential Questions Journal** — To begin to build a response to the unit Essential Question, go to your **Essential Questions Journal.**

# Unit 5
# The Judicial Branch

**Essential Question** What should be the role of the judicial branch?

517

## Government Online Resources

Government Online Teacher Center at **PearsonSchool.com/phgovt** includes
- Online Teacher's Edition with lesson planner and lecture notes
- Teacher's Resource Library with All-in-One Resources, Color Transparencies, Adequate Yearly Progress Monitoring, and an alternative lesson plan for each chapter
- SuccessTracker Assessment

Government Online Student Center at **PearsonSchool.com/phgovt** includes
- Interactive textbook with audio
- American Government Essential Questions Video
- Chapter-level WebQuests
- Guided Audio Tours and Interactivities
- Student Self-Tests

**ESSENTIAL QUESTION PERSPECTIVES**

Essential questions frame each unit and chapter of study, asking students to consider big ideas about government. The question for this unit—**What should be the role of the judicial branch?**—demands that students ask further questions. What is the role of the judicial branch? Is an independent judiciary essential to the success of our government? Should the Supreme Court have the final word in interpreting the Constitution? How should the courts make judgments when presented with two or more equally valid points of view?

To begin this unit, assign the Unit 5 Warmup Activity on page 148 of the **Essential Questions Journal.** This will help students start to consider their position on the **Unit 5 Essential Question: What should be the role of the judicial branch?**

Show the **Unit 5 American Government Essential Questions Video** to help students begin thinking about the unit Essential Question and designate a classroom bulletin board for students to post news articles related to the unit Essential Question. Use the Conversation Wall strategy (p. T27) to encourage students to post articles and comments on other students' postings.

Later, students will further explore the chapter-level essential questions:

*Chapter 18:* **Does the structure of the federal court system allow it to administer justice effectively?**

*Chapter 19:* **How can the judiciary balance individual rights with the common good?**

*Chapter 20:* **To what extent has the judiciary protected the rights of privacy, security, and personal freedom?**

*Chapter 21:* **Why are there ongoing struggles for civil rights?**

Use the **Essential Questions Journal** throughout the program to help students consider these and other big ideas about government.

# Introduce the Chapter

## Essential Questions:

**UNIT 5**

What should be the role of the judicial branch?

**CHAPTER 18**

Does the structure of the federal court system allow it to administer justice effectively?

### ACTIVATE PRIOR KNOWLEDGE

Have students examine the image and the quotation on these pages. Ask: **What do the photo and quotation suggest about the federal court system?** *(that the judicial branch has the power to "say what the law is")* In this chapter, students will learn about the structure of the federal court system. Then tell students to begin to explore the federal court system by completing the Chapter 18 **Essential Questions Journal.** Discuss their responses as a class.

### BEFORE READING

**L2** **ELL Differentiate** Chapter 18 Prereading and Vocabulary Worksheet (Unit 5 All-in-One, p. 9)

### SUCCESSNET STUDENT AND TEACHER CENTER

Visit **PearsonSchool.com/phgovt** for downloadable resources that allow students and teachers to connect with government "on the go."

### DIGITAL LESSON PRESENTATION

The digital lesson presentation supports the print lesson with activities and summaries of key concepts. Activities for this chapter include:

- **Types of Jurisdiction: Which Court?**
- **Who Is on the Court Today?**

## SKILLS DEVELOPMENT

### DECISION MAKING

You may wish to teach decision making as a distinct skill within Section 3 of this chapter. Use the Chapter 18 Skills Worksheet (Unit 5 All-in-One, p. 41) to help students learn the steps in making a decision. The worksheet asks students to read an excerpt from the *Plessy* v. *Ferguson* decision of 1896 and to answer questions about it. For L2 and L1 students, assign the adapted Skill Activity (Unit 5 All-in-One, p. 42).

**WebQuest online** The chapter WebQuest challenges students to answer the chapter Essential Question by asking them about the federal court system.

518

## Block Scheduling

**BLOCK 1:** Teach these parts of the Section 1 lesson: Analyze the Framers' Intentions (Transparency 18A), Differentiate Types of Federal Courts, Chart Federal Court Jurisdiction, Core Worksheet 18.1, and Extend Worksheet 18.1. Discuss Transparency 18B. Have students complete first two Strategies for Remediation.

**BLOCK 2:** Teach the Section 2 lesson, including Core Worksheet 18.2. Allow time for students to prepare courtroom skits. Skip to Section 4 and teach Chart Special Courts' Jurisdiction and Trace Appeals Through Special Courts.

**BLOCK 3:** Have students perform their courtroom skits. Allow one hour for Core Worksheet 18.3A discussion. Distribute Core Worksheet 18.3B for groups to comprise majority opinions. Conclude by assigning the second Remediation activity in Section 3 (writing a booklet) and the Assess activity in Section 4 (pyramid chart).

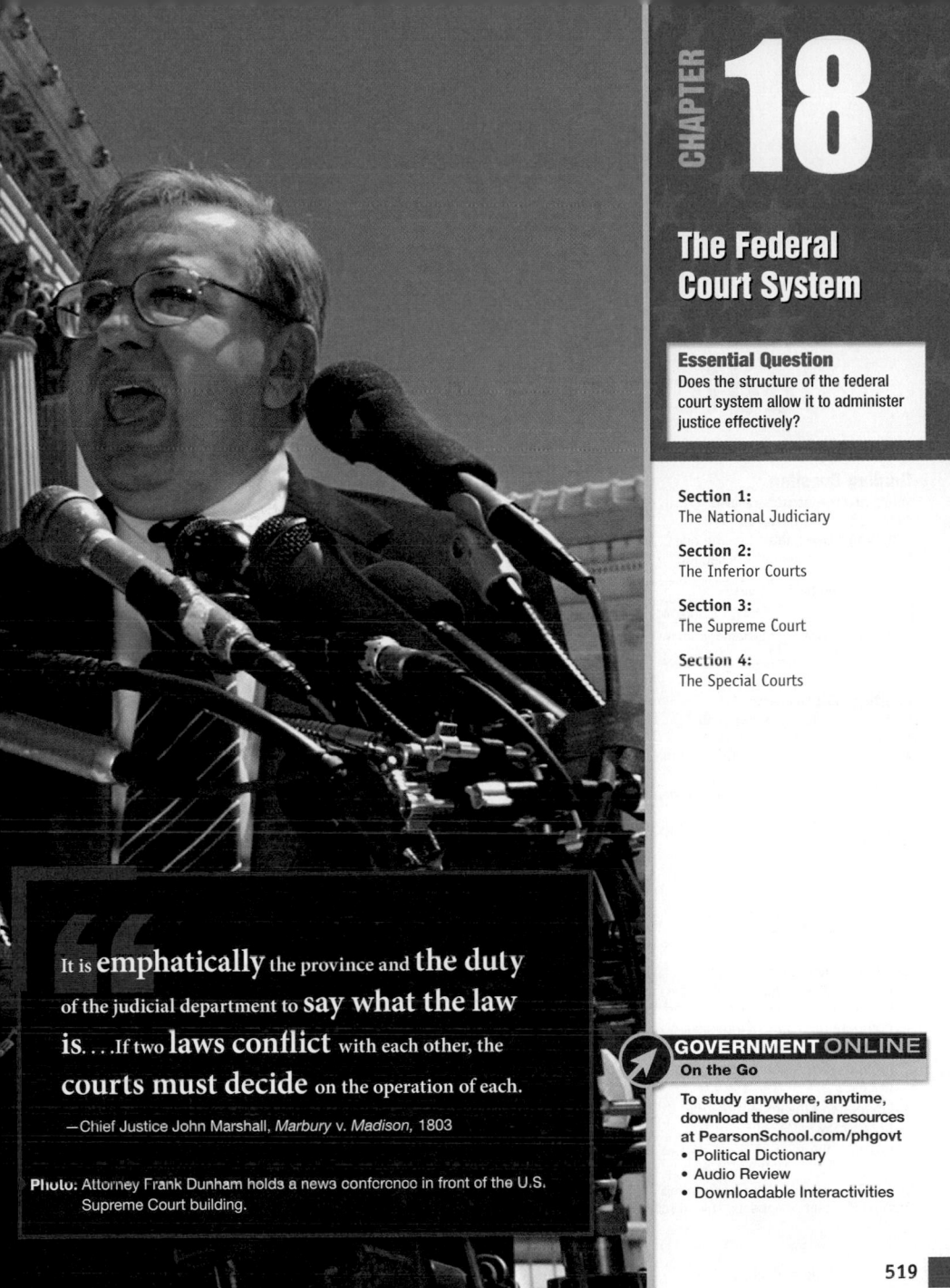

# 18

## The Federal Court System

**Essential Question**
Does the structure of the federal court system allow it to administer justice effectively?

**Section 1:**
The National Judiciary

**Section 2:**
The Inferior Courts

**Section 3:**
The Supreme Court

**Section 4:**
The Special Courts

"It is **emphatically** the province and **the duty** of the judicial department to **say what the law is**....If two **laws conflict** with each other, the **courts must decide** on the operation of each."

—Chief Justice John Marshall, *Marbury* v. *Madison*, 1803

**Photo:** Attorney Frank Dunham holds a news conference in front of the U.S. Supreme Court building.

**GOVERNMENT** ONLINE
**On the Go**

To study anywhere, anytime, download these online resources at PearsonSchool.com/phgovt
• Political Dictionary
• Audio Review
• Downloadable Interactivities

519

## Lesson Goals

**SECTION 1**
Students will . . .
• learn the Framers' intentions for the national judiciary by analyzing an excerpt from *The Federalist* No. 78.
• comprehend the structure and role of the federal courts by completing a jurisdiction T-chart and filling in a Venn diagram with examples of exclusive and concurrent cases.
• identify the skills, term, pay, and selection of federal judges by creating a classified advertisement for a judge.

**SECTION 2**
Students will . . .
• identify the structure of the inferior constitutional courts by completing a chart highlighting the various courts and their jurisdictions.
• understand how inferior constitutional courts function by constructing paths of appeals for various case scenarios.

**SECTION 3**
Students will . . .
• learn about the scope of the Supreme Court's jurisdiction by analyzing a political cartoon showing the power of judicial review, and by identifying the Court's original and appellate jurisdiction.
• identify how the Supreme Court operates by sequencing the appeals process, by reading a transcript of a real case, and by formulating opinions on controversial cases.

**SECTION 4**
Students will . . .
• identify the special courts by completing a chart highlighting the various courts' jurisdictions.
• understand how special courts function by constructing paths of appeals for case scenarios.
• analyze the constitutionality of military commissions by studying opinions for and against them.

## Pressed for Time

Display Transparency 18E to give students an overview of the federal courts and their appellate path. Have students briefly study it, especially the "Key to Courts." Then organize the students into four groups, with each group assigned to a section of the chapter. Groups must change each heading or subheading in their section into a question, and then answer the question. They should use these questions/answers to teach an overview of their section to the other groups. Fill in vital information that students overlook, or distribute copies of the Facts and Enduring Understandings. Finally, have each student re-create the transparency diagram, adding specific information to each level and type of courts.

**DIFFERENTIATED INSTRUCTION KEY**

Look for these symbols to help you adjust steps in each lesson to meet your students' needs.

**L1** Special Needs
**L2** Basic
    **ELL** English Language Learners
    **LPR** Less Proficient Readers
**L3** All Students
**L4** Advanced Students

## What are the structure and function of the national judiciary?

| The National Judiciary | |
| --- | --- |
| **Structure** | **Types of Jurisdiction** |
| • Dual court system | • Exclusive jurisdiction |
| • Supreme Court | • Concurrent jurisdiction |
| • Constitutional courts | • Original jurisdiction |
| • Special courts | • Appellate jurisdiction |

# Get Started

## LESSON GOALS

Students will . . .

- learn the Framers' intentions for the national judiciary by analyzing an excerpt from *The Federalist* No. 78.
- comprehend the structure and role of the federal courts by completing a jurisdiction T-chart and filling in a Venn diagram with examples of exclusive and concurrent cases.
- identify the skills, term, pay, and selection of federal judges by creating a classified advertisement for a judge.

## BEFORE CLASS

Assign the section, the graphic organizer in the text, and Reading Comprehension Worksheet (Unit 5 All-in-One, p. 13) before class.

**L2 Differentiate** Reading Comprehension Worksheet (Unit 5 All-in-One, p. 15)

## SKILLS DEVELOPMENT

### ANALYZE GRAPHIC DATA

Before students examine the "Types of Federal Courts" diagram in this section, you may want to review tips on analyzing graphic data in the Skills Handbook, p. S26.

---

SECTION 1

# The **National Judiciary**

**Guiding Question**
What are the structure and function of the national judiciary? Use a table like the one below to take notes on the section.

| The National Judiciary | |
| --- | --- |
| **Structure** | **Types of Jurisdiction** |
| • Dual court system | • Exclusive jurisdiction |
| • | • |

**Political Dictionary**
- inferior courts
- jurisdiction
- concurrent jurisdiction
- plaintiff
- defendant
- original jurisdiction
- appellate jurisdiction
- judicial restraint
- precedent
- judicial activism

**Objectives**
1. Explain why the Constitution created a national judiciary, and describe its structure.
2. Identify the criteria that determine whether a case is within the jurisdiction of a federal court, and compare the types of jurisdiction.
3. Outline the process for appointing federal judges, and list their terms of office.
4. Understand the impact of judicial philosophy.
5. Examine the roles of court officers.

**Image Above:** Judge Maryanne Trump Barry, U.S. Court of Appeals, Third Circuit

Joe steals a sports car in Chicago. Two days later, he is stopped for speeding in Atlanta. Where, now, will he be tried for car theft? In Illinois, where he stole the car? In Georgia, where he was caught? Joe may be on the verge of learning something about the federal court system—and about the Dyer Act of 1925, which makes it a federal crime to transport a stolen vehicle across a State line.

## Creation of a National Judiciary

During the years the Articles of Confederation were in force (1781–1789), there were no national courts and no national judiciary. The laws of the United States were interpreted and applied as each State saw fit, and sometimes not at all. Disputes between States and between persons who lived in different States were decided, if at all, by the courts in one of the States involved.[1] Often, decisions by the courts in one State were ignored by courts in the other States.

Alexander Hamilton spoke to the point in *The Federalist* No. 22. He described "the want of a judiciary power" as a "circumstance which crowns the defects of the Confederation." Arguing the need for a national court system, he added, "Laws are a dead letter without courts to expound and define their true meaning and operation." The Framers created a national judiciary for the United States in a single sentence in the Constitution:

**FROM THE CONSTITUTION**

**The judicial Power of the United States shall be vested in one supreme Court, and in such inferior Courts as the Congress may from time to time ordain and establish.**

—Article III, Section 1

Congress also is given the expressed power "to constitute Tribunals inferior to the supreme Court"—that is, create the rest of the federal court system—in Article I, Section 8, Clause 9.

---

1 The Articles of Confederation did provide (in Article IX) a very complicated procedure for the settlement of such disputes, but it was rarely used.

# Focus on the Basics

**FACTS:** • The national judiciary consists of a Supreme Court and inferior courts. • Congress created two kinds of inferior courts. • Federal courts have exclusive jurisdiction over some cases and concurrent jurisdiction in others. • The President appoints federal judges, who are subject to confirmation by the Senate. • Judges' philosophies influence their decisions.

**CONCEPTS:** checks and balances, federalism, role of government in public policy

**ENDURING UNDERSTANDINGS:** • The Constitution created the Supreme Court, its jurisdiction, and the manner and terms of federal judicial appointments. • The U.S. has dual national and State court systems. • Federal judges often shape public policy.

**A Dual Court System** Keep in mind this important point: There are *two* separate court systems in the United States.[2] On one hand, the national judiciary spans the country with its more than 100 courts. On the other hand, each of the 50 States has its own system of courts. Their numbers run well into the thousands, and most of the cases that are heard in court today are heard in those State, not federal, courts.

**Two Kinds of Federal Courts** The Constitution establishes the Supreme Court and leaves to Congress the creation of the **inferior courts**—the lower federal courts, those beneath the Supreme Court. Over the years, Congress has created two distinct types of federal courts: (1) the constitutional courts,

and (2) the special courts. See the diagram "Types of Federal Courts" below.

The constitutional courts are those federal courts that Congress has formed under Article III to exercise "the judicial Power of the United States." Together with the Supreme Court, they now include the courts of appeals, the district courts, and the U.S. Court of International Trade. The constitutional courts are also called the regular courts and, sometimes, Article III courts.

The special courts do not exercise the broad "judicial Power of the United States." Rather, they have been created by Congress to hear cases arising out of some of the expressed powers given to Congress in Article I, Section 8. The special courts hear a much narrower range of cases than those that may come before the constitutional courts.

These special courts are also called the legislative courts and, sometimes, Article I courts. Today, they include the U.S. Court of Appeals for the Armed Forces, the U.S. Court of Appeals for Veterans Claims, the U.S. Court of Federal Claims, the U.S. Tax

2  Federalism does not require two court systems. Article III provides that Congress "may" establish lower federal courts. At its first session in 1789, Congress decided to construct a complete set of federal courts to parallel those of the States. In most of the world's other federal systems, the principal courts are those of the states or provinces; typically, the only significant federal court is a national court of last resort, often called the supreme court.

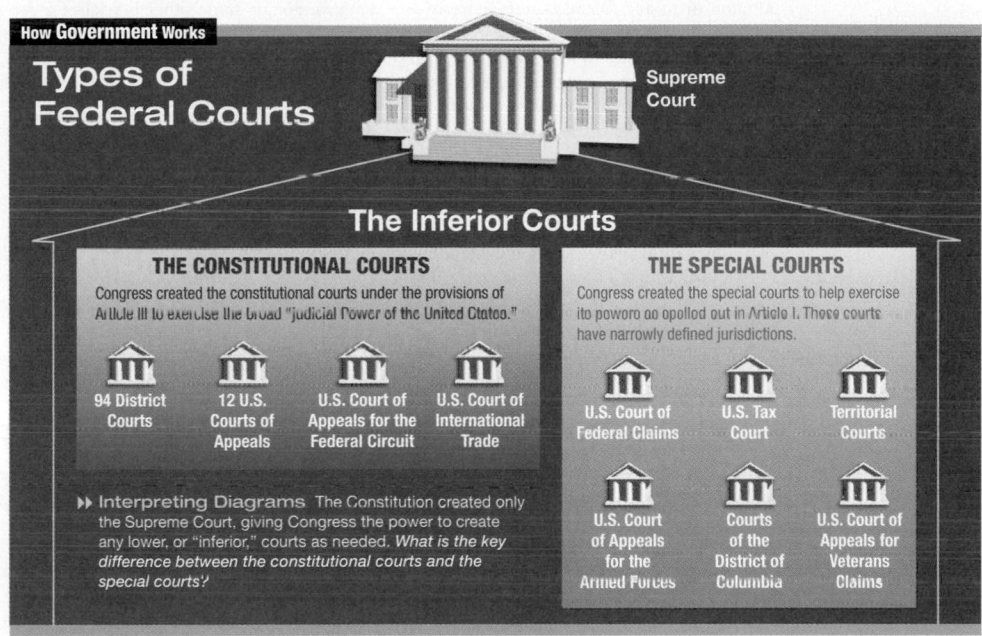

**How Government Works**

**Types of Federal Courts**

Supreme Court

**The Inferior Courts**

**THE CONSTITUTIONAL COURTS**
Congress created the constitutional courts under the provisions of Article III to exercise the broad "judicial Power of the United States."

- 94 District Courts
- 12 U.S. Courts of Appeals
- U.S. Court of Appeals for the Federal Circuit
- U.S. Court of International Trade

**THE SPECIAL COURTS**
Congress created the special courts to help exercise its powers as spelled out in Article I. These courts have narrowly defined jurisdictions.

- U.S. Court of Federal Claims
- U.S. Tax Court
- Territorial Courts
- U.S. Court of Appeals for the Armed Forces
- Courts of the District of Columbia
- U.S. Court of Appeals for Veterans Claims

▶▶ **Interpreting Diagrams** The Constitution created only the Supreme Court, giving Congress the power to create any lower, or "inferior," courts as needed. *What is the key difference between the constitutional courts and the special courts?*

---

**BELLRINGER**
Write the following quote and questions on the board:

**"The judiciary . . . has no influence over either the sword or the purse; . . . It may truly be said to have neither FORCE nor WILL, but merely judgment."**

—Alexander Hamilton, *The Federalist* No. 78

**What is Hamilton saying about the function of the judicial branch? What does he imply are NOT functions of the judicial branch?**

Have students write answers to the questions in their notebooks.

**L1 L2 Differentiate** Have students look up definitions of the terms *sword* and *purse*. Discuss how Hamilton is using nonliteral meanings of these words.

# Teach

To present this topic using online resources, use the lesson presentations at **PearsonSchool.com/phgovt.**

**REVIEW BELLRINGER ANSWERS**

Have volunteers share their answers to the Bellringer questions. Hamilton states that the function of the judicial branch is to judge. The judiciary has no power to make (the "will") or to enforce (the "force") laws.

**L2 ELL Differentiate** Ask students how Hamilton refers to the executive and legislative branches. Why does he refer to them this way? *(He refers to the executive branch as the "sword" and the "force" because it has the power to implement laws. The legislative branch is the "purse" and the "will" because it makes the laws and must authorize all government spending.)*

# Differentiated Resources

The following resources are located in the All-in-One, Unit 5, Chapter 18, Section 1:

- **L2** Prereading and Vocabulary Worksheet (p. 9)
- **L3** Reading Comprehension Worksheet (p. 13)
- **L2** Reading Comprehension Worksheet (p. 15)
- **L3 L2** Core Worksheets (pp. 17, 18)
- **L2** Extend Activity (p. 22)
- **L3 L4** Extend Worksheet (p. 20)
- **L3** Quiz A (p. 23)
- **L2** Quiz B (p. 24)

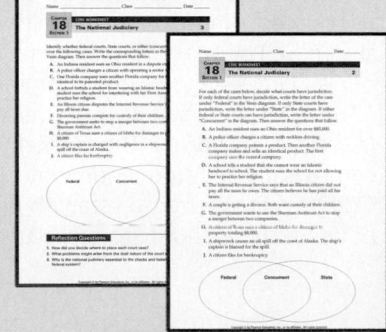

## Answers

**Interpreting Diagrams** Constitutional courts were created to exercise broad judicial powers, whereas special courts were created to exercise narrowly defined powers.

Display Transparency 18A, which includes another excerpt from *The Federalist* No. 78. After a volunteer reads the excerpt aloud, ask: **What does Hamilton say is the exclusive province of the judiciary?** *(the power to interpret laws)* **Does this function make the judicial branch more powerful than the legislative branch?** *(no)* **What protects the people from unconstitutional statutes of the legislature?** *(Judges must interpret the legislature's laws through the fundamental laws of the Constitution.)*

**L2 ELL Differentiate** Point out that the word *province* in this context means "function" or "scope." In addition, the phrase *power of the people* can be interpreted as "rights of the people."

**L4 Differentiate** Have students paraphrase the excerpt from *The Federalist* No. 78.

## DIFFERENTIATE TYPES OF FEDERAL COURTS

Display Transparency 18B and have students study the *How Government Works* diagram "Types of Federal Courts." Ask: **Which is the only court mentioned in the Constitution?** *(the Supreme Court)* **What are the two levels of federal courts?** *(the Supreme Court and inferior courts)* **How are the inferior courts further delineated?** *(as constitutional courts and special courts)* **Which type of inferior courts were created by Congress?** *(both the constitutional courts and the special courts)*

**L2 LPR Differentiate** Have students re-create the "Types of Federal Courts" diagram in their notebooks, labeling the two levels of federal courts, the two general types of inferior courts, the specific courts in each type, and the other names of the inferior courts *(constitutional courts: regular or Article III; special courts: legislative or Article I).*

## Answers

**Checkpoint** the United States or one of its officers or agencies; an ambassador, consul, or other foreign official; a State if it is suing another State, a citizen of another State, or a foreign government or subject; a citizen of one State suing a citizen of another State; a U.S. citizen suing a foreign government or subject; citizens of the same State if both claim land under grants from different States

---

**tribunal**
*n.* a judicial body, a court

**infringement**
*n.* violation

Court, the various territorial courts, and the courts of the District of Columbia. You will look at the unique features of these tribunals later in this chapter.

## Federal Court Jurisdiction

The constitutional courts hear most of the cases tried in the federal courts. That is to say, those courts have jurisdiction over most federal cases. **Jurisdiction** is defined as the authority of a court to hear (to *try* and to *decide*) a case. The term means, literally, the power "to say the law."

The Constitution gives federal courts jurisdiction over only certain cases. Recall, most cases heard in court in the United States are heard in State, not federal, courts. Article III, Section 2 provides that the federal courts may hear cases either because of (1) the *subject matter* or (2) the *parties* involved in those cases.

**Subject Matter** In terms of subject matter, the federal courts may hear a case if it involves a "federal question"—that is, the interpretation and application of a provision in the Constitution or in any federal statute or treaty—or a question of admiralty or maritime law. Admiralty law relates to matters that arise on the high seas or the navigable waters of the United States, such as a collision at sea or a crime committed aboard a ship. Maritime law relates to matters that arise on land but are directly related to the water, such as a contract to deliver ship supplies at dockside.

The Framers purposefully gave the federal courts exclusive jurisdiction in all admiralty and maritime cases in order to ensure national supremacy in the regulation of all waterborne commerce.

**Parties** A case falls within the jurisdiction of the federal courts if one of the parties involved in the case is (1) the United States or one of its officers or agencies; (2) an ambassador, consul, or other official representative of a foreign government; (3) one of the 50 States suing another State, a resident of another State, or a foreign government or one of its subjects; (4) a citizen of one State suing a citizen of another State; (5) an American citizen suing a foreign government or one of its subjects; or

(6) a citizen of a State suing another citizen of that same State where both claim title to land under grants from different States.

These criteria for determining which cases can be heard in the federal courts may seem quite complicated, and they are. But the matter is also a reflection of federalism and, so, of the dual system of courts in this country. To put the whole point of the jurisdiction of the federal courts the other way around: Those cases that are not heard by the federal courts fall within the jurisdiction of the State courts.

## Types of Jurisdiction

Still more must be said on this quite complex matter of federal court jurisdiction. The federal courts exercise both *exclusive* and *concurrent* jurisdiction and, also, original and appellate jurisdiction.

**Exclusive and Concurrent Jurisdiction** Most of the cases that can be heard in the federal courts fall within their exclusive jurisdiction. That is, they can be tried *only* in the federal courts. Thus, a case involving an ambassador or some other official of a foreign government cannot be heard in a State court; it *must* be tried in a federal court. The trial of a person charged with a federal crime, or a suit involving the infringement of a patent or a copyright, or one involving any other matter arising out of an act of Congress is also within the exclusive (sole) jurisdiction of the federal courts.

Some cases may be tried in either a federal *or* a State court. Then, the federal and State courts have **concurrent jurisdiction,** meaning they share the power to hear these cases. Disputes involving citizens of different States are fairly common examples of this type of case. Such cases are known in the law as cases in diverse citizenship.[3]

Congress has provided that a federal district court may hear a case of diverse citizenship only when the amount of money

---

[3] Congress first gave the federal courts concurrent jurisdiction in these cases in 1789, out of a perceived need for a neutral forum to settle disputes between residents of different States. Early on, it was feared that State courts (and their juries) might be prejudiced against "foreigners," people from other States. There seems little likelihood of such bias today.

---

# Background

**FEDERAL CRIMES** The federal courts hear cases concerning federal crimes. The Constitution gives the National Government the authority to punish certain crimes, such as counterfeiting, crimes committed on the high seas, and treason. "The Congress shall have Power . . . To provide for the Punishment of counterfeiting; . . . To define and punish Piracies and Felonies committed on the high Seas. . . ." (Article I, Section 8). "The Congress shall have Power to declare the Punishment of Treason. . . ." (Article III, Section 3). The authority of the National Government to punish other crimes is implied from enumerated powers. For example, the Constitution grants Congress the power to establish post offices (Article I, Section 8). Implied in this power is the authority to prosecute mail fraud.

## Types of Jurisdiction

# Which Court?

Two separate court systems, federal and State, hear and decide cases in the United States. Their jurisdictions and examples of types of cases that would be heard in each are shown in this Venn diagram. **How does the structure of this illustrated diagram explain the types of jurisdictions?**

**GOVERNMENT** ONLINE
For **interactive** scenarios, visit
PearsonSchool.com/phgovt

**Scenario:**
**Citizen X of Michigan** sues **Citizen Y of Massachusetts** for $80,000 in damages caused as a result of a car accident.

**Jurisdiction: Concurrent**

**Why?** When a citizen from one State sues a citizen of another State for damages greater than $75,000, the case can be heard in either a federal or a State court.

**Scenario:**
**Citizen M** robs a bank in California.

**Jurisdiction: Federal**

**Why?** Bank robbery violates a federal law, regardless of the State in which the crime is committed.

**Scenario:**
**Citizen Z of Ohio** has her car repaired at AJ's, the local repair shop. Her car breaks down on her way home. She sues the repair shop for breach of contract.

**Jurisdiction: State**

**Why?** This is a purely local matter. Nothing in the facts of the case support federal court jurisdiction.

---

involved in that case is at least $75,000. In such a case, the **plaintiff**—the person who files the suit—may bring the case in the proper State or federal court, as he or she chooses. If the plaintiff brings the case in a State court, the **defendant**—the person against whom the complaint is made—can have the trial moved, under certain circumstances, to the federal district court.

**Original and Appellate Jurisdiction** A court in which a case is first heard is said to have **original jurisdiction** over that case. That court, the trial court, is often described as "the court of first instance." A court that hears a case on appeal from a lower court exercises **appellate jurisdiction** over that case.

Appellate courts do not retry cases. Rather, they determine whether a trial court

has acted in accord with applicable law. The higher court—the appellate court—may uphold, overrule, or in some way modify the decision appealed from the lower court.[4]

In the federal judiciary, the district courts have only original jurisdiction, and the courts of appeals have only appellate jurisdiction. The Supreme Court exercises both original and (most often) appellate jurisdiction.

## Federal Judges

The manner in which federal judges are chosen, the terms for which they serve, and even the salaries they are paid are vital parts of the Constitution's design of an independent

[4] Appellate comes from the Latin word *appellare*, meaning "to speak to, to call upon, to appeal to."

---

Tell students to go to the Interactivity for scenarios about types of jurisdiction.

### DEFINE *JURISDICTION*

Have a student find the meaning of *jurisdiction* in the textbook (the authority of a court to hear a case; literally, the power to "say the law"). Ask another student to look up the word in the dictionary for additional meanings. (the authority of a sovereign power to govern or legislate; the power or right to exercise authority or control; the limits or territory within which authority may be exercised)

**L2 Differentiate** Ask students to provide samples of various jurisdictions outside the realm of the courts. For example, what are the jurisdictions of the principal and assistant principal? (*One may handle issues of truancy and failing grades; the other may handle issues of discipline.*) How far does the jurisdiction of coastal countries extend into the ocean or sea? (*Many countries claim the waters 200 nautical miles from their coasts as exclusive economic zones.*)

### CHART FEDERAL COURT JURISDICTION

On the board, draw a T-chart like the one below. Have students copy the T-chart in their notebooks and work in pairs to fill in the information on both sides of the T.

| Federal Court Jurisdiction | |
|---|---|
| Exclusive jurisdiction (definition) | Subject Matter |
| | Parties Involved |
| Concurrent jurisdiction (definition) | Types of cases |
| Original jurisdiction (definition) | Which federal courts have? |
| Appellate jurisdiction (definition) | Which federal courts have? |

**L2 Differentiate** Model note-taking skills by asking volunteers to write the information on the board.

---

# Constitutional Principles

**SEPARATION OF POWERS** In *The Federalist* No. 78, Alexander Hamilton discussed the importance of offering life tenure for judges. Besides enabling justices to remain independent of legislative and executive intrigue, life tenure was needed to attract qualified attorneys: " . . . [I]t will readily be conceived from the variety of controversies which grow out of the folly and wickedness of mankind, that the records of . . . precedents [and rules] must unavoidably swell to a very considerable bulk, and must demand long and laborious study to acquire a competent knowledge of them. Hence it is, that there can be but few men in the society who will have sufficient skill in the laws to qualify them for the stations of judges. . . . [A] temporary duration in office . . . would naturally discourage such characters from quitting a lucrative line of practice to accept a seat on the bench. . . ."

## Answers

**Which Court?** In some areas, federal and State jurisdiction are distinct, whereas in other areas they overlap.

## DISTRIBUTE CORE WORKSHEET

Distribute the Chapter 18 Section 1 Core Worksheet (Unit 5 All-in-One, p. 17). Have students work in pairs to complete the Venn diagram by identifying federal, State, and concurrent jurisdiction, and then to answer the Reflection Questions. After the worksheets are finished, discuss why each dispute or case had its particular jurisdiction.

**L2 L3 ELL Differentiate** For these students, distribute the adapted Core Worksheet (Unit 5 All-in-One, p. 18).

**L4 Differentiate** Ask students to research current cases in the news and determine which court(s) would hear the cases, and why.

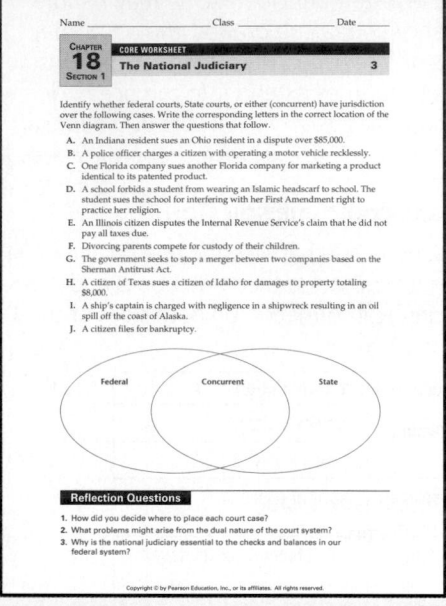

### WRITE A CLASSIFIED AD FOR A JUSTICE

Have students study samples of newspaper job ads, especially the wording of the skills required of applicants. Then ask students to write their own ads for the position of Supreme Court justice. Although the Constitution lists no formal requirements, students should list the skills and experience they believe justices should have. The ads should also list pay and other benefits. Students should provide "applicants" with information on the judicial selection process and why the presidential nomination/Senate approval process is a form of checks and balances.

## Answers

**Checkpoint** the Senate, especially influential senators from the nominee's home State and members of the Senate Judiciary Committee; the President's closest legal and political aides, especially the Attorney General; interest groups

---

judicial branch. The Constitution declares that the President

> ### FROM THE CONSTITUTION
>
> **shall nominate, and by and with the Advice and Consent of the Senate, shall appoint . . . Judges of the supreme Court . . .**
>
> –Article II, Section 2, Clause 2

First, in the Judiciary Act of 1789, and ever since, Congress has provided the same procedure for the selection of all federal judges.

**jurist**
*n.* an expert in the law, especially a judge or legal scholar

**Selection of Judges** The Senate has a major part in the selection of every federal judge. In effect, the Constitution says that the President can name to the federal bench anyone whom the Senate will confirm. Recall the practice of senatorial courtesy. It gives great weight to the wishes of the senators from a State in which a federal judge is to serve. In short, that unwritten rule means that the President almost always selects someone the senators from that State recommend.

The Constitution sets no age, residence, or citizenship requirements for federal judges. Nor does it require that a judge have a professional background in the law.

The President's closest legal and political aides, especially the Attorney General, take the lead in selecting federal judges. Influential senators—especially those from the nominee's home State and members of the Judiciary Committee, the President's allies and supporters in the legal profession, and various other personalities in the President's political party also play a major role in selecting judges. Several interest groups are also quite interested in the process.

**premise**
*n.* reason that forms the basis of an argument or conclusion

Today, an increasing number of those persons who are appointed to the federal bench have had prior judicial experience. Most federal judges are drawn from the ranks of leading attorneys, legal scholars and law school professors, former members of Congress, and State court judges. Elective office (in particular, a seat in the U.S. Senate) was once a well-traveled path to the Supreme Court; now, most justices reach the High Court from the courts of appeals.

To this point (2011), only four of the now 112 Supreme Court justices have been women: Sandra Day O'Connor was the first, appointed in 1981. The other three now sit on the Court: Ruth Bader Ginsburg (1993), Sonia Sotomayor (2009), and Elena Kagan (2010). Justice Sotomayor is also the Court's first Hispanic member. Only two African Americans have thus far become justices: Thurgood Marshall (appointed in 1967) and Clarence Thomas (1991).

From George Washington's day, Presidents have looked to their own political party to fill judgeships. Republican Presidents consistently choose Republicans; Democrats usually pick Democrats. Every President knows that judges may serve for decades. So chief executives regularly look for jurists who tend to agree with their own views.

**The Impact of Judicial Philosophy** Another major impact on the judicial selection process is judicial philosophy—in particular, the concepts of judicial restraint and judicial activism. All federal judges make decisions in which they must interpret and apply provisions in the Constitution and acts of Congress. That is, they often decide questions of public policy—and, in doing so, they inevitably *shape* public policy.

The proponents of **judicial restraint** believe that judges should decide cases on the basis of (1) the original intent of the Framers or those who enacted the statute(s) involved in a case, and (2) **precedent**—a judicial decision that serves as a guide for settling later cases of a similar nature. They say that the courts should defer to policy judgments made in the legislative and executive branches of the government and, in so doing, honor the basic premise of self-government: the right of the majority to determine public policy. In short, they argue that elected legislators, not appointed judges, should make law.

Those who support **judicial activism** take a much broader view of judicial power. They argue that provisions in the Constitution and in statute law should be interpreted and applied in the light of ongoing changes in conditions and values—especially in cases involving civil rights and social welfare issues. They,

## Background

**SWING VOTE** When Ronald Reagan, a conservative President, appointed Sandra Day O'Connor to the Supreme Court in 1981, most observers expected her to act according to judicial restraint, the more conservative philosophy. Instead, she emerged as a moderate voice on a sharply divided Court. Often during her 24-year tenure, she served as the "swing vote"—casting the deciding vote in 5–4 decisions on many controversial issues. She used her strategic role as swing vote to moderate the extreme positions of other justices. For example, she helped to limit the right to abortion, yet she also blocked attempts by more conservative justices to overturn that right altogether. When Justice O'Connor announced her retirement in 2005, President George W. Bush nominated Samuel Alito, a conservative, to replace her.

too, insist on the fundamental importance of majority rule and the value of precedents, but they believe that the courts should not be overly <u>deferential</u> to existing legal principles or to the judgments of elected officials.

**Terms and Pay of Judges** Article III, Section 1 of the Constitution reads, in part: "The Judges, both of the supreme and inferior Courts, shall hold their Offices during good Behaviour. . . ." This means that the judges of the constitutional courts are appointed for life; they serve until they resign, retire, or die in office. The Framers provided for what amounts to life tenure for these judges quite purposefully, to ensure the independence of the federal judiciary.

The very next words of the Constitution are directed to that same purpose. Article III, Section 1 continues: "and [they] shall, at stated Times, receive for their Services, a Compensation, which shall not be diminished during their Continuance in Office."

Federal judges may be removed from office only through the impeachment process. In 180 years, only 15 have ever been impeached. Of that number, seven were convicted and removed by the Senate, including three in the recent past.[5]

Those judges who sit in the special courts are not appointed for life. They are named, instead, to terms of 8 to 15 years—and may be, but seldom are, reappointed. In the District of Columbia, Superior Court judges are chosen for four-year terms; those who sit on the district's Court of Appeals are chosen for a period of eight years.

Congress sets the salaries of federal judges and has provided a generous retirement for

[5] The judges removed from office were John Pickering of the district court in NH, for judicial misconduct and drunkenness (1804); West H. Humphreys of the district court in TN, for disloyalty (1862); Robert W. Archbald of the old Commerce Court, for improper relations with litigants (1913); Halsted L. Ritter of the district court in FL, on several counts of judicial misconduct (1936); Harry E. Claiborne of the district court in NV for filing false income tax returns (1986); Alcee Hastings of the district court in FL, on charges of bribery and false testimony (1989); and Walter Nixon of the district court in MS, for perjury (1989). Four other federal judges were impeached by the House but acquitted by the Senate. Three district court judges, impeached by the House, resigned and so avoided a Senate trial. And the Senate vote is pending in the case of Louisiana district judge Thomas Porteous, impeached in early 2010.

✔ **Checkpoint**
How do the terms of office differ for judges of the constitutional courts and the special courts?

**deferential**
*adj.* respectful

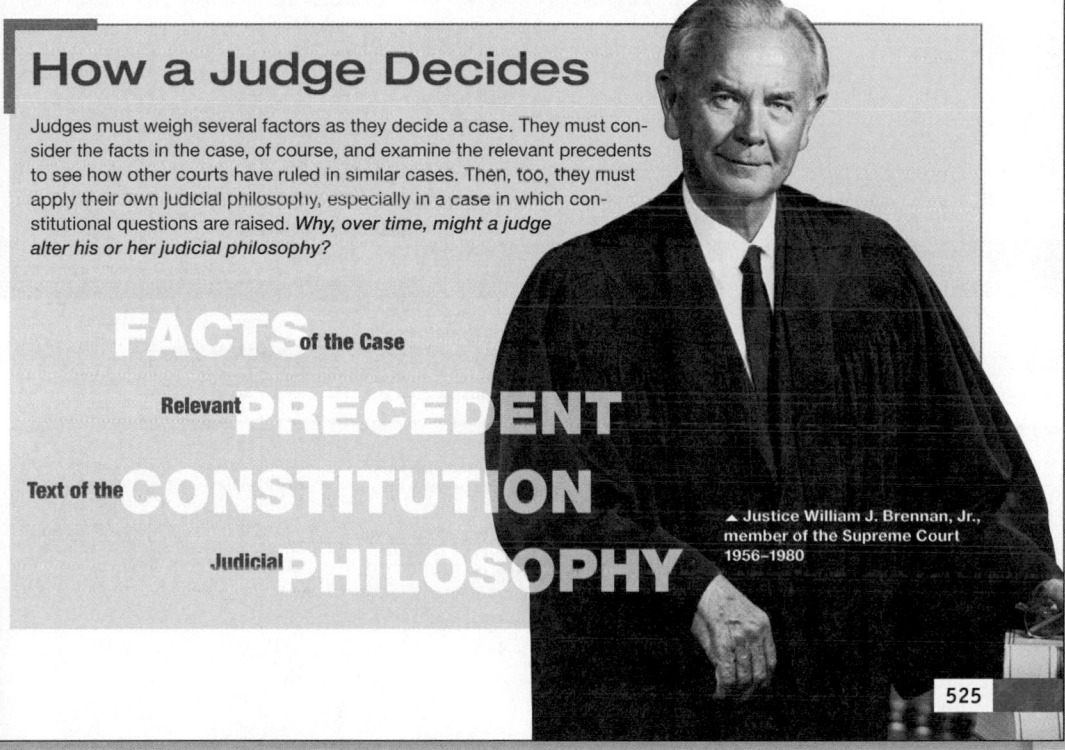

# How a Judge Decides

Judges must weigh several factors as they decide a case. They must consider the facts in the case, of course, and examine the relevant precedents to see how other courts have ruled in similar cases. Then, too, they must apply their own judicial philosophy, especially in a case in which constitutional questions are raised. *Why, over time, might a judge alter his or her judicial philosophy?*

FACTS of the Case

Relevant PRECEDENT

Text of the CONSTITUTION

Judicial PHILOSOPHY

▲ Justice William J. Brennan, Jr., member of the Supreme Court 1956–1980

525

# Political Cartoon Mini-Lesson

Transparency 18C features a political cartoon about filling a vacancy on the Supreme Court. Display the transparency as you discuss the selection of judges with the class. Ask: **What is the subject of this cartoon?** (*filling a vacancy on the Supreme Court*) **Whom does the person speaking represent? How do you know?** (*the President; because the President has the power to appoint someone to fill a vacancy on the Court*) **What is the cartoonist saying will happen?** (*The President will appoint a conservative judge from the "right" to fill the vacancy.*) **What is the impact of the President's power to appoint judges?** (*The power to appoint judges enables the President to influence the philosophical direction of the Court, and thereby steer public policy toward the President's views.*)

**EXTEND THE LESSON**

**L3** **L4** **Differentiate** Have students read the article "Chief Justice Urges Pay Raise for Judges" on the Chapter 18 Section 1 Extend Worksheet (Unit 5 All in-One, p. 20). After answering the questions, have students debate a pay raise for federal judges, with half the class supporting and half the class opposing an increase.

**L1** **L2** **Differentiate** Pair students who have written expression difficulties with study partners to complete the Chapter 18 Section 1 Extend Activity, "Your Role in the Legal System" (Unit 5 All-in-One, p. 22).

**L4** **Differentiate** Have students reread this section's Guiding Question and then the chapter's Essential Question. Point out that the structure of the national judiciary could *not* function effectively without the thousands of court officers who perform administrative duties, which allows federal judges to preside over cases. Have students select one of the court officers discussed later in this section, or distribute slips of paper with each identifying one officer. Tell students to research their chosen or assigned officer, including required education, the duties and terms of the job, which federal court they work for (if specific), and the pay. Then have students state their findings and have the rest of the class guess which court officer is being described.

## Answers

**Checkpoint** Judges of the constitutional courts are appointed for life terms, serving until they resign, retire, or die in office. Judges of the special courts are appointed for 8- to 15-year terms.

**How a Judge Decides** A judge may change his or her philosophy because new cases may require a reinterpretation of the Constitution.

# Assess and Remediate

**L3** Have students draw a graphic organizer or other visual that shows the checks and balances the judicial branch has over the executive and legislative branches, and vice versa. Assess students' participation using the Rubric for Assessing a Graph, Chart, or Table (Unit 5 All-in-One, p. 240).

**L3** Assign the Section 1 Assessment questions.

**L3** Section Quiz A (Unit 5 All-in-One, p. 23)

**L2** Section Quiz B (Unit 5 All-in-One, p. 24)

Have students complete the review activities in the digital lesson presentation and continue their work in the **Essential Questions Journal.**

## REMEDIATION

| If Your Students Have Trouble With | Strategies For Remediation |
|---|---|
| The structure and function of the federal judiciary (Questions 1, 6) | Have students make a tree diagram showing the structure of the federal court system. Within their diagrams, students should include the specific wording of the Constitution that grants each type its powers. |
| The jurisdiction of the federal courts (Questions 2, 4) | Have each student create a quiz describing ten scenarios in which someone breaks a federal or State law. Have students complete each other's quizzes by naming each case's jurisdiction. |
| Judicial philosophy (Questions 3, 5) | Organize students into groups and have them make a list of qualifications the President might consider when selecting a justice for the Supreme Court. Have the groups rank their list of items in order from most to least important, and then defend their rankings to the class. |

## Answers

**Checkpoint** U.S. Attorneys are the government's prosecutors, bringing to trial persons charged with federal crimes. They also represent the United States in all civil actions brought by or against the Federal Government in their districts.

---

them. They may retire at age 70, and if they have served for at least 10 years, receive full salary for the rest of their lives. Or, they may retire at full salary at age 65, after at least 15 years of service. The Chief Justice may call any retired judge back to temporary duty in a lower federal court at any time.

## Court Officers

Today, federal judges have little involvement in the day-to-day administrative operations of the courts over which they preside. Their primary mission is to hear and decide cases. A clerk, several deputy clerks, bailiffs, court reporters and stenographers, probation officers, and others provide support services.

The judges of each of the 94 district courts appoint one or more United States magistrates, of which there are now more than 400. They are appointed to eight-year terms and handle a number of legal matters once dealt with by the judges themselves. They issue warrants of arrest, and often hear evidence to decide whether or not a person who has been arrested on a federal charge should be held for action by a grand jury. They also set bail in federal criminal cases, and even have the power to try those who are charged with certain minor offenses.

Each federal judicial district also has at least one bankruptcy judge. These judges handle bankruptcy cases under the direction of the district court to which they are assigned.[6] There are now some 300 bankruptcy judges, all of them appointed to 14-year terms by the judges of each federal court of appeals.

The President and the Senate appoint a United States Attorney for each federal judicial district. The U.S. Attorneys and their many deputies are the government's prosecutors. They work closely with the FBI and other law enforcement agencies, and they bring to trial those persons charged with federal crimes. They also represent the United States in all civil actions brought by or against the Federal Government in their districts.

The President and Senate also select a United States marshal to serve each of the district courts. These marshals, and their several deputy U.S. marshals, perform duties much like those of a county sheriff. They make arrests in federal criminal cases, hold accused persons in custody, secure jurors, serve legal papers, keep order in courtrooms, and execute court orders and decisions. They also respond to such emergency situations as riots, mob violence, and other civil disturbances, as well as terrorist incidents. All United States Attorneys and marshals are appointed to four-year terms.

---

6 Recall that bankruptcy is a legal proceeding in which a debtor's assets are distributed among those to whom the bankrupt person, business, or other organization owes money. Although some bankruptcy cases are heard in State courts, nearly all of them fall within the jurisdiction of the federal district courts.

---

**Essential Questions Journal** To continue to build a response to the chapter Essential Question, go to your **Essential Questions Journal.**

## SECTION 1 ASSESSMENT

1. **Guiding Question** Use your completed graphic organizer to answer this question: What are the structure and function of the national judiciary?

**Key Terms and Comprehension**

2. (a) What is the difference between **original jurisdiction** and **appellate jurisdiction**? (b) What kind of jurisdiction does the Supreme Court have?

3. (a) What is a **precedent**? (b) Write a sentence using the word **precedent**

to illustrate why it is important in the judicial system.

4. Under what circumstances do federal courts have **jurisdiction** in a case?

**Critical Thinking**

5. **Demonstrate Reasoned Judgment** What role should judicial philosophy play in the selection of judges?

6. **Predict Consequences** What do you think are the consequences of life tenure for federal judges?

### Quick Write

**Explanatory Essay: Choose a Topic** Do preliminary research online or at the library to choose one of the following Supreme Court cases: *South Carolina* v. *United States*, 1905; *Brandenburg* v. *Ohio*, 1969; or *City of Boerne* v. *Flores*, 1997. Then write a paragraph to summarize the case you chose. Include details such as who, what, when, where, and why.

---

# Assessment Answers

**1. Structure:** more than 100 courts nationwide; Supreme Court at top; inferior courts include constitutional courts and special courts. **Function:** Supreme Court and other constitutional courts exercise broad "judicial Power of the United States"; special courts hear cases arising out of expressed powers given to Congress in Article I.

**2.** (a) **original jurisdiction:** held by court in which a case is first heard; **appellate jurisdiction:** held by the court that hears a case on appeal from lower court (b) both

**3.** (a) judicial decision that serves as a guide for justices to follow in similar cases (b) Judges look at precedents to see how courts have ruled in the past.

**4.** if the case involves an interpretation of the Constitution or federal statute or treaty, or relates to admiralty or maritime law; if one of the parties is: the United States or one of its officers or agencies; a foreign government or official; a State if it is suing another State, a citizen of another State, or a foreign government or subject; a citizen of one State suing a citizen of another

State; a U.S. citizen suing a foreign government or subject; citizens of the same State if both claim land under grants from different States

**5.** A President is apt to choose nominees who agree with his or her view of strict v. liberal construction of the Constitution.

**6.** ensures judiciary independence and allows judges to make decisions without fear of political reprisals

**QUICK WRITE** A strong assignment will show evidence of research and answers to the questions of who, what, when, where, and why.

# Judicial Restraint vs. Activism

## ▶ Track the Issue

**The Court's power** of judicial review has long been an important part of the governing process in this country. But from *Marbury* on, this question has been the subject of intense debate: What is the appropriate role for the Supreme Court? Throughout its history, it has exercised both judicial restraint and judicial activism.

### 1819

In *McCulloch* v. *Maryland,* the Court exercised judicial activism, expanding constitutional provisions without citing precedent.

### 1849

The Court's decision in *Luther* v. *Borden* is one of the earliest cases of judicial restraint.

### 1954

The decision in *Brown* v. *Board of Education* provides a major example of judicial activism.

### 1969–1986

The Burger Court exercised a combination of judicial restraint and activism.

### Today

Although extremely conservative, the Roberts Court has been far more judicially active than restrained in its decisions to this point.

Chief Justice John Roberts ▶

## ▶▶ Perspectives

**There are two camps in the debate** over judicial decision making. One side supports judicial restraint; its proponents believe that judges should consistently follow the letter of the law and apply precedent. The other supports judicial activism; its proponents think that judges should indeed consider precedent, but that they should also be willing to go further and play an active, creative role in the shaping of public policies. Time has proven that rarely can the Court exercise but one method of decision making. How might you describe the Court today?

"In our democratic system, responsibility for policy making properly rests with those branches that are responsible . . . to the people. It was . . . because the Framers intended the judiciary to be insulated from popular political pressures that the Constitution accords judges tenure during good behavior. . . . To the extent the term "judicial activism" is used to describe unjustified intrusions by the judiciary into the realm of policy making, the criticism is well-founded. . . . It is not part of the judicial function to make the law . . . or to execute the law."
—**John Roberts** at his Senate confirmation hearing, 2005

"We are under a Constitution, but the Constitution is what the judges say it is, and the judiciary is the safeguard of our liberty and of our property under the Constitution."
—*Charles Evan Hughes, Chief Justice of the United States 1930–1941*

## ▶▶ Connect to Your World

1. **Understand (a)** What reasons does Justice Roberts cite for supporting judicial restraint? **(b)** How does Justice Hughes support his argument for judicial activism?
2. **Synthesize Information** To which of these competing positions—judicial restraint or judicial activism—do you think a judge should subscribe?

**GOVERNMENT** ONLINE
**In the News**
To find out more about judicial decision making, visit
**PearsonSchool.com/phgovt**

527

## Background

***LUTHER* v. *BORDEN*** In 1841, Rhode Island was still ruled by a charter government with limited suffrage. Opposing groups held a convention, which drafted a new constitution and elected a governor. The existing charter government opposed the new government, however, and declared martial law. One of the dissidents brought suit, claiming the old government was not "a republican form of government" and was therefore invalid. In *Luther* v. *Borden,* 1849, the Supreme Court held that federal courts had no jurisdiction over the establishment of State governments: "The Constitution of the United States has . . . placed the power of recognizing a State government in the hands of Congress. . . ."

---

## LESSON GOAL

• Students will contrast the "restraint" and "activism" roles of the Supreme Court.

## Teach

### DEFINE TERMS

Have students provide synonyms for *restraint* (limit, restrict, curb, self-control) and *activism* (to change, innovate, create, revise).

### DISTINGUISH ACTIVISM AND RESTRAINT

Ask: **What types of Supreme Court decisions would show judicial restraint?** *(upholding a State law or a lower court's decision; following precedent; refusal to rule on a case, claiming it is the jurisdiction of the State or another branch of government)* **What decisions of the Court would show judicial activism?** *(changing a previous Supreme Court ruling; overturning a lower court's decision; halting or requiring legislative, executive, and/or State action)*

### CLASSIFY COURT CASES

Have students classify the following cases as judicial restraint or judicial activism.

• The Court upholds laws requiring racially segregated facilities, *Plessy* v. *Ferguson,* 1896. [restraint]
• The Court declares that freedom of speech and press cannot be denied by either the National Government or State governments, *Gitlow* v. *New York,* 1925. [activism]

## Assess and Remediate

Have students answer the Connect to Your World questions. For further clarification, discuss why the *McCulloch* and *Brown* cases are considered activism, and the *Luther* case (see background note) is considered restraint.

---

## Answers

### CONNECT TO YOUR WORLD

1. (a) Policymaking rests with branches that are responsible to the people (legislative and executive). It is not part of the judicial function to make or execute the law. (b) Hughes states that judges say what the Constitution is.
2. A strong answer will provide supportive statements of an opinion either for or against restraint or activism.

## What are the structure and jurisdiction of the inferior courts?

| The Inferior Courts | |
| --- | --- |
| **Structure** | **Jurisdiction** |
| • District courts | • Original jurisdiction |
| • Courts of appeals | • Appellate jurisdiction within circuit |
| • Court of International Trade | • Original jurisdiction on trade issues |

# Get Started

## LESSON GOALS

Students will . . .

- identify the structure of the inferior constitutional courts by completing a chart highlighting the various courts and their jurisdictions.
- understand how inferior constitutional courts function by constructing paths of appeals for various case scenarios.

## BEFORE CLASS

Assign the section, the graphic organizer in the text, and Reading Comprehension Worksheet (Unit 5 All-in-One, p. 25) before class.

**L2 Differentiate** Reading Comprehension Worksheet (Unit 5 All-in-One, p. 26)

## BELLRINGER

Write the following on the board, and have students answer the questions in their notebooks: **The DA obtained an indictment from the grand jury today in *Joe Smith* v. *United States*. What type of court is hearing this case? How do you know? Is this a criminal case or a civil case?**

# SKILLS DEVELOPMENT

## GIVE A MULTIMEDIA PRESENTATION

Before students turn their Core Worksheet cases into classroom skits, you may want to review tips on giving a multimedia presentation in the Skills Handbook, p. S21.

---

## SECTION 2

# The **Inferior Courts**

### Guiding Question

**What are the structure and jurisdiction of the inferior courts?** Use a table like the one below to take notes on the structure and jurisdiction of the inferior courts.

| The Inferior Courts | |
| --- | --- |
| **Structure** | **Jurisdiction** |
| • | • |
| • | • |
| • | • |

### Political Dictionary

- criminal case
- civil case
- docket
- record

### Objectives

1. Describe the structure and jurisdiction of the federal district courts.
2. Describe the structure and jurisdiction of the federal courts of appeals.
3. Describe the structure and jurisdiction of the two other constitutional courts.

**Image Above:** An attorney for Napster, Inc., the online music firm, outside the 9th Circuit Court of Appeals

**Y**ou know that the particular meaning of a word often depends on the context—the setting—in which it is used. Thus, *pitch* can be either a baseball term or a musical term; it can also refer to setting up a tent or to a high-pressure sales talk. The word *inferior* also has various meanings. Here, it describes the lower federal courts, those courts created by act of Congress to function beneath the Supreme Court. The inferior courts handle nearly all of the cases tried in the federal courts.

## The District Courts

The United States district courts are the federal trial courts. Their 667 judges handle more than 300,000 cases per year, about 80 percent of the federal caseload. The district courts were first created by Congress in the Judiciary Act of 1789. There are now 94 of them.

**Federal Judicial Districts** The 50 States are divided into 89 federal judicial districts, and there are also federal district courts for Washington, D.C., Puerto Rico, the Virgin Islands, Guam, and the Northern Mariana Islands. Each State forms at least one judicial district. Some are divided into two or more districts, however—usually because of the larger amount of judicial business there. At least two judges are assigned to each district, but many districts have several. Thus, New York is divided into four judicial districts; one of them, the United States Judicial District for Southern New York, now has 44 judges.

Cases tried in the district courts are most often heard by a single judge. However, certain cases may be heard by a three-judge panel. Chiefly, these are cases that involve congressional districting or State legislative apportionment questions; those arising under the Civil Rights Act of 1964 or the Voting Rights Acts of 1965, 1970, 1975, and 1982; and certain antitrust actions.

Two little-known multi-judge panels—made up entirely of judges drawn from the district courts—play a key role in ongoing efforts to combat terrorism in this country and abroad. Both are shrouded in secrecy. One is the Foreign Intelligence Surveillance Court, created by Congress in 1978. It is often called the "FISA court" and is composed of 11 federal district court judges, who are appointed to seven-year terms by the Chief Justice of

# Focus on the Basics

**FACTS:** • The 94 U.S. district courts have original jurisdiction over most federal criminal and civil cases. • The 12 federal courts of appeals hear cases on appeal within their circuit. • The Court of Appeals for the Federal Circuit has nationwide appellate jurisdiction. • The Court of International Trade hears tariff and trade cases.

**CONCEPTS:** federalism, role of the judiciary

**ENDURING UNDERSTANDINGS:** • Civil and criminal laws are put in place to provide order, protect society, and settle conflicts. • Law officers have the duty to enforce the laws, and courts have the duty to interpret the law and decide punishment for those found guilty of breaking the laws. • The inferior constitutional courts form the core of the federal judicial system, hearing nearly all of the cases tried in federal courts.

the United States. The court, which meets in secret, has the power to issue secret search warrants—court orders that allow the FBI and other federal law enforcement agencies to conduct covert surveillance of persons suspected of being spies or members of terrorist organizations.

The other is the Alien Terrorist Removal Court, created by Congress in 1996. It is made up of five district court judges, appointed by the Chief Justice to five-year terms. This court has the power to decide whether those persons identified as "alien terrorists" by the Attorney General of the United States should be expelled from this country.

**District Court Jurisdiction** The district courts have original jurisdiction over more than 80 percent of the cases that are heard in the federal court system. The only federal cases that do not begin in the district courts are those few that fall within the original

jurisdiction of the Supreme Court and those cases heard by the Court of International Trade or by one of the special courts. Thus, the district courts are the principal trial courts, the "courts of first instance," in the federal judiciary.

District court judges hear a wide range of both criminal cases and civil cases. In the federal courts, a **criminal case** is one in which a defendant is tried for committing some action that Congress has declared by law to be a federal crime. A federal **civil case** involves some noncriminal matter—say, a dispute over the terms of a contract or a suit in which the plaintiff seeks damages (money) for some harm done by the defendant.

The United States is always a party to a federal criminal case, as the prosecutor. Most civil cases are disputes between private parties, but here, too, the United States may be a <u>litigant</u>, as either the plaintiff or the defendant.

✔ **Checkpoint**
What is the principal role of the federal district courts?

**litigant**
*n.* party to a case, either plaintiff or defendant

## Federal Court Circuits and Districts

**GOVERNMENT ONLINE**
**Audio Tour**
Listen to a guided audio tour of the map at **PearsonSchool.com/phgovt**

▸▸ **Interpreting Maps** Each State comprises at least one United States judicial district. The nation is divided into 13 judicial circuits, including the Court of Appeals for the District of Columbia and the Court of Appeals for the Federal Circuit, as shown on the map. *Which States are in the Fifth Circuit?*

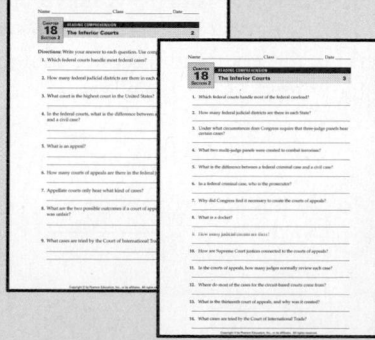

SOURCE: www.uscourts.gov

KEY
1 Judicial Circuit
District Court boundaries
C, E, M, N, S, W central, eastern, middle, northern, southern, western districts

## Differentiated Resources

The following resources are located in the All-in-One, Unit 5, Chapter 18, Section 2:

- **L3** Reading Comprehension Worksheet (p. 25)
- **L2** Reading Comprehension Worksheet (p. 26)
- **L3** Core Worksheet (p. 27)
- **L2** Extend Activity (p. 28)
- **L3** Quiz A (p. 29)
- **L2** Quiz B (p. 30)

# Teach

To present this topic using online resources, use the lesson presentations at **PearsonSchool.com/phgovt**.

### REVIEW BELLRINGER ANSWERS

Discuss students' answers to the Bellringer: What type of court is hearing this case? *(a U.S. district court)* Is this a criminal case or a civil case? *(It is probably a criminal case, because the U.S. is always a party in federal criminal cases. However, the U.S. also may be a litigant in a civil case, so the case could be either.)*

### CHART INFERIOR CONSTITUTIONAL COURTS

Refer students back to the Section 1 diagram "Types of Federal Courts" or display Transparency 18B. Ask a volunteer to identify the inferior constitutional courts shown in the diagram. *(district courts, courts of appeals, Court of Appeals for the Federal Circuit, U.S. Court of International Trade)* Draw a chart on the board like the one below. Have students work in pairs to complete the columns. Then discuss the chart.

| Name of Court (and Number) | No. of Judges on Each | Type of Jurisdiction |
|---|---|---|
| District courts (94) | 2–28 | *Federal trial courts; original jurisdiction over more than 80 percent of federal criminal and civil cases* |
| Courts of Appeals (12) | 6–28 (plus a Supreme Court justice assigned to each circuit) | *Appellate jurisdiction over the district courts within their circuit; also hear appeals from U.S. Tax Court, territorial courts, and federal regulatory agencies* |
| Court of Appeals for the Federal Circuit | 12 | *Nationwide appellate jurisdiction over Court of International Trade, Court of Federal Claims, Court of Appeals for Veterans Claims, and patent or copyright appeals from 94 district courts* |
| U.S. Court of International Trade | 9 | *Trial court; original jurisdiction over civil cases concerning customs and trade-related laws* |

### ANALYZE CIRCUITS AND DISTRICTS MAP

Have students look at the map "Federal Court Circuits and Districts" in their text or on Transparency 18D. Ask them to use the Chapter 18 Section 2 Extend Activity "The Federal District Courts in Your State" (Unit 5 All-in-One, p. 28) to identify their circuit and district.

**L3** **Differentiate** Ask students to research the names of their circuit and district judges, and to describe the cases they have ruled on recently.

Tell students to go to the Audio Tour for a guided audio tour of the Federal Court Circuits and Districts map.

## Answers

**Checkpoint** as federal trial courts

**Interpreting Maps** Texas, Louisiana, and Mississippi

Tell students to go to the Audio Tour for a guided audio tour of the appellate path.

**TRACE THE APPELLATE PATH**

Guide students through the appellate path. Display Transparency 18E, The Appellate Path in Federal Courts. Explain that students should focus only on the constitutional courts. Then present the cases below. Students should answer the questions and show where on the transparency each case would move in the appellate path.

**CASE A:** A citizen is accused of counterfeiting. Where does the case begin? *(district court)* What type of case is this? *(criminal case)* What is the first step in the case? *(indictment by a grand jury)* What is the next step? *(verdict by a petit jury)* Assuming the case is appealed, where would the case go next? *(court of appeals)*

**CASE B:** An American importer of fish claims that the U.S. Department of Commerce placed an unusually high tariff on fillets from Vietnam. Where does this case begin? *(U.S. Court of International Trade)* What type of case is this? *(civil case)* The case is lost by the American importer and then appealed. Where does the case go next? *(U.S. Court of Appeals for the Federal Circuit)*

**CASE C:** An Ohio company claims that a Florida company produced an identical product and files for copyright infringement. Where does the case begin? *(district court)* What type of case is this? *(civil case)* The Ohio company loses the case and appeals. Where does the case go next? *(U.S. Court of Appeals for the Federal Circuit)*

**DISTRIBUTE CORE WORKSHEET**

Distribute the Chapter 18 Section 2 Core Worksheet (Unit 5 All-in-One, p. 27). Students should work in groups to create a fictional federal case and its path of appeal to the Supreme Court. Then ask students to read the description of their cases aloud. Have the class identify the types of courts that should hear the case in its original and appellate forms.

**EXTEND THE LESSON**

**L3 Differentiate** Have students turn their fictional Core Worksheet cases into two courtroom skits. In the trial portion of the case, students should create roles for the plaintiffs, defendants, witnesses, attorneys, and judges. In the appeals portion of the case, speaking roles should be created only for attorneys and judges.

**L1 L2 Differentiate** For these students, distribute the Extend Activity entitled "The Federal District Courts in Your State" (Unit 5 All-in-One, p. 28).

---

**Answers**

**Interpreting Diagrams** possible answer: district courts and courts of appeals

---

## The Appellate Path in the Federal Courts

**GOVERNMENT** ONLINE
**Audio Tour**
Listen to a guided audio tour of the appellate path at PearsonSchool.com/phgovt

Supreme Court

Appeals from the Highest State Courts

U.S. Court of Appeals for the Armed Forces

Military Courts

U.S. Court of Appeals for the Federal Circuit

U.S. Court of International Trade

U.S. Court of Federal Claims

U.S. Court of Appeals for Veterans Claims

12 U.S. Courts of Appeals

Appeals from Federal Regulatory Agencies

94 District Courts

U.S. Tax Court

Territorial Courts

Courts of the District of Columbia

KEY TO COURTS
Constitutional Courts
Special Courts
Other Courts

▶▶ **Interpreting Diagrams** This diagram shows how cases originating in various courts can be appealed to the U.S. Supreme Court. *From what you have read, which two or three of the inferior courts do you think handle the largest number of cases in the federal judiciary?*

---

The district courts try criminal cases ranging from bank robbery, kidnapping, and mail fraud to counterfeiting, terrorism, and tax evasion. They hear civil cases arising under bankruptcy, postal, tax, public lands, civil rights, and other laws of the United States. These trial courts are the only federal courts that use grand juries to <u>indict</u> defendants, and petit juries to determine their guilt or innocence.

Most of the decisions made in the 94 federal district courts are final. That is, most federal cases not only begin in those courts, they end there as well. Losing parties do not often appeal a decision to a higher court. Still, a few cases are taken to the court of appeals in that judicial circuit or, in a few instances, directly to the Supreme Court.

**indict**
*v.* accuse, bring charges against

---

### The Courts of Appeals

The courts of appeals were created by Congress in 1891. They were established as "gate-keepers" to relieve the Supreme Court of much of the burden of hearing appeals from the decisions of the district courts. Those appeals had become so numerous that the High Court was more than three years behind its **docket**—its list of cases to be heard.

There are now 13 courts of appeals in the federal judiciary.[7] As the map on page 529 indicates, the country is divided into 12 judicial circuits, including the District of Columbia. There is one court of appeals for each of those circuits, and they hear cases on appeal from the various district courts within their circuit. The Court of Appeals for the Federal Circuit is the thirteenth of these appellate tribunals. It sits in the District of Columbia, but its jurisdiction is nationwide and it is mostly concerned with appeals of decisions in patent, copyright, and international trade cases.

---

7 These tribunals were originally called the circuit courts of appeals. Before 1891, each Supreme Court justice "rode circuit," hearing appeals from the district courts within that geographic area. Congress renamed these courts in 1948, but they still are often called the "circuit courts."

---

## Teacher-to-Teacher Network

**ALTERNATE LESSON PLAN** Hollywood has long been fascinated with courtroom drama. Have students watch a film you have prescreened, such as *To Kill a Mockingbird, Runaway Jury,* or *Twelve Angry Men.* Lead a discussion about whether students think the courtroom scenes they viewed appeared realistic. Did the movie seem true to what students have learned about the court system?

To see this lesson plan, go to

**Teacher Center**
at PearsonSchool.com/phgovt

**Appellate Court Judges** Each of these courts is composed of from 6 to 28 judges (179 in all). In addition, a justice of the Supreme Court is assigned to each. For example, the United States Court of Appeals for the Eleventh Circuit covers Alabama, Florida, and Georgia. The court is composed of 12 circuit judges and Associate Justice Clarence Thomas of the Supreme Court. The judges hold their sessions in a number of major cities within the circuit.

Each court of appeals usually sits in three-judge panels. Occasionally, however, and especially for an important case, a court will sit *en banc*—that is, with all of the judges on that court participating.

**Appellate Court Jurisdiction** The 13 courts of appeals have only appellate jurisdiction. For the 12 circuit-based courts, most cases come to them from the district courts within their circuit, but some are appealed from the Tax Court and some from the territorial courts. Recall, they are also empowered to hear appeals from the decisions of several federal regulatory agencies—for example, the Federal Trade Commission and the National Labor Relations Board.

Unlike the 12 circuit-based courts, the jurisdiction of the thirteenth, the Court of Appeals for the Federal Circuit, is nationwide in scope. Congress created it in 1982, with the special purpose of centralizing and speeding up the handling of appeals in certain types of federal civil cases.

The Court of Appeals for the Federal Circuit hears appeals from the decisions rendered in several different courts. Many of its cases come from the other constitutional court, the Court of International Trade, and still others come from two of the special courts: the Court of Federal Claims and the Court of Appeals for Veterans Claims. It also hears the appeals taken in any patent, copyright, or trademark case decided in any of the 94 federal district courts.

Again, these 13 tribunals are appellate courts. They do not conduct trials or accept new evidence in the cases they hear. Instead, they review the **record,** the transcript of proceedings made in the trial court, and they ponder the oral and written arguments (the briefs) submitted by attorneys representing parties to a case. The fact that less than one percent of their decisions are appealed to the Supreme Court underscores the importance of the place these tribunals occupy.

## Court of International Trade

Congress has established one other Article III court, the Court of International Trade. Often called the Trade Court, this body was originally created in 1890, and was restructured as a constitutional court in 1980.

The Trade Court now has nine judges, including its chief judge, appointed by the President and the Senate. Like the 94 district courts, it is a federal trial court, a court of first instance. It tries all civil (but not criminal) cases that arise out of the nation's customs and other trade-related laws. Its judges sit in panels of three and often hold jury trials in such major ports as New Orleans, San Francisco, Boston, and New York.

**✔ Checkpoint**
Which inferior court hears appeals related to patents and copyrights?

---

**Essential Questions Journal** To continue to build a response to the chapter Essential Question, go to your **Essential Questions Journal.**

---

## SECTION 2 ASSESSMENT

**1. Guiding Question** Use your completed graphic organizer to answer this question: What are the structure and jurisdiction of the inferior courts?

**Key Terms and Comprehension**

**2.** What is the difference between a **criminal case** and a **civil case?**

**3.** When and why were the courts of appeals created?

**Critical Thinking**

**4. Draw Conclusions** Why do you think so many of the courts in the federal judiciary are appellate courts?

**5. Predict Consequences** What do you think might be the consequences if Congress were to follow the lead of several States by reducing or eliminating the role of the grand jury in federal criminal cases?

**Quick Write**

**Explanatory Essay: Research the Topic** Research to gather more details on the Supreme Court case you chose in Section 1. Focus especially on the path the case took to reach the Supreme Court.

---

## Assess and Remediate

**L2** Have students re-create from memory the diagram "The Appellate Path in the Federal Courts," but with just the constitutional courts. Underneath each court, have students list examples of the types of cases heard in that court.

**L3** Collect the Core Worksheets and assess the students' class participation using the Rubric for Assessing Performance of an Entire Group (Unit 5 All-in-One, p. 241).

**L3** Assign the Section 2 Assessment questions.

**L3** Section Quiz A (Unit 5 All-in-One, p. 29)

**L2** Section Quiz B (Unit 5 All-in-One, p. 30)

Have students complete the review activities in the digital lesson presentation and continue their work in the **Essential Questions Journal.**

### REMEDIATION

| If Your Students Have Trouble With | Strategies For Remediation |
|---|---|
| The structure and functions of district courts (Questions 1, 2) | Have students draw a web diagram with "District Courts" in the center oval. In at least five outer ovals, students should list important characteristics about the structure and functions of district courts. |
| The structure and jurisdiction of appeals courts (Questions 3, 4, 5) | Have students make an appellate flowchart from the court of first instance to the Supreme Court for these scenarios: (1) a patent dispute; (2) an appeal from the Nuclear Regulatory Commission; (3) a federal civil case in New Mexico; (4) a federal criminal case tried in Guam; and (5) a U.S. citizen sues the federal government after her exporters' license is revoked. |

## Answers

**Checkpoint** Court of Appeals for the Federal Circuit

---

## Assessment Answers

**1.** 94 district courts with original jurisdiction in criminal and civil cases; 12 judicial circuits have their own courts of appeals with appellate jurisdiction; Court of Appeals for the Federal Circuit has nationwide appellate jurisdiction; Court of International Trade has original jurisdiction on all civil cases arising from the nation's customs and other trade-related issues

**2. criminal case:** one in which a person is tried for committing an illegal action; **civil case:** one that involves a noncriminal matter, such as a dispute between parties

**3.** in 1891; to relieve the overloaded Supreme Court docket of appeals from district courts

**4.** The U.S. judicial process includes many opportunities for decisions to be reviewed.

**5.** U.S. attorneys would have to file cases rather than grand juries being responsible for indictments. In addition, the constitutionality of such a move might be questioned.

**QUICK WRITE** A strong assignment will show evidence of additional research and details, including the constitutional grounds on which each side based its arguments, specific arguments each side presented, and the verdict/opinions of the courts.

## What is the Supreme Court's jurisdiction, and how does the Court operate?

I. The Supreme Court
  A. Judicial review
    1. Established in Marbury v. Madison, 1803
    2. Supreme Court may declare laws unconstitutional
  B. Jurisdiction
    1. original on cases involving States or public ministers
    2. appellate most common
  C. How cases reach Court
    1. writ of certiorari
    2. certificate
  D. How Court operates
    1. reviews briefs
    2. hears oral arguments
    3. meets in conference
    4. announces decision, with one or more written opinions

# Get Started

## LESSON GOALS

Students will . . .

- learn about the scope of the Supreme Court's jurisdiction by analyzing a political cartoon showing the power of judicial review, and by identifying the Court's original and appellate jurisdiction.

- identify how the Supreme Court operates by sequencing the appeals process, reading a transcript of a real case, and formulating opinions on controversial cases.

## SKILLS DEVELOPMENT

### DECISION MAKING

To practice decision making in this section, use the Chapter 18 Skills Worksheet (Unit 5 All-in-One, p. 41). You may teach the skills explicitly either before or after students work on Core Worksheet B. For L2 and L1 students, assign the adapted Skill Activity (Unit 5 All-in-One, p. 42).

---

SECTION 3

# The Supreme Court

## Guiding Question

**What is the Supreme Court's jurisdiction, and how does the Court operate?** Use an outline like the one below to take notes on the Supreme Court.

I. The Supreme Court
  A. Judicial review
    1. **Established in** *Marbury* v. *Madison,* 1803
    2. _____
  B. _____
    1. _____
    2. _____

## Political Dictionary

- writ of certiorari
- certificate
- brief
- majority opinion
- concurring opinion
- dissenting opinion

## Objectives

1. Define the concept of judicial review.
2. Outline the scope of the Supreme Court's jurisdiction.
3. Examine how cases reach the Supreme Court.
4. Summarize the way the Court operates.

**Image Above:** John Marshall, Chief Justice of the United States, 1801–1835

The eagle, the flag, Uncle Sam—you almost certainly recognize these symbols. They are used widely to represent the United States. You probably also know the symbol for justice: the blindfolded woman holding a balanced scale. She represents what is perhaps this nation's loftiest goal: equal justice under the law. Indeed, those words are chiseled in marble above the entrance to the Supreme Court building in Washington, D.C.

The Supreme Court of the United States is the only court specifically created by the Constitution, in Article III, Section 1. The Court is made up of the Chief Justice of the United States, whose office is also established by the Constitution,[8] and eight associate justices.[9]

The Framers quite purposely placed the Court on an equal plane with the President and Congress. As the highest court in the land, it stands as the court of last resort in all questions of federal law. That is, the Supreme Court of the United States is the final authority in any case involving any question arising under the Constitution, an act of Congress, or a treaty of the United States.

## Judicial Review

Remember, most courts in this country, both federal and State, may exercise the critically important power of judicial review. They have the extraordinary power to decide the constitutionality of an act of government, whether executive, legislative, or judicial. The ultimate exercise of that power rests with the Supreme Court of the United States. That single fact makes the Supreme Court the final authority on the meaning of the Constitution.

The Constitution does not, in so many words, provide for the power of judicial review. Nevertheless, there is little doubt that the Framers intended that the federal courts—and, in particular, the Supreme Court—should have this power.[10]

---

8 Article I, Section 3, Clause 6.
9 Congress sets the number of associate justices and thus the size of the Supreme Court. The Judiciary Act of 1789 created a Court of six justices, including the Chief Justice. The Court was reduced to five members in 1801 but increased to seven in 1807, to nine in 1837, and to 10 in 1863. It was reduced to seven in 1866 and increased to its present size of nine in 1869.
10 See Article III, Section 2, setting out the Court's jurisdiction, and Article VI, Section 2, the Supremacy Clause.

# Focus on the Basics

**FACTS:** • The Court first asserted its power of judicial review—the power to decide the constitutionality of an act of government—in *Marbury* v. *Madison.* • The Supreme Court is the only court created by the Constitution. • The Supreme Court has both original and appellate jurisdiction, but usually hears cases on appeal. • The Supreme Court studies written briefs; hears oral arguments; meets in conference to discuss the cases; and renders majority, concurring, and dissenting opinions.

**CONCEPTS:** federalism, judicial review, checks and balances

**ENDURING UNDERSTANDINGS:** • The Supreme Court is the final authority on questions arising under the Constitution, an act of Congress, or a treaty of the U.S. • The power of judicial review established in *Marbury* v. *Madison* laid the foundation for the judicial branch's key role in government.

**Marbury v. Madison** The Court first asserted its power of judicial review in *Marbury* v. *Madison* in 1803.[11] (See the Landmark Decisions of the Supreme Court feature, Chapter 3.) Recall that the case arose in the aftermath of the stormy elections of 1800. Thomas Jefferson had won the presidency and control of both houses of Congress. The outgoing Federalists, stung by their defeat, then tried to pack the judiciary with loyal party members. Congress created several new federal judgeships in the early weeks of 1801, and President John Adams quickly filled those posts with Federalists.

William Marbury had been appointed a justice of the peace for the District of Columbia. The Senate had promptly confirmed his appointment, and late on the night of March 3, 1801, President Adams signed the commissions of office for Marbury and a number of other new judges. The next day, Jefferson became President and discovered that

Marbury's commission and several others had not been delivered.

Angered by the Federalists' attempted court-packing scheme, President Jefferson instructed James Madison, the new secretary of state, not to deliver those commissions. William Marbury then went to the Supreme Court, seeking a writ of mandamus to force delivery.[12] Marbury based his suit on the Judiciary Act of 1789, in which Congress had created the federal court system. That law gave the Supreme Court the right to hear such suits in its original jurisdiction (not on appeal from a lower court).

In a unanimous opinion written by Chief Justice John Marshall, the Court refused Marbury's request. It did so because it found the section of the Judiciary Act on which Marbury had based his case to be in conflict with Article III in the Constitution and, therefore, void.

**The Effects of *Marbury*** With the Court's decision, Chief Justice Marshall claimed for the Supreme Court the right to declare acts

✓ **Checkpoint**
What is the significance of the case *Marbury* v. *Madison?*

**aftermath**
*n.* result or consequence

---

[11] It is often mistakenly said that the Court first exercised the power in this case, but in fact the Court did so at least as early as *Hylton* v. *United States* in 1796. In that case it upheld the constitutionality of a tax Congress had laid on carriages. It found that the tax was not a direct tax and so was not one that had to be apportioned among the States in accord with Article I, Section 2, Clause 3 of the Constitution.

[12] A writ of mandamus is a court order compelling an officer of government to perform an act that the officer has a clear legal duty to perform.

# Packing the Court

The Judiciary Act of 1789 created a Supreme Court of six justices, including the Chief Justice. The Court's size has fluctuated over time, reaching its present size of nine in 1869. In 1937, President Franklin D. Roosevelt asked Congress to increase the size of the Court, proposing that one additional justice be added for each sitting justice over age 70, to a maximum of 15 members. FDR claimed that his plan would make the Court a more efficient body. In reality, however, the proposal—which became known as "the Court-packing scheme"—was born out of the fact that the then-current Court had found several key pieces of New Deal legislation to be unconstitutional. Despite FDR's popularity, his plan was widely opposed, and it was roundly defeated in Congress, thereby protecting the separation of powers. *Why must a President be closely interested in the composition of the Supreme Court?*

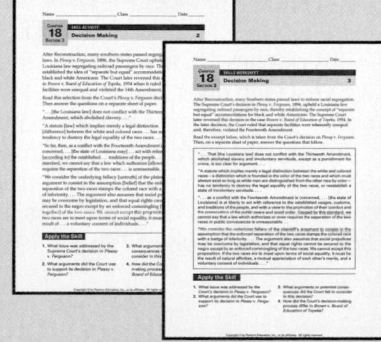

ALL I SAID WAS 'GIMME SIX MORE JUSTICES!'

---

Assign the section, the graphic organizer in the text, and Reading Comprehension Worksheet (Unit 5 All-in-One, p. 31) before class.

**L2 Differentiate** Reading Comprehension Worksheet (Unit 5 All-in-One, p. 33)

**BELLRINGER**

Check students' prior knowledge of the Supreme Court by writing these questions on the board: **(1) How many justices are on the Supreme Court? (2) How is the number of justices determined? (3) Does the Court have original or appellate jurisdiction or both? (4) Must the Court decide cases by a unanimous vote? Answer in your notebook.**

# Teach

To present this topic using online resources, use the lesson presentations at **PearsonSchool.com/phgovt.**

**REVIEW BELLRINGER ANSWERS**

Discuss students' Bellringer answers. *(1. nine 2. The Constitution established the position of Chief Justice; Congress sets the number of associate justices. 3. both 4. no, just a majority vote)*

**ANALYZE *MARBURY* v. *MADISON***

Have students reread the Chapter 3 discussion of judicial review. Review *Marbury* v. *Madison*. Have students create a storyboard of major events leading to the Court's exercise of this power.

**L4 Differentiate** Have students draw and analyze political cartoons illustrating the power of the Supreme Court to declare acts of Congress or the President unconstitutional through judicial review. Have the class analyze the cartoons.

# Differentiated Resources

The following resources are located in the All-in-One, Unit 5, Chapter 18, Section 3:

**L3** Reading Comprehension Worksheet (p. 31)
**L2** Reading Comprehension Worksheet (p. 33)
**L3** Core Worksheet A (p. 35)
**L3** Core Worksheet B (p. 40)
**L3** Skills Worksheet (p. 41)
**L2** Skill Activity (p. 42)
**L3** Quiz A (p. 43)
**L2** Quiz B (p. 44)

# Answers

**Checkpoint** The Court is thought to have first asserted its power of judicial review.

**Packing the Court** By appointing more like-minded justices, the President could steer the Court to support the administration's programs.

## IDENTIFY SUPREME COURT JURISDICTION

Have students draw a pyramid. In the bottom part, they should list the inferior constitutional courts and write the subject matter and parties involved in cases that fall within the exclusive jurisdiction of these courts. Refer students to Section 1 for this information. *(Subject matter: if the case involves an interpretation of the Constitution or federal statute or treaty, or relates to admiralty or maritime law; Parties: the U.S. or one of its officers or agencies; a foreign government or official; a State if it is suing another State, a citizen of another State, or a foreign government or subject; a citizen of one State suing a citizen of another State; a U.S. citizen suing a foreign government or subject; citizens of the same State if both claim land under grants from different States)*

In the top part of the pyramid, have students write the two classes of cases heard by the Supreme Court in its original and exclusive jurisdiction. *(all controversies involving two or more States, and all cases brought against ambassadors or other public ministers)* Ask: **What type of jurisdiction does the Supreme Court utilize the most, by far?** *(appellate)* **About how many cases does the Court hear each year?** *(a few hundred)*

**L3 Differentiate** State the Essential Question of this chapter. Ask students to write a paragraph answering this question after viewing the pyramid.

---

**Government** online *All print resources are available on the Teacher's Resource Library CD-ROM and online at PearsonSchool.com/phgovt.*

---

## Answers

**Checkpoint** cases in which a State is a party; and those affecting ambassadors, other public ministers, and consuls

---

✔ **Checkpoint**
In which two types of cases does the Supreme Court have original jurisdiction?

of Congress unconstitutional, and so laid the foundation for the judicial branch's key role in the development of the American system of government.

The dramatic and often far-reaching effects of the Supreme Court's exercise of the power of judicial review tend to overshadow much of its other work. Each year, it hears dozens of cases in which questions of constitutionality are not raised, but in which federal law is interpreted and applied. Thus, many of the more important statutes that Congress has passed have been brought to the Supreme Court time and again for decisions. So, too, have many of the lesser ones. In interpreting those laws and applying them to specific situations, the Court has had a real impact on both their meaning and their effect.

### Supreme Court Jurisdiction

The Supreme Court has both original and appellate jurisdiction. Most of its cases, however, come on appeal—from the lower federal courts and from the highest State courts. Article III, Section 2 of the Constitution spells out two classes of cases that may be heard by the High Court in its original jurisdiction: (1) those to which a State is a party, and (2) those affecting ambassadors, other public ministers, and consuls.

Congress cannot enlarge on this constitutional grant of original jurisdiction. Recall, that is precisely what the Supreme Court held in *Marbury*. If Congress could do so, it would in effect be amending the Constitution. Congress can **implement** the constitutional provision, however, and it has done so. It has provided that the Supreme Court shall have original and exclusive jurisdiction over (1) all controversies involving two or more States, and (2) all cases brought against ambassadors or other public ministers, but not consuls.

The Court may choose to take original jurisdiction over any other case covered by the broad wording in Article III, Section 2 of the Constitution. Almost without exception, however, those cases are tried in the lower courts. The Supreme Court hears only a very small number of cases in its original jurisdiction—in fact, no more than a case or two each term.

**implement**
*v.* to carry out, to put into effect

### How Cases Reach the Court

More than 8,000 cases are now appealed to the Supreme Court each term. Of these, the Court accepts only a few hundred for decision. In most cases, petitions for review are denied, usually because most of the justices agree with the decision of the lower court or believe that the case involves no significant point of law.

In short, the High Court is in the somewhat enviable position of being able to set its own agenda. It decides what it wants to decide. The Court selects those cases that it does hear according to "the rule of four": At least four of its nine justices must agree that a case should be put on the Court's docket.

More than half the cases decided by the Court are disposed of in brief orders. For example, an order may remand (return) a case to a lower court for reconsideration in light of some other recent and related case decided by the High Court. All told, the Court now decides, after hearing arguments and with full opinions, fewer than 80 cases per term.

Most cases reach the Supreme Court by **writ of certiorari** (from the Latin, meaning "to be made more certain"). This writ is an order by the Court directing a lower court to send up the record in a given case for its review. Either party to a case can petition the Court to issue a writ. But, again, "cert" is granted in only a very limited number of instances—typically, only when a petition raises some important constitutional question or a serious problem in the interpretation of a statute.

When certiorari is denied, the decision of the lower court stands in that particular case. Note, however, that the denial of cert is not a decision on the merits of a case. All a denial means is that, for whatever reason, four or more justices could not agree that the Supreme Court should accept that particular case for review.

A few cases do reach the Court in yet another way: by **certificate.** This process is used when a lower court is not clear about the procedure or the rule of law that should apply in a case. The lower court asks the Supreme Court to certify the answer to a specific question in the matter.

---

# Myths and Misperceptions

**JUDICIAL REVIEW** Contrary to popular belief, judicial review involves more than simply determining whether a law "matches" the Constitution. Supreme Court justices are often unsure of what is and is not constitutional. According to Justice Charles Evans Hughes, "The history of scholarship is a record of disagreements. And when we deal with questions relating to the principles of law and their applications, we do not suddenly rise into the stratosphere of icy certainty." Justices must interpret the Constitution as it applies to each case. Sometimes interpretations change, and the Court overturns a ruling of an earlier Court. For example, in *Plessy* v. *Ferguson,* 1896, the Court upheld racial segregation. A later Court reversed this decision in *Brown* v. *Board of Education of Topeka,* 1954.

Most cases that reach the Court do so from the highest State courts and the federal courts of appeals. A very few do come from the federal district courts and an even smaller number from the Court of Appeals for the Armed Forces.

## How the Court Operates

The Supreme Court sits from the first Monday in October to sometime the following June or July. Each term is identified by the year in which it began. Thus, the 2011 term runs from October 3, 2011, into the early summer of 2012.

**Oral Arguments** Once the Supreme Court accepts a case, it sets a date on which that matter will be heard. As a rule, the justices consider cases in two-week cycles from October to early May. They hear oral arguments in several cases for two weeks; then recess for two weeks to consider those cases and handle other Court business.

On those days on which the Court hears arguments, it convenes at 10:00 A.M. on Mondays, Tuesdays, Wednesdays, and sometimes Thursdays. At those public sessions, the lawyers, representing the parties of those cases the Court has accepted, make their oral arguments. Their presentations are almost always limited to 30 minutes.

The justices usually listen to an attorney's arguments and sometimes interrupt them with pointed questions. After 25 minutes, a white light flashes at the lectern from which an attorney addresses the Court. Five minutes later, a red light signals the end of the presentation and it must stop, even if the lawyer is in mid-sentence.

**Briefs** Each party files detailed written statements—**briefs**—with the Court before they present their oral arguments. These detailed statements spell out the party's legal position and are built largely on relevant facts and the citation of precedents. Briefs often run to hundreds of pages.

The Court may also receive *amicus curiae* (friend of the court) briefs. These are briefs filed by persons or groups who are not actual parties to a case but who nonetheless have a substantial interest in its outcome. Thus, for

**GOVERNMENT** ONLINE
**Audio Tour**
Listen to a guided audio tour of an appeal reaching the Supreme Court at **PearsonSchool.com/phgovt**

## How a Case Reaches the Supreme Court

**STEP 1:**
Case is filed in a federal district court.

**STEP 2:**
Case is appealed to a federal court of appeals.

**STEP 3:**
Case is appealed to the United States Supreme Court, which does one of three things:

**STOP**
The Supreme Court allows the lower court ruling to stand.

**GO BACK**
The Supreme Court remands the case—sends it back to the lower court for reconsideration.

**GO FORWARD**
The Supreme Court decides the case.

▶▶ **Interpreting Diagrams**
This diagram shows the typical route (though not the only one) a case might take to the Supreme Court. *Why do you think this process involves so many steps, often at great expense and time to the parties involved?*

Tell students to go to the Audio Tour for a guided audio tour of an appeal reaching the Supreme Court.

### STUDY THE COURT IN ACTION

Ask students to read the Chapter 18 Section 3 Core Worksheet A (Unit 5 All-in-One, p. 35). Students will read excerpts of the oral arguments in the case *Ward v. Rock Against Racism,* 1989. The case deals with the issue of time, place, and manner of protected speech. (Does New York City have the power to control the mix and volume of a rock concert?) Have students read the excerpts aloud, taking turns playing the parts of the justices and attorneys.

Note that there is audio on the Internet of the actual case being argued in the Supreme Court. You may locate the Web site, which has the audible and complete written transcript of the case. Students can hear the attorneys argue their cases and the justices interrupt them with questions and comments. You can also direct students to another Web site for the full text of the opinion of the Court, including concurring and dissenting opinions.

**L2 Differentiate** If students listen to the audio only, ask them if the Court proceedings surprised them in any way. Which questions by the justices do students think were the most important in defining the heart of the issue? How would students have ruled on the case if they had been on the Court?

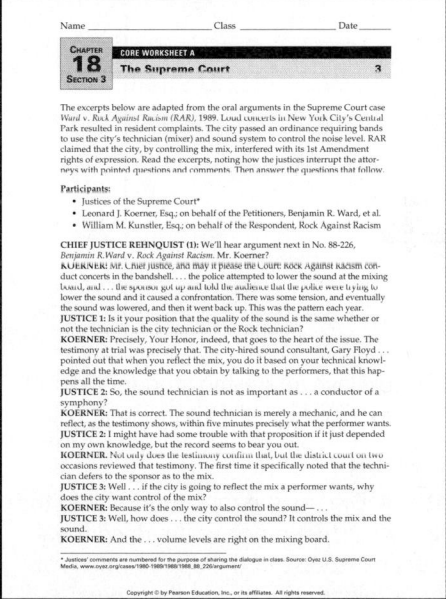

# How Government Works

**DIAGRAM THE APPEALS PROCESS** Have students analyze the *How Government Works* diagram, "How a Case Reaches the Supreme Court," on this page or on Transparency 18G. Working in groups, have students create a flowchart showing the path taken by a specific case from a federal district court to the Supreme Court. They should include the date and place where the case originated, the decision made by each court, how the case reached the Supreme Court, and the final decision made by the Court in the case. Suggest these cases to diagram (they are discussed in Chapter 19): *Engel* v. *Vitale, Tinker* v. *Des Moines School District, Gregory* v. *Chicago, Hazelwood School District* v. *Kuhlmeier,* and *Wisconsin* v. *Yoder.*

## Answers

**Interpreting Diagrams** Because the Supreme Court has time to hear only a limited number of cases, those cases must be significant. Inferior courts and the Supreme Court discourage frivolous cases from reaching the Court through this lengthy and expensive process.

Tell students to go to the Online Update for additional information on the Court.

## DISTRIBUTE CORE WORKSHEET B

Ask students to work in odd-numbered groups to complete the Chapter 18 Section 3 Core Worksheet B (Unit 5 All-in-One, p. 40). They will formulate opinions on controversial issues before the Supreme Court. Each group must come to a majority opinion. Tabulate the statements and opinions.

**L1 L2 Differentiate** Have students work individually and select one issue on Core Worksheet B that interests them. Students should analyze and make notes about their opinions. Then discuss the issues as a class.

**L3 L4 Differentiate** Have student pairs take opposing sides on one issue on Core Worksheet B. Students should research the issue and debate it in class. Then have the class discuss how the evidence influenced their opinion.

**L4 Differentiate** Have interested students identify the actual case described by each statement.

## EXTEND THE LESSON

**L3 Differentiate** Discuss the role of gender in the Supreme Court. Ask students to write an editorial describing how an increase in the appointment of women might or might not change the Court.

**L4 Differentiate** Display and discuss Transparencies 18H and 18I. Ask students to research the justices' nomination process and write a newspaper article on the confirmation of John Roberts or Elena Kagan.

## Answers

**Who Is on the Court Today?** A new case or an overruled precedent may require a justice to reevaluate his or her position on some laws.

The Federal Court System

---

**Update**
For online updates and additional information on the Court, go to PearsonSchool.com/phgovt

# Who Is On the Court Today?

| Justice | Age When Appointed | Appointed by (Year) | Previous Years as a Judge |
|---------|--------------------|--------------------|---------------------------|
| Chief Justice John G. Roberts, Jr. | 50 | G.W. Bush (2005) | 2 |
| Antonin Scalia | 50 | Reagan (1986) | 4 |
| Anthony M. Kennedy | 51 | Reagan (1988) | 13 |
| Clarence Thomas | 43 | G.H.W. Bush (1991) | 2 |
| Ruth Bader Ginsburg | 60 | Clinton (1993) | 13 |
| Stephen G. Breyer | 55 | Clinton (1994) | 14 |
| Samuel A. Alito, Jr. | 55 | G.W. Bush (2006) | 16 |
| Sonia Sotomayor | 55 | Obama (2009) | 17 |
| Elena Kagan | 50 | Obama (2010) | 0 |

A President seeks to appoint justices who share his or her political stance, but justices' views may change over time in unpredictable ways. Today's Supreme Court has a conservative majority and is often divided in its decisions, likely due to the controversial nature of the cases that it hears. The Court has recently made 5–4 decisions on topics such as public school affirmative action programs and capital punishment for juvenile offenders. *What might lead a justice to change his or her basic position in some area of the law?*

Front row: Clarence Thomas, Antonin Scalia, Chief Justice John Roberts, Anthony Kennedy, Ruth Bader Ginsberg
Back row: Sonia Sotomayor, Stephen Breyer, Samuel Alito, Elena Kagan

example, cases involving such highly charged matters as abortion or affirmative action regularly attract a large number of *amicus* briefs. Notice, however, that these briefs can be filed only with the Court's permission or at its request.

The solicitor general, a principal officer in the Department of Justice, is often called the Federal Government's chief trial lawyer. He—and, certainly, one day she—represents the United States in all cases to which it is a party in the Supreme Court and may appear and argue for the government in any federal or State court.[13]

The solicitor general also has another extraordinary responsibility. He decides which cases the government should ask the Supreme Court to review and what position the United States should take in those cases it brings before the High Court.

---

[13] The Attorney General may argue the government's position before the Supreme Court but rarely does so.

**The Court in Conference** On most Fridays through a term, the justices meet in conference. There, in closest secrecy, they consider the cases in which they have heard oral arguments; and there, too, they decide which new cases they will accept for decision.

Only the Chief Justice, who presides, and the eight other members of the Court are present at the conference. The Chief Justice leads the discussion of each case to be considered—stating the facts, summarizing the questions of law involved, and usually indicating how he thinks the Court should dispose of that case. Then each of the associate justices, in order of seniority, present their views and conclusions. A majority must decide which party wins or loses a case and whether a lower court's decision in that matter is to be affirmed or reversed.

About a third of the Court's decisions are unanimous, but most find the Court divided. The High Court is sometimes criticized for its split decisions. However, most of the cases

The Federal Court System

---

# Myths and Misconceptions

**RISING TO THE TOP** In the federal inferior courts, a judge rises to the position of chief judge based on seniority. For example, when the chief judge of a federal circuit court steps down, the position goes to the judge who has served on the court for the longest time, is 64 years old or younger, and has not previously served as chief judge. Contrary to popular belief, the top judge on the highest court in the land—the Chief Justice of the U.S. Supreme Court—does not necessarily rise to the position through long years of service. The President may elevate any associate justice to Chief Justice or appoint someone directly to the position from outside the Court. Chief Justice John Roberts had no experience on the U.S. Supreme Court before President George W. Bush appointed him to the top position.

it hears pose difficult and complicated questions, and many present questions on which lower courts have disagreed. In short, most of the Court's cases excite controversy; the easy cases seldom get that far.

**The Court's Opinions** Once a case has been considered and decided in conference, the Court announces its decision in the matter and, with it, issues one or more written opinions. The decision indicates which party has won the dispute and by what margin among the justices. Where the decision is unanimous, the Chief Justice most often writes the Court's opinion. If there has been a split decision, the Chief Justice may write the majority opinion, or he may assign that task to another justice in the majority. When the Chief Justice is in the minority, the senior justice in the majority makes that assignment.

The **majority opinion,** officially called "the Opinion of the Court," sets out the facts in a case, identifies the issues it presents, and details the reasons that <u>underpin</u> the majority's decision.[14]

The Court's opinions are exceedingly valuable. Its majority opinions stand as precedents. The lower courts, both federal and State, are expected to follow precedent—that is, decide cases of like nature in a manner consistent with previous rulings.[15]

One or more of the justices on the majority side may write a **concurring opinion,** usually to make some point not made or not emphasized in the majority opinion. In effect, a justice who writes a concurring opinion agrees with (concurs in) the majority decision as to the winner of a case but offers different reasons for reaching that conclusion.

One or more **dissenting opinions** may be written by those justices who do not agree with the Court's majority decision. Those dissents do not become precedent. They are, instead, expressions of opposition to the majority's views in a case. Chief Justice Charles Evans Hughes once described dissenting opinions as "an appeal to the brooding spirit of the law, to the intelligence of a future day." Rarely, the High Court does reverse itself—and so minority opinion of today could become the Court's majority position on some distant tomorrow.

---

**14** Most majority opinions, and many concurring and dissenting opinions, run to dozens of pages. Some Supreme Court decisions are issued with very brief, unsigned opinions. These *per curiam* (for the court) opinions seldom run more than a paragraph or two and usually dispose of relatively uncomplicated cases. All of the High Court's opinions in every case are published online and in the *United States Reports,* the official printed record of its decisions.

**15** The doctrine of precedent is often identified as *stare decisis*—Latin for "let the decision stand," or adhere to decided cases.

✔ **Checkpoint**
What happens once a case has been decided?

**underpin**
*v.* to support or strengthen

---

**Essential Questions**
**Journal**

To continue to build a response to the chapter Essential Question, go to your **Essential Questions Journal.**

## SECTION 3 ASSESSMENT

1. **Guiding Question** Use your completed graphic organizer to answer this question: What is the Supreme Court's jurisdiction, and how does the Court operate?

**Key Terms and Comprehension**

2. **(a)** What does a **writ of certiorari** have in common with a **certificate?** **(b)** How do the two differ?

3. What is **majority opinion** and why is it important?

4. Explain briefly how most cases reach the Supreme Court.

**Critical Thinking**

5. **Summarize** Why was the Court's decision in *Marbury* v. *Madison* one of the most important cases ever decided by the Supreme Court?

6. **Determine Cause and Effect** How does the power of judicial review place the judicial branch on an equal plane with the other branches of the Federal Government?

**Quick Write**

**Explanatory Essay: Create a Flowchart** Using your research from Section 2, create a flowchart to show the path the case you selected took to reach the Supreme Court. Be sure to use arrows or lines so that the sequence is clear.

---

## Assess and Remediate

**L3** Ask students to sketch the Supreme Court building. On at least eight "pillars" of the building, have them write facts about the Court. For example, students could write out Article III, Section 1 of the Constitution, which created the Court; the Court's jurisdiction as spelled out in Article III, Section 2; the number of justices and their names; and so on.

**L3** Collect Core Worksheet B and assess students' participation using the Rubric for Assessing Performance of an Entire Group (Unit 5 All-in-One, p. 241).

**L3** Assign the Section 3 Assessment questions.

**L3** Section Quiz A (Unit 5 All-in-One, p. 43)

**L2** Section Quiz B (Unit 5 All-in-One, p. 44)

Have students complete the review activities in the digital lesson presentation and continue their work in the **Essential Questions Journal.**

### REMEDIATION

| If Your Students Have Trouble With | Strategies For Remediation |
|---|---|
| The scope of the Supreme Court's jurisdiction (Questions 1, 5, 6) | Have students turn each heading and subhead in this section into a question, and then answer the questions. For example, the heading "Judicial Review" in this section could be rewritten as the question "What is judicial review?" or "How did the Court obtain the power of judicial review?" |
| How the Supreme Court operates (Questions 1, 2, 3, 4) | Have students write and illustrate books for elementary school children that explain how a case works its way to the Supreme Court. The books should include definitions; the purpose of briefs and oral arguments; what justices do in conference; and the purpose of majority, concurring, and dissenting opinions. |

## Answers

**Checkpoint** The Court announces its decision and issues one or more written opinions.

---

## Assessment Answers

**1.** It has both original and appellate jurisdiction, but most of its cases come on appeal. It has original and exclusive jurisdiction over cases involving two or more States and all cases involving ambassadors or other public ministers. The Court studies briefs and hears oral arguments before meeting in conference to consider decisions.

**2.** (a) Both are ways for a case from a lower court to reach the Supreme Court. (b) **writ of certiorari:** requested by either party in the case;

**certificate:** requested by the lower court

**3.** A **majority opinion** sets out the facts in a case, identifies the issues, details the reasons that underpin the majority's decision, and becomes a precedent that lower courts are expected to follow.

**4.** A case is tried in a district court or highest State court and appealed to a court of appeals. It is then appealed to the Supreme Court. At least four justices must agree before a case is put on the docket. Most cases reach the Court by a writ of certiorari; a few reach the Court by certificate.

**5.** It established the Court's right to exercise the power of judicial review and ensured the independence and equal footing of the judicial branch with the legislative and executive branches.

**6.** It gives the judicial branch the authority to declare acts of Congress and executive actions unconstitutional.

**QUICK WRITE** A strong flowchart should include the trial court of original jurisdiction, the appellate court, and the path of the appeal to the Supreme Court.

## GUIDING QUESTION

## What are the special courts, and what are the jurisdictions of each?

## Get Started

### LESSON GOALS

Students will . . .

- identify the special courts by completing a chart highlighting the various courts' jurisdictions.
- understand how special courts function by constructing paths of appeals for case scenarios.
- analyze the constitutionality of military commissions by studying opinions for and against them.

### BEFORE CLASS

Assign the section, the graphic organizer in the text, and Reading Comprehension Worksheet (Unit 5 All-in-One, p. 45) before class.

**L2** **Differentiate** Reading Comprehension Worksheet (Unit 5 All-in-One, p. 46)

### BELLRINGER

Display Transparency 18J. Have students write answers to the questions in their notebooks.

## SKILLS DEVELOPMENT

### ANALYZE POLITICAL CARTOONS

To help students learn to analyze political cartoons, have them turn to the Skills Handbook, p. S22, and use the information there to complete the Bellringer activity.

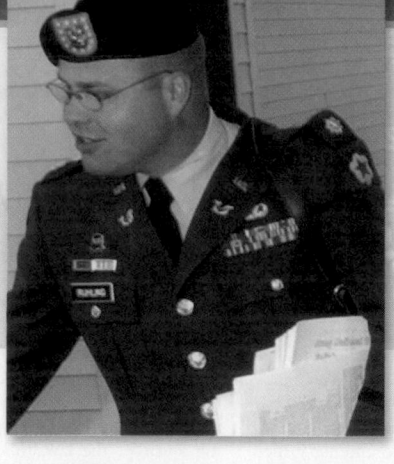

SECTION 4

# The Special Courts

## Guiding Question

What are the special courts, and what are the jurisdictions of each? Use a concept web to take notes on the special courts.

### Political Dictionary

- court-martial
- civilian tribunal
- redress

### Objectives

1. Contrast the jurisdiction of the Court of Appeals for the Armed Forces and the Court of Appeals for Veterans Claims.
2. Explain how a citizen may sue the United States government in the Court of Federal Claims.
3. Examine the roles of the territorial courts and those of the District of Columbia courts.
4. Explain what types of cases are brought to the Tax Court.

**Image Above:** U.S. Army attorney before a court-martial

Recall, the national court system is made up of two quite distinct types of federal courts. They are (1) the constitutional courts, sometimes called the regular or Article III courts, discussed over the last several pages, and (2) the special courts, also known as the legislative or Article I courts.

Each of the special courts was established by Congress acting under the authority delegated to it in Article I, Section 8 of the Constitution—not under the power given to it in Article III to create courts to exercise the broad "judicial Power of the United States." That is to say, each of these courts has a very narrow jurisdiction; each hears only those cases that fall into a very limited class. And the special courts differ from the constitutional courts in one other important regard. Although their judges are all appointed by the President and Senate, they serve for a fixed term—not for life "during good Behaviour."

## Military and Veterans Claims Courts

Beginning in 1789, Congress has created a system of military courts for each branch of the nation's armed forces, as an exercise of its expressed power to "make Rules for the Government and Regulation of the land and naval Forces."[16] These military courts—**courts-martial**—serve the special disciplinary needs of the armed forces and are *not* a part of the federal court system. Their judges, prosecutors, defense attorneys, court reporters, and other personnel are all members of the military; most of them are officers. They conduct trials of those members of the military who are accused of violating military law. Today, the proceedings in a court-martial are fairly similar to the trials held in civilian courts across the country. There are some important differences, however. For example, at a court-martial, only two thirds of the panel (the jury in the case) must agree on a guilty verdict, in contrast to the unanimous verdict usually required in cases tried in the civilian courts.

---

**16** Article I, Section 8, Clause 14. This provision allows Congress to provide for the regulation of the conduct of members of the armed forces under a separate, noncivil legal code. The present-day system of military justice has developed over more than 230 years. Today, the Uniform Code of Military Justice, enacted by Congress in 1950, and the Military Justice Acts of 1968 and 1983 are the principal statutes that set out the nation's military law.

## Focus on the Basics

**FACTS:** • The Court of Appeals for the Armed Forces is a civilian tribunal that hears appeals of courts-martial. • The Court of Appeals for Veterans Claims hears claims regarding veterans' benefits. • The Court of Federal Claims hears claims for damages against the Federal Government. • Congress created federal courts for U.S. territories and the District of Columbia. • The Tax Court is part of the legislative branch and hears civil cases concerning tax law.

**CONCEPTS:** federalism, role of the judiciary

**ENDURING UNDERSTANDINGS:** • Congress has created many special courts to handle specific types of cases. • The National Government can be taken to court only in cases in which Congress declares the U.S. to be open to suit.

**The Court of Appeals for the Armed Forces** In 1950, Congress created the Court of Military Appeals, now titled the Court of Appeals for the Armed Forces, to review the more serious court-martial convictions of military personnel. This appellate court is a **civilian tribunal,** a part of the judicial branch, entirely separate from the military establishment. Appeals from the court's decisions can be taken to the Supreme Court. It is, then, the court of last resort in most cases that involve offenses against military law.

**The Court of Appeals for Veterans Claims** Acting under its power (Article I, Section 8, Clause 9) to "constitute Tribunals inferior to the supreme Court," Congress created the Court of Veterans Appeals in 1988 and changed its name in 1999 to the Court of Appeals for Veterans Claims.

This court has the power to hear appeals from the decisions of an administrative agency, the Board of Veterans' Appeals in the Department of Veterans Affairs (VA). Thus, this court hears cases in which individuals claim that the VA has denied or otherwise mishandled <u>valid</u> claims for veterans' benefits. Appeals from the decisions of the Court of Appeals for Veterans Claims can be taken to the Court of Appeals for the Federal Circuit.

**Military Commissions** In 2001, President Bush issued a controversial executive order creating several military commissions. These court-like bodies were set up, outside the regular courts-martial system, to try "unlawful enemy combatants"—suspected terrorists captured by American forces in Iraq and Afghanistan. Some 770 of those captives were held over a seven-year period in a military prison at the American naval base at Guantanamo Bay, Cuba.

Recall that in 2006, the Supreme Court found that those military commissions had been improperly established, *Hamdan* v. *Rumsfeld*; see page 402. The Court held that a chief executive could create such tribunals but only if authorized to do so by an act of Congress. Congress responded with the Military Commissions Act of 2006, but the

commissions accomplished very little over the next three years.

Upon taking office, President Obama suspended the tribunals and ordered the closure of the Guantanamo Bay facility. Congressional resistance soon derailed those plans, however, and the daunting problem of the fate of some 170 detainees still held there remains.

## Other Special Courts

The other special courts also have very narrow jurisdictions. They include the Court of Federal Claims, the territorial courts, the District of Columbia courts, and the U.S. Tax Court.

**The Court of Federal Claims** The United States government cannot be sued by anyone, in any court, for any reason, without its consent.[17] The government may be taken to court

---

[17] The government is shielded from suit by the doctrine of sovereign immunity. The doctrine comes from an ancient principle of English public law: "The King can do no wrong." The rule is not intended to protect public officials from charges of wrongdoing; rather it is intended to prevent government from being hamstrung in its own courts. Congress has long since agreed to a long list of legitimate court actions against the government.

**valid**
*adj.* legitimate, well-grounded

▸ **Analyzing Political Cartoons** Military tribunals have been established at various times in America's past—during the Mexican-American War, the Civil War, and World War II. *How do the bystanders in this cartoon view the military commissions at Guantanamo Bay?*

---

## Differentiated Resources

The following resources are located in the All-in-One, Unit 5, Chapter 18, Section 4:

- **L3** Reading Comprehension Worksheet (p. 45)
- **L2** Reading Comprehension Worksheet (p. 46)
- **L3** Core Worksheet (p. 47)
- **L2** Core Worksheet (p. 49)
- **L3** Quiz A (p. 51)
- **L2** Quiz B (p. 52)
- **L3** Chapter Test A (p. 53)
- **L2** Chapter Test B (p. 56)

---

# Teach

To present this topic using online resources, use the lesson presentations at **PearsonSchool.com/phgovt.**

### REVIEW BELLRINGER ANSWERS

Discuss the political cartoon that students analyzed for the Bellringer. *(Answers: 1. Internal Revenue Service, collect taxes; 2. Students may scan the text to find the answer: United States Tax Court.)*

### CHART SPECIAL COURTS' JURISDICTION

Display Transparency 18E, The Appellate Path in Federal Courts. Ask a volunteer to identify the special courts on the transparency. Draw a chart on the board like the one below. Have students work in pairs to complete the information. Then discuss the chart.

| Name of Court | Jurisdiction |
| --- | --- |
| Court of Appeals for the Armed Forces | *Appellate jurisdiction over court-martial convictions* |
| Court of Appeals for Veterans Claims | *Appellate jurisdiction over denied or mishandled veterans' claims arising from the Department of Veterans Affairs* |
| Court of Federal Claims | *Hears claims against the Federal Government* |
| Territorial Courts | *Hear cases in the Virgin Islands, Guam, and Northern Mariana Islands* |
| District of Columbia Courts | *Trial and appellate courts for residents of Washington, D.C.* |
| U.S. Tax Court | *Hears civil cases involving disputes of tax laws* |

### TRACE APPEALS THROUGH SPECIAL COURTS

As students answer the questions in the cases below, have them point out how on Transparency 18E each case would move along the appellate path.

**CASE A:** A citizen in Guam is accused of kidnapping. Where does the case begin? *(territorial court)* The defendant is found guilty and appeals. Where does the case go? *(Court of Appeals for the Ninth Circuit)*

**CASE B:** A citizen claims that the U.S. Forest Service harmed his crops, and sues for redress. Where does this case begin? *(Court of Federal Claims)* The case is lost by the citizen and then appealed. Where does the case go next? *(U.S. Court of Appeals for the Federal Circuit)*

### DISTRIBUTE CORE WORKSHEET

Have students work in groups to complete the Chapter 18 Section 4 Core Worksheet (Unit 5 All-in-One, p. 47). Students will form opinions on the constitutionality of military tribunals.

---

# Answers

**Analyzing Political Cartoons** as a "black hole," or something that swallows up detainees' rights in a mysterious, comprehensive way

Ask students to write a radio program discussing the procedures set out in the Military Commissions Act of 2006. They should write a script that might be used to interview a politician or member of the military.

# Assess and Remediate

**L3** Have students create a pyramid chart (or expand upon the pyramid they created in Section 3) to illustrate the different levels of the federal court system. They should label the top of the pyramid "Supreme Court," and complete the rest of the chart with the appropriate inferior court titles and jurisdictions at each level.

**L3** Assign the Section 4 Assessment questions.

**L3** Section Quiz A (Unit 5 All-in-One, p. 51)

**L2** Section Quiz B (Unit 5 All-in-One, p. 52)

Have students complete the review activities in the digital lesson presentation and continue their work in the **Essential Questions Journal.**

## REMEDIATION

| If Your Students Have Trouble With | Strategies For Remediation |
|---|---|
| The jurisdiction of special courts (Questions 1, 3, 4, 6) | Ask students to briefly identify the function of each special court (and the other inferior courts) on a slip of paper. Collect and read aloud the slips for a "Which Court Am I?" quiz. |
| The functions of military courts and commissions (Questions 2, 5) | Have students describe characteristics of courts-martial and the Court of Appeals for the Armed Forces. Ask them to write their descriptions as part of a political cartoon or other visual that shows how appeals of courts-martial go to a civilian court. |

## Answers

**Checkpoint** claims for damages against the Federal Government

---

only in cases in which Congress has declared the United States to be open to suit. Originally, any person with a money claim against the United States could secure **redress**—satisfaction of a claim, payment—only by an act of Congress. In 1855, however, Congress set up the Court of Claims to hear such pleas.[18] That body was renamed the United States Court of Federal Claims in 1992.

The Court of Federal Claims holds trials throughout the country, hearing claims for damages against the Federal Government. Those claims it upholds cannot in fact be paid until Congress appropriates the money, which it does almost as a matter of standard procedure. Appeals from the court's decisions may be carried to the Court of Appeals for the Federal Circuit.

Occasionally, those who lose in the Claims Court still manage to win some compensation. Some years ago, a Puget Sound mink rancher lost a case in which he claimed that low-flying Navy planes had frightened his animals and caused several of the females to become sterile. He asked $100 per mink. He lost, but then his congressman introduced a private bill that eventually paid him $10 for each animal.

**The Territorial Courts** Acting under its power (Article IV, Section 3, Clause 2) to "make all needful Rules and Regulations respecting the Territory . . . belonging to the United States," Congress has created courts for the nation's territories. These courts sit in the Virgin Islands, Guam, and the Northern Mariana Islands. They function much like the local courts in the 50 States.

**The District of Columbia Courts** Acting under its power to "exercise exclusive Legislation in all Cases whatsoever, over such District . . . as may . . . become the Seat of the Government of the United States" (Article I, Section 8, Clause 17), Congress has set up a judicial system for the nation's capital. Both the federal district court and the federal Court of Appeals for the District of Columbia hear cases as constitutional courts. Congress has also established two local courts, much like the courts in the States: a superior court, which is the general trial court, and a court of appeals.

**The United States Tax Court** Acting under its power to tax (Article I, Section 8, Clause 1), Congress created the United States Tax Court in 1969 as "an independent judicial body" in the legislative branch. It is not, in fact, a part of the federal court system. The Tax Court hears civil but not criminal cases involving disputes over the application of the tax laws. Most of its cases, then, are generated by the Internal Revenue Service and other Treasury Department agencies. Its decisions may be appealed to the federal courts of appeals.

---

18 Congress acted under its expressed power to pay the debts of the United States, Article I, Section 8, Clause 1.

---

**Essential Questions Journal** To continue to build a response to the chapter Essential Question, go to your **Essential Questions Journal.**

## SECTION 4 ASSESSMENT

1. **Guiding Question** Use your completed graphic organizer to answer this question: What are the special courts and what are the jurisdictions of each?

**Key Terms and Comprehension**

2. What is the difference between **civilian tribunals** and **courts-martial?**

3. What does it mean to seek **redress** in a court?

4. How do the special courts differ from the constitutional courts?

**Critical Thinking**

5. **Synthesize Information** When, if ever, do you think the establishment of a military commission is justified?

6. **Determine Relevance** Why do you think Congress has created the several special courts, rather than simply providing that all federal cases are to be tried in the regular courts?

### Quick Write

**Explanatory Essay: Write a Thesis Statement** A thesis states specifically what you will cover in your essay. Write a thesis statement for an explanatory essay on your chosen case's path to the Supreme Court. You will use your thesis as a guide to develop an organizational plan for your essay.

---

# Assessment Answers

**1.** The special courts (and their jurisdictions): courts-martial (trial courts for the military), Court of Appeals for the Armed Forces (reviews court-martial convictions), Court of Appeals for Veterans Claims (hears appeals regarding VA benefits), military commissions (try "unlawful enemy combatants"), Court of Federal Claims (hears claims against the Federal Government), territorial courts (courts in U.S. territories), District of Columbia courts (trial and appellate courts in Washington, D.C.), U.S. Tax Court (civil cases involving disputes over tax laws).

**2. civilian tribunals:** appellate courts, separate from the military, which review serious court-martial convictions; **courts-martial:** courts composed of military personnel that try cases concerning military law

**3.** satisfaction or payment of a claim

**4.** Special courts have a narrower jurisdiction, and judges serve a fixed term, not for life.

**5.** Some students might support military commissions for terrorists; others might say terrorists should be tried in federal district courts.

**6.** Special courts relieve caseload in constitutional courts. Congress wanted courts with special expertise.

**QUICK WRITE** Thesis statements may include the general constitutional grounds on which the cases worked their way to the Supreme Court.

# Quick Study Guide

**GOVERNMENT** ONLINE
**On the Go**
To review anytime, anywhere, download these online resources at **PearsonSchool.com/phgovt**
Political Dictionary, Audio Review

**Guiding Question**
**Section 2** What are the structure and jurisdiction of the inferior courts?

**Guiding Question**
**Section 3** What is the Supreme Court's jurisdiction, and how does the Court operate?

**Guiding Question**
**Section 1** What are the structure and function of the national judiciary?

**CHAPTER 18**
**Essential Question**
Does the structure of the federal court system allow it to administer justice effectively?

**Guiding Question**
**Section 4** What are the special courts, and what are the jurisdictions of each?

## Political Dictionary

inferior courts p. 521
jurisdiction p. 522
concurrent jurisdiction p. 522
plaintiff p. 523
defendant p. 523
original jurisdiction p. 523
appellate jurisdiction p. 523
judicial restraint p. 524
precedent p. 524
judicial activism p. 524
criminal case p. 529
civil case p. 529
docket p. 530
record p. 531
writ of certiorari p. 534
certificate p. 534
brief p. 535
majority opinion p. 537
concurring opinion p. 537
dissenting opinion p. 537
court-martial p. 538
civilian tribunal p. 539
redress p. 540

### The Federal Courts

**U.S. Supreme Court**

**Inferior Courts**

**Constitutional Courts**
- District Courts
- U.S. Courts of Appeals
- U.S. Court of Appeals for the Federal Circuit
- U.S. Court of International Trade

**Special Courts**
- U.S. Court of Appeals for the Armed Forces
- U.S. Court of Appeals for Veterans Claims
- U.S. Court of Federal Claims
- Territorial Courts
- Courts of the District of Columbia
- U.S. Tax Court

### How Cases Reach the Court

Original jurisdiction → Writ of certiorari → On appeal

**U.S. Supreme Court**

---

# For More Information

To learn more about the federal court system, refer to these sources or assign them to students:

**L1** **McElroy, Lisa.** *Sandra Day O'Connor: Supreme Court Justice.* Millbrook Press, 2003.

**L2** **January, Brendan.** *The Supreme Court.* Franklin Watts, 2005.

**L3** **Jacobs, Thomas A.** *Teens Take It to Court: Young People Who Challenged the Law—and Changed Your Life.* Free Spirit Publishing, 2006.

**L4** **Trachtman, Michael G.** *The Supremes' Greatest Hits: The 34 Supreme Court Cases that Most Directly Affect Your Life.* Sterling, 2006.

---

Have students download the digital resources available at Government on the Go for review and remediation.

**STUDY TIPS**

**Set Goals for Study Sessions** Setting goals can help students achieve both long- and short-term goals. Setting goals for study sessions makes it more likely that students will stay on task and accomplish the necessary work. Ask students to write down a study goal for each subject for the week. Then ask them to write down a study goal for today's study session. Goals should keep in mind upcoming tests and assignments that are due. Explain that it is important to prioritize tasks for each study session, in order to meet the goal for that session. It can be helpful to assign a length of time to each task, both to organize study time effectively and to help with concentration. Remind students to make goals realistic. For example, a study goal for one session might be to read the chapter, or to review the class notes for the day. Have students create a "goal chart" that lists today's study goals and the priority of each, as well as the length of time to complete the task. Suggest that students reward themselves for meeting each day's goals with something they enjoy doing.

**ASSESSMENT AT A GLANCE**

**Tests and Quizzes**
Section Assessments
Section Quizzes A and B, Unit 5 **All-in-One**
Chapter Assessment
Chapter Tests A and B, Unit 5 **All-in-One**
Document-Based Assessment
Progress Monitoring Online
Exam*View* Test Bank

**Performance Assessment**
Essential Questions Journal
Extend the Lesson, p. 530
Assessment Rubrics, **All-in-One**

# Chapter Assessment

## COMPREHENSION AND CRITICAL THINKING

### SECTION 1

**1.** (a) to define and apply laws in a uniform way for all States (b) Possible answer: An independent judiciary keeps the separation and balance of power in government, thus assuring fair trials as well as judicial decisions not dependent on political pressure.

**2.** (a) subject matter a "federal question" and parties involved (b) Some students may note that the Constitution kept the principles purposefully broad to allow for interpretation. Other students may note that the principles are too broad and should be narrowed to reduce the federal caseload. Still others may find the principles not broad enough, citing cases heard in State courts that would be better tried by a nonelected judge in the federal judiciary.

**3.** (a) The President nominates, and the Senate confirms. The President usually nominates judges recommended by that State's senators. (b) Possible answer: If either the executive or legislative branch had the sole power to appoint a judge, the other branch would always suspect a lack of impartiality and would not support the work of the judge.

### SECTION 2

**4.** (a) The room is in disorder, and the justices are frazzled and overwhelmed. (b) The court is beset with cases it cannot hear.

**5.** (a) both civil and criminal cases (b) More than 80 percent of federal cases are tried in district courts.

**6.** (a) They hear appeals from the decisions of the district courts. (b) They were created to relieve the Supreme Court of its overloaded docket.

### SECTION 3

**7.** (a) the power to decide the constitutionality of an act of government (b) yes, because judicial review serves as a check on actions of all three branches of government

**8.** (a) both original and appellate jurisdiction (b) "Easy" cases involve simple points of law, or their decisions are not appealed. The Supreme Court hears only those cases that it feels involve significant points of law or that were not decided properly in the lower court.

---

# Chapter Assessment

**GOVERNMENT** ONLINE
Self-Test
To test your understanding of key terms and main ideas, visit
PearsonSchool.com/phgovt

## Comprehension and Critical Thinking

### Section 1

**1.** (a) Why did the Framers see a need for a national court system? (b) Why did the Framers believe that an independent judiciary was so important?

**2.** (a) What are the two general principles that determine whether the federal courts have jurisdiction over a case? (b) Do you think these principles are broad enough? Why or why not?

**3.** (a) Outline the process by which most federal judges are nominated and approved. (b) Why did the Framers create a system of judicial selection that requires the cooperation of the President and the Senate?

### Section 2

**4.** **Analyze Political Cartoons** (a) What is happening in this scene? (b) What point is the cartoonist making?

### Apply What You've Learned

**13.** **Essential Question** **Activity** Interview a federal judge or lawyer who has experience with federal cases. Ask:
(a) What do you think is the purpose of the law?
(b) What is the role of the courts in our system of government?
(c) What do you think are the advantages of trying a case in federal court, as compared to a State or local court? The disadvantages?

**14.** **Essential Question** **Assessment** Based on the interview you conducted and the content you have

**5.** (a) What kinds of cases do the district courts hear? (b) Why can it be said that the federal district courts are the principal trial courts in the national judiciary?

**6.** (a) What is the principal role of the courts of appeals? (b) Why were they a necessary creation?

### Section 3

**7.** (a) What is judicial review? (b) Is the power of judicial review consistent with the basic principles of democracy? Why or why not?

**8.** (a) What is the jurisdiction of the Supreme Court? (b) For what reasons do you think the "easy" cases do not reach the Supreme Court?

**9.** (a) What is a concurring opinion? What is a dissenting opinion? (b) Why do Supreme Court justices often write concurring and/or dissenting opinions in a case?

### Section 4

**10.** (a) What are the special courts? Cite two examples and the jurisdiction of each. (b) What does it mean to say these courts have a very narrow jurisdiction?

**11.** (a) What is the function of a civilian tribunal? (b) Why do you think Congress established a civilian tribunal to hear the appeals of serious courts-martial convictions?

### Writing About Government

**12.** Use your Quick Write exercises from this chapter to write an explanatory essay about the path your chosen case took to reach the Supreme Court. Be sure to write an introduction that has a strong and clear purpose, a body that identifies the steps in the process and shows how each step relates to the overall process, and a conclusion that synthesizes the information. See pp. S3–S5 in the Skills Handbook.

learned in this chapter, write an op-ed that helps to answer the Essential Question: **Does the structure of the federal court system allow it to administer justice effectively?** An op-ed is an opinion piece that you could submit to your local newspaper for publication. Op-eds present an informed view and should be engaging. Include facts and statistics to support your opinion.

| **Essential Questions** **Journal** | To respond to the chapter Essential Question, go to your **Essential Questions Journal.** |
|---|---|

---

**9.** (a) **concurring:** written by a judge who agrees with the majority decision but offers different reasons for reaching that conclusion; **dissenting:** explanation written by a justice who does not agree with the Court's majority decision (b) Possible answer: Concurring and dissenting opinions enable justices to express different points of view; in future cases, they may form the basis for majority opinions.

### SECTION 4

**10.** (a) The special courts (and their jurisdictions) include courts-martial (trial courts for the

military); Court of Appeals for the Armed Forces (reviews courts-martial convictions); Court of Appeals for Veterans Claims (hears appeals regarding VA benefits); military commissions (try "unlawful enemy combatants"); Court of Federal Claims (hears claims for damages against the Federal Government); territorial courts (courts in U.S. territories); District of Columbia courts (trial and appellate courts in Washington, D.C.); and U.S. Tax Court (hears civil cases involving disputes over tax laws). (b) Each of these courts hears only those cases that fall into a very limited class.

# Document-Based Assessment

## Term Limits for Federal Judges

Over recent years, many have questioned the wisdom of the provision of life tenure for federal judges, as illustrated in Document 1 below. The debate has often focused on the Supreme Court. Article III, Section 1 of the Constitution gives Supreme Court justices lifetime appointments. A Framer's viewpoint is set out in Document 2. Any change in the tenure of Supreme Court justices would require a constitutional amendment. Although both supporters and opponents of such an amendment agree that one is unlikely any time soon, the issue has led to lively debate.

### Document 1

"[L]ifetime tenure should be abolished. . . . [A]s the judiciary has become almost as polarized [divided] along partisan lines as the elective branches, Presidents have been seeking out younger and younger judge-ship appointees at every level of the judiciary, hoping to influence the courts long after they [the Presidents] leave the White House.

The insularity [isolation] produced by lifetime tenure, combined with youthful appointment and long service, often means that senior judges represent the views and outlooks of past generations better than the current day.

Therefore, a nonrenewable term of fifteen years is an attractive innovation. . . . This is a long time to serve—nearly four current presidential terms. . . . At the same time, it is short enough to prevent justices from becoming too detached and generationally removed from the American mainstream.

—Larry J. Sabato, *A More Perfect Constitution*, 2007

### Document 2

"The standard of good behavior for the continuance in office of the judicial magistracy [judges], is certainly one of the most valuable of the modern improvements in the practice of government. In a monarchy it is an excellent barrier to the despotism of the prince; in a republic it is a no less excellent barrier to the encroachments and oppressions of the representative body. And it is the best expedient which can be devised in any government, to secure a steady, upright, and impartial administration of the laws.

—Alexander Hamilton, *The Federalist* No. 78, 1788

Use your knowledge of the terms of Supreme Court justices and Documents 1 and 2 to answer Questions 1–3.

1. What concern does the author of Document 1 have about life tenure for judges?
   - **A.** Justices who are appointed to the Court at a young age lack the knowledge and experience of older justices.
   - **B.** Justices should be required to retire from the Court at a specified age.
   - **C.** Justices who serve long terms on the Court can become out of touch with the challenges of society today
   - **D.** Justices who have life tenure do not understand the concerns of young people.

2. What reasons does the author of Document 2 give for his opinion about lifetime tenure for justices?

3. **Pull It Together** Would you support or oppose term limits for Supreme Court justices? Why or why not?

### GOVERNMENT ONLINE
**Documents**
To find more primary sources on judges' term limits, visit
PearsonSchool.com/phgovt

---

## DOCUMENT-BASED ASSESSMENT

1. C

2. Lifetime tenure is a barrier to the encroachments and oppressions of the representative body; and it secures a steady, upright, and impartial administration of the laws.

3. A strong essay will include a thesis statement and a summary of the writer's opinion in the first paragraph. The second paragraph should include relevant support information and points that address counterarguments.

**L2 Differentiate** Students use all the documents on the page to support their thesis.

**L3 Differentiate** Students include additional information available online at **PearsonSchool.com/phgovt.**

**L4 Differentiate** Students use materials from the textbook, the online information at **PearsonSchool.com/phgovt,** and do additional research to support their views.

**Go Online to PearsonSchool.com/phgovt** for a student rubric and extra documents.

---

11. (a) to hear appeals of serious courts-martial convictions (b) Possible answer: to introduce impartiality by having nonmilitary personnel review the appeal

### WRITING ABOUT GOVERNMENT

12. Have students refine their explanatory essays before submitting them. They should be sure each paragraph has a topic sentence and supporting sentences, and that all related points are grouped together into one paragraph. They should also review sentence patterns, adding variety by inserting a short sentence between two long ones or by combining two short sentences into one longer, compound sentence. Finally, have them look for vague words and replace them with more concise, active (not passive) terms.

### APPLY WHAT YOU'VE LEARNED

13. Students should write a list of open-ended, neutral questions before the interview. Researching the subject's background will direct students to a thoughtful line of questioning. During the interview, students should listen closely for central ideas and what seems important to the interviewee. Have students clarify any misunderstanding by restating in their own words the subject's responses.

14. Students' op-eds should answer the Essential Question using facts and statistics for support. Ask for volunteers to read their pieces to the class, followed by discussion, or to stage a debate using pro and con arguments.

# Introduce the Chapter

## Essential Questions:

**UNIT 5**

What should be the role of the judicial branch?

**CHAPTER 19**

How can the judiciary balance individual rights with the common good?

### ACTIVATE PRIOR KNOWLEDGE

Have students examine the photo and quotation on these pages. Ask: **What do the photo and quotation suggest about civil liberties?** *(that Americans have had to fight for civil liberties)* In this chapter, students will learn about First Amendment freedoms. Then tell students to begin to further explore civil liberties by completing the Chapter 19 Essential Question Warmup activity in their **Essential Questions Journal.** Discuss their responses as a class.

### BEFORE READING

**L2 ELL Differentiate** Chapter 19 Prereading and Vocabulary Worksheet (Unit 5 All-in-One, p. 68)

### SUCCESSNET STUDENT AND TEACHER CENTER

Visit **PearsonSchool.com/phgovt** for downloadable resources that allow students and teachers to connect with government "on the go."

### DIGITAL LESSON PRESENTATION

The digital lesson presentation supports the print lesson with activities and summaries of key concepts. Activities for this chapter include:

• **The *Lemon* Test**

• **Freedoms of Speech and Press**

## SKILLS DEVELOPMENT

### ANALYZE SOURCES

You may wish to teach analyzing sources as a distinct skill within Section 1 of this chapter. Use the Chapter 19 Skills Worksheet (Unit 5 All-in-One, p. 77) to help students learn the steps in analyzing sources. The worksheet asks students to read and identify two sources as primary or secondary, to find the main idea, and to evaluate the sources for point of view and bias. For L2 and L1 students, assign the adapted Skill Activity (Unit 5 All-in-One, p. 78).

**WebQuest online** The chapter WebQuest challenges students to answer the chapter Essential Question by asking them about civil liberties.

544

# Block Scheduling

**BLOCK 1:** Teach Section 1 lesson, including Core Worksheet 19.1 and the Strategies for Remediation. Begin Section 2 Lesson, including Bellringer and Draw a Wall of Separation. Assign Core Worksheet 19.2; have students discuss it.

**BLOCK 2:** Review Transparency 19C. Begin Section 3; discuss Bellringer and Chart Restrictions on Speech. Allow time for groups to complete Core Worksheet 19.3. Discuss the rulings. Go over Recognize Limits and Protections of the Media; organize groups for dramatizations.

**BLOCK 3:** Have groups dramatize their media cases. Display and discuss Transparency 19F. Introduce Section 4 with Transparency 19G and Identify Time-Place-Manner Rules. Distribute Core Worksheet 19.4; have students prepare their scenarios. Present cases before "judges." Complete Strategies for Remediation.

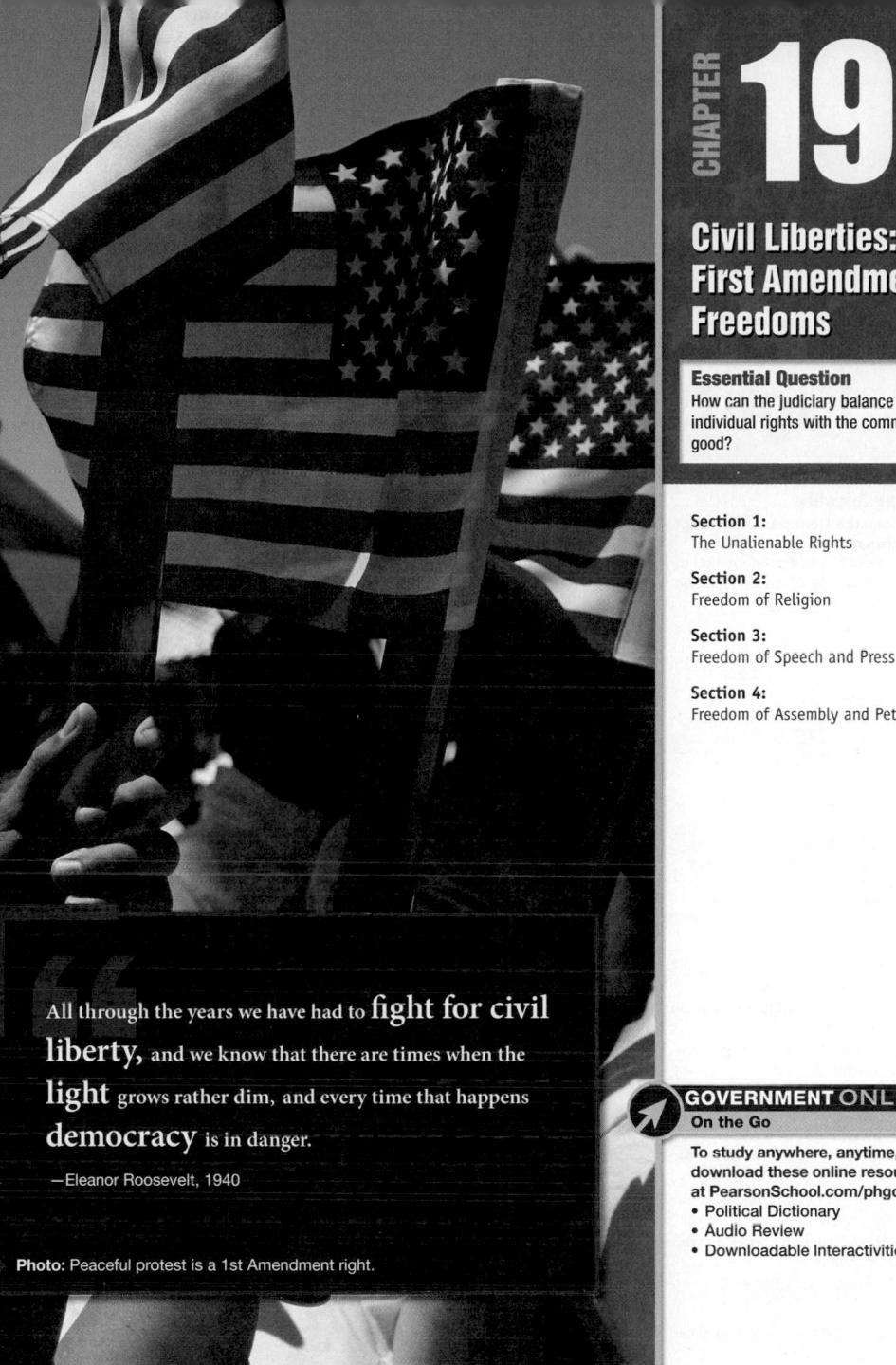

## Civil Liberties: First Amendment Freedoms

### Essential Question
How can the judiciary balance individual rights with the common good?

**Section 1:**
The Unalienable Rights

**Section 2:**
Freedom of Religion

**Section 3:**
Freedom of Speech and Press

**Section 4:**
Freedom of Assembly and Petition

"
All through the years we have had to **fight for civil liberty,** and we know that there are times when the **light** grows rather dim, and every time that happens **democracy** is in danger.

—Eleanor Roosevelt, 1940

**Photo:** Peaceful protest is a 1st Amendment right.

**GOVERNMENT** ONLINE
On the Go

To study anywhere, anytime, download these online resources at PearsonSchool.com/phgovt
• Political Dictionary
• Audio Review
• Downloadable Interactivities

## Lesson Goals

### SECTION 1
Students will…

• identify liberties guaranteed by the Bill of Rights by analyzing photographs and political cartoons.

• understand that rights are not absolute by debating issues in which rights and interests must be balanced.

• describe how the Constitution protects the rights of individuals by creating a diagram.

### SECTION 2
Students will…

• clarify the meaning of the Establishment Clause and its "wall of separation" by completing a diagram and chart concerning cases on freedom of religion.

• learn how the Supreme Court has interpreted the Establishment Clause and Free Exercise Clause by evaluating scenarios about freedom of religion conflicts.

### SECTION 3
Students will…

• identify the limits and protections of freedom of speech by charting restrictions on different forms of expression, analyzing prior restraint, summarizing court rulings on student speech, and interpreting political cartoons.

• identify the limits and protections of freedom of the press by researching media cases.

### SECTION 4
Students will…

• distinguish the conflicting but essential nature of the right to assemble by participating in scenarios about freedom of assembly and petition conflicts.

• understand the restrictions on assembly and petition by identifying and applying time-place-manner regulations and content neutrality to assembly situations.

## Pressed for Time

Have students read the Bill of Rights, and then write a matching quiz listing the first ten amendments in Column 1 and their corresponding rights (out of order) in Column 2. Ask students to exchange and complete the quizzes. Reproduce and distribute the Facts and Enduring Understandings from each section opener of the Teacher Edition. Using the information from their quizzes and the Facts and Enduring Understandings, have students create an illustrated "Know Your Rights" Guide to the Bill of Rights that briefly explains what each right includes as well as what limitations it puts on government.

**DIFFERENTIATED INSTRUCTION KEY**

Look for these symbols to help you adjust steps in each lesson to meet your students' needs.

**L1** Special Needs

**L2** Basic

    **ELL** English Language Learners

    **LPR** Less Proficient Readers

**L3** All Students

**L4** Advanced Students

## How does the Constitution protect the rights of individuals against government?

Answers may include any three of the following:

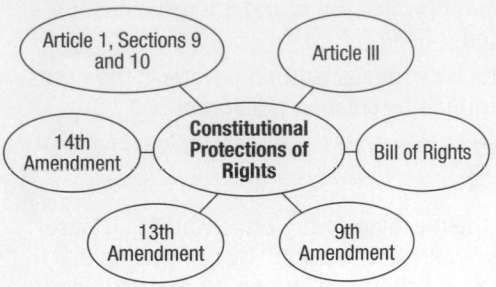

Article 1, Sections 9 and 10 — Article III — 14th Amendment — **Constitutional Protections of Rights** — Bill of Rights — 13th Amendment — 9th Amendment

# Get Started

## LESSON GOALS

Students will . . .

- identify liberties guaranteed by the Bill of Rights by analyzing photographs and political cartoons.
- understand that rights are not absolute by debating issues in which rights and interests must be balanced.
- describe how the Constitution protects the rights of individuals by creating a diagram.

## BEFORE CLASS

Assign the section, the graphic organizer in the text, and the Reading Comprehension Worksheet (Unit 5 All-in-One, p. 72) before class.

**L2 Differentiate** Reading Comprehension Worksheet (Unit 5 All-in-One, p. 74)

# SKILLS DEVELOPMENT

## ANALYZE SOURCES

To practice analyzing sources in this section, use the Chapter 19 Skills Worksheet (Unit 5 All-in-One, p. 77). You may wish to teach the skill explicitly before you discuss the Bill of Rights. For L2 and L1 students, assign the adapted Skill Activity (Unit 5 All-in-One, p. 78).

---

## SECTION 1

# The **Unalienable Rights**

### Guiding Question

**How does the Constitution protect the rights of individuals against government?** Use a concept web to identify three parts of the Constitution that protect individual rights.

Constitutional Protections of Rights

### Political Dictionary

- Bill of Rights
- civil liberties
- civil rights
- alien
- Due Process Clause
- process of incorporation

### Objectives

1. Explain how Americans' commitment to freedom led to the creation of the Bill of Rights.
2. Understand that the rights guaranteed by limited government are not absolute.
3. Show how federalism affects individual rights.
4. Describe how the 9th Amendment helps protect individual rights.

**Image Above:** James Madison, author of the Bill of Rights

Have you ever heard of Walter Barnette? How about Toyosaburo Korematsu? Dollree Mapp? Clarence Earl Gideon? Walter Barnette was a Jehovah's Witness in West Virginia who told his children not to salute the American flag or to recite the Pledge of Allegiance in school. Toyosaburo Korematsu was an American citizen interned by the Federal Government during World War II. Dollree Mapp was jailed for keeping "lewd and lascivious books" in her boarding house in Ohio. Clarence Earl Gideon went to prison for breaking into a poolroom in Florida. You will encounter these names again as you read this chapter and the next one. Each of these people played an important part in building and protecting the rights of all Americans.

## A Commitment to Freedom

A commitment to personal freedom is deeply rooted in America's colonial past. For centuries, the people of England waged a continuing struggle for individual rights, and the early colonists brought a dedication to that cause with them to America.

Their commitment to freedom took root here, and it flourished. The Revolutionary War was fought to preserve and expand those very rights: the rights of the individual against government. In proclaiming the independence of the new United States, the founders of this country declared:

> **PRIMARY SOURCE**
> We hold these truths to be self-evident, that all men are created equal, that they are endowed by their Creator with certain unalienable Rights, that among these are Life, Liberty and the pursuit of Happiness. That to secure these rights, Governments are instituted among Men. . . .
>
> —Declaration of Independence

The Framers of the Constitution repeated the justification for the existence of government in the Preamble to the Constitution. That document, they said, was written to "secure the Blessings of Liberty to ourselves and our Posterity."

---

# Focus on the Basics

**FACTS:** • The first ten amendments to the Constitution are known as the Bill of Rights. • Individual rights are not absolute. • The 14th Amendment's Due Process Clause prevents the States from abridging rights guaranteed by the Bill of Rights. • The 9th Amendment declares that people have rights in addition to those listed in the Constitution.

**CONCEPTS:** limited government, individual rights, federalism, due process of law

**ENDURING UNDERSTANDINGS:** • The guarantees in the Bill of Rights reflect the nation's commitment to personal freedom and to the principle of limited government. • The Due Process Clause of the 14th Amendment ensures that State governments do not limit or take away rights given to citizens by the National Government.

The Constitution, as it was written in Philadelphia, contained a number of important guarantees. The most notable of these can be found in Article I, Sections 9 and 10, and in Article III. Unlike many of the first State constitutions, however, the new National Constitution did not include a general listing of the rights of the people.

That omission raised an outcry. The objections were so strong that several States ratified the Constitution only with the understanding that a listing of rights would soon be added. The first session of the new Congress proposed a series of amendments. Ten of them, known as the **Bill of Rights,** were ratified by the States and became a part of the Constitution on December 15, 1791. Later amendments, especially the 13th and the 14th, have added to the Constitution's guarantees of personal freedom.

The Constitution guarantees both rights and liberties to the American people. The distinction between civil rights and civil liberties is murky at best. Legal scholars often disagree on the matter, and the two terms often are used interchangeably.

Think of the distinction this way: In general, **civil liberties** are protections *against government.* They are guarantees of the safety of persons, opinions, and property from <u>arbitrary</u> acts of government. Thus, freedom of religion, freedom of speech and press, and the guarantees of fair trial are prime examples of civil liberties.

In contrast, **civil rights** are often associated with *positive acts of government* that seek to make constitutional guarantees a reality for all people. Viewed from this perspective, laws against discrimination on the basis of race, sex, religious belief, or national origin set out in the Civil Rights Act of 1964 are leading examples of civil rights.

## Limited Government

Remember, government in the United States is limited. The Constitution is filled with examples of this fact. Chief among them are its many guarantees of personal freedom. Each of those guarantees is either an outright

prohibition or a restriction on the power of government to do something.

All governments have and use authority over individuals. The all-important difference between a democratic government and a dictatorial one lies in the extent of that authority. In a dictatorial <u>regime</u>, the government's powers are practically unlimited. The government regularly suppresses dissent, often harshly. In the United States, however, governmental authority is strictly limited. As Justice Robert H. Jackson once put the point:

### " PRIMARY SOURCE

**If there is any fixed star in our constitutional constellation, it is that no official, high or petty, can prescribe what shall be <u>orthodox</u> in politics, nationalism, religion, or any other matters of opinion or force citizens to confess by word or act their faith therein.**

—*West Virginia Board of Education* v. *Barnette,* **1943**

**Rights Are Relative, Not Absolute** The Constitution guarantees many rights to everyone in the United States. Still, no one has the right to do anything he or she pleases. Rather, all persons have the right to do as they please as long as they do not infringe on the rights of others. That is, each person's rights are *relative* to the rights of every other person.

To illustrate the point: Everyone in the United States has a right of free speech, but no one enjoys absolute freedom of speech. A person can be punished for

✔ **Checkpoint**
**How does the Bill of Rights limit government in the United States?**

**regime**
*n.* a government

**orthodox**
*adj.* standard, recognized, accepted

**arbitrary**
*adj.* random

No one has a right to play loud music if doing so infringes on the rights of others. ▼

547

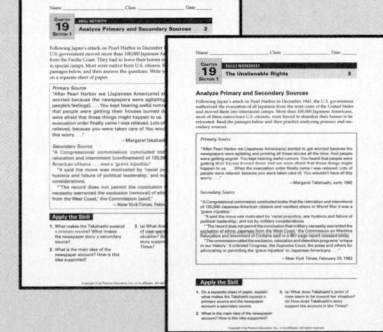

**BELLRINGER**

Write the following on the board: **Is it important to protect the right to protest? Explain. Write your answer in your notebook.**

# Teach

To present this topic using online resources, use the lesson presentations at **PearsonSchool.com/phgovt.**

### INTRODUCE THE TOPIC

Write these terms on the board and ask students to define them in their notebooks: *civil liberties* (guarantees of the safety of persons, opinions, and property from the arbitrary acts of government); *Bill of Rights* (the first ten amendments to the Constitution); *unalienable rights* (rights that cannot be taken away; life, liberty, and the pursuit of happiness). Work with the class to agree on definitions and write them on the board. Next, have students name the 1st Amendment rights and freedoms. *(freedom of religion, speech, and press; the right to assemble and to petition the government for redress of grievances)*

**L3** **Differentiate** Ask students why they think this section is titled "The Unalienable Rights." *(It covers the most basic of rights—the 1st Amendment freedoms.)* Can students think of additional rights they consider unalienable?

**L1 L2** **Differentiate** Have students create an acrostic poem or mnemonic device to help them remember the 1st Amendment freedoms.

### REVIEW BELLRINGER ANSWERS

Discuss the Bellringer question. *(Sample answer: Yes. The right to protest acts as a safeguard against government power, helps inform lawmakers of citizens' concerns, and allows the minority opinion to be heard.)* Ask students to consider what might happen if people were not allowed to protest *(only the majority voice would be heard),* or if protesters demonstrated in a country that had unlimited government. *(In dictatorships, protests against the government are usually put down forcibly.)*

**L3 L4** **Differentiate** Ask students to identify demonstrations that have had an impact on the United States or other countries. *(protests against the Vietnam War or war in Iraq, Tiananmen Square, Myanmar)* Ask: **What prevents police from dispersing the protesters?** *(The 1st Amendment gives U.S. citizens the right to peaceably protest.)*

# Answers

**Checkpoint** by either prohibiting or restricting certain actions of government

## DISTRIBUTE CORE WORKSHEET

Distribute Chapter 19 Section 1 Core Worksheet (Unit 5 All-in-One, p. 76). Explain that students will analyze a political cartoon related to the Bill of Rights.

**L2** **L1** **Differentiate** Have students work together to identify the rights portrayed and opinions expressed.

**L4** **Differentiate** Have students select one right in the Bill of Rights and create political cartoons that show the interests the Supreme Court must balance when ruling on cases related to this right. Have students explain their cartoons to the class. Evaluate students' work with the Rubric for Assessing Political Cartoons (Unit 5 All-in-One, p. 244).

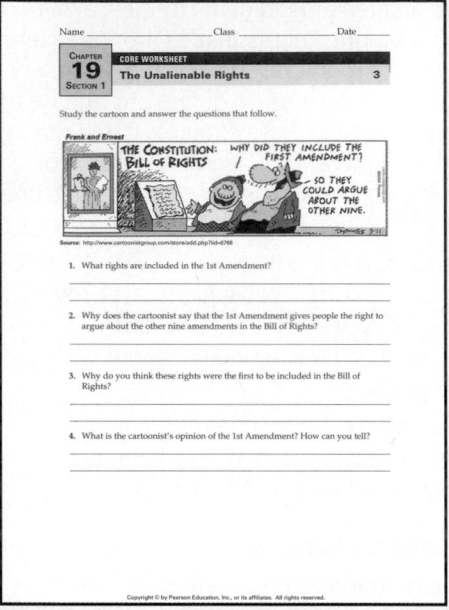

## DISCUSS AND DEBATE BALANCING RIGHTS

Write on the board: **Rights are relative, not absolute.** Ask students to explain. *(Individuals can exercise their rights only as long as their actions do not infringe on the rights of others.)* Organize student groups to debate Issue 1 or Issue 2 below. Each debate should include a For and an Against position and a discussion of the conflicting rights.

**Issue 1** The government should pass a law limiting the use of cell phones in public places.

**Issue 2** Before entering a mall, people must show an identification card and pass through a metal detector.

## Answers

**Checkpoint** Possible response: The right to free speech does not allow one person to slander another.

---

✔ **Checkpoint**
Cite an example that illustrates the point that rights are relative.

**vulgarity**
*n.* an offensive or indecent act or expression

**stringent**
*adj.* strict, rigid, narrow

using obscene language, or for using words in a way that causes someone to commit a crime—to riot or to desert from the military, for example. The Supreme Court dealt with this point most recently in *Federal Communications Commission* v. *Fox Television Stations*, 2009. There, 5–4, it upheld the FCC's controversial policy of punishing broadcasters for even the one-time use of gross <u>vulgarities</u> on the air.

In this oft-quoted line, Justice Oliver Wendell Holmes put the relative nature of each person's rights in this way:

> ❝ **PRIMARY SOURCE**
> **The most <u>stringent</u> protection of free speech would not protect a man in falsely shouting fire in a theatre and causing a panic.**
> —*Schenck* v. *United States*, 1919

**When Rights Conflict** On occasion, different guarantees of rights come into conflict with one another. For example, cases involving freedom of the press versus the right to a fair trial are not at all uncommon.

In one famous case, Dr. Samuel Sheppard of Cleveland, Ohio, had been convicted of murdering his wife. His lengthy trial was widely covered in the national media. On appeal, Sheppard claimed that the highly sensational coverage had denied him a fair trial. The Supreme Court agreed. In *Sheppard* v. *Maxwell*, 1966, the Court rejected the free press argument, overturned Sheppard's conviction, and ordered a new trial.

**To Whom Are Rights Guaranteed?** Most constitutional rights are extended to all persons. The Supreme Court has often held that "persons" includes **aliens**, people who are not citizens of the country in which they live. Not *all* rights are given to aliens, however. The right to travel freely throughout the country is guaranteed to all citizens, for example, but travel by aliens can be restricted.[1]

---

1 See the two Privileges and Immunities clauses, in Article IV, Section 2, and the 14th Amendment. The guarantee does not extend to citizens under some form of legal restraint—for example, in jail or out on bail awaiting trial.

After the bombing of Pearl Harbor by Japan in 1941, all persons of Japanese descent living on the Pacific Coast were evacuated—forcibly moved—inland. Many suffered economic and other hardships. In 1944, the Supreme Court reluctantly upheld the forced evacuation as a reasonable wartime emergency measure.[2] Still, the relocation was strongly criticized over the years. In 1988, the Federal Government admitted that the wartime relocation had been both unnecessary and unjust. Congress voted to pay $20,000 to each living internee. It also declared, "the Congress apologizes on behalf of the nation."

The current war on terrorism has created a political climate similar to that of the early days of World War II. Did the mistreatment of Japanese Americans then provide a lesson for today? Will the rights of Muslims and others of Middle Eastern descent be respected by government as it fights terrorism here and abroad?

## Federalism and Individual Rights

Federalism is a complicated governmental arrangement. It produces any number of problems—including a very complex pattern of guarantees of individual rights in the United States.

**The Bill of Rights** Remember, the first ten amendments to the Constitution were originally intended as restrictions on the new National Government, not on the already existing States. And that remains the fact of the matter today.[3]

To illustrate this important point: The 5th Amendment says that no person can be charged with "a capital, or otherwise infamous crime" except by a grand jury. As a part of the Bill of Rights, this provision applies

---

2 *Korematsu* v. *United States*, 1944. However, on the same day the Court held, in *Ex parte Endo*, that once the loyalty of any citizen internee had been established, no restriction could be placed on that person's freedom to travel that was not legally imposed on all other citizens.

3 The Supreme Court first held that the provisions of the Bill of Rights restrict only the National Government in *Barron* v. *Baltimore*, 1833. This was the first case in which the point was raised. The Supreme Court has followed that holding (precedent) ever since.

---

# Background

**DUE PROCESS CLAUSE** Congress rejected much of the original draft of the Bill of Rights, which contained restrictions on both National and State governments. In the late 1700s, many Americans trusted their State governments far more than the National Government. For many decades, however, some States continued to have State-supported churches because their constitutions pre-dated the federal constitution. Decades after the Civil War ended, many southern States ignored the 14th Amendment, which was intended to protect the rights of former slaves. According to political science professor Richard Cortner, through the incorporation process the Court turned the Due Process Clause of the 14th Amendment into a "second bill of rights" more applicable "to the liberty of the average American than the one . . . ratified by the states in 1791."

## The 14th Amendment's Due Process Clause
# Incorporation of Rights

- Provisions of the **Bill of Rights INCORPORATED** into the 14th Amendment's Due Process Clause

**1st AMENDMENT**
- Freedom of speech
- Freedom of press
- Freedom of assembly, petition
- Free Exercise Clause
- Establishment Clause

**2nd AMENDMENT**
- Right to keep, bear arms

**4th AMENDMENT**
- No unreasonable searches, seizures

**5th AMENDMENT**
- No self-incrimination
- No double jeopardy

**6th AMENDMENT**
- Right to counsel
- Right to confront and obtain witnesses
- Speedy trial
- Trial by jury in criminal cases

**8th AMENDMENT**
- No cruel, unusual punishments

- Provisions of the **Bill of Rights NOT INCORPORATED** into the 14th Amendment's Due Process Clause

**3rd AMENDMENT**
- No quartering of troops

**5th AMENDMENT**
- Grand jury

**7th AMENDMENT**
- Trial by jury in civil cases

▶▶ **Interpreting Charts** This chart shows which rights the Supreme Court has "nationalized" by incorporating them into the meaning of the Due Process Clause in the 14th Amendment. *Why do you think that some, but not all, rights have been incorporated into the 14th Amendment's Due Process Clause?*

only to the National Government. The States may use the grand jury to bring accusations of serious crime—or, if they prefer, they can use some other process to do so. The grand jury is a part of the criminal justice system in all but two States and the District of Columbia, however. For additional information, see the coverage of the grand jury in the next chapter and also in Chapter 24.

**The Modifying Effect of the 14th Amendment** Again, the provisions of the Bill of Rights apply against the National Government, not against the States. This does *not* mean, however, that the States can deny basic rights to the people.

In part, the States cannot do so because each of their own constitutions contains a bill of rights. In addition, they cannot deny these basic rights because of the 14th Amendment's **Due Process Clause.** It says

" **FROM THE CONSTITUTION**

**No State shall . . . deprive any person of life, liberty, or property, without due process of law. . . .**
—14th Amendment, Section 1

The Supreme Court has often said that the 14th Amendment's Due Process Clause means that no State can deny to any person any right that is "basic or essential to the American concept of ordered liberty."

But what specific rights are "basic or essential"? The Supreme Court has answered that question in a long series of cases in which it has held that most (but not all) of the protections in the Bill of Rights are also covered by the 14th Amendment's Due Process Clause, and so apply against the States. In deciding those cases, the Court has engaged in what has come to be called the **process of incorporation.** It has incorporated—merged,

# Constitutional Principles

**JUDICIAL REVIEW** In *Gitlow* v. *New York,* 1925, the Supreme Court established that the Due Process Clause prevented States from impairing personal freedoms. However, the decision upheld Gitlow's conviction. Justice Holmes, in dissent, went one step further in arguing that the conviction be overturned. His dissent addressed the New York attorneys' claim that Gitlow's actions were an incitement. "It is said that this manifesto was more than a theory, that it was an incitement. Every idea is an incitement. . . . The only difference between the expression of an opinion and incitement in the narrower sense is the speaker's enthusiasm for the result."

Tell students to go to the Audio Tour for a listing of rights incorporated in the 14th Amendment's Due Process Clause.

**CREATE A DIAGRAM**

Have a volunteer read aloud the 14th Amendment's Due Process Clause from the textbook. Ask: **From what or whom does the 14th Amendment protect citizens' rights?** *(State governments)* **Why does the Bill of Rights not protect citizens against the States?** *(The Bill of Rights applies only to the National Government.)* **What are some other rights that U.S. citizens have that are not specifically listed in the Constitution?** *(Provide students with prompts, such as the right to move from one State to another or the right to change jobs without government permission.)* **How are these unspecified rights protected?** *(9th Amendment)* Have students use this information to create a diagram or other visual that illustrates how individuals' rights are protected in "layers" by various parts of the Constitution.

**L3** **Differentiate** Display Transparency 19B, and have students select one of the Court cases to research. They should explain in a paragraph how the case incorporated a Bill of Rights guarantee into the 14th Amendment's Due Process Clause.

**EXTEND THE LESSON**

**L3** **Differentiate** Have students create an illustrated "Know Your Rights" Guide to the Bill of Rights that briefly explains what each right includes and the limits it puts on government. Students can use print or online resources to find examples of citizens exercising these rights.

**L2** **Differentiate** Distribute the Extend Activity entitled "The Bill of Rights" (Unit 5 All-in-One, p. 79).

# Assess and Remediate

**L2** **L3** Ask students to list ten things they have the right to do without government interference. Then ask them to note whether each right listed is protected by the 1st Amendment, the 9th Amendment, the 14th Amendment, or some other part of the Constitution.

## Answers

**Interpreting Charts** Sample answer: Quartering of troops is obsolete. States should be allowed to decide on the jury process that works best for them. The right to bear arms is too controversial to be nationalized.

## Answers

**Checkpoint** The case began the incorporation of 1st Amendment rights into the 14th Amendment's Due Process Clause.

---

combined—most of the guarantees in the Bill of Rights into the 14th Amendment's Due Process Clause.

The Court began that historic incorporation in *Gitlow* v. *New York*, 1925. That landmark case involved Benjamin Gitlow, a Communist, who had been convicted of criminal anarchy in the State courts. He had made several speeches and published a pamphlet calling for the violent overthrow of government in this country.

On appeal, the Court upheld Gitlow's conviction and the State law under which he had been tried. In deciding the case, however, the Court made this crucial point: Freedom of speech and press, which the 1st Amendment says cannot be denied by the National Government, are also "among the fundamental personal rights and liberties protected by the Due Process Clause of the 14th Amendment from impairment by the States."

Soon after *Gitlow*, the Court held each of the 1st Amendment's other guarantees to be covered by the 14th Amendment. It struck down State laws involving speech (*Fiske* v. *Kansas*, 1927; *Stromberg* v. *California*, 1931), the press (*Near* v. *Minnesota*, 1931), assembly and petition (*DeJonge* v. *Oregon*, 1937), and religion (*Cantwell* v. *Connecticut*, 1940). In each of those cases, the Court declared a State law unconstitutional as a violation of the 14th Amendment's Due Process Clause.

In the 1960s, the Court extended the scope of the 14th Amendment's Due Process Clause even further, and in 2010 it added the 2nd Amendment to that coverage. We shall look at incorporation of the 1st Amendment's guarantees in this chapter and examine the inclusion of the others in Chapter 20.

## The 9th Amendment

The Constitution does *not* contain a complete catalog of all the rights held by Americans. The little-noted 9th Amendment says that there are, in fact, some guarantees beyond those set out in the Constitution:

> **FROM THE CONSTITUTION**
>
> **The enumeration in the Constitution, of certain rights, shall not be construed to deny or disparage others retained by the people.**
>
> —9th Amendment

Over the years, the Supreme Court has found a number of other rights "retained by the people." They include, most notably, the guarantee that an accused person will not be tried on the basis of evidence unlawfully gained, and the right of a woman to choose to have an abortion without undue interference by government.

---

**Essential Questions Journal** To continue to build a response to the chapter Essential Question, go to your **Essential Questions Journal.**

## SECTION 1 ASSESSMENT

1. **Guiding Question** Use your completed graphic organizer to answer this question: How does the Constitution protect the rights of individuals against government?

**Key Terms and Comprehension**

2. What is the **Bill of Rights,** and why did its omission from the original Constitution raise such an outcry?

3. Compare and contrast **civil liberties** and **civil rights.**

4. **(a)** What is the **process of incorporation? (b)** What guarantees in the Bill of Rights are covered by the 14th Amendment's **Due Process Clause?**

**Critical Thinking**

5. **Draw Inferences (a)** Why are individual rights not absolute? **(b)** Cite two examples of the fact that rights may come into conflict with one another.

6. **Predict Consequences** How do you think life in this country might be different today if the Court had not applied the process of incorporation to the 14th Amendment?

**Quick Write**

**Persuasive Essay: Choose a Topic** To write a persuasive essay, one that convinces others to accept your views, you should select a topic that you feel strongly about. Read through this section and identify a topic on which you might write such an essay—for example, proper limits on freedom of speech.

# Assessment Answers

**1.** Guarantees are written into Article I, Sections 9 and 10; Article III; the Bill of Rights, and most notably Amendments 9, 13, and 14. These guarantees either prohibit or limit the power of government to do something.

**2.** The Bill of Rights is the first ten amendments to the Constitution. People wanted specific, written protection against abuses of government.

**3.** Civil liberties are protections against arbitrary acts of government; civil rights are positive acts of government that seek to make constitutional guarantees for all people.

**4. (a)** The process of incorporation is the judicial process that has combined most of the Bill of Rights guarantees into the 14th Amendment's Due Process Clause. Incorporating these guarantees nationalizes them—making them apply to the States as well as to the National Government. **(b)** everything in the 1st, 4th, 6th, and 8th and part of the 5th amendments

**5. (a)** Individual rights cannot be absolute because they must not infringe upon the rights of others. **(b)** Sample answers: Freedom of the press may conflict with the right to a fair trial;

freedom of speech may conflict with the right to privacy.

**6.** Possible answer: Without the process of incorporation, the rights of citizens might vary from State to State.

**QUICK WRITE** Students must select an issue with at least two sides. At this stage of the writing process, have students think about the various strategies they may use to persuade their audience—for example, emotion, logic or reason, and statistics for and against.

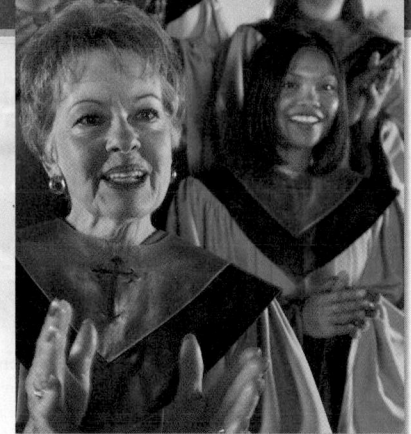

## SECTION 2

# Freedom
## of Religion

### Guiding Question

**How does the 1st Amendment protect the freedom of religion?**
Use a chart like the one below to take notes on five Supreme Court cases that protect the freedom of religion.

| Freedom of Religion | |
|---|---|
| **Case** | **Ruling** |
| • *Pierce* v. *Society of Sisters*, 1925 | • |
| • | • |
| • | • |

### Political Dictionary
- Establishment Clause
- Free Exercise Clause
- parochial

### Objectives
1. Examine why religious liberty is protected in the Bill of Rights.
2. Describe the limits imposed by the Establishment Clause of the 1st Amendment.
3. Summarize the Supreme Court rulings on religion and education as well as other Establishment Clause cases.
4. Explain how the Supreme Court has interpreted and limited the Free Exercise Clause.

**Image Above:** Freedom of religion is among the most important of the rights guaranteed by the Constitution.

---

In the early 1830s, a Frenchman, Alexis de Tocqueville, came to America to observe life in the young country. He is said to have later written in his classic, *Democracy in America,* that he had searched for the greatness of America in many places: in its large harbors and deep rivers, in its fertile fields and boundless forests, in its rich mines and vast world commerce, in its public schools and institutions of higher learning, and in its democratic legislature and matchless Constitution. Yet it was not until he went into the churches that Tocqueville said he came to understand the genius and the power of this country.

### Religious Liberty

The 1st Amendment sets out *two* guarantees of religious freedom. It prohibits (1) "an establishment of religion" (in the **Establishment Clause**), and (2) any arbitrary interference by government with "the free exercise thereof" (in the **Free Exercise Clause**). And, recall, both protections are extended against the States by the Due Process Clause in the 14th Amendment.[4]

These constitutional guarantees were born out of decades of colonial opposition to established churches—to official government-sponsored churches in the colonies. The Virginia Statute for Religious Freedom, adopted in 1786, was the immediate basis for the 1st Amendment. Drafted by Thomas Jefferson, that law provided for absolute religious freedom in Virginia. It declared that that State could not require that any person profess any set of religious beliefs nor support any religious institution.

### Separation of Church and State

The Establishment Clause sets up, in Thomas Jefferson's words, "a wall of separation between church and state." That wall is not infinitely high, however, and it is not impenetrable. Church and government are constitutionally separated in this country, but they are neither enemies nor even strangers to one another.

---

4 Also, Article VI, Section 3 provides that "no religious Test shall ever be required as a Qualification to any Office or public Trust under the United States." In *Torcaso* v. *Watkins*, 1961, the Supreme Court held that the 14th Amendment puts the same restriction on the States.

Chapter 19 • Section 2 **551**

---

# Focus on the Basics

**FACTS:** • The 1st Amendment's Establishment Clause prohibits government from establishing or aiding religion. • Most Establishment Clause cases involve religion and education. • The 1st Amendment's Free Exercise Clause guarantees individuals the right to believe as they choose in matters of religion. • The 14th Amendment's Due Process Clause extends 1st Amendment protections against the States.

**CONCEPTS:** individual rights and responsibilities, limited government, judicial review

**ENDURING UNDERSTANDINGS:** • The Establishment Clause sets up "a wall of separation between church and state." • The Free Exercise Clause protects religious beliefs but does not protect religious actions that violate laws or threaten safety.

---

**GUIDING QUESTION**

## How does the 1st Amendment protect the freedom of religion?

| Freedom of Religion (Sample Answers) | |
|---|---|
| **Case** | **Ruling** |
| *Pierce* v. *Society of Sisters*, 1925 | struck down law requiring children to attend public (not parochial) schools |
| *Everson* v. *Board of Education*, 1947 | upheld tax-supported busing of parochial school students |
| *Westside Community Schools* v. *Mergens*, 1990 | upheld law requiring schools to allow student religious groups to meet on same terms as other student groups |
| *Epperson* v. *Arkansas*, 1968 | struck down law banning teaching of evolution |
| *Lemon* v. *Kurtzman*, 1971 | bans government sponsorship, financing, and active involvement in religious activity |

## Get Started

### LESSON GOALS

Students will . . .

- clarify the meaning of the Establishment Clause and its "wall of separation" by completing a diagram and chart concerning cases on freedom of religion.
- learn how the Supreme Court has interpreted the Establishment Clause and Free Exercise Clause by evaluating scenarios about freedom of religion conflicts.

### BEFORE CLASS

Assign the section, the graphic organizer in the text, and the Reading Comprehension Worksheet (Unit 5 All-in-One, p. 82) before class.

**L2 Differentiate** Reading Comprehension Worksheet (Unit 5 All-in-One, p. 84)

## SKILLS DEVELOPMENT

### DECISION MAKING

Before students begin analyzing the various scenarios presented in this lesson, you may want to review tips on decision making in the Skills Handbook, p. S18.

Chapter 19 • Section 2 **551**

# Teach

To present this topic using online resources, use the lesson presentations at **PearsonSchool.com/phgovt.**

### BELLRINGER

Write on the board: **In what ways is freedom of religion limited in public schools? Answer in your notebook.**

**L2 Differentiate** Provide prompts, such as focus on prayer, the Bible, group meetings, religious artifacts, and religious clothing.

### REVIEW BELLRINGER ANSWERS

Ask students to share their answers to the Bellringer question. Possible responses:

- School-sponsored prayer or "moments of silence" are prohibited.
- Observances of religious holidays are prohibited.
- Religious groups cannot use public school facilities during school hours.
- Bible study is prohibited in classrooms.
- The Ten Commandments and religious icons cannot be posted in classrooms.

**L2 Differentiate** Have students define the term *icons* (visual representations of gods, saints, and other religious entities).

**L3 Differentiate** Ask: **Why do you think government prohibits these forms of religious expression in public schools?** *(Guide students to conclude that limiting government support for and opposition to all religions protects minority religions and free expression for all people.)*

**L2 L3 Differentiate** Demonstrate the sensitive nature of personal belief. First, ask students to raise their hands if they have brown eyes; do the same with blue-eyed and green-eyed students. Explain to students in the minority that they will have to purchase and wear [brown] contact lenses to "fit in." Now loosely apply this reasoning to religion. Ask students how comfortable they would be if they were asked which religion, if any, they and their family follow. Point out that anyone who follows a minority religion would be "different." In many countries, they would be harassed. In the United States, however, their beliefs are protected.

**L3 Differentiate** Ask: **What aspects of religion do you think *are* allowed in public schools?** *(Examples: Individuals can pray when and as they choose in any place. The Bible can be studied as a literary or historical piece. Religious groups may use public school facilities after school.)*

---

## Answers

**Checkpoint** The 1st Amendment requires the government to maintain strict neutrality, neither aiding nor opposing religion.

---

**sect**
*n.* a religious group

Government has done much to encourage churches and religion in the United States. Nearly all property of and contributions to religious <u>sects</u> are free from federal, State, and local taxation. Chaplains serve with each branch of the armed forces. Most public officials take an oath of office in the name of God. Sessions of Congress, most State legislatures, and many city councils open with prayer. The nation's anthem and its coins and currency make reference to God.

The limits imposed by the Establishment Clause remain a matter of continuing and often heated controversy. The Supreme Court did not hear its first Establishment Clause case until 1947. A few earlier cases did involve government and religion, but none of them involved a direct consideration of the "wall of separation."

The most important of those earlier cases was *Pierce* v. *Society of Sisters,* 1925. There, the Court held an Oregon compulsory school attendance law unconstitutional. That law required parents to send their children to *public* schools. It was purposely intended to eliminate private and especially **parochial** (church-related) schools.

In striking down the law, the Court did not address the Establishment Clause question. Instead, it found the law to be an unreasonable interference with the liberty of parents to direct the upbringing of their children—and so in conflict with the Due Process Clause of the 14th Amendment.

## Religion and Education

The Court's first direct ruling on the Establishment Clause came in *Everson* v. *Board of Education,* a 1947 case often called the New Jersey School Bus Case. The Court upheld a State law that provided for the public, tax-supported busing of students attending any school in the State, including parochial ones.

Critics had attacked the law as a support of religion. They maintained that it relieved parochial schools of the need to pay for busing and so freed their money for other, including religious, purposes. The Court disagreed; it found the law to be a safety measure intended to benefit children, no matter what schools they might attend. Since that decision, the largest number of the Court's Establishment Clause cases have involved, in one way or another, religion and education.

**Released Time** "Released time" programs allow public schools to release students during school hours to attend religious classes. In *McCollum* v. *Board of Education,* 1948, the Court struck down the released time program then in place in Champaign, Illinois, because the program used public facilities for religious purposes.

Yet in *Zorach* v. *Clauson,* 1952, the Court upheld New York City's released time program. It did so because that program required religious classes to be held in private places off school grounds.

**Prayers and the Bible** The Court has now decided seven major cases involving prayer and the reading of the Bible in public schools. In *Engel* v. *Vitale,* 1962, the Court outlawed the use, even on a voluntary basis, of a prayer written by the New York State Board of Regents. The prayer read: "Almighty God, we acknowledge our dependence upon Thee, and we beg Thy blessings upon us, our parents, our teachers, and our country."

In striking down the prayer, the Supreme Court held that:

> ❝
> **PRIMARY SOURCE**
> [T]he constitutional prohibition against laws respecting an establishment of religion must at least mean that, in this country, it is no part of the business of government to compose official prayers for any group of the American people to recite as part of a religious program carried on by government.
> —Justice Hugo L. Black

The High Court extended that holding in two 1963 cases. In *Abington School District* v. *Schempp,* it struck down a Pennsylvania law requiring that each school day begin with readings from the Bible and a recitation of the Lord's Prayer. In *Murray* v. *Curlett,* the Court erased a similar rule in Baltimore. In both cases, the Court found violations of

---

# Differentiated Resources

The following resources are located in the All-in-One, Unit 5, Chapter 19, Section 2:

**L3** Reading Comprehension Worksheet (p. 82)
**L2** Reading Comprehension Worksheet (p. 84)
**L3** Core Worksheet (p. 86)
**L3** Quiz A (p. 88)
**L2** Quiz B (p. 89)

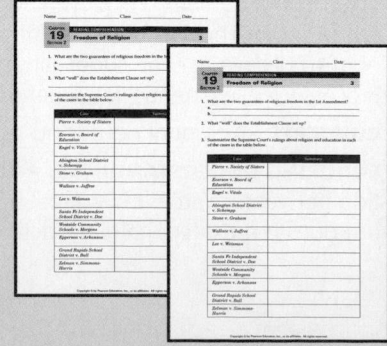

## 1st Amendment

"Congress shall make no law respecting an establishment of religion, or prohibiting the free exercise thereof; or abridging the freedom of speech, or of the press; or the right of the people peaceably to assemble, and to petition the Government for a redress of grievances.

# FROM THE CONSTITUTION

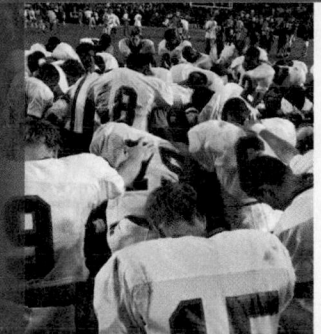

**Ruling on Religion** The Court has held that public schools cannot sponsor religious exercises. It has not ruled, however, that individuals cannot pray when and as they choose in schools or in any other place. Nor has it held that students cannot study the Bible in a literary or historical context in school. The Court's rulings have nevertheless been widely criticized. Many critics have proposed that the Constitution be amended to allow voluntary group prayer in public schools. Despite the Court's decisions, both organized prayer and Bible readings are found in many public school classrooms today.

**Constitutional Principles** How does the separation of church and state reflect the principle of limited government?

▲ Public schools cannot sponsor prayer at school-related events.

"the command of the 1st Amendment that the government maintain strict neutrality, neither aiding nor opposing religion."

Since then, the Supreme Court has found the following to be unconstitutional:

• a Kentucky law that ordered the posting of the Ten Commandments in all public school classrooms, *Stone* v. *Graham*, 1980;

• Alabama's "moment of silence" law, *Wallace* v. *Jaffree*, 1985, which provided for a one-minute period for "meditation or voluntary prayer" at the start of each school day;

• the offering of prayer as part of a public school graduation ceremony, in a Rhode Island case, *Lee* v. *Weisman*, 1992;

• a Texas school district's policy that permitted student-led prayer at high school football games, *Santa Fe Independent School District* v. *Doe*, 2000.

**Student Religious Groups** The Equal Access Act of 1984 declares that any

public high school that receives federal funds (nearly all do) must allow student religious groups to meet in the school on the same terms that it sets for other student organizations. The Supreme Court found that the law does not violate the Establishment Clause in a Nebraska case, *Westside Community Schools* v. *Mergens*, 1990. There, several students had tried to form a Christian club at the high school. The students had to fight the school board in the federal courts in order to win their point.

The High Court has since gone much further than it did in *Mergens*—in a case from New York, *Good News Club* v. *Milford Central School*, 2001. There, a school board had refused to allow a group of grade-school students to meet after school to sing, pray, memorize scriptures, and hear Bible lessons. The school board based its action on the Establishment Clause. The Court, however, held that the board had violated Good News Club members' 1st and 14th amendment rights to free speech.

## Background

**BUILDING THE "WALL"** In 1787, the Constitution's only mention of religion was a statement that there could be no religious requirements for holding federal office. Thomas Jefferson, unlike many leaders of his day, was committed to a "wall of separation between church and state." He resisted declaring a national day of prayer and thanksgiving. With this unpopular action, he broke a tradition begun by George Washington. Despite the 1st Amendment ban on the establishment of religion, some States continued to ignore the Bill of Rights on this issue. In the early 1800s, some States taxed their citizens to support their State's Christian churches. Several State constitutions prohibited non-Christians from holding public office or refused to allow them to vote. The "wall of separation" grew more quickly after the incorporation process of the 14th Amendment began in the twentieth century.

## CLARIFY "ESTABLISHMENT" AND "FREE EXERCISE"

Have a volunteer read aloud the 1st Amendment in the textbook feature. Ask: **Which part of the 1st Amendment addresses freedom of religion?** Be sure students understand that the constitutional guarantee of religious freedom has two parts: the Establishment Clause *(creates a "wall of separation between church and state" by prohibiting government from passing any law that establishes a State or national religion or favors one religion over another)* and the Free Exercise Clause *(guarantees all people the right to believe whatever they choose in matters of religion)*.

**L2 ELL Differentiate** Explain that the term *church* refers to all religions and *state* refers to local, State, and National Government.

**L2 Differentiate** Point out that another way to think of the Establishment Clause is as an "anti-Establishment Clause"—the government *cannot* establish or favor a religion.

## DRAW A "WALL OF SEPARATION"

The "height" of the wall of separation—the limits imposed by the Establishment Clause—varies. Have students draw, in pencil, a five-paneled wall and the labels "church" in the foreground and "state" in the background. On the board, list these Establishment Clause cases (but not the height of the panels):

• *Engel* v. *Vitale*, 1962 (high panel)
• *Wallace* v. *Jaffree*, 1985 (high panel)
• *Committee for Public Education and Religious Liberty* v. *Regan*, 1980 (medium panel)
• *County of Allegheny* v. *ACLU*, 1989 (high panel)
• *March* v. *Chambers*, 1983 (low panel)

Have students label their panels with the cases and their rulings. Students should read about each case, decide whether the Court placed a high or low wall of separation, adjust the panel height accordingly, and explain their reasoning.

**L2 Differentiate** Instead of actual cases, write the following issues on the board, and have students apply them to their walls. These issues correspond to the cases above.

• School-sponsored prayer (high panel)
• State-sponsored "moment of silence" (high panel)
• State support for standardized testing in parochial schools (medium panel)
• Seasonal displays of a single religious doctrine at government buildings (high panel)
• Group prayer in State legislatures (low panel)

## Answers

**Constitutional Principles** It limits government interference and prevents the government from favoring one religion over another.

## SUMMARIZE ESTABLISHMENT CLAUSE CASES

Display the first column and row of Transparency 19C, which focuses on five Supreme Court cases that examine issues related to religion in schools. Working in groups of five, have students copy the chart into their notebooks, with each student completing Columns 2–4 for a single case. After students have completed their own rows, they should share their information with other group members.

When all groups are finished, uncover one row on the transparency at a time, and discuss each case. Ask: **Which cases limit free expression of religion?** (Abington, Lee, *and* Epperson) **Which cases support the view that the wall of separation between church and state is "not impenetrable"?** *(Students may cite* Everson *and* Good News Club. *In both cases, the Supreme Court declared the actions of lower courts unconstitutional.)* **In which cases do you agree with the ruling? Explain.**

**L2 LPR Differentiate** Instead of displaying Transparency 19C, draw the chart on the board. Work as a class to find the specific information in the text. Review unfamiliar words. Model note-taking skills by filling in the correct answers on the board.

## ANALYZE CONFLICTS OF RELIGIOUS FREEDOM

Distribute the Chapter 19 Section 2 Core Worksheet (Unit 5 All-in-One, p. 86), which presents four conflicts about religious freedom. Have students work in groups to analyze the scenarios.

**L2 ELL Differentiate** Assign only Scenario D.

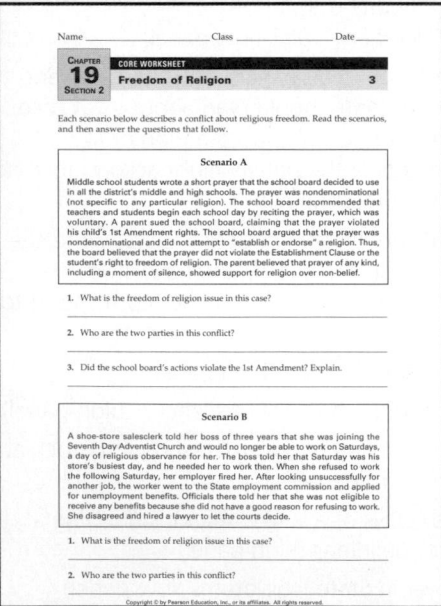

## Answers

**Checkpoint** to determine whether or not a State law or State aid to parochial schools amounts to an establishment of religion

**554** Civil Liberties: First Amendment Freedoms

---

✔**Checkpoint**
What is the purpose of the *Lemon* test?

**Evolution** In *Epperson* v. *Arkansas,* 1968, the Court struck down a State law forbidding the teaching of the scientific theory of evolution. It held that the Constitution

> " **PRIMARY SOURCE**
> **forbids alike the preference of a religious doctrine or the prohibition of theory which is deemed antagonistic to a particular dogma. . . . 'The State has no legitimate interest in protecting any or all religions from views distasteful to them.'**
> —Justice Abe Fortas

The Court found a similar law to be unconstitutional in 1987. In *Edwards* v. *Aguillard,* it voided a 1981 Louisiana law that provided that whenever teachers taught the theory of evolution, they also had to offer instruction in "creation science."

**Aid to Parochial Schools** Most recent Establishment Clause cases have centered on this highly controversial question: What forms of State aid to parochial schools are constitutional? Several States give help to private schools, including schools run by church organizations, for transportation, textbooks, standardized testing, and much else.

Those who support this aid argue that parochial schools enroll many students who would otherwise have to be educated at public expense. They also point out that parents have a legal right to send their children to those schools—as, recall, the Court held in *Pierce* v. *Society of Sisters,* 1925.

To give that right real meaning, they say, the State should give some aid to parochial schools in order to relieve parents of some of the double burden they carry because they must pay taxes to support the public schools their children do not attend. Advocates also insist that schools run by religious organizations pose no real church-state problems because they devote most of their time to <u>secular</u> subjects rather than to <u>sectarian</u> ones.

Several States give aid to parochial schools for such things as student transportation.

<u>secular</u>
*adj.* nonreligious

<u>sectarian</u>
*adj.* religious

Opponents of aid to parochial schools argue that parents who send their children to parochial schools should accept the financial consequences of that choice. Many of these critics also insist that it is impossible to draw clear lines between secular and sectarian courses in parochial schools. They say that religious beliefs are bound to have an effect on the teaching of nonreligious subjects.

**The *Lemon* Test** The Court applies a three-pronged standard, the *Lemon* test, to decide whether a State law amounts to an "establishment" of religion. That standard states: (1) a law must have a secular, not religious, purpose; (2) it must neither advance nor inhibit religion; and (3) it must not foster an "excessive entanglement" of government and religion.

The test stems from *Lemon* v. *Kurtzman,* 1971. There, the Supreme Court held that the Establishment Clause is designed to prevent three main evils: "sponsorship, financial support, and active involvement of the sovereign in religious activity." It struck down a Pennsylvania law that provided for reimbursements (money payments) to private schools to cover their costs for teachers' salaries, textbooks, and other teaching materials in nonreligious courses.

The Court held that the State's program was of direct benefit to parochial schools, and so to the churches sponsoring them. It also found that the Pennsylvania program required such close State supervision that it produced an excessive entanglement of government with religion.

More often than not, the Court has ruled unconstitutional those laws that provide some form of public aid to church-related schools. Thus, it ruled in an Ohio case that public funds cannot be used to pay for such things as field trips for parochial school students, *Wolman* v. *Walter,* 1977. Nor can tax monies be used to pay any part of the salaries of parochial school teachers, even those who teach only secular courses, *Grand Rapids School District* v. *Ball,* 1985. In this Michigan case, the Supreme Court noted that while the contents of, say, a textbook used in a course might be checked easily, the way a teacher handles that course cannot. And the Court invalidated a New York law that created a small school

**554** Civil Liberties: First Amendment Freedoms

---

# Debate

Use the statement below to initiate a debate in your class. Use the debate rules on page T25 to structure the class.

**Allowing a moment of silent prayer in the public school classroom does/ does not violate the Establishment Clause.**

# The *Lemon* Test

The courts determine whether State aid to parochial schools is constitutional by applying the *Lemon* test. **How does the Lemon test support the Court's rulings in** Wolman v. Walter **and** Mueller v. Allen?

1. Secular purpose
2. Neutral toward religion
3. No "excessive" entanglement

Constitutional

district to benefit handicapped school children in a tight-knit community of Hasidic Jews, *Board of Education of Kiryas Joel v. Grumet,* 1994.

Some State laws have passed the *Lemon* test, however. The Court has held that New York can pay church-related schools what it costs them to administer the State's standardized tests, *Committee for Public Education and Religious Liberty v. Regan,* 1980. In a 1993 case from Arizona, *Zobrest v. Catalina Foothills School District,* it said that the use of public money to provide an interpreter for a deaf student in a Catholic high school does not violate the Establishment Clause. The Constitution, said the Court, does not place an *absolute* barrier to the placing of a public employee in a religious school.

In 1973, the Court struck down a New York law that reimbursed parents for the tuition they paid to religious schools, *Committee for Public Education* and *Religious Liberty v. Nyquist.* But in *Mueller v. Allen,* 1983, it upheld a Minnesota tax law that really accomplishes the same end.

The Minnesota law gives parents a State income tax deduction for the costs of tuition, textbooks, and transportation. Most public school parents pay little or nothing for those items, so the law is of particular benefit to parents with children in private, mostly parochial, schools. The Court found that the law meets the *Lemon* test, and it relied on this point: The tax deduction is available to all parents with children in school.

The High Court went much further in *Zelman v. Simmons-Harris* in 2002. There, it upheld Ohio's experimental "school choice" plan. Under that plan, parents in Cleveland can receive vouchers (grants for tuition payments) from the State and use them to send their children to private schools. Nearly all families who take the vouchers send their children to parochial schools. The Court found, 5–4, that the Ohio program is not intended to promote religion but, rather, to help children from low-income families.

## Other Establishment Cases

Most church-state controversies have involved public education. Some Establishment Clause cases have arisen in other policy areas, however.

**Seasonal Displays** Many public organizations sponsor celebrations of the holiday season with street decorations, programs in public schools, and the like. Can these publicly sponsored observances properly include expressions of religious belief?

In *Lynch v. Donnelly,* 1984, the Court held that the city of Pawtucket, Rhode Island, could include the Christian nativity scene in its holiday display, which also featured nonreligious objects such as Santa's sleigh and reindeer. That ruling, however, left open this question: What about a public display made up *only* of a religious symbol?

The Court faced that question in 1989. In *County of Allegheny v. ACLU,* it held that the

✔ **Checkpoint**
Why did the Supreme Court rule in favor of a law that gave an income tax deduction for parochial tuition?

---

Tell students to go to the Audio Tour for a guided tour on the *Lemon* test.

**REVEAL THE CORE WORKSHEET SCENARIO RULINGS**

Ask: **How do you think the Supreme Court or lower courts might rule in these cases? Explain your reasoning.** As you share the actual rulings, ask for a show of hands of those who agree or disagree with the ruling, and why.

- **Scenario A** is based on *Engel* v. *Vitale,* 1962. The Supreme Court ruled that the school board could not sponsor prayers and similar religious activities because they violated the Establishment Clause of the 1st Amendment.

- **Scenario B** is based on *Hobbie* v. *Unemployment Appeals Commission of Florida,* 1987. The Court ruled in favor of the worker: "To condition the availability of benefits upon this appellant's unwillingness to violate a cardinal principle of her religious faith effectively penalizes the free exercise of her constitutional liberties."

- **Scenario C** is based on *Doe* v. *Porter,* 2004, argued in the 6th District Court of Appeals. The judge ruled that the school board violated the Establishment Clause by allowing the college students to conduct Bible classes during school time, and the program failed the *Lemon* test.

- **Scenario D** is based on the Eastern District of Oklahoma case *Hearn, et al.* v. *Muskogee Public School District,* 2004. The U.S. government intervened on behalf of the student, identifying the issue as a civil rights issue of equal protection. The school district agreed to revise its dress code to allow exceptions for religious reasons.

---

# Background

**HISTORY OF RELIGIOUS LIBERTY** At the beginning of the Revolution in 1775, there were official, State-supported churches in at least eight former colonies. Because of growing opposition, most established churches did not survive the revolutionary period. Jefferson, with Patrick Henry and George Mason, led the effort to disestablish the Church of England in Virginia (1779). Jefferson also wrote the Virginia Statute of Religious Liberty (1786), which provided for absolute religious freedom and equality and was a precursor to the 1st Amendment. It declared that the State could not require that any person profess any set of religious beliefs nor could it support any religious institution. An insistence upon religious freedom was also written into the Northwest Ordinance (1787). Article VI of the Constitution, written that same year, prohibited any religious test as a qualification for public office in the United States.

---

# Answers

**The Lemon Test** *Wolman:* public funding of parochial field trips violates neutrality; *Mueller:* no violation—tax deduction available to all parents

**Checkpoint** The deduction is available to all parents with children in school.

Ask students to define the Free Exercise Clause. *(guarantees to each person the right to practice whatever he or she chooses in matters of religion)* What does the Free Exercise Clause not protect? *(religious actions that violate criminal laws, offend public morals, or threaten community safety)*

Write the following scenarios on the board. Have students categorize each scenario as "Limiting Free Exercise" or "Upholding Free Exercise."

- **The use of poisonous snakes is forbidden in religious rituals.** *(limiting) Bunn v. North Carolina,* 1949

- **Individuals do not have to salute the flag.** *(upholding) West Virginia Board of Education v. Barnette,* 1943

- **Animals may be sacrificed in church services.** *(upholding) Lukumi Babalu Aye v. City of Hialeah,* 1993

- **A permit is required to hold a religious parade on public property.** *(limiting) Cox v. New Hampshire,* 1941

- **Amish children cannot be forced to attend school beyond the 8th grade.** *(upholding) Wisconsin v. Yoder,* 1972

- **The Federal Government can draft those who have religious objections to military service.** *(limiting) Welsh v. United States,* 1970

**L3 Differentiate** Have students identify the case associated with each scenario.

**L2 Differentiate** Ask students to select one of these scenarios and write a paragraph explaining why they agree or disagree with the Court's ruling.

**Government** online *All print resources are available on the Teacher's Resource Library CD-ROM and online at PearsonSchool.com/phgovt.*

---

## Answers

**Checkpoint** Seasonal displays: Christmas trees and other secular decorations do not violate the Establishment Clause. Chaplains: Legislative sessions opening with prayer are constitutional, because legislators are not "susceptible to religious indoctrination or peer pressure." The Ten Commandments: Rulings vary on whether the original display was set among other historical and cultural markers.

---

**Establishment Clause Cases**
# How Did the Court Rule?

**Seasonal Displays**
A Christmas tree sparkles in front of the California State Capitol. The Court has ruled that "government may celebrate Christmas in some manner and form, but not in a way that endorses Christian doctrine."

**Chaplains**
A chaplain offers the opening prayer in both houses of Congress and most State legislatures (shown here). The Court has ruled that this practice, unlike organized prayers in public schools, is constitutionally permissible.

✔ **Checkpoint**
How do each of the situations described here and in the photos above exemplify the Establishment Clause?

**endorsement**
*n.* approval or backing of

county's seasonal display "endorsed Christian doctrine," and so violated the 1st and 14th amendments. The county courthouse had a large display celebrating the birth of Jesus and a banner proclaiming "Glory to God in the Highest."

At the same time, the Court upheld another holiday display in *Pittsburgh* v. *ACLU.* The city's display consisted of a Christmas tree, an 18-foot menorah, and a sign declaring the city's dedication to freedom.

**Chaplains** Daily sessions of both houses of Congress and most of the State legislatures begin with prayer. In Congress, and in many States, chaplains paid with public funds offer the opening prayer.

The Supreme Court has ruled that this practice, unlike prayers in the public schools, is constitutionally permissible. The ruling was made in a case involving Nebraska's one-house legislature, *Marsh* v. *Chambers,* 1983.

The Court rested its distinction between school prayers and legislative prayers on two points. First, prayers have been offered in the nation's legislative bodies "from colonial times through the founding of the Republic and ever since." Second, legislators, unlike

schoolchildren, are not "susceptible to 'religious indoctrination,' or peer pressure."

**The Ten Commandments** Public displays of the Ten Commandments have ignited controversy in several places in recent years. The High Court decided its first case on the matter, *Stone* v. *Graham,* in 1980. It ruled on two other similar cases in 2005.

In *Van Orden* v. *Perry,* the Court held that the Ten Commandments monument located on the grounds of the Texas State Capitol in Austin does not violate the 1st and 14th amendments. The Court found that the monument (1) was erected in 1961 as part of a private group's campaign against juvenile delinquency, (2) is set among 37 other historical and cultural markers, and (3) had gone unchallenged for some 40 years. In short, the Court found the monument's overall message to be secular rather than religious and therefore acceptable.

In *McCreary County* v. *ACLU of Kentucky,* a differently divided 5–4 majority ruled that the display of the Ten Commandments in Kentucky county courthouses was unacceptable. They were, said the Court, an impermissible endorsement of religion by government.

---

## Supreme Court Notes

**LIMITS ON FREE EXERCISE** In *Oregon* v. *Smith,* 1990, the Court upheld Oregon's denial of unemployment benefits to a man who had been fired by a private drug counseling group because he had smoked peyote in violation of the State's drug laws—even though the man had done so as part of a ceremony conducted by his Native American Church. However, Congress reacted to that decision by passing the Religious Freedom Restoration Act of 1993. In effect, that law permits the use of peyote, and other controlled substances, when that use occurs as part of a legitimate religious ceremony.

**The Ten Commandments**

A tablet of the Ten Commandments is removed from a public building. The Court has ruled variously depending on whether the display is designed to promote religion.

Framed copies of the Commandments were first posted in county courthouses in 1999. Nonreligious documents, including the Bill of Rights, were added to the displays some years later, but only after the original displays' content had been challenged. The Supreme Court found that the original displays had a clear religious purpose. The later additions were merely "a sham," an attempt to mask that unconstitutional religious purpose.

## The Free Exercise Clause

The second part of the constitutional guarantee of religious freedom is set out in the 1st Amendment's Free Exercise Clause, which guarantees to each person the right to believe whatever he or she chooses to believe in matters of religion. No law and no other action by any government in this country can violate that absolute constitutional right. It is protected by both the 1st and the 14th amendments.

No person has an absolute right to act as he or she chooses, however. The Free Exercise Clause does *not* give anyone the right to violate criminal laws, offend public morals, or threaten community safety.

The Supreme Court laid down the basic shape of the Free Exercise Clause in the first case it heard on the issue, *Reynolds* v. *United States*, 1879. Reynolds, a Mormon, had two wives. That practice, polygamy, was allowed by his church but prohibited by federal law in any territory of the United States.

Reynolds was convicted under the law. On appeal, he argued that the law violated his right to the free exercise of his religious beliefs. The Supreme Court disagreed. It held that the 1st Amendment does not forbid Congress the power to punish those actions that are "violations of social duties or subversive of good order."

**Limits on Free Exercise** Over the years, the Court has approved many regulations of human conduct in the face of free exercise challenges. For example, it has upheld laws that require the vaccination of schoolchildren, *Jacobson* v. *Massachusetts*, 1905; laws that forbid the use of poisonous snakes in religious rites, *Bunn* v. *North Carolina*, 1949; and laws that require certain businesses to be closed on Sundays ("blue laws"), *McGowan* v. *Maryland*, 1961.

A State can require religious groups to have a permit to hold a parade on public streets, *Cox* v. *New Hampshire*, 1941; and organizations that enlist children to sell religious literature must obey child labor laws, *Prince* v. *Massachusetts*, 1944. The Federal Government can draft those who have religious objections to military service, *Welsh* v. *United States*, 1970.

The Court has also held that the Air Force can deny an Orthodox Jew the right to wear his yarmulke (skull cap) while on active duty, *Goldman* v. *Weinberger*, 1986. The U.S. Forest Service can allow private companies to build roads and cut timber in national forests that Native Americans have traditionally used for religious purposes, *Lyng* v. *Northwest Indian Cemetery Protective Association*, 1988.

**Free Exercise Upheld** Over time, however, the Court has found many actions by governments to be incompatible with the free exercise guarantee. The Court did so for the first time in one of the landmark Due Process cases cited earlier in this chapter,

✔ **Checkpoint**
What acts are not protected by the Free Exercise Clause?

## Supreme Court Notes

**FREE EXERCISE UPHELD** A State cannot forbid ministers to hold elected public offices (*McDaniel* v. *Paty*, 1978). Nor can a State deny unemployment compensation benefits to a worker who quit a job because it involved a conflict with his or her religious beliefs (*Sherbert* v. *Verner*, 1963; *Thomas* v. *Indiana*, 1981; *Hobbie* v. *Florida*, 1987; *Frazee* v. *Illinois*, 1989).

## REVISITING THE ESSENTIAL QUESTION

Write the chapter's Essential Question on the board: **How can the judiciary balance individual rights with the common good?** Ask students to write a paragraph applying this question to religious rights. *(To protect people's right to practice their religion, the judiciary must uphold laws that ensure each individual is free to follow his or her own religious beliefs or to have no religious beliefs at all. To protect the common good, the judiciary must uphold laws that ensure that individuals practice their religions in ways that do not violate the rights of others in the community.)*

**L2 ELL Differentiate** Discuss the meaning of the term *common good*.

### EXTEND THE LESSON

Display Transparency 19D, and discuss the three standards of the *Lemon* test. Then have students work in pairs to write a brief that applies the three-part *Lemon* test to one of the cases discussed in the text. Tell students to use the Internet and other resources to learn more about the case they have chosen. Explain that student papers should include these parts of a typical brief for appealing a case to a higher court:

1. **Statement of Facts:** a short summary of the facts in the case;
2. **Statement of Issues:** the main issues or questions in the case;
3. **Arguments:** a list of reasons why the actions in this case do or do not pass the *Lemon* test, and a list of three related cases that provide precedents for arguments;
4. **Conclusion:** one or two sentences that ask the Court to affirm or overturn a lower court ruling or to issue a ruling prohibiting an existing program from continuing.

**L2 Differentiate** Have students make a T-chart listing arguments for and against providing public aid to parochial schools.

## Assess and Remediate

**L3** Have students work in groups to rewrite each head and subhead in this section of the textbook as a newspaper headline—for example, "Religious Liberty Protected by 1st Amendment."

## Answers

**Checkpoint** acts that violate criminal laws, offend public morals, or threaten community safety

■L3 Collect the Core Worksheets and assess the students' class participation using the Rubric for Assessing Performance of an Entire Group (Unit 5 All-in-One, p. 241).

■L3 Assign the Section 2 Assessment questions.

■L3 Section Quiz A (Unit 5 All-in-One, p. 88)

■L2 Section Quiz B (Unit 5 All-in-One, p. 89)

Have students complete the review activities in the digital lesson presentation and continue their work in the **Essential Questions Journal.**

## REMEDIATION

| If Your Students Have Trouble With | Strategies For Remediation |
|---|---|
| Understanding the Establishment Clause and the "wall of separation" (Questions 1, 2, 3, 5) | Have students write ten Establishment Clause cases on ten index cards. On another ten cards, have them write what these cases uphold or prohibit. Students should turn the cards facedown and mix them up in four rows of five cards each. Then have them play the Memory game, matching the cases with their rulings. |
| Understanding the Free Exercise Clause (Questions 1, 4, 6) | Have groups of five students write a newscast summarizing five Free Exercise Clause cases. Then, in character as reporters or anchors, students should answer the questions *Who? What? When?* and *Where?* for each case in a 2- to 3-minute news story. As a conclusion, students should explain why these cases are considered Free Exercise cases. |

## Answers

**Checkpoint** The *Gobitis* decision upheld a compulsory flag-salute law; the *Barnette* decision struck down a similar law.

---

✔**Checkpoint**
How did the decision in *Barnette* differ from the decision in *Gobitis*?

*Cantwell* v. *Connecticut*, 1940. There, the Court struck down a law requiring a person to obtain a license before soliciting money for a religious cause. The Court reaffirmed that holding in an Ohio case, *Watchtower Bible and Tract Society* v. *Village of Stratton*, 2002.

The Supreme Court has decided a number of other cases in a similar way. Thus, Amish children cannot be forced to attend school beyond the 8th grade, because that sect's centuries-old "self-sufficient agrarian lifestyle is essential to their religious faith and is threatened by the exposure of their children to modern educational influences," *Wisconsin* v. *Yoder*, 1972. On the other hand, the Amish, who provide support for their own elderly or disabled people, must pay Social Security taxes, as all other employers do, *United States* v. *Lee*, 1982.

The Court has often held that "only those beliefs rooted in religion are protected by the Free Exercise Clause," *Sherbert* v. *Verner*, 1963. So what beliefs are "rooted in religion"? Clearly, religions that seem strange to most Americans are as entitled to constitutional protection as are the more traditional ones. For example, in *Lukumi Babalu Aye* v. *City of Hialeah*, 1993, the High Court struck down a Florida city's ordinance that outlawed animal sacrifices as part of any church services.

The Jehovah's Witnesses have carried several important religious freedom cases to the High Court. Perhaps the stormiest controversy resulting from these cases arose out of the Witnesses' refusal to salute the flag because they see such conduct as a violation of the Bible's commandment against idolatry. In *Minersville School District* v. *Gobitis*, 1940, the Court upheld a Pennsylvania school board regulation requiring students to salute the flag each morning. Walter Gobitis instructed his children not to do so, and the school expelled them. He went to court, basing his case on the constitutional guarantee.

Gobitis finally lost in the Supreme Court, which declared that the board's rule was not an infringement of religious liberty. Rather, it found the rule a lawful attempt to promote patriotism and national unity.

Three years later, in the midst of World War II, the Court reversed that decision. In *West Virginia Board of Education* v. *Barnette*, 1943, it held a compulsory flag-salute law unconstitutional. Justice Robert H. Jackson's words below are from the Court's powerful opinion in that case.

**PRIMARY SOURCE**
To believe that patriotism will not flourish if patriotic ceremonies are voluntary and spontaneous, instead of a compulsory [forcibly required] routine, is to make an unflattering estimate of the appeal of our institutions to free minds.

—Justice Robert H. Jackson

**Essential Questions Journal** To continue to build a response to the chapter Essential Question, go to your **Essential Questions Journal.**

## SECTION 2 ASSESSMENT

1. **Guiding Question** Use your completed graphic organizer to answer this question: How does the 1st Amendment protect the freedom of religion?

**Key Terms and Comprehension**
2. **(a)** What is the **Establishment Clause? (b)** How does it provide for a separation of church and state?
3. **(a)** What does the *Lemon* test evaluate? **(b)** How did the test originate?

4. What does the 1st Amendment's **Free Exercise Clause** guarantee?

**Critical Thinking**
5. **Draw Inferences** Why do you think the doctrine of separation between church and state is a continuing issue?
6. **Identify Central Issues** Some critics feel that Supreme Court decisions such as *Engel* v. *Vitale* and *Murray* v. *Curlett* limit people's free exercise of religion. Do you agree or disagree?

**Quick Write**

**Persuasive Essay: Gather Evidence** Based on the topic you chose in Section 1, gather evidence to support your position. In addition, gather information on the other side of the issue. Make a Pro and Con chart to list arguments on both sides.

## Assessment Answers

**1.** The 1st Amendment prohibits government from establishing or aiding religion, and guarantees to each person the free exercise of religion.

**2. (a)** a statement in the 1st Amendment forbidding Congress from making any law that establishes a religion **(b)** It protects religion from interference by government.

**3. (a)** The *Lemon* test evaluates laws that provide aid to parochial schools. **(b)** *Lemon* v. *Kurtzman*, 1971

**4.** that each person has the right to believe whatever he or she wants to in matters of religion without interference from government

**5.** Possible answer: The exact nature of separation cannot be pinned down, which leads to reinterpretation. In addition, religion is a sensitive topic for many Americans.

**6.** Students should recognize that in these two cases, the Supreme Court struck down laws requiring prayer in schools. Students should provide reasons for their opinions.

**QUICK WRITE** Students must gather information about both sides of the issue. Have them ask questions as they research to determine the most relevant facts and data and to anticipate opposing arguments.

# Freedom of Speech and Press

**Guiding Question**
**What are the limits on the guarantees of free speech and free press?** Use a table like the one below to take notes on how freedom of expression is limited in the various types of speech and media.

| Type of Expression | Limitation |
|---|---|
| Seditious speech | |
| | |
| | |
| | |

**Political Dictionary**
- libel
- slander
- sedition
- seditious speech
- prior restraint
- injunction
- shield law
- symbolic speech
- picketing

**Objectives**
1. Explain the importance of the two basic purposes served by the guarantees of free expression.
2. Summarize how the Supreme Court has limited seditious speech and obscenity.
3. Examine the issues of prior restraint and press confidentiality, and describe the limits the Court has placed on the media.
4. Define symbolic and commercial speech; describe the limits on their exercise.

**Image Above:** Network television news anchor Katie Couric

Think about this children's verse: "Sticks and stones may break my bones, but names will never hurt me." This rhyme says, in effect, that acts and words are separate things, and that acts can harm but words cannot.

Is that really true? Certainly not. You know that words can and do have consequences, sometimes powerful consequences. Words, spoken or written, can make you happy, sad, bored, informed, or entertained. They can also expose you to danger, deny you a job, or lead to other serious events.

## Free Expression

The guarantees of free speech and press in the 1st and 14th amendments serve two fundamentally important purposes: (1) to guarantee to *each* person a right of free expression, in the spoken and the written word, and by all other means of communication; and (2) to guarantee to *all* persons a wide-ranging discussion of public affairs. That is, the 1st and 14th amendments give people the right to have their say *and* the right to hear what others have to say.

The American system of government depends on the ability of the people to make sound, reasoned judgments on matters of public concern. The people can best make such judgments when they know all the facts and can hear all the available interpretations of those facts.

Keep two other points in mind: First, the guarantees of free speech and press are intended to protect the expression of unpopular views. The opinions of the majority need little or no constitutional protection. These guarantees ensure, as Justice Holmes put it, "freedom for the thought that we hate," (dissenting opinion, *Schwimmer* v. *United States*, 1929). Second, some forms of expression are not protected by the Constitution. No person has an unbridled right of free speech or free press. Reasonable restrictions can be placed on those rights. Think about Justice Holmes's comment about restricting the right to falsely shout "Fire!" in a crowded theater. Or consider this restriction: No person has the right to libel or slander another. **Libel** is the false and malicious use of printed words; **slander** is the false and malicious use of spoken words.[5]

---

[5] Both libel and slander involve the use of words maliciously—with vicious purpose, to injure a person's character or reputation; or to expose that person to public contempt, ridicule, or hatred.

## What are the limits on the guarantees of free speech and free press?

| Type of Expression | Limitation |
|---|---|
| Seditious speech | crime if words trigger clear and present danger of criminal acts or advocate government overthrow |
| Obscenity | may not disseminate materials average person would judge as appealing to prurient interest; depicts sexual conduct dealt with in anti-obscenity law; and lacks literary, artistic, political, scientific value |
| Media | prior restraint only in war, obscenity, or incitement to violence; reporters must testify unless protected by shield law |
| Movies | rating system |
| Radio, TV | licensing; no indecent language |
| Internet | public libraries must filter access to pornographic sites |
| Symbolic speech | illegal or violent picketing; dissent that government has constitutional power to restrict, restriction is reasonable, and intent is not to squelch dissent |
| Commercial speech | advertising may not be false or misleading or advertise illegal goods |

## Get Started

**LESSON GOALS**

Students will . . .

- identify the limits and protections of freedom of speech by charting restrictions on different forms of expression, analyzing prior restraint, summarizing court rulings on student speech, and interpreting political cartoons.

- identify the limits and protections of freedom of the press by researching media cases.

## SKILLS DEVELOPMENT

**GIVE A MULTIMEDIA PRESENTATION**

Before students dramatize freedom of press cases in this lesson, you may want to review tips on giving a multimedia presentation in the Skills Handbook, p. S21.

## Focus on the Basics

**FACTS:** • The 1st and 14th Amendment guarantees of free speech and press protect a person's right to speak freely and to hear what others have to say. • The Supreme Court has limited seditious speech and obscenity but seldom allows prior restraint. • Radio and television are subject to more regulation because they use public airwaves. • Symbolic speech and commercial speech are protected by the Constitution but can be limited under certain circumstances.

**CONCEPTS:** individual rights and responsibilities, limited government

**ENDURING UNDERSTANDINGS:** • The guarantees of free speech and press are intended to protect the expression of unpopular views. • The government cannot place prior restraint on spoken or written words.

Assign the section, the graphic organizer in the text, and the Reading Comprehension Worksheet (Unit 5 All-in-One, p. 90) before class.

**L2** **Differentiate** Reading Comprehension Worksheet (Unit 5 All-in-One, p. 91)

**BELLRINGER**

Write the following on the board, and have students answer in their notebooks:

**"One man's vulgarity is another's lyric."**
**—Supreme Court Justice John M. Harlan**
**1. What did Harlan mean by this remark?**
**2. How does his comment capture the fundamental issue of freedom of speech?**

# Teach

To present this topic using online resources, use the lesson presentations at **PearsonSchool.com/phgovt.**

**DISCUSS BELLRINGER QUESTIONS**

Students should infer from the quote that the definition of *vulgarity* (obscenity) varies according to opinion. The fundamental issue is protecting the minority voice.

## Answers

**Caption** a 1917 law that made it a crime to encourage disloyalty, interfere with the draft, obstruct recruiting, incite insubordination in the armed forces, hinder the sale of government bonds, or utter or print disloyal or abusive language about the U.S. government

**560** Civil Liberties: First Amendment Freedoms

---

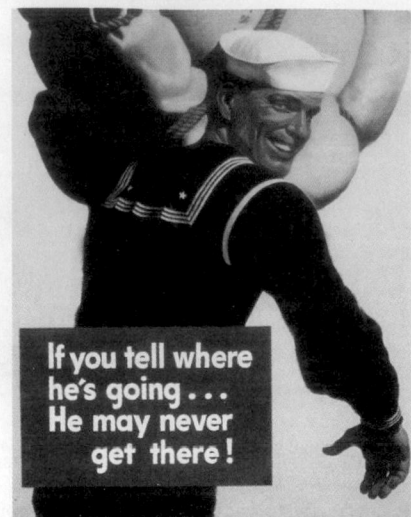

This World War II poster warned of the dangers of careless talk and espionage. **What was the Espionage Act?** ▶

**run afoul of**
*v.* to come into conflict with, become entangled with

**insubordination**
*n.* rebellion or disobedience

**scurrilous**
*adj.* insulting or scandalous

Truth is generally an adequate defense against a claim of libel or slander. The law does not shield public officials nearly as completely as it protects private persons, however. In *New York Times* v. *Sullivan,* 1964, the Supreme Court held that public officials cannot recover damages for a published criticism, even if it is exaggerated or false, "unless that statement was made with actual malice—that is, knowledge that it was false or with a reckless disregard of whether it was false or not."

Several later decisions have extended that ruling to cover "public figures" and even private persons who simply happen to become involved in some newsworthy event.

Similarly, the law prohibits the use of obscene words, the printing and distributing of obscene materials, and false advertising. It also condemns the use of words to prompt others to commit a crime—for example, to riot or to attempt to overthrow the government by force.

### Seditious Speech

**Sedition** is the crime of attempting to overthrow the government by force or to disrupt its lawful activities by violent acts.[6] **Seditious speech** is the advocating, or urging, of such conduct. It is not protected by the 1st Amendment.

**The Alien and Sedition Acts** Congress first acted to curb opposition to government in the Alien and Sedition Acts of 1798. Those acts gave the President the power to deport undesirable aliens and made "any false, scandalous, and malicious" criticism of the government a crime. The laws were meant to stifle the opponents of President John Adams.

The Alien and Sedition Acts were undoubtedly unconstitutional, but that point was never tested in the courts. Some 25 persons were arrested for violating them; of those, 10 were convicted. The Alien and Sedition Acts expired before Thomas Jefferson became President in 1801, and he soon pardoned those who had <u>run afoul of</u> them.

**Sedition Act of 1917** Congress passed another sedition law during World War I, as part of the Espionage Act of 1917. That law made it a crime to encourage disloyalty, interfere with the draft, obstruct recruiting, incite <u>insubordination</u> in the armed forces, or hinder the sale of government bonds. The act also made it a crime to "willfully utter, print, write, or publish any disloyal, profane, <u>scurrilous</u>, or abusive language about the form of government of the United States."

More than 1,000 persons were convicted for violating the Espionage Act. The constitutionality of the law was upheld several times, most importantly in *Schenck* v. *United States,* 1919. Charles Schenck, an officer of the Socialist Party, had been found guilty of obstructing the war effort. He had sent fiery leaflets to some 15,000 draftees, urging them to resist the call to military service.

The Supreme Court upheld Schenck's conviction. The case is particularly noteworthy because the Court's opinion, written by Justice Oliver Wendell Holmes, established the "clear and present danger" rule:

---

6 Espionage, sabotage, and treason are often confused with sedition. Espionage is spying for a foreign power. Sabotage involves an act of destruction intended to hinder a nation's war or defense effort. Treason can be committed only in times of war and can consist only of levying war against the United States or giving aid and comfort to its enemies.

---

# Differentiated Resources

The following resources are located in the All-in-One, Unit 5, Chapter 19, Section 3:

**L3** Reading Comprehension Worksheet (p. 90)
**L2** Reading Comprehension Worksheet (p. 91)
**L3** Core Worksheet (p. 92)
**L3** **L4** Extend Worksheet (p. 95)
**L2** Extend Activity (p. 96)
**L3** Quiz A (p. 97)
**L2** Quiz B (p. 98)

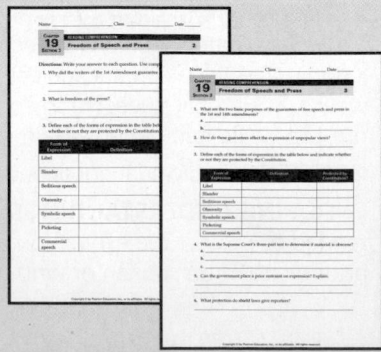

"
The question in every case is whether the words used are used in such circumstances and are of such nature as to create a clear and present danger that they will bring about the substantive evils that Congress has a right to prevent.

—Justice Oliver Wendell Holmes

In short, the rule says that words can be outlawed. Those who utter them can be punished if there is an immediate danger that criminal acts will follow.

**The Smith Act of 1940** Congress passed the Smith Act in 1940, just over a year before the United States entered World War II. That law is still on the books. It makes it a crime for anyone to advocate the violent overthrow of the government of the United States, to distribute any material that teaches or advises violent overthrow, or to knowingly belong to any group with such an aim.

The Court upheld the Smith Act in *Dennis* v. *United States*, 1951. There, 11 Communist Party leaders had been convicted of advocating the overthrow of the Federal Government. On appeal, the Communist leaders argued that the Smith Act violated the 1st Amendment. They also claimed that no actions of theirs constituted a clear and present danger to this country. The Court disagreed.

Later, however, the Supreme Court modified the *Dennis* ruling in several cases. In *Yates* v. *United States*, 1957, for example, the Court overturned the Smith Act convictions of several Communist Party leaders. It held that merely to urge someone to *believe* something, in contrast to urging that person to *do* something, cannot be made illegal. In *Yates* and other Smith Act cases, the Court upheld the constitutionality of the law, but interpreted its provisions so that enforcing the Smith Act became practically impossible.

## Obscenity

Both federal and State laws have made the <u>dissemination</u> of obscene material illegal, and the courts have generally agreed

that obscenity is not protected by the 1st and 14th amendments. But what, exactly, is *obscenity*? Lawmakers and judges have wrestled with that question for decades. The Supreme Court's Justice Potter Stewart once famously said that, although he could not define the term, "I know it when I see it," *Jacobellis* v. *Ohio*, 1964.

A large part of the problem in defining *obscenity* lies in the fact that moral standards vary from time to time, place to place, and person to person. To illustrate that point: Much of what appears on television today would, in fact, have been banned as obscenity only a few decades ago.

In 1872, Congress passed the first in a series of laws that prevent the mailing of obscene matter. The current postal law, upheld in *Roth* v. *United States*, 1957, excludes "obscene, lewd, lascivious, or filthy" material from the mail. The Court found the law a proper exercise of the postal power (Article I, Section 8, Clause 7) and so not prohibited by the 1st Amendment. *Roth* marked the Court's first attempt to define obscenity.

Today, the leading case is *Miller* v. *California*, 1973. There the Court laid down a three-part test to define obscenity. A book, film, recording, or other piece of material is legally obscene if (1) "the average person applying contemporary [local] community standards" finds that the work, taken as a whole, "appeals to the prurient interest"— that is, tends to excite lust; (2) "the work depicts or describes, in a patently offensive way," a form of sexual conduct specifically dealt with in an anti-obscenity law; and (3) "the work, taken as a whole, lacks serious literary, artistic, political, or scientific value."

In recent years, the Court has heard only a handful of cases involving questions of obscenity. As you will see shortly, those cases have all involved the Internet.

## Prior Restraint

The Constitution allows government to punish some <u>utterances</u> after they are made—for example, in cases involving libel or slander, or obscenity. With almost no exceptions, however, government cannot curb ideas *before* they are expressed. That is, except in

**utterance**
*n.* remark, statement
**dissemination**
*n.* distribution

---

| Type of Speech (definition) | Restrictions |
|---|---|
| seditious speech (advocating the overthrow of government by force or the disruption of its lawful activities by violent acts) | *Schenck* v. *United States*: seditious words can be outlawed if they present a "clear and present danger" of criminal acts; Smith Act: made it a crime to advocate the overthrow of the U.S. government, to distribute material that teaches or advises violent overthrow, or to knowingly belong to any group with this aim |
| obscenity (objectionable or offensive words or materials) | Mailing of obscene materials prohibited; *Miller* v. *California*: laid down three-part test to determine what is and is not obscenity; public libraries that receive federal aid must block computer access to pornographic sites; FCC bans indecent language on radio and network TV |
| symbolic speech (expression by conduct) | Picketing "set in background of violence" is prohibited; *U.S.* v. *O'Brien*: cannot burn draft cards; *Virginia* v. *Black*: cannot burn a cross as an act of intimidation |
| commercial speech (business purposes, advertising) | False and misleading advertising is prohibited, as is advertising for illegal goods and services; tobacco ads on radio and TV are prohibited |

---

# Background

**SEDITIOUS SPEECH** The Alien and Sedition Acts of 1798, the Sedition Act of 1918, and the Smith Act all led to heated debate on the constitutional limits of political dissent. Congress passed the Alien and Sedition Acts in 1798 at a time when Americans feared that war was about to break out between France and the United States. Most Federalists supported the act, arguing that criticism of government would endanger the nation's safety. Jeffersonians, who largely opposed the acts, believed they exceeded the powers given by the Constitution to the National Government. The Sedition Act of 1918 was passed during World War I, when there was small but vocal opposition to U.S. participation in the war. The Smith Act was passed soon after World War II began in Europe. Federal prosecutors first applied this law to members of the Socialist Workers Party and then to Communist Party members.

## Answers

**Checkpoint** illegal to advocate violent overthrow of government, distribute materials teaching or advising violent overthrow, or knowingly belong to a group with such an aim

Read aloud this quote from Thomas Jefferson:

"We have nothing to fear from the demoralizing reasonings of some, if others are left free to demonstrate their errors and especially when the law stands ready to punish the first criminal act produced by the false reasonings; these are safer corrections than the conscience of the judge." (This quote also appears in the Document-Based Assessment at the end of Chapter 19.)

Then ask students to infer answers to the following questions: **Does Jefferson believe in prior restraint of unpopular views or words that incite violence?** *(No; he says there is nothing to fear from "demoralizing reasonings.")* **What two actions does Jefferson believe will counteract unpopular opinions?** *(others who are also free to voice their opinions, and laws that will punish criminal acts that arise from the speech)* **Do you agree with Jefferson's quote? Why or why not? What if the "demoralizing reasoning" incites people to commit acts of terrorism? Should we wait for the first criminal act to occur, or should the speaker be censored? Explain.**

**L2 ELL Differentiate** Before reading the passage, review the meaning of *prior restraint* by asking students to predict what it means based on the meaning of each word.

**L2 LPR Differentiate** Have students review the text material under "Prior Restraint" and point out the exceptions to prior restraint on publications. *(such extreme situations as wartime or when a publication is obscene or incites its readers to acts of violence)* **What prior restraints has the Court approved?** *(cases regarding political literature on military bases, publications about the CIA, certain publications in prisons, and student speech)* **Do you think Jefferson would agree with these examples of prior restraint? Why or why not?**

**L4 Differentiate** To have students realize the importance of no prior restraint in a democracy, ask them to research control of the press in Nazi Germany or the Soviet Union. Have them compare government censorship and propaganda at that time with the ability of Americans to speak openly about government actions. Ask students to use this information to write a poem or rap comparing speech in a totalitarian versus a democratic society.

## Answers

**Supreme Court at a Glance** The ruling in the case made it illegal for public officials to stop the publication of outrageous or insulting information. Such prior restraint is unconstitutional.

**SUPREME COURT at a glance**

▶ **Case:** *Near v. Minnesota*, 1931
▶ **Constitutional Principle:** Limited Government
▶ **Decision:** Local public officials relied on a State law to prevent a newspaper from printing scandalous information about them. The Supreme Court struck down the State law. The Court ruled that freedom of the press does not allow such prior restraint on publications.

Articles in the *Saturday Press* in the late 1920s prompted a landmark decision in *Near v. Minnesota*, 1931. **What is the significance of the ruling in this case?**

the most extreme situations, government cannot place any **prior restraint** on written or spoken expression.

The concept of prior restraint is basic to the meaning of the 1st and 14th amendment protections of freedom of expression. *Near v. Minnesota,* 1931, is a leading case in point. There, the Supreme Court struck down a State law that allowed local public officials to prevent the publication of any "malicious, scandalous, and defamatory" periodical. Acting under that law, a local court had issued an order forbidding the publication of the *Saturday Press.* That Minneapolis newspaper had published a series of articles charging public corruption and attacking local officials as "grafters" and "Jewish gangsters."

The Court held that the guarantee of a free press does not allow a prior restraint on publication—*except* in such extreme situations as wartime, or when a publication is obscene or incites its readers to acts of

violence. Even "miscreant purveyors of scandal" and anti-Semitism are entitled to constitutional protection, said the Court.

The Constitution does not forbid any and all forms of prior censorship, but "any prior restraint on expression comes to this Court with a 'heavy presumption' against its constitutional validity," *Nebraska Press Association v. Stuart,* 1976.[7] The Court has used that general rule several times—for example, in the famous Pentagon Papers Case, *New York Times v. United States,* 1971.

In that case, several newspapers had obtained copies of a set of classified documents, widely known as the Pentagon Papers. Officially titled *History of U.S. Decision-Making Process on Viet Nam Policy,* those documents had been stolen from the Defense Department and then leaked to the press.

The Nixon administration sought an **injunction** (a court order) to bar their publication, arguing that national security was at stake and the documents (government property) had been stolen. The newspaper argued the "public right to know," and it insisted that the 1st Amendment protected its right to publish the papers. The Court found that the government had not shown that printing the documents would endanger the nation's security. The government, in effect, had not overcome the "heavy presumption" against prior censorship.

The few prior restraints the Supreme Court has approved include:

• regulations prohibiting the distribution of political literature on military bases without the approval of military authorities, *Greer v. Spock,* 1976;

• a Central Intelligence Agency (CIA) rule that agents must never publish anything about the agency without the CIA's express permission, *Snepp v. United States,* 1980;

• a federal prison rule that allows officials to prevent an inmate from receiving publications considered "detrimental to the security, good order, or discipline" of the prison, *Thornburgh v. Abbott,* 1989.

7 There, a State judge had ordered the media not to report certain details of a murder trial. The Court found the judge's gag order to be unconstitutional.

## Supreme Court Notes

**FIGHTING WORDS** "Fighting words" are not protected by the 1st Amendment. In *Chaplinsky v. New Hampshire,* 1942, the Supreme Court held: "There are certain well defined and narrowly limited classes of speech, the prevention and punishment of which have never been thought to raise any Constitutional problem. These include the lewd and obscene, the profane, the libelous, and the insulting or 'fighting' words—those which, by their very utterance, inflict injury or tend to incite an immediate breach of the peace. . . . Resort to epithets or personal abuse is not in any proper sense communication of information or opinion safeguarded by the Constitution, and its punishment as a criminal act would raise no question under that instrument."

The Court has also said that public school officials have a broad power to censor school newspapers, plays, and other "school-sponsored expressive activities." It did so in a case from Missouri, *Hazelwood School District* v. *Kuhlmeier*, 1988. There, the principal of a St. Louis high school had prohibited the publication of a series of articles written by student reporters for their school's paper. Those articles explored the impact that various events, among them pregnancy and parents' divorces, can have on teenagers. Three students sued, but they finally lost their case when the High Court held that school administrators can exercise "editorial control over the style and content of student speech in school-sponsored expressive activities so long as their actions are reasonably related to legitimate pedagogical concerns."

## The Media

The 1st Amendment stands as a monument to the central importance of the media in a free society. That raises this question: To what extent can the media—whether print, radio, television, or the Internet—be regulated by government?

**Confidentiality** Can news reporters be forced to testify before a grand jury in court or before a legislative committee? Can those government bodies require journalists to name their sources and reveal other confidential information? Many reporters and news organizations insist that they must have the right to refuse to testify in order to protect their sources. They argue that without this right they cannot assure confidentiality, and therefore many sources will not reveal important, sensitive information.

Both State and federal courts have generally rejected the news media argument. In recent years, several reporters have refused to obey court orders directing them to give information, and they have gone to jail, thus testifying to the importance of these issues.

In the leading case, *Branzburg* v. *Hayes*, 1972, the Supreme Court held that reporters, "like other citizens, [must] respond to relevant questions put to them in the course of a valid grand jury investigation or criminal

trial." If the media are to receive any special exemptions, said the Court, they must come from Congress and the State legislatures.

To date, Congress has not acted on the Court's suggestion, but some 30 States have passed so-called **shield laws.** These laws give reporters some protection against having to disclose their sources or reveal other confidential information in legal proceedings in those States.

**Motion Pictures** The Supreme Court took its first look at motion pictures early in the history of the movie industry. In 1915, in *Mutual Film Corporation* v. *Ohio*, the Court upheld a State law that barred the showing of any film that was not of a "moral, educational, or amusing and harmless character." The Court declared that "the exhibition of moving pictures is a business, pure and simple," and "not . . . part of the press of the country." With that decision, nearly every State and thousands of communities set up movie review (really movie censorship) programs.

The Court reversed itself in 1952, however. In *Burstyn* v. *Wilson*, a New York censorship case, it found that "liberty of expression by means of motion pictures is guaranteed by the 1st and 14th amendments." Still, the Court has never held that the Constitution grants the film industry the same level of protection against prior restraint that it gives to newspapers. In fact, it has upheld a requirement that films be submitted to official censors so long as those censors are required to act reasonably and their decisions are subject to speedy court review, *Freedman* v. *Maryland*, 1965.

Very few of the once-common movie review boards still exist. Most people now rely on the film industry's own rating system and on the comments of movie critics to guide their viewing choices.

**Radio and Television** Both radio and television broadcasting are subject to extensive federal regulation. Most of this regulation is based on the often-amended Federal Communications Act of 1934, which is administered by the Federal Communications Commission (FCC). As the Supreme Court noted in

✔ **Checkpoint**
How has the Supreme Court ruled on student speech?

**pedagogical**
*adj.* educational, academic, instructional

## Constitutional Principles

**JUDICIAL REVIEW** Although the law protects most people against libel and slander, public officials are less protected. In *New York Times* v. *Sullivan*, 1964, the Supreme Court held that public officials cannot recover damages for published criticisms even if exaggerated or false, unless the criticism was made "with actual malice." The Court ruled that debate on public issues is critical to democracy, and that lawsuits discourage future criticism of government officials. Later decisions extended that ruling to other public figures, such as actors and private individuals involved in newsworthy events. Actress Carol Burnett proved malice and won a libel case in 1983 against the *National Enquirer*. However, in *Hustler Magazine* v. *Falwell*, 1988, the Court affirmed the right to make fun of public figures in political cartoons and satire, noting that both have played a key role in "public and political debate."

---

### EXPLAIN RESTRICTIONS ON SCHOOL SPEECH

The Supreme Court and lower courts have ruled that student rights are limited by the "special characteristics of the school environment." Ask: **What might these "special characteristics" be?** *(atmosphere in the school; impact of students' actions on normal school routine; effects of student speech on classroom instruction and other activities in the school building; impact of students' actions on the rights of others)* Explain that school officials must be able to show that student conduct or opinions have disrupted class work, led to disorder in the school, or restricted the rights of other students. Ask: **Do these special characteristics support the chapter Essential Question: How can the judiciary balance individual rights with the common good?**

### DISTRIBUTE CORE WORKSHEET

Distribute the Chapter 19 Section 3 Core Worksheet (Unit 5 All-in-One, p. 92), which analyzes cases related to freedom of speech in schools. Organize students into six groups, and assign each group a different case. Groups can use the Jigsaw strategy (p. T27) to analyze their cases and share their information and opinions with the class.

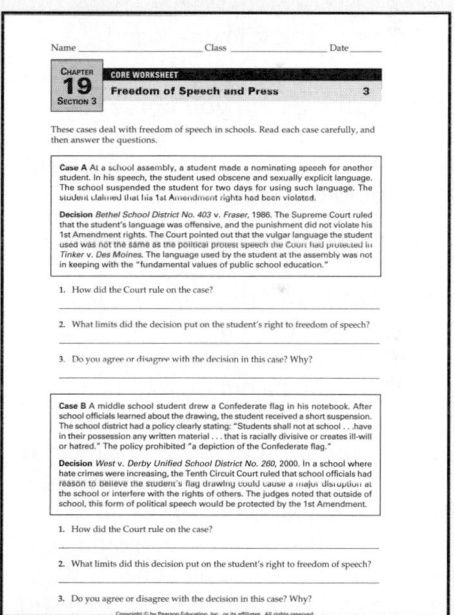

**L1 L2 Differentiate** Choose one of the Core Worksheet cases to read aloud. State the facts in the case, but do not indicate how the courts ruled. Ask the class if they think the ruling will favor the school district or the student, and why.

### Answers

**Checkpoint** School officials may exercise editorial control over style and content of student speech in school-sponsored expressive activities reasonably related to pedagogical concerns.

## RECOGNIZE LIMITS AND PROTECTIONS OF THE MEDIA

Ask students to raise their hands if they think the following statements are TRUE:

- Public officials are allowed to prevent the publication of malicious and defamatory periodicals. *(false; Near v. Minnesota)*

- Reporters are protected against having to reveal their sources during testimony. *(false; Branzburg v. Hayes)*

- Any radio station that allows a personal attack on a public figure must alert that person about the attack and allow him or her to respond to the attack at no charge. *(true; Red Lion Broadcasting Co., Inc. v. FCC)*

- No Internet site may knowingly transmit obscene or indecent speech or images to any person under age 18. *(false; Reno v. American Civil Liberties Union)*

- The government has the right to prevent publication of material that it asserts to be harmful to national security. *(false; New York Times v. United States)*

- Newspapers may advertise abortion services. *(true; Bigelow v. Virginia)*

- Newspapers may not print State liquor prices. *(false; 44 Liquormart, Inc. v. Rhode Island)*

Ask: **Were you surprised by any of these rulings? With which rulings did you agree? Disagree? Why?**

### DRAMATIZE FREEDOM OF PRESS CASES

Organize students into five groups: three newspaper groups, one radio and television group, and one Internet group. Assign each group one of the first five Supreme Court cases listed above that pertains to its particular medium. Each group should research details of its case and the majority, concurring, and dissenting opinions of the Court. Then have each group present its information to the rest of the class in the form of its medium; for example, the three groups researching newspaper issues should present their cases in newspaper form. The radio group could present its information in an "on-air" newscast. The Internet group could construct a bulletin-board display of its home page and "link" pages that describe the aspects of its case.

## Answers

**Freedoms of Speech and Press** because they both use public airwaves

**564** Civil Liberties: First Amendment Freedoms

---

Freedoms of Speech and Press

# Rules of the Road

The 1st Amendment stands as a monument to the central importance of free speech and the media in a free society. Various forms of speech are regulated by government, however. *Why are radio stations and network television subjected to wide-ranging federal regulation?*

**The Supreme Court has ruled** that school administrators can exercise "editorial control over the style and content of student speech in school-sponsored expressive activities...."

**The Federal Communications Act,** administered by the FCC, bans the use of indecent language on the radio and on network television, and may deny violators a renewal of their operating licenses.

**The Children's Internet Protection Act** (CIPA) requires public libraries that receive federal money to use filters to block their computers' access to pornographic sites on the Internet.

*FCC* v. *Pacifica Foundation,* 1978: "Of all forms of communication, broadcasting has the most limited 1st Amendment protection."

The Court has several times upheld this wide-ranging federal regulation as a proper exercise of the commerce power. Unlike newspapers and other print media, radio and television use the public's property—the public airwaves—to distribute their materials. They have no right to use the limited broadcast frequencies without the public's permission in the form of a proper license, said the Court in *National Broadcasting Co.* v. *United States,* 1943.

The Court has regularly rejected the argument that the 1st Amendment prohibits such regulations. Instead, it has said that regulation of this industry implements the constitutional guarantee. In *Red Lion Broadcasting Co.* v. *FCC,* 1969, the Court held that there is no "unabridgeable 1st Amendment right to broadcast comparable to the right of every individual to speak, write, or publish." However, "this is not to say that the 1st Amendment is irrelevant to public broadcasting.... It is the right of the viewers and the listeners, not the right of the broadcasters..."

The Federal Communications Act forbids prior censorship—and so the FCC cannot censor the content of programs before they are broadcast. However, the law does permit the FCC to ban the use of indecent language, and the Court has held that it can take violations of that ban into account when a station applies for the renewal of its operating license, *FCC* v. *Pacifica Foundation,* 1978.

In several recent decisions, the Supreme Court has given cable television somewhat broader 1st Amendment freedoms than those enjoyed by traditional network television. *United States* v. *Playboy Entertainment Group,* 2000, is fairly typical. There, the Court struck down an attempt by Congress to force many cable systems to limit sexually explicit

---

# Teacher-to-Teacher Network

**ALTERNATE LESSON PLAN** Have students read the Alien and Sedition Acts, as well as the Smith Act of 1940. Have students debate whether laws like these should be strengthened in times of war and what effects such laws would have on society.

To see this lesson plan, go to

**Teacher Center**

at PearsonSchool.com/phgovt

**Except in the most extreme** situations, government cannot place any prior restraint on the content of newspapers and other print media.

channels to confine their programs to late night hours. The Court agreed that shielding children from such programming is a worthy goal; nevertheless, it found the 1996 law to be a violation of the 1st Amendment.

**The Internet** The Internet has generated only a handful of Supreme Court cases—and each of them has involved attempts by Congress to regulate access to pornographic matter on the World Wide Web. Congress first attempted to protect minors from that material in the Communications Decency Act of 1996. That law made it a crime to "knowingly" transmit any "obscene or indecent" speech or image that is "patently offensive as measured by contemporary community standards" to any person under the age of 18.

The Court promptly declared that law unconstitutional in *Reno* v. *American Civil Liberties Union,* 1997. A majority of the justices found that the words "indecent" and "patently offensive" were too vague and that the overall effect of that law was to deny to adults materials that are protected by the 1st Amendment. "Regardless of the strength of the government's interest in protecting children," said the Court, "the level of discourse reaching a mailbox cannot be limited to that which would be suitable for a sandbox."

The Supreme Court did uphold an act of Congress dealing with pornography, the Internet, and public libraries in *United States* v. *American Library Association,* 2003. There, a majority could find no constitutional fault in the Children's Internet Protection Act (CIPA) of 2002. That law provides that those public libraries that receive federal money—nearly all of them do—must use filters to block their computers' access to pornographic sites on the Internet.

## Symbolic Speech

People also communicate ideas by their conduct, by the way they do a particular thing. Thus, a person can "say" something with a facial expression or a shrug of the shoulders, or by carrying a sign or wearing an armband. This expression by conduct is known as **symbolic speech.**

Clearly, not all conduct amounts to symbolic speech. If it did, murder or robbery or any other crime could be excused on grounds that the person who committed the act meant to say something by doing so.

Just as clearly, however, some conduct does express opinion. Take picketing in a labor dispute as an example. **Picketing** involves the patrolling of a business site by workers who are on strike. By their conduct, picketers attempt to inform the public of the controversy and to persuade others not to deal with the firm involved. Picketing is, then, a form of expression. If peaceful, it is protected by the 1st and 14th amendments.

The leading case on the point is *Thornhill* v. *Alabama,* 1940. There, the Court struck down a State law that made it a crime to loiter about or to picket a place of business in order to influence others not to trade or work there. Picketing that is "set in a background of violence," however, can be prevented. Even peaceful picketing can be restricted if it is

**✓ Checkpoint**
What is symbolic speech?

## ANALYZE LIMITATIONS ON MEDIA

Display Transparency 19E. Ask: **Which type of speech is most limited?** *(student speech)* **What regulatory agency functions as a watchdog over radio and network television?** *(Federal Communications Commission)* **What is the purpose of the Children's Internet Protection Act of 2002?** *(to block children's access to Internet pornographic sites at public libraries)* **Which types of media have little or no prior restraint?** *(newspapers and other print media; the Internet)*

## INTERPRET SYMBOLIC SPEECH

Ask students for examples of symbolic speech, and write them on the board. *(textbook examples include picketing, burning draft cards, burning a cross, wearing armbands to protest war, flag burning)* **Which of these forms of symbolic speech are not protected by the 1st Amendment?** *(picketing if it is violent, burning draft cards, and burning a cross if it is used to intimidate a person)* Lead to a discussion of whether students think burning the U.S. flag should be protected by the 1st Amendment. Display Transparency 19F. **What opinion does Cartoon 1 convey?** *(Cartoon 1 supports flag burning as protected free speech. The cartoonist uses satire to point out that by calling for a ban on flag burning, the Congressman is actually attacking the 1st Amendment.)* **What opinion does Cartoon 2 display?** *(Cartoon 2 is similar to Cartoon 1 in its satire. It, too, calls for a ban on burning the American flag and shows the man is ready to attack the First Amendment.)*

**L3 Differentiate** Create a classroom Blogger Bulletin Board related to this issue. Post the following statement on the bulletin board: "The United States needs a constitutional amendment making the burning of a U.S. flag a crime." Choose two students with opposing points of view to post opinions about this statement on the bulletin board. Encourage other students to write their own reactions or responses to the original question or student responses on note cards and post them on the board.

Tell students to go to the Interactivity for more examples of the freedoms of speech and press.

# Background

**CAMPAIGN FINANCE AS "SPEECH"** In *Buckley* v. *Valeo,* 1976, the Court found that campaign contributions are "a symbolic expression of support" for candidates, and therefore the making of those contributions is entitled to constitutional protection. Both federal and State laws regulate campaign contributions, but the fact that in politics "money is speech" greatly complicates the whole matter of campaign finance regulation.

## Answers

**Checkpoint** expression by conduct, such as carrying a sign, wearing an armband, or using facial expressions

**L3 Differentiate** Have students debate the following statement: "Violence on television and in movies is a threat to society and should be censored." Both sides should research statistics and information supporting or opposing the statement. (If pressed for time, have each student write a paragraph as homework, agreeing or disagreeing with the statement, and explaining why.)

**L2 Differentiate** Have students work in groups to make a list of rules for speech on the Internet. The class might be divided into such topics as regulation of libel, seditious speech, and obscenity. Others might prepare rules about prior restraint and whether some Web sites should be completely censored. Then have students decide how these rules might be enforced.

**L3 L4 Differentiate** Have students complete the Chapter 19 Extend Worksheet (Unit 5 All-in-One, p. 95). They will use library resources or the Internet to research the school freedom of speech and press case *Hazelwood School District* v. *Kuhlmeier,* 1988. In this case, the Supreme Court ruled that school officials may censor school-sponsored newspapers because they are part of the school curriculum rather than a forum for public expression. The case is often cited as precedent in other cases involving the 1st Amendment rights of students.

**L2 Differentiate** Have students complete the Chapter 19 Extend Activity entitled "Freedom of the Press" (Unit 5 All-in-One, p. 96).

# Assess and Remediate

**L3** Have students identify what they believe are the three most important cases that have guaranteed freedom of speech to Americans. Ask them to work in pairs to identify the constitutional issue of each case and then summarize the Court's rulings. When finished, students should explain why they gave these cases most-important status.

**L4** Restate the chapter Essential Question: **How can the judiciary balance individual rights with the common good?** Do students believe that the Supreme Court rulings discussed in this section have done a fair job of balancing rights with the common good? Have students draw a sketch of "blind justice," with one of her scales labeled "individual rights" and the other labeled "common good." Students should list guarantees of speech and press in the appropriate scale.

## Answers

**Checkpoint** when the object of the protest is within the constitutional powers of government, the restriction is no greater than necessary in the circumstances, and the government's interest in the matter is not to squelch dissent

---

✔ **Checkpoint**
When are acts of dissent by conduct punished?

**squelch**
*v.* to silence or smother

The Supreme Court ruled in favor of John and Mary Beth Tinker (shown here), emphasizing that students' 1st Amendment rights could not be abridged just because students are on school property. ▼

566

conducted for an illegal purpose—for example, forcing someone to do something that is itself illegal.

**Other Symbolic Speech Cases** The Court has been sympathetic to the symbolic speech argument, but it has not given blanket 1st Amendment protection to that means of expression. Note these cases:

*United States* v. *O'Brien,* 1968, involved four young men who had burned their draft cards to protest the war in Vietnam. A court convicted them of violating a federal law that makes that act a crime. O'Brien appealed, arguing that the 1st Amendment protects "all modes of communication of ideas by conduct." The Court disagreed, saying: "We cannot accept the view that an apparently limitless variety of conduct can be labeled 'speech' whenever the person engaging in the conduct intends thereby to express an idea."

The Court also held that acts of dissent by conduct can be punished if: (1) the object of the protest is within the constitutional powers of the government; (2) whatever restriction is placed on expression is no greater than necessary; and (3) the government's real interest in the matter is not to squelch dissent.

Using that three-part test, the Court has sometimes denied claims of symbolic speech. Thus, in *Virginia* v. *Black,* 2003, it upheld a State law that prohibits the burning of a cross as an act of intimidation, a threat that can make a person fear for his safety. The Court

also made this point: Those who burn crosses at rallies or parades as acts of political expression (acts not aimed at a particular person) cannot be prosecuted under the law.

*Tinker* v. *Des Moines School District,* 1969, on the other hand, is one of several cases in which the Court has come down on the side of symbolic speech. In *Tinker,* several students who had worn black armbands to school to dramatize their opposition to the war in Vietnam had been suspended by the district.

The Court found that school officials had overstepped their authority and violated the students' right to free expression. Said the Court: "It can hardly be argued that either students or teachers shed their constitutional rights to freedom of speech or expression at the schoolhouse gate."[8]

The Court first recognized campaign contributions as protected speech in *Buckley* v. *Valeo* in 1976—and it did so again in *Citizens United* v. *FEC* in 2010. See Chapter 7.

**Flag Burning** A sharply divided Court has twice held that burning the American flag as an act of political protest is expressive conduct protected by the 1st and 14th amendments. In *Texas* v. *Johnson,* 1989, a 5–4 majority ruled that State authorities had violated a protester's rights by prosecuting him under a law that forbids the "desecration of a venerated object." Johnson had set fire to an American flag during an anti-Reagan demonstration at the Republican National Convention in Dallas in 1984. Said the Court:

> **" PRIMARY SOURCE**
> If there is a bedrock principle underlying the 1st Amendment, it is that the government may not prohibit the expression of an idea simply because society finds the idea itself offensive. . . . We do not consecrate the flag by punishing its

8 Do not read too much into this, for the Court noted that it "has repeatedly emphasized the need for affirming the comprehensive authority of the States and of school officials, consistent with fundamental constitutional safeguards, to prescribe and control conduct in the schools." The fact that in *Tinker* the students' conduct did not cause a substantial disruption of normal school activities was an important factor in the Court's decision.

# Background

**COMMERCIAL SPEECH** One of the Court's first commercial speech cases had an interesting twist. In *Wooley* v. *Maynard,* 1977, the Court held that a State cannot force its citizens to act as "mobile billboards." At least, a State cannot do so when the words used conflict with its citizens' religious or moral beliefs. The Maynards, who were Jehovah's Witnesses, objected to the New Hampshire State motto on their automobile license plates. The words *Live Free or Die* clashed with their belief in everlasting life, and so they covered those words with tape. For this, Maynard was arrested three times. On appeal, the Supreme Court sided with Maynard.

idea itself offensive. . . . We do not consecrate the flag by punishing its desecration, for in doing so we dilute the freedom that this cherished emblem represents.

—Justice William J. Brennan, Jr.

The Supreme Court's decision in *Johnson* set off a firestorm of criticism around the country and prompted Congress to pass the Flag Protection Act of 1989. It, too, was struck down by the Court, 5–4, in *United States* v. *Eichman*, 1990. The Court based its decision on the same grounds as those set out a year earlier in *Johnson*. Since *Johnson* and *Eichman*, Congress has rejected several attempts to propose a constitutional amendment to outlaw flag burning.

## Commercial Speech

Commercial speech is speech for business purposes; the term refers most often to advertising. Until the mid-1970s, it was thought that the 1st and 14th amendments did not protect such speech. In *Bigelow* v. *Virginia*, 1975, however, the Court held unconstitutional a State law that prohibited the newspaper advertising of abortion services. The following year, in *Virginia State Board of Pharmacy* v. *Virginia Citizens Consumer Council*, it struck down another Virginia law forbidding the advertisement of prescription drug prices.

Not all commercial speech is protected, however. Government can and does prohibit false and misleading advertisements, and the advertising of illegal goods or services.

In fact, government can even forbid advertising that is neither false nor misleading. In 1970, Congress banned cigarette ads on radio and television. In 1986, it extended the ban to include chewing tobacco and snuff.

In most of its commercial speech cases, the Court has struck down arbitrary restrictions on advertising. In *44 Liquormart, Inc.* v. *Rhode Island*, 1996, the Court voided a State law that prohibited ads in which liquor prices were listed. In *Greater New Orleans Broadcasting Association* v. *United States*, 1999, it struck down a federal law that prohibited casino advertising on radio or television.

More recently, the Court dealt with limits on smokeless tobacco and cigar advertising. Massachusetts had barred outdoor ads for these <u>commodities</u> within 1,000 feet of any school or playground. The Court held that the limit was a violation of the 1st and 14th amendments' guarantee of free speech, *P. Lorillard Co.* v. *Reilly*, 2001.

> **✔ Checkpoint**
> Why, according to Justice Brennan, is flag burning protected by the 1st and 14th amendments?

**commodity**
*n.* article that can be bought or sold

**Essential Questions Journal** To continue to build a response to the chapter Essential Question, go to your **Essential Questions Journal**.

## SECTION 3 ASSESSMENT

1. **Guiding Question** Use your completed graphic organizer to answer this question: What are the limits on the guarantees of free speech and free press?

**Key Terms and Comprehension**

2. **(a)** What is **libel?** **(b)** What is **slander?** How do the two differ?

3. Why does the government restrict **seditious speech?**

4. **(a)** What are **shield laws?** **(b)** Why have some States passed these laws?

**Critical Thinking**

5. **Draw Inferences** What do you think are the advantages and disadvantages of a free press?

6. **Identify Central Issues** The Constitution makes a particular effort to protect the expression of unpopular views. **(a)** Why is this important? **(b)** Do you think even racist or sexist expressions should be protected? Why or why not?

**Quick Write**

**Persuasive Essay: Develop a Thesis** Based on the topic you chose in Section 1 and the evidence you gathered in Section 2, identify your argument in a thesis statement, which expresses the main idea of your persuasive essay. All information that follows should support or elaborate on this statement.

---

**L3** Collect the Core Worksheets and assess the students' class participation using the Rubric for Assessing Performance of an Entire Group (Unit 5 All-in-One, p. 241).

**L3** Assign the Section 3 Assessment questions.

**L3** Section Quiz A (Unit 5 All-in-One, p. 97)

**L2** Section Quiz B (Unit 5 All-in-One, p. 98)

Have students complete the review activities in the digital lesson presentation and continue their work in the **Essential Questions Journal.**

### REMEDIATION

| If Your Students Have Trouble With | Strategies For Remediation |
|---|---|
| Freedom of speech limits and protections (Questions 1, 2, 3, 6) | Have students make a poster titled "Free Speech." Underneath this title, ask them to write two subtitles: "Know Your Rights" and "Know Your Limits." Then ask them to list or illustrate the rights and limits on freedom of speech. Students should also include limits that are particular to student speech. |
| Freedom of press limits and protections (Questions 1, 4, 5) | Have students draw a web diagram with "Freedom of the Press" in the center oval. In the outer ovals, ask students to identify at least five facts (cases, issues, examples) that protect freedom of the press and at least three facts (exceptions) that allow prior restraint on publications. |

## Answers

**Checkpoint** An important principle that flag burning represents is freedom of speech, even if offensive. If flag burning is punished, then the principle of free speech for which it stands is undercut.

---

# Assessment Answers

**1.** Libel, slander, seditious speech, words prompting others to commit a crime, disseminating obscene materials, illegal or violent picketing, some forms of dissent, false and misleading advertising, and advertising illegal goods are not protected by the 1st Amendment. The FCC regulates radio and television.

**2. (a)** false and malicious use of printed words **(b)** false and malicious use of spoken words; libel is printed, whereas slander is spoken

**3.** The Supreme Court determined that seditious speech could provide a "clear and present danger" that criminal acts will follow.

**4. (a)** laws that give reporters some protection against having to disclose their sources or reveal other confidential information in legal proceedings **(b)** to assure confidentiality so that sources will reveal vital information

**5.** Possible answers: **advantages:** citizens have the right to free expression and to read what others have to say; minority opinions can be heard; a free press can act as a watchdog on conduct in government and business;

people can be more fully informed; **disadvantages:** some printed material might be offensive or reveal potentially damaging information

**6. (a)** Protecting unpopular views means that every citizen has a voice and can participate in public affairs. **(b)** Some students might argue that even offensive speech is protected. Others might say that sexist and racist speech is intimidating and should be limited.

**QUICK WRITE** Have students review the effectiveness of their thesis statements with these questions: What detail does the statement provide? What does it prompt readers to ask?

## LESSON GOAL

- Students will research an issue and participate in a classroom debate.

## Teach

### READ AND BRAINSTORM

Have students read the feature. Brainstorm possible responses to the issue of extending the school year.

### WRITE SPEECH FOR PUBLIC DEBATE

Pose this issue to students for debate: **Song lyrics promoting violence or defaming women should NOT be protected by the 1st Amendment.** Have students research the issue and write a speech. Explain that speeches should begin with a position statement for or against followed by evidence. Students must also address objections to their arguments. Tell them to bring up points that seem to be against their views, and then explain why those points are wrong. Students should conclude their speeches by forcefully restating their position.

### DELIVER PUBLIC DEBATE SPEECHES

Have students deliver one-minute speeches. Provide these tips for effective public speaking: (1) Raise and lower your voice to stress key points. (2) Make eye contact with the audience. (3) Use gestures to emphasize main points. (4) Avoid distracting gestures, looking down, or saying "um," "like," and "you know."

## Assess and Remediate

Peer-assess speeches using this checklist:
- \_\_ Had strong opening position statement
- \_\_ Included supporting arguments
- \_\_ Provided arguments against other positions
- \_\_ Used facts from research in arguments
- \_\_ Summarized position in a logical conclusion
- \_\_ Modulated tone, pitch, and volume
- \_\_ Engaged audience with eye contact

## Answers

1. State Department of Education, local school board, superintendent, principal, teachers

2. short-term goals: persuading others to join the cause, or a promise by a public official to investigate the matter; possible long-term goals: progress on a public issue, identifying problems and solutions, learning to speak well in public

3. Students should include a position statement, arguments for and against, and a conclusion.

---

# Participating in Public Debate

Dear Student,

Our State Department of Education has instituted new requirements for the current school year. Effective immediately, the school year will be lengthened from 180 days to 200 days, and each school day will be extended one additional hour. The DOE feels strongly that this decision is necessary in order to remain competitive in the global economy. Statistics show that schools in China and India are in session 225–250 days a year. Students in those countries are well on their way to outperforming American students.

Thank you for your cooperation,
George Carruthers, Principal

Your right to participate in public debate is central to the founding principles of our country. If you received a letter from your school like the one above, you would probably have strong feelings about it. One way to express your views is by participating in public debate. You might speak at a city council or town hall meeting, or address your local school board. Use these opportunities to voice your opinions by following these steps:

1. **Choose an issue of concern to you, and then find out whom to contact.** Your opinion counts most when you express it to those people who have some authority or influence in the matter. That could be city council members, a private lobbying group, a school board, or a media outlet.

2. **Organize your arguments.** Decide on the best way to get your ideas across. Create an outline or a list of talking points to organize your thoughts. Think of supporting details for each point, and then identify the most important points, which you will emphasize to influence your particular audience. You might want to make these points the first few lines of your speech. Most important, rehearse what you will say.

3. **Present your ideas.** Speak in a loud, clear voice when you present your ideas. Keep your speech lively and exciting, and be precise with the words you use. If you conduct yourself with civility and respect to win the hearts and minds of other citizens, you will persuade them to take up your cause.

### ▸▸ What do you think?

1. Whom might you contact to express your views in the situation presented here?

2. What short-term and long-term goals might you seek through participating in public debate?

3. **You Try It** Follow the steps above to develop a strategy for airing your views about the issue presented here. Prepare a one-minute oral argument on the issue and present it to your peers.

> **GOVERNMENT** ONLINE
> **Citizenship Activity Pack**
> For activities on participating in public debate, go to **PearsonSchool.com/phgovt**

568

## Citizenship Activity Pack

If your students need extra support, use the Citizenship Activity Pack lesson *How to Participate in Public Debate.* It includes a lesson plan for you and eleven tent cards and two posters for students. Each tent card describes characteristics of a participant in a town meeting about an issue illustrated in the posters. While eleven students play roles in the town meeting debate, the remaining students serve as interested observers. Students may also access the Citizenship Activity Pack online for activities on How to Participate in Public Debate at **PearsonSchool.com/phgovt.**

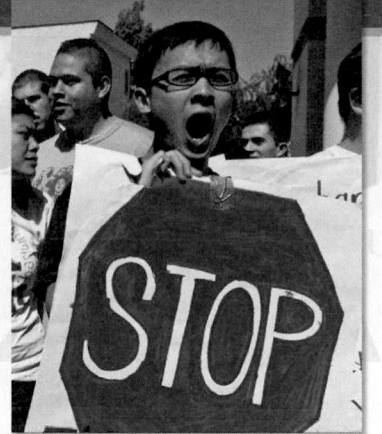

# SECTION 4

# Freedom of Assembly and Petition

### Guiding Question
**How has the Supreme Court ruled on assembly and petition cases?**
Use a table like the one below to take notes on important Supreme Court cases involving freedom of assembly.

| Case | Issue | Ruling |
|------|-------|--------|
|      |       |        |
|      |       |        |
|      |       |        |
|      |       |        |

### Political Dictionary
• assemble          • content neutral
• petition           • right of
• civil               association
  disobedience

### Objectives
1. Explain the Constitution's guarantees of assembly and petition.
2. Summarize how government can limit the time, place, and manner of assembly.
3. Compare and contrast the freedom-of-assembly issues that arise on public versus private property.
4. Explore how the Supreme Court has interpreted freedom of association.

**Image Above:** The 1st Amendment protects the people's right to assemble and protest peaceably.

A noisy street demonstration by gay rights activists or neo-Nazis; a candlelight vigil by opponents of the death penalty; pro-life supporters picketing an abortion clinic; pro-choice supporters on the steps of the State capitol . . . these are all everyday examples of freedom of assembly and petition.

## The Constitution's Guarantees

The 1st Amendment guarantees "the right of the people peaceably to assemble, and to petition the Government for a redress of grievances." The 14th Amendment's Due Process Clause also protects those rights of assembly and petition against actions by the States or their local governments, *DeJonge* v. *Oregon*, 1937.

The Constitution protects the right of the people to **assemble**—to gather with one another—to express their views. It protects their right to organize to influence public policy, whether in political parties, interest groups, or other organizations. It also protects the people's right to **petition**—to bring their views to the attention of public officials by such varied means as written petitions, letters, or advertisements; lobbying; and parades or marches.

Notice, however, that the 1st and 14th amendments protect the rights of *peaceable* assembly and petition. The Constitution does not give to anyone the right to incite others to violence, block a public street, close a school, or otherwise endanger life, property, or public safety.

Note this important point as well: A significant part of the history of this country can be told in terms of **civil disobedience.** That is to say that much of our history has been built out of incidents in which people have purposely violated the law—nonviolently, but nonetheless deliberately, as a means of expressing their opposition to some particular law or public policy.

Do the 1st and 14th amendment guarantees of freedom of assembly and petition include a right of civil disobedience? That thorny question cannot be answered absolutely or without qualification because of the very nature of civil disobedience: those acts are expressions of opinion on some public matter.

Still, courts have consistently held that, as a general rule, civil disobedience is not a constitutionally protected right. Those who choose to take part

## Focus on the Basics

**FACTS:** • The 1st Amendment guarantees the right to assemble peacefully and to petition the government for a redress of grievances. • Government can reasonably regulate the time, place, and manner of assembly, but those regulations must be content neutral. • The Supreme Court distinguishes between the rights of citizens to assemble in public places and on private property. • The guarantees of assembly and petition include the right of association.

**CONCEPTS:** individual rights and responsibilities, democratic principles

**ENDURING UNDERSTANDINGS:** • The rights of peaceable assembly and petition, basic to democracy, protect the people's right to bring their views to the attention of public officials.

**GUIDING QUESTION**

## How has the Supreme Court ruled on assembly and petition cases?

| Case | Issue | Ruling |
|------|-------|--------|
| *Delonge* v. *Oregon* | Do assembly and petition apply to State governments? | yes, by Due Process Clause |
| *Gregory* v. *Chicago* | demonstrators arrested; bystanders caused disorder | convictions overturned; demonstrators acted peacefully |
| *Cox* v. *Louisiana* | parade near courthouse | banned if intended to influence court |
| *Coates* v. *Cincinnati* | groups gathering on street were annoying | struck down law due to vague wording |
| *Forsyth County* v. *Nationalist Movement* | Can assembly be regulated based on what might be said there? | no—not content neutral |

## Get Started

### LESSON GOALS
Students will . . .

• distinguish the conflicting but essential nature of the right to assemble by participating in scenarios about freedom of assembly and petition conflicts.

• understand the restrictions on assembly and petition by identifying and applying time-place-manner regulations and content neutrality to assembly situations.

## SKILLS DEVELOPMENT

### DRAW INFERENCES AND CONCLUSIONS
To teach the skill of drawing inferences and conclusions, have students read Draw Inferences and Conclusions in the Skills Handbook, p. S19. Then have them do the Bellringer activity.

## BEFORE CLASS

Assign the section, the graphic organizer in the text, and the Reading Comprehension Worksheet (Unit 5 All-in-One, p. 99) before class.

**L2 Differentiate** Reading Comprehension Worksheet (Unit 5 All-in-One, p. 100)

## BELLRINGER

Display Transparency 19G. Have students read the quote and answer the questions in their notebooks.

# Teach

To present this topic using online resources, use the lesson presentations at **PearsonSchool.com/phgovt.**

### REVIEW BELLRINGER RESPONSES

Discuss students' answers to the Bellringer questions. *(1. Demonstrations may disrupt daily routines and individual freedoms. 2. It may cause inconveniences, but limiting the right to assemble would be harmful to democracy.)*

### INTRODUCE THE TOPIC

Display Transparency 19H. Have students complete these statements:

- **Freedom of assembly gives me the right to...**
- **Freedom of assembly does not give me the right to...**

Responses should indicate that freedom of assembly gives people the right to come together in public places to express their opinions on issues and encourage others to join them. This right is limited by time-place-manner regulations, public safety concerns, and public versus private property restrictions. Ask: **What are some examples of assembly?** *(demonstration or march, picketing, prayer vigil)* **What are the advantages of joining a group to protest a policy or express an opinion?** *(A group has more clout than an individual protester. A large group is also more likely to get media coverage.)*

## Answers

**Checkpoint** Possible answers: If the assembly disrupts school or courthouse activities; permits must be obtained for public demonstrations.

---

✔ **Checkpoint**
How has the Supreme Court limited the time, place, and manner of assembly?

**inherent**
*adj.* natural to or basic

in such activities are often aware of that fact, and they are usually willing to accept the consequences of their conduct.

## Time-Place-Manner Rules

Government can make and enforce reasonable rules covering the time, place, and manner of assemblies. Thus, in *Grayned* v. *City of Rockford*, 1972, the Court upheld a city ordinance that prohibits making a noise or any other diversion near a school if that action has a disruptive effect on school activities. It has also upheld a State law that forbids parades near a courthouse when they are intended to influence court proceedings, *Cox* v. *Louisiana*, 1965.

Rules for keeping the public peace must be more than just reasonable, however. They must also be precisely drawn and fairly administered. In *Coates* v. *Cincinnati*, 1971, the Court struck down a city ordinance that made it a crime for "three or more persons to assemble" on a sidewalk or street corner "and there conduct themselves in a manner annoying to persons passing by, or occupants of adjacent buildings." The Court found the wording of the ordinance much too vague and therefore unconstitutional.

Government's rules must be **content neutral.** That is, although government can regulate assemblies on the basis of time, place, and manner, it cannot regulate gatherings on the basis of what might be said there. Thus, in *Forsyth County* v. *Nationalist Movement*, 1992, the Court threw out a Georgia county's ordinance that levied a fee of up to $1,000 for public demonstrations.

The law was contested by a white supremacist group seeking to protest the creation of a holiday to honor Martin Luther King, Jr. The Court found the ordinance not to be content neutral, particularly because county officials had unlimited power to set the exact fee to be paid by any group.

## Public Property

Over the past several years, most of the Court's freedom of assembly cases have involved organized demonstrations. Demonstrations are, of course, assemblies.

Most demonstrations take place in public places—on streets and sidewalks, in parks or public buildings, and so on. This is the case because it is the *public* the demonstrators want to reach.

Demonstrations almost always involve some degree of conflict. Most often, they are held to protest something, and so there is an inherent clash of ideas. Many times there is also a conflict with the normal use of streets or other public facilities. It is hardly surprising, then, that the tension can sometimes rise to a serious level.

Given all this, the Supreme Court has often upheld laws that require advance notice and permits for demonstrations in public places. In an early leading case, *Cox* v. *New Hampshire*, 1941, it unanimously approved a State law that required a license to hold a parade or procession on a public street.

Right-to-demonstrate cases raise many difficult questions. How and to what extent can government regulate demonstrators? Does the Constitution require that police officers allow an unpopular group to continue to demonstrate even when its activities have excited others to violence? When, in the name of public peace and safety, can police order demonstrators to disband?

***Gregory* v. *Chicago*** A leading and illustrative case is *Gregory* v. *Chicago*, 1969. While under police protection, comedian Dick Gregory and others marched while singing, chanting, and carrying placards, from city hall to the mayor's home some five miles away. Marching in the streets around the mayor's house, they demanded the firing of the city's school superintendent and an end to de facto segregation in the city's schools.

A crowd of several hundred people, including many residents of the all-white neighborhood, quickly gathered. Soon, the bystanders began throwing insults and threats, as well as rocks, eggs, and other objects. The police tried to keep order, but after about an hour, they decided that serious violence was about to break out. At that point, they ordered the demonstrators to leave the area. When Gregory and others failed to do so, the police arrested them and charged them with disorderly conduct.

---

# Differentiated Resources

The following resources are located in the All-in-One, Unit 5, Chapter 19, Section 4:

**L3** Reading Comprehension Worksheet (p. 99)
**L2** Reading Comprehension Worksheet (p. 100)
**L3** Core Worksheet (p. 101)
**L2** Core Worksheet (p. 105)
**L3** Quiz A (p. 109)
**L2** Quiz B (p. 110)
**L3** Chapter Test A (p. 111)
**L2** Chapter Test B (p. 114)

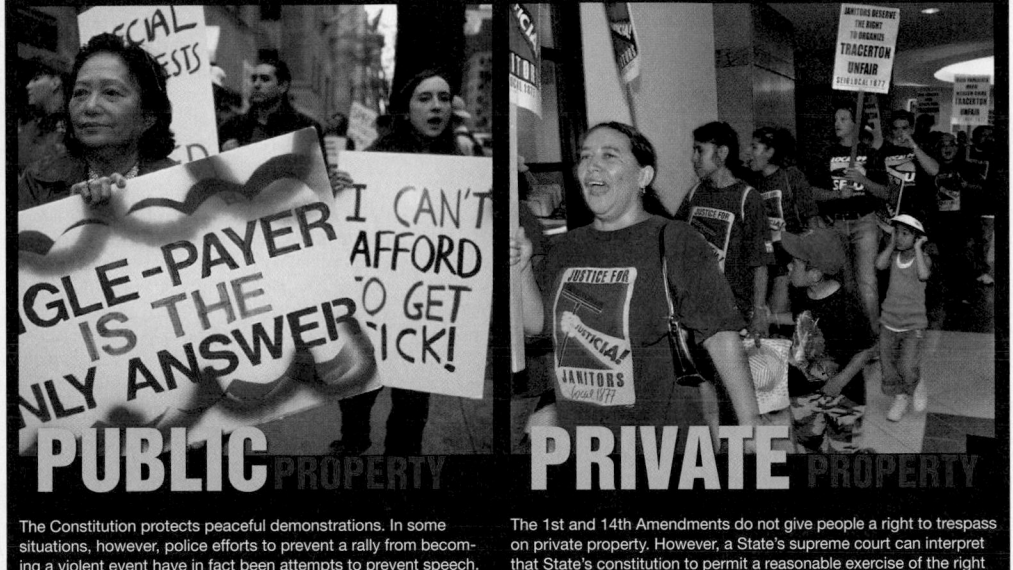

The Constitution protects peaceful demonstrations. In some situations, however, police efforts to prevent a rally from becoming a violent event have in fact been attempts to prevent speech. The line between crowd control and thought control can be very thin, indeed.

The 1st and 14th Amendments do not give people a right to trespass on private property. However, a State's supreme court can interpret that State's constitution to permit a reasonable exercise of the right of petition on private property. **Why has the Court ruled differently on public and private property demonstrations?**

The convictions of the demonstrators were unanimously overturned by the Court. It noted that the marchers had exercised their constitutional rights of assembly and petition. The bystanders, not the demonstrators, had caused the disorder. As long as the demonstrators acted peacefully, they could not be punished for disorderly conduct.

**Recent Cases** Over recent years, many of the most controversial demonstrations have been those held by anti-abortion groups. For the most part, their efforts have been aimed at discouraging women from seeking the services of abortion clinics, and those efforts have generated many lawsuits.

There have been two particularly notable cases to date. In the first one, *Madsen v. Women's Health Services, Inc.*, 1994, the Supreme Court upheld a Florida judge's order directing protesters not to block access to an abortion clinic. The judge's order had drawn a 36-foot buffer zone around the clinic. The

High Court found that to be a reasonable limit on the demonstrators' activities.

The other major case is *Hill v. Colorado*, 2000. There, the Court upheld, 5–4, a State law that limits "sidewalk counseling" at clinics where abortions are performed. That statute creates an eight-foot buffer zone around anyone who wants to enter. No one may make an "unwanted approach" to talk, hand out a leaflet, or wave a sign.

The Court found that the Colorado law does not deal with the content of abortion protestors' speech. It is aimed, instead, at *where*, *when*, and *how* their message is delivered.

### Private Property

What about demonstrations on private property—at shopping centers, for example? The Court has said that the 1st and 14th Amendment rights of assembly and petition do not give people a right to trespass on private property, even to express political views.

# Background

**RIGHT OF ASSOCIATION CASES** In 1995, the Court ruled that a Boston veterans' group did not have to include gay marchers in its St. Patrick's Day parade. The justices ruled that being forced to do so would interfere with the group's social and religious purposes. Other Supreme Court decisions have made associations more inclusive. Court decisions in the 1980s opened many formerly all-male civic organizations, such as the Rotary Club and Jaycees, to women. In these cases, the Court ruled that admitting women would not prevent these groups from carrying out their educational, charitable, and community service goals. There is no absolute right of association, however. For example, Congress can forbid federal employees to do such things as engage in partisan election campaigns or hold a leadership position in a political party organization, *Harris v. United States*, 1954.

## IDENTIFY TIME-PLACE-MANNER RULES

Ask a volunteer to define what is meant by "time, place, and manner." *(reasonable government limits on when, where, and how an assembly may be conducted)* Read aloud the situations below, and have students identify whether they follow a time-place-manner restriction or are unconstitutional.

- The mayor rejected a rally permit for the local chapter of the Ku Klux Klan. *(unconstitutional)*
- The State's highest court ruled that shopping malls are not public places where citizens can distribute political pamphlets as they please. *(time-place-manner restriction)*
- Various injunctions have barred youths identified by the authorities as gang members from sitting in parks. *(unconstitutional)*
- A permit to march against police brutality was denied by New York City, citing rush hour congestion. *(time-place-manner restriction)* Yet the entire area was closed to traffic to celebrate the World Series victory. *(This knowledge makes the denial of the permit unconstitutional.)*

## COMPLETE CORE WORKSHEET

Organize students into these six groups:

- Group 1: Peace Up, plaintiff
- Group 2: Town, defendant
- Group 3: Parents Against Violent Video Games (PAVVG), plaintiff
- Group 4: Mall Owner, defendant
- Group 5: Three judges, Peace Up v. Town
- Group 6: Three judges, PAVVG v. Mall Owner

Distribute the Chapter 19 Section 4 Core Worksheet (Unit 5 All-in-One, p. 101). Each group will analyze a scenario in which the rights of assembly and petition must be weighed against the government's responsibility to protect the rights of the community or private property. Have Groups 1–4 study their scenarios and answer the questions. These will be used as briefs explaining the facts in the case, the constitutional issue, precedents that support their position, and counterarguments. Groups 5 and 6 should also study their scenarios and identify precedents for the judgments they will make after hearing the cases. Have Groups 1–4 choose "attorneys" to present their briefs to the Group 5 or Group 6 judges. Each attorney has five minutes to present arguments. The judges can interrupt to ask questions. After hearing the cases, Groups 5 and 6 will write opinions on their cases, explaining their reasons.

## Answers

**Caption** Assembly and petition guarantees for public demonstrations do not give people a right to trespass on private property.

**L3 Differentiate** Have students go online or to the office of their mayor or city manager to find the local regulations for obtaining a demonstration permit. Ask students to analyze the regulations for constitutionality.

# Assess and Remediate

**L3** Collect the Core Worksheets and assess the students' class participation using the Rubric for Assessing Performance of an Entire Group (Unit 5 All-in-One, p. 241).

**L3** Assign the Section 4 Assessment questions.

**L3** Section Quiz A (Unit 5 All-in-One, p. 109)

**L2** Section Quiz B (Unit 5 All-in-One, p. 110)

Have students complete the review activities in the digital lesson presentation and continue their work in the **Essential Questions Journal.**

## REMEDIATION

| If Your Students Have Trouble With | Strategies For Remediation |
|---|---|
| Protections on the rights to assemble and petition (Questions 2, 3, 4, 5) | Have students list the cases identified in this section. Next to each case, students should write the effect of the ruling on the rights to assemble and petition. |
| Limits to the freedoms of assembly and petition (Questions 1, 6) | Have students use the textbook to find and list time-place-manner rules applied to organized demonstrations to keep the public peace. |

## Answers

**Checkpoint** right to join with others to promote political, economic, and social causes

---

Privately owned shopping centers are not "places of public assembly." Thus, no one has a constitutional right to do such things as hand out political leaflets or ask people to sign petitions in those places, according to the leading case on the subject, *Lloyd Corporation* v. *Tanner*, 1972.

## Freedom of Association

The guarantees of freedom of assembly and petition include a **right of association**—the right to join with others to promote political, economic, and social causes. That right is not set out in so many words in the Constitution. However, in *National Association for the Advancement of Colored People* v. *Alabama*, 1958, the Supreme Court said, "it is beyond debate that freedom to engage in association for the advancement of beliefs and ideas is an inseparable aspect" of the Constitution's guarantees of free expression.

The case just cited is one of the early right-to-associate cases. There, a State law required the Alabama branch of the NAACP to disclose the names of all its members in that State. When the organization refused a court's order to do so, it was found in contempt of court and fined $100,000.

The Supreme Court overturned the contempt conviction. It said that it could find no legitimate reason why the State should have the NAACP's membership list.

A person cannot be fired from a job because of political associations—for example, membership in a political party, *Brown* v. *Socialist Workers '74 Campaign Committee*, 1982. And a person cannot be required to disclose his or her political associations in order to be licensed to practice law, *Gibson* v. *Florida*, 1966. On the other hand, the State of Washington's publication of the names of those registered voters who signed initiative petitions to put a measure on the general election ballot does not violate the Constitution's guarantee of a right of association, *Doe* v. *Reed*, 2010.

There is no absolute right of association, however. In *Boy Scouts of America* v. *Dale*, 2000, the Supreme Court held that the Boy Scouts have a constitutional right to exclude gays from their organization. The Court noted that opposition to homosexuality is a part of the Boy Scout organization's "expressive association"— that is, what they stand for.

The decision overturned a ruling by the New Jersey Supreme Court. That court had applied the State's anti-discrimination law against the Scouts. It ordered a New Jersey troop to readmit James Dale, an Eagle Scout, whom the troop had dismissed when it learned he was gay. The Court ruled that a State cannot force an organization to accept members when that action would contradict what the organization professes to believe.

---

**Essential Questions Journal** To continue to build a response to the chapter Essential Question, go to your **Essential Questions Journal.**

# SECTION 4 ASSESSMENT

1. **Guiding Question** Use your completed graphic organizer to answer this question: How has the Supreme Court ruled on assembly and petition cases?

**Key Terms and Comprehension**

2. What do the guarantees of freedom of assembly and petition intend to protect?

3. **(a)** What is **civil disobedience? (b)** Is it constitutionally protected? Why or why not?

4. How does the **right of association** extend the right of assembly?

**Critical Thinking**

5. **Draw Conclusions (a)** Why are the freedom to assemble peacefully and the freedom of association important to a democratic society? **(b)** What might happen if people were denied these rights?

6. **Demonstrate Reasoned Judgment** Why do you think the government can regulate assemblies based on time, place, and manner, but not on the basis of what might be said there?

**Quick Write**

**Persuasive Essay: Provide Elaboration** In a persuasive essay, you can build a strong case for your position by stating facts, providing statistics, and including details. Conduct research to find this information on the topic you chose in Section 1. Take notes on index cards to help you organize your persuasive essay.

---

# Assessment Answers

**1.** The Court applies time-place-manner restrictions to assembly and petition cases. It has upheld laws that require advance notice and permits for demonstrations. Government's rules must be content neutral. Demonstrators cannot be punished for disorder if they act peacefully. Protesters may not block access to abortion clinics or approach people entering. Demonstrators do not have the right to trespass on private property. Guarantees of freedom of assembly and petition include the right of association.

**2.** the right of people to organize to influence public policy and to bring their views to the attention of public officials

**3. (a)** the act of purposefully but nonviolently disobeying the law as a means of expressing an opinion on some particular law or public policy **(b)** No; it is not considered part of the right of assembly or petition.

**4.** It stipulates the right to associate with others to promote political, economic, and social causes.

**5. (a)** Assembling to promote causes is a

primary means for people to express their opinions and influence policy, which is vital to any democracy. **(b)** Only the majority voice would be heard.

**6.** Regulating assemblies based on what is said there would be limiting freedom of speech.

**QUICK WRITE** Remind students to support their persuasive arguments with relevant statistics and details. If a clear connection cannot be made between the main idea and the statistics, students should continue researching to find other supportive facts.

# Quick Study Guide

**GOVERNMENT** ONLINE
**On the Go**
To review anytime, anywhere, download these online resources at **PearsonSchool.com/phgovt**
Political Dictionary, Audio Review

CHAPTER **19**

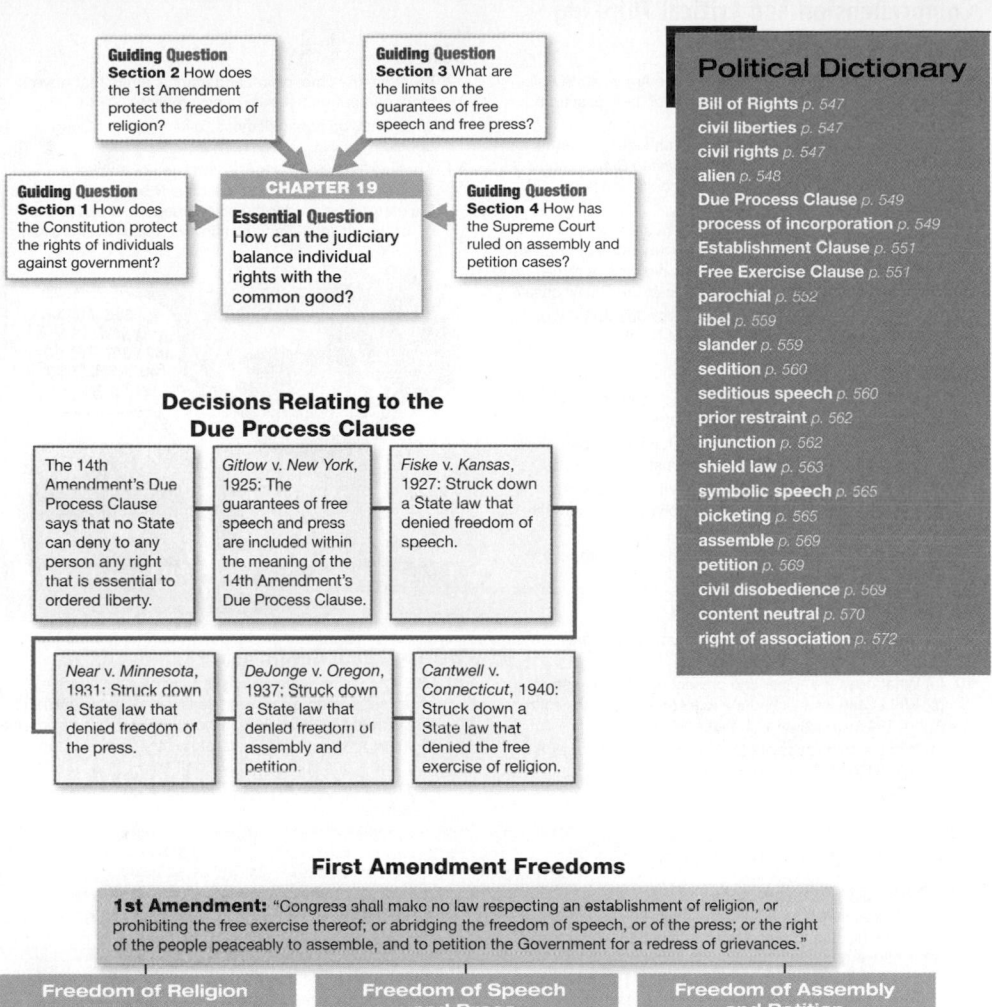

**Guiding Question**
**Section 2** How does the 1st Amendment protect the freedom of religion?

**Guiding Question**
**Section 3** What are the limits on the guarantees of free speech and free press?

**Guiding Question**
**Section 1** How does the Constitution protect the rights of individuals against government?

**CHAPTER 19**
**Essential Question**
How can the judiciary balance individual rights with the common good?

**Guiding Question**
**Section 4** How has the Supreme Court ruled on assembly and petition cases?

## Political Dictionary

**Bill of Rights** p. 547
**civil liberties** p. 547
**civil rights** p. 547
**alien** p. 548
**Due Process Clause** p. 549
**process of incorporation** p. 549
**Establishment Clause** p. 551
**Free Exercise Clause** p. 551
**parochial** p. 552
**libel** p. 559
**slander** p. 559
**sedition** p. 560
**seditious speech** p. 560
**prior restraint** p. 562
**injunction** p. 562
**shield law** p. 563
**symbolic speech** p. 565
**picketing** p. 565
**assemble** p. 569
**petition** p. 569
**civil disobedience** p. 569
**content neutral** p. 570
**right of association** p. 572

### Decisions Relating to the Due Process Clause

The 14th Amendment's Due Process Clause says that no State can deny to any person any right that is essential to ordered liberty.

*Gitlow* v. *New York*, 1925: The guarantees of free speech and press are included within the meaning of the 14th Amendment's Due Process Clause.

*Fiske* v. *Kansas*, 1927: Struck down a State law that denied freedom of speech.

*Near* v. *Minnesota*, 1931: Struck down a State law that denied freedom of the press.

*DeJonge* v. *Oregon*, 1937: Struck down a State law that denied freedom of assembly and petition.

*Cantwell* v. *Connecticut*, 1940: Struck down a State law that denied the free exercise of religion.

### First Amendment Freedoms

**1st Amendment:** "Congress shall make no law respecting an establishment of religion, or prohibiting the free exercise thereof; or abridging the freedom of speech, or of the press; or the right of the people peaceably to assemble, and to petition the Government for a redress of grievances."

**Freedom of Religion**
- Creates a separation of church and state (Establishment Clause)
- Protects people's right to believe what they choose in matters of religion (Free Exercise Clause)

**Freedom of Speech and Press**
- Guarantee the right to speak, write, and otherwise communicate most ideas
- Ensure the people's right to hear the ideas of others

**Freedom of Assembly and Petition**
- Protect people's right to assemble peaceably to express their views
- Ensure people's right to bring their views to public attention

## For More Information

To learn more about civil liberties, refer to these sources or assign them to students:

**L1** **Smith, Rich.** *First Amendment: The Right of Expression.* ABDO & Daughters, 2007.

**L2** **Dudley, William, ed.** *The Bill of Rights—Freedom of Speech.* Greenhaven Press, 2005.

**L3** **Gottfried, Ted.** *Homeland Security vs. Constitutional Rights.* Lerner Publishing Group, 2003.

**L4** **Lewis, Anthony.** *Freedom for the Thought That We Hate: A Biography of the First Amendment.* Basic Books, 2007.

---

Have students download the digital resources available at Government on the Go for review and remediation.

### STUDY TIPS

**Cornell Notes** The Cornell note-taking strategy involves several distinct and easy steps. First, students should divide their paper into 3 sections, with horizontal lines near the top and bottom of the page, and a vertical line running from the top horizontal line to the bottom horizontal line that divides the main body of the paper into a narrow and a wide column. Write "First Amendment Freedoms" and the date at the top of the paper. Next, use the "5Rs": record, reduce, recite, reflect, and review. **Record:** Have students use the wide column for taking notes as they read the chapter, using abbreviations and shorthand whenever possible. **Reduce:** Have students identify main ideas, key points, dates, people, and vocabulary in their notes and write them in the narrow column. They will use these to write a summary of the main points in the bottom section of the paper. **Recite:** Direct students to study their notes. Cover up the wide column and respond to the key points listed in the narrow column and the summary. **Reflect:** Are there any parts of their notes that students don't understand? **Review:** Suggest that students spend 10 minutes per week reviewing their notes.

### ASSESSMENT AT A GLANCE

**Tests and Quizzes**
Section Assessments
Section Quizzes A and B, Unit 5 **All-in-One**
Chapter Assessment
Chapter Tests A and B, Unit 5 **All-in-One**
Document-Based Assessment
Progress Monitoring Online
Exam*View* Test Bank

**Performance Assessment**
Essential Questions Journal
Debates, pp. 548, 554
Dramatize Freedom of Press Cases, p. 564
Assessment Rubrics, **All-in-One**

# Chapter Assessment

## COMPREHENSION AND CRITICAL THINKING

### SECTION 1

1. **(a)** life, liberty, and the pursuit of happiness **(b)** by legalizing them in the Bill of Rights

2. **(a)** must not infringe on others' rights **(b)** the right to freedom of speech would not protect a person who falsely shouts "fire" in a crowded theater **(c)** right to a fair trial versus freedom of the press

3. **(a)** Federalism means that restrictions on the National Government concerning individual rights do not apply to the States. **(b)** The 14th Amendment applied the restrictions of the National Government to the States. **(c)** The Court declared many State laws unconstitutional as a violation of the 14th Amendment's Due Process Clause.

4. **(a)** that rights exist beyond those listed in the Constitution **(b)** because the Framers realized that the Constitution could not possibly list all the rights retained by the people

### SECTION 2

5. Nearly all property of and contributions to religious sects are free from federal, State, and local taxation. Chaplains serve with each branch of the armed forces. Most public officials take an oath of office in the name of God. Sessions of Congress, most State legislatures, and many city councils open with prayer. The nation's anthem and its coins and currency make reference to God.

6. **(a)** parochial schools enroll large numbers of students who would otherwise have to be educated at public expense; to relieve parents who pay taxes to support the public schools their children do not attend **(b)** parents who send their children to parochial schools should accept the financial consequences of that choice; it is impossible to draw clear lines between secular and sectarian courses in parochial schools

7. **(a)** Prayers have been offered in the nation's legislative bodies "from colonial times through the founding of the Republic and ever since." Legislators, unlike schoolchildren, are not "susceptible to religious indoctrination or peer pressure." **(b)** Answers will vary.

8. Religious practices must not violate criminal laws, offend public morals, or threaten community safety.

---

# Chapter Assessment

## Comprehension and Critical Thinking

### Section 1

1. **(a)** For what unalienable rights was the American Revolution fought? **(b)** How did the Framers of the Constitution guarantee those rights?

2. **(a)** What general limitation is placed on individual rights? **(b)** What example does *Schenck* v. *United States* cite to explain this limitation? **(c)** To which conflicting rights did *Sheppard* v. *Maxwell* apply?

3. **(a)** How does federalism complicate guarantees of individual rights? **(b)** How does the 14th Amendment address this complication? **(c)** On what basis did the Supreme Court strike down many State laws after the *Gitlow* case?

4. **(a)** What does the 9th Amendment provide? **(b)** Why do you think it was included in the Bill of Rights?

### Section 2

5. List five examples of the ways in which government encourages religion in the United States.

6. **(a)** Cite two arguments for allowing State aid to parochial schools. **(b)** Cite two arguments against this practice.

7. **(a)** Why has the Court allowed legislative prayers but not organized school prayers? **(b)** Do you agree with the Court's rationale? Why or why not?

8. Identify three ways in which government may properly restrict the exercise of religious belief.

### Section 3

9. What two basic purposes do the guarantees of free expression serve?

10. **(a)** What does the "clear and present danger" rule say? **(b)** What case established the rule? **(c)** How is the Smith Act of 1940 consistent with that rule?

11. **(a)** What is prior restraint? **(b)** In what situations does the Supreme Court allow prior restraint?

### Section 4

12. What are the time, place, and manner limits that government can put on freedom of assembly?

13. What limits on public demonstrations has the Court upheld?

14. **Analyze Political Cartoons** How do you think the Supreme Court might rule in a case like the one shown in the cartoon below: for the boys (freedom of association) or for the girl (anti-discrimination)? Explain your answer.

### Writing About Government

15. Use your Quick Write exercises to write a persuasive essay supporting a civil liberties issue. Write an introduction with at least two sides, a body that provides evidence to support your position and refutes the opposing position, and a conclusion that strengthens your argument. See pp. S9–S10 in the Skills Handbook.

---

### Apply What You've Learned

16. **Essential Question Activity** Not all assembly is protected by the 1st and 14th Amendments. Suppose you are helping to organize a demonstration for a political cause. Write three to five questions you should ask to determine if the Supreme Court would consider your demonstration to be constitutionally protected.

17. **Essential Question Assessment** Based on the questions you wrote and the content of this chapter, create a brochure for participants that helps to answer the Essential Question: **How can the judiciary balance individual rights with the common good?** Consider the freedoms of speech, press, and assembly and petition. Include examples from the chapter that show how individual rights are balanced by the courts to ensure relative guarantees for the public (the common good).

**Essential Questions Journal** To respond to the chapter Essential Question, go to your **Essential Questions Journal.**

---

### SECTION 3

9. to guarantee each person a right of free expression and to ensure all persons a full discussion of public affairs

10. **(a)** that words can be outlawed if they trigger an immediate danger of criminal acts **(b)** *Schenck* v. *United States* **(c)** The Smith Act makes it a crime to advocate violent overthrow of the government. Such advocacy would create clear and present danger.

11. **(a)** restricting spoken or written words before they are expressed **(b)** in such extreme situations as wartime, or when a publication is obscene or incites its readers to acts of violence

### SECTION 4

12. Government can set limits on when, where, and how assemblies take place. However, government rules must be precisely drawn, fairly administered, and content neutral.

13. Laws can require advance notice and permits for demonstrations in public places.

14. for the boys, because their clubhouse is a private organization

# Document-Based Assessment

## Freedom of Speech and Assembly

Citizens burn the American flag in a protest and the Ku Klux Klan parades along Main Street. Both these controversial actions are protected by the 1st and 14th Amendments. Some Americans believe such actions should not be protected. From America's earliest days, public and judicial opinion have been divided over the extent of free speech and assembly, as shown in the documents below.

### Document 1

"We have nothing to fear from the demoralizing reasonings of some, if others are left free to demonstrate their errors and especially when the law stands ready to punish the first criminal act produced by the false reasonings; these are safer corrections than the conscience of the judge."

—Thomas Jefferson, July 3, 1801

### Document 2

### Document 3

"[F]reedom of speech which is secured by the Constitution does not confer an absolute right to speak, without responsibility, whatever one may choose, . . . a State in the exercise of its police power may punish those who abuse this freedom by . . . tending to incite to crime, disturb the public peace, or endanger the foundations of organized government. . . ."

—*Whitney* v. *California*, 1927

### Document 4

"[T]he constitutional guarantees of free speech and free press do not permit a State to forbid or proscribe advocacy of the use of force or of law violation except where such advocacy is directed to inciting or producing imminent lawless action and is likely to incite or produce such action. . . . [T]he mere abstract teaching . . . of the moral propriety or even moral necessity for a resort to force and violence is not the same as preparing a group for violent action and steeling it to such action. . . ."

—*Brandenburg* v. *Ohio*, 1969

---

**Use your knowledge of 1st Amendment freedoms and Documents 1–4 to answer these questions.**

1. According to Document 1, which of these should be punished?
   A. violent ideas
   B. "demoralizing reasonings"
   C. criminal acts produced by violent ideas
   D. speech whose purpose is to incite fear

2. What comment does the cartoon make about some of the Court's 1st Amendment decisions?

3. According to Document 3, when may a State exercise its police power in order to limit freedom of speech and assembly?

4. According to Document 4 (a case that overturned *Whitney*), when may speech and assembly be properly limited?

5. **Pull It Together** Which documents support tightening limits on speech and assembly? With which documents do you agree? Why?

 **GOVERNMENT** ONLINE
**Documents**
To find additional primary sources on 1st Amendment freedoms, visit PearsonSchool.com/phgovt

---

## DOCUMENT-BASED ASSESSMENT

1. C

2. The cartoonist believes that the Court has trampled on 1st Amendment freedoms, or has allowed others to do so.

3. when someone abuses this freedom by "tending to incite to crime, disturb the public peace, or endanger the foundations of organized government"

4. only when the use of force or of law violation is directed to inciting or producing imminent lawless action and is likely to incite or produce such action

5. Documents 2 and 3. Students should provide valid reasons for their responses.

**L2 Differentiate** Students use all the documents on the page to support their opinion.

**L3 Differentiate** Students include additional information available online at **PearsonSchool.com/phgovt.**

**L4 Differentiate** Students use materials from the textbook, the online information at **PearsonSchool.com/phgovt,** and do additional research to support their views.

**Go Online to PearsonSchool.com/phgovt** for a student rubric and extra documents.

---

### WRITING ABOUT GOVERNMENT

15. Have students proofread and refine their persuasive essays before submitting them.

### APPLY WHAT YOU'VE LEARNED

16. Possible questions: Does our action violate any laws? Would our demonstration endanger public safety? Can we ensure that our demonstrators will remain peaceful? Did we get the proper permit? Will we be trespassing on private property?

17. Each part of the brochure should include examples of conflicts between individual rights and the common good, and present a solution to the conflict that creates a fair balance.

# Introduce the Chapter

## Essential Questions:

**UNIT 5**

What should be the role of the judicial branch?

**CHAPTER 20**

To what extent has the judiciary protected the rights of privacy, security, and personal freedom?

**ACTIVATE PRIOR KNOWLEDGE**

Have students examine the photo and quotation on these pages. Ask: **What does the image represent?** *(justice)* **What is the significance of the scale?** *(fair treatment for all under the law)* **According to Ronald Reagan, what is the government's responsibility toward constitutional rights?** *(to restore rights unjustly denied)* In this chapter, students will learn about constitutional liberties related to legal proceedings. Have students begin to further explore civil liberties by completing the Chapter 20 Essential Question Warmup activity in their **Essential Questions Journal.**

**BEFORE READING**

**L2 ELL Differentiate** Chapter 20 Prereading and Vocabulary Worksheet (Unit 5 All-in-One, p. 126)

**SUCCESSNET STUDENT AND TEACHER CENTER**

Visit **PearsonSchool.com/phgovt** for downloadable resources that allow students and teachers to connect with government "on the go."

**DIGITAL LESSON PRESENTATION**

The digital lesson presentation supports the print lesson with activities and summaries of key concepts. Activities for this chapter include:

• **Rights of the Accused: Steps of Justice**

## SKILLS DEVELOPMENT

**DECISION MAKING**

You may wish to teach decision making as a distinct skill within Section 2 of this chapter. Use the Chapter 20 Skills Worksheet (Unit 5 All-in-One, p. 142) to help students learn about decision making. The worksheet asks students to decide whether to vote for or against the USA Patriot Act. For L2 and L1 students, assign the adapted Skill Activity (Unit 5 All-in-One, p. 143).

**WebQuest** **online** The chapter WebQuest challenges students to answer the chapter Essential Question by asking them about the judiciary.

576

## Block Scheduling

**BLOCK 1:** Teach the Section 1 lesson, including the Bellringer and Due Process activities. Discuss Core Worksheet 20.1. Teach the Section 2 lesson, including the Bellringer (Transparency 20B), Cover Search-and-Seizure Basics, Core Worksheet 20.2, and the Exclusionary Rule activities. Choose one of the Extend options to conclude the lesson.

**BLOCK 2:** Teach the Section 3 lesson, including the Bellringer (Transparency 20E), Clarify Rights of the Accused, Diagram Rights of the Accused (Transparency 20F), and Evaluate the Miranda Rule (Core Worksheet 20.3B). Teach the Section 4 lesson, including the Bellringer (Transparency 20G), Analyze Court Decisions, and Core Worksheets 20.4A and 20.4B. Conclude with the Political Cartoon Mini-Lesson (Transparency 20H).

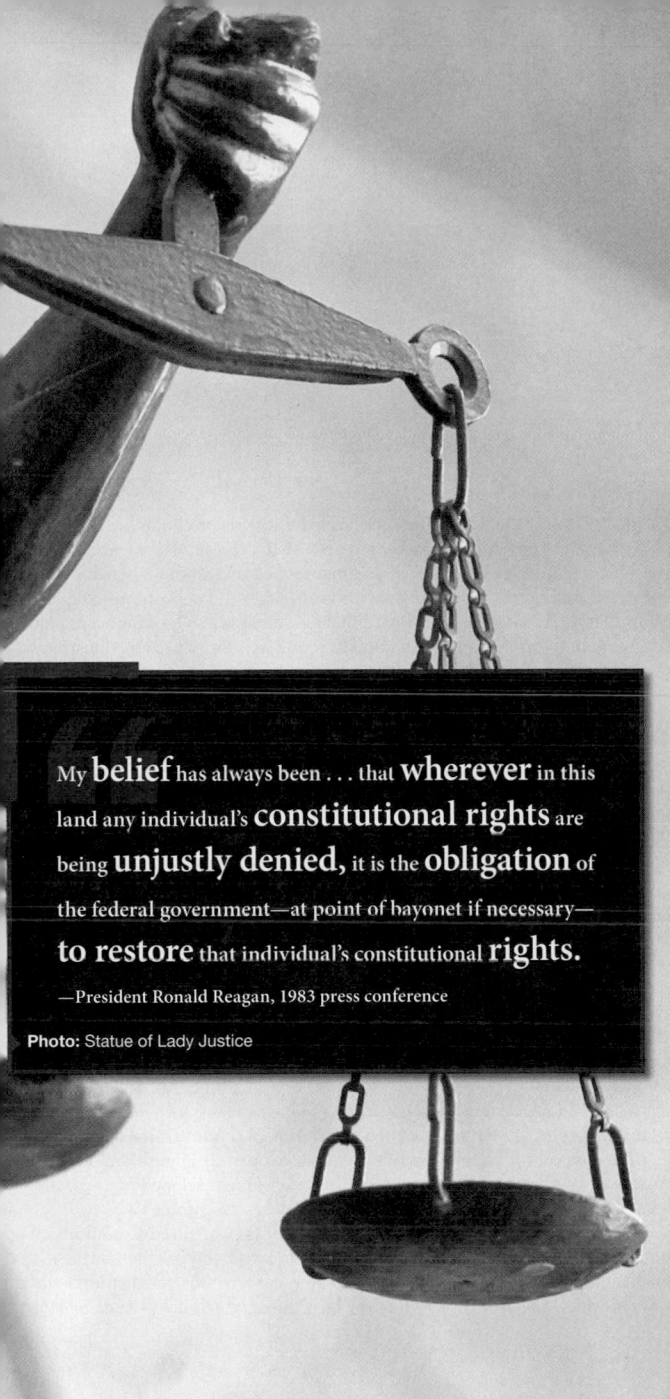

**Essential Question**
To what extent has the judiciary protected the rights of privacy, security, and personal freedom?

My **belief** has always been . . . that **wherever** in this land any individual's **constitutional rights** are being **unjustly denied**, it is the **obligation** of the federal government—at point of bayonet if necessary— **to restore** that individual's constitutional **rights.**

—President Ronald Reagan, 1983 press conference

**Photo:** Statue of Lady Justice

**GOVERNMENT** ONLINE
**On the Go**

To study anywhere, anytime, download these online resources at PearsonSchool.com/phgovt
- Political Dictionary
- Audio Review
- Downloadable Interactivities

## Lesson Goals

**SECTION 1**

Students will . . .

- understand the importance of due process by analyzing examples of when due process was and was not followed and by considering how government might function without due process.

- evaluate how government balances its police power with individual freedoms by summarizing scenarios in which society's well-being conflicts with a person's rights.

**SECTION 2**

Students will . . .

- understand 4th Amendment guarantees against unreasonable search and seizure by discussing proper procedures of police officers and by completing a chart on court decisions in related cases.

- identify how Supreme Court rulings have narrowed the meaning of the exclusionary rule by defining the rule and analyzing Court opinions related to it.

**SECTION 3**

Students will . . .

- identify the rights of people accused of crimes by note-taking, completing a tree diagram, and discussing a case related to habeas corpus.

- evaluate the guarantee against self-incrimination by participating in simulations and analyzing a case related to the Miranda rule.

**SECTION 4**

Students will . . .

- examine how the Court's interpretation of "cruel and unusual punishment" has changed over time by analyzing court cases on the death penalty.

- analyze and evaluate arguments on the constitutionality of juvenile capital punishment by analyzing Supreme Court opinions and editorials on this issue.

## Pressed for Time

Explain that due process of law requires that government act fairly and in accordance with established rules. Have students create a timeline that charts the development and expansion of due process in the United States. Timelines should begin with the Civil War period and continue to the present. Tell students to scan the chapter to find key Supreme Court cases that addressed due process guarantees regarding security of the person and rights of the accused, and which limited both the Federal Government and State governments. Have students note the cases on their timelines, including explanations of their significance.

**DIFFERENTIATED INSTRUCTION KEY**

Look for these symbols to help you adjust steps in each lesson to meet your students' needs.

**L1** Special Needs

**L2** Basic

    **ELL** English Language Learners

    **LPR** Less Proficient Readers

**L3** All Students

**L4** Advanced Students

# Why is the concept of due process important to a free society?

| Due Process of Law | |
|---|---|
| **Restrictions on Government** | **Benefits to Individuals** |
| • must act fairly and in accord with established rules when enforcing laws<br>• laws must also be fair | • life, liberty, and property cannot be taken unfairly or arbitrarily<br>• civil liberties are protected by government following established procedures |

# Get Started

## LESSON GOALS

Students will . . .

- understand the importance of due process by ana-lyzing examples of when due process was and was not followed and by considering how government might function without due process.
- evaluate how government balances its police power with individual freedoms by summarizing scenarios in which society's well-being conflicts with a person's rights.

## BEFORE CLASS

Assign the section, the graphic organizer in the text, and the Reading Comprehension Worksheet (Unit 5 All-in-One, p. 130) before class.

**L2 Differentiate** Reading Comprehension Worksheet (Unit 5 All-in-One, p. 131)

## SKILLS DEVELOPMENT

### DRAW INFERENCES AND CONCLUSIONS

Before students begin the Core Worksheets in this lesson, you may want to review tips on drawing inferences and conclusions in the Skills Handbook, p. S19.

---

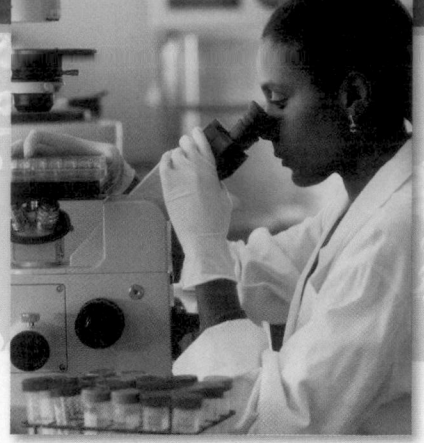

## SECTION 1

# Due Process of Law

### Guiding Question

**Why is the concept of due process important to a free society?** Use a chart like the one below to take notes on due process.

| Due Process of Law | |
|---|---|
| **Restrictions on Government** | **Benefits to Individuals** |
| •<br>• | •<br>• |

### Political Dictionary

- due process
- procedural due process
- substantive due process
- police power
- search warrant

### Objectives

1. Explain the meaning of due process of law as set out in the 5th and 14th amendments.
2. Define police power and under-stand its relationship to civil rights.
3. Describe the right of privacy and its origins in constitutional law.

**Image Above:** Evidence in a criminal case is tested in a laboratory.

**D**id you know that DNA evidence has led to the reversal of more than 200 wrongful convictions in recent years? That the use of evidence drawn from the scientific study of body tissues has proved that all those persons were convicted, and served time in prison, for crimes they did *not* commit? Did you know that there is a strong likelihood that an untold number of innocent persons remain in prison today? As you will soon see, this point alone illustrates the importance of due process of law.

## What Due Process Means

The Constitution contains two due process clauses. The 5th Amendment declares that the Federal Government cannot deprive any person of "life, liberty, or property, without due process of law." The 14th Amendment places that same restriction on every one of the States—and, very importantly, on their local governments, as well. A thorough grasp of the meaning of these provisions is absolutely essential to an understanding of the American concept of civil rights and liberties.

It is impossible to define the two due process guarantees in exact and complete terms. The Supreme Court has consistently and purposely refused to do so. Instead, it has relied on finding the meaning of due process on a case-by-case basis. The Court first described that approach in *Davidson* v. *New Orleans*, 1878, as the "gradual process of inclusion and exclusion, as the cases presented for decision shall require."

Fundamentally, however, the Constitution's guarantee of **due process** means this: In whatever it does, government must act fairly and in accord with established rules. It may not act unfairly, arbitrarily, or unreasonably.

The concept of due process began and developed in English and then in American law as a procedural concept. That is, it first developed as a requirement that government act fairly, use fair procedures, to enforce law.

Fair procedures are of little value, however, if they are used to administer unfair laws. The Supreme Court recognized this fact toward the end of the nineteenth century. It began to hold that due process requires that both the ways in which government acts *and* the laws under which it acts must be fair.

---

# Focus on the Basics

**FACTS:** • The 5th and 14th amendments guarantee that the National, State, and local governments cannot deprive a person of life, liberty, or property without due process of law. • Substantive due process guarantees that laws will be fair. • Procedural due process guarantees that laws will be enforced in a fair and equal manner. • The States' reserved powers include the police power. • The Court has held that constitutional guarantees of due process create a right of privacy.

**CONCEPTS:** limited government, due process of law, individual rights and responsibilities

**ENDURING UNDERSTANDINGS:** • Due process requires government to act fairly and according to established rules. • When the use of police power conflicts with civil liberties, courts must balance society's needs with individual freedoms.

Thus, the Court added the idea of substantive due process to the original notion of procedural due process.

In short, **procedural due process** has to do with the *how* (the procedures, the methods) of governmental action. **Substantive due process** involves the *what* (the substance, the policies) of governmental action.

**Examples of Due Process** Any number of cases may be used to illustrate these two elements of due process. Take a classic case, *Rochin* v. *California,* 1952, to exemplify procedural due process.

Rochin was a suspected narcotics dealer. Acting on a tip, three Los Angeles County deputy sheriffs went to his rooming house. They forced their way into Rochin's room, found him sitting on a bed, and spotted two capsules on a nightstand. When one of the deputies asked, "Whose stuff is this?" Rochin popped the capsules into his mouth. Although all three officers jumped him, Rochin managed to swallow the pills.

The deputies took Rochin to a hospital, where his stomach was pumped. The capsules were recovered and found to contain morphine. The State then prosecuted and convicted Rochin for violating the State's narcotics laws.

The Supreme Court unanimously held that the deputies had violated the 14th Amendment's guarantee of procedural due process. Said the Court:

### PRIMARY SOURCE

**This is conduct that shocks the conscience. Illegally breaking into the privacy of the petitioner, the struggle to open his mouth and remove what was there, the forcible extraction of his stomach's contents—this course of proceeding by agents of government to obtain evidence is bound to offend even hardened sensibilities. They are methods too close to the rack and the screw. . . .**
—Justice Felix Frankfurter

The case *Pierce* v. *Society of Sisters,* 1925, illustrates substantive due process. In 1922, Oregon's voters had adopted a new compulsory school-attendance law that required all persons between the ages of 8 and 16 to attend *public* schools. The law was purposely written to destroy private, especially parochial, schools in the State.

A Roman Catholic order challenged the law's constitutionality, and the Supreme Court held that its provisions violated the 14th Amendment's Due Process Clause. The Court did not find that the State had enforced the law unfairly. Rather, it held that the law itself, in its contents, "unreasonably interferes with the liberty of parents to direct

## Due Process

This basic limit is placed on the Federal Government in the **5th Amendment,** and on State and local governments in the **14th Amendment:**

> **Government cannot deprive any person of life, liberty, or property without due process of law.**

Both the **procedures** and the **laws** of government must be in accord with due process. *Why are procedural and substantive due process both necessary?*

**PROCEDURAL**
Due Process
The procedures, the methods, the *how* of governmental action must be fair.

**SUBSTANTIVE**
Due Process
The substance, the meaning, the *what* of a law or action of government must be fair.

## Differentiated Resources

The following resources are located in the All-in-One, Unit 5, Chapter 20, Section 1:

- **L3** Prereading and Vocabulary Worksheet (p. 126)
- **L3** Reading Comprehension Worksheet (p. 130)
- **L2** Reading Comprehension Worksheet (p. 131)
- **L3** Core Worksheet A (p. 132)
- **L3** Core Worksheet B (p. 134)
- **L3** Quiz A (p. 135)
- **L2** Quiz B (p. 136)

Write these examples of arbitrary laws and the following question on the board: **(1) Only students who drive red or blue cars can park in the school parking lot. (2) On Mondays and Wednesdays, brown-eyed students cannot eat in the cafeteria. (3) Police officers can search your home whenever they feel like it. What is wrong with these laws? Answer in your notebook.**

## Teach

To present this topic using online resources, use the lesson presentations at **PearsonSchool.com/phgovt.**

### REVIEW BELLRINGER ANSWERS

Ask students to share their answers to the Bellringer question. Students should infer that the laws are unfair and arbitrary. Then ask: **Why is it important that laws not only be fair but also consistent, regular, or uniform across all situations and classes of people?** *(Consistent, predictable laws and law enforcement procedures promote order and stability.)* **What prevents governments from passing unfair laws or applying laws in an arbitrary manner?** *(due process of law)*

**L2** **L3** **Differentiate** Have groups list characteristics of a fair law. *(applied equally regardless of race, gender, religious beliefs, or income; easy to understand; enforceable; not vague; clearly states what is and is not legal)* Then ask groups to write a law concerning curfew for teenagers, drug testing for athletes, or mandatory sentencing for criminals. When finished, have groups use their lists of fair characteristics to critique one another's laws.

### INTRODUCE DUE PROCESS

Explain that due process originated as early as 1215 in the Magna Carta. Display Transparency 20A, Protecting Individual Rights, and have a volunteer read aloud the quote. Then ask: **According to the document, what factors will determine a person's imprisonment?** *(judgment by one's peers or by the law of the land)* **How did government by "law of the land" differ from previous government?** *(Absolute monarchs ruled according to their whims, not by laws.)*

Have a student read aloud the 5th Amendment and Section 1 of the 14th Amendment. Ask: **What limits do the amendments place on government?** *(National and State governments cannot deprive any person of life, liberty, or property without following fair laws and procedures.)*

## Answers

**Due Process** to ensure not only that procedures are fair, but also that the laws they administer are fair

**L2 Differentiate** Students who have difficulty grasping the concept of due process may find it easier to think of limits on government as the "law of the land."

**L2 ELL Differentiate** Explain these words in the 5th and 14th amendments: *jeopardy* (danger or risk), *deprive* (remove or take away), *compensation* (payment or reimbursement), *abridge* (reduce or cut), *arbitrary* (random).

**L3 Differentiate** Have students consider what might result from the following actions *without* fair laws or due process of law: someone criticizes the government *(banishment, execution);* shoplifting *(hand cut off, other torture punishment exceeding the crime);* a suspect without an attorney is tried only by a judge, not by a jury *(sham trial with rigged witnesses).*

**IDENTIFY DUE PROCESS PROCEDURES**

Distribute the Chapter 20 Section 1 Core Worksheet A (Unit 5 All-in-One, p. 132). Students will identify due process procedures that were or were not followed in a trial.

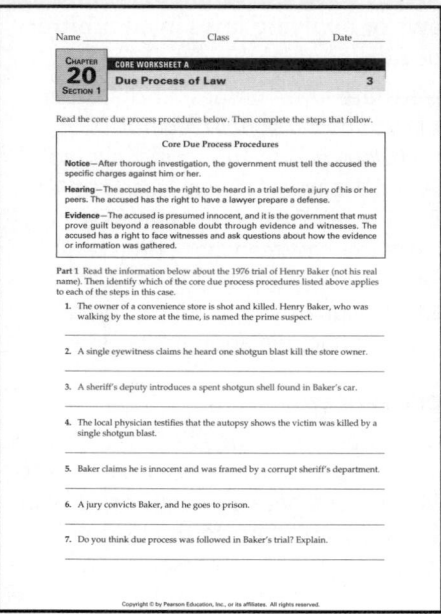

**L2 Differentiate** Have students complete the worksheet using the Think-Pair-Share strategy (p. T22).

## Answers

**Checkpoint** the authority of each State to protect and promote the public health, safety, morals, and general welfare of its people

**Interpreting Political Cartoons** Possible answer: No. Due process guarantees a fair trial, not acquittal.

---

the upbringing and education of children under their control.

**The 14th Amendment and the Bill of Rights** Recall these crucial points from Chapter 19: The provisions of the Bill of Rights apply against the National Government *only.* However, the Supreme Court has held that the 14th Amendment's Due Process Clause includes within its meaning most of the protections set out in the Bill of Rights.

In a long series of decisions dating from 1925, the Court extended the protections of the Bill of Rights against the States through the 14th Amendment's Due Process Clause. The chart on page 549 lists those amendments that have been incorporated—and with them the four provisions in the Bill of Rights that have not been incorporated.

The key 1st Amendment cases were discussed in Chapter 19. Those involving the 4th through the 8th amendments are treated in Sections 2, 3, and 4 of this chapter.

**compulsory**
*adj.* forced, obligatory

*"What's so great about due process? Due process got me ten years."*

▶▶ **Interpreting Political Cartoons** *Is it possible that the prisoner's complaint is justified? Explain your answer.*

### The Police Power

In the federal system, the reserved powers of the States include the broad and important **police power**. The police power is the authority of each State to act to protect and promote the public health, safety, morals, and general welfare. In other words, it is the power of each State to safeguard the well-being of its people.

**The Police Power and Civil Liberties** The use of the police power often produces conflicts with civil liberty protections. When it does, courts must strike a balance between the needs of society, on the one hand, and of individual freedoms on the other. Any number of cases can be used to illustrate the conflict between police power and individual rights. Take as an example a matter often involved in drunk-driving cases.

Every State's laws allow the use of one or more tests to determine whether a person arrested and charged with drunk driving was in fact drunk at the time of the incident. Some of those tests are simple: walking a straight line or touching the tip of one's nose, for example. Some are more sophisticated, however, notably the breathalyzer test and the drawing of a blood sample.

Does the requirement that a person submit to such a test violate his or her rights under the 14th Amendment? Does the test involve an unconstitutional search for and seizure of evidence? Does it amount to forcing a person to testify against himself or herself (unconstitutional compulsory self-incrimination)? Or is that requirement a proper exercise of the police power?

Time after time, State and federal courts have come down on the side of the police power. They have supported the right of society to protect itself against drunk drivers and rejected the individual rights argument.

The leading case is *Schmerber* v. *California,* 1966. There, the Court found no objection to a situation in which a police officer had directed a doctor to draw blood from a drunk-driving suspect. The Court emphasized these points: The blood sample was drawn in accord with accepted medical practice. The officer had reasonable grounds

## Background

**MAGNA CARTA** When rebellious barons forced King John to sign the Magna Carta in 1215, they intended to secure rights for the powerful families in feudal England—not for everyone. However, in negotiating the wording, they changed "any baron" to "any freeman." This change, minor at the time, would later be used to apply the charter to broader society. In the 17th century, Edward Coke, an English lawyer, reinterpreted the Magna Carta, arguing that it established universal rights that kings and acts of Parliament could not void. American colonists wrote these views into the legal codes of the colonies. They cited the Magna Carta to condemn the Stamp Act as against "the natural rights of Englishmen." In the Constitution, "all freemen" would become "we the people." Just as the Magna Carta could not be canceled by later English laws, the U.S. Constitution would become "the Supreme Law of the Land."

to believe that the suspect was drunk. Further, had the officer taken the time necessary to secure a **search warrant**—a court order authorizing a search—whatever evidence was present could have disappeared from the suspect's system.

**Protecting the Public** Legislators and judges have often found the public's health, safety, morals, and/or welfare to be of overriding importance. For example:

**1.** To promote health, States can limit the sale of alcoholic beverages and tobacco, make laws to combat pollution, and require the vaccination of schoolchildren.

**2.** To promote safety, States can regulate the carrying of concealed weapons, require the use of seat belts, and punish drunk drivers.

**3.** To promote morals, States can regulate gambling and outlaw the sale of obscene materials and the practice of prostitution.

**4.** To promote the general welfare, States can enact compulsory education laws, provide help to the medically needy, and limit the profits of public utilities.

Clearly, governments cannot use the police power in an unreasonable or unfair way, however. In short, they cannot violate the 14th Amendment's Due Process Clause.

## The Right of Privacy

The constitutional guarantees of due process create a right of privacy—"the right to be free, except in very limited circumstances, from unwanted governmental intrusions into one's privacy," *Stanley* v. *Georgia*, 1969.[1] It is, in short, "the right to be let alone."[2]

The Constitution makes no specific mention of the right of privacy, but the Supreme Court declared its existence in *Griswold* v. *Connecticut*, 1965. That case centered on a State law that outlawed birth-control counseling and prohibited the use of all birth-control devices. The Court held the law to be a violation of the 14th Amendment's Due Process Clause—and noted that the State had no business policing the marital bedroom.

*Roe* v. *Wade* The most controversial applications of the right of privacy have come in cases that raise this question: To what extent can a State limit a woman's right to an abortion? The leading case is *Roe* v. *Wade*, 1973. There, the Supreme Court struck down a Texas law that made abortion a crime except when necessary to save the life of the mother.

In *Roe*, the Court held that the 14th Amendment's right of privacy "encompass[es] a woman's decision whether or not to terminate her pregnancy." More specifically, the Court ruled that:

**1.** In the first trimester of pregnancy (about three months), a State must recognize a woman's right to an abortion; it cannot interfere with medical judgments in that matter during that period.

**2.** In the second trimester, a State, acting in the interest of women who undergo abortions, can make reasonable regulations about how, when, and where abortions can be performed but cannot prohibit the procedure.

**3.** In the final trimester, a State, acting to protect the unborn child, can choose to prohibit all abortions except those necessary to preserve the life or health of the mother.

**Challenges to *Roe*** In several later cases, the Court rejected a number of challenges to its basic holding in *Roe*. As the composition of the Court has changed, however, so has the Court's position on abortion. That shift can be seen in the Court's decisions in later cases on the matter.

In *Webster* v. *Reproductive Health Services*, 1989, the Court upheld two key parts of a Missouri law. Those provisions prohibit abortions, except those that preserve the

CELL PHONE USE WHILE DRIVING PROHIBITED

> Promoting safety is one of the States' police powers. *In what ways do States promote morality?*

---

[1] *Stanley* involved the possession of obscene materials in one's own home. In a more recent right to privacy case, the Court struck down a Texas law that made sexual relations between consenting gay adults a crime, *Lawrence* v. *Texas*, 2003.

[2] Justice Louis D. Brandeis, dissenting in *Olmstead* v. *United States*, 1928.

## Background

**DNA AND DUE PROCESS** After his conviction for rape, James Harvey maintained his innocence for more than ten years. In 2001, a federal judge ruled for the first time that Harvey, and other convicted felons, have a constitutional right to have their DNA tested to try to prove their innocence. An appeals court later overturned this ruling. Still, this case helped pave the way for The Innocence Protection Act (2001). This law was designed to reduce the risk that innocent people might be executed. Among other protections, it guarantees convicted offenders the right to DNA testing. But DNA can help convict as well as exonerate. Since passage of the act, law enforcement agencies in some States have expanded the collection of DNA samples from not only convicted felons but also from arrestees. Critics argue that this practice erodes due process by denying citizens the right to keep their genetic information private.

## ANALYZE STATES' POLICE POWER

Organize students into pairs. Distribute the Chapter 20 Section 1 Core Worksheet B (Unit 5 All-in-One, p. 134), which asks students to analyze scenarios that pit individual rights against the public good. Discuss Situation 1 before pairs work independently to complete the worksheet.

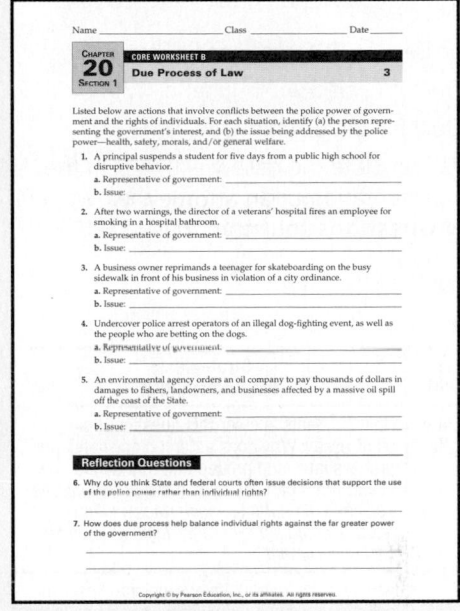

**L2 ELL Differentiate** Clarify for students that *police power* refers to the reserved power of the States, not to the actions of police officers.

**L3 Differentiate** Ask students to role-play a conversation between an offender and a representative of the government's interest. Each should explain his or her side, and individuals should ask for explanations of their due process rights.

### EXTEND THE LESSON

**L3 Differentiate** Have students research a case in this section. Ask them to draw a flowchart showing the due process procedures followed. Questions that could be answered in the flowchart include: What are the facts in the case? What due process rule, law, or policy was followed or violated? How was it violated? How was evidence or information gathered?

**L4 Differentiate** Have students research one of these cases and write a newspaper editorial explaining whether they agree or disagree with the Court's ruling: In *Chicago* v. *Morales*, 1999, the Court struck down an antigang loitering ordinance. In *Lee* v. *Kemna*, 2002, the Court ruled that the defendant was denied his due process rights.

---

## Answers

**Caption** States regulate gambling and outlaw the sale of obscene materials and the practice of prostitution.

# Assess and Remediate

**L3** Have students write a journal entry explaining whether they agree or disagree with this statement: The right to due process has been called the greatest protection in the Constitution from the abuse of power by government.

**L3** Collect Core Worksheet B and assess students' work.

**L3** Assign the Section 1 Assessment questions.

**L3** Section Quiz A (Unit 5 All-in-One, p. 135)

**L2** Section Quiz B (Unit 5 All-in-One, p. 136)

Have students complete the review activities in the digital lesson presentation and continue their work in the **Essential Questions Journal.**

## REMEDIATION

| If Your Students Have Trouble With | Strategies For Remediation |
|---|---|
| Due Process of law (Questions 1, 2, 3) | Have students answer this question in a short essay: Why does a democracy need due process laws and procedures that define how government can use its power? *(If democratic societies did not have such rules, political leaders could act arbitrarily, leading to unlimited government.)* |
| Police power of government (Questions 4, 5, 6) | Ask students to make a two-column chart. In column one, have them list ten problems in the United States: social, environmental, economic, urban, rural, etc. In column two, next to each problem, have students list the police power that attempts to address that problem. |

## Answers

**Checkpoint** A State may place reasonable limits on a woman's right to have an abortion, but restrictions cannot impose an "undue burden" on this right.

---

✓ **Checkpoint**
How has the Court modified its *Roe* v. *Wade* ruling in later decisions?

mother's life or health, (1) in any publicly operated hospital or clinic in that State, and (2) when the mother is 20 or more weeks pregnant and tests show that the fetus is viable (capable of sustaining life outside the mother's body).

Two cases in 1990 addressed the issue of minors and abortion. In those cases, the Court said that a State may require a minor (1) to inform at least one parent before she can obtain an abortion, *Ohio v. Akron Center for Reproductive Health*, and (2) to tell both parents of her plans, except in cases where a judge gives permission for an abortion without parental knowledge, *Hodgson v. Minnesota.*

The Court's most important decision on the issue since *Roe* v. *Wade* came in *Planned Parenthood of Southeastern Pennsylvania v. Casey* in 1992. There, the Court announced this rule: A State may place reasonable limits on a woman's right to have an abortion, but these restrictions cannot impose an "undue burden" on her choice of that procedure.

In *Casey*, the Court applied that new standard to Pennsylvania's Abortion Control Act. It upheld several sections of the law, finding that they did not place "a substantial obstacle in the path of a woman seeking an abortion of a non-viable fetus." Those provisions, it said, do not impose an "undue burden" on a woman's choice.

The Supreme Court did strike down another key part of the Pennsylvania law in *Casey*, however. That provision required that a married woman tell her husband of her plan to have an abortion. That requirement, said the Court, did indeed amount to an "undue burden."

**Recent Cases** The High Court has decided only two abortion cases since 1992. Its 5–4 vote in the most recent one effectively overturned its 5–4 decision in the earlier case. Together, the two cases underscore the impact that changes in the composition of the Court can have on the outcome of cases that come before it.

In *Gonzales* v. *Carhart*, 2007, the justices applied *Casey's* "undue burden" rule to an act of Congress, the Partial Birth Abortion Ban Act of 2003, and found it constitutional. That statute prohibits a particular method of abortion, a medical procedure that opponents of abortion call "partial birth abortion." In fact, that operation had been performed in very few instances.

In the earlier case, *Stenberg* v. *Carhart*, 2000, the Court had applied *Casey* to strike down a Nebraska law that also banned partial birth abortions, and in language very nearly identical to that used by Congress when it passed the federal law in 2003.

**Essential Questions Journal** To continue to build a response to the chapter Essential Question, go to your **Essential Questions Journal.**

## SECTION 1 ASSESSMENT

1. **Guiding Question** Use your completed graphic organizer to answer this question: Why is the concept of due process important to a free society?

### Key Terms and Comprehension

2. **(a)** What does the phrase **due process** of law mean? **(b)** Why has the Supreme Court purposefully not defined due process exactly?

3. How do **procedural due process** and **substantive due process** differ?

4. **(a)** What is the **police power** reserved to the States? **(b)** What is the relationship between the police power and due process of law?

### Critical Thinking

5. **Draw Conclusions** Considering the constitutional right of privacy, is it proper for a State to use its police power to protect and promote morals among its citizens? Explain your answer.

6. **Demonstrate Reasoned Judgment** The right of privacy is not found in the Constitution. **(a)** How did Justice Brandeis define the right of privacy? **(b)** Do you think a constitutional amendment is needed to guarantee an individual's right to privacy? Why or why not?

### Quick Write

**Research Essay: Choose a Topic** Scan the chapter for two or three Supreme Court cases. Research the cases online, and write a summary paragraph of each case that includes the facts and issues. Select the case that most interests you.

---

# Assessment Answers

**1.** Procedural due process and substantive due process act as safeguards on the rights of citizens and as restraints on the power of government officials. Life, liberty, and property cannot be taken away by unfair laws or unfair administration of laws.

**2. (a)** Government must act fairly and in accord with established rules and laws. **(b)** Justices do not see due process as absolute and unyielding; rather, they feel it is relative and should be decided on a case-by-case basis.

**3. procedural:** refers to the *how (the procedures, methods)* of government action; **substantive:** refers to the *what (the substance, policies)* of government action

**4. (a)** the authority to protect and promote public health, safety, morals, and general welfare **(b)** When using police power to protect society, States cannot violate the due process rights of individuals.

**5.** Possible answers: Yes, protection of morals falls within a State's police power. No, right of privacy limits the right of government to deem actions immoral.

**6. (a)** "the right to be let alone" **(b)** Answers will vary. Some students may believe the right is already protected sufficiently through the Supreme Court rulings. Others may feel an amendment is necessary.

**QUICK WRITE** Refer students to the Web site "Oyez: U.S. Supreme Court Media" to help them write their case summaries.

## SECTION 2

# Freedom and Security of the Person

**Political Dictionary**
- involuntary servitude
- discrimination
- writs of assistance
- probable cause
- exclusionary rule

**Objectives**
1. Outline Supreme Court decisions regarding slavery and involuntary servitude.
2. Explain the intent and application of the 2nd Amendment's protection of the right to keep and bear arms.
3. Summarize the constitutional provisions designed to guarantee security of home and person.

**Image Above:** Police must have probable cause when they stop a vehicle.

The Constitution of the United States is, in very large part, a statement of limited government. Many of the restrictions it puts on governmental power are intended to protect the right of every American to be free. That is, those restrictions guard the right of individuals to be free from physical restraints, to be secure in their persons, and to be secure in their homes.

## Slavery and Involuntary Servitude

The 13th Amendment was added to the Constitution in 1865, ending over 200 years of legalized slavery in America. Section 1 of the amendment declares: "Neither slavery nor involuntary servitude, . . . shall exist within the United States, or any place subject to their jurisdiction." Importantly, Section 2 of this amendment gives Congress the expressed power "to enforce this article by appropriate legislation."

Until 1865, each State could decide for itself whether to allow slavery within its borders. With the 13th Amendment, that power was denied to them, and to the National Government, as well.

**The 13th Amendment: Section 1** As a widespread practice, slavery disappeared in the United States more than 140 years ago. There are still occasional cases of it, however. Most often, those cases have involved **involuntary servitude**—that is, forced labor. An 1867 federal law, the Anti-Peonage Act, makes it a crime to force someone to work for another in order to fulfill a contract or satisfy a debt. Several times, the Supreme Court has struck down State laws making it a crime for any person to fail to work after having received money or other benefits by promising to do so.

The 13th Amendment does not forbid all forms of involuntary servitude, however. Thus, in 1918, the Supreme Court drew a distinction between "involuntary servitude" and "duty" in upholding the constitutionality of the selective service system (the draft).[3] Nor does imprisonment for crime violate the amendment; and those who are convicted of crime can be forced to work. Finally, note this important point: Unlike any other provision in the Constitution,

---
3 *Selective Draft Law Cases*, 1918.

## Focus on the Basics

**FACTS:** • The 13th Amendment prohibits slavery and involuntary servitude. • The 2nd Amendment preserves the right of States to keep militias. • The 4th Amendment prohibits unreasonable searches and seizures. • The Supreme Court adopted the controversial exclusionary rule, which says that evidence gained as the result of an illegal act by police cannot be used in court.

**CONCEPTS:** due process of law, individual rights and responsibilities, limited government

**ENDURING UNDERSTANDINGS:** • The 4th Amendment protects one from arbitrary searches and seizures. It requires police officers, except in special circumstances, to have a search warrant that was obtained with probable cause.

---

**GUIDING QUESTION**

## How does the Constitution protect the freedom and security of the person?

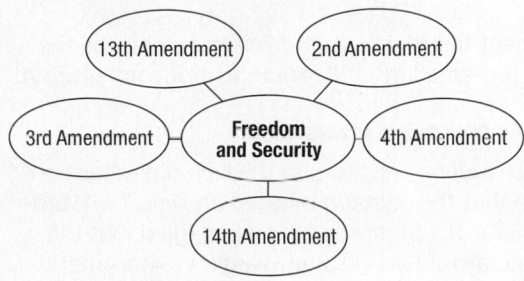

## Get Started

**LESSON GOALS**

Students will . . .

- understand 4th Amendment guarantees against unreasonable search and seizure by discussing proper procedures of police officers and by completing a chart on Court decisions in related cases.

- identify how Supreme Court rulings have narrowed the meaning of the exclusionary rule by defining the rule and analyzing Court opinions related to it.

**BEFORE CLASS**

Assign the section, the graphic organizer in the text, and the Reading Comprehension Worksheet (Unit 5 All-in-One, p. 137) before class.

**L2 Differentiate** Reading Comprehension Worksheet (Unit 5 All-in-One, p. 139)

## SKILLS DEVELOPMENT

**DECISION MAKING**

To practice decision making in this section, use the Chapter 20 Skills Worksheet (Unit 5 All-in-One, p. 142). You may teach the skill explicitly before students do the Core Worksheet. For L2 and L1 students, assign the adapted Skill Activity (Unit 5 All-in-One, p. 143).

Display Transparency 20B, Search-and-Seizure Scenario, which describes a search-and-seizure situation. Have students answer the question in their notebooks.

# Teach

To present this topic using online resources, use the lesson presentations at **PearsonSchool.com/phgovt.**

### DISCUSS BELLRINGER ANSWERS

Discuss students' answers to the Bellringer question. Explain that the scenario is based on *Illinois* v. *Wardlow,* 2000. The State supreme court ruled that the stop and arrest had violated Wardlow's 4th Amendment rights. Upon appeal, however, the Supreme Court ruled that flight can be an important factor in deciding whether police have "reasonable suspicion" to stop a suspect. The Court also noted that flight from the police will not always justify a stop or that it will never do so. Ask students whether they agree or disagree with the Court's decision, and why.

### INTRODUCE THE 4TH AMENDMENT

Ask a student to read the 4th Amendment aloud. Tell students that in this lesson, they will look at the rules and standards that the Supreme Court uses to examine the 4th Amendment rights of citizens and the responsibility of police to use proper procedures in search-and-seizure cases.

**L2** **ELL Differentiate** As students read the 4th Amendment, point out that the prefix *un-* means "not." Write the word *unreasonable* on the board, and ask students to explain what it means. (You also may want to explain that *seizure* in this case means "to arrest or detain.") Ask: **What is an unreasonable search and seizure?** *(one in which the police search a suspect or take the suspect's belongings without a warrant or without adequate reason for believing that a crime is about to be or already was committed)*

## Answers

**Caption** The selective service system may draft people into military service; convicts can be forced to work.

---

the prohibitions in the 13th Amendment cover the conduct of private individuals as well as the behavior of government.

**The 13th Amendment: Section 2** Shortly after the Civil War, Congress passed several civil rights laws based on the 13th Amendment. The Supreme Court, however, sharply narrowed the scope of federal authority in several cases, especially the *Civil Rights Cases,* 1883. In effect, the Court held that racial **discrimination** (prejudice, unfairness) against African Americans by *private individuals* was allowed. Private discrimination, ruled the Court, did not place the "badge of slavery" on African Americans nor keep them in servitude.

The 13th Amendment abolished slavery in 1865. *What types of involuntary servitude are permitted today?*

As a result, Congress soon repealed most of the civil rights laws based on the 13th Amendment. The enforcement of the few laws that remained was at best unimpressive. For years, it was generally thought that Congress did not have the power, under either the 13th or 14th Amendment, to act against those who practiced race-based discrimination.

Nearly a century later, however, in *Jones* v. *Mayer,* 1968, the Supreme Court breathed new life into the 13th Amendment. The case centered on one of the post-Civil War acts Congress had not repealed. Passed in 1866, that almost-forgotten law provided in part that:

> **PRIMARY SOURCE**
> [All] citizens of the United States; . . . of every race and color, . . . shall have the same right, in every State and Territory of the United States, . . . to inherit, purchase, lease, sell, hold, and convey real and personal property, . . . as is enjoyed by white citizens, . . .
> — Civil Rights Act of 1866

Jones, an African American, had sued because Mayer had refused to sell him a home, solely because of his race. Mayer contended that the 1866 law was unconstitutional, since it sought to prohibit private racial discrimination.

The Supreme Court upheld the 1866 law, declaring that the 13th Amendment abolished slavery and also gave Congress the power to abolish "the badges and incidents of slavery." Said the Court:

> **PRIMARY SOURCE**
> At the very least, the freedom that Congress is empowered to secure under the 13th Amendment includes the freedom to buy whatever a white man can buy, the right to live wherever a white man can live.
> —Justice Potter Stewart

The Court affirmed that decision in several later cases. Thus, in *Runyon* v. *McCrary,* 1976, two private schools had refused to admit two African American students. By doing so, the schools had refused to enter into a contract of admission—a contract they had advertised to the general public. The Court found that the schools had violated another provision of the 1866 law, providing that: "[All] citizens of the United States, . . . of every race and color, . . . shall have the same right, . . . to make and enforce contracts . . . as is enjoyed by white citizens. . . ."

The Court has also ruled that the Civil Rights Act of 1866 protects all "identifiable classes of persons who are subjected to intentional discrimination solely because of their ancestry or ethnic characteristics"—for example Jews, *Shaare Tefila Congregation* v. *Cobb,* 1987, and Arabs, *St. Francis College* v. *Al-Khazraji,* 1987.

More recently, the Court has backed off a bit. In *Patterson* v. *McLean Credit Union,* 1989, it declared that although the 1866 law does prohibit racial discrimination in a contract of employment, any on-the-job discrimination should be handled in accord with the Civil Rights Act of 1964. (See Chapter 21.) Nevertheless, the Court has several times held that the 13th Amendment gives Congress

# Differentiated Resources

The following resources are located in the All-in-One, Unit 5, Chapter 20, Section 2:

**L3** Reading Comprehension Worksheet (p. 137)
**L2** Reading Comprehension Worksheet (p. 139)
**L3** Core Worksheet (p. 141)
**L3** Skills Worksheet (p. 142)
**L2** Skill Activity (p. 143)
**L3** **L4** Extend Worksheet (p. 144)
**L3** Quiz A (p. 146)
**L2** Quiz B (p. 147)

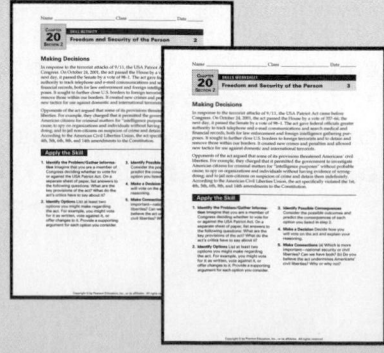

significant power to attack "the badges and incidents of slavery," from whatever source they may come.

## Right to Keep and Bear Arms

The 2nd Amendment was added to the Constitution to protect the concept of the citizen-soldier. It reads:

> ### FROM THE CONSTITUTION
> A well regulated Militia, being necessary to the security of a free State, the right of the people to keep and bear Arms, shall not be infringed.

What, exactly, do these words mean? Do they protect *only* the right of each State to keep a militia, especially against encroachments by the Federal Government? Or, does the 2nd Amendment do that *and also* give to individuals a right to keep and bear arms—just as, say, the 1st Amendment protects free speech?

For decades, the Supreme Court refused to accept the latter interpretation. In its one really important 2nd Amendment ruling, in *United States* v. *Miller,* 1939, the Court rejected the individual right argument. It upheld a section of the National Firearms Act of 1934 that made it a crime to ship sawed-off shotguns or submachine guns across State lines unless the shipper had a federal license to do so. The Court said that it could find no valid link between the shotgun involved in the case and "the preservation . . . of a well-regulated militia."

The High Court has substantially reshaped the 2nd Amendment in its most recent 5–4 decisions. In *District of Columbia* v. *Heller,* 2008, it struck down the District's very strict gun control ordinance—finding that there is, in fact, a 2nd Amendment guarantee of the right of individuals to keep and bear arms for self-defense. And in *McDonald* v. *Chicago,* 2010, it went a step further, incorporating the 2nd Amendment into the 14th Amendment's Due Process Clause. Recall, the Court began that lengthy process of incorporation nearly 100 years ago, in 1925.

Still, the Court said in both *Heller* and *McDonald* that those cases do not overrule

"long-standing prohibitions on the possession of firearms by felons or the mentally ill or laws forbidding the carrying of firearms in sensitive places such as schools and government buildings, or laws imposing conditions and qualifications on the commercial sale of arms."

Clearly, both federal and State courts will hear any number of cases challenging the many State and federal laws that limit an individual's right to keep and bear arms.

## Security of Home and Person

The 3rd and 4th amendments say that government cannot violate the home or person of anyone in this country without just cause.

**The 3rd Amendment** This amendment forbids the quartering (housing) of soldiers in private homes in peacetime without the owner's consent and not in wartime except "in a manner to be prescribed by law." The guarantee was added to prevent what had been British practice in colonial days.[4] The 3rd Amendment has had little importance since 1791 and has never been the subject of a Supreme Court case.

**The 4th Amendment** The 4th Amendment also grew out of colonial practice. It was designed to prevent the use of **writs of assistance**—blanket search warrants with which British customs officials had invaded private homes to search for smuggled goods.

Each State constitution contains a similar provision. The guarantee also applies to the States through the 14th Amendment's Due Process Clause, *Mapp* v. *Ohio,* 1961. Unlike the 3rd Amendment,

This statue, called *The Minuteman,* honors the colonial militia. **Why was the 2nd Amendment added to the Constitution?**

**encroachment**
*n.* intrusion, invasion

---

4  Recall that among the king's many "repeated injuries and usurpations [seizures]" set out in the Declaration of Independence was that of "quartering large bodies of troops among us." See page 45.

---

**COVER SEARCH-AND-SEIZURE BASICS**

Point out that 4th Amendment search-and-seizure restrictions apply to law enforcement officials. Ask:

• **How do warrants protect the rights of citizens against unreasonable search and seizure?** *(They reduce the chance that law enforcement will act arbitrarily or make a mistake in the person, place, or thing to be searched or seized.)*

• **Why do you think the Supreme Court uses the principle of probable cause to analyze search-and-seizure cases?** *(Probable cause provides standards for police conduct and admissible evidence, which support fair courts, trials, and procedures.)*

• **How does the requirement to show probable cause limit police in search-and-seizure actions?** *(Probable cause states that a warrant can be obtained only when there are reasonable grounds to believe that a crime has been or is about to be committed, and the person, place, or thing to be searched or seized is related to that crime.)*

Explain that courts usually decide if a search was "reasonable" by looking at the evidence that was available to police at the time of the incident and by asking these questions:

1. Did the police have enough evidence to justify stopping the suspect?

2. Was the scope of the police search reasonably related to the suspected crime? For example, police looking for a stolen car would not need to look inside the suspect's home or conduct a "pat-down" or body search.

**L2** **Differentiate** Ask students to consider types of behavior that would lead police to have a reasonable suspicion that a crime has occurred or is about to occur. Refer students to the "From the Constitution—4th Amendment" feature in this section of the text. After students read the feature, have them complete this prompt: "I was surprised to learn that . . . "

# Background

**WRITS OF ASSISTANCE** By the early 1700s, the New England colonies had a thriving rum trade. To make the rum, they imported molasses from the British, French, and Spanish islands in the West Indies. To raise money and force the colonies to buy only from British growers, Parliament passed the Molasses Act in 1733, placing a heavy tax on foreign molasses. The colonists avoided the tax by smuggling the less-costly French and Spanish molasses. At first, the British made little effort to enforce the act. In 1764, realizing the extent of lost revenue, Parliament passed the Sugar Act, with strong enforcement measures. Britain issued writs of assistance, allowing customs agents unlimited power to search homes, ships, and warehouses for smuggled goods. The colonists challenged these writs in court in all 13 colonies. This strong opposition led the Framers to ban general warrants in the 4th Amendment.

---

## Answers

**Caption** to protect the right of each State to maintain a militia

## DISTRIBUTE CORE WORKSHEET

Organize students into five groups. Distribute the Chapter 20 Section 2 Core Worksheet (Unit 5 All-in-One, p. 141), which asks students to summarize Supreme Court rulings in search and seizure cases, to evaluate each ruling's impact on 4th Amendment rights, and to decide whether they agree with the decisions.

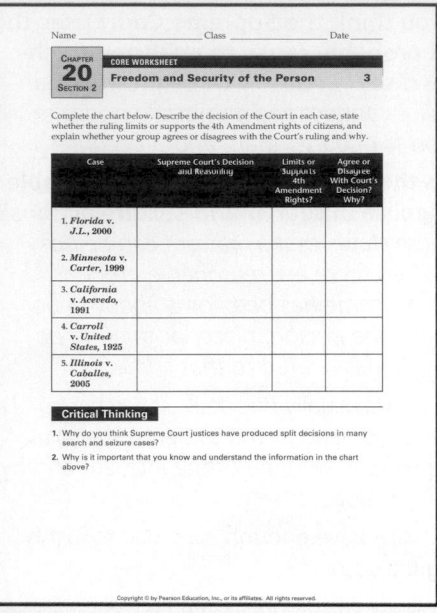

**L2** **LPR Differentiate** Have each group complete one case on the chart and explain it to the class.

## DEFINE EXCLUSIONARY RULE

Ask students to define the exclusionary rule. *(Evidence gained by police as the result of an unreasonable or illegal act cannot be used at the trial of the person from whom it was seized.)* Ask: **Is the exclusionary rule found in the Constitution?** *(It is not. The Supreme Court developed this rule through its decisions over the years in a wide variety of cases.)* **What is the purpose of the exclusionary rule?** *(to prevent law enforcement officers from obtaining evidence illegally)*

**L2** **ELL Differentiate** Ask students for synonyms of *exclude*. *(keep out, reject, prevent)* Then ask students why this rule is called the exclusionary rule. *(It rejects unlawfully obtained or tainted evidence.)* Ask: **What does the word *tainted* mean?** *(damaged or rotten)* **What does "tainted evidence" refer to?** *(evidence that has been illegally gathered without a warrant or probable cause)*

## Answers

**Constitutional Principles** Americans have the constitutional right against unreasonable searches and seizures and probable cause is an indispensable extension of that guarantee.

---

## 4th Amendment

"The right of the people to be secure in their persons, houses, papers, and effects, against unreasonable searches and seizures, shall not be violated, and no Warrants shall issue, but upon probable cause, supported by Oath or affirmation, and particularly describing the place to be searched, and the persons or things to be seized.

# FROM THE CONSTITUTION

**Probable Cause** The 4th Amendment holds that police must show probable cause to obtain a search warrant. However, officers may stop and frisk a person without a warrant if they have a reasonable suspicion that a crime is about to be committed. What constitutes *probable cause* and *reasonable suspicion?* Chief Justice William Rehnquist answered that question this way: "They are commonsense, nontechnical conceptions that deal with the factual and practical considerations of everyday life on which reasonable and prudent men, not legal technicians, act." Actions that the Court has accepted as justifying a stop and frisk include fleeing from the police, "casing" a store, and an officer's belief that a person is armed and dangerous.

**Constitutional Principles** Is probable cause an indispensable part of the guarantee against unreasonable searches and seizures?

▲ The Supreme Court has ruled that "a police officer's decision [to stop and frisk] must be based on more than a hunch or speculation," *Arizona* v. *Gant*, 1994.

the 4th Amendment has proved a highly important guarantee. See the text of the 4th Amendment above.

**Probable Cause** The basic rule laid down by the 4th Amendment is this: Police officers have no general right to search for evidence or to seize either evidence or persons. Except in special circumstances, they must have a proper warrant (a court order). That warrant must be obtained with **probable cause**—that is, a reasonable suspicion of crime.

*Florida* v. *J.L.,* 2000, illustrates the rule. There, Miami police received a tip that a teenager was carrying a concealed weapon. Two officers went to the bus stop where the tipster said the young man could be found. The police located him, searched him, pulled a gun from his pocket, and arrested him.

The Court held that the police acted illegally because they did not have a proper warrant. All they had was an anonymous tip,

unsupported by any other evidence. Their conduct amounted to just the sort of thing the 4th Amendment was intended to prevent.

Police do not always need a warrant, however—for example, when evidence is "in plain view." Thus, the Court upheld a search and seizure involving two men who were bagging cocaine. A policeman spotted them through an open window, entered the apartment, seized the cocaine, and arrested them. The Court upheld their conviction, rejecting a claim to 4th Amendment protection, *Minnesota* v. *Carter,* 1999.

Many 4th Amendment cases are complicated. In *Lidster* v. *Illinois,* 2004, for example, the Court upheld the use of so-called "informational roadblocks." In 1997, police had set up barriers on a busy highway near Chicago, hoping to find witnesses to a recent hit-and-run accident. When Robert Lidster was stopped, an officer smelled alcohol on him. Lidster failed several sobriety tests and

# Supreme Court Notes

***NIX V. WILLIAMS*** A young girl disappeared from a YMCA. After finding items of her clothing several miles away, police organized 200 volunteers to search the area. Meanwhile, Robert Williams surrendered to local police. In conversing with the officer on the drive back to the city, without an attorney present, Williams gave information leading officers to the girl's body. Williams was convicted. On appeal, Williams' lawyer argued to exclude the body as evidence because Williams' statement was illegally obtained. The Supreme Court ruled the evidence was admissible, because the volunteers would have found the body without the statement. "If the prosecution can establish . . . that the information ultimately or inevitably would have been discovered by lawful means—here, the volunteers' search—then . . . the evidence should be received." This ruling established the inevitable discovery exception.

was arrested on a drunk-driving charge. Lidster's attorney filed a motion to quash (set aside) that arrest. The lawyer argued that Lidster was forced to stop by officers who, before they stopped him, had no valid reason (no probable cause) to believe that he had committed any crime.

Lidster lost that argument. The Court upheld both his conviction and the use of informational roadblocks. Lidster had simply run afoul of the long arm of coincidence.

**Arrests** An arrest is the seizure of a person. When officers make a lawful arrest, they do not need a warrant to search "the area from within which [the suspect] might gain possession of a weapon or destructible evidence."[5] In fact, most arrests take place without a warrant. Police can arrest a person in a public place without one, provided they have probable cause to believe that person has committed or is about to commit a crime.[6]

*Illinois* v. *Wardlow*, 2000, illustrates this point. There, four police cars were patrolling a high-crime area in Chicago. When Wardlow spotted them, he ran. An officer chased him down an alley, caught him, and found that Wardlow was carrying a loaded pistol. The Court held, 5–4, that Wardlow's behavior—his flight—gave the police "common sense" grounds on which to believe that he was involved in some criminal activity. (Note, however, that the Court did not hold that police have a blanket power to stop anyone who flees at the sight of a police officer.)

When, exactly, does the 4th Amendment protection come into play? The Court has several times held that this point is reached "only when the officer, by means of physical force or show of authority, has in some way restrained the liberty of a citizen," *Terry* v. *Ohio*, 1968.

**Automobiles** The Court has long had difficulty applying the 4th Amendment to automobiles. It has several times held that an officer needs no warrant to search an automobile, a boat, an airplane, or some other vehicle, when there is probable cause to believe that it is involved in illegal activities—because such a "movable scene of crime" could disappear while a warrant was being sought.

*Carroll* v. *United States*, 1925, is an early leading case on the point. There, the Court emphasized that "where the securing of a warrant is reasonably practicable, it must be used, . . . In cases where seizure is impossible except without a warrant, the seizing officer acts unlawfully and at his peril unless he can show the court probable cause."

The Court overturned a long string of automobile search cases in 1991. Before then, it had several times held that a warrant was usually needed to search a glove compartment, a paper bag, luggage, or other "closed containers" in an automobile. But, in *California* v. *Acevedo*, 1991, the Court set out what it called "one clear-cut rule to govern automobile searches." Whenever police lawfully stop a car, they do not need a warrant to search anything in that vehicle that they have reason to believe holds evidence of a crime. "Anything" includes a passenger's belongings, *Wyoming* v. *Houghton*, 1999.

Police, upon making a routine traffic stop, do not need to secure a warrant in order to use a trained dog to sniff around (search) the outside of a car for narcotics, *Illinois* v. *Caballes*, 2005. When officers make a traffic stop, the Constitution protects passengers as well as drivers against an illegal search or seizure, *Brendlin* v. *California*, 2007. And when police stop a car and arrest the driver, they may search inside the car only if they have reason to believe that the car contains evidence of the crime for which that arrest was made, *Arizona* v. *Gant*, 2009.

## The Exclusionary Rule

The heart of the guarantee against unreasonable searches and seizures lies in this question: If an unlawful search or seizure does occur, can that "tainted evidence" be used in court? If it can be used, the 4th Amendment offers no real protection to a person accused of crime.

> ✔ **Checkpoint**
> What rule regarding automobile searches was established in *California* v. *Acevedo*?

> **tainted**
> *adj.* spoiled, tarnished, flawed

---

**IDENTIFY EXCLUSIONARY RULE LIMITS**

Read aloud the following situations regarding the exclusionary rule. Have students raise their hands if they think the statements are true. You may want to have students skim the text and identify the specific cases as you read the statements.

• Police may introduce evidence gathered by illegal means, if they can prove that they eventually would have found this evidence legally. *(True—*Nix *v.* Williams*)*

• Evidence can be admissible if it was obtained by police officers who thought they had a valid search warrant but which was later found to be faulty. *(True—*United States *v.* Leon*)*

• A warrantless search for a specific item turns up other, different illegal materials, which can be used at a trial. *(False—*Mapp *v.* Ohio*)*

• Tainted evidence found through an honest mistake is admissible in court. *(True—*Maryland *v.* Garrison*)*

• Evidence obtained by police who did not knock before forcing their way into a residence can still be used in a trial. *(True—*Hudson *v.* Michigan*)* See the political cartoon mini-lesson.

**L2 LPR Differentiate** Display Transparency 20C, Exceptions to the Exclusionary Rule, and discuss each limit on the exclusionary rule as the statements above are read. Less-proficient readers may be prompted to contribute by guiding them to complete a diagram or flowchart for each case.

---

# Political Cartoon Mini-Lesson

Display Transparency 20D, 4th Amendment Rights, about the knock-and-announce rule. Ask: **Who are the two men, and what are they preparing to do?** *(police officers; break down the door of someone's home)* **Which case is depicted in this cartoon?** *(Hudson v. Michigan, 2006)* **How did the Court rule on the case?** *(Evidence seized without giving prior notice is still admissible in a trial.)* **What was the Court's reasoning behind its decision?** *(The knock-announce-wait rule is not intended to give people time to hide evidence.)* **The cartoonist does not show a search warrant. Does that affect the way you interpret the Court's ruling? Explain.** *(Leaving out the search warrant makes the actions of the police officers illegal and might make the viewer more likely to disagree with the Court's decision. The police in this case did have a search warrant, however.)*

---

## Answers

**Checkpoint** Whenever police lawfully stop a car, they do not need a warrant to search anything in that vehicle that they have reason to believe holds evidence of a crime.

**L3** **L4** **Differentiate** Distribute the Chapter 20 Extend Worksheet (Unit 5 All-in-One, p. 144), which describes a search and seizure case that took place in a public high school in 1985. Begin by asking students to identify the constitutional issue in the case. After studying the case, students can discuss how they think the Court should rule and then prepare their own summary with the reasons for their opinion. Use Think-Write-Pair-Share (p. T22) to give students a chance to verbalize their thoughts before they write their summaries.

After students have completed their worksheets and shared their summaries with the class, tell them that in *T.L.O.* v. *New Jersey,* the Supreme Court ruled that the vice principal's decision to search the students' belongings was "reasonable." He did not need to show probable cause or get a warrant. Students' privacy and 4th Amendment rights must be weighed against the school's interest in preventing the use of illegal drugs. The Supreme Court stated that the New Jersey supreme court had been wrong to suppress the evidence found by the vice principal. Administrators and teachers have the authority, in order to maintain discipline and order, to take immediate action in certain situations.

**L4** **Differentiate** Have students research two cases related to school drug-testing programs: *Vernonia School District* v. *Acton* and *Board of Education of Independent School District No. 92 of Pottawatomie County* v. *Earls.* After completing their research, have students give a short speech that:

• identifies the issues each case raises about students' 4th Amendment rights;

• compares and contrasts the facts and the rulings in the two cases;

• explains whether the student agrees or disagrees with the Supreme Court's decision in each case.

**L2** **Differentiate** Have students conduct a citizens' rights poll. Questions may include: (1) What does the 4th Amendment guarantee? (2) May an officer arrest a suspect without a warrant? (3) May an officer search a driver and passenger if their vehicle is pulled over? Have students summarize the findings of the poll on a poster.

To meet that problem, the Supreme Court has adopted, and is still refining, the **exclusionary rule.** Essentially, the rule is this: Evidence gained as the result of an illegal act by police cannot be used at the trial of the person from whom it was seized.

The rule was first laid down in *Weeks* v. *United States,* 1914. In that narcotics case, the Court held that evidence obtained illegally by federal officers could not be used in the federal courts. For decades, however, the Court left questions of the use of such evidence in State courts for each State to decide for itself.

**SUPREME COURT**
at a glance

▶ **Case:** *Mapp* v. *Ohio,* 1961
▶ **Issue:** States' use of illegally obtained evidence
▶ **Decision:** After a warrantless search of Dollree Mapp's house, police officers turned up "lewd and lascivious material" and used it as evidence to convict Mapp. The Supreme Court struck down Mapp's conviction, holding that evidence seized illegally could not be used in either federal or State courts.

*Mapp* **v.** *Ohio* The exclusionary rule was finally extended to the States in *Mapp* v. *Ohio,* 1961. There, the Court held that the 14th Amendment forbids unreasonable searches and seizures by State and local officers just as the 4th Amendment bars such actions by federal officers. It also held that the fruits of an unlawful search or seizure cannot be used in the State courts, just as they cannot be used in the federal courts.

In *Mapp,* Cleveland police had entered Dollree Mapp's home, forcibly and without a warrant. They claimed to be searching for both a fugitive in a bombing case and evidence of gambling. Their lengthy search found nothing on either count. But they did turn up some "dirty books." Mapp was then convicted of the possession of obscene materials and sentenced to jail. The Court overturned that conviction, holding that the evidence against her had been found illegally and so could not be used at her trial.

**Cases Narrowing the Rule** The exclusionary rule has always been controversial. It was intended to put teeth into the 4th Amendment, and it has. It says to police: As you enforce the law, obey the law. The rule seeks to prevent, or at least deter, police misconduct.

Critics of the rule say that it means that some persons who are clearly guilty nonetheless go free. Why, they ask, should criminals be able to "beat the rap" on "a technicality"?

The Court has narrowed the scope of the rule most notably in the four cases in the feature on the next page.

**Drug Testing Programs** Federal drug-testing programs involve searches of persons, so are covered by the 4th Amendment. To date, however, the Court has held that those programs can be conducted without warrants or even any indication of drug use by those who must take the tests. It did so in two 1989 cases. One involved the mandatory testing of those drug enforcement officers of the U.S. Customs Service (now Immigration and Customs Enforcement) who carry firearms, *National Treasury Employees Union* v. *Von Raab.* The other had to do with the testing of railroad workers after a train accident, *Skinner* v. *Railway Labor Executives' Association.* In effect, the Court said in both cases that the violations of privacy involved were outweighed by a legitimate governmental interest—for example, in *Skinner,* discovering the cause of a train accident.

The Court has also upheld two local school districts' drug-testing programs, both covered by the 14th Amendment's Due Process Clause. It sustained an Oregon school district's program that requires all students who take part in school sports to agree to be tested for drug use, *Vernonia School District* v. *Acton,* 1995. That ruling was extended in a case from Oklahoma, *Board of Education of Independent School District No. 92 of Pottawatomie County* v. *Earls,* 2002. There, the Court upheld the random testing of students who want to participate in *any* competitive extracurricular activity. In both of these cases, the Court said that "a warrant and finding of probable cause are unnecessary in the public school context because [they] would unduly interfere with . . . swift and informal disciplinary procedures."

**The Patriot Act** The USA Patriot Act, commonly called the Patriot Act, is officially the Uniting and Strengthening America by Providing Appropriate Tools Required to Intercept and Obstruct Terrorism Act of 2001. It was passed by Congress and signed by President George W. Bush just six weeks after the terrorist attacks of 9/11. That 342-page statute

# Debate

Since *Pottawatomie,* drug testing of students participating in extracurricular activities has expanded, leading to court challenges. A Pennsylvania school tested Kimberly and Jennifer Theodore. School officials did not suspect the girls of drug use or have any evidence of use. The girls were student leaders, and the school tested them to set an example. Their parents felt the test was an invasion of privacy, and sued. In *Theodore* v. *Delaware Valley School District,* 2003, the Pennsylvania supreme court ruled for the parents. In the opinion, Justice Ronald D. Castille wrote: "The [school's] theory apparently is that, even in the absence of any suspicion of drug or alcohol abuse, it is appropriate to single these students out and say, in effect: 'Choose one: your Pennsylvania constitutional right to privacy or the chess club.'" To begin a class debate, ask: **Should schools be allowed to conduct "suspicionless" drug tests?**

## Exceptions to the Exclusionary Rule

In recent decades, the Supreme Court has narrowed the scope of the exclusionary rule by allowing evidence to be admissible in situations that it previously had not. *What is the purpose of that rule?*

◄ Evidence bag

**GOVERNMENT** ONLINE

INTERACTIVE

For an **interactive** exploration of these cases, visit
PearsonSchool.com/phgovt

### Inevitable Discovery

Tainted evidence can be used in court if it "inevitably would have been discovered by lawful means." In *Nix* v. *Williams*, 1984, the defendant claimed the evidence against him had been found only after his confession was illegally obtained. **The Court ruled that the evidence ultimately would have been found without the defendant's statement.**

### Knock-and-Announce Violation

The centuries-old "knock-and-announce" rule requires that police announce their presence before serving a warrant. The rule is intended to give residents a chance to open the door, not hide evidence. **The Court found that the rule is meant to protect persons and property from violence when police arrive,** *Hudson* v. *Michigan*, 2006.

### Good Faith

In *United States* v. *Leon*, 1984, agents thought they were using a proper warrant. Their warrant was later shown to be faulty, but the Court upheld their actions nonetheless: **"When an officer acting with objective good faith has obtained a search warrant . . . and acted within its scope . . . there is nothing to deter."**

### Honest Mistakes

**The Court allowed the use of evidence seized in the mistaken search of an apartment,** *Maryland* v. *Garrison*, 1987. Officers had a warrant to search for drugs in an apartment on the third floor of a building. Not realizing that there were two apartments, they entered and found drugs in the wrong apartment—the one for which they did not have a warrant.

## Evidence is admissible

---

was renewed, after some contentious debate and with some modifications, in 2006.

The law provides for greatly increased governmental powers to combat domestic and international terrorist activities. Its major provisions focus on three broad areas: surveillance and investigation, immigration, and the financing of terrorist groups. Several provisions raise significant civil liberties issues that, over time, will be tested in the courts.

Of particular 4th Amendment concern are the act's provisions that allow the secret "sneak-and-peek searches." Under the statute, federal agents, acting with a warrant, may enter a person's home or office when no one is present and conduct a search—making notes, taking photos, and so on. The agents need not notify the person who is the subject of the search for weeks or even months—and so they are able to continue their investigation without that person's knowledge.

**Wiretapping** Electronic eavesdropping, such as wiretapping, videotaping, and other more sophisticated means of "bugging," is now quite widely used in the United States. These various techniques of discovery present difficult search and seizure questions that the authors of the 4th Amendment could not possibly have foreseen.

## Background

**4TH AMENDMENT PROTECTIONS** The Court has decided only a handful of eavesdropping cases since *Katz*. In 1999 it held that "a reasonable expectation of privacy" had been violated when police officers invited reporters and photographers to go with them into a man's home to witness their search and his arrest, *Wilson* v. *Layne*. And it has ruled that federal agents must secure a warrant before they can use heat-sensing devices to look inside a person's home to find evidence of drug law violations, *Kyllo* v. *United States*, 2001.

---

Tell students to go to the Interactivity to learn more about the Exclusionary Rule.

## Assess and Remediate

**L3** Tell students that a foreign exchange student needs to know her 4th Amendment rights against unreasonable searches and seizures. Have students develop a brochure or draw an illustrated guide showing law enforcement actions that are limited by the 4th Amendment and the exclusionary rule. Law enforcement actions that are upheld by Court rulings should also be included.

**L3** Collect the Core Worksheets and assess student work using the Rubric for Assessing a Graph, Chart, or Table (Unit 5 All-in-One, p. 240).

**L3** Assign the Section 2 Assessment questions.

**L3** Section Quiz A (Unit 5 All-in-One, p. 146)

**L2** Section Quiz B (Unit 5 All-in-One, p. 147)

Have students complete the review activities in the digital lesson presentation and continue their work in the **Essential Questions Journal.**

## Answers

**Exceptions to the Exclusionary Rule** The exclusionary rule was intended to make 4th Amendment protections meaningful by preventing the use of illegally obtained evidence in court.

| If Your Students Have Trouble With | Strategies For Remediation |
|---|---|
| 13th Amendment protections (Question 2) | Have students make a timeline showing the changes in application of the 13th Amendment as discussed in this section. |
| 2nd Amendment protections (Question 3) | Ask students to write two editorials on gun control, one from the point of view of gun-control advocates (such as the Fraternal Order of Police) and one from the point of view of gun-control opponents (such as the National Rifle Association). |
| 4th Amendment protections (Questions 1, 4, 5, 6) | Have students draw a two-column chart. In the first column, they should list at least ten Court cases discussed in the text regarding the 4th Amendment. In the second column, next to each case, students should write the constitutional guarantees that resulted from or were narrowed by the case in column one. |

## Answers

**Checkpoint** In *Olmstead,* the Court ruled that wiretapping did not involve a search and, therefore, needed no warrant. *Katz* overruled *Olmstead,* stating that wiretapping a phone booth violated a person's 4th Amendment right to privacy.

✔ **Checkpoint**
How did the Court's ruling in *Katz* v. *United States* differ from its ruling in *Olmstead* v. *United States*?

The 4th Amendment has always applied to "searches" that involve a physical intrusion—for example, a police officer entering a building or reaching inside a car. The amendment has also always applied to "seizures" that produce some tangible object—for example, a gun or a packet of methamphetamines found inside a car. Listening in on a conversation electronically, from afar, is a quite different matter.

In fact, in its first eavesdropping case, *Olmstead* v. *United States,* 1928, the Court held that the wiretapping there did not constitute a "search." The case arose when federal agents tapped a Seattle bootlegger's telephone calls. Their bugs produced evidence that led to Olmstead's conviction under the National Prohibition Act. The Court upheld that conviction. It found that, although the agents had not secured a warrant, there had been no "actual physical invasion" of Olmstead's home or office, and so no violation of the 4th Amendment because the phone lines had been tapped *outside* those places.

*Olmstead* stood for nearly forty years. It was finally overruled in what remains the leading case today, *Katz* v. *United States,* 1967. Katz had been convicted of transmitting gambling information across State lines. He had used a public phone booth in Los Angeles to call his contacts in Boston and Miami. Much of the evidence against him had come from an electronic tap placed on the roof—outside—of the phone booth.

The Court ruled that the bugging evidence could not be used against Katz. Despite the fact that he was in a public, glass-enclosed phone booth, he was entitled to make a *private* call, from a place where he had "a reasonable expectation of privacy." Said the Court: The 4th Amendment protects "persons, not just places." It noted, however, that the requirements of the amendment can be satisfied in such situations if police obtain a proper warrant before they install a listening device.

Congress responded to the Court's decision in *Katz* in a provision in the Omnibus Crime Control and Safe Street Act of 1968. There, Congress prohibited any wiretapping for domestic purposes except that authorized by a warrant issued by a federal judge.

Soon after September 11, President George W. Bush directed the National Security Agency (NSA), acting in secret and without court-approved warrants, to monitor the international telephone calls and e-mails of Americans with suspected ties to terrorists. The public did not become aware of that monitoring program until late 2005, and its disclosure brought a storm of protest. Many insist that this NSA activity is illegal. However, the Bush administration defended it as an appropriate exercise of the President's power as commander in chief.

**Essential Questions Journal** To continue to build a response to the chapter Essential Question, go to your **Essential Questions Journal.**

## SECTION 2 ASSESSMENT

1. **Guiding Question** Use your completed graphic organizer to answer this question: How does the Constitution protect the freedom and security of the person?

**Key Terms and Comprehension**

2. **(a)** What does the 13th Amendment guarantee? **(b)** How did the *Civil Rights Cases,* 1883, undermine those guarantees?

3. **(a)** How does the 4th Amendment limit government? **(b)** When does the 4th Amendment come into play during an arrest?

**Critical Thinking**

4. **Express Problems Clearly (a)** What does the exclusionary rule exclude? **(b)** Does the exclusionary rule serve the interests of justice? Answer this question first as the defendant in a criminal trial, and then as an arresting police officer.

5. **Identify Central Issues (a)** Why did the Court overturn the conviction in *Katz* v. *United States?* **(b)** Do you agree with the Court's decision? Why or why not?

**Quick Write**

**Research Essay: Organize Your Notes** Research to find additional information on the case you selected in Section 1, taking notes as you read. Then organize your notes under main headings. Scan the material for subtopics. Subtopics may include *What is this case about? How did it change an existing law? Why it is important to individual rights today?* Under your subtopics, write related details.

## Assessment Answers

**1.** through the 2nd, 3rd, 4th, 13th, and 14th amendments

**2. (a)** the end to slavery and involuntary servitude **(b)** by allowing racial discrimination against African Americans by private individuals

**3. (a)** by requiring officers to show probable cause to obtain a warrant to search for or seize evidence or a suspect **(b)** when an officer has in some way restrained the liberty of a citizen

**4. (a)** evidence gained as a result of an illegal act by police **(b)** Possible answers: Defendant's view: Yes. The rule protects the accused and prevents police misconduct. Police view: No. The rule unreasonably restricts the ability of police officers to gather evidence to convict a guilty person.

**5. (a)** The police illegally tapped a phone booth in which Katz had a "reasonable expectation of privacy." **(b)** Possible answer: Yes. Tapping phones is an invasion of privacy that should be illegal unless supported by a warrant.

**QUICK WRITE** Students should organize ideas from their notes by the main headings and subtopics they identify.

# ISSUES OF OUR TIME

## Balancing Security and Liberty

### ▶ Track the Issue

As contact among nations expanded in the 20th century, so too did government surveillance.

**1908**
**The Bureau of Investigation** (BOI) is formed and becomes the Federal Bureau of Investigation (FBI) in 1935.

**1947**
**The National Security Act** establishes the Central Intelligence Agency (CIA) to coordinate intelligence affecting national security.

**1978**
**The Foreign Intelligence Surveillance Act (FISA)** is passed. Any monitoring of suspected terrorists in the U.S. must be based on warrants issued by the FISA Court.

**2001**
**The Patriot Act** is passed, allowing the National Security Agency (NSA) to monitor Americans secretly and without court-approved warrants.

**Today**
**The Federal Government** is making efforts to protect the nation's security without undo infringement on citizens' freedoms.

Secretary of Homeland Security Janet Napolitano ▶

### ▶ Perspectives

**Soon after September 11,** President G.W. Bush directed the National Security Agency to begin the secret, warrantless monitoring of all international telephone and e-mail communications by persons within the United States. At the time, many believed that practice to be in the nation's best interest, but it was also highly criticized as a violation of fundamental rights. Balancing national security and American freedoms remains a challenging task today.

"While effective and efficient information sharing among law enforcement agencies is an important goal, we must remember that U.S. intelligence activities have too often targeted political dissent as a threat to security, which has led to misguided investigations that violated rights [and] chilled free expression . . . . Establishing new information collection and sharing authorities for the federal, state and local law enforcement poses significant risks to our individual liberties, our democratic principles and, ironically, even our security."

—*Caroline Fredrickson, Director, ACLU, 2009*

"We frequently hear about a simple inverse relationship between security and liberty. . . . If one is embraced, the other must be sacrificed. . . . The description doesn't do justice to the relationship between security and other values. . . . Security is interrelated with our core values, and among the aspects of the homeland that must be made secure are our fundamental rights and freedoms. . . . The threats we face are very unpredictable, but we can predict. . . . that securing ourselves against them will often present us with challenges and difficult decisions."

—*Secretary of Homeland Security Janet Napolitano, 2010*

### ▶ Connect to Your World

1. **Understand (a)** According to Ms. Fredrickson, what civil rights are violated by information sharing? **(b)** To what do you think Secretary Napolitano is referring in her reference to "difficult decisions"?
2. **Synthesize Information (a)** When do you think it might be necessary for national security to override personal liberties? **(b)** How difficult do you think it would be to regain any rights that may have been suspended at the time?

**GOVERNMENT ONLINE**
**In the News**
To find out more about balancing security and liberty, visit
**PearsonSchool.com/phgovt**

591

## Background

**ATTACKING TERRORIST COMMUNICATIONS** A fundamental goal of U.S. intelligence agencies is to infiltrate communications networks of terrorists. According to the *National Strategy for Combating Terrorism:* "The methods by which terrorists communicate are numerous and varied. Our enemies rely on couriers and face-to-face contacts with associates and tend to use what is accessible in their local areas as well as what they can afford. They also use today's technologies with increasing acumen and sophistication. This is especially true with the Internet, which they exploit to create and disseminate propaganda, recruit new members, raise funds and other material resources, provide instruction on weapons and tactics, and plan operations. Without a communications ability, terrorist groups cannot effectively organize operations, execute attacks, or spread their ideology."

## LESSON GOAL

- Students will analyze points of view on the issue of protecting national security while guarding individual liberties.

## Teach

### STUDY THE TIMELINE

Draw a horizontal line on the board. As volunteers read aloud the entries under "Track the Issue," write the years and general events in the appropriate place on the timeline. Then, between the 1947 and 1978 entries, write "1967 The Supreme Court rules that bugging is illegal without a search warrant, *Katz* v. *United States.*" Ask: **How does knowledge of this event affect your perception of the 2001 and 2008 events?**

### ANALYZE HISTORICAL PERSPECTIVE

Write these quotes by James Madison on the board:

- **It is a universal truth that the loss of liberty at home is to be charged to the provisions against danger, real or pretended, from abroad.**

- **The means of defense against foreign danger historically have become the instruments of tyranny at home.**

Discuss how Madison's statements support the comment by Caroline Fredrickson in the feature. Ask whether Madison's statements are applicable to today's war on terrorism. Why or why not?

**L2** **ELL Differentiate** Define *dissent* (to disagree with a widely held opinion), *misguided* (mistaken, inappropriate), *inverse* (involving two variables in a relationship that when one increases, the other decreases), and *sacrifice* (giving up something valuable or important).

## Assess and Remediate

Refer students to the Document-Based Assessment at the end of this chapter. Discuss reasons why the Patriot Act is so controversial. Then have students draw a political cartoon reflecting their own opinions about the Patriot Act.

## Answers

1. **(a)** free speech, security of person and property **(b)** decisions that may require the limitation of civil liberties and civil rights to ensure national security
2. Students should support their responses.

## What protections does the Constitution set out for persons accused of crimes?

| Rights of the Accused | |
|---|---|
| 5th Amendment | 6th Amendment |
| • grand jury in federal criminal cases<br>• no double jeopardy<br>• no self-incrimination | • speedy and public trial<br>• impartial jury<br>• adequate defense<br>• informed of nature and cause of accusation<br>• confront witnesses<br>• subpoena favorable witnesses<br>• assistance of counsel |

# Get Started

## LESSON GOALS

Students will . . .

- identify the rights of people accused of crimes by note-taking, completing a tree diagram, and discussing a case related to habeas corpus.
- evaluate the guarantee against self-incrimination by participating in simulations and analyzing a case related to the Miranda rule.

## BEFORE CLASS

Assign the section, the graphic organizer in the text, and the Reading Comprehension Worksheet (Unit 5 All-in-One, p. 148) before class.

**L2 Differentiate** Reading Comprehension Worksheet (Unit 5 All-in-One, p. 149)

## SKILLS DEVELOPMENT

### GIVE A MULTIMEDIA PRESENTATION

Before the debate in this lesson, you may want to review tips on giving a multimedia presentation in the Skills Handbook, p. S21.

---

## SECTION 3

# Rights of the Accused

### Guiding Question

**What protections does the Constitution set out for persons accused of crimes?** Use a table to take notes on the section.

| Rights of the Accused | |
|---|---|
| 5th Amendment | 6th Amendment |
| •<br>•<br>• | •<br>•<br>• |

### Political Dictionary

- writ of habeas corpus
- bill of attainder
- ex post facto law
- grand jury
- indictment
- presentment
- information
- double jeopardy
- bench trial
- Miranda rule

### Objectives

1. Define writ of habeas corpus, bills of attainder, and ex post facto laws.
2. Outline how the right to a grand jury and the guarantee against double jeopardy help safeguard the rights of the accused.
3. Describe issues that arise from guarantees of speedy and public trials.
4. Determine what constitutes a fair trial by jury.
5. Examine the right to an adequate defense and the guarantee against self-incrimination.

**Image Above:** A suspect must be brought before the court and informed of the charges against him.

---

Think about this statement: "It is better that ten guilty persons go free than that one innocent person be punished." That maxim expresses one of the bedrock principles of the American legal system.

Of course, society must punish criminals in order to preserve itself. However, the law intends that any person who is suspected or accused of a crime must be presumed innocent until proven guilty by fair and lawful means.

## Habeas Corpus

The **writ of habeas corpus,** sometimes called the writ of liberty, is intended to prevent unjust arrests and imprisonments.[7] It is a court order directed to an officer holding a prisoner. It commands that the prisoner be brought before the court and that the officer show cause—explain, with good reason—why the prisoner should not be released.

The right to seek a writ of habeas corpus is protected against the National Government in Article I, Section 9 of the Constitution. That right is guaranteed against the States in each of their own constitutions.

The Constitution says that the right to the writ cannot be suspended, "unless when in Cases of Rebellion or Invasion the public Safety may require it." President Abraham Lincoln suspended the writ in 1861 during the Civil War. His order covered various parts of the country, including several areas in which war was not then being waged. Chief Justice Roger B. Taney, sitting as a circuit judge, held Lincoln's action unconstitutional, *Ex parte Merryman,* 1861.

Taney ruled that the Constitution gives the power to suspend the writ to Congress alone. Congress then passed the Habeas Corpus Act of 1863. It gave the President the power to suspend the writ when and where, in his judgment, that action was necessary. In *Ex parte Milligan,* 1866, the Supreme Court ruled that neither Congress nor the President can suspend the writ in those locales where there is no actual fighting nor the likelihood of combat.

The right to the writ has been suspended only once since the Civil War and the Reconstruction Period that followed it. The territorial governor of Hawaii

---

7 The phrase *habeas corpus* comes from the Latin, meaning "you should have the body," and those are the opening words of the writ.

## Focus on the Basics

**FACTS:** • Rights of the accused include the writ of habeas corpus and a constitutional ban on bills of attainder and ex post facto laws. • Persons accused of serious federal crimes have the right to a grand jury proceeding. • Accused persons are guaranteed a speedy and public trial by jury, the right to an adequate defense, and a guarantee against self-incrimination and double jeopardy. • Suspects must be told of their constitutional rights before police questioning.

**CONCEPTS:** individual rights and responsibilities, due process of law, limited government

**ENDURING UNDERSTANDINGS:** • In the American judicial system, any person accused of a crime is presumed innocent until proven guilty. • The 5th and 6th amendments contain provisions guaranteeing rights to people accused of crimes.

did so following the Japanese attack on Pearl Harbor in December 1941. The Supreme Court later ruled that the governor did not have the power to take that action, *Duncan* v. *Kahanamoku*, 1946.

In 2008, the Supreme Court held, for the first time, that foreign prisoners being held as enemy combatants at the U.S. naval base at Guantanamo Bay, Cuba, have a constitutional right to challenge their detention—that is, a right to seek writs of habeas corpus—in the federal courts, *Boumediene* v. *Bush* and *Al Odah* v. *United States*. The Bush administration had vigorously opposed that 5–4 ruling, but the Obama administration generally supports it. See page 539.

## Bills of Attainder

A **bill of attainder** is a legislative act that provides for the punishment of a person without a court trial. The Constitution prohibits Congress from passing any such measure in Article I, Section 9, and it places the same prohibition on the States in Section 10.

The Framers wrote the ban on bills of attainder into the Constitution because Parliament and several of the colonial legislatures had passed many such bills. They have been quite rare in our national history, however.

The denial of the power to pass bills of attainder is both a protection of individual freedom and one of the Constitution's several provisions for separation of powers. In effect, the ban says to members of Congress and to the States' lawmakers: Be legislators, not judges. A legislative body can pass laws that define crime and set the penalties for violations of them. But it cannot pass a law that declares a person or identifiable group of persons guilty of a crime and provides for his or their punishment.

*United States* v. *Lovett*, 1946, is one of the few attainder cases ever decided by the Supreme Court. That case involved a provision in a law appropriating funds for the army that declared that none of the monies could be used to pay the salaries of three named persons. Several members of the House thought that those three were "subversive," and they urged the President to discharge them. The Court found that provision to be a bill of attainder.

In another similar case, *United States* v. *Brown*, 1965, the Court overturned a provision in the Landrum-Griffin Act of 1959. That provision made it a federal crime for a member of the Communist Party to serve as an officer of a labor union.

## Ex Post Facto Laws

The Constitution, in Article I, Sections 9 and 10, prohibits Congress and the States from enacting ex post facto laws. An **ex post facto law** is a law applied to an act committed before the passage of that law. The phrase *ex post facto* is from the Latin, meaning "after the fact." An ex post facto law (1) is a criminal law—one defining a crime and/or providing for its punishment; (2) applies to an act committed before its passage; and (3) works to the disadvantage of the accused.

For example, a law making it a crime to sell marijuana cannot be applied to a sale that occurred before that law was passed. Or, a law that changes the penalty for murder from life in prison to death cannot be used to sentence a person who committed a murder before the punishment was made more severe.

Retroactive civil laws are *not* forbidden. Thus, a law raising income tax rates could be passed in November and applied to income earned through the whole year.

After the Japanese bombed Pearl Harbor, the governor of Hawaii suspended the writ of habeas corpus. **Who has the power to suspend the writ?**

593

---

## Differentiated Resources

The following resources are located in the All-in-One, Unit 5, Chapter 20, Section 3:

**L3** Reading Comprehension Worksheet (p. 148)

**L2** Reading Comprehension Worksheet (p. 149)

**L3** **L2** Core Worksheet A (pp. 151, 155)

**L3** **L2** Core Worksheet B (pp. 153, 158)

**L3** Quiz A (p. 161)

**L2** Quiz B (p. 162)

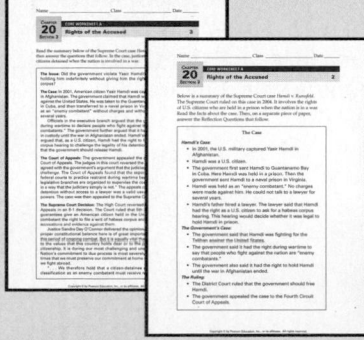

## BELLRINGER

Display Transparency 20E, 5th Amendment Rights, which tests students' prior knowledge about the Miranda rights and "taking the Fifth." Have students answer the questions in their notebooks.

## Teach

To present this topic using online resources, use the lesson presentations at **PearsonSchool.com/phgovt.**

### REVIEW BELLRINGER ANSWERS

Discuss the Bellringer questions. (1) What "rights" is the man in Cartoon A requesting? *(From movies and television, students may know the Miranda rights: right to remain silent; anything you say can and will be used against you in a court of law; right to an attorney; if you cannot afford one, an attorney will be appointed for you.)* (2) In Cartoon B, what does "take the Fifth" mean? *(Students may know that "taking the Fifth" means remaining silent or not answering any questions that may lead to self-incrimination.)* (3) How are these cartoons related? *(Both deal with rights of the accused.)* Ask: **When are the Miranda rights usually read to someone?** *(Students should infer from the cartoon that the rights are read to someone who has "done something wrong"; legally, after arrest and before interrogation.)*

### CLARIFY RIGHTS OF THE ACCUSED

Introduce this activity by asking students: **What is the underlying principle toward the accused in the U.S. justice system?** *(that people are innocent until proven guilty)* **Who has the burden of proving guilt?** *(the prosecution or government)* Then organize students into seven groups. Assign each group one of these topics: (a) habeas corpus; (b) grand jury; (c) double jeopardy; (d) speedy and public trial; (e) trial by jury; (f) right to an adequate defense; (g) guarantee against self-incrimination.

Each group should use the text to record the following: (1) the exact wording of the amendment or part of the Constitution where this right is found; (2) definition of the right in their own words; (3) how this right protects a person accused of a crime; (4) what responsibilities this right puts on the judicial system; (5) Supreme Court precedents related to this right and how the decision in each case limited or expanded this guarantee; and (6) how the criminal justice system would be different if people accused of crimes did not have this right.

**L2** **ELL Differentiate** Before beginning the group work, have volunteers find and read the definitions of these words in the dictionary: *habeas corpus, jeopardy, self-incrimination.*

---

## Answers

**Caption** Congress

## SHARE NOTES USING JIGSAW STRATEGY

After groups have completed the discussion and notes of their assigned topic (see Clarify Rights of the Accused on the previous page), use the Jigsaw strategy (p. T27), which allows students to teach the other groups what they have learned. Conclude by asking students in their second groups to pick the three rights of the accused they think are most important. Ask each group to share its choices and reasons with the class.

## DIAGRAM RIGHTS OF THE ACCUSED

Display Transparency 20F, Rights of the Accused, which shows the How Government Works diagram "Steps of Justice." Then draw a tree diagram on the board to help students categorize and review the rights of the accused. Label the four squares "At Arrest," "Before Trial," "During Trial," and "After Trial." Students should put each of the rights listed on the transparency into the appropriate part of the diagram. Explain that "After Trial" rights will be discussed in Section 4. "No excessive fines or cruel and unusual punishment" and "right to appeal" should be written in that part of the diagram.

| Rights of the Accused | | | |
|---|---|---|---|
| At Arrest | Before Trial | During Trial | After Trial |
| | | | |

## Answers

**Steps of Justice** officers must have warrant or act on probable cause; no unreasonable search or seizure; accused may request writ of habeas corpus; accused must be informed of right to counsel and to remain silent; no third degree methods or coerced confession; accused may be charged by indictment or presentation; no excessive bail; public trial by impartial jury; accused may request change of venue; assistance of counsel guaranteed; no self-incrimination; favorable witnesses may be subpoenaed, opposing witnesses confronted; jury verdict to convict must be unanimous; no double jeopardy

---

### Rights of the Accused
# Steps of Justice

Any person accused of a crime is presumed to be innocent until proven guilty. *What protections does the Constitution extend to those accused of crime?*

### Arrest
- Officers must have a warrant or act on probable cause.
- No unreasonable search or seizure.
- Accused may request writ of habeas corpus to challenge detention.

### Interrogation
- Accused must be informed of the right to counsel and the right to remain silent.
- No third degree methods or coerced confession.

### Grand Jury Proceeding
- Grand jury weighs evidence provided by prosecutor.
- Accused may be charged by indictment or presentment.
- Bail, if required, cannot be excessive.

## Grand Jury

The 5th Amendment to the Constitution declares that

> ### FROM THE CONSTITUTION
> **No person shall be held to answer for a capital, or otherwise infamous crime, unless on a presentment or indictment of a Grand Jury. . . .**

The **grand jury** is the formal device by which a person can be accused of a serious crime—that is, any offense for which the punishment is death or imprisonment.[8] In federal cases, the grand jury is a body of from 16 to 23 persons drawn from the area of the district court that it serves. The votes of at least 12 of the grand jurors are needed to return an indictment or to make a presentment.

An **indictment** is a formal complaint that the prosecutor lays before a grand jury. It charges the accused with one or more crimes. If the grand jury finds that there is enough evidence to justify a trial, it returns a "true bill of indictment." The accused person is then held for prosecution. If the grand jury does not make such a finding, the charge is dropped and the accused is set free.

A **presentment** is a formal accusation brought by the grand jury on its own motion, rather than that of the prosecutor. It is rarely used in federal courts.

A grand jury's proceedings are not a trial. Since unfair harm could come if they were public, its sessions are secret. They are also one-sided—in the law, an *ex parte* judicial proceeding. That is, only the prosecution, not the defense, is present.

---

8 The 5th Amendment declares that the guarantee of grand jury does not extend to "cases arising in the land or naval forces." The conduct of members of the armed forces is regulated under a code of military law enacted by Congress, now the Uniform Code of Military Justice.

---

# Background

**EX POST FACTO LAWS** Ex post facto cases do not come along very often. The Court decided its most recent one, *Carmell* v. *Texas,* in 2000. There, the Court overturned a man's sexual abuse conviction because of a change in State law. That change had made it easier for the prosecution to prove its charge than was the case when the abuse was committed.

GOVERNMENT ONLINE
Audio Tour
To learn more about the rights of the accused, visit
PearsonSchool.com/phgovt

## Trial

- Public trial by an impartial jury within 100 days of arrest.
- Accused may request a change of venue.
- Assistance of counsel guaranteed.
- No self-incrimination.
- Favorable witnesses may be subpoenaed, opposing witnesses confronted.
- Jury's verdict to convict must be unanimous.
- No double jeopardy.

## Punishment
### (if found guilty)

- No excessive fine.
- No cruel and unusual punishment.

## Appeals

- Either side may appeal a verdict against it.

---

The right to grand jury is intended as a protection against overzealous prosecutors. Critics say that it is too time-consuming, too expensive, and too likely to follow the dictates of the prosecutor.

The 5th Amendment's grand jury provision is the only part of the Bill of Rights relating to criminal prosecution that the Supreme Court has not brought within the coverage of the 14th Amendment's Due Process Clause. In the majority of States today, most criminal charges are not brought by grand jury indictment. They are brought, instead, by an **information,** an affidavit in which the prosecutor swears that there is enough evidence to justify a trial. (See Chapter 24.)

## Double Jeopardy

The 5th Amendment's guarantee against double jeopardy is the first of several protections in the Bill of Rights especially intended to

ensure fair trials in the federal courts.[9] Fair trials are guaranteed in State courts by each State's constitution and, also, recall, by the 14th Amendment's Due Process Clause.

The 5th Amendment says in part that no person can be "twice put in jeopardy of life or limb." Today, this prohibition against **double jeopardy** means that once a person has been tried for a crime, he or she cannot be tried again for that same crime. The Constitution's ban of double jeopardy applies against the States through the 14th Amendment's Due Process Clause, *Benton* v. *Maryland,* 1969.

A person can violate both a federal *and* a State law in a single act, however—for example, by selling narcotics. That person can then be tried for the federal crime in a federal court and for the State crime in a State court. Thus, a single act can also result in several criminal charges. A person who breaks into a

---

9 See the 4th, 5th, 6th, 7th, and 8th amendments and Article III, Section 2, Clause 3.

---

Tell students to go to the Audio Tour to learn more about the rights of the accused.

### ANALYZE HABEAS CORPUS ISSUES

Distribute the Chapter 20 Section 3 Core Worksheet A (Unit 5 All-in-One, p. 151). Explain that students will look at the challenges the courts face in balancing due process rights of the accused with national security during wartime. They will analyze the Supreme Court case *Hamdi* v. *Rumsfeld,* 2004. Before students begin the worksheet, review the definition of *habeas corpus* in Article 1 of the Constitution. Remind students that the right to a writ of habeas corpus can be suspended "when in Cases of Rebellion or Invasion the public Safety may require it."

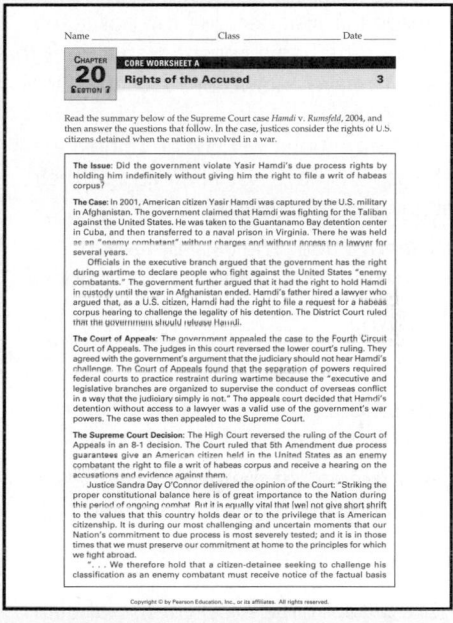

**L2 Differentiate** Distribute the adapted Chapter 20 Section 3 Core Worksheet A (Unit 5 All-in-One, p. 155).

**L4 Differentiate** Have students write an essay based on this quote from the Roman statesman and philosopher Cicero: "In time of war, the laws are silent." Students should explain what they think Cicero means and how it relates to the habeas corpus cases discussed in the text and on Core Worksheet A.

---

# Teacher-to-Teacher Network

**ALTERNATE LESSON PLAN** "If you haven't done anything wrong, why not answer the police officer's questions?" To help students answer this question, provide them with a brief historical overview of the 5th Amendment. Then discuss the importance of the 5th Amendment protection against self-incrimination. Have students write an essay or give an oral presentation about the trade-off between the need for law enforcement and protection of individual rights, such as the right to privacy.

To see this lesson plan, go to

Teacher Center

at PearsonSchool.com/phgovt

Ask students to define *self-incrimination* (acting as a witness against oneself in a criminal case). Then organize students into three groups. Have each group research and simulate one of the cases below, showing how it has affected the guarantee against self-incrimination. Simulations may take the form of a police drama, a documentary, or a radio or TV broadcast about the case.

• *Escobedo* v. *Illinois*, 1964: A confession cannot be used against a defendant if the confession was obtained by police who refused to allow the defendant to see an attorney or if the accused was not told that he or she had a right to refuse to answer questions. The Court's ruling extended the exclusionary rule to confessions obtained by unconstitutional means.

• *Miranda* v. *Arizona*, 1966: Because the police did not tell Miranda that he had a constitutional right to remain silent and to have an attorney present during interrogation, his rights were violated and his conviction overturned. Convictions will not be upheld in cases in which suspects have not been told of their constitutional rights before questioning.

• *Missouri* v. *Seibert*, 2006: The case outlawed two-step interrogations or "rehearsed confessions" if the accused was intentionally not given Miranda warnings until after the police had questioned the accused for the first time.

**ASSESSMENT RUBRIC** Explain to students that an excellent simulation will meet these standards:

**1.** *Research:* All members of the group conducted thorough research. Research was detailed and showed a deep understanding of the guarantee against self-incrimination.

**2.** *Planning:* The group made excellent use of planning time, sharing the writing and incorporating peer feedback. The selection of information used was well thought out and insightful.

**3.** *Presentation:* The simulation was creative, interesting, organized, focused on topic, and an appropriate length. Group members worked together harmoniously and dynamically. Actors were well rehearsed. The dialog was presented clearly and flowed logically.

---

## Answers

**Checkpoint** Excessive media coverage can jeopardize the right to a fair trial.

---

store, steals liquor, and sells it can be tried for illegal entry, theft, and selling liquor without a license.

In a trial in which a jury cannot agree on a verdict (a hung jury), there is no jeopardy. It is as though no trial had been held. Nor is double jeopardy involved when a case is appealed to a higher court.[10]

Several States allow the continued confinement of violent sex predators after they have completed a prison term. The Court has twice held that that confinement is not punishment—and so does not involve double jeopardy. Rather, the practice is intended to protect the public from harm, *Kansas* v. *Hendrick*, 1987, and *Seling* v. *Young*, 2001.

## Speedy and Public Trial

The 6th Amendment commands that:

> ❝
> **FROM THE CONSTITUTION**
>
> **In all criminal prosecutions, the accused shall enjoy the right to a speedy and public trial, . . .**

**Speedy Trial** The guarantee of a speedy trial is meant to ensure that the government will try a person accused of crime within a reasonable time and without undue delay. But how long a delay is too long? The Supreme Court has recognized that each case must be judged on its own merits.

In a leading case, *Barker* v. *Wingo*, 1972, the Court listed four criteria for determining if a delay has violated the constitutional protection. They are (1) the length of the delay, (2) the reasons for it, (3) whether the delay has in fact harmed the defendant, and (4) whether the defendant had asked for a prompt trial.

The Speedy Trial Act of 1974 says that the time between a person's arrest and the beginning of his or her federal criminal trial cannot be more than 100 days. The law does allow for some exceptions, however—for

example, when the defendant must undergo extensive mental tests, or when the defendant or a key witness is ill.

The 6th Amendment guarantees a prompt trial in *federal* cases. The Supreme Court first applied this right against the States as part of the 14th Amendment's Due Process Clause in *Klopfer* v. *North Carolina*, 1967.

**Public Trial** The 6th Amendment says that a trial must also be public. The right to be tried in public is also part of the 14th Amendment's guarantee of procedural due process, *In re Oliver*, 1948.

A trial must not be too speedy or too public, however. The Supreme Court threw out an Arkansas murder conviction in 1923 on just those grounds. The trial had taken only 45 minutes, and it had been held in a courtroom packed by a threatening mob.

Within reason, a judge can limit both the number and the kinds of spectators who may be present at a trial. Those who seek to disrupt a courtroom can be barred from it. A judge can order a courtroom cleared when the expected testimony may be embarrassing to a witness or to someone else who is not a party to the case.

Many questions about how public a trial should be involve the media—especially newspapers and television. The guarantees of fair trial and free press often collide in the courts. On the one hand, a courtroom is a public place where the media have a right to be present. On the other hand, media coverage can jeopardize a defendant's right to a fair trial. The Supreme Court has often held that the right to a public trial belongs to the defendant, not to the media.

What about televised trials? Television cameras are barred from all federal courtrooms. Yet most States do allow some form of in-court television reporting. Can televising a criminal trial violate a defendant's rights?

In an early major case, *Estes* v. *Texas*, 1965, the Supreme Court reversed the conviction of an oil man charged with swindling investors and others out of millions of dollars. The Court found that the media coverage of his trial had been so "circus-like" and disruptive that Estes had been denied his right to a fair trial.

---

**10** The Organized Crime Control Act of 1970 allows federal prosecutors to appeal sentences they believe to be too lenient. The Supreme Court has held that such appeals do not violate the double jeopardy guarantee, *United States* v. *Di Francesco*, 1980.

---

# Debate

Organize students into two groups to debate this topic: **The Court has gone too far in expanding the rights of the accused.** Both sides should research the following points to prepare arguments for and against the topic:

• Explain the effects criminal acts have on their intended victims.

• Explain the different types of defenses used by perpetrators of crime.

• Cite the number of people wrongfully accused and incarcerated.

Sixteen years later, the Court held in *Chandler* v. *Florida,* 1981, that nothing in the Constitution prevents a State from allowing the televising of a criminal trial. At least, televising is not prohibited as long as steps are taken to avoid too much publicity and to protect the defendant's rights.

## Trial by Jury

The 6th Amendment also says that a person accused of a federal crime must be tried "by an impartial jury." This guarantee reinforces an earlier one set out in the Constitution, Article III, Section 2. The right to trial by jury is also binding on the States, but only in cases involving "serious" crimes, *Duncan* v. *Louisiana* (1968).[11] The trial jury is often called the petit jury. *Petit* is the French word for "small."

The 6th Amendment adds that the members of a federal court jury must be drawn from "the State and district wherein the crime shall have been committed, which district shall have been previously ascertained by law." This stipulation gives the defendant any benefit there might be in having a jury familiar with the people and problems of the area.

A defendant may ask to be tried in another place—seek a "change of venue"—on grounds that the people of the locality are so prejudiced in the case that an impartial jury cannot be drawn. The judge must decide whether a change of venue is justified.

A defendant may also <u>waive</u> the right to a jury trial. However, he or she can do so only if the judge is satisfied that the defendant fully understands what that action means. In fact, a judge can order a jury trial even when a defendant does not want one. If a defendant waives the right, a **bench trial** is held, which means that a judge alone hears the case. (Of course, a defendant can plead guilty and so avoid any trial.)

---

**11** In *Baldwin* v. *New York*, 1970, the Court defined serious crimes as those for which imprisonment for more than six months is possible.

**12** The 14th Amendment does not say that there cannot be juries of fewer than 12 persons, *Williams* v. *Florida*, 1970, but it does not allow juries of fewer than six members, *Ballew* v. *Georgia*, 1978. Nor does it prevent a State from providing for a conviction on a less than unanimous jury vote, *Apodaca* v. *Oregon*, 1972. But if a jury has only six members, it may convict only by a unanimous vote, *Burch* v. *Louisiana*, 1979.

In federal practice, the jury that hears a criminal case must have 12 members. However, some federal civil cases are tried before juries of as few as six members. Several States now provide for smaller juries, often of six members, in both criminal and civil cases.

In the federal courts, the jury that hears a criminal case can convict the accused only by a unanimous vote. Most States follow the same rule.[12]

In a long series of cases, dating from *Strauder* v. *West Virginia*, 1880, the Supreme Court has held that a jury must be "drawn from a fair cross section of the community." A person is denied the right to an impartial jury if he or she is tried by a jury from which members of any groups "playing major roles in the community" have been excluded, *Taylor* v. *Louisiana*, 1975. In short, no person can be kept off a jury on such grounds as race, color, religion, national origin, or gender.

## Adequate Defense

Every person accused of a crime has the right to the best possible defense that circumstances will allow. In *Gideon* v. *Wainwright*, 1963, the Court held that an attorney must be furnished to a defendant who cannot afford one. In many places, a judge assigns a lawyer from the local community,

✓ **Checkpoint**
What are the advantages of having a local jury? Of having a change in venue?

**waive**
*v.* to give up or forgo

**SUPREME COURT**
at a glance

▸ **Case:** *Gideon v. Wainwright,* 1963
▸ **Issue:** 6th Amendment right to counsel
▸ **Decision:** Clarence Earl Gideon (below) defended himself at his trial and was found guilty. He wrote to the Supreme Court, saying that he had been unconstitutionally denied counsel. The Court agreed and ordered a new trial, holding that an attorney must be provided to those who cannot afford one.

597

---

**EVALUATE THE MIRANDA RULE**

Distribute the Chapter 20 Section 3 Core Worksheet B (Unit 5 All-in-One, p. 153), which examines the case of *Dickerson* v. *United States,* 2000. The case focuses on police use of Miranda warnings, as well as the separation of power between the legislative and judicial branches. After students complete their analysis of the case, discuss the Reflection Questions as a class.

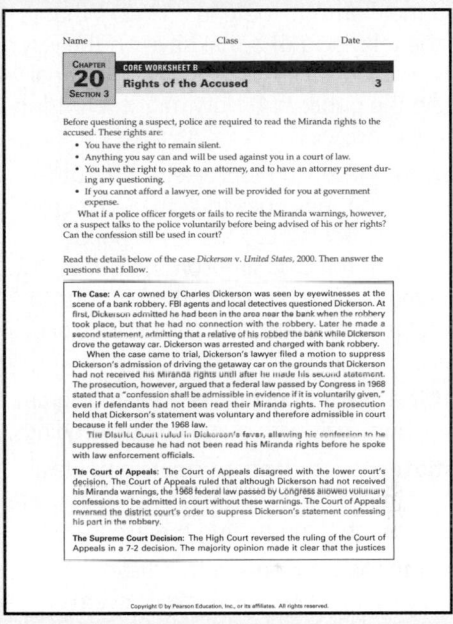

**L2 Differentiate** Distribute the adapted Chapter 20 Section 3 Core Worksheet B (Unit 5 All-in-One, p. 158).

## Supreme Court Notes

**IMPARTIAL JURY** As the Court has put it in several recent decisions on jury selection: Both the 5th and the 14th amendments mean that jury service cannot be determined by "the pigmentation of skin, the accident of birth, or the choice of religion." In *Miller-El* v. *Dretke,* 2005, Miller-El claimed that the prosecution purposefully excluded blacks from the jury in his capital murder trial. The Court held that Miller-El deserved to win his appeal because the jury selection was discriminatory. The Court noted that prosecutors excluded 91 percent of the eligible black prospective jurors, "a disparity unlikely to have been produced by happenstance." Two eliminated black prospective jurors were compared to similar white jurors who were not eliminated, and the Court concluded that the "selection process was replete with evidence that prosecutors were selecting and rejecting potential jurors because of race."

## Answers

**Checkpoint** A local jury may be advantageous because the jurors are familiar with the people and problems of the area. A change of venue may be advantageous when the local people are so prejudiced that an impartial jury cannot be drawn.

**L3 Differentiate** The 6th Amendment commands that the accused shall have the right to a public trial. Have students hold a debate on this question: **Should television cameras be allowed in courtrooms holding criminal trials?** Although more than 35 States allow State criminal trials to be televised, the broadcasting of federal criminal trials has been prohibited since 1946. To prepare for the debate, have students answer the following questions: (1) Does the televising of a trial harm the defendant? (2) What effect might the televising of a trial have on the jury? On judges and witnesses? (3) Does televising a trial in any way help the public? (4) How might televising a trial affect the outcome?

**L3 Differentiate** Have students research a 20th-century trial, such as the Scopes trial, the Lindbergh kidnapping trial, the Scottsboro trials, the Sacco and Vanzetti trial, or the O.J. Simpson trial. Have them explain whether the 6th Amendment right to a public trial helped or harmed the defendants or proceedings.

**L2 Differentiate** Have students use a Venn diagram to compare petit jury trials with grand jury proceedings.

**L4 Differentiate** Ask students to create a political cartoon that addresses this topic: The Court has gone too far/not far enough in protecting the accused.

**L3 Differentiate** Ask students with artistic skills to draw a graphic novel depicting the major events in the case *Gideon* v. *Wainwright*.

# Assess and Remediate

**L3** Have students suppose that a friend has just been arrested. Ask them to diagram in a flowchart the due process rights the accused is entitled to at arrest, before trial, and during the trial. Encourage students to provide a step-by-step analysis of legal proceedings and the accused friend's rights that are associated with each step.

**L3** Collect the Core Worksheets and assess students' participation using the Rubric for Assessing a Writing Assignment (Unit 5 All-in-One, p. 242).

**L3** Assign the Section 3 Assessment questions.

**L3** Section Quiz A (Unit 5 All-in-One, p. 161)

**L2** Section Quiz B (Unit 5 All-in-One, p. 162)

Have students complete the review activities in the digital lesson presentation and continue their work in the **Essential Questions Journal.**

## Answers

**Caption** refusing to speak or incriminate oneself

▲ The guarantee against self-incrimination does not prevent the fingerprinting of a suspect. **What does "taking the Fifth" mean?**

**subpoena**
*v.* to legally summon, order to appear

or a private legal aid association provides counsel.

The 6th Amendment says that a defendant has the right (1) "to be informed of the nature and cause of the accusation," (2) "to be confronted with the witnesses against him" and question them in open court, (3) "to have compulsory process for obtaining witnesses in his favor" (that is, favorable witnesses can be <u>subpoenaed,</u> and (4) "to have the Assistance of Counsel for his defense."

These key safeguards apply in the federal courts. Still, if a State fails to honor any of them, the accused can appeal a conviction arguing that the 14th Amendment's Due Process Clause has been violated. The Supreme Court protected the right to counsel in *Gideon* v. *Wainwright,* 1963; the right of confrontation in *Pointer* v. *Texas,* 1965; and the right to call witnesses in *Washington* v. *Texas,* 1967.

These guarantees are intended to prevent the cards from being stacked in favor of the prosecution. One of the leading right-to-counsel cases, *Escobedo* v. *Illinois,* 1964, illustrates this point.

Chicago police picked up Danny Escobedo for questioning in the death of his brother-in-law. On the way to the police station, and then while he was being questioned there, he asked several times to see his lawyer. The police denied those requests.

They did so even though his lawyer was in the police station and was trying to see him, and the police knew the lawyer was there. Through a long night of questioning, Escobedo made several damaging statements. Prosecutors later used those statements in court as a major part of the evidence that led to his murder conviction.

The Supreme Court ordered Escobedo freed from prison four years later. It held that he had been improperly denied his 14th Amendment right to counsel.

## Self-Incrimination

The guarantee against self-incrimination is among the several protections set out in the 5th Amendment. That provision declares that no person can be "compelled in any criminal case to be a witness against himself." This protection must be honored in both the federal and State courts, *Malloy* v. *Hogan,* 1964.

In a criminal case, the burden of proof is always on the prosecution. The defendant does not have to prove his or her innocence. The ban on self-incrimination prevents the prosecution from shifting the burden of proof to the defendant.

**Applying the Guarantee** The language of the 5th Amendment suggests that the guarantee against self-incrimination applies only to criminal cases. In fact, it covers any governmental proceeding in which a person is legally compelled to answer any question that could lead to a criminal charge. Thus, a person may claim the right ("take the Fifth") in a variety of situations: in a divorce proceeding (which is a civil matter), before a legislative committee, at a school board's disciplinary hearing, and so on.

The courts, not the individuals who claim it, decide when the right can be properly invoked. If the plea of self-incrimination is pushed too far, a person can be held in contempt of court.

The guarantee against self-incrimination is a personal right.[13] One can claim it only

---

13 With this major exception: A husband cannot be forced to testify against his wife, or a wife against her husband, *Trammel* v. *United States,* 1980. One can testify against the other voluntarily, however.

# Supreme Court Notes

**MIRANDA V. ARIZONA** Chief Justice Earl Warren provided historical context in his opinion: "From extensive factual studies undertaken in the early 1930's . . . it is clear that police violence and the 'third degree' flourished at that time. In a series of cases decided by this Court long after these studies, the police resorted to physical brutality—beating, hanging, whipping—and to sustained and protracted questioning incommunicado in order to extort confessions. . . . The examples given above are undoubtedly the exception now, but they are sufficiently widespread to be the object of concern. Unless a proper limitation upon custodial interrogation is achieved such as these decisions will advance there can be no assurance that practices of this nature will be eradicated in the foreseeable future."

for oneself. It cannot be invoked in someone else's behalf; a person can be forced to "rat" on another.

The privilege does not protect a person from being fingerprinted or photographed or required to submit a handwriting sample or appear in a police lineup. And, recall, it does not mean that a person does not have to submit to a blood test in a drunk-driving situation, *Schmerber* v. *California*, 1966.

A person cannot, however, be forced to confess to a crime under duress—that is, as a result of torture or other physical or psychological pressure. In *Ashcraft* v. *Tennessee*, 1944, for example, the Supreme Court threw out the conviction of a man accused of hiring another person to murder his wife. The confession on which his conviction rested had been secured only after some 36 hours of continuous, threatening interrogation. The questioning was conducted by officers who worked in shifts because, they said, they became so tired that they had to rest.

***Miranda* v. *Arizona*** In a truly historic decision, the Court refined the Escobedo holding in *Miranda* v. *Arizona*, 1966. (See the Landmark Decisions of the Supreme Court feature on the next two pages.) In this case, a mentally challenged man, Ernesto Miranda, had been convicted of kidnapping and rape. Ten days after the crime, the victim picked Miranda out of a police lineup. After two hours of questioning, during which the police did not tell him of his rights, Miranda confessed.

The Supreme Court struck down Miranda's conviction. More importantly, it said that it would no longer uphold convictions in cases in which suspects had not been told of their constitutional rights before police questioning. It thus laid down the **Miranda rule**—the requirement that police must read a suspect his or her rights before any questioning occurs.

The Supreme Court is still refining the rule on a case-by-case basis. Most often the rule is closely followed. But there are exceptions. Thus, the Court has held that once police have read a suspect his rights and questioning has begun, it is up to the person in custody to very clearly assert his right to remain silent, *Berghuis* v. *Thompkins*, 2010.

The Miranda rule has always been controversial. Critics say that it "puts criminals back on the streets." Others applaud the rule, arguing that criminal law enforcement is most effective when it relies on independently secured evidence, rather than on confessions gained by questionable tactics from defendants who do not have the help of a lawyer.

✔ **Checkpoint**
What does the Miranda rule require of police officers?

## REMEDIATION

| If Your Students Have Trouble With | Strategies For Remediation |
|---|---|
| Rights of the accused (Questions 1–6) | Have students write all the headings from the section on a sheet of paper, leaving room under each for notes. (The text under each heading in this section explains a right.) Have students fill in information under each heading that explains why that right is vital to people accused of crime. |
| Protection against self-incrimination (Question 7) | Ask students to write 10 quiz questions related to the guarantee against self-incrimination. For example, What does it mean to "take the Fifth"? Who can decide when an individual may claim the Fifth? Does the 5th Amendment prohibit being fingerprinted or appearing in a police lineup? Then have students exchange and complete one another's quizzes. |

---

Essential Questions Journal — To continue to build a response to the chapter Essential Question, go to your Essential Questions Journal.

## SECTION 3 ASSESSMENT

1. **Guiding Question** Use your completed graphic organizer to answer this question: What protections does the Constitution set out for persons accused of crimes?

**Key Terms and Comprehension**

2. **(a)** What does a **writ of habeas corpus** require? **(b)** When has the writ been suspended?

3. What are the three characteristics of an **ex post facto law?**

4. **(a)** Who bears the burden of proof in criminal cases? **(b)** What constitutional guarantee enforces this?

5. What rights to fair trial are guaranteed by the 6th Amendment?

**Critical Thinking**

6. **Express Problems Clearly (a)** What rights may come into conflict when a trial is televised? **(b)** Should television cameras be allowed in the courtroom? Why or why not?

7. **Identify Arguments** Why has the Miranda rule been both criticized and applauded?

**Quick Write**

**Research Essay: Paraphrasing** As you take notes on the case you selected in Section 1, paraphrase the source information by restating it in your own words. If you use the author's words, use quotation marks. You should cite your source even if you do not include direct quotes from them.

## Answers

**Checkpoint** to read a suspect his or her constitutional rights before questioning

## Assessment Answers

1. **5th Amendment:** grand jury in federal criminal cases, no double jeopardy, no self-incrimination; **6th Amendment:** right to speedy and public trial, impartial jury, adequate defense, be informed of nature and cause of accusation, confront witnesses, subpoena favorable witnesses, have access to a lawyer

2. **(a)** that a prisoner be brought before the court and that the holding officer show cause for not releasing the prisoner **(b)** during the Civil War and after the Japanese attack on Pearl Harbor

3. criminal law, applies to an act committed before its passage, works to the disadvantage of the accused

4. **(a)** the prosecution **(b)** 5th Amendment (no person can be "compelled in any criminal case to be a witness against himself")

5. right to prompt trial, right to public trial by an impartial jury, right to know charges, right to face witnesses, right to legally summon favorable witnesses, right to legal counsel

6. **(a)** fair trial versus freedom of the press **(b)** Students should provide reasons for their responses.

7. Critics say it puts criminals back on the streets. Supporters applaud reliance on independently secured evidence rather than on a coerced confession.

**QUICK WRITE** Remind students to limit direct quotes. Wording like "According to Jane Smith . . ." makes it clear that students are paraphrasing someone else's idea, but then they need to rewrite the idea in their own words.

- Students will analyze the initial reaction to the Miranda rule, when it must be used, and why.

## Teach

Have students read the feature as homework or at the beginning of class.

### IDENTIFY MIRANDA RIGHTS

Have students draw a web diagram in their notebooks, with "Miranda Rights" in the center oval. Ask students to write, from memory, four Miranda rights in surrounding ovals. Point out that a fifth right is often added: "You may bring police questioning to an end at any time." (See the Supreme Court Notes below.)

### DISCUSS INITIAL REACTION

The Miranda rule is commonplace now. When the Supreme Court ruled on the case in 1966, however, the police community and citizens were outraged. Justice White, in a dissenting opinion, even stated: "I have no desire whatsoever to share the responsibility for any such impact on the present criminal process." Ask students why they think this ruling caused such outrage. *(Criminals appeared to be set free on legal technicalities.)* Then pose these questions for discussion: **Can a society have too many rights? Is societal order more important than individual liberty?**

## SKILLS DEVELOPMENT

### PROBLEM SOLVING

Before students begin the brainstorming activity in this lesson, you may want to review the tips on problem solving in the Skills Handbook p. S17.

---

**Landmark Decisions of the SUPREME COURT**    *Miranda v. Arizona,* 1966

# What Are the Rights of the Accused?

- You have the right to remain silent.
- Anything you say can and will be used against you in a court of law.
- You have the right to an attorney.
- If you cannot afford an attorney, one will be appointed for you.

These words have been made famous by countless television dramas over the past forty years. They stem from the 5th and 6th amendments: "nor shall [any person] be compelled in any criminal case to be a witness against himself," and "[the accused] shall have the Assistance of Counsel for his defence." Often called the Miranda rights, they must be spoken to suspects before police interrogation.

In 1963, Ernesto Miranda was arrested at his home in Phoenix, Arizona. Accused of kidnapping and rape, he was questioned at the police station by two police officers. After two hours of interrogation, he signed a written confession. That confession was used at his trial, where Miranda was found guilty and sentenced to 20 to 30 years in prison. Miranda's attorney appealed to the Supreme Court of Arizona, claiming that Miranda had not been informed of his right to remain silent or to have an attorney present during the interrogation. The Arizona Court upheld the conviction, however, noting that Miranda had not requested an attorney. The case was then appealed to the United States Supreme Court.

In a 5–4 decision, the Supreme Court overturned Miranda's conviction. Chief Justice Earl Warren wrote the majority opinion, which centered on what happens when a suspect is taken into custody: "Today, then, there can be no doubt that the 5th Amendment privilege is available outside of criminal court proceedings and

The Supreme Court overturned the conviction of Miranda (right). He was retried without his confession but with witnesses and other evidence. Found guilty, he served 11 years.

Justice Harlan, dissenting, wrote: "The social costs of crime are too great to call the new rules anything but a hazardous experimentation."

600

## Supreme Court Notes

**HALTING THE INTERROGATION** If individuals waive their right to be silent or to have counsel, they may change their mind later. "Once warnings have been given, the subsequent procedure is clear. If the individual indicates in any manner, at any time prior to or during questioning, that he wishes to remain silent, the interrogation must cease. At this point he has shown that he intends to exercise his Fifth Amendment privilege; any statement taken after the person invokes his privilege cannot be other than the product of compulsion, subtle or otherwise. Without the right to cut off questioning, the setting of in-custody interrogation operates on the individual to overcome free choice in producing a statement after the privilege has been once invoked. If the individual states that he wants an attorney, the interrogation must cease until an attorney is present." (Chief Justice Earl Warren, *Miranda* v. *Arizona*) serves to protect persons in all settings in which their freedom of action is curtailed in any significant way from being compelled to incriminate themselves. We have concluded that without proper safeguards the process of in-custody interrogation of persons suspected or accused of crime contains inherently compelling pressures which work to undermine the individual's will to resist and to compel him to speak where he would not otherwise do so freely. In order to combat these pressures and to permit a full opportunity to exercise the privilege against self-incrimination, the accused must be adequately and effectively apprised of his rights and the exercise of those rights must be fully honored."

⊘ GOVERNMENT ONLINE
In the News
To learn more about the relevance of the case today, go to
PearsonSchool.com/phgovt

### Arguments for Miranda

- Miranda was poor and uneducated. He did not know of his 5th Amendment right to remain silent nor his 6th Amendment right to counsel.
- Arizona ignored both the *Escobedo* rule (evidence obtained from an illegally obtained confession is inadmissible in court) and the *Gideon* rule (all felony defendants have the right to an attorney).
- Miranda's confession was illegally obtained and should be thrown out.
- Miranda's conviction was faulty, and he deserves a new trial.

### Arguments for Arizona

- Miranda was no stranger to police procedures. He negotiated with police officers with intelligence and understanding.
- Miranda signed his confession of guilt willingly.
- The prosecution was proper, his conviction was based on Arizona law, and his imprisonment was just.
- The Arizona Supreme Court upheld his conviction and the rejection of its decision would cripple the work of police.

---

**Thinking Critically**

1. Is it essential that a person be given the right to counsel during police interrogation as well as during trial? Why or why not?
2. **Constitutional Principles** How does this case reflect the principle of limited government?

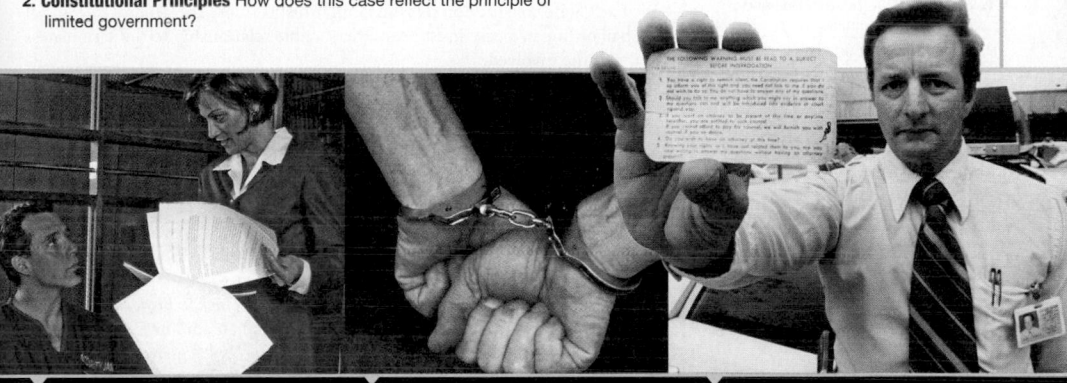

In *Miranda*, the Court said: "With a lawyer present the likelihood that the police will practice coercion is reduced."

The Miranda rights must be read to a suspect as soon as possible after he or she has been restrained.

The Miranda rule has "become part of our national culture," *Dickerson* v. *United States*, 2000.

601

---

## Supreme Court Notes

**REFINING THE MIRANDA RULE** *Missouri* v. *Seibert*, 2004, centered on what lately had become fairly common police practice: two-step interrogations, also known as "rehearsed confessions." Police officers had questioned Patrice Seibert, drawing out details of the fire she had set to cover up the murder of her son. *Then* she was told of her Miranda rights—and questioned again. That second round was taped, and she was asked questions based on the incriminating statements she had made in the first—untaped, unwarned—round. She confessed again. The Supreme Court found that her confession had been coerced and so was invalid. It struck down the two-step practice, saying that it threatened the very purpose of *Miranda*.

---

### SPECIFY IN-CUSTODY INTERROGATION

Ask: **When must the Miranda rights be read to a suspect?** *(before in-custody interrogation)* **Must the Miranda rights be stated before questioning witnesses to a crime?** *(no)* **Why not?** *(because witnesses are not under restraint or in police custody)* **Why do you think in-custody interrogation requires extra rights?** Read aloud Chief Justice Warren's statement: "An individual swept from familiar surroundings into police custody, surrounded by antagonistic forces . . . cannot be otherwise than under compulsion to speak."

### BRAINSTORM ALTERNATIVE METHODS

Have students brainstorm possible alternative rules that would allow police to better obtain confessions constitutionally. Before students brainstorm, write this statement on the board:

**The quality of a nation's civilization can be largely measured by the methods it uses in the enforcement of its criminal law. (W.V. Schaefer, *Harvard Law Review*, 1956)**

**L1 L2 Differentiate** Have students raise their hands when they have a point they wish to make. Call on lower-level students first to ensure that they participate in the discussion.

### EXTEND THE LESSON

**L3 L4 Differentiate** Assign the Landmark Decisions of the Supreme Court Worksheet (Unit 5 All-in-One, p. 173).

**L2 Differentiate** Assign the adapted Landmark Decisions of the Supreme Court Worksheet (Unit 5 All-in-One, p. 175).

## Assess and Remediate

Have students write several paragraphs describing (1) what the Miranda rights are; (2) when they must be stated and why; and (3) whether they think the Miranda rule does more good in protecting criminals or more harm in neglecting crime victims.

### IN THE NEWS

Students can learn more about *Miranda* v. *Arizona* by visiting **PearsonSchool.com/phgovt**.

---

### Answers

1. Yes. The presence of a lawyer during interrogation will reduce the possibility of police coercion.
2. by requiring government (law enforcement) to use proper procedures to solve crime

## How does the Constitution set limits on punishments for crime?

| Punishment |
| --- |
| **8th Amendment Limits**<br>• "Excessive bail shall not be required, nor excessive fines imposed. . . ."<br>• forbids "cruel and unusual punishment" |

# Get Started

## LESSON GOALS

Students will . . .

- examine how the Court's interpretation of "cruel and unusual punishment" has changed over time by analyzing court cases on the death penalty.

- analyze and evaluate arguments on the constitutionality of juvenile capital punishment by analyzing Supreme Court opinions and editorials on this issue.

## BEFORE CLASS

Assign the section, the graphic organizer in the text, and the Reading Comprehension Worksheet (Unit 5 All-in-One, p. 163) before class.

**L2 Differentiate** Reading Comprehension Worksheet (Unit 5 All-in-One, p. 164)

## BELLRINGER

Display Transparency 20G, Death Penalty in the United States. Have students answer the questions in their notebooks.

# SKILLS DEVELOPMENT

## ANALYZE POLITICAL CARTOONS

To help students learn to analyze political cartoons, have them turn to the Skills Handbook, p. S22, and use the steps explained there to complete the Political Cartoon Mini-Lesson.

---

SECTION 4

# Punishment

## Guiding Question

**How does the Constitution set limits on punishments for crime?** Use a table like the one below to take notes on the section.

| Punishment |
| --- |
| **8th Amendment Limits** |
| • |
| • |

## Political Dictionary

- bail
- preventive detention
- capital punishment
- treason

## Objectives

1. Explain the purpose of bail and preventive detention.
2. Describe the Court's interpretation of cruel and unusual punishment.
3. Outline the history of the Court's decisions on capital punishment.
4. Define the crime of treason.

**Image Above:** A lawyer reviews her client's paperwork before a bail hearing.

Again, think about this proposition: "It is better that ten guilty persons go free than that one innocent person be punished." How do you react to that comment now, after reading about the rights of persons accused of crime? Consider those persons who are found guilty, those who do not go free but are instead punished. How should they be treated? The Constitution gives its most specific answers to that question in the 8th Amendment.

## Bail and Preventive Detention

The 8th Amendment says, in part:

> **FROM THE CONSTITUTION**
>
> **Excessive bail shall not be required, nor excessive fines imposed, . . .**

Each State constitution sets out similar restrictions. The general rule is that the bail or fine in a case must bear a reasonable relationship to the seriousness of the crime involved.

**Bail** The sum of money that the accused may be required to post (deposit with the court) as a guarantee that he or she will appear in court at the proper time is called **bail**. The use of bail is justified on two bases: First, that a person should not be jailed until his or her guilt has been established; and second, that a defendant is better able to prepare for trial outside of a jail.

Note that the Constitution does not say that all persons accused of a crime are automatically entitled to bail. Rather, it guarantees that, where bail is set, the amount will not be excessive.

The leading case on bail in the federal courts is *Stack* v. *Boyle,* 1951. There, the Court ruled that "bail set at a figure higher than an amount reasonably calculated" to assure a defendant's appearance at a trial "is 'excessive' under the 8th Amendment." In *Stack,* 12 persons had been accused of violating the Smith Act of 1940, which, recall, made it a federal crime for any person to advocate the violent overthrow of government in the United States. (See Chapter 19, Section 3.)

# Focus on the Basics

**FACTS:** • The 8th Amendment addresses the issue of punishment for crime. • The Supreme Court has consistently held that the death penalty is constitutional if it is applied fairly. • The crime of treason is specifically defined in Article III of the Constitution to prevent its use for political purposes.

**CONCEPTS:** individual rights, due process of law, judicial review

**ENDURING UNDERSTANDINGS:** • The 8th Amendment bans excessive bail and fines and cruel and unusual punishment. • Although the Supreme Court has ruled that the death penalty does not constitute cruel and unusual punishment, the question of capital punishment continues to be debated.

A defendant can appeal the denial of release on bail or the amount of bail. Bail is usually set in accordance with the severity of the crime charged and with the reputation and financial resources of the accused. People with little or no income often have trouble raising bail. Therefore, the federal and most State courts release many defendants "on their own recognizance"—that is, on their honor. Failure to appear for trial, "jumping bail," is itself a punishable crime.

**Preventive Detention** In 1984, Congress provided for the **preventive detention** of some people accused of federal crimes. A federal judge can order that the accused be held, without bail, when there is good reason to believe that he or she will commit another serious crime before trial. Critics of the law claim that preventive detention amounts to punishment before trial. They say it undercuts the presumption of innocence to which all defendants are entitled.

The Supreme Court upheld the 1984 law, 6–3, in *United States* v. *Salerno*, 1987. The majority rejected the argument that preventive detention is punishment. Rather, it found the practice a legitimate response to a "pressing societal problem." And the Court has recently upheld a federal law that allows the government to keep those inmates who are deemed "sexually dangerous" behind bars even though they have served their sentenced time, *United States* v. *Comstock*, 2010.

## Cruel and Unusual Punishment

The 8th Amendment also forbids "cruel and unusual punishment." The 14th Amendment extends that prohibition against the States, *Robinson* v. *California*, 1962.

The Supreme Court decided its first cruel and unusual case in 1879 in *Wilkerson* v. *Utah*. There, a territorial court had sentenced a convicted murderer to death by a firing squad. The Court held that this punishment was not forbidden by the Constitution. The kinds of penalties the Constitution intended to prevent, said the Court, were such barbaric tortures as burning at the stake, crucifixion,

drawing and quartering, "and all others in the same line of unnecessary cruelty." The Court took the same position a few years later when, for the first time, it upheld the electrocution of a convicted murderer in a case from New York, *In re Kemmler*, 1890.

Since then, the Court has heard only a handful of cruel and unusual cases, except for those relating to capital punishment. More often than not, it has rejected the cruel and unusual punishment argument.[14] *Louisiana* v. *Resweber*, 1947, is fairly typical. There, the Court found that it was not unconstitutional to subject a convicted murderer to a second electrocution after the chair had failed to work properly on the first occasion. And in *Rhodes* v. *Chapman*, 1980, it held that putting two inmates in a cell that had been designed to hold only one did not violate the constitutional command.

The Court also denied the cruel and unusual claim in its most recent 8th Amendment case not involving the death penalty,

[14] The prohibition of cruel and unusual punishments is limited to criminal matters. It does not forbid paddling or similar punishments in the public schools, *Ingraham* v. *Wright*, 1977.

**legitimate**
*adj.* valid, sound, lawful

*"OVERCROWDED—I'll say it's OVERCROWDED!"*

▶▶ **Analyzing Political Cartoons** The 8th Amendment forbids cruel and unusual punishment. **What point is the cartoonist making here?**

## Differentiated Resources

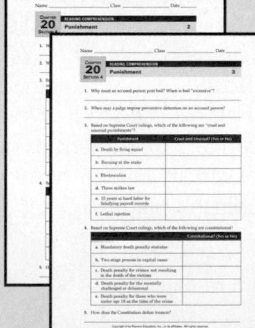

# Teach

To present this topic using online resources, use the lesson presentations at **PearsonSchool.com/phgovt.**

### REVIEW BELLRINGER ANSWERS

Have students discuss the Bellringer questions. Ask: **What can you infer about American attitudes toward the death penalty?** *(Almost three fourths of the States have the death penalty for people convicted of murder. Students may infer that almost 75 percent of Americans favor the death penalty. However, a recent Gallup poll showed these results: 47 percent prefer the death penalty; 48 percent prefer life without parole; and 5 percent had no opinion.)* **Does your State have the death penalty?** Have students discuss their thoughts about this situation.

### DEFINE "CRUEL AND UNUSUAL"

Have students define what they consider cruel and unusual punishment regarding sentencing for persons convicted of crime. Use a Think-Write-Pair-Share strategy (p. T22) to give students a chance to express their thoughts. After students have discussed the issue with a partner, have each pair share its opinions with the class. Then ask students to arrive at a consensus definition of *cruel and unusual punishment*.

### DISCUSS CHANGES IN PUNISHMENT

Point out that the Supreme Court's interpretation of what constitutes "cruel and unusual punishment" has changed over time. List on the board these forms of punishment commonly used in the American colonies: whipping, branding a hand with a *T* for thief or *M* for manslaughter, cutting off ears, standing in stocks, public hangings. Ask: **Which of these would have been considered "cruel and unusual punishment" in early colonial America?** *(none of them)* **Which of these punishments would be considered cruel and unusual today?** *(all of them)* **Why do you think attitudes about what constitutes cruel and unusual punishment have changed over time?** *(possible answers: reformers publicized the ineffectiveness of various punishments as a deterrent to crime; the perception that electrocution or lethal injection is a more clinical and humane form of capital punishment)*

## Answers

**Caption** that being incarcerated in an overcrowded prison would not qualify as "cruel and unusual punishment"

## ANALYZE COURT DECISIONS

Ask these questions to help students understand how judicial decisions have helped define what is and is not cruel and unusual punishment.

• *Wilkerson* v. *Utah*, 1879: **How did the Court define cruel and unusual punishment in this case?** *(burning at the stake, crucifixion, drawing and quartering, other forms of "unnecessary cruelty")*

• *In re Kemmler*, 1890, and *Louisiana* v. *Resweber*, 1947: **How were the rulings in these cases similar?** *(In both cases, the justices ruled that electrocution was not cruel and unusual punishment.)*

• *Weems* v. *United States*, 1910, and *Robinson* v. *California*, 1962: **In what ways were the rulings in these cases similar?** *(The Court ruled that the actions taken by the government were cruel and unusual punishment. Weems was given 15 years hard labor chained at ankle and wrist. Robinson was imprisoned for narcotics addiction.)*

• *Coker* v. *Georgia*, 1977, *Atkins* v. *Virginia*, 2002, *Roper* v. *Simmons*, 2005: **Did the Supreme Court's rulings in these cases expand or limit capital punishment?** *(limit; ruled that the death penalty can be imposed only in murder cases and cannot be imposed on people who are mentally challenged or were under age 18 when they committed crimes)*

Then ask: **What conclusion can you draw about the makeup of the Court and the definition of cruel and unusual punishment?** *(Students should conclude that judicial philosophy affects Court decisions on this controversial issue.)*

## DISCUSS JUVENILE CAPITAL PUNISHMENT

Use an Opinion Line (p. T26) as a starting point for a discussion of capital punishment for juveniles. Put up signs at the beginning, middle, and end of the line that say: Limited Sentence with Parole, Life Sentence without Parole, and Death Penalty. Ask students to stand closest to the sign that expresses their opinion about sentencing for convicted murderers age 18 and younger. Ask volunteers to explain why they have chosen their positions.

## ANALYZE A JUVENILE CAPITAL CASE

Distribute the Chapter 20 Section 4 Core Worksheet A (Unit 5 All-in-One, p. 165), which presents the majority and dissenting opinions in *Roper* v. *Simmons*. Have students answer the questions on the worksheet and discuss the opinions as a class.

## Answers

**Checkpoint** It struck down all of the then-existing State laws providing for the death penalty because they gave too much discretion to judges or juries in deciding whether to impose the death penalty.

---

**capriciously**
*adv.* unpredictably; erratically, without reason

*Lockyer* v. *Andrade*, 2003. That case centered on California's "three strikes" law. That statute provides that any person convicted of a third crime must be sentenced to at least 25 years in prison. Leandro Andrade had received 50 years for stealing $153.54 worth of children's videos from two K-Mart stores. The K-Mart thefts were treated as separate offenses and he had an earlier burglary conviction on his record, as well.

The Court has held some punishments to be cruel and unusual, but only a very few. It did so for the first time in *Weems* v. *United States* in 1910. There, the Court overturned the conviction of a Coast Guard official who had been found guilty of falsifying government pay records. He had been sentenced to 15 years at hard labor, constantly chained at wrist and ankle. In *Robinson* v. *California*, 1962, the Court ruled that a State law that defined narcotics addiction as a crime to be punished, rather than an illness to be treated, violated the 8th and 14th amendments.[15]

## Capital Punishment

Laws providing for **capital punishment**—the death penalty—date back to at least the 18th century B.C. and the Code of Hammurabi, which set death as the penalty for more than 25 different offenses.[16] The punishment has been a part of American law since the colonial period, and both the Federal Government and 35 States provide for it today.

Over time, the Supreme Court was reluctant to face this highly charged question: Is capital punishment cruel and unusual and therefore prohibited by the 8th Amendment?

**State Laws Struck Down** The Court did meet the issue, finally, and more or less directly, in *Furman* v. *Georgia*, 1972. There, it struck down all of the then-existing State laws providing for the death penalty—but not because that punishment is cruel and unusual.

Rather, the Court voided those laws because they gave too much discretion to judges or juries in deciding whether to impose the ultimate penalty. The Court found that of all the people convicted of capital crimes, only "a random few," most of them African American or poor, or both, were "capriciously selected" for execution.

Immediately, most States and Congress began to write new capital punishment laws. Those new statutes took one of two forms. Several States made a death sentence mandatory for certain crimes—for example, the killing of a police officer or a murder committed during a rape, kidnapping, or arson. Others provided, instead, for a two-stage process in capital cases: first, a trial to settle the question of guilt or innocence; then, for those convicted, a second proceeding to decide if the circumstances involved in the crime justify a sentence of death.

In considering scores of challenges to these new laws, the Supreme Court found mandatory death penalty statutes unconstitutional. In *Woodson* v. *North Carolina*, 1976, it ruled that those statutes were "unduly harsh and rigidly unworkable." They were, said the Court, simply attempts to "paper over" the decision in *Furman*.

**Two-Stage Approach Upheld** The two-stage approach was found to be constitutional in *Gregg* v. *Georgia*, 1976. There, the Court held for the first time that the "punishment of death does not invariably violate the Constitution." It declared that well-drawn two-stage laws could practically eliminate "the risk that it [the death penalty] would be inflicted in an arbitrary or capricious manner."

**Later Cases** Opponents of the death penalty continue to appeal capital cases to the Supreme Court, but to no real avail. Most of their cases have centered on the application, not the constitutionality, of the punishment. The more important of those several cases have resulted in these rulings: The death penalty can be imposed only for "crimes resulting in the death of the victim," *Coker* v. *Georgia*, 1977. That penalty cannot be imposed on those who are mentally challenged, *Atkins* v. *Virginia*, 2002, or on those who were

---

15 But, notice, that does not mean that buying, selling, or possessing narcotics cannot be made a crime. Laws that criminalize such conduct are designed to punish persons for their behavior, not for being ill.

16 The phrase "capital punishment" comes from the Latin *caput*, meaning "head"; in many cultures, the historically preferred method for execution was beheading (decapitation).

---

# Background

**ELECTROCUTION** Before 1888, hanging was the most common way in which those on death row were executed. Some considered it a form of "cruel and unusual punishment." The electric chair was developed in 1887 as a result of a rivalry between Thomas Edison and Westinghouse. In trying to promote his DC electricity, Edison proved that AC electricity, used by Westinghouse, could easily kill people and animals exposed to it. While doing this, he proposed the idea for an "electric chair" for capital punishment using AC, thinking that people would not want the same type of electricity in their homes. Electrocution was adopted by many States, yet contrary to Edison's plans, AC still became the main type of current used across the country.

# Capital Punishment Debate

**GOVERNMENT** ONLINE
**Audio Tour**
For additional information on capital punishment, visit
**PearsonSchool.com/phgovt**

Capital punishment has a lengthy history, and so does the controversy surrounding it. The punishment has been a part of American law since the colonial period, and 35 States provide for it today. More than 1,200 persons have been executed in this country since the Supreme Court reinstated capital punishment in 1976. Since 2000, an average of 40 percent of death sentences imposed are ever carried out. Fifty-two persons were executed in 11 States in 2009. Some 3,300 persons sit on death row in American prisons today. *Do you think the maximum penalty for murder should be death or, instead, life without the possibility of parole? Explain.*

## 47% prefer death penalty — Public Opinion — 48% prefer life without parole

SOURCE: Gallup poll, 2006

" Although some of the studies suggest that the death penalty may not function as a significantly greater deterrent than lesser penalties, there is no convincing empirical evidence either supporting or refuting this view. We may nevertheless assume safely that there are murderers, such as those who act in passion, for whom the threat of death has little or no deterrent effect. But for many others, the death penalty undoubtedly is a significant deterrent.

—Justice Potter Stewart, Gregg v. Georgia, 1976

" One area of law more than any other besmirches the constitutional vision of human dignity. . . . The barbaric death penalty violates our Constitution. Even the most vile murderer does not release the state from its obligation to respect dignity, for the state does not honor the victim by emulating his murderer. Capital punishment's fatal flaw is that it treats people as objects to be toyed with and discarded. . . . One day the Court will outlaw the death penalty. Permanently.

—William J. Brennan, former U.S. Supreme Court Justice, 1996

---

under the age of 18 when their crimes were committed, *Roper* v. *Simmons*, 2005.

The question of whether the ultimate penalty is to be imposed must be decided by the jury that convicted the defendant, not the judge who presided at the trial, *Ring* v. *Arizona*, 2002.

And, most recently, these holdings: A delusional person who cannot understand why he has been sentenced to death cannot be executed, *Panetti* v. *Quarterman*, 2007. Execution by lethal injection, the method most widely used today, does not violate the 8th Amendment, *Baze* v. *Rees*, 2008. The sum of the Court's many decisions over the past thirty years or so comes down to

this: The death penalty, fairly applied, is constitutional.

**Continuing Controversy** Even so, capital punishment remains controversial. Public opinion polls do show that there is support for it. However, many of those supporters express misgivings about the fairness with which it is applied.

Clearly, the application of the death penalty must be closely monitored to protect the innocent and prevent wrongful convictions. The Death Penalty Information Center reports that over the past 30 years, some 125 persons who had been sentenced to death have been exonerated and released from prison.

**exonerate**
*v.* to declare innocent, absolve, free of blame

---

# Political Cartoon Mini-Lesson

Point out that when deciding whether a punishment is cruel and unusual, the Supreme Court considers what Chief Justice Earl Warren described as "evolving standards of decency in a civilized society." Justices often look at the laws on capital punishment passed by State legislatures, at how juries have voted in death penalty cases, and at the results of opinion polls that reflect society's views on the death penalty. Display Transparency 20H, featuring two political cartoons with different views toward punishment. Ask: **What is the message in Cartoon A?** (*pro-punishment; Victims of crime should be treated justly and their plight acknowledged.*) **In Cartoon B?** (*anti-punishment; All capital punishment, and lethal injection, is murder.*) **Which recent case considered the cruel-and-unusual aspect of lethal injection?** (*Baze v. Rees*) Have students write a journal entry describing their opinions on the death penalty.

---

Tell students to go to the Audio Tour for a guided audio tour of the capital punishment arguments.

## EVALUATE EDITORIALS

Organize students into four groups. Distribute Chapter 20 Section 4 Core Worksheet B (Unit 5 All-in-One, p. 167), and assign each group one of the editorials based on skill level: Editorial A is for L3 students; Editorial B is for L4 students; Editorials C and D are for L2 students. Each group should analyze its editorial and answer the worksheet questions on a separate sheet of paper. Have a spokesperson from each group explain its editorial to the rest of the class. Ask students whether they agree or disagree with the editorials as they are presented.

**L3 Differentiate** After all groups have completed their worksheets, write "Juvenile Capital Punishment" on the board. Underneath, make two columns labeled "Arguments For" and "Arguments Against." Ask each group to list statements from its editorial in the appropriate column.

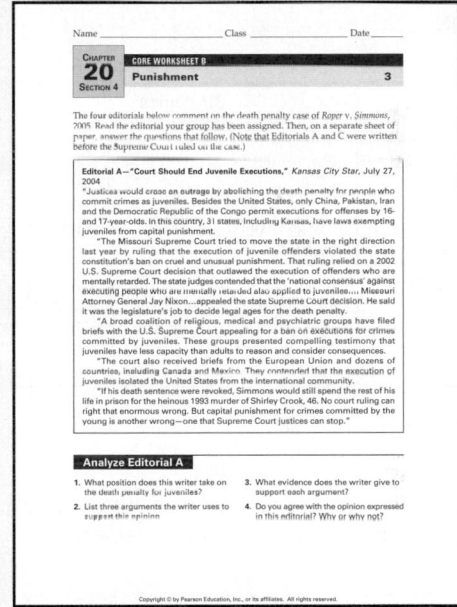

## EXTEND THE LESSON

**L3 Differentiate** Ask students to act out two scenarios in pairs. In the first scenario, one student will be a lawyer explaining to a suspected client his or her right to bail as well as possible preventive detention. In the second scenario, students will switch roles. The lawyer will explain possible penalties to the client if he or she is convicted. In their role as lawyers, students should cite cases from the text.

---

## Answers

**Capital Punishment Debate** Answers will vary, but students' opinions should show evidence of careful reasoning.

**L2 Differentiate** Have volunteers poll others about whether they are for or against the death penalty for juveniles convicted of murder. Pollsters should include the age and gender of each respondent. Have students present their findings in a bar graph, noting whether age or gender made a difference in responses.

# Assess and Remediate

**L3** Ask students to summarize the 8th Amendment and Article III, Section 3, in their own words.

**L3** Collect the Core Worksheets and assess students' work.

**L3** Assign the Section 4 Assessment questions.

**L3** Section Quiz A (Unit 5 All-in-One, p. 171)

**L2** Section Quiz B (Unit 5 All-in-One, p. 172)

Have students complete the review activities in the digital lesson presentation and continue their work in the **Essential Questions Journal.**

## REMEDIATION

| If Your Students Have Trouble With | Strategies For Remediation |
|---|---|
| Punishments set by the Constitution (Questions 1, 2, 5, 6) | Have students research to find answers to these questions: Who sets the amount of bail? In what situations is bail denied? Who determines preventive detention and treason? |
| The debate over capital punishment (Questions 3, 4, 7) | Ask students to write a true-or-false quiz with ten questions concerning Supreme Court rulings on capital punishment. Have students exchange and complete one another's quizzes. |

## Answers

**Checkpoint** all U.S. citizens at home or abroad and all permanent resident aliens; the death penalty

---

As retired Supreme Court Justice Sandra Day O'Connor has observed: "If statistics are any indication, the system may well be allowing some innocent defendants to be executed."

That fact has also prompted many who support capital punishment to insist that the remedies for whatever problems there may be in the administration of the penalty should not be found in its abolition. They should be found, instead, in the continuing improvement of the processes by which the ultimate penalty is imposed.

## Treason

Treason against the United States is the only crime defined in the Constitution. The Framers provided a specific definition of the crime because they knew that the charge of treason has long been a favorite weapon in the hands of tyrants.

**Treason,** says Article III, Section 3, can consist of only two things: either (1) levying war against the United States or (2) "adhering to their Enemies, giving them Aid and Comfort." And the Constitution adds that no person can be convicted of the crime of treason "unless on the Testimony of two Witnesses to the same overt Act, or on Confession in open Court."

The law of treason covers all citizens of the United States, at home or abroad, and all permanent resident aliens. Congress has set death as the maximum sentence for someone convicted of the federal crime but no person has ever, in fact, been executed for that offense. Indeed, the death penalty was not imposed in a federal treason case until as recently as 1942. Then, four German-born American citizens were sentenced to be hanged for aiding a group of Nazi saboteurs who had been landed on the East Coast by a German submarine. But those sentences were never carried out.[17]

Treason can only be committed in wartime. But Congress has made it a crime, during times of either peace or war, to commit either espionage or sabotage, to attempt to overthrow the government by force, or to conspire to do any of these things.

Most State constitutions also condemn treason. The fabled abolitionist John Brown was hanged as a traitor by Virginia after his raid on Harpers Ferry in 1859. He is believed to be the only person ever executed for treason against a State.

---

[17] The sentence of one of the traitors was commuted to life in prison; he was later denaturalized and then deported. The other three appealed their convictions and won new trials. One of them was again convicted of treason but this time sentenced to life in prison; the other two pleaded guilty to lesser charges and received five-year prison terms.

---

**Essential Questions Journal** To continue to build a response to the chapter Essential Question, go to your **Essential Questions Journal.**

## SECTION **4** ASSESSMENT

1. **Guiding Question** Use your completed graphic organizer to answer this question: How does the Constitution set limits on punishments for crime?

**Key Terms and Comprehension**

2. **(a)** Define **bail. (b)** What is its purpose? **(c)** When is the use of bail justified?

3. What penalties has the Supreme Court considered cruel and unusual?

4. **(a)** When did the Supreme Court first hear a **capital punishment** case? What was the ruling in that case? **(b)** What is the two-stage process?

5. **(a)** Define **treason. (b)** Why does the Constitution contain a specific definition of treason?

**Critical Thinking**

6. **Identify Point of View** Why do some oppose preventive detention? **(b)** Why has the Supreme Court upheld it? **(c)** With which point of view do you agree? Why?

7. **Demonstrate Reasoned Judgment (a)** In capital cases, who cannot be sentenced to death? **(b)** Do you agree with the Court's ruling that mandatory death sentences are unconstitutional? Why or why not?

**Quick Write**

**Research Essay: Opening Statement** Write an opening statement, or hook, for an essay on the case you selected in Section 1. A hook should grab readers' interest. Various types of hooks motivate further reading. These include (1) a statement that hints at what is to come; (2) a fascinating description of an exciting event or action; or (3) a question that will be answered later in the essay. Your hook should connect smoothly to the introduction and the body of your essay.

---

# Assessment Answers

**1.** The 8th Amendment prohibits excessive bail and fines and forbids cruel and unusual punishment.

**2. (a)** sum of money the accused is required to deposit with the court **(b)** to guarantee that the person will appear in court at the proper time **(c)** when it is not excessive

**3.** barbaric tortures such as burning at the stake, crucifixion, drawing and quartering

**4. (a)** 1972, in *Furman* v. *Georgia;* the Court struck down all of the then-existing State laws providing for the death penalty **(b)** a trial to settle guilt or innocence; after conviction, a proceeding to decide if the crime justifies death sentence

**5. (a)** levying war against the U.S. or giving aid and comfort to enemy **(b)** The Framers knew that a charge of treason was a favorite weapon in the hands of tyrants.

**6. (a)** They claim it is punishment before trial. **(b)** as a legitimate response to a pressing societal problem **(c)** Answers will vary.

**7. (a)** those who are mentally challenged, under age 18, or delusional **(b)** Possible answer: A mandatory death sentence for a particular crime does not allow the court to consider the circumstances involved in individual cases, such as self-defense.

**QUICK WRITE** After writing their opening statement, students should review its effectiveness by asking themselves these questions: What question does the hook prompt readers to ask? How does it connect to the rest of the story?

## Quick Study Guide

**GOVERNMENT** ONLINE
**On the Go**
To review anytime, anywhere, download these online resources at **PearsonSchool.com/phgovt**
Political Dictionary, Audio Review

CHAPTER **20**

**Guiding Question**
**Section 2** How does the Constitution protect the freedom and security of the person?

**Guiding Question**
**Section 3** What protections does the Constitution set out for persons accused of crimes?

**Guiding Question**
**Section 1** Why is the concept of due process important to a free society?

**CHAPTER 20**
**Essential Question**
To what extent has the judiciary protected the rights of privacy, security, and personal freedom?

**Guiding Question**
**Section 4** How does the Constitution set limits on punishments for crime?

### Political Dictionary

due process *p. 578*
procedural due process *p. 579*
substantive due process *p. 579*
police power *p. 580*
search warrant *p. 581*
involuntary servitude *p. 583*
discrimination *p. 584*
writs of assistance *p. 585*
probable cause *p. 586*
exclusionary rule *p. 588*
writ of habeas corpus *p. 592*
bill of attainder *p. 593*
ex post facto law *p. 593*
grand jury *p. 594*
indictment *p. 594*
presentment *p. 594*
information *p. 595*
double jeopardy *p. 595*
bench trial *p. 597*
Miranda Rule *p. 599*
bail *p. 602*
preventive detention *p. 603*
capital punishment *p. 604*
treason *p. 606*

### Protections of Freedom and Security

**13th Amendment:**
"Neither slavery nor involuntary servitude, . . . shall exist within the United States, or any place subject to their jurisdiction."

**2nd Amendment:**
"A well regulated Militia, being necessary to the security of a free State, the right of the people to keep and bear Arms, shall not be infringed."

**4th Amendment:**
"The right of the people to be secure in their persons, houses, papers, and effects, against unreasonable searches and seizures, shall not be violated, and no Warrants shall issue, but upon probable cause, supported by Oath or affirmation, and particularly describing the place to be searched, and the persons or things to be seized."

**14th Amendment's Due Process Clause:**
"No State shall . . . deprive any person of life, liberty, or property, without due process of law . . . "

### Limits on Punishment

**8th Amendment**

"Excessive bail shall not be required, nor excessive fines imposed. . . ."

Forbids "cruel and unusual punishment"

Have students download the digital resources available at Government on the Go for review and remediation.

### STUDY TIPS

**Taking Multiple Choice Tests** When taking multiple choice tests, students should scan the entire document before they begin, noting the number of questions and their point values. They can then use this information to pace themselves. For each question, caution students to read all the choices before selecting an answer, eliminating those choices they know to be wrong. Suggest the following strategy: Cover up the answers and try to anticipate the correct answer. If your answer is among the choices, circle it but then read the others to make sure none is better. When "all of the above" is a choice, it is probably the correct answer if at least two choices are correct. Recommend that students not skip questions they are unsure about, however—this increases the chances of forgetting to go back and answer some questions. Instead, have them answer as best they can and then mark the question to return to if time permits.

### ASSESSMENT AT A GLANCE

**Tests and Quizzes**
Section Assessments
Section Quizzes A and B, Unit 5 **All-in-One**
Chapter Assessment
Chapter Tests A and B, Unit 5 **All-in-One**
Document-Based Assessment
Progress Monitoring Online
Exam*View* Test Bank

**Performance Assessment**
Essential Questions Journal
Debates, pp. 588, 596
Assessment Rubrics, **All-in-One**

## For More Information

To learn more about civil liberties, refer to these sources or assign them to students:

**L1** **Smith, Rich.** *Fifth Amendment: The Right to Fairness.* ABDO & Daughters, 2007.

**L2** **Winters, Robert, ed.** *The Bill of Rights—Freedom from Unfair Searches and Seizures.* Gale Group, 2005.

**L3** **Orth, John V.** *Due Process of Law: A Brief History.* University Press of Kansas, 2003.

**L4** **Zimring, Franklin E.** *The Contradictions of American Capital Punishment.* Oxford University Press, 2004.

# Chapter Assessment

**COMPREHENSION AND CRITICAL THINKING**

## SECTION 1

1. **(a)** to secure due process rights at both the federal and State government levels **(b)** police officers acting on a tip instead of probable cause; violating privacy without a warrant; attempting to obtain evidence by attacking the suspect and by forcing the suspect to submit to stomach pumping

2. **(a)** States **(b)** Students should provide examples of the use of the police power to promote their own health, safety, morals, and general welfare.

3. **(a)** issues of abortion **(b)** Answers will vary.

## SECTION 2

4. **(a)** 4th Amendment **(b)** Officers must obtain a search warrant based on probable cause before a search and seizure.

5. **(a)** Court ruled that the 13th Amendment did not prohibit discrimination by individuals. **(b)** Court strengthened the 13th Amendment by holding that discrimination was a badge of slavery and, so, illegal.

6. **(a)** yes, if they have probable cause **(b)** no **(c)** *California* v. *Acevedo; Brendlin* v. *California*

7. **arguments for:** requires police to obey the law and deters police misconduct; **arguments against:** allows criminals to "beat the rap" on a technicality

## SECTION 3

8. **(a)** legislative act that provides for the punishment of a person without a court trial **(b)** requires that an accused person be punished after breaking a law but not be punished by a law itself; also enforces that the accused receive a fair trial

9. **(a) grand jury:** 16 to 23 jurors in a federal case; jurors must be drawn from the district court area that it serves; at least 12 jurors needed to return an indictment; sessions are secret; only the prosecution presents before the grand jury; **petit jury:** jurors must be drawn from the district where crime was committed; must have 12 members in a federal criminal case; must convict by a unanimous vote; members must be drawn from a fair cross section of the community **(b)** Answers will vary.

10. **(a)** Police must read a suspect his or her constitutional rights before questioning. **(b)** 5th and 6th amendments

---

CHAPTER **20** **Chapter Assessment**

**GOVERNMENT** ONLINE
Self-Test
To test your understanding of key terms and main ideas, visit
PearsonSchool.com/phgovt

## Comprehension and Critical Thinking

### Section 1

1. **(a)** Why are there two due process clauses in the Constitution? **(b)** In *Rochin* v. *California*, what particular actions by the deputies constituted violations of due process?

2. **(a)** Which level of government has the police power in the federal system? **(b)** Provide at least four examples of the ways in which exercises of the police power affect you.

3. **(a)** In what area has the right to privacy been most controversial? **(b)** Should the right to privacy be applied to the Census Bureau, credit card companies, and Internet sites as they collect personal information? Why or why not?

### Section 2

4. **Analyze Political Cartoons (a)** Which amendment is involved in the events described in this cartoon? **(b)** What is the basic rule laid down by that amendment?

"Yes, the search was totally by-the-book. I recall covering my eyes and counting to 100 before I began looking."

5. **(a)** How did the Court apply the 13th Amendment in the late 1800s? **(b)** How did its ruling in *Jones* v. *Mayer*, 1968 revise the meaning of the 13th Amendment?

6. **(a)** Can police search a vehicle during a routine traffic stop? **(b)** Can they search both the driver and passengers? **(c)** Cite two cases to support your answers.

7. What arguments can be made for and against the exclusionary rule?

### Section 3

8. **(a)** What is a bill of attainder? **(b)** How does the ban on bills of attainder protect individual freedoms?

9. **(a)** Describe five characteristics of a grand jury and four characteristics of a petit jury. **(b)** On which type of jury would you prefer to serve? Why?

10. **(a)** What is the Miranda rule? **(b)** From which two amendments is the rule drawn?

### Section 4

11. **(a)** What are the constitutional guarantees regarding bail? **(b)** How is the amount of bail set? **(c)** What happens if a defendant cannot raise bail?

12. **(a)** What was the significance of *Furman* v. *Georgia*? **(b)** How does the Supreme Court view capital punishment today?

### Writing About Government

13. Use your Quick Write exercises from each Section Assessment to write a research essay about the case you selected in Section 1. Use an informative writing style that describes what happened, when and where it happened, why it happened, and who was involved. Present the facts in an objective way without displaying emotion or injecting your opinion in the essay. See pp. S6–S8 in the Skills Handbook.

---

## Apply What You've Learned

14. **Essential Question Activity** Scan the newspaper for articles concerning any guarantees of the rights of the accused shown in the illustration in Section 3 of this chapter. Prepare a brief report describing the article and the right(s) in question. Indicate how you think the issue or case should be resolved and why.

15. **Essential Question Assessment** Based on the brief report you wrote and the content of this chapter, create a poster that helps to answer the Essential Question: **To what extent has the judiciary protected the rights of privacy, security, and personal**

**freedom?** Your poster should list the rights of privacy, security, and/or personal freedom related to your everyday life—that is, in your home, automobile, on your computer and/or phone. On a separate piece of paper, write a paragraph that outlines the extent to which each of these freedoms is protected.

**Essential Questions Journal** To respond to the chapter Essential Question, go to your **Essential Questions Journal.**

---

## SECTION 4

11. **(a)** Where bail is set, the amount shall not be excessive. **(b)** in accordance with the severity of the crime charged and with the reputation and financial resources of the accused **(c)** The defendant either remains in jail or the courts may release a defendant on his or her own recognizance, or honor.

12. **(a)** It struck down all the then-existing State laws providing for the death penalty. **(b)** The death penalty, if applied fairly, is constitutional.

## WRITING ABOUT GOVERNMENT

13. Remind students that an informative writing style includes answers to these questions: What happened? Who was involved? Where did this occur? When did it occur? Why did it happen? Students should also include answers to this question: How did it affect the rights of the accused?

## APPLY WHAT YOU'VE LEARNED

14. Students' reports should focus on the rights of the accused. Summaries should be accurate and include all relevant points; opinions should be backed with precedents.

# Document-Based Assessment

## The Patriot Act

The Patriot Act was enacted "to deter and punish terrorist acts in the United States and around the world, to enhance law enforcement investigatory tools, and for other purposes." Debate centers around whether it provides a balance between national security and the Constitution's guarantees of individual freedom, as shown in the documents below.

### Document 1

The law allows our intelligence and law enforcement officials to continue to share information. It allows them to continue to use tools against terrorists that they . . . use against drug dealers and other criminals. It will improve our nation's security while we safeguard the civil liberties of our people. The legislation strengthens the Justice Department so it can better detect and disrupt terrorist threats.

—President George W. Bush, March 2006

### Document 2

Just 45 days after the September 11 attacks, with virtually no debate, Congress passed the USA PATRIOT Act. There are significant flaws in the Patriot Act, flaws that threaten your fundamental freedoms by giving the government the power to access your medical records, tax records, information about the books you buy or borrow without probable cause, and the power to break into your home and conduct secret searches without telling you for weeks, months, or indefinitely.

—American Civil Liberties Union, 2003

### Document 3

Delayed notification search warrants are a long-existing, crime-fighting tool upheld by courts nationwide for decades in organized crime, drug cases and child pornography. The Patriot Act simply codified the authority law enforcement had already had for decades. This tool is a vital aspect of our strategy of prevention-detecting and incapacitating terrorists before they are able to strike.

—U.S. Department of Justice, 2003

### Document 4

'I need to get a bigger bat.'

---

**Use your knowledge of the Patriot Act and Documents 1–4 to answer the following questions.**

1. Document 1 implies that the overriding goal of the Patriot Act is to
   A. strengthen the Justice Department.
   B. allow law enforcement and intelligence officials to share information.
   C. safeguard civil liberties.
   D. improve the nation's security.
2. According to Document 2, what does the Patriot Act give government the power to do?
3. How does Document 3 justify the use of delayed notification search warrants?
4. What is the cartoonist saying about the Patriot Act in Document 4?
5. **Pull It Together** How do these documents illustrate the difficulty of striking a proper balance between national security and individual rights?

 **GOVERNMENT** ONLINE
**Documents**
To find additional primary sources on the Patriot Act, visit
**PearsonSchool.com/phgovt**

---

**DOCUMENT-BASED ASSESSMENT**

1. D
2. access your medical records, tax records, information about the books you buy or borrow without probable cause, and the power to break into your home and conduct secret searches without telling you for weeks, months, or indefinitely
3. It says that delayed notification search warrants have long existed and been upheld by courts in other criminal cases.
4. The Patriot Act has broken civil liberties (the home furnishings) in its attempt to strike at terrorists (the wasp). In other words, the act is both excessive and ineffective.
5. Students should summarize excerpts from the documents in their responses.

**L2 Differentiate** Students use all the documents on the page to support their thesis.

**L3 Differentiate** Students include additional information available online at **PearsonSchool.com/phgovt.**

**L4 Differentiate** Students use materials from the textbook, the online information at **PearsonSchool.com/phgovt,** and do additional research to support their views.

**Go Online to PearsonSchool.com/phgovt** for a student rubric and extra documents.

---

15. Students should scan the chapter for court cases that guaranteed the rights of privacy, security, and/or personal freedom related to a home, a vehicle, a computer and/or phone, and their person. For example, officers need a warrant before searching a home. A phone cannot be tapped or bugged without a warrant as well. Vehicles may be stopped and searched without a warrant but with probable cause. A suspect must be told of the charges against him or her, and is guaranteed the right against self-incrimination.

# Introduce the Chapter

## Essential Questions:

**UNIT 5**

What should be the role of the judicial branch?

**CHAPTER 21**

Why are there ongoing struggles for civil rights?

### ACTIVATE PRIOR KNOWLEDGE

Have students examine the image and quotation on these pages. Point out that Amendments 13, 14, and 15 ended slavery and extended the rights of citizenship to African Americans. Ask: **Why was the civil rights movement necessary?** *(because discriminatory laws and practices still existed in society, which worked to deny equal rights; for example, poll taxes and intimidation limited the ability of African Americans to vote, and segregation in schools denied them equal access to education)* Then tell students to begin to further explore civil rights by completing the Chapter 21 Essential Question Warmup activity in their **Essential Questions Journal.** Discuss their responses as a class.

### BEFORE READING

**L2 ELL Differentiate** Chapter 21 Prereading and Vocabulary Worksheet (Unit 5 All-in-One, p. 192)

### SUCCESSNET STUDENT AND TEACHER CENTER

Visit **PearsonSchool.com/phgovt** for downloadable resources that allow students and teachers to connect with government "on the go."

### DIGITAL LESSON PRESENTATION

The digital lesson presentation supports the print lesson with activities and summaries of key concepts.

## SKILLS DEVELOPMENT

### ANALYZE IMAGES

You may wish to teach analyzing images as a distinct skill within Section 3 of this chapter. Use the Chapter 21 Skills Worksheet (Unit 5 All-in-One, p. 217) to help students learn how to analyze images. The worksheet asks students to study two photographs and analyze them in terms of content, emotions, context, and purpose. For L2 and L1 students, assign the adapted Skill Activity (Unit 5 All-in-One, p. 218).

**WebQuest online** The Chapter WebQuest challenges students to answer the chapter Essential Question by asking them about civil rights.

610

## Block Scheduling

**BLOCK 1:** Teach Section 1 lesson, including Transparencies 21A and 21B, Core Worksheet 21.1, and the Assess activity. Begin Section 2, including Bellringer and Compare/Apply Rational Basis/Strict Scrutiny activities. Discuss Transparency 21C and assign Create a Timeline of Civil Rights.

**BLOCK 2:** Have students complete Core Worksheet 21.2 and Extend Worksheet. Begin Section 3; discuss Bellringer and Relate Actions to Legislation. Allow time for groups to complete Core Worksheet 21.3. Organize groups for Debate Affirmative Action.

**BLOCK 3:** Have groups debate. Introduce Section 4 with Transparency 21F and Analyze Line Graph. Distribute Core Worksheet 21.4A; have students take the citizenship test. Assign Understand Immigration Arguments and Core Worksheet 21.4B. End the lesson with Strategies for Remediation.

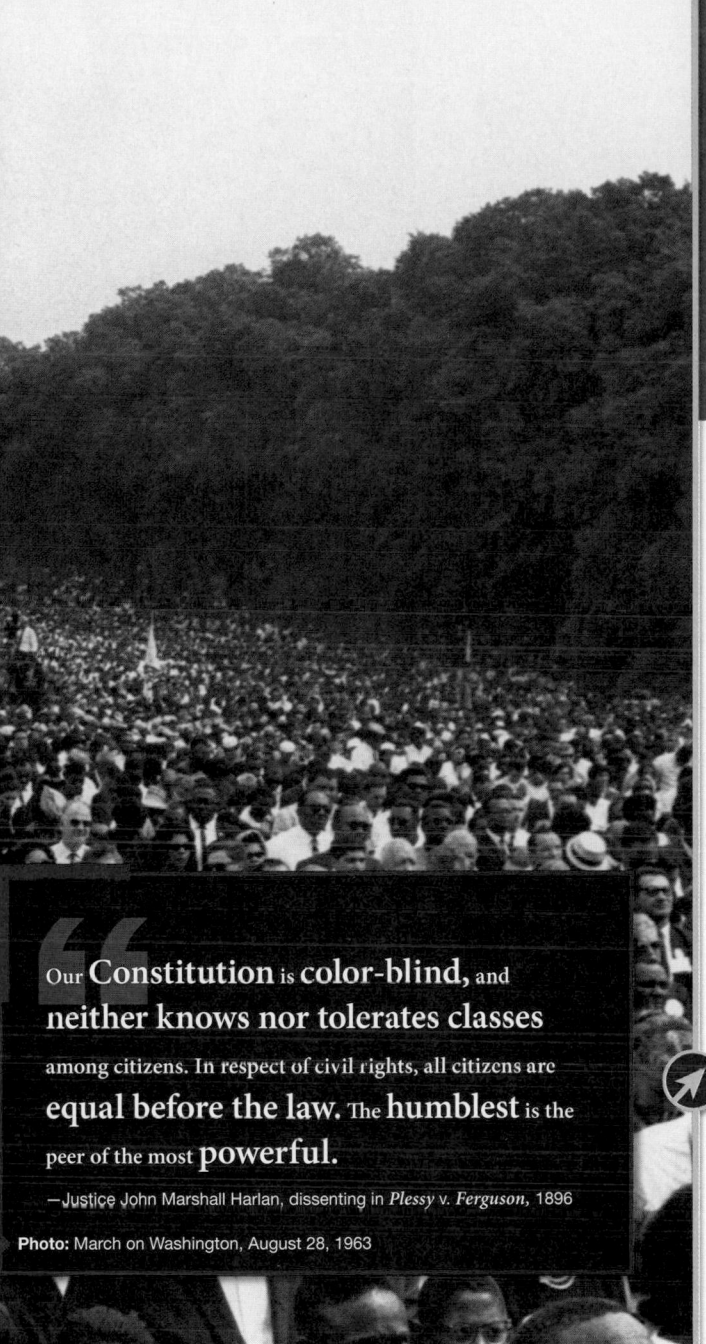

CHAPTER

# 21

## Civil Rights: Equal Justice Under Law

**Essential Question**
Why are there ongoing struggles for civil rights?

**Section 1:**
Diversity and Discrimination

**Section 2:**
Equality Before the Law

**Section 3:**
Federal Civil Rights Laws

**Section 4:**
American Citizenship

> "Our **Constitution** is **color-blind,** and **neither knows nor tolerates classes** among citizens. In respect of civil rights, all citizens are **equal before the law.** The **humblest** is the peer of the most **powerful.**
>
> —Justice John Marshall Harlan, dissenting in *Plessy v. Ferguson,* 1896

**Photo:** March on Washington, August 28, 1963

**GOVERNMENT ONLINE**
**On the Go**

To study anywhere, anytime, download these online resources at PearsonSchool.com/phgovt
• Political Dictionary
• Audio Review
• Downloadable Interactivities

611

## Lesson Goals

### SECTION 1

Students will . . .

• identify ways that increasing diversity is changing American society by analyzing data on the ethnic composition of the United States.

• summarize the history of race- and gender-based discrimination in the United States by completing a chart on events and laws or policies that affected minority groups and women.

### SECTION 2

Students will . . .

• understand how the Supreme Court interprets "equal protection of the laws" by analyzing and applying the tests it uses to decide cases.

• trace the history of segregation in public schools by creating a timeline of cases related to school integration.

• examine changing attitudes about school integration by evaluating a political cartoon on this topic.

### SECTION 3

Students will . . .

• trace the development of civil rights legislation by relating it to historical actions of States designed to nullify African Americans' rights.

• analyze the policy of affirmative action and why it is controversial by studying political cartoons and by exploring the issues surrounding it.

### SECTION 4

Students will . . .

• summarize ways that individuals become citizens in the United States.

• analyze the controversy over immigration in the United States by preparing arguments for and against opinions on the topic.

## Pressed for Time

Have students prepare a handbook that recent immigrants could use to help them prepare for American citizenship. Students should include a historical perspective of civil rights legislation that applies to new citizens. Encourage students to illustrate their handbooks and provide the names and phone numbers of important local government resources. Handbooks should also include a citizenship study guide and test.

**DIFFERENTIATED INSTRUCTION KEY**

Look for these symbols to help you adjust steps in each lesson to meet your students' needs.

**L1** Special Needs

**L2** Basic

　**ELL** English Language Learners

　**LPR** Less Proficient Readers

**L3** All Students

**L4** Advanced Students

How have various minority groups in American society been discriminated against?

| African Americans | Native Americans | Hispanic Americans | Asian Americans |
|---|---|---|---|
| • Slavery<br>• Civil rights gains<br>• Discrimination ongoing | • Disease decimated population<br>• Driven from lands<br>• Forced relocation to reservations<br>• Poverty, joblessness, alcoholism | • Largest minority in U.S.<br>• Mexican Americans in Southwest<br>• Puerto Ricans in Northeast<br>• Cuban Americans in South Florida | • Resentment of Chinese workers led to violence<br>• Chinese Exclusion Act<br>• Japanese relocation camps during World War II |

# Get Started

## LESSON GOALS

Students will . . .

- identify ways that increasing diversity is changing American society by analyzing data on the ethnic composition of the United States.

- summarize the history of race- and gender-based discrimination in the United States by completing a chart on events and laws or policies that affected minority groups and women.

## SKILLS DEVELOPMENT

### ANALYZE GRAPHIC DATA

Since there are several instances of graph use in this section, have students read about analyzing graphic data in the Skills Handbook, p. S26.

---

## SECTION 1

# Diversity and Discrimination

### Guiding Question

**How have various minority groups in American society been discriminated against?** Use a table like the one below to take notes on the section.

| African Americans | Native Americans | Hispanic Americans | Asian Americans |
|---|---|---|---|
| • | • | • | • |
| • | • | • | • |
| • | • | • | • |

### Political Dictionary

- heterogeneous
- immigrant
- reservation
- refugee
- assimilation

### Objectives

1. Understand what it means to live in a heterogeneous society.
2. Summarize the history of race-based discrimination in the United States.
3. Examine discrimination against women in the past and present.

**Image Above:** The United States takes pride in its diversity.

Have you read George Orwell's classic, *Animal Farm?* Even if you have not, you may have heard its most oft-quoted line: "All animals are created equal, but some animals are more equal than others." You might keep Orwell's comment in mind as you read this chapter.

## A Heterogeneous Society

The term **heterogeneous** is a compound of two Greek words: *hetero,* meaning "other or different," and *genos,* meaning "race, family, or kind." Something that is heterogeneous is composed of dissimilar parts, made up of elements that are unrelated to or unlike one another—in short, something composed of a mix of ingredients. "We the People of the United States" are a heterogeneous lot, and we are becoming more so, year to year.

The population of the United States is predominantly white. It is today and, as you can see in the circle graph on page 614, it has been historically. The first census in 1790 reported that there were 3,929,214 people living in this country. More than four out of five were white. African Americans made up the remaining 19 percent of the population counted in that census. As the nation's population grew over the decades, so, too, did the proportion of the American people who were white—until recently.

Today, the ethnic composition of the population is strikingly different from what it was only a generation ago. **Immigrants**—those aliens legally admitted as permanent residents—have arrived in near-record numbers every year since the mid-1960s. Over that period, the nation's African American, Hispanic American, and Asian American populations have grown at rates several times that of the white population. Indeed, the minority population now exceeds the white population in four States: California, Hawaii, New Mexico, and Texas.

A look at gender balance in the population reveals that females are more numerous than males. This has been the case for more than half a century.

As a result of these changes in the American population, the United States is more heterogeneous today than ever before. That fact is certain to have a profound effect on the American social, political, and economic landscape on through the twenty-first century.

---

## Focus on the Basics

**FACTS:** • The United States is a diverse nation made up of people from many different backgrounds. • African Americans, Native Americans, Hispanic Americans, Asian Americans, and other minority groups have suffered from discrimination. • Women of all backgrounds have experienced gender discrimination, especially in wages.

**CONCEPTS:** equal protection

**ENDURING UNDERSTANDINGS:** • The Declaration of Independence declares that "all men are created equal," but our nation still struggles to meet the ideal of equality for all. • Race-based and gender-based discrimination has declined but not disappeared in this country.

## Race-Based Discrimination

White Americans have been historically reluctant to yield to nonwhite Americans a full and equal place in the social, economic, and political life of this nation. Over time, the principal targets of that ethnic prejudice have been African Americans, Native Americans, Asian Americans, and Hispanic Americans. The white-male-dominated power structure has also been slow to recognize the claims of women to an equal place in American society.

**African Americans** Much of what you will read in these pages focuses on discrimination against African Americans. There are three principal reasons for this focus. First, African Americans have been the victims of consistent and deliberate unjust treatment for a longer time than any other minority group of Americans.[1] The ancestors of most African Americans came to this country in chains. Over a period of some two hundred years, tens of thousands of Africans were kidnapped, crammed aboard sailing ships, brought to America, and then sold in slave markets. As slaves, they were the legal property of other human beings. They could be bought and sold and forced to do their owners' bidding, however harsh the circumstances.

It took a civil war to end more than two centuries of slavery in this country. The 13th Amendment finally abolished slavery in 1865. Still, the Civil War and the ratification of that amendment did not end widespread racial discrimination in the United States.

Second, African Americans constitute a huge minority group in the United States. They number well over 40 million today, over 13 percent of all of the American people.

Finally, most of the gains the nation has made in translating the Constitution's guarantees of equality into a reality for all persons have come out of efforts made by and on behalf of African Americans. Recall that, for example, the struggles of Martin Luther King, Jr., and others resulted in the Civil Rights Act of 1964 and then the Voting Rights Act of 1965. See Chapter 6, Section 3.

[1] Slavery first came to what was to become the United States in 1619; in August of that year, 20 Africans were sold to white settlers at Jamestown in colonial Virginia.

America is now an inescapably multi-racial society. Still, unlike whites, African Americans live with the consequences of America's history of racial discrimination every day of their lives. Of course, this is not to say that other groups of Americans have not also suffered the effects of discrimination. Clearly, many have.

**Native Americans** White settlers first began to arrive in America in relatively large numbers in the mid-1600s. At the time, some one million Native Americans were living in territory that was to become the United States.[2] By 1900, however, their number had fallen to less than 250,000.

Diseases brought by white settlers decimated those first Americans. So, too, did the succession of military campaigns that accompanied the westward expansion of the United States. To quote one leading commentator:

"'The only good Indian is a dead Indian' is not simply a hackneyed expression from cowboy movies. It was part of the strategy of westward expansion, as settlers and U.S. troops mercilessly drove the eastern Indians from their ancestral lands to the Great Plains and then took those lands too."

—**Thomas E. Patterson,**
*The American Democracy*

Today, about 3 million Native Americans live in this country. More than a third of them live on or near **reservations,** which are public lands set aside by government for use by Native American tribes.

[2] An estimated 8 to 10 million Native Americans lived in all of North and South America in the mid-1600s.

✓ **Checkpoint**
What was the impact of the 13th Amendment on racial discrimination?

Native Americans comprise a large number of ethnic groups and distinct tribes, representing a diversity of nations and lifestyles. ▼

613

## Differentiated Resources

The following resources are located in the All-in-One, Unit 5, Chapter 21, Section 1:

**L2** Prereading and Vocabulary Worksheet (p. 192)

**L3** Reading Comprehension Worksheet (p. 196)

**L2** Reading Comprehension Worksheet (p. 197)

**L3** Core Worksheet (p. 198)

**L3** Quiz A (p. 199)

**L2** Quiz B (p. 200)

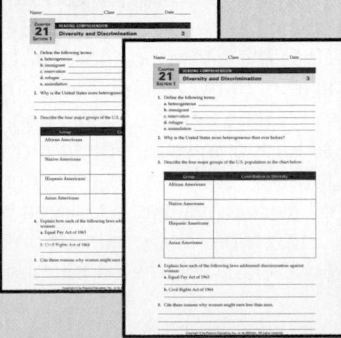

### BEFORE CLASS

Assign the section, the graphic organizer in the text, and the Reading Comprehension Worksheet (Unit 5 All-in-One, p. 196) before class.

**L2 Differentiate** Reading Comprehension Worksheet (Unit 5 All-in-One, p. 197)

### BELLRINGER

Write on the board: **How has cultural diversity in the United States affected the foods you eat? Sports you play or watch? Holidays you celebrate? List examples in your notebook.**

# Teach

To present this topic using online resources, use the lesson presentations at **PearsonSchool.com/phgovt.**

### DISCUSS BELLRINGER RESPONSES

Have students share their answers to the Bellringer questions. Point out that the United States is among the most heterogeneous societies in the world. Ask students to guess other heterogeneous countries. *(Canada, for example, has more than 200 ethnic groups. Nigeria is made up of more than 250 ethnic groups.)* Have students name countries with homogeneous societies. *(Han Chinese make up 92 percent of China's population. Egypt is 98 percent Egyptian.)*

**L2 ELL Differentiate** Have students look up the meaning of the words *hetero-* (other, different), *homo-* (same, like), and *-genos* (race, family, kind) in the dictionary. Ask non-native students to discuss how heterogeneous their home country is compared to the United States.

### DISCUSS DIVERSITY

Display Transparency 21A, Cultural Diversity, which shows the ethnic composition of the United States. Ask: **What two ethnic groups were counted in the 1790 census?** *(White and African American)* **What is the fastest-growing minority group?** *(Hispanic Americans)* Ask volunteers among your minority students to discuss diversity within their group. For example, what countries of origin are represented among your Asian students? Do individuals consider themselves "Chicano," "Latino," or some other designation? Is the diversity within these groups reflected in different forms of dress, foods, or customs? Be mindful of students' privacy by respecting their decision not to participate. If your class contains no minority students, lead a general class discussion on diversity within minority groups.

## Answers

**Checkpoint** It had no effect on racial discrimination.

## IDENTIFY BENEFITS/CHALLENGES OF DIVERSITY

Ask: **In what ways might diversity change U.S. politics?** *(may lead to varied voting blocs and more diverse groups of candidates and elected officials)* **What challenges might growing diversity create?** *(possible answers: increased misunderstanding or conflict among people whose social, cultural, and religious beliefs differ; resentment from whites who feel their dominant position is threatened)* **Is increasing diversity likely to make Americans more or less tolerant? Explain.** *(Some may say that having more frequent contact with diverse peoples will increase tolerance; others might argue that greater diversity will cause intolerance or bigotry by introducing people to beliefs or practices that they disagree with or find threatening.)*

## PREDICT ASSIMILATION PATTERNS

Review the definitions of *discrimination* (prejudice against) and *assimilation* (merge into). Point out that in the early 1900s, Americans often referred to the nation as a "melting pot," in which immigrants worked hard to assimilate. Today the United States with its many distinctive racial and ethnic groups is instead compared to a "salad bowl" or "marble cake," in which each of the ingredients retains its separate color, texture, and flavor within the "whole." Have students write a paragraph answering this question and giving reasons for their opinion: **What will American culture resemble by 2050?**

## INTRODUCE THE TOPIC OF DISCRIMINATION

Display Transparency 21B, Preventing Discrimination. Then ask: **What are some situations in which withholding information about a person's age, gender, and race is appropriate?** *(applications for jobs, school, or housing)* **What are some situations in which providing this information may be appropriate? Why?** *(applying for certain vocational or educational scholarships or medical benefits set aside for particular races or ages, or for certain athletic competitions in which men and women compete separately or in age categories)*

Explain that diversity is reflected not only in age, gender, ethnicity, and race, but also in religious beliefs and practices, languages spoken, country of origin, income, marital status, and education. Have students describe situations in which a group might face discrimination based on any of these characteristics. As each is described, have students suggest laws, rules, or procedures that act as protections against discrimination.

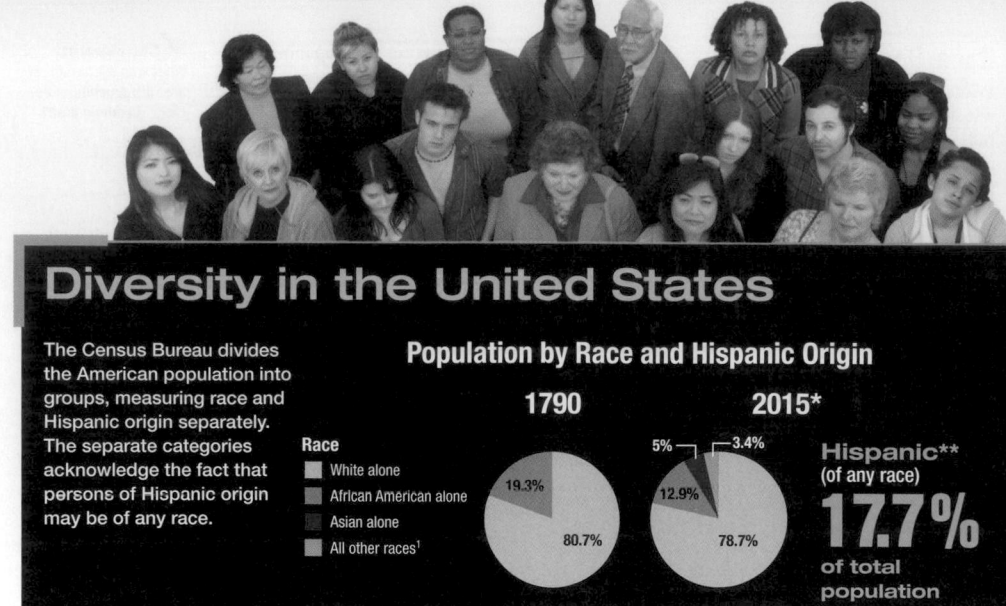

# Diversity in the United States

The Census Bureau divides the American population into groups, measuring race and Hispanic origin separately. The separate categories acknowledge the fact that persons of Hispanic origin may be of any race.

## Population by Race and Hispanic Origin

**Race**
- White alone
- African American alone
- Asian alone
- All other races[1]

**1790**
- 19.3%
- 80.7%

**2015***
- 5%
- 3.4%
- 12.9%
- 78.7%

**Hispanic**** (of any race)

**17.7%** of total population

---

Like African Americans, Native Americans have been the victims of overwhelming discrimination. The consequences of that bias have been appalling, and they remain evident today. Poverty, joblessness, and alcoholism plague many reservations. The Indian Education Act of 1972 attempted to remedy the cycle of continual poverty by providing financial assistance to local educational agencies for Native American children and adult programs. Still, the life expectancy of Native Americans living on reservations today is ten years less than the national average, and the Native American infant mortality rate is one and a half times that of white Americans.

**Hispanic Americans** Hispanic Americans are those in this country who have a Spanish-speaking background; many prefer to be called *Latinos*. Hispanics may be of any race. According to the Bilateral Commission on the Future of United States–Mexican Relations, Hispanic Americans "are among the world's most complex groupings of human beings. [The largest number] are white, millions . . . are mestizo,

nearly half a million in the United States are black or mulatto."[3]

Today, the number of Hispanic Americans approaches 50 million and they constitute the largest minority group in this country, having surpassed African Americans sometime around the year 2000. They are also the nation's fastest-growing population group. Hispanic Americans can generally be divided into four main subgroups:

**1.** *Mexican Americans* Well over half of all Hispanics in the U.S., some 32 million persons, were either born in Mexico or trace their ancestry there. Those born in this country of Mexican parents are often called *Chicanos*.

Most of the Mexican American population lives in the States of California, Arizona, New Mexico, and Texas, but that population is spreading throughout much of the country. A majority of the residents of such large cities as El Paso and San Antonio in Texas are

---

**3** A *mestizo* is a person of both Spanish or Portuguese and Native American ancestry. A *mulatto* is a person of African and white ancestry.

# Background

**INDIAN EDUCATION ACT** The Department of Education has recognized that Native Americans had unique educational, linguistic, and cultural academic needs. Thus, the Indian Education Act of 1972 "provides federal assistance in education . . . to help close the gap which now exists between Indian education and the general educational level of the United States. The Act further creates a new Office of Indian Education within the Office of Education. . . . The new Act created the National Advisory Council for Indian Education to provide policy direction and guidance to the Congress and those responsible for implementing the Act. The Council is comprised of 15 Indian or Alaskan Natives appointed by the President from a select list recommended by Indian tribes and organizations throughout the Country." (*Journal of American Indian Education:* Volume 14, Number 2)

## Population Increase, 2010–2020*

**Race**
- White alone
- African American alone
- Asian alone
- Hispanic of any race**
- All other races[1]

Although the population of the United States remains predominantly white, minority populations are growing at a faster rate than the majority population. *What is the rate of growth for Asian Americans? What are the benefits of diversity in a community?*

8%    11.2%    30.1%    33.5%    29.0%

**Hispanic**
(of any race)

## 33.5%
population increase

*Projected; **The Census Bureau added the classification of "Hispanic of any race" to better reflect the growing diversity of the nation's population.
[1]Includes American Indian and Alaska Native alone, Native Hawaiian and Other Pacific Islander alone, and Two or More Races. SOURCE: Census Bureau

---

Hispanic today, and such smaller border cities as Laredo and Brownsville in Texas are now over 90 percent Latino.

**2.** *Puerto Ricans* Another large group of Hispanics has come to the mainland from the island of Puerto Rico. The population of the United States now includes about four million Puerto Ricans. Most of them have settled in New York and New Jersey, and in other parts of the Northeast.

**3.** *Cuban Americans* The Hispanic population also includes some 1.7 million Cuban Americans. They are mostly people who fled the Castro dictatorship in Cuba, and their descendants. A majority of them have settled in Miami and elsewhere in South Florida.

**4.** *Central and South Americans* The fourth major subgroup of Hispanic Americans came here from Central and South America, many as refugees. A **refugee** is one who seeks protection (refuge) from war, persecution, or some other danger. Nearly 7 million persons have emigrated to the United States from Central and South American countries

over the past 30 years or so; they have arrived in the largest numbers from Nicaragua, El Salvador, Guatemala, Colombia, and Chile. Many have also come from the Dominican Republic, an island nation in the Caribbean.

**Asian Americans** The story of white America's mistreatment of Asians is a lengthy one, too. Asians have faced discrimination from the first day they arrived. As with all immigrant groups, assimilation into the white-dominated population has been difficult. **Assimilation** is the process by which people of one culture merge into and become part of another.

Chinese laborers were the first Asians to come to the United States in large numbers. They were brought here in the 1850s to 1860s as contract laborers to work in the mines and to build railroads in the West. Many white Americans, both native-born and immigrants, resented the competition of what they called "coolie labor." Their resentments were frequently expressed in acts of violence toward Asians.

Congress brought Chinese immigration to a near halt with the Chinese Exclusion

**✔ Checkpoint**
What is a refugee?

---

## Background

**CHINESE EXCLUSION ACT** The Chinese Exclusion Act of 1882 barred Chinese immigrants because "in the opinion of the Government of the United States the coming of Chinese laborers to this country endangers the good order of certain localities...." Events leading to this discriminatory law began in the mid-1800s when the California Gold Rush drew waves of Chinese immigrants hoping to work in the mines. Many new arrivals found jobs building railroads. In 1870, Chinese laborers agreed to work on the Union Pacific in Wyoming for $32.50 per month. White workers earned $52 per month for the same job. White workers resented the competition for jobs and blamed the Chinese for depressing wages. Many Americans also believed that the physical and cultural differences of Asians made assimilation impossible. After the act passed, violence against Chinese people in the United States increased.

---

Tell students to go to the Audio Tour for data on the ethnic composition of the U.S. population and the rate of growth of ethnic populations.

### DISTRIBUTE CORE WORKSHEET

Organize students into small groups and distribute the Chapter 21 Section 1 Core Worksheet (Unit 5 All-in-One, p. 198), which asks students to identify historical events and laws that perpetuated or removed discrimination against minority groups in the United States. Ask students to complete the chart based on information in the text and then to answer the Reflection Questions. Point out that the impact of discrimination on each of these groups has varied over time, increasing or decreasing based in part upon historical events as well as government policies. Discuss students' responses to the Reflection Questions, particularly number 3, which focuses on the judiciary's proper role in battling discrimination.

**L2 Differentiate** Fill in the first row of the chart for students, ask a volunteer to fill in the second row, and then have students work independently or in pairs to complete the remainder of the chart.

Name _____ Class _____ Date _____

**CHAPTER 21 SECTION 1**
**CORE WORKSHEET**
**Diversity and Discrimination**    3

Use information in your textbook to complete the chart below. Then answer the questions that follow.

| Minority Group | Historical Event(s) that Influenced Treatment | Government Policies or Laws that Resulted from Historical Events | Effects of Government Policies |
|---|---|---|---|
| African Americans | | | |
| Native Americans | | | |
| Hispanic Americans | | | |
| Asian Americans | | | |

1. Based on this chart, how responsive would you say Congress has been in dealing with discrimination?

2. Why do you think the heterogeneous makeup of the American population will have an important effect on American society, politics, and economics in the years to come?

3. What do you think should be the role of the judiciary in responding to the types of discrimination described in the chart?

4. What does the passage of civil rights and voting rights laws suggest about how public attitudes about discrimination against African Americans have changed over time?

---

## Answers

**Analyzing Graphs** 30.1 percent; possible benefits of diversity: more opportunity for social and cultural exchange and expression; multiple perspectives and skill sets to contribute to business and society; greater variety in music, dance, theater, architectural styles, cuisine, fashion

**Checkpoint** a person who seeks protection in a new country from war, persecution, or some other danger in the home country

**L3 Differentiate** Have students research the immigration of refugees from a particular country or countries. Ask them to prepare a report that identifies the country or countries the immigrants came from, why they left their home country, the obstacles they faced in getting out of the country of origin or into the United States, how they obtained refugee status in the United States, and, if known, where large numbers of this group have settled in the United States.

## Assess and Remediate

**L2** Have students create a timeline showing the history of discrimination against minority groups and women in the United States.

**L3** Collect the Core Worksheets and assess the students' work.

**L3** Assign the Section 1 Assessment questions.

**L3** Section Quiz A (Unit 5 All-in-One, p. 199)

**L2** Section Quiz B (Unit 5 All-in-One, p. 200)

Have students complete the review activities in the digital lesson presentation and continue their work in the **Essential Questions Journal.**

**Government online** *All print resources are available on the Teacher's Resource Library CD-ROM and online at PearsonSchool.com/phgovt.*

## Answers

**Analyzing Graphs** Sample answer: Women have not yet achieved equality in the workforce based on pay.

---

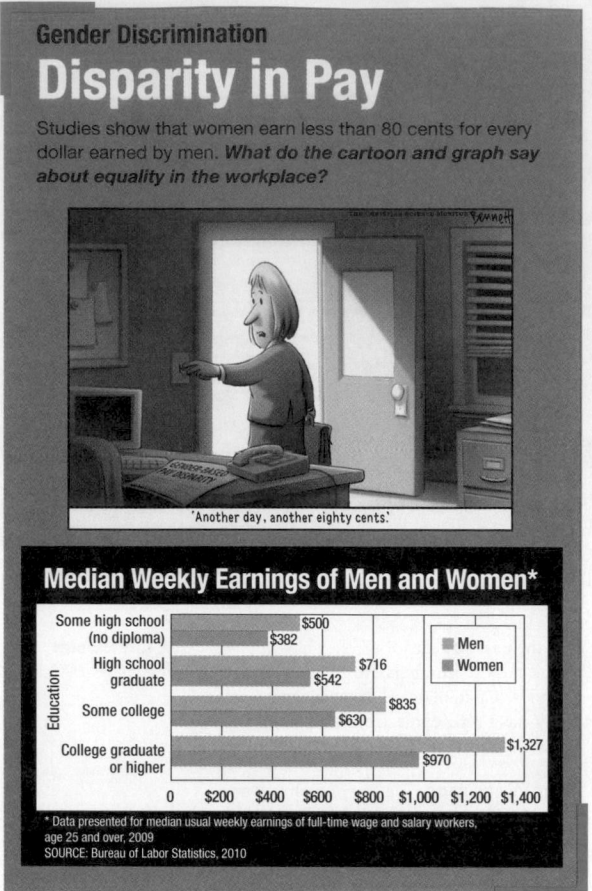

### Gender Discrimination
# Disparity in Pay

Studies show that women earn less than 80 cents for every dollar earned by men. **What do the cartoon and graph say about equality in the workplace?**

'Another day, another eighty cents.'

**Median Weekly Earnings of Men and Women***

| Education | Men | Women |
|---|---|---|
| Some high school (no diploma) | $500 | $382 |
| High school graduate | $716 | $542 |
| Some college | $835 | $630 |
| College graduate or higher | $1,327 | $970 |

*0 $200 $400 $600 $800 $1,000 $1,200 $1,400*

\* Data presented for median usual weekly earnings of full-time wage and salary workers, age 25 and over, 2009
SOURCE: Bureau of Labor Statistics, 2010

**virulent**
*adj.* bitterly antagonistic, spiteful

Act of 1882. Because of this and other governmental actions, only a very small number of Chinese, Japanese, and other Asians were permitted to enter the United States for more than 80 years.

Early in World War II, the Federal Government ordered the evacuation of all persons of Japanese descent from the Pacific Coast. Some 120,000 people, two thirds of them native-born American citizens, were forcibly removed to inland "war relocation camps." Years later, the government conceded that this action had been both unnecessary and unjust.

Congress made dramatic changes in American immigration policies in 1965. Since then, some ten million Asian immigrants have come to this country, mostly from the Philippines, China, Korea, Vietnam, and India. The term "Asian American" encompasses an ever more diverse population. Asian Americans represent a tremendous variety of languages, religions, and cultures, and many recent immigrants from Asia have little in common with one another.

Today, Asian Americans number some 15 million. Asian Americans now live in every part of the United States. They constitute some 40 percent of the population in Hawaii and more than 10 percent of the population in California. New York City boasts the largest Chinese community outside Asia.

### Discrimination Against Women

Unlike the several ethnic groups described thus far, women are not a minority in the United States. They are, in fact, a majority group. Still, traditionally in American law and public policy, women have not enjoyed the same rights as men. Their status was even lower, in many instances, than men who were themselves the target of virulent discrimination. Women have been treated as less than equal in a great many matters—including, for example, property rights, education, and employment opportunities.

Organized efforts to improve the place of women in American society date from July 19, 1848. On that day, a convention on women's rights met in Seneca Falls, New York, and adopted a set of resolutions that deliberately echoed the words of the Declaration of Independence. It began:

> **PRIMARY SOURCE**
> When, in the course of human events, it becomes necessary for one portion of the family of man to assume among the people of the earth a position different from that which they have hitherto occupied, . . . We hold these truths to be self-evident: that all men and women are created equal . . .
> —Declaration of Sentiments, 1848

---

## Background

**ANTISLAVERY AND WOMEN'S RIGHTS** The antislavery movement spurred the women's rights movement, as many abolitionists were women. At the second women's rights convention, which was held in 1850 at Salem, Ohio, speaker J. Elizabeth Jones noted: "It is not Woman's *Rights* of which I design to speak, but of Woman's *Wrongs*. I shall claim nothing for ourselves because of our sex—I shall demand the recognition of no rights on the ground of our womanhood. In the contest which is now being waged in behalf of the enslaved colored man in this land, I have yet to hear the first word in favor of his rights as a colored man; the great point which is sought to be established is this, that the colored man is a human being, and as such, entitled to the free exercise of all the rights which belong to humanity. And we should demand *our* recognition as equal members of the human family. . . ."

Those who fought and finally won the long struggle for women's suffrage believed that, with the vote, women would soon achieve other basic rights. That assumption proved to be false. Although more than 51 percent of the population is now female, women have held only a minor fraction of the nation's top public offices since 1789.

Even today, women hold less than 20 percent of the 535 seats in Congress and a little less than 25 percent of the 7,382 seats in the 50 State legislatures. Only six of the 50 State governors today are female. Women are also hugely underrepresented at the upper levels of corporate management and other power groups in the private sector. Fewer than 20 percent of the nation's doctors, lawyers, and college professors are women.

It is illegal to pay women less than men for the same work. The Equal Pay Act of 1963 requires employers to pay men and women the same wages if they perform the same jobs in the same establishment under the same working conditions. The Civil Rights Act of 1964 also prohibits job discrimination based on sex. Yet, more than 45 years after Congress passed those laws, working women earn, on the average, less than 80 cents for every dollar earned by working men. See the cartoon and graph on page 616.

Women earn less than men for a number of reasons—including the fact that the male

workforce is, overall, better educated and has more job experience than the female workforce. (Note that these factors themselves can often be traced to discrimination.) In addition, some blame the so-called "Mommy track," in which women put their careers on hold to have children or work reduced hours to juggle child-care responsibilities. Others claim that a "glass ceiling" of discrimination in the corporate world and elsewhere, invisible but impenetrable, prevents women from rising to their full potential.

Certainly it is true that until quite recently women were limited to a fairly narrow range of jobs. In many cases, women were encouraged not to work outside the home once they were married. Even now, many jobs held by women are in low-paying clerical and service occupations. The Bureau of Labor Statistics reports that 97 percent of all secretaries today are women; so too are 95 percent of all child-care workers, 92 percent of all registered nurses, 92 percent of all bookkeepers and auditing clerks, 90 percent of all hairdressers and cosmetologists, and 87 percent of all dieticians and nutritionists.

Efforts on behalf of equal rights for women have gained significant ground in recent years. But, recall, that significant ground has not included an Equal Rights Amendment to the Constitution.

✔ **Checkpoint**
What was the significance of the Declaration of Sentiments?

**Essential Questions Journal** To continue to build a response to the chapter Essential Question, go to your **Essential Questions Journal.**

## SECTION 1 ASSESSMENT

1. **Guiding Question** Use your completed graphic organizer to answer this question: How have various minority groups in American society been discriminated against?

**Key Terms and Comprehension**

2. Who are **immigrants?**

3. What event and which amendment outlawed slavery in this country?

4. How are **refugees** similar to and different from other **immigrants?**

5. (a) Identify and describe two laws intended to improve women's wages. (b) Summarize three reasons why women still earn less than men.

**Critical Thinking**

6. **Predict Consequences (a)** What is assimilation? **(b)** What could be the consequences of assimilation on a minority group?

7. **Express Problems Clearly (a)** What problems have Native Americans faced? **(b)** Does the Federal Government have a responsibility to remedy that situation? Why or why not?

**Quick Write**

**Problem-Solution Essay: Identify a Problem** Scan the chapter for a challenge that immigrants, minority Americans, or women face. Write a summary paragraph or two that includes a statement of the problem or challenge and an explanation of why and for whom it is a problem. Look at society as a whole as you consider the matter.

## Answers

**Checkpoint** It was created as a result of the first organized effort to improve the place of women in American society.

# Assessment Answers

1. African American slavery and ongoing discrimination; Native Americans driven from lands by settlers and military and moved to reservations; violence against Chinese immigrant workers in mid-1800s; Chinese Exclusion Act stopped almost all Chinese immigration; Japanese relocation camps during World War II

2. aliens legally admitted as permanent residents

3. Civil War and 13th Amendment

4. **refugees:** forced to leave home country

because of war, persecution, or other danger; **immigrants:** leave home country, but do so voluntarily without seeking refuge

5. **(a) Equal Pay Act of 1963:** Employers must pay men and women the same wages if they perform the same jobs in the same establishment under the same working conditions. **Civil Rights Act of 1964:** prohibits job discrimination based on sex **(b)** Male work force is, overall, better educated with more experience; women put careers on hold to raise children; "glass ceiling" prevents women from rising to their full potential.

6. **(a)** process by which people of one culture merge into and become part of another culture **(b)** may lose cultural history, identity, and values

7. **(a)** poverty, joblessness, alcoholism, lower life expectancy, higher infant mortality **(b)** Answers will vary.

**QUICK WRITE** Remind students to consider the cascading effects on society, such as intolerance or fear, associated with the problem or challenge they identify.

How has the interpretation of the guarantee of equal rights changed over time?

| Equal Protection Clause: | Reasonable Classification: | Rational Basis Test: |
|---|---|---|
| 14th Amendment; no State shall deny to any person the equal protection of the laws | government may classify, but not unreasonably | classification must be reasonably related to achieving proper government purpose |

| Strict Scrutiny Test: | Separate-but-Equal Doctrine: | De Jure, De Facto Segregation: |
|---|---|---|
| in equal protection cases involving fundamental rights or suspect classifications, a "compelling government interest" must justify class distinctions | ruling in *Plessy* v. *Ferguson* that segregation does not violate equal protection if the separate facilities are equal | de jure: segregation authorized by law; de facto: segregation that exists in fact, even if no law requires it |

# Get Started

## LESSON GOALS

Students will . . .

- understand how the Supreme Court interprets "equal protection of the laws" by analyzing and applying the tests it uses to decide cases.

- trace the history of segregation in public schools by creating a timeline of cases related to school integration.

- examine changing attitudes about school integration by evaluating a political cartoon on this topic.

## SKILLS DEVELOPMENT

### ANALYZE TIMELINES

Before students create a timeline of civil rights in this section, you may want to review information on analyzing timelines in the Skills Handbook, p. S29.

---

## SECTION 2

# Equality Before the Law

### Guiding Question

How has the interpretation of the guarantee of equal rights changed over time? Use a flowchart like the one below to take notes on the section.

| Equal Protection Clause | Reasonable Classification | Rational Basis Test |
|---|---|---|

| Strict Scrutiny Test | Separate-but-Equal Doctrine | De Jure, De Facto Segregation |
|---|---|---|

### Political Dictionary

- rational basis test
- strict scrutiny test
- segregation
- Jim Crow
- separate-but-equal doctrine
- integration
- de jure
- de facto

### Objectives

1. Explain the importance of the Equal Protection Clause.
2. Describe the history of segregation in America.
3. Examine how classification by gender relates to discrimination.

**Image Above:** The statue *Freedom*, atop the nation's Capitol

The huge bronze statue of *Freedom* has stood atop the nation's Capitol in Washington, D.C., for about 150 years now. That bold figure is meant to symbolize the basic ideas upon which the United States exists—the concepts of individual liberty, of self-government, and of equal rights for all.

The irony is that records recently unearthed by the Architect of the Capitol show that at least 400 slaves worked on the construction of the Capitol from 1792 to its opening in 1800. And that those slaves cast the huge sculpture of *Freedom*, and even hoisted it atop the new building. Those old documents also record payments to several local slave owners—for example, "To Joseph Forest, for the hire of the Negro Charles." The owners were paid $5 a month for each slave who worked on the project.

## Equal Protection Clause

The equality of all persons, proclaimed so boldly in the Declaration of Independence, is not set out in so many words in the Constitution. Still, that concept pervades the document.

The closest approach to a literal statement of equality is found in the 14th Amendment's Equal Protection Clause. It declares that "No State shall . . . deny to any person within its jurisdiction the equal protection of the laws."

Those words, added to the Constitution in 1868, were originally meant to benefit newly freed slaves. Over time, they have come to mean that the States (and their local governments) cannot draw unreasonable distinctions between any classes of persons. The Supreme Court has often held that the 5th Amendment's Due Process Clause puts the same restriction on the Federal Government.

**Reasonable Classification** Government must have the power to classify, to draw distinctions between persons and groups. Otherwise, it could not possibly regulate human behavior. That is to say, government must be able to *discriminate*—and it does. For example, those who rob banks fall into a special class, and they receive special treatment by government. Clearly, that sort of discrimination is reasonable.

# Focus on the Basics

**FACTS:** • The 14th Amendment guaranteed "equal protection of the laws" to all Americans in 1868, yet many States adopted laws allowing race- and gender-based discrimination. • The Supreme Court established the separate-but-equal doctrine in *Plessy* v. *Ferguson,* but then reversed it in *Brown* v. *Board of Education.* • Since 1971, most laws that treat women differently from men have been successfully challenged in the courts.

**CONCEPTS:** individual rights and responsibilities, equal protection

**ENDURING UNDERSTANDINGS:** • The Constitution describes the equality of all persons in general terms, but the concept pervades the document. • The nation has not yet achieved complete integration of educational systems, but legally enforced racial segregation in public life has been eliminated.

Government may not discriminate *unreasonably*, however. Every State taxes the sale of cigarettes, and so taxes smokers but not non-smokers. No State can tax only blonde smokers, however, or only male smokers.

Over time, the Supreme Court has rejected many equal protection challenges to a wide variety of actions by government. More often than not, however, the Supreme Court has found that what those governments have done is, in fact, constitutional.

**The Rational Basis Test** The Supreme Court most often decides equal protection cases by applying a standard known as the **rational basis test.** This test asks: Does the classification in question bear a reasonable relationship to the achievement of some proper governmental purpose?

A California case, *Michael M.* v. *Superior Court*, 1981, illustrates that test. California law says that a man who has sexual relations with a girl under 18 to whom he is not married can be prosecuted for statutory rape. However, the girl cannot be charged with that crime, even if she is a willing partner. The Court found the law to bear a reasonable relationship to a proper public policy goal: preventing teenage pregnancies.

**The Strict Scrutiny Test** The Court imposes a higher standard in some equal protection cases, however. This is especially true when a case deals with (1) such "fundamental rights" as the right to vote, the right to travel between the States, or 1st Amendment rights; or (2) such "suspect classifications" as those based on race, sex, or national origin.

In these instances, the Court has said that a law must meet a higher standard than the rational basis test: the **strict scrutiny test.** A State must be able to show that some "compelling governmental interest" justifies the distinctions it has drawn between classes of people. Thus, in an alimony case, *Orr* v. *Orr*, 1979, an Alabama law that made women but not men eligible for alimony was held unconstitutional, as a denial of equal protection—because the law's distinction between men and women did not serve any compelling governmental interest.

## Segregation by Race

Beginning in the late 1800s, nearly half the States—including some outside the South—passed racial segregation laws. Used in this context, **segregation** refers to the separation of one group from another on the basis of race. Most of those statutes were **Jim Crow** laws—laws aimed at African Americans in particular. Some were also drawn to affect Mexican Americans, Asian Americans, and Native Americans. They regularly required segregation by race in the use of both public and private facilities: schools, parks and playgrounds, hotels and restaurants, streetcars and railroads, public drinking fountains, restrooms, and cemeteries. Many also prohibited interracial marriages.

**The Separate-but-Equal Doctrine** The Supreme Court provided a constitutional basis for Jim Crow laws by creating the **separate-but-equal doctrine** in 1896. In *Plessy* v. *Ferguson*, the Court upheld a Louisiana law that required segregation in railroad coaches. It ruled that the law did not violate the Equal Protection Clause because the *separate* seating provided for African Americans was *equal* to the seating provided for whites.

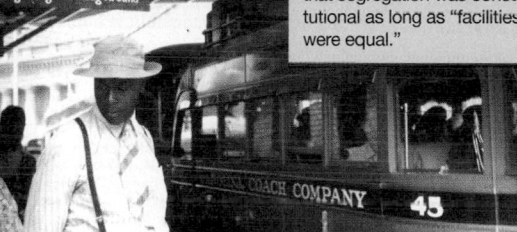

✔ **Checkpoint**
What were Jim Crow laws?

### SUPREME COURT
#### at a glance

▶ **Case:** *Plessy* v. *Ferguson*, 1896
▶ **Issues:** equal protection, constitutionality of segregation
▶ **Decision:** A Louisiana law stated that railway companies had to "provide equal but separate accommodations for the white and colored races." Homer Plessy, who was one-eighth African American, was arrested for refusing to move from a whites-only coach. On appeal, the Supreme Court upheld the law, 7–1, ruling that segregation was constitutional as long as "facilities were equal."

**BEFORE CLASS**

Assign the section, the graphic organizer in the text, and the Reading Comprehension Worksheet (Unit 5 All-in-One, p. 201) before class.

**L2** **Differentiate** Reading Comprehension Worksheet (Unit 5 All-in-One, p. 204)

**BELLRINGER**

Write on the board: **"Our Constitution is color-blind, and neither knows nor tolerates classes among citizens. . . . The humblest is the peer of the most powerful." —Justice John Marshall Harlan, dissenting in *Plessy* v. *Ferguson*, 1896**

**L2** **ELL Differentiate** Explain that one meaning of the word *peer* is "equal."

# Teach

To present this topic using online resources, use the lesson presentations at **PearsonSchool.com/phgovt.**

**DISCUSS THE BELLRINGER**

Ask: **Why is the Constitution "color-blind"?** *(Its laws are to be applied equally, regardless of a person's race or ethnicity.)* Have students paraphrase the second sentence. *(Poor people have the same rights as rich people.)*

**COMPARE RATIONAL BASIS TO STRICT SCRUTINY**

On the board, draw a T-chart like the one below. Have students compare and contrast the two tests the Supreme Court uses to decide whether a law is discriminatory toward one classification (group) or provides equal protection.

| Rational Basis Test | Strict Scrutiny Test |
| --- | --- |
| • least strict or lowest level of scrutiny<br>• Questions considered: Is there a good reason for this law? Does applying this law meet a legitimate or reasonable social or economic purpose that is a goal of government?<br>• The Court rarely overturns legislation using the rational basis test. | • most strict or highest level of scrutiny<br>• Questions considered: Does the law infringe on a fundamental or basic constitutional right? Does the law or policy include a "suspect" or suspicious classification based on race, gender, or national origin? If so, the law is invalid unless the government can show it serves a compelling governmental interest, such as national security.<br>• The Court often overturns laws using the strict scrutiny test. |

# Differentiated Resources

The following resources are located in the All-in-One, Unit 5, Chapter 21, Section 2:

**L3** Reading Comprehension Worksheet (p. 201)
**L2** Reading Comprehension Worksheet (p. 204)
**L3** Core Worksheet (p. 207)
**L3** **L4** Extend Worksheet (p. 208)
**L3** Quiz A (p. 210)
**L2** Quiz B (p. 211)

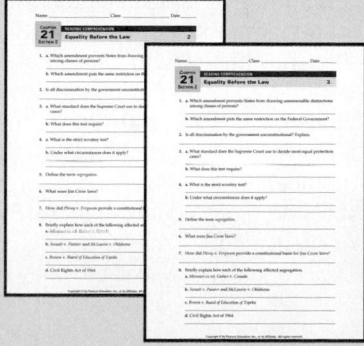

## Answers

**Checkpoint** laws that required segregation by race in public and private facilities

## APPLY RATIONAL BASIS AND STRICT SCRUTINY

Distribute the Chapter 21 Section 2 Core Worksheet (Unit 5 All-in-One, p. 207) or read aloud the following laws or cases and ask students to determine which test the Court would use to analyze them under the Equal Protection Clause. Have students explain their answers.

**1. Seatbelts are mandatory.** *(rational basis; social goal of safety)*

**2. Japanese Americans must relocate to internment camps.** *(strict scrutiny; suspect classification discriminates against national origin and denies freedom of movement; ruling upheld based on national security)*

**3. Virginia law makes interracial marriages illegal.** *(strict scrutiny; suspect classification discriminates against race; law overturned)*

**4. The legal drinking age is raised to 21 years old.** *(rational basis; social goals of health and safety)*

**5. A State law excludes women from jury duty.** *(strict scrutiny; suspect classification discriminates against gender; law overturned because it served no compelling governmental interest)* NOTE: Explain to students that cases involving women's rights were analyzed under the rational basis test from 1789 to the 1970s. The Court followed social norms, which assumed it was rational to protect women and keep them in their "proper sphere."

**6. A white male fights affirmative action policies of law school registration.** *(strict scrutiny; suspect classification discriminates against race)*

**7. Law requires States to use social security numbers when administering welfare benefits.** *(rational basis; economic regulation)*

**8. U.S. Forest Service harvests timber in the National Forest, which disturbs Native American burial grounds.** *(rational basis; economic goal of utilizing federal lands; Court decided that the case did not interfere with fundamental religious rights of Native Americans and so did not warrant strict scrutiny.)*

**L4 Differentiate** Have students research *Korematsu v. United States* (case 2 above), one of the few cases in which the Court allowed a suspect classification to stand. Have students answer these questions: **What justification did the majority give for its decision to allow race-based classification? What was the suspect classification in this case? Do you think the action would pass the strict scrutiny test today? Why or why not?**

---

## Answers

**Checkpoint** Schools had to desegregate.

---

The doctrine was soon extended to other fields. And it stood, largely unchallenged, for nearly 60 years.

**Early Challenges** The Supreme Court first began to chip away at the separate-but-equal doctrine in *Missouri ex rel. Gaines v. Canada* in 1938. Lloyd Gaines, an African American, was denied admission to the law school at the all-white University of Missouri. Gaines was fully qualified for admission—except for his race. The State did not have a separate law school for African Americans. However, it did offer to pay his tuition at a public law school in any of the four neighboring States, which did not discriminate by race. Gaines, however, insisted on a legal education in his home State.

The Court held that the separate-but-equal doctrine left Missouri with two choices: admit Gaines to the State's one law school or establish a separate-but-equal school for him. The State gave in. Gaines was admitted to the university's law school.

Over the next several years, the Court began to insist on equality of separate facilities. Thus, in 1950 the Court decided two major cases in line with its holding in Gaines: *Sweatt v. Painter* and *McLaurin v. Oklahoma.* Both cases involved African American university students for whom a State had provided separate educational facilities. The Court found that, in both instances, those separate facilities were, in fact, far from equal. Still, in neither of these cases did the Court reexamine the validity of the separate-but-equal doctrine.

***Brown v. Board of Education*** Finally, in 1954, the Court reversed *Plessy v. Ferguson.* In *Brown v. Board of Education of Topeka,* it struck down the laws of four States requiring or allowing separate public schools for white and African American students.[4]

Unanimously, the Court held segregation by race in public education to be invalid:

---

4 Kansas, Delaware, South Carolina, and Virginia. On the same day, the High Court also struck down racially segregated public schools in the District of Columbia as a violation of the 5th Amendment, *Bolling v. Sharpe*, 1954.

---

---

**" PRIMARY SOURCE**

**Does segregation of children in public schools solely on the basis of race, even though the physical facilities and other 'tangible' factors may be equal, deprive the children of the minority group of equal educational opportunities? We believe that it does.**

**. . . To separate them from others of similar age and qualifications solely because of their race generates a feeling of inferiority as to their status in the community that may affect their hearts and minds in a way unlikely ever to be undone. . . . Separate educational facilities are inherently unequal.**

**—Chief Justice Earl Warren**

In 1955 the Court directed the States to make "a prompt and reasonable start" to end segregation and to accomplish that goal "with all deliberate speed."

A "reasonable start" was made in Baltimore, Louisville, St. Louis, and elsewhere. In most of the Deep South, however, "massive resistance" soon developed. State legislatures passed laws, and school boards worked to block **integration**—the process of desegregation, of bringing a previously segregated group into the mainstream of society. Most of those efforts were clearly unconstitutional, but challenging them in court proved both costly and slow.

The pace of desegregation quickened after Congress passed the Civil Rights Act of 1964. That act forbids the use of federal funds to aid any State or local activity in which racial segregation is practiced. The statute also directed the Justice Department to file suits to spur desegregation efforts.

The Supreme Court hastened the process in 1969. In a case from Mississippi, *Alexander v. Holmes County Board of Education,* it ruled that, after 15 years, the time for "all deliberate speed" had ended. Said a unanimous Court: "[C]ontinued operation of segregated schools under a standard of allowing 'all deliberate speed' . . . is no longer constitutionally permissible."

---

# Background

**JIM CROW LAWS** From the 1880s into the 1960s, many States enacted Jim Crow laws to promote racial segregation. Here are some samples. "No person . . . shall require any white female nurse to nurse in wards . . . in which negro men are placed." (Alabama) "[I]t shall be unlawful for any amateur colored baseball team to play baseball in any vacant lot or baseball diamond within two blocks of any playground devoted to the white race." (Georgia) "Books shall not be interchangeable between white and colored schools . . . ." (North Carolina) "Any instructor who shall teach in any school . . . where members of the white and colored race are . . . enrolled . . . shall be guilty of a misdemeanor . . . ." (Oklahoma) "Any person . . . who shall be guilty of printing, publishing or circulating . . . matter urging or presenting . . . arguments or suggestions in favor of social equality . . . shall be guilty of a misdemeanor." (Mississippi)

# De Jure Segregation

When the Supreme Court held separate-but-equal facilities to be constitutional in *Plessy* in 1896, the States had the law on their side. Jim Crow laws, named for a character in minstrel shows, limited voting rights and required separate facilities for African Americans. Similar laws legalized Mexican American segregation in Texas and throughout the Southwest. **What federal law quickened the pace of desegregation?**

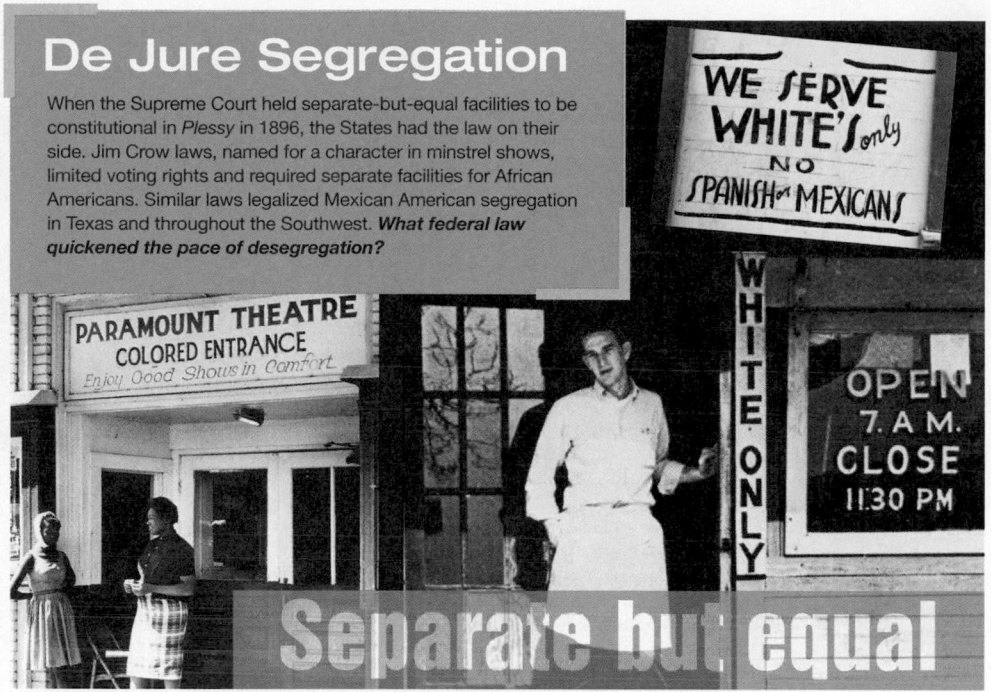

**De Jure, De Facto Segregation** By the fall of 1970, school systems characterized by de jure segregation—segregation authorized by law—had been abolished. That is not to say that desegregation had been fully accomplished, however—far from it.[5]

Many recent integration controversies have arisen in places where the schools have never been segregated by law. They have occurred, instead, in communities in which de facto segregation has long been present, and continues. **De facto** segregation is segregation that exists in fact, even if no law requires it. Housing patterns have most often been its major cause. The concentration of African Americans in certain sections of cities inevitably led to local school systems in

which the student bodies of some schools are largely African American. That condition is quite apparent in many northern as well as southern communities today.

Efforts to desegregate those school systems have taken several forms over recent decades. Thus, for example, school district lines have been redrawn and the busing of students out of racially segregated neighborhoods has been tried. Those efforts have brought strong protests in many places and violence in some of them.

The Court first sanctioned busing in a North Carolina case, *Swann* v. *Charlotte-Mecklenburg Board of Education*, 1971. There it held that: "Desegregation plans cannot be limited to the walk-in school." Busing has been used since then to increase the racial mix in many school districts across the country— in some by court order, in others voluntarily.

In recent years, a growing number of school systems have turned to socioeconomic status—

**sanction**
*v.* to authorize or permit

**socioeconomic**
*adj.* social and economic

---

[5] Some States, several school districts, and many parents and private groups sought to avoid integrated schools through established or, often, newly created private schools. On this point, see the Court's holding in *Runyon* v. *McCrary*, 1976, page 584.

# Background

**INTEGRATING CENTRAL HIGH** Ernest Green, the first black student to graduate from Central High School in Little Rock, Arkansas, recalled his experience: "The *Brown* decision made me feel that the U.S. Constitution was finally working for me. . . . I could believe I was a full citizen, not a second class citizen as segregation had made me feel. . . . Initially, a number of students signed up to enroll, but . . . only nine . . . survived the pressure to quit. . . . [W]hen we tried to attend school, we were met by an angry white mob and armed soldiers. . . . Finally, President Dwight Eisenhower called out the [army] to protect us. . . . Once we got inside, it was like being in a war zone. We were harassed, our books were destroyed. . . . [At graduation] I knew that not only had I achieved something for myself, but I had broken a barrier as well." (Ernest Green, *Perspectives: Readings on Contemporary American Government*)

## ANALYZE A MAP OF SEGREGATION LAWS

Display Transparency 21C, Segregation in 1954. Then ask:

- **How did historical events influence the pattern of segregation?** *(Prior to and during the Civil War, antislavery sentiment was strong in the North. Slavery was critical to the economy of the South, and race-based discrimination was a social norm. After slavery was abolished, State laws mandating segregation continued.)*

- **Where would you expect de jure segregation to be strongest?** *(in the South)*

- **Why do you think the States had many different policies on segregation?** *(Policies reflected local conditions and attitudes toward segregation.)*

- **How did the Court's decision in the *Brown* case change the pattern of regional variations in laws on segregation?** *(made all forms of de jure segregation illegal)*

- **Do you think voluntary desegregation would have occurred over time? Why or why not?**

## CREATE A TIMELINE OF CIVIL RIGHTS

Organize students into six groups to create an illustrated timeline of civil rights. Assign each group one of the cases below. Groups should research, illustrate, and write an extended caption that describes the issues of the case and how it changed the interpretation of "equal protection."

- *Plessy* v. *Ferguson*, 1896 *(ruled that 14th Amendment guarantee of equal protection required equal public facilities for the two races, not equal access to the same facilities)*

- *Missouri ex rel. Gaines* v. *Canada*, 1938 *(acknowledged that separate schools were not equal; required Missouri to admit Gaines to the State's one law school or establish a separate but equal school for Gaines)*

- *Sweatt* v. *Painter*, *McLaurin* v. *Oklahoma*, 1950 *(determined that separate educational facilities were not equal)*

- *Brown* v. *Board of Education*, 1954 *(overruled Plessy v. Ferguson; ruled that racial segregation was inherently unequal)*

- *Alexander* v. *Holmes County Board of Education*, 1969 *(required States to stop delaying and act more aggressively to end segregation; time for "all deliberate speed" was over)*

- *Swann* v. *Charlotte-Mecklenburg Board of Education*, 1971 *(allowed use of busing to increase racial diversity in public schools)*

---

## Answers

**Caption** Civil Rights Act of 1964

**L3** **L4** Have students complete the Chapter 21 Extend Worksheet (Unit 5 All-in-One, p. 208), which compares the dissenting opinion of Justice Harlan in *Plessy* v. *Ferguson* with the majority opinion of Chief Justice Earl Warren in *Brown* v. *Board of Education of Topeka.*

✔**Checkpoint**
Where does the Constitution specifically reference gender?

in particular, to income rather than race—in assigning students to schools within the district. That is, they have tried to promote schools with economically diverse student bodies. The results appear to be promising, both in terms of maintaining integrated schools and in improving the performance of disadvantaged students.

**Segregation in Other Fields** Public schools have not been fully integrated. But legally enforced racial segregation in all other areas of life has been eliminated. In the process, many State and local laws have either been repealed or they have been struck down by the courts.

The Supreme Court took a leading role in that process—holding in a number of cases that segregation by race is unconstitutional in other areas as well. Thus, it has held that the 14th Amendment's Equal Protection Clause forbids segregation in public swimming pools and all other public recreational facilities, *Baltimore* v. *Dawson,* 1955; local transportation, *Gayle* v. *Browder,* 1956; and State prisons and local jails, *Lee* v. *Washington,* 1968.[6] The High Court struck down all State miscegenation laws (statutes forbidding interracial marriages) in *Loving* v. *Virginia,* 1967.

## Classification by Gender

The Constitution speaks of the civil rights of "the people," "persons," and "citizens." Nowhere does it make its guarantees only to "men" or separately to "women." Its only reference to gender is in the 19th Amendment, which forbids denial of the right to vote "on account of sex." Gender has long been used as a basis of classification in the law, however. That practice reflected society's long-held view of the "proper" role of women. Most often, laws that treated men and women differently were intended to protect "the weaker sex." Over the years, the Court read that view into the 14th Amendment.

▲ In response to *United States* v. *Virginia,* 1996, women now attend the Virginia Military Institute.

**First Tests** In the first case to challenge sex discrimination, *Bradwell* v. *Illinois,* 1873, the Court upheld a State law barring women from the practice of law. In that case, Justice Joseph P. Bradley wrote that:

**PRIMARY SOURCE**
**The civil law, as well as nature herself, has always recognized a wide difference in the respective spheres and destinies of man and woman. Man is, or should be, woman's protector and defender. The natural and proper timidity and delicacy which belongs to the female sex evidently unfits it for many of the occupations of civil life.**

—Concurring Opinion

Even as late as 1961, in *Hoyt* v. *Florida,* the Court could find no constitutional fault with a law that required men to serve on juries, but gave women the choice of serving or not.

**Circumstances Today** Matters are far different today. The Court now takes a very close look at cases involving claims of sex discrimination. It first did so in *Reed* v. *Reed,* 1971; there, it struck down an Idaho law that

---

6 *Gayle* v. *Browder* stemmed from the lengthy bus boycott in Montgomery, Alabama—the event that first brought Dr. Martin Luther King, Jr., to national attention.

# Teacher-to-Teacher Network

**ALTERNATE LESSON PLAN** Have your students read Dr. Martin Luther King, Jr.'s "I Have a Dream" speech and his "Letter from Birmingham Jail." Students can work in groups to identify reasons why mainstream society wanted to take desegregation slowly, and reasons why King wanted to speed up the process.

To see this lesson plan, go to

at PearsonSchool.com/phgovt

## Answers

**Checkpoint** only in the 19th Amendment, which forbids denial of the right to vote "on account of sex" gave fathers preference over mothers in the administration of their children's estates.

Since then, the Supreme Court has found a number of sex-based distinctions to be unconstitutional. In *Taylor* v. *Louisiana*, 1975, it held that the 14th Amendment's Equal Protection Clause forbids the States to exclude women from jury service. Among other examples of that line of cases, it struck down an Oklahoma law that prohibited the sale of beer to males under 21 and to females under 18, *Craig* v. *Boren*, 1976. And the Court found the practice of refusing to admit women to the rigorous citizen-soldier program offered by a public institution, the Virginia Military Institute, to be constitutionally unacceptable, *United States* v. *Virginia*, 1996.

The Court's changed attitude in cases involving sex-based discrimination was put this way in the majority opinion in *Frontiero* v. *Richardson* in 1973:[7]

---

[7] In this case, the Court for the first time struck down a federal law providing for sex-based discrimination, as a violation of the 5th Amendment's Due Process Clause. That law gave various housing, medical, and other allowances to a serviceman for his wife and other dependents, but it made those same allowances available to a servicewoman only if her husband was dependent on her for more than half of his support.

Not all sex-based distinctions are unconstitutional, however. The Court has upheld a Florida law that gives an extra property tax exemption to widows, but not to widowers, *Kahn* v. *Shevin*, 1974; an Alabama law forbidding women to serve as prison guards in all-male penitentiaries, *Dothard* v. *Rawlinson*, 1977; and the federal selective service law that requires only men to register for the draft and excludes women from any future draft, *Rostker* v. *Goldberg*, 1981.

In effect, these cases say this: Classification by gender is not in and of itself unconstitutional. However, laws that treat men and women differently will be overturned by the courts unless (1) they are intended to serve an "important governmental objective" and (2) they are "substantially related" to achieving that goal.

**✓ Checkpoint**
What does the Court say today about gender-based discrimination?

---

# SECTION 2 ASSESSMENT

**Essential Questions Journal** To continue to build a response to the chapter Essential Question, go to your **Essential Questions Journal.**

1. **Guiding Question** Use your completed graphic organizer to answer this question: How has the interpretation of the guarantee of equal rights changed over time?

**Key Terms and Comprehension**

2. **(a)** What does the 14th Amendment's Equal Protection Clause say? **(b)** To whom was it originally directed?

3. **(a)** What two tests does the High Court use when deciding equal protection cases? **(b)** How do the tests differ? **(c)** Summarize two cases that illustrate those tests.

4. **(a)** What is **integration? (b)** Which Supreme Court case led to public school integration?

5. **(a)** What is the difference between **de jure** and **de facto** segregation?

**(b)** What actions have school systems taken, voluntarily or otherwise, to end de facto segregation?

**Critical Thinking**

6. **Draw Conclusions (a)** Why do you think the Supreme Court was vague about the time frame in which to end segregation ("with all deliberate speed")? **(b)** How did the Civil Rights Act of 1964 speed up the process of integration?

7. **Recognize Bias (a)** What do you suppose Justice Bradley meant by separate "spheres and destinies of man and woman"? **(b)** Which gender-based distinctions are considered constitutional today? **(c)** Do you agree or disagree with those distinctions?

**Quick Write**

**Problem-Solution Essay: Consider Solutions** Use the problem you identified in Section 1 and research possible solutions to that problem. What solutions have been tried successfully? Unsuccessfully? Construct a chart to evaluate the pros and cons of each solution.

---

# Assess and Remediate

**L3** Collect the Core Worksheet and assess students' work.

**L3** Assign the Section 2 Assessment questions.

**L3** Quiz A (Unit 5 All-in-One, p. 210)

**L2** Quiz B (Unit 5 All-in-One, p. 211)

Have students complete the review activities in the digital lesson presentation and continue their work in the **Essential Questions Journal.**

**REMEDIATION**

| If Your Students Have Trouble With | Strategies For Remediation |
|---|---|
| Understanding equal protection issues (Questions 1, 2, 3) | Have students select five cases in the Supreme Court Glossary and determine which test the Court would use to analyze them under the Equal Protection Clause. Remind students that economic or social regulations generally fall under the rational basis test; constitutional or racial issues receive strict scrutiny. |
| History and types of segregation (Questions 4, 5, 6) | Have students illustrate a "path" of desegregation, beginning with *Plessy* v. *Ferguson* and citing the cases and acts in this section. |
| Gender-based discrimination (Question 7) | Ask students to modernize the "separate spheres" argument by finding photos or drawings showing then and now images of women in the home, school, workplace, sports, and so on. Students should label the visuals with cases that expanded women's rights. |

---

# Answers

**Checkpoint** It must serve an "important governmental objective" and be "substantially related" to achieving that goal.

---

# Assessment Answers

1. Historically, *equal rights* applied only to white males. Today the phrase applies to minorities and women as well.

2. **(a)** "No State shall . . . deny to any person within its jurisdiction the equal protection of the laws." **(b)** newly freed slaves

3. **(a)** rational basis and strict scrutiny **(b)** rational basis: applied to cases that achieve a governmental purpose or public policy goal; strict scrutiny: applied to cases about fundamental rights or suspect classifications **(c)** *Michael M.* v. *Superior Court*, 1981, based on goal of preventing teenage pregnancies; *Orr* v. *Orr*, 1979, alimony only for women held unconstitutional, does not serve compelling governmental interest

4. **(a)** process of desegregation **(b)** *Brown* v. *Board of Education of Topeka*, 1954

5. **(a)** de jure: segregation by law; de facto: segregation in fact, even if no law requires it **(b)** school district lines redrawn, students bused out of segregated neighborhoods, assigning students to schools based on socioeconomic status to achieve economic diversity

6. **(a)** possible answer: to allow local communities time to develop orderly plans to implement desegregation smoothly **(b)** forbade the use of federal funds to any State or local activity in which racial segregation was practiced

7. **(a)** possible answer: each gender group has its own place in society **(b)** extra property tax exemption to widows, women forbidden to serve as prison guards in all-male penitentiaries, women excluded from the draft **(c)** Answers will vary.

**QUICK WRITE** Remind students to list both strengths and weaknesses of possible solutions.

# Get Started

## LESSON GOAL

- Students will examine the Supreme Court case *Brown* v. *Board of Education* by analyzing the arguments from both sides and considering initial reactions to the Court's ruling.

## BEFORE CLASS

Have students read the feature as homework or at the beginning of class.

# Teach

### STUDY AND BRAINSTORM ARGUMENTS

Have volunteers read aloud the arguments in the text for Brown and then for the Board of Education. Ask: **Which single argument would most compel you to support one side or the other? Why?** Then ask students to brainstorm additional arguments for Brown, and list these on the board. Do the same for Board of Education. The 14th Amendment states that people should be treated equally; it does not state that people should be treated the same. Ask: **How would you refute each argument from the opposing side?**

## SKILLS DEVELOPMENT

### COMPARE VIEWPOINTS

Before students discuss reactions to the *Brown* ruling, you may want to review information on comparing viewpoints in the Skills Handbook p. S15.

---

# Is Segregation in Schools Constitutional?

The Supreme Court ruled unanimously that it was not. Third-grader Linda Brown who lived in Topeka, Kansas, had to walk a mile through a dangerous railroad yard and then take a bus to get to school. There was another school much closer to her home, but school officials would not allow her to attend that school because it was reserved for white students only. Separate elementary schools for whites and nonwhites were maintained by Topeka's Board of Education.

Oliver Brown, Linda's father, turned to the local chapter of the National Association for the Advancement of Colored People (NAACP) for help. The Topeka chapter of the NAACP believed it had the "right plaintiff at the right time," and used Brown's complaint, along with those of 13 other African American parents in Topeka, to take the case for school desegregation to the United States District Court for the District of Kansas. In the early 1950s, segregation of the races was legal, and in some States, required. Kansas gave local school districts a choice of integrating their schools. Like many States at the time, however, it chose segregation with the condition that the minority schools were to be equal to the white schools. The District Court felt "compelled" to rule in favor of the Board of Education, citing *Plessy* v. *Ferguson,* which allowed separate but equal facilities. The NAACP appealed the case to the Supreme Court, where it was combined with three other cases calling for school desegregation in Delaware, South Carolina, and Virginia.

In a unanimous 9–0 decision, the Supreme Court overturned the "separate but equal" doctrine. Chief Justice Earl Warren delivered the opinion of the Court: "we

Before *Brown,* schools designated for African Americans were separate but definitely not equal in such terms as buildings, library resources, and teachers' salaries.

Linda Brown was the subject of the landmark case. The case was a class action suit, but Oliver Brown was deliberately named plaintiff because he was male.

# Supreme Court Notes

**CONNECTION TO *PLESSY*** Although many editorials at the time hailed the Supreme Court decision in *Brown* as a healing democratic action, others were bitter that the Court dared to legislate social norms. This attitude had been introduced in Justice Henry Brown's majority opinion in *Plessy* v. *Ferguson* 60 years earlier. He stated that Plessy's argument "assumes that social prejudices may be overcome by legislation, and that equal rights cannot be secured to the Negro except by an enforced commingling of the two races. We cannot accept this proposition. If the two races are to meet upon terms of social equality, it must be the result of natural affinities, a mutual appreciation of each other's merits, and a voluntary consent of individuals."

cannot turn the clock back to 1868 when the [14th] Amendment was adopted, or even to 1896 when *Plessy v. Ferguson* was written. We must consider public education in the light of its full development and its present place in American life throughout the Nation. Only in this way can it be determined if segregation in public schools deprives these plaintiffs of the equal protection of the laws. . . .

We come then to the question presented: Does segregation of children in public schools solely on the basis of race, even though the physical facilities and other 'tangible' factors may be equal, deprive the children of the minority group of equal educational opportunities? We believe that it does. . . . To separate them from others of similar age and qualifications solely because of their race generates a feeling of inferiority as to their status in the community that may affect their hearts and minds in a way unlikely ever to be undone. . . . We conclude that in the field of public education the doctrine of 'separate but equal' has no place. Separate educational facilities are inherently unequal."

**GOVERNMENT** ONLINE
**In the News**
To learn more about the relevance of the case today, go to
**PearsonSchool.com/phgovt**

### Arguments for Brown

- Segregating African American students from white students makes them feel inferior.
- A sense of inferiority affects a child's motivation to learn.
- Segregation results in the fundamentally unequal education of minority students.

### Arguments for Board of Education of Topeka

- Minority schools in Topeka are equal in every way to, and sometimes have better programs than, schools for whites.
- There is no conclusive evidence that segregation by race affects the education of children.
- Segregated schools prepare black children for the segregated society they will face in adulthood.

**Thinking Critically**

1. On what basis did the District Court reach its decision? On what basis did the Supreme Court reach its decision?
2. **Constitutional Principles** How does this case reflect the principle of equal protection?

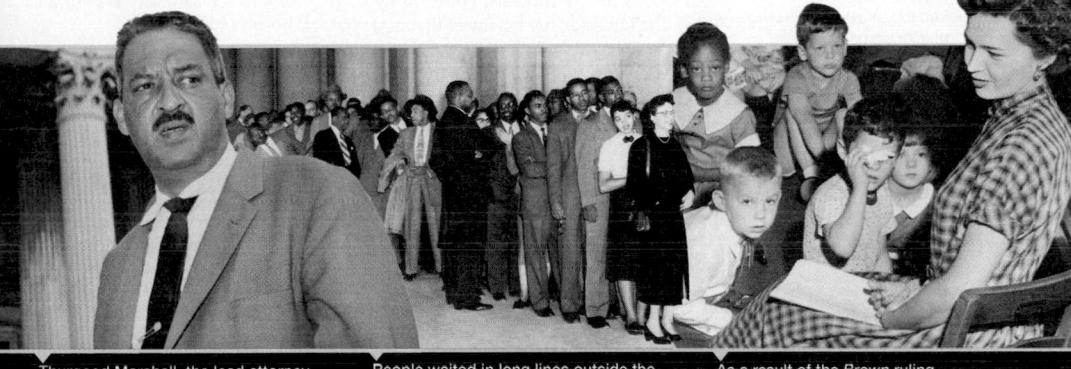

Thurgood Marshall, the lead attorney who argued for desegregation, would become the first African American Supreme Court justice in 1967.

People waited in long lines outside the Supreme Court building, hoping for the opportunity to hear the Court deliver its opinion in this landmark case.

As a result of the *Brown* ruling, classrooms across the country were required to desegregate.

625

## Background

**THE DOLL TEST** In its argument before the Court, the NAACP introduced many sociological tests to prove that school segregation was psychologically harmful to African American children. In Footnote 11 of the *Brown* opinion, Dr. Kenneth Clark is listed. In the early 1950s, he and his wife Mamie performed a series of tests involving black and white dolls. African American children were asked to point to the "good" doll, and the majority pointed to the white doll. The tests had an impact on the Court's decision. The sociological tests are controversial today, however, with historians citing their use as nonscientific.

### DISCUSS INITIAL REACTION

Ask students what they think initial white reactions were to the *Brown* ruling. *(Many in the South were shocked and angered.)* Have students consider reaction to the ruling from an African American student who would face prejudice at a desegregated school, and from an African American teacher who likely faced unemployment.

**L3 Differentiate** Have students suppose that they are parents of a minority high school student who enters a formerly segregated school. Ask them to answer the following question: **How would you prepare your child to face a racially charged environment?**

### RESEARCH ACCOMPANYING CASES

Organize students into three groups, and have each group research the following cases that were ultimately combined with *Brown:* in Delaware, *Gebhart v. Belton;* in South Carolina, *Briggs v. Elliott;* and in Virginia, *Davis v. County School Board of Prince Edward County.* Groups should provide information regarding the plaintiffs, their actions, and the case's path to the Supreme Court.

**L3 Differentiate** Have groups present their cases as interviews or oral histories. The Web site of the University of Michigan Digital Archive: *Brown v. Board of Education* has sample oral histories.

### EXTEND THE LESSON

**L3 L4 Differentiate** Assign the Landmark Decisions of the Supreme Court Worksheet (Unit 5 All-in-One, p. 229).

**L2 Differentiate** Assign the adapted Landmark Decisions of the Supreme Court Worksheet (Unit 5 All-in-One, p. 231).

## Assess and Remediate

Have students summarize the majority opinion of the Court. Ask them to explain the significance of the unanimous ruling of the justices.

Correct students' answers to the Thinking Critically questions.

### IN THE NEWS

Students can learn more about *Brown v. Board of Education* at **PearsonSchool.com/phgovt**

### Answers

1. the *Plessy v. Ferguson* precedent that allowed separate but equal facilities; on intangible factors such as segregation generating feelings of inferiority
2. By desegregating schools, all students are provided with equal access to education.

## What is the history of civil rights legislation from Reconstruction to today?

Sample answers for timeline:

**1964** Civil Rights Act

**1968** Civil Rights Act (Open Housing Act)

**1972** Title IX of Education Amendments

**1978** *Regents of the University of California v. Bakke*

# Get Started

## LESSON GOALS

Students will . . .

- trace the development of civil rights legislation by relating it to historical actions of States designed to nullify African Americans' rights.

- analyze the policy of affirmative action and why it is controversial by studying political cartoons and by exploring the issues surrounding it.

## BEFORE CLASS

Assign the section, the graphic organizer in the text, and the Reading Comprehension Worksheet (Unit 5 All-in-One, p. 212) before class.

**L2 Differentiate** Reading Comprehension Worksheet (Unit 5 All-in-One, p. 213)

## BELLRINGER

Check students' prior knowledge by displaying Transparency 21D, which is a quote from President Lyndon Johnson. Have students answer the questions in their notebooks.

## SKILLS DEVELOPMENT

## ANALYZE IMAGES

To practice analyzing images in this section, use the Chapter 21 Skills Worksheet (Unit 5 All-in-One, p. 217). You may want to teach the skill explicitly before discussing civil rights and voter rights legislation. For L2 and L1 students, assign the adapted Skill Activity (Unit 5 All-in-One, p. 218).

---

SECTION 3

# Federal Civil Rights Laws

### Guiding Question

**What is the history of civil rights legislation from Reconstruction to today?** Use a timeline like the one below to take notes on the section.

| 1964 | 1968 | 1972 | 1978 |

### Political Dictionary

- affirmative action
- quota
- reverse discrimination

### Objectives

1. Outline the history of civil rights legislation from the Reconstruction period on to today.
2. Explore the issues surrounding affirmative action.

**Image Above:** Dr. Martin Luther King, Jr., acknowledges the crowd at his "I Have a Dream" speech, August 28, 1963.

Those who, for one reason or another, oppose the enactment of civil rights legislation often rely on this observation: "You can't legislate morality." That is, racism, sexism, and other forms of discrimination will not be eliminated by simply passing a law.

The Reverend Dr. Martin Luther King, Jr., responded to that contention this way: "Judicial decrees," he said, "may not change the heart, but they can restrain the heartless." Clearly, Congress has agreed with Dr. King—as it has enacted a number of civil rights laws over the past 40 years or so.

## Civil Rights: Reconstruction to Today

From the 1870s to the late 1950s, Congress did not pass a single piece of meaningful civil rights legislation. Several factors contributed to that fact. Among the major ones: Through that period, the nation's predominantly white population was generally unaware of or little concerned with the plight of African Americans, Native Americans, or other nonwhites in this country. And southern white Democrats, bolstered by such devices as the seniority system and the filibuster, held many of the most strategic posts in Congress.

That historic logjam was finally broken in 1957, largely as a result of the pressures brought to bear by the civil rights movement led by Dr. King (see Chapter 6, Section 3). Beginning in that year, Congress passed a number of civil rights laws—notably, the Civil Rights Acts of 1957, 1960, 1964, and 1968; the Voting Rights Acts of 1965, 1970, 1975, 1982, and 2006; and Title IX in the Education Amendments of 1972.[8]

**The Civil Rights Act of 1964** The 1964 law is the most far-reaching of those statutes. It was passed after the longest debate in Senate history (83 days), and only after the Senate invoked cloture (limited debate) to kill a filibuster.

---

8 The 1957 and 1960 laws set up modest safeguards for the right to vote. You considered the voting rights provision in those statutes in Chapter 6, Section 3. The 1957 law created the U.S. Commission on Civil Rights. The commission is an independent eight-member executive branch agency that is supposed to monitor the enforcement of the various civil rights laws, investigate cases of alleged discrimination, and report its findings to the President, Congress, and the public.

---

# Focus on the Basics

**FACTS:** • Beginning in 1957, Congress passed several acts to guarantee the civil rights of African Americans, other minorities, and women. • The policy of affirmative action requires most employers to take positive steps to remedy the effects of past discrimination. • Supporters and critics of affirmative action have taken their debate to the Supreme Court, Congress, State legislatures, and the voting booth.

**CONCEPTS:** individual rights and responsibilities, equal protection

**ENDURING UNDERSTANDINGS:** • Congress passed civil rights laws to carry out the Constitution's insistence on the equality of all before the law. • The controversy surrounding affirmative action continues today.

Beyond its voting rights provisions, the 1964 law outlaws discrimination in a number of areas. With its several later amendments, the law's major sections now:

• provide that no person may be denied access to or refused service in various "public accommodations"—hotels, motels, restaurants, theaters, and the like—because of race, color, religion, national origin, or physical disability (Title II).[9]

• prohibit discrimination against any person on grounds of race, color, religion, national origin, sex, or physical disability in any program that receives any federal funding (Title VI).

• forbid both employers and labor unions to discriminate against any person on grounds of race, color, religion, sex, physical disability, or age in job-related matters (Title VII).[10]

**The Civil Rights Act of 1968** The Civil Rights Act of 1968 is often called the Open Housing Act. With minor exceptions, it forbids anyone to refuse to sell or rent a dwelling to any person on grounds of race, color, religion, national origin, sex, or disability. It also forbids refusal to sell or rent to a family with children.

At first, the burden of enforcing the law fell on those persons who claimed to be victims of housing discrimination; they could seek damages from alleged offenders. Congress finally strengthened the law in 1988, to allow the Justice Department to bring criminal charges against those who violate its terms. Still, housing remains among the most segregated areas of American life today.

**Title IX** In Title IX of the Education Amendments of 1972, Congress added a key gender-based guarantee to the provisions of the Civil Rights Act of 1964. Title IX forbids discrimination on the basis of gender "in any education program or activity receiving Federal financial assistance." The statute intends to ensure that women receive equal treatment in all aspects of education. Its provisions apply to all schools, public and private, that receive federal funds, and nearly all of them do.

Since its passage, Title IX has had its most telling effect on school athletics programs, especially at the college level, by requiring roughly equal funding and opportunities for women and men. The law has been in effect for nearly four decades now; still, it continues to generate controversy.

## Affirmative Action

These civil rights statutes all come down to this: Discriminatory practices based on such factors as race, color, national origin, sex, or disability are illegal. But what about the effects of *past* discrimination? Consider an African American who, for no reason of his or her own making, did not get a decent education and so today cannot get a decent job. Of what real help to that person are all of those laws that make illegal today what was done years ago?

So far, the Federal Government's chief answer to this troubling question has been a policy of **affirmative action**. That approach requires that most employers take positive steps (affirmative action) to remedy the effects of past discriminations. The policy applies to all agencies of the Federal Government, States and their local governments, and private employers who sell goods or services to any agency of the Federal

✔**Checkpoint**
What is the Civil Rights Act of 1968?

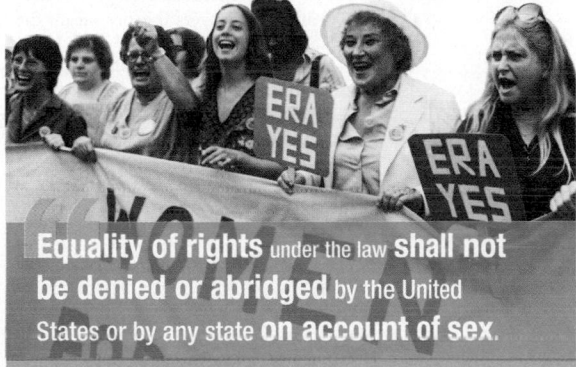

These words would have been added to the Constitution if three additional States had ratified the Equal Rights Amendment (ERA). *Why do you think the ERA was not ratified?*

Equality of rights under the law **shall not be denied or abridged** by the United States or by any state **on account of sex.**

---

[9] Congress based this section of the law on its commerce power. See Chapter 11, Section 1. Title II covers those places in which lodgings are offered to transient guests and those where a significant portion of the items sold have moved in interstate commerce. The Supreme Court upheld Title II and the use of the Commerce Clause as a basis for civil rights legislation in *Heart of Atlanta Motel, Inc. v. United States,* 1964.

[10] The five-member Equal Employment Opportunity Commission (EEOC), an independent executive branch agency, enforces Title VII.

---

# Differentiated Resources

The following resources are located in the All-in-One, Unit 5, Chapter 21, Section 3:

---

# Teach

To present this topic using online resources, use the lesson presentations at **PearsonSchool.com/phgovt.**

### DISCUSS BELLRINGER RESPONSES

Have students share their answers to the Bellringer. *(1. civil rights demonstrations; 2. African Americans were not "trained" for the "race" and so should be given an advantage now. 3. affirmative action)*

### RELATE ACTIONS TO LEGISLATION

Ask: **Why were so many civil rights and voting rights laws needed?** Discuss the actions that States took to nullify African American voting and other rights: poll taxes; literacy tests; vouchers of "good character" needed; the white primary; voter registration grandfather clauses; gerrymandered or annexed election districts to reduce African American voting strength and to minimize the number of black elected officials. Then have students cite federal legislation and Court cases from the section that tried to remedy this discrimination. On the board, list students' citations as well as the legislation below. Point out how federal responses to these actions began slowly on a case-by-case basis before being expanded to nationwide jurisdiction.

**Civil Rights Act of 1957:** Attorney General given authority to begin lawsuits against local violations of the 15th Amendment

**Civil Rights Act of 1960:** federal courts could appoint referees to conduct voter registration, but only after a judicial finding of voting discrimination

**Voting Rights Act of 1965:** strengthened enforcement of the 15th Amendment nationwide; prohibited all literacy requirements for voting; federal examiners ensured registration; federal observers oversaw elections; in certain jurisdictions, any changes in voting procedures had to be approved by the Federal Government

**1975:** amendments to 1965 law added voting protections for Hispanic, Asian, and Native American citizens

---

# Answers

**Checkpoint** called Open Housing Act; forbids anyone to refuse to sell or rent a dwelling to any person on grounds of race, color, religion, national origin, sex, disability, or families with children

**Caption** because women's rights were already protected as "citizens' rights"

Organize students into four groups, and have them prepare to debate the issue of affirmative action from one of these points of view:

• Dr. Martin Luther King, Jr.
• Allan Bakke
• White high school senior who wants to enter college
• Minority high school senior who wants to enter college

Have students use the Debate strategy (p. T25) to formulate their arguments. Distribute the Chapter 21 Section 3 Core Worksheet (Unit 5, All-in-One, p. 215), which helps students prepare for the debate. Groups should summarize the validity of affirmative action from their point of view. Students should make strong arguments with supporting information from the Constitution and Court precedents. After the debate, debrief the activity, allowing students to state which perspectives used the best evidence to prove their point.

## Answers

**Analyzing Timelines** By holding that race could be a narrowly tailored factor in affirmative action decisions, the Court left the door open to future interpretations.

# Equal Rights and Affirmative Action

## 1900s

**1954** In *Brown* v. *Board of Education*, the Court overrules *Plessy*, holding that separate-but-equal public schools are unconstitutional.

**1964** Civil Rights Act of 1964 outlaws discrimination in several key areas.

**1965** Voting Rights Act protects minorities against racial discrimination in voting.

**1965** President Johnson's Executive Order 11246 requires equal opportunity in federal hiring practices.

**1972** Title IX of the Education Amendments forbids gender discrimination in all federally funded educational programs.

**1978** In *Regents of the University of California* v. *Bakke*, the Court rules that affirmative action is acceptable, but strict quotas are not.

▲ Martin Luther King, Jr. leads a march in Washington, D.C. to promote equal rights in 1963.

▸▸ **Analyzing Timelines** Affirmative action programs arose in the 1960s to help rectify the harm suffered by minorities as a result of discrimination. *How did the two Michigan cases in 2003 leave the legal status of affirmative action unsettled?*

Government. The Federal Government began to demand the adoption of affirmative action programs in 1965.

To illustrate the policy, take the case of a company that does business with the Federal Government. It must adopt an affirmative action plan designed to make its workforce reflect the general makeup of the population in its locale. The plan must include steps to correct or prevent inequalities in such matters as pay, promotions, and fringe benefits.

For many employers this has meant that they must hire and/or promote more workers with minority backgrounds and more females. The share of a group necessary to satisfy a particular affirmative action requirement—say, the number of females in a company's workforce or the number of African Americans in a school's student body—is often called a **quota.**

**Reverse Discrimination?** Affirmative action policies remain highly controversial today. This is principally because those policies necessarily involve race-based and/or gender-based classifications.

Critics argue that affirmative action programs amount to **reverse discrimination,** or discrimination against the majority group. Affirmative action demands that preference be given to females and/or nonwhites solely on the basis of sex or race. Critics say that the Constitution requires that all public policies be "color blind."

The opponents of affirmative action have attacked the policy at the State and local levels in several places in recent years. Most often, they have relied primarily on the reverse discrimination argument as they have done so.

In 1996, California's voters gave overwhelming approval to a measure that eliminated nearly all affirmative action programs conducted by public agencies in that State. Since then, the voters in Washington (in 1998), Michigan (in 2004), and Nebraska (in 2008) have adopted measures similar to California's.

**The Bakke Case** The Supreme Court decided its first major affirmative action case, *Regents of the University of California* v. *Bakke*, in 1978. Allan Bakke, a white male, had been denied admission to the university's medical school at Davis. The school had set aside 16 of the 100 seats in each year's entering class for nonwhite students. He sued the university, charging it with reverse discrimination and,

# Political Cartoon Mini-Lesson

**THE EQUAL RIGHTS AMENDMENT** Congress passed the ERA in 1972 with a seven-year deadline for ratification. A three-year extension was added in 1979. Only 35 of the required 38 States approved it, however, so the ERA failed. Display Transparency 21E, Equal Rights Amendment. Ask: **Why do you think some women opposed the ERA?** *(They believed the ERA would take away traditional women's rights, such as alimony and all-female colleges. They also believed women might get drafted into the armed forces.)* **According to the cartoon, what is ironic about the ERA's failure to pass from the point of view of one woman's employment?** *(She must go to her low-paying, menial job cleaning the floors.)* Have students debate this topic: **Does the United States still need an Equal Rights Amendment to guarantee the rights of women?**

▲ Title IX increased opportunities for women to participate in sports.

## 2000s

**2003** The Court finds that a State university may take race into account in admitting students, *Grutter* v. *Bollinger*, but it may not blindly give extra weight to race in that process, *Gratz* v. *Bollinger*.

**2007** In *Parents Involved* v. *Seattle School District* and *Meredith* v. *Jefferson County*, Court overturns school integration policies that it holds, 5–4, rely too heavily on race.

**2009** The Court bans the use of race as the sole factor in promotions, *Ricci* v. *DeStefano*.

**1990** Americans with Disabilities Act prohibits discrimination on the basis of disability.

**1995** In *Adarand Constructors* v. *Pena*, the Court finds that affirmative action programs will be upheld only if shown to serve some "compelling government interest."

**GOVERNMENT** ONLINE
For an **interactive** version of this timeline, visit PearsonSchool.com/phgovt
INTERACTIVE

so, a violation of the Equal Protection Clause. By a 5–4 majority, the Court held that Bakke had been denied equal protection and should be admitted to the medical school.

A differently composed 5–4 majority made the more far-reaching ruling in the case, however. Although the Constitution does not allow race to be used as the *only* factor in the making of affirmative action decisions, that majority of the justices held that both the Constitution and the 1964 Civil Rights Act do allow its use as one among several factors in such situations.

**Later Cases** The Supreme Court has decided several affirmative action cases since *Bakke*. In some of them it has upheld quotas, especially in such industries as construction, where longstanding discrimination was involved. The High Court has also held, however, that quotas can be used in only the most extreme situations. Thus, the Court held in *Richmond* v. *Croson*, 1989, that the city of Richmond, Virginia, had not shown that its minority set-aside policy was justified by a record of past discrimination by the city.

This approach has become steadily more apparent in recent affirmative action decisions. In 1995, for example, the Court's decision in *Adarand Constructors* v. *Pena*

marked a major departure from its previous rulings in such cases. *Adarand* arose when a white-owned Colorado company, Adarand Constructors, Inc., challenged a federal affirmative action policy. Under that policy, the government gave bonuses to highway contractors if 10 percent or more of their construction work was subcontracted to "socially and economically disadvantaged" businesses, including those owned by racial minorities.

Until *Adarand*, the Court had regularly upheld affirmative action laws, regulations, and programs as mild but necessary restraints on behavior. In this case, however, the Court held that henceforth all affirmative action cases will be reviewed under strict scrutiny— that is, affirmative action programs will be upheld only if it can be shown that they serve some "compelling government interest." (See page 619.)

"The Constitution protects persons, not groups," wrote Justice Sandra Day O'Connor in the majority opinion. "Whenever the government treats any person unequally because of his or her race, that person has suffered an injury" covered by "the Constitution's guarantee of equal treatment." Affirmative action programs must be "narrowly tailored" to overcome specific cases of discrimination.

## Background

**AMERICANS WITH DISABILITIES** Inspired by the civil rights movement, people with disabilities pushed for equal treatment. Their efforts led to passage of the Individuals with Disabilities Education Act (IDEA) in 1975 (revised substantially in 1997 and 2004). IDEA guarantees free appropriate public education to children with disabilities. The law guides schools in crafting an individualized education program (IEP) for each child with a disability. In 1990, Congress passed the Americans with Disabilities Act (ADA), banning discrimination against people with disabilities in employment, public services, public accommodations, and telecommunications. The law requires employers to make "reasonable accommodation," which may include making existing facilities accessible (such as by installing a wheelchair ramp), modifying the job or work schedule, acquiring devices, or modifying equipment and training.

Tell students to go to the Interactivity for an interactive version of the timeline regarding equal rights and affirmative action.

### EXTEND THE LESSON

**L3 Differentiate** Have students work in pairs to research the annual increase in African American voter registration after 1965, following the passage of the Civil Rights Acts and Voting Rights Acts. Students should put the information they find into a bar graph on poster board with an appropriate title.

**L2 LPR ELL Differentiate** Provide students with the statistics below showing changes in voter registration from 1965 to 1988. Have them calculate the "gap" columns. Ask: **Which State had the largest gap in 1965?** *(Mississippi)* **in 1988?** *(North Carolina)*

| | Voter Registration Rates (1965 vs. 1988) | | | | | |
|---|---|---|---|---|---|---|
| | March 1965 | | | November 1988 | | |
| | Black | White | Gap | Black | White | Gap |
| AL | 19.3 | 69.2 | 49.9 | 68.4 | 75.0 | 6.6 |
| GA | 27.4 | 62.6 | 35.2 | 56.8 | 63.9 | 7.1 |
| LA | 31.6 | 80.5 | 48.9 | 77.1 | 75.1 | -2.0 |
| MS | 6.7 | 69.9 | 63.2 | 74.2 | 80.5 | 6.3 |
| NC | 46.8 | 96.8 | 50.0 | 58.2 | 65.6 | 7.4 |
| SC | 37.3 | 75.7 | 38.4 | 56.7 | 61.8 | 5.1 |
| VA | 38.3 | 61.1 | 22.8 | 63.8 | 68.5 | 4.7 |

Adapted from *Minority Representation and the Quest for Voting Equality* by Bernard Grofman, Lisa Handley and Richard G. Niemi (New York: Cambridge Press, 1992).

## Assess and Remediate

**L3** Ask students to write a paragraph answering the Chapter Essential Question: **Why are there ongoing struggles for civil rights?** Have students consider such factors as political, economic, or security concerns; the emergence of minority leaders with the determination, skills, and resources to work for change; and the role of the media in making the public aware of discrimination or the effects of discrimination.

**L3** Collect the Core Worksheets and assess students' responses to the questions.

**L3** Assign the Section 3 Assessment questions.

**L3** Quiz A (Unit 5 All-in-One, p. 219)

**L2** Quiz B (Unit 5 All-in-One, p. 220)

Have students complete the review activities in the digital lesson presentation and continue their work in the **Essential Questions Journal.**

| If Your Students Have Trouble With | Strategies For Remediation |
|---|---|
| Civil rights legislation (Questions 1, 2, 5) | Have students create annotated timelines of civil rights legislation from Reconstruction to today. Timelines should include brief descriptions of each law or act, how it was decided, and how it relates to other laws or acts on the timeline. |
| Affirmative action policies (Questions 3, 4, 6) | Have students add the section's affirmative action cases and rulings to their civil rights timelines (see above). |

**Government online**
All print resources are available on the Teacher's Resource Library CD-ROM and online at PearsonSchool.com/phgovt.

## Answers

**Checkpoint** The Court moved away from regularly upholding affirmative action programs and instead ruled that those programs must prove to serve some "compelling government interest."

---

✔ **Checkpoint**
What was the significance of the Court's ruling in *Adarand*?

**The Future of Affirmative Action** As controversy continued to rage over the place of affirmative action in the twenty-first century, the Court's ruling in two Michigan cases signaled a continuation of the move away from this policy. The resolution of two cases, *Gratz* v. *Bollinger* and *Grutter* v. *Bollinger*, 2003, marked the High Court's most important statement on affirmative action since its decision in *Bakke* in 1978.

The cases involved the admissions policies of the University of Michigan. Jennifer Gratz applied for admission to the University as a freshman in 1997, and Barbara Grutter sought to enter the University's law school that same year. Both women are white, and both were rejected in favor of minority applicants with lower grade point averages and lower entry test scores. Both women sued the university. After losing in the lower courts, each appealed to the Supreme Court.

In deciding the cases, a majority of the Court found that the State of Michigan (and all the States) has a compelling interest in the diversity of the student bodies of its public educational institutions. That compelling interest justifies the narrowly tailored use of race as one factor in the student admissions policies of those institutions.

However, Justice Sandra Day O'Connor, writing for the majority, predicted that affirmative action would become unnecessary in the coming years. "We expect that 25 years from now, the use of racial preferences will no longer be necessary."

A 2007 Supreme Court decision underscored this trend away from affirmative action. *Parents Involved* v. *Seattle School District* and *Meredith* v. *Jefferson County Board of Education* both centered on this question: To what extent can public school officials use race as a factor in assigning students to particular schools as they seek to maintain racially integrated student bodies?

The Court split 5–4 in the two cases. The majority found that the student assignment policies in both districts relied too heavily on race and so ran afoul of the 14th Amendment's Equal Protection Clause. In fact, four of the five justices in the majority favored the total elimination of race as a factor in school admission decisions.

It seems clear that the days of affirmative action programs are drawing to a close. That point was made again in *Ricci* v. *DeStefano*, 2009. In this case, a group of white and Hispanic firefighters sued the city of New Haven, Connecticut. They claimed that they had been the victims of reverse discrimination when the results of an exam were discarded after few minority firefighters qualified for a promotion. The Court ruled, 5–4, in favor of the firefighters. It said, in effect, that race could not be used as the sole factor in promotions.

## SECTION 3 ASSESSMENT

**Essential Questions Journal** To continue to build a response to the chapter Essential Question, go to your **Essential Questions Journal**.

1. **Guiding Question** Use your completed timeline to answer this question: What is the history of civil rights legislation from Reconstruction to today?

**Key Terms and Comprehension**
2. Cite the three major provisions of the Civil Rights Act of 1964.
3. **(a)** What does the policy of **affirmative action** require? **(b)** Who must abide by the policy?
4. Under what circumstances has the Supreme Court upheld the use of **quotas?**

**Critical Thinking**
5. **Demonstrate Reasoned Judgment (a)** What does Title IX provide? **(b)** In what situation has it been most controversial? **(c)** Do you agree with the law? Why or why not?
6. **Synthesize Information** Some nations, such as France, require *gender parity* in government; that is, a certain number of candidates or elected leaders must be women. **(a)** How is this similar to a quota system? **(b)** Do you think the United States should adopt that system? Why or why not?

**Quick Write**
**Problem-Solution Essay: Select the Best Solution** Decide which one of the solutions you researched in Section 2 would solve the problem you identified in Section 1. Using supporting facts and details, make a list that evaluates the solution's effectiveness in achieving both short-term gains and long-term goals.

---

## Assessment Answers

**1.** No meaningful legislation passed from the 1870s to the 1950s. First far-reaching law was the Civil Rights Act of 1964, which bans discrimination in public accommodations, in federally funded programs, and in jobs. Title IX (1972) bans gender-based discrimination in education. In 1965, the Federal Government began demanding affirmative action programs to reduce the effects of past discrimination. In the *Bakke* case (1978), the court ruled that affirmative action is acceptable, but strict quotas are not. In *Adarand* (1995), the Court ruled that future affirmative action cases would be judged under the higher standard of strict scrutiny.

**2.** Discrimination based on race, color, religion, national origin, or physical disability is banned in public accommodations, in any program that receives any federal funding, and by employers and labor unions in job-related matters.

**3. (a)** employers to take positive steps to remedy effects of past discrimination **(b)** all agencies of the Federal Government, all States and local governments, all private employers who sell goods or services to any federal agency

**4.** in extreme situations where longstanding, flagrant discrimination was involved

**5. (a)** equal treatment for women in all aspects of education **(b)** school athletics programs, especially in colleges **(c)** Answers will vary.

**6. (a)** It requires that a share of a group be a certain gender. **(b)** Answers will vary.

**QUICK WRITE** Have students incorporate their lists into a flowchart showing how the solution moves from a short-term gain to a long-term goal.

# CITIZENSHIP 101

## Writing a Letter to the Editor

**Editor:**

Regarding the article on additional budget cuts to public education ("Governor Proposes Slashing School Funding," May 9), I believe that every penny spent is a necessary investment in the future of this community. As a junior at Westfield High School, I know that these cuts would place students' futures in greater jeopardy. Last year, 15 percent of the teaching staff and 10 percent of all elective courses were eliminated due to severe reductions in funding. These cuts ultimately impacted the quality of our education, and that is a sacrifice this town should not be willing to make again.

—Thomas Grey, St. Clairsville

The Constitution guarantees all people the right to express their views. Writing a letter to the editor of your local newspaper is your chance to share your opinion about important issues that affect you and your community. Follow these steps to write an effective letter:

1. **Briefly summarize the issue.** A good letter to the editor should be brief and to the point. Begin your letter by clearly identifying the issue. If you are responding to an article published in the paper, mention the article by title and publication date in the first sentence. State your opinion up-front.

2. **Explain your position.** You should explain why you feel the way you do about the issue. Support your explanation with at least one or two specific examples. If you feel particularly passionate about the issue, let your emotions come through in your letter but remember to be civil. Never resort to name-calling or vulgar language. If you do, few people will take your letter seriously.

3. **Make a suggestion.** The main point of your letter might be to express your opinion, but you could also include suggestions for future actions. If you are writing about a problem in your community, explain what you think can be done to fix it.

4. **Identify yourself.** Sign your letter with your real name, and provide contact information. Most editors will not print anonymous letters, and they must be able to verify your identity. You can also mention any experiences you have had that are relevant to the issue.

### ▶▶ What do you think?

1. When writing a letter to the editor, why do you think you should be brief and to the point?

2. Why would adding suggestions for action make your letter more effective?

3. **You Try It** Choose an issue that interests you and write a letter to the editor of your local newspaper.

**GOVERNMENT ONLINE**
**Citizenship Activity Pack**
For activities on writing a letter to the editor, go to
**PearsonSchool.com/phgovt**

631

## Citizenship Activity Pack

**L1** **L2** If your students need extra support, use the Citizenship Activity Pack lesson *How to Write a Letter to the Editor*. It includes a lesson plan, four sample editorials as handouts, and a model for analyzing the elements of an editorial. Students will work in groups to analyze one of the editorials, write a one-sentence response, and present their work orally to the class. At the end of the lesson, students will have an opportunity to write their own letter to the editor. Students may also access the Citizenship Activity Pack online for activities on writing letters to the editor at **PearsonSchool.com/phgovt**.

## Teach

### READ AND IDENTIFY PARTS OF A LETTER

Have students read the Citizenship 101 feature. As a class, identify the various parts of the letter and their purpose.

### ANALYZE LETTERS IN NEWSPAPERS

Bring to class enough newspaper editorial sections for each student to have one. Have students analyze the editorials and highlight the main point the writer is trying to make. Then have them place a checkmark next to each criticism the writer makes, and circle each suggestion for action. Finally, have students rate the editorials from best to worst, explaining what made the best one successful in their opinion.

### WRITE A LETTER TO THE EDITOR

Have students write their own letters to the editor in response to a news story or letter in the newspaper sections they analyzed in the activity above.

## Assess and Remediate

Have students read aloud their letters. Peer-assess the letters using this checklist:

__ Had quickly identifiable issue

__ Included up-front opinion

__ Provided several explanations for opinion

__ Included suggestions for future action

__ Tone was forceful but civil

## Answers

1. possible answers: to hold readers' attention; to fit the newspaper's limited space for letters

2. Adding suggestions for action shows readers that you have carefully and extensively thought this issue through.

3. Letters will vary but should include an opinion, arguments or explanations supporting the opinion, and a suggestion for action.

How can American citizenship be attained and how has immigration policy changed over the years?

I. Citizenship
   A. By Birth
      1. jus soli—place of birth
      2. jus sanguinis—parentage
   B. By Naturalization
      1. individual
      2. collective
II. Immigration
   A. Regulation
      1. by Congress only
      2. encouraged when workers needed
      3. exclusion based on personal traits
   B. Quotas
      1. number limits based on country of origin
      2. favored northern and western Europe
      3. Immigration Act of 1965—limit not based on country
   C. Present Policies
      1. Immigration Act of 1990 increased quota
      2. preference to family members
      3. preference to aliens with needed skills
   D. Undocumented Aliens
      1. enter illegally (or legally and overstay)
      2. often hired at substandard pay
      3. strain public services
      4. Immigration Reform and Control Act of 1986—amnesty; crime to hire illegals
      5. Illegal Immigration Restrictions Act of 1996—deportation easier; public services restricted

## SKILLS DEVELOPMENT

### DRAW INFERENCES AND CONCLUSIONS

Before students research immigration issues and prepare arguments for and against, you may want to review information on drawing inferences and conclusions in the Skills Handbook, p. S19.

SECTION 4

# American Citizenship

## Guiding Question

**How can American citizenship be attained and how has immigration policy changed over the years?**
Use an outline like the one below to take notes on the section.

I. Citizenship
  A. By Birth
    1. _____
    2. _____
  B. _____
  C. _____
II. Immigration

## Political Dictionary
• citizen                • alien
• jus soli               • expatriation
• jus sanguinis          • denaturalization
• naturalization         • deportation

## Objectives
1. Describe how people become American citizens by birth and by naturalization.
2. Explain how an American can lose his or her citizenship.
3. Illustrate how the United States is a nation of immigrants.
4. Compare and contrast the status of undocumented aliens and legal immigrants.

**Image Above:** New citizens take the oath during a naturalization ceremony in Miami, Florida.

**C**itizenship is the badge of membership in a political society.[11] Today, every state in the world has rules by which citizenship is determined. And much can be learned about the basic nature of a government by examining those rules. Who are and who may become citizens? Who are excluded from citizenship, and why?

## The Constitution and Citizenship

An American **citizen** is one who owes allegiance to the United States and is entitled to both its protection and the privileges of its laws. As it was originally written, the Constitution referred to both "citizens of the United States" and "citizens of the States." Neither of those phrases was defined, however. Throughout much of our earlier history, it was generally agreed that national citizenship followed that of the States. That is, a person who was a citizen of, say, Maryland, was also thought to be a citizen of the United States.

Actually, the question was of little importance before the 1860s. Much of the population was the product of recent immigration, and little distinction was made between citizens and those who were not. The Civil War and the adoption of the 13th Amendment in 1865 raised the need for a constitutional definition, however.[12] The 14th Amendment met that need in 1868:

### FROM THE CONSTITUTION

**All persons born or naturalized in the United States and subject to the jurisdiction thereof, are citizens of the United States and of the State wherein they reside.**

—14th Amendment, Section 1

11 The concept of citizenship—of the free inhabitants of a city—was developed by the ancient Greeks and Romans. It replaced the earlier concept of kinship—of the blood relationships of the family and the tribe—as the basis for community.
12 In the Dred Scott case (*Scott* v. *Sandford*) in 1857, the Supreme Court had ruled that neither the States nor the National Government had the power to confer citizenship on African Americans—slave or free. The dispute over that matter was one of the several causes of the Civil War.

## Focus on the Basics

**FACTS:** • A person can become an American citizen either at birth or through the process of naturalization. • Several million Americans have become citizens through naturalization. • Congress has the exclusive power to regulate immigration. • Most immigrants to the United States have come through official channels, but many arrive illegally. • Aliens may be subject to deportation.

**CONCEPTS:** citizenship

**ENDURING UNDERSTANDINGS:** • The United States is a nation of immigrants. • As immigration to the United States has surged over the past few decades, record numbers of immigrants have become American citizens. • Current immigration policy is controversial.

Thus, the Constitution declares that a person may become an American citizen in either of two ways: by birth or by naturalization. The feature on page 634 summarizes the means by which American citizenship can be acquired.

## Citizenship by Birth

More than 260 million Americans—nearly 90 percent—are citizens simply because they were born in this country. Another several million are also citizens by birth, although they were born outside the United States.

Two basic rules determine citizenship at birth: jus soli and jus sanguinis. According to **jus soli**—the law of the soil—citizenship is determined by place of birth, by *where* one is born.

Notice that the 14th Amendment awards American citizenship according to the location of one's birth: "All persons born . . . in the United States . . ." Congress has defined the United States to include, for purposes of citizenship, the 50 States, the District of Columbia, Puerto Rico, Guam, the Virgin Islands, and the Northern Mariana Islands, and all American embassies and all public vessels of the United States, wherever they might be.[13] Just how broad the 14th Amendment's statement of jus soli is can be seen from a leading case on citizenship, *United States* v. *Wong Kim Ark*, 1898.

Wong Kim Ark was born in San Francisco in 1873 to parents who were citizens of China. He made a brief trip to China in 1895. Upon Wong Kim Ark's return, he was refused entry to the United States by immigration officials at San Francisco. They insisted that the 14th Amendment should not be read so literally as to mean that he had become an American citizen at birth. They declared that he was an alien and so was denied entry by the Chinese Exclusion Act of 1882. The Supreme Court held, however, that under the clear wording of the 14th Amendment, he was indeed a native-born citizen of this country and so not subject to the terms of the Chinese Exclusion Act.

[13] Until 1924, Native Americans born to tribal members on reservations did not become citizens at birth. They were, instead, wards (persons under legal guardianship) of the government. In that year, Congress finally did grant citizenship to all Native Americans who did not already possess it.

[14] Article I, Section 8, Clause 4.

A very small number of persons who are born *physically* in the United States do not in fact become citizens at birth. They are those few who are born not "subject to the jurisdiction of the United States"—for example, children born to foreign diplomatic officials.

According to **jus sanguinis,** the law of the blood, citizenship at birth may also be determined by parentage, to *whom* one is born. Thus, it is altogether possible for one to become a citizen at birth even when that birth occurs outside the United States. A child born abroad can become a citizen at birth under circumstances set out in the feature on page 634. The 14th Amendment does not provide for jus sanguinis. However, Congress first recognized the doctrine in 1790 and its constitutionality has never been challenged.

## Citizenship by Naturalization

**Naturalization** is the legal process by which a person can become a citizen of another country at some time after birth. Congress has the exclusive power to provide for naturalization.[14] No State may do so.

**Individual Naturalization** Naturalization is most often an individual process, conducted by a court. Generally, any person eligible to

✔ **Checkpoint**
What does the 14th Amendment say about citizenship?

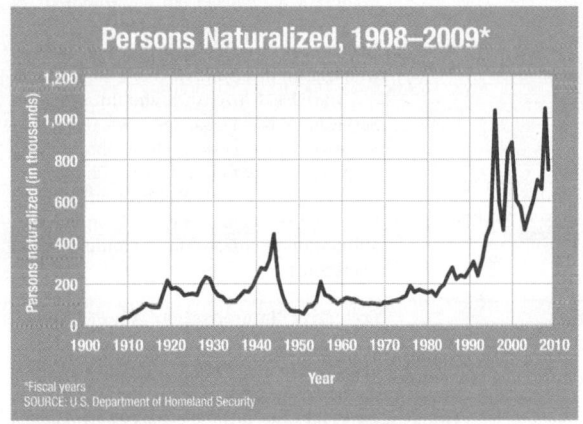

**Persons Naturalized, 1908–2009***

*Fiscal years
SOURCE: U.S. Department of Homeland Security

▶▶ **Analyzing Graphs** *In what year were the greatest number of persons naturalized? The fewest?*

---

### LESSON GOALS

Students will . . .

- summarize ways that individuals become citizens in the United States.
- analyze the controversy over immigration in the United States by preparing arguments for and against opinions on the topic.

### BEFORE CLASS

Assign the section, the graphic organizer in the text, and the Reading Comprehension Worksheet (Unit 5 All-in-One, p. 221) before class.

**L2 Differentiate** Reading Comprehension Worksheet (Unit 5 All-in-One, p. 222)

### BELLRINGER

Display Transparency 21F, Naturalization, and write on the board: **1. Which requirement do you think is most difficult to evaluate? 2. What requirements should be added or removed? 3. How did the original Texans become U.S. citizens? 4. Who are the most recent "collective" citizens? Answer in your notebook.**

## Teach

To present this topic using online resources, use the lesson presentations at **PearsonSchool.com/phgovt.**

### ANALYZE LINE GRAPH

Have students study the graph "Persons Naturalized, 1908–2009" in their textbook. Ask students to use their knowledge of history to explain the spikes, dips, and other trends in the graph. *(For example, a spike occurs after World War I ends in 1918; immigration dips during the Great Depression of the 1930s, and it spikes again after World War II ends in 1945.)* Have students note the spike in the 1990s, which resulted from the naturalization of some 1 million undocumented aliens who became legalized under the Immigration Reform and Control Act of 1986.

## Differentiated Resources

The following resources are located in the All-in-One, Unit 5, Chapter 21, Section 4:

**L3** Reading Comprehension Worksheet (p. 221)
**L2** Reading Comprehension Worksheet (p. 222)
**L3** Core Worksheet A (p. 223)
**L3** **L2** Core Worksheets B (pp. 225, 226)
**L3** Quiz A (p. 227)
**L2** Quiz B (p. 228)
**L3** Chapter Test A (p. 233)
**L2** Chapter Test B (p. 236)

## Answers

**Checkpoint** that any person born in the U.S. or naturalized becomes a U.S. citizen

**Analyzing Graphs** 2008; 1908

Have students share their Bellringer answers. *(1. possible answer: evaluating whether someone is "of good moral character"; 2. Answers will vary. Direct students to consider adding education or skills requirements. 3. by a joint resolution of Congress in 1845; 4. citizens of the Northern Mariana Islands)*

**L2 ELL Differentiate** Ask students to provide synonyms for the word *renounce* (give up, reject, relinquish, disown).

**L2 Differentiate** Have students list characteristics of a person "of good moral character." Write these on the board. Then ask students to rate the characteristics from "most important" to "least important" and explain their ratings.

## DISCUSS ACQUIRING CITIZENSHIP

Review the ways to gain citizenship. Ask: **What are two ways to acquire citizenship?** *(by birth and by naturalization)* **In what two ways can a person become a citizen by birth?** (jus soli: *citizenship is determined by where one is born;* jus sanquinis: *citizenship is determined by to whom one is born)*

Now display Transparency 21F (Bellringer) again and ask: **What are the various ways groups have become collectively naturalized in the United States?** *(through treaties, a joint resolution of Congress, acts of Congress, and a constitutional amendment)*

# Acquiring Citizenship

Most Americans acquire citizenship at birth. *How else can one acquire American citizenship?*

**Birth**

**Naturalization**

**Jus Soli:** Law of Soil
- A child becomes an American citizen if born in the United States, Puerto Rico, Guam, Virgin Islands, Northern Mariana Islands, any U.S. embassy, or aboard a U.S. public vessel anywhere in the world.

**Jus Sanguinis:** Law of Blood

A child born to an American citizen on foreign soil becomes a citizen if:
- both parents are American citizens, and at least one has lived in the United States or an American territory at some time.
- one parent is an American citizen who has lived in the U.S. for at least 5 years, 2 of them after age 14, and the child has lived in the U.S. continuously for at least 5 years between the ages of 14 and 28.

**Individually**
- Naturalization of both parents (one parent if divorced or the other is deceased) automatically naturalizes children under age 16 who reside in the U.S. Adopted children born abroad are automatically naturalized if under age 18 when adoption becomes final.

**Collectively**
- Collective naturalization—when entire groups are naturalized—usually occurs by treaty or by act or joint resolution of Congress.

**petition**
*n.* formal request, application

enter the United States as an immigrant may become a naturalized citizen. Hundreds of thousands of aliens are now naturalized each year. An **alien** is a citizen of a foreign state who lives in this country.

The U.S. Citizenship and Immigration Services in the Department of Homeland Security investigates each applicant, and then reports its findings to the judge with whom a petition for naturalization has been filed. If the judge is satisfied, an oath or affirmation of citizenship is administered in open court.

**Collective Naturalization** At various times, entire groups have been naturalized *en masse.* This has most often happened when the United States has acquired new territory. Those living in the areas involved were naturalized by a treaty or by an act or a joint resolution passed by Congress.

The largest single instance of collective naturalization came with the ratification of the 14th Amendment, however. The most recent instance occurred in 1977, when Congress gave citizenship to the more than 16,000 native-born residents of the Northern Mariana Islands.

## Loss of Citizenship

Although it rarely happens, every American citizen, whether native-born or naturalized, has the right to renounce—voluntarily abandon—his or her citizenship. **Expatriation** is the legal process by which a loss of citizenship occurs.

The Supreme Court has several times held that the Constitution prohibits automatic expatriation. That is, Congress cannot take away a person's citizenship for something he or she has done. Thus, actions such

# Background

**EXPATRIATION** Any party claiming that a person has abandoned his U.S. citizenship must establish three elements. First, the person must have taken one of the acts of expatriation stated by law, such as "obtaining naturalization in" or "taking an oath or making an affirmation or other formal declaration of allegiance to a foreign state" after reaching the age of 18, "entering, or serving in, the armed forces of a foreign state . . . engaged in hostilities against the United States," or formal renunciation before an appropriate United States official. Second, he must have acted "voluntarily." Third, he must have acted "with the intention of relinquishing United States nationality." An individual who voluntarily "enter[s], or serve[s] in, the armed forces of a foreign state" may be expatriated, "if (A) such armed forces are engaged in hostilities against the United States, or (B) such persons serve as a commissioned or non-commissioned officer."

## Answers

**Acquiring Citizenship** through naturalization, either individually or collectively as committing a crime, voting in a foreign election, or serving in the armed forces of another country are not grounds for automatic expatriation.[15]

Naturalized citizens can lose their citizenship involuntarily. However, this process—**denaturalization**—can occur only by court order and only after it has been shown that the person became an American citizen by fraud or deception.

A person can neither gain nor lose American citizenship by marriage. The only significant effect that marriage has is to shorten the time required for the naturalization of an alien who marries an American citizen.

## A Nation of Immigrants

We are a nation of immigrants. Except for Native Americans—and even they may be the descendants of earlier immigrants—all of us have come here from abroad or are descended from those who did.

**Regulation of Immigration** Congress has the exclusive power to regulate the crossing of this nation's borders, both inward (immigration) and outward (emigration). It alone has the power to decide who may be admitted to the country and under what conditions. In an early leading case on the point, the Court ruled that the power of the United States to "exclude aliens from its territory is . . . not open to controversy," *Chae Chan Ping* v. *United States*, 1889. The States have no power in the field, *The Passenger Cases*, 1849.

There were only some 2.5 million people in the United States when independence was declared in 1776. Since then, the population has grown more than a hundredfold, to well over 300 million today. That extraordinary population growth has come from two sources: births and immigration. Some 70 million immigrants have come here since 1820, the year when such figures were first recorded.

Congress made no serious attempt to regulate immigration for more than a century after

---

15 A person convicted of a federal or a State crime may lose some of the privileges of citizenship, however, either temporarily or permanently—for example, the right to travel freely or to vote or hold public office.

independence. As long as land was plentiful and expanding industry demanded more and still more workers, immigration was actively encouraged.

By 1890, however, the open frontier was a thing of the past, and labor was no longer in short supply. Then, too, the major source of immigration had shifted. Until the 1880s, most immigrants had come from the countries of northern and western Europe. The "new immigration" from the 1880s onward came mostly from southern and eastern Europe. All these factors combined to bring major changes in the traditional policy of encouraging immigration. Ultimately, the policy was reversed.

Congress placed the first major restrictions on immigration with the passage of the Chinese Exclusion Act in 1882. At the same time, it barred the entry of convicts, "lunatics," paupers, and others likely to become public charges. Over the next several years, a long list of "undesirables" was added to the law. Thus, contract laborers were excluded in 1885, immoral persons and anarchists in 1903, and illiterates in 1917. By 1920, more than 30 groups were denied admission on the basis of personal traits.

The tide of newcomers continued to mount, however. In the 10 years from 1905 through 1914, an average of more than a million persons, most of them from southern and eastern Europe, came to this country each year.

**Quotas** Congress responded to pressure for tighter regulation by adding quantitative limits (numerical ceilings) to the qualitative restrictions (personal characteristics) already in place. The Immigration Acts of 1921 and 1924 and the National Origins Act of 1929 assigned each country in Europe a quota—a limit on the number of immigrants who could enter the United States from that country each year. Altogether, only 150,000 quota immigrants could be admitted in any one year.

The quotas were purposely drawn to favor northern and western Europe. The quota system was not applied to the Western Hemisphere, but immigration from Asia, Africa, and elsewhere was generally prohibited.

✔ **Checkpoint**
When and why did Congress first begin to regulate immigration?

## Debate

Have students debate the following statement: **Loss of U.S. citizenship should be a penalty in the American system of justice.**

Have students provide reasons for and against using the threat of losing one's citizenship as a punishment for criminal acts. In addition, students should note which acts would warrant loss of citizenship.

---

**TAKE A CITIZENSHIP TEST**

Distribute the Chapter 21 Section 4 Core Worksheet A (Unit 5 All-in-One, p. 223), which includes questions from the U.S. Citizenship and Immigration Services (USCIS) test that individuals take as part of the process of becoming an American citizen. Have students answer as many questions as they can in ten minutes. Quickly review the answers. Then ask: **Do you think any of the questions are unusual or difficult? Which ones? What is the general focus of most of the questions the USCIS thinks every new citizen should know?** (citizenship, civic rights and responsibilities) **What questions would you add to the test?**

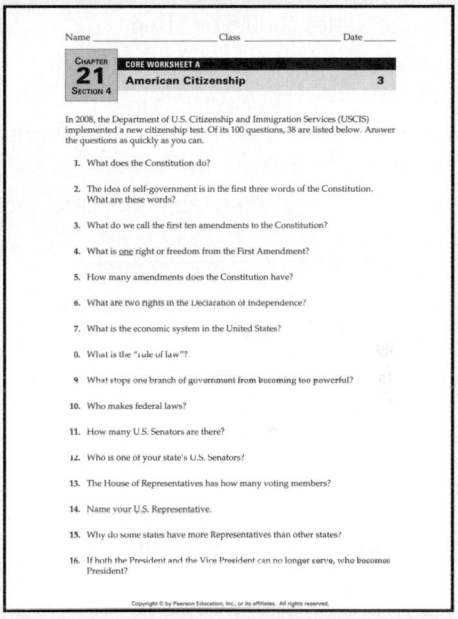

**L3 Differentiate** Ask: **Why is it important that new citizens know about and understand U.S. history and government?**

---

## Answers

**Checkpoint** By 1890, the open frontier was gone and labor was no longer in short supply. New immigrants were coming mostly from southern and eastern Europe. The Chinese Exclusion Act was passed in 1882 to restrict Chinese immigrants. Other "undesirables" were added to the law based on personal traits. In the 1920s, immigration was restricted to favor people from northern and western Europe.

Tell students to go to the Audio Tour to hear where immigrants settle in the United States.

## UNDERSTAND IMMIGRATION ARGUMENTS

In this activity, students will gain an understanding of why immigration is so controversial. Have students work in pairs to research the opinions about immigration listed below. Pairs should write at least three arguments supporting the opinion and three refuting it. Have pairs share their arguments with the class. Point out that the opinions and arguments are similar to discussions that take place in Congress.

- America should more effectively militarize its borders to keep undocumented immigrants out.

- Quotas limiting the number of people that may enter the United States should be lifted.

- Undocumented immigrants are necessary to do the jobs that Americans do not want to do.

- Amnesty should be given to immigrants who have been in the country illegally for five years.

- Granting permanent legal status to undocumented immigrants who attend two years of college or military service is wasting American money.

- Harsher immigration policies are needed in the United States to fight terrorism.

- Refugees and others seeking asylum should have to provide evidence of the dangerous situation in the countries they are fleeing.

## Answers

**Analyzing Maps** California, Nevada, Florida, New York, New Jersey, Hawaii

**Checkpoint** Congress eliminated it in the Immigration Act of 1965.

# Immigrants in the U.S.

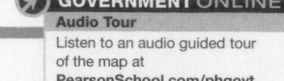
**GOVERNMENT** ONLINE
Audio Tour
Listen to an audio guided tour of the map at
PearsonSchool.com/phgovt

▶▶ **Analyzing Maps** The Immigration Act of 1990 allows 675,000 immigrants to enter the U.S. each year. The percentage of foreign-born people living in each State in 2009 ranged from less than 2 percent to more than 25 percent. *Which States have the largest immigrant populations?*

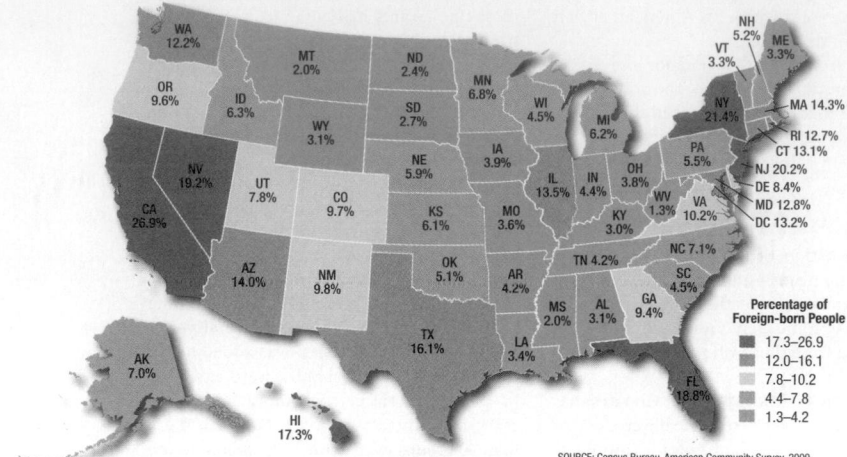

SOURCE: Census Bureau, American Community Survey, 2009

✔ **Checkpoint**
What happened to the country-based quota system?

In 1952, Congress passed yet another basic law, the Immigration and Nationality Act. That statute modified the quota system, extending it to include every country outside the Western Hemisphere.

Congress finally eliminated the country-based quota system in the Immigration Act of 1965. That law allowed as many as 270,000 immigrants to enter the United States each year, without regard to race, nationality, or country of origin. The 1965 law gave special preference to immediate relatives of American citizens or of aliens legally residing in this country.

**Present Immigration Policies** Today, the Immigration Act of 1990 governs the admission of aliens to the United States. Like its predecessors, it was adopted only after years of intense debate, and many of its provisions are the subject of continuing controversy.

The 1990 law provided for a substantial increase in the number of immigrants who may enter the United States each year. The annual ceiling is now set at 675,000. It also continues the family-preference policy first put in place in 1965; at least one third of those persons admitted under its terms must be the close relatives of either American citizens or resident aliens. Those immigrants who have occupational talents which are in short supply in the United States (notably, highly skilled researchers, engineers, and scientists) also receive special preference.

Only those aliens who can qualify for citizenship can be admitted as immigrants. The law's list of "excludable aliens"—those barred because of some personal characteristic—is extensive. Among those excluded are: criminals (including suspected terrorists), persons with communicable diseases, drug abusers and addicts, illiterates, and mentally disturbed persons who might pose a threat to the safety of others.

# Background

**DUAL CITIZENSHIP** Dual citizenship has become much more common in recent years. Although the U.S. State Department does not officially recognize dual citizenship, it does not specifically prohibit it under some circumstances. There are certain rules for becoming a legal citizen of the United States and another country. The most basic rule is that a person who has United States citizenship by birth may later apply for citizenship in another country, without losing his or her American citizenship. A naturalized citizen, however, is required to renounce his or her foreign citizenship when granted American citizenship.

Some 20 million persons—nonimmigrants—come here each year for temporary stays. They are mostly tourists, students, and people traveling for business reasons.

**Deportation** Most of the civil rights set out in the Constitution are guaranteed to "persons"—a term that covers aliens as well as citizens. In one important respect, however, the status of aliens is altogether unlike that of citizens: Aliens may be subject to **deportation,** a legal process by which aliens are legally required to leave the country.

The Supreme Court has long held that the United States has the same almost-unlimited power to deport aliens as it has to exclude them. In an early major case, the Court ruled that deportation is an inherent power, arising out of the sovereignty of the United States, and that deportation is not criminal punishment, and so does not require a criminal trial, *Fong Yue Ting* v. *United States,* 1893.

An alien may be deported on any one of several grounds. The most common is illegal entry. Thousands of aliens who enter with false papers, sneak in by ship or plane, or slip across the border at night are caught each year and deported. Many of them are repeat offenders who will soon make yet another attempt to cross the border.

Conviction of any serious crime, federal or State, usually leads to a deportation order. In recent years, several thousand aliens have been expelled on the basis of their criminal records, especially narcotics violators. The war on terrorism has also quickened the pace of deportations. Because deportation is a civil, not a criminal, matter, several constitutional safeguards do not apply—for example, bail and the ban on ex post facto laws.

## Undocumented Aliens

No one knows just how many undocumented aliens reside in the United States today. Best estimates put their total at about 12 million.

The Department of Homeland Security reports that there are some 11 million undocumented aliens in this country today. Most entered the country by slipping across the Mexican or Canadian borders, usually at night. Some come with forged papers. Many others are

aliens who entered legally, as nonimmigrants, but then overstayed their legal welcomes.

Well over half of all aliens who are here illegally have come from Mexico; most of the others come from other Latin American countries and from Asia. A majority of the Mexicans stay here only some four to six months a year, working on farms or in other seasonal jobs, and then return home. Most others hope to remain here permanently.

**A Troublesome Situation** Once here, many of these aliens find it easy to become "invisible," especially in larger cities, and law-enforcement agencies find it very difficult to locate them. Even so, immigration officials have apprehended more than a million undocumented aliens in each of the last several years. Nearly all are sent home. Most go voluntarily, but some leave only as the result of formal deportation proceedings.

The presence of so many undocumented persons has caused a number of nagging problems. Those problems have grown worse over the past several years and, until recently, not much had been done to solve them.

Consider this: Ever since 1987, it has been illegal for an employer to hire an undocumented alien to perform work anywhere in the United States. Even so, some four million persons who now hold jobs in this country came here illegally. Some employers still hire aliens who are often willing to work for substandard wages and in substandard conditions.

No one knows just how many undocumented aliens have taken jobs on farms or become day laborers. Or how many have become janitors or dishwashers, or seamstresses in sweatshops, or have found other <u>menial</u> work. However many they are, their presence has multiplied the burdens of already strained public school systems and welfare services of an increasing number of States, most notably California, Arizona, Texas, and Florida.

**Current Law** The problems posed by undocumented aliens trouble and divide many different interests in American politics—chief among them labor, farm, business, religious, ethnic, and civil rights organizations. After wrestling with the matter for years,

✔ **Checkpoint**
For what reasons may a person be deported?

**menial**
*adj.* unskilled, humble, lowly

# Background

**BEHIND THE SCENES** Three bureaus in the Department of Homeland Security regulate immigration. United States Citizenship and Immigration Services (USCIS) adjudicates applications for benefits and services; United States Immigration and Customs Enforcement (ICE) is the law enforcement arm of the old INS; and United States Customs and Border Protection (CBP) is responsible for inspecting immigrants at entry and for border patrol. These bureaus are working to secure the nation's borders against both terrorists and undocumented immigrants. Their planned tactics include building fences and other barriers along the borders. Virtual fencing, or radiation detection equipment, sensors, cameras, and other high-tech tools, are being implemented.

## TRACE ATTITUDES TOWARD IMMIGRATION

Distribute the Chapter 21 Section 4 Core Worksheet B (Unit 5 All-in-One, p. 225), which shows a political cartoon about attitudes toward immigration in the 1890s. Students will learn that immigration policies were controversial even then. Have students answer the questions and discuss them in class.

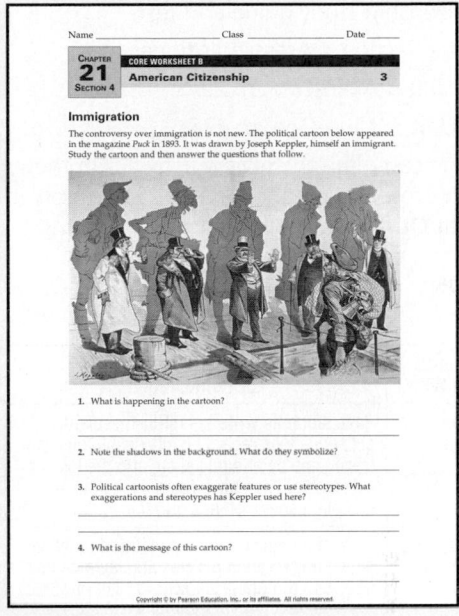

**L1 L2 Differentiate** For these students, distribute the adapted Chapter 21 Section 4 Core Worksheet B (Unit 5 All-in-One, p. 226).

### EXTEND THE LESSON

**L3 Differentiate** Have students interview a relative or a family friend who moved to the United States from another country. Provide students with the following questions to initiate the interviews:

- **Do you have any personal stories that capture a sense of your experience?**
- **Do you believe your experiences were typical?**
- **How do you feel about television and film portrayals of immigrants' lives?**
- **What lesson would you like to convey to members of my generation?**

Then have students use their notes from the interview to write a short public-interest piece for a magazine or a newspaper.

**L2 Differentiate** If students are comfortable discussing their ancestors, chart how many students are first-generation through tenth-generation (or more) Americans.

## Answers

**Checkpoint** illegal entry, conviction of a serious federal or State crime

# Assess and Remediate

**L3** Have students prepare a citizenship and naturalization handbook that recent immigrants could use to help them prepare for American citizenship. Encourage students to illustrate their handbooks and provide the names and phone numbers of important local government resources. Handbooks should also include a citizenship study guide and test.

**L3** Assign the Section 4 Assessment questions.

**L3** Quiz A (Unit 5 All-in-One, p. 227)

**L2** Quiz B (Unit 5 All-in-One, p. 228)

Have students complete the review activities in the digital lesson presentation and continue their work in the **Essential Questions Journal.**

## REMEDIATION

| If Your Students Have Trouble With | Strategies For Remediation |
|---|---|
| Citizenship requirements (Questions 1, 2, 3, 5) | Have students write ten fill-in-the-blank quiz questions regarding citizenship by birth, citizenship by naturalization, and the loss of citizenship. Then have them exchange and complete one another's quizzes. |
| Immigration laws and policies (Questions 1, 4, 6) | Have students create an annotated timeline noting immigration policies and laws beginning with the Chinese Exclusion Act of 1882. |

## Answers

**Analyzing Political Cartoons** Congress should address the issue because it is not going away.

---

Congress was finally able to pass the Immigration Reform and Control Act of 1986. Then, it enacted the Illegal Immigration Reform and Immigrant Responsibility Act of 1996.

The 1986 law did two major things. First, it established a one-year amnesty program under which many undocumented aliens could become legal residents. More than two million aliens used the process to legalize their status. Second, that law made it a crime to hire any person who is in this country illegally. Any employer who knowingly hires an undocumented alien can be fined from $250 to as much as $10,000. Repeat offenders can be jailed for up to six months.

The 1996 law made it easier to deport illegal aliens by streamlining the deportation process. It also toughened the penalties for smuggling aliens into this country, prevented undocumented aliens from claiming Social Security or public housing benefits, and allowed State welfare agencies to check the legal status of any alien who applies for any welfare benefit. The statute also doubled the size of the Border Patrol—which is, today, the largest of the several federal law enforcement agencies.

Congress has not been able to enact any meaningful immigration reform legislation for more than a decade now, however. The principal reason for the impasse is a continuing dispute over how best to approach the matter.

Many in and out of Congress insist that securing the nation's borders—stemming the flow of illegal entries—should be the nation's first concern. That thorny matter should be addressed, they say, before anything is done to meet the problems posed by the undocumented aliens already in this country. Many others argue that the need to confront these problems should not be put off to another day. In particular, many of them want to make it possible for large numbers of undocumented aliens to become legal residents and, eventually, citizens of the United States.

"ANYBODY HOME?"

▸▸ **Analyzing Political Cartoons** *What does the cartoonist say about Congress and the immigration issue?*

**Essential Questions Journal** To continue to build a response to the chapter Essential Question, go to your **Essential Questions Journal.**

## SECTION **4** ASSESSMENT

1. **Guiding Question** Use your completed outline to answer this question: How can American citizenship be attained and how has immigration policy changed over the years?

**Key Terms and Comprehension**

2. **(a)** In what two ways may a person become a U.S. **citizen? (b)** What is the difference between **jus soli** and **jus sanguinis?**

3. **(a)** What is **naturalization? (b)** About how many **aliens** are naturalized in this country each year?

**Critical Thinking**

4. **Demonstrate Reasoned Judgment (a)** Should U.S. citizenship be considered a right or a privilege? **(b)** Do you think citizens by birth should meet the same requirements as those set for naturalized citizens? Why or why not? **(c)** What actions, if any, do you think should result in an individual's involuntary expatriation?

5. **Identify Alternatives (a)** What did the Illegal Immigration Reform and Immigrant Responsibility Act of 1996 provide? **(b)** Do you think these provisions have been successful? Why or why not? **(c)** What changes, if any, do you think should be made to the law?

**Quick Write**

**Problem-Solution Essay: Implement the Solution** Write a specific proposal or action plan to implement the solution you selected in Section 3. Identify the steps needed to solve the problem, and then write an outline of your solution.

---

# Assessment Answers

**1.** by birth if born to a U.S. citizen or if born in the U.S.; by naturalization through the courts or if both parents are naturalized; first major restriction was Chinese Exclusion Act of 1882; by 1920 more than 30 groups denied on basis of personal traits; each European country assigned a quota in the 1920s; quota system eliminated in 1965; annual ceiling now 675,000

**2. (a)** by birth or naturalization **(b) jus soli:** citizenship determined by where one is born; **jus sanguinis:** citizenship determined by parentage

**3. (a)** legal process by which a person can become a citizen of another country **(b)** hundreds of thousands

**4. (a)** and **(b)** Answers will vary. **(c)** possible answers: terrorist activities, helping a country at war with the U.S.

**5. (a)** made it easier to deport undocumented aliens, toughened penalties for smuggling aliens into this country, prevented undocumented aliens from claiming Social Security benefits or public housing, allowed State welfare agencies to check the legal status of

any alien who applies for any welfare benefit, doubled the size of the Border Patrol **(b)** Answers will vary, but students should realize that the issue of illegal immigration remains problematic. **(c)** Answers will vary.

**QUICK WRITE** Students should include specific details about implementing the solution funds needed, time allotment, and so on.

# Quick Study Guide

**GOVERNMENT** ONLINE
**On the Go**
To review anytime, anywhere, download these online resources at **PearsonSchool.com/phgovt**
Political Dictionary, Audio Review

CHAPTER 21

**Guiding Question**
**Section 1** How have various minority groups in American society been discriminated against?

**Guiding Question**
**Section 2** How has the interpretation of the guarantee of equal rights changed over time?

**Guiding Question**
**Section 3** What is the history of civil rights legislation from Reconstruction to today?

**CHAPTER 21**
**Essential Question**
Why are there ongoing struggles for civil rights?

**Guiding Question**
**Section 4** How can American citizenship be attained and how has immigration policy changed over the years?

## Political Dictionary

**heterogeneous** *p. 612*
**immigrant** *p. 612*
**reservation** *p. 613*
**refugee** *p. 615*
**assimilation** *p. 615*
**rational basis test** *p. 619*
**strict scrutiny test** *p. 619*
**segregation** *p. 619*
**Jim Crow** *p. 619*
**separate-but-equal doctrine** *p. 619*
**integration** *p. 620*
**de jure** *p. 621*
**de facto** *p. 621*
**affirmative action** *p. 627*
**quota** *p. 628*
**reverse discrimination** *p. 628*
**citizen** *p. 632*
**jus soli** *p. 633*
**jus sanguinis** *p. 633*
**naturalization** *p. 633*
**alien** *p. 634*
**expatriation** *p. 634*
**denaturalization** *p. 635*
**deportation** *p. 637*

## Segregation in American Society

**Late 1800s:** Nearly half the States pass segregation (Jim Crow) laws.

**1896:** The Supreme Court establishes the separate-but-equal doctrine in *Plessy* v. *Ferguson*.

**1954:** The Supreme Court rules in *Brown* v. *Board of Education* that the separate-but-equal doctrine is unconstitutional.

**1955:** Public schools begin to desegregate.

**1960s:** Major civil rights legislation is passed, including the Civil Rights Act of 1964.

## Affirmative Action

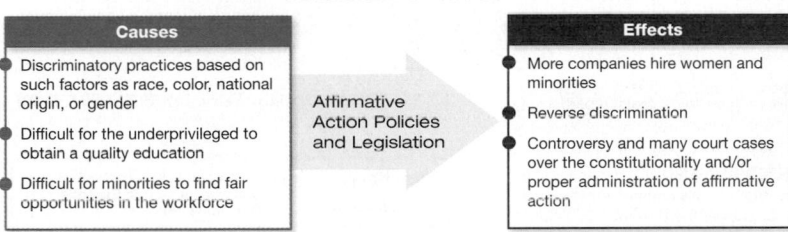

**Causes**
- Discriminatory practices based on such factors as race, color, national origin, or gender
- Difficult for the underprivileged to obtain a quality education
- Difficult for minorities to find fair opportunities in the workforce

Affirmative Action Policies and Legislation

**Effects**
- More companies hire women and minorities
- Reverse discrimination
- Controversy and many court cases over the constitutionality and/or proper administration of affirmative action

Chapter 21 Assessment **639**

---

Have students download the digital resources available at Government on the Go for review and remediation.

### STUDY TIPS

**Predict Test Questions** Predicting with accuracy what will be on a test can lead to more focused studying and better grades. Suggest the following prediction strategies to students: Above all, pay attention to those things the teacher emphasizes in class. If a particular point is repeated; written on the board, on an overhead, or in a Power Point presentation; or appears in a study guide, chances are it will resurface on the test. In addition, suggest that students take note of questions asked by the teacher during class. A review of old tests and quizzes will reveal the types of questions and content the teacher stresses. Advise students to predict both lower- (factual recall) and higher-order (critical thinking) questions. Students can create their own study guide by writing a few possible questions after every class.

### ASSESSMENT AT A GLANCE

**Tests and Quizzes**
Section Assessments
Section Quizzes A and B, Unit 5 **All-in-One**
Chapter Assessment
Chapter Tests A and B, Unit 5 **All-in-One**
Document-Based Assessment
Progress Monitoring Online
Exam*View* Test Bank

**Performance Assessment**
Essential Questions Journal
Debate, p. 635
Assessment Rubrics, **All-in-One**

---

# For More Information

To learn more about civil rights, refer to these sources or assign them to students:

**L1** **Johnson, Troy R.** *Red Power: The Native American Civil Rights Movement.* Chelsea House Publications, 2007.

**L2** **Friedman, Lauri S., ed.** *Discrimination (Issues That Concern You).* Greenhaven Press, 2007.

**L3** **McNeese, Tim.** *The Civil Rights Movement: Striving for Justice.* Chelsea House Publications, 2007.

**L4** **Kellough, J. Edward.** *Understanding Affirmative Action: Politics, Discrimination, and the Search for Justice.* Georgetown University Press, 2006.

# Chapter Assessment

**COMPREHENSION AND CRITICAL THINKING**

## SECTION 1

1. **(a)** It is made up of a mix of races and nationalities. **(b)** In colonial times, 80 percent of the population was white; 20 percent African American. Today the ethnic composition includes many nationalities, with whites making up about 65 percent of the population. **(c)** Hispanic Americans and Asian Americans

2. **(a)** by providing financial assistance to educational programs for Native American children and adults **(b)** Answers will vary.

3. **(a)** 1850s to 1860s; to work as contract laborers in mines and on railroads **(b)** Chinese immigration came to a halt with the Chinese Exclusion Act of 1882. When immigration policies were changed in 1965, Chinese immigration increased dramatically.

4. **(a)** an invisible but impenetrable barrier that prevents women from rising in the corporate world **(b)** reverse discrimination **(c)** The character laments that a male bee cannot obtain the highest position; usually, gender-based discrimination complaints are made by women.

## SECTION 2

5. Answers will vary. Possible response: Government may tax smokers. Burglars fall into a criminal classification.

6. **(a)** to keep African Americans segregated from whites **(b)** *Plessy* v. *Ferguson;* that separate facilities for African Americans were equal **(c)** Answers will vary. Possible response: No. Separate facilities are inherently unequal because separation implies inferiority of those set apart.

7. **(a)** Possible answers: *Reed* v. *Reed* struck down a law that gave fathers preference in the administration of children's estates; *Taylor* v. *Louisiana* forbids States to exclude women from jury duty **(b)** Students should respond to the Court's gender classifications that gender-based laws must be (1) intended to serve an "important governmental objective" and (2) are "substantially related" to achieving that goal.

## SECTION 3

8. **(a) 1964:** outlaws discrimination in a number of areas, including various "public accommodations," in any program that receives any federal funding, or in job-related matters; **1968:** forbids anyone to refuse to sell or rent a dwelling to people

---

# Chapter Assessment

## Comprehension and Critical Thinking

### Section 1

1. **(a)** What does it mean to say that the population of the United States is heterogeneous? **(b)** How does the ethnic balance in the United States today differ from that of colonial times? **(c)** Which ethnic groups are experiencing the most rapid population growth?

2. **(a)** How did the Indian Education Act of 1972 attempt to reduce poverty on and near reservations? **(b)** Do you think that laws can fix the damage done to Native Americans? Why or why not?

3. **(a)** When and why did Asians first come to the United States? **(b)** How did Asian immigration change after 1882? After 1965?

4. **Analyze Political Cartoons** Study the cartoon below. **(a)** What does "glass ceiling" mean? **(b)** What form of discrimination is targeted by this cartoon? **(c)** How does the cartoon reverse the usual situation?

### Section 2

5. Cite an example of what you consider to be reasonable discrimination by government.

6. **(a)** What was the intent of Jim Crow laws? **(b)** What landmark Supreme Court case upheld Jim Crow laws and on what basis? **(c)** Do you think facilities can be "separate but equal"? Why or why not?

7. **(a)** Cite two cases in which the Supreme Court found sex-based distinctions to be unconstitutional. **(b)** Do you think the parameters that the Supreme Court uses when ruling on laws regarding the treatment of men and women are fair? Explain.

### Section 3

8. **(a)** What do the Civil Rights Acts of 1964 and 1968 prohibit? **(b)** How was enforcement of the 1968 act given added strength?

9. **(a)** What was the first major affirmative action case ruled on by the Supreme Court? **(b)** How did the Supreme Court rule in the case? **(c)** What arguments do critics use when they claim that affirmative action is unconstitutional?

### Section 4

10. **(a)** How does the 14th Amendment define citizenship? **(b)** In what circumstances may a child born abroad become an American citizen at birth?

11. **(a)** Why was immigration restricted in the 1880s and again in the 1920s? **(b)** Outline present immigration policy. **(c)** Who is excluded from entering the United States today?

### Writing About Government

12. Use your Quick Write exercises from each Section Assessment to write a problem-solution essay about the topic you selected in Section 1. Begin with an interesting detail that grabs readers' attention, then explain the problem. Describe the pros and cons of two solutions, using supporting facts and details to outline the steps of what you consider to be the best proposal. Proofread and revise your rough draft into final manuscript. See pp. S3–S5 in the Skills Handbook.

## Apply What You've Learned

13. **Essential Question Activity** Research major civil rights leaders in the United States, looking particularly for information on their ideals, struggles, and successes. Jot down notes as you work.

14. **Essential Question Assessment** Based on your research and the content of this chapter, create a timeline that helps to answer the Essential Question:

**Why are there ongoing struggles for civil rights?** Your timeline should include civil rights legislation and court cases, as well as quotes from famous civil rights leaders.

**Essential Questions Journal** To respond to the chapter Essential Question, go to your **Essential Questions Journal.**

---

on grounds of race, color, religion, national origin, sex, disability, or whether they have children **(b)** The Justice Department was given authority to bring criminal charges against those who violate its terms.

9. **(a)** *Regents of the University of California* v. *Bakke* **(b)** It held that *Bakke* had been denied equal protection and should be admitted to the medical school. **(c)** Critics say that the Constitution requires all public policies to be "color blind."

## SECTION 4

10. **(a)** as "all persons born or naturalized in the United States and subject to the jurisdiction thereof" **(b)** if both parents are American citizens, and at least one has lived in the United States or an American territory at some time; or if one parent is an American citizen who has lived in the United States for at least 5 years, 2 of them after age 14, and the child has lived in the United States continuously for at least 5 years between the ages of 14 and 28

11. **(a)** In the 1880s, the open frontier was gone and labor was no longer in short supply, and new immigrants were coming mostly from southern and eastern Europe.

# Document-Based Assessment

## Liberty, Equality, and Justice

For a very long time, the words "All men are created equal" meant little to African Americans who faced de jure segregation in the South and de facto segregation in the North. These documents show that Dr. Martin Luther King, Jr., who emerged as the leader of the civil rights movement, inspired Americans to press the struggle for civil rights.

### Document 1

**Section 1** That all men are by nature equally free and independent and have certain inherent rights, of which, when they enter into a state of society, they cannot, by any compact, deprive or divest their posterity; namely, the enjoyment of life and liberty, with the means of acquiring and possessing property, and pursuing and obtaining happiness and safety.

—**Virginia Declaration of Rights, 1776**

### Document 2

I say to you today, my friends, so even though we face the difficulties of today and tomorrow, I still have a dream. It is a dream deeply rooted in the American dream.

I have a dream that one day this nation will rise up and live out the true meaning of its creed: 'We hold these truths to be self-evident: that all men are created equal.'

I have a dream that one day on the red hills of Georgia the sons of former slaves and the sons of former slave owners will be able to sit down together at the table of brotherhood. . . .

I have a dream that my four little children will one day live in a nation where they will not be judged by the color of their skin but by the content of their character.

—**Martin Luther King, Jr., "I Have a Dream,"
August 28, 1963**

### Document 3

### Document 4

Injustice anywhere is a threat to justice everywhere. We are caught in an inescapable network of mutuality, tied in a single garment of destiny. Whatever affects one directly, affects all indirectly. Never again can we afford to live with the narrow, provincial 'outside agitator' idea. Anyone who lives inside the United States can never be considered an outsider anywhere within its bounds.

—**Martin Luther King, Jr., "Letter From Birmingham
Jail," April 16, 1963**

**Use your knowledge of civil rights and Documents 1–4 to answer the following questions.**

1. Which statement best summarizes Document 4?
   A. Never stop fighting for your rights.
   B. We are all afflicted by injustice.
   C. Search your heart for the truth.
   D. All Americans should enjoy happiness and safety.
2. According to Document 1, what are the inherent rights of the American people?
3. From which founding document does Dr. King quote in Document 2?
4. What method of protest is illustrated in Document 3?
5. **Pull It Together** What is the common thread that is woven through these documents? Explain.

**GOVERNMENT** ONLINE
**Documents**
To find additional primary sources about civil rights, visit
**PearsonSchool.com/phgovt**

---

**DOCUMENT-BASED ASSESSMENT**

1. B
2. life, liberty, property, happiness, and safety
3. the Declaration of Independence
4. nonviolent or peaceful picketing
5. All Americans are inherently equal, and all should receive equal justice and liberty.

**L2 Differentiate** Students use all the documents on the page to support their thesis.

**L3 Differentiate** Students include additional information available online at **PearsonSchool.com/phgovt.**

**L4 Differentiate** Students use materials from the textbook, the online information at **PearsonSchool.com/phgovt,** and do additional research to support their views.

**Go Online to PearsonSchool.com/phgovt** for a student rubric and extra documents.

---

In the 1920s, immigration was restricted to favor people from northern and western Europe. **(b)** The annual ceiling is set at 675,000 immigrants. Relatives of American citizens or resident aliens and immigrants with needed occupational talents are given priority. **(c)** criminals, suspected terrorists, persons with communicable diseases, drug abusers and addicts, illiterates, and mentally disturbed persons who might pose a threat to the safety of others

**WRITING ABOUT GOVERNMENT**

12. Students' essays should show evidence that they have researched pros and cons to plan and organize their steps toward solutions. A solid essay will utilize this research, with paragraphs organized by main ideas and supporting details. If students need help, guide them during the planning stage, using questions to draw out details for their solutions.

**APPLY WHAT YOU'VE LEARNED**

13. Students' notecards should include civil rights leaders of various races, ethnicities, and gender. Encourage students to locate and read the complete text of "Letter From Birmingham Jail" by Martin Luther King, Jr.

14. Students should scan the chapter for important civil rights legislation. Timelines should include brief descriptions of each law, how it was decided, and how it relates to other laws on the timeline.

Before assigning these questions, distribute the Rubric for Assessing a Writing Assignment (Unit 5 All-in-One, p. 242). Use the criteria and the guidelines below to grade students' answers to the Essential Question Warmup questions. Then send students to the **Essential Questions Journal** to answer the unit Essential Question.

**1.** According to this quote from *The Federalist* No. 78, Hamilton believed that the role of the judicial branch was to define and interpret the laws.

**2.** To answer this question successfully, students must demonstrate that they understand the premise of constitutionality. They will also make a clear statement of position and defend it with evidence.

**3.** A good answer will articulate an opinion about the role of the judicial branch in settling disputes related to new technology and situations that the Framers could not have foreseen when the Constitution was written. It will offer concrete examples to support the thesis.

**4.** To answer this question successfully, students must state a position on whether judges should be guided by personal views and support that position with evidence and examples.

## Essential Question
# What should be the role of the judicial branch?

Whether the role of the judicial branch should be to make law, apply law, or explain the law has been debated throughout history. The following examples each offer a perspective on the answer.

**" ON JUDICIAL ACTIVISM:**

We want courts to settle the question of whether someone has exceeded the limits set by the law. And we want judges to be free of essential dependence upon the wielders of power so that they can do what they are supposed to do without being intimidated.

—Joseph Tussman, *Judicial Activism and the Rule of Law—Toward a Theory of Selective Intervention*

**" ON THE IMPLICATIONS OF LAWS WITHOUT COURTS:**

Laws are dead letters without courts to expound and define their true meaning and operation.

—Alexander Hamilton, *The Federalist* No. 78, 1788

**ON HOW JUSTICES RULE:**

*Frank and Ernest*

### Essential Question Warmup

Throughout this unit, you studied the judicial branch. Use what you have learned and the quotations and opinions above to answer the following questions. Then go to your **Essential Questions Journal.**

**1.** What did Hamilton think should be the role of the judicial branch?

**2.** Are all laws completely constitutional or unconstitutional?

**3.** Should the role of the judicial branch change to adapt to changing times? Explain.

**4.** Should judges allow their personal views to guide their decisions? Why or why not?

**Essential Questions Journal** — To continue to build a response to the unit Essential Question, go to your **Essential Questions Journal.**

642

# Assessment Resources

Unit 5 AYP Monitoring Assessment
Exam*View* Test Bank CD-ROM
SuccessTracker Assessment
Online Student Self-Tests
Chapter Tests
Section Quizzes
Chapter-level Document-Based Assessment

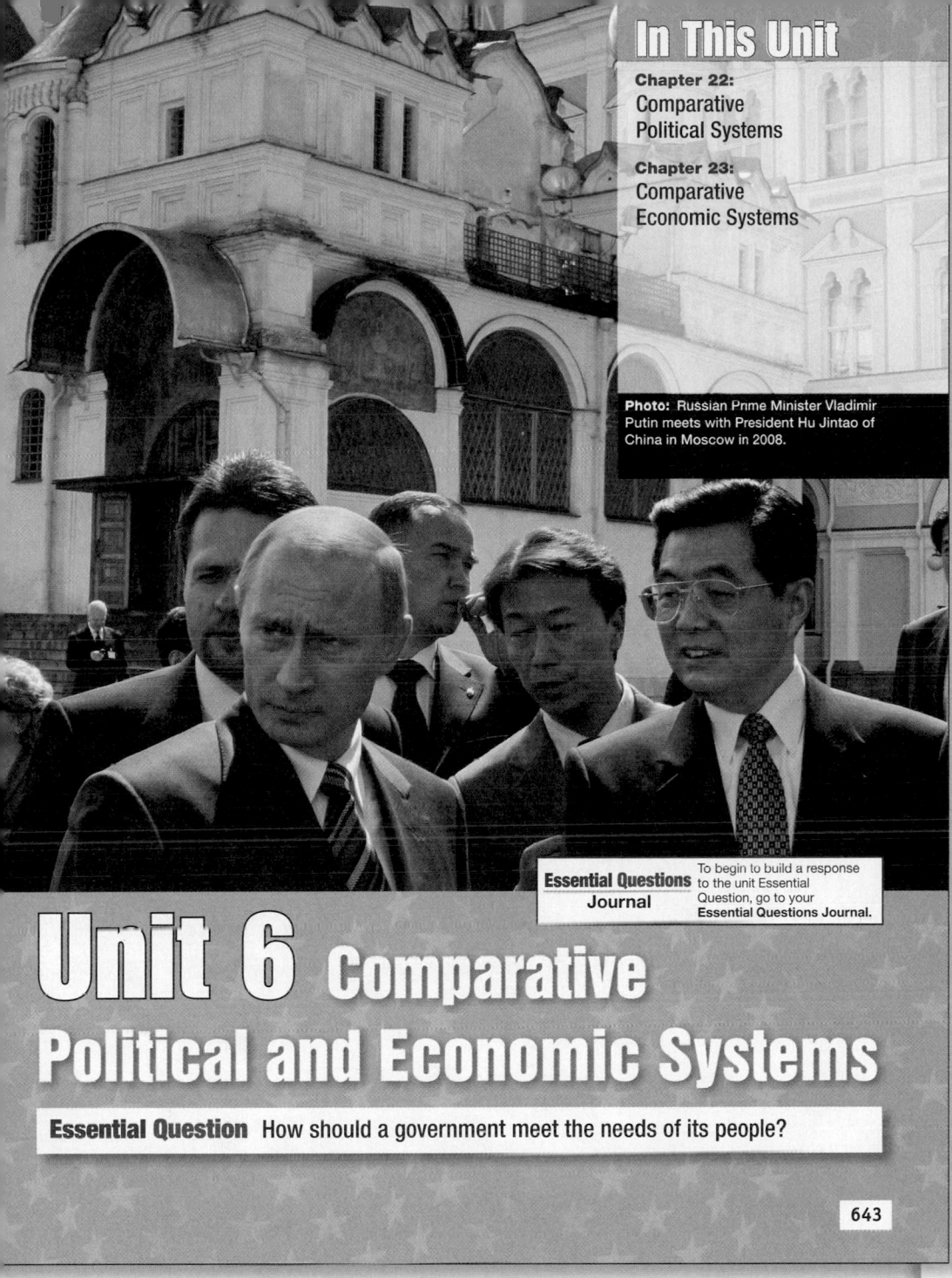

**Photo:** Russian Prime Minister Vladimir Putin meets with President Hu Jintao of China in Moscow in 2008.

**Essential Questions Journal**

To begin to build a response to the unit Essential Question, go to your **Essential Questions Journal.**

# Unit 6 Comparative Political and Economic Systems

**Essential Question** How should a government meet the needs of its people?

## Government Online Resources

Government Online Teacher Center at **PearsonSchool.com/phgovt** includes
- Online Teacher's Edition with lesson planner and lecture notes
- Teacher's Resource Library with All-in-One Resources, Color Transparencies, Adequate Yearly Progress Monitoring, and an alternative lesson plan for each chapter
- SuccessTracker Assessment

Government Online Student Center at **PearsonSchool.com/phgovt** includes
- Interactive textbook with audio
- American Government Essential Questions Video
- Chapter-level WebQuests
- Guided Audio Tours and Interactivities
- Student Self-Tests

## ESSENTIAL QUESTION PERSPECTIVES

Essential questions frame each unit and chapter of study, asking students to consider big ideas about government. The question for this unit—**How should a government meet the needs of its people?**—demands that students ask further questions. How should a government identify and define the people's needs? Is there a difference between political needs and economic needs? What should be the balance between meeting needs and allowing the market to work? How do governments measure their success in meeting its people's needs?

To begin this unit, assign the Unit 6 Warmup Activity on page 185 of the **Essential Questions Journal.** This will help students start to consider their position on the **Unit 6 Essential Question: How should a government meet the needs of its people?**

Show the **Unit 6 American Government Essential Questions Video** to help students begin thinking about the unit Essential Question and designate a classroom bulletin board for students to post news articles related to the unit Essential Question. Use the Conversation Wall strategy (p. T27) to encourage students to post articles and comments on other students' postings.

Later, students will further explore the chapter-level essential questions:

*Chapter 22:* **How should you measure different governments?**

*Chapter 23:* **To what extent should governments participate in the economy?**

Use the **Essential Questions Journal** throughout the program to help students consider these and other big ideas about government.

# Introduce the Chapter

## Essential Questions:

### UNIT 6

How should a government meet the needs of its people?

### CHAPTER 22

How should you measure different governments?

### ACTIVATE PRIOR KNOWLEDGE

Have students examine the image and quotation on these pages. Ask: **What form of government does China have?** *(Communist)* **Based on the quotation, do you think Winston Churchill would consider China's government effective? Explain.** *(No. The quote suggests that Churchill considers democracy more effective than communism.)* In this chapter, students will learn about democracy: its roots, its different forms, and the difficulties of achieving it. Tell students to begin to explore democracy by completing the Chapter 22 Essential Question Warmup activity in their **Essential Questions Journal.** Discuss their responses as a class.

### BEFORE READING

**L2** **ELL Differentiate** Chapter 22 Prereading and Vocabulary Worksheet (Unit 6 All-in-One, p. 9)

### SUCCESSNET STUDENT AND TEACHER CENTER

Visit **PearsonSchool.com/phgovt** for downloadable resources that allow students and teachers to connect with government "on the go."

### DIGITAL LESSON PRESENTATION

The digital lesson presentation supports the print lesson with activities and summaries of key concepts.

## SKILLS DEVELOPMENT

### ANALYZE TIMELINES

You may wish to teach analyzing timelines as a distinct skill within Section 1 of this chapter. Use the Chapter 22 Skills Worksheet (Unit 6 All-in-One, p. 20) to help students learn how to analyze timelines. The worksheet asks students to use information about African independence to create a vertical timeline. For L2 and L1 students, assign the adapted Skill Activity (Unit 6 All-in-One, p. 22).

**WebQuest online** The chapter WebQuest challenges students to answer the chapter Essential Question by asking them about different forms of government.

> "No one pretends that democracy is perfect or all-wise. Indeed, it has been said that democracy is the worst form of government except all those other forms that have been tried from time to time.
>
> —Winston Churchill, 1947

**Photo:** China's Premier Wen Jiabao opens the National People's Congress in Beijing.

644

## Block Scheduling

**BLOCK 1:** Teach the Section 1 lesson, and omit the Core Worksheet activity and Extend options. Teach the Section 2 and 3 lessons, omitting the Core Worksheet activity in Section 2 and the Extend options in both sections.

**BLOCK 2:** Have students create a Venn diagram to compare and contrast the governments of the UK and Mexico.

# Comparative Political Systems

**Essential Question**
How should you measure different governments?

**GOVERNMENT** ONLINE
On the Go

To study anywhere, anytime, download these online resources at PearsonSchool.com/phgovt
• Political Dictionary
• Audio Review
• Downloadable Interactivities

645

## Pressed for Time

To cover the chapter quickly, read aloud the primary source in the Section 1 Core Worksheet and discuss the questions. If time permits, discuss Transparency 22A, Legitimacy. For Section 2, have students complete the concept web on Enlightenment ideas in the Bellringer activity. Follow the discussion in the lesson to compare paths to popular sovereignty taken by Britain, France, and Latin America. In Section 3, discuss and list the factors that lead to democracy and the factors that cause failed states. Use the feature "What Makes Democracy Succeed" in the text to discuss democratic consolidation. In Section 4, display and discuss Transparency 22G, Two Modern Democracies, and Transparency 22H, Election Process in the United Kingdom.

## Lesson Goals

**SECTION 1**
Students will . . .
• compare the governments of ancient Athens and Rome by completing a pro/con chart.
• use a primary source to analyze the government of the Roman Republic and identify elements of it in the U.S. government.
• discuss legitimacy using a transparency and apply the concept to the Declaration of Independence.

**SECTION 2**
Students will . . .
• complete a concept web to review Enlightenment ideas.
• use the Think-Write-Pair-Share strategy to write a summarizing sentence connecting Enlightenment ideas with the spread of popular sovereignty.
• discuss the reasons for different paths toward popular sovereignty.
• create a political cartoon to illustrate the relationship of fascism or communism to the concept of popular sovereignty.

**SECTION 3**
Students will . . .
• discuss the challenges to democratic transitions.
• complete a chart to list the factors contributing to greater democracy and to failed democracy.
• analyze how Haiti and Iraq could succeed or fail in their transitions to democracy.

**SECTION 4**
Students will . . .
• recognize variations in democracies by comparing features of the governments of the UK and Mexico in a transparency.
• understand the UK's general election processes by examining a flowchart.
• compare and contrast the governments of the UK, Mexico, and the United States by playing a fact game.

**DIFFERENTIATED INSTRUCTION KEY**

Look for these symbols to help you adjust steps in each lesson to meet your students' needs.

**L1** Special Needs

**L2** Basic

**ELL** English Language Learners
**LPR** Less Proficient Readers

**L3** All Students

**L4** Advanced Students

## On what early political ideas and traditions was modern government founded?

I. Ancient Foundations
    A. Athens: The First Democracy
    B. Roman Republic
    C. Feudalism
II. Rise of Sovereign State
    A. Commercial revolution
    B. Towns
    C. Rise of Monarchies
III. Legitimacy
    A. People believe government has right to make public policy
    B. Established by tradition, power of personality, or rule of law
    C. Divine right of kings—traditional belief that God granted monarchs authority to rule
IV. Colonialism
    A. Spread laws and religious beliefs
    B. Mercantilism emphasized accumulation of precious metals to increase state's wealth and power
    C. Mercantilist policies involved monarch and state in economy
    D. Monarchs set up companies to monopolize trade with and tap wealth of colonies
    E. British colonial efforts led to creation of constitutional government of United States

## SKILLS DEVELOPMENT

### ANALYZE TIMELINES

To practice analyzing timelines in this section, use the Chapter 22 Skills Worksheet (Unit 6 All-in-One, p. 20). You may want to teach the skill before discussing the historical aspects of early governments. For L2 and L1 students, assign the adapted Skill Activity (Unit 6 All-in-One, p. 22).

---

SECTION 1

# Origins of the Modern State

### Guiding Question
**On what early political ideas and traditions was modern government founded?** Use an outline to take notes on the roots of modern American democracy.

I. Ancient Foundations
   A. Athens: The First Democracy
     1. _____
     2. _____
   B. _____
     1. _____
     2. _____

### Political Dictionary
- patricians
- plebeians
- feudalism
- sovereignty
- legitimacy
- divine right of kings
- colonialism
- mercantilism

### Objectives
1. Identify the ancient foundations of the state in Athens, in Rome, and in the feudal system.
2. Analyze the rise of sovereign states.
3. Explain how governments can achieve legitimacy.
4. Understand why European nations turned to colonialism.

**Image Above:** The *agora*, a large public space, was the ancient home of Athenian democracy.

**A**s you know, government is among the oldest of all human inventions. It emerged long before the dawn of recorded history, when human beings first realized that they could not survive without it—that is, without some means by which they could regulate their own and their neighbors' behavior. The earliest evidences of government date back some 3,000 years, but clearly the institution is much older than that.

An uncountable number of governments of various forms have appeared, and disappeared, through the centuries in Europe, Asia, Africa, and the Americas. Those that survived for any length of time were those that could adapt to major changes in their environments.

The roots of democratic government in today's world—including government in the United States—lie deep in human history. They reach back most particularly to ancient Greece and Rome and also to later beliefs and practices that emerged elsewhere in Europe.

## Ancient Foundations

Those who built a governmental system for the newly independent United States in the late 1700s were, on the whole, well educated. They were quite familiar with the political institutions of their day and, importantly, those of ancient Greece and Rome, as well.

**Athens: The First Democracy** Greek civilization began to develop some 700 to 800 years before the birth of Christ, and it reached its peak in the fourth century B.C. The Greece of that time was a loose collection of many small, independent, and somewhat isolated city-states[1]—a pattern dictated by the geography of the region, where every island, valley, and plain is cut off from its neighbors by the sea or by mountain ranges.

The concept of democracy was born in those city-states, most notably in Athens. Like the other city-states, Athens began as a monarchy. By the sixth century B.C., however, the Athenians had overthrown monarchical rule, and

---

1 Originally, the city-state (*polis*) was a defensible location to which those who lived in a particular locale could retreat when attacked. Over time, towns grew up around those defensible places.

# Focus on the Basics

**FACTS:** • Democracy was born in ancient Athens. • Representative government developed in the ancient Roman Republic. • Feudalism was a system of loose alliances between lords and vassals in medieval Europe. • In the late 1400s and the 1500s, European nations began colonizing other lands. • Colonial powers adopted mercantilism to control and profit from their colonies.

**CONCEPTS:** forms of government, role of government

**ENDURING UNDERSTANDINGS:** • The roots of modern democracies, including the United States, reach back to ancient Greece and Rome. • *Sovereignty* is the utmost authority to make decisions and maintain order. • All governments seek legitimacy through tradition, a charismatic leader, or the rule of law.

they soon replaced it with what they called *demokratia*—literally, "rule by the people."

Athenian democracy was, at base, direct democracy. Its central feature was an Assembly (the *Ecclesia*) composed of male citizens at least 18 years of age.[2] The Assembly met 40 times a year to debate public matters and make law. Decisions in the Assembly were made by majority vote.

The Assembly's agenda was set by a Council of Five Hundred (the *boule*). That body was composed of 500 citizens who were chosen randomly, served one-month terms, and did the routine day-to-day work of government. Courts (*dikastria*) were staffed by judges who were at least 30 years of age. They, too, were chosen randomly, served one-year terms, and settled both public and private disputes.

Athens reached the peak of its glory in art, literature, and philosophy in the fifth century B.C., but it had been severely weakened by the long Peloponnesian War (431–404 B.C.) and later conquest by the Macedonians. What remained of Athenian democracy was <u>extinguished</u> by the Romans who overran Greece in 146 B.C.

**The Roman Republic** At about the time that glimmers of democracy first appeared in Greece, they began to emerge as well in Rome on the Italian peninsula. Rome was founded in 753 B.C. and, like Athens, was originally a city-state ruled by a monarchy. Monarchical rule was overthrown in 509 B.C. and was soon replaced by a rude form of popular government. The Romans referred to their new system as *res publica*, a republic.[3] The Roman Republic was to last for some 400 years, until it became the Roman Empire at the end of the first century B.C. Over that period, Rome, involved in almost continuous military conflict, expanded its domain to include most of the lands surrounding the Mediterranean Sea and nearly all of Western Europe.

2  Neither political rights nor citizenship were granted to women, slaves, or males born to noncitizens. In all, only some 30,000 of Athens' estimated 250,000 inhabitants were citizens in the fourth century B.C.

3  From the Latin *res*, meaning "thing" or "matter," and *publicus* or *publica*, meaning "the public"—thus, "the public's thing," a thing belonging to the public

In Latin, SPQR stands for "the Senate and the people of Rome," the source of all government authority in the Roman Republic. ***How well did the Senate represent the people of Rome?***

**extinguish**
v. end, destroy

The Republic was far from democratic in the modern sense. It did introduce the concept of representation, however. Much of the political history of the republican period revolved around an often violent struggle between two social classes: the **patricians,** mostly rich upper-class, landowning aristocrats; and the **plebeians,** the common folk. The Romans did hold elections to choose some public officials, but women, slaves, and the foreign-born could not participate.

Government was centered in the Senate, composed of some 300 members, and two consuls chosen by the Senate. Senators were elected by the citizenry. The patricians dominated that body, but, over time, an increasing number of plebeians were elected to the Senate and to a number of lesser assemblies. The consuls were, effectively, the heads of state. They commanded the army and conducted foreign affairs. The consuls also presided over the Senate and enforced its decrees. Interestingly, each consul had the power to veto the other's decisions. In times of crisis, the Senate could appoint a

# Get Started

## LESSON GOALS

Students will . . .

- compare the governments of ancient Athens and Rome by completing a pro/con chart.

- use a primary source to analyze the government of the Roman Republic and identify elements of it in the U.S. government.

- discuss legitimacy using a transparency and apply the concept to the Declaration of Independence.

## BEFORE CLASS

Assign the section, the graphic organizer in the text, and the Reading Comprehension Worksheet (Unit 6 All-in-One, p. 13) before class.

**L2 Differentiate** Reading Comprehension Worksheet (Unit 6 All-in-One, p. 14)

## BELLRINGER

Write on the board: **Would you prefer to have lived under the government of ancient Athens or the Roman Republic? In your notebook, briefly explain why.**

**L2 Differentiate** Students may list a few reasons why they would prefer one system over the other.

# Differentiated Resources

The following resources are located in the All-in-One, Unit 6, Chapter 22, Section 1:

**L2** Prereading and Vocabulary Worksheet (p. 9)

**L3** Reading Comprehension Worksheet (p. 13)

**L2** Reading Comprehension Worksheet (p. 14)

**L3 L2** Core Worksheets (pp. 16, 18)

**L3 L2** Skills Worksheets (pp. 20, 22)

**L3 L4** Extend Worksheet (p. 24)

**L3** Quiz A (p. 26)

**L2** Quiz B (p. 27)

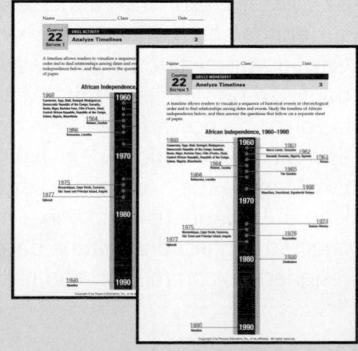

# Answers

**Caption** Possible response: For the time, the Senate was relatively representative; but from a modern perspective, it was not. It represented only the views of the male patricians, not the lower classes or women.

# Teach

To present this topic using online resources, use the lesson presentations at **PearsonSchool.com/phgovt**.

## INTRODUCE THE TOPIC

Tell students that the topic of this lesson is early types of government—particularly those that form the roots of modern democracies. Several basic concepts on which the United States government is based developed in ancient Athens and the Roman Republic. (Clarify that democracy was specific to Athens; for example, Sparta was a monarchy.)

## CREATE PRO/CON CHARTS

Write *direct democracy* and *republic* on the board. Ask volunteers to define each term. *(Direct democracy is a system, developed in ancient Athens, in which citizens participate directly in the government. A republic is a representative government, developed in ancient Rome, in which citizens elect officials to make laws and run the government.)* Ask students which type of government they chose in the Bellringer, and why. Discuss what life would have been like under each—for example, would they have had any say in the government or any rights at all? Were there benefits in either system for females? Count to see how many students chose each system. Ask: **What are some positive and negative aspects of each system?** *(Students may note that neither government was very responsive to most of the residents. Citizenship was very limited in Athens and to some extent in Rome. In Athens, people had a direct say in the government. In Rome, the patricians dominated the senate, although some plebeians were eventually elected to the senate and to lesser assemblies. Direct democracy is not very efficient and could not work in a large country. A republic is more efficient, but the people give up some of their power to those who rule for them.)* Record students' responses in pro/con charts on the board.

**L2 ELL Differentiate** Encourage students to share the words in their native languages for democracy and republic.

## Answers

**Checkpoint** Athens pioneered democratic government; Rome introduced representative government and the rule of law.

**648** Comparative Political Systems

---

✔ **Checkpoint**
What did Athens and Rome contribute to modern government?

**epochal event**
*n.* beginning of an era marked by notable happenings

**catalyst**
*n.* something that prompts, brings about, change

dictator to serve in place of the consuls and exercise absolute power, but for no longer than six months.[4]

**Feudalism** The decline and fall of the Roman Empire in the fifth century A.D. marked the beginning of the Middle Ages—the period from that <u>epochal event</u> on to the 16th century. It also marked the collapse of centralized authority and organized government over vast stretches of the western world. For more than a thousand years, that world would know little or nothing of government in the modern sense of the term.

The feudal system was born in response to that chaos and disorder. It developed in fits and starts and came to hold sway over much of Europe from the ninth through the twelfth centuries. **Feudalism** was a loosely organized system in which powerful lords divided their lands among other, lesser lords. Those with land and power agreed to protect others in exchange for their loyalty, their military service, and a share of the crops they produced. The basic economic units in the feudal system were the lords' manors. Each manor contained all of a lord's land holdings, which often included a town or village, as well.

The primary relationship in the feudal chain was that between a lord and his vassals, lesser lords who pledged their loyalty to the ranking lord—who was, in some places, a monarch. The lord ruled and the vassals served him, watching over the lands in their section of the manor.

The lord did perform some functions of the state in the modern world. He provided protection for his vassals and administered a rough form of justice. In return, the vassals supported the lord's decisions and served under his military command when necessary. The lord-vassal relationship was but one part of a large complex of relationships. Often, a vassal was himself a lord to other, less powerful vassals, and a lord was sometimes a vassal under an even more powerful lord.

Serfs, the bulk of the population, lived at the bottom of the chain of feudal relationships. They were peasants, bound to the land they farmed. The serfs gave a share of what they grew to their vassals in return for protection in times of war. They led harsh lives. None could leave the land without the lord's permission, and their children inherited their ties and responsibilities to the lord. Most died young, never having journeyed more than a few miles from the lord's manor.

**The Roman Catholic Church** As the Roman Empire had spread across Western Europe, so had Roman Catholicism. The Church survived the collapse of imperial rule and now, in concert with feudalism, it provided some measure of government-like order to life in the Europe of the Middle Ages.

The Roman Catholic Church, now nearly 2,000 years old, traces its origins to the birth of Christianity and to the death of Jesus in Jerusalem, in the Roman province of Judea, in A.D. 33. Catholicism managed to overcome three centuries of often violent persecution by a succession of hostile emperors. In A.D. 380, the Roman Catholic Church became the official church of the Roman Empire.

As most of Europe was converted to Christianity—that is, as most Europeans became Catholics—the Roman Catholic Church became increasingly powerful. By the late Middle Ages, the pope and his bishops ruled vast land holdings, and they frequently vied with monarchs and lords for political as well as religious influence over people's lives.

## Rise of the Sovereign State

Feudalism was, at best, a loose, makeshift basis for government. As cracks emerged in the system—between Catholics and Protestants and the feudal manor and the marketplace—the need for a more structured arrangement became apparent. The outlines of the modern, sovereign nation-state began to emerge.

**The Commercial Revolution** By the end of the Middle Ages, a commercial revolution began to change the ways in which people lived and did business. A horrific plague, the Black Plague of the 1340s, was a major <u>catalyst</u> of that revolution. In all, it killed a third of Western Europe's population. The

---

4 The word *dictator* comes from the Latin *dictare*, meaning "to say or pronounce."

**648** Comparative Political Systems

---

# Background

**AMERICAN CINCINNATUS** Around 458 B.C., Lucius Quinctius Cincinnatus was plowing his field when a messenger arrived. The Roman consul and his legions were surrounded by the Aequi tribe and faced annihilation. The senate had appointed Cincinnatus dictator, and he was charged with rescuing the army. Cincinnatus departed his farm immediately and soon defeated the enemy. The crisis over, he resigned his powerful position and returned to his home. Legend honors Cincinnatus as a model of patriotism. Inspired by this story, many people have called George Washington the "American Cincinnatus." Washington accepted his country's call to lead the Continental Army in a time of crisis. When the Revolution ended, Washington rejected suggestions that he become king of the new nation. Like Cincinnatus, he resigned his commission and returned to his farm, instead of taking power.

# Roots of the Sovereign State

The defining elements of sovereign states developed over time and in different lands. *What characteristics define the United States as a sovereign state?*

**GOVERNMENT** ONLINE
**Audio Tour**
Listen to a guided audio tour on sovereignty at
PearsonSchool.com/phgovt

### Ancient Athens

The Athenians introduced direct democracy. Citizens debated public questions and decided them by majority vote. Courts administered justice.

### Roman Republic

The Roman Republic gave decision-making power to an elite Senate and consuls who could check each other and, in theory, represented the people. The laws of Rome were written for all to see.

### Feudalism

In the Feudal Era, Europe's first parliaments emerged and began to limit the powers of kings. England provided for trial by a jury of one's peers.

### 17th century

Sovereignty emerged in the 17th century, with states with fixed borders, a national identity, and a centralized government with broad authority.

Above. The Norman Invasion of 1066 brought feudalism to England.

Plague itself did not destroy the feudal system. Rather its far-reaching effects undercut that system.

After the plague, the manors still depended on the same amount of work, but from the smaller number of serfs who had survived. Serfs and free peasants found strength in the high value of their labor and began to demand higher wages and better conditions.

Because of the vast decrease in population caused by the plague, the prices of food crops fell, and so the lords made less money from their manorial lands. Merchants and artisans became increasingly wealthy and more powerful. The economy became increasingly based on money and trade, rather than land.

**The Influence of Towns** As you know, feudalism relied on personal relationships and agreements in which people exchanged work and food for security and justice. Over time,

lords had to find new ways to gather money. Some lords accepted money from their vassals in place of military service. Others allowed free people to set up towns on their land for a fee under a charter. In this way, towns began to spring up across Europe. Those towns were centers of trade and freedom that tested the limits of feudalism.

The most important of these towns were found in northern Italy, northern Germany, and the Netherlands. Their income came from trade with Central Europe and Asia. The merchants in these towns had uneasy relationships with the lords. Although the merchants were free, they had to pay money to lords for protection, duties on their trade goods, and the right to use roads, rivers, and bridges. Many lords tried to extend their system of justice to the towns. They often failed, because they depended on the merchants and bankers of the towns for loans. Trade <u>guilds</u> also developed

✔ **Checkpoint**
Why did feudalism endure?

**guild**
*n.* association of craftsmen or merchants

# Background

**THEOCRACY** Religion has influenced governments throughout history. A *theocracy* is a government run by religious leaders or clergy. The term originated with Jewish historian Flavius Josephus in the first century A.D. In describing God's laws revealed to the Israelites, he used the Greek word *theokratia,* meaning "rule of God." One of colonial America's first governments was a Puritan theocracy in Massachusetts Bay Colony. Only believers in the Puritan faith could vote and govern. Roger Williams objected to this and went to what is now Rhode Island to start his own colony. Display Transparency 22B, In Puritan Theocracy Dissenter. Ask: **What is the main idea of this excerpt?** *(to keep religion and government separate)* Few theocracies exist today, but some governments rule under the Sharia, or Islamic law. A modern example is Iran, in which a powerful cleric serves as head of state.

## DISTRIBUTE THE CORE WORKSHEET

Distribute the Chapter 22 Section 1 Core Worksheet (Unit 6 All-in-One, p. 16), which contains an excerpt about the government of the Roman Republic. Point out that the Framers of the U.S. Constitution were familiar with Roman political institutions and used some of these ideas in creating the U.S. government. Have students read the excerpt and then answer the questions.

**L1 L2 ELL Differentiate** Distribute the adapted Core Worksheet (Unit 6 All-in-One, p. 18). Have students work in small groups to answer the questions.

**L4 Differentiate** Have students do research on the government of ancient Athens. Ask them to work together to prepare a presentation explaining the basic elements of the Athenian government and the concepts the U.S. Framers may have drawn from it.

## COMPARE AND CONTRAST SYSTEMS

Have students share their answers to the Core Worksheet with the class. Draw a Venn diagram on the board, with the following labels: "Roman Republic," "United States," and "Both." Students should work with you to fill in the diagram with details to compare and contrast the governmental systems. Then have students identify specific features in the U.S. government that were drawn from the Roman Republic.

Tell students to go to the Audio Tour for a guided tour of the roots of the sovereign state.

## Answers

**Roots of the Sovereign State** fixed borders, a national identity, centralized government with complete authority

**Checkpoint** Feudalism provided stability and security.

## DISCUSS LEGITIMACY

Ask: **What is *legitimacy*?** Explain that the root of *legitimacy* is from the Latin word *lex,* which means "law." Ask students how this might relate to the meaning of *legitimacy.* (*Legitimacy is literally "legal rule."*) Clarify that *legitimacy* is the right to rule, granted by the ruled to the rulers. Tell students that even a government that rules by force seeks legitimacy. Ask: **Why is legitimacy important to a government?** (*The government will be more stable and likely to last if the people believe it has the right to rule them.*)

Display Transparency 22A, Legitimacy. Ask: **Which types of legitimacy did the Athenian democracy have?** (*traditional, rule of law*) **the Roman Republic?** (*traditional, rule of law*) **feudalism?** (*traditional, power of personality*) **absolute monarchy?** (*traditional/divine right, power of personality*) **the United States government?** (*rule of law*)

**L1** **L2** **ELL Differentiate** Pronounce *legitimacy* for students. Clarify that *legitimacy* is a noun and *legitimate* is the related adjective, meaning that it describes a government that has legitimacy, as in "a legitimate government." Ask students if they know the verb that means "to make legitimate." (*legitimize*) Be sure that students see the common root in these words.

## EXTEND THE LESSON

**L3** **Differentiate** Distribute the Chapter 22 Section 1 Extend Worksheet (Unit 6 All-in-One, p. 24). Tell students that the worksheet provides parts of the Declaration of Independence. As they read it, they should identify key phrases that relate to legitimacy and then use these phrases to help them answer the question that follows.

**L4** **Differentiate** Have students read the full version of the Declaration of Independence reproduced in their textbook and answer the worksheet question based on the entire document.

**L1** **L2** **ELL Differentiate** Read through the worksheet excerpts as a class. Pause after reading each paragraph to have students identify phrases concerning the right to rule and restate the phrases in their own words.

---

in the cities and towns, and their members demanded a say in government.

**The Rise of Monarchies** All of these factors began to undermine the feudal system, weakening the power of the lords. At the same time, the leaders of the towns began to appreciate the benefits of supporting a central authority and they allied themselves with monarchs. The monarchs, in turn, saw the towns as a source of wealth that could free them from dependence on their vassals.

Therefore, by the late 1400s the powers of the monarchs were expanding, and feudalism was fast disappearing. In nations such as England, Spain, and France, rulers centralized power, establishing national governments with national legal systems, national identities, and, most important for the monarchs, national taxes. Warfare now was between national armies, not between powerful nobles. Monarchs, whose power was absolute or nearly so, no longer needed the lords to support them and could also ignore popular representative assemblies, if they wished, for long periods of time.

To help manage the national government, monarchs hired loyal civil servants typically born in the towns and educated at local universities. Their perspectives were

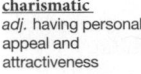
**charismatic**
*adj.* having personal appeal and attractiveness

▲ In the 1400s, King Ferdinand and Queen Isabella united their lands in marriage into what became the Kingdom of Spain. The unification of power in Spain, France, and England led to the establishment of colonies overseas.

national, not regional. The state, in the person of the monarch, now had **sovereignty,** or the utmost authority in decision making and in maintaining order. Everyone, including the nobles, was subordinate to that authority.

Because monarchs already existed within the feudal system, they enjoyed the benefits and respect of tradition. A monarch was now recognized as the strongest individual who could best govern a state and protect the people from harm. With sovereignty, the monarch now had the right to make laws for the entire nation and all its people.

## Legitimacy

The development of the sovereign state was useful in creating political organization, but claiming sovereignty alone does not establish government. All governments must have legitimacy to rule.

Rulers have strong reasons to seek consent for their rule. This consent is known as **legitimacy,** the belief of the people that a government has the right to make public policy. A legitimate government is one that is accepted by its people and other governments as the sovereign authority of a nation. Leaders may use force to keep power. However, force is difficult to maintain over time.

Governments may gain legitimacy in several ways. One is by tradition. In this case, people accept a certain form of government because their society has long been governed in that way, and people expect their institutions and traditions to be carried on into the future. One type of traditional legitimacy is known as the **divine right of kings.** For hundreds of years, European monarchs based their right to rule on this belief that God had granted them that authority. To disobey a monarch was to deny the natural order of society and to commit a sin against God. In theory, monarchs who ruled by divine right did not have to answer to parliaments or to the people, only to God. The divine right of kings drew its claim to legitimacy from Europe's deep-rooted Christian values.

Another way for a government, and in particular one leader, to win legitimacy is through the power of personality. A <u>charismatic</u> person with strong leadership skills can often win

---

# Teacher-to-Teacher Network

**ALTERNATE LESSON PLAN** Have students work in groups to create an informational display about one of these forms of government: Athenian democracy, the Roman Republic, feudalism, or a seventeenth-century absolute monarchy. Each display should point out concepts and practices that form the roots of democratic government today. Students should enhance their display with images of political leaders and other appropriate visuals.

To see this lesson plan, go to

**Teacher Center**
at PearsonSchool.com/phgovt

popular support. The people agree to allow this person to rule them.

The final and most durable form of legitimacy is created when a government binds itself to the rule of law. The law must be seen as fair and effective in order for people to trust their government. Constitutional government in the United States is an excellent example of this form of legitimacy.

## Colonialism

Beginning in the late 1400s and early 1500s, several European monarchies embarked on a policy of **colonialism**—the control of one nation over lands abroad. European settlers, laws, and religious beliefs spread around the world as rival nations competed for colonial possessions.

Colonial trade and its wealth brought newfound power to merchants, and monarchs adopted mercantilism to control and profit from that situation. **Mercantilism** is an economic and political theory emphasizing money as the chief source of wealth to increase the absolute power of the monarchy and the nation. The policy stressed the accumulation of precious metals, like gold and silver. It also called for the establishment of colonies and a merchant marine and the development of industry and mining to build a favorable balance of trade with other countries. Mercantilist policies brought the monarchy and the state deep into the economy. Monarchs taxed imports heavily to protect locally produced goods. Foreigners were required to buy licenses from the state in order to trade with local merchants. Monarchs sought to fill their treasuries and enhance their own and their nations' power.

Mercantilism expanded when European explorers reached the Western Hemisphere. Their explorations there opened new opportunities for trade and farming, but only monarchs had the wealth and power to establish and control new colonies.

The high cost of exploration allowed monarchs to control overseas commerce by setting up companies to monopolize trade with the new regions. The company system allowed monarchs to tap new sources of wealth from distant gold and silver mines and from far-flung trade.

European colonization brought about new developments in modern government. Britain's colonial efforts led to the American Revolution and the creation of the United States and its constitutional government. The experiences of other countries originally colonized by Spain, France, Portugal, and even Great Britain, however, differed in several ways from the American experience.

✔ **Checkpoint**
Why is legitimacy important?

**monopolize**
v. prevent others from sharing; control, dominate

---

**Essential Questions Journal**

To continue to build a response to the chapter Essential Question, go to your Essential Questions Journal.

## SECTION 1 ASSESSMENT

1. **Guiding Question** Use your completed outline to answer this question: On what early political ideas and traditions was modern government founded?

**Key Terms and Comprehension**

2. How did the Athenian *Ecclesia* differ from the Roman Senate?

3. What were the main elements of **feudalism**?

4. How did the power of monarchs change over time?

**Critical Thinking**

5. **Understanding Cause and Effect** How did the rise of towns and the commercial revolution contribute to the decline of the feudal system?

6. **Drawing Inferences** Why is it necessary for a government to gain legitimacy?

**Quick Write**

**Expository Writing: Select a Topic** The goal of a compare-and-contrast essay is to analyze similarities and differences between two topics. Select two systems of government or examples of nations that developed into democracies to compare and contrast in your essay. As you read, use a Venn diagram to record similarities and differences between your two selections.

---

## Assess and Remediate

**L3** Collect the Core Worksheets and assess the students' work.

**L3** Assign the Section 1 Assessment questions.

**L3** Section Quiz A (Unit 6 All-in-One, p. 26)

**L2** Section Quiz B (Unit 6 All-in-One, p. 27)

Have students complete the review activities in the digital lesson presentation and continue their work in the **Essential Questions Journal.**

### REMEDIATION

| If Your Students Have Trouble With | Strategies For Remediation |
|---|---|
| Elements of ancient Athenian and Roman governments (Questions 1, 2) | Have students write a summary of the main parts of the government in ancient Athens and Rome under the Republic. |
| Aspects of the feudal system (Questions 3, 5) | Ask students to make a pyramid showing the hierarchical relationships under feudalism, with the monarch at the top and the serfs at the bottom. |
| Changes in the power of European monarchs (Question 4) | Have students make a flowchart that describes changes in monarchies from the feudal period to the seventeenth century. |
| The concept of legitimacy (Question 6) | With students, create a class concept web that records ideas about legitimacy—its forms and purpose. |

## Answers

**Checkpoint** Legitimacy allows governments to rule without violence and with the respect of the people. It also ensures a more stable and successful government.

---

# Assessment Answers

**1.** The U.S. was founded on principles of democracy, legitimacy, and representative government that have their roots in ancient Athens and the Roman Republic. Ancient Greeks practiced direct democracy and majority rule. The Roman Republic introduced representative government and the veto to check power. Monarchs at the end of the Middle Ages centralized power and established a national government, national legal system, and national identity, leading to the state as the sovereign entity.

**2.** Both were the central lawmaking body. However, the *Ecclesia* was based on direct democracy. The Roman senate was a representative government.

**3.** Lords protected and gave land to vassals in exchange for loyalty, labor, military service, and part of the crop. The lords' manors were the basic economic units. Serfs farmed the land and received protection from their vassals in exchange for a share of their crop.

**4.** Under feudalism, monarchs were usually the most powerful lords. As the Black Plague, commercial revolution, and rise of towns eroded feudalism, monarchs centralized power, creating sovereign states.

**5.** Towns and the commercial revolution weakened feudalism by offering people a way to live freely outside the feudal structure. It also increased the power of landless townspeople through wealth that they lent to the monarchs.

**6.** If citizens do not view their government as legitimate, they may disobey or overthrow it.

**QUICK WRITE** Students should create Venn diagrams to compare and contrast two systems of government discussed in the chapter.

# Teach

## BRAINSTORM

Have students brainstorm a list of specific news-oriented sites, such as local or network television sites, e-zines, government sites, and online newspapers. Discuss sites such as blogs and wikis. Explain that these must be carefully evaluated because they rely on individuals' contributions, with little or no oversight.

## DEVELOP AN EVALUATION CHECKLIST

List the criteria below on the board. Tell students that they can evaluate the reliability of an Internet source by asking the following questions.

- **Authorship**—Who wrote the site content?
- **Credentials**—Where does the site content originate?
- **Currency**—How up-to-date is the content?
- **Purpose**—Why has the content been created?
- **Accuracy**—Are there grammar, spelling, or factual errors?

# Assess and Remediate

Collect students' research results and grade them. You may also wish to have them answer the What Do You Think questions.

## Answers

1. Sample response: Focusing your search saves time. Search terms that are too broad can return thousands of possible sites. Terms that are too narrow might return none.

2. You can compare the information to the same information at a trustworthy Web site. Also, you can trust government sites and reputable news sources, such as *Newsweek* and the BBC.

3. A strong result will include a focused search topic and trustworthy Web sources.

---

## CITIZENSHIP 101

# Using the Internet as a News Source

Suppose your teacher gave you the following assignment in Government class: Write a report on this week's visit of the Japanese prime minister to the United States. Include major locations where the prime minister spoke and the significance of his meetings with the President.

When researching current events, such as the visit of a foreign leader to the United States, Internet news sources are extremely helpful—provided you are careful about evaluating the sources you use. Major television networks, newspapers, and news magazines all have Web sites, and they are usually quite reliable—for example: CNN, the BBC, National Public Radio, *The Wall Street Journal*, and *The New York Times*. Government Web sites are also useful sources.

To use the Internet as a news source, follow these steps:

1. **Determine your search term(s).** To search most effectively on the Internet, you need to determine a specific term or topic. Searching for a broad subject can yield too many responses that do not address your questions. For example, "Japan prime minister" will yield thousands of results and take a great deal of time to sift through. In this case, you might use the prime minister's name and "U.S. visit."

2. **Use a search engine to find information on your topic or to locate specific news sources.** Type in the search term for your topic or the name of a specific news organization, such as *Newsweek*, if you already have one in mind. You can also simply type "news" into a search engine, but it will take you much longer to locate specific information on your topic. News sources that are local to the event may provide unique information and coverage.

3. **Be sure that your sources have a reputation for accurate news coverage.** Some news organizations have better reputations for accuracy and objectivity than others, but findings from all sources should be confirmed with at least a second source. If you are unsure of a source's reliability, compare its information with similar information from a source you know to be trustworthy.

### ▸▸ What do you think?

1. Why is it important to determine your topic or search terms before you begin an Internet search?
2. How can you determine the reliability of a news source?
3. **You Try It** Choose a current topic in the news related to the government or politics of one of the nations covered in this chapter. Determine your search terms, and type them into a search engine. Follow the results from reliable news sources. Take notes about the information you find at each of at least three Web sites you think are trustworthy—reports, editorials, photographs, video, and so on.

**GOVERNMENT** ONLINE
**Citizenship Activity Pack**
For an activity to help you use the Internet for research, go to **PearsonSchool.com/phgovt**

652

# Citizenship Activity Pack

**L1** **L2** If your students need extra support, use the Citizenship Activity Pack lesson *How to Use the Internet as a News Source*. It includes a lesson plan for you, worksheets that help students analyze Web sites, assessment rubrics, and posters that represent Web sites covering one story in different ways. Students may also access the Citizenship Activity Pack online for activities on How to Use the Internet as a News Source at **PearsonSchool.com/phgovt**.

# SECTION 2

# Ideas and Revolutions

## Guiding Question

**How have some nations expanded popular sovereignty?** Use a flowchart similar to the one below to record information about how different nations have expanded popular sovereignty.

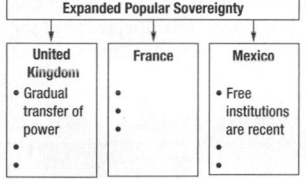

**Expanded Popular Sovereignty**

| United Kingdom | France | Mexico |
|---|---|---|
| • Gradual transfer of power | • | • Free institutions are recent |
| • | • | • |
| • | • | • |

## Political Dictionary

- *encomienda*
- *guerrilla warfare*
- *fascism*
- *communism*

## Objectives

1. Understand how Enlightenment helped influence the expansion of popular sovereignty.
2. Analyze the role of popular sovereignty in England, France, and around the world.
3. Describe events in Latin America, Asia, and Africa that expanded popular sovereignty.
4. Examine how fascism and communism distort the concept of popular sovereignty.

**Image Above:** Simón Bolívar led many South American nations to independence from Spain in the early 1800s.

In the previous section, you traced the development of governments in Europe from ancient Greece and Rome to the rise of the sovereign state and absolute monarchies. You also discovered how sovereign states gain legitimacy. In this section, you will see how legitimacy can lead to stable government. You will also discover how governments that lack legitimacy can fall to revolutions and descend into tyranny.

## The Enlightenment

By the beginning of the eighteenth century, scientific discoveries and new thinking had led to an intellectual movement based on reason and known as the Enlightenment. Some of the most important ideas about modern government, economics, and society were developed at the time, as people began to discuss the rights of individuals to control their own fates and to have a meaningful say in their governance.

Early in the movement, English political theorist John Locke (1632–1704) put forth the notion of the natural rights of all human beings, including the rights to life, liberty, and property—ideas that later formed the basis for the Declaration of Independence. He built on the view of fellow Englishman Thomas Hobbes (1588–1679): that the people and their rulers are parties to a social contract that defines the rights and powers of each. Economists, including Adam Smith (1723–1790) and David Ricardo (1772–1823), criticized those economic policies that had helped monarchs grow wealthier while most of their subjects became steadily poorer and less free.

In France, the philosopher François-Marie Arouet (1694–1778), known as Voltaire, advocated reason, freedom of religion, the importance of scientific observation, and the idea of human progress. The ideas of the Baron de Montesquieu (1689–1755) were crucial to political theory during the Enlightenment. His theories about the separation of the powers of government, so that the different branches might check and balance one another, were integral to what was to become the Constitution of the United States.

As reason and secular thinking began to supersede religious belief, monarchs lost some of their divine legitimacy, and their God given sovereignty

---

# How have some nations expanded popular sovereignty?

**Expanded Popular Sovereignty**

| United Kingdom | France | Mexico |
|---|---|---|
| • Gradual transfer of power | • French Revolution | • Free institutions are recent |
| • Magna Carta | • The Terror | • Agustin de Iturbide engineered independence and became emperor; later overthrown |
| • Charles I overthrown | • Rise of Napoleon | • Periods of civil war through nineteenth century |
| • Petition of Right | • War with rest of Europe | • Stability under President Porfirio Diaz's harsh rule |
| • Bill of Rights | • Historic institutions destroyed and replaced by new ones | • Revolt and civil war |
| • Parliament used power of purse to gain power over monarch | • Several revolutions and changes in government | • New constitution 1910 |
| • Laws gradually expanded suffrage | | • Reform under Institutional Revolutionary Party |
| • Historic institutions preserved | | |

# Get Started

## LESSON GOALS

Students will . . .

- complete a concept web to review Enlightenment ideas.
- use the Think-Write-Pair-Share strategy to write a summarizing sentence connecting Enlightenment ideas with the spread of popular sovereignty.
- discuss the reasons for different paths toward popular sovereignty.
- create a political cartoon to illustrate the relationship of fascism or communism to popular sovereignty.

## SKILLS DEVELOPMENT

### ANALYZE POLITICAL CARTOONS

Before students use this section's Core Worksheet to create political cartoons about fascism or communism, have them turn to the Skills Handbook, p. S22, to learn more about political cartoons.

---

# Focus on the Basics

**FACTS:** • Enlightenment thinkers developed new ideas about the relationship between government and the governed. • Popular sovereignty in Britain was based on the Magna Carta, Petition of Right, and Bill of Rights. • Fascist governments glorify the state over the individual. • Communist governments control the economy without regard for individual liberty.

**CONCEPTS:** types of government systems, popular sovereignty

**ENDURING UNDERSTANDINGS:** • The Enlightenment emphasized reason and scientific inquiry. • Britain achieved popular sovereignty gradually, while France underwent a bloody revolution. • Nations in Latin America, Asia, and Africa struggled to maintain democracy after independence. • Communist and fascist governments emphasize popular sovereignty but distort the concept.

Assign the section, the graphic organizer in the text, and the Reading Comprehension Worksheet (Unit 6 All-in-One, p. 28) before class.

**L2 Differentiate** Reading Comprehension Worksheet (Unit 6 All-in-One, p. 30)

**BELLRINGER**

Display Transparency 22C, Enlightenment Web, which is a blank concept web with the center oval labeled "Enlightenment Ideas." Instruct students to fill in the concept web based on their reading.

**L1 L2 ELL Differentiate** Direct students to begin the concept web by recording the names of thinkers mentioned on the first page of the section. Point out that the text discusses the ideas of Smith and Ricardo together, so students should combine them in the concept web.

---

## Answers

**Checkpoint** Popular sovereignty means that all power comes from the people. Democracy is based on the principle of popular sovereignty.

**Two Revolutions** The French transition resulted in significant bloodshed and the destruction of its historic institutions. Britain's transition preserved many of its institutions and minimized bloodshed.

---

✔ **Checkpoint**
What is popular sovereignty and why is it important?

came into question. More and more people began to feel that even monarchs governed only because the people granted them the power to do so. If a monarch abused his or her power, he or she broke the social contract with the people and no longer deserved to rule. In this way, popular sovereignty became increasingly important, even in a monarchy. Recall that popular sovereignty is the idea that governments can exist only with the consent of the governed.

Popular sovereignty would eventually form the basis for the many republics and democracies in the world today. Since the eighteenth century, almost every government has had to address issues of popular sovereignty in one way or another.

## Two Roads to Popular Sovereignty

Two leading monarchies in Western Europe, Britain and France, took very different paths to popular sovereignty. In Britain, popular sovereignty was achieved gradually. As one of the first modern countries where the people began to have a say in their government,

Britain blended popular sovereignty with deep-seated cultural traditions. Meanwhile, France took a revolutionary route to popular sovereignty and rejected many longstanding traditions.

**Democracy in Britain** Great Britain, now the United Kingdom, is today a constitutional monarchy. Yet that nation functions as a democracy much like the United States. Britons elect a government that is responsible to them and which draws its legitimacy from their votes and support. Great Britain was not always democratic, however. How did a country once ruled by powerful monarchs become a vibrant democracy?

The UK's history is marked by the gradual transfer of sovereignty from the monarchy to the people. The Magna Carta in 1215 was the first move toward a constitutional monarchy. In the 1640s, the English people went to war against their monarch, King Charles I. He was tried, found guilty, and executed as a tyrant and traitor in 1649. The Petition of Right of 1628 and the Bill of Rights of 1689 took more authority from the monarch and gave it to Parliament, which represented the people. Parliament controlled "the power of

# Two Revolutions

Monarchies in Britain and France adapted to popular sovereignty—one nation peacefully, the other violently. Each country's transition began with a revolutionary moment that determined the shape of future events. *What were the effects of each form of revolution?*

### The French Revolution

**1789–1794** The French revolutionary government violently overthrew King Louis XVI, the nobility, and the Church, creating a new republic with new institutions that did not last very long.

### Britain's Glorious Revolution

**1688** Parliament invited William and Mary (above) to peacefully replace King James II on condition that they recognize the authority of Parliament and the rights of individuals.

---

# Differentiated Resources

The following resources are located in the All-in-One, Unit 6, Chapter 22, Section 2:

**L3** Reading Comprehension Worksheet (p. 28)

**L2** Reading Comprehension Worksheet (p. 30)

**L3** Core Worksheet (p. 32)

**L3** Quiz A (p. 34)

**L2** Quiz B (p. 35)

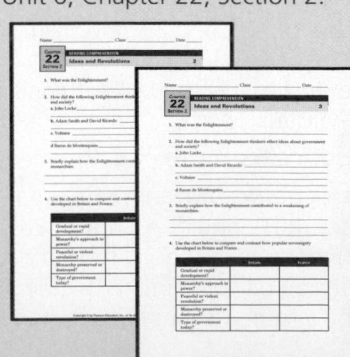

the purse," the right to tax people to fund the government. Through this lever, this representative body gained more and more power over the monarchy.

The conception of exactly who "the people" are has also evolved in the UK as it has in the United States. Well into the nineteenth century, only male property owners could vote, and only those who belonged to officially recognized Protestant churches could hold public office. At times, some of the largest cities in Great Britain had no representation in Parliament at all.

Far-sighted members of Parliament recognized the need for change. In the 1800s, Parliament passed several laws to expand the right to vote. A law passed in 1829 allowed Roman Catholics to hold public office. Landmark parliamentary acts in 1832, 1867, and 1885 reduced and then removed property restrictions. Women gained the right to vote in 1918. By adapting its government to embrace popular sovereignty, Great Britain protected many of its institutions, including the monarchy, Parliament, the legal system, and the Church of England. These institutions have changed to meet the needs of a modern economy and diverse society, but they preserve a link to Britain's past.

**Revolution in France** France took a very different route toward popular sovereignty. While the British monarchy compromised with nobles and Parliament gained power, the French monarchy expanded and centralized its authority. Royal power reached its peak under Louis XIV (1643–1715), who famously and accurately proclaimed, "L'état, c'est moi." ("I am the state.") He was the <u>epitome</u> of the absolute monarch. The continuing concentration of power in the monarchy set the stage for a violent reaction led by those who adopted the concept of popular sovereignty based on reason and the natural rights of the governed.

The French Revolution of 1789 would see the end, temporarily, of the French monarchy, followed by a period of confusion and fear known as The Terror. This period was soon followed by the rise of the empire of Napoleon and war with the rest of Europe. Historic institutions like the monarchy, nobility, church, and law were destroyed and

replaced by new ones. France has undergone a number of revolutions and changes in government since the Revolution of 1789. Today, it is a representative, constitutional democracy, much like the United States, with no monarch.

Does the experience of Britain or France serve as a better model for those countries currently seeking to increase popular sovereignty? The British example was accomplished more slowly and with less bloodshed, but it took hundreds of years before all adult Britons had the right to vote. On the other hand, the instability of a revolution, as in the French model, can lead to chaos and abuse of power. In 1959, for example, many cheered when Fidel Castro overthrew the corrupt dictatorship of Fulgencio Batista in Cuba. However, the destruction of Cuba's old political system created a vacuum that Castro then filled with his own absolute authority, and Cuba is today as far from a democracy as it has ever been.

Political events in Europe significantly influenced the course of political development in Latin America, Asia, and Africa. However, the colonies in those regions would have very different experiences from those of the European states or of the 13 British colonies that became the United States.

## Latin America

Spain, which controlled large portions of North and South America and the Caribbean into the 1800s, established a different system of government in its colonies than did other nations. To control the Indian population and force its subjects to labor in mining and agriculture, the Spanish crown instituted a system called the **encomienda.** Under this system, the monarch granted control of Indians living in a specific area to a settler. The grant did not include ownership of any land, but the settler could demand tribute and work from the Indians he controlled. In return, the settler was supposed to protect the Indians and see that they were instructed in the Catholic faith.

The *encomienda* system basically failed. Settlers took over Indian lands and worked the people to death in virtual slavery. The

✓ **Checkpoint**
How did democracy in the UK differ from democracy in France?

**epitome**
*n.* perfect representation, model

# Teach

To present this topic using online resources, use the lesson presentations at **PearsonSchool.com/phgovt**.

**DISCUSS THE ENLIGHTENMENT**
Display Transparency 22D, Enlightenment Web, which is a completed version of the Bellringer concept web. Use this transparency to discuss Enlightenment ideas. Ask: **Who were some major figures of the Enlightenment?** *(Thomas Hobbes, John Locke, Voltaire, Montesquieu, Adam Smith, David Ricardo)* **What were some of the main ideas of Enlightenment thinkers?** *(Locke: the natural rights of all people; Hobbes: the social contract between the ruler and the ruled; Voltaire: an emphasis on reason, freedom of religion, scientific observation, and human progress; Montesquieu: separation of powers and checks and balances; Smith and Ricardo: economic freedom)* **Why might absolute rulers have viewed Enlightenment ideas as a threat?** *(Sample response: Enlightenment ideas emphasized reason, which eroded public acceptance of divine right. The ideas of natural rights, social contract, and separation of powers would place limits on a monarch's power and would ultimately make the monarch answerable to the people. Reforming economic policies would remove a source of wealth for the monarch.)* **Why was the Enlightenment important to United States history?** *(These ideas influenced the Framers of the U.S. Constitution and became the foundation of our democracy.)*

# Background

**COALITION FOR REFORM** England had a revolution and beheaded a king. This violence led to the English Bill of Rights, which gave Parliament superiority over the king, but gave no rights to the common people. In 1800, fewer than five percent of the British people could vote. The coalition that pressed for reform in Parliament in the 1800s included Enlightenment thinkers who favored a more rational system, middle-class leaders who wanted more representation for the new industrial middle class, and radical leaders supported by workers. Revolts in Europe also emphasized the urgency of reform. Although it took a century to achieve universal suffrage, Britain was one of the few countries in Europe to avoid revolution in the 19th century. Democratic reforms in many countries have been made by similar coalitions of interests.

# Answers

**Checkpoint** Democracy evolved gradually in the UK, while in France, it came through revolution.

## ENLIGHTENMENT AND POPULAR SOVEREIGNTY

Write *popular sovereignty* on the board. Remind students that they learned about this concept earlier in the textbook. Underline *popular* and explain that it means "of the people," and then underline the term *sovereignty* and explain that it is the authority to rule. Therefore, *popular sovereignty* means "rule by the consent of the people." Have students work in pairs to use the Think-Write-Pair-Share strategy (p. T22) to write a summarizing statement explaining how the Enlightenment relates to the spread of popular sovereignty in Britain and France.

**L2 ELL Differentiate** Explain that *popular* has a different meaning in *popular sovereignty* from the one with which students might be more familiar—"being liked by many people." Have students write a sentence using each meaning. Alternatively, write two sentences on the board and have students explain the meaning used in each. For example: "The candidate won the *popular* vote, but did not win the electoral vote." "The new candidate is more *popular* than the current President."

Tell students to go to the Audio Tour to listen to a guided audio tour of the map of Latin American independence.

**Government** online *All print resources are available on the Teacher's Resource Library CD-ROM and online at PearsonSchool.com/phgovt.*

# Latin American Independence

▸▸ **Interpreting Maps** Most countries in the Western Hemisphere won their independence from Spain or Portugal, which practiced a different form of colonial rule than had Britain in North America. *How did Spanish colonial rule continue to influence governments in Latin America after independence?*

**KEY**
- former British colony
- former French colony
- former Portuguese colony
- former Spanish colony
- British colony
- Dutch colony
- French colony
- Spanish colony

Dates shown are dates of independence

**GOVERNMENT ONLINE**
Audio Tour
Listen to a guided audio tour of this map at
PearsonSchool.com/phgovt

When Spain was conquered by Emperor Napoleon of France in the early 1800s, Latin America began to move toward independence. Many colonial elites rejected Napoleon's choice for the Spanish throne, his brother Joseph I, and remained loyal to the deposed Ferdinand VII. Other colonials, most notably Simón Bolívar, were inspired by the same Enlightenment ideas that gave rise to the American and French revolutions. They sought to create a new political order in Latin America, based on popular sovereignty.

**Independence** When Ferdinand VII regained the Spanish crown in 1814, he agreed to grant greater power to parliament and place some restrictions on the Church. His conservative supporters in the colonies felt betrayed. Thus, in Mexico, Agustín de Iturbide engineered that country's independence in 1821 and had himself crowned its emperor. Iturbide soon would be forced to give up his throne, and Mexico, like many of the new states of Latin America, would fall into periods of civil war throughout the nineteenth century. Most of Latin America similarly won independence from Spain (and Brazil from Portugal) in the decades after Napoleon conquered Spain and left the country too weak to control its colonies.

**Obstacles to Stability** It was difficult for democracy to take root in the region, however. As in Mexico, political stability was rare in most of what was postcolonial Spanish America.

Why were the new states of Latin America less able to maintain popular sovereignty than the colonies that became the United States? A main reason lay in that those 13 colonies were British, and Great Britain had

*encomienda* system was eventually replaced by *haciendas*, large estates to which workers were tied, like serfs. These extensive landholdings would emerge as nearly self-sufficient centers of political and economic power throughout much of Latin America.

# Background

**SIMÓN BOLÍVAR** Born into wealth and educated in Europe, Simón Bolívar personally led the liberation of Venezuela, Colombia, Ecuador, Peru, and Bolivia. Before achieving any of these successes, he wrote a letter in which he anticipated the difficulties Latin America would face after independence. He noted that colonialism, in which Latin Americans held "a position in society no better than that of serfs," had kept them "in a sort of permanent infancy with regard to public affairs." He wondered how people who had never even voted would be able to fill "the eminent roles of legislator, magistrate, minister of the treasury, diplomat, general, and every position of authority, supreme or subordinate, that comprises the hierarchy of a fully organized state." Near the end of his life, discouraged by the failure of democracy in Latin America, Bolívar wrote, "We have achieved our independence at the expense of everything else."

## Answers

**Interpreting Maps** Spain and Portugal were ruled by absolute monarchs, so the colonists had no tradition of popular sovereignty to draw on. The encomienda system, later replaced by the hacienda system, created a powerful elite who worked against popular sovereignty.

a tradition of limited representative government, an expanding sense of popular sovereignty, and a population greatly influenced by the Enlightenment. The British colonists, therefore, had existing ideas that formed a basis for wanting and for justifying independence. Although the British monarch was very powerful, there was a belief among Britons that they had certain rights in the face of tyranny. Also, there were no all-powerful elites in the British colonies, as there were in Latin America, to struggle against independence.

In Latin America, social, political, and cultural traditions originated in Spain and Portugal—nations that at that time had not embraced ideas of popular sovereignty. Those nations were ruled by absolute monarchs, with little popular representation. The Catholic Church also had enormous influence and supported the status quo. There was little in the history or traditions of these colonials, for the most part, to help them foster or maintain democratic institutions.

Hacienda landowners were a powerful barrier to popular sovereignty. They did not want to give up their authority, property, and privileges, and they fought among themselves for control of the central government. Once in government, they faced new rebellions because they did little to solve the economic and social problems. This cycle of political disorder was common throughout Latin America well into the twentieth century.

Latin America's political troubles slowed its economic development, while relative political stability allowed countries such as Britain, France, Germany, and the United States to embrace the Industrial Revolution and the economic growth that followed.

**The Mexican Revolution** Throughout the 1800s, Mexico's leaders grappled, often violently, with a number of questions. Should there be a centralized or, instead, a federal government? How much power should a single political leader have? How could Mexico remain independent from its powerful neighbor to the north and other major world powers?

President Porfirio Díaz brought the Republic of Mexico its first long period of stability and economic growth, from 1876 to 1910. His economic plan was based on using cheap labor to work the mineral wealth and large farms of Mexico, and inviting large foreign firms to invest in the exploitation of the country's natural resources. Those policies benefited few Mexicans. In time, the people revolted against Díaz's harsh rule, and so began a long period of civil war.

In 1917, the revolutionaries won and wrote a new constitution in which the government played a more active role in promoting the quality of Mexican social, economic, and cultural life. Though revolutionaries Emilio Zapata and Pancho Villa were assassinated, the new government absorbed their call for extensive reform in a state-supported political party. The National Revolutionary Party was formed in 1929, but later changed its name to the Institutional Revolutionary Party (PRI). The PRI controlled the government and politics of Mexico until 2000.

**Latin America in the Modern Era** While Mexico remained stable under the control of the PRI, the period of the 1960s to 1980s proved to be violent elsewhere in Latin America. Throughout the nineteenth century and the first half of the twentieth century, most countries experienced cycles of dictatorship and military control, with wealth and land concentrated in the hands of a few. Democracy sprouted in the region during the 1950s, but continued economic decline and growing inequality fueled demands for real reforms. Many were inspired by the Cuban Revolution in 1959, which, based on communist ideology, promised to attend to the basic needs of the people. They often resorted to guerrilla warfare in an attempt to topple their governments. **Guerrilla warfare** is fighting carried out by small groups in hit-and-run raids.

The threat that communist guerrillas and others posed in the 1960s and 1970s led the national armed forces to take more active roles in several countries. Military leaders believed that Latin America's continued economic problems stemmed from the endless debate and corruption of politicians. In its view, the political class had to be curbed and the armed forces had to seize power to strengthen the economy and restore political

✔ **Checkpoint**
How did Spanish colonialism shape government in Latin America?

**status quo**
*n.* condition that currently exists

**grapple**
*v.* struggle, wrestle with

**COMPARE PATHS TO POPULAR SOVEREIGNTY**

Discuss the different paths nations took toward popular sovereignty. Ask: **How did Britain advance toward popular sovereignty?** *(through a gradual transfer of power from the monarchy to the people)* **How did France make this transition?** *(violently, through revolution)* **Why did these nations follow different paths?** *(The British monarchy compromised with the nobles through the Magna Carta, Petition of Right, and Bill of Rights. Parliament took further power from the monarchy through the power of the purse and passed laws to expand suffrage. In contrast, the French monarchy expanded and centralized its authority. This concentration of power set the stage for a violent reaction from supporters of the Enlightenment ideas of popular sovereignty and natural rights.)* **How did Latin America's colonial history influence its path to popular sovereignty?** *(These colonists came from Spain and Portugal—countries ruled by absolute monarchs who did not embrace popular sovereignty. Therefore, these colonists had no history or tradition to support a move toward democracy. Also, the encomienda and hacienda systems created an elite ruling class that formed a powerful barrier to popular sovereignty.)*

# Political Cartoon Mini-Lesson

Display Transparency 22E, Promised Land of Marxism, as an example to help students create their own political cartoon in the core activity. Ask: **Who is the man with the white beard?** *(Karl Marx)* **What is he doing?** *(pointing the way for his followers)* **What does the sun represent?** *(the goals of Marxism—liberté, egalité, fraternité, which means liberty, equality, brotherhood)* **Why do you think Marxism appealed to many working-class people, especially during hard economic times?** *(People who are unemployed or living in poverty would be attracted to promises of a better life.)* **What promise appears on the largest sail?** *(universal suffrage)* **Do Communist governments fulfill this promise?** *(No. In Communist states, all sovereignty lies with the government, not the people.)*

## Answers

**Checkpoint** Spanish colonial policy left new countries with few democratic institutions, leading to unstable governments and a cycle of violence.

## INTRODUCE THE ACTIVITY

Distribute the Chapter 22 Section 2 Core Worksheet (Unit 6 All-in-One, p. 32) and the Rubric for Assessing a Political Cartoon (Unit 6 All-in-One, p. 101). Tell students that in this activity, they will create a political cartoon about fascism or communism and its relationship to popular sovereignty. Students may work individually or with a partner.

Before students begin, brainstorm some ideas about the relationship between these two ideologies and popular sovereignty. Ask students to consider how fascist or Communist governments have made it appear that they ruled by the will of the people. Encourage students to suggest, or give them time to research, slogans or episodes from history demonstrating that fascist or Communist dictators acknowledged the idea of popular sovereignty. When cartoons are complete, have students explain them to the class. Have the class vote on the best one and explain the reasons for their choices.

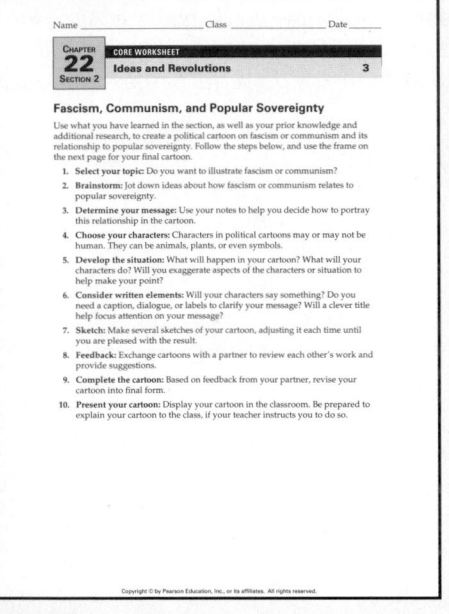

## Answers

**Interpreting Political Cartoons** Possible response: The European powers wanted Africa for its resources. The cake represents the resources that the Europeans intended to divide up among themselves and consume.

**658** Comparative Political Systems

---

peace. Only then would Latin America prosper. Democracy could come later.

Despite these struggles, the idea of popular sovereignty—government in the name of the people—remained important. Every military leader who intervened in a crisis claimed to be working toward democracy. Nonetheless, military rule soon led to tyranny. Innocent civilians were caught up in heavy-handed efforts to defeat the guerrilla groups.

The events that unfolded in Latin America over this period received little official criticism from abroad. During the Cold War, the United States was concerned chiefly with the spread of the Soviet Union's communist influence in the Americas. The end of the Cold War brought new opportunities for democracy in Latin America.

### Asia and Africa

Unlike Latin America, where most countries had won independence by 1830, some of Asia and most of Africa remained under

▶▶ **Interpreting Political Cartoons** The borders of many modern African nations still follow the lines drawn by European colonizing powers at the Conference of Berlin in 1884–1885. *Why is Africa (Afrique in French) represented by a cake in this cartoon?*

colonial control through the mid-twentieth century. In theory, by this time, the ruling nations of Europe were preparing colonies in these regions for democracy. In practice, they governed with little respect for native cultures and did not provide the structures the colonies would need to thrive after independence.

The main goal of colonialism was always the control of distant lands to extract resources that would enrich the parent country. At the Conference of Berlin (1884–1885), major European powers carved nearly the entire continent of Africa into colonial holdings, with artificial boundaries that often divided tribal lands or forced diverse groups into a single colony. Not infrequently, a colonial power would favor one segment of the population over another to advance its own interests. These "divide and rule" techniques would leave lasting legacies in many places. In Rwanda, efforts by the Belgians to pit Hutus against Tutsis created tensions that exploded in the mass killings of the 1990s, more than 30 years after independence.

Economically, each colony was directed to export a few specific resources to Europe. After independence, countries often found that reliance on one or a few cash crops or raw materials could drive their economies through cycles of prosperity and depression from year to year. Thus, a fall in the world price for coffee or oil could bring tremendous hardship to an entire country.

Another major problem facing the former colonies in Africa and Asia was that most won their independence in the 1950s and 1960s, at the height of the Cold War. Many countries, such as the former French colony Vietnam, were drawn into the Cold War when the Soviet Union and United States provided arms and money to different sides fighting for control of the newly independent countries.

Under these conditions, it is not surprising that democracy failed to take hold in many newly independent nations. Countries that combined many ethnic groups had few common traditions to build upon. Conflict and mistrust made it difficult to adopt a legal system on which everyone could agree. The only way for a government to gain legitimacy was to improve the lives of the people and bring peace quickly. Unfortunately, this left

**658** Comparative Political Systems

---

## Debate

After students have studied various ways in which nations have tried to achieve popular sovereignty, use the following quotation to start a debate.

"Those who make peaceful revolution impossible will make violent revolution inevitable."

—President John F. Kennedy

Ask: **Do you agree or disagree with President Kennedy?** As an alternative to an oral debate, you could ask students to write their response in their journals.

governments vulnerable to economic crises and appealing figures who easily became dictators. Because most former colonies had underdeveloped economies, there was no large middle class to balance the interests of the vast numbers of poor and of the few elite. The military often stood as the only recognizable national institution, so it could intervene in a crisis with much popular support. However, in almost every case, the military then refused to give up power after the crisis and repressed its critics.

## Fascism and Communism

The experience of dictatorship has been common throughout the world. Two of the political philosophies that created the most powerful and destructive dictatorships, particularly in Europe and Asia, are fascism and Communism. **Fascism** describes a centralized, authoritarian government with policies that glorify the state over the individual. **Communism** is principally an economic theory, and you will read more about the economics of Communist states in the next chapter. In the context of government, communism describes a state based on the idea of complete government control of the economy to serve the welfare of workers, without regard for individual liberty. Although the two political movements are quite distinct, they share some traits.

Both Communist and fascist governments go to great lengths to address the idea of popular sovereignty, though in doing

✔ **Checkpoint**
What factors affected government in newly independent countries in Asia and Africa?

---

# Fascism and Communism

⊙ **GOVERNMENT** ONLINE
**Audio Tour**
Listen to a guided audio tour of this diagram at
**PearsonSchool.com/phgovt**

Fascism and communism are totalitarian political systems in which the state has complete control over society, but they differ in some goals and economic policies. *How did fascist and Communist governments benefit from identifying and attacking an "enemy of the people"?*

## Similarities

- One-party states with no free elections or fair courts
- People gathered into a mass movement against an enemy
- A strong military and militarized society
- Government-controlled media broadcasting propaganda and censored news

Nazi youth parade in Germany ▶

## Differences

### Fascist state

- Nation defined on racial or ethnic terms
- Foreign powers and minorities are the enemy
- State-directed economy with private enterprise
- Some religions tolerated but strictly controlled

Adolf Hitler,
Fascist dictator
Germany, 1933–1945

### Communist state

- State based on a glorified working class
- Global capitalism is the enemy
- State-controlled economy
- Religion discouraged or outlawed

Josef Stalin,
Communist dictator
Soviet Union, 1924–1953

---

## Background

**BENITO MUSSOLINI** World War I left Italy's economy in ruins. Backed by many unemployed war veterans, Benito Mussolini organized the Fascist Party. He formed armed groups called Black Shirts, who terrorized political opponents. In 1922, the Black Shirts marched on Rome, bringing Mussolini to power. He set about removing all institutions of democratic government. Mussolini was wildly popular at first. He promised to restore Italy to the glory of Rome. He built roads, restored Roman statues, and made the trains run on time. He had his photo hung in every classroom with the caption "Mussolini is always right." Mussolini held power through intimidation and carefully crafted propaganda. During World War II, Mussolini joined Adolf Hitler in the Pact of Steel. However, as the Allies advanced into Italy, Mussolini was overthrown by members of his own Fascist party and later shot by his fellow Italians.

---

## EXTEND THE LESSON

**L3** **Differentiate** Have each student sign up to research a country in Latin America, Africa, or Asia that experienced dictatorship in the twentieth century. Have students make a chart identifying the forms of illegitimate power that dictators used to gain and hold office. For each illegitimate form of power, have students (a) describe it, (b) identify conditions and interests that supported it, and (c) describe its effects on the people. Then have students who researched each continent get together and create a three-column chart on all the countries with the information they collected. Have them present their chart to the class and discuss any patterns that emerge.

**L2** **ELL Differentiate** Have students create a circular flowchart of the cycle of disorder, military control, and dictatorship in Latin America in the nineteenth century. Then have them create a second flowchart showing how the cycle changed in the twentieth century with the addition of communism and guerrilla warfare.

**L4** **Differentiate** This section poses the question of whether revolutionary political change opens the door to abuse of power. Have students research at least five revolutions on different continents, including the American and French revolutions. Have them use the evidence from those revolutions to write an essay answering the question. Essays should suggest the best ways to avoid abuse of power in the transition to democracy.

Tell students to go to the Audio Tour to listen to a guided audio tour of the "Fascism and Communism" diagram.

---

## Answers

**Checkpoint** Colonialism introduced and worsened ethnic conflicts within states, oriented national economies to serve the colonizing power's market, and left countries unprepared for self-government. Cold War conflicts created additional problems.

**Fascism and Communism** Possible response: This tactic rallied the people to support the government in fighting the common enemy while diverting attention away from the nation's problems and government abuses.

# Assess and Remediate

**L3** Collect the Core Worksheets and assess the students' work using the Rubric for Assessing a Political Cartoon (Unit 6 All-in-One, p. 101).

**L3** Assign the Section 2 Assessment questions.

**L3** Section Quiz A (Unit 6 All-in-One, p. 34)

**L2** Section Quiz B (Unit 6 All-in-One, p. 35)

Have students complete the review activities in the digital lesson presentation and continue their work in the **Essential Questions Journal.**

## REMEDIATION

| If Your Students Have Trouble With | Strategies For Remediation |
|---|---|
| The concept of popular sovereignty (Questions 1, 6) | Work with students to create a continuum that shows the development of popular sovereignty from a dictatorship to a modern democracy. |
| Enlightenment ideas (Question 2) | Tell students to review their concept webs from the lesson and review the text to add any additional details. |
| Causes of instability in post-colonial Latin American nations (Questions 3, 4, 5) | With students, create a cause-and-effect chart that lists causes and effects of instability in post-colonial Latin American nations, such as Mexico. |

## Answers

**Checkpoint** Both are authoritarian systems of government built around an all-powerful state. Fascism is a nationalist, racist ideology, while communism is an economic ideology built on Marx's ideas of the class struggle.

---

✔ **Checkpoint**
How are fascism and communism different and alike?

so they distort that concept significantly. As radical movements, they raise some concerns also found in the French Revolution, most notably: Does revolution open the door to the abuse of power?

**Fascist Governments** Historic examples of fascism include Adolf Hitler's Germany, (1933–1945), Benito Mussolini's Italy (1922–1943), and Francisco Franco's Spain (1936–1975). These regimes embraced a right-wing, militaristic, ultranationalist ideology that, especially in Germany, included intense racist elements. Typically, a charismatic leader heads an all-powerful political party that incites violence against all who disagree with the party or with the ruling clique. The leader also heads a state that assumes control over social and economic policy in the supposed interests of the nation. "The people" is narrowly defined to exclude cultures and ethnic groups outside the national majority, most infamously in Nazi Germany. Democratic processes are viewed with suspicion, as they lead to debate and perceived delays that prevent the government from working to help "the people." Needless to say, fascist governments rarely helped the people as much as they had promised to do.

It is not a coincidence that these governments emerged out of the economic depressions of the 1920s and the 1930s. In such difficult times, people often look for scapegoats, and, as in Latin America in later decades, they hope for a strong military hand to restore order and prosperity. Hence, in Nazi Germany, Hitler pointed to the Jews as the source of German woes, and, in Italy, many supported Mussolini because they were pleased by the fact that he "made the trains run on time."

**Communist Governments** Communist states promote a left-wing ideology based on the theories of Karl Marx. Marx believed that the workers of the world would overthrow the capitalist free-market system and replace it with their own rule. Unlike fascist governments, communist regimes downplay the importance of the nation in lieu of "the people," representing farmers and workers. However, they too promote a one-party rule and a strong military.

Like fascism as it was practiced in Italy and Germany, the tremendous decision-making power given to government "in the name of the people" in a communist state regularly leads to repression and suspension of civil rights. All sovereignty lies with the government and none with the people. You will read more about communism's economic goals in Chapter 23.

**Essential Questions Journal** To continue to build a response to the chapter Essential Question, go to your Essential Questions Journal.

## SECTION 2 ASSESSMENT

1. **Guiding Question** Use your completed flowchart to answer this question: How have some nations expanded popular sovereignty?

**Key Terms and Comprehension**

2. What major ideas relating to government developed during the Enlightenment period?

3. Why were Latin American countries unable to found stable democracies after independence?

4. How does **guerrilla warfare** often lead to the strengthening of militaristic governments?

**Critical Thinking**

5. **Express Problems Clearly** Why did Mexico face difficulties in creating a successful democracy following independence in 1821?

6. **Draw Inferences** Why do fascist and communist governments claim that they govern by the consent of their people?

**Quick Write**

**Expository Writing: Research for Examples and Details** When writing a compare-and-contrast essay, you should include details that support the comparisons and contrasts you drew. Use your textbook, the library, and reliable Internet sources to add details and examples to the notes you made in your Venn diagram in Section 1. Review the notes to delete details that are unimportant or do not relate to both systems.

---

# Assessment Answers

**1.** Some nations, such as Britain, underwent gradual changes that transferred power from monarchs to the people with minimal bloodshed or destruction of institutions. Other nations, such as France and former colonies in Latin America, experienced violent change that did away with the monarchy and most traditional institutions. They experienced civil wars and political and economic instability on their path toward popular sovereignty.

**2.** that all human beings have natural rights, including the rights to life, liberty, and property; that the people and their ruler are parties to a social contract that defines the rights and powers of each; the importance of a separation of powers in government; that monarchs governed only because the people granted them that power

**3.** existing social and political structures prevented democracy from taking root

**4.** The military used the chaos and threat of guerilla warfare to justify repression and violent military campaigns, strengthening their power.

**5.** Mexico's social, political, and cultural traditions originated in Spain, a nation that had not embraced ideas of popular sovereignty. The colonists had little history or tradition to help them create a successful democracy. Also, the hacienda landowners worked against popular sovereignty. The elite fought among themselves to control government and did little to solve social and economic problems, resulting in cycles of political disorder.

**6.** to help them claim legitimacy

**QUICK WRITE** Students should include details about the two selected systems of government.

## SECTION 3

# Transitions to Democracy

### Guiding Question
**How successfully have some nations achieved democratic government?** Use a table similar to the one below to record information about modern transitions to democracy.

| Russia | Iraq | Yugoslavia |
|---|---|---|
| • 1985—soft-liner Gorbachev becomes general secretary | • | • |
| • | • | • |
| • | | • |

### Political Dictionary
- hard-liners
- soft-liners
- democratization
- democratic consolidation
- genocide
- failed states

### Objectives
1. Understand how regimes can change from dictatorship to democracy.
2. Describe the fall of the Soviet Union in the late 1980s and early 1990s.
3. Explain the factors necessary for democratic consolidation.
4. Analyze why some countries experience setbacks or failed transitions to democracy.

**Image Above:** Germans celebrate the fall of the Berlin Wall in November 1989.

When the political scientist Samuel Huntington studied the rise of democracy through history, he noticed an interesting pattern: Democratization tends to happen in waves across the world. The good news from Huntington's study is that the number of democracies rises gradually over time. However, this news is tempered by his other major conclusion—that not all those countries swept up by a democratic wave achieve a stable democracy. Some do fall back into authoritarianism.

## Openings for Democracy

Democracy takes root when competing groups cede the power to control a society and agree to compromise and cooperate with one another to make government work. In the modern era, new democracies have often been born out of toppled dictatorships.

Dictatorships often find themselves on the defensive in today's world. The principle of popular sovereignty forces dictators to explain why they put limits on basic freedoms. Some dictators argue that the state must be strong enough to create a better society in the long run. Others point to foreign enemies or domestic unrest to justify their repressive acts, and some lay the blame on the lack of economic development.

Both internal and external pressures can create splits and discord within a dictatorial regime. **Hard-liners,** who fight to maintain the status quo, may do battle with **soft-liners,** who want to reform governmental policies or procedures but keep the current governmental system in place.

Interestingly, soft-liners do not always prefer democratic government. Many support reforms meant to strengthen their hold on power. Nevertheless, the splits they provoke can create opportunities for change. Influential individuals can then lead social movements to bring about real reform.

Individuals from all walks of life influence democratization. Lech Walesa, a labor organizer whose struggles led to the peaceful end of communism in Poland in mid-1989, worked in a shipyard. Vaclav Havel, an intellectual, poet, and playwright, led a march to democracy in late 1989 and became president of his country, Czechoslovakia, and, later, the Czech Republic.

## How successfully have some nations achieved democratic government?

| Electoral College | | |
|---|---|---|
| **Russia** | **Iraq** | **Yugoslavia** |
| • 1985: Gorbachev becomes general secretary<br>• reforms based on *perestroika* and *glasnost*<br>• Yeltsin declares Russian Republic sovereign<br>• 1991: coup against Gorbachev fails<br>• Soviet Union breaks into independent republics<br>• 1991: Gorbachev resigns<br>• new Russian constitution proclaims a democratic republic, with individual rights and freedoms<br>• Putin concentrates power and restricts civil liberties | • 2003: U.S. topples Hussein<br>• 2005: Iraqis elect a parliament<br>• Iraqis approve new constitution<br>• success depends on three competing groups working together to build democratic institutions | • Communist rule weakens<br>• Regional leaders inflame ethnic differences for personal gain<br>• Provinces declare independence and fight with each other for land<br>• Bosnian genocide<br>• NATO intervenes to end fighting<br>• Yugoslavia ceases to exist |

## Get Started

### LESSON GOALS

Students will . . .

- discuss the challenges to democratic transitions.
- complete a chart to list the factors contributing to greater democracy and to failed democracy.
- analyze how Haiti and Iraq could succeed or fail in their transitions to democracy.

### SKILLS DEVELOPMENT

#### DRAW INFERENCES AND CONCLUSIONS

This section's Core Worksheet asks students to list factors affecting democratic transitions in Haiti and Iraq, and to predict whether those transitions will be successful. To assist students, you can refer them to the Skills Handbook, p. S19, to learn more about drawing inferences and conclusions.

## Focus on the Basics

**FACTS:** • *Democratization* is a change from dictatorship to democracy. • Democratic consolidation occurs when a country firmly establishes a free press, a multi-party system, civilian control of the military, interest groups, economic opportunity, and a professional civil service. • Russia has made the transition to democracy, but is showing signs of a return to centralized power. • Iraq and Haiti have not achieved democratic consolidation. • Sudan, Afghanistan, and Somalia are examples of failed states.

**CONCEPTS:** democracy, role of government

**ENDURING UNDERSTANDINGS:** • For democracy to succeed, democratic consolidation must follow democratization. • Democracy takes root when competing groups cooperate to make government work. • All democracies are based on popular sovereignty. • Failed states can become a refuge for terrorists.

Assign the section, the graphic organizer in the text, and the Reading Comprehension Worksheet (Unit 6 All-in-One, p. 36) before class.

**L2** **Differentiate** Reading Comprehension Worksheet (Unit 6 All-in-One, p. 37)

**BELLRINGER**

Write on the board: **High school graduation is a major transition. What changes will you need to make and what new responsibilities will you have to accept to make that transition successful? How can having more freedom be a challenge? Respond in your notebook.**

# Teach

To present this topic using online resources, use the lesson presentations at **PearsonSchool.com/phgovt.**

**DISCUSS DEMOCRATIC TRANSITIONS**

Explain that this lesson is about transition from one type of government to another—to more democratic government—and the challenges nations face when they attempt this change. Clarify that a *transition* is a major change. Discuss students' answers to the Bellringer. Especially focus on how more freedom can be challenging. Ask: **How can a transition from dictatorship or colonial rule to democracy be difficult, even though it is a positive development?** *(More freedom means more responsibility. Instead of being told what to do, citizens in a democracy must participate in the government, take responsibility for voting and overseeing the acts of their government, and think for themselves.)* Draw a chart like the one below on the board, and have students answer these questions: **What factors lead to more democracy? What factors lead to the failure of democracy?**

| Transition to Democracy | |
|---|---|
| Factors Leading to More Democracy | *push for popular sovereignty, hardliner-softliner clashes, strong leaders, free press, multiple parties, civilian control over the military, interest groups, economic opportunities, fair and open economic system, professional civil service, common trust among citizens* |
| Factors Leading to Failure of Democracy | *civil war, distrust, competition among groups for power, ethnic violence, independent and powerful military, no history of free institutions, weak economy* |

## Answers

**Checkpoint** Soft-liners work to reform government from within, while hard-liners try to hold power and prevent change.

**Caption** Putin was able to revive Russia's flagging economy.

---

✔**Checkpoint**
What do hard-liners and soft-liners do?

Other individuals avoid politics but still influence public opinion. Russian author Alexander Solzhenitsyn wrote *The Gulag Archipelago* to expose the network of prison camps in his country and spurred the cause of human rights in the Soviet Union.

Then, too, some individuals are able to encourage democracy from beyond the borders of their own country. Pope John Paul II, a native of Poland, inspired the people of his homeland and maintained pressure on Eastern European countries to move them toward democracy.

## Fall of the Soviet Union

The collapse of the Communist regimes in Eastern Europe contributed to the fall of the world's first Communist superpower, the Soviet Union, which was the successor to the Russian empire. From the Revolution of 1917 until 1990, the Communist Party was the only political party allowed to operate in the Soviet Union.

A new stage of Soviet government began in 1985 when Mikhail Gorbachev became general secretary of the party. As a soft-liner, Gorbachev undertook a reform program that rested on the principles of *perestroika* and *glasnost. Perestroika* called for a wide-ranging restructuring of political and economic life. *Glasnost* was the policy of openness, under which the government increased its tolerance of dissent and of freedom of expression.

**flagging**
*adj.* lagging, losing energy

Prime Minister Vladimir Putin (right) of Russia reversed many democratic reforms of the 1990s and effectively chose his own replacement as President, Dmitry Medvedev. *Why was Putin able to assert strong control over Russia?*

**Transition to Democracy** Changes occurred rapidly after Boris Yeltsin was elected president of Russia in 1991. Russia was then still a republic within the Soviet Union. Although it was not independent, Yeltsin used his position to confront Gorbachev, resigning from the Communist Party and declaring the laws of the Russian Republic sovereign over Russia's population and its territory.

In August 1991, Gorbachev and his wife were vacationing when a group of hardline Communist Party leaders placed him under house arrest. They wanted a return to the policies of the old Soviet government.

When the Russian public heard of this attempted coup, thousands of protesters took to the streets of Moscow, led by Yeltsin. After several tense days, the conspirators surrendered. The coup had failed. Extraordinary events followed. The three Baltic Soviet republics of Estonia, Latvia, and Lithuania were the first to depart from the Soviet Union. Soon, the remaining 12 left the Union as well.

As the elected leader of the dominant Soviet republic of Russia, Boris Yeltsin's power overshadowed that of Gorbachev. Recognizing reality, Gorbachev resigned on December 25, 1991. By the end of the year, the Soviet Union had ceased to exist.

**Independent Russia** A new constitution was approved in a national referendum in late 1993. It proclaims the Russian Federation to be "a democratic, federal legally based state with a republican form of government." It also set out a new governmental structure and contains an extensive list of individual rights and freedoms.

Boris Yeltsin kept his presidential role under the new constitution, and he was reelected in 1996. Soon thereafter, the economy began to spiral downward. Yeltsin suffered serious health problems and was accused of corruption in his inner circle.

In a surprise move, Yeltsin resigned at the end of December 1999, yielding the presidency to his prime minister, Vladimir Putin. Putin won election on his own in 2000 and again in 2004. Though Putin's reputation as a political strongman allowed him to revive the flagging economy, that same reputation drew criticism as he increasingly concentrated

---

# Differentiated Resources

The following resources are located in the All-in-One, Unit 6, Chapter 22, Section 3:

**L3** Reading Comprehension Worksheet (p. 36)

**L2** Reading Comprehension Worksheet (p. 37)

**L3** Core Worksheet (p. 38)

**L2** Extend Activity (p. 39)

**L3** Quiz A (p. 40)

**L2** Quiz B (p. 41)

power in the presidency and restricted civil liberties. In 2007, Putin's United Russia Party took control of the legislature in a questionable election. Putin announced he would serve as prime minister and engineered the election of an ally, Dmitry Medvedev, to the presidency, leading some observers to wonder if dictatorship had not returned to Russia.

## Democratic Consolidation

So far, you have read about the process of democratization, studying the example of the Soviet Union. **Democratization** refers to the change from dictatorship to democracy and is marked by the holding of free and fair elections. What must happen, once change occurs, to ensure that democracy takes root?

**Essentials of Democracy** As opposed to democratization, **democratic consolidation** is a much longer process that takes place as a country firmly establishes all those factors considered necessary for a democracy to survive. These factors include a free press, a true multiparty system, civilian control over the military, a vibrant collection of interest groups, an economic system that offers clear opportunities for advancement, and a professional civil service. Some of these elements may not be present in the early stages of transition. Many take time to become firmly established.

Most of all, democratic consolidation occurs when a society establishes a sense of common trust among its citizens. Because many transitions take place following a civil war or a dictatorship that pitted one group against another, mutual trust can be difficult to establish. However, when it is achieved, democracy stands on a solid footing.

**Haiti** The political history of the Caribbean nation of Haiti has been very troubled. It is the poorest country in the Western Hemisphere, and the process of democratization has been extremely difficult.

The Duvalier family, which ruled the country brutally for 29 years, fled in 1986. After four years of provisional governments, a presidential election was held, and Jean-Bertrand Aristide took office. Members of the armed forces still loyal to the Duvaliers

promptly overthrew Aristide. The international community cut off aid to Haiti and called for Aristide's return, and the military rulers finally withdrew in 1994. In 1996, Aristide handed over power to his political ally, René Préval. However, Aristide and Préval each led large blocs of supporters in Haiti's parliament and refused to work together. Both sides were accused of corruption.

When Aristide recaptured the presidency in 2000 in a rigged election, the United States and other countries threatened new sanctions if democratic procedures were not followed. Instead, Aristide, once a champion of democracy, became more of a dictator. In 2004, an

✔ **Checkpoint**
What is democratic consolidation?

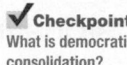 **GOVERNMENT**ONLINE
For an **interactive** exploration on how democracies succeed, visit
PearsonSchool.com/phgovt

### Democratic Consolidation

## What Makes Democracy Succeed?

Several factors must be in place in order for a democratic system of government to take root and flourish. *Which of these factors do you think is most important? Explain.*

| Factors | Why they matter |
|---|---|
| A **free press** | The media reports on the government's actions and regularly communicates ideas for change. |
| **Multiple parties** | Competition forces the government to listen to voters. |
| **Civilian control** of the military | Clear control prevents the military from taking power. |
| **Economic opportunity** for all | Education and hard work reward people for working within the law. |
| Professional **civil service** | Bureaucrats are less likely to be corrupt and keep government functioning when changes in leadership occur. |
| Common **trust** among citizens | Everyone shares a wish for the government to thrive and settle disputes peacefully. |

## Background

**DEMOCRATIZATION** Political scientist Samuel Huntington identified three waves of democratization: 1828 to 1926, 1943 to 1962, and the 1970s and 1980s. Huntington saw five reasons for the latest wave: the lack of legitimacy of dictatorships facing military defeat and economic woes, better standards of living that led to better education and rising expectations, pressure from religious institutions, pressure from the world community, and the snowballing effect of democratization in other countries. Conditions he viewed as favoring democratic consolidation include previous efforts to democratize, strong economic development, support from the international community, internal sources of the drive to democratize, and a peaceful transition.

**L2** **ELL Differentiate** Clarify the difference between *democratization* and *democratic consolidation*. Tell students that *democratization* is the initial move toward democracy. For example, a nation might hold free and fair elections for the first time. *Democratic consolidation* is a later and longer process of firmly establishing the democratic factors, so that democracy will last. For example, it takes time to build mutual trust among rival groups following a civil war.

### DISTRIBUTE CORE WORKSHEET

Distribute the Chapter 22 Section 3 Core Worksheet (Unit 6 All-in-One, p. 38). Students will complete the chart on the worksheet to list factors that could lead to the success of democratization and factors that could lead to failure in Haiti and Iraq.

**L3** **L4** **Differentiation** Students can research the current situation in these countries relating to factors necessary to democratic consolidation.

### WRAP UP

As a class, review students' work on the Core Worksheet. Which factors might help Haiti and Iraq be successful in their transitions to democracy and which factors could cause them to fail? Ultimately, do students think that Haiti and Iraq will succeed?

## Answers

**Checkpoint** Democratic consolidation is the strengthening of democracy and the establishment of democratic institutions within a country.

**What Makes Democracy Succeed?** Possible response: Common trust is most important, because everyone must believe in democracy and work together to preserve it for democratic consolidation to occur.

**L3** **Differentiate** Divide students into four groups assigned to Czechoslovakia, Hungary, Poland, and the Soviet Union. Have students in each group research and create a large flowchart showing how the country became Communist, how the Communist government maintained control, and how the Communist government ended. Have them illustrate the flowchart with art or clippings from magazines.

**L1** **Differentiate** Have students research and prepare a short illustrated booklet for younger students on a person who influenced a change from communism to democracy, such as Lech Walesa, Vaclav Havel, Alexander Solzhenitsyn, or Pope John Paul II.

**L2** **Differentiate** Distribute the Extend Activity entitled "Foreign Governments" (Unit 6 All-in-One, p. 39), which asks students to select a foreign government and conduct research to learn information about its people, government, and economy.

**L4** **Differentiate** Divide students into an even number of small teams. Assign equal numbers of teams to debate for and against the idea that one country can export democracy to another. Have pairs of teams take turns debating. Then poll the class on which were the best arguments and whether or not the debate changed anyone's mind. You may wish to have students use the Debate strategy (p. T25).

Tell students to go to the Online Update for current information about Iraq.

## Divisions in Iraq

▸▸ **Interpreting Maps** A large majority of Iraq's inhabitants are Muslim, but they adhere to different forms of Islam and belong to many different ethnic groups speaking different languages. *How can religious and linguistic divides pose challenges for an emerging democracy?*

**KEY**
- Kurd
- Sunni Arab
- Sunni Arab/Kurd mix
- Shia Arab
- Shia/Sunni Arab mix
- Sunni Turkoman
- Sparsely populated

SOURCE: Central Intelligence Agency

**GOVERNMENT** ONLINE
**Update**
For current information about Iraq, visit
PearsonSchool.com/phgovt

armed revolt ousted Aristide and a provisional government and a UN peacekeeping force stepped in. In 2006, René Préval was returned to the presidency in a disputed election.

Progress was made in some areas in subsequent years, but lawlessness and poverty still plagued Haiti. In the midst of this tenuous situation, a major setback struck in 2010, when a tragic earthquake destroyed the capital city and killed more than 200,000 people. The resulting upheaval left the future of Haiti very much in doubt.

**Iraq** In 2003, the United States led an invasion that toppled Saddam Hussein's brutal dictatorship in Iraq and began attempts to build a democracy amid the strife and sectarian violence there.

The few instances in which one or more countries have attempted to establish democratic institutions in another country have been filled with difficulties. There have been spectacular successes, notably in Japan and Germany in the years following World War II, but what does the future hold for Iraq?

As a country with no history of free institutions upon which a democracy might be built, Iraq faces enormous challenges. The people of Iraq comprise many ethnic groups and religious traditions, and there are few significant unifying traditions to bring the nation's diverse Kurdish, Shia Arab, and Sunni Arab populations together as a tolerant and peaceful whole.

However, the people of Iraq have a common interest in reducing violence and restoring order in the country. Iraq has large oil reserves that could help the country to recover economically if peace returns. In 2005, Iraqis elected an interim parliament that drafted a new constitution. Iraqi voters approved the constitution, creating the basis for a new democratic government. The success of Iraqi democracy depends on the ability of the three competing groups to work together and build democratic institutions acceptable to all.

### Setbacks and Failed Transitions

While some countries have successfully established democratic governments, and many others have begun the democratization process, a third group of countries has failed.

The costs of failure are great. Many countries today find that they must confront new problems, previously hidden by dictatorial rule, when they attempt to move toward democracy. Countries that fail to transition to democracy can pose a threat to other

## Answers

**Interpreting Maps** Possible response: Diverse languages and religious backgrounds make it difficult to bring the people together into a tolerant and peaceful whole. Different factions may compete for dominance rather than work together to build democratic institutions that is acceptable to all.

countries if they open safe havens for international terrorist groups.

**Ethnic Violence** The country of Yugoslavia no longer exists. Founded in 1918, Yugoslavia included people from three major religions and many ethnic groups.

When Communist rule began to weaken in the late 1980s, regional political leaders inflamed ethnic differences for their own personal gain. By playing up old battles, they hoped to position themselves as the leaders who could correct past wrongs. The country split apart. Several provinces of Yugoslavia declared independence and went to war with one another for control of land that multiple ethnic groups believed was theirs by right or by history. The province of Bosnia-Herzegovina, peopled with a mix of Muslims, Serbians, and Croatians, was targeted by forces supported by neighboring Serbia and Croatia. This province saw the most intense fighting, and Bosnians suffered **genocide,** or the attempted extermination of a cultural, racial, or national group. About 200,000 civilians were killed, and many more were forced to flee the country. The conflict ended in 1995, but only after NATO intervened to stop the fighting. Instead of leading to democracy, the end of dictatorship in Yugoslavia triggered the bloody breakup of the country into at least five independent states.

**Failed States** Other countries remain similarly troubled. Their inability to find stability has even raised security concerns for other states. Countries such as Sudan and Afghanistan include large regions that remain outside the control of their own governments. Somalia, in East Africa, does not have a functioning government, and most of the country is ruled by warlords. These countries are known as **failed states.** In most of these areas, security is nonexistent, the economy has collapsed, the healthcare and school systems are in shambles, and corruption flourishes.

International terrorist groups have found refuge in these lawless lands, and have used them as bases to plan and train for acts of violence. The Soviet Union occupied Afghanistan in the 1980s. Withdrawing in 1989, it left the country utterly devastated. Groups of Afghans who had fought against the Soviets now turned their arms against one another for control of provinces, and Afghanistan became a failed state. The anarchy provided a haven for Osama bin Laden and his al Qaeda terrorist network to plan their attacks on the United States on September 11, 2001. In response to those attacks, a coalition of troops led by the United States moved into Afghanistan with the hope of creating a fledgling democratic government. However, large portions of the country remain outside the control of the central government. In 2009, President Obama increased U.S. troop levels in Afghanistan, in hopes of reducing civilian casualties, bringing Taliban leaders to justice, and affording some measure of stability to the struggling nation.

✓ **Checkpoint**
What can happen when democracies fail?

**Essential Questions Journal** To continue to build a response to the chapter Essential Question, go to your **Essential Questions Journal.**

## SECTION 3 ASSESSMENT

1. **Guiding Question** Use your completed table to answer this question: How successfully have some nations achieved democratic government?

**Key Terms and Comprehension**

2. What role can **soft-liners** often play in a dictatorship?
3. What is the importance of **democratic consolidation?**

**Critical Thinking**

4. **Making Comparisons** Why have Iraq and Russia experienced different outcomes in their respective transitions to democracy?
5. **Drawing Inferences** How might the United States help other countries as they seek to build strong, independent democratic institutions?

**Quick Write**

**Expository Writing: Write a Thesis Statement** As in other types of essays or reports, you need to formulate a thesis statement to direct your thinking, research, and writing. Review your notes from Sections 1 and 2 to find one overarching concept that connects your categories and questions. Write a thesis statement that expresses that concept.

---

# Assess and Remediate

**L3** Collect the Core Worksheets and assess students' work.

**L3** Assign the Section 3 Assessment questions.

**L3** Section Quiz A (Unit 6 All-in-One, p. 40)

**L2** Section Quiz B (Unit 6 All-in-One, p. 41)

Have students complete the review activities in the digital lesson presentation and continue their work in the **Essential Questions Journal.**

### REMEDIATION

| If Your Students Have Trouble With | Strategies For Remediation |
|---|---|
| Democratization (Questions 1, 2, 3, 4, 5) | Have students work with a partner to outline the section; tell them to include definitions of key terms in their outlines. Then review the outlines as a class. |

## Answers

**Checkpoint** Failed democracies can lead to dictatorships or failed states and an increase in violence.

---

# Assessment Answers

**1.** Although it is a very difficult process, a few nations, such as Poland and the Czech Republic, have been very successful at achieving democratic government. For other nations, such as Iraq, where the struggle continues, and in failed states, such as Afghanistan, the effort has been very challenging or has failed entirely.

**2.** Soft-liners support reforms, but not always democratic reforms. They can, however, create openings for the opposition to push for democracy.

**3.** Unless democratic consolidation occurs, democracy will not endure.

**4.** Possible answer: After the fall of the U.S.S.R., Russians quickly wrote a constitution for the new nation and the first President, Boris Yeltsin, stayed true to its principles. Also, there is a stronger tradition of popular sovereignty—at least the idea if not the practice—in Russia. In Iraq, which has no such history or tradition, with its infrastructure destroyed and fighting in the streets, much work remains in securing just basic necessities, which must occur before true democracy can be established.

**5.** Answers may include offering economic or technical support, supplying peacekeeping forces, or using economic or political pressures to discourage dictatorship.

**QUICKWRITE** Students' thesis statements should express their essays' main concept in one clear sentence.

# What form does democratic government take in the UK and in Mexico?

**United Kingdom**
- Constitutional monarchy
- Unitary system
- Parliamentary system
- Constitution—written and unwritten parts
- Monarch reigns but does not rule
- Real power lies with prime minister
- Parliament—House of Lords; House of Commons
- Prime minister—no term limits
- Crown Court—serious crimes
- Magistrates' courts—less serious cases
- No power of judicial review
- General election at least every five years for all seats in Commons
- Devolved regional governments in Scotland, Wales, Northern Ireland

**Both**
- Bicameral legislature
- Multi-party system

**Mexico**
- Federal system
- Written constitution
- President popularly elected to one six-year term
- General Congress—Senate, Chamber of Deputies
- Chamber elected through mix of direct and proportional representation
- State and federal court systems
- Supreme Court

## SKILLS DEVELOPMENT

### ANALYZE GRAPHIC DATA

Before displaying Transparency 22G, Two Modern Democracies, and discussing the election process in the United Kingdom, you may want to review with students the information in the Skills Handbook, p. S26, on analyzing graphic data.

---

SECTION **4**

# Case Studies in Democracy

## Guiding Question

**What form does democratic government take in the UK and in Mexico?** Use a Venn diagram to record information about the modern governments of the UK and Mexico.

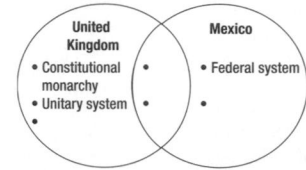

**United Kingdom**
- Constitutional monarchy
- Unitary system

**Mexico**
- Federal system

## Political Dictionary
- coalition
- ministers
- shadow cabinet
- devolution

## Objectives
1. Examine elements of the United Kingdom's parliamentary democracy.
2. Describe regional and local government in the United Kingdom.
3. Analyze the federal government of Mexico.

**Image Above:** President Felipe Calderón of Mexico

A majority of the states in the world today are representative and democratic. Each of them has developed its own set of distinctive institutions, however. The United Kingdom and Mexico present two different approaches to democratic government in today's world.

## The United Kingdom: A Constitutional Monarchy

Like the United States, the United Kingdom, the UK, is a democracy. Indeed, the roots of American government are buried deep in British political and social history. Yet there are important differences between the two systems of government. Unlike government in the United States, where it is federal and presidential, government in the UK is unitary and parliamentary and rests upon an unwritten constitution.

The British constitution is not entirely unwritten. However, there is no single constitutional document, as there is in the United States. Many historic documents figure in the written portions of the UK's constitution. Especially important are the Magna Carta of 1215 and the Bill of Rights of 1689. Certain acts of Parliament also form a basic part of the British constitution.

Additionally, centuries of court decisions have created a body of law covering nearly every aspect of human conduct. Such decisions make up the common law. The truly unwritten part of the British constitution consists of the customs and practices of British politics. The written parts are called "the law of the constitution" and the unwritten parts are called "the conventions of the constitution."

In formal terms, all acts of the British government are performed in the name of the monarch. Queen Elizabeth II has been the UK's monarch since 1952. However, the prime minister and other high officials exercise the real power to govern. The monarch appoints the prime minister (traditionally the leader of the majority party in the House of Commons), but her choice is subject to the approval of that house. She has no power to dismiss the prime minister or any other government official. She has no veto power over acts of Parliament. In short, today's monarch reigns but does not rule.

---

# Focus on the Basics

**FACTS:** • The UK has a unitary, constitutional monarchy, with a bicameral Parliament, led by the prime minister • Mexico has a federal government, with three independent branches, a bicameral legislature, and a powerful President. • Mexico became a true democracy when free and fair elections were held in 2000.

**CONCEPTS:** forms of government, democracy

**ENDURING UNDERSTANDINGS:** • Democracies take different forms. • The UK and Mexico are both democracies, despite many differences in their governments. • The UK has devolved, or delegated, authority from the central government to regional governments in Scotland, Northern Ireland, and Wales.

## British Government

Britain's storied Parliament is the core institution of government in the UK. It holds both the legislative and the executive powers of the nation—powers that in the United States are divided between separate branches of the government. It is also a bicameral body, made up of the House of Lords and the House of Commons. The latter is by far the more significant of its two chambers.

**The House of Lords** Historically, the House of Lords was largely composed of hereditary peers—members who inherited noble titles and, with them, seats in Parliament. Today, that largely powerless chamber's seats are held by some 700 members appointed by the Queen on the advice of the prime minister. They hold their positions mostly on the basis of their individual accomplishments in the sciences, literature, the arts, politics, or business.

The Lords have only meager law-making power: Any measure passed by the Commons but then rejected by the Lords has only to be approved a second time by the Commons in order to become law.

**The House of Commons** The House of Commons has 650 members today. All of them are popularly elected from single-member districts (constituencies) of roughly equal populations. There are now 533 constituencies in England, 59 in Scotland, 40 in Wales, and 18 in Northern Ireland.

The majority party in the House of Commons controls the work of that chamber. It selects the prime minister and the members of the cabinet who, together, form "the government." Its (usually) ten or so committees are generalist in nature—that is, the Speaker can refer a bill to any of those committees. All bills sent to committee must be reported to the floor, where each of them is voted up or down on a party-line basis.

**The Prime Minister** The prime minister, although formally appointed by the monarch, is in fact responsible to the House of Commons. When a single party holds a majority in the House of Commons, as is usually the case, that party's leader becomes prime minister. If no single party holds a majority, a coalition must be formed. A **coalition** is a temporary alliance of parties for the purpose of forming a government. Two or more parties must agree on a common choice for prime minister and on a joint slate of cabinet members.

There are no term limits on the post of prime minister. William Gladstone held the position four times from 1868 to 1894. Once a member of the Conservative Party, he broke ranks to create the Liberal Party and presided over voting reforms that expanded the electorate. Winston Churchill may be the most famous prime minister, remembered for his inspiring leadership during World War II. Margaret Thatcher, Britain's first female prime minister, led the government from 1979 to 1990 and oversaw the denationalization of many of Britain's coal, steel, and other basic industries. Gordon Brown served as prime minister from 2007 until 2010, when he stepped down and was replaced by the current prime minister, David Cameron.

**The Cabinet** The prime minister selects the members of the cabinet, or **ministers,** from the House of Commons, although a few may sit in the House of Lords. Collectively, the prime minister and the cabinet provide

**✔ Checkpoint**
What type of government does the UK have?

**denationalization**
*n.* the transfer of a public enterprise to private owners

At the annual opening of Parliament, the British monarch reads a Speech from the Throne outlining her government's goals. The speech is written by the prime minister and cabinet. *How does that speech symbolize the roles of the prime minister and the monarch in British government?*

---

# Differentiated Resources

The following resources are located in the All-in-One, Unit 6, Chapter 22, Section 4:

- **L3** Reading Comprehension Worksheet (p. 42)
- **L2** Reading Comprehension Worksheet (p. 43)
- **L3** Core Worksheet (p. 44)
- **L3** Quiz A (p. 46)
- **L2** Quiz B (p. 47)
- **L3** Chapter Test A (p. 48)
- **L2** Chapter Test B (p. 51)

---

# Get Started

## LESSON GOALS

Students will . . .

- recognize variations in democracies by comparing features of the governments of the UK and Mexico in a transparency.
- understand the UK's general election processes by examining a flowchart.
- compare and contrast the governments of the UK, Mexico, and the United States by playing a fact game.

## BEFORE CLASS

Assign the section, the graphic organizer in the text, and the Reading Comprehension Worksheet (Unit 6 All-in-One, p. 42) before class.

**L2 Differentiate** Reading Comprehension Worksheet (Unit 6 All-in-One, p. 43)

## BELLRINGER

Have students write a response to these questions: **What are some advantages of a written constitution? What are some disadvantages? Answer in your notebook.**

**L2 ELL Differentiate** Students may make a pro/con list instead of writing out an answer.

---

# Answers

**Checkpoint** The UK has a constitutional monarchy.

**Caption** In giving the Throne Speech, the monarch is serving as the ceremonial leader. The prime minister, who holds the real power, writes the speech.

# Teach

To present this topic using online resources, use the lesson presentations at PearsonSchool.com/phgovt.

## REVIEW BELLRINGER ACTIVITY

The United Kingdom and Mexico are democracies, yet their governments differ a great deal. Ask: **How do the constitutions of these two nations differ?** *(Mexico's constitution is written. The UK's is mostly unwritten. Its government is based on historic documents, acts of Parliament, common law, customs, and traditional practices.)* Have students share their answers to the Bellringer activity. Ask: **What are some advantages of a written constitution?** *(can serve as clear statement of the supreme law of the land; can be used as a concise standard for judging the validity of government's laws and actions; lengthy amendment process protects against ill-considered changes)* **What are some disadvantages?** *(less flexible because amendment process is more lengthy and difficult than change through court precedent or legislative acts; can contain provisions that no longer apply to the modern world)*

## EXAMINE VARIATIONS IN DEMOCRACIES

Ask students to offer some main facts about the systems of government in the UK and Mexico. Then display Transparency 22G, Two Modern Democracies. Explain that a *constitutional monarchy* has a hereditary ruler whose power is restricted by the constitution and laws of the land. Ask: **How is the role of chief of state different from head of government?** *(Chief of state is a largely ceremonial or figurehead role; the head of government holds the real power.)* **How do these roles differ between the UK and Mexico?** *(The UK has a ceremonial monarch and a powerful prime minister. In Mexico, the President serves in both roles.)* **Is the government of the UK or Mexico most like the government of the United States?** *(Mexico)* **Name some similarities.** *(federalism, written constitution, powerful President, popularly elected President, bicameral legislature, state and federal courts, Supreme Court)*

Tell students to go to the Audio Tour for a guided tour of the government in the UK.

## Answers

**United Kingdom** All acts of British government are performed in the name of the monarch, but the monarch holds no real political power. The monarch formally appoints the prime minister, but the choice is actually made by the House of Commons, to whom the prime minister is responsible. The monarch has no power to dismiss the prime minister or any other government official, nor any power to veto acts of Parliament.

---

# United Kingdom

GOVERNMENT ONLINE
Audio Tour
Listen to an audio guided tour about government in the UK at PearsonSchool.com/phgovt

Britain's constitutional monarchy is based on a largely unwritten constitution. The prime minister is responsible to the House of Commons and is the real head of government. *Cite examples from the text to support this statement: The British monarch reigns but does not rule.*

| Form of government | Constitutional Monarchy |
|---|---|
| Constitution | Unwritten; partly statutes, partly common law and practice |
| Chief of state | Queen Elizabeth II |
| Head of government (Party) | Prime Minister David Cameron (Conservative Party) |
| Executive branch | Prime Minister is head of majority party in House of Commons |
| Legislative branch | Bicameral Parliament consists of House of Lords and House of Commons |
| Judicial branch | Crown Courts/UK Supreme Court |

political leadership, both in making and carrying out public policy. Individually, cabinet ministers head the various executive departments, such as Defense, the Exchequer (the treasury), or Health.

The opposition parties appoint their own teams of potential cabinet members. Each opposition MP watches, or shadows, one particular member of the cabinet. If an opposition party should succeed in gaining a majority, its so-called **shadow cabinet** would then be ready to run the government.

**The Courts** The UK has three separate court systems—one for England and Wales, one in Northern Ireland, and one in Scotland. In England and Wales, most civil cases are tried in county courts. Serious (indictable) criminal cases are tried in the Crown Courts and less serious criminal cases in the magistrates' courts.

Judges and juries try the more serious criminal cases in the Crown Court, while judges alone hear the majority of civil disputes and less serious criminal cases. The House of Lords serves as the final court of appeal in a hierarchy of appellate courts. The court system in Northern Ireland is similar to the system in England and Wales, but the Scottish system is simpler, with fewer hierarchical layers.

Courts in the UK decide cases on the basis of (1) the common law—that is, law that has been established by judicial precedent, and (2) acts of Parliament. In the most serious cases, appeals may now be taken to a new court of last resort, the Supreme Court of the UK. That 11-judge tribunal, created by Parliament, began to hear cases in 2009. Recall, none of the courts in the UK, including the new Supreme Court, possess the power of judicial review.

---

# Background

**CONVENTIONS OF THE CONSTITUTION** Unwritten rules, or conventions, govern many of the practices of British politics. For example, no written account says that Parliament must meet in yearly sessions. It just does. Also, no written rule gives the House of Commons the power to force the government to resign. These central features of British government developed over centuries and are today a matter of custom. With its open-ended constitution, the UK has a flexible, always-evolving set of rules. A majority vote in Parliament can alter any provision of the constitution. This flexibility can be very useful. Without the delays and safeguards of a system like that of the United States, however, the danger of ill-considered and hasty action that might fundamentally alter the people's rights is ever present.

## The Election Process

In marked contrast to the practice in the United States, the UK does not have a fixed date for the holding of elections. Instead, the law requires only that a general election—an election in which all the seats in the Commons are at stake—be held at least once every five years. If an MP dies or resigns, a special election, called a by-election, is held in that constituency to choose a replacement.

**Calling Elections** Customarily, the prime minister calls an election when the political climate favors the majority party. Occasionally, an election is triggered by quite different circumstances—when the government falls because it has lost the confidence, that is, the support, of the House. This can occur if the government is defeated on a critical vote; it loses the confidence of the Commons and falls. The prime minister must then ask the monarch to dissolve Parliament (end its sessions) and call a new general election. The ability to change governments in this way means that a prime minister who becomes either ineffective or unpopular can be removed before his or her actions cause serious damage to the political system. It also means that an effective prime minister can stay in office until his or her goals are met.

**Political Parties** Two parties have dominated British politics in recent decades: the Conservative Party (historically known as the Tory Party or the Tories) and the Labour Party. The Conservatives have long drawn support from middle- and upper-class Britons. They tend to favor private economic initiatives over governmental involvement in the nation's economic life. The Labour Party has regularly found most of its support among working-class voters. Labour tends to favor government involvement in the economic system and a more socially equal society. Historically, the party preached doctrinaire socialism, but it moderated its views under the leadership of Prime Minister Tony Blair (1997–2007). Most recently, the Liberal Democratic Party has emerged as an alternative that blends left-wing and moderate views without the Labour Party's ties to unions.

British parties are more highly organized and centrally directed than the major parties in American politics. High levels of party loyalty and party discipline characterize the British party system. Voters regularly select candidates for the House of Commons on the basis of the candidates' party membership, not their individual qualifications.

✔ **Checkpoint**
How are governments formed in the UK?

## Regional and Local Government

Recall, the United Kingdom has a unitary government. This means that there is no constitutional division of powers between the national government and regional or local governments, as in the American federal system. All power belongs to the central government. To whatever extent local governments deliver services or do anything else, they can do so only because the central government has created them, given them powers, and financed them.

**Regional Government** The United Kingdom is composed of four separate nations with different histories, cultures, and traditions. To provide for the distinctive governmental needs of the people of Scotland, Wales, and Northern Ireland, the United Kingdom has recently undergone a process of **devolution**—the delegation of authority from the central government back to regional governments.

▴ Scotland's Parliament flies the flags of the UK, Scotland, and the European Union.

**DISCUSS ELECTIONS IN THE UK**

Display Transparency 22H, Election Process in the United Kingdom. Ask: **What is a general election in the UK?** *(an election in which all seats in the House of Commons are at stake)* **Why do you think the majority party often remains in power for a long time?** *(There is no fixed date for elections. The prime minister can choose to call a general election at a time when his or her party is popular and therefore likely to win the most seats.)* **Under what circumstances does the opposition party become the majority party in the UK?** *(When the ruling party loses the confidence of the House of Commons, the government is dissolved, and the opposition party usually wins the most seats in the general election that follows.)* **How does the election process in the UK differ from that of the U.S.?** *(Possible response: The U.S. has fixed dates for elections and term limits for the President. The UK does not.)*

## Political Cartoon Mini-Lesson

Display Transparency 22I, Trouble for the British Labour Party, when you discuss the British election process. Point out that the man in the cartoon represents British Prime Minister Gordon Brown. Ask: **Based on your reading of the text, what is a by-election?** *(a special election to replace a member of Parliament who resigns or dies)* **What is the woman in the cartoon doing?** *(reading a greeting card to Gordon Brown)* **What sentiment does the card express?** *(joy that Brown might resign and be replaced in a "bye-bye election")* **What is the message in the woman's comment that "It could have come from anyone"?** *(This comment suggests that Brown is very unpopular, because many people could have been the source of the card's message.)* **What is Brown's political party? How do you know?** *(Labour Party. The newspaper headline suggests that the Labour Party is in trouble.)*

## Answers

**Checkpoint** Voters elect members of Parliament who then choose a government from among themselves.

## DISTRIBUTE THE CORE WORKSHEET

Distribute the Chapter 22 Section 4 Core Worksheet (Unit 6 All-in-One, p. 44). Tell students that in this activity they will make up question cards and play a fact game. Each question will cover a fact about the government of the UK, Mexico, or the United States. Point out that some facts may describe the government of more than one of these nations. In these cases, the answer should include all nations to which the fact applies.

Depending on the size of your class, divide the class into an even number of teams of four to five students each. Provide 22 index cards to each team. This will give each team two cards to label categories and four or five cards per student to write questions. Have each team follow the steps on the worksheet. After the teams create and arrange their game cards, pair the teams to play the game.

**L1 L2 ELL Differentiate** Allow students to write fewer questions.

**L4 Differentiate** Have students work individually to prepare their cards. Then pair individual students to play the game.

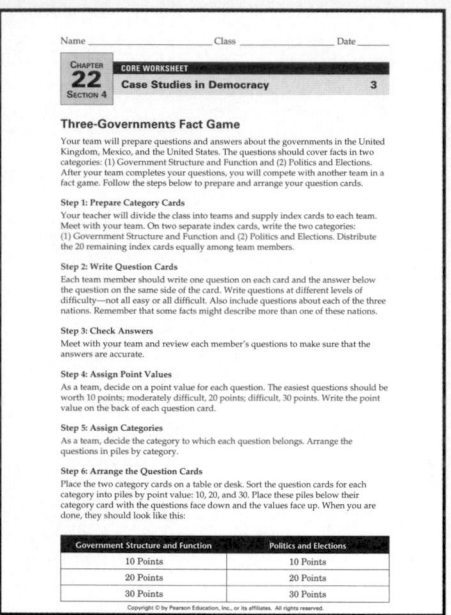

Tell students to go to the Audio Tour for a guided tour of the government in Mexico.

## Answers

**Mexico** A single party, the PRI, had dominated the government in Mexico for decades, squelching opposition through patronage and repression. Victories by PAN candidates Fox and Calderón marked the emergence of a true multi-party system in Mexico.

---

Although the British Parliament has assigned many responsibilities to the devolved bodies, such as the Scottish Parliament that was reestablished in 1998, it has reserved for itself the exclusive power to legislate on several matters that affect the whole of the United Kingdom. These include defense, foreign policy, and macroeconomic policy. The British Parliament also continues to legislate more broadly for England, which does not have a devolved assembly.

**Local Government** Local government bodies have been a feature of the British political landscape for much longer than the recently established regional assemblies. Today, there are some 470 local authorities of varying types in the UK. Much as in the United States, local governments in the United Kingdom perform a broad range of functions,

**entity**
*n.* object, element

from running local schools and libraries to collecting trash and maintaining roads.

## Mexico: A Federal System

Mexico has a political system similar in form to the United States. In operation, however, it is the product of a unique combination of Mexico's history and the cultural makeup of its people.

**Three Branches of Government** Mexico's Constitution of 1917 established a national government with three independent branches. The executive branch is headed by the president, the legislature is bicameral, and the judiciary is an independent <u>entity</u>. While this sounds much like the American political system, a major distinction can be found in the greater power of the executive branch in Mexico compared to the other branches of government.

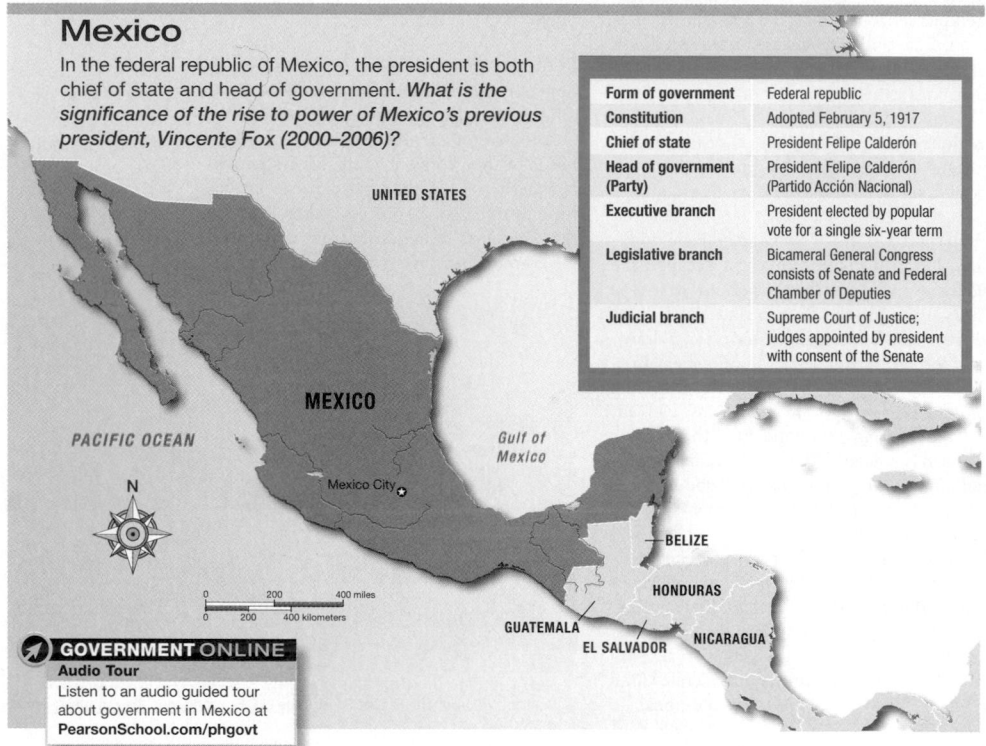

### Mexico

In the federal republic of Mexico, the president is both chief of state and head of government. *What is the significance of the rise to power of Mexico's previous president, Vincente Fox (2000–2006)?*

| | |
|---|---|
| **Form of government** | Federal republic |
| **Constitution** | Adopted February 5, 1917 |
| **Chief of state** | President Felipe Calderón |
| **Head of government (Party)** | President Felipe Calderón (Partido Acción Nacional) |
| **Executive branch** | President elected by popular vote for a single six-year term |
| **Legislative branch** | Bicameral General Congress consists of Senate and Federal Chamber of Deputies |
| **Judicial branch** | Supreme Court of Justice; judges appointed by president with consent of the Senate |

**GOVERNMENT ONLINE**
**Audio Tour**
Listen to an audio guided tour about government in Mexico at **PearsonSchool.com/phgovt**

## Myths and Misconceptions

**TWO HEADS** Many Americans may believe that it is old-fashioned to have both a head of state, such as a monarch, with mainly ceremonial duties, and a head of government, such as a prime minister. In fact, most democracies worldwide have both a President and a prime minister. Often the President is elected, while the prime minister is the leader of the majority party in the parliament. In most countries, including Germany, Ireland, India, Israel, and Singapore, the President is mainly a ceremonial position. However, in Israel and Indonesia, the President can dissolve the parliament. In other countries, such as France and Russia, the President has as much or more power than the prime minister.

**The President** The president of Mexico is popularly elected and serves one six-year term. The one-term limit is intended to prevent a popular leader from becoming a dictator by winning several reelections.

The president selects the members of the council of ministers (the cabinet) and other top civilian officers of government. He also appoints the senior officers of the armed forces and all federal judges.

In addition to the power usually held by a nation's chief executive, Mexico's president has the power to propose amendments to the constitution. Those amendments must be ratified at both the national and state levels, by a two-thirds vote in each house of Congress, and by a majority (at least 16) of the state legislatures. The president also has the power to enact laws through executive decree in some economic matters.

**The Legislature** The bicameral national legislature, called the General Congress, is composed of the Senate and the Chamber of Deputies. There are 64 senators—two from each of the 31 Mexican states and two from the Federal District, which includes Mexico City. Senators are elected to six-year terms. Half are elected at the time of the presidential election and half at a midterm election three years later.

The Chamber's 500 members are elected to three-year terms and cannot be reelected. Of those, 300 are directly elected from districts of more than 300,000 people. The other seats are filled from the ranks of the various political parties, based on their shares of the total vote in the national election. Thus, the Chamber is elected in a mixed system of direct and proportional representation.

The Congress meets from September 1 to December 31 each year. The combination of term limits and a short session gives the General Congress a far less significant role than that played by the Congress in the United States. Moreover, a lack of resources limits the ability of the Mexican Congress to exercise its powers. Its committees are poorly funded and understaffed, which also contributes to the dominant position of the presidency in the governmental system.

**The Judicial System** Mexico's independent judicial system is very similar to that of the United States. However, one difference of note is that trial is by a judge alone in most criminal cases, rather than by jury. Two systems of courts—state and federal—operate within the Mexican federal system.

The federal judiciary consists of district and circuit courts that function under the Supreme Court. These <u>tribunals</u> hear all cases that arise under federal law, including those that raise constitutional issues. The 31 separate state court systems are composed of trial and appellate courts. They hear civil and criminal cases in a judicial system headed by a state Supreme Court of Justice.

**Regional and Local Governments** As you know, Mexico is divided into 31 states and one Federal District. The Federal District includes the capital, Mexico City, and is administered by a governor appointed by the president. Each of the 31 state constitutions provides for a governor, unicameral legislature, and state courts. Each governor is elected to a single six-year term. Legislators are elected to three-year terms. The governors appoint judges. The states have the power to legislate on local matters and to levy taxes, but most of their funding comes from the national government.

## National Politics in Mexico

Mexico has a multiparty system. However, as you have read, it was dominated for decades by the PRI, which won every presidential election from 1929 until 2000. In fact,

In Mexico City, voters protested alleged election fraud after their party's candidate narrowly lost the 2006 presidential election. **Why is election fraud a concern in Mexico?**

<u>tribunal</u>
*n.* court

**EXTEND THE LESSON**

**L3 Differentiate** Have students write a paragraph explaining whether they think it is best for the legislative branch to have more power, for the executive branch to have more power, or for all three branches to have equal power, and why, using the UK and Mexico as examples.

**L2 ELL Differentiate** Have students create a political cartoon about the 2006 election in Mexico, using the criteria in the Rubric for Assessing a Political Cartoon (Unit 6 All-in-One, p. 101). Have students show and explain their political cartoons to the class. Have students vote on the most creative.

**L4 Differentiate** Mexico, and the UK as well, have recently made changes that have increased the level of democracy in each nation: the advent of free and fair elections in Mexico and Britain's enactment of the House of Lords Act, the Human Rights Act, and devolution. Have students research and write an essay on the conditions and pressures that led to these changes in each country. Encourage them to draw conclusions about lessons other democracies might learn from these examples.

# Background

**SAFEGUARDING MEXICO'S DEMOCRACY** Mexico's Federal Electoral Institute (IFE) was part of the executive branch until 1996, when reforms transformed it into an independent agency. Free from ruling-party control, the IFE succeeded for the first time in preventing election fraud—rampant for decades in Mexico. For the 2000 election, voters were required to show their identification cards. They marked their ballots in private booths. The ballot boxes were transparent, so that independent observers could verify that voters cast only one ballot, correcting past practices of ballot-box stuffing. Voters' thumbs were then marked with indelible ink to make sure no one voted more than once—a common practice in previous elections. The election processes the IFE established in 2000 proved their value in 2006, when Felipe Calderón's victory was challenged, and the IFE was called on to declare a winner.

## Answers

**Caption** Fraudulent elections in Mexico had allowed the PRI to retain its control over the nation for decades.

# Assess and Remediate

**L3** Collect the game questions and assess students' work.

**L3** Assign the Section 4 Assessment questions.

**L3** Section Quiz A (Unit 6 All-in-One, p. 46)

**L2** Section Quiz B (Unit 6 All-in-One, p. 47)

Have students complete the review activities in the digital lesson presentation and continue their work in the **Essential Questions Journal.**

## REMEDIATION

| If Your Students Have Trouble With | Strategies For Remediation |
|---|---|
| Government system of the United Kingdom (Questions 1, 2, 5) | Work with students to complete a concept web in which you record what they have learned about the government of the United Kingdom. |
| Government system of Mexico (Questions 1, 3, 6) | Have students complete a Venn diagram comparing Mexico's government to the U.S. Government. |
| NAFTA (Question 4) | Have students write a summary of the information about NAFTA in this section. |

## Answers

**Checkpoint** PAN, PRI, and PRD

---

✓ **Checkpoint**
What are Mexico's main political parties?

because the PRI retained its position through patronage, and opposition movements were often repressed, Mexico was not generally considered to be democratic until 2000.

**The PRI** The PRI's dominant position began to erode in the 1980s. The government borrowed heavily during the 1970s, expecting that oil prices would remain high. When oil prices declined sharply worldwide, the country plunged into economic chaos. Debt problems led to severe cutbacks in government programs and undermined the PRI's patronage system. Prices soared and investment capital fled the country.

The PRI made its worst showing ever in the elections of 1988. The party barely maintained control of the government, when presidential candidate Carlos Salinas de Gortari won that year. Allegations of fraud were widespread.

President Salinas pursued broad-based economic, social, and electoral reforms. He also backed the North American Free Trade Agreement (NAFTA). This agreement, about which you will learn more in the next chapter, removed trade and investment restrictions among the United States, Canada, and Mexico. In the close elections of 1994, the PRI's presidential candidate, Ernesto Zedillo, won 48.8 percent of the total vote, and the PRI retained control of the legislature.

**Multiparty Democracy** In the 1990s, candidates from the conservative National Action Party (PAN) and leftist Democratic Revolutionary Party (PRD) had won increasing numbers of federal, state, and local offices. Both parties took aim at the nation's highest office in 2000. Public opinion and world attention forced the PRI to guarantee a fraud-free presidential contest. When all the votes had been counted, the PAN candidate, Vicente Fox, had won with 45 percent of the vote.

Fox initially held approval ratings of over 70 percent, but those ratings later dipped below 50 percent. President Fox may have been a victim of unmet, or even unrealistic, expectations. His political rise marked a dramatic event in Mexican politics, but for many Mexicans socioeconomic conditions did not improve under his tenure. As a sign of the growing discontent, the PRI seemed to be experiencing a resurgence. Midterm elections allowed it to shore up its majority in the Senate and it almost gained a majority in the Chamber of Deputies, as well. However, PAN candidate Felipe Calderón narrowly won the presidency in the contentious 2006 election over Andrés Manuel López Obrador of the PRD. The PRI's candidate, Roberto Madrazo, came in third. PAN also gained control of both houses of Congress in that election.

> **Essential Questions Journal** To continue to build a response to the chapter Essential Question, go to your **Essential Questions Journal.**

## SECTION 4 ASSESSMENT

1. **Guiding Question** Use your completed Venn diagram to answer this question: What form does democratic government take in the United Kingdom and in Mexico?

**Key Terms and Comprehension**

2. Under what circumstances would a **coalition** government be formed in the United Kingdom?

3. In what major ways are the three branches of Mexican government similar to those in the United States?

4. What is the significance to Mexico of the North American Free Trade Agreement (NAFTA)?

**Critical Thinking**

5. **Making Comparisons** What are the major differences between **(a)** the British Parliament and the U.S. Congress? **(b)** the British prime minister and the American President?

6. **Drawing Inferences** Which form of presidential tenure do you think is preferable: the Mexican model, with one six-year term, or the American model, with a four-year term and the possibility of a second term? Explain your reasoning.

**Quick Write**

**Expository Writing: Create an Outline** To help structure your compare-and-contrast essay, create an outline in which you identify each area of comparison and contrast in a single phrase. When you are ready to write your essay, you can use the outline as a guide. Alternatively, you may create a flowchart to help you organize and order your ideas.

Comparative Political Systems

---

# Assessment Answers

**1.** United Kingdom: unitary, parliamentary, constitutional monarchy; Mexico: federal republic

**2.** A coalition government would be formed if no single party held a majority in the House of Commons.

**3.** Like the United States, Mexico has three independent branches consisting of an executive branch headed by a president, a bicameral legislative branch, and a judicial branch composed of federal and state systems and a Supreme Court.

**4.** NAFTA removed trade and investment restrictions among the United States, Mexico, and Canada, thus increasing trade across the borders of those countries.

**5. (a)** Congress only holds legislative power; Parliament also holds executive (House of Commons) and judicial (House of Lords) power, and members of the House of Lords are not elected. **(b)** The prime minister is not elected but is appointed by the monarch, is head of the majority party of the House of Commons, and has both executive and legislative powers.

**6.** Possible answer: I think the Mexican model is more effective because it gives the President time to achieve his or her goals. However, if the President is not effective, the people must wait longer than they do in the United States to vote him or her out of office.

**QUICK WRITE** A good assignment will show a series of points, in correct outline format, that compare and contrast two forms of government.

Comparative Political Systems

# Quick Study Guide

**GOVERNMENT ONLINE**
On the Go
To review anytime, anywhere, download these online resources at **PearsonSchool.com/phgovt**
Political Dictionary, Audio Review

**CHAPTER 22**

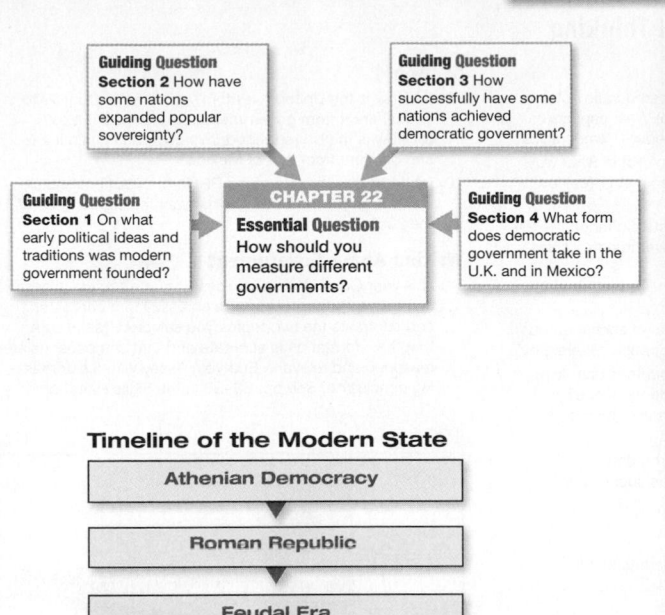

**Guiding Question**
Section 2 How have some nations expanded popular sovereignty?

**Guiding Question**
Section 3 How successfully have some nations achieved democratic government?

**Guiding Question**
Section 1 On what early political ideas and traditions was modern government founded?

**CHAPTER 22**
Essential Question
How should you measure different governments?

**Guiding Question**
Section 4 What form does democratic government take in the U.K. and in Mexico?

### Timeline of the Modern State

Athenian Democracy

↓

Roman Republic

↓

Feudal Era

↓

Sovereign States and Colonialism

↓

Popular Sovereignty

### Political Dictionary

patricians *p. 647*
plebeians *p. 647*
feudalism *p. 648*
sovereignty *p. 650*
legitimacy *p. 650*
divine right of kings *p. 650*
colonialism *p. 651*
mercantilism *p. 651*
encomienda *p. 655*
guerrilla warfare *p. 657*
fascism *p. 659*
communism *p. 659*
hard-liners *p. 661*
soft-liners *p. 661*
democratization *p. 663*
democratic consolidation *p. 663*
genocide *p. 665*
failed states *p. 665*
coalition *p. 667*
ministers *p. 667*
shadow cabinet *p. 668*
devolution *p. 669*

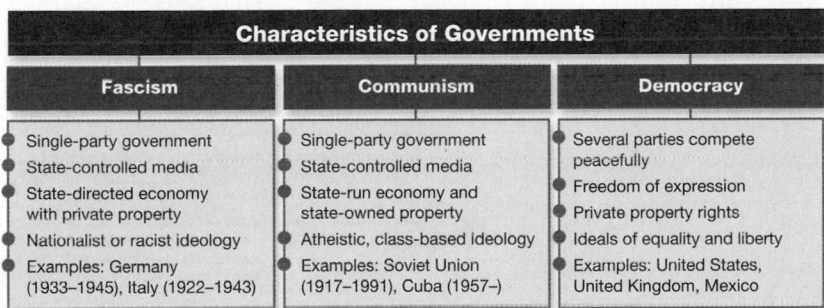

### Characteristics of Governments

| Fascism | Communism | Democracy |
|---|---|---|
| • Single-party government | • Single-party government | • Several parties compete peacefully |
| • State-controlled media | • State-controlled media | • Freedom of expression |
| • State-directed economy with private property | • State-run economy and state-owned property | • Private property rights |
| • Nationalist or racist ideology | • Atheistic, class-based ideology | • Ideals of equality and liberty |
| • Examples: Germany (1933–1945), Italy (1922–1943) | • Examples: Soviet Union (1917–1991), Cuba (1957–) | • Examples: United States, United Kingdom, Mexico |

Have students download the digital resources available at Government on the Go for review and remediation.

**STUDY TIPS**

**Rewrite and Color-Code Notes** While rewriting notes is time-consuming, it is also an excellent way to review. By rewriting their notes, students can make them neater and better organized. As they rewrite, they may see relationships among ideas that they missed in class, and they can refer to their reading assignments to help fill in gaps in their notes or clarify a troublesome point. Suggest that students rewrite their notes as soon as possible after class, while the lecture is still fresh in their minds. Color-coding can make rewriting more fun and can also help to organize material. Students might consider using different colors for different types of information (i.e., terms or dates), to highlight important information, or to show relationships among ideas.

**ASSESSMENT AT A GLANCE**

**Tests and Quizzes**
Section Assessments
Section Quizzes A and B, Unit 6 **All-in-One**
Chapter Assessment
Chapter Tests A and B, Unit 6 **All-in-One**
Document-Based Assessment
Progress Monitoring Online
Exam*View* Test Bank

**Performance Assessment**
Essential Questions Journal
Debate, p. 658
Assessment Rubrics, **All-in-One**

# For More Information

To learn more about different governments, refer to these sources or assign them to students:

**L1** **Padrino, Mercedes.** *Feudalism and Village Life in the Middle Ages.* World Almanac Library, 2006.

**L2** **Mellor, Ronald and Marni McGee.** *The Ancient Roman World.* Oxford University Press, USA, 2004.

**L3** **Arnold, James R.** *The Aftermath of the French Revolution.* Twenty-First Century Books, 2008.

**L4** **Paxton, Robert O.** *The Anatomy of Fascism.* Vintage, 2005.

# Chapter Assessment

## COMPREHENSION AND CRITICAL THINKING

### SECTION 1

1. **(a)** direct democracy, legislative assembly, majority vote, separate judiciary **(b)** legislative assembly, top executives, written laws, representative government, elections, the veto, checks on power

2. **(a)** It developed after the fall of the Roman Empire to provide a governmental system for Western Europe. **(b)** Power was not held by central, national governments. Feudalism was a loosely organized system of powerful lords who developed relationships of mutual dependence with vassals and serfs. **(c)** Feudalism filled the need for some kind of government after the fall of the Roman Empire. The feudal system provided economic and social stability, protection for the people, and a rough form of justice.

3. **(a)** Government became more centralized and nation-based. Monarchies held absolute power and did not need to recognize popular sovereignty, in some nations, to any degree at all. **(b)** through tradition (such as divine right), through the power of personality (such as strong charisma of the leader), and through binding government to the rule of law

### SECTION 2

4. **Britain:** benefits: gradual change, not as violent or destructive of traditional institutions; drawbacks: slow, true democracy did not appear until fairly late. **France:** benefits: achieved popular sovereignty very rapidly; drawbacks: was extremely violent, destroyed all traditional institutions, did not last long initially.

5. **(a)** The colonists in Latin America came from Spain and Portugal—countries ruled by absolute dictators who did not embrace popular sovereignty. Therefore, these colonists had no history or tradition to support a move toward democracy. Also, the encomienda and hacienda systems created an elite ruling class that formed a powerful barrier to popular sovereignty. **(b)** Colonialism left bitter tensions by creating artificial boundaries that broke up tribal lands and forcibly combined diverse groups into a single state. The colonial power often favored one segment of the population over another, creating tensions among groups that would explode later into conflict. The colonial powers directed each colony to export a few raw resources, which

---

CHAPTER 22 **Chapter Assessment**

**GOVERNMENT ONLINE**
Self-Test
To test your understanding of key terms and main ideas, visit
PearsonSchool.com/phgovt

## Comprehension and Critical Thinking

### Section 1

1. **(a)** What aspects of ancient Athenian democratic government exist in modern democracies? **(b)** What aspects of ancient Roman government exist in modern democracies?
2. **(a)** Why did the feudal system develop? **(b)** In what way was it a decentralized system of government? **(c)** How did feudalism meet the needs of its time?
3. **(a)** How did the rise of the sovereign state change the role of government? **(b)** How did these governments achieve legitimacy?

### Section 2

4. What were the benefits and drawbacks of each method used by Britain and France to adopt popular sovereignty?
5. **(a)** Why were many Latin American countries unable to establish stable democracies after independence? **(b)** What obstacles to stability were caused by the former colonial system in Africa?
6. **(a)** What are the goals of fascist governments? **(b)** Must governments have goals to be successful? If so, what should those goals be?

### Section 3

7. **(a)** Describe the difference between democratization and democratic consolidation. **(b)** How is each one important to the success of a government?
8. **Analyzing Cartoons** Study the cartoon at right. **(a)** What form of government does the hammer represent? **(b)** What is this cartoonist saying about that form of government? **(c)** From your reading and understanding of history, is this cartoon fair? Explain.

### Section 4

9. **(a)** How is the United Kingdom's government similar to and different from government in the United States? **(b)** How is the United Kingdom's government similar to and different from that of Mexico?
10. **(a)** What was the role of the PRI in Mexican political life up through the 1990s? **(b)** What was the significance of the 2000 election?

## Writing About Government

11. Use your Quick Write exercises from the section assessments in this chapter to write an essay that compares and contrasts the two topics you selected. Make sure that the information is accurate and that comparisons are reasoned and relevant. End your essay with a summarizing conclusion. See pp. S3–S5 in the Skills Handbook.

HUMAN RIGHTS

## Apply What You've Learned

12. **Essential Question Activity** Speak with an immigrant to the United States or someone who has known an immigrant well and can answer as that person might answer. Ask:
    **(a)** Why did you come to the United States?
    **(b)** How do you view the government of your native country? What do you think worked well? How well did it meet citizens' needs? How democratic do you think it is?
    **(c)** How do you view the government of the United States in comparison to that of your native country?

13. **Essential Question Assessment** Based on the interview you conducted and what you have learned about democracy and American government, write a guide to the government of this country designed to help immigrants learn about its basic structure and functions in comparison with other countries. Your guide should help you answer the Essential Question: **How should you measure different governments?**

**Essential Questions Journal** To respond to the chapter Essential Question, go to your **Essential Questions Journal.**

---

after independence led to weak economies dependent on one or a few cash crops or raw materials.

6. **(a)** Fascist governments win power with ultranationalist, racist ideology; a charismatic dictator; violent suppression of dissent; totalitarian; policies glorify the state over the individual; unite people against common enemy—foreign powers or minorities; and promises to promote the people's welfare. **(b)** Possible answer: I think governments must have goals—general, such as maintaining order, civil rights, and justice—and specific, such as passing

laws and other activities that protect and serve its citizens.

### SECTION 3

7. **(a)** Democratization is the change from dictatorship to democracy, marked by the holding of free and fair elections. Democratic consolidation is the much longer process of firmly establishing the factors necessary for democracy to succeed. **(b)** Democratization is the first step in shifting from a dictatorship to a democracy, but democratic consolidation must follow to ensure that democracy will last into the future.

# Document-Based Assessment

## Fascism and Communism

Communist and fascist leaders claimed to meet the needs of the people and to rule on the basis of popular sovereignty. However, communist governments, such as those in the Soviet Union and China, and fascist governments, as in Italy and Germany, became dictatorships. How did these governments use propaganda to legitimize their rule?

### Document 1

"

Fascism conceives of the State as an absolute, in comparison with which all individuals or groups are relative, only to be conceived of in their relation to the State. . . . The Fascist State organizes the nation, but leaves a sufficient margin of liberty to the individual; the latter is deprived of all useless and possibly harmful freedom, but retains what is essential; the deciding power in this question cannot be the individual, but the State alone. . . . Fascism is the doctrine best adapted to represent the tendencies and the aspirations of a people, like the people of Italy, who are rising again after many centuries of abasement and foreign servitude. But empire demands discipline, the coordination of all forces and a deeply felt sense of duty and sacrifice.

—Benito Mussolini, from "What Is Fascism?" 1932

### Document 2

"

We hold these Truths to be self-evident, that all Men are created equal, that they are endowed by their Creator with certain unalienable Rights, that among these are Life, Liberty, and the Pursuit of Happiness.

—Declaration of Independence,1776

### Document 3

This Chinese Communist Party poster of 1974 calls on "workers, peasants, and soldiers" to criticize the philosopher Confucius and a discredited communist leader, Lin Biao.

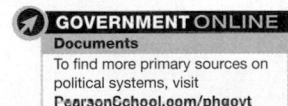

---

**Use your knowledge of fascism and communism and Documents 1–3 to answer Questions 1–3.**

1. In his description of fascism, Mussolini says that
   A. the people have liberty only in relation to the state.
   B. the people have absolute power over the state.
   C. the state receives its authority directly from the people.
   D. the state is democratic and has little power over the people.

2. How does Mussolini's description of freedom differ from that set out in the Declaration of Independence?

3. **Pull It Together** Italy under Mussolini and China under Mao were both authoritarian dictatorships. However, both Documents 1 and 3 make appeals to popular sovereignty. How are these appeals the same and different in each document?

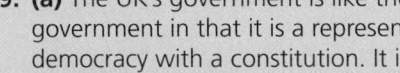

**GOVERNMENT** ONLINE
**Documents**
To find more primary sources on political systems, visit
**PearsonSchool.com/phgovt**

---

1. A

2. Possible response: The Declaration of Independence holds that all people have rights that no one, including the state, can take away. This philosophy places the people above the state. Mussolini holds the opposite—that the state is supreme and the people receive whatever liberties the state chooses to give them.

3. Both documents refer to the importance of "the people." Fascism, however, holds that the state grants liberty to the people, while communism downplays the importance of the state compared with the people.

**L2** **Differentiate** Students use all the documents on the page to support their thesis.

**L3** **Differentiate** Students include additional information available online at **PearsonSchool.com/phgovt.**

**L4** **Differentiate** Students use materials from the textbook, the online information at **PearsonSchool.com/phgovt,** and do additional research to support their views.

**Go Online to PearsonSchool.com/phgovt** for a student rubric and extra documents.

---

8. **(a)** Communist government in the Soviet Union **(b)** that it brutally suppresses human rights **(c)** Possible response: Yes. Although Communist governments claim to rule in the people's name, they have regularly led to repression. Rule by a single party, supported by a strong military, places all decision-making power with the government.

### SECTION 4

9. **(a)** The UK's government is like the U.S. government in that it is a representative democracy with a constitution. It is different in that it is a unitary system under a constitutional monarch, and the constitution is mostly unwritten. It is led by a prime minister, who is the party head, not by a popularly elected President. **(b)** The UK's government has the same similarities and differences with Mexico as with the U.S., since Mexico and the U.S. have a federal government under a popularly elected President and a written constitution.

10. **(a)** Although the PRI still dominated Mexican politics in the 1990s, its hold was slipping. **(b)** Public opinion and world attention forced the PRI to guarantee a fraud-free election in 2000. PAN candidate Vicente Fox won, marking the end of the PRI's 70-year political domination.

### WRITING ABOUT GOVERNMENT

11. Essays should compare and contrast the topics selected and end with a summarizing conclusion.

### APPLY WHAT YOU'VE LEARNED

12. Responses should summarize the interviewee's answers.

13. Students' guides should accurately describe the U.S. federal system of government and its three branches.

# Introduce the Chapter

## Essential Questions:

**UNIT 6**

How should a government meet the needs of its people?

**CHAPTER 23**

To what extent should governments participate in the economy?

### ACTIVATE PRIOR KNOWLEDGE

Have students examine the image and quotation on these pages. Ask: **How do you think political freedom relates to economic freedom?** *(Possible answer: In a free democracy, people are allowed to make their own economic choices. This increases opportunities and quality of life.)* In this chapter, students will learn about three economic systems—capitalism, socialism, and communism—and how the U.S. government is involved in the modern global economy. Tell students to begin to further explore economic systems by completing the Chapter 23 Essential Question Warmup activity in their **Essential Questions Journal.** Discuss their responses as a class.

### BEFORE READING

**L2** **ELL Differentiate** Chapter 23 Prereading and Vocabulary Worksheet (Unit 6 All-in-One, p. 61)

### SUCCESSNET STUDENT AND TEACHER CENTER

Visit **PearsonSchool.com/phgovt** for download-able resources that allow students and teachers to connect with government "on the go."

### DIGITAL LESSON PRESENTATION

The digital lesson presentation supports the print lesson with activities and summaries of key concepts.

## SKILLS DEVELOPMENT

### ANALYZE GRAPHIC DATA

You may wish to teach analyzing graphic data as a distinct skill within Section 3 of this chapter. Use the Chapter 23 Skills Worksheet (Unit 6 All-in-One, p. 88) to help students learn how to analyze graphic data. The worksheet asks students to interpret two graphs and then draw conclusions about them. For L2 and L1 students, assign the adapted Skill Activity (Unit 6 All-in-One, p. 90).

**WebQuest online** The chapter WebQuest challenges students to answer the chapter Essential Question by asking them about governments and economies.

676

## Block Scheduling

**BLOCK 1:** Teach the Section 1 lesson, and omit the Extend options.

**BLOCK 2:** Teach the Section 2 and 3 lessons, omitting the Core Worksheet activity in Section 3 and the Extend options in both sections.

## Comparative Economic Systems

### Essential Question
To what extent should governments participate in the economy?

**Section 1:**
Capitalism

**Section 2:**
Socialism and Communism

**Section 3:**
The U.S. in a Global Economy

> **Freedom** in **economic arrangements** is itself a component of **freedom** broadly understood. . . . **Economic freedom** is . . . an **indispensable** means toward the **achievement** of **political freedom.**
>
> —Milton Friedman, 1962

**Photo:** Traders buy and sell at the Chicago Mercantile Exchange.

**GOVERNMENT** ONLINE
On the Go

To study anywhere, anytime, download these online resources at PearsonSchool.com/phgovt
• Political Dictionary
• Audio Review
• Downloadable Interactivities

677

## Lesson Goals

### SECTION 1
Students will . . .

• examine the factors of production and the fundamental factors of free enterprise by completing concept webs.

• discuss and vote on what they feel is the proper level of government control in the economy.

• work in groups to create and present arguments advocating the free enterprise system.

### SECTION 2
Students will . . .

• use a transparency to discuss the theories of Karl Marx.

• complete a chart that compares and contrasts economic systems.

• role-play and write a dialogue to compare and contrast life under capitalism and communism.

• write a journal entry evaluating economic systems.

### SECTION 3
Students will . . .

• list ways in which government regulation of the economy affects their own lives.

• complete a concept web about the role of the Federal Government in the economy at home and abroad.

• summarize economic news reports to present to the class in a mock television program.

## Pressed for Time

To cover the chapter quickly, have students complete the Reading Comprehension Worksheet for Section 1. Then ask them to complete the Bellringer Worksheet from Section 2. Review the answers to the worksheet as a class. Then have students complete the concept web activity from the Section 3 lesson on government involvement in the economy. Finally, have students make a pro/con chart on the issue of free trade.

**DIFFERENTIATED INSTRUCTION KEY**

Look for these symbols to help you adjust steps in each lesson to meet your students' needs.

**L1** Special Needs

**L2** Basic

    **ELL** English Language Learners

    **LPR** Less Proficient Readers

**L3** All Students

**L4** Advanced Students

# What is the role of government in the American economy?

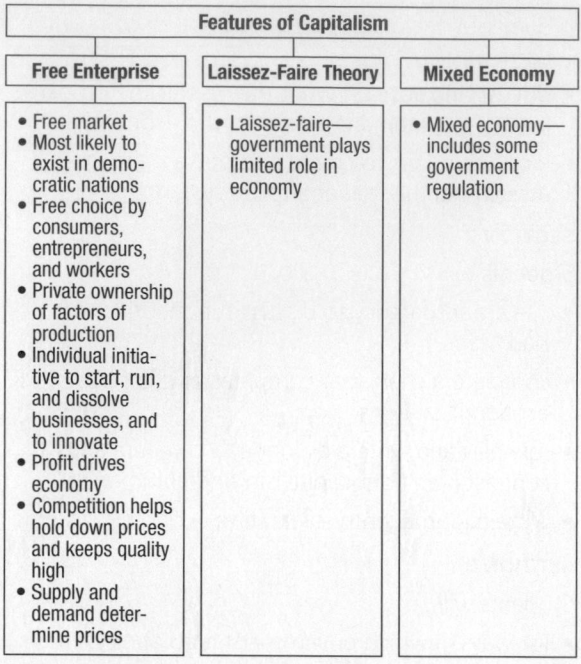

| Features of Capitalism | | |
|---|---|---|
| **Free Enterprise** | **Laissez-Faire Theory** | **Mixed Economy** |
| • Free market<br>• Most likely to exist in democratic nations<br>• Free choice by consumers, entrepreneurs, and workers<br>• Private ownership of factors of production<br>• Individual initiative to start, run, and dissolve businesses, and to innovate<br>• Profit drives economy<br>• Competition helps hold down prices and keeps quality high<br>• Supply and demand determine prices | • Laissez-faire—government plays limited role in economy | • Mixed economy—includes some government regulation |

## SKILLS DEVELOPMENT

### ANALYZE CAUSE AND EFFECT

Before students do the Bellringer in this section, you may want to review information on analyzing cause and effect in the Skills Handbook, p. S16.

---

**SECTION 1**

# Capitalism

### Guiding Question

**What is the role of government in the American economy?** Create a chart similar to the one below to record information from the section on features of capitalism.

| Features of Capitalism | | |
|---|---|---|
| **Free Enterprise** | **Laissez-Faire Theory** | **Mixed Economy** |
| • Private ownership<br>• Individual initiative<br>• | • Government plays a limited role in economy<br>• | •<br>• |

### Political Dictionary

- capitalism
- factors of production
- capital
- entrepreneur
- free enterprise system
- free market
- law of supply and demand
- monopoly
- laissez-faire theory

### Objectives

1. Identify the factors of production.
2. Describe the free enterprise system and laissez-faire theory.
3. Analyze the role of government in a mixed economy.
4. Compare and contrast three types of business organizations.
5. Explain the role of profit and loss in a free enterprise system.

**Image Above:** Small businesses are an essential part of a free enterprise system.

You have confronted these questions several times in this book: What are the functions a government ought to undertake? What should it have the power to do? What should it not be allowed to do? Certainly these questions can be asked of just about all areas of human activity, but they are raised very significantly in the realm of economic affairs.

Questions of politics and economics are inseparable. The most important economic questions faced by a nation are also political questions. For example: Who should decide what goods will be produced? How should goods and services be distributed and exchanged within a nation? What types of income or property ought to be taxed? What social services should a government provide to its citizens?

Capitalism provides one response to all of these questions. **Capitalism** is an economic system in which individuals are free to own the means of production and maximize profits. Many aspects of capitalism will be familiar to you because the United States and most other nations in the world today have adopted this economic system.

## Factors of Production

Certain resources are necessary to any nation's economy, no matter what economic system is in place. Economists call these basic resources, which are used to make all goods and services, the **factors of production.**

**Land** Land, which in economic terms includes all natural resources, is an important factor of production. Land has a variety of economic uses, such as agriculture, mining, and forestry. Along with farms and other property, economists categorize the water in rivers and lakes and the coal, iron, and petroleum found beneath the ground as part of the land itself.

**Capital** A second factor of production is **capital**—all the human-made resources that are used to produce goods and services. Physical capital (also called "capital goods") includes the buildings, machines, computers, and other materials workers need to turn land and another factor, labor, into goods and

---

# Focus on the Basics

**FACTS:** • Entrepreneurs bring together the factors of production to create goods and services. • The laws of supply and demand determine market prices. • Laissez-faire theory holds that the government should play a very limited role in society. • Three types of businesses exist in the U.S.: sole proprietorships, partnerships, and corporations.

**CONCEPTS:** economic systems, laissez-faire theory, role of government

**ENDURING UNDERSTANDINGS:** • The United States has a mixed economy in which private enterprise and governmental participation coexist. • In a free enterprise system, consumers, entrepreneurs, and workers enjoy freedom of choice. • Capitalist economies are driven by the desire to make a profit.

services. Note that capital is a product of the economy that is then put back into the economy.

**Labor** Yet another factor of production is a human resource—labor. Men and women who work in mines, factories, offices, hospitals, and other places all provide labor that is an essential part of a nation's economy. In a capitalist, or free market, economy, individuals "own" their labor and can sell it to any employer. Human capital includes the knowledge and skills that workers gain from their work experiences—an investment in themselves.

One who owns capital and puts it to productive use is called a capitalist. That term is applied to people who own large businesses or factories as well as investors and the owners of small businesses. The American economy is called capitalistic because its growth depends very largely on the energy and drive of thousands of individual capitalists, not the government.

**The Role of the Entrepreneur** To actually produce goods and services, someone must bring together and organize the factors of production. An **entrepreneur**—literally, an "enterpriser"—is an individual with the drive and ambition to combine land, labor, and capital resources to produce goods or offer services, and is willing to risk losses and failure. Entrepreneurs start businesses and make them grow, creating jobs and goods and services that contribute to a high standard of living.

## Free Enterprise System

Capitalism is frequently referred to as a **free enterprise system,** which is an economic system characterized by private ownership of capital and by investments that are determined by private decision, not by public authorities. This system needs a **free market,** a market in which buyers and sellers are free to buy and sell as they wish. A free market is most likely to exist in a democratic nation, such as the United

✓ **Checkpoint**
Why are the factors of production important?

# Factors of Production

Land, labor, and capital are the building blocks of the economy known as the factors of production. The entrepreneur brings these three factors together to create something consumers will buy. *Look up "land" and "capital" in the dictionary. How do economists' definitions differ from what you found?*

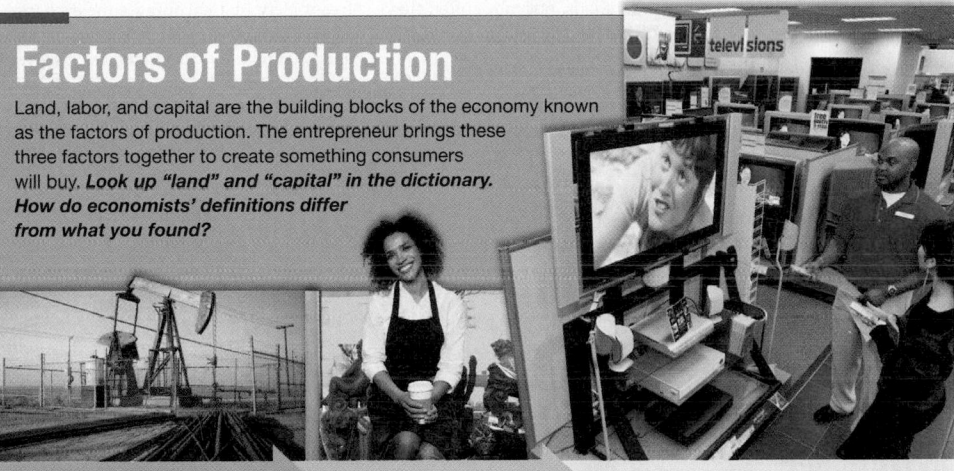

**Land** includes property and the resources found in nature.

**Labor** describes the work of individuals.

**Capital** includes the tools, money, and human expertise that turn labor and land into goods and services.

**Entrepreneurs** are risk-taking individuals who have the skill and drive to create new products or services for the market.

**Goods and Services** are the items people buy and the things one does for another or for the community.

# Differentiated Resources

The following resources are located in the All-in-One, Unit 6, Chapter 23, Section 1:

**L2** Prereading and Vocabulary Worksheet (p. 61)
**L3** Reading Comprehension Worksheet (p. 65)
**L2** Reading Comprehension Worksheet (p. 67)
**L3** Core Worksheet (p. 69)
**L3** **L4** Extend Worksheet (p. 70)
**L3** Quiz A (p. 71)
**L2** Quiz B (p. 72)

**LESSON GOALS**

Students will . . .

- examine the factors of production and the fundamental factors of free enterprise by completing concept webs.
- discuss and vote on what they feel is the proper level of government control in the economy.
- work in groups to create and present arguments advocating the free enterprise system.

**BEFORE CLASS**

Assign the section, the graphic organizer in the text, and the Reading Comprehension Worksheet (Unit 6 All-in-One, p. 65) before class.

**L2 Differentiate** Reading Comprehension Worksheet (Unit 6 All-in-One, p. 67)

**BELLRINGER**

Display the blank Concept Web Graphic Organizer transparency and write on the board: **Look at the "Factors of Production" diagram in your textbook. Then create and complete a concept web about the factors.**

## Answers

**Checkpoint** because they are the basic resources that are used to make all goods and services

**Factors of Production** Economists include all natural resources, including water, in "land," not just the part of the earth's surface not covered by water. The dictionary defines "capital" as wealth in money or property. Economists consider "capital" to be all human-made resources put to productive use and then reinvested in the economy, including physical goods, such as machines and materials.

# Teach

To present this topic using online resources, use the lesson presentations at **PearsonSchool.com/phgovt.**

## INTRODUCE THE TOPIC

Explain that this lesson is about capitalism, or the free enterprise system, and how that system works in the United States. Begin by reviewing the Bellringer activity. Point out that the factors of production *(land, labor, and capital)* are the basic resources *(rivers, workers, and tools)* required to make goods and services in all economic systems, including capitalism. In a free enterprise system, entrepreneurs bring these resources together to make goods and services. Ask: **If you were an American entrepreneur starting a new restaurant, what factors of production would you need?** *(land: a space for the restaurant and parking; labor: chef, waitpersons, cashier, bus persons, hosts or hostesses, dishwashers; capital: money, computers, a building, meal preparation appliances, ingredients for food preparation, skills/ knowledge)*

Next, draw or display a blank transparency of a concept web. Label the web "The Free Enterprise System." Work with students to complete the concept web through discussion of the features of capitalism. Ask: **What are the four fundamental factors in a free enterprise system?** *(private ownership, individual initiative, profit, and competition)* Add ovals for each of these factors. Ask: **How would these factors of the free enterprise system encourage entrepreneurs, like the restaurant owner, to start new businesses?** *(The free enterprise system allows private ownership of the factors of production and the freedom to choose how to use them to produce goods and services. Entrepreneurs who have drive, talent, and a willingness to accept the risk of loss can use their factors of production to start a business and keep the profits they earn. Competition encourages business owners to improve goods and services and hold prices down, which benefits consumers.)*

## Answers

**Checkpoint** an economic system characterized by private ownership of capital and by investments that are determined by private decision, not by public authorities

**Elements of Free Enterprise** possible response: preserve competition by preventing monopolies and trusts that interfere with the free market; supply justice system to protect private property

**680** Comparative Economic Systems

---

✔ **Checkpoint**
What is the free enterprise system?

**just compensation**
*n.* fair payment for loss

States, where security and the rule of law are protected by the government.

A free enterprise system lets consumers, entrepreneurs, and workers enjoy freedom of choice. Consumers can choose from a variety of products and services. Entrepreneurs can switch from one business to another. Workers can quit their jobs and seek new ones, and they can choose to organize labor unions as a way to bargain for better working conditions or benefits.

A capitalistic system—a free enterprise system—is based on four fundamental factors: private ownership, individual initiative, profit, and competition.

**Private Ownership** In a capitalistic system, private individuals and companies own most of the factors of production—the basic resources used to produce goods and services. They decide how this productive property will be used—for example, to build a business or invest in technology. What the property produces is theirs, as well. The owners of productive property are sometimes individuals, but more often they are groups of people who share ownership of a company.

In a free enterprise system, individuals own the right to their own labor. They sell that labor by taking a job, and the pay they receive represents the price paid for their work. In other economic systems, workers may have little choice as to the kinds of work they will do and little opportunity to change jobs or pay.

The protection of the rights of private ownership is also important, particularly in the United States. The 5th and 14th amendments declare that no person may be deprived "of life, liberty, or property, without due process of law." The 5th Amendment also says that "just compensation" must be paid to owners when their private property is taken for some public use.

**Individual Initiative** In our economy, entrepreneurs are an essential factor in the production of goods and services. Under a free enterprise system, all individuals are free to start and run their own businesses (their own enterprises). They are also free to dissolve those businesses. Importantly, the atmosphere of a free market, as well as a free society that encourages the exchange of ideas, can and often does lead to innovation and scientific and technological discoveries.

## Elements of Free Enterprise

A free market economy cannot succeed without these four basic elements: private ownership, individual initiative, profit, and competition. Supported by the rule of law and by the people, these factors allow for the many market transactions that define a free enterprise economy. *What is the role of government in preserving the elements of free enterprise?*

Private ownership

UNDER NEW MANAGEMENT
NOW OPEN
COFFEE C

Profit

Individual initiative

**680** Comparative Economic Systems

---

# Constitutional Principles

**LIMITED GOVERNMENT** Adam Smith's book *The Wealth of Nations* introduced not only laissez-faire capitalism, but also the idea of economics as a separate discipline. Smith advocated severe limits on government intervention in the economy. He was specifically responding to the English government's practice at that time of forming monopolies and granting exclusive trading rights to certain companies. However, Smith's ideas also stemmed from his belief that people's capacity for reason regulated their actions and could influence the economy more than government could.

These promote growth in the economy and often improve the quality of everyday life.

That is not necessarily true in other economic systems. In some countries, government planners decide what will be produced and how it will be made. There, centralized decision making, not individual initiative, controls the production and distribution of goods and services.

**Profit** Just as individuals are free to choose how they will spend or invest their capital in a free enterprise system, they are also entitled to benefit from whatever their investment or enterprise earns or gains in value. The "profit motive" is the desire to gain from business dealings. It drives entrepreneurs to create goods and services people will want to buy, and is a major reason why entrepreneurs are willing to take risks.

**Competition** The freedom to enter or start a new business at any time leads to competition. Competition is a situation in which a number of companies offer similar products or services. They must compete against one another for customers. In a free enterprise system, competition often helps to hold down

Competition

prices and keep quality high. This is usually the case because customers are likely to buy from the company with the best product at the lowest price. Competition promotes efficiency; the producer has the incentive (more sales) to keep costs low.

Under these competitive conditions, the **law of supply and demand** determines the market price for goods or services. Supply is the quantity of goods or services available for sale at a range of prices. As the price increases, more of a product will be offered for sale. Demand is buyers' desire and ability to purchase a good or service. As the price falls, more of a product will be demanded by buyers. If supply increases and demand remains the same, prices will fall. If demand decreases and supply stays the same, prices will also fall. On the other hand, if demand increases and supply remains the same, prices will rise.

Competition does not always work smoothly. Sometimes a single business becomes so successful that all its rivals go out of business. A firm that is the only source of a product or service is called a **monopoly**. Monopolies can be very powerful in the marketplace. Practically speaking, they can charge as much as they want for a product. Since there is no other supplier of that good or service, the consumer must pay the monopoly's price or do without.

In the late nineteenth century, political leaders in the United States gradually became convinced that certain monopolies were stifling competition and interfering with the free market. They were especially concerned about a type of monopoly called a *trust*. A trust exists when several corporations in the same line of business work together to eliminate competition from the market and regulate prices. By the latter part of the nineteenth century, trusts had gained tight-fisted control over the markets for petroleum, steel, coal, beef, sugar, and other commodities.

In response, Congress passed the Sherman Anti-Trust Act of 1890, which remains the basic law to curb monopolies today. It prohibits "every contract, combination in the form of a trust or otherwise, or conspiracy in restraint of trade or commerce among the several States, or with foreign nations."

✔ **Checkpoint**
Why is competition important?

**L2 ELL Differentiate** Write *enterprise* and *entrepreneur* on the board. Clarify that an *enterprise* is a new business or project. Pronounce the word *entrepreneur*. Explain that it is a French word with the same root as *enterprise,* and underline *enter-/entre-* in the two words. Tell students that both words are from an Old French verb meaning "to begin or undertake." Remind students that *entrepreneur* means "an enterpriser, or a person who starts a new business."

**DISCUSS THE LAISSEZ-FAIRE THEORY**

Write *laissez-faire theory* on the board, and pronounce it for students. Ask a volunteer to define the term. Tell students that although the trend over the last 100 years has been toward more government control and the United States has a mixed economy, some people believe that the government should have little or no role in the economy—that the "invisible hand" of the market should be left to work on its own.

Discuss with students how freely they think the economy should be allowed to operate. Use the Think-Pair-Share strategy (p. T22) to generate a class list of ways in which the government currently controls or manages the economy. For example, government controls interest rates to stabilize the economy and minimize inflation; regulates business practices to promote fair competition, ensure product safety and truthful labeling, and protect the environment; provides Social Security and Medicare/Medicaid; oversees the stock market; taxes some goods, such as gasoline; and taxes income. List each example students offer and then for each, ask: **How would life for Americans be different if the government did not carry out this activity?**

When you have finished the discussion, take a vote on what level of control the government should have. Tell students to raise both hands if they think that the government should be more laissez-faire, raise one hand if they think government involvement is about right, and raise no hands if they think there should be more government control. Take a count and then ask students from each group to explain their viewpoint.

**L2 ELL Differentiate** Ask students from different countries to compare and contrast an aspect of government control of the economy in the United States to government control of the economy in their countries of origin.

## Answers

**Checkpoint** Competition often helps hold down prices and keep quality high.

## INTRODUCE THE ACTIVITY

Tell students to suppose that a nation has just won independence and its leaders are trying to determine what type of economic system to establish. Students will act as economic advisers and pitch to that nation's leaders the concept of a mixed economy, with an emphasis on free enterprise.

### DISTRIBUTE THE CORE WORKSHEET

Divide the class into small groups. Distribute the Chapter 23 Section 1 Core Worksheet (Unit 6 All-in-One, p. 69). Assign each group one aspect of the free enterprise system—private ownership, individual initiative, profit, and competition; assign two other groups to present facts about the benefits of mixed economies and types of business organizations. Students will make their presentations to the whole class. Tell students they will use the worksheet to organize their presentations. To engage them in active listening, tell students that they will use the evaluation part of the worksheet to judge the effectiveness of each group's presentation.

**L2 Differentiate** Review the outline format. Then walk through the worksheet as a class, rather than letting students work on their own, outlining the main points for each assignment on the board. Be sure to give students a few minutes to think about it on their own before you begin.

Name _____ Class _____ Date _____

**CHAPTER 23 SECTION 1** | CORE WORKSHEET
**Capitalism** 3

**Presentation on the Free Enterprise System**
Follow these steps to create a presentation on the free enterprise system.
1. Divide up tasks for researching, outline writing, preparing visuals, and presenting.
2. Gather information about your topic from the textbook and other sources.
3. Use the information to create an outline.
4. As a group, review the outline and revise it, based on members' feedback.
5. Create a first draft of the presentation based on the final outline.
6. Prepare relevant visuals, such as charts, graphs, and photographs.
7. Rehearse the presentation with your group and collect members' feedback.
8. Use the feedback to revise the presentation into final form.
9. Make your presentation to the class.

**Presentation Evaluation**
Evaluate the effectiveness of other groups' presentations. Note any suggestions you would offer to the group.

Group: _____ Topic: _____

**Content:** Did the presentation include all key points?

**Organization:** Was the presentation well organized and easy to follow?

**Visuals:** Were the visuals relevant and interesting?

**Effectiveness:** If you were a leader of the new nation, would this presentation help convince you to adopt the free enterprise system? Why or why not?

Copyright © by Pearson Education, Inc., or its affiliates. All rights reserved.

---

## Answers

**Checkpoint** Monopolies can threaten competition in a market, leaving consumers to either pay high prices or do without.

**682** Comparative Economic Systems

---

✔ **Checkpoint**
What is a disadvantage of monopolies?

The Anti-Trust Division in the Department of Justice watches business activities to determine whether competition within an industry is threatened. It can, for example, stop the sale or merger of a company if that move threatens competition in a particular market. On rare occasions, the Justice Department has acted to break up a monopoly to restore competition.

### Laissez-Faire Theory

Early capitalist philosophers believed that, if only government did not interfere, the free enterprise system would work automatically. Adam Smith presented the classic expression of that view in his book, *The Wealth of Nations*, in 1776. Smith wrote that when all individuals are free to pursue their own private interests, an "invisible hand" works to promote the general welfare. In short, Smith introduced laissez-faire capitalism.[1]

**Laissez-faire theory** holds that government should play only a very limited, hands-off role in society. Governmental activity should be confined to: (1) foreign relations and national defense, (2) the maintenance of police and courts to protect private property and the health, safety, and morals of the people, and (3) those few other functions that cannot be performed by private enterprise at

Amtrak is an example of a federally owned and run enterprise.

---

1 *Laissez-faire* is a French idiom meaning "to let alone."

a profit. The proper role of government in economic affairs should be restricted to functions intended to promote and protect the free play of competition and the operation of the laws of supply and demand.

Laissez-faire capitalism has never in fact operated in this country. The concept has had, nevertheless, and still has, a profound effect on the structure of the economic system in the United States.

### A Mixed Economy

Although the American economic system is essentially private in character, government has always played a large part in it. Economists usually describe an economy in which private enterprise and governmental participation coexist as a mixed economy.

Government at every level regulates the various features of American economic life. Among its many other functions, government prohibits trusts, protects the environment, and ensures the quality of the food we eat.

Government also promotes many aspects of American economic life. It constructs roads and highways, provides such services as public health programs, the census, and weather reports, and operates Social Security and other insurance programs. And it also offers a number of subsidies and various loan programs to help entrepreneurs and businesses prosper.

Federal, State, and local governments conduct some enterprises that might well be operated privately—for example, public education, the postal system, and municipal water and power systems. It has also assumed some functions that have proved unprofitable to private enterprise—for example, many local transit systems and waste disposal and recycling projects. These sorts of public efforts are sometimes called "ash-can socialism."

Mixed economies are common in Europe and in most former communist countries. In Britain, the government provides free medical care to all. The government of the People's Republic of China owns steel mills and factories. Germany's federal government requires large companies to give workers representation on managing boards, and France once banned most companies from asking

**682** Comparative Economic Systems

---

## Background

**CONTROLLING MONOPOLIES** Even when the Department of Justice fails to win an antitrust case, it can change an industry. Thirty years ago, computers were big, expensive, and nearly always manufactured by IBM. Federal lawyers pursued IBM for 13 years, forcing the company to deal very carefully with companies that wrote software for its machines. The United States abruptly dropped its lawsuit in 1982; but by that time, technology and IBM's weaknesses had reshaped the computer market. Today, IBM is one of many computer manufacturers. Microsoft, the software company that used IBM's troubles to set the standard in operating systems, was itself tried and found guilty of violating the Sherman Anti-Trust Act.

## Supply and Demand

# How are prices set in a free market?

**GOVERNMENT** ONLINE

For an **interactive** exploration of supply and demand, visit
**PearsonSchool.com/phgovt**

INTERACTIVE

In general, suppliers will produce more goods when prices are high and fewer goods when prices fall. Consumers usually seek to purchase (demand) more of a commodity at low prices and less at high prices. Where people enjoy the freedom to trade, they will find the market price that suits both sides. *What is a market signal that a price is too high?*

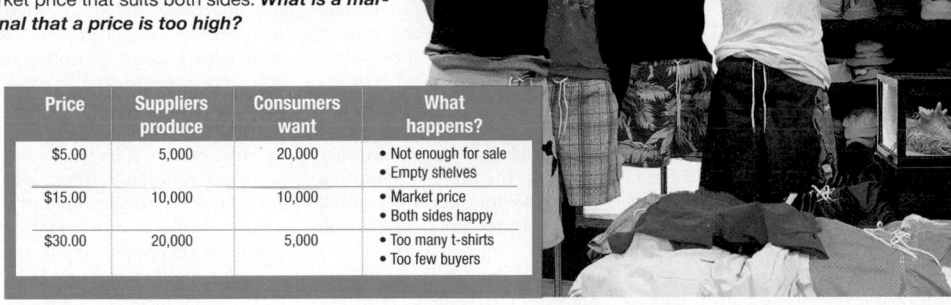

| Price | Suppliers produce | Consumers want | What happens? |
|-------|-------------------|----------------|---------------|
| $5.00 | 5,000 | 20,000 | • Not enough for sale<br>• Empty shelves |
| $15.00 | 10,000 | 10,000 | • Market price<br>• Both sides happy |
| $30.00 | 20,000 | 5,000 | • Too many t-shirts<br>• Too few buyers |

employees to work more than 35 hours per week. In each of these mixed economies, government intervention coexists with independent companies and market forces.

## Types of Business Organizations

The American economy contains a number of gigantic companies with thousands of employees and factories or offices all over the world. Still, most businesses in the United States are relatively small. Some 85 percent of all businesses in this country employ fewer than 20 people. Three basic types of business organizations exist: sole proprietorships, partnerships, and corporations. Each has advantages and disadvantages.

**Sole Proprietorships** Businesses owned by a single individual are called sole proprietorships. Typical businesses in this category include such enterprises as hair salons, auto repair shops, and dentists' offices. About three quarters of all businesses in this country are sole proprietorships. However,

because most sole proprietorships are small, they produce only a minor fraction of annual sales in the United States.

Sole proprietorships are the most flexible form of business organization. Their major advantage is that the single owner can make decisions quickly. He or she has full control of the company and can draw a salary or close the business without consulting others. A major disadvantage is that the owner is personally liable for the debts the business might acquire. Sole proprietorships are also limited by the owner's ability to contribute resources and manage the business.

**Partnerships** Businesses owned by two or more individuals, called partners, are known as partnerships. Lawyers and architects are among those professionals who often work together in partnerships.

One advantage of a partnership is that it can draw on the resources of more than one person for the capital necessary to start or expand a business. Different people bring different strengths and perspectives to a business, and a partnership can provide a

✔ **Checkpoint**
What are the three basic types of business organizations?

**liable**
*adj.* responsible, obligated

Chapter 23 • Section 1 **683**

---

Tell students to go to the Interactivity to learn more about Supply and Demand.

**EXTEND THE LESSON**

**L3 L4 Differentiate** Assign the Extend Worksheet (Unit 6 All-in-One, p. 70), which is an excerpt from Adam Smith's *Wealth of Nations*. After students have answered the questions on the worksheet, have them summarize the selection in a paragraph, using their own words. Then ask them to find specific examples in the passage that refer to the idea of limited government involvement in the economy.

**L2 ELL Differentiate** Have students work in small groups to create a collage about the free enterprise system that includes images describing or depicting the concepts of private ownership, individual initiative, profit, and competition. Students should draw or collect images from the Internet, magazines, or newspapers that express these ideas. Have a volunteer from each group present the collage to the class.

**L2 Differentiate** Ask students to use a local phone book or the Internet and list two businesses from your community under each of the following categories, and identify what good or service it produces: sole proprietorship, partnership, and corporation. Tell students to decide, based on their research, which type of business seems to be the most common in your community.

**L4 Differentiate** Have students locate, read, and write a report on a nonfiction book about the American free enterprise system, an American entrepreneur, or how an American business operates. Reports should include an analysis of the author's main points, conclusions, and biases. Students should state whether they agree or disagree with the author, and assess the book's reliability and interest value to a general reader.

---

# Background

**SUPPLY AND DEMAND** Use Transparency 23B to show how supply and demand work together to set prices in a free market. This transparency shows in graph form the hypothetical data in the text feature "Supply and Demand." Ask: **At $5, how many T-shirts will shirt makers supply?** *(5,000)* **How many will consumers want to buy?** *(20,000)* **Faced with such great demand for their shirts, how do you think shirt makers will adjust their price?** *(raise it)* **Suppose they raise the price to $30. How many T-shirts will makers supply and consumers buy?** *(20,000; 5,000)* **How will makers adjust price based on sagging demand?** *(lower it)* **At $15, how many T-shirts will makers supply and consumers demand?** *(10,000)* The price at which the supply and demand lines intersect is the market price—the price at which the quantity supplied equals the quantity demanded.

# Answers

**Supply and Demand** Demand for the product falls, so that supply exceeds demand.

**Checkpoint** sole proprietorships, partnerships, and corporations

# Assess and Remediate

**L3** Collect the Core Worksheet and assess the students' work, using the criteria on the Presentation Evaluation Worksheet (Unit 6 All-in-One, p. 69).

**L3** Assign the Section 1 Assessment questions.

**L3** Section Quiz A (Unit 6 All-in-One, p. 71)

**L2** Section Quiz B (Unit 6 All-in-One, p. 72)

Have students complete the review activities in the digital lesson presentation and continue their work in the **Essential Questions Journal**.

## REMEDIATION

| If Your Students Have Trouble With | Strategies For Remediation |
|---|---|
| The role of the U.S. government in the economy (Questions 1, 4, 6) | Ask students to write a few sentences or words that summarize the role of the government in the U.S. economy. |
| Factors of production (Question 2) | Review the information from concept webs students created in the lesson. Have students add additional specific examples of the factors of production. |
| The role of entrepreneurs (Question 3) | Ask students to re-read the information under "The Role of the Entrepreneur," and write a job description for an entrepreneur. |
| Types of business organizations (Question 5) | Have students re-read "Types of Business Organizations" and make a bulleted list of the features of each type. |

## Answers

**Checkpoint** Partnerships can draw on the resources of more than one person for capital, and different people bring different strengths to the business. However, these differences can lead to conflict.

---

✔ **Checkpoint**
What are the advantages and disadvantages of a partnership?

useful framework for entrepreneurs to use their skills to create a small business. These differences can also lead to conflict among partners, however; and partnerships may dissolve if one of the partners leaves or dies.

**Corporations** Corporations include both very small companies and large multinational firms. Unlike partnerships, corporations almost always have many owners, called shareholders. A share is a fraction of ownership in the corporation, and a shareholder is any person or group owning one or more shares. A corporation can continue indefinitely because a shareholder's death does not affect the legal status of the corporation. In other words, the corporation exists as its own legal entity, independent from the existence of any shareholders. The Supreme Court has often held that, under the 14th Amendment, a corporation occupies the same legal position as a person.

Corporations can draw their capital from hundreds and even thousands of investors. This characteristic enables them to finance such costly projects as artificial satellites or oil pipelines. Shareholders are responsible only for the amount of money they have invested. If the business fails, they can lose that amount, but no more. Shareholders have limited liability and are not held responsible for any debts the corporation might have.

Corporations suffer this disadvantage: The income they produce is taxed twice. First, the corporation pays a tax on its profits. Then, individual shareholders pay a tax on the dividends they receive.

## Profit and Loss

What drives the capitalist economy? The best answer, most often, is profit.

To understand what profit is, you must first understand the idea of investment. An investment is a sum of money—capital—that is put into a business enterprise. For example, if you buy a van to start an express delivery business, what you pay for the van is an investment in the business.

Your profit will be the amount of money you earn from the business, after you have subtracted the costs involved in making that money—in this case, the purchase of the van and the costs of operating it, plus whatever you pay yourself. If earnings are less than the costs, the business has not made a profit; it has, instead, suffered a loss.

Taking risks and making investments are, therefore, an essential part of the capitalist system. Every year, many businesses fail because they do not produce a profit. The businesses that survive tend to be those whose owners have learned to make the most efficient use of the factors of production.

---

**Essential Questions Journal** To continue to build a response to the chapter Essential Question, go to your **Essential Questions Journal**.

## SECTION 1 ASSESSMENT

1. **Guiding Question** Use your completed chart to answer this question: What is the role of government in the American economy?

**Key Terms and Comprehension**

2. **(a)** What is physical **capital?** **(b)** What is human capital? **(c)** How do economists define land as a **factor of production?**

3. Why are **entrepreneurs** important?

4. What is the role of government in a mixed economy?

**Critical Thinking**

5. **Make Comparisons** Which type of business organization would be most appropriate for: **(a)** a large bus company? **(b)** a nonchain coffee shop? Explain.

6. **Draw Conclusions** Identify two arguments that can be made for and two against government participation in a free enterprise economy.

**Quick Write**

**Expository Writing: Select a Topic and Record Details** The goal of a compare-and-contrast essay is to analyze similarities and differences between two topics. In this chapter, you will learn about different economic systems: capitalism, socialism, and communism. As you read the chapter, use a Venn diagram to record similarities and differences between two of these systems.

---

# Assessment Answers

**1.** The U.S. government regulates parts of the economy to, for example, prohibit trusts, protect the environment, and ensure food quality. Government participates in the economy by providing roads, public health programs, loans, and public education.

**2. (a)** human-made goods, such as buildings, machines, and materials, that workers use to turn labor and land into goods and services **(b)** knowledge and skills that workers gain from their work experience **(c)** all natural resources

**3.** because they start businesses and make them grow, creating jobs, goods, and services that contribute to a high standard of living

**4.** The government regulates and participates in parts of the economy. For example, government prohibits trusts, protects the environment, ensures food quality, operates social insurance programs, provides loans, and conducts postal service and public education.

**5. (a)** a corporation **(b)** a sole proprietorship or partnership. The first company is very large with many employees, so would benefit from

a corporate structure for management and from money from shareholders for growth. The coffee shop is a very small company with few employees and could be financed and managed by one or a few people.

**6. for:** to ensure market fairness and to protect consumers; **against:** the free market operates best with few controls and people should make their own economic choices

**QUICK WRITE** Students' Venn diagrams should compare and contrast two economic systems.

## SECTION 2

# Socialism and Communism

### Guiding Question

**What is the role of government under socialism and communism?**
Create a table similar to the table below to record information about the role of government under socialism and communism.

| Role of Government | |
| --- | --- |
| **Socialism** | **Communism** |
| • State owns largest industries | • |
| • | • |
| • | • |

### Political Dictionary

- *The Communist Manifesto*
- socialism
- communism
- welfare state
- command economy
- five-year plan
- collectivization
- privatization
- Great Leap Forward

### Objectives

1. Summarize the theories of Karl Marx and their roots.
2. Identify important characteristics of socialist economies.
3. Outline the characteristics of communist economies.
4. Describe socialism and communism in action today.
5. Evaluate the effects of socialism and communism.

**Image Above:** Communist artwork often celebrated workers in industry and agriculture.

Y ou know that in the United States everyone is entitled to the equal protection of the law. Political equality, of course, is not the same as economic equality. The capitalist system of the United States allows some to achieve greater financial rewards than others are able to. However, other economic systems—socialism and communism—do seek to distribute wealth more evenly across the society.

## Karl Marx's Theory

Karl Marx (1818–1883), the father of modern socialism and communism, was the most significant critic of capitalism as it developed during the early stages of the Industrial Revolution. Numerous observers of working conditions in nineteenth-century factories were appalled by what they found. Those conditions led many of them to seek social and economic reforms. Marx and his colleague Friedrich Engels (1820–1895) argued for much more radical change than did most of their contemporaries.

**Writings** Marx and Engels first published their basic concepts in *The Communist Manifesto* in 1848. That political document condemned the miseries of the Industrial Revolution and called upon oppressed workers throughout Europe to free themselves from "capitalist enslavement." The Manifesto ended with this rallying cry:

> **PRIMARY SOURCE**
>
> **The proletarians have nothing to lose but their chains. They have a world to win. Workingmen of all countries, unite.**
>
> —*The Communist Manifesto*

*The Communist Manifesto* and Marx's later multivolume work, *Das Kapital*, published in 1867, 1885, and 1894, were based on four closely related concepts: Marx's theory of history, the labor theory of value, the role of institutions, and the dictatorship of the proletariat.

## Focus on the Basics

**FACTS:** • Socialism and communism are based on theories of Karl Marx. • Socialist economies involve some nationalization, broad public welfare, high taxes, and some central planning. • Communist governments control most aspects of economic, social, intellectual, and religious life.

**CONCEPTS:** economic systems, role of government

**ENDURING UNDERSTANDINGS:** • Under socialism and communism, the government has much more active and direct control over the economy than under capitalism. • Communism failed in Russia; the few remaining Communist nations are loosening economic controls.

## What is the role of government under socialism and communism?

| Role of Government | |
| --- | --- |
| **Socialism** | **Communism** |
| • State owns largest industries<br>• State provides pensions, universal health care, free university education, housing<br>• State collects high taxes<br>• State makes many economic decisions | • Communist Party holds decision-making power in government and economy<br>• State controls social, intellectual, and religious life<br>• State makes all economic decisions—plans and supervises production in factories, farms, and stores<br>• Five-year plans set goals for growth in industry and agriculture, what individual businesses should produce, prices, and distribution<br>• State ownership of means of production<br>• State-owned, collective farms<br>• State-owned industry and transportation<br>• In some Communist states, local governments own housing, banks, hospitals, and stores |

## Get Started

### LESSON GOALS

Students will . . .

- use a transparency to discuss the theories of Karl Marx.
- complete a chart that compares and contrasts economic systems.
- role play and write a dialogue to compare and contrast life under capitalism and communism.
- write a journal entry evaluating economic systems.

### SKILLS DEVELOPMENT

#### DECISION MAKING

To help students learn decision making, have them turn to the Skills Handbook, p. S18, and use the information there to help them when discussing the four Marxist concepts in this section.

Assign the section, the graphic organizer in the text, and the Reading Comprehension Worksheet (Unit 6 All-in-One, p. 73) before class.

**L2** **Differentiate** Reading Comprehension Worksheet (Unit 6 All-in-One, p. 75)

**BELLRINGER**

Distribute the Bellringer Worksheet (Unit 6 All-in-One, p. 77). Have students complete the chart, based on their reading.

**L2** **ELL Differentiate** To help them complete the worksheet, allow students to choose one column or row to fill in.

---

**✓Checkpoint**
Why was Karl Marx important?

**1.** *Marx's View of History.* To Marx, all of history was a story of class struggle—of social classes competing for the control of labor and productive property. One class was the oppressor; the other, the oppressed. In the modern world, the bourgeoisie—the capitalists—oppressed the proletariat—the workers. According to Marx, the class struggle in the modern era would become so intense that, inevitably, the masses would revolt and bring down the bourgeoisie.

**2.** *The Labor Theory of Value.* Marx rejected the free enterprise ideas of profit and competition. In his view, the value of a commodity was set by the amount of labor put into it. A pair of shoes or a rebuilt bicycle is worth a certain amount because it takes that much labor to produce it. Marx argued that the laborer should receive that value in full.

**commodity**
*n.* anything bought or sold

**3.** *The Role of Institutions.* Marx saw the state and its government as tools by which capitalists maintained their power and privileges. Other social institutions also played a role in enforcing capitalist control over the masses. Marx described religion as "the opiate of the people"—a drug that persuades workers to tolerate their harsh lot in this life in the hope that someday they will gain what Marx called a "fictional afterlife."

**4.** *The Dictatorship of the Proletariat.* Marx did not believe that revolution would automatically bring about the final goal of communism—the classless society. First, he predicted a transitional phase during which an authoritarian state would represent and enforce the interests of the masses. This he called the "dictatorship of the proletariat." Once the goal of classlessness was realized, the state, he said, would "wither away."

**authoritarian**
*adj.* demanding total obedience

Based on these four concepts, Marx envisioned a "free, classless society." Social classes would vanish and the people would own all property in common. Exploitation of labor and unemployment would disappear. Abundant goods would be available to all according to their needs, not necessarily how much work they contributed. Marx also expected that workers in different countries—for example, France and Germany—would share a bond far stronger than national loyalties.

Thus, he theorized that communism would also bring an end to nationalism, a major cause of European wars.

**Socialists and Communists** Many European workers and thinkers of the middle and late nineteenth century accepted Marx's criticisms of capitalism. His followers were deeply divided, however, by the question of how best to achieve a more equitable economy. Some argued that economic equality could be attained by peaceful, democratic means. Today, the terms **socialism** and *socialist* are usually used to identify those evolutionary ideals and the people who support them. Others argued that a fair society could come only out of a violent revolution, born out of class struggle. Over time, those who took that more strictly Marxist view came to be called communists, the advocates of **communism.**

## Characteristics of Socialist Economies

Countries with a socialist government typically enact one or more of a set of public policies to achieve the basic aims of socialism. These policies include nationalization, broadening of public services, high taxation, and a command economy.

**Nationalization** Placing enterprises under governmental control, often by taking over privately owned industries, is called nationalization. In a socialist society, nationalization rarely includes all businesses within the country. Socialist governments usually want to control only certain segments of the economy—those having many workers, a few dominant firms, and great importance to other businesses—particularly, utilities, transportation, and steel. Many smaller companies remain in private hands. The government may also want industries that are based on new technologies to remain in private hands. It often does because individual initiative and entrepreneurship are so vital in the early phases of the development of a business.

Many socialist governments want to give each company's workers a say in deciding how a company is to be managed. Elected

---

# Differentiated Resources

The following resources are located in the All-in-One, Unit 6, Chapter 23, Section 2:

**L3** Reading Comprehension Worksheet (p. 73)

**L2** Reading Comprehension Worksheet (p. 75)

**L3** Bellringer Worksheet (p. 77)

**L3** Core Worksheet (p. 78)

**L2** Core Worksheet (p. 79)

**L3** Section Quiz A (p. 80)

**L2** Section Quiz B (p. 81)

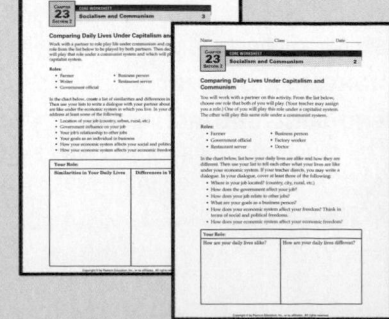

---

## Answers

**Checkpoint** Possible answer: Marx's theories have affected the lives of millions of people during and after his lifetime.

worker representatives now sit on the boards of directors of many major companies in both Sweden and Germany.

**Public Welfare** Socialists aim to guarantee the public welfare by providing for the equal distribution of such necessities and services as retirement pensions, universal healthcare, free university education, and housing. Any country that provides extensive social services at little or no direct cost to consumers is a **welfare state.**

In a welfare state, medical and dental services often are provided free or at a small charge. People who lose their jobs or who are physically unable to work receive government payments that are nearly as high as their former wages. All those who reach retirement age receive government pensions. Parents are often paid a benefit for each child until that child reaches the age of 18. Workers in several European nations receive paid maternity leave, often for both parents, and several weeks of paid vacation each year, considerably more than most American workers receive.

**Taxation** All governments in both capitalist and socialist states are funded by taxation. Because social welfare services are quite expensive, taxes in socialist countries tend to be relatively high. Taxes regularly take as much as 50 or 60 percent of an individual's yearly income. Socialists tend to place most of the tax burden on the upper and middle classes, in line with their aim to achieve a more equal distribution of wealth. However, gasoline and consumer goods are also subject to high taxes.

**A Command Economy** Economies can be divided into several categories, depending on how basic economic decisions are made. Under capitalism, key decisions are made by thousands of private individuals and companies through the give-and-take of the marketplace. Under socialism, and even more so under communism, economic decision making is more centralized. In a **command economy,** government bureaucrats plan for the development of the economy over a period of years. They set targets for production and direct investments to specific industries.

### National Healthcare
# What Is the Cost of Free Healthcare?

In the UK, all citizens are entitled to free, government-funded healthcare. In 2009–2010, both the pros and cons of the British system became part of a debate over healthcare reform in the U.S. With the passage of the Affordable Care Act in 2010, supporters hoped to incorporate some of the benefits of the British system (top) without its drawbacks (bottom). *What might the law of supply and demand predict for a free healthcare system?*

"WHAT I DON'T UNDERSTAND IS WHY PEOPLE IN ENGLAND ARE HEALTHIER THAN PEOPLE IN THE UNITED STATES."

YOUR INJURY IS IMPORTANT TO US. ALL OUR DOCTORS ARE BUSY HELPING OTHER CUSTOMERS. PLEASE WAIT, YOU ARE ADVANCING IN THE QUEUE AND YOU WILL BE SEEN AS SOON AS A DOCTOR BECOMES AVAILABLE.

BILL PROUD

## Socialism Today

At various times in recent history, elected socialist parties have controlled governments and instituted socialist programs through democratic means. Gradually, however, most socialist parties in Europe have given up such traditional goals as nationalizing industries. And many socialist parties in Britain, France, and Germany have

✓ **Checkpoint**
What defines a socialist economy?

# Debate

**SOCIALIST IN THE SENATE** In 2006 Bernie Sanders became the first self-described socialist to win a seat in the U.S. Senate. When interviewer Amy Goodman asked him the meaning of *socialist,* Sanders replied: "Well, I think it means the government has got to play a very important role in making sure that as a right of citizenship, all of our people have healthcare; that as a right, all of our kids, regardless of income, have quality childcare, are able to go to college without going deeply into debt; that it means we do not allow large corporations and moneyed interests to destroy our environment; that we create a government in which it is not dominated by big money interest." ("Vermont's Bernie Sanders Becomes First Socialist Elected to U.S. Senate," from *Democracy Now*) Read this quotation to the class. Then have students debate this question: **How would you contrast Sanders's views with those of Adam Smith?**

# Teach

To present this topic using online resources, use the lesson presentations at **PearsonSchool.com/phgovt.**

**INTRODUCE THE TOPIC**

Explain that this lesson is about two main economic systems with common roots: socialism and communism. Both systems grew out of the ideas of economist and philosopher Karl Marx (1818–1883) and his writing partner, Friedrich Engels (1820–1895). Display Transparency 23C, Four Major Marxist Concepts.

Divide the class into four discussion groups and assign each group one of the four concepts. Then come together again as a class. Ask: **Do you agree that history is a series of class struggles and that all conflicts are based on economics? Why or why not?** (Sample response: I think that many conflicts are about economic issues and class struggle, but often people are in conflict over power or jealousy or something other than material goods or gain.) **Do you think that laborers should receive the full value of the goods they produce? What about the role of the entrepreneur and the profit motive in this system?** (Sample response: I do not think that a worker can get the full value of the goods he or she produces unless the person works alone and owns the business. If a person is an entrepreneur and creates a business and hires workers, then that person needs some of the profits to pay employees and him- or herself, and to purchase more materials and grow the business.) **Do you think that the U.S. government is controlled by capitalists?** (Sample response: I think that to some extent, the U.S. government is controlled by rich and powerful people, but because we have the power to vote, other groups of Americans can change that if they want to.) **What might be the drawback of the proletarian dictatorship, even if it is a transitional phase?** (Sample response: Any dictatorship is unfair, because it is undemocratic and does not represent the interests of all people. Just because a group was oppressed, it should not then become the oppressor.)

Remind students that these concepts grew out of Marx's analysis of existing conditions at the birth of the Industrial Revolution, when working conditions were generally terrible. Workers were moving from "cottage industries," where they owned the factors of production and their labor, to factories in which their labor was "human capital" for someone else.

# Answers

**National Healthcare** The more people who use the free healthcare system, the more it will cost the government to meet that demand.

**Checkpoint** nationalization, public welfare, high taxation, and a command economy lost power or have abandoned some of their socialist objectives that have become too expensive and unpopular to maintain.

Socialism has won a large following in developing countries in Africa and more recently in Latin America. One reason for its appeal in those nations is that large existing industries have often been owned by foreign companies. By nationalizing a foreign-owned industry and placing local people in charge, a political leader can win broad public support. He or she can also gain power by promising to provide socialist-style, "cradle-to-grave" services and to redistribute land from large land owners to the poor.

For example, after he came to power in 1999, Venezuela's President Hugo Chávez and his nationalist-socialist party, Movement for the Fifth Republic (MVR) nationalized the oil industry and used the profits to fund free education, healthcare, and low-cost housing. Chávez has also nationalized the telecommunications and electricity industries. These moves have brought support for Chávez, especially among the urban poor, and have helped him retain power, despite broad resistance to many of his socialist, or even communist, goals. Meanwhile, Venezuela's economy has experienced inflation and shortages as a result of Chávez's actions.

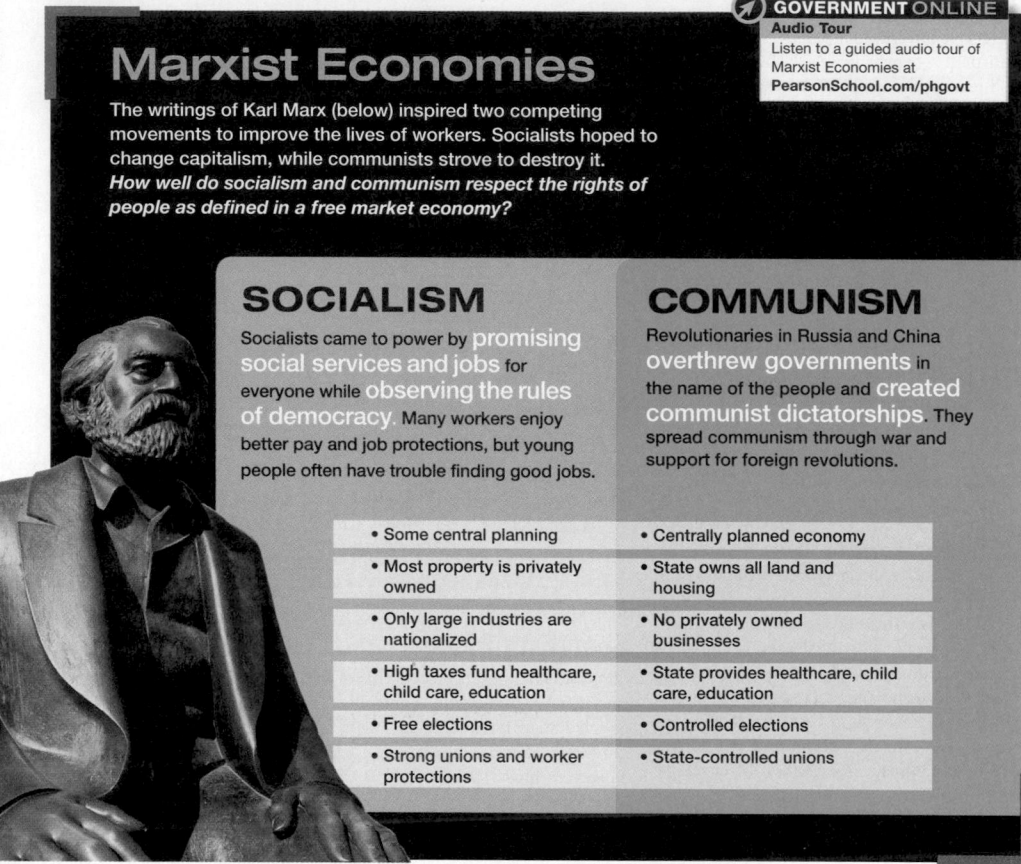

**GOVERNMENT** ONLINE
**Audio Tour**
Listen to a guided audio tour of Marxist Economies at **PearsonSchool.com/phgovt**

## Marxist Economies

The writings of Karl Marx (below) inspired two competing movements to improve the lives of workers. Socialists hoped to change capitalism, while communists strove to destroy it. *How well do socialism and communism respect the rights of people as defined in a free market economy?*

### SOCIALISM

Socialists came to power by **promising social services and jobs** for everyone while **observing the rules of democracy**. Many workers enjoy better pay and job protections, but young people often have trouble finding good jobs.

### COMMUNISM

Revolutionaries in Russia and China **overthrew governments** in the name of the people and **created communist dictatorships**. They spread communism through war and support for foreign revolutions.

| SOCIALISM | COMMUNISM |
|---|---|
| • Some central planning | • Centrally planned economy |
| • Most property is privately owned | • State owns all land and housing |
| • Only large industries are nationalized | • No privately owned businesses |
| • High taxes fund healthcare, child care, education | • State provides healthcare, child care, education |
| • Free elections | • Controlled elections |
| • Strong unions and worker protections | • State-controlled unions |

## Background

**GENERAL STRIKE OF 1926** Decades of industrial disputes in Great Britain reached a climax in 1926. Miners joined with the Trade Union Congress to reject wage cuts instituted by mine owners and supported by the prime minister, Stanley Baldwin. The owners locked out the miners, who were supported by an estimated 1.75 million other workers, in what became known as the General Strike of 1926. The strike came to a halt when the Trade Union Congress ended it after nine days, saying that the government was too well-prepared to concede. Though the miners tried to continue the strike alone, it failed. The strike divided the nation sharply along class lines and ushered in a period of government intolerance of union activities and the struggle for workers' rights.

## Characteristics of Communist Economies

Socialism represents one path from Karl Marx's theories to a modern economy. Communism describes a more dramatic and frequently violent approach, one that dominated large parts of the world in the twentieth century. In practice, communism has been less successful than socialism, and has generally led to the formation of totalitarian regimes. Marx's theories did not provide a blueprint for the formation of a communist society, and communism has taken different forms in different places. However, certain common characteristics can be seen.

**1.** *Role of the Communist Party.* In any communist-run nation, the Communist Party holds the decision-making power in both the government and the economy. Party leaders also hold the top government positions. From top to bottom, the two institutions run parallel to one another. Inevitably, such centralized political and economic control has meant control over social, intellectual, and religious life, as well.

**2.** *Central Planning.* Because government makes all economic decisions, bureaucrats in a command economy must plan and supervise the production of all factories, farms, and stores in the country. Typically, a **five-year plan** plays a key role, outlining how the government wants the economy to develop. The plan sets economic goals that dictate where to emphasize growth in industry or agriculture and what and how much each individual factory and farm must produce. It also sets prices and decides how goods and services will be distributed.

**3.** *Collectivization.* Collective ownership—state ownership—of the means of production is a fundamental pillar of communist doctrine. The merger of small private farms into large government-owned agricultural enterprises is a major step in the creation of a communist economy. The process of **collectivization** may be voluntary in theory, but in many countries, peasant farmers were forced to give up their land. Millions died resisting collectivization in the Soviet Union.

**4.** *State Ownership.* Industrial enterprises, transportation, and other segments of the economy are state-owned. This aspect of the system varies greatly from country to country. In China, for example, provincial and municipal governments, not a central government ministry, own enterprises such as housing, banks, hospitals, and stores.

✔ **Checkpoint**
What defines a communist economy?

## The Soviet Union

Marx believed that the revolution would come first in industrialized countries with large working-class populations—in particular, France, Germany, Great Britain, and then the United States. Ironically, the revolution occurred first in Russia, then an undeveloped, mainly agricultural nation, in 1917. V.I. Lenin and his followers began immediately to build a communist state in the new Soviet Union. By the time of Lenin's death in 1924, the Soviet Union had become a one-party state in control of the country's social, political, and economic institutions. Lenin's successor, Josef Stalin, tightened that control and built a totalitarian dictatorship.

**The Soviet Union Under Stalin** Stalin introduced centralized planning. The First Five-Year Plan (1928–1933) demanded collectivization of agriculture and a heightened production of chemicals, petroleum, and steel. Later five-year plans also emphasized heavy industry, and the Soviet Union achieved rapid, if uneven, industrialization. Unfortunately, those advances came at great cost in the form of scarce consumer goods, housing, and urban services.

The Soviet Union did provide its citizens with free education, medical care, and even summer youth camps. It was far from a classless society, however. An elite class owed its privileged status to the Communist Party. In addition, many free government services were either unavailable or of poor quality.

**Transition to a Free Market** By the late 1980s, under Mikhail Gorbachev's policies of *glasnost* (openness) and *perestroika* (restructuring), the Soviet Union began to dismantle the political and economic structures of communism. In 1991, the Soviet

---

Tell students that they will now consider what living under communism might be like and how it might compare to daily life under capitalism. Divide the class into pairs and distribute the Chapter 23 Section 2 Core Worksheet (Unit 6 All-in-One, p. 78). Tell students that they will role play a specific individual with a partner to develop ideas of what life might be like under each economic system. Then they will write a dialogue about daily life under communism or capitalism. Explain that partners must play the same role, but will select to write about capitalism or communism.

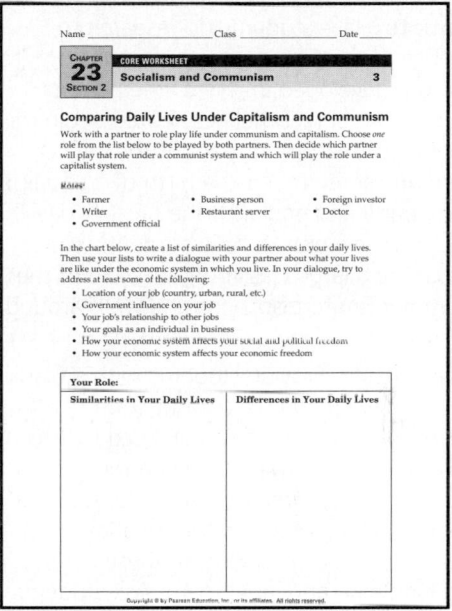

**L2** **Differentiate** For these students, distribute the adapted Core Worksheet (Unit 6 All-in-One, p. 79). If students have trouble with writing the dialogue, have them create a list of key points that they can use to tell their stories to partners. They may also tell their story in illustrated panels, if time allows.

---

# Background

**INFLUENCE OF KARL MARX** Most Americans view communism, and its father, Karl Marx, as colossal failures. With its troubles and eventual widespread collapse, communism as implemented in the 20th century was, indeed, largely a disaster. However, Karl Marx himself (whose conception of communism bears little resemblance to the way it was practiced) is arguably one of the most influential thinkers of all time. At its apex, the number of people who considered themselves followers of Marx approached 1.5 billion. This is a greater number of followers and a greater percentage of the world's population than any other ideology has had in the history of the world.

---

## Answers

**Checkpoint** centralized economic control by the Communist Party, central planning, collectivization, and state ownership

## FOLLOW UP

When students have completed their dialogues, group three sets of partners in different roles to act out their dialogues. Then re-form as a class and draw a graphic organizer on the board in which students list features of life under each system. Next, have students write a journal entry about their overall impression of life under communism compared to capitalism. Have them state in which system they would prefer to live. What would they like and dislike about it? Remind students to support their choice with logical reasoning.

## EXTEND THE LESSON

**L3 Differentiate** Have students do research to create a timeline of the history of socialism or communism as it developed in one of the nations mentioned in this section. Timelines should begin with the revolution that brought about the institution of a Communist regime or the birth of a socialist or Communist party and end with the present day. Alternatively, you may wish to have students work in groups to create a large classroom timeline of the history of communism to display on the walls around the room.

**L2 ELL Differentiate** Provide students with a blank world map and a world atlas or current country map to share. Have students skim textbook Section 2 to find the names of the five remaining communist countries. *(China, Cuba, Vietnam, Laos, North Korea)* Have them identify these countries in an atlas or on a world map. Then they should locate these countries on the blank map and label them. Ask students to create a color key for "Communist States" and "Capitalist States" and color the map according to the key.

**L4 Differentiate** Have students do research to create an in-depth report comparing and contrasting economic facts about the United States with one socialist country, such as Sweden, and one Communist country, such as China or North Korea. Facts might include GDP, literacy rate, mortality, average work week, vacation time, income, and national tax rates. Encourage students to arrange some of the data in graphs or tables. Tell students to complete the assignment with a written summary that draws conclusions about the relative socio-economic status of citizens of the three nations they analyzed.

▲ Although China still identifies itself as a communist state, private enterprise and investment have achieved remarkable growth in recent years.

Union dissolved into 15 independent countries. The largest and most populous of them was Russia.

Many state-owned companies in Russia were privatized. **Privatization** is the process of returning nationalized enterprises to private ownership. Today, Russia is a country with some features of free enterprise but also extensive state intervention in the economy.

## China

Mao Zedong, the founder of the People's Republic of China, was a Marxist. However, he believed the peasantry, not industrial workers, were the key to a successful communist revolution in agricultural China.

After Mao took control of the country in 1949, China developed its own version of a command economy. Despite its huge population, the country lacked skilled workers. The government improved technical and scientific educational opportunities and then assigned workers to jobs in the state sector. The government regulated the labor market, giving people little choice about where or for whom they worked.

**The Great Leap Forward** The five-year plan for 1958, the **Great Leap Forward,** was a drastic attempt to modernize China quickly. All elements of free enterprise were eliminated. Collective farms were brought together into larger units, communes. Communes grew into self-sufficient bodies run by Communist Party officials. These officials oversaw farms, industries, and government in a region, and they also managed social policy. Workers received the same rewards no matter how much they produced, so there were few incentives to work hard. The Great Leap Forward was a disastrous failure and was followed by a severe famine.

**Deng Xiaoping's Reforms** A new leader, Deng Xiaoping, came to power in 1977 and made great changes in the economy. Deng's program of the "Four Modernizations" was aimed at improving agriculture, industry, science and technology, and defense. He began to move China from a command economy to a market economy and opened the country to foreign investment.

Today, China's economic system is a maze of different levels of governmental bodies and economic units. Although the Communist Party remains in power and directs economic growth, the state-owned sector has shrunk. The government encourages private enterprise and investment and China has enjoyed many years of strong economic growth.

## Other Communist Nations

Very few communist economies exist today. Most communist nations, like China, have incorporated elements of free enterprise into their economic systems.

Cuba, led by Fidel Castro from 1959 to 2008, developed a communist economy heavily dependent on Soviet economic aid during the Cold War. As a result, the fall of the Soviet Union caused an economic crisis in Cuba. Despite modest reforms, most Cubans still live and work within the state-controlled economy.

In Southeast Asia, Vietnam and Laos are also ruled by communist parties and have centrally planned economies. However, since the late 1980s, both nations have instituted

# Teacher-to-Teacher Network

**ALTERNATIVE LESSON PLAN** Some of your classes may already have a basic knowledge of capitalism, socialism, and communism. Help these students increase their understanding by having them compare the three economic systems. Divide students into three groups, and assign each group one of the economic systems. Ask each group to create a poster-sized table describing their assigned system in terms of such factors as government control, price systems, and distribution of goods and services. Display the tables, and lead a class discussion about the differences among the three systems.

To see this lesson plan, go to

Teacher Center

at PearsonSchool.com/phgovt

free-market reforms to open their domestic markets and promote growth and encourage investment.

Communist North Korea has achieved little growth. Its economy, army, and all civil institutions are under the total control of dictator Kim Jong-Il, and severe food shortages plague the country.

## Evaluating Command Economies

Both free market and command economies have their strengths and their weaknesses. For the supporters of capitalism, it is easy to see the weaknesses in the theory and practice of socialism and communism. To the supporters of those two systems, capitalism seems filled with faults.

Critics argue that the many layers of bureaucracy in socialist countries complicate decision making and have a depressing effect on individual initiative. As a result, command economies are slow to take advantage of new technologies. In addition, many say, the smooth running of an economy is too complex to be directed by central planners. Too many unpredictable events are involved, and too many clashing interests are at stake. For all its faults, they argue, the invisible hand of the free-market economy works more efficiently than the ever-present hand of central planning.

Command economies are also criticized because they deprive people of the freedom to decide for themselves how to use their income. Since workers get to keep only a part of their earnings after taxes, they have little incentive to work harder and earn more, and no incentive to innovate or create new products. Why work hard when your basic needs will be taken care of anyway?

In response, socialists and communists say that it is fairer to supply everyone with such basic needs as medical care, housing, and education. They point to the inequalities of wealth and power that exist under capitalism. In their view, socialism makes political democracy work more smoothly by meshing it with economic democracy.

Defenders of socialism and communism also argue that these systems give workers and other ordinary citizens more control over their daily lives. Under capitalism, they say, a company's management can abruptly decide to close an unprofitable factory, even though such a decision can put thousands out of work and disrupt an entire community. This could not happen in a socialist or communist state, the argument goes. Workers and community leaders on the company's board would help decide what is best for the entire workforce and community—not just for the company's investors and shareholders.

✓ **Checkpoint** How successful have communist economies been?

---

**Essential Questions Journal** To continue to build a response to the chapter Essential Question, go to your **Essential Questions Journal**.

## SECTION 2 ASSESSMENT

1. **Guiding Question** Use your completed chart to answer this question: What is the role of government under socialism and communism?

**Key Terms and Comprehension**

2. How did Karl Marx's theories lead to **socialism** and **communism?**
3. What role does the government play in a **command economy?**
4. In your own words, describe how **communism** is intended to work.

**Critical Thinking**

5. **Make Comparisons** How might a capitalist, socialist, and communist government each interact with small businesses?
6. **Make Decisions** Do you think the government should have the responsibility of ensuring that every citizen has a job? Why or why not?

**Quick Write**

**Expository Writing: Research for Examples and Details** When writing a compare-and-contrast essay, you should include details that support the comparisons and contrasts you discuss. Use your textbook, the library, and reliable Internet sources to add details and examples to the notes you have made in your Venn diagram. Review the notes to delete details that are unimportant or do not relate to both systems.

---

# Assess and Remediate

**L3** Collect the Core Worksheet and assess the students' work, using the Rubric for Assessing a Writing Assignment (Unit 6 All-in-One, p. 102).

**L3** Assign the Section 2 Assessment questions.

**L3** Section Quiz A (Unit 6 All-in-One, p. 80)

**L2** Section Quiz B (Unit 6 All-in-One, p. 81)

Have students complete the review activities in the digital lesson presentation and continue their work in the **Essential Questions Journal**.

**REMEDIATION**

| If Your Students Have Trouble With | Strategies For Remediation |
|---|---|
| The role of government under socialism and communism (Questions 1, 3, 4, 5, 6) | Draw a Venn diagram on the board. Have students offer details from the text, their notes, and their dialogues to compare and contrast government's role under the two systems. |
| The theories of Karl Marx (Question 2) | Have students review the four main Marxist concepts and write or give an oral summary in their own words of each concept. |

## Answers

**Checkpoint** Very few communist economies exist today. Most communist nations have incorporated elements of free enterprise into their economic systems.

---

# Assessment Answers

1. **under socialism:** to ensure that all citizens are decently housed and fed and have medical care and to plan the growth of many parts of the economy; **under communism:** to manage all means of production and distribution of goods and services, to make all economic decisions, and to ensure the health and welfare of all citizens

2. Marx predicted that the workers would overthrow the capitalist bourgeoisie and take over the government, ensuring economic equality for all. This led leaders and thinkers to try to reform or revolutionize the government to redistribute wealth and provide more services to the workers.

3. One ruling party plans all aspects of the economy, oversees collectivization of agriculture, and runs major industries.

4. Communism is supposed to be a fair, open system under which all people are supplied with the goods and services they need to live well, including housing, jobs, healthcare, and retirement pensions. It is supposed to ensure that wealth and power are shared equally among all citizens.

5. **capitalist:** some oversight to maintain fairness in the marketplace and to ensure fair and safe treatment of workers; **socialist:** run some major industries and ensure workers' health and fair wages; **communist:** run all major industries and ensure that all workers are employed and paid fairly

6. Accept all logical responses.

**QUICK WRITE** A strong assignment will include details related to the two economic systems and go beyond the information in the Venn diagram.

## LESSON GOAL

- Students will create a pro/con chart to examine the effects of globalization.

## Teach

### INTRODUCE THE TOPIC

Explain that many people feel that the United States must be competitive in the global economy. Others think globalization harms the American economy. Ask volunteers to summarize the arguments in the feature.

### COMPLETE A PRO/CON CHART

Ask: **How can free trade help Americans? How can it hurt them?** Have students answer these questions by completing a pro-con chart as a class. Encourage students to use information from the quotations on this page and their prior knowledge of the effects of free trade or global competition, such as factory closings or new job creation. *(sample responses: pro—stronger U.S. economy leading to more American jobs, more access to foreign goods at lower prices; higher standard of living in developing nations can increase security; con—jobs outsourced to countries with lower wages; more family members have to work; loss of economic stability)*

### DRAW A CONCLUSION

Ask students to use the pro/con chart to draw a written conclusion about whether free trade is beneficial or harmful overall.

## Assess and Remediate

Have students decide which quotation they think made the strongest argument and explain why.

---

## Answers

1. Answers will vary.
2. **(a)** It says communities as well as individuals are affected, tax revenues fall, public assistance needs rise, and national competitiveness is at risk. **(b)** He believes that free trade will make the U.S. economy stronger and Americans more prosperous. **(c)** Students' answers should demonstrate an understanding of the issue and should clearly illustrate their point of view.

# ISSUES OF OUR TIME

## Globalization and Free Trade

### ▶▶ Track the Issue

**Until the 1940s,** the United States followed protectionist policies rather than free trade.

**1789**
**Congress passes the first Tariff Act,** providing the new Federal Government with its main source of revenue.

**1930**
**Smoot-Hawley Tariff Act** raises tariffs on imports to historically high levels.

**1948**
**The General Agreement on Tariffs and Trade (GATT)** is signed, opening a new era of lower tariffs.

**1994**
**The North American Free Trade Agreement (NAFTA)** takes effect, reducing trade barriers among the United States, Canada, and Mexico.

**1995**
**The World Trade Organization** replaces GATT, aiming to expand global trade and resolve disputes.

**Today**
**The United States** remains committed to opening markets and expanding business opportunities through new trade agreements.

Federal Reserve Chairman Ben S. Bernanke ▶

### ▶▶ Perspectives

The growth of free trade has brought both benefits and challenges to Americans. While trade has expanded in some areas and the United States remains the world's largest exporter, there have also been painful job losses. What economic and social issues do government leaders need to consider in drafting free trade agreements?

"Trade-related job loss does not just hurt individual workers and their families. Entire communities are affected negatively as tax revenues fall, dependency on public assistance increases, and incomes stagnate. And as the off-shoring and job loss spreads to sectors with higher technology and skills that drive innovation and productivity, it puts the long-term competitiveness of the American economy at risk."

—AFL-CIO, "Exporting America", 2010

With our strong institutions, deep capital markets, flexible labor markets, technological leadership, and penchant [like] for entrepreneurship and innovation, no country is better placed than the United States to benefit from increased participation in the global economy. If we resist protectionism and isolationism while working to increase the skills and adaptability of our labor force, the forces of globalization and trade will continue to make our economy stronger and our citizens more prosperous.

—Federal Reserve Chairman Ben S. Bernanke, 2007

### ▶▶ Connect to Your World

1. **Understand (a)** Identify five items you use each day. Where were these goods made? **(b)** How does trade affect your community in terms of jobs and the goods people buy?
2. **Compare and Contrast (a)** What does the AFL-CIO say are the negative effects of free trade? **(b)** Why does Chairman Bernanke think that globalization and free trade are good for the American economy? **(c)** With whom do you agree? Why?

**GOVERNMENT ONLINE**
**In the News**
To find out about free trade and globalization, visit
**PearsonSchool.com/phgovt**

**692**

## Background

**SECURITY AND PROSPERITY PARTNERSHIP OF NORTH AMERICA** In 2005, leaders of Mexico, Canada, and the United States launched the Security and Prosperity Partnership of North America (SPP). The SPP is an initiative to increase security and prosperity among the three nations through greater cooperation and information sharing. Its working groups discuss shared issues such as terrorism, smuggling, and trade. The SPP is not a signed agreement or treaty, and therefore contains no legally binding obligations. However, this also means that the organization operates outside of congressional oversight. Critics fear that the SPP's ultimate goal is political and economic integration, creating a North American Union (NAU) with blurred borders and a shared currency. Official sources call such fears conspiracy theory. The fact that the NAU myth persists may reflect the public's apprehension about globalization.

# The U.S. in a Global Economy

## How does the Federal Government support economic growth at home and abroad?

I. The Domestic Economy
 A. Supports free enterprise
 B. Federal Reserve System
  1. uses monetary policy to promote price stability, full employment, and economic growth
  2. adjusts federal funds rate to expand or contract the economy
 C. Security and Exchange Commission
  1. oversees the stock markets
  2. prevents insider trading, fraudulent accounting, and false information to investors
 D. Department of Labor
  1. protects rights of workers and oversees workplace fairness and safety
  2. Occupational Safety and Health Administration oversees workplace safety
  3. Employment Standards Administration promotes fairness in contracts, benefits, and wages
  4. Bureau of Labor Statistics tracks employment statistics used to evaluate economy
II. The Global Economy
 A. Protects American producers and consumers
  1. tariff increases price of imported good to protect domestic industry
  2. quota limits amount of commodity that can be imported
  3. embargo bans trade with a nation as diplomatic pressure
 B. Supports trade
  1. North American Free Trade Agreement eliminated trade barriers among U.S., Mexico, and Canada
  2. trade agreements with countries of Latin America and Asia
III. International Organizations
 A. World Trade Organization works to increase trade
 B. World Bank makes loans to poor countries to build infrastructure
 C. International Monetary Fund helps countries whose financial systems are in trouble
 D. Group of 8 discuss world affairs and crises

## Guiding Question

**How does the Federal Government support economic growth at home and abroad?** Use an outline to take notes on the ways in which the government takes part in both the domestic and global economies.

I. The Domestic Economy
 A. Supports free enterprise
  1. _____
  2. _____
 B. _____

## Political Dictionary

- globalization
- protectionism
- tariff
- import quota
- trade embargo
- NAFTA
- World Trade Organization (WTO)

## Objectives

1. Describe the role of government in the domestic economy.
2. Understand the reasons why nations participate in trade.
3. Describe the role of the Federal Government in the global economy.
4. Explain the causes of globalization and its effects on the American economy.

**Image Above:** Traders signal an offer on the exchange floor of the Chicago Board of Trade.

Since 1789, the government of the United States has become increasingly involved in protecting, managing, and regulating this nation's economic life. With the rise of worldwide markets, free trade agreements, multinational corporations, and the use of off-shore labor—known as outsourcing—the Federal Government's participation in the economy is now more crucial than ever. Today, it has a great deal to say about how the economy operates at home and abroad. It also works to protect the economic interests of its citizens.

## The Domestic Economy

For the first 120 years or so of its existence, the Federal Government played only a very limited role in the economy and in the economic well-being of the American people. However, by the early twentieth century, due to repeated economic "panics" and recessions, culminating in the Great Depression of the 1930s, the amount of governmental involvement began to change.

A vital free enterprise system fosters competition and entrepreneurship. The Federal Government tries to support this system by attempting to ensure fairness in the market place, and, with it, the health and well-being of both consumers and workers.

Recall, there are a number of independent agencies within the executive branch of the government. Many of them have an important role in the regulation of economic activities within the United States. Among the most important of them are the Federal Reserve System, the Securities and Exchange Commission (SEC), and such organizations as the Occupational Safety & Health Administration (OSHA) in the Department of Labor.

**The Federal Reserve System** Known as "the Fed," the Federal Reserve System is one of the most powerful tools the Federal Government uses to regulate the nation's economy. The Fed was established by Congress in 1913 to become the central banking system for the United States. It consists of a Board of Governors appointed by the President (one of whom is appointed to act as the chairperson), 12 regional banks, and many other member banks. The main purpose of the Fed is to use the tools of monetary policy to promote price stability, full employment, economic growth, and other national economic goals.

## SKILLS DEVELOPMENT

### ANALYZE GRAPHIC DATA

To practice analyzing graphic data in this section, use the Chapter 23 Skills Worksheet (Unit 6 All-in-One, p. 88). You may want to teach the skill before discussing issues of global trade. For L2 and L1 students, assign the adapted Skill Activity (Unit 6 All-in-One, p. 90).

## Focus on the Basics

**FACTS:** • Through various agencies, the Federal Government regulates the economy to ensure fairness, economic stability, and growth. • The United States is the world's largest importer and exporter. • The main U.S. trade partners are Canada, China, Mexico, Japan, and Germany. • Tariffs, import quotas, and embargoes create trade barriers, often to protect domestic industry. • The United States, Canada, and Mexico formed NAFTA to eliminate trade barriers among themselves.

**CONCEPTS:** role of government in economic policy, globalization

**ENDURING UNDERSTANDINGS:** • Advances in communication and transportation technologies have enabled economic interdependence. • Globalization has been good for the U.S. economy in some areas, but has cost American jobs.

# Get Started

## LESSON GOALS

Students will . . .

- list ways in which government regulation of the economy affects their own lives.
- complete a concept web about the role of the Federal Government in the economy at home and abroad.
- summarize economic news reports to present to the class in a mock television program.

## BEFORE CLASS

Assign the section, the graphic organizer in the text, and the Reading Comprehension Worksheet (Unit 6 All-in-One, p. 82) before class.

Tell students to look through print or online sources for brief news items about the U.S. government and some aspect of the domestic or global economy and bring them to class for this lesson. Each student should bring in at least two items.

**L2 Differentiate** Reading Comprehension Worksheet (Unit 6 All-in-One, p. 84)

## BELLRINGER

Write on the board: **In your notebook, describe three ways in which you participate in the economy and three ways in which the U.S. government affects that participation.**

**L2 Differentiate** Have students list only the three ways in which they take part in the U.S. economy or the three government effects.

Tell students to go to the Audio Tour to listen to a guided audio tour of the Federal Reserve System.

## Answers

**The Federal Reserve System** The 12 bank directors based in different regions of the country can give feedback as to conditions in their regions.

**Checkpoint** the nation's central banking system and a powerful tool used by the Federal Government to regulate the nation's economy

---

# The Federal Reserve System

Twelve regional banks make up the Federal Reserve System, known as the Fed. The banks' directors and an appointed Board of Governors make important decisions that affect the national and global economy. *Why does including the regional directors improve the Fed's decisions?*

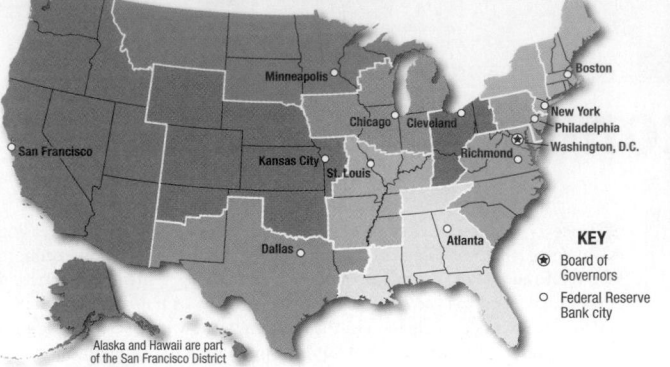

Minneapolis
Boston
Chicago · Cleveland
New York
Philadelphia
San Francisco
Kansas City · St. Louis · Richmond · Washington, D.C.
Dallas
Atlanta

**KEY**
⊛ Board of Governors
○ Federal Reserve Bank city

Alaska and Hawaii are part of the San Francisco District

**The Fed's Responsibility: Set interest rates to encourage steady economic growth**

If the Fed sets interest rates too **High**
- businesses will not borrow and invest
- the economy slows
- people lose jobs

If the Fed sets interest rates too **Low**
- too much money is borrowed
- businesses make risky investments
- prices rise quickly

---

✔ **Checkpoint**
What is the Federal Reserve System?

**fraudulent**
*adj.* false, dishonest

Mainly, this means adjusting the federal funds rate—an interest rate at which banks lend money to other banks on a daily basis. The Fed does this to either contract or expand the amount of money in the economy in response to changes in inflation or unemployment. Raising interest rates makes money more expensive to borrow, and so, in theory, contracts the economy. Lowering interest rates makes money less expensive to borrow, and so tends to expand the economy. The rate adjustments that the Fed makes can affect other lending rates, foreign exchange rates, and the levels of money and credit available in the economy, as well as employment and prices. In 2008 on into 2009, the Fed took several actions to avert a panic in the financial markets. You can read more about the importance of the Fed in Chapter 16.

**The Securities and Exchange Commission** The Securities and Exchange Commission (SEC) is a federal regulatory agency consisting of five commissioners appointed by the President, who also selects the SEC's chairperson from among those five commissioners. Congress created the SEC in 1934 in the aftermath of the stock market crash that contributed to the Great Depression.

The commission's central task is to oversee the nation's stock markets and ensure that corporations do not engage in such abuses as insider trading, which is the practice of buying or selling stock based on company information not known to other investors. The SEC also ensures that publicly traded companies truthfully disclose their finances. It brings court actions against those who violate securities laws—for example, through insider trading, <u>fraudulent</u> accounting practices, or providing false information to investors.

**The Department of Labor** The Federal Government provides protections for the basic rights of workers and oversees issues of fairness and safety in the workplace. Much of this is accomplished by the Department of Labor.

---

# Differentiated Resources

The following resources are located in the All-in-One, Unit 6, Chapter 23, Section 3:

- **L3** Reading Comprehension Worksheet (p. 82)
- **L2** Reading Comprehension Worksheet (p. 84)
- **L3** Core Worksheet (p. 86)
- **L3** Skills Worksheet (p. 88)
- **L2** Skill Activity (p. 90)
- **L3** Quiz A (p. 92)
- **L2** Quiz B (p. 93)
- **L3** Chapter Test A (p. 94)   **L2** Chapter Test B (p. 97)

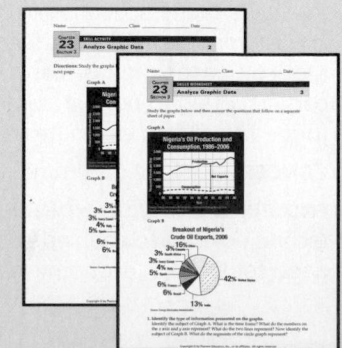

To meet these aims, the Department works through its various agencies. For example, since the Occupational Safety & Health Administration (OSHA) was established in 1971, its inspectors have worked with employers and employees to decrease deaths in the workplace by 60 percent. The Employment Standards Administration (ESA) monitors fairness in contracts, benefits, and wages. The Bureau of Labor Statistics plays the important role of tracking major economic statistics, such as the unemployment rate and the consumer price index. These data are used to evaluate the health of the nation's economy.

## A Global Economy

There is a growing economic <u>interdependence</u> among nations of the world. This interdependence, often called **globalization**, has been both driven and enabled by many remarkable advancements in communication and transportation technologies. Everything from the enormous increase in computing power, the Internet, communications satellites, and even the building of larger ships has increased the flow of goods, and, as well, the flow of information that connects world markets. Globalization has also developed out of the drive for increased international trade promoted by the United States in the years since the Great Depression.

**The Purpose of Trade** All nations engage in trade. Trade is one of the <u>hallmarks</u> of civilization, and it has been for thousands of years. However, improvements in transportation and communication technologies and the pressure to find new markets have spurred the growth of worldwide markets.

The United States produces a great many different goods, but it does not produce everything this country needs. No country does because of the unequal distribution of natural resources and other factors of production, such as skilled workers, among countries. The unequal distribution of factors of production means that one nation can more effectively specialize in producing certain goods—for example, petroleum or computer chips. That nation will then

export petroleum or computer chips and use the profits to purchase, or import, goods from other nations who have an advantage in the production of, for example, food stuffs or automobiles.

Trade allows Americans to acquire the goods they want, but which this nation cannot produce as cost-effectively or efficiently as it does other goods. It is the role of the Federal Government to support trade and other economic opportunities around the world, while at the same time, protecting American producers and consumers.

**American Trade Partners** Today, as it has been for several decades, Canada is the United States' chief trade partner. After the North American Free Trade Agreement (NAFTA) became effective in 1994, Mexico moved up in rank to second among the United States' main trade partners. However, by the end of 2004, China had surpassed Mexico to become the United States' second leading trading partner. This remains true today.

The United States is the largest exporter of goods and services in the world. Major American exports include such goods as telecommunications, aerospace, medical, and military equipment. This country also exports soybeans, corn, fruit, automobiles, and a great many other products. Service exports are a large and quickly growing sector of world trade. The United States leads there, as well, in exporting education, information, data processing, financial services, and medical care.

The United States is also the world's number one importer of goods and services. More than $2 trillion in goods and services enter this country each year. That is nearly 15 percent of all the world's imports, and includes such consumer goods as clothing, toys, and electronics, as well as capital goods, which include computers, electronic parts, and industrial machinery. Another import category is food and beverages, including animal feed. Automobiles and auto parts constitute a fourth import category.

However, the largest category of imported goods is industrial supplies and materials, including crude oil. The United States is the largest importer of crude oil in the world,

✔ **Checkpoint**
What is the goal of globalization?

**interdependence**
*n.* dependence upon one another

**hallmark**
*n.* distinguishing feature

## Political Cartoon Mini-Lesson

Display Transparency 23E, The Federal Reserve Takes Action, when you discuss the role of the Federal Reserve in regulating the economy. To make sure all students recognize the cartoon character, ask a volunteer to explain who Popeye is and what happens when he eats spinach. *(Popeye is a cartoon sailor who gains strength by eating spinach.)* Ask: **What does Popeye represent in the cartoon?** *(the economy)* **What does the can of spinach represent?** *(interest rate cuts made by the Federal Reserve)* **How are interest rate cuts supposed to affect the economy?** *(Interest rate cuts are supposed to strengthen the economy. Lower interest rates add money— in this case, spinach—to the economy by making loans less expensive. Businesses will then borrow more and expand.)* **Is the Fed's action working in this case? How do you know?** *(Not yet. Popeye's bicep is sagging, so he is not gaining strength.)*

# Teach

To present this topic using online resources, use the lesson presentations at **PearsonSchool.com/phgovt**.

### GOVERNMENT'S ROLE IN THE ECONOMY

Explain that this lesson is about the ways in which the Federal Government acts to regulate or support economic life in the United States. Review the students' responses to the Bellringer activity. *(Students might note that when the Federal Reserve adjusts interest rates, students make less interest on savings. Other examples include income and other taxes they pay, OSHA and worker safety, the minimum wage, unemployment benefits, and Social Security.)*

Remind students that the U.S. has a mixed economy, in which the free market operates with government oversight. The government takes actions that affect the economy at home, but it also takes actions that influence the global economy. In turn, the global economy affects the U.S. economy.

Begin a concept web like the one below. Have students offer examples for each part of the web. *(At Home examples include: activities of the Federal Reserve, Securities and Exchange Commission, and Department of Labor—OSHA, ESA, and the Bureau of Labor Statistics. International examples include: trade barriers—tariffs, quotas, and embargoes; free-trade agreements—NAFTA and APEC; and international organizations—World Trade Organization and the World Bank.)*

Challenge students to think about the U.S. government's activities in the global sphere and how they may affect Americans. Examples include: free-trade agreements, such as NAFTA, might mean job losses or lower prices for goods imported from Canada and Mexico; tariffs and other protectionist tools mean higher prices for imported goods but protections for American jobs; conflicts, such as the war in Iraq, increase government debt, which can lead to higher taxes. Conflicts also often lead to shortages or higher prices for goods, such as oil.

## Answers

**Checkpoint** to achieve economic interdependence among the world's nations

Write the term *globalization* and its definition (worldwide economic interdependence) on the board, and display Transparency 23D, Top U.S. Trade Partners. Tell students to work with a partner to write three questions and answers about the United States position and activities in the global economy, based on information in the text or on the transparency. Example: Why do you think that Canada and Mexico are major trade partners? *(They are our nearest neighbors and also are now members of NAFTA.)* Have pairs exchange questions, and then check each other's work.

**L2 Differentiate** Verify that students understand the graph by asking: **What does "total trade" mean in this graph?** *(all transfers of goods or services between the United States and the rest of the world)* **Which country does the most trade with the United States?** *(Canada)* **How do you know?** *(It has the largest piece of the pie representing all U.S. trade with other nations.)*

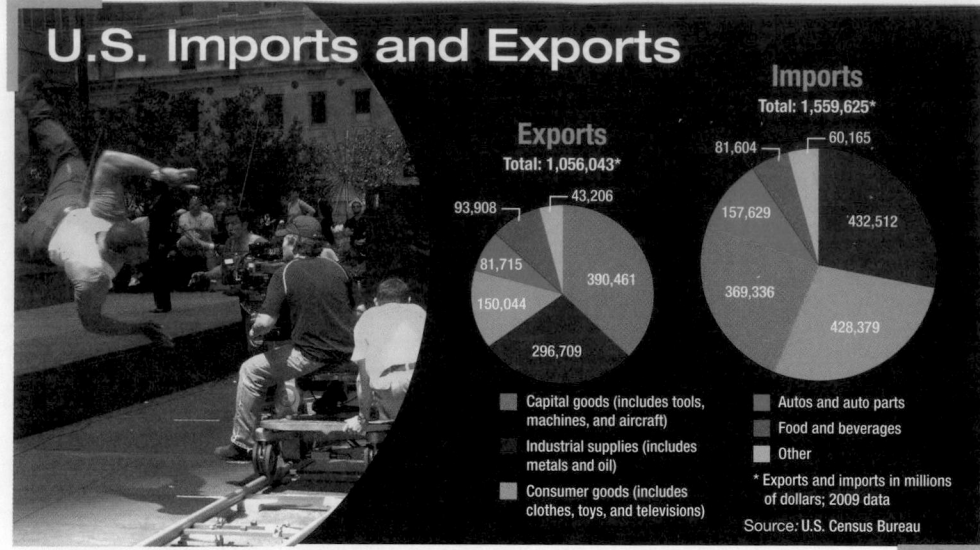

## U.S. Imports and Exports

**Exports** Total: 1,056,043*

93,908 — 43,206
81,715
150,044
390,461
296,709

**Imports** Total: 1,559,625*

81,604 — 60,165
157,629
432,512
369,336
428,379

- Capital goods (includes tools, machines, and aircraft)
- Industrial supplies (includes metals and oil)
- Consumer goods (includes clothes, toys, and televisions)
- Autos and auto parts
- Food and beverages
- Other

*Exports and imports in millions of dollars; 2009 data

Source: U.S. Census Bureau

▶▶ **Analyzing Charts** The United States imports more goods and services than it exports, although film and television programs (above left) are an exception to this pattern. *According to the charts, how do you suppose oil influences the trade balance of imports and exports?*

✔ **Checkpoint**
What are the main imports of the United States?

*jeopardize*
*v.* to risk, put in danger

accounting for some 12 percent of all oil imports. Most of that oil comes from the countries of Canada, Saudi Arabia, Mexico, Venezuela, and Iraq.

### U.S. Trade Policies

One goal of the Federal Government has often been to protect American producers and workers by keeping prices, and therefore profits, high, while minimizing competition from imports. The government must do this through such agencies as the Department of Commerce and the International Trade Commission without <u>jeopardizing</u> relationships with its trade partners. It has employed several tools for this tricky task.

**Economic Policy Tools** Most national governments try to control imports to protect native industries from foreign competition. The goals of this practice, known as **protectionism,** include safeguarding of jobs,

protecting emerging or weakened industries, and enhancing national security. Governments often pursue these goals with trade barriers that hinder free trade and raise the prices consumers must pay for imported goods. These trade barriers are generally of three types: tariffs, import quotas, and trade embargoes.

A **tariff** is a tax on imported goods. A tariff increases the cost of an imported item and makes American-made products more attractive to the domestic customer. The government regularly places high tariffs on goods that are produced by important American industries. For example, the tariff on steel is relatively high because Americans produce a great deal of it and the steel industry is considered vital to national security, so the government does not wish cheaper imports to put domestic steel mills out of business.

An **import quota** is a limit put on the amount of a commodity that can be imported into a country. While recently limited by international agreements, import quotas are

## Background

**WORLD TRADE ORGANIZATION** Most of the world's trading nations negotiated and signed agreements that form the foundation of the World Trade Organization (WTO). The members established trade rules that all agreed to follow. Members also set up a systematic process for resolving trade disputes. When a member believes a nation has broken a rule, it can take its case to the WTO. The process begins with the two sides trying to settle their problem by talking. If talking fails, the WTO appoints a panel of experts to make a ruling. If the panel concludes that a nation has violated a rule, that nation must correct its policy, or the WTO will allow the complaining nation to impose trade penalties, such as tariffs on imports from the offending nation. In 2007, the U.S. charged that China's weak copyright laws have led to unlawful copying of U.S. movies and music. A WTO panel is now considering the case.

## Answers

**Analyzing Charts** Oil is the largest import for the U.S. and the second-largest export.

**Checkpoint** consumer goods, capital goods, food and beverages, automobiles and auto parts, industrial supplies and materials still in place in the United States on such items as cotton, sugar, and milk. Many European nations have put a quota on American films and television shows to encourage the production of their own features and to protect national cultures.

A more significant trade barrier—and one that is more often used to apply diplomatic pressure or as a punishment rather than as an economic tool—is the trade embargo. A **trade embargo** is a ban on trade with a particular country or countries. An embargo might be placed on all goods or only specific items. It can be placed on exports or, separately, on imports. The United States has used trade embargoes largely to promote its foreign policy positions. For example, the United States has maintained a complete economic embargo on Communist Cuba since the early 1960s. Embargoes can be effective, but notice that they may also hurt the domestic economy of the nation imposing them.

**NAFTA** The North American Free Trade Agreement, known as **NAFTA,** became effective in 1994. NAFTA established free trade among the United States, Canada, and Mexico, and intended to eliminate, in steps, all tariffs and other barriers to trade by 2009. It created what amounts to the world's largest free trade zone.

NAFTA was approved only after a great deal of controversy and resistance, especially in the United States. Opponents of the agreement were concerned that American manufacturing operations would be moved to Mexico, where wages are lower and regulations are fewer, and lead to huge job losses. Others worried that imports without tariffs would put American businesses at a huge disadvantage. Supporters insisted that the expected increase in exports to Canada and Mexico would mean an increase in American jobs. They also argued that an improved economy would create greater prosperity and stability in Mexico, and so reduce illegal immigration from that country.

Today, nearly all <u>facets</u> of NAFTA are in place; the results seem to indicate that the pact was on the whole good for U.S. trade and investment, but not positive for all American workers. Although the long-term results

are hard to distinguish from other trends, it appears that NAFTA accelerated the loss of high-paying manufacturing jobs. For example, jobs in the American textile and clothing sectors, already in decline, decreased steeply. However, many manufacturing jobs that have left the U.S. have moved to countries other than Mexico or Canada.

On the positive side, trade—in agricultural products especially—has increased dramatically with the elimination of nearly all trade barriers. Between 1993 and 2008, United States exports to Mexico rose from $41 billion to nearly $130 billion.

While NAFTA affects only trade with Canada and Mexico, it provides a model for freer trade between the United States and other countries. The United States has signed similar treaties with many other countries in Latin America and Asia involving much smaller trade flows.

## International Organizations

The United States employs the tools of protectionism to support industries and workers at home. It also uses them to enlarge economic opportunities, strengthen international ties, and open new markets abroad. It often does this through membership in free trade agreements and international alliances and organizations.

**Protecting the Global Economy** The **World Trade Organization (WTO)** was created in 1995 to help carry out and extend the goals of a 1948 treaty, the General Agreement on Tariffs and Trade (GATT) intended to increase trade. With 153 members, the WTO provides a set of rules for international commerce, a forum for the creation of new trade agreements, and an arena in which to resolve trade issues.

The United States is also a member of, and the largest shareholder in, the World Bank. The goal of this institution is to reduce poverty and raise the standard of living around the world by making loans to poor nations to build infrastructure or reduce debt and by providing advice and training.

The International Monetary Fund (IMF) is, like the World Bank, headquartered in

<u>facet</u>
*n.* aspect, piece, side

---

## INTRODUCE THE ACTIVITY

Tell students that in this activity they will take on the role of reporters for a fictitious economics television network. They will work in groups to plan a program that includes at least three reports on the U.S. government activities that affect the global or domestic economy. Their reports will be brief summaries of the news items they brought to class.

## DISTRIBUTE THE CORE WORKSHEET

Divide the class into small groups and distribute one copy of the Chapter 23 Section 3 Core Worksheet (Unit 6 All-in-One, p. 86) to each group. Tell students that the worksheet has two parts. The first part consists of step-by-step guidelines to help them create their program. The second part is a programming schedule where they will list and briefly describe each news report they plan to give during their group's program. To begin each presentation, one student will serve as the news anchor and read the schedule. Then individual members will present their reports to the class in the style of television news reporters.

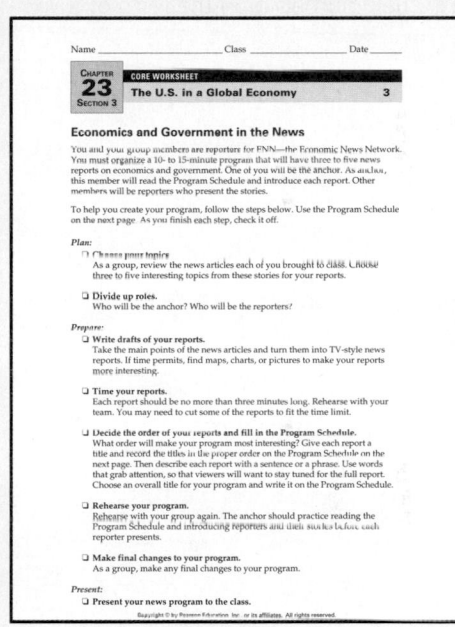

# Background

**THE CASE FOR FREE TRADE** Support for free trade rests on the economic principle of comparative advantage: Nations benefit from producing what they do best and trading for products that other countries do best. For example, coffee grows very well in Brazil. It makes no economic sense for the United States to restrict imports of coffee from Brazil and try to grow it ourselves. American resources can be employed more efficiently to produce, say, software and financial services. Free trade increases competition, which lowers prices for consumers. Competition also forces producers to become more efficient and improve their products to attract buyers. Competition from Japanese cars prompted U.S. automakers to produce better cars at lower prices. Statistics support the case for free trade. As tariffs fell after World War II, world economic growth rose sharply, leading to higher living standards for many nations.

**L3 Differentiate** As an alternate approach, organize students into groups well before class. Assign each group a broad topic or theme, such as protectionism, consumer and worker protection, international trade alliances and organizations, the domestic economy and government, U.S. trade partners, or U.S. economic policy and foreign relations. Have each group search for news items related to their topic to summarize for their news program.

**L3 Differentiate** If a video camera is available, you may wish to have students tape their reports.

**L2 ELL Differentiate** If students have difficulty with English language skills or writing, suggest that they research or create supporting visuals for their group's reports.

### WRITE A FOLLOW-UP JOURNAL ENTRY

After all groups have presented their programs, have students write a journal entry describing one thing they learned from the reports and one thing about which they would like to know more. Encourage students to research that topic and write about what they learned in their journals or in the form of a short report.

## Answers

**Top U.S. Trade Partners** China

**698** Comparative Economic Systems

---

Washington, D.C. It was established in 1945 to promote a healthy global economy and to prevent crises in the international monetary and financial systems. While the World Bank lends money to developing countries to build bridges, dams, and other tangible improvements, the IMF helps countries whose financial or banking systems are in trouble.

Another important group to which the United States belongs is the Group of 8, or "the G8," an annual meeting of the leaders of eight wealthy and industrialized nations: the United States, Canada, France, Germany, Italy, Japan, Russia, and the United Kingdom. The group has no rigid structure and leaders meet as representatives of their governments to discuss world affairs and crises.

**Other Trade Alliances** The European Union (EU) is the most successful of the world's free trade organizations. It is also responsible for setting policies in other areas of common concern to its members, including social issues and security. The evolution of the EU began in 1957, when six European nations established the European Common Market to coordinate economic policies and trade. Over time, most Western European nations joined the group. In 1986, they created the European Economic Community (EEC) and, in an historic step, eliminated all tariffs on trade between EU members.

In 1993, the organization went even further to blur international boundaries by forming the European Union. The EU operates much like a weak federal government, with its own parliament, its own flag, and even an anthem. Citizens of most member nations can now travel as tourists or workers across national borders freely, without a passport. In 2002, twelve of the member nations gave up their individual currencies and replaced them with the euro, which is the EU's currency. The EU is now comprised of 27 nations, including many of the former Soviet republics.

Inspired by the success of the EU, other nations have formed mostly regional trade alliances. One of the largest is the Asian-Pacific Economic Cooperation (APEC). Its 21 members include nations on the Pacific Rim, such as the United States, Japan, Canada, Chile, and China. The Southern Common Market, or MERCOSUR, is a regional trade bloc established by Brazil, Argentina, Paraguay, and Uruguay.

**tangible**
*adj.* real, physical, touchable

# Top U.S.Trade Partners

The United States trades most heavily with countries in North America, East Asia, and Europe. However, we import more from each of our six largest trade partners than we export to them, leading to trade deficits. *With which country does the United States have the largest trade deficit?*

EXPORTS to U.S. and IMPORTS from U.S. in billions of dollars

| Canada | China | Mexico | Japan |
|---|---|---|---|
| EXPORTS to U.S. 224.9 | EXPORTS to U.S. 296.4 | EXPORTS to U.S. 176.5 | EXPORTS to U.S. 95.9 |
| IMPORTS from U.S. 204.7 | IMPORTS from U.S. 69.6 | IMPORTS from U.S. 129.0 | IMPORTS from U.S. 51.2 |
| **16.4%** | **14%** | **11.7%** | **5.6%** |
| TOTAL U.S. TRADE | TOTAL U.S. TRADE | TOTAL U.S. TRADE | TOTAL U.S. TRADE |

SOURCE: U.S. Census, 2009 data

**698** Comparative Economic Systems

## Background

**THE CASE AGAINST FREE TRADE** The U.S. government sets standards to protect its citizens and the environment. For example, the government requires safety equipment for workers, sets a minimum wage, and requires companies to practice pollution control. These protective measures often raise the costs of production. Some other nations do not have strict standards. These nations can produce less expensively by paying low wages, allowing unsafe working conditions, and polluting the environment. Without tariffs, these exports will sell at lower prices in the U.S. than will the American-made versions, depressing U.S. industry and costing jobs. Free trade agreements have encouraged U.S. manufacturers to relocate abroad, where they can avoid the costs of meeting U.S. standards. The result is millions of American jobs lost, eroding U.S. wages, exploited foreign workers, and environmental damage.

## Impact of Trade

For the most part, a global economy seems to be a positive development. It means that more goods are available to more consumers, and that there are more markets in which producers can sell goods. Globalization and international partnerships also help developing nations to expand their economies and raise their standards of living by enabling them to sell goods to more affluent countries.

And, clearly, competition in a global market lowers the price of goods. Goods made overseas, unblocked by tariffs, are less expensive and become more affordable for Americans. Increases in jobs and higher wages, in turn, allow consumers in developing nations to buy American goods and services, and this helps to increase or at least maintain American jobs. Additionally, new, creative approaches to outsourcing may actually create new American jobs by lowering costs so that corporations are able to use the savings to grow and develop innovative products and services. Importantly, increased economic interdependence may lead to more political cooperation and so to fewer conflicts.

**GOVERNMENT** ONLINE
**Audio Tour**
Listen to an audio guided tour on trade at
PearsonSchool.com/phgovt

**Germany**
EXPORTS to U.S. 71.3
IMPORTS from U.S. 43.3
**4.4%**
TOTAL U.S. TRADE

**United Kingdom**
EXPORTS to U.S. 47.5
IMPORTS from U.S. 45.7
**3.6%**
TOTAL U.S. TRADE

However, with interdependence comes risk. A crisis in another nation on which Americans depend for an important commodity can have quick, profound, and direct economic effects. Thus, in recent years, war in Iraq and instability in Nigeria—both major oil-producing nations—contributed to higher oil and gas prices in the United States.

Some people worry that international trade agreements may affect a nation's sovereignty if they have to get "permission" from partner nations to make decisions about such matters as civil rights, defense, or the environment. With <u>instantaneous</u> communications, economic downturns or market fluctuations in one part of the world now cause instability in other markets within hours.

The United States is also moving from a manufacturing economy to a service economy, in large part because American workers cannot compete with workers in other nations who are paid much less. The loss of high-paying manufacturing jobs is painful to the individuals involved, and if these workers are not retrained to begin new jobs with comparable wages, the transition will also hurt both the local and the national economy. In addition, the growth of the service sector has created many new, high-paying jobs that did not exist a decade ago, but often in different locations from where workers live.

The United States is also adversely affected by trade deficits. For example, the United States buys much more from China than China buys from the United States, and so an enormous trade deficit has developed. China has financed the deficit by lending the United States government money and by buying American assets. This means that China, along with Japan and many oil-exporting countries, owns a portion of the American economy, with implications for the economic health and future of this nation.

## Tomorrow's Marketplace

As you have seen, the trend today in the world economy is toward greater interdependence among nations—

✔ **Checkpoint**
What is the purpose of the European Union?

**instantaneous**
*adj.* happening in an instant

---

Tell students to go to the Audio Tour to listen to a guided audio tour of Top U.S. Trade Partners.

**EXTEND THE LESSON**

**L3 Differentiate** Have students work in pairs or small groups to create an informational poster or brochure about one of the international organizations to which the United States belongs, such as the World Trade Organization or the World Bank. Have students present their work to the class.

**L3 Differentiate** Ask students to do research and create a circle graph showing on which nations the United States is most dependent for petroleum and the percentages Americans import from each nation. Have students write a summary about how this dependency might affect U.S. relations and policy with these nations.

**L3 ELL Differentiate** Tell students to draw a political cartoon about some aspect of the U.S. government's role in the economy and explain it in annotations or in a summarizing caption.

**L2 ELL Differentiate** Give students an outline map of the world. Have them color in the six top trade partners of the United States and label each nation.

**L4 Differentiate** Ask students to research and write a report on the subject of the U.S. trade imbalance. Tell students to focus on the causes and effects of large trade imbalances—for example, the trade imbalance with China—on the American economy.

**L4 Differentiate** Instruct students to hold a mock trial of NAFTA. The goal is to determine if the agreement is guilty or not guilty of being bad for the American economy. Students may take the roles of defense attorney, prosecuting attorney, judge, witnesses, and jury. Tell students that the jury must weigh the evidence presented by both sides and reach a verdict with which a majority agrees.

**Government** online *All print resources are available on the Teacher's Resource Library CD-ROM and online at PearsonSchool.com/phgovt.*

## Debate

Free trade is a contentious issue. The economic gains do not benefit everyone equally: some individuals may rise from poverty, while others lose their jobs. Organize the class into teams to debate this issue. Ask: **Is the growth of free trade a positive or negative development?** Assign each team to debate from one of these points of view: U.S. auto workers facing plant closings; U.S. farmers receiving government subsidies; top managers of a U.S. factory that makes weapons for the military; free-market economists; entrepreneurs in Africa; workers in U.S. textile factories operating in Mexico; or owners of U.S. textile factories operating in Mexico. Have students do research to prepare their case. Ask them to conduct the debate in character.

## Answers

**Checkpoint** The European Union is a free trade organization that sets policies in other areas of common concern to its members.

# Assess and Remediate

**L3** Collect the Core Worksheets and assess the students' work, using the Rubric for Assessing Individual Performance in a Group (Unit 6 All-in-One, p. 103).

**L3** Assign the Section 3 Assessment questions.

**L3** Section Quiz A (Unit 6 All-in-One, p. 92)

**L2** Section Quiz B (Unit 6 All-in-One, p. 93)

Have students complete the review activities in the digital lesson presentation and continue their work in the **Essential Questions Journal.**

## REMEDIATION

| If Your Students Have Trouble With | Strategies For Remediation |
|---|---|
| The role of the U.S. government in the domestic and global economy (Questions 1, 3, 5) | Draw a two-column chart on the board to list the activities of the U.S. government in the economy "At Home" and "Globally." Have students offer details from their reading and class work to complete the chart. |
| The structure and function of the Federal Reserve (Question 2) | Draw a pyramid on the board to show the structure of the Fed, with the Chairman of the Board of Governors at the top. Then ask students to help you list the main ways in which the Fed regulates the U.S. economy. |
| The goals and effects of NAFTA (Question 4) | Have students draw a simple cause-and-effect diagram. Ask them to complete the chart by listing the goals of NAFTA as causes and its effects. |

## Answers

**Analyzing Charts** These jobs require either college degrees or training beyond high school to meet the qualifications.

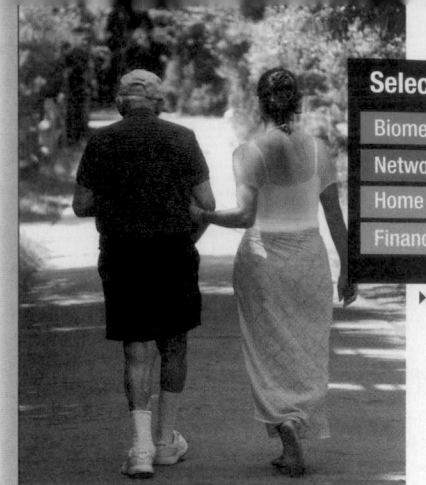

## Selected Fast-Growing Occupations Projected increase 2008–2018

| | |
|---|---|
| Biomedical engineer +11,600 | +72% |
| Network systems and data communications analyst +156,000 | +53% |
| Home health aide +461,000 | +50% |
| Financial examiners +11,100 | +41% |

**Source:** The Bureau of Labor Statistics

▶▶ **Analyzing Charts** The Bureau of Labor Statistics estimates that these occupational fields will see high growth over this ten-year period. *How can education help people prepare to fill these jobs?*

increased globalization. Along with the United States, most nations are joining multiple trade alliances, such as NAFTA and the EU, to open new markets and promote free trade. Developing nations are working to diversify their economies and open their markets. The United States continues to build partnerships by establishing new trade agreements with nations such as Peru, South Korea, Singapore, and Colombia and working with China to lower the U.S. trade deficit with that nation.

The good news for Americans is that the huge increase in the demand for services worldwide means that the United States will probably continue to see an increase in service exports and retain its position as the global leader in that area. Unfortunately,

the increase in free trade and outsourcing to emerging nations means further loss of manufacturing jobs. Although economic analysts have mixed views about the overall cost in American jobs due to outsourcing, thousands or even millions of jobs could move overseas in the coming years. Federal programs such as Trade Adjustment Assistance, which retrains workers who are laid off due to outsourcing or foreign competition, will help American workers deal with this challenge.

As the economy shifts toward services, the United States will need to rely on intellectual property as much as on exported goods. Among other important challenges and issues the United States government must face in the future are the protection of American copyrights and patents against piracy and the need to foster stability in oil-producing nations and regions.

**Essential Questions Journal** To continue to build a response to the chapter Essential Question, go to your **Essential Questions Journal.**

## SECTION 3 ASSESSMENT

1. **Guiding Question** Use your completed outline to answer this question: How does the Federal Government support economic growth at home and abroad?

### Key Terms and Comprehension

2. What is the basic structure and role of the Federal Reserve System?

3. Briefly identify and define the three main **protectionist** tools available to a national government.

### Critical Thinking

4. **Summarize (a)** What are the goals of NAFTA? **(b)** How has NAFTA affected different people in different ways?

5. **Draw Inferences** How might the U.S. benefit from participating in the World Bank, the G8, and the WTO?

### Quick Write

**Expository Writing: Create an Outline** To help you structure a compare-and-contrast essay on two different economic systems, create an outline in which you identify each area of comparison and contrast in a single phrase. When you are ready to write your essay, you can use the outline as a guide. Or, you may create a flowchart to help you organize and order your ideas.

**700** Comparative Economic Systems

---

# Assessment Answers

**1.** Through various departments and agencies, the U.S. government regulates the economy. For example, the Federal Reserve uses monetary policy to promote price stability, full employment, and economic growth. The Securities and Exchange Commission oversees stock markets. The Department of Labor ensures workplace fairness and safety. The Federal Government uses tariffs and quotas to protect domestic industry. It also works through free-trade agreements and membership in several international organizations, such as the World Bank, to expand global trade and strengthen the U.S. economy.

**2.** The Federal Reserve is run by a board of governors appointed by the President, one of whom is the chairperson. It consists of 12 regional banks and many other member banks. Its main role is to promote price stability, full employment, economic growth, and other national economic goals.

**3. tariff:** a tax on imported goods; **import quota:** a limit on the amount of a commodity that may be imported; **trade embargo:** a ban on trade with one or more countries

**4. (a)** to create a free-trade zone in North

America **(b)** It was good for trade and investment, but not positive for many American workers, especially in manufacturing, although trade in agricultural products increased.

**5.** The U.S. can benefit by having a say in important international activities and agreements regulating or increasing global trade, which will keep its economy strong.

**QUICK WRITE** Outlines should be in correct outline form and cover the comparisons and contrasts between the two economic systems appropriately and logically.

# Quick Study Guide

**GOVERNMENT** ONLINE
**On the Go**
To review anytime, anywhere, download these online resources at **PearsonSchool.com/phgovt**
Political Dictionary, Audio Review

**CHAPTER 23**

**Guiding Question**
**Section 2** What is the role of government under socialism and communism?

**Guiding Question**
**Section 1** What is the role of government in the American economy?

**CHAPTER 23**
**Essential Question**
To what extent should governments participate in the economy?

**Guiding Question**
**Section 3** How does the Federal Government support economic growth at home and abroad?

**Free Enterprise**
- Private ownership of land, labor, and capital
- Limited government participation
- Free markets and prices
- Competition among entrepreneurs

**Socialism**
- Some private businesses, property
- Democratic government

**Communism**
- No private property or businesses
- Dictatorship

- State owns big industries
- Welfare state
- Planned economy

### Political Dictionary

capitalism *p. 678*
factors of production *p. 678*
capital *p. 678*
entrepreneur *p. 679*
free enterprise system *p. 679*
free market *p. 679*
law of supply and demand *p. 681*
monopoly *p. 681*
laissez-faire theory *p. 682*
*The Communist Manifesto* *p. 685*
socialism *p. 686*
communism *p. 686*
welfare state *p. 687*
command economy *p. 687*
five-year plan *p. 689*
collectivization *p. 689*
privatization *p. 690*
Great Leap Forward *p. 690*
globalization *p. 695*
protectionism *p. 696*
tariff *p. 696*
import quota *p. 696*
trade embargo *p. 697*
NAFTA *p. 697*
World Trade Organization (WTO) *p. 697*

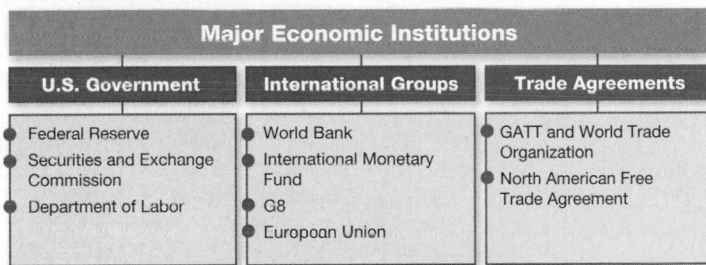

### Major Economic Institutions

| U.S. Government | International Groups | Trade Agreements |
|---|---|---|
| • Federal Reserve | • World Bank | • GATT and World Trade Organization |
| • Securities and Exchange Commission | • International Monetary Fund | • North American Free Trade Agreement |
| • Department of Labor | • G8 | |
| | • European Union | |

## For More Information

To learn more about comparative economic systems, refer to these sources or assign them to students:

**L1 Jarnow, Jesse.** *Socialism: A Primary Source Analysis.* Rosen Publishing Group, 2004.

**L2 Kowalski, Kathiann M.** *Free Trade* (Open for Debate). Marshall Cavendish Children's Books, 2007.

**L3 Marx, Karl, Friedrich Engels, and Gareth Stedman Jones, ed.** *The Communist Manifesto.* Penguin Classics, 2002.

**L4 Gregory, Paul R.** *The Political Economy of Stalinism: Evidence from the Soviet Secret Archives.* Cambridge University Press, 2003.

Have students download the digital resources available at Government on the Go for review and remediation.

### STUDY TIPS

**Consistent Notebook Organization** An organized notebook is an important study tool. Suggest that students consider using one large notebook with dividers. The advantage of this approach is less time spent searching for the right notebook or discovering that students have left the notebook they need at home, at school, or in their lockers. Many find that a three-ring binder works best, because pages can easily be added or removed, and homework papers and tests can be punched for inclusion. Make sure students use the tab dividers in the notebook so they can easily find the subject they need; organizing the sections in order of their schedule is one option. Recommend that students include a separate section for listing homework assignments, so they don't have to page through each subject to find their assignments. A front pocket is handy for keeping homework assignments. Have students go through their notebooks weekly to discard old papers and make sure the pages are in the right sections.

### ASSESSMENT AT A GLANCE

**Tests and Quizzes**
Section Assessments
Section Quizzes A and B, Unit 6 **All-in-One**
Chapter Assessment
Chapter Tests A and B, Unit 6 **All-in-One**
Document-Based Assessment
Progress Monitoring Online
Exam*View* Test Bank

**Performance Assessment**
Essential Questions Journal
Debates, pp. 687, 699
Assessment Rubrics, **All-in-One**

# Chapter Assessment

**COMPREHENSION AND CRITICAL THINKING**

## SECTION 1

**1. (a)** land, labor, and capital **(b)** The factors of production are the basic resources used to make all goods and services in any economic system.

**2. (a)** Competition keeps prices low and quality high. **(b)** Businesses may become monopolies, which can lead to higher prices and less innovation. **(c)** It can regulate the market to prevent the formation of monopolies and price fixing.

**3. (a)** carry out foreign relations and defend the country; protect private property, public health, safety, and morals; carry out other tasks that private companies cannot carry out profitably **(b)** Answers will vary; students should support their opinions with reasoned arguments and details from the text.

## SECTION 2

**4. (a)** Under capitalism, the proletariat—workers—are oppressed by the bourgeoisie—those who own the capital. Capitalists maintain their power and privilege through the state, its government, and social institutions. **(b)** Both systems seek to redistribute wealth that, in capitalism, is concentrated in one group, establish economic equality, and see to it that all citizens have their basic needs met.

**5. (a)** Answers include: nationalization of industries, a welfare state, high tax rates, and central planning. **(b)** a strong Communist Party, central planning, collective agriculture, and state ownership of industry and property **(c)** In a Communist country, government does not just participate, it controls the economy to a much greater degree than in a socialist country.

**6. (a)** Possible response: Yes. Profit motivates individuals to show initiative, take risks, and work hard. Under communism and, to a lesser extent socialism, people keep little of what they earn and their basic needs are met without taking initiative, so they are less motivated to do so. **(b)** Answers will vary but might allude to the removal of individual choice in a command economy, in which the government controls the economy and how it will develop.

## SECTION 3

**7. (a)** Through various departments and agencies, the U.S. government regulates

---

# Chapter Assessment

## Comprehension and Critical Thinking

### Section 1

1. **(a)** What are the three **factors of production?** **(b)** What role do the factors of production play in the economy?

2. **(a)** Why is competition important in a **free market** economy? **(b)** What might happen in a market without competition? **(c)** How might government promote competition?

3. **(a)** According to **laissez-faire theory,** what are the three major concerns of government? **(b)** Do you think this amounts to too little, too much, or just about the right amount of involvement by government? Why?

### Section 2

4. **(a)** Briefly explain Karl Marx's basic ideas about **capitalism.** **(b)** In what sense are **socialism** and **communism** a response to capitalism?

5. **(a)** What are three characteristics of socialist countries? **(b)** What are four characteristics of communist countries? **(c)** How does government participation in the economy vary in the two systems?

6. **(a)** Many people say that **socialism** and **communism** discourage individual initiative. Is this criticism valid? Why or why not? **(b)** How does **capitalism** differ from **command economies** in the treatment of the individual?

### Section 3

7. **(a)** Summarize the role of the Federal Government in the American economy. **(b)** Describe how three institutions of the Federal Government help carry out this role.

8. **Analyzing Cartoons** This cartoon features a candidate's stand on tariffs on steel. **(a)** Why would steel workers and auto workers have different views on steel tariffs? **(b)** What does this say about the effect of tariffs on jobs? **(c)** Does the cartoon take a favorable, an opposed, or a neutral position on free trade?

ARE YOU FOR STEEL TARIFFS TO HELP THE STEEL WORKERS OR AGAINST THEM TO HELP THE AUTO WORKERS?

### Writing About Government

9. Use your Quick Write exercises from the section assessments in this chapter to write an essay that compares and contrasts the two topics you selected. Make sure that the information is accurate and that comparisons are reasoned and relevant. End your essay with a summarizing conclusion. See pp. S3–S5 in the Skills Handbook.

### Apply What You've Learned

10. **Essential Question Activity** In small groups, meet with a business owner in your community. Ask:
    **(a)** How do you think the American system of government supports or encourages economic freedom?
    **(b)** How does a free market help your business?
    **(c)** In what ways do you think your life and your business would be different in a socialist or communist system?
    **(d)** Do you think that the Federal Government should be more or less involved in the economy, workers' rights, and social welfare?

11. **Essential Question Assessment** Based on the interview you conducted, write a political statement that expresses the views of this business owner about the relationship between economic and political freedom and the role of government in the economy. Discuss your ideas with your classmates to help you answer the Essential Question: **To what extent should governments participate in the economy?**

**Essential Questions Journal** To respond to the chapter Essential Question, go to your **Essential Questions Journal.**

---

the domestic marketplace to ensure fairness, workplace safety, a minimum wage, and fair hiring practices, and it regulates prices and inflation via the Federal Reserve. It also works through its membership in several international organizations, such as the World Bank, to expand global trade to increase jobs and strengthen the U.S. economy. **(b)** Possible response: The Federal Reserve promotes price stability, full employment, and economic growth mainly through adjusting the federal funds rate. The Security and Exchange Commission oversees the nation's stock markets to prevent abuses such as insider trading. The Department of Labor provides protections for the rights of workers and oversees fairness and safety in the workplace.

**8. (a)** The steel tariff is relatively high so that the U.S. steel industry and its workers are protected. However, a high steel tariff could lead to higher auto prices, which could hurt autoworkers. **(b)** A tariff could have both positive and negative effects on jobs, depending on the industries involved. **(c)** Possible answer: The cartoon is neutral because it recognizes that free trade has both positive and negative effects.

# Document-Based Assessment

## Government and the Economy

As the United States approached its entry into World War II, President Franklin Roosevelt defined "four freedoms" government should protect, as shown in Document 1. While many question how far the government should intervene in the economy, the Federal Government often acts to influence business trends, as in Document 3.

### Document 1

"[W]e look forward to a world founded upon four essential human freedoms. The first is freedom of speech and expression—everywhere in the world. The second is freedom of every person to worship God in his own way—everywhere in the world. The third is freedom from want—which, translated into world terms, means economic understandings which will secure to every nation a healthy peacetime life for its inhabitants—everywhere in the world. The fourth is freedom from fear—which, translated into world terms, means a world-wide reduction of armaments to such a point and in such a thorough fashion that no nation will be in a position to commit an act of physical aggression against any neighbor—anywhere in the world.

—President Franklin D. Roosevelt,
"The Four Freedoms" State of the Union Address,
January 6, 1941

### Document 2

I'm going to cut taxes, increase social spending and balance the budget. All you have to do is turn rocks into gold.

© Thaves THAVES

### Document 3

*In 2008, President George W. Bush sought to boost the nation's flagging economy by sending most American taxpayers a payment of several hundred dollars.*

"This growth package must be big enough to make a difference in an economy as large and dynamic as ours . . . This growth package must be built on broad-based tax relief that will directly affect economic growth—and not the kind of spending projects that would have little immediate impact on our economy. This growth package must be temporary and take effect right away—so we can get help to our economy when it needs it most. And this growth package must not include any tax increases. . . . We're in the midst of a challenging period, and I know Americans are concerned about our economic future. But our economy has seen challenging times before—and it is resilient. In a vibrant economy, markets rise and decline. We cannot change that fundamental dynamic. As a matter of fact, eliminating risk altogether would also eliminate the innovation and productivity that drives the creation of jobs and wealth in America.

— Presidential address, January 18, 2008

Use your knowledge of government's role in the economy and Documents 1, 2, and 3 to answer Questions 1–3.

1. In his speech, Franklin Roosevelt expressed the idea that
   A. all nations should govern their people in the same way as does the United States.
   B. the most important long-term goal of all nations should be rearmament.
   C. it is the responsibility of government to ensure the welfare of all of its citizens.
   D. the global political situation is very dangerous and no one is secure.

2. How did President Bush characterize downturns in the American economy?

3. **Pull It Together** Do you think that Mr. Bush's economic growth plan met the third freedom described by FDR? Why or why not?

 **GOVERNMENT ONLINE**
**Go Online**
To find more primary sources about the economy, visit
PearsonSchool.com/phgovt

---

## DOCUMENT-BASED ASSESSMENT

1. C

2. He sees economic downturns as part of the rise and fall of markets in a vibrant economy, and believes that risk is necessary to achieve innovation and productivity.

3. Possible answer: I believe that Bush's plan is less far-reaching and temporary, compared to Roosevelt's idea that government has the responsibility to intervene in the economy in order to ensure citizens' welfare.

**L2 Differentiate** Students use all the documents on the page to support their thesis.

**L3 Differentiate** Students include additional information available online at **PearsonSchool .com/phgovt.**

**L4 Differentiate** Students use materials from the textbook, the online information at **PearsonSchool .com/phgovt,** and do additional research to support their views.

**Go Online to PearsonSchool.com/phgovt** for a student rubric and extra documents.

---

## WRITING ABOUT GOVERNMENT

9. Essays should compare and contrast two economic systems and end with a summarizing conclusion.

## APPLY WHAT YOU'VE LEARNED

10. Responses should summarize the interviewee's answers.

11. Students' statements should include the views of the interviewee on economic freedom and the role of the government in the economy, as well as their own ideas about the connections between economic and political freedom.

Before assigning these questions, distribute the Rubric for Assessing a Writing Assignment (Unit 6 All-in-One, p. 102). Use the criteria and the guidelines below to grade students' answers to the Essential Question Warmup questions. Then send students to the **Essential Questions Journal** to answer the unit Essential Question.

**1.** A strong answer will give a coherent and well-considered definition of needs.

**2.** A strong answer will demonstrate the student's understanding of various political systems and historical events. It will also explain how specific leaders or nations approached the well-being of the people.

**3.** A good answer will state a position on whether a single person or party can understand and identify the needs of a people and why it would or would not. It will explain the reasons why such governments have often been unresponsive to people's needs in the past.

**4.** To answer this question successfully, students must identify the aspects of a free market system that address the collective needs. Further, students may find it necessary to address the definition of *need* in context.

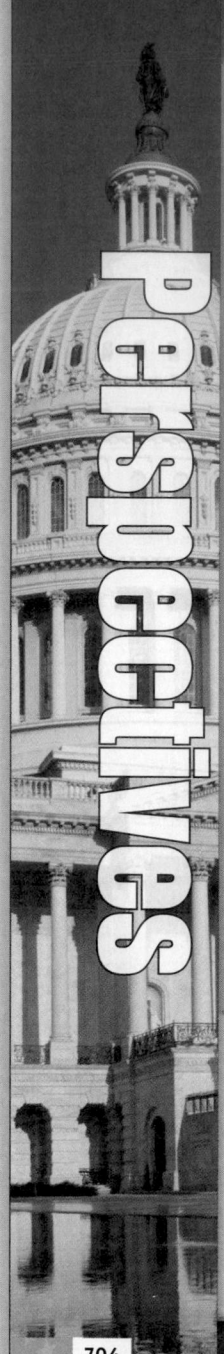

### Essential Question

# How should a government meet the needs of its people?

The nearly 200 sovereign states in the world today identify the needs of their people in different ways and disagree on how or to what extent government should attempt to meet those needs.

#### ON THE LIMITS OF GOVERNMENT:

Conservatives know that governments don't have all the answers. But if they govern with the right values, they can make a real difference.

—UK Conservative Party Manifesto, 2005

#### ON MEASURING THE IMPROVEMENT IN LIVES:

## Prosperity Indicators, U.S.

|  | 1950 | 2009 |
|---|---|---|
| Life Expectancy at Birth (years) | 68.2 | 78.2 (est.) |
| Per Capita Gross Domestic Product (constant 2000 dollars) | $11,720* | $46,000 |
| Population with Bachelor's Degree or higher, ages 25 and up | 6.2% | 29.5% |

*approximate

By most measures, Americans are healthier, better educated, and more affluent today than in the past.

#### ON THE RESPONSIBILITIES OF A COMMUNIST PARTY:

Without the efforts of the Chinese Communist Party . . . as the mainstay of the Chinese people, China can never achieve independence and liberation, or industrialization and the modernization of her agriculture.

—Mao Zedong, 1945

### Essential Question Warmup

Throughout this unit, you studied the history and ideas behind political systems and economic systems around the world. Use what you have learned and the quotations, data, and opinions above to answer the following questions. Then go to your **Essential Questions Journal.**

**1.** How would you define "the needs of the people"?

**2.** How might other nations, and specific leaders in history, define "the needs of the people" differently?

**3.** Can a country led by a single party or person successfully represent a country's people?

**4.** How does a free market economy help meet people's needs?

| **Essential Questions Journal** | To continue to build a response to the chapter Essential Question, go to your **Essential Questions Journal.** |
|---|---|

# Assessment Resources

Unit 6 AYP Monitoring Assessment
Exam*View* Test Bank CD-ROM
SuccessTracker Assessment
Online Student Self-Tests
Chapter Tests
Section Quizzes
Chapter-level Document-Based Assessment

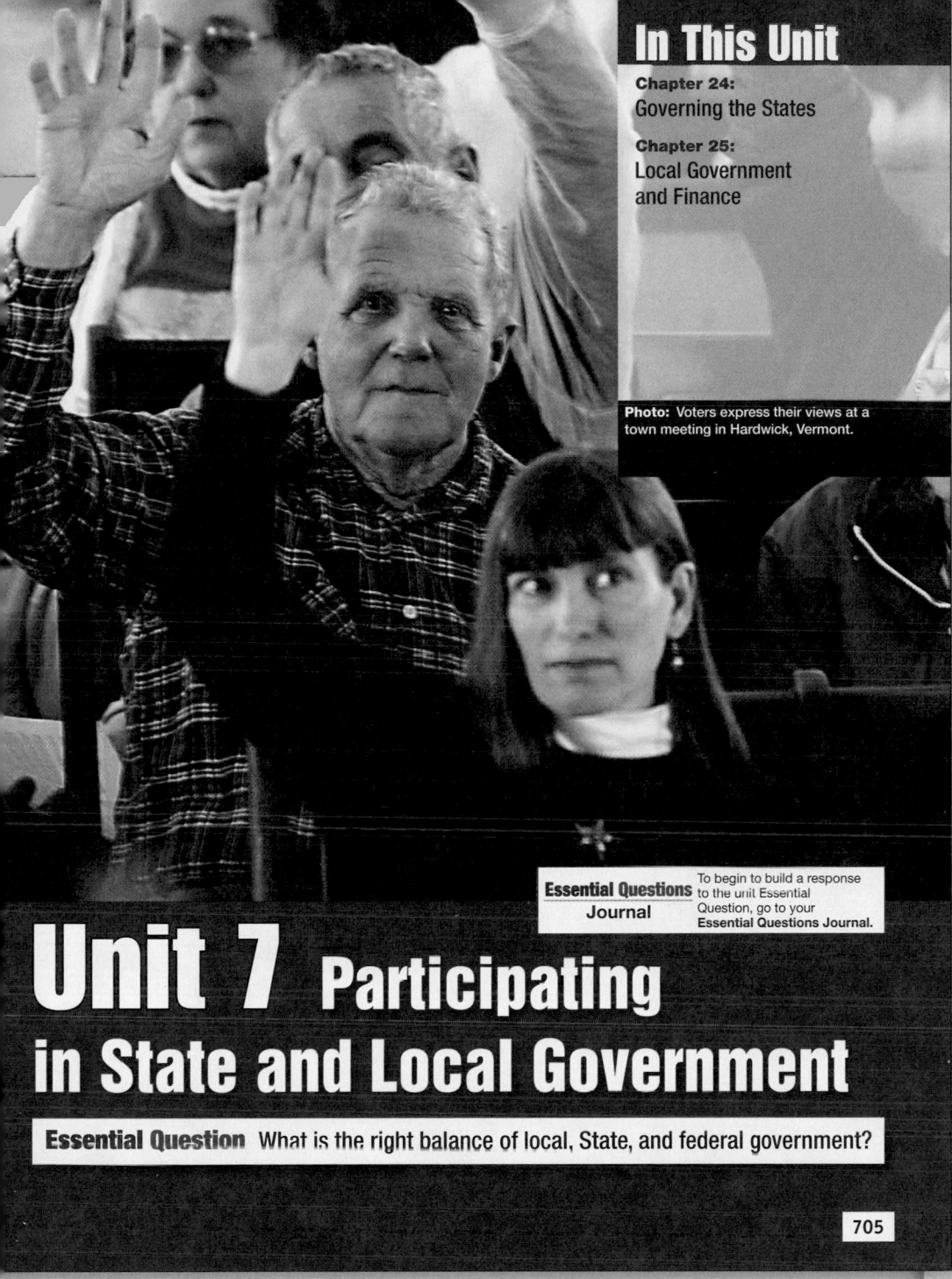

## In This Unit

**Chapter 24:**
Governing the States

**Chapter 25:**
Local Government
and Finance

**Photo:** Voters express their views at a town meeting in Hardwick, Vermont.

**Essential Questions Journal**

To begin to build a response to the unit Essential Question, go to your **Essential Questions Journal.**

# Unit 7 Participating in State and Local Government

**Essential Question** What is the right balance of local, State, and federal government?

## Government Online Resources

Government Online Teacher Center at **PearsonSchool.com/phgovt** includes
- Online Teacher's Edition with lesson planner and lecture notes
- Teacher's Resource Library with All-in-One Resources, Color Transparencies, Adequate Yearly Progress Monitoring, and an alternative lesson plan for each chapter
- SuccessTracker Assessment

Government Online Student Center at **PearsonSchool.com/phgovt** includes
- Interactive textbook with audio
- American Government Essential Questions Video
- Chapter-level WebQuests
- Guided Audio Tours and Interactivities
- Student Self-Tests

**ESSENTIAL QUESTION PERSPECTIVES**

Essential questions frame each unit and chapter of study, asking students to consider big ideas about government. The question for this unit—**What is the right balance of local, State, and federal government?**—demands that students ask further questions. What does each level of government do now? How responsive is each level of government to citizens? How do different levels of government work with or against each other? How and why has the balance of power evolved over time?

To begin this unit, assign the Unit 7 Warmup Activity on page 202 of the **Essential Questions Journal.** This will help students start to consider their position on the **Unit 7 Essential Question: What is the right balance of local, State, and federal government?**

Show the **Unit 7 American Government Essential Questions Video** to help students begin thinking about the unit Essential Question and designate a classroom bulletin board for students to post news articles related to the unit Essential Question. Use the Conversation Wall strategy (p. T27) to encourage students to post articles and comments on other students' postings.

Later, students will further explore the chapter-level essential questions:

*Chapter 24:* **How much power should State government have?**

*Chapter 25:* **How local should government be?**

Use the **Essential Questions Journal** throughout the program to help students consider these and other big ideas about government.

# Introduce the Chapter

## Essential Questions:

**UNIT 7**

What is the right balance of federal, State, and local government?

**CHAPTER 24**

How much power should State government have?

**ACTIVATE PRIOR KNOWLEDGE** Have students examine the photo and quotation on these pages. Ask: **What do the photo and quotation suggest about the relationship between State governments and the Federal Government?** *(that strong State governments together create a strong Federal Government)* In this chapter, students will learn about the elements of State governments. Then tell students to begin to further explore these topics by completing the Chapter 24 Essential Question Warmup activity in their **Essential Questions Journal.** Discuss their responses as a class.

**BEFORE READING**

**L2** **ELL Differentiate** Chapter 24 Prereading and Vocabulary Worksheet (Unit 7 All-in-One, p. 11)

**SUCCESSNET STUDENT AND TEACHER CENTER**

Visit **PearsonSchool.com/phgovt** for downloadable resources that allow students and teachers to connect with government "on the go."

**DIGITAL LESSON PRESENTATION**

The digital lesson presentation supports the print lesson with activities and summaries of key concepts.

---

## SKILLS DEVELOPMENT

### PROBLEM SOLVING

You may wish to teach problem solving as a distinct skill within Section 3 of this chapter. Use the Chapter 24 Skills Worksheet (Unit 7 All-in-One, p. 37) to help students learn how to solve problems. The worksheet asks students to explore issues of public trust in State government. For L2 and L1 students, assign the adapted Skill Activity (Unit 7 All-in-One, p. 38).

**WebQuest online** The chapter WebQuest challenges students to answer the chapter Essential Question by asking them about State governments.

706

## Block Scheduling

**BLOCK 1:** Teach the Section 1, 2, and 3 lessons, omitting the Section 1 discussion of federalism and the Section 2 discussion of legislative and non-legislative powers. In Section 3, omit the mock executive meeting. Omit the Extend options for all sections.

**BLOCK 2:** Teach the Section 4 and 5 lessons, omitting the Extend options for Section 4. Assign the Extend option for Section 5.

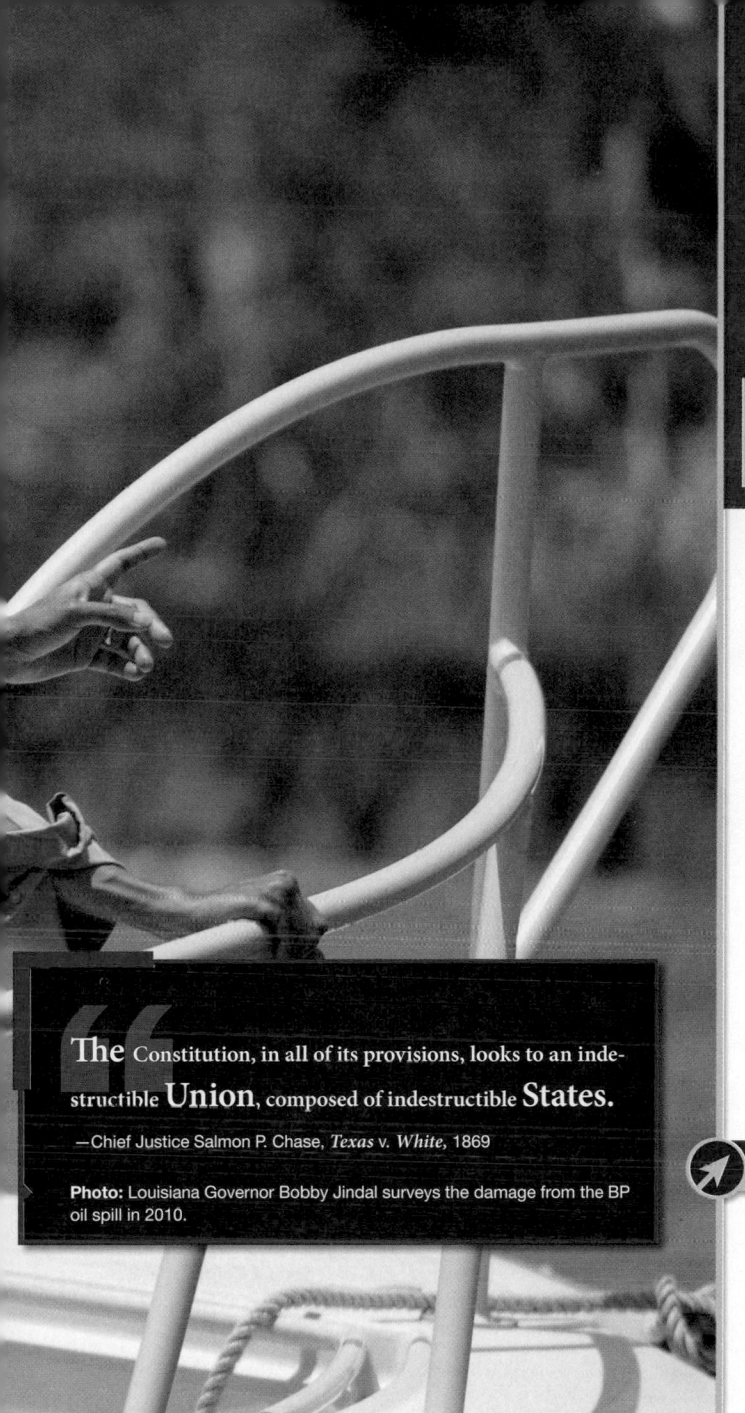

" The Constitution, in all of its provisions, looks to an inde-structible Union, composed of indestructible States.

—Chief Justice Salmon P. Chase, *Texas v. White*, 1869

**Photo:** Louisiana Governor Bobby Jindal surveys the damage from the BP oil spill in 2010.

### GOVERNMENT ONLINE
On the Go

To study anywhere, anytime, download these online resources at PearsonSchool.com/phgovt
• Political Dictionary
• Audio Review
• Downloadable Interactivities

707

## Lesson Goals

**SECTION 1**

Students will . . .

- examine the origins, features, and purposes of State constitutions through discussion of the six main principles of State constitutions.
- analyze their State constitution and complete a chart identifying areas for reform.
- discuss federalism and locate supporting information in the U.S. Constitution.

**SECTION 2**

Students will . . .

- compare and contrast features of State legislatures with those of the U.S. Congress.
- identify and rank the main powers of State legislatures and provide examples of each.
- discuss how State legislatures influence the lives of citizens and how citizens influence lawmaking.

**SECTION 3**

Students will . . .

- complete a chart to examine the powers of a State governor.
- complete a worksheet to compare and contrast State governorships with the U.S. presidency.
- participate in a mock meeting to investigate the roles and responsibilities of State executive officers.

**SECTION 4**

Students will . . .

- demonstrate knowledge of the five forms of law by completing a concept web.
- compare and contrast features of criminal versus civil law.
- analyze summaries of court cases.

**SECTION 5**

Students will . . .

- discuss the positive and negative aspects of electing or appointing judges.
- evaluate methods of judge selection by reading primary sources and through participation in a Socratic Dialogue.

## Pressed for Time

To cover the chapter quickly, have students describe the basic structure and function of the Federal Government (the three branches, the executive leader, the courts, and so on). As they do so, create a concept web on the board. As you discuss each part of the structure, describe how that structure applies to State governments, including the fact that each is based on a written constitution. Explain the powers of each branch of State government. Ask students to re-create the concept web from the board in their notebooks, title it "State Governments," and add details to each part as they read Sections 2–5.

---

**DIFFERENTIATED INSTRUCTION KEY**

Look for these symbols to help you adjust steps in each lesson to meet your students' needs.

**L1** Special Needs

**L2** Basic

  **ELL** English Language Learners
  **LPR** Less Proficient Readers

**L3** All Students

**L4** Advanced Students

## What are the defining features of State constitutions?

I. The First State Constitutions
  A. Independence
    1. first modeled on colonial charters
    2. most today became effective after popular vote
  B. Principles of State constitutions
    1. popular sovereignty; limited government
    2. bill of rights; separation of powers; checks and balances; bicameral
II. State Constitutions Today
  A. Basic Principles
    1. popular sovereignty and limited government
    2. separation of powers; checks and balances
  B. Bill of rights
  C. Structure of State and local government
  D. Powers and processes
  E. Process for constitutional change
  F. Miscellaneous provisions
    1. preamble—purpose
    2. schedule for putting into effect
    3. dead letter provisions—no current effect
III. Constitutional Change
  A. Procedures for Change
    1. steps: proposal; then ratification
    2. conventions for revision
    3. amendment proposed by legislature or initiative
  B. Ratification of Amendments—usually majority vote
IV. Need for Reform
  A. many State constitutions are too long
  B. fail to distinguish fundamental from statutory law
  C. outdated

## SKILLS DEVELOPMENT

### ANALYZE SOURCES

To help students learn to analyze sources, have them turn to the Skills Handbook, p. S14, and use the information there to assist them in examining their State constitution for the Extend Worksheet activity.

---

SECTION **1**

# State Constitutions

## Guiding Question

**What are the defining features of State constitutions?** Use an outline to take notes on the defining qualities of State constitutions.

**I. The First State Constitutions**
  **A. Independence**
    1. _____
    2. _____
  **B.** _____
    1. _____
    2. _____

## Political Dictionary

- popular sovereignty
- limited government
- fundamental law
- initiative
- statutory law

## Objectives

1. Examine the history, content, and significance of the first State constitutions.
2. Describe the basic principles common to all State constitutions today.
3. Explain the procedures used to change State constitutions.
4. Analyze why State constitutions are in need of reform.

**Image Above:** Massachusetts constitution of 1780

Not very many people have ever seen a State constitution, let alone read one. Join a rather exclusive club and look at your State's document. This step should prove useful as you read this chapter.

A State constitution is that State's supreme law. It sets out the ways in which the government of the State is organized, and it distributes powers among the various branches of that government. It authorizes the exercise of power by government and, at the same time, puts limits on the exercise of power by government. Every State's constitution is superior to any and all other forms of State and local law within that State.

Recall, however: Each State's constitution is subordinate to the Constitution of the United States. No provision in any State's constitution may conflict with any form of federal law.

## The First State Constitutions

Each of the 50 States has a *written* constitution. From the beginning, government in this country has been based on written constitutions.

Our experience with such documents dates from 1606, when King James I granted a charter to the Virginia Company. That act led to the settlement at Jamestown in the following year and, with it, the first government in what would become British North America. Later, each of the other English colonies was also established and governed on the basis of a written charter.

**Independence** When the 13 colonies became independent, each faced the problem of establishing a new government. On May 15, 1776, the Second Continental Congress, meeting in Philadelphia, advised each of the new States to adopt

"such governments as shall, in the opinion of the representatives of the people, best conduce to the happiness and safety of their constituents in particular, and America in general."

—Second Continental Congress

---

# Focus on the Basics

Here is the information that your students need to learn in this section.

**FACTS:** • The first State constitutions emerged from colonial charters and the revolutionary experience. • State constitutions outline the governments' basic principles, protect civil rights, define the structure of State government and its functions, and include procedures for amendment. • State constitutions can be changed by formal amendment or revision, usually with approval by popular vote.

**CONCEPTS:** constitutional government, fundamental law, initiative

**ENDURING UNDERSTANDINGS:** • Every State has a unique written constitution that defines the State's government and values. • Many State constitutions need reform to remove outdated and confusing provisions.

Most of the colonial charters served as models for the first State constitutions. Indeed, in Connecticut and Rhode Island, the charters seemed so well suited to the needs of the day that they were carried over into statehood as constitutions almost without change.[1]

The earliest State constitutions were adopted in a variety of ways. However, the people played no direct part in the process in any State.

Six of the revolutionary legislatures drew up new documents and proclaimed them in force in 1776. In none of those States—Maryland, New Jersey, North Carolina, Pennsylvania, South Carolina, and Virginia—was the new constitution offered to the people for their judgment.

In Delaware and New Hampshire in 1776, and in Georgia and New York in 1777, the constitutions were prepared by conventions called by the legislature. In each case, the new document had to be approved by the legislature in order to become effective, but in none was popular approval required.

In 1780, a popularly elected convention prepared a new constitution for Massachusetts. It was then ratified by a vote of the people. Thus, Massachusetts set the pattern of popular participation in the constitution-making process, a pattern generally followed among the States ever since.[2]

Assemblies representing the people drafted all of the present State constitutions; most of them became effective only after a popular vote. Only the present-day documents of Delaware (1897), Mississippi (1890), South Carolina (1895), and Vermont (1793) came into force without popular ratification.

### Principles of State Constitutions

Because the first State constitutions came out of the same revolutionary <u>ferment</u>, they shared many basic features. Each proclaimed

the principles of **popular sovereignty** and **limited government.** That is, in each of them the people were recognized as the sole source of authority for government, and the powers given to the new government were closely limited. Seven documents began with a lengthy bill of rights. All of them made it clear that the sovereign people held "certain unalienable rights" that government must respect.

The doctrines of separation of powers and checks and balances were also built into each of the new constitutions. In practice, however, the memory of the hated royal governors was still fresh. Thus, most of the authority that each State government had was given to the legislature. For example, only New York, Massachusetts, and South Carolina allowed the governor to veto acts of the legislature. In all the States except Georgia (until 1789) and Pennsylvania (until 1790), the legislature was bicameral.[3]

For their time, the early State constitutions were fairly democratic. Each however, contained several provisions (and some important omissions) that were quite undemocratic by today's standards. Thus, none of them provided for full religious freedom. Each one set rigid qualifications for voting and for officeholding, and all gave property owners a highly favored standing.

### State Constitutions Today

The present-day State constitutions are the direct descendants of those earlier documents. Only 17 of the current State constitutions were written after 1900, and nearly all have been amended dozens of times.

Subject only to the broad limitations set out in the Federal Constitution, the people of each State can create whatever kind of "Republican Form of

✔ **Checkpoint**
Who drafted the first State constitutions?

<u>ferment</u>
*n.* a state of great change

State constitutions often specify designs for State symbols, including the State seal.

---

1 Connecticut's legislature did not write a new document until 1818, and Rhode Island's waited until 1842.

2 As we noted in Chapter 2, with independence Massachusetts relied on the colonial charter in force there prior to 1691 as its first State constitution. When New Hampshire adopted its second and (present) constitution in 1784, it followed the Massachusetts model of popular convention and popular ratification.

3 Vermont, which became the 14th State in 1791, had a unicameral legislature until 1830. Only Nebraska has a one-house legislative body today, and it has had one since 1937.

---

## Differentiated Resources

The following resources are located in the All-in-One, Unit 7, Chapter 24, Section 1:

**L2** Prereading and Vocabulary Worksheet (p. 11)

**L3** Reading Comprehension Worksheet (p. 15)

**L2** Reading Comprehension Worksheet (p. 16)

**L3** Core Worksheet (p. 17)

**L3 L4** Extend Worksheet (p. 19)

**L2** Extend Activity (p. 20)

**L3** Quiz A (p. 21)

**L2** Quiz B (p. 22)

---

# Get Started

### LESSON GOALS

Students will . . .

- examine the origins, features, and purposes of State constitutions through discussion of the six main principles of State constitutions.

- analyze their State constitution and complete a chart identifying areas for reform.

- discuss federalism and locate supporting information in the U.S. Constitution.

### BEFORE CLASS

Assign the section, the graphic organizer in the text, and the Reading Comprehension Worksheet (Unit 7 All-in-One, p. 15) before class.

**L2 Differentiate** Reading Comprehension Worksheet (Unit 7 All-in-One, p. 16)

### BELLRINGER

In their notebooks, ask students to answer this question: **Why do we have State constitutions as well as a U.S. Constitution?**

**L2 Differentiate** Rephrase the directions. Ask: **What does a State constitution do that the U.S. Constitution does not?** Allow students to use their textbooks for ideas.

**L2 ELL Differentiate** Suggest that students create a concept web to record their ideas about why we have State constitutions.

# Teach

To present this topic using online resources, use the lesson presentations at **PearsonSchool.com/phgovt.**

### INTRODUCE THE TOPIC

Ask students to share their ideas from the Bellringer activity about why State constitutions are needed. Examples may include: to set up State government, regulate the safety and welfare of citizens at the State level, limit the power of the State government, and pass and execute laws at the local level. Display Transparency 24A, Six Principles of State Constitutions. Have students describe each principle and explain why it is important for each to operate at the State level.

**L1 L2 ELL Differentiate** Clarify that a *principle* is "an important basic belief or idea." Point out the difference in spelling between *principle* and *principal.*

---

## Answers

**Checkpoint** Most were based on colonial charters and written by legislatures or conventions, without popular approval.

## DISTRIBUTE THE CORE WORKSHEET

Divide the class into pairs. Distribute copies of your State's constitution to students. (You may obtain copies of the constitution from governmental offices, such as the secretary of state, or online.) Then distribute Chapter 24 Section 1 Core Worksheet (Unit 7 All-in-One, p. 17). Either assign different sections of the constitution to each pair, or have all pairs read the entire document. Explain that they will learn about the nature of State constitutions and why reforms are needed by analyzing the constitution or their assigned section and completing the chart in the Core Worksheet.

**L1 L2 ELL Differentiate** You may wish to assign partners so that advanced or proficient students are paired with English language learners or less-proficient students. Check that students are sharing tasks fairly.

---

Name _____ Class _____ Date _____

**CHAPTER 24 SECTION 1** | CORE WORKSHEET
**State Constitutions** 3

**Analyzing a State Constitution**

Read the State constitution, or portion of it, that your teacher has assigned. As you read, analyze the document to identify areas where you think it should be changed or updated. Write your ideas in the chart below. Then answer the following questions.

| Suggested Change | Location in Constitution | Reason for Change |
|---|---|---|
|  |  |  |
|  |  |  |
|  |  |  |

1. When was this constitution written?

2. What historical events may have influenced the writers' feelings about government?

3. What rights are specifically protected?

4. What sort of language is used in this constitution? Is it difficult to understand? Who is the audience?

5. Does the document contradict itself? Explain.

6. What beliefs about society and government are reflected in this constitution?

Copyright © by Pearson Education, Inc., or its affiliates. All rights reserved.

---

**L3 Differentiate** Display Transparency 24B, The Appeals Process for appeals. Discuss with students how a State's constitution grants power to the courts and establishes processes for appeals. Ask students to speculate how the issue in the cartoon could be resolved by a State's constitution. *(The constitution could set limits on appeals.)*

## Answers

**Analyzing Charts** They all include basic principles of popular sovereignty, separation of powers, checks and balances; a bill of rights; structure and processes of government; powers of each branch; amendment process; and a preamble.

**Checkpoint** Most were written before 1900 and are direct descendants of earlier documents.

---

# Elements of State Constitutions

**PRINCIPLES**
- Popular sovereignty; power comes from the people
- Separation of powers
- Checks and balances

**CIVIL RIGHTS**
- Similar to U.S. Bill of Rights
- May guarantee right to education or gender equality

**STRUCTURE**
- Outline of State and local government
- Structure of governorship, legislature, and courts

▶▶ **Analyzing Charts** *How are the several State constitutions similar to the federal Constitution?*

✓ **Checkpoint**
When were most current State constitutions adopted?

Government" they choose. Unique provisions can be found in each of the 50 present-day State constitutions. Still, all of them are quite similar in general outline.

**Basic Principles** Every State's constitution is built on the principles of popular sovereignty and limited government. Each of them recognizes that government exists only with the consent of the people, and that it must operate within certain, often closely defined, bounds. In every State, the powers of government are divided among executive, legislative, and judicial branches. Each branch has powers with which it can restrain the actions of the other two. That is, each of the 50 documents proclaims separation of powers and, with it, checks and balances. Each also provides, either expressly or by implication, for the power of judicial review.

**Protections of Civil Rights** Each document features a bill of rights, a listing of the rights that individuals hold against the State and its officers and agencies. Most constitutions set out guarantees much like those in the first ten amendments to the national Constitution. Several of them include a number of other guarantees as well—for example, the right to self-government, to be safe from imprisonment for debt, and to organize labor unions and bargain collectively.

**Governmental Structure** Every State constitution deals with the structure of government at both the State and the local levels, including all three branches of State government and the organization of counties and local governments. A few follow the national pattern, providing only a broad outline. Most, however, cover the subject in considerable and often quite specific detail.

**Governmental Powers and Processes** Each document lists, in detail, the powers vested in the executive branch (the governor and other executive officers), the legislature, the courts, and the units of local government. The powers to tax, spend, borrow, and provide for education are very prominent. So, too, are such processes as elections, legislation, judicial procedures, and intergovernmental (State–local) relations.

**Constitutional Change** Constitutions are the product of human effort. None are perfect. Sooner or later, changes become necessary, or at least desirable. So, each State constitution sets out the means by which it may be revised or amended. Constitutions are **fundamental laws**—laws of such basic and lasting importance they cannot be changed as ordinary law can be. Constitutional changes are more difficult to bring about, as you shall see.

## Constitutional Principles

**LIMITED GOVERNMENT AND COLONIAL RULE** The principle of limited government in American State and National constitutions can be traced back to oppressive policies of British colonial rule. For example, the British Parliament claimed the right to impose taxes on the colonists, despite the fact that the colonists could not elect officials to represent them in the British Parliament. Britain required the colonists to house British troops in their homes. When the assembly in New York refused to agree to follow through with this demand, Parliament threatened to dissolve the assembly. For many colonists, the main purpose of the struggle for independence was to free themselves from what they saw as illegal and unfair policies. As a result, the colonists wrote many limits into the State and National constitutions to make sure that their new governments could not encroach on their rights in these ways.

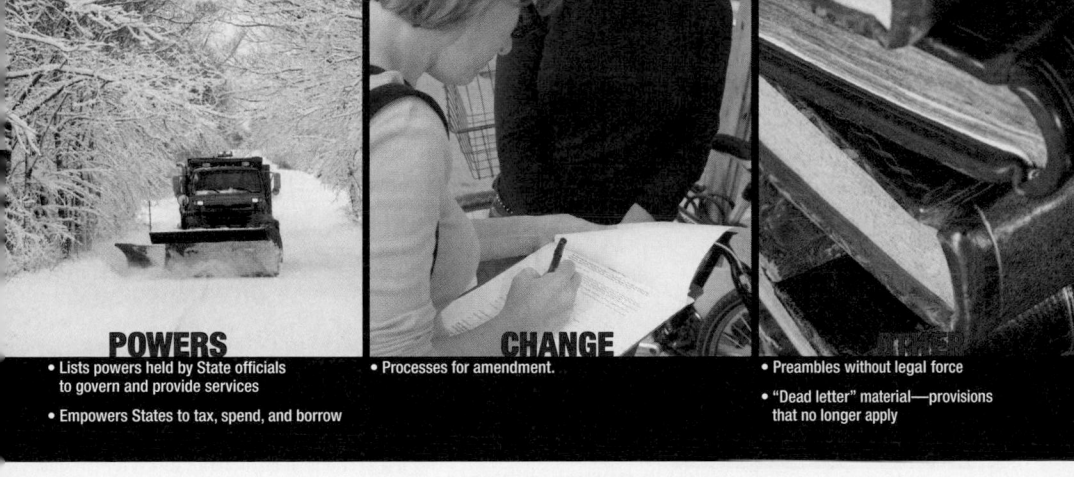

**POWERS**
- Lists powers held by State officials to govern and provide services
- Empowers States to tax, spend, and borrow

**CHANGE**
- Processes for amendment.

- Preambles without legal force
- "Dead letter" material—provisions that no longer apply

**Miscellaneous Provisions** Every State constitution contains several sections of a miscellaneous character. Thus, most begin with a preamble, which has no legal force but does set out the purposes of those who drafted and adopted the document. Most also contain a schedule, a series of provisions for putting a new document into effect and for avoiding conflicts with its predecessor. And most include a number of "dead letter" provisions, items that have no current force or effect but nonetheless remain a part of the constitution.

## Constitutional Change

Like the national Constitution, the State constitutions have been altered over time by formal amendment and by such other processes as court decisions and custom. However, those other processes have not been nearly so important at the State level as at the national level.

State constitutions are much less flexible, and much more detailed, than the national document. Constitutional change and development at the State level has come about mostly through formal amendment rather than by other means.

Two kinds of formal changes have been used: amendments, which usually deal with one or a few provisions in a constitution; and revisions, the term usually used to refer to changes of a broader scope. Revisions might

include, for example, an entirely new document. Most of the formal changes made in State constitutions are made by amendment.

**Procedures for Change** The process of formal change involves two basic steps: proposal and then ratification. Proposals for change can be made by a constitutional convention, the legislature, or (in several States) by the voters themselves. Ratification is by popular vote in every State except Delaware.

The constitutional convention is the usual device by which new constitutions have been written and older ones revised. More than 200 such conventions have been held. In every State the legislature has the power to call a convention, and that call is generally subject to voter approval. In 14 States the question of calling a convention must be submitted to the voters at regular intervals.[4] Conventions can also propose amendments. However, because they are both costly and time-consuming, conventions are most often used for the broader purpose of revision.

Most amendments are proposed by the legislature. The process is comparatively simple in some States, while it is quite difficult in others. In Massachusetts, an amendment must

---

[4] Every 20 years in Connecticut, Illinois, Maryland, Missouri, Montana, New York, Ohio, and Oklahoma; every 16 years in Michigan; every 10 years in Alaska, Iowa, New Hampshire, and Rhode Island; and every 9 years in Hawaii

✔**Checkpoint**
What are the six elements of State constitutions?

**miscellaneous**
*adj.* varying; not belonging to a single category

---

**DISCUSS FEDERALISM**
Wrap up this activity by discussing federalism and the need for both State and National governments. Have students examine the U.S. Constitution to identify at least five areas that outline or support the federal system. They should look for articles and amendments that describe the powers granted and denied to the National Government and powers reserved to the State Governments.

**EXTEND THE LESSON**

**L3** **L4** **Differentiate** Have students work individually or with a partner to complete Chapter 24 Section 1 Extend Worksheet (Unit 7 All-in-One, p. 19).

**L2** **Differentiate** Have students create a timeline that includes main events in the history and development of your State's constitution or the main events in the passage of a recent amendment. Timeline items might include the date when the constitution was ratified and the dates of major amendments or updates.

**L2** **ELL Differentiate** Have visual learners or English language learners design a mural that illustrates all six elements of State constitutions. For "miscellaneous provisions," encourage students to study your State's constitution for ideas.

**L2** **Differentiate** Distribute the Extend Activity "Finding Information About Your State" (Unit 7 All-in-One, p. 20), which has students research for data about their State.

## Background

**OLDEST AND NEWEST STATE CONSTITUTIONS** The Massachusetts constitution of 1780 and New Hampshire's constitution of 1784 are the oldest State constitutions still in force. In fact, the constitutions of these two States are older than all other written constitutions in effect in the world today. At the other extreme, Louisiana has adopted a new constitution 11 times since statehood in 1812, most recently in 1974. Georgia adopted its tenth and current constitution in 1983.

## Answers

**Checkpoint** basic principles of popular sovereignty and limited government; protections of civil rights; governmental structure; governmental powers and processes; methods for constitutional change; miscellaneous provisions

Tell students to go to the Audio Tour to listen to a guided audio tour of the "How Government Works: Amending State Constitutions" diagram.

## Assess and Remediate

**L3** Collect the Core Worksheets and assess students' work using the Rubric for Assessing a Graph, Chart, or Table (Unit 7 All-in-One, p. 124).

**L3** Assign the Section 1 Assessment questions.

**L3** Section Quiz A (Unit 7 All-in-One, p. 21)

**L2** Section Quiz B (Unit 7 All-in-One, p. 22)

Have students complete the review activities in the digital lesson presentation and continue their work in the **Essential Questions Journal.**

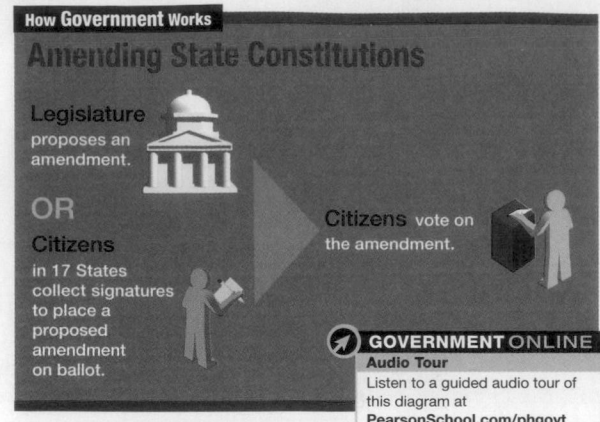

**How Government Works**

## Amending State Constitutions

**Legislature** proposes an amendment.

**OR**

**Citizens** in 17 States collect signatures to place a proposed amendment on ballot.

**Citizens** vote on the amendment.

**GOVERNMENT** ONLINE
Audio Tour
Listen to a guided audio tour of this diagram at
**PearsonSchool.com/phgovt**

▶▶ **Analyzing Diagrams** *How does the process for amending State constitutions reflect the idea of popular sovereignty?*

✔ **Checkpoint**
Describe the procedure for changing a State's constitution.

**obsolete**
*adj.* out of date

be approved by the legislature at two successive annual sessions before it goes to the voters for approval or rejection. In California, a proposal must be approved by the legislature at a single session before being sent on to the voters. Not surprisingly, more amendments are proposed (and adopted) in those States with simpler processes, such as California, than in States such as Massachusetts.

In 18 States the voters themselves can propose constitutional amendments through the **initiative,** a process in which a certain number of qualified voters sign petitions in favor of a proposal. The proposal then goes directly to the ballot, for approval or rejection by the people.

**Ratification of Amendments** In every State except Delaware, an amendment must be approved by vote of the people in order to become part of the constitution. The ratification process, like the proposal process, varies among the States.[5]

---

**5** In Delaware, if an amendment is approved by a two-thirds vote in each house of the legislature at two successive sessions, it becomes effective. In South Carolina, final ratification, after a favorable vote by the people, depends on a majority vote in both houses of the legislature. Both the Alabama and South Carolina constitutions provide that amendments of local, as opposed to Statewide, application need be approved only by the voters in the affected locale.

Typically, the approval of a majority of those voting on an amendment adds it to the State constitution, though some States require a majority of all who vote in an election. On many occasions, in several States, amendments have been defeated though they received more *yes* votes than *no* votes. Most often, this happens because many voters fail to vote on all or at least some ballot measures.

### The Need for Reform

Almost without exception, State constitutions are in urgent need of reform. The typical document is cluttered with unnecessary details, burdensome restrictions, and obsolete sections. It also carries much repetitious, even contradictory, material. Moreover, it fails to deal with many of the pressing problems that the States and their local governments currently face.

Even the newest and most recently rewritten constitutions tend to carry over a great deal of material from earlier documents and suffer from these same faults. The need for reform can be demonstrated in several ways. Looking at the documents from two standpoints, their lengths and their ages, can produce some useful insights.

**The Problem of Length** Length was not a problem for the first State constitutions. They were quite short, ranging from New Jersey's 1776 document (2,500 words) to the 1780 Massachusetts constitution (12,000 words). Those early constitutions were meant simply to be statements of basic principle and organization. Purposely, they left to the legislature—and to time and practice—the task of filling in the details as they became necessary.

Through the years, however, State constitutions have grown and grown. Most today are between 15,000 and 40,000 words. The shortest are those of New Hampshire (1784), with some 9,200 words, and Vermont (1793), with just over 10,200 words. At the other extreme, Alabama's 1901 constitution now runs to more than 340,000 words. A leading cause of this expansion is popular distrust of government, a historical and continuing fact of American political life. That distrust has often led to the insertion into State constitutions of detailed

## How Government Works

**PROPOSING A STATE CONSTITUTIONAL AMENDMENT** Have students apply the *How Government Works* diagram, "Amending State Constitutions," on this page to their own State. Working with the same partner, have student pairs select a proposed constitutional change they identified in their Core Worksheet. Ask them to write a description of the change on the form of proposed legislation. Then have them write a justification for the change that they would present to the voters to urge them to approve the amendment. For an interactive version of "Amending State Constitutions," go to **PearsonSchool.com/phgovt.**

---

## Answers

**Analyzing Diagrams** Amendments can be proposed by legislators, who are elected by the people, or by the people themselves. The people then vote on the proposed amendments.

**Checkpoint** Proposals for change can be made by a constitutional convention, the legislature, or an initiative of the people, with ratification by popular vote in every State except Delaware.

provisions aimed at preventing the misuse of government power.

Many restrictions on that power, which could be set out in ordinary law, have been purposely written into the State constitution, where they cannot be easily ignored or readily, and quietly, changed. Special interest groups learned long ago that public policies of particular benefit to them are much more secure in the State constitution than in a mere statute.

There has been a marked failure in every State to distinguish *fundamental law*, that which is basic and of lasting importance and should be in the constitution, from **statutory law,** that which should be enacted as ordinary law by the legislature. The line separating fundamental and statutory law may be blurry in some cases. But who can seriously argue that fundamental law includes the regulation of the length of wrestling matches, as in California's constitution, or the problem of off-street parking in the city of Baltimore, as in Maryland's document?

Two other factors have contributed to the growth of State constitutions. First, the functions performed by the States, and by most of their local governments, have multiplied over recent decades. That development has prompted many new constitutional provisions. Second, the "people" have not been stingy in the use of the initiative in those States where it is available.

**The Problem of Age** Most State constitutions are severely outdated. They were written for another time and are in urgent need of revision. All too often, their many amendments have aggravated the problem, adding to the clutter of the document.

The Oregon constitution provides a typical example of the situation. It was written by delegates to a territorial convention in 1857 and became effective when Oregon entered the Union in 1859. It has been amended more than 240 times; it now contains more than 55,000 words and includes *two* Articles VII and *seventeen* Articles XI!

Like most of the other State charters, the Oregon document is overloaded with statutory material. One of those Article XIs devotes nearly 2,000 words to a closely detailed treatment of veterans' farm and home loans. The document also contains a number of obsolete provisions, including one that bars any person who has ever engaged in a duel from holding any public office in the State.

Some States' charters have proved to be more stable than others. The oldest of all the constitutions are those in Massachusetts (1780), New Hampshire (1784), and Vermont (1793). Nineteen States still have the constitutions with which they entered the Union and, all told, 35 have documents that are now more than 100 years old.

A number of States have had several constitutions. Louisiana holds the record, with eleven. Georgia's current charter, its tenth, is the most recently rewritten document; it was adopted in 1982 and became effective the following year.

✓ **Checkpoint**
What are the two main problems of State constitutions today?

**REMEDIATION**

| If Your Students Have Trouble With | Strategies For Remediation |
|---|---|
| The defining features of State constitutions (Questions 1, 2) | Display Transparency 24A, Six Principles of State Constitutions. Have students copy the concept web in their notebooks and add details from the textbook. |
| Methods for changing State constitutions (Question 3) | Tell students to review the How Government Works diagram on page 712, "Amending State Constitutions." Ask them to summarize in their own words what the diagram shows. Alternatively, students may draw a flowchart with labels in their notebooks. |
| The basis of early State constitutions and governments (Question 4) | Describe some events and feelings that led to the American Revolution—the resentment over taxation without representation and other forced measures of the British government—and how those events affected those who wrote the new State constitutions. |
| Need for reform in State constitutions (Question 5) | Have students review the material under "The Need for Reform" and write a main idea for each paragraph. |

**Essential Questions Journal** To continue to build a response to the chapter Essential Question, go to your **Essential Questions Journal.**

# SECTION 1 ASSESSMENT

1. **Guiding Question** Use your completed outline to answer this question: What are the defining features of State constitutions?

**Key Terms and Comprehension**

2. Explain the concept of **popular sovereignty** as it applies to State governments.

3. (a) List and explain three ways changes to State constitutions may be proposed. (b) How are proposed changes ratified?

**Critical Thinking**

4. **Predict Consequences** Would early State governments have developed differently if they had not grown out of the experiences of the American Revolution?

5. **Draw Inferences** Why do you think that many State constitutions remain so lengthy and unnecessarily detailed and have so many outdated provisions?

**Quick Write**

**Explanatory Writing: Explore a Topic** Based on your prior knowledge and what you have read in this section, write at least three questions that explore the ways in which State governments affect your life. (You may also want to preview Sections 2–5 for additional questions.) For example, you might ask: Which have the most direct effect on individual citizens, State laws or federal laws?

## Answers

**Checkpoint** too long and out of date

# Assessment Answers

**1.** popular sovereignty and limited government; protection of civil rights; governmental structure; governmental powers and processes; process for constitutional change; miscellaneous provisions

**2.** The people of the State are the source of authority for the State's government.

**3. (a) By convention:** The legislature calls a constitutional convention to write a new State constitution or revise the existing one. **By the legislature:** The State legislature proposes amendments. **By initiative:** A specified number of voters signs a petition to put a proposal on the ballot, and voters either accept or reject it. **(b)** by voters in every State except Delaware

**4.** Students may suggest that the struggle to win freedom from an oppressive British government led States to establish many limits on government power and protect civil liberties and popular sovereignty.

**5.** The constitutional change process is cumbersome; the changes are often not a high priority for either government officials or the public.

**QUICK WRITE** A strong answer will relate questions to the content of the sections and to students' lives.

## What are the defining traits and purpose of State legislatures?

| Purpose/Structure | Powers | Organization |
|---|---|---|
| • Purpose is to make the law<br>• 49 are bicameral<br>• 30–50 members in most upper houses<br>• 100–150 members in most lower houses<br>• elected from districts | • all those not granted to executive, courts, or local government<br>• all those not denied by State or U.S. constitutions<br>• tax, spend, borrow, establish courts/jurisdiction, define crimes/punishment, regulate commerce, maintain schools<br>• police power<br>• approve or reject appointments<br>• discipline and impeach<br>• constituent power | • speaker presides in lower house<br>• president of senate is lieutenant governor in 23 States<br>• president *pro tempore* serves in lieutenant governor's absence<br>• standing committee of each house organized by subject<br>• bills introduced by legislators, but may come from agencies, local governments, interest groups, public |

# Get Started

## LESSON GOALS

Students will . . .

• compare and contrast features of State legislatures with those of the U.S. Congress.

• identify and rank the main powers of State legislatures and provide examples of each.

• discuss how State legislatures influence the lives of citizens and how citizens influence lawmaking.

## SKILLS DEVELOPMENT

### ANALYZE POLITICAL CARTOONS

To help students learn to analyze political cartoons, have them turn to the Skills Handbook, p. S22, and use the steps explained there to complete the Political Cartoon Mini-Lesson.

**SECTION 2**

# State
# Legislatures

## Guiding Question

**What are the defining traits and purpose of State legislatures?** Use a table similar to the one below to record the main facts about State legislatures.

| Purpose/Structure | Powers | Organization |
|---|---|---|
| • Purpose is to make the law<br>• 49 are bicameral | •<br>•<br>• | •<br>•<br>• |

## Political Dictionary

• police power
• constituent power
• referendum

## Objectives

1. Describe State legislatures.
2. Explain the election, terms, and compensation of legislators.
3. Examine the powers and organization of State legislatures.
4. Describe how voters may write and pass laws through direct legislation.

**Image Above:** Virginia's House of Delegates

In every State, the legislature, whatever it is called, is the lawmaking branch of State government. So, its basic function goes to the very heart of democratic government: It is charged with translating the public will into the public policy of the State.

## The Legislature

Several features of their lawmaking bodies vary among the 50 States. This is notably true with regard to both name and size.

**Name and Structure** Just over half the States call their lawmaking body, officially, the "legislature." In 19 States it is known as the "General Assembly," in two States it is called the "Legislative Assembly," and in two others the "General Court."

All but one of the 50 State legislatures are bicameral, having two chambers. The upper house is known everywhere as "the Senate." The lower house is most commonly titled "the House of Representatives," but may also be "the Assembly," "the General Assembly," or "the House of Delegates." Nebraska, the only State with a one-house legislature, calls it "the Legislature."

As with Congress, bicameralism came to the States' legislative bodies out of the colonial experience. Unicameralism is regularly cited as one of the most significant steps that could be taken to improve State legislatures. Despite its apparent successes in Nebraska, efforts to accomplish it elsewhere have been notably unsuccessful. Those who defend bicameralism usually claim that one house can and does act as a check on the other, and so prevent the passage of unwise legislation. Whether that widely held view is justified or not, it has proved a major barrier to the spread of one-chamber lawmaking bodies.

**Size** There may be no ideal size for a legislative body, but two basic considerations are important. First, a legislature, and each of its houses, should not be so large as to hamper the orderly conduct of the people's business. Second, it should not be so small that the many views and interests within the State cannot be adequately represented.

# Focus on the Basics

Here is the information that your students need to learn in this section.

**FACTS:** • State laws must not conflict with the U.S. Constitution. • Like Congress, nearly all legislatures are bicameral and have presiding officers and committees. • The 50 State constitutions set very different qualifications, terms, pay, and work calendars for their legislators. • In some States, voters can propose bills through initiatives or approve or defeat legislative bills through a referendum vote.

**CONCEPTS:** representative government, legislative branch, initiative and referendum

**ENDURING UNDERSTANDINGS:** • State constitutions set up their legislatures according to citizens' views on the relative power of government. • The initiative and referendum give voters a role in lawmaking.

The upper house in most States has from 30 to 50 members, with as few as 20 senators in Alaska and as many as 67 in Minnesota. The lower house usually ranges between 100 and 150 members. However, there are only 40 seats in Alaska's lower chamber, and New Hampshire's has a whopping 400!

## State Legislators

Today, there are 7,382 State legislators—5,411 representatives and 1,971 senators—among the 50 States. Nearly all of them are Republicans or Democrats; fewer than 20 belong to a minor party or are independents.

As you read these pages, keep this point in mind: To really understand your own State's lawmaking body and how it operates, and its members and the ways in which they behave, you have to know a good deal about that institution and those people that you will not find in a textbook. As one widely respected authority on State government and politics tells us,

"[Y]ou need to know about all sorts of things . . . which party is in control and by how much . . . who the governor is, and how he gets along with the legislators . . . what sorts of people those legislators are: not just what they say but how long they have been there, where they come from, what they did before they ran for office and how they got elected. . . the communities that produced them, the families that raised them and the other families they were close to; where they went to school. . . ."

—**Alan Ehrenhalt, "Clueless in Boise,"** *Governing* **magazine**

**Qualifications** Every State's constitution sets out formal requirements of age, citizenship, and residence for legislators. Most everywhere, a representative must be at least 21 years old and senators must be at least 25. The realities of the politics of the State add informal qualifications far more difficult to meet. They have to do with a candidate's vote-getting abilities, and are based on such things as occupation, name recognition, party, race, religion, national origin, and the like.

**Election** Everywhere, legislators are chosen by popular vote and, almost everywhere, candidates for the legislature are nominated at party primaries. Nominees are picked by conventions in only a few States. In Nebraska, the unicameral legislature is organized on a <u>nonpartisan</u> basis. Candidates are nominated at nonpartisan primaries, and they are not identified by party in the general election.

In most States, the lawmakers are elected in November of even-numbered years. In four States, however—Mississippi, New Jersey, Virginia, and Louisiana—they are chosen in the odd-numbered years, in the hope of separating State and local issues from those in national politics.

**Districts** Every State's constitution requires that legislators be chosen from districts within the State, and nearly all are now elected from single-member districts. Those districts are drawn by the legislature itself in most States, and they are redrawn (reapportioned) every ten years, in line with the federal census. Gerrymandering is quite common.

Most State legislatures were long dominated by the rural, less populated areas of the State. In *Baker v. Carr*, 1962, however, the United States Supreme Court held the unfair, unequal distribution of State legislative seats to be a violation of the Equal Protection Clause of the 14th Amendment. That historic

✔ **Checkpoint**
What are the qualifications for State legislators?

<u>nonpartisan</u>
*adj.* not belonging to or favoring any political party

State representatives Alisha Thomas Morgan of Georgia (left) and Justin Davis of South Dakota (right) were in their early 20s when first elected. *What valuable perspectives might young legislators bring to State government?*

715

## Differentiated Resources

The following resources are located in the All-in-One, Unit 7, Chapter 24, Section 2:

- **L3** Reading Comprehension Worksheet (p. 23)
- **L2** Reading Comprehension Worksheet (p. 25)
- **L3** Core Worksheet (p. 27)
- **L2** Extend Activity (p. 28)
- **L3** Quiz A (p. 29)
- **L2** Quiz B (p. 30)

Assign the section, the graphic organizer in the text, and the Reading Comprehension Worksheet (Unit 7 All-in-One, p. 23) before class.

**L2** **Differentiate** Reading Comprehension Worksheet (Unit 7 All-in-One, p. 25)

**BELLRINGER**

Write on the board: **How are State legislatures similar to the U.S. Congress? How are they different? Answer in your notebook.**

## Teach

To present this topic using online resources, use the lesson presentations at **PearsonSchool.com/phgovt.**

**COMPARE AND CONTRAST**

Distribute the Chapter 24 Section 2 Core Worksheet (Unit 7 All-in-One, p. 27). Draw a large Venn diagram on the board—or display the Venn Diagram graphic organizer transparency—and label it in the same way as the one on the Core Worksheet. With students, analyze features of State legislatures by comparing and contrasting them with the U.S. Congress. Have students complete their Venn diagram on the Core Worksheet as you discuss each feature. You may want to compare and contrast the following topics:

- Purpose
- Structure
- Member qualifications
- Election process
- Terms
- Compensation
- Powers

**L3** **Differentiate** Refer students to the chapter on the U.S. Congress if they need help recalling its features.

**L2** **Differentiate** Remind students to use the headings in the section to locate information they may need to fill in the Venn diagram.

**L1** **ELL Differentiate** Check that students understand the meanings of the key terms before you begin. Pronounce the more challenging terms, such as *constituent.* Suggest that students add their own phonetic respellings to the definitions they record in their notebooks.

## Answers

**Checkpoint** Representatives must be at least 21 and senators at least 25. There are usually other formal requirements of age, citizenship, and residence.

**Caption** Young legislators can represent views of younger constituents and might bring fresh ways of approaching problems.

Have students identify the legislative and nonlegislative powers of the State legislatures. With students, list the powers on the board. Have volunteers offer an example of an application of each power. Then ask: **Which power do you think is the most important and why?** Have the class rank the powers in order of importance by voting on each one. Some students may identify police power as the most important. Explain that although the U.S. Congress has taken on some police power over time, this power is still largely reserved to the States.

**L1 L2 ELL Differentiate** Clarify that *police* in *police power* does not mean the same as "the police." The meaning here is more closely related to the term *policy*, which is "a plan or set of laws designed to solve a problem."

**L2 Differentiate** Have students rank the powers on their own and use the Think-Pair-Share strategy (p. T22) to let them explain their answers to a partner before sharing with the class.

STUDENT DRIVER    MINIMUM WAGE

State law governs many areas of daily life, including, for example, the regulation of drivers' licenses and minimum wage rates above the federal level. *Why are these policies determined at the State level?*

✔**Checkpoint**
How long do legislators serve?

**turnover**
*n.* rate at which people enter and leave a group

decision was soon followed by *Reynolds* v. *Sims* in 1964. There, the Court held that the Equal Protection Clause requires every State to draw its legislative districts on the basis of population equality.

**Terms** Legislators are elected to either two-year or four-year terms. Representatives serve two-year terms in 44 States and four-year terms in Alabama, Louisiana, Maryland, Mississippi, and North Dakota. Senators win four-year terms in 38 States (including Nebraska), and only two-year stints in the other 12.

Fifteen States now limit the number of terms any person can serve. In most, the limit is placed on service in each chamber, separately. In a few, the restriction is applied to total legislative service in either house.

The rate of turnover in legislative seats is fairly high, although it tends to vary from State to State and time to time. In a given year, some 20 percent of all lawmakers around the country are serving their first term in office. The major reasons for that turnover appear to be low pay, political instability, and term limits. Lawmakers tend to remain in office longer in those States that pay higher salaries and where one party regularly wins elections.

**Compensation** Far too often, capable men and women refuse to run for seats in the legislature because of the financial sacrifices that service usually entails. Legislative pay varies considerably and so the situation is more trying in some States than others. California now pays lawmakers $95,291 per year, plus benefits. Oregon provides a more typical example of the compensation package. There, the total compensation per member comes to just over $30,000 per year.

Clearly, decent salaries in line with the responsibilities of the job will not automatically bring the most able men and women into State legislatures. Certainly, better pay can make public service much more appealing to qualified people, however.

**Sessions** Little more than a generation ago, only a handful of State legislatures met in regular sessions each year, and then usually for only a few months or so. Most met only every other year. It has long since become apparent that the legislature's workload cannot be properly handled on so limited a basis.

Today, 44 State lawmaking bodies hold their regular sessions annually, and most of those sessions run for three to five months or more. Several legislatures are now in session nearly year-round.

In every State, the governor, and in three fourths of them the legislature itself, can call the body into special session. Those meetings, most common in States where legislators meet infrequently, allow lawmakers to take up urgent matters between their regularly scheduled sessions.

# Background

**NEBRASKA'S UNIQUE LEGISLATURE** Nebraska's unicameral, nonpartisan legislature resulted largely from the reform efforts of George Norris, who represented Nebraska in the U.S. Congress for more than 40 years. "[T]here is no sense or reason in having the same thing done twice, especially if it is to be done by two bodies of men elected in the same way and having the same jurisdiction," he insisted. Norris argued that the State supreme court and the governor would provide sufficient checks and balances. Also, unlike the closed-door secrecy of bicameral conference committees, the unicameral legislature would conduct all activities in open forum. In this way, the press and public opinion could check possible abuses. When Nebraska's unicameral amendment took effect in 1937, it abolished one house, reducing the number of legislators on the payroll from 133 to 43—a cost savings of nearly 70 percent.

## Answers

**Caption** Possible response: so that regulations can meet local conditions and needs (For example, States that have difficulty filling entry-level jobs may choose to pay a higher minimum wage.)

**Checkpoint** Either two- or four-year terms; 15 States have term limits.

## Powers of the Legislature

No State's constitution lists all of the powers vested in the legislature—nor could it. In each State, the legislature has all of those powers that (1) the State constitution does not grant exclusively to the executive or judicial branches or to local governments, and (2) neither the State constitution nor the United States Constitution denies to it. In effect, most of the powers held by a State are vested in its legislature.

**Lawmaking Powers** The fact that the legislature can enact any law that does not conflict with any provision in federal law or in the State constitution means that there can be no all-inclusive list of the legislature's powers. Its more important powers are usually set out in the State constitution, however. Those most often mentioned include the powers to tax, spend, borrow, establish courts and fix their jurisdiction, define crimes and provide for their punishment, regulate commercial activities, and maintain public schools.

Every State's legislature possesses the **police power**—the State's hugely important power to protect and promote the public health, public safety, public morals, and the general welfare. Recall, most of what government does in this country today is done by the States (and their local governments), and most of what they do is done through the exercise of the police power. In short, that extraordinarily broad authority is the power to <u>safeguard</u> the welfare of the people of the State, and it is the basis for much of what State legislatures do.

**Nonlawmaking Powers** All 50 State legislatures possess certain nonlegislative powers, in addition to those they exercise when they make a law.

In the separation of powers and checks and balances scheme, the legislature exercises some *executive* powers—for example, it has the power to approve or reject the governor's appointment of a number of officials. In some States, the legislature itself appoints various executive officers.

The legislature also has certain *judicial* powers, capped by the power of impeachment. In every State except Oregon, the legislature can remove any State officer in the executive

or judicial branch through that process. Each chamber also has the power to discipline and even expel one of its own members.

Recall that the legislature plays a significant role in both constitution-making and the constitutional amendment process. When, for example, it proposes an amendment to the State's constitution, it is not making law. It is, instead, exercising a nonlegislative power: the **constituent power.**

## Organization and Lawmaking

Both the organization and procedures of State legislatures are similar to those found in Congress. Much of their work centers around presiding officers and a committee system.

**Presiding Officers** Those who preside over the sessions of the States' lawmaking chambers are almost always powerful political figures, not only in the legislature itself but elsewhere in State politics.

The lower house in each of the 49 bicameral bodies elects its own presiding officer, known everywhere as the speaker. The senate chooses its own presiding officer in 23 States; in the other 27, including Nebraska, the lieutenant governor has the authority to serve as president of the senate in various capacities. Where the lieutenant governor does preside, the senate selects a president *pro tempore* to serve in the lieutenant governor's absence.

Except for the lieutenant governors, each of these presiding officers is chosen by a vote on the floor of his or her chamber. In fact, the majority party's caucus usually picks those who fill the leadership posts, just before the legislature begins a new term.

The chief duties of these presiding officers revolve around the conduct of the legislature's floor business. They refer bills to committee, recognize members who seek the floor, and interpret and apply the rules of their chamber to its proceedings.

Unlike the Speaker of the House in Congress, the speaker in nearly every State appoints the chair and other members of each house committee. The senate's president or president *pro tem* has that same power in just over half the States. The presiding officers

✔ **Checkpoint**
Why is the police power important?

**safeguard**
*v.* to protect or ensure

---

## Political Cartoon Mini-Lesson

Display the political cartoon Transparency 24C, Ballot Initiatives, when you discuss direct participation of voters in the lawmaking process. This cartoon illustrates why government officials might be less than thrilled with the initiative process. Ask: **Whom do the people in the cartoon represent?** (a king and queen or, more broadly, powerful government officials) **What is happening to these people?** (They are imprisoned in shackles.) **What does the cartoon suggest about why government officials might oppose ballot initiatives?** (Through initiatives, voters can restrain governmental power.)

---

### DISCUSS THE ESSENTIAL QUESTION

Write the Unit 7 Essential Question on the board: **What is the right balance of local, State, and federal government?** Discuss students' ideas about how the State and the National governments affect their lives directly and which level affects them more. Tell students to recall that the police power is reserved to State governments. Ask: **How does the police power affect the lives of the State's citizens?** *(gives State legislatures broad control over local issues of safety and public welfare, giving them great influence over citizens' lives)* **On what level of government do you think most citizens have the greatest impact?** *(Most students will say State and local government.)* **Do citizens have the most control where government has the greatest impact on their lives?** Discuss the importance in a democracy of this relationship between citizens and government.

### DISCUSS CITIZEN PARTICIPATION

Discuss the voters' direct role in the legislative process at the State level. Have volunteers name the two types of *initiatives (direct and indirect)* and the three types of *referenda (mandatory, optional, and popular)* as you write them on the board. (Point out the plural, *referenda*.) Ask: **What types of laws do voters usually want to change? Why do you think this is?** Ask students what types of laws they would like to add or change in their State.

**L1** **L2** **ELL Differentiate** Define *referendum* (a process in which a legislature refers a measure to voters for final approval or rejection) and *initiative* (a process in which voters sign petitions to suggest a law) for the class.

**L3** **L4** **Differentiate** Ask students to write a journal entry that examines the reasons why the initiative and referendum are not used at the national level.

---

### Answers

**Checkpoint** It is the broad authority reserved to the States that has the greatest effect on the daily lives of citizens because it involves issues of public health, safety, morals, and general welfare.

**L3** Have students make a fact sheet about their State's legislature, including its origins, official name, structure, qualifications and election of members, terms, and compensation.

**L3 Differentiate** Display Transparency 24D, Factors Influencing State Legislators, and discuss key influencing factors regarding an issue. Ask: **Which major factor shown here influences decisions State legislators must make about issues?** (responsibility to many [five] groups)

**L1 L2 ELL Differentiate** Ask students to draw a concept web titled "Sources of Bills" using the information under that heading in the text.

**L2 Differentiate** Distribute the Extend Activity "The State Legislature and You" (Unit 7 All-in-One, p. 28), which asks students to write to their State legislators about issues important to them.

**L2 L3 Differentiate** Have students work in pairs to design and create a graphic representation of the powers of State legislatures.

**L4 Differentiate** Instruct students to research the origins, provisions, and status of a bill currently active in their State legislature and report their findings to the class. Ask them to include the source of the bill and who is sponsoring it.

**L4 Differentiate** Tell students to review the material on the police power in their textbook. Explain that since the New Deal, the U.S. Congress has taken on the police power in certain circumstances. Have students do research and write a short report on one example of when Congress has exercised the police power.

Tell students to go to the Audio Tour to listen to a guided audio tour of the *How Government Works* diagram, "Initiative and Referendum."

## Answers

**Initiative and Referendum** Legislators may view initiatives as intruding on their power or as interference by people who do not understand the full consequences of their proposals.

**Checkpoint** refer bills to committee, recognize members who seek the floor, interpret and apply rules of chamber and its proceedings, appoint committee members and chairs

GOVERNMENT ONLINE
Audio Tour
Listen to an audio guided tour on these processes at
PearsonSchool.com/phgovt

How Government Works

# Initiative and Referendum

Voters in many States can write new laws or prevent laws from taking effect through the initiative and the referendum. *Why do you think many legislators oppose the initiative process?*

**Initiative takes two forms**

1. Voters write a new law and gather signatures in its support.
2. The proposed law goes directly to the ballot. OR The proposed law goes to the legislature.
3. Voters approve or reject the measure. OR Legislature approves it or sends to voters.

**Referendum takes one form**

1. The legislature proposes a new law.
2. The proposed law goes to the ballot.
3. Voters approve or reject the measure.

✓**Checkpoint**
What do a legislature's presiding officers do?

**sift**
*v.* to sort or pick through carefully

regularly use this power much as they do their other powers: to reward their friends, punish their enemies, and otherwise work their influence on the legislature and its product.

**Committees** Several hundred or, in many larger States, several thousand measures are introduced at each session of the legislature. That flood of bills makes the committee system as practical and necessary at the State level as it is in Congress. Much of the work of the legislature is done in committee, where members sift through that pile of proposed legislation, deciding which bills will go on to floor consideration and which will fall by the wayside.

The standing committees of each house are regularly organized on a subject-matter basis—as committees on finance, education, highways, and so on. A bill referred to one of these committees may be amended or even largely rewritten there. Or, as frequently happens, it may be ignored altogether.

"Pigeonholing" occurs in the States as in Congress. In fact, in most States one of the standing committees in each house is usually the "graveyard committee." Bills are sent there to be buried. The judiciary committee, to which bills may be referred "on grounds of doubtful constitutionality," often fills this role.[6]

**Sources of Bills** Legally, only a member may introduce a bill in either house in any State's legislature. So, in the strictest sense, legislators themselves are the source of all measures the legislature considers. In broader terms, however, the lawmakers are the authors of only a handful of bills.

A large number of measures come from public sources, from officers and agencies in the State executive branch, and from local governments. Every State governor has a legislative program, often extensive and bold.

Many bills come from the private sector. Indeed, interest groups appear to be the

---

6 A striking illustration of a graveyard committee existed for several years in landlocked Oklahoma: the Committee on Deep Sea Navigation.

# How Government Works

**INITIATIVES** Have students apply the *How Government Works* diagram, "Initiative and Referendum," on this page to your State or another specific State. Have students identify a State in which voters may propose constitutional amendments or legislation through the initiative process. Ask them to write a brief description of a specific initiative proposed by the people of the State, and answer these questions: **How many supporting signatures were required? Did the initiative go directly to the ballot or to the legislature? Would you support or oppose this initiative? Why? What was the outcome?** For an audio tour of the "Initiative and Referendum" diagram, go to **PearsonSchool.com/phgovt**.

largest single source of proposed legislation. Remember, those groups and the lobbyists who represent them exist for one overriding purpose: to influence public policy to the benefit of their own particular interests. Of course, some measures do originate with private individuals—business owners, farmers, union members, and other citizens—who, for one reason or another, think, "There ought to be a law. . . ."

## Direct Legislation

In several States, voters themselves can take a direct part in the lawmaking process. The main vehicles for that participation are the initiative and the referendum.

**Initiative** Through the initiative process, voters in 18 States can propose amendments to the State's constitution. In 21 States, they can also use that process to propose ordinary statutes. The initiative takes two quite different forms: the more common direct initiative and the little-used indirect initiative.

In both forms, a certain number of qualified voters (which varies from State to State) must sign petitions to <u>initiate</u> a law. Where the direct initiative is in place, a measure with sufficient signatures goes directly to the ballot, usually in the next general election. If voters approve the measure, it becomes law. If not, it dies. Where the indirect form is found,

a proposed measure goes first to the legislature for its consideration. If the lawmakers approve the measure, it becomes law. If the legislature fails to pass it, the measure then goes to the voters.

**Referendum** A **referendum** is a process in which the legislature refers a measure to the voters for final approval or rejection. The referendum takes three different forms: mandatory, optional, and popular.

A *mandatory referendum* occurs in those situations in which the legislature must send a measure to the voters. Recall, in every State except Delaware, a proposed constitutional amendment must be submitted to the electorate. In several States some other measures, such as those providing for the borrowing of funds, must also go to the voters.

An *optional referendum* involves a measure that the legislature has referred to the voters voluntarily. Such measures are rare. They usually involve "hot potato" issues: issues that lawmakers would prefer not to take direct responsibility for deciding themselves.

Under the *popular referendum*, a group of citizens may demand by petition that a measure passed by the legislature be referred to the voters for final action. Most attempts to use this form of the referendum fail. Most often, the opponents of a particular measure simply cannot gather the required number of signatures to force a popular vote on the target of their <u>ire</u>.

✓ **Checkpoint**
What is direct legislation?

**initiate**
*v.* to begin, launch, set in motion

**ire**
*n.* anger, outrage

---

# Assess and Remediate

**L3** Check students' work on the Core Worksheet. (Unit 7 All-in-One, p. 27)

**L3** Assign the Section 2 Assessment questions.

**L3** Section Quiz A (Unit 7 All-in-One, p. 29)

**L2** Section Quiz B (Unit 7 All-in-One, p. 30)

Have students complete the review activities in the digital lesson presentation and continue their work in the **Essential Questions Journal.**

## REMEDIATION

| If Your Students Have Trouble With | Strategies For Remediation |
|---|---|
| The defining traits and purposes of State legislatures (Questions 1, 2, 3, 5) | On the board, draw a table similar to the one in the section opener. Review with students the information they recorded on State legislatures about their structure, powers, and features. Tell students to add any information they did not already have in their own charts. |
| Compensation of State legislators (Question 4) | Have groups find out how much the legislators are paid in their State and then compare the legislators' pay rates with those of other jobs. |

---

# SECTION 2 ASSESSMENT

**Essential Questions Journal** To continue to build a response to the chapter Essential Question, go to your **Essential Questions Journal.**

1. **Guiding Question** Use your completed table to answer this question: What are the defining traits and purpose of State legislatures?

**Key Terms and Comprehension**

2. What are the major purposes of the **police power**?

3. What three types of nonlegislative powers does a State legislature have?

**Critical Thinking**

4. **Demonstrate Reasoned Judgment** Do you think that State legislators should be paid a generous salary? Why or why not?

5. **Analyze Information** Would you support an amendment to your State's constitution to provide for a unicameral legislature? Why or why not?

**Quick Write**

**Explanatory Writing: Organize Your Ideas** Review your list of questions and loosely categorize them under various topics, such as "State Legislatures" or "Powers of the Executive." Select two or three categories that relate most closely to the concept of the effects of State governments on the lives of citizens. Use your textbook or other resources to take notes to answer each of the questions under your selected categories.

---

## Answers

**Checkpoint** the direct participation of voters in the lawmaking process

---

# Assessment Answers

**1.** State legislatures are the lawmaking bodies in the States. They vary in size and structure. All but Nebraska are bicameral. Legislators are selected by popular vote. Qualifications, terms, and compensation vary, as do the length and frequency of sessions. State legislatures have legislative powers—especially the police power, which is reserved to them—as well as nonlegislative powers, which include executive powers, judicial powers, and constituent powers. State legislatures are organized much as the U.S.

Congress is, with presiding officers and a committee system.

**2.** to protect and promote public health, safety, morals, and general welfare

**3.** executive powers, such as approval of governor's appointments; judicial powers, such as the power of impeachment; constituent powers, such as revising and amending the State's constitution

**4.** Answers will vary. Students may cite the need to attract the best candidates for these important positions with appropriate compensation.

**5.** Answers should consider the main argument on both sides: in a bicameral legislature, one house acts as a check on the other; in a unicameral legislature, lawmaking might be more efficient.

**QUICK WRITE** A strong assignment will include reasonable categories and answers relating State government actions to the lives of citizens.

## What are the roles and powers of a governor?

| Roles and Responsibilities | | |
|---|---|---|
| Executive | Legislative | Judicial |
| • carry out laws<br>• appoint/remove subordinates<br>• supervise executive branch<br>• prepare budget<br>• commander in chief of State's National Guard | • recommend legislation<br>• call special sessions<br>• veto legislation | • powers of clemency: pardon, commute, reprieve, parole |

# Get Started

## LESSON GOALS

Students will . . .

- complete a chart to examine the powers of a State governor.
- complete a worksheet to compare and contrast State governorships with the U.S. presidency.
- participate in a mock meeting to investigate the roles and responsibilities of State executive officers.

## BEFORE CLASS

Assign the section, the graphic organizer in the text, and Reading Comprehension Worksheet (Unit 7 All-in-One, p. 31) before class.

**L2 Differentiate** Reading Comprehension Worksheet (Unit 7 All-in-One, p. 33)

# SKILLS DEVELOPMENT

## PROBLEM SOLVING

To practice problem solving in this section, use the Chapter 24 Skills Worksheet (Unit 7 All-in-One, p. 37). You may teach the skill explicitly before students begin studying about State governors. For L2 and L1 students, assign the adapted Skill Activity (Unit 4 All-in-One, p. 38).

---

SECTION **3**

# The **Governor** and State **Administration**

**What are the roles and powers of a governor?** Use a chart to identify the roles and responsibilities of a governor.

| Roles and Responsibilities | | |
|---|---|---|
| Executive | Legislative | Judicial |
| • Carry out laws<br>•<br>• | •<br>•<br>• | •<br>•<br>• |

## Political Dictionary

- recall
- item veto
- clemency
- pardon
- commutation
- reprieve
- parole

## Objectives

1. Describe the main features of the office of governor.
2. Summarize a governor's roles, powers, duties, and the limitations of the office.
3. List and describe the other executive offices at the State level.

**Image Above:** Governor of Louisiana Piyush "Bobby" Jindal

The governor is the principal executive officer in each of the 50 States. He or she is always a central figure in State politics and is often a well-known national personality as well. Governors today occupy an office that is the direct descendant of the earliest public office in American politics, the colonial governorship, first established in Virginia in 1607.

## The Governorship

In colonial America, the actions of the royal governors inspired much of the resentment that fueled the Revolution. That attitude was carried over into the first State constitutions. Most of the powers of government were given to the legislatures; the new State governors, for the most part, had little real authority. In every State except Massachusetts and New York, the governor was chosen by the legislature, and in most of them only for a one-year term. And only in three States did the governor have a veto power.

That original separation of powers soon proved unsatisfactory. Many of the State legislatures abused their powers. Several fell prey to special interests, and the governors were unable to respond. So, as new constitutions were written, and the older ones revised, the powers of the legislatures were curbed and the powers of the governors generally increased.

Beginning with Illinois in 1917, most States have redesigned and strengthened the executive branch to make the governor the State's chief executive in more than name. Some States have gone further than others in this direction, but, overall, governors are much more powerful figures today than in decades past.

**Qualifications** Anyone who wants to become the governor of a State must be able to satisfy a set of formal qualifications. Typically, he or she must be an American citizen, of at least a certain age (usually 25 or 30), have lived in the State for a given period of time (most often for at least five years), and be a qualified voter.

Clearly, these formal qualifications for office are not very difficult to meet. It is the informal qualifications that have real meaning. To become a governor, a person must have those characteristics that will first attract a party's nomination, and then attract the voters in the general election. Those characteristics

---

# Focus on the Basics

Here is the information that your students need to learn in this section.

**FACTS:** • The governor leads the State's executive branch. • State constitutions have strengthened the job of governor over time. • In addition to executive powers, the governor has legislative and judicial powers.• In most States, the governor shares executive power with other elected officials, such as the lieutenant governor, secretary of state, state treasurer, and attorney general.

**CONCEPTS:** separation of powers, federalism, leadership

**ENDURING UNDERSTANDINGS:** • The presidency and governorships have many similarities, but most governors share executive power with other elected officials. • Governors possess some legislative and judicial powers.

vary from State to State, and even from election to election within a State. Race, sex, religion, name recognition, personality, party identification, experience, ideology, the ability to use television effectively—these and several other factors are all part of the mix.

Today, most governors are attorneys in their 40s and 50s. Nearly all of them were State legislators or held another elective office in the State, such as lieutenant governor, attorney general, or mayor of a large city. California's "governator," Arnold Schwarzenegger, is a leading illustration of the fact that someone who has never held public office does sometimes win a governorship.

The first <u>gubernatorial</u> elections occurred in 1775 and more than 2,500 persons have now served as governors of the various States. To this point (2011), only 34 of those governors have been women.

Two women succeeded their husbands as governor in 1924: Nellie Taylor Ross in Wyoming and Miriam "Ma" Ferguson in Texas. Over the past 30 years or so, a growing number of women have won the office. Six currently serve: Jan Brewer (R., Arizona), Susana Martinez (R., New Mexico), Beverly Perdue (D., North Carolina), Mary Fallin (R., Oklahoma), Nikki Haley (R., South Carolina), and Christine Gregoire (D., Washington). Governor Haley, who captured the office in 2010, is the nation's first female Indian American governor.

Only three African Americans have ever held the office: Douglas Wilder (D., Virginia, 1989); Deval Patrick (D., Massachusetts), chosen in 2006 and again in 2010; and David Patterson (D., New York), who succeeded to the post in 2008. Bobby Jindal (R., Louisiana; 2007) is the nation's first Indian American governor.

**Selection** The governor is chosen by popular vote in every State. In all but five, only a <u>plurality</u> is needed for election. If no candidate wins a clear majority in Arizona, Georgia, or Louisiana, the two top vote-getters meet in a runoff election. If no one wins a majority in Mississippi, the lower house of the legislature picks the new governor. In Vermont, both houses make the choice.

The major parties' gubernatorial candidates are usually picked in primaries. In a few States, however, conventions choose the nominees. Nearly half the States now provide for the joint election of the governor and the lieutenant governor. In those States, each party's candidates for those offices run as a team, and the voter casts one vote to fill both posts.

**Term** The one-year gubernatorial term has long since disappeared. Governors are now chosen to four-year terms nearly everywhere. Thirty-six States limit the number of terms a chief executive may serve, most often to two terms. Those governors who seek reelection usually do so successfully.[7]

**Succession** Governors are mortal. Occasionally, one of them dies in office. Many of them are also politically ambitious. Every so often, one resigns in midterm—to become a United States senator or accept an appointment to the President's Cabinet, for example.

When a vacancy does occur, it sets off a game of political musical chairs in the State. The political plans and timetables of ambition of a number of public personalities are affected by the event. No matter what causes a vacancy, every State's constitution provides for a successor. In 44 States the lieutenant governor is first in line. In Maine, New Hampshire, and West Virginia, the president of the senate succeeds. In Arizona, Oregon, and Wyoming, the office passes to the secretary of state.

**Removal** The governor may be removed from office by impeachment in every State except Oregon. Only six governors have been impeached and removed since the <u>turbulent</u> Reconstruction years after the Civil War. The most recent to suffer that fate: Rod Blagojevich (D., Illinois) in 2009.

In 18 States, the governor may be recalled by the voters.[8] The **recall** is a petition procedure by which voters may remove an elected official from office before the completion of

7 The all-time record for both gubernatorial service and electoral success belongs to George Clinton of New York. He sought and won seven three-year terms as governor and held the office from 1777 to 1795 and again from 1801 to 1804. He was later Vice President of the United States, from 1805 to 1812.

8 Alaska, Arizona, California, Colorado, Georgia, Idaho, Kansas, Louisiana, Michigan, Minnesota, Montana, Nevada, New Jersey, North Dakota, Oregon, Rhode Island, Washington, Wisconsin.

---

✔ **Checkpoint**
What are common characteristics of governors?

**gubernatorial**
*adj.* of or relating to a governor

**turbulent**
*adj.* disorderly, stormy

**plurality**
*n.* the largest total, not necessarily a majority

# Differentiated Resources

The following resources are located in the All-in-One, Unit 7, Chapter 24, Section 3:

- **L3** Reading Comprehension Worksheet (p. 31)
- **L2** Reading Comprehension Worksheet (p. 33)
- **L3** Core Worksheet A (p. 35)
- **L3** Core Worksheet B (p. 36)
- **L3** Skills Worksheet (p. 37)
- **L2** Skill Activity (p. 38)
- **L3** Quiz A (p. 39)
- **L2** Quiz B (p. 40)

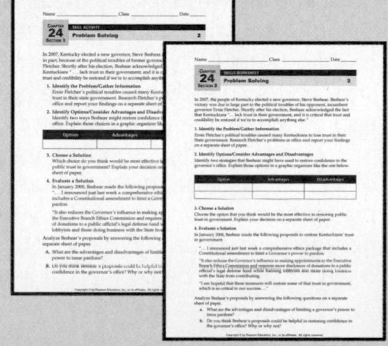

---

**BELLRINGER**

Write the following on the board: **A majority of U.S. presidential candidates and many Presidents have been governors. Why do you think voters often select former governors as President? Answer in your notebook.**

**L2 Differentiate** Rephrase the directions. Ask: **Do you think a governor or a U.S. Senator would make a better President? Explain your choice in your notebook.**

# Teach

To present this topic using online resources, use the lesson presentations at **PearsonSchool.com/phgovt.**

### INTRODUCE THE TOPIC

Tell students that they will discuss the main executive officers at the State level, including the governor. On the board, draw a three-column chart titled "Powers of a State Governor." Label the sections "Executive Powers," "Legislative Powers," and "Judicial Powers." Have students complete the chart by adding examples of each type of power mentioned in the text. Discuss with students how these powers enable a governor to run a State.

**L2 ELL Differentiate** Have students create vocabulary flash cards for terms in the Political Dictionary, with the term on one side and the definition from the Glossary on the other, and work with partners to test their knowledge.

### COMPARE A GOVERNORSHIP AND THE PRESIDENCY

Remind students of the role of the executive branch in the National Government—that the President is *the* executive in the National Government, while a governor is the *chief* executive in the State's government. Based on their answers to the Bellringer question, discuss with students how being a governor might prepare a person to be President. Have students identify powers listed in the chart that both positions share, and circle them.

**L1 L2 Differentiate** Tell students to copy the chart in their notebooks to help them study for assessments on the topic.

---

## Answers

**Checkpoint** attorneys in their 40s and 50s, former State legislators or holders of other elective State offices, male, white

Distribute Chapter 24 Section 3 Core Worksheet A (Unit 7 All-in-One, p. 35). Explain to students that they will use the worksheet to compare and contrast the job of a governor and that of the U.S. President. Students should complete the chart and formulate an answer to the worksheet question. If your classroom has Internet access, you may wish to have students complete the chart using specific information for your State.

Name _____ Class _____ Date _____

**CHAPTER 24 SECTION 3** | **CORE WORKSHEET A**
**The Governor and State Administration** | 3

**The National and State Chief Executives**

Complete the chart below to compare and contrast roles, duties, and other features of the U.S. presidency and a State governorship. Then answer the questions that follow.

| | President | State Governor |
|---|---|---|
| Qualifications | | |
| Selection | | |
| Term | | |
| Main roles | | |
| Succession | | |
| Executive or cabinet departments | | |

In general, how is a State governorship similar to the presidency? How is it different?

_____
_____
_____

Copyright © by Pearson Education, Inc., or its affiliates. All rights reserved.

**Government** online All print resources are available on the Teacher's Resource Library CD-ROM and online at PearsonSchool.com/phgovt.

## Answers

**Analyzing Political Cartoons** to emphasize the ridiculousness of having so many candidates and to poke fun at the politically ambitious pretenders

▶▶ **Analyzing Political Cartoons** In 2003, California voters had to choose whether to recall the governor and, if so, which of 135 candidates should replace him. *Why did the cartoonist include a clown among the candidates?*

**intangible**
*n.* something not concrete or easily defined

**fragmented**
*adj.* split, separated into many pieces

his or her regular term. The process generally works this way: If a certain number of qualified voters—usually 25 percent of the number who voted in the last election held for the office—sign recall petitions, a special election must be held in which the voters decide whether to remove or instead, retain, the officeholder.

To this point, only two governors have ever been recalled: Governor Lynn J. Frazier of North Dakota, a Republican, in 1921, and Governor Gray Davis of California, a Democrat, in 2003.

**Compensation** In many respects, a governor's job is not unlike that of the chief executive officer of one of the nation's larger corporations. Both administer hugely complex organizations, manage the work of thousands of employees, and oversee the spending of incredible amounts of money. Governors are not paid nearly so well as the CEOs of large companies, however. The latter make tens of millions of dollars per year in salary and benefits.

In contrast, most governors earn little more than $120,000 per year. Salaries now range from $70,000 per year in Maine and $87,352 in Arkansas to $179,000 in New York. Most States provide their chief executive with an official residence, often called a

governor's mansion, and money for travel and other expenses.

To the governor's salary and other material compensations must be added the intangibles of honor and prestige that go with the office. It is this factor, and a sense of public duty, that often persuades many of our better citizens to seek the post. Several Presidents were governors before reaching the White House—most recently, Bill Clinton and George W. Bush.

## A Governor's Many Roles

Much like the President, a governor plays a number of different roles. He or she is, simultaneously, an executive, an administrator, a legislator, a party leader, an opinion leader, and a ceremonial figure. What the office amounts to depends, in no small part, on how well the governor plays each—and all—of these roles. And that must depend, in turn, on his or her personality, political muscle, and overall abilities.

Many of a governor's formal powers are hedged with constitutional and other legal restrictions. Nonetheless, the powers a governor does have, together with the prestige of the office, make it quite possible for a capable, dynamic person to be a "strong" governor, one who can accomplish much for the State and for the public good.

## Executive Powers

The presidency and the governorships are similar in several ways, but the comparison can be pushed too far. Remember, the Constitution of the United States makes the President *the* executive in the National Government. State constitutions, on the other hand, regularly describe the governor as the *chief* executive in the State's government. The distinction here, between *the* executive and the *chief* executive, is a critical one. The executive authority is fragmented in most States, but it is not at the national level.

In nearly every State, the executive authority is shared by a number of "executive officers"—a secretary of state, an attorney general, a treasurer, and so on. Most of these executive officers are, like the governor,

## Background

**SUCCESSION** Before 2005, New Jersey had no lieutenant governor. A vacancy in the governorship was filled by the president of the senate, who continued to serve as senator—thus sidestepping the separation of powers. In those cases, the same person could sponsor a bill and then sign it into law. When Governor Christie Whitman stepped down early, the senate president served as acting governor until his term expired a week before newly elected Governor James McGreevey was sworn in. The new senate president should have filled the governor's role until McGreevey took office, but because the legislature was evenly divided between parties, the senate presidency was shared. The two men agreed to split the week, each serving as governor for three and a half days. Four governors in one week prompted officials to move toward creating the position of lieutenant governor.

popularly elected, and for that reason, very largely beyond the governor's direct control.

In short, most State constitutions so divide the executive authority that the governor can best be described as a "first among equals." Yet, whatever the realities of the distribution of power, the people look to the governor for leadership in State affairs. It is also the governor whom they hold responsible for the conduct of those affairs and for the overall condition of the State.

The governor's basic legal responsibility is regularly found in a constitutional provision that directs the chief executive to "take care that the laws be faithfully executed." Though the executive power may be divided, the governor is given a number of specific powers with which to accomplish that task.

**Appointment and Removal** The governor can best execute the law with subordinates of his or her own choosing. Hence, the powers of appointment and removal are, or should be, among the most important.

A leading test of any administrator is his or her ability to select loyal and able assistants. Two major factors work against the governor's effectiveness here, however. First is the existence of those other elected executives; the people choose them and the governor cannot remove them. Second, the State's constitution and statutes place restrictions on the governor's power to hire and fire. Most State constitutions require that the majority of the governor's major appointees be confirmed by the State senate.

Moreover, the legislature often sets qualifications that must be met by the governor's appointees. In a vigorous two-party State, for example, the law often requires that not more than a certain number of the members of each board or commission be from the same political party. Thus, a governor must appoint some members of the opposing party to posts.

**Administering the Executive Branch** The governor is the State's chief administrator. Alone and unaided, he or she could not possibly "take care that the laws be faithfully executed." The day-to-day work of enforcing the State's laws, of performing its many functions, and of delivering its many services is done by the thousands of men and women in all of the agencies that make up the executive branch. The governor must supervise that work.

Here again, the constitution and statutes of the State often limit a governor's authority. Many agencies are subject to his or her direct control, but many are not. That situation puts a <u>premium</u> on the governor's powers of persuasion and on his or her ability to operate through such informal channels as party leadership and appeals to the public.

**The Budget** Always remember: A government's budget is much more than a mere bookkeeping exercise. It is a political document, a statement of public policy. Its numbers, its dollar figures, reflect the struggle over "who gets what" and who doesn't.

In most States the governor prepares the budget that goes to the legislature. The lawmakers can and do make changes in the governor's financial plan. Still, the governor's recommendations carry a great deal of weight.

✔ **Checkpoint**
What are a governor's executive powers?

**premium**
*n.* high value

### Party Control of Governorships, 2011

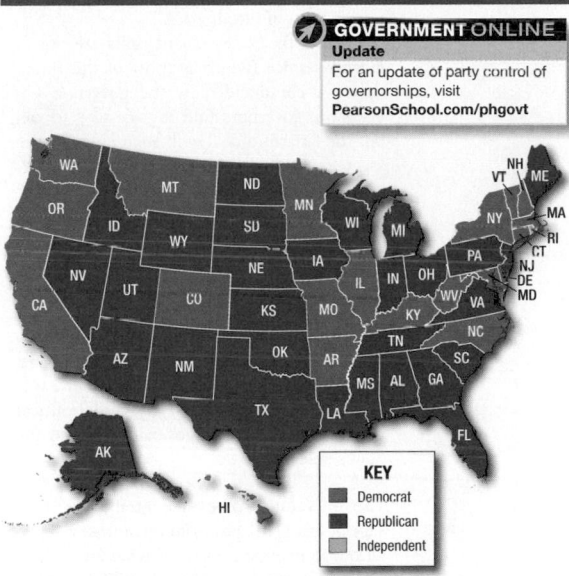

**GOVERNMENT** ONLINE
**Update**
For an update of party control of governorships, visit
**PearsonSchool.com/phgovt**

**KEY**
■ Democrat
■ Republican
□ Independent

▶▶ **Analyzing Maps** The two major parties compete in gubernatorial elections in every State. *Which party holds a majority of the State governorships today?*

Chapter 24 • Section 3 **723**

# Political Cartoon Mini-Lesson

Display the political cartoon Transparency 24E, Man in Charge, when you discuss the executive powers of the governor. This cartoon shows the massive Arnold Schwarzenegger facing a devastated California treasury. Ask: **Who is the man in charge?** *(Governor Arnold Schwarzenegger of California)* **What major problem does he face?** *(The State treasury is in ruins, meaning that funds are short.)* **What executive power of the governor will this problem affect most?** *(budget preparation)*

### HOLD MOCK EXECUTIVE BRANCH MEETINGS

Assemble the class into five groups, each representing one of the five State government executive officers mentioned in the text: governor, lieutenant governor, secretary of state, treasurer, and attorney general. Have students create a list of questions that will help them to define the role of their subject, such as:

- **Does this executive office exist in your State?**
- **Is the officer elected or appointed?**
- **How long is the term?**
- **What are the main duties and concerns of this officer?**
- **Which departments does the person oversee or interact with?**
- **What are the legislative involvements, if any?**

Then distribute Chapter 24 Section 3 Core Worksheet B (Unit 7 All-in-One, p. 36) to all students. Assign one student from each group to a mini-meeting of the executive branch. Tell students to suppose that this is the first meeting of a new administration. Have students role play, explaining their main responsibilities and at least one thing they want to accomplish or the main problem they want to solve while in office.

As students meet in their groups, circulate around the classroom to keep students on task and to ensure that each student in the group has a chance to present. Remind students that they must fill in their worksheet charts as each group member speaks.

### EVALUATE THE MEETINGS

When the mini-meetings are concluded, have each group name the three top projects or items they wanted to address first and list them on the board. Compare and discuss each group's items. Are there any similarities? Was it hard for group members to come to an agreement on which problems to address first? How did the roles and responsibilities of each member direct his or her priorities? Which officers were more likely to work together? Which were least likely?

Tell students to go to the Online Update for an update of party control of governorships.

## Answers

**Checkpoint** execute laws; appoint and remove subordinates; supervise executive branch; prepare the budget; commander in chief of State's National Guard

**Analyzing Maps** the Republican Party

**L3** **L4** **Differentiate** Have students research to gather data about all the women who have ever served as a State governor. Then have students use that data to make a map titled "Women Governors in U.S. History." Students should also design a key for their maps.

**L1** **Differentiate** Direct students to create a "My State's Governor" information sheet, in which they list the governor's name, party, date elected to office, length of term, number of terms so far, and at least three major initiatives or accomplishments. Have students complete the activity by answering these questions: **Has this governor done a good job? Why or why not?**

**L2** **ELL Differentiate** Tell students to make a chart like the one on Core Worksheet A that compares the job of one of the State officers covered in this section to positions with parallel roles or titles in the federal government. For example, students might compare the roles of the U.S. Attorney General with the role of a State attorney general or lieutenant governor to Vice President.

**L2** **Differentiate** Ask students to find a news story about your State's governor. Tell them to write a phrase or sentence identifying any powers mentioned in the article that they learned about in this section and tell how they are being applied.

**L4** **Differentiate** Have students analyze the prior jobs of all U.S. Presidents and group them into categories. For example, which U.S. Presidents had been governors, Senators, military leaders, or "other"? Tell students to use the data to create a bar graph or circle graph, and write a summary to explain what it shows about who becomes a U.S. President. Encourage students to analyze their findings and explain any changes that may have occurred throughout U.S. history.

The governor's budget-making power can be a highly effective tool with which to control State administration. Although unable to appoint or remove the head of a particular agency, for example, the governor can use the budget-making power to affect that agency's programs and have a real impact on those who work in that agency.

**Military Powers** Every State's constitution makes the governor the commander in chief of the State militia—in effect, of the State's units of the National Guard. The National Guard is the organized part of the State militia. In a national emergency, the National Guard may be "called up," ordered into federal service by the President.

All of the States' National Guard units were federalized in 1940 and served as part of the nation's armed forces in World War II. Many units also saw combat duty in Korea, Vietnam, and the Persian Gulf War. Today, National Guard units are on duty in such far-flung places as Bosnia, Kosovo, Afghanistan, and Iraq. Indeed, the Defense Department has relied very heavily on the Guard in the prosecution of recent wars.

When the State's Guard units are not in federal service (which is most of the time), they are commanded by the governor. On occasion, governors find it necessary to call out the Guard to deal with such emergencies as prison riots, to help fight a dangerous forest fire, to aid in relief and evacuation after a flood, to prevent looting during and after some other natural disaster, and so on.

**reluctant**
*adj.* hesitant, unwilling

## Legislative Powers

The State's principal executive officer exercises three significant legislative powers. Those powers, together with the chief executive's personality, popularity, and political muscle, can make the governor, in fact, the State's chief legislator.

**The Message Power** Essentially, the message power is the power to recommend legislation. Remember, much of what lawmakers do is prompted by what the governor has urged them to do. The most effective governors push their wish lists by combining their use of the formal message power with such informal tactics as close contacts with key legislators and appeals to the public.

**Special Sessions** The governor in every State has the power to call the legislature into special session. As you know, that power is meant to permit the State to meet extraordinary situations. It can also be an important part of the governor's legislative arsenal. On many occasions, governors have persuaded reluctant lawmakers to pass a particular bill by threatening to call them back in a special session if they adjourn their regular meeting without having approved that measure.

**The Veto Power** Every governor can veto measures enacted by the legislature. The veto power—including the timely use of threats to invoke the power—can be very useful to the governor as he or she tries to influence what the legislature does or doesn't do.

In most States, the governor has only a very few days in which to sign or veto a bill—most often, five. If no action is taken within the prescribed period, the measure becomes law without his or her signature.

Only 11 States give the governor a pocket veto.[9] So, in most States, those bills a governor neither signs nor vetoes become law. Forty-four States give the governor the **item veto**—the power to eliminate one or more items from a bill without rejecting the entire measure. It is used most often on spending measures.

As in the Federal Government, the legislature may attempt to override a veto. In most States, a veto requires a two-thirds majority in both houses.

## Judicial Powers

In every State the chief executive has some authority of a judicial nature. Principally, the governor has various powers of executive **clemency:** powers of mercy that may be shown to persons convicted of crime.

With the power of **pardon**, the governor may relieve someone of the legal consequences of a crime. In most States, a pardon

9 Alabama, Delaware, Iowa, Kansas, Massachusetts, New Mexico, New York, Ohio, Oklahoma, Vermont, Virginia

# Background

**THE WALLACES OF ALABAMA** Lurleen Wallace of Alabama was the third female governor ever elected in the United States. Oddly enough, her term fell between two of her husband's. George Wallace was governor of Alabama for two terms, including terms both before and after Mrs. Wallace's term. When he was elected, Alabama State law prohibited a governor from serving two consecutive terms in office. As a result, Mrs. Wallace ran for office as a representative of her husband, intending to carry out all his policies for him. Although she did accomplish this, she also pushed for several of her own programs, including more funding for State mental hospitals.

## How Government Works

# Choosing Executive Officers

**GOVERNMENT** ONLINE
**Audio Tour**
Listen to a guided audio tour of this diagram at
PearsonSchool.com/phgovt

Many jobs that are filled by presidential appointment in the Federal Government are decided by elections at the State level. *How does the direct election of executive officers empower voters in State government?*

**Federal Government**

The **voters** choose presidential electors who then elect the President and Vice President.

**President**  **Vice President**

The **President** chooses the members of the Cabinet, usually from among his or her supporters.

**Cabinet Members**

**State Government**

The **voters** elect the governor. In most States, they also elect several other executive officers.

**Governor**  **Lieutenant Governor**

**Attorney General**  **Secretary of State**  **State Treasurer**

---

may be full or conditional, and usually it can be granted only after conviction. The power of **commutation** may be used to commute a sentence imposed by a court. Thus, a death sentence might be commuted to life in prison, or a sentence might be commuted to "time served," which leads to the release of a prisoner from custody.

The power to **reprieve** can be used to postpone the execution of a sentence. Reprieves are normally granted for very brief periods—for example, to allow time for an appeal or because of the late discovery of new evidence in a case. The power of **parole** permits the release of a prisoner short of the completion of a sentence.

The governor may have some or all of these powers of executive clemency. They

are often shared, however. For example, the governor may share the power to pardon with an appointed board of pardons.

Governors have not often abused their clemency powers, but in her first term (1925–1927), Governor Miriam "Ma" Ferguson of Texas pardoned 3,737 convicted felons, an average of more than five per day.[10] The pardons came so thick and fast that several Texas

**commute**
*v.* to reduce, make less severe

10 Governor James "Pa" Ferguson was impeached and removed by the Texas legislature in 1917. He was later pardoned by the legislature and soon announced that he would run for the governorship again. The State Supreme Court ruled the legislative pardon unconstitutional, however. All of that prompted "Ma" Ferguson to run for governor in 1924. She vented her anger over the treatment of her husband in other ways, too—for example, by refusing any and all extradition requests from other States. Mrs. Ferguson was defeated for reelection in 1926, but did win another two-year term in 1932.

---

# Background

**ATTRACTING JOBS** For governors, persuading corporations to locate in their State means jobs for their constituents and a boost for the State's economy. In recent years, Michigan has experienced one of the nation's highest unemployment rates. Governor Jennifer Granholm set her sights on easing this problem. In 2005, she traveled to Nagoya, Japan, to try to entice Toyota to build its planned new factory in Michigan, the heart of America's depressed auto industry. To sweeten the deal, the State legislature authorized $50 million in incentives. Granholm also used her influence to help Toyota obtain the land it wanted to expand its technical center in Ann Arbor. However, in late 2007, Toyota selected Mississippi for its new factory to open in 2010, lured by Governor Haley Barbour and incentives worth $296 million.

---

Tell students to go to the Audio Tour to listen to a guided audio tour of the *How Government Works* diagram, "Choosing Executive Officers."

# Assess and Remediate

**L3** Collect and grade students' work on Core Worksheets A and B using the Rubric for Assessing Performance of an Entire Group (Unit 7 All-in-One, p. 125).

**L3** Assign the Section 3 Assessment questions.

**L3** Section Quiz A (Unit 7 All-in-One, p. 39)

**L2** Section Quiz B (Unit 7 All-in-One, p. 40)

Have students complete the review activities in the digital lesson presentation and continue their work in the **Essential Questions Journal.**

---

## Answers

**Choosing Executive Officers** Direct election makes top officials accountable to the voters. Appointees are more accountable to the executive who appointed them.

| If Your Students Have Trouble With | Strategies For Remediation |
|---|---|
| Roles and responsibilities of a governor (Questions 1, 2, 3) | Make a table on the board listing the roles and powers—executive, legislative, and judicial—of a governor. Ask for examples of gubernatorial actions under each. |
| Changes in the position and power of the governor since the first State constitutions were written (Question 4) | Have students work with partners and make a before/after chart. They should scan the text under "The Governorship" and record information in the chart about changes in the roles and powers of governors from the early history of the nation. |
| Appointment of executive officers (Question 5) | Have students reread the text under the heading "Appointment and Removal." In small groups, have students debate whether or not executive officers should be appointed or elected. As part of the discussion, have groups make a pro/con chart on the issue. |

## Answers

**Checkpoint** grants pardons, commutes court sentences, grants reprieves, and paroles prisoners

---

✔ **Checkpoint**
What are a governor's judicial duties?

newspapers ran daily "pardon columns" rather than separate news stories.

## Miscellaneous Duties

In addition to the exercise of executive, legislative, and judicial powers, every chief executive must perform several other, often time-consuming duties. These duties are only hinted at by a listing of the powers of the office.

Among many other things, the governor receives official visitors and welcomes other distinguished personalities to the State, dedicates parks and public and private buildings, opens the State fair, and addresses countless organizations and public gatherings. Beyond those chores, he or she is often called upon to settle labor disputes, travel elsewhere in the country and sometimes abroad to promote the State and its trade interests, endorse any number of worthy causes, and on and on.

## Other Executive Officers

In nearly every State, the governor must share control of the administration with a number of other executive officers. Most of those other officials are, like the governor, chosen by voters. The following four positions are found in most, but not all, State governments today.

The lieutenant governor must be ready to succeed to the governorship should a vacancy occur, and, in half the States, presides over the senate. The office can be a stepping-stone to the governorship by succession or by future elections. It remains, in many places, not much more than a part-time job.

The secretary of state serves as the State's chief clerk and records-keeper. He or she has charge of a great variety of public documents, records the official acts of the governor and the legislature, and usually administers the election laws.

The treasurer is the custodian of State funds, often the State's chief tax collector, and regularly the State's paymaster. Other names for this position include chief financial officer, director of finance, the commissioner of finance, and the comptroller of public accounts. The treasurer's major job is to make payments out of the State treasury to pay salaries and bills associated with State government.

The attorney general is the State's chief lawyer. He or she acts as the legal advisor to State officers and agencies as they perform their official functions, represents the State in court, and oversees the work of local prosecutors as they try cases on behalf of the State.

Much of the power of the office centers on the attorney general's formal written interpretations of constitutional and statutory law. These interpretations, called opinions, are issued to answer questions raised by officials regarding the lawfulness of their actions or proposed actions.

---

**Essential Questions Journal** To continue to build a response to the chapter Essential Question, go to your **Essential Questions Journal.**

## SECTION 3 ASSESSMENT

1. **Guiding Question** Use your completed chart to answer this question: What are the roles and powers of a governor?

### Key Terms and Comprehension
2. What executive powers do most governors have?
3. Briefly explain each of a governor's judicial powers: **clemency, pardon, commutation, reprieve,** and **parole.**

### Critical Thinking
4. **Summarize** How has the position and power of the governor relative to the legislature evolved since the first State constitutions were written?
5. **Identify Central Issues** Should the governor of your State be able to appoint the other executive officers now chosen by voters? Why or why not?

### Quick Write

**Explanatory Writing: Research for Examples and Details** When writing an explanatory essay, you should include examples illustrating the concepts or processes you discuss. Use your textbook, the library, or reliable Internet sources to add details and examples to the notes you have made about each of your categories. As you read each section of this chapter and learn new information, you may also want to add or replace questions.

---

## Assessment Answers

**1. Executive:** carry out laws, appoint/remove subordinates, supervise executive branch, prepare budget, commander in chief of State's National Guard; **Legislative:** recommend legislation, call special sessions, veto; **Judicial:** grant clemency; **Miscellaneous:** receive visitors, dedicate public spaces, open State fair, give speeches, help settle labor disputes, represent State interests, endorse causes

**2.** appointment and removal, supervising the executive branch, budget-making, and being commander of the State's National Guard

**3.** *Clemency* is mercy shown to a person convicted of a crime. *Pardon* is relieving a person of the legal consequences of a crime. *Commutation* is reducing a sentence imposed by a court. *Reprieve* is postponing the execution of a sentence. *Parole* is allowing the release of a prisoner short of completing a sentence.

**4.** Because the early State constitutions were based on events leading to the American Revolution, most governors had limited power and many were chosen by the legislature. This original separation of powers proved unsatisfactory,

and as time passed, constitutions were changed to increase the power of the governors.

**5.** possible answers: no, because appointment by the governor would place too much control in the hands of the executive; yes, because authority would be less fragmented and the governor might be able to accomplish more working with people he or she had appointed

**QUICK WRITE** A strong assignment will include many examples and details about the influence of the State government on the students' lives in support of their selected questions.

# In the Courtroom

## SECTION 4

## How do State and local courts apply different types of law?

| State and Local Courts | | |
|---|---|---|
| **Kinds of Law** | **Criminal and Civil Law** | **Jury System** |
| • constitutional<br>• statutory—written laws<br>• administrative—rules of government officials<br>• common—unwritten, judge-made laws<br>• equity—preventative; fairness | • felony—greater crime<br>• misdemeanor—lesser crime<br>• tort—civil; injury to person, property, reputation<br>• contract—agreement to do something for another | • jury—hears evidence; decides cases<br>• grand jury—decides if evidence justifies trial<br>• petit jury—trial jury; civil and criminal<br>• information—charge filed by prosecutor<br>• bench trial—case heard by judge |

### Guiding Question

**How do State and local courts apply different types of law?** Use a flowchart similar to the one below to explain the significance of elements of the legal system.

| State and Local Courts | | |
|---|---|---|
| Kinds of Law | Criminal and Civil Law | Jury System |
| •<br>•<br>• | •<br>•<br>• | •<br>•<br>• |

### Political Dictionary

- common law
- precedent
- criminal law
- felony
- misdemeanor
- civil law
- tort
- contract
- jury
- information
- bench trial

### Objectives

1. Identify and define the kinds of law applied in State courts.
2. Compare and contrast criminal law and civil law.
3. Describe the types and purposes of juries and juror selection.

**Image Above:** Jury trial

The principal function of the State courts is to decide disputes between private parties and between private parties and government. In addition, because nearly all of these courts have the power of judicial review, they act as checks on the conduct of all other agencies of both State and local government.

### Kinds of Law Applied in State Courts

The law is the code of conduct by which society is governed.[11] It is made up of several different forms, including constitutional law, statutory law, administrative law, common law, and equity.

The highest form of law in this country is *constitutional law*. It is based on the United States Constitution and the State constitutions and on judicial interpretations of those documents. *Statutory law* consists of the statutes (laws) enacted by legislative bodies, including the United States Congress, the State legislature, the people, and local governments. *Administrative law* is composed of the rules, orders, and regulations issued by federal, State, or local executive officers, acting under proper constitutional and/or statutory authority.

**Common Law** The common law makes up a large part of the law of each State except Louisiana.[12] **Common law** is unwritten, judge-made law that has developed over centuries from those generally accepted ideas of right and wrong that have gained judicial recognition. It covers nearly all aspects of human conduct. State courts apply common law except when it is in conflict with written law.

The common law originated in England. It grew out of the decisions made by the king's judges on the basis of local customs. It developed as judges, coming upon situations similar to those found in earlier cases, applied and reapplied the rulings from those earlier cases. Thus, little by little, the law of those cases

---

11 In its overall sense, the term *law* may be defined as the whole body of "rules and principles of conduct which the governing power in a community recognizes as those which it will enforce or sanction, and according to which it will regulate, limit, or protect the conduct of its members"; *Bouvier's Law Dictionary*, 3rd revision, Vol. II.
12 Because of an early French influence, Louisiana's legal system is largely based on French legal concepts, derived from Roman law. Nevertheless, the common law has worked its way into Louisiana law.

## Get Started

### LESSON GOALS

Students will . . .

- demonstrate knowledge of the five forms of law by completing a concept web.
- compare and contrast features of criminal versus civil law.
- analyze summaries of court cases.

### SKILLS DEVELOPMENT

### DRAW INFERENCES AND CONCLUSIONS

Before students work on the Core Worksheet in this lesson, you may want to review tips on drawing inferences and conclusions in the Skills Handbook, p. S19.

## Focus on the Basics

Here is the information that your students need to learn in this section.

**FACTS:** • The law is the code of conduct by which society is governed. • The principles of common law and equity derive from English legal traditions, while constitutional law and statutory law are based in written documents. • Criminal law defines crimes and punishments. • Civil law applies to noncriminal disputes. • The jury system includes the grand jury and the petit jury.

**CONCEPTS:** precedent, jury trial, judicial branch

**ENDURING UNDERSTANDINGS:** • Each form of law applies to its own category of disputes and legal questions. • The jury system follows a clear and complicated process to guarantee justice to all.

Assign the section, the graphic organizer in the text, and the Reading Comprehension Worksheet (Unit 7 All-in-One, p. 41) before class.

**L2 Differentiate** Reading Comprehension Worksheet (Unit 7 All-in-One, p. 42)

**BELLRINGER**

Write the following on the board: **Create a concept web titled "The Five Forms of Law," based on information from this section. Include words that describe the features of each form.**

**L1 L2 Differentiate** Tell students that a concept web is built on details that support a main idea. Display the blank Concept Web transparency.

# Teach

To present this topic using online resources, use the lesson presentations at **PearsonSchool.com/phgovt.**

**DISCUSS THE FIVE FORMS OF LAW**

Draw a concept web on the board or display the Concept Web graphic organizer transparency to record information about the five forms of law as a class: constitutional, statutory, administrative, common, and equity.

Have students add their information from the Bellringer to the whole-class concept web. Tell students to record any new information from this discussion in their individual concept webs.

**L2 Differentiate** Display Transparency 24F, Five Forms of Law Applied in State Courts, for group discussion.

**CONTRAST CIVIL AND CRIMINAL LAW**

Write the categories "Civil Law" and "Criminal Law" on the board. For each category, have students suggest reasons why people are taken to court. *(civil: breach of contract, dispute over property ownership, divorce; criminal: murder, theft, trespassing, speeding)* Ask students to explain how the two categories are different. *(civil law—disputes between people and between people and the government not covered by criminal law; criminal law—felonies and misdemeanors—public wrongdoing prohibited by written law)* Ask volunteers to categorize crimes into felonies and misdemeanors. *(felonies: murder, theft, arson, manslaughter; misdemeanors: traffic violations, trespassing)*

**L1 ELL Differentiate** Pronounce and define *misdemeanor* and *felony* for students.

## Answers

**Checkpoint** constitutional, statutory, administrative, common, and equity

---

**✓ Checkpoint**
What forms of law are practiced in State courts?

**compelling**
*adj.* very good; powerful

became *common* throughout England and, in time, throughout the English-speaking world.

American courts generally follow that same rule. A decision, once made, becomes a **precedent,** a guide to be followed in all later, similar cases, unless <u>compelling</u> reasons call for either an exception or its abandonment and the setting of a new precedent.

The common law is extremely important. Statutory law does override common law, but many statutes are based on the common law. A great many statutes are, in effect, common law translated into written law.

**Equity** This branch of the law supplements common law. It developed in England to provide equity—"fairness, justice, and right"—when remedies under the common law fell short of that goal.

The common law is mostly remedial, while equity is preventative. Thus, the common law applies to or provides a remedy for matters after they have happened; equity seeks to stop wrongs before they occur.

Suppose your neighbors plan to add a room to their house. You think that a part of the planned addition will be on your land and will destroy your rose garden. You can prevent the construction by getting an injunction, a court order prohibiting a specified action by the party named in the order.

A court is likely to grant the injunction for two reasons: (1) the immediacy of the threat to your property, and (2) the fact that the law can offer no fully satisfactory remedy once your garden has been destroyed. No money award can give back the pride or the pleasure your roses now give you.

At first, different courts administered equity and common law. In time, most States provided for the administration of both forms by the same courts, and the procedural differences between the two are disappearing.

## Criminal and Civil Law

The law as it is applied by courts in this country can also be described as either criminal or civil law. **Criminal law** is that branch of the law that regulates human conduct. It identifies and defines those actions that are crimes and provides for their punishment. A crime is a

public wrong considered so damaging to society at large that it has been prohibited by law. The government (State or federal) is always a party to a criminal case, as prosecutor.

Crimes are of two kinds. A **felony** is the greater offense, punishable by a heavy fine, imprisonment, or even death—for example, murder, robbery, assault, or kidnapping. A **misdemeanor** is a lesser wrong and may be punished by a lighter fine and/or a shorter jail term—for example, a traffic violation, underage drinking, or disorderly conduct.

**Civil law** relates to that human conduct that is not criminal in nature, to those disputes between private persons and between private persons and government that are not covered by criminal law. Civil law involves a wide range of issues, including divorce and custody disputes, torts, and contracts.

Both tort law and contract law are major and often-used branches of civil law. A **tort** is a wrongful act that involves injury to one's person, property, or reputation in a situation not covered by the terms of a contract—for example, an automobile accident, product liability, or libel. A **contract** is a legally binding agreement in which one party agrees to do something with or for another party—for example, an agreement covering the sale of property or the terms of employment.

## The Jury System

A **jury** is a body of persons selected according to law to hear evidence and decide questions of fact in a court case. There are two basic types of juries in the American legal system: (1) the grand jury and (2) the petit jury.

The major function of the grand jury is to determine whether the evidence against a person charged with a crime is sufficient to justify a trial. The grand jury is used only in criminal proceedings. The petit jury is the trial jury, and it is used in both civil and criminal matters.

**The Grand Jury** The grand jury has from 6 to 23 persons, depending on the State. Where larger juries are used, generally at least 12 jurors must agree that an accused person is probably guilty before a formal accusation is made. Similarly, with smaller juries, an

---

# Differentiated Resources

The following resources are located in the All-in-One, Unit 7, Chapter 24, Section 4:

**L3** Reading Comprehension Worksheet (p. 41)

**L2** Reading Comprehension Worksheet (p. 42)

**L3** Core Worksheet (p. 43)

**L2** Core Worksheet (p. 46)

**L3** Quiz A (p. 49)

**L2** Quiz B (p. 50)

extraordinary majority is needed to indict, which means to bring the formal charge.

When a grand jury is <u>impaneled</u>, the judge instructs the jurors to find a true bill of indictment against any and all persons whom the prosecuting attorney brings to their attention and whom they think are probably guilty. The judge also instructs them to bring a presentment, an accusation, against any persons whom they, of their own knowledge, believe have violated the State's criminal laws.

The grand jury meets in secret. The prosecuting attorney presents witnesses and evidence against persons suspected of crime. The jurors may question those witnesses and may also <u>summon</u> others to testify against a suspect. After receiving the evidence and hearing witnesses, the grand jury deliberates alone and in secret. They then move to the courtroom where their report, including any indictments they may have returned, is read in their presence.

The grand jury is expensive and time-consuming. Therefore, most of the States today depend more heavily on a much simpler process of accusation: the information.

**The Information** An **information** is a formal charge filed by the prosecutor, without the action of a grand jury. It is used for most minor offenses and, in many States, for some serious cases. It is far less costly and time-consuming than a grand jury. Also, since grand juries most often follow the prosecutor's

✓ **Checkpoint**
What does a jury do?

**impaneled**
v. enrolled; established

**summon**
v. call, send for

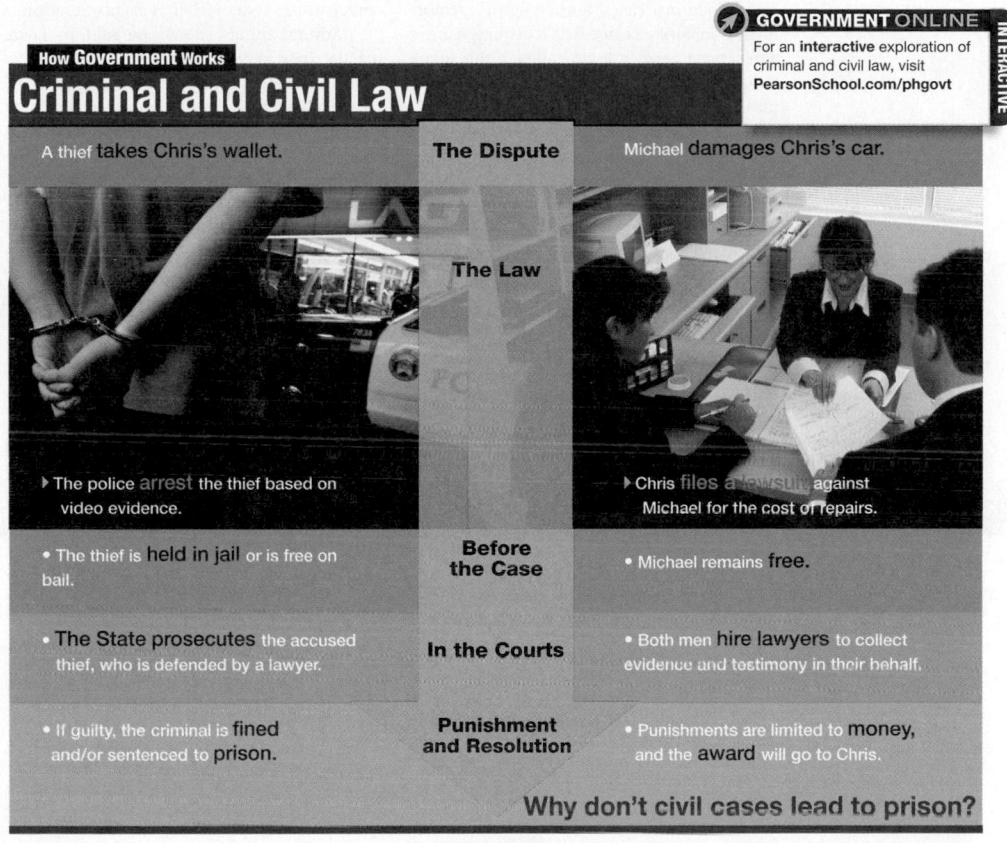

**How Government Works**
# Criminal and Civil Law

GOVERNMENT ONLINE
For an **interactive** exploration of criminal and civil law, visit PearsonSchool.com/phgovt

A thief takes Chris's wallet.

**The Dispute**

Michael damages Chris's car.

**The Law**

▸ The police arrest the thief based on video evidence.

▸ Chris files a lawsuit against Michael for the cost of repairs.

• The thief is held in jail or is free on bail.

**Before the Case**

• Michael remains free.

• The State prosecutes the accused thief, who is defended by a lawyer.

**In the Courts**

• Both men hire lawyers to collect evidence and testimony in their behalf.

• If guilty, the criminal is fined and/or sentenced to prison.

**Punishment and Resolution**

• Punishments are limited to money, and the award will go to Chris.

**Why don't civil cases lead to prison?**

Chapter 24 • Section 4 **729**

# Teacher-to-Teacher Network

**ALTERNATE LESSON PLAN** Have students compare legal systems from other countries, possibly from countries represented in the makeup of the class. In this lesson plan, students will research and present the historical background or foundation of that particular legal system and explain how it is similar to or different from the system found in the United States.

To see this lesson plan, go to

**Teacher Center**
at PearsonSchool.com/phgovt

---

## Answers

**Checkpoint** hears evidence and decides questions of fact in a court case

**Criminal and Civil Law** Civil cases deal with disputes rather than crimes.

Chapter 24 • Section 4  **729**

# Assess and Remediate

**L3** Collect and grade students' work on the Core Worksheet (Unit 7 All-in-One, p. 43).

**L3** Assign the Section 4 Assessment questions.

**L3** Section Quiz A (Unit 7 All-in-One, p. 49)

**L2** Section Quiz B (Unit 7 All-in-One, p. 50)

## REMEDIATION

| If Your Students Have Trouble With | Strategies For Remediation |
|---|---|
| Types of laws and juries in the States (Questions 1, 2, 3) | Make a flowchart on the board similar to the one in the Section Opener. Have students provide information from their own flowcharts to help complete this one. List the five forms of law, differences and definitions of criminal and civil law, and information on the two types of juries. Have students record any new information in their own charts. As you work, give students opportunities to ask questions about anything they still do not understand. |
| The secrecy of grand juries (Question 4) | Tell students to review the text under the heading "The Grand Jury." Ask them to record details about the grand jury process in a concept web. |
| The purpose of an injunction (Question 5) | Write the word *injunction* and its definition on the board. Clarify that its purpose is to stop activity that might cause damage that cannot be repaired later. Point out the example in the text. Ask students to use the Think-Pair-Share strategy to brainstorm situations when an *injunction* might be requested. |

## Answers

**Checkpoint** to decide if the evidence justifies a trial

---

**verdict**
*n.* decision or judgment

recommendations, many argue that a grand jury is really unnecessary. Others feel that the grand jury prevents prosecutors from abusing their powers.

**The Petit Jury** The petit jury, or trial jury, hears the evidence in a case and decides the disputed facts. In very few instances, it may also have the power to interpret and apply the law. That, however, is usually the function of the judge.

The number of trial jurors may vary. As it developed in England, the jury consisted of "12 men good and true." Although 12 is the usual total, a lesser number, often six, now fills jury boxes in several States.

In more than a third of the States, jury verdicts need not be unanimous in civil and minor criminal cases. Rather, some extraordinary majority is needed. If a jury cannot agree on a verdict (a so-called hung jury), either another trial with a new jury takes place or the matter is dropped.

Misdemeanor cases and civil proceedings in which only minor sums are involved are often heard without a jury, in a **bench trial,** by the judge alone. In several States, even the most serious crimes may be heard without a jury if the accused, fully informed of his or her rights, waives the right to trial by jury.

**Selection of Jurors** Jurors are picked in more or less the same way in most States. Periodically, a county official or special jury commissioners prepare a list of persons eligible for jury service, with names drawn from poll books, tax rolls, driver's license records, or other sources.[13] The sheriff serves each person with a court order to appear. After eliminating those who, for good reason, cannot serve, the judge prepares a list of those who can. Persons under 18 and over 70 years of age, illiterates, the ill, and criminals are commonly excluded. Those in occupations vital to the public interest or for whom jury service would mean real hardship are often excused, too.

As with the grand jury, the States are moving away from the use of the trial jury. Leading reasons are the greater time and cost of jury trials. The competence of the average jury and the impulses that may lead it to a verdict are often questioned, as well. Much criticism of the jury system is directed not so much at the system itself as at its operation.

Several things should be said in favor of the jury system, however. It has a long and honorable place in the development of Anglo-American law. Its high purpose is to promote a fair trial, by providing an impartial body to hear the charges brought against the accused. A jury tends to bring the common sense of the community to bear on the law and its application. Finally, the jury system gives citizens a chance to take part in the administration of justice, and it fosters a greater confidence in the judicial system.

---

**13** It may be the clerk of the court, the sheriff, the county governing body, or the presiding judge; in New England, it is officers of the town.

---

## SECTION 4 ASSESSMENT

**Essential Questions Journal**
To continue to build a response to the chapter Essential Question, go to your **Essential Questions Journal.**

1. **Guiding Question** Use your completed flowchart to answer this question: How do State and local courts apply different types of law?

### Key Terms and Comprehension

2. Define **common law, criminal law,** and **civil law.**

3. Identify two types of **juries** and explain what they do.

### Critical Thinking

4. **Check Consistency** Most government processes in this country must take place in public, but a grand jury does its work in secret. **(a)** Why do you think this is? **(b)** Is this secrecy a good idea? Why or why not?

5. **Identify Alternatives** Describe a situation in which someone might seek an injunction. Then write a brief argument in favor of granting the injunction and a brief argument against it.

### Quick Write

**Explanatory Writing: Write a Thesis Statement** As in other types of essays or reports, you need to formulate a thesis statement to direct your thinking, research, and writing. Review your notes to find one main concept that connects your categories and questions. Write a thesis statement that expresses that concept.

---

# Assessment Answers

**1.** They apply five types of law: constitutional, statutory, administrative, common, and equity. Laws are either criminal or civil. In serious cases, a grand jury decides whether to indict, sending the case to a petit jury trial. For minor and some serious offenses, the prosecutor files an information, without a grand jury. In cases involving misdemeanors or minor sums, a judge decides in a bench trial, without a petit jury.

**2.** Common law is unwritten, judge-made law, developed over centuries from generally accepted ideas of right and wrong. Criminal law defines those actions that are crimes and provides for their punishment. Civil law relates to disputes between private parties or private parties and government.

**3. grand jury:** determines whether evidence against a person charged with a crime is sufficient to justify a trial; **petit jury:** a trial jury that hears evidence and decides disputed facts

**4. (a)** Students may suggest that the jury hears much unsupported evidence that if false or misleading could ruin a person's reputation even without indictment or conviction. Secrecy also protects jurors from outside influences or retribution. **(b)** Answers should reflect sound reasoning.

**5.** Example answer: A woman seeks an injunction to stop a former boyfriend from following her. Argument for: The woman fears for her life. Argument against: The man has committed no crime at this point.

**QUICK WRITE** A strong thesis statement should be a complete sentence that expresses one clear goal for the explanatory essay.

# Serving on a Jury

**Someday, you may have the chance to participate directly in the American justice system. The right to be tried by a jury of one's peers is one of the fundamental rights afforded to citizens of a democracy, and is guaranteed by the Constitution. As a juror, you will become a major participant in the American judicial system with a duty to ensure that a fellow citizen receives justice.**

How can you be selected as a potential juror? Most are chosen from voting lists, from State departments of motor vehicles, or tax rolls. How long your jury service may last can vary depending on the nature and complexity of the case involved and whether or not you are actually chosen to serve on a jury panel. Some people are excused from duty due to health issues or other hardships.

You may also be dismissed without having served at all. If you are chosen to move on to the jury selection phase, known as *voir dire*, lawyers on both sides will have questions for the potential jurors as they try to select a jury that they hope will favor their case. You may be rejected.

If chosen, you and the other jurors will receive instructions prior to the beginning of the trial. These may include:

1. **Do not be influenced by bias.** Your decision in a case should not be affected by sympathies or antipathies you may have for the defendant, the plaintiff, or their attorneys.

2. **Follow the law exactly as it is explained to you.** Your job as a juror is to determine whether or not someone broke the law, regardless of whether you approve of the law or not.

3. **Remember that the defendant is presumed innocent.** The government has the burden of proving a defendant guilty "beyond a reasonable doubt." If it fails to do so, the jury verdict must be "not guilty." If you feel that the government did make its case, then you must find the defendant "guilty."

4. **Keep an open mind.** Do not form or state any opinions about the case until you have heard all the evidence, the closing arguments of the lawyers, and the judge's instructions on the applicable law.

5. **During the trial, do not discuss the case.** Do not permit anyone to talk about the case with you or in your presence, except with the court's permission. Avoid media coverage of the case once the trial has begun.

## ▶▶ What do you think?

1. What does the concept "reasonable doubt" mean to you?

2. Why do you think jurors are instructed not to discuss a case and to avoid media coverage of it during the trial?

3. **You Try It** Create a jury simulation. Work in groups of six students to prepare a list of evidence related to a theoretical crime. After each team has completed its list, exchange lists. Following the instructions above, each team will then act as a jury to reach a verdict in another team's case. Ask each jury to discuss its verdict with the team that created the evidence.

### 🡒 GOVERNMENT ONLINE
**Citizenship Activity Pack**
For activities on serving on a jury, go to
**PearsonSchool.com/phgovt**

731

## Citizenship Activity Pack

**L1** **L2** If your students need extra support, use the Citizenship Activity Pack lesson *How to Serve on a Jury.* It includes a lesson plan for you, a poster outlining the development of the jury system, 28 character descriptions for prospective jurors, and case briefs containing scripts for the defendant's team and for the plaintiff's team. Students will hold a mock juror selection. Students may also access the Citizenship Activity Pack online for activities on How to Serve on a Jury at **PearsonSchool.com/phgovt.**

## LESSON GOAL

- Students will work in groups to take part in a jury simulation.

# Teach

### REVIEW THE JURY INSTRUCTIONS

Have students read aloud each instruction to the jury from the feature, as you write it on the board. Ask students if they have any questions about any of the instructions before they begin the simulation.

### DEVELOP EVIDENCE LISTS

Discuss the types of evidence that might be included in a particular trial, such as a criminal trial for robbery. For example, there may be witness or victim statements, videotape from surveillance cameras, a police report, DNA or other forensic evidence, and so on. Give groups time to determine the subjects of their cases and to develop their lists of evidence. Lists should be detailed and include at least five items, as well as a brief description of the case.

### DECIDE A VERDICT AND DISCUSS IT

You may want to assign groups for the exchange of evidence. In their groups, students should discuss the evidence and come to a verdict, which they should write on a piece of paper. Tell students that if their case is a murder, they must be unanimous in their decision. If their case is not a murder, a majority can decide the verdict. When verdicts and intergroup discussions are complete, ask students to each write a summary about their jury experience.

# Assess and Remediate

Collect students' evidence lists and summaries and grade them. You may also wish to have them answer the What Do You Think questions.

## Answers

**1.** Students should suggest that absolute certainty may not be possible but that if the prosecution makes its case, little doubt should remain as to the defendant's guilt.

**2.** Opinions of individuals and the media who are not privy to all the evidence could be inaccurate or biased; their ideas could sway a juror away from his or her true opinion.

**3.** A strong evidence list will include at least five relevant items and a description of the case. A strong summary will accurately present key points and explain the process that led to the verdict.

## How are State and local courts organized and staffed?

| Municipal Courts | Juvenile Courts | Justices and Magistrates' Courts |
|---|---|---|
| • citywide jurisdiction<br>• divisions: civil, criminal, small claims, traffic, probate | • minors under age 18<br>• rehabilitation<br>• may assign serious cases to adult court | • Justices: misdemeanors, small civil suits, warrants, preliminary hearings, marriages<br>• Magistrates: urban version of JPs<br>• both popularly elected |

# Get Started

## LESSON GOALS

Students will . . .

- discuss the positive and negative aspects of electing or appointing judges.
- evaluate methods of judge selection by reading primary sources and through participation in a Socratic Dialogue.

## BEFORE CLASS

Assign the section, the graphic organizer in the text, and the Reading Comprehension Worksheet (Unit 7 All-in-One, p. 51) before class.

**L2 Differentiate** Reading Comprehension Worksheet (Unit 7 All-in-One, p. 52)

## SKILLS DEVELOPMENT

### COMPARE VIEWPOINTS

To teach the skill of comparing viewpoints, have students read Compare Viewpoints in the Skills Handbook, p. S15. Then have them read and evaluate the two editorials in this lesson's Core Worksheet.

## SECTION 5

# State Courts and Their Judges

### Guiding Question

**How are State and local courts organized and staffed?** Use a table similar to the one below to record information about the types of State and local courts.

| Municipal Courts | Juvenile Courts | Justice and Magistrates' Courts |
|---|---|---|
| • | • | • |
| • | • | • |
| • | • | • |

### Political Dictionary

- justice of the peace
- warrant
- preliminary hearing
- magistrate
- appellate jurisdiction

### Objectives

1. Explain how State courts are organized and describe the work that each type of court does.
2. Examine and evaluate the different methods by which judges are selected among the States.

**Image Above:** Leah Sears, Chief Justice of the Georgia Supreme Court and first African American woman to hold that position, 2005–2009

They deal with everything from traffic tickets to murder, from disputes over nickels and dimes to settlements involving millions. They are the State and local courts and the judges who sit in them. Here, you will look at the way these courts are organized and how they conduct their business.

## Organization

Each of the State constitutions creates a court system for that State. Some of the documents deal with the courts at great length, but most of them leave much of the detail of judicial organization and procedure to the legislature.

**Justices of the Peace** Justices of the peace—JPs—stand on the lowest rung of the State judicial ladder. They preside over what are commonly called justice courts.

JPs were once found nearly everywhere in the country. In their day, they seemed well-suited to their purpose. In justice courts, people could obtain a hearing for minor offenses quickly. JPs and their justice courts have been done away with in several States. However, they can still be found in many smaller towns and rural areas.

JPs are usually popularly elected. For the most part, they try misdemeanors—that is, cases involving such petty offenses as traffic violations, disturbing the peace, public drunkenness, and the like. JPs can almost never settle civil disputes involving more than a few hundred dollars. They do issue certain kinds of warrants, hold preliminary hearings, and often perform marriages.

A **warrant** is a court order authorizing, or making legal, some official action. Search warrants and arrest warrants are the most common of these documents. A **preliminary hearing** is generally the first step in a major criminal prosecution. There, the judge decides if the evidence is, in fact, enough to hold that person—bind that person over—for action by the grand jury or the prosecutor.

In some places, JPs are still paid out of the fines they take in. The more fines they impose, the higher their incomes. This "fee system" can lead to any number of abuses and raises serious questions about the fairness of the treatment a defendant can expect.[14]

# Focus on the Basics

Here is the information that your students need to learn in this section.

**FACTS:** • State courts are classified by location, the community they serve, and the types of cases they resolve. • Court cases can be appealed to appellate courts and to the State supreme court. • Most State and local judges are directly elected. • Others are named by legislatures, governors, or by a combination of elected officials and voters.

**CONCEPTS:** judicial branch

**ENDURING UNDERSTANDINGS:** • Local courts serve a defined community and deal with a wide range of case types. • Cases involving difficult points of law rise to appellate courts or State supreme courts on appeal. • Any method of choosing judges raises questions about the independence and quality of the people selected.

**Magistrates' Courts** Magistrates are the city cousins of JPs. For the most part, magistrates handle those minor civil complaints and misdemeanor cases that arise in an urban setting. They preside over what often are called magistrates' courts or police courts. Magistrates, like JPs, are usually popularly elected for fairly short terms.

**Municipal Courts** Municipal courts were first established in Chicago in 1906. They are now found in most large cities and many smaller ones.

The jurisdiction of municipal courts is citywide. They can often hear civil cases involving several thousands of dollars as well as the usual run of misdemeanors. Many municipal courts are organized into divisions, which hear cases of a given kind—for example, civil, criminal, small claims, traffic, and probate divisions.

Consider the small claims division, often called the small claims court. Many people cannot afford the costs of suing for the collection of a small debt. A newspaper carrier, for example, can hardly afford a lawyer to collect a month's subscription from a customer. The owner of a two-family house may have the same problem with a tenant's back rent, and many merchants are forced to forget an overdue bill or sell it to a collection agency.

Small claims courts are designed for just such situations. There, a person can bring a claim for little or no cost. The proceedings are usually informal, and the judge often handles the matter without attorneys for either side.

**Juvenile Courts** Individuals under 18 years of age are generally not subject to the jurisdiction of the courts in which adults are tried. Minors who are arrested for some offense, or who otherwise come to the attention of the police or other authorities, may appear in juvenile courts.

The juvenile justice system is designed to address the special needs and problems of young people. This system generally emphasizes <u>rehabilitation</u> more than punishment. However, under some circumstances, juvenile courts do refer certain offenders to a regular criminal court for trial.

Recently, most States have responded to juvenile crime with tougher criminal laws. Often these statutes make it easier to try juveniles as adults when they are charged with serious crimes. In 46 States, juvenile court judges may assign certain cases involving juveniles to adult courts. In several States, cases that meet certain standards must be tried in adult courts.

**General Trial Courts** Most of the more important civil and criminal cases are heard in the States' general trial courts. Every State is divided into a number of judicial districts, or circuits, each generally covering one or more counties. For each district there is a general trial court, which may be known as a district, circuit, chancery, county, or superior court, or as a court of common pleas.

These general trial courts are courts of "first instance." That is, they exercise original jurisdiction over most of the cases they hear. Most legal actions brought under State law begin in these courts. When cases do come to them on appeal from some lower court, a new trial (a trial *de novo*) is usually held.

The cases heard in trial courts are tried before a single judge. Most often a petit jury (the trial jury) hears and decides the facts at issue in a case, and the judge interprets and applies the law involved. Criminal cases are presented for trial either by a grand jury or, most often, on motion of the prosecuting attorney.

The trial court is seldom limited as to the kinds of cases it may hear. Although this court's decision on the facts in a case is usually final, disputes over questions of law may be carried to a higher court.

✔ **Checkpoint**
What are the responsibilities of JPs, magistrates' courts, and municipal courts?

**rehabilitation**
*n.* the act of restoring, transforming one to a useful, lawful life

**probate**
*adj.* the official proving, verifying, of a will

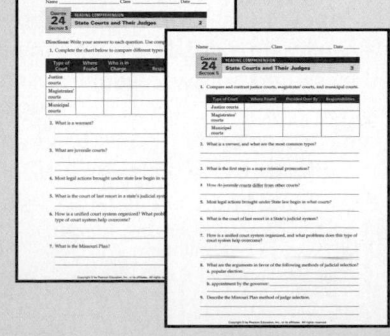
A municipal court might handle appeals of parking tickets.▼

---

14 Many insist that the fee system means that "JP" really stands for "judgment for the plaintiff." The practice also encourages "fee splitting"—an arrangement in which judges can increase the number of misdemeanors they hear by agreeing to share their fees with those arresting officers who bring such cases to them. The "speed trap" is probably the best known and most common result of a fee-splitting situation.

# Differentiated Resources

The following resources are located in the All-in-One, Unit 7, Chapter 24, Section 5:

- **L3** Reading Comprehension Worksheet (p. 51)
- **L2** Reading Comprehension Worksheet (p. 52)
- **L3** Core Worksheet (p. 53)
- **L3** Quiz A (p. 57)
- **L2** Quiz B (p. 58)
- **L3** Chapter Test A (p. 59)
- **L2** Chapter Test B (p. 62)

Write on the board: **How are judges selected in our State? How fair and effective is this method? Answer in your notebook.**

**L1 L2 ELL Differentiate** Suggest that students write their ideas in the form of a two-column advantages/drawbacks chart about the method used in your State to select judges.

# Teach

To present this topic using online resources, use the lesson presentations at **PearsonSchool.com/phgovt.**

## MATCH TYPES OF COURTS WITH CASES

Draw a two-column chart on the board. Have students help you to list the seven main types of courts that may be found in a State's judicial system in the first column. In the second column, ask students to provide examples of the types of cases that might appear in each court. *(examples: JP and magistrates' courts—traffic violations; juvenile courts—vandalism by a minor; municipal courts—a lawsuit over unpaid rent; general trial courts—burglary trial; appellate and State supreme courts—appeal of a case questioning the constitutionality of a State law)*

**L1 L2 Differentiate** Write example cases on the board and have students match each example to the appropriate court.

## EVALUATE METHODS USED TO SELECT JUDGES

Display Transparency 24H, Selection of Judges. Ask: **What are the three main ways of selecting judges in the States?** *(election, appointment by the governor, and appointment by the State legislature)* Tell students that the Missouri Plan is in place in a little over half the States. Election is the method most often used, while appointment by the State legislature is used least. **Why do few people favor appointment by the State legislature?** *(State legislators might select judges biased toward their party's views, not based on judicial merit.)* **How does the Missouri Plan make use of checks and balances?** *(The governor's choice has to be approved by the people, who act as a check on the choice.)* Ask: **Why do you think judges are selected differently at the State and national levels?** *(It could be too cumbersome a process to have national elections for federal judges or people might not know enough to make informed voting decisions.)*

**L2 Differentiate** Have students use the Think-Pair-Share method to answer this question.

---

# Answers

**Checkpoint** JPs and magistrates: misdemeanors, small civil suits, warrants, preliminary hearings, marriages; municipal courts: civil cases of several thousand dollars, misdemeanors, small claims, traffic, probate

## DISTRIBUTE THE CORE WORKSHEET

Distribute Chapter 24 Section 5 Core Worksheet (Unit 7 All-in-One, p. 53), which contains editorials written by retired U.S. Supreme Court Justice Sandra Day O'Connor and J. Karl Miller, a staff writer for the *Columbia Missourian* newspaper. Both editorials give opinions on how judges are selected. Have students read the selections and answer the questions that follow. Tell students that they will use the information and opinions in these selections to participate in a Socratic Dialogue.

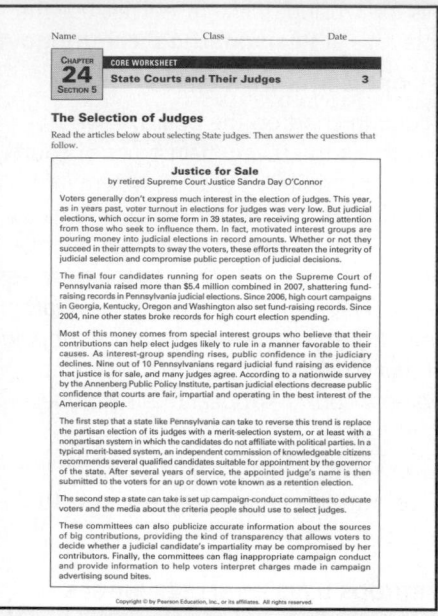

**L2** **ELL Differentiate** If students are having difficulty reading the primary sources on the Core Worksheet, pair them with a more proficient reader to help explain difficult words or concepts.

## Answers

**Juvenile Justice** Juveniles may lack adult judgment in determining right from wrong. Influence from adult inmates could turn juvenile offenders into hardened criminals or be dangerous. Juvenile justice should focus on rehabilitation.

# Juvenile Justice

Juvenile courts arose from decades of struggle at the State level to adapt and reform the criminal justice system. *Why do you think reformers sought separate jails and prisons for young people?*

**1800s** Common law preferred to have parents discipline children for most crimes. Young people accused of serious crimes were jailed with adults, and those as young as seven could be tried and sentenced in criminal courts.

**1899** Cook County, Illinois, creates the first juvenile court on the principle of "the state as parent." The court protects both public safety and the needs of the juveniles accused of crimes.

**1974** Congress passes the Juvenile Justice and Delinquency Prevention Act requiring that young people be jailed separately from adults and encouraging states to develop alternatives to prisons.

**Today** While juvenile courts still flourish, States increasingly allow juveniles accused of serious crimes to be tried and sentenced in adult courts.

**Intermediate Appellate Courts** Most States now have one or more intermediate appellate courts. They are courts of appeal that stand between the trial courts and the State's supreme court. These appellate courts act as "gatekeepers" to ease the burden of the State's highest court.

The appellate courts have different names among the States, but they are most often called the court of appeals.[15] Most of their work involves the review of cases decided in the trial courts. That is, these appeals courts exercise mostly **appellate jurisdiction.** Their original jurisdiction, where it exists, is limited to a few specific kinds of cases—election disputes, for example.

In exercising their appellate jurisdiction, these courts do not hold trials. Rather, they hear oral arguments from attorneys, study the briefs (written arguments) that attorneys submit, and review the record of the case in the lower court.

Ordinarily, an intermediate appellate court does not concern itself with the facts in a case. Rather, its decision turns on whether the law was correctly interpreted and applied in the court below. Its decision may be reviewed by the State's high court; its disposition of a case is usually final, however.

**The State Supreme Court** The State's supreme court is the highest court in its judicial system.[16] Its major function is to review the decisions of lower courts in those cases that appealed to it.

The size of each State supreme court is fixed by that State's constitution, usually at five or seven justices. A chief justice presides over the sessions of each State's top court.

The governor appoints the justices in just over half of the States. The voters elect them elsewhere, except in two States where the legislature chooses.

The State supreme court is the court of last resort in the State's judicial system. It has the final say in all matters of State law. The United States Supreme Court *may* review some State supreme court decisions touching on federal law. But not very many State decisions actually go to the federal Supreme Court.[17] Recall

---

15 In New York, the general trial court is called the supreme court, or the county court; the intermediate appellate court is the appellate division of the supreme court; the State's highest court is known as the Court of Appeals.

16 The State's highest court is known as the Supreme Court in 45 States. But in Maine and Massachusetts it is called the Supreme Judicial Court; in Maryland and New York, the Court of Appeals; and in West Virginia, the Supreme Court of Appeals. Oklahoma and Texas have two high courts: the Supreme Court is the highest court in civil cases, and a separate Court of Criminal Appeals is the court of last resort in criminal cases.

17 Many of the cases that have reached the Supreme Court involved the 14th Amendment's Due Process and Equal Protection clauses.

# Background

**JUVENILE COURT MOVEMENT** For over 100 years from its inception, the United States treated juvenile offenders no differently from adult offenders. In 1899, for example, 322 boys ages 9 to 16 were imprisoned in the city of Chicago for crimes ranging from assault with a deadly weapon to picking up coal on the railroad tracks. In prison, they shared cells with adult criminals. This raised an outcry for a new system, and the Illinois Juvenile Court Act of 1899 established the first separate, noncriminal court for the children of the State. The juvenile court movement spread rapidly, due largely to the influence and philosophy of Judge Ben Lindsey of Colorado, and by the 1920s every State had some legal provision for delinquent youth.

that an appeal from a State's highest court will be heard in the federal Supreme Court only if (1) a "federal question"—some matter of federal law—is involved in the case and (2) the Supreme Court agrees to hear that appeal. In short, most State supreme court decisions are final.[18]

**Unified Court Systems** The typical State court system is organized geographically rather than by types of cases. In these map-based systems, a judge must hear cases in nearly all areas of the law. A <u>backlog</u> of cases can and often does build up in some courts while judges sit with little to do in others. Moreover, uneven interpretations and applications of the law may and sometimes do occur from one part of the State to another. To overcome these difficulties, a number of States have turned to a unified court system—one that is organized on a functional, or case-type, basis.

In a completely unified court system, there is technically only one court for the entire State. It is presided over by a chief judge or judicial council. There are a number of levels within the single court, such as supreme, intermediate appellate, and general trial sections. At each level within each section, divisions are established to hear cases in certain specialized or heavy-caseload areas of the law—criminal, juvenile, family relations, and other areas that need special attention.

In such an arrangement, a judge can be assigned to that section or division to which his or her talents and interests seem best suited. To relieve overcrowded dockets, judges may be moved from one division to another.

## Selection of Judges

Clearly, the quality of any court system—indeed, the quality of justice itself—depends in large measure on the selection of competent,

---

18 State law regularly gives its lower courts final jurisdiction over many types of minor cases. That is, review cannot be sought in a higher State court. In those cases, the lower court is the State's court of last resort. If any review is to be had, it can be only in the United States Supreme Court. Such reviews are extremely rare.

19 Alabama, Illinois, Kentucky, Michigan, Minnesota, Nevada, New Mexico, North Carolina, North Dakota, Pennsylvania, Wisconsin.

---

well-trained judges. More than 15,000 judges now sit in the States' various trial and appellate courts. Nearly all of them came to office in one of three ways: (1) by popular election, (2) by appointment by the governor, or (3) by appointment by the legislature.

Popular election is by far the most widely used method of judicial selection. In fact, the only way to become a judge in 11 States is by popular election.[19] Midterm vacancies, caused by death or resignation, provide the only exception to that blanket rule; those vacancies are usually filled by gubernatorial appointment. Roughly half of all judicial elections are nonpartisan contests today.

Selection by the legislature is the method least often used. The lawmakers now choose all or at least most judges in only two States: South Carolina and Virginia.

Governors now select nearly a fourth of all State judges. In five States, the chief executive appoints them all. In several others, the governor has the power to appoint all or at least many judges, but under a Missouri Plan arrangement, as you will see.

**How Should Judges Be Selected?** Most people believe that judges should be independent, that they should "stay out of politics."

"My basic judicial philosophy is 'Guilty.'"

▶▶ **Analyzing Political Cartoons** *What does this cartoon suggest about electing judges based on their judicial philosophy?*

---

✔ **Checkpoint**
Why do some States have a unified court system?

**backlog**
*n.* a build-up of unfinished work

---

## MAKE A DECISION USING A SOCRATIC DIALOGUE

Discuss students' answers to the Bellringer questions. Then discuss their reactions to the primary source readings and ask whether either source changed their ideas about appointment versus election of judges. Ask: **How does the election of judges help or hurt the judicial system?** *(More competent judges might be chosen through appointment, but election ensures accountability to the people.)* **Selecting judges through popular election is more democratic, but does it create a stronger or weaker judicial system?** Tell students that they will have 15 minutes to choose whether they think election or appointment is the best method. Remind them to consider the advantages and disadvantages of both. Have them use a Socratic Dialogue (p. T24) to decide.

### FOLLOW UP THE DISCUSSION

Give students a few minutes to reflect on the results of the Socratic Dialogue in a journal entry. If they agreed on a method, have students answer these questions: **What criteria were important in your choice? Is one method overwhelmingly better than another? Is one method best for all cases?**

If they were unable to agree, have students answer these questions: **Why were you not able to agree on a method? Do you think the class could have settled on a method for specific government levels or specific types of courts?**

### EXTEND THE LESSON

Have students investigate the types of courts in your State's judicial system. Ask them to use the information they find to create an informational poster that explains each type of court, each level of authority, and how each court's judges are selected.

---

## Answers

**Checkpoint** to spread caseloads more evenly and to make interpretations and applications of law more uniform across the State

**Analyzing Political Cartoons** that the elected judge's judicial philosophy could be positive or negative

# Assess and Remediate

**L3** Assess students' class participation using the Rubric for Assessing Individual Performance in a Group (Unit 7 All-in-One, p. 126).

**L3** Assign the Section 5 Assessment questions.

**L3** Section Quiz A (Unit 7 All-in-One, p. 57)

**L2** Section Quiz B (Unit 7 All-in-One, p. 58)

Have students complete the review activities in the digital lesson presentation and continue their work in the **Essential Questions Journal.**

## REMEDIATION

| If Your Students Have Trouble With | Strategies For Remediation |
|---|---|
| The organization of the State courts (Questions 1, 2, 3) | List the seven main types of courts at the State level on the board. Ask students to supply details about each type, including their main functions and the kinds of cases they hear. |
| How judges are selected (Question 4) | Write the three methods of judge selection on the board in the form of a pro/con chart. Based on their reading and their own thinking, ask students to suggest the benefits and drawbacks of each method. |
| Qualifications for judges (Question 5) | Have students create a résumé that represents someone they would consider to be a highly qualified judge. Tell students to work in groups of three to compare the types of experience they listed. |

## Answers

**Checkpoint** by popular election or by gubernatorial appointment

---

✔ **Checkpoint**
What are the two main ways that judges are selected?

**proponent**
*n.* one who is actively in favor of something; a supporter

Whatever method of selection is used should be designed with that goal in mind.

Nearly all authorities agree that selection by the legislature is the most political of all the methods of choice. Few favor it. So, the question really becomes: Which is better, the popular election of judges or their appointment by the governor?

Those who favor popular election generally make the democratic argument. Because judges "say the law" (interpret and apply it), they should be chosen by and answer directly to the people. Some also argue that the separation of powers is undercut if the executive names the members of the judicial branch.

Those who favor appointment by the governor argue that the judicial function should be carried out only by those who are well qualified. The fact that a person has the support of a political party or is a good vote-getter does not mean that person has the capacity to be a good judge. Proponents of executive appointment insist that it is the best way to ensure that those persons who preside in courts will have the qualities most needed in that role: absolute honesty and integrity, fairness, and the necessary training and ability in the law.

Deciding between these two positions is difficult at best. The people have often made excellent choices, and governors have not always made wise and nonpolitical ones. Still, most authorities come down on the side of gubernatorial appointment—largely because those characteristics that make a good judge and those that make a good candidate are not too often found in the same person.

Popular election is both widely used and widely supported by citizens and party organizations. So, most moves to revise methods of judicial selection have kept at least some element of voter choice.

**The Missouri Plan** For most of the past century, the American Bar Association (ABA) has sponsored an approach that combines election and appointment. The method is often called "the Missouri Plan," and some form is now in place in just over half the States.

In Missouri's version of this method, the governor appoints the seven justices of the State supreme court, the 32 judges of the court of appeals, and all judges who sit in the trial courts in the most heavily populated parts of the State. The governor must make each appointment from a panel, or list, of three candidates recommended by a judicial nominating commission. The commission is made up of a sitting judge, several members of the bar, and private citizens.

Each judge named by the governor serves until the first general election after he or she has been in office for at least a year. The judge's name then appears on the ballot without opposition. The voters decide, in a retain-reject election, whether or not that judge should be kept in office. Should the voters reject a sitting judge, the process begins again.

**Essential Questions Journal** To continue to build a response to the chapter Essential Question, go to your **Essential Questions Journal.**

## SECTION **5** ASSESSMENT

**1. Guiding Question** Use your completed table to answer this question: How are State and local courts organized and staffed?

**Key Terms and Comprehension**

**2. (a)** What is **appellate jurisdiction?** **(b)** Which State courts have this jurisdiction?

**3.** Describe the work of the general trial courts.

**Critical Thinking**

**4. Demonstrate Reasoned Judgment** How do you think judges should be selected? Choose one method described in this section and create a strong, well-supported argument for that method.

**5. Draw Inferences** What qualifications do you think a good judge should have? Write a help-wanted advertisement for your ideal candidate.

**Quick Write**

**Explanatory Writing: Create an Outline** To help you structure an explanatory essay on the differences in power between the national and State governments, create an outline in which you identify each topic and subtopic in a single phrase. When you are ready to write your essay, you can use the outline as a guide. Alternatively, you may create a flowchart to help you organize and order your ideas.

---

# Assessment Answers

**1.** Main types of State courts: Justice of the Peace courts (misdemeanors, small civil suits, warrants, preliminary hearings, marriages); magistrates' courts (urban version of JPs); municipal courts (civil, criminal, small claims, traffic, probate); juvenile courts (minors under age 18); general trial courts (most of the more important civil and criminal cases); intermediate appellate courts (appeals from trial courts); supreme court (appeals from lower courts). Some States have a unified court system with a chief judge or council and several levels. Divisions within each level hear cases in specialized or heavy-caseload areas, such as criminal, juvenile, and family relations. Judges in the States may be elected, appointed by the governor, or appointed by the legislature. The Missouri Plan combines election and appointment.

**2. (a)** review of the interpretation and application of law in cases decided by lower courts **(b)** intermediate appellate courts and the State supreme court

**3.** General trial courts exercise original jurisdiction, and hear both criminal and civil cases.

**4.** Strong answers should focus on the goal of keeping judges independent of politics as much as possible.

**5.** Answers will vary but might include knowledge of the law and judicial processes, good judgment, honesty, integrity, and fairness.

**QUICK WRITE** Outlines should be presented in correct outline format and cover the topic of the differences in power between the State and national governments appropriately and logically.

# Quick Study Guide

**GOVERNMENT** ONLINE
**On the Go**
To review anytime, anywhere, download these online resources at **PearsonSchool.com/phgovt**
Political Dictionary, Audio Review

**CHAPTER 24**

**Guiding Question**
**Section 2** What are the defining traits and purpose of State legislatures?

**Guiding Question**
**Section 3** What are the roles and powers of a governor?

**Guiding Question**
**Section 4** How do State and local courts apply different types of law?

**Guiding Question**
**Section 1** What are the defining features of State constitutions?

**CHAPTER 24**
**Essential Question**
How much power should State government have?

**Guiding Question**
**Section 5** How are State and local courts organized and staffed?

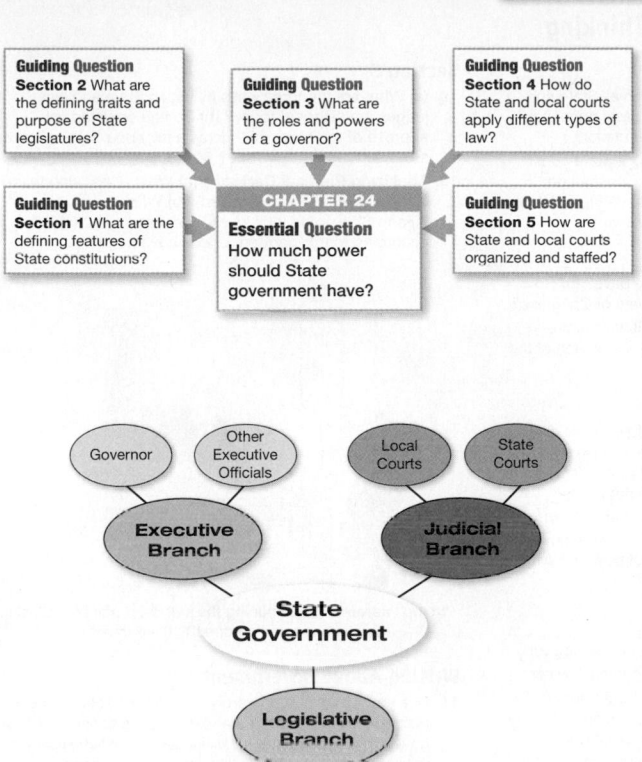

## Political Dictionary

**popular sovereignty** *p. 709*
**limited government** *p. 709*
**fundamental law** *p. 710*
**initiative** *p. 712*
**statutory law** *p. 713*
**police power** *p. 717*
**constituent power** *p. 717*
**referendum** *p. 719*
**recall** *p. 721*
**item veto** *p. 724*
**clemency** *p. 724*
**pardon** *p. 724*
**commutation** *p. 725*
**reprieve** *p. 725*
**parole** *p. 725*
**common law** *p. 727*
**precedent** *p. 728*
**criminal law** *p. 728*
**felony** *p. 728*
**misdemeanor** *p. 728*
**civil law** *p. 728*
**tort** *p. 728*
**contract** *p. 728*
**jury** *p. 728*
**information** *p. 729*
**bench trial** *p. 730*
**justice of the peace** *p. 732*
**warrant** *p. 732*
**preliminary hearing** *p. 732*
**magistrate** *p. 733*
**appellate jurisdiction** *p. 734*

## Legal Terms

| Term | Purpose |
|------|---------|
| Jury | To reach a just decision |
| Common law | To guide a judge's decisions with past examples |
| Equity | To stop wrongs before they occur |
| Criminal law | To protect the public order |
| Civil law | To resolve disputes between people and between people and the government |

## For More Information

To learn more about governing the states, refer to these sources or assign them to students:

**L1** **De Capua, Sarah.** *Being a Governor.* Children's Press, 2004.

**L2** **Marvis, B., Austin Sarat, and Leslie Berger.** *Grand Jury.* Chelsea House Publishers, 2000.

**L3** **Braunstein, Richard.** *Initiative and Referendum Voting: Governing Through Direct Democracy in the United States.* LFB Scholarly Publishing LLC, 2004.

**L4** **Tarr, G. Alan.** *Understanding State Constitutions.* Princeton University Press, 2000.

---

Have students download the digital resources available at Government on the Go for review and remediation.

### STUDY TIPS

**SQ3R** SQ3R stands for "Survey, Question, Read, Recite, Review." Explain to students that SQ3R is a reading method that will help them organize and remember information. When they sit down to read a section of their textbook using this method, students will first **survey** the section. This means skimming the headings, subheadings, and captions in the section, as well as introductory and concluding paragraphs. Students should then skim the section again, this time asking themselves **questions** such as "What is this section about?" and turning the headings and subheadings into questions. After considering these questions briefly, students should **read** the section, looking for the answers. While reading, students should also note key terms and review graphic organizers. When reading is complete, students **recite** information from the section. To do this, they can ask themselves questions aloud or summarize aloud what they've read or jot down key points in their own words. The **review** part of the method is ongoing over several days. To review what they have read, students can write questions about the content, skim the material, or create graphic organizers to summarize the material in the section. Students might also make flash cards of key points in the section that they can use while studying.

### ASSESSMENT AT A GLANCE

**Tests and Quizzes**
Section Assessments
Section Quizzes A and B, Unit 7 **All-in-One**
Chapter Assessment
Chapter Tests A and B, Unit 7 **All-in-One**
Document-Based Assessment
Progress Monitoring Online
Exam*View* Test Bank

**Performance Assessment**
Essential Questions Journal
Extend the Lesson, p. 711
Assessment Rubrics, **All-in-One**

# Chapter Assessment

**COMPREHENSION AND CRITICAL THINKING**

## SECTION 1

1. **(a)** popular sovereignty, limited government, separation of powers, checks and balances **(b)** The early constitutions arose from the experiences of the American Revolution and reflect the goals of the revolutionaries. After throwing off the tyranny of the British government, Americans wanted to set limits and checks within their constitutions to protect basic rights and ensure that the people remained the supreme authority and that their governments could not oppress them again.

2. **(a)** Amending State constitutions requires a proposal from a constitutional convention, the legislature, or popular initiative followed by ratification by popular vote, typically by a majority of those voting. Amending the U.S. Constitution is more difficult. There is no initiative process, and proposals and ratification require greater support than a majority vote. **(b)** The process of formal change for State constitutions involves proposal by the legislature, which can be simple in some States or difficult in others. In 18 States, the voters themselves can propose constitutional amendments through the initiative, a process in which voters sign petitions in favor of a proposal that goes on the ballot for approval or rejection by the people. Over the years, State constitutions have grown in size and complexity, with outdated provisions and unnecessary details.

## SECTION 2

3. **(a)** all powers not granted to another branch or denied by State or U.S. constitutions; pass laws that do not conflict with federal law or the State constitution; tax, spend, borrow, establish courts/jurisdiction, define crimes/punishment, regulate commerce, maintain schools; police power; approve appointments; impeach; propose State constitutional amendments **(b)** State legislatures basically have the same powers as Congress, but they also have the police power, which is reserved to them.

4. **(a)** Voters can propose and force a vote on an amendment or a law by initiative. In a referendum, the legislature decides to refer the measure to the voters. **(b)** Students should support their positions with details from the text.

---

# Chapter Assessment

## Comprehension and Critical Thinking

### Section 1

1. **(a)** What are the basic principles on which all State constitutions are based? **(b)** How do these basic principles reflect the origins of the first State constitutions?

2. **(a)** Explain how the process of amending a State constitution differs from amending the federal Constitution. **(b)** How might the two basic methods for changing State constitutions contribute to the need for reform?

### Section 2

3. **(a)** What powers does a State legislature have? **(b)** How are those powers different from the powers of Congress?

4. **(a)** What is the difference between an initiative and a referendum? **(b)** Is the initiative process a reflection of the principle of representative government?

### Section 3

5. **(a)** How does the governor's role as chief executive differ from the President's role as head of the executive branch? **(b)** Should the formal and informal qualifications for a governorship differ from those for the presidency? Why?

6. **(a)** Which of the governor's executive powers is most important? Explain. **(b)** Do the governor's judicial powers conflict with the principle of separation of powers? Why or why not?

### Section 4

7. **(a)** What is common law and what are its origins? **(b)** Why do you think that it remains important to our legal system?

8. **(a)** What does the use of juries tell you about traditional American views of the proper role of citizens and government officials in the judicial process? **(b)** What does the trend away from jury trials say about trends in the American system of justice?

### Section 5

9. **(a)** What are the three ways by which State and local judges are selected today? **(b)** Do you or would you approve of the Missouri Plan as a fair and effective way to select judges in your State? Why or why not?

10. **Analyzing Political Cartoons (a)** What does "streamlining the judicial process" mean? **(b)** What are the benefits to States and individuals of streamlining? **(c)** What, according to this cartoon, is a disadvantage?

"In the interest of streamlining the judicial process, we'll skip the evidence and go directly to sentencing."

### Writing About Government

11. Use your Quick Write exercises from the section assessments to write an essay that explains the aspect of State government you selected. Make sure the body supports your thesis with accurate information and reasoned arguments. See pp. S3–S5 in the Skills Handbook.

---

## Apply What You've Learned

12. **Essential Question Activity** Speak with a State legislator, legislative aide, or employee of State government. Ask:

   **(a)** How does State government most directly affect people's lives?

   **(b)** Is State government as responsible to voters as it should be?

   **(c)** If you could change the structure of State government, what would you do?

13. **Essential Question Assessment** Use the interview you conducted to write an editorial that helps you answer the Essential Question: **How much power should State government have?** In your editorial, propose what you think is the one most important reform that should be made to your State's government. Explain your reasoning and include information from your interview to help persuade readers of the benefits of your suggested reform.

**Essential Questions**
**Journal**
To respond to the chapter Essential Question, go to your **Essential Questions Journal.**

---

## SECTION 3

5. **(a)** A governor shares power with other State executives. The President is alone at the top. **(b)** Some students may feel that since both positions require similar responsibilities, the qualifications should be the same. Others may feel that President is a broader and more crucial job requiring more experience and greater qualifications.

6. **(a)** Students should choose one of the executive powers and support their choice. **(b)** The governor can alter judicial decisions, thereby checking the power of the judicial branch, by using the powers of pardon, commutation, reprieve, and parole. The governor cannot remove a judge or jury or decide a case, but only change a decision and probably would not do this lightly because of public opinion.

## SECTION 4

7. **(a)** The common law is unwritten, judge-made law developed over centuries from generally accepted ideas of right and wrong that have gained judicial recognition. It originated in England. **(b)** Possible answer: It is important because it is the

# Document-Based Assessment

## Direct Democracy in the States

The initiative and referendum are crucial tools of direct democracy that grew out of the Populist and Progressive reform movements of the nineteenth and early twentieth centuries as indicated in Document 1. These reforms increased control of government by the voters, but some critics wonder how effective they really are, as shown in Document 2.

### Document 1

" Corruption dominates the ballot-box, the Legislatures, the Congress, and touches even. . . the bench. The people are demoralized; . . . [t]he newspapers are largely subsidized or muzzled, public opinion silenced, business [exhausted], homes covered with mortgages, labor impoverished, and the land concentrating in the hands of capitalists. . . . From the same [fertile] womb of governmental injustice we breed the two great classes—tramps and millionaires. . . . We have witnessed for more than a quarter of a century the struggles of the two great political parties for power and plunder, while grievous wrongs have been inflicted upon the suffering people. We charge that the controlling influences dominating both these parties have permitted the existing dreadful conditions to develop without serious effort to prevent or restrain them. Neither do they now promise us any substantial reform. . . . They propose to sacrifice our homes, lives, and children on the altar of mammon; to destroy the multitude in order to secure [corrupt] funds from the millionaires. . . . RESOLVED, that we commend to the favorable consideration of the people and the reform[ist] press the legislative system known as the initiative and referendum.

—The Populist Party Platform, 1892

### Document 2

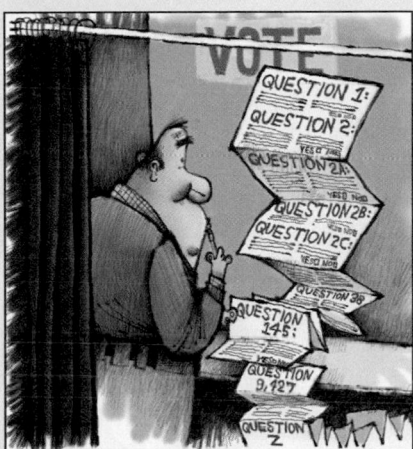

Use your knowledge of the police power and Documents 1 and 2 to answer Questions 1–3.

1. Through the initiative and referendum, the Populist Party hoped to
   A. redistribute money and land to promote the economic equality of all Americans
   B. create long and confusing ballots designed to trick voters.
   C. give Americans more faith in their powerful and wealthy leaders.
   D. take power away from the wealthy and special interests and restore it to the common people.

2. What concern about ballot reforms is the cartoonist expressing in Document 2? Explain.

3. **Pull It Together** Do you think that initiatives and referenda are still effective ways for voters to influence or control government in the States? Explain.

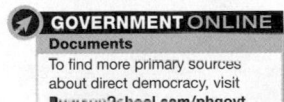 **GOVERNMENT** ONLINE
**Documents**
To find more primary sources about direct democracy, visit
Pearson3chool.com/phgovt

---

## DOCUMENT-BASED ASSESSMENT

1. D

2. Reforms will result in so many initiatives that the ballot will become overly long and complicated.

3. Answers should reflect an understanding of the need to give reasonable voice to ordinary citizens without overcomplicating elections. Students should recognize that voters have an important role in a democracy, whether exercised indirectly through elected officials or directly through initiative and referendum.

**L2 Differentiate** Students use all the documents on the page to support their thesis.

**L3 Differentiate** Students include additional information available online at **PearsonSchool.com/phgovt.**

**L4 Differentiate** Students use materials from the textbook, the online information at **PearsonSchool.com/phgovt,** and do additional research to support their views.

 **Go Online to PearsonSchool.com/phgovt** for a student rubric and extra documents.

---

tradition on which many written laws and judicial decisions today are based.

8. **(a)** possible answer: faith in ordinary citizens and suspicion of government **(b)** Possible answer: It may indicate a desire for fast, inexpensive results and more efficient government; less confidence in the motivation and competence of jurors and more confidence in professional jurists.

### SECTION 5

9. **(a)** popular election, appointment by governor, appointment by legislature **(b)** Students should support their opinion.

10. **(a)** simplifying the trial process **(b)** a quicker, less costly resolution of a trial **(c)** the possibility that critical evidence would not be heard and a fair judgment might not be reached

### WRITING ABOUT GOVERNMENT

11. Essays should be well-organized and clearly explain the concept or process students worked to develop throughout the chapter.

### APPLY WHAT YOU'VE LEARNED

12. Responses should summarize the interviewee's answers.

13. Students' editorials should contain well-organized, informative details presented in an effective, persuasive style.

# Introduce the Chapter

## Essential Questions:

**UNIT 7**

What is the right balance of federal, State, and local government?

**CHAPTER 25**

How local should government be?

### ACTIVATE PRIOR KNOWLEDGE

Have students examine the photo and quotation on these pages. Ask: **What do the photo and quotation suggest about the importance of local governments in citizens' lives?** *(Local governments can be agents of change for their citizens.)* In this chapter, students will learn how State and local governments serve citizens. Tell students to further explore local governments by completing the Chapter 25 Essential Question Warmup activity in their **Essential Questions Journal.** Discuss their responses.

### BEFORE READING

**L2 ELL Differentiate** Chapter 25 Prereading and Vocabulary Worksheet (Unit 7 All-in-One, p. 74)

### SUCCESSNET STUDENT AND TEACHER CENTER

Visit **PearsonSchool.com/phgovt** for downloadable resources that allow students and teachers to connect with government "on the go."

### DIGITAL LESSON PRESENTATION

The digital lesson presentation supports the print lesson with activities and summaries of key concepts. Activities for this chapter include:

- **Municipalities and Townships**
- **State and Local Spending**

## SKILLS DEVELOPMENT

### ANALYZE CAUSE AND EFFECT

You may wish to teach analyzing cause and effect as a distinct skill within Section 2 of this chapter. Use the Chapter 25 Skills Worksheet (Unit 7 All-in-One, p. 94) to help students learn how to analyze cause and effect. The worksheet asks students to read an excerpt and then explain how highway construction is described as both a cause and an effect. For L2 and L1 students, assign the adapted Skill Activity (Unit 7 All-in-One, p. 95).

**WebQuest online** The chapter WebQuest challenges students to answer the chapter Essential Question by asking them about local government.

740

## Block Scheduling

**BLOCK 1:** Teach the Section 1 lesson and assign the L3 Extend option. Teach the Section 2 lesson, omitting the city planning activity and the Extend options.

**BLOCK 2:** Teach the Section 3 and 4 lessons, omitting the Extend options.

CHAPTER

# 25

## Local Government and Finance

**Essential Question**
How local should government be?

Section 1:
Counties, Towns, and Townships

Section 2:
Cities and Metropolitan Areas

Section 3:
Providing Vital Services

Section 4:
Financing State and Local Government

> **Now,** we find ourselves on the brink of **great change** and we stand at **the edge of greatness**. ... We can choose to try **new ideas,** new approaches, **new ways** of doing things.

—Philadelphia Mayor Michael Nutter

**Photo:** Mayor Nutter in Philadelphia's City Hall, 2008

**GOVERNMENT** ONLINE
On the Go

To study anywhere, anytime, download these online resources at PearsonSchool.com/phgovt
• Political Dictionary
• Audio Review
• Downloadable Interactivities

741

# Lesson Goals

**SECTION 1**

Students will . . .

• use a transparency to discuss the typical structure and variations in county governments.
• work with a partner to debate the need for county government.
• investigate their own local government structure to complete an informational diagram.

**SECTION 2**

Students will . . .

• compare and contrast the three basic forms of city government using a transparency.
• experience the planning function of city government by planning a city square.

**SECTION 3**

Students will . . .

• list and categorize services that they receive from State and local governments.
• role-play to complete a worksheet ranking the importance of State and local services from various perspectives.
• compare their rankings of State services against actual State and local spending.

**SECTION 4**

Students will . . .

• list and categorize taxes as progressive or regressive.
• use a bar graph to discuss sources of State and local revenue.
• evaluate different types of State and local taxes based on four criteria describing "a good tax."

# Pressed for Time

To cover the chapter quickly, have students complete the Reading Comprehension worksheets for Section 1 and Section 2. Write each type of local government—counties, towns, townships, and cities—on the board, and ask students to volunteer features of each. Clarify the type of local government in your community. Define and describe the structure of the types of local government. Ask students to suggest the types of services that each needs to provide. Discuss how local governments raise money to pay for these services. Conclude by emphasizing this importance of local government, and have students write a journal entry to answer this question: **Would it be possible for a nation as large as the United States to meet the needs of its citizens without local governments?** Have students provide reasoned arguments and details to support their positions.

**DIFFERENTIATED INSTRUCTION KEY**

Look for these symbols to help you adjust steps in each lesson to meet your students' needs.

**L1** Special Needs
**L2** Basic
**ELL** English Language Learners
**LPR** Less Proficient Readers
**L3** All Students
**L4** Advanced Students

What are the similarities and differences of local governments, special districts, and tribal governments?

| Types of Local Government | | |
|---|---|---|
| **Counties** | **Towns** | **Townships** |
| • New England: serve as judicial districts<br>• South and West: main unit in rural areas<br>• Elements: governing body, several boards or commissions, appointed bureaucrats, elected officials<br>• Governing body usually has executive and legislative powers<br>• Boards of commissioners: include fair board, planning commission, board of health<br>• Administer State and county laws; keep peace; maintain jails; assess property for taxes; collect taxes; spend county funds; maintain roads, bridges, schools; record deeds, marriage licenses, other documents; issue licenses; administer elections; care for poor; safeguard health | • Found in New England<br>• Major unit of local government in New England<br>• Include rural and urban areas<br>• Deliver services provided by cities and counties elsewhere<br>• Town meeting open to all eligible voters—levies taxes, makes spending and policy decisions, elects officials<br>• Board of selectmen/selectwomen manages town business<br>• Direct democracy replaced by representative government in larger towns | • Mid-Atlantic and Midwest: share government with counties<br>• About half have annual township meetings<br>• Others have elected board of trustees or supervisors<br>• Municipality—separate urban unit within township<br>• Townships tend to be rural |

# SECTION 1
# Counties, Towns, and Townships

### Guiding Question

**What are the similarities and differences of local governments, special districts, and tribal governments?** Use a chart similar to the one below to record facts about local governments.

| Types of Local Government | | |
|---|---|---|
| **Counties** | **Towns** | **Townships** |
| • Major unit of local government | • Found in New England<br>• | •<br>• |

**Political Dictionary**
- county
- township
- municipality
- special district

**Objectives**
1. Describe the typical county, its governmental structure, and functions.
2. Analyze the need for reform in county government.
3. Identify the responsibilities of tribal governments.
4. Examine the governments of towns, townships, and special districts.

**Image Above:** Local governments provide fire protection and many other essential services.

You know that the Census Bureau is in the people-counting business. Do you know that it also counts a great many other things—including units of government? The Bureau's Census of Governments found an astounding 89,527 governments in the United States. In 2007, it counted the Federal Government, 50 States, and 89,476 local governments across the country.

Those local units come in many different shapes and sizes. Some have only a handful of employees and operate with only meager budgets. Others have tens of thousands of employees and budgets of a billion dollars or more. Many perform only a single public function, such as providing fire protection or water service. Others, including nearly all cities and most urban counties, deliver a long list of services, limited only by budgetary and legal restraints.

The Constitution of the United States says nothing about local governments. So, cities, towns, counties, school districts, and all other local governments, unlike the Federal Government and the 50 States, have no independent constitutional standing. They are, instead, creatures of the States.

Recall that each of the 50 States is a *unitary* government. Each one of them has the reserved power to create local governments and structure them in whatever ways it chooses—and also to abolish them, if it chooses to do so.[1] Whether they are providing services, regulating activities, collecting taxes, or doing anything else, local governments can only act because the State that established them has given them the power to do so.

## Counties

A **county** is a major unit of local government in most States. Like all local governments, it is created by the State. There are 3,028 county governments in the United States today. No close relationship exists between the size of any given State and the number of counties in that State. The number of county governments per State ranges from none in Connecticut and Rhode Island and three in Delaware to as many as 254 in Texas.

---

[1]  The Census Bureau found 116,756 local units in its first Census of Governments, in 1952. There are, then, more than 27,000 fewer units of local government than there were a half century ago. The Bureau conducts the Census of Governments in every fifth year ending in 2 or 7.

# Focus on the Basics

Here is the information that your students need to learn in this section.

**FACTS:** • Counties exist in most States. • County responsibilities may include building and maintaining roads, sewers, and other public works; operating jails; keeping public records; and safeguarding health. • Towns and townships are found in the Northeast and Midwest. • Special districts serve specific functions at the local level.

**CONCEPTS:**  types of governments, role of government

**ENDURING UNDERSTANDINGS:** • Local governments supply basic services of daily life. • County, town, and township governments offer many of the same services. • Special districts are created where other boundaries don't correspond with the area in need of services. • Federally recognized Native American tribal governments are sovereign.

In Louisiana, units of government known elsewhere as counties are called parishes. In Alaska, they are known as boroughs. In addition to the entire States of Connecticut and Rhode Island, several other places across the country have no organized county government. About 10 percent of the nation's population lives in those areas today.

The functions of counties vary, often widely, from region to region. They serve almost solely as judicial districts in some of the New England States. There, towns carry out most of the functions undertaken by counties elsewhere in the country. In many mid-Atlantic and Midwestern States, counties are divided into subdivisions called **townships.** In those States, counties and townships share the functions of rural local government. In the South and the West, counties are the major governing unit in rural areas.

In terms of area, San Bernardino County in California is the largest in the continental United States; it spreads across 20,105 square miles. Kalawao County in Hawaii is the smallest; it covers just 13 square miles. Counties within each State often vary widely in area.

Counties also differ greatly in terms of population. Nearly 10 million people now live in Los Angeles County in Southern California, but census takers could find only 67 residents of Loving County, Texas, in 2000. Almost three quarters of all counties serve populations of fewer than 50,000 today.

## County Government Structure

The structures of county government differ, too, and often considerably. Even so, a county typically has four major elements: a governing body, a number of boards or commissions, appointed bureaucrats, and a variety of elected officials.

**The Governing Body** The county's governing body is frequently called the county board. It is also known as the board of commissioners, board of supervisors, police jury, assembly, legislature, and board of chosen freeholders, among other names.

The members of this governing body are almost always popularly elected. Terms of office run from two to six years, but four-year terms are the most common. Board members are usually chosen from districts within the county rather than on an at-large basis.

Generally, county boards can be grouped into two types: boards of commissioners and boards of supervisors. The board of commissioners is the smaller, more common type. It is found everywhere in the South and West, and it is also well known elsewhere. A board of commissioners most often has three or five members, but some have seven or more.

The board of supervisors is typically a much larger body. It averages about 15 members but can run to 80 or more. The supervisors are elected from single-member districts in the county. Each supervisor may be an officer of his or her township, as well as a member of the countywide governing body.

The State constitution and acts of the State legislature spell out the powers held by county governing bodies. Those powers are usually both executive and legislative, despite the American tradition of separation of powers.

County governments' most important legislative powers deal with finance. Everywhere, county boards levy taxes, appropriate funds, and can <u>incur</u> limited debts. They also have a number of other legislative powers— for example, in the fields of public health and corrections.

✔ **Checkpoint**
In what ways do counties vary across the country?

<u>incur</u>
v. invite, bring about

The county courthouse is the center of county government, as in Sevier County, Tennessee.

## Get Started

### LESSON GOALS

Students will . . .

- use a transparency to discuss the typical structure and variations in county governments.
- work with a partner to debate the need for county government.
- investigate their own local government structure to complete an informational diagram.

### BEFORE CLASS

Assign the section, the graphic organizer in the text, and the Reading Comprehension Worksheet (Unit 7 All-in-One, p. 77) before class.

**L2 Differentiate** Reading Comprehension Worksheet (Unit 7 All-in-One, p. 79)

### BELLRINGER

Write on the board: **What types of local government exist in our area? What are the names of the governmental units that apply to you? Write your answers in your notebook.**

**L2 ELL Differentiate** Suggest that students create a concept web to record the information.

## Differentiated Resources

The following resources are located in the All-in-One, Unit 7, Chapter 25, Section 1:

**L2** Prereading and Vocabulary Worksheet (p. 74)

**L3** Reading Comprehension Worksheet (p. 77)

**L2** Reading Comprehension Worksheet (p. 79)

**L3** Core Worksheet (p. 81)

**L2** Core Worksheet (p. 82)

**L2** Extend Activity (p. 84)

**L3** Quiz A (p. 85)

**L2** Quiz B (p. 86)

## Answers

**Checkpoint** Counties vary in size and number, with some States having none. Counties serve almost solely as judicial districts in New England. In mid-Atlantic and midwestern States, counties share rural government responsibilities with townships. In the South and West, counties are the main rural government.

# Teach

To present this topic using online resources, use the lesson presentations at **PearsonSchool.com/phgovt.**

### INTRODUCE THE TOPIC

Explain to students that this lesson is about the forms of local government in the United States. Draw a simple flowchart on the board to show the levels of government in a typical State: State, county, town/township. Include tribal government if applicable.

```
UNITED          ┌──────────┐
STATES   ─────▶ │  TRIBAL  │
                └──────────┘
  │
  ▼
┌──────────┐    ┌──────────────┐
│ State:   │    │ Special      │
│ [Ohio]   │───▶│ Districts:   │
└──────────┘    │ [Sycamore    │
  │             │ School       │
  ▼             │ District]    │
┌──────────┐    │              │
│ County:  │    │ [Metropolitan│
│[Hamilton]│    │ Sewer        │
└──────────┘    │ District]    │
  │             └──────────────┘
  ▼
┌──────────┐
│ Town/    │
│Township: │
│[Sycamore]│
└──────────┘
```

Discuss aspects of each specific form of local government in your State, and have students use the information from the Bellringer activity to fill in details on the flowchart for the area in which they live. Students may come from different towns or counties, which can all be listed on the flowchart. It may be helpful to display a map showing towns and counties in your State. Help students identify your county on the map.

**L2 ELL Differentiate** Clarify that the word *county* is different from *country*, and make sure that students understand that a county is an area within a State. You may wish to show an outline map of the United States to clarify *country* and a map of your region with county boundaries to clarify *county*.

## Answers

**County Government Structure** Students will likely note that the school superintendent has the greatest impact on their lives.

---

# County Government Structure

A typical county government is made up of a governing body, often known as a county board, and several appointed and elected officials with assigned responsibilities. *Which local government officials have the greatest impact on your daily life?*

| County Official Duties | |
|---|---|
| County Board | Levies taxes and sets spending |
| | Administers roads, county buildings, and programs |
| | Appoints boards and officials |
| Sheriff | Runs county jail |
| | Provides rural police protection |
| | Carries out court orders |
| | May collect taxes |
| Clerk | Registers and records documents for property, birth, and death |
| | Runs county elections |
| Assessor | Sets the value of taxable property |
| | Collects property taxes |
| Treasurer | Keeps county funds |
| Auditor | Keeps financial records |
| District Attorney | Conducts criminal investigations |
| | Prosecutes criminal cases |
| School Superintendent | Administers public schools |
| Coroner | Investigates violent deaths |
| | Certifies causes of death |

An elected county board (above) holds broad powers over budgets and programs. Such officers as the county assessor (left) may be elected or appointed.

Most boards also carry out a number of administrative functions. They supervise the county road program and manage county property, including the courthouse, jails, hospitals, and parks. They are often responsible for the administration of welfare (cash assistance) programs and the conduct of elections. They are also responsible for the hiring of most county employees—from a few dozen or so in many rural places to several thousand in most metropolitan areas. And, importantly, they determine the pay of nearly all of the people who work for the county.

**Other Elements** In addition to its governing body, the typical county's government regularly includes a number of other elected officials—as you can see in the chart on this page.

Then, too, county governments usually feature several boards and commissions, whose members are also sometimes elected. Those agencies frequently include a fair board, a planning commission, a board of health, a library board, and a board of road viewers. Altogether, the nation's 3,028 counties now employ some three million men and women who do the day-to-day work of those units of local government.

## Functions of Counties

Because counties are creations of the State, they are responsible for the administration of State laws. They also administer such county laws as the State's constitution and legislature allow their governing bodies to make.

Historically, nearly all counties have been institutions of rural government. Most remain rurally oriented today. Although there are some differences from State to State, the major functions of counties still reflect their rural character.

Their most common functions are to keep the peace and maintain jails and other

---

# Background

**SOCIOECONOMIC INTEGRATION** Inequality among school districts remains a problem. With forced racial integration meeting increased opposition, schools are trying new approaches. One approach, called "socioeconomic integration," assigns children to schools based on income level rather than on race. In this way, students from lower-income areas have access to the educational opportunities found in schools in higher-income areas. In the early 1990s, the La Crosse, Wisconsin, school district became the first in the nation to integrate students from different economic groups. Since then, test scores in La Crosse have risen and dropout rates have fallen. Observing this success in La Crosse, other schools began similar plans. According to researcher Richard Kalenberg, socioeconomic integration works because, "the obstacles to good schooling . . . track much more closely along economic lines than racial lines."

correctional facilities; assess property for tax purposes; collect taxes and spend county funds; build and repair roads, bridges, drains, and other public works; and maintain schools. Counties record deeds, mortgages, marriage licenses, and other documents; issue licenses for such things as hunting, fishing, and marriage; administer elections; care for the poor; and work to safeguard the health of the people who live in the county.

Many counties have taken on other functions as they have become more urban. Several of these more heavily populated counties now offer many of the public services and facilities that are usually found in cities. They provide water and sewer service; have professionally trained police, fire, and medical units; and operate airports and mass transit systems. Some also enforce zoning and other land-use regulations. Many have built and now operate auditoriums, stadiums, golf courses, and other recreational facilities.

## The Need for Reform

County organization is often chaotic. In the typical county, no single official can really be called the *chief* administrator. Rather, authority is divided among a number of elected boards and officials, each largely independent of the others. Too often, it is impossible to identify who is responsible for inefficiency or inaction (or worse) in the conduct of county affairs.

The large number of popularly elected officials adds to the chaos. Faced with the typical county's long ballot, voters are often hard-pressed to make informed choices. Also, many of those elected officials have no basic public policy-making responsibilities. Many people are convinced that popular election is not the best way to fill those offices.

The size and the number of counties in most States are another source of weakness. Nearly every county now in existence was laid out in the days of the horse and the stagecoach. Then, it made good sense to draw county lines so that no one lived more than a dozen miles or so from the county seat. Today, however, most counties are geographically ill-suited to the realities of the modern world.

One way in which many States have attempted to reform county government is through county home rule. That is, those 37 States allow some or all of their counties, subject to approval by the local voters, to decide the details of their own governmental structure.

Another approach to reform seeks to deal with the fragmented authority of counties. It does so by creating the position of county manager, modeled along the lines of the council-manager form of city government. Still another approach is county-city consolidation—where a major city and the county around it join into a single unit of government. San Francisco, California, and Nashville, Tennessee are leading examples.

## Tribal Governments

Tribal governments exist as a distinct form of government. Unlike State, county, or community governments, however, the governments of recognized Native American nations have a unique "government-to-government" relationship with the United States. These Native American tribes are considered sovereign nations, with the right to govern their own people on their own territories unless otherwise specified by treaty or acts of Congress.

Official recognition by the Federal Government is crucial for tribal governments because it establishes their sovereignty and exempts them from State or local control. For example, some tribes have established gambling casinos on their reservations even though the territory lies within States that do not allow that type of gambling. Because the officially recognized tribes are sovereign, they are not subject to State laws and regulations. Also, recognized tribes are eligible to receive federal funds that can be used to provide local services. Today, there are some 560 federally recognized tribal governments in this country, with authority over the lives of some 1.9 million people.

Typically, a tribal government has an elected leader called a chief or chairman. Most tribes also have a council, which can vary in size from only two or three to almost 100 members. Other than these common

**✔ Checkpoint**
Why do most county governments need reform?

---

### DISCUSS THE ROLE OF COUNTY GOVERNMENT

Display Transparency 25A, Typical County Government Structure. Have students compare and contrast the information on the transparency with information about your area. For example, does your county have a county board? Which officials are elected and which are appointed? Ask: **Which officials do voters elect in the county government shown in this transparency?** *(members of the county board and officials such as the sheriff, district attorney, clerk, school superintendent, and coroner)* **Who selects the members of the planning commission and budget committee?** *(county board)* Discuss why certain officials might be appointed, while others are elected.

### INTRODUCE THE ACTIVITY

Explain that the county is a very old government unit. It dates back to Anglo-Saxon times in England, where it was first called a *shire*. (You may want to share the fact that the word *sheriff* is derived from *shire-reeve*, the main official of the shire.) In some cases, counties were established in the United States largely because they were a traditional and familiar unit of government to settlers from England. As students have read, county government today is often chaotic, outdated, overlaps with town and city governments, or has a very narrow jurisdiction. In some States, county government has been abolished altogether.

---

# Background

**TOWN MEETING DAY** The first Tuesday of March is Town Meeting Day in Vermont. It is a holiday for State government employees. Almost all Vermont towns practice direct democracy—all eligible voters may attend town meetings and vote. At least 30 days before the meeting, the "warning" is posted, which gives the time and place and lists the "articles" (topics) to be discussed. First the meeting elects a moderator, who calls the meeting to order and reads the first article. Following Robert's Rules of Order, participants raise their hands to present their views. The vote is taken by voice ("yea" or "nay") or hand-raising. However, if seven voters move to "divide the assembly," the vote proceeds by paper ballot. The town clerk records the results, and the moderator moves to the next article. Town meetings also serve a social function; they strengthen community ties as people work together to solve problems.

---

## Answers

**Checkpoint** Most counties have no chief administrator and fragmented authority, creating unclear accountability. The large number of elected officials overwhelms voters. Also, counties are geographically ill-suited to today's world.

Divide the class into pairs and distribute the Chapter 25 Section 1 Core Worksheet (Unit 7 All-in-One, p. 81). Tell students they will use the worksheet to formulate their arguments for a written debate with their partner on whether or not county government is useful in your State—or in cases where it has been abolished, if it should be reestablished to serve some particular purposes.

**L1 L2 Differentiate** Go through the worksheet as a class, rather than letting students work on their own, outlining the arguments on the board. Be sure to give students a few minutes to think about it on their own before you begin.

# Native American Reservations

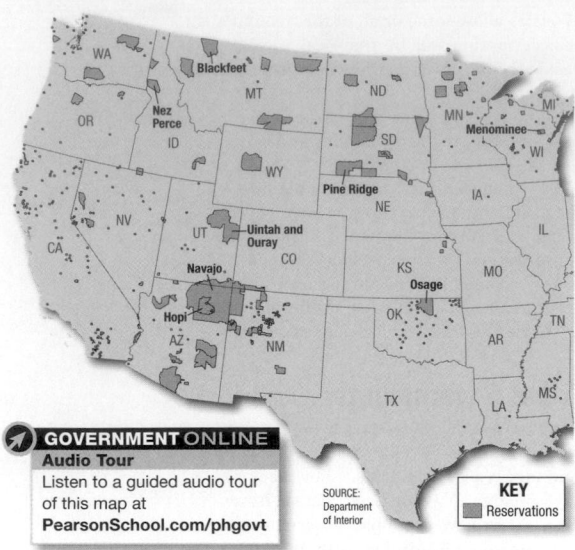

**GOVERNMENT ONLINE**
**Audio Tour**
Listen to a guided audio tour of this map at
PearsonSchool.com/phgovt

SOURCE: Department of Interior

**KEY**
☐ Reservations

▶▶ **Analyzing Maps** Native American governments enjoy a sovereign status and a special relationship with the federal and State governments. *Why are reservations organized differently from other forms of local government?*

✔ **Checkpoint**
How do tribal governments relate to State governments?

**vehicle**
*n.* agent through which something is accomplished

**constable**
*n.* local police officer

features, tribal governments vary widely in size and structure. Some, such as the Cherokee and Navajo tribes, have a written code or constitution that provides for a State-like government with executive, legislative, and judicial branches. Others are small and loosely organized.

Like State and county governments, tribal governments use federal funds and tax revenue to provide services. These services depend on the size, history, and needs of the tribe. Many tribes have executive officers or departments that oversee policy and manage funds to provide health care, education, and welfare to tribe members. They also oversee cultural events and sites as well as distribute information about the tribe. Even smaller tribal governments provide some services, especially housing and health and education information and support.

## Towns and Townships

Towns and townships exist in nearly half the States. They are little known in the South or West but are commonly found from New England to the Midwest.[2]

**The New England Town** In New England, the town is a major unit of local government. Except for a few major cities, each of the six States in the region is divided into towns. Each town generally includes all of the rural and the urban areas within its boundaries. The town delivers most of the services that are the responsibility of cities and counties elsewhere around the country.

The roots of the New England town reach back to the early colonial period. The Pilgrims landed at Plymouth Rock in 1620 as an organized congregation. They quickly set up a close-knit community in which their church and their government were almost one. Other Puritan congregations followed the Pilgrims' pattern.

At least in form, much of town government today is little changed from colonial times. The main feature is a town meeting, long praised as the ideal <u>vehicle</u> of direct democracy. The town meeting is an assembly open to all the town's eligible voters. It meets yearly, and sometimes more often, to levy taxes, make spending and other policy decisions, and elect officers for the next year.

Between town meetings, the board of selectmen/selectwomen chosen at the annual meeting manages the town's business. Typically, the board is a three-member body and has responsibilities for such things as roads, schools, care of the poor, and sanitation. Other officers regularly selected at the annual meeting include the town clerk, a tax assessor, a tax collector, a <u>constable</u>, road commissioners, and school board members.

The ideal of direct democracy is still alive in many smaller New England towns. It has given way, however, to the pressures

---

2 The term *town* is used in some States as the legal designation for smaller urban places; it is also sometimes used as another word for township. Township is also a federal public lands survey term, used to identify geographic units (often called congressional townships), each having exactly 36 square miles (36 sections).

## Answers

**Analyzing Maps** because each tribe is sovereign and may set up its government as it chooses

**Checkpoint** Tribal governments are usually exempt from State laws and regulations.

of time, population, and the complexities of public problems in many of the larger towns. There, representative government has largely replaced it. Town officers are often elected before the yearly gathering. Many of the decisions once made by the assembled voters are now made by the selectmen and selectwomen. In recent years, several towns have gone to a town manager system for the day-to-day administration of local affairs.

**Townships** Townships are units of local government found principally in the Northeast and the Midwest. Nowhere do townships blanket an entire State, however.

In New York, New Jersey, and Pennsylvania, townships were formed as areas were settled and the people needed the services of local government. Consequently, the township maps of those States often resemble crazy quilts. From Ohio westward, they mostly follow the regular lines drawn in federal public land surveys. Many are perfect squares.

About half of these States provide for annual township meetings, like those held in New England towns. Otherwise, the governing body is usually a three- or five-member board, generally called the board of trustees or board of supervisors. Its members are elected for fixed terms or serve because they hold other elected township offices. Township offices often include a supervisor, a clerk, a treasurer, an assessor, a constable, a justice of the peace, and a body of road commissioners.

A **municipality** is an urban political unit within a township that usually exists as a separate governmental <u>entity</u>. As a result, township functions tend to be rural. They regularly involve such matters as roads, cemeteries, drainage, and minor law enforcement. In some States, however, the township is also the basic unit of public school administration.

Many people believe that townships have outlived their usefulness. More than half the States get along without them. Many rural townships have been abolished as a result

**entity**
*n.* unit, thing, element

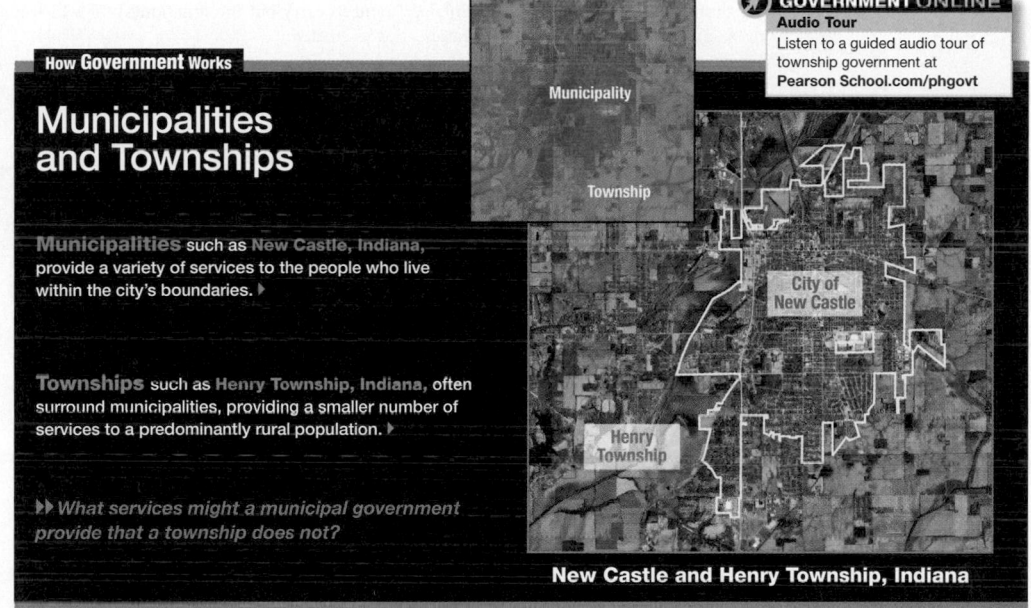

**How Government Works**

## Municipalities and Townships

**Municipalities** such as New Castle, Indiana, provide a variety of services to the people who live within the city's boundaries. ▶

**Townships** such as Henry Township, Indiana, often surround municipalities, providing a smaller number of services to a predominantly rural population. ▶

▶▶ *What services might a municipal government provide that a township does not?*

Municipality

Township

City of New Castle

Henry Township

**New Castle and Henry Township, Indiana**

**GOVERNMENT** ONLINE
**Audio Tour**
Listen to a guided audio tour of township government at Pearson School.com/phgovt

## Background

**CITY OF MIAMI** Government at the county level can sometimes seem like an attractive option. With 375,000 residents, Miami, Florida, came dangerously close to disappearing in September 1997. The city faced $68 million in debt, and top officials were serving sentences in federal prison for corruption. Angry Miamians launched a ballot initiative to dissolve Miami's city government and pass all responsibilities and authority to Dade County. However, on Election Day, voters chose by a landslide to keep Miami intact.

---

**EXTEND THE LESSON**

**L3** **Differentiate** Have students work in small groups to create an informational diagram showing the major elements of your county or local government. The chart should include information about the governing body, boards and commissions, appointed bureaucrats, and elected officials. Encourage students to include the real names of each official and details about his or her roles and responsibilities.

**L2** **Differentiate** Distribute the Extend Activity "Write a Letter to a Local Official" (Unit 7 All-in-One, p. 84), which has students contact local government to suggest improvements for their community.

**L4** **Differentiate** Tell students that the variations in the structure and power of local government exist due to each region's history. Have students do research and write a report or create an informational pamphlet that compares and contrasts the origins and development of government structure below the State level in the Northeast, the South, the Midwest, and the West.

**Government** online  *All print resources are available on the Teacher's Resource Library CD-ROM and online at PearsonSchool.com/phgovt.*

Tell students to go to the Audio Tour to listen to a guided tour on municipalities and townships.

## Assess and Remediate

**L3** Collect the Core Worksheets and assess the students' debates, using the Rubric for Assessing a Debate (Unit 7 All-in-One, p. 127).

**L3** Assign the Section 1 Assessment questions.

**L3** Section Quiz A (Unit 7 All-in-One, p. 85)

**L2** Section Quiz B (Unit 7 All-in-One, p. 86)

Have students complete the review activities in the digital lesson presentation and continue their work in the **Essential Questions Journal.**

---

**Answers**

**Municipalities and Townships** A municipal government might be more urban-oriented, while township functions tend to be rural.

| If Your Students Have Trouble With | Strategies For Remediation |
|---|---|
| Roles and functions of local governments (Questions 1, 2, 4, 5) | On the board, draw a chart like the one in the section opener. Add *municipalities* and *special districts* to it. With students, fill in the chart with details from students' original charts and from the text. |
| Understanding the weaknesses of county government (Question 3) | Have students re-read the text under the heading "The Need for Reform," and write a main idea for each paragraph. |

## Answers

**Checkpoint** A municipality serves the urban population within a township.

---

✔ **Checkpoint**
What is the purpose of a municipality?

**sidestep**
*v.* avoid, get around

of declining populations, improvements in transportation, and other factors.

Some of the more densely populated townships appear to have brighter futures than their country cousins, however. This seems especially true in the suburban areas around some larger cities. Some States, such as Pennsylvania, now allow townships to exercise many of the powers and furnish many of the services once reserved for cities.

## Special Districts

There are now tens of thousands of special districts across the country. A **special district** is an independent unit created to perform one or more related governmental functions at the local level. These districts are found in mind-boggling variety and in every State. School districts—some 13,000 of them—are by far the most common example. More than 37,000 other special districts also blanket the country, and their numbers are growing.

Special districts are found most often, but not always, in rural and suburban areas. Many have been created to provide water, sewage, or electrical service; to furnish fire or police protection; and to build and maintain bridges, airports, swimming pools, libraries,

or parks. Others have been created for such purposes as soil conservation, housing, public transportation, irrigation, or reforestation. There are even, in many places, special districts for dog or mosquito control purposes.

A leading reason for the creation of special districts has been the need to provide a particular service in a wider or a smaller area than that covered by a county or a city. For example, a special district might be needed to handle pollution in the several counties through which a river flows. On the other hand, a special district might be set up to provide fire or police protection in some out-of-the-way locale.

In many cases, special districts have been formed because other local governments could not, or would not, provide the services desired. Others have been created to sidestep constitutional limits on the size of a city's or a county's debt; to finance a public service out of users' fees instead of general tax revenue; and to take advantage of some federal grant program.

The governing body for a special district is almost always an elected board. It has the power to lay taxes (usually on property) or charge fees, as well as the powers to spend and to carry out the function(s) for which it was created.

**Essential Questions Journal** To continue to build a response to the chapter Essential Question, go to your **Essential Questions Journal**.

## SECTION 1 ASSESSMENT

1. **Guiding Question** Use your completed chart to answer this question: What are the similarities and differences of local governments, special districts, and tribal governments?

**Key Terms and Comprehension**

2. What is the main purpose of **(a)** a **township? (b)** a **special district?**
3. What factors generally make county governments inefficient?

**Critical Thinking**

4. **Identifying Assumptions** Consider the concept of the New England town meeting. What does this form of local government assume about the citizens of the town?
5. **Drawing Inferences** Review the functions of county and town or township government. List and describe at least three examples that show how these governing bodies affect the day-to-day lives of people in your community.

**Quick Write**

**Writing for Assessment: Develop the Main Points** When writing for assessment, carefully plot your response *before* you begin writing. Select one of the questions below. In a chart or outline, develop at least three major points that you might cover to answer that question.
**(a)** How do county and township governments differ from one another?
**(b)** What are the strengths and weaknesses of the different forms of city government?

## Assessment Answers

**1.** A county is a unit of local government below the State and consisting of several towns or townships. County organization is often chaotic because no single official can be called the chief administrator. Towns are smaller units of local government. In New England they are the major form of local government and are governed by a board of selectpersons and through town meetings of all voters. Townships are the major form of local government in New York, New Jersey, and in the Midwestern States. They are also generally administrated by an elected board. A special district is an

independent unit of government created for a particular governmental function. Tribal governments are sovereign, if federally recognized, and may operate like small nations outside the control of federal and State governments.

**2. (a)** to provide rural areas with local services such as roads, cemeteries, drainage, and minor law enforcement; basic unit of public school administration in some States **(b)** to perform governmental functions at the local level, such as to administer school districts or provide water, sewage, or electrical service

**3.** chaotic organization; no single chief administrator; authority divided among boards and officials; difficult to identify accountability; geographically ill-suited to today's realities

**4.** It assumes that they are informed and interested in participating in town issues.

**5.** possible response: provide essential services, such as water and sewer; administer schools; provide protective services

**QUICK WRITE** Students should write three important points related to answering their question.

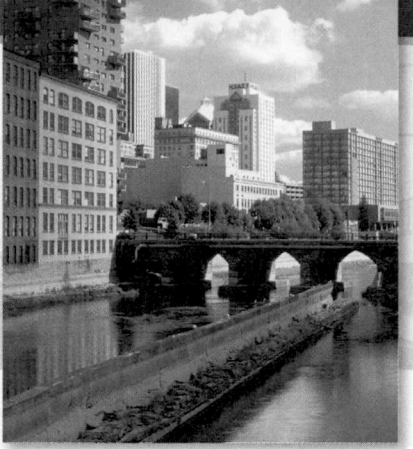

SECTION **2**

# Cities and Metropolitan Areas

## Guiding Question
**How do city governments serve the needs of residents and other Americans?** Use an outline to take notes about the ways in which city governments serve people.

I. America's Rural-Urban Shift
II. Incorporation and Charters
III. Forms of City Government
  A. Mayor-Council Form
    1. _____
    2. _____

## Political Dictionary
- incorporation
- charter
- mayor-council government
- strong-mayor government
- weak-mayor government
- commission government
- council-manager government
- zoning
- metropolitan area

## Objectives
1. Explain the process of incorporation and the function of city charters.
2. Contrast the major forms of city government.
3. Evaluate the need for city planning and list some major municipal functions.
4. Outline the challenges that face suburbs and metropolitan areas.

**Image Above:** City of Rochester on Lake Ontario in upstate New York

**W**e are fast becoming a nation of city dwellers. Where once our population was small, mostly rural, and agricultural, it is now large, mostly urban, and dominated by technology, manufacturing, and service industries. In 1790, a mere 5 percent of the population lived in the nation's few cities. Today, some 235 million people—more than 75 percent of the population—live in the nation's cities and their surrounding suburbs.[3] For local governments, that change has had dramatic consequences.

The larger the number of people living in close contact with one another, the greater the strains on local governments. The larger the population, the greater the problems in providing water, police and fire protection, sewers, waste removal, streets and traffic regulation, public health services, schools, recreational facilities, and more. The larger the population, the more extensive—and expensive—all of this becomes.

## Incorporation and Charters
Remember, each of the 50 States is a unitary government. That means that each State has complete control over all of the units of local government within its borders. All those units, including cities, were created by the State, received their powers from the State, and are subject to a variety of limitations imposed by the State.

The process by which a State establishes a city as a legal body is called **incorporation.**[4] Each State sets out in its constitution, or by statute, the conditions and the procedures under which a community may become an incorporated municipality. Typically, a State requires that a minimum number of persons live within a given area before incorporation can take place.

The fact that cities are incorporated highlights an important difference between city and county government. Cities are created largely at the request of their residents, because residents want certain public services. Counties,

3 Depending on local custom and State law, municipalities may be known as cities, towns, boroughs, or villages. The use and meaning of these terms vary among the States. The larger municipalities are known everywhere as cities, and the usual practice is to use that title only for those communities with significant populations.
4 The term *incorporation* comes from the Latin words *in* (into) and *corpus* (body).

## How do city governments serve the needs of residents and other Americans?

I. America's Rural-Urban Shift
II. Incorporation and Charters
  A. Cities incorporated to provide public services to residents
  B. Charter sets out city's form of government and powers
III. Forms of City Government
  A. Mayor-Council Form
    1. Council: elected legislature, often nonpartisan
    2. Mayor: elected or chosen by council
  B. Commission Form
    1. Elected commissioners carry out legislative and executive functions
    2. Each commissioner heads department; one serves as mayor with no extra power
  C. Council-Manager Form
    1. Strong council, weak mayor
    2. Council chooses professionally trained manager to be chief administrator
    3. Council makes policy; manager carries out
IV. City Planning
  A. Planning commission to manage growth
  B. Zoning (residential, commercial, industrial) sets rules for land use
V. Municipal Functions
  A. Police and fire protection
  B. Build and maintain streets, sidewalks, bridges, street lights, parks, libraries, hospitals, schools, jails, sports arenas
  C. Furnish public health and sanitation services
  D. Operate water, gas, electric, transportation systems
  E. Regulate traffic, building codes, pollution, public utilities
VI. Metropolitan Areas
  A. Movement to suburbs removing resources from cities while creating greater need for city services
  B. Metropolitan districts cut across county and city lines to provide specific services

## SKILLS DEVELOPMENT

### ANALYZE CAUSE AND EFFECT
To practice analyzing cause and effect in this section, use the Chapter 25 Skills Worksheet (Unit 7 All-in-One, p. 94). You may teach the skill explicitly either before or after teaching the lesson. For L2 and L1 students, assign the adapted Skill Activity (Unit 7 All-in-One, p. 95).

# Focus on the Basics

Here is the information that your students need to learn in this section.

**FACTS:** • Most Americans today live in or near cities. • States create city governments through incorporation. • City governments take one of three forms: mayor-council, commission, or council-manager. • Cities manage their growth by zoning land for specific uses. • Annexation, special districts, and increased county authority are ways to provide services to suburban residents.

**CONCEPTS:** types of governments, role of government

**ENDURING UNDERSTANDINGS:** • Local governments provide a wide range of public services to residents. • As the population shifted from rural to urban and then to suburban, different forms of local government arose to serve the population.

# Get Started

## LESSON GOALS

Students will . . .

- compare and contrast the three basic forms of city government using a transparency.
- experience the planning function of city government by planning a city square.

## BEFORE CLASS

Assign the section, the graphic organizer in the text, and the Reading Comprehension Worksheet (Unit 7 All-in-One, p. 87) before class.

**L2 Differentiate** Reading Comprehension Worksheet (Unit 7 All-in-One, p. 89)

## BELLRINGER

Display Transparency 25C, City Government. Write on the board: **List five characteristics that make [insert name of your city] a "city."** If the school is not located in a city, insert the name of the city nearest you.

---

## Answers

**Checkpoint** A State establishes a city through the process of incorporation, once the community meets the conditions required under the State's laws and constitution.

**Analyzing Tables** Possible answer: Writing the budget allows a mayor to implement city policies and programs that are priorities of his or her administration.

---

**vest**
*v.* granted to, bestowed upon

▸ **Analyzing Tables** *Why is the power to write the budget a critically important power?*

on the other hand, exist largely to serve the administrative needs of the State. Cities do act as agents of the State, of course—for example, in law enforcement and public health. But the principal reason for the existence of a city is for the convenience of those who live there.

The **charter** is a city's basic law, its constitution. Its contents may vary from city to city, but commonly the charter names the city, describes its boundaries, and declares it to be a municipal corporation. As a municipal corporation, a city has the right to sue and be sued in the courts; to have a corporate seal; to make contracts; and to acquire, own, manage, and dispose of property.

Generally, the charter sets out the other powers <u>vested</u> in the city and outlines its form of government. It also provides how and for what terms its officers are to be chosen, outlines their duties, and deals with finances and other matters.

## Forms of City Government

Although variations can and do exist, each city has one of three basic forms of government. A city has either (1) a mayor-council, (2) a commission, or (3) a council-manager form of government.

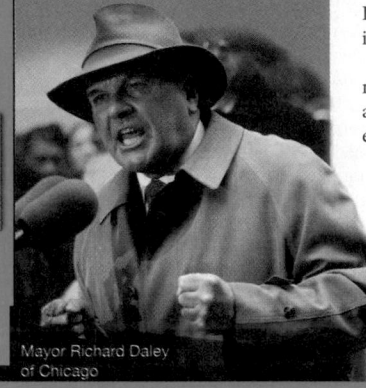

# What does a mayor do?

The mayor is the official representative and face of the city. In a **strong-mayor government,** the mayor has the power to

- recommend or veto city laws
- preside over council meetings
- hire and fire city employees
- write the budget

The more common **weak-mayor government** assigns most of those powers to other elected officials or the city council.

Mayor Richard Daley of Chicago

**The Mayor-Council Form** The **mayor-council government** is the oldest and still the most widely used type of city government. It features an elected mayor as the chief executive and an elected council as its legislative body.

*The council.* The council is almost always unicameral and typically has five, seven, or nine members. Some larger cities have more. New York City has the largest council, with 51 members. Members of the council are popularly elected, almost always from districts (wards) within the city. Terms of office vary from one to six years. Four-year terms are the most common.

A move to nonpartisan city government began in the early 1900s. Its champions believed that (1) political parties were a major source of corruption in city government, and (2) partisan contests at the State and national levels have little to do with municipal problems and local issues. Today, less than one third of all cities still run their elections on a partisan basis.

*The mayor.* Generally, the voters elect the mayor. In some places, however, the council chooses one of its members to serve as mayor. The mayor presides at council meetings, usually may vote only to break a tie, and may recommend—and often veto—ordinances. In most cities, the council can override the veto.

Mayor-council governments are often described as either of the strong-mayor or the weak-mayor type, depending on the powers given to the mayor. This classification is useful for purposes of description. It blurs the importance of informal power in city politics, however.

In a **strong-mayor government,** the mayor heads the city's administration, usually has the veto power, can hire and fire employees, and prepares the budget. Typically, the mayor is able to exercise strong leadership in making city policy and running the city's affairs.

In a **weak-mayor government,** the mayor has much less formal power. Executive duties are shared with other elected officials—for example, a clerk, treasurer, city engineer, police chief, and even council members.

---

# Differentiated Resources

The following resources are located in the All-in-One, Unit 7, Chapter 25, Section 2:

- **L3** Reading Comprehension Worksheet (p. 87)
- **L2** Reading Comprehension Worksheet (p. 89)
- **L3** Core Worksheet (p. 91)
- **L2** Extend Activity (p. 96)
- **L3** Skills Worksheet (p. 94)
- **L2** Skill Activity (p. 95)
- **L3** Quiz A (p. 97)
- **L2** Quiz B (p. 98)

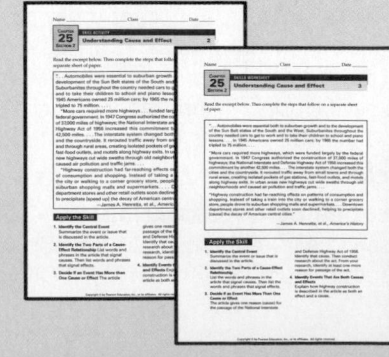

Powers of appointment, removal, and budget are shared with the council or exercised by that body alone. The mayor seldom has a veto power.

Most mayor-council cities operate under the weak-mayor rather than the strong-mayor plan. The strong-mayor form is most often found in larger cities.

The success of the mayor-council form depends in very large measure on the power, ability, and influence of the mayor. In weak-mayor cities, responsibility for action or inaction is hard to assign. The strong-mayor plan helps to solve the problems of leadership and responsibility. Still, the mayor-council form has three large defects:

1. It depends quite heavily on the capacities of the mayor.

2. An ongoing dispute between the mayor and the council can stall the workings of a city's government.

3. It is quite complicated and, so, is often little understood by the average citizen.

**The Commission Form** The **commission government** is simple in structure. Three to nine, but usually five, commissioners are popularly elected. Together, they form the city council, pass ordinances, and control the purse strings. Individually, they head the different departments of city government: police, fire, public works, finance, parks, and so on. Thus, both legislative and executive powers are centered in one body.

The commission form was born in Galveston, Texas, in 1901, after a tidal surge had devastated the city. When the existing mayor-council government proved unequal to the task, the Texas legislature gave Galveston a new charter, providing for five commissioners to make and enforce law in the stricken city. Intended to be temporary, the arrangement proved so effective that it soon spread to other communities across the country.

Depending on the city, either the voters or the commissioners themselves choose one of the commissioners to serve as the mayor. Like the other commissioners, the mayor heads one or more of the city's departments. He or she also presides at council meetings and represents the city for ceremonial purposes.

The mayor generally has no more authority than the other commissioners and rarely has a veto power.

Although many reformers supported the commission form at first, experience pointed up serious defects in the system, and its popularity fell off rapidly. Only a very few American cities have a commission form of government today.

The commission form suffers from three chief defects:

1. The lack of a single chief executive makes it difficult to assign responsibility. This can also mean that the city has no effective political leadership.

2. A built-in tendency toward "empire building" often surfaces. Each commissioner tries to draw as much of the city's money and influence as possible to his or her own department.

3. A lack of coordination plagues the topmost levels of policymaking and administration. Each commissioner is likely to equate the city-wide public good with the particular interests and functions of his or her department.

**The Council-Manager Form** The **council-manager government** is a modification of the mayor-council form. Its main features are (1) a strong council of usually five or seven members elected at-large on a nonpartisan ballot; (2) a weak mayor chosen by the voters; and (3) a manager, the city's chief administrative officer, named by the council.

The form first appeared in Ukiah, California. In 1904, that city's council appointed an "executive officer" to direct the work of city government. The first charter expressly providing for the council-manager form was granted to the city of Sumter, South Carolina, in 1912.

The council is the city's policymaking body. The manager carries out the policies the council makes. He or she is directly responsible to that body for the efficient administration of the city. The manager serves at the council's pleasure and may be dismissed at any time and for any reason.

Today, most city managers are professionally trained career administrators. As chief administrator, the manager directs the

✔**Checkpoint**
What are the strengths and weaknesses of commission government?

**plagues**
*v.* disturbs, negatively affects

**purse strings**
*n.* access to financial resources

# Teach

To present this topic using online resources, use the lesson presentations at **PearsonSchool.com/phgovt.**

### UNDERSTAND FORMS OF CITY GOVERNMENT

Have students read their list of characteristics from the Bellringer activity. Discuss what a city is and how it is different from a town or township. Work with the class to agree on a definition of a city. (*Sample answer: A* city *is a community where a large number of people live, which is incorporated and has a charter from the State.*)

Display Transparency 25D, Three Forms of City Government. Use the diagrams to compare and contrast the three forms. Ask: **In which form of government do the voters directly elect the department heads?** (*commission form*) **How is the council-manager form the same as and different from the strong mayor form?** (*The voters elect the council and the mayor in both, but in the council-manager form, the manager—not the mayor—is the chief administrator.*)

**L2 ELL Differentiate** Clarify that *municipality, urban area,* and *municipal area* generally have the same meaning as *city.* You may also want to clarify the meanings of the terms *council, mayor,* and *manager,* to be sure that students understand the roles of each in the various types of city governments.

### EVALUATE THE FORMS AND VOTE

Discuss the three forms of city government. Have students work with a partner or work as a whole class to create a list of advantages and disadvantages of each form, based on students' reading. Then ask: **What form of city government do you think would be the most effective for our community? Why?** Ask students to vote by a show of hands. Have volunteers explain why they voted the way that they did. Ask them to write a journal entry that predicts what might happen if a city has an ineffective government.

# Myths and Misconceptions

**THE LAND OF CITIES** Which State has the most cities? Asked this question, Americans are likely to name the largest or most populous States: New York, California, Texas, Florida, or even Alaska. The surprising answer to the question is—Illinois. With nearly 1,300 incorporated municipalities, the "Land of Lincoln" is also the land of cities—about 1 out of every 14 cities in the entire United States is located in Illinois. However, this count is based on the fact that what constitutes a "city" differs from State to State. For example, Illinois counts many small municipalities as cities, while Juneau, Alaska, could be considered the largest city in the nation because it includes an area of several hundred square miles.

# Answers

**Checkpoint** strengths: simple structure, individual commissioners responsible for specific departments; weaknesses: lack of chief executive weakens leadership and accountability, individual commissioners tend to compete for money and influence, lack of coordination

## INTRODUCE THE ACTIVITY

Ask students to suppose that a main square in a city has become run down, with several vacant and dilapidated buildings, and therefore needs to be redeveloped. Ask: **What needs must a city square meet to be a successful space?** *(ways for people to get there, attractions to draw people there, and basic needs such as food, water, and restrooms)* **What types of buildings and other features would help provide these needs?** *(Students might suggest popular restaurants and shops, hotels, attractive landscaping, benches or picnic tables, parking spaces, bike lanes, water fountains, and restrooms.)*

## DISTRIBUTE CORE WORKSHEET

Distribute the Chapter 25 Section 2 Core Worksheet (Unit 7 All-in-One, p. 91). Explain that students will work in small groups and use this worksheet to develop a plan for a city square. Review the steps listed on the worksheet. Remind them that in brainstorming, they should record all ideas. They will evaluate these ideas and select the best ones in the next step.

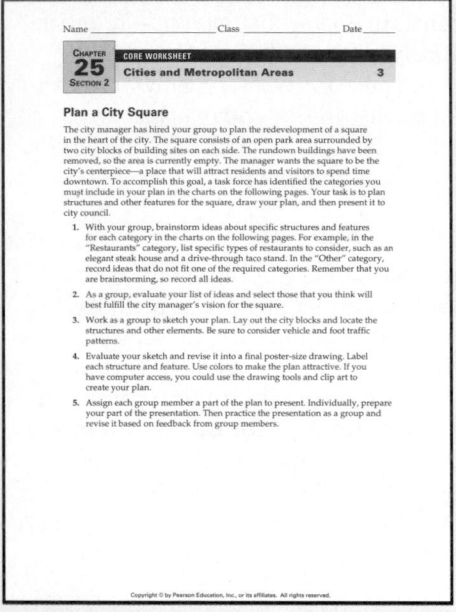

Tell students to go to the Audio Tour to listen to a guided audio tour of city governments.

## Answers

**Alternate Forms of City Government** Commission: Each commissioner heads a department. Council-Manager: Manager is chief executive, but serves at the Council's pleasure.

---

work of all city departments and has the power to hire and fire all city employees. The manager also prepares the budget for council consideration and controls the spending of the funds the council appropriates.

The council-manager plan has the backing of nearly every expert on municipal affairs, and its use has spread widely. It is now found in more than 8,000 communities, including most of those cities with populations between 25,000 and 250,000.

The council-manager plan has three major advantages over other forms of city government:

**1.** It is simple in form.

**2.** It is fairly clear who is responsible for policy, on the one hand, and for its application, on the other.

**3.** It relies on highly trained experts who are skilled in modern techniques of budgeting, planning, computerization, and other administrative tools.

**expendable**
*adj.* disposable, replaceable

In theory, the nonpolitical manager carries out the policies enacted by the council. Yet, in practice, sharp distinctions between policymaking and policy-application seldom exist. The manager is very often the chief source for new ideas and fresh approaches to the city's problems. On the other hand, the city council often finds it politically useful to share the responsibility for controversial decisions with the "expendable" city manager.

Some critics of the council-manager form hold that it is undemocratic because its chief executive is not popularly elected. Others say that it lacks strong political leadership. This is a particular shortcoming, they argue, in larger cities, where the population is often quite diverse and there can be many competing interests. Support for this view can be seen in the fact that only a handful of cities with more than a half a

**GOVERNMENT** ONLINE
**Audio Tour**
For a guided tour of city government, visit
**PearsonSchool.com/phgovt**

**How Government Works**

# Alternate Forms of City Government

The commission (left) and council-manager (right) forms of city government provide alternatives to the traditional roles of the mayor and city council. *How does each form of government divide executive power?*

The people elect the **Board of Commisioners.**

Public Works     Finance

Public Safety     Mayor     Education

Each commissioner is responsible for the conduct of particular city functions.

**Commission**

The people elect the **Council and Mayor.**

The council appoints the **City Manager.**

The city manager carries out the council's policies and administers the day-to-day work of city government.

**Council-Manager**

## Background

**SPRAWL** While the media and city planners have often lamented sprawl, it is sometimes hard for the average person to see the overall problems that result from a lack of city planning and zoning. *A Field Guide to Sprawl,* by Dolores Hayden (with photographs by Jim Wark), remedies this situation. In a series of photographs and simple explanations, Hayden shows examples of how sprawl affects the environment and reveals names given to various types of land-use practices. Terms such as "snout house" (a house where a garage is dominant and projecting) and "zoomburb" demonstrate why city planning is so important in today's growing communities. Ms. Hayden's Web site provides a Sprawl Quiz based on the book, which students may find interesting.

million residents have a council-manager government in place today.

## City Planning

With few exceptions, most American cities developed haphazardly, without a plan, and with no eye to the future. The results of this shortsightedness can be seen in what is often called the core area or the inner city. These are often the older and usually overcrowded central sections of larger cities.

Industrial plants were placed anywhere their owners chose to build them. Rail lines were run through the heart of the community. Towering buildings shut out the sunlight from the narrow streets below. Main roads were laid out too close together and sometimes too far apart. Schools, police and fire stations, and other public buildings were squeezed onto cheap land or put where the political organization could make a profit. The many examples of this shortsightedness are nearly endless.

**Planning Growth** Fortunately, many cities have seen the need to create order out of their random growth. Most have established some sort of planning agency, supported by a trained professional staff.

A number of factors have prompted this step. The need to correct past mistakes has often been a compelling reason, of course. Also, many cities have recognized both the advantages that can result, and the pitfalls that can be avoided, through well-planned and orderly development. Importantly, the Federal Government has spurred cities on. Most federal grant and loan programs require that cities that seek aid must first have a master plan as a guide to future growth.

**City Zoning** The practice of dividing a city into a number of districts, or zones, and regulating the uses to which property in each of them may be put is called **zoning.** Generally, a zoning ordinance places each parcel of land in the city into one of three spheres: residential, commercial, or industrial zones.

Each of these zones is then divided into subzones. For example, each of several residential zones may be broken down into several areas. One may be reserved for single-family residences, another may allow one-family and two-family dwellings, and a third, large apartment buildings.

Most zoning ordinances also <u>prescribe</u> limits on the height and area of buildings, determine how much of a lot may be occupied by a structure, and set out several other such restrictions on land use. They often have "setback" requirements, providing that structures must be placed at least a certain distance from the street and from other property lines.

Zoning still meets opposition from many who object to this interference with their right to use their property as they choose. Even so, nearly every city of any size in the United States is zoned today. The city of Houston, where zoning was turned down three times by popular vote, remains the only major exception.

Zoning ordinances must be reasonable. Remember that the 14th Amendment prohibits any State, and thus its cities, from depriving any person of life, liberty, or property without due process of law. Each of the 50 State constitutions contains a similar provision.

Clearly, zoning does deprive a person of the right to use his or her property for certain purposes. Thus, if an area is zoned for single-family dwellings only, one cannot build an apartment house or a service station on property in that zone. Zoning can also reduce the value of a particular piece of property. A choice corner lot, for example, may be much more valuable with a drive-through restaurant or gas station on the property rather than a house.[5]

While zoning may at times deprive a person of liberty or property, the key question is always this: Does it do so without due process? That is, does it do so unreasonably?

The question of reasonableness is one for the courts to decide. The Supreme Court first upheld zoning as a proper use of the police power in *Euclid* v. *Amber Realty Co.,* 1926, a case involving an ordinance enacted by the city council of Euclid, Ohio.

---

[5] Nonconforming uses in existence before a zoning ordinance is passed are almost always allowed to continue. Most ordinances give the city council the right to grant exceptions, called variances, in those cases where property owners might suffer undue hardship.

✔ **Checkpoint**
How do cities plan for the future?

**prescribe**
*v.* order, set down, specify

---

## Background

**MODERN-DAY CITY PLANNING** Modern-day city planning has reached its boldest extreme in fast-growing Portland, Oregon. In 1995, regional leaders adopted the 2040 Growth Concept to curb traffic and preserve Portland's natural beauty and neighborhoods. The 2040 Growth Concept focuses development on urban centers inside a line called the Urban Growth Boundary. Houses and apartments are built close to one another and to commercial buildings. Inside the line, public transportation, walking, and bicycling are attractive alternatives to driving. Outside the line, development is strictly limited.

---

**FOLLOW UP AND VOTE**

Have the groups present their finished plans to the class. Then have the class vote by secret ballot to select the overall best plan. Discuss with the class what was so attractive about the winning design. Ask: **Does the winning design best meet the city manager's goal? Why or why not? If not, what other features should it have?**

**L3 Differentiate** Post the groups' plans around the room with a blank piece of paper next to each one. Allow time for students to look at other groups' work and comment on it in a Conversation Wall (p. T27). After students have commented, give groups time to read the comments on their work, respond, and make improvements to their plans.

**MAKE A JOURNAL ENTRY**

Have students complete the activity by writing a journal entry about the process of their city square planning. Ask them to consider the following questions: **Did the group work well together? Did all members contribute? Were the priorities the same for everyone? Were you satisfied with the final plan? Why or why not? What comments by other students did you find helpful? What changes, if any, did you make to your group's plan based on peer feedback?**

---

## Answers

**Checkpoint** They establish some sort of planning agency and zoning ordinances.

**L3 Differentiate** Tell students to research and write a report on the development of a planned city of the past, such as Washington, D.C., or a modern planned community, such as Celebration, Florida. Reports should focus on the goals of the designers and whether or not students think those goals were achieved.

**L2 ELL Differentiate** Have students use mapping and satellite photography software, such as Google Maps, to analyze your community. Ask them to print out their neighborhoods and label different zones: residential, commercial, and industrial.

**L2 Differentiate** Have students research and report on one zoning law in your community. Students should summarize for the class the purpose of the zoning law and what it allows, establishes, or restricts.

**L2 Differentiate** Distribute the Extend Activity "Your City Government" (Unit 7 All-in-One, p. 96), which has students attend a local government meeting and report on it to the class.

**L4 Differentiate** Remind students that American cities have been the breeding ground for powerful political machines. Ask students to report on the history and influence of political machines such as the Tammany Hall machine in New York City or the Daley machine in Chicago. Students should investigate the means by which these machines obtained and retained power over city government and beyond. Encourage students to research the events that brought about the decline of the machines' power. Allow students to present their findings in a variety of ways.

**L4 Differentiate** Have students work in pairs or small groups to research and report to the class on an area that has been a target of community planning in the last five years in their own, or in a nearby, community. (To avoid duplication, pre-approve topics before work begins.) Reports should include the project's history and current status. Students should analyze it from start to finish and evaluate its success. Alternatively, you may ask students to create annotated timelines giving details of the project. Encourage students to interview participants and to include maps and images of the project—before and after.

## Answers

**Farms, Cities, Suburbs** rural settlement: people largely self-sufficient, with local government providing few services to widely dispersed population; urban settlement: local government provides wide range of services to large, densely packed population; suburban settlement: city, county, and special district governments provide services to broad metropolitan areas

**Checkpoint** Accept any applicable function of city government

---

# Farms, Cities, Suburbs

The United States began as a rural nation, but factories and new opportunities drew millions to cities in the 1800s and early 1900s. Today, about half of all Americans live in suburbs that bridge the gap between country and city. *How do different forms of settlement affect the responsibilities of local government?*

## 1790    1920    Today

| Nearly all Americans live on farms or in small towns. | For the first time, more Americans live in cities than in the countryside. | Suburbs are home to half of all Americans. |

SOURCE: U.S. Census

✔ **Checkpoint**
What are some of the functions of city governments?

## Municipal Functions

The services a city provides day in and day out are so extensive that it is almost impossible to catalog them. Most larger cities, and many smaller ones, issue annual reports on the city's condition. These are often book-length publications.

Consider just a few of the many things that most or all cities do. They provide police and fire protection. They build and maintain streets, sidewalks, bridges, street lights, parks and playgrounds, swimming pools, golf courses, libraries, hospitals, schools, correctional institutions, day-care centers, airports, public markets, parking facilities, auditoriums, and sports arenas. They furnish public health and sanitation services, including sewers and wastewater treatment, garbage collection and disposal, and disease prevention programs.

Cities operate water, gas, electrical, and transportation systems. They regulate traffic, building codes, pollution, and public utilities. Many cities also build and manage public housing projects, provide summer youth camps, build and operate docks and other harbor facilities, and maintain tourist attractions.

## Metropolitan Areas

The growth of urban areas has raised many problems for city dwellers. Urban growth also affects residents of nearby suburbs.

**The Suburban Boom** About half of all Americans now live in suburbs. The nation's suburbs first began to grow rapidly in the years after World War II, and that growth has continued. As suburban populations have mushroomed, many of the nation's larger cities have actually lost residents.

These dramatic population shifts stemmed, in large part, from peoples' desire for more room, cheaper land, greater privacy, and less smoke, dirt, noise, and congestion. Many have also sought less crime, newer and better schools, safer streets and playing conditions, lower taxes, and higher social status. The car and the freeway turned millions of rooted city dwellers into mobile suburbanites.

Businesses followed customers to the suburbs, often clustering in shopping centers or malls instead of traditional downtowns. Many industries moved from the central city in search of cheaper land, lower taxes, and a more stable labor supply. Industries also

---

# Teacher to Teacher Network

**ALTERNATE LESSON PLAN** Mayors sometimes take on politically controversial issues, such as the environment, climate change, and gun control. Have students research initiatives that a mayor in their area is working on and select one to look into further. They should describe the issue, explain the mayor's plan for addressing it, present the arguments for and against the plan, and assess the success of the plan to date. Student groups could focus on different initiatives.

To see this lesson plan, go to

at PearsonSchool.com/phgovt

sought an escape from city building codes, health inspectors, and other regulations.

This "suburbanitis" has added to city-dwellers' woes. As high-income families have moved out, they have taken their civic, financial, and social resources with them. They have left behind center cities with high percentages of older people, low-income families, and minorities. Both the need for, and the stress on, city services have multiplied.

**Metropolitan Areas** Suburbanites face their share of problems, too, including the need for water supplies, sewage disposal, police and fire protection, transportation, and traffic control. Duplication of such functions by city and suburb or by city and county can be wasteful, even dangerous. More than one fire has raged while neighboring fire departments quibbled over the responsibility for fighting it.

Attempts to meet the needs of the nation's **metropolitan areas**—cities and the areas around them—have taken several forms. Over the years, annexation has been the standard means. Outlying areas have simply been brought within a city's boundaries. Many suburbanites resist annexation, however, and many cities have been hesitant to take on the burdens involved.

Another approach has been to create special districts designed to meet the problems of heavily populated urban areas. Their boundaries frequently cut across county and city lines to include an entire metropolitan area. They often are called metropolitan districts and can serve one purpose (for example, maintaining parks) or many.

In Oregon, a regional agency known as Metro manages several activities in an area that includes Portland, the State's largest city, and 23 other municipalities. Within this region, Metro is responsible for land-use and transportation planning, solid-waste disposal programs, and the operation of the Oregon Convention Center, the Oregon Zoo, and other facilities.

Yet another approach to the challenges facing metropolitan areas is increasing the authority of counties. Among local governments around the country, counties are generally the largest in area and are most likely to include those places demanding new and increased services. In Miami-Dade County, Florida, a countywide metropolitan government took responsibility for areawide functions following a 1957 charter. Responsibilities include fire and police protection; an integrated water, sewer, and drainage system; zoning; and expressway construction. Miami and the county's other 34 municipalities continue to perform strictly local functions and services.

**woe**
*n.* problem

**duplication**
*n.* doubling

Portland's metropolitan government operates a popular regional transit system. ▾

**Essential Questions Journal** To continue to build a response to the chapter Essential Question, go to your **Essential Questions Journal.**

## SECTION 2 ASSESSMENT

1. **Guiding Question** Use your completed outline to answer this question: How do city governments serve the needs of residents and other Americans?

**Key Terms and Comprehension**
2. What are the key differences between a **strong-mayor** and a **weak-mayor government**?
3. List at least five functions of municipal government.

**Critical Thinking**
4. **Comparing Points of View** Zoning may be used to exclude businesses popular with young people from residential neighborhoods. **(a)** Why do you think this is so? **(b)** Is this a fair use of a local government's police power? Why or why not?
5. **Determining Cause and Effect** How have shifts in the American population led to changes in the responsibilities and organization of local government?

**Quick Write**

**Writing for Assessment: Gather Details** Reread the question you have chosen and the main points you developed in Section 1. Gather details from the text that support each of the main points to answer the question. Briefly check your final list to delete unnecessary details.

---

# Assess and Remediate

**L3** Collect the Core Worksheets and assess the students' plans, using the Rubric for Assessing the Performance of an Entire Group (Unit 7 All-in-One, p. 125).

**L3** Assign the Section 2 Assessment questions.

**L3** Section Quiz A (Unit 7 All-in-One, p. 97)

**L2** Section Quiz B (Unit 7 All-in-One, p. 98)

Have students complete the review activities in the digital lesson presentation and continue their work in the **Essential Questions Journal.**

## REMEDIATION

| If Your Students Have Trouble With | Strategies For Remediation |
|---|---|
| Roles and responsibilities of city government (Questions 1, 3, 5) | Draw a concept web on the board. With students fill in the web with details from their section outlines on the roles and responsibilities of city government. |
| Differences between the two types of mayoral government (Question 2) | Display Transparency 25D and have students work in pairs to quiz each other about the structure of types of city government. |
| Functions of zoning and city planning (Question 4) | Have students re-read the text under the heading "City Planning," and write a summary of the purpose of zoning. |

---

# Assessment Answers

**1.** City governments manage growth through zoning, create and manage the budget, and provide important public services. City governments also make and enforce regulations (such as traffic laws, building codes, and pollution laws).

**2.** A strong mayor can exercise strong leadership in making city policy and running the city's affairs. A weak mayor has much less formal power and shares executive duties with other elected officials.

**3.** provide police and fire protection; build and maintain streets, bridges, and libraries; furnish public health and sanitation facilities; operate water, gas, electric, and transportation systems; build and maintain public housing

**4. (a)** Local government makes rules based on the interests of the entire neighborhood, not just a segment of it. **(b)** Yes. The interests of different segments of a community often conflict, and it is an appropriate role of local government to settle such conflicts with rules that benefit the community as a whole.

**5.** Possible answer: The population shift from farms to cities created a need for city governments to provide a wide range of services and plan for orderly growth. The movement to the suburbs gave rise to special districts and broader county authority to provide essential services to wider metropolitan areas.

**QUICK WRITE** Students should list details that support the main idea in the answer to their question. For example, students addressing the second question should provide specific details about the benefits and drawbacks of each form of city government.

# What services do State and local governments provide?

# Get Started

## LESSON GOALS

Students will . . .

- list and categorize services that they receive from State and local governments.
- role play to complete a worksheet ranking the importance of State and local services from various perspectives.
- compare their rankings of State services against actual State and local spending.

## BEFORE CLASS

Assign the section, the graphic organizer in the text, and the Reading Comprehension Worksheet (Unit 7 All-in-One, p. 99) before class.

**L2** **Differentiate** Reading Comprehension Worksheet (Unit 7 All-in-One, p. 100)

## SKILLS DEVELOPMENT

### COMPARE VIEWPOINTS

Before students complete the Core Worksheet in this section, you may want to review tips on comparing viewpoints in the Skills Handbook, p. S15.

---

SECTION **3**

# Providing **Vital Services**

**What services do State and local governments provide?** Use a concept web similar to the one below to record information about State and local government services.

**Political Dictionary**
- Medicaid
- welfare
- entitlement

**Objectives**

1. Explain why State and local governments have a major role in providing important services.
2. Identify State and local services in the fields of education, public welfare, public safety, and highways.

**Image Above:** Educational spending includes computers, books, and salaries.

The 50 State governments and their tens of thousands of local governments are principally responsible for many of the public services with which most Americans are familiar. The many differences among States means that there can be variations in both the quantity and the quality of those public services, but they include, especially, those in the areas of education, public safety, welfare, streets and highways, and public health. The several States deliver services to their residents in two ways: (1) directly, through State agencies conducting State-operated programs, and (2) through the many local governments the States have created.

## Education

Public education is among the oldest of all State responsibilities. Boston Latin School, in Massachusetts, is the oldest public school in continuous existence in the United States; it opened its doors in 1635. The State of New York created the first school districts in 1812. Today, public education is also among the most important of all State responsibilities. This is reflected in the fact that education is the most expensive item in every State's budget, accounting for about 30 percent of all State spending.

Funding for public education has risen sharply over recent decades, and the recent downturn in the nation's economy has almost certainly brought only a temporary dip in that trend. The amount of money spent per pupil in public schools has nearly doubled over the past 25 years.

Primary and secondary public education is largely the responsibility of local governments. Local taxes, especially property taxes, provide much of the funding for schools.

Of course, the States do provide some financial assistance to their local governments for education. The level of that aid varies, however. Some States contribute well over half the cost of primary and secondary education. Others provide only a minor fraction of the cost.

In addition, States set guidelines in order to promote quality in the schools. For example, State laws establish teacher qualifications, curricula, quality standards for educational materials, and the length of the school year.

---

# Focus on the Basics

Here is the information that your students need to learn in this section.

**FACTS:** • Under the federal system, States and local governments provide many important services. • State and local governments provide education, help ensure public welfare and safety, and build and maintain highways. • State and local governments vary widely in the number, extent, and types of services they provide.

**CONCEPTS:** types of governments, purpose of government, federalism

**ENDURING UNDERSTANDINGS:** • The U.S. Constitution reserves to the States all powers not delegated to the Federal Government or not denied to the States. • Education is the largest spending category for State and local governments.

State interest and involvement in those matters have intensified in recent years. Most States have established "curriculum frameworks" or "content standards" outlining the material that must be covered in core subjects. Every State now has an extensive Statewide testing program, fueled by the No Child Left Behind Act signed by President Bush in 2002.

At the college and university levels, the States also play a major role. States understand that, in order for businesses to succeed in the State, a ready supply of highly trained college graduates is key. Every State has a public higher education system, which may include universities, technical schools, and community colleges. Education at State universities and colleges is generally much less expensive than at private institutions. On average, tuition at four-year public colleges and universities is about one fourth that of private four-year schools. Nevertheless, many public institutions—for example, the University of California at Berkeley—are ranked among the world's finest schools.

## Public Welfare

States take an active role in promoting the health and welfare of their residents. They pursue that goal by a variety of means.

**Public Health** Most States fund ambitious public health programs. States operate public hospitals and offer direct care to millions of citizens. They immunize children against dangerous childhood diseases, such as measles and mumps. With the Federal Government, they administer such programs as **Medicaid,** which provides medical care and some other health services to low-income families. Recent soaring costs in the health-care industry have placed a great strain on many States' budgets.

**Cash Assistance** Another major area in which States contribute to the well-being of their citizens is cash assistance to the poor, commonly called **welfare.** States now take a leading role in this area.

**✓ Checkpoint**
What are a State's responsibilities for education?

**tuition**
*n.* fee paid for schooling

**GOVERNMENT**ONLINE
For an **interactive** exploration of state and local expenditures, visit PearsonSchool.com/phgovt

**How Government Works**

# State and Local Spending

Public schools account for nearly three in every ten dollars spent by State and local governments. *How are the different responsibilities of State and local government versus the Federal Government reflected in these categories of spending?*

- 6% Other
- 6% Transportation
- 7% Environment/Housing
- 7% Healthcare
- 7% Utilities
- 8% Unemployment/Worker's Comp/Retirement
- 29% Education
- 14% Public welfare
- 8% Public safety
- 14% Other

**6%** TRANSPORTATION needs drive governments to build and maintain roads, bridges, and trains. ▲

**8%** PUBLIC SAFETY expenditures protect people from fires and crime.

**7%** HEALTHCARE spending includes Medicaid for low-income Americans. ▶
SOURCE: U.S. Census

CHICAGO POLIC[E]

# Differentiated Resources

The following resources are located in the All-in-One, Unit 7, Chapter 25, Section 3:

- **L3** Reading Comprehension Worksheet (p. 99)
- **L2** Reading Comprehension Worksheet (p. 100)
- **L3** Core Worksheet (p. 101)
- **L3** Quiz A (p. 102)
- **L2** Quiz B (p. 103)

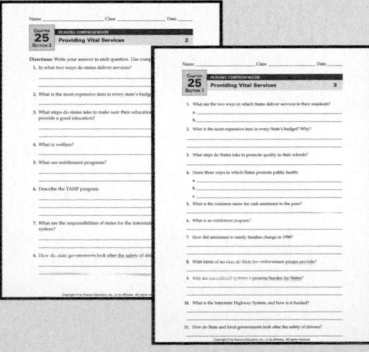

Write on the board: **List ten services that State and local governments provide that directly affect your life.**

**L1** **Differentiate** Ask students to provide five, instead of ten, services.

**L2** **ELL Differentiate** Tell students to review the main headings/topics in the section, to help generate items for their lists.

# Teach

To present this topic using online resources, use the lesson presentations at **PearsonSchool.com/phgovt**.

**CATEGORIZE THE BELLRINGER RESPONSES**

Write these headings on the board: **Education, Public Welfare, Public Safety, Public Health, Roads.** Have students read the services they listed in the Bellringer activity and sort them under the appropriate category. Also, ask students to identify which level of government provides each service. Ask: **Why are these services provided at the State or local level and not by the National Government?** *(Local governments have better knowledge about how to meet the needs of their citizens.)*

**RANK THE IMPORTANCE OF SERVICES**

Divide the class into seven groups. Assign each group one of the following roles: (1) student in the local high school; (2) parent of three school-age children; (3) police officer; (4) taxi driver; (5) carpenter; (6) elderly resident; (7) worker who lives outside the community.

Tell students that they will complete a worksheet from the perspective of their assigned role by ranking various services provided by State and local governments. They will also explain their reasoning based on the role they are playing.

**L3** **Differentiate** Students may work individually or in their role groups to complete the worksheet.

**L1** **L2** **ELL Differentiate** You may want to assign these students more straightforward or familiar roles, such as the student or parent.

Tell students to go to the Interactivity for current information on State and local spending.

## Answers

**Checkpoint** to help fund schools and to set guidelines to promote quality education; to help support a system of State colleges and universities

**State and Local Spending** Federal spending focuses on programs benefiting the nation as a whole, such as the military, whereas State and local spending supports programs for the local community, such as schools, assistance to needy citizens, and police and fire protection.

**DISTRIBUTE CORE WORKSHEET**

Distribute the Chapter 25 Section 3 Core Worksheet (Unit 7 All-in-One, p. 101). Give students time to complete the first column on their own.

**L1** **L2** **ELL Differentiate** Before beginning, review the service categories on the worksheet and offer examples of each to clarify.

**FOLLOW UP—COMPARE PERSPECTIVES**

After students complete their own ranking, have them work in groups of students assigned to the same role to reach a consensus on the rankings. Then ask them to post their rankings around the room, as well as to explain their choice for their number one ranking. Discuss any differences in the rankings from group to group. Then ask students to vote to create a class ranking. Have students record class rankings on the Core Worksheet.

**L3** **Differentiate** Have students write a journal entry explaining why they agree or disagree with the class ranking.

Display Transparency 25E, State and Local Spending. Ask: **How closely do State and local spending align with your rankings?** For example, did most students feel that education was the most important service? Were parks and recreation the least important?

**EXTEND THE LESSON**

**L3** **Differentiate** Have students find one or two recent articles that describe a difference of opinion on how to fund public schools. Ask them to summarize in a bulleted list the main arguments from the different viewpoints. Then ask them to take a position and write a paragraph supporting their position.

## Answers

**Caption** Possible response: Local governments are best able to judge where roads in their jurisdiction are most needed.

**Checkpoint** to provide cash assistance to needy citizens for up to five years while they work or receive training to become self-sufficient

The Federal Government shares the cost of highway projects like Boston's Big Dig with the States and counties where they are built. *Why do local governments make most decisions about road building?*

✔ **Checkpoint**
What is the purpose of public welfare spending?

**entitled**
*adj.* eligible for, qualified to receive

**recipient**
*n.* one who receives

the federal grant, plus the State funds they are obliged to contribute, to design and implement their own welfare programs. TANF limits recipients to a total of five years of assistance during the course of their lifetimes, and recipients must work or participate in some form of vocational training or community service.

The number of families on welfare has plunged since the mid-1990s. Many who remain on welfare must overcome a number of barriers, such as physical or mental disabilities or substance abuse, in order to obtain and hold jobs. Now that States have the primary responsibility for welfare, it is their task to find ways to help these families.

**Other Efforts** States do much more to promote their citizens' health and welfare. They make and enforce antipollution laws to protect the environment; they inspect factories and other workplaces to protect worker safety; they license healthcare practitioners to ensure quality care; and the list goes on and on.

## Public Safety

One of the oldest law-enforcement groups, the legendary Texas Rangers, was established in 1835. Today, a variety of police forces, from the local sheriff to academy-trained State police, operate in every State to preserve law and order.

The State police are perhaps the most visible group, since they patrol the State's roads and highways. State law-enforcement forces perform other vital services, as well. They may function as the primary police force in rural communities, investigate crimes, provide centralized files for fingerprints and other information, and provide training and many other services to support local law-enforcement agencies.

Each State has its own corrections system for dealing with those convicted of State crimes. States operate prisons, penitentiaries, and other correctional facilities, including those for juvenile offenders.

Operating these disciplinary systems is a growing burden for States. Today, more than 2.3 million people are incarcerated, more than half of them in State prisons.

Between 1936 and 1996, the Federal Government provided cash assistance to needy families through the Aid to Families with Dependent Children (AFDC) program.[6] AFDC was an **entitlement** program, which means that anyone who met the eligibility requirements was entitled to receive benefits under the program. The Federal Government and the States shared the costs of providing AFDC benefits.

Critics of AFDC pointed to soaring costs, expanding caseloads, and the absence of time limits on benefits as serious problems with the program. Because of these issues, critics argued that the program encouraged people to depend on government assistance rather than become self-supporting.

In 1996, AFDC was replaced with a new and strikingly different program, Temporary Assistance to Needy Families (TANF). Unlike AFDC, TANF is a block grant program: The Federal Government gives States a fixed amount of money each year, regardless of whether the number of TANF recipients rises or falls. The States are then free to use

6 AFDC was authorized by Title IV of the Social Security Act of 1935. Until 1962, the program was named Aid to Dependent Children, as the 1935 act was aimed simply at needy dependent children.

Two leading causes of booming prison populations are (1) increases in the number of people sentenced for violent crimes and (2) the increasing length of the average prison sentence. One result is prison overcrowding. Another result is rising State corrections spending, which has more than doubled over the past 20 years. The States now spend more than $40 billion each year to build, staff, and maintain prisons and to house prisoners.

In an effort to expand their prison capacity more affordably, many States have hired private contractors to operate some of their prisons. More than 5 percent of all State prisoners are now held in private facilities.

## Highways and Other Services

Building and maintaining roads and highways is an enormous job. It regularly ranks among the most expensive of all the many items in State budgets.

Again, the Federal Government is a partner with the States in funding highways. The most impressive example is the Interstate Highway System, a network of high-speed roadways that spans the length and breadth of the continental United States. Construction of the system began with the 1956 Federal-Aid Highway Act and continues to this day.

The Interstate Highway System, now officially known as the Dwight D. Eisenhower System of Interstate and Defense Highways, is 99 percent finished. When finally complete, it will total some 45,000 miles. The Federal Government has paid roughly 90 percent of its total cost.

While the interstate system is a magnificent achievement, it constitutes only a tiny fraction of the nation's more than 4 million miles of roads. Many roadways are built with State, not federal, funds; and the States maintain those roads, as well.

State and local governments must also look after the physical safety of drivers on thousands of miles of roads and highways. Besides patrolling the roads, State and local governments set speed limits. The States license drivers to ensure their competence, and many States require periodic safety inspections of vehicles.

As indicated earlier, the many services the States and their local units provide are really far too numerous to be recounted here. That these services are not detailed here does not discount the importance of such functions as the setting aside of public lands for purposes such as conservation and recreation, the regulation of business practices, and the protection of consumers from a variety of dangers and inconveniences.

✔ **Checkpoint**
How do State and local governments ensure the safety of the people?

**capacity**
n. ability to hold

**Essential Questions Journal** To continue to build a response to the chapter Essential Question, go to your **Essential Questions Journal.**

## SECTION 3 ASSESSMENT

1. **Guiding Question** Use your completed concept web to answer this question: What services do State and local governments provide?

**Key Terms and Comprehension**

2. What are the three largest spending categories in State and local budgets?

3. How is an **entitlement** program different from other spending programs?

**Critical Thinking**

4. **Drawing Inferences** Why do you think that many States asked the Federal Government to give them block grants to create their own welfare programs?

5. **Expressing Problems Clearly** What challenges do State and local governments face in providing for public welfare and safety? How are governments meeting these challenges?

**Quick Write**

**Writing for Assessment: Write a Strong Opening Statement** When writing for assessment, the opening statement should set forth the main idea of your response in an interesting and clear manner. Review your question and list of main points from Sections 1 and 2 and write an opening statement. Check it against your main idea and main points to be sure that all parts of your response are closely related.

---

# Assess and Remediate

**L3** Collect the Core Worksheets and assess the students' class participation, using the Rubric for Assessing Individual Performance in a Group (Unit 7 All-in-One, p. 126).

**L3** Assign the Section 3 Assessment questions.

**L3** Section Quiz A (Unit 7 All-in-One, p. 102)

**L2** Section Quiz B (Unit 7 All-in-One, p. 103)

Have students complete the review activities in the digital lesson presentation and continue their work in the **Essential Questions Journal.**

### REMEDIATION

| If Your Students Have Trouble With | Strategies For Remediation |
|---|---|
| Services provided by State and local governments (Questions 1, 2, 3, 5) | Draw a concept web on the board like the one on the first page of the section. With students, fill in the web with details about State and local government services. Tell students to add any additional details they did not have to their own concept webs. |
| Understanding block grants (Question 4) | Direct students to re-read the text about TANF and federal block grants and summarize that paragraph. |

## Answers

**Checkpoint** by maintaining police forces and corrections systems, inspecting workplaces for safety, and licensing health-care providers

---

# Assessment Answers

1. State and local governments provide services such as education, public health programs (including Medicaid), and welfare. They promote public safety by maintaining police forces and correctional institutions, making antipollution laws, inspecting factories, licensing health-care providers, setting speed limits, licensing drivers, and requiring vehicle inspections. They build and maintain roads, set aside public lands, regulate businesses, and protect consumers from dangerous products.

2. education, other, public welfare

3. An entitlement program provides benefits to everyone who meets the eligibility requirements, and it is a form of social welfare.

4. possible response: so that the States could design welfare programs according to the needs and wishes of their own citizens

5. Possible response: The main challenge is lack of funds. In the case of the corrections system, many States have hired private contractors to operate some prisons. Also, TANF limits welfare recipients to five years of assistance during their lifetimes.

**QUICK WRITE** Students should write an opening statement containing the main idea in their response to the question they selected. Sample opening statement: Each form of city government has its strengths and weaknesses based on the relationship between the executive and the other parts of the government.

- Students will examine issues surrounding State budgets by balancing a sample budget.

## Teach

### INTRODUCE THE TOPIC

Tell students that a major challenge facing State leaders is to balance the budget. The main issue is how to pay for all the State's services while keeping taxes, fees, and debt low. Elected officials know that voters do not want services cut, but neither do they want higher taxes. Have students read the feature and answer the questions.

**L2** **ELL Differentiate** Explain that a *shortfall* is another way of saying *deficit*, in other words a falling short of an amount needed.

### BALANCE A SAMPLE STATE BUDGET

Distribute the worksheet for this feature (Unit 7 All-in-One, p. 104). Tell students that they will work in pairs to balance a simplified sample State budget. If possible, furnish calculators.

### FOLLOW UP

When students have completed their worksheets, have them share their outcomes. Ask: **Were you able to balance the budget? Why or why not? What did you find most challenging about the activity?** Explain that a negative ending balance in the worksheet represents a negative deficit—in other words, a surplus. A *surplus* is extra money that can be saved for future spending.

## Assess and Remediate

Have students write a main idea sentence for each quotation and then explain which one they agree with most, and why.

## Answers

1. **(a)** possible answer: because governments provide more services to more people than ever before **(b)** Possible answer: People want services, but no tax increases to pay for them. Therefore, officials risk losing reelection if they either cut services or raise taxes.

2. **(a)** Sample answer: No, the reforms would have been as undesirable as the taxes, but increased taxes might have been preferred over reduced services. **(b)** Sample answer: Yes, his emphasis on the importance of education today as well as in the future would garner support. **(c)** Answers will vary.

# ISSUES OF OUR TIME

## State Taxation and Spending

### ▶▶ Track the Issue

**The United States** was founded, in part, on opposition to taxes. Nonetheless, governments have found many ways to raise money.

**1646**

**The Massachusetts Bay Colony** establishes the first property tax in the 13 colonies.

**1765**

**Prompted by the Stamp Act,** the colonists declare "taxation without representation" to be unfair.

**1862**

**The Federal Government** provides for a temporary income tax to meet the costs of the Civil War.

**1911**

**Wisconsin** establishes the first State income tax.

**1964**

**New Hampshire** institutes the first modern-day State lottery to pay for public programs.

**1970s to Today**

**Voters in several States rebel** against rising property taxes with laws limiting tax increases.

Governor Pat Quinn (R, Illinois) ▶

### ▶▶ Perspectives

Many Americans complain that the government takes too much money out of their pockets. However, limits on taxes have contributed to deficit spending or cuts in services in the States. The current economic recession has put a great deal of pressure on State governments to adopt budgets that cut whatever spending they can while continuing to provide those services their citizens expect. What issues do State government officials and taxpaying citizens need to consider when trying to balance budgets?

"A number of solutions were proposed that would have addressed the budget shortfall without increasing taxes, such as reforming workers' compensation, reducing unemployment insurance premiums, and providing regulatory reforms. Unfortunately, those ideas were shut out of the process. Instead, the entire debate . . . focused on tax increases. Now we're close to the end of a . . . special session with no budget reforms . . . as . . . lawmakers seek to tax the state out of the shortfall at the expense of jobs and taxpayers. . . ."

—Republican Illinois State Representative Dan Roach, 2010

"I am challenging you today to consider a wise and responsible alternative to damaging cuts in education funding. My alternative is a one percent income tax surcharge for education. That . . . will be enough to restore our education budget to current levels—and allow us to get caught up on some of the millions of dollars we owe to our . . . schools, . . . We must invest in the future—even in these tough economic times. . . . We cannot walk away from teaching our kids. . . . [W]e adults sacrifice some of our present in order to help our children's future."

—Democratic Governor of Illinois Pat Quinn, 2010

### ▶▶ Connect to Your World

1. **Understand (a)** Why do you think that taxes have increased in both number and rates since independence? **(b)** What is the central conflict in the relationship between taxation and government services?

2. **Drawing Conclusions (a)** Would Representative Roach's proposed reforms have been more acceptable to taxpayers than a tax increase? **(b)** Do you think Governor Quinn's impassioned plea for education will attract public support? **(c)** How do these excerpts illustrate the challenges the States face as they make their budgets?

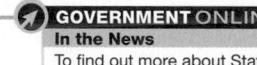
**GOVERNMENT ONLINE**
**In the News**
To find out more about State revenues and spending, visit **PearsonSchool.com/phgovt**

**760**

## Background

**TAX REVOLT IN ARIZONA** The economic downturn in 2008 strained the budgets of families and States. In Arizona, Governor Janet Napolitano vetoed a proposed law that would reduce property taxes. Outraged citizens decided to bypass the legislative process and fight for tax relief directly through the ballot. Citizen organizations, such as The Sun City Taxpayers Association, began gathering signatures to put initiatives on the ballot. These initiatives prohibit new taxes on property sales and require voter approval for new tax propositions. Property taxes hit retirement communities, such as Sun City, especially hard. Most retirees are living on fixed incomes—their incomes do not rise to cover tax increases. The property tax initiative passed, but it could cause Arizona to sink deeper into its budget deficit.

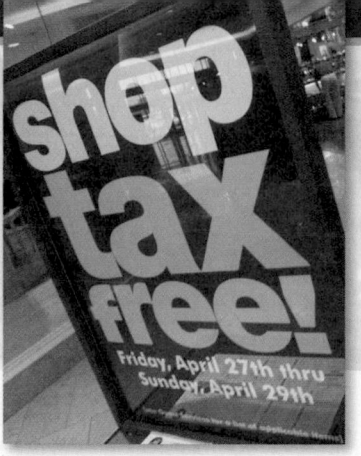

**shop tax free!**
Friday, April 27th thru Sunday, April 29th

## SECTION 4

# Financing State and Local Government

### Guiding Question

**How do State governments raise money to pay for services?** Use a chart similar to the one below to record information about the sources of State revenue.

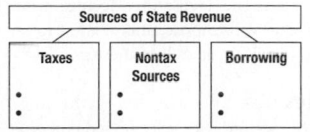

| Sources of State Revenue | | |
|---|---|---|
| Taxes | Nontax Sources | Borrowing |
| • | • | • |
| • | • | • |

### Political Dictionary

- sales tax
- regressive tax
- income tax
- progressive tax
- property tax
- assessment
- inheritance tax
- estate tax
- budget

### Objectives

1. Describe the major federal and State limits on raising revenue.
2. List the four principles of sound taxation.
3. Identify major tax and nontax sources of State and local revenue.
4. Explain the State budget process.

**Image Above:** Sales taxes are a major source of revenue for State and local governments.

**A**ltogether, despite the recent recession, the 50 States and their thousands of local governments take in and spend well over $2 *trillion* per year. If you were to place 2 trillion dollar bills end to end, they would extend more than 185 million miles—farther than the distance from Earth to the planet Venus. Where do those governments get all that money, and what do they do with it?

## Limits on Raising Revenue

The States now take in well over $750 billion in taxes a year. And their local governments collect some 550 billion tax dollars every year. Those two basic levels of government also receive more than $1 trillion from several nontax sources, too—much of it from the Federal Government.

The power to tax is one of the major powers of the States in the federal system. In a strictly legal sense, then, their taxing power is limited only by the restrictions imposed by the Federal Constitution and those imposed by a State's own fundamental law.[7]

**Federal Limitations** The Federal Constitution does place some restrictions on the taxing abilities of State and local government. Although few in number, those limits do have a major impact.

The Constitution prohibits the States from taxing interstate and foreign trade. Remember, the Supreme Court's decision in *McCulloch* v. *Maryland*, in 1819, bars States from taxing the Federal Government or any of its agencies or functions.

The 14th Amendment's Due Process and Equal Protection clauses place important limits on the power to tax at the State and local levels. Essentially, the Due Process Clause requires that taxes be (1) imposed and administered *fairly*, (2) not so heavy as to actually confiscate property, and (3) imposed only for *public* purposes.

The Equal Protection Clause forbids the making of unreasonable classifications for the purpose of taxation. The clause thus forbids tax classifications

---

7 Remember, the power to tax is also limited by any number of practical considerations—including, especially, economic and political factors.

---

## How do State governments raise money to pay for services?

| Sources of State Revenue | | |
|---|---|---|
| **Taxes** | **Nontax Sources** | **Borrowing** |
| • sales | • Federal Government grants | • bonds |
| • income | • business enterprise and user fees | |
| • property | • court fines | |
| • inheritance | • sales and lease of public lands | |
| • estate | • interest from loans, investments, and late tax payments | |
| • severance | • lotteries | |
| • license (business) | | |
| • documentary and stock transfer | | |
| • capital stock | | |
| • payroll | | |
| • amusement | | |
| • license (non-business) | | |

## Get Started

### LESSON GOALS

Students will . . .

- list and categorize taxes as progressive or regressive.
- use a bar graph to discuss sources of State and local revenue.
- evaluate different types of State and local taxes based on four criteria describing "a good tax."

**ANALYZE SOURCES**

To help students learn to analyze sources, have them turn to the Skills Handbook, p. S14 and use the steps explained there to complete the Extend Worksheet.

---

## Focus on the Basics

Here is the information that your students need to learn in this section.

**FACTS:** • The federal Constitution and State constitutions restrict State and local taxing powers. • Adam Smith identified four principles of sound taxation: equality, certainty, convenience, and economy. • The Due Process Clause requires taxes to be imposed fairly, in reasonable amounts, and only for public purposes.

**CONCEPTS:** taxation, Due Process Clause, Equal Protection Clause, budget

**ENDURING UNDERSTANDINGS:** • Progressive taxes rise along with ability to pay, while regressive taxes fall most heavily on low-income individuals. • Sources of State and local funding include taxes, nontax sources (especially federal grants), and borrowing. • The State budget is the plan for the control and use of public money.

Assign the section, the graphic organizer in the text, and the Reading Comprehension Worksheet (Unit 7 All-in-One, p. 105) before class.

**L2 Differentiate** Reading Comprehension Worksheet (Unit 7 All-in-One, p. 107)

## BELLRINGER

Create a two-column chart on the board, with the headings "Progressive" and "Regressive." Write on the board: **Categorize these taxes: sales tax, income tax, property tax, tax on movie tickets, and tax on drivers' licenses.**

**L1 L2 ELL Differentiate** Remind students that a *progressive tax* requires people with higher incomes to pay more than those with lower incomes. A *regressive tax* is not based on ability to pay.

## Answers

**Checkpoint** States may not tax interstate or foreign trade, tax the Federal Government or any of its agencies or functions, impose unfair or unreasonably heavy taxes, impose taxes for purposes other than public purposes, or make unreasonable classifications for tax purposes.

---

✔**Checkpoint**
What are the federal constitutional limits on State taxes?

**arbitrary**
*adj.* unfairly determined by chance

**contrived**
*adj.* carefully planned, skillfully designed

**exemption**
*n.* freed, excused from a duty

based on race, religion, nationality, political party membership, or any other factors beyond what is reasonable.

Most tax laws do involve some form of classification, however. Thus, a cigarette tax is collected only from those who buy cigarettes, a classification most people agree is a reasonable one.

**State Limitations** Each State's constitution limits a State's taxing powers. State constitutions also limit the taxing powers of their local governments, often in great detail.

Most State constitutions create tax <u>exemptions</u> for religious and other nonprofit groups. State codes often set maximum rates for levies such as sales taxes or local property taxes. Some States prohibit certain taxes—for example, a general sales tax or a personal income tax.

Since local governments have no independent powers, the only taxes they can impose are those that the State allows them to levy. States have been restrictive in the matter. Even local units with home-rule charters are closely limited as to what and how they can tax.

## Principles of Sound Taxation

Any tax, if taken by itself, can be shown to be unfair. If a government's total revenues were to come from one tax—say, a sales, an income, or a property tax—its tax system would be very unfair. Some people would bear a much greater burden than others, and some would bear little or none. Each tax should thus be defensible as part of a tax system.

In his classic 1776 work, *The Wealth of Nations*, Scottish economist Adam Smith laid out four principles of a sound tax system, which tax experts still cite today:

**PRIMARY SOURCE**

**1. The subjects of every state ought to contribute towards the support of the government as nearly as possible, in proportion to their respective abilities; that is, in proportion to the revenue which they respectively enjoy under the protection of the state.**

**2. The tax which each individual is bound to pay ought to be certain, and not <u>arbitrary</u>.**

**3. Every tax ought to be levied at the time, or in the manner, in which it is most likely to be convenient for the contributor to pay it.**

**4. Every tax ought to be so <u>contrived</u> as to both take out and to keep out of the pockets of the people as little as possible over and above what it brings into the public treasury. . . .**

—*The Wealth of Nations*

Shaping a tax system that meets those standards of equality, certainty, convenience, and economy is just about impossible. Still, that goal should be pursued.

## Sources of Revenue

Beyond the limits noted, a State can levy taxes as it chooses. The legislature decides what taxes the State will impose, and at what rates. It decides, too, what taxes localities can levy.[8]

**The Sales Tax** The sales tax is the most productive source of State-levied income today. It accounts for about a third of all tax monies the several States now collect.

A **sales tax** is a tax placed on the sale of various commodities; the purchaser pays it. It may be either *general* or *selective* in form. A general sales tax is one applied to the sale of most commodities. A selective sales tax is one placed on the sale of only certain commodities.

In 1932, Mississippi became the first State to levy a sales tax. Today, 45 States do so.[9] The rates range from 2.9 percent in Colorado to as much as 8.25 percent in California; most States now peg the rate at 5 or 6 percent. Some things are exempted from the tax almost everywhere—most commonly, food, medicine, and newspapers. A growing number of

---

[8] Some State constitutions do grant certain taxing powers directly to some local governments, but this is not common practice.

[9] Only Alaska, Delaware, Montana, New Hampshire, and Oregon do not levy general sales taxes, but each does impose various selective sales taxes.

---

# Differentiated Resources

The following resources are located in the All-in-One, Unit 7, Chapter 25, Section 4:

cities, and some urban counties, also levy sales taxes today—a "piggy-back tax," added on to and collected with the State tax.

All 50 States impose a selective sales tax on gasoline, alcoholic beverages, cigarettes, and insurance policies. Many of them also place selective sales taxes on such things as hotel and motel accommodations, restaurant meals, and theater and other amusement admissions.

Sales taxes are widely used for two major reasons: They are easy to collect, and they are dependable revenue producers. Yet a sales tax is a **regressive tax**—that is, it is not levied according to a person's ability to pay. The tax falls most heavily on those least able to pay it.

States are prohibited from collecting the sales taxes on most Internet purchases. That is because products made in one State are sold online to customers across the country. As more and more people shop via the Internet, the States complain that the drain on their sales tax receipts could very well lead to a reduction of public services and/or an increase in their sales tax and other tax rates. Congress, acting under its commerce power, put a temporary <u>moratorium</u> on State taxation of e-commerce in 1998 and renewed it most recently in 2007.

**The Income Tax** The **income tax**, which is levied on the income of individuals and/or corporations, yields another one third of State tax revenues today. Wisconsin enacted the first State income tax in 1911. Today, 43 States levy an individual income tax; 46 have some form of corporate income tax.[10]

The individual income tax is usually a **progressive tax**—that is, the higher your income, the more tax you pay. Income tax rates vary among the States, from 1 or 2 percent on lower incomes in most States to 9

---

10 Nevada, Texas, Washington, and Wyoming levy neither type of income tax. Alaska, Florida, and South Dakota impose only the corporate tax.

✔ **Checkpoint**
What are the benefits and drawbacks of the sales tax?

**moratorium**
*n.* freeze, suspension

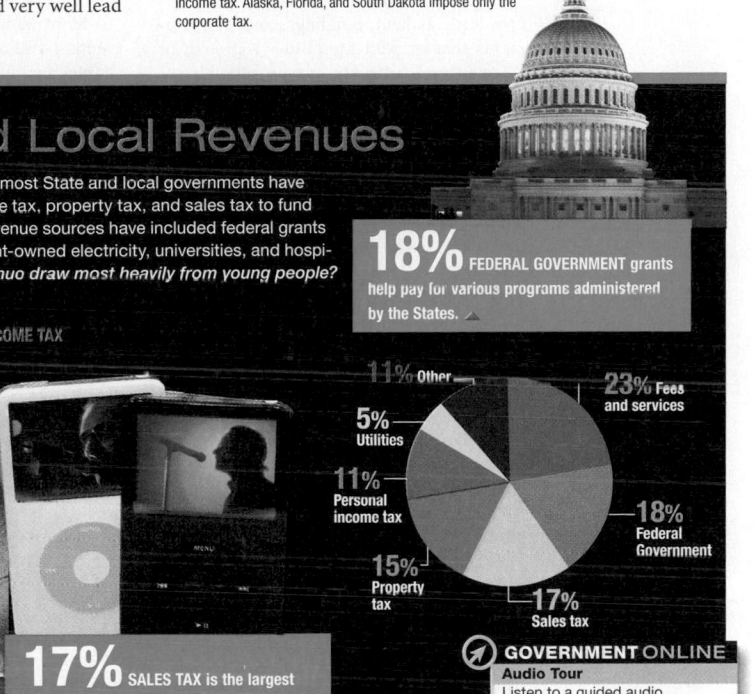

**How Government Works**

# State and Local Revenues

Over the past several years, most State and local governments have relied on a balance of income tax, property tax, and sales tax to fund their expenditures. Other revenue sources have included federal grants and income from government-owned electricity, universities, and hospitals. *Which sources of revenue draw most heavily from young people?*

**11%** PERSONAL INCOME TAX is levied by 43 States.

**18%** FEDERAL GOVERNMENT grants help pay for various programs administered by the States.

- 11% Other
- 5% Utilities
- 11% Personal income tax
- 15% Property tax
- 23% Fees and services
- 18% Federal Government
- 17% Sales tax

**17%** SALES TAX is the largest source of tax revenue for State and local governments.

**GOVERNMENT** ONLINE
**Audio Tour**
Listen to a guided audio tour of this diagram at PearsonSchool.com/phgovt

SOURCE: U.S. Census

---

# Teach

To present this topic using online resources, use the lesson presentations at **PearsonSchool.com/phgovt.**

## REVIEW THE TWO TYPES OF TAXES

Ask students to share their charts from the Bellringer activity and record their responses on the board in the two-column chart. *(regressive: sales tax, property tax, tax on movie tickets, tax on drivers' licenses; progressive: income tax)* Discuss why States levy different kinds of taxes. *(Any one tax places a larger burden on some people than on others. A variety of taxes spreads the burden, making the tax system as a whole more fair.)* Ask: **Do you think progressive or regressive taxes are more fair? What are the benefits and drawbacks of each type?** *(Some students may feel that progressive taxes are more fair because they are based on ability to pay, while others may feel that regressive taxes are fair because they affect only those who use the taxed items.)*

## DISCUSS STATE AND LOCAL REVENUE SOURCES

Point out that State and local governments do not rely solely on taxes for revenue. Display Transparency 25G, State and Local Revenue, and discuss the data. Ask: **Which sources produced the most and the least revenue for State and local governments?** *(most: Charges and Misc.; least: Utilities)* **About how much did the Federal Government provide to State and local governments?** *(about $438 billion)* Tell students to raise their hands when you name each revenue source if they have ever contributed to that source directly. If your State has a sales tax, most students will have paid that. Some students with jobs may also pay a State income tax, and they may have paid fees for the use of parks. Ask students if they feel that the taxes they pay are fair, and ask them to explain their opinions.

Tell students to go to the Audio Tour to explore how different States raise money.

---

# Background

**REGRESSIVE TAX** A regressive tax takes a larger percentage of income from low-income people than from high-income people. For example, suppose Jay pays a $1 sales tax when he buys a DVD. His income is $100. This tax represents 1% of Jay's income ($1/$100). Now suppose Keisha, whose income is $1,000, buys the same DVD and pays the $1 tax. The tax represents 0.1% of her income ($1/$1,000). This regressive tax puts a heavier burden on Jay, because it takes a larger percentage of his income than it does of Keisha's. Property taxes are typically regressive as well. While people with higher incomes tend to have more expensive homes and therefore pay more property tax, the tax is not based on income. Suppose two people in the same locality own homes valued at $200,000. The property tax rate is $10 per $1,000 assessed value. Both will pay $2,000 ($10 × 200), regardless of their income.

---

# Answers

**Checkpoint** benefits: easy to collect, dependable source of revenue; drawbacks: regressive, difficult to apply to Internet sales

**State and Local Revenues** sales tax and personal income tax if the young person has a job

## INTRODUCE THE ACTIVITY

Distribute the Chapter 25 Section 4 Core Worksheet (Unit 7 All-in-One, p. 109). Refer students to Adam Smith's four criteria on the worksheet or in the textbook. Tell students that they will work in pairs to evaluate different State and local taxes based on these criteria.

**L1** **L2** **ELL Differentiate** Before beginning this portion of the lesson, have students read aloud each criterion and then restate it in their own words.

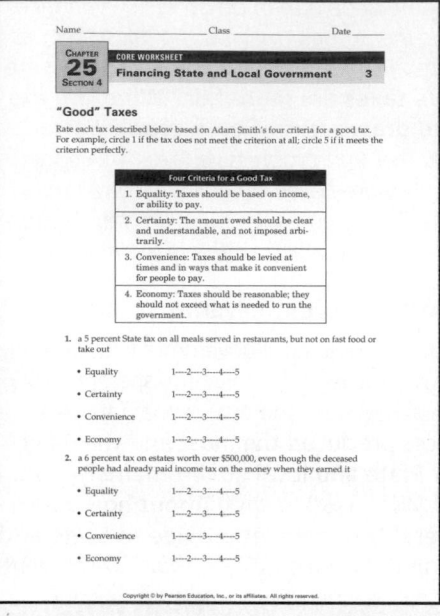

## Answers

**Checkpoint** a tax levied based on the income of individuals and sometimes on corporations

---

**beneficiary**
*n.* one who benefits

**graduated**
*adj.* scaled

**enterprise**
*n.* initiative, drive, determination

percent or more on the highest incomes in a few States. Those who pay the tax receive various exemptions and deductions in calculating their taxable income.

Corporate income tax rates are usually a uniform (fixed) percentage of income. Only a few States set the rates on a graduated basis.

The progressive income tax is held by many to be the fairest—or the least unfair—form of taxation, because it can be geared to a person's ability to pay. If the rates are too high, however, the tax can discourage individual enterprise.

**The Property Tax** Property taxes have been a major source of governmental revenue since the early colonial period. Once the major source of State revenue, they are now levied almost exclusively at the local level. They provide roughly three fourths of all local governmental income today.

A **property tax** is a levy on (1) real property, such as land, buildings, and improvements that go with the property if sold; or (2) personal property, either tangible or intangible. Tangible personal property is movable wealth that is visible and the value of which can be easily assessed—for example, computers, cars, and books. Intangible personal property includes such things as stocks, bonds, mortgages, and bank accounts.

The process of determining the value of the property to be taxed is known as **assessment**. An elected county, township, or city assessor usually carries out the task.

Supporters of the property tax argue that, because government protects property and often enhances its value, property owners can logically be required to contribute to the support of government. They note that the rate at which the tax is levied can be readily adjusted to meet governmental needs.

Critics insist that the property tax is not progressive, not geared to one's ability to pay. They also argue that it is all but impossible to set the value of all property on a fair and equal basis. They also note that personal property is easily hidden from assessors.

**Inheritance or Estate Taxes** Every State has some form of inheritance or estate tax, sometimes called the "death tax." An

inheritance tax is levied on the beneficiary's (heir's) share of an estate. An **estate tax** is one levied directly on the full estate itself.

**Business Taxes** A variety of business taxes, in addition to the corporate income tax, are important sources of revenue in most States. More than half the States impose severance taxes, levies on the removal of natural resources such as timber, oil, minerals, and fish from the land or water.

Every State has various license taxes that permit people to engage in certain businesses, occupations, or activities. For example, all States require that corporations be licensed to do business in the State. Certain kinds of businesses—chain stores, amusement parks, taverns, and transportation lines—must have an additional operating license. Most States also require the licensing of doctors, lawyers, hairdressers, plumbers, electricians, insurance agents, and a host of others.

Many States have levies known as documentary and stock transfer taxes. These are charges made on the recording, registering, and transfer (sale) of such documents as mortgages, deeds, and securities. Some States also impose capital stock taxes, which are levied on the total assessed value of the shares of stock issued by a business.

**Other Taxes** A variety of other taxes are imposed by the States and their local governments in order to raise revenues. As a leading example, payroll taxes produce huge sums; the monies generated by those taxes are held in trust funds to pay the benefits provided by unemployment assistance, accident insurance, and retirement programs. Most States levy amusement taxes for admission to theaters, sports events, circuses, and the like. Every State imposes license taxes for various nonbusiness purposes—notably, on motor vehicles and drivers, and for such things as hunting, fishing, and marriage.

**Nontax Sources** Taxes have never been very popular, and so State and local officials have long looked for nontax revenue sources. Today, the States and their many local governments take in more than a trillion dollars a year from these sources. Much

## Background

**VALUING PROPERTY FOR TAXES** Outdated property taxes drove Nassau County, New York, into bankruptcy in 2000. The county valued each house according to the cost of building that house—in 1938, when a movie ticket cost 20 cents and a nickel bought a hotdog. Another problem was that a house in a desirable town could sell for twice or three times as much as a house in a distressed town, but both owners paid property taxes at the same rate. As long as some voters benefited from the system, the county refused to update assessments, which led to bankruptcy. Nassau County has since gone through a reassessment that brought property taxes in line with current market values.

Property taxes may be charged on real estate, such as houses (left), and on personal property, which includes cars (right). **Why do you think real estate is easier for governments to value and tax than purchases or income?**

of that huge amount comes as grants from the Federal Government.

*Business enterprises and user fees.* State and local governments also make money from a variety of publicly operated business enterprises. Toll roads and bridges are especially popular in the East. Several States, notably Washington, are in the ferry business. North Dakota markets a baking flour, sold under the brand name "Dakota Maid," and is also in the commercial banking business. Eighteen States are in the liquor business, selling alcohol in State-operated stores.[11]

Many cities own and operate their water, electric power, and bus transportation systems. Some cities operate farmers' markets; rent space in their office buildings, warehouses, and housing projects; and operate dams and wharves. Receipts from such businesses support the local governments that own them. Other nontax sources include court fines, sales and lease of public lands, and interest from loans, investments, and late tax payments. Among the many public services for which those who use them must now pay a fee are hospitals, airports, parks, water, sewers, and garbage disposal.

*Lotteries.* For many years, nearly all forms of gambling were outlawed in every State except Nevada. Most States have relaxed their anti-gambling laws, hoping to attract dollars, jobs, and tourists. Today, only Hawaii and Utah do not permit any kind of gambling.

State-run lotteries net some $18 billion per year for 43 States, the District of Columbia, Puerto Rico, and the U.S. Virgin Islands.[12] Lotteries provide revenue without raising taxes. Supporters note that they are popular, voluntary, and offer an alternative to illegal gambling. Opponents say that lotteries prey on the poor and encourage compulsive gambling. Lottery proceeds are used for a number of purposes among the States. About half of the States with lotteries earmark all or most of their revenue for education. Some channel the money directly to the State's general fund, while others dedicate most of it to economic development.

**Borrowing** The States and many of their local governments regularly borrow money to pay for such large undertakings as the construction of schools, highways, hospitals, sports facilities, and college dormitories. Much of that borrowing is done by issuing bonds, much as the Federal Government does. Generally, State and local bonds are fairly easy to market because the interest paid on them is not subject to State or federal income taxes.

**earmark**
*v.* set aside for a specific purpose

11 Those states are Alabama, Idaho, Iowa, Maine, Michigan, Mississippi, Montana, New Hampshire, North Carolina, Ohio, Oregon, Pennsylvania, Utah, Vermont, Virginia, Washington, West Virginia, and Wyoming. North Carolina's stores are operated by the counties; Wyoming's liquor monopoly operates only at the wholesale level.

12 Seven States do not operate lotteries: Alabama, Alaska, Hawaii, Mississippi, Nevada, Utah, and Wyoming.

# Political Cartoon Mini-Lesson

Display Transparency 25H, The Shortfall, when you discuss State budgets. This cartoon depicts a budget crisis. Ask: **Whom do the people represent?** *(the citizens of the State)* **What are they doing?** *(waiting to be fed)* **How does the cartoonist depict revenues?** *(as the promise of food to feed the citizens)* **What problem does the State have?** *(Its revenues are much smaller than its overall budget and insufficient to support the citizens of the State.)* **How does the dining scene contribute to the meaning of the cartoon?** *(The dining scene makes the point that revenues are a necessity of life for the State—like food.)*

## FOLLOW UP THE ACTIVITY

Discuss students' evaluations of the taxes. Ask students to raise their hands for "best" or "worst" as you name each tax on the worksheet, and record the vote on the board. Is there a general agreement on these designations? If so, have volunteers explain why they selected the tax they did for the best and worst. If there was no consensus, discuss with students why there is so much difference of opinion among the class on what is a good tax. Ask students to explain what so many differences of opinion in your classroom might indicate about the difficulties of establishing tax policies in the larger world.

**L3 Differentiate** Tell students that some people believe that there should be few or no federal taxes—only State or only local taxes. Have students write a journal entry that uses what they have learned about State and local taxes to address the Chapter Essential Question: How local should government be? Students should explore whether they think federal taxes are "fair," if people in one State pay for services or expenditures in another State.

**Government** online — *All print resources are available on the Teacher's Resource Library CD-ROM and online at PearsonSchool.com/phgovt.*

## EXTEND THE LESSON

**L3 L4 Differentiate** Have students read "Estates of Pain" in the Extend Worksheet (Unit 7 All-in-One, p. 112) and answer the questions.

**L3 Differentiate** Have students do research to identify a State with a tax initiative on the ballot in 2008. Have them summarize the purpose of the initiative and provide the results of the vote.

**L1 L2 Differentiate** Ask students to create a concept web to show the various sources of State and local revenue, including the different types of taxes, borrowing, and other means of generating income.

**L4 Differentiate** Separate students into groups of three or four. Have them research to find State and community government resources that provide information about specific revenue sources. Ask each group to create circle graphs illustrating (1) the sources of your State's revenues and (2) how those revenues are distributed to and spent in your community. Tell students to include a summary explaining each graph.

## Answers

**Caption** Real estate transactions are public, recorded, and visible, and therefore easier to access.

# Assess and Remediate

**L3** Collect the Core Worksheets and assess the students' work.

**L3** Assign the Section 4 Assessment questions.

**L3** Section Quiz A (Unit 7 All-in-One, p. 115)

**L2** Section Quiz B (Unit 7 All-in-One, p. 116)

Have students complete the review activities in the digital lesson presentation and continue their work in the **Essential Questions Journal.**

## REMEDIATION

| If Your Students Have Trouble With | Strategies For Remediation |
|---|---|
| State revenues (Questions 1, 5) | Display Transparency 25G. Review with students each bar on the graph and check understanding by asking them to make one true statement about the graph. |
| Progressive and regressive taxes (Question 2) | Tell students to make a Venn diagram to compare and contrast features of progressive and regressive taxes, including examples of each. |
| Limits on State taxes (Question 3) | Have students work with a partner to make an outline of the text under the heading "Limits on Raising Revenue." |
| Adam Smith's four principles of sound taxation (Question 4) | Have students rewrite each of Smith's principles in their own words in their notebooks. |

## Answers

**Checkpoint** to pay for large undertakings, such as the construction of schools, highways, hospitals, and sports facilities

---

✓ **Checkpoint**
How and why do State and local governments borrow money?

**default**
*v.* fail to pay

At various times in the past, many State and local governments <u>defaulted</u> on their debts. Thus, most State constitutions now place quite detailed limits on the power to borrow. Altogether, the 50 States' debts now total about a trillion dollars, and local governments owe more than $1.5 trillion.

## State Budgets

A public **budget** is much more than bookkeeping entries and dollar signs. It is a financial plan, a plan for the control and use of public money, public personnel, and public property. It is also a political document, a highly significant statement of public policy. Here, in its budget, the State establishes its priorities and decides who gets what, and who doesn't.

For more than 150 years, State budgets were the product of haphazard and uncoordinated steps centered in the legislature. Various State agencies appeared before legislative committees, each seeking its own funding, often in fierce competition with one another. Their chances of success depended far less on need or merit than on whatever political muscle they could bring to bear. When the legislature adjourned, no one had any real idea of how much had been appropriated or for what. Inevitably, extravagance and waste, unresolved problems, debt, favoritism, and graft were all parts of the process.

State budgets are strikingly different things today. They remain highly charged political documents, but they are the end products of what is, by and large, an orderly and systematic process.

All but three States have now adopted the executive budget, which gives the governor two vital powers: (1) to prepare the State's budget, and, after the legislature has acted upon his or her recommendations, (2) to manage the spending of the monies set aside by the legislature.[13] The basic steps in the budget process are much the same at the State, local, and federal levels:

1. Each agency prepares estimates of its needs and proposed expenditures in the upcoming fiscal period.

2. Those estimates are reviewed by an executive budget agency.

3. Revised estimates, with supporting information, are brought together in a consolidated financial plan, the budget, which the governor then presents to the legislature for its consideration.

4. The legislature reacts to the proposed budget, part by part, appropriates the funds it deems necessary to pay for governmental activities, and enacts whatever revenue measures may be needed.

5. The governor supervises the execution of the budget—the actual spending of the funds provided by the legislature.

6. The execution of the budget is subject to an independent check—a postaudit.

---

[13] In Mississippi, South Carolina, and Texas, budget making is shared by the governor and the legislature.

---

**Essential Questions Journal** To continue to build a response to the chapter Essential Question, go to your **Essential Questions Journal.**

## SECTION 4 ASSESSMENT

1. **Guiding Question** Use your completed chart to answer this question: How do State governments raise money to pay for services?

### Key Terms and Comprehension
2. Explain why **income taxes** are generally described as progressive taxes.
3. What limits does the U.S. Constitution put on the States' ability to tax?

### Critical Thinking
4. **Determining Relevance (a)** What are Adam Smith's four principles of sound taxation? **(b)** What do you think makes each principle important?
5. **Identifying Alternatives** What might be the advantages and disadvantages of raising revenue through **(a)** A State-run lottery? **(b)** A State-run business? **(c)** A State-wide property tax?

### Quick Write

**Writing for Assessment: Write a Summation** Assessment essays often end with a summation. The summation should restate, briefly, your main points and echo the opening statement. Write a summation for the question you chose in Section 1. Check your summation against your main points to be sure that all are closely related.

---

# Assessment Answers

**1.** State governments raise money through a variety of taxes, such as sales, income, property, inheritance, estate, and various business taxes. Nontax sources include Federal Government grants, court fines, sales and lease of public lands, interest, and lotteries. States borrow funds by issuing bonds.

**2.** Income taxes are progressive because they are levied according to a person's ability to pay. The higher the income, the more tax is paid.

**3.** States cannot tax interstate or foreign trade, or tax the Federal Government or any of its agencies or functions. Taxes must be fair, not so heavy as to confiscate property, and imposed only for public purposes. States may not make unreasonable classifications for tax purposes.

**4. (a)** (1) Citizens should contribute to government revenues in proportion to their income. (2) The tax amount should be clear. (3) Paying taxes should be convenient. (4) The tax amount should not exceed what is necessary to run the government. **(b)** People are more likely to accept taxes that are fair, clear, convenient, and not excessive.

**5. (a)** Lotteries raise money without raising taxes, but people who participate are often those least able to afford to do so. **(b)** State-run businesses raise money without raising taxes, but government monopolies on certain businesses can lead to higher prices. **(c)** Property taxes can be fair because the people with the most highly valued property pay the most taxes. However, high property taxes can make home ownership unaffordable.

**QUICK WRITE** Students should write a summation that concludes their response to the question.

# Quick Study Guide

## GOVERNMENT ONLINE
**On the Go**
To review anytime, anywhere, download these online resources at **PearsonSchool.com/phgovt**
Political Dictionary, Audio Review

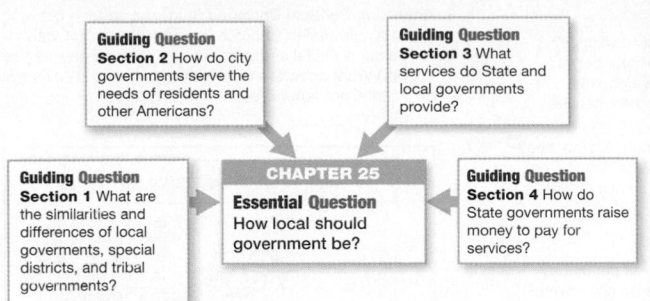

**Guiding Question**
**Section 2** How do city governments serve the needs of residents and other Americans?

**Guiding Question**
**Section 3** What services do State and local governments provide?

**Guiding Question**
**Section 1** What are the similarities and differences of local governments, special districts, and tribal governments?

**CHAPTER 25**
**Essential Question**
How local should government be?

**Guiding Question**
**Section 4** How do State governments raise money to pay for services?

## Political Dictionary

county *p. 742*
township *p. 743*
municipality *p. 747*
special district *p. 748*
incorporation *p. 749*
charter *p. 750*
mayor-council government *p. 750*
strong-mayor government *p. 750*
weak-mayor government *p. 750*
commission government *p. 751*
council-manager government *p. 751*
zoning *p. 753*
metropolitan area *p. 755*
Medicaid *p. 757*
welfare *p. 757*
entitlement *p. 758*
sales tax *p. 762*
regressive tax *p. 763*
income tax *p. 763*
progressive tax *p. 763*
property tax *p. 764*
assessment *p. 764*
inheritance tax *p. 764*
estate tax *p. 764*
budget *p. 766*

## Local government responsibilities

- Provide essential services including education, security, road upkeep, and public records
- Conduct elections
- Administer justice
- Plan for future growth and development
- Collect taxes for local services

## Revenues and Expenditures

| Revenues | | Expenditures |
|---|---|---|
| Federal Government | | Education |
| Fees for services | State and Local Government | Public welfare |
| Sales tax | | Public safety |
| Property tax | | Healthcare |
| Income tax | | Roads and transportation |

# For More Information

To learn more about local governments, refer to these sources or assign them to students:

**L1** **Silate, Jennifer.** *Your Mayor: Local Government in Action.* The Rosen Publishing Group, Inc., 2004.

**L2** **Snedden, Robert.** *Growth of Cities (Earth's Changing Landscape).* Franklin Watts Ltd, 2007.

**L3** **Duany, Andres, Elizabeth Plater-Zyberk, and Jeff Speck.** *Suburban Nation: The Rise of Sprawl and the Decline of the American Dream.* North Point Press, 2001.

**L4** **Morgan, David R., Robert E. England, and John P. Pelissero.** *Managing Urban America.* CQ Press, 2006.

---

Have students download the digital resources available at Government on the Go for review and remediation.

## STUDY TIPS

**Learning Styles** Explain that figuring out their particular way of absorbing information can go a long way toward helping students study more effectively. The simplest and most useful grouping of learning styles divides people into visual, auditory, and kinesthetic/tactile learners. Have students consider the following questions to help them recognize their preferred learning style: Do they remember information best when they read it, hear it, or take notes about it? When learning new vocabulary, do they tend to visualize the word, sound out the word, or write the word down? Are they likely to forget names but remember faces? Remember names but forget faces? Remember what they were doing or where they were when meeting someone new? These examples illustrate visual, auditory, and kinesthetic learners, in that order. Visual learners need quiet study time and learn well using outlines. Auditory learners do well with group discussions and audiotapes. Kinesthetic learners benefit from short study sessions and role playing

## ASSESSMENT AT A GLANCE

### Tests and Quizzes
Section Assessments
Section Quizzes A and B, Unit 7 **All-in-One**
Chapter Assessment
Chapter Tests A and B, Unit 7 **All-in-One**
Document-Based Assessment
Progress Monitoring Online
Exam*View* Test Bank

### Performance Assessment
Essential Questions Journal
Presentation of Small-Group Plans, p. 752
Assessment Rubrics, **All-in-One**

**COMPREHENSION AND CRITICAL THINKING**

### SECTION 1

1. **(a)** A county is a unit of local government that consists of several towns or townships. Counties, unlike towns or townships, tend to have larger groups of administrators, with no chief administrator. Towns are smaller units. In New England, they are the major form of local government, and are governed by a board of selectpersons and through town meetings. Townships are the major form of local government in New York, New Jersey, and the Midwestern States. They are also generally administrated by an elected board. **(b)** Like the Federal Government, recognized tribal governments are sovereign and may operate like small nations outside of the control of Federal and State governments. Unlike the Federal Government, tribes require federal recognition for sovereign status. **(c)** Like State governments, tribal governments are subordinate to the Federal Government in some ways. Tribal governments use federal funds and tax revenues to provide services. Also, they are responsible for geographic units within the U.S. However, tribal governments have more autonomy than do State governments.

2. **(a)** to include all the town's eligible voters in decisions that affect the town **(b)** One benefit is that town meetings are a form of direct democracy, where all voters have a say in how the town is run. It is a very fair and open form of government. A drawback is that as populations grow and problems become more complex, it can be difficult to make decisions in such a wide-open forum with so many people involved. **(c)** Possible responses: Yes. Our community is small enough that direct citizen participation is practical. OR: No. Our city is too large for all citizens to meet at once. Also, the problems are too complex for many people to solve efficiently.

### SECTION 2

3. **(a)** City governments provide police and fire protection, sewer and water, sanitation, public health, planning, and zoning. They maintain schools, libraries, roads, bridges, and parks. **(b)** City leaders deal with issues that come with large populations that might not occur in more rural or suburban areas. These include issues of higher crime, traffic management, public

---

CHAPTER **25** **Chapter Assessment**

> **GOVERNMENT** ONLINE
> Self-Test
> To test your understanding of key terms and main ideas, visit
> PearsonSchool.com/phgovt

## Comprehension and Critical Thinking

### Section 1

1. **(a)** How do counties differ from towns or townships? **(b)** What similarities and differences are there between the Federal Government and a tribal government? **(c)** What similarities and differences are there between tribal and State governments?

2. **(a)** What is the purpose of a New England town meeting? **(b)** What are its benefits and limitations? **(c)** Would it be a good form of government for your community? Why or why not?

### Section 2

3. Think about large cities as opposed to less populous communities. **(a)** What types of services do city governments provide? **(b)** What types of special issues or problems do city leaders deal with?

4. Voters in a few cities have rejected zoning with noticeable results. **(a)** What do you think those results are? **(b)** How might a lack of zoning affect your quality of life?

### Section 3

5. **(a)** What powers are delegated to the States that are denied to the Federal Government? **(b)** Does this division of powers make public services less efficient or more efficient, in your opinion?

6. **(a)** In what ways do States try to ensure the public safety of their citizens? **(b)** What challenges do States face in ensuring public safety?

### Section 4

7. Some States are turning increasingly to nontax revenue sources. **(a)** Why do you think States prefer nontax revenues to taxes? **(b)** Some people are critical of using a lottery as a method for raising State revenue. Why do you think this is the case? Do you agree or disagree?

8. **Analyzing Political Cartoons** Study the cartoon below about a man making a purchase over the Internet with his personal digital assistant. **(a)** Why must he pay a sales tax? **(b)** What does this cartoon imply about the sales tax as a State, not federal, source of revenue?

CONCERNED CITIZENS WANT TO KNOW

IF I DRIVE OVER THE STATE LINE AND USE MY P.D.A. TO MAKE AN ON-LINE PURCHASE IN A THIRD STATE, DO I OWE SALES TAX IN MY HOME STATE?

STATE LINE

### Writing About Government

9. Use your Quick Write exercises from the section assessments in this chapter to write a three-paragraph essay that answers your question about local government and finance. The question should be answered in at least three paragraphs—one for each of your main points—including a strong opening statement and a clear summation. Make sure that your essay is concise, correctly spelled, and demonstrates an understanding of correct grammar. See pp. S11–S12 of the Skills Handbook.

---

## Apply What You've Learned

10. **Essential Question Activity** Research your local community or county government structure and budget. Answer the following questions:
    **(a)** What positions in local government are elected and what positions are appointed?
    **(b)** What are the most costly programs in the local government budget?
    **(c)** Which officials have the greatest authority over the budget?
    **(d)** What responsibilities does the State require of local government?

11. **Essential Question Assessment** Use the results of your research to prepare an election brochure that helps you answer the Essential Question: **How local should government be?** Create a brochure for a fictional candidate for local office explaining the responsibilities of the office and including specific promises to the voters, a description of the goals of local government, and how the candidate hopes to work with State government and other local officials.

> **Essential Questions Journal** To respond to the chapter Essential Question, go to your **Essential Questions Journal.**

---

transportation, overcrowding and housing, pollution, and disease prevention.

4. **(a)** various kinds of homes and businesses in the same areas; lack of open space **(b)** Unplanned growth could create parking problems, traffic congestion, and lack of green space for residents to enjoy.

### SECTION 3

5. **(a)** all powers not expressly delegated to the National Government in the Constitution **(b)** Possible response: More efficient; the United States is too large and diverse for one huge government to provide all

services. Local governments understand the needs of their communities and can focus their funds on the services their citizens need most.

6. **(a)** State police and law-enforcement services; State corrections systems **(b)** booming prison populations and insufficient funds

### SECTION 4

7. **(a)** possible answer: because tax increases tend to be unpopular, and officials who propose them risk losing the next election **(b)** Possible response: Some people are against lotteries on moral grounds,

# Document-Based Assessment

## State Safety Laws and the Police Power

According to the Federal Constitution, the police power is reserved to the States. As these documents show, many question how far a State can go in legislating citizens' personal safety before it begins to intrude on personal privacy and choice.

### Document 1

In 1987, Iowan John Hartog received a ticket for not wearing his seat belt. Hartog argued that Iowa's seat-belt law was unconstitutional because it violated rights to privacy and equal protection and went beyond the State's authorized police power. The following excerpt from the case transcript supports the court's finding that the seat-belt law was not unconstitutional.

" The government provides roads as a service to its citizens, and part of that service is assuring that these roads will be safe and efficient. The motorist is not being overly imposed upon when asked to comply with minimal standards of behavior designed to reduce the dangers of his driving to other drivers. It is also difficult to object to the State's attempt to stop an individual from making the rest of society pay for the consequences of his risk-taking. . . . our government provides services from the ambulance that delivers the injured motorist to the hospital to disability insurance. Having to buckle up may be inconvenient, but it is not an unreasonable price to pay for the use of public roads.

—from State of Iowa v. John Hartog, 1989

### Document 2

---

Use your knowledge of the police power and Documents 1 and 2 to answer Questions 1–3.

1. What is the main point of Document 1?
   A. Seat-belt laws are unconstitutional because they interfere with the right to privacy and to equal protection.
   B. Seat-belt laws are inconvenient and the State has no right to impose safety laws on individuals.
   C. Seat-belt laws are reasonable because the government bears costs incurred by injured people who were not wearing belts.
   D. Seat-belt laws are necessary to prevent accidents on public roads and to promote public safety.

2. What opinion about State regulations does Document 2 express?

3. **Pull It Together** Do you think that seat-belt laws and other public safety laws are a reasonable use of a State's police power? Do they intrude on individual rights? Why or why not?

 **GOVERNMENT** ONLINE
**Documents**
To find more primary sources on police power, visit PearsonSchool.com/phgovt

---

## DOCUMENT-BASED ASSESSMENT

1. C

2. The cartoon implies that with no seat belt law, the driver is at least free of one State regulation under the police power.

3. Some students might say that as long as society must pay the price of a citizen's poor choices, government has a right to legislate public safety. Other students might say that such legislation can go too far and must be assessed on a case-by-case basis. Too much government control can turn our society into a police state.

**L2 Differentiate** Students use all the documents on the page to support their thesis.

**L3 Differentiate** Students include additional information available online at **PearsonSchool.com/phgovt.**

**L4 Differentiate** Students use materials from the textbook, the online information at **PearsonSchool.com/phgovt,** and do additional research to support their views.

 **Go Online to PearsonSchool.com/phgovt** for a student rubric and extra documents.

---

because they believe that gambling is just wrong; others think it is wrong because usually those who play are the people who can least afford to, so it becomes an unfair tax. I do not agree. I think lotteries are great ways for States to raise large sums of money to pay for important services or to lower taxes. People who buy into lotteries do it based on their own free will.

8. **(a)** The cartoon implies that the man must pay a sales tax if he makes an online purchase. **(b)** Internet sales cross State lines. If sales taxes were federal, then taxes on Internet sales would be easy to collect.

However, because sales taxes are imposed by States, and they vary from State to State, it is confusing and hard to apply the taxes to Internet sales.

### WRITING ABOUT GOVERNMENT

9. Responses should be well-organized, demonstrate attention to grammar, spelling, and style, and address the question students selected and worked to answer throughout the chapter.

### APPLY WHAT YOU'VE LEARNED

10. Students should adequately research their

selected government structure and budget in order to answer the questions in the activity.

11. Students' brochures should be detailed enough to cover the responsibilities of the office, should describe the goals of local government, and should realistically explain how their candidates will work with State and local officials.

Before assigning these questions, distribute the Rubric for Assessing a Writing Assignment (Unit 7 All-in-One, p. 128). Use the criteria and the guidelines below to grade students' answers to the Essential Question Warmup questions. Then send students to the **Essential Questions Journal** to answer the unit Essential Question.

**1.** Students should present a list of issues that reflect the current division of responsibilities for services among the three levels. A strong answer will provide reasons why each level of government is best suited to handle certain responsibilities.

**2.** A strong answer will recognize that revenues and responsibilities are shared among different levels of government so they must work together to provide efficient taxation and services and prevent conflicts between governments.

**3.** Students should state a position on whether one level of government is more responsive than others and support that position with facts and examples.

**4.** To answer this question successfully, students should explain several advantages and disadvantages of centralizing power. The explanations should demonstrate that students understand the challenges of balancing local, State, and federal governments.

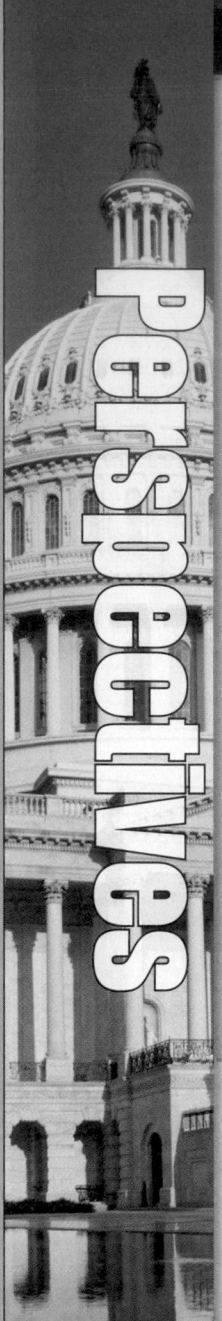

Perspectives

## Essential Question
# What is the right balance of local, State, and Federal government?

The U.S. federal system divides power between two levels of government. Elected officials at each level have sought more power and authority for their governments—or to spread responsibilities to others.

### ON THE ROLE OF THE FEDERAL GOVERNMENT:

"It is my intention to curb the size and influence of the Federal establishment and to demand recognition of the distinction between the powers granted to the Federal Government and those reserved to the States or to the people. All of us need to be reminded that the Federal Government did not create the States; the States created the Federal Government.

—Ronald Reagan, First Inaugural Speech, 1981

### ON THE KEY ISSUES FACING THE STATES:

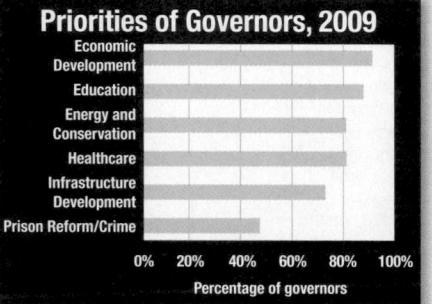

**Priorities of Governors, 2009**

Each year, the National Governors Association tracks the governors' State of the State addresses and identifies the subjects mentioned most often by the most governors.

### ON THE VALUE OF MAYORS:

"As CEOs of the nation's cities, mayors know all too well the challenges American families face daily, so we are in the best position to offer solutions to local problems.

—Mayor Douglas Palmer, Trenton, New Jersey, 2007

### Essential Question Warmup

Throughout this unit, you studied the roles, responsibilities, and powers of State and local government. Use what you have learned and the quotations, data, and opinions above to answer the following questions. Then go to your **Essential Questions Journal.**

**1.** Which issues are best handled at the local, State, and federal levels, respectively?

**2.** How do taxes, spending, and various programs link different levels of government?

**3.** Is any level of government more responsive and democratic than any other level?

**4.** What are the advantages and disadvantages of centralizing power?

**Essential Questions Journal** To continue to build a response to the chapter Essential Question, go to your **Essential Questions Journal.**

# Assessment Resources

Unit 7 AYP Monitoring Assessment
ExamView Test Bank CD-ROM
SuccessTracker Assessment
Online Student Self-Tests
Chapter Tests
Section Quizzes
Chapter-level Document-Based Assessment

# Reference

# The United States: A Statistical Profile

| State | Capital | Population (in thousands) Year 2000 | % Urban | African American | Hispanic Origin | % Foreign Born | Land Area in Sq. Mi. | Population per Sq. Mi |
|---|---|---|---|---|---|---|---|---|
| United States | Washington, D.C. | 281,422 | 80.1 | 34,862 | 31,337 | 7.9 | 3,536,278 | 79.6 |
| Alabama | Montgomery | 4,447 | 70.1 | 1,139 | 45 | 1.1 | 50,750 | 87.6 |
| Alaska | Juneau | 627 | 41.5 | 24 | 25 | 4.5 | 570,374 | 1.1 |
| Arizona | Phoenix | 5,131 | 87.8 | 176 | 1,084 | 7.6 | 113,642 | 45.2 |
| Arkansas | Little Rock | 2,673 | 48.6 | 411 | 54 | 1.1 | 52,075 | 51.3 |
| California | Sacramento | 33,872 | 96.7 | 2,487 | 10,460 | 21.7 | 155,973 | 217.2 |
| Colorado | Denver | 4,301 | 84.0 | 176 | 604 | 4.3 | 103,729 | 41.5 |
| Connecticut | Hartford | 3,406 | 95.6 | 309 | 279 | 8.5 | 4,845 | 703.0 |
| Delaware | Dover | 784 | 81.6 | 149 | 28 | 3.3 | 1,955 | 401.0 |
| Florida | Tallahassee | 15,982 | 93.0 | 2,333 | 2,334 | 12.9 | 53,937 | 296.3 |
| Georgia | Atlanta | 8,186 | 68.9 | 2,236 | 240 | 2.7 | 57,919 | 141.3 |
| Hawaii | Honolulu | 1,212 | 73.1 | 34 | 95 | 14.7 | 6,423 | 188.7 |
| Idaho | Boise | 1,294 | 38.3 | 8 | 93 | 2.9 | 82,751 | 15.6 |
| Illinois | Springfield | 12,419 | 84.5 | 1,854 | 1,276 | 8.3 | 55,593 | 223.4 |
| Indiana | Indianapolis | 6,080 | 71.7 | 498 | 154 | 1.7 | 35,870 | 169.5 |
| Iowa | Des Moines | 2,926 | 44.6 | 58 | 62 | 1.6 | 55,875 | 52.4 |
| Kansas | Topeka | 2,688 | 56.4 | 157 | 148 | 2.5 | 81,823 | 32.9 |
| Kentucky | Frankfort | 4,042 | 48.3 | 288 | 35 | 0.9 | 39,732 | 101.7 |
| Louisiana | Baton Rouge | 4,469 | 75.2 | 1,415 | 119 | 2.1 | 43,566 | 102.6 |
| Maine | Augusta | 1,275 | 35.8 | 6 | 9 | 3.0 | 30,865 | 41.3 |
| Maryland | Annapolis | 5,296 | 92.7 | 1,454 | 199 | 6.6 | 9,775 | 541.8 |
| Massachusetts | Boston | 6,349 | 96.1 | 405 | 391 | 9.5 | 7,838 | 810.0 |
| Michigan | Lansing | 9,938 | 82.6 | 1,415 | 276 | 3.8 | 56,809 | 174.9 |
| Minnesota | St. Paul | 4,919 | 70.1 | 149 | 93 | 2.6 | 79,617 | 61.8 |
| Mississippi | Jackson | 2,845 | 35.9 | 1,010 | 24 | 0.8 | 46,914 | 60.6 |
| Missouri | Jefferson City | 5,595 | 68.0 | 617 | 91 | 1.6 | 68,898 | 81.2 |

| State | Capital | Population (In thousands) | | | | % Foreign Born | Land Area in Sq. Mi. | Population per Sq. Mi |
| --- | --- | --- | --- | --- | --- | --- | --- | --- |
| | | Year 2000 | % Urban | African American | Hispanic Origin | | | |
| Montana | Helena | 902 | 33.4 | 3 | 16 | 1.7 | 145,556 | 6.2 |
| Nebraska | Lincoln | 1,711 | 51.8 | 68 | 77 | 1.8 | 76,878 | 22.3 |
| Nevada | Carson City | 1,998 | 86.1 | 140 | 304 | 8.7 | 109,806 | 18.2 |
| New Hampshire | Concord | 1,236 | 60.2 | 9 | 20 | 3.7 | 8,969 | 137.8 |
| New Jersey | Trenton | 8,414 | 100.0 | 1,197 | 1,027 | 12.5 | 7,419 | 1,134.1 |
| New Mexico | Santa Fe | 1,819 | 57.0 | 46 | 708 | 5.3 | 121,364 | 15.0 |
| New York | Albany | 18,976 | 91.9 | 3,222 | 2,661 | 15.9 | 47,224 | 401.8 |
| North Carolina | Raleigh | 8,049 | 67.1 | 1,686 | 176 | 1.7 | 48,718 | 165.2 |
| North Dakota | Bismarck | 642 | 43.1 | 4 | 7 | 1.5 | 68,994 | 9.3 |
| Ohio | Columbus | 11,353 | 81.0 | 1,304 | 185 | 2.4 | 40,953 | 277.2 |
| Oklahoma | Oklahoma City | 3,451 | 60.5 | 262 | 137 | 2.1 | 68,679 | 50.2 |
| Oregon | Salem | 3,421 | 72.7 | 62 | 213 | 4.9 | 96,002 | 35.6 |
| Pennsylvania | Harrisburg | 12,281 | 84.5 | 1,170 | 326 | 3.1 | 44,820 | 274.0 |
| Rhode Island | Providence | 1,048 | 93.8 | 50 | 69 | 9.5 | 1,045 | 1,002.9 |
| South Carolina | Columbia | 4,012 | 70.0 | 1,157 | 54 | 1.4 | 30,111 | 133.2 |
| South Dakota | Pierre | 755 | 34.0 | 5 | 9 | 1.1 | 75,896 | 9.9 |
| Tennessee | Nashville | 5,689 | 67.8 | 913 | 67 | 1.2 | 41,219 | 138.0 |
| Texas | Austin | 20,852 | 84.5 | 2,470 | 6,045 | 9.0 | 261,914 | 79.6 |
| Utah | Salt Lake City | 2,233 | 76.7 | 19 | 151 | 3.4 | 82,168 | 27.2 |
| Vermont | Montpelier | 609 | 27.9 | 3 | 5 | 3.1 | 9,249 | 65.8 |
| Virginia | Richmond | 7,079 | 78.1 | 1,385 | 266 | 5.0 | 39,598 | 178.8 |
| Washington | Olympia | 5,894 | 82.9 | 204 | 377 | 6.6 | 66,581 | 88.5 |
| West Virginia | Charleston | 1,808 | 41.9 | 56 | 10 | 0.9 | 4,087 | 75.1 |
| Wisconsin | Madison | 5,364 | 67.8 | 293 | 140 | 2.5 | 54,314 | 98.8 |
| Wyoming | Cheyenne | 494 | 29.6 | 4 | 29 | 1.7 | 97,105 | 5.1 |
| Washington, D.C. | | 572 | 100.0 | 319 | 38 | 9.7 | 61 | 9,377.0 |

George Washington  Zachary Taylor  Abraham Lincoln  Ulysses S. Grant  Chester A. Arthur

# Presidents of the United States

| Name | Party | State [a] | Entered Office | Age On Taking Office | Vice President(s) |
|---|---|---|---|---|---|
| **George Washington** (1732–1799) | Federalist | Virginia | 1789 | 57 | John Adams |
| **John Adams** (1735–1826) | Federalist | Massachusetts | 1797 | 61 | Thomas Jefferson |
| **Thomas Jefferson** (1743–1826) | Dem-Rep[b] | Virginia | 1801 | 57 | Aaron Burr/George Clinton |
| **James Madison** (1751–1836) | Dem-Rep | Virginia | 1809 | 57 | George Clinton/Elbridge Gerry |
| **James Monroe** (1758–1831) | Dem-Rep | Virginia | 1817 | 58 | Daniel D. Tompkins |
| **John Q. Adams** (1767–1848) | Dem-Rep | Massachusetts | 1825 | 57 | John C. Calhoun |
| **Andrew Jackson** (1767–1845) | Democrat | Tennessee (SC) | 1829 | 61 | John C. Calhoun/Martin Van Buren |
| **Martin Van Buren** (1782–1862) | Democrat | New York | 1837 | 54 | Richard M. Johnson |
| **William H. Harrison** (1773–1841) | Whig | Ohio (VA) | 1841 | 68 | John Tyler |
| **John Tyler** (1790–1862) | Democrat | Virginia | 1841 | 51 | none |
| **James K. Polk** (1795–1849) | Democrat | Tennessee (NC) | 1845 | 49 | George M. Dallas |
| **Zachary Taylor** (1784–1850) | Whig | Louisiana (VA) | 1849 | 64 | Millard Fillmore |
| **Millard Fillmore** (1800–1874) | Whig | New York | 1850 | 50 | none |
| **Franklin Pierce** (1804–1869) | Democrat | New Hampshire | 1853 | 48 | William R. King |
| **James Buchanan** (1791–1868) | Democrat | Pennsylvania | 1857 | 65 | John C. Breckinridge |
| **Abraham Lincoln** (1809–1865) | Republican | Illinois (KY) | 1861 | 52 | Hannibal Hamlin/Andrew Johnson[c] |
| **Andrew Johnson** (1808–1875) | Democrat | Tennessee (NC) | 1865 | 56 | none |
| **Ulysses S. Grant** (1822–1885) | Republican | Illinois (OH) | 1869 | 46 | Schuyler Colfax/Henry Wilson |
| **Rutherford B. Hayes** (1822–1893) | Republican | Ohio | 1877 | 54 | William A. Wheeler |
| **James A. Garfield** (1831–1881) | Republican | Ohio | 1881 | 49 | Chester A. Arthur |
| **Chester A. Arthur** (1829–1896) | Republican | New York (VT) | 1881 | 51 | none |
| **Grover Cleveland** (1837–1908) | Democrat | New York (NJ) | 1885 | 47 | Thomas A. Hendricks |
| **Benjamin Harrison** (1833–1901) | Republican | Indiana (OH) | 1889 | 55 | Levi P. Morton |
| **Grover Cleveland** (1837–1908) | Democrat | New York (NJ) | 1893 | 55 | Adlai E. Stevenson |

William Howard Taft    Harry S Truman     Lyndon B. Johnson     Ronald Reagan     Barack Obama

| Name | Party | State [a] | Entered Office | Age On Taking Office | Vice President(s) |
|---|---|---|---|---|---|
| William McKinley (1843–1901) | Republican | Ohio | 1897 | 54 | Garret A. Hobart/ Theodore Roosevelt |
| Theodore Roosevelt (1858–1919) | Republican | New York | 1901 | 42 | Charles W. Fairbanks |
| William H. Taft (1857–1930) | Republican | Ohio | 1909 | 51 | James S. Sherman |
| Woodrow Wilson (1856–1924) | Democrat | New Jersey (VA) | 1913 | 56 | Thomas R. Marshall |
| Warren G. Harding (1865–1923) | Republican | Ohio | 1921 | 55 | Calvin Coolidge |
| Calvin Coolidge (1872–1933) | Republican | Massachusetts (VT) | 1923 | 51 | Charles G. Dawes |
| Herbert Hoover (1874–1964) | Republican | California (IA) | 1929 | 54 | Charles Curtis |
| Franklin Roosevelt (1882–1945) | Democrat | New York | 1933 | 51 | John N. Garner/ Henry A. Wallace/Harry S Truman |
| Harry S Truman (1884–1972) | Democrat | Missouri | 1945 | 60 | Alben W. Barkley |
| Dwight D. Eisenhower (1890–1969) | Republican | New York (TX) | 1953 | 62 | Richard M. Nixon |
| John F. Kennedy (1917–1963) | Democrat | Massachusetts | 1961 | 43 | Lyndon B. Johnson |
| Lyndon B. Johnson (1908–1973) | Democrat | Texas | 1963 | 55 | Hubert H. Humphrey |
| Richard M. Nixon (1913–1994) | Republican | New York (CA) | 1969 | 56 | Spiro T. Agnew [d]/Gerald R. Ford [e] |
| Gerald R. Ford (1913–2006) | Republican | Michigan (NE) | 1974 | 61 | Nelson A. Rockefeller [f] |
| James E. Carter (1924– ) | Democrat | Georgia | 1977 | 52 | Walter F. Mondale |
| Ronald W. Reagan (1911–2004) | Republican | California (IL) | 1981 | 69 | George H. W. Bush |
| George H.W. Bush (1924– ) | Republican | Texas (MA) | 1989 | 64 | J. Danforth Quayle |
| William J. Clinton (1946– ) | Democrat | Arkansas | 1993 | 46 | Albert Gore, Jr. |
| George W. Bush (1946– ) | Republican | Texas | 2001 | 54 | Richard B. Cheney |
| Barack Obama (1961– ) | Democrat | Illinois (HI) | 2009 | 47 | Joseph R. Biden |

[a] State of residence when elected; if born in another State, that State in parentheses.
[b] Democratic-Republican
[c] Johnson, a War Democrat, was elected Vice-President on the coalition Union Party ticket.
[d] Resigned October 10, 1973.

[e] Nominated by Nixon, confirmed by Congress on December 6, 1973.
[f] Nominated by Ford, confirmed by Congress on December 19, 1974.

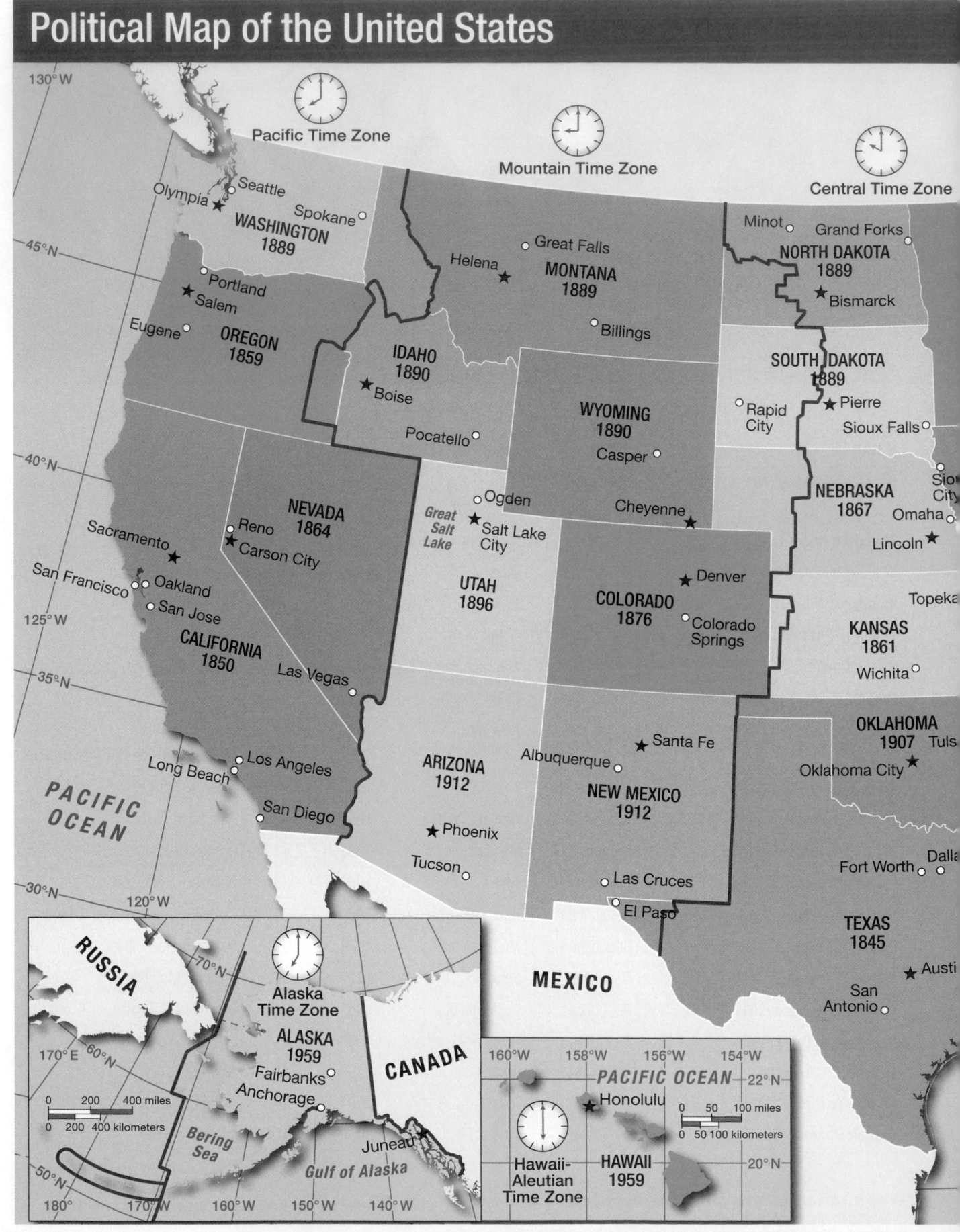

# Political Map of the United States

Pacific Time Zone

Mountain Time Zone

Central Time Zone

130°W

Olympia ★  ○ Seattle
                  Spokane ○
WASHINGTON
1889

45°N

Portland ○
★ Salem
Eugene ○        OREGON
                1859

Great Falls ○
Helena ★        MONTANA
                1889

○ Billings

IDAHO
1890
★ Boise

Pocatello ○

WYOMING
1890
Casper ○

○ Ogden
Great
Salt
Lake        Salt Lake
            ★ City

40°N

NEVADA
1864
Reno ○
★ Carson City

Sacramento ★

San Francisco ○  ○ Oakland
                 ○ San Jose

125°W

UTAH
1896

Cheyenne
★

Denver ★
COLORADO
1876
○ Colorado
  Springs

Minot ○  ○ Grand Forks
NORTH DAKOTA
1889
★ Bismarck

SOUTH DAKOTA
1889
Rapid ○      ★ Pierre
City         Sioux Falls ○

NEBRASKA        Sio
1867            City
            Omaha
Lincoln ★

Topeka

KANSAS
1861

CALIFORNIA
1850

35°N

Las Vegas
○

Long Beach ○  ○ Los Angeles

ARIZONA
1912

San Diego ○

PACIFIC
OCEAN

30°N

120°W

Albuquerque ○

★ Santa Fe

Wichita ○

OKLAHOMA
1907  Tuls

Oklahoma City ★

NEW MEXICO
1912

★ Phoenix

Tucson ○

○ Las Cruces
○ El Paso

Fort Worth ○  Dalla

TEXAS
1845

★ Austi

San
Antonio ○

MEXICO

RUSSIA

70°N

Alaska
Time Zone

ALASKA
1959

170°E  60°N

CANADA

Fairbanks ○
Anchorage ○

0    200    400 miles
0    200  400 kilometers

Bering
Sea

50°N

180°    170°W    160°W    150°W    140°W

Gulf of Alaska

Juneau ★

160°W    158°W    156°W    154°W
PACIFIC OCEAN  22°N

Honolulu ★

0    50    100 miles
0  50 100 kilometers

Hawaii-
Aleutian
Time Zone

HAWAII
1959

20°N

CANADA

Lake Superior

**MINNESOTA 1858**
Duluth

St. Paul ★
Minneapolis ○

**WISCONSIN 1848**
Green Bay ○
Madison ★   Milwaukee ○

**IOWA 1846**
Des Moines ★

**MICHIGAN 1837**
Lake Michigan
Lake Huron
Grand Rapids ○
Lansing ★
Detroit ○

Chicago ○
Gary ○
Peoria ○
Toledo ○
Ft. Wayne ○

**ILLINOIS 1818**
Springfield ★
Indianapolis ★

**INDIANA 1816**

**OHIO 1803**
Columbus ○
Cincinnati ○
Cleveland ○
Akron ○
Lake Erie

Kansas City ○
Jefferson ★ St. ○
City   Louis

**MISSOURI 1821**
Springfield ○

Louisville ○
Frankfort ★
Lexington ○

**KENTUCKY 1792**

Huntington ○
Charleston ○

**WEST VIRGINIA 1863**

Pittsburgh ○
Harrisburg ○

**PENNSYLVANIA 1787**
Philadelphia ○
Trenton ○
Newark ○

**Eastern Time Zone**

**VERMONT 1791**
Montpelier ★
Burlington ○

**NEW YORK 1788**
Rochester ○
Buffalo ○
Albany ○
Lake Ontario

Hartford ★

**Atlantic Time Zone**

**MAINE 1820**
Bangor ○
Augusta ★
Lewiston ○

**NEW HAMPSHIRE 1788**
Concord ★
Manchester ○
Portland ○

**MASSACHUSETTS 1788**
Boston ★
Providence ★

**RHODE ISLAND 1790**
**CONNECTICUT 1788**

New York ○
Jersey City ○

**NEW JERSEY 1787**

Wilmington ○
Dover ★

**DELAWARE 1787**

Baltimore ○
Washington, D.C. ✪
Annapolis ★

**MARYLAND 1788**

Richmond ★
Norfolk ○

**VIRGINIA 1788**

N

Fort Smith ○
Little Rock ★

**ARKANSAS 1836**

Nashville ★
Memphis ○

**TENNESSEE 1796**

Winston-Salem ○
Knoxville ○
Charlotte ○
Greensboro ○
Raleigh ★

**NORTH CAROLINA 1789**

ATLANTIC OCEAN

Shreveport ○

**MISSISSIPPI 1817**
Jackson ★

Birmingham ○

**ALABAMA 1819**
Montgomery ★
Macon ○
Columbus ○

**GEORGIA 1788**
Atlanta ★
Columbia ★
Charleston ○

**SOUTH CAROLINA 1788**

Savannah ○

**LOUISIANA 1812**
Baton Rouge ★

Mobile ○
Pensacola ○
Tallahassee ★

Jacksonville ○

Houston ○
Lake Pontchartrain
New Orleans ○

**Gulf of Mexico**

Tampa ○

**FLORIDA 1845**

Lake Okeechobee

Miami ○

**BAHAMAS**

Tropic of Cancer

**CUBA**

60° W
45° N
65° W
40° N
35° N
70° W   30° N
75° W
25° N
80° W
85° W
90° W
95° W

0    200    400 miles
0    200    400 kilometers

**KEY**
✪ National capital
★ State capital
○ Other city
1787 Year of admission to the Union
— Time Zone boundary

**Europe**

0   200   400 miles
0   200  400 kilometers

**West Africa**

0   200   400 miles
0   200  400 kilometers

## KEY
- ⊙ National capital
- ○ Other city

0    1,000    2,000 miles
0    1,000    2,000 kilometers

### Middle East

0    400 miles
0    400 kilometers

# Analyzing Documents

**1.** crime, unfair business practices, debt, marriage, and punishment

**2.** The laws were written down and codified to ensure that judgments were consistent throughout the land and that all citizens were aware of the laws and the punishments associated with them.

# ▶ The Code of Hammurabi

The Code of Hammurabi, believed to date before 1750 B.C., is a series of laws decreed by Hammurabi, the ruler of Babylon when that ancient city was at the peak of its power. Inscribed on stone columns over seven feet high, the Code consisted of 280 sections. Selected sections are excerpted below:

- If a man practice (robbery) and be captured, that man shall be put to death. . . .
- If a man has come forward in a lawsuit for the witnessing of false things, and has not proved the thing that he said, if that lawsuit is a capital case, that man shall be put to death. If he came forward for witnessing about corn or silver, he shall bear the penalty (which applies to) that case.
- If a man has concealed in his house a lost slave or slave-girl belonging to the Palace or to a subject, and has not brought him (or her) out at the proclamation of the Crier, the owner of the house shall be put to death.
- If a fire has broken out in a man's house, and a man who has gone to extinguish it has cast his eye on the property of the owner of the house and has taken the property of the owner of the house, that man shall be thrown into the fire.
- If a man is subject to a debt bearing interest, and Adad (the Weather-god) has saturated his field or a high flood has carried (its crop) away, or because of lack of water he has not produced corn in that field, in that year he shall not return any corn to (his) creditor. He shall . . . not pay interest for that year.
- If a man has donated field, orchard or house to his favourite heir and has written a sealed document for him (confirming this), after the father has gone to his doom, when the brothers share he (the favorite heir) shall take the gift that his father gave him, and apart from that they shall share equally in the property of the paternal estate.
- If an artisan has taken a child for bringing up, and has taught him his manual skill, (the child) shall not be (re)claimed. If he has not taught him his manual skill, that pupil may return to his father's house.
- If a man aid a male or female slave . . . to escape from the city gates, he shall be put to death. . . .

- If a man be in debt and sell his wife, son, or daughter, or bind them over to service, for three years they shall work in the house of the purchaser or master; in the fourth year they shall be given their freedom. . . .
- If a builder has made a house for a man but has not made his work strong, so that the house he made falls down and causes the death of the owner of the house, that builder shall be put to death. If it causes the death of the son of the owner of the house, they shall kill the son of the builder.
- If a man would put away [divorce] his wife who has not borne him children, he shall give her money to the amount of her marriage settlement and he shall make good to her the dowry which she brought from her father's house and then he may put her away.
- If a son has struck his father, they shall cut off his hand.
- If a man has destroyed the eye of a man of the "gentleman" class, they shall destroy his eye. If he has broken a gentleman's bone, they shall break his bone. If he has destroyed the eye of a commoner or broken a bone of a commoner, he shall pay one mina [about $300] of silver. If he has destroyed the eye of a gentleman's slave, he shall pay half the slave's price.
- If a gentleman's slave strikes the cheek of a man of the "gentleman" class, they shall cut off (the slave's) ear.
- If a gentleman strikes a gentleman in a free fight and inflicts an injury on him, that man shall swear "I did not strike him deliberately," and he shall pay the surgeon.

▲ Stone pillar with Hammurabi's Code

## Analyzing Documents

Use the passage on this page to answer the following questions.
1. With what general topics is the Code concerned?
2. Why do you suppose the laws were written down and codified?

# ▶Magna Carta

Signed by England's King John in 1215, the Magna Carta (Great Charter) was the first document to limit the power of England's monarchs. The Magna Carta established the principle that rulers are subject to law—a major step toward constitutional government.

W e . . . by this our present Charter have confirmed, for us and our heirs forever—

**1.** That the English Church shall be free and shall have her whole rights and her liberties inviolable. . . .

**9.** Neither we nor our bailiffs shall seize any land or rent for any debt while the chattels [possessions] of the debtor are sufficient for the payment of the debt. . . .

**12.** No scutage [tax] or aid [subsidy] shall be imposed in our kingdom, unless by the common counsel of our kingdom. . . .

**14.** And also to have the common council of the kingdom to assess and aid, . . . and for the assessing of scutages, we will cause to be summoned the archbishops, bishops, abbots, earls, and great barons, . . . And besides, we will cause to be summoned . . . all those who hold of us in chief, at a certain day    . and to a certain place; and in all the letters of summons, we will express the cause of the summons; and the summons being thus made, the business shall proceed on the day appointed, according to the counsel of those who shall be present, although all who have been summoned have not come.

**39.** No free-man shall be seized, or imprisoned, or dispossessed, or outlawed, or in any way destroyed; nor will we condemn him, nor will we commit him to prison, excepting by the legal judgment of his peers, or by the laws of the land.

**40.** To none will we sell, to none will we deny, to none will we delay right or justice.

▲ King John signs the Magna Carta.

**41.** All merchants shall have safety and security in coming into England, and going out of England, and in staying and in traveling through England . . . to buy and sell, . . . excepting in the time of war, and if they be of a country at war against us. . . .

**42.** It shall be lawful to any person to go out of our kingdom . . . and to return safely and securely, by land or by water, saving his allegiance to us, unless it be in time of war, for some short space, for the common good of the kingdom. . . .

**52.** If any have been disseised [deprived] or dispossessed by us, without a legal verdict of their peers, of their lands, castles, liberties, or rights, we will immediately restore these things to them. . . .

**63.** Wherefore our will is . . . that the men in our kingdom have and hold the aforesaid liberties, rights, and concessions . . . fully and entirely, to them and their heirs, . . . in all things and places forever.

## Analyzing Documents

Use the passage on this page to answer the following questions.

1. What basic American right has its origins in Article 39 of the Magna Carta?
2. Which article provides the basis for the Fifth Amendment to the Constitution, which states that no person can "be deprived of life, liberty, or property, without due process of law"?
3. What limits does Article 12 place on the king's power to tax?

## Analyzing Documents

**1.** The basic American right that has its origins in Article 39 of the Magna Carta is found in the 5th Amendment: criminal proceedings, including the right to be tried in court by an impartial jury.

**2.** Article 52

**3.** A tax will not be imposed unless decided by the "common counsel" (the people).

## Analyzing Documents

**1.** to enact fair and equal laws that would be followed by all the settlers to ensure the settlement's survival

**2.** The document was necessary because it provided the settlers with an agreed-upon governmental authority that they consented to obey; the settlers would not have been able to survive if they had not banded together in an orderly manner.

**3.** Sample answer: Without the compact, it is possible that there would be strife between settlers and discord about who or what had the authority to make laws for the colony, which may eventually have led to the settlement's failure.

# ▶ Mayflower Compact

The *Mayflower* landed in present-day Cape Cod in November, 1620. The document that became know as the Mayflower Compact contained the first written laws for the new land and established a government created by those who were to be governed. It was signed by 41 adult men.

In the name of God, Amen. We, whose names are underwritten, the Loyal Subjects of our dread Sovereign Lord, King James, by the Grace of God, of England, France and Ireland, King, Defender of the Faith, e&.

Having undertaken for the Glory of God, and Advancement of the Christian Faith, and the Honour of our King and Country, a voyage to plant the first colony in the northern parts of Virginia; do by these presents, solemnly and mutually in the Presence of God and one of another, covenant and combine ourselves together into a civil Body Politick, for our better Ordering and Preservation, and Furtherance of the Ends aforesaid; And by Virtue hereof to enact, constitute, and frame, such just and equal Laws, Ordinances, Acts, Constitutions and Offices, from time to time, as shall be thought most meet and convenient for the General good of the Colony; unto which we promise all due submission and obedience.

In Witness whereof we have hereunto subscribed our names at Cape Cod the eleventh of November, in the Reign of our Sovereign Lord, King James of England, France and Ireland, the eighteenth, and of Scotland the fifty-fourth. Anno Domini, 1620.

### Analyzing Documents

Use the passage on this page to answer the following questions.
1. What goals are laid out in this document?
2. Why was this document necessary?
3. What might have happened if the Mayflower Compact had not be written?

Selected signatures on the Mayflower Compact

Signing the Mayflower Compact aboard ship ▶

# ▶ English Bill of Rights

When the Catholic king, James II, was forced from the English throne in 1688, Parliament offered the crown to his Protestant daughter Mary and her husband, William of Orange. Parliament, however, insisted that William and Mary submit to a bill of rights. This document sums up the powers that Parliament had been seeking since the Petition of Right in 1628.

Whereas, the late King James II . . . did endeavor to subvert and exirpate [eliminate] the Protestant religion and the laws and liberties of this kingdom . . . and whereas the said late king James II having abdicated the government, and the throne being vacant. . . .

The said Lords [Parliament] . . . being now assembled in a full and free representative [body] of this nation . . . do in the first place . . . declare

- That the pretended [untruthfully claimed] power of suspending the laws or the execution of laws by regal authority without consent of Parliament is illegal;
- That the pretended power of dispensing with laws or the execution of laws by regal authority, as it hath been assumed and exercised of late, is illegal; . . .
- That levying money for or to the use of the Crown by pretence of prerogative, without grant of Parliament, for longer time, or in other manner than the same is or shall be granted, is illegal;
- That it is the right of the subjects to petition the king, and all commitments and prosecutions for such petitioning are illegal;
- That the raising or keeping a standing army within the kingdom in time of peace, unless it be with consent of Parliament, is against law;
- That the subjects which are Protestants may have arms for their defence suitable to their conditions and as allowed by law;
- That election of members of Parliament ought to be free;
- That the freedom of speech and debates or proceedings in Parliament ought not to be impeached or questioned in any court or place out of Parliament;
- That excessive bail ought not to be required, nor excessive fines imposed, nor cruel and unusual punishments inflicted;
- That jurors ought to be duly impaneled and returned, and jurors which pass upon men in trials for high treason ought to be freeholders [property owners with unconditional rights];

▲ Mary and William

- That all grants and promises of fines and forfeitures of particular persons before conviction are illegal and void;
- And that for redress of all grievances, and for the amending, strengthening and preserving of the laws, Parliaments ought to be held frequently.

## Analyzing Documents

Use the passage on this page to answer the following questions.
1. Which rights and freedoms listed above do you think are most important? Explain your choices.
2. Review the American Declaration of Independence. What similarities do you see between the two documents?
3. What is the importance of this document for American government?

## Analyzing Documents

**1.** Accept any response that is backed by logical reasoning. Sample answer: I think "That excessive bail ought not to be required, nor excessive fines imposed, nor cruel and unusual punishments inflicted . . ." is the most important right because otherwise, judges could hand down unfair or disproportionate punishments based on revenge or their own personal convictions.

**2.** Similarities include the sovereignty of the people and the importance of representative, freely elected government.

**3.** The importance of this document is that much of American government and politics today is based on these early English ideas.

## Analyzing Documents

**1.** the freedom to be absolutely in charge of their lives and possessions without answering to anyone

**2.** With all people living in perfect freedom, an individual's rights and property are at risk for destruction and seizure by others.

**3.** Governments are formed by the consent of individuals as a community to willingly give up their perfect freedoms and place themselves under a government to preserve their life, liberty, and property.

**4.** In order to preserve life, liberty, and property, governments require individuals to submit to the power of someone other than themselves; the governed must bear the responsibility of the community as a whole.

# ▶Second Treatise on Government

In 1690, English philosopher John Locke (1632–1704) produced two treatises (essays) on government. In his second treatise, he discussed the responsibilities of a government and claimed that the people have the right to overthrow an unjust government. Locke's ideas greatly influenced Thomas Jefferson and other supporters of the American Revolution. In this selection, Locke explains why people form governments.

To understand political power aright . . . we must consider what estate all men are naturally in, and that is, a state of perfect freedom to order their actions, and dispose of their possessions and persons as they think fit, within the bounds of the law of nature, without asking leave or depending upon the will of any other man. . . .

Men being . . . by nature, all free, equal and independent, no one can be put out of this estate and subjected to the political power of another without his own consent, which is done by agreeing with other men, to join and unite into a community for their comfortable, safe and peaceable living, one amongst another, in a secure enjoyment of their properties, and a greater security against any that are not of it. . . .

When any number of men have, by the consent of every individual, made a community, they have thereby made that community one body, with a power to act as one body, which is only by the will and determination of the majority. . . . . And thus every man, by consenting with others to make one body politic under one government, puts himself under an obligation to every one in that society to submit to the determination of the majority, and to be concluded by it. . . .

If man in the state of nature . . . be absolute lord of his own person and possessions, equal to the greatest and

▲ John Locke

subject to nobody, why will he part with his freedom, this empire, and subject himself to the dominion and control of any other power? . . . It is obvious to answer that though in the state of nature he hath such a right, yet the enjoyment of it is very uncertain and constantly exposed to the invasion of others; for all being kings as much as he, every man his equal, . . . the enjoyment of the property he has in this state is very unsafe, very insecure. This makes him willing to quit this condition which, however free, is full of fears and continual dangers; and it is not without reason that he seeks out and is willing to join in society with others . . . for the mutual preservation of their lives, liberties and estates, which I call by the general name—property.

The great and chief end, therefore, of men uniting into commonwealths, and putting themselves under government, is the preservation of their property. . . .

### Analyzing Documents

Use the passage on this page to answer the following questions.
1. According to Locke, what freedoms did people have before the founding of governments?
2. What are the potential dangers of a person living in what Locke called "perfect freedom"?
3. According to Locke, how are governments formed?
4. What trade-off does Locke say occurs when people live under government?

# ▶Virginia Declaration of Rights

The Virginia Declaration of Rights was largely the work of George Mason (1725–1792), one of Virginia's wealthiest planters and a neighbor and friend of George Washington. The Declaration was adopted unanimously by the Virginia Convention of Delegates on June 12, 1776, and was later incorporated within the Virginia State Constitution. It influenced a number of later documents, including the Declaration of Independence and the Bill of Rights.

A declaration of rights made by the representatives of the good people of Virginia, assembled in full and free convention; which rights do pertain to them and their posterity, as the basis and foundation of government.

**I** That all men are by nature equally free and independent, and have certain inherent rights, of which, when they enter into a state of society, they cannot, by any compact, deprive or divest their posterity; namely, the enjoyment of life and liberty, with the means of acquiring and possessing property, and pursuing and obtaining happiness and safety.

**II** That all power is vested in, and consequently derived from, the people; that magistrates are their trustees and servants, and at all times amenable to them.

**III** That government is, or ought to be, instituted for the common benefit, protection, and security of the people, nation or community; of all the various modes and forms of government that is best, which is capable of producing the greatest degree of happiness and safety and is most effectually secured against the danger of maladministration; and that, whenever any government shall be found inadequate or contrary to these purposes, a majority of the community hath an indubitable, unalienable, and indefeasible right to reform, alter or abolish it, in such manner as shall be judged most conducive to the public weal.

**IV** That no man, or set of men, are entitled to exclusive or separate emoluments or privileges from the community, but in consideration of public services; which, not being descendible, neither ought the offices of magistrate, legislator, or judge be hereditary.

**V** That the legislative and executive powers of the state should be separate and distinct from the judicative; and, that the members of the two first may be restrained from oppression by feeling and participating the burthens of

▲ George Mason

the people, they should, at fixed periods, be reduced to a private station, return into that body from which they were originally taken, and the vacancies be supplied by frequent, certain, and regular elections in which all, or any part of the former members, to be again eligible, or ineligible, as the laws shall direct.

**VI** That elections of members to serve as representatives of the people in assembly ought to be free; and that all men, having sufficient evidence of permanent common interest with, and attachment to, the community have the right of suffrage and cannot be taxed or deprived of their property for public uses without their own consent or that of their representatives so elected, nor bound by any law to which they have not, in like manner, assented, for the public good.

**VII** That all power of suspending laws, or the execution of laws, by any authority without consent of the representatives of the people is injurious to their rights and ought not to be exercised.

**VIII** That in all capital or criminal prosecutions a man hath a right to demand the cause and nature of his accusation to be confronted with the accusers and witnesses, to call for evidence in his favor, and to a speedy trial by an impartial jury of his vicinage, without whose unanimous consent he cannot be found guilty, nor can he be compelled to give evidence against himself; that no man be deprived of his liberty except by the law of the land or the judgement of his peers.

**IX** That excessive bail ought not to be required, nor excessive fines imposed; nor cruel and unusual punishments inflicted.

**X** That general warrants, whereby any officer or messenger may be commanded to search suspected places without evidence of a fact committed, or to seize any person or persons not named, or whose offense is not

## Analyzing Documents

**1.** The Declaration of Independence and the Bill of Rights echo several phrases and sentiments contained in the Virginia Declarations of Rights, such as "That all men are by nature equally free and independent, and have certain inherent rights"; "That all power is vested in, and consequently derived from, the people"; "That a well regulated militia, composed of the body of the people, trained to arms, is the proper, natural and safe defense of a free state"; and "That excessive bail ought not to be required, nor excessive fines imposed; nor cruel and unusual punishments inflicted." They both delineate such basic rights as freedom of the press and freedom of religion.

**2.** Accept any answers that are supported with solid reasoning. Sample answer: I feel that the rights of the accused, which are described in Articles VIII and IX, are extremely important civil rights. The legal system at certain times in history has been such that the accused was not innocent until proven guilty and punished without just cause or due process. Defining these rights prevents judicial abuses and unfair trials. Delineated by the Bill of Rights and clarified by decisions handed down by the Supreme Court, the rights of the accused remain an important part of the American judicial system and our democratic society.

particularly described and supported by evidence, are grievous and oppressive and ought not to be granted.

**XI** That in controversies respecting property and in suits between man and man, the ancient trial by jury is preferable to any other and ought to be held sacred.

**XII** That the freedom of the press is one of the greatest bulwarks of liberty and can never be restrained but by despotic governments.

**XIII** That a well regulated militia, composed of the body of the people, trained to arms, is the proper, natural, and safe defense of a free state; that standing armies, in time of peace, should be avoided as dangerous to liberty; and that, in all cases, the military should be under strict subordination to, and be governed by, the civil power.

**XIV** That the people have a right to uniform government; and therefore, that no government separate from, or independent of, the government of Virginia, ought to be erected or established within the limits thereof.

**XV** That no free government, or the blessings of liberty, can be preserved to any people but by a firm adherence to justice, moderation, temperance, frugality, and virtue and by frequent recurrence to fundamental principles.

**XVI** That religion, or the duty which we owe to our Creator and the manner of discharging it, can be directed by reason and conviction, not by force or violence; and therefore, all men are equally entitled to the free exercise of religion, according to the dictates of conscience; and that it is the mutual duty of all to practice Christian forbearance, love, and charity towards each other.

### Analyzing Documents

Use the passage on these pages to answer the following questions.

1. What similarities do you see in language and ideas between the Virginia Declaration of Rights and the Declaration of Independence? Between the Virginia Declaration of Rights and the Bill of Rights?

2. Choose one of the articles from the Virginia Declaration and explain the importance of the right that it describes using examples from your reading and general knowledge.

# ▶Articles of Confederation

The Articles of Confederation were approved on November 15, 1777, and were in effect from March 1, 1781, when they were finally ratified by all 13 States, until March 4, 1789. They established a weak central government, which led to conflicts among the States. Demand soon grew for a stronger central government, leading to the creation of the United States Constitution.

To all to whom these Presents shall come, we the undersigned Delegates of the States affixed to our Names send greeting. Whereas the Delegates of the United States of America in Congress assembled did on the fifteenth day of November in the Year of our Lord One Thousand Seven Hundred and Seventy seven, and in the Second Year of the Independence of America agree to certain articles of Confederation and perpetual Union between the States of New Hampshire, Massachusetts Bay, Rhode Island and Providence Plantations, Connecticut, New York, New Jersey, Pennsylvania, Delaware, Maryland, Virginia, North Carolina, South Carolina and Georgia in the Words following, viz. "Articles of Confederation and perpetual Union between the states of New Hampshire, Massachusetts Bay, Rhode Island and Providence Plantations, Connecticut, New York, New Jersey, Pennsylvania, Delaware, Maryland, Virginia, North Carolina, South Carolina and Georgia.

**[ART. I.]** The Stile of this confederacy shall be "The United States of America."

**[ART. II.]** Each state retains its sovereignty, freedom and independence, and every Power, Jurisdiction and right, which is not by this confederation expressly delegated to the United States, in Congress assembled.

**[ART. III.]** The said states hereby severally enter into a firm league of friendship with each other, for their common defence, the security of their Liberties, and their mutual and general welfare, binding themselves to assist each other, against all force offered to, or attacks made upon them, or any of them, on account of religion, sovereignty, trade, or any other pretence whatever.

**[ART. IV.]** The better to secure and perpetuate mutual friendship and intercourse among the people of the different states in this union, the free inhabitants of each of these states, paupers, vagabonds and fugitives from

Justice excepted, shall be entitled to all privileges and immunities of free citizens in the several states; and the people of each state shall have free ingress and regress to and from any other state, and shall enjoy therein all the privileges of trade and commerce, subject to the same duties, impositions and restrictions as the inhabitants thereof respectively, provided that such restriction shall not extend so far as to prevent the removal of property imported into any state, to any other state of which the Owner is an inhabitant; provided also that no imposition, duties or restriction shall be laid by any state, on the property of the united states, or either of them.

If any Person guilty of, or charged with treason, felony, or other high misdemeanor in any state, shall flee from Justice, and be found in any of the united states, he shall upon demand of the Governor or executive power, of the state from which he fled, be delivered up and removed to the state having jurisdiction of his offence.

Full faith and credit shall be given in each of these states to the records, acts and judicial proceedings of the courts and magistrates of every other state.

**[ART. V.]** For the more convenient management of the general interests of the united states, delegates shall be annually appointed in such manner as the legislature of each state shall direct, to meet in Congress on the first Monday in November, in every year, with a power reserved to each state, to recall its delegates, or any of them, at any time within the year, and to send others in their stead, for the remainder of the Year.

No state shall be represented in Congress by less than two, nor by more than seven Members; and no person shall be capable of being a delegate for more than three years in any term of six years; nor shall any person, being a delegate, be capable of holding any office under the united states, for which he, or another for his benefit receives any salary, fees or emolument of any kind.

Each state shall maintain its own delegates in a meeting of the states, and while they act as members of the committee of the states.

In determining questions in the united states, in Congress assembled, each state shall have one vote.

Freedom of speech and debate in Congress shall not be impeached or questioned in any Court, or place out of Congress, and the members of congress shall be protected in their persons from arrests and imprisonments, during the time of their going to and from, and attendance on congress, except for treason, felony, or breach of the peace.

**[ART. VI.]** No state without the Consent of the united states in congress assembled, shall send any embassy to, or receive any embassy from, or enter into any conference, agreement, or alliance or treaty with any King, prince or state; nor shall any person holding any office of profit or trust under the united states, or any of them, accept of any present, emolument, office or title of any kind whatever from any king, prince or foreign state; nor shall the united states in congress assembled, or any of them, grant any title of nobility.

No two or more states shall enter into any treaty, confederation or alliance whatever between them, without the consent of the united states in congress assembled, specifying accurately the purposes for which the same is to be entered into, and how long it shall continue.

No state shall lay any imposts or duties, which may interfere with any stipulations in treaties, entered into by the united states in congress assembled, with any king, prince or state, in pursuance of any treaties already proposed by congress, to the courts of France and Spain.

No vessels of war shall be kept up in time of peace by any state, except such number only, as shall be deemed necessary by the united states in congress assembled, for the defence of such state, or its trade; nor shall any body of forces be kept up by any state, in time of peace, except such number only, as in the judgment of the united states, in congress assembled, shall be deemed requisite to garrison the forts necessary for the defence of such state; but every state shall always keep up a well regulated and disciplined militia, sufficiently armed and accounted, and shall provide and constantly have ready for use, in public stores, a due number of field pieces and tents, and a proper quantity of arms, ammunition and camp equipage.

No state shall engage in any war without the consent of the united states in congress assembled, unless such state be actually invaded by enemies, or shall have received certain advice of a resolution being formed by some nation of Indians to invade such state and the danger is so imminent as not to admit of a delay, till the united states in congress assembled can be consulted: nor shall any state grant commissions to any ships or vessels of war, nor letters of marque or reprisal, except it be after a declaration of war by the united states in congress assembled, and then only against the kingdom or state and the subjects thereof, against which war has been so declared, and under such regulations as shall be established by the united states in congress assembled, unless such state be infested by pirates, in which case vessels of war may be fitted out for that occasion, and kept so long as the danger shall continue, or until the united states in congress assembled shall determine otherwise.

**[ART. VII.]** When land-forces are raised by any state for the common defence, all officers of or under the rank of colonel, shall be appointed by the legislature of each state respectively by whom such forces shall be raised, or in such manner as such state shall direct, and all vacancies shall be filled up by the state which first made the appointment.

**[ART. VIII.]** All charges of war, and all other expences that shall be incurred for the common defence or general welfare, and allowed by the united states in congress assembled, shall be defrayed out of a common treasury, which shall be supplied by the several states, in proportion to the value of all land within each state, granted to or surveyed for any Person, as such land and the buildings and improvements thereon shall be estimated according to such mode as the united states in congress assembled, shall from time to time direct and appoint. The taxes for paying that proportion shall be laid and levied by the authority and direction of the legislatures of the several states within the time agreed upon by the united states in congress assembled.

**[ART. IX.]** The united states in congress assembled, shall have the sole and exclusive right and power of determining on peace and war, except in the cases mentioned in the sixth article—of sending and receiving ambassadors—entering into treaties and alliances, provided that no treaty of commerce shall be made whereby the legislative power of the respective states shall be restrained from imposing such imposts and duties on foreigners, as their own people are subjected to, or from prohibiting the exportation or importation of any species of goods or commodities whatsoever—of establishing rules for deciding in all cases, what captures on land or water shall be legal, and in what manner prizes taken by land or naval forces in the service of the united states shall be divided or appropriated—of granting letters of marque and reprisal in times of peace—appointing courts for the trial of piracies and felonies committed on the high seas and establishing courts for receiving and determining finally appeals in all cases of captures, provided that no member of congress shall be appointed a judge of any of the said courts.

The united states in congress assembled shall also be the last resort on appeal in all disputes and differences now subsisting or that hereafter may arise between two or more states concerning boundary, jurisdiction or any other cause whatever; which authority shall always be exercised in the manner following. Whenever the legislative or executive authority or lawful agent [of any] state in controversy with another shall present a petition to congress stating the matter in question and praying for a hearing, notice thereof shall be given by order of congress to the legislative or executive authority of the other state in controversy, and a day assigned for the appearance of the parties by their lawful agents, who shall then be directed to appoint by joint consent, commissioners or judges to constitute a court for hearing and determining the matter in question; but if they cannot agree, congress shall name three persons out of each of the united states, and from the list of such persons each party shall alternately strike out one, the petitioners beginning, until the number shall be reduced to thirteen; and from that number not less than seven, nor more than nine names as congress shall direct, shall in the presence of congress be drawn out by lot, and the persons whose names shall be so drawn or any five of them, shall be commissioners or judges, to hear and finally determine the controversy, so always

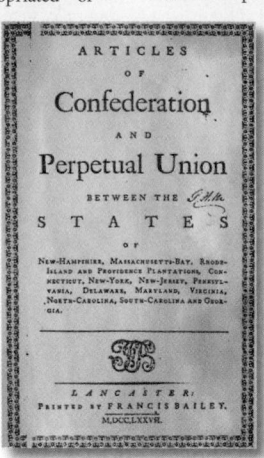

Cover of the Articles of Confederation

as a major part of the judges who shall hear the cause shall agree in the determination: and if either party shall neglect to attend at the day appointed, without shewing reasons, which congress shall judge sufficient, or being present shall refuse to strike, the congress shall proceed to nominate three persons out of each state, and the secretary of congress shall strike in behalf of such party absent or refusing; and the judgment and sentence of the court to be appointed, in the manner before prescribed, shall be final and conclusive; and if any of the parties shall refuse to submit to the authority of such court, or to appear to defend their claim or cause, the court shall nevertheless proceed to pronounce sentence, or judgment, which shall in like manner be final and decisive, the judgment or sentence and other proceedings being in either case transmitted to congress, and lodged among the acts of congress for the security of the parties concerned: provided that every commissioner, before he sits in judgment, shall take an oath to be administered by one of the judges of the supreme or superior court of the state, where the cause shall be tried, "well and truly to hear and determine the matter in question, according to the best of his judgment, without favour, affection or hope of reward;" provided also that no state shall be deprived of territory for the benefit of the united states.

All controversies concerning the private right of soil claimed under different grants of two or more states, whose jurisdictions as they may respect such lands, and the states which passed such grants are adjusted, the said grants or either of them being at the same time claimed to have originated antecedent to such settlement of jurisdiction, shall on the petition of either party to the congress of the united states, be finally determined as near as may be in the same manner as is before prescribed for deciding disputes respecting territorial jurisdiction between different states.

The united states in congress assembled shall also have the sole and exclusive right and power of regulating the alloy and value of coin struck by their own authority, or by that of the respective states—fixing the standard of weights and measures throughout the united states—regulating the trade and managing all affairs with the Indians, not members of any of the states, provided that the legislative right of any state within its own limits be not infringed or violated—establishing and regulating post-offices from one state to another, throughout all the united states, and exacting such postage on the papers passing thro' the same as may be requisite to defray the expences of the said office—appointing all officers of the land forces, in the service of the united states, excepting regimental officers—appointing all the officers of the naval forces, and commissioning all officers whatever in the service of the united states—making rules for the government and regulation of the said land and naval forces, and directing their operations.

The united states in congress assembled shall have authority to appoint a committee, to sit in the recess of congress, to be denominated "A Committee of the States," and to consist of one delegate from each state; and to appoint such other committees and civil officers as may be necessary for managing the general affairs of the united states under their direction—to appoint one of their number to preside, provided that no person be allowed to serve in the office of president more than one year in any term of three years; to ascertain the necessary sums of Money to be raised for the service of the united states, and to appropriate and apply the same for defraying the public expences—to borrow money, or emit bills on the credit of the united states, transmitting every half year to the respective states an account of the sums of money so borrowed or emitted—to build and equip a navy—to agree upon the number of land forces, and to make requisitions from each state for its quota, in proportion to the number of white inhabitants in such state; which requisition shall be binding, and thereupon the legislature of each state shall appoint the regimental officers, raise the men and clothe, arm and equip them in a soldier like manner, at the expence of the united states, and the officers and men so clothed, armed and equipped shall march to the place appointed, and within the time agreed on by the united states in congress assembled. But if the united states in congress assembled shall, on consideration of circumstances judge proper that any state should not raise men, or should raise a smaller number than its quota, and that any other state should raise a greater number of men than the quota thereof, such extra number shall be raised, officered, clothed, armed and equipped in the same manner as the quota of such state, unless the legislature of such state shall judge that such extra number cannot be safely spared out of the same, in which case they shall raise, officer, clothe, arm and equip as many of such extra number as they judge can be safely spared. And the officers and men so clothed, armed and equipped, shall march to the place appointed, and within the time agreed on by the united states in congress assembled.

The united states in congress assembled shall never engage in a war, nor grant letters of marque and reprisal in time of peace, nor enter into any treaties or alliances, nor coin money, nor regulate the value thereof, nor ascertain the sums and expences necessary for the defence and welfare of the united states, or any of them, nor emit bills, nor borrow money on the credit of the united states, nor appropriate money, nor agree upon the number of vessels of war, to be built or purchased, or the number of land or sea forces to be raised, nor appoint a commander in chief of the army or navy, unless nine states assent to the same: nor shall a question on any

other point, except for adjourning from day to day be determined, unless by the votes of a majority of the united states in congress assembled.

The congress of the united states shall have power to adjourn to any time within the year, and to any place within the united states, so that no period of adjournment be for a longer duration than the space of six Months, and shall publish the Journal of their proceedings monthly, except such parts thereof relating to treaties, alliances or military operations as in their judgment require secrecy; and the yeas and nays of the delegates of each state on any question shall be entered on the Journal, when it is desired by any delegate; and the delegates of a state, or any of them, at his or their request shall be furnished with a transcript of the said Journal, except such parts as are above excepted, to lay before the legislatures of the several states.

**[ART. X.]** The committee of the states, or any nine of them, shall be authorised to execute, in the recess of congress, such of the powers of congress as the united states in congress assembled, by the consent of nine states, shall from time to time think expedient to vest them with; provided that no power be delegated to the said committee, for the exercise of which, by the articles of confederation, the voice of nine states in the congress of the united states assembled is requisite.

**[ART. XI.]** Canada acceding to this confederation, and joining in the measures of the united states, shall be admitted into, and entitled to all the advantages of this union: but no other colony shall be admitted into the same, unless such admission be agreed to by nine states.

**[ART. XII.]** All bills of credit emitted, monies borrowed and debts contracted by, or under the authority of congress, before the assembling of the united states, in pursuance of the present confederation, shall be deemed and considered as a charge against the united states, for payment and satisfaction whereof the said united states, and the public faith are hereby solemnly pledged.

**[ART. XIII.]** Every state shall abide by the determinations of the united states in congress assembled, on all questions which by this confederation are submitted to them. And the Articles of this confederation shall be inviolably observed by every state, and the union shall be perpetual; nor shall any alteration at any time hereafter be made in any of them; unless such alteration be agreed to in a congress of the united states, and be afterwards confirmed by the legislatures of every state.

And whereas it hath pleased the Great Governor of the World to incline the hearts of the legislatures we respectively represent in congress, to approve of, and to authorize us to ratify the said articles of confederation and perpetual union. Know ye that we the undersigned delegates, by virtue of the power and authority to us given for that purpose, do by these presents, in the name and in behalf of our respective constituents, fully and entirely ratify and confirm each and every of the said articles of

# Analyzing Documents

**1.** Contributing factors to the establishment of a loose confederation include the desire not to have a powerful central authority like the government from which the colonists had just gained their independence; the need to provide a central authority without undermining the authority and sovereignty of each State; and the necessity of meeting the demands of the ideological differences of each State.

**2.** Any three of the following is acceptable: each State no matter its size had only one vote; Congress could not levy or collect taxes; Congress was not able to regulate foreign or interstate commerce; there was no executive in place to enforce the acts of Congress; there was no national court system; amending the Articles of Confederation could occur only with the consent of all States; a 9/13 majority was required to pass laws; and the Articles were only "firm league of friendship."

**3.** Accept any answers that are supported with solid reasoning. Sample answer: The subservient nature of Congress to the States seems to be the greatest flaw in the Articles of Confederation. In order for the 13 colonies to work together as a nation, instead of 13 individual nations, there needed to be a central authority that was charged with the responsibility of looking out for the country as a whole without deference to the particular needs of a given State. A central government would have the authority to create and implement national laws, levy taxes to pay for government and governmental programs, and provide for the defense of the nation. Without a powerful central government, the confederation would eventually become weakened by in-fighting and dissent so that nothing would be accomplished and the "united states" would ultimately divide and become individual nations.

confederation and perpetual union, and all and singular the matters and things therein contained: And we do further solemnly plight and engage the faith of our respective constituents, that they shall abide by the determinations of the united states in congress assembled, on all questions, which by the said confederation are submitted to them. And that the articles thereof shall be inviolably observed by the states we respectively represent, and that the union shall be perpetual. In Witness whereof we have hereunto set our hands in Congress. Done at Philadelphia in the state of Pennsylvania the ninth Day of July in the Year of our Lord one Thousand seven Hundred and Seventy-eight, and in the third year of the independence of America.

JOSIAH BARTLETT
JOHN WENTWORTH JUNR
AUGUST 8TH 1778
On The Part & Behalf Of
The State Of New Hampshire

JOHN HANCOCK
SAMUEL ADAMS
ELBRIDGE GERRY
FRANCIS DANA
JAMES LOVELL
SAMUEL HOLTEN
On The Part And Behalf Of
The State Of Massachusetts Bay

WILLIAM ELLERY
HENRY MARCHANT
JOHN COLLINS
On The Part And Behalf
Of The State Of Rhode Island
And Providence Plantations

ROGER SHERMAN
SAMUEL HUNTINGTON
OLIVER WOLCOTT
TITUS HOSMER
ANDREW ADAMS
On The Part And Behalf Of
The State Of Connecticut

JAS DUANE
FRAS LEWIS
WM DUER.
GOUV MORRIS
On The Part And Behalf Of
The State Of New York

JNO WITHERSPOON
NATHL SCUDDER
On The Part And In Behalf Of
The State Of New Jersey.
Novr 26, 1778.—

ROBT MORRIS
DANIEL ROBERDEAU
JONA BAYARD SMITH.
WILLIAM CLINGAN
JOSEPH REED
22D JULY 1778
On The Part And Behalf Of
The State Of Pennsylvania

THO MCKEAN
FEBY 12 1779
JOHN DICKINSON
MAY 5TH 1779
NICHOLAS VAN DYKE,
On The Part & Behalf Of
The State Of Delaware

JOHN HANSON
MARCH 1 1781
DANIEL CARROLL DO
On The Part And Behalf
Of The State Of Maryland

RICHARD HENRY LEE
JOHN BANISTER
THOMAS ADAMS
JNO HARVIE
FRANCIS LIGHTFOOT LEE
On The Part And Behalf Of
The State Of Virginia

JOHN PENN
JULY 21ST 1778
CORNS HARNETT
JNO WILLIAMS
On The Part And Behalf
Of The State Of No Carolina

HENRY LAURENS
WILLIAM HENRY DRAYTON
JNO MATHEWS
RICHD HUTSON.
THOS HEYWARD JUNR
On The Part & Behalf Of
The State Of South Carolina

JNO WALTON
24TH JULY 1778
EDWD TELFAIR.
EDWD LANGWORTHY
On The Part And Behalf Of
The State Of Georgia

## Analyzing Documents

Use the passage on these pages to answer the following questions.
1. What factors explain why the first government of the United States was a loose confederation of individual States?
2. List three reasons why the Articles of Confederation failed to establish a lasting government.
3. What do you think was the greatest flaw in the Articles? Why?

# ▶ *The Federalist* No. 10

One of the 29 essays believed to have been written by James Madison, the tenth of *The Federalist* papers presents Madison's observations on dealing with the "mischiefs of faction" and the advantages of a republican (representative) form of government over that of a pure democracy. This essay was first published on November 23, 1787.

Among the numerous advantages promised by a well-constructed Union, none deserves to be more accurately developed than its tendency to break and control the violence of faction. The friend of popular governments never finds himself so much alarmed for their character and fate as when he contemplates their propensity to this dangerous vice. He will not fail, therefore, to set a due value on any plan which, without violating the principles to which he is attached, provides a proper cure for it. The instability, injustice, and confusion introduced into the public councils have, in truth, been the mortal diseases under which popular governments have everywhere perished; as they continue to be the favorite and fruitful topics from which the adversaries to liberty derive their most specious declamations.

The valuable improvements made by the American constitutions on the popular models, both ancient and modern, cannot certainly be too much admired; but it would be an unwarrantable partiality to contend that they have as effectually obviated the danger on this side, as was wished and expected. Complaints are everywhere heard from our most considerate and virtuous citizens, equally the friends of public and private faith, and of public and personal liberty, that our governments are too unstable, that the public good is disregarded in the conflicts of rival parties, and that measures are too often decided, not according to the rules of justice and the rights of the minor party, but by the superior force of an interested and overbearing majority. However anxiously we may wish that these complaints had no foundation, the evidence of known facts will not permit us to deny that they are in some degree true.

It will be found, indeed, on a candid review of our situation, that some of the distresses under which we labor have been erroneously charged on the operation of our governments; but it will be found, at the same time, that other causes will not alone account for many of our heaviest misfortunes; and, particularly, for that prevailing and increasing distrust of public engagements, and alarm for private rights, which are echoed from one end of the continent to the other. These must be chiefly, if not wholly, effects of the unsteadiness and injustice with which a factious spirit has tainted our public administrations.

By a faction, I understand a number of citizens, whether amounting to a majority or minority of the whole, who are united and actuated by some common impulse of passion, or of interest, adversed to the rights of other citizens, or to the permanent and aggregate interests of the community.

There are two methods of curing the mischiefs of faction: the one, by removing its causes; the other, by controlling its effects.

There are again two methods of removing the causes of faction: the one, by destroying the liberty which is essential to its existence; the other, by giving to every citizen the same opinions, the same passions, and the same interests.

It could never be more truly said than of the first remedy that it was worse than the disease. Liberty is to faction what air is to fire, an ailment without which it instantly expires. But it could not be less folly to abolish liberty, which is essential to political life, because it nourishes faction, than it would be to wish the annihilation of air,

Madison warned of "factions" leading to violence.

which is essential to animal life, because it imparts to fire its destructive agency.

The second expedient is as impracticable as the first would be unwise. As long as the reason of man continues fallible, and he is at liberty to exercise it, different opinions will be formed. As long as the connection subsists between his reason and his self-love, his opinions and his passions will have a reciprocal influence on each other; and the former will be objects to which the latter will attach themselves. The diversity in the faculties of men, from which the rights of property originate, is not less an insuperable obstacle to a uniformity of interests. The protection of these faculties is the first object of government. From the protection of different and unequal faculties of acquiring property, the possession of different degrees and kinds of property immediately results; and from the influence of these on the sentiments and views of the respective proprietors ensues a division of the society into different interests and parties.

The latent causes of faction are thus sown in the nature of man; and we see them everywhere brought into different degrees of activity, according to the different circumstances of civil society. A zeal for different opinions concerning religion, concerning government, and many other points, as well of speculation as of practice; an attachment of different leaders ambitiously contending for preeminence and power; or to persons of other descriptions whose fortunes have been interesting to the human passions, have, in turn, divided mankind into parties, inflamed them with mutual animosity, and rendered them much more disposed to vex and oppress each other than to cooperate for their common good. So strong is this propensity of mankind to fall into mutual animosities that, where no substantial occasion presents itself, the most frivolous and fanciful distinctions have been sufficient to kindle their unfriendly passions and excite their most violent conflicts. But the most common and durable source of factions has been the various and unequal distribution of property.

Those who hold and those who are without property have ever formed distinct interests in society. Those who are creditors and those who are debtors fall under a like discrimination. A landed interest, a manufacturing interest, a mercantile interest, a moneyed interest, with many lesser interests, grow up of necessity in civilized nations and divide them into different classes, actuated by different sentiments and views. The regulation of these various and interfering interests forms the principal task of modern legislation and involves the spirit of party and faction in the necessary and ordinary operations of the government.

No man is allowed to be a judge in his own cause, because his interest would certainly bias his judgment and, not improbably, corrupt his integrity. With equal, nay, with greater reason, a body of men are unfit to be both judges and parties at the same time; yet what are many of the most important acts of legislation but so many judicial determinations, not indeed concerning the rights of single persons, but concerning the rights of large bodies of citizens? And what are the different classes of legislators but advocates and parties to the causes which they determine? Is a law proposed concerning private debts? It is a question to which the creditors are parties on one side and the debtors on the other. Justice ought to hold the balance between them. Yet the parties are, and must be, themselves the judges; and the most numerous party or, in other words, the most powerful faction must be expected to prevail.

Shall domestic manufactures be encouraged, and in what degree, by restrictions on foreign manufactures? [These] are questions which would be differently decided by the landed and the manufacturing classes, and probably by neither with a sole regard to justice and the public good. The apportionment of taxes on the various descriptions of property is an act which seems to require the most exact impartiality; yet there is, perhaps, no legislative act in which greater opportunity and temptation are given to a predominant party to trample on the rules of justice. Every shilling with which they overburden the inferior number is a shilling saved to their own pockets.

It is in vain to say that enlightened statesmen will be able to adjust these clashing interests and render them all subservient to the public good. Enlightened statesmen will not always be at the helm. Nor, in many cases, can such an adjustment be made at all without taking into view indirect and remote considerations, which will rarely prevail over the immediate interest which one party may find in disregarding the rights of another or the good of the whole. The inference to which we are brought is that the causes of faction cannot be removed and that relief is only to be sought in the means of controlling its effects.

If a faction consists of less than a majority, relief is supplied by the republican principle, which enables the majority to defeat its sinister views by regular vote. It may clog the administration, it may convulse the society; but it will be unable to execute and mask its violence under the forms of the Constitution. When a majority is included in a faction, the form of popular government, on the other hand, enables it to sacrifice to its ruling passion or interest both the public good and the rights of other citizens. To secure the public good and private rights against the danger of such a faction, and at the same time to preserve the spirit and the form of popular government, is then the great object to which our inquiries are directed. Let me add that it is the great desideratum by which this form of government can be rescued from the opprobrium under which it has so long labored and be recommended to the esteem and adoption of mankind.

By what means is this object attainable? Evidently by one of two only. Either the existence of the same passion or interest in a majority at the same time must be prevented, or the majority, having such coexistent passion or interest, must be rendered, by their number and local situation, unable to concert and carry into effect schemes of oppression. If the impulse and the opportunity be suffered to coincide, we well know that neither moral nor religious motives can be relied on as an adequate control. They are not found to be such on the injustice and violence of individuals and lose their efficacy in proportion to the number combined together, that is, in proportion as their efficacy becomes needful.

From this view of the subject it may be concluded that a pure democracy, by which I mean a society consisting of a small number of citizens who assemble and administer the government in person, can admit of no cure for the mischiefs of faction. A common passion or interest will, in almost every case, be felt by a majority of the whole; a communication and concert result from the form of government itself; and there is nothing to check the inducements to sacrifice the weaker party or an obnoxious individual. Hence it is that such democracies have ever been spectacles of turbulence and contention; have ever been found incompatible with personal security or the rights of property; and have in general been as short in their lives as they have been violent in their deaths. Theoretic politicians, who have patronized this species of government, have erroneously supposed that by reducing mankind to a perfect equality in their political rights, they would, at the same time, be perfectly equalized and assimilated in their possessions, their opinions, and their passions.

A republic, by which I mean a government in which the scheme of representation takes place, opens a different prospect and promises the cure for which we are seeking. Let us examine the points in which it varies from pure democracy, and we shall comprehend both the nature of the cure and the efficacy which it must derive from the Union.

The two great points of difference between a democracy and a republic are: first, the delegation of the government, in the latter, to a small number of citizens elected by the rest; secondly, the greater number of citizens, and greater sphere of country, over which the latter may be extended.

The effect of the first difference is, on the one hand, to refine and enlarge the public views by passing them through the medium of a chosen body of citizens, whose wisdom may best discern the true interest of their country, and whose patriotism and love of justice will be least likely to sacrifice it to temporary or partial considerations. Under such a regulation, it may well happen that the public voice, pronounced by the representatives of the people, will be more consonant to the public good than if pronounced by the people themselves, convened for the purpose. On the other hand, the effect may be inverted. Men of factious tempers, of local prejudices, or of sinister designs may, by intrigue, by corruption, or by other means, first obtain the suffrages, and then betray the interests of the people. The question resulting is, whether small or extensive republics are more favorable to the election of proper guardians of the public weal; and it is clearly decided in favor of the latter by two obvious considerations:

In the first place, it is to be remarked that, however small the republic may be, the representatives must be raised to a certain number, in order to guard against the cabals of a few; and that, however large it may be, they must be limited to a certain number, in order to guard against the confusion of a multitude. Hence, the number of representatives in the two cases not being in proportion to that of the two constituents, and being proportionally greater in the small republic, it follows that, if the proportion of fit characters be not less in the large than in the small republic, the former will present a greater option, and consequently a greater probability of a fit choice.

In the next place, as each representative will be chosen by a greater number of citizens in the large than in the small republic, it will be more difficult for unworthy candidates to practice with success the vicious arts by which elections are too often carried; and the suffrages of the people being more free, will be more likely to center in men who possess the most attractive merit and the most diffusive and established character.

It must be confessed that in this, as in most other cases, there is a mean, on both sides of which inconveniences will be found to lie. By enlarging too much the number of electors, you render the representative too little acquainted with all their local circumstances and lesser interests; as by reducing it too much, you render him unduly attached to these and too little fit to comprehend and pursue great and national objects. The federal Constitution forms a happy combination in this respect: the great and aggregate interests being referred to the national, the local and particular to the state legislatures.

The other point of difference is the greater number of citizens and extent of territory which may be brought within the compass of republican than of democratic government; and it is this circumstance principally which renders factious combinations less to be dreaded in the former than in the latter. The smaller the society, the fewer probably will be the distinct parties and interests composing it; the fewer the distinct parties and interests, the more frequently will a majority be found of the same party; and the smaller the number of individuals composing a majority, and the smaller the compass within which they are placed, the more easily will they concert and execute their plans of oppression. Extend the sphere and you take in a greater variety of parties and interests; you make it less probable that a majority of the whole will have a common motive to invade the rights of other citizens; or if such a common motive exists, it will be more difficult for all who feel it to discover their own strength and to act in unison with each other. Besides other impediments, it may be remarked that, where there is a consciousness of unjust or dishonorable purposes, communication is always checked by distrust in proportion to the number whose concurrence is necessary.

Hence, it clearly appears that the same advantage which a republic has over a democracy, in controlling the effects of factions, is enjoyed by a large over a small republic—is

## Analyzing Documents

**1.** The number of factions, or groups, was causing instability, injustice, and confusion.

**2.** Madison supports a republican form of government over a pure democracy because in a pure democracy, "measures are too often decided, not according to the rules of justice and the rights of the minor party, but by the superior force of an interested and overbearing majority." In other words, factions and individuals will tyrannize minorities.

**3.** Sample answer: Yes, because when there are too many groups with differing opinions, it is difficult to arrive at an equitable consensus. In addition, majority rule is inherently unrepresentative if one party is able to outnumber and oppress the rest.

enjoyed by the Union over the States composing it. Does the advantage consist in the substitution of representatives whose enlightened views and virtuous sentiments render them superior to local prejudices and to schemes of injustice? It will not be denied that the representation of the Union will be most likely to possess these requisite endowments. Does it consist in the greater security afforded by a greater variety of parties, against the event of any one party being able to outnumber and oppress the rest? In an equal degree does the increased variety of parties comprised within the Union increase this security? Does it, in fine, consist in the greater obstacles opposed to the concert and accomplishment of the secret wishes of an unjust and interested majority? Here, again, the extent of the Union gives it the most palpable advantage.

The influence of factious leaders may kindle a flame within their particular States but will be unable to spread a general conflagration through the other States. . . . A rage for paper money, for an abolition of debts, for an equal division of property, or for any other improper or wicked project will be less apt to pervade the whole body of the Union than a particular member of it; in the same

proportion as such a malady is more likely to taint a particular county or district than an entire State.

In the extent, and proper structure of the Union, therefore, we behold a republican remedy for the diseases most incident to republican government. And according to the degree of pleasure and pride we feel in being republicans, ought to be our zeal in cherishing the spirit and supporting the character of Federalists.

### Analyzing Documents

Use the passage on these pages to answer the following questions.
1. What does Madison mean by "the mischief of faction"?
2. Why does Madison support a republican form of government over a pure democracy?
3. Do you agree with Madison's point of view? Explain your answer.

## ▶ *The Federalist* No. 51

In the passage below, first published on February 8, 1788, Madison discusses the need for a system of checks and balances to guard against "a gradual concentration of the same powers [of the new government] in the same department."

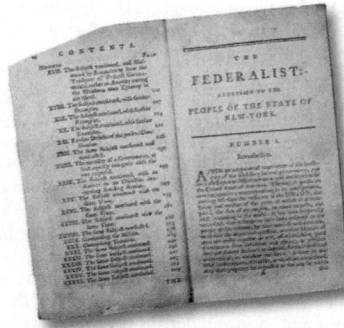

To what expedient, then, shall we finally resort, for maintaining in practice the necessary partition of power among the several departments as laid down in the Constitution? The only answer that can be given is that as all these exterior provisions are found to be inadequate the defect must be supplied, by so contriving the interior structure of the government as that its several constituent parts may, by their mutual relations, be the means of keeping each other in their proper places. Without presuming to undertake a full development of this important idea, I will hazard a few general observations which may perhaps place it in a clearer light, and enable us to form a more correct judgment of the principles and structure of the government planned by the convention.

In order to lay a due foundation for that separate and distinct exercise of the different powers of government, which to a certain extent is admitted on all hands to

be essential to the preservation of liberty, it is evident that each department should have a will of its own; and consequently should be so constituted that the members of each should have as little agency as possible in the appointment of the members of the others. Were this principle rigorously adhered to, it would require that all the appointments for the supreme executive, legislative, and judiciary magistracies should be drawn from the same fountain of authority, the people, through channels having no communication whatever with one another. Perhaps such a plan of constructing the several departments would be less difficult in practice than it may in contemplation appear. Some difficulties, however, and some additional expense would attend the execution of it. Some deviations, therefore, from the principle must be admitted. In the constitution of the judiciary department in particular, it might be inexpedient to insist rigorously on the principle; first, because peculiar qualifications being essential in the members, the primary consideration ought to be to select that mode of choice which best secures these qualifications; secondly, because the permanent tenure by which the appointments are held in that department must soon destroy all sense of dependence on the authority conferring them.

It is equally evident that the members of each department should be as little dependent as possible on those of the others for the emoluments annexed to their offices. Were the executive magistrate, or the judges, not independent of the legislature in this particular, their independence in every other would be merely nominal.

But the great security against a gradual concentration of the several powers in the same department consists in giving to those who administer each department the necessary constitutional means and personal motives to resist encroachments of the others. The provision for defense must in this, as in all other cases, be made commensurate to the danger of attack. Ambition must be made to counteract ambition. The interest of the man must be connected with the constitutional rights of the place. It may be a reflection on human nature that such devices should be necessary to control the abuses of government. But what is government itself but the greatest of all reflections on human nature? If men were angels, no government would be necessary. If angels were to govern men, neither external nor internal controls on government would be necessary. In framing a government which is to be administered by men

James Madison

over men, the great difficulty lies in this: You must first enable the government to control the governed; and in the next place, oblige it to control itself. A dependence on the people is, no doubt, the primary control on the government; but experience has taught mankind the necessity of auxiliary precautions.

This policy of supplying, by opposite and rival interests, the defect of better motives might be traced through the whole system of human affairs, private as well as public. We see it particularly displayed in all the subordinate distributions of power; where the constant aim is to divide and arrange the several offices in such a manner as that each may be a check on the other—that the private interest of every individual may be a sentinel over the public

rights. These inventions of prudence cannot be less requisite in the distribution of the supreme powers of the State.

But it is not possible to give to each department an equal power of self-defense. In republican government, the legislative authority necessarily predominates. The remedy for this inconveniency is to divide the legislature into different branches; and to render them, by different modes of election, and different principles of action, as little connected with each other as the nature of their common functions and their common dependence on the society will admit. It may even be necessary to guard against dangerous encroachments by still further precautions. As the weight of the legislative authority requires that it should be thus divided, the weakness of the executive may require, on the other hand, that it should be fortified. An absolute negative on the legislature appears, at first view, to be the natural defense with which the executive magistrate should be armed. But perhaps it would be neither altogether safe nor alone sufficient. On ordinary occasions it might not be exerted with the requisite firmness, and on extraordinary occasions it might be perfidiously abused. May not this defect of an absolute negative be supplied by some qualified connection between this weaker department and the weaker branch of the stronger department, by which the latter may be led to support the constitutional rights of the former, without being too much detached from the rights of its own department?

If the principles on which these observations are founded be just, as I persuade myself they are, and they be applied as a criterion to the several State constitutions, and to the federal Constitution, it will be found that if the latter does not perfectly correspond with them, the former are infinitely less able to bear such a test.

There are, moreover, two considerations particularly applicable to the federal system of America, which place that system in a very interesting point of view.

*First.* In a single republic, all the power surrendered by the people is submitted to the administration of a single government; and the usurpations are guarded against by a division of the government into distinct and separate departments. In the compound republic of America, the power surrendered by the people is first divided between two distinct governments, and then the portion allotted to each subdivided among distinct and separate departments. Hence a double security arises to the rights of the people. The different governments will control each other, at the same time that each will be controlled by itself.

## Analyzing Documents

**1.** through a system of checks and balances

**2.** The government will be divided into different branches that will be independent of one another.

**3.** "Double security" refers to first, the power of the people being divided between two distinct governments (State and federal), and second, subdividing that power among distinct and separate departments.

*Second.* It is of great importance in a republic not only to guard the society against the oppression of its rulers, but to guard one part of the society against the injustice of the other part. Different interests necessarily exist in different classes of citizens. If a majority be united by a common interest, the rights of the minority will be insecure. There are but two methods of providing against this evil: The one by creating a will in the community independent of the majority—that is, of the society itself; the other, by comprehending in the society so many separate descriptions of citizens as will render an unjust combination of a majority of the whole very improbable, if not impracticable. The first method prevails in all governments possessing an hereditary or self appointed authority. This, at best, is but a precarious security; because a power independent of the society may as well espouse the unjust views of the major as the rightful interests of the minor party, and may possibly be turned against both parties. The second method will be exemplified in the federal republic of the United States. Whilst all authority in it will be derived from and dependent on the society, the society itself will be broken into so many parts, interests, and classes of citizens, that the rights of individuals, or of the minority, will be in little danger from interested combinations of the majority. In a free government the security for civil rights must be the same as that for religious rights. It consists in the one case in the multiplicity of interests, and in the other in the multiplicity of sects. The degree of security in both cases will depend on the number of interests and sects; and this may be presumed to depend on the extent of country and number of people comprehended under the same government. This view of the subject must particularly recommend a proper federal system to all the sincere and considerate friends of republican government, since it shows that in exact proportion as the territory of the Union may be formed into more circumscribed Confederacies, or States, oppressive combinations of a majority will be facilitated: the best security, under the republican forms, for the rights of every class of citizens, will be diminished; and consequently, the stability and independence of some member of the government, the only other security, must be proportionally increased. Justice is the end of government. It is the end of civil society. It ever has been and ever will be pursued until it be obtained, or until liberty be lost in the pursuit. In a society under the forms of which the stronger faction can readily unite and oppress the weaker, anarchy may as truly be said to reign as in a state of nature, where the weaker individual is not secured against the violence of the stronger: And as, in the latter state, even the stronger individuals are prompted by the uncertainty of their condition to submit to a government which may protect the weak as well as themselves. So, in the former state, will the more powerful factions or parties be gradually induced, by a like motive, to wish for a government which will protect all parties, the weaker as well as the more powerful. It can be little doubted that if the State of Rhode Island was separated from the Confederacy and left to itself, the insecurity of rights under the popular form of government within such narrow limits would be displayed by such reiterated oppressions of factious majorities that some power altogether independent of the people would soon be called for by the voice of the very factions whose misrule had proved the necessity of it. In the extended republic of the United States, and among the great variety of interests, parties, and sects which it embraces, a coalition of a majority of the whole society could seldom take place on any other principles than those of justice and the general good; whilst there being thus less danger to a minor from the will of the major party, there must be less pretext, also, to provide for the security of the former, by introducing into the government a will not dependent on the latter; or, in other words, a will independent of the society itself. It is no less certain that it is important, notwithstanding the contrary opinions which have been entertained, that the larger the society, provided it lie within a practicable sphere, the more duly capable it will be of self-government. And happily for the *republican* cause, the practicable sphere may be carried to a very great extent by a judicious modification and mixture of the *federal principle*.

## Analyzing Documents

Use the passage on these pages to answer the following questions.
1. How will the new government guard against placing too much power in the hands of one individual or government body?
2. How will checks and balances be achieved in the new government?
3. What is the "double security" that Madison refers to in this passage?

# ▶ *The Federalist* No. 78

*The Federalist* papers were the brainchild of Alexander Hamilton, who conceived them and recruited James Madison and John Jay to the project. Hamilton is usually credited as the author of 51 of the 85 essays in the collection. Here, he discusses the national judiciary to be established by Article III in the proposed Constitution. He emphasizes the vital need for an independent judiciary and its role in the interpretation of laws and the determination of their constitutionality. First published April 11, 1788.

We proceed now to an examination of the judiciary department of the proposed government. In unfolding the defects of the existing Confederation, the utility and necessity of a federal judicature have been clearly pointed out. It is the less necessary to recapitulate the considerations there urged as the propriety of the institution in the abstract is not disputed; the only questions which have been raised being relative to the manner of constituting it, and to its extent. To these points, therefore, our observations shall be confined.

The manner of constituting it seems to embrace these several objects: 1st. The mode of appointing the judges. 2nd. The tenure by which they are to hold their places. 3rd. The partition of the judiciary authority between different courts and their relations to each other.

*First.* As to the mode of appointing the judges: this is the same with that of appointing the officers of the Union in general and has been so fully discussed in the two last numbers that nothing can be said here which would not be useless repetition.

*Second.* As to the tenure by which the judges are to hold their places: this chiefly concerns their duration in office, the provisions for their support, the precautions for their responsibility.

According to the plan of the convention, all judges who may be appointed by the United States are to hold their offices during good behavior; which is conformable to the most approved of the State constitutions, and among the rest, to that of this State. Its propriety having been drawn into question by the adversaries of that plan is no light symptom of the rage for objection which disorders their imaginations and judgments. The standard of good behavior for the continuance in office of the judicial magistracy is certainly one of the most valuable of the modern improvements in the practice of government. In a monarchy it is an excellent barrier to the despotism of the prince; in a republic it is a no less excellent barrier to the encroachments and oppressions of the representative body. And it is the best expedient which can be devised in any government to secure a steady, upright, and impartial administration of the laws.

Whoever attentively considers the different departments of power must perceive that, in a government in which they are separated from each other, the judiciary, from the nature of its functions, will always be the least dangerous to the political rights of the Constitution; because it will be least in a capacity to annoy or injure them. The executive not only dispenses the honors but holds the sword of the community. The legislature not only commands the purse but prescribes the rules by which the duties and rights of every citizen are to be regulated. The judiciary, on the contrary, has no influence over either the sword or the purse; no direction either of the strength or of the wealth of the society, and can take no active resolution whatever.

This simple view of the matter suggests several important consequences. It proves incontestably that the judiciary is beyond comparison the weakest of the three departments of power; that it can never attack with success either of the other two; and that all possible care is requisite to enable it to defend itself against their attacks. It equally proves that though individual oppression may now and then proceed from the courts of justice, the general liberty of the people can never be endangered from that quarter; I mean so long as the judiciary remains truly distinct from both the legislature and the executive. For I agree that "there is no liberty if the power of judging be not separated from the legislative and executive powers." And it proves, in the last place, that as liberty can have nothing to fear from the judiciary alone, but would have everything to fear from its union with either of the other departments; that as all the effects of such a union must ensue from a dependence of the former on the latter, notwithstanding a nominal and apparent separation; that as, from the natural feebleness of the judiciary, it is in continual jeopardy of being overpowered, awed, or influenced by its coordinate branches; and that as nothing can contribute so much to its firmness and independence as permanency in office, this quality may therefore be justly regarded as an indispensable ingredient in its constitution, and, in a great measure, as the citadel of the public justice and the public security.

The complete independence of the courts of justice is peculiarly essential in a limited Constitution. By a limited Constitution, I understand one which contains certain specified exceptions to the legislative authority; such, for instance, as that it shall pass no bills of attainder, no ex post facto laws, and the like. Limitations of this kind can be preserved in practice no other way than through the medium of courts of justice, whose duty it must be to declare all acts contrary to the manifest tenor of the Constitution void. Without this, all the reservations of particular rights or privileges would amount to nothing.

Some perplexity respecting the rights of the courts to pronounce legislative acts void, because contrary to the Constitution, has arisen from an imagination that the doctrine would imply a superiority of the judiciary to the legislative power. It is urged that the authority which can declare the acts of another void must necessarily be superior to the one whose acts may be declared void. As this doctrine is of great importance in all the American constitutions, a brief discussion of the grounds on which it rests cannot be unacceptable.

There is no position which depends on clearer principles than that every act of a delegated authority, contrary to the tenor of the commission under which it is exercised, is void. No legislative act, therefore, contrary to the Constitution, can be valid. To deny this would be to affirm that the deputy is greater than his principal; that the servant is above his master; that the representatives of the people are superior to the people themselves; that men acting by virtue of powers may do not only what their powers do not authorize, but what they forbid.

If it be said that the legislative body are themselves the constitutional judges of their own powers and that the construction they put upon them is conclusive upon the other departments, it may be answered that this cannot be the natural presumption where it is not to be collected from any particular provisions in the Constitution. It is not otherwise to be supposed that the Constitution could intend to enable the representatives of the people to substitute their will to that of their constituents. It is far more rational to suppose that the courts were designed to be an intermediate body between the people and the legislature in order, among other things, to keep the latter within the limits assigned to their authority. The interpretation of the laws is the proper and peculiar province of the courts. A constitution is, in fact, and must be regarded by the judges as, a fundamental law. It therefore belongs to them to ascertain its meaning as well

Alexander Hamilton

as the meaning of any particular act proceeding from the legislative body. If there should happen to be an irreconcilable variance between the two, that which has the superior obligation and validity ought, of course, to be preferred; or, in other words, the Constitution ought to be preferred to the statute, the intention of the people to the intention of their agents.

Nor does this conclusion by any means suppose a superiority of the judicial to the legislative power. It only supposes that the power of the people is superior to both, and that where the will of the legislature, declared in its statutes, stands in opposition to that of the people, declared in the Constitution, the judges ought to be governed by the latter rather than the former. They ought to regulate their decisions by the fundamental laws rather than by those which are not fundamental.

This exercise of judicial discretion in determining between two contradictory laws is exemplified in a familiar instance. It not uncommonly happens that there are two statutes existing at one time, clashing in whole or in part with each other and neither of them containing any repealing clause or expression. In such a case, it is the province of the courts to liquidate and fix their meaning and operation. So far as they can, by any fair construction, be reconciled to each other, reason and law conspire to dictate that this should be done; where this is impracticable, it becomes a matter of necessity to give effect to one in exclusion of the other. The rule which has obtained in the courts for determining their relative validity is that the last in order of time shall be preferred to the first. But this is a mere rule of construction, not derived from any positive law but from the nature and reason of the thing. It is a rule not enjoined upon the courts by legislative provision but adopted by themselves, as consonant to truth and propriety, for the direction of their conduct as interpreters of the law. They thought it reasonable that between the interfering acts of an equal authority that which was the last indication of its will should have the preference.

But in regard to the interfering acts of a superior and subordinate authority of an original and derivative power, the nature and reason of the thing indicate the converse of that rule as proper to be followed. They teach us that the prior act of a superior ought to be preferred to the subsequent act of an inferior and subordinate authority; and that accordingly, whenever a particular statute contravenes the Constitution, it will be the duty of the judicial tribunals to adhere to the latter and disregard the former.

It can be of no weight to say that the courts, on the pretense of a repugnancy, may substitute their own pleasure to the constitutional intentions of the legislature. This might as well happen in the case of two contradictory statutes; or it might as well happen in every adjudication upon any single statute. The courts must declare the sense of the law; and if they should be disposed to exercise will instead of judgment, the consequence would equally be the substitution of their pleasure to that of the legislative body. The observation, if it prove anything, would prove that there ought to be no judges distinct from that body.

If, then, the courts of justice are to be considered as the bulwarks of a limited Constitution against legislative encroachments, this consideration will afford a strong argument for the permanent tenure of judicial offices, since nothing will contribute so much as this to that independent spirit in the judges which must be essential to the faithful performance of so arduous a duty.

This independence of the judges is equally requisite to guard the Constitution and the rights of individuals from the effects of those ill humors which the arts of designing men, or the influence of particular conjunctures, sometimes disseminate among the people themselves, and which, though they speedily give place to better information, and more deliberate reflection, have a tendency, in the meantime, to occasion dangerous innovations in the government, and serious oppressions of the minor party in the community. Though I trust the friends of the proposed Constitution will never concur with its enemies in questioning that fundamental principle of Republican government which admits the right of the people to alter or abolish the established Constitution whenever they find it inconsistent with their happiness; yet it is not to be inferred from this principle that the representatives of the people, whenever a momentary inclination happens to lay hold of a majority of their constituents incompatible with the provisions in the existing Constitution would, on that account, be justifiable in a violation of those provisions; or that the courts would be under a greater obligation to connive at infractions in this shape than when they had proceeded wholly from the cabals of the representative body. Until the people have, by some solemn and authoritative act, annulled or changed the established form, it is binding upon themselves collectively, as well as individually; and no presumption, or even knowledge of their sentiments, can warrant their representatives in a departure from it prior to such an act. But it is easy to see that it would require an uncommon portion of fortitude in the judges to do their duty as faithful guardians of the Constitution, where legislative invasions of it had been instigated by the major voice of the community.

But it is not with a view to infractions of the Constitution only that the independence of the judges may be an essential safeguard against the effects of occasional ill humors in the society. These sometimes extend no farther than to the injury of the private rights of particular classes of citizens, by unjust and partial laws. Here also the firmness of the judicial magistracy is of vast importance in mitigating the severity and confining the operation of such laws. It not only serves to moderate the immediate mischiefs of those which may have been passed but it operates as a check upon the legislative body in passing them; who, perceiving that obstacles to the success of iniquitous intention are to be expected from the scruples of the courts, are in a manner compelled, by the very motives of the injustice they mediate, to qualify their attempts. This is a circumstance calculated to have more influence upon the character of our governments than but few may be aware of. The benefits of the integrity and moderation of the judiciary have already been felt in more States than one; and though they may have displeased those whose sinister expectations they may have disappointed, they must have commanded the esteem and applause of all the virtuous and disinterested. Considerate men of every description ought to prize whatever will tend to beget or fortify that temper in the courts; as no man can be sure that he may not be tomorrow the victim of a spirit of injustice, by which he may be a gainer today. And every man must now feel that the inevitable tendency of such a spirit is to sap the foundations of public and private confidence and to introduce in its stead universal distrust and distress.

That inflexible and uniform adherence to the rights of the Constitution, and of individuals, which we perceive to be indispensable in the courts of justice, can certainly not be expected from judges who hold their offices by a temporary commission. Periodical appointments, however regulated, or by whomsoever made, would, in some way or other, be fatal to their necessary independence. If the power of making them was committed either to the executive or legislature there would be danger of an improper complaisance to the branch which possessed it; if to both, there would be an unwillingness to hazard the displeasure of either; if to the people, or to persons chosen by them for the special purpose, there would be too great a disposition to consult popularity to justify a reliance that nothing would be consulted but the Constitution and the laws.

There is yet a further and a weighty reason for the permanency of the judicial offices which is deducible from the nature of the qualifications they require. It has been frequently remarked with great propriety that a voluminous code of laws is one of the inconveniences necessarily connected with the advantages of a free government. To avoid an arbitrary discretion in the courts, it is indispensable that they should be bound down by strict rules and precedents which serve to define and point out their duty in every particular case that comes before them; and it will readily be conceived from the variety of controversies which grow out of the folly and wickedness of mankind that the records of those precedents must unavoidably swell to a very considerable bulk and must demand long and laborious study to acquire a competent knowledge of them. Hence it is that there can be but few men in the society who will have suf-

## Analyzing Documents

**1.** According to Hamilton, the term of a judge should be the length of the judge's lifetime as long as he exhibits good behavior.

**2.** Judges are to be an intermediary between the people and the legislature, checking the legislature when it oversteps its bounds. They should remain independent of the other branches of government with regard to decision making, and should regard the Constitution as the nation's fundamental law, deferring to it when making decisions.

**3.** Sample answer: I believe Hamilton would be generally pleased with the judicial system as it exists today. Many of the fundamental principles he puts forth in *The Federalist* No. 78 are visible in our judiciary. Hamilton might frown on the election of judges and those who are seen as "activist." However, he would probably approve of the idea that many judges are free of political constraints and that they still hold the Constitution as the fundamental law of the land.

ficient skill in the laws to qualify them for the stations of judges. And making the proper deductions for the ordinary depravity of human nature, the number must be still smaller of those who unite the requisite integrity with the requisite knowledge. These considerations apprise us that the government can have no great option between fit characters; and that a temporary duration in office which would naturally discourage such characters from quitting a lucrative line of practice to accept a seat on the bench would have a tendency to throw the administration of justice into hands less able and less well qualified to conduct it with utility and dignity. In the present circumstances of this country and in those in which it is likely to be for a long time to come, the disadvantages on this score would be greater than they may at first sight appear; but it must be confessed that they are far inferior to those which present themselves under the other aspects of the subject.

Upon the whole, there can be no room to doubt that the convention acted wisely in copying from the models of those constitutions which have established *good behavior* as the tenure of their judicial offices, in point of duration; and that so far from being blamable on this account, their plan would have been inexcusably defective if it had wanted this important feature of good government. The experience of Great Britain affords an illustrious comment on the excellence of the institution.

### Analyzing Documents

Use the passage on these pages to answer the following questions.
1. According to Hamilton, how long should judges stay in office?
2. What does Hamilton say is the role of judges?
3. What might Hamilton say about the judicial system as it exists today?

## ▶The Emancipation Proclamation

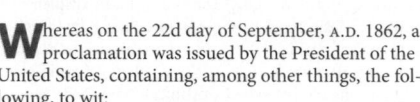

President Abraham Lincoln issued the Emancipation Proclamation on January 1, 1863, at the beginning of the third year of the bloody Civil War. The proclamation declared "that all persons held as slaves" within the rebellious states "are, and henceforward shall be free." Although the Emancipation Proclamation applied to a limited geographical area, it fundamentally changed the nature of the war to a conflict focused on freedom for all.

**W**hereas on the 22d day of September, A.D. 1862, a proclamation was issued by the President of the United States, containing, among other things, the following, to wit:

"That on the 1st day of January, A.D. 1863, all persons held as slaves within any State or designated part of a State the people whereof shall then be in rebellion against the United States shall be then, thenceforward, and forever free; and the Executive Government of the United States, including the military and naval authority thereof, will recognize and maintain the freedom of such persons and will do no act or acts to repress such persons, or any of them, in any efforts they may make for their actual freedom.

"That the executive will on the 1st day of January aforesaid, by proclamation, designate the States and parts of States, if any, in which the people thereof, respectively, shall then be in rebellion against the United States; and the fact that any State or the people thereof shall on that day be in good faith represented in the Congress of the United States by members chosen thereto at elections wherein a majority of the qualified voters of such States shall have participated shall, in the absence of strong countervailing testimony, be deemed conclusive evidence that such State and the people thereof are not then in rebellion against the United States."

Now, therefore, I, Abraham Lincoln, President of the United States, by virtue of the power in me vested as Commander-in-Chief of the Army and Navy of the United States in time of actual armed rebellion against the authority and government of the United States, and as a fit and necessary war measure for suppressing said rebellion, do, on this 1st day of January, A.D. 1863, and in accordance with my purpose so to do, publicly proclaimed for the full period of one hundred days from the first day above mentioned, order and designate as the States and parts of States wherein the people thereof, respectively, are this day in rebellion against the United States the following, to wit:

Arkansas, Texas, Louisiana (except the parishes of St. Bernard, Plaquemines, Jefferson, St. John, St. Charles, St. James, Ascension, Assumption, Terrebonne, Lafourche, St. Mary, St. Martin, and Orleans, including the city of New Orleans), Mississippi, Alabama, Florida, Georgia, South Carolina, North Carolina, and Virginia (except the forty-eight counties designated as West Virginia, and also the counties of Berkeley, Accomac, Northhampton, Elizabeth City, York, Princess Anne, and Norfolk, including the cities of Norfolk and Portsmouth), and which excepted parts are for the present left precisely as if this proclamation were not issued.

And by virtue of the power and for the purpose aforesaid, I do order and declare that all persons held as slaves within said designated States and parts of States are, and henceforward shall be, free; and that the Executive Government of the United States, including the military and naval authorities thereof, will recognize and maintain the freedom of said persons.

And I hereby enjoin upon the people so declared to be free to abstain from all violence, unless in necessary self-defense; and I recommend to them that, in all cases when allowed, they labor faithfully for reasonable wages.

And I further declare and make known that such persons of suitable condition will be received into the armed service of the United States to garrison forts, positions, stations, and other places, and to man vessels of all sorts in said service.

And upon this act, sincerely believed to be an act of justice, warranted by the Constitution upon military necessity, I invoke the considerate judgment of mankind and the gracious favor of Almighty God.

## Analyzing Documents

Use the passage on these pages to answer the following questions.
1. Recall the eight roles and the powers of the President. Which role and which power allow Lincoln to proclaim freedom for slaves?
2. In addition to proclaiming an end to slavery, what other action does the Proclamation declare? Why is this action significant?
3. Why was the Proclamation important even though no slaves were freed immediately?

Over the course of the Civil War, nearly 180,000 African Americans wore the Union uniform. ▶

HISTORICAL DOCUMENTS

## Analyzing Documents

**1.** role: chief executive; power: ordinance power

**2.** In addition to ending slavery, the Proclamation declares that "military and naval authorities will recognize and maintain the freedom of said persons."

**3.** It changed the nature of the Civil War to a conflict focused on freedom for all, instead of a war about slavery.

# ▶Declaration of Sentiments

Elizabeth Cady Stanton and Lucretia Mott, two activists in the movement to abolish slavery, called together the first conference to address women's rights and issues in Seneca Falls, New York, in 1848. Using the Declaration of Independence as a model, the Declaration of Sentiments demanded that the rights of women be acknowledged and respected.

When, in the course of human events, it becomes necessary for one portion of the family of man to assume among the people of the earth a position different from that which they have hitherto occupied, but one to which the laws of nature and of nature's God entitle them, a decent respect to the opinions of mankind requires that they should declare the causes that impel them to such a course.

We hold these truths to be self-evident: that all men and women are created equal; that they are endowed by their Creator with certain inalienable rights; that among these are life, liberty, and the pursuit of happiness; that to secure these rights governments are instituted, deriving their just powers from the consent of the governed. Whenever any form of government becomes destructive of these ends, it is the right of those who suffer from it to refuse allegiance to it, and to insist upon the institution of a new government, laying its foundation on such principles, and organizing its powers in such form, as to them shall seem most likely to effect their safety and happiness. Prudence, indeed, will dictate that governments long established should not be changed for light and transient causes; and accordingly all experience hath shown that mankind are more disposed to suffer. while evils are sufferable, than to right themselves by abolishing the forms to which they are accustomed. But when a long train of abuses and usurpations, pursuing invariably the same object, evinces a design to reduce them under absolute despotism, it is their duty to throw off such government, and to provide new guards for their future security. Such has been the patient sufferance of the women under this government, and such is now the necessity which constrains them to demand the equal station to which they are entitled. The history of mankind is a history of repeated injuries and usurpations on the part of man toward woman, having in direct object the establishment of an absolute tyranny over her. To prove this, let facts be submitted to a candid world.

- He has never permitted her to exercise her inalienable right to the elective franchise.
- He has compelled her to submit to laws, in the formation of which she had no voice.
- He has withheld from her rights which are given to the most ignorant and degraded men—both natives and foreigners.
- Having deprived her of this first right of a citizen, the elective franchise, thereby leaving her without representation in the halls of legislation, he has oppressed her on all sides.
- He has made her, if married, in the eye of the law, civilly dead.
- He has taken from her all right in property, even to the wages she earns.
- He has made her, morally, an irresponsible being, as she can commit many crimes with impunity, provided they be done in the presence of her husband. In the covenant of marriage, she is compelled to promise obedience to her husband, he becoming, to all intents and purposes, her master—the law giving him power to deprive her of her liberty, and to administer chastisement.
- He has so framed the laws of divorce, as to what shall be the proper causes, and in case of separation, to whom the guardianship of the children shall be given, as to be wholly regardless of the happiness of women—the law, in all cases, going upon a false supposition of the supremacy of man, and giving all power into his hands.
- After depriving her of all rights as a married woman, if single, and the owner of property, he has taxed her to support a government which recognizes her only when her property can be made profitable to it.
- He has monopolized nearly all the profitable employments, and from those she is permitted to follow, she receives but a scanty remuneration.
- He closes against her all the avenues to wealth and distinction which he considers most honorable to himself. As a teacher of theology, medicine, or law, she is not known.
- He has denied her the facilities for obtaining a thorough education, all colleges being closed against her.
- He allows her in church, as well as state, but a subordinate position, claiming apostolic authority for her exclusion from the ministry, and, with some exceptions, from any public participation in the affairs of the church.

Lucretia Mott ▶

◀ Elizabeth Cady Stanton

- He has created a false public sentiment by giving to the world a different code of morals for men and women, by which moral delinquencies which exclude women from society, are not only tolerated, but deemed of little account in man.

- He has usurped the prerogative of Jehovah himself, claiming it as his right to assign for her a sphere of action, when that belongs to her conscience and to her God.

- He has endeavored, in every way that he could, to destroy her confidence in her own powers, to lessen her self-respect, and to make her willing to lead a dependent and abject life.

Now, in view of this entire disfranchisement of one-half the people of this country, their social and religious degradation—in view of the unjust laws above mentioned, and because women do feel themselves aggrieved, oppressed, and fraudulently deprived of their most sacred rights, we insist that they have immediate admission to all the rights and privileges which belong to them as citizens of the United States.

## Analyzing Documents

Use the passage on these pages to answer the following questions.

1. Why did Mott and Stanton base their Declaration on the Declaration of Independence? What additional goals does the Declaration of Sentiments include?

2. The Declaration of Sentiments attracted much controversy when it was first published. Why might this have been so?

3. Why is the Declaration of Sentiments an important document in the history of securing rights for all Americans?

## Analyzing Documents

**1.** Sample answer: Mott and Stanton based their declaration on the Declaration of Independence to show the omission of "women" alongside "men are created equal" in the Declaration of Independence. That document also lent their declaration weightiness and authority. Additional goals included a desire for an equal station in government, a voice in the formation of laws, and a thorough education. They wanted immediate admission to all the rights and privileges that belonged to them as citizens.

**2.** Sample answer: At the time, it was a radical idea to think of women having an equal place in society and enjoying the full rights of citizenship.

**3.** The Declaration of Sentiments demands equality regardless of gender, and the same could be said for other groups who have experienced discrimination.

## Analyzing Documents

**1.** The following rights are also reflected in the Bill of Rights: prohibition of cruel and unusual punishment, freedom of religion, freedom of opinion and expression, and freedom of peaceful assembly and association.

**2.** Additional rights that are not included in the U.S. Constitution include free choice of employment, the right to an adequate standard of living, and the right to education. Sample answer: These rights are most likely not spelled out in the Constitution because they are inherent to our democratic system of government.

**3.** Sample answer: The existence of this declaration would put pressure on oppressive regimes to provide basic liberties and freedoms.

**HISTORICAL DOCUMENTS**

# ▶ Universal Declaration of Human Rights

The General Assembly of the United Nations adopted this declaration on December 10, 1948. The document sets forth the basic liberties and freedoms to which all people are entitled.

**Article 1** All human beings are born free and equal in dignity and rights. They are endowed with reason and conscience and should act toward one another in a spirit of brotherhood.

**Article 2** Everyone is entitled to all the rights and freedoms set forth in this Declaration, without distinction of any kind, such as race, colour, sex, language, religion, political or other opinion, national or social origin, property, birth or other status. . . .

**Article 3** Everyone has the right to life, liberty and security of person.

**Article 4** No one shall be held in slavery or servitude. . . .

**Article 5** No one shall be subjected to torture or to cruel, inhuman or degrading treatment or punishment.

**Article 9** No one shall be subjected to arbitrary arrest, detention or exile.

**Article 13** Everyone has the right to freedom of movement. . . .

**Article 18** Everyone has the right to freedom of thought, conscience and religion. . . .

**Article 19** Everyone has the right to freedom of opinion and expression. . . .

**Article 20** Everyone has the right to freedom of peaceful assembly and association. . . .

**Article 23** Everyone has the right to work, to free choice of employment, to just and favourable conditions of work and to protection against unemployment. . . .

**Article 25** Everyone has the right to a standard of living adequate for the health and well-being of himself and of his family, including food, clothing, housing and medical care and necessary social services, and the right to security in the event of unemployment, sickness, disability, widowhood, old age or other lack of livelihood in circumstances beyond his control.

**Article 26** Everyone has the right to education. Education shall be free, at least in the elementary and fundamental stages. . . .

## Analyzing Documents

Use the passage on this page to answer the following questions.
1. Which of the above rights are reflected in the Bill of Rights in the U.S. Constitution?
2. What additional rights are included in these excerpts? Why do you think these rights are not spelled out in the U.S. Constitution?
3. In what ways might the existence of this declaration benefit people living under an oppressive regime?

▲ A young girl carries water in Chennai, India

# Supreme Court Glossary

### *Abrams* v. *United States* (1919)

*Decision:* The Court ruled 7-2 that Congress could make it illegal to criticize the United States government and to encourage others not to obey the laws. When the defendants were convicted of distributing pamphlets that opposed certain U.S. military policies during World War I and urging people not to participate in the war effort, they were sentenced to 20 years imprisonment. The Court upheld their convictions. In his dissent, Justice Oliver Wendell Holmes argued that "the surreptitious publishing of a silly leaflet by an unknown man" did not create a clear and imminent danger to the United States and therefore should be protected by the First Amendment. The case was essentially overruled 50 years later in *Brandenburg* v. *Ohio*, which held that "mere advocacy" is constitutionally protected unless it is actually likely to produce imminent lawless action.

### *Agostini* v. *Felton* (1997)

*Decision:* The Court decided that it was appropriate to reconsider *Aguilar* v. *Felton* as subsequent cases had undermined several of the assumptions, for example that public employees placed at parochial schools would "inevitably inculcate religion," upon which the decision was based. The Court then found that New York City's Title I Program did not violate any of the criteria used "to evaluate whether government aid has the effect of advancing religion: it does not result in governmental indoctrination; define its recipients by reference to religion; or create an excessive entanglement." As a result, the Court concluded that "a federally funded program providing supplemental, remedial instruction to disadvantaged children on a neutral basis is not invalid under the Establishment Clause when such instruction is given on the premises of sectarian schools by government employees pursuant to a program containing safeguards" against excessive entanglement between government and religion.

### *Alden* v. *Maine* (1999)

*Decision:* In a 5-4 decision, the Court held that Congress does not have the power to force States to submit to being sued in their own courts without their consent. The structure of the Constitution and the Eleventh Amendment give the States "sovereign immunity" that allows the States to prevent people from suing them in their own courts, and Congress does not have the power to override this immunity.

### *American Insurance Association* v. *Garamendi* (2003)

*Decision:* California's Holocaust Victim Insurance Relief Act interferes with the President's conduct of the nation's foreign policy and is therefore unconstitutional. Although the executive agreements do not specifically prohibit State action, they do pre-empt (override) the State's authority to act on the same subject matter, even in the absence of any direct conflict.

### *Baker* v. *Carr* (1962)

*Decision:* Although in past decisions, the Court had called apportionment cases a "political thicket" and declined to intervene, in *Baker*, the Court held that it was within the scope of the judicial branch of government to rule on matters of legislative apportionment. The Court further ruled that Baker and other Tennessee citizens were entitled to a trial deciding whether their constitutionally guaranteed right to equal protection of the law (14th Amendment) had been denied. *Baker* opened the door to later cases on apportionment which led to the eventual reapportioning of nearly every State legislature according to population.

### *Board of Estimate of City of New York* v. *Morris* (1989)

*Decision:* The reapportionment requirement of "one-person, one-vote" applies to the Board of Estimate. The Board has sufficient legislative functions that its composition must fairly represent city voters on an approximately equal basis. The fact that some members are elected city-wide is one factor to be considered in evaluating the fairness of the electoral structure, but it is not determinative. The City's expressed interests—that the Board be effective and that it accommodate natural and political boundaries as well as local interests—does not justify the size of the deviation from the "one-person, one-vote" ideal. The City could structure the Board in other ways that would further these interests while minimizing the discrimination in voting power.

### *Bob Jones University* v. *United States* (1983)

(14th Amendment in conflict with 1st Amendment) Bob Jones University, a private school, denied admission to applicants in an interracial marriage or who "espouse" interracial marriage or dating. The Internal Revenue Service then denied tax exempt status to the school because of racial discrimination. The university appealed, claiming their policy was based on the Bible. The Court upheld the IRS ruling, stating that ". . . Government has a fundamental overriding interest in eradicating racial discrimination in education."

### *Brandenburg* v. *Ohio* (1969)

*Decision:* The Court ruled unanimously that advocacy is protected under the First Amendment "except where such advocacy is directed to inciting or producing imminent lawless action and is likely to incite or produce such action." Therefore a Ku Klux Klan leader could not be convicted under an Ohio statute that prohibited advocating violence. The opinion effectively overruled prior Supreme Court cases such as *Whitney v. California* and *Abrams v. United States* that had allowed criminal convictions merely for urging violence or other unlawful acts.

### Brown v. Board of Education of Topeka (1954)
(14th Amendment, Equal Protection Clause) Probably no twentieth century Supreme Court decision so deeply stirred and changed life in the United States as *Brown*. A 10-year-old Topeka girl, Linda Brown, was not permitted to attend her neighborhood school because she was an African American. The Court heard arguments about whether segregation itself was a violation of the Equal Protection Clause and found that it was, commenting that "in the field of public education the doctrine of 'separate but equal' has no place. . . . Segregation is a denial of the equal protection of the laws." The decision overturned *Plessy v. Ferguson*, 1896.

### City of Boerne, Texas v. Flores (1997)
*Decision:* A 6-3 majority ruled that the Religious Freedom Restoration Act was unconstitutional. The majority concluded that the Act was not a legitimate attempt by Congress to implement the Free Exercise Clause of the First Amendment but was really an attempt to change constitutional law as previously determined by the Court. The Act therefore violated separation of powers.

### The Civil Rights Cases (1883)
(14th Amendment, Equal Protection Clause) The Civil Rights Act of 1875 included punishments of businesses that practiced discrimination. The Court ruled on a number of cases involving the Acts in 1883, finding that the Constitution, "while prohibiting discrimination by governments, made no provisions . . . for acts of racial discrimination by private individuals." The decision limited the impact of the Equal Protection Clause, giving tacit approval for segregation in the private sector.

### Cruzan v. Missouri (1990)
(14th Amendment, Due Process Clause) After Nancy Beth Cruzan was left in a "persistent vegetative state" by a car accident, Missouri officials refused to comply with her parents' request that the hospital terminate life-support. The Court upheld the State policy under which officials refused to withdraw treatment, rejecting the argument that the Due Process Clause of the 14th Amendment gave the parents the right to refuse treatment on their daughter's behalf. Although individuals have the right to refuse medical treatment, "incompetent" persons are not able to exercise this right; without "clear and convincing" evidence that Cruzan desired the withdrawal of treatment, the State could legally act to preserve her life.

### Dennis v. United States (1951)
(1st Amendment, freedom of speech) The Smith Act of 1940 made it a crime for any person to work for the violent overthrow of the United States in peacetime or war. Eleven Communist party leaders, including Dennis, had been convicted of violating the Smith Act, and they appealed. The Court upheld the Act.

### District of Columbia v. Heller (2008)
*Decision:* The Court ruled 5 to 4 that Washington, D.C.'s gun law was unconstitutional. The majority concluded that the Second Amendment "right of the people to keep and bear Arms" meant that individuals could have weapons for self-defense. An outright ban on gun ownership was therefore unconstitutional. In addition, since dismantled or disabled weapons would not be useful for self-defense, the part of the law requiring that all guns, including shotguns and rifles, be kept unloaded and either taken apart or disabled by a trigger lock was also unconstitutional. In dissent, Justice Breyer suggested a balancing test, under which gun control laws could be constitutional when they supported a compelling governmental interest in preventing crime.

### Dred Scott v. Sandford (1857)
(5th Amendment, individual rights) This decision upheld property rights over human rights by saying that Dred Scott, a slave, could not become a free man just because he had traveled in "free soil" States with his master. A badly divided nation was further fragmented by the decision. "Free soil" federal laws and the Missouri Compromise line of 1820 were held unconstitutional because they deprived a slave owner of the right to his "property" without just compensation. This narrow reading of the Constitution, a landmark case of the Court, was most clearly stated by Chief Justice Roger B. Taney, a States' rights advocate.

### Edwards v. South Carolina (1963)
(1st Amendment, freedom of speech and assembly) A group of mostly African American civil rights activists held a rally at the South Carolina State Capitol, protesting segregation. A hostile crowd gathered and the rally leaders were arrested and convicted for "breach of the peace." The Court overturned the convictions, saying, "The Fourteenth Amendment does not permit a State to make criminal the peaceful expression of unpopular views."

### Engel v. Vitale (1962)
(1st Amendment, Establishment Clause) The State Board of Regents of New York required the recitation of a 22-word nonsectarian prayer at the beginning of each school day. A group of parents filed suit against the required prayer, claiming it violated their 1st Amendment rights. The Court found New York's action to be unconstitutional, observing, "There can be no doubt that. . . religious beliefs [are] embodied in the Regent's prayer."

### Escobedo v. Illinois (1964)

(6th Amendment, right to counsel) In a case involving a murder confession by a person known to Chicago-area police who was not afforded counsel while under interrogation, the Court extended the "exclusionary rule" to illegal confessions in State court proceedings. Carefully defining an "Escobedo Rule," the Court said, "where. . . the investigation is no longer a general inquiry . . . but has begun to focus on a particular suspect . . . (and where) the suspect has been taken into custody . . . the suspect has requested . . . his lawyer, and the police have not . . . warned him of his right to remain silent, the accused has been denied . . . counsel in violation of the Sixth Amendment."

### Ex parte Milligan (1866)

(Article II, executive powers) An Indiana man was arrested, treated as a prisoner of war, and imprisoned by a military court during the Civil War under presidential order. He claimed that his rights to a fair trial were interfered with and that military courts had no authority outside of "conquered territory." He was released because, "the Constitution . . . is a law for rulers and people, equally in war and peace, and covers . . . all . . . men, at all times, and under all circumstances." The Court held that presidential powers to suspend the writ of habeas corpus in time of war did not extend to creating another court system run by the military.

### Flast v. Cohen (1968)

*Decision:* The Supreme Court concluded that the rule announced in *Frothingham* v. *Mellon* expressed a practical policy of judicial self-restraint rather than an absolute constitutional limitation on the power of federal courts to hear taxpayer suits. While mere status as a federal taxpayer ordinarily will not give sufficient "standing" to allow a person to challenge the constitutionality of a federal law, there may be times when taxpayers are appropriate plaintiffs. *Flast* v. *Cohen*, in which plaintiffs argued that the First Amendment specifically prohibited taxing them in order to support religious activities, was one in which their role as taxpayers was well suited to the challenge they sought to assert. The Court ruled that they had standing to sue, and allowed them to proceed with their case.

### Furman v. Georgia (1972)

(8th Amendment, capital punishment) Three different death penalty cases, including *Furman,* raised the question of racial imbalances in the use of death sentences by State courts. Furman had been convicted and sentenced to death in Georgia. In deciding to overturn existing State death-penalty laws, the Court noted that there was an "apparent arbitrariness of the use of the sentence. . . ." Many States rewrote their death-penalty statutes and these were generally upheld in *Gregg* v. *Georgia,*1976.

### Gibbons v. Ogden (1824)

(Supremacy Clause) This decision involved a careful examination of the power of Congress to "regulate interstate commerce." Aaron Ogden's exclusive New York ferry license gave him the right to operate steamboats to and from New York. He said that Thomas Gibbons's federal "coasting license" did not include "landing rights" in New York City. The Court invalidated the New York licensing regulations, holding that federal regulations should take precedence under the Supremacy Clause. The decision strengthened the power of the United States to regulate any interstate business relationship. Federal regulation of the broadcasting industry, oil pipelines, and banking are all based on *Gibbons*.

### Gideon v. Wainwright (1963)

(6th Amendment, right to counsel) In 1961 a Florida court found Clarence Earl Gideon guilty of breaking and entering and sentenced him to five years in prison. Gideon appealed his case to the Supreme Court on the basis that he had been unconstitutionally denied counsel during his trial due to Florida's policy of only providing appointed counsel in capital cases. The Court granted Gideon a new trial, and he was found not guilty with the help of a court-appointed attorney. The "Gideon Rule" upheld the 6th Amendment's guarantee of counsel of all poor persons facing a felony charge, a further incorporation of Bill of Rights guarantees into State constitutions.

### Gitlow v. New York (1925)

(1st Amendment, freedom of speech) A New York socialist, Gitlow, was convicted under a State law on "criminal anarchy" for distributing copies of a "left-wing manifesto." For the first time, the Court considered whether the 1st Amendment applied to State laws. The case helped to establish what came to be known as the "incorporation" doctrine, under which, it was argued, the provisions of the 1st Amendment were "incorporated" by the 14th Amendment, thus applying to State as well as federal laws. Although New York law was not overruled in this case, the decision clearly indicated that the Supreme Court could make such a ruling. See also *Powell* v. *Alabama,* 1932.

### Goss v. Lopez (1975)

(14th Amendment, Due Process Clause) Ten Ohio students were suspended from their schools without hearings. The students challenged the suspensions, claiming that the absence of a preliminary hearing violated their 14th Amendment right to due process. The Court agreed, holding that "having chosen to extend the right to an education. . . Ohio may not withdraw that right on grounds of misconduct, absent fundamentally fair procedures to determine whether the misconduct has occurred, and must recognize a student's legitimate entitlement to a public education as a property interest that is protected by the Due Process Clause."

### Gregg v. Georgia (1976)

(8th Amendment, cruel and unusual punishment) A Georgia jury sentenced Troy Gregg to death after finding him guilty on two counts each of murder and armed robbery. Gregg appealed the sentence, claiming that it violated the "cruel and unusual punishment" clause of the 8th Amendment and citing *Furman* v. *Georgia*, 1972, in which the court held that Georgia's application of the death penalty was unfair and arbitrary. However, the Court upheld Gregg's sentence, stating for the first time that "punishment of death does not invariably violate the Constitution."

### Griswold v. Connecticut (1965)

(14th Amendment, Due Process Clause) A Connecticut law forbade the use of "any drug, medicinal article, or instrument for the purpose of preventing conception." Griswold, director of Planned Parenthood in New Haven, was arrested for counseling married persons and, after conviction, appealed. The Court overturned the Connecticut law, saying that "various guarantees (of the Constitution) create zones of privacy..." and questioning, "...would we allow the police to search the sacred precincts of marital bedrooms...?" The decision is significant for raising for more careful inspection the concept of "unenumerated rights" in the 9th Amendment, later central to *Roe* v. *Wade*, 1973.

### Grutter v. Bollinger; Gratz v. Bollinger (2003)

*Decision:* (*Gratz*) The policy of the University of Michigan, giving undergraduate applicants twenty points just for being a member of a racial or ethnic group, violates the Equal Protection Clause of the 14th Amendment. The policy discriminates on the basis of race, but is not narrowly tailored to create a diverse student body. (*Grutter*) The policy of the University of Michigan's law school, considering an applicant's racial or ethnic background as just one factor in attempting to admit a diverse student body, is constitutional. Because the law school considers each applicant individually, and does not assign an inflexible value for race, the policy creates a diverse student body without discriminating on the basis of race.

### Hazelwood School District v. Kuhlmeier (1988)

(1st Amendment, freedom of speech) In 1983, the principal of Hazelwood East High School in Missouri removed two articles from the upcoming issue of the student newspaper, deeming their content "inappropriate, personal, sensitive, and unsuitable for student readers." Several students sued, claiming that their right to freedom of expression had been violated. The Court upheld the principal's action: "a school need not tolerate student speech that is inconsistent with its basic educational mission, even though the government could not censor similar speech outside the school." School officials had full control over school-sponsored activities "so long as their actions are reasonably related to legitimate pedagogical concerns...."

### Heart of Atlanta Motel, Inc. v. United States (1964)

*Decision:* The Court ruled that Congress could outlaw racial segregation of private facilities that are engaged in interstate commerce. The Court's decision stated, "If it is interstate commerce that feels the pinch, it does not matter how 'local' the operation which applies the squeeze.... The power of Congress to promote interstate commerce also includes the power to regulate the local incidents thereof, including local activities... which have a substantial and harmful effect upon that commerce."

### Hutchinson v. Proxmire (1979)

*Decision:* The Court held that the Speech or Debate Clause gives members of Congress immunity from suit for defamatory statements made within the legislative chambers, but the privilege does not extend to comments made in other locations, even if they merely repeat what was said in Congress. The newsletters and press release were not within the deliberative process nor were they essential to the deliberation of the Senate. They also were not part of the "informing function" of members of Congress, since they were not a part of legislative function or process. The comments were merely designed to convey information on the Senator's individual positions and beliefs. Finally, although Hutchinson had received extensive attention in the media as a result of his receipt of the Golden Fleece Award, he was not a public figure prior to that controversy and thus is entitled to the greater protection against defamation that is extended to non-public figures. The fact that the public may have an interest in governmental expenditures does not make Hutchinson himself a public figure.

### Illinois v. Wardlow (2000)

*Decision:* The Supreme Court refused to say that flight from the police will always justify a stop or that it will never do so. Instead, the Court ruled that flight can be an important factor in determining whether police have "reasonable suspicion" to stop a suspect. The trial court will have to determine in each case whether the information available to the police officers, including the fact of a suspect's flight, was sufficient to support the stop.

### In Re Gault (1966)

(14th Amendment, Due Process Clause) Prior to the *Gault* case, proceedings against juvenile offenders were generally handled as "family law," not "criminal law" and provided few due process guarantees. Gerald Gault was assigned to six years in a State juvenile detention facility for an alleged obscene phone call. He was not provided counsel and not permitted to confront or cross-examine the principal witness. The Court overturned the juvenile proceedings and required that States provide juveniles "some of the due process guarantees of adults," including a right to a phone call, to counsel, to cross-examine, to confront their accuser, and to be advised of their right to silence.

### Johnson v. Santa Clara Transportation Agency (1987)

(Discrimination) Under their affirmative action plan, the Transportation Agency in Santa Clara, California, was authorized to "consider as one factor the sex of a qualified applicant" in an effort to combat the significant underrepresentation of women in certain job classifications. When the Agency promoted Diane Joyce, a qualified woman, over Paul Johnson, a qualified man, for the job of road dispatcher, Johnson sued, claiming that the Agency's consideration of the sex of the applicants violated Title VII of the Civil Rights Act of 1964. The Court upheld the Agency's promotion policy, arguing that the affirmative action plan created no "absolute bar" to the advancement of men but rather represented "a moderate, flexible, case-by-case approach to effecting a gradual improvement in the representation of minorities and women . . . in the Agency's work force, and [was] fully consistent with Title VII."

### Korematsu v. United States (1944)

*Decision:* The Court upheld the military order in light of the circumstances presented by World War II. "Pressing public necessity may sometimes justify the existence of restrictions which curtail the civil rights of a single racial group." The Court noted, however, that racial antagonism itself could never form a legitimate basis for the restrictions.

### Lemon v. Kurtzman (1971)

(1st Amendment, Establishment Clause) In overturning State laws regarding aid to church-supported schools in this and a similar Rhode Island case, the Court created the Lemon test limiting ". . . excessive government entanglement with religion." The Court noted that any State law about aid to religion must meet three criteria: (1) purpose of the aid must be clearly secular, (2) its primary effect must neither advance nor inhibit religion, and (3) it must avoid "excessive entanglement of government with religion."

### Mapp v. Ohio (1962)

(4th and 14th Amendments, illegal evidence and Due Process Clause) Admitting evidence gained by illegal searches was permitted by some States before *Mapp*. Cleveland police raided Dollree Mapp's home without a warrant and found obscene materials. She appealed her conviction, saying that the 4th and 14th Amendments protected her against improper police behavior. The Court agreed, extending "exclusionary rule" protections to citizens in State courts, saying that the prohibition against unreasonable searches would be "meaningless" unless evidence gained in such searches was "excluded." *Mapp* developed the concept of "incorporation" begun in *Gitlow* v. *New York,* 1925.

### Marbury v. Madison (1803)

(Article III, judicial powers) After defeat in the 1800 election, President Adams appointed many Federalists to the federal courts, but James Madison, the new secretary of state, refused to deliver the commissions. William Marbury, one of the appointees, asked the Supreme Court to enforce the delivery of his commission based on a provision of the Judiciary Act of 1789 that allowed the Court to hear such cases on original jurisdiction. The Court refused Marbury's request, finding that the relevant portion of the Judiciary Act was in conflict with the Constitution. This decision, written by Chief Justice Marshall, established the evaluation of federal laws' constitutionality, or "judicial review," as a power of the Supreme Court.

### McCulloch v. Maryland (1819)

(Article I, Section 8, Necessary and Proper Clause) Called the "Bank of the United States" case. A Maryland law required federally chartered banks to use only a special paper to print paper money, which amounted to a tax. James McCulloch, the cashier of the Baltimore branch of the bank, refused to use the paper, claiming that States could not tax the Federal Government. The Court declared the Maryland law unconstitutional, commenting ". . . the power to tax implies the power to destroy."

### Miranda v. Arizona (1966)

(5th, 6th, and 14th Amendments, rights of the accused) Arrested for kidnapping and sexual assault, Ernesto Miranda signed a confession including a statement that he had "full knowledge of [his] legal rights. . . ." After conviction, he appealed, claiming that without counsel and without warnings, the confession was illegally gained. The Court agreed with Miranda that "he must be warned prior to any questioning that he has the right to remain silent, that anything he says can be used against him in a court of law, that he has the right to. . . an attorney and that if he cannot afford an attorney one will be appointed for him. . . ." Although later modified by *Nix* v. *Williams,* 1984, and other cases, *Miranda* firmly upheld citizen rights to fair trials in State courts.

### New Jersey v. T.L.O. (1985)

(4th and 14th Amendments) After T.L.O., a New Jersey high school student, denied an accusation that she had been smoking in the school lavatory, a vice-principal searched her purse and found cigarettes, marijuana, and evidence that T.L.O. had been involved in marijuana dealing at the school. T.L.O. was then sentenced to probation by a juvenile court, but appealed on the grounds that the evidence against her had been obtained by an "unreasonable" search. The Court rejected T.L.O.'s arguments, stating that the school had a "legitimate need to maintain an environment in which learning can take place," and that to do this "requires some easing of the restrictions to which searches by public authorities are ordinarily subject. . ." The Court thus created a "reasonable suspicion" rule for school searches, a change from the "probable cause" requirement in the wider society.

### New York Times v. Sullivan (1964)

*Decision:* A unanimous Court announced that a public official could not win a suit for defamation (false statement) unless the statement was made with "actual malice," meaning either with the knowledge that it was false or with "reckless disregard" of the truth. The Court found a national commitment to "uninhibited, robust, and wide-open" debate on issues of public concern—even when this included "vehement, caustic, and sometimes unpleasantly sharp attacks on government and public officials." Without an "actual malice" standard, citizens might be unwilling to criticize elected officials for fear of being sued if something they said turned out to be inaccurate.

### New York Times v. United States (1971)

(1st Amendment, freedom of the press) In 1971 The New York Times obtained copies of classified Defense Department documents, later known as the "Pentagon Papers," which revealed instances in which the Johnson Administration had deceived Congress and the American people regarding U.S. policies during the Vietnam War. A U.S. district court issued an injunction against the publication of the documents, claiming that it might endanger national security. On appeal, the Supreme Court cited the 1st Amendment guarantee of a free press and refused to uphold the injunction against publication, observing that it is the obligation of the government to prove that actual harm to the nation's security would be caused by the publication. The decision limited "prior restraint" of the press.

### Nixon v. Fitzgerald (1982)

*Decision:* The Court ruled that a President or former President is entitled to absolute immunity from liability based on his official acts. The President must be able to act forcefully and independently, without fear of liability. Diverting the President's energies with concerns about private lawsuits could impair the effective functioning of government. The President's absolute immunity extends to all acts within the "outer perimeter" of his duties of office, since otherwise he would be required to litigate over the nature of the acts and the scope of his duties in each case. The remedy of impeachment, the vigilant scrutiny of the press, the Congress, and the public, and presidential desire to earn reelection and concern with historical legacy all protect against presidential wrongdoing.

### Nixon v. Shrink Missouri Government PAC (2000)

*Decision*: In *Buckley* v. *Valeo*, 1976, the Supreme Court had upheld a $1000 limit on contributions by individuals to candidates for federal office. In *Nixon* v. *Shrink Missouri Government PAC*, the Court concluded that large contributions will sometimes create actual corruption, and that voters will be suspicious of the fairness of a political process that allows wealthy donors to contribute large amounts. The Court concluded that the Missouri contribution limits were appropriate to correct this problem and did not impair the ability of candidates to communicate their messages to the voters and to mount an effective campaign.

### Olmstead v. United States (1928)

(4th Amendment, electronic surveillance) Olmstead was engaged in the illegal sale of alcohol. Much of the evidence against him was gained through a wiretap made without a warrant. Olmstead argued that he had "a reasonable expectation of privacy," and that the *Weeks* v. *United States* decision of 1914 should be applied to exclude the evidence gained by the wiretap. The Court disagreed, saying that Olmstead intended "to project his voice to those quite outside . . . and that . . . nothing tangible was taken." Reversed by subsequent decisions, this case contains the first usage of the concept of "reasonable expectation of privacy" that would mark later 4th Amendment decisions.

### Oregon v. Mitchell (1970)

*Decision:* The Supreme Court was unable to issue a single opinion of the Court supported by a majority of the justices. However, in a series of separate opinions, differing majority groups agreed that (1) the 18-year-old minimum-age requirement of the Voting Rights Act Amendments is valid for national elections but not for State and local elections; (2) the literacy test provision is valid in order to remedy discrimination against minorities; and (3) the residency and absentee balloting provisions are a valid congressional regulation of presidential elections.

### Plessy v. Ferguson (1896)

(14th Amendment, Equal Protection Clause) A Louisiana law required separate seating for white and African American citizens on public railroads, a form of segregation. Homer Plessy argued that his right to "equal protection of the laws" was violated. The Court held that segregation was permitted if facilities were equal. The Court interpreted the 14th Amendment as "not intended to give Negroes social equality but only political and civil equality. . . ." The Louisiana law was seen as a "reasonable exercise of (State) police power. . ." Segregated public facilities were permitted until *Plessy* was overturned by the *Brown* v. *Board of Education* case of 1954.

### Powell v. Alabama (1932)

(6th Amendment, right to counsel) The case involved the "Scottsboro boys," seven African American men accused of sexual assault. This case was a landmark in the development of a "fundamentals of fairness" doctrine of the Court over the next 40 years. The Scottsboro boys were quickly prosecuted without the benefit of counsel and sentenced to death. The Court overturned the decision, stating that poor people facing the death penalty in State courts must be provided counsel, and commenting, ". . . there are certain principles of Justice which adhere to the very idea of free government, which no [State] may disregard." The case was another step toward incorporation of the Bill of Rights into State constitutions.

## Printz v. United States (1997)

*Decision:* The Court ruled that the Brady Act's interim provision requiring certain State or local law enforcement agents to perform background checks on prospective handgun purchasers was unconstitutional. Although no provision of the Constitution deals explicitly with federal authority to compel State officials to execute federal law, a review of the Constitution's structure and of prior Supreme Court decisions leads to the conclusion that Congress does not have this power.

## Reno v. American Civil Liberties Union (1997)

*Decision:* The Supreme Court unanimously ruled that the anti-obscenity provisions of the Communications Decency Act (CDA) abridged the freedom of speech protected under the First Amendment. Those parts of the CDA were intended to keep minors from "patently offensive" or "indecent" communications on the Internet. While the Court recognized the importance of Congress's goal of protecting children, it concluded that the terms "patently offensive" and "indecent" were too vague to be enforceable, especially since information on the Internet is easily transmitted to many different parts of the country where community standards of decency may vary. The decision suggested that the Court saw the Internet as more like books or newspapers, which have high First Amendment protection, rather than like radio and television, where content can be more closely regulated by the government.

## Reno v. Condon (2000)

*Decision:* The Court upheld the federal law that forbids States from selling addresses, telephone numbers, and other information that drivers put on license applications. They agreed with the Federal Government that information, including motor vehicle license information, is an "article of commerce" in the interstate stream of business and therefore is subject to regulation by Congress. The Court emphasized that the statute did not impose on the States any obligation to pass particular laws or policies and thus did not interfere with the States' sovereign functions.

## Republican Party of Minnesota v. White (2002)

*Decision:* The Supreme Court decided that the State prohibition on "announcing" a judicial candidate's views violates the 1st Amendment. It unduly restricts the candidates' rights of free speech without adequately furthering the expressed goal of improving judicial impartiality and the appearance of impartiality. The government may not restrict speech based on its content, as this rule does. In addition, the government may not restrict speech about candidates' qualifications for office, which the rule also does. In addition, the rule is not well designed to preserve impartiality,

since it has no effect on the candidate's beliefs. Finally, the lack of any longstanding tradition of such a rule shows there is no historical presumption of constitutionality.

## Roe v. Wade (1973)

(9th Amendment, right to privacy) A Texas woman challenged a State law forbidding the artificial termination of a pregnancy, saying that she "had a fundamental right to privacy." The Court upheld a woman's right to choose in this case, noting that the State's "important and legitimate interest in protecting the potentiality of human life" became "compelling" at the end of the first trimester, and that before then, ". . . the attending physician, in consultation with his patient, is free to determine, without regulation by the State, that . . . the patient's pregnancy should be terminated." The decision struck down the State regulation of abortion in the first three months of pregnancy and was modified by *Planned Parenthood of Southeastern PA v. Casey,* 1992.

## Rostker v. Goldberg (1981)

*Decision:* The Court ruled that women did not have to be included in the draft registration. The purpose of having draft registration was to prepare for the actual draft of combat troops if they should be needed. Since Congress and the President had both consistently decided not to use women in combat positions, it was not necessary for women to register either. The Court also noted that the role of women in the armed services had been debated extensively in the Congress, and concluded that the legislature had reached a thoughtful, reasoned conclusion on this issue.

## Roth v. United States (1951)

(1st Amendment, freedom of the press) A New York man named Roth operated a business that used the mail to invite people to buy materials considered obscene by postal inspectors. The Court, in its first consideration of censorship of obscenity, created the "prevailing community standards" rule, which required a consideration of the work as a whole. In its decision, the Court defined as obscene that which offended "the average person, applying contemporary community standards." In a case decided the same day, the Court applied the same "test" to State obscenity laws.

## Rush Prudential HMO, Inc. v. Moran (2002)

*Decision*: The Supreme Court decided that ERISA does not preempt the Illinois medical-review statute. The statute regulates insurance, which is one of the functions HMOs perform. Although HMOs provide healthcare as well as insurance, the statute does not require choosing a single or primary function of an HMO. Congress has long recognized that HMOs are risk-bearing organizations subject to state regulation. Finally, allowing States to regulate the insurance aspects of HMOs will not interfere with the desire of Congress for uniform national standards under ERISA.

### Schenck v. United States (1919)

(1st Amendment, freedom of speech) Charles Schenck was an officer of an antiwar political group who was arrested for alleged violations of the Espionage Act of 1917, which made active opposition to the war a crime. He had urged thousands of young men called to service by the draft act to resist and to avoid induction. The Court limited free speech in time of war, stating that Schenck's words, under the circumstances, presented a "clear and present danger. . . ." Although later decisions modified the decision, the *Schenck* case created a precedent that 1st Amendment guarantees were not absolute.

### School District of Abington Township, Pennsylvania v. Schempp (1963)

(1st Amendment, Establishment Clause) A Pennsylvania State law required reading from the Bible each day at school as an all-school activity. Some parents objected and sought legal remedy. When the case reached the Court, the Court agreed with the parents, saying that the Establishment Clause and Free Exercise Clause both forbade States from engaging in religious activity. The Court created a rule holding that if the purpose and effect of a law "is the advancement or inhibition of religion," it "exceeds the scope of legal power."

### Shelley v. Kraemer (1948)

*Decision:* The Court ruled that "in granting judicial enforcement of the restrictive agreements . . . the States have denied petitioners the equal protection of the laws. . . ." No individual has the right under the Constitution to demand that a State take action that would result in the denial of equal protection to other individuals. The Court rejected the respondents' argument that, since State courts would also enforce restrictive covenants against white owners, enforcement of covenants against black owners did not constitute a denial of equal protection. "Equal protection of the laws is not achieved through indiscriminate imposition of inequalities."

### Sheppard v. Maxwell (1966)

(14th Amendment, Due Process Clause) Dr. Samuel Sheppard was convicted of murdering his wife in a trial widely covered by national news media. Sheppard appealed his conviction, claiming that the pretrial publicity had made it impossible to get a fair trial. The Court rejected the arguments about "press freedom," overturned his conviction, and ordered a new trial. As a result of the *Sheppard* decision, some judges have issued "gag" orders limiting pretrial publicity.

### Tahoe-Sierra Preservation Council v. Tahoe Regional Planning Agency (2002)

*Decision:* The 32-month moratorium imposed by the Tahoe Regional Planning Agency on development in the Lake Tahoe Basin between Nevada and California is not a taking of property for which compensation is required. It is impossible in the abstract to say how long a restriction would be permissible. Although 32 months is a long moratorium, it is not unreasonable in this case and does not restrict the property owners' economic use of their property sufficiently to amount to a taking for which compensation must be paid.

### Tennessee Valley Authority v. Hill (1978)

(Article I, Section 8, Necessary and Proper Clause) In 1975 the secretary of the interior found that the Tennessee Valley Authority's work on the Tellico Dam would destroy the endangered snail darter's habitat in violation of the Endangered Species Act of 1975. When the TVA refused to stop work on the project, local residents sued and won an injunction against completion of the dam from the federal court of appeals. The TVA appealed, arguing that the project should be completed since it had already been underway when the Endangered Species Act had passed and, with full knowledge of the circumstances of the endangered fish, Congress had continued to appropriate money for the dam in every year since the Act's passage. However, the Supreme Court found the injunction against the TVA's completion of the dam to be proper, stating "examination of the language, history, and structure of the legislation . . . indicates beyond doubt that Congress intended endangered species to be afforded the highest of priorities."

### Texas v. White (1869)

*Decision:* The Court held, in a 5–3 decision, that Texas had the right to bring suit as a "State" in the Supreme Court, even though it had claimed to secede from the United States in 1862. Writing after the end of the Civil War, with military rule imposed in Texas under the Reconstruction Acts of 1867, the majority concluded that the United States was "an indestructible Union, composed of indestructible States," so that Texas had never actually left the Union.

### Tinker v. Des Moines School District (1969)

*Decision:* The Court upheld the students' First Amendment rights. Because students do not "shed their constitutional rights to freedom of speech or expression at the schoolhouse gate," schools must show a possibility of "substantial disruption" before free speech can be limited at school. Students may express personal opinions as long as they do not materially disrupt classwork, create substantial disorder, or interfere with the rights of others. In this case, the wearing of black armbands was a "silent, passive expression of opinion" without these side effects and thus constitutionally could not be prohibited by the school.

### U.S. Term Limits, Inc. v. Thornton (1995)

*Decision:* The Arkansas amendment preventing any person who had already served three terms as U.S. representative or two terms as U.S. senator from being listed on the ballot violates Article I, Section 2, Clause 2 and Section 3, Clause 3 of the Federal Constitution. The Arkansas law in effect established term limits for members of Congress, but the Constitution is the sole source of qualifications for membership. Such limits can only be set by an amendment to the Federal Constitution.

### United States v. American Library Association (2003)

*Decision:* Requiring public libraries to install filters to block obscene or pornographic Internet sites as a condition for obtaining federal funds for Internet access does not violate the 1st Amendment. Congress's substantial interest in protecting children from harmful materials justifies the minimal interference with free speech caused when library users are forced to request access to a specific site.

### United States v. Amistad (1841)

In 1839 two Spaniards purchased a group of kidnapped Africans and put them aboard the schooner *Amistad* for a journey from Cuba to Principe. The Africans overpowered the ship's crew, killing two men, and ordered the Spaniards to steer towards Africa. The crew steered instead toward the United States coast, where the U.S. brig *Washington* seized the ship, freeing the Spaniards and imprisoning the Africans. A series of petitions to the courts ensued, in which the Spaniards claimed the Africans as their property, and the Americans who had seized the ship claimed a share of the cargo, including the Africans, as their lawful salvage. The Court, however, declared that the Africans were not property and issued a decree that the unlawfully kidnapped Africans "be and are hereby declared to be free."

### United States v. Eichman (1990)

*Decision:* The Court agreed with the trial courts' rulings that the Flag Protection Act violated the 1st Amendment. Flag-burning constitutes expressive conduct, and thus is entitled to constitutional protection. The Act prevents protesters from using the flag to express their opposition to governmental policies and activities. Although the protesters' ideas may be offensive or disagreeable to many people, the government may not prohibit them from expressing those ideas.

### United States v. General Dynamics Corp. (1974)

A deep-mining coal producer, General Dynamics Corp., acquired control of a strip-mining coal producer, United Electric Coal Companies. The Government filed suit against the company, claiming that the acquisition violated the Clayton Act by limiting competition in coal sales and production. The Court rejected the Government's argument, finding that, although the acquisition may have increased concentration of ownership, it did not threaten to substantially lessen competition and was therefore not in violation of the Clayton Act.

### United States v. Leon (1984)

(4th Amendment, exclusionary rule) Police in Burbank, California, gathered evidence in a drug-trafficking investigation using a search warrant issued by a State court judge. Later a District Court found that the warrant had been improperly issued and granted a motion to suppress the evidence gathered under the warrant. The Government appealed the decision, claiming that the exclusionary rule should not apply in cases where law enforcement officers acted in good faith, believing the warrant to be valid. The Court agreed and established the "good-faith exception" to the exclusionary rule, finding that the rule should not be applied to bar evidence "obtained by officers acting in reasonable reliance on a search warrant issued by a detached and neutral magistrate but ultimately found to be invalid."

### United States v. Lopez (1990)

(Article I, Section 8, Commerce Clause) Alfonzo Lopez, a Texas high school student, was convicted of carrying a weapon in a school zone under the Gun-Free School Zones Act of 1990. He appealed his conviction on the basis that the Act, which forbids "any individual knowingly to possess a firearm at a place that [he] knows . . . is a school zone," exceeded Congress's legislative power under the Commerce Clause. The Court agreed that the Act was unconstitutional, stating that to uphold the legislation would "bid fair to convert congressional Commerce Clause authority to a general police power of the sort held only by the States."

### United States v. Nixon (1974)

(Separation of powers) During the investigation of the Watergate scandal, in which members of President Nixon's administration were accused of participating in various illegal activities, a special prosecutor subpoenaed tapes of conversations between Nixon and his advisors. Nixon refused to release the tapes but was overruled by the Court, which ordered him to surrender the tapes, rejecting his arguments that they were protected by "executive privilege." The President's "generalized interest in confidentiality" was subordinate to "the fundamental demands of due process of law in the fair administration of criminal justice."

### Wallace v. Jaffree (1985)

(1st Amendment, Establishment Clause) An Alabama law authorized a one-minute period of silence in all public schools "for meditation or voluntary prayer." A group of parents, including Jaffree, challenged the constitutionality of the statute, claiming it violated the Establishment Clause of the 1st Amendment. The Court agreed with Jaffree and struck down the Alabama law, determining that "the State's endorsement . . . of prayer activities at the beginning of each schoolday is not consistent with the established principle that the government must pursue a course of complete neutrality toward religion."

### *Walz* v. *Tax Commission of the City of New York* (1970)

(1st Amendment, Establishment Clause) State and local governments routinely exempt church property from taxes. Walz claimed that such exemptions were a "support of religion," a subsidy by government. The Court disagreed, noting that such exemptions were just an example of a "benevolent neutrality" between government and churches, not a support of religion. Governments must avoid taxing churches because taxation would give government a "control" over religion, prohibited by the "wall of separation of church and state" noted in *Everson* v. *Board of Education*, 1947.

### *Watchtower Bible & Tract Society* v. *Village of Stratton* (2001)

*Decision:* The Court ruled the Village's ordinance requiring canvassers to get a permit to be unconstitutional. Although a municipality may have a legitimate interest in regulating door-to-door solicitation, there must be a balance between furthering that interest and restricting 1st Amendment rights. The ordinance restricts religious or political speech, and thus needs strong justification to be valid. Because the ordinance is not restricted to commercial activities, it is broader than necessary to protect fraud. Residents have other ways to protect their privacy—they can post "no solicitation" signs or refuse to talk with unwelcome visitors. Finally, the 1st Amendment protects the right to anonymous expressions of religious or political belief.

### *Watkins* v. *United States* (1957)

*Decision:* The Court held that Watkins was not given a fair opportunity to determine whether he was within his rights in refusing to answer the Committee's questions. Congress has no authority to expose the private affairs of individuals unless justified by a specific function of Congress. Congress's investigative powers are broad but not unlimited, and must not infringe on 1st Amendment rights of speech, political belief, or association. When witnesses are forced by subpoena to testify, the subject of Congressional inquiry must be articulated in the Committee's charter or explained at the time of testimony if 1st Amendment rights are in jeopardy.

### *West Virginia Board of Education* v. *Barnette* (1943)

(1st Amendment, freedom of religion) During World War II the West Virginia Board of Education required all students to take part in a daily flag-saluting ceremony or else face expulsion. Jehovah's Witnesses objected to the compulsory salute, which they felt would force them to break their religion's doctrine against the worship of any "graven image." The Court struck down the rule, agreeing that a compulsory flag salute violated the 1st Amendment's exercise of religion clause and stating that "No official, high or petty, can prescribe what shall be orthodox in politics, nationalism, religion, or other matters of opinion. . . ."

### *Board of Education of Westside Community Schools* v. *Mergens* (1990)

(1st Amendment, Establishment Clause) A request by Bridget Mergens to form a student Christian religious group at school was denied by an Omaha high school principal. Mergens took legal action, claiming that a 1984 federal law required "equal access" for student religious groups. The Court ordered the school to permit the club, stating, "a high school does not have to permit any extracurricular activities, but when it does, the school is bound by the . . . [Equal Access] Act of 1984. Allowing students to meet on campus and discuss religion is constitutional because it does not amount to 'State sponsorship of a religion.' "

### *Wisconsin* v. *Yoder* (1972)

(1st Amendment, Free Exercise Clause) Members of the Amish religious sect in Wisconsin objected to sending their children to public schools after the eighth grade, claiming that such exposure of the children to another culture would endanger the group's self-sufficient agrarian lifestyle essential to their religious faith. The Court agreed with the Amish, while noting that the Court must move carefully to weigh the State's "legitimate social concern when faced with religious claim for exemption from generally applicable educational requirements."

# English and Spanish Glossary

## A

**absentee voting** provisions made for those unable to get to their regular polling places on election day (p. 195)
**voto en ausencia** medidas para que voten, el día de las elecciones, aquellas personas que no puedan hacerlo en su lugar habitual de votación

**acquit** find not guilty of a charge (p. 319)
**absolver** determinar que alguien no es culpable de un delito

**act of admission** congressional act admitting a new State to the Union (p. 106)
**decreto de admisión** ley del Congreso mediante la cual se admite a un nuevo estado dentro de la Unión

**adjourn** suspend, as in a session of Congress (p. 271)
**aplazamiento** suspender, por ejemplo, una sesión del Congreso

**administration** the officials in the executive branch of a government and their policies and principles (p. 428)
**administración** funcionarios del poder ejecutivo de un gobierno, así como sus políticas y sus directores

**affirmative action** a policy that requires most employers take positive steps to remedy the effects of past discriminations (p. 627)
**acción afirmativa** política que exige que la mayoría de los empleadores lleven a cabo ciertas acciones para remediar los efectos de discriminaciónes pasadas

**Albany Plan of Union** plan proposed by Benjamin Franklin in 1754 that aimed to unite the 13 colonies for trade, military, and other purposes; the plan was turned down by the colonies and the Crown (p. 37)
**Plan de Unión Albany** proyecto propuesto por Benjamín Franklin en 1754 cuyo objetivo era unir a las 13 colonias en cuanto a asuntos comerciales, militares, así como para otros propósitos; las colonias y la Corona rechazaron el plan

**alien** a foreign-born resident, or noncitizen (pp. 156, 548, 634)
**extranjero** persona residente nacida en otro país o que no se ha nacionalizado

**ambassador** an official representative of the United States appointed by the President to represent the nation in matters of diplomacy (p. 485)
**embajador** funcionario oficial designado por el Presidente para representar a la nación en asuntos diplomáticos

**amicus curiae brief** legal Latin term meaning "friend of the court;" a document that consists of written arguments presented to a court in support of one side in a dispute (p. 257)
**alegato amicus curiae** término legal en latín que significa "amigo de la corte;" documento presentado ante la corte que expone argumentos escritos en defensa de una de las partes en una disputa

**amendment** a change in, or addition to, a constitution or law (p. 78)
**enmienda** cambio o adición a la Constitución o a una ley

**amnesty** a blanket pardon offered to a group of law violators (p. 420)
**amnistía** perdón general que se ofrece a un grupo de personas que han violado la ley

**Anti-Federalists** those persons who opposed the ratification of the Constitution in 1787–1788 (p. 59)
**Anti-federalistas** aquellas personas que se opusieron a la ratificación de la Constitución entre 1787 y 1788

**appellate jurisdiction** the authority of a court to review decisions of inferior (lower) courts; see original jurisdiction (pp. 523, 734)
**jurisdicción de apelación** autoridad de una corte para revisar decisiones de cortes inferiores; ver original jurisdiction/jurisdicción original

**apportion** distribute, as in seats in a legislative body (p. 273)
**prorrateo** distribuir, por ejemplo, los escaños de un cuerpo legislativo

**appropriate** assign to a particular use (p. 316)
**asignar** destinar a un uso particular

**Articles of Confederation** plan of government adopted by the Continental Congress after the American Revolution; established "a firm league of friendship" among the States, but allowed few important powers to the central government (p. 48)
**Artículos de la Confederación** plan de gobierno adoptado por el Congreso Continental, después de la Independencia de los Estados Unidos; se enunciaron como "un vínculo firme de amistad" entre los estados, pero le delegaron pocos poderes importantes al gobierno central

**assemble** to gather with one another in order to express views on public matters (p. 569)
**congregar** reunirse con otras personas para expresar puntos de vista sobre asuntos públicos

**assessment** the process of determining the value of property to be taxed (p. 764)
**valuación** proceso para determinar el valor de una propiedad que será gravada

**assimilation** the process by which people of one culture merge into, and become part of, another culture (p. 615)
**asimilación** proceso mediante el cual las personas de una cultura se integran en otra cultura y se convierten en parte de ella

**at-large election** election of an officeholder by the voters of an entire governmental unit (e.g., a State or country) rather than by the voters of a district or subdivision (p. 275)
**elección general** elección de un funcionario público por los votantes de una unidad gubernamental completa (por ejemplo, un estado o país), en vez de por los votantes de un distrito o subdivisión

**Attorney General** the head of the Department of Justice (p. 435)
**Procurador General** funcionario más alto del Departamento de Justicia

**autocracy** a form of government in which a single person holds unlimited political power (p. 14)
**autocracia** forma de gobierno en la que una sola persona tiene poder político ilimitado

## B

**bail** a sum of money that the accused may be required to post (deposit with the court) as a guarantee that he or she will appear in court at the proper time (p. 602)
**fianza** suma de dinero que se exige que el acusado pague (en la corte) como garantía de que se presentará en dicha corte en la fecha señalada

**balance the ticket** when a presidential candidate chooses a running mate who can strengthen his chance of being elected by virtue of certain ideological, geographic, racial, ethnic, gender, or other characteristics (p. 372)

**designar al compañero de fórmula** acción que ejerce un candidato presidencial cuando elige al candidato a la vicepresidencia que refuerza sus oportunidades de ganar las elecciones, gracias a sus características ideológicas, geográficas, raciales, étnicas, de género, u otras virtudes

**ballot** the device voters use to register a choice in an election (p. 194)

**papeleta electoral** medio que los votantes utilizan para indicar su preferencia en una elección

**ballot fatigue** the phenomenon by which voters cast fewer votes for offices listed toward the bottom of the ballot (p. 171)

**fatiga al votar** fenómeno que se presenta cuando los votantes marcan menos casillas hacia el final de la papeleta electoral

**bankruptcy** the legal proceeding by which a bankrupt person's assets are distributed among those to whom he or she owes debts (p. 302)

**bancarrota** procedimiento legal mediante el cual los bienes de una persona se distribuyen entre las personas con las que tiene deudas

**battleground States** States in which the outcome of an election is too close to call and either candidate could win (p. 386)

**estados reñidos** estados donde los resultados de las elecciones indican que cualquier candidato podría ser el ganador

**bench trial** a trial in which the judge alone hears the case (pp. 597, 730)

**juicio ante judicatura** proceso en en el cual sólo el juez escucha el caso

**bicameral** an adjective describing a legislative body composed of two chambers (pp. 33, 268)

**bicameral** adjetivo que describe un cuerpo legislativo formado por dos cámaras

**bill** a proposed law presented to a legislative body for consideration (pp. 287, 343)

**proyecto de ley** ley propuesta que se presenta ante un cuerpo legislativo para su consideración

**Bill of Attainder** a legislative act that inflicts punishment without a court trial (p. 593)

**Escrito de proscripción y confiscación** acto legislativo que inflige un castigo sin que haya un juicio ante un jurado

**Bill of Rights** the first ten amendments to the Constitution (pp. 82, 547)

**Declaración de derechos** las primeras diez enmiendas a la Constitución

**bipartisan** supported by two parties (p. 127)

**bipartidista** apoyado por dos partidos

**blanket primary** a voting process in which voters receive a long ballot containing the names of all contenders, regardless of party, and can vote however they choose (p. 189)

**elecciones primarias generales** proceso de elección en el que los votantes reciben una papeleta electoral grande que contiene los nombres de todos los candidatos, independientemente del partido, y en el cual pueden elegir libremente

**block grant** one type of federal grants-in-aid for some particular but broadly defined area of public policy; *see* grants-in-aid (p. 109)

**subsidio en conjunto** tipo de subsidio público federal que se ofrece para un área particular pero definida en términos generales; *ver* grants-in-aid program/programa de subvención de fondos públicos

**briefs** detailed written statements filed with the Court before oral arguments are presented (p. 535)

**alegato** reseña detallada presentada ante la Corte antes de dar un argumento oral

**budget** a financial plan for the use of money, personnel, and property (p. 766)

**presupuesto** plan financiero para el uso del dinero, el personal y la propiedad

**bureaucracy** a large, complex administrative structure that handles the everyday business of an organization (p. 426)

**burocracia** estructura administrativa grande y compleja que gobierna los negocios cotidianos de una organización

**bureaucrat** a person who works for a bureaucratic organization; *see* bureaucracy (p. 426)

**burócrata** persona que trabaja en una organización burocrática; *ver* bureaucracy/burocracia

# C

**Cabinet** presidential advisory body, traditionally made up of the heads of the executive departments and other officers (p. 87)

**Gabinete** cuerpo consultivo del Presidente que tradicionalmente está formado por los funcionarios más altos de los departamentos ejecutivos y otros agentes

**capital** all the human-made resources that are used to produce goods and services (p. 678)

**capital** todos los recursos creados por el hombre que se utilizan para producir bienes y servicios

**capital punishment** the death penalty (p. 604)

**pena capital** la pena de muerte

**capitalism** economic system in which individuals are free to own the means of production and maximize profits (p. 678)

**capitalismo** sistema económico en el que individuos tienen la libertad de poseer los medios de producción y de aumentar sus ganancias

**categorical grant** one type of federal grants-in-aid; made for some specific, closely defined, purpose; *see* grants-in-aid (p. 108)

**subsidio categórico** tipo de subsidio público federal; proporcionado para un propósito específico y rigurosamente definido; *ver* grants-in-aid program/programa de subvención de fondos públicos

**caucus** as a nominating device, a group of like-minded people who meet to select the candidates they will support in an upcoming election (pp. 185, 381)

**junta de dirigentes** en función de instrumento nominativo, grupo de personas que comparten la misma ideología y que se reúnen para seleccionar a los candidatos que apoyarán en una elección

**censure** issue a formal condemnation (p. 320)

**amonestación** pronunciamiento de una condena formal

**certificate** a method of putting a case before the Supreme Court; used when a lower court is not clear about the procedure or rule of law that should apply in a case and asks the Supreme Court to certify the answer to a specific question (p. 534)

**certificación** método de remitir un caso a la Corte Suprema; se utiliza cuando una corte inferior no está segura de qué procedimiento o regla deberá aplicar en un caso y consulta a la Corte Suprema para que certifique una respuesta a una pregunta específica

**charter** a city's basic law, its constitution; a written grant of authority from the king (pp. 33, 750)

**carta constitucional** ley básica de una ciudad, su constitución; concesión de autoridad escrita otorgada por el rey

**checks and balances** system of overlapping the powers of the legislative, executive, and judicial branches to permit each branch to check the actions of the others; *see* separation of powers (p. 72)

**sistema de frenos y contrapesos** sistema de equilibrio entre los poderes; mecanismo mediante el cual se traslapa la autoridad del poder legislativo, el poder ejecutivo y el poder judicial para permitir que cada poder verifique las acciones de los otros dos; *ver* separation of powers/separación de poderes

**chief administrator** term for the President as head of the administration of the Federal Government (p. 365)

**administrador en jefe** nombre que se le da al Presidente por ser el jefe de la administración del gobierno federal

**chief citizen** term for the President as the representative of the people, working for the public interest (p. 365)

**primer ciudadano** nombre que se le da al Presidente por ser representante del pueblo y trabajar por el interés público

**chief diplomat** term for the President as the main architect of foreign policy and spokesperson to other countries (p. 365)

**diplomático titular** nombre que se le da al Presidente por ser el arquitecto principal de la política exterior y un vocero ante otros países

**chief executive** term for the President as vested with the executive power of the United States (p. 364)

**primer mandatario** nombre que se le da al Presidente porque está investido con el poder ejecutivo de los Estados Unidos

**chief legislator** term for the President as architect of public policy and the one who sets the agenda for Congress (p. 365)

**legislador en jefe** nombre que se le da al Presidente por ser arquitecto de la política pública y por ser la persona que determina la agenda del Congreso

**chief of party** term for the President as the leader of his or her political party (p. 365)

**jefe del partido** nombre que se le da al Presidente por ser el líder de su partido político

**chief of state** term for the President as the ceremonial head of the United States, the symbol of all the people of the nation (p. 364)

**jefe de estado** nombre que se le da al Presidente por ser el funcionario ceremonial de los Estados Unidos, el símbolo de toda la gente de la nación

**citizen** a member of a state or nation who owes allegiance to it by birth or naturalization and is entitled to full civil rights (pp. 23, 632)

**ciudadano** miembro de un estado o nación por nacimiento o naturalización, que se beneficia de todos los derechos civiles y que le debe lealtad a ese estado o nación

**civil case** a case involving a noncriminal matter such as a contract dispute or a claim of patent infringement (p. 529)

**caso civil** caso relacionado con un asunto no criminal, como un litigio por contrato o una demanda por violación de patentes

**civil disobedience** a form of protest in which people deliberately but non-violently violate the law, as a means of expressing their opposition to some particular law or public policy (p. 569)

**resistencia pasiva** forma de protesta en la cual las personas violan la ley de una manera no violenta, como método para expresar su oposición a una ley o política pública

**civil law** the portion of the law relating to human conduct, to disputes between private parties, and to disputes between private parties and government not covered by criminal law (p. 728)

**ley civil** área de la ley que se relaciona con la conducta humana, con litigios entre entidades privadas, así como entre partes privadas y el gobierno, que no están cubiertos bajo la ley penal

**civil liberties** the guarantees of the safety of persons, opinions, and property from the arbitrary acts of government, including freedom of speech and freedom of religion (p. 547)

**libertades civiles** garantías que protegen la seguridad, las opiniones y la propiedad de las personas de actos arbitrarios del gobierno; entre ellas están la libertad de expresión y la libertad de religión

**civil rights** a term used for those positive acts of government that seek to make constitutional guarantees a reality for all people, e.g., prohibitions of discrimination (p. 547)

**derechos civiles** término que designa actos positivos del gobierno con el objetivo de hacer realidad las garantías constitucionales para todo el pueblo, por ejemplo la prohibición de la discriminación

**civil service** those civilian employees who perform the administrative work of government (p. 443)

**servicio civil** grupo de empleados civiles que desempeñan el trabajo administrativo del gobierno

**civilian** nonmilitary (p. 435)

**civil** que no es militar

**civilian tribunal** a court operating as part of the judicial branch, entirely separate from the military establishment (p. 539)

**tribunal civil** corte que actúa como parte del poder judicial y que está separado por completo de la institución militar

**clemency** mercy or leniency granted to an offender by a chief executive; *see* pardon and reprieve (pp. 419, 724)

**clemencia** misericordia o piedad que dispensa el Presidente a un delincuente; *ver* pardon/perdón y reprieve/suspensión

**closed primary** a party nominating election in which only declared party members can vote (p. 188)

**elección primaria cerrada** elecciones para una nominación de un partido en la que sólo los miembros declarados del partido pueden votar

**cloture** procedure that may be used to limit or end floor debate in a legislative body (p. 353)

**limitación del debate** procedimiento que puede utilizarse para restringir o terminar un debate verbal de un cuerpo legislativo

**coalition** a temporary alliance of several groups who come together to form a working majority and so to control a government (pp. 128, 667)

**coalición** alianza temporal de varios grupos que se juntan para alcanzar el poder mayoritario y controlar el gobierno

**coattail effect** the effect of a strong candidate running for an office at the top of a ballot helping to attract voters to other candidates on the party's ticket (p. 195)

**efecto de refilón** efecto que produce la presencia de un candidato fuerte en la parte superior de una papeleta electoral y que ayuda a atraer votantes hacia otros candidatos de su mismo partido

**cold war** a period of more than 40 years during which relations between the two superpowers were at least tense, and often hostile. A time of threats and military build up (p. 498)

**guerra fría** período de más de 40 años en el que las relaciones entre las dos superpotencias fueron por lo menos tensas, y a menudo hostiles; época de amenazas y de desarrollo armamentista

**collective security** the keeping of international peace and order (p. 498)

**seguridad colectiva** conservación de la paz y el orden internacionales

**collectivization** collective or state ownership of the means of production (p. 689)

**colectivización** hacer colectivos o propiedad del estado los medios de producción

**colonialism** the control of one nation over foreign lands (p. 651)

**colonialismo** control que tiene una nación sobre tierras extranjeras

**command economy** system in which government bureaucrats plan and direct most economic activity (p. 687)

**economía dirigida** sistema en el cual los burócratas del gobierno planean y dirigen la mayor parte de la actividad económica

**commander in chief** term for the President as commander of the nation's armed forces (p. 364)

**comandante en jefe** nombre que se le da al Presidente por ser el comandante de las Fuerzas Armadas de la nación

**Commerce and Slave Trade Compromise** an agreement during the Constitutional Convention protecting slave holders; denied Congress the power to tax the export of goods from any State, and, for 20 years, the power to act on the slave trade (p. 56)

**Avenencia de comercio y trata de esclavos** acuerdo durante la Convención Constitucional que protegió los intereses de los dueños de esclavos, al negarle al Congreso el poder de gravar la exportación de bienes desde cualquier estado y el poder de actuar, durante 20 años, en contra de la trata de esclavos

**commerce power** exclusive power of Congress to regulate interstate and foreign trade (p. 297)

**poder mercantil** poder exclusivo que tiene el Congreso para regular el comercio interestatal e internacional

**commission government** a government formed by commissioners, heads of different departments of city government, who are popularly elected to form the city council and thus center both legislative and executive powers in one body (p. 751)

**junta municipal** gobierno formado por comisionados, funcionarios altos de distintos departamentos del gobierno de la ciudad, que se eligen por voto popular para formar el Consejo de la ciudad y, por consiguiente, reúnen los poderes legislativos y ejecutivos en un solo cuerpo

**committee chairman** member who heads a standing committee in a legislative body (p. 336)

**presidente de comisión** miembro que encabeza una comisión permanente en un cuerpo legislativo

**common law** an unwritten law made by a judge that has developed over centuries from those generally accepted ideas of right and wrong that have gained judicial recognition (p. 727)

**derecho consuetudinario** ley que no ha sido sancionada por un juez y se ha desarrollado a lo largo de los siglos, con base en ideas generalmente aceptadas de lo bueno y lo malo que se han ganado un reconocimiento judicial

**communism** an ideology which calls for the collective, or state, ownership of land and other productive property (pp. 659, 686)

**comunismo** ideología que exige la propiedad colectiva, o estatal, de la tierra y de otros medios de producción

***Communist Manifesto, The*** a political document written by Karl Marx and Friedrich Engels that urged workers to free themselves from "capitalist enslavement" (p. 685)

***El manifiesto comunista*** documento político escrito por Karl Marx y Friedrich Engels en el cual se urge a los trabajadores a que se liberen de ser esclavizados por el capitalismo

**commutation** the power to reduce (commute) the length of a sentence or fine for a crime (pp. 420, 725)

**conmutación** poder de reducir (conmutar) la duración de una sentencia o el monto de la multa por haber cometido un crimen

**compromise** an adjustment of opposing principles or systems by modifying some aspect of each (p. 22)

**transigencia** acuerdo intermedio entre principios o sistemas opuestos, al que se llega mediante la modificación de algún aspecto de cada uno de ellos

**concurrent jurisdiction** power shared by federal and State courts to hear certain cases (p. 522)

**jurisdicción coincidente** poder compartido por cortes federales y estatales para atender ciertos casos

**concurrent powers** those powers that both the National Government and the States possess and exercise (p. 100)

**poderes concurrentes** aquellos poderes que el gobierno nacional y los estados poseen y ejercen

**concurrent resolution** a statement of position on an issue used by the House and Senate acting jointly; does not have the force of law and does not require the President's signature (p. 344)

**resolución conjunta** enunciado de una opinión sobre un asunto utilizado por la Cámara de Representantes y el Senado al actuar conjuntamente; no tiene el poder de la ley y no requiere la firma del Presidente

**concurring opinion** written explanation of the views of one or more judges who support a decision reached by a majority of the court, but wish to add or emphasize a point that was not made in the majority decision (p. 537)

**opinion coincidente** explicación escrita de los puntos de vista de uno o más jueces quienes apoyan una decisión alcanzada por una mayoría en la corte, pero desean añadir o recalcar un punto que no se remarcó en la decisión mayoritaria

**confederation** a joining of several groups for a common purpose (pp. 16, 37)

**confederación** unión de diversos grupos para un propósito común

**conference committee** temporary joint committee created to reconcile any differences between the two houses' versions of a bill (p. 342)

**comité de consulta** comité conjunto temporal formado para reconciliar cualquier diferencia entre las versiones de un proyecto de ley propuesto por las dos cámaras legislativas

**Connecticut Compromise** agreement during the Constitutional Convention that Congress should be composed of a Senate, in which States would be represented equally, and a House, in which representation would be based on a State's population (p. 56)

**Acuerdo de Connecticut** acuerdo alcanzado durante la Convención Constitucional que estableció que el Congreso debería estar integrado por un Senado donde cada estado estuviera representado de manera equitativa, y una Cámara de Representantes en la que la representación estuviera basada en la población de cada estado

**consensus** general agreement among various groups on fundamental matters; broad agreement on public questions (pp. 127, 314)

**consenso** acuerdo general entre diversos grupos sobre temas fundamentales; acuerdo general sobre asuntos públicos

**constituency** the people and interests that an elected official represents (p. 283)

**circunscripción electoral** las personas e intereses que un funcionario elegido representa

**constituent power** the non-legislative power of Constitution-making and the constitutional amendment process (p. 717)

**poder constituyente** poder no legislativo de la elaboración de la Constitución y del proceso de enmiendas constitucionales

**constitution** the body of fundamental laws setting out the principles, structures, and processes of a government (p. 5)

**constitución** cuerpo de leyes fundamentales que definen los principios, las estructuras y los procesos de gobierno

**constitutionalism** basic principle that government and those who govern must obey the law; the rule of law; *see* limited government (p. 70)

**constitucionalismo** principio básico que establece que el gobierno y los gobernantes deben obedecer la ley; el gobierno de la ley; *ver* limited government/gobierno limitado

**containment** a policy based in the belief that if communism could be kept within its existing boundaries, it would collapse under the weight of its internal weaknesses (p. 500)

**contención** Política basada en la creencia de que si se pudiera evitar la expansión del régimen comunista, éste colapsaría debido a la fragilidad de su estructura interna

**content neutral** the government may not regulate assemblies on the basis on what might be said (p. 570)

**voto neutral** el gobierno no regulará a las asambleas en lo concerniente a lo que se expresará en ellas

**continuing resolution** a measure that allows agencies to continue working based on the previous year's appropriations (p. 471)

**resolución ininterrumpida** medida que permite que las agencias continúen funcionando basándose en de las asignaciones del año anterior

**continuous body** governing unit (e.g. the United States Senate) whose seats are never all up for election at the same time (p. 283)

**cuerpo legislativo ininterrumpido** unidad gubernamental (por ejemplo, el Senado de los Estados Unidos) cuya totalidad de escaños nunca se elige al mismo tiempo

**contract** a legally binding agreement in which one party agrees to do something with or for another party (p.728)

**contrato** acuerdo legal mediante el cual una parte se compromete a actuar con o para otra parte

**controllable spending** an amount decided upon by Congress and the President to determine how much will be spent each year on many individual government expenditures, including environment protection programs, aid to education, and so on (p. 468)

**gasto controlable** cantidad de dinero determinada por el Congreso y el Presidente, que indica el monto anual de muchos gastos gubernamentales individuales, como programas para la protección del ambiente, ayuda a la educación, y otros

**convene** to begin a new session of Congress (p. 271)

**convocar** empezar una nueva sesión del Congreso

**copyright** the exclusive, legal right of a person to reproduce, publish, and sell his or her own literary, musical, or artistic creations (p. 307)

**derechos de autor** derechos legales y exclusivos de una persona para reproducir, publicar y vender su trabajo creativo literario, artístico o musical

**council-manager government** a modification of the mayor-council government, it consists of a strong council of members elected on a non-partisan ballot, a weak mayor, elected by the people, and a manager, named by the council; *see* mayor-council government; *see also* weak mayor government (p. 751)

**gobierno de consejo-superintendente** modificación del gobierno de consejo-alcalde, que consiste en un vigoroso consejo de miembros elegidos mediante un sufragio no partidista; un alcalde débil, elegido por el pueblo y un superintendente nombrado por el consejo; *ver* mayor-council government/gobierno de consejo-alcalde; *ver también* weak-mayor government/gobierno de alcalde débil

**county** a major unit of local government in most States (p. 742)

**Condado** unidad importante de gobierno local en gran parte de los estados

**court-martial** a court composed of military personnel, for the trial of those accused of violating military law (p. 538)

**Corte marcial** corte integrada por personal militar para juzgar a quienes han sido acusados de violar la ley militar

**criminal case** a case in which a defendant is tried for committing a crime as defined by the law (p. 529)

**caso criminal** caso en el que se juzga al acusado por cometer un crimen, tal y como éste se define de acuerdo a la ley

**criminal law** the portion of the law that defines public wrongs and provides for their punishment (p. 728)

**derecho penal** área de la ley que define los agravios públicos y que establece su castigo

**custom duty** a tax laid on goods brought into the United States from abroad, also known as tariffs, import duties, or imposts (p. 462)

**derecho de aduana** impuesto sobre los bienes traídos a los Estados Unidos desde el exterior, también se conoce como arancel, impuesto sobre importaciones o tasa sobre importaciones

## D

**de facto segregation** segregation even if no law requires it, e.g., housing patterns (p. 621)

**discriminación de facto o de hecho** segregación, incluso sin que la ley lo exija, como en la asignación de viviendas

**de jure segregation** segregation by law, with legal sanction (p. 621)

**discriminación de jure o de ley** segregación con base en la ley, que implica una sanción legal

**defendant** in a civil suit, the person against whom a court action is brought by the plaintiff; in a criminal case, the person charged with the crime (p. 523)

**acusado** en un juicio civil, es la persona en contra de quien el demandante pide ejecutar una acción judicial; en un caso criminal, es la persona acusada de un crimen

**deficit** the yearly shortfall between revenue and spending (p. 463)

**déficit** diferencia anual entre los ingresos y los egresos

**deficit financing** practice of funding government by borrowing to make up the difference between government spending and revenue (p. 301)

**financiamiento del déficit** práctica que consiste en subvencionar al gobierno mediante préstamos, a fin de compensar la diferencia entre los gastos y los ingresos gubernamentales

**deflation** a general decrease in prices (p. 474)

**deflación** disminución general de los precios

**delegated powers** those powers, expressed, implied, or inherent, granted to the National Government by the Constitution (p. 96)

**poderes delegados** poderes explícitos, implícitos o inherentes que la Constitución transfiere al gobierno nacional

**delegates** representatives; members of Congress who cast votes based on the wishes of their constituents (pp. 37, 287)

**delegados** representantes; miembros del Congreso que votan según los deseos de sus constituyentes

**demand-side economics** the theory that the higher employment that results from government borrowing will produce higher tax revenues (p. 464)

**economía de demanda** teoría que establece que un alza de los empleos debido a préstamos del gobierno producirá un incremento en los ingresos tributarios

**democracy** a form of government in which the supreme authority rests with the people (p. 5)

**democracia** forma de gobierno en la cual la autoridad suprema reside en el pueblo

**democratic consolidation** the process of establishing the factors considered necessary for a democracy to succeed (p. 663)

**consolidación democrática** proceso mediante el cual se establecen los factores necesarios para el éxito de una democracia

**democratization** the change from dictatorship to democracy, marked by the holding of free and fair elections (p. 663)

**democratización** cambio de una dictadura a una democracia mediante elecciones libres y justas

**denaturalization** the process through which naturalized citizens may involuntarily lose their citizenship (p. 635)

**desnaturalización** proceso mediante el cual los ciudadanos naturalizados pueden perder su ciudadanía de manera involuntaria

**deportation** a legal process in which aliens are legally required to leave the United States (p. 637)

**deportación** proceso legal mediante el cual se exige a los extranjeros que abandonen los Estados Unidos

**détente** a relaxation of tensions (p. 501)

**relajamiento** disminución de las tensiones

**deterrence** the policy of making America and its allies so militarily strong that their very strength will discourage, or prevent, any attack (p. 498)

**disuasión** política que consiste en convertir a los Estados Unidos y sus aliados en una fuerza militar tan poderosa que su fortaleza desaliente, o prevenga, cualquier ataque

**devolution** the delegation of authority from the central government to regional governments (p. 670)

**delegación** transferencia de la autoridad del gobierno central a los gobiernos regionales

**dictatorship** a form of government in which the leader has absolute power and authority (p. 5)

**dictadura** forma de gobierno en la que el líder ejerce poder y autoridad absolutos

**diplomatic immunity** when an ambassador is not subject to the laws of the state to which they are accredited (p. 486)

**inmunidad diplomática** condición en la que un embajador no está sujeto a las leyes del estado anfitión

**direct popular election** proposal to do away with the electoral college and allow the people to vote directly for President and Vice President (p. 392)

**elección popular directa** propuesta para abolir el colegio electoral y permitir que la gente elija de manera directa al Presidente y al Vicepresidente

**direct primary** an election held within a party to pick that party's candidates for the general election (p. 187)

**elecciones primarias directas** elecciones realizadas dentro de un partido para escoger a los candidatos del partido para las elecciones generales

**discharge petition** a procedure enabling members to force a bill that has been pigeonholed in committee onto the floor for consideration (p. 345)

**petición de exoneración** procedimiento que permite a los miembros reiniciar la discusión para considerar una propuesta de ley que se había suspendido en una comisión de debate

**discount rate** the rate of interest a bank must pay when it borrows money from a Federal Reserve Bank (p. 476)

**tasa de descuento** tasa de interés que debe pagar un banco que toma un préstamo del Banco de la Reserva Federal

**discrimination** bias, unfairness (p. 584)

**discriminación** prejuicio, injusticia

**disenfranchised** denied the right to vote (p.153)

**privación del derecho al voto** acción que consiste en negarle a alguien el derecho de votar

**dissenting opinion** written explanation of the views of one or more judges who disagree with (dissent from) a decision reached by a majority of the court; *see* majority opinion (p. 537)

**opinión disidente** explicación escrita de los puntos de vista de uno o más jueces que está(n) en desacuerdo con una decisión tomada por la mayoría de la corte; *ver* majority opinion/opinión mayoritaria

**district plan** proposal for choosing presidential electors by which two electors would be selected in each State according to the Statewide popular vote and the other electors would be selected separately in each of the State's congressional districts (p. 391)

**plan de distrito** propuesta para elegir a los electores presidenciales, mediante la cual se seleccionarían dos electores en cada estado, de acuerdo con el voto popular de todo ese estado, y los otros electores se elegirían de manera separada en cada uno de los distritos del Congreso de ese estado

**divine right of laws** the belief that God grants authority to a government (p. 650)

**derecho divino** creencia de que Dios le concede autoridad a un gobierno

**division of powers** basic principle of federalism; the constitutional provisions by which governmental powers are divided on a geographic basis (in the United States, between the National Government and the States) (pp. 16, 95)

**división de poderes** principio básico del federalismo; estipulaciones constitucionales que establecen que los poderes gubernamentales están separados según la ubicación geográfica (en los Estados Unidos, se dividen entre el gobierno nacional y los estados)

**docket** a court's list of cases to be heard (p. 530)

**agenda** lista de casos por atender en una corte

**domestic affairs** all matters not directly connected to the realm of foreign affairs (pp. 434, 482)

**asuntos internos** todas cuestiones no relacionadas con el campo de los asuntos exteriores

**double jeopardy** part of the 5th Amendment which says that no person can be put in jeopardy of life or limb twice. Once a person has been tried for a crime, he or she cannot be tried again for the same crime (p. 595)

**doble juicio** parte de la 5ª enmienda que establece que no se puede poner en riesgo la vida de una persona o su integridad física dos veces. Una vez que se ha juzgado por un crimen a una persona, no puede volvérsele a juzgar por el mismo delito

**draft** conscription, or compulsory military service (p. 445)

**reclutamiento** conscripción o servicio militar obligatorio

**due process** the government must act fairly and in accord with established rules in all that it does (pp. 31, 578)

**proceso legal establecido** el gobierno debe actuar con justicia y de acuerdo con las reglas establecidas en todo lo que hace

**Due Process Clause** part of the 14th Amendment which guarantees that no state deny basic rights to its people (p. 549)

**Cláusula del proceso** parte de la 14ª enmienda que garantiza que ningún estado negará los derechos básicos a su pueblo

# E

**economic protest parties** parties rooted in poor economic times, lacking a clear ideological base, dissatisfied with current conditions and demanding better times (p. 138)

**partidos de protesta económica** partidos surgidos en tiempos de descontento económico, que carecen de una base ideológica bien definida, están insatisfechos por las condiciones presentes y exigen mejoras

**electoral college** group of persons chosen in each State and the District of Columbia every four years who make a formal selection of the President and Vice President (pp. 87, 375)

**colegio electoral** grupo de personas (electores presidenciales) elegidos cada cuatro años en todos los estados y en el Distrito de Columbia a fin de elegir formalmente al Presidente y Vicepresidente

**electoral votes** votes cast by electors in the electoral college (p. 375)

**votos electorales** votos emitidos por los electores en el Colegio electoral

**electorate** all of the people entitled to vote in a given election (pp. 132, 152)

**electorado** todas las personas que tienen derecho a votar en una elección determinada

**eminent domain** power of a government to take private property for public use (p. 308)

**dominio supremo** poder de un gobierno de expropiar la propiedad privada para uso público

**enabling act** a congressional act directing the people of a United States territory to frame a proposed State constitution as a step towards admission to the Union (p. 106)

**ley de habilitación** ley del Congreso que orienta al pueblo de un territorio de los Estados Unidos para que redacte una propuesta de la constitución para el estado, como un paso hacia la admisión de dicho estado dentro de la Unión

**encomienda** a system instituted by the Spanish crown in which the monarch granted control of Indians to settlers for forced labor for mining and agriculture (p. 655)

**encomienda** sistema instituido por la corona española en el que el monarca les otorga a los colonos el control de los indígenas para ser forzados a trabajar en minas y en agricultura

**English Bill of Rights** document written by Parliament and agreed on by William and Mary of England in 1689, designed to prevent abuse of power by English monarchs; forms the basis for much in American government and politics today (p. 31)

**Declaración inglesa de los derechos** documento redactado por el Parlamento y aceptado por William y Mary de Inglaterra en 1689, elaborado para evitar el abuso de poder por parte de los monarcas ingleses; constituye la base de grande parte del gobierno y la política estadounidenses actuales

**engross** to print a bill in its final form (p. 349)

**transcribir** imprimir un proyecto de ley en su forma final

**entitlement** a benefit that federal law says must be paid to all those who meet the eligibility requirements, e.g., Medicare, food stamps, and veterans' pension (pp. 467, 758)

**derecho** beneficio que la ley federal establece que se debe pagar a todos los que cumplan los requisitos para ser elegibles, por ejemplo: el seguro médico, los bonos de comida y los pensión para los veteranos

**entrepreneur** an individual with the drive and ambition to combine land, labor, and capital resources to produce goods or offer services (p. 679)

**empresario** individuo con el impulso y la ambición de combinar los recursos de la tierra, la mano de obra y el capital para producir bienes u ofrecer servicios

**espionage** spying (p. 492)

**espionaje** acto de espiar

**Establishment Clause** separates church and state (p. 551)

**Cláusula del establecimiento** separa a la Iglesia del Estado

**estate tax** a levy imposed on the assets of one who dies (pp. 461, 764)

**impuesto testamentario** gravamen sobre los bienes de una persona que muere

**ex post facto law** a law applied to an act committed before its passage (p. 593)

**ley ex post facto** ley que se aplica a un acto cometido con anterioridad a la aprobación de la ley

**excise tax** a tax laid on the manufacture, sale, or consumption of goods and/or the performance of services (p. 461)

**impuesto al consumo** gravamen sobre la manufactura, venta o consumo de bienes y/o al suministro de servicios

**exclusionary rule** evidence gained as the result of an illegal act by police cannot be used against the person from whom it was seized (p. 588)

**regla de exclusión** evidencia obtenida como resultado de una acción ilegal de la policía y que no puede utilizarse contra la persona arrestada

**exclusive powers** those powers that can be exercised by the National Government alone (p. 99)

**poderes exclusivos** poderes que sólo el gobierno nacional puede ejercer

**executive agreement** a pact made by the President directly with the head of a foreign state; a binding international agreement with the force of law but which (unlike a treaty) does not require Senate consent (pp. 87, 413)

**acuerdo ejecutivo** pacto establecido de manera directa entre el Presidente y otro jefe un estado extranjero; pacto internacional obligatorio que tiene el poder de una ley pero que no requiere, a diferencia de un tratado, de la aprobación del Senado

**Executive Article** Article II of the Constitution. Establishes the presidency and gives the executive power of the Federal Government to the President (p. 400)

**Artículo del ejecutivo** el segundo artículo de la Constitución. Define la presidencia y le otorga el poder ejecutivo del gobierno federal al Presidente

**executive departments** often called the Cabinet departments, they are the traditional units of federal administration (p. 435)
**oficinas del poder ejecutivo** a menudo llamadas oficinas del gabinete; son las unidades tradicionales de la administración federal

**Executive Office of the President** an organization of several agencies staffed by the President's closest advisors (p. 431)
**Oficina ejecutiva del Presidente** organización compleja, que abarca diversas oficinas separadas, cuyo personal está integrado por los consejeros y asistentes más cercanos al Presidente

**executive order** directive, rule, or regulation issued by a chief executive or subordinates, based upon constitutional or statutory authority and having the force of law (p. 406)
**orden ejecutiva** directiva, regla o reglamento expedido por un primer mandatario o sus subordinados, con base en su autoridad estatutaria o constitucional, y que tiene el poder de una ley

**executive power** the power to execute, enforce, and administer law (p. 5)
**poder ejecutivo** poder para ejecutar, administrar y obligar al cumplimiento de la ley

**executive privilege** the President's power to refuse to disclose information (p. 409)
**privilegio ejecutivo** poder que tiene el Presidente para rehusarse a revelar información

**expatriation** the legal process by which a loss of citizenship occurs (p. 634)
**expatriación** proceso legal mediante el cual ocurre la pérdida de ciudadanía

**expressed powers** those delegated powers of the National Government that are spelled out, expressly, in the Constitution; also called the "enumerated powers" (pp. 96, 296)
**poderes explícitos** aquellos poderes delegados del gobierno nacional que se señalan explícitamente en la Constitución; también se conocen como los "poderes ennumerados"

**extradition** the legal process by which a fugitive from justice in one State is returned to that State (p. 113)
**extradición** proceso legal a través del cual un fugitivo de la justicia de un estado se retorna a ese estado

# F

**faction** a conflicting group (p. 131)
**facción** un grupo disidente

**factors of production** basic resources which are used to make all goods and services (p. 678)
**factores de producción** recursos básicos que se utilizan para elaborar todos los bienes y servicios

**failed states** nations in which security is nonexistent, the economy has collapsed, healthcare and school systems are in shambles, and corruption flourishes (p. 665)
**estados fallidos** Países con un sistema de seguridad nulo, una economía muy deteriorada, sistemas de asistencia de salud y de educación en crisis y donde prospera la corrupción

**fascism** a system of government characterized by a centralized, authoritarian government with policies that glorify the state over the individual (p. 659)
**fascismo** Sistema político caracterizado por un gobierno centralizado y autoritario con políticas que destacan al estado por encima del individuo

**federal budget** a detailed financial document containing estimates of federal income and spending during the coming fiscal year (p. 433)
**presupuesto federal** documento financiero detallado que contiene las estimaciones de las recaudaciones y gastos que anticipan los ingresos y egresos federales durante el año fiscal venidero

**Federal Government** a form of government in which powers are divided between a central government and several local governments (p. 16)
**Gobierno Federal** forma de gobierno en la que los poderes están divididos entre un gobierno central y diversos gobiernos locales

**federalism** a system of government in which a written constitution divides power between a central, or national, government and several regional governments (pp. 75, 94)
**federalismo** sistema de gobierno en el que una constitución escrita divide los poderes del gobierno, entre un gobierno central (o nacional) y diversos gobiernos regionales

**Federalists** those persons who supported the ratification of the Constitution in 1787–1788 (p. 59)
**Federalistas** personas que apoyaron la ratificación de la Constitución entre 1787 y 1788

**felony** a serious crime which may be punished by a heavy fine and/or imprisonment or even death (p. 728)
**felonía** un crimen grave que puede castigarse con una gran multa, la prisión o incluso la muerte

**feudalism** a loosely organized system in which powerful lords divided their lands among other, lesser lords (p. 648)
**feudalismo** sistema relativamente organizado en el cual los grandes señores les concedían sus tierras a otros señores de menor autoridad

**filibuster** various tactics (usually long speeches) aimed at defeating a bill in a legislative body by preventing a final vote; associated with the U.S. Senate; *see* cloture (p. 352)
**obstrucción** tácticas diversas (por lo general, prolongar el debate verbal) con el objetivo de derrotar una propuesta de ley en un cuerpo legislativo, evitando que se tenga un voto final; a menudo se asocia con el Senado de los Estados Unidos; *ver* cloture/limitación del debate

**fiscal policy** the various means the government uses to raise and spend money (pp. 456, 474)
**política económica** métodos varios que usa el gobierno para obtener y gastar dinero

**fiscal year** the 12-month period used by a government and the business world for its record-keeping, budgeting, revenue-collecting, and other financial management purposes (p. 433)
**año fiscal** período de 12 meses utilizado por el gobierno y el mundo de los negocios para su contabilidad, presupuesto, recaudación de ingresos y otros propósitos financieros

**five-year plan** a plan which projects economic development over the next five years (p. 689)
**plan quinquenal** plan que hace proyecciones sobre el desarrollo económico durante los siguientes cinco años

**floor consideration** the process by which proposed laws are considered and acted upon by the full membership of the House or Senate (p. 287)
**consideración de la sala** proceso mediante el cual la Cámara de Representantes o el Senado consideran y reaccionan a las leyes propuestas

**floor leaders** members of the House and Senate picked by their parties to carry out party decisions and steer legislative action to meet party goals (p. 336)

**líderes de fracciones partidistas** miembros de la Cámara de Representantes y del Senado elegidos por sus partidos con el objeto de llevar a cabo las decisiones partidistas e impulsar la acción legislativa a fin de que se cumplan los propósitos partidistas

**foreign affairs** a nation's relationships with other countries (p. 482)
**asuntos exteriores** relaciones de una nación con otros países

**foreign aid** economic and military aid to other countries (p. 505)
**ayuda extranjera** auxilio militar y económico a otros países

**foreign policy** a group of policies made up of all the stands and actions that a nation takes in every aspect of its relationships with other countries; everything a nation's government says and does in world affairs (p. 483)
**política exterior** conjunto de políticas conformado por todas las posturas y acciones que una nación asume en cada uno de los aspectos de sus relaciones con otros países; todo lo que el gobierno de una nación expresa y hace respecto a los asuntos mundiales

**formal amendment** change or addition that becomes part of the written language of the Constitution itself through one of four methods set forth in the Constitution (p. 79)
**enmienda formal** cambio o adición que se convierte en parte del lenguaje escrito de la Constitución misma, mediante uno de los cuatro métodos enunciados de la Constitución

**Framers** group of delegates who drafted the United States Constitution at the Philadelphia Convention in 1787 (p. 52)
**Redactores** grupo de delegados que esbozaron la Constitución de los Estados Unidos en la Convención de Filadelfia en 1787

**franchise** the right to vote (p. 152)
**sufragio** derecho a votar

**franking privilege** benefit allowing members of Congress to mail letters and other materials postage-free (p. 289)
**exención de franquicia** beneficio otorgado a los miembros del Congreso que les permite enviar por correo cartas y otros materiales gratis

**free enterprise system** an economic system characterized by private or corporate ownership of capital goods; investments that are determined by private decision rather than by state control, and determined in a free market (pp. 23, 679)
**sistema de libre empresa** sistema económico caracterizado por la propiedad privada o corporativa de los bienes de capital; inversiones que están determinadas por una decisión privada, en vez del control estatal, y están sujetas a un mercado libre

**Free Exercise Clause** the second part of the constitutional guarantee of religious freedom, which guarantees to each person the right to believe whatever he or she chooses to believe in matters of religion (p. 551)
**Cláusula de la libertad de cultos** segunda parte de la garantía constitucional de libertad religiosa, que garantiza a todos el derecho de creer en lo que se escoja en cuestiones de religión

**free market** a market in which buyers and sellers are free to buy and sell as they wish (p. 679)
**mercado libre** mercado en el cual los compradores y vendedores tienen la libertad de comprar y vender como lo deseen

**Full Faith and Credit Clause** Constitution's requirement that each State accept the public acts, records, and judicial proceedings of every other State (p. 112)
**Cláusula de fe y crédito cabal** requisito constitucional (Artículo IV, Sección 1) según el cual cada estado acepta (da "fe y crédito cabal") los actos públicos, documentos y procedimientos judiciales de cualquier otro estado

**fundamental law** laws of basic and lasting importance which may not easily be changed (p. 710)
**ley fundamental** leyes de importancia primordial y duradera que no se cambiarán con facilidad

# G

**gender gap** measurable differences between the partisan choices of men and women today (p. 174)
**brecha de género** diferencias medibles entre las elecciones partidistas actuales de los hombres y las mujeres

**general election** the regularly scheduled election at which voters make a final selection of officeholders (p. 185)
**elecciones generales** elecciones programadas regularmente en la que los votantes hacen una selección final de los funcionarios públicos

**genocide** the attempted extermination of a cultural, racial, or national group (p. 664)
**genocidio** intento de aniquilar a un grupo cultural, racial o nacional

**gerrymandering** the drawing of electoral district lines to the advantage of a party or group (pp. 165, 277)
**demarcación arbitraria** establecimiento de los límites de los distritos electorales de modo que den ventaja a un partido

**gift tax** a tax on a gift by a living person (p. 461)
**impuesto a los regalos** gravamen sobre los regalos que una persona viva otorga

**globalization** economic interdependence among nations of the world (p. 695)
**globalización** interdependencia económica entre naciones del mundo

**government** the institution through which a society makes and enforces its public policies (p. 4)
**gobierno** institución mediante la cual una sociedad lleva a cabo y hace cumplir sus políticas públicas

**government corporation** corporations within the executive branch subject to the President's direction and control, set up by Congress to carry out certain business-like activities (p. 448)
**corporación gubernamental** instituciones del poder ejecutivo que están sujetas a la dirección y el control del Presidente, formadas por el Congreso para que realicen determinadas actividades de tipo empresarial

**grand jury** the formal device by which a person can be accused of a serious crime (p. 594)
**gran jurado** dispositivo formal a través del cual puede acusarse a una persona de un crimen serio

**grants-in-aid program** grants of federal money or other resources to States, cities, counties, and other local units (p. 107)
**programa de subvención de fondos públicos** subvenciones de dinero o de otros recursos federales para los estados, sus ciudades, condados y otras unidades locales

**grass-roots pressures** pressures on public officials from members of an interest group or the people at large (p. 257)
**presión popular** presión que los miembros de un grupo de interés o la población en general ejercen sobre funcionarios públicos

**Great Leap Forward** the five-year plan for 1958 which was an attempt to quickly modernize China (p. 690)
**Gran Salto Hacia Adelante** plan quinquenal de 1958 que fue un intento de modernizar rápidamente a China

**gross domestic product (GDP)** the total amount of goods and services produced in a country each year (p. 473)

**producto interno bruto (PIB)** cantidad total de bienes y servicios producidos por un país cada año

**guerilla warfare** fighting carried out by small groups in hit-and-run raids (p. 657)

**conflicto guerrillero armado** lucha de golpe y fuga entre grupos pequeños

## H

**hard money** campaign money that is subject to regulations by the FEC (p. 208)

**fondos fiscalizados** dinero de campaña que está sujeto a las regulaciones de la FEC

**hardliners** those who fight to maintain the status quo (p. 661)

**radical** los que luchan por mantener el status quo

**heterogeneous** of another or different race, family or kind; composed of a mix of elements (p. 612)

**heterogéneo** de diferente raza, familia o especie; compuesto por una mezcla de elementos

## I

**ideological parties** parties based on a particular set of beliefs, a comprehensive view of social, economic, and political matters (p. 137)

**partidos ideológicos** partidos que se basan en un conjunto determinado de creencias, un punto de vista exhaustivo sobre asuntos sociales, económicos y políticos

**immigrant** those people legally admitted as permanent residents of a country (p. 612)

**inmigrante** persona que es admitida legalmente en calidad de residente permanente de un país

**impeach** to bring formal charges against a public official; the House of Representatives has the sole power to impeach civil officers of the United States (p. 319)

**impugnar** presentar cargos formales en contra de un funcionario público; la Cámara de Representantes tienen el exclusivo poder de impugnar a los funcionarios públicos de los Estados Unidos

**imperial presidency** term used to describe a President as an "emperor" who acts without consulting Congress or acts in secrecy to evade or deceive Congress; often used in reference to Richard Nixon's presidency (p. 403)

**presidencia imperial** término utilizado para describir a un Presidente como "emperador", quien actúa sin consultar al Congreso o de manera secreta para evadirlo o engañarlo

**implied powers** those delegated powers of the National Government that are suggested by the expressed powers set out in the Constitution; those "necessary and proper" to carry out the expressed powers; *see* delegated powers, expressed powers (pp. 96, 296)

**poderes implícitos** aquellos poderes delegados del gobierno nacional que se sugieren o están implícitos por los poderes explícitos; aquellos que son "necesarios y pertinentes" para realizar los poderes explícitos; *ver* delegated powers/poderes delegados, expressed powers/poderes explícitos

**import quota** a limit put on the amount of a commodity that can be imported into a country (p. 696)

**cuota de importación** límite sobre la cantidad de un producto que se puede importar a un país

**income tax** a tax levied on the income of individuals and/or corporations (p. 763)

**impuesto sobre la renta** gravamen sobre el ingreso de los individuos y/o corporaciones

**incorporation** the process by which a State establishes a city as a legal body (p. 749)

**incorporación** proceso mediante el cual un estado establece a una ciudad como un cuerpo legal

**incumbent** the current officeholder (pp. 131, 280)

**titular** funcionario público actual

**independent agencies** additional agencies created by Congress located outside the Cabinet departments (p. 441)

**oficinas independientes** agencias adicionales creadas por el Congreso y que se ubican fuera de los departamentos del Gabinete

**independent executive agencies** agencies headed by a single administrator with regional subunits, but lacking Cabinet status (p. 442)

**oficinas ejecutivas independientes** agencias dirigidas por un solo administrador que tiene subunidades operativas regionales pero que carecen del estatus del Gabinete

**independent regulatory commissions** independent agencies created by Congress, designed to regulate important aspects of the nation's economy, largely beyond the reach of presidential control (p. 445)

**comisiones regulatorias independientes** agencias independientes cuya función es regular aspectos importantes de la economía de la nación, en su mayoría fuera del control y dirección del Presidente

**Independents** a term used to describe people who have no party affiliation (p. 177)

**Independientes** término usado para describir a las personas que no están afiliadas a un partido

**indictment** a formal complaint before a grand jury which charges the accused with one or more crimes (p. 594)

**denuncia** queja formal que el fiscal expone ante un gran jurado, que incluye cargos al acusado por uno o más crímenes

**inferior courts** the lower federal courts, beneath the Supreme Court (p. 521)

**cortes inferiores** las cortes federales menores, que están por debajo de la Corte Suprema

**inflation** a general increase in prices throughout the economy (p. 474)

**inflación** incremento general de precios en la economía

**information** a formal charge filed by a prosecutor without the action of a grand jury (pp. 595, 729)

**información** acusación oficial presentada por un acusador sin acción de parte del jurado

**inherent powers** powers the Constitution is presumed to have delegated to the National Government because it is the government of a sovereign state within the world community (pp. 97, 296)

**poderes inherentes** aquellos poderes delegados del gobierno nacional que le pertenecen de manera inherente, debido a que es el gobierno de un estado soberano de la comunidad mundial

**inheritance tax** a tax levied on the beneficiary's share of an estate (p. 764)

**impuesto sobre la herencia** gravamen sobre lo que hereda un beneficiario

**initiative** a process in which a certain number of qualified voters sign petitions in favor of a proposed statute or constitutional amendment, which then goes directly to the ballot (p. 712)

**iniciativa** proceso en el que determinado número de votantes calificados firman peticiones a favor de una propuesta que se pasa después directamente a la papeleta electoral

**injunction** a court order that forces or limits the performance of some act by a private individual or by a public official (pp. 165, 562)

**mandato** orden judicial que fuerza o limita el desempeño de determinado acto, mediante la intervención de un particular o un funcionario público

**integration** the process of bringing a group into equal membership in society (p. 620)

**integración** proceso mediante el cual se ofrece a un grupo participación igualitaria dentro de la sociedad

**interest** a charge for borrowed money, generally a percentage of the amount borrowed (p. 462)

**interés** cargo que se hace por el dinero prestado, por lo general es un porcentaje de la cantidad prestada

**interest group** private organizations whose members share certain views and work to shape public policy (pp. 221, 242)

**grupo de interés** organizaciones privadas cuyos miembros comparten determinados puntos de vista y trabajan para dar forma a las políticas públicas

**interstate compact** formal agreement entered into with the consent of Congress, between or among States, or between a State and a foreign state (p. 111)

**pacto interestatal** acuerdo formal suscrito con el consentimiento del Congreso, entre dos estados o entre un estado y un estado extranjero, el cual está autorizado por la Constitución (Artículo I, Sección 10)

**involuntary servitude** forced labor (p. 583)

**servidumbre involuntaria** trabajo forzado

**isolationism** a purposeful refusal to become generally involved in the affairs of the rest of the world (p. 482)

**aislacionismo** rechazo voluntario a verse involucrado, de manera general, en los asuntos del resto del mundo

**item veto** a governor may veto one or more items in a bill without rejecting the entire measure (p. 724)

**veto de artículo** un gobernador puede vetar uno o más artículos de una propuesta de ley, sin rechazar toda la medida

# J

**Jim Crow law** a law that separates people on the basis of race, aimed primarily at African Americans (p. 619)

**Ley Jim Crow** ley que separa a un grupo de personas del resto de la gente con base en la raza, dirigido principalmente a los afroamericanos

**joint committee** legislative committee composed of members of both houses (p. 341)

**comité conjunto** comité legislativo compuesto por miembros de ambas cámaras

**joint resolution** a proposal for action that has the force of law when passed; usually deals with special circumstances or temporary matters (p. 344)

**resolución conjunta** propuesta de acción que tiene el poder de una ley cuando se aprueba; a menudo tiene que ver con circunstancias especiales o asuntos temporales

**judicial activism** a judicial philosophy in which supporters believe that judges should interpret and apply provisions in the Constitution and in statute law in the light of ongoing changes in conditions and values (p. 524)

**activismo judicial** filosofía judicial que argumenta que los

jueces deberían interpretar y aplicar las condiciones de la Constitución y del derecho escrito considerando los cambios progresivos de condiciones y valores

**judicial power** the power to interpret laws, to determine their meaning, and to settle disputes within the society (p. 5)

**poder judicial** poder para interpretar las leyes, determinar su significado y resolver las disputas que surgen dentro de la sociedad

**judicial restraint** a judicial philosophy in which supporters believe that judges should decide cases based on the original intent of the Framers or those who enacted the statute(s) involved in a case, or on precedent (p. 524)

**restricción judicial** filosofía judicial que argumenta que los jueces deberían tomar decisiones sobre sus casos basándose en la intención original de los creadores de la Declaración de Derechos o los que promulgan los estatutos del caso, o en el precedente

**judicial review** the power of a court to determine the constitutionality of a governmental action (p. 73)

**revisión judicial** poder de una corte para determinar la constitucionalidad de una acción gubernamental

**jurisdiction** the authority of a court to hear a case (p. 522)

**jurisdicción** autoridad de una corte para atender (juzgar y decidir) un caso

**jury** a body of persons selected according to law who hear evidence and decide questions of fact in a court case (p. 728)

**jurado** conjunto de personas seleccionadas de acuerdo con la ley para que escuchen la evidencia y decidan cuestiones de hecho en un caso de la corte

**jus sanguinis** the law of blood, which determines citizenship based on one's parents' citizenship (p. 633)

**jus sanguinis** ley de la sangre que define la ciudadanía con base en la ciudadanía de los padres

**jus soli** the law of soil, which determines citizenship based on where a person is born (p. 633)

**jus soli** ley del territorio que determina la ciudadanía con base en el lugar de nacimiento de la persona

**justice of the peace** a judge who stands on the lowest level of the State judicial system and presides over justice courts (p. 732)

**Juez de paz** juez que está en el nivel inferior del sistema judicial estatal y preside las cortes de justicia.

# K

**keynote address** speech given at a party convention to set the tone for the convention and the campaign to come (p. 383)

**discurso de apertura** alocución dada en una convención de partido para establecer el tono de la convención y de la futura campaña

# L

**labor union** an organization of workers who share the same type of job, or who work in the same industry, and press for government policies that will benefit their members (p. 248)

**sindicato laboral** organización de trabajadores que comparten el mismo tipo de trabajo, o que laboran en la misma industria y que busca impulsar políticas gubernamentales que beneficien a sus miembros

**laissez-faire theory** a theory which suggests that government should play a very limited role in society (p. 682)

**teoría del dejar hacer** teoría que sugiere que el gobierno debería desempeñar un papel limitado dentro de la sociedad

**law of supply and demand** a law which states that when supplies of goods and services become plentiful, prices tend to drop. When supplies become scarcer, prices tend to rise (p. 681)

**ley de la oferta y la demanda** ley que establece que cuando los suministros de bienes y servicios son abundantes, los precios tienden a bajar; cuando los suministros escasean, los precios tienden a subir

**legal tender** any kind of money that a creditor must, by law, accept in payment for debts (p. 303)

**moneda de curso legal** cualquier moneda que un acreedor debe aceptar, por ley, como pago de una deuda

**legislative power** the power to make a law and to frame public policies (p. 5)

**poder legislativo** poder para hacer una ley y redactar políticas públicas

**legitimacy** the belief of the people that a government has the right to make public policy (p. 650)

**legitimidad** crencia que un gobierno tiene el derecho de crear políticas públicas

**libel** false and malicious use of printed words (p. 559)

**libelo** utilización falsa y maliciosa de la palabra impresa

**liberal constructionist** one who argues a broad interpretation of the provisions of the Constitution, particularly those granting powers to the Federal Government (p. 314)

**construccionista liberal** aquel que argumenta una amplia interpretación de las estipulaciones de la Constitución, en particular las que otorgan poderes al gobierno federal

**limited government** basic principle of American government which states that government is restricted in what it may do, and each individual has rights that government cannot take away; *see* constitutionalism, popular sovereignty (pp. 31, 69, 709)

**gobierno limitado** principio básico del sistema estadounidense de gobierno que establece que el gobierno tiene restricciones en cuanto a lo que puede hacer, y en el cual cada individuo tiene ciertos derechos que el gobierno no puede enajenar; *ver* constitutionalism / constitucionalismo, popular sovereignty/soberanía popular

**line agency** an agency which performs the tasks for which the organization exists (p. 430)

**agencia del ramo** oficina que desempeña las tareas para las que la organización existe

**line-item veto** a President's cancellation of specific dollar amounts (line items) from a congressional spending bill; instituted by a 1996 congressional act, but struck down by a 1998 Supreme Court decision (p. 418)

**veto de partida** cancelación presidencial de ciertas cantidades de dólares (partidas) de una cuenta de gastos del Congreso; este veto se instituyó en 1996 mediante una ley del Congreso, pero la Suprema Corte lo derogó en 1998

**literacy** a person's ability to read or write (p. 161)

**alfabetismo** capacidad de una persona para leer o escribir

**lobbying** activities by which group pressures are brought to bear on legislators, the legislative process, and all aspects of the public-policy-making process (p. 254)

**cabildeo** actividades mediante las que un grupo aplica presión a los legisladores; al proceso legislativo, y a todos los aspectos del proceso de creación de políticas públicas

**lobbyist** a person who tries to persuade public officials to do those things that interest groups want them to do (p. 254)

**cabildero** persona que intenta persuadir a funcionarios a realizar cosas que ciertos grupos de interés quieren que se lleven a cabo

# M

**magistrate** a justice who handles minor civil complaints and misdemeanor cases that arise in an urban setting (p. 733)

**magistrado** juez que atiende demandas civiles menores y casos de faltas leves que surgen en un contexto urbano

**Magna Carta** Great Charter forced upon King John of England by his barons in 1215; established that the power of the monarchy was not absolute and guaranteed trial by jury and due process of law to the nobility (p. 31)

**Carta Magna** constitución que los barones impusieron al rey John de Inglaterra en 1215; estableció el principio de que el poder del monarca no era absoluto y garantizó los derechos fundamentales, como el de un juicio con jurado y procesos establecidos legales para la nobleza

**majority leader** the floor leader of the party that holds the majority of seats in each house of Congress (p. 336)

**líder mayoritario** portavoz del partido político que posee la mayor cantidad de escaños en cada cámara del Congreso

**majority opinion** officially called the Opinion of the Court; announces the Court's decision in a case and sets out the reasoning upon which it is based (p. 537)

**opinión mayoritaria** llamada oficialmente Opinión de la Corte; anuncia la decisión de la Corte sobre el caso y describe el razonamiento sobre el que ésta se basa

**majority rule** in a democracy, the majority of the people will be right more often than they will be wrong, and will be right more often than will any one person or small group (p. 21)

**gobierno por mayoría** en una democracia, la mayoría de personas estarán en lo correcto con más frecuencia, y estarán en lo correcto con más frecuencia que una sola persona o un grupo pequeño

**mandate** the instructions or commands a constituency gives to its elected officials (p. 220)

**mandato** las intrucciones u órdenes que un grupo de votantes da a sus funcionarios electos

**mass media** those means of communication that reach large audiences, especially television, radio, printed publications, and the Internet (p. 217)

**medios masivos de comunicación** aquellos medios de comunicación que llegan a grandes audiencias, sobre todo la radio, televisión, publicaciones impresas e Internet

**mayor-council government** the oldest and most widely used type of city government—an elected mayor as the chief executive and an elected council as its legislative body (p. 750)

**gobierno de consejo-alcalde** el más antiguo y más utilizado tipo de gobierno municipal: un alcalde electo como Presidente y un consejo electo como su cuerpo legislativo

**Medicaid** a program administered by the State to provide medical insurance to low-income families (p. 757)

*Medicaid* programa administrado por el Senado para proporcionar seguro médico a las familias de bajos ingresos

**medium** a means of communication; something that transmits information (p. 228)

**medio** un medio de comunicación; algo que transmite información

**mercantilism** an economic and political theory emphasizing money as the chief source of wealth to increase the absolute power of the monarchy and the nation (p. 651)

**mercantilismo** teoría económica y política que destaca el dinero como la fuente primaria de riqueza para incrementar el poder absoluto de la monarquía y de la nación

**metropolitan area** a city and the area around it (p. 755)

**area metropolitana** la ciudad y el área que le circunda

**minister** cabinet members, most commonly of the House of Commons (p. 667)

**ministro** miembro del gabinete, y más frecuentemente de la Cámara de los Comunes

**minority leader** the floor leader of the party that holds the minority of seats in each house of Congress (p. 336)

**líder minoritario** portavoz del partido político que posee la menor cantidad de escaños en cada cámara del Congreso

**Miranda Rule** the constitutional rights which police must read to a suspect before questioning can occur (p. 599)

**Ley Miranda** derechos constitucionales que la policía debe especificar a un sospechoso antes de que se le pueda interrogar

**misdemeanor** a lesser offense, punishable by a small fine and/or a short jail term (p. 728)

**falta leve** delito menor que se castiga mediante una pequeña multa o un breve período de encarcelamiento

**monetary policy** a process through which the government can influence the nation's economy through changes in the money supply and the availability of credit (p. 475)

**política monetaria** proceso mediante el cual el gobierno toma decisiones que afectan a la economía del país mediante cambios en la oferta monetaria y la disponibilidad de crédito

**monopoly** a firm that is the only source of a product or service (p. 681)

**monopolio** empresa que es la única fuente de un producto o servicio

**municipality** an urban political unit within a township that usually exists as a separate government entity (p. 747)

**municipalidad** unidad política urbana dentro de un municipio que por lo general existe como una entidad gubernamental independiente

# N

**NAFTA** (North American Free Trade Agreement) an agreement which removed trade restrictions among the United States, Canada, and Mexico, thus increasing cross-border trade (p. 697)

**NAFTA** (Tratado de Libre Comercio de América del Norte) acuerdo que elimina las restricciones comerciales entre los Estados Unidos, Canadá y México, con lo cual se incrementa el comercio transfronterizo

**national convention** meeting at which a party's delegates vote to pick their presidential and vice-presidential candidates (p. 381)

**convención nacional** Reunión en la que los delegados de un partido votan para elegir a sus candidatos a la presidencia y vicepresidencia

**national popular vote plan** proposal for electing the President whereby each State's election laws would provide for all of the State's electoral votes to be awarded to the winner of the national popular vote and enter into an interstate compact agreeing to elect the President by national popular vote (p. 393)

**plan para el voto nacional popular** propuesta para elegir al Presidente de la nación mediante la cual las leyes electorales de cada Estado decretan que los votos electorales sean otorgados al ganador del voto popular nacional y que de esta manera se llegue a un acuerdo interestatal donde se elija al presidente por voto popular

**NATO** (North American Treaty Organization) an alliance formed to protect the freedom and security of its members through political and military action (p. 506)

**OTAN** (Organización del Tratado del Atlántico Norte) alianza formada para proteger la libertad y seguridad de sus miembros a través de medidas políticas y militares

**naturalization** the legal process by which citizens of one country become citizens of another (pp. 309, 633)

**naturalización** proceso legal mediante el cual los ciudadanos de un país se convierten en ciudadanos de otro

**Necessary and Proper Clause** constitutional clause that gives Congress the power to make all laws "necessary and proper" for executing its powers; *see* implied powers (p. 312)

**Cláusula de necesidad y conveniencia** cláusula constitucional que otorga al Congreso el poder de expedir leyes "necesarias y pertinentes" para el ejercicio de sus poderes; *ver* implied powers/poderes implícitos

**New Jersey Plan** plan presented as an alternative to the Virginia Plan at the Constitutional Convention; called for a unicameral legislature in which each State would be equally represented (p. 55)

**Plan Nueva Jersey** plan presentado en la Convención Constitucional como una alternativa al Plan Virginia; proponía una legislatura unicameral en la que cada estado estuviera representado de forma equitativa

**nomination** the process of candidate selection in an electoral system (p. 184)

**nominación** proceso de selección de candidatos en una democracia

**nonpartisan election** election in which candidates are not identified by party labels (p. 190)

**elección no partidista** elección en la que los candidatos no están identificados por afiliaciones partidarias

# O

**off-year election** congressional election that occurs between presidential election years (pp. 170, 275)

**elección intermedia** elección del Congreso que ocurre entre las elecciones presidenciales

**oligarchy** a form of government in which the power to rule is held by a small, usually self-appointed elite (p. 14)

**oligarquía** forma de gobierno en la que el poder de gobernar lo ejerce una elite pequeña y por lo general autonombrada

**open market operations** the processes by which the Federal Reserve buys or sells government securities from and to the nation's banks in order to alter the money supply (p. 476)

**operaciones de mercado abierto** proceso por el cual la Reserva Federal compra y vende valores del Estado a los bancos del país para controlar la cantidad de dinero en circulación

**open primary** a party-nominating election in which any qualified voter can take part (p. 188)

**elección primaria abierta** elección partidista de nominación en la que cualquier votante calificado puede tomar parte

**opinion leader** any person who, for any reason, has an unusually strong influence on the views of others (p. 218)

**líder de opinión** cualquier persona que por alguna razón tiene una poderosa influencia en los puntos de vista de otras

**ordinance power** power of the President to issue executive orders; originates from the Constitution and acts of Congress (p. 406)

**poder de decreto** poder del Presidente de emitir órdenes ejecutivas; se fundamenta en la Constitución y en los actos del Congreso

**original jurisdiction** the power of a court to hear a case first, before any other court (p. 523)

**jurisdicción original** poder de una corte de atender un caso antes que otra corte

**oversight function** review by legislative committees of the policies and programs of the executive branch (p. 288)

**función de vigilancia** revisión de las políticas y los programas de la rama ejecutiva por parte de los comités legislativos

# P

**pardon** release from the punishment or legal consequences of a crime, by the President (in a federal case) or a governor (in a State case) (pp. 419, 724)

**perdón** exoneración que lleva a cabo el Presidente (en el caso federal) o el gobernador (en el caso estatal) del castigo o de las consecuencias legales de un crimen

**parliamentary government** a form of government in which the executive branch is made up of the prime minister, or premier, and that official's cabinet (p. 18)

**gobierno parlamentario** forma de gobierno en la que la rama ejecutiva está conformada por el primer ministro, o premier, y el gabinete oficial

**parochial** church-related, as in a parochial school (p. 552)

**parroquial** relacionado con la iglesia, como las escuelas parroquiales

**parole** the release of a prisoner short of the complete term of the original sentence (p. 725)

**liberación bajo palabra** libertad condicional de un prisionero poco antes de que termine el lapso de su sentencia original

**partisan** lawmaker who owes his/her first allegiance to his/her political party and votes according to the party line (p. 287)

**partidista** legislador que le debe fidelidad, en primer lugar, a su partido político, por lo que vota de acuerdo con la línea del partido

**partisanship** government action based on firm allegiance to a political party (p. 124)

**partidarismo** acción gubernamental basada en la vigorosa fidelidad a un partido político

**party caucus** a closed meeting of a party's House or Senate members; also called a party conference (p. 334)

**junta de dirigentes de partido** reunión cerrada de los miembros de la Cámara de Representantes o del Senado; también se conoce como Conferencia de partido

**party identification** loyalty of people to a political party (p. 177)

**identificación con el partido** lealtad de la gente hacia un partido político

**passport** a legal document issued by a state that identifies a person as a citizen of that state and permits travel to and from that state (p. 487)

**pasaporte** documento legal emitido por el estado que identifica a una persona como ciudadano de un país y le permite viajar al exterior y regresar

**patent** a license issued to an inventor granting the exclusive right to manufacture, use, or sell his or her invention for a limited period of time (p. 307)

**patente** licencia expedida a un inventor para garantizar el derecho exclusivo de manufactura, uso o venta de su invento, durante un tiempo limitado

**patrician** rich upper-class, landowning aristocrat of ancient Rome (p. 646)

**patricio** aristócrata propietario de tierras en la antigua Roma

**patronage** the practice of giving jobs to supporters and friends (p. 443)

**patrocinio** práctica de dar trabajo a los simpatizantes y amigos

**payroll tax** a tax imposed on nearly all employers and their employees, and on self-employed persons—the amounts owed by employees withheld from their paychecks (p. 460)

**impuesto sobre la nómina** gravamen tasado a casi todos los empleadores y sus empleados, así como a las personas autoempleadas; cantidad debida por los empleados que se les descuenta de su salario

**peer group** people with whom one regularly associates, including friends, classmates, neighbors, and co-workers (p. 218)

**grupo de camaradas** gente con la que uno se asocia regularmente y que incluye a socios, amigos, compañeros de clase, vecinos y compañeros de trabajo

**perjury** the act of lying under oath (p. 320)

**perjurio** mentir bajo juramento

**persona non grata** an unwelcome person; used to describe recalled diplomatic officials (p. 414)

***persona non grata*** una persona que no es bienvenida; se utiliza para describir a los funcionarios diplomáticos destituidos

**petition** a citizen's right to bring his or her view to the attention of public officials by such means as written petitions, letters, lobbying, and marches (p.569)

**petición** derecho de un ciudadano a presentar su opinión ante funcionarios públicos, por medio de escritos, cartas, el cabildeo y marchas

**Petition of Right** document prepared by Parliament and signed by King Charles I of England in 1628; challenged the idea of the divine right of kings and declared that even the monarch was subject to the laws of the land (p. 31)

**Solicitud de Derecho** documento preparado por el Parlamento y firmado por el rey Charles I de Inglaterra en 1628; cuestionó la idea del derecho divino de los reyes y declaró que incluso el monarca está sujeto a las leyes de la tierra

**picketing** patrolling of a business site by workers who are on strike (p. 565)

**vigilancia** manifestación de los trabajadores en el sitio donde están en huelga

**pigeonholed** expression describing how most bills introduced in each session of Congress are buried, put away, or never acted upon (p. 345)

**dar carpetazo** expresión que describe cómo proyectos de ley que se presentan ante el Congreso se olvidan, se ponen a un lado o nunca se llevan a cabo

**plaintiff** in civil law, the party who brings a suit or some other legal action against another (the defendant) in court (p. 523)

**demandante** en el derecho civil, la parte que entabla un juicio u otra acción legal contra otra (el demandado) en una corte

**platform** a political party's formal statement of basic principles, stands on major issues, and objectives (p. 382)

**plataforma** un enunciado formal por parte de un partido político respecto a sus principios básicos, opiniones sobre cuestiones políticas importantes y objetivos

**plebeians** the common folk in the Roman Republic (p. 647)

**plebeyos** personas que pertenecían a la plebe en la República Romana

**plurality** in an election, the number of votes that the leading candidate obtains over the next highest candidate (p. 127)

**mayoría** en una elección, el número de votos que el candidato que va a la punta tiene de ventaja sobre su competidor más cercano

**pocket veto** type of veto a chief executive may use after a legislature has adjourned; when the chief executive does not sign or reject a bill within the time allowed to do so; *see* veto (pp. 356, 418)

**veto indirecto** tipo de veto que el Presidente puede utilizar después de que una legislatura se suspende; se aplica cuando un Presidente no firma formalmente o rechaza una propuesta de ley, dentro del tiempo comprendido para eso; *ver* veto

**police power** the authority of each State to act to protect and promote the public health, safety, morals, and general welfare of its people (pp. 580, 717)

**facultad policial** autoridad de cada estado para proteger y promover la salud pública, la seguridad, la moral y el bienestar general de su pueblo

**political action committee** the political extension of special-interest groups which have a major stake in public policy (p. 202)

**comité de acción política** extensión política de grupos de interés especial, los cuales tienen un gran interés en la política pública

**political efficacy** one's own influence or effectiveness on politics (p. 172)

**eficacia política** la influencia o eficacia individual en la política

**political party** a group of persons who seek to control government through the winning of elections and the holding of public office (p. 122)

**partido político** grupo de personas que buscan controlar el gobierno mediante el triunfo en las elecciones y ejerciendo puestos públicos

**political socialization** the process by which people gain their political attitudes and opinions (p. 173)

**socialización política** proceso mediante el que la gente obtiene sus actitudes y opiniones políticas

**political spectrum** the range of political views (p. 123)

**espectro político** gama de perspectivas políticas

**politico** lawmaker who attempts to balance the basic elements of the trustee, delegate, and partisan roles; *see* trustee, delegates, partisan (p. 287)

**político** legislador que intenta balancear sus responsabilidades como legislador independiente, partidario político y delegado; *ver* trustee/independiente, delegats/delegads, partisan/partidista

**poll book** list of all registered voters in each precinct (p. 159)

**padrón electoral** lista de todos los votantes registrados en cada distrito

**poll tax** a special tax, demanded by States, as a condition of voting (p. 154)

**impuesto sobre el padrón electoral** gravamen especial, exigido por los estados como una condición para votar

**polling place** the place where the voters who live in a certain precinct go to vote (p. 195)

**casilla electoral** lugar donde los votantes que viven en cierto distrito acuden a votar

**popular sovereignty** basic principle of the American system of government which asserts that the people are the source of any and all governmental power, and government can exist only with the consent of the governed (pp. 41, 69, 709)

**soberanía popular** principio básico del sistema estadounidense de gobierno que establece que el pueblo es la fuente de todos los poderes gubernamentales, y que el gobierno sólo puede existir con el consentimiento de los gobernados

**precedent** court decision that stands as an example to be followed in future, similar cases (pp. 524, 728)

**precedente** decisión judicial que se toma como un ejemplo a seguir en el futuro para casos similares

**precinct** the smallest unit of election administration; a voting district (pp. 146, 195)

**circunseripción** unidad mínima de la administración electoral; distrito de votación

**preclearance** mandated by the Voting Rights Act of 1965, the prior approval by the Justice Department of changes to or new election laws by certain States (p. 167)

**preautorización** ordenada por la Ley de Derechos de Votos de 1965, respecto a la aprobación anterior, por parte del Departamento de Justicia, de los cambios en las leyes electorales existentes o nuevas en ciertos estados

**preliminary hearing** the first step in a major criminal prosecution where the judge decides if the evidence is enough to hold the person for action by the grand jury or the prosecutor (p. 732)

**audiencia preliminar** el primer paso del procesamiento de un crimen mayor, en el que el juez decide si la evidencia basta para que la persona comparezca ante el gran jurado o ante el fiscal para ser sujeto de una acción

**presentment** a formal accusation brought by the grand jury on its own motion, rather than that of the prosecutor (p. 594)

**declaración del Jurado** una acusación formal hecha por el jurado de acusación en vez del acusador

**President of the Senate** the presiding officer of a senate; in Congress, the Vice President of the United States; in a State's legislature, either the lieutenant governor or a senator (p. 333)

**Presidente del Senado** funcionario que preside un Senado; en el Congreso es el Vicepresidente de los Estados Unidos; en la legislatura estatal, cualquier vicegobernador o un senador

**President *pro tempore*** the member of the United States Senate, or of the upper house of a State's legislature, chosen to preside in the absence of the president of the Senate (p. 334)

**Presidente *pro tempore*** miembro del Senado de Estados Unidos, o de la cámara superior de la legislatura estatal, elegido para ser Presidente, en caso de ausencia del Presidente del Senado

**presidential elector** a person elected by the voters to represent them in making a formal selection of the Vice President and President (p. 374)

**elector presidencial** persona elegida por los votantes para representarlos en la selección formal del Presidente y Vicepresidente

**presidential government** a form of government in which the executive and legislative branches of the government are separate, independent, and coequal (p. 17)

**gobierno presidencial** forma de gobierno en la que las ramas ejecutivas y legislativas del gobierno están separadas, son independientes y están en la misma jerarquía

**presidential primary** an election in which a party's voters (1) choose State party organization's delegates to their party's national convention, and/or (2) express a preference for their party's presidential nomination (p. 378)

**elección presidencial primaria** elección en la que los votantes de un partido: (1) eligen a varios o a todos los delegados de la organización partidista estatal para la convención nacional de su partido, y/o (2) expresan una preferencia por alguno de los distintos contendientes para la nominación presidencial de su partido

**presidential succession** scheme by which a presidential vacancy is filled (p. 370)
  **sucesión presidencial** plan mediante el cual se resuelve la vacante presidencial

**Presidential Succession Act of 1947** law specifying the order of presidential succession following the Vice President (p. 370)
  **Ley para la sucesión presidencial de 1947** ley que especifica el orden para la sucesión presidencial, después del Vicepresidente

**preventive detention** a law which allows federal judges to order that an accused felon be held, without bail, when there is good reason to believe that he or she will commit yet another serious crime before trial (p. 603)
  **arresto preventivo** ley que permite a los jueces federales ordenar que un acusado de felonía sea arrestado, sin derecho a fianza, cuando existen buenas razones para creer que cometerá otro crimen grave antes del juicio

**prior restraint** the government cannot curb ideas before they are expressed (p. 562)
  **prohibición anticipada** el gobierno no puede reprimir las ideas antes de que se expresen

**privatization** the process of returning national enterprises to private ownership (p. 690)
  **privatización** regresar las empresas nacionales a la iniciativa privada

**Privileges and Immunities Clause** constitution's stipulation (Article IV, Section 2) that all citizens are entitled to certain "privileges and immunities," regardless of their State of residence; no State can draw unreasonable distinctions between its own residents and those persons who happen to live in other States (p. 114)
  **Cláusula de privilegios e inmunidades** estipulación constitucional (Artículo IV, Sección 2), en que se conceden ciertos "privilegios e inmunidades" a los ciudadanos, sin importar su estado de residencia; ningún estado puede hacer distinciones no razonables entre sus propios residentes y aquellas personas que vivan en otros estados

**probable cause** reasonable grounds, a reasonable suspicion of crime (p. 586)
  **causa probable** fundamentos razonables, sospecha razonable de un crimen

**procedural due process** the government must employ fair procedures and methods (p. 579)
  **procesos legales establecidos** el gobierno debe emplear procedimientos y métodos justos

**process of incorporation** the process of incorporating, or including, most of the guarantees in the Bill of Rights into the 14th Amendment's Due Process Clause (p. 549)
  **proceso de incorporación** proceso de integrar, o incluir, la mayor parte de las garantías de la Declaración de los derechos en la Cláusula de proceso legal establecido de la 14a enmienda

**progressive tax** a type of tax proportionate to income (pp. 459, 763)
  **impuesto progresivo** tipo de impuesto que es proporcional con el ingreso

**project grant** one type of federal grants-in-aid; made for specific projects to States, localities, and private agencies who apply for them (p. 109)
  **subvención de proyecto** tipo de subvención de fondos públicos; proporcionada para proyectos específicos de los estados, las localidades y las oficinas privadas que la solicitan

**property tax** a tax levied on real and personal property (p. 764)
  **impuesto a la propiedad** gravamen sobre los bienes raíces y la propiedad personal

**proportional plan** proposal by which each presidential candidate would receive the same share of a State's electoral vote as he or she received in the State's popular vote (p. 392)
  **plan proporcional** propuesta para seleccionar electores presidenciales, mediante la cual cada candidato recibiría la misma cantidad de votos electorales de un estado que recibió durante la votación popular del estado

**proportional representation** rule applied in Democratic primaries whereby any candidate who wins at least 15 percent of the votes gets the number of State Democratic convention delegates based on his or her share of that primary vote (p. 379)
  **regla de la representación proporcional** procedimiento aplicado en las elecciones primarias del partido Demócrata, en el cual cualquier candidato que gane al menos el 15% de los votos emitidos en una elección primaria, obtiene el número de delegados a la convención estatal demócrata, que le corresponda a esa proporción de las primarias

**proprietary** organized by a proprietor (a person to whom the king had made a grant of land) (p. 33)
  **propiedad** organizada por un dueño (persona a quien el rey le ha otorgado tierras)

**prorogue** adjourn, as in a legislative session (p. 271)
  **prórroga** aplazamiento, por ejemplo, de una sesión legislativa

**protectionism** the practice of national governments trying to control imports to protect native industries from foreign competition (p. 696)
  **proteccionismo** práctica en la que gobiernos nacionales tratan de controlar las importaciones para proteger a sus industrias de la competencia extranjera

**public affairs** those events and issues that concern the people at large; e.g., politics, public issues, and the making of public policies (pp. 215, 245)
  **asuntos públicos** aquellos acontecimientos y asuntos que importan al público en general, por ejemplo: la política, los temas públicos y la determinación de las políticas públicas

**public agenda** the public issues on which the people's attention is focused (p. 234)
  **agenda pública** asuntos públicos sobre los cuales está enfocada la atención de las personas

**public debt** all of the money borrowed by the government and not yet repaid, plus the accrued interest on that money; also called the national debt or federal debt (pp. 301, 466)
  **deuda pública** todo el dinero que ha pedido prestado el gobierno a lo largo de los años y que todavía no paga, además del interés acumulado sobre ese capital; también se conoce como deuda nacional o deuda federal

**public-interest group** an interest group that seeks to institute certain public policies of benefit to all or most people in this country, whether or not they belong to or support that organization (p. 252)
  **grupo de interés público** grupo de interés que busca instituir determinadas políticas públicas de beneficio para la mayoría de las personas de su país, sin importar si pertenecen o apoyan a la organización

**public opinion** the complex collection of the opinions of many different people; the sum of all their views (p. 215)
  **opinión pública** colección compleja de opiniones de diversas personas; la suma de todos sus puntos de vista

**public opinion poll** device that attempts to collect information by asking people questions (p. 222)

**encuestas de opinión pública** dispositivos que intentan recolectar información al hacerle preguntas a las personas

**public policy** all of the many goals that a government pursues in all of the many areas of human affairs in which it is involved (pp. 4, 242)

**políticas públicas** todas las metas que un gobierno se fija, así como los distintos cursos de acción que toma en sus intentos por llevar a cabo esos objetivos

**purge** the process of reviewing lists of registered voters and removing the names of those no longer eligible to vote; a purification (p. 159)

**purga** proceso de revisión de las listas de los votantes registrados y de la eliminación de los nombres que ya no son elegibles para votar; una depuración

# Q

**quorum** least number of members who must be present for a legislative body to conduct business; majority (p. 348)

**quórum** mínimo número de miembros que debe estar presente para que un cuerpo legislativo funcione; mayoría

**quota** a rule requiring certain numbers of jobs or promotions for members of certain groups (p. 628)

**cuota** regla que requiere que determinado número de trabajos o ascensos se den a miembros de ciertos grupos

**quota sample** a sample deliberately constructed to reflect several of the major characteristics of a given population (p. 224)

**muestra de cuota** muestra deliberadamente hecha para reflejar ciertas características importantes de una determinada población

# R

**random sample** a certain number of randomly selected people who live in a certain number of randomly selected places (p. 224)

**muestra aleatoria** determinado número de gente seleccionada al azar y que vive en ciertos lugares seleccionados de manera aleatoria

**ratification** formal approval, final consent to the effectiveness of a constitution, constitutional amendment, or treaty (pp. 48, 79)

**ratificación** aprobación formal, consentimiento definitivo de la eficacia de una constitución, de una enmienda constitucional o de un tratado

**rational basis test** a test less intensive than the strict scrutiny test that the Supreme Court uses to decide equal protection cases; the test asks whether the classification in question bears a reasonable relationship to the achievement of some proper governmental purpose (p. 619)

**prueba de razonamiento básico** examen menos intenso que el examen judicial riguroso que implementa la Corte Suprema para tomar decisiones en casos de protección equitativa; el examen pregunta si hay una relación razonable entre la clasificación en cuestión y el logro de algún propósito gubernamental

**reapportion** redistribute, as in seats in a legislative body (p. 274)

**reasignación** redistribución, como los escaños en un cuerpo legislativo

**recall** a petition procedure by which voters may remove an elected official from office before the completion of his or her regular term (p. 721)

**retirada inesperada** procedimiento de petición por el que los votantes puedan destituir a un funcionario oficial antes de terminar su mandato

**recess** a time when both houses of Congress temporarily suspend business (p. 271)

**receso** período en que ambas cámaras del Congreso suspenden actividades temporalmente

**recession** an absence of economic growth (p. 474)

**recesión** ausencia de crecimiento económico

**recognition** the exclusive power of a President to legally recognize (establish formal diplomatic relations with) foreign states (p. 414)

**reconocimiento** el poder exclusivo de un Presidente para reconocer (establecer relaciones diplomáticas) a estados extranjeros

**record** a transcript of proceedings made in trial court (p. 531)

**registro** trasunto de los procesos llevados a cabo en una corte tribunal

**redress** satisfaction of a claim payment (p. 540)

**resarcir** satisfacer una queja, por lo general mediante un pago

**referendum** a process by which a legislative measure is referred to the State's voters for final approval or rejection (p. 719)

**referendo** proceso mediante el cual una medida legislativa se consulta con los votantes de los estados para su aprobación o rechazo final

**refugee** one who leaves his or her homeland to seek protection from war, persecution, or some other danger (p. 615)

**refugiado** persona que abandona su hogar para buscar protección contra la guerra, la persecución o algún otro peligro

**regional security alliances** treaties in which the U.S. and other countries involved have agreed to take collective action to meet aggression in a particular part of the world (p. 506)

**alianzas regionales de seguridad** tratados mediante los cuales los Estados Unidos y otros países han acordado actuar colectivamente para enfrentar una agresión en una determinada parte del mundo

**registration** a procedure of voter identification intended to prevent fraudulent voting (p. 158)

**registro** procedimiento de identificación del votante para evitar votaciones fraudulentas

**regressive tax** a tax levied at a flat rate, without regard to the level of a taxpayer's income or ability to pay (pp. 461, 763)

**impuesto regresivo** gravamen con una tasa semejante, sin considerar el nivel de ingreso de los contribuyentes o su capacidad para pagarlo

**representative government** system of government in which public policies are made by officials selected by the voters and held accountable in periodic elections; *see* democracy (p. 31)

**gobierno representativo** sistema de gobierno en el que las políticas públicas están elaboradas por funcionarios elegidos por los votantes y que rinden cuentas en elecciones periódicas; *ver* democracy/democracia

**reprieve** an official postponement of the execution of a sentence; *see* pardon (pp. 419, 725)

**suspensión** un aplazamiento oficial de la ejecución de una sentencia; *ver* pardon/perdón

**reservation** public land set aside by a government for use by Native American tribes (p. 613)

**reservación** terrenos públicos que un gobierno reserva para el uso de las tribus nativas estadounidenses

**reserve requirement** the amount of money the Federal Reserve determines banks must keep in reserve with one of the Federal Reserve Banks (p. 476)

**reserva obligatoria** cantidad de dinero que la Reserva Federal determina que los bancos deben mantener en reserva con uno de los Bancos de la Reserva Federal

**reserved powers** those powers that the Constitution does not grant to the National Government and does not deny to the States (p. 99)

**poderes reservados** aquellos poderes que la Constitución no otorga al gobierno nacional, pero que tampoco niega a los estados

**resolution** a measure relating to the business of either house or expressing an opinion; does not have the force of law and does not require the President's signature (p. 344)

**resolución** medida relativa al funcionamiento de cualquier Cámara, o una expresión de opinión sobre un asunto; no tiene la fuerza de una ley y no requiere la firma del Presidente

**reverse discrimination** discrimination against the majority group (p. 628)

**discriminación inversa** segregación en contra del grupo mayoritario

**rider** unpopular provision added to an important bill certain to pass so that it will "ride" through the legislative process (p. 344)

**cláusula adicional** provisión poco probable de ser aprobada por méritos propios, que se agrega a un proyecto de ley importante que se tiene la seguridad que será aprobado, así que dicha cláusula "cabalga" por todo ese proceso legislativo

**right of association** the right to associate with others to promote political, economic, and other social causes (p. 572)

**derecho de asociación** derecho de asociarse con otros para promover causas políticas, sociales, económicas y de otra índole

**right of legation** the right to send and receive diplomatic representatives (p. 485)

**derecho de legación** derecho a enviar y recibir representantes diplomáticos

**rule of law** concept that government and its officers are always subject to the law (p. 70)

**gobierno de la ley** el concepto en que el gobierno y sus oficiales estan sujetos a la ley

**runoff primary** a primary in which the top two vote-getters in the first direct primary face one another (p. 190)

**elección primaria complementaria** elección primaria en la que los dos candidatos con más votos en la elección primaria directa se enfrentan; el ganador de esa votación se convierte en el nominado

# S

**sales tax** a tax placed on the sale of various commodities, paid by the purchaser (p. 762)

**impuesto a las ventas** gravamen sobre las ventas de distintos bienes, el cual paga el comprador

**sample** a representative slice of the public (p. 224)

**muestra** una porción representativa del público

**search warrant** a court order authorizing a search (p. 581)

**orden de allanamiento** autorización judicial para registrar algo

**secretary** an official in charge of a department of government (p. 435)

**secretario** funcionario a cargo de un departamento de gobierno

**sectionalism** a narrow-minded concern for, or devotion to, the interests of one section of a country (p. 133)

**regionalismo** preocupación estrecha, o devoción por los intereses de una región del país

**Security Council** a 15-member panel that bears the UN's major responsibility for keeping international peace (p. 509)

**Consejo de Seguridad** panel de 15 miembros de la ONU que tiene la máxima responsabilidad para la conservación de la paz internacional

**sedition** the crime of attempting to overthrow the government by force, or to disrupt its lawful activities by violent acts (p. 560)

**sedición** crimen de intentar derrocar al gobierno mediante la fuerza, o de interrumpir las actividades legales por medio de actos violentos

**seditious speech** the advocating, or urging, of an attempt to overthrow the government by force, or to disrupt its lawful activities with violence (p. 560)

**discurso sedicioso** la convocatoria o el apoyo a un intento de derrocar al gobierno mediante la fuerza, o a la interrupción de actividades legales por medio de la violencia

**segregation** the separation of one group from another (p. 619)

**segregación** separación de un grupo respecto a otro

**select committee** legislative committee created for a limited time and for some specific purpose; also known as a special committee (p. 340)

**comité selecto** comité legislativo creado por un tiempo limitado y para algún propósito específico; también se conoce como comité especial

**senatorial courtesy** custom that the Senate will not approve a presidential appointment opposed by a majority-party senator from the State in which the appointee would serve (p. 88)

**cortesía senatorial** costumbre de que el Senado no aprobará una nominación presidencial, si esa designación no es aprobada por el senador del partido mayoritario de ese estado, en donde la persona designada habría de servir

**seniority rule** unwritten rule in both houses of Congress reserving the top posts in each chamber, particularly committee chairmanships, for members with the longest records of service (p. 337)

**regla de antigüedad** regla no escrita de ambas Cámaras del Congreso, de acuerdo con la cual, los puestos más altos de cada una de ellas los ocuparán aquellos miembros que tengan un historial de servicio más antiguo; se aplica de forma más estricta a las presidencias de los comités

**separate-but-equal doctrine** a constitutional basis for laws that separate one group from another on the basis of race (Jim Crow Laws) (p. 619)

**doctrina de iguales pero separados** base constitucional para leyes que segregan a un grupo respecto a otro, con base en la raza (Leyes Jim Crow)

**separation of powers** basic principle of American system of government that the executive, legislative, and judicial powers are divided among three independent and coequal branches of government; *see* checks and balances (p. 70)

**separación de poderes** principio básico del sistema de gobierno estadounidense, según el cual los poderes ejecutivo, legislativo y judicial están divididos en tres ramas independientes e iguales; *ver* checks and balances/pesos y contrapesos

**session** period of time during which, each year, Congress assembles and conducts business (p. 270)

**sesión** período regular durante el cual se reúne el Congreso para atender a asuntos oficiales

**shadow cabinet** members of opposition parties who watch, or shadow, particular Cabinet members, and who would be ready to run the government (p. 668)

**gabinete alterno** miembros de los partidos de oposición que vigilan, o supervisan, a un miembro particular del gabinete, y que estarían listos para ejercer el gobierno

**shield law** a law which gives reporters some protection against having to disclose their sources or reveal other confidential information in legal proceedings (p. 563)

**ley Escudo** ley que ofrece a los periodistas cierta protección contra la revelación de sus fuentes o la publicación de otra información confidencial durante los procedimientos legales

**single-issue parties** parties that concentrate on only one public policy matter (p. 137)

**partidos de un único asunto** partidos que se concentran en un solo aspecto de la política pública

**single-member district** electoral district from which one person is chosen by the voters for each elected office (pp. 127, 275)

**distrito de un solo miembro** distrito electoral en donde los votantes eligen, en la papeleta electoral, una sola persona para cada cargo

**slander** false and malicious use of spoken words (p. 559)

**calumnia** utilización falsa y maliciosa del discurso hablado

**socialism** a philosophy based on the idea that the benefits of economic activity should be fairly distributed (p. 686)

**socialismo** filosofía basada en la idea de que los beneficios de la actividad económica deben distribuirse de manera equitativa a toda la sociedad

**soft-liners** those who want to reform governmental policies or procedures (p. 661)

**blandos** quienes quieren reformar las políticas o procesos gubernamentales

**soft money** money given to State and local party organizations for voting-related activities (p. 208)

**fondos no fiscalizados** fondos otorgados al estado y a organizaciones partidistas locales para actividades relacionadas con el voto, por ejemplo: registro de votantes, envío de propaganda por correo, anuncios

**sound bite** short, sharply focused report that can be aired in 30 or 45 seconds (p. 235)

**informe sucinto** informaciones breves y concisas que pueden despacharse en 30 ó 45 segundos

**sovereign** having supreme power within one's own territory; neither subordinate nor responsible to any other authority (pp. 7, 649)

**soberano** tener poder supremo y absoluto dentro de su propio territorio; no estar subordinado ni ser responsable ante ninguna otra autoridad

**sovereignty** utmost authority in decision making and in maintaining order of a state (p. 650)

**soberanía** autoridad suprema para tomar desiciones y mantener el orden en un estado

**Speaker of the House** the presiding officer of the House of Representatives, chosen by and from the majority party in the House (p. 332)

**Vocero de la Cámara** funcionario que preside la Cámara de Representantes y que es electo por el partido mayoritario en la Cámara, al cual pertenece

**special district** an independent unit created to perform one or more related governmental functions at the local level (p. 748)

**distrito especial** unidad independiente creada para llevar a cabo una o más funciones gubernamentales relacionadas a nivel local

**special session** an extraordinary session of a legislative body, called to deal with an emergency situation (p. 271)

**sesión especial** sesión extraordinaria de un cuerpo legislativo, convocada para tratar una situación de emergencia

**splinter parties** parties that have split away from one of the major parties (p. 138)

**partidos de escisión** partidos formados por la fractura de uno de los principales partidos; la mayor parte de los partidos pequeños importantes en el ámbito político estadounidense son partidos de escisión

**split-ticket voting** voting for candidates of different parties for different offices at the same election (p. 177)

**voto diferenciado** votar, en la misma elección, por candidatos de distintos partidos para puestos diferentes

**spoils system** the practice of giving offices and other favors of government to political supporters and friends (pp. 132, 443)

**sistema de prebendas** práctica de ofrecer cargos y otros favores gubernamentales a los simpatizantes y amigos políticos

**staff agency** an agency that supports the chief executive and other administrators by offering advice and other assistance in the management of the organization (p. 430)

**oficina de apoyo** tipo de agencia cuya función es dar respaldo al Presidente y a otros administradores, ofreciendo consejos y otro tipo de asistencia en la administración de la organización

**standing committee** permanent committee in a legislative body to which bills of a specified subject matter are referred; *see* select committee (p. 338)

**comisión permanente** comité permanente de un cuerpo legislativo al que se presentan las propuestas de ley sobre una materia específica; *ver* comité selecto

**state** a body of people living in a defined territory who have a government with the power to make and enforce law without the consent of any higher authority (p. 5)

**estado** conjunto de personas que viven en un territorio definido y que tienen un gobierno con el poder de legislar y de hacer cumplir la ley, sin tener el consentimiento de una autoridad superior

**statutory law** a law passed by the legislature (p. 713)

**ley estatuida** ley aprobada por los legisladores

**straight-ticket voting** the practice of voting for candidates of only one party in an election (p. 177)

**voto duro** práctica de votar en una elección por los candidatos de un solo partido

**straw vote** poll that seeks to read the public's mind by asking the same question of a large number of people (p. 222)

**encuesta pre-electoral** encuestas que pretenden conocer la opinión de la gente haciendo simplemente la misma pregunta a una gran cantidad de personas

**strict constructionist** one who argues a narrow interpretation of the Constitution's provisions, in particular those granting powers to the Federal Government (p. 313)

**construccionista estricto** persona que defiende una interpretación estrecha de las estipulaciones de la Constitución, en particular las referentes al otorgamiento de poderes al gobierno federal

**strict scrutiny test** a higher standard than the rational basis test a law must meet in equal protection cases (p. 619)

**examen judicial riguroso** estándar más alto que la prueba de fundamento razonable que una ley debe honrar en casos de protección equitativa

**strong-mayor government** a type of government in which the mayor heads the city's administration (p. 750)
  **gobierno de alcalde vigoroso** tipo de gobierno en el que el alcalde encabeza la administración de la ciudad

**subcommittee** division of existing committee that is formed to address specific issues (p. 340)
  **subcomité** división de un comité existente que se forma para atender asuntos específicos

**subpoena** an order for a person to appear and to produce documents or other requested materials (p. 322)
  **citación** orden para que se presente una persona o para que se presenten documentos u otros materiales solicitados

**subsidy** a grant of money, usually from a government (p. 207)
  **subsidio** una subvención de dinero, por lo general por un gobierno

**substantive due process** the government must create fair policies and laws (p. 578)
  **proceso legal duradero** el gobierno debe crear políticas y leyes justas

**successor** a person who inherits a title or office (p. 319)
  **sucesor** persona que hereda un título o un cargo

**suffrage** the right to vote (p. 152)
  **sufragio** el derecho de votar

**supply-side economics** the assumption that tax cuts increase the supply of money in private hands and stimulate the economy (p. 464)
  **economía de oferta** idea que supone que la reducción de impuestos aumenta el dinero de entidades privadas y estimula la economía

**Supremacy Clause** a provision of the U.S. Constitution that states that the Constitution, federal law, and treaties of the United States are the "supreme Law of the Land" (p. 101)
  **Cláusula de Supremacía** Cláusula de la Constitución de los Estados Unidos que estipula que la Constitución, la ley federal y los tratados de los Estados Unidos son la "ley suprema del país"

**surplus** more income than spending (p. 463)
  **superávit** cuando hay más ingresos que gastos

**swing voters** members of the electorate who have not made up their minds at the start of a campaign and are open to persuasion by either side (p. 386)
  **votantes indecisos** miembros del electorado que no han tomado una decisión al comienzo de una campaña y están dispuestos a inclinarse hacia cualquiera de los candidatos

**symbolic speech** expression by conduct; communicating ideas through facial expressions, with body language, or by carrying a sign or wearing an armband (p. 565)
  **discurso simbólico** expresión mediante la conducta; comunicación de ideas a través de expresiones faciales, lenguaje corporal o mediante el uso de un letrero o portando una banda en el brazo

# T

**tariff** a tax on imported goods (p. 696)
  **arancel** impuesto que se aplica a las importaciones

**tax** a charge levied by government on persons or property to meet public needs (p. 300)
  **impuesto** cargo gravado por el gobierno a las personas o propiedades, con el objeto de satisfacer las necesidades públicas

**term** two-year period of time during which Congress meets (p. 270)

**término** lapso especificado durante el cual se desempeñará en el cargo un funcionario elegido

**territory** part of the United States that is not admitted as a State and has its own government (p. 308)
  **territorio no incorporado** territorio de los Estados Unidos que no tiene calidad de estado y que tiene su propio gobierno

**terrorism** the use of violence to intimidate a government or society (p. 492)
  **terrorismo** el uso de violencia para intimidar a un gobierno o sociedad

**Three-Fifths Compromise** an agreement at the Constitutional Convention to count a slave as three-fifths of a person when determining the population of a State (p. 56)
  **Avenencia de las tres quintas partes** acuerdo logrado en la Convención Constitucional respecto a que un esclavo debería contarse como tres quintas partes de una persona, para propósitos de determinar la población de un estado

**tort** a wrongful act that involves injury to one's person, property, or reputation in a situation not covered by the terms of a contract (p. 728)
  **entuerto** acto injusto que incluye daño a la propiedad de una persona, su reputación o a la persona en sí en una situación que no está cubierta por un contrato

**township** a subdivision of a county (p. 743)
  **municipio** división de un condado

**trade association** interest group within the business community (p. 248)
  **asociación comercial** grupos de interés dentro de la comunidad de los negocios

**trade embargo** a ban on trade with a particular country or particular countries (p. 697)
  **embargo comercial** prohibición de comerciar con un país o varios países en particular

**transient** person living in a State for only a short time, without legal residence (p. 157)
  **transeúnte** persona que vive en un estado sólo por un breve tiempo, sin residencia legal

**treason** betrayal of one's country; in the Constitution, by "levying war against the United States or offering comfort or aid to its enemies" (p. 606)
  **alta traición** deslealtad hacia el país propio; en la Constitución, librar una guerra en contra de los Estados Unidos, proporcionar aliento u ofrecer ayuda a sus enemigos

**treaty** a formal agreement between two or more sovereign states (pp. 87, 412)
  **tratado** acuerdo formal entre dos o más estados soberanos

**trustee** lawmaker who votes based on his or her conscience and judgment, not the views of his or her constituents (p. 287)
  **independiente** legislador que vota en cada asunto de acuerdo con su conciencia y su juicio independiente, sin considerar las opiniones de sus electores o de otros grupos

# U

**unconstitutional** contrary to constitutional provision and so illegal, null and void, of no force and effect (p. 73)
  **inconstitucional** contrario a las estipulaciones constitucionales y, por lo tanto, ilegal, nulo e inválido, que no tiene fuerza ni efecto

**uncontrollable spending** spending that Congress and the President have no power to change directly (p. 468)
  **gasto incontrolable** gastos que ni el Congreso ni el Presi-

**gasto incontrolable** gastos que ni el Congreso ni el Presidente tienen el poder de cambiar de manera directa, incluyendo los intereses de la deuda

**unicameral** an adjective describing a legislative body with one chamber; *see* bicameral (p. 34)

**unicameral** adjetivo que describe un cuerpo legislativo con una sola Cámara; *ver* bicameral

**unitary government** a centralized government in which all government powers belong to a single, central agency (p. 14)

**gobierno unitario** gobierno centralizado en el que los poderes ejercidos por el gobierno pertenecen a una única oficina central

**United Nations** a league of nations, with 192 members, that accepts the obligations of the United Nations Charter, a treaty drafted in 1945 (p. 508)

**Naciones Unidas** grupo de naciones compuesto por 192 miembros, que acepta las obligaciones de la Carta de las Naciones Unidas, tratado redactado en el año 1945

**universe** a term used in polling that refers to the whole population that the poll aims to measure (p. 224)

**universo** término que se usa en asuntos de elecciones que se refiere a la población entera que se intenta medir mediante una encuesta

# V

**veto** chief executive's power to reject a bill passed by a legislature; literally (Latin) "I forbid"; *see* pocket veto (pp. 72, 356)

**veto** poder del Presidente para rechazar un proyecto de ley aprobado por una legislatura; literalmente (latín) "Prohíbo"; *ver* pocket veto/veto indirecto

**Virginia Plan** plan presented by delegates from Virginia at the Constitutional Convention; called for a three-branch government with a bicameral legislature in which each State's membership would be determined by its population or its financial support for the central government (p. 54)

**Plan Virginia** proyecto presentado por los delegados de Virginia en la Convención Constitucional; proponía un gobierno con tres poderes y una legislatura bicameral en la que la representación de cada estado estuviera determinada por su población o por su apoyo financiero al gobierno central

**visa** a permit to enter another country, obtained from the country one wishes to enter (p. 487)

**visa** permiso para entrar a otro país, otorgado por el país al cual se desea entrar

# W

**ward** a unit into which cities are often divided for the election of city council members (p. 146)

**barrio** unidad en la que suelen dividirse las ciudades para la elección de los miembros del consejo municipal

**warrant** a court order authorizing, or making legal, some official action, such as a search or an arrest (p. 732)

**mandamiento** orden judicial que autoriza o hace legal alguna acción oficial, como la orden de allanamiento o la orden de arresto

**weak-mayor government** a type of government in which the mayor shares his or her executive duties with other elected officials (p. 750)

**gobierno de alcalde débil** tipo de gobierno en el que el alcalde comparte las obligaciones ejecutivas con otros funcionarios electos

**weblogs (blogs)** Web site postings usually devoted to a specific subject, often allowing visitors to post comments (p. 233)

**blogs** listados en un sitio web que por lo general se enfocan en un tema en específico y que muchas veces permite a los visitantes poner sus comentarios

**welfare** cash assistance to the poor (p. 757)

**beneficencia** ayuda en efectivo a los pobres

**welfare state** country that provides extensive social services at little or no cost to the users (p. 687)

**estado benefactor** países que ofrecen una amplia gama de servicios sociales a un bajo costo o de manera gratuita para los usuarios

**whips** assistants to the floor leaders in the House and Senate, responsible for monitoring and marshaling votes (p. 336)

*whips* auxiliares de los líderes de las fracciones partidistas en la Cámara de Representantes y el Senado que son responsables de vigilar y ordenar los votos

**winner-take-all** an almost obsolete system whereby a presidential aspirant who won the preference vote in a primary automatically won all the delegates chosen in the primary (p. 379)

**el ganador se lleva todo** sistema casi obsoleto en donde un aspirante presidencial que ganaba la preferencia del voto en las elecciones primarias, automáticamente obtenía el apoyo de todos los delegados elegidos en dichas elecciones

**World Trade Organization (WTO)** organization created in 1995 to increase trade (p. 697)

**Organización Mundial del Comercio (OMC)** organización creada en 1995 para aumentar el comercio

**writ of assistance** blanket search warrant with which British custom officials had invaded private homes to search for smuggled goods (p. 585)

**auto de ayuda** orden general de allanamiento con la que los funcionarios aduanales británicos invadían los hogares privados en busca de bienes de contrabando

**writ of certiorari** an order by a higher court directing a lower court to send up the record in a given case for review; from the Latin meaning "to be more certain" (p. 534)

**auto de avocación *o certiorari*** orden emitida por una corte superior dirigida a una corte inferior para que remita el expediente de un determinado caso para su revisión; el significado en latín de la expresión es "tener mayor certeza"

**writ of habeas corpus** a court order which prevents unjust arrests and imprisonments (p. 592)

**auto de *habeas corpus*** orden judicial que evita arrestos y encarcelamientos injustos

# Z

**zoning** the practice of dividing a city into a number of districts and regulating the uses to which property in each of them may be put (p. 753)

**zonificación** práctica de dividir a una ciudad en determinado número de distritos y de regular los usos que se dará a la propiedad en cada uno de ellos

# Index

Items in blue refer to Teacher's Edition pages. Note: Entries with a page number followed by a (c) denote reference to a chart on that page; those followed by a (p) denote a photo; those followed by a (m) denote a map; those followed by a (g) denote a graph.

INDEX

**INDEX**

**INDEX**

# Acknowledgments

The people who made up the **Magruder's American Government** team—representing design services, editorial, editorial services, education technology, fact-checking, library services, manufacturing and inventory planning, market research, marketing services, product management, production, planning and coordination, and technical operations—are listed below. Boldface type denotes the core team members.

**Courtney Alexander, Alyssa Boehm,** Kristen Braghi, **Peter Brooks,** Lynn Burke, Todd Christy, **Lori-Anne Cohen,** Brett Creane, Michael Di Maria, Laura Edgerton-Riser, Thomas Ferreira, Patricia Fromkin, Andrea Golden, Shelby Gragg, Thomas Guarino, Susan Hersch, Paul Hughes, Katharine Ingram, Stephanie Krol, Courtney Markham, **Dotti Marshall, Grace Massey,** Laurie McKenna, Angelina Mendez, Jennifer Paley, **Gabriela Perez Fiato,** Judi Pinkham, Charlene Rimsa, Amanda Seldera, Alexandra Sherman, **Mark Staloff,** Kara Stokes, Kristen VanEtten, Paula Wehde

## Art Credits

Maps: XNR Productions, Inc.

## Cover Image

Stockbyte/Thinkstock

## Illustration

Kenneth Batelman, Kerry Cashman, Daniel Guidera, Gillian Kahn, Rich McMahon, Jen Paley, Cyndy Patrick, Ted Smykal, Robin Storesund

## Picture Research

Kara Stokes

## Photography

Every effort has been made to secure permission and provide appropriate credit for photographic material. The publisher deeply regrets any omission and pledges to correct errors called to its attention in subsequent editions.

Unless otherwise acknowledged, all photographs are the property of Pearson Education, Inc.

Photo locators denoted as follows: Top (T), Center (C), Bottom (B), Left (L), Right (R), Background (Bkgd)

**FRONT MATTER Title page** Stockbyte/Thinkstock; **v** Catherine Karnow/Corbis; **vi** (R) Jason Reed/Reuters Media; **vii** David Noble Photography/Alamy Images; **viii** ©Doug Mills/AP Images; **ix** Catherine Karnow/Corbis; **x** Zhukov Sergei/ITAR-TASS/Corbis; **xi** ©Toby Talbot/AP Images; **xiii** Danny Kerr/Authentic Education; **xiv** (T) Inti St Clair/Getty Images, (C, B) iStockphoto; **xvii** (B) Flip Schulke/Black Star; **xxvi** (T) Swim Ink 2, LLC/Corbis; **C04** Daniel Webster addressing the United States Senate, in the Great Debate on the Constitution and the Union in 1850, 1860 (engraving) (b&w photo), American School, (19th century)/Library of Congress, Washington D.C., USA,/Bridgeman Art Library, (B) Greg Pease/Getty Images; **C05** (R) Greg Pease/Getty Images; **C06** (BCR) ©The Granger Collection, NY, (L) Bettmann/Corbis, (TR) Courtesy of the U.S. Department of the Treasury, (BR) JUPITERIMAGES/Comstock Images/Alamy, (TC) The Trustees of the British Museum/Art Resource, NY; **C09** Scott J. Ferrell/Congressional Quarterly/Getty Images; **C10** (BL) Ron Edmonds/AP Images; **C11** Stockbyte/Getty Images; **C14** ©The Granger Collection, NY; **C15** ©The Granger Collection, NY; **C17** Ron Chapple/Taxi/Getty Images; **C18** ©Ron Edmonds/AP Images; **C20** (R) David J. & Janice L. Frent Collection/Corbis, (L) Drug Enforcement Administration; **S00** Corbis; **S01** JUPITERIMAGES/BananaStock/Alamy; **S03** Grapheast/Alamy; **S06** Tetra Images/Alamy; **S13** Blend Images/Getty Images; **S14** (L) Corbis; **S17** PHOVOIR/FCM Graphic/Alamy; **S19** Digital Vision/Alamy; **S20** Juliet Brauner/Alamy Images; **S22** Ed Fischer/The Post-Bulletin; **S24** Red Chopsticks/Getty Images; **S28** (R) ©David J. & Janice L. Frent Collection/Corbis

**UNIT 1 Page 1** Catherine Karnow/Corbis; **2** Larry Chiger/SuperStock; **4** (TL) Klaus Hackenberg/zefa/Corbis, (TR) Romilly Lockyer/The Image Bank/Getty Images; **5** (T) Mark Wilson/Getty Images, (C) SANDY SCHAEFFER/MAI/Landov LLC, The Collection of the Supreme Court of the United States; **7** (R) Atlantide Phototravel/Corbis, (L) REUTERS/Victor Fraile/Landov LLC; **8** (T) Archive Photos/Getty Images, (TC) Bridgeman Art Library/Bridgeman Art Library, (BC) Joseph Werner/Bridgeman Art Library/Getty Images,

(B) Library of Congress; **9** By permission of Johnny Hart and Creators Syndicate, Inc./Creators Syndicate; **10** Mike Lutz/U.S. Coast Guard via/Getty Images; **11** Ed Fischer/Cartoon Stock; **12** (R, Bkgd) Tim Graham/Getty Images; **13** (B) ©Harry Cabluck/AP Images, (T) ©Toby Talbot/AP Images; **15** (R) Alain Evrard/Impact Photos/Imagestate Media, (L) Christy Bowe/Corbis; **18** ©Benny Gool/AP Images; **19** ©Mike Stone/AP Images; **20** (R, Bkgrd) Richard B. Levine/Ambient Images, Inc.; **21** (R, L) Bettmann/Corbis; **22** Steve Artley/Artley Cartoons; **26** Baloo-Rex May/Cartoon Stock; **27** (L) Bust of Aristotle (384–322 BC) (marble) (bw photo), Roman Museo Nazionale Romano, Rome, Italy, Alinari/Bridgeman Art Library, (R) Bust of Plato (c. 427–347 BC) (stone) (bw photo), Greek Vatican Museums and Galleries, Vatican City, Italy, Alinari/Bridgeman Art Library; **28** The Battle of Lexington, 19th April 1775, 1910 (oil on canvas), Wollen, William Barnes (1857–1936) National Army Museum, London,/Bridgeman Art Library; **30** (R) ©The Granger Collection, NY; **31** The Trustees of the British Museum/Art Resource, NY; **32** William Sumits/Time Life Pictures/Getty Images; **35** (TL) Ehsan Maleki/Sipa Press/NewsCom, (B) AFP PHOTO/FILES/NewsCom, (TR) ©Jeff Widener/AP Images; **36** (R) HIP/Art Resource, NY; **37** (T) American Antiquarian Society, Worcester, Massachusetts, USA,/Bridgeman Art Library, (B) Library of Congress; **38** (CR, CL, C) ©The Granger Collection, NY, (L) British Library Board/Bridgeman Art Library, (R) The Art Archive; **39** (R) ©The Granger Collection, NY, (C) Bunker's Hill, 1775, c.1900 (wc on paper), Simkin, Richard (1840–1926) National Army Museum, London,/Bridgeman Art Library, (L) HIP/Art Resource, NY; **41** ©Bettmann/Corbis; **42** (R) Bill Brooks/Alamy Images, (L) English School/Bridgeman Art Library/Getty Images; **43** Thomas Jefferson Writing the Declaration of Independence, from 'The Story of the Revolution' by Henry Cabot Lodge (1850–1924), published in Scribner's Magazine, March 1898 (oil on canvas), Pyle, Howard (1853–1911) Delaware Art Museum, Wilmington, USA, Howard Pyle Collection/Bridgeman Art Library; **45** (L) Bettmann/Corbis, (R) Eric Van Den Brulle/Riser/Getty Images; **47** (R) Bettmann/Corbis, (L) Todd Gipstein/National Geographic/Getty Images; **48** (R) ©The Granger Collection, NY, (L) Federal Reserve Bank of San Francisco; **49** ©The Granger Collection, NY; **51** Russell Kord/Alamy Images; **52** (R, L) The Granger Collection, NY; **53** (TC) ©The Granger Collection, NY, Bettmann/Corbis, (TR) Burazin/Getty Images, (BR) Photo by George Skadding/Time & Life Pictures/Getty Images, (L) Purestock/Getty Images, (BC) Visions of America/Joe Sohm/Getty Images; **55** (TR) Bust of Charles de Secondat (1689–1755) Baron de Montesquieu, 1767 (marble), Lemoyne, Jean Baptiste II (1704–78) Musee des Arts Decoratifs, Bordeaux, France, Lauros Giraudon/Bridgeman Art Library, (BL) Bust of Jean Jacques Rousseau (1712–78) (terracotta), Houdon, Jean-Antoine (1741–1828) Musee des Beaux-Arts, Orleans, France, Giraudon/Bridgeman Art Library, (TL) John Locke (1632–1704) (plaster), English School, (19th century) Yale Center for British Art, Paul Mellon Collection, USA,/Bridgeman Art Library, (BR) Library of Congress; **57** (L, Bkgrd) The Granger Collection, New York; **58** Courtesy, Independence National Historical Park ; **59** (L) Garry Black/Masterfile Corporation, (R) Picture History; **60** (L) Stock Montage/Getty Images, (R) The Granger Collection, New York; **61** American Antiquarian Society; **64** Library of Congress; **65** Getty Images; **66** age fotostock/SuperStock; **68** (R, L) ROBERTO SCHMIDT/AFP/Getty Images; **69** Visions of America, LLC/Alamy; **70** (R, L, C) Steve Artley/Artley Cartoons; **71** (R, L, C) Steve Artley/Artley Cartoons; **76** (BR, BC) ©The Granger Collection, NY, (BL) James Madison (oil on canvas), American School, (19th century) Musee Franco-Americaine, Blerancourt, Chauny, France, Giraudon/Bridgeman Art Library, (L) Purestock/Getty Images; **77** Bettmann/Corbis; **78** (R, Bkgrd) Bettmann/Corbis; **80** (R) Bettmann/Corbis, (C) Smithsonian Institution/Corbis, (L) The Granger Collection, NY; **81** (R, L) Bettmann/Corbis; **83** reprint by permission/Mark Parisi; **84** image100/Corbis; **85** (R, Bkgrd) Tom Fox/Dallas Morning News/Corbis; **86** ©AP Images; **88** ©Gerald Herbert/Associated Press; **90** Baloo-Rex May/Cartoon Stock; **91** (B) ©The Granger Collection, NY, (T) New York Public Library/Art Resource, NY; **92** EMMANUEL DUNAND/AFP/Getty Images; **94** (R, Bkgrd) ©Denis Poroy/Associated Press; **95** ©Chris Polk/AP Images; **97** (R) ©Bettmann/Corbis, (L) Carlos Barria/Reuters Media; **98** (B) SERGEI ILNITSKY/EPA/Landov LLC; **100** (L) David R. Frazier/Photo Researchers, Inc., (R) LUKE FRAZZA/AFP/Getty Images; **101** ©The Granger Collection, NY; **103** (R, Bkgrd) ©Nancy Bannick Collection, Hawaii State Archives/AP Images; **106** (R) Connie Ricca/Corbis, (L) Tony Freeman/PhotoEdit, Inc.; **108** (L) Bob Daemmrich/PhotoEdit, Inc., (C) ©Ric Dugan/Herald-Mail/AP Images, (R) Richard T. Nowitz/Corbis; **110** (TR) age fotostock/SuperStock, (TL) Mark Constantini/San Francisco Chronicle/Corbis, (B) SEAN GARDNER/Reuters/Landov LLC; **111** (R, L) Corbis/SuperStock; **113** Bettmann/Corbis; **116** Mischa Richter/Cartoon Bank/Conde Nast Publications; **117** (R) Getty Images, (L) Stock Montage/SuperStock; **118** (L) Gary Blakeley/Shutterstock;

**UNIT 2 Page 119** Jason Reed/Reuters Media; **120** ©Stephan Savoia/Associated Press; **122** (R, L) ©Victoria Arocho/AP Images; **123** (B) EPA/TANNEN MAURY/Landov LLC; **125** (TR) Carolyn Chappo, (BL) Democratic National Committee, (T) RICH GLICKSTEIN/MCT/Landov LLC; **129** J.B.

Handelsman/Cartoon Bank/Conde Nast Publications; **130** (C) James Madison (1751–1836) (colour litho), American School, (19th century) Private Collection, Peter Newark American Pictures/Bridgeman Art Library, (Bkgrd) Library of Congress, SuperStock; **131** (R) Library of Congress; **133** (R, L) ©The Granger Collection, NY, (CR, CL) Beathan/Corbis; **134** (C) ©Private Collection/Christie's Images/Bridgeman Art Library, (L) ©The Granger Collection, NY, (CL) Brooklyn Museum/Corbis, (R) Minnesota Historical Society/Corbis, (CR) Poster depicting Abraham Lincoln, the White House and the log cabin in which he was born (colour litho), American School/ Private Collection/Bridgeman Art Library; **135** (R) ©Jean-Pierre Lescourret/ Corbis, (C) Bettmann/Corbis, (BL) President Franklin D. Roosevelt (1882–1945) c.1941 (photo), American Photographer, (20th century) Private Collection, Peter Newark American Pictures/Bridgeman Art Library; **137** (R) ©Bettmann/Corbis, (L) Three Lions/Getty Images; **139** (TR, TL) David J. & Janice L. Frent Collection/Corbis, Niday Picture Library/Alamy Images; **140** Underwood And Underwood/Time & Life Pictures/Getty Images; **141** ©Kevork Djansezian/AP Images; **142** (R, Bkgrd) Chris Kleponis/Zuma/ Corbis; **143** Gary Markstein/Copley Service/Creators Syndicate; **144** (BR) Democratic National Committee, (TR) JASON REED/Reuters/Corbis, (Bkgrd) MedioImages/Corbis; **146** ©Kiichiro Sato/AP Images; **148** Mischa Richter/ Cartoon Bank/Conde Nast Publications; **149** Jeff Parker/Florida Today/ Cagle Cartoons, Inc.; **150** ©Springfield News-Leader, Christina Dicken/ AP Images; **152** (R, Bkgrd) LOU DEMATTEIS/Reuters/Corbis; **153** (R) ©AP Images, (L) George Caleb Bingham/Bridgeman Art Library/Getty Images, (C) The Granger Collection, NY; **155** Bettmann/Corbis; **156** (R, Bkgrd) Barbara Davidson/Dallas Morning/Corbis; **157** (L) ©Chuck Burton/AP Images, (R) ©Khampha Bouaphanh/AP Images; **158** Bettmann/Corbis; **159** (C) ©Bill Waugh/AP Images, (L) Jonathan Nourok/PhotoEdit, Inc., (Bkgrd) ©Ric Feld/ AP Images, (T) ©Robert E. Klein/AP Images; **160** (T) ©Craig Fritz/AP Images, (B) ©Ric Feld/AP Images; **163** ©Bob Adelman/Magnum Photos, Spencer Platt/Getty Images; **164** (R, Bkgrd) Bettmann/Corbis; **166** (R) ©AP Images, (C) Corbis, (L) The Granger Collection, New York; **167** (L) ©AP Images, (R) Jacques M. Chenet/Corbis; **169** Jim West/Alamy Images; **170** (R, L) Peter Turnley/Corbis; **172** Gary Varvel/Creators Syndicate; **175** (R) Kara Stokes; **176** 2008 Jeff Parker/Cagle Cartoons, Inc.; **177** EMMANUEL DUNAND/AFP/ Getty Images; **180** (R) Marshall Ramsey/NewsCom; **181** Library of Congress; **182** ©Elaine Thompson/AP Images; **184** (R, Bkgrd) ERIC MILLER/REUTERS/ Landov LLC; **185** Jack Ohman/Tribune Media Services; **186** (B) ©Amy E. Powers/AP Images, (T) David R. Frazier Photolibrary, Inc./Alamy Images, (C) REUTERS/Eric Miller/Landov LLC; **188** JIM WATSON/AFP/Getty Images; **189** (TR) ©Chris Carlson/AP Images, (BL) J. Scott ©Applewhite/AP Images; **193** (R, L) ©Mark Humphrey/AP Images; **194** ©Elaine Thompson/AP Images; **196** Getty Images, Inc./Getty Images; **198** ©Jamie-Andrea Yanak/AP Images; **200** (TR) ©David Crenshaw/AP Images, (TL) KYU OH/Getty Images, (B) The Collection of the Supreme Court of the United States; **201** (R, Bkgrd) ©Ben Margot/AP Images; **203** (R, C) Jason Reed/Reuters/Corbis, (L) Richard Ellis/Getty Images; **204** (R, L) Joe Raedle/Getty Images; **206** ©Josh Reynolds/AP Images; **207** Steve Artley/Artley Cartoons; **210** Steve Kelley/ Creators Syndicate/Cartoonist Group; **212** Mario Tama/Getty Images; **214** (R, Bkgrd) Alex Wong/Getty Images; **217** (TR) Comstock Select/Corbis, (BL) Image Source/Corbis; **218** Dave Carpenter/Cartoon Stock; **219** Minnesota Historical Society/Corbis; **220** (R, Bkgrd) Billy E. Barnes/PhotoEdit, Inc.; **221** (R) ©Shawn Patrick Ouellette/AP Images; **222** Gary Varvel/Creators Syndicate; **227** (B) Tom Carter/PhotoEdit, Inc.; **228** (R, Bkgrd) ©Masterfile Royalty-Free; **230** ©The Granger Collection, NY; **232** (L) Bettmann/Corbis, (R) Yale Joel/Time Life Pictures/Getty Images; **233** att Campbell/epa/Corbis; **234** (L) Harley Schwadron/Cartoon Stock, (R) Leo Cullum/Cartoon Bank/ Conde Nast Publications; **238** Adey Bryant/Cartoon Stock; **239** Ray Jelliffe/ Cartoon Stock; **240** ©Jonathan Alcorn/Zuma Press, Inc.; **242** (R, Bkgrd) Frances Roberts/Richard B. Levine; **243** Dave Coverly/Cartoonist Group; **244** (R) ©The Granger Collection, NY, (TL) J. R. Eyerman/Time Life Pictures/ Getty Images, (TCL) Library of Congress, (BL) Minnesota Historical Society/ Minnesota Historical Society, (BCL) Photography Collection, Miriam and Ira D. Wallach Division of Art, Prints and Photographs/New York Public Library Picture Collection; **246** A. Ramey/PhotoEdit, Inc.; **247** (R, Bkgrd) ©Mike Groll/AP Images; **249** (T) Bettmann/Corbis, Blend Images/SuperStock; **251** (T) ©Gary Dineen/Getty Images, (B) Scott Nelson/Getty Images; **253** (TL) Catherine Karnow/Corbis, (TR) Michael Geissinger/The Image Works, Inc., (B) UPI Photo/Roger L. Wollenberg/NewsCom; **254** (R, Bkgrd) Getty Images; **255** ©Charles Dharapak/AP Images; **258** (BC) Alan Schein Photography/ Corbis, (Bkgrd) Momatiuk-Eastcott/Corbis, (B) Polka Dot Images/ SuperStock, (TC) Ryan McVay/Getty Images, (T) Spencer Jones/Jupiter Images; **259** Lynne Fernandes/The Image Works, Inc.; **260** Mike Keefe/ The Denver Post/dePIXion Studios, Inc.; **262** Cartoon Bank/Conde Nast Publications; **263** Ann Telnaes/Cartoonist Group; **264** (R)Charles Barsotti/ Cartoon Bank/Conde Nast Publications, (L) Gary Blakeley/Shutterstock;

**UNIT 3 Page 265** David Noble Photography/Alamy Images; **266** Shawn Thew/epa/Corbis; **268** (R, Bkgrd) Olivier Douliery/Abaca Press/MCT/ NewsCom; **269** Brad Markel/Getty Images; **272** Bonnie Kamin/PhotoEdit, Inc.; **273** (R, Bkgrd) Stefan Zaklin/epa/Corbis; **278** Bettmann/Corbis; **279** (R) ©Times-News, Mike Dirks/AP Images, (L) Courtesy of Ileana Ros-Lehtinen; **281** (R, Bkgrd) Kevin Dietsch/UPI/NewsCom; **282** (L) ©Jackie Johnston/AP Images, (TR) Jason Reed/Reuters/Landov LLC; **283** Matthew Cavanaugh/ epa/Corbis; **284** Bernard Schoenbaum/Cartoon Bank/Conde Nast

Publications; **285** (R, Bkgrd) ©J. Scott Applewhite/AP Images; **287** KEVIN LAMARQUE/Reuters/Landov LLC; **288** DON EMMERT/AFP/Getty Images; **289** Joseph Farris/Cartoon Bank/Conde Nast Publications; **292** Library of Congress; **294** Mark Wilson/Getty Images; **296** (R, Bkgrd) ©LM Otero/AP Images; **298** (R) ©Free Agents Limited/Corbis, (L) Bill Frymire/Masterfile Corporation; **299** (L) David Pollack/Corbis, (C) Photofusion Picture Library/ Alamy Images; **300** Robert Weber/Cartoon Bank/Conde Nast Publications; **304** (R, Bkgrd) Harris and Ewing/Corbis; **305** James Madison (1751–1836) published by Nathaniel Currier (1813–88) (colour litho), Stuart, Gilbert (1755–1828) (after) Private Collection, Peter Newark American Pictures/ Bridgeman Art Library; **306** (C) DK Stock/Getty Images, (L) UpperCut Images/Getty Images; **307** (R) ©Eg Project/Photonica/Getty Images, (L) Corbis/Alamy, (C) Getty Images, Inc./Getty Images; **308** (TL) David R. Frazier Photolibrary, Inc./Alamy Images, (TR) Don Smetzer/Alamy Images, (B) Paul Springett/Alamy; **310** (BC) Alexander Hamilton, c. 1804 (oil on canvas), Trumbull, John (1756–1843) Collection of the New York Historical Society, USA,/Bridgeman Art Library, (BL) Corbis/Alamy, (BR) Courtesy of the American Numismatic Association, (L) Purestock/Getty Images; **311** (L) ©Private Collection/Christie's Images/Bridgeman Art Library, (C) Courtesy of the American Numismatic Association, (R) Sandy Felsenthal/ Corbis; **312** (R, Bkgrd) ©Khampha Bouaphanh/AP Images; **314** ©A.Y. Owen/ Time Life Pictures/Getty Images; **315** (L) ©Jason Hunt/AP Images, (R) Jeff Greenberg/PhotoLibrary Group, Inc.; **316** J.B. Handelsman/Cartoon Bank/ Conde Nast Publications; **317** (TL) ©AP Images, (B) MIKE SEGAR/Reuters/ Landov LLC, (TR) SHAMIL ZHUMATOV/Reuters/Corbis; **318** (Bkgrd) ©AP Images, (R) ©Joe Marquette/AP Images; **320** ©AP Images; **321** (R) George Waldman/Getty Images, (CR) ©Khue Bui/AP Images, (B) Mark Wilson/ Getty Images, (TR, TL) Najlah Feanny/Corbis, (CL) Wally McNamee/Corbis; **322** (R) LUKE FRAZZA/AFP/Getty Images, (L) UPI Photo/Landov LLC; **323** (L) Brandi Simons/Getty Images, (R) Paul Katz/Getty Images; **324** Ed Stein The Rocky Mountain News Dist. by United Feature Syndicate, Inc./ United Media; **327** Bob Artley/Worthington Daily Globe; **328** Scott J. Ferrell/Congressional Quarterly/Getty Images; **330** (Bkgrd) EPA/MICHAEL REYNOLDS/Landov LLC; **331** Corbis; **333** (TL, CL, BCL) Courtesy of U. S. House of Representatives, Office of Senator Inouye, Photo courtesy Office of Representative Kevin McCarthy, (CR, BR, BCR) United States Senate; **336** Harley Schwadron/Cartoon Stock; **338** (R, Bkgrd) Ken Cedeno/Corbis; **342** Rafael Suanes/MCT/NewsCom; **343** (Bkgrd) Brooks Kraft/Corbis, (R) Scott J. Ferrell/Congressional Quarterly/NewsCom; **344** Mark Wilson/Getty Images; **347** (L) ©Tim Sloan/AFP/Getty Images, (R) Chip Somodevilla/ Getty Images; **348** Cartoon Bank/Conde Nast Publications; **350** (B) CHUCK KENNEDY/KRT/NewsCom, (TL) Scott J. Ferrell/Congressional Quarterly/ Getty Images, (TR) William Thomas Cain/Getty Images; **351** (R, Bkgrd) Scott J. Ferrell/Congressional Quarterly/NewsCom; **352** NewsCom/NewsCom; **354** Mark Kauffman/Time Life Pictures/Getty Images; **355** (C) Courtesy of U. S. House of Representatives, (T, B) Scott J. Ferrell/Congressional Quarterly/Getty Images; **356** ©Haraz N. Ghanbari/Associated Press; **358** John Cole, The Scranton Times-Tribune/Cagle Cartoons, Inc.; **359** Bob Englehart/Cagle Cartoons, Inc.; **360** (L) Gary Blakeley/Shutterstock, (R) Nick Anderson/Washington Post Writers Group/Cartoonist Group;

**UNIT 4 Page 361** ©Doug Mills/AP Images; **362** Jim Young/Reuters Media; **364** (R, Bkgrd) David Hume Kennerly/Getty Images; **365** Reuters/Corbis; **367** (L) ©AP Images; **368** Brooks Kraft/Corbis; **369** Michael Newman/ PhotoEdit, Inc.; **370** (R, Bkgrd) Bettmann/Corbis; **371** National Archives/ Handout/Getty Images; **372** Peter Steiner/Cartoon Bank/Conde Nast Publications; **373** ©Terry Ashe (BIDEN CHOICE)/AP Images; **374** (L) Bettmann/Corbis, (R) Bristol City Museum and Art Gallery, UK/Bridgeman Art Library, (C) Private Collection/Peter Newark American Pictures/Bridgeman Art Library; **377** (R, Bkgrd) Spencer Platt/Getty Images; **380** Jack Ohman/ All rights reserved. Reprinted with permission/Tribune Media Services; **381** ©Chris Carlson/AP Images; **384** (R) Paul Drinkwater/NBC/Getty Images, (L) ©Reed Saxon/AP Images; **386** (R, Bkgrd) Kayte Deioma/PhotoEdit, Inc.; **390** (L) REUTERS/Colin Braley/Corbis, (R) Robert King/Newsmakers/ Getty Images; **391** DAEMMRICH BOB/Corbis; **393** (BR) ©Carolyn Kaster/AP Images, (L) Dave Granlund, (TR) JEFF HAYNES/AFP/Getty Images; **396** Tony Auth 1986 The Philadelphia Inquirer/Universal Uclick; **398** Bettmann/Corbis; **400** (R) Christie's Images/Corbis, (Bkgrd) Paul Damien/NGS/Getty Images; **402** (R) ©The Granger Collection, NY, (L) Library of Congress; **403** Harris & Ewing, Inc./Corbis; **404** (TL) Brooks Kraft/Corbis, (TR) NSA/Getty Images, (B) UPI/Kevin Dietsch/NewsCom; **405** (R, Bkgrd) ©Ron Edmonds/AP Images; **406** Cynthia Johnson/Time Life Pictures/Getty Images; **408** 2005 Dwayne Booth/Cagle Cartoons, Inc.; **410** (C) ©AP Images, (BL) Joseph Sohm/ Visions of America/Corbis, (TL) Purestock/Getty Images, (R) ©The Herald-Sun, Christine T. Nguyen/AP Images; **411** (R) Bettmann/Corbis, (L) Owen Franken/Corbis, (C) ©White House/AP Images; **412** (R) Bettmann/Corbis, (Bkgrd) Dirck Halstead/Getty Images; **413** LUKE FRAZZA/AFP/Getty Images; **414** Bettmann/Corbis; **415** Kevin Lamarque/REUTERS/Corbis; **417** (R, Bkgrd) TIM SLOAN/MAI/Landov LLC; **419** Bettmann/Corbis; **422** Rex Babin/ The Sacramento Bee/Rex Babin; **424** Melanie Steton Freeman/The Christian Science Monitor via Getty Images/Getty Images; **426** (R, Bkgrd) UPI Photo/ Roger L. Wollenberg/Landov LLC; **427** ©Clay Bennett/Christian Science Monitor; **429** Jon Arnold Images Ltd/Alamy Images; **431** (R, Bkgrd) Pete Souza/White House/Handout/Corbis; **432** ©Brooks Kraft/Corbis; **433** SAUL LOEB/AFP/Getty Images; **435** (R, Bkgrd) Photoshot/NewsCom; **436** (L)

Bettmann/Corbis, (C) DK Images, (R) H. Armstrong Roberts/Retrofile/Getty Images; **437** (R) C. Sherburne/PhotoLink/Getty Images, (L) Philip Nealey/Digital Vision/Getty Images; **439** (B) Bettmann/Corbis, (T) Chuck Kennedy/White House/Sipa Press/0909141931/NewsCom; **440** Bettmann/Corbis; **441** (R, Bkgrd) ©Diane Bondareff, Pool/AP Images; **443** (BR) ©Eugene Hoshiko/AP Images, (L) Helen Ashford/Jupiter Images, (C) Popperfoto/Getty Images; **444** (C) Adam Jones/DanitaDelimont/NewsCom, (R) REUTERS/Bob Care Florida Keys News Bureau/HO/Landov LLC, (L) REUTERS/Jessie Cohen/Smithsonian's National Zoo/Landov LLC; **447** (L) Brooks Kraft/Sygma/Corbis, (T) Comstock/Corbis, (R) David Frazier/PhotoEdit, Inc., (B) ©Keith Srakocic/AP Images; **448** Bob/Thom Thaves/Cartoonist Group; **450** (B) Carrie Devorah/WENN/NewsCom, (TR) Chris Howes/Wild Places Photography/Alamy Images, (TL) Walter Bibikow/Corbis; **452** Gary McCoy/Cagle Cartoons, Inc.; **454** GREG DERR photos/The Patriot Ledger; **456** (R, Bkgrd) Monika Graff/Getty Images; **457** Harley Schwadron/Cartoon Stock; **459** (CC) Bryan Mullennix/Getty Images, (T) Don Farrall/Getty Images, (B) Large blue and white Ming vase with the Hsuan Te mark, 1426–35 (porcelain), Chinese School, (15th century) Private Collection,/Bridgeman Art Library, (TC) PM Images/Getty Images, (CC) Scott Kleinman/Getty Images, (BC) Stockbyte/Getty Images; **463** (R, Bkgrd) Minnesota Historical Society/Corbis; **465** Bryan Mitchell/Getty Images; **467** (R, Bkgrd) Najlah Feanny/Corbis; **471** Paul Morigi/WireImage/Getty Images; **472** C Squared Studios/Getty Images; **473** (R, Bkgrd) Scott J. Ferrell/Congressional Quarterly/Getty Images; **474** (B) ©Ed Reinke/AP Images, (T) LARRY DOWNING/Reuters/Landov LLC; **475** David Horsey/Seattle Post-Intelligencer; **478** Steve Kelley/Creators Syndicate/Cartoonist Group; **480** Bettmann/Corbis; **482** (R, Bkgrd) Howard Sochurek/Time Life Pictures/Getty Images; **483** ©2010 Luojie, China Daily, China/Cagle Cartoons, Inc.; **484** (BR) ©Dimas Ardian/Getty Images, (TR) Courtesy United States Government/U.S. Department of State, Martin Shields/Alamy Images, (TL) Marwan Assaf/REUTERS/Corbis; **485** U.S. Department of State; **486** (T) ©MPI/Getty Images, (B) Library of Congress; **487** (R) Breck P. Kent/Breck P. Kent Natural History Photography, (L) Sarah-Maria Vischer/The Image Works, Inc.; **488** (R, Bkgrd) Shawn Thew/AFP/Getty Images; **491** Brad Loper/Dallas Morning News/Corbis; **493** (BR) ©U.S. Coast Guard/Getty Images, (BC) Brooks Kraft/Corbis, (T) Gerald French/Corbis, (BL) Tom Pennington/Fort Worth Star-Telegram/MCT/NewsCom; **494** Momatiuk-Eastcott/Corbis; **495** (R, Bkgrd) Library of Congress; **496** (L) Bettmann/Corbis, (R) Culver Pictures/The Art Archive; **497** Library of Congress; **500** Popperfoto/Getty Images; **501** (T) Bettmann/Corbis, (B) ©Joe Marquette/AP Images; **502** Darren McCollester/Getty Images; **504** (B) AFP PHOTO/POOL/JIM WATSON/NewsCom, (TL) ACOB J. KIRK/US NAVY NEWS PHOTO/NewsCom, (TR) RomeoRanoco/Reuters/Landov LLC; **505** (R, Bkgrd) ©Bettmann/Corbis; **508** REUTERS/Paco Sanseviero/Corbis; **510** (T) Bettmann/Corbis, (BR) Dimas Ardian/Getty Images, (BL) Dung Vo Trung/Sygma/Corbis, (BC) Tetra Images/Corbis; **514** Robert Mankoff/Cartoon Bank/Conde Nast Publications; **516** (L) Gary Blakeley/Shutterstock, (R) John Deering;

**UNIT 5 Page 517** Catherine Karnow/Corbis; **518** ©Evan Vucci/AP Images; **520** (Bkgrd) Gaetano/Corbis, (R) SCOTT J. FERREL/Congressional Quarterly Inc./NewsCom; **525** Corbis/Corbis; **527** (TL) Barros & Barros/Getty Images, (B) Image by Ron Sachs/CNP/Corbis, (TR) Richard Cummins/SuperStock; **528** (R, Bkgrd) Jerry Talfer/San Francisco Chronicle/Corbis; **532** (R) ©Stock Montage/Getty Images, (Bkgrd) Digital Vision/Alamy; **533** ©The Granger Collection, NY; **536** (T) The Collection of the Supreme Court of the United States; **538** (R, Bkgrd) ©U.S. Army, Pvc Ben Brody/AP Images; **539** 2007 Paresh Nath/Cagle Cartoons, Inc.; **542** Bettmann/Corbis; **543** picturehistory/NewsCom; **544** JOSHUA LOTT/Reuters/Landov LLC; **546** (R, Bkgrd) ©AP Images; **547** Michael Newman/PhotoEdit, Inc.; **551** (R, Bkgrd) JUPITERIMAGES/Brand X/Alamy; **553** ©Douglas C. Pizac/AP Images; **554** Peter Titmuss/Alamy Images; **556** (R) ©Mike Groll/AP Images, (L) ©Steve Yeater/AP Images; **557** ©The News Tribune, Bob King/AP Images; **559** (R, Bkgrd) New York Times Pictures/Redux Pictures; **560** Al Freni/Library Of Congress/Time Life Pictures/Getty Images; **562** (TR, TL) Minnesota Historical Society; **566** Bettmann/Corbis; **568** Tony Freeman/PhotoEdit, Inc.; **569** (R, Bkgrd) ©Nick Ut/AP Images; **571** (L) Najlah Feanny/Corbis, (R) ©Ric Francis/AP Images; **574** Steve Artley/Artley Cartoons; **575** Doug Marlette, Tallahassee Democrat/Tribune Media Services; **576** Steve Hamblin/Alamy; **578** (Bkgrd) Alfred Pasieka/Photo Researchers, Inc., (R) Mark Harmel/Getty Images; **579** (T) Jon Shireman/Getty Images, (B) Stockbyte/Getty Images; **580** The New Yorker Collection 1970, J.B. Handelsman from cartoonbank/Cartoon Bank/Conde Nast Publications; **581** Gunter Marx/Alamy Images; **583** (R, Bkgrd) William Fritsch/Harper Fritsch Studios; **584** Manuscripts, Archives and Rare Books Division, Schomburg Center for Research in Black Culture, The New York Public Library, Astor, Lenox and Tilden Foundations/New York Public Library Picture Collection; **585** Rolf Richardson/Alamy Images; **586** Susan Van Etten/PhotoEdit, Inc.; **588** ©AP Images; **589** William Whitehurst/Corbis; **591** (B) AFP PHOTO/Mandel NGAN/NewsCom, (TR) Ralf-Finn Hestoft/Corbis, (TL) William Foley/Time Life Pictures/Getty Images; **592** (R, Bkgrd) ©Douglas C. Pizac-Pool/Getty Images; **593** (T) American Stock/Getty Images, (B) ©AP Images; **597** Flip Schulke/Black Star; **598** (T) David R. Frazier Photolibrary, Inc./Alamy Images, (B) Thinkstock/Alamy; **600** (BL) Bettmann/Corbis, (BR) John Loengard/Time Life Pictures/Getty Images, (L) Purestock/Getty Images; **601** (BC) Digital Vision/Getty Images, (BL) Michael Newman/PhotoEdit, Inc., (BR) ©Robert Houston/AP Images;

**602** (R, Bkgrd) ©Nathan Martin/AP Images; **603** Dave Parker/Cartoon Stock; **608** Mike Baldwin/Cartoon Stock; **609** ©Clay Bennett/Christian Science Monitor; **610** ©Bruce Davidson/Magnum Photos; **612** (R, Bkgrd) ©Chuck Savage/Corbis; **613** Alison Wright/Corbis; **614** Digital Vision/Getty Images; **615** Digital Vision/Getty Images; **616** ©Clay Bennett/Christian Science Monitor; **618** (R, Bkgrd) ©Marcy Nighswander/AP Images; **619** Library of Congress; **621** (BR) ©Hulton Archive/Getty Images, (L) ©New York Times Co./Getty Images, (TR) The Lee Russell Photo Collection/Dolph Briscoe Center for American History; **622** Alex Wong/Getty Images; **624** (BR) Carl Iwasaki/Time Life Pictures/Getty Images, (TL) Purestock/Getty Images; **625** (L) ©AP Images, (R) Bettmann/Corbis, (C) Bettmann/Corbis; **626** (R, Bkgrd) AP Images; **627** Bettmann/Corbis; **628** Robert W. Kelley/Time Life Pictures/Getty Images; **629** Doug Pensinger/Getty Images; **631** Newmann/zefa/Corbis; **632** (R, Bkgrd) Carlos Barria/Reuters/Corbis; **634** (L) Bruce Forster/Getty Images, (R) Jeff Greenberg/Alamy Images; **638** ©2010 RJ Matson, The St. Louis Post Dispatch/Cagle Cartoons, Inc.; **640** Steve Artley/Artley Cartoons; **641** ©The Granger Collection, NY; **642** (R) Bob/Tom Thaves/Cartoonist Group, (L) Gary Blakeley/Shutterstock;

**UNIT 6 Page 643** Zhukov Sergei/ITAR-TASS/Corbis; **644** Lan Hongguang/Xinhua Press/Corbis; **646** (R, Bkgrd) Jon Arnold Images Ltd/Alamy Images; **647** Justin Kase Threez/Alamy; **649** Hulton Archive/Getty Images; **650** MPI/Getty Images; **652** Picture Partners/Alamy Images; **653** (R, Bkgrd) ©The Granger Collection, NY; **654** (R) Ceiling of the Painted Hall, detail of King William III (1650–1702) and Queen Mary II (1662–94) Enthroned, 1707–14 (see 2080–87), Thornhill, Sir James (1675–1734) Royal Naval College, Greenwich, London, UK, Photo: James Brittain/Bridgeman Art Library, (L) The Art Archive/Musée Carnavalet Paris/Gianni Dagli Orti/The Art Archive; **659** (L, BR) Bettmann/Corbis, (TR) Stapleton Collection/Corbis; **661** (R, Bkgrd) ©Lionel Cironneau/AP Images; **662** ©Dmitry Lovetsky/AP Images; **666** (R, Bkgrd) Erich Schlegel/Dallas Morning/Corbis; **667** ©Russell Boyce/Reuters/Corbis; **669** Yerbury Photography/Alamy Images; **671** ©Gregory Bull/AP Images; **674** Ed Fischer/Omaha World-Herald; **675** ©The Granger Collection, NY; **676** ©M. Spencer Green, file/AP Images; **678** (R, Bkgrd) Don Mason/Corbis; **679** (C) Cultura/Corbis, (R) Rick Friedman/Corbis, (L) Sean Masterson/epa/Corbis; **680** (C) ©Mark Lewis/Getty Images, (R) Robin Nelson/PhotoEdit, Inc., (L) Tony Freeman/PhotoEdit, Inc.; **681** Image Source/SuperStock; **682** (B) Brian Rybolt/PhotoLibrary Group, Inc.; **683** Shutterstock/Shutterstock; **685** (R, Bkgrd) Swim Ink 2, LLC/Corbis; **687** (B) Bill Proud/Cartoon Stock, (T) Bob Englehart/Cagle Cartoons, Inc.; **688** Gerd Schnuerer/Getty Images; **690** Robert Van Der Hilst/Getty Images; **692** (TL) ©Masterfile Royalty-Free, (TR) Keith Dannemiller/Corbis, (B) TIM SHAFFER/Reuters/Landov LLC; **693** (R, Bkgrd) Frank Polich/Reuters/Landov LLC; **696** Bobby Bank/WireImage/Getty Images; **700** Ed Kashi/Corbis; **702** Chip Bok/Creators Syndicate/Cartoonist Group; **703** Bob Thaves/Cartoonist Group; **704** (L) Gary Blakeley/Shutterstock;

**UNIT 7 Page 705** ©Toby Talbot/AP Images; **706** Steven Johnson/Miami Herald/MCT/NewsCom; **708** (R, Bkgrd) Kara Stokes; **710** (L) ©Eckehard Schulz/AP Images, (C) ©Kevin P. Casey/AP Images, (R) VisionsofAmerica/Joe Sohm/Getty Images; **711** (R) capt.digby/Alamy Images, (C) Jeff Greenberg/PhotoEdit, Inc., (L) Steven Puetzer/Getty Images; **714** (R, Bkgrd) ©Richmond Times-Dispatch, Bob Brown/AP Images; **715** (R) ©Doug Dreyer/AP Images, (L) ©Ric Feld/AP Images; **716** (L) Somos Images/Corbis, (R) ©The Hawk Eye, John Lovretta)/AP Images; **720** (R, Bkgrd) ©Judi Bottoni/Associated Press; **722** 2003 Monte Wolverton/Cagle Cartoons, Inc.; **727** (R, Bkgrd) Alan Klehr/Getty Images; **728** (L) Ruaridh Stewart/ZUMA/Corbis; **729** (R) David Young-Wolff/PhotoEdit, Inc.; **731** Michael Kelley/Getty Images; **732** (Bkgrd) ©Jim McKnight/AP Images, (R) ©Ric Feld/AP Images; **734** Bettmann/Corbis; **735** Leo Cullum/Cartoon Bank/Conde Nast Publications; **738** J.B. Handelsman/Cartoon Bank/Conde Nast Publications; **740** ©Matt Rourke/AP Images; **742** (R, Bkgrd) First Light/Corbls; **743** Jeff Greenberg/PhotoEdit, Inc.; **744** (T) ©Charles Rex Arbogast/AP Images, (B) photocritic/Alamy Images; **749** (R, Bkgrd) Andre Jenny/Alamy Images; **750** Scott Olson/Getty Images/Getty Images; **754** (C) Comstock/Thinkstock, (L) Michael Freeman/Corbis, (R) VisionsofAmerica/Joe Sohm/Getty Images; **755** Bruce Forster/NewsCom; **756** (R, Bkgrd) Thomas Barwick/Digital Vision/Getty Images; **757** (TR) ©Beth A. Keiser/Corbis, (BL) Andersen Ross/Stockbyte/Getty Images, (BR) Ed Kashi/Corbis; **758** ©Angela Rowlings/AP Images; **760** (TR) ©Paul Sakuma/AP Images, (B) UPI Photo/Kevin Dietsch/NewsCom, (TL) Zbigniew Bzdak/Chicago Tribune/MCT/NewsCom; **761** (R, Bkgrd) ©The Tennessean, Sanford Myers/AP Images; **763** (BL) Momentum Creative Group/Alamy, (BR) Ruaridh Stewart/ZUMA/Corbis, (TR) Wes Thompson/Corbis; **765** (R) David Young-Wolff/PhotoEdit, Inc., (L) Steve Dunwell/The Image Bank/Getty Images; **768** Chip Bok/Creators Syndicate/Cartoonist Group; **769** Mike Marland, Concord Monitor; **770** (L) Gary Blakeley/Shutterstock; **771** Ron Watts/Corbis; **772** Jose Luis Pelaez, Inc./Corbis; **774** (R, CL) Bettmann/Corbis, (L) Christie's Images/Corbis, (CR, C) Corbis; **775** (C) Arnold Newman/Corbis, (L, CL) Bettmann/Corbis, The White House, (CR) Wally McNamee/Corbis; **780** Mansell/Time Life Pictures/Getty Images; **781** King John signing the Magna Carta reluctantly (colour litho), Michael, A.C. (fl.1903–28) Private Collection, The Stapleton Collection/Bridgeman Art Library; **782** (R) ©The Granger Collection, NY, (L) Three Lions/Getty Images; **783** Ceiling of the Painted

Hall, detail of King William III (1650–1702) and Queen Mary II (1662–94) Enthroned, 1707–14 (see 2080–87), Thornhill, Sir James (1675–1734) Royal Naval College, Greenwich, London, UK, Photo: James Brittain/Bridgeman Art Library; **784** ©The Granger Collection, NY; **785** ©The Granger Collection, NY; **788** The Granger Collection, NY; **791** ©The Granger Collection, NY; **794** The Granger Collection, NY; **795** James Madison (1751–1836) (colour litho), American School, (19th century) Private Collection, Peter Newark American Pictures/Bridgeman Art Library; **798** Stock Montage/Getty Images; **800** Stock Montage/Getty Images; **801** MPI/Getty Images; **803** (R) ©The Granger Collection, NY, (L) National Portrait Gallery, Smithsonian Institution/Art Resource, NY; **804** Tai Power Seeff/The Image Bank/Getty Images.

**END MATTER** 772–773, Jose Luis Pelaez, Inc./Corbis; **774 L,** Christie's Images/Corbis; **774 ML,** Bettmann/Corbis; **774 M,** Corbis; **774 MR,** Corbis; **774 R,** Bettmann/Corbis; **775 L,** Bettmann/Corbis; **775 ML,** Bettmann/Corbis; **775 M,** Corbis; **775 MR,** Wally McNamee/Corbis; **775 R,** Courtesy barackobama.com; **780,** Time Life Pictures/Mansell/Time Life Pictures/Getty Images; **781,** King John signing the Magna Carta reluctantly (colour litho), Michael, A.C. (fl. 1903–28)/Private Collection, The Stapleton Collection/The Bridgeman Art Library; **782 L,** Three Lions/Getty Images; **782 R,** The Granger Collection, New York; **783,** Ceiling of the Painted Hall, detail of King William III (1650–1702) and Queen Mary II (1662–94) Enthroned, 1707–14 (see 2080–87), Thornhill, Sir James (1675–1734)/Royal Naval College, Greenwich, London, UK, Photo: James Brittain/The Bridgeman Art Library; **784,** The Granger Collection, New York; **785,** The Granger Collection, New York; **788,** The Granger Collection, New York; **791,** The Granger Collection, New York; **794,** The Granger Collection, New York; **795,** James Madison (1751–1836) (colour litho), American School, (19th century)/Private Collection, Peter Newark American Pictures/The Bridgeman Art Library; **798,** Stock Montage/Stock Montage/Getty Images; **800,** Stock Montage/Stock Montage/Getty Images; **801,** MPI/Getty Images; **803 L,** National Portrait Gallery, Smithsonian Institution/Art Resource, NY; **803 R,** The Granger Collection, New York; **804,** Tai Power Seeff/The Image Bank/Getty Images; **809,** Tai Power Seeff/The Image Bank/Getty Images.

## Text Acknowledgments

Grateful acknowledgment is made to the following for copyrighted material:

**American Civil Liberties Union** "Protecting National Security and Civil Liberties: Strategies for Terrorism Information Sharing." Statement of Caroline Fredrickson, Director of American Civil Liberties Union Washington Legislative Office before the Subcommittee on Terrorism and Homeland Security Senate Committee on the Judiciary, April 21, 2009.

**The Associated Press** "School's Integration Legacy Looms Large" by Andrew DeMillo from *The Associated Press, September 22, 2007*. Copyright © The Associated Press. Used by permission. All rights reserved.

**CNN** "Myanmar's Ruler Warns Against External Interference" from *cnn.com, March 27, 2010*. Copyright © Cable News Network.

**Congressional Quarterly, Inc.** "Clueless in Boise" by Alan Ehrenhalt from *www.governing.com*. Copyright © Congressional Quarterly Inc.

**Industrial Minerals Association** "Letter to the White House on Lobbying Reform, February 3, 2010" by Darrell K. Smith from *www.ima-na.org*. Copyright © Industrial Minerals Association.

**The Irrawaddy** "Than Shwe Signals a 'No' Vote to Election Observers" by Prakash B. Das from *The Irrawaddy, April 22, 2010*. Copyright © Irrawaddy Publishing Group.

**The New York Times** "Fewer Youths Jump Behind the Wheel at 16" by Mary M. Chapman and Micheline Maynard from The New York Times, February 25th, 2008. Copyright © 2008 by The New York Times. All rights reserved. Used by permission and protected by the Copyright Laws of the United States. The printing, copying, redistributing, or retransmission of the Material without express written permission is prohibited.

**The San Francisco Chronicle** "Homeless project's army of citizens calls year success" by Kevin Fagan from The San Francisco Chronicle, October 19th, 2005. Copyright © The San Francisco Chronicle. Used by permission.

**Writers House** "I have a dream" by Dr. Martin Luther King Jr. Copyright © 1963 Dr. Martin Luther King Jr.; copyright © renewed 1991 Coretta Scott King. Used by arrangement with The Heirs to the Estate of Martin Luther King Jr., c/o Writers House as agent for the proprietor New York, NY.

Note: Every effort has been made to locate the copyright owner of material reproduced on this component. Omissions brought to our attention will be corrected in subsequent editions.

## Teacher's Edition Photo Acknowledgments

**Page T0,** Hollingsworth/Photodisc/Getty Images, inc.; **T2,** Courtesy Dan M. Shea; **T3,** Tom Carter/PhotoEdit Inc.; **T6 L,** istockphoto.com; **T6 R,** Pearson Education, screenshot; **T8,** Courtesy Grant Wiggins; **T10,** L. Clarke/Corbis; **T14,** Neil Overy/Getty Images, Inc.; **T16,** istockphoto.com/René Mansi; **T17,** William Casey/Shutterstock, Inc.; **T19,** Michael Newman/PhotoEdit; **T20,** istockphoto.com; **T21,** Michael Newman/PhotoEdit; **T23,** istockphoto.com/Chris Schmidt; **T24,** istockphoto.com/René Mansi; **T26 L,** istockphoto.com/Joshua Blake; **T26 M,** istockphoto.com/Chris Schmid, **T26R,** istockphoto.com/Chris Schmidt; **T33,** Jose Luis Pelaez, Inc./Corbis.